R745.1075
K849k
2014

P9-DNO-203
3 5674 05167849 9

46TH EDITION

KOVELS'
Antiques &
Collectibles
PRICE GUIDE 2014

CHASE BRANCH LIBRARY
17731 W. SEVEN MILE RD.
DETROIT, MI 48235
578-8002

BLACK DOG
& LEVENTHAL
PUBLISHERS
NEW YORK

OCT 2013

R
CH
cont

Copyright © 2013 by Terry Kovel and Kim Kovel

All rights reserved. No part of this book, either text or illustrations,
may be used or reproduced in any form without
the prior written permission of the publisher.

Published by
Black Dog & Leventhal Publishers, Inc.
151 W. 19th Street
New York, NY 10011

Distributed by
Workman Publishing Company
225 Varick Street
New York, NY 10014

Designed by Sheila Hart Design, Inc.
Manufactured in the United States of America

ISBN-978-1-57912-947-7
Library of Congress Cataloging-in-Publication Data is available on file at
the offices of the publisher.

Paperback
b d f h g e c a

Front cover photographs, from top to bottom:
Lamp, electric, Prairie School
Bottle, scent, Turkish princess, Jacob Petit
Furniture, sideboard, neoclassical, mahogany

On the spine:
Furniture, sofa, Federal, c.1810

Back cover photographs, from top to bottom:
Toy, boat, ocean liner, windup, Bing
Roseville, Foxglove, vase, blue green, tapered, angular handles
Advertising, tray, Buffalo Brewing Co., Sacramento
Silver, creamer, pedestal, Philadelphia

Authors' photographs © Molly Nook (top) and Alex Montes de Oca (bottom)

BOOKS BY RALPH AND TERRY KOVEL

American Country Furniture, 1780–1875

A Directory of American Silver, Pewter, and Silver Plate

Kovels' Advertising Collectibles Price List

Kovels' American Antiques 1750–1900

Kovels' American Art Pottery

Kovels' American Collectibles 1900–2000

Kovels' American Silver Marks, 1650 to the Present

Kovels' Antiques & Collectibles Fix-It Source Book

Kovels' Antiques & Collectibles Price Guide

Kovels' Bid, Buy, and Sell Online

Kovels' Book of Antique Labels

Kovels' Bottles Price List

Kovels' Collector's Guide to American Art Pottery

Kovels' Collectors' Guide to Limited Editions

Kovels' Collectors' Source Book

Kovels' Depression Glass & Dinnerware Price List

Kovels' Dictionary of Marks— Pottery and Porcelain, 1650 to 1850

Kovels' Guide to Selling, Buying, and Fixing Your Antiques and Collectibles

Kovels' Guide to Selling Your Antiques & Collectibles

Kovels' Illustrated Price Guide to Royal Doulton

Kovels' Know Your Antiques

Kovels' Know Your Collectibles

Kovels' New Dictionary of Marks— Pottery and Porcelain, 1850 to the Present

Kovels' Organizer for Collectors

Kovels' Price Guide for Collector Plates, Figurines, Paperweights, and Other Limited Edition Items

Kovels' Quick Tips: 799 Helpful Hints on How to Care for Your Collectibles

Kovels' Yellow Pages: A Resource Guide for Collectors

The Label Made Me Buy It: From Aunt Jemima to Zonkers— The Best-Dressed Boxes, Bottles, and Cans from the Past

INTRODUCTION

The past year has been another year of the weak "collecting" economy that started in 2008 (but this year prices are a little better than last). Still, many record prices were set as bidders fought for the best of the best. (See page vi for a list of this year's record prices.) It was another year of great changes in the way antiques are collected, thanks to the Internet, cell phones, iPads and other electronic ways to buy and sell. Since 1953, the year we published our first book, the antiques world went from one or two antiques shows in a city per year to one almost every week. But with so many new online ways to buy or sell antiques—and the weak economy—many have been discontinued. Auctions of expensive antiques used to be held in a few large cities; small towns had "farm auctions" often held outside a farmhouse. Or a local auctioneer who sold antiques often sold the stuff in the barn, too. There were no antiques malls and no Internet shops, sales, or auctions. Collectors went on antiquing trips to look for the furniture, pottery, or glass they found in a few shops in each town, so buying was limited to a small geographic area and a few items. Today the New York auction houses run regular sales at their galleries along with online auctions that reach buyers in every country. And major auctions are also online from London, Paris, Hong Kong, and sometimes from the sale site of a special collection. You can even watch live auctions and bid from your computer.

When we wrote our first book, *Kovels' Dictionary of Marks: Pottery & Porcelain*, it was one of just 60 titles about antiques announced that year. In 1969 there were about 200. Then several publishers started to offer picture-price books about a single type of collectible. Soon hundreds of books for collectors filled shelves at bookstores across the country. Now fewer new books about collectibles and antiques are published, but much old and new information is found on the Internet. And much of the information found in old books, even old company catalogs and advertisements, can be found by searching online. Our old newspaper columns, newsletters, special reports, books of marks, and other writings are now easily found via an Internet search.

The economic problems that started with the stock market crash and housing bust late in 2008 spread to other investments, including antiques and collectibles. There is still a myth that if you buy antiques, they will go up in value every year and therefore are a good investment. That is only half true. If you buy the right antiques and sell at the right time, they sell for higher prices than you paid, even when you factor in inflation. Consider this: Our first price book lists a Diamond Dyes cabinet for $50. In the early months of 2008, the same cabinet sold for $1,112 to $2,633. In 2012, two Diamond Dyes cabinets were listed in the Advertising category, one at $540 and the other at $550, very low prices. In 2013, the most common Diamond Dyes cabinets in good condition were $407, $1,320, and $1,540. The ongoing worldwide recession is still affecting the values of antiques, but prices are starting to go up, show organizers are seeing better attendance, and there are many more auction bidders—because most auctions today are online and international, so bids come from phones, computers, and those in the room. Final prices show that the average auction ends with many unsold lots, but the auction makes enough money to stay in business.

Prices for items offered by people on eBay are still low, and many items do not sell at all. In 2012, prices had gone up for some things with international appeal, like Chinese porcelain and ivory. But in 2013, Chinese bidding slowed down for all but top-quality pieces. Hummel and Royal Doulton figurines, "country furniture" with peeling paint, and "brown furniture" like period Chippendale desks and 1890s oak dining tables have gone down in value. Prices for Japanese antiques are down because buyers in Japan are showing less interest in Satsuma, Nippon, and other Japanese porcelains. Prices for large advertising signs and rock posters are up. Through it all, malls, shows, and shops have seen fewer buyers and lower prices than they could get five years ago. But we talk to collectors and dealers, and most agree that "good stuff sells" and well-run shows, shops, and sales are doing "OK." Usable furniture in good condition and "smalls" are selling for expected prices, and the "best" of every type of antique or collectible is still in demand. Auction prices are closer to retail than they were before because of the large, worldwide pool of bidders.

One influence in this decade's market was the demand for Asian antiques. Jade, ivory, and cloisonné made in

China, Japan, Korea, and other Asian countries were selling for many times estimate until about a year ago, but that's changed because China's economy is suffering and laws protecting endangered species are being enforced. The laws forbid the sale of elephants (ivory), rhinoceros (horns), eagles (feathers), tigers (skins), and even some types of turtles (shells). An auction that advertises top-quality Asian items often is visited by buyers and appraisers who travel to the United States from China to see pieces at previews before bidding way over estimated prices. Do Asian buyers know more than Americans do about the age and quality of these pieces? Or are they eager to bring their culture back home, no matter what the price? A few items estimated to be worth thousands have sold for millions of dollars. Unfortunately, there is a growing problem with bids from China. Some bidders refuse to honor their bid and ask for a large reduction or just don't pick up the piece. Often this "sale" is reported at the time of the auction, but there is rarely a public announcement that the bid was not honored.

Kovels' Antiques and Collectibles Price Guide 2014 still has current, reliable information, plus two generations of Kovels editing the content. The book has 2,500 color photographs, 35,000 prices, over two hundred facts of interest, and tips about care and repair. Each photograph is shown with a complete caption that includes the price and the source. The book has color tabs and color-coded paragraphs that make it easy to find listings and it has a modern, readable typestyle. There are more than seven hundred categories with introductory paragraphs that include company history. We make some changes in the paragraphs every year to indicate new owners, new distributors, or new information about production dates. This year we made fifty-three updates to paragraphs, many of which tell of the sale or closing of a company, and added three new categories. All of the antiques and collectibles priced here were offered for sale during the past year, most of them in the United States. Other prices came from sales that accepted bids from all over the world. Almost all auction prices given include the buyer's premium, because that is part of what the buyer paid. None include local sales tax.

READ THIS FIRST

This is a book for the collector. We check prices, visit shops, shows, and flea markets, read hundreds of publications and catalogs, check Internet sales and other online services, and decide which antiques and collectibles are of most interest to most collectors. We concentrate on the average pieces in any category. Sometimes high-priced items are included so you can see that special rarities are very valuable. Prices of some items were very high because major collections of top-quality pieces were auctioned. This year, these collections included toy cars, advertising, art glass, Shaker furniture, and bottles.

Most listed pieces cost less than $10,000. The highest price in this book is $239,000 for a Babe Ruth baseball cap. The lowest price, $1, is for a Harker saucer. The largest is an architectural cherry backbar in Eastlake style with mirrors, doors, and drawers made in the 1880s. It is 192 by 112 inches and cost $11,750. The smallest is a button that looks like a plastic dice cube, ⅜ of an inch square. It sold for the small price of $5.

Many unusual, unique, and weird things are included. This year we have listed a vampire killing kit ($14,800), a salesman's sample casket with a window ($825), and a leather pirate's arm with a Captain Hook's hook made about 1855 ($944). We also list the prop horse head used in 1972's The Godfather movie ($11,500), a pair of iron horse's legs ($825), a cut glass toupee stand from the American Brilliant period ($590), and the uniform of a prison road gang ($219).

There are still bargains to be had, some that have been emerging as "collectibles" over the last five years. Most are in newer categories, like modernist jewelry and twentieth-century studio pottery. Big is still "big." Small sets of figurines or plates are very hard to sell. But large-scale accent pieces with colors and lines that blend in with modern furnishings—pieces like huge crocks, floor vases, centerpieces, and garden statuary—attract decorators as well as the owners of large homes. Shocking pink, orange, and chartreuse are popular colors this year, so decorators are buying colorful pottery from Czechoslovakia and large glassware like Blenko. Anything from clothes and glass to ceramics and furniture that was in the "newest style" between the 1950s and the 1990s is hot. Also wanted are very large beige pots from the 1960s that can be displayed on the floor. And some old standbys, like toy cars, mechanical banks, shaving mugs, and war and political memorabilia, are going up in price. They are attracting new, younger buyers. Of major interest today are antique guns and ammunition and, surprisingly, anything made of iron, like bookends and doorstops. But costume jewelry is the most popular item we see selling at shows. Prices for pieces marked with important makers' names can sell for as much as $1,500. A few very popular collectibles of the past, like Roseville pottery and wicker furniture, have come down in price. The biggest change is silver tableware. The high meltdown price of sterling silver made it more profitable to melt some pieces than to sell them as antiques. But the price for meltdown has dropped a lot for gold and some for silver, so less is being destroyed. Hundreds of coin silver items, especially spoons, and no-name sterling serving dishes and flatware disappeared in the meltdown craze. But sterling by well-known companies or designers like Tiffany, Georg Jensen, or Paul Storr still get top dollar. The June 2013 auction of a 1934 silver coffee service by a famous American silversmith, Paul Lobel (1899-1983), showed the level of recent interest in 20th-century silversmiths. It sold for $449,000. Quality sells high—because collectors consider it an "investment" that will increase in value.

This book seems to have gotten younger over the past forty-six years. Most items in our original book were made before 1860. Today we list pieces made as recently as the twenty-first century, and there is great interest in furniture, glass, ceramics, and good design made since 1950.

The book is more than 680 pages long and crammed full of prices and photographs. We try to have a balanced format—not too many items that sell for over $5,000. We list a few very expensive pieces so you can realize that a great paperweight may cost $9,000 but an average one only $25. Nearly all the prices are from the American market for the American market. Only a few European sales are reported. We don't include prices we think result from "auction fever." We do list verified bargains.

The index is computer-generated. Use it often. It includes categories and much more. For example, there is a category for Celluloid. Most celluloid will be there, but a toy made of celluloid will be listed under Toy and also indexed under Celluloid. There are also cross-references in the listings and in the paragraphs. But some searching must be done. For example, Barbie dolls are in the Doll category; there is no Barbie category. And when you look at "doll, Barbie," you find a note that "Barbie" is under "doll, Mattel, Barbie" because Mattel makes Barbie dolls and most dolls are listed by maker.

All photographs and prices are new. Antiques and collectibles pictured are items that were offered for sale or sold for the amount listed in 2012-13. Auction prices include the buyer's premium. Wherever we had extra space on a page, we filled it with tips about the care of collections and other useful information. Don't discard this book. Old Kovels' price guides can be used for future reference and for tax, estate, and appraisal information.

The prices in this book are reports of the general antiques market. As we said, every price in the book is new. We do not estimate or "update" prices. Prices are either realized prices from auctions or completed sales or they're asking prices. We know that a buyer may have negotiated an asking price to a lower selling price, but we report asking prices. We do not pay dealers, collectors, or experts to estimate prices. If the price is from an auction, it includes the buyer's premium if one was charged; but like all the prices, it does not include sales tax. If a price range is given, at least two identical items were offered for sale at different prices. Price ranges are found only in categories like Pressed Glass, where identical items can be identified. Some prices in Kovels' Antiques & Collectibles Price Guide may seem high and some low because of regional variations, but each price is one you could have paid for the object somewhere in the United States. Some Internet prices from sellers' ads or listings are avoided. Because so many non-collectors sell online but know little about the objects they are describing, there can be inaccuracies in descriptions. Sales from well-known Internet sites, shops, and sales, carefully edited, are included.

If you are selling your collection, do not expect to get retail value unless you are a dealer. Wholesale prices for antiques are usually 40 to 50 percent of retail prices. The antiques dealer must make a profit or go out of business. Internet auction prices are less predictable—because of an international audience and "auction fever," prices can be higher or lower than retail.

RECORD PRICES

Record prices for antiques and collectibles make news every year. We report those that relate to the entries in this book. We do not include record prices for works of art that are often seen in museums, like oil paintings, antique sculptures, or very recent work by modern artists. Our list is a snapshot of the collectors' market. This year we include the Chippendale block-front desk and bookcase that sold for over a million dollars, an Apple 1 computer, a small Lutz marble, a silver spice container, a Ty Cobb bat, a Honus Wagner baseball card, a toy carousel, and three banks.

CLOCKS

E. Howard clock: $230,100 for an E. Howard walnut regulator clock, No. 46, with reverse-painted glass astronomical dial, roman numerals, 8-day brass weight-driven time-only movement, signed, 126 x 41 in., *Fontaine's Auction Gallery*.

Southern clock: $271,400 for a tall-case Virginia clock known as the "John Cole" clock, cherry and tulip poplar, carved and decorated with inlays and turnings, tombstone-shape door, and moon phase dial, c.1810, 105 x 24 x 14 in., *Quinn & Farmer Auctions*.

DECOY

Chauncey Wheeler works: $63,250 for a mallard drake decoy by Chauncey Wheeler, Guyette, Schmidt & Deeter.

Crowell miniature decoy: $31,050 for a miniature great blue heron carved by A. Elmer Crowell, mounted on carved rock-form base, 8 in., *Decoys Unlimited*.

FURNITURE

Massachusetts tea table: $962,500 for a Queen Anne carved mahogany tea table with slides, Boston, 1740-60, 26 ¾ x 30 x 18 ¾ in., *Christie's*.

Any piece of Connecticut furniture: $1,082,500 for a Samuel Talcott Chippendale block-front desk and bookcase, cherry, with original finish, cast-brass hardware, and finials, c.1765-75, 97 ½ x 43 ¼ x 25 ¼ in., *Sotheby's*.

Diego Giacometti work: $1,762,500 for a Diego Giacometti console table, glass top, bronze frame sculpted with trees and a family of deer, Chevreuil, Biche et Bambi, c.1975, 31 ¾ x 67 x 15 in., *Doyle New York*.

English glass decanters: $47,400

GLASS & BOTTLES

Arlington Bar amber whiskey flask: $7,289 for a pair of amber whiskey flasks, with the slug inscribed, "Arlington M.A. Lindberg Prop. Bakersfield, Cal.," with a footed base and single collar, 1878-82, pint, *Holabird-Kagin Americana*.

Cameo glass: $263,000 for the cameo glass plaque, "The Attack," by Thomas and George Woodall, dark amethyst glass overlaid with white carved Pompeian scene of two cupids surprising an undressed maiden, 17 ¼ in., *Bonhams*.

Works by Attilio Spaccarelli: $39,775 for a Venetian cameo glass vase by Attilio Spaccarelli, amphora shape, cobalt blue overlaid in white, carved, four figures of satyrs and a maiden, flowers, vines and scroll borders, signed, 1887, 9 ¼ in., *Bonhams*.

Santa Cruz flask: $2,989 for a Pacific Ocean House EJS Santa Cruz flask, clear glass picnic style, footed base, and applied single collar, 1878-85, *Holabird-Kagin Americana*.

English glass decanters: $47,400 for a pair of English cut glass presentation decanters decorated with transparent enamel, scene of a queen on a throne, sunburst stoppers, one titled "Europe," the other "America," made by William Collins for the Duke of Sussex, 1810-20, 13 ½ in., *Kaminski Auctions*.

Apothecary bottle: $4,780 for a G.P. Morrill, Virginia City, green apothecary bottle, 1863, *Holabird-Kagin Americana*.

MISCELLANEOUS

Apple 1 computer: $671,000 for the Apple 1 computer, the first desktop computer created by Steve Wozniak and Steve Jobs, including all the system components plus the original manual and a letter to the original owner signed by Wozniak, *Auction Team Breker*.

Presentation silver ingot: $103,695 for a silver anniversary ingot presented to "St. Bernard Commandery No. 35, Chicago, For Efficiency Exhibition Drill, Denver, August 10th 1892," an engraved scene of Mount of the Holy Cross on the front and a list of Chamber of Commerce Committee members, *Holabird-Kagin Americana*.

Scrimshaw: $324,000

Jonas Weber dresser box: $159,975

Presentation candlestick: $51,385 for a presentation candlestick made in Canon City State Penitentiary by a blacksmith named Cox, nickel-silver-plated spike and hook, solid nickel and silver handle and thimble, with engravings and inlays, c.1920, 16 ¾ in., *Holabird-Kagin Americana.*

Marble less than 1 in.: $25,800 for a pink opaque Lutz marble with green lines, handmade in Germany, ⅞ in., *Morphy Auctions.*

Scrimshaw: $324,000 for a whale's tooth engraved on one side with a fully rigged ship, whaleboats, whales, and albatrosses, the other side with a Federal house, foliage, crescent moon, 5-point star, and sun, 8 in., *Northeast Auctions.*

Jonas Weber dresser box: $159,975 for a Jonas Weber dresser box, dark blue painted pine with lift lid, original wire hinges and tin hasp, signed by Weber, dated 1845, 10 in. x 5 ¾ in. x 5 ¾ in., *Pook & Pook.*

PAPER

Adolphe Mouron Cassandre poster: $156,000 for the Adolphe Mouron Cassandre L.M.S. Best Way travel poster, for the London, Midland and Scottish Railway, 1928, 41 ½ x 50 in., *Swann Auction Galleries.*

Sam Hyde Harris travel poster: $9,600 for the Sam Hyde Harris Southern Pacific's New Daylight travel poster, 1937, 23 x 16 in., *Swann Auction Galleries.*

PHOTOGRAPHY

Photograph by Man Ray: $1,203,750 for Man Ray's "Untitled Rayograph," 1922, unique gelatin silver (photogram), signed in pencil, 14 x 10 ⅝ in., *Christie's.*

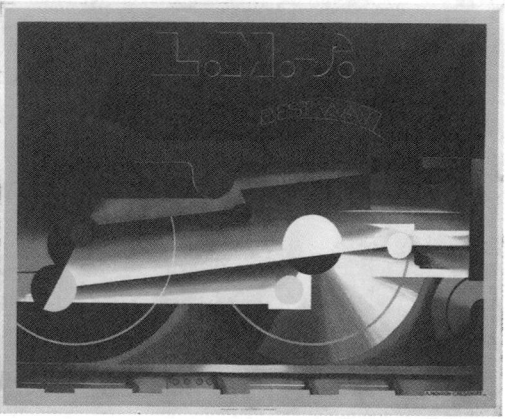

Adolphe Mouron Cassandre poster: $156,000

Full-plate daguerreotype: $106,200 for a cased full-plate daguerreotype, picturing four men in matching uniforms in front of crossed American flags, hand-colored, 1840s, 8 ¼ x 6 ¼ in., in original embossed leather case, 9 ⅛ x 7 ⅛ in., *Eldred's.*

Herbert Bayer: $1,482,500 for the gelatin-silver print photomontage, "The Lonely Metropolitan," by Herbert Bayer, with gouache and airbrush, 1932, 16 ¼ x 11 ⅞ in., *Sotheby's.*

László Moholy-Nagy: $1,482,500 for a photogram titled "Fotogramm," by László Moholy-Nagy, signed, dated, and inscribed in pencil and red crayon, studio stamp on reverse, frame, 1925, 9 ⅜ x 7 ⅛ in., *Sotheby's.*

POTTERY & PORCELAIN

Chinese porcelain from Kangxi period: $9,537,832 for a Chinese porcelain bowl, ruby red ground with double lotus blooms in yellow, blue, pink and white, thin rounded sides, straight foot, and enameled six-character blue Kangxi yuzhi mark, 1662-1722, 4 ⅜ in., *Sotheby's.*

SILVER

Spice container: $337,900 for a Polish parcel-gilt silver spice container, four tiers tall with clock tower, lion-shaped flag at top, gilt masks, ball and claw pedestal, male figures, hinged door, lock and working key, 18th century, 15 in., *Kestenbaum & Co.*

SPORTS

Ty Cobb baseball bat: $253,000 for a game-used Ty Cobb Louisville Slugger baseball bat, c.1919-1922, along with two letters of provenance written by Cobb, *Hunt Auctions.*

Honus Wagner baseball card: $2,105,770 for a 1909 T206 Honus Wagner baseball card, graded EX 5 (MC) by PSA, referred to as "The Jumbo Wagner" because of the unusually wide border, reverse advertisement for Sweet Caporal cigarettes, *Goldin Auctions.*

Ernest Holzman salmon reel: $8,050 for a salmon reel made by Ernest Holzman of Brooklyn, New York, c.1900, *Crossroads Angling Auctions.*

Fly-tying vise: $6,900 for a fly-tying vise owned by Theodore Gordon, marked "L. Hugoniot-Tisso," *Crossroads Angling Auctions.*

Duck call: $103,500 for walnut duck call by James Beckhart with four carved panels, alligator, shotgun, dog chasing a duck and dead game, 1905, *Guyette, Schmidt & Deeter.*

American Indian war shirt: $877,500

TEXTILE

American Indian war shirt: $877,500 for an American Indian poncho-style war shirt made of two soft skins with beadwork and geometric designs, belonging to Chief Joseph of the Nez Perce tribe, *Coeur d'Alene Art Auction.*

TOYS, DOLLS & BANKS

German doll: $212,800 for a Kammer & Reinhardt Model 104 character doll, smiling child, blond mohair wig, painted blue eyes, closed mouth, composition and wood ball-jointed body, marked, 1910, 20 in., *Theriault's.*

Marklin carousel: $218,500 for a Marklin tin musical carousel with original cloth canopy, painted pennants, embossed shields, scalloped rounding boards, floral decals, red bullion trim, and central mirrored column, eight girl and four boy riders, ten additional figures watching, propelled by hand with drive wheel and wooden crank, allows for power to be supplied by steam engine, Germany, c.1910, 16 x 21 in., *Noel Barrett.*

Marklin toy bi-plane: $20,700 for a c.1910 German Marklin tin and celluloid toy bi-plane with two passengers, *White's Auctions.*

Madame Alexander/Any American dolls: $96,560 for a set of six "Mystery Portrait" dolls by Madame Alexander, each hard plastic with socket head, sleep eyes, closed mouth, five-piece body and variations of painted facial features, hair color, costume and hair ornamentation, 1951, 21 in., *Theriault's.*

Lenci "Equestrienne" doll: $30,240 for a Lenci "Equestrienne" doll with pressed felt swivel head, painted facial features, pale blue eyes, closed mouth, blond mohair wig, and felt body jointed at shoulders and hips, marked, c.1930, 17 in., *Theriault's.*

Madame Alexander/Any American dolls: $96,560

Santa with tree mechanical bank: $22,050 for a cast-iron Santa mechanical bank with removable wire tree, Ives, Blakeslee, & Co., c.1890, *RSL Auction Co.*

Black character bank known as "Snowflake": $9,493 for the spelter bank of the European black character known as "Snowflake," Germany, c.1915, *RSL Auction Co.*

"1905 Bank": $20,825 for the "1905 Bank," a replica of an old-fashioned bank building with domed roof and five spires, cast iron, *RSL Auction Co.*

KOVELS HAVE OTHER PRICE INFORMATION SOURCES

Website: Kovels.com

Join the community of collectors at Kovels.com to keep up on more in the buy-sell world of antiques. Register; there is no charge for most of the information on the site, including our directory of services for collectors and dealers and hundreds of thousands of searchable prices from past years. Other information, including a database of pottery and porcelain marks and makers and another of silver marks and makers, is available for a fee.

Newsletter: Kovels on Antiques and Collectibles

You already know this is a great overall price guide for antiques and collectibles. Each entry is current, every photograph is new, and all prices are accurate. There is also another Kovel publication designed to keep you up-to-the-minute in the world of collecting. Things change quickly. Important sales produce new record prices. Fakes appear. Rarities are discovered. To keep up with developments, you can read Kovels on Antiques and Collectibles, our monthly newsletter. It is now available by subscription in two forms, a print edition that is mailed and an electronic format that is available via an online subscription at Kovels.com. Both provide the identical newsletter, with current information and photos so useful to collectors. The electronic edition gives you access to newsletter archives. Each newsletter is filled with color photographs, about forty per issue. The newsletter reports prices, trends, auction results, Internet sales, and other news for collectors (see back page to order).

There are a few rules for using this book. Each listing is arranged in the following manner: CATEGORY (such as Pressed Glass), OBJECT (such as vase), DESCRIPTION (as much information as possible about size, age, color, and pattern). Some types of glass, pottery, and silver are exceptions to this rule. These are listed CATEGORY, PATTERN, OBJECT, DESCRIPTION. All items are presumed to be in good condition and undamaged, unless otherwise noted. In most sections, if a maker's name is easily recognized, like Gustav Stickley, we include it near the beginning of the entry. If the maker is obscure, the name may be near the end.

- You will find silver flatware in either Silver Flatware Plated or Silver Flatware Sterling. There is also a section for Silver Plate, which includes coffeepots, trays, and other plated hollowware. Most solid or sterling silver is listed by country, so look for Silver-American, Silver-Danish, Silver-English, etc. Silver jewelry is listed under Jewelry. Most pottery and porcelain is listed by factory name, such as Weller; by item, such as Calendar Plate; in sections like Dinnerware or Kitchen; or in a special section, such as Pottery-Art, Pottery-Contemporary, Pottery-Midcentury, etc.

- Sometimes we make arbitrary decisions. Fishing has its own category, but hunting is part of the larger category called Sports. We have omitted most guns except toy guns; these are listed in the Toy category. It is not legal to sell weapons without a special license, so guns are not part of the general antiques market but are often seen at auctions. Air guns, BB guns, rocket guns, and others are listed in the Toy section. Everything is listed according to the computer alphabetizing system. We have made several editorial decisions. A butter dish is a "butter." A salt dish is called a "salt" to differentiate it from a saltshaker. It is always "sugar and creamer," never "creamer and sugar." Where one dimension is given, it is the height; or if the object is round, it's the diameter. The height of a picture is listed before width. Glass is clear unless a color is indicated.

- Some antiques terms, such as "Sheffield" or "Pratt," have two meanings. Read the paragraph headings to know the definition being used. All category headings are based on the vocabulary of the average person, and we use terms like "mud figures" even if not technically correct.

- This book does not include price listings for fine art paintings, antiquities, stamps, coins, or most types of books. Comic books are listed only in special categories like Superman, but original comic art and cels are listed in their own categories.

- Prices for items pictured can be found in the appropriate category. Look for the matching entry with the abbreviation "Illus." The photograph will be nearby.

- Because of the computer, the book can be produced quickly. The last entries are added in June; the book is available in August. But human help finds prices and checks accuracy. We read everything at least five times, sometimes more. We edit more than 50,000 entries down to the 35,000 entries found here. We correct spelling, remove incorrect data, write category paragraphs, and decide on new categories. We proofread copy and prices many times, but there will always be some misspelled words and other errors. Information in the paragraphs is updated each year and this year more than fifty updates and additions were made.

- Prices are reported from all parts of the United States, Canada, and Europe, converted to U.S. dollars at the time of the sale. The average rate of exchange in June 2013 was $1 U.S. to about $1.02 Canadian, €0.75 (Euro), and £0.64 (British Pound). Prices are from auctions, shops, Internet sales, and shows. Every price is checked for accuracy, but we are not responsible for errors.

- We cannot answer your letters asking for price information, but please write if you have any requests for categories to be included or any corrections to the paragraphs or prices. You may find the answers to your questions at Kovels.com.

- When you see us at shows auctions, house sales, and flea markets, please stop and say hello. Don't be surprised if we ask for your suggestions. You can write to us at P.O. Box 22192-K, Beachwood, OH 44122, or visit us on our website, www.Kovels.com.

TERRY KOVEL AND KIM KOVEL
July 2013

ACKNOWLEDGMENTS

Our publisher, Black Dog & Leventhal, and its president, J.P. Leventhal, have continued to suggest and implement improvements to this book. There are also improvements in design and technology that add to the speed of production and ease of use. Thanks to J.P. Leventhal; Lisa Tenaglia, our editor; Pamela Schechter, production editor; and Stephanie Sorenson and Audrey Gibbons, publicity. Mary Flower, Robin Perlow, and Cynthia Schuster Eakin did copyediting and proofreading for the entire book and found the tiniest of errors.

Thanks to Sheila Hart and her assistant, Mike Levay, who put all the prices, photographs, and paragraphs together and created the look and layout of Kovels' Antiques & Collectibles Price Guide 2014.

The details and hard work required to record prices, assemble photos and information, check accuracy and spelling, and solve many other problems are all done by our Kovel staff. We thank Mary Ellen Brennan, Grace DeFrancisco, Marcia Goldberg, Katie Karrick, Liz Lillis, Tina McBean, Renee McRitchie, Erika Risley, and Cherrie Smrekar. Special thanks to Carmie Amata, who helped with the Charlie Chaplin and Movie categories, and Lee Markley, who helped proofread the glass categories, including carnival glass. Photographs came from many sources, and they were all sized and digitally enhanced by our photo editor and house photographer, Janet Dodrill, and her staff, Carolyn K. Lewis, Liz Blankschaen, and Stan Bujak. Gay Hunter, our in-house editor, always worries the most about the book. She kept detailed records and made sure all of us were on track and on schedule. She read and reviewed pages of prices, corrected our spelling errors, and handled computer problems. And during the final proofing and re-proofing, she kept finding minor errors. Together we updated paragraph information when a company closed or was purchased. Thanks to all of them. We have what we are sure is our best book ever. We know that the book is possible only because of the group effort, even though it is our names that appear on the cover.

The world of antiques and collectibles is filled with people who have answered our every request for help. Dealers, auction houses, and shops have given advice and opinions, supplied photographs and prices, and made suggestions for changes. Special thanks to all of them: A.H. Wilkens, Aleph-Bet Books, Allard Auctions, American Bottle Auctions, Anderson Americana, Bertoia Auctions, Bloomsbury House, Bonhams, Brian Lebel's Old West Show & Auction, Brunk Auctions, Charlton Hall Auctions, Conestoga Auction Co., Copake Auction, Cottone Auctions, Cowan's Auctions, Cowans + Clark + DelVecchio, Doyle New York, DuMouchelles Art Gallery, Early Auction Co., Eldred's Auction, Elite Decorative Arts, Fox Auctions, Garth's Auctioneers, Glass Works Auctions, Gray's Auctioneers, Hake's Americana & Collectibles, Heritage Auctions, Hollywood Poster, Humler & Nolan, Ivey-Selkirk Auctioneers, James D. Julia Auctioneers, Jeffrey S. Evans & Associates, Lang's Sporting Collectibles, Leslie Hindman Auctioneers, Los Angeles Modern Auctions, Matthews Auctions, McMasters Harris Auction Co., Morphy Auctions, Mosby & Co. Auctions, Neal Auction Co., New Orleans Auction Galleries, Norman C. Heckler & Co., Old Barn Auction, Palm Beach Modern Auctions, Past Tyme Pleasures, Rago Arts & Auctions Center, Rich Penn Auctions, RSL Auction, Ruby Lane, Seeck Auctions, Showtime Auction Services, Skinner Inc., Sloans & Kenyon, Sotheby's, The Stein Auction Co., Theriault's, Treadway Toomey Galleries, V & M, Victorian Casino Antiques, William Morford Antiques, Willis Henry Auctions, Woody Auction, Wright.

To the others who knowingly or unknowingly contributed to this book, we say thank you: American Glass Gallery, Aspire Auctions, Auction Gallery of the Palm Beaches, Auction Team Breker, Austin Auction Co., Belhorn Auction Services, Bob Courtney Auctions, Bruhns Auction Gallery, Buffalo Bay Auction Co., Burchard Galleries, Capo Auction, Christie's, CRN Auctions, Crocker Farm, Crown Jewels of the Wire, Dallas Auction Gallery, Dirk Soulis Auctions, Don Presley Auction, Early American History Auctions, Fenton Art Glass Collectors of America, Freeman's Auctioneers, Great Gatsby's Fine Antiques, Great Vintage Jewelry, Griswold & Cast Iron Cookware Association, Heisey Collectors of America, Hill House Wares, Jackson's International Auctioneers, Kamelot Auctions, Kaminski Auctions, Ken Farmer Auctions, Keno Auctions, Leighton Galleries, Leland Little Auctions, Maine Antique Digest, Manor Auctions, Morton Kuehnert Auctioneers, Noel Barrett Antiques & Auctions, Northeast Auctions, O'Gallerie Auctioneers, Passion for Perfume, Pole Top Discoveries, Political Bandwagon, Pook & Pook, Potteries Specialist Auctions, Quinn's Auction Galleries, Richard Opfer Auctioneering, Roland Antiques, Simpson Galleries, SM Publications, Sotheby's, Stair Galleries, Stevenson's Auction, Strawser Auctions, Swann Auction Galleries, Tea Leaf Club International, Tradewinds Antiques & Auctions, Treadway Gallery, Vectis Auctions, Vintage Jewelry Online, Watt Pottery Shop, Weschler's Auctioneers, William H. Bunch Auctions, William J. Jenack Auctioneers, Woodbury Auction.

A. **WALTER** made pate-de-verre glass under contract at the Daum glassworks from 1908 to 1914. He decorated pottery during his early years in his studio in Sevres, where he also developed his formula for pale, translucent pate-de-verre. He started his own firm in Nancy, France, in 1919. Pieces made before 1914 are signed *Daum, Nancy* with a cross. After 1919 the signature is *A. Walter Nancy*.

Dish, Crayfish, Translucent, Amber, Marked, Berge, 1920s, 5 ¾ x 5 In.	1323.00
Dish, Vide De Poch, Capricorn Beetle, Mottled, Red Fusion, 5 x 3 ⅜ In.	1179.00
Dresser Tray, Dragon Fly, Amber To Clear, Signed, 4 ½ x 2 ¼ In.	2900.00
Figurine, Baby Chick, Blue, Square Base, 4 ¼ In.	3100.00
Figurine, Frog, Green, 1920s, 1 ¾ x 2 In.	688.00
Paperweight, Mouse, White, Green Base, Henri Berge, 3 ½ x 3 In.	813.00

ABC plates, or children's alphabet plates, were most popular from 1780 to 1860, but are still being made. The letters on the plate were meant as teaching aids for children learning to read. The plates were made of pottery, porcelain, metal, or glass. Mugs and other items were also made with alphabet decorations.

Cup & Saucer, Rooster, Pink Border, Germany	49.00
Cup, Nesting Birds, Sterling Silver, Straight-Sided, Scroll Handle, Wm. Kerry, c.1890, 4 In.	550.00
Cup, Sterling Silver, Blocks, Oval Cartouche, Monogram, Handle, c.1920, 2 In.	175.00
Mug, Bullfinch, Brown, Staffordshire, 3 In.	98.00
Plate, 3 Men, Catching Fish, Red Trim, Staffordshire, 1800s, 5 ⅛ In.	175.00
Plate, Abraham Lincoln, Transfer, Black, 6 In.	1114.00
Plate, Alphabet, Numbers, Calendar, Clock, Red, Staffordshire, 1888, 7 ½ In.	175.00
Plate, Baked Taters All Hot, Red Center, Blue Rim, England, 7 In.	30.00
Plate, Baseball Players, Embossed, 7 ¼ In.	160.00
Plate, Boy & Girl, Alphabet Border, Buffalo Pottery, c.1935, 7 ½ In.	35.00
Plate, Boy Holding Y, Red Transfer, 19th Century, 6 ¼ In.	165.00
Plate, Boy, Dog, Scalloped Blue Edge, 7 ½ In.	40.00
Plate, Boy, Dog, Staffordshire, c.1850, 6 ⅞ In.	180.00
Plate, Boys Playing Rugby, Brown Transferware, Staffordshire, 7 ⅝ In.	130.00
Plate, Bunny, Speckled Pottery, Signed, T. Grey, 8 ½ In.	11.00
Plate, Center Clock Face, Scalloped & Numbered Border, Ripley Glass Co., c.1880, 7 In.	38.00
Plate, Clock Face, Children Playing, Wheelbarrow, Staffordshire, England, c.1880, 7 ⅜ In.	140.00
Plate, Dutch Boy & Girl, Animals, Windmill, Multicolor, Germany, c.1920, 6 ½ In.	52.00
Plate, Dutch Girls Playing, Braille Alphabet, H. Aynsley & Co., c.1904, 6 In.	84.00
Plate, Horses, Riders, Brown, White, Staffordshire, 7 In.	45.00
Plate, Lion, Transfer, Brownsville Pottery, c.1870, 7 ½ In.	50.00
Plate, Little Girl, Chasing Pigs, 6 ½ In.	37.00
Plate, Manhattan Beach Hotel, Staffordshire, c.1870, 6 ⅞ In.	40.00
Plate, Mary, Sister, Lambs, Transfer, Staffordshire, England, c.1860, 7 ½ In.	140.00
Plate, Oxen Pulling Plow, Staffordshire, c.1860, 7 ⅛ In.	65.00
Plate, Robinson Crusoe, Pets, Transfer, Brownsville Pottery Co., 19th Century, 8 In.	185.00
Plate, Seal Hunting, Staffordshire, c.1870, 7 In.	260.00
Plate, Tea Party, Sign Language, Brown, H. Aynsley & Co., c.1870, 6 ¼ In.	295.00
Plate, Tin, Empty Center, c.1926, 6 In.	50.00
Plate, Wisdom Saying, Couple, Preacher, 19th Century, 7 ⁷⁄₁₆ In.	65.00

ABINGDON POTTERY was established in 1908 by Raymond E. Bidwell as the Abingdon Sanitary Manufacturing Company. The company started making art pottery in 1934. The factory ceased production of art pottery in 1950.

Candleholder, 2-Light, Art Nouveau, White, Gold, 4 x 3 x 6 In.	23.00
Cookie Jar, Mammy, Hand On Hip, Flower Basket, Impressed, 9 In.	83.00
Cookie Jar, Mammy, Holding Flower Basket, Hand On Hip, 9 In.	36.00
Lamp, Drape & Tassel, Green, Metal Base, 12 ½ In.	95.00
Planter, 2 Handles, Pink, Star Flower, Leaves, Footed, 6 ¼ In.	30.00
Planter, Pink Matte Glaze, 14 x 9 x 2 In.	19.00
Planter, Shell Shape, Green, 7 In.	25.00
Vase, Art Deco, V-Shape Top, Flared, Blue, Marked 512, 6 ¾ In.	42.00
Vase, Cornucopia, Pink, Star Flower, Base, 3 ½ In., Pair	64.00
Vase, Peach, Stylized Handles, Leafy Branches, 10 ¾ In.	30.00
Wall Pocket, Open Book Shape, Cookbook, Raised Blue Letters, White Ground, 7 x 6 x 4 In.	75.00
Wall Shelf, White, Scrolled Edge, Tapered Body, Acanthus Leaf Bottom, 8 x 7 x 4 In.	175.00

Advertising, Banner, Circus, Spidora Alive, Canvas, Leather, Snap Wyatt, Tampa, c.1945, 116 x 92 In.
$632.00

James D. Julia Auctioneers

Advertising, Bowl, Quaker Oats, Quaker Character, Oats Design Border, Porcelain, 7 ½ In.
$55.00

Wm Morford Antiques

Advertising, Box, Display, Adam's Gum, Tutti Frutti, Cardboard, Glass Lift Lid, 9 ⅞ x 4 ¼ In.
$88.00

Wm Morford Antiques

The edited listings of the current prices in this *Kovels' Antiques & Collectibles Price Guide* aren't available on any website. Readers can visit **Kovels.com** to check thousands of past prices and sign up for free information on trends, tips, reproductions, marks, and more.

Advertising, Box, Over-Sea Rolled Oats, Cardboard, Train, Plane, Bridge, Cylindrical, 1 ¼ Lb., 7 ⅜ x 4 In. $330.00

Wm Morford Antiques

Advertising, Bucket, Candy, Underwood Talmage Co., Dayton, Ohio, Cardboard, 30 Lb., 12 x 13 In. $880.00

Wm Morford Antiques

Advertising, Cabinet, Diamond Dyes, Children With Balloon, Embossed Tin, c.1911, 25 x 15 In. $896.00

Victorian Casino Antiques

The First Cereal Premium
Kellogg's offered the first cereal premium in 1909, the Funny Jungleland Moving Pictures Booklet, available with the purchase of two boxes of Kellogg's Corn Flakes.

ADAMS china was made by William Adams and Sons of Staffordshire, England. The firm was founded in 1769 and became part of the Wedgwood Group in 1966. The name *Adams* appeared on various items through 1998. All types of tablewares and useful wares were made. Other pieces of Adams may be found listed under Flow Blue and Tea Leaf Ironstone.

Bowl, Adam's Rose, Rainbow, Red, Blue, Sponge, 1800s, 5 In.	182.00
Bowl, Gray Rabbit, Friends, Under Tree, 6 In.	21.00
Chamber Pot, Rose, Red Flowers, Green Leaves, 9 In.	91.00
Charger, Rabbitware, Frog Center, Adam's Rose Border, c.1870, 13 In.	1180.00
Coffeepot, Jeddo, Panel Gothic, Blue, White, 8 ¾ In.	345.00
Cup & Saucer, Chusan, Zigzag Border, Blossoms	17.00
Cup & Saucer, Cries Of London	35.00
Cup & Saucer, Lowestoft, Paneled	28.00
Gravy Boat, Underplate, Chusan	75.00
Plate, Bread & Butter, Chusan, Green Border, Trees, 6 ¼ In.	8.00
Plate, Dinner, Chusan, 10 ¼ In.	25.00
Plate, Rabbitware, Adam's Rose Center, Frog Border, Spatterware, c.1880, 9 In.	235.00
Plate, Rainbow, Scallop Edge, Concentric Color Bands, Spatterware, c.1830, 10 In.	176.00
Plate, Salad, Chusan, 8 ¼ In.	10.00
Platter, Adam's Rose, Flowers, Red, Green, Blue, Rabbit, Frog, Cabbage Border, 14 x 10 In.	375.00
Platter, Adam's Rose, Red, Sponge, c.1850, 10 ¼ x 13 ½ In.	516.00
Platter, Country Estate, Figures, Rounded Rectangle, Blue Transfer, 1800s, 19 x 14 ¾ In.	360.00
Platter, Empress, White, Octagonal, Oval, 11 ¾ x 8 ⅝ In.	15.00
Sugar, Lid, Adam's Rose, Black, Brown Bands, Red, Roses, Flared, 4 ¼ x 4 ¾ In.	59.00

ADVERTISING containers and products sold in the old country store are now all collectibles. These stores, with crackers in a barrel and a potbellied stove, are a symbol of an earlier, less hectic time. Listed here are many advertising items. Other similar pieces may be found under the product name, such as Planters Peanuts. We have tried to list items in logical places, so enameled tin dishes will be found under Graniteware, auto-related items in the Auto category, paper items in the Paper category, etc. Store fixtures, cases, signs, and other items that have no advertising as part of the decoration are listed in the Store category. The early Dr Pepper logo included a period after "Dr," but it was dropped in 1950. We list all Dr Pepper items without a period so they alphabetize together. For more prices, go to kovels.com.

Apron, Grocer's, Post Toasties Corn Flakes, White Cotton, Cereal Box Photo, 1930s, 22 x 35 In.	115.00
Apron, Wall Street Journal, Cloth, Canvas, 27 x 20 In.	132.00
Ashtray, Bowling Countertop Figure, Fan Fare, Gutter Gus, Engraved, c.1949	48.00
Ashtray, Nathan's Famous Hot Dogs, Restaurant, Cream & Gold, Logo On Apron, 6 ⅝ In.	160.00
Ashtray, RCA Nipper Dog, Cast Metal, Applied Pressed Brass, 1930s, 6 ½ x 6 ½ In.	158.00
Banner, Circus, Spidora Alive, Canvas, Leather, Snap Wyatt, Tampa, c.1945, 116 x 92 In. .....*Illus*	632.00
Banner, Hanging, Olympia Beer, Cloth, It's The Water, Olympia Brewing Co., 9 ½ x 12 In.	60.00
Barrel, Fred Neesemann's Enamel Paints, Wood, Black, Red, Gilt, c.1850, 12 ½ x 9 In.	6683.00
Barrel, Liggetts' Root Beer, Tap, Wood Lid, Claw Feet, 15 In.	715.00
Bench, Nunn-Bush Shoes, Foot Rest, Metal, 25 In.	36.00
Bin, Cherry Diamond Cigar, Tin, 17 ½ x 10 In.	275.00
Bin, Honest Scrap Tobacco, Tin, 2 Dogs Playing, 18 x 12 In.	1020.00
Blackboard, Kibbe's Candies, Horses, Wagon, Sheet Steel, Lithograph, 28 x 19 In.	201.00
Blotter, Hendrick Hudson Garage, N.Y., Car Shape, 1938 Calendar, Celluloid Holder, 8 x 3 In.	60.00
Books may be included in the Paper category.	
Bootjack, Use Musselman's Boot-Jack Plug Tobacco, Flowers, c.1890, 9 ½ In.	288.00
Bottles are listed in their own category.	
Bottle Openers are listed in their own category.	
Bowl, Cereal, Wheaties Premium, Milk Glass, Silhouettes Of Sports Stars, 1930s	45.00
Bowl, Quaker Oats, Quaker Character, Oats Design Border, Porcelain, 7 ½ In. ....*Illus*	55.00
Box, see also Box category.	
Box, Baltimore Biscuit Co., Wood, Painted Lettering, c.1910, 21 ½ x 13 In.	86.00
Box, Cereal, Cap'N Crunch, Shooting Cannon, Holding Sword, Prototype, c.1968, 9 x 12 ¾ In.	345.00
Box, Cereal, Wheaties, Musketeer Record, 78 RPM, Donald Duck's Song, 1956, 11 x 18 In.	175.00
Box, Display, Adam's Gum, Tutti Frutti, Cardboard, Glass Lift Lid, 9 ⅞ x 4 ¼ In. ....*Illus*	88.00
Box, Display, Castile Soap, Wood, Trademark Eagle, McKeone, Van Haagen & Co., c.1875, 11 x 4 In.	385.00
Box, Display, Kurly Kate Stainless Pot Cleaner, 24 Red Scrubbers, 1940s, 11 x 8 ¾ In.	295.00
Box, Great China Tea Co., Cardboard, Green Paper, Asian Symbols, Figures, c.1850, 8 x 8 In.	58.00
Box, Holiday Set, American Tobacco Co., 5 Packs Of Cigarettes, 1958, 10 ¼ x 8 ¼ In.	63.00
Box, Over-Sea Rolled Oats, Cardboard, Train, Plane, Bridge, Cylindrical, 1 ¼ Lb., 7 ⅜ x 4 In...*Illus*	330.00
Box, Rowntree Dairy Chocolates, Wood & Wire, Christmas Wrap, 1950s, 29 x 13 In.	225.00
Box, Super Suds Detergent, Suds For Dishes & Duds, Blue, White Letters, 1930, Lb.	20.00

Box, Watkins Pure Fruit Pectin, Housewife, Recipes, Unopened, 1920s, 3 ⅜ x 5 ⅛ In.................	45.00
Bucket, Candy, Underwood Talmage Co., Dayton, Ohio, Cardboard, 30 Lb., 12 x 13 In.....*Illus*	880.00
Cabinet, Ace Combs, Wood & Glass, Spins, Display, 11 x 14 In..	224.00
Cabinet, Display, Carter's, Ideal, Typewriter Tins, Oak, Decals, 10 ¼ x 12 ½ x 15 In.	275.00
Cabinet, Diamond Dyes, Children With Balloon, Embossed Tin, c.1911, 25 x 15 In.........*Illus*	896.00
Cabinet, Diamond Dyes, Governess, Children Playing, Fitted Interior, Wood, Tin, 29 ¾ x 23 In.	1560.00
Cabinet, Diamond Dyes, Washer Woman, Embossed Tin, 22 x 30 In.............................*Illus*	720.00
Cabinet, Dr. Daniels' Veterinary Medicines, Oak, Tin Litho Door, c.1900, 29 x 21 In.................	648.00
Cabinet, Harper & Cosgrove Amazon Spice, Tin, Countertop, Zanesville, Ohio, 24 x 13 In.......	294.00
Cabinet, Humphrey's Veterinary, Horse Head, Cardboard Door, Embossed, Wood Case, 33 In. .	6600.00
Cabinet, Putnam Fadeless Dyes, Tin, Monroe Chemical Co., Quincy, Ill., 19 x 15 In................	220.00
Cabinet, Sen-Sen Chewing Gum, 5 Cent, Door, Wood, Etched Glass, 30 x 16 x 14 In.	784.00
Cabinet, Spool, Clark's, Mahogany, 6 Drawers, Ruby Glass Inserts, 23 x 19 In........................	1116.00
Cabinet, Spool, Coats & Clark Sewing Thread, 6 Drawers, Bins, Thread Spools, Counter, 16 x 27 In.	71.00
Cabinet, Spool, Corticelli, Spool Silk, Curved Glass Front, Decal, Hardware, 21 x 18 x 16 In.....*Illus*	3600.00
Cabinet, Spool, J. & P. Coats' Spool Cotton, Maple, 6 Drawers, Logo Lithograph, 22 x 26 In.....	531.00
Cabinet, Spool, J. & P. Coats', Shape Of Horizontal Spool, 4 Drawers, Painted, 18 x 22 In.	420.00
Cabinet, Spool, Oak, Merrick's Six Cord, 15 ¼ x 22 ½ In.	240.00
Calendars are listed in their own category.	
Can, Kentucky Rifle Gunpowder, Paper Label, Hazard Powder Co., c.1865, Lb., 4 x 5 ½ In. *Illus*	112.00
Can, Reading's Original Quinlan's Cheese Sticks, Boy Logo, Round, Metal, 6 Lb.	59.00
Canisters, see introductory paragraph to Tins in this category.	
Cards are listed in the Card category.	
Carrier, Sealshipt, National Oyster Carrier Co., Porcelain, 1913, 20 ½ x 18 In........................	1980.00
Case, Display, Freihofer's Quality Cakes, Faux Mahogany, Paint, Sheet Metal, Glass, 28 x 15 In.	413.00
Case, Display, Krementz Collar Button, c.1920s, 11 ¼ In...	450.00
Case, Display, Nightingale Miniatures Cigar, Glass, Tin, 8 ½ x 8 ½ In..	60.00
Case, Display, Parker Fountain Pen, Oak, Etched Glass	168.00
Case, Display, Refill Pencils, A.W. Faber Castell, Silk Screen, 2 Tiers, Hinged Lid, 1930s, 2 x 7 x 14 In.	115.00
Case, Display, Sanford's Inks, Wood, Gingerbread Top, Glass Panels, Stencil, 34 In...................	995.00
Case, J.C. Primley's California Fruit & Pepsin Gum, Etched Curved Glass Front, 19 x 12 In.	540.00
Chair, Piedmont, Smoke The Cigarette Of Quality, Wood, Enameled Sign Back, 31 In.............	71.00
Change Receiver, see Tip Tray in this category.	
Charger, Buffalo Brewing Co., Sacramento, Round, Tin, Oak Frame, 31 In.	15400.00
Charger, Hodico Whiskey, Every Drop A Pleasure, Marcelle Portrait, Round, Tin, c.1910, 19 In.	770.00
Cigar Cutter, Blue Seal, Cast Iron, Brunhoff Mfg. Co., 9 x 6 ½ In.	358.00
Cigar Cutter, El Roi-Tan Perfect Cigars, Silvered Brass, Movable Blade, c.1913, 1 ⁵⁄₁₆ In.........	95.00
Cigar Cutter, Five Bro's Tobacco W'Ks, Cast Iron, 19 In..	90.00
Cigar Cutter, Harvester, Milwaukee, Wis., Fay Lewis & Bros. Co., Brunhoff Mfg. Co., Windup...*Illus*	1020.00
Cigar Cutter, Judge Howell E. Jackson, Cast Iron, Crane Factory Makers, 4 ¾ x 3 ½ In............	420.00
Cigar Cutter, La Cinceridad, Embossed, Iron, Nickel Plating, Brunhoff Mfg. Co., 9 x 7 In.	360.00
Cigar Cutter, Niles & Moser's Chancellor, Mild, Fragrant, Scrolled Cast Iron	173.00
Cigar Cutter, Opia, Smoker's Dream, Iron, Brunhoff Mfg. Patent 1902, 9 x 7 ½ In....................	1052.00
Cigar Cutter, Peerless Tobacco, Black Enamel, Cast Iron, Patent 1914, 16 x 7 ½ In..................	240.00
Cigar Cutter, Pointer's, 5 Cent, Cast Iron, North Western Novelty Co., 1909, 6 x 7 x 8 In.	330.00
Cigar Cutter, Que Placer Havana, Cast Iron, Brunhoff Mfg. Co., 1902, 6 x 8 ¾ In....................	358.00
Cigar Cutter, Robert Burns Cigars, Geo. L. Storm & Co., Cast Iron, Ornate, 1904	384.00
Cigar Cutter, Simon & Son Cigars, Iron, Embossed, Chrome Plated, 1914, 8 x 15 x 4 In...........	176.00
Cigar Cutter, Smoke Morey's Fat Hog Cigars, Pig, Standing, Rectangular Base	448.00
Clocks are listed in their own category.	
Container, Bassett's Egg Shampoo Cream, Egg Shape, Tin Lithograph, 1906, 2 ¾ x 1 ¾ In. *Illus*	123.00
Cooler, Gnome Beverages Ice Cold, Oak, Paint, Metal, c.1850, 32 x 32 In.	325.00
Cooler, Picnic, Yellow & Red Metal, Spout, 18 x 16 In.	196.00
Cuspidor, Red Skin Chewing Tobacco, Brass, Flared Rim, c.1970	40.00
Dispenser, Cardinal Cherry, Birds, Leaves, Red, Green, Round, Ceramic, c.1920, 9 In.	5700.00
Dispenser, Chocolat Menier, Parisian Kiosk Replica, 6-Sided, Tin, France, c.1895, 10 In.........	2576.00
Dispenser, Diamond Matches, Books, One Cent, Round Top	364.00
Dispenser, Drink Hires, It Is Pure, Porcelain, Cinched Waist, Raspberry Pump	448.00
Dispenser, Hires Rootbeer, Ugly Kid, Urn, Blue Trim, c.1900, 15 ½ In..............................*Illus*	39675.00
Dispenser, Ideal Sanitary Toothpicks, Take One, Press Bar, Rectangular, c.1926......................	1200.00
Dispenser, Matches, Baking Powder, Best Up To Date, Iron, Hamilton Brass Mfg. Co.......*Illus*	1008.00
Dispenser, Nesbitt Fruit Products, Chrome, Glass, Attaches To Counter.................................	140.00
Dispenser, Orange Crush, Round, Ceramic, 1920s	660.00
Dispenser, Paper Cup, Vortex Cups, Aluminum, Glass Tube, Wall Mount	164.00
Dispenser, Paper Roll, Barber Shop, Scroll, Round Base, Cast Iron, Counter, 1920s................	280.00

Advertising, Cabinet, Diamond Dyes, Washer Woman, Embossed Tin, 22 x 30 In.
$720.00

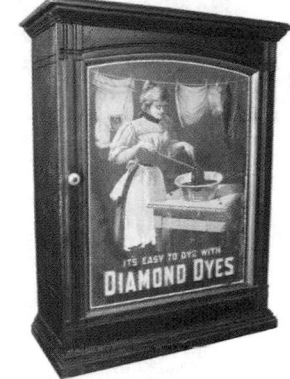

Showtime Auction Services

Advertising, Cabinet, Spool, Corticelli, Spool Silk, Curved Glass Front, Decal, Hardware, 21 x 18 x 16 In.
$3,600.00

Showtime Auction Services

Advertising, Can, Kentucky Rifle Gunpowder, Paper Label, Hazard Powder Co., c.1865, Lb., 4 x 5 ½ In.
$112.00

Past Tyme Pleasures

Advertising, Cigar Cutter, Harvester, Milwaukee, Wis., Fay Lewis & Bros. Co., Brunhoff Mfg. Co., Windup
$1,020.00

Victorian Casino Antiques

A

Advertising, Container, Bassett's Egg Shampoo Cream, Egg Shape, Tin Lithograph, 1906, 2 ¾ x 1 ¾ In. $123.00

Past Tyme Pleasures

Advertising, Dispenser, Hires Rootbeer, Ugly Kid, Urn, Blue Trim, c.1900, 15 ½ In. $39,675.00

James D. Julia Auctioneers

Advertising, Dispenser, Matches, Baking Powder, Best Up To Date, Iron, Hamilton Brass Mfg. Co. $1,008.00

Victorian Casino Antiques

Advertising, Dispenser, Ward's Orange Crush, Figural, Pump, c.1920, 8 ½ x 13 In. $805.00

James D. Julia Auctioneers

Dispenser, Ward's Lemon Crush, Lemon Shaped, Pump, Porcelain, c.1920, 10 ½ x 13 ½ In. ...	1093.00
Dispenser, Ward's Lime Crush, Round, 1920s, 12 In.	4500.00
Dispenser, Ward's Orange Crush, Figural, Pump, c.1920, 8 ½ x 13 In. ....*Illus*	805.00
Dispenser, Ward's Orange Crush, Orange With Blossoms, Glazed China, c.1900, 7 ½ x 9 ½ In.	291.00
Display, 20 Mule Team Borax Soap Chips Box, Pacific Coast Borax Co., 14 x 20 In.	1210.00
Display, B-1 Lemon-Lime, Tin, Embossed, 28 x 8 In.	200.00
Display, Blue Crown Spark Plugs, Tin, Get More Pep, Save Gas, Counter, 1950s, 16 x 10 In.	450.00
Display, Boye Safety Pins, Guarded Coil, Rust Proof, Stepped, Wood	224.00
Display, Buss Fuses, Why Be Helpless When Fuses Blow?, Tin Litho, 1950s, 9 ⅝ x 6 x 4 In.	110.00
Display, Carter's Ideal Typewriter Ribbons & Carbon Paper, Oak, 4 Drawers, 10 x 12 ½ In.	275.00
Display, Carter's Ideal Typewriter Ribbons & Carbon Paper, Wood, 3 Shelves, Drawer.............	180.00
Display, Carter's Inks, Oak Frame, Stenciled, Hinged Door, 1890, 21 x 14 In. ....*Illus*	644.00
Display, Christian Dior, Stylized Head, On Gloves, Plaster, 1950s, 22 In.	660.00
Display, Clutch Fish Hook Store, Tubes, Hooks, Green Paint, Metal, Thomas Jolley, 12 x 9 In. ..	649.00
Display, Drink Nochal Kola, Bottle Shape, Tin, Embossed, 24 x 8 In.	118.00
Display, Dubonnet, Man, Glass In Hand, Striped Awning, Paint, Wood, 1950s, 12 ¼ In.............	510.00
Display, Franco American Coffee, Blond Woman, Coffee Can, Cardboard	600.00
Display, Hand With Bottle, Leinenkugel's Beer, Here's The Best In The House, Plaster..............	112.00
Display, Hand, Whistle Soda, Black, Cast Iron, 1930s, 10 ½ In.	720.00
Display, Hills Bros. Coffee, Die Cut, Easel Back, 1931, 19 ½ x 20 ¾ In.	303.00
Display, Hires Root Beer, Barrel, Tap, Paw Feet, Counter, 23 ½ x 13 ½ In.	450.00
Display, Hobner Harmonica, Wood, Wind-Up, Hand Crank, Numbered, Tapered, 11 x 32 In....	510.00
Display, Light Bulb, Mazda Lamps, General Electric, Papier-Mache, 31 In. ....*Illus*	390.00
Display, Light Bulbs, Edison Mazda Lamps, Metal Rack, Counter...................................	1568.00
Display, Light Bulbs, Westinghouse Mazda Lamps, Do You Need Lamps, Counter, Metal, Glass	1344.00
Display, Lowenbrau, Munich, Lion, Sitting With Beer Bottle, Made In W. Germany, 14 In........	137.00
Display, Lucky Strike, Hardboard, Die Cut, Red, Yellow, 23 x 29 In.	550.00
Display, Munyon's Homoeopathic, Tin Litho, American Art Works, c.1900, 11 x 14 In. ....*Illus*	316.00
Display, Nebraska Seed Co., Omaha, Neb., Tangier Brand, Seed Packets, Decal, 28 ¾ x 45 In.....*Illus*	840.00
Display, Old Valley Whiskey Bottle, Golden Amber, Sloping Double Collar, 25 In....................	1170.00
Display, OTC Truss, Doctor, Holding Surgical Device, 1930s, 25 In.	150.00
Display, Phillip's Shoe Repair, Man, Holding Heel, Paint, Composition, 12 In......................	120.00
Display, Pixie-Dixon, Soda Fountain, Flavors, Bottles & Pumps, White & Blue, Counter	672.00
Display, Plessis Liquor, Bottle Body, Legs, Cane, Hat, 1950s, 12 In.	1080.00
Display, Princess Youth, Undergarment Form, Composition, c.1950, 32 In.	300.00
Display, Ringling Bros. & Barnum & Bailey Circus, Die Cut, Standee, 1944, 17 x 22 In............	380.00
Display, Store, Confections, Asian Man, Canister, Papier-Mache, Paint, c.1915, 28 In..............	2280.00
Display, Tape Dispenser, Alka-Seltzer, Metal, Counter, c.1950s....................................*Illus*	140.00
Display, Truck, Old Gold Cigarette, 2-Sided Picture Of Cigarettes, 1930s, 4 x 11 In................	175.00
Display, Whitman's Chocolates, Santa, With Sign, Die Cut, Standee, Easel Back, c.1939, 26 x 31 In.	158.00
Display, Window, Fairbanks Tar Soap, 5 Cents, Die Cut, 35 x 59 In. ....*Illus*	9600.00
Display, Winston, Cigarette Pack Shape, 2-Sided, Cigarettes Sold Here, Tin, Red & White, 17 x 34 In.	112.00
Dolls are listed in their own category.	
Door Pull, Richardson Root Beer, Porcelain, Chrome Handle, c.1945, 12 In., 3 Piece	570.00
Door Push, Canada Dry Spur, Embossed Tin Litho, Big 12 Oz. Bottle, 5 Cents, 1950s, 3 x 9 In.	135.00
Door Push, Rainbow Is Good Bread, Oval, Blue, White, Red, Yellow, Steel, c.1950, 3 x 26 In...	224.00
Door Push, Star Weekly, On Sale Here, Red, White, Porcelain, 10 x 2 In.	198.00
Dress, Souper Dress, Andy Warhol, Campbell's Soup Campaign, Cellulose Paper, 1969, 38 In...*Illus*	1565.00
Fans are listed in their own category.	
Fan Pull, Ruhf's Cigars, Man, Holding Open Umbrella, Cardboard, Die Cut, 2 x 3 In...............	110.00
Figure, ABC Man On Phone, By Microphone, White Dinner Jacket, Plaster, 1930s, 11 In..........	240.00
Figure, Airway Suspenders, Man, Mechanical, Composition, Wood, 1940s, 21 In.	1140.00
Figure, Alligator Raincoats, Man, Coat & Hat, Flat Back, Carved Wood, 1930s, 18 In.	1440.00
Figure, Barbisio Menswear, Man's Head, Hat Model, Composition, Wood Base, 14 In.	90.00
Figure, Borden, Elsie The Cow, Composition, 1940s, 8 x 10 In......................................*Illus*	316.00
Figure, Boston Terrier, Bryant Pup, Bryant Gas Heating Co., Papier-Mache, 20 x 10 ¾ In........	384.00
Figure, Bostonians Men Shoe, Man, Metal, Wood Base, c.1950, 17 In.	1440.00
Figure, Boy, Tyrolean, Swinging From Rope, Wood, Paint, Germany, c.1890, 35 In.................	420.00
Figure, BPR Whiskies, Man In Tux, Holding Sign, Rubber Composition, 1930s, 15 ½ In............	960.00
Figure, Buxton Wallets, Tuxedo, Key Holder, Wallet, Paint, Wood, 1930s, 12 ½ In...............	480.00
Figure, Climatic Raincoat Man, Hat, Holding Book, Paint, Composition, 1940s, 17 ½ In...........	510.00
Figure, Cora Vermouth, Miss Cora, Green Dress, Mask, Hard Rubber, 18 ½ In.....................	390.00
Figure, Corn Plaster Man, Mechanical, Papier-Mache, Germany, 1920s, 26 In......................	2700.00
Figure, Der Darotti-Mehr White Prince Tea, Indian Carrying Plate, Ceramic, 1930s, 12 In......	90.00
Figure, Energizer Batteries, Bunny, With Drum, Plastic, Counter, 20 In............................	58.00
Figure, Enro Shirts, Man, Standing, Shirt, Tie, Composition, 1940s, 16 ½ In......................	240.00

Figure, Esquire Man, Bust, Handlebar Mustache, Navy Uniform, Plaster, 19 In.		1920.00
Figure, Esquire Man, Esky In Summerwear, Hat, Jacket, Composition, Rubber, 1940s, 24 In.		960.00
Figure, Esquire Man, Hat, Suit, Coat, Eyeglasses, 1940s, 24 In.		19200.00
Figure, Fakir Nail Man, Paint, Papier-Mache, 1920s, 25 In.		1320.00
Figure, Florsheim Shoes Man, Putting On Shoe, Head Rocks, Clockwork, c.1925, 29 In.		510.00
Figure, Fruit Of The Loom, Woman, Nightgown, Composition, 49 In.		510.00
Figure, Gossard Girdle Girl, Kneeling Woman, Composition, Wood Base, 1930s, 17 In.		1080.00
Figure, Heinz 57, Tomato Head, Top Hat, Hard Rubber, Painted, 5 ¾ In. ....*Illus*		165.00
Figure, Heinz's Tomato Ketchup, Bottle, Glass, 26 ½ x 6 ¼ In. ....*Illus*		2310.00
Figure, Hills Bros. Coffee, Mechanical, Turbaned Man, Pours Coffee, Drinks, 1950s, 30 In.		660.00
Figure, Hindelang, Girl, German Folk Dress, Paint, Plaster, 1940s, 21 In.		120.00
Figure, Hollywood Vassarette Girl, Red Gloves, Shoes, Plastic, Hartland, 1950s, 8 ½ In.		780.00
Figure, I Saw It In Esquire, Mascot Man, Dark Suit, Hat, Composition, 1940s, 8 ½ In.		540.00
Figure, Imperial Corset, Woman, Hands On Hips, Plaster, c.1900, 21 In.		510.00
Figure, Ingersoll, Man, Straw Hat, White Coat, Composition, Electric, 39 ½ In.		180.00
Figure, Jacquin's Cordials, Man, Bug-Eyed, Tuxedo, Top Hat, Bottles, Plaster, 1940s, 15 In.		180.00
Figure, Joe Camel Cigarette, Torso In Suit, Arms Crossed, Plastic, 1980s, 20 In.		390.00
Figure, Keen's Corn Cure, Foot, Open Mouth, Composition, King Kole Tag, 18 In.		2280.00
Figure, Komorin Tea, Man, Seated, Conical Hat, Paint, Papier-Mache, 29 ½ In.		2040.00
Figure, Koroseal Raincoat Woman, Removable Coat, Composition, 1940s, 16 ½ In.		390.00
Figure, Kyanize Heat Resistant Radiator, Boy, Standing By Radiator, Plaster, 1930s, 10 In.		90.00
Figure, Mannequin, Singer Sewing Machine Co., Rubber, Painted Hair, Jointed Arms, 1949, 12 In.		75.00
Figure, Martel Cognac Man, Brandy Glass Face, Cigarette, Toasting, Ceramic, 1950s, 10 In.		180.00
Figure, Michelin Man, Seated, Plaster, 1930s, 13 In.		840.00
Figure, National Tailor, Man, Tuxedo, Top Hat, Embossed Sides, 1930s, 30 In.	840.00 to 1440.00	
Figure, Nipper, Dog, Seated, Cocked Ear, RCA, Paint, Composition, 36 In.		510.00
Figure, Nipper, Painted, 39 In.		259.00
Figure, Nipper, RCA Dog, Molded Resin, Sticker, 18 In. ....*Illus*		288.00
Figure, Nipper, RCA, Victrola, Papier-Mache, Glass Eyes, Label, Old King Cole Co., 1920s, 42 In.		2178.00
Figure, Old Crow, Wearing Tux, Top Hat, Plastic, 1950s, 31 In.		150.00
Figure, Palm Beach Menswear Tailored By Goodall, Man, Composition, 1930s, 18 In		1440.00
Figure, Palm Beach Menswear, Man, Seated, White Suit, Composition, 11 In.		1320.00
Figure, Palm Beach Menswear, Man, White Suit, Composition, 1930s, 18 ½ In.		1200.00
Figure, Philip Morris, Johnny Goes Places, Bellhop, Suitcase, Composition, c.1938, 13 In.		900.00
Figure, Rabhor Pajamas, Man, Bathrobe, Ascot, Paint, Composition, 1930s, 27 ½ In.		1200.00
Figure, Railway Express Serviceman, Composition, Wood Base, 1930s, 19 In.		1320.00
Figure, Reddy Kilowatt, Clear Red Lucite With Glow In Dark Head, Hands & Feet, 1950s, 5 In.		195.00
Figure, Reddy Kilowatt, Mazda Lamps, Holding Lamps, Porcelain, 38 In.		978.00
Figure, Ronald McDonald, Plastic, Stand-Up, Flange, 66 In.		180.00
Figure, Ronald McDonald, Waving, Wood, Painted, Pole Mounted, Cone Base, 78 In.		403.00
Figure, Saxon Slacks, Man, Standing, Composition, 1950s, 15 ½ In.		240.00
Figure, Schrank Nurse, Uniform, Cap & Cape, 28 ½ In.		570.00
Figure, Shar-Loo Women's Fashions, Woman, Gold, Cream, Composition, 1940s, 25 In.		1200.00
Figure, Shell Butagas Mascot, Gas Tank Body, Spring Arms, Legs, Metal, 1940s, 15 In.		1080.00
Figure, Silver Top Gum, Wood, Boy, Holding Gum Packages, 9 x 9 x 6 In.		412.00
Figure, Stanley Tool Man, Holding Tape, Hand To Head, Composition, Paint, 1960s, 18 In.		210.00
Figure, Stork, Holding Sign, Castle Hall Twin Cigars, Papier-Mache, 25 In.		390.00
Figure, Stow-A-Way Rain Coats, Man, Tan Suit, Holding Packet, Hard Rubber, 1940s, 17 In.		150.00
Figure, Van Heusen Shirts, Man, Pointing, 1950s, 16 ¾ In.		360.00
Figure, Wayfarer Raincoat Couple, Papier-Mache, Plastic, Paint, 1930s, 25 In.		2700.00
Figure, White Eagle, Gas Station, Cast Aluminum, 34 In.		1560.00
Figure, Willy Wirehand, Midwest Gas & Electric Mascot, Vinyl, Wood Base, 13 In.		780.00
Figure, Window, Shoes By Wienberg, Man, Seated, Plaster, 1930s, 23 ½ In.		1800.00
Figure, Wolverine Robes, Woman, Short Bathrobe, Paint, Composition, 1930s, 25 ½ In.		660.00
Firecrackers, Gorilla, 50 Pack, Made In China, 6 ½ x 3 ½ In.		1560.00
Floaty Pen, Airco Welding & Gas, Welding Tank, Secretary Pen Co., Union, N.J., 5 ¼ In.		45.00
Flour Receiver, Telescope, Marked 50 Lb. & 100 Lb., 40 x 18 ½ In. ....*Illus*		2040.00
Game, Ronald McDonald Head, Resin, Multicolor Hair, Target...................*Illus*		120.00
Globe, We Recommend Chicago Solvay Cole Fuel, Milk Glass, Round, 13 In.		660.00
Goodyear Lifeguards, Porcelain, Diamond Shape, 2-Sided, Blue, Orange, 27 x 47 In.		660.00
Handbag, Cut Plug Tobacco, Tin, Handle, 7 x 6 x 4 ¼ In. ....*Illus*		83.00
Hatchet, Karadam Tobacco, Iron Head, Wood Handle, 16 In.		510.00
Horse Tether, Amex Co., Cast Iron, 7 ¾ x 3 In.		330.00
Indian, Figural, Plaster, Cigar Counter Statue, Havana, 18 x 28 In.		660.00
Jar, Chico's, 5 Cent, Spanish Peanuts, Yellow & Black, Glass, Tin Lid		532.00
Jar, Thompson's Double Malted Milk, Porcelain, T Logo Crest, 1920s, 5 ¼ x 10 ¼ In.		190.00

Advertising, Display, Carter's Inks, Oak Frame, Stenciled, Hinged Door, 1890, 21 x 14 In.
$644.00

Norman C. Heckler & Company

The Flying Red Horse

Mobil gasoline's flying red horse logo, called Pegasus, changed directions. The sign introduced in 1931 had the head at the left when you viewed it. After 1965 the head was to the right. But many reproductions of the sign used the head-left form, which can confuse collectors.

Advertising, Display, Light Bulb, Mazda Lamps, General Electric, Papier-Mache, 31 In.
$390.00

Victorian Casino Antiques

Advertising, Display, Munyon's Homoeopathic, Tin Litho, American Art Works, c.1900, 11 x 14 In.
$316.00

Hake's Americana & Collectibles

TIP
Avoid shopping in stores with unpriced items. If you look eager or affluent, you may be charged more.

Advertising, Display, Nebraska Seed Co., Omaha, Neb., Tangier Brand, Seed Packets, Decal, 28 ¾ x 45 In. $840.00

Showtime Auction Services

Advertising, Display, Tape Dispenser, Alka-Seltzer, Metal, Counter, c.1950s $140.00

Victorian Casino Antiques

Advertising, Display, Window, Fairbanks Tar Soap, 5 Cents, Die Cut, 35 x 59 In. $9,600.00

Showtime Auction Services

6

Keg, Barrel, Hagerstown Br'G Co., Wood, Iron Bands, Blue Paint, c.1890, 16 ¼ In.	173.00
Keg, Birch-O Draft Style Birch Beer, Wood Keg, Oak, Staved, Iron Hoops, Plug, Spigot, 14 x 14 In.	118.00
Keg, Dickinson's Witch Hazel, Blue Paint, 21 ½ x 14 In.	385.00
Label, Cigar Box, Arizona, Indian, Profile, Teepee, Sample, 9 x 6 ¾ In.	165.00
Label, Cigar Box, Cosmopolitan, Saloon, Black, White, J.C. Harrison & Sons, 9 x 7 In.	83.00
Label, Cigar Box, Fire King, Pumper, Rescue, Lithograph, Schmidt & Co., c.1895, 7 x 4 ½ In.	138.00
Label, Cigar Box, Golf Nugget, Prospector, 6 ⅝ x 4 ⅝ In.	165.00
Label, Cigar Box, Great Catch, Woman, Man, Fishing, O.L. Schwencke Litho Co., 8 x 5 ½ In.	193.00
Label, Cigar Box, Happy John Salesman Sample, c.1890, 9 x 12 In.	90.00
Label, Cigar Box, Key West Flyer, O.L. Schwencke, Land, Seas Scene, Lithograph, 9 x 5 ⅞ In.	110.00
Label, Cigar Box, Manila Rose, Woman, Lithograph, Geo. Harris & Sons, 8 x 6 In.	55.00
Label, Cigar Box, McCormick's Harvester, Field Scene, Factory Proof, 10 x 6 ¾ In.	120.00
Label, Cigar Box, Midland Trail, Standard Of The West, Shield Shape, J.W. Sink Co., 4 ½ In.	60.00
Label, Cigar Box, Our Brownies, Color Lithograph, O.L. Schwencke, 8 ⅛ x 6 In.	330.00
Label, Cigar Box, Our Fire Laddies, Fires Scene, Horses, Wagons, Litho, Kruger & Braun, 8 x 5 In.	240.00
Label, Cigar Box, Pedigree, Horse Head, Gold Embossed, Geo. Harris & Sons, 8 x 4 ¾ In.	28.00
Label, Cigar Box, Red Boot, 7 ¼ x 5 ⅜ In.	165.00
Label, Cigar Box, Seal Of The Golden West, California Symbols, 1901, 7 ⅜ x 5 ¼ In.	248.00
Label, Cigar Box, The Alerts, Color Lithograph, Geo. Harris & Sons, 6 ⅝ x 3 ¾ In.	120.00
Label, Express Cigar, Witsch & Schmitt Litho Co., 1899, 7 ⅜ x 4 ⅝ In. ....*Illus*	193.00
Label, Firecrackers, Anchor Brand, 50-Pack, 6 In.	30.00
Label, Firecrackers, Animal Crackers, Light Their Tails & Run, 5 ⅝ x 3 ½ In.	270.00
Label, Firecrackers, Black Prince, 20-Pack, E-Wo Yeung Hong, Chinese, 1941, 10 ⅝ x 6 ½ In. ....*Illus*	360.00
Label, Firecrackers, Buffalo Brand, 60-Pack, Made In Macau, 7 ½ x 3 ¼ In.	570.00
Label, Firecrackers, Carnival Scene, Merry-Go-Round Brand, Chinese, 3 ¼ x 2 ½ In.	3000.00
Label, Firecrackers, China Bride, Hong Kong, 16-Pack, 3 ¼ x 2 In.	1080.00
Label, Firecrackers, Columbia Brand, Statue Of Liberty, Chinese, 1937, 5 ⅜ x 3 ⅜ In.	2040.00
Label, Firecrackers, Cowboy 24-Pack, Contents, E-Wo Yeung Hong, Chinese, 3 ⅜ x 3 In. .*Illus*	180.00
Label, Firecrackers, Crax Boy, 50-Pack, Chan Tai Kee, Chinese, 3 ⅛ x 3 In. ....*Illus*	330.00
Label, Firecrackers, Crown Brand, 16-Pack, Made In China, 3 x 2 In.	780.00
Label, Firecrackers, Dwarf Ladycrackers, Seven Dwarfs, Chinese, 1 ¼ x 4 ⅜ In.	1200.00
Label, Firecrackers, Foxhound Brand, Dog, 8-Pack, Made In China, 2 x 1 ⅝ In.	1560.00
Label, Firecrackers, Giant Panda Brand, Bear, 50-Pack, 6-Sided, 2 ⅜ In.	240.00
Label, Firecrackers, Lobster Brand, 50-Pack, Made In Macau, 6 x 3 In.	390.00
Label, Firecrackers, Peacock Brand, 60-Pack, 8 ⅜ x 3 ⅜ In.	720.00
Label, Firecrackers, Raven & Bell, Wing Lee Hong, Chinese, 3 ¼ x 2 ⅝ In. ....*Illus*	150.00
Label, Firecrackers, Skipper Crackers, 32-Pack, Consigned Sales Co., Macau, 4 ¼ x 3 ⅛ In.. *Illus*	1200.00
Label, Firecrackers, Spirit Of 76, 20-Pack, Pensick & Gordon, Chinese, 3 x 2 ⅜ In..........*Illus*	210.00
Label, Firecrackers, Squirrel, 20-Pack, Made In Macau, 3 x 2 ½ In.	390.00
Label, Firecrackers, Tin Shing, Boy & Girl Shaking Hands, Chinese, 5 ⅛ x 4 ⅞ In. ....*Illus*	270.00
Label, Red Rooster California's Best, Paper, Glass, 10 x 10 In.	283.00
Lamps are listed in the Lamp category.	
Lantern, None Such, Halloween, Patriotic, Tin, Reverse Painted Glass, 1900, 7 x 7 x 17 In.....*Illus*	6900.00
Ledger Marker, Queen Insurance Co., Tin Lithograph, 12 x 3 In.	187.00
Lunch Boxes are also listed in their own category.	
Mason's Blacking, Box, 1800s, 2 ¾ x 11 ¾ In.	59.00
Menu, Bob's Big Boy, Cardboard, 1961	196.00
Mileage Meter, Holiday Inn, Miles To Cities, Plastic, Willard C. George, 1950s, 7 x 10 In.	750.00

Advertising mirrors of all sizes are listed here. Pocket mirrors range in size from 1 ½ to 5 inches in diameter. Most of these mirrors were given away as advertising promotions and include the name of the company in the design.

Mirror, Acme Harvester, Farmer On Binder, Horses, Celluloid, Whitehead & Hoag, c.1900, 2 ⅛ In.	316.00
Mirror, Buckeye Fence, 4 Quadrants, Women Dressed For 4 Seasons, 2 ⅛ In.	221.00
Mirror, Cash Your Checks At Happy Bill's Grill, Nude Woman, Black & White, Oval, c.1900, 2 ¾ In.	141.00
Mirror, Dr. Van Dyke's Holland Bitters, Headless Body, Tan, Brown, 1 ½ In.	78.00
Mirror, Drink Golden Grain Belt Beer, Hold To Light, Woman, Flowers, Tin Rim, Pocket, 1 ⅞ In.. *Illus*	158.00
Mirror, Falcon Bee Supplies, Stenciled, Painted, c.1910, 9 x 9 In.	207.00
Mirror, Fleischmann's Yeast, Horse, Wagon, Pocket, 1 ¾ In.	121.00
Mirror, Good For 10 Cents In Trade, F.S. Pattridge, Round, Photo, Young Woman, c.1900, 2 ¼ In.	285.00
Mirror, Hires Root Beer, Woman, Put Roses In Your Cheeks, Celluloid, c.1910, 2 ⅞ In.	313.00
Mirror, Old Manse, Canadian Sap Maple Syrup, Celluloid, 2 ⅛ In. ....*Illus*	605.00
Mirror, Raphael Beck Exposition, Brass, 1901, 1 ¾ In.	98.00
Mirror, Stephenson Union Suits, Gymnasts, Celluloid, 2 ⅞ x 1 ¾ In..................*Illus*	935.00

Mirror, Wheat Bitters, Cherub On Cart With Bottle, Tan, Black, Blue Border, 2 In.	101.00
Nodder, K-C Pistons, Let Casey Go To Bat For You, 1960s, 7 In.	240.00
Nut Cup, Cream Dove Brand Salted Peanuts, Tin Litho, 2 ⅛ x 2 ¼ In. ....*Illus*	220.00
Pails are also listed in the Lunch Box category.	
Pail, Albany Pressure Grease, Albany Lubricating Compound, Tin Lithograph, 5 Lb., 8 x 6 In.....*Illus*	77.00
Pail, Brotherhood Tobacco, Orange, Black, Handle, Lunch, 7 ½ x 4 In.	90.00
Pail, Cookie, Sunshine Biscuit Inc., Red, White & Blue, Pictures Cookies, c.1950, 11 Oz..........	70.00
Pail, Country Club Kentucky Long Cut Tobacco, Handle, Scotten Tobacco Co., 7 x 5 In.	90.00
Pail, Lovell & Covel Co., Hard Candy, Colonial Scenes, Tin Lithograph, 2 ⅞ x 2 ⅞ In.	143.00
Pail, Ojibwa Fine Cut Chewing Tobacco, Indian Brave, Scotten-Dillon Co., 6 ¼ x 5 ½ In.	270.00
Pail, Old Soldier Tobacco, Union Soldier, Goodrich & Co., Milwaukee, 6 x 5 ½ In.	185.00
Pail, Squirrel Brand Peanut Butter, Bail Handle, Image Of Squirrel, Orange, Tin, 1920s, Lb. ..	175.00
Pail, Squirrel Brand Peanut Butter, Squirrel, Eating Peanut, Red, Yellow Black, Tin, 3 Lb.	715.00
Pail, Wilson's Peanut Butter, Nursery Rhyme Images, Tin Lithograph, Handle, 3 ⅛ x 3 ⅝ In.....*Illus*	440.00
Pin, Comfort Soap, Save The Wrappers, It's Allright, Youngster, Missing Teeth, c.1900, 1 ¾ In.	460.00
Pin, Convention, Ohio Hardware Assn., Frog On Lily Pad, Celluloid, c.1899, 1 ¾ In.	144.00
Pin, Dent's Dog Remedies, Pair Of Setters, Shaded Black & White, Round, c.1898	201.00
Pin, Egg-O-See, Figural, Resembles Product Package, Aluminum, Early 1900s, 1 ¾ In.	63.00
Pin, Emergency Fuse Holder, Whitbread & Hoag, Back Paper, 1 ¼ In.	69.00
Pin, Farmall Tractioneer, Tractor, Round, Red, White, Black, 1930s, 2 In.	105.00
Pin, Filmore East, Rock Venue, Yellow, Green Lettering, Bill Graham, 1968-71, 2 ⅛ In.	94.00
Pin, Johnson's Axle Grease, Girl, Dog, Paper Clip, Celluloid, Kishwaukee, Ill., 2 ¼ x 1 ¾ In.	69.00
Pin, King Tomato Filler, Early Canning Machine, W&H Backpaper, 1 ¾ In.	71.00
Pin, Kis-Me-Gum, Stylish Woman Logo, White, Red Checkerboard, 1920s, ⅞ In.	52.00
Pin, Mitchell & Co., Horse Drawn Hearse, Ingersoll, Ontario, 1 ¼ In.	190.00
Pin, Nabisco, I Signed Up, Boy In Rain Jacket & Hat, Holding Savings Bond, 1 ¼ In.	25.00
Pin, Oz, Department Store, Your Dollars Will Work Magic In Hecht Month, 1939, 1 ¼ In.	252.00
Pin, P.B. Ale, Oh Be Jolly, Scary Clown, Blue Ground, W&H Backpaper, c.1912....................	101.00
Pin, Pyramid Soap Powder, Multicolor Egyptian Scene, W&H Backpaper, c.1900, 1 ¾ In.	70.00
Pin, Red Indian Cut Plug, The Finest Yet, Pack Of Cigarettes, Indian Chief, c.1900, 1 ¾ In.	155.00
Pin, Superb Farm Equipment, Advance Thresher Co., Oval, Knight, Holding Banner, 1 In.	158.00
Pin, Vote For Col. Sanders, Blue & White, Portrait, Round, 1972, 1 ½ In.	49.00
Pin, Welcome Home Wright Brothers, Compliments, James M. Cox, 1 ¾ In.	5750.00
Pin, WIIK Radio, Good Guys, I'm For The Monkees, Cleveland, Tin Litho, 1960s, 2 In.	52.00
Pin, Yellow Kid, Close Shave, No. 81, Celluloid, 1 ¼ In.	54.00
Pin, Yellow Kid, Yeller Dress, Harp, No. 28, Celluloid, 1 ¼ In.	17.00
Plaque, Admiration Cigars, Plaster, Multicolor, 15 x 11 In.	282.00
Plaque, Face, Early Sensation Cigar, Smiling, Winking, Composition, Chain, 9 In.	360.00
Plaque, Fire Insurance, Friendship, Inst. Augst. 18th, 1796, Bronze, Oval, 8 x 11 In.	1098.00
Plaque, Whitman's Chocolates, Wilson's Pharmacy, Green, Imperial Brass Co., 21 x 5 In........	259.00
Plate, El Gallo Cigars, Tin, Cockerel In Center, Chromolitho, Vienna Art, 10 In.	81.00
Plate, Farrel, Herring & Co., Safe Maker's, Brass, Marked May 18th 1852, 7 x 5 In, ...	295.00
Plug Cutter, Drummond's Good Luck Tobacco, Cast Iron, 16 x 2 ½ In.	94.00
Poster, Hood's Sarsaparilla, Woman, Red Hair, Toasting, William Bradley, 1896, 41 x 26 In....	2600.00
Poster, Horse Sense, Stewart Clipping Machine, Horse Looking At Billboard, Lithograph, 24 x 18 In.	118.00
Poster, Little Giant Mower & Reaper, 4 Pictures, Graham, Emlen & Passmore, 25 ½ x 20 ½ In.	36.00
Rack, Bissell Carpet Sweeper, Oak, Cyco Ball Bearings, 48 In...	504.00
Rack, Dr. Scholl's Zino Pads, Tin, 2 Drawers...	112.00
Rack, National Biscuit Company, Oak, 4 Shelves, 55 x 46 x 10 In.......................................	168.00
Record Holder, Nipper, RCA Dog, Cast Iron	25.00
Ring, Kool-Aid, Treasure Hunt, Silver Luster, Text, Round, 1940..	94.00
Rug, Old Dutch Cleanser, Store Promotion, Woman, Stick, Yellow, 1930s, 17 x 29 In.............	95.00
Salt & Pepper Shakers are listed in their own category.	
Scales are listed in their own category.	
Shade, Old Dutch Cleanser, Paper, Cardboard, c.1920, 6 ½ In.	120.00
Shoehorn, St. Mungo Mfg. Co., Golf Ball, Golfer, Celluloid, 4 ¾ In.	110.00
Shoehorn, W.L. Douglas, World's Greatest Shoemaker, Tin Litho, 4 x 1 ⅝ In. ....*Illus*	99.00
Showcase, 20 Mule Team, Model, Wood, Lucite, 45 x 7 x 5 ½ In..	220.00
Sign, 7Up Float, Bottles, Glasses, Frame, c.1960, 34 x 21 In.	71.00
Sign, 7Up, Orange, Rolled Edges, Black, White, Porcelain, 12 x 14 In.	148.00
Sign, 7Up, Your Fresh Up, Hand Holding Bottle, Green, Tin, Stout, c.1946, 32 x 56 In.	920.00
Sign, 20 Mule Team Borax, Out Of Death Valley, Wagon Train, Paper, Frame, 15 x 39 In.	443.00
Sign, A & W Root Beer Ice Cold, Round, Red, Tan, Tin, 35 In.	502.00
Sign, A. Scheffman's, Butcher, 2-Sided, 3 Sections, Steer Head, Banners, 35 x 46 In.	41300.00
Sign, Abingdon Hotel, New York, Tin, Lithograph, Frame, c.1910, 22 ¼ x 28 ½ In.	1573.00
Sign, Ace In The Hole Saloon & Gambling Room, Wood, Painted, Cards, 32 x 21 In.................	1020.00

Advertising, Dress, Souper Dress, Andy Warhol, Campbell's Soup Campaign, Cellulose Paper, 1969, 38 In. $1,565.00

Hake's Americana & Collectibles

Advertising, Figure, Borden, Elsie The Cow, Composition, 1940s, 8 x 10 In. $316.00

Hake's Americana & Collectibles

Advertising, Figure, Heinz 57, Tomato Head, Top Hat, Hard Rubber, Painted, 5 ¾ In. $165.00

Hake's Americana & Collectibles

Snapp!
In 1932, Snapp!, a small gnome wearing a baker's cap and carrying a spoon, was the first gnome to be featured on Kellogg's Rice Krispies.

Advertising, Figure, Heinz's Tomato Ketchup, Bottle, Glass, 26 ½ x 6 ¼ In.
$2,310.00

Wm Morford Antiques

Advertising, Figure, Nipper, RCA Dog, Molded Resin, Sticker, 18 In.
$288.00

Victorian Casino Antiques

Advertising, Flour Receiver, Telescope, Marked 50 Lb. & 100 Lb., 40 x 18 ½ In.
$2,040.00

Showtime Auction Services

Advertising, Game, Ronald McDonald Head, Resin, Multicolor Hair, Target
$120.00

Victorian Casino Antiques

Advertising, Handbag, Cut Plug Tobacco, Tin, Handle, 7 x 6 x 4 ¼ In.
$83.00

Showtime Auction Services

Advertising, Label, Express Cigar, Witsch & Schmitt Litho Co., 1899, 7 ⅜ x 4 ⅝ In.
$193.00

Showtime Auction Services

Advertising, Label, Firecrackers, Black Prince, 20-Pack, E-Wo Yeung Hong, Chinese, 1941, 10 ⅝ x 6 ½ In.
$360.00

Morphy Auctions

Advertising, Label, Firecrackers, Cowboy 24-Pack, Contents, E-Wo Yeung Hong, Chinese, 3 ⅜ x 3 In.
$180.00

Morphy Auctions

Advertising, Label, Firecrackers, Crax Boy, 50-Pack, Chan Tai Kee, Chinese, 3 ⅛ x 3 In.
$330.00

Morphy Auctions

Advertising, Label, Firecrackers, Raven & Bell, Wing Lee Hong, Chinese, 3 ¼ x 2 ⅝ In.
$150.00

Morphy Auctions

Advertising, Label, Firecrackers, Skipper Crackers, 32-Pack, Consigned Sales Co., Macau, 4 ¼ x 3 ⅛ In.
$1,200.00

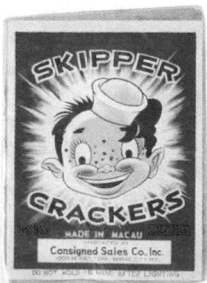

Morphy Auctions

A

Sign, Adams' Pepsin, Tutti Frutti Sold Here, Glass, Mirror Back, Frame, 10 x 21 In.	504.00
Sign, Agency Sanderson's Express, 2-Sided, Porcelain, 24 x 15 In.	570.00
Sign, Air France, Eiffel Tower, Plane, Bernard Villemot, Paris, 1952, 39 x 24 In.	600.00
Sign, Air France, L'Amerique Du Nord, Map Of U.S., Paris, 1951, 39 x 24 In.	425.00
Sign, Alba Grand Vin Moussseux, Flapper, Pouring Wine In Elephant, Marseille, 62 x 45 In.	1200.00
Sign, Albana Cigarettes, Color Lithograph, France, Frame, 51 x 36 In.	426.00
Sign, Alioto's Barber Shop, Board, Paint, Black, White, c.1910, 24 ½ x 38 In.	237.00
Sign, Alka-Seltzer, Neon, Etched Glass, Metal, Box Style, 8 x 27 In.	330.00
Sign, Allen & Ginter, Reverse Glass, Frame, 46 x 28 In.	330.00
Sign, American Express, Money Orders, Travelers Cheques, Shield, Tin, 35 x 26 In.	1800.00
Sign, Anheuser-Busch, Custer's Last Fight, Cardboard, U.S. Cavalry, Print, Frame, 46 x 36 In....*Illus*	672.00
Sign, Anheuser-Busch, Custer's Last Fight, Frame, 42 x 33 In.	420.00
Sign, Apothecary, Mortar Shape, Ross Johnson Drug Co., c.1924, 34 x 24 In.	7200.00
Sign, Approved Campground, AAA, 2-Sided, Red & White, Metal, 28 x 28 In.	110.00
Sign, Armour's Old Black Joe Fertilizer, Multicolor, Tin, 1950s, 18 x 31 In.	420.00
Sign, Ax Shape, 2-Sided, Parade Prop, Wood, Red, Black Paint, 43 x 12 In.	326.00
Sign, Ayer's Cherry Pectoral, Santa, Green Suit, Brown Fur, Sleigh, Cardboard, Cutout, 11 ¾ In.	300.00
Sign, Ayer's Sarsaparilla, Purifying Blood, Parlor Scene, Yellow, Blue, Tin, 1800s, 14 x 20 In.	805.00
Sign, Baltimore Oysters, H. McWilliams & Co., Train, Lithograph, 24 x 18 In.	4130.00
Sign, Bec-Kina Aperitif Des Sportifs, Rugby Players, Holding Bottle, Mich., c.1920, 62 x 46 In.	1100.00
Sign, Beech-Nut Gum, Die Cut, Stand-Up, Woman Playing Drums, 38 x 14 ½ In.	303.00
Sign, Beech-Nut Gum, Woman, Handing Out Gum, Cardboard, Stand-Up, Die Cut, 38 x 14 In.. *Illus*	303.00
Sign, Bickmore Easy Shave Cream 35 Cents, Die Cut, Cardboard, Frame, 24 x 34 In.	252.00
Sign, Billiards, Leaded Glass, Red & Green, White Ground, 82 ¾ x 15 ½ In.	3630.00
Sign, Bitter Campari, Clown, Peel, Bottle, Leonetto Cappiello, 1921, 38 x 27 In.	5000.00
Sign, Blaze Of Athlone, Finest Dublin Stout, Man, Horse, Wood, Paint, 24 x 36 In.	130.00
Sign, Blue Gap Cigar, Tin, Embossed, 5 x 14 In.	83.00
Sign, Blue Grotto Oyster & Chop House, Oval, Wood, Light-Up, 50 x 68 In.	448.00
Sign, Bluff City Beer, Brewery, Round, Reverse On Glass, 18 In.	3920.00
Sign, Boot, Miller Bros., Wood, Boot With Heel, Wrought Iron Hanging Rings, 1800s, 47 In. .... *Illus*	911.00
Sign, Boots Shoes & Rubbers, Wood Panel, Molding, White & Black Paint, c.1895, 14 ¾ x 39 ¾ In.	1659.00
Sign, Borax Dry Soap, Embossed, Tin, 24 x 7 In.	480.00
Sign, Borden's Eagle Brand Condensed Milk, Mother, 3 Girls, Frame, 15 x 10 In.	367.00
Sign, Borden's Ice Cream, Elsie The Cow, Tin, 12 x 24 In.	224.00
Sign, Boyce Motometer, Man, Car Hood, Tin, Cardboard Back, 27 x 19 In.	6050.00
Sign, Broadleaf Cigars, La Flor De Ampere, Cardboard, Frame, 24 x 32 In.....................*Illus*	84.00
Sign, Bromo Quinine, Red Letters, Pointing Hand, Chain, Celluloid, 18 x 5 ¾ In.	468.00
Sign, Buckeye Beer, Diamond Lite, Light-Up, Cincinnati, Oh., 18 ½ x 7 In.	240.00
Sign, Budweiser, Help Yourself To Good Cheer, Bearded Chef, Food, 1940s, 60 x 29 ½ In.	180.00
Sign, Bus, Greyhound, Logo, Metal, Red, White & Blue, Attached Pole, 24 x 48 In.	600.00
Sign, Butcher, Bull's Head, Cast Iron, Faneuil Hall Market, c.1765, 18 x 14 In.	1416.00
Sign, Buy OshKosh B'Gosh Overalls, Uncle Sam, Cardboard, Patent 1918, 14 x 30 In.	800.00
Sign, Buy U.S. Savings Bonds, America's Opportunity Drive, Lithograph, 26 x 19 In.	177.00
Sign, C.W. Fifield Optometrist, Glasses Fitted, Lens, Eyeball, Round, Glass, Tin, Wood, c.1850, 30 In.	823.00
Sign, C.W. Parker Leavenworth, Carousel, Steam Riding Gallery, Double Cylinder Engine, 29 x 22 In.	1080.00
Sign, Cab Stand, No Parking, Taxi, Sidewalk, Cast Iron, Black & Yellow, 48 In.	390.00
Sign, California's Favorite Dessert, Ice Cream Sundae, Porcelain, Blue, White, 10 x 8 In.	523.00
Sign, Canada Dry Beverages, Porcelain, 7 x 24 In.	177.00
Sign, Cape Cod, Fish, Wood, Paint, c.1955, 14 x 48 In.	474.00
Sign, Carnival Arcade, 25 Cents, Red, White Paint, Wood, Round, 21 ½ In.	201.00
Sign, Carnival Arcade, Glass Pitch, Wood Panel, c.1930s, 28 x 14 In.	259.00
Sign, Carpeting, Shaped Wood Panel, 2-Sided, Gilt Lettering, Black, c.1895, 24 x 9 Ft.	948.00
Sign, Castle Hall Twin Cigars, String Hanger, Papier-Mache Stork, 25 In......................*Illus*	358.00
Sign, Cetacolor, Prevents Wash Goods From Fading, Canvas, Acme, Dayton, Ohio, 37 x 26 In. ..*Illus*	280.00
Sign, Cherry Blossom Boot Polish, Kittens In Work Boots, Sheet Steel, 28 x 19 In.	325.00
Sign, Chesterfield Cigarettes, True Individuality, Seated Woman, Frame, 10 x 20 In.	115.00
Sign, Chew Mail Pouch Tobacco, Civil War Soldiers, Camel, Cardboard, Die Cut, 34 In.	153.00
Sign, Chiquita Banded Bananas, Out Of This World, Earth, Banana In Dress, c.1950, 20 x 28 In.	500.00
Sign, Choice Cigars & Tobacco, Snuff, Pipes, Wood, Blue, Yellow, c.1895, 60 x 20 In.	13035.00
Sign, Cigarette, Chesterfield, Light One For Me, Swimmer, Couple By Shore, c.1930, 21 x 10 In.	450.00
Sign, Clean Rest Rooms, 2-Sided, Flange, Blue & White, Porcelain, 24 x 12 In.	192.00
Sign, Clement Cycles, Cock, Sunrise, Linen, La Berceuse, 21 x 28 In.	295.00
Sign, Clicquot Club Pale Dry Ginger Ale, Tin Litho Cardboard, Eskimo Holding Bottle, 6 x 9 In.	127.00
Sign, Clothier For Men, Shoes For Men & Women, Wood, c.1890, 7 x 61 In.	316.00
Sign, Club Harlem, Greatest Sepia Floor Show Ever, Paint, Tin, c.1925, 11 x 6 In.	863.00
Sign, Club Manhattan Cocktails, Tin, Man Smoking & Drinking, Frame, c.1894, 12 x 17 In......*Illus*	672.00

Advertising, Label, Firecrackers, Spirit Of 76, 20-Pack, Pensick & Gordon, Chinese, 3 x 2 ⅜ In.
$210.00

Morphy Auctions

Advertising, Label, Firecrackers, Tin Shing, Boy & Girl Shaking Hands, Chinese, 5 ⅛ x 4 ⅞ In.
$270.00

Morphy Auctions

Advertising, Lantern, None Such, Halloween, Patriotic, Tin, Reverse Painted Glass, 1900, 7 x 7 x 17 In.
$6,900.00

James D. Julia Auctioneers

Advertising, Mirror, Drink Golden Grain Belt Beer, Hold To Light, Woman, Flowers, Tin Rim, Pocket, 1 ⅞ In.
$158.00

Hake's Americana & Collectibles

Advertising, Mirror, Old Manse, Canadian Sap Maple Syrup, Celluloid, 2 ⅛ In.
$605.00

Wm Morford Antiques

Advertising, Mirror, Stephenson Union Suits, Gymnasts, Celluloid, 2 ⅞ x 1 ¾ In.
$935.00

Wm Morford Antiques

Advertising, Nut Cup, Cream Dove Brand Salted Peanuts, Tin Litho, 2 ⅛ x 2 ¼ In.
$220.00

Wm Morford Antiques

Advertising, Pail, Albany Pressure Grease, Albany Lubricating Compound, Tin Lithograph, 5 Lb., 8 x 6 In.
$77.00

Wm Morford Antiques

Sign, Collector Car Sales, Antiques Classics, Wood, 73 x 49 In.	504.00
Sign, Coppertone, Girl On Beach, Dog Pulling Suit, Cardboard, Frame, 32 x 22 In.	252.00
Sign, Cove Forge Blacksmithing, Anvil, 2 Chains, Iron, Sheet Metal, Mass., c.1930, 44 In.	668.00
Sign, Craps, Star, Dice, Blue Ground, Oval, Light-Up, Frame	84.00
Sign, Cruwell-Tobak, Indian, Holding Pipe, Feather Headdress, Germany, 1930s, 9 x 14 In.	168.00
Sign, Cunard Line New York, Boston, Liverpool, Ship, O. Rosenvinge, c.1907, 40 x 25 In.	4400.00
Sign, Cycles Sirius, Woman, Seminude, On Bicycle, Pointing At Star, France, Frame, 14 x 18 In.	301.00
Sign, Dad's Old Fashioned Root Beer, Big Junior, Tin, Embossed, Self-Framed, 14 x 29 In.*Illus*	300.00
Sign, Danderine, Cardboard, Die Cut, Easel Back, 34 x 24 In.*Illus*	168.00
Sign, Deer Run Whiskey, Deer, Aug. Baetzhold, Buffalo, N.Y., Tin, Round, 12 In.	504.00
Sign, Dentist Trade, Tooth, Wood, Gilt, Carved, c.1890, 16 In.	4029.00
Sign, Devilish Good Cigar, None Better, 5 Cents, Embossed, Tin Litho, 9 ⅞ x 13 ¾ In.*Illus*	412.00
Sign, Diamonds, NYC Jewelry District, Paint, Wood, c.1935, 19 x 49 ½ In.	374.00
Sign, Dominion Tubular Lamp Co., Station Lamps, Lantern Display, Canada, c.1875, 22 x 17 In.	104.00
Sign, Dr. D. Jaynes Family Medicines, Flemish Bride, Litho, Gold Frame, 23 x 19 In.	527.00
Sign, Dr. Pierce's Medical Discovery, Man On Old Fashioned Telephone, Frame, 23 x 34 In.	180.00
Sign, Dr. Schenck's Mandrake Liver Pills, Grandmother & Children, Frame, 19 x 30 In.*Illus*	1150.00
Sign, Drink A Punch & Judy Cocktail, It Recuperates, Cameo Inset, Celluloid, 11 ¾ x 7 In.	2415.00
Sign, Drink Broadway Dry Ginger Ale, Bottle, Embossed, Green, Red, 1920s, 11 x 23 In.	127.00
Sign, Drink Brownie Chocolate It's Delicious, Brownie, Embossed Tin, Self-Framed, 20 x 28 In.	266.00
Sign, Drink Cheer Up, Tin, Embossed, 7 x 19 In.	130.00
Sign, Drink Royal Crown Cola, Take Home A Carton, Tin, Frame, 54 x 18 In.	390.00
Sign, Drink Squeeze, Embossed, Tin Litho, JV Reed, Louisville, 1930s, 10 x 28 In.*Illus*	267.00
Sign, Driver Ed. Car, Wood, White, Black Paint, Curved, U.S.A., 1900s, 6 x 39 ½ In.	119.00
Sign, Dun Workin, Wood, Black & White Paint, Panel, Applied Molding, c.1900, 9 ¼ x 27 In.	770.00
Sign, Dutch Boy Paints, Lewis White Lead, Lithographed Steel, 2-Sided, 26 x 15 In.	4720.00
Sign, E A T, Sheet Iron, Painted, c.1950	4030.00
Sign, Eagle Beers, Made In Utica, N.Y., Corner, Glass, Reverse Painted, 19 x 15 In.	1008.00
Sign, Eastside Beer, Make Every Meal A Party, Beer Can, Confetti, Paper, 1950s, 42 x 29 In.	30.00
Sign, Eat More Jolly Time Pop Corn, Metal, Glass, Light-Up, 8 x 12 In.	560.00
Sign, Eberhardt & Ober Brewing Company, Allegheny, Pa., Factory Scene, c.1895, 42 x 26 In.*Illus*	700.00
Sign, Egyptienne Luxury Cigarettes, Cardboard, Woman, Pink Bonnet & Dress, 1890s, 21 x 17 In.	775.00
Sign, El Guardo Cigars, Catches On, Chromolithograph, On Board, Frame, 10 ¾ x 15 In.	109.00
Sign, El Rancho Vegas, Motor Inn, Piece Of Picket Fence Surrounding Property, Tin	633.00
Sign, Elephant Head Rubber Boots, Man, Standing In River, Woonsocket Co., 1911, 20 x 30 In.	935.00
Sign, Emerson Pianos, Reverse Painted, Girls, Letters, Frame, c.1890, 22 x 30 In. *Illus*	900.00
Sign, Enameline Stove Polish, Girl, Blue Dress, Paper, Frame, 1890s, 26 x 15 ½ In.	360.00
Sign, Enjoy Grapette Soda, Bottle Cap Shaped, Stout Sign Co., Tin, 38 In. Diam.	224.00
Sign, Ethan Allen Clothier, Marshall, Delighted With The Clothes, Die Cut, 38 x 14 In.	150.00
Sign, Eveready Battery, Bellhop, With Flashlight, Arabic Script, Porcelain, 17 ¾ x 11 ¾ In.	90.00
Sign, Eveready Flashlights & Batteries, Man, Alligator, Paper, Frame, 1930s, 28 x 20 In.	210.00
Sign, Ever-Ready Safety Razor, Oval, Razors, Blades, Boxes, Frame, Tin, 14 x 11 In.	826.00
Sign, Everything's Jantzen, Latex, Woman In Red Swimsuit, 1950s, 21 x 48 In.	300.00
Sign, Exit, McDonald's, Neon, Yellow, Golden Arches, Red, Black, 2-Sided, 36 x 38 In.	448.00
Sign, F. & J. Smith, Smiling Black Man, Best Think Black Tobacco, Chromolithograph, 26 x 21 In.	391.00
Sign, F.W. Young Woolen Co., Painted, Ram, Arched Top, c.1875, 18 x 73 In.	1150.00
Sign, Fada Radio, Black, Red, 17 ½ x 9 In.	201.00
Sign, Farm Bureau, Round, Red, White, Blue, 2-Sided, Tin, 18 In.	200.00
Sign, Fehr's Malt Tonic, Woman, Cherubs, Reaching For Bottle, Tin, c.1911, 28 In.	2400.00
Sign, Figural, Dutch Shoe Pipe, Wood, Olympiade 1928 Amsterdam, 1 ¼ x 2 ½ In.	141.00
Sign, Figural, Turtle, Pattern & Flask Lumber, Iron, Celluloid Top, 2 ⅝ x 1 ⅝ In.	187.00
Sign, Fire-Chief Gasoline, 2-Sided, Gas Price, Metal, 30 x 38 In.	224.00
Sign, Fire-Chief Gasoline, Texaco, Fireman's Hat, Logo, Red, White, Black, 1948, 12 x 18 In.	158.00
Sign, Flintlock Musket, Giltwood Carved, Mounted On Board, 1700s, 26 x 61 In.	1071.00
Sign, Flor De Franklin Cigars, Cardboard, Hanging String, Frame, Wholesale Cigars, 23 x 16 In.	440.00
Sign, Florence & Howe Sewing Machines, Right & Left Facing, Painted, 35 x 30 In., 2 Piece	472.00
Sign, Foster's Ice Cream, Porcelain, Blue, White, 11 x 6 In.	440.00
Sign, Fowler's Cherry Smash Soda Fountain, Round Top, Menu Sign, Tin, 9 x 18 In.	460.00
Sign, Frank Polk, Maker Of Exclusive Gambling Devices, 3-D, Wood, Indians, Slots, 42 x 24 In.	390.00
Sign, Fresh Up With 7Up, You Like It, It Likes You, Oval, Tin, Embossed, 1950s, 40 In.	1200.00
Sign, G.K. Basset Soap, Wooden, Gray & Black Paint, Shaped Rectangle, c.1890, 11 ¾ x 30 In.	780.00
Sign, Gas Today, Drink Ice Cold Nehi, Sold Here, Tin, Yellow, Red, 42 x 15 In.	560.00
Sign, GE, Neon, Orange, White, Blue, 2-Sided, 41 x 56 x 15 In.	5400.00
Sign, Geo. Hocker's Fine Shoes, Tin, Gold, Silver Gilt, Frame, c.1885, 15 x 23 In.*Illus*	2818.00
Sign, George Strait, Bud Light, Cowboy Hat, Neon, Light-Up, 30 x 30 In.	150.00
Sign, Gibson's Rip Van Winkle Whiskey, Paper, 1882, 20 In.	468.00

Sign, Gloves, Watches, Jewelry, Cutlery, Fancy Goods, White, Red, c.1900, 32 ¾ x 17 ¾ In.	2015.00
Sign, Golfology Quality Cigar, Golfer, Cardboard, Die Cut, Easel Back, 25 x 37 In.	360.00
Sign, Good Enough Sulky Plow, Moline Plow Co, Paper, Frame, 20 x 15 In.	138.00
Sign, Granite State Fire Insurance, Portsmouth, N.H., Train, Reverse Glass, 42 ½ x 30 ½ In. ....*Illus*	3300.00
Sign, Grape-Nuts Cereal, Snow White & Seven Dwarfs, 1938, 20 x 11 ½ In.	540.00
Sign, Grape-Nuts, Girl, Red Cape, Dog, Tin Lithograph, Self-Framed, 30 x 20 In.	8910.00
Sign, Gray-Seal Paints, Distributor, Progress Enamels, Sheet Steel, 2-Sided, Flange, 13 ½ x 18 In.	71.00
Sign, Green River Whiskey, Black Man, Horse With Jug, Outside Inn, Tin, 1899, 32 x 44 ½ In.	900.00
Sign, Greensmith's Derby Dog Biscuits, Cardboard, Clown, Dog Jumping Through Hoops, 24 x 19 In.	358.00
Sign, Greyhound Lines, Ticket Office, Clock, Light-Up, Ohio Display Co., c.1920s, 25 x 19 In.	1650.00
Sign, Greyhound, Dog Running, Mounted On Board, 62 x 19 In.	275.00
Sign, Greyhound, Dog Running, Red Rim, 2-Sided, 40 x 24 In.	900.00
Sign, Grovedale Tourists Accommodated Over Night, Metal, Oak Frame, 63 x 37 In.	492.00
Sign, Guinness, Parrot, Neon	201.00
Sign, Harness Shop, Wood, Paint, c.1915, 63 x 8 ½ In.	345.00
Sign, Heinz Hot Dog, Multicolor, Hooks For Hanging, 42 In.	288.00
Sign, Henry George 5 Cent Cigar, Tin, Embossed Wood Frame, 24 x 17 In.	1680.00
Sign, Hershey's Ice Cream, Menu, Prices, Famous For Quality Since 1894, Tin, 26 x 11 In.	316.00
Sign, Hershey's Milk Chocolate, Tin Litho, Logo, Frame, 7 x 11 In. ....*Illus*	468.00
Sign, Hires For Pleasure & Thirst, Round, Embossed Tin, Blue, Black, White, 24 In.	266.00
Sign, Hires In Bottles, Black, Orange, Gold, Bottle, Tin, 28 x 10 In.	112.00
Sign, Hires Root Beer, Route 66, Drive-In, Embossed, Tin, Frame, 1950s, 56 x 31 In.	504.00
Sign, Hires Root Beer, Trademark Kid, Die Cut, 13 ¾ In.	385.00
Sign, Hires, So Refreshing, Blue, White, Tin, 12 x 14 In.	165.00
Sign, Holiday Orders Taken Now, Wood, Paint, c.1920, 31 x 7 ¾ In.	130.00
Sign, Horn & Hardart Automat, Boy, Round, Plastic, Blue, Yellow, c.1950, 30 In. Diam.	533.00
Sign, Horse & Buggy, David L. Adams, Metal	22.00
Sign, Horse, Black Hawk, Stud Service, Clarson & Fitch Belvidere, 1834, 21 x 16 In.	1126.00
Sign, Hot Soda, Wood, Cut Corners, Molding, Black Lettering, c.1895, 12 ¾ x 72 In.	4148.00
Sign, Howel's Root Beer, Bottle Shaped, Yellow, Red, Embossed, Tin, 16 x 57 In.	420.00
Sign, Hutchinson Optometrist Glasses Fitted & Repaired, Paint, 2-Sided, c.1910	144.00
Sign, I Just Love Moxie, It's So Delicious, Embossed, Die Cut Cardboard, 10 x 4 ¾ In. ......*Illus*	495.00
Sign, I.W. Harper Whiskey, Nelson Co., Ky., Glass, Reverse Painted, 21 x 16 In.	1456.00
Sign, Ice Cold Frostie, You'll Love It, Bottle, Bear, Motor, Ice, Vacuform, 1960s, 13 x 15 In.	137.00
Sign, Ice Cream Centerville Ice Co., Sheet Metal, Paint, 28 x 20 In.	207.00
Sign, Ingram's Carbolated Witch Hazel Salve, Machinist, Injured Arm, Celluloid, 13 ¾ x 19 ¾ In.	4888.00
Sign, International Tailoring Pleasures Of A Man, N.Y., Oval, Frame, 17 x 26 In.	1540.00
Sign, Iroquois Brewing Co., Buffalo, N.Y., Factory Scene, Paper Litho, Frame, 27 ¾ x 37 In....*Illus*	8690.00
Sign, It's A Dilley For Thirst, Tin, 12 x 36 In.	218.00
Sign, J. Ramsey Watch Repair, Union St., Pocket Watch, Sheet Metal, Crate Lid, 28 x 24 In.	115.00
Sign, J.I. Case Co., Eagle, On Sphere, Old Abe, c.1890, 27 x 9 ½ In.	2360.00
Sign, J.W. Mallett, Sign Painter, Wood, Black, Red Letters, Gold, 28 x 18 In.	1440.00
Sign, Jack Frost Cane Sugars, Dessert, Boy, Sugar, Cardboard, Hanging, 1940s, 10 x 10 In.	95.00
Sign, Je Ne Fume Que Le Nil, Paper, Leonetto Cappiello, 1912, 45 x 62 In.	900.00
Sign, Joe's Road House, Casino & Saloon, Clock Center, Neon, 3 Colors, 41 In.	1120.00
Sign, John Strootman Fine Shoes, Buffalo, N.Y., Reverse Painted Glass, 24 x 31 In.	1120.00
Sign, Johnson Halter, Tavern, Horse Head, Papier-Mache, Black, c.1910, 20 In.	1150.00
Sign, Jubilee Crawford Stoves, Black & White, Frame, 21 ¾ x 13 ½ In.	59.00
Sign, Just Say Triple AAA Root Beer, Bottle, Tin Litho Red, Yellow, 1950s, 19 x 27 In.	127.00
Sign, Just Whistle, Sparkling Orange Goodness, Bottle, Tin, Embossed, 32 x 56 In.	896.00
Sign, Justin Gates Traveling Drug Store, Covered Wagon, Logo, Lithograph, 21 x 18 In.	561.00
Sign, Ken-L-Products, Silk Screen, Sheet Metal, Flange, 27 x 18 In.	201.00
Sign, Kenwick Whiskey, Floating Nude Woman, Reverse Painted, Fetcheimer, Hart & Co.	3300.00
Sign, Kerosene Lamp Co., c.1875, 17 ½ x 11 ½ In.	196.00
Sign, Key Shape, Die Cut, Tin Lithograph, Independent Lock Co., 32 In.	403.00
Sign, Key Shape, Orange Paint, Steel, Hanging, 68 In.	472.00
Sign, Kickapoo Joy Juice, Li'l Abner Holding Sign, Life Size, 62 x 31 In.	995.00
Sign, Kina Lillet, Woman, Grape Vines, Raised Glass, Paper, Robert Wolf, 1937, 78 x 50 In.	950.00
Sign, Kis-Me, Woman, Gum Package, Tin, Self-Framed, 17 x 14 In.	728.00
Sign, Lacquerwax Car Polish, Lasts Twice As Long, Tin, Embossed, 1930s, 14 x 19 In.	850.00
Sign, Ladies & Gents Lunchrooms, 2-Sided, Paint, Wood, c.1900, 19 ¾ x 48 In.	4740.00
Sign, Lakefront Brewery, Inc., 2-Sided, Light-Up, 16 x 19 ½ In.	155.00
Sign, L'Alsacienne Verft Alle Stoffen, Linen, Signed Dorf, France, c.1910, 52 x 68 In.	450.00
Sign, Le Tulmulte Noir, Black Man, Cane, Hat, Paul Colin, 1929, 18 x 12 In.	1000.00
Sign, Learn It Right Springfield Business College, Embossed Tin, Frame, c.1910, 15 x 12 In.	90.00
Sign, Lemp Beer, St. Louis, Teddy Roosevelt, Tin Litho, Die Cut, 13 ⅝ x 9 In. ....*Illus*	5500.00

Advertising, Pail, Wilson's Peanut Butter, Nursery Rhyme Images, Tin Lithograph, Handle, 3 ⅛ x 3 ⅝ In. $440.00

Wm Morford Antiques

Advertising, Shoehorn, W.L. Douglas, World's Greatest Shoemaker, Tin Litho, 4 x 1 ⅝ In. $99.00

Wm Morford Antiques

Advertising, Sign, Anheuser-Busch, Custer's Last Fight, Cardboard, U.S. Cavalry, Print, Frame, 46 x 36 In. $672.00

Victorian Casino Antiques

Advertising, Sign, Beech-Nut Gum, Woman, Handing Out Gum, Cardboard, Stand-Up, Die Cut, 38 x 14 In. $303.00

Wm Morford Antiques

Advertising, Sign, Boot, Miller Bros.,
Wood, Boot With Heel, Wrought Iron
Hanging Rings, 1800s, 47 In.
$911.00

Garth's Auctioneers & Appraisers

Advertising, Sign, Broadleaf Cigars,
La Flor De Ampere, Cardboard, Frame,
24 x 32 In.
$84.00

Victorian Casino Antiques

Advertising, Sign, Castle Hall Twin
Cigars, String Hanger, Papier-Mache
Stork, 25 In.
$358.00

Showtime Auction Services

Advertising, Sign, Cetacolor, Prevents
Wash Goods From Fading, Canvas, Acme,
Dayton, Ohio, 37 x 26 In.
$280.00

Victorian Casino Antiques

Sign, Levi's Blue Jeans, Mine Shaft, Denim Mountains, Frame, 28 x 20 In.	130.00
Sign, Lightning Mouse Trap, Never Fails, Embossed, Tin, c.1900, 9 x 6 In.	3900.00
Sign, Lillibridge Chocolates, Die Cut, Woman's Head, Embossed, c.1906, 15 x 11 In.	577.00
Sign, Lime Kiln Club Cigars, Boisterous Lodge Meeting, Paper, 25 x 30 In.	224.00
Sign, Lincoln Bouquet Cigars, Pride Of All Domestic Goods, Chromolitho, Frame, 22 x 19 In.	495.00
Sign, Lions International, L In Center, Porcelain, Round, Metal Frame, 1930s, 30 In.	392.00
Sign, Liquor Cordial Medoc, Clown, Glass, Bottle, Frame, France, c.1935	177.00
Sign, Livery Trade, Horse Head, Cast Zinc, J.W. Friske, 1800s, 33 x 26 ½ In.	4374.00
Sign, Locksmith Trade, Eagle Lock Co., Wood, Paint, c.1915, 8 ¾ x 6 ½ In.	356.00
Sign, London Life Cigarettes, Tin, Multicolor, Wood Grain Frame, c.1910, 39 x 28 In.	431.00
Sign, Look Out For The Locomotive, 2-Sided, Shield Shape, Star, Iron, c.1890, 22 x 22 In.	780.00
Sign, Lorillard's Climax Plug Tobacco, Laughing Woman, I Should Smile, Cardboard, 13 x 9 In.	112.00
Sign, Love Nest, Best Eating Candy Bar In The World, 5 Cent, Embossed Tin Litho, 1930s, 10 x 28 In.	121.00
Sign, Lowe Brothers Vernicol, Floor & Varnish Stain, Wood, Hooks, 5 x 43 In.	29.00
Sign, Lucky Strike Cigarettes, Die Cut, Cardboard, c.1940, 13 x 8 In.	75.00
Sign, Lucky Strike Cigarettes, It's Toasted, Die Cut, Board, Round Target, Color, 23 x 29 In.	550.00
Sign, M.W. Fisher, Stopwatch Shaped, Zinc, Black & Red, U.S.A., c.1895, 28 x 19 In.	588.00
Sign, Maine Coast Fly Way Birds, Duck Decoy Shaped, Canvas, c.1950, 6 x 13 In.	830.00
Sign, Mandeville King Flower Seeds, 18th Century Couple In Garden, H.G. Ferris, 17 x 26 In.	300.00
Sign, Marquette Pure Rye, Reverse On Glass, Frame, 17 x 8 In. ....*Illus*	540.00
Sign, Ma's Cola, Tin, Embossed, 12 x 28 In.	189.00
Sign, Masury's Pure Colors Paint, Tin Litho, Sentenne & Green, N.Y., 23 x 17 In. ....*Illus*	1416.00
Sign, Maxwell House Coffee, Dripping Coffee Cup, Double Sided, Steel Flange, 27 In.	4235.00
Sign, McCormick For 1891, 2-Horse Team & Driver, Lithograph, Frame, 15 x 21 In.	531.00
Sign, McCormick Harvester Machines, Wood, 2-Sided, 36 x 11 ¼ In.	550.00
Sign, Mecca Cigarettes Perfect Satisfaction, Earl Christy, Frame, c.1912, 10 x 19 In.	115.00
Sign, Medo-Land Ice Cream, Cone Shape, c.1955, 38 In.	650.00
Sign, Menu, Borden's, Blue, White, Red, Cardboard, Wood Frame, 26 x 14 In.	150.00
Sign, Michelin Pneumatic Velo, Red Bicycle, Bonetti Milano, France, 28 x 21 In.	236.00
Sign, Mickey Mouse Slip-Overs For Boys & Girls, Cardboard, Easel Back, 1920, 20 x 12 In.	630.00
Sign, Miller High Life Beer, Black, Red, Gold, Light-Up, Brunhoff, 1940s, 20 x 16 In.	1440.00
Sign, Miss Teenage America, Enter Now, Lithograph Print, Dr Pepper Sponsor, c.1964, 25 x 15 In.	59.00
Sign, Monarch Pool Table, Porcelain, Brunswick & Balke Co. Billiards, 29 x 39 In.	509.00
Sign, Monogram Whiskey, Bottle, Reverse Painted Glass, Frame, Chain Border, 14 In.	870.00
Sign, Moore, Scroll Design, Boot Shaped, Wood, Yellow Paint, Leather Strap, c.1890, 25 x 14 ¾ In.	600.00
Sign, Munsingwear, Girls, Wearing Union Suit Underwear, Cutout, Tin, c.1910, 24 x 15 In.	1020.00
Sign, Nehi Beverages, Bottle Logo, Embossed Tin, 11 x 27 In.	248.00
Sign, Neon, Schlitz Beer, Everbrite Electric Signs Inc., Harbor City, Ca., 23 x 9 In.	120.00
Sign, New Haven Dairy Ice Cream Cones, 5 Cent, Red & White, Porcelain, 21 x 27 In.	600.00
Sign, O.F.C. Bourbon, Stag In Landscape, Tin, Haeusermann, Frame, 41 x 30 In.	1120.00
Sign, Old Boone Distillery, Log Cabin Scene, Tin, 1904, 28 x 36 In.	1560.00
Sign, Old Dutch Cleanser, 10 Cents, Chases Dirt, Woman, Curved, Porcelain, 28 x 12 In.	240.00
Sign, Old English, Curve Cut Pipe Tobacco, Round, Multicolor, c.1905, 24 In.	449.00
Sign, Old Gold, Pack, Majorette, Trumpet, Tastiest Cigarette, Cardboard, 49 x 35 In.	560.00
Sign, Old Quaker Rye Whiskey, Quaker, Men Drinking, Lithograph, Frame, 19 x 26 In.	295.00
Sign, Old Schenley Whiskey, Davy Crockett, I've Struck The Trail, River, Tin, 25 x 33 In.	990.00
Sign, Omar Turkish Blend Cigarettes, Chromolithograph, Embossed, Frame, 21 x 14 ¾ In.	150.00
Sign, One For Breakfast, Shakespeare Tackle Co, Fisherman, In Water, Pole, Net, 27 x 20 In.	560.00
Sign, Only Zenith Has It, Chromacolor, Moving Lights, 1970s, 11 x 20 In.	144.00
Sign, Optometry Trade, Spectacle, Cobalt Blue Lenses, Gilt Iron, c.1850, 14 x 26 In.	1337.00
Sign, Orange Crush, Bathing Girl, Beach, Cardboard, Frame, 1920s, 20 x 198 In.	3000.00
Sign, Orlando Buffet & Wine, Budweiser Served Exclusively, R.S. Meech & Co., 36 x 62 In.	880.00
Sign, Out Of This World, Energy Rich Chocolate, Man In Spacesuit, Cardboard, 1950s, 11 x 21 In.	143.00
Sign, OVB Tools & Cutlery, Wood Sand, 70 ½ x 10 ½ In.	3025.00
Sign, Oyster House & Cafe, Girl, Stroller, Doll, Cardboard, Lithograph, Die Cut, 13 x 9 In.	132.00
Sign, Pabst Blue Ribbon Beer On Draft, Metal Stand, Edgebright, 15 ¾ In.	780.00
Sign, Pabst Blue Ribbon, On The Air, Reverse Painted Glass, 13 x 13 In.	130.00
Sign, Pabst Brewing Co., Spreadwing Eagle, Leaf In Red Circle, Bottle, Tin, c.1892, 24 x 17 In.	3738.00
Sign, Parrot, Say Gear-Ar-Delly, Ghirardelli's Chocolate, Cardboard, Die Cut, 21 In.	226.00
Sign, Paul A. Kuhns Purina Chows, Boy In Overalls, Frame, 18 ⅝ x 14 ⅝ In.	95.00
Sign, Paul Jones Whiskey, Temptation Of St. Anthony, Litho, Oak Plate, c.1900, 20 x 14 In.	660.00
Sign, Peaches For Sale, Paint, Wood, c.1920, 10 x 18 In.	92.00
Sign, Pee Gee Paint Service, Can Of Paint, Porcelain, 2-Sided, Flange, 14 x 16 In.	1375.00
Sign, Penn Esther Kitchen Range, Cooking Scene, Embossed Tin, Reading, Pa., c.1890, 9 x 8 In.	660.00
Sign, Pepsin Punch, Asti, Woman's Portrait, Ideal Soda-Fount Beverage, 5 Cents, 22 x 28 In.	510.00
Sign, Peters Ammunition, Growling Bear, Frank Ross, 1930s, 21 x 13 In.	448.00

Sign, Peters Big Game Ammunition, Bears On Mountain, Foam Backboard, 1911, 30 x 20 In.		3696.00
Sign, Petro Oil Burner, Porcelain, Tanker Truck, 30 x 21 In.		4950.00
Sign, Philco Balanced, Unit Radio, Light-Up Box, 19 x 7 In.		364.00
Sign, Pianos Daude Sonorite Remarquable, France, Frame, 1960s, 49 x 65 In.		354.00
Sign, Pick A Pack Of Jic Jac, 6 Pack, Stops Thirst Good Mixer, 1950s, 12 x 31 In.		115.00
Sign, Piedmont Cigarettes, Washington, Return To Mt. Vernon, Tin, Frame, c.1916, 30 x 24 In.		219.00
Sign, Pince Nez, 2 Different Eyes In Lenses, Neon, Box Frame, 10 x 23 In.		1080.00
Sign, Pipe Shape, Wood, Canvas, Gold, Black Paint, Tobacco Shop, Ohio, c.1900, 19 ½ x 73 In.		452.00
Sign, Pittsburgh Paint, House Shape, Glass, Save With Pittsburgh Paints, 1930s, 3 ½ In.		75.00
Sign, PKZ, Well Suited Man, Hat, Paper, Ernest Kretschmann, Zurich, 1924, 50 x 36 In.		1600.00
Sign, Plaque, Furs, Inscribed, Carved, Painted, 31 x 40 In.		3318.00
Sign, Player's Country Life, Tobacco & Cigarettes, Sheet Iron, Enamel, c.1900, 17 x 57 In.		230.00
Sign, Pleasant Hours, Wood, Gilt Lettering, 2-Sided, Shaped, Jagged Ends, c.1895, 16 ½ In.		444.00
Sign, Pocket Watch, Marked Max J. Egge, Paint, 2-Sided, 34 x 41 In.		1840.00
Sign, Pocket Watch, Wood, Black, Gilt Paint, Inscribed C.H. Priest, 1800s, 27 x 18 In.		4266.00
Sign, Post Lanterns, Iron, 2-Sided, c.1900, 12 x 16 In.		196.00
Sign, Pozzoni's Medicated Complexion Powder, Girl, Flowers, Frame, Baxter & Co., 1886, 24 x 31 In.		220.00
Sign, Pratt & Lambert Paint & Varnish, Red White, Porcelain, 2-Sided, 17 x 28 In.		330.00
Sign, Pretzel, Wood, Carved, Painted, Trade, c.1860, 12 ½ x 19 In.		546.00
Sign, Prevent Forest Fires, Yellow, Embossed, Tin, Maine Forest Service, 9 ¾ x 14 In.		55.00
Sign, Prisco Lantern, Cardboard, Pritchard-Strong Co., Frame, c.1920, 17 x 12 In.		173.00
Sign, Prunier, Livre Vite Et Bien, Chef, Fish, Bird, Basket On Head, Paper, c.1932, 86 x 52 In.		2000.00
Sign, Pub, Puppy, Holding Umbrella, British Flag, Frame, c.1850, 25 In.		885.00
Sign, Pub, The Parson's Daughter, Wines & Ales, Black Paint, Red, Woman, 1900s, 49 x 35 In.		236.00
Sign, Quaker Maid Milk, First In Quality, Porcelain, Die Cut, 24 x 41 In.		450.00
Sign, Que Placer Cigars, Multicolor, Tin, Self-Framed, American Art Works, c.1910, 19 x 13 In.		173.00
Sign, Quick Refreshing Lift, Ice Skaters, Bottle, c.1958, 33 x 21 In.		59.00
Sign, Radio 1310 K-BUK, Tin, Embossed, Self-Framed, San Antonio, 4,000 Watts, 35 x 24 In.		173.00
Sign, Rams Head Ale, Tin Litho Over Cardboard, Graphic Bottle, Sandwich On Dish, 1930s, 9 x 13 In.		202.00
Sign, Raven & Ring, 2-Sided, Shaped, Tavern, Carved Black Bird, Ring, 1900s, 47 x 32 In.		8295.00
Sign, RCA Victor, Red Letters, Light-Up, Neon, Metal Box, 10 x 33 In.		224.00
Sign, Reach For Sunbeam Bread, Blond Girl Eating, 19 x 54 In.		345.00
Sign, Red Diamond Overalls Workshirts, Cardboard, 11 x 13 In.		390.00
Sign, Red Lobster Restaurant, Call Ahead, Fisherman, Megaphone, Wood, Paint, 31 x 25 In.		130.00
Sign, Red Man Cigar Leaf, Finest In America, Metal, Painted, AAA Sign Co., 17 x 11 In.		210.00
Sign, Red Rose Coffee, Pretty Woman Sitting, Oval, Wood Frame, c.1940, 33 x 30 In.		420.00
Sign, Reddy Kilowatt, Electric Company, Red, White Figure, Porcelain, Die Cut, 19 x 28 In.		550.00
Sign, Remington Cutlery, DuPont, Reverse Painted, Electric, Black, Green, Red, 7 x 13 In.		443.00
Sign, Remington UMC Nitro Club Gameload Shells, Rice Paper Back, 16 x 8 In.		195.00
Sign, Rendering Company, We Pay For Dead Stock, Tin Litho, Quick, Reliable, 1930s, 9 x 14 In.		115.00
Sign, Rest Rooms, White, Colored, Arrows Pointing To Segregated Rooms, Glass, 1929, 12 x 4 In.		288.00
Sign, Rexall, Watson Drugs, Orange, Blue, White, 2-Sided, 48 x 72 x 5 In.		600.00
Sign, Ricardo Llacer E Hijos, Oranges In Cart, Duck, Spain, 22 x 31 In.		266.00
Sign, Richfield, Flying Bird, Oil Company, Die Cut Plastic, Neon, 22 x 22 In.		364.00
Sign, Rockford Railroad Watch, Time For A Lifetime, Station, Wife, Child, Husband, 15 x 21 In.		690.00
Sign, Rocky Ford Cigars, Embossed Die Cut, 2-Sided, Indian Hunter, 5 Cents, c.1900, 9 x 11 In.		173.00
Sign, Rose Standish House, Resort, Ferries, Boston Wharf, Color Litho, Frame, 23 x 31 In.		1170.00
Sign, Roth's Hy-Quality Coffee, Woman On Swing, Cardboard, Die Cut, 37 x 16 In.		392.00
Sign, Routh's Ice Cream, 25 Cents, Couples, With Cones, Paint, Wood, 1900s, 72 x 24 In.		1984.00
Sign, Royal Crown Cola, Embossed, Bottle Shape, Tin, 12 x 3 In.		153.00
Sign, Royal Electric Cleaner, Milk Glass Letters, Light-Up, 40 x 120 In.		1425.00
Sign, Rubberset Brushes, Tin, 2-Sided, Flange, 19 ¼ x 12 In.	*Illus*	1045.00
Sign, Russells' Ales, The Beer From The Country, Men, Barrels, 21 x 29 In.		336.00
Sign, Sanford's Inks Mucilage, Embossed, Tin, Self-Framed, Tuscarora Co., Oh., 20 x 14 In.	*Illus*	8250.00
Sign, Satin Skin Powder, Smiling Woman, 2 Powder Jars, Paper, c.1904, 28 x 42 In.		72.00
Sign, Saw Blade, Buy Henery Disston & Sons Saws, Files, Phila., Penna., U.S.A., 27 In.	*Illus*	112.00
Sign, Schiltz, Atlas, Reverse Glass, Chain, 24 x 14 ¾ In.		2200.00
Sign, Schlitz Atlas Brau, On Draught, Chain, 24 x 14 ¾ In.	*Illus*	2200.00
Sign, Schorn Paint, Blue White, Painter's Head, 44 ½ x 32 In.		295.00
Sign, Scissors, W.C. Heimerbinger, Zinc, 22 In.		468.00
Sign, Scott Bicycle Tyres, Woman, Police, Look Here Miss, Cardboard, c.1900, 16 x 20 In.		90.00
Sign, Selz Shoes, Sole Of Honor, Hand, Holding Shoe, Die Cut, Cardboard, 12 x 15 In.		180.00
Sign, Senior, Teapot Shaped, Cast Iron, Painted, Hanging, U.S.A., c.1900, 20 In.		1778.00
Sign, Sen-Sen Chewing Gum, Japanese Woman, Parasol, Cardboard, Frame, 31 x 22 In.		600.00
Sign, Sergeant's Dog Care, 2 Cocker Spaniel Puppies, Easel Back, 24 ¾ x 21 In.		176.00
Sign, Shell, Die Cut, Embossed Porcelain, Shell Shape, Yellow, Red Neon, 53 x 52 In.		2240.00

Advertising, Sign, Club Manhattan Cocktails, Tin, Man Smoking & Drinking, Frame, c.1894, 12 x 17 In.
$672.00

Victorian Casino Antiques

Advertising, Sign, Dad's Old Fashioned Root Beer, Big Junior, Tin, Embossed, Self-Framed, 14 x 29 In.
$300.00

Victorian Casino Antiques

Advertising, Sign, Danderine, Cardboard, Die Cut, Easel Back, 34 x 24 In.
$168.00

Victorian Casino Antiques

TIP

For every 24 inches of horizontal shelving in your bedroom, den, or library, fill the space with about 20 books. Books need air.

ADVERTISING

Advertising, Sign, Devilish Good Cigar, None Better, 5 Cents, Embossed, Tin Litho, 9 ⅞ x 13 ¾ In.
$412.00

Wm Morford Antiques

Advertising, Sign, Dr. Schenck's Mandrake Liver Pills, Grandmother & Children, Frame, 19 x 30 In.
$1,150.00

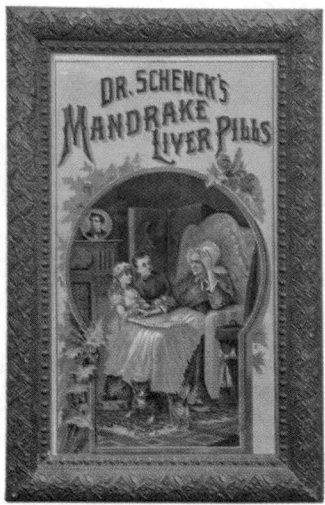

Victorian Casino Antiques

Advertising, Sign, Drink Squeeze, Embossed, Tin Litho, JV Reed, Louisville, 1930s, 10 x 28 In.
$267.00

Hake's Americana & Collectibles

Advertising, Sign, Eberhardt & Ober Brewing Company, Allegheny, Pa., Factory Scene, c.1895, 42 x 26 In.
$700.00

Past Tyme Pleasures

Advertising, Sign, Emerson Pianos, Reverse Painted, Girls, Letters, Frame, c.1890, 22 x 30 In.
$900.00

Cowan's Auctions

Advertising, Sign, Geo. Hocker's Fine Shoes, Tin, Gold, Silver Gilt, Frame, c.1885, 15 x 23 In.
$2,818.00

James D. Julia Auctioneers

Advertising, Sign, Granite State Fire Insurance, Portsmouth, N.H., Train, Reverse Glass, 42 ½ x 30 ½ In.
$3,300.00

Showtime Auction Services

Advertising, Sign, Hershey's Milk Chocolate, Tin Litho, Logo, Frame, 7 x 11 In.
$468.00

Wm Morford Antiques

Advertising, Sign, I Just Love Moxie, It's So Delicious, Embossed, Die Cut Cardboard, 10 x 4 ¾ In.
$495.00

Wm Morford Antiques

Advertising, Sign, Iroquois Brewing Co., Buffalo, N.Y., Factory Scene, Paper Litho, Frame, 27 ¾ x 37 In.
$8,690.00

Wm Morford Antiques

Advertising, Sign, Lemp Beer, St. Louis, Teddy Roosevelt, Tin Litho, Die Cut, 13 ⅝ x 9 In.
$5,500.00

Wm Morford Antiques

Sign, Sheridan's Cavalry Condition Powders, Horses, Wagon, Paper, Litho, 16 x 21 In............. 826.00
Sign, Ship Stores, Black Paint, Gilt Stencil, 11 x 84 In.............. 11328.00
Sign, Signal Lubrication, Black, Yellow, Red Border, Porcelain, 140 x 12 In. 952.00
Sign, Silsby Steam Engine, Color Fire Scenes, 10 x 12 In.............. 358.00
Sign, Simonds Saw, Old Man, Fingering Saw, Cardboard, Paper, 12 x 16 In.............. 385.00
Sign, Smoke Old Virginia Cheroots, Cake Walk, Chromolitho, Frame, c.1899, 17 x 17 In......... 253.00
Sign, Smoke Porto Rico Cigars, Seated Woman, Bird, Man, Cardboard, Frame, 13 x 17 In. 280.00
Sign, Smoking Moon Face, Winking, Caricature, Cast Aluminum, 10 In. Diam. 3738.00
Sign, Snag-Proof Lambertville Rubbers, Brownies, Boots, Paper, Frame, 18 x 27 In. 825.00
Sign, Snider's Tomato Catsup, Embossed, Snider Preserve Co., Chicago, 11 x 16 ¾ In. .....*Illus* 600.00
Sign, Soapine, Toilet & Laundry Soaps, Reverse Painted, Silver Foil, Mother-Of-Pearl, 23 x 30 In..*Illus* 6900.00
Sign, Soda, Sarsaparilla & Ginger Ale, 5 Cent, Oil On Canvas, 13 x 21 In.............. 310.00
Sign, Soo Ice Cream, Light-Up, Indian Chief, Mulholland-Harper, 24 x 14 In. 240.00
Sign, Springfield Republican, All The News & The Truth About It, c.1850, 30 x 16 In.............. 1007.00
Sign, Spud Cigarettes, America's Most Refreshing Cigarette, Woman, Man, Frame, 14 x 24 In. . 112.00
Sign, Squeeze That Distinctive Orange Drink, Children, Tin, Embossed, 14 x 26 In. 212.00
Sign, Squirt, Boy With Bottle, Just Call Me Squirt, Porcelain, Die Cut, Painted, 16 x 10 In. 480.00
Sign, Standing Hay, Wood, Paint, c.1920, 30 x 6 ½ In............ 144.00
Sign, Star Soap, Paper, Woman Dressed In Pink, Schultz & Co., Frame, 14 x 30 In. 715.00
Sign, Star Soap, Sleeping Children, Mother Hovering, Paper, Frame, 1890s, 32 x 24 In. 90.00
Sign, Steam Gauge & Lantern Co., Paper, 50 Lanterns, Frame, c.1885, 41 x 28 In. 489.00
Sign, Stephano Cigarettes, Color Litho, Silvertone Frame, France, 44 x 29 In. 391.00
Sign, Stop At The Palace Hotel, Missoula Mont., Embossed Tin, Black, Orange, 27 x 9 In.......... 336.00
Sign, Subway, Boston, Stations' Order, To Dorchester, Cambridge, Steel, Frame, c.1910, 21 x 12 In.. 1534.00
Sign, Sunbeam Bread, For Freshness' Sake, Girl, Tin, Embossed, Self-Framed, 30 x 12 In........ 230.00
Sign, Tab, Flavor In-Calorie Out, Tin, 12 x 32 In............ 123.00
Sign, Tavern, Maison Eugene Fietres, Wood, Painted, Grape Clusters, 1900s, 27 x 32 In. 173.00
Sign, Thermometer, Mail Pouch Tobacco, Treat Yourself To The Best, Porcelain, Frame, 20 x 73 In.. 960.00
Sign, This Island Self Service, Enco, Porcelain, Gas Station, 14 x 28 In. 210.00
Sign, Thompson's Clam Bar, Lobster, Carved, Red, Black, White Paint, 13 x 112 In. 1534.00
Sign, Thorsen Ice Cream, Ellsworth, Maine, 2-Sided, Porcelain, Cobalt Blue, Gray, 24 x 17 ½ In. 118.00
Sign, Tin Flange, Scarce Case Agency, Eagle On Globe, 24 x 16 In. 8250.00
Sign, Tip-Top Bread, Navy With Loaf Of Bread, Red & White Lettering, 1950s, 12 x 30 In. 198.00
Sign, To Auburn Shoe City Of Maine Chamber Of Commerce, Tie Shoe, Wood, c.1910, 9 x 24 In. 3555.00
Sign, Topsy Tobacco, Black Woman, Holding Package, Paper, Frame, c.1900, 59 x 45 In. 1920.00
Sign, Towle's Log Cabin Syrup, Syrup Camp, Woodsy Scene, Cardboard, 26 x 31 In............ 805.00
Sign, Tractors With Lugs Prohibited, Embossed Heavy Metal, Black & White, 18 x 24 In.. 336.00
Sign, Trolley, Cleveland Baking Powder, Cardboard, Image Of Muffins, 1920s, 12 x 22 In........ 90.00
Sign, Tropical Heavy Duty Paints, Hippo, Tin, 2-Sided, Flange, 16 x 12 In.......................*Illus* 248.00
Sign, Turkey Red Cigarettes, Red Woman, Cardboard Lithograph, Oak Frame, c.1915, 34 x 24 In. 345.00
Sign, Union Must & Shall Be Preserved, U.S., Cutwork, Painted, 1861, 13 x 22 In.............*Illus* 5100.00
Sign, Union Shop, Celluloid, Cardboard Back, 9 x 8 In.............. 173.00
Sign, Valvoline, Marine Products, Convex, Tin, 20 x 28 In............ 354.00
Sign, Velvet Ice Cream, 2-Sided, Red, White, Porcelain, 20 x 28 In. 283.00
Sign, Village Optical, Wood, Carved, Painted, c.1850, 29 x 40 In............ 356.00
Sign, Volunteer Bible Class, Black Paint, White Stenciled Letters, c.1900, 15 x 25 In.............. 460.00
Sign, W.R. Hayes' Office, Painted & Gilded, Wood, Molding, Black, c.1895, 5 x 50 In.............. 533.00
Sign, W.S. Doake, Wood, Gilt Lettering & Border, Black Paint, Signed, c.1895, 18 x 10 In......... 356.00
Sign, Warning, Watch Out, Men Working Above, American Bridge, Stand Alone Safety Worker 224.00
Sign, Washing In Six Minutes With A 1900 Washer, Tin, On Cardboard, 19 x 13 In................... 1440.00
Sign, Watertite, Paint For Every Surface, 2-Sided, Painter With Can, Steel, c.1950, 28 x 20 In. 590.00
Sign, We Fix Zippers, Paint, Tin, 25 ½ x 37 ½ In. 316.00
Sign, We Give Yellow Trading Stamps, Yellow Ground, Black Lettering, 24 x 20 In.................... 59.00
Sign, We Have Garson Vending Machine Here, Selling Cigars Of Higher Quality, Frame, 25 x 23 In. 1644.00
Sign, Wear Candee Rubbers, Woman, Reclining, Reading Paper, Gown, Cardboard, 48 x 18 In.. 2040.00
Sign, Western Cartridge Co., New Chief Powder Shells, Husband, Wife, Dog, Boy, Rifle, 19 x 27 In.... 3680.00
Sign, Western Union, 3-Sided, Pole, Light-Up, Viking Sign Co., Counter, 26 In. 2520.00
Sign, Western Union, Bronze, Glass, Light-Up, Counter, 26 In............ 1416.00
Sign, Whiskey, Monticello Distilling, Home Of Thomas Jefferson, Tin Litho, c.1910, 28 x 39 In. . *Illus* 263.00
Sign, Whistle, Thirsty?, Sparkling Orange Goodness, Orange, Blue, Tin, Frame, c.1950, 56 x 32 In... 575.00
Sign, White King Soap, Tin, c.1920, 14 x 9 ¾ In............ 120.00
Sign, White Label Soup, Armour Packing Co., Tin, 23 ½ x 18 In............ 385.00
Sign, Who's Your Druggist?, H. Dale, Owl Holding Sign, Paint, Tin, c.1850, 26 x 11 In.............. 259.00
Sign, Wiard Plow Co., Outdoor, Wood Stand, 74 x 11 ½ In. 358.00
Sign, Wingo, Ellett & Crump Footwear, Reverse Glass, Gesso Frame, c.1900, 21 x 27 In. 150.00

Watch out for Flour Dust
Cadwallader C. Washburn started the Minneapolis Milling Company in 1856. In 1880 his mills and five others were destroyed when flour dust caused an explosion. He immediately built a new, modern mill and won awards for his Gold Medal flour.

Advertising, Sign, Marquette Pure Rye, Reverse On Glass, Frame, 17 x 8 In. $540.00

Victorian Casino Antiques

Advertising, Sign, Masury's Pure Colors Paint, Tin Litho, Sentenne & Green, N.Y., 23 x 17 In. $1,416.00

James D. Julia Auctioneers

Advertising, Sign, Rubberset Brushes, Tin, 2-Sided, Flange, 19 ¼ x 12 In. $1,045.00

Showtime Auction Services

Advertising, Sign, Sanford's Inks Mucilage, Embossed, Tin, Self-Framed, Tuscarora Co., Oh., 20 x 14 In.
$8,250.00

Showtime Auction Services

Advertising, Sign, Saw Blade, Buy Henery Disston & Sons Saws, Files, Phila., Penna., U.S.A., 27 In.
$112.00

Victorian Casino Antiques

Advertising, Sign, Schlitz Atlas Brau, On Draught, Chain, 24 x 14 ¾ In.
$2,200.00

Showtime Auction Services

Advertising, Sign, Snider's Tomato Catsup, Embossed, Snider Preserve Co., Chicago, 11 x 16 ¾ In.
$600.00

Showtime Auction Services

Sign, Wise Potato Chips, Table With Soup & Chips, Easel Back, 1954, 15 x 14 In.	145.00
Sign, Wool Soap, Best For Toilet & Bath, It Floats, 2 Children, Tin, 8 x 15 In.	180.00
Sign, Ye Old Trail Inn, Wood, Tin, Mountain, Indian, Teepees, 41 x 29 In.	1003.00
Sign, Yuengling Premium Beer, Red, Cream, c.1955, 25 x 11 In.	210.00
Stand, Smoking, Drink Moxie, Butler, Holding Tray, Wood, Painted, 32 In.	798.00
Stringholder, Goose, Red Goose Shoes, Green Base, Removable Side Panel, c.1920, 16 In. *Illus*	2360.00
Sugar & Creamer, Borden's Elsie & Elmer, Manufactured By F & F, 1950s, 4 ½ In.	175.00
Tap Handle, Catamount Brewing Co., Lion's Head	40.00
Tap Handle, Mother Pumpkin Ale, Blue Point Brewing Co., 10 In.	33.00
Tap Handle, Spotted Cow Beer, New Glarus Brewing Co., White, 10 In.	35.00
Tether, Borden, Octagonal, Cast Iron, 6 x 3 ½ In.	440.00
Thermometers are listed in their own category.	

Advertising tin cans or canisters were first used commercially in the United States in 1819 and were called tins. Today the word *tin* is used by most collectors to describe many types of containers, including food tins, biscuit boxes, roly poly tobacco containers, gunpowder cans, talcum powder sprinkle-top cans, cigarette flat-fifty tins, and more. Beer Cans are listed in their own category. Things made of undecorated tin are listed under Tinware.

Tin, 2 Orphans, 50 Cigars, 5 x 5 In.	248.00
Tin, 3 Bears Honey, Papa, Mama, Baby, Key, R.D. Bradshaw & Sons, 1949, 4 ⅝ x 4 In.	40.00
Tin, Babbitt's Cleanser, Cardboard, Tin Top, Uniformed Man Holding Brush, Canister, 1930s, 5 x 3 In.	55.00
Tin, Bank Roll Cigar, Round, 50 Cigars, 5 x 5 ½ In.	420.00
Tin, Beech Nut Stogies, Round, Yellow Ground, 50 Cigars, 6 x 4 In.	30.00
Tin, Biscuit, Bookstand, Lithograph, Embossed Panels, Huntley & Palmers, c.1905, 6 ½ x 5 In. *Illus*	143.00
Tin, Biscuit, Golf Bag, Golf Club Lid, Embossed, Tin Litho, Robertson Bros. Ltd., c.1913, 10 ½ In. *Illus*	590.00
Tin, Biscuit, Hansel & Gretel, Cottage, Witch Door, Dutch, 10 ½ x 8 In. *Illus*	690.00
Tin, Biscuit, Row Of Books Shape, Bound With Belt, 6 x 6 In.	70.00
Tin, Blanke's Coffee, Red & Gold Ground, World's Fair Brand, 1903, 10 In.	264.00
Tin, Blue Bird Coffee, White, Bail Handle, 5 Lb., 7 ½ x 9 In. *Illus*	431.00
Tin, By-Lo Talcum Powder, Violet, Lithograph, Oval, Gould Co., N.Y., 4 ½ x 2 In. *Illus*	413.00
Tin, Cadette Borated Baby Talc, Toy Soldier, Lithograph, 7 ⅜ x 2 In. *Illus*	143.00
Tin, Castle Brand Tea, Pry Lid, Castles, Lithograph, 7 x 6 x 7 In.	88.00
Tin, Cigar, Gobblers, The Latest Smoke, Turkey, 50 Cigars, 5 x 5 In. *Illus*	440.00
Tin, Cigar, Orioles, Multicolor, C.E. Acton, Belmont, Oh., 5 ¼ x 5 In.	358.00
Tin, Cigar, Red Feather, Duquesne Cigar Co., Pittsburg Mkrs., 5 x 5 ¼ In.	220.00
Tin, Cigar, Sky Rambler, Above Them All, Cherub On Eagle, Kipp Cigar Co., Hastings, Nebr., 5 x 4 In.	510.00
Tin, Cigar, Yocum Brothers, La Cubana Cigar Factory, Color Lithograph, 5 ½ x 6 In.	59.00
Tin, Coffee, Fairway, Tin Lithograph, Key Wind, Lb., 4 x 5 In. *Illus*	495.00
Tin, Coffee, Leggett's Champion Java, Tin Lithograph, Ginna Co., 3 Lb., 9 x 5 x 5 In. *Illus*	187.00
Tin, Coffee, No. 1, Convention Hall, Ridenour-Baker Grocery Co., Kansas City, 4 x 6 In.	1560.00
Tin, Columbus Stogies, Commercial Cigar Co., 25 Cigars, 6 x 4 In.	660.00
Tin, Custom House Cigar, 50 Cigars, 5 x 5 ½ In.	138.00
Tin, Cut Plug Tobacco, Faux Leather Finish, Handle, Handbag Shape, 7 x 6 In.	83.00
Tin, Daily Habit The Cigar Of Merit, Round, 50 Cigars, 5 x 5 ½ In.	360.00
Tin, Dan Patch Tobacco, Lithograph, Race Horse, Yellow, Red, 3 x 6 x 3 In.	330.00
Tin, Dandy Lyne Pencil, White, Green Dandy Lions, c.1925, 2 x 7 In.	45.00
Tin, De Soto Cigar, 50 Cigars, 5 ½ x 5 ½ In.	90.00
Tin, El Corsocano, Southwest Cigar Co., 25 Cigars, 5 ¾ x 4 ¾ In.	83.00
Tin, El Producto Cigar, Woman, Garden, Lute, Blue Ground, Round, 5 ¾ x 5 ½ In.	120.00
Tin, Elm 5 Cent Cigar, Embossed, Tax Stamps, 50 Cigars, 5 x 5 In.	138.00
Tin, Elm 5 Cent Cigar, Round, 50 Cigars, 5 x 5 ½ In.	30.00
Tin, Even Steven Cigar Tin, C.E. Bair & Sons, 25 Cigars, 3 x 5 ¼ In.	600.00
Tin, Fall-Leaf Coffee, Lithograph, Soodman & Co., Lb., 6 x 4 In. *Illus*	770.00
Tin, Flick & Flock 5 Cent Cigar, Oval, Roby Cigar Co., Barnesville, Ohio, 5 Cigars, 6 x 6 In.	715.00
Tin, Flor De Haynie 10 Cent Straight Cigar, Portraits, Round, Liberty Can Co., 5 x 5 In.	275.00
Tin, Franklin Coffee, Ben Franklin, Lithograph, 3 Lb., 6 x 9 In. *Illus*	345.00
Tin, Frings 3 Bros. Cigar, Orange Liberty Can Co., 50 Cigars, 5 ½ x 5 ⅞ In.	138.00
Tin, Gold Dust Tobacco, Worth Its Weight In Gold, 3 Miners, Canada, Pocket, 4 x 3 In.	1485.00
Tin, Gold Leaf Tobacco, Woman Holding Flag, Leaning On Globe, Label, 6 x 5 In. *Illus*	198.00
Tin, Henrietta Cigar, Ostrich, Otto Eisenlohr & Bros, 50 Cigars, 5 x 5 ¼ In.	220.00
Tin, Hitts Fireworks Co., Car Flares, Devil, Car, Tin Lithograph, Cylindrical, 13 In.	253.00
Tin, Hoffmann's Old Time Coffee, Pry Lid, 3 Lb., 9 ¾ x 5 ½ In. *Illus*	330.00
Tin, Home Run Cigar, Baseball Game Scene, Round, 50 Cigars, 5 ¾ x 4 ¾ In.	5400.00
Tin, Hoopers, Fatal Food, Bug Killer, Woman, Bugs On Floor, Paper Label Over Tin, 5 x 2 In. *Illus*	242.00
Tin, Idols Hand Made Cigar, Multicolor, 3 x 4 ⅞ In.	55.00
Tin, John Storm 5 Cent Cigar, Man's Portrait, Tin, Sepia, 50 Cigars, 6 x 5 ½ In.	120.00

Advertising, Sign, Soapine, Toilet & Laundry Soaps, Reverse Painted, Silver Foil, Mother-Of-Pearl, 23 x 30 In.
$6,900.00

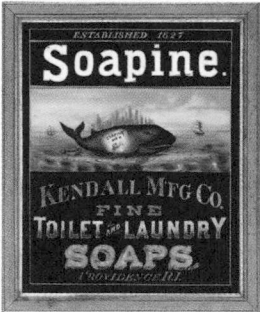

James D. Julia Auctioneers

Advertising, Sign, Tropical Heavy Duty Paints, Hippo, Tin, 2-Sided, Flange, 16 x 12 In.
$248.00

Showtime Auction Services

Advertising, Sign, Union Must & Shall Be Preserved, U.S., Cutwork, Painted, 1861, 13 x 22 In.
$5,100.00

Skinner, Inc.

Advertising, Sign, Whiskey, Monticello Distilling, Home Of Thomas Jefferson, Tin Litho, c.1910, 28 x 39 In.
$263.00

Hake's Americana & Collectibles

Advertising, Stringholder, Goose, Red Goose Shoes, Green Base, Removable Side Panel, c.1920, 16 In.
$2,360.00

Bertoia Auctions

Advertising, Tin, Biscuit, Bookstand, Lithograph, Embossed Panels, Huntley & Palmers, c.1905, 6 ½ x 5 In.
$143.00

Wm Morford Antiques

Advertising, Tin, Biscuit, Golf Bag, Golf Club Lid, Embossed, Tin Litho, Robertson Bros. Ltd., c.1913, 10 ½ In.
$590.00

Bertoia Auctions

Advertising, Tin, Biscuit, Hansel & Gretel, Cottage, Witch Door, Dutch, 10 ½ x 8 In.
$690.00

James D. Julia Auctioneers

Advertising, Tin, Blue Bird Coffee, White, Bail Handle, 5 Lb., 7 ½ x 9 In.
$431.00

Bertoia Auctions

Advertising, Tin, By-Lo Talcum Powder, Violet, Lithograph, Oval, Gould Co., N.Y., 4 ½ x 2 In.
$413.00

Wm Morford Antiques

Advertising, Tin, Cadette Borated Baby Talc, Toy Soldier, Lithograph, 7 ⅜ x 2 In.
$143.00

Wm Morford Antiques

A

Advertising, Tin, Cigar, Gobblers, The Latest Smoke, Turkey, 50 Cigars, 5 x 5 In.
$440.00

Showtime Auction Services

Advertising, Tin, Coffee, Fairway, Tin Lithograph, Key Wind, Lb., 4 x 5 In.
$495.00

Wm Morford Antiques

Advertising, Tin, Coffee, Leggett's Champion Java, Tin Lithograph, Ginna Co., 3 Lb., 9 x 5 x 5 In.
$187.00

Wm Morford Antiques

Advertising, Tin, Fall-Leaf Coffee, Lithograph, Soodman & Co., Lb., 6 x 4 In.
$770.00

Wm Morford Antiques

Tin, Jumbo Dixie Salted Peanuts, Multicolor Label, 9 ½ In., 10 Lb.	1080.00
Tin, Kipling Cut Plug Tobacco, 4 ½ x 2 ⅝ In.	30.00
Tin, Klein's Breakfast Cocoa, Tin Litho, Parrot, Pry Lid, ½ Lb., 4 ½ x 3 In. ....*Illus*	303.00
Tin, La Flor De Portuondo Cigar, Plantation, Round, Liberty Can Co., 50 Cigars, 5 x 4 ⅞ In.	523.00
Tin, La Primadora Coronations, O.I.C. Co 31, Man, Basket On Head, Rounded, 50 Cigars	150.00
Tin, Little Teazer Twist Tobacco, Red, Rectangular, Roth Tobacco Co., Mo., 8 x 5 In.	150.00
Tin, Mackintosh's Rag-Time Candy, Black Couple, Dancing, Banjo, Lift Top, England, 9 ¾ x 6 In.	120.00
Tin, Madame Butterfly, Ritter Can Co., Phila., 5 x 5 ½ In.	138.00
Tin, Martinez Cigar, Blue, Round, 50 Cigars, 5 x 5 ½ In.	55.00
Tin, Master Stogies Cigar, Hound Dog, Pail, 100 Cigars, 6 x 6 In.	150.00
Tin, Meditation Cigar, Woman, Rowboat, Moon, Round, 50 Cigars, 5 x 5 In.	630.00
Tin, Miners, Puddlers Smoking Tobacco, Pail, Handle, 6 ½ x 5 ⅜ In.	440.00
Tin, Nebraska Blossom Cigar, Woman, Frontier Hat, Round, Heekin Can, Ohio, 25 Cigars, 5 x 4 In.	360.00
Tin, Nic Nac Chewing Tobacco, Dog, Pack On Back, B. Leidersdorf Co., 5 Lb., 11 ⅝ x 8 In.....*Illus*	2860.00
Tin, North Pole Cut Plug Tobacco, United States Tobacco Co., Richmond, Va., 6 x 3 In.	90.00
Tin, Old English Curve Cut Tobacco, A Slice To A Pipeful, Fits The Pocket, 13 x 8 ½ In.	210.00
Tin, Old Partner Tobacco Smoking & Chewing, Pail, American Can Co., 6 x 5 In.	303.00
Tin, Old Rip Smoking Tobacco, Red, Allen & Ginter, American Tobacco Co.	120.00
Tin, Orange Flower, 5 Cent Cigar, 5 x 5 ½ In.	165.00
Tin, Orioles Cigar, Round, C.E. Acton, Belmont, Ohio, 50 Cigars, 5 x 4 ⅞ In.	358.00
Tin, Planters Popcorn Seasoning Oil, Cardboard, Uncle Sam, Red Letters, 1918, 13 x 29 In.	800.00
Tin, Poker Club Mixture, Square Corner, S.F. Hess & Co., 4 x 2 In.	480.00
Tin, Pride Of The Chesapeake Oyster, Bail Handle, Orange Ground, c.1910, 7 In.	173.00
Tin, Prince Albert Tobacco, Indian Chief, R.J. Reynolds Tobacco Co., 19 x 25 In.	1870.00
Tin, Red Feather, Green, Duquesne Cigar Co., Pittsburg Makers, 50 Cigars, 5 x 5 In.	220.00
Tin, Robert Fulton 5 Cent Cigar, Liberty Can Co., Medals, Portrait, 50 Cigars, 6 x 5 In.	270.00
Tin, Rose-O-Cuba, Round, Woman, Portrait, Lace Veil, 50 Cigars, 5 x 5 ½ In.	138.00
Tin, Sky Rambler Cigar, Cherub, Riding Eagle, Round, Heekin Can Co., 25 Cigar, 5 x 4 In.	510.00
Tin, Sphinx Mixture, United States Tobacco Co., 4 ½ x 3 In.	390.00
Tin, Sweet Cuba Fine Cut Tobacco, Yellow Ground, 18 x 12 In.	540.00
Tin, Switch Cigar, Railroad Switching Station, 50 Cigars, 5 ½ x 5 ¼ In.	125.00
Tin, Telegrafo Tobacco Very Mild, Professor Morse Image, 5 ⅞ x 5 ¼ In.	193.00
Tin, Tennyson, 5 Cent Cigar, Mazer Cressman Cigar Co., Detroit, Cadillac Can Co., 3 x 5 ⅝ In.	83.00
Tin, Three Ears Honey, Key Wind, Mama & Pap & Baby In Tree, 2 ½ Lb.	42.00
Tin, Three Kings Tobacco Mixture, Monte Cristo Filmy Cut, Wm. Kimball & Co.	60.00
Tin, Tiz 5 Cent Havana Segars, Round, Tiz Real Cardenas & Co., Liberty Can Co., 5 x 5 ⅜ In.	275.00
Tin, Tobacco Girl 5 Cent Cigar, Square, Liberty Can Co., 25 Cigars, 3 ½ x 5 ½ In.	523.00
Tin, Tobacco Girl 5 Cent Cigar, Square, Liberty Can Co., 50 Cigars, 6 ½ x 5 ½ In.	660.00
Tin, Tobacco, City Club, Man Smoking Pipe, Newspaper, Burley Tobacco Co., 3 ⅝ x 2 ¾ In. .....*Illus*	303.00
Tin, Tobacco, Sure Shot Chewing, It Touches The Spot, Indian With Bow, 15 x 10 In.	448.00
Tin, Tobacco, Washington Mixture, George Washington, 44 Star Flag, c.1891, 3 x 4 In. ...*Illus*	303.00
Tin, Torpedo Special Short Cut Smoking Tobacco, Litho, Rock City Tobacco Co., 4 x 3 In.....*Illus*	2530.00
Tin, Virginity Smoking Tobacco, Women, Yellow, Ginna & Co., N.Y., 7 x 3 ¾ In.	303.00
Tin, Yankee Notions Cigar, Liberty Can Co., 50 Cigars, 5 ⅜ x 4 ⅝ In.	120.00

Advertising tip trays are decorated metal trays less than 5 inches in diameter. They were placed on the table or counter to hold either the bill or the coins that were left as a tip. Change receivers could be made of glass, plastic, or metal. They were kept on the counter near the cash register and held the money passed back and forth by the cashier. Related items may be listed in the Advertising category under Change Receiver.

Tip Tray, Bromo-Seltzer, Cures All Headaches, Red Lettering, Steel, Round, 4 In.	106.00
Tip Tray, C.D. Kenny & Co., Thanksgiving Greetings, Girl On Knees Praying, Fruit On Rim, 4 In.	118.00
Tip Tray, Carnation Gum, Tin Lithograph, Carnations, Pink, 4 ⅜ In.	77.00
Tip Tray, Grin & Begin To Win, Billiken, Chromolithograph, Steel, C.D. Kenny Co., 4 In....*Illus*	106.00
Tip Tray, Katz's Export Lager, York Brewing Co., Lithograph, Steel, Round, 4 In.	71.00
Tip Tray, National Brewing Company, Shooting Cowboy, Round, Tin, c.1910, 4 ½ In.	660.00
Tobacco Cutter, Dominion Tobacco Co., Cast Iron, Nickel, Paint, c.1890, 6 x 16 In.	127.00
Token, Columbia Bicycles, Celluloid, Compass, 1892, 1 ½ In.	69.00
Tray, Adolph Coors, Mountain Scene, Tin, Round, 13 In., Pair	266.00
Tray, Anheuser-Busch, Cherubs, Scrolled Border, Tin Lithograph, Oval, 13 x 16 In.	825.00
Tray, Arctic Ice Cream, Cream Supreme, Polar Bear, Tin Litho, 13 ⅝ In. ....*Illus*	688.00
Tray, Billings Brewing Co., Litho, Depicting Lower Yellowstone Falls, Round, c.1900, 12 In.	2912.00
Tray, Buffalo Brewing Co., Sacramento, Tin, Kaufmann & Strauss Co., N.Y., c.1916, 12 In. ... *Illus*	270.00
Tray, Cabello Cigar, Oval, Woman, Rose In Hair, 13 x 17 In.	364.00
Tray, Central Brewing Co., River, Boats, Buildings, Oval, Tin Lithograph, 13 x 16 In.	1760.00

Tray, Charles Valley Brewing Co., Export, Oval, Woman, Holding Bottle, 14 x 17 In. 540.00
Tray, Christian Feigenspan Brewing, Woman's Profile, Round, Tin, 13 In. 60.00
Tray, Climax Stoves, Soldier, Holding Flame, Tin Lithograph, Multicolor, 13 In. Diam. 413.00
Tray, Clysmic, King Of Table Waters, Oval, Seminude Woman, Elk, By Water, 13 x 16 In. 364.00
Tray, Dr. Bouvier's Buchu Gin, Grandpa's Story, Tin Litho, c.1910, 16 x 13 ¾ In. 195.00
Tray, Drink Dr Pepper, You'll Like It Too, Woman, Holding 2 Bottles, 1939, 10 ½ x 13 In. 147.00
Tray, Frank C. Hicks, Wholesale Liquor, Tin Lithograph, Horses, Stable Door, 1908, 13 In. 649.00
Tray, Gal Liker's Ice Cream, Mother Feeding Son, Art Nouveau Rim, Round, 1916, 13 In. 115.00
Tray, Hires Root Beer, Hires To Your Health, Boy, Serving, 12 In. Diam. 115.00
Tray, Hires Root Beer, Ugly Kid, The Best Drink On Earth, Early 1900s, 12 In. 230.00
Tray, Hires, Ugly Kid, Say!, Drink Hires Root Beer, Red, Black, 12 In. Diam. 144.00
Tray, Juicy Fruit Gum, Girl, St. Bernard Dog, Donkey, Round, Blue, Gold Border, c.1905, 10 In. 518.00
Tray, Kaiser Beer, Mahanoy City, Pa., Woman, Horse, Oval, Tin, 16 ½ In. 180.00
Tray, Magnus Beck Beer, Buffalo's Best Beer, Factory, Eagle, Tin Litho, 12 x 17 In. 578.00
Tray, Merry Widow Rolls Her Cigarettes, From Old North State, Tin, c.1908, 13 In. 420.00
Tray, Old Saratoga Whiskey, Dogs Playing Poker, Tin, Ruska, Gerstein & Co., 13 In. *Illus* 224.00
Tray, Rainier Beer, Gibson Girl, Evelyn Nesbitt, Tin Lithograph, 1903, 13 In. *Illus* 2035.00
Tray, Rose Of Killarney, A. Mesh's Sons, Buffalo, American Art Works, 1910, 13 In. 120.00
Tray, Serving, Hires Root Beer, Ugly Kid, The Best Drink On Earth, 1900s, 12 In. 230.00
Tray, Serving, Orange Crush Soda, Orange, White & Blue, Ask For Crush, 1946, 12 In. 155.00
Tray, Steamier Beer Factory, Exterior Industrial View, Round, Tin, 1920s, 12 In. 150.00
Tray, The West End Brewing Co., Utica, New York, Wuerzburger, Round, 13 In. Diam. 570.00
Tray, Walter Bros. Brewing Co., Gold Label Beer, Oval, Wheat, 17 x 14 In. 420.00
Tray, York Brewing Co., Eagle On Keg, Spread Wings, Wheat, Green Rim, York, Pa., 13 In. 2478.00
Tray, Yuengling's Ice Cream Pottsville, Maid Serving, Round, Haskell Coffin, 13 In. 510.00
Tray, Zipp's Cherri-O, Bird, On Branch, Glass, Tin, 1920s, 12 In. 1080.00
Tray, Tip, see Tip Trays in this category.
Trunk, Russian Liqueurs, 12 Embossed Tin Panels, Domed Hinged, 42 ½ x 20 ½ In. 3630.00
Vase, Spaulding & Merrick Sunny Bank, Chicago, Grapes, Flowers, D.F. Haynes, c.1890, 7 In. 115.00
Vest, Planet Hollywood, Space & Island Design, Multicolor, Large, X-Large 29.00
Woman In Bathtub, Metal, Copper Patina, Kercher Baths, Glass Well, Footed, 2 ¾ x 4 In. 413.00

AGATA glass was made by Joseph Locke of the New England Glass Company of Cambridge, Massachusetts, after 1885. A metallic stain was applied to New England Peachblow, which the company called Wild Rose, and the mottled design characteristic of agata appeared. There are a few known items made of opaque green with the mottled finish.

Bowl, Rose To Pink, Gold & Amethyst Staining, Undulating Inverted Rim, Squat, 3 ½ x 7 ½ In. 575.00
Cruet, Wild Rose, Amber, Amethyst Staining, New England, 6 In. 403.00
Pitcher, Cream, Bulbous Square Mouth, Wild Rose, Amethyst Staining, 4 In. 920.00
Salt & Pepper, Wild Rose, Purple & Amber Staining, Cylindrical, Ring Neck, 4 ½ In. 776.00
Saltshaker, Cylindrical Ring Neck Shape, New England, 4 In. 230.00
Tumbler, Pink To Cream, Gold Bubbly Mottling, Cylindrical, 3 ⅞ In. 219.00
Tumbler, Rose To Pink, Oil Staining, Cylindrical, 3 ¾ In. 115.00
Vase, Lily, Pink To Fuchsia, Trumpet Shape, Flower Petal Rim, Amethyst & Amber Staining, 6 In. 518.00
Vase, Lily, Wild Rose To Pale Pink, Amethyst Staining, Trumpet Shape, Ruffled Rim, Round Foot, 8 In. 403.00
Vase, Pink, Purple & Amber Stain, Pinched Sides, Ribbed Ruffled Rim, 4 ¾ In. 403.00

AKRO AGATE glass was founded in Akron, Ohio, in 1911 and moved to Clarksburg, West Virginia, in 1914. The company made marbles and toys. In the 1930s it began making other products, including vases, lamps, flowerpots, candlesticks, and children's dishes. Most of the glass is marked with a crow flying through the letter *A*. The company was sold to Clarksburg Glass Co. in 1951. Akro Agate marbles are listed in this book in the Marble category.

Ashtray, Shell Shape, Blue 9.00
Bowl, Dart Pattern, Orange, White, Flared, 6 x 3 In. 20.00
Cornucopia, Ribbed, Base, White, Green, 3 In. 15.00
Cup & Saucer, Demitasse, Blue & White, Marbleized 28.00
Cup, Concentric Rings, Transparent Blue 65.00
Flowerpot, Ribbed Band, Orange, Miniature, 2 ⅜ x 2 ⅝ In. *Illus* 8.00
Pitcher, Child's, Stippled Band, Topaz 42.00
Planter, Daffodils, Blue, Footed, 5 ½ x 3 In. 14.00
Planter, Narcissus, Yellow, Orange, White, Marked, 5 x 3 x 2 In. 47.00
Powder Dish, Scottish Terrier, Pink Slag, 2 x 4 In. 35.00
Powder Jar, Figural, Colonial Woman, Blue, 6 ¼ In. 95.00
Thumb Pot, Ribbed Rim, Marbleized, Jadite Green, 1 ¼ In. 45.00
Vase, Ribbed, Footed, Tab Handles, White, Blue, 3 In. 15.00

Advertising, Tin, Franklin Coffee, Ben Franklin, Lithograph, 3 Lb., 6 x 9 In.
$345.00

Bertoia Auctions

Advertising, Tin, Gold Leaf Tobacco, Woman Holding Flag, Leaning On Globe, Label, 6 x 5 In.
$198.00

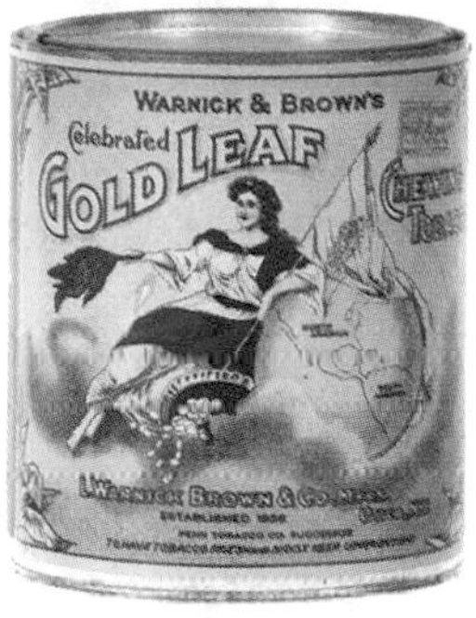

Wm Morford Antiques

Advertising, Tin, Hoffmann's Old Time Coffee, Pry Lid, 3 Lb., 9 ¾ x 5 ½ In.
$330.00

Wm Morford Antiques

Dr. Kellogg's Breakfast
Although he invented Granola and Corn Flakes, Dr. John Harvey Kellogg ate seven graham crackers for breakfast everyday.

Advertising, Tin, Hoopers, Fatal Food, Bug Killer, Woman, Bugs On Floor, Paper Label Over Tin, 5 x 2 In.
$242.00

Wm Morford Antiques

Advertising, Tin, Klein's Breakfast Cocoa, Tin Litho, Parrot, Pry Lid, ½ Lb., 4 ½ x 3 In.
$303.00

Wm Morford Antiques

Advertising, Tin, Nic Nac Chewing Tobacco, Dog, Pack On Back, B. Leidersdorf Co., 5 Lb., 11 ⅝ x 8 In.
$2,860.00

Wm Morford Antiques

Advertising, Tin, Tobacco, City Club, Man Smoking Pipe, Newspaper, Burley Tobacco Co., 3 ⅝ x 2 ¾ In.
$303.00

Wm Morford Antiques

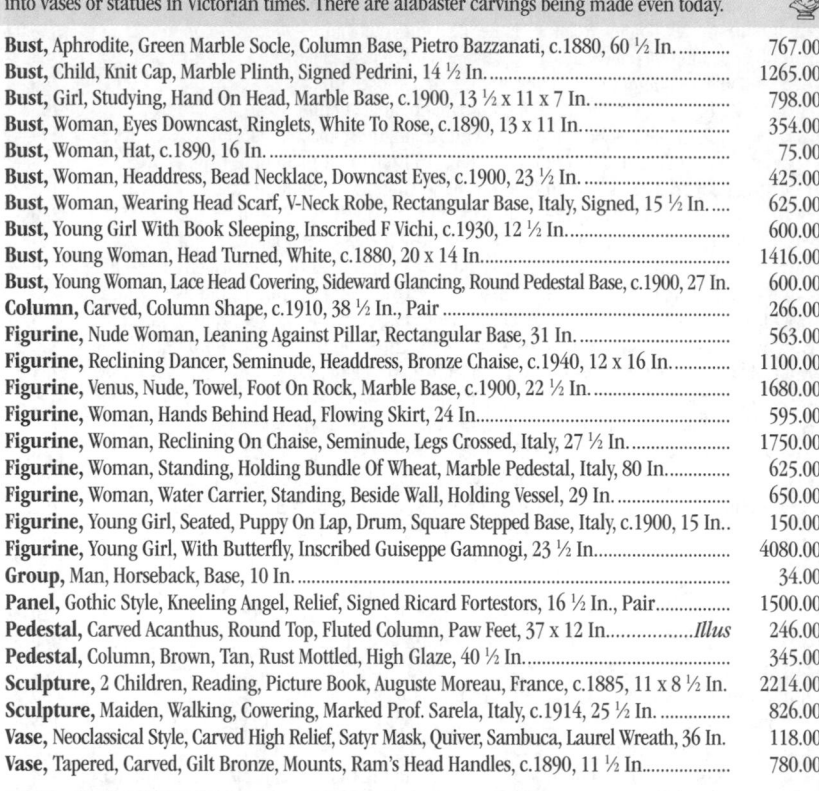

ALABASTER is a very soft form of gypsum, a stone that resembles marble. It was often carved into vases or statues in Victorian times. There are alabaster carvings being made even today.

Bust, Aphrodite, Green Marble Socle, Column Base, Pietro Bazzanati, c.1880, 60 ½ In.	767.00
Bust, Child, Knit Cap, Marble Plinth, Signed Pedrini, 14 ½ In.	1265.00
Bust, Girl, Studying, Hand On Head, Marble Base, c.1900, 13 ½ x 11 x 7 In.	798.00
Bust, Woman, Eyes Downcast, Ringlets, White To Rose, c.1890, 13 x 11 In.	354.00
Bust, Woman, Hat, c.1890, 16 In.	75.00
Bust, Woman, Headdress, Bead Necklace, Downcast Eyes, c.1900, 23 ½ In.	425.00
Bust, Woman, Wearing Head Scarf, V-Neck Robe, Rectangular Base, Italy, Signed, 15 ½ In.	625.00
Bust, Young Girl With Book Sleeping, Inscribed F Vichi, c.1930, 12 ½ In.	600.00
Bust, Young Woman, Head Turned, White, c.1880, 20 x 14 In.	1416.00
Bust, Young Woman, Lace Head Covering, Sideward Glancing, Round Pedestal Base, c.1900, 27 In.	600.00
Column, Carved, Column Shape, c.1910, 38 ½ In., Pair	266.00
Figurine, Nude Woman, Leaning Against Pillar, Rectangular Base, 31 In.	563.00
Figurine, Reclining Dancer, Seminude, Headdress, Bronze Chaise, c.1940, 12 x 16 In.	1100.00
Figurine, Venus, Nude, Towel, Foot On Rock, Marble Base, c.1900, 22 ½ In.	1680.00
Figurine, Woman, Hands Behind Head, Flowing Skirt, 24 In.	595.00
Figurine, Woman, Reclining On Chaise, Seminude, Legs Crossed, Italy, 27 ½ In.	1750.00
Figurine, Woman, Standing, Holding Bundle Of Wheat, Marble Pedestal, Italy, 80 In.	625.00
Figurine, Woman, Water Carrier, Standing, Beside Wall, Holding Vessel, 29 In.	650.00
Figurine, Young Girl, Seated, Puppy On Lap, Drum, Square Stepped Base, Italy, c.1900, 15 In.	150.00
Figurine, Young Girl, With Butterfly, Inscribed Guiseppe Gamnogi, 23 ½ In.	4080.00
Group, Man, Horseback, Base, 10 In.	34.00
Panel, Gothic Style, Kneeling Angel, Relief, Signed Ricard Fortestors, 16 ½ In., Pair	1500.00
Pedestal, Carved Acanthus, Round Top, Fluted Column, Paw Feet, 37 x 12 In. .....*Illus*	246.00
Pedestal, Column, Brown, Tan, Rust Mottled, High Glaze, 40 ½ In.	345.00
Sculpture, 2 Children, Reading, Picture Book, Auguste Moreau, France, c.1885, 11 x 8 ½ In.	2214.00
Sculpture, Maiden, Walking, Cowering, Marked Prof. Sarela, Italy, c.1914, 25 ½ In.	826.00
Vase, Neoclassical Style, Carved High Relief, Satyr Mask, Quiver, Sambuca, Laurel Wreath, 36 In.	118.00
Vase, Tapered, Carved, Gilt Bronze, Mounts, Ram's Head Handles, c.1890, 11 ½ In.	780.00

ALUMINUM was more expensive than gold or silver until the 1850s. Chemists learned how to refine bauxite to get aluminum. Jewelry and other small objects were made of the valuable metal until 1914, when an inexpensive smelting process was invented. The aluminum collected today dates from the 1930s through the 1950s. Hand-hammered pieces are the most popular.

Ashtray, McDonald's, Arches, Stamped, 1970s, 3 ½ In. Diam.	9.00
Basket, Curled Handle, Embossed, Fruit, Flowers, c.1940, 9 In. Diam.	18.00
Biscuit Cutter, 1950s, 3 x 2 In.	8.00
Bowl, Scalloped, Scroll, Incised, Krischer Metal, 8 x 13 In.	19.00
Butter, Cover, Hammered Look, Dome, Finial, Glass Insert, 6 ½ In. Diam.	48.00
Candleholder, Snuffer, Hammered, Flowers, B. Quenilum	25.00
Coaster, Duck, 3 ¼ In.	4.00
Cocktail Shaker, 1950s, 10 ¼ In.	5.00
Colander, 7 Stars, 6 Points, 3-Footed, c.1950, 9 x 5 In.	20.00
Double Boiler, Mirro Aluminum Co., 1 ½ Qt.	23.00
Figurine, Girl, Jumping Rope, Signed Christian Petersen, 1973, 10 In.	48.00
Ice Bucket, Hammered, Swing Handle, c.1950, 12 x 7 In.	25.00
Lazy Susan, Embossed Candies, Fruits, c.1960, 15 In.	35.00
Letter Opener, Ruler Measurements, 12 In.	25.00
Mobile, Dancer, Orange, Black, Red, Painted, Signed Max Papart, France, 17 x 28 In.	336.00
Mold, Muffin, Card Symbols, 13 x 6 In.	36.00
Napkin Holder, Embossed, Flowers, Ribbon, Crimped, Leaf Feet, 1950s, 6 In.	35.00
Pan, Bundt, West Bend, c.1960, 10 In.	27.00
Pitcher, Water, Hammered, Gailstyn, c.1960, 8 In.	30.00
Planter, Women, Flowers Relief, Art Nouveau, 10 ½ x 9 In.	406.00
Plate, Metropolitan Presidents, Map, Bahamas, Wendell August, 1971, 8 In.	17.00
Reamer, Handle, Pat. 61609, Mpls., Minn., c. 1955, 2 x 4 x 8 In.	15.00
Sculpture, Woman's Torso, Classical, Iron Brace Stand, 49 x 14 In.	480.00
Silent Butler, Etched Flowers, Hammered Lid, Rippled Rim, Twisted Handle, c.1945, 12 ¼ In.	23.00
Tea & Coffee Set, Picuot Ware, Brushed, Maple, Formica, Teapot, Coffeepot, Sugar, Creamer, Tray	540.00
Tea Set, Teapot, Sugar, Salt & Pepper, Tray, Flying Saucer Style, Gold Banding, 16 ½ In.	266.00
Teapot, Bulbous, Red Handle, WearEver, c.1940, 13 x 9 In.	105.00
Tray, Hammered, Braided Handles, Marked, Rodney Kent, c.1950, 10 x 8 In.	30.00
Tray, Hammered, Fruit, Scalloped Rim, Square Handles, c.1945, 21 x 12 In.	85.00
Tray, Overlapping Running Horses, Scalloped Rim, 14 In.	30.00

AMBER, *see Jewelry category.*

AMBER GLASS is the name of any glassware with the proper yellow-brown shading. It was a popular color just after the Civil War and many pressed glass pieces were made of amber glass. Depression glass of the 1930s–50s was also made in shades of amber glass. Other pieces may be found in the Depression Glass, Pressed Glass, and other glass categories. All types are being reproduced.

Vase, Embossed Art Deco Flowers, Ribbed Sides, Oval, 7 x 7 In.	108.00

AMBERINA, a two-toned glassware, was originally made from 1883 to about 1900. It was patented by Joseph Locke of the New England Glass Company, but was also made by other companies and is still being made. The glass shades from red to amber. Similar pieces of glass may be found in the Baccarat, Libbey, Plated Amberina, and other categories. Glass shaded from blue to amber is called *Blue Amberina* or *Bluerina*.

Basket, Thumbprint, Amber, Orange, Egg Shape, Ruffled Rim, Handles, Applied Leaf Feet, 12 In.	891.00
Basket, Thumbprint, Egg Shape, Ruffled Rim, Applied Leaf Feet, Thorn Handles, 12 In.	891.00
Berry Set, Daisy & Button, Master Bowl, 6 Square Bowls, Hobbs, Brockunier, 9 & 5 In.	201.00
Bowl, Coin Spot, Squat, Flaring Crimped Rim, 8 ½ In.	719.00
Bowl, Diamond-Quilted, Fuchsia To Amber, Inverted Rim, 4 ½ In.	58.00
Bowl, Ribbed, Yellow To Rose, 5 In.	4600.00
Bowl, Rippled Rim, Applied Mid Ring Amber Scallop Shells, 2 ¾ x 6 In.	24.00
Box, Lid, Tapered, Ribbed, Amber Spear Finial, Signed, 4 ½ In.	1035.00
Butter, Cover, Coin Spot, Reeded Snail Formed Finial, 7 In.	144.00
Creamer, Coin Spot Translucent, Reeded Clear Handle, 4 ½ In.	29.00
Creamer, Cranberry To Amber, Thumbprint, Amber Twist Handle, 4 In.	230.00
Creamer, Lincoln Drape Pattern, Fuchsia To Amber, Reeded Loop Handle, 5 In.	115.00
Cruet, Diamond Optic, Ruffled Rim, Round Faceted Amber Stopper, 12 In.	144.00
Cruet, Flower Design, Amber, Green, Signed, 7 In.	62.00
Cruet, Swirled, Faceted Stopper, 6 ½ In. ....*Illus*	144.00
Pitcher, Water, Herringbone, Melon Ribbed, 8 ¼ In. ....*Illus*	345.00
Rose Bowl, Cranberry To Amber, Diamond-Quilted, Oval, Reeded Feet, Trifold Rim, 6 In.	403.00
Salt & Pepper, Coin Spot, Footed, 4 ½ In., Pair	173.00
Saltshaker, Inverted Honeycomb, Multicolor Enameled Flowers, 3 ½ In.	86.00
Syrup, Cranberry To Amber, Ball Shape, Coin Spot, Silver Plate Flip Lid & Handle, 5 ½ In.	690.00
Toothpick Holder, Diamond-Quilted, Amber To Red, Smokestack Shape, 2 ½ In.	259.00
Tumbler, Cranberry To Amber, Intaglio Cut Band, Blossoms & Leaves, 3 ¾ In.	144.00
Tumbler, Cranberry To Fuchsia To Yellow, Wide Ribbing, 3 ¾ In.	1725.00
Vase, Cranberry To Yellow, Round Foot, Flower Shaped Rim, Swollen Reeded Body, 8 In.	863.00
Vase, Fan, Graf Harrach, Swirled Body, Amber Rigaree Feet, Enamel Flower Rim, 11 In.	345.00
Vase, Lily, Amber To Fuchsia, Optic Ribbed, Disc Foot, Trumpet, Flower Petal Rim, 8 ¼ In.	259.00
Vase, Lily, Cranberry To Amber, Swirled Ribbed Stem, Round Foot, Trifold Rim, 10 In.	288.00
Vase, Lily, Disc Foot, Trifold Rim, 10 In.	5463.00

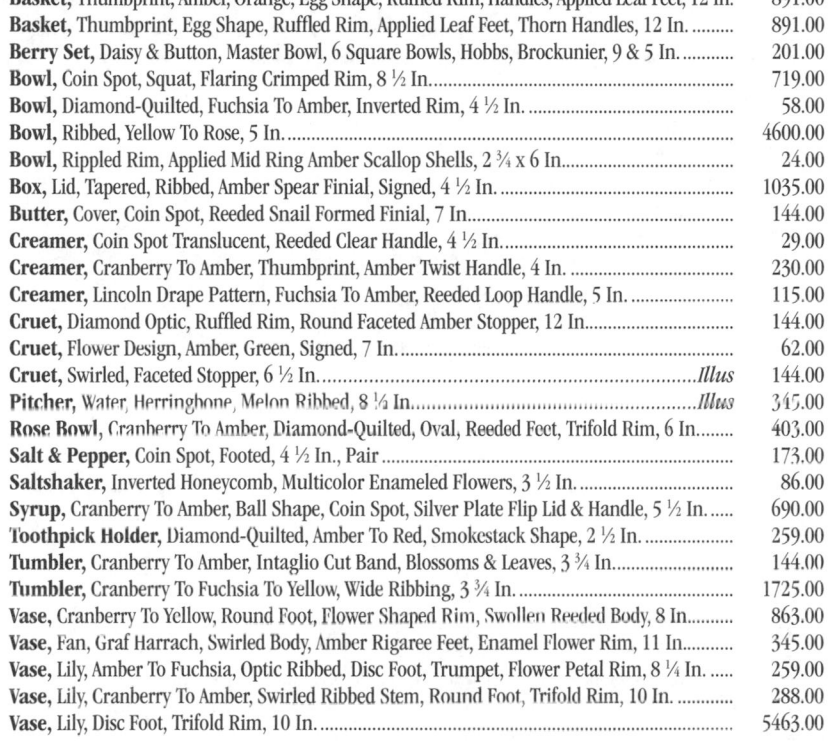

AMERICAN DINNERWARE, *see Dinnerware.*

AMERICAN ENCAUSTIC TILING COMPANY was founded in Zanesville, Ohio, in 1875. The company planned to make a variety of tiles to compete with the English tiles that were selling in the United States for use in fireplaces and other architectural designs. The first glazed tiles were made in 1880, embossed tiles in 1881, faience tiles in the 1920s. The firm closed in 1935 and reopened in 1937 as the Shawnee Pottery.

Dish, Figural, Seminude Woman, Basket, Green Glaze, 7 ¼ x 5 ½ In.	293.00
Tile, Entwined Circle, Flower, Green, Brown, Zanesville, Ohio, c.1910, 12 In.	180.00

AMETHYST GLASS is any of the many glasswares made in the dark purple color of the gemstone amethyst. Included in this category are many pieces made in the nineteenth and twentieth centuries.

Beverage Set, Decanter, Stopper, Silver Band, 6 Footed Cordials, Faceted, 8 In. Decanter	179.00
Bowl, Melon Ribbed, Blown, U.S.A., c.1840, 3 ¾ x 4 ¾ In.	499.00
Bowl, Paneled, 5 ¼ x 9 In.	127.00
Candlestick, Hexagonal, Urn Socket, Double Knob Stem, c.1850, 7 ½ x 4 In., Pair	316.00
Cordial Set, Blown, Silver Applique, Stopper, Colonial Couple, 14 & 3 ¼ In., 7 Piece	71.00
Creamer, Medial Shoulder, Handle Feather Terminal, Rough Pontil, Pa., c.1825, 5 In.	2070.00
Creamer, Vertical Ribs, Waisted Globular, Handle Curl, Rough Pontil, c.1900, 4 x 2 ⅞ In.	345.00
Decanter, 8-Flute, Applied Bar Lip, Polished Pontil, Stopper, Pressed, c.1860, 10 ¼ x 3 ¾ In., Qt.	1035.00

Advertising, Tin, Tobacco, Washington Mixture, George Washington, 44 Star Flag, c.1891, 3 x 4 In.
$303.00

Wm Morford Antiques

Advertising, Tin, Torpedo Special Short Cut Smoking Tobacco, Litho, Rock City Tobacco Co., 4 x 3 In.
$2,530.00

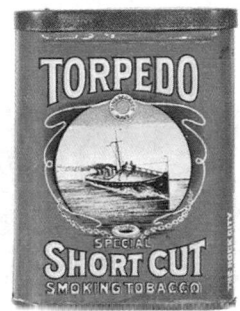

Wm Morford Antiques

Advertising, Tip Tray, Grin & Begin To Win, Billiken, Chromolithograph, Steel, C.D. Kenny Co., 4 In.
$106.00

Conestoga Auction Co., Inc.

Advertising, Tray, Arctic Ice Cream, Cream Supreme, Polar Bear, Tin Litho, 13 ⅝ In.
$688.00

Wm Morford Antiques

Advertising, Tray, Buffalo Brewing Co., Sacramento, Tin, Kaufmann & Strauss Co., N.Y., c.1916, 12 In.
$270.00

Advertising, Tray, Old Saratoga Whiskey, Dogs Playing Poker, Tin, Ruska, Gerstein & Co., 13 In.
$224.00

Victorian Casino Antiques

Advertising, Tray, Rainier Beer, Gibson Girl, Evelyn Nesbitt, Tin Lithograph, 1903, 13 In.
$2,035.00

Wm Morford Antiques

Akro Agate, Flowerpot, Ribbed Band, Orange, Miniature, 2 ⅜ x 2 ⅝ In.
$8.00

Ruby Lane, Inc.

Decanter, Syrup, 8-Panel, Tapered Cylinder, Ring Neck, Silver Nozzle, c.1860, 11 x 3 In., Pair..	403.00
Pitcher, Coin Spot, Bulbous, Ruffled Rim, Clear Reeded Loop Handle, 9 In.	58.00
Tumbler, Ring Framed Ovals, 6-Sided Bowl, Stem, Foot, c.1865, 5 x 3 ½ In.	92.00
Vase, 3-Printie, Milk Striations, 6-Petal Rim, Raised, Flared 6-Sided Base, New Eng., c.1860, 9 x 4 In.	259.00
Vase, Melon Ribbed, Raised Round Foot, Rounded Square, 7 ½ In.	575.00
Vase, Painted Iris, Blown, Signed, 12 x 7 In.	270.00
Vase, Silver Flower Overlay, 14 x 10 In.	119.00

AMPHORA *pieces are listed in the Teplitz category.*

ANDIRONS *and related fireplace items are included in the Fireplace category.*

ANIMAL TROPHIES, such as stuffed animals, rugs made of animal skins, and other similar collectibles made from animal, fish, or bird parts, are listed in this category. Collectors should be aware of the endangered species laws that make it illegal to buy and sell some of these items. Any eagle feathers, many types of pelts or rugs (such as leopard), ivory, and many forms of tortoiseshell can be confiscated by the government. Related trophies may be found in the Fishing category. Ivory items may be found in the Scrimshaw or Ivory categories.

Antelope Head, Antlers, Mounted, 32 In.	98.00
Bear, Standing On Hind Legs, Stuffed, 84 In.	1320.00
Black Bear Hide, With Head, Red & Black Felt Backing, 64 x 60 In.	443.00
Brown Bear Hide, With Head, Peach & Brown Felt Backing, 90 x 86 In.	590.00
Buffalo Head, Stuffed, 36 In.	336.00
Cape Buffalo, Shoulder Mount	240.00
Chucker Birds, Naturalistic Setting, Glass Lighted Display Case, 69 x 23 x 17 In.	633.00
Cow Horns, Polished, Steel Base, 31 ½ In., Pair	587.00
Deer Head, Carved, Painted, Oak Leaves, Acorns, 39 In.	504.00
Deer, 10-Point Buck, Albino, Full Body Mount, Glass Case, 53 x 46 In.	2185.00
Elk, 12-Point Antlers, Mounted, 54 x 48 x 42 In. ....*Illus*	500.00
Impala Head, Horns, Mounted, 37 ½ In.	403.00
Kudu, Shoulder Mount	600.00
Longhorn Horns, Leather Mounts, Inscribed, 1971, 93 In.	354.00
Moose Head, Alaska, 1900s, 65 x 67 In. ....*Illus*	2115.00
Moose Head, Antlers, 1900s, 58 x 60 In. ....*Illus*	2468.00
Owl, White, Mounted On Plants & Leaves, Plexiglas Case, c.1850, 17 ½ x 14 ½ In. ....*Illus*	1722.00
Prong Horn Antelope, Shoulder Mount, 30 x 12 In.	708.00
Ram's Head, Horns, Mounted, 14 x 18 ½ In.	132.00
Rug, Bear Skin, Blond, Light Brown Fur, Head, Legs, Claws, Felt Back, Jonas Bros., 80 x 84 In.	3300.00
Rug, Brown Bear, Full Body Mount, Red Wood Felt Border, c.1910, 74 x 60 In.	826.00
Rug, Cheetah Head, Cloth Lining, Tag, Dr. James L. Clark, 76 In. ....*Illus*	1270.00
Rug, Leopard Head & Body, 78 x 40 In.	1534.00
Rug, Polar Bear, Alaska, 1959, 95 x 101 In.	7475.00
Rug, Zebra Skin, Black Wool Backing, c.1900, 132 x 87 In.	944.00
Sable, Shoulder Mount, 57 In.	840.00
Stag, Antlers, Black Forest Mount, Shield Shape Plaque, c.1890, 61 x 42 In.	1955.00
Stag, Molded Plastic, Real Antlers, Painted, Brown Glass Eyes, 1900s, 20 ½ In.	230.00
Tarpon, Mounted, 66 In.	180.00
Water Buck, Shoulder Mount	150.00

ANIMATION ART collectibles include cels that are painted drawings on celluloid needed to make animated cartoons shown in movie theaters or on TV. Hundreds of cels were made, then photographed in sequence to make a cartoon showing moving figures. Early examples made by the Walt Disney Studios are popular with collectors today. Original sketches used by the artists are also listed here. Modern animated cartoons are made using computer-generated pictures. Some of these are being produced as cels to be sold to collectors. Other cartoon art is listed in Comic Art and Disneyana.

Cel, Charlie Brown, Good Grief Expression, Peanuts, 9 x 10 In.	1200.00
Cel, Pinocchio, Holding Apple & Book, Figaro, Steps, 7 ¼ x 7 ¼ In.	2645.00
Cel, Snow White, Doves On Windowsill, Mat, Frame, 1930s, 17 ¾ x 17 ⅞ In. ....*Illus*	3105.00
Cel, Winnie The Pooh New Adventures, Production, Color, Frame, c.1988, 7 x 9 & 9 x 11 In., Pair	765.00
Cel, Yellow Submarine, Nowhere Man, Jeremy Hilary Boob, Waving, Reading Book, 1968, 11 x 14 In.	1500.00
Drawing, Sleeping Beauty, Eyes Closed, Pencil, Disney, 1958, 10 x 12 In.	1200.00
Fan Card, Mickey Mouse, Walking & Waving, Ink, Watercolor, 1935, 10 x 12 ½ In.	1968.00

Preliminary Art, Donald Duck, Better Self, Devil & Angel, Pencil, 1938, 10 x 12 In.......... 835.00
Preliminary Art, Little Hiawatha, Good Housekeeping, Pencil, 1937, 10 x 12 In. 345.00
Production Drawing, Mickey Mouse, Fiddling Around, Pencil, 1930, 9 ½ x 12 In. 230.00
Production Drawing, Steamboat Willie, Mickey Mouse With Mallets, Pencil, 1928, 9 ½ x 12 In. 2038.00
Production Drawing, Tortoise & Hare, Ready To Run, Pencil, 1935, 9 x 12 In., Pair.............. 316.00

ANNA POTTERY was started in Anna, Illinois, in 1859 by Cornwall and Wallace *Anna Pottery*
Kirkpatrick. They made many types of utilitarian wares, bricks, drain tiles, and
giftware. The most collectible pieces made by the pottery are the pig-shaped bottles and jugs with special
inscriptions, applied animals, and figures. The pottery closed in 1894.

Bottle, Pig, Bennington Glaze, Sanford Wells & Co., St. Louis, Mo., c.1872, 7 In. 4600.00
Bottle, Pig, Dark Brown Albany Glaze, Incised, Good Old Rye, 1876, 7 In................................. 2070.00
Bottle, Pig, Eastern Route Railroad & River Guide, Incised, Brown Albany Glaze, c.1870, 7 ¾ In.. *Illus* 4025.00
Bottle, Pig, Figural, Horace Greely, Albany Slip Glaze, c.1872, 8 In. 21850.00
Bottle, Pig, Gray Salt Glaze, Cobalt Blue Letters, J.O. Sanders, 1883, 6 ½ In. 13800.00
Bottle, Pig, Midwest Map, Albany Slip Glaze, Kirkpatrick, St. Louis, c.1880, 8 In. 3450.00
Bottle, Pig, Railroad Guide, Kansas City & Northern R.Y., Salt Glaze, J.O. Sanders, 6 ¼ In... *Illus* 8050.00
Death Mask, Abraham Lincoln, Salt Glaze, Paint, 2 Holes To Base, Kirkpatrick, 1877, 13 ¾ In. 4600.00
Flask, Pig, Albany Slip Glaze, Chicago World's Fair, 1893, 6 In. 4888.00
Flask, Pig, Incised Face, Hooves, Round Opening, St. Louis, Future Capital, Anna Pottery, c.1880, 8 In. 1265.00
Flask, Pig, Railroad Map, Brown To Amber Albany Glaze, c.1870, 6 ½ In. 2280.00
Inkwell, Frog, On Clamshell, Cobalt Spots, Salt Glaze, Kirkpatrick Bros., 1881, 3 ⅜ x 3 ¾ In.. 5750.00
Urn, Salt Glaze, Wide Rim, Incised Allen Huckleberry, 1886, Kirkpatrick Bros., Ill., 15 x 19 In... 2070.00

ARABIA began producing ceramics in 1874. The pottery was established in Helsinki, Finland,
by Rörstrand, a Swedish pottery that wanted to export porcelain, earthenware, and other
pottery from Finland to Russia. Most of the early workers at Arabia were Swedish. Arabia
started producing its own models of tiled stoves, vases, and tableware c.1900. Rörstrand sold its interest
in Arabia in 1916. By the late 1930s, Arabia was the largest producer of porcelain in Europe. Most of its
products were exported. A line of stoneware was introduced in the 1960s. Arabia worked in cooperation
with Rörstrand from 1975 to 1977. Arabia was bought by Hackman Group in 1990 and Hackman was
bought by Iittala Group in 2004. Arabia is now a brand owned by Iittala Group.

ARABIA
FINLAND

Plaque, Vase, Flowers, Blue, 9 x 4 In. 41.00
Vase, 6-Sided, Green, Flared, Marked 45.00

ARCHITECTURAL antiques include a variety of collectibles, usually very large, that
have been removed from buildings. Hardware, backbars, doors, paneling, and even old
bathtubs are now wanted by collectors. Pieces of the Victorian, Art Nouveau, and Art Deco
styles are in greatest demand.

Arch, Oak, Carved, Armorial Shield, Shells, Putti, Garland, c.1890, 20 ½ x 54 ½ In. 3360.00
Backbar, Mirror, Cast Iron, Galleried, Arched Top, Casting, 45 x 28 In. 300.00
Backbar, Oak, San Domingo Model, Brunswick Balke Collender, 18 x 9 ½ Ft. 22000.00
Backbar, Rothchild, Eastlake Style, Cherry, Mirrors, Doors, Drawers, 1880s, 192 x 112 In....... 11750.00
Balcony Panel, Iron, Art Nouveau, Stylized Scrolls, Flowers, France, c.1910, 39 x 59 In., Pair.. 1800.00
Balcony Panel, Iron, Leaf, Scroll Design, Bombe Shape, Paint, c.1890, 37 x 57 In., Pair 900.00
Bank Teller's Cage, No, 5, Door With Bars, Glass Window, Virginia City, Nevada, 20 x 40 In... 259.00
Bathtub, Metal, Tin Claw Feet..*Illus* 168.00
Bathtub, Zinc, Neoclassical Style, Tapered Body, Handles, 1800s, 26 x 65 In. ....*Illus* 427.00
Beam, Bronze, Eagle, Shield, Deus Meus Et Omnia, Crucifix, Olive Branches, 1800s, 17 x 30 In. 431.00
Bell Ringer, Bronze, Raised Stars, Push Button, c.1900, 6 ½ x 3 ¼ In....................................... 413.00
Bracket, Butcher Trade Sign, Black Paint, Cast Iron, 24 x 28 In..*Illus* 3300.00
Bracket, Corner, Giltwood, Acanthus Leaves, Round Shelf, Flower Swags, c.1885, 16 x 11 In.. 492.00
Bracket, Fluted, Curved Capital, Platform Covered In Green Felt, 8 ¼ x 6 ¼ In., 4 Piece 288.00
Bracket, Gilt, Carved, 10 ½ x 10 ¾ In.. 25.00
Bracket, Gilt, Rococo Revival, Oval Top, Scrolled Supports, Grapes, Leaves, c.1865, 18 x 20 In. 676.00
Bracket, Giltwood, Eagle, Spread Wings, Pinecone Finial, Shelf, c.1885, 18 x 20 In., Pair 1599.00
Bracket, Giltwood, Georgian Style, Scrolls, Leaves, Carved, c.1910, 10 ½ In............................ 948.00
Bracket, Giltwood, Rococo Style, Pierced C-Scrolls, Shelf, Notch Corners, 10 x 8 In., Pair 110.00
Bracket, Louis XIV, Walnut, Galleried Top, Leafy Scroll, c.1700, 14 x 14 In., Pair 1100.00
Bracket, Louis XV, Silver Clad, Bombe Shape, Leaves, Scrolls, Swags, c.1765, 12 x 18 In......... 738.00
Bracket, Oak, Renaissance Style, Putti, C-Scroll, Roses, Stippled, c.1885, 21 x 4 In., Pair 738.00
Bracket, Wall, Gilt, Pheasant, On Branch, Serpentine Shelves, Leaves, 18 x 19 In., Pair 1599.00
Bracket, Wall, Gilt, Rococo, Half Round Shelf, Carved C-Scrolls, Drop, c.1890, 16 ½ x 23 In... 492.00
Bracket, Wood, Carved, Masks, Blossoms, Leaves, Shield Shape, Paint, 19 x 17 In., Pair......... 500.00

Alabaster, Pedestal, Carved Acanthus,
Round Top, Fluted Column, Paw Feet,
37 x 12 In.
$246.00

Skinner, Inc.

Amberina, Cruet, Swirled, Faceted
Stopper, 6 ½ In.
$144.00

Early Auction Co.

Amberina, Pitcher, Water, Herringbone,
Melon Ribbed, 8 ½ In.
$345.00

Early Auction Co.

**Hang a Horseshoe for
Good Luck**
When you hang a horseshoe
today for good luck, you
hang it so the opening faces
the ceiling. In earlier days,
you wanted the horseshoe
opening to face the floor.
During the Depression of
the 1930s, the superstition
changed and the idea was to
hold the luck in, not let it
run to the floor.

Animal Trophy, Elk, 12-Point Antlers, Mounted, 54 x 48 x 42 In.
$500.00

Rago Arts & Auction Center

Animal Trophy, Moose Head, Alaska, 1900s, 65 x 67 In.
$2,115.00

Garth's Auctioneers & Appraisers

Animal Trophy, Moose Head, Antlers, 1900s, 58 x 60 In.
$2,468.00

Garth's Auctioneers & Appraisers

> **TIP**
> *Clean the feathers on a stuffed bird with chunks of fresh white bread. After cleaning, spray lightly with hair spray.*

Cherub Head, Wood, Paint, Gilt, Carved, c.1790, 13 ½ x 21 In.	805.00
Column Capital, Wood Blocks, Carved, Rustic Painted, 10 ½ x 10 In., Pair	173.00
Column Panel, Buddhist Temple, Carved, Chinese Characters, Gilt, Black, 1800s, 97 x 12 In., Pair	920.00
Column, Faux Sienna Marble, Tapered, Square Base, Capital, 1900s, 96 ½ x 9 In.	295.00
Column, Half, Wood, Carved, Honey Finish, 88 In., Pair	495.00
Column, Parcel Gilt, Paint, Cylindrical, Ionic Capital, Carved, Square Base, 73 In., Pair	750.00
Column, Pine, Poplar, Tapered, Scroll Top, Square Base, 1800s, 46 ½ In., Pair	472.00
Corbel, Oak, Carved, Griffin, Baring Teeth, Paw Foot, 36 x 6 In.	1560.00
Cornice, Giltwood, Gesso, Carved Leaves, 10 x 55 In.	210.00
Cornice, Wood, Orb, Cross Finial, Carved, c.1860, 25 ½ x 20 In.	295.00
Crest, Door Frame, Giltwood, Leaves, Prince Of Wales Feathers, 39 x 28 ½ In., Pair	6457.00
Door Handle, Iron, Hand Forged, Tulip Terminal, 10 In.	237.00
Door Hinge, Wrought Iron, Early 19th Century, 22 In., Pair	1007.00
Door Lock, Wrought Iron, Cast Iron Key, 8 x 13 In.	325.00
Door Pull, Hand Wrought Monel, Geometrics & Flowers, Samuel Yellin, 10 ½ In. ....*Illus*	1652.00
Door, 7 Doors, Wood, Label, Salesman's Sample, 11 x 9 x 4 In.	1020.00
Door, Cabinet, Wrought Iron Springlock, Engraved Hinges, Painted, c.1820, 26 x 51 In.	276.00
Door, Entry, Cross Over Bible, Paneled, Dog Ear Frame, Butt Hinges, 79 x 48 In.	58.00
Door, Iron, Arch Transom, Scrolls, Wrought, Paint, c.1920, 116 x 44 In., Pair	720.00
Door, Iron, Gothic Style, Glass Transom, Scrolls, Leaves, c.1880, 94 x 62 In., Pair	1440.00
Door, Molded Cornice, Dentil, Painted, Side Columns, Gilt, Continental, 1800s, 100 x 78 In. .... *Illus*	3068.00
Door, Oak, Etched Glass Panel, Woman In Garden, c.1890, 26 x 11 In.	1725.00
Door, Pine, 6 Recessed Panels, Carved, Egg & Dart, Leaves, Berries, 77 x 33 In., Pair	2106.00
Door, Pine, Georgian Style, Turned Panels, c.1860, 84 x 48 In., Pair	510.00
Door, Saloon, Oak, Leaded Glass Window, Arched Top, Hinges, 54 x 65 In., Pair	770.00
Door, Stable, Green Paint, Free Swinging Top & Bottom, c.1900, 48 x 27 In.	230.00
Door, Stained Glass, Tiles, Art Nouveau, Fleur-De-Lis, Multicolor, c.1890, 120 x 41 In.	2300.00
Doorbell, Wrought Iron, Brass, Rectangular, S-Scrolls, 10 Brass Bells, Crank, 16 x 11 In.	805.00
Doorknob, Oak Mount, Louis Sullivan, Wainwright Building, St. Louis, Mo., 1891, 4 x 13 In.	732.00
Doorknocker, Brass, Cuffed Hand, Holding Sphere, Green Paint Stand, England, 7 ½ In.	590.00
Doorknocker, Brass, Hand Holding Ball, Mounted, Wooden Block, 1800s, 6 ⅝ In.	767.00
Doorknocker, Cast Iron, Fish, Gothic, 9 In.	138.00
Doorknocker, Cast Iron, Ram's Head, 10 ¾ In.	90.00
Doorknocker, Cast Iron, Rose Bowl, Bow, Painted, Cream & Pink Medallion, Box, Hubley, 4 In.	118.00
Doorknocker, Iron, Egyptian Bust, Plate Mount, Bell Button, 8 x 5 In.	1495.00
Doorknocker, Iron, Owl, On Branch, Back Plate, Painted, 5 In. ....*Illus*	443.00
Doorknocker, Iron, Parrot, Wreath Perch, Painted, Oval Back Plate, Hubley, 4 ½ In.	47.00
Doorknocker, Iron, Trotting Horse, Red Paint, 13 In.	207.00
Doorway, Pine, Federal, Fan Light, Pilasters, Carved, White Paint, Md., c.1800, 128 x 82 In.	3720.00
Downspout, Copper, Federal Style Eagle, Numeral, c.1799, 19 ½ x 21 ¾ In.	1020.00
Downspout, Tin, Painted, Inscribed 1850, C.L., 21 x 11 In.	504.00
Eagle, Copper, Spread Wings, On Sphere, 1800s, 31 x 70 In.	4740.00
Eagle, Copper, Spread Wings, Orb, Stand, Fiske, 14 ½ x 11 ½ In.	236.00
Eagle, Giltwood, Spread Wings, Holding Shield, Red, White, Blue, c.1900, 12 x 35 In.	1625.00
Eagle, Iron, Spread Wings, c.1850, 7 ½ x 15 In.	474.00
Eagle, Iron, Spread Wings, Half Sphere, Gold Paint, Base, 1800s, 52 x 45 In.	558.00
Exit Sign, Theater, Ruby Glass, 5 ½ x 11 In., Pair	935.00
Fence, Iron, Bent Rods, Scalloped Top, 6 Sections, c.1900, 43 x 85 In.	323.00
Fence, Iron, Neoclassical, Scrolls, Flowers, Ball Finials, Cast, c.1880, 31 x 61 In., 10 Piece	7200.00
Figure, Putti, Wood, Carved, 1800s, 14 In.	345.00
Finial, Devil, Carnival Wagon, Iron, J.W. Leach, 1870s, 5 x 5 ½ In.	303.00
Finial, Iron, Pineapple, Pedaled Urn, Ogee Base, Gray Paint, 21 In., Pair	590.00
Finial, Sheet Zinc, Galvanized Metal, Baluster Shaft, Star, Embossed Flowers, c.1875, 46 In.	1067.00
Fireplace Surround, Double Over Panels, Fluted Columns, 1800s, 75 x 92 In.	443.00
Fireplace Surround, Federal, Poplar, Molded Edge, Rounded Corners, Columns, 51 x 77 In.	584.00
Fireplace Surround, Mantel, Federal, Carved, Swags, Paint, Salem, Mass., c.1795, 58 x 80 In.	5270.00
Fireplace Surround, Mirror, Mahogany, Burl, Marquetry, c.1870, 104 x 72 In.	8750.00
Fireplace Surround, Oak, Oval Mirror, Flower Carved Panels, Columns, c.1900, 72 x 60 In.	207.00
Fireplace Surround, Oak, Victorian, Wreath, Carved, 4-Column Base, c.1890, 78 x 60 In.	660.00
Fireplace Surround, Victorian, Panel Frieze, Scroll Carvings, 51 x 60 In.	184.00
Fireplace Surround, Wood Carving, Federal, Egg & Dart, Urns, Garland, c.1900, 61 x 60 In.	360.00
Flagpole Bracket, Wrought Iron, Scroll & Arrow Design, Stamped, S. Yellin, 9 ½ In.	1416.00
Fragment, Concrete, Coca-Cola Bottle, Scroll Design, Frame, White, Black, c.1900, 30 x 27 In.	1778.00
Fragment, Wood, Carved, Man, On Keg Drinking, Dragon, Carved, 11 ¼ In.	96.00
Frieze, Neogothic Style, Scrolling, 14 x 30 ½ In.	210.00
Gargoyle, Iron, Winged, Seated, 42 x 41 ½ In.	1200.00

Gate, Cast Iron, 4-Part Panel, Lion Of Venice, Kneeling Bishop, Italy, 1800s, 66 x 57 In............	7475.00
Gate, Entry, Iron, Black Paint, c.1900, 61 x 88 In..	240.00
Gate, Farm, Wood Slats, Steel Hardware, Latch, Swivel Base, Stenciled, 16 x 34 In....................	863.00
Gate, Gilt Iron, Bronze, Scrollwork, Twist Columns, Shells, c.1940, 71 ⅝ x 29 ⅝ In., Pair........	6300.00
Gate, Iron, Allover Scrolls, Gilt, Wrought, c.1940, 68 x 52 In., Pair................................	840.00
Gate, Walnut, Picket Style, c.1850, 15 x 14 In..	504.00
Gate, Wrought Iron, 2 Panel, Arched, Applied Grape Leaves, Shields, c.1910, 78 In...................	3360.00
Gate, Wrought Iron, Bronze Lion, Scrollwork, 83 x 62 In., Pair....................................	1020.00
Griffin, Mahogany, Carved, c.1800, 9 x 9 In..	144.00
Handrail, Wrought Iron, Cross Design Mounts, Yellin, 46 ½ In...................................	1770.00
Hinge, Wrought Iron, Bat Wing Shape, Die Cut Flange, Rolled Hinge Socket, 7 In., Pair..........	118.00
Indian, Sheet Iron, Bow, Arrow, Black Paint, c.1880, 36 In......................................	11160.00
Lamp Post, Column, Attached Scrolls, Stepped Base, Acanthus Feet, Iron, 1800s, 61 x 20 In....	210.00
Lion's Head, Cast Iron, 13 In..	690.00
Lion's Head, Copper, c.1890, 22 x 20 In..	5925.00
Lock Plate, Sheet Iron, Hammered, Pierced, 1600s, 17 x 8 ½ In................................	1872.00
Locker, Metal, c.1930, 69 x 47 In., 4 Piece..	450.00
Manhole Cover, Iron, Indian, Soldier, Shield, State Office Building, Marietta, c.1930, 18 In.....	267.00
Mantel, Bleached Walnut, Adams Style, Mirror, Shelves, Carvings, England, 1800s, 83 x 41 In...	633.00
Mantel, Federal, Pine, Columns, Stepped, Pierced, Carved, Blue Paint, 62 x 69 ½ In.............	1422.00
Mantel, Fireplace, Pine, Shelf, Moldings, Reeded Square Columns, 1800s, 53 x 69 In............	264.00
Mantel, George III Style, Molded & Beaded Cornice, Fluted Columns, c.1900, 47 x 63 In........	492.00
Mantel, Mixed Woods, Classical Pilasters, White, Gray, Chillicothe, O., c.1800, 52 x 63 In........	176.00
Mantel, Mixed Woods, Oak Graining, Fluted Pilasters, c.1850, 52 x 45 In........................	118.00
Mantel, Oak, Scroll Leaf Cornices, Beveled Mirror, Shelves, Tile Insert, c.1890, 84 x 60 In.......	660.00
Mantel, Pine, Carved, Scroll Cutout, Columns, 1800s, 52 x 60 In................................	30.00
Mantel, Pine, Federal Style, Sponged Paint, Applied Flat Columns, c.1850, 38 x 52 ½ In........	345.00
Mantel, Pine, Federal, Carved, Fan Panels, Reeded Pilasters, Cartouches, c.1810, 58 x 88 In...	4740.00
Mantel, Pine, Federal, Carved, Green Paint, Kentucky, c.1810, 58 x 67 In.......................	1541.00
Mantel, Pine, Federal, Carved, White Paint, c.1810, 59 x 75 In.................................	474.00
Mantel, Pine, Federal, Figure, Swag Carved, Philadelphia, c.1805, 58 ¼ x 82 ¼ In..............	4503.00
Mantel, Rouge Griotte Marble, Molded Top & Surround, 43 x 49 x 14 In.........................	777.00
Mantel, Wood, Gesso Paint, Applied Gilt Urn, Swag, 1800s, 48 ½ x 49 In........................	826.00
Model, Hardwood, Spiral Staircase, One Turn, 31 ½ In..	185.00
Model, House, 2 Story, 3 Chimney, Picket Fence, Painted, 26 x 37 x 35 In.......................	767.00
Model, House, Pittsburg, Gables, Double Level Porches, Victorian, c.1890, 38 x 27 In...........	1936.00
Model, Mahogany, Spiral Staircase, Triple Turn, 42 In..	1230.00
Newel Post, Brass, Lobed, c.1900, 3 ½ In..	84.00
Newel Post, Faceted Crystal, Sphere Shape, Bronze Mounted, c.1920, 6 In.......................	540.00
Niche, Giltwood, Faux Marble, Corner, Half Dome, Arched, Italy, c.1800, 88 x 54 In.............	1200.00
Overmantel Mirror, Federal, Giltwood, Divided Panes, c.1820, 24 ½ x 59 In...................	119.00
Overmantel Mirror, Gilt Federal, Diamond Shapes, Dots, Landscape Eglomise, 25 x 49 In...	2655.00
Overmantel Mirror, Giltwood, Georgian Style, C-Scroll, Leaves, Phoenix, 1800s, 46 x 56 In..	2370.00
Overmantel Mirror, Giltwood, Row Of Spherules, Corinthian Columns, 52 In....................	550.00
Overmantel Mirror, Regency, Egyptian Busts, Divided, Beaded Frieze, Column, 32 x 55 In....	8125.00
Panel, Brass, Art Deco, Scrolls, Flowers, Mythical Animal, 23 x 10 In., Pair.....................	72.00
Panel, Circus Wagon, Parcel Gilt, Carved, Gray, c.1905, 46 x 34 In., Pair.......................	403.00
Panel, Iron, Art Deco, c.1900, 18 x 27 ½ In., Pair..	240.00
Panel, Iron, Art Nouveau, Flower Detail, France, c.1930, 20 x 73 In., Pair......................	420.00
Panel, Oak, Black Forest Style, Lion's Head Mask, Flowers, Swiss, 24 ¾ x 21 ½ In., Pair	660.00
Panel, Oak, Carved, Fish, Fowl, Blossoms, Raised Molded Border, Italy, 1800s, 22 x 24 In., Pair	540.00
Panel, Oak, Wainscoting, Columns, Arch, Carved, c.1890, 40 ½ x 58 In., 6 Piece...............	5040.00
Panel, Ventilation, Sandstone, Stylized Lion, Mexico, 18th Century, 17 x 25 In.................	649.00
Panel, Walnut, Berry & Leaf Clusters, Scrollwork, Molded Border, Italy, 1800s, 7 x 28 In., Pair .	330.00
Panel, Walnut, Carved Fruit Bowl, Pedestal Center, Reeded Border, 1800s, 20 x 23 In., Pair	450.00
Panel, Wood, Carved Trompe L'Oeil, Putto Head, Scrolls, Gray, White, c.1800, 22 x 46 In., Pair.	1610.00
Panel, Wood, Carved, Lion Face, Leaves, Scallop Rim, 27 x 28 ¼ In..............................	936.00
Panel, Wrought Iron, Bronze Leaf & Branch, France, 63 x 18 In., 6 Piece........................	2800.00
Panel, Wrought Iron, Scrolls, Pods, c.1910, 75 x 14 In., Pair....................................	840.00
Pedestal, Brass, Classical Women, Fruits, Vine Panels, 45 x 15 In., Pair.........................	893.00
Pedestal, Gilt, Neoclassical, Scrolled Capital, Fluted Column, Round Base, Italy, 47 x 12 In., Pair	625.00
Pedestal, Giltwood, Carved, Cherub Masks, Leaves, Octagon, Venice, 1800s, 16 x 20 In.........	1725.00
Pedestal, Marble, Column, Removable Top, 42 In..	179.00
Pedestal, Wood, Empire Style, Reeded, Fluted, Scroll Feet, Painted, 48 x 12 In., Pair	875.00
Pedestal, Wood, Marble Inset, Round, Pierced Frieze, Cabriole Legs, Chinese, 43 In., Pair.......	1573.00
Pediment, Broken Arch, Carved, Fluted, 18th Century, 20 x 53 In................................	545.00

Animal Trophy, Owl, White, Mounted On Plants & Leaves, Plexiglas Case, c.1850, 17 ½ x 14 ½ In.
$1,722.00

New Orleans Auction Galleries, Inc.

Animal Trophy, Rug, Cheetah Head, Cloth Lining, Tag, Dr. James L. Clark, 76 In.
$1,270.00

Leslie Hindman Auctioneers

Animation Art, Cel, Snow White, Doves On Windowsill, Mat, Frame, 1930s, 17 ¾ x 17 ⅞ In.
$3,105.00

Humler & Nolan

Anna Pottery, Bottle, Pig, Eastern Route Railroad & River Guide, Incised, Brown Albany Glaze, c.1870, 7 ¾ In.
$4,025.00

Glass Works Auctions

The edited listings of the current prices in this *Kovels' Antiques & Collectibles Price Guide* aren't available on any website. Readers can visit *Kovels.com* to check thousands of past prices and sign up for free information on trends, tips, reproductions, marks, and more.

A

Anna Pottery, Bottle, Pig, Railroad Guide, Kansas City & Northern R.Y., Salt Glaze, J.O. Sanders, 6 ¼ In. $8,050.00

Glass Works Auctions

TIP

Window sash locks are available at hardware stores for less than $10 each. Keep your windows closed and locked when you are out of the house.

Architectural, Bathtub, Metal, Tin Claw Feet $168.00

Victorian Casino Antiques

Architectural, Bathtub, Zinc, Neoclassical Style, Tapered Body, Handles, 1800s, 26 x 65 In. $427.00

Neal Auction Co.

Architectural, Bracket, Butcher Trade Sign, Black Paint, Cast Iron, 24 x 28 In. $3,300.00

Showtime Auction Services

Pediment, Wood, Carved, Paint, c.1890, 31 x 96 In.	1080.00
Plaque, Eagle, Spread Wings, Shield, Carved, Painted, 14 x 43 In.	2232.00
Plaque, Gilt, Sunburst, Continental, 56 In.	3125.00
Porch Support, Wood, Woman Shape, Arms Up, White Paint, c.1940, 40 In.	1736.00
Screens are also listed in the Fireplace and Furniture categories.	
Screen, Leaded Glass, Bowed Top, Rabbit, Running, c.1910, 6 x 12 In.	1375.00
Shield, Sheet Metal, Copper, Iron, Union, 33 Stars, Stripes, Eagle, c.1860, 41 x 25 In.......*Illus*	9600.00
Shutter, Wood, Blue Paint, Crescent Moon, U.S.A., 1800s, 63 x 24 In., Pair	460.00
Shutter, Wood, Louvered, Arched White, 32 ¼ x 31 ½ In.	7703.00
Shutter, Wood, Louvered, Green, Iron Strap Hinges, c.1810, 56 ½ x 18 ½ In., 6 Pair	226.00
Shutter, Wood, Louvered, Rayed Gothic Arch, Painted Green, 1800s, 32 x 37 In.	1659.00
Sign, Street, Intersection, S. Jefferson St., E. 3rd St., Iron, 1930s.....................*Illus*	210.00
Spiral Staircase, Wrought Iron, 20 Oak Treads, 160 x 68 In.	1020.00
Staircase, Oak, Lacquered Metal, Ladder Shape, France, c.1960, 87 x 116 In.	1500.00
Stanchion, Cast Iron, Horse Hoof, Leg, 26 In., Pair	1560.00
Strap Hinge, Tulip Terminal, Iron, Pa., c.1800, 24 ¾ In., Pair	5214.00
Streetlight, Tin, Canted Sides, Glass Panels, Electrified, c.1825, 38 In. ....*Illus*	59.00
Tieback, Portrait, Washington, Color Porcelain, Brass Shank, Round, 2 ¾ In., Pair	4025.00
Tieback, Pressed Glass, Opalescent, Flower Shape, 1800s, 4 ½ In., 5 Piece	240.00
Tieback, Sandwich Glass, Opalescent Rosette, 1800s, 8 Piece	237.00
Valance, Giltwood, Carved, Empire Revival, Lapettes, Flower Crest, France, c.1860, 53 x 9 In.	1080.00
Valance, Wood, Painted, Stenciled, Fruit, Flowers, Lyre, Gilt, Scrolled, 7 x 41 In., 3 Piece	889.00
Windmill, Model M, Beard Mfg. Company, Angola, Ind., Salesman's Sample, 19 ½ In.	10200.00
Windmill, Smith & Pomeroy, Wooden Wheel, Cast Iron Hood, Salesman's Sample, Case, 19 In. *Illus*	8400.00
Window Grate, Iron, Flowers, France, 10 ½ x 34 ½ In.	397.00
Window Grate, Iron, Wirework, Paint, c.1895, 48 x 32 In.	444.00
Window, Stained, 2 Angels, Pointed Arch, Blue, Purple, Red, Green, 1800s, 42 ½ x 34 In.	1180.00
Window, Stained, Arched Top, Church Lamb Of God, Rosette, Wood Frame, c.1900, 39 x 46 In.	718.00

AREQUIPA POTTERY was produced from 1911 to 1918 by the patients of the Arequipa Sanatorium in Marin County, north of San Francisco. The patients were trained by Frederick Hurten Rhead, who had worked at the Roseville Pottery.

Bowl, Green Matte Glaze, Squat, Rounded Shoulder, Flat Wide Rim, Marked, 4 ½ In.	316.00
Vase, Holly Leaves & Berries, Squeezebag, Green, White, Bulbous, F.H. Rhead, 4 x 4 In.	6875.00
Vase, Leaf Blades, Irises, Green, Pink, Cream Color, Shouldered, Tapered, 5 ⅛ In.	1725.00
Vase, Peacock Feathers, Squeezebag, Frederick Rhead, c.1911-13, 5 ¾ x 3 In.................*Illus*	18750.00
Vase, Purple Matte Glaze, Brown Raised Organic Design, Swollen, 4 x 7 In.	5625.00

ARGY-ROUSSEAU, *see G. Argy-Rousseau category.*

ARITA is a port in Japan. Porcelain was made there from about 1616. Many types of decorations were used, including the popular Imari designs, which are listed under Imari in this book.

Boat, Blue & White, Raised Wave Designs, 19th Century, 14 In..................*Illus*	72.00

ART DECO, or Art Moderne, a style started at the Paris Exposition of 1925, is characterized by linear, geometric designs. All types of furniture and decorative arts, jewelry, book bindings, and even games were designed in this style. Additional items may be found in the Furniture category or in various glass and pottery categories, etc.

Bowl, Silvered Metal, Brass Cover, M. Brandt, Impressed Bauhaus, Germany, c.1924, 44 In.	34375.00
Box, Glass, Green Swirl, Singing Pierrot Top, Round, 4 In.	179.00
Paperweight, Nude Woman, Seated, Ivory Matte Glaze, Rectangular Base, 1930, 4 In.	196.00

ART GLASS, *see Glass-Art category.*

ART NOUVEAU is a style of design that was at its most popular from 1895 to 1905. Famous designers, including Rene Lalique and Emile Galle, produced furniture, glass, silver, metalwork, and buildings in the new style. Ladies with long flowing hair and elongated bodies were among the more easily recognized design elements. Copies of this style are being made today. Many modern pieces of jewelry can be found. Additional Art Nouveau pieces may be found in Furniture or in various glass categories.

Frame, Silvered Bronze, Maiden Figureheads In Corners, Flowing Hair, 8 x 6 In.	800.00

ART POTTERY, *see Pottery-Art category.*

ARTS & CRAFTS

ARTS & CRAFTS was a design style popular in American decorative arts from 1894 to 1923. In the 1970s collectors began to rediscover Mission furniture, art pottery, metalwork, linens, and light fixtures from this period. The interest has continued. Today everything from this era is collectible, including jewelry, graphics, and silverware. Additional items may be found in the Furniture category and other categories.

Ashtray, Embossed Insects, Copper, 4 ½ x 2 In.	28.00
Bowl, Mixed Metals, Fishing Scene, Interior Applied Fish, Gorham, c.1880, 2 x 5 In.	625.00
Bowl, Mixed Metals, Roses, Bird In Flight, Hammered, Gorham, c.1880, 1 ¾ x 5 In.	875.00
Humidor, Stand, Iron, Applied Heart Shape, 20th Century, 34 x 17 ½ In.	119.00
Lamp, Landscape, Brown, Tan, Reverse Painted Glass Shade, Base, Handles, Pittsburg, 18 x 22 In.	2750.00
Mirror, Copper, Repousse, Beveled Glass, c.1905, 17 x 24 In.	800.00
Vase, Copper, Repousse Flower Design, Square, Flared, Footed, England, 9 ¾ In., Pair	500.00

AURENE pieces are listed in the Steuben category.

AUSTRIA is a collecting term that covers pieces made by a wide variety of factories. They are listed in this book in categories such as Royal Dux or Porcelain.

AUTO

AUTO parts and accessories are collectors' items today. Gas pump globes and license plates are part of this specialty. Prices are determined by age, rarity, and condition. Signs and packaging related to automobiles may also be found in the Advertising category. Lalique hood ornaments will be listed in the Lalique category.

Award, Chevrolet Gogetter Salesman, Man, Briefcase, Walking On Book, Metal, 8 In.	390.00
Award, Oscar Esso Award, Hand Raised, Brass, Onyx Base, c.1955, 8 ½ In.	390.00
Banner, Cities Service Koldpruf Anti-Freeze, Dog Sled Team, Penguin, Yellow, Navy, 34 x 55 In.	118.00
Banner, Packard Anti-Freeze, Winterize Your Car, Cloth, Red, Blue, 34 x 112 In.	148.00
Banner, Pontiac 1950, Why Pay More?, Why Take Less?, Canvas, Green, Yellow, White, 38 x 56 In.	392.00
Bottle Carrier, Mobiloil, Pegasus Logo, Red Metal, Holds 6 Oil Bottles	540.00
Button, Ford, Stylized Model T Made Out Of Letters, White, Blue, Celluloid, 2 ¼ In.	45.00
Can, Beaver-Penn Motor Oil, Beaver, Blue, Yellow, Metal, Qt.	295.00
Can, Ben Hur Motor Oil, Round, Metal, Red, White, Qt.	236.00
Can, Big Chief Supreme Quality, Indian Graphics, Black, Red, Qt.	300.00
Can, Blakely Heavy Duty Motor Oil, Race Car, Rocket Logo, Round, Metal, Qt.	325.00
Can, Crozoil Motor Oil, Bird, Orange, White, Metal, Qt.	944.00
Can, En-Ar-Co Motor Oil, Round, Metal, Bail Handle, 5 Imperial Gal.	177.00
Can, Freedom Perfect Motor Oil, Bull Dog, Yellow, Blue, Metal, Qt.	443.00
Can, Frontier Econo Lube Motor Oil, Round, Metal, Light Blue, Red, Qt.	47.00
Can, Gree-Scoff Automobile Soap, Early Car, Green, Yellow, Round, Tin	384.00
Can, Heavy Duty Reclaimed Motor Oil, Elephant, Qt.	142.00
Can, Indian Premium Motorcycle Oil, Round Metal, Red, Yellow, Qt.	165.00
Can, Mobil, Gargoyle Mobiloel A F, Tin Lithograph, Germany, 12 ⅛ x 4 In. .... *Illus*	440.00
Can, Mobiloil Arctic Light Medium Body, Gargoyle, Square, Metal, 5 Gal.	89.00
Can, Mona Motor Oil, Red, Rocker, 5 Gal.	275.00
Can, Mountain Motor Oil, Tin Litho, Mountain Tire & Gas Co., Colorado Springs, Gal. ..... *Illus*	1925.00
Can, Oilzum, Underseat, Oswald Mascot Face At Ends, Orange, Black Metal, 1920s, 13 In.	150.00
Can, Oneida Motor Oil, Time Tested, Indian Graphics, Round, Metal, Yellow, Qt.	175.00
Can, Penn-Bee Motor Oil, Bee Graphics, Yellow, Black	225.00
Can, Pep Boys Motor Oil, Pure Gold, Red, Yellow, Black, Metal, 2 Gal.	120.00
Can, Power-Lube Motor Oil, Tiger, Round, Metal, Rocker, 5 Gal.	354.00
Can, Progress Motor Oil, Round, Man Running, Blue, Metal, Qt.	675.00
Can, Quaker State Medium Oil, Metal, Flat, 5 Qt.	125.00
Can, Red Indian Motor Oil, Indian, Headdress, Round, Metal, Imperial Qt.	118.00
Can, Snow Flake, Axle Grease, Tin Lithograph Label, Fitchburg, Mass., 1880s, 4 x 5 ½ In.	67.00
Can, Speedway Motor Oil, Checkered Flag, Rectangular, Metal, Red, White, Gal.	153.00
Can, Thorobred Motor Oil, Horse, Rectangular, Metal, Red, Cream, 2 Gal.	118.00
Can, Vanderbilt Motor Oil, Leopard, Yellow, Black, Red, Metal, Qt.	826.00
Can, Whippet Motor Oil, Greyhound, Green, Orange, Metal, Qt.	1416.00
Can, Whiz 30 Degree Below Zero Motor Oil, Winter Scenes, Car, Blue, Black, Metal, Qt.	148.00
Car Front, Mercury, Front Lights, Red Paint, Chrome, c.1970, 80 In.	411.00
Clock, Dash, Iron, Round Case, Black Dial, White Numerals, Waltham, c.1920, 3 In.	46.00
Clock, Oilzum Motor Oil Telechron, Capped Attendant's Face, Light-Up, Electric, 15 In.	1593.00
Desert Water Bag, Linen, Miner's Shovel, Pan, Pick, Neville Co., San Francisco, 10 x 12 In., Gal.	308.00
Dispenser, Shell Motor Oil, Logo, Painted Orange & Red, Pump Top, 1930s, 49 In.	336.00
Display, Bosch Auto Battery Man, Composition, Paint, Batteries, c.1955, 25 In.	840.00
Display, Edison Mazda Super Auto Lamps, Image Of Car, Die Cut Cardboard, 11 x 16 x 5 In.	3410.00

Architectural, Door Pull, Hand Wrought Monel, Geometrics & Flowers, Samuel Yellin, 10 ½ In.
$1,652.00

Brunk Auctions

Architectural, Door, Molded Cornice, Dentil, Painted, Side Columns, Gilt, Continental, 1800s, 100 x 78 In.
$3,068.00

Brunk Auctions

Architectural, Doorknocker, Iron, Owl, On Branch, Back Plate, Painted, 5 In.
$443.00

Bertoia Auctions

Architectural, Shield, Sheet Metal, Copper, Iron, Union, 33 Stars, Stripes, Eagle, c.1860, 41 x 25 In.
$9,600.00

Skinner, Inc.

Architectural, Sign, Street, Intersection, S. Jefferson St., E. 3rd St., Iron, 1930s
$210.00

Victorian Casino Antiques

Architectural, Streetlight, Tin, Canted Sides, Glass Panels, Electrified, c.1825, 38 In.
$59.00

Garth's Auctioneers & Appraisers

Architectural, Windmill, Smith & Pomeroy, Wooden Wheel, Cast Iron Hood, Salesman's Sample, Case, 19 In.
$8,400.00

Showtime Auction Services

Arequipa, Vase, Peacock Feathers, Squeezebag, Frederick Rhead, c.1911-13, 5 ¾ x 3 In.
$18,750.00

Rago Arts & Auction Center

Display, Flying A Tires, Metal, 8 x 15 In.	212.00
Display, Ford Ribbon, Black, Red, Yellow, Masonite, Wood, 47 x 36 In.	708.00
Display, Hanging, Ford Asbestos Transmission Lining, Tin, Red, White, 18 x 12 In.	1652.00
Display, Michelin Man, Cast Iron, Paint, 22 x 9 ½ In.	960.00
Display, Texaco Havoline Formula 3 Motor Oil Hanging Rack, Tin, 11 x 18 In.	41.00
Display, Tire Stand, Seiberling, Metal, Yellow, Black, Red, 9 x 17 In.	59.00
Display, Trico Wiper Washer Service, 2-Sided, Red Paint, Tin, 48 x 14 In.	118.00
Doorstop, Texaco Scottie Dogs, Listen Tags, Cast Iron, Black Paint	94.00
Furnace, Gas Station, Michelin, Bibendum, Michelin Man Logo, Iron, 17 x 18 In.	1770.00
Gas Pump Globe, Hustol, Black, Gold, White, 13 ½ In.	325.00
Gas Pump Globe, Johnson, Time Tells Gasoline, Single Lens, 15 In.	4675.00
Gas Pump Globe, Texaco, Red, Round Base, Visible, Cylindrical	1120.00
Gas Pump Globe, Texaco, Star, Red, Green, White, Glass, 13 ½ In.	384.00
Gas Pump Nozzle, Working Lever, Made By Buckeye, Brass, Dated 1926, 7 x 15 In.	175.00
Gas Pump Sign, Calso Gasoline, Porcelain, 14 x 11 In.	325.00
Gas Pump, Curb, Wayne No. 2, Pale Yellow, Round Base, c.1905	3360.00
Globe, Holder, Wall Mount, Cast Iron, 12 x 16 In.	94.00
Hat, Goodyear, Station Attendant, Woven Wicker Band, 5 x 10 ¾ In. *Illus*	176.00
Hood Ornament, Cadillac, Chrome, 1932	120.00
Hood Ornament, Indian Chief Head, Chrome, Plastic, Light-Up, Box, 1950s, 4 x 2 x 4 In.	467.00
Lapel Stud, Automobile Show, Mythical Driver, Winged Helmet, 1911, 1 In.	40.00
Letters & Stars, Texaco, Porcelain, Red, 21 In., 7 Piece	436.00
Letters, Texaco, Brass, 15 In., 6 Piece	118.00
License Plate Holder, Hood Tires, Man In Uniform, Holding Flag, Tin, 4 ½ In.	605.00
License Plate, Illinois, 1947, Fiberboard, Black, White Numbers	50.00
License Plate, Massachusetts, 1915, Porcelain Over Tin, White Letters, Blue Ground, 14 In.	53.00
License Plate, Pennsylvania, 1912, Faux Grain, Label Brilliant Mfg. Co., 6 x 14 In.	35.00
License Plate, Pennsylvania, 1913, Enamel, Stenciled Label, Brilliant Mfg. Co., 6 x 14 In., Pair	236.00
Manual, 1948 Hudson Motor Car, Illustrations, Photos, Instructions, Foldout, 72 Pages	95.00
Paperweight, Exide Battery, For Electric Cars, Photo, Battery, Interior Images, c.1920, 2 ¾ x 4 ¼ In.	86.00
Paperweight, Ford Headquarters, Crystal, Laser Engraved, Case, 4 ½ x 7 In.	180.00
Pencil Box, Richfield Oil, Race Car Shape, Copper, Over Plaster, 1920s, 9 ¾ In.	960.00
Photograph, 3 Men Posing With Auto, S.C.B. Publicity Tour, Round, 1915, 1 ¾ In.	52.00
Pin, Buick Greets You, Photo, Car, Black & White, Gold, 1930s, 1 ½ In.	104.00
Pin, Buy It Now 1915 Regal, Round, Black & Yellow, Car, 1 ¼ In.	116.00
Pin, Chrysler, Sign Of Quality, Used Cars, Black, Orange, Celluloid, c.1950, 1 ½ In.	213.00
Pin, Esso Gasoline, Plush Tiger, Can I Get In Your Tank, 1960s, 1 ⅜ & 3 In., 2 Piece	139.00
Poster, Atlantic Gasoline, Season's Greetings, Santa Claus, Atlantic Theme Toys, c.1957, 28 x 44 In.	173.00
Poster, Ce Michelin Est Indechirable, Paper, Maxime Fraikin, 1907, 47 x 31 In.	1100.00
Poster, Graham Crusader, Yellow Car, 1937, 48 x 37 In.	950.00
Poster, Peugeot, African Native Couple, Car, Rene Vincent, Draeger, Paris, c.1925, 37 x 54 In.	3000.00
Poster, Sebring 60/12 Hour, Grand Prix Of Endurance, 1960, 22 x 15 In.	3510.00
Pressure Gauge, Screw-On Bezel, Brass Cased, U.S. Gauge Co., c.1953, 11 In.	119.00
Pump Plate, Diesel 2 Fuel, Porcelain, 11 x 9 In.	295.00
Pump Plate, Gulf, No-Nox, Porcelain, 9 x 11 In.	130.00
Pump Plate, Gulf, No-Nox, Red, White, Blue, Porcelain, 12 x 18 In.	177.00
Pump Plate, Mobilgas, Pegasus, Shield Shape, Porcelain, 12 x 12 In.	295.00
Pump Plate, Sav'n Sam's Regular Gasoline, Cowboy, Round, Porcelain, 9 ½ In.	2360.00
Pump Plate, Texaco, Fire Chief Gasoline, Fireman Helmet, White T, Porcelain, 12 x 8 In.	266.00
Pump Plate, Texaco, Sky Chief With Petrox, White T, Porcelain, Green, Red, 22 x 12 In.	325.00
Pump Plate, Texaco, Wide Spray Diesel Chief, Porcelain, White T, 1942, 18 x 12 In.	1888.00
Pump Plate, Union 76 Gasoline, Round, Porcelain, White, Red, Black, 11 In.	236.00
Pump Plate, Veltex Super Ethyl Gasoline Fletcher Oil, Orange, Navy, Porcelain, 15 x 13 In.	826.00
Sign, AAA Emergency Service, 2-Sided, Blue, White, Red, Porcelain, 1950s, 22 ⅜ In.	230.00
Sign, AAA Emergency Service, 2-Sided, Oval, Navy, White, Porcelain, 17 x 23 In.	295.00
Sign, AAA, NYSAA Official Service Station & Automobile Club, New York, Oval, Porcelain, 17 x 23 In.	295.00
Sign, Ace High Motor Oil, Car, Airplane, Embossed, Tin, 14 x 20 In.	4130.00
Sign, Aristo Motor Oil, Union Oil Company Of Arizona, Best All Ways, Neon, Tin, 26 x 25 In.	560.00
Sign, Ask For Wolf's Head Oil, Red, White, Green, 2-Sided, Tin, Round, 36 In.	472.00
Sign, Atlantic Motor Oil, Ask For Atlantic Keeps Upkeep Down, Tin, 15 x 21 In.	207.00
Sign, Atlantic, Credit Cards Honored Here, 2-Sided, Tin, 10 x 15 In.	266.00
Sign, Atlantic, White Flash, Porcelain, 17 x 13 In.	271.00
Sign, B.F. Goodrich Tires, White, Blue, Red, Tin, 26 x 60 In.	12.00
Sign, Banner, Red Hat Motor Oil, Uniform, Dependable, Linen, Frame, 1930s, 60 ⅓ x 24 ¼ In.	1020.00
Sign, Brown's Oyl, For Fords, Brownie, Embossed, Tin, 20 x 13 In.	325.00
Sign, Chevrolet Convertible, Yellow 1949 Styleline Deluxe Convertible, Easel Back, 14 x 22 In.	450.00

Sign, Chevrolet, OK Used Cars Authorized Dealer, Porcelain, Neon, 38 x 45 In.	6490.00
Sign, Chevrolet, Oldsmobile, 2-Sided Porcelain, 34 x 96 In.	3245.00
Sign, Chrysler Plymouth Approved Service, Masonite, Paint, Black, Red, 12 x 13 In.	384.00
Sign, Chrysler, Porcelain, 2-Sided, White, Navy, 24 x 36 In.	708.00
Sign, Cities Service, Hanger, Black, White, 2-Sided, Porcelain, 56 x 48 In.	1770.00
Sign, Clean Rest Room, Blue, White, Round, 2-Sided, Porcelain, 30 In.	354.00
Sign, Curb, Conoco Germ Processed Motor Oil, Logo, Porcelain, 2-Sided, Cast Iron Base, 22 x 27 In.	2655.00
Sign, Curb, Mobil Oil, Pegasus, Die Cut, Porcelain, 2-Sided, 32 x 36 In.	944.00
Sign, Dayton Tires Finest Safest, Horse Logo, Red, Yellow, White, Tin, 2-Sided, 32 x 44 In.	89.00
Sign, Derby Gasoline, 2-Sided, Round, Star, White, Red, Black, Porcelain, 48 In. Diam.	1232.00
Sign, Englebert Tires, Boy Airing Tire, Rolled Edge, Porcelain, 34 x 14 In.	207.00
Sign, Esso, Red, White, Oval, Porcelain, 60 ½ x 91 ½ In.	360.00
Sign, Exide Batteries Recharging, Rental, Black, White, Tin, 2-Sided, 20 x 26 In.	354.00
Sign, Ford, V8, Genuine Parts, Logo, V-Shape, Neon, 34 In.	560.00
Sign, Genuine Ford Parts, Oval, Porcelain, Blue, White, 24 x 30 In.	570.00
Sign, Get Atlantic Car Condition Service, 1950s Car, Cardboard Winter Front, Red, Yellow, 11 x 18 In.	89.00
Sign, GM, Hydromatic Drive, Skeleton, Neon, 26 x 36 In.	325.00
Sign, GMC, The Truck People, Spinning, 32 x 22 In.	260.00
Sign, Goodrich Automobile Tires, Regular Clincher, Woman Wearing Hat, Paper, Frame, 36 x 44 In.	112.00
Sign, Goodrich Silvertowns, Banner Shape, Porcelain, Flange, 19 x 24 In.	325.00
Sign, Goodyear Shoe With Wing, Die Cut, Porcelain, 46 x 17 In.	616.00
Sign, Goodyear Tire Sales, Blue, White, Yellow, Metal, 1970s, 24 x 18 In.	180.00
Sign, Gulf, Red, Black, White, Round, Porcelain, c.1955, 73 x 79 In.	1320.00
Sign, H-C Sinclair Gasoline, Porcelain, Black, Red, White, Round, 2-Sided, 48 In.	431.00
Sign, Hudson, Parts Service, Porcelain, Blue, Red, Neon, 30 x 42 In.	1180.00
Sign, Husky Tri-Power, Dog Logo, Red, White, 12 x 12 In.	1400.00
Sign, Indiana Gasoline, Art Deco Design, Curved, Green, White, Porcelain, 18 x 12 In.	236.00
Sign, Johnson Gasoline, Logo, Cardboard Winter Front, Black, Yellow, 12 x 20 In.	177.00
Sign, Kelly Balloon Tires, Mascot Lotta Miles, Holding Wrench, Porcelain, 35 x 33 In.	5500.00
Sign, Keystone Automobile Club, Largest In The East, Porcelain, 2-Sided, 1920s, 29 ¾ x 33 ¾ In.	417.00
Sign, Keystone Oil Sold Here, With Pennsylvania Permit Seal, Oval, Porcelain, 11 x 18 In.	443.00
Sign, Let Us Marfak Your Car, Tin, 1939, 18 x 30 In.	236.00
Sign, Life Gasoline Barnett Oil Co., Elf, Red, Yellow, Tin, 10 x 8 In.	1416.00
Sign, Loyal-Penn Red Hat Royal 400, Cardboard Winter Front, Green, Orange, White, 18 x 20 In.	325.00
Sign, Mercedes-Benz Original Parts, Blue, Silver, Porcelain, 30 x 23 In.	1180.00
Sign, Michelin Man, Blue Porcelain, France, c.1965, 31 ½ x 31 ½ In.	480.00
Sign, Miller Tires, Wood, 20 x 60 In.	600.00
Sign, Mobil, Flag, Shield Shape, Pegasus, Red, White, 17 x 25 In.	153.00
Sign, Mobil, Xl Pegasus, Red, Die Cut, Porcelain, 1950s, 70 x 90 In.	3600.00
Sign, Mobilgas, Porcelain, Round, Pegasus Logo, 12 In.	144.00
Sign, Mobilgas, Red Pegasus & Cloud Outline, Neon, 30 x 24 In.	345.00
Sign, Mobiloil, Red Pegasus, Lollipop, Blue, White, 2-Sided, Porcelain, 37 x 33 In.	690.00
Sign, Mother Penn All Pennsylvania Motor Oil, White, Red, Black, Porcelain, c.1935, 8 ½ x 6 In.	1200.00
Sign, Oakland Pontiac, Products Of General Motors, Blue, Porcelain, 28 x 84 In.	1456.00
Sign, Obey The Motor Vehicle Law, Wood, Painted, Flange, 12 x 20 In.	616.00
Sign, Office, Texaco Gasoline Motor Oil, Round, Porcelain, Hand Painted, 1974, 42 In.	413.00
Sign, Oilzum Motor Oil, Company Mascot Oswald, Triangle, Orange, Black, White, 1953, 17 In.	1920.00
Sign, Oilzum Motor Oil, Ralph McCook, Brass, Oak Frame, Worcester, Mass., 32 x 22 In.	3300.00
Sign, Oilzum, Cutout, Orange, Black, White, Tin, 1940s, 48 x 33 In.	660.00
Sign, Oilzum, Face Of Goggled Driver, Round, Brown, Yellow, Paint, Tin, 1930s, 9 In.	480.00
Sign, Oilzum, Lollipop Shape, Round Base, Black, Orange, Tin, 2-Sided, 1937, 61 ½ In.	7200.00
Sign, Oilzum, Orange, Black, Tin Flange, 15 x 6 In.	1680.00
Sign, OK, Chevrolet, Round, Orange, Red, Porcelain, 30 In.	1298.00
Sign, Oldsmobile, Service, World Logo, Round, Porcelain, Neon, 2-Sided, 1953, 54 In.	1888.00
Sign, Our Weighing Service Is Rendered By Toledo Scales, No Springs, Porcelain, 11 x 18 In.	236.00
Sign, Packard, Approved Services, Round, Neon, 42 In.	4130.00
Sign, Pan-Am Motor Oil, Round, Green, Red, White, Porcelain, 15 In.	1475.00
Sign, Penn Empire Gasoline, 2-Sided, Ethyl Logo, Multicolor, Round, 30 In.	6875.00
Sign, Penn Empire Motor Oil, More Miles-Less Cost, Cardboard, 30 x 21 In.	148.00
Sign, Pennzoil Safe Lubrication, Sound Your Z, Red Ball, Die Cut, Tin, 2-Sided, 12 x 17 In.	207.00
Sign, Pennzoil, Supreme Quality, Safe Lubrication, Oval, 2-Sided, Tin, Yellow, Black, c.1974, 31 x 18 In.	140.00
Sign, Pirelli Tires, Shield Logo, Yellow, Blue, Red, Porcelain, 23 x 23 In.	443.00
Sign, Plymouth Service, Ship, Navy Blue, White, Porcelain, 2-Sided, 22 x 18 In.	1416.00
Sign, Pontiac Authorized Service, Indian Profile, Tin, 2-Sided, c.1935, 42 ½ In.	3300.00
Sign, Pottstown Labor Day Races, Paper, Oak Frame, 30 x 26 In.	826.00
Sign, Quaker State Cold Test Oil For Winter Driving, Porcelain, 2-Sided, 6 x 26 In.	354.00

Arita, Boat, Blue & White, Raised Wave Designs, 19th Century, 14 In.
$72.00

Sloans & Kenyon

Auto, Can, Mobil, Gargoyle Mobiloel A F, Tin Lithograph, Germany, 12 ⅛ x 4 In.
$440.00

Wm Morford Antiques

Auto, Can, Mountain Motor Oil, Tin Litho, Mountain Tire & Gas Co., Colorado Springs, Gal.
$1,925.00

Wm Morford Antiques

Auto, Hat, Goodyear, Station Attendant, Woven Wicker Band, 5 x 10 ¾ In.
$176.00

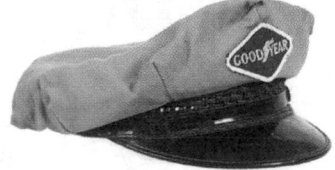

Wm Morford Antiques

Auto, Sign, Top Quality Iso=Vis D Motor Oil, Porcelain, Rolled Edges, 1920s, 15 ¾ x 60 In.
$513.00

Hake's Americana & Collectibles

Baccarat, Atomizer, Green To Clear, Laurel Leaf Band, Arched Panels, Metal Top, 10 In.
$161.00

Humler & Nolan

Baccarat, Decanter, Wine, Stopper, Stamped, Baccarat, France, 12 In.
$168.00

Victorian Casino Antiques

Sign, Railway Express Agency, Masonite, Black, Yellow, 14 x 65 In.	413.00
Sign, Registered Rest Room, Texaco Dealer Service, Navy, Tin, 2-Sided, 38 x 30 In.	295.00
Sign, Rider, Oilzum America's Finest Oil, Orange, Black, Porcelain, 2-Sided, 1930s, 46 In.	5400.00
Sign, Route 66, Neon, 19 x 18 In.	460.00
Sign, Rover, Viking Ship Logo, Die Cut, Black, Red, Porcelain, 24 x 18 In.	826.00
Sign, Shell, Clam Shape, Orange, Red, Porcelain, 2-Sided, 48 x 48 In.	2596.00
Sign, Sinclair Credit Card Honored, Porcelain, 2-Sided, 14 x 23 In.	590.00
Sign, Sky Chief Gasoline, Texaco Driving Area, Rack Top, Tin, Red, Green, 18 x 16 In.	148.00
Sign, Summit Tires, Red, White, Tin, 16 x 48 In.	59.00
Sign, Texaco Certified Lubrication, Red, White, Porcelain, 1930s, 38 ¾ 8 ¾ In.	900.00
Sign, Texaco Fire Chief Gasoline, Fireman's Helmet, White T, Porcelain, Curved, 1940, 18 x 12 In.	236.00
Sign, Texaco Gas, Red, White, Round, Porcelain, 1930s, 42 In.	840.00
Sign, Texaco Havoline Ford Thunderbird NASCAR, Light-Up, Plastic, Box, 26 x 44 In.	177.00
Sign, Texaco Mail Port, Flags, Porcelain, 17 x 23 In.	826.00
Sign, Texaco Motor Oil, Clean Clear, Golden, Poured Oil, Porcelain, 16 x 16 In.	2360.00
Sign, Texaco Motor Oil, Red, White, Metal, Marked, E-8-36, 36 x 22 ½ In.	780.00
Sign, Texaco No Smoking, Porcelain, 4 x 23 In.	177.00
Sign, Texaco Sea Chief, Tin, Embossed, Black, White, Gold, 10 x 16 In.	266.00
Sign, Texaco, Easy Pour Can, Hand, Can, Black T, Porcelain 16 x 15 In.	9440.00
Sign, Toll Gate, Automobiles & Motor Cycles Must Stop, Wood, Painted, 1918, 30 In.	944.00
Sign, Top Quality Iso=Vis D Motor Oil, Porcelain, Rolled Edges, 1920s, 15 ¾ x 60 In. ...*Illus*	513.00
Sign, U.S. Tires, Embossed, Tin, Frame, c.1984, 146 x 36 In.	476.00
Sign, United Motors Service, Touring Car, Orange, Navy, Oval, Neon, Porcelain, 14 x 28 In.	6490.00
Sign, Vita Lube, Hanging, Cream, Black, Tin, Iron Bracket, c.1935, 15 x 9 In.	4200.00
Sign, Wasatch Gasoline, Indian Chief, Profile, Headdress, Tin, 24 In. Diam.	960.00
Sign, We Install The Boyce Motor Meter, Man, Gauge, Tin, Cardboard Back, 27 x 19 In.	6490.00
Sign, We Sell Socony Motor Gasoline, Standard Oil Of N.Y., Porcelain, c.1930, 24 x 20 In.	1080.00
Sign, Wolf's Head Motor Oil, Hatted Wolf, Oval, Black, Red, Tin, 2-Sided, 30 x 22 In.	236.00
Thermometer, Veedol Motor Oil, Winged V, Porcelain, Yellow, 1961, 36 x 12 In.	531.00
Thimble, This Is A Studebaker Year, Silver Metal, 1950s, ¾ x ¾ In.	15.00
Tin, Pep Boys 600 Transmission Oil, Orange, Art Deco Diamond Design, 1920s, 9 x 9 In.	335.00
Tire Gauge, Schrader Universal, c.1916, 2 ½ In.	20.00
Toy, Fire Chief Hat, Texaco, Plastic, Box, 14 x 11 In.	83.00
Toy, Gas Pump, Texaco Sky Chief, Wood, Metal, 12 x 31 In.	295.00
Traffic Light, Hanging, Red, Yellow, Green, Turn Signals, 42 ½ x 13 ½ In.	144.00
Wax Seal, Miracle Car Polish, Tin Flange, 14 x 17 In.	189.00

AUTUMN LEAF pattern china was made for the Jewel Tea Company beginning in 1933. Hall China Company of East Liverpool, Ohio, Crooksville China Company of Crooksville, Ohio, Harker Potteries of Chester, West Virginia, and Paden City Pottery, Paden City, West Virginia, made dishes with this design. Autumn Leaf has remained popular and was made by Hall China Company until 1978. Some other pieces in the Autumn Leaf pattern are still being made. For more prices, go to kovels.com.

Bean Pot, Lid	99.00
Bowl, Cereal, 6 In.	14.00
Bowl, Vegetable, Oval, 10 ¼ In.	21.00
Bowl, Vegetable, Ruffled, 10 ⅜ In.	18.00
Bowl, Vegetable, Ruffled, Divided, 10 ⅜ In.	80.00
Butter, Cover, Ruffled Grip	349.00
Cake Plate, 9 ½ In.	20.00
Cookie Jar, Handles, Eva Zeisel, c.1957, 9 ⅝ In.	135.00
Creamer, Fluted, 3 ¼ In.	70.00
Creamer, Ribbed, Gilt	45.00
Creamer, Ruffled, 3 ⅛ In.	20.00
Cup & Saucer	10.00
Jam Dish, 3 ½ In.	48.00
Jam Jar, Underplate, 4 ½ In.	31.00
Mug, Irish Coffee, 1966, 6 In.	60.00
Pitcher, Water, 7 In.	84.00
Plate, Bread & Butter, 6 ⅛ In.	8.00
Plate, Dessert, 7 ¼ In.	10.00
Plate, Dinner, 10 ⅛ In.	34.00
Platter, Oval, 11 ⅜ In.	24.00
Platter, Oval, 13 ⅝ In.	28.00
Salt & Pepper, Ruffled Bottom, 2 ½ In.	45.00
Sugar, Lid, 3 x 4 In.	32.00
Teapot, Aladdin Shape, Diffuser, Swirl Lid	49.00

AVON bottles are listed in the Bottle category under Avon.

AZALEA dinnerware was made for Larkin Company customers from 1918 to 1941. Larkin, the soap company, was in Buffalo, New York. The dishes were made by Noritake China Company of Japan. Each piece of the white china was decorated with pink azaleas.

Bowl, Vegetable, Divided, 10 ¼ In.	209.00
Bowl, Vegetable, Oval, 9 In.	38.00
Bowl, Vegetable, Oval, Handles, Gold Accents, 10 ½ In.	60.00
Butter Pat, 3 ¼ In.	65.00
Cake Plate, Open Handles, 9 ¾ In.	34.00
Creamer, Gold Trim, 8 Oz., 3 ¼ In.	44.00
Cup & Saucer	14.00
Eggcup, 3 ⅛ In.	27.00
Gravy Boat, Underplate	40.00
Jam Jar, Underplate, Lid	140.00
Nut Dish, Footed, Handle	42.00
Plate, 7 ⅝ In.	11.00
Plate, Dinner, 9 ⅞ In.	25.00
Plate, Scalloped Edge, 7 x 7 In.	43.00
Platter, Oval, 10 ¼ In.	139.00
Platter, Oval, 16 ¼ In.	379.00
Relish, 2 Section, Loop Handle, 7 ¾ In.	209.00
Relish, 8 ¼ In.	18.00
Salt & Pepper, Bell Shape	40.00
Salt & Pepper, Bulbous	18.00
Teapot, Cover, Gold Finial, 3 Cup, 4 In.	339.00
Toothpick Holder, 6-Sided, Footed, 2 ½ In.	60.00
Whipped Cream Bowl, 3 Ball Feet, 4 ½ In.	16.00

BACCARAT glass was made in France by La Compagnie des Cristalleries de Baccarat, located 150 miles from Paris. The factory was started in 1765. The firm went bankrupt and began operating again about 1822. Cane and millefiori paperweights were made during the 1845 to 1880 period. The firm is still working near Paris making paperweights and glasswares.

Atomizer, Green To Clear, Laurel Leaf Band, Arched Panels, Metal Top, 10 In. ....*Illus*	161.00
Bowl, Centerpiece, Amethyst To Clear, Fleur-De-Lis, 8 ½ x 12 In.	840.00
Candelabrum, 3-Light, Baluster, Scrolling Arms, Wall Prisms, Amethyst Color, Clear, 21 In., Pair	4000.00
Candlestick, Clear, Flared Base, Marked, 6 In., Pair	107.00
Candlestick, Regence Louis XIV, Crystal, Box, 7 ½ In., Pair	300.00
Candlestick, Swirl Foot, Twist Standard, Tulip Cup, 9 x 5 In., Pair	240.00
Centerpiece, Gilt, Ribbed Bowl, Frame, Feet, Flower Swags, Putti Handles, c.1915, 7 x 15 In.	2214.00
Centerpiece, Lobed, Oval, Gilt Bronze Holder, Leafy Handles & Feet, 9 x 20 In.	2032.00
Decanter, Faceted, Plum Color Band, Flowers, Gilt, Stopper, Acid Etched Mark, 12 In.	196.00
Decanter, Millefiori Stopper, Clear, Box, 9 ¾ In.	158.00
Decanter, Octagonal, Rectangular Shape Stopper, 10 ½ In.	120.00
Decanter, Stopper, Etched, Lafrance, 8 ½ In.	147.00
Decanter, Stopper, Ribbed, Clear, Box, 12 ½ In.	96.00
Decanter, Wine, Stopper, Stamped, Baccarat, France, 12 In. ....*Illus*	168.00
Figurine, Boar, Acid Mark, 4 x 6 In.	96.00
Figurine, Cat, Black, Resting, Acid Etched Mark, 3 In.	132.00
Figurine, Cat, Egyptian, Black Glass, 6 In.	570.00
Figurine, Cat, Egyptian, Seated, Round, Acid Etched Mark, 6 ⅛ In.	110.00
Figurine, Chow Dog, Box, 4 x 4 ½ In.	173.00
Figurine, Dabbling Duck, Frosted Crystal, Detailed Face, Logo On Base, 1 ½ x 5 In.	115.00
Figurine, Dog, Clear, 4 x 4 In.	83.00
Figurine, Dog, Labrador, Reclining, Clear, 5 x 7 In.	570.00
Figurine, Eagle, Clear, 7 In.	540.00
Figurine, Falcon, Clear, Marked, 10 In.	387.00
Figurine, Koi Fish, Green Satin Glass, Acid Etched Mark, 3 ¾ In.	69.00
Figurine, Shell, Snail, Clear & Frosted, 6 x 5 In.	960.00
Goblet, Wine Set, Montaigne, Optic White, 5 ½ In., 12 Piece	360.00
Ice Bucket, Clear, Tapered, Paneled, Bronze Swing Bail Handle, Marked, 6 In.	420.00
Paperweight, 2 White Flowers, Ladybug, Signed 1976 B, 3 ¾ In.	266.00
Paperweight, Flowers, Blue Ground, White Honeycomb, Signed, 1986, 3 ¼ In.	325.00
Paperweight, Flowers, Multicolor, Amethyst Ground, Signed, 1982, 3 In.	266.00
Paperweight, Millefiori, Horoscope Animals, Faceted, Figures, c.1967, 2 In.	316.00

Baccarat, Urn, Intaglio, Scroll & Flower Mounts, Gilt Bronze, Mark, 1800s, 17 ½ In.
$12,980.00

Brunk Auctions

Badge, City Marshal, Gold, Engraved, Enamel, R.M. Calahan, Inscribed, T-Bar Pinback, 1898, 2 In.
$9,775.00

Brian Lebel's Old West Show & Auction

Badge, Texas Ranger Force, Capt. Frank Johnson, Presentation, Gold, T-Bar, 1909, 2 In.
$25,875.00

Brian Lebel's Old West Show & Auction

Bank, Bank Building, Columbia, Cast Iron, Silver Paint, Kenton, 7 In.
$460.00

Bertoia Auctions

Bank, Bank Building, Domed Roof, 5 Spires, Iron, c.1905 $20,825.00

RSL Auction

Bank, Bank Building, State, Cast Iron, Japanned, Gold & Bronze, Straight Letters, Kenton, 4 ½ In. $201.00

Bertoia Auctions

Bank, Black Boy, Snowflake, Spelter, Germany, c.1915 $9,494.00

RSL Auction

Bank, Bust, F.D. Roosevelt, New Deal, Nickel Finish, Kenton, 5 In. $144.00

Bertoia Auctions

Paperweight, Multicolor Canes, Animals, Geometrics, Latticinio, Signed, 1849, 2 ½ In.	1062.00
Paperweight, Poinsettia, Faceted, 2 ⅝ In.	4095.00
Paperweight, Purple, Yellow Pansy, Leaves, Red, White Canes, Star Cut Base, 1800s, 1 ¾ x 2 In.	885.00
Paperweight, Scattered Millefiori, Deer, Goat, Dog, Rooster, Pelican, Ground, 1848, 1 ¾ x 2 In.	1298.00
Urn, Intaglio, Scroll & Flower Mounts, Gilt Bronze, Mark, 1800s, 17 ½ In. ....*Illus*	12980.00
Vase, Amethyst & Clear, Oval, 6-Sided, 8 In.	784.00
Vase, Amethyst Crystal, Black, Impressed, Flared, Signed, Label, 8 ½ In.	125.00
Vase, Clear, Ribbed, Etched Round Mark, 10 In., Pair	238.00
Vase, Faceted, Tapered, c.1950, 9 ½ x 9 ½ In.	369.00

BADGES have been used since before the Civil War. Collectors search for examples of all types, including law enforcement and company identification badges. Well-known prison or law enforcement badges are most desirable. Most are made of nickel or brass. Many recent reproductions have been made.

American Legion, Emblem, Lincoln Profile, Illinois, St. Louis, C-Clasp, Metal, 1935, 1 x 2 In. .	19.00
Bowling, Jacob Bruegger, Highest Average, Banner, Pins, Ball, Shield, c.1896, 2 ⅛ In.	190.00
Chauffeur, Illinois, C-Clasp, 1930, 1 ¼ x 1 In.	110.00
City Marshal, Gold, Engraved, Enamel, R.M. Calahan, Inscribed, T-Bar Pinback, 1898, 2 In.*Illus*	9775.00
Conductor, C. & O. RY, Embossed, Enamel, Beveled Edge, Gold Tone, c.1900, 4 x 1 In.	125.00
Convention, Coal Miners & Operators, Coal Mountain, Railroad Coal Car, Brass, c.1906, 3 ⅜ In..	75.00
Davey Adams, Shipmates Club, Secret Compartment, Decoder, Brass, 1939, 1 ⅞ In.	144.00
Deputy Sheriff, Teller Co., Colo., Enameled Letters, Starburst, Pinback, 1 ¾ In.	3163.00
Director, Prospect Park Fair Ground Assoc., Jockey, Horse, Blue Enamel, Brass Finish, 2 In....	140.00
Elocution, Star Shape, 10K Gold, Wreath, Engraved, Louis V. Hamman, 1893, 2 ¾ In.	190.00
Employee, Weyerhaeuser Timber Co., Longview, Washington, Metal, 1 ⅜ In.	15.00
Fireman, Shield, Jackson Engine 3, N.F.D., Leather, 6 ¼ x 4 ½ In.	25.00
Harvard Aeronautical Society, Ribbon, Contest Com., 1911, 3 ¾ In.	75.00
Latin Prize, Keystone Academy, Cross Shape, 10K Gold, Black Enameling, June 1889, 2 In.	153.00
Order Of Charity, Star Shape, Gold, Ruby Enamel, Green Garland, Diamonds, Ottoman, c.1900, 3 In..	5500.00
Police, Sheriff, Tolland Co., Conn., 14K Yellow Gold, 1915	4500.00
Postal Telegraph, All America Cables, Globe, Triangular, Blue, White Cloisonne, 2 x 1 ⅞ In..	44.00
Press, International Livestock Expo, Building, Green Enamel, 1927, 1 In. Diam.	65.00
Special Police, Star, 6-Point, Ball Ends, Pinback, 1920s	175.00
Swiss Red Cross, Male Nude, Volcanoes, Hans Frei, Copper Plated, 1947, 1 x ⅞ In.	45.00
Taxi Service, Wings, Cab, No. 24, Stainless Steel, 1940s	30.00
Texas Ranger Force, Capt. Frank Johnson, Presentation, Gold, T-Bar, 1909, 2 In...........*Illus*	25875.00
U.S. Military, West Point, Eagle, Helmet, Brass, Screw Back, 1 ⅞ x 1 ⅞ In.	75.00
United States Coast Guard, Anchor Border, No. 1790, 2 x 2 In.	35.00

BANKS of metal have been made since 1868. There are still banks, mechanical banks, and registering banks (those that show the total money deposited on the face of the bank). Many old iron or tin banks have been reproduced since the 1950s in iron or plastic. Some old reproductions marked *Book of Knowledge, John Wright,* or *Capron* may be listed. Pottery, glass, and plastic banks are also listed here. Mickey Mouse and other Disneyana banks are listed in Disneyana. We have added the M numbers based on *The Penny Bank Book: Collecting Still Banks* by Andy and Susan Moore and the R numbers based on *Coin Banks by Banthrico* by James L. Redwine.

Airplane, Spirit Of Savings, c.1927, 6 ½ In.	450.00
Apple, Chalkware, Yellow Paint, Red Blush, Wood Stem, 4 In.	71.00 to 153.00
Aunt Jemima, Hands On Hips, Red Dress, White Apron, Cast Iron, c.1900, 7 In.	180.00
Bank Building, Belfry, 4 Columns, Cast Iron, Japanned, Kenton, M 1233, 8 In.	2185.00
Bank Building, Columbia Nickel Savings, Eagle & Liberty, Red, White & Blue, 1920s, 4 In.	1620.00
Bank Building, Columbia, Cast Iron, Silver Paint, Kenton, 7 In. ....*Illus*	460.00
Bank Building, Domed Roof, 5 Spires, Iron, c.1905 ....*Illus*	20825.00
Bank Building, Eagle, Cast Iron, 2 Chimneys, Painted, c.1875, 9 ¾ x 5 ¼ x 5 In.	889.00
Bank Building, Property Of Home Savings, Detroit, Chimney, Cast Iron, Nickel Finish, 10 ½ In..	345.00
Bank Building, State, Cast Iron, Japanned, Gold & Bronze, Straight Letters, Kenton, 4 ½ In.....*Illus*	201.00
Bank Building, State, Cast Iron, Japanned, Gold, Bronze, Key Lock Door, Kenton, 8 ¾ In.	1035.00
Bank Building, State, Cast Iron, Japanned, Gold, Bronze, Straight Letters, Kenton, 6 ½ In.	690.00
Bank Building, Traders Bank Of Canada, Yonge St. Colburne St., Nickle Plated, Iron, 8 x 10 In.	325.00
Baseball Player, Holding Bat, Blue, Red Paint, Cast Iron, A.C. Williams, 5 ¾ In.	354.00
Bear, Honey Pot, Brown, Hubley, 6 ½ In.	175.00
Bear, Standing, Cast Iron, Stencil, Yellowstone Park, John Harper, 6 In.	173.00
Beehive, Stepped Finial, Crimped Moldings, Amber Glaze, Redware, c.1855, 6 ½ In.	1035.00
Black Boy, Snowflake, Spelter, Germany, c.1915.................................*Illus*	9494.00
Boat, Battleship Maine, Cast Iron, Japanned, Gold Highlights, Grey Iron Casting, 4 ½ In.	259.00

B

Boat, Battleship Oregon, Iron, Painted, Gold, J. & E. Stevens, 1896-1906, M 1451, 5 x 4 In.	316.00
Boy, Comic Character, Yellow Kid, Head Slot, Victorian, c.1890, 5 In.	173.00
Buffalo Billy, Christmas Figure, Cardboard Body, Wooden Arms, 1958, 4 x 7 In.	75.00
Buffalo Billy, Elf, Spring Bobbing Head, Red, 1958, Buffalo Savings Bank, 5 x 7 In.	80.00
Building, Belfry, Cupola, Cast Iron, Japanned, 8 In.	2185.00
Building, Chocolat Menier, Tin Litho, 6-Sided, Dome Top, Chocolate Dispenser, France, 10 In.	518.00
Building, Cupola, Cast Iron, Paint, J.& E. Stevens, 5 ½ In.	563.00
Building, High Rise, Gray Paint, Cast Iron, c.1900, M 1217, 5 ½ x 2 ½ In.	59.00
Building, Old South Church, Cast Iron, Gray, Gold Trim On Spire, 9 ¾ In.	3163.00
Bust, F.D. Roosevelt, New Deal, Nickel Finish, Kenton, 5 In. ....*Illus*	144.00
Buster Brown, Tige, Cast Iron, Painted, Full Figure, A.C. Williams, c.1910, 3 ¼ x 5 In.	139.00
Caboose, Majolica, Red Roof, France, c.1920, 3 ⅛ x 4 ⅛ In.	62.00
Car, Nash, Ceramic, Green, U.S.A., c.1950, 6 In.	50.00
Cash Register, Easy Saver, Coin Registers, Buddy L	20.00
Cat, Arched Back, Pottery, Brown, Austria, c.1920, 4 ⅛ x 5 In.	112.00
Chest Of Drawers, 4 Drawers, Scroddleware, England, 1800s, 6 x 7 In.	237.00
Circus Elephant, Clown Outfit, Cast Iron, Hubley, M 462, 3 ⅞ In.	230.00
Clock, Street, Cast Iron, Red, Gold Face, Tall Stand, Pressed Steel Back, A.C. Williams, M 1548, 6 In.	230.00
Coconut, Carved, Pierced, Round, 3 x 4 In.	360.00
Columbia Nickel Savings Bank, Lady Liberty, Eagle & Shield On Side, c.1910, 4 In.	1620.00
Columbia Tower, 3 Tiers, Japanned, Embossed, Gray Iron Casting Co., M 118, 7 In.	472.00
Cottage Building, Painted, Stenciled, Dormers, Red Roof, Tin, George Brown, Fence, 6 ¼ In.	1298.00
Cottage, 2-Story White Tudor, Moss On Base & Roof Edges, Staffordshire, 1800s, 5 ½ x 3 In.	155.00
Cottage, Cast Iron, Green Embossed People On Porch, Grey Iron Casting, M 999, 4 In.	86.00
Cottage, Gingerbread, Tin, Painted, George Brown, 6 In.	1154.00
Cottage, Yellow, Green Paint, Cast Iron, 4 In.	150.00
Devil Head, On Chest, Ceramic, Germany, c.1920, 4 ¾ x 3 ⅜ In. ....*Illus*	168.00
Dog Head, Bisque, Brown, White, Staffordshire, 2 ¼ In.	59.00
Dog, Lost Dog, Seated, Howling, Embossed, Iron, H.L. Judd, 5 ½ In. ....*Illus*	403.00
Dog, Nipper, RCA, Pot Metal, Textured Flocking, Painted Collar & Eyes, 1930s, M 376, 6 In.	445.00
Dog, Orange, Cast Iron, Arcade, 3 ½ In.	83.00
Dog, Reclining, Black & White Paint, Cast Iron, c.1910, 10 In.	325.00
Dog, Spaniel, Chalkware, Painted Trim, Slot On Neck, 12 x 12 In.	35.00
Dog, Spaniel, Seated, Octagonal Base, Yellow & Brown Slip Glaze, Redware, 1800s, 4 In.	173.00
Dog, Terrier, Seated, Gray Paint, Cast Iron, c.1900, 4 ½ x 4 ½ In.	30.00
Donkey, Green Paint, Cast Iron, A.C. Williams, M 499, 4 In.	71.00
Doughboy, Cast Iron, Grey Iron Casting, M 48, c.1917, 7 In.	115.00
Flat Limousine Cab, Cast Iron, Black, Orange, Nickel Lights, Rear Spare Tire, Arcade, M 1480, 8 In.	5750.00
Florida Orange Juice, Plastic, Promotional Bird, Big Orange Head, 4 x 3 In.	14.00
G.E. Refrigerator, Monitor Top, White Iron, Hubley, c.1930, M 1331, 4 x 2 ½ In.	185.00
Gas Pump, Cast Iron, Red, Gold Globe, Hose On Side, U.S., 5 ¾ In.	230.00
General Butler, Caricature Face, Frog Body, J. & E. Stevens, M 54, 6 ½ In. ....*Illus*	1035.00
Globe, Electroplated, Round Door, Combination Lock, Ball & Claw Feet, c.1889, 5 In.	230.00
Golden Possum, Standing, Cast Iron, A.C. Williams, 4 ½ In.	420.00
Goose, Red Goose School Shoes, Iron, Red, Silver Beak, 3 ⅜ In.	345.00
Horse, Brown Paint, Cast Iron, Arcade, 4 In.	35.00
House, Mahogany, Painted Windows, Door, c.1880, 5 x 7 In.	178.00
Independence Hall, Copper, Bronze Paint, Enterprise Mfg. Co., 1876, M 1202, 9 x 6 x 6 In.	948.00
Jukebox, Plastic, Coin Slot In Front, Windup, Ideal, 1930s, 6 ½ In.	85.00
Lincoln's Log Cabin, Ceramic, Van Dyk Tea, Austria, c.1920, 2 ½ x 3 ¾ In.	28.00
Lion, Cast Iron, Green Paint, Arcade, 4 ¾ In.	345.00
Lion, Gold Paint, Cast Iron, 5 x 6 In.	24.00
Lion, On Wheels, Cast Iron, Gold, A.C. Williams, c.1920, M 760, 4 ½ In.	450.00

Mechanical banks were first made about 1870. Any bank with moving parts is considered mechanical. The metal banks made before World War I are the most desirable. Copies and new designs of mechanical banks have been made in metal or plastic since the 1920s. The condition of the paint on the old banks is important. Worn paint can lower a price by 90 percent. In 2012 there was an auction of mechanical banks that had almost all of their original paint. These banks sold for thousands of dollars.

Mechanical, 2 Frogs, Cast Iron, Painted	711.00
Mechanical, Afghanistan, Stone Wall, Heart, Gate, 2 Animals, Cast Iron, Copper, 3 ½ In.	5100.00
Mechanical, Artillery, Cast Iron, Nickel Plated, Shepard Hardware, 1892, 6 ½ In.	1093.00
Mechanical, Artillery, Union Soldier, Painted, Cast Iron, J. & E. Stevens, 8 In.	728.00 to 1440.00
Mechanical, Baby In Egg, Die Cast, Trap On Bottom, Black Paint ....*Illus*	345.00
Mechanical, Bad Accident, Iron, Black Man, Cart, Donkey, J. & E. Stevens, c.1890, 10 In.	863.00 to 2400.00

Bank, Devil Head, On Chest, Ceramic, Germany, c.1920, 4 ¾ x 3 ⅜ In. $168.00

Mosby & Co. Auctions

Bank, Dog, Lost Dog, Seated, Howling, Embossed, Iron, H.L. Judd, 5 ½ In. $403.00

Bertoia Auctions

Bank, General Butler, Caricature Face, Frog Body, J. & E. Stevens, M 54, 6 ½ In. $1,035.00

James D. Julia Auctioneers

Few Cars, Low Wages
When the Model T Ford was invented in 1909, there were only about 8,000 cars in the world. The average wage was 22 cents an hour.

Bank, Mechanical, Baby In Egg, Die Cast, Trap On Bottom, Black Paint $345.00

Bertoia Auctions

Bank, Mechanical, Darktown Battery, Baseball Players, Cast Iron, J. & E. Stevens, 1888 Patent $1,610.00

Bertoia Auctions

Bank, Mechanical, Elephant, Howdah, Pull Tail, Cast Iron, 5 x 7 ¾ In. $118.00

Bank, Mechanical, I Always Did 'Spise A Mule, Bench, J. & E. Stevens, 1897 $1,093.00

Bertoia Auctions

> **TIP**
> *Don't repaint old metal toys. It lowers the value.*

Mechanical, Bank Building, Cashier Takes Coin, J. & E. Stevens	863.00
Mechanical, Bank Building, Presto, Iron, Japanned, Red Roof & Door, Kyser & Rex	230.00
Mechanical, Beehive, Text, Scrollwork, Nickel Plated, Cast Iron, Arthur Golton, 1892, 7 x 7 In.	560.00
Mechanical, Billiards Player, Blue Jacket, Germany, 6 In.	316.00
Mechanical, Black Man, Holding Top Hat, Tin Lithograph, Striped Pants, 7 In.	632.00
Mechanical, Boy Stealing Watermelon, Paint, Cast Iron, Kyser & Rex, 6 ½ In.	6600.00
Mechanical, Boy, On Trapeze, Paint, Cast Iron, J. Barton Smith Co., 9 ½ In.	1800.00
Mechanical, Bulldog Savings Bank, Coin In Man's Hand, Dog Jumps, Ives	6900.00
Mechanical, Bulldog, Coin On Nose, Blanket, Pull Tail, Cast Iron, J. & E. Stevens	460.00
Mechanical, Cabin, Black Man Kicks Coin, Yellow Shed, Iron, J. & E. Stevens	288.00 to 510.00
Mechanical, Calamity, 3 Football Players, Cast Iron, J. & E. Stevens, 1904	1888.00 to 4025.00
Mechanical, Cat & Mouse, Cat, Painted, Cast Iron, J. & E. Stevens, 11 ½ In.	10285.00
Mechanical, Cat & Mouse, Painted, Cast Iron, J. E. Stevens, 11 ¾ In.	1320.00
Mechanical, Chief Big Moon, Indian Squaw, Frog, Pond, Iron, Painted, J. & E. Stevens	978.00 to 1416.00
Mechanical, Clown On Globe, Painted, Cast Iron, J. & E. Stevens, 9 In.	19360.00
Mechanical, Creedmoor, Hunter With Rifle, Tree Stump, Iron, J. & E. Stevens, 1877	259.00 to 575.00
Mechanical, Darktown Battery, Baseball Players, Cast Iron, J. & E. Stevens, 1888 Patent... *Illus*	1610.00
Mechanical, Darktown Battery, Cast Iron, Reproduction, 1950s-60s, 9 ½ x 6 In.	316.00
Mechanical, Darky In The Cabin, Cast Iron, J. & E. Stevens, 1880s, 4 x 4 In.	1295.00
Mechanical, Dinah, Green Dress, Cast Iron, Painted, c.1920, 6 ½ In.	150.00
Mechanical, Dog On Turntable, Cast Iron, Japanned, H. L. Judd, 1870s	460.00 to 504.00
Mechanical, Eagle & Eaglets, Coin In Beak, Iron, Painted, c.1883, 5 ¾ x 8 ½ In.	420.00
Mechanical, Eagle & Eaglets, Painted, Cast Iron, Green Base, J. & E. Stevens, 8 In.	2280.00
Mechanical, Eagle, Eaglets, Cast Iron, Tan Base, J. & E. Stevens, 8 In.	1093.00
Mechanical, Elephant & 3 Clowns, Cast Iron, Blue Base, J. & E. Stevens, 1883	2588.00
Mechanical, Elephant, Howdah, Pull Tail, Cast Iron, 5 x 7 ¾ In.	*Illus* 118.00
Mechanical, Fidelity Trust, Brown Paint, Cast Iron, J. & E. Stevens, 6 ½ In.	510.00
Mechanical, Frog On Lattice, Eyes Wink, Lavender Base, Cast Iron, J. & E. Stevens	316.00
Mechanical, Frog On Lattice, Eyes Wink, Red Base, Cast Iron, J. & E. Stevens	575.00
Mechanical, Globe Savings Fund, Drawer, Red, Black Paint, Cast Iron, 7 ¼ In.	3900.00
Mechanical, Globe, Cast Iron, Blue, Red Base, Eagle Finial, Enterprise	2185.00
Mechanical, Guard, Cast Iron, Red, Green, c.1875, 6 ¼ In.	1659.00
Mechanical, Hall's Excelsior, Cast Iron, Tan, J. & E. Stevens	259.00
Mechanical, Humpty Dumpty, Clown, Open Mouth, Shepherd Hardware, 7 ½ In.	480.00
Mechanical, I Always Did 'Spise A Mule, Bench, J. & E. Stevens, 1897	*Illus* 1093.00
Mechanical, Indian Shooting Bear, Cast Iron, J. & E. Stevens, c.1900	3738.00
Mechanical, Jolly Nigger, Bowtie, Eyes Roll, John Harper	201.00
Mechanical, Jolly Nigger, Eyes Roll, Cast Iron, Shepard Hardware, c.1882, 7 x 6 In.	138.00 to 207.00
Mechanical, Jonah & The Whale, Painted, Iron, Shepherd Hardware, 10 In.	1265.00 to 2280.00
Mechanical, Leap Frog, 2 Boys, Tree Stump, Shepard Hardware	863.00 to 1840.00
Mechanical, Lion & Monkeys, Double Peanut, Cast Iron, Kyser & Rex	863.00 to 1452.00
Mechanical, Magic Bank Building, Cashier, Cast Iron, J. & E. Stevens	1840.00
Mechanical, Magician, Cast Iron, J. & E. Stevens, 1901	1955.00
Mechanical, Mama Katzenjammer, Eyes Roll, Cast Iron, Kenton, c.1910	*Illus* 3163.00
Mechanical, Mammy & Child, With Spoon, Dress, Kyser & Rex, 1884 Patent	*Illus* 1380.00
Mechanical, Mason, 2 Men, Brick Wall, Cast Iron, Shepard Hardware, c.1887	1265.00
Mechanical, Minstrel, With Verse, Tin Lithograph, c.1925, 7 In.	*Illus* 403.00
Mechanical, Monkey & Coconut, Brown, Green Paint, Cast Iron, J. & E. Stevens	1610.00 to 2700.00
Mechanical, Monkey, Coin In Mouth, Monkey Jumps, Coin Falls In Organ, Hubley	345.00 to 780.00
Mechanical, Old Time Uncle Sam, Plastic, Push Button Coin In Bag, 1974, 8 ¾ In.	40.00
Mechanical, Organ Grinder & Performing Bear, Yellow House, Kyser & Rex	4312.00
Mechanical, Organ, Cat & Dog, Cast Iron, Kyser & Rex, c.1882	672.00 to 748.00
Mechanical, Organ, Cat, Dog, Monkey, Cast Iron, 1882, 4 x 7 ¼ In.	421.00
Mechanical, Organ, Monkey Dancing Figures, Iron, Pat June 13, 1882, Crank, 7 In.	157.00
Mechanical, Owl, Turns Head, Gold, Paint, Cast Iron, J. & E. Stevens, 7 ½ In.	316.00 to 840.00
Mechanical, Pegleg Beggar, Painted, Cast Iron, H.L. Judd, 5 In.	908.00
Mechanical, Pelican, Man Thumbs Nose Inside Beak, Cast Iron, J. & E. Stevens	1380.00
Mechanical, Pelican, Rabbit In Bill, Painted, Cast Iron, J. & E. Stevens, 7 ½ In.	10200.00
Mechanical, Picture Gallery, Painted, Cast Iron, Shepherd Hardware, 8 ¼ In.	4500.00
Mechanical, Professor Pug Frog's Great Bicycle Feat, J. & E. Stevens Co., 1886	5015.00
Mechanical, Punch & Judy, Painted, Cast Iron, Shepherd Hardware, 1894, 7 ½ In.	1020.00 to 1815.00
Mechanical, Reclining Chinese Man, Shows Cards, Salutes, J. & E. Stevens, c.1885	1840.00
Mechanical, Rooster, Painted, Cast Iron, Kyser & Rex, 6 ¼ In.	1200.00
Mechanical, Santa Claus, Chimney, Shephard Hardware	3250.00
Mechanical, Scotchman, Verse, Tin, Selhumer & Strauss, Germany	*Illus* 460.00
Mechanical, Smyth X-Ray, Optical Illusion, Iron, Angled Mirrors, Henry Hart Mfg. Co., 1898	5900.00

Mechanical, Speaking Dog, Cast Iron, Shepard Hardware, 1885, 7 ½ In.	2300.00
Mechanical, Stump Speaker, Black Man, Carpet Bag, Iron, Shepard Hardware, 1886, 9 In.	1020.00
Mechanical, Stump Speaker, Black Man, Green Jacket, Cast Iron, Shepherd Hardware, 10 In.	2400.00
Mechanical, Tammany, Brown Pants, Yellow Vest, Red Buttons, Cast Iron, J. & E. Stevens, 5 ½ In.	514.00
Mechanical, Tammany, Cast Iron, J. & E. Stevens, c.1873	252.00
Mechanical, Tammany, Coin In Hand, Goes In Pocket, Gray Pants, J. & E. Stevens, c.1873	575.00
Mechanical, Teddy & The Bear, Painted, Cast Iron, J. & E. Stevens, 10 In.	900.00 to 3025.00
Mechanical, Thrifty Scotchman, Man, House, Paint, Wood, 9 x 8 In.	35.00
Mechanical, Tommy, Soldier, Lying Down, Rifle, Stump, Painted, Cast Iron, John Harper, England	7800.00
Mechanical, Trick Dog, Clown With Hoop, Dog Jumps, Hubley, 1906, 8 ¾ In.	374.00 to 570.00
Mechanical, Trick Dog, Clown, Cast Iron, Hubley, 7 ½ In.	472.00
Mechanical, Trick Elephant, Tin, Red, Green Paint, Saalheimer & Strauss, 5 ½ In.	570.00
Mechanical, Trick Pony, Flips Coin Manger, Shepard Hardware, 7 ½ In.	6000.00
Mechanical, Two Frogs, Green Paint, Cast Iron, J. & E. Stevens, 9 In.	3328.00
Mechanical, William Tell, Boy, Apple On Head, Iron, Painted, 10 In.	1430.00
Mechanical, Wimbledon, Harper Manufacturing, London, 12 In.	6000.00
Mechanical, World's Fair, Columbus, Indian Chief, Peace Pipe, Cast Iron, J. & E. Stevens	1725.00
Mechanical, Yellow Cab, Red & Black Trim, Cast Iron, Hubley, 8 In.	856.00
Mermaid, Child In Boat, Holding Fish, Cast Iron, Gold Paint, M 3, 4 ⅝ x 4 ⅜ In.	209.00
Middy, Boy, Cast Iron, Painted Black, Red Lips, Embossed Base, c.1887, M 36, 5 ¼ In.	59.00
Model T Ford, White Rubber Tires, Cast Iron, Arcade, M 1484, 6 ½ In.	570.00
Mosque, Domed, Gray Paint, Cast Iron, c.1905, 4 ½ In.	356.00
Nipper, RCA Dog, Cast Iron, 10 In.	70.00
Nodder, Black Boy Holding Apple & Banana, 1950s, 6 In.	55.00
Olympics, Porcelain, Embossed Nazi Eagle, Brandenburg Gate, Germany, 1936, 4 x 4 In.	157.00
Pabst Blue Ribbon Beer, Can Shape, 1950s, 3 ½ In.	45.00
Palace, Tower, Cast Iron, Ives, c.1890, M 1116 .... *Illus*	19600.00
Parrot, Porcelain, Painted, Japan, Art Deco, c.1930, 4 ⅛ x 2 ⅞ In. .... *Illus*	56.00
Pig, Pink, Blue, Glossy, Forward Ears, Cork Nose, Hull, 1957, 7 x 5 In.	117.00
Pig, Stoneware, Molded Ears, Eyeholes, Manganese Glaze, 5 ¾ x 6 ¾ In. .... *Illus*	443.00
Pigeon, On Tree Stump, Leaves, Chalkware, Painted, 11 In.	47.00
Piggy, Sitting, Cast Iron, c.1910, 5 ¾ In.	24.00
Piggy, Standing, Cast Iron, Marked Deckers, Iowa, 4 x 2 ½ In.	30.00
Policeman, Blue Uniform, Gold Buttons, Cast Iron, 5 ¾ In.	288.00
Policeman, Mulligan, Paint, Cast Iron, A.C. Williams, M 177, 5 ¾ In.	201.00
Policeman, Mulligan, Painted, Holding Club, Cast Iron, A.C. Williams, 5 ¾ In. .... *Illus*	201.00
Prussian Soldier, Bust, Gold Accents, Ceramic, 6 In. .... *Illus*	94.00
Radio, 3 Nickel Dials, Cast Iron, Red, Kenton, M 828, 4 ½ In.	115.00
Reindeer, Cast Iron, Nickel Plated, A.C. Williams, M 736, 6 In.	978.00
Reindeer, On Base, Cast Iron, Painted, John Wright, M 735, 10 ¼ In.	345.00
Rooster, Cast Iron, Painted, Black, Red, White, Arcade, c.1910, M 547, 4 ¾ In.	450.00
Rooster, Full Figure, Cast Iron, A.C. Williams, 1920s, M 548, 4 ¾ In. .... *Illus*	144.00
Saddle Horse, Paint, Cast Iron, A.C. Williams Co., c.1934, M 523, 3 x 3 In.	81.00
Safe, Army Safe, Cast Iron, Nickel Plated, 4 ¼ In.	173.00
Safe, Bank Of Commerce & Savings, Woman, Anchor, Iron, Nickel Finish, Kenton, 7 In.	201.00
Safe, Bank Of Industry, Iron, Red, Nickel Door, Blacksmith, Anvil, Kenton, 5 ½ In.	115.00 to 173.00
Safe, Black, Cast Iron, 4 In.	120.00
Safe, Cast Iron, Embossed Animals On Door, Scrolls, Black, Gold Trim, 1881, 3 In.	374.00
Safe, Coin Deposit Bank, Cast Iron, Embossed, Combination Dial On Door, 6 ¾ In.	230.00
Safe, Combination Lock, Cast Iron, Salesman's Sample, 6 x 8 ¼ In.	480.00
Safe, Combination Lock, Embossed Cast Iron, Ideal Security, c.1910, 6 x 4 In.	89.00
Safe, Embossed Horse Heads, Cast Iron, 5 ½ x 3 In.	118.00
Safe, Green Paint, Fitted Interior, Ryan & Williams, c.1915, 66 x 38 In.	920.00
Safe, Safe Deposit, Iron, Black, Stencils, Side Handles, Henry C. Hart Mfg., 5 In.	144.00
Sailor, Saluting, Gray Paint, Cast Iron, Hubley, c.1910, M 27, 5 ¼ In.	201.00
Sandpiper, Embossed Feathers, Beak, Lifts Head, Key, Germany, M 663, 4 ½ In. .... *Illus*	1180.00
Santa Claus, Holding Staff, Bag Over Shoulder, Lead, Painted, Germany, 6 ¼ In.	8625.00
Santa Claus, Holding Wreath, Cast Iron, Hubley, c.1906, 6 In.	650.00
Santa Claus, Red Robe, Gold Boots, Holding Tree, Iron, Wing, 5 In. .... *Illus*	460.00
Santa Claus, Removable Wire Tree, Multicolor, Iron, Ives, c.1890 .... *Illus*	22050.00
Satyr Head, Porcelain, Green, Europe, c.1890, 2 ¾ x 3 ¾ In.	142.00
Save & Smile Money Box, Cast Iron, Harper, 4 ¼ In.	270.00 to 350.00
Scrappy Bank, Boy, Leather, Brass Corners, People Life Insurance Co., 3 ½ x 4 In.	95.00
Shake Buddy!, Tin Lithograph, Glass Jar, Marx, 4 ¼ In. .... *Illus*	295.00
Ship, Maine, Japanned Gold, Grey Iron Casting Co., 4 ½ x 4 ¾ In.	61.00 to 270.00

B

TIP

*For best results, have
your house sale on
the 1st or 15th of the
month (near payday),
but not during holiday
weekends.*

Bank, Mechanical, Mama
Katzenjammer, Eyes Roll, Cast Iron,
Kenton, c.1910
$3,163.00

Bertoia Auctions

Bank, Mechanical, Mammy & Child,
With Spoon, Dress, Kyser & Rex,
1884 Patent
$1,380.00

Bertoia Auctions

Bank, Mechanical, Minstrel, With Verse,
Tin Lithograph, c.1925, 7 In.
$403.00

James D. Julia Auctioneers

Bank, Mechanical, Scotchman, Verse, Tin, Selhumer & Strauss, Germany $460.00

Bertoia Auctions

Bank, Palace, Tower, Cast Iron, Ives, c.1890, M 1116 $19,600.00

RSL Auction

Bank, Parrot, Porcelain, Painted, Japan, Art Deco, c.1930, 4 ⅛ x 2 ⅞ In. $56.00

Mosby & Co. Auctions

Bank, Pig, Stoneware, Molded Ears, Eyeholes, Manganese Glaze, 5 ¾ x 6 ¾ In. $443.00

Conestoga Auction Co., Inc.

Singer Electric Sewing Machine, Table Model, Tin, Iron, Germany, c.1925, M 1369, 5 In. ...	144.00
Skyscraper, Cast Iron, A.C. Williams, M 1240, 5 ½ In.	83.00
Smokey Bear, Painted, Ceramic, Rubber Stopper, 9 ¼ x 4 In. *Illus*	99.00
Statue Of Liberty, Cast Iron, Painted Silver, Kenton, M 1166, 9 ⅝ In.	748.00
Steamboat, Cast Iron, Silver Paint, Paddle Wheels, Arcade, M 1461, 8 In.	115.00
Stop Sign, Stop, Save, Iron, Gray, Red & Green Signal, Dent, M 1481, 5 ¾ In.	288.00
Teddy Roosevelt, Bust, Uniform, Iron, Brass Finish, A.C. Williams, c.1919, 5 In. ..	143.00 to 172.00
Time Zones, 6 Dials, Cast Iron, 4 ¼ In.	180.00
Tommy In Tank, Pottery, Pink, c.1914, M 297, 3 ⅞ x 4 In.	112.00
Tower, Black, Cast Iron, 9 ½ In.	330.00
Tower, Blackpool Tower, Iron, Japanned, Chamberlain & Hill, England, M 984, 7 ⅜ In.	230.00
Tower, Columbia Tower, 3 Levels, Windows, Iron, Grey Iron Casting, M 1118, 7 ¼ In.	863.00
Trolley, Cast Iron, Silver Paint, Kenton, M 1474, 5 ¼ In.	431.00
U.S. Bank, Letter Box, Eagle Finial, Cast Iron, Brown, Spread Foot Base, 1881, M 859, 9 ½ In.	978.00
V For Victory, Blue, Ceramic, Paper Label, Richard Nelson Co., c.1941, 5 ⅜ x 4 In. *Illus*	140.00
White City Puzzle Barrel, On Hand Cart, Cast Iron, Nickel Plated, c.1894, 5 In.	431.00
Woolworth Building, Bronze, Cast Iron, By A.C. Williams, Ravenna, Ohio, 1920s, 8 In.	155.00
Yellow Cab, Driver, Black, Orange, Cast Iron, Arcade, 7 ⅞ In.	546.00
Yellow Cab, Flat Top, Orange, Black, Stenciled, Cast Iron, Rubber Tires, Arcade, 8 In.	1150.00
Yellow Cab, Orange, Black Paint, Cast Iron, c.1905, 7 ¾ In.	334.00
Yellow Cab, Orange, Silver, Black, Driver, Cast Iron, Rubber Tires, Hubley, 8 In.	460.00

BARBER collectibles range from the popular red and white striped pole that used to be found in front of every shop to the small scissors and tools of the trade. Barber chairs are wanted, especially the older models with elaborate iron trim.

Chair, Archer, 3-Legged Stool, Wood, Iron, Red Velvet Fabric, c.1894	180.00
Chair, Berninghaus Hercules, Shamrock Brand None Better, Strap, Porcelain, Leather	600.00
Chair, Hair Dryer, Art Deco, Modecraft Rayette, Adjustable Hood, Mechanical Footrest, Vinyl ..	47.00
Chair, Hercules, White Porcelain, Black Leather, Round Back	1200.00
Chair, Kochs, Chicago, Porcelain, Blue Leather	1295.00
Chair, Kochs, Oak, Carved, Red Velvet Cushions, Kandle Head Rest Co.	826.00
Chair, Kochs, Oak, Tufted Leather, Hydraulic, Restored, Salesman's Sample, 17 x 9 In.	3850.00
Chair, Kochs, Round Seat, Black & Maroon, Oxblood Leather, Copper Flashing	3080.00
Chair, Kochs, White Porcelain, Blue Velvet Cushions	1080.00
Chair, Koken, Cowhide Upholstery, Oak, c.1895	1320.00
Chair, Koken, Oak, Black Leather, Button Tufted Back & Seat	2750.00
Chair, Koken, Oak, Black Upholstery, Nickel Plated Patina, Porcelain Base	1180.00
Chair, Koken, Round Seat, Square Back, White Porcelain, Nickel Plate	672.00
Chair, Koken, Swivel, Leather, 1950s	2385.00
Chair, Lion, Converted From Carousel, Carved By Heyn, J.L. Hudson Co., 42 In. *Illus*	4200.00
Chair, Mahogany, Adjustable Headrest, Lever-Operated Tilt Mechanism, c.1850, 45 In. *Illus*	369.00
Chair, Porcelain, Ornamental Metal, Wood, Leather, Swivel Type, 1940s	3490.00
Chair, Raised Pad, Foot Stand, No Back, Marked Archer, 1878 Patent, 26 ½ In.	120.00
Chair, Walnut, Burl, Mechanical Foot Pump, Turned Legs, Child's, c.1880, 36 In.	678.00
Coat Rack, Haircut & Shave, 25 Cent, Cast Iron, Scrolls, Wall Mount, 4 Hooks	224.00
Fan, Handheld, Wood Grips, Metal Cage, Spring Mechanism, 10 ½ In.	660.00
Footrest, Cast Iron, Embossed, Wood Base, Koken	150.00
Globe, Barber & Beauty Shoppe, Red Arrows, Milk Glass, Electric, 14 x 15 In.	440.00
License, Illinois, Chas. W. Baker, 1920, 3 x 6 In.	81.00
Pole, Column Shape, Red, White, Blue, Glass Casing, Spins, c.1911, 82 ½ In.	1180.00
Pole, Kochs, Light-Up, Globe Top, Spiral Stripes, Porcelain, Wood Mount, Marvy, No. 2	448.00
Pole, Marvy, Wall Mount, Model 506, Light-Up, Chrome, Wood, 33 In.	316.00
Pole, Oak, Paint, c.1910, 28 ¼ In., Pair	972.00
Pole, Pine, Red, White, Blue Stripe, Gold Top Orb, Paint, c.1850, 91 In.	889.00
Pole, Pine, Turned, Red, White, Blue Painted, c.1890, 30 In., Pair	2607.00
Pole, Porcelain, Stain Glass, Black & White Stripes, c.1925, 35 In.	960.00
Pole, Red, White Stripes, Gold Ball Finial, Paint, 58 In.	604.00
Pole, Rotating, Clear Red Glass Globe, Red, White, Blue Stripes, Metal, 38 In.	499.00
Pole, Star Painted Base, Applied Columns, c.1860, 72 In.	805.00
Pole, Turned, Red, White, Blue, Gold Ball Finial, c.1900, 49 In., Pair	8320.00
Pole, Turned, Red, White, Blue, Paint, c.1880, 53 In.	444.00
Pole, Wall Mount, Electric, William Marvy Co., 26 x 9 In.	600.00
Pole, Wall Mount, Theo. A. Kochs Co. *Illus*	288.00
Pole, Wall, Glass, Porcelain, White Finial, Koken, 10 ½ x 42 In.	825.00

Pole, Wood, Cannon Ball Finial, Red, White Paint, c.1925, 60 In.	345.00
Pole, Wood, Carved, Paint, Black, White Stripes, Gray Acorn Finials, Iron Mounts, 35 In.	1725.00
Pole, Wood, Freestanding, Red, White, Blue, Lamb's Tongue Base, c.1900, 95 In. *Illus*	2585.00
Pole, Wood, Half Column, Red, White, Blue, Paint, Spiral Stripes, 1800s, 54 In. *Illus*	1007.00
Pole, Wood, Painted Red, Blue Stripes, Black Stand, c.1885, 36 x 42 ½ In.	230.00
Pole, Wood, Painted, Gilt Acorn Terminals, Black & White Stripes, Square Base, c.1870, 35 x 2 ½ In.	837.00
Pole, Wood, Painted, Red, White, Blue Spiral Stripes, Yellow Ball Finial, 1900s, 90 x 8 In.	935.00
Pole, Wood, Red & White Stripes, Turned Half Column, c.1920, 78 In.	323.00
Pole, Wood, Red, White, Blue, Cone Finial, Gilt, Freestanding, c.1910, 68 x 80 In. *Illus*	529.00
Pole, Wood, Turned & Painted, Red White & Blue, Mustard Yellow, c.1900, 41 x 3 In.	2015.00
Pole, Wood, Turned, Baluster, Gold Finial, Red, White, Blue, 64 ½ In.	1007.00
Pole, Wood, Turned, Red, White, Gilt, Tin Mounting Arms, 19th Century, 39 ½ In.	2450.00
Rack, Mug, Oak, 42 Mug Spaces, 35 x 32 In.	660.00
Rack, Occupational Mug, Oak, Carved, 40 Compartments, 44 ½ x 41 ½ In.	880.00
Sign, Ask For Wildroot, Tin, Embossed, 10 x 28 In.	330.00
Sign, Barber Shop Men's Room, Brown, Gold, Paint, Wood, c.1910, 25 x 6 In.	144.00
Sign, Barber Shop Pole, Porcelain, Stripes, Globe Top, Theo. A. Kochs Co.	672.00
Sign, Barber Shop Pole, Stained Glass, Globe Top, Cylindrical Base, 15 x 71 In.	2520.00
Sign, Barber Shop, 2-Sided, Porcelain, Flange, Red, White, Blue, 24 x 12 In.	140.00
Sign, Barber Shop, Porcelain, Flange, 12 x 24 In.	130.00
Sign, Barber Shop, Shaving 10 Cents, Hair Cut 15 Cents, Barber Pole, c.1885, 36 x 24 In. *Illus*	4025.00
Sign, Globe, Barber Shop, Hand Lettered, White, 16 ½ In.	210.00
Sign, Goods Of Honor, Straight Razor, Wood, John Primble India Steel Works Blade, 32 In.	4675.00
Sign, Leaded Glass Globe, Cast Iron Wall Bracket, 15 ½ x 11 ½ In. *Illus*	900.00
Sign, Trade, Scissors, Metal, 24 In.	248.00
Sign, Trade, Scissors, Zinc, Paint, W.C. Heimmerbinger, 22 In.	468.00

BAROMETERS are used to forecast the weather. Antique barometers with elaborate wooden cases and brass trim are the most desirable. Mercury column barometers are also popular with collectors. It is difficult to find someone to repair a broken one, so be sure your barometer is in working condition.

Aneroid, Calibrated Semicircle Gauge, Ogee Wood Base, Round, Germany, c.1920, 7 x 4 ½ In.	495.00
Aneroid, Thermometer, Round Dial, Gilt Flowers & Ribbons, Columns, 1800s, 39 In.	652.00
Banjo, Huddleston, Federal, Mahogany, Boston, c.1830, 40 In.	296.00
Banjo, Mahogany, Line Inlay, Scrolled Pediment, Urn Finial, England, 1800s, 38 ¾ In.	201.00
Banjo, Negretti & Zambra, Rosewood, Mother-Of-Pearl, Engraved Steel, London, c.1885, 44 In. *Illus*	1107.00
Banjo, Orteily & Co., Mahogany, Signed, London, c.1810, 37 In.	182.00
Banjo, William IV, Mahogany, Patera Inlay, Thermometer, Ebony Ringed Mirror, c.1835, 43 In.	492.00
Gimbaled, Mahogany, Brass, Spencer, Browning & Co., London, c.1890, 37 In.	625.00
Holosteric, Street Linder & Propert, Philadelphia, France, 5 In.	119.00
Kendall Bros., Mahogany, Beaded, Rippled Moldings, New York, c.1850, 38 ½ In.	944.00
Louis Philippe, Giltwood, Blowing Winds, Painted, c.1840, 43 x 35 ½ In.	1195.00
Louis XVI Style, Giltwood, Globe, Flower & Leaf Carved Crest, Painted Dial, 35 In.	938.00
Mahogany, Inlaid, Broken Arch Pediment, Convex, c.1800, 38 ½ In.	413.00
Marine, Kew Pattern, Mark IV, Fitted Wood Case, Royal Navy, c.1940, 36 In.	345.00
Mercury, Admiral Fitzroy, Paper Scale, Thermometer, Glazed Case, c.1890, 43 In.	380.00
Oak, Admiral Fitzroy's, No. 367-815, 1870, 9 ½ x 47 ¼ In.	900.00
Regency, Rosewood Veneer, Mother-Of-Pearl Buttons, Ivory Adjustor, 40 In.	531.00
Rosewood, Brass Gimbal Mounted, 37 In.	5265.00
Stick, Admiral Fitzroy, Oak, 1870s, 9 ½ x 47 In.	900.00
Stick, Altria, Mahogany, Swan's Neck Pediment, Brass Finial, Ivory Medallions, 40 In.	615.00
Stick, B. Conti, Mahogany, Glasgow, Scotland, 38 In.	770.00
Stick, C. Alietti, Mahogany, Broken Arch, Metal Dial, Marked, England, c.1850, 43 In.	264.00
Stick, Charles Wilder, Mahogany, Rosewood, Silvered Scale, Woodruff's Patent, c.1860, 36 x 3 In.	230.00
Stick, Exposed Tube, Veneered Panel, Blond Wood, Inlay, Brass Urn Finial, Regency, 39 In.	322.00
Stick, Hugh Jones, Bettws-Gwerfyl-Goch, Walnut Wales, c.1800, 37 In.	177.00
Stick, J. King, Mahogany, Etched Ivory Registers, Ivory Knob, England, c.1835, 37 In.	474.00
Stick, L. Casella, Fruitwood, Narrow, London, England, 35 In.	472.00
Stick, L. Casella, Mahogany, Arch Crest, Round Terminal, Eng., 36 In.	561.00
Stick, Mahogany, Broke Scroll Pediment, Silvered Dial, George III, 41 In.	531.00
Stick, Marine, Brass, Engraved Steel Face, Weighted Stem, Portugal, c.1895, 37 In.	1541.00
Stick, Saunders & Cooke, Regency Style, Bowfront, Temperature Gauge, Swan Neck, 1900s	759.00
Surveyor's, Pocket, Round Brass Case, Signed A. & N.C.O.S.L., Leather Box, 1 ¾ In.	299.00
Thermometer, John Merrick & Co., Timby's Patent, Wood, Cylindrical, c.1860, 37 ½ In.	356.00

Bank, Policeman, Mulligan, Painted, Holding Club, Cast Iron, A.C. Williams, 5 ¾ In.
$201.00

Bertoia Auctions

Bank, Prussian Soldier, Bust, Gold Accents, Ceramic, 6 In.
$94.00

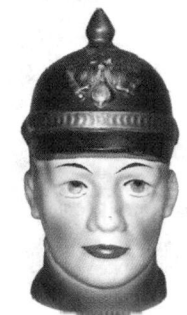

Mosby & Co. Auctions

Bank, Rooster, Full Figure, Cast Iron, A.C. Williams, 1920s, M 548, 4 ¾ In.
$144.00

Hake's Americana & Collectibles

Bank, Sandpiper, Embossed Feathers, Beak, Lifts Head, Key, Germany, M 663, 4 ½ In.
$1,180.00

Bertoia Auctions

Bank, Santa Claus, Red Robe, Gold Boots, Holding Tree, Iron, Wing, 5 In. $460.00

Bertoia Auctions

Bank, Santa Claus, Removable Wire Tree, Multicolor, Iron, Ives, c.1890 $22,050.00

RSL Auction

Bank, Shake Buddy!, Tin Lithograph, Glass Jar, Marx, 4 ¼ In. $295.00

Bertoia Auctions

Bank, Smokey Bear, Painted, Ceramic, Rubber Stopper, 9 ¼ x 4 In. $99.00

Wm Morford Antiques

Thermometer, Mahogany, Line Inlay, Columns, Brass Urn Finial, c.1800, 38 ¾ In.	460.00
Thermometer, Par L. Monty, Giltwood, Round Dial, Garland, Vines, Louis XV, 40 In.......*Illus*	2040.00
Walnut, Doves, Rams Head, Carved, France, 19th Century, 44 x 19 In.	956.00
Wheel, F. Belloni, Mahogany, Blond Banding, Hygrometer, Temp Gauge, Brass, Swan Neck, 40 In..	460.00
Wheel, Leveling Dial, Mahogany, String Inlay Borders, Ivory Knob, England, c.1850, 42 In. ...	296.00
Wheel, Mercury Thermometer, Rosewood, Carved, C Scrolls, Starburst Dial, c.1880, 40 In......	380.00
Wheel, Thermometer, Mahogany, Silvered Dial, Ivory Knob, Leveling Window, c.1800, 39 In..	470.00

BASALT is a special type of ceramic invented by Josiah Wedgwood in the eighteenth century. It is a fine-grained, unglazed stoneware. Some pieces are listed in that section. The most common type is black, but many other colors were made. It was made by many factories. Some pieces are listed in the Wedgwood section.

Teapot, Cylindrical, Loop Handle, Straight Spout, Relief Band, Lid, Sibyl Finial, c.1800, 4 ½ In.....	176.00

BASEBALL *collectibles are in the Sports category, except for baseball cards, which are listed under Baseball in the Card category.*

BASKETS of all types are popular with collectors. American Indian, Japanese, African, Nantucket, Shaker, and many other kinds of baskets can be found. Of course, baskets are still being made, so a collector must learn to judge the age and style of a basket to determine its value. Also see Purse.

Berry, Splint, Oak, Tall, Square, Arched Handle, Appalachia, c.1890, 11 ½ x 8 In.	127.00
Berry, Woven, Multicolor Bands, Looped Rim, Aleutian, c.1900, 8 x 9 In.	575.00
Buttocks, Bentwood Handle, New England, c.1850, 16 ½ x 21 ½ In.	201.00
Buttocks, Splint, 2 Lids, Woven Handle, 23 x 24 In.	266.00
Buttocks, Woven Splint, Painted Chrome Yellow Over Green, New England, c.1850, 11 x 13 In. ...	661.00
Cheese, Open Hexagonal, Split Woven, 1800s, 22 ¾ In.	207.00
Cheese, Splint, Oak, Round, Openwork, 8 x 19 In.	207.00
Cheese, Woven Splint, Salmon, New England, c.1850, 4 x 11 In.	863.00
Egg, Oak, Ribbed, Arched Handle, Shelton Sisters, No. Carolina, c.1925, 6 x 3 ½ In.	4025.00
Egg, Splint, Oak, Kidney Shape, Arch Handle, Green Paint, Va., c.1875, 10 x 5 ½ In.	489.00
Egg, Splint, Oak, Kidney Shape, Ribbed, Double Rim, Arch Handle, c.1910, 5 x 3 ½ In.	518.00
Egg, Splint, Oak, Melon Shape, God's-Eye Supports, Arch Handles, c.1925, 4 ½ x 3 In.	127.00
Egg, Splint, Oak, Ribbed, Double Rim, Arched, Paint, Virginia, c.1900, 7 x 4 ½ In.	920.00
Egg, Splint, Oak, Round, Red, Green Paint, Arched Handle, Va., c.1900, 8 ½ x 4 ½ In.	518.00
Field, Splint, Oak, X-Wrapped Rim, Handles, Va., c.1940, 19 ½ x 17 In.	374.00
Gathering, Rye Straw, Round, Carved Oak Handles, Wrapped Rim, 16 x 14 ½ In.	35.00
Gathering, Rye Straw, Twig Handles, Pa., 8 x 19 In.	152.00
Gathering, Splint, Oak, Tapered, Arched Handle, Double Rim, Va., c.1870, 12 x 15 In.	374.00
Gathering, Splint, Oak, X-Wrapped Rim, Arch Handle, Green, c.1940, 13 x 7 ½ In.	690.00
Gathering, Split Ash, Hand Holes, Wrapped Shaved Branch Rim, Flat Bottom, 29 x 25 In.	35.00
Gathering, White Oak, Red, Green, God's-Eye Loop Handle, Ribbed, 16 x 13 In.	295.00
Hamper, Coiled Rye Straw, Lid, Ash Strip, Flat Bottom, 11 ¼ x 12 ½ In.	130.00
Hamper, Lid, Split Ash, Drop Handle, Wide Splints, Some Dyed Red, 24 x 18 In.	12.00
Kingwood, Satinwood, Parquetry, Panels, Gilt Metal Handles, Round, 1895, 4 ½ x 8 In.	531.00
Lapped Seam, Lozenge Shape Slatted Staves, Bent Hardwood Hoops, Paint, 8 ½ x 25 In.	1007.00
Laundry, Wood, Picket Fence Design, Oval, Slatted, Double Swing Handles, c.1890, 15 x 17 In.	235.00
Nantucket, Friendship, Ivory Whale On Lid, Latch Strap, Signed, Jose Formoso Reyes, 6 x 7 In.....	2819.00
Nantucket, Light Ship, Swing Handle, Inscribed Bartel, 6 x 5 In.	2108.00
Nantucket, Oval, Swing Handle, Wood Base, 2 ½ x 7 ¾ In.	2714.00
Nantucket, Round, Swing Handle, Turned Base, 5 x 8 In.	2596.00
Nantucket, Rounded, Swing Handle, 7 ½ x 8 ¾ In.	767.00
Nantucket, Turned, Swing Handle, Ferdinand Sylvaro, c.1920, 8 ¾ x 5 ½ In.	590.00
Oak, Round, Green Paint, Handle, Pa., 11 ½ x 12 In.	1185.00
Pack, Lid, Splint, Painted, c.1900, 18 ½ In.	563.00
Picnic, Coracle Wicker, Hinged Lid, Fitted Interior, 6 Settings, 7 ¾ x 26 ½ In.	338.00
Rinsing, Hickory, Footed Stretcher Base, 1800s, 20 x 30 In.	1067.00
Round, Split Ash, Cross Weaving, Twig Reinforced Rim, Bentwood, Swing Handle, 10 x 8 In. *Illus*	142.00
Rye Straw, Coarse Wrap, Oval, Dome, Lid, 17 ½ In.	885.00
Rye Straw, Flared, Ribbed Handles, Double Foot, 8 ½ x 15 ½ In.	189.00
Rye Straw, Wrapped, Wrapped Coil Foot Bead, Oval, 28 x 24 In.	324.00
Rye, Bentwood Handles, Oval, Pa., 1800s, 6 ½ x 18 In.	948.00
Splint, 2 Lids, Bentwood Handle, 16 x 23 ¾ In.	561.00
Splint, Lid, Handle, Potato Stamped, Red, Yellow Ground, c.1880, 15 ½ x 11 ½ In.	237.00
Splint, Lid, Red, Green, Blue Paint, Loop Handles, Maine, c.1890, 10 x 12 ½ In.	365.00
Splint, Oak, Corn, Bentwood Handles, Pa., 1800s, 13 ½ x 19 In.	89.00

Splint, Oak, Lid, Footed Cross Stretcher Base, 1800s, 12 ½ x 20 In.	356.00
Splint, Oak, Melon, God's-Eye Handle, 8 ½ x 12 In.	533.00
Splint, Oak, Red Paint, c.1865, 9 In.	486.00
Splint, Potato Stamp Flowers, Red, Yellow, Green Paint, Handles, Maine, c.1890, 7 x 11 In.	1304.00
Splint, Potato Stamp, Red Paint, Loop Handles, Maine, c.1890, 6 ½ x 13 In.	148.00
Splint, Round, Carved Handles, Dome Lid, 1800s, 16 x 23 In.	148.00
Splint, Round, Handle, Green Paint, c.1850, 10 ½ x 8 ½ In.	374.00
Splint, Winnowing, Wood Lapped Sides, Pierced, Carved Handles 30 ½ In.	531.00
Splint, Woven, Paint, Round, Domed Center, 2 Carved Handles, U.S.A., 1800s, 7 x 13 In.	4148.00
Splint, Woven, Square, Bentwood Handle, Round Lid, 18 ¾ In.	236.00
Storage, Lid, Open Weave, Multicolor Birds, Ovoid, Hooper Bay, 11 x 7 In.	219.00
Storage, Splint, Curved Ends, Notched Hickory Handles, c.1850, 18 x 41 In.	1035.00
Storage, Splint, Oak, Tapered Cylinder, V-Wrapped Rim, Paint, Lid, c.1900, 31 x 13 ½ In.	489.00
Sweetgrass, Dark Blue Squares, Red Ground, Oval, 4 ¾ In.	90.00
Tobacco, Intertwined Reeds, Square, Pa., 1800s, 37 ¾ x 38 ½ In.	152.00
Water, Woven Reed, Wood, Round Bottom, Strip Rim, Overlapping Wood Handle, 25 x 15 In.	71.00
Wedding, Bamboo, Woven, Brass Mounts, 4-Tier, Handles, Chinese, 39 x 34 In.	354.00
Woven, Lid, Silk Threads, Hearts & Flowers, Aleutian, c.1890, 5 x 6 In.	1150.00

BATCHELDER products are made from California clay. Ernest Batchelder established a tile studio in Pasadena, California, in 1909. He went into partnership with Frederick Brown in 1912 and the company became Batchelder and Brown. In 1920 he built a larger factory with a new partner. The Batchelder-Wilson Company made all types of architectural tiles, garden pots, and bookends. The plant closed in 1932. In 1936 Batchelder opened Batchelder Ceramics, also in Pasadena, and made bowls, vases, and earthenware pots. He retired in 1951 and died in 1957. Pieces are marked *Batchelder Pasadena* or *Batchelder Los Angeles*.

BATCHELDER LOS ANGELES

Tile, Hands, Scrolls, Flowers, Green, Marked, 5 ¾ In.	115.00
Tile, Knight, Horse, Castle, Blue Highlights, Impressed, 8 x 8 In.	375.00

BATMAN and Robin are characters from a comic strip by Bob Kane that started in 1939. In 1966, the characters became part of a popular television series. There have been radio and movie serials that featured the pair. The first full-length movie was made in 1989.

Action Figure, Bend'n Flex, Posable, Mego, Card, 1972, 5 In.	158.00
Action Figure, Robin, Posable, Box, 1972, 8 In.	318.00
Bath Sponge, Batman Face, Logo, Bag, Color Header Card, Jak Pak, 1970s, 5 In., 3 Piece	115.00
Belt, Leather, Metal Buckle, Gold Luster, Logo, City Skyline, Header Card, 1966, Size 24	323.00
Comic Book, No. 64, February-March 1966, 6 ¾ x 10 ¼ In.	25.00
Comic Book, No. 193, July-August 1967, 7 x 10 In.	18.00
Flashlight, Bat Lite, Bat Shape, Projects Bat Signal, Bag, Header Card, 1960s, 6 x 7 ½ In.	138.00
Life Magazine Issue, Leaping Batman, Cast Signed, 1966	438.00
Pajamas, Short Sleeve, Long Leg, Logo, c.1966, 10 x 14 In., Size 10	115.00
Pencil Box, Gun Shape, Plastic, On Card, 1966, 8 ¾ x 11 In.	104.00
Rain Cape, Hood, Snap Down Mask, Text, Vinyl, 1966, 46 In.	138.00
Statue, Arms Folded, Cold Cast, Hand Painted, Round Base, 1989, 9 In.	369.00
Toothbrush, Batman & Robin, Battery-Operated, 2 Brushes, Box, 1970s, 7 x 10 In.	561.00
Toy, Batmobile, Bump & Go, Tin Litho, Lights, Battery Operated, Box, Aoshin, 1966, 4 x 12 In.	949.00
Toy, Batmobile, Tin Litho, Plastic Canopy, Batman & Robin Figures, Red, Box, 1970s, 12 In.	696.00
Toy, Walking, Arms Move, Glows, Battery, Tin Litho, Cloth, Vinyl, Nomura, 1966, 12 In.	2530.00
Watch, Gilbert Action, Bat Shape Plastic Case, Bat Wing Hands, Box, 1966, 1 ½ x 2 ¾ In.	773.00
Watch, Running Batman On Dial, Plastic, Teaches Time, Marx, 1975, 5 x 9 ½ In.	145.00
Wristwatch, Logo, Batman Leaping Forward, Lightning Bolt Hands, N.P.P. Inc., 1971, 1 ¼ In.	557.00

BATTERSEA enamels, which are enamels painted on copper, were made in the Battersea district of London from about 1750 to 1756. Many similar enamels are mistakenly called Battersea.

Box, Courting Couple Lid, Period Dress, 1700s, 1 ½ x 3 ¼ In.	516.00
Box, Floors Castle, Oval, Crummles & Co., 2 x 1 ½ x 1 In.	129.00
Box, Heart Shape, Two Bunches A Penny, Primroses, Girl, Mother, 2 ¾ x 2 ¼ In.	375.00
Candlestick, Baluster Stem, Shaped Foot, Flowers, c.1765, 12 In., Pair	2250.00
Counter Tray, Couple, Tree, Lake, Pierced, 18th Century, 4 x 3 x 1 In.	485.00
Dish, Jack Of Clubs Card, Pierced, Quatrefoil, Pink, c.1775, 3 In., Pair	2450.00
Patch Box, Boat, Mast, Steps, Men, Yellows, Lavender, Oval, c.1780, 1 ¾ In.	345.00
Scent Bottle, Flowers, Multicolor, White Ground, Cylindrical, c.1800, 3 ½ In.	645.00
Snuffbox, Putti, Reading Letter, Diamond Shape, 3 ⅛ x 2 ¼ x 1 ¼ In.	295.00
Tieback, Buildings, On River, 18th Century, 2 ½ In., Pair	495.00

Bank, V For Victory, Blue, Ceramic, Paper Label, Richard Nelson Co., c.1941, 5 ⅜ x 4 In.
$140.00

Mosby & Co. Auctions

Barber, Chair, Lion, Converted From Carousel, Carved By Heyn, J.L. Hudson Co., 42 In.
$4,200.00

DuMouchelles Art Gallery

Barber, Chair, Mahogany, Adjustable Headrest, Lever-Operated Tilt Mechanism, c.1850, 45 In.
$369.00

Neal Auction Co.

B

Barber, Pole, Wall Mount,
Theo. A. Kochs Co.
$288.00

Victorian Casino Antiques

Barber, Pole, Wood, Freestanding,
Red, White, Blue, Lamb's Tongue Base,
c.1900, 95 In.
$2,585.00

Garth's Auctioneers & Appraisers

Barber, Pole, Wood, Half Column,
Red, White, Blue, Paint, Spiral Stripes,
1800s, 54 In.
$1,007.00

Skinner, Inc.

BAUER pottery is a California-made ware. J.A. Bauer bought Paducah Pottery in Paducah, Kentucky, in 1885. He moved the pottery to Los Angeles, California, in 1909. The company made art pottery after 1912 and introduced dinnerware marked *Bauer* in 1930. The factory went out of business in 1962 and the molds were destroyed. Since 1998, a new company, Bauer Pottery Company of Los Angeles, has been making Bauer pottery using molds made from original Bauer pieces. The pottery is now made in Highland, California. Most pieces are marked "2000." Original pieces of Bauer pottery are listed here. See also the Russel Wright category.

Cal-Art, Candlestick, Double Holder, Pink, Pair	125.00
Cal-Art, Planter, Swan, Satin White, 10 In.	90.00
Kitchenware, Mixing Bowl, No. 12, Green	109.00
Kitchenware, Mixing Bowl, No. 9, Yellow	110.00
Ring, Pitcher, Orange, Copper Handle, Raffia Wrapped, 7 ½ In.	495.00
Ring, Vase, Green, Flared, 4 ⅝ In.	85.00
Strawberry Pot, Black Matte Glaze, Bulbous, 9 x 10 In.	100.00 to 122.00

BAVARIA is a region in Europe where many types of porcelain were made. In the nineteenth century, the mark often included the word *Bavaria*. After 1871, the words *Bavaria, Germany,* were used. Listed here are pieces that include the name *Bavaria* in some form, but major porcelain makers, such as Rosenthal, are listed in their own categories.

Plate, Bacchus & Ariadne, Green Band, Gold Rim, F. Morelli, 12 ½ In.	86.00
Platter, Iris Design, Green Ground, Gold Border, Round, 13 In.	23.00

BEADED BAGS *are included in the Purse category.*

BEATLES collectors search for any items picturing the four members of the famous music group or any of their recordings. Because these items are so new, the condition is very important and top prices are paid only for items in mint condition. The Beatles first appeared on American network television in 1964. The group disbanded in 1971. Ringo Starr and Paul McCartney are still performing. John Lennon died in 1980. George Harrison died in 2001.

Binder, Portrait Photo, 3-Ring, Vinyl, Nems Enterprises, 1964, 10 ½ x 11 ½ In. ....*Illus*	144.00
Disk-Go-Case, Blue, String Tag, Insert, Plastic, Holds 45 RPM Records, 1966, 7 ½ x 8 ½ In.	253.00
Dolls, Instruments, Oversized Heads, Remco, c.1964, 5 In., 4 Piece	290.00
Dress, Fabric, Crossed Gold Guitars, Face Images, Fabric Belt, Holland, 1964, Size 38	345.00
Glass Set, Individual Images, Gold Accent Top Rim, J & L Co. Ltd., 1964, 4 In., 4 Piece	380.00
Guitar, Cream & Orange, 4-Color Strings, Butterfly Pegs, Plastic, Selcol, 1964, Full Size	495.00
Guitar, Junior, Hard Plastic, Instruction Folder, Graphics, Mastro, c.1964, 14 ½ & 4 x 6 In.	291.00
Jackknife, 4 Images, 1960s	113.00
Jacket, Authentic Mod Fashions, Houndstooth, Gabardine, 9th Street East Ltd., 1966, 26 In.	115.00
Lunch Box, Blue, Aladdin, 1965	450.00
Lunch Box, Tin, Plastic, White, Embossed, 8 ½ x 6 ¾ x 3 ¾ In.	35.00
Lunch Box, Yellow Submarine, Thermos, Scenes, King-Seeley, 1968, 7 x 8 ¾ In.	448.00
Magazine, How You Can Become A Beatle, 1964, 8 x 10 ¾ In.	55.00
Poster, Magical Mystery Tour, Fab 4 Frolicking, 1967, 31 x 23 In.	150.00
Purse, Cloth, Clutch, Leather Handle, Zipper, Faces, Tag, 5 ½ x 9 ½ In.	253.00
Purse, Clutch, Vinyl, Orange, Cloth Lined, Brass Handles, Reverse Zipper Pouch, 10 x 10 In.	229.00
Puzzle, Yellow Submarine, Old Fred, Box, 1968, 8 x 9 ½ In.	115.00
Record, Help, Cover, 33 ½ RPM, Capitol Records, 1965	180.00
Record, Meet The Beatles, Cover, 33 ½ RPM, Capitol Records, 1960s	45.00
Record, The Beatles Again, Apple Records, 33 ⅓ RPM, 1970	80.00
Sheet Music, Abbey Road, 1969	20.00
Shirt, Meet The Beatles, Knit, 3 Buttons, Portrait, Piping, Collar, 1964, Size L	115.00
Stationery Set, Yellow Submarine, 6 Different Designs, Box, Unicorn Creations, 1968	127.00
Ticket Stub, J.F.K. Stadium, Philadelphia, August 16, 1966, $5.00, Band Photo, 1 ½ x 3 ¼ In.	522.00
Toy, Guitar, Beatle, Portraits, Shoulder Strap, Hard Plastic, Pink, c.1964, 10 ¾ x 30 In.	519.00
Toy, Guitar, New Sound, Cream, Orange, Plastic, Selcol Ind., England, 1964, 23 In.	495.00
Wig, Die Cut Head Card, Graphic, Bag, Lowell Toy Mfg. Corp., 1964, 9 ¾ x 12 In.	139.00

BEEHIVE, Austria, or Beehive, Vienna, are terms used in English-speaking countries to refer to the many types of decorated porcelain bearing a mark that looks like a beehive. The mark is actually a shield, viewed upside down. It was first used in 1744 by the Royal Porcelain Manufactory of Vienna. The firm made what collectors call Royal Vienna porcelains until it closed in 1864. Many other German, Austrian, and Japanese factories have reproduced Royal Vienna wares, complete with the original shield or beehive mark. This listing includes the expensive, original Royal Vienna porcelains and many other types of beehive porcelain. The Royal Vienna pieces include that name in the description.

Charger, Stencil, Cobalt Blue Border, Gilt, Daisy Rim, Classical Figures, Footed, Royal Vienna, 17 In.	276.00

Dresser Box, Figural, Hound Dog, Resting On Pink Cushion, Tassel Feet, Vienna, 5 ½ x 14 In.	1495.00
Plate, Daphne, Leaf Garland In Hair, Multicolor Border, Signed Wagner, Vienna, 9 ½ In.	1094.00
Plate, Woman, Classical, Blue, Gilt Scroll Rim, L. Scholtz, Vienna, c.1890, 9 ½ In.	590.00
Tazza, Una, Woman, Yellow Drape, Pink Roses, Cherubs Border, Scalloped, Pedestal, 3 ¼ In.	863.00
Tray, Satyr & Diana, Gilt, Signed, K. Otto, Marked, Royal Vienna, 13 x 17 In. ....*Illus*	1800.00
Urn, Classical Scene, Blue, Bronze Ormolu Mounts, Gilt Details, Royal Vienna, c.1905, 16 In.	472.00
Urn, Landscape, Family Scenes, Blue, Gilt Mask Handles, Lid, Royal Vienna, c.1890, 15 In.	502.00
Urn, Lid, Encrusted Flowers, Fruit, Parrot Finial, Branch Handle, Royal Vienna, c.1850, 20 ½ In.	826.00
Urn, Lid, Red, Gilt, Scene, Medallions, Inscribed Sommer, Royal Vienna, c.1890, 22 In. ....*Illus*	896.00
Urn, Lid, Square Base, Transfer Vignette, 3 Women Playing Instruments, Royal Vienna, 15 ½ In.	150.00
Urn, Lid, Women In Conversation, Egyptian Mask Handles, Royal Vienna, 22 In.	2588.00
Urn, Stand, Presentation, Emperor Franz Joseph I Of Austria, Portrait, Royal Vienna, c.1886 .	12000.00
Vase, Classical Figures, Handles, Royal Vienna, Blue Underglaze Mark, 14 In..................*Illus*	188.00
Vase, Courting Couple, Gilt Bronze Mount, Shaped Base, Royal Vienna, 42 In.	11500.00
Vase, Cupid & Maiden, Cobalt Blue Ground, Urn Shape, Gilt Handles, Royal Vienna, 11 In., Pair ..	1955.00
Vase, Nude Woman, Sitting, Lily Pond, Beaded Rim, Tapered, Ring Foot, 18 In.	7475.00
Vase, Portrait, Oval Reserve, Woman, Mounted As Lamp, Richter, Royal Vienna, 15 x 34 In.	3300.00

BEER BOTTLES *are listed in the Bottle category under Beer.*

BEER CANS are a twentieth-century idea. Beer was sold in kegs or returnable bottles until 1934. The first patent for a can was issued to the American Can Company in September of that year, and Gotfried Kruger Brewing Company, Newark, New Jersey, was the first to use the can. The cone-top can was first made in 1935, the aluminum pop-top in 1962. Collectors should look for cans in good condition, with no dents or rust. Serious collectors prefer cans that have been opened from the bottom.

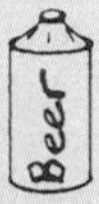

Black Label, Carling, Red, White, Black, Flat Top	6.00
Budweiser Light, Flat Top, Red, Blue Silver, St. Louis Missouri, 1981	80.00
Coors, Adolph Coors Brewing, Flat Top, 7 Oz.	20.00
Crystal Rock Pilsener, White, Blue, Flat Top, Sandusky Brewing Co., 12 Oz.	18.00
Dixie Beer, Straight, Steel, Green, White	3.00
Dottie Seattle Lager, Woman, Sitting, Holding Glass, Emerald City Beer Co., 16 Oz.	37.00
Drewry's Extra Dry Beer, Green, White, Black, Horoscope Set, Piece	87.00
Fox Head 400 Beer, Waukesha, Wisconsin	4.00
Gilley's, Outline Of Texas, 4 ½ In.	7.00
Hampden Mild Ale, Flat Top, Yellow, Green, Flat Top, c.1947, 12 Oz.	26.00
Hanley's Extra Ale, Cone Top, Silver, Blue, 12 Oz.	100.00
Leinenkugel's Chippewa Pride, Flat Top, Yellow Ground, 1940s	4.80
National Bohemian, Natty Boh, Cone Top	275.00
Old Imperial, Cone Top, Brown, Red, Rahr's Brewing Co., 1940s	180.00
Olde Frothingslosh, Pull Tab, 1969, 12 Oz.	5.00
Phoenix Premium Beer, Blue, White, Phoenix Brewing Co., Flat Top, 12 Oz.	32.00
Reserve Of Wisconsin, Flat Top Beer, Red, White	43.00
Rheingold Extra Dry Lager, Suzy Ruel, Flat Top, Red, White, 12 Oz.	136.00
Schlitz, Flat Top, 1949	13.00
Tennent's Girl, Lorraine, Scotland, 15 ½ Oz.	12.00

BELL collectors collect all types of bells. Favorites include glass bells, figural bells, school bells, and cowbells. Bells have been made of porcelain, china, or metal through the centuries.

Brass, Champagne Bottle Shaped, Figural, 5 ¼ x 2 ⅛ In.	165.00
Brass, Graduated Set, Black Wood Handles, Cast Iron Clapper, Wire Link, 6 To 2 In., 4 Piece ..	59.00
Brass, Hotel Counter, Turtle Shape, Press Tail Or Head To Ring, Signed CSS, Germany, c.1910, 2 x 7 In. .	775.00
Brass, School, 1884, 19 ¼ In.	173.00
Brass, Sleigh, 13 Bells, 2 Leather Straps, Scrolled Leaves, 24 In.	460.00
Brass, Sleigh, Leather Strap, 17 Bells, c.1890	180.00
Brass, Strap, 25 Sleigh Bells, 96 In.	354.00
Bronze, 11 Bells, Leather Strap, Spain, 18 x 6 In.	518.00
Bronze, Cast, Pierced Back Plate, Fleur-De-Lis, Hinged Armature, Swan, Gloria Ad Mogore, 13 x 8 In..	213.00
Bronze, Church, Leaves, Inscribed Jesus Maria Joseph, France, c.1693, 11 ¼ In.	1960.00
Bronze, C-Scroll, Cherubs, c.1900, 4 In.	330.00
Bronze, Gold, Black Lacquer, Buddhist Angels Design, Lucite Stand, Thailand, 1800s, 14 x 10 ½ In..	1107.00
Bronze, Horse, 5 Extending Round Bells, Stylized Raised Flowers, 4 ⅜ In.	830.00
Bronze, Iron Yoke, U.S.A., 1800s, 13 In.	2032.00
Bronze, Leather Strap, Brass Buckle, Spain, 17 x 6 In.	575.00

Billy Beer Is a Bust
The Billy Beer can, made when Jimmy Carter, Billy's brother, was president, is now worth about a dollar.

Barber, Pole, Wood, Red, White, Blue, Cone Finial, Gilt, Freestanding, c.1910, 68 x 80 In.
$529.00

Garth's Auctioneers & Appraisers

Barber, Sign, Barber Shop, Shaving 10 Cents, Hair Cut 15 Cents, Barber Pole, c.1885, 36 x 24 In.
$4,025.00

James D. Julia Auctioneers

Barber, Sign, Leaded Glass Globe, Cast Iron Wall Bracket, 15 ½ x 11 ½ In.
$900.00

Showtime Auction Services

Barometer, Banjo, Negretti & Zambra, Rosewood, Mother-Of-Pearl, Engraved Steel, London, c.1885, 44 In.
$1,107.00

New Orleans Auction Galleries, Inc.

Barometer, Thermometer, Par L. Monty, Giltwood, Round Dial, Garland, Vines, Louis XV, 40 In.
$2,040.00

Skinner, Inc.

Basket, Round, Split Ash, Cross Weaving, Twig Reinforced Rim, Bentwood, Swing Handle, 10 x 8 In.
$142.00

Conestoga Auction Co., Inc.

Bronze, Neoclassical, Putti, Iron Stand, Clapper, Vanduzen & Tift, Ohio, 1865, 20 In.......*Illus*	3055.00
Bronze, Scroll Hook, Marked, Stanley, U.S.A., 1800s, 16 ½ In.	1320.00
Bronze, Scrolled Wrought Iron Bracket, 3 Graduated Bells, c.1650, 23 ½ x 15 In.	1840.00
Bronze, Service, Hotel Front Desk, Match Holder Bottom	112.00
Bronze, Temple, Animals, Chinese Characters, Bats, Dragons, Stand, Qing Dynasty, 40 In.....*Illus*	1298.00
Bronze, Yoke, Stamped, John Wilbank, Philadelphia, 1836, 18 ½ In.	2645.00
Cast Iron, Alarm, Dome, Plated, Reciprocating Electro-Magnet Ringer, 14 In.	59.00
Glass, Fenton, Lily-Of-The-Valley, Blue Opalescent, 5 ¼ In.	23.00
Glass, Roses, Vines, Medallions, Cambridge Glass, c.1940, 6 In.	155.00
Iron, Chant, Gilt, Impressed Symbols, Deity Head, Tibet, 6 ¾ x 3 ⅞ In.	2925.00
Iron, Farm, Frame, Ringer Handle, c.1890, 15 In.	115.00
Iron, Hotel, Owl, Figural, Key Wind Clockwork, Countertop, 4 ½ x 3 In.	660.00
Iron, Marked, C.S. Bell Co., 1886, 19 In. Diam.	431.00
Iron, Turtle, Green, Painted, Frog On Back, 6 ¾ In.	230.00
Mahogany, Hand, Turned, Brass, Engraved, U.S.A., c.1895, 16 ¼ In.	178.00
Metal, Cow, Holstein, No. 4, Blum Mfg., Salesman's Sample, 4 ½ x 10 ½ In.	2090.00
Metal, Cow, Leather Strap, Russia, 22 In.	460.00
Metal, Cow, Yoke, Painted Strap, Flowers, Geometric, 1800s, 13 x 13 In.	118.00
Metal, Cyrillic Decoration, Medallions, Brothers V.B. Molovih, Russia, 1876, 4 x 5 In.	190.00
Metal, Hotel Desk, Bull Dog Face, Yellow Glass Eyes, 1880s, 4 ½ In.	1140.00
Metal, Town Crier, Cherry Handle, Hingham, Massachusetts, 13 In.	1930.00
Metal, Verdigris, Meneely Co., Troy, New York, In Memory Of Daniel P. Woodin 1920	546.00
Milk Glass, Hobnail, Fenton, Squared Handle, c.1960, 5 ½ In.	15.00
Sterling Silver, Dinner, Imp, Blowing Horn, 3 ½ In.	126.00

BELLEEK china was made in Ireland, other European countries, and the United States. The glaze is creamy yellow and appears wet. The first Belleek was made in 1857. All pieces listed here are Irish Belleek. The mark changed through the years. The first mark, black, dates from 1863 to 1890. The second mark, black, dates from 1891 to 1926 and includes the words *Co. Fermanagh, Ireland.* The third mark, black, dates from 1926 to 1946 and has the words *Deanta in Eirinn.* The fourth mark, same as the third mark but green, dates from 1946 to 1955. The fifth mark (second green mark) dates from 1955 to 1965 and has an *R* in a circle added in the upper right. The sixth mark (third green mark) dates from 1965 to 1981 and the words *Co. Fermanagh* have been omitted. The seventh mark, gold, was used from 1981 to 1992 and omits the words *Deanta in Eirinn.* The eighth mark, used from 1993 to 1996, is similar to the second mark but is printed in blue. The ninth mark, blue, includes the words *Est. 1857* and the words *Co. Fermanagh Ireland* are omitted. The tenth mark, black, is similar to the ninth mark but includes the words *Millennium 2000* and *Ireland.* It was used only in 2000. The eleventh mark, similar to the millennium mark but green, was introduced in 2001. The twelfth mark, black, is similar to the eleventh mark but has a banner above the mark with the words "Celebrating 150 Years." It was used in 2007. The thirteenth trademark, used from 2008 to 2010, is similar to the twelfth but is brown and has no banner. The fourteenth mark, the Classic Belleek trademark, is similar to the twelfth but includes Belleek's website address. The Belleek Living trademark was introduced in 2010 and is used on items from that giftware line. The word *Belleek* is now used only on the pieces made in Ireland even though earlier pieces from other countries were sometimes marked *Belleek.* These early pieces are listed by manufacturer, such as Ceramic Art Co., Haviland, Lenox, Ott & Brewer, and Willets.

Basket, Lid, Reticulated, Branch Handles, Applied Flowers, Oval, 6 x 9 x 6 ¾ In.	705.00
Basket, Open Weave, Wavy Rim, Oval, Flowers, Ireland, 7 ¼ In.	40.00
Biscuit Jar, Lid, Diamond Pattern, Pink Trim, Black Mark, 7 In.	57.00
Biscuit Jar, Lid, White, 7 In.	69.00
Bowl, Clematis, Yellow Daisies, Brown, Wavy Rim, 10 In.	173.00
Cake Plate, Twig, 4-Strand, Marked Fermanach, Ireland, 10 In.	84.00
Cup & Saucer, Sea Shell, Green Mark, Ireland, 6 x 2 ½ In.	17.00
Dish, Heart Shape, Pink Roses, Leaves, Gilt Edge, 6 In.	200.00
Figurine, Maiden, Draped, Standing At Wall, Gathering Water, Pitcher At Feet, c.1890, 15 In..	7620.00
Figurine, Pig, Sitting, Yellow Iridescent, c.1965, 3 In.	28.00
Flowerpot, Applied Flowers, Flared Scalloped Rim, Green Mark, Ireland, 3 ½ In.	34.00
Honey Pot, Beehive Shape, On Stand, White Ground, Clover, Bees, c.1910, 6 x 5 In. 210.00 to 240.00	
Salt, Shell Shape, 3 ¼ x 2 ¼ In.	30.00
Sugar & Creamer, Ivy, Twisted Handles, Yellow Iridescent	68.00
Sugar & Creamer, Lily, Black Mark, Ireland, 2 ½ x 3 ¼ In.	28.00
Teapot, Grass Pattern, Pink, Red, Green, Side & Top Handle, Black Mark, c.1875, 6 x 8 In.	170.00
Vase, Kingfisher, Flying, Reeds, 12 In.	550.00
Vase, Triple Bud Vase, Tree Trunk Shape, Clovers, c.1960, 6 In.	55.00

B

BENNINGTON ware was the product of two factories working in Bennington, Vermont. Both the Norton Company and Lyman Fenton & Company were out of business by 1896. The wares include brown and yellow mottled pottery, Parian, scroddled ware, stoneware, graniteware, yellowware, and Staffordshire-type vases. The name is also a generic term for mottled brownware of the type made in Bennington.

Bottle, Coachman, Flint Enamel, Impressed, c.1855, 10 ¾ In.	150.00
Bottle, Coachman, Rockingham Glaze, Impressed Lyman Fenton Co., 1849, 10 ¼ In.	295.00
Bowl, Mixing, Flint Enamel, Green, Ocher, Yellow, Brown, Footed, c.1850, 15 ⅜ In.	472.00
Box, Toilette, Rockingham Glaze, Coffin Shape, 8 ¼ In.	118.00
Churn, Cobalt Blue Flowers, Applied Handles, Impressed E. Norton & Co., Bennington, 18 In.	411.00
Crock, Cobalt Blue Brushed Leaves, Pressed Label, Stoneware, E.& L.P. Norton, Vt., c.1860, 2 In.	323.00
Crock, Cobalt Blue Flower, Cylindrical, Tooled, Handles, E. & L.P. Norton, c.1875, 3 Gal.	115.00
Crock, Stoneware, Blue Slip Trail Flower, Cylinder, Handles, J. Norton & Co., c.1850, 2 Gal.	316.00
Crock, Stoneware, Cobalt Blue Bird, Cylindrical, Lug Handles, c.1850, 2 Gal.	575.00
Figurine, Dog, Poodle, Opposing, Coleslaw Lion Clip, Holding Fruit Basket, 1850s, 8 In., Pair	4720.00
Figurine, Dog, Spaniel, Seated, Flint Glaze, Creamware Pottery Ground, c.1850, 7 In.	150.00
Figurine, Lion, Standing, Paw On Globe, Flint, Lyman Fenton & Co., c.1850, 10 x 11 In.	10073.00
Jug, Cobalt Blue, Pheasant, Stump, Sloped Shoulder, Stoneware, J. & E. Norton, c.1855, 2 Gal.	1668.00
Jug, Stoneware, Cobalt Blue Flower Spray, Spots, Slope Shoulder, J. Norton & Co., c.1850, 2 Gal.	431.00
Jug, Stoneware, Cobalt Blue Pheasant, Slip Trail, Rounded, Stamped J. & E. Norton, c.1855, 4 Gal.	4313.00
Jug, Stoneware, Cobalt Blue, Double Pheasant, J. & E. Norton, c.1855, 16 In., 3 Gal.	6325.00
Pipkin, Rockingham Glaze, Alternate Rib, Paper Label, 1849-58, 5 ½ In.	472.00
Pitcher, Charter Oak, Impressed U.S.P. Ribbon Mark, c.1855, 8 ¾ In.	502.00
Pitcher, Washbowl, Flint Enamel, Alternate Rib, c.1850.	118.00
Snuff Jar, Toby, Rockingham Glaze, Impressed 1849 Mark, 4 ¼ In.	260.00
Soap Dish, Glaze Earthenware, Hollow, Pierced Drainage Bed, Leaf Base, 8 x 6 In.	12.00
Stoneware, Jar, Blue Flowers, Sloped Cylinder, Stamped Julius Norton, c.1845, 2 Gal.	201.00
Toilet Box, Flint Enamel, Alternate Rib, 1847-58, 8 In.	325.00
Toilet Box, Rockingham Glaze, Knop, Canted Corners, Impressed 1849 Mark, 8 In.	118.00

BERLIN, a German porcelain factory, was started in 1751 by Wilhelm Kaspar Wegely. In 1763, the factory was taken over by Frederick the Great and became the Royal Berlin Porcelain Manufactory. It is still in operation today. Pieces have been marked in a variety of ways.

Plaque, Gypsy Woman, Tambourine, Harp, Stone Wall, Mountain, Frame, c.1900, 10 x 7 In.	1348.00
Plaque, Woman, Blue Gown, Red Hat, Red Cloth Mat, Wood Frame, 6 ½ In.	115.00

BESWICK started making earthenware in Staffordshire, England, in 1936. The company is now part of Royal Doulton Tableware, Ltd. Figurines of animals, especially dogs and horses, Beatrix Potter animals, and other wares are still being made.

Beatrix Potter, Figurine, Amiable Guinea Pig, BP 2A, 2 ½ x 3 In.	83.00
Beatrix Potter, Figurine, Diggory Diggory Delvet, BP 3B, 2 ¾ In.	60.00
Beatrix Potter, Figurine, Duchess With Pie, BP 3B, 4 In.	173.00
Beatrix Potter, Figurine, Head Gardener, BP 11A, 3 ½ In.	232.00
Beatrix Potter, Figurine, Jeremy Fisher, Gold Buttons, 3 In.	77.00
Beatrix Potter, Figurine, Little Pig Robinson Spying, BP 3B, 3 In.	48.00
Beatrix Potter, Figurine, Mrs. Tiggy Winkle, Silver Iron, BP 1B, 3 In.	1194.00
Beatrix Potter, Figurine, Mrs. Tittlemouse, BP 2B, 3 ½ In.	140.00
Beatrix Potter, Figurine, Peter & The Red Pocket Handkerchief, BP 9D, 4 ¾ In.	38.00
Beatrix Potter, Figurine, Peter Rabbit, BP 2A, 3 ½ In.	98.00
Beatrix Potter, Figurine, Peter Rabbit, Running, Base, Circular Gold Stamp, 1948 ....*Illus*	357.00
Beatrix Potter, Figurine, Pickles, BP 3B, 4 ½ In.	96.00
Beatrix Potter, Figurine, Simpkin, BP 3B, 4 In.	134.00
Beatrix Potter, Figurine, Sir Isaac Newton, BP 3B, 4 In.	96.00
Beatrix Potter, Figurine, Susan, BP 3B, 4 In.	106.00
Beatrix Potter, Group, Flopsy, Mopsy & Cottontail, Box, BP 2, 2 ½ x 3 In.	232.00
Beatrix Potter, Group, Hiding From The Cat, Box, BP 8C, 5 In.	77.00
Beatrix Potter, Group, Tom Kitten & Moppet, Box, No. 3792, 7 In.	66.00
Figurine, Ayrshire Bull, No. 1454B, 5 ¼ In.	163.00
Figurine, Ayrshire Cow, No. 1350, 5 In.	163.00
Figurine, Belted Boar, No. 1512, 2 ¾ In.	384.00
Figurine, Bird, Bald Eagle, No. 1018, 7 ¼ In.	77.00
Figurine, Bird, Golden Eagle, Matte Glaze, No. 2062, 9 ½ In.	77.00
Figurine, Bird, Pair Of Grouse, No. 2063, 5 ½ In.	345.00
Figurine, Bird, Penguin Chick, No. 2398, 7 In.	464.00

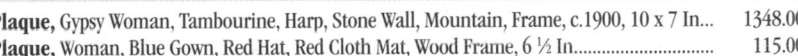

B

Beatles, Binder, Portrait Photo, 3-Ring, Vinyl, Nems Enterprises, 1964, 10 ½ x 11 ½ In.
$144.00

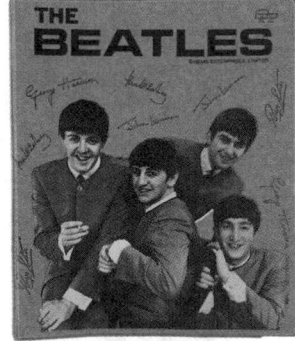

Hake's Americana & Collectibles

Beehive, Tray, Satyr & Diana, Gilt, Signed, K. Otto, Marked, Royal Vienna, 13 x 17 In.
$1,800.00

DuMouchelles Art Gallery

Beehive, Urn, Lid, Red, Gilt, Scene, Medallions, Inscribed Sommer, Royal Vienna, c.1890, 22 In.
$896.00

Sloans & Kenyon

TIP

Remove traces of gum, adhesive tape, and other sticky tape by rubbing the glue with lemon juice.

Beehive, Vase, Classical Figures, Handles, Royal Vienna, Blue Underglaze Mark, 14 In.
$188.00

Leslie Hindman Auctioneers

Bell, Bronze, Neoclassical, Putti, Iron Stand, Clapper, Vanduzen & Tift, Ohio, 1865, 20 In.
$3,055.00

Garth's Auctioneers & Appraisers

Bell, Bronze, Temple, Animals, Chinese Characters, Bats, Dragons, Stand, Qing Dynasty, 40 In.
$1,298.00

Brunk Auctions

Figurine, Bird, Songthrush, No. 2308, 5 ¾ In.	66.00
Figurine, Bird, Turkey, No. 1957, 7 ¼ In.	806.00
Figurine, Camel Foal, No. 1043, 5 In.	106.00
Figurine, Canadian Mounted Cowboy, No. 1377, 8 ¾ In.	1349.00
Figurine, Cardy The Million Dollar Pacer, No. 2340, 20 ½ In.	617.00
Figurine, Dairy Shorthorn Bull, No. 1504, 5 In.	655.00
Figurine, Dairy Shorthorn Calf, No. 1406, 3 In.	576.00
Figurine, Dairy Shorthorn Cow, No. 1510, 4 ¾ In.	1155.00
Figurine, Dog, Blue Mountain Greta, No. 1202, 5 ½ In.	58.00
Figurine, Dog, English Setter, No. 1220, 8 In.	1002.00
Figurine, Fish, Perch, No. 1875, 6 ¼ In.	303.00
Figurine, Fish, Trout, No. 1032, 6 ¼ In.	86.00
Figurine, Fox, Curled, No. 1017, 1 ¾ In.	96.00
Figurine, Fox, Standing, No. 1016A, 5 ½ In.	96.00
Figurine, Galloway Bull, Silver Dunn, No. 1746C	1580.00
Figurine, Giraffe, No. 853, 7 ¼ In.	96.00
Figurine, Goat, No. 1035, 5 ½ In.	116.00
Figurine, Hereford Bull, No. 949, 5 ¾ In.	9634.00
Figurine, Hereford Calf, No. 901A, 4 In.	1155.00
Figurine, Huntslady On Gray Horse, No. 1730, 8 ¼ In.	462.00
Figurine, Indian On Skewbold Horse, No. 1391, 6 ½ In.	388.00
Figurine, Kangaroo, No. 1160, No. 5 ¾ In.	134.00
Figurine, Kid, No. 1036, 2 ½ In.	66.00
Figurine, Leopard, Seated, No. 841, 6 ¼ In.	684.00
Figurine, On Skewbold Horse, No. 1373, 6 ½ In.	365.00
Figurine, Racehorse, Gray, No. 1564, 11 ¼ In.	96.00
Figurine, Rocking Horse Gray, No. 1197, 5 ½ In.	887.00
Figurine, Springbok, No. 1048, 7 ¼ In.	384.00
Plaque, Horse & Horseshoe, Looking Left & Right, No. 806, No. 807, 7 ¼ x 6 In., Pair	116.00
Vase, Fan, Green, Blue, Gold Glaze, Stylized Leaves, c.1940, 7 In.	95.00
Wall Pocket, Boy's Head, No. 612, 7 ¼ In.	163.00
Wall Pocket, Girl With Black Beret, No. 197, 6 ½ In.	106.00
Wall Pocket, Girl With Black Beret, No. 314, 9 ¼ In.	134.00
Wall Pocket, Girl With Bonnet & Green Scarf, No. 380, 9 In.	124.00
Wall Pocket, Girl With Green Beret, No. 314, 9 ¼ In.	173.00
Wall Pocket, Girl With Headdress, Art Deco, No. 483, 9 In.	866.00
Wall Pocket, Lady With Polka Dot Scarf, No. 449, 12 ½.	58.00

BETTY BOOP, the cartoon figure, first appeared on the screen in 1931. Her face was modeled after the famous singer Helen Kane and her body after Mae West. In 1935, a comic strip was started. Her dog was named Bimbo. Although the Betty Boop cartoons ended by 1938, there was a revival of interest in the Betty Boop image in the 1980s and new pieces are being made.

Button, Posed Between Stage Curtains, White, Black, Yellow, 1930s, 1 ¼ In.	690.00
Charm, Blue Dress, Square, Atlantic City, Silvered Brass, Enameled, 1 ⁷⁄₁₆ In.	115.00
Figure, Wood Joint, Applied Decal Face, Leatherette Curls, 1930s, 7 In.	1222.00
Pencil Case, Celluloid Case, Applied Face, Painted Details, 1930s, 2 ⅜ x 8 ¾ In.	173.00
Toy, Betty Boop Trapeze, Celluloid, Wire, Key Wind, Kuramochi, Japan, 1930s, 9 In.	259.00
Ukulele, Koko, Bimbo, Wood, c.1930, 21 In.	173.00
Wristwatch, Boop Boop Be-Boop, Moving Eyes, Brass, Musical Notes, 1970s, 1 ¼ In.	139.00

BICYCLES were invented in 1839. The first manufactured bicycle was made in 1861. Special ladies' bicycles were made after 1874. The modern safety bicycle was not produced until 1885. Collectors search for all types of bicycles and tricycles. Bicycle-related items are also listed here.

American Rambler, Hard Tire Safety, Men's, Sprung Frame, c.1890, Wheel 26 x 30 In.	4830.00
AMF Roadmaster, Luxury Liner, Boy's, Black, Chrome, Spring Front Suspension, 1960, 26 In.	300.00
AMF Roadmaster, Luxury Liner, Boy's, Chrome, Black, Red, White Wall Tires, 26 In.	360.00
AMF Roadmaster, Luxury Liner, Cleveland Welding, 1950s	250.00
Bell, Bicycle Club, All Heil, Rider, Footed, Germany, 19th Century	425.00
Bell, Cast Bronze, Clip On, c.1885, 2 ½ In.	325.00
Bell, Century, Brass, c.1900, 2 ⅛ In.	225.00
Bell, Eagle, c.1897, 2 ¼ In.	70.00
Boneshaker, Bronze Pedals, c.1865, 33 ½ In.	4200.00
Boneshaker, Child's, Red, Gray, c.1878, Wheels 24 In. & 20 In.	3910.00
Boneshaker, Wire, Miniature, c.1920, 6 In.	558.00
Columbia, Light Roadster, Hard Tires, c.1890	5200.00

Columbia, Model 704, Men's, Chainless, Blue, c.1917	2070.00
Columbia, Pope Manufacturing Co., Pneumatic Safety, Mother-Of-Pearl Grips, 1890s	1000.00
Columbia, Sidewalk, 1930s	173.00
Dedemstaart Union, Folding, Netherlands, c.1950	1006.00
EC Meacham Arms, St. Louis, Safety, Hard Tire, 1891, 22-In. Wheel	6000.00
Heifmann, Balloon, Germany, 1950	201.00
High Wheel, American Safety, Gormully & Jeffery, c.1887	25000.00
High Wheel, Columbia, Ordinary, Standard, c.1884, 54 In.	2645.00
High Wheel, Safety, Springfield Roadster, c.1889, 46 In.	7763.00
High Wheel, Safety, Telegram, c.1892, Wheels 30 x 24 In.	26800.00
High Wheel, Victor, Junior, c.1888, 50 In.	2645.00
Indian, Pneumatic, Tank Model, Head Lamp, Hendee, Mass., c.1915	3565.00
Ingo-Bike, Ingersoll Div., Borg Warner Corp., c.1933	978.00
Irish Mail, Quadracycle, Wheel, Differential Steering, Transmission, 1930s	201.00
Irish Mail, Quadracycle, Wood, Scooter, Hill Standard Indiana, c.1910	661.00
J.C. Higgins, Deluxe Balloon, Red, Speedometer, 1957	1840.00
Keating, Pneumatic, Men's, c.1894	1725.00
League, Shaft Drive, Chainless, Commercial, 1895	7750.00
Light, Phareluisant, Battery, Nickel, c.1900, 5 In.	450.00
Monark, Firestone Balloon, Tank Model, Woman's, Lime Green, c.1957	374.00
Monark, Silver King Balloon, Flo Cycle, Aluminum, Speedometer, Headlight, 1937	3105.00
Moulton, Folding, Front Suspension, White, 1960	374.00
Murray, Jet Fire X-65, Boy's, Chrome Fenders, Black, Red, White, 1960s, 26 In.	150.00
Pedal, Rat Trap Pattern, Victor, c.1900, Pair	160.00
Peugeot, Wood Fenders, Whitewall Tires, France, 38 x 68 In.	360.00
Pneumatic Safety, Scorcher Style, Rear Step, Coaster Pegs, c.1898	725.00
Pneumatic, Sidecar, Red Cover, c.1915	2415.00
Poster, Pierce Cycles, Woman, Bike, Cow Chasing, Frame, Niagara Lith. Co., N.Y., 1898, 81 x 41 In.	9200.00
Queen City, Pneumatic, Truss Frame, Elmira, N.Y., 1920s	604.00
Racing, Champion, Men's, Heil Brothers, 1920	489.00
Rack & Chalkboard, Wood Slats, Trestle Base, Pa., 26 x 47 ½ In.	690.00
Raleigh, Twenty, Folding, 3-Speed, Rear Rack, 1960s	175.00
Saddle, Bicycle, Christy, Woman's, No. 9	546.00
Schwinn, Black Phantom, Boy's Balloon, c.1955, 20 In.	4025.00
Schwinn, Hornet, Fender Lamp, Horn, c.1940	650.00
Schwinn, Racer, Boy's, Light Weight, 1960s	115.00
Schwinn, Sting-Ray, c.1970	250.00
Schwinn, Sting-Ray, Pea Picker, 5-Speed Stick	949.00
Schwinn, Super Sport, Men's, 10-Speed, Molybdenum, 1970s	125.00
Schwinn, Tandem, Town & Country, Male, Female, c.1960	200.00
Schwinn, Tornado, 1970s	125.00
Scooter, Balloon Tire, Burgundy Frame, 1940	104.00
Spalding, Chainless, Pneumatic Safety, 1899	1400.00
Stoffard, Tigress, Woman's, Pneumatic, Lamp, c.1897	2760.00
Tandem, Latonia, Boren Bicycle Co.	500.00
Tandem, Stearns, Yellow Fever, Convertible, Dual Steer, Plunger Brake, c.1898	2875.00
Terrot, Pneumatic, 2-Speed, Retro-Direct Pedaling, Men's, c.1904	5520.00
Tricycle, 1915, 22 In. ....Illus	468.00
Tricycle, American, Painted Red, White, Spoke Wheels, Black Rubber Tires, 28 x 35 In.	71.00
Tricycle, Invalid's, Wicker Seat, Bell, c.1890	891.00
Tricycle, Metal, Pedal Kids, 1930s ....Illus	300.00
Tricycle, Oilzum, Racer Plaque, Orange Paint	150.00
Tricycle, Rachet Drive, Red, Yellow, 1930	92.00
Tricycle, Tiller, Worthington Co., Cloth Seat, c.1899	300.00
Tricycle, Victorian, Cast Metal, Wood Handles, 30 In.	180.00

BING & GRONDAHL is a famous Danish factory making fine porcelains from 1853 to the present. Underglaze blue decoration was started in 1886. The annual Christmas plate series was introduced in 1895. Dinnerware, stoneware, and figurines are still being made today. The firm has used the initials B & G and a stylized castle as part of the mark since 1898. The company became part of Royal Copenhagen in 1987.

B&G
KBENHAVN
MADE IN
DENMARK

Figurine, Kissing Couple, Mark, 7 ½ In.	35.00
Figurine, Penguin, Black, White, No. 1822, 9 ½ In.	189.00
Figurine, Polar Bear, Signed, 11 ½ In.	173.00
Plaque, Parian, Relief Nymph, Cherub, Attendant, Stamped, 11 ¼ In.	121.00
Plate, Christmas, 1964, Fir Tree	5.00

B

Beswick, Beatrix Potter, Figurine, Peter Rabbit, Running, Base, Circular Gold Stamp, 1948
$357.00

Bloomsbury House

Bicycle, Tricycle, 1915, 22 In.
$468.00

Showtime Auction Services

Bicycle, Tricycle, Metal, Pedal Kids, 1930s
$300.00

Victorian Casino Antiques

TIP
If two tumblers get stuck when stacked, try putting cold water into the inside glass, then put both into hot water up to the lower rim.

Birdcage, Mahogany, Carved, Tiers, Dome Top, Stand, 83 x 26 ¾ In. $330.00

DuMouchelles Art Gallery

Birdcage, Wood, Asian Style, 3 Metal Dragons, Maitland-Smith, 27 x 24 In. $120.00

DuMouchelles Art Gallery

Black, Ashtray, Amos 'n' Andy, I'se Regusted, Plaster, Slots, Cigarette, Barrel, 1930s, 7 ½ In. $171.00

Hake's Americana & Collectibles

Plate, Jule After, 1967, 6 In.	16.00
Plate, Yard & Washhouse, Reticulated Border, c.1978, 8 In.	48.00
Sculpture, Water Mother, Reclining, Nursing 2 Babies, K. Nielsen, c.1925, 12 x 20 In.	546.00
Vase, Windjammer Collection, 9 ½ In.	84.00

BINOCULARS of all types are wanted by collectors. Those made in the eighteenth and nineteenth centuries are favored by serious collectors. The small, attractive binoculars called opera glasses are listed in their own category.

Barr & Stroud, British Pat. No. 435220, 1940s, 10 x 7 In.	145.00
Bausch & Lomb, Army Signal Corp, Stereo Prism, Case, c.1920, 5 x 7 x 3 ¼ In.	75.00
Bushnell, 7x35, Black, Plastic Case, c.1950	18.00
Legendre Grands Oculaires, Night Hawk, Paris, c.1940	45.00
Pride, Stainless Steel, Leather Case, Japan, 3 ½ x 1 ¾ In.	38.00
Signal Glass, Day Night, Enamel, Gutta Percha Rotating Knob, Leatherette, Civil War	225.00
Talbot Reel & Mfg. Co., World War I, Military Stereo, Leather Strap & Case	130.00
Wardavoir, World War I, Leather Bound, Edwardian, 4 ¼ x 3 ¾ In.	65.00

BIRDCAGES are collected for use as homes for pet birds and as decorative objects of folk art. Elaborate wooden cages of the past centuries can still be found. The brass or wicker cages of the 1930s are popular with bird owners.

Art Nouveau Style, Wall, Molded Hardwood, Hourglass Shape, 1900s, 34 In.	403.00
Chrome, Wall, Art Deco, Blue Porcelain Bird, Glass Panels, Paris, c.1950, 29 x 15 In.	575.00
Hendryx, Brass, Seed Tray, Carved Wood Curved Pole	518.00
Iron, Painted, Fleur-De-Lis Finials, Rope Twist, Tassels, Dome Top, c.1915, 46 x 21 In.	461.00
Mahogany, Carved, Tiers, Dome Top, Stand, 83 x 26 ¾ In. *Illus*	330.00
Mahogany, Walnut, George III Style, Double House Shape, Stand, 65 x 42 In.	1188.00
Metal, Mansion Shaped, 4 Doors, Turreted, Victorian, c.1890, 30 x 39 In.	184.00
Metal, Patinated, Tiers, Dome Top, Square Legs, Finial, 37 x 18 x 10 In.	120.00
Pine, Broken Arch Pediment, Parquetry Inlay Panel, 1800s, 11 x 8 In.	118.00
Victorian House Shape, Spires, Octagonal, Bird Finial, Iron, c.1880, 13 In.	1659.00
Victorian Style, Wire, Wood, Dome Top, 46 x 36 In.	702.00
Wood, Asian Style, 3 Metal Dragons, Maitland-Smith, 27 x 24 In. *Illus*	120.00
Wood, Wire, Dome Top, Wire Loop Feeders, Painted Blue, 1800s, 21 x 24 In.	118.00
Wood, Wire, House Form, Painted, Gray Ground, Faux Windows & Door, 37 x 32 In.	767.00
Wood, Wire, Sheet Metal, Yellow, Red, Arched Windows, Doors, Victorian, 38 x 28 In.	516.00

BISQUE is an unglazed baked porcelain. Finished bisque has a slightly sandy texture with a dull finish. Some of it may be decorated with various colors. Bisque gained favor during the late Victorian era when thousands of bisque figurines were made. It is still being made. Additional bisque items may be listed under the factory name.

Bust, Classical Man, 17 In.	236.00
Bust, Hermes, Curly Hair, Olympian God, Integral Socle, c.1850, 9 ¾ x 6 ¾ In.	492.00
Figure Group, Hunters, Dogs, Game Birds, Gilt Accents, Continental, c.1840, 7 x 7 In.	72.00
Figurine, Girl With Ice Skates, Giuseppe Armani, c.1989, 15 x 9 In.	96.00
Figurine, Pierrot & Columbine, Limoges, France, c.1900, 20 ½ In., Pair	375.00
Figurine, Rabbit, Standing, Easter Egg In Paw, Marolin, Germany, 6 ½ In.	34.00
Figurine, Woman, On Pedestal, 2 Courting Couples, 1700s Attire, 12 In.	219.00
Group, Boy & Girl Under Umbrella, Holding Basket, Germany, 10 ½ In.	46.00
Humidor, Taupe, Gloss Glaze, Dancers In Reserves, Buddha Finial, Germany, 7 ½ In.	132.00
Toothbrush Holder, 3 Little Pigs, Musical Instruments, Japan, 1940s, 4 x 3 ¾ In.	85.00
Vase, Green, Porcelain Relief, Angelic Scene, Putto, Marked Germany, c.1895, 11 In.	480.00

BLACK memorabilia has become an important area of collecting since the 1970s. The best material dates from past centuries, but many recent items are also of interest. F & F is the mark used on plastic made by Fiedler & Fiedler Mold & Die Works, Inc. in the 1930s and 1940s. Objects that picture a black person may also be listed in this book under Advertising, Sign; Bank; Bottle Opener; Cookie Jar; Doll; Salt & Pepper; Sheet Music; Toy; etc.

Ashtray, Amos 'n' Andy, I'se Regusted, Plaster, Slots, Cigarette, Barrel, 1930s, 7 ½ In. *Illus*	171.00
Automaton, Man, Black Face, Bellman Cap, Bowtie, Jacket, Glass Eyes, Key, Windup, c.1910, 26 In.	3850.00
Book, Pore Li'l Mose His Letters To His Mammy, Grand Union Tea Co., c.1902, 10 ½ x 15 In.	779.00
Boot Scraper, Aunt Jemima, Standing On Trestle, Painted, c.1900, 13 ¾ x 15 x 9 In. *Illus*	1062.00
Broadside, Fugitive Slave Reward, 400 Dollars, Samuel Sayers, Kentucky, 1844, 10 x 7 ½ In.	1528.00
Bust, Ceramic, Black Gentleman, Riverboat Croupier, Shirt, Top Hat, Bowtie, Base, c.1860, 27 In.	5900.00
Bust, Man Wearing Floppy Hat, Who Said Chicken?, Plaster, 1902, 17 In.	3300.00

Bust, Man, Striped Jacket, Cigar, Top Hat, Paint, Tin Cutout, 29 ½ In.	1440.00
Button, Black Boy, Urinating, Attacked By Goose, Landscape, Celluloid, Round, c.1915, 9 In.	104.00
Cane, Man's Head, Brown Hair, Glass Eyes, Red Lips, Hardwood, Ivory, Brass, c.1900, 36 In.	431.00
Card Carrier, Blackamoor, Child, Carrying Brass Framed Shell, Gilt, Bronze, 9 In.	1107.00
Cigar Box, Cast Iron, Man, Top Hat, Polka Dot Tie, c.1875, 8 x 6 x 4 In.	1840.00
Cigarette Stand, Man Holding Tray, Jacket, Tie, Cast Iron, Art Deco, 34 In.	1176.00
Cigarette Stand, Porter, Holding Tray, Wood, Uniform, Paint, c.1940, 35 In.	115.00
Clown, Papier-Mache, Holds Globe Light, 63 In.	168.00
Cookie Jars are listed in the Cookie Jar category.	
Doll, Bisque Head, Brown Sleep Eyes, Jointed, Composition, Schoenau & Hoffmeister, c.1923, 16 In.	424.00
Doll, Bisque Shoulder Head, Brown Set Eyes, Open Mouth, Cloth, Composition, 14 In.	1243.00
Doll, Bisque Socket Head, Set Eyes, Open Mouth, Composition, Paint, Unis, 60, France, 13 In.	116.00
Doll, Cloth, Stockinet Body, Weighted, Embroidered Features, Jewelry, Apron & Scarf, c.1935, 24 In.	264.00
Doll, Composition Head, Cloth Body, Glass Eyes, Mohair Wig, Closed Mouth, 15 In.	174.00
Doll, Slave, Wood, Carved, Leather Skirt, c.1850, 7 ¾ In.	326.00
Doll, Socket Head, Brown Paperweight Eyes, Cork Pate, Pink Dress, Bebe, Jumeau, 18 In.	2034.00
Doorstop, Minstrel, Sitting On Cotton Bale, Cast Iron, 9 In.	4313.00
Figurine, Aunt Chloe, From Uncle Tom's Cabin, Holding Basket, Multicolor, Gilt, 8 ¼ In.	196.00
Figurine, Boy, Playing Banjo, White Metal, Painted Bronze, c.1890, 8 In.	415.00
Figurine, Boy, Seated On Barrel, Crossed Legs, Turned Hat, Paint, Plaster, c.1900, 23 In.	259.00
Figurine, Girl, Dancing, Holding Tambourine Over Head, Multicolor, 8 ½ In.	247.00
Figurine, Man's Head, Carved Labradorite, Enamel, Gemset, Patriotic Collar, c.1900, 1 ¾ In.	1080.00
Figurine, Native, Female, Quiver Of Arrows, Lion, Elephant, Porcelain, 1800s, 14 In. ......*Illus*	11950.00
Figurine, Uncle Tom, Eva, Cotton Bales, Holding Bible, Blowing Scarf, Multicolor, Gilt, 11 x 6 In.	253.00
Game, Dandy Ball Toss, Man, Bull's-Eye Stomach, Papier-Mache, Germany, c.1895, 24 x 19 In. . *Illus*	8575.00
Game, Nodding Nancy Party, Black Mammy, Hoops, Parker Brothers, c.1900, 12 x 5 ¾ In.	90.00
Hitching Post, Man, Yellow, Pink, Green Paint, Mott Iron Works, N.Y.C., c.1850, 31 In.	2415.00
Incense Burner, Baby On Chamber Pot, Metal, Signed National Prod. Inc., 6 In.	149.00
Lamp, Mammy Base, Woman's Smiling Face, Porcelain, Printed Kerchief, Shade, 16 x 10 In.	165.00
Match Strike, Seated Boy, Pipe, Majolica, Multicolor, 7 In.	81.00
Night-Light, Cast Iron, Boy Holding Lantern, Painted, c.1945, 12 In.	400.00
Picture, Boys Eating Watermelon Slices, Watermelon Shape Frame, 17 x 23 In.	531.00
Postcard, Cotton Ginning Day, Georgia, Black Wagon Drivers, 1936, 5 ½ x 3 In.	23.00
Poster, Theater, Come Steben, Come Leben, South Before The War, Harry Martell, 28 x 21 In.	165.00
Puzzle, Mammy, Eating Blackberries, 7 Pieces, 6 ½ x 7 ¾ In.	90.00
Quilt, Doll, 12 Blocks, Stylized Figures, Calico Dresses, Red Border, Frame, 20 x 23 In.	460.00
Recipe Box, Aunt Jemima, Yellow Plastic, Aunt Jemima On Front, Red Bandana, 6 x 3 In.	295.00
Slave Bracelet, Double Rattle, Wrought Iron, Child's, 3 ¼ x 2 ¼ In.	189.00
Slave Collar, Leather, Brass Band, Ruth, 9 Yrs., House Girl, Charleston, 1857, 22 In. ......*Illus*	266.00
Slave Tag, Copper, Cut Corners, Stamped, Charleston, 1825, Porter, 629, P. Lafar, 2 In.	3240.00
Smoking Set, Man, Seated, Baskets, White Metal, 5 ½ x 6 ½ In. ......*Illus*	231.00
Smoking Stand, Butler, Black Suit & Tie, Holds Tray, Figural, Cast Iron, 35 In.	224.00
Smoking Stand, Porter, Man, Elongated Legs, Plays Music, Moves Head, Wood	4500.00
Sprinkler, Lawn, Sambo, Tin, Painted, 34 ½ In.	118.00
Stringholder, Mammy, Yellow Dress, Occupied Japan, 6 ¼ In.	130.00
Tobacco Jar, Boy, Reclining On Melon, Majolica, Multicolor, 1890s, 9 ¼ x 6 ½ In.	230.00
Toothbrush Holder, Mammy, Pottery, c.1940, 5 In.	55.00
Toy, Sambo, Pull Cart, Cord, Wood, Paint, 14 ½ In.	330.00
Toy, Tombo, Yellow Hat, Dancing Figure, Square Base, Tin, Clockwork, F. Strauss, 10 ¼ In.	345.00
Vending Machine, Peanut, Smilin' Sam, 1 Cent, Bald Head, Tongue Sticks Out, 1931	5480.00
Whirligig, Man, Composition Face, Hair, Pine, Paint, S. Polaha, 18 In.	504.00

BLENKO GLASS COMPANY is the 1930s successor to several glassworks founded by William John Blenko in Milton, West Virginia. In 1933, his son, William H. Blenko Sr., took charge. The company made tablewares and vases in classical shapes. In the late 1940s it hired talented designers and made innovative pieces. The company made a line of reproductions for Colonial Williamsburg. It is still in business and is best known today for its decorative wares and stained glass. All products are made to order.

BLENKO – HANDCRAFT

Ashtray, Amber, Bowl Style, Ruffled Rim, 3 x 6 In.	18.00
Bookends, Owl, Label, 7 In.	85.00
Bottle, Stopper, Pillow Shape, Amethyst Glass, 13 In.	46.00
Bowl, Asymmetrical, Olive Green, 17 x 12 In.	185.00
Bowl, Yellow, Pebbled Texture, Scalloped, 1960s, 11 x 4 In.	48.00
Candleholder, Emerald Green, Round Block, 1950s, 1 ¾ x 3 In.	22.00
Candlestick, Amethyst, Applied Punts, Foot Ring, 3 ¼ In., Pair.	125.00

Black, Boot Scraper, Aunt Jemima, Standing On Trestle, Painted, c.1900, 13 ¾ x 15 x 9 In.
$1,062.00

Brunk Auctions

Black, Figurine, Native, Female, Quiver Of Arrows, Lion, Elephant, Porcelain, 1800s, 14 In.
$11,950.00

Neal Auction Co.

Black, Game, Dandy Ball Toss, Man, Bull's-Eye Stomach, Papier-Mache, Germany, c.1895, 24 x 19 In.
$8,575.00

RSL Auction

Black, Slave Collar, Leather, Brass Band, Ruth, 9 Yrs., House Girl, Charleston, 1857, 22 In.
$266.00

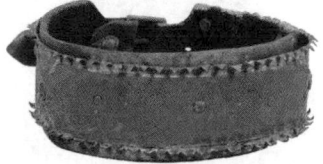

Conestoga Auction Co., Inc.

Black, Smoking Set, Man, Seated, Baskets, White Metal, 5 ½ x 6 ½ In. $231.00

Wm Morford Antiques

Boch Freres, Vase, Grapes, Leaves, Glazed, Charles Catteau, Belgium, 1920s, 9 ½ x 5 In. $2,875.00

Rago Arts & Auction Center

Boch Freres, Vase, Tulips, Flowers, Multicolor, Crackle, Marked, 12 ½ In. $230.00

Humler & Nolan

Boehm, Great Horned Owl, Fledgling, 10 In. $120.00

Cowan's Auctions

Centerpiece, Trumpet, Plum, Amber Foot, 7 ½ In.	110.00
Cobalt Glass, Shell Shape, 6 ½ In.	23.00
Compote, Azure & Emerald, Ribbed, 14 x 6 In.	100.00
Decanter, Squat, Wheat Color, Lollipop Stopper, 10 In.	149.00
Figurine, Elephant, Amber, Sticker, Signed	54.00
Jug, Crackle, Amber, Pontil, Kiwanis International Sticker, 1971, 6 In.	25.00
Lamp, Plastic, Black, White, Egg Shape, 1960s, 13 In., Pair	87.00
Paperweight, Clear, Amber Shadow & Bubbles, Cylindrical, 4 In.	50.00
Top Hat, Ebony, 7 ¾ x 11 In.	325.00
Vase, Crackled, Turquoise Rosettes, Flared, 9 In.	95.00
Vase, Fish Shape, 1962, 12 x 9 In.	85.00
Vase, Green, Flared Cylinder, 10 In.	30.00
Vase, Heart Shape, Amethyst, 4 x 4 x 2 In.	125.00
Vase, Oval, Flat, Center Hole, Blue To Green, Bubbles, 6 x 10 x 3 In.	75.00
Vase, Purple Optic, Applied Leaf, 5 In.	32.00
Vase, Round, Green, Optic, Ribbed, 1952, 11 In.	950.00
Vase, Square, Amber, Ruffled Rim, 9 ½ In.	125.00

BLOWN GLASS, see Glass-Blown category.

BLUE GLASS, see Cobalt Blue category.

BLUE ONION, see Onion category.

BLUE WILLOW, see Willow category.

BOCH FRERES factory was founded in 1841 in La Louviere in eastern Belgium. The wares resemble the work of Villeroy & Boch. The factory closed in 1985. M.R.L. Boch took over the production of tableware, but went bankrupt in 1988. Le Hodey took over Boch Freres in 1989, using the name Royal Boch Manufacture S.A. It went bankrupt in 2009. A new managing director is now running the company.

Vase, Flowers, Art Deco, Blue, Yellow, White Ground, Mark, 1920s, 8 ½ In.	230.00
Vase, Grapes, Leaves, Glazed, Charles Catteau, Belgium, 1920s, 9 ½ x 5 In. ......*Illus*	2875.00
Vase, Oranges, Leaves, Lines, Cobalt Blue, Shouldered, Marked, c.1925, 14 In., Pair	875.00
Vase, Tulips, Flowers, Multicolor, Crackle, Marked, 12 ½ In. ......*Illus*	230.00
Vase, Yellow To Green, High Shoulder, Tapered, Marked, 6 ¼ In.	92.00

BOEHM is the collector's name for the porcelains of Edward Marshall Boehm. In 1953 the Osso China Company was reorganized as Edward Marshall Boehm, Inc. The company is still working in England and New Jersey. In the early days of the factory, dishes were made, but the elaborate and lifelike bird figurines are the best-known ware. Edward Marshall Boehm, the founder, died in 1969, but the firm has continued to design and produce porcelain. Today, the firm makes both limited and unlimited editions of figurines and plates.

American Redstarts, 1 On Branch, 1 In Nest, Square Stepped Base, Marked, 11 ½ In.	240.00
Baby Blue Jay, 4 ¼ In.	185.00
Baby Buntings, Cuddled In Nest, c.1970, 2 x 3 ½ In.	350.00
Baby Cedar Waxwing, Sitting On Leaves, 3 In.	125.00
Baby Chickadee, 4 In.	80.00
Baby Goldfinch, 4 ½ In.	90.00
Baby Mockingbird, On Branch, Red Berries, 5 ⅝ In.	95.00
Baby Wood Thrush, Butterfly In Mouth, 4 ½ In.	250.00
Bald Eagle, On Rock, c.1950, 9 ¾ In.	385.00
Bittern, Standing, Branch, Snail, c.1992, 14 x 9 In.	540.00
Black Capped Baby Chickadee, Branch, Pinecones, c.1964, 3 ½ In.	300.00
Black Capped Chickadee & Holly, 1976, 13 ½ In.	450.00
Blackburnian Warbler, c.1960, 4 In.	395.00
Blue Jay, Where's Ma, 4 ½ In.	58.00
Common Fern, 16 In.	367.00
Crested Flycatcher, Perched On Leafy Branch, Marked, 18 ¾ In.	450.00
Cygnet, Sitting On Leaf, c.1974, 6 x 4 In.	200.00
Dove, Wedding, Spread Wing, Branch, Marked, c.1992, 12 In.	240.00
Downy Woodpeckers, No. 427, 13 ½ In.	189.00
Eastern Kingbird, 20 In.	570.00
Fledgling Kingfisher, 5 ⅞ In.	65.00
Golden Crowned Kinglets, 10 ½ x 7 ¼ In.	497.00

Great Horned Owl, Fledgling, 10 In. ....*Illus*	120.00
Lion Cubs, Rolled Together, c.1982, 3 In. Diam.	350.00
Magpie Fledging, 5 ½ In.	125.00
May Warbler, 1977, 9 ½ In.	270.00
Meadowlark, Marked 435, 9 x 8 x 6 In. ....*Illus*	936.00
Morning Doves, Perched On Branch, Round Base, Signed, 14 ¾ In. ..	240.00
Nonpariel Buntings, 9 In.	527.00
Northwood Rose, 3 Buds, c.1884, 9 x 7 In.	480.00
Parula Warblers, On Leaf-Covered Branches, Pink Blossoms, Signed, 15 ¾ In.	570.00
Peking Robin, 1975, 17 ½ In.	1140.00
Polar Bear, Cubs, On Iceberg, 6 x 12 In.	149.00
Rhododendron Fastousom With Butterflies, 1976, 8 In.	240.00
Rufous Hummingbirds, 15 x 8 ½ x 7 ¼ In.	936.00
Rufous Hummingbirds, Yellow Flower, Removable, Green Leaves, 15 In.	450.00
Swan, c.1979, 6 ½ x 5 ½ In.	300.00
Tree Sparrow, On Branch, c.1972, 8 In.	550.00
Tufted Titmice, Perched On Berry Branches, Snow Covered, 13 ¼ In.	270.00
Varied Bunting, Flower Mount, Orange Blossoms, Signed, 23 In. ..	900.00
Western Bluebirds, c.1975, 17 ¼ In.	780.00

BONE includes those articles made of bone not listed elsewhere in this book.

Box, Casket Shape, Sailor Carved, Crosshatch, Slide Lid, 1800s, New England, 5 ⅞ In.	1007.00
Brush Holder, Carved, Natural Shape, Pierced Designs, Figure, Cloud, Landscape, 6 ¾ x 3 In..	109.00
Brushpot, Carved, Mt. Fuji Scene, Cylindrical, Pinched Collar, Japan, 1900s, 4 In.	72.00 to 85.00
Figurine, Horse, Chinese, 13 x 13 In.	188.00
Game Box, Carved, Lovebirds, Piercework, Slide Lid, Game Pieces, POW, c.1805, 3 ½ In.	2360.00

BONE DISHES were considered a necessary part of a table setting for the Victorian table. The crescent-shaped dish was kept at the edge of the dinner plate so the bones removed from the fish could be stored away from the uneaten food. Some bone dishes were made in more fanciful shapes and many resemble fish.

Angelus Shape, Pink Flower Swag, Gilt Trim, Homer Laughlin, c.1900, 5 In.	8.00
Crescent, Scalloped, Green Flowers, Transfer, Gilt Trim, John Maddock & Sons, 5 ¾ In.	38.00
Fish Shape, Blue, Slip Glaze, Stoneware, Japan, 4 ¼ In.	6.00
Gold Trim, Shell Shape, White, 5 ½ x 4 ½ In.	17.00
Half Moon, Blue & White, Trees, River, Royal Staffordshire, 6 ¾ x 3 ¾ In.	28.00
Half Moon, White, Embossed, Scalloped Rim, Wheat, Royal Crownford, 6 ⅝ In.	17.00
Leaf Shape, Violets, Purple, Gilt Scrolls, Limoges, France	12.00
Moon Shape, Gilt Trim, Magenta Roses, Porcelain, 6 ½ In.	7.00
Moon Shape, Raised Gilt Edge, Henry Alcock & Co., c.1890, 6 ½ In.	12.00
Pink Bouquets, C. Ahrenfeldt, Limoges, France, 6 ¾ In.	15.00
Scalloped, Half Moon, Gilt Flowers, Green, Trim, Knowles, c.1909, 6 ½ In.	11.00

BOOKENDS have probably been used since books became inexpensive. Early libraries kept books in cupboards, not on open shelves. By the 1870s bookends appeared, especially homemade fret-carved wooden examples. Most bookends listed in this book date from the twentieth century. Bookends are also listed in other categories by manufacturer or material. All bookends listed here are pairs.

American Indian, Head, Feathered Headdress, Sewer Tile, c.1900, 5 ½ In.	59.00
Amish Couple, Seated, Cast Iron, Paint, 5 In.	71.00
Arrows, Aluminum, Brass, Signed, C. Jere, 4 ½ In.	438.00
Asian Man, Standing By Fountain, Palm Trees, Bronze, Cold Painted, Stamped, Austria, 6 In...	1063.00
Bell, Embossed Town Crier, Metal, Provincetown, Ma., 7 ¼ In. ..	189.00
Bird, Blue Matte Glaze, Rectangular Base, Pottery, c.1922, 5 In.	230.00
Blacksmith In Workshop, Cast Iron, Bracket Shape, Copper Patina Finish, 6 ½ x 5 ¼ In.	69.00
Book Shape, Marble Carved, Plum Color, White, Gray Veining, 6 x 2 ¾ x 5 In.	150.00
Bulldog, Standing, Collar, Rectangular Base, Bradley & Hubbard, Impressed, c.1900, 5 x 5 In..	533.00
Cat, Arched Back, Bronze, Stamped Tiffany, c.1915, 6 In.	1770.00
Cats, Stylized, Art Deco, Green Painted Metal, 6 ½ In.	296.00
Charles Lindbergh Portrait, Bronze Plate, 6 In.	210.00
Chinese Boys, Porcelain, Black, Red Clothing, Raised Hands, 4 ¼ In.	142.00
Cranes, Bronze, Judd Co., Late 19th Century, 5 ¼ x 4 ½ In.	330.00
Dante, Bust, Bronze, Bradley & Hubbard, 5 ½ In.	153.00

Boehm, Meadowlark, Marked 435, 9 x 8 x 6 In.
$936.00

Charlton Hall Auctions

Bookends, Stylized Horse, Nickel Plated Metal, Cast Mark, Russel Wright, c.1927, 5 x 6 ½ In., Single
$4,000.00

Los Angeles Modern Auctions (LAMA)

TIP
If you find an old bottle with an unwanted old cork inside, pour ammonia into the bottle until it covers the cork. The cork will dissolve.

Bottle, Beer, Staudingers New York, Yellow Olive, Applied Collar, Stoddard, N.H., c.1865, 9 ½ In.
$585.00

Norman C. Heckler & Company

B

Bottle, Bininger, A.M. & Co., 19 Broad St., N.Y., Knickerbocker, Amber, Pontil, Handle, c.1860, 6 ⅝ In.
$575.00

Glass Works Auctions

Bottle, Bininger, A.M. & Co., 375 Broadway, N.Y., Topaz, Applied Tapered Collar, Partial Label, 9 ⅝ In.
$978.00

Glass Works Auctions

Bottle, Bitters, Big Bill Best, Embossed, Yellow Amber, Smooth Base, c.1900, 12 ⅛ In.
$633.00

Glass Works Auctions

Deer, Patinated Metal, Seated, Marble Base, 6 ⅞ In.	625.00
Dog, Terrier, Running, Verdigris Patina, E.B. Parsons, Gorham, c.1940, 8 In.	1888.00
Egyptian Figure, Pushing, Pot Metal, Stamped L. Maronson, 1924, 6 ½ In.	165.00
Elephant Head, Brass, Rocky Base, Weighted, P. Johnson, 1900s, 6 1/16 In.	504.00
Elephant, Standing, Trunk Down, Dark Glaze, Cliftwood, 6 In.	29.00
Elephant, Trunk Up, Bronze, Paul Herzel, c.1945, 7 ½ x 6 ¾ In.	295.00
Fairy, Seated, Rectangular Marble Base, Bronze, 9 ¼ x 5 ½ In.	329.00
Fish, Orange, Black, Cast Iron, AT & M Co., 3 ⅝ x 3 ½ In.	316.00
Football Player, Cast Iron, Painted, Holding Football, Arm Out, Brown, Green, c.1900, 5 In.	207.00
Foundry Worker, Pouring Molten Metal, Bronze, Relief, Arched, 6 ¾ x 5 ½ In.	98.00
Fox Hunt, Embossed, Bronze, Cast Iron, Bradley & Hubbard, 5 In.	173.00
Franklin D. Roosevelt, White Metal, c.1933, 4 ¼ x 6 ¼ In.	85.00
Gargoyle, Terra-Cotta, Mottled Green Over Brown Matte Glaze, 7 x 4 ¾ x 3 In.	406.00
Harlequin Riding Donkey, Cast Metal, 7 In.	104.00
Indian Chief Head, Headdress, Cast Bronze, Bracket Shape, Brown Patina, 4 ½ x 4 In.	161.00
Ionic Columns, Pediment, Stepped Base, Cast Metal, Brown Patina, 4 ½ x 7 In.	86.00
Lighthouse, Cast Iron, c.1925, 7 ¾ x 4 ¾ In.	474.00
Lion, Reclining, Marble Base, Gilt, Paper Label, Bradley & Hubbard, 7 x 3 x 5 In.	75.00
Lions, Resting, Gold Paint, Marble Base, Paper Label, Bradley & Hubbard, 7 x 3 In.	92.00
Lovebird, Cast Iron, Painted, 2 Birds On Leafy Branch, Red, Brown, Yellow, c.1900, 7 In.	267.00
Man, Athlete, Leaning Forward, Head Bowed, Bronze, Art Deco, 6 ⅝ In.	3125.00
Merchant Figure, Seated, Jars, Ivory, Bronze, Scrimshaw, Japan, 7 In.	774.00
Parrot, Perched On Book, Atlas Of The World, Bronze, 9 In.	431.00
Pouter Pigeon, Paden Glass Co., 6 ¼ In.	200.00
Queen At Temple Gate, Enamel, Glass, Egyptian Revival, Ronson, 7 x 6 ¾ In.	466.00
Racing Sailing Sloops, Aluminum, Wendell August, 5 x 5 In.	18.00
Raggedy Ann & Andy, Cast Iron, Painted, PF Volland & Co., 1931, 3 ½ In.	1180.00
Sad Dog, Bronze, Verdigris, Marked, McClelland Barclay, 5 ½ In.	142.00
Stylized Horse, Nickel Plated Metal, Cast Mark, Russel Wright, c.1927, 5 x 6 ½ In., Single .. *Illus*	4000.00
Venus & Poseidon, Bronze, Round Black Marble Base, Signed, 1922, 9 In.	5192.00
Vulture, Seated, Patinated Metal, Verdigris, Glass Eyes, H. Moreau, c.1930, 5 ½ In.	219.00
Woman, Art Deco Style, Seated, Spelter & Faux Ivory, Marble Base, 8 ½ In.	151.00
Woman, Son, Lotus Leaves, Waves, Bone, Carved, Copper Base, Chinese, c.1890, 7 x 7 In.	690.00

BOOKMARKS were originally made of parchment, cloth, or leather. Soon woven silk ribbon, thin cardboard, celluloid, wood, silver, tortoiseshell, and metals were used. Examples made before 1850 are scarce, but there are many to be found dating before 1920.

Blue Ribbon, Sterling Silver Angel At Each End, James Avery	95.00
Celluloid, Sterling Book Charm, c.1900, 4 ¼ In.	185.00
Celluloid, White Flower, Books Of The Bible, c.1910, 4 ⅝ In.	18.00
Ivory, Monkey, Wasps, Japan, c.1900, 4 In.	85.00
Pacific Coast Biscuit Co., Boy, Violets, Cardboard, Victorian, c.1890, 5 In.	12.00
Paper, Eilers Bookmark Of International Sunday School Lessons, Tassel, 1886	16.00
Paper, Fraktur, Watercolor, Ink, Arched Columns, Frame, Johannes Mayer, 1785, 5 ½ x 3 In.	3081.00
Paper, Lilacs, Little Girl, Die Cut, 6 x 2 In.	18.00
Sterling Silver, Cornucopia, Reed & Barton, c.1950, 2 ¾ x 1 ¾ In.	35.00
Sterling Silver, Flower & Leaf Wreath, Blue Tassel, c.1940, 2 ¼ In.	75.00
Sterling Silver, Guilloche Enamel, Flowers, c.1940, 3 ½ In.	155.00
Sterling Silver, Iconic Mayan Figure, Blue & Black Enamel, Mexico, 3 ⅞ In.	60.00
Sterling Silver, Pierced & Carved Top, Ribbon, Whiting, 4 ½ In.	52.00
Sterling Silver, Scottie Dog, Frank Smith Silver Co., c.1910, 3 ⅞ In.	95.00
Sterling Silver, Tiffany & Co., c.1970, 2 In.	60.00
Woven Silk, George Washington, 1776-1876 Centennial, Framed, 13 In.	125.00

BOSSONS character wall masks (heads), plaques, figurines, and other decorative pieces **BOSSONS** were made by W.H. Bossons, Limited, of Congleton, England. The company was founded in 1946 and closed in 1996. Dates shown are the date the item was introduced.

Wall Mask, Bust, Sikhs, c.1963, 6 In.	150.00
Wall Mask, Eskimo, England, c.1970, 8 In.	200.00
Wall Mask, Himalayan, 1966, 5 ½ In.	48.00
Wall Mask, Javanese, c.1959, 7 In.	175.00
Wall Mask, Life Boatman, c.1965, 4 ¾ In.	43.00
Wall Mask, Mr. Pickwick, c.1964, 4 ¾ x 3 ¼ In.	25.00
Wall Mask, Old Salt, Pipe, 1971	27.00
Wall Mask, Old Timer, 5 ½ In.	26.00

Wall Mask, Pancho, 1960, 7 ½ x 6 ½ In.	50.00
Wall Mask, Rawhide	35.00
Wall Mask, Romani, 12 In.	100.00
Wall Mask, Sea Captain	40.00
Wall Plaque, Boxer, Collar, 4 In.	95.00
Wall Plaque, Clovelly Up-A-Long Devon, Fishing Village, c.1956, 18 x 12 In.	125.00
Wall Plaque, English Spaniel, Black, White, Tag, 5 In.	95.00
Wall Plaque, Golden Labrador, 4 In.	95.00
Wall Plaque, Poodle, Black, 5 In.	95.00

BOSTON & SANDWICH CO. *pieces may be found in the Sandwich Glass category.*

BOTTLE collecting has become a major American hobby. There are several general categories of bottles, such as historic flasks, bitters, household, and figural. ABM means the bottle was made by an automatic bottle machine after 1903. Pyro is the shortened form of the word *pyroglaze,* an enameled lettering used on bottles after the mid-1930s. This form of decoration is also called ACL or applied color label. For more prices, go to kovels.com. Several major bottle collections were auctioned in 2012. Records were set. Some are listed in the introduction to this book.

Apothecary, Lid, Pure Drugs Reverse Painted, Eagle, Shield, c.1890.25 ½ In.	711.00

Avon started in 1886 as the California Perfume Company. It was not until 1929 that the name Avon was used. In 1939, it became Avon Products, Inc. Avon has made many figural bottles filled with cosmetic products. Ceramic, plastic, and glass bottles were made in limited editions.

Avon, Automobile, Brown Glass, Paper Label	20.00
Avon, Bell, Ribbed, Gold Tone Plastic Handle, Box, 1968, 6 In.	20.00
Avon, Bowling Pin, Milk Glass, Red Stripe, 1978, 7 In.	12.00
Avon, Candle, Box, 1977, 4 ⅝ In.	17.00
Avon, Cannonball Express Locomotive, 1970s, 6 ½ x 2 ¾ In.	6.00
Avon, Car, Black Green, Paper Label, 6 ½ In.	12.00
Avon, Little Worm, 2 In.	10.00
Avon, Nearness, Round, Clear, Blue Ribbed Lid, c.1945, 4 ¾ In.	35.00
Avon, Pheasant, 1972, 6 ½ x 7 In.	15.00
Avon, Swordfish, Blue Glass, 1972, 10 ½ x 5 In.	12.00
Barber, Clam Broth, Witch Hazel, Silver Trim, Marked, 7 In.	95.00
Barber, Cobalt Blue, Girl In Meadow, Holding Flower, 9 In.	209.00
Barber, Cranberry Swirl, Ribbed, Fluted, Silvered Spout, c.1870, 8 ¼ In.	86.00
Barber, Cut Glass, Green To Clear, Silver Top, 6 ¾ In.	65.00
Barber, Heather Bloom Toilet Water, Koken, St. Louis, Embossed, Label Under Glass, 7 ¾ In.	660.00
Barber, Milk Glass, Ball Shape, Embossed Lion's Head, Gold Paint, 6 ½ In.	22.00
Barber, Milk Glass, Swirl, Leaves, Blue, Gold, 11 ½ In.	45.00
Barber, Yellow Amber, Silver Overlay, Flowers, Leaves, Lattice Pattern, Footed, c.1900, 11 In.	100.00

Beam bottles were made to hold Kentucky Straight Bourbon, made by the James B. Beam Distilling Company. The Beam series of ceramic bottles began in 1953.

Beam, Antique Trader, 11th Anniversary, 1968, 11 x 9 In.	35.00
Beam, Arizona, Grand Canyon, 1968, 12 In.	24.00
Beam, Florida, Seashell Headquarters Of The World, 1968, 9 ½ In.	19.00
Beam, Harold's Club, Reno, Nevada, Slot Machine, 1968, 10 x 5 x 3 In.	17.00
Beam, Harold's Club, Reno, Nevada, Stagecoach, 1969, 7 ¾ In.	16.00
Beam, King Kamehameha, 1971, 11 x 6 In.	28.00
Beam, New Hampshire, Granite State, Live Free Or Die, 1960s, 13 In.	24.00
Beam, Olympian, Slag Milk Glass, Pedestal, 2 Handles, 1970s, 13 ½ In.	55.00
Beam, Professional Baseball, 100th Anniversary, 10 ½ x 7 In.	15.00
Beam, San Francisco, Side Car, Tram, Green, 1968, 4 x 6 x 8 In.	23.00
Beam, Tower Of The Americas, San Antonio Hemisfair, 1968, 15 In.	75.00
Beer, Bay View Brewing Co., Seattle, Wash., Green, Applied Collar, Qt.	392.00
Beer, Buffalo Brewing Co., SF Agency, Applied Double Collar, Pt.	240.00
Beer, G.W. Hoxie's Premium, Blue Green, Sloping Collar, 6 ¾ In.	316.00
Beer, Kensington Brown Stout, Emerald Green, Squat, Double Collar, 6 ⅞ In.	276.00
Beer, Rainier Beer Bottling Works, Reno, Nev., Tooled Crown Top, Pt.	110.00
Beer, Sierra Bottling Co., Weiland's Best, Jamestown, Cal., Tooled Top, Pt.	650.00
Beer, Staudingers New York, Yellow Olive, Applied Collar, Stoddard, N.H., c.1865, 9 ½ In. … *Illus*	585.00
Beer, Yellow Olive, Cylindrical, Sloping Collar, 7 ⅝ In.	2808.00
Bininger, A.M. & Co., 19 Broad St., N.Y., Knickerbocker, Amber, Pontil, Handle, c.1860, 6 ⅝ In. …*Illus*	575.00

Bottle, Bitters, Celebrated Nectar Stomach, Nerve Tonic, Toledo, O., Green, c.1900, 9 ⅜ In.
$1,265.00

Glass Works Auctions

Bottle, Bitters, Chalmer's Catawba Wine, Sutters Old Mill, Spruance Stanley & Co., Applied Top
$12,880.00

American Bottle Auctions

Bottle, Bitters, Dr. Loew's Celebrated Stomach, Aromatic Tonic, Cleveland, O., Green, c.1900, 9 In.
$345.00

Glass Works Auctions

The edited listings of the current prices in this *Kovels' Antiques & Collectibles Price Guide* aren't available on any website. Readers can visit **Kovels.com** to check thousands of past prices and sign up for free information on trends, tips, reproductions, marks, and more.

B

Bottle, Bitters, Drake's Plantation, 6 Log, Medium Blue Green, Patented 1862, 10 In.
$46,000.00

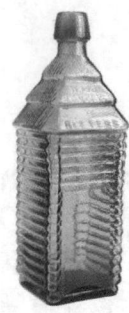

Glass Works Auctions

Bottle, Bitters, Fish, W.H. Ware, Patented 1866, Amber, Applied Lip, 11 ¾ In.
$265.00

Glass Works Auctions

Bottle, Bitters, Kelly's Old Cabin, Patented 1863, Cabin, Green
$50,400.00

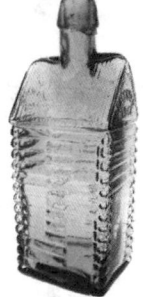

American Bottle Auctions

Bottle, Bitters, Old Cabin, Amber, Applied Mouth, Patented 1863, 9 ½ In.
$2,875.00

Glass Works Auctions

Bininger, A.M. & Co., 375 Broadway, N.Y., Topaz, Applied Tapered Collar, Partial Label, 9 ⅝ In... *Illus*	978.00
Bininger, A.M. & Co., Old London Dock Gin, Yellow, Olive Tone, Case, 9 ½ In.	257.00
Bininger, Peep-O'-Day, No. 19 Broad St., N.Y., Golden Amber, Double Collar, Pt.	585.00
Bitters, A.T. & Co., Amber, 3-Piece Mold, Double Collar, 10 ¼ In.	2016.00
Bitters, A.T. & Co., Olive Green, Double Collar, 10 ¼ In.	2464.00
Bitters, A.T. & Co., Yellow, Double Collar, 10 ¼ In.	3136.00
Bitters, Alpine Herb, Monogram, Amber, Arched Panels, Sloping Collar	896.00
Bitters, Atwood's, Cylindrical, Tooled Top, Label, 6 ¾ In.	78.00
Bitters, Baker's Orange Grove, Topaz Puce, Roped Corners, 9 ½ In.	1344.00
Bitters, Baker's Orange Grove, Yellow Green, Roped Corners, 9 ½ In.	1568.00
Bitters, Berkshire, Amann & Co., Cincinnati, O., Deep Amber, Squat, 9 ½ In.	3075.00
Bitters, Berkshire, Amann & Co., Cincinnati, O., Pig Shape, Tobacco Amber, 10 ⅜ In.	6325.00
Bitters, Big Bill Best, Embossed, Yellow Amber, Smooth Base, c.1900, 12 ⅛ In. *Illus*	633.00
Bitters, Bitter Witch, Horseshoe, Yellow Olive, Arched Shoulders, Double Roll Collar	2912.00
Bitters, Bourbon Whiskey, Barrel, Pink Puce, Squared Collar, 9 ¼ In.	3584.00
Bitters, Brown's Castilian, Honey Amber, Bell Shape, Double Collar, 10 ⅝ In.	202.00
Bitters, Brown's Celebrated Indian Herb, Patented 1867, Golden Amber, Rolled Lip, 12 In.	560.00
Bitters, Bryant's Stomach, Yellow Green, 8 Sides, Lady's Leg Neck, Sloping Collar	3808.00
Bitters, Caldwell's Herb, Yellow Amber, 12 In.	310.00
Bitters, Canteen, For All Disorders Of The Stomach, Lancaster, Pa., Blue Green, 10 In.	3450.00
Bitters, Celebrated Nectar Stomach, Nerve Tonic, Toledo, O., Green, c.1900, 9 ⅜ In. *Illus*	1265.00
Bitters, Chalmer's Catawba Wine, Sutters Old Mill, Spruance Stanley & Co., Applied Top ....*Illus*	12880.00
Bitters, Doctor Fisch's, W.H. Ware, Fish Shape, Patented 1866, Amber, 11 ½ In.	374.00
Bitters, Dr. C.W. Roback's Stomach, Cincinnati, O., Honey, Barrel, Sloping Collar, 9 In.	364.00
Bitters, Dr. Henley's Wild Grape Root IXL, Light Green, Applied Lip	840.00
Bitters, Dr. Henley's Wild Grape Root, IXL In Circle, Aqua, Applied Lip	280.00
Bitters, Dr. Henley's Wild Grape Root, IXL In Circle, Green	2240.00
Bitters, Dr. Herbert John's Indian, Square, Beveled Corners, Indented Panels, 8 ½ In.	702.00
Bitters, Dr. J. Hostetter's Stomach, Applied Lip	375.00
Bitters, Dr. J. Hostetter's Stomach, Dark Amber, Sloping Collar, 9 ⅞ In.	6160.00
Bitters, Dr. Loew's Celebrated Stomach, Aromatic Tonic, Cleveland, O., Green, c.1900, 9 In...*Illus*	345.00
Bitters, Dr. Renz's Herb, Olive Green, Arched Sides, Double Collar, 1868-1881	672.00
Bitters, Dr. S. Cropper's Stomach, Medium Green, 1860s, 9 ⅝ In.	6000.00
Bitters, Dr. Soule Hop, 1872, Semi-Cabin, Light Green, Sloping Collar, 9 ¾ In.	504.00
Bitters, Dr. Wonser's U.S.A. Indian Root, Amber, Fluted Neck With Rings	12376.00
Bitters, Dr. Zabriskie's, Jersey City, N.J., Moonstone, Indented Panels, Flattened Rim, 6 In.	1456.00
Bitters, Drake's Plantation, 6 Log, Copper Puce, Sloping Collar, 10 In.	672.00
Bitters, Drake's Plantation, 6 Log, Golden Amber, Sloping Collar, 10 In.	504.00
Bitters, Drake's Plantation, 6 Log, Medium Blue Green, Patented 1862, 10 In. *Illus*	46000.00
Bitters, Drake's Plantation, 6 Log, Peach Apricot, Sloping Collar, 9 ¾ In.	2800.00
Bitters, Drake's Plantation, 6 Log, Puce, Amber & Apricot Tones, 10 In.	146.00
Bitters, Drake's Plantation, 6 Log, Yellow Green, Sloping Collar, 10 In.	1456.00
Bitters, Electric, Yellow Green, Applied Collar, c.1895	1500.00
Bitters, Excelsior, Amber, Recessed Panels, Sloping Collar, 8 ¾ In.	672.00
Bitters, Fish, W.H. Ware, Patented 1866, Amber, Applied Lip, 11 ¾ In. *Illus*	265.00
Bitters, German Hop, Dr. C.D. Warner's, Semi-Cabin, Amber, Arched Panels, 8 In.	532.00
Bitters, Greeley's Bourbon, Barrel, Olive Green, Squared Collar, 9 ¼ In.	8400.00
Bitters, Greeley's Bourbon, Barrel, Smoky Puce, Applied Lip, 9 ¼ In.	1064.00
Bitters, Greeley's Bourbon, Barrel, Smoky Topaz, 9 ¼ In.	1568.00
Bitters, Greeley's Bourbon, Barrel, Smoky Yellow Olive, 9 ⅛ In.	4600.00
Bitters, Greeley's Bourbon, Barrel, Strawberry Amber, Applied Lip, 9 ¼ In.	325.00
Bitters, Greeley's, Barrel, Peach Puce, Flattened Square Collar, 9 In.	380.00
Bitters, H. Pharazyn, Phila, Indian Queen, Amber, Rolled Lip	2688.00
Bitters, H.P. Herb Wild Cherry, Reading, Pa., Tree, Semi-Cabin, Amber, Roped, 10 In.	560.00 to 952.00
Bitters, Hibernia, Golden Amber, Arched Panels, Sloping Collar	952.00
Bitters, Hierapicra, Extract Of Figs, Botanical Society, California, Blue, Applied Top	1000.00
Bitters, Holtzermann's Patent Stomach, Cabin, Shaded Amber, Sloping Collar, 9 ⅜ In.	1792.00
Bitters, Jackson's Aromatic Life, Olive Green, Recessed Panels, Sloping Collar, 9 In.	6160.00
Bitters, John W. Steele's Niagara Star, Semi-Cabin, Amber, Shaded, Flat Ring, 10 In.	1456.00
Bitters, Kelly's Old Cabin, Cabin, Amber, 9 In.	560.00
Bitters, Kelly's Old Cabin, Patented 1863, Cabin, Green *Illus*	50400.00
Bitters, Kimball's Jaundice, Apricot, Backwards S, 7 In.	1456.00
Bitters, Kimball's Jaundice, Yellow Olive, Sloping Shoulder & Collar, 7 In.	995.00
Bitters, Lacour's Sarsapariphere, Lighthouse, Light To Medium Amber, Applied Lip, 9 In.	3584.00
Bitters, Lash's Kidney & Liver, Best Cathartic & Blood Purifier, Red Amber, Panels.	364.00

Bitters, M.G. Landsberg, Chicago, Eagle, 1776 In Sunburst, Honey, Diamond Shoulders	532.00
Bitters, Mist Of The Morning, S.M. Barnett & Company, Barrel, Amber, 10 In.	560.00
Bitters, National, Ear Of Corn, Golden Amber, Sloping Collar, 12 ¼ In.	468.00
Bitters, National, Ear Of Corn, Patent 1867 On Base, Amber, Applied Lip	450.00
Bitters, National, Ear Of Corn, Patent 1867, Apricot, Double Collar, 12 ¼ In.	1344.00
Bitters, National, Ear Of Corn, Patent 1867, Straw Yellow, Sloping Collar, 12 ½ In.	2128.00
Bitters, National, Ear Of Corn, Patent 1867, Yellow Brown, Applied Lip	1500.00
Bitters, National, Ear Of Corn, Patent 1867, Yellow, Green Tone, 12 ¼ In.	2912.00
Bitters, National, Ear Of Corn, Yellow Amber, Sloping Collar, 12 ⅝ In.	374.00
Bitters, Old Cabin, Amber, Applied Mouth, Patented 1863, 9 ½ In. ....*Illus*	2875.00
Bitters, Old Homestead Wild Cherry, Cabin, Golden Amber, Sloping Collar, 9 ½ In.	1456.00
Bitters, Old Homestead Wild Cherry, Cabin, Honey Amber, Sloping Collar, 9 ¼ In.	420.00
Bitters, Old Homestead Wild Cherry, Cabin, Yellow, Lime Tone, 10 In.	3136.00
Bitters, Old Homestead Wild Cherry, Yellow Green, Applied Collar	4000.00
Bitters, Old Sachem & Wigwam Tonic, Barrel, Cherry Puce, Square Collar, 9 ⅜ In.	633.00
Bitters, Old Sachem & Wigwam Tonic, Barrel, Golden Amber, Squared Collar, 9 ¾ In.	504.00
Bitters, Old Sachem & Wigwam Tonic, Barrel, Yellow Olive, Square Collar, 9 ⅜ In.	2185.00
Bitters, Perrine's Apple Ginger, Phila, Cabin, Golden Amber, Roped Corners, 9 ⅞ In.	392.00
Bitters, Pig, Berkshire, Amann & Co., Cincinnati, O., Pottery, Brown Glaze, 8 In. ....*Illus*	276.00
Bitters, Pineapple, W & Co., N.Y., Blue Green, Applied Mouth, Pontil, 8 ½ In. ....*Illus*	6325.00
Bitters, Pineapple, W & Co., N.Y., Green, Double Ring Collar, Pontil, 9 In. 4700.00 to 6164.00	
Bitters, Prickly Ash, Amber, Square, Beveled Corners, Applied Collar, Label, 9 ⅛ In. ....*Illus*	140.00
Bitters, Rising Sun, John C. Hurst, Philada, Yellow, Sloping Collar, 9 ⅜ In.	235.00
Bitters, Roback's, Light To Medium Amber, Iron Pontil, 9 ¾ In.	500.00
Bitters, Sazerac Aromatic, Lady's Leg, Milk Glass, Embossed, Applied Mouth, Ring, 10 In. .. *Illus*	257.00
Bitters, Schiedam, New York, Amber, Arched Panels, Sloping Collar, 9 In.	200.00
Bitters, Sir Robert Edgar's English Life, Crown, Rutland, Vt., Amber, 8 ⅝ In.	2223.00
Bitters, Solomons' Strengthening & Invigorating, Savannah, Ga., Cobalt Blue, 9 ½ In.	1344.00
Bitters, Suffolk, Philbrook & Tucker, Boston, Pig, Yellow Amber, Double Collared Mouth, 10 In. *Illus*	995.00
Bitters, Tip Top, II.R. & Co., Golden Amber, Cylindrical, Squat, Long Neck, Seal, 9 In	364.00
Bitters, Tippecanoe, II.II. Warner, Golden Amber, Textured, Mushroom Top, 9 In	235.00
Bitters, William Allen's Congress, Semi-Cabin, Emerald Green, Sloping Collar, 10 In.	3920.00
Bitters, Wormser Bros., San Francisco, Amber, Applied Lip	650.00
Bitters, Wormser Bros., San Francisco, Barrel, Honey Amber, Sloping Collar, 9 ¾ In.	1904.00
Black Glass, Flattened Pancake, Onion, Deep Yellow Olive, Sheared, String Lip, 5 In.	1053.00
Black Glass, Olive Green, Oval, Tall Neck, Tooled Spout, c.1790, 10 ¾ In.	345.00
Blown, Chestnut, Amber, Flat Oval, Sloping Collar, Kick Up Base, c.1850, 10 ¾ x 6 ½ In.	196.00
Blown, Chestnut, Light Green, Bubbles, Flat Oval, Rolled Mouth, Kick Up Base, c.1805, 9 In.	150.00
Blown, Chestnut, Olive Amber, Flattened Oval, Rolled Mouth, Kick Up Base, c.1815, 8 x 5 ¼ In.	403.00
Blown, Globular, Light Blue Green, Kick Up Base, Pontil, c.1800, 11 ½ In.	316.00
Blown, Globular, Shaft & Globe, Forest Green, Medium Neck, Applied Lip, Domed Base, c.1860, 6 In.	230.00
Blown, Globular, Tapered, Deep Olive Amber, Applied Mouth, Pontil, England, c.1800, 10 ¾ In.. *Illus*	633.00
Coca-Cola bottles are listed in the Coca-Cola category.	
Cognac Jacquet, Peacock, Bouchet, c.1925, 62 x 46 In.	1100.00
Cologne, 6-Sided, Amber, Elongated Loop, Flange Skirt, Stopper, c.1865, 7 In., Pair	259.00
Cologne, 8 Ribs, Canary Yellow, Squat, Pillar Mold, c.1880, 5 In.	230.00
Cologne, 8-Sided, Opaque Yellow, Swirled, Threaded Neck, Britannia Cap, c.1860, 2 ½ In.	518.00
Cologne, 12-Sided, Sapphire Blue, Ovoid, Outward Rolled Mouth, Pontil, 7 ½ In.	202.00
Cologne, Bunker Hill Monument, Cobalt Blue, Flared Mouth, 12 In.	1170.00
Cologne, Emerald, Flattened Round, Lunettes, Quatrefoils, Brass Hinged Lid, c.1850, 2 ¾ x 2 In.	184.00
Cologne, Overlay, Blue Over Clear, Diamond, Cylindrical, Finial, Star Cut Base, c.1865, 5 ¾ In.	219.00
Cologne, Overlay, Red Over Clear, Octagon Diamond, Cylindrical, Finial, Star Cut Base, c.1865, 4 In.	207.00
Cologne, Paneled, Translucent Starch Blue, Pebbles, Ruffled Rim, Flower Stopper, c.1860, 7 ½ In.	288.00
Cologne, Pinched Waist, Cobalt Blue, Panels, Inward Rolled Flared Mouth, 6 In.	585.00
Cologne, Pinched Waist, Paneled, Electric Blue, Tooled Flared Mouth, 5 ⅞ In. ....*Illus*	1404.00
Cologne, Ribs, Translucent Pale Blue, Rounded Shoulder, Cylindrical, Stopper, c.1860, 4 ½ In., Pair	259.00
Cologne, Ruby, Cut To Clear, Engraved Grapes, Bell Shape, Trefoil, Draped, Stopper, c.1880, 7 ½ In. .	115.00
Cologne, Sapphire Blue, Squat, 8 Protruding Cabochons, Long Neck, Steeple Stopper, c.1875, 7 ½ In.	138.00
Cordial, Wishart's Pine Tree Tar, Patent 1859, Embossed Tree, Apple Green, 8 In.	202.00
Cordial, Wishart's Pine Tree Tar, Phila, Embossed Tree, Emerald Green, 9 ⅜ In.	235.00
Cordial, Wishart's Pine Tree Tar, Phila, Embossed Tree, Sloping Collar, 9 ¾ In.	1232.00
Cosmetic, A.B. Moore Rose Hair Gloss, B.G. Noble, Buffalo, Aqua, Indented Panels, 7 In.	532.00
Cosmetic, Bear's Oil Label, Bear, Clear, C. Knapp, Philada, 3 ¾ In.	1955.00
Cosmetic, Bear's Oil, Arched, Blue Aqua, Inward Rolled Lip, Open Pontil, 3 In.	978.00
Cosmetic, Bear's Oil, Walking Bear, Rectangular, Squat, 3 In.	1093.00

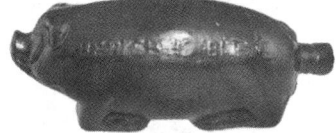

Bottle, Bitters, Pig, Berkshire, Amann & Co., Cincinnati, O., Pottery, Brown Glaze, 8 In.
$276.00

Glass Works Auctions

Bottle, Bitters, Pineapple, W & Co., N.Y., Blue Green, Applied Mouth, Pontil, 8 ½ In.
$6,325.00

Glass Works Auctions

Bottle, Bitters, Prickly Ash, Amber, Square, Beveled Corners, Applied Collar, Label, 9 ⅛ In.
$140.00

Norman C. Heckler & Company

TIP
Want a hot collectible? Try pepper sauce bottles. Old ones are found at bottle shows, new ones in grocery stores.

Bottle, Bitters, Sazerac Aromatic, Lady's Leg, Milk Glass, Embossed, Applied Mouth, Ring, 10 In. $257.00

Norman C. Heckler & Company

Bottle, Bitters, Suffolk, Philbrook & Tucker, Boston, Pig, Yellow Amber, Double Collared Mouth, 10 In. $995.00

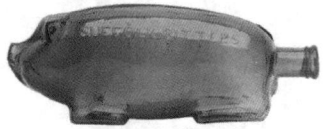

Norman C. Heckler & Company

Bottle, Blown, Globular, Tapered, Deep Olive Amber, Applied Mouth, Pontil, England, c.1800, 10 ¾ In. $633.00

Glass Works Auctions

Bottle, Cologne, Pinched Waist, Paneled, Electric Blue, Tooled Flared Mouth, 5 ⅞ In. $1,404.00

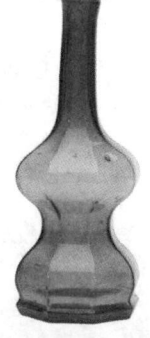

Norman C. Heckler & Company

Cosmetic, Dr. Graham's Tonic Hair Balm, Rochester, N.Y., Aqua, Flared Lip, Pontil, 4 In.	1680.00
Cosmetic, Genuine Bear's Oil, Standing Bear, Green Aqua, Inward Rolled Lip, Label, Pontil, 2 ⅝ In.	1380.00
Cosmetic, J.L. Giofray & Co. Hair Renovator, Red Amber, Indented Panels, 8 In.	3510.00
Cosmetic, Slipper, Bear's Oil, Clear, Label, 4 ⅝ In.	978.00
Cosmetic, Winans Bear's Oil, Blue Aqua, Inward Rolled Lip, Pontil, 2 ⅞ In.	1093.00
Cure, Dr. Hand's Colic Mixture, Wind Colic, Sour Stomach, c.1891, 5 ¾ In.	32.00
Cure, Humphrey's Cold Medication, Cylindrical, 1800s, 4 In.	200.00
Cure, Owbridge's Stomachic, Greenish Aqua, 5 ½ In.	32.00
Cure, Piso's For Consumption, Hazeltine & Co., Deep Aqua, 5 In.	29.00
Cure, Rhodes' Fever & Ague, Antidote To Malaria, Aqua, Sloping Collar, Label, 8 ¼ In.	308.00
Cure, Sanford's Radical, Straight Neck, Cobalt Blue, 7 ½ In.	70.00
Cure, Warner's Safe Diabetes, Safe, Rochester, N.Y., Amber, 9 ⅝ In.	170.00
Cure, Warner's Safe Diabetes, Safe, Rochester, N.Y., Slug Plate, Red Amber, 9 ¾ In.	400.00
Cure, Warner's Safe, Frankfurt, Safe, Emerald Green, 9 ⅜ In.	425.00
Cure, Witt's Colic & Cholera, Chicago, USA, Aqua, 5 In.	39.00
Cure, Wynkoop & Co.'s Tonic Mixture, Warranted To Cure Fever & Ague, Blue, 6 ½ In.	8400.00
Decanter, 3-Piece Mold, Geometric, Olive Green, Sheared & Tooled Lip, Keene, Qt. *Illus*	316.00
Decanter, 8 Ribs, Cone Shape, Cobalt Blue, Neck Ring, Pontil, c.1860, 10 ⅜ x 5 ¼ In.	1035.00
Decanter, Cruciform, Clear, Tooled Mouth, Applied String Rim, c.1760, 9 x 4 In., Pair	920.00
Decanter, Diamond Diaper Band, Swirls, Vertical Flutes, Yellow Olive, 3-Piece Mold, Pt.	4680.00
Decanter, Silver Overlay, Pierced & Scrolled Star Etching, England, 1899, 7 ¾ In., Pair	847.00
Decanter, Spirits, Blown, Red Amber, Silver Overlay & Stopper, Clasped Hands, 11 In. *Illus*	403.00
Decanter, Sunburst, Geometrics, Club Form, Wafer Stopper, Pt.	213.00
Demijohn, Golden Yellow, Tooled Lip, 15 In.	157.00
Demijohn, Green, Applied Ring, Blown, Marked, Nienburg, Germany, 1800s, 24 In.	294.00
Demijohn, Olive Amber, Bulbous, Squat, 17 ¼ In.	590.00
Demijohn, Olive Green, Flat High Shoulders, Sloping Mouth, Kick Up Base, c.1830, 17 ¼ x 12 In.	138.00
Demijohn, Olive Green, Pontil, 12 In.	460.00
Fire Grenade, Hayward's Hand, Cobalt Blue, Sheared & Ground Lip, 1875-1900, 6 In. *Illus*	173.00
Fire Grenade, Healy's Hand, Golden Yellow Amber, Applied Mouth, 1880-1900, 11 In. *Illus*	1150.00
Flask, 16 Ribs, Swirled To Right, Beehive, Aqua, 8 In.	146.00
Flask, 16 Ribs, Vertical, Amethyst, Flattened, Sheared Mouth, Pontil, 5 ¼ In.	952.00
Flask, 16 Ribs, Vertical, Green Aqua, Flattened, Sheared Mouth, Pontil, Pocket, 5 In.	202.00
Flask, 24 Ribs, Vertical, Golden Amber, Flattened, Sheared Mouth, Pontil, Pocket, 4 ⅝ In.	308.00
Flask, 24 Ribs, Vertical, Pumpkinseed, Amber, Sheared Lip, Pontil, 5 In.	246.00
Flask, Anchor & Phoenix, Resurgam, Yellow Topaz, Sheared Lip, Pt.	616.00
Flask, Byron & Scott, Yellow Olive, Sheared Mouth, Pontil, ½ Pt.	364.00
Flask, Chestnut, 10 Diamond, Golden Amber, Shaded, Sheared Mouth, Pocket, 4 ¾ In.	840.00
Flask, Chestnut, 16 Ribs, Vertical, Lavender, Sheared Mouth, Pontil, 6 In.	672.00
Flask, Chestnut, 20 Ribs, Deep Plum Amethyst, Sheared Mouth, Pocket, 6 ¼ In.	896.00
Flask, Chestnut, Amber, Applied Lip, 1780-1820, 8 ½ In.	532.00
Flask, Chestnut, Amber, Sheared Mouth, Pontil, Pocket, 5 In.	213.00
Flask, Chestnut, Lime Green, Bubbles, Applied Flared Lip, 5 ¼ In.	246.00
Flask, Chestnut, Olive Green, Applied Lip, 7 In.	308.00
Flask, Columbia & Eagle, 13 Stars, Cornflower Blue, Blown, Eagle, Clear, Blue, Pontil, 7 x 4 In.	24800.00
Flask, Concentric Ring Eagle, NG Co., Shaded Yellow Green, Canteen, Pt.	22230.00
Flask, Concentric Ring Eagle, NG Co., Yellow Green, Olive Tone, Canteen, Pt.	19890.00
Flask, Corn For The World, Monument, Baltimore, Apricot Puce, Double Collar, Qt.	2808.00
Flask, Corn For The World, Monument, Baltimore, Apricot, Squared Collar, Qt.	2457.00
Flask, Corn For The World, Monument, Baltimore, Golden Topaz, Applied Band, Qt.	1232.00
Flask, Corn For The World, Monument, Baltimore, Olive Green, Pontil, 1840-60, ½ Pt. *Illus*	6435.00
Flask, Corn For The World, Monument, Baltimore, Pale Aqua, Pt.	380.00
Flask, Corn For The World, Monument, Baltimore, Peacock Blue, Sloping Collar, Qt.	9360.00
Flask, Corn For The World, Monument, Baltimore, Yellow Amber, Sloping Collar, Qt.	4972.00
Flask, Cornucopia & Medallion, Olive Amber, Sheared Mouth, Pontil, 1 ½ Pt.	17550.00
Flask, Cornucopia & Urn, Blue Green, Sheared Mouth, Pontil, Pt.	476.00
Flask, Cornucopia & Urn, Blue Green, Sloping Collar, Pt.	1755.00
Flask, Cornucopia & Urn, Olive, Sheared Lip, Pontil, c.1830, 5 ½ In., ½ Pt.	115.00 to 127.00
Flask, Cornucopia Medallion, Pale Green, Sheared Mouth, 1 ½ Pt.	8190.00
Flask, Diamonds, Amethyst, Oval, Narrow Rim, 1800s, 5 In.	173.00
Flask, Double Eagle, Blue Aqua, Corrugated Edge, Sheared Lip, Open Pontil, Pt.	364.00
Flask, Double Eagle, Forest Green, Sheared Mouth, Qt.	6435.00
Flask, Double Eagle, Light Green, Vertical Ribs, Round Collar, Oval, Pt.	43290.00
Flask, Double Eagle, Ribbed, Emerald Green, Applied Double Collar Mouth, Louisville, Qt. *Illus*	2415.00
Flask, Double Eagle, Teal, Vertical Ribs, Applied Ring Collar, Pontil, Qt.	6160.00
Flask, Double Eagle, Yellow Olive, Kentucky Glassworks, c.1850, 8 ½ In.	4977.00

Flask, Double Masonic, Hourglass, Crescent Moon, Yellow Olive, ½ Pt. 21060.00
Flask, Eagle & Anchor, Aqua, 9 Stars Over Eagle, Double Collar, ½ Pt. 702.00
Flask, Eagle & Anchor, Blue Green, 7 Stars Over Eagle, Sheared Mouth, Pontil, Pt. 4095.00
Flask, Eagle & Banner, Aqua, Ring Collar, Pt. 585.00
Flask, Eagle & Cornucopia, Apple Green, Sheared Mouth, Pontil, ½ Pt. 1456.00
Flask, Eagle & Cornucopia, J.P.F. In Frame, Yellow Olive, Corrugated Sides, Pontil, Pt. 25740.00
Flask, Eagle & Cornucopia, Teal, Sheared Lip, Pontil, ½ Pt. 1232.00
Flask, Eagle & Cornucopia, Yellow Olive Amber, Sheared Mouth, Pt. 168.00
Flask, Eagle & Cornucopia, Yellow Olive, Corrugated Sides, ½ Pt. .... 9945.00 to 17550.00
Flask, Eagle & Lafayette, Aqua, Sheared Lip, Kensington Glass Works, c.1850, 6 ½ In., Pt. 288.00
Flask, Eagle & Louisville, Aqua, Vertical Ribs, Eagle With Ribbon, Flattened Lip, Pt. 123.00
Flask, Eagle & Louisville, Root Beer Amber, 5 Stars Over Eagle, Vertical Ribs, ½ Pt. 448.00
Flask, Eagle & Oak Tree, Amber, Tobacco Shaded To Golden, ½ Pt. 3136.00
Flask, Eagle & Oak Tree, Clambroth, ½ Pt. 2464.00
Flask, Eagle & Oak Tree, Tobacco Amber, ½ Pt. 2912.00
Flask, Eagle & Oak Tree, Tobacco Amber, Sheared Mouth, ½ Pt. 2464.00
Flask, Eagle & Oak Tree, Yellow Green, Shaded, Sheared Mouth, ½ Pt. 5558.00
Flask, Eagle & Ravenna, Aqua, Rolled Collar, Iron Pontil, Pt. 280.00
Flask, Eagle & Willington, Green, Sheared Lip, Open Pontil, ½ Pt. .... 633.00 to 728.00
Flask, Eagle & Willington, Yellow Olive, Double Collar, ½ Pt. 420.00
Flask, Eagle & Willington, Yellow Olive, Double Collar, Pt. 269.00
Flask, Eagle, Coffin & Hay, Blue Green, Sheared Mouth, Pontil, Qt. 11200.00
Flask, Eagle, Concentric Ring, Yellow Green, Canteen Sheared Mouth, Pontil, c.1820, Pt.*Illus* 4973.00
Flask, Eagle, Louisville Glass Works, Vertical Ribs, Aquamarine, c.1860, ½ Pt. 384.00
Flask, Flag & New Granite Glass Works, Stoddard, Golden Amber, Sheared Mouth, Pt. 3510.00
Flask, Flora Temple, Blue Green, Applied Mouth With Ring, Pt. 1404.00
Flask, Flora Temple, Harness Trot, Embossed Horse, Smoky Olive, c.1860, 8 ½ In. ....*Illus* 1610.00
Flask, For Pike's Peak, Prospector, Eagle, Apple Green, Applied Collar, Pt. 213.00
Flask, Granite Glass Co., Stoddard, N.H., Yellow Olive Amber, Sheared, Pt. 672.00
Flask, Harrison & Log Cabin, Light Blue Green, Sheared Mouth, Pt. 19890.00
Flask, Horse Pulling Cart & Eagle, Olive Amber, Sheared Mouth, Pt. 420.00
Flask, Hunter & Fisherman, Calabash, Apricot, Sloping Collar, Qt. 644.00
Flask, Jackson & Flowers, Green Aqua, Sheared Mouth, Pt. 5265.00
Flask, Jenny Lind & Glasshouse, Calabash, Blue Green, Applied Mouth, c.1850, Qt. ....*Illus* 1989.00
Flask, Jenny Lind & Glasshouse, Calabash, Ribbed, Yellow Green, Qt. 878.00
Flask, Jenny Lind & Glasshouse, Calabash, Sapphire Blue, Striations, Qt. 4680.00
Flask, Jenny Lind & Lyre, Green Aqua, Qt. 761.00
Flask, Jenny Lind, Calabash, Fislerville Glass Works, Fluted Sides, Qt., 9 ½ In. 59.00
Flask, Kossuth & Frigate, Calabash, Blue Green, Sloping Collar, Qt. 819.00
Flask, Lafayette & Clinton, Coventry, Olive Amber, Sheared Mouth, Pontil, Pt. 235.00
Flask, Lafayette & Clinton, Coventry, Yellow Olive, Sheared Mouth, Pontil, Pt. 819.00
Flask, Lafayette & Clinton, Coventry, Yellow Olive, Sheared Mouth, Pt. 1755.00
Flask, Lafayette & Clinton, C-T, Yellow Olive, Sheared Mouth, Pontil, ½ Pt. 15210.00
Flask, Lafayette & Clinton, Green Amber, ½ Pt. ....*Illus* 12880.00
Flask, Lafayette & Clinton, Yellow Olive, Sheared Mouth, Pontil, c.1824, Pt. ....*Illus* 995.00
Flask, Lafayette & Liberty, 11 Stars, Yellow Amber, Sheared Mouth, Pontil, Pt. 1755.00
Flask, Lafayette & Liberty, No Stars, Yellow Olive, Sheared Mouth, Pontil, ½ Pt. 16380.00
Flask, Lafayette & Masonic, 3 Stars, Olive Green, Sheared Mouth, Pontil, ½ Pt. 13440.00
Flask, Lafayette & Masonic, 3 Stars, Yellow Olive, Sheared Mouth, Pontil, ½ Pt. 8190.00
Flask, Lafayette & Masonic, Forest Green, Sheared Mouth, Pontil, Pt. 9360.00
Flask, Lafayette & Masonic, Light Apple Green, Sheared Mouth, Pontil, ½ Pt. ....*Illus* 47970.00
Flask, Lafayette & Masonic, Sun & Moon, Olive Green, Pontil, Pt. 11200.00
Flask, Lafayette & Masonic, Sun & Moon, Yellow Olive, Sheared, Pontil, Pt. 11700.00
Flask, Log Cabin & Flag, Hard Cider, Ice Blue, Sheared Mouth, Pt. 23400.00
Flask, Masonic & Eagle, Elongated Star In Oval Frame, Yellow Olive, Sloping Collar, ½ Pt. 18720.00
Flask, Masonic & Eagle, Head Turned To Left, Blue Green, Sheared Flared Mouth, Pt. 497.00
Flask, Masonic & Eagle, Head Turned To Right, T.W.D. In Frame, Aqua, Pt. 392.00
Flask, Masonic & Eagle, Initials IP Joined Together, Amethyst Shaded To Cobalt, Pt. 17360.00
Flask, Masonic & Eagle, KCCNC In Oval Frame, Olive Amber, Sheared Lip, Keene, Pt. 476.00
Flask, Masonic & Eagle, KCCNC In Oval Frame, Olive Amber, Sheared Mouth, Pontil, Pt. 308.00
Flask, Masonic & Eagle, Star In Oval Frame, Aqua, Sheared Mouth, Pontil, ½ Pt. 3360.00
Flask, Masonic & Seeing Eye, Yellow Olive, Sheared Mouth, Pt. 644.00
Flask, Masonic, Star & Crossed Keys, Backwards G, Olive Yellow, Pontil, c.1920, ½ Pt. .....*Illus* 22230.00
Flask, Medallion, Jared Spencer, Diamond Diaper, Light Yellow Olive, Pitkin Glass, c.1820, Pt. ....*Illus* 109980.00
Flask, Medallions & Rings & Diamond Diaper, Yellow Olive, Pitkin Glass, c.1815, Pt. ....*Illus* 111150.00
Flask, Medallions, Pearls, Diamond Diaper, Yellow, Pitkin Glass, 1815-30, Pt. ....*Illus* 78390.00

Bottle, Decanter, 3-Piece Mold, Geometric, Olive Green, Sheared & Tooled Lip, Keene, Qt.
$316.00

Glass Works Auctions

Bottle, Decanter, Spirits, Blown, Red Amber, Silver Overlay & Stopper, Clasped Hands, 11 In.
$403.00

Glass Works Auctions

Bottle, Fire Grenade, Hayward's Hand, Cobalt Blue, Sheared & Ground Lip, 1875-1900, 6 In.
$173.00

Glass Works Auctions

Bottle, Fire Grenade, Healy's Hand, Golden Yellow Amber, Applied Mouth, 1880-1900, 11 In.
$1,150.00

Glass Works Auctions

Bottle, Flask, Corn For The World, Monument, Baltimore, Olive Green, Pontil, 1840-60, ½ Pt.
$6,435.00

Norman C. Heckler & Company

Bottle, Flask, Double Eagle, Ribbed, Emerald Green, Applied Double Collar Mouth, Louisville, Qt.
$2,415.00

Glass Works Auctions

Flask, Merry Christmas, Happy New Century, Pocket Watch, Milk Glass, 5 In.	374.00
Flask, Merry Christmas, Happy New Year, Hotel Emrich, Label Under Glass, 1880-90, ½ Pt.... *Illus*	468.00
Flask, Monument & Fell's Point, Yellow Topaz, Sheared Mouth, ½ Pt.	3510.00
Flask, Moon, Porcelain, Famille Jaune, Flattened, Cylindrical, Neck, Dragon Handles, 1900s, 14 ⅝ In.	738.00
Flask, Nailsea Type, 13 Ribs, Swirled To Right, Olive Amber, Swirled White Flecks, 5 In.	448.00
Flask, Pitkin Type, 10 Ribs, Vertical, Over 19 Ribs, Swirled To Right, Green, Flattened Pear, 7 In...	616.00
Flask, Pitkin Type, 30 Ribs, Vertical, Over 30 Ribs, Swirled To Right, Sea Green, Sheared, 7 In..	308.00
Flask, Pitkin Type, 32 Ribs, Swirled To Left, Olive Amber, Sheared Mouth, 3 ¾ In.	5265.00
Flask, Pitkin Type, 32 Ribs, Swirled To Right, Amber, Olive Tone, Sheared Lip, Pontil, 5 ½ In..	672.00
Flask, Pitkin Type, 32 Swirled Ribs, Turquoise Green, 6 ¾ In.	616.00
Flask, Pitkin Type, 36 Ribs, Swirled To Left, Light Yellow Olive, Sheared Mouth, 5 ¾ In.	1053.00
Flask, Pitkin Type, 36 Ribs, Vertical, Over 36 Ribs, Swirled To Left, Tobacco Amber, 5 ½ In.	784.00
Flask, Pitkin Type, 36 Swirled Ribs, Yellow Amber, 5 In.	672.00
Flask, Porcelain, Moon Shape, Flowers, Dragons, Yellow, Turquoise, Lizard Handles, c.1890, 12 In.	516.00
Flask, Pottery, Cobalt Blue, Blossoms, Gilt Scroll Handles At Neck, Tapered, 13 x 8 In.	1045.00
Flask, Remember The Maine, Label Under Glass, 5 In. *Illus*	504.00
Flask, S.F. Rose, Straight Goods From The Wood, Vallejo, Cal., Pumpkinseed, ½ Pt.	672.00
Flask, Scroll & Anchor, Fleur-De-Lis, Aqua, Sheared, Pontil, ½ Pt.	3640.00
Flask, Scroll, Acanthus, Blue Aqua, Pinched Waist, Pt.	1008.00
Flask, Scroll, Cobalt Blue, Rough Sheared Lip, Pontil, Pt. *Illus*	3450.00
Flask, Scroll, Fleur-De-Lis, Pinched Waist, Blue Aqua, Sheared Lip, Open Pontil, Pt.	1680.00
Flask, Scroll, JR & Son, Ice Green, Pinched Waist, Sheared Lip, Pt.	1680.00
Flask, Soldier & Hound, Light Blue Green, Ringed Mouth, Qt.	281.00
Flask, Spirits, Cobalt Blue, 24 Ribs, Pinched, Pontil, German Alpine Region, c.1810, 8 ⅝ In. *Illus*	575.00
Flask, Spirits, Sapphire Blue, Fern Loops, Sheared Mouth, Pewter Collar, Cap, c.1800, 7 ½ In. *Illus*	1287.00
Flask, Spring Garden & Anchor, Golden Amber, Double Collar, Pt.	1521.00
Flask, Steamboat & Sheaf Of Rye, Light Green, Sheared Mouth, Pt.	30420.00
Flask, Stiegel Type, Amethyst, Diamond Daisy, Sheared Mouth, Pocket, 4 In.	702.00
Flask, Stoneware, Brown Glaze, Flower Design, Chinese, 8 ½ In.	184.00
Flask, Success To The Railroad, Horse Pulling Cart, Yellow Olive Amber, Sheared Mouth, Pt...	364.00
Flask, Success To The Railroad, Locomotive, Golden Amber, Sheared Mouth, Pontil, Pt.	6435.00
Flask, Success To The Railroad, Locomotive, Teal, Sheared Lip, Pontil, Pt.	3360.00
Flask, Sunburst, 24 Rays, Vertical Ribs, Shaded Copper, Sheared Mouth, ½ Pt.	8960.00
Flask, Sunburst, Keen P & W, Yellow Olive Green, Embossed, c.1830, 5 ¾ In.	748.00
Flask, Sunburst, Olive, Keen, c.1840, ½ Pt., 5 ½ In.	881.00
Flask, Sunburst, Rays, Ribbed, Pale Aqua, Sheared Mouth, Pontil, ½ Pt.	364.00
Flask, Taylor, Eagle, Aqua, Beaded Sides, Pt.	16380.00
Flask, The Monte Carlo, Parker & Clifford, Bakersfield, Cal., Pumpkinseed, Rolled Lip, ½ Pt...	728.00
Flask, Union, Clasped Hands & Cannon, Ice Blue, Applied Collar, Pt.	258.00
Flask, Union, Clasped Hands & Eagle, Etched, 5 ¾ In.	144.00
Flask, Union, Clasped Hands & Eagle, Light Green, Applied Band, Qt.	784.00
Flask, Washington & Eagle, Blue Aqua, Sheared Lip, Open Pontil, Pt.	4480.00
Flask, Washington & Eagle, Light Green, Sheared Lip, Pontil, c.1850, 6 ⅞ In., Pt. . 518.00 to 560.00
Flask, Washington & Jackson Never Surrenders, Puce, Applied Tapered Collar, Qt. *Illus*	19550.00
Flask, Washington & Jackson, Olive Green, Sheared, Tooled Lip, Keene Marlboro, Pt...*Illus*	575.00
Flask, Washington & Monument, Aqua, Pontil, Pt.	280.00
Flask, Washington & Taylor, 4 Buttons On Coat, Tangerine, Double Collar, Qt.	7020.00
Flask, Washington & Taylor, A Little More Grape, Cobalt Blue, Sheared Mouth, Pontil, Qt. .	5265.00
Flask, Washington & Taylor, A Little More Grape, Turquoise, Amber Lip, Pontil, Qt.	1872.00
Flask, Washington & Taylor, Apricot, Shaded, Sloping Collar, Qt.	6160.00
Flask, Washington & Taylor, Deep Wine, Sheared Mouth, Pontil, Qt.	5850.00
Flask, Washington & Taylor, Green, Applied Ring Mouth, c.1865, Qt. *Illus*	1638.00
Flask, Washington & Taylor, I Have Endeavour'd To Do My Duty, Gray Blue, Striations, Qt.	23400.00
Flask, Washington & Taylor, I Have Endeavour'd To Do My Duty, Yellow Olive, Pontil, Qt.	5850.00
Flask, Washington & Taylor, Yellow, Olive Tone, Sheared, Pontil, ½ Pt.	5265.00
Flask, Washington & Tree, Calabash, Aqua, Sloping Collar, c.1860, 9 In.	150.00
Flask, Washington Bust, Ginger Ale, No Inscription, Dyottville, c.1850 *Illus*	6325.00
Flask, Washington, Father Of His Country, Blue Green, Applied Lip, Pontil, Qt.	616.00
Flask, Washington, Father Of His Country, Green, Round Collar, Qt.	878.00
Flask, Wheat Price & Co., Bust, Bushy Hair, Fair View Works, Blue Aqua, Ribbing, Pt.	15210.00
Flask, Wheat Price & Co., Bust, Fair View Works, Blue Green, Ribbing, Pt.	11115.00
Flask, Whiskey, Pennsylvania Pure Rye, Columbus, Yellow Amber, Pumpkinseed, Flask, ½ Pt.	468.00
Flask, Whiskey, Pretzel Shape, Ceramic, 5 ¾ In.	83.00
Food, Moutarde Diaphane, Louit Freres, Barrel, Clear, Applied Rolled Lip, Pontil, 5 In.	67.00
Fruit Jar, Aqua Lighting, 8 In.	20.00
Fruit Jar, Atlas, Good Luck, Shamrock, Qt.	18.00

Bottle, Flask, Eagle, Concentric Ring, Yellow
Green, Canteen Sheared Mouth, Pontil, c.1820, Pt.
$4,973.00

Norman C. Heckler & Company

Bottle, Flask, Flora Temple, Harness Trot,
Embossed Horse, Smoky Olive, c.1860, 8 ½ In.
$1,610.00

Glass Works Auctions

Bottle, Flask, Jenny Lind & Glasshouse,
Calabash, Blue Green, Applied Mouth, c.1850, Qt.
$1,989.00

Norman C. Heckler & Company

Bottle, Flask, Lafayette & Clinton, Green
Amber, ½ Pt.
$12,880.00

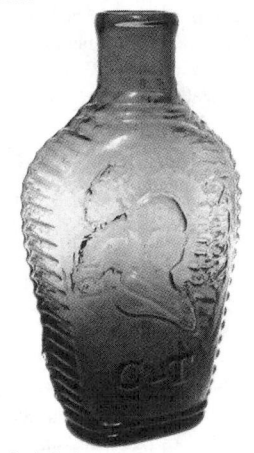

American Bottle Auctions

Bottle, Flask, Lafayette & Clinton, Yellow
Olive, Sheared Mouth, Pontil, c.1824, Pt.
$995.00

Norman C. Heckler & Company

Bottle, Flask, Lafayette & Masonic,
Light Apple Green, Sheared Mouth,
Pontil, ½ Pt.
$47,970.00

Norman C. Heckler & Company

Bottle, Flask, Masonic, Star & Crossed Keys,
Backwards G, Olive Yellow, Pontil,
c.1920, ½ Pt.
$22,230.00

Norman C. Heckler & Company

Bottle, Flask, Medallion, Jared Spencer,
Diamond Diaper, Light Yellow Olive,
Pitkin Glass, c.1820, Pt.
$109,980.00

Norman C. Heckler & Company

Bottle, Flask, Medallions & Rings & Diamond
Diaper, Yellow Olive, Pitkin Glass, c.1815, Pt.
$111,150.00

Norman C. Heckler & Company

Bottle, Flask, Medallions, Pearls, Diamond Diaper, Yellow, Pitkin Glass, 1815-30, Pt.
$78,390.00

Norman C. Heckler & Company

Bottle, Flask, Merry Christmas, Happy New Year, Hotel Emrich, Label Under Glass, 1880-90, ½ Pt.
$468.00

Norman C. Heckler & Company

Bottle, Flask, Remember The Maine, Label Under Glass, 5 In.
$504.00

American Bottle Auctions

Bottle, Flask, Scroll, Cobalt Blue, Rough Sheared Lip, Pontil, Pt.
$3,450.00

Glass Works Auctions

Fruit Jar, Ball Mason, Aqua, No. 13 Jar, No.13 Zinc Lid, 7 x 3 ½ In.	75.00
Fruit Jar, Beaver, ½ Gal.	115.00
Fruit Jar, E.C. Flaccus Co., Stag Head, Yellow Amber, Starburst, Rough Sheared Lip, Pt. *Illus*	575.00
Fruit Jar, Josee Johnson, Cylindrical, Iron Lid, Wood Frame, Pat'd May 16-65, ½ Gal.	3080.00
Fruit Jar, Lafayette & Bust, Aquamarine, Ground Mouth, 3-Piece Closure, c.1870, Pt. *Illus*	4973.00
Fruit Jar, Leader, Yellow Amber, Ground Lip, Embossed Lid, Wire Clamp, Qt. *Illus*	184.00
Fruit Jar, Mason Patent No. 30th 1858, Aqua, Cross Emblem, 2 Qt.	15.00
Fruit Jar, Mason, Aqua, No. 13 Zinc Lid, 7 x 3 ½ In.	75.00
Fruit Jar, Mason, Atlas, Strong Shoulder Mason, Cornflower Blue, Zinc Lid, ½ Gal.	25.00
Fruit Jar, Mason, Lynchburg, Standard, No. 5, c.1924, Qt.	39.00
Fruit Jar, Mason's Patent Nov. 30th, 1858, Green, 9 In.	42.00
Fruit Jar, Ne Plus Ultra, Bodine & Bros., Applied Wax Sealer, ½ Gal., 9 ¼ In.	1232.00
Fruit Jar, Sapphire Blue, Wax Sealer, W. McCully & Co., c.1860, 7 ¼ In.	345.00
Fruit Jar, Stoneware, Brown, Tan, Marked, Qt., 1899.	40.00
Fruit Jar, Van Vliet Of 1881, Aqua, Embossed, Thumbscrew Closure, c.1865, Qt. *Illus*	633.00
Gin, Case, Charles' London Cordial, Olive Amber, Sloping Collar, 8 ¼ In.	1064.00
Gin, Case, Charles' London Cordial, Olive Amber, Sloping Collar, 9 ½ In.	1521.00
Gin, Case, Cobalt Blue, Sloping Collar, 10 In.	1093.00
Gin, Case, Teal Blue, Cobalt Blue Mouth, Sloping Collar, 10 In.	374.00
Gin, J.T. Daly, Club House, Case, Backwards S, Amber Olive, Applied Lip.	220.00
Gin, London Jockey Club House, Horse & Rider, 7Up Green, Rounded Shoulders	3136.00
Gin, London Jockey Club House, Horse & Rider, Turquoise, Sloping Collar, 9 ¾ In.	2464.00
Gin, London Jockey Club House, Horse & Rider, Yellow Amber, Sloping Collar, 9 ¾ In.	5600.00
Ginger Beer, Barnum's Brewed, Niagara Falls, N.Y., Stencil, Stoneware, Oatmeal, 7 ⅝ In.	101.00
Ginger Beer, Daly & Day, Cape Town, Neptune, Stoneware, Cream, Caramel Shoulder, Blob Top.	168.00
Household, Albany Blacking, Blue Green, Oval, Sheared Wide Mouth, Pontil, 6 ½ In.	840.00
Household, Blacking, Shaded Olive Amber, Concave Corners, Sheared Mouth, 5 ½ In.	476.00
Household, Gutta Percha Oil Blacking, Yellow Olive, Rectangular, Indented Panels, 5 In.	5558.00
Household, Hutchins & Mason Waterproof Blacking, Yellow Olive, Square, 5 ½ In.	1112.00
Household, Liquid Mirror, Metallic, Elisha Waters, Olive, Men Racing Label, c.1865, 6 In. *Illus*	1755.00
Household, Race & Sheldon's Magic Waterproof Boot Polish, Teal, 10-Sided, 7 ¾ In.	8960.00
Ink, 12 Ribs, Cobalt Blue, Round, Squat, Domed Lid, Finial, 2 In.	560.00
Ink, 12-Sided, Blue Green, Sheared Mouth, Pontil, 1 ⅞ In.	258.00
Ink, 28 Vertical Ribs, Yellow Olive, Pontil, 1 ¾ x 2 ¾ In.	7020.00
Ink, Cobalt Blue, Cylindrical, Applied Double Collar, Pontil, Master, 7 ¼ In.	728.00
Ink, Cone, Draped, Cobalt Blue, Double Collar, Pontil, 3 ⅝ In.	1232.00
Ink, Cylindrical, Rounded Shoulder, Narrow Spout, Wavy Stripes & Spots, Redware, c.1815, 4 ¾ In.	1840.00
Ink, Cylindrical, Yellow Olive, Sloping Collar, Applied Ring, Spout, Pontil, Master, 12 In.	1287.00
Ink, E. Waters, Troy, N.Y., Yellow Green, Cylindrical, Fluted, Applied Mouth, Master, 6 In.	2576.00
Ink, Farley's, 8-Sided, Yellow Olive Amber, Sheared Mouth, Pontil, 1 ¾ In.	952.00
Ink, Farley's, 8-Sided, Yellow Olive, Amber Tone, Flared Mouth, Pontil, Master, 3 ¾ In.	1232.00
Ink, Farley's, 8-Sided, Yellow Olive, Sheared Mouth, 2 x 2 In.	761.00
Ink, Fred. D. Alling's, Stoneware, Tan Glaze, Cylindrical, Flared Mouth, Pour Spout, 9 In.	56.00
Ink, Geometric, 14 Diamond, Medium To Deep Olive, Cylindrical, 3-Piece Mold, Pontil, 2 x 2 ⅝ In.	202.00
Ink, Geometric, Olive Amber, Blown, Tooled Mouth, Pontil, Keene Glass, c.1825, 2 In. *Illus*	460.00
Ink, Harrison's Columbian, 12-Sided, Aqua, Double Collar, Pontil, Master, 5 ⅞ In.	202.00
Ink, Hover, Phila., Yellow Olive, Cylindrical, Flanged Mouth, Pontil, Master, 5 In.	448.00
Ink, J.K. Palmer Chemist, Boston, Yellow Olive, Cylindrical, Spout, Master, 9 In.	761.00
Ink, Log Cabin, Smooth Base, Sheared, Ground Lip, c.1885, 3 ¼ In. *Illus*	1840.00
Ink, Master, E. Waters, Troy, N.Y., Aquamarine, Petalled Shoulders, Iron Pontil, 6 ⅜ x 4 In. *Illus*	1638.00
Ink, Olive Green, Ringed Base, Pontil, c.1830, 1 ¾ x 2 ⅝ In.	127.00
Ink, S. Fine, Green, Cylindrical, Inward Rolled Mouth, Pontil, 2 ⅞ In.	190.00
Ink, Stafford's, Teal, Qt.	40.00
Ink, Teakettle, 8-Sided, Medium Green, Concave Panels, Sheared Mouth, c.1850, 1 ½ In.	316.00
Ink, Teakettle, 8-Sided, Milk Glass, Blue Opalescent, Sheared, Brass Neck Ring, 2 ⅜ In. *Illus*	230.00
Ink, Umbrella, 8-Sided, Amethyst, Shaded, Inward Rolled Mouth, 2 ⅜ In.	2240.00
Ink, Umbrella, 8-Sided, Amethyst, Sheared Mouth, 2 ¾ x 2 ½ In.	1232.00
Ink, Umbrella, 8-Sided, Blue Green, Inward Rolled Mouth, Pontil, 2 In.	308.00
Ink, Umbrella, 8-Sided, Olive Green, Inward Rolled Mouth, Pontil, 2 In.	308.00
Ink, Umbrella, 8-Sided, Sapphire Blue, Baltimore Star, Concave Panels, Sheared Mouth, 2 In.	1344.00
Ink, Umbrella, 8-Sided, Sapphire Blue, Sheared, Tooled Lip, Concave Panels, Baltimore, 2 ½ In.	1610.00
Ink, Umbrella, 16-Sided, Olive Green, Sheared & Polished Mouth, 2 ¼ In.	2352.00
Ink, Umbrella, Superior Black, 8-Sided, Olive Green, Inward Rolled Mouth, Label, 2 ¼ In.	728.00
Ink, Umbrella, Waters, Troy, N.Y., 6-Sided, Aqua, Squat, Rolled Mouth, 3 x 2 ⅜ In.	527.00
Ink, Yellow Slip, Cone Shape, Redware, 1800s, 2 ¾ In.	230.00
Jar, Globe Tobacco Co., Detroit & Windsor, Pat. Oct. 10th 1882, Yellow, Barrel, Qt.	146.00

B

Jar, Storage, Golden Yellow, Topaz Tone, 12-Sided, Inward Rolled Mouth, 5 x 2 ½ In.	468.00
Jar, Storage, Olive Green, Bulbous, Long Neck, Tooled Mouth, String Lip, 9 ¼ In.	2106.00
Jar, Storage, Yellow Olive, 8-Sided, Sloping Double Collar, Pontil, 6 ¼ In.	322.00
Jug, Bellarmine, Brown, Smiling Face, Coat Of Arms Belly, Stoneware, c.1600, 8 ⅛ In. .....*Illus*	345.00
Medicine, Alden's Extract Of Coffee, Green, Cylindrical, Sloping Collar, Spout, 7 In.	468.00
Medicine, Alterative Syrup, Pike & Osgood, Boston, Olive Amber, Rectangular, 8 ⅜ In.	2223.00
Medicine, American Liniment, Auburn, N.Y., Rolled Lip, Pontil, Label, 5 In.	1120.00
Medicine, Bear's Oil, Beveled Corners, Green Aquamarine, Pontil, c.1850, 2 ¾ In. ....*Illus*	878.00
Medicine, Beekman's Pulmonic Syrup, New York, Yellow Olive, 8-Sided, 7 ¼ In.	2925.00
Medicine, Beekman's Pulmonic Syrup, Olive Green, 8-Sided, Double Collar, 7 ¼ In.	5750.00
Medicine, Burrington's Vegetable Croup Syrup, Providence, Aqua, Cylindrical, 5 ½ In.	276.00
Medicine, Byrd Antarctic Expedition, Fluted Shoulders, 1929, 5 ⅝ In. .... 336.00 to 527.00
Medicine, C. Brinckerhoff's Health Restorative, Price $1.00, New York, Olive, 7 In.	1093.00
Medicine, Chapman's Genuine, Salem St., Boston, Yellow Olive, Flattened Collar, 8 In.	936.00
Medicine, Cook's Balm Of Life, Sapphire Blue, Oval, Strap Sides, Squared Collar, 8 ¾ In.	224.00
Medicine, Delmonico's Syrup Pectoral, New York, Aqua, Indented Panels, Pontil, 7 In.	748.00
Medicine, Dr. Browder's Compound Syrup Of Indian Turnip, Aqua, Sloping Collar, 7 In.	207.00
Medicine, Dr. C. Freeman, Indian Specific For Coughs, Light Aqua, Flared Lip, 5 In.	316.00
Medicine, Dr. D. Jayne's Life Preservative, Aqua, Paneled, Flared Lip, Pontil, 5 ½ In.	1400.00
Medicine, Dr. E.J. Cox, New Orleans, Light Green, Round, Panel, Pontil, 7 ¼ In.	489.00
Medicine, Dr. Edward's Tar Wild Cherry & Naptha Cough Syrup, Aqua, Rolled Lip, 5 In.	168.00
Medicine, Dr. J. Webster's, Cerevisia, Anglicana Duplex, Emerald Green, Pontil, c.1850, 7 ⅜ In... *Illus*	3738.00
Medicine, Dr. J.A. Burgoon's System Renovator, Medicine Man In Top Hat, Aqua, 8 ¼ In.........	840.00
Medicine, Dr. Larooka's Indian Vegetable Pulmonic, Green Aqua, Syrup	45.00
Medicine, Dr. Mitchell Ox Gall & Arnica, Liniment, Aqua, Cylindrical, Rolled Lip, 4 ⅝ In........	750.00
Medicine, Dr. Rall Liniment, Aqua, Rolled Lip, Pontil, 4 ¼ In.	325.00
Medicine, Dr. Rose's, Philada, Blue Green, Rectangular, Beveled Corners, 5 ¼ In.....................	134.00
Medicine, E.S. Green's Flesh & Blood Liniment, Aqua, 6-Sided, Pontil, 4 ½ In.	850.00
Medicine, Friedenwald's Buchu Gin, For Kidney & Liver Troubles, 7Up Green, 9 ¾ In.	213.00
Medicine, G.W. Merchant, Lockport, N.Y., Blue Green, Rectangular, Sloping Collar, 5 In.,........	190.00
Medicine, Hampton's V Tincture, Mortimer & Mowbray, Balto., Copper Topaz, 6 ⅜ In.............	1495.00
Medicine, Houchin's Corn Solvent, Aqua, Outward Rolled Lip, 2 ½ In...............................	130.00
Medicine, Howard's Vegetable Cancer & Canker Syrup, Yellow Amber, Squared Rim, 7 In.......	5558.00
Medicine, L.P. Dodge, Rheumatic Liniment, Newburg, Chocolate Amber, 5 ¾ In.	1120.00
Medicine, Longley's Panacea, Olive Green, Shaded, Rectangular, Beveled Corners, 6 In.	1120.00
Medicine, Morse's Celebrated Syrup, Prov., R.I., Green, Rounded Shoulders, Pontil, 9 In.	1680.00
Medicine, Olive Amber, Rectangular, Beveled Corners, Sloping Collar, 7 ⅞ In.	672.00
Medicine, Preston's Veg Purifying Catholicon, Portsm. N.II., Aqua, Oval, 9 ⅝ In.	550.00
Medicine, Rabenau's Rheumatic Remedy, Pottsville, Pa., Crow In Branch, Aqua, 6 In...............	123.00
Medicine, S.M. Kier Petroleum, Pittsburgh, Aqua, Recessed Panels, Open Pontil, 6 ½ In.	179.00
Medicine, Seaver's Joint & Nerve Liniment, Yellow Amber, Flared Lip, Pontil, 4 In.	863.00
Medicine, Skerrett's Oil, B. Wheeler, W. Henrietta, Mon. Co., N.Y., Teal, 6 In.	1904.00
Medicine, Swaim's Panacea, Genuine, Philadelphia, Aqua, Arched Sides, Pontil, 8 In.	896.00
Medicine, Swaim's Panacea, Genuine, Philadelphia, Blue Green, Round, Paneled, 7 ¾ In......	364.00
Medicine, Tonic, Dr. T.G. Evans, Brownsville, Pa., Sovereign Tonic For Fever, Apple Green, 6 In. ...	448.00
Medicine, Turlington's, Balsam Of Life, London, Kings Royal Patent, Aqua, Stepped Sides, 2 ½ In.	123.00
Medicine, U.S.A. Hosp. Dept., Olive Amber, Double Collar, 9 In.	1568.00
Medicine, University Free, Philada., Aqua, 6 Panels, Flared Lip, Pontil, Label, 5 ½ In.	532.00
Medicine, Vaughn's Vegetable Lithontriptic Mixture, Buffalo, Aqua, Indented Panels, 8 In......	316.00
Medicine, Westlake's Vegetable Ointment, Lima, N.Y., Cornflower Blue, Rolled Lip, 3 In.	130.00
Medicine, Whitwell's Original Opodeldoc, Aqua, Cylindrical, Flattened Lip, 4 ½ In.	202.00
Medicine, Winant's Relief Liniment, Blue Aqua, Rolled Lip, 4 ¼ In.	275.00
Milk, Big Elm Dairy Co., Yellow Green, ABM Lip, 9 ⅛ In., Qt...*Illus*	184.00
Milk, Dixie Dairies, Macon, Ga., c.1935, ½ Qt.	30.00
Milk, Elmview Jersey Farm Dairy, Columbus, Penn., Orange Graphics, ½ Gal.	39.00
Milk, Golden Cream Dairy, Galesburg, Ill., Embossed, Qt.	28.00
Milk, Lionberger's Dairy Products, Hermann, Missouri, Red Letters, 1950s, Qt........................	20.00
Milk, Pevely Dairy, St. Louis, 2 Qt., 10 ½ In...	15.00
Milk, Robertson's Dairy, Kernersville, N.C., Cow, Red Paint, Qt..	65.00
Milk, Ronny Brook Dairy, Square, Lid, 1950s, 16 Oz.	16.00
Milk, Schramm Cry Co., Farmington Missouri, Duraglass, Green Letters, 1946, 9 ½ In.	15.00
Milk, Whiting Milk Companies, 1930s, ½ Pt.	15.00
Mineral Water, A.W. Rapp, New York, Dyottville Glass Works, Sapphire Blue, 7 ⅝ In.	1265.00
Mineral Water, B & G, San Francisco, Superior Mineral Water, Mug Base, Iridescent......*Illus*	2128.00
Mineral Water, Caledonia Springs, Wheelock, Vt., Golden Amber, Double Collar, Qt...............	819.00

Bottle, Flask, Spirits, Cobalt Blue, 24 Ribs, Pinched, Pontil, German Alpine Region, c.1810, 8 ⅝ In.
$575.00

Glass Works Auctions

Bottle, Flask, Spirits, Sapphire Blue, Fern Loops, Sheared Mouth, Pewter Collar, Cap, c.1800, 7 ½ In.
$1,287.00

Norman C. Heckler & Company

Bottle, Flask, Washington & Jackson Never Surrenders, Puce, Applied Tapered Collar, Qt.
$19,550.00

Glass Works Auctions

B

Bottle, Flask, Washington & Jackson, Olive Green, Sheared, Tooled Lip, Keene Marlboro, Pt.
$575.00

Glass Works Auctions

Bottle, Flask, Washington & Taylor, Green, Applied Ring Mouth, c.1865, Qt.
$1,638.00

Norman C. Heckler & Company

Bottle, Flask, Washington Bust, Ginger Ale, No Inscription, Dyottville, c.1850
$6,325.00

Glass Works Auctions

Bottle, Fruit Jar, E.C. Flaccus Co., Stag Head, Yellow Amber, Starburst, Rough Sheared Lip, Pt.
$575.00

Glass Works Auctions

Mineral Water, Champion Spouting Spring, Saratoga, Blue Aqua, Sloping Collar, Pt.	90.00
Mineral Water, Chase & Co., San Francisco, Applied Top, Iron Pontil	200.00
Mineral Water, Clarke & Co., New York, Shaded Teal, Sloping Collar, Pontil, Pt.	180.00
Mineral Water, Clarke & White, C, New York, Dark Olive Green, Sloping Collar, Pt.	2016.00
Mineral Water, Congress & Empire Spring Co., C, Amber, Double Collar, Pt.	234.00
Mineral Water, Congress & Empire Spring Co., C, Olive Green, Double Collar, Pt.	168.00
Mineral Water, Congress & Empire Spring Co., E, Golden Amber, Pt.	448.00
Mineral Water, Congress & Empire Spring Co., E, Green, Shaded, Double Collar, Pt.	560.00
Mineral Water, Congress & Empire Spring Co., E, Saratoga, N.Y., Emerald Green, Pt.	90.00
Mineral Water, Congress & Empire Spring Co., Honey Yellow, Sloping Collar, Qt.	476.00
Mineral Water, Congress & Empire Spring Co., Hotchkiss' Sons, E, Orange Amber, Pt.	308.00
Mineral Water, Congress & Empire Spring Co., Yellow Olive, Sloping Collar, Qt.	420.00
Mineral Water, Congress & Empire Spring, Hotchkiss' Sons, E, Saratoga, Red Amber, Pt.	257.00
Mineral Water, Congress Spring Co., C, Saratoga, N.Y., Congress Water, Blue Green, Pt.	67.00
Mineral Water, Covert, Morristown, N.J., Superior, Cobalt Blue, Mug Base, Pontil, 7 In.	460.00
Mineral Water, D.A. Knowlton, Saratoga, N.Y., Seedy Olive Green, Sloping Collar, Qt.	112.00
Mineral Water, G. Gent, New York, Pale Aqua, Blob Top, Iron Pontil, 7 In.	173.00
Mineral Water, G.A. Cook & Bro., Philipsburg, N.J., Slug Plate, Emerald Green, 7 ½ In.	460.00
Mineral Water, G.A. Kohl, Cobalt Blue, Sloping Collar, Pontil, 7 ½ In.	489.00
Mineral Water, Ghirardelli's Branch, Oakland, Cobalt Blue, Sloping Collar, 7 ½ In.	532.00
Mineral Water, Haas Bros., Natural, Napa Soda, Blue, Blob Top, 7 ¼ In.	202.00
Mineral Water, Hamilton & Church, Excelsior, Brooklyn, Blue Green, 8-Sided, 7 In.	805.00
Mineral Water, J. Boardman & Co., 8-Sided, Cobalt Blue, Applied Tapered Collar Mouth, 7 ¾ In. *Illus*	230.00
Mineral Water, John Clarke, New York, Green, Sloping Collar, Iron Pontil, Pt.	258.00
Mineral Water, John J. Staff, New York, Orange Amber, Sloping Double Collar, 7 ⅝ In.	1035.00
Mineral Water, Lamoille Spring, Milton, Vt., Golden Amber, Sloping Double Collar, Qt.	2223.00
Mineral Water, Lynch & Clarke, New York, Dark Olive Green, Sloping Collar, 7 ¼ In.	896.00
Mineral Water, Lynch & Clarke, New York, Olive Amber, Sloping Collar, Pt.	1792.00
Mineral Water, Lynde & Putnam, Applied Lip, Graphite Pontil	250.00
Mineral Water, Middletown Healing Springs, Grays & Clark, Blue Green, Double Collar, Qt.	575.00
Mineral Water, Napa Soda, Phil Caduc, Natural Mineral Water, Teal, Blob Top, 7 In.	157.00
Mineral Water, S S Smith, Auburn, N.Y., Cobalt Blue, 10-Sided, Blob Top, 7 In.	489.00
Mineral Water, S. Keys, Burlington, N.J., Cobalt Blue, Blob Top, Iron Pontil, 7 In.	633.00
Mineral Water, S. Smith's Knickerbocker, Emerald Green, Sloping Collar, 7 In.	1093.00
Mineral Water, Sage's Pacific Congress Springs, Deer, Green, Sloping Collar, 8 In.	3360.00
Mineral Water, Saratoga A Spring Co., N.Y., Olive Yellow, Applied Mouth, c.1870, Pt. *Illus*	1380.00
Mineral Water, Summit, Applied Top, Teal Green	170.00
Mineral Water, Summit, J.H., Green, Blob Top, 1870s, 7 ½ In.	448.00
Mineral Water, Syracuse Springs, D, Excelsior, Golden Amber, Sloping Collar, Pt.	1053.00
Mineral Water, Tahoe Soda Springs, Blob Top, 1880s	600.00
Mineral Water, Vermont Spring Saxe & Co., Sheldon, Vt., Pink, Sloping Collar, c.1865, Qt. *Illus*	1989.00
Mineral Water, W.M. Fraser & Co., Improved, Green, Sloping Collar, Pontil, 7 In.	546.00
Pepper Sauce, Straight Neck, Ribbed, Amethyst, c.1900, 8 ¼ In.	40.00
Pepper Sauce, W.K. Lewis, 8 Panel, Aqua, Tapered Collar, Open Pontil, c.1850, 8 In.	80.00
Pepper Sauce, Western Spice Mills, Cathedral, 4-Sided, Yellow, Double Collar, 8 ¾ In.	12320.00
Perfume bottles are listed in their own category.	
Pickle, 12 Shoulder Panels, 14 Base Panels, Blue Aqua, Rolled Rim, Iron Pontil, 12 In.	374.00
Pickle, Cathedral, 6-Sided, Turquoise, Applied Mouth, Metal & Cork Closure, 13 ¼ In.	1100.00
Pickle, Cathedral, Amber, Rolled Lip, Willington Glass, Conn., c.1850, 8 ¼ In.	2240.00
Pickle, Cathedral, Aqua, Applied Mouth, Pontil, 11 ¾ In. *Illus*	265.00
Pickle, Cathedral, Aqua, Arched Panels, Outward Rolled Mouth, 13 In.	527.00
Pickle, Cathedral, Blue Green, Gothic Arches, Scallops, Rolled Collar, 11 ½ In.	616.00 to 920.00
Pickle, Cathedral, Blue Green, Iron Pontil, 11 ⅜ In.	1150.00
Pickle, Cathedral, E.H.V.B., N.Y., Blue Green, 6-Sided, Iron Pontil, c.1855, 11 ½ In. *Illus*	138.00
Pickle, Cathedral, Wm. Bodmann, Baltimore, Aqua, Outward Folded Mouth, Pontil, 1840s, Qt. *Illus*	10640.00
Pickle, Golden Amber, Vertical Lobes, Applied Mouth, New Hampshire, 1865-72, 8 ⅛ In. *Illus*	1989.00
Pickle, Skilton Foot & Co., Bunker Hill, Embossed Barrels & Bunker Hill Monument, 11 In.	1500.00
Poison, Coffin, Amber, Diamonds On 3 Sides, Ring Lip, Label, 25 Tablets, 3 ½ In.	213.00
Poison, Coffin, Sapphire Blue, Diamonds On 3 Sides, Ring Lip, 3 ½ In.	112.00
Poison, Embossed Poison, Golden Amber, Square, Prunts Along Corners, 3 ¼ In.	224.00
Poison, Embossed Poison, Yellow Amber, Raised Dots On Sides, Rolled Lip, 2 ⅝ In.	112.00
Poison, Embossed Skull & Crossbones, 5-Point Star, Cobalt, Rolled Lip, 2 In.	67.00
Poison, Embossed Skull & Crossbones, Star, Lattice & Diamonds, Honey Amber, Oval, 4 In.	476.00
Poison, H.K. Mulford Co., Chemists, Philadelphia, Skull & Crossbones, Amber, Label, 3 In.	280.00
Poison, H.K. Mulford Co., Chemists, Philadelphia, Skull & Crossbones, Blue, 3 ¼ In.	157.00
Poison, Ice Blue, Hobnail, Flattened Horseshoe Flask, Sheared Mouth, Pontil, ½ Pt.	1680.00

Poison, Jacobs' Bichloride Tablets, Skull & Crossbones, Orange Amber, 8-Sided, 2 In.	1680.00
Poison, Lattice & Diamond, Cobalt Blue, Cylindrical, Flattened Rim, ½ Gal., 10 ¾ In.	476.00
Poison, Lattice & Diamond, Cobalt Blue, Tooled Lip, 1890-1910, 11 ½ In. *Illus*	374.00
Poison, Rhode Island Hospital, External Use, Lattice & Diamond, Blue, Label, 4 ½ In.	90.00
Poison, Skull, Cobalt Blue, Tooled Lip, 1890-1905, 4 ⅛ In.	952.00
Poison, Tincture Of Iodine, Lattice & Diamond, Cobalt Blue, Cylindrical, Label, 3 ⅝ In.	112.00
Sarsaparilla, Dr. Townsend's, Albany, N.Y., Blue Green, Square, Beveled, Sloping Collar, 9 In.	878.00
Sarsaparilla, Dr. Townsend's, Albany, N.Y., Green, Arched Sides, Sloping Collar, 9 ¾ In.	392.00
Sarsaparilla, Dr. Townsend's, Albany, N.Y., Yellow Green, Sloping Collar, 9 ⅜ In.	364.00
Sarsaparilla, Log Cabin, Rochester, N.Y., Amber, 8-Sided, Applied Lip, Box, 9 In.	500.00
Sarsaparilla, Wynkoop's Katharismic Honduras, Cobalt Blue, Indented Panels, 10 In.	8625.00
Scent, Peasant Girl & Boy, Porcelain, Enamel, Gilt, Scroll Base, France, c.1840, 11 ⅜ In., Pair .	582.00
Scent, Scrolls, Shells, Black, Pilgrim Flask Shape, Stopper Jacob Petit, France, c.1850, 9 ¾ In., Pair ..	690.00
Scent, Sterling Silver, Flowers, Scrolling Leaves, Enamel, Persian Style, Topper, 5 ½ In.	267.00
Scent, Sterling Silver, Hammered, Dragonfly, Leaves, Engraved, 3 ¾ In.	459.00
Scent, Turkish Prince & Princess, Porcelain, Marked, Jacob Petit, c.1850, 7 x 5 ½ In., Pair... *Illus*	1912.00
Seal, Crown, N, Deep Yellow Olive, Sheared Mouth, Applied String Lip, 9 In.	2106.00
Seal, Green, Natichitoches, Gegrundel, 1811, Manufacture De Tabac, Label, Ship, City, 9 In.	1673.00
Seal, Jade, Round Top, Carved Lions, Paws On Ball, Engraved Characters, Chinese, 3 In.	184.00
Seal, W. Daubeny, 1776, Deep Yellow Olive, Shouldered, Sheared, String Lip, 9 In.	11700.00
Snuff, Agate, Amber Stopper, Chinese, 3 In.	452.00
Snuff, Agate, Amber, Carved Peanuts, Oval, Coral Stopper, 2 In.	922.00
Snuff, Agate, Black Veiling, Green Stone Stopper, Footed, Oval, Spoon, 2 ⅝ In.	868.00
Snuff, Agate, Carved, Beast Mask Handle, Chinese, 3 In.	663.00
Snuff, Agate, Carved, Landscape, Chinese, 3 In.	823.00
Snuff, Agate, Carved, Stepped Shoulder, Carnelian Stopper, Chinese, 2 ½ In.	241.00
Snuff, Agate, Faux Chicken Blood Stone, Mottled, Red & Green, Chinese, 19th Century, 3 In.	1687.00
Snuff, Agate, Gray, Orange Highlights, Flat Oval, c.1890, 3 In.	384.00
Snuff, Agate, Lapis Lazuli Stopper, 3 In.	331.00
Snuff, Agate, Mottled, Bulbous, Fiery Stopper, Chinese, 3 ½ In.	392.00
Snuff, Agate, Relief Carved, Cranes, Pine Tree, Gray & White, 1900s, 2 ¾ In.	338.00
Snuff, Agate, Yellow Carved, Carnelian Stopper, Chinese, 20th Century, 3 ½ In.	331.00
Snuff, Amber, 3 Carved Kittens, Amber Stopper, Spoon, 2 ⅛ In.	190.00
Snuff, Amber, Peaches, Pomegranates, Buddha's Hand, Flattened Baluster Handles, 1800s, 3 ⅛ In.	356.00
Snuff, Amethyst, Mythical Frog Shape, Aventurine Stopper, Chinese, 1800s, 2 ½ In.	5060.00
Snuff, Aquamarine, Carved, 3 Figures, Pine Trees, Lion & Cup Finial, Chinese, 1800s, 5 In.	1067.00
Snuff, Blue Enamel, Buddhist Symbols, Eternity Knot, Couch Shell, Beaded Stopper, Spoon, 2 ⅝ In..	293.00
Snuff, Blue Glass, Reverse Painted, Warriors On Horses, 3 ¾ In.	120.00
Snuff, Bone, Carved, Relief Figures, Courtyard, Tapering Flattened Shape, 3 ⅛ x 2 In.	29.00
Snuff, Carnelian, Carved, Birds, Flowers, Chinese, 1800s, 3 ¼ In.	230.00
Snuff, Carnelian, Carved, Swirling Design, Peanuts, Coral Stopper, 1800s, 1 ¾ In.	922.00
Snuff, Celadon, Lobed, Chinese, 2 In.	522.00
Snuff, Cinnabar, Carved, Mountain Village Scene, Ch'ien Lung Mark, 1700s, 2 ¼ In.	1955.00
Snuff, Cinnabar, Carved, Phoenixes, Clouds, Thunder Border, c.1800, 3 In.	345.00
Snuff, Cinnabar, Children Playing, Foo Dog Handles, Chrysanthemum Stopper, c.1800, 3 In....*Illus*	748.00
Snuff, Cinnabar, Lacquered, Melon Plants, Grapes, Squirrel, Symbols, Stopper, 1800s, 2 ½ In. ...	1067.00
Snuff, Cloisonne, Bird, Perched On Tree, Peonies, Gilt, Rectangular, Cut Corners, 1800s, 2 ¼ In...	889.00
Snuff, Cloisonne, Butterfly, Bird, Flowers, Chinese, 19th Century, 2 ¾ In.	482.00
Snuff, Cloisonne, Yellow, 100 Antiques, Turquoise Borders, Flowers, Coral Stopper, 1800s, 2 ⅓ In.	115.00
Snuff, Coral Glaze, White Rim, Cylindrical, c.1900, 3 In., Pair	345.00
Snuff, E. Roome, Troy, New York, Green Glass, Rectangular, Flared Lip, Pontil	728.00
Snuff, Glass, Elephant, Standing, Red, Carved, Knopped Finial Stopper, Spoon, India, 3 In.	247.00
Snuff, Glass, Enameled, Dog Walking In Grass, Round, Flattened, Marked, Red Stopper, 2 ¾ In..	948.00
Snuff, Glass, Landscape, Lappets, Scrolls, Rectangular, Marked, Green Stopper, Chinese, 1900s, 3 In.	1304.00
Snuff, Glass, Olive Green, Square, Arched Shoulders, Beveled Corners, Dip Mold, 4 In.	336.00
Snuff, Glass, Relief Carved, 100 Antiques Design, Pear Shape, Stopper, Chinese, 1900s, 2 ¾ In.	615.00
Snuff, Glass, Reverse Painted, Woman Leaning On Tree, Characters, Jade Stopper, 2 ¾ In.	1293.00
Snuff, Green Quartz, Fish Shape, Stopper In Mouth, Chinese, 2 ¾ In.	777.00
Snuff, Hardstone, Ivory, Overlapping Lines, Carved, Silver Mount, Chinese, c.1890, 3 ¾ In.	500.00
Snuff, Horn, Carved Shou-Lao, Deer, Waves, Scrolls, Flattened Shouldered, Domed Stopper ...	1067.00
Snuff, Hornbill Beak, Carved Scenes, Black Detail, Stopper, Spoon, 3 ½ In.	293.00
Snuff, Hornbill, Carved Figures In Pavilion, Dragons On Sides, Chinese, 2 ⅜ In.	1800.00
Snuff, Ivory, Carved Landscape, Figures, Metal Base & Lid, Marked, Maquet, 4 ⅝ In.	605.00
Snuff, Ivory, Carved Lily, Rondel, Calligraphy, Vining, Multicolor, 2 ½ In.	259.00
Snuff, Ivory, Carved, Inked Scenes, Stag, Man Fishing, Spoon, Chinese, 3 ½ x 2 In.	120.00
Snuff, Ivory, Ear Of Corn, Mouse, Patina, Chinese, c.1910, 3 ¼ In. *Illus*	230.00

Bottle, Fruit Jar, Lafayette & Bust, Aquamarine, Ground Mouth, 3-Piece Closure, c.1870, Pt.
$4,973.00

Norman C. Heckler & Company

Bottle, Fruit Jar, Leader, Yellow Amber, Ground Lip, Embossed Lid, Wire Clamp, Qt.
$184.00

Glass Works Auctions

Bottle, Fruit Jar, Van Vliet Of 1881, Aqua, Embossed, Thumbscrew Closure, c.1865, Qt.
$633.00

Glass Works Auctions

Bottle, Household, Liquid Mirror, Blacking, Elisha Waters, Olive, Men Racing Label, c.1865, 6 In.
$1,755.00

Norman C. Heckler & Company

Bottle, Ink, Geometric, Olive Amber, Blown, Tooled Mouth, Pontil, Keene Glass, c.1825, 2 In.
$460.00

Glass Works Auctions

Bottle, Ink, Log Cabin, Smooth Base, Sheared, Ground Lip, c.1885, 3 ¼ In.
$1,840.00

Glass Works Auctions

Bottle, Ink, Master, E. Waters, Troy, N.Y., Aquamarine, Petalled Shoulders, Iron Pontil, 6 ⅜ x 4 In.
$1,638.00

Norman C. Heckler & Company

Bottle, Ink, Teakettle, 8-Sided, Milk Glass, Blue Opalescent, Sheared, Brass Neck Ring, 2 ⅜ In.
$230.00

Glass Works Auctions

Bottle. Jug, Bellarmine, Brown, Smiling Face, Coat Of Arms Belly, Stoneware, c.1600, 8 ⅛ In.
345.00

Glass Works Auctions

Bottle, Medicine, Bear's Oil, Beveled Corners, Green Aquamarine, Pontil, c.1850, 2 ¾ In.
$878.00

Norman C. Heckler & Company

Bottle, Medicine, Dr. J. Webster's, Cerevisia, Anglicana Duplex, Emerald Green, Pontil, c.1850, 7 ⅜ In.
$3,738.00

Glass Works Auctions

Bottle, Milk, Big Elm Dairy Co., Yellow Green, ABM Lip, 9 ⅛ In., Qt.
$184.00

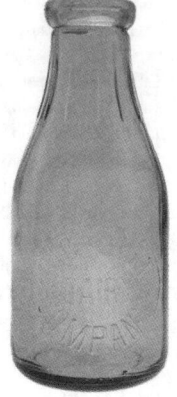

Glass Works Auctions

Bottle, Mineral Water, B & G, San Francisco, Superior Mineral Water, Mug Base, Iridescent
$2,128.00

American Bottle Auctions

Bottle, Mineral Water, J. Boardman & Co., 8-Sided, Cobalt Blue, Applied Tapered Collar Mouth, 7 ¾ In.
$230.00

Glass Works Auctions

Snuff, Ivory, Empress, Riding Elephant, Multicolor, Japan, 3 In. 146.00
Snuff, Ivory, Figural, Carved, Emperor, Empress, Signed, 3 In., Pair 293.00
Snuff, Ivory, Landscape, Carved, Chinese, Late 1800s, 2 ½ In. 353.00
Snuff, J.J. Mapes, 61 Front St., N. York, Rounded Corners, Yellow Olive, 4 ½ In. 187.00
Snuff, Jade, Carved Peony, Round, Tourmaline & Gilt Stopper, c.1890, 2 ¼ In. 472.00
Snuff, Jade, Chicken Blood, Squat, Flattened Circle, Stopper, 1800s, 2 ½ In. 288.00
Snuff, Jade, Cranes, Landscape, Russet Skin, Chinese, c.1800, 3 ½ In. 1837.00
Snuff, Jade, Gray, Mottled Brown, Coral & Brass Top, Metal Spoon, c.1890, 2 ⅜ In. 354.00
Snuff, Jade, Jadeite Stopper, Double Gourd, Gray, White, c.1800, 2 ¾ In. 1375.00
Snuff, Jade, Lemon, Oval, Black Stopper, 1800s, 2 ½ In. 403.00
Snuff, Jade, Openwork Scroll Design, Revolving, Rounded Square, Red Dome Stopper, 3 ½ In. 296.00
Snuff, Jade, Pebble Of Gray, Mottled Brown, Peach Shape, Leaves, Coral Stopper, Chinese, 1800s, 2 In. 1007.00
Snuff, Jade, Pebble, 1700s, 2 ¾ In. 3062.00
Snuff, Jade, White, Carved, Scholars, Pine Trees, Leaves, Red Stopper, Chinese, c.1800, 2 ¾ In. 2818.00
Snuff, Jade, White, Cicada Shape, Coral Stopper, Chinese, Late 19th Century 5581.00
Snuff, Lapis Lazuli, Bird Perched On Rock, Peonies, Relief, Chinese, 3 In. *Illus* 200.00
Snuff, Lapis Lazuli, Flattened Cylinder, Veining, Chinese, 2 ¼ In. 230.00
Snuff, Leonard Appleby Railroad Mills, Red Amber, Flared Lip, 4 ½ In. 460.00
Snuff, Leonard Appleby Railroad Mills, Yellow Amber, Rectangular, Flared Lip, 5 In. 2223.00
Snuff, Malachite, Monster Masks, Chilong Playing With Ball, Flattened Pear, 1900s, 2 In. 119.00
Snuff, Milk Glass, Green Medallions, Flat Oval, Loop Handles, Blue Glass Top, Brass Mounts, 2 ¾ In. 502.00
Snuff, Mother-Of-Pearl, Bird On Branch, Relief Carved, Chinese, 2 ⅝ In. 240.00
Snuff, Peking Glass, Bat, Horse, Tree, Flattened Globular, Sepia Overlay, Opaque, 1800s, 2 ¼ In. 368.00
Snuff, Peking Glass, Purple, Carved Coral Stopper, 19th Century, 3 ¼ In. 1326.00
Snuff, Peking Glass, Turquoise, Wavy Carving, Bulbous, Carnelian Stopper, 3 In. 603.00
Snuff, Porcelain, Copper Red, Dragon, Rouleau Shape, Green Jade Stopper, 1800s, 3 ½ In. 299.00
Snuff, Porcelain, Famille Verte, Painted Deer, In Woods, Teardrop Shape, Green Stone Stopper, 3 ¼ In. 86.00
Snuff, Puddingstone, Flattened Oval, Coral Stopper, 1800s, 3 ¼ In. 518.00
Snuff, Puddingstone, Green & Black, Flattened Oval, Stopper, Chinese, 1800s, 2 ⅝ In. 304.00
Snuff, Puddingstone, Purple, Pink, Flattened Oval, c.1890, 2 ¾ In. 148.00
Snuff, Rock Crystal, Carved, Bulbous, Pink Stone Stopper, Chinese, 3 In. 961.00
Snuff, Sodalite, Relief Carved Fish In Waves, Pink Quartz Stopper, Spoon, 2 ¾ In. 132.00
Snuff, Spinach Jade, Mottled Green Texture, Hardwood Stand, Chinese, 2 ½ In. 345.00
Snuff, Stoneware, Salt Glaze, Bowers 3 Thistles, Brown Albany Slip, Cobalt Blue Letters, 14 ½ In. *Illus* 288.00
Snuff, Suzhou School, Green Rim, Pink Quartz Stopper, Chinese, 2 ½ In. 353.00
Snuff, Tiger Eye, Floater, Round, Flattened, Oval Foot, Ivory Spoon, 2 ¾ In. 384.00
Snuff, Turquoise, Deeply Carved Bird & Fish, Chinese, 19th Century, 2 ½ In. 452.00
Snuff, Turquoise, Flattened Shape, Figures, Relief Carved, 2 In. *Illus* 374.00
Soda Water, Taylor & Co., San Francisco, Eureka, Applied Top, Iron Pontil 550.00
Soda Water, Williams & Severance, San Francisco, Cal., Blue Applied Top, 1850s 425.00
Soda, B.J. McGee, Benicia, Teal, Blob Top, 7 ¼ In. 560.00
Soda, B.W. & Co., New York, Cobalt Blue, Applied Blob Mouth, 7 ⅝ In. *Illus* 518.00
Soda, Babe Ruth, All American Athlete, Label, Tin Lid, 4 ½ In., 5 Piece *Illus* 392.00
Soda, Bay City Soda Water Co., Star, Applied Top 550.00
Soda, Bonanza Bottling Co., Dawson, N.W.T., Aqua, Blob Top, 7 ¾ In. 896.00
Soda, Bostwick's, New York, Shaded Emerald Green, Sloping Collar, Pontil, 6 ⅝ In. 1955.00
Soda, Breig & Schafer, Embossed Fish, S.F., Light Green Aqua, Blob Top 110.00
Soda, C. & K., Eagle Works, Sac City, Blue, Sloping Collar, 7 ¼ In. 420.00
Soda, C. Freeman, Bottler, Buffalo, N.Y., Golden Amber, Squat, Sloping Collar, ½ Pt. 1755.00
Soda, Crystal Bottling Works, Lehigh, I.T., Route 290 On Base, Aqua, Blob Top 616.00
Soda, Crystal Soda Works, Honolulu, H.I., Blue Aqua, Torpedo, Blob Top 420.00
Soda, Decatur Bottling Works, DBCO In Diamond, Decatur, Ill., Teal, Hutchinson, Pt. 168.00
Soda, Donald Duck Lime Cola, Cardboard Carrier, Image Of Donald, W.D., 7 Oz. 165.00
Soda, E.L. Billings, Sac City, Geyser Soda On Reverse, Applied Top, Aqua 475.00
Soda, Eureka California Soda Water Co., S.F., Embossed Eagle, Amethyst, Blob Top, 6 ¾ In. 728.00
Soda, F & B, Boston, A.D.C. Co., New Haven, Pat. Jan. 5th 1864, Aqua, Blob Top 560.00
Soda, F. Knebel, 1860, Brooklyn, Aqua, Blob Top, Wire Bail, 7 ½ In. 179.00
Soda, G.A. Cook & Bro, Philipsburg, N.J., Green, Sloping Collar, Pontil, ½ Pt. 322.00
Soda, Geo. Cleminden, Savannah, Geo., Eagle & Flag, Teal, Blob Top, 7 ¼ In. 616.00
Soda, H. Nash & Co., Root Beer, Cincinnati, Cobalt Blue, 12-Sided, Iron Pontil, 8 ¾ In. 1380.00
Soda, H.O. Kreuger, Grand Forks, Dak., Aqua, Hutchinson, 7 ¼ In. 420.00
Soda, Heiss, Philada., Script H, Cobalt Blue, Sloping Collar, 7 ½ In. 345.00
Soda, J. Nevin, 1861, Brooklyn, Aqua, Blob Top, 7 ½ In. 112.00
Soda, J.T. Brown Chemist, Boston, Green, Torpedo, Blob Top 448.00
Soda, Jackson Napa Soda, Mineral Water On Reverse 400.00
Soda, Koca Nola, J. Esposito, Philada., Yellow Amber, Blob Top, Hutchinson, 7 ¾ In. 1120.00

Bottle, Mineral Water, Saratoga A Spring Co., N.Y., Olive Yellow, Applied Mouth, c.1870, Pt.
$1,380.00

Glass Works Auctions

Bottle, Mineral Water, Vermont Spring Saxe & Co., Sheldon, Vt., Pink, Sloping Collar, c.1865, Qt.
$1,989.00

Norman C. Heckler & Company

Bottle, Pickle, Cathedral, Aqua, Applied Mouth, Pontil, 11 ¾ In.
$265.00

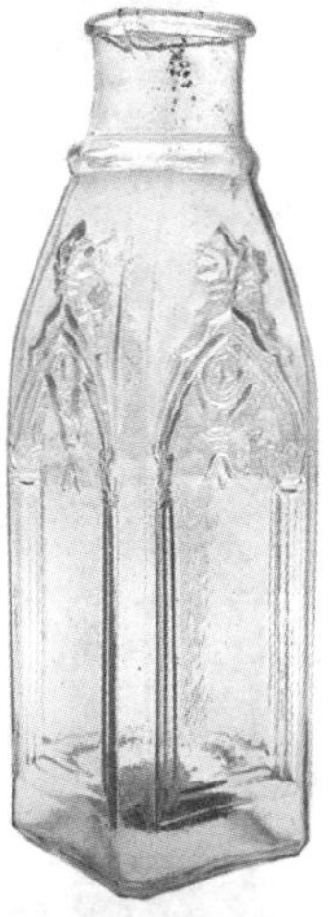

Glass Works Auctions

Bottle, Pickle, Cathedral, E.H.V.B., N.Y., Blue Green, 6-Sided, Iron Pontil, c.1855, 11 ½ In.
$138.00

Glass Works Auctions

Bottle, Pickle, Cathedral, Wm. Bodmann, Baltimore, Aqua, Outward Folded Mouth, Pontil, 1840s, Qt.
$10,640.00

American Bottle Auctions

Bottle, Pickle, Golden Amber, Vertical Lobes, Applied Mouth, New Hampshire, 1865-72, 8 ⅛ In.
$1,989.00

Norman C. Heckler & Company

Bottle, Poison, Lattice & Diamond, Cobalt Blue, Tooled Lip, 1890-1910, 11 ½ In.
$374.00

Glass Works Auctions

Soda, Leland Ice & Cold Storage Co., Leland, Miss., Blue Aqua, Blob Top, 7 ¼ In.	90.00
Soda, Napa Soda, Phil Caduc, Natural, Blue, Blob Top, 1871-1883	392.00
Soda, Owen Casey, Eagle Soda Works, Sac City On Reverse, Applied Top	220.00
Soda, Owen Casey, Eagle Soda Works, Steel Blue, Blob Top, 7 In.	336.00
Soda, P. Kellett, Newark N.J., K, 1857, Teal, Blob Top, Iron Pontil, 7 ½ In.	168.00
Soda, Pacific Soda Works, Claussen & Co., San Francisco, Teal, Blob Top, 6 ¾ In.	179.00
Soda, Pearson Bros., Bodie, Aqua, Gravitating Stopper, 1882-1891, 7 ¼ In.	3136.00
Soda, Property Of Monterey Soda Works, Tooled Top, Cal. Hutchinson	150.00
Soda, R. Robinson, 376 Bowery, N.Y., Script R, Green, Blob Top, 7 ¼ In.	213.00
Soda, Richmond Soda Works, R.S.W., Aqua, Blob Top, 1902-1915, 7 In.	476.00
Soda, S. Grossman, Monogram, Philada, Lime Green, Mug Base, Hutchinson, 7 ¾ In.	863.00
Soda, S. Smith's Knickerbocker, New York, Blue Green, Sloping Collar, 6 ¾ In.	784.00
Soda, Star Bottling Works, Anadarko, O.T., Amethyst Tint, Blob Top, 6 ⅞ In.	896.00
Soda, Steam Bottling Works, Shawnee, O.T., Embossed Anchor, Aqua, Hutchinson, 6 ¾ In.	728.00
Soda, Tahoe Soda Springs, Mineral Water, Carnelian Bay, Tooled Top, 1880	600.00
Soda, Taylor & Co., Valparaiso, Green, Blob Top, 7 ½ In.	308.00
Soda, Ukiah Soda Works, Ukiah, Cal., Aqua, Blob Top, Hutchinson, 7 In.	135.00
Soda, Union Soda Works, B & B, Yellow Amber, Blob Top	2688.00
Soda, Wm. S. Ford, Brooklyn, N.Y., Root Beer, Shield, Inverted Heart, Aqua, Blob Top, 10 In.	112.00
Stiegel Type, Lavender Amethyst, Diamond Pattern Above Vertical Flutes, Pocket, 4 ¾ In.	8775.00
Tantalus, Mahogany, Boulle, Tortoiseshell Inlays, Clear Glass Decanters, Cordials, 10 x 12 ¾ In.	431.00
Target Ball, Bogardus, Pat'd Apr 10 1877, Amethyst, 2 ¼ Oz.	1200.00
Target Ball, Bogardus, Pat'd Apr 10 1877, Diamond, Blue Green, Olive Swirl, 2 ⅝ In.	1093.00
Target Ball, Bogardus, Pat'd Apr 10 1877, Diamond, Pink Amethyst, Shaded, 2 ⅝ In.	2070.00
Target Ball, Bogardus, Pat'd Apr 10 1877, Diamond, Yellow Amber, 2 ⅝ In.	374.00
Target Ball, Bogardus, Pat'd Apr 10 1877, Diamond, Yellow Amber, Sheared, 2 ⅝ In.	276.00
Target Ball, Bogardus, Pat'd Apr 10 1877, Jade Green, 2 ½ Oz.	1000.00
Target Ball, Bogardus, Pat'd Apr 10 1877, Jade Green, 3 Oz.	1500.00
Target Ball, Bogardus, Pat'd Apr 10 1877, Lattice, Yellow Amber, Burst Lip, 2 ⅝ In.	560.00
Target Ball, Charlottenburg Glasshutten, Dr. A. Frank, Diamond, Yellow Olive, 2 ¾ In.	265.00
Target Ball, Cobalt Blue, 5-Piece Mold, Sheared Mouth, 2 ⅝ In.	115.00
Target Ball, Ira Paine's Filled Ball, Pat. Oct 23 1877, Yellow, Amber Tone, 2 ⅝ In.	288.00
Target Ball, J.H. Johnston, Great Western Gun Works, Pittsburgh, Purple, 2 ¾ In.	12880.00
Target Ball, Man, Shooting, Diamond, Cobalt Blue, England, c.1890, 2 ⅝ In.	978.00
Target Ball, Man, Shooting, Diamond, Moss Green, England, 2 ⅝ In.	345.00
Target Ball, Mauritz, Wid'fors, Yellow Amber, Sheared Mouth, 2 ⅝ In.	805.00
Target Ball, Stars & Bars, Yellow Amber, 2 ⅝ In.	2875.00
Tonic, B. Stafford's Celebrated Indian Hair Tonic, Olive, 3 Indented Panels, 8 ½ In.	878.00
Tonic, Rohrer's Expectoral Wild Cherry, Honey Amber, Pyramid, 10 ⅜ In.	896.00
Tonic, Rohrer's Expectoral Wild Cherry, Yellow Amber, Tapered, 10 ½ In.	575.00
Tonic, Spooners Hygeian, New York, Price $1.00, Yellow Olive, 8-Sided, 6 In.	3218.00
Whiskey, Backbar, S.B. Rothenberg, Label Under Glass, c.1890, Port, Rum, Gin, Sherry, 4 Piece... *Illus*	20160.00
Whiskey, Bennett & Carrol, Pittsburg, Barrel, Honey Amber, Squared Collar, 9 ¼ In.	3080.00
Whiskey, Boulevard Bourbon, Buneman Mercantile Co., Amber, Tooled Lip, Fifth.	258.00
Whiskey, Callahan's Old Cabin, Amber, Applied Mouth, Smooth Base, Pa., c.1870, 9 In...*Illus*	23000.00
Whiskey, Cantwell & Keefer, One Quart, Philadelphia, Cylindrical, Dark Olive, 11 ⅝ In.	920.00
Whiskey, Casper's, Made By Honest North Carolina People, Blue, Fluted Neck	650.00 to 672.00
Whiskey, Choice Old Cabinet, Ky. Bourbon, Embossed Crown, Applied Top, Amber *Illus*	1456.00
Whiskey, Corn Shape, Amber, Applied Lip, 9 ¼ In.	325.00
Whiskey, Cutter OK, J.H. Cutter Old Bourbon, Crown, Barrel, Amber, Sloping Collar, Fifth	235.00
Whiskey, Goudie & McKelvy Pepper Tree Saloon, Amber, Coffin Flask, Tooled Lip, ½ Pt.	1792.00
Whiskey, H & D, Monogram, Squat, Aqua, Applied Top, Iron Pontil, 6 In.	350.00
Whiskey, H. Pharazyn, Indian Maiden, Yellow Amber, Inward Rolled Mouth, 12 In.	322.00
Whiskey, IXL, Valley, EB Bevan, Pittston, Pa., Root Beer Amber, 8-Sided, Squat, 7 In.	2875.00
Whiskey, J.H. Cutter Old Bourbon, E. Martin & Co. Sole Agents, Crown, Sloping Collar	420.00
Whiskey, Jockey Club, G.W. Chesley & Co., S.F., Olive Amber, Sloping Collar, Fifth.	5152.00
Whiskey, Jug, Copper Puce, Shaded, Pear Shape, Curled Handle, Blob Top, Pontil, 7 ¾ In.	448.00
Whiskey, Jug, Golden Amber, Apricot Tone, Pear Shape, Curled Handle, Sloping Collar, 6 In.	235.00
Whiskey, Jug, Golden Amber, Cylindrical, Urn Form, Blob Top, Pontil, 9 ½ In.	213.00
Whiskey, Jug, Golden Honey, Cylindrical, Urn Form, Rigaree On Handle, 9 In.	146.00
Whiskey, Jug, Old Mountain Dew, Thomas Oates & Co., Multicolor Distillery Scenes, 7 ½ In... *Illus*	1495.00
Whiskey, Jug, Red Plum, Curled Handle, Rigaree, Sloping Collar, Pontil, 9 ½ In.	476.00
Whiskey, Jug, Strawberry Puce, Pear Shape, Curled Handle, Sloping Collar, Pontil, 6 ¼ In.	258.00
Whiskey, Lilienthal & Co., Distillers, Monogram, Amber, Coffin Flask, Tooled Lip, ½ Pt.	448.00
Whiskey, Louis Taussig & Co., 26 & 28 Main St., S.F., Golden Amber, Flask, Pt., 7 In.	672.00
Whiskey, Merry Christmas, Happy New Year, Woman, Rooster, Half Barrel, Amber, 6 In.	230.00

Whiskey, Miller's Extra Old Bourbon, Trade Mark, E. Martin & Co., Applied Collar, 1871-75.... *Illus*	6720.00
Whiskey, Mohawk, Pure Rye, Indian Queen, Tomahawk On Shield, Golden Amber	4032.00
Whiskey, Mohawk, Pure Rye, Pat Feb 11 1868, Indian Queen, Yellow Amber, 12 ⅜ In.	345.00
Whiskey, Nabob, Yellow, Amber Tint, Sloping Collar, Fifth	476.00
Whiskey, Old Gilt Edge, OK Bourbon, Crown, Monogram, Amber, Sloping Collar, Fifth	1120.00
Whiskey, Peach Apricot, Square, Beveled Corners, Sloping Collar, 9 ½ In.	101.00
Whiskey, Pig, Duffy Crescent Saloon, Louisville, Rooster, Golden Amber, 7 ½ In.	1840.00
Whiskey, Pig, Good Old Bourbon In A Hog's, Finger Painting, Honey Amber, 6 ¾ In.	489.00
Whiskey, S.M. & Co., N.Y., Seal, Amber, Applied Handle, 3 Ridges, Pontil, 7 ¾ In.	1344.00
Whiskey, Selzer & Miller, Amber, Slug Plate, Sloping Collar, 9 ¾ In.	35.00
Whiskey, Simmond's Nabob, Embossed, Man At Table, Amber, Fifth	1008.00
Whiskey, Simmond's Nabob, In Circle, Amber, Sloping Collar, Fifth	123.00
Whiskey, Strawberry Puce, Square, Beveled Corners, Sloping Collar, 8 In.	504.00
Whiskey, Teakettle Old Bourbon, Embossed Teakettle, Amber, Sloping Collar, Fifth	1568.00
Whiskey, Tippecanoe, North Bend, Cabin, Emerald Green, Sloping Collar, c.1840, 5 In.	38610.00
Whiskey, W & Co., N.Y., Pineapple, Golden Amber, Double Collar, 8 ½ In.	644.00
Whiskey, W. Wolf, Pittsburgh, Squat Barrel, Cornflower Blue, Double Collar, 7 ¾ In.	25760.00
Whiskey, Weeks & Gilson, Olive Amber, 3-Piece Mold, Double Collar, Stoddard, 11 In.	117.00
Wine, Crescent, Los Angeles, Cal., Crescent Moon, Amber, Fifth	336.00
Wine, Mallet, Yellow Olive, Shaded, Applied String Lip, 7 ⅜ x 4 ¾ In.	995.00
Zanesville, 24 Ribs, Swirled To Right, Aqua, Globular, Outward Folded Mouth, 7 In.	420.00
Zanesville, 30 Ribs, Swirled To Left, Golden Amber, Globular, Rolled Collar, Pontil, 12 In.	7605.00
Zanesville, Yellow Olive, Globular, Pinched Strap Handle, Outward Folded Lip, 5 ¼ In.	1344.00

BOTTLE CAPS for milk bottles are the printed cardboard caps used since the 1920s. Crown caps, used after 1892 on soda bottles, are also popular collectibles. Unusual mottoes, graphics, and caps from bottlers that are out of business bring the highest prices.

Donald Duck Ginger Ale, Cork Lined, Yellow, Green	9.00
Fresca, Cork Lined, Silver, Green	3.00
Paper, Mellin's Food, For Infants & Invalids, Black, White, 1 ⁵⁄₁₆ In.	10.00
Paper, Sanitarium & School Dairy, Pasteurized, Red, Green, White Ground, 2 ¼ In.	5.00
Pop's Root Beer, Cork Lined, Red & Blue Bubbles, Yellow Ground	3.00

BOTTLE OPENERS are needed to open many bottles. As soon as the commercial bottle was invented, the opener to be used with the new types of closures became a necessity. Many types of bottle openers can be found, most dating from the twentieth century. Collectors prize advertising and comic openers.

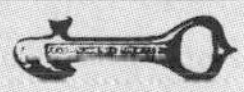

Acorn, Sterling Silver, Georg Jensen, 6 ¼ In.	125.00
Alligator, Cast Iron, 6 In.	16.00
Antler Handle, John Hasselbring, c.1940, 7 In.	149.00
Bakelite, Ribbed, Red, 4 ½ In.	25.00
Dolphin, Chrome, 6 ½ In.	12.00
Drunk Man, Wall On Palm Tree, Cast Iron, John Wright, c.1930	115.00
Elephant, Brass, Thailand, 4 x 3 In.	20.00
Gnome, Black Forest Wood, Germany, 7 ½ In.	68.00
Lobster, Goldtone, Rhinestones, 4 In.	25.00
Mermaid, Cast Iron, Furled Tail, 7 In.	30.00
Pabst Blue Ribbon Beer, Keychain, Logo, Aluminum, 2 In.	35.00
Parrot, On Perch, Brass, 5 In.	65.00
Rooster, Cast Iron, Painted, 3 x 2 ½ In.	38.00
Spoon, Waldorf Astoria, 7 In.	75.00

BOXES of all kinds are collected. They were made of thin strips of inlaid wood, metal, tortoiseshell, embroidery, or other material. Additional boxes may be listed in other sections, such as Advertising, Battersea, Ivory, Shaker, Tinware, and various Porcelain categories. Tea Caddies are listed in their own category.

Altar, Giltwood, Carved, Pierced, Foo Dog Supports, Bird & Flower Painted, Chinese, 10 ¾ x 17 ¼ In.	259.00
Apple, Bird's-Eye Maple, Dovetail, Canted Sides, Flat Bottom, c.1800, 3 x 8 x 8 In.	948.00
Ballot, Walnut, Blackball, Drawer, Turned Funnel, Brass Knob, c.1825, 4 x 8 In.	316.00
Band, Blue, Roses & Leaves Painted On Lid, 1800s, 4 ⅞ In. ....*Illus*	200.00
Band, Cardboard, Yellow, Gray Wallpaper, Flowers, Fish, Round, U.S.A., c.1850, 7 In.	382.00
Band, Pine, Oval, Birds, Stars, Stripes, Swags, Painted, Lid, New England, 1800s, 3 x 6 ½ In.	3081.00
Band, Wallpaper, Flowers, Rounded Corners, Lid, c.1850, 10 ½ x 14 In.	353.00

Bottle, Scent, Turkish Prince & Princess, Porcelain, Marked, Jacob Petit, c.1850, 7 x 5 ½ In., Pair
$1,912.00

Neal Auction Co.

Bottle, Snuff, Cinnabar, Children Playing, Foo Dog Handles, Chrysanthemum Stopper, c.1800, 3 In.
$748.00

James D. Julia Auctioneers

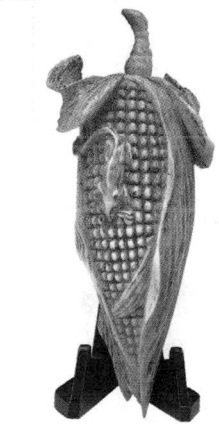

Bottle, Snuff, Ivory, Ear Of Corn, Mouse, Patina, Chinese, c.1910, 3 ¼ In.
$230.00

James D. Julia Auctioneers

Bottle, Snuff, Lapis Lazuli, Bird Perched On Rock, Peonies, Relief, Chinese, 3 In.
$200.00

Skinner, Inc.

Bottle, Snuff, Stoneware, Salt Glaze, Bowers 3 Thistles, Brown Albany Slip, Cobalt Blue Letters, 14 ½ In. $288.00

Glass Works Auctions

Bottle, Snuff, Turquoise, Flattened Shape, Figures, Relief Carved, 2 In. $374.00

Cottone Auctions

Bottle, Soda, B.W. & Co., New York, Cobalt Blue, Applied Blob Mouth, 7 ⅝ In. $518.00

Glass Works Auctions

Bottle, Soda, Babe Ruth, All American Athlete, Label, Tin Lid, 4 ½ In., 5 Piece $392.00

Garth's Auctioneers & Appraisers

Band, Wallpaper, Wagon, Dove, Camel, Oval, Lid, Henry Cushing & Co., R.I., c.1850, 10 x 16 In. ..	411.00
Bible, Oak, Carved Front Panel, Wrought Iron Strap Hinges, 1600s, 9 x 24 In.	588.00
Bible, Oak, Carved Panels, Iron Hardware, England, c.1700, 9 x 25 In.	646.00
Bible, Oak, Chip Carved Design, Hinged Lid, England, 1600s, 8 x 25 In.	474.00
Bible, Walnut, Carved, Painted, Wrought Iron Handle, Spain, c.1690, 20 x 16 ¼ In.	1035.00
Bowl, Magic, Islamic Script Panels, Raised Rondel, Footed, Middle East, 7 ½ In. Diam.	676.00
Brass, Casket Shape, Dragon Feet, Scrollwork, Woman On Horseback, Warrior, Griffin, 5 ½ x 10 ½ In.	369.00
Brass, Fruitwood, Ebonized Wood, Oval, Raised Handles, Branch Lid Handle, Scotland, c.1850, 5 In.	384.00
Brass, Inset Corners, Exotic Birds, Cloud Banding, Lid, Bird Finial, Ivory, 1800s, 1 ¾ x 4 ½ In. ...	177.00
Bride's, Lapped Seam, Painted, Man Hunter, Shooting Stag, Verse, c.1890, 7 x 13 x 20 In.	415.00
Bride's, Man, Woman, Flower Border, Continental, c.1800, 6 ½ x 19 In.	889.00
Campaign, Stand, Burl Walnut, Brass Bound, Fitted Interior, 21 ¾ x 12 In.	590.00
Candle, Mahogany, Slide Lid, Dovetailed, Ivory Edged, Round Crest, Compass Star, 1800s, 19 x 6 In.	1763.00
Candle, Mahogany, Slide Lid, Lollipop Hanger, New England, c.1790, 18 x 4 ¾ In.	652.00
Candle, Pine, Black Graining, Red, Dovetailed, Slide Lid, Penn., c.1913, 4 ¾ x 13 ¾ In.	764.00
Candle, Pine, Chip Carved Pinwheel, Red Paint, Pa., c.1810, 12 In.	531.00
Candle, Pine, Painted Green, Chamfered, Slide Lid, Teardrop Thumb Grip, c.1810, 15 x 7 In.	230.00
Candle, Pine, Painted, Dovetailed Drawer, Heart Pierced Handle, Blue, Yellow, c.1850, 10 x 7 In.	531.00
Candle, Pine, Woman Carrying Buckets, Paint, Scandinavia, 18 In.	474.00
Candle, Red & White Tulips, Yellow, Green, Black Ground, Slide Lid, Heinrich Bucher, 9 x 6 In.	165.00
Candle, Wall, Cherry, Slide Lid, Raised Panel, Paddle Shape Crest, c.1810, 20 x 6 x 5 In.	805.00
Candle, Wall, Walnut, Incised Flower Pinwheels, 1800s, 7 x 12 ½ In.	1126.00
Candle, Walnut, Flower Row, Chip Carved, New England, c.1790, 6 x 11 ¾ In.	830.00
Candle, Walnut, Lollipop Finials, Peaked Scalloped Rim, Pa., c.1810, 18 x 9 In.	1067.00
Carved, Cigar Boxes, Birds, Folk Art, U.S.A., 1800s, 5 ½ x 7 In.	118.00
Cigar, Bronze, Art Nouveau, Flowers, Camphor Wood Lining, Lid, c.1900, 3 ½ x 8 ¾ In...*Illus*	615.00
Cigar, Mixed Metal, Marble, Silver Gilt Edged, France, c.1900, 1 ¾ x 6 ⅜ In.	1541.00
Cigar, Silver, Engraved Crest, Ram, Oak Branch, Soyez Juste, Shield, c.1917, 3 x 9 In.	1000.00
Cigarette, Art Deco, Boy, Grapes, Deer, Brass Plate, Wood Liner, Rockwell Kent, 6 ½ x 5 ⅜ In.	184.00
Coin, Hardwood Veneer, Locked Hinged Lid, Black Glass Handle, 4 Interior Coin Trays, 7 ½ x 7 ⅜ In.	59.00
Cutlery, Marquetry, Hinged Sloped Lid, Putti, Floral Sprays, Flower Basket, c.1780, 12 ½ x 9 In.	345.00
Cutlery, Pine, Painted, Blue, Yellow Striping, Pa., Mid 19th Century, 7 x 13 ¾ x 9 ½ In.	1067.00
Cutlery, Wood, 2 Sections, Canted Sides, Footed Base, Handle, Green Paint, c.1815, 14 ¼ In. ...	144.00
Document, Basswood, Red Grain Paint, New England, c.1860, 6 x 14 In.	119.00
Document, Huanghuali, Plank Top, U-Shape Handles, Lotus Escutcheon, Lid, 1600s, 5 x 7 In.	7110.00
Document, Leather Covered, Scrollwork, Flowers, Leaves, Strap Hinges, c.1715, 7 x 11 ¾ In.	799.00
Document, Mixed Woods, Green Paint, Chippendale Brass Handle, Dome Lid, c.1850, 9 ½ x 18 In.	176.00
Document, Pine, Blue, Green Smoke Decorated, New England, 19th Century, 7 x 17 In.	119.00
Dresser, Brass, Beveled Glass, Filigree, Rose Medallion, Paw Feet, 5 x 9 In. .....*Illus*	210.00
Dresser, Federal, Cherry, Eagle Inlay, c.1810, 4 ¾ x 12 ½ In.	474.00
Dresser, Lid, Oval, Winged Cherubs, Scrolls, Fruits & Flowers, c.1899, 1 x 2 ¾ In.	178.00
Dresser, Metal, 5 Porcelain Panels, Cherubs, Flowers, 6 In. .....*Illus*	776.00
Dresser, Pine, Red Tulip, Farmhouse, Yellow, Red Paint, Jonas Weber, c.1840, 4 x 6 In.	45030.00
Dresser, Wood, Inlay, Ormolu Trim, Shaped Lid, French Feet, France, c.1835, 7 ½ x 12 ½ In. .	470.00
Dressing Case, Leather, Flowers, Leaves, Mirror, Tray, Pouches, Lid, Mexico, c.1950, 7 x 14 In. ...	123.00
Flatware, Cherry, Lift Lid, Shaped & Pierced Handle, Dovetailed, Hinged Lids, 9 x 14 ¾ In.	245.00
Game, Rosewood, Brass Inlay, Civil War Designs, G.W. Williams, N.Y., 4 x 19 x 10 In.	1035.00
Gold, Nosegay, Enamel, Diamond Centers, Hardstone Base, Hinged Lid, Round, 2 In.	3480.00
Gold, Tricolor, 14K Yellow, Green, Pink Gold, Engraved Geometrics, Flowers, Scrolls, 3 x 2 ¼ In.	2760.00
Hat, Leather, Beaver Skin Hat, Stovepipe, Lock & Key, Taylor, 1890s .....*Illus*	270.00
Hat, Lid, Wallpaper Covered, Yellow, Red & Gold Tulips & Vines, Oval, 10 x 15 x 11 In.	354.00
Hat, Poplar, Blue, Black, Yellow Paint, Hinged Dome Top, c.1850, 16 ½ x 14 ½ In.	345.00
Hat, Resistol Cowboy Hats, Cardboard, Ranch Scenes, 16 ½ x 8 ¼ x 15 ½ In. .....*Illus*	48.00
Hat, Wallpaper, Birds, Landscape Scene, Blue, Oval, 12 ½ In.	620.00
Hat, Wallpaper, Blue & White, Top Hat Shape, Belfast, 9 x 13 x 11 ½ In.	1093.00
Hat, Wallpaper, Blue Flowers, Oval, 5 ½ x 10 In.	767.00
Hat, Wallpaper, Blue, White Paper Lining, 9 x 13 x 11 ½ In.	47.00
Hat, Wallpaper, Chintz, Orange, Blue, Green Flowers, Birds, Oval, c.1850, 7 x 11 In.	1007.00
Hat, Wallpaper, Fox Hunt Scene, c.1810, 12 ½ x 16 ¾ In.	504.00
Honor, Brass, Handle, Ball Feet, Marked, Rich's Patent, 1800s, 7 In. .....*Illus*	885.00
Humidor, Mahogany, Hinged Lid, Porcelain Interior, Filter, c.1900, 12 ¾ x 7 ½ In.	29.00
Incense, Lacquer, Octagonal, Mother-Of-Pearl Seashell Design, Signed, c.1900, 1 ½ In.	486.00
Jewelry, 18K Gold, Line-Engraved Squares, Sapphire Clusters, Van Cleef & Arpels, 1 ½ x 1 In.	2760.00
Jewelry, Burled Circassian Walnut Veneer, String Inlay, Hinged Lid, Ivory Mounts, c.1850, 15 x 10 In.	1840.00
Jewelry, Gilt Brass, Glass, Pierced, Beading, Flowers, Maidens, Eagle, Paw Feet, c.1900, 2 x 6 In.	338.00

Jewelry, Papier-Mache, Mother-Of-Pearl, Greek Key Border, Landscape, c.1850, 4 x 10 ½ In. ..	338.00
Jewelry, Regency, Leather, 2 Doors, Interior Drawers, Hinged Lid, Brass Mounted, 13 x 12 In..	1610.00
Jewelry, Rosewood, Deer & Pine Tree, Soapstone Inlay, 1900s, 2 ½ x 7 ¾ In.	144.00
Jewelry, Round, Inlaid Jade & Coral, Silver Filigree, Masks, Figures, Footed, 1800s, 5 x 7 In....	1380.00
Knife, Federal, Urn Shape, Vertical Bands, Square Base, Ogee Bracket Feet, c.1850, 27 In........	944.00
Knife, George III, Mahogany Veneer, Serpentine Front, Banding, Hinged, Inlay, 14 x 9 In., Pair	483.00
Knife, George III, Mahogany, Molded, Inlays, c.1805, 15 x 11 In., Pair	1840.00
Knife, George III, Serpentine, Mahogany, Crossbanded, Sawtooth, Ball Feet, c.1775, 16 x 8 x 13 In.	399.00
Knife, Georgian, Serpentine, Painted, Side Handles, Ivory Ball Feet, 13 ½ x 8 In.	403.00
Knife, Mahogany, George III Style, String & Banded Inlay, Oval Patera, Urn, 1900s, 15 ½ In., Pair.	3540.00
Knife, Pine, Canted Sides, Divider, Cutout Handle, c.1800, 8 x 7 x 15 In.	356.00
Knife, Wall, Carved, Slotted Compartments, Shaped Leather Lid, H.B. Crosby, 17 x 6 In.	748.00
Lacquer, Chrysanthemum Shape, Incised, Dragons, Flaming Pearl, Gilt Mark, 9 x 20 In. ....*Illus*	7768.00
Lacquer, Lid, Evening Sleigh Ride, Red Interior, Russia, 1900s, 3 ⅜ x 5 ¾ In.	356.00
Lacquer, Troika, 3 Horses Pulling Sleigh, Driver, Seated Man, Woman, Russia, Signed, 4 x 3 In. ..	120.00
Letter, Marquetry Inlay, Hexagonal Pearl Insets, Interior Tray, Hinged Lid, 5 ½ x 11 In..........	240.00
Letter, Pine, 2 Tiers, Black Pinstripes, Red Paint, Cutouts, c.1840, 19 x 14 In........................	770.00
Letter, Regency, Mahogany, Pierced Brass Rail, 2 Stamp Drawers, England, c.1860, 10 x 12 In.	360.00
Liquor, Mahogany, Inlaid Lid, Shell, Brass Carrying Handles, Silk Lining, c.1800, 12 x 14 ½ In.	1180.00
Lock, Lift Lid, Pine, Painted, Flowers, Hinged, Continental, c.1810, 12 ¼ x 27 ¾ In..............	356.00
Lock, Ocher Grain Paint, Looped Line Design, New England, c.1850, 9 x 18 In.	122.00
Lock, Pine, Flame Grain Paint, Beveled Lid, Divided Interior, Ohio, c.1865, 4 x 12 In..............	118.00
Lock, Pine, Painted Green, G.L.O. 1846-47 In Yellow, General Land Office, New England, 10 x 19 In.	267.00
Lock, Walnut, Line & Berry, Ball Feet, Auspitz, York, Pa., 15 x 25 ½ In.	474.00
Lock, Yewwood, Inlaid Pinwheels, Continental, 1700s, 6 ¾ x 15 ¾ In.	326.00
Love Token, Pine, Heart, Hands, Doves, True Love Letters Carved, Hinged Lid, c.1930, 6 x 5 ¾ In..	81.00
Mahogany, Chest Of Drawers Shape, Inlays, Lift Lid, c.1810, 5 ¾ x 4 ¼ In..........................	531.00
Mechanics, Pine, Hinged Top, Iron Handle, Red, White, Blue Paint, c.1890, 8 ½ x 16 In........	230.00
Oak, Pinwheels, Stars, Carved, Slide Lid, Initialed IB, 4 ¾ x 9 In..	593.00
Pencil, Walnut, Slide Lid, Locking, Signed, Dated 1818, 8 ⅜ x 1 ⅝ In..............................	130.00
Picnic, Brass, Engraved Landscape, Pierced Lid, Fretwork Border, 2 Swing Handles, 7 ¼ In.	236.00
Picnic, Hardwood, 2 Tiers, Iron Mounted Frame, Handle, 1800s, 20 ½ x 20 ½ In.	600.00
Picnic, Hardwood, 3 Tiers, Conforming Stand, Chinese, c.1800, 10 x 15 In.	1080.00
Pine, Black, Gold, Brown Panels, Slide Lid, Pa., c.1840, 3 ½ x 7 ¼ In.	652.00
Pine, Blue, Orange Paint, Slide Lid, Marked A. H. D., 1826, 8 ¾ x 25 In...............................	356.00
Pine, Eagle & Banner, Green Paint, Lift Lid, c.1850, 6 x 29 In..	325.00
Pine, Mahogany Grain Paint, Black Stencil Border, Stringing, Dome Lid, c.1815, 12 x 31 In...	480.00
Pine, Painted Multicolor Geometric Designs, Relief Carved Rosettes, Borders, 1800s, 6 ½ x 8 x 17 In..	4148.00
Pine, Painted, Slide Lid, Scandinavia, c.1850, 11 x 14 In.	207.00
Poplar, Bird, Flowers, Blue Ground, Gilt Pinstripes, Paint, Pa., Furniture, c.1850, 5 x 12 In. ..	178.00
Poplar, Wall, Red Paint, Carved Back, Lift Lid, Drawer, Pa., 1800s, 14 x 11 ½ In.....................	1422.00
Red, White Stylized Flowers, Blue Ground, Dome Lid, Compass Artist, Pa., c.1820, 10 x 11 ¾ In...	9480.00
Regency, Rolled Paper Filigree, Red, Gold Flowers, Blue, Satinwood, Round, c.1780, 4 In.	413.00
Rosewood, Ivory, Lift Lid, Piano Shape, Keys, 7 ½ x 9 In.	177.00
Schoolgirl, Burgundy Paint, Mustard Decoration, Lucia, Pinstripe, Hinged Lid, 1800s, 14 x 9 ½ In.	115.00
Shoe Shine, 10 Cents, Sloped, Wood, Painted Tin, c.1860, 18 x 8 In.	633.00
Storage, Brass, Jade, Quatrefoil, Engraved, Conforming Lid, Inset Plaque, 1900s, 5 x 6 In., Pair..	3198.00
Storage, Case Of Drawers, Poplar, Grain Paint, Ripple Molded Lid, U.S.A., c.1865, 7 x 13 In....	452.00
Storage, Cherry, Stamped J. Fisher, c.1805, 4 ½ x 11 In..	122.00
Storage, Cranberry Carrier, Bentwood Oak Handle, Iron Swing Handle, Lid, Cape May, 11 x 10 In.	345.00
Storage, Grain Painted, Fan & Eye Shape Knot Design, Hinged Lid, Latch, 1800s, 10 x 5 In.....	144.00
Storage, Pine, Dovetailed, Green Paint, Yellow Flowers, Stars, Dome Top, U.S.A., 1800s, 12 x 24 In.	323.00
Storage, Pine, Grain Design, Dovetailed, Lid, Brass Bail Handle, U.S.A., c.1850, 9 ½ x 20 In. ..	206.00
Storage, Pine, Grain Paint, Dome Lid, New England, c.1810, 10 ½ x 24 In.	207.00
Storage, Pine, Paneled, Grain Painted, Hinged Lid, c.1835, 23 ½ x 22 ¼ In...........................	1067.00
Storage, Pine, Putty Paint, Brass Swing Handle, Iron Latch, Dome Lid, U.S.A., c.1825, 5 ¾ x 12 In.	2844.00
Storage, Shaped Circular, Dragon, Clouds, Landscapes, Lid, Stand, c.1890, 27 x 20 In.	922.00
Storage, Tiger Maple, Banded Inlay, Hinged Dome Lid, Brass Swing Handles, 1800s, 6 x 11 ½ In..	490.00
Storage, Wallpaper, Square Wire Handle, Rectangular, Swags, Black, Pink, Dome Lid, c.1815, 3 ⅜ In.	960.00
Storage, Walnut, Tab Pull Slide Lid, Dovetail & Rosehead Design, c.1800, 4 ½ x 10 ½ In.	265.00
Storage, Wood, Leaf & Berry Design, Yellow Paint, Slide Lid, U.S.A., c.1800, 4 x 11 ¾ In.........	2133.00
Storage, Wood, Feet, Flags, Leaves, Hinged Lid, Fort Hancock, U.S.A., c.1900, 8 x 9 In..............	1080.00
Strong, Brass & Steel, Lid, Gothic Strapwork, Flowers, Bail Handle, Flowers, c.1850, 4 ½ x 8 ½ In..	553.00
Strong, Iron, Cube Shape, 2 Hinged Lids, Strap, Spain, 17th Century, 16 ½ 13 ¼ In.	3000.00
Tobacco, Brass, Engraved, Coat Of Arms, Cityscape, Amsterdam, 18th Century, Oval................	145.00

Bottle, Whiskey, Backbar, S.B. Rothenberg, Label Under Glass, c.1890, Port, Rum, Gin, Sherry, 4 Piece
$20,160.00

American Bottle Auctions

Bottle, Whiskey, Callahan's Old Cabin, Amber, Applied Mouth, Smooth Base, Pa., c.1870, 9 In.
$23,000.00

Glass Works Auctions

Bottle, Whiskey, Choice Old Cabinet, Ky. Bourbon, Embossed Crown, Applied Top, Amber
$1,456.00

American Bottle Auctions

Bottle, Whiskey, Jug, Old Mountain Dew, Thomas Oates & Co., Multicolor Distillery Scenes, 7 ½ In.
$1,495.00

Glass Works Auctions

Bottle, Whiskey, Miller's Extra Old Bourbon, Trade Mark, E. Martin & Co., Applied Collar, 1871-75
$6,720.00

American Bottle Auctions

Box, Band, Blue, Rose & Leaves Painted On Lid, 1800s, 4 7/8 In.
$200.00

Conestoga Auction Co., Inc.

Box, Cigar, Bronze, Art Nouveau, Flowers, Camphorwood Lining, Lid, c.1900, 3 1/2 x 8 3/4 In.
$615.00

New Orleans Auction Galleries, Inc.

Box, Dresser, Brass, Beveled Glass, Filigree, Rose Medallion, Paw Feet, 5 x 9 In.
$210.00

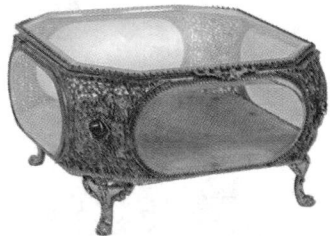

DuMouchelles Art Gallery

Trinket, 2 Birds, Heart Border, Fannie C. Hunt, Aug. 28th 1912, 7 x 4 x 3 In.	142.00
Trinket, Octagonal, Central Panel, Hardstone Birds, Flowering Branches, Lid, 3 1/4 x 7 1/2 In.	575.00
Trinket, Orange & Brown Wavy Grain Paint, Removable Lid, Folk Art, c.1850, 4 1/4 x 8 1/4 In.	86.00
Trinket, Pine, Blue, Orange, Yellow Paint, Scandinavia, c.1850, 5 x 12 1/2 In.	152.00
Trinket, Pine, Painted Tulip, Dome Lid, c.1810, 3 3/4 x 7 3/4 In.	1067.00
Trinket, Pine, Slide Chamfered Lid, Finger Hold, Dovetailed, Painted, c.1800, 3 x 5 x 4 In.	948.00
Trinket, Stylized Flower, Blue, Compass Artist, Paint, Lancaster County, Pa., c.1800, 6 x 7 1/4 In.	8295.00
Trinket, Tulip, Leaf, Landscape Painted, Green Ground, Jonas Weber, Pa., c.1840, 2 x 3 1/2 In.	4740.00
Trinket, Wood, Book Shape, Carved & Painted, Gilt Edges, Slide Lid, c.1800, 7 x 3 3/4 In.	420.00
Trinket, Wood, Grain Painted, Bird On Branch Design, Handle, 1800s, 12 1/2 In.	144.00
Vampire Killing Kit, Wood, Hinged Lid, 20 Pieces, Fitted Compartments, c.1885, 17 x 9 1/2 In.	14800.00
Vanity, Travel, Rosewood, Mother-Of-Pearl, 1800s, 6 3/8 x 12 In. ....*Illus*	420.00
Wall, Maple, Dovetailed, Pierced Shaped Back, Drawer, Slant Lid, U.S.A., 1800s, 11 1/4 x 11 In.	246.00
Wall, Parquetry Inlay, Walnut, Mirror, c.1850, 20 1/2 x 9 1/2 In.	119.00
Wall, Pine, Drawer, Cutout Holder, Pa., 12 3/4 x 10 In.	356.00
Wall, Poplar, Love Birds, Flowers, c.1830, 7 3/4 x 13 In.	9480.00
Wall, Spoon Rack, Wood, Star Cutout, Red Ocher Paint, Pa., c.1820, 25 x 13 In.	2607.00
Wall, Walnut, Hinged, Slant Lid, Cutout Wall Hole, Virginia, c.1850, 7 3/4 x 12 In.	259.00
Wall, Walnut, Lollipop Hanger, 3 Drawers, Pa., c.1850, 22 x 8 In.	1126.00
Wall, Wood, 2 Knobbed Drawers, Painted, Red, Yellow, Lift Lid, 12 x 13 1/2 In.	4248.00
Wallpaper, Birds, Flowers, Blue Ground, Round, 1800s, 5 x 6 1/4 In.	4740.00
Wallpaper, Blue Flowers, Orange Ground, c.1850, 3 1/2 x 7 3/4 In.	533.00
Wallpaper, Fabric, Brown, Tan Design, Vase Shape, Red Ribbon, c.1850, 4 3/4 In.	444.00
Wallpaper, Flowers, Yellow, Brown, Salmon Ground, Round, Lid, c.1850, 2 3/4 x 3 In.	1659.00
Wallpaper, Geometric, Blue On Yellow Ground, Pa., 7 x 13 1/4 In.	1067.00
Wallpaper, Orange Leaves, Blue Ground, Oval, Pa., c.1850, 6 x 8 In.	474.00
Wallpaper, Orange, Black Flowers, Salmon Ground, 19th Century, 3 3/4 x 5 1/2 In.	593.00
Wallpaper, Orange, Green Flowers, White Ground, Oval, Lid, New England, c.1859, 3 x 7 In.	243.00
Wallpaper, White Fruit, Green, Yellow, Blue Ground, Oval, Lid, c.1850, 4 1/2 x 8 In.	770.00
Wallpaper, Yellow & Orange Flowers, Blue Ground, Round, c.1850, 4 x 6 1/4 In.	1304.00
Walnut, Pine, Slide Lid, 3 Lids, Brass Knob, Pa., c.1845, 4 1/2 x 14 In.	518.00
Wood, Cutout Handle, Green Paint, 9 x 14 In.	1304.00
Wood, Dovetailed, Red Paint, Slide Lid, 6 Compartments, 2 x 10 x 5 In.	142.00
Wood, Painted, Boys In Landscape, River, Horn, Hat, Hinged Lid, Folk Art, c.1840, 4 3/4 x 11 5/8 In.	1185.00
Wood, Tin, Repousse Flowers, Birds, Bustamante, 15 x 32 1/2 In., Pair	1200.00
Writing, Mahogany, Brass Bound, Portable, Fitted Interior, Slanted, Eng., 8 1/2 In., 21 x 13 In.	413.00
Writing, Rosewood, Fitted Interior, Inlaid Birds, Flowers, 12 x 4 In.	266.00
Writing, Sheraton, Mahogany, Drawer, Reeded Stop, Tabletop, c.1805, 8 x 15 1/2 In.	237.00

BOY SCOUT collectibles include any material related to scouting, including patches, manuals, and uniforms. The Boy Scout movement in the United States started in 1910. The first Jamboree was held in 1937. Girl Scout items are listed under their own heading.

Book, Little Cub Scout, By Mabel Watts, Rand McNally Elf Book, 1964	20.00
Booklet, Boy Scout Plan, Flags, Celluloid, c.1915, 2 3/4 In., 4 Pages	60.00
Button, Norman Rockwell Illustration, Fort Orange Council, 1934 & 1936, 1 1/4 In., 2 Piece	114.00
Compass, Silva System, Tin, Attached To Acrylic Board, 1960s, 4 x 3 In.	20.00
Explorer Manual, 1957	12.00
Handbook, 1960	15.00
Hunting Knife, RH-51, Logo, Sheath, Remington, 7 5/8 In.	135.00
Pin, Circus Arena, St. Louis, Scout Figure, Waving, 1940, 1 1/4 In.	82.00
Plate, Our Heritage, Boy Scout With Cub Scout, Norman Rockwell, 1950, 8 In.	29.00
Watch, Jamboree, Scoutmaster Moving Arm Up & Down, Smith's, England, 1950s	150.00
Watch, Scout Slogans Around Dial, Ingersoll, 1937, Pocket	600.00

BRADLEY & HUBBARD is a name found on many metal objects. Walter Hubbard and his brother-in-law, Nathaniel Lyman Bradley, started making cast iron clocks, tables, frames, andirons, bookends, doorstops, lamps, chandeliers, sconces, and sewing birds in 1854 in Meriden, Connecticut. The company became Bradley & Hubbard Manufacturing Company in 1875. Charles Parker Company bought the firm in 1940. Bradley & Hubbard items may be found in other sections that include metal.

Chandelier, 3-Light, 8-Panel Slag Glass Shade, Flower & Swag Overlay, 15 x 14 In.	230.00
Lamp, Brass, Duplex Burner, Etched Shade, Signed, c.1800, 21 x 8 In.	354.00
Lamp, Brass, Embossed, Footed Lizard Base, Etched White Globe, Paneled, 8 x 24 In.	990.00
Lamp, Caramel Slag Glass, Geometric Border, Paneled Metal Base, 22 In.	1020.00
Lamp, Figural, Partly Clad Man, Holding Pink Glass Globe, Roses, 32 x 17 In.	767.00

Lamp, Filigree Metal Town Scene, Over Slag Glass Shade, 4 Sockets, 23 x 13 ¾ In.		920.00
Lamp, Green Glass Shade, Embossed Base, 18 ½ In.		201.00
Lamp, Yellow Ball Shade, Ornate Cast Metal, 37 In.		209.00
Mirror, Flower Openwork, Marked, 16 ¼ x 13 ¾ In.		148.00
Stand, Brass, Square Top, Enamel Tile, Leaf Design, Flowers, Fans, c.1870, 32 In.		2726.00

BRASS has been used for decorative pieces and useful tablewares since ancient times. It is an alloy of copper, zinc, and other metals. Additional brass items may be found under Bell, Candlestick, Tool, or Trivet.

Alms Dish, Repousse, Depicting Louis XV, Continental, 17 ¼ In.		59.00
Ashtray, Devil Dragon, Hinged Jaw, 3 ½ x 4 x 8 In.		55.00
Ashtray, Man In The Moon, 3 ¼ x 4 ¾ In.		33.00
Baker's Rack, 3 Shelves, 96 x 32 In.		210.00
Basket, Hammered, Ribbed, Fluted, Handle, Josef Hoffman, Wiener Werkstatte, Vienna, 8 x 7 In. *Illus*		6000.00
Bed Warmer, Baluster Turnings, Hinged Pierced Lid, Flower Design, c.1800, 44 ½ In.		267.00
Bed Warmer, Copper Rim, Wood Turned Handle, c.1855, 42 In.		89.00
Bed Warmer, Engraved Bird, Flowers, Turned Cherry Handle, Iron, c.1830, 44 In.		385.00
Bed Warmer, Engraved Lid, Wrought Iron Handle, Engraved Scrolls, Lion Head, 1800s, 44 In.		181.00
Bed Warmer, Engraved, Turned Wood Handle, 48 In.		94.00
Bed Warmer, Maple Handle, Hinged Lid, Punch Design, Bird, Flowers, Scrolls, 1800s, 42 ½ In.		200.00
Bed Warmer, Pan, Pierced Lid, Turned Handle, U.S.A., 1800s, 53 In.		176.00
Bed Warmer, Punched Bird, c.1810, 43 In.		182.00
Bible Stand, Cloisonne, Pierced Apron, Gothic Pattern, Jesus, Lamb, Paw Feet, c.1900, 6 ¾ x 14 In.		1353.00
Bible Stand, Ratcheted, Pierced Skirt, Scrolls, Rope Twist Turnings, Paw Feet, c.1900, 6 ¼ x 11 ½ In.		492.00
Box, Cigarette, Diving Helmet, Air Tank, Lighter, Oval Walnut Base, 8 x 9 In.		215.00
Brazier, Stamped, Engraved, Pierced Flowers, Scrolls, Oval, Raised Paw Feet, 1700s, 12 x 17 In.		944.00
Bucket, 3 Bands, Oak, Scroll Side Handles, England, 10 x 20 In.		293.00
Bucket, 4 Bands, Oak Barrel Shape, Swing Handle, England, 17 x 11 In.		293.00
Bucket, Mahogany, Hammered Swing Handle, Banding, Pail Liner, England, c.1815, 17 x 15 In.		1968.00
Bucket, Turned Wood, Tapered Ringed Bowl, Ebonized Wood, Swing Handle, 14 x 12 In.		644.00
Candle Reflector, 3 Footed, England, 18th Century, 7 In.		295.00
Casket, Hinged Lid, Engraved Exterior Designs, Wood Lined Interior, Persia, 5 x 3 ½ In.		63.00
Charger, Embossed Tavern Scene, 24 ½ In.		18.00
Cigar Box, Humidor, Hinged Compartments, c.1900, 3 x 8 ½ In. *Illus*		60.00
Coffeepot, Stand, Cylindrical, Filigree Spigot, Lid, Ventilated Base, 1800s, 12 In.		207.00
Coffeepot, Turned Walnut Side Handle, Hinged Lid, Cone Shape, 9 ¼ In.		518.00
Cuspidor, Dragon, Figural, Flip Top		504.00
Cuspidor, Figural, Crab, Jewel Eyes, 15 x 12 In.		715.00 to 900.00
Cuspidor, Turtle, Figural, Flip Top		780.00
Doorknocker, Late Georgian, Cast Iron Trim, c.1800, 7 x 5 ¾ In.		184.00
Ewer, Chased Arabesque Design, Bird Finial, Bulbous, Spread Foot, Square Handle, Turkey, 19 ½ In.		389.00
Ewer, Hand Chased, Teardrop Shape, Hinged Lid, S-Shape Handle, Footed, India, 1700s, 10 ½ In.		115.00
Figurine, Asian Boy, Art Deco, Stylized, Holding Box, Cast, Cold Painted, Ivoreen Hands, 9 x 3 In.		144.00
Figurine, Buddha, Seated, Pierced Base, Dogs, Birds, Man, 14 ⅝ In. *Illus*		83.00
Figurine, Dog, Whippet, Seated, Holding Card, Oval Marble Base, Victorian, 14 x 6 In.		461.00
Figurine, Grecian Fairy, Seminude Woman, Crouching, Wings, Marble Base, 9 ¼ In.		443.00
Figurine, Horse, Rearing, Stamped, Franz & Karl Hagenauer, Austria, 1930s, 21 x 8 In. *Illus*		2875.00
Figurine, Peacock, Enameled, Detachable Fan Tail, Round Base, Asia, 26 ¾ x 23 ¾ In.		118.00
Figurine, Stylized Dancer, Marked Hagenauer, 3 x 4 ¼ In.		366.00
Figurine, Stylized Dancer, Wood Dress, Marked Hagenauer, 8 x 10 In.		2562.00
Flask, Round Shaped, Crowned 2-Headed Eagle, Flared Feet, Russia, 4 ¾ In.		191.00
Footbath, Georgian, Oval, Banded, Seamed, Rolled Rim, c.1815, 9 x 19 ¼ In.		492.00
Frame, Cast, French Style, Scrolling Leaves, Vines, Tabletop, 11 ½ x 8 In.		150.00
Frame, Gilt, Cherubs, Bows Border, Easel Back, Victorian, 11 x 9 In.		387.00
Frame, Gilt, Jewels, Paint, Leaves, Scrolls, Easel Back, Victorian, 9 ½ x 7 ½ In.		357.00
Gorget, Leather Backed Brass, Stamped Crown, Initials, Leaves, 6 x 6 In.		345.00
Helmet, Officer's, Acanthus Crest, Louis Philippe, Rooster Roundel, Feather Plume, 1820s, 13½ In. *Illus*		1195.00
Horn, Hunter's, Brass, France, c.1750, 16 ½ In.		518.00
Jam Hooks, Ball & Urn Finials, 4 In., Pair		118.00
Jardiniere, Empire, Gadrooned Body, Paw Feet, Lion's Head Ring Handles, Scrolls, c.1850, 8 x 18 In.		531.00
Jardiniere, Flared Rim, Cylindrical Body, Tree Branch Handles, Turtles, Footed, 14 x 12 In.		180.00
Jardiniere, Lion Masks, Leaf Feet, Imperial Russia, Tula City Mark, c.1910, 12 x 14 In.		391.00
Jardiniere, Louis XVI Style, Tray Shape, Footed, Pierced, Arches, Flowers, Handles, c.1900, 6 x 19 In.		430.00
Jardiniere, Panels, Flowers, Engraved, Lion's Head Ring Handles, Paw Feet, c.1900, 14 x 15 In.		522.00
Jardiniere, Stand, Hammered, Border, Foo Dog Handles, Pierced, Cabriole Legs, c.1890, 38 x 23 In.		1107.00

Box, Dresser, Metal, 5 Porcelain Panels, Cherubs, Flowers, 6 In.
$776.00

Early Auction Co.

Box, Hat, Leather, Beaver Skin Hat, Stovepipe, Lock & Key, Taylor, 1890s
$270.00

Showtime Auction Services

Box, Hat, Resistol Cowboy Hats, Cardboard, Ranch Scenes, 16 ½ x 8 ¼ x 15 ½ In.
$48.00

Showtime Auction Services

Box, Honor, Brass, Handle, Ball Feet, Marked, Rich's Patent, 1800s, 7 In.
$885.00

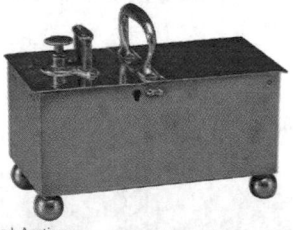

Brunk Auctions

TIP
Brass tarnishes more quickly in direct sunlight.

B

Box, Lacquer, Chrysanthemum Shape, Incised, Dragons, Flaming Pearl, Gilt Mark, 9 x 20 In.
$7,768.00

Neal Auction Co.

Box, Vanity, Travel, Rosewood, Mother-Of-Pearl, 1800s, 6 ⅜ x 12 In.
$420.00

DuMouchelles Art Gallery

Brass, Basket, Hammered, Ribbed, Fluted, Handle, Josef Hoffman, Wiener Werkstatte, Vienna, 8 x 7 In.
$6,000.00

DuMouchelles Art Gallery

Brass, Cigar Box, Humidor, Hinged Compartments, c.1900, 3 x 8 ½ In.
$60.00

DuMouchelles Art Gallery

Jewelry Casket, Relief Cherubs, Hinged Lid, Velvet Lining, Stamped Germany, 7 ¾ x 6 In.	132.00
Kettle Stand, Iron, Cutout Design, c.1850, 12 ½ x 9 ½ In.	30.00
Kettle, Coffee, Scrolling Handle, S-Handle, Urn Finial, Persia, 1800s, 14 In.	81.00
Kettle, Dovetail, Bail Handle, 17 x 27 ½ In.	83.00
Letter Holder, Cast, Acanthus Leaf, Griffin, Winged Women Creatures, 3 Slots, Victorian, 11 x 15 In.	420.00
Mailbox, Cutout Design, Monogram, Newcomb College, c.1915, 11 x 9 In. ....*Illus*	896.00
Milk Can, Collar Neck, Applied Copper Flowers, Strap Handle, Dutch, 22 x 14 In.	1265.00
Mirror, Neoclassical, Embossed Armor, Arms, Busts, Repousse, Round, c.1890, 27 In.	72.00
Ornament, Helmet, Deep Sea Diver's, Glass Inserts, MGM Studios, 3 ¾ In.	173.00
Planter, On Stand, Lotus Design, Fish Relief, Hexagonal Pedestal, Key Fret Edge, Domed Base, 30 In.	207.00
Plate Pail, George III, Mahogany, Tapered Cylinder, 3 Bands, Swing Handle, 16 ½ x 14 ¾ In.	1170.00
Pot, Footed, Squat, 2-Headed Eagle, 3 Lion's Head & Ring Handles, Paw Feet, Russia, 1800s, 14 In.	115.00
Pot, Molded Rim, Swing Handle, 6 x 12 In.	62.00
Samovar, Conical, Gadroons, Openwork Scroll Handles, Hoofed Feet, Russia, c.1900, 20 x 15 In.	492.00
Samovar, Cylindrical Smoke Stack, Ring Handles, Spout, Square Base, Ball Feet, 21 In.	150.00
Samovar, Hinged Lid, Tab & Seam Construction, Shaped Spout, Handle & Collar Base, 11 In.	12.00
Sculpture, Puzzle, Figural, Male Torso, Torero, Stamped, M. Berrocal, Spain, 1972, 11 x 8 In.	3000.00
Sculpture, Stylized Bird, Wooden Stand, Hans Christensen, 22 In.	2530.00
Shot Holder, Steel, Revolutionary War Era, 4 In.	96.00
Stand, Magazine, Victorian, Folding, Easel Shape, 3 Shelves, 33 In.	72.00
Standish, Urn Standard, Scalloped Edge, 3 Containers, Candlestick Holder, Bell, 1800s, 8 In.	472.00
Tazza, Classical Style, Bronze, Cast Iron Base, Woman's Head Medallion, Floral Stem, 4 ¼ x 5 ⅜ In.	12.00
Tazza, Copper, Column, Center Reserve, Relief Design, Classical Roman Scenes, 6 x 7 In., Pair	177.00
Teapot, Bottle, Handle, Straight Spout, Dome Cap, Hunters On Horseback, Scroll, 18 ½ In.	584.00
Teapot, Lid, Silvered, Repousse, Hounds Chasing Stag, Swan Swimming, Eagle Knop, 9 ½ In.	207.00
Tinder Box, Candle Socket Lid, Damper, Flint, Steel, Hollow Handle, Wall Ring, c.1810, 9 In.	294.00
Urn, Lid, Samurai Finial, Dragon Handles & Legs, Round Base, Birds, c.1900, 25 In., Pair	850.00
Valance, Embossed, Victorian, 65 In., Pair	89.00

BRASTOFF, *see Sascha Brastoff category.*

BREAD PLATE, *see various silver categories, porcelain factories, and pressed glass patterns.*

BRIDE'S BOWLS OR BASKETS were usually one-of-a-kind novelties made in American and European glass factories. They were especially popular about 1880 when the decorated basket was often given as a wedding gift. Cut glass baskets were popular after 1890. All bride's bowls lost favor about 1905. Bride's bowls and baskets may also be found in other glass sections. Check the index at the back of the book.

Amber, Glass, Spiral Handle, Tiffin, 10 ¼ In.	48.00
End-of-Day Glass, Cased, Ruffled, Silver Mica Highlights, Silver Plated Frame, 11 x 7 ½ In. ... *Illus*	75.00
Flowers, Griffins, Pink, White, Tooled Ruffled Rim, Cameo, Mt. Washington, c.1890, 4 x 8 In., Pair	546.00
Glass, Molded, Fern Leaves, Bent Glass Handle, 10 x 13 In.	60.00
Peach Glass, Applied Wavy Amber Rim, Scrolled Metal Frame, Victorian, 12 ½ In.	316.00
Peachblow, Ruffled Rim, Victorian, 6 ½ In.	201.00
Pink & White Cased, Ruffled, Enamel, Silver Plated Frame .....*Illus*	275.00
Pink Opalescent, Ruffled Edge, Silver Plate Frame, c.1890, 11 x 12 In.	83.00
Pink Opalescent, Scalloped Ruffled Top, 9 ½ In.	73.00
Ruby Thumbprint, Engraved Flowers, Silver Plated Frame, 12 x 10 In. ....*Illus*	125.00
Silver Plate, Art Glass, Ruffle Rim, Waisted, Flower Bands, Pink, Yellow, c.1885, 11 x 10 ¾ In.	246.00
Silver, Reticulated, Flowers, Ribbons, Swing Handle, Oval Foot, George Roth, c.1860	387.00
Sterling Silver, Scrollwork, Pierced Design, Leaves, Trumpet Foot, c.1900, 16 x 12 ½ In.	1659.00
Webb Peachblow, Tricolor, Gold Enameling, 3 Cherubs, Silver Plated Frame, 12 ½ x 10 ½ In. ...*Illus*	2250.00
Yellow & Russet Swirl Pattern, White Interior, Tight Ruffled Rim, 10 In. Diam.	518.00

BRISTOL glass was made in Bristol, England, after the 1700s. The Bristol glass most often seen today is a Victorian, lightweight opaque glass that is often blue. Some of the glass was decorated with enamels.

Basket, Flowers, Butterflies, Enamel, Overlay, Gilt, c.1880, 12 x 7 In. .....*Illus*	150.00
Bowl, Blue, White, Figures, Flowers, Scalloped Rim, Melon Shape, c.1770, 16 ¼ In.	885.00
Charger, Blue, Flowers, c.1805, 13 ¼ In.	118.00
Shaker, Gray, Multicolor Flowers, Ring Based, 4 ½ In., Pair	23.00
Vase, Pink, Glass Plate Over White, Raised Gilt Leaves, Flowers, c.1885, 12 In., Pair	110.00
Vase, Portrait Medallions, Woman, Daughter, Blue Ground, Gilt, Tapered, Footed, 10 In., Pair	130.00
Vase, White Translucent, Baluster Shape, Painted, Peach, Bird, Branches, 6 x 4 In., Pair	81.00

BRITANNIA, *see Pewter category.*

BRONZE is an alloy of copper, tin, and other metals. It is used to make figurines, lamps, and other decorative objects. Bronze lamps are listed in the Lamp category. Pieces listed here date from the eighteenth, nineteenth, and twentieth centuries.

Ashtray, Cigar, Devil, Embossed, 2 ½ x 4 In.	138.00
Bowl Stand, French Empire Style, Dore, 3 Griffin Shape Legs, Sienna Marble Base, 7 In.	828.00
Bowl, Lotus, 3 Toad Footed Stand, Cast, Patinated, Japan, 8 ¼ In.	354.00
Bracket, Shaped Shelf, Fluted Support, Dolphins, Plaques Of Cavaliers, c.1890, 16 x 15 In., Pair	896.00
Brush Rest, 5 Peaked Mountain Shaped, Chinese, 1800s, 3 ½ In.	153.00
Bulb Tray, Relief Irises, Tin Inset, Oval, 4 Scrolled Feet, Dragon Handles, 8 x 5 In.	138.00
Bust, Carrier, A., Young Woman, Bark Brown Patina, Inscribed, 16 ¾ In.	1320.00
Bust, Carrier-Belleuse, Albert, William Shakespeare, Green Marble Pedestal, c.1880, 9 ½ In.	1185.00
Bust, Colombo, R., Napoleon, Signed, Italy, c.1885, 22 In.	1968.00
Bust, Dante, Cap, Clock, Gazing Ahead, Marble Oval Base, c.1925, 8 ¼ In.	375.00
Bust, Fraikin, C.A., Jeune, Dove On Shoulder, Hair With Grapevines, Signed, C.A., 1800s, 10 ½ x 7 In.	676.00
Bust, Menelaus, Sideward Glancing, Helmut, Pedestal, Square Base, 20 In.	956.00
Bust, Muller, H., Ludwig Von Beethoven, Paint, Marble Base, Signed, Austria, c.1920, 18 In.	250.00
Bust, Muller, H., Woman, Art Nouveau Style, Printemps On Plaque, 9 x 10 In. ....*Illus*	450.00
Bust, Orlando, Jay Smith, Jacket, Vest, Roman Bronze Works, 1901, 24 ½ In.	500.00
Bust, Scipio, Marble Socle, Bald Head, Draped Robe, c.1890, 24 x 11 In.	1168.00
Bust, Villanis, Emmanuel, Byzance, Woman, Headband, Large Earrings, Roman Fibula, 21 ½ In.	6250.00
Bust, Weisse, Henry, Gypsy, ¾ Profile, Square Base, 26 In.	813.00
Cannon, Signal, Breech Loading, Mahogany Carriage, Wheels, Strong Firearms Co., 10 ½ In....*Illus*	3450.00
Casket, Gabled Roof, Double Hasp, Birds, Bracket Feet, Handle, c.1775, 13 x 9 x 7 In.	1534.00
Censer, 3 Arms, Swag, Acanthus Leaf Embossed, Chains, c.1920, 28 x 11 In.	150.00
Censer, Bamboo Leaves, Twisted Bamboo Feet & Handles, Foo Dog Knop, c.1900, 20 ¾ x 10 In.	1476.00
Censer, Compressed Oval, Column Feet, Taotie Masks, Lion Mask Lugs, Dome Wood Lid, 1800s, 7 In.	2844.00
Censer, Compressed, Scroll Designs, Animal Mask Feet, Beast Handles, Domed Lid, 10 ¾ In.	450.00
Censer, Dragon Pierced Lid, 2 Figures Over Cooking Pot, Foo Dog Head Handles, Finial, 20 x 12 In.	369.00
Censer, Dragon Shape, Loose Ring Handles, Squat, Carved Wood Stand, 1800s, 15 In. Diam.	717.00
Censer, Figural, Reclining Cat, Glass Eyes, Enamel Work Collar, Chinese, 1800s, 6 ½ x 10 In.	1150.00
Censer, Incised Figures, Rustic Landscape, Foo Dog Mask Handles, Marked, Chinese, 3 x 5 In...*Illus*	325.00
Censer, Loop Handles, Gold Splashed Design, Splay Feet, Chinese, 3 ¾ x 8 ¼ In.	1896.00
Censer, Lotus Blooms, Scrolling Leaves, Elephant Head Handles, Upturned Snouts, Dome Lid, 13 In.	1215.00
Censer, Mask & Animal Shape Handles, Dragons, Serpents, Rosewood Lid, Jade Finial, 1800s, 6 ½ In.	3163.00
Censer, Oval, 2 Oblong Handles, Landscape, Geometric Ground, Footed, 1800s, 9 x 12 In.	375.00
Censer, Oval, Birds, Flowers, Dragon, Openwork Clouds, Bird Head Handles, Crane Finial, 43 In.	1215.00
Censer, Peach Shape, Leaves, Branch Shape Handle, 5 In.	1195.00
Censer, Rectangular, Lotus Legs, Molded Handles, Reticulated Lid, Dragon Finial, 1900s, 19 ½ In.	270.00
Censer, Relief Bands, Tripod Shaped, Signed, Toun, 5 ⅞ In.	573.00
Censer, Splayed Lip, Constricted Neck, Twisted Handles, Drum Belly, Marked, Chinese, 3 ¼ In.	2607.00
Censer, Spread Foot, Squat, C-Scroll Handles, Landscape, Trees, Gilded, 3 ½ x 4 ½ In.	4860.00
Censer, Squat, Tripod, Rope Shaped Handles, Scrolling, Banded Center, 6 ¼ x 7 ½ In.	826.00
Censer, Squat, Waisted Neck, Tripod Feet, Chinese, 1800s, 5 In. Diam.	304.00
Censer, Stand, 3 Parts, Root Openwork Lid, Conforming Base, Handle, Pierced Stand, 1800s, 25 In.	750.00
Censer, Tripod Feet, Upright Ear Lugs, Pierced Dome Lid, Foo Dog Knop, 1800s, 14 x 9 In.	354.00
Censer, Urn Shape, Mythical Figure, Dragons, Carved, Openwork, Lotus Clouds, Lid, c.1900, 36 In.	5581.00
Centerpiece, 2 Elephants, Playing, Round Onyx Base, Cold Painted, Austria, 1920s, 6 x 12 ¾ In.	625.00
Centerpiece, Gilt, Reticulated, 3 Graces, Winged Sphinx, Tripartite Base, 17 ¼ In.	1500.00
Centerpiece, Pan, 1 Foot Stance, On Edge Of Bowl, Head Bowed, Arms Spread, c.1925, 20 x 20 In.	6875.00
Chalice, Silvered, Gilt, Urn Shape, Naturalistic Vine Handles, Bacchus Masks, 6 In.	426.00
Charger, Repousse Style, Putti, Crabs, Exotic Birds, Francis I Medallion, Continental, 25 In.	420.00
Cigar Box, Casket Shape, Battle Scenes, Inscribed, Dutch, c.1900, 3 ½ x 8 In.	369.00
Cigar Tray, Embossed, 8 x ¾ In.	540.00
Compote, Gilt, Flared, 18 Inset Malachite Cabochons, Rope Twist Edge, 4 x 12 In.	633.00
Cooler, Champagne, Brass Geared Crank, c.1910, 21 ¼ In.	180.00
Cross, Processional, Victorian, Gilt, Leaf Molded Base, England, c.1885, 71 ½ In.	430.00
Crucifix, Processional, Gothic Style, France, c.1900, 38 In.	1320.00
Cup, Presentation, Silvered Inside, Lid, Soldier, Shield, Inscription, Pedestal, E.C. Lentz, 1793	307.00
Desk Clip, Setter Running, Cold Painted, Spring Mounted, Mahogany Base, Vienna, 12 In.	1076.00
Dish, Round, Beaded, Ring Inset, Silver Geometric Pattern, Wide Mouth, Flared Foot, 1800s, 12 ½ In.	200.00
Encrier, Eagle, Patinated, Gilt Shaped Base, 2 Glass Cups, c.1900, 10 x 17 ¾ In.	375.00
Encrier, Grand Tour, Molded, Scrolls, Mask Under Handle, Italy, c.1885, 5 ¼ x 6 In.	430.00
Ewer, Baluster, Medallions, Cupids, Handle, Wide Spout, Putto & Dolphin Finial, c.1895, 34 In.	1320.00

Brass, Figurine, Buddha, Seated, Pierced Base, Dogs, Birds, Man, 14 ⅝ In. $83.00

Conestoga Auction Co., Inc.

Brass, Figurine, Horse, Rearing, Stamped, Franz & Karl Hagenauer, Austria, 1930s, 21 x 8 In. $2,875.00

Rago Arts & Auction Center

Brass, Helmet, Officer's, Acanthus Crest, Louis Philippe, Rooster Roundel, Feather Plume, 1820s, 13 ½ In. $1,195.00

Neal Auction Co.

Brass, Mailbox, Cutout Design, Monogram, Newcomb College, c.1915, 11 x 9 In. $896.00

Neal Auction Co.

Bride's Basket, End-of-Day Glass, Cased, Ruffled, Silver Mica Highlights, Silver Plated Frame, 11 x 7 ½ In. $75.00

Woody Auction

Bride's Basket, Pink & White Cased, Ruffled, Enamel, Silver Plated Frame $275.00

Woody Auction

Bride's Basket, Ruby Thumbprint, Engraved Flowers, Silver Plated Frame, 12 x 10 In. $125.00

Woody Auction

Ewer, Cast, Relief Meandering Scroll, Cherubs, Scroll Handle With Rabbit, Mask, 8 x 3 ¾ In. .	92.00
Ewer, Classical Style, Cast, Lioness Shape Handle, Fruiting Olive Branches, c.1800, 7 ½ In.	173.00
Ewer, Neoclassical Style, Bacchantes, Grapes, Handle, Reclining Putto, 1800s, 21 In., Pair	1778.00
Ewer, Putti, Chariots, Grapes, Vined, Ram's Head Mask Handles, 21 x 37 In., Pair..................	298.00
Ewer, Renaissance Revival, Putti, Figural Handle, Ram's Head, Cherub, France, 17 In., Pair ..	360.00
Finial, Griffin, Spread Wings, Ornate, 10 ½ x 8 In.	220.00
Flower Holder, Jewett, Maude Sherwood, Bacchante, Man, Woman, 1924, 10 In. ....*Illus*	3900.00
Frame, Copper, Silver Doors, Caryatids, Putto, Figures, Stones, Caldwell & Co., c.1920, 18 x 12 In.	10625.00
Frame, Mother-Of-Pearl Flowers, Arched Crest, Easel Back, France, B. Altman, c.1905, 10 x 7 ½ In.	3600.00
Frame, Picture, Porcelain, Mother-Of-Pearl, Scrollwork, Plaques, Instruments, c.1900, 8 x 6 In.	1168.00
Furniture Mounts, French Empire, Gilt, Pharaoh Heads, 6 ¼ x 4 In., Pair....................	239.00
Garniture, Neoclassical Revival, Figures, Flame, Winged Woman, c.1890, 17 x 6 In., Pair......	2952.00
Gong, Hammered, Open Oval, Red Lacquer & Hide Strike, Buddhist, Japan, 1800s, 12 x 15 In....	2300.00
Gong, Round, Hand Hammered, Carved, Gilt Stand & Strike, Vietnam, 45 ½ x 38 ¼ In.	374.00
Group, Cossack After Battle, Soldier, Horse, Marble Base, Russia, 18 x 16 In.	1190.00
Group, Ronde Damours, Pan, Playing Pipes, 5 Dancing Putto, Holding Hands, c.1890, 17 In.	750.00
Hand Warmer, Pierced Flowers, Geometrics, Swing Handle, Japan, 6 x 7 ½ In.	826.00
Ikebana Stand, 3 Parts, Birds, Rabbits Leaping Through Waves, Japan, 15 In. Diam............	748.00
Incense Burner, Bulbous, 2 Loop Handles, 3 Cone Shape Feet, 17th Century, 3 ¾ In. Diam...	1968.00
Incense Burner, Indian Chief, Cross Legged, 4 x 3 x 3 In., 2 Piece.............................	154.00
Incense Burner, Serpent Handles, Foo Dogs, Frog Finial, 3-Footed, Chinese, 7 x 6 In.	210.00
Jardiniere, Cast Pheasant, Horse, Flowers, Fretwork, Ring Handles, Chinese, 25 ½ x 29 In..	10350.00
Jardiniere, Classical, Verdigris Patina, Pedestal Base, Figures, Flower Swags, Paw Feet, 37 x 20 In......	1236.00
Jardiniere, Napoleon III Style, Hardwood, Turned Feet, Columns, Swags, Bands, 8 x 15 In.....	615.00
Jardiniere, Panels, Dragons, Swimming In Sea, Molded Mushrooms, Swing Handles, 9 x 15 In...	215.00
Jardiniere, Pine Trees & Swallows, Bamboo, Mountains, 12 ½ In..............................	276.00
Jardiniere, Urn Shape, Winged Putti, On Lion Mask Handles, Gilt, Pedestal Base, c.1920, 37 x 30 In.	3840.00
Letter Rack, 4 Steeplechase Riders, Fences, Cold Painted, c.1900, 7 x 8 x 4 ½ In.	4313.00
Mirror Plateau, Rocky Border, Mahogany Base, Turned Wooden Feet, c.1900, 2 ½ x 15 In.. *Illus*	354.00
Mirror, French Empire, Round, Swivel Top, Cupid Standard, Pedestal Base, 16 ¼ In.	413.00
Mirror, Hand, Cast Relief, Fruit Trees, Landscape, Chinese Characters, Lacquered Box, 10 x 6 In. .	35.00
Mirror, Hand, Obverse Cranes, Pine Forest, Round, Japan, 1800s, 9 ¾ x 6 In.	288.00
Mirror, Water Chestnut Flower Shaped, Phoenixes, Scrolls, Flower Heads, 8 ⅞ In.	2370.00
Monstrance, Glass Window, Gilt Rays, Putti, Clouds, Grapes, Raised Base, c.1890, 17 In.	865.00
Monstrance, Sunburst, Cherubs, Hinged Door, Window, Cross Finial, 1800s, 25 In.	2280.00
Monstrance, Sunburst, Flowers, Cross, Gilt, c.1875, 17 ½ In...............................	767.00
Paperweight, Fish, Gilt Accents, Red, Japan, 1800s, 4 ¼ In.	288.00
Pitcher, Art Nouveau, Bacchus Mask Under Spout, Mermaids, Merman, Fish, Relief, c.1910, 8 In. *Illus*	1107.00
Pitcher, Figural, Elephant, 7 In.	590.00
Planter, Kettle Well, Tripod Downswept Legs, Raised Base, Castors, c.1920, 33 x 13 In.	450.00
Planter, Oval, Relief Hawk, Engraved, Japan, 13 ½ x 17 In..................................	633.00
Plaque, Figures, Man & Woman, Holding Jug & Shield, Green, Art Deco, 22 x 21 In.	1380.00
Plaque, Fredericks, Marshall, Philosopher Chimpanzee, 10 ½ x 8 In.	6000.00
Plaque, Napoleon, Profile, Relief, Emp. Et Roi, Maire, Fecit 1814, Round, Self-Framed, c.1900, 6 In. .	184.00
Plaque, Neoclassical Style, Woman, ¾ Profile, Rectangular, 21 ½ x 14 ¾ In.	438.00
Plaque, Royal Crest, Falcon, 3 Crown, 18 ½ x 21 In.	708.00
Plaque, Savage Bros. Co., Indian Head, 11 x 8 ½ In.	412.00
Replica, Napoleon's Tomb, Cold Painted, Bicorn Hat, Sword, Laurel Branch, Marble Base, 7 x 5 In.	656.00
Sculpture, 2 Dolphins, Jumping, Water, Marble Oval Base, 1900s, 26 ¼ In.	108.00
Sculpture, 2 Grappling Horses, Naturalistic Base, Signed, 1901, 16 x 18 ½ In.	850.00
Sculpture, 3 Cranes, Wood Base, 25 In.	480.00
Sculpture, Abraham Lincoln, Rail Splitter, Jacket Holding, Hatchet, Base, c.1911, 20 In.	6518.00
Sculpture, Aegina, Zeus As Eagle, Cup, Oval Black Marble Plinth, 13 In.	1063.00
Sculpture, Aichele, Paul, Maiden, Seated, Snail, Cast, Brown Patina, Marble Base, 15 x 14 In.	2961.00
Sculpture, Alligator, Head Turned, Jaws Open, 25 x 71 In. ....*Illus*	7170.00
Sculpture, Alonzo, D., Medieval Woman, Staircase, Ivory, Marble Base, Signed, 11 ⅝ In...*Illus*	2160.00
Sculpture, Angel, Seminude, Arm Stretched Above Head, Sphere Of Clouds, c.1900, 24 In.	650.00
Sculpture, Arab, On Horse, Barye, Antoine-Louis, Cold Painted, Signed, 29 ½ x 23 x 11 ½ In.	1265.00
Sculpture, Argentinian Dance, Woman, Gilt, Ivory, Wood, Onyx, Base, c.1925, 19 In..............	8750.00
Sculpture, Art Deco, Nude Dancer, Black Belgian Marble Base, c.1920, 26 In.	1440.00
Sculpture, Aube, Jean Paul, Girl With Roses, Cast, Brown Patina, Gilt, Round Base, 24 ¼ In..	920.00
Sculpture, Aurora, Holding Scarf Above Head, 1800s, 32 In.	8050.00
Sculpture, Bald Eagle, In Flight, Silver Gilt Head, Feathers, 33 ¼ In.	431.00
Sculpture, Ball, Thomas, Daniel Webster, Brown Patina, Signed, 30 In....................	1062.00
Sculpture, Barbedienne, Bull, Taureau Debout, Seconde Version, c.1890, 7 ¼ x 11 In...........	4000.00
Sculpture, Baroque, Putto, Arms Raised, Black Socle, 13 x 4 In...........................	936.00

Sculpture, Bartholome, Nude Woman, Mourning, Dore, Incised, France, c.1900, 2 ¼ x 6 ½ In.....	460.00
Sculpture, Barye, Bull Elk, Oval Base, 16 x 13 In..	480.00
Sculpture, Barye, Elk, Standing, Raised Leg, Head Up, Rectangular Base, France, Signed, 18 x 21 In.	1168.00
Sculpture, Barye, Lion, Lion Qui Marche, Inscribed, c.1955, 8 ¾ x 15 In..................	500.00
Sculpture, Bayer, Antoine-Louis, Panther, Eating Its Prey, France, Signed, c.1825, 12 In.........	2015.00
Sculpture, Bear, c.1960, 19 x 12 In..	316.00
Sculpture, Bear, Rampant, Standing, Front Paws Up, Rectangular Base, Signed, 6 ½ x 6 ½ In.	356.00
Sculpture, Bergman, Arab Child, Reclining, Smoking, Head Scarf, Austria, c.1900, 6 In.........	480.00
Sculpture, Bergman, Arab Rider, Donkey, Multicolor, Saddle, Blanket, Signed, 5 ¼ x 5 ½ In..	805.00
Sculpture, Bergman, F.X., Woman, Partly Clad, Child, Cold Painted, Carpet, Austria, c.1910, 6 x 5 In..	1770.00
Sculpture, Bergman, Franz Xavier, Dancer, Woman Holding Skirt, c.1900, 11 In...................	2806.00
Sculpture, Bergman, Franz Xavier, Dancer, Woman, Holding Short Skirt, Bare Waist, c.1900, 11 In.	2806.00
Sculpture, Bergman, Franz Xavier, Girl With Tray, On Rug, c.1900, 9 ½ In.	1098.00
Sculpture, Bergman, Franz Xavier, Woman, Carrying Jar On Head, c.1900, 10 ½ In.............	2562.00
Sculpture, Bergman, Franz, Woman, Attendant, Hinged Arm Reveals Nude, Namgreb, 11 In. *Illus*	2300.00
Sculpture, Bergman, Franz, Kingfisher, Cold Painted, Stamped, 7 ½ In........................	305.00
Sculpture, Bergman, Rug Merchant, Man, Turban, Holding Rug, Cold Painted, c.1925, 7 x 8 ¼ In..	625.00
Sculpture, Berlini, W. Rogel, Eagle, Wings Up, Oval Base, Signed, 5 x 14 In.....................	472.00
Sculpture, Bianchi, A., Dog, Crouching, Signed, 1864, 8 ¼ x 12 ¾ In.	500.00
Sculpture, Bissell, George, Abraham Lincoln, Standing, Emancipation Paper, c.1898, 8 ¼ In.	1416.00
Sculpture, Black Shoeshine Boy, Cold Painted, c.1900, 3 ½ In.	911.00
Sculpture, Blackamoor, Sewing Jacket, Seated On Rug, Cold Painted, Austria, 4 x 4 In..........	265.00
Sculpture, Blossom, Lotus, Kannon, Standing Man, Outstretched Arm, Drapery, 1800s, 21 In.	711.00
Sculpture, Bonheur, I., Jockey On His Horse, Inscribed, 28 ¼ x 30 ½ In......................	1035.00
Sculpture, Bonheur, Isidore, Charging Bull, Patina, Oval Marble Base, Signed, 14 x 21 In.	900.00
Sculpture, Boobis Chanin, Man, Standing, Signed, 15 In....................................	327.00
Sculpture, Botzaris, Sava, Nude, Woman, Recumbent, Patinated, England, c.1950	5625.00
Sculpture, Boxing Rabbit, Stand, Dark Patina, 31 ¾ In.	690.00
Sculpture, Boy, Seated, Marble Base, c.1900, 4 ¾ In.	1215.00
Sculpture, Boy, Singing, Seminude, Holding Stringed Instrument, 29 In........................	1400.00
Sculpture, Buddha Guardian, On Rock, Military Uniform, Lion Heads, Holding Sword, 14 In.	7290.00
Sculpture, Buddha, 4 Faces, 8 Arms, Seated, Lotus Throne, 18th Century, 11 ⅜ In. ....*Illus*	12000.00
Sculpture, Buddha, 4-Armed Manjushri, Seated, Crown, Lotus Flower Base, Nepal, 1900s, 14 In.	584.00
Sculpture, Buddha, Crown, Draped Robe, Earrings, Fulfilling Of Vow Mudra, Lotus Base, 7 In. ...	3949.00
Sculpture, Buddha, Seated In Lotus Position, Snail Hair, Hollow Cast, Applied Gilt, 14 In.	207.00
Sculpture, Buddha, Seated, Double Lotus Throne, Hand In Mudra, Gilt, Chinese, c.1900, 50 ⅞ In.	4148.00
Sculpture, Buddha, Seated, Double Lotus Throne, Legs Crossed, Robes, 9 In.....................	1380.00
Sculpture, Buddha, Seated, Lotus Shaped Base, Shakyamuni, c.1900, 6 ¼ In.	382.00
Sculpture, Buddha, Seated, Robes, Stepped Oval Base, Burma, 16 In...........................	598.00
Sculpture, Buddha's Hand, Hollow, Applied Gilt, Wood Mount, 12 x 6 ½ In....................	949.00
Sculpture, Buffalo, Laying, Wood Stand, Chinese, c.1850, 2 ½ x 5 In........................	1960.00
Sculpture, Buffalo, Walking, Molded, Shaped Wooden Base, Signed Japan, c.1900, 9 x 17 In.	646.00
Sculpture, Bust, Minerva, Sideward Glancing, Helmet, Pedestal, Square Base, 19 ½ In..........	1830.00
Sculpture, Cain, Auguste, Dogs, 2 Labradors, Seduisant Et Lumineau, 1800s, 12 x 16 In........	2091.00
Sculpture, Calandra, D., Horse, Standing, Patinated, 1913, 26 ½ x 29 x 7 In..................	2832.00
Sculpture, Campbell, Neil, Dogs, Running, Signed, c.1950, 9 x 11 In.........................	125.00
Sculpture, Carrier, A., Sculptor, Descending Stairs, Holding Ecorche, Signed, 1855, 25 ½ In...	1000.00
Sculpture, Carrier, Albert, Dante Alighien, Seated, Holding Book, Divine Comedy, 1856, 26 In..	3213.00
Sculpture, Cartier, T., Dog, Seated, Signed, 1913, 12 In.	575.00
Sculpture, Cartinet, Discus Thrower, Man, Standing, Hardstone Base, 9 ⅝ In.	375.00
Sculpture, Chimpanzee, Seated, 12 x 11 In. ....*Illus*	390.00
Sculpture, Chiparus, Dancing Girl, Arms Over Head, Signed, Art Deco, 57 x 10 In..................	531.00
Sculpture, Chiparus, Dourga, Arms Up, On Toes, Gilt, Ivory, Onyx, Art Deco, c.1925, 25 In.	31250.00
Sculpture, Circus Clown, Standing, Head Down, Open Arms, Granite Stand, 1900s, 28 In.......	8260.00
Sculpture, Cleopatra's Needle, Hieroglyphics, Cast, Brown Patina, Slate Base, Fence, 8 ⅜ In..	483.00
Sculpture, Clesinger, A., Woman, Bitten By Snake, c.1870, 8 ½ x 22 ½ In...................	6040.00
Sculpture, Clodion, Bacchanalia, 2 Women, Dancing, Sheer Dresses, Signed, 1762, 23 In......	1845.00
Sculpture, Clodion, Bacchus With Children, Signed On Base, 15 In...........................	540.00
Sculpture, Collet, Edouard Louis, Nocturne, Female Nude, Both Hands Held Up Behind Head, 40 In..	1440.00
Sculpture, Cosimo De Medici, Seated, Pondering, 16 In.....................................	266.00
Sculpture, Cossack Couple, Horse, Rifle, Sabre, Russia, c.1960, 11 ½ In.....................	2000.00
Sculpture, Cotterill, Tim, Frog, Enameled, On Reed, With Lady Bug, Signed, 6 x 14 In..........	1298.00
Sculpture, Cougar, Walking Stance, Marble Base, Plaque, 15 x 24 In.........................	1476.00
Sculpture, Crane, Standing, Base, Looking Up, Curved Back Neck, 51 ¾ In., Pair..................	837.00
Sculpture, Crossing The Balkans, 3 Men, 4 Horses, Rocks, Oval Green Marble Base, 17 ½ In.	1250.00
Sculpture, Cuevas, Jorge Luis, Nude, Seated, Wood Base, 1977, 14 ½ In....................	8750.00

Bride's Basket, Webb Peachblow, Tricolor, Gold Enameling, 3 Cherubs, Silver Plated Frame, 12 ½ x 10 ½ In. $2,250.00

Woody Auction

Bristol, Basket, Flowers, Butterflies, Enamel, Overlay, Gilt, c.1880, 12 x 7 In. $150.00

DuMouchelles Art Gallery

Bronze, Bust, Muller, H., Woman, Art Nouveau Style, Printemps On Plaque, 9 x 10 In. $450.00

DuMouchelles Art Gallery

Bronze, Cannon, Signal, Breech Loading, Mahogany Carriage, Wheels, Strong Firearms Co., 10 ½ In. $3,450.00

James D. Julia Auctioneers

Bronze, Censer, Incised Figures, Rustic Landscape, Foo Dog Mask Handles, Marked, Chinese, 3 x 5 In.
$325.00

Skinner, Inc.

Bronze, Flower Holder, Jewett, Maude Sherwood, Bacchante, Man, Woman, 1924, 10 In.
$3,900.00

Skinner, Inc.

Bronze, Mirror Plateau, Rocky Border, Mahogany Base, Turned Wooden Feet, c.1900, 2 ½ x 15 In.
$354.00

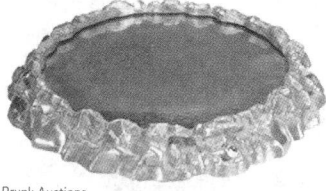

Brunk Auctions

Bronze, Pitcher, Art Nouveau, Bacchus Mask Under Spout, Mermaids, Merman, Fish, Relief, c.1910, 8 In.
$1,107.00

Skinner, Inc.

Sculpture, Cupid, Seated, Pedestal, Holding Gilt Bow, Rectangular, Marble Base, c.1910, 17 ¾ In. | 1750.00
Sculpture, Dancer, Castanets, Stepped Marble Base, 27 x 21 In. | 2250.00
Sculpture, Dancer, Standing, Arms Out, Flowing Skirt, Round Marble Base, Art Deco, Signed, 11 In. | 2875.00
Sculpture, Dancers, Pas De Deux, On Point, Cast, Polished, Black Granite Base, American, 37 In. | 316.00
Sculpture, David, Fernand, Woman, Nude, Stretching Arms Upwards, Standing On Toes, 30 x 32 In. | 2185.00
Sculpture, De Bologne, Giovanni, Mercury, North Wind Allegory, Brown Patina, Marble Base, 35 In. | 661.00
Sculpture, De Portugal, A.C., La Caceria, The Hunt, Horse, Rider, Prey, A.C., Spain, c.1980, 17 x 18 In. | 1416.00
Sculpture, Deity, Seated, Taoist Divinity, Dragon, Parcel Gilt, Chinese, 1900s, 11 In. | 922.00
Sculpture, Delabrierre, E., Dog, English Setter, Partridge, Gilt, France, Signed, 8 ½ x 13 ½ In. | 522.00
Sculpture, Delabrierre, Paul-Edouard, Dog, Setter, On Point, Patina, 7 ⅜ x 11 In. ....*Illus* | 2360.00
Sculpture, Deluca, Fernando, Woman, Seated, Painted, c.1915, 29 ½ In. | 678.00
Sculpture, Der Sklavin Los, Nude Slave Girl, Being Auctioned, Man, Seated, Germany, c.1900, 9 In. | 671.00
Sculpture, Diety, Longevity God, Staff, Scroll, Brown Patina, Japan, 10 In. | 201.00
Sculpture, Discus Thrower, Applied Verdigris Finish, Gilt Finish On Loin Cloth, 20 x 10 In. | 299.00
Sculpture, Dog, Doberman Pinscher, Standing, Ears Up, Rectangular Base, 36 x 40 In. | 1344.00
Sculpture, Dog, Mastiff, Reclining, Mottled Black Marble Base, c.1900, 4 ½ x 10 ¼ In., Pair. | 1845.00
Sculpture, Dog, Pug, Seated, Leash, In Mouth, Wearing Collar, Head Turned To Side, c.1915, 4 x 3 In. | 153.00
Sculpture, Dog, Terrier, Pawing At Crab, Rounded Rectangular Marble Base, Signed, 7 ½ x 3 ½ In. | 577.00
Sculpture, Dolphins, Leaping From Water, Round Black Marble Plinth, 23 ½ In. | 316.00
Sculpture, Dondeur, F. Barbedienne, Diana, Nude, Bow In Hand, Inscribed, 32 In. | 1875.00
Sculpture, Driscoll, S. Wiggins, Indian, Deer Hat, Crouching, Mahogany Base, Signed, c.1960, 17 In. | 210.00
Sculpture, Driscoll, S. Wiggins, Indian, Paddling Canoe, Base, Signed, c.1970, 6 ½ x 24 In. | 590.00
Sculpture, Drouot, E., Girl With Goat, Signed, c.1900, 24 In. | 1785.00
Sculpture, Drouot, E., The Eagle Attacks, Man, Birds, Hand On Nest, c.1900, 33 ¾ In. | 3125.00
Sculpture, Eagle Attacking Hare, Inscribed Signature, Black Marble Stand, 5 ¾ x 6 In. | 1170.00
Sculpture, Eagle, In Flight, Cold Painted, Japan, 29 x 28 ½ In. | 1188.00
Sculpture, Eagle, Taking Dove On Rocky Outcrop, c.1900, 50 x 38 In. | 2460.00
Sculpture, Eagle, Wings Spread, Cold Paint, Austria, 8 In. | 413.00
Sculpture, Elephant, Walking, Raised Trunk, Ivory Tusks, Wood Base, Japan, c.1900, 13 x 19 In. | 482.00
Sculpture, Embossed Women Holding Hands, Gilt Snakes, c.1930, 17 In., Pair. | 1625.00
Sculpture, Equestrian Napoleon, Cast, Rearing Horse, Brown Patina, Amber Marble Base, 12 x 10 In. | 1277.00
Sculpture, Erte, Evening In 1921, Woman, Art Deco Attire, Gilt, Painted, Verdigris, c.1980, 16 In. | 1725.00
Sculpture, Erte, Tanagra, Impressed 7 Arts Ltd., c.1988, 20 ½ In. | 2645.00
Sculpture, Face & Hand Smoking Cigar, Cement Base, 18 In. | 230.00
Sculpture, Falguiere, A., Man, Nude, Holding Rooster, Base, Signed, c.1890, 34 In. | 2600.00
Sculpture, Faun, Dancing, Signed Fond A. Sommey, Naples, Italy, 27 ½ x 8 ¼ In. | 1989.00
Sculpture, Fish, Caught, Lure In Mouth, Waves, Persistent Devil, Wood Base, 1976, 15 In. | 750.00
Sculpture, Flora, Standing, Holding Basket Of Fruit On Head, France, 1800s, 24 In. | 2300.00
Sculpture, Franeschi, G., Hebe, Jupiter, As An Eagle, Domed Foot, 26 In. | 5000.00
Sculpture, Frazier, Elk, Bugling, Rocky Base, 15 x 16 In. | 472.00
Sculpture, Fredericks, Marshall, The Thinker, Chimpanzee, 13 In. | 26400.00
Sculpture, Fremiet, E., 2 Hounds, Tethered, Round Red Marble Base, c.1900 | 2360.00
Sculpture, Fremiet, E., Dog, Whippet, Mottled Base, Signed, 9 ½ x 12 In. | 236.00
Sculpture, Fremiet, E., Sister Of Charity, Brown Patina, c.1900, 8 ¾ x 3 ½ In. | 874.00
Sculpture, Freres, Raingo, Le Messager, Woman, Classical Attire, Bird On Hand, France, c.1890, 27 In. | 4688.00
Sculpture, Frishmuth, Harriet Whitney, The Star, Nude Woman, Marble Base, 1918, 19 In. .. *Illus* | 45000.00
Sculpture, Gallo, Ignacio, Nude Woman, Dog, Art Deco, Patina, White Metal Base, 11 x 7 In. | 150.00
Sculpture, Gaudez, A. & Belleuse, A. Carrier, La Melodie, Woman, Lyre, Marble Base, France, 34 ¼ In. | 5520.00
Sculpture, Germain, J.B., Nymph, Standing, Instrument, Stepped Base, France, c.1900, 38 In. | 2337.00
Sculpture, Gerome, J.L., Napoleon, Hat Raised, On Horse, J.L., c.1945, 36 ¾ x 34 ¾ In. | 4063.00
Sculpture, Group, Lion, Tiger, Fighting, Japan, c.1900, 4 ½ x 12 ¾ In. | 660.00
Sculpture, Group, Neoclassical, 2 Wrestlers, Shaped Naturalistic Base, 29 ½ In. | 3750.00
Sculpture, Group, Neoclassical, Pankration Wrestlers, Naturalistic Shaped Base, 15 In. | 1524.00
Sculpture, Grouse, Cold Painted, Vienna, 2 ½ x 5 In. | 322.00
Sculpture, Guandi, Military Armor, Long Robe, Dragons, Head Scarf, Stroking His Beard, 1700s, 9 In. | 1896.00
Sculpture, Guanyin, Reclining Against Box, Fret Design, Robes, Topknot, 9 ¾ In. | 5036.00
Sculpture, Guanyin, Seated, Double Lotus Throne, Crown, Necklaces, Chinese, 10 In. | 711.00
Sculpture, Guanyin, Standing, Base, Robe, Bead Necklace, Holding Scroll, c.1900, 31 In. | 8664.00
Sculpture, Guanyin, Thousand Arm, 11 Heads, 5 Levels, On Lotus Throne, Holding Items, 42 In. | 3555.00
Sculpture, Hagenauer, Greyhound, Nickel-Plated, Marked, 1930s, 6 x 20 In. | 2125.00
Sculpture, Hagenauer, Javelin Thrower, Nickel-Plated, Stamped, c.1930, 9 x 11 x 3 In. | 1375.00
Sculpture, Hagenauer, Karl, Hunter, On Horse, 2 Hounds, Austria, Signed, c.1930, 8 ¼ x 13 In. | 2844.00
Sculpture, Hagenauer, Tennis Player, Nickel Plated, 1930s, 11 ¾ x 9 In. | 1250.00
Sculpture, Harlequin, Standing, Arms Crossed, Square Footed Base, c.1890, 34 In. | 2400.00
Sculpture, Hebe, Atop Jupiter's Eagle, Holding Bow & Arrow, Rock Base, Silvered, 18 In. | 800.00
Sculpture, Holland, T., Polo Players, 2 Horse Mounted Men, Oval Base, Inscribed, 1960, 20 In. | 270.00

B

Sculpture, Hopkins, Mark, Mountain Lion, Head, Paw, Branch, Signed, 1992, 13 ¾ x 11 In. ..	236.00
Sculpture, Horse, Bridled, Standing, Rectangular Naturalistic Base, c.1835, 24 ½ In.	3000.00
Sculpture, Horse, Marley, On Hind Legs, Flowing Mane, Leafy Ground, 1800s, 15 ½ x 14 In., Pair....	840.00
Sculpture, Horse, Rearing, Green Base, c.1900, 13 ½ In..................................	1000.00
Sculpture, Horse, Running, Jockey, Wire, Oval Horse Scene Carved Base, 19 ¼ x 22 In.	2375.00
Sculpture, Horse, Trotting, Silvered, Marble Base, France, c.1910, 19 In..................	646.00
Sculpture, Houdon, Jean-Antoine, Bust, Diana, ¾ Profile, 27 In........................	1375.00
Sculpture, Hunting Party, Hounds, Horses, Octagonal Base, 1900s, 10 ⅜ x 15 ¾ In................	2390.00
Sculpture, Huntington, Anna Vaughn Hyatt, Yawning Tiger, Out Stretched, Signed, 13 ¼ x 4 In..	1725.00
Sculpture, Ihlenfeld, Klaus, Ancient Gateway Design, Shaped Base, Rays Design, 10 ½ x 8 ½ In..	1000.00
Sculpture, Imperial Guard, Standing, Armored Robes, Holding Staff, Octagonal Base, Chinese, 65 In.	570.00
Sculpture, Indian Chief, Standing, Full Dress, Patinated, Incised, 30 x 11 In.	518.00
Sculpture, Kaesbach, R., Athlete, Bending, Stone Plinth, c.1910, 12 ½ In.........................	403.00
Sculpture, Kauba, Carl, Dancer, Woman, Stepped Round Marble Base, Signed, c.1900, 12 In.	3294.00
Sculpture, Kauba, Carl, Indian Chief, Amerika, Headdress, Shield, Paint, Austria, c.1900, 20 In. .	7080.00
Sculpture, Kauba, Carl, Indian With Canoe, Multicolor, Gazing Into Distance, 8 x 9 ½ In......	1323.00
Sculpture, Kauba, Carl, Indian, Seated, Blanket Wrapped, Marble Plinth, Signed, 5 ½ x 4 In.	115.00
Sculpture, Kelety, A., Dancer, Holding Cloth, Arms Up, Marble Base, Art Deco, c.1930, 13 In...	1375.00
Sculpture, Knight, Medieval, Credo Banner, F. Barbedienne Fondeur, Red Marble Base, 16 In. .	875.00
Sculpture, Knight, Standing, Holding Sword Before Him, Octagonal Base, Austria, c.1900, 29 In.	1000.00
Sculpture, L. Moreau, Alerta, Inscribed, c.1880, 29 In.	2640.00
Sculpture, La Source Du Pactole, Laborer, Seated, Hammer, Coins, c.1900, 23 ¾ In...............	1750.00
Sculpture, L'Acquaiola, Boy, Leaning Forward, Holding Jug, Ball, 1881, 21 In........................	2790.00
Sculpture, Lady Godiva, On Horseback, Sidesaddle, Marble Base, 21 ½ x 18 ½ In....................	1016.00
Sculpture, Laurent, E., La Fileuse, Standing Girl, Folded Hands, Bent Knee, France, 1800s, 27 x 26 In.	1968.00
Sculpture, L'Aveau-Salon Des Breaux Arts, Embracing Couple, Base, c.1900, 27 ½ In.............	4674.00
Sculpture, Lebroc, Jean Baptiste, Putto, Playing Bagpipes, Marble Pedestal, Signed, 12 ½ In...*Illus*	885.00
Sculpture, Leducq, M., Seagull, Patinated, c.1955, 11 ½ x 31 ½ In................................	750.00
Sculpture, Lerrat, Devil, Winged, Marble Base, France, 4 ½ x 6 In...................	165.00
Sculpture, Lion, Reclining, Sideward Glancing, Cold Painted, Marble Base, Austria, 1900s, 4 x 8 In.	354.00
Sculpture, Lion, Renaissance Style, Rampant Pose, Both Paws Up, c.1980, 8 ¾ In.	184.00
Sculpture, Lion, Snarling, Attacking Snake, Marble Round Base, 9 x 11 In....................	360.00
Sculpture, Lioness, Stalking, Green Patina, Rocky Marble Stand, 9 ¾ x 15 In................	702.00
Sculpture, Lizard, Cold Painted, Initialed, Austria, 8 ½ In.	1265.00
Sculpture, Lorenzl, J., Woman, Apron, Standing, Hands On Hips, Signed, Austria, c.1920, 14 In.	1534.00
Sculpture, Lorenzl, J., Woman, Leg Lifted, Short Green Skirt, Ivory, Carved, Austria, c.1930, 12 ½ In.	2252.00
Sculpture, Ludwig, Eduard, Eagle, Spread Wing, On Flag, Wreath, Signed, c.1880, 26 x 38 In..	17775.00
Sculpture, Madonna, Child, Seated, Gilt, Wood Plinth, France, c.1870, 10 In.................	360.00
Sculpture, Manjusri, Seated, Royal Ease Pose, Atop Lion, Hand In Karana Mudra, Chinese, 13 In....	5333.00
Sculpture, Mansion, Asclepius, Hygeia, Man, Woman, Cow, Snake, Signed, France, c.1800, 15 In..	1875.00
Sculpture, Manzel, Ludwig, Allegory Of Sea, Tiffany & Co., Germany, 21 ½ x 24 ½ In.....*Illus*	1298.00
Sculpture, Marioton, Eugene, Hercules, Dark Patina, France, c.1920, 29 ½ In..................	2450.00
Sculpture, Marquel, A., Girl, Nude, Looking At Rose On Base, Dore, Signed, 27 x 9 In.	1320.00
Sculpture, McVey, Seated Lion, Stylized, Verdigris, Black Marble Base, Signed, 10 x 3 ¼ In.	546.00
Sculpture, McVey, William Mozart, McDog, Sculpture, Brown Patina, Black Marble Base, 10 x 6 ½ In.	604.00
Sculpture, McVey, William Mozart, Seated Lion, Brown Finish, Black Marble Base, 10 x 3 In.	690.00
Sculpture, Mene, P.J., 3 Goats, Standing, Reclining, Triangle Color, Oval Base, Signed, 4 ½ x 8 ½ In.	799.00
Sculpture, Mene, P.J., Dog, French Setter, Fabio, Oval Base, Signed, France, 6 x 5 In............	1168.00
Sculpture, Mene, P.J., Highlander, Fox, Hound, France, c.1850, 19 ½ In................	2844.00
Sculpture, Mene, P.J., Horse, Standing, c.1850, 7 ½ In..........................	615.00
Sculpture, Mene, P.J., Rabbit Chase, France, c.1850, 7 ½ x 14 In.	948.00
Sculpture, Merciere, A., David, Standing On Goliath's Head, Signed, 73 In............................	1230.00
Sculpture, Mercury, Atlanta, Standing On One Foot, Arm Up, Marble Base, c.1900, 21 In., Pair..	922.00
Sculpture, Mercury, Wing Footed God, Balancing On Zephyr Head, Marble Base, Italy, 1800s, 20 ¾ In.	1168.00
Sculpture, Mermaid, Nude Woman, Emerging From Water, Signed Ikart, 18 ¼ In.	382.00
Sculpture, Moigniez, Jules, Cattle Grazing, Red Marble Plinth, 11 x 18 In..............	1652.00
Sculpture, Monkey Group, Fruit Branch, Silvered, Japan, 16 ⅝ In.	2057.00
Sculpture, Monkey, Seated, Folded Arms, Crossed Legs, Round Marble Base, 14 In.	600.00
Sculpture, Monkey, Seated, Holding Crab, Japan, 1800s, 28 x 11 In.	4600.00
Sculpture, Montagne, Pierre, Marius, Hermes, Patina, Signed, 1800s, 33 In...................*Illus*	8850.00
Sculpture, Moor Warrior, Astride Camel, Holding Staff, c.1900, 8 ¾ In.	1045.00
Sculpture, Moreau, Classical Woman, Seated, Dore, Wood Lamp Base, Impressed, 16 In.	327.00
Sculpture, Moreau, Louis Auguste, Girl In A Swing, Cast, Brown & Verdigris Patina, Signed, 10 x 5 In.	242.00
Sculpture, Morin, Georges, Woman, Hoop Dancer, Classical Dress, Cold Paint, Ivory, c.1925, 10 In..	1875.00
Sculpture, Morion, A., Woman, Seated, Nuzzling Deer, Stepped Marble Base, c.1930, 12 x 24 In..	1375.00
Sculpture, Mother & Child, Flowing Dress, Walking, Round Stepped Base, France, 20 ¼ In....	1750.00

TIP

Old furs oxidize and change color. Dark furs darken, light furs turn yellow, brown furs often turn reddish brown.

Bronze, Sculpture, Alligator, Head Turned, Jaws Open, 25 x 71 In.
$7,170.00

Neal Auction Co.

Bronze, Sculpture, Alonzo, D., Medieval Woman, Staircase, Ivory, Marble Base, Signed, 11 ⅝ In.
$2,160.00

Skinner, Inc.

Bronze, Sculpture, Bergman, Franz, Woman, Attendant, Hinged Arm Reveals Nude, Namgreb, 11 In.
$2,300.00

James D. Julia Auctioneers

Bronze, Sculpture, Buddha, 4 Faces, 8 Arms, Seated, Lotus Throne, 18th Century, 11 ⅜ In.
$12,000.00

Skinner, Inc.

Bronze, Sculpture, Chimpanzee, Seated, 12 x 11 In.
$390.00

DuMouchelles Art Gallery

Bronze, Sculpture, Delabrierre, Paul-Edouard, Dog, Setter, On Point, Patina, 7 ⅜ x 11 In.
$2,360.00

Brunk Auctions

TIP

When ordering antiques by mail, do not send cash; send a check or charge them. Keep a copy of your order.

Sculpture,	Murmann, Jozsef A., Hope, Nude, Woman, Seated, Patinated, c.1920, 16 ½ x 16 ¼ In.	1125.00
Sculpture,	Napoleon, Military Attire, On Rearing Horse, Rectangular Base, c.1890, 25 x 21 In.	3125.00
Sculpture,	Nenikhkamen, Male, Nude, Messenger, Arm Raised, Red Marble Base, 24 x 18 In.	1000.00
Sculpture,	Nevelson, Louise, Block Figure, Running, Black Enamel Base, 15 ¾ x 16 In.	3750.00
Sculpture,	Nobleman, Standing, 1700s Attire, Misanthrope Scroll, France, 15 In.	1000.00
Sculpture,	Nude, Wearing Sash, Leaning On Tree Stump, Square Base, Stamped, 27 ½ In.	1875.00
Sculpture,	Owl, Spread Wings, Landing On Branch, Round Marble Base, France, c.1850, 34 ½ In.	2006.00
Sculpture,	Paillet, C.H., Dog, Marked, c.1920, 12 ½ x 5 ¾ In.	1610.00
Sculpture,	Panther & Snake, Salan Des Beaux Art, 8 ½ x 15 ½ In.	115.00
Sculpture,	Panther, Open Mouth, Stalking Position, Asian, 25 ¼ x 10 In.	726.00
Sculpture,	Pealle, R., Boy, Puppies, Duck, Signed, 28 x 20 In.	179.00
Sculpture,	Pheasant, Perched On Rocks, Lizard, Round Stepped Base, c.1855, 27 In.	1528.00
Sculpture,	Pheasants, Gilt, Crested, Poised To Walk, Feathers Ruffled, c.1910, 9 ¾ x 3 In., Pair	799.00
Sculpture,	Philippe, P., Harem Dancer, Radha, Red Marble Plinth, c.1935, 22 ¾ In.	5463.00
Sculpture,	Picault, Emile-Louis, Perseus, Pegasus, Copper Finish, Base, c.1888, 21 x 18 In.	311.00
Sculpture,	Pilet, Leon, Hager & Ishmael, Gilt Patina, Marked, 16 ½ In.	960.00
Sculpture,	Polk, F., One Armed Bandit, Standing Man, Cowboy Hat, Signed, c.1978, 16 In.	1120.00
Sculpture,	Porcupine, Brown Patina, Cold Paint, Multicolor Quills, Austria, c.1910, 6 In. *Illus*	1680.00
Sculpture,	Prisoner, Nude Man, Chained To Rock, Black Marble Base, c.1900, 23 In.	700.00
Sculpture,	Psyche, Holding Oil Lamp, Dagger At Feet, Stepped Round Base, 14 ⅝ In.	1000.00
Sculpture,	Puppy, Rotund, Seated On Haunches, Floppy Ears, Signed, Chinese, 1900s, 7 In.	338.00
Sculpture,	Putnam, Arthur, Crouching Panther, Cast, Brown Patina, Signed, c.1911, 12 ½ x 8 In.	5463.00
Sculpture,	Rabbit, Teaching Music, 4 Bunnies, Cold Paint, Cabinet, Austria, c.1900, 2 ½ In.	660.00
Sculpture,	Ram's Head, Cast, Continental, c.1900, 6 In. *Illus*	1121.00
Sculpture,	Reusch, Friedrich J., Steel Worker, Man, Holding Tools, Brown Patina, c.1900, 26 ½ In.	510.00
Sculpture,	Reveil, Female Nude, Standing, 1 Hand To Hear, Other Arm Outstretched, 18 x 5 In.	390.00
Sculpture,	Richele, R., Diana, Standing, Nude, Waving Arms, Rocky Base, Signed, 1900s, 31 In.	575.00
Sculpture,	Roberts, Gilroy, Eagle, Spread Wings, Black Plinth, c.1975, 20 In.	300.00
Sculpture,	Roncourt, J., Man, Throwing Spear, Marble Base, 1900s, 22 x 32 In.	2875.00
Sculpture,	Saint Holding 2 Children, C.J. Barnhorn, Roman Bronze Works, 1898, 12 In.	1763.00
Sculpture,	Sakyamuni, Child, Apron, Double Lotus, Hands Pointing To Sky & Earth, c.1900, 12 In.	948.00
Sculpture,	Salmones, Victor, Male Nude Dancer, Stretching, 11 x 12 In.	480.00
Sculpture,	Salome, Standing, Flowing Robes, Holding Sword, France, 33 In.	2100.00
Sculpture,	Sappho, Seat, On Stool, Holding Leg, Marble Base, Susse Frees, 16 In.	938.00
Sculpture,	Sauvage, R., Venus De Milo, Patinated, Signed, France, 34 ¾ In.	1320.00
Sculpture,	Schmiemann, A., Blacksmith, Black Marble Base, Signed, 24 ¾ In. *Illus*	1652.00
Sculpture,	Scholtz, H.K., Girl, Deer, 1919, 16 ¾ In.	1944.00
Sculpture,	Seidel, E.P., Dancer, Flapper, c.1925, 14 In.	885.00
Sculpture,	Shrady, Henry Merwin, Horse Head, Marble Base, Signed, c.1900, 16 In. *Illus*	3995.00
Sculpture,	Soldier, Spanish, On Horseback, Black Marble Base, c.1905, 17 ½ x 8 In.	396.00
Sculpture,	St. Francis, Standing, Wearing Robes, Wolf & Sheep, Round Base, Signed, 1900s, 13 ½ In.	705.00
Sculpture,	Steiner, Leopold C., Girl, Washbasin, c.1880, 9 In.	325.00
Sculpture,	Stekol, Bird, Wings Folded Inward, Wood Base, 1958, 12 In.	51.00
Sculpture,	Swanson, G., Falcon, Perched On Rocks, Painted, Wood Base, Signed, 18 ½ In.	900.00
Sculpture,	Tereszcuk, Paul, Woman, Combing Hair, Cast, Patina, Ivory Face, Chest, Round Base, 7 In.	374.00
Sculpture,	Tereszcuk, Paul, Woman, Ermine Cape, Cast, Patina, Ivory Head, Base, 8 In.	316.00
Sculpture,	Terrier Grouping, Stamped Cartier, c.1920, 15 ½ In.	570.00
Sculpture,	Tiger, Growling, Prancing, Etched Stripes, Wood Base, Japan, c.1900, 9 x 20 In.	904.00
Sculpture,	Toulgouat, P., 2 Rugby Players, Falling, Ball, Nickeled, France, c.1970, 8 x 14 In.	3555.00
Sculpture,	Tovar, Soto, 2 Lovers, 1963, 12 x 8 In.	329.00
Sculpture,	Turtle, Dragon Head, Atop Pile Of Coins, Chinese, 15 x 10 In.	600.00
Sculpture,	Vacossin, G., Dog, Setter, Leg Raised, Sniffing, Oval Base, France, Signed, 5 x 8 ¼ In.	430.00
Sculpture,	Valenta, J., 2 Crouched Players, Running, Marked, Austria, c.1920, 8 ½ x 8 In.	413.00
Sculpture,	Vendome Column, Napoleon On Top, White Marble Base, 10 ⅞ x 3 ½ In.	1112.00
Sculpture,	Volk, L.W., Abraham Lincoln, Impressed, c.1880, 21 x 11 ½ In.	1404.00
Sculpture,	Wagon, Cattle Drawn, Rider Trying To Free Wagon From Mud, c.1900, 41 ½ In.	490.00
Sculpture,	Walker, W.A., 4 Aces, Man, Top Hat, Playing Cards In Hand, Signed, 32 In.	1180.00
Sculpture,	Waltzing Couple, Woman Leaning Back, Round Base, Gold Finish, Signed, c.1900, 17 In.	353.00
Sculpture,	Wegner, Paul, Morning Glory, Nude Woman, Holding Vine, Flower, Painted, 1986, 19 ¼ In.	708.00
Sculpture,	Wernekinck, Sigismund, Parakeet, Cast, Painted, Marble Base, Signed, c.1900, 12 In.	863.00
Sculpture,	Woman, Classical Nude, Running, Holding Ribbon, Round Embossed Base, c.1960, 24 In.	367.00
Sculpture,	Woman, Classically Dressed, Hand To Chin, Rock Base, Barbedienne, c.1890, 10 In.	295.00
Sculpture,	Woman, Nude, Standing On Tiptoes, Stretching, Base, c.1925, 16 In.	1800.00
Sculpture,	Woman, Nude, Standing, Arm Raised Overhead, Closed Eyes, Square Base, 1925, 38 ½ In.	5334.00
Sculpture,	Woman, Nude, Standing, Arms Up, Long Hair, Round Base, 37 In.	1560.00
Sculpture,	Woman, Standing With Mandolin, Ivory Head, Marble Base, Austria, c.1900	863.00

Sculpture, Women, Nude, Holding Grapes, Arms Crossed, Standing, Onyx Bowl, France, 14 ½ In..	953.00
Sculpture, Young Mozart, Tuning Violin, Standing On Scroll Of Sheet Music, c.1800s, 21 In..	1600.00
Spoon, Jade Insert, Animal Head Shape, Chinese, 13 In.	119.00
Table, Side, Seandel, Sila, Textured, Block Shaped, 1980s, 23 x 13 In.	1625.00
Tazza, Gilt Bowl, Handles, Green Marble Base, France, c.1790, 12 x 8 ½ In., Pair	3000.00
Tazza, Gilt, Vine & Fruit Around Stem, Ormolu, Applied Serpent Double Handles, 4 ⅜ x 6 In..	311.00
Teapot, Gilt Finial, Embossed Leaf, Flower Panels, Japan, c.1900, 4 ¼ In.	365.00
Tray, Hurley, E.T., Round, Fat Spider, Sitting In Web, Bugs, E.T., 3 ¾ In. Diam.	546.00
Tray, Perrin, Art Nouveau, Flowering Branch, Handle, Patina, Incised, c.1910, 16 ¾ In...*Illus*	1200.00
Umbrella Stand, Whippet Shaped, Seated, Quirt In Mouth, 29 ½ x 10 In.	922.00
Urn, Baluster, Spire Finial, Handles, Maiden Masks, Scrolls, Flowers, 19 In., Pair	450.00
Urn, Cast, Relief Birds, Flowering Bushes, Applied Foot, 10 ⅜ x 8 ½ In.	83.00
Urn, Chariot, Figural Scenes, Applied Grapes, Cherubs, On Handle, c.1900, 22 In., Pair	266.00
Urn, Louis XIV Style, Bacchanalian Heads, Flowers, Boar's Head Handles, Gilt, c.1890, 19 In., Pair	813.00
Urn, Napoleon III, Marble, Gilt Dolphins Holding Bowl, Scrollwork Handles, c.1865, 6 x 8 In.	738.00
Urn, Neoclassical Style, Figures, Scrolled Handles, 13 ¾ In.	375.00
Urn, Neoclassical Style, Ormolu, Gilt Cherubs, Tambourine, Pan Flute, 11 x 7 ½ In., Pair	253.00
Urn, Roman Revival, Wreath Edge, Nymph Handles, Vine & Berry Column, c.1800, 12 In.	400.00
Urn, Satyr's Mask, Marble, Flowers, Garland, Fluted, Acorn Finial, 1900s, 17 ½ In., Pair	375.00
Urn, Verdigris Patinated, Octagon Top, c.1930, 19 ½ x 20 In.	660.00
Vase, Applied Cherry Blossoms & Birds, Japan, 12 ¼ In., Pair	300.00
Vase, Bacchic Putti, Lion Masks, Fluted Marble Pedestal, 1900s, 17 In.	325.00
Vase, Cloisonne, Eagle, Waves, Flower Basket, Scrolls, Squat, Shaped Handles, Footed, 3 ¾ In.	400.00
Vase, Coiled Dragon, Wavy Background, Japan, 1800s, 12 In.	2775.00
Vase, Coiled Dragon, Wavy Sea, Gilt Highlights, Baluster, Round Foot, Japan, 12 In.	2280.00
Vase, Dragon, Engraved Flowers, Seal Mark, Chinese, c.1910, 13 ¼ In.	345.00
Vase, Dragons, Flaming Pearl Bottle Shape, Flared Lip, Handles At Neck, 11 In., Pair	269.00
Vase, Moreau, Aug., Applied Cupid, Cone Shape, Red Marble Plinth, Inscribed, c.1905, 7 x 7 ¼ In.	420.00
Vase, Nesting Cranes, Cylindrical Foot, Stylized Handles, Bulbous Pear Shape, c.1900, 8 In.	148.00
Vase, Pear Shape, Elongated Foot, Flared Rim, Gold Splashes, 4 Flanges, 6 ⅞ In.	1422.00
Vase, Phoenix, Flying, Clouds, Rolling Waves, Compressed Globular, Flared Rim, 1800s, 6 x 8 ½ In..	504.00
Vase, Stylized Mask Faux Handles, Baluster, Cast, Chinese, 7 x 2 ¾ In.	144.00
Vase, Wood Nymph, Holding Conical Cup, Gilt Leaf Footed, Victorian, 10 ¼ In.	270.00
Wine Bucket, Empire Style, Glass, Diamond Cut, Grapes, Lion's Head Ring Pull, France, 9 x 8 In.	861.00

BROWNIES were first drawn in 1883 by Palmer Cox. They are characterized by large round eyes, downturned mouths, and skinny legs. Toys, books, dinnerware, and other objects were made with the Brownies as part of the design.

Bowling Pin Figure, From 9 Pins Set, Wood, Paper Image, c.1892, 12 ½ In., 5 Piece	348.00
Button, Calendar, January '97, 8 Figures, Snow Accented Fence, W&H Backpaper, 1 ¼ In.	152.00
Figure, Waist Up, Bald Headed, Orange Body, Hands Rested On Stomach, Conte & Bohme, 5 In.	132.00
Ornament, Patriotic Figure, Composition, Strung Arms & Legs, Germany, 3 ½ In. ....*Illus*	413.00
Ring, Brass, Side Brownies, Adjustable, 1930s	150.00
Salt & Pepper, Pillar, Brownies Working, Opalescent, Metal Caps, Mt. Washington ....*Illus*	805.00
Saltshaker, Cylindrical, Ring Neck, 2 Scottish Brownies, Dancing Jig, 4 In.	316.00
Saltshaker, Police Man, Napoli, Translucent, Raised Gilt Honeycomb, Mt. Washington, 3 In..	1380.00
Saltshaker, Postman, Napoli, Translucent, Raised Gilt Honeycomb, Mt. Washington, 3 In.	1035.00
Shaker, Opal, Leaf Embossed Silver Plate Caddy, Oval, 5 ½ In., Pair	863.00
Target Set, Brownie Artillery, Wood, Paper Images, Dovetailed Box, 8 x 12-In. Box, 9 ¾ In., 10 Piece	575.00
Toothpick Holder, 3 Figures, Opal, Mt. Washington, 2 ½ In.	316.00
Uncle Sam, Top Hat, Bow Tie, Stripe Pants, Palmer Cox, R.J. Wright, No. 176/250, 9 In.	435.00
Uniform, 3 Snaps, Belt, Hat, Cotton, Felt, Terri Lee, 1950s	50.00

BRUSH-MCCOY, *see Brush category and related pieces in McCoy category.*

BRUSH POTTERY was started in 1925. George Brush first worked in 1901 in Zanesville, Ohio. He started his own pottery in 1907, but it burned to the ground soon after. In 1909 he became manager of the J.W. McCoy Pottery. In 1911, Brush and J.W. McCoy formed the Brush-McCoy Pottery Co. After a series of name changes, the company became The Brush Pottery in 1925. It closed in 1982. Old Brush was marked with impressed letters or a palette-shaped mark. Reproduction pieces are being made. They are marked in raised letters or with a raised mark. Collectors favor the figural cookie jars made by this company. Because there was a company named Brush-McCoy, there is great confusion between Brush and Nelson McCoy pieces. Most collectors today refer to Brush pottery as Brush-McCoy. See McCoy category for more information.

Cookie Jar, Humpty Dumpty, Beanie, Bowtie, c.1958, 10 In.	295.00
Jardiniere, Majolica, Green, Drip Glaze, 6 ¼ In.	10.00

Bronze, Sculpture, Frishmuth, Harriet Whitney, The Star, Nude Woman, Marble Base, 1918, 19 In.
$45,000.00

DuMouchelles Art Gallery

Bronze, Sculpture, Lebroc, Jean Baptiste, Putto, Playing Bagpipes, Marble Pedestal, Signed, 12 ½ In.
$885.00

Brunk Auctions

Bronze, Sculpture, Manzel, Ludwig, Allegory Of Sea, Tiffany & Co., Germany, 21 ½ x 24 ½ In.
$1,298.00

Brunk Auctions

The edited listings of the current prices in this *Kovels' Antiques & Collectibles Price Guide* aren't available on any website. Readers can visit **Kovels.com** to check thousands of past prices and sign up for free information on trends, tips, reproductions, marks, and more.

Bronze, Sculpture, Montagne, Pierre, Marius, Hermes, Patina, Signed, 1800s, 33 In.
$8,850.00

Brunk Auctions

Bronze, Sculpture, Porcupine, Brown Patina, Cold Paint, Multicolor Quills, Austria, c.1910, 6 In.
$1,680.00

Cowan's Auctions

Bronze, Sculpture, Ram's Head, Cast, Continental, c.1900, 6 In.
$1,121.00

Brunk Auctions

Bronze, Sculpture, Schmiemann, A., Blacksmith, Black Marble Base, Signed, 24 ¾ In.
$1,652.00

Brunk Auctions

Lawn Ornament, Frog, Green, Brush-McCoy, 7 ½ In.	29.00
Lawn Ornament, Frog, Seated, Green, Brush-McCoy, 16 In.	69.00
Lawn Ornament, Turtle, Green, Brush-McCoy, 15 In.	127.00
Navarre, Jardiniere, Green, Cream, Woman & Running Border, 10 ¼ x 8 ¼ In.	104.00
Oil Jar, Black Squiggle Design, Yellow, Handles, Brush-McCoy, 18 In.	69.00
Pedestal, Dark Brown, Green, Ridged Mouth, Brush-McCoy, 12 ¾ In.	23.00
Planter, Figural, Frog, Black, Tan, Brush-McCoy, 5 ¼ In.	35.00
Planter, Figural, Frog, Resting On Side, Green, Black, White, Brush-McCoy, 10 In.	58.00
Planter, Figural, Horse, Cream, Brush-McCoy, 4 In.	81.00
Planter, Frog Shape, Green, Brush-McCoy, 5 ½ In.	12.00
Umbrella Stand, Liberty Bell, Independence Hall, Dark Green, Cylinder, Brush-McCoy, 23 In.	86.00
Umbrella Stand, Yellow Flowers, Black Ground, Brush-McCoy, 17 ¼ In.	150.00
Vase, Bittersweet Double Cornucopia, Brush-McCoy, 11 ¾ In.	6.00

BUCK ROGERS was the first American science fiction comic strip. It started in 1929 and continued until 1967. Buck has also appeared in comic books, movies, and, in the 1980s, a television series. Any memorabilia connected with the character Buck Rogers is collectible.

25th Century Laboratory, Test Tubes, Telescope, Microscope, Box, Porter Chemical Co., 31 x 17 In.	6050.00
Adventure Book, Cutout, Multicolor, Cocomalt Premium, 1933, 9 ¼ x 12 ¼ In.	3163.00
Badge, Chief Explorer, Red Paint, 1936, 1 ½ In.	150.00
Badge, Solar Scouts Member, Brass, 1936, 1 ½ In.	60.00
Badge, Space Ship Commander, Solar Scouts, Silver, Metallic Blue, Cream Of Wheat, 1936, 1 ⅝ In.	173.00
Button, Member, Buck Rogers Club, Helmet, Red, White, Blue, High Gloss, c.1937, 1 In.	345.00
Card, Satellite Pioneers Member, 1957, 3 ¾ x 2 ¼ In.	60.00
Clock, Wall, Action Scene, White Rim, Round, Box, 1990, 10 ½ x 9 In.	90.00
Game, 25th Century A.S., Rocket, Box, 1934, 9 ½ x 13 ½ In.	443.00
Gum Book, The Fight Beneath The Sea, Big Thrill Chewing Gum, 1937, 3 x 2 ½ In.	150.00
Holster, Wilma Rogers, 1935, 9 In.	240.00
Interplanetary Navigation Helmet, Suede, Graphic Box, c.1934, 8 x 5 ½ In.	460.00
Interplanetary Telescope, Metal, Fins, Green Fabric, Red, Yellow, Creamsicle Premium, 1939, 6 ½ In.	1150.00
Jigsaw Puzzle, Buck, In Rocket Ship, 1945, 11 x 8 ½ In.	360.00
Leaflet, Radio Program, Blue, Gray, 1934, 5 ¾ x 5 In.	120.00
Picture, Matt Crowley, CNS Radio Voice, Dixie Ice Cream, 8 x 10 In.	120.00
Pin, Buck Rogers Buffalo Evening News, Cream, Blue, Round, 1930s, 1 ¼ In.	90.00
Pin, Buck Rogers In The 25th Century, Profile, Celluloid, 1935, 1 In.	60.00
Pocket Knife, 2 Blades, Celluloid Grips, Camillus Cutlery Company, 1935, 3 In.	403.00
Ranger Dog Tag, Premium, Aluminum Plate, Impressed Text, Black Accents, c.1935, 1 x 2 In.	1725.00
Ring Of Saturn, Glow-In-Dark, Instructions, Mailer, Premium, Post Corn Toasties, 1946, 3 x 5 In.	895.00
Ring, Glow In Dark Ring Of Saturn, Cereal Radio Premium, Red, White, 1946, 1 In.	240.00
Ring, Repeller Ray, Supreme Inner Circle, Manual, Mailer, Cream Of Wheat, 1936 ...	1150.00 to 2530.00
Rocket Pistol, XZ-31, Blue Steel, Nickel Plated Rocket Nozzle, Deflector, Daisy, 1934, 9 ½ In.	306.00
Space Ranger Kit, Punch-Out, Helmet, Compass, Phones, Badge, Sylvania TV Premium, 1952	127.00
Toy, Rocket Ship, Tin Lithograph, Windup, Marx, 12 In.	600.00
Toy, Rocket, Police Patrol, Buck Riding, Holding Gun, Tin Lithograph, Windup, 1939, 12 In.	479.00
Watch, Space Character, Copper Lightning Bolt Hands, Ingraham, 1935	420.00
Whistle, Commander, 1936, 1 ¾ In.	150.00

BUFFALO POTTERY was made in Buffalo, New York, after 1902. The company was established by the Larkin Company, famous manufacturers of soap. The wares are marked with a picture of a buffalo and the date of manufacture. Deldare ware is the most famous pottery made at the factory. It has either a khaki-colored or green background with hand-painted transfer designs.

BUFFALO POTTERY

Bowl, Cereal, Green Stripes, 5 In.	14.00
Bowl, Girl, Boy, Broken Doll, Stamped, 7 ¾ In.	29.00
Charger, Monks, Fishing, Mustard Color, Blue, Thursday, Marked, 1917, 13 ¼ In.	575.00
Cup & Saucer, Chinese Maiden, Willow, 1911	60.00
Cup & Saucer, Restaurant, Flowers, Blue, Lune Restaurant	18.00
Pitcher, Buffalo Hunt, Indians, Horseback, Buffalo	383.00
Pitcher, Deer Hunter Pattern, Flowers, Dog Chasing Deer, 1907, 6 ½ In.	207.00
Pitcher, George Washington, Blue, White, 8 In.	81.00
Pitcher, Geraniums, Cobalt Blue, 5 ¼ In.	345.00
Pitcher, Roosevelt Bears, Bear Riding Giraffe, Auto Scene, 1907, 8 In.	944.00 to 1995.00
Pitcher, Willow, Cobalt Blue, Gold Trim, 1907, 7 x 7 ½ In.	350.00

Plate, Faneuil Hall, Boston, Green Transfer, Wild Flower Border, 10 ¼ In. *Illus* 11.80
Plate, Niagara Falls, Green, c.1900, 7 ½ In. 55.00
Plate, Restaurant Scene, Blue, 1909, 9 ⅜ In. 95.00
Plate, Restaurant, Flowers, Blue, Lune Restaurant, 10 In., 5 Piece 95.00
Plate, Teddy B & Teddy G, Gold Sponge Rim, Hunting Pose, c.1906, 10 ¼ In. 354.00
Plate, Wild Ducks, Marsh, Clouds, Green, c.1907, 9 In. 50.00
Plate, Woodman Of America, Buffalo, Green, 1911, 7 ½ In. 78.00
Platter, Flowers, Blue, Lune Restaurant, 10 ½ In., Pair 75.00
Platter, Willow, 1908, 14 ⅛ x 11 ⅛ In. 185.00 to 195.00
Platter, Willow, c.1911, 14 x 11 In. 60.00
Sugar, Lid, Flowers, Blue, Lune Restaurant 35.00

BUFFALO POTTERY DELDARE

Bowl, Footed, Fallowfield Hunt, Horse, Resting Dogs, 1909, 9 x 3 In. 395.00
Candlestick, Hexagonal, Figures, Houses, 8 ¾ In. 235.00
Charger, An Evening At Ye Lion Inn, 1908, 13 ¾ In. 250.00
Chop Plate, An Evening At Ye Lion Inn, 1908, 13 ½ In. 350.00
Dresser Box, White Flowers, Green Ground, Round, 1911, 3 x 4 ½ In. 313.00
Pitcher, 8-Sided, Fallowfield Hunt, The Return, 1908, 8 In. 349.00
Pitcher, Dr. Syntax, Bound To Tree, Woman On Horses, Dog, c.1911, 8 x 7 In. 720.00
Pitcher, Octagonal, Vicar Of Wakefield, 1908, 9 In. 399.00
Plate, Advertising, 3 Buildings, Marked M.H., 6 ½ In. 438.00
Plate, Bread & Butter, Ye Lion Inn, Signed, c.1908, 6 ¼ In. 225.00
Plate, Fallowfield Hunt, Breaking Lid, 1909, 7 ½ In. 180.00
Plate, Ye Olden Times, Signed, 1909, 9 ¼ In. 85.00
Plate, Ye Town Crier, 1908, 9 ½ In. 115.00
Sugar & Creamer, Colonial Couple, Stone Walks, 1925 225.00

BUNNYKINS, *see Royal Doulton category.*

BURMESE GLASS was developed by Frederick Shirley at the Mt. Washington Glass Works in New Bedford, Massachusetts, in 1885. It is a two-toned glass, shading from peach to yellow. Some pieces have a pattern mold design. A few Burmese pieces were decorated with pictures or applied glass flowers of colored Burmese glass. Other factories made similar glass also called Burmese. Related items may be listed in the Fenton category and under Webb Burmese.

Biscuit Jar, Salmon Pink To Yellow, Enamel, Flowers, Butterflies, Silver Plate Lid, Bail Handle, 8 In. 460.00
Bowl, Peach To Yellow, Optic Ribbing, Bulbous, Wavy Rim, Rigaree Collar, Bow Tie, 4 In. 1035.00
Bride's Bowl, Melon Ribbed, Dolphin, Gundersen, Meriden Silver Plated Frame, 9 ¾ x 8 ¾ In. *Illus* 3500.00
Creamer, Peach To Yellow, Tapered, Loop Handle, Crimped Rim, Ring Foot, 6 In. 173.00
Creamer, Satin Finish, Applied Amber Handle, 5 ½ In. 225.00
Cruet, Melon Ribbed, Teardrop Stopper, Mt. Washington, 7 In. *Illus* 259.00
Ewer, Queen's Lace, Rosettes, Flowers, Scrolling, Gold Handle, Mt. Washington, 12 In. *Illus* 4600.00
Jar, Temple, Lid, Tiny White Flowers, Green Leaves, c.1885 1872.00
Potpourri, Peach To Yellow, Enameled Blossoms & Leaves, Gold Mottled Lid, Slot Insert, 5 In. 920.00
Shade, Peach, Yellow, Bulbous, 5 Point Crimped Rim, 2 ¼ In. 58.00
Syrup, Daisy, Gold Tracery, Applied Handle, 6 ¼ In. 2760.00
Toothpick Holder, Cylindrical, Optic Diamond, Yellow To Peach, Raspberries, Leaves, 3 In. 403.00
Toothpick Holder, Diamond-Quilted, Peach To Yellow, Square Rim, 2 ¾ In. 144.00
Toothpick Holder, Optic Diamond, Blue Stippling, Leaves, Mt. Washington, 3 In. *Illus* 431.00
Toothpick Holder, Optic Diamond, Rigaree Collar, Glossy, Ruffled Rim, 2 ½ In. 575.00
Toothpick Holder, Peach To Yellow, Diamond-Quilted, Rigaree Collar, Ruffled Rim, 3 In. 748.00
Vase, 2 Owls, Perched On Pine Branch, Trifold Ruffled Rim, Round Bottom, Yellow To Pink, 3 In. 719.00
Vase, Applied Poppies, Ribbed, Folded Tricorner Rim, Mt. Washington, 5 x 5 In. 1638.00
Vase, Bud, Peach To Yellow, Cylindrical, Spreading Crimped Rim, Round Pedestal Foot, 6 In. 115.00
Vase, Ducks, Gilt Sun, Flask Shape, Yellow To Pink, Mt. Washington, Frank Guba, 11 In. *Illus* 4485.00
Vase, Fish In Net, Enamel, Applied Gold Netting, Mottled Neck, Mt. Washington, 9 ¾ In. *Illus* 2243.00
Vase, Gourd, Stylized Gilt Medallions, Trifold Rim, Mt. Washington, 12 In. 6038.00
Vase, Jack-In-The-Pulpit, Peach To Yellow, Crimped Rim, Round Foot, 13 ½ In. 345.00
Vase, Leaves, Trailing Stem, Berries, Bulbous, Stick Neck, Blue Stippling, Yellow To Peach, 10 In. 460.00
Vase, Monkey, Enamel, Bamboo Shoots, Gold, Scalloped Rim, Mt. Washington, 13 ¼ In. *Illus* 28750.00
Vase, Peach To Yellow, Cone Shape, Folded Rim, Round Pedestal Foot, 4 In. 173.00
Vase, Peach To Yellow, Elongated Oval, Handles At Neck, Rolled Rim, Ruffled Base, 10 ½ In. 230.00
Vase, Peach To Yellow, Enameled Branches, Gold Accents, Bulbous, Stick Neck, 12 In. 920.00
Vase, Peach, Pouch Shape, Footed, Flowers, Leaves, Drip Collar, Rectangular Mouth, 8 In. 13800.00
Vase, Pink To Yellow, Egg Shape, Ring Foot, 4-Point Inverted Rim, 6 ½ In. 173.00

B

Bronze, Sculpture, Shrady, Henry Merwin, Horse Head, Marble Base, Signed, c.1900, 16 In.
$3,995.00

Garth's Auctioneers & Appraisers

Bronze, Tray, Perrin, Art Nouveau, Flowering Branch, Handle, Patina, Incised, c.1910, 16 ¾ In.
$1,200.00

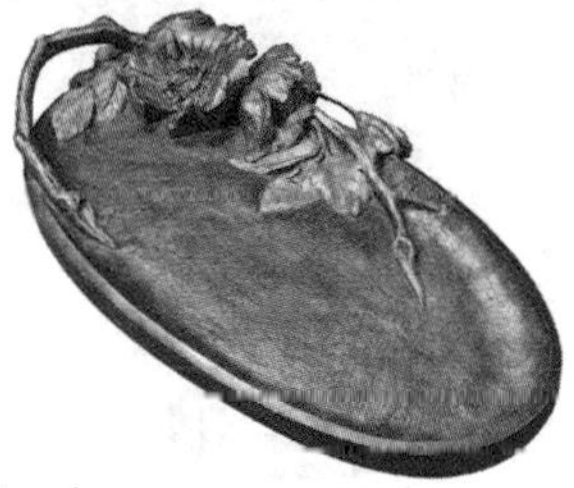

Skinner, Inc.

Brownies, Ornament, Patriotic Figure, Composition, Strung Arms & Legs, Germany, 3 ½ In.
$413.00

Bertoia Auctions

Brownies, Salt & Pepper, Pillar, Brownies Working, Opalescent, Metal Caps, Mt. Washington
$805.00

Early Auction Co.

Buffalo Pottery, Plate, Faneuil Hall, Boston, Green Transfer, Wild Flower Border, 10 ¼ In.
$11.80

Conestoga Auction Co., Inc.

Burmese, Bride's Bowl, Melon Ribbed, Dolphin, Gundersen, Meriden Silver Plated Frame, 9 ¾ x 8 ¾ In.
$3,500.00

Woody Auction

Burmese, Cruet, Melon Ribbed, Teardrop Stopper, Mt. Washington, 7 In.
$259.00

Early Auction Co.

Save the Label
Save all labels and written information found on antiques to help determine the history of the object. Do not remove labels. To copy a bottle label, you can try rolling the bottle on a scanner bed at the scan speed. It is easier than it sounds. Put a wide rubber band on the bottle if it has embossed lettering. It helps make a smoother roll.

BUSTER BROWN, the comic strip, first appeared in color in 1902. Buster and his dog, Tige, remained a popular comic and soon became even more famous as the emblem for a shoe company, a textile firm, and other companies. The strip was discontinued in 1920. Buster Brown sponsored a radio show from 1943 to 1955 and a TV show from 1950 to 1956. The Buster Brown characters are still used by Brown Shoe Company, Buster Brown Apparel, Inc., and Gateway Hosiery.

Bank, Tige, Horse, Horseshoe, Cast Iron, Arcade Toy Co., c.1920, 4 x 4 In.	249.00
Bell Ringer, Buster Brown, Tige, Lamp Pole, String, Tin, Paint, Windup, Germany, c.1900, 8 In.	1955.00
Bench, Brown's Shoes, Oak, Buster Brown & Tige, Cabriole Legs, Arms, c.1910, 36 x 58 In. ..... *Illus*	1293.00
Book, Buster Brown Goes Swimming, 21 Pages, Cupples & Leon, N.Y., 1907, 6 x 7 In.	45.00
Button, Buster Brown Shoes, Buster & Tige, Celluloid, Bastian, Backpaper, c.1915, 1 ½ In. ..... *Illus*	115.00
Button, Pinback, Buster, Tige, Member Buster Brown Gang, Celluloid, ¾ In.	27.00
Camera, Instruction Booklet, Box, 1900s, 6 x 4 x 4 In.	425.00
Display, Buster & Tige, Seated, Holding Sign, Blue Bow, 2 Parts, Tin, Easel, 8 x 12 In.	1495.00
Display, Buster Holding Treat For Jumping Tige, 2 Parts, Tin, Die Cut, 20 ¾ x 39 In.	1840.00
Display, Shoe Store, Buster Brown, Rubber Figure, Molded, Red Outfit, Tige, 29 In. ....*Illus*	196.00
Doll, Purple Cloth, Long Arms & Legs, Ads On Front & Back, 1930s, 28 In.	125.00
Game, Card, Circus Characters, Animals, Yellow Kid, Billy Bear, Topsy, Box, c.1904, 5 ¾ x 7 ½ In..	269.00
Lantern, Papier-Mache, Paint, Head, Bail Wire Handle, 3 ¾ In.	1035.00
Mirror, Buster, Holding Shoe, Celluloid, Pocket, 1 ¼ In.	1760.00
Plate, Buster, Tige, Teapot, Scroll & Beaded Edge, Flowers, 7 In.	20.00
Sewing Kit, Brass, Bullet Shape, Thimble, Thread, Needle, 2 In.	45.00
Sign, Buster, Tige, Paper, On Masonite, c.1955, 14 ½ x 13 ¾ In.	36.00
Tin, Cigar, 2 For 5 Cents, Buster Brown & Tige, Man Seated, 50 Cigars, 5 x 5 In..............*Illus*	600.00
Toothpick Holder, Bisque, Mary Jane, Tige, 4 In.	85.00
Toy, Buster Brown, Tige, Pole Climbing, Drop, Tin, Painted, Windup, Germany, 13 In.	4485.00
Toy, Buster Brown, Winking Eye, Juggling, Tin, Windup, Painted, Germany, 6 ½ In. ....*Illus*	1322.00
Toy, Roly Poly, 8 In.	325.00
Watch, Pocket, Ansonia, Box, 1929	510.00
Wristwatch, Buster & Tige Playing Tug Of War, 17 Jewel, Goldtone, Windup, 1950s	275.00
Yo-Yo, Tin, Image Of Buster & Tige, Japan, 1 x 2 In.	35.00

BUTTER CHIPS, or butter pats, were small individual dishes for butter. They were the height of fashion from 1880 to 1910. Earlier as well as later examples are known.

Blue Willow, Royal Winton, Octagonal	45.00
Chinese, Pat Allerton	30.00
Princess, Haviland	19.00

BUTTER MOLDS *are listed in the Kitchen category under Mold, Butter.*

BUTTON collecting has been popular since the nineteenth century. Buttons have been used on clothing throughout the centuries, and there are millions of styles. Gold, silver, or precious stones were used for the best buttons, but most were made of natural materials, like bone or shell, or from inexpensive metals. Only a few types favored by collectors are listed for comparison.

Bakelite, 4-Leaf Clover Shape, Shank Back, 1 ½ In.	40.00
Bakelite, Bow, Figural, Aqua, 1 x 1 ½ In.	12.00
Bakelite, Dog Shape, Shank Back, 1 ¾ In.	30.00
Bakelite, Toggle, Red, Center Hole, 1 ⅛ In., 12 Piece	41.00
Black Glass, Triangular, Faceted, Victorian, 2 ¼ x 1 ½ In.	18.00
Brass & Enamel, Steel Cut Border, Domed, ⁹⁄₁₆ In.	26.00
Brass & Enamel, Woven Ribbons, Roses, Leaves, Domed, c.1870, 1 In.	30.00
Brass Finish, Openwork, Rhinestones, Domed, 1960s, 1 ½ In.	5.00
Brass Open Work, Purple & White Enamel Leaves, Marcasite Accents, 1 ¼ In.	60.00
Brass, Domed, Rosebuds, c.1890, ⅞ In.	52.00
Brass, Enamel, White Star, Rosebuds, Leaves, Pink, Green, Cobalt Blue Ground, ⅝ In.	55.00
Brass, Flowers, Stamped, Wire Loop Shank, ¾ In.	9.00
Brass, Punched Woman's Portrait, 1 ¼ In.	42.00
Celluloid, Art Deco, Gray, Black Cut To Ivory, 1930s, 2 In.	6.00
Celluloid, Noodle, Square, 1 In.	12.00
Celluloid, Tortoise-Like Design, Green Border, Domed, Wire Shank, Victorian, 1 In.	18.00
Crystal, Sterling, Reverse Painted, Horse Head, ½ In., 4 Piece	68.00
Enamel, Cut Steel Border, Wreath Of Roses, Leaves, c.1895, 1 In.	100.00

B

Enamel, Flowers, Purple, Pink, Gold Painted Border, c.1910, ⅞ In.	22.00
Glass Rhinestones, 1950s, 1 ¼ In.	7.00
Glass, Barbell Style, Double End, Goldtone, Openwork Setting, 1 ⅜ x ½ In.	26.00
Glass, Black, Hand With Flowers, Lace Sleeve, ¾ In.	8.00
Gutta Percha, Black, Victorian, 1 ½ In.	39.00
Jet, Carved, Curling Pattern Border, Mother-Of-Pearl Center, c.1850, 1 ½ In.	100.00
Lucite, Knight, Armor, Metal Repousse, 1940s, 1 ¾ In.	18.00
Metal, Charlemagne, Warning Angel, 1 ⅜ In.	12.00
Metal, Glass, Faceted, Opalescent, ½ In.	50.00
Metal, Goldtone, Anchor, Old Dominion Steamship Co., ¾ In.	15.00
Metal, Goldtone, Coco Chanel Profile, ⅝ In.	45.00
Metal, Railroad Agent, Stars, Goldtone, ¾ In.	18.00
Papier-Mache, Mother-Of-Pearl Flower Inlay, ¾ In.	15.00
Plastic, Dice Cube, Black, White, ⅜ x ⅜ In.	5.00
Porcelain, Roses, Square, ⅞ In.	50.00
Red, Plastic, Textured, Faceted, Metal Shank, 5 ⅛ In, 4 ¾ In., 9 Piece	34.00
Rhinestone, Red, 4-Leaf Clover, Topaz Center, ¾ In.	5.00
Rhinestones, Goldtone Metal, 1940s, 1 1/16 In.	6.00
Silver Plate, Embossed Packard, 1910, 1 ⅛ In.	25.00
Steel, Pearl Cameo, Riveted Border, ¾ In.	35.00
Sterling Silver, Concave, Turquoise Central Stone, 1 ½ In.	65.00
Sulfide, Cobalt Blue, Sailboat, Theresa Raring, ½ In.	36.00
Wizard Of Oz, Characters, 1939, 1 ¼ In., Set Of 5	501.00
Wood, Set, Oval, Black, White Stripes, Carded, ¾ x ½ In.	10.00

BUTTONHOOKS have been a popular collectible in England for many years and are now gaining the attention of American collectors. The buttonhooks were made to help fasten the many buttons of the old-fashioned high-button shoes and other items of apparel.

Celluloid, Double Ended, Metal, D. Bachanan Leeds, c.1900, 3 ¾ In.	30.00
Celluloid, Green Marbleized, Black Trim, 7 ⅜ In.	12.00
Celluloid, Metal, c.1930, 4 In.	25.00
Metal, Hand Shape, Hutzler Brothers, c.1900, 4 ¼ In.	24.00
Silvertone, Art Nouveau, 5 ¼ In.	10.00
Sterling Silver, Chain Links, Tiffany, c.1880, 6 In.	125.00
Sterling Silver, Oval, 1902, 2 1/16 In.	125.00
Sterling Silver, Repousse Rose, Scrolls, Swirls, Art Nouveau, 2 ⅝ In.	27.00

BYBEE POTTERY of Bybee, Kentucky, was started by Webster Cornelison. The company claims it started in 1809, although sales records were not kept until 1845. The pottery is still operated by members of the sixth generation of the Cornelison family. The handmade stoneware pottery is sold at the factory. Various marks were used, including the name *Bybee*, the name *Cornelison*, or the initials *BB*. Not all pieces are marked. A mark shaped like the state of Kentucky with the words *Genuine Bybee* and similar marks were also used by a different company, Bybee Pottery Company of Lexington, Kentucky. It was a distributor of various pottery lines from 1922 to 1929.

Crock, Vinegar, Globular, Blue Splotches, Pint	15.00
Pitcher, Dark Green Glaze, 6 ¾ In.	23.00
Vase, 2 Handles, Green, Footed, 1930s, 8 ½ In., Pair	1295.00

CALENDARS made to hang on the wall or to be displayed on a desk top have been popular since the last quarter of the nineteenth century. Many were printed with advertising as part of the artwork and were given away as premiums. Calendars with guns, gunpowder, or Coca-Cola advertising are most prized.

1869, Commerce Insurance Co., Albany, N.Y., Oct.-Dec., 4 x 5 In.	45.00
1888, Scott's Emulsion, Girl, Holding Dog & Cat, Full Pad, 7 ¾ x 4 ¾ In.	35.00
1890, W.F. Moody & Co., Dealer In Fine Footwear, Nov., Dec. Pages, 7 x 9 In.	240.00
1900, Hood's Sarsaparilla, America's Greatest Medicine, Maud Humphrey, 6 x 5 In.	25.00
1902, Port Huron Engine & Thresher Co., Tractor, The New Rusher, Michigan, 13 ¾ x 32 In.	767.00
1905, H.H. Kramer Dept. Store, Batesville, Ind., Girl, Flower In Hair, Feb.-Dec. Pages, 8 x 12 In.	150.00
1906, C.A. McElhinney Morning Sun, Cardboard, Embossed, Basket, Young Girl, 20 x 22 In.	308.00
1906, Mother Goose, Little Bo Peep, Simple Simon, Full Pad, 14 x 22 In.	395.00
1906, Peake & Levi, Babies On Swings, Die Cut, July-Dec., 7 ½ x 5 In.	26.00
1908, National Stoves & Ranges, Blond Girl, Red Hood, Gray Kitten, 13 x 9 In.	69.00

TIP

Old Burmese glass will fluoresce yellow-green under a black light. Recent reproductions will not.

Burmese, Ewer, Queen's Lace, Rosettes, Flowers, Scrolling, Gold Handle, Mt. Washington, 12 In.
$4,600.00

Early Auction Co.

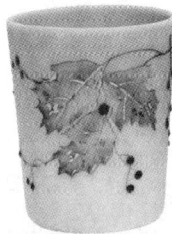

Burmese, Toothpick Holder, Optic Diamond, Blue Stippling, Leaves, Mt. Washington, 3 In.
$431.00

Early Auction Co.

Burmese, Vase, Ducks, Gilt Sun, Flask Shape, Yellow To Pink, Mt. Washington, Frank Guba, 11 In.
$4,485.00

Early Auction Co.

Burmese, Vase, Fish In Net, Enamel, Applied Gold Netting, Mottled Neck, Mt. Washington, 9 ¾ In.
$2,243.00

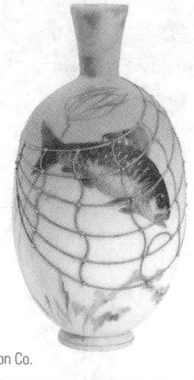

Early Auction Co.

Burmese, Vase, Monkey, Enamel, Bamboo Shoots, Gold, Scalloped Rim, Mt. Washington, 13 ¼ In.
$28,750.00

James D. Julia Auctioneers

Buster Brown, Bench, Brown's Shoes, Oak, Buster Brown & Tige, Cabriole Legs, Arms, c.1910, 36 x 58 In.
$1,293.00

Garth's Auctioneers & Appraisers

Buster Brown, Button, Buster Brown Shoes, Buster & Tige, Celluloid, Bastian, Backpaper, c.1915, 1 ½ In.
$115.00

Hake's Americana & Collectibles

1910, Swift's Lowell Fertilizer Co., 2 Smiling Girls, Wheat Sheaf, Dec. Page, 14 x 21 In............	138.00
1911, Hill's Cascara Quinine Bromide, Girl, Flower On Head, Die Cut, Cardboard, Frame, 9 x 13 In.	168.00
1912, Woman, Roses, Embossed, Multicolor, Die Cut Cardboard, Sept.-Dec., 11 x 10 In.	56.00
1913, Heart's Desire, Knapp Litho Co., New York, Woman In Hat, Frame, 41 x 24 In.	224.00
1914, Laflin & Rand, Smokeless Powder For Rifles, Hunter, Snowshoes, Frank Stick, 9 x 18 In.	2296.00
1914, Milwaukee Harvesting Machines, Friend Of Forest, Spiegle, Feb.-Dec., Frame, 12 x 21 In.	275.00
1916, P. Squillan Grocer, Providence, R.I., Girl, In 1700s Men's Attire, Metal Bands..................	150.00
1917, Grocer, John F. Pimentel, North Tiverton, R.I., Spanish, Partial Pad, 19 ¾ x 14 In..*Illus*	303.00
1918, Bristol Steel Fishing Rods, Horton Mfg. Co., Bristol, Conn., Partial Pad, 16 x 31 In.*Illus*	1064.00
1918, James Cardi Bread Co., Baker Giving Cookies To Customers, Full Pad, 21 x 15 In...........	175.00
1920, Pennsylvania, 2 Children, Spinning Wheel, Multicolor, Full Pad, 21 ½ x 12 In...............	231.00
1921, Selz Shoes, Selz Schwab & Co., Metal Strips, Yard Long...................................*Illus*	252.00
1922, Glamour Girls, J. Knowles Hare, Full Pad, 8 x 14 In.	65.00
1923, Henry Richter, Girl, Blond, Flowers, Basket, Die Cut, Cardboard, Frame, 16 x 24 In.	280.00
1923, Selz Shoes, Woman, Orange Dress, Standing By Stairs, 37 x 10 In.	390.00
1924, Remington Fire Arms & Ammunition, Old Mike Series, Partial Pad, 28 x 15 In......*Illus*	2800.00
1925, Selz Shoes, Blue Dress, Hat, Walking Cane, 37 x 10 In.	390.00
1926, Compliments Of Stefani & Feretti, Nude Woman, Blue Scarf, Full Pad	28.00
1926, Edison Mazda Lamps, Woman, Sitting By Fountain, Maxfield Parrish, 18 x 38 In.	360.00
1926, Home Sweet Home, Die Cut, Cabin, Snow, Germany, 14 x 9 In.....................................	60.00
1927, First National Bank, Girl, Flower Basket, Full Pad, 9 ½ x 7 In.	35.00
1927, Hercules Powder, Pals, Full Pad, William Eaton, 29 x 13 In.	560.00
1927, Selz Shoes, Woman, Kimono, McClelland Barclay, 37 x 10 In.	270.00
1927, Texas Bottling Works, Girl, Drinking With Straw, Jan., 12 x 23 In.................................	115.00
1928, Selz Shoes, Woman, Satin Gown, Christy, 30 ¼ x 12 In.	300.00
1929, Winchester Store, Old West Couple, Waving Guns, Pony Express, 17 x 27 In..................	201.00
1931, Hardesty & Stineman, Baker's Supplies, Flapper In Pink, Priceless Jewels, 28 x 15 In. ...	12.00
1935, Chilean Natural Nitrate, Boy, Playing Banjo, Dog, Black Man, 21 x 10 In.	95.00
1935, Gerlach Barklow Co., Franklin Roosevelt Portrait, Border Of Past Presidents, 44 x 21 In.	200.00
1939, Budweiser, Vintage Woman, Captivating, Full Pad, 11 x 5 In.	40.00
1946, Cheltenham National Bank, Spirit Of America, Illustrated, Shrink Wrapped, 42 ½ x 31 In. .	35.00
1946, Varga Pinup, Full Pad, 12 x 8 In..	450.00
1950, General Electric, Month To Month Electricity Usage Photos, Full Pad, 30 x 16 In...........	70.00
1951, H.H. Van Luven Mfg., Earl Moran Pinup, January, Top & Bottom Metal Strips, 33 x 16 In.....	201.00
1952, Neff's Supermarket, May-Dec.	5.00
1955, Radio & TV Clinic, Nude Marilyn Monroe, January & February Only, 21 In.....................	336.00
1957, Conyers Flowers, Thermometer, Desktop, Full Pad	12.00
1965, Peace, Red, White Blue, Peace Symbol, Ring Bound, 8 x 11 In.	28.00
1965, Timken Co., Fashionable Woman, Full Pad, 20 x 16 In.	250.00
1969, Truckee Tahoe Fuel Co., Road Along River, Trees, Full Pad, 11 x 7 In.	175.00
1980, Eden Hashish Centre, Katmandu, Nepal, Let Us Take You Higher, Lotus, Frame, 16 x 26 In.	112.00
Perpetual, Gilt Metal, Silver Tone Stem, Round Wood Base, Stamped Pope Gregorio VII, 15 ½ In.	426.00
Perpetual, Wood, Painted, Black Top, c.1900, 8 x 5 x 3 In...	125.00

CALENDAR PLATES were popular in the United States as advertising giveaways from 1906 to 1929. Since then, a few plates have been made every year. A calendar and the name of a store, a picture of flowers, a girl, or a scene were featured on the plate.

1910, Center Pink Rose, 9 ¼ In.	65.00
1911, Arizona Country Scene, Acorn Border, Dresden, 8 ½ In..	25.00
1912, American Flags, Martyred Presidents, Gilt Trim, 8 ⅛ In..	150.00
1912, Flags, Our Martyrs, Log Cabin Foods, Gilt, 8 ⅛ In..	150.00
1914, Boy, Swiss Alps Mountain Scene, 8 ¼ In..	50.00
1916, Dutch Boy & Girl, Bluebirds, 8 ¼ In...	180.00
1919, Silver Creek, Nebraska, U.S. Flag, D.E. McNicol, 8 ¼ In...	23.00
1923, Norwalk, Connecticut, Flowers, River Scene, 9 In...	35.00
1956, Gilt Flowers, Scrolls, Windmill, Ship Scene, Taylor, Smith & Taylor, 10 In......................	30.00
1959, Lincoln Sesquicentennial, Black White Ground, 10 In...	11.00
1964, God Bless Our House, Brown Transfer, House, Flag, Royal Staffordshire, 9 In...............	11.00
1965, Zodiac, Town Meeting House, Brown, Royal Staffordshire, 9 In....................................	25.00
1967, French Poodle Head, Compliments Walter's Auction Gallery, 9 In................................	14.00
1967, Spaniel Head, 9 ¼ In...	17.00
1971, God Bless Our House, Mulberry, A. Meakin, Staffordshire, 9 In....................................	11.00
1974, Currier & Ives, Central Wreath, Blue, Royal China, 10 In..	20.00

CAMARK POTTERY started out as Camden Art Tile and Pottery Company in Camden, Arkansas. Jack Carnes founded the firm in 1926 in association with John Lessell, Stephen Sebaugh, and the Camden Chamber of Commerce. Many types of glazes and wares were made. The company was bought by Mary Daniel in the early 1960s. Production ended in 1983.

Figurine, Cat, Sitting, Black, Glossy, Impressed, Mark, 10 In.	46.00
Vase, Elk, Pine Trees, Metallic Gold Luster Glaze, Black Ground, Incised Lessell, 12 ⅞ In...*Illus*	2760.00
Vase, Light Overflow, Paper Label, Gray, Black, 5 In.	17.00
Vase, Overflow, Orange, Green, Pinched Rim, Label, 5 ½ In.	29.00
Vase, Overflow, Orange, Green, Wavy Rim, Footed, 6 In.	29.00

CAMBRIDGE GLASS COMPANY was founded in 1901 in Cambridge, Ohio. The company closed in 1954, reopened briefly, and closed again in 1958. The firm made all types of glass. Its early wares included heavy pressed glass with the mark *Near Cut*. Later wares included Crown Tuscan, etched stemware, and clear and colored glass. The firm used a *C* in a triangle mark after 1920.

Aero Optic, Tumbler, Green, Footed, 6 Oz., 3 ¾ In.	14.00
Aero Optic, Tumbler, Pink, 4 ⅜ In.	20.00
Azurite, Candlestick, Blue, Laurel Leaf Etching, Gilt, c.1925, 7 In., Pair	65.00
Azurite, Console Set, 2 Candlesticks, Bowl, Gilt Laurel Etching, 7 x 3 ¾ & 8 ½ x 2 ¾ In.	100.00
Azurite, Console, Blue, Laurel Leaf Etching, Gilt, c.1925, 8 In.	45.00
Caprice, Bowl, Handles, 1940s, 7 In.	25.00
Caprice, Bowl, Moonlight Blue, Alpine Frost, 13 In.	95.00
Caprice, Cigarette Set, Dolphin Footed Box, 4 Shell Ashtray, 1949, 6 Piece	150.00
Caprice, Cruet, Geometric Handle, Stopper, c.1940, 4 ¾ In.	30.00
Caprice, Relish, 6 Sections, 11 ½ In.	185.00
Caprice, Sugar & Creamer, 4 ¼ x 2 ⅝ & 3 ⅝ x 3 In.	18.00
Cascade, Goblet, Wine, Label, 3 ¾ In., 4 Piece	22.00
Chantilly, Cake Plate, Handle, 13 In.	85.00
Chantilly, Goblet, Water, 9 Oz., 7 ⅞ In.	44.00
Chantilly, Sherbet, 7 Oz., 5 ⅞ In.	24.00
Chrysanthemum, Tumbler, Amber, 12 Oz., 5 ⅛ In.	20.00
Cleo, Decanter, Pink, 7 ¾ x 12 In.	75.00
Compact, Purple, Powder, Puff, Rouge, Lipstick Compartments, c.1929, 8 ½ x 3 ½ In.	128.00
Crown Tuscan, Candlestick, White, Nude Woman Base, 9 ½ In., Pair	275.00
Crown Tuscan, Plate, Seashell, Charleton Roses & Bows, 7 x 7 In.	45.00
Crown Tuscan, Vase, Bud, Peach, 1930s, 10 In., Pair	45.00
Crown Tuscan, Vase, Bud, Peach Pink, 10 ¼ In., Pair	45.00
Daffodil, Goblet, Water, 7 ¾ In.	69.00
Daffodil, Relish, 3 Sections, Handle, 9 ¾ In.	59.00
Daffodil, Sherbet, 4 ½ In.	14.00
Diane, Ashtray, Round, 3 In.	28.00
Diane, Goblet, Water, 10 Oz., 7 ¼ In.	35.00
Diane, Parfait, 6 ¼ In.	38.00
Diane, Tumbler, 10 Oz., 4 ⅛ In.	74.00
Dish, Mayonnaise, Emerald Green, Bowl, Underplate, Ladle, 1930s, 3 Piece	125.00
Doric Ram's Head, Bowl, Azurite, 1921-29, 8 ¼ x 10 In.	120.00
Dover, Finger Bowl, 4 ⅜ In.	40.00
Dover, Goblet, Water, 7 ½ In.	28.00
Dover, Wine, 5 ⅝ In.	30.00
Elaine, Compote, Keyhole Stem, 5 ¾ x 7 ½ In.	65.00
Elaine, Relish, Handles, 3 Section, c.1940, 8 In.	40.00
Everglade, Plate, Amber, 8 ½ In.	50.00
Florentine, Candlestick, Amber Gold, Gold Encrusted, 1920s, 9 ½ x 2 ¼ In., Pair	55.00
Gloria, Tumbler, Yellow, Footed, 10 Oz., 6 ⅜ In.	50.00
Harvest, Plate, Salad, 7 ½ In.	12.00
Harvest, Relish, 5 Sections, 11 In.	56.00
Laurel Wreath, Compote, 4 ½ In.	41.00
Laurel Wreath, Cordial, 4 ½ In.	35.00
Laurel Wreath, Plate, Bread & Butter, 6 ⅜ In.	20.00
Lion, Bookend, Crystal, Paper Label, 1950s, 6 ½ In.	125.00
Lynbrook, Cordial, 3 ⅝ In.	35.00
Lynbrook, Cruet, Stopper, 6 In.	69.00
Lynbrook, Goblet, Water, 5 ⅞ In.	20.00
Marjorie, Sherbet, 3 ⅜ In.	15.00
Marjorie, Tumbler, 12 Oz., 5 ¾ In.	27.00
Minuet, Cordial, 5 ¼ In.	49.00

Buster Brown, Display, Shoe Store, Buster Brown, Rubber Figure, Molded, Red Outfit, Tige, 29 In.
$196.00

Victorian Casino Antiques

Cambridge Glass After 1958
Cambridge Glass Company went out of business in 1958 and the molds were sold to the Imperial Glass Company and later to other glass factories. Many pieces have been reproduced.

Buster Brown, Tin, Cigar, 2 For 5 Cents, Buster Brown & Tige, Man Seated, 50 Cigars, 5 x 5 In.
$600.00

Showtime Auction Services

Buster Brown, Toy, Buster Brown, Winking Eye, Juggling, Tin, Windup, Painted, Germany, 6 ½ In.
$1,322.00

James D. Julia Auctioneers

Calendar, 1917, Grocer, John F. Pimentel, North Tiverton, R.I., Spanish, Partial Pad, 19 ¾ x 14 In. $303.00

Wm Morford Antiques

Calendar, 1918, Bristol Steel Fishing Rods, Horton Mfg. Co., Bristol, Conn., Partial Pad, 16 x 31 In. $1,064.00

Past Tyme Pleasures

TIP

Never laminate a paper collectible, whether it's a document, photo, letter, press pass, cut autograph, or baseball card. Lamination is permanent, and permanently decreases value.

Minuet, Goblet, Water, 7 ¾ In.	41.00
Montrose, Bowl, Crimped, Round, 11 ¾ In.	55.00
Montrose, Plate, Salad, 7 ½ In.	14.00
Montrose, Wine, 5 ½ In.	30.00
Mt. Vernon, Creamer, Carmen Red	20.00
Mt. Vernon, Cup & Saucer	9.00
Mt. Vernon, Tumbler, Footed, 2 Oz., 3 ¼ In.	8.00
Nude Stem, Ashtray, 6 ½ In.	189.00
Nude Stem, Cigarette Box, 7 ½ In.	209.00
Nude Stem, Goblet, Water, 9 In.	139.00
Nude Stem, Wine, 7 ¾ In.	128.00
Pristine, Ice Bucket, Tab Handles, 4 ⅜ In.	56.00
Pristine, Tumbler, Footed, 6 In.	14.00
Pristine, Wine, 5 ¾ In.	36.00
Rose Point, Cake Plate, Footed, Handle, Clear, 11 ¾ In.	119.00
Rose Point, Candlestick, Winged, 6 ¾ x 7 In.	124.00
Rose Point, Celery Dish, 3 Parts, Scrolling Handle, Scalloped, 12 x 7 In.	70.00
Rose Point, Goblet, Water, Clear, 10 Oz., 8 ⅜ In.	46.00
Rose Point, Plate, Buffet, Patterned Edge, 18 In.	258.00
Rose Point, Plate, Dinner, Clear, 10 ½ In.	209.00
Rose Point, Sugar, 2 Handles, 4 ¾ x 2 ½ In.	9.00
Rose Point, Vase, Bud, Blue, 1930s, 10 In., Pair	45.00
Roxbury, Cake Plate, Handle, 13 ¾ In.	49.00
Roxbury, Cordial, 4 ¾ In.	40.00
Roxbury, Goblet, Water, 7 ¼ In.	22.00
Star, Candleholder, Block, c.1950, 4 x 1 In., Pair	16.00
Swan, Black Milk Glass, Signed C In Triangle, 12 x 7 In.	400.00
Swan, Light Green, Signed C In Triangle, 12 ½ x 7 In.	400.00
Virginia, Cake Stand, Brandy Well In Center, 1940s, 8 x 11 In.	200.00
Wildflower, Candlestick, Double Light, Clear	47.00
Wildflower, Jug, Ball, Clear, 80 Oz., 9 ¼ In.	209.00
Wildflower, Tumbler, Footed, Clear, 10 Oz., 7 In.	27.00

CAMBRIDGE POTTERY was made in Cambridge, Ohio, from about 1895 until World War I. The factory made brown glazed decorated artwares with a variety of marks, including an acorn, the name *Cambridge,* the name *Oakwood,* and the name *Terrhea.*

Pitcher, Green Matte Glaze, Molded Leaves & Berries, 6 ¼ x 4 In.	250.00
Tile, Green Gloss Glaze, Molded Torches, Flowers, Ribbons, 6 ¼ x 6 ¼ In.	30.00
Vase, Arts & Crafts, Green Trial Glaze, 6 In.	495.00
Vase, Poppies, Standard Glaze, Bulbous, c.1906, 7 ½ In.	275.00

CAMEO GLASS was made in much the same manner as a cameo in jewelry. Parts of the top layer of glass were cut away to reveal a different colored glass beneath. The most famous cameo glass was made during the nineteenth century. Signed cameo glass pieces are listed under the glasswork's name, such as Daum, Galle, Legras, Mt. Joye, Webb, and others.

Bell, Red Satin, White, Cascading Leafy Flowering Vine, 6 ½ In.	2070.00
Bowl, Meandering Flowers, Swag At Lip, Green Leaves, Amethyst Blossom, 4 ¼ x 2 ½ In.	759.00
Bowl, Trefoil, Opaque Cutting Over Prussian Blue Ground, 5 x 2 ¾ In.	173.00
Lamp, Oxblood Brown To Tan, Domed Shade & Standard Landscape, Tapered, Metal Base, 20 In.	275.00
Perfume Bottle, Blue, White Flowers & Leaves, Elongated Teardrop, Laydown, Twist Lid, 8 ½ In.	1380.00
Perfume Bottle, Cascading Berry Branch, Squat, Stick Neck, 9 ½ In.	403.00
Perfume Bottle, Gourd Shape, Red Glass, Flowers, Flip Sterling Lid, Crystal Stopper, 3 ½ In.	1265.00
Pitcher, Red, White Blossoming Branches, Loop Handle, Wide Spout, 6 In.	1380.00
Plaque, Classical Maiden, Fruit Tray, Raisin Tint, Signed, G. Woodall, 6 x 4 ½ In. ...*Illus*	29900.00
Vase, Amber Overlay Flowers, Gilt Highlights Cut To Clear Ground, c.1910, 10 In.	474.00
Vase, Blue Dog, Limited Edition, Marked, Pilgrim Glass, 1994, 10 ¾ x 6 ½ In. ...*Illus*	11438.00
Vase, Blue, Squat, Leafy Flowering Branch, Full Bloom, Sawtooth Rim, 5 ½ In.	805.00
Vase, Citron Green, White Flower Blossoms, Scrolls, Elongated Pear, Trumpet Neck, Ring Foot, 9 ¼ In.	2300.00
Vase, Citron Yellow, Red & White Flowers, Banding, Shouldered, Flared Rim, 6 ¼ In.	1495.00
Vase, Citron Yellow, White Flowers, Butterflies, Bulbous, Tapering Stick Neck, 11 ½ In.	1265.00
Vase, Cut Iris, Leaves, Flared Top, Base, Gilt Rim, Victorian, 16 In.	98.00
Vase, Dark Flower, Leaf, Green Ground, Etched D. Christian Meisenthal, c.1900, 4 In.	1500.00
Vase, Enameled Greyhounds, Acid Cut, Tapered, France, 12 In.	863.00
Vase, Frosted Purple, Stemmed Flowers, Icicle Border, Bell Shape, Ring Foot, Rolled Rim, 3 In.	805.00
Vase, Iris, Pantin Glass, Orange, Cream, 13 ¼ In., Pair	1422.00

Vase, Landscape, Yellow To Brown, Rounded Rim, Footed, 14 ¼ In.	185.00
Vase, Purple Flowers, Frosted Ground, Flared, Purple Foot, c.1900, 4 x 4 ½ In.	240.00
Vase, Red Leaves, Pink Mottled Ground, Crumpled Rim, France, c.1900, 4 In.	960.00
Vase, Red, White Oak Leaves, Acorns, Stems, Bulbous, Shouldered, Flat Collar, Banding, 3 ½ In.	2760.00
Vase, Roman Gladiator Embracing Maiden, Yellow, Handles, Burgun, Schverer & Co., 9 In... *Illus*	5750.00
Vase, Stick, Smokestack Bottom, Ruffled Rim, Landscape, France, c.1910, 12 x 5 ½ In.	531.00
Vase, Vines, Grape Pods, Leaves, Green, Amber, Swollen, Spread Foot, 11 In.	230.00
Vase, White Floral Vines, Green Ground, Geometric Bands, Bulbous, Long Neck, 9 In.	1200.00
Vase, Yellow, White, Blossoms, Butterflies, Scrolling, Shouldered, Cylindrical Neck, 9 In.	1725.00

CAMPAIGN *memorabilia are listed in the Political category.*

CAMPBELL KIDS were first used as part of an advertisement for the Campbell Soup Company in 1904. The kids were created by Grace Drayton, a popular illustrator of the day. The kids were used in magazine and newspaper ads until about 1951. They were presented again in 1966; and in 1983, they were redesigned with a slimmer, more contemporary appearance.

Dish, ABC, Standing In Flowering Field, 7 ½ In.	130.00
Doll, Composition, Painted Hair, Painted Eyes, c.1928, 12 In.	250.00
Ornament, Round, Glass, Kids Decorating Tree, 1986, 3 In.	12.00
Pillowcase, Embroidered, Watering Garden, Butterfly, 30 x 21 In.	15.00
Spoon Rest, Ceramic, c.1955, 4 In., Pair	29.00

CANDELABRUM refers to a candleholder with more than one arm to hold many candles; a candlestick is designed to hold one candle. The eccentricity of the English language makes the plural of candelabrum into candelabra.

2-Light, Beaded Scroll Arms, Swags Of Prisms, Tapered Glass Finial, 19 x 12 In., Pair	246.00
2-Light, Brass, Iron, Georgian Style, Tripod Base, Scrolled Arms, Standing, 50 In.	338.00
2-Light, Bronze, Louis XVI Style, Scrolled Arms, Flower Swags, c.1910, 18 In., Pair	450.00
2-Light, Bronze, Marble, Louis XVI, Cherub, Holding Torch, Pedestal, Base, 18 x 7 ½ In., Pair	4973.00
2-Light, Bronze, Marble, Sprays Of Prisms, Tulip Shaped Cups, c.1889, 12 ½ In., Pair	98.00
2-Light, Gilt Bronze, Figural, Putto, Scrolling Arms, Stepped Base, 12 ½ In., Pair	826.00
2-Light, Gilt Bronze, Louis XVI Style, Leaves, Flowers, Scrolled Arms, Beaded, c.1885, 14 In., Pair	738.00
2-Light, Gilt Bronze, Rococo, Scrolled Arms, Footed Base, France, 1800s, 7 ½ In., Pair	354.00
2-Light, Gilt Bronze, Scrolled Arms, Bell Shape Base, Snuff, Victorian, 18 ½ In., Pair	120.00
2-Light, Gilt Metal, Engraved Flowers, Beads, Spiral Fluted Domed Base, 7 ½ In., Pair	118.00
2-Light, Gilt, Bronze, Putto, Scrolling Arms, Columnar Stem, Paw Feet, Empire, 16 ¼ In., Pair	1000.00
2-Light, Glass, Hanging Prisms, Round Swirl Foot, 16 In., Pair	431.00
2-Light, Patinated Bronze, Winged Victory, Holding Gilt Cups, Empire Style, c.1860, 20 In., Pair	3125.00
2-Light, Silver, Acorn, Curved Branches, Round Base, Harald Nielsen, 1930, 6 In., Pair	13800.00
2-Light, Silver, Neoclassical, Scrolled Arms, Italy, c.1910, 15 ½ In., Pair	2478.00
2-Light, Silver, P. Lopez G., Mexico, 9 ½ In., Pair	600.00
2-Light, Silver, Scrolling Arms, Urn Shape Nozzle, Round Foot, Peru, 5 ¾ In., Pair	388.00
2-Light, Silver, Stylized J Shape, Rectangular Base, P.G. Lopez, Mexico, 9 In., Pair	660.00
2-Light, Tapered, Fluted, Silver, J. Parsons & Co., c.1790, 20 x 17 In., Pair	4025.00
2-Light, Wrought Iron, Tripod Foot, 1900s, 23 In., Pair	474.00
3-Light, Antler, Fallow, Brass Base, J. Anthony Redmile, 27 ½ In., Pair	920.00
3-Light, Baluster Stem, Domed Foot, Silver, Shreve & Co., 19 x 17 In., Pair	5000.00
3-Light, Brass, Pierced Leafy Standard, Flower Nozzle, c.1895, 13 ½ In., Pair	4720.00
3-Light, Bronze, Glass, Lotus Shape Standard, Eagle, Flowers, Swags, Hanging Prisms, 21 x 15 In.	922.00
3-Light, Bronze, Louis XIV, Flower Scrolled Arms, Stepped Marble Base, France, 16 x 9 In., Pair	177.00
3-Light, Bronze, Marble, Louis XV Style, Putti, Scroll Branches, Fluted Candle Cup, 23 ¾ In., Pair	2460.00
3-Light, Bronze, Marble, Woman, Cornucopia, Scrolling Arms, Bird Heads, 1800s, 39 In., Pair	8050.00
3-Light, Bronze, Tree Shape, Hawk Finial, Applied Foxes, c.1800s, 27 ½ In.	472.00
3-Light, Enamel, Ruby Glass, Spear Shape, Drop Prisms, Flower Shape Cups, 21 In., Pair	173.00
3-Light, Gilt Bronze, Directoire, Patinated, Applied Animal Heads, Scrolls, c.1795, 23 ½ In., Pair	5000.00
3-Light, Gilt Bronze, Electrified, Louis XVI Style, Scroll Arms, Fruit Knop, 14 ¼ x 14 In., Pair	936.00
3-Light, Gilt Bronze, Putti, Fluted Cylindrical Pedestal, Marble Base, Branch Arms, c.1915, 25 In., Pair	1722.00
3-Light, Gilt Bronze, Round Foot, Quiver Shape Stem, Arrow Top Finial, Leaves, c.1885, 8 ½ In., Pair	338.00
3-Light, Gilt Metal, Louis XVI Style, Acanthus Stem, France, 23 ¼ In., Pair	270.00
3-Light, Girandole, Gilt Brass, Glass, Marble, Rococo Revival, Paul & Virginia, 15 & 17 In., 3 Piece	148.00
3-Light, Girandole, Silver Baluster Stem, Pierced Base, Scroll Arms, Prisms, Candles, c.1915, 33 x 14 In., Pair	2337.00
3-Light, Molded Glass, Hexagonal Base, Grooves, Baluster Shaft, Prisms, 21 x 14 In., Pair	357.00
3-Light, Oak, Brass, Barley Twist Stem, Round Dished Foot, 15 ¾ In., Pair	250.00
3-Light, Patinated Bronze, Louis XVI, Ormolu, Woman, Holding Cornucopia, 1780, 36 In., Pair	6000.00
3-Light, Pillar Molded Standard, Amberina Bobeches, Spear Prisms, Round Base, c.1900, 21 In., Pair	2214.00

C

Calendar, 1921, Selz Shoes, Selz Schwab & Co., Metal Strips, Yard Long
$252.00

Victorian Casino Antiques

TIP

If you find an old seed catalog or recipe pamphlet with a cover you want to frame, don't tear off the cover. Frame the whole catalog.

Calendar, 1924, Remington Fire Arms & Ammunition, Old Mike Series, Partial Pad, 28 x 15 In.
$2,800.00

Past Tyme Pleasures

85

Camark, Vase, Elk, Pine Trees, Metallic Gold Luster Glaze, Black Ground, Incised Lessell, 12 ⅞ In.
$2,760.00

Humler & Nolan

Cameo Glass, Plaque, Classical Maiden, Fruit Tray, Raisin Tint, Signed, G. Woodall, 6 x 4 ½ In.
$29,900.00

Early Auction Co.

Cameo Glass, Vase, Blue Dog, Limited Edition, Marked, Pilgrim Glass, 1994, 10 ¾ x 6 ½ In.
$11,438.00

New Orleans Auction Galleries, Inc.

Cameo Glass, Vase, Roman Gladiator Embracing Maiden, Yellow, Handles, Burgun Schverer & Co., 9 In.
$5,750.00

Humler & Nolan

3-Light, Porcelain, Cherubs, Holding Paddle, Roses & Leaves, Scroll Feet, 21 ½ In., Pair	173.00
3-Light, Porcelain, Figural, Man, Woman, Flowers, Leaves, Sitzendorf, c.1880, 18 In., Pair	115.00
3 Light, Porcelain, Regency, Prisms, Round Base, c.1850, 25 In., Pair	395.00
3-Light, Scroll Arms, Reeded Round Foot, Tapered Shaft, 12 ½ In., Pair	115.00
3-Light, Sheffield Plate, Tapered Stem, Calyx, Fluted Banding, Scrolling Arms, c.1815, 26 In., Pair	4674.00
3-Light, Silver Plate, Scrolling Arms, Gadrooned Round Foot, Shell Design, c.1898, 22 ½ In., Pair	480.00
3-Light, Silver Plate, Sweeping Arms, Friedman Silver Co., England, 16 x 13 In., Pair	390.00
3-Light, Silver Plate, Trumpet Shaped Shaft, Reeded Twisting Arms, Gadrooned, 1800s, 19 In., Pair	717.00
3-Light, Silver, Francis I, Scrolled, Reed & Barton, 13 ¼ In., Pair	1770.00
3-Light, Silver, Francis I, Sterling, Reed & Barton, 1956, 15 ⅔ In., Pair	3422.00
3-Light, Silver, Multi-Knopped Standard, Scrolled Branches, Mexico, 11 ¾ x 12 ¾ In., Pair	2500.00
3-Light, Silver, Rococo Style, Figural, Putto, Domed Base, Openwork Feet, 8 ½ x 8 ⅛ In., Pair	1722.00
3-Light, Silver, Rouchambeau, Sterling, Convertible, Bobeches, Mueck-Carey Co., c.1940, 15 In., Pair	1320.00
3-Light, Silver, Scroll Branch, Stepped Round Foot, Mexico, 11 ¾ x 11 ½ In., Pair	2500.00
3-Light, Silver, Scroll, Straight Arms, Sweden, 1927, 13 ⅝ In., Pair	1652.00
3-Light, Silver, Scroll, Turned, Redlich & Co., 6 x 10 In.	117.00
3-Light, Silver, Scrolled Branch Arm, Palette Base, J.L. Reyes, Mexico, 7 In., Pair	885.00
3-Light, Wrought Iron, Twisted Shaft, Hanging Loop, Swivel, Split Socket, Round Drip Cup, 20 x 8 In.	295.00
4-Light, Brass, Louis XVI Style, Leaves, Bellflowers, Scrolled Arms, Hanging Prisms, 27 In., Pair	2460.00
4-Light, Bronze, Egyptian Style, Urn, Flame Finial, Women's Heads, Round Base, c.1890, 24 In., Pair	2460.00
4-Light, Bronze, Marble, Louis XV Style, Satyrs, Pan Pipes, Grapes, Fluted, c.1915, 17 x 9 ½ In., Pair	1476.00
4-Light, Bronze, Patina, Egyptian Woman, Gilt Flowers, Sphinx, France, c.1900, 30 In., Pair	1140.00
4-Light, Gilt Bronze, Cut Glass, Baluster, Scrolling Arms, Hanging Prisms, Amethyst, 35 In., Pair	1524.00
4-Light, Gilt Bronze, Louis XV Style, Twisted Arms, Leaves, France, c.1900, 12 ½ In., Pair	944.00
4-Light, Louis XVI Style, Urn Body, Ram's Head Handles, Rose Stem Sockets, Gilt, 16 In., Pair	1125.00
4-Light, Meissen Style, Flowers, Man, Woman, 22 In., Pair	325.00
4-Light, Metal, Empire Style, Column Standard, Scrolled Branches, Flame Finial, 28 In., Pair	250.00
4-Light, Porcelain, Figural, Maiden, Cherub, Leaning On Tree, Leaves, Roses, c.1880, 21 In., Pair	316.00
4-Light, Porcelain, Maiden Leaning On Tree, Cherub, Flowers, Germany, c.1880, 21 In., Pair	316.00
4-Light, Silvered Metal, Modeled Oak Tree, 3 Branches, Leaves, Acorns, c.1890, 25 In.	978.00
4-Light, Tin, Wirework Basket Support, Columnar Stem, Footed Round Dish Base, c.1815, 16 In.	660.00
5-Light, Beehive Stem, Scrolled Pierced Arms, Domed Base, c.1915, 18 ½ In., Pair	307.00
5-Light, Bronze Dore, Glass, Flower Arms, Baluster Standard, Leaf Handles, Swags, 42 x 17 In., Pair	4305.00
5-Light, Bronze, Classical Woman Support, Holders Overhead, c.1900, 26 x 15 In., Pair	1560.00
5-Light, Bronze, Flower Design Arms, Seated Putti, France, 1800s, 31 In., Pair	2963.00
5-Light, Bronze, Malachite, Tapered Square Shape, Square Footed Base, France, 1900s, 20 In., Pair	1380.00
5-Light, Bronze, Putto, Holding Cornucopia, Leg On Torch, Flowering Stems, 1800s, 21 ¼ In., Pair	1778.00
5-Light, Bronze, Ram's Head Design, Leaves, Round Foot, 1800s, 29 In., Pair	748.00
5-Light, Bronze, Rococo Style, Spiral Stem, Baluster Standard, Tripod Base, 1800s, 24 In.	615.00
5-Light, Carved & Gilded, Rococo Style, Scrolled Support, Rosettes, Italy, 1800s, 28 In., Pair	3050.00
5-Light, Chantilly Duchess, Silver, Gorham, 13 x 11 In., Pair	531.00
5-Light, Cut Glass, Tapered, Honeycomb, Petal Base, Spear Prisms, c.1885, 24 In., Pair	1968.00
5-Light, Descending Beaded Scales, Tapered Shafts, Louis XVI Style, 1800s, 19 In.	1180.00
5-Light, Faux Stone, Wirework, Urn Shape Stem, Twisted Branches, 22 x 21 ½ In., Pair	215.00
5-Light, Gilt Bronze, Column Standard, Curved, Stiff Arms, Square Base, c.1850, 23 ¼ In., Pair	2500.00
5-Light, Gilt Bronze, Empire, Column Support, Scrolled Arms, 32 x 12 In., Pair	600.00
5-Light, Gilt Bronze, Leafy Branches, Glass Drops, Rosettes, Spear Finial, c.1900, 29 x 14 In., Pair	2214.00
5-Light, Gilt Bronze, Louis Philippe, Column Stem, Curved Arms, Square Base, c.1850, 23 In., Pair	2500.00
5-Light, Gilt Bronze, Louis XV Style, Scroll Leaf Standard, Flame Finial, Pierced Base, 25 In., Pair	677.00
5-Light, Gilt Bronze, Marble, Flame Finial, Leaves, Fluted Base, 15 ¾ In., Pair	1000.00
5-Light, Gilt Metal, Baroque Style, Scrolling Arms, Shields, Paw Feet, Knopped, 1900s, 23 ½ In., Pair	203.00
5-Light, Gilt Metal, Marble, Downswept Stems, Urn Shape Standard, Stepped Base, 21 In., Pair	306.00
5-Light, Napoleon III, Bronze, Woman Standard, Cornucopia, Flowers, 28 In., Pair	2250.00
5-Light, Porcelain, Cherubs, Flowers, Von Schierholtz, Germany, 22 x 18 In., Pair	259.00
5-Light, Porcelain, Ormolu, Putto Support, Paneled Base, 25 In., Pair	2015.00
5-Light, Silver, Scroll Arms, Adjustable, Cartier, 17 x 13 In., Pair	1033.00
5-Light, Silver, Serpentine Arms, Rope Trim, Round Foot, 12 ¾ In., Pair	460.00
5-Light, Wrought Iron, Gothic Style, Arched Supports, Tripod Feet, Floor, France, 61 In., Pair	711.00
5-Light, Wrought Iron, Scrolls, Twisted Post, c.1940, 48 x 32 In.	2880.00
6-Light, Brass, Marble, Cherub, Floral Swag Mount, Contemporary, 28 In., Pair	176.00
6-Light, Bronze, Figural, 3-Part, Paw Feet, Lotus Leaf Branches, Reeded, 26 x 10 In., Pair	1230.00
6-Light, Bronze, Scrolled Arms, Grape Clusters, Columnar Stem, Pedestal Base, 27 In., Pair	478.00
6-Light, Bronze, Shaped Stem, Dolphins, Scrolls, Gadrooned, 1800s, 21 In., Pair	325.00
6-Light, Gilt Bronze, Louis XVI Style, Hanging Prisms, Stepped Arms, Bead Swags, 28 In., Pair	1107.00
6-Light, Gilt Bronze, Louis XVI Style, Scroll Arms, Torch Finial, Open Stem, Onyx Base, 20 In., Pair	1063.00
6-Light, Gilt Bronze, Marble, 3 Parts, Base, Leaf Molded Sockets, Scroll Arms, c.1835, 34 In., Pair	2091.00

<table>
<tr><td>6-Light, Gilt Bronze, Marble, Figural, Putto, Leaf Scroll, Columns, Top Shape Feet, 23 In., Pair....</td><td>3750.00</td></tr>
<tr><td>6-Light, Gilt Bronze, Pierced & Molded, Plumes, Ribbed, Paw Feet, c.1900, 23 ½ x 11 ¾ In., Pair.</td><td>369.00</td></tr>
<tr><td>6-Light, Gilt Bronze, Round Foot, Beaded, Rope Twist Scroll Arms, Leaves, c.1885, 30 In., Pair.</td><td>1476.00</td></tr>
<tr><td>6-Light, Gilt Bronze, Urn, Acanthine Arms, Triangular Standard, Shaped Base, c.1850, 23 In., Pair ..</td><td>1912.00</td></tr>
<tr><td>6-Light, Gilt Metal, Figural, Musician, Sculptor, Griffin Base, 27 In., Pair ....</td><td>344.00</td></tr>
<tr><td>6-Light, Porcelain, Scrolling Leaves, Bouquets, Leaf Handles, Maroon, Gilt, 28 In., Pair ....</td><td>460.00</td></tr>
<tr><td>6-Light, Silver Plate, Figural, Fortuna, Flowing Robes, Cornucopia, Scrolls, c.1885, 27 x 10 In.</td><td>3567.00</td></tr>
<tr><td>7-Light, Brass, Paw Footed Base, Pierced Branches, Lilies, Pineapple Cups, c.1895, 32 x 18 In..</td><td>215.00</td></tr>
<tr><td>7-Light, Bronze Dore, Porcelain Flowers, Putti, Torch, 1900s, 35 x 17 In., Pair.........................</td><td>3000.00</td></tr>
<tr><td>7-Light, Bronze, Marble, Empire, Triangle Base, Leaf Mounts, Electric, France, 39 x 13 In., Pair ..</td><td>6325.00</td></tr>
<tr><td>7-Light, Gilt Bronze, Napoleon III, Reeded Ball Feet, Leafy Scrolls, Shells, 27 ¾ x 17 In. ....</td><td>738.00</td></tr>
<tr><td>7-Light, Gilt Metal, Standing Knight, Dragon Finial, Roundel, Crocket Base, c.1850, 34 x 12 In., Pair</td><td>4392.00</td></tr>
<tr><td>7-Light, Metal, Hammered, Gunmetal Finish, Round Domed Base, 10 ¾ x 21 In. ....</td><td>69.00</td></tr>
<tr><td>7-Light, Silver, Scrolling Arms, Stems, Leaves, Round Stepped Base, Shells, c.1900, 24 In., Pair</td><td>5875.00</td></tr>
<tr><td>8-Light, Brass, Glass, Scroll Arms, Beaded Swags, Hanging Prisms, Faux Candles, c.1900, 40 In., Pair</td><td>2460.00</td></tr>
<tr><td>10-Light, Gilt Bronze, Napoleon III, Pierced Feet, Putti, Swags, Banana Trees, c.1865, 26 x 16 In., Pair</td><td>2337.00</td></tr>
<tr><td>11-Light, Bronze, Ecclesiastical, 3-Footed, 40 In., Pair...</td><td>660.00</td></tr>
<tr><td>17-Light, Tin, Cylindrical Holders, Folk Art, 23 x 13 In. ....</td><td>518.00</td></tr>
</table>

CANDLESTICKS were made of brass, pewter, glass, sterling silver, plated silver, and all types of pottery and porcelain. The earliest candlesticks, dating from the sixteenth century, held the candle on a pricket (sharp pointed spike). These lost favor because in times of strife the large church candlesticks with prickets became formidable weapons, so the socket was mandated. Candlesticks changed in style through the centuries, and designs range from Classical to Rococo to Art Nouveau to Art Deco.

<table>
<tr><td>Antler, Weighted Base, Marked J. T., 5 ¾ x 7 ½ In., Pair ....</td><td>826.00</td></tr>
<tr><td>Brass, Altar, Twisted Embossed Stem, Gargoyles, Flared Scallop Rim, Fleur-De-Lis, c.1885, 25 In., Pair</td><td>584.00</td></tr>
<tr><td>Brass, Art Nouveau, Exotic Seminude Woman Holding Flower Overhead, Gilt, 9 ½ In. ....</td><td>210.00</td></tr>
<tr><td>Brass, Arts & Crafts, Tall Standard, Round Base, 8 x 18 In...</td><td>325.00</td></tr>
<tr><td>Brass, Beehive Standard, Scallop Edge Pan, Diamond Pattern Knop, Ribbed Dome Base, 18 In., Pair .</td><td>98.00</td></tr>
<tr><td>Brass, Beehive Turned Standard, Ribbed Domed Foot, Flared Rim, c.1887, 17 ¼ In., Pair.......</td><td>215.00</td></tr>
<tr><td>Brass, Bell Foot, Tapered Turned Standard & Cups, Mid Ribs, c.1885, 10 ½ In., Pair.........</td><td>276.00</td></tr>
<tr><td>Brass, Bronze, Cold Paint, Column Standard, Leaf Separator, Talon Foot, c.1920, 8 In., Pair ..</td><td>1375.00</td></tr>
<tr><td>Brass, Capstan, Cylindrical Spread Foot, Tray, Socket, Stem Peened To Base, 1600s, 4 ¾ In.....</td><td>499.00</td></tr>
<tr><td>Brass, Classical Male Figures, Urn Shape Socket, 1800s, 12 In., Pair ....Illus</td><td>84.00</td></tr>
<tr><td>Brass, Columnar, Slide Ejector, Handle, England, 10 ½ In., Pair................................</td><td>590.00</td></tr>
<tr><td>Brass, Delta, Jarvie, 4 ½ x 11 In., Pair...</td><td>671.00</td></tr>
<tr><td>Brass, Domed Base, Extractor Socket Holds, Threaded Posts, Solder, c.1690, 8 & 9 In., 2 Piece</td><td>294.00</td></tr>
<tr><td>Brass, Double Twist, 1800s, 12 In., Pair...</td><td>72.00</td></tr>
<tr><td>Brass, Edwardian, Corinthian Column, Gilt Stand, Velvet Lining, c.1815, 8 In., Pair..............</td><td>307.00</td></tr>
<tr><td>Brass, Empire, Fluted Stem, Flared Cup, Round Foot, France, 11 ½ In., Pair ....</td><td>748.00</td></tr>
<tr><td>Brass, Flemish Baroque, Capstan, Drip Pan, Bell Shape Base, 5 ¼ In., Pair ....</td><td>944.00</td></tr>
<tr><td>Brass, French Punched, Engraved, 6 ½ In., Pair..</td><td>413.00</td></tr>
<tr><td>Brass, Frog, Doing Headstand On Turtle, Cup Balanced On Feet, Painted, c.1910, 7 In., Pair ..</td><td>4030.00</td></tr>
<tr><td>Brass, George III, Beaded Trim Base, Tapered Fluted Shaft, c.1915, 10 ¼ In., Pair ....</td><td>307.00</td></tr>
<tr><td>Brass, George III, Knopped Stem, Scallop Edged Base, Push-Up, c.1780, 7 ¾ In., Pair ....</td><td>177.00</td></tr>
<tr><td>Brass, George III, Lobe Side Cut Base, England, 6 ¼ In...</td><td>708.00</td></tr>
<tr><td>Brass, Georgian, Petal Base, Scallops, Baluster Stem, Turned Cup, c.1735, 8 ¾ In., Pair.........</td><td>922.00</td></tr>
<tr><td>Brass, Girandole, Rococo Revival, Gilt, Marble Base, Figures, Putti, c.1850, 13 ½ In................</td><td>148.00</td></tr>
<tr><td>Brass, Gothic Revival, Altar Stick, Pierced Cross, Quatrefoil, Windows, Spires, c.1885, 18 In., Pair</td><td>153.00</td></tr>
<tr><td>Brass, Heemskerk, Nozzle Holes, Dutch, 7 ¾ In., Pair...</td><td>885.00</td></tr>
<tr><td>Brass, Heraldic Eagle, Spread Wings, Serpent In Mouth, 7 In., Pair.............................</td><td>3081.00</td></tr>
<tr><td>Brass, Iota, Swollen Cup, Spread Foot, Arts & Crafts, Jarvie, 14 x 7 In., Pair......................</td><td>3500.00</td></tr>
<tr><td>Brass, Knopped Stem, Round Dished Base, England, c.1720, 4 ¾ In. ....</td><td>119.00</td></tr>
<tr><td>Brass, Louis XV, Domed Base, Stepped, Vase Shape Standard, Tulip Cup, c.1765, 9 In., Pair.....</td><td>276.00</td></tr>
<tr><td>Brass, Mahogany, Fluted Stem, Square Cup, Spiral Turnings, Round Base, c.1914, 14 In., Pair</td><td>184.00</td></tr>
<tr><td>Brass, Octagonal Petal Base, 7 ½ In...</td><td>767.00</td></tr>
<tr><td>Brass, Octagonal Standard, c.1800, 9 ½ In., Pair..</td><td>188.00</td></tr>
<tr><td>Brass, Petal Base, Knopped Stem, England, 1700s, 7 ½ In., Pair ....</td><td>267.00</td></tr>
<tr><td>Brass, Pricket Stick, Triangular Base, Paw Feet, Spain, c.1715, 14 In., 4 Piece ....</td><td>235.00</td></tr>
<tr><td>Brass, Pricket, Fleur-De-Lis, 3 Paw Feet, France, 1800s, 31 In., Pair..............................Illus</td><td>270.00</td></tr>
<tr><td>Brass, Pricket, Northern European, Domed Base, 8 ½ In., Pair ....</td><td>649.00</td></tr>
<tr><td>Brass, Pricket, Repousse, c.1880, 39 In., Pair...</td><td>780.00</td></tr>
<tr><td>Brass, Queen Anne, Flared Rim, Knopped Stem, Notched Corner, Dished Base, c.1700, 7 In., Pair..</td><td>563.00</td></tr>
<tr><td>Brass, Queen Anne, Knopped Stem, Petal Shape Bobeche, Stepped Base, c.1760, 8 ½ In., Pair</td><td>1126.00</td></tr>
</table>

Candlestick, Brass, Classical Male Figures, Urn Shape Socket, 1800s, 12 In., Pair
$84.00

DuMouchelles Art Gallery

Candlestick, Brass, Pricket, Fleur-De-Lis, 3 Paw Feet, France, 1800s, 31 In., Pair
$270.00

DuMouchelles Art Gallery

Candlestick, Enamel, Georgian, White, Flower Sprigs, Vignettes, 1700s, 9 In., 4 Piece
$2,510.00

Neal Auction Co.

Candy Container, Airplane, Liberty Motor, Flag, Tin, Stamped, Borgfeldt
$1,035.00

James D. Julia Auctioneers

Candy Container, Boob McNutt, Glass, Original Closure
$1,840.00

James D. Julia Auctioneers

Candy Container, Flossie Fisher's, Sideboard, Tin
$402.00

James D. Julia Auctioneers

Candy Container, Gentleman, Wearing Suit, Jointed Arms, Germany, 5 ¾ In.
$173.00

Bertoia Auctions

Candy Container, Goblin Head, Painted Glass, Original Closure
$402.00

James D. Julia Auctioneers

Brass, Renaissance Revival, Griffin, Holding Torch, Pierced Cup, Eagle Feet, c.1890, 9 In., Pair....	307.00
Brass, Repousse, Silver Plate, Urn Shape Columns, Dome Base, 3 Shields, Prague, 1800s, 13 ½ In. ...	63.00
Brass, Riveted Posts, Mid Drip Pans, Extractor Holes, Dutch, 1600s, 8 ½ In., Pair	904.00
Brass, Sausage Turned Neck, Trumpet Base, Mid Drip, England, 17th Century, 5 In................	230.00
Brass, Side Ejector, Cylindrical, Urn Standard, Beaded Border, Dish Base, England, 8 ½ In., Pair..	295.00
Brass, Tube Shape, Round Foot, Ringed Shaft, Side Ejector, 7 ¾ In.	46.00
Brass, Turned Standard, Domed Base, Incised Ribbing, Flared Candlecup, c.1850, 12 In., Pair.	215.00
Brass, Turned Standard, Round Base, c.1790, 12 In., Pair	81.00
Brass, Turned Standard, Shaped Raised Base, France, c.1790, 12 In., Pair........................	345.00
Brass, Turned Stem, Central Knop Of Incised Bull's-Eye, Beading, Square Base, 1800s, 12 ½ In., Pair	369.00
Brass, Turned Stem, Flared Lip, Petal Base, England, c.1750, 7 ½ In., Pair	345.00
Brass, Turned Stem, Round Petal Base, Wavy Rim Cup, England, c.1750, 6 In.	356.00
Brass, Turned, Tulip Candle Cup, Round Drip Pan, Baluster, Urn, Triangular Footed, 53 In., Pair	472.00
Brass, Woman, Holding Socket On Head, Stone Column & Plinth Base, 24 In., Pair	71.00
Brass, Zeta, Flared Cup, Tapered Foot, Angular Handle, Jarvie, 6 x 6 In.	625.00
Bronze, Cherubs, Holding Lily, Marble Plinth, c.1845, 11 In., Pair...........................	390.00
Bronze, Crane, On Turtle's Back, Gilt Flowers & Cup, c.1860, 36 In., Pair	6875.00
Bronze, Dolphin, Tail Up, Supporting Candle Cup, Mouth Open, c.1885, 6 ½ x 4 ½ In.	430.00
Bronze, Gilt, Louis XVI Style, Fluted Shaft, Round Base, Leaves, Beaded, c.1865, 11 In., Pair ..	984.00
Bronze, Gilt, Oval Center, Masks, Putto Finial, Hoof Feet, Henri Picard, c.1850, 24 In., Pair....	3000.00
Bronze, Gothic Revival, Column Standard, Octagonal Drip Cup, 22 ½ In., Pair	938.00
Bronze, Neoclassical, Gilt, Urn, Sun Face Medallion, Stepped Base, Lamp Mount, c.1824, 11 In., Pair	2000.00
Bronze, Nude, Carrying Urn On Shoulder, Round Marble Base, Couple, 17 ¼ In., Pair...........	
1150.00 **Bronze,** Pierced Pagoda Shape, Panel Shaft, Picket, Chinese, 13 ½ In., Pair	345.00
Bronze, Pierced, Relief Designs, Chinese, 23 ¼ In.	81.00
Bronze, Pricket, Inverted Bell Shape, Drip Pan, Columnar, Dragons, c.1855, 19 In., Pair........	20910.00
Bronze, Salamander Shape, Ruby Eyes, Scroll Mounted, c.1885, 4 x 4 ½ In.	399.00
Bronze, Sconce, 2-Light, Lyre Form, Leafy Arms, France, 7 ½ x 4 ½ In., 4 Piece	5676.00
Bronze, Shaped, Leaves, Winged Putti, Tripod Base, Medallions, Paw Feet, c.1795, 14 In., Pair .	830.00
Chased Flowers, Weighted, S. Kirk & Sons, 3 ⅝ In., Pair..	188.00
Copper, Altar, Cylindrical, Wheat & Grapes, Beaded, Leaves, c.1915, 31 In., Pair................	153.00
Enamel, Copper, Painted Flowers, White, Gilt Metal Scalloped Base, Eng., 9 ⅜ In., Pair	708.00
Enamel, Georgian, White, Flower Sprigs, Vignettes, 1700s, 9 In., 4 Piece..........................*Illus*	2510.00
Enamel, Renaissance Style, Blue, Portraits, Medallions, Octagonal Base, Limoges, 1800s, 6 In.	413.00
Enamel, Turquoise Blue, Porcelain Landscape Cartouches, c.1910, 14 ¼ In........................	1701.00
Gilt Bronze, Altar, Fluted Stem, Ribbed Pan, 3-Sided Base, Medallion Portraits, 18 In., Pair...	72.00
Gilt Bronze, Column Standard, Berry & Leaf Cast, France, 1800s, 12 In., Pair	750.00
Gilt Bronze, Embossed Leaves, Column Standard, Round Foot, 12 In., Pair......................	750.00
Gilt Bronze, Fluted Stem, Swans, Shell Molded Base, Egg & Dart Pans, c.1890, 10 ¼ In., Pair	430.00
Gilt Bronze, Regency Style, Cast Shells, Profiles, Strapwork, Square Foot, c.1800, 9 In., Pair..	4688.00
Gilt Bronze, Rock Crystal, Beading, Molded Leaves, Reeded Stem, Round Base, c.1890, 7 ¾ In., Pair	1045.00
Gilt Gesso, Flower & Leaf Prickets, Urn Shape, Carved, Spain, c.1790, 31 x 15 In., Pair...........	2478.00
Gilt, Carved, 2 Headed Eagle, Inset Round Mirror, Square Base, Footed, c.1800, 17 ½ In., Pair	546.00
Giltwood, Carved Stem, Ruffle Rim, Scrolling, Paw Feet, Italy, 1700s, 42 In.	450.00
Glass, Cobalt Blue, Swollen Stem, Pinched Neck, Flared Rim, Round Foot, 16 In., Pair	374.00
Glass, Green Stems, Amethyst Socle, Round Foot, Cylindrical, Chatham Glass Co., 6 ½ In., Pair...	150.00
Glass, Pink & Clear, Flower Shaped Cups, Petals, Footed Stem, 11 In., Pair.....................	374.00
Mahogany, Brass, Georgian Style, Reeded Urns, Fluted Stem, Tapered, 14 ¼ In., Pair.............	53.00
Marble, Metal, Scroll Feet, Cartouches, Putti, 16 ¼ x 8 ½ In., Pair	984.00
Metal, Patinated, Whippet, Seated, Holding Torch, 13 x 7 ⅔ In., Pair	325.00
Paktong, George III, Columnar, Square Base, c.1760, 10 ½ In., Pair...........................	4266.00
Pewter, Shaped Baluster Stem, Round Foot, Flared Rim, Flagg & Homan, Ohio, c.1850, 8 In., Pair..	206.00
Plaster, Bronze Finish, Gilt Highlights, Carved Swollen Stem, Tripod Scroll Feet, 25 In., Pair .	240.00
Porcelain, Blanc De Chine, Sphinx Shape, Dome Base, Fitz & Floyd, 10 In., Pair...................	81.00
Porcelain, Figural, Maiden, Gold Draped Gown, Cornucopia, Amphora, Footed Base, 19 In., Pair....	115.00
Pricket, Baroque Style, Patinated Metal, Cartouche 3-Part Base, Medallions, 16 In., Pair	2950.00
Repousse Flowers, Cylindrical, Footed, Silver, S. Kirk & Son, 10 In., 4 Piece...........................	1998.00
Repousse, Flowers & Leaves, Baluster, Silver, S. Kirk & Son, 10 In., Pair	1320.00
Silver, Aqua Swirl Glass Shade, Gorham, 13 In., Pair.......................................	149.00
Silver, Baluster Standard, Putti, Shaped Square Base, Pierced, Scrolls, Germany, c.1915, 11 In., Pair.	584.00
Silver, Baluster Stem, Urn Shape Nozzle, Gadroon Banding, 1947, 12 In., Pair.......................	1168.00
Silver, Baluster, Embossed, Chased Design, Paw Feet, c.1800, 9 ½ In., Pair	940.00
Silver, Baluster, Knopped Standard, Chased, Repousse, Austria-Hungary, c.1850, 11 ½ In., Pair....	813.00
Silver, Bronze Patinated, Charles X, Ormolu, Raised Feet, c.1825, 13 In., Pair................	1250.00
Silver, Chased, Column Shape, Knopped Stem, Domed Base, Twig Feet, Poland, c.1892, 13 In., Pair.	2813.00
Silver, Cherub, Dolphin, Winged Angel Thumb Piece, Shaped Base, Round Foot, 1800s, 5 In..	270.00

C

Silver, Corinthian Column, Square Stepped Base, Elkington, 1913, 11 In., Pair	531.00
Silver, Corinthian, Leaf & Scroll, Ribbons, Swags, Flowers, Tiered Base, 11 ⅝ In., Pair	4148.00
Silver, Curvilinear Arms, Center Scroll, Tulip & Ball, Alphonse Lapaglia, 8 x 11 In., Pair	1944.00
Silver, Embossed, Baluster Shape, Paw Feet, c.1840, 9 ½ In., Pair	1015.00
Silver, Figural, Dolphin Standard, Beaded Cavetto Domed Base, Italy, c.1965, 7 ½ x 4 In., Pair.	799.00
Silver, Fluted, Stepped Base, E. Hutton, 1893, 12 x 4 ¾ In.	413.00
Silver, George II Style, Tapered, Weighted, S. Kirk & Sons, Baltimore, c.1955, 9 In.	540.00
Silver, George V, Tapered, Stepped Base, England, 10 In., Pair	575.00
Silver, Horse Hoof Base, Inscribed Sir Julian, England, c.1890, 7 In., Pair	1180.00
Silver, Knopped Column, Cased Leaves, 10 ½ In., Pair	1000.00
Silver, Leaves, Incised Veins, 3 Tiers, Holder, H. Petzal, 1968, 4 x 10 In.	4800.00
Silver, Maintenon Pattern, Tapered, Urn Cup, Gorham, 1920s, 11 In., 4 Piece	3660.00
Silver, Petals, Blossoms, Hollow Knopped Standard, Germany, Schott, 11 ⅜ In., Pair	1000.00
Silver, Rococo, Shaped Bobeche, Base, Shells, Knopped Baluster Stems, c.1750, 10 In., 4 Piece.	13035.00
Silver, Scrolled, Embossed, Weighted, Russia, c.1910, 13 ¾ In., Pair	790.00
Silver, Squared Column, Engraved Monogram, Webster Co., 5 ½ In., Pair	178.00
Silver, Swags, Masks, Tapered Square Column, Urn Socket, Footed, Crichton, c.1917, 10 In., Pair	1625.00
Silver, Tapered, Gadrooned, Acanthus Calyx, Urn Shape Nozzle, Round Foot, 9 In., Pair	338.00
Silver, Tapering Concave Standard, Domed Foot, Inverted Bell Nozzle, c.1927, 12 In., Pair	615.00
Silver Plate, Anthemion & Palmette Design Stem, Spread Foot, c.1800, 13 In., Pair	538.00
Silver Plate, Art Nouveau, Bobeche, Barbour, c.1902, 10 ½ In., Pair	71.00
Silver Plate, Detachable Nozzle, Sheffield, England, c.1810, 11 ¼ In., 4 Piece	384.00
Silver Plate, Elongated Octagon, Tapered Stem, Domed Foot, Reeded, c.1885, 12 ¾ In., Pair.	153.00
Silver Plate, George V, Baluster Stem, Domed Foot, Thistle Shape Nozzle, c.1935, 12 In., Pair..	430.00
Silver Plate, George V, Baluster, Cavetto Domed Foot, Inverted Bell Nozzle, c.1935, 10 In., Pair ...	184.00
Silver Plate, Georgian Style, Oval, Fluted, 11 ½ In., Pair	63.00
Silver Plate, Paneled, Stepped, Gallia, Christofle, France, 6 In., Pair	472.00
Silver Plate, Wood, Spiral, Arts & Crafts, England, c.1920, 9 In., Pair	325.00
Tavern, Inset Bells, Turned Shaft & Foot Supports, c.1850, 15 In., Pair	276.00
Walnut, Turned Baluster Columns, Ring Base, White, Gilt, 1700s, 23 In., Pair	475.00
Wood, Angel, Carved, Paint, Holding Pricket, 1800s, 19 In., Pair	1375.00
Wood, Baroque Women, Pricket, Paint, c.1850, 19 ½ In., Pair	1750.00
Wood, Blackamoor, Carved, Glass Eyes, Holding Scalloped Tole Tray, 15 In., Pair	4700.00
Wood, Paint Design, Shaped Stem, Tripod Base, Paw Feet, 18th Century, 16 ½ In., Pair	748.00
Wood, Paint, Altar, Carved, Fluted, Gilt Leaves, Paw Feet, Black Platform, c.1815, 38 In., Pair	1968.00
Wood, Turned, Green Paint, Round Stepped Base, Red & Yellow Striping, 11 In., Pair	326.00
Wood, Walnut, Torchere, Angel, Carved, Pricket, Italy, c.1800, 42 In., Pair	3750.00
Wood, White Paint, Gold Leaf, Curl Footed, 36 x 11 In., Pair	600.00
Wrought Iron, 2 Sockets, Floor, Tripod Base, c.1890, 58 ½ In.	264.00
Wrought Iron, Cylindrical Stem, Round Foot, Ball In Open Circle, 1950s, 42 x 11 ¾ In., Pair.	813.00
Wrought Iron, Flared Top & Bottom, Strip Of Metal Design, 17 In., Pair	295.00
Wrought Iron, Hanging, J-Shape, Twisted Shaft, Curled Tip, c.1790, 15 ½ In.	230.00
Wrought Iron, Hog Scraper, Riveted Base, U.S.A., c.1800, 7 In., Pair	705.00
Wrought Iron, Miner, Spike, Black Paint, c.1800, 11 ½ In.	201.00

CANDLEWICK *items may be listed in the Imperial Glass and Pressed Glass categories.*

CANDY CONTAINERS have been popular since the late Victorian era. Collectors have long favored the glass containers, but now all types, including tin and papier-mache, are collected. Probably the earliest glass container sold commercially was the Liberty Bell made in 1876 for sale at the Centennial Exposition. Thousands of designs were made until the cost became too high in the 1960s. By the late 1970s, reproductions were being made and sold without the candy. Containers listed here are glass unless otherwise described. A Belsnickle is a nineteenth-century figure of Father Christmas. Some candy containers may be listed in Toy or in other categories.

Airplane, Liberty Motor, Flag, Tin, Stamped, Borgfeldt.............................*Illus*	1035.00
Ax, Cardboard, Patriotic, Red, White, Blue, Germany, 7 In.	29.00
Baby Shoe, Papier-Mache, Chenille, Pink, 4 x 2 In.	45.00
Baseball Player With Bat, Glass, 3 ¼ x 4 x 2 In.	1100.00
Belsnickle, Blue Robe, Rabbit Hair Beard, Fir Tree, Germany, 30 In.	6600.00
Boob McNutt, Glass, Original Closure.............................*Illus*	1840.00
Boy, Sitting On Rabbit, Carrot In Mouth, Glass Eyes, Bisque, Felt, c.1900, 8 x 9 In.	2450.00
Bull, Papier-Mache, Wide Eyed, Smiling, Coiled Horns, Germany, 4 ½ In.	45.00
Chick, Yellow, Metal Legs, Porcelain, c.1900, 2 ½ x 3 In.	75.00
Chicken, On Nest, Papier-Mache, White, Red, 1924, 7 x 6 x 4 In.	125.00
Chicken, Pushing Cart, Wood, Metal Wheels, Germany, c.1950, 6 x 3 ¾ In.	75.00

Candy Container, Halloween, Black Cat, Composition, Papier-Mache, Fur, Glass Eyes, Germany, 10 In.
$1,652.00

Bertoia Auctions

Candy Container, Halloween, Jack-O'-Lantern, Composition, Painted Face, Stem, Germany, 5 ½ In.
$708.00

Bertoia Auctions

Candy Container, Halloween, Pumpkin-Head Vegetable Man, Composition, Molded Head, 1920s, 5 ¾ In.
$506.00

Hake's Americana & Collectibles

Candy Container, Hot Doggie, Glass, Original Closure, 5 ⅝ In.
$288.00

James D. Julia Auctioneers

Candy Container, Reindeer Head, Cracker Body, Applied Antlers & Ears, Hanging Loop, Dresden, 6 In. $885.00

Bertoia Auctions

Candy Container, Santa Claus, Feather Tree, Composition, Painted, 1920s, 7 ½ In. $171.00

Hake's Americana & Collectibles

Candy Container, Store, 5 & 10 Cent, Tin $805.00

James D. Julia Auctioneers

Candy Container, Toonerville Trolley, Glass, Paint Traces, 3 ¼ In. $690.00

Bertoia Auctions

Choir Boy, Robe, Papier-Mache, Chenille Muff, Nodder, Germany, 5 ½ In.	55.00
Clown, Brown Cone Hat, Composition, 4 ¾ In.	90.00
Devil Head, Horns, Composition, Germany, c.1920, 6 In.	95.00
Dog, Glass, Clear, Federal Glass Co., c.1930, 3 ⅛ In.	15.00
Doll, Composition Boy Head, Yellow, Brown Clothing, c.1910, 10 ¼ In.	96.00
Donkey, Barrel Wagon, Glass, Screw Lid, c.1900, 4 ½ x 2 ¾ In.	50.00
Drum, Brass Hoops, Wire Rope, Drum Sticks On Rim, Kepi, Stopper, 2 x 1 ½ In.	384.00
Duck, Sitting On Egg, Spring-Loaded Head, Yellow, Green, 7 In.	165.00
Easter Bunny, Standing, Basket On Back, Glass Eyes, 11 In.	89.00
Egg, Papier-Mache, Children, Ducks, Bunnies, Gold Ground, Germany, 4 x 6 In.	19.00
Egg, Papier-Mache, Rabbits In Car, Chicks, Echt Erzgebirge, Germany, 10 In.	50.00
Egg, Teddy Bears, Dresden, Germany, 2 ¾ In.	266.00
Elephant, In Egg, Glass Eyes, Bobble Ears, Tail, Tusks, Germany, 5 ½ In.	384.00
Father Christmas, Red Robe, Snow Flecked, White Trim, Composition, Tree Sprig, 13 In.	472.00
Felix The Cat, Walking Position, Round Tapered Pedestal, 3 In.	4025.00
Flossie Fisher's, Sideboard, Tin *Illus*	402.00
Flossie Fisher's, Table, Round Top, Cylindrical Pedestal, Yellow & Black	1035.00
Gas Pump, Tin Closure, Raised Lettering, 23 Cents To-Day, 1920-30s, 2 x 4 ¼ In.	230.00
Gentleman, Wearing Suit, Jointed Arms, Germany, 5 ¾ In. *Illus*	173.00
Gingerbread Boy, Cardboard, Painted, Base, Germany, c.1925, 5 x 3 In.	110.00
Girl, Chalkware, Green Bonnet, Polka Dot Dress, Germany, 4 ¾ In.	65.00
Goblin Head, Painted Glass, Original Closure *Illus*	402.00
Greyhound Bus, Glass, Embossed, Dog, 5 x 1 ¾ In.	231.00
Halloween, Black Cat, Composition, Papier-Mache, Fur, Glass Eyes, Germany, 10 In. *Illus*	1652.00
Halloween, Jack-O'-Lantern, Bell Shape, Tin Closure, Paint, Glass, 3 ¾ In.	480.00
Halloween, Jack-O'-Lantern, Composition, Painted Face, Stem, Germany, 5 ½ In. *Illus*	708.00
Halloween, Jack-O'-Lantern, Man Playing Accordion, Plastic, 1950s, 3 x 5 In.	125.00
Halloween, Jack-O'-Lantern, Playing Accordion, Orange, Blue & White, Tico Toys, 1950s	125.00
Halloween, Jack-O'-Lantern, Smiling, On Back Of Black Cat, Plastic, 1960s, 2 x 3 In.	28.00
Halloween, Jack-O'-Lantern, Watermelon, Composition, Multicolor, Germany, 2 ½ In.	649.00
Halloween, Pumpkin-Head Boy, Squats, Kneels, Mechanical, 4 ½ In.	300.00
Halloween, Pumpkin-Head Vegetable Man, Composition, Molded Head, 1920s, 5 ¾ In. *Illus*	506.00
Halloween, Veggie Man, Composition, Painted, Pumpkin Body, Lemon Head, Germany, 7 In.	1416.00
Hansel & Gretel, Witch's House, Cylindrical, Cardboard, Germany, 5 ¼ In.	45.00
Hat, Fedora, Glass, Clear, 4 ½ x 2 x 4 In.	25.00
Horn, Plastic, Glass, Spiral, Whistle Mouthpiece, J.H. Millstein Co., 1948, 7 In.	45.00
Hot Doggie, Glass, Original Closure, 5 ⅝ In. *Illus*	288.00
Kaleidoscope, Tin & Glass, Moving Pictures Decal, Cylindrical, Box, c.1913, 7 x 3 In.	13800.00
Kangaroo, Standing, Glass, Round Pedestal, 5 ¼ In.	403.00
Lantern, Glass, Red Metal, Marked, USA, 3 ½ In.	20.00
Oyster Shell Ornament, Golden, Pink Silk Bag, Dresden, Germany, 2 ½ In.	207.00
PEZ, Batman, Blue Cowl, Cape, Removable, c.1966, 4 In.	178.00
PEZ, Olympic Snowman, Red, White Plastic, 4 ¾ In.	390.00
PEZ, Snoopy, Black & White, 12 In.	26.00
PEZ, Space Gun, Silver, Red, Raised Design, Permits, Instruction Sheet, 5 In., 2 Piece	348.00
PEZ, Speedy Alka-Seltzer, White, Tablet Hat, Red Hair, Feet, 4 ¼ In.	191.00
PEZ, Yoko Wolf, Red Plastic, 4 ¾ In.	330.00
Phone, Glass, Clear, Wood Receiver, 4 ½ In.	55.00
Phonograph, Glass Body, Square Base, Horn, 3 ⅝ In.	230.00
Piano, Black, Red, Gladys, c.1913	518.00
Pumpkin Head, Glass, Metal Handle, Paint, 4 ¾ In.	450.00
Pumpkin Head, Holding Accordion, Wooden Arms, Legs, 5 ½ In.	720.00
Purse, Clear Textured Glass, Handle, Red Tag, Eagle Bend	173.00
Rabbit, In Egg, Papier-Mache, Glass Eye, 1920s, 7 ¾ In.	75.00
Ram's Head, Silver, Extended Ears, Full Horns, Red Silk Bag, 5 In.	1298.00
Reindeer Head, Cracker Body, Applied Antlers & Ears, Hanging Loop, Dresden, 6 In. *Illus*	885.00
Rooster, Cock-Of-The-Walk, Composition, Glass Eyes, Multicolor, Germany, 7 In.	236.00
Santa Claus, Black, Composition Face, Hands, Wood Base, Green Robe, White Trim, 21 In.	384.00
Santa Claus, Chimney, Sack, Lowney's, Scotland, 10 In.	90.00
Santa Claus, Composition Face, Hands, Rabbit Fur Beard, Holding Basket, 22 In.	5100.00
Santa Claus, Eating Sweets, Tin, Red, England, 1940s, 2 ⅞ In., Diam.	48.00
Santa Claus, Feather Tree, Composition, Painted, 1920s, 7 ½ In. *Illus*	171.00
Santa Claus, Head, Winking, Handle, Celluloid, 1 ½ x 2 ½ In.	9.00
Santa Claus, In Sleigh, Reindeer, Wood, Composition, Rabbit Fur Beard, Feather Tree Sprig, 17 In.	885.00
Santa Claus, Paper, Fur Beard, Bobble Head, Red, 12 In.	150.00
Santa Claus, Red Cape, Hood, Crepe Paper, Papier-Mache, Composition, Germany, 14 In.	270.00
Santa Claus, Red Felt, Leather Belt, Fir Tree, Standing, Germany, 13 In.	1020.00

Santa Claus, Reindeer, Removable Antlers, Glass Eyes, Composition, 16 In.	5900.00
Santa Claus, Sleigh, Composition, Wood Sled, Fur Beard, Feather Tree Sprig, 5 ½ In.	118.00
Ship, Milk Glass, c.1950, 6 ½ x 3 ½ In.	83.00
Shoe, Glass, Clear, Heal, c.1960, 2 ⅞ In.	32.00
Soldier, Standing By Tent, Glass, 3 ¼ In.	2645.00
Store, 5 & 10 Cent, Tin. *Illus*	805.00
Telephone, Glass, Brass Receiver, Paper Label, c.1930, 1 ¾ x 2 ½ In.	43.00
Telephone, Redlich, Bell, Wood Handle, 6 ¼ In.	316.00
Toonerville Trolley, Glass, Paint Traces, 3 ¼ In. *Illus*	690.00
Turkey, Composition, Painted, Lead Feet, Head Separates, Germany, 8 ¼ In.	413.00
Uncle Sam, Red, White, Blue, Stars, Movable Wood Arms, 10 ¾ In.	80.00
Wagon, Hello Express, Children Playing, 1920s, 6 x 3 In.	360.00
Wedding Silver, Silver, Silk Bag, Dresden, Germany, 3 ¾ In.	238.00
Whip, Clear Handle, Tapered Shaft, 5 ½ In.	1495.00
Windmill, Glass, Red & Green, 4 In.	374.00
Windmill, Golden Blades Turn, Embossed Shingles, Dresden, Germany, 3 ½ In.	1121.00

CANES and walking sticks were used by every well-dressed man in the nineteenth century, but by World War I the style had changed. Today canes are used by few but the infirm. Collectors prize old canes made with special features, like hidden swords, whiskey flasks, or risqué pictures seen through peepholes. Examples with solid gold heads or made from exotic materials are among the higher-priced canes. See also Scrimshaw.

Amethyst Quartz Handle, Purple, Off-White, Gold Filled Collar, Snakewood, c.1900, 37 In.	1265.00
Blowgun, Wood, Brass Collar, Ferrule, Continental, c.1880	863.00
Bone, Silver Head, Horse Shape, Glass Eye, Silver Bridle, Wood Shaft, Bone Tip, 36 In.	885.00
Cat, Seated, Amber, Yellow & Black Eyes, Black Polished Handle, Ebony Shaft, 35 ½ In.	368.00
Cat, Smoky Quartz, Enamel, Furry Face, Sapphire Eyes, Purple Enamel, Horn, c.1900, 36 In.	4888.00
Dagger, Man's Head, Boxwood, Mutton Chop Beard, Top Hat, Branch Nib Release, c.1865, 29 In.	1495.00
Dog Head, Gutta Percha, Remington Dog, Ferrous Metal Ferrule, c.1875, 34 In.	316.00
Ebony, Art Nouveau, Butterfly, Flowers, Silver Loop, Brass & Iron Ferrule, c.1895, 34 In.	460.00
Folding Seat, Horse's Fetlock, Hoof, Brass Horseshoe, Nickel Metal Seat Opens, c.1892, 37 In.	345.00
Fruitwood, Boar's Tusk, Sterling Collar, Embossed, Tapering Shaft, Steel Ferrule, 34 ¾ In.	344.00
Gambler's, Ivory, Receptacle Holds Dice, Spinner, Pencil, Brass Fitting, Exotic Wood, c.1915, 35 In.	920.00
Gold, 14K, Bone Handle, Walnut Shaft, c.1850, 35 In.	443.00
Gold, Jade, Duck Head Handle, Glass Eyes, Wicker Cane, Rose Gold Band, Lady's, 37 In.	1778.00
Gold, Scrolls & Flowers, Presentation In Cartouche, 40th Regiment, 35 In.	480.00
Gun, Breech Load, Dumonthier, Horn Handle, Brass Collar, Drop Down Trigger, c.1880, 35 In.	1725.00
Ivory Handle, Scrolled, Copper Mounts, Wood Shaft, Black Paint, c.1900, 29 In.	130.00
Ivory, Blackamoor Handle, Man's Head, Bulging Pear Set Eyes, Ebony, 36 ½ In.	276.00
Ivory, Skeleton, Standing On Plinth, Silver Collar, Bamboo Shaft, Brass Ferrule, c.1895, 36 In.	1265.00
Jade, Australian Wild Parakeet, Horn Ferrule, Mahoganized Hardwood Shaft, c.1870, 36 In.	345.00
Parrot, Ivory, On Perch, Gold Collar, Rosewood, Brass Ferrule, c.1885, 37 In.	3220.00
Porcelain, Ball & Stem, Painted, Blue, Courting Couple, Period Clothes, Ebony, c.1900, 37 In.	489.00
Porcelain, Blue Rosette, Gold Overlay, Blue Scrolls, Flowers, Umber, Gold, Chestnut, c.1885, 36 In.	1955.00
Porcelain, Mephistopheles, Ringed Brass Snake Collar, Black Hardwood, Horn Ferrule, c.1900, 36 In.	546.00
Root Carved, Lizard Handle, Ohio, c.1900, 32 ½ In.	259.00
Rosewood, Cow's Head Handle, Horn Tip, Bone, 19th Century, 38 ½ In.	326.00
Rosewood, Rose Quartz, Cylindrical, Flat Panels, Vermeil Silver Collar, Brass Ferrule, c.1895, 36 In.	460.00
Shaving Kit, Silver Knob, Hinged Lid, Horsehair, Sterling Brush, Razor, Malacca, Brass, c.1932, 34 In.	690.00
Shillelagh, Blackthorn, Leather Wrist Strap, c.1890, 22 ½ In.	69.00
Silver Head, Golf Club Head, Wood Shaft, Monogram, England, 36 In.	413.00
Silver Knob, Rose Boughs, Repousse, Flowers, Insects, Conifer Wood, Brass, France, c.1895, 35 In.	374.00
Silver, Ebonized, Figural Handle, Leda Embracing Swan, Tapering Shaft, 38 ⅜ In.	349.00
Sword, Hazelwood, Crook Handle, Steel Blade, Engraved, Metal Ferrule, c.1910, 37 In.	690.00
Telescope, Compass, Wood Ball Handle, Removable Cap, Brass Collar, Wood, c.1910, 38 In.	1150.00
Tool Kit, Rosewood Knob Handle, Concealed Tools, Pressure Fitting, Brass, 1900s, 36 In.	633.00
Undertaker's Coffin Measure, Bamboo, Root Handle, Swing-Out Arm, c.1880, 37 In.	1610.00
Walking Stick, Antler Handle, Black Trim, Nickel Silver Cap, c.1885, 36 In.	184.00
Walking Stick, Bearded Man's Handle, Carved, Pa., 34 ½ In.	237.00
Walking Stick, Bird, Carved, Stippled Yellow Paint, Branch Form, 34 In.	413.00
Walking Stick, Bone, Tapered, Turned Ivory Knob, c.1875, 35 ¾ In.	711.00
Walking Stick, Carved, Painted, Indian Head Knob, 1912, 36 In.	324.00
Walking Stick, Daisy Knob, Carved Rock Crystal, Gold, Diamond Center, Ebony, 36 In.	1800.00
Walking Stick, Eagle's Head, Glass Eyes, Spiral Reeding, Stars & Stripes, Walnut Shaft, 33 In.	413.00
Walking Stick, Entwined Snake, Carved, 37 In.	561.00

Canton, Chestnut Basket, Pierced, Landscape, Cloud & Rain Border, Handles, 1800s, 5 x 9 In.
$173.00

James D. Julia Auctioneers

Canton, Platter, Water Landscape, Chamfered, 17 ¼ x 14 ½ In.
$480.00

DuMouchelles Art Gallery

Canton, Tank, Pagodas, Boats, Mountains, Wave Design Rim, Drain Hole, 1800s, 8 In.
$4,800.00

Skinner, Inc.

TIP
If you are installing a dead-bolt lock on your door for added security, be sure the screws are at least 1 inch long. It is best to use a screw 1½ to 2 inches long. In a break-in attempt where force is used against the outside of the door, a short screw in the strike plate will tear away, allowing the door to be opened.

Canton, Tray, River Scene, Oblong, c.1900, 7 In.
$120.00

DuMouchelles Art Gallery

Canton, Tureen, Soup, Lid, Pagoda, River, Boats, Bridge, Boar Head Handles, 1800s, 9 x 13 In.
$390.00

Cowan's Auctions

Capo-Di-Monte, Charger, Armorial, Bird, Crown, Gilt, Flowers, Scrolls, Figures, Marked, 1800s, 16 In.
$649.00

Brunk Auctions

Capo-Di-Monte, Figurine, Satyr Drinking Wine, Seminude Female Holding Grapes, Marked, c.1800, 12 ½ In., Pair
$826.00

Brunk Auctions

Walking Stick, Frog Handle, Pink Quartz, Ruby Eyes, Guilloche Collar, Ebony Shaft, 36 In. .. 2280.00
Walking Stick, Gold Mounted, Repousse Handle, Shells, Flower Garlands, Horn Tip, c.1800 .. 418.00
Walking Stick, Horse Head, Rooster Handle, Pa., c.1895, 34 In. ... 415.00
Walking Stick, Ivory Handle, Stallion's Head, Mouth Open, c.1890, 33 In. ... 960.00
Walking Stick, Ivory Lady's Leg Handle, c.1890, 28 ¼ In. ... 720.00
Walking Stick, Mahogany, Brass Inlaid Knob, Tapered, 35 ¼ In. ... 236.00
Walking Stick, Snake Wrap, Wood, Painted, Black, Brown & Yellow Rattler, 34 In. ... 354.00
Walking Stick, Tree Branch, Knob, Pommel Handle, Metal Tip, 34 In. ... 24.00
Walking Stick, Whalebone, Baleen Spacer, Scrimshaw, Clasped Fist, Snake Pommel, 33 ½ In. 3068.00
Walking Stick, Whalebone, Baleen, Scrimshaw, Hand Clasping Ball Pommel, 36 ½ In. ... 1180.00
Walking Stick, Whalebone, Carved, Embossed Metal, Tapered, c.1840, 36 In. ... 2133.00
Walking Stick, Whalebone, Ivory, Baleen, Abalone Design, Sailor Made, 36 ¼ In. ... 6372.00
Walking Stick, Whalebone, Ivory, Turned Knob, c.1870, 35 In. ... 944.00
Walking Stick, Wood, Ivory Cue Ball Handle, Silver Disk, Engraved Boston Red Sox, c.1900, 34 In. 783.00
Walking Stick, Wood, Man's Bald Head, Large Parrot-Like Nose, Carved, Victorian ... 270.00
Walking Stick, Wood, Roses, Parade Figure, Tree, Book, Rifle, Sun, Soldier, c.1870, 36 In. ... 3100.00
Walking Stick, Wrought Iron, Twisted Shaft, Openwork Basket Weave Tip, D. Merkel, 36 ¾ In. 295.00
Walrus Ivory Handle, Dog-Like Head, Glass Eyes, Wood Shaft, Brass, Silver Mounts, c.1885, 34 In... 325.00
Whimsy, 10 Balls In Chamber, 1-Piece Conifer Wood, Handle, White Metal Ferrule, c.1890, 34 In. 690.00
Whimsy, Wood, Carved, Chip Carved, 2 Free Moving Balls In Handle, c.1927, 5 ¾ In. ... 599.00
Wood, Applied Dogs, Pig, Opossum, Carved, Painted, 1888, 37 In. ... 5214.00
Wood, Art Nouveau, Silver Base, Vermeil Flowers, Reticulated Leaves, Brass, Iron, c.1900, 37 In.... 1380.00
Wood, Bearded Man's Head, Arms & Hands Holding Under His Chin, Carved, 39 In. ... 130.00
Wood, Bird Whistle Handle, Carved, Painted, Schtockschnitzler Simmons, Pa., c.1900, 37 In. 3081.00
Wood, Bird Whistle Handle, Carved, Schtockschnitzler Simmons, Pa., c.1885, 34 ½ In. ... 1033.00
Wood, Bird, Flags, Masonic Emblems, Trolley Car, Couple In Bed, Indians, J.P. Zweizig, c.1910, 35 In. 1304.00
Wood, Bird, Mask Handle, Carved, Red, Black Paint, Ribbed, Bally, 39 In. ... 5214.00
Wood, Dog Head Handle, Eagle, Steer, Horse Shaft, Carved, Pa., c.1895, 36 In. ... 1007.00
Wood, Dog Head Handle, Glass Eye, c.1890, 32 ½ In. ... 236.00
Wood, Dog Head Handle, Horse, Stag, Vine, Flower Carved Shaft, 33 1/13 In. ... 1778.00
Wood, Dog Head Handle, Rooster Grip, Carved, Pa., c.1890, 31 ½ In. ... 415.00
Wood, Dog, Man's Figure, Carved, Painted Red, Signed H. Bleck, c.1870, 34 ½ In. ... 1185.00
Wood, Donkey Head, Handle, Glass Eyes, Side Button Controls Tongue, Ear, c.1890, 37 In. ... 944.00
Wood, Eagle, Stag, Figures, Carved, Marked JMP 1890, 37 ⅜ In. ... 889.00
Wood, Horn, Art Nouveau, Maiden, Flowers In Hair, Vines, Mucha Style, 1890s, 36 In. ... 1725.00
Wood, Indian Head, Handle, Carved, Dartmouth College, 37 ½ In. ... 153.00
Wood, Man's Head Handle, Wearing Jockey Cap, Riding Crop Carved From Root, c.1850, 26 In. ... 118.00
Wood, Martyred Presidents, 1865-1902, Carved, Checkerboard Ground, c.1915, 36 ½ In. ... 3081.00
Wood, Parrot, Carved, Ebonized, Multicolor, 36 In. ... 178.00
Wood, Pig Head Handle, Carved, Painted, c.1900, 36 In. ... 178.00
Wood, Snake, Entwined Around Staff, Carved, Painted, 35 In. ... 207.00
Wood, Snake, Turtle, Bust Of Woman Handle, Carved, Pa., c.1890, 36 In. ... 444.00
Wood, Snake-Wrapped Shaft, Painted, U.S.A., c.1900, 39 In. ... 600.00
Wood, Spread Wing Eagles, Turtle, Stars, Violin, Carved, GAR, c.1875, 34 In. ... 948.00

CANTON CHINA is blue-and-white ware made near the city of Canton, in China, from about 1795 to the early 1900s. It is hand decorated with a landscape, building, bridge, and trees. There is never a person on the bridge. The "rain and cloud" border was used. It is similar to Nanking ware, which is listed in this book in its own category.

Basket, Fruit, Stand, Reticulated, c.1870, 10 x 9 ¾ In. ... 885.00
Bidet, Pagoda, River Landscape, Flower Medallion, 24 ¼ In. ... 3776.00
Bowl, Blue, White, Square, Cut Corners, c.1860, 4 ½ x 10 ¼ In. ... 266.00
Bowl, Lid, Seascape, Knob Finial, Pinched Rectangle Shape, c.1860, 9 ¾ In. ... 165.00
Bowl, Salad, Cut Corners, c.1850, 9 ½ x 9 ¼ In. ... 708.00
Bowl, White Ground, Cobalt Blue Glaze, Footed, 7 ¾ x 2 ¼ In. ... 121.00
Charger, Courtyard Scene, Blue & White, Gilt Rim, 1800s, 14 ½ In. ... 300.00
Chestnut Basket, Pierced, Landscape, Cloud & Rain Border, Handles, 1800s, 5 x 9 In. ...*Illus* 173.00
Cream Jug, Snout Nose, c.1850, 4 ¾ In. ... 118.00
Creamer, Helmet Shape, c.1860, 5 In. ... 295.00
Dish, Boat, River, House Scene, 10 ½ x 13 ½ In. ... 189.00
Dish, Hot Water, Cover, Pod Finial, c.1850, 15 In. ... 561.00
Dish, Sweetmeat, Scholars & Students, 9 Sections, 10 ¾ x 10 ¾ In. ... 767.00
Drainer, Meat Platter, 16 In. ... 1062.00
Ginger Jar, Lid, Blue & White, Landscape, Urn Shape, 7 In. ... 81.00
Ginger Jar, Lid, Bulbous, White, Cobalt Blue Scene, Garden Gazebo, Mountains, 8 x 7 In. ... 130.00

Ginger Jar, Lid, Gasket, Oval, White, Blue, 1800s, 6 In.	115.00
Jug, Lid, Foo Dog Finial, Strap Handle, c.1850, 8 In.	1534.00
Mug, Strap Handle, c.1860, 4 ¼ In.	472.00
Pitcher, Water, 7 ¾ In.	384.00
Platter, Landscape, Canted Rectangle, c.1850, 18 In.	590.00
Platter, Water Landscape, Chamfered, 17 ¼ x 14 ½ In. ......*Illus*	480.00
Platter, White Ground, Cobalt Blue Glaze, Canted Corners, 16 x 12 ½ In.	115.00
Punch Bowl, Pastoral, Water Landscape, Cloud Border, Wide Rim, Ring Foot, 1800s, 6 x 16 In.	1150.00
Serving Dish, Lid, c.1850, 8 ¼ In., Pair	561.00
Stand, Tureen, c.1850, 14 In.	384.00
Tank, Pagodas, Boats, Mountains, Wave Design Rim, Drain Hole, 1800s, 8 In. ......*Illus*	4800.00
Tea Canister, Lid, Rectangular, 8 In.	1652.00
Teapot, Lid, c.1850, 5 ½ In.	189.00 to 826.00
Teapot, Lid, c.1850, 9 ½ In.	1180.00
Tray, Landscape, Leaf Shape, c.1860, 7 ¼ In., Pair	165.00
Tray, River Scene, Oblong, c.1900, 7 In. ......*Illus*	120.00
Tureen, Lid, Boar's Head Handles, 12 ½ In.	472.00
Tureen, Lid, c.1850, 8 ¼ In.	148.00
Tureen, Lid, Chamfered, Raised Foot, Boar's Head Handles, Shaped Knop, c.1890, 8 ½ x 13 In.	246.00
Tureen, Lid, White, Cobalt Blue Glaze, Boar's Head Handles, Stem Knop, 12 x 8 ¾ In.	150.00
Tureen, Sauce, Lid, Lug Handles, c.1850, 13 In.	354.00
Tureen, Soup, Lid, Pagoda, River, Boats, Bridge, Boar Head Handles, 1800s, 9 x 13 In.....*Illus*	390.00
Tureen, Soup, Lid, Riverscape, Houses, Boar's Head Handles, c.1860, 8 x 13 In.	354.00
Vase, Octagonal, River Mountain, Poem, 12 ¾ In.	826.00

CAPO-DI-MONTE porcelain was first made in Naples, Italy, from 1743 to 1759. The factory moved near Madrid, Spain, and operated there from 1771 until 1821. The Ginori factory of Doccia, Italy, acquired the molds and began using the crown and *N* mark. It eventually became the modern-day firm known as Richard Ginori, often referred to as Ginori or Capo-di-Monte. This company also used the crown and *N* mark. Richard Ginori went into bankruptcy in 2013.

Basket, Floral Encrusted, Branch Handle, Legs, 6 ¼ x 7 ½ In.	35.00
Box, Cupids Arranging Flowers, Fired Gold, Bronze Rim, France, c.1930, 5 ½ x 4 In.	180.00
Cake Stand, Cherubs, Flowers, 3 Layers, Gold Trim Rims, 20 x 14 In.	82.00
Charger, Armorial, Bird, Crown, Gilt, Flowers, Scrolls, Figures, Marked, 1800s, 16 In. ......*Illus*	649.00
Ewer, Bas Relief, Cherubs, Scroll Handle, c.1905, 10 In.	1560.00
Figurine, Hobo On Bench, 10 In.	240.00
Figurine, Satyr Drinking Wine, Seminude Female Holding Grapes, Marked, c.1800, 12 ½ In., Pair.*Illus*	826.00
Figurine, Soldier, Gilt, Silver Helmet & Chest Armor, Marked, 12 In. ......*Illus*	169.00
Figurine, Woman, On Pedestal, Short Sleeved Dress, Flowered Skirt, Train, 10 ¼ In.	165.00
Jewelry Box, Oval, Mythological Figures Design, Gilt Accents, 1800s, 6 x 8 In.	1150.00
Lavabo, Angel Heads, Flowers, Multicolor, 2 Sections, 14 x 13 & 6 x 14 In.	330.00
Lipstick Holder, Musical, 13 In.	158.00
Plate, Bacchanal Procession, Multicolor, Gilt Trim, 9 ½ In., 12 Piece	837.00
Table Casket, Quatrefoil Shaped, Figures In Relief Design, 8 ¾ In.	889.00
Urn, Lid, Classical Figures, Gilt, Finial, Bacchus Head Handles, 1900s, 22 In., Pair.........*Illus*	944.00
Urn, Lid, Flowers, Cherubs, Climbing, Flying, Climbing, 17 ½ x 8 ½ In.	82.00
Vase, Cherubs, Seated On Chariot, Flowers, Painted, Wheels, 15 x 12 ½ In.	223.00

CAPTAIN MARVEL was introduced in February 1940 in Whiz comic books. An orphan named Billy Batson met the wizard, Shazam, and whenever he said the magic word he was transformed into a superhero. A movie serial was released in 1940. The comic was discontinued in 1954. A second Captain Marvel appeared in 1966, a third in 1967. Only the original was transformed by shouting "Shazam."

Button, Pinback, Club Member, Shazam, Red, Blue, White Ground, 1941, ⅞ In.	18.00
Figure, Plaster, Painted, Yellow, Red, c.1940, 15 In.	115.00
Poster, Adventures, Hoisting Giant Scorpion, Linen Back, 1941, 6 Sheet, 79 x 79 In.	7475.00

CAPTAIN MIDNIGHT began as a network radio show in September 1940. The first comic book appeared in July 1941. Captain Midnight was really the aviator Captain Albright, who was to defeat the Nazis. A movie serial was made in 1942 and a comic strip was published for a short time. The comic book version of Captain Midnight ended his career in 1948. Radio premiums are the prized collector memorabilia today.

Code Key, Brass, 1949, ¾ In.	115.00
Decoder Badge, Revolving Red & Clear Plastic Center Wheel, Ovaltine, 1945, 2 ½ In.	86.00

TIP

Got bubble gum on your sports cards? Rub them gently with a nylon stocking.

C

Capo-Di-Monte, Figurine, Soldier, Gilt, Silver Helmet & Chest Armor, Marked, 12 In. $169.00

Theriault's

Capo-Di-Monte, Urn, Lid, Classical Figures, Gilt, Finial, Bacchus Head Handles, 1900s, 22 In., Pair $944.00

Brunk Auctions

TIP

Dirty or warped cards should be wiped with a sponge dipped in a mild solution of detergent and water. The detergent will help make the cards cleaner and more pliable. Warped cards should be wiped, dried, then put under a heavy weight for a few days.

C

Card, Greeting, Valentine, Scherenschnitte, Pen & Ink, Miss Mary A. Starling, Frame, 13 x 13 In.
$323.00

Garth's Auctioneers & Appraisers

Carnival Glass, Beaded Cable, Rose Bowl, Aqua Opal
$170.00

Seeck Auctions

Carnival Glass, Dragon & Lotus, Bowl, Amethyst, Footed
$60.00

Seeck Auctions

Carnival Glass, Grape & Cable, Dresser Tray, Purple
$140.00

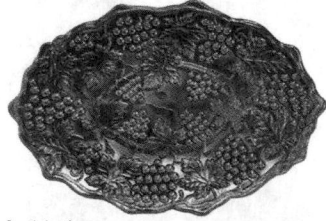

Seeck Auctions

Premium, 3-Way Mystery Dog-Whistle, 1941, 5 ⅛ In.	195.00
Ring, Flight Commander, Eagle, Shield, Propeller, Wing Emblem, Super Code 3, 1941	230.00
Ring, Flight Commander, SQFC, Jet Plane, Plastic, Silver, 1957	288.00
Ring, Mystic Sun God, Brass, Aztec Design, Ruby Red Colored Plastic Stone, 1946	506.00
Ring, Ovaltine, Initial J, Brass, Removable Cover, Clock Face Logo, Initials CM, 1948	115.00
Secret Squadron Decoder, Key, Manual, Ovaltine Premium, 1949, 3 Piece	190.00
Treasure Hunt, Map, Secret Letter, Skelly Oil Premium, 1939, 8 ½ x 11 In., 3 Piece	278.00

CARAMEL SLAG, *see Imperial Glass category.*

CARDS listed here include advertising cards (often called trade cards), baseball cards, playing cards, and others. Color photographs were rare in the nineteenth century, so companies gave away colorful cards with pictures of children, flowers, products, or related scenes that promoted the company name. These were often collected and stored in albums. Baseball cards also date from the nineteenth century, when they were used by tobacco companies as giveaways. Gum cards were started in 1933, but it was not until after World War II that the bubble gum cards favored today were produced. Today over 1,000 cards are issued each year by the gum companies. Related items may be found in the Christmas, Halloween, Movie, Paper, and Postcard categories.

Baseball, Cleveland Baseball Club, Supplement Photo, Hall Of Famers, 1892, 6 ½ x 9 ½ In.	345.00
Baseball, Don Drysdale, Topps, No. 18, 1957	175.00
Baseball, Gil Hodges, Topps, No. 295, 1960	19.00
Baseball, Hank Sauer, No. 4, Topps, 1954, 2 x 3 In.	10.00
Baseball, John Henry Lloyd, Punch Cigarros, Without Backing, Cuba, 1910, 1 ¼ x 1 ⅞ In.	94875.00
Baseball, Juan Marichal, Topps, No. 370, 1969	12.00
Baseball, Lamar Newsom, National Chicle Fine Pen, No. 88, 1936	15.00
Baseball, Lou Gehrig, Goudey, No. 160, 1933	995.00
Baseball, Rival All Stars, Mantle & Boyer, Topps, No. 160, 1960	60.00
Baseball, Sherry Magee, Error Magie, Piedmont, c.1910	17950.00
Baseball, Willie Mays, Topps, No. 200, 1960, 2 ½ x 3 ½ In.	25.00
Candy, Minute Biographies, Federal Sweets & Wafer Co., 1930s, 1 x 3 ½ In., 19 Piece	209.00
Football, Dick Lane, Topps, No. 85, 1957	50.00
Football, Four Horseman, Notre Dame, Topps, No. 68, 1955	145.00
Football, Joe Montana, Topps, No. 157, 1986	9.00
Football, Johnny Unitas, Topps, No. 455, 1973	12.00
Football, Len Szafaryn, Bowman, No. 86, 1955	20.00
Football, Leo Nomellini, Topps, No. 74, 1956	17.00
Football, Leon Hart, Topps, No. 104, 1956	7.00
Football, O.J. Simpson, Rookie, Topps, No. 90, 1970, 2 ½ x 3 ½ In.	25.00
Football, Randall Cunningham, Topps, No. 296, 1987	6.00
Football, Washington Redskins, Topps, No. 132, 1960	80.00
Football, Willard Sherman, Topps, No. 66, 1958	8.00
Greeting, Birthday, Holly Hobbie, Flying Kite, 1970s, 5 x 7 In.	6.00
Greeting, Easter, Boy, Basket Of Eggs, Rooster Pulling Pants, c.1930	6.00
Greeting, Valentine, Boy In Overalls, Straw Hat, Head Raises When Ax Is Moved, 1941, 6 ⅞ In.	10.00
Greeting, Valentine, Die Cut, Mechanical, Boy & Girl, On Seesaw, 1920s, 8 x 6 In.	22.00
Greeting, Valentine, Googly-Eye Girl, Apron, Chef's Hat, You're Sweet As Pie, 1939, 4 ⅞ In.	10.00
Greeting, Valentine, Granddaughter, Girl, Bonnet, Apron, American Greetings, 1940s, 6 x 4 In.	11.00
Greeting, Valentine, Scherenschnitte, Heart, Geometric Cutouts, Watercolor, c.1810, 12 ½ In.	266.00
Greeting, Valentine, Scherenschnitte, Pen & Ink, Miss Mary A. Starling, Frame, 13 x 13 In...*Illus*	323.00
Gum, Horrors Of War, No. 1-48, 1938, 2 ½ x 3 ⅛ In., 48 Piece	190.00
Gum, Mars Attacks, Topps, 1962, 2 ½ x 3 ½ In., 55 Piece	2024.00
Playing, American Manufacture, c.1805, 52 Piece	504.00
Playing, Film Stars, Chariot Race Design, Movie Souvenir Card Co., 1916, 3 ¾ x 2 ¾ In.	540.00
Trade, Ideal Cash Register Co., Black Man, Holding Ideal Razor, 4 x 6 ¾ In.	248.00
Trade, Royal Ham's, Man, Sitting On Globe Holding Ham	35.00
Trade, Woolson Spices, Sleeping Girl, Dreaming Of Easter Bunnies, 1893, 7 x 5 In.	18.00

CARDER, *see Aurene and Steuben categories.*

CARLTON WARE was made at the Carlton Works of Stoke-on-Trent, England, beginning about 1890. The firm traded as Wiltshaw & Robinson until 1957. It was renamed Carlton Ware Ltd. in 1958. The company went bankrupt in 1995, but the name is still in use.

Figurine, Bird Of Paradise, Nude Woman, 7 ½ In.	86.00
Figurine, Butterfly Garden Fairy, 9 ½ In.	182.00
Figurine, Hollyhocks Girl, 9 In.	173.00
Figurine, Mephesto, 10 ¼ In.	94.00
Figurine, Pink Buttercup, Nude Woman, 11 In.	86.00

Figurine, Sunflower, 10 ½ In.	94.00
Figurine, Sunflower, Woman In Red Bathing Suit, 10 ½ In.	115.00
Ginger Jar, Lid, Galleons On High Seas, Blue Ground, 12 In.	499.00

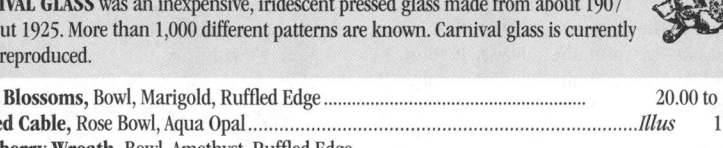

CARNIVAL GLASS was an inexpensive, iridescent pressed glass made from about 1907 to about 1925. More than 1,000 different patterns are known. Carnival glass is currently being reproduced.

Apple Blossoms, Bowl, Marigold, Ruffled Edge	20.00 to 56.00
Beaded Cable, Rose Bowl, Aqua Opal ....*Illus*	170.00
Blackberry Wreath, Bowl, Amethyst, Ruffled Edge	40.00
Blackberry Wreath, Bowl, Green, Ruffled Edge, 10 In.	55.00
Blackberry, Compote, Green, Miniature	100.00
Captive Rose, Plate, Green, 9 In.	1250.00
Cherry Pattern, Bowl, 12 In.	93.00
Chesterfield, Sugar, Breakfast, White	75.00
Christmas Giant, Compote, Marigold	700.00
Christmas Giant, Compote, Purple	2600.00
Colonial, Candlestick, White, 8 ½ In., Pair	725.00
Concave Diamonds, Tumbler, Russet	50.00 to 450.00
Concave Diamonds, Tumbler, Vaseline	35.00 to 50.00
Concord, Plate, Amethyst, 9 In.	575.00
Concord, Plate, Green, 9 In.	525.00
Cosmos & Cane, Cuspidor, Honey Amber, Ladies	2150.00
Dandelion, Tumbler, Ice Blue	105.00
Diamond Band & Fan, Wine, Marigold	35.00
Diamonds, Tumbler, Green	25.00
Diamonds, Tumbler, Russet	50.00
Dragon & Lotus, Bowl, Amethyst, Footed ....*Illus*	60.00
Farmyard, Bowl, Purple, Ruffled Edge	3500.00
Field Thistle, Tumbler, Marigold	10.00
Fisherman's, Mug, Marigold	10.00
Fisherman's, Mug, Peach Opal	475.00
Fisherman's, Mug, Purple	25.00
Five Bubbles, Candlestick, Marigold, 7 In.	15.00
Flute No. 3, Tumbler, Aqua	27.00
Forget-Me-Not, Tumbler, Blue Enameled	25.00
Four Seventy Four, Cordial, Marigold, 3 In.	375.00
Four Seventy Four, Vase, Emerald Green, 12 ½ In.	21000.00
Freefold, Vase, Purple, 12 In.	77.00
Good Luck, Bowl, Blue, Ruffled Edge, Ribbed Back	190.00
Good Luck, Bowl, Purple, Ruffled Edge	160.00
Grape & Cable, Bowl, Green, Crimped, 8 In.	40.00
Grape & Cable, Dresser Tray, Purple ....*Illus*	140.00
Grape & Cable, Pitcher, Amethyst, 64 Oz.	78.00
Grape & Cable, Plate, Blue, Footed, 9 In. ....*Illus*	40.00
Grape & Cable, Sauce, Marigold	20.00
Grape & Cable, Sweetmeat, Purple ....*Illus*	100.00
Grape & Cable, Tumbler, Amethyst, 8 Oz.	40.00
Grape & Cable, Tumbler, Marigold, 8 Oz.	32.00
Grapevine Lattice, Tumbler, Purple	25.00
Hattie, Rose Bowl, Purple	498.00
Heavy Diamonds, Breakfast Set, Marigold	10.00
Heavy Grape, Nappy, Amethyst	32.00
Heavy Grape, Plate, Amber, Scalloped Rim, 8 In.	55.00
Heavy Grape, Plate, Marigold, 8 In.	260.00
Heavy Grape, Plate, Smoke, 8 In.	275.00
Imperial Grape, Cup & Saucer, Marigold	45.00
Imperial Grape, Plate, Lime Green, 6 In.	55.00
Imperial Grape, Tumbler, Green	10.00
Lattice & Daisy, Tumbler, Blue	20.00
Leaf Chain, Bowl, Green, Ruffled Edge, 9 ½ In.	1322.00
Luster Rose, Pitcher, Marigold, 54 Oz.	26.00
Maple Leaf, Water Set, Amethyst, Striped Veined Ground, 1912, 7 Piece	640.00
Octagon, Toothpick Holder, Marigold, Curved-In Lip, Imperial Glass Co., 2 ½ In.	35.00
Orange Tree, Mug, Aqua, Small	65.00
Orange Tree, Mug, Loop Handle, White	240.00
Orange Tree, Mug, Marigold, Souvenir Of Newark, N.J.	55.00

Carnival Glass, Grape & Cable, Plate, Blue, Footed, 9 In.
$40.00

Seeck Auctions

Carnival Glass, Grape & Cable, Sweetmeat, Purple
$100.00

Seeck Auctions

Carnival Glass, Persian Medallion, Bowl, 3-In-1 Edge, Blue, 10 In.
$95.00

Seeck Auctions

TIP

Do not display carnival glass made before 1910 in direct sunlight. The glass will turn purple or brown and the iridescent finish may fade.

Carousel, Horse, Jumper, Flowing Mane, Armitage-Herschell, New York, c.1897, 70 x 50 In. $6,150.00

New Orleans Auction Galleries, Inc.

Carousel, Rooster, Runner, Cast Aluminum, Painted, c.1900, 40 ½ In. $470.00

Garth's Auctioneers & Appraisers

Carriage, Baby Buggy, Wicker, Adjustable Hood & Footboard, Hand Brake, Heywood-Wakefield $83.00

Conestoga Auction Co., Inc.

Bisque Doll Heads
Bisque is unglazed porcelain that may be tinted or painted and used for dolls' heads and perhaps hands and bodies. It is also used for figurines and dishes.

Orange Tree, Mug, White	240.00
Orange Tree, Spooner, Cobalt Blue	2500.00
Palm Beach, Table Set, Honey Amber, 4 Piece	400.00
Palm Beach, Table Set, White, 4 Piece	450.00
Peacock At The Fountain, Punch Cup, Cobalt	46.00
Peacock At The Fountain, Table Set, Blue, 4 Piece	425.00
Peacock At The Fountain, Table Set, Ice Blue, 4 Piece	750.00
Peacock At The Fountain, Table Set, Purple, 4 Piece	325.00
Peacock At The Fountain, Table Set, White, 4 Piece	375.00
Peacock At Urn, Compote, Aqua, Ruffled Edge	40.00
Peacock At Urn, Sauce, Purple	55.00
Persian Medallion, Bowl, 3-In-1 Edge, Blue, 10 In. ......*Illus*	95.00
Persian Medallion, Plate, Blue, 6 In.	130.00
Pine Cone, Plate, Green, 6 In.	120.00
Pony, Bowl, Amethyst, Ruffled Edge, 10 In.	105.00
Poodle, Powder Jar, Marigold & Black	40.00
Poppy, Dish, Pickle, Aqua	110.00 to 500.00
Poppy, Dish, Pickle, Blue	85.00
Poppy, Dish, Pickle, Green	165.00
Poppy, Dish, Pickle, Iridized Custard	1550.00
Poppy, Dish, Pickle, Purple	180.00
Poppy, Dish, Pickle, White	225.00
Princess, Punch Cup, Green	5.00
Prism, Butter, Marigold	10.00
Rose Show, Bowl, Sapphire, Ruffled Edge	525.00
Rose Show, Plate, Ice Blue, 9 In.	210.00
Rustic, Vase, Green, 14 In.	52.00
Shell & Sand, Plate, Purple, 9 In.	700.00
Shell & Sand, Plate, Smoke, 9 In.	575.00
Singing Birds, Mug, Aqua Opal	600.00
Singing Birds, Mug, Purple	20.00
Smooth Rays, Plate, Purple, Ruffled Edge, 6 In.	20.00
Stag & Holly, Serrated, Scalloped Rim, 3 Scrolled, Paneled Feet, Marigold, 3 ¾ x 10 ½ In.	12.00
Star Of David, Bowl, Purple, Ruffled Edge	250.00
Stippled Good Luck, Bowl, Blue, Ruffled Edge	190.00
Stippled Singing Birds, Mug, Marigold	15.00
Stippled Three Fruits, Bowl, Ribbed, Apple Green, Ruffled Edge	1700.00
Ten Mums, Tumbler, Marigold	25.00
Three Fruits, Plate, Purple, 9 In.	95.00
Tree Bark, Pitcher, Marigold, 48 Oz.	58.00
Tree Bark, Tumbler, Marigold, 6 Oz.	18.00
Twist, Bobeche, Candlestick, Vaseline, 9 ½ In.	150.00
Vintage, Goblet, Marigold	18.00
Vintage, Nappy, Ruffled Edge, Marigold	30.00
Vintage, Plate, Green, 7 In.	70.00
Water Lily, Table Set, Marigold, 4 Piece	130.00
Windmill, Bowl, Smoke, Ruffled Edge	21.00
Windmill, Water Set, Marigold Over Clear, 10 Piece	400.00

CAROUSEL or merry-go-round figures were first carved in the United States in 1867 by Gustav Dentzel. Collectors discovered the charm of the hand-carved figures in the 1970s, and they were soon classed as folk art. Most desirable are the figures other than horses, such as pigs, camels, lions, or dogs. A jumper is a figure that was made to move up and down on a pole; a stander was placed in a stationary position.

Cow, Paint, Wood, Brass Horn, Neck Metal Hold Bar, 47 In.	1331.00
Donkey, Nodding, Hollow Carved, Molded Brass Detail, Painted, France, c.1900, 50 x 64 In.	2300.00
Horse, Glass Eyes, Carved, Painted, Tan, Brown, c.1960, 50 ½ x 42 In.	177.00
Horse, Jumper, Flowing Mane, Armitage-Herschell, New York, c.1897, 70 x 50 In. ....*Illus*	6150.00
Horse, Jumper, Inner Ring, Carved, Painted, Philadelphia Toboggan Co., c.1930, 50 ½ In.	500.00
Horse, Jumper, Ivory Paint, Cast Iron Pedestal Base, 39 ½ In.	575.00
Horse, Oak Stand, Twist Pole, Restored, Frederick Heintz, 48 x 76 In.	1760.00
Horse, Pine, Carved, Painted, Pole, c.1910, 51 x 58 In.	516.00
Horse, Prancer, Narra Wood, Carved, 52 x 9 ½ In.	230.00
Horse, Prancer, On Wood Rockers, Open Mouth, Raised Bent Front Legs, c.1890, 45 x 50 In.	345.00
Horse, Prancer, Pine, Painted, Charles Carmelt, Philadelphia Toboggan Co., c.1900, 51 x 58 In.	8888.00
Horse, Prancer, Wood, Carved, Pole, Paint, Signed, 1982, 64 In.	708.00
Horse, Rearing, Wood, Carved, Glass Eyes, Horsehair Tail, Stand, 44 ⅔ In.	277.00

Horse, Runner, Carved, Herschell-Spillman, c.1915, 38 x 62 In.		6600.00
Horse, Stander, Wood, Carved, W.P. Wilcox, Brass Pole & Stand, 63 In.		660.00
Model, Fairground, Horses, Swing Coaches, Gondolas, Wood, Metal, Electric, Germany, 24 x 28 In.		771.00
Model, Fairground, Merry-Go-Round, Wood, Metal, Painted, Electric Light, Motor, 19 x 19 In.		462.00
Pig, Runner, Pink, Blue, Red Paint, Carved, Wood, 25 ½ In.		960.00
Rooster, Pine, Carved, Painted, Gilt, 50 x 35 In.		1298.00
Rooster, Runner, Cast Aluminum, Painted, c.1900, 40 ½ In.	*Illus*	470.00
Seat, Swan, White, Yellow Paint, Wood, 34 x 24 In.		4255.00
Tiger, Stander, Outside Row, White, Black, Red Paint, Glass Eyes, c.1910, 52 ½ x 59 In.		33180.00
Zebra, Runner, Black, White Paint, Wood, 45 In.		580.00

CARRIAGE means several things, so this category lists baby carriages, buggies for adults, horse-drawn sleighs, and even strollers. Doll-sized carriages are listed in the Toy category.

Baby Buggy, Whitney, Wicker, 37 x 46 In.		177.00
Baby Buggy, Wicker, Adjustable Hood & Footboard, Hand Brake, Heywood-Wakefield	*Illus*	83.00
Bench, Pine, Wire, Metal Supports, c.1850, 33 ¾ x 42 In.		267.00
Buggy Wagon, Pedal Pumper, Steer With Feet, Herman Vaughan, 1898, 46 In.		4200.00
Child's, Wicker, Paint, Brown, Wire Wheels, Nickel Hubcaps, Pull, c.1910, 20 x 31 x 24 In.		375.00
Child's, Wicker, Rubber Wheels, Movable Hood, 26 x 38 In.		125.00
Child's, Wicker, Wire Wheels, c.1890, 53 x 24 x 42 In.		575.00
Child's, Wood, Paint, Red, Scrolls, Fringe, 19th Century, 26 x 24 x 35 In.		795.00
Perambulator, Black Canvas Top, 3 Port Windows, Painted Green, 4 Spoke Wheels, 60 x 44 x 25 In.		414.00
Sleigh, Open, Wood, Black, Metal Rails, Single Seat, 1800s, 44 ½ x 41 In.		750.00
Sleigh, Wood, Leather Tufted Seat, Paint, W.B. Doolittle, Springwater, N.Y., 45 ½ x 71 In.		1304.00
Stroller, Wood, Carved, Scrolls, Red Paint, Gold, Black Pinstripes, Canopy, c.1890, 34 ½ In.		2844.00
Wagon Seat, Cast Iron, Wire Shock Absorbers, Red & Yellow Paint, Foot Board, 9 x 10 In.		978.00
Whip, Bone Handle, Carved Flowers, Leather Case, c.1890, 50 In.		196.00
Wicker, Iron Wheels, Turned Wood Handle, Adjustable Back & Feet, c.1885, 43 x 33 x 22 In.		1449.00

CASH REGISTERS were invented in 1884 because an eye on the cash was a necessity in stores of the nineteenth century, too. John and James Ritty invented a large model that resembled a clock and kept a record of the dollars and cents exchanged in the store. John Patterson improved the cash register with a paper roll to record the money. By the early 1900s, elaborate brass registers were made. More modern types were made after 1920.

American, Candy Store Model, Extended Keys, Embossed, Brass, White Marble		2400.00
National, Model 5, Nickel Finish, Side Clock		1792.00
National, Model 6, Oak, Extended Key Arms, Embossed Quality Ice Cream		3300.00
National, Model 8, Clock, Embossed, Brass, Marble		1320.00
National, Model 33, Brass, Embossed, c.1895, 18 x 15 In.		300.00
National, Model 37, Brass, Top Sign, Embossed, 1897		978.00
National, Model 39 3/4-2-2, Saloon, Double Door, Embossed, Brass, Marble		1210.00
National, Model 47 1/4-2-2, Amount Purchased, Bar Counter, 2 Drawers		1680.00
National, Model 79, Series 400, Crank, 4 Rows Of Keys, Printer, c.1900		844.00
National, Model 250, Top Sign, Keys, Restored	*Illus*	900.00
National, Model 313, Brass, D. Feidler, 21 x 10 In.		327.00
National, Model 313, Brass, Marble Sill, Oak Base, c.1910, 17 x 10 ½ In.		885.00
National, Model 313, Brass, Top Plaque, Say Hires Root Beer	*Illus*	1120.00
National, Model 313, Brass, Topper Sign, 21 x 16 In.		900.00
National, Model 313, Candy Store, Bronze, White Marble Shelf		460.00
National, Model 313, Candy Store, Copper	*Illus*	672.00
National, Model 317, Brass, Copper Finish, Oak Base		840.00
National, Model 332, Brass, Top Sign		908.00
National, Model 349-2-2, Side By Side Drawers, Keys, Restored	*Illus*	1920.00
National, Model 451, Receipt Cage, Amount Purchased Top Sign, Oak Base		720.00
National, Model S88019, Candy Store, Cast Metal, Marble Shelf, 10 x 16 In.		406.00
National, Wood Grain Painted, Metal, Mechanical, 23 x 24 In.		94.00
Western, Nickel Plate, Cherub, Burdick-Corbin Co., Detroit, Mich., 12 x 21 x 14 In.		1469.00

CASTOR JARS for pickles are glass jars about six inches in height, held in special metal holders. They became a popular dinner table accessory about 1890. Each jar had a top that was usually silver or silver plate. The frame, also of a silver metal, had a handle that arched above the jar and a hook that held a pair of tongs. By 1900, the pickle castor was out of fashion. Many examples found today have reproduced glass jars in old holders. Additional pickle castors may be found in the various Glass categories.

Pickle, Cranberry Glass, Diagonal Swirl, Silver Tong Holder, 11 In.		115.00
Pickle, Cranberry Glass, Thumblift, Enameled Flowers, Wilcox Silver Stand, Lid, Tongs, 12 In.		420.00

Cash Register, National, Model 250, Top Sign, Keys, Restored
$900.00

Showtime Auction Services

Cash Register, National, Model 313, Brass, Top Plaque, Say Hires Root Beer
$1,120.00

Victorian Casino Antiques

Cash Register, National, Model 313, Candy Store, Copper
$672.00

Victorian Casino Antiques

Cash Register, National, Model 349-2-2, Side By Side Drawers, Keys, Restored $1,920.00

Showtime Auction Services

Castor, Pickle, Daisy & Fern, Apple Blossom, Blue, Silver Plate Holder, Northwood, 12 In. $316.00

Early Auction Co.

Celadon, Cadogan Pot, Glazed, c.1830, 5 ½ x 7 ½ In. $960.00

DuMouchelles Art Gallery

Celluloid, Mirror, Nude Women, Bedroom Scene, Pocket, c.1910, 1 ¾ In. $95.00

Hake's Americana & Collectibles

Pickle, Cranberry Glass, Thumblift, Silver Cover & Tongs, Victorian, 9 ½ In.	108.00
Pickle, Daisy & Fern, Apple Blossom, Blue, Silver Plate Holder, Northwood, 12 In. ....*Illus*	316.00
Pickle, Double, Silver Plate, Embossed Flowers, Viking Legs, Rogers, Smith & Co., c.1877, 10 In...	725.00
Pickle, Silver Plate, Victorian, Tongs, Meriden Silverplate Co., c.1870, 11 In.	260.00
Pickle, Silver, Arched Pierced Flower Crest, Ornate Feet, c.1875, 11 ⅞ In.	650.00

CASTOR SETS holding just salt and pepper castors were used in the seventeenth century. The sugar castor, mustard pot, spice dredger (shaker), bottles for vinegar and oil, and other spice holders became popular by the eighteenth century. These sets were usually made of sterling silver. The American Victorian castor set, the type most collected today, was made of silver plated Britannia metal. Colored glass bottles were introduced after the Civil War. The sets were out of fashion by World War I. Be careful when buying sets with colored bottles; many are reproductions. Other castor sets may be listed in various porcelain and glass categories in this book.

3 Bottles, Twisted Wire Stand, 3-Footed, 5 ½ x 2 ¾ In.	85.00
4 Bottles, Cruets, Shakers, Cranberry Glass, Electroplate Silver, England, c.1890, 11 In.	150.00
4 Bottles, Silver Plate, Pedestal, McGee Glass Co., 10 In.	140.00
5 Bottles, Silver Plate, Bird Head Handle, Meriden Britannia Co., c.1875, 14 x 8 In.	245.00

CATALOGS *are listed in the Paper category.*

CAULDON Limited worked in Staffordshire, Great Britain, and went through many name changes. John Ridgway made porcelain at Cauldon Place, Hanley, until 1855. The firm of John Ridgway, Bates and Co. of Cauldon Place worked from 1856 to 1859. It became Bates, Brown-Westhead, Moore and Co. from 1859 to 1862. Brown-Westhead, Moore and Co. worked from 1862 to 1904. About 1890, this firm started using the words *Cauldon* or *Cauldon Ware* as part of the mark. Cauldon Ltd. worked from 1905 to 1920, Cauldon Potteries from 1920 to 1962. Related items may be found in the Indian Tree category.

Plate Set, Flower Reserves In Gilt Rim, Marked Cowell & Hubbard Co., 10 ½ In., 12 Piece	581.00

CELADON is the name of a velvet-textured green-gray glaze used by Chinese, Japanese, Korean, and other factories. The name refers both to the glaze and to pieces covered with the glaze. It is still being made. Only celadon-colored ceramics are listed here.

Bowl, Bats, Clouds, Shou Characters, Chinese, 1800s, 2 ¼ x 11 ½ In.	345.00
Bowl, Flared, Undulating Rim, Wire Crackle, Rosewood Stand, 19th Century, 6 In.	676.00
Bowl, Flying Bat, Fruit, Leaves, Carved, Chinese, 4 ¾ In.	2596.00
Bowl, Overall Gray Green, Molded Flower Sprig, 3 x 13 In.	345.00
Bowl, Round, Flared, Turned Out, Crackled, 10 ½ In. Diam.	184.00
Cadogan Pot, Glazed, c.1830, 5 ½ x 7 ½ In. ....*Illus*	960.00
Censer, Bulbous, Footed, Beast Shape Handles, Rings, Lid, Dragon Finial, Wood Stand, 1900s, 4 ½ In...	390.00
Charger, Green, Scalloped, Embossed Chinese, c.1890, 16 ¼ In.	7670.00
Charger, Reeded Interior, Flowering Branch, Rolled Wide Rim, 13 In. Diam.	896.00
Charger, Scalloped Border, 3 ½ x 19 In.	126500.00
Dish, Chrysanthemum, Scalloped & Fluted Edge, Flower Petal Shaped, Marked, 7 In.	633.00
Incense Burner, Tripod, 2 Biscuit Dragons, 7 ½ In. Diam.	155.00
Jar, Dome Lid, Urn Shape, Quilin Finial, Flowers, Leaves, Round Foot, 19 ¾ x 8 ½ In., Pair	480.00
Plate, Barbed Rim, Footed, Incised Key Fret Rim, Cavetto, Lotus Flower, Chinese, 11 In.	891.00
Seal, Foo Dog, Calligraphy, Rectangular, Chinese, 2 ½ In.	1573.00
Vase, Bottle Shape, Elongated Neck, Raised Rings, Reeded Band, 9 ½ In.	167.00
Vase, Crackle Glaze, Square Oval, Tubular Handles, Marked, 1900s, 12 In.	3200.00
Vase, Double Gourd, Black Splotch Design, Raised Foot Rim, Stand, 6 In.	403.00
Vase, Raised Archaic Design, Enameled Dragon, Footed, Gloss, Glaze, Wood Base, Kangxi, 10 In.	518.00
Vase, Rectangular, Elephant Head Handles, Guanyin & Buddhist Design, Pierced Brass Base, 25 ½ In.	492.00
Vase, Scenic Landscape Band, Handles, Lappets, Trumpet Rim, Ring Foot, 1918, 1800s, 15 In.	5310.00
Vase, Turned Out Rim, Tapering Body, Dragon, Flame, Clouds, Sea, Round Foot, 1800s, 11 In...	250.00

CELLULOID is a trademark for a plastic developed in 1868 by John W. Hyatt. Celluloid Manufacturing Company, the Celluloid Novelty Company, Celluloid Fancy Goods Company, and American Xylonite Company all used celluloid to make jewelry, games, sewing equipment, false teeth, and piano keys. The name *celluloid* was often used to identify any similar plastic. Celluloid toys are listed under Toy.

Box, Card Holder, Sterling Trim, Nautical Design, Unger Brothers, 4 x 3 x 1 In.	275.00
Box, Ring, Scroll Design, 3 In., Diam.	70.00

Button, Apollo 11, We Landed Men On The Moon For Peace, Moon, Eagle, 3 ½ In.	37.00
Button, Friendship Flyers, Amelia Earhart, Wilmer Stutz, Lou Gordon, Photo, 1 ¼ In.	76.00
Button, Halley's Comet, Streaking Comet, Green Ground, 1985-1986, 3 ½ In.	8.00
Button, Saint Anne, Mary, Pinback, Diedrich Schaefer Co., 3 In.	12.00
Cigarette Holder, Case, Flowers, Multicolor, Telescoping, 1930s, 7 In.	65.00
Collar Box, Dancing Figures, Double Hinged, 11 In.	113.00
Draw Pulls, Red, Cream, 1950s, 4 In., 8 Piece	40.00
Dresser Box, Neckties, Woman, Seated On Bench, Drawer, 15 In.	124.00
Dresser Set, Orange, Black, Chinese Design, Mirror, Box, Buffer, 1930s, 3 Piece	165.00
Figurine, Cow, Gray, Cream, Red Glass Eye, Hollow, Japan, 1940s, 5 ½ In.	15.00
Figurine, Rickshaw, Japan, 1 ½ In.	25.00
Glove Stretcher, Sterling, Unger Brothers, 8 x 3 ¼ In.	95.00
Hair Comb, Amber, Rhinestones, U Shape, c.1920, 5 x 3 In.	40.00
Hair Comb, Blue, Rhinestones, Pierced Lace Design, c.1900, 4 ½ x 3 In.	55.00
Hair Comb, Butterfly, Pierced, Blue, Green, Rhinestones, c.1910, 7 x 5 In.	145.00
Mirror, Nude Women, Bedroom Scene, Pocket, c.1910, 1 ¾ In. ....*Illus*	95.00
Photo Album, Victorian, Winter Scene, Bears, Pulling Sled, 9 x 11 In.	226.00
Pin, Rolling Stones, Original 5, Black & White Photo, 3 ½ In.	122.00
Rattle, Baby Head, Googly Eye, c.1910, 3 ½ In.	45.00
Toothpick Holder, Man Shape, Maroon, Cream, Press Tab Causes Genitals To Extend, 3 In.	82.00
Watch Fob, Arkansas Brick & Manufacturing Co., Brick, W&H, c.1907, 1 ½ x 2 In. ....*Illus*	52.00

CELS *are listed in this book in the Animation Art category.*

CERAMIC ART COMPANY of Trenton, New Jersey, was established in 1889 by Jonathan Coxon and Walter Scott and was an early producer of American belleek porcelain. It became Lenox, Inc. in 1906. Do not confuse this ware with the pottery made by the Ceramic Arts Studio of Madison, Wisconsin.

Mug, Berries, Leaves, Barrel Shape, 5 In.	55.00
Mug, Corn On The Cob, Barrel Shape, Brown, Yellow, Green, 4 ⅞ In.	55.00
Mug, Hops, Brown, Green, Mary Chase Perry, Belleek Blank, Signed, 5 ½ In. ....*Illus*	333.00
Mug, Strawberries, Green Leaves, 5 x 4 ¾ In.	85.00
Stein, Rugby Players, Blue, Marked, 7 In.	1250.00
Vase, Ivory, Roses, Bees, Raised Gold Detail, Squat Gourd Shape, Strap Handles, 7 ¾ x 7 ½ In.	900.00
Vase, Painted, Boy & Girl, Signed L. Schantz, 18 x 8 In.	325.00
Vase, Painted, Red & Yellow Roses, Gold Handles, 6 x 6 ½ In.	135.00
Vase, Purple Flowers, White, Scroll Handles, Gilt Cherub Head Finials, Marked, 8 ⅛ In.	230.00

CHALKWARE is really plaster of Paris decorated with watercolors. One type was molded from Staffordshire and other porcelain models and painted and sold as inexpensive decorations in the nineteenth century. This type is very valuable today. Figures of plaster, made from about 1910 to 1940 for use as prizes at carnivals, are also known as chalkware. Kewpie dolls made of chalkware will be found in their own category.

Bust, Abraham Lincoln, 31 In.	425.00
Bust, Admiral Oliver Perry, c.1830, 13 In.	1062.00
Bust, Eastern Woman, Intaglio Cut Eyes, Headpiece, Coin Necklaces, Victorian, 26 ½ x 17 In....*Illus*	575.00
Bust, Milton, c.1855, 18 In.	122.00
Cardholder, Entryway, Figural, Woman, Partly Clothed, 31 x 16 In.	495.00
Compote, Fruit Painted, Red, Yellow, Green, c.1850, 13 ¼ In.	652.00
Figurine, Billy Goat, Red Yoke, Pa., 1800s, 8 ¼ In.	2360.00
Figurine, Bulldog, Nodding, Standing, Painted, 1800s, 7 ¾ In.	590.00
Figurine, Bunny, Seated, Painted, Red, Green, Yellow, Flower Medallion, 1800s, 5 In.	354.00
Figurine, Cat, Mold Cast, Painted, Yellow, Red Dots, Slashes, Black Whiskers, Round Base, 13 ½ In.	1534.00
Figurine, Cat, Reclining, Yellow Glass Eyes, c.1900, 14 In.	4722.00
Figurine, Cat, Seated, Hollow Cast, Black, Red, Brown, Brown & Yellow Stripes, 13 ½ In.	11210.00
Figurine, Cat, Seated, Smiling, Long Eyelashes, Painted, 1800s, 4 ¾ In.	531.00
Figurine, Cat, Sitting, White, Black Spots, Detail, 1800s, 15 ½ In.	826.00
Figurine, Cat, White Ground, Multicolor, Pa., 1800s, 9 In.	2844.00
Figurine, Chicken, Red & Yellow Tail & Wings, Black Beak, Cone Shape Base, 6 In.	165.00
Figurine, Dog, Collie, Off-White On White, Black & Brown Accents, Red Ribbon, 15 In.	35.00
Figurine, Dog, Collie, White, Tan & Gold Highlights, 17 ¾ x 23 In.	24.00
Figurine, Dog, Poodle, Red, Green & Yellow Dots, Black Ears, 6 x 5 In.	189.00
Figurine, Dog, Pug, Painted, Standing, Studded Collar, c.1915, 13 ½ x 16 In.	153.00
Figurine, Dog, Shaggy, Seated, Painted, U.S.A., c.1890, 9 In.	382.00

Celluloid, Watch Fob, Arkansas Brick & Manufacturing Co., Brick, W&H, c.1907, 1 ½ x 2 In.
$52.00

Hake's Americana & Collectibles

Ceramic Art Co., Mug, Hops, Brown, Green, Mary Chase Perry, Belleek Blank, Signed, 5 ½ In.
$333.00

Humler & Nolan

Chalkware, Bust, Eastern Woman, Intaglio Cut Eyes, Headpiece, Coin Necklaces, Victorian, 26 ½ x 17 In.
$575.00

James D. Julia Auctioneers

TIP
If you leave salty food on a chrome plate, it may corrode the chrome. The only "cure" for this is re-plating.

Charlie Chaplin, Toy, Charlie, Wire Cane, Tin Litho, Windup, Key, Gunthermann, Germany, c.1920, 8 ½ In. $670.00

Hake's Americana & Collectibles

Charlie Chaplin, Toy, Cymbal Player, Squeeze, Tin Lithograph, Distler, Germany, c.1920, 7 In. $374.00

Bertoia Auctions

Charlie Chaplin, Toy, Walker, Cane, Cloth Suit, Tin Face & Hat, Roller Bars, Clockwork, 8 In. $2,360.00

Bertoia Auctions

Figurine, George Washington, On Horseback, c.1850, 11 ¾ In.		593.00
Figurine, Girl, Traditional Dress, Painted, 1800s, 9 ⅞ In.		384.00
Figurine, Lovebirds, Painted, 19th Century, 3 ¼ In.		383.00
Figurine, Mourning Dove, Perched On Stump, Cherry Branch, 1800s, 11 In.		856.00
Figurine, Pinecone, On Pedestal Finial, Painted, Green, Ocher, Brown, 1800s, 9 ¼ In.		472.00
Figurine, Ram, 2 Heads, Knobby Body, Black Paint Accents, 8 x 7 In.		213.00
Figurine, Ram, Black Paint, Silver Trim, Ribbon Collar, 7 ½ x 10 In., Pair		153.00
Figurine, Rooster, Multicolor Plumage, Pa., 1800s, 6 ¼ In.		885.00
Figurine, Rooster, Painted, c.1840, 5 In.		295.00
Figurine, Rooster, Painted, c.1850, 7 In.		1126.00
Figurine, Sheep & Lamb, Multicolor Spots, c.1860, 7 ½ In.		294.00
Figurine, Sheep & Lamb, Reclining, Red Painted Ears, Brown Banded Base, 6 x 9 In.		118.00
Figurine, Squirrel, Holding Nut, Yellow, Black & Red Accents, 6 ½ In.		767.00
Figurine, Squirrel, Seated, Eating Nut, Painted, 1800s, 6 In.		649.00
Figurine, Stag, Seated, Pa., 1800s, 10 ¼ x 9 ¾ In.		356.00
Figurine, Woman, Painted, Provincial Attire, 1800s, 9 ½ In.		504.00
Figurine, Woman, Standing, Red, Yellow & Brown Painted Stripes, Hat, 10 In.		236.00
Fruit Garniture, Painted, c.1870, 10 ½ In., Pair		1116.00
Horse Head, Hollow Cast, Painted, White, Black Spatter, Black Mane, Ears, Eyes, 9 ½ x 6 x 10 In.		165.00
Indian, Cigar Countertop, Standing, Legs Crossed, 20 In.		990.00
Potholder Hooks, Creole Couple, Wedge Of Watermelon, Painted, 1950s, 4 x 4 In., Pair		35.00
Shelf, Eagle Support, Spread Wing, Paint, c.1890, 12 x 14 In.		89.00
Watch Hutch, Multicolor, Waltham Pocket Watch, Pa., 1800s, 9 In.		444.00
Watch Hutch, Napoleonic Figure In Alcove, Columns, Domed Pediment, 12 In.		1062.00

CHARLIE CHAPLIN, the famous comedian, actor, and filmmaker, lived from 1889 to 1977. He made his first movie in 1913. He did the movie *The Tramp* in 1915. The character of the Tramp has remained famous, and in the 1980s appeared in a series of television commercials for computers. Dolls, candy containers, and all sorts of memorabilia with the image of Charlie's Tramp are collected. Pieces are being made even today.

Button, Citylights, Warren Theatre, Starting April 5th, Black & White, 1931, 1 ½ In.		114.00
Doll, Cloth, Metal Ball Jointed, Composition, Swiss, Bucherer, 7 ½ In.		345.00
Doll, Walking, Composition Head & Hands, Painted, Cloth, Paper Shirt, 6 ⅝ In.		472.00
Figure, Tumbler, Composition, Wood, Cloth Suit, 9 ½ In.		316.00
Game, Ball Toss, Die Cut Image Of Charlie, Moving Eyes, Cigar, 23 In.		978.00
Toy, Charlie, Wire Cane, Tin Litho, Windup, Key, Gunthermann, Germany, c.1920, 8 ½ In.	*Illus*	670.00
Toy, Cymbal Player, Squeeze, Tin Lithograph, Distler, Germany, c.1920, 7 In.	*Illus*	374.00
Toy, Riding Bicycle, Smoking Cigar, Tin Lithograph, c.1920, 7 ½ x 7 In.		190.00
Toy, Walker, Cane, Cloth Suit, Tin Face & Hat, Roller Bars, Clockwork, 8 In.	*Illus*	2360.00

CHARLIE MCCARTHY was the ventriloquist's dummy used by Edgar Bergen from the 1930s. He was famous for his work in radio, movies, and television. The act was retired in the 1970s.

Cigarette Carton, Your Christmas Chesterfield, Souvenir Match Lot, 1950s, 3 x 11 In.		95.00
Doll, Composition, Movable Jaw, Pull String, Monocle, Tuxedo, Box, c.1938, 20 In.		531.00
Doll, Composition, Wearing Top Hat, Suit, Effanbee, Box, c.1930, 20 In.		304.00
Doll, Mortimer Snerd, Ventriloquist Dummy, Cloth Body, Vinyl Head, Juro Novelty Co., 1950s, 29 In.		85.00
Doll, Wearing Tuxedo, Top Hat, Monocle, 1930s, 12 ½ In.		225.00
Pencil Sharpener, Bakelite, Butterscotch, Graphic Image, 1 ⅝ x ½ In.		41.00
Radio, Art Deco, White Plastic Case, Charlie Seated In Speaker, Majestic, c.1938, 5 ⅜ x 7 In.		826.00
Toy, Benzine Mobile, Tin, Clockwork, Louis Marx, 7 In.		345.00
Toy, Walker, Tin Lithograph, Clockwork, Louis Marx, 8 ¼ In.		230.00
Toy, Walker, Top Hat, Tux, Duck, Suitcase, Tin Lithograph, Clockwork, Marx, 8 In.		230.00

CHELSEA porcelain was made in the Chelsea area of London from about 1745 to 1769. Some pieces made from 1770 to 1784 are called Chelsea Derby and may include the letter *D* for *Derby* in the mark. Ceramic designs were borrowed from the Meissen models of the day. Pieces were made of soft paste. The gold anchor was used as the mark, but it has been copied by many other factories. Recent copies of Chelsea have been made from the original molds. Do not confuse Chelsea porcelain with Chelsea Grape, a white pottery with luster grape decoration. Chelsea Keramic is listed in the Dedham category.

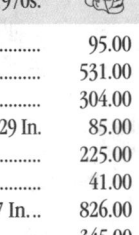

Figurine, Bullfinch, Perched On Stump, Cherry Branches, Painted, Red Anchor Mark, c.1760, 8 In.		3540.00
Figurine, Maiden, Playing Triangle, Drummer, Flowering Hedges, 1700s, 10 x 6 In., Pair		480.00
Vase, Red Flowers, Brown Ground, Round, Footed, 7 ¼ In.		20.00

CHELSEA GRAPE pattern was made before 1840. A small bunch of grapes in a raised design, colored with purple or blue luster, is on the border of the white plate. Most of the pieces are unmarked. The pattern is sometimes called Aynsley or Grandmother. Chelsea Sprig is similar but has a sprig of flowers instead of the bunch of grapes. Chelsea Thistle has a raised thistle pattern. Do not confuse these Chelsea patterns with Chelsea Keramic Art Works, which can be found in the Dedham category, or with Chelsea porcelain, the preceding category.

Plate, Dessert, Copper Luster, c.1835, 7 ¼ In. 20.00

CHINESE EXPORT porcelain comprises the many kinds of porcelain made in China for export to America and Europe in the eighteenth, nineteenth, and twentieth centuries. Other pieces may be listed in this book under Canton, Celadon, Nanking, Rose Canton, Rose Mandarin, and Rose Medallion.

Bodhisattva, On Lotus Base, Famille Rose, Character Marks, 1900s, 12 In. 176.00
Bottle, Water, White Flowers, Blue Ground, c.1860, 13 ½ In. 767.00
Bowl, Battles Of The Saintes, Panorama, c.1784, 15 ¾ In. 32500.00
Bowl, Blue & White, Figure, Bridge, Landscape, c.1750, 5 ⅞ In., 4 Piece 472.00
Bowl, Blue, White, Cranes, Clouds, Octagonal Reserves, Tapered, c.1900, 6 ½ x 11 ½ In. 360.00
Bowl, Canton Waterfront Scene, Flags, Figures, Red Ground, Flowers, 16 In. 104500.00
Bowl, Famille Rose, Birds, Flowers, Gold Mille Fleurs, Ring Foot, Wide Rim, c.1900, 2 ½ x 7 ½ In. 345.00
Bowl, Famille Rose, Ceremonial Scenes, Painted Border, Animals, Carved Stand, 21 In. 30680.00
Bowl, Famille Rose, Chrysanthemum, Blue Asters, Yellow, Green, Pink, Zitan Stand, c.1930, 6 ⅜ In. 307.00
Bowl, Famille Rose, Courtyard Scene, Leaves, Canted Rectangle, 9 In., Pair 438.00
Bowl, Famille Rose, Cross Edge Design, Flowers, Branches, Inverted Bell Shape, c.1930, 13 ⅞ In. . 676.00
Bowl, Famille Rose, Dragon & Phoenix, Clouds, Pearls, Greek Key Borders, 3 ⅓ x 8 ¼ In. 590.00
Bowl, Famille Rose, Dragon, Flaming Pearl, Multicolor, Chinese, c.1720, 8 ½ In. 4537.00
Bowl, Famille Rose, Dragon, Flowers, 9 ½ In. 119.00
Bowl, Famille Rose, Eggshell, Qianlong Style, Dragon, Flowers, Blue, Marked, 9 ½ In. 117.00
Bowl, Famille Rose, Figures, Blue Border, 1700s, 8 In. 246.00
Bowl, Famille Rose, Figures, Gilt Highlights, c.1850, 7 x 15 ½ In. .... *Illus* 1534.00
Bowl, Famille Rose, Flared Bell Shape, Turquoise Glaze, Dragons, Flowers, Birds, c.1930, 7 In. . 738.00
Bowl, Famille Rose, Flowers, Fence, c.1780, 11 ½ In. 472.00
Bowl, Famille Rose, Fluted, Round Foot, Applied Lotus Branches, c.1745, 4 ⅝ In. 359.00
Bowl, Famille Rose, Gilt Bronze, Flowers, Scroll Handles, Pierced Round Foot, 1800s, 11 x 16 In. . 3540.00
Bowl, Famille Rose, Horizontally Lobed, Ring Foot, Wide Rim, Ducks, Lotus, Peonies, 1800s, 7 In. 148.00
Bowl, Famille Rose, Iron Red, Flowering Branches, Round Foot, 4 ½ In. 359.00
Bowl, Famille Rose, Panels, Figures, Bouquets, Birds, 1800s, 5 ¼ x 13 In. 708.00
Bowl, Famille Rose, Pink Ground, Flowers, Gilt Rim, Round Foot, Wide Rim, 3 x 5 ¾ In., Pair . 403.00
Bowl, Famille Rose, Square Shaped, Cut Corners, Woman & Children Design, 1700s, 10 x 10 In... 215.00
Bowl, Famille Rose, Vases & Flowers, Rondels, Wide Rim, Ring Foot, c.1900, 3 ¼ x 7 ⅝ In. 288.00
Bowl, Famille Rose, Yellow Ground, Bats, Peaches, Ring Foot, c.1900, 4 ¼ In. Diam. 1380.00
Bowl, Famille Rose, Yellow Ground, Flowers, Calligraphy, Round Foot, 6 ⅜ In. 777.00
Bowl, Famille Verte, Lobed, Flowers, Butterfly, Turquoise Inside, 2 ¼ x 9 In. 81.00
Bowl, Flowers, Symbols Of Luck, Recessed Base, 1900s, 15 ⅞ In. .... *Illus* 500.00
Bowl, Flowers, Urns, c.1795, 5 x 11 In. 992.00
Bowl, Rice, Famille Rose, 2 Peasants, Rockwork, Flowering Trees, Plants, c.1830, 5 ⅞ In. 307.00
Bowl, Rice, Famille Rose, Blue & White, Lotus Blossoms, Scrolling Leaves, c.1900, 6 ¼ In. Diam... 430.00
Box, Famille Rose, Butterflies, Melons, Birds, Leaf Shape, Pierced Cover, 1 ¾ x 5 In. 120.00
Brushpot, Famille Rose, Flower Panels, Hexagonal, c.1860, 5 In. 2125.00
Brushpot, Famille Rose, Immortals, Attendants, Garden, Bell Shape, Wide Rim, c.1908-49, 8 ¾ In. 738.00
Buddha, Famille Rose, Yellow, Green Robes, Seated, Impressed Mark, 10 x 9 In., Pair 11136.00
Cachepot, Underplate, Famille Noir, Black, Prunus, c.1920, 6 x 6 In., Pair 540.00
Charger, Famille Rose, Peonies, Prunus Branches, Yellow Ground, 1800s, 14 In. 316.00
Charger, Famille Verte, Armorial, Arms Of France, Lotus, 1705, 12 ¼ In. 5975.00
Chocolate Pot, Bulbous, Cone Shape Lid, Strawberry Knop, Strap Handle, 9 ¼ In. 259.00
Coffeepot, Flower Medallion, Pomegranate Knop, Blue, Gilt, Lighthouse Shape, 9 In. 750.00
Cup, Ship, American Flags, Sails, Interior Flowers, Garland, Wide Rim, Ring Foot, c.1800, 3 ½ In. 529.00
Cup, Wine, Iron Red, Inverted Bell Shape, Dragons, Flaming Pearl, Waves, Marked, 2 x 2 ¼ In. 492.00
Dish, Famille Rose, Maiden On Flat Boat, Lotus Pond, Holding Bamboo Pole, Iron Red, 2 x 12 In. 837.00
Dish, Famille Verte, Bird On Rock, Flared Sloping Sides, Foot Ring, c.1800, 8 In. 538.00
Dish, Musicians, Blue & White, c.1700, 13 ½ In. 17500.00
Dish, Shaped, Blue Borders, Gilt Ecclesiastical Center Arms, 1700s, 7 x 8 In. 221.00
Figurine, Cockerels, Blue, Yellow, Purple, c.1880, 5 In., Pair 826.00
Figurine, Crane, Cocked Head, Black, White, Rockwork, 20 ¼ In. 35000.00
Fruit Basket, Stand, Famille Rose, Oval, Fleurette Handles, Reticulated, 1800s, 10 ¼ In. 553.00
Ginger Jar, Blue & White, Waterway Scene, Carved Wood Cover & Stand, c.1890, 11 ⅜ In. 533.00

TIP
If you live in a damp climate, keep a small lightbulb lit in each closet to retard mildew.

Chinese Export, Bowl, Famille Rose, Figures, Gilt Highlights, c.1850, 7 x 15 ½ In.
$1,534.00

Brunk Auctions

Chinese Export, Bowl, Flowers, Symbols Of Luck, Recessed Base, 1900s, 15 ⅞ In.
$500.00

Skinner, Inc.

Chinese Export, Plate, Figures, Actors, Script Panels, c.1825, 8 In., Pair
$1,121.00

James D. Julia Auctioneers

The edited listings of the current prices in this *Kovels' Antiques & Collectibles Price Guide* aren't available on any website. Readers can visit **Kovels.com** to check thousands of past prices and sign up for free information on trends, tips, reproductions, marks, and more.

Chinese Export, Punch Bowl, Famille Rose, Bird, Flowers, Panels, Wood Stand, 1800s, 13 x 5 In.
$610.00

Neal Auction Co.

Chinese Export, Tureen, Lid, Pigeon, Pink Roses, Blue & White Nest, 1800s, 3 ¾ x 6 ¾ In.
$900.00

Cowan's Auctions

Chinese Export, Vase, Double Gourd, 3 Children Supports, Marked, 5 ½ In.
$748.00

James D. Julia Auctioneers

Chocolate Glass, Cactus, Tumbler, Greentown, 4 In.
$35.00

Early Auction Co.

TIP
Never scrub porcelain dolls.

Ginger Jar, Famille Verte, Phoenix, Flowers, Iron Red, Green, Wood Stand, 10 ¾ x 12 ¼ In., Pair.	702.00
Ginger Jar, Lid, Famille Rose, Birds, Flowers, 17 In., Pair	119.00
Jar, Famille Rose, Baluster, Shaped Panels, Birds, Flowering Branches, c.1890, 15 ¼ In.	799.00
Jar, Lid, Famille Rose, Globular, Flowers, Ruyi Heads, Lapped Border, c.1915, 9 ½ In., Pair	676.00
Jar, Lid, Famille Rose, Pheasant, Rocks, Flowers, Baluster Shape, c.1850, 12 ½ In., Pair	3835.00
Jar, Lid, Famille Rose, Procession, Honoring Boy, Hand Painted, Hardwood Stand, c.1910, 9 ¾ In.	510.00
Jar, Lid, Famille Rose, Scholar, Garden, Multicolor, c.1905, 9 In.	104.00
Jar, Lid, Famille Verte, Birds, Flowers, Branches, Oval, Chinese, 1800s, 12 ¼ In., Pair	1089.00
Jardiniere, Blue, White, Blossoms, Branches, c.1860, 9 x 10 In.	590.00
Jardiniere, Famille Rose, Figures, Flowers, Blossoms, Rosewood Stand, c.1915, 7 ½ In., Pair	3250.00
Jardiniere, Famille Rose, Foo Dog-Mask Ring Handles, Flared Rim, 1700s, 24 In., Pair	146500.00
Jardiniere, Famille Rose, Tapered, Squat, In-Curved Rim, Lotus, Scrolling Leaves, c.1900, 11 ⅞ In.	1476.00
Jardiniere, Famille Verte, Butterflies, Flowers, Lappet & Brocade Borders, 1800s, 14 x 16 In.	1168.00
Jardiniere, Famille Verte, Pavilions, Landscapes, Turquoise Ground, 13 In.	826.00
Lamp, Famille Verte, Baluster Shape, Wood Base, 16 ⅜ In., Pair	384.00
Mug, 3-Masted Ship, Flags, Green, Interlaced Strap Handle, c.1790, 4 ⅜ In.	11875.00
Pheasant, Famille Rose, Mottled Rockwork, Red, Gilt, 1700s, 13 In., Pair	74500.00
Plaque, Famille Rose, Birds & Flowers, 13 ½ In.	448.00
Plate, American Eagle, E Pluribus Unum, Fitzhugh, Orange, c.1800, 9 ¾ In. Diam.	2952.00
Plate, Apple Pickers, Orange, Green, Gilt, c.1790, 8 ¾ In., Pair	1067.00
Plate, Cape Of Good Hope, Dutch Ships, c.1740, 9 In.	13750.00
Plate, Famille Rose, Depicting Flower Seller, 6 Character Mark, 10 In.	590.00
Plate, Famille Rose, Octagonal, Bok Choy, Flowering Trees, 1700s, 8 ⅝ In. Diam., Pair	676.00
Plate, Figures, Actors, Script Panels, c.1825, 8 In., Pair...............................*Illus*	1121.00
Plate, Fish, Famille Rose, Dragon, Phoenix, c.1875, 11 x 16 In.	1225.00
Plate, Fitzhugh, Orange, c.1850, 8 In., 12 Piece	3540.00
Plate, Fitzhugh, Orange, Green, c.1820, 9 ¾ In., Pair	9440.00
Plate, Fitzhugh, Rose, Horse, Cart, Landscape, c.1815, 9 ¾ In.	9440.00
Plate, Grape Borders, Phoenix, Flowering Peony, c.1850, 9 ⅝ In.	215.00
Plate, Luncheon, Fitzhugh, Green, c.1830, 8 ¾ In. Diam.	110.00
Plate, Okeover Arms, Cartouches, Crest, c.1743, 9 In.	9375.00
Plate, Portrait, European Man, Flower Borders, c.1900, 8 In. Diam.	522.00
Plate, Shipping, St. Albans, Battle Of The Saintes, c.1784, 8 ⅝ In.	5625.00
Plate, Soup, Fitzhugh, Green, 10 In.	708.00
Plate, War-Like Figures, Actors, Lines From Plays, Multicolor, c.1800, 8 In. Diam., Pair	590.00
Platter, Blue & White, River Scene, Cantered Rectangle, c.1850, 10 ½ In.	189.00
Platter, Blue & White, Woman, Child In Garden, Oval, 15 In., Pair	1534.00
Platter, Blue Bands, Gilt Diaperwork Banding, Faux Bamboo Stand, Oval, 13 x 18 In.	403.00
Platter, Famille Rose, Flower Sprays, Swags, Blossoms On Rim, 13 ⅛ In., Pair	313.00
Platter, Famille Rose, Reticulated Border, Arm Of Pakenham, c.1785, 7 ¾ In.	1195.00
Platter, Famille Rose, Tobacco Leaf, Scalloped Rim, c.1775, 18 ½ In.	15000.00
Platter, Fitzhugh, Orange, Oval, c.1850, 17 In.	1534.00
Platter, Table Base, Multicolor, Figures Playing Chess, Musicians, 1700s, 13 ¼ & 16 ½ In.	2160.00
Punch Bowl, Famille Rose, Bird, Flowers, Panels, Wood Stand, 1800s, 13 x 5 In.............*Illus*	610.00
Punch Bowl, Famille Rose, Figures In Landscapes, Armor Pattern, 1700s, 10 ¼ In., Pair	922.00
Punch Bowl, Famille Rose, Figures In Palace Garden, 1700s, 15 ⅝ In.	1599.00
Punch Bowl, Famille Rose, Figures, Garden Scenes, Armor Pattern Ground, 1700s, 10 ⅜ In.	307.00
Punch Bowl, Famille Rose, Figures, Landscape, 1700s, 12 ¼ In. Diam.	215.00
Punch Bowl, Famille Rose, Figures, Landscapes, Diapered Ground, Flower Border, 1700s, 10 ¼ In.	399.00
Punch Bowl, Famille Rose, Figures, Musical Instruments, Plants, Fish, Gilt Rim, c.1850, 13 ½ In.	4838.00
Punch Bowl, Famille Rose, Figures, Palace Scene, Leaf Borders, Gilt, 1700s, 15 ¼ In. Diam.	2214.00
Punch Bowl, Famille Rose, Hunt Scene, c.1850, 13 ⅝ In.	2375.00
Punch Bowl, Flowers, Garland, Footed, 19th Century, 5 x 11 In.	504.00
Punch Bowl, Multicolor, Gray Brothers Square, Copenhagen, Flowers, c.1775, 12 ½ In.	74500.00
Punch Bowl, Pheasant, Flowers, Scholars, Inscriptions, Iron Red, 1800s, 16 In.	1180.00
Punch Bowl, Rouge De Fer, Red, Gold, Black Diaper, Reserves, Scrolling, 12 ½ x 5 ½ In.	1380.00
Punch Pot, Gilt Handle & Spout, Scrolls, Mandarin Figures, Ho Ho Birds, c.1750, 8 x 12 In.	1168.00
Saucer, Famille Rose, Deer, Flower Borders, Butterflies, c.1800, 6 In. Diam., Pair	246.00
Serving Dish, Famille Rose, Figures, Garden, Pavilion, Flower Band, c.1890, 7 ⅞ In.	153.00
Tankard, Armorial, Cylindrical, Gilt Fret Border, Arms Of Talbot, c.1790, 6 In.	307.00
Tankard, Armorial, White Ground, 19th Century, 6 ½ In.	213.00
Tea Bowl, Famille Rose, Iron Red Bats, Flying, Clouds, c.1900, 3 ⅝ In. Diam.	246.00
Teapot, Famille Rose, Round Lobed, Loop Handle, Lotus, Flowers, c.1730, 4 ½ In.	896.00
Tureen, Famille Rose, Notched Corners, Boar's Head Handles, Scrolled Knop, c.1790, 9 x 12 ½ In.	1722.00
Tureen, Lid, Famille Rose, Peaches, Guava, Buddha's Hand, c.1875, 10 x 13 In.	678.00
Tureen, Lid, Pigeon, Pink Roses, Blue & White Nest, 1800s, 3 ¾ x 6 ¾ In.........*Illus*	900.00

C

Tureen, Lid, Stand, Court Figures, Dragons, Flaming Pearl, Gilt, Jin Neng Heng, c.1840 .... 10000.00
Urn, Lid, Classical Shape, Waisted, Pedestal Base, Squared Plinth, Scrolled Handles, 15 In., Pair... 334.00
Vase, Apple Green Glaze, Flower Sprays, Enamel Overglaze, Marked, 11 In. 1150.00
Vase, Blossoms, Branches, Gray Ground, Enamel Copper Champleve, Sloped, Oval, c.1890, 21 In. 480.00
Vase, Blue & White, Man, Woman, Children, Gate, 11 ¾ In. 531.00
Vase, Blue & White, Sleeve Shape, Court Figure, Attendants, Willow Tree, 1600s, 17 ½ In. 40000.00
Vase, Bottle Shape, Famille Rose, Multicolor Enamels, Flowers, Birds, 1900s, 17 In. 82.00
Vase, Double Gourd, 3 Children Supports, Marked, 5 ½ In. .... *Illus* 748.00
Vase, Famille Jaune, Flowers, Scrolls, Octagonal, c.1850, 23 ½ In. 4248.00
Vase, Famille Jaune, Hexagonal, Trumpet Rim, Yellow, 1900s, 16 ½ x 8 In., Pair 600.00
Vase, Famille Noir, Peonies, Scrolling Vines, Seal Mark, 17 In., Pair 3540.00
Vase, Famille Noir, Square Beaker, Tapering Sides, Birds, Flowers, Marked, c.1898, 16 ½ In. ... 546.00
Vase, Famille Rose, 7 In., Pair 590.00
Vase, Famille Rose, 9 Peaches, Rouleau, 13 ½ In. 330.00
Vase, Famille Rose, Baluster, Flared Shoulder, Dragon, Mille Fleur Design, c.1890, 11 ⅛ In. ... 676.00
Vase, Famille Rose, Baluster, Lion Head Handles, Flowers, Butterflies, Gilt, 1900s, 21 ½ In. 307.00
Vase, Famille Rose, Birds, Flowers, Blue Ground, c.1875, 24 In. 3675.00
Vase, Famille Rose, Birds, Flowers, Ruby Ground, Bat Shape Handles, Baluster, c.1890, 12 ¾ In.... 1353.00
Vase, Famille Rose, Bottle Shape, Cranes, Clouds, Lotus Flowers, Gilt Borders, c.1900, 15 ½ In.. 593.00
Vase, Famille Rose, Bottle Shape, Elongated Neck, Foo Lions, Scrolling Lotus, c.1900, 15 ⅛ In.. 1422.00
Vase, Famille Rose, Bottle Shape, Landscape, Mountains, River, Boats, Round Foot, c.1900, 9 ¼ In. 474.00
Vase, Famille Rose, Cylindrical, Flared Rim, Landscape, c.1900, 9 ½ In., Pair 900.00
Vase, Famille Rose, Flowers, Dragons, Green Ground, High Shoulder, 7 x 5 In. 1062.00
Vase, Famille Rose, Mother, Children, Flared Rim, Baluster, c.1850, 9 In., Pair 690.00
Vase, Famille Rose, Peony Blossoms, Short Neck, c.1920, 16 ½ In., Pair 540.00
Vase, Famille Rose, Rose Peonies, Cylindrical, Flared Rim, 19th Century, 7 ¾ In. 264.00
Vase, Famille Rose, Scrolling Lotus, Pink, Gilt, Bell Shape Base, Trumpet Rim, 1800s, 9 ¾ In. 2066.00
Vase, Famille Rose, Tobacco Leaf, Gilt Highlights, Flowers, Trumpet Shape, Splay Base, 7 ⅞ In., Pair. 584.00
Vase, Famille Rose, Urn Shape, Narrow Mouth, Turquoise, Flowers, 8 ⅜ In. 657.00
Vase, Famille Verte, Beaker Shape, Birds, Scrolling Flowers, Chinese, 1800s, 17 ½ In. 1150.00
Vase, Famille Verte, Landscape, Scholar Scene, White Ground, Pear Shape, c.1780, 9 ½ In...... 11500.00
Vase, Famille Verte, Phoenix, Peony Green Enamel Ground, c.1830, 9 ½ In. 780.00
Vase, Famille Verte, Tapered Baluster, Mythological Panels, Green Grid Ground, c.1850, 13 ¾ In. 2160.00
Vase, Floor, Famille Rose, 37 x 13 In. 600.00
Vase, Mandarin Lotus, Lotus Pod Handles At Neck, c.1860, 24 In. 1840.00
Vase, Moon Flask, Handles, Blue & White, c.1850, 17 In. 4375.00
Vase, Serpentine Sides, Orange Diapering, Blue Panels, c.1795, 12 x 5 ¼ In. 1107.00
Vase, Temple, Famille Rose, Mythological Figure Handles, Palace Figures, c.1920, 53 In. 13750.00
Washbasin, Famille Rose, Dragon Spewing Vapors To Sea, Carp, Crab, Buddhist Symbols, 14 ⅜ In. .. 307.00
Washbasin, Famille Rose, Figures, Landscape, Butterflies, Flowers, Gilt, 1800s, 13 ¾ In. Diam. 984.00
Washbowl, Famille Rose, U-Shape, Flared Rim, Figures, Birds, Insects, 1800s, 5 x 16 In. 275.00
Wine Cooler, Famille Rose, Scalloped Rim, Leaf Swags, Intertwined Handles, Splayed Foot, 6 ½ In. .. 1250.00
Wine Pot, Cadogan, Cobalt Blue Flowers, Square Handle, S-Spout, Round Foot, 1800s, 6 x 8 In. .. 518.00

CHINTZ is the name of a group of china patterns featuring an overall design of flowers and leaves. The design became popular with English makers about 1928. A few pieces are still being made. The best known are designs by Royal Winton, James Kent Ltd., Crown Ducal, and Shelley. Crown Ducal and Shelley are listed in their own sections.

Apple Blossom, Creamer, James Kent, 2 ½ In. 116.00
Apple Blossom, Plate, Salad, Pink, Scalloped, James Kent, 7 ⅞ In. 68.00
Ascot, Plate, Dessert, Gilt Trim, Crown Ducal, 6 x 6 In. 39.00
Ascot, Plate, Multicolor, Crown Ducal, 9 ¾ In. 134.00
Balmoral, Creamer, Royal Winton, Multicolor Flowers, Black Ground, Footed 70.00
Balmoral, Plate, Dinner, Royal Winton, Flowers, Black Ground, 10 In. 140.00
Beeston, Vase, Royal Winton, Orange & Pink Flowers, Black Ground, 4 ⅞ In. 130.00
Cheadle, Relish, Royal Winton, Rounded Handles, 11 x 5 In. 65.00
DuBarry, Creamer, James Kent, Footed, Oval, 6 Oz., 2 ¾ In. 119.00
DuBarry, Cup & Saucer, Footed, James Kent 83.00
DuBarry, Plate, Dinner, James Kent, 9 In. 107.00
Lady Gay, Plate, Green Trim, Square, Royal Albert, 8 ¾ In. 24.00
Mayfair, Ashtray, Royal Winton, Blue & Pink Flowers, Leaves, 3 x 3 In. 43.00
Old Cottage, Sugar & Creamer, Royal Winton 120.00
Pekin, Cup & Saucer, Royal Winton, Black Ground 86.00
Queen Anne, Cup & Saucer, Royal Winton .... 50.00 to 69.00
Queen Anne, Plate, Dinner, Royal Winton, 10 In. 97.00
Rosalynde, Plate, Dinner, James Kent, 9 ¾ In. 128.00

TIP
Don't try to wash and clean vintage glass Christmas ornaments. The paint could easily flake off. Just dust.

C

Christmas, Belsnickle, Blue Coat, Papier-Mache, 10 ½ In.
$660.00

Morphy Auctions

Christmas, Belsnickle, Blue Coat, Red Trim, Black Boots, Tree, Chalkware, 14 ¾ In.
$3,835.00

Bertoia Auctions

TIP
Don't stack boxes of Christmas ornaments. The weight may break some of the glass ornaments.

Christmas, Belsnickle, Holding Basket, Composition Face, Rabbit Fur Beard, 12 In.
$2,280.00

Morphy Auctions

Christmas, Label, Firecracker, Santa Claus, 50-Roll Pack, Him Shun, Chinese, 2 ⅜ x 2 ⅛ In.
$1,320.00

Morphy Auctions

Christmas, Label, Firecracker, Santa Claus, Him Shun, 20-Pack, Chinese, 3 ⅛ x 2 ½ In.
$90.00

Morphy Auctions

Rosalynde, Sugar, Lid, James Kent, 2 ⅜ In.	62.00
Royal Gay, Sugar, Paneled, Royal Albert	53.00
Summertime, Bowl, Roses, Daisies, c.1940, 4 x 4 In., Pair	89.00
Trellis Rose, Gravy Boat, James Kent, Footed	127.00
Trellis Rose, Plate, Bread & Butter, James Kent, Scalloped, 8 In.	20.00

CHOCOLATE GLASS, sometimes mistakenly called caramel slag, was made by the Indiana Tumbler and Goblet Company of Greentown, Indiana, from 1900 to 1903. It was also made at other National Glass Company factories. Fenton Art Glass Co. made chocolate glass from about 1907 to 1915. More recent pieces have been made by Imperial and others.

Cactus, Tumbler, Greentown, 4 In. ....*Illus*	35.00
Chrysanthemum Leaf, Syrup, Greentown, 6 ½ In.	460.00
Cruet, Leaf Bracket, Greentown, 6 In., Pair	115.00
Feather, Cruet, Cream To Chocolate Brown, Stopper, 5 ½ In.	58.00
Geneva, Bowl, Oval, Scalloped Rim, Footed, 9 ½ In.	58.00

CHRISTMAS collectibles include not only Christmas trees and ornaments listed below, but also Santa Claus figures, special dishes, and even games and wrapping paper. A Belsnickle is a nineteenth-century figure of Father Christmas. A kugel is an early, heavy ornament made of thick blown glass, lined with zinc or lead, and often covered with colored wax. Christmas cards are listed in this section under Greeting Card. Christmas collectibles may also be listed in the Candy Container category. Christmas trees are listed in the section that follows.

Bank, Mechanical, Santa Claus At Chimney, Paint, Cast Iron, Shepherd Hardware, 6 In.	3000.00
Belsnickle, Blue Coat, Papier-Mache, 10 ½ In. ....*Illus*	660.00
Belsnickle, Blue Coat, Red Trim, Black Boots, Tree, Chalkware, 14 ¾ In. ....*Illus*	3835.00
Belsnickle, Brown Robe, Red Trim, Wood Switches, Pennsylvania Dutch, 7 ¾ In.	1140.00
Belsnickle, Holding Basket, Composition Face, Rabbit Fur Beard, 12 In. ....*Illus*	2280.00
Belsnickle, Papier-Mache, Feather Tree, Germany, c.1800, 6 ½ In.	281.00
Belsnickle, Red, White Robe, Hood, Fir Tree, Standing, 2 ¾ In.	120.00
Belsnickle, Yellow Robe, Red Trim, Fir Tree, Germany, 11 ¼ In.	660.00
Belsnickle, Yellow, Red Pipe Cleaner Trim, Feather Tree Sprig, Mica Base, Germany, 14 ½ In.	1416.00
Book, Christmas ABC, Little Golden Book, 22 Pages, 1962	15.00
Bottle, Blown, Santa, Climbing From Chimney, Amber, c.1890, 5 ¾ x 2 ¼ In.	150.00
Candy Containers are listed in the Candy Container category.	
Cracker, Snapping, Paper Die Cut Images, Sailors, Composition Head, Box, 9 In.	115.00
Creche Set, Mary, Joseph, Baby, Painted, Terra-Cotta, Cloth, Glass Eyes, Basket, c.1890, 14 In.	1534.00
Decoration, Pyramid, 4 Tiers, Candle Powered, Carved, Painted, c.1900, 41 ½ In.	326.00
Diorama Pyramid, Wood, Multicolor, Candle Powered, Dresden Star, Erzgebirge, 11 In.	472.00
Display, Santa Claus, Walking Stick, Tree, Dolls, Pressed Cardboard, Germany, 1920s, 26 In.	191.00
Figurine, Angel, December, Napco, 4 In.	29.00
Label, Firecracker, Santa Claus, 50-Roll Pack, Him Shun, Chinese, 2 ⅜ x 2 ⅛ In. ....*Illus*	1320.00
Label, Firecracker, Santa Claus, Him Shun, 20-Pack, Chinese, 3 ⅛ x 2 ½ In. ....*Illus*	90.00
Nodder, Santa Claus, Celluloid, Japan, c.1935, 7 In.	180.00
Nodder, Santa Claus, On Donkey, Holding Fur, Composition Face, 11 In.	510.00
Nodder, Santa Claus, On Elephant, Composition Face & Hands, 8 ½ In.	720.00
Pin, Santa Claus Club, Have You Read It?, Celluloid, W&H, c.1905, 1 ½ In. ....*Illus*	475.00
Pin, Santa Claus, I Am At Wanamaker's, Round, Wreath Border, c.1910, 1 ¼ In.	168.00
Pin, Santa Claus, On Phone, Call Me At Wanamaker's, Keystone Backpaper, 1915, 1 In.	86.00
Plates that are limited edition are listed in the Collector Plate category or in the correct factory listing.	
Postcard, Art Deco, Festive Flowers, Fringe Lamp, 1936, 5 ½ x 3 ½ In.	5.00
Poster, Schribners, Maxfield Parrish, 1897, 21 x 13 In.	850.00
Santa Claus, In Wood Sleigh, Multicolor, 10 ¼ In.	150.00
Santa Claus, Mechanical, Feather Tree, Lantern, Composition, 25 In.	4029.00
Santa Claus, On Reindeer, Composition, Wire, Coat, Pants, Feather Sprig, Germany, 13 In.	2006.00
Santa Claus, On Skis, Composition Face & Hands, Japan, 5 ¾ In. ....*Illus*	120.00
Santa Claus, On Sleigh, Composition Face, Japan, 4 ½ In. ....*Illus*	90.00
Santa Claus, Papier-Mache Face, Cotton Beard, Composition Hands, Fir Tree, 21 In. ......*Illus*	1440.00
Santa Claus, Redware, Mold Cast, Amber Sponge, Glaze, 1988, 17 x 8 ½ In.	48.00
Santa Claus, Riding Reindeer, Glass Eyes, Saddle, Leather Antlers, Fir Tree, 11 In.	1440.00
Santa Claus, Riding Reindeer, Holding Fir Tree, Lead Antlers, Composition, 7 In.	450.00
Santa Claus, Riding Sheep, Blue Collar, Bell, Leather Ears, Feather Tree, 10 In.	330.00
Santa Claus, Riding Sleigh, Moss, Wicker, Germany, 11 ½ In.	150.00
Santa Claus, Rosy Cheeks, Teeth Showing, Painted, c.1970, 8 ½ In.	75.00
Santa Claus, Sled, Reindeer, Wheeled Platform, Cloth, Metal, Celluloid, 25 ½ In.	272.00

C

Sign, Bond Bread, Santa Claus, Easel Back, Die Cut, c.1930, 15 x 8 ¾ In........................*Illus*	176.00
Toy, Flying Santa Claus, Branch, Tin, Painted, Clockwork Propeller, Distler, c.1900, 6 ¾ In.....	1116.00
Toy, Santa Claus Open Auto, Tin Litho, Graphics, Feather Tree, Tippco, Germany, c.1928, 12 In.....	28910.00
Toy, Santa Claus, Head Moves, Windup, Celluloid, 6 ½ In..	210.00
Toy, Santa Claus, Holding Gift, Walker, Tin, J. Chein, 1930s, 5 ½ In.................................	540.00
Toy, Santa Claus, On Mechanical Bear, Robe, Pants, Fur Beard, Windup, 7 ½ In.......................	649.00
Toy, Santa Claus, On Rocking Horse, Wood, Composition, Windup, Germany, c.1920, 10 x 9 In.	259.00
Toy, Santa Claus, Riding In Car, Fir Tree, Wood Wheels, Headlight, Dresden Germany, 7 In.....	510.00
Toy, Santa Claus, Riding Nodding Elephant, Fir Tree, Composition, Wood, Pull, 8 ½ In.	240.00
Toy, Santa Claus, Riding White Sheep, Bell, Fir Tree, Metal Wheels, Pull, 7 In....... 420.00 to 510.00	
Toy, Santa Claus, Sleigh, Reindeer, Paint, Cast Iron, Hubley, 15 ½ In.................................	1200.00
Toy, Santa Claus, Walking, Windup, Tin, Lithograph, Japan, Box, 7 In................................	420.00
Toy, Santa Claus, Windup, Tin, Lithograph, Chein, 5 ½ In..	450.00
Toy, Santee Claus, Santa In Sleigh, 2 Reindeer, Tin, Clockwork, Strauss, 10 ¾ In....................	863.00
Toy, Santee Claus, Toy, Sleigh, Reindeer, Windup, Tin, Strauss, 11 ¼ In..............................	840.00
Trinket Box, Tree Shape, Cardinal, Holly, Red Berries, 3 ½ In..	28.00

CHRISTMAS TREES made of feathers and Christmas tree decorations of all types are popular with collectors. The first decorated Christmas tree in America is claimed by many states, including Pennsylvania (1747), Massachusetts (1832), Illinois (1833), Ohio (1838), and Iowa (1845). The first glass ornaments were imported from Germany about 1860. Dresden ornaments were made about 135 years ago of paper and tinsel. Manufacturers in the United States were making ornaments in the early 1870s. Electric lights were first used on a Christmas tree in 1882. Character light bulbs became popular in the 1920s, bubble lights in the 1940s, twinkle bulbs in the 1950s, plastic bulbs by 1955. In this book a Christmas light is a holder for a candle used on the tree. Other forms of lighting include light bulbs. Other Christmas collectibles are listed in the preceding section.

Aluminum, 31 Branches, Tubes, Stand, Box, c.1950, 4 Ft..	180.00
Aluminum, 55 Branches, Tripod Stand, Box, c.1960, 6 ½ Ft......................................	300.00
Bottle Brush, Glitter Paper, Crinkled, Mercury Glass Beads, 3 In. Diam........................	30.00
Bottle Brush, Gold Flocked & Glittered, Lights, 1960s, 13 In...................................	48.00
Bottle Brush, Red Wooden Base, 5 ½ In..	10.00
Feather, New Growth Branches, Red Berries, Master Geschttzt, Germany, 54 In..................	561.00
Feather, Red Berries, Wood Base, c.1900, 12 In...	99.00
Feather, Spun Cotton Candles, Ornaments, 1930s, 4 In...	49.00
Flocked, Green, Glass & Beaded Ornaments, Wood Stand, 1950s, 6 In.............................	60.00
Kugel, Golden Amber, Brass Hanger, Germany, c.1890, 9 ½ In..........................*Illus*	331.00
Kugel, Orange Shape, Silver, Textured, Stem Indent, Germany, 3 ¾ In...........................	885.00
Kugel, Tramp Art Base, Birds, Green Crepe Paper Branches, 25 In...............................	89.00
Light Bulb, Figural, Santa Claus, Milk Glass, 2-Sided, 3 In..................................	6.00
Light Set, Wonder Stars, Matchless Electric Co., Box, 11 Lights, 10 x 7 ¼ In..................	1020.00
Ornament, Angel Bell, Embossed Stars, White Bisque, Goebel, 1977, 3 In.......................	16.00
Ornament, Angel, Playing Harp, Red & White, Josef, 4 In......................................	45.00
Ornament, Bell, Red Holly, Berries, Lefton, 3 ¼ In...	14.00
Ornament, Blown Glass, Boy Clown Head, Indent Ball, Germany, 5 ½ In..........................	207.00
Ornament, Blown Glass, Gramophone, Wire Wrap, Red Horn, Germany, 4 In........................	354.00
Ornament, Blown Glass, Keystone Kop, Extended Legs, Germany, 4 ¾ In.................*Illus*	384.00
Ornament, Frog, Green Iridescent, Gold Detail, Dresden, 2 In.................................	502.00
Ornament, Glass, Frosted, Baby In Cradle..	32.00
Ornament, Glass, Longshoreman, Extended Legs, Germany, 5 In..........................*Illus*	561.00
Ornament, Golden Flounder, Open Mouth, Full Figure, Dresden, Germany, 4 ¾ In.................	531.00
Ornament, Horse, Prancing, Gold Pressed Paper, Silver Saddle, Highlights, 3 ½ In.............	295.00
Ornament, Icicle, Pressed Cotton, Mica Snow, 7 In., 4 Piece..................................	148.00
Ornament, Peacock, Green Iridescent, Gold Trim, Dresden, Germany, 4 ¼ In.....................	266.00
Ornament, Pirate, Cotton, Crepe Paper, Parrot On Shoulder, Dresden Face, Germany, 4 In......	1121.00
Ornament, Rabbit, Angel, Duck, Cat, Horse, Lamb, Lion, Painted, Meringue, 2 To 3 In., 7 Piece ...	12.00
Ornament, Raggedy Ann, Wreath, Bobbs Merrill Co., 1975, 3 In.................................	12.00
Ornament, Wax Angel, Spun Glass Wings, Skirts, 4 ½ In., 6 Piece..............................	384.00
Skirt, Felt, Green, Red Pompom Border, Fringe, 1960s, 42 In. Diam............................	34.00
Stand, Cast Iron, 3 Legs, North Brothers Mfg., 10 In...	100.00
Stand, Cast Iron, Bells In Ovals, Starburst, Green, Gilt, c.1910, 10 In. Diam................	78.00
Stand, Cast Iron, Green Gold, Embossed, Season's Greetings, Bells, c.1960, 13 In.............	68.00
Stand, Cast Iron, Green, Cherub, Germany, 1903, 10 x 9 In....................................	185.00
Stand, Cast Iron, Santa Claus Figure, Red Robe, Multicolor, Germany, 10 x 10 In.............	266.00
Stand, Enameled Steel, Safe-T Tree, White, Precision Products, Box, c.1965, 17 In...........	36.00

Christmas, Pin, Santa Claus Club, Have You Read It, Celluloid, W&H, c.1905, 1 ½ In. $475.00

Hake's Americana & Collectibles

Christmas, Santa Claus, On Skis, Composition Face & Hands, Japan, 5 ¾ In. $120.00

Morphy Auctions

Christmas, Santa Claus, On Sleigh, Composition Face, Japan, 4 ½ In. $90.00

Morphy Auctions

Christmas, Santa Claus, Papier-Mache Face, Cotton Beard, Composition Hands, Fir Tree, 21 In. $1,440.00

Morphy Auctions

Christmas, Sign, Bond Bread, Santa Claus, Easel Back, Die Cut, c.1930, 15 x 8 ¾ In.
$176.00

Wm Morford Antiques

Christmas Tree, Kugel, Golden Amber, Brass Hanger, Germany, c.1890, 9 ½ In.
$331.00

Garth's Auctioneers & Appraisers

Christmas Tree, Ornament, Blown Glass, Keystone Kop, Extended Legs, Germany, 4 ¾ In.
$384.00

Bertoia Auctions

Christmas Tree, Ornament, Glass, Longshoreman, Extended Legs, Germany, 5 In.
$561.00

Bertoia Auctions

Stand, Metal, 3-Footed, Lifetime, Box, 8 x 5 In.	25.00
Stand, Musical, Monopol, 4 Bells, 36-Tooth Steel Comb, Disc, Attachment, Leipziger Muskiwerke.	1540.00
Stand, Musical, Turns, 3 Saucer Bells, Clockwork Mechanism, J.C. Eckardt, c.1900, 11 In.	445.00
Stand, Wood, Plated Brass Dome Cover, Rotating, Musical, Windup, 4 Tunes, 3 ¾ x 13 In.	189.00
Tinsel, Gold, Pixie Elves, Glass Beads, Wood Base, Japan, Box, 1960s, 18 In.	52.00
Topper, Angel, Burlap, Jute, Taiwan, 1970s, 11 ½ In.	30.00
Topper, Angel, Halo, Plastic, Tinsel, Hands Clasped, Electric, Box, c.1964, 9 x 7 In.	39.00
Topper, Blown, Triple Indent, Rotating Stripes, Multicolor, 1930s, 11 ½ In.	35.00
Topper, Plastic, Sphere, Red, Blue, White, Italy, c.1960, 12 x 2 In.	18.00
Topper, Plastic, White, Red Trim, Electric, Gem, Box, 1950s, 11 x 8 In.	48.00
Topper, Star, Tinsel, Green, Silver, Germany, 9 x 11 ½ In.	45.00
Topper, Star, Tinsel, Reflector Center, c.1940, 7 x 6 In.	34.00

CHROME AND STAINLESS STEEL items in the Art Deco style became popular in the 1930s. Collectors are most interested in high-style pieces made by the Connecticut firms of Chase Brass & Copper Co., Manning-Bowman & Co., and others. In about 1920, stainless steel became available to artists and manufacturers, who used it to make many decorative items.

Ashtray, Chrome, 2 Open Beaked Birds, c.1950, 6 In. Diam.	22.00
Ashtray, Chrome, Mack Truck, Bulldog, c.1930, 5 ½ In., Diam.	75.00
Bottle Opener, Ribbed Handle, 1950s, 6 In.	25.00
Bowl Set, Stainless Steel, Abstract Leaf Shape, Georg Jensen, 3 ⅞, 8 ¾, 5 In., 3 Piece	148.00
Bowl, Stainless Steel, Boat Shape, Tapered Ends, Satinsteel, England, 1960s	38.00
Butter, Cover, Chrome, Glass Liner, Scalloped Rim, Finial, Sheltonware, 7 x 4 In.	15.00
Cocktail Pick Holder, Chrome, Enamel, Ebony, Bakelite Bottle-End Metal Picks, c.1930, 5 ½ In.. *Illus*	220.00
Cocktail Shaker, Chrome, Zeppelin Shape, Wheels, 12 ½ In.	725.00
Cocktail Shaker, Tray, Chrome, Cylindrical, Ribbed, Stepped Edge, Bel Geddes, 13-In. Shaker.	510.00
Dish, Party, Stainless Steel, Textured, 7 Compartments, Box, Rectangular, 1960s	30.00
Figure, Chrome, Woman, Outstretched Arms, Holding Gong & Hammer, Round Pedestal, c.1925, 8 In.	365.00
Flask, Chrome, Hammered, Cartouche, West Germany, 1950s, 10 Oz., 7 In.	30.00
Flatware, Stainless Steel, Blue Shark, Marked, Georg Jensen, 1900s, 59 Piece	*Illus* 1888.00
Holder, Wine Bottle, Stainless Steel, Copper, Pedestal Shape, Culinox, Switzerland	24.00
Ice Bucket, Chrome, Applied Panel, Man Holding Grapes, Loop Handles, Rockwell Kent, 9 ¼ In. .	385.00
Martini Caddy, Chrome, Round Frame, Feet, Wood Handle, 4 Glasses, Shaker, 12 ¾ x 8 ¾ In.	167.00
Sculpture, Stainless Steel, Flame, Triangular, Cut Angles, Signed Pohowsky, 62 x 32 In.	488.00
Siphon, Chrome, Soda King, Pat. 20535, Norman, Bel Geddes, c.1937, 9 ¾ In.	40.00
Smoking Stand, Plated Steel, Clock, Nightlight, Ash Pots, Cache, Lighted Base, 31 x 13 In.	106.00
Sugar & Creamer, Stainless Steel, Round, Hinged Flip Top, Logo, Alessi	24.00
Table, Side, Chrome Plated Brass, Adjustable Airplane, Electrified Base, c.1940s, 34 x 15 In. . *Illus*	590.00
Table, Stainless Steel, Industrial Style, Round Top, Rod Legs, Lower Shelf, 20 x 16 In.	24.00
Tea Set, Stainless Steel, Danish Style, Teak Lids, Cylindrical, Squared Handles, Box, 1960s, 4 Piece	45.00
Toast Rack, Stainless Steel, 6 Slots, Cylinder Line, Arne Jacobsen, Stelton, England	42.00
Vase, Chrome, Cone Shape, Twisting Spiral Lines, Stepped Base, England, 6 In., Pair	60.00
Vase, Chrome, Elongated Cylindrical Body, Round Foot, Hagenauer, Werkstatten, Vienna, 19 In.	356.00

CIGAR STORE FIGURES of carved wood or cast iron were used as advertisements in front of the Victorian cigar store. The carved figures are now collected as folk art. They range in size from counter type, about three feet, to over eight feet high.

Gentleman, Cigar & Feathers, Wood, Paint, 30 x 17 In.	6325.00
Headdress, Carved, Painted, 47 In.	192.00
Indian Princess, Tobacco Leaf Headdress, Iron, Bronze, Hollow Cast, c.1890, 27 In. *Illus*	7800.00
Indian, Bust, Red Feather Headdress, Plaster, 22 In.	480.00
Indian, Bust, Red Indian Tobacco, 5 Cts., Plaster, 30 In.	960.00
Indian, Chief, Full Headdress, Cigar Bundle, Pine, Carved, Multicolor, 74 In.	575.00
Indian, Countertop, Chalkware, 20 In.	990.00
Indian, Feather Headdress, Holding Cigars, Painted, c.1890, 27 x 11 In. *Illus*	3851.00
Indian, Feather Headdress, Wolf Skin Cape, Shield, Tunic, Carved, c.1860, 64 x 76 In.	6900.00
Indian, Full Headdress, Holding Cigars, Carved Wood, c.1955, 51 In.	345.00
Indian, Headdress, Hand On Forehead, Carved, Painted, Round Base, c.1950, 73 x 22 In.	944.00
Indian, Headdress, Smoke Shop, Samuel Robb, Wood, Painted, 1880s, 78 In. *Illus*	77000.00
Indian, Holding Tobacco Leaf, Cigars, Painted, 1800s, 49 In.	2832.00
Indian, Looking Up, Plaster, Painted, 20 In.	96.00
Indian, Maiden, 5 Feather Headdress, Berries, Cigars, Blue Tunic, c.1860, 70 x 78 In.	31050.00
Indian, Profile, Plaster, Painted, Havana, 18 x 28 In.	660.00
Punch, Cigar In Mouth, Painted, Zinc, William Demuth	37290.00

CINNABAR is a vermilion or red lacquer. Pieces are made with tens to hundreds of thicknesses of the lacquer that is later carved. Most cinnabar was made in the Orient.

Boat, Emblems Of Immortals, 1800s, 7 ¾ x 3 ⅓ In.	2013.00
Box, 2 Figures In Garden, c.1900, 1 ¾ x 4 In.	98.00
Box, Lid, Butterfly Shaped, Carved, Mountains, Children, Marked, 1 ⅞ x 6 In.	460.00
Box, Lid, Carved, Brass Trim, Mountain Scene, c.1790, 1 ¾ x 5 ½ In.	118.00
Box, Lid, Dragon, Carved, China, Late 1800s, 2 x 3 In.	235.00
Box, Lid, Relief Carved, Scholars, Mountain Forest Landscape, 2 x 5 ¾ In., Pair	115.00
Inro, Hexagonal, Barrel Shape, Carved, 1800s, 3 In.	115.00
Snuff Bottle, Carved, Landscape, Figures, Trees, Marked, 1800s, 3 ⅛ In. ......*Illus*	245.00
Trinket Box, Round, Clouds, 2 Lions, Brocade Ball, Leaping Fish, Peaches, Leaves, 1800s, 4 x 3 ½ In.	1896.00
Vase, Carved Landscapes, Black Geometric, Brass Rim, Chinese, c.1910, 8 In., Pair	575.00
Vase, Green, Chrysanthemums, Lotus Scrolls, Baluster, Spread Foot, 1900s, 15 In., Pair	922.00
Vase, Handles, Black Interior, Carved Leaves, Geometrics, Landscapes, Figures, 10 In.	185.00
Vase, Landscape, Carved, Swollen Middle, Flared Neck, China, 19th Century, 10 In.	499.00

CIVIL WAR mementos are important collectors' items. Most of the pieces are military items used from 1861 to 1865. Be sure to avoid any explosive munitions.

Badge, G.A.R., Ribbon, Maimed Soldiers, Only A Few Of Us Left, Celluloid, 1897, 4 In.	111.00
Badge, Post Identification, GAR Merriam Post, No. 8, Color Litho, Oak Frame, 27 x 14 In.	71.00
Badge, Reunion, Bucktails, 12th, Celluloid, Brass, Pinback, Col. Thomas Kane, 1898, 7 x 2 In..	413.00
Broadside, To Laboring Men Of New York, Stop & Think, Draft Riots, 1863, 11 x 18 In.	7050.00
Broadside, Union Meeting, Chazy, N.Y., Eagle, Banner, 9 ¼ x 12 1/12 In.	1058.00
Button, General Robert E. Lee, 1807-1907, Photo, ⅞ In.	95.00
Button, McKinley, Soldier, Eagle, Flags, 1896, 1 In.	144.00
Button, U.C.V., Confederate Veterans, Soldiers, Shaking Hands, Flags, 1907, 1 ¼ In.	127.00
Camp Chair, Pine, Woven Seat, Tacks, Gen. H. F. Clarke, Gettysburg, 34 In.	588.00
Canteen, G.A.R., 26th Annual Encampment, Cobalt Blue Trim, Badge, Wentz, Post No. 1, 1900, 3 In.	165.00
Canteen, G.A.R., 26th Annual Encampment, Nickel Plated Tin, Copper Medallions, 1892, 4 In.	130.00
Cap, Kepi, Officer's, 40th Alabama Confederate, Wool, Leather, Lt. E. Gulley	9600.00
Cup, G.A.R., Tin Plated Steel, Loop Handle, 24th Encampment, Plymouth, Mass., 2 ¾ x 3 ¾ In..	83.00
Kerchief, G.A.R. Union Corps Badges, Blue, White, Flag, Circle Of Stars, Frame, 26 x 26 In.....	142.00
Membership Certificate, G.A.R., Watercolor, Soldiers, Eagle, Badge, David N. Curtis, Frame .	71.00
Memorial, G.A.R., Painted, Green Ribbon, Wreath, Giltwood Frame, 15 ½ x 11 ½ In.	177.00
Mug, G.A.R., White Stoneware, Joseph Cocks, Gilt Letters, Color Enamel Image, 3 ½ In.	177.00
Plate, Dinner, G.A.R., White Ironstone, Purple Band, Transfer, Members Medal, Post 71, 1884, 8 In.	12.00
Ribbon Badge, United Confederate Veterans Reunion, Brass Bar Pin, Celluloid, 1907, 2 x 2 In.....	95.00
Ribbon, Reunion, Old Bucktails, 13th Annual, 5th Corps., Philadelphia, 1899, 7 x 2 In.	165.00
Ribbon, Reunion, Old Bucktails, 17th Annual, Eagle Pinback, Harrisburg, 1903, 9 x 3 In.......	177.00
Saber, Cavalry, Brass Hilt, Wire Wrapped Grip, Marked 55, 30 ¼ In.	685.00
Socks, Wool, Flag Design, Related Newspaper Article, c.1861, 19 x 21 In.	2760.00

CKAW, *see Dedham category.*

CLARICE CLIFF was a designer who worked in several English factories, including A.J. Wilkinson Ltd., Wilkinson's Royal Staffordshire Pottery, Newport Pottery, and Foley Pottery after the 1920s. She is best known for her brightly colored Art Deco designs, including the Bizarre line. She died in 1972. Reproductions have been made by Wedgwood.

Bizarre, Bowl, Saucer Shape, Geometric Design, Blue, Purple, Orange, Tripod, Fruit, Twigs, 12 In......	504.00
Bizarre, Charger, Rhodanthe Pattern, Mark, Wilkinson Ltd., 1900s, 18 In. ......*Illus*	1422.00
Bizarre, Jug, Lotus, Pine Grove Pattern, Ribbed, Back Stamp, 1900s, 11 ⅜ In.......*Illus*	1126.00
Bizarre, Jug, Ribbed Body, Geometric Pattern, Diamonds, Loop Handle, 1900s, 11 In...........	376.00
Bizarre, Pot, Lid, Ball Finial, Bulbous, Wicker Handle, Pansies, 1900s, 6 In.	385.00
Bizarre, Vase, Tulip Shape, Scalloped Rim, Rounded Bottom, Ring Foot, Geometric, 1900s, 8 In. .	652.00
Crocus, Cup & Saucer, Wilkinson's	171.00
Delecia, Bowl, Pansies, Ribbed Sides, 1900s, 9 ¼ In.	296.00
Fantasque, Vase, Broth Pattern, Green, Red, Black, Cylindrical, Banding, c.1900, 11 In.	1304.00
Fantasque, Vase, Brown Lily, Multicolor Banding, Spread Foot, 1900s, 5 ⅞ In.	415.00
Fantasque, Vase, Trees, House, c.1930, 9 ¾ x 6 ½ In.......*Illus*	2250.00
House & Bridge, Plate, Tree, Hills, Orange, Yellow, Black Border, 1900s, 10 In.	415.00
Lotus, Vase, Multicolor, Baluster, 2 Loop Handles, 1900s, 9 ⅝ In.	1067.00
Rhodanthe, Bowl, Ring Foot, Cream Ground, Orange & Yellow Blossoms, 1900s, 8 ½ In........	296.00
Rhodanthe, Vase, Cream, Orange, Yellow, Brown, Flare Rim, 10 ⅝ In.	593.00
Tonquin, Bone Dish, Crescent Shape, Green, c.1930, 6 ⅝ x 3 ¾ In.	15.00

Chrome, Cocktail Pick Holder, Enamel, Ebony, Bakelite Bottle-End Metal Picks, c.1930, 5 ½ In.
$220.00

Heritage Auctions

Chrome, Flatware, Blue Shark, Stainless Steel, Marked, Georg Jensen, 1900s, 59 Piece
$1,888.00

Brunk Auctions

Chrome, Table, Side, Chrome Plated Brass, Adjustable Airplane, Electrified Base, c.1940s, 34 x 15 In.
$590.00

Brunk Auctions

TIP
Do not soak stainless steel flatware for a long time.

Cigar Store Figure, Indian Princess, Tobacco Leaf Headdress, Iron, Bronze, Hollow Cast, c.1890, 27 In. $7,800.00

Skinner, Inc.

Cigar Store Figure, Indian, Feather Headdress, Holding Cigars, Painted, c.1890, 27 x 11 In. $3,851.00

Skinner, Inc.

Cigar Store Figure, Indian, Headdress, Smoke Shop, Samuel Robb, Wood, Painted, 1880s, 78 In. $77,000.00

Showtime Auction Services

Tonquin, Platter, Royal Staffordshire, Blue & White, 11 ¼ In.		35.00
Turkey Platter, Strutting Turkey, Royal Staffordshire, 20th Century, 19 x 15 In.		125.00
Woodland, Planter, Tree, Hanging Leaves, Cream, Orange, Green, Black, 3 Feet, 7 ½ In.		365.00

CLEWELL was made in limited quantities by Charles Walter Clewell of Canton, Ohio, from 1902 to 1955. Pottery was covered with a thin coating of bronze, then treated to make the bronze turn different colors. Pieces covered with copper, brass, or silver were also made. Mr. Clewell's secret formula for blue patinated bronze was burned when he died in 1965.

Bowl, Copper Clad, Verdigris Patina, Folded In Sides, 3 ½ x 9 In.		313.00
Bowl, Copper To Green, Squat, 3 Ball Feet, Marked, 2 ⅞ x 7 ¼ In.		138.00
Bowl, Embossed Fruit, Copper Clad, 8 x 3 In.		375.00
Bowl, Matte Glaze, Faux Rivets, Brown Matte Glaze, Round, 4 In.		63.00
Urn, Bronze, Verdigris Patina, Swollen Neck, 2 Angular Handles, Spread Foot, 9 In.		2000.00
Vase, Copper Clad, Bronze & Verdigris Patina, Barrel Shape, Flared Rim, 8 x 6 In.		875.00
Vase, Copper Clad, Bronze & Verdigris Patina, Tapered, 13 x 4 In.		3625.00
Vase, Copper Clad, Bulbous Base, Elongated Neck, 10 ¼ In.		382.00
Vase, Copper Clad, Bulbous, Green, 5 x 5 ½ In.		313.00
Vase, Copper Clad, Deep Green Patina, Shouldered, Stand-Up Rim, 17 x 10 In.		1250.00
Vase, Copper Clad, Patina, Marked, 11 ¾ x 6 ¾ In.	*Illus*	2625.00
Vase, Copper Clad, Verdigris Patina, Flared, Spread Foot, 7 ½ x 3 In., Pair		500.00
Vase, Copper Clad, Verdigris Patina, Marked, 1920s, 15 x 7 In.	*Illus*	2500.00
Vase, Copper Clad, Verdigris Patina, Oval, Shouldered, 8 ½ x 7 In.		1375.00
Vase, Copper Clad, Verdigris Patina, Swollen Shape, 12 ½ x 5 ½ In.		531.00
Vase, Copper Clad, Verdigris Patina, Tapered, 10 x 5 ½ In.		563.00
Vase, Grapes, Copper Clad, Cylindrical, 4 x 9 In.		125.00
Vase, Rust, Turquoise, Footed Cylinder, Marked, 8 ½ In.		633.00
Vase, Shouldered, Ring Foot, Copper, Dark Green, c.1920, 8 ½ x 5 ¾ In.		1188.00
Vase, Shouldered, Spread Foot, Copper, Green Patina, c.1920, 9 ½ x 5 In.		2250.00
Vase, Swollen, Curved Rim, Copper Clad, 7 x 9 In.		250.00

CLIFTON POTTERY was founded by William Long in Newark, New Jersey, in 1905. He worked there until 1909 making lines that included Crystal Patina and Clifton Indian Ware. Clifton Pottery made art pottery until 1911 and then concentrated on wall and floor tile. By 1914, the name had been changed to Clifton Porcelain and Tile Company. Another firm, Chesapeake Pottery, sold majolica marked *Clifton Ware*.

Clifton

Jardiniere, Cylindrical Pedestal, Spread Foot, American Indian Design, 10 ⅞ x 14 In.		374.00
Vase, Bud, Crystal Patina, Silver Overlay, Signed, 1906, 5 x 4 In.	*Illus*	1125.00
Vase, Dripped Glaze, Brown, Green, Yellow, Incised, 1906, 13 ⅛ In.	*Illus*	345.00

CLOCKS of all types have always been popular with collectors. The eighteenth-century tall case, or grandfather's, clock was designed to house a works with a long pendulum. The name on the clock is usually the maker but sometimes it is a merchant or other craftsman. In 1816, Eli Terry patented a new, smaller works for a clock, and the case became smaller. The clock could be kept on a shelf instead of on the floor. By 1840, coiled springs were used and even smaller clocks were made. Battery-powered electric clocks were made in the 1870s. A garniture set can include a clock and other objects displayed on a mantel.

Advertising, Airmaid Nylons, For Your Convenience, Yellow, Cream, Plastic, Metal, Light-Up, 18 In.		480.00
Advertising, Borax Is King, Wall, Oak, Galleried Top, Round Dial, Davis Sales Co.		300.00
Advertising, Bulova Watch Repair, Reverse Painted, Electric, Pam Clock Co., 15 x 5 In.		98.00
Advertising, Calumet Baking Powder, Oak Case, Sessions, c.1915, 34 x 18 In.		767.00
Advertising, Chappaqua Shoes, Button Top Shoe Shape, Metal, 9 x 9 x 5 In.		154.00
Advertising, Charlie The Tuna, Starkist, Alarm, Blue, Gold, 6 In.		125.00
Advertising, Davis Of Baltimore Paint, Brush & Can, Light-Up, 1960s, 15 ¾ In. Diam.		115.00
Advertising, Diamond Black Leather Oil, Figure 8, Baird Adv. Clock Co., c.1910, 31 In.		1778.00
Advertising, Dr Pepper, Drink A Bite To Eat, Pam Style, Light-Up, 15 In.	*Illus*	300.00
Advertising, Dr Pepper, Good For Life, Bubble, Light-Up, Yellow, Red, 15 In. Diam.		360.00
Advertising, Dr Pepper, Good For Life, Round, Green Composition, 1930s, 14 ¾ x 2 ½ In.		115.00
Advertising, Dr Pepper, Green, Yellow, Round, Fiberboard, Tin, Telechron, 1930s, 14 ½ In.		330.00
Advertising, Durham Cigar, Figural, Bull, Hettermann Bros. Co., Louisville, Ky., 12 x 9 ½ In.	*Illus*	660.00
Advertising, Elgin Jewelers, Reverse Painted, Black Ground, Electric, S.S. Jewelers, 15 x 15 In.		46.00
Advertising, Ever-Ready Safety Razor, Man Shaving, Tin, Embossed, c.1910, 14 ¾ x 12 ½ In.		1560.00
Advertising, Ever-Ready Safety Razor, Man Shaving, Wood, Pendulum, 22 x 18 x 4 In.		1430.00
Advertising, Fisk Tires, Tire Shape, Rubber, Glass Over Metal, Folding Stand, 6 In.		880.00
Advertising, G.E. Lamps, Round, Light-Up, 15 In.		150.00

C

Advertising, Gem Damaskeene Razor, Man Holding Baby, Shaving, Wood, Crest, Key.............		1920.00
Advertising, Gem Damaskeene Razor, Pendulum...*Illus*		1320.00
Advertising, Gillette Razor Blade, Wood, Man's Face, Shaving Cream, Round, 1930s.............		390.00
Advertising, Gleem Paints, Reverse Painted, White, Red, Blue, Aluminum, Round, 15 In.......		94.00
Advertising, Headlight Work Clothes, Neon, 1940s, 15 x 15 In.		575.00
Advertising, L.B. Rocke Jewelers, Round Face, Square Wood Case, General Electric, 15 x 15 In.		12.00
Advertising, Light N' Lively Milk, Square, Carton, Light-Up, Pam Style, 15 x 15 In.		168.00
Advertising, Nature's Remedy Vegetable Laxative, Gilbert, Early 1900s, 31 In.		425.00
Advertising, None Such Mince Meat, Pumpkin Shape, Cardboard, Tin, Embossed, 9 ½ In......		300.00
Advertising, Sabin Robbins Paper, Square, Salesman, Light-Up, 1960s, 15 ¼ In...................		115.00
Advertising, Save Movie Stamps, Black, White, Neon, Glo Dial, c.1935, 21 In.		330.00
Advertising, Savers Flavorings & Extracts, Regulator, New Haven Clock Co., c.1910, 41 x 17 In. ...		570.00
Advertising, Starkist Tuna, Charlie, Mechanical Alarm, Box...		135.00
Advertising, Super Sue Ice Cream, Double Bubble, Cone, Light-Up, 1950s, 16 x 16 In.		795.00
Advertising, Wolverine Shell Horse Hide, Soles, Red, White, Yellow, Round, 15 In.		303.00
Advertising, Woolf Clothiers, Round, Metal, Painted, Baird, 18 ½ x 30 ½ In.		1920.00
Advertising, Wurlitzer Music, Round, Motion, 14 In. Diam.		600.00
American Clock Co., Shelf, Iron, Mother-Of-Pearl, Painted, Pendulum, c.1860, 18 x 14 In.....		184.00
Angevin A Paris, Empire Style, Bronze, Apollo, Lyre, Symbols, 13 x 10 In........................		688.00
Ansonia, Art Nouveau, Cast Metal, Gold Paint, White Porcelain Dial, Curved Feet, 7 ¾ In.		94.00
Ansonia, Black Belgian Marble, Gilt, White Face, Roman Numerals, c.1890, 10 x 9 In.		360.00
Ansonia, Bouncing Doll, Jumper No. 2, Cast Metal Body, Key Wind, 1886, 14 ½ In...............		483.00
Ansonia, Regulator, Mahogany, 22 ½ x 12 ½ In.		180.00
Ansonia, Regulator, Open Escapement, Brass, Crystal, 11 In.		186.00
Ansonia, Rococo Revival, Gilt, Nymph Crest, Flowers, Scrolls, c.1890, 12 ¾ In.		240.00
Ansonia, Santa Fe, Oak, Paper On Zinc Dial, 8-Day, Brass Weights, c.1890, 46 In............*Illus*		1185.00
Ansonia, School, Calendar, Oak, Brass Pendulum, 32 x 18 In.		115.00
Ansonia, Shelf, Porcelain, Rustic, Flowers, Green, Gilt Ground, c.1890, 10 ¾ In...................		178.00
Ansonia, Shelf, Regulator, Crystal, Gilt Bronze, Molded Cornice, Bracket Feet, c.1895, 10 In...		210.00
Ansonia, Shelf, Urn Pedestal, Gilt, Flowers, Scrolls, 15 ½ In.......................................		384.00
Ansonia, Swinging Arm, Fisher Woman, Spelter, Spring Driven, c.1900, 24 In...................		1323.00
Art Nouveau, Shelf, Mahogany, Inlaid Flowers, Balloon Case, c.1900, 18 x 10 In.................		633.00
Banjo, Aaron Willard, Federal, Mahogany, Acorn Finial, Giltwood, Mt. Vernon, c.1820, 41 In..		1195.00
Banjo, E. Howard, Rosewood Case, Red, Black, Gold Eglomise Panels, Weight Driven, 38 In...		3304.00
Banjo, Elnathan Taber, Mahogany, Line Inlay, Eglomise Panels, Gilt, c.1820, 33 ½ In		5310.00
Banjo, Federal, Gilt, Eglomise Panels, Red, Gold, Rural Landscape, Mass., 33 In.		2478.00
Banjo, Federal, Mahogany, Gilt, Eagle Finial, Enameled Panel, Philip Stolze, N.Y., 44 ½ In...		2607.00
Banjo, Federal, Mahogany, Giltwood, Eagle Finial, Landscape Panels, New England, c.1815, 40 In.		444.00
Banjo, Federal, Mahogany, Round Face, Ball & Spire Finial, Box Bottom, Mass., 34 ½ In.		649.00
Banjo, Gilbert, Mahogany, Brass Eagle Finial, Engraved, 8-Day, Barometer, 1900s, 18 In.		178.00
Banjo, Howard & Davis, Cherry, Rosewood Graining, Marked, c.1860, 32 In.		1645.00
Banjo, Howard & Davis, Cherry, Weight Movement, c.1850, 30 x 11 In.		767.00
Banjo, J.L. Dunning, Giltwood, Fluted, Eglomise Panel, Fruit, Urn, Ship, Knob Finial, 39 In...		1080.00
Banjo, Killam & Co., Mahogany, Giltwood, Eagle Finial, Green & Red Painted Panel, c.1860, 43 In....		2844.00
Banjo, Mahogany, Onion Finial, Eglomise Panel, Gilt, Red Pendant Spray, 1800s, 34 x 8 x 10 In..		403.00
Banjo, Mahogany, Reverse Print Under Glass, Boston Statehouse, 42 In................................		660.00
Banjo, Reverse Painted Naval Battle, Eagle, Shield, Giltwood, c.1820, 42 ½ In......................		649.00
Banjo, S. Whiting, Federal, Eglomise Panel, Chariot, Winged Horses, 35 In............................		1298.00
Banjo, Sessions, Mahogany, Pendulum, Eagle Finial, Reverse Painted Door, 26 x 9 In.............		58.00
Banjo, Waterbury, Mahogany Case, Brass Spire, Naval Scene, Reverse Painted, c.1910, 44 x 10 In.		1265.00
Bark, Elov, Spring Driven, Pendulum, Giltwood Case, Sweden, c.1925, 30 In..		307.00
Behrens, Synchron, Copper, Glass, Enamel, Metal, Marked AEG, Germany, 1910s, 4 ¼ x 12 ½ In..*Illus*		5000.00
Biedermeier Style, Rosewood, Enamel Face, Roman Numerals, Weight, Vienna, c.1875, 37 x 12 In.		900.00
Bigelow Kennard, Shelf, Black Marble, Gilt Accents, France, 1800s, 12 ½ x 8 In.		237.00
Bigelow Kennard, Shelf, Morning & Night, Slate, Relief, Rooster, Owl, 10 x 22 In...................		413.00
Birge & Fuller, Shelf, Mahogany, Double Steeple, Painted Flower Panel, c.1850, 26 In.............		1126.00
Birge & Fuller, Shelf, Mahogany, Wagon Spring, 8-Day, Frosted Tablet, Mirror, c.1845, 27 In..*Illus*		1541.00
Black Forest, Cuckoo, Carved Walnut, Stag, Crossed Gun Crest, Horn, c.1890, 41 In.		1422.00
Black Forest, Shelf, Carved Gnome, c.1900, 13 ¼ In...		273.00
Black Forest, Shelf, Stag, On Rockwork, Oak Leaves, Ferns, Branches, c.1860, 33 x 28 In.......		5865.00
Black Forest, Shelf, Walnut, Brass Dial, 15 In.		110.00
Black Forest, Stag's Head, Antlers, Carved, Cartouche, Oak Leaf, Acorns, c.1880, 28 x 21 In...		805.00
Blinking Eye, Black Banjo Player, Red Hat, Yellow Shirt, Green Pants, Cast Iron, 16 In.		2478.00
Boston Clock Co., Shelf, Onyx, Gilt Metal, Carved, Painted Swags, c.1880, 10 x 14 In.		177.00
Bracket, Asselin, George I, Japanned, Brass Face, Musical Works, London, c.1710, 20 In.........		10665.00
Bracket, Bronze, Ebonized, Mask, Cornucopia, Mercury Finial, Chimes, c.1900, 23 x 13 In.		3444.00

Cinnabar, Snuff Bottle, Carved, Landscape, Figures, Trees, Marked, 1800s, 3 ⅛ In.
$245.00

Skinner, Inc.

Clarice Cliff, Bizarre, Charger, Rhodanthe Pattern, Mark, Wilkinson Ltd., 1900s, 18 In.
$1,422.00

Skinner, Inc.

Clarice Cliff, Bizarre, Jug, Lotus, Pine Grove Pattern, Ribbed, Back Stamp, 1900s, 11 ⅜ In.
$1,126.00

Skinner, Inc.

Clarice Cliff, Fantasque, Vase, Trees, House, c.1930, 9 ¾ x 6 ½ In.
$2,250.00

Rago Arts & Auction Center

Clewell, Vase, Copper Clad, Patina, Marked, 11 ¾ x 6 ¾ In. $2,625.00

Rago Arts & Auction Center

Clewell, Vase, Copper Clad, Verdigris Patina, Marked, 1920s, 15 x 7 In. $2,500.00

Rago Arts & Auction Center

Clifton, Vase, Bud, Crystal Patina, Silver Overlay, Signed, 1906, 5 x 4 In. $1,125.00

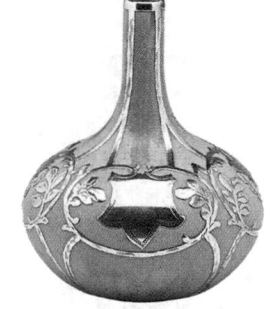

Rago Arts & Auction Center

Clifton, Vase, Dripped Glaze, Brown, Green, Yellow, Incised, 1906, 13 ⅛ In. $345.00

Humler & Nolan

Bracket, Faux Tortoiseshell, Gilt Bronze, Jewel Bezel, Tiffany & Co., c.1900, 8 ½ x 3 ¾ In.	1380.00
Bracket, George III, Burl Walnut, Arched Case, Brass Handle, Enamel Face, 1700s, 17 In.	1416.00
Bracket, Georgian, Mahogany, 8-Day Movement, c.1790, 15 ½ x 9 ½ In.	948.00
Bracket, Strapwork, Gilt Putto Finial, Justice Cartouche, Masks, Scroll Feet, c.1715, 41 ½ In.	3690.00
Brewster & Ingraham, Shelf, Gothic, Rosewood Veneer, 2 Steeples, Onion Top, 1800s, 20 In.	449.00
Brown, J.C., Shelf, Gothic, Rosewood, Molded, Zinc Dial, Etched Tablet, c.1845, 20 In. *Illus*	1823.00
Caldwell, J.E, Shelf, Louis XV Style, Gilt Bronze, Shell Crest, Painted, c.1900, 14 In.	1353.00
Carriage, Brass, Bowed, Latticework, Enamel Dial, Scroll Handle, France, c.1815, 6 x 3 ¼ In.	307.00
Carriage, Brass, Engraved Flower, Cartouches, Beveled Glass, Repeating, c.1890, 5 In.	1298.00
Carriage, Bronze, Chased, Arabesques, Flowers, Beveled Glass Panels, France, 5 ½ In.	1800.00
Carriage, Gilt Brass, Porcelain, Engraved, Repeating, France, 1870-80, 8 In.	28320.00
Carriage, Porcelain, Painted, Flowers, Butterflies, Children, Repeater, France, c.1885, 5 ½ x 3 ½ In.	861.00
Cartel, Gilt Bronze, Cartouche Case, White Enamel Dial, Torch Finial, 27 x 11 In.	625.00
Cartel, Louis XVI Style, Gilt Bronze, Mask, Laurel Swags, Urn, Pendulum, France, 25 x 13 In.	604.00
Cartier, Blue Guilloche Enamel, Strike & Repeat, Rectangular, c.1905, 3 In.	14900.00
Chelsea Clock Co., Tambour, Silvered Brass, 8-Day, Spaulding & Co., 13 ½ In. *Illus*	1126.00
Crane, Aaron, Shelf, Torsion Pendulum, Pillars, Gilt	6545.00
Durfee, Walter H., Girandole, Carved, Gilt Eagle, Eglomise, Battle Scene, War Of 1812, 46 In.	27140.00
Egyptian Revival, Slate, Onyx, 8-Day Time & Strike, Garniture, 1800s, 17 In., 3 Piece *Illus*	2400.00
Empire, Rosewood, Gilt, Columns, Flowers & Leaves, Bun Feet, France, 1800s, 19 ½ In.	956.00
Eureka, Shelf, Mahogany, Light Wood Inlay, Battery Operated, England, c.1910, 15 x 9 In. *Illus*	1298.00
Farcot, Shelf, Swinging Putto Pendulum, 8-Day, S-Scroll Mounts, Paw Feet, 1800s, 9 x 9 In.	920.00
Farret, Shelf, Gutenberg Figure, Printing Press, Cast Metal, Slate Case, Paris, 22 x 12 In.	944.00
Figural, Elephant, Bronze, Seated Chinese Man, Saddle, Openwork, 1800s, 16 ½ In.	4253.00
Figural, Monk Sitting On Barrel, Drinking, Plastic, 25 In.	168.00
Figural, Reclining Woman, Gilt Bronze, Round Dial, France, 16 In.	826.00
Forestville Hardware & Clock Co., Iron, Pearl, Zinc Dial, 30-Hour, c.1855, 13 In. *Illus*	2400.00
Forestville Mfg. Co., Shelf, Beehive, Mahogany, Ripple Front, Painted Dial, c.1840, 19 x 10 ½ In.	652.00
Foster, Edward, Mahogany, Brass Dial, Calendar Ring, 8-Day Time & Strike, Alarm, c.1765, 15 In. *Illus*	3998.00
French Empire Style, Marble, Bronze Mount, Enamel Dial, Sonnerie, 23 x 11 In.	2400.00
French, Blanchet, Rosewood, Ivory, Round Face, Rectangular Base, c.1830, 6 In.	540.00
French, Bracket, White Marble, Bronze Dore Columns & Swags, c.1885, 18 x 9 In.	450.00
French, Gilt Brass, Woman, Seated, Enameled Dial, Garlands, 8-Day, c.1875, 18 In. *Illus*	1580.00
French, Regulator, Alabaster, Ormolu, Urn Finial, Flower, Scrolls, c.1890, 15 In.	649.00
French, Shelf, Brass, Bronze Patina, Hand-Hammered Dome, Embossed Flowers, c.1860, 17 In.	472.00
French, Shelf, Brass, Enamel Trim, Columns, Pineapple Finials, Flowers, c.1915, 13 x 6 In.	5412.00
French, Shelf, Bronze, Flower Basket Crest, Porcelain Dial, Lion & Portrait Masks, 12 In.	176.00
French, Shelf, Bronze, Marble, Bust Of Flower Girl, Oval Base, c.1885, 26 x 16 ¾ In.	1476.00
French, Shelf, Burl Wood, Carved, Bronze Ormolu, Brass Movement, c.1935, 27 x 14 In.	300.00
French, Shelf, Empire Style, Red Paint, Casket Shape, Arc Of Bronze Stars, 9 x 4 In.	1230.00
French, Shelf, Empire, Gilt Bronze, Woman, With Lyre, Footed, Enamel Dial, c.1800, 13 x 9 ¾ In.	826.00
French, Shelf, Gilt Bronze, Figural Draped Woman, Cupid, Bow, 2 Doves, 17 x 16 In.	2540.00
French, Shelf, Louis XV Style, Red Faux Tortoiseshell, Enamel Dial, Gilt Mounts, 10 In.	374.00
French, Shelf, Louis XVI, Gilt Bronze, Urns, Scrolls, Marble Base, Brass Silk Movement, 21 In.	1680.00
French, Shelf, Marble, Bronze Finish, Winged Female, Garlands, Scroll Feet, c.1885, 27 x 14 In.	1107.00
French, Shelf, Marble, Bronze Mount, Eagle, Tapered Columns, Porcelain Dial, 15 In.	1470.00
French, Shelf, Marble, Bronze, Handled Tazza, Scroll Leaves, Garland, Scroll Feet, c.1800, 19 In.	360.00
French, Shelf, Ormolu, Green Onyx, Porcelain Dial, Urn Finial, Scroll Handles, 16 x 10 In.	590.00
French, Shelf, Porcelain, Gilt, Asian Man, Dagger, Enameled Dial, Flower Bouquets, 21 In.	8750.00
French, Shelf, Spelter, Marble, Woman & Cherub, Ormolu Mount, 1800s, 22 In.	390.00
Frodsham & Co., Shelf, French Empire, Marble, Embossed, Paris, c.1870, 16 x 12 In.	1121.00
German, Shelf, Mahogany, Inlaid Satinwood, Mother-Of-Pearl, 8-Day, Key Wind, 1900s, 17 x 11 In.	300.00
Gilbert, Wood, Gingerbread, Gold Bird Detail, Pendulum	58.00
Gothic Style, Regulator, Astronomical, Mercury Pendulum, Weight, c.1860, 90 In.	6613.00
Harris Strong, Walnut Veneer, Ceramic Tile, Chapters, 3 Bands, 1966, 42 x 11 In. *Illus*	240.00
Herman Miller, Burled Wood, Chrome Trim, G. Rohde, 1930s, 13 x 2 ½ In.	2063.00
Herman Miller, Chrome, Stainless Steel Base, Signed Face, G. Rohde, 1930s, 6 x 2 In.	1875.00
Herman Miller, Chrome Plated Ball Shape, Curved Bronze Base, Black, G. Rohde, 11 x 5 In.	8125.00
Herman Miller, Enameled, Chrome Plated Steel, Aluminum, G. Rohde, c.1933, 6 ½ x 12 In.	5313.00
Herman Miller, Wall, Art Deco, Black Enamel Case, Chrome Trim, 21 In.	2625.00
Herschede, Shelf, Mahogany, Dual Chime, No. 10, 18 In.	255.00
Hoadley, Silas, Shelf, Franklin Alarm, Wood Case, Works, Stenciled Eagle, Reverse Painted, 38 x 17 In.	144.00
Howard Miller, Art Deco, Chrome, Square, G. Rohde, 1930s, 8 x 6 ½ In.	1037.00
Howard Miller, Birch, Brass Spokes, Red Second Hand, G. Nelson, 13 In.	427.00
Howard Miller, Black, White Body, Birch Cone Base, G. Nelson, 5 ¾ x 6 ¾ In.	4688.00
Howard Miller, Flock Of Butterflies, Brushed Metal, Enamel, Painted, G. Nelson, 1950s, 24 In. *Illus*	3125.00
Howard Miller, Multicolor, Brass, Wood, Round Center, G. Nelson, 1950s, 13 In. Diam.	1375.00

Howard Miller, Shelf, Walnut, Brass, Enameled, Watermelon Shape, G. Nelson, c.1954, 4 ¾ x 8 In..	3125.00
Howard Miller, Star, Wood, Metal, Painted Black, Metal Hands, G. Nelson, 15 In......................	1440.00
Howard, E., No. 5, Rosewood Grained, Reverse Painted, Gilt Glass, 28 ¾ In. ....*Illus*	1896.00
Howard, E., Regulator, No. 12, Black Walnut, 8-Day, Weight, Pendulum, c.1875, 62 In....*Illus*	26070.00
Ingersoll, Art Deco, Beige, Celluloid, Windup, c.1930, 4 ¼ x 4 ½ x 1 In..................................	55.00
Ingraham, Admiral Dewey, Low Relief, Cannon, Flag, Gingerbread, 23 x 14 In..................	173.00
Ingraham, Calendar, Dew Drop, Rosewood, 24 In..	182.00
Ingraham, E., Shelf, Oak, Carved Crest, Half Columns, Victorian, 16 In.......................	116.00
Ingraham, Shelf, Oak, Carved Flowers, Gold Stenciled Garland, Victorian, 22 x 15 In.....	35.00
International Time Recorder, Oak, c.1890, 47 In..	236.00
International Time Recording Co., Wall, Oak, Endicott, N.Y., 43 In...........................	24.00
Ithaca Calendar Clock Co., 2 Paper Dials, 8-Day, c.1890, 28 In. ....*Illus*	356.00
Ithaca Calendar Clock Co., Shelf, Walnut, Octagon Crest, c.1890, 18 In.	826.00
Ives, J., Shelf, Triple Deck, Mahogany Veneer, Gilt Eagle Crest, c.1820, 37 x 17 In.	390.00
Ives, Joseph, Mahogany, Scroll Top, Painted Dial, Reverse Painted, 8-Day, c.1820, 56 In. ....*Illus*	2370.00
Japy Freres, Shelf, Black, Red Marble, c.1885, 9 ½ In..	237.00
Jennings Brothers, Shelf, Cast Metal, Painted, Porcelain Dial, 2 x 8 In........................	94.00
Jerome & Co., Botsford Improved Patent Lever, Glass Dome, 30-Hour, c.1850, 12 In.......*Illus*	2205.00
Jerome & Co., Shelf, Ogee Wood Case, Reverse Painted, c.1850, 26 In..........................	63.00
Jerome & Darrow, Shelf, Empire, Mahogany, Carved, 3 Landscape Panels, c.1835, 40 x 18 In.	385.00
Jones, George, Wall, Regulator, Carved Wood, Pendulum, 1880, 47 In............................	2700.00
Junghans, Shelf, Mahogany, 17 In..	207.00
Junghans, Walnut, Regulator, Porcelain, Brass Pendulum, Columns, c.1860, 30 x 11 In.	270.00
Kemp & Wilcox, Shelf, Oak, Carved, Brass Handle, Flambeau Finials, England........................	7592.00
Krober, Shelf, Walnut, Carved Crest, Columns, Brass Pendulum, c.1875, 23 x 16 In................	767.00
Kruger, Gottfried, Table, Engraved Brass, Silvered, Hexagonal Case, Ball, 17th Century, 4 x 6 In. ..	8050.00
Lantern, Brass, Chapter Ring, England, c.1800, 15 ½ In.	688.00
Lantern, Brass, Chapter Ring, Scrolling Acanthus, Iron Hands, Pierced Fret, 15 In................	944.00
Lantern, Brass, Egg & Dart Borders, Urn Finials, Bracket Feet, 1800s, 15 ¾ In.	649.00
Lantern, Moorish Temple, Gilt Bronze, Enameled Face, Brass Works, Marked F. Bohler, Key, 13 In.*Illus*	590.00
Lawson Time, Digital, Chrome Plated Steel, Bakelite, K.E.M. Weber, 1933, 3 x 8 In.........*Illus*	813.00
LeCoultre, Atmos, Brass, Glass Case, 9 ¼ In.	708.00
LeRoy, Julian, Bronze Dore, Cherub Playing Lyre, Scrolls, Key Wind, France, 13 In.............	360.00
Liberty & Co., Tudric, Pewter, Enamel, Stamped, c.1910, 7 In..............................*Illus*	6050.00
Liberty & Co., Tudric, Pewter, Hammered, Blue, Green Enameled Face, c.1920, 6 In.	2125.00
Lighthouse, Mahogany, Single Train Movement, 19 ¼ In.	1298.00
Loring, Joseph, Shelf, Cherry, Fret Top, 8 Day, Pendulum, French Feet, c.1800, 38 In.	5925.00
Louis Philippe, Gilt Bronze, Seated Sultan, Leaf & Scroll Carved Plinth, c.1850, 23 In.	1625.00
Louis XIV Style, Marquetry, With Pedestal, 20th Century, 75 x 16 In.................................	270.00
Louis XV Style, Shelf, Bronze, Porcelain Urn Finial & Dial, Putto, Flowers, France, 1800s, 22 In...	460.00
Louis XVI Style, Gilt Bronze, Enamel Face, Laurel Wreath, Cornucopia, Swag, 1800s, 16 In...	1003.00
Lux, Black Man's Face, Smiling, Eyes Move With Tie Pendulum, Paint, 4 ½ x 9 In.	510.00
Lyre, French Empire, Ebony Veneer, Gilt Bronze, Egyptian Revival Columns, 24 x 10 In.	518.00
Lyre, Mahogany, Recessed Panels, Pendulum, 20th Century, 40 In......................................	770.00
Lyre, Shelf, Cut Glass, Gilt, Lotus Leaves, Reeded Base, Sunburst Finial, c.1885, 24 In.	3198.00
Lyre, Shelf, Empire, Marquetry, Scrolling Vines, Leaves, Flower Crest, France, 25 In..............	460.00
Morbier, Musical Movement, Swiss Cylinder, Louis Plantier A Bourg Argental........................	2147.00
Morbier, Pressed Brass, Steel Face, Pendulum, Enameled, 59 x 13 In.................................	414.00
Morbier, Shelf, Louis XVI Style, Embossed, Flowers, Bell, Calendar, France, 60 x 12 In.	236.00
Moreau, Shelf, Bronze, Classical Warrior, Marble Base, France, c.1900, 37 In........................	2813.00
Morel, Shelf, Portico, Gilt Metal, Rosewood, Marquetry, Signed, Paris, c.1890, 18 In..............	354.00
Munger, Asa, Shelf, Mahogany, Carved Columns, Flat Top, N.Y., c.1835, 37 ½ In..................	1763.00
New Haven, Empire, Ogee Mahogany Case, Reverse Painted, c.1950, 19 x 12 In. ....*Illus*	60.00
New Haven, Shelf, Aesthetic Revival, Stag, Dogs, Birds, Flowers, Cast Iron, 15 x 13 In.	109.00
New Haven, Shelf, Black Steel Case, Cast Brass, Ormolu, Enameled Dial, 13 x 9 In.	59.00
New Haven, Shelf, Cottage, Rosewood Veneer, 30-Hour Time & Strike, c.1870, 14 x 10 In.	225.00
Patek Philippe, Solar Panel, 5 ½ x 5 ½ In.	2400.00
Portico, Bronze Dore, Engine Turned Mid Rib, Columns, Bun Feet, Berries, c.1835, 20 ¼ In. ..	2091.00
Portico, Napoleon III, Gilt Metal, Black Paint, Round Dial, Bun Feet, 20 x 10 In.	406.00
Portico, Neoclassical Bronze, Green Marble, Enameled Dial, Pendulum, Sonnerie, 23 x 11 In.	2400.00
Portico, Renaissance Style Inlay, Gilt Bronze, Columns, Enameled Face, Mirror, 1800s, 19 ½ In. *Illus*	177.00
Raingo Freres, Shelf, Cathedral, Silk Thread Movement, Porcelain, Paris, c.1835, 24 In...*Illus*	15535.00
Raingo Freres, Shelf, Neoclassical, Bronze, Goddess Bust Crest, Brown Patina, 1850s, 10 x 19 In.	1035.00
Regency, Wood, Urn Shape, Gilt Bronze Pedestal, Finial, England, 14 In..........................	840.00
Regulator, Vienna, Glass Door, Porcelain Dial, Finials, Pendulum, c.1860, 51 In.	161.00
Regulator, Vienna, Walnut, Carved Columns, c.1850, 35 ½ In.	148.00

C

Clock, Advertising, Dr Pepper, Drink A Bite To Eat, Pam Style, Light-Up, 15 In.
$300.00

Victorian Casino Antiques

Clock, Advertising, Durham Cigar, Figural, Bull, Hettermann Bros. Co., Louisville, Ky., 12 x 9 ½ In.
$660.00

Showtime Auction Services

Clock, Advertising, Gem Damaskeene Razor, Pendulum
$1,320.00

Victorian Casino Antiques

TIP

Don't put an old clock that is wound near a heat or air-conditioning duct. The air will dry out the oil used in the clock. Fireplaces and wood-burning stoves can also dry the works, and the clock may not keep correct time—or could stop.

Clock, Ansonia, Santa Fe, Oak, Paper On Zinc Dial, 8-Day, Brass Weights, c.1890, 46 In. $1,185.00

Skinner, Inc.

Clock, Behrens, Synchron, Copper, Glass, Enamel, Metal, Marked AEG, Germany, 1910s, 4 ¼ x 12 ½ In. $5,000.00

Rago Arts & Auction Center

Clock, Birge & Fuller, Shelf, Mahogany, Wagon Spring, 8-Day, Frosted Tablet, Mirror, c.1845, 27 In. $1,541.00

Skinner, Inc.

Regulator, Wall, Wood, Enameled Dial, Reeded Columns, Stepped Cornice, c.1900, 28 In.	138.00
Reouvier, Shelf, Louis XIV Style, Marble, Bronze, Urn, Scroll Handles, c.1880, 16 x 9 In.	354.00
Russel Wright, White Clover, Meadow Green, GE, Harker, 8 In.	85.00
Sessions, Aviator, Airplane Shape, Carved Wood, Cockpit Windows Light, 10 x 21 In.	71.00
Sessions, Clinton, Oak, White Face, 27 x 17 In.	60.00
Sessions, Shelf, Cathedral Gong, 10 In.	41.00
Seth Thomas, Oak, Regulator, 8-Day, Deadbeat Escape, No. 2, c.1890, 36 In.	1067.00
Seth Thomas, Regulator, Rosewood, Round Top, Mirror Door, 19th Century, 32 x 15 In.	480.00
Seth Thomas, Shelf, Adamantine, Rosewood Veneer, Pediment, Cornice, c.1880, 11 x 8 In.	63.00
Seth Thomas, Shelf, Flowers, Inlaid Crest, 19 ½ In.	162.00
Seth Thomas, Shelf, Hardwood, Chiming, Key, c.1950, 14 ½ In.	118.00
Seth Thomas, Shelf, Mahogany Veneer, Chime, Key Wind, 9 x 20 In.	236.00
Seth Thomas, Shelf, Mahogany, Dome Top, 9 In.	46.00
Seth Thomas, Shelf, Mahogany, Half Pilaster, Painted Rose Tablet, 25 In.	52.00
Seth Thomas, Shelf, Mahogany, Pillar & Scroll, Reverse Painted, c.1820, 31 ¾ x 18 In.	1121.00
Seth Thomas, Shelf, Mahogany, Sonora Chime, Dome Top, 14 In.	244.00
Seth Thomas, Shelf, Regulator, 8-Day Strike Movement, c.1915, 14 In.	288.00
Seth Thomas, Shelf, Rosewood, 12 ½ In.	58.00
Seth Thomas, Shelf, Rosewood, Corinthian Columns, Sonora Chimes, c.1900, 14 x 15 In.	450.00
Seth Thomas, Travel, Plastic, Alarm, Folding, Brazil, 2 ¾ x 1 x 3 ¼ In.	9.00
Shelf, Alabaster, Ogee Scroll Supports, Girl, On Swing Pendulum, Glass Dome, c.1865, 12 In.	1353.00
Shelf, Alabaster, Ormolu, Putto, C-Scrolls, Woman, Urn Finial, Shaped Base, 13 In.	385.00
Shelf, Arts & Crafts, Copper, Brass Wash, Enamel, Glass, c.1900, 10 x 16 In.	1500.00
Shelf, Beehive, Mahogany, Wooden Dial, Buildings, Pillar & Scroll, Urn Finials, c.1825, 31 In.	770.00
Shelf, Beehive, Walnut Veneer, Reverse Painted, Time & Strike, Alarm, Pendulum, c.1840, 10 x 12 In.	46.00
Shelf, Blue Enamel, Snuffbox Shape, Brass Figural Supports, c.1890, 4 ¼ In.	1062.00
Shelf, Bronze, Flared, Ram's Heads, Flowers, Figures, Griffins, c.1900, 14 x 11 In.	3000.00
Shelf, Bronze, Man Of Science, Black Marble Base, Gilt Numerals, Signed VE, c.1870, 20 x 18 In.	649.00
Shelf, Bronze, Porcelain, Enamel, Cherubs, Lovebird Finials, 19 x 15 In.	1298.00
Shelf, Bronze, Venus, Griffin, Cupid, Bow, Centaur, Paw Feet, 1800s, 20 x 15 In.	3250.00
Shelf, Bronze, Woman Pouring Oil In Lamp, Pedestal, Square Base, c.1825, 15 ½ x 11 ½ In.	2074.00
Shelf, Cast Iron, Gilt Incised Case, Winged Caryatids Handles, c.1885, 11 x 15 In.	276.00
Shelf, Chinoiserie, Bronze, Marble, Woman In Pagoda, Openwork, Columns, 1800s, 20 In.	3851.00
Shelf, Cloisonne, Curved, 4 Reeded Columns, Handled Urn Finial, Spread Feet, 1900s, 9 In.	108.00
Shelf, Directoire, Gilt Bronze, Marble, Oak Leaves, Vases Of Wheat, Mask, c.1815, 22 x 12 In.	1722.00
Shelf, Ebonized Wood, Gilt Metal Mount, Gilt Brass Face, Chimes, Victorian, 22 In.	826.00
Shelf, Empire Style, Gilt Bronze, White Enamel Dial, 2 Griffins, Cut Glass Base, 11 ⅜ In.	1188.00
Shelf, Empire, Mahogany, Carved Crest & Columns, Paw Feet, N.Y., c.1835, 39 ½ In.	1058.00
Shelf, Federal Style, Inlaid Mahogany, Painted Dial, Gilt, Eagle Finial, 33 ½ In.	1180.00
Shelf, Federal, Mahogany Inlay, Painted Cornucopia On Face, Footed, 34 ½ In.	325.00
Shelf, French Empire, Gilt Bronze, Cut Glass Columns, Eagles, Putti, 1800s, 24 In.	5500.00
Shelf, French Empire, Marble, Scroll Supports, Marked Graverand, c.1835, 17 In.	590.00
Shelf, Fruitwood, Carved, Flame Finials, Ormolu Mounts, Italy, c.1790, 19 In.	3081.00
Shelf, Gilt Brass, Enamel, Pierced Skirt, Columns, Bow Crest, Scroll Feet, c.1900, 17 x 8 In.	1168.00
Shelf, Gilt Bronze, Arts & Sciences Symbols, Woman At Table, Cherubs, Scrolled, c.1860, 18 In.	1140.00
Shelf, Gilt Bronze, Cavalier Reclining On Cannon, Plumed Hat, 20 x 13 In.	1875.00
Shelf, Gilt Bronze, Napoleon On Horse, Eagles, Garland, Paw Feet, c.1835, 18 x 13 In.	5904.00
Shelf, Gilt Bronze, Snarling Dragon, Pierced Scrollwork, Cupid, c.1865, 26 In.	3936.00
Shelf, Gilt Bronze, Stepped Corners, Round Dial, Columns, Square Base, 19 ¾ In.	875.00
Shelf, Gilt Bronze, Woman, Holding Lute, Leaf Base, Scroll Feet, 1800s, 17 x 14 In.	950.00
Shelf, Linet Aime, Ebony, Fruitwood, 4 Columns, Pendulum, 1880-1900, 18 x 12 In.	420.00
Shelf, Louis XVI Style, Bronze, Marble, Putti, Flowers, Hourglass, c.1850, 15 x 18 In.	1500.00
Shelf, Louis XVI Style, Gilt Bronze, Corset Shape, Scroll Leaves, Cherub, 1800s, 15 ½ In.	600.00
Shelf, Louis XVI Style, Gilt Bronze, Porcelain, Pink, Rose Plaques, c.1865, 14 x 15 In.	1107.00
Shelf, Louis XVI Style, Porcelain, Gilt, Dancing Woman, Flowers, Lovebirds, c.1890, 19 In.	2706.00
Shelf, Louis XVI, Gilt Bronze, Alabaster, Urn Shape, Putto Drinking Finial, c.1890, 24 In.	2880.00
Shelf, Mahogany, Pillar & Scroll, Eglomise, Broken Arch, Columns, c.1800, 31 x 17 In.	430.00
Shelf, Mahogany, Plaque, Bell, Lion Holding Shield, Bull's-Eye Glass, c.1900, 22 In.	1353.00
Shelf, Mixed Woods, Fernware, Columns, Porcelain Dial, Slogan, England, c.1890, 18 x 13 In.	472.00
Shelf, Neoclassical, Parcel Gilt, Reclining Figure, c.1790, 13 x 14 ⅞ In.	750.00
Shelf, Porcelain, Bronze, Urn Shape, Scrolls, Ram Mask Handles, 22 In.	2794.00
Shelf, Queensware, Flowers, Gilt Leaves, Footed, Shaped Crest, c.1873, 12 In.	889.00
Shelf, Rococo Revival, Porcelain, Scrolled & Pierced, Flowers, Gilt Scroll Base, c.1850, 14 In.	461.00
Shelf, Silver Plate, Carriage, Columns, Scrolled Top Handle, Leather Case, 1800s, 3 x 2 In.	4313.00
Shelf, Slate, Malachite, L. Mart, France, c.1850, 19 ¾ x 15 In.	267.00

Clock, Brown, J.C., Shelf, Gothic, Rosewood, Molded, Zinc Dial, Etched Tablet, c.1845, 20 In. $1,823.00

Skinner, Inc.

Clock, Chelsea Clock Co., Tambour, Silvered Brass, 8-Day, Spaulding & Co., 13 ½ In. $1,126.00

Skinner, Inc.

Clock, Egyptian Revival, Slate, Onyx, 8-Day Time & Strike, Garniture, 1800s, 17 In., 3 Piece $2,400.00

Cowan's Auctions

Clock, Eureka, Shelf, Mahogany, Light Wood Inlay, Battery Operated, England, c.1910, 15 x 9 In. $1,298.00

Brunk Auctions

Clock, Forestville Hardware & Clock Co., Iron, Pearl, Zinc Dial, 30-Hour, c.1855, 13 In. $2,400.00

Skinner, Inc.

Clock, Foster, Edward, Mahogany, Brass Dial, Calendar Ring, 8-Day Time & Strike, Alarm, c.1765, 15 In. $3,998.00

Skinner, Inc.

Clock, French, Gilt Brass, Woman, Seated, Enameled Dial, Garlands, 8-Day, c.1875, 18 In. $1,580.00

Skinner, Inc.

Clock, Harris Strong, Walnut Veneer, Ceramic Tile, Chapters, 3 Bands, 1966, 42 x 11 In. $240.00

Skinner, Inc.

Clock, Howard Miller, Flock Of Butterflies, Brushed Metal, Enamel, Painted, G. Nelson, 1950s, 24 In. $3,125.00

Rago Arts & Auction Center

Clock, Howard, E., No. 5, Rosewood Grained, Reverse Painted, Gilt Glass, 28 ¾ In. $1,896.00

Skinner, Inc.

Clock, Howard, E., Regulator, No. 12, Black Walnut, 8-Day, Weight, Pendulum, c.1875, 62 In.
$26,070.00

Skinner, Inc.

Clock, Ithaca Calendar Clock Co., 2 Paper Dials, 8-Day, c.1890, 28 In.
$356.00

Skinner, Inc.

Clock, Ives, Joseph, Mahogany, Scroll Top, Painted Dial, Reverse Painted, 8-Day, c.1820, 56 In.
$2,370.00

Skinner, Inc.

Clock, Jerome & Co., Botsford Improved Patent Lever, Glass Dome, 30-Hour, c.1850, 12 In.
$2,205.00

Skinner, Inc.

Clock, Lantern, Moorish Temple, Gilt Bronze, Enameled Face, Brass Works, Marked F. Bohler, Key, 13 In.
$590.00

Brunk Auctions

Clock, Lawson Time, Digital, Chrome Plated Steel, Bakelite, K.E.M. Weber, 1933, 3 x 8 In.
$813.00

Los Angeles Modern Auctions (LAMA)

> ### TIP
> *Antique clocks should be level both back to front and side to side to keep correct time*

Clock, Liberty & Co., Tudric, Pewter, Enamel, Stamped, c.1910, 7 In.
$6,050.00

DuMouchelles Art Gallery

Clock, New Haven, Empire, Ogee Mahogany Case, Reverse Painted, c.1950, 19 x 12 In.
$60.00

DuMouchelles Art Gallery

Clock, Portico, Renaissance Style Inlay, Gilt Bronze, Columns, Enameled Face, Mirror, 1800s, 19 ½ In.
$177.00

Brunk Auctions

Shelf, Theodore Roosevelt, Rough Rider, Cast Iron, Windup, 1899, 8 x 10 x 3 In.	1278.00
Shelf, Wood, Reeded Edge, Scalloped Backboard, Gray Paint, 23 x 12 In.	443.00
Skeleton, Brass, Pierced Dial, Bell, Glass Dome, Faux Marble Base, 9 ½ In.	236.00
Skeleton, Brass, Silvered Metal Face, Glass Dome, Fusee Movement, Marble Base, 17 x 11 In.	604.00
Skeleton, Louis XVI, Directoire, Ormolu, Enamel, Marble, Striking, c.1800	27000.00
Skeleton, Wood & Onyx Base, c.1900, 15 x 13 In.	1320.00
Star Brass Mfg., Wall, Brass, Round, Boston, 1899, 10 ½ x 7 In.	649.00
Tall Case, Abraham Shaw, English Oak, Mahogany, Broken Scroll, England, 86 In.	590.00
Tall Case, Arts & Crafts, Oak, Leaded Glass Door, Monitor Works, c.1910, 78 In.	1875.00
Tall Case, Benjamin Swan, Federal, Mahogany, Moon Phase Dial, Augusta, Me., 93 In.	10325.00
Tall Case, Black Forest, Cherry, Scroll Top, Arched Hood, 30-Hour, c.1830, 100 In.	415.00
Tall Case, Blumfield, Mixed Woods, Bonnet Top, Fluted Columns, England, c.1820, 91 In.	885.00
Tall Case, Broken Arch Pediment, Flowers, Inscription, Orange Paint, Sweden, c.1870, 83 In. ..	384.00
Tall Case, Carved Hood, Fluted Columns, Glass Door, Brass Dial, 11 x 20 In.	1869.00
Tall Case, Cherry, Carved, Swan's Neck Crest, Brass Finials, Tombstone Door, c.1795, 89 In.	948.00
Tall Case, Cherry, Maple, Broken Arch, Painted Dial, Inscribed Griffith Owen, Phila., c.1785, 100 In.	7110.00
Tall Case, Cherry, Reeded Columns & Finials, Fretted Crest, c.1800, 94 In.	1800.00
Tall Case, Chippendale, Cherry, Heart Cutouts, Brass Works, David Blaisdell, N.H., c.1770, 83 In..	7080.00
Tall Case, Chippendale, Mahogany, Broken Arch, Floral Rosettes, John Fissler, 1790, 102 In....	4995.00
Tall Case, Chippendale, Walnut, 30-Hour, John Murphy, Northampton, Pa., 1793, 96 In.	3402.00
Tall Case, Chippendale, Walnut, Broken Arch, 8-Day, Brass Face, B. Chandlee, c.1770, 95 In. .	7703.00
Tall Case, Chippendale, Walnut, Carved Pediment, Columns, 8-Day Works, Va., c.1799, 99 x 21 In..	26450.00
Tall Case, Chippendale, Walnut, Flame Finials, Flower Carved Bonnet, c.1790, 102 In.	1541.00
Tall Case, Clarke & Bilbie, Jacobean Style, Oak, Carved, Phoenix Birds, c.1885, 81 x 18 In......	1230.00
Tall Case, Durfee, Renaissance Revival, Oak, Beveled Glass, 9 Tubes, Tiffany & Co., 104 In... *Illus*	13750.00
Tall Case, Edwardian, Mahogany, 5-Tube, Broken Arch Pediment, Brass Steeple Finial, c.1885, 94 In.	2337.00
Tall Case, Federal Style, Mahogany, Fretwork, Ship, French Feet, c.1920, 52 In.	6463.00
Tall Case, Federal, Cherry, Arch Bonnet, 8-Day, Painted Dial, Mid-Atlantic, c.1810, 90 In.	652.00
Tall Case, Federal, Cherry, Burl Maple, Broken Arch, Rosettes, c.1820, 93 In.	3254.00
Tall Case, Federal, Cherry, Carved Feathers, Arched Pediment, Urn Finials, 1800s, 86 x 18 In. ..	767.00
Tall Case, Federal, Cherry, Carved, String Inlay, Arched, Reeded Columns, c.1805, 95 In.	13035.00
Tall Case, Federal, Cherry, Pa., Early 19th Century, 85 In.	563.00
Tall Case, Federal, Cherry, Pine, Arched Hood, Cutout Feet, Landscape Dial, c.1800, 87 In.	1293.00
Tall Case, Federal, Cherry, Pine, Scroll Crest, Eagle Finial, Fluted Columns, c.1815, 87 In.......	2350.00
Tall Case, Federal, Cherry, Walnut Inlay, 30-Hour, Brass Movement, c.1810, 96 In. ....*Illus*	1763.00
Tall Case, Federal, Cherry, Walnut Inlay, Broken Arch, Painted & Gilt Dial, 1800s, 97 x 18 In. ..	3450.00
Tall Case, Federal, Mahogany, 8-Day, Waisted, Pinwheel Rosettes, c.1800, 86 In.	2242.00
Tall Case, Federal, Mahogany, Broken Arch, Carved Roses, String Inlay, c.1800, 95 In.	2468.00
Tall Case, Federal, Mahogany, Waisted, Broken Arch Pediment, c.1800, 91 x 20 In.	944.00
Tall Case, Federal, Walnut, Broken Arch, Quatrefoil Panel, Sun, Moon Dial, c.1800, 96 In.	1175.00
Tall Case, Federal, Walnut, Shaped Pediment, 8-Day, Pa., 90 In.	770.00
Tall Case, George II, Burl, Walnut, Flat Bonnet, Fretwork, Columns, Putto, c.1745, 89 x 21 In..	3690.00
Tall Case, George III Style, Pine, Scrolling Broken Pediment, Arched Door, 89 x 20 In.	1230.00
Tall Case, George III, Mahogany, Broken Arch Pediment, Eagle Finial, c.1800, 93 x 24 In.......	1476.00
Tall Case, George III, Mahogany, Broken Arch, Roses, Scrollwork, Columns, c.1790, 96 x 23 In. ..	1845.00
Tall Case, George III, Mahogany, String Inlay, Broken Arch, Ogee Bracket Feet, c.1790, 94 x 23 In....	1045.00
Tall Case, George III, Oak, Broken Swan's Neck Pediment, Columns, 87 x 17 In.	850.00
Tall Case, Georgian Style, Mahogany, Brass Dial, Broken Pediment, Finial, c.1900, 58 x 11 In. .	1150.00
Tall Case, Georgian, Chinoiserie, Inlay, Oriental Scenes, Arched, England, 90 In.	1770.00
Tall Case, Georgian, Mahogany Inlay, Swan's Neck Pediment, Brass Finials, 85 In.	1476.00
Tall Case, Georgian, Mahogany, Painted Dial, Barr Castle, Galston, 8-Day, 1800s, 91 In...*Illus*	1416.00
Tall Case, Gothic Revival, Spires, Floral Painted Dial	2200.00
Tall Case, Hans Telerud, Knotty Pine, Brass Dial, Medallion, Pendulum, c.1753, 80 x 18 In....	600.00
Tall Case, Henry Hahn, Walnut, 8-Day, Reading, Pa., c.1810, 100 In.	3792.00
Tall Case, Herschede, Blond Finish, Lunar Movement, 9 Tubes, 3 Chimes, c.1925, 86 In. ..*Illus*	1320.00
Tall Case, Howard Miller, Burl, Arched Crown Molding, Brass, Moon Phase, c.1890, 87 x 27 In. ...	540.00
Tall Case, Howard Miller, Carved Crest, Fluted Columns, 83 x 27 In.	384.00
Tall Case, J. & R. Twiss, Pine, Wood Works, Swan's Neck Pediment, Signed, Canada, 1800s, 83 In.	889.00
Tall Case, Jacob Eby, Federal, Cherry, Broken Arch, Urn Finials, Brass Works, c.1810, 89 In. ...	4425.00
Tall Case, James Bennett, Walnut, Calendar, Moon Phase, 13 Bells, Engraved Dial, c.1780, 96 In.	6900.00
Tall Case, Louis XVI, Oak, Urn & Wreath Carved Hood, Basket, France, 1800s, 87 x 19 In........	944.00
Tall Case, Mahogany, Brass Dial, Moon, 12 Tubes, Chimes, 8-Day, Germany, c.1900, 101 In...*Illus*	7110.00
Tall Case, Mahogany, Broken Pediment, Eagle Finial, Gilt, 8-Day, Pendulum, Ireland, c.1775, 96 In.	2160.00
Tall Case, Mahogany, Small Round Dial, Tapered Case, Plinth, Scotland, c.1830, 90 In............	10030.00
Tall Case, Mahogany, Stepped Hood, Brass Face, 3 Finials, Wavy Skirt, Spade Feet, 100 x 24 In.	2750.00
Tall Case, Maple, Tombstone Door, Arched Top, Fretwork, Urn Finials, Columns, c.1810, 91 In. ...	5925.00
Tall Case, Neoclassical, Mahogany, Arched, Columns, Brass Movement, Frank Herschede, 92 In..	1175.00

Clock, Raingo Freres, Shelf, Cathedral, Silk Thread Movement, Porcelain, Paris, c.1835, 24 In.
$15,535.00

Neal Auction Co.,

Clock, Tall Case, Durfee, Renaissance Revival, Oak, Beveled Glass, 9 Tubes, Tiffany & Co., 104 In.
$13,750.00

Leslie Hindman Auctioneers

TIP
Old clocks should be oiled every four to six years and cleaned every six to eight months.

115

Clock, Tall Case, Federal, Cherry, Walnut Inlay, 30-Hour, Brass Movement, c.1810, 96 In.
$1,763.00

C

Garth's Auctioneers & Appraisers

Clock, Tall Case, Georgian, Mahogany, Painted Dial, Barr Castle, Galston, 8-Day, 1800s, 91 In.
$1,416.00

Brunk Auctions

Clock, Tall Case, Herschede, Blond Finish, Lunar Movement, 9 Tubes, 3 Chimes, c.1925, 86 In.
$1,320.00

DuMouchelles Art Gallery

Clock, Tall Case, Mahogany, Brass Dial, Moon, 12 Tubes, Chimes, 8-Day, Germany, c.1900, 101 In.
$7,110.00

Skinner, Inc.

Clock, Tall Case, Peter Schwartz, Brass Dial, 8-Day Time & Strike, Brass, York, Pa., 1773, 98 In.
$4,600.00

Cottone Auctions

Clock, Tall Case, Stephen Taber, Mahogany, Iron Dial, Moon, Inlay, 8-Day, c.1800, 89 In.
$18,960.00

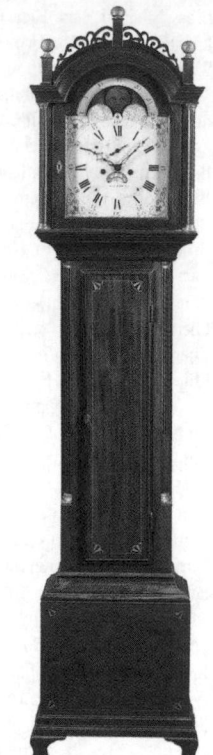

Skinner, Inc.

Clock, Tall Case, Thomas McCredie, 8-Day, Hour Strike, Calendar, Bowed, Scotland, 1840s, 87 In.
$1,008.00

Cowan's Auctions

Tall Case, Oak, Bird's-Eye Maple Dial, Recoil Escapement, Pendulum, Pedestal, 1800s, 78 In. 690.00
Tall Case, Paulus Bramer, Walnut, Gilt, Arch Hood, Painted Scene, Amsterdam, c.1800, 111 In.... 10625.00
Tall Case, Peter Schwartz Queen Anne, Mahogany, Embossed Surround, York, Pa., c.1750, 84 In. 2370.00
Tall Case, Peter Schwartz, Brass Dial, 8-Day Time & Strike, Brass, York, Pa., 1773, 98 In...... *Illus* 4600.00
Tall Case, Pine, Painted Dial, Wood Works, 2 Weights, Bell Strike, Ohio, c.1815, 7 Ft. 863.00
Tall Case, R. Whiting, Pine, Red Stain, Multicolor, Gilt, White Wood Dial, Village Scene, c.1810, 86 In. 1185.00
Tall Case, R. Whiting, Wood, Flat Top, Red Stain, Inscribed 1831, 87 In. 3081.00
Tall Case, Radio, Atwater Kent, Bailey Banks & Biddle, 68 In. 533.00
Tall Case, Riley Whiting, Federal, Grain Painted, Scroll & Urn Finials, Winchester, 86 In. 236.00
Tall Case, Riley Whiting, Federal, Rosewood, Carved Crest, Conn., 80 In. 1298.00
Tall Case, Robertson, Mahogany, Round Dial, Signed, England, 81 In. 649.00
Tall Case, Rococo Revival, Mahogany, Flowers, Brass & Steel Sun & Moon Dial, 96 In. 7050.00
Tall Case, Sheraton, Curly Maple, Pine, Banding, Turned Finials, Reeded, c.1820, 100 In. 4465.00
Tall Case, Silas Hoadley, Grain Painted, Conn., 85 In. 767.00
Tall Case, Stephen Taber, Mahogany, Iron Dial, Moon, Inlay, 8-Day, c.1800, 89 In. *Illus* 18960.00
Tall Case, Thomas McCredie, 8-Day, Hour Strike, Calendar, Bowed, Scotland, 1840s, 87 In. ... *Illus* 1008.00
Tall Case, Thomas Shaw, George III, Mahogany, Brass Face, Lancaster, c.1790, 85 ½ In.... *Illus* 1058.00
Tall Case, Waltham, Mahogany, Glass Door, Moon Phase, 9 Chimes, c.1905, 80 In. 3068.00
Tall Case, Willard, Federal, Cherry, Fretwork Hood, c.1795, 80 In. 4406.00
Telechron, Refrigerator Shape, General Electric, Monitor Top, 8 In. 144.00
Terry & Andrews, Rosewood, Eglomise Door, Open Window, Pendulum, 26 x 15 In. 120.00
Terry, Eli, Pillar & Scroll, Mahogany, Flower Dial, Reverse Painted, Brass Finials, c.1910, 29 In..... 413.00
Terry, Eli, Shelf, Carved Eagle Crest, Pillar, Landscape Tablet, 29 In. 244.00
Terry, Eli, Shelf, Empire, Mahogany, Stencil Crest, Reverse Painted, c.1835, 31 In. 295.00
Terry, Eli, Shelf, Mahogany, Pillar & Scroll, Gilt, 30-Hour, Reverse Painted, c.1820, 30 In... *Illus* 474.00
Terry, Eli, Shelf, Pillars, Swan's Neck Pediment, Brass Urn Finials, Reverse Painted, 1800s, 32 In.. 531.00
Tiffany & Co., Angelus, Descodate, Bronze, Swiss, Stamped 732, 5 ½ x 5 In. 120.00
Tiffany & Co., Carriage, Gilt Bronze, Handles, Repeater, c.1901, 6 ¼ In. 875.00
Tiffany & Co., Gilt Metal, Quartz, Rounded, Roman Numerals At Quarter Hour, Swiss, 6 x 5 In... 96.00
Tiffany & Co., Lyre, Shelf, Louis XVI Style, Bronze, White Marble, Inset Stones, Sun Finial, 18 In. 4688.00
Tiffany & Co., Regulator, Brass, Beveled Glass, Columns, Champleve, 8-Day, c.1890, 16 In....... *Illus* 9840.00
Tiffany & Co., Shelf, French Empire Style, Marble, Ormolu, Daubref Movement, 11 x 10 In... 1783.00
Tiffany & Co., Silver Dial, Alarm, Seconds Dial, Key Wind, c.1910, 3 In. 115.00
Tiffany clocks that are part of desk sets made by Louis Comfort Tiffany are listed in the Tiffany category. Clocks sold by the store Tiffany & Co. are listed here.
Tiffany Reed & Co., Carriage, Gilt Metal, Champleve, Turquoise Vines, France, 5 x 4 In. 4095.00
Travel, Hook & Spike, Brass, Steel, Alarm, Roman Numerals, England, c.1690, 5 In. 679.00
Udall & Ballou, Art Deco, Mother-Of-Pearl, Gilt, Convex Glass, Enameled, 3 ½ In. 265.00
Vermont Clock Co., Carriage, Brass, Beveled Glass, Enameled Dial, 8-Day, 4 ½ x 3 In. 132.00
Wag-On-Wall, Brass, Repousse, Enameled Dial, 2-Weight, Wichelmann, 58 x 14 In. 176.00
Wall, Empire Style, Brass, Enamel Face, Pocket Watch Shape, Swiss, c.1900, 7 x 5 In. 184.00
Wall, Eye Shape, Walnut, Brass, Enameled Aluminum, c.1957, 13 ½ x 30 ¼ In. 3750.00
Wall, Oak, Regulator, Calendar, Reeded, Stepped Cornice, Shaped Apron, c.1900, 38 In. 84.00
Wall, Porcelain, Gilt, Round, Acorn Shape, Windmills, Handles, c.1885, 17 In. 584.00
Wall, Stromberg, Roman Numerals, Pendulum, Maple, 31 In. 178.00
Wall, Sunburst, Wood, Gilt, c.1960, 26 In. 1188.00
Wall, Walnut, Lion Mask, Finials, Turned Columns, Cream Dial, c.1900, 39 x 15 ½ In. 375.00
Wall, Wood, Dutch Painted, White Face, Roman Numerals, Exposed Weights, 9 ½ x 7 In. 180.00
Waltham, Girandole, Painted Scene, Eagle Finial, c.1900, 48 x 15 In. 17255.00
Waterbury, Oak, Octagonal, Roman Numerals, c.1890, 9 In. 84.00
Waterbury, Shelf, Eastlake Style, Oak, Carved, 21 x 15 In. 96.00
Waterbury, Shelf, Mahogany Inlay, Round Face, Convex Glass Door, 1800s, 14 In. 508.00
Waterbury, Shelf, Mahogany Stain, Gilt Brass Mounts, Lion Heads, c.1898, 17 x 11 In. 86.00
Waterbury, Shelf, Marble Slate, Porcelain Dial, Time & Strike, c.1890, 11 x 10 In. 118.00
Waterbury, Shelf, Oak, Gold Highlights, Allover Carvings, 22 In. 70.00
Welch, Shelf, Oak, Carved Spanish-American War Themes, 24 In. 313.00
Welch, Spring & Co., Perpetual Calendar, Rosewood, c.1875, 53 x 24 In. 1560.00
Willard, Aaron, Shelf, Federal, Mahogany, Urn Finials, Glazed Door, Inscribed Dial, 23 In..... 3540.00
Willats, John, Bracket Stepped Top, Brass Carrying Handle, Arched Gilt Brass Face, c.1750, 18 ¼ In.. 3186.00
Wittner, Simon, School Regulator, Mahogany, Blown Glass, Pendulum, c.1900, 22 x 12 In. ... 42.00

CLOISONNE enamel was developed during the tenth century. A glass enamel was applied between small ribbons of metal on a metal base. Most cloisonne is Chinese or Japanese. Pieces marked *China* are twentieth-century examples.

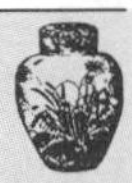

Bowl, Butterfly & Moth Design, 9 ½ In. Diam 2530.00
Bowl, Dome Lid, Spread Foot, Flowers, Scrolling, Finial, Wood Stand, 8 In., Pair 837.00

Clock, Tall Case, Thomas Shaw, George III, Mahogany, Brass Face, Lancaster, c.1790, 85 ½ In.
$1,058.00

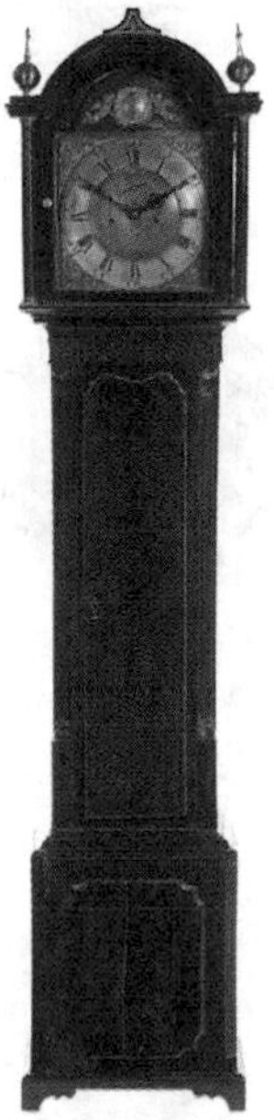

Garth's Auctioneers & Appraisers

Clock, Terry, Eli, Shelf, Mahogany, Pillar & Scroll, Gilt, 30-Hour, Reverse Painted, c.1820, 30 In.
$474.00

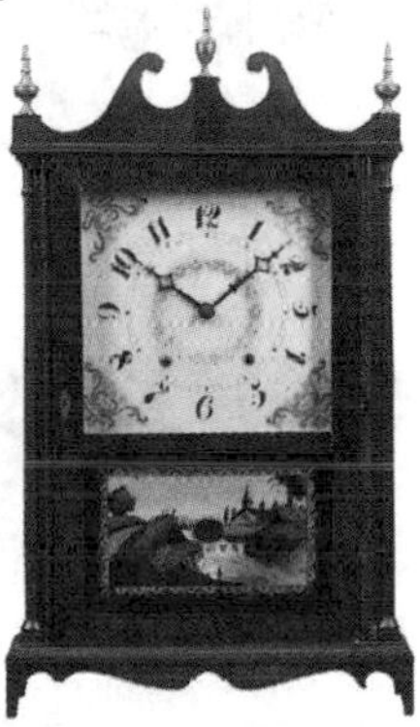

Skinner, Inc.

Clock, Tiffany & Co., Regulator, Brass, Beveled Glass, Columns, Champleve, 8-Day, c.1890, 16 In.
$9,840.00

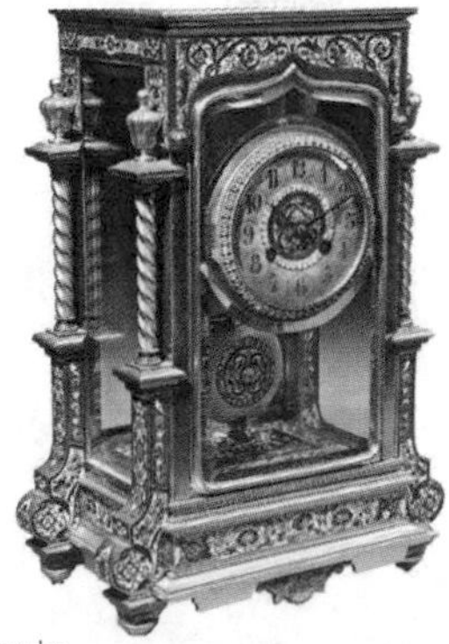

Skinner, Inc.

CLOISONNE

C

Cloisonne, Vase, Bottle Shape, Turquoise, Leaf Scrolls, Central Lotus Flowers, Chinese, 1662-1722, 14 ⅛ In. $79,625.00

Skinner, Inc.

Cloisonne, Vase, Butterflies, Peonies, Lotus, Gilt Mouth & Foot, Marked, Chinese, c.1900, 13 In. $2,370.00

Skinner, Inc.

Clothing, Belt, Concha, Silver, Buckle Stamped LC Sterling, 42 In. $660.00

Old Barn Auction

Clothing, Collars & Display Case, Silver Brand, Copper, Etched Glass, 15 x 51 x 9 In. $2,700.00

Showtime Auction Services

118

Bowl, Exotic Fish Scene, Water Lilies, Roses, Gilt Sculpted Figural Fish Shape Feet, 1900s, 12 ½ In.....	390.00
Bowl, U Shape, Foot Ring, Qilin, Foo Dog, Twin Fish, 3 ⅞ x 9 In.	1554.00
Box, Canted Lid, Flowers, Leaves, Scrolls, c.1900, 2 ¼ x 4 In.	215.00
Box, Cinquefoil Shape, Prunus Blossoms, Namikawa Sosuke, c.1900, 1 x 3 In.	19000.00
Box, Dome Lid, Birds, Bamboo, Flowers, Blue Ground, Japan, 2 x 5 In..........	268.00
Box, Dome Lid, Painted, Birds, Bamboo, Flowers, Japan, 2 x 5 In.	225.00
Box, Dome Lid, Round, Lotus Flowers, Leaves, Gilded Dragons, Pearl, c.1900, 3 ½ In..........	533.00
Box, Double, 2 Compartments, Center Handle, Meandering Flowers, Blossoms, Green, 8 x 4 In.....	121.00
Box, Egg Shape, Pedestal Base, Turquoise, Cobalt Blue, Green, Flowers, 1880, 4 In.	500.00
Box, Lid, Cylindrical, Hundred Antiques Design, Bat, 1800s, 4 In.	115.00
Box, Lid, Fan Shape, Shou Character, Bats, Lotus Flowers, Gilt, c.1900, 2 ⅜ x 8 In., Pair.........	3437.00
Box, Lid, Round, Gilded Dragons, Flames, Lotus, Leaves, Cabriole Legs, c.1900, 4 In.	2370.00
Box, Oval, Flower Blossoms, Siren, Giltwashed Interior, c.1890, 2 ¾ In..........	425.00
Brushpot, Cylindrical, Shaped Feet, Lotus Scrolls, Turquoise, Marked, 1900s, 3 x 3 ½ In.	4674.00
Candleholder, Pricket, Flared Drip Pan, Splayed Foot, Lotus Blossoms, Gilt, 1800s, 3 In., Pair	1164.00
Censer, Bombe Shape, Upright Handles, Flowers, Footed, 5 In..........	6573.00
Censer, Dome Lid, Foo Dog Finial, Flowers, Scrolling Vines, Wood Stand, Handles, 7 ⅛ In.	2988.00
Censer, Duck, Blue, Green, Red, Dragon's Mask Handle, Flowers & Leaves, Gilt Feet, 19 ½ In..	3851.00
Censer, Gilt, Turquoise, Flowers, Dragon Shape Handles & Finial, Animal Feet, 1900s, 7 In. ...	148.00
Censer, Peach Branch Legs, Scrolling Lotus, Gilt Trim, Loop Handles, c.1800, 4 In.	830.00
Censer, Ruyi Handles, Animal Feet, Lotus, Pierced Lid, Gilt Finial, c.1900, 27 x 12 In.	4130.00
Censer, Squat, Footed, Stylized Lotus Flowers, Multicolor, Marked, c.1900, 6 In.	472.00
Charger, 2 Boys Crossing River, 1800s, 12 In. Diam.	288.00
Charger, 2 Cranes, Grass, Mountains, Japan, c.1890, 17 ⅞ In..........	354.00
Charger, 2 Quail, Flowers, Blue, Signed, 1800s, 14 ½ In..........	575.00
Charger, Flowers, White, Blue On Reverse, Rosewood Reticulated Stand, Chinese, 8 In.	48.00
Charger, Multicolor Rim, Repeating Design, White Cranes, Blue, Foot Ring, 5 ½ x 36 In........	1416.00
Charger, Quail, Flowers, Leaves, Turquoise, Stylized Pattern Border, 1800s, 14 In. Diam........	575.00
Cigarette Case, Cartouche, Flowers, Turquoise Border, Russia, 1892, 3 ½ x 2 In..........	1200.00
Cigarette Case, Central Medallion, Scrolls, Rectangular, Russia, 4 ⅛ x 3 ¼ In.	750.00
Cigarette Case, Flowers, Scrolls, Turquoise, Green, White, Russia, 4 x 3 In.	1625.00
Cigarette Case, Napoleon, Scrolled Leaves, Multicolor, Russia, 4 ⅜ x 3 ¼ In.	6875.00
Compote, Tulip, Leaves, Chinese Blue Ground, 9 ½ x 6 In.	124.00
Egg, Multicolor Flowers, Beading, Silver Gilt, Stippled, Moscow, c.1915, 2 ½ In.	3600.00
Egg, Silver, Geometric Design, Multicolor Enamel, Russia, 1908-17, 2 ½ In.	7110.00
Ewer, Lid, Jade Panels, Gilt, Dragon Handle & Spout, Finial, 1800s, 18 In.	2950.00
Figurine, Bodhisattva, 16 Arms, Cross Legged, Lotus Base, c.1950, 20 ½ x 20 In.........	840.00
Figurine, Buddha, Gilt Bronze, Standing, Wearing Robe, Flowers, c.1900, 22 ½ In.	177.00
Figurine, Dragon, S-Curve Shape, Raising Head, Wings, Base, Sprays Of Water, 11 In.	911.00
Figurine, Foo Dog, Female With Pup, Male With Ball, 31 x 22 x 17 In., Pair..........	9440.00
Figurine, Horse, Blue, Yellow Saddle, Brown Flowing Mane, Upturned Tail, 14 x 14 ¾ In........	374.00
Figurine, Horse, Prancing, Wood Base, Chinese, 19 x 18 ½ In..........	205.00
Figurine, Kylin, Standing, Blue Scales, Gilt Accents, c.1735, 8 ¼ x 11 ½ In., Pair..........	7072.00
Figurine, Male Foo Dog, Seated On Haunches, Foot On Ball, Stepped Base, 1900s, 21 In........	1599.00
Figurine, Parrot, Perched On Rockwork, Blue, Green, Marked, c.1900, 9 ¾ In..........	531.00
Goblet, Saucer, Silver, Flowers, Scrolls, Inset Stones, Blue, Green, White, Red, Russia, 5 In......	2125.00
Jar, Barrel Shape, Flowering Branches, White Ground, Finial, c.1900, 6 ½ In.	239.00
Jar, Lid, Figural, Flowers, Birds, 8 In., Pair..........	117.00
Jardiniere, Cranes, Peonies, Diaper Borders, Turquoise, Interior, 12 x 14 In.	357.00
Jardiniere, Metal, Flowers, Vases, Lappet Bands, Blue, Wood Stand, Chinese, 34 In., Pair........	1250.00
Kovsh, Scrolling Flowers, Giltwashed, Russia, c.1905, 2 ¾ x 8 In.	4000.00
Planter, Round, Branch Shaped Feet, Peaches & Bats, Blue, Greek Key Rim, 1900s, 8 In........	1416.00
Plaque, Riverscape Scene, Pagoda, Mountains, Chinese, 15 x 12 In..........	1135.00
Pricket Stand, Figural, Ram, Standing, Head Turned Over Backside, Saddle, 12 x 6 ½ In., Pair ...	976.00
Spoon, Elliptical Bowl, Spiral Twist Stem, Geometric Banding, 1888, 7 In.	615.00
Stand, Gilt, Lotus Scrolls, Pierced Base, Dragon Brackets, Zigzag Rim, 1700s, 2 x 7 In.	1180.00
Tureen, Lid, Oval, Raised Fish, Aquatic Plants, Foo Dog Handles, 5 ¾ x 13 In..........	215.00
Urn, Lid, Flowers, Green, Red, White Panels, Signed, Yasuyuki, c.1900, 4 In.	7200.00
Vase, Blue Dragon, Bulbous, Tapered Neck, Gilt Bands, Chinese, 12 x 6 In., Pair	150.00
Vase, Blue, Peony, Crane, Baluster Shape, Flared Neck, Recessed Foot, 9 ¼ x 5 ½ In..........	230.00
Vase, Bottle Shape, Multicolor, 10 ⅜ In..........	173.00
Vase, Bottle Shape, Raised Foot, Emblems, Scrolling Lotus, Gilt, c.1900, 10 In., Pair..........	1778.00
Vase, Bottle Shape, Turquoise, Leaf Scrolls, Central Lotus Flowers, Chinese, 1662-1722, 14 ⅛ In... *Illus*	79625.00
Vase, Bottle, Pear Shape, Funnel Neck, Splayed Foot Ring, Wood Stand, 15 In., Pair	657.00
Vase, Bronze, Diaper Pattern, Rounded Square Shape, Foot, Rolled Rim, c.1900, 9 ½ In.	120.00
Vase, Bronze, Phoenix, Flowers, Drilled For Lamp, Japan, 14 ½ In.	360.00

Vase, Butterflies, Peonies, Lotus, Gilt Mouth & Foot, Marked, Chinese, c.1900, 13 In........*Illus*	2370.00
Vase, Dragon, Blue Ground, Bulbous, Tapered Neck, Early 20th Century, 24 x 7 In....................	840.00
Vase, Elongated Oval, Spread Foot, Round Handles, Turquoise, Scrolling Lotus, 1700s, 10 In..	3540.00
Vase, Flared Neck & Foot, Dragon, Phoenix, Red, Black, Blue, Green, Gilt, 12 In......................	1422.00
Vase, Flattened Heart Shape, Quatrefoil Mouth, Silver Wirework, Phoenix, Kylin, c.1890, 8 In. .	920.00
Vase, Flowers, Animals, Blue, Landscape, Bird Wing Handles, Oval, Chinese, 13 x 18 In..........	2400.00
Vase, Foo Dogs, Flowers, Blue Ground, Bulbous, 1700s, 13 In.	1960.00
Vase, Genie Bottle, Round Foot, Flowers, Blue Ground, 12 ¾ In., Pair................................	2988.00
Vase, Gilt Peacock Forming Handle, Peonies, Flared Rim, Gilt Trim, c.1900, 13 In.	4444.00
Vase, Goldstone, Bands Of 3 Clawed Dragons, Phoenix Birds, 1800s, 40 In.	338.00
Vase, Leaves, Insects, Dragons & Phoenix, c.1900, 7 ½ In.	475.00
Vase, Long Neck, Orange Fish, White Ground, Japan, 12 In...	1815.00
Vase, Masks, Scrolling Lotus, Turquoise Ground, Marked, 1900s, 11 In...........................	4674.00
Vase, Oval, Bird, Flowers, Branches, 12 In., Pair...	478.00
Vase, Pear Shape, Beast Handles At Neck, Round Foot, Archaic Designs, c.1900, 11 In.	120.00
Vase, Phoenix, Yellow Ground, Chinese, 8 ¼ In..	7080.00
Vase, Pink, White Flowers, Dark Blue Ground, Japan, c.1900, 35 ½ In.............................	666.00
Vase, Serpentine Dragon, Black, Red, Brown, Shouldered, Ring Foot, Pinched Neck, 6 In.......	219.00
Vase, Slender Tapering Neck, Turned In Rim, S-Scroll Handles, Flowers, c.1900, 8 ½ In.	750.00
Vase, Square, Narrow Neck, Round Foot, Flowers, Chinese, 24 In.	359.00
Vase, Taotie, Monkey, Fruit Tree, Robin's Egg Blue Ground, Japan, 12 ½ In......................	3840.00
Vase, Teal Ground, Prunus Tree, Birds, Japan, 7 ½ In..	173.00
Vase, White Ground, Black Flowers, Gold Rim, Chinese, 1800s, 8 In..............................	96.00
Vase, White, Purple Wisteria, Green Ground, Long Neck, 12 ¼ In., Pair..........................	480.00

CLOTHING of all types is listed in this category. Dresses, hats, shoes, underwear, and more are found here. Other textiles are to be found in the Coverlet, Movie, Quilt, Textile, and World War I and II categories.

Belt, Art Deco, Black Snakeskin, Cabochon Clad Buckle, Stamped Judith Leiber......................	420.00
Belt, Brass, Niello, Silvered Medallions, Hinged, Bow Clasp, Tassels, 28 In.	144.00
Belt, Concha, Silver, Buckle Stamped LC Sterling, 42 In...*Illus*	660.00
Belt, Enamel Spade Shape Buckle, Glass, 2 Headed Eagle, Filigree, c.1900, 31 In.................	1778.00
Belt, Leather, Red, Goldtone Hardware, Dust Bag, Siso, Italy, Woman's, 35 In....................	48.00
Belt, Needlework, Carriage Design, Black Ground, 2 Tassels, Label Hermes, Paris, 44 In.........	295.00
Belt, Pebble Grain, Chestnut Brown, Gold Chain, Stamped Chanel, 39 ½ In........................	184.00
Belt, Persian Style, Linked Cast Plaques, Clasp, Brass Tone, Brown Patina, 29 In................	69.00
Belt, Silver, Alligator Leather, Barry Kieselstein-Cord, 1986, 34 In.............................	179.00
Boots, Cowboy, Red, White Spread Eagles, Tulips, Number 76, Signed Tony Lama, El Paso......	770.00
Boots, Flowers, Horses, Embroidery, Silk, Tan, Orange, Wood Soles, Frame, 22 x 16 In., Pair ..	141.00
Bra, Backless, Strapless, Ecru Color, Lace Cups, Strouse Adler Company, 1970s, 36B	18.00
Caftan, Gray, Brown, Tan Geometrics, Emilio Pucci, Saks Fifth Avenue, 1980s	298.00
Cape, Lamb's Wool & Cashmere, Faux Fur Collar, Jimmy Hourihan, 3 Buttons, Size 42, 39 In...	480.00
Cardigan, Evening, Silver Knit, Metallic & Lurex-Shot, 1 Hook, St. John, Size 4	338.00
Chemise, Black & White Check, Wool, Jewel Neck, Pockets, Buttoned Cuffs, Valentino, Size 46..	338.00
Christening Grown & Slip, Cartridge Pleating, Drawstring, 2 Buttons In Back, c.1860	395.00
Coat, Dark Brown, Mink, Hillis Of Vail, 47 x 18 In.	655.00
Coat, Fox, Lined, 18 x 28 In., Size 6-8	47.00
Coat, Fur, 2-Tone Brown, 50 x 19 In...	327.00
Coat, Fur, Blue Mink, Full-Length, Rolled Cuffs, Flower Print Lining, Size 10	1440.00
Coat, Fur, Fox, Gray, Wide Rolled Collar, Arpin, 30 In. Long	450.00
Coat, Fur, Leopard, Fitted Waist, Georgeou Westchester Label, 40 In............................	173.00
Coat, Fur, Light Beige To Dark Brown, Full-Length, Woman's, 50 x 19 In.........................	322.00
Coat, Fur, Mink, Dark Brown, Woman's, 45 x 20 In..	322.00
Coat, Fur, Raccoon, Full-Length, Bricker-Tunis, 51 In. Long....................................	480.00
Coat, Fur, Silver Fox, Black & White, Clasp Closures, Pockets, ¾ Length	489.00
Coat, Mink, Black, Hooded, Ranch Style, Sash, Satin Lining, Full-Length, Size 12	1599.00
Coat, Mink, Brown, Leather Belt, Pockets, Size 6-8 Petite..	625.00
Coat, Mink, Brown, Swing, Raglan Sleeves, Full-Length, Geoffrey Beene, Size 4-6, 49 In.........	1722.00
Coat, Mink, Mahogany, Fox Trim, Denmark, Flemington Furs, Size 14, 40 x 18 In.	1190.00
Coat, Mink, Mahogany, Hillis Of Vail, Full-Length, 47 In..	774.00
Coat, Mink, Stroller, Brown, Stand-Up Collar, Bishop's Sleeve, Size 4-6, 27 In.	553.00
Coat, Ranch Mink, Carolina Herrera, Blackglama, Opera Length, Size 16, 51 In.	3900.00
Coat, Seal, Red Fox Collar, Bell Sleeves, Snap Belt, Georgeou Westchester Label, 38 x 18 In.....	144.00
Coat, Swing, Evening, Black, Flower Form Beads, Sequins, Diana Frels, 1970s, Size 4-6..........	246.00
Coat, Tailcoat, Wool, Black, Double-Breasted, Men's, c.1840, 36-In. Chest	495.00

Clothing, Handkerchief, Duck, Cotton, Child's, Square, 8 In.
$18.00

Clothing, Robe, Kesi, 8 Dragons, Flaming Pearls, Clouds, Buddhist Emblems, Woven, Woman's, Chinese
$3,900.00

Skinner, Inc.

Clothing, Robe, Silk, Dragon, Cloud Band, Embroidered, Metallic Thread, Chinese, 54 In.
$2,588.00

James D. Julia Auctioneers

Clothing, Shoes, Sneakers, Canvas, Rubber Soles, Peter Max, Box, Randy Mfg., c.1972, 10 In.
$822.00

Hake's Americana & Collectibles

C

Clothing, Suit, Boucle, Cloth Buttons, Pockets, Pleated Skirt, Jeunes Filles, Jacques Heim, 1960s
$60.00

Sloans & Kenyon

Clothing, Surcoat, Silk, Embroidered, Roundels, Flowers, Butterflies, Chinese, 1900s, 41 In.
$1,000.00

Skinner, Inc.

Cluthra, Vase, Blue, Mottled, Bubbles, Acid Stamp, Steuben, Fleur-De-Lis, 6 ¼ In.
$748.00

Humler & Nolan

Coat, Wool Boucle, Miss Bergdorf Label, Pink, 1960s	96.00
Coat, Wool, Double-Breasted, Powder Blue, Rhinestone Collar, Julius Garfinckel & Co., c.1963	90.00
Coat, Wool, Flare Cut, Peter Pan Collar, Kimono Sleeves, Pink, 1950s, XL	85.00
Cocktail Dress, Black Velvet, Sequins, Drop Waist, Long Sleeves, Carlina Herrera, Size 12	123.00
Collars & Display Case, Silver Brand, Copper, Etched Glass, 15 x 51 x 9 In..................*Illus*	2700.00
Dress, Brown & White Checked, Cotton, 1800s, Child's, 22 In.	142.00
Dress, Chiffon, Green, Gold Beads, c.1921, 49 In.	3000.00
Dress, Cocktail, Black, Strapless, Beading At Bust Line, Bustle Bow, 1950s, Size 6	210.00
Dress, Cocktail, Rhinestones, Feathers, Stop Senes, Rome, 36 In.	179.00
Dress, Evening, Beaded, Taffeta, Black Straps, White Bodice, Flowing Skirt, De La Renta	240.00
Dress, Evening, Polyester, Beaded, Black, Bob Mackie, Size 8	119.00
Dress, Evening, Silk, Strapless, Mermaid Style, Navy, Calvin Klein, 49 In.	83.00
Dress, Flapper, Sleeveless, Silk, Battaglia Factory, N.Y., 1920s, 38 x 13 In.	100.00
Dress, Green Cotton, Red, Blue Floral, Cap Sleeves, Glass Buttons, Child's, 1800s, 22 In.	83.00
Dress, Red Silk, Sleeveless, Red Sequins, 7 Layers Petticoat, Label Christian Dior, 1961	1440.00
Dress, Strappy Sheath, Black Knit & Rhinestone, Full-Length, St. John, 1980s, Size 12	184.00
Dress, White, Cotton Organdy, Orange, Green, Embroidery, Sleeveless, Norell, c.1954, 47 In.	2400.00
Dress, Wool Blend, Navy, A-Line, Concealed Pockets, Logo Button, Chanel Boutique, Size 38	1200.00
Handkerchief, Calendar, 1965, Alternating Squares, 13 x 12 In.	38.00
Handkerchief, Duck, Cotton, Child's, Square, 8 In......................*Illus*	18.00
Handkerchief, George Washington, Horse, Liberty Bell, Shields, Cotton, c.1876, 23 ¾ x 17 ¼ In.	660.00
Hat, Cartwheel, Black Felt, Wide Brim, Yellow & Orange Flower, Roberta Bernay, 1940s	155.00
Hat, Furry, Pompom Ties, White, Leather Lined, Lord Taylor, Italy, 1940s	20.00
Hat, Parade Stovepipe, Tin, Black Paint, 1864 Newspaper Lining, 7 In.	593.00
Hat, Top, Beaver, Philipp Neubauer, Berlin, Leather Banding, Box, 5 ½ x 10 In.	180.00
Hat, Top, Dunlop & Co., Ibex Hat Box, 9 x 14 In.	152.00
Hat, Velvet Crown, Egret Feathers, Stretch Band, Lily Dache Label, c.1940	676.00
Headdress, Mardi Gras, Red Bird, In Green Tree, Sequins, 22 In.	94.00
Helmet, Parade, Brass, Hair Crest, Red, White, Blue Plume, France, c.1860	1416.00
Helmet, Steel, Domed, Spiked Top, Chainmail Skirt, Middle Eastern, 19 ½ In.	313.00
Insole, Polar, Patented Nov. 13, 1817, J.K. Gittens, Salesman's Sample, 3 ⅞ In., Pair	55.00
Jacket, Black Sueded Deer Hide & Persian Lamb, Set-In Sleeves, Military Style, Chanel	492.00
Jacket, Blue Denim, Long Sleeves, Pockets, Chanel, France, Size 40	70.00
Jacket, Chinese Silk, Embroidered, Multicolor Flowers, Butterflies, Bats, 1800s, 30 In.	173.00
Jacket, Lace, Morning, Rose Pattern, Metallic Thread Trim, c.1890	189.00
Jacket, Leather Exterior, Beaver Fur Lining, Hook & Eye Closure, ¾ Length, 37 In.	120.00
Jacket, Mink, Sheared, Animal Print, Finland, 30 x 17 In.	536.00
Jacket, Rabbit Fur, Collar, Elastic Bottom, Cuffs, Zipper, Lined, Rein & Moriber, 27 In.	300.00
Jacket, Smoking, Man's, Cotton, Red, Black Print, Black Sash Belt, State O Maine Co., Large	145.00
Kerchief, Silk, Purple, Multicolor Binding, Shaker, 32 ½ x 32 ½ In.	2164.00
Kimono, Blue Silk, White, Yellow, Pink Mums, Ivory Lining, Full-Length	71.00
Kimono, Green, Red, Gold, Silver Cranes, Japan, 1900s	242.00
Kimono, Red Silk, Embroidered, Birds In Flight, Clouds, Japan	480.00
Kimono, Sash, Silk, Blue Field, Flowers, Birds, Red Lining, 60 In.	403.00
Kimono, Silk, Metallic Eagle & Dragon, Embroidered, c.1970	210.00
Kimono, Wedding, Embroidered, Cream Color, Flowers, Birds, Leaves	240.00
Mittens, Blue, Red Snowflake, Cross, Diamond, Multicolor Cuff, Knitted, Wool, 10 In.	115.00
Mittens, Knit, Wool, Crossed Block Pattern, Green, White, Lancaster County, 10 In.	12.00
Necktie, Leaf Design, Brown Weave, Small Square, Blue Accents, Derry Spun, 1940s	48.00
Robe, Black Satin, Spaghetti Straps, Fitted Bust, Kimono Sleeves, Tootsie's Houston, Size 4	123.00
Robe, Ceremonial, Silk Brocade, Red 5-Claw Dragon Design, 51 In.	2588.00
Robe, Embroidered, Dragons, Flaming Pearls, Clouds, Brown, Gold, Horseshoe Cuffs, Chinese, 1800s	770.00
Robe, Embroidered, Gold Dragons, Clouds, Waves, Rocks, Border, Chinese, c.1900, 46 In.	2187.00
Robe, Embroidered, Red, Blue, Gold, Dragons, Pearls, Clouds, Wide Arms, Chinese, c.1900	1353.00
Robe, Embroidered, Silk, Ivory, Prunus Flowers, Chinese, c.1920, 48 In.	345.00
Robe, Embroidered, Woven Panels, Latticework, Flower Heads, Black, Mideastern, Size 44	58.00
Robe, Kesi, 8 Dragons, Flaming Pearls, Clouds, Buddhist Emblems, Woven, Woman's, Chinese..*Illus*	3900.00
Robe, Silk, Dragon, Cloud Band, Embroidered, Metallic Thread, Chinese, 54 In.............*Illus*	2588.00
Robe, Silk, Embroidered Flowers, Cream, Yellow, Aqua, Ribbons, Chinese, 39 In.	590.00
Robe, Silk, Embroidered, Butterflies, Clouds, Purple, Peach & Cream Sleeves, Chinese, 53 In.	2952.00
Robe, Silk, Embroidered, Dragons, Flaming Pearls, Yellow, Chinese, c.1900, 50 x 44 In.	12000.00
Robe, Silk, Red Embroidered Design, Gold Thread Borders, Chinese, c.1800, 56 In.	1725.00
Sailor Suit, Blue, Wool, Brass Buttons, Bamberger & Hertz, Child's	150.00
Scarf, Candace Sturgill, Kentucky Derby, Frame, 37 x 38 In.	390.00
Scarf, Caraibes, White Ground, Blue Border, Silk, Hermes, 34 x 35 In.	136.00
Scarf, Compass, Blue, Original Tag, Hermes, 36 x 36 In.	132.00
Scarf, Early America, Silk, Lady & General George Washington, Hermes, 35 x 35 In.	450.00

Scarf, Erte, Man In Top Hat, Silk, Signed, Frame, 35 x 35 In.	360.00
Scarf, Harnais De Ceremonie, Coach, Horses Harnesses, Tack, White, Hermes, 35 x 32 In.	295.00
Scarf, Les Rubans Di Cheval, Silk, Hermes, 35 x 35 In.	136.00
Scarf, Orange & Black Plumes, Orange Border, Signed Paoli, 1960s	20.00
Scarf, Pasementerie, Multicolor Tassels, Ivory Ground, Hermes, Paris, 35 x 32 In.	325.00
Scarf, Pierres D'Orient Et D'Occident, Blue Flowers, Black, Hermes, Paris, 35 x 34 In.	413.00
Scarf, Pierres D'Orient Et D'Occident, Multicolor, Gold Border, Hermes, 36 x 36 In.	495.00
Scarf, Silk, Flowers, Dark Blue Ground, Gucci, 33 In.	413.00
Scarf, Silk, La Cle Des Champs, Birds, Rococo Scroll, Blue, Hermes, Paris, 34 In.	443.00
Scarf, Silk, Louveterie, Hunt Scenes, Hermes, Paris, 34 In.	201.00
Scarf, Silk, Napoleon, Life Scene Ovals, Hermes, Paris, 34 x 35 In.	354.00
Scarf, Silk, Printed Design, Gabor Petredi, Tina Lesser, Frame, 1950s, 21 x 21 In.	242.00
Scarf, Tabriz, Cashmere, Silk, Hermes, Box, 55 x 55 In.	1200.00
Shawl, Kashmir Jamawar, Woven, Paisley Borders, Fringe, India, 60 x 128 In.	69.00
Shawl, Silk, Multicolor Embroidered Flowers, Black Ground, Fringe, 54 x 53 In.	53.00
Shirt, Bowling, Women's, Orange, Embroidered Bowler On Collar, Pins On Pocket, 1950s	75.00
Shirt, Evening, Gold Beaded, Sleeveless, Made By Cashmere, 1940s, Size 40	60.00
Shoes, Color Block, Black, Magdesian's Of California, 1960s, Size 6 ½	35.00
Shoes, Heels, Platform, Snakeskin, Ankle Strap, Yellow, Blue, Pink, White, DeHavilland, 1970s	295.00
Shoes, Pump, Leather, Black Patent, Silvertone Buckle, Gucci, Size 8	36.00
Shoes, Sneakers, Canvas, Rubber Soles, Peter Max, Box, Randy Mfg., c.1972, 10 In. ....*Illus*	822.00
Skirt, Embroidered, Green Silk, Dragon & Phoenix, Scrolling Leaves, 1800s	307.00
Skirt, Linen, Linsey-Woolsey, Straps, Brown, Full, Bucks County, Pa., 1800s	326.00
Spats, Woman's, Weedies Bootops, Wool, Buttons, Metal Eyes, 1915, 10 x 7 In.	65.00
Stole, Mink, Black, Brown, Gathered Ends, Tail Tassels, Silk Lined, Size 4, 68 In.	738.00
Suit, Black Knit, Skirt, Multicolor Sequin Jacket, Marie Gray, St, John Evening, Size 4	270.00
Suit, Boucle, Cloth Buttons, Pockets, Pleated Skirt, Jeunes Filles, Jacques Heim, 1960s....*Illus*	60.00
Suit, Man's, Linen, White, Cuffed Pants, Button Fly, Tailored By Goodall, 1930s, Size 30	295.00
Suit, Navy Blue, Rayon Blend, Skirt, Classico Gold Silk Blouse, Giorgio Armani, Size 10	360.00
Suit, Wool, Wool Blend, Skirt, Cream Jacket, Black Trim, Skirt, Chanel Boutique, Size 40-42	780.00
Surcoat, Silk, Embroidered, Roundels, Flowers, Butterflies, Chinese, 1900s, 41 In. ....*Illus*	1000.00
Tailcoat, Men's, Black Wool, 2 Pockets In Tail, Double-Breasted, 1840s, 36 In. Chest	495.00
Tunic, Black Silk, Gauze Medallions, Gold Embroidered Panels Of Phoenix, Chinese, 36 In.	118.00
Tunic, Chainmail, Wide Sleeves, Front Slit Opening, Felt Collar, Persia, 30 x 39 In.	762.00
Uniform, Prison, Road Gang, Stripped Shirt, Drawstring, Pants, Virginia, c.1920, 28 In.	219.00

CLUTHRA glass is a two-layered glass with small bubbles and powdered glass trapped between the layers. The Steuben Glass Works of Corning, New York, first made it in 1920. Victor Durand of Kimball Glass Company in Vineland, New Jersey, made a similar glass from about 1925. Durand's pieces are listed in the Durand category. Related items are listed in the Steuben category.

Goblet, Fuchsia To White, Hexagonal Mouth, Tapered, Stamped, 6 ½ In.	690.00
Vase, Amethyst Glass, Oval, Steuben, 6 ½ In.	518.00
Vase, Blue Mottled To White, Rounded Square Shaped, Ring Foot, Air Trap, 7 In.	575.00
Vase, Blue Shaded To White, Trapped Bubbles, Inverted Rim, Steuben, 6 ½ In.	288.00
Vase, Blue, Mottled, Bubbles, Acid Stamp, Steuben, Fleur-De-Lis, 6 ¼ In. ....*Illus*	748.00
Vase, Blue, Mottled, Shouldered, Tapered, Marked, 8 ½ In.	805.00
Vase, Blue, Oval, Shouldered, Steuben, 11 In. ....*Illus*	1725.00
Vase, Bright Green, Oval, Flared Rim, Steuben, c.1920, 8 ¼ x 7 In.	900.00
Vase, Bud, 3 Stems, Green, Clear Foot, Steuben, 9 ½ In.	748.00
Vase, Bud, 3 Stems, Pink, Clear Foot, Steuben, 10 ½ In.	805.00
Vase, Bulbous, Flared Rim, Allover Green Tones, Internal Bubbles, Steuben, 8 ⅛ In. ....*Illus*	1270.00
Vase, Gold Ruby Glass, Pink, Bubbles, Bulbous, Shouldered, Flare Rim, 10 ½ In.	3335.00
Vase, Green, Mottled, Shouldered, Rolled Rim, Signed, 6 ½ In.	460.00
Vase, Green, Shouldered, Steuben, 1920s, 12 x 10 ½ In.	1125.00
Vase, Green, Urn, Shape, Shaped Opalescent Handles, Carder, Steuben 10 ⅝ In.	1080.00
Vase, Mottled Green, Shouldered, Tapered, Flared Rim, Stamped, 12 In.	207.00
Vase, Mottled Plum, Opalescent M-Handles, Shouldered, Ring Foot, Rolled Rim, 10 ¼ In.	1725.00
Vase, Pink, White Mottled, Suspended Bubbles, Shouldered, Oval, Steuben, 8 ½ In.	805.00
Vase, Strawberry, Glossy, Oval, Flared, Steuben, 8 ½ In.	748.00
Vase, White, Opalescent, Shouldered, Rolled Rim, 8 ½ In.	460.00

COALBROOKDALE was made by the Coalport porcelain factory of England during the Victorian period. Pieces are decorated with floral encrustations.

Dresser Jar, Flowers, Rocaille Gold Designs, Handles, c.1850, 6 ½ In.	385.00
Sucrier, Flowers, Butterflies, Ladybugs, c.1850, 7 ½ x 6 In.	1025.00

Cluthra, Vase, Blue, Oval, Shouldered, Steuben, 11 In.
$1,725.00

Early Auction Co.

Cluthra, Vase, Bulbous, Flared Rim, Allover Green Tones, Internal Bubbles, Steuben, 8 ⅛ In.
$1,270.00

Leslie Hindman Auctioneers

Coalport, Tureen, Lid, Stand, Cabbage, 1800s, 5 ½ In.
$420.00

Cowan's Auctions

Coca-Cola, Blotter, Duster Girl, c.1910, 3 ½ x 5 ½ In.
$300.00

DRINK BOTTLED
Coca-Cola
Delightfully Carbonated
and
So Easily Served

Victorian Casino Antiques

Coca-Cola, Calendar, 1921, Autumn Girl, Garden Scene, Paper, No Pad, Frame, 28 ½ x 13 ¾ In.
$330.00

Wm Morford Antiques

Coca-Cola, Cooler, Drink Coca-Cola, Serve Yourself, Vendo Junior, Coin-Operated, 1930s-40s
$960.00

Victorian Casino Antiques

TIP
Rusted toys have very low value.

Vase, 3-Footed, Handles, Flowers, Leaves, Scalloped, Pierced Rim, c.1891, 9 In.	350.00
Vase, Flowers, Multicolor, Leaves, Footed, Handles, c.1830, 11 ¾ In.	375.00

COALPORT ware was made by the Coalport Porcelain Works of England beginning about 1795. Early pieces were unmarked. About 1810–25 the pieces were marked with the name *Coalport* in various forms. Later pieces also had the name *John Rose* in the mark. The crown mark was used with variations beginning in 1881. The date 1750 is printed in some marks, but it is not the date the factory started. Coalport was bought by Wedgwood in 1967. Coalport porcelain is no longer being produced. Some pieces are listed in Indian Tree.

Bowl, Flowers, Cobalt Blue, White, 8 ½ In., Pair	37.00
Cup & Saucer, Wenlock Fruit, Gadroon Shape	50.00
Figurine, Crooked Cottage, Pastilles, c.1960, 4 In.	77.00
Plate, Red, Gilt Border, 9 In., 17 Piece	1094.00
Plate, Yellow Border, Dark Blue Edge, Gilt Scrolls, 10 ¼ In., 12 Piece	295.00
Saucer, Green Border, Multicolor Flowers, Fluted Gilt Rim, Marked, 5 ½ In., Pair	23.00
Tureen, Lid, Stand, Cabbage, 1800s, 5 ½ In. *Illus*	420.00
Vase, Enameled, Moorish Design, Medallion, Golden Orb, c.1875, 6 x 5 ½ In., Pair	270.00

COBALT BLUE glass was made using oxide of cobalt. The characteristic bright dark blue identifies it for the collector. Most cobalt glass found today was made after the Civil War. There was renewed interest in the dark blue glass in the late 1930s and dinnerware were made.

Bowl, Double Ogee Shape, 10 Ribs, Rough Pontil, c.1900, 2 x 6 ½ In.	403.00
Bowl, Finger, Diamond Rows, Plain Rim, Polished Pontil, c.1855, 3 ½ x 4 ¾ In.	81.00
Bowl, Finger, Free-Blown, Grapevine, Flower Engraved, Polished Pontil, c.1860, 3 x 4 In., Pair.	69.00
Compote, Vertical Ribs, Folded Rim, Knob, c.1835, 4 ¾ x 4 ¾ In.	173.00
Creamer, Tall Neck, Solid Handle, Applied Flared Foot, c.1840, 4 ½ x 2 ¼ In.	58.00
Pitcher, Medial Shoulder, Tooled Rim, Pa., c.1840, 5 ⅜ In.	1610.00
Salt, Cast Ram's Mask, Vine Silver Frame, Paw Feet, Marked, Germany, c.1890, 3 ⅞ In., 4 Piece	944.00
Salt, Footed, Double Ogee Shape, Diamond Rows, Short Stem, c.1840, 2 ¾ In.	288.00
Sugar, Applied Stem, Stepped Foot, Folded Rim, c.1810, 4 ¾ x 4 ¼ In.	81.00
Sugar, Diamond Rows, Flared Foot, c.1825, 2 ¾ x 4 In.	150.00
Sugar, Lid, Urn Shape, 8-Petal Rim., 8-Sided Stem, Footed, 6-Sided Finial, c.1860, 8 x 6 In.	1035.00
Tumbler, Colonial, Hexagonal, Rough Pontil, c.1860s, 3 ¾ x 3 ¼ In.	460.00
Whimsy, Horn, 12 Ribs, Swirled, Tooled Mouth, c.1850, 8 ½ x 2 ⅝ In.	288.00

COCA-COLA was first served in 1886 in Atlanta, Georgia. It was advertised through signs, newspaper ads, coupons, bottles, trays, calendars, and even lamps and clocks. Collectors want anything with the word *Coca-Cola*, including a few rare products, like gum wrappers and cigar bands. The famous trademark was patented in 1893, the *Coke* mark in 1945. Many modern items and reproductions are being made.

Ax, Coca-Cola For Sportsman, Wood Handle, c.1929, 13 ½ In.	4130.00
Banner, Drink A Bottle Of Delicious & Refreshing, Canvas, 1910, 16 x 138 In.	4720.00
Baseball Glove, Coca-Cola, Selling Points For Cooler On Fingers, Leather, 1930s, 7 In.	2714.00
Bell, Embossed Bottled Coca-Cola, Metal, Wood Handle, c.1920, 3 ¼ In.	944.00
Billboard, Roadside, Girls, Shopping, Linen, Paper, 1954, 9 x 20 Ft.	4425.00
Blotter, Duster Girl, c.1910, 3 ½ x 5 ½ In. *Illus*	300.00
Bookmark, Girl Drinking Coca-Cola, Heart Shape, Celluloid, 2 ¼ In.	600.00
Bookmark, Girl, Evening Attire, Heart Shape, Celluloid, 1896, 2 ¼ x 2 In.	1118.00
Bookmark, Owl, Book, What Shall We Drink?, Drink Coca-Cola 5 Cents, Celluloid, 1906, 3 In..	840.00
Bottle Holder, Logo, While You Shop, Metal, Holds 2 Bottles	140.00
Bottle Opener, Knife, Logo, 5 Cents, 3 ⅜ In.	15.00
Bottle, 6-Pack, Coca-Cola Diamonds, Filled, 1960s	1534.00
Bottle, Clear Glass, Binghamton, N.Y., 28 Oz., 11 ½ In.	36.00
Bottle, Coca-Cola, Birmingham Hutchinson Co., Embossed, c.1894, 6 ¾ In.	708.00
Bottle, E.L. Husting Co., Green Glass, c.1910	720.00
Bottle, Green Glass, Lowell, Mass., 28 Oz., 11 In.	120.00
Bottle, Lead Glass, Light-Up, Metropolitan Art Glass Co., 1920, 36 In.	76700.00
Bottle, Syrup, Clear, 1920s, 12 ½ In.	8850.00
Bus, Volkswagen, Tippco., Tin Lithograph, Friction, 6 Bottle Crates, c.1960, 9 In.	9568.00
Calendar, 1908, Lady In Red, March, Frame, 14 x 6 ¾ In.	3540.00
Calendar, 1913, Hamilton King, 22 ½ x 13 ½ In.	3068.00
Calendar, 1920, Golfer Girl, Yellow Dress, Wide Brim Hat, Frame, 32 ½ x 19 ½ In.	1062.00
Calendar, 1921, Autumn Girl, Garden Scene, Paper, No Pad, Frame, 28 ½ x 13 ¾ In. *Illus*	330.00
Calendar, 1931, Barefoot Boy, Dog, Norman Rockwell, 11 ¾ x 24 ¼ In.	345.00

Calendar, 1937, Fishing Hole, Boy, Fishing Pole, Frame, 32 ½ x 19 ½ In.	1888.00
Calendar, 1940, Girl In Red Dress, Seated, 32 ½ x 19 ½ In.	1416.00
Calendar, 1943, Girl In Aviator Jumpsuit, Holding Bottle, 25 x 19 In.	120.00
Calendar, 1944, Girl Holding Bottle, Soldier, With Picnic Basket, Spanish, 31 x 18 In.	1140.00
Calendar, 1947, Girl With Skis, Coke, 22 x 13 In.	330.00
Calendar, 1949, Girl, Winter Coat, Scarf, Holding Bottle, Mexico, 29 x 15 ½ In.	1920.00
Carrier, 6 Indents, Handle, Aluminum, Acton, 6 ¼ In.	48.00
Carrier, 6-Pack, Red Lettering, Wood, 7 ½ In.	120.00
Carrier, Aluminum, Handle, 6 Openings, c.1950	40.00
Carrier, Red, Tan, Cardboard, 1920s, 8 x 7 ¼ In.	24.00
Carrier, Refresh Yourself Drink Coca-Cola, 6-Bottle, Wood, Rope Handle, 1920s, 5 x 8 In.	649.00
Chair, Porch, Metal, Drink Coca-Cola, Round Back, Square Seat, Arms, Red, White, 1950s, Pair	633.00
Cigarette Case, 50th Anniversary Coca-Cola 1886-1936, Frosted, Embossed Glass, 5 ½ In.	300.00
Clock, Aluminum, Painted Case, Paper Dial, Wood Back, Winsted, 1950s, 15 x 4 In.	173.00
Clock, Coca-Cola, Delicious Refreshing, Tin, Wood, Baird, 29 x 18 In.	6490.00
Clock, Coca-Cola, Neon, Spinning Illusion Wheel, Round, c.1939, 18 In.	2124.00
Clock, Coca-Cola, The Ideal Brain Tonic, Baird, 31 x 18 ½ In.	7670.00
Clock, Drink Coca-Cola, 5 Cents, Red, Porthole Shape, Swivel Base, Countertop, 15 x 17 In.	450.00
Clock, Drink Coca-Cola, Plastic Front, Metal Frame, Light-Up, 1960s, 24 x 40 In.	354.00
Clock, Drink Coca-Cola, Square, Metal, Fishtail Logo, Light-Up, 1960s, 11 x 12 In.	175.00
Clock, Electric, Sign, Brass Border, Square, Pam Mfg., 15 In.	148.00
Clock, Ice Cold, Neon, Octagonal, Green, Orange, Red, 18 x 18 In.	630.00
Clock, Light-Up, Aluminum, Chrome Plate, Glass Dome, Red, Green Edge, Round, 1950s, 14 In.	538.00
Clock, Light-Up, Drink Coca-Cola, Aluminum, Round, Red, Green, Florescent, 1960s, 14 In. Diam.	201.00
Cooler, Cavalier, c.1950, 41 In.	2950.00
Cooler, Drink Coca-Cola, 5 Cent, Hand Holding Bottle, Red, Coin-Operated	1008.00
Cooler, Drink Coca-Cola, Glascock, Junior, 18 x 30 In.	1888.00
Cooler, Drink Coca-Cola, Serve Yourself, Vendo Junior, Coin-Operated, 1930s-40s.......*Illus*	960.00
Cooler, Floor, Single Case, Drink Coca-Cola Ice Cold, Red, 1930s, 35 ½ In.	450.00
Cooler, Metal Frame, Tin, Embossed, c.1928	708.00
Cooler, Serve Yourself, Galvanized, Shaped Apron, Square Legs, Wheels, 1920s	1680.00
Coupon, 2 Free Glasses Of Coca-Cola, 1890s, 3 x 5 In.	4720.00
Cutout, Refreshment Worth Carrying, Girl, Shopping Basket, Frame, 1944, 67 x 31 In.	450.00
Display Rack, 6-Pack, Sign Top, Logo, Take Home A Carton, Metal	300.00
Display, Coca-Cola, Meet Your Friends Here, Boy & Girl, Cardboard, Cutout, 1944, 16 x 19 In.	1062.00
Display, Girl, Drinking Coca-Cola, Cutout, 1940, 43 x 32 ½ In.	1652.00
Display, Have A Coke, Girl At Counter, Die Cut, Cardboard, c.1946, 30 x 44 In.	900.00
Display, School Crossing Guard, Slow 15 MPH, School, Embossed Metal, Cut Out, 77 In.	1904.00
Display, Service Girl, Cardboard, Cutout, 1943, 65 x 24 In.	944.00
Door Insert, Ice Cold Drink Coca-Cola, Thermometer, Other Side Thanks, c.1940, 5 ¾ x 9 In.	1121.00
Door Pull, Drink Coca-Cola, Bottle Shaped, Aluminum, 1930s, 3 ¼ x 10 ¾ In.	288.00
Door Push, Drink Coca-Cola, Delicious & Refreshing, 5 Cents, Aluminum, 1905, 2 x 8 In.	460.00
Door Push, Ice Cold Coca-Cola In Bottles, Red & White Porcelain, Embossed	280.00
Fan, Coca-Cola Cures Headaches, Reverse Side Multicolor Birds, Seth Fowle & Sons, 1894, 12 x 8 ½ In.	5900.00
Festoon, Snow, Ice, Girl Drinking Coke, 1937, 12 In.	944.00
Glass Holder, Coca-Cola Engraved, Pewter, c.1896, 2 ¾ In.	767.00
Hat, Deliveryman's, White, Green Strips, Reads Brookfield Uniform, Mo., 1950s, Size 7	225.00
Ice Box, Hand Holding Bottle, Footed, Red & White	448.00
Ice Chest, Drink Coca-Cola In Bottles, Red Metal, Shelf, Handle, 19 x 12 In.	390.00
Ink Blotter, Chew This Coca-Cola Gum, Red, Cream, c.1915, 6 x 3 ¾ In.	660.00
Ink Blotter, Coca-Cola Chewing Gum, Best, Sanitary, Made To Chew, c.1915, 9 ½ x 4 In.	390.00
Lamp, Bottle, Acid Stain, 1930s, 20 ½ In.	2006.00
Lamp, Globe Shade, Coca-Cola, Red, White, Green Tiles, Leaded Glass, c.1920, 12 In.	59000.00
Lamp, Hanging, Frosted Globe, c.1925, 14 In.	3540.00
Lamp, Leaded Glass, Patinated Metal Base, 21 x 10 ½ x 16 In.	180.00
Lampshade, Coca-Cola, Leaded Glass, 1920s, 18 In.	4720.00
Lampshade, Leaded Glass, Scalloped Top, Red, White, Green, 1920s, 16 In. Diam.	3220.00
Logo, Driver's Hat, Brass, Script, Cutout, 1 ¼ x 4 In.	590.00
Match Striker, Red, White, c.1940, 4 ½ x 4 ½ In.	660.00
Menu Board, Drink Coca-Cola Be Really Refreshed, Metal, Glass, 19 x 37 In.	826.00
Menu Board, Logo, Bottle, Item Lines, Laminate, Wood, 1930s, 25 ¾ x 36 In.	330.00
Menu Card, Hilda Clark, Sipping Coca-Cola, 1903, 6 x 4 In.	2400.00
Mirror, 1907, Pocket, 2 ¾ x 1 ¾ In.	561.00
Mirror, Bottle At Each Side, Metal Holder, Mounting Holes, 7 x 3 In.	118.00
Mirror, Calendar Girl, Large Hat, Flowers, Celluloid, 1911, Pocket, 2 ¾ x 1 ¾ In.......*Illus*	176.00

TIP

Fasten hooks and eyes before washing vintage dresses.

Coca-Cola, Mirror, Calendar Girl, Large Hat, Flowers, Celluloid, 1911, Pocket, 2 ¾ x 1 ¾ In.
$176.00

Wm Morford Antiques

Coca-Cola, Mirror, Drink Coca-Cola, Girl Holding Glass, Celluloid, c.1908, Pocket, 2 ¾ x 1 ¾ In.
$963.00

Wm Morford Antiques

Coca-Cola, Sign, Drink Coca-Cola, Fountain Dispenser, Porcelain, 2-Sided, 1940, 25 x 26 In.
$3,192.00

Hake's Americana & Collectibles

Coca-Cola, Sign, Girl With Parasol, Bottle, Die Cut, Easel Back, Snyder & Black, 1931, 10 x 18 ⅜ In.
$1,150.00

James D. Julia Auctioneers

Coca-Cola, Sign, Girl, Carrying 6-Pack Coca-Cola & Groceries, Cardboard, Niagara Litho., 1943, 15 x 27 In.
$230.00

James D. Julia Auctioneers

Coca-Cola, Thermometer, Bottle Shape, Embossed, Tin Lithograph, c.1930s, 17 x 4 ⅞ In.
$275.00

Wm Morford Antiques

Mirror, Drink Coca-Cola, Girl Holding Glass, Celluloid, c.1908, Pocket, 2 ¾ x 1 ¾ In......*Illus*	963.00
Mirror, Girl, Beach, Drinking From Bottle, Umbrella, Oval, Pocket, 1922, Pocket, 2 ¾ In........	900.00
Painting, Barn, Drink Coca-Cola In Bottles On Side, Canvas, Frame, 39 x 49 In.	84.00
Playing Cards, Girl Sipping From Straw, Green Yellow, Complete Deck, 1928, 4 x 2 In............	600.00
Poster, Drink Coca-Cola Take Some Home Today, Girl, Dress, Paper, Frame, 1950, 32 x 21 In.	660.00
Poster, The Answer To Thirst, Coca-Cola, Girl Studying, Paper, Frame, 1945, 37 ½ x 24 In......	480.00
Seat Cushion, Drink In Bottles, Round, Strap, Canvas, c.1925, 15 x 2 In...........................	443.00
Sidewalk Sign, Enjoy Coca-Cola While We Check Your Tires, Round, Rack, Tin, Metal	672.00
Sign, 1 Billionth Gallon Of Coca-Cola Syrup, White, Red & Black, Cardboard, 1944, 11 x 14 In.....	230.00
Sign, 1908, Drink Coca-Cola In Bottles, Tin, Embossed, 12 x 36 In.	1121.00
Sign, 1942, Drink Coca-Cola, Girl, Boy, Sun, Tin, 1942, 32 x 56 In.	531.00
Sign, 5 Cents Ice Cold, Bottle, Red, Green, Raised Border, Tin, c.1936, 18 x 53 ½ In.	690.00
Sign, 50th Anniversary Coca-Cola, 1886-1936, Embossed, Red, Kay, 16 In......................	540.00
Sign, Answer To Thirst, 5 Cents Coca-Cola, Girl, Water Skiing, Cardboard, 1920s, 45 x 31 In......	4100.00
Sign, Ball Park Vendor, Cardboard, Cutout, 1926, 18 In....................................	6490.00
Sign, Bartender On Duty We Proudly Serve Coca-Cola, c.1960, 11 x 14 In........................	413.00
Sign, Blinking Coca-Cola Logo, Bulbs, Light-Up, Metal, c.1935, 5 x 18 Ft.	46200.00
Sign, Cabins, Gas & Oil, Boats & Motors, Tackle & Supplies, 2-Sided, c.1962, 30 x 54 In.	1680.00
Sign, Cap, Arrow, Drink Coca-Cola, Red, Silver, Button, 1949, 19 ½ In...........................	330.00
Sign, Cap, Coca-Cola, Bottle, Store Front, Porcelain, Button, Mountings, 36 In. Diam.	1080.00
Sign, Cap, Coca-Cola, Round, Porcelain, Button, 1950s, 48 In................ 420.00 to 510.00
Sign, Cap, Drink Coca-Cola In Bottles, Button, Tin, 1953, Tin, 12 In.........................	300.00
Sign, Cap, Drink Coca-Cola Serve Yourself, Button, Aluminum, 1950s, 16 In.....................	300.00
Sign, Cap, Logo, Porcelain, Button, 25 In.	280.00
Sign, Cap, Silver Arrow, Drink Coca-Cola, Sign Of Good Taste, Button, Tin, 1950s, 20 ½ In......	420.00
Sign, Cap, White Ground, Button, 36 In..	660.00
Sign, Chinese Script, Chinese Girl, Blue Dress, Paper, 1936, 14 x 23 In.	4130.00
Sign, Clown On Finger Balancing Coca-Cola Cap & Bottles, Cardboard, 1950s, 48 In............	1652.00
Sign, Coca-Cola Bottle, Tin, Embossed, 1932, 39 x 12 In.	1416.00
Sign, Coca-Cola Cola Ask For It Either Way, Celluloid, Round, 1940s, 9 In......................	767.00
Sign, Coca-Cola Delicious Ice Cold Drinks, Plastic Front, Tin, Light-Up, 1960s, 15 x 17 In......	2006.00
Sign, Coca-Cola, Tin, Oval, 1926, 7 ½ x 10 ½ In...	1770.00
Sign, Coke & Food Go Together, Girl, Shopping Cart, Cutout, 1956, 60 x 30 In...................	3304.00
Sign, Coke For Me Too, Young Couple, Bottle & Hotdog, Cardboard, Frame, 1945, 24 x 37 In..	531.00
Sign, Cooler, Coca-Cola Boy, Arrow Shape, c.1945, 31 In.......................................	12000.00
Sign, Counter, Drink Coca-Cola, Price Bros., Light-Up, Round, 1950s, 11 In.	1180.00
Sign, Cutout, Masonite, Man, Hat, Holding Glass, 1940s, 48 x 48 In.............................	560.00
Sign, Delicious Refreshing, 5 Cents, All Soda Fountains, Red, Green, Tin, c.1899, 17 x 25 ¾ In.	1265.00
Sign, Delicious, Refreshing, Drink Coca-Cola, 5 Cents, In Bottles, Red, Green, Tin, 1902, 13 x 9 In......	575.00
Sign, Drink Coca-Cola Highballs, Celluloid, Tin, Black, Gold Letters, String Hanger, 1921	5900.00
Sign, Drink Coca-Cola In Bottles, 5 Cents, Red, Gold, Paper, Frame, c.1918, 38 x 16 In............	330.00
Sign, Drink Coca-Cola In Bottles, 5 Cents, Red, White, Embossed, Tin, 1922, 23 x 6 In............	403.00
Sign, Drink Coca-Cola In Bottles, Red, White Letters, Porcelain, 24 x 68 In......................	224.00
Sign, Drink Coca-Cola In Bottles, Tin, Embossed, c.1910, 11 ½ x 35 ½ In.........................	4130.00
Sign, Drink Coca-Cola Refreshing, Cardboard, Paper, c.1907, 18 x 30 In..........................	1888.00
Sign, Drink Coca-Cola, Button & Arrow, Drink Coca-Cola, Tin, 1950s, 12 x 20 In.	1298.00
Sign, Drink Coca-Cola, Cardboard, Red, 1940s, 4 x 8 In...	708.00
Sign, Drink Coca-Cola, Delicious & Refreshing, Red, Porcelain, 1930s, 4 x 8 Ft..................	8850.00
Sign, Drink Coca-Cola, Dispenser, Porcelain, Red, Yellow, 1940, 25 x 26 In.....................	2360.00
Sign, Drink Coca-Cola, Fountain Dispenser, Porcelain, 2-Sided, 1940, 25 x 26 In...........*Illus*	3192.00
Sign, Drink Coca-Cola, Fountain Service, Green, Red, Yellow, Porcelain, 1950s, 12 x 28 In......	450.00
Sign, Drink Coca-Cola, Girl, Glass, Flowers, Die Cut, Cardboard, c.1933, 37 x 27 In.	644.00
Sign, Drink Coca-Cola, Ocean Waves, Girl In Pink Hat, Die Cut, c.1936, 39 x 25 In.	448.00
Sign, Drink Coca-Cola, Please Pay When Served, Glass, Light-Up, Price Bros., 7 x 10 In.	660.00
Sign, Drink Coca-Cola, Relieves Fatigue, Sold Everywhere 5 Cents, Girl, Hat, 14 x 22 In.	6900.00
Sign, Drink Coca-Cola, Stadium Girl, Red Suit, Hat, Football Game, c.1940, 30 x 50 In.	201.00
Sign, Drink Coca-Cola, Tin, Diamond Shape, 1939, 76 x 76 In...................................	3540.00
Sign, Drugstore, Drink Coca-Cola, Delicious & Refreshing, Porcelain, Frame, c.1933, 96 x 56 In..	1120.00
Sign, Enjoy Coca-Cola, Coke Adds Life To Everything Nice, Tin, 20 x 40 In.	112.00
Sign, Enjoy Coca-Cola, Golf Ball On Tee Shape, Masonite, Cutout, c.1955, 47 x 30 In.	767.00
Sign, Family Riding Bikes, Multicolor, Die Cut, Cardboard, Frame, 51 x 33 In.	476.00
Sign, Flapper, Dress, Glass, Sitting In Frame, Cardboard, Frame, 1924, 45 ¾ x 28 In..............	3600.00
Sign, For People On The Go, Drink Coca-Cola, World War II Marine, Cardboard, 1944, 16 x 27 In.....	288.00
Sign, Fountain Luncheon, Drink Coca-Cola, 2-Sided, Porcelain, Metal Frame, Scrolling, 46 x 53 In..	1080.00
Sign, Fountain Service, Drink Coca-Cola, Shield Shape, Porcelain, 1938, 14 x 27 In...............	1080.00

Sign, Girl With Parasol, Bottle, Die Cut, Easel Back, Snyder & Black, 1931, 10 x 18 ⅜ In.... *Illus* 1150.00
Sign, Girl, Carrying 6-Pack Coca-Cola & Groceries, Cardboard, Niagara Litho., 1943, 15 x 27 In. *Illus* 230.00
Sign, Girl, Holding Bottle, Barbeque, Picnic Items, House, Paper, Frame, 1955, 28 x 20 In. 330.00
Sign, Go Refreshed Coca-Cola, Winged Hand, Bottle, Stamped Cardboard, Round, 1941, 8 ½ In.. 2478.00
Sign, Hanger, Drink Coca-Cola, Black, Celluloid, Round, 1902, 6 In. 9440.00
Sign, Hanger, Drink Coca-Cola, Delicious Beverage, Turtle, Red, Green, Tin, 1920s, 20 x 15 In.. 1150.00
Sign, Hanger, Drink Coca-Cola, Drugstore, 2-Sided, Porcelain, c.1935, 63 x 42 In. 1920.00
Sign, Hanger, Girl, Striped Dress, Offering Coca-Cola, Tin, 8 x 11 In. 1652.00
Sign, Hanger, Refreshing, Wood, Applied Lettering, 1940s, 8 x 24 In. 144.00
Sign, Hanger, String, Coca-Cola, Hand Holding Bottle, Cardboard, Cutout, 1926, 12 x 16 In. .. 2006.00
Sign, Have A Coke, Bottle, Sea Of Icebergs, Cardboard, Frame, 1944, 39 x 24 ½ In. 472.00
Sign, Have A Coke, Hand, Coming From Water, Easel Back, Cardboard, 1950, 24 In. 330.00
Sign, Home Refreshment, Blond Girl, Bottle, Tulips, Cardboard, Frame, 1950s, 37 x 24 In. 345.00
Sign, I Am Heading For Coca-Cola, Stewardess Leaving Plane, Paper, 1942, 27 x 6 In. 510.00
Sign, Ice Cold Coca-Cola Sold Here, Tin, Embossed, Round, 1932, 19 ½ In. 1770.00
Sign, Ice Cold Coca-Cola, Cup, Tin, 1960s, 28 x 20 In. 708.00
Sign, Ice Cold, Sign Of Good Taste, Bottle, Fishtail Design, Tin, Frame, 54 x 18 In. 316.00
Sign, June Collyer At Home, Keep It In Your Home, Cutout, Cardboard, Frame, 1932, 22 x 18 In.. 1140.00
Sign, Man, Towel, Girl, White Bathing Suit, Cardboard, Frame, 1934, 56 ¾ x 35 ½ In. 1200.00
Sign, Pause & Refresh, Drink Coca-Cola, Serve Yourself, Waterfall, Countertop, Light-Up, 19 x 9 In... 460.00
Sign, Pause, Go Refreshed, Celluloid, Round, 1942, 9 In. 2478.00
Sign, Play Refreshed Name The Game, Cardboard, 1958, 29 x 50 In. 443.00
Sign, Play Refreshed, Carousel Ride, Blond Girl Seated On Horse, c.1948, 30 x 50 In. 540.00
Sign, Refresh Yourself Drink Coca-Cola, Light-Up, Glow, Hanover Neon Co., c.1960, 10 x 17 In. 2006.00
Sign, Refreshment Right Out Of A Bottle, Girl, Bottle, Roller Skates, Cardboard, 1941, 16 x 27 In.. 885.00
Sign, Relieves Fatigue, Drink Coca-Cola, Man, Straw Hat, 1907, 11 x 21 In. 3068.00
Sign, Sandwiches, Drink Coca-Cola, Delicious & Refreshing, Green, Red, Porcelain, 1930s, 45 x 60 In.. 780.00
Sign, Santa Claus, Playing With Train, Helicopter, Coca-Cola In Hand, Cardboard, 1960s, 48 In. .. 660.00
Sign, Serve Coca-Cola Sign Of Good Taste, Black Family, Cardboard, 1950s, 20 x 36 In. 885.00
Sign, Serve Ice Cold, 6-Pack, Arctic Water King, Easel Back, Cardboard, 1953, 21 ½ In. 210.00
Sign, Sidewalk, Drink Coca-Cola, Chalkboard, Tin, Metal Frame, Bottle, 21 x 33 In. 230.00
Sign, Slow, Children, Drink Coca-Cola In Bottles, School Crossing, 1950s, 21 x 36 In............. 944.00
Sign, Starburst Lighted Motion, 1960s, 16 ½ x 14 In. 210.00
Sign, Startup's Coca-Cola Chocolates, Cardboard, 1908, 7 x 11 In. 944.00
Sign, Sundblom Girl & Horse, Cardboard, 1937, 32 x 49 In. 2006.00
Sign, Take Home A Carton, 6-Pack, Tin, Frame, 20 x 29 In. 308.00
Sign, Take Home A Carton, Tin Rack, Round, c.1942, 13 In. 590.00
Sign, Take Home The New Home Case, Masonite, c.1945, 18 x 48 In............................. 1416.00
Sign, Talk About Refreshing, 2 Girls At Beach, Cardboard, c.1943, 34 x 63 In................... 360.00
Sign, Thirst Asks Nothing More, Man, Woman, Dispenser, Cardboard, Frame, 1940, 33 x 21 In. 720.00
Sign, Triangular, Ice Cold, Porcelain, 2-Sided, 1934, 22 x 24 In. 18880.00
Sign, Trolley, Delicious & Refreshing, 5 Cents At Fountains, In Bottles, Cardboard, 21 x 11 In. .. 2128.00
Sign, Truck Cab, Drink Coca-Cola Ice Cold, Porcelain, c.1945, 9 ¾ x 51 In. 649.00
Sign, Wall, Bottle, Tin, Paint, Neon, 1950s, 72 x 21 In. 3835.00
Sign, Yes!, Girl, Handed A Bottle, Green, Yellow, Red, Frame, 1944, 62 x 34 In. 460.00
Sofa, Cooler Couch, Drink Coca-Cola, Square Shape, Arms, Red Vinyl, 1950s 900.00
Stamp Holder, Compliments Of Coca-Cola Co., Celluloid, 1902, 1 ½ x 2 ½ In. 502.00
Stand, Music, Folding, c.1963, 24 x 25 In. 590.00
Syrup Bottle, Wreath, Drink Coca-Cola, Glass, Metal Cap, c.1910, 12 ½ x 3 ¼ In. 358.00
Syrup Dispenser, Knop Top, 8-Sides, Metal, Red Paint, 20 In. 1140.00
Thermometer, Bottle Shape, Embossed, Tin Lithograph, c.1930s, 17 x 4 ⅞ In................*Illus* 275.00
Thermometer, Drink Coca-Cola, Metal, Red, White, Oval, 1950s, 29 x 8 In. 330.00
Thermometer, Things Go Better With Coke, Round, 1960s, 18 In. 531.00
Tip Tray, 1907, Relieves Fatigue, Drink Coca-Cola, Girl, Holding Glass, Oval, 6 In................ 1062.00
Tip Tray, 1914, Betty, Lace Bonnet, Drink Coca-Cola Delicious & Refreshing, Oval, 6 In. 767.00
Topper, Carton, Image Of Eddie Fisher Smiling, Now On Radio, 1954, 20 x 12 In. 475.00
Toy, Airplane, Spirit Of St. Louis, Envelope, Frame, 1928, 10 In. 1121.00
Toy, Stove, Drink Coca-Cola, Metal, Paint, Cord, c.1932, 8 ¾ x 8 ½ In........................... 1416.00
Toy, Truck, Cast Resin, Wood, Smith Miller, 1980s, 10 ½ x 24 ½ In.............................. 649.00
Toy, Truck, Red, Yellow, Steel, Marx Canada, 20 In.. 502.00
Toy, Truck, Wood, Buddy L, 1948, 19 In... 1534.00
Tray, 1901, Girl, With Roses, Round, 5 ⅝ In. 7670.00
Tray, 1904, Lillian Nordica, With Bottle, 13 x 10 In.................................*Illus* 1320.00
Tray, 1908, Topless, Where Ginger Ale Seltzer Or Soda Is Good, Tin, 12 In............*Illus* 2420.00
Tray, 1916, Elaine, Basket Of Flowers, 19 x 8 ½ In. 295.00

TIP
Coca-Cola will remove stains from glazed china.

C

Coca-Cola, Tray, 1904, Lillian Nordica, With Bottle, 13 x 10 In.
$1,320.00

Victorian Casino Antiques

Coca-Cola, Tray, 1908, Topless, Where Ginger Ale Seltzer Or Soda Is Good, Tin, Western Coca-Cola Bottling, 12 In.
$2,420.00

Showtime Auction Services

Coca-Cola, Tray, 1928, Soda Jerk, White Uniform, Red Rim, 13 ¼ x 10 ½ In.
$259.00

James D. Julia Auctioneers

The edited listings of the current prices in this *Kovels' Antiques & Collectibles Price Guide* aren't available on any website. Readers can visit **Kovels.com** to check thousands of past prices and sign up for free information on trends, tips, reproductions, marks, and more.

Coffee Mill, Elgin National, 2 Wheels, Cast Iron, Woodruff & Edwards Co. $450.00

Victorian Casino Antiques

Coffee Mill, Enterprise, Iron, Decals, 28 x 17 x 19 In. $420.00

DuMouchelles Art Gallery

Coffee Mill, Fairbanks Morse & Co., Model 15, 2 Wheels, Cast Iron, Floor $1,096.00

Victorian Casino Antiques

TIP
Never bid at an auction if you have not previewed the items.

Tray, 1925, Party Girl, Holding Glass, Turban, Fur Drape, Pink Dress, 13 x 10 ½ In.	300.00
Tray, 1927, Car Hop At Drive-In, Curb Service, 10 x 13 In.	200.00
Tray, 1928, Soda Jerk, White Uniform, Red Rim, 13 ¼ x 10 ½ In. ....*Illus*	259.00
Tray, 1929, Girl, Yellow Bathing Suit, Towel, Seated, Class, 13 x 10 ½ In.	210.00
Tray, 1930, Telephone Girl, Red, Black, Yellow, 10 ½ x 13 ¼ In.	173.00
Tray, 1934, Tarzan, Johnny Weissmuller & Maureen O'Sullivan, 10 ½ x 13 In.	2714.00
Tray, 1938, Girl In Yellow Hat, 13 ¼ x 10 ½ In.	173.00 to 354.00
Truck, Delivery, Bronze, Mounted On Wood Base, Award, 16 In.	115.00
Truck, Goso, Metal, Key Wind, 1949, 8 In.	1534.00
Vending Machine, Drink Coca-Cola In Bottles, 1950s, 64 x 33 In.	826.00
Vending Machine, Drink Coca-Cola, Vendorlator 27, Mailbox Shape, c.1948	1440.00
Vending Machine, Here's The Real Thing, Enjoy Coke, 5 Cent, Red, Round Top, 54 x 28 In.	1400.00
Vending Machine, Red, White Lettering, Front Bottle Opener, 10 Cent, Vendo Model F39B5, 1940s	1560.00
Vending Machine, Vendo, Model 44, Drink Coca-Cola, 5 Cent, Red, White, c.1956	3360.00
Vending Machine, Vendo, Red, Drink, Logo, Hand Holding Bottle, 10 Cent, Key	2688.00
Watch Fob, Brass, Bottle, 5 Cents, Raised	45.00
Watch Fob, Drink Coca-Cola In Bottles, 1912, 1 ½ In.	5605.00
Window Trim, Man, Girl, Flowers, Branches, Paper, c.1917, 34 x 14 In., Pair	15340.00

COFFEE MILLS are also called coffee grinders, although there is a difference in the way each grinds the coffee. Large floor-standing or counter-model coffee mills were used in the nineteenth-century country store. Small home mills were first made about 1894. They lost favor by the 1930s. The renewed interest in fresh-ground coffee has produced many modern electric mills and hand mills and grinders. Reproductions of the old styles are being made.

American Duplex Electric Coffee Cutter, Louisville, Kentucky, Pot Shape	1456.00
Elgin National, 2 Wheels, Cast Iron, Woodruff & Edwards Co. ....*Illus*	450.00
Enterprise, 2 Wheels, Cast Iron, Red Paint, c.1845, 12 In.	889.00
Enterprise, 2 Wheels, Painted Red, Cast Iron, Drawer, Pat. July 12 1898, 16 In.	300.00
Enterprise, 2 Wheels, Red Paint, Drawer, c.1900, 15 In.	288.00
Enterprise, 2 Wheels, Red Paint, Wood Drawer, Eagle Finial, 1898, 23 In.	390.00
Enterprise, 2 Wheels, Red, Cast Iron, 1800s, 15 In.	533.00
Enterprise, Iron, Decals, 28 x 17 x 19 In. ....*Illus*	420.00
Enterprise, No. 2, 2 Wheels, Cast Iron, Painted Red, Gold Trim, Drawer, 12 In.	2240.00
Enterprise, No. 2, 2 Wheels, Cast Iron, Painted, Red, Blue, Drawer, Countertop	325.00
Enterprise, No. 3, 2 Wheels, Cast Iron, Painted Red, Wood Base, Drawer	575.00
Enterprise, No. 4, 2 Wheels, 12 ½ In.	237.00
Enterprise, No. 8, 2 Wheels, Drawer, Cast Iron, 15 ½ In.	132.00
Enterprise, No. 212, Cast Iron, Painted, 2 Wheels, 44 In.	638.00
Enterprise, No. 218, Cast Iron, Brass, 81 In.	567.00
Enterprise, Painted Red, Stencils, Drawer, 12 ½ x 10 ¼ In.	690.00
Fairbanks Morse & Co., Model 15, 2 Wheels, Cast Iron, Floor ....*Illus*	1096.00
Hobart, Model 2040, Commercial Size For Store, 1920s	224.00
Landers, Frary & Clark, 2 Wheels, Painted Red, Wood Base	330.00
Landers, Frary & Co., Cast Iron, 2 Wheels, Red	411.00
Lane Bros., Swift Mill, No. 13, Iron, Paint, Compass Design Wheel Spokes, 18 x 11 ¾ In. ...*Illus*	413.00
Mr. Dudley International, 1 Wheel, Cast Iron, Wood Base, Drawer, 12 In.	176.00
Star, No. 10, 2 Wheels, Cast Iron, Aluminum Bean Hopper, Philadelphia, 15 x 15 In.	207.00
Wood, Iron & Tin, Image Of Teddy Roosevelt, Bronson Co., 1930s, 10 ½ In.	205.00

COIN-OPERATED MACHINES of all types are collected. The vending machine is an ancient invention dating back to 200 B.C., when holy water was dispensed in a coin-operated vase. Smokers in seventeenth-century England could buy tobacco from a coin-operated box. It was not until after the Civil War that the technology made modern coin-operated games and vending machines plentiful. Slot machines, arcade games, and dispensers are all collected.

Arcade, English Execution, Trap Door Opens, Man Is Hung, Mahogany Case, 1928, 30 x 75 In.	9196.00
Arcade, Game, Pinball, World's Fair, Jigsaw, 5 Cent, Rock-Ola Mfg., 1933	2400.00
Arcade, Iron Claw, 5 Cent, Digger Machine, Wood, Carved Crest, Square Feet, c.1930	2400.00
Arcade, Match Maker, Who's Your Perfect Mate, 25 Cent, Light-Up	280.00
Arcade, Pinball, Spit Fire, 5 Cent, Genco, c.1935	3000.00
Arcade, Questions & Answers, Watling, Have You Gained Or Lost Weight?, Mirrors	1110.00
Arcade, Rock-Ola, Five Jacks, 1 Cent, Silver, Orange, Wood Base, c.1930, 16 x 20 In.	2185.00
Arcade, Skipper, Puppet, Peppy The Clown, Token Play, Blue, Glass, 26 x 72 In.	448.00
Arcade, Strength Tester, Grip, 1 Cent, Red, 14 In.	360.00
Arcade, Strength Tester, Tropic, 5 Cent, Monkey Climbs Palm Tree, Squeeze Handle, Key	1150.00

Arcade, Target, 1 Cent, Embossed Indians, Silver Finish, Wood Panel, Key, 16 x 11 In. .....*Illus*	472.00
Arcade, Test Your Love, Measure Sex Appeal, 10 Cent, Squeeze Handle, Floor Model	1140.00
Arcade, View Machine, Flip Card, Buxom Babes Of Barbary Coast, 5 Cent, c.1905, 20 x 48 In.	2040.00
Arcade, View Machine, Hootchie Cootchie, 5 Cent, Gypsy Oak, Iron, Music, 10 x 17 In............	7920.00
Dispenser, Scup, Matches, 1 Cent, Cast Iron, Japanned, Cigar Cutter, 14 x 5 ¾ In. ....*Illus*	1180.00
Fortune Teller, Crystal Gazer, 10 Cent, Red, Blue, Counter, c.1929	560.00
Fortune Teller, Position Hand, Carmen Will Do The Rest Talks, Compuvend, 15 In.	168.00
Fortune Teller, Prophecy Of The Pharaoh, Crystal Ball, 1 Dollar, American Sammy.............	3000.00
Fortune Teller, Wizard, Mills, Wood Case, Cast Metal Front, 19 In..	1815.00
Fortune Teller, Wizard's Pen, 5 Cent, Palm Reading, Wood, Yellow, Key, 20 x 69 In.	3080.00
Gambling, Barnyard Golf Poker, 1 Cent, Farmer Playing Golf, Wood Cabinet, Metal Front, 17 ½ In..	1815.00
Gambling, Bones, 5 Cent, Red, Black, Wood Base, Buckley, 15 x 13 In...	2300.00
Gambling, Horse Race, Pace's Races, Wood, Glass Side Panel, Pace, c.1934	14560.00
Gambling, Wheel, Stick Match Holder, Wine & Grape Harvest, Brass, Iron, France................	1560.00
Graphophone, Cylinder, Oak, Curved Glass Case, Horn, The Eagle, c.1897, 15 x 12 In.	4800.00
Gumball, Basketball Hoop, Metal, Glass, 1 Cent, 13 x 9 x 6 In..	468.00
Gumball, Penny, Columbus, Red Metal Base, Restored, 15 ½ In..	300.00
Music Box, Automated Dancers, Walnut Case, Turned Columns & Feet, Cylinder, 8 Tunes, 32 x 25 In.	5750.00
Music Box, Walnut Case, Carved, Double Comb, 19 Discs, Komet, 55 x 30 In. ....*Illus*	4600.00
Music, Graphophone, 5 Cent, Marquee, Horn, Cylinder, Wood, Glass, Metal	3360.00
Mutoscope, Doctor's Office, Clam Shell Lion Design, Castle Park, 18 ½ x 76 x 20 In.......*Illus*	6000.00
Mutoscope, Flip Card Movie, Cast Iron, Crank, c.1900...	12650.00
Mutoscope, Hoochie Coochie Dancer, Flip Card, Reel	784.00
Mutoscope, Hoot Gibson Movie Cowboy, 5 Cent, Crank Handle, Steel, Iron, Cobalt Blue, Red, 52 In...	1298.00
Napkin Holder, Answer Box, 1 Cent, Chrome, Key, 1950s, 7 x 9 In...	300.00
Ragtime Band Organ, 25 Cent, Oak, Beveled & Leaded Glass, 8 Instruments........................	5100.00
Ride, Tooner Ville Trolley, 10 Cent, Li'l Abner, Daisy Mae, Pops, Keys, 1950s ....*Illus*	767.00
Scale, Cast Iron, Porcelain Face, Correct Weight, 1 Cent, National Automatic Weighing Machine, 1900	2300.00
Scale, Weighing, Caille Bros. Peerless, 1 Cent, Porcelain, Cast Iron, Keys, Floor..............*Illus*	1725.00
Scale, Weighing, Exact Weight, 1 Cent, Cast Iron, Green, E.A. Burkhart, Reading, Penn., 72 In.	1920.00
Scale, Weighing, Mint Green Color, Floor Model, O.D. Jennings..	280.00
Skill, Alcohol Meter, Are You A Safe Driver, 5 Cent	720.00
Skill, Basketball, Junior Basket Ball, Flip Ball, Peo. Mfg. Co., c.1949	7840.00
Skill, Basketball, Vest Pocket, 1 Cent, Flip Ball, c.1929, 9 x 16 In.	952.00
Skill, Bat-A-Penny, 1 Cent, Baseball, Light-Up, Cast Iron, Red, c.1926, 13 x 16 In.	2016.00
Skill, Boxing, Deliver The Punch, Punch Bag, Wood, Cast Iron, Mills, 1903, 79 In....................	6440.00
Skill, Challenger, Pistol Target, 1 Cent, A.B.T. Mfg. Co., c.1946...	364.00
Skill, Crane, Engineer Operator, 10 Cent, Williams, c.1955...	1206.00
Skill, Golf Ball Putter, Aristocrat, 5 Cent, Mills, c.1931...	1918.00
Skill, Ice Hockey, Goalie, 2 Players, Wood, Chicago Coins, c.1945...	11200.00
Skill, Lucky Coin Tosser, 1 Cent, Penny Flip, c.1934, 6 x 13 In.	1120.00
Skill, Lung Strength, Caille Hygiene Exercises, Blow Hose, Marble Stand, 72 In.........................	3920.00
Skill, Play Football, 10 Cent, Mechanical Players, Carved Crest, Block Feet, c.1924, 46 x 70 In..	3080.00
Skill, Play Football, Wood, Miniature Players, Chester-Pollard, c.1924...	1320.00
Skill, Play Hi-Li, Spanish, Wood & Glass Case, Turned Legs, Carved Crest, c.1932, 26 x 30 In..	3562.00
Skill, Real Ten Pin, Bowling, 1 Cent, Gumball, Wood, 8 x 21 In..	1456.00
Skill, Skipper, 5 Cent, Pinball Style, Wood Case, c.1933, 19 x 11 x 6 In..	1080.00
Skill, Strength, Try Your Grip, Oak, Squeeze Handle, Gatter Novelty Co., c.1925.........................	3738.00
Skill, Target Practice, Mills, 1 Cent, Key, 12 x 18 In..	3575.00
Skill, Target, Big Game Hunter, 1 Cent, A.B.T., Key, 10 ½ x 18 In..	1650.00
Skill, Test Your Blow, 1 Cent, Wall Mount, Punch Machine, Cast Iron, c.1939	2040.00
Slot, 5 Cent, Jennings Club Chief, c.1920, 27 x 16 In..	1121.00
Slot, 10 Cent, Jennings Standard Chief, c.1920, 27 x 17 In.	767.00
Slot, Baseball, 3-Reel, 5 Cent, Key, Mills Novelty Co...*Illus*	4950.00
Slot, Brownie Jackpot, 5 Cent, Wheel, Counter, c.1918, 19 x 29 In.	8400.00
Slot, Caille Big Six, 5 Cent, Upright, Music & Keys ....*Illus*	29900.00
Slot, Cherry Bell, 3-Reel, Jackpot, Wood Case, Metal Front, Mills Chicago, 1937......................	1186.00
Slot, Club Chief, 25 Cent, Chinese Front, On Stand, Jennings, 61 In.	2400.00
Slot, Dictator, 5 Cent, Black, Silver, Key, Caille Bros., c.1934...	1680.00
Slot, Golden Nugget, 5 Cent, Sun Chief, Light-Up, Red, Blue, c.1947	2520.00
Slot, Hi-Top Bandit, 25 Cent, 1-Arm Cowboy, Figural, Round Base, c.1952	3000.00
Slot, Little Duke, 3-Reel, 1 Cent, Aluminum, Multicolor, Oak Cabinet, Jennings, 22 x 17 In....	2013.00
Slot, Little Duke, Art Deco Case, Aluminum, Tin Litho, O.D. Jennings Co., Chicago, 1931........	1227.00
Slot, Mills Novelty, Elk, Poker Hand Reel, 5 Cent, Keys, c.1906...	4760.00
Slot, Mills, Black Cherry, Red Cherries, 5 Cent, Aluminum, c.1938, 16 x 23 In.	575.00
Slot, Mills, Brownie, 5 Cent, Oak, Nickel Plated Iron, Token Payout, 21 x 29 x 11 In........*Illus*	9775.00

C

Coffee Mill, Lane Bros., Swift Mill, No. 13, Iron, Paint, Compass Design Wheel Spokes, 18 x 11 ¾ In. $413.00

Conestoga Auction Co., Inc.

Coin-Operated Machine, Arcade, Target, 1 Cent, Embossed Indians, Silver Finish, Wood Panel, Key, 16 x 11 In. $472.00

Bertoia Auctions

Coin-Operated Machine, Dispenser, Scup, Matches, 1 Cent, Cast Iron, Japanned, Cigar Cutter, 14 x 5 ¾ In. $1,180.00

Conestoga Auction Co., Inc.

COIN-OPERATED MACHINE

Coin-Operated Machine, Music Box, Walnut Case, Carved, Double Comb, 19 Discs, Komet, 55 x 30 In.
$4,600.00

James D. Julia Auctioneers

Coin-Operated Machine, Mutoscope, Doctor's Office, Clam Shell Lion Design, Castle Park, 18 ½ x 76 x 20 In.
$6,000.00

Showtime Auction Services

Coin-Operated Machine, Ride, Tooner Ville Trolley, 10 Cent, Li'l Abner, Daisy Mae, Pops, Keys, 1950s
$767.00

Victorian Casino Antiques

Coin-Operated Machine, Scale, Weighing, Caille Bros. Peerless, 1 Cent, Porcelain, Cast Iron, Keys, Floor
$1,725.00

Victorian Casino Antiques

Coin-Operated Machine, Slot, Baseball, 3-Reel, 5 Cent, Key, Mills Novelty Co.
$4,950.00

Showtime Auction Services

Coin-Operated Machine, Slot, Caille Big Six, 5 Cent, Upright, Music & Keys
$29,900.00

Victorian Casino Antiques

Coin-Operated Machine, Slot, Mills, Brownie, 5 Cent, Oak, Nickel Plated Iron, Token Payout, 21 x 29 x 11 In.
$9,775.00

James D. Julia Auctioneers

Coin-Operated Machine, Slot, Mills, Little Six, 5 Cent, Single Wheel, Oak, Keys, Counter, 30 x 19 In.
$6,720.00

Victorian Casino Antiques

Coin-Operated Machine, Slot, Novelty, Cherry, 5 Cent, Half-Top, Key, Mills, c.1939
$1,120.00

Victorian Casino Antiques

Slot, Mills, Bursting Cherry Diamond Bell, Cash Box, 10 Cent, 26 In.	1020.00
Slot, Mills, Castle Front, 5 Cent, Blue, 26 In.	1200.00
Slot, Mills, Castle Front, Jackpot, 5 Cent, Blue Panel, Key, c.1937	896.00
Slot, Mills, Diamond Front, 10 Cent, Gray, 26 In.	960.00
Slot, Mills, Hi-Top, Bonus, 10 Cent, 3-Reel, Table Top, Pull Lever, c.1952	1120.00
Slot, Mills, Hi-Top, Golden Nugget, 25 Cent, Yellow, Black, Knob Handle, c.1955	1456.00
Slot, Mills, Judge, 5 Cent, Wood, Silver, Paper Wheel, Crank Handle, c.1899, 63 In.	6000.00
Slot, Mills, Little Six, 5 Cent, Single Wheel, Oak, Keys, Counter, 30 x 19 In. ....*Illus*	6720.00
Slot, Mills, Melon Bell, 25 Cent, Wood Case, 25 ½ In.	1200.00
Slot, Mills, Oak Case, Countertop, Square Box, Dome Cover, 5 Card Dials, 11 x 11 In.	885.00
Slot, Mills, Poinsettia, 5 Cent, c.1929	364.00
Slot, Mills, Poinsettia, 25 Cent, Aluminum, Flowers, Wood Sides, 24 In.	863.00
Slot, Mills, Silent F.O.K., 5 Cent, 1931, 16 x 27 In.	1017.00
Slot, Novelty, Cherry, 5 Cent, Half-Top, Key, Mills, c.1939 ....*Illus*	1120.00
Slot, Rol-A-Top, 1 Cent, Twin Jackpot, Front Coin Slot, Coin Design, Square Base, Yellow, c.1936...	5040.00
Slot, Rol-A-Top, 5 Cent, Jackpot, Front Hand Load, Yellow, Eagle, c.1935	3640.00
Slot, Stand, Wood, Lead Glass, Aluminum Feet, 33 ½ In.	240.00
Slot, Superior, 4-Reel, 25 Cent, Callie, 24 ½ In.	1920.00
Slot, Thunderbird Hotel, 25 Cent, Sun Chief, Light-Up, Keys, c.1949	3920.00
Slot, Tic-Tac-Toe, 25 Cent, Light-Up, Red, O.D. Jennings, c.1961, Keys	2520.00
Slot, Twenty-One, 5-Reel, Wood Cabinet, Key, 13 x 11 ½ In.	540.00
Slot, Victory, 5 Cent, Cast Iron, Scrolls, Caille, c.1925	5754.00
Slot, Watling, Baseball, 5 Cent, 3-Reel, Blue Seal, Key	6000.00
Slot, Watling, Rol-A-Top, 5 Cent, Coin Front, Twin Jackpot, c.1935	3300.00
Slot, Watling, Rol-A-Top, 25 Cent, Cash Box, 26 ½ In.	2400.00
Slot, Wheel, Horseshoe & Playing Cards, 5 Cent, D.N. Schall Co., c.1898, 16 x 22 In.	3024.00
Stereo Viewer, Mills, 5 Cent, Wood Cabinet, Owl Head Side Handles, 49 x 17 In.	3933.00
Stereoscope, Mills, 1 Cent, Flip Card View, Bow Front, Oak, Iron, Crank, c.1905	5100.00
Trade Stimulator, 1 Cent, Gumball, Cigarette, 3-Reel, Silver, Square Base, Groetchen, Keys ..	570.00
Trade Stimulator, 21 Vendor, Gumball, 5-Reel, Key, Groetchen Tool & Mfg. Co., c.1932 .*Illus*	1680.00
Trade Stimulator, Admiral Dewey, 1 Cent, Pinfield, Oak, Jonas D. Bell & Co., 20 x 10 In.*Illus*	3240.00
Trade Stimulator, American Eagle, 1 Cent, Fruit, 3-Reel, Daval Mfg., c.1940	224.00
Trade Stimulator, Bar Boy, Garden City Novelty, 3-Reel, Key, c.1936	1560.00
Trade Stimulator, Bartender, 1 Cent, 3-Reel, Gumball, Groetchen	633.00
Trade Stimulator, Bell Slide, Gumball, 5-Reel, Key, Daval Mfg. Co., c.1938.....................*Illus*	1440.00
Trade Stimulator, Bicycle, 5 Cent, Cigar Payout, Sun Manufacturing, 20 x 13 In...........*Illus*	9200.00
Trade Stimulator, Bicycle, Wood Cabinet, Sun Manufacturing, c.1895, 17 ½ x 13 In.	6650.00
Trade Stimulator, Board Of Craps, Gum Machine, 5 Cent, Spin Dice, c.1907, 18 x 17 In.	1206.00
Trade Stimulator, Boomer, 5 Cent, Wheel, Inlaid Wood Case, Round, Footed, c.1897, 13 x 13 In.	1008.00
Trade Stimulator, Centasmoke, Cigarette, 3-Reel, c.1935	1041.00
Trade Stimulator, Chicago Club-House, Poker Hand, 5-Reel, Daval Mfg., c.1933	896.00
Trade Stimulator, Cigar, 5 Cent, Cast, Oak Cabinet, Caille, 12 ½ x 23 In.	4125.00
Trade Stimulator, Cigarette, 1 Cent, Groetchen, Woman Blowing Kiss, Deluxe Mercury, c.1940..	288.00
Trade Stimulator, Crystal Gazer Tells Your Fortune, 1 Cent, Spin Dice, Electric, 8-Sided	896.00
Trade Stimulator, Elk, Cigar & Fortune, Reel, Cast Iron Case, c.1904, 14 x 17 In.	2128.00
Trade Stimulator, Fairest Wheel No. 2, 5 Cent, Decatur, 1900s.....................*Illus*	863.00
Trade Stimulator, Favorite, Horse Race Theme, Aluminum, Penny Drop, Jennings, 20 x 14 In...	2300.00
Trade Stimulator, Foot Ease, Vitalizer, 10 Cent, Exhibit Supply, Chicago, c.1941.............*Illus*	420.00
Trade Stimulator, Gum Ball, 1 Cent, Metal, Key, 11 x 12 ½ In.	825.00
Trade Stimulator, Gyroscore, Pinball, 1 Cent, 8 x 14 In.	3575.00
Trade Stimulator, Hol-E-Smokes, Cigarette, Gumball, 3-Reel, 1 Cent, c.1931, 9 x 11 In.	767.00
Trade Stimulator, Honest John, 1 Cent, Skill, Falling Gumball, c.1929, 12 x 17 In.	2466.00
Trade Stimulator, Improved Roulette, 5 Cent, Cigar, Oak Case, c.1894, 11 x 11 In.	3738.00
Trade Stimulator, Jumping Jack, Spin Dice, Gumball, Blue, c.1933	1035.00
Trade Stimulator, King Six Jr., 5 Cent, Dice Spin, Wood Case, c.1938, 12 x 17 x 10 In.	690.00
Trade Stimulator, La Comete, Single Reel, Cast Iron, Mills Novelty, c.1906	2880.00
Trade Stimulator, Magic Clock, Gumball, Wood Case, Eclipse Design, c.1933, 12 x 14 In.	448.00
Trade Stimulator, Make Penny Wiggle, Double Or Triple Your Candy Money, 1 Cent, Keys.....	270.00
Trade Stimulator, Marvel, 1 Cent, Cigarette, Red Knob, 3-Reel, Daval Mfg., Key, c.1940	360.00
Trade Stimulator, Official Sweepstakes, Horse Race, Gumball, c.1928	2875.00
Trade Stimulator, On The Level, Dice Spinner, Key, Chas. Faye, 10 x 13 In. ....*Illus*	4400.00
Trade Stimulator, Penny Pack Cigarette, 1 Cent, 3-Reel, Gumball, Swivel Base, c.1936	780.00
Trade Stimulator, Penny Smoke Cigar, 1 Cent, 3-Reel, Groetchen Tool Co.	900.00
Trade Stimulator, Poker Hand, Flip Card, 5-Reel, Cast Iron, Mills Commercial, 1904	4200.00
Trade Stimulator, Poker, 5 Cent, 5-Reel, Iron, Oak, Caille Bros., Key, 12 ½ x 23 In.	4125.00
Trade Stimulator, Poker, Cigar, 1 Cent, 5-Reel, No. 6, Key, Mills Novelty Co., c.1905.......*Illus*	4370.00
Trade Stimulator, Ring His Bell, Hitler, 1 Cent, Pin Field, Keys	1560.00

Coin-Operated Machine, Trade Stimulator, 21 Vendor, Gumball, 5 Reel, Key, Groetchen Tool & Mfg. Co., c.1932
$1,680.00

Victorian Casino Antiques

Coin-Operated Machine, Trade Stimulator, Admiral Dewey, 1 Cent, Pinfield, Oak, Jonas D. Bell & Co., 20 x 10 In.
$3,240.00

Victorian Casino Antiques

Coin-Operated Machine, Trade Stimulator, Bell Slide, Gumball, 5 Reel, Key, Daval Mfg. Co., c.1938
$1,440.00

Victorian Casino Antiques

Coin-Operated Machine, Trade Stimulator, Bicycle, 5 Cent, Cigar Payout, Sun Manufacturing, 20 x 13 In.
$9,200.00

James D. Julia Auctioneers

Coin-Operated Machine, Trade Stimulator, Fairest Wheel No. 2, 5 Cent, Decatur, 1900s
$863.00

Victorian Casino Antiques

Coin-Operated Machine, Trade Stimulator, Foot Ease, Vitalizer, 10 Cent, Chicago, c.1941
$420.00

Victorian Casino Antiques

Coin-Operated Machine, Trade Stimulator, On The Level, Dice Spinner, Key, Chas. Faye, 10 x 13 In.
$4,400.00

Showtime Auction Services

Trade Stimulator, Rock-Ola, Horse Race, 1 Cent, Wheel, Wood Case, c.1933, 15 x 12 In.	5400.00
Trade Stimulator, Skipper, Penny Drop, Countertop, 1940s, 6 ¾ x 14 x 15 ½ In.	459.00
Trade Stimulator, Smiling Joe, 1 Cent, Skill, Flip Ball, Gumball, c.1925	1232.00
Trade Stimulator, Smoke Reels, 1 Cent, Cigarette, Wood, Metal Swivel Base, c.1938, 10 x 12 In.	356.00
Trade Stimulator, Star, Red Star, Cast Iron, Pearsall & Findbeine, 1898	14300.00
Trade Stimulator, Steeple Chase, 1 Cent, Spinning Horse Skill, c.1933, 7 x 14 In.	3617.00
Trade Stimulator, Target Practice, 1 Cent, Aluminum, Ad-Lee Novelty Co., c.1928	420.00
Trade Stimulator, Target, 1 Cent, Coin Drop, Skill, Indians, Bow & Arrow, c.1926, 12 x 17 In.	600.00
Trade Stimulator, Triograph, 5 Cent, Cigar, Peep Show, Oak Case, Clockwork, c.1889	16800.00
Trade Stimulator, Triple Roll, 5, 10, 25 Cent, Roulette Style, 6 Slots, Cast Iron, c.1914, 10 x 13 In.	6160.00
Trade Stimulator, Whiz Ball, 1 Cent, Wood Base, Pace Mfg. Co., c.1931	720.00
Vending, 7Up, 10 Cent, Vendorlator VMC, 81 Bottle, c.1950s	4920.00
Vending, Adams' Pepsin, Tutti-Frutti Gum, Chocolate, 1 Cent, Porcelain, c.1898, 11 x 29 In.	7840.00
Vending, Auto Doctor, Audoco Preparations, Oak Cabinet, 12 x 17 In.	7800.00
Vending, Candies, Select-O-Vend, 1 Cent, Red Painted Steel Case, 18 x 8 In.	106.00
Vending, Candy Bar, 5 Cent, 8 Column, Metal, Art Deco Style, 1950s, Key	1232.00
Vending, Chicken Egg, Chocolate, 5 Cent, Cast Iron, Seated Hen, Floor Model, Square Base, c.1900	5100.00
Vending, Chlorophyll, 5 Cent, Cash Tray, Metal, Glass, Abby Mfg. Co., c.1948	168.00
Vending, Cigarettes, Lucky Strike, Coin, Built In Table, C.B. Howard Co., 1930s, 29 ¾ In.	300.00
Vending, Cigaromat, Cigars, 6 Column, Wood, Footed	2520.00
Vending, Condom, 50 Cent, Wall, Woman, Long Blond Hair, c.1981, Keys	120.00
Vending, Cooler, Eskimo Pie, 5 Cent, Sun Setting	150.00
Vending, Cornets Aspirin, 5 Cent, Cylindrical, Cast Iron Base, c.1932, 7 x 10 In.	1206.00
Vending, Diamond Matches, 1 Cent, Lucky Strike Cigarettes, Round, Pyramid Base	700.00
Vending, Double Balloon, Stand, Pump, Red, Clown	252.00
Vending, Fresh Confections, 1 Cent, Double Bin, Side By Side, Metal, Red, 19 x 8 In.	266.00
Vending, Gem Confection, Gum, 1 Cent, Indian Head, Metal, Glass, c.1930, 12 x 17 In.	986.00
Vending, Golf Balls, Sportsman, 25 Cent, 3-Reel, Slot Top, Wood, Jennings, c.1934	5754.00
Vending, Gum & Music, Regina Music & Pepsin Gum, 3 Discs, Oak, c.1906	8960.00
Vending, Gum, 5 Cent, Aluminum, Glass Globe, Lid, Key, Regal, 1940s ....*Illus*	196.00
Vending, Gum, 5 Cent, Red Base, Columbus, 15 In.	450.00
Vending, Gum, Baker Boy, Sanitary, 1 Cent, Green, Red, Manikin Vendor Co., c.1929	3000.00
Vending, Gum, Chicago Gum & Candy Co., 6 Selections, 5 Cent, 15 ¼ In.	210.00
Vending, Gum, Chicklets, Chocolate, 4 Columns, Red Porcelain, Autosales, 1920s	720.00
Vending, Gum, Home Run Ball, Red, Lights, 26 In.	330.00
Vending, Gum, Pulver, 1 Cent, Clown Inside, Crinkle Paint, Keys, c.1950 ....*Illus*	1096.00
Vending, Gum, Pulver, Delivers A Tasty Chew, 1 Cent, Short Case, c.1950	1232.00
Vending, Gumball, 1 & 5 Cent, Moon Rocket Shaped, Take Off, Red & White, Keys, c.1959	1568.00
Vending, Gumball, 1 Cent, Bluebird 1-2-3, Oh Boy, 6 Balls 3 Cent, c.1915	767.00
Vending, Hershey's Chocolate, 1 Cent, Steel, 2-Sided Case, Shipman Mfg., 19 ¼ x 9 ¼ In.	649.00
Vending, Hot Nut, 5 Cent, Glass Cup Holder, Metal Stand, Silver King, c.1947	180.00
Vending, Hot Nut, Aluminum, 8-Sided Glass Globe, Blinking Light, c.1946	560.00
Vending, Jergens Lotion, Liquid Soap, 1 Cent, Art Deco Aluminum Case, 1937	672.00
Vending, Kay Salted Nut, Counter Display, Double, Blue Metal Base, 4 Glass Bins, 17 x 19 In.	71.00
Vending, Master Prophylactic, 10 Cent, Aluminum, Norris Mfg., 1920s	4200.00
Vending, Matchbox, 1 Cent, Embossed, Nickel Plated, Red Paint, Keys	1320.00
Vending, Matches, 1 Cent, Cigar Cutter, Cast Iron, Art Nouveau, Northwestern, c.1912	1008.00
Vending, Matches, 1 Cent, Diamond Match Co., c.1928	280.00
Vending, Nut, Asco Hot Nut Dispenser, Cup Attachment, 23 In.	330.00
Vending, Nut, Hawk Eye, 1 Cent, Bell Ringer, Porcelain	330.00
Vending, Parker Pencil Service, 5 Cent, Aluminum Case, c.1927, 10 x 9 In.	548.00
Vending, Peanut & Candy, 1 Cent, Freeport Peanut, Embossed Cast Iron, c.1905, 7 x 16 In.	7280.00
Vending, Peanut, Log Cabin Duplex, Clear, 1 Cent, Lock, Key	480.00
Vending, Peanut, Smilin' Sam From Alabam', 1 Cent, Red Man's Head ....*Illus*	1120.00
Vending, Peanut, Smiling Sam, Aluminum, Red, 13 ½ In.	420.00
Vending, Pencil, 5 Cent, Harmon Machine Co., Blue, 13 ½ In.	480.00
Vending, Perfume, Bull's Head, Pull Horns To Spray, 5 Cent, Iron, c.1904, 9 x 14 In.	11200.00
Vending, Pocket Comb, WC Brand, 10 Cent, Metal, Wall Mount, Key	224.00
Vending, Popcorn, Pop Corn Sez, It's Hot 'N Fresh, Clear Dome Top, Key	960.00
Vending, Postage Stamp, 2 Columns, Cast Iron, Glass Case, Kone Klutch, c.1911	728.00
Vending, Postage Stamp, 5 & 10 Cent, Porcelain, Keys, Shipman Mfg. Co., c.1938 ....*Illus*	300.00
Vending, Postage Stamp, 5 & 10 Cent, Schermack Cabinet, Arched Skirt, Square Feet, 39 x 62 In.	448.00
Vending, Postage Stamp, Oak Case, Beveled Mirror, Shield, Stars & Stripes, Keys, c.1915	2040.00
Vending, Postage Stamp, Red, White, Blue, Metal, Uncle Sam, 5 & 10 Cent, 20 x 8 In.	71.00
Vending, Pulver Chewing Gum, Delivers A Tasty Chew, 1 Cent, Red Porcelain, 9 x 20 In.	784.00

C

Vending, Razor Blade, 10 Cent, Nickel Plated, Cast Iron, Chum, c.1927	658.00
Vending, Razor Blade, Vend-O-Blade, Genuine Crescent, 10 Cent, Metal	210.00
Vending, Razor Blades, Gillette Razor, 50 Cent, Push Lever, 18 In.	210.00
Vending, Red Cross Pepsin Gum, 1 Cent, Red Porcelain Case, c.1910, 10 x 25 In.	7672.00
Vending, Roth's Pansy Gum, Fortune & Love Letter, 1 Cent, Stenciled Tin, Blue, c.1905, 5 x 20 In.	6160.00
Vending, Scup, Matches, 1 Cent, Cast Iron, Filigree, Cigar Cutter, Match Holder, c.1910, 6 x 13 In.	896.00
Vending, Shaeffer Script, Fountain Pen Ink, 1 Cent, Cast Iron Case, Wall Mount, Key, 6 x 8 x 17 In.	954.00
Vending, Spray Perfume, 1 Cent, Benedict, 3 Columns, Oak Case, c.1904, 16 x 27 In.	2040.00
Vending, Stamps, U.S. Postage, Porcelain, Monro-Matlack Co., Cleveland, Oh., 7 ½ x 16 In.. *Illus*	420.00
Vending, Towel & Soap, 1 Cent, Sanitary, Embossed, 1930s, 6 x 19 In.	1904.00
Vending, Towel & Soap, 5 Cent, Wood Case, Porcelain, c.1904, 9 x 31 In.	7200.00
Vending, Whiffs Of Fragrance, 1 Cent, Spray Handkerchief, Oak, c.1916, 12 x 17 In.	10800.00
Vending, Wildroot, 5 Cent, Lotion Dispenser, Green, 1950s, 8 x 11 In.	952.00
Weighing, Peerless, Honest Weight, 1 Cent, White Porcelain, Lollipop Shape, Floor Model, 1930s .	540.00
Weighing, Tom Thumb, How Much Do You Weigh, No Springs, Red, White, 1930s	270.00
Weighing, Watling Mfg. Co., Guess Your Weight, Oak, Mirror, Iron Base, 1 Cent, Chicago, 88 In.	3835.00
Weight, Guess Your Weight, Nickel Scale, Watling Mfg. Co., 1902, 69 In.	8800.00

COLLECTOR PLATES are modern plates produced in limited editions. Some may be found listed under the factory name, such as Bing & Grondahl, Royal Copenhagen, Royal Doulton, and Wedgwood.

Christmas 1992, Christmas Eve, Girl, Tree, P. Buckley Moss, Box, 8 In.	95.00
Gorham, Firelight, Rose Of The Year, 1971, 10 ¾ In.	25.00
Hamilton Collection, Sara & Marie, Timeless Friends, Karen Noles, 1987, 8 ½ In.	45.00
Hank Ketchum, Dennis The Menace, Mom, Dad, Decorating Tree, 1977, 9 In.	15.00
Knowles, Rhett, Gone With The Wind, c.1981, 8 ½ In.	24.00
Lenox, Redstart Birds, Pink Dogwood Tree, Boehm, 1975, 10 ¾ In.	46.00
Norman Rockwell, Big Brother, Boy, Girl, Dog, Japan, 6 ⅜ In.	15.00
Norman Rockwell, Toymaker, 1980, 7 ¾ In.	15.00
Orrefors, Westminster Abbey, Famous Places Of Worship, Gold Design & Rim, 1971, 9 ½ In.	49.00
Studio Dante Di Volteradici, Serene Madonna, Living Madonna Series, 3-D, 1979, 8 ½ In.	53.00
Thomas Kinkade, Warm Welcome Home, Home Is Where The Heart Is, Lighted Windows, 8 ¼ In.	30.00
W.S. George, Moonlight Retreat, Wings Of Winter, Cardinals In Tree, Cabin, 8 ½ In.	25.00

COMIC ART, or cartoon art, is a relatively new field of collecting. Original art for comic strips, magazine covers, and even printed strips are collected. The first daily comic strip was printed in 1907. The paintings on celluloid used for movie cartoons are listed in this book under Animation Art.

Comic Strip, Blondie, 4 Panels, She's Not The Neat & Orderly Type, Chic Young, 1948, 5 x 17 ⅝ In.	168.00
Drawing, Dick Tracy, Talking To Man On Wrist TV, Chester Gould, Frame, 1964, 16 x 16 ¾ In..	557.00
Drawing, Lurch, Addams Family, Cold Press Art Board, India Ink, Tempera, Pencil, Signed, 5 x 5 ¾ In.	458.00
Drawing, Panoramic, Mexican Soldiers, Charge, Sergio Aragones, Frame, 1974, 11 x 29 In. ..	629.00
Drawing, Uncle Fester, Addams Family, Art Board, India Ink, Tempera, Pencil, Signed, 5 x 6 In.	730.00
Illustration, Conan, With Sword, Art Board, India Ink, Frank Frazetta, 1970s, 13 ½ x 16 ½ In.	1740.00
Illustration, Swords Of Mars, Synthetic Men Of Mars, Frank Frazetta, John Carter, 12 x 12 In., 2 Piece	2627.00
Promo Sheet, Pin The Hat On Jiggs, San Francisco Examiner, 1930s, 17 x 22 In.	115.00
Strip, Blondie & Dagwood, Art Board, India Ink, 4 Panels, Sept. 20 1963, 5 x 17 ½ In.	154.00
Strip, Bringing Up Father, Get Out Of This House, Art Board, Ink, Signed, 1930, 4 x 17 In.	357.00
Strip, Dick Tracy, Bandaged Karpse In Hospital, Art Board, India Ink, Signed, Dec. 12 1938, 7 x 23 In.	575.00
Strip, Howdy Doody, Art Board, India Ink, 11 Panels, Sunday, Dec. 10 1950, 17 x 24 In.	230.00
Strip, Peanuts, Lucy, Linus, Charles Schulz, Sunday, February 9, 1964	24860.00

COMMEMORATIVE items have been made to honor members of royalty and those of great national fame. World's Fairs and important historical events are also remembered with commemorative pieces. Related collectibles are listed in the Coronation and World's Fair categories.

Badge, Queen Victoria, Jubilee, Brass, Crown & Star, Round Photo, 1897, 2 ⅛ In.	115.00
Badge, United Daughters Of The Confederacy, 10K Gold, Enamel, 1 ¾ In.	139.00
Bar Pin, Czech Freedom Tank, Breaking Through Iron Curtain, Metal, 1 ½ In.	52.00
Goblet, Otto Von Bismark, 1815-1898, Enamel Crest, Vine, Bohemian Glass, Tapered Stem, 8 In. .	123.00
Mug, Franz Josef, Elizabeth, 1854, White, Gilt Trim, Footed, 5 In.	750.00
Pin, Comstock Carnival, Virginia Nevada, Mining Symbols, Multicolor, 1903, 1 ¾ In.	75.00
Pin, Pioneer House, Little Town On The Prairie, Old Settlers Day, Desmet, S.D., 1911, 1 ¾ In..	57.00
Pin, Ribbon, John Glenn Smiling, Homecoming, Welcome Back To Earth, 1962, 1 ¾ In.	69.00

Coin-Operated Machine, Trade Stimulator, Poker, Cigar, 1 Cent, 5 Reel, No. 6, Key, Mills Novelty Co., c.1905
$4,370.00

Victorian Casino Antiques

Coin-Operated Machine, Vending, Gum, 5 Cent, Aluminum, Glass Globe, Lid, Key, Regal, 1940s
$196.00

Victorian Casino Antiques

Coin-Operated Machine, Vending, Gum, Pulver, 1 Cent, Clown Inside, Crinkle Paint, Keys, c.1950
$1,096.00

Victorian Casino Antiques

What's a Can Without an Opener
The can opener was invented 48 years after the can.

TIP

Don't scour a seasoned iron pan to clean it. Scrape off any particles with a spoon.

Coin-Operated Machine, Vending, Peanut, Smilin' Sam From Alabam', 1 Cent, Red Man's Head
$1,120.00

Victorian Casino Antiques

Coin-Operated Machine, Vending, Postage Stamp, 5 & 10 Cent, Porcelain, Keys, Shipman Mfg. Co., c.1938
$300.00

Victorian Casino Antiques

TIP

Crayons are wax, so crayon marks can be removed by melting the wax and blotting it away.

Pin, Stafford Co. Fair Association, Beautiful Kansas, 2nd Annual, 1901, 1 ¾ In.	180.00
Plaque, Ambassador Bridge, Classical Woman, With Shields, U.S., Canada, 1930, 4 x 2 ¾ In.	390.00
Plate, Elizabeth II, Silver Anniversary, Coat Of Arms, Banner, 1947-1972, 8 In., Pair	531.00
Print, Queen Victoria, 60 Years, Gilt Maple Frame, 27 x 21 In.	130.00

COMPACTS hold face powder. A woman did not powder her face in public until after World War I. By 1920, the beauty parlor, permanent waves, and cosmetics had become acceptable. A few companies sold cake face powder in a box with a mirror and a pad or puff. Soon the compact was designed by jewelers and made of gold, silver, and precious materials. Cosmetic companies began to sell powder in attractive compacts of less valuable metal or plastic. Collectors today search for Art Deco designs, commemorative compacts from World's Fairs or political events, and unusual examples. Many were made with companion lipsticks and other fittings.

Bucheron, Gold, Openwork Butterflies & Flowers, Cabochon Rubies, 3 x 2 ¼ In.	1845.00
Cartier, 14K Gold, Engine-Turned Lines, Monogram, 3 x 2 ⅜ In.	2726.00
Cartier, Sterling Silver, U.S. Cities, Round, Mirror Inside, 3 ⅜ In.	504.00
Diamond Melee, Woven Design, Clip Closure, 18K Gold, Marchak, Paris, 3 In.	8295.00
Elgin, Silver, Blue Enamel, Chain, Ring Loop, Monogram, Round, 1915, 1 ¾ In.	150.00
Mary Garden Rigaud, Brass, Embossed, Woman's Profile, Paris, c.1920, 1 ½ In.	29.00
Schlumberger, Basket Weave, 18K Bicolor Gold, Blue Enamel & Diamond Flowers	7821.00
Silver, Emerald Green Enamel, Ray Pattern, Round, Continental, 1 ⅝ In.	240.00
Silver, Engraved Flowers, Scrolls, Lines, Round, Rex Label, c.1940, 4 In.	150.00
Silver, Pale Yellow Enamel, Embossed Roses, Round, Stamped Austria, c.1905, 2 ¾ In.	150.00
Stratton, Pink Flamingos, Blue, Green Ground, Mirror, c.1950, 3 ⅛ In.	80.00
Tiffany & Co., 14K Gold, Line Engraving, Palmette Edges, Black Enamel Border	2880.00

CONSOLIDATED LAMP AND GLASS COMPANY of Coraopolis, Pennsylvania, was founded in 1894. The company made lamps, tablewares, and art glass. Collectors are particularly interested in the wares made after 1925, including black satin glass, Cosmos (listed in its own category in this book), Martele (which resembled Lalique), Ruba Rombic (1928–32 Art Deco line), and colored glasswares. Some Consolidated pieces are very similar to those made by the Phoenix Glass Company. The colors are sometimes different. Consolidated made Martele glass in blue, crystal, green, pink, white, or custard glass with added fired-on color or a satin finish. The company closed for the final time in 1967.

Jardiniere, Pink, Leaf Molded Pattern, Gold Trim, Flat Rim, 8 In.	104.00
Lamp, Figural, Santa Claus Shade, Pair Of Shoes Base, 9 ½ In. ....*Illus*	2760.00
Syrup, Crisscross, Cranberry Opalescent, Metal Lid, 7 In. ....*Illus*	690.00
Vase, Art Deco, Dancing Nudes, Scarves, Satyr Playing Instrument, 12 In. ....*Illus*	115.00
Vase, Blue, Impressed Tropical Fish, 8 ½ x 6 ¾ In.	77.00
Vase, Embossed Flowers, Satin, Gilt Cherub Handles, Footed	148.00
Vase, Lovebirds, Molded, Frosted, Blue, c.1920, 10 ½ In.	150.00

CONTEMPORARY GLASS, *see Glass-Contemporary.*

COOKBOOKS are collected for various reasons. Some are wanted for the recipes, some for investment, and some as examples of advertising. Cookbooks and recipe pamphlets are included in this category.

365 Cookies You Can Bake, 230 Pages, Copyright 1990 Outlet Book Co., Inc.	10.00
A World Of Good Eating, Phillips Publishers, 128 Pages, 1951, 8 x 6 In.	30.00
Approved Recipes From Mirro Test Kitchen, 284 Pages, 1937	21.00
Better Homes & Garden Cookbook, Cookies & Candies, 90 Pages, 1968	12.00
Betty Crocker, Hardcover, Western Publishing, 1976, 208 Pages	38.00
Blueberry Hill Cookbook, Elsie Masterton, Hard Cover, 302 Pages, 1959	48.00
Calumet Advertising Recipe Book, Copyright G.F. Corporation, 1931, 30 Pages	15.00
Cooking Made Easy For Children, 48 Pages, Vintage Books, 1985	10.00
General Foods Kitchens, Hard Cover, Random House, 436 Pages, 1959, 9 x 9 In.	28.00
General Foods, All About Home Baking, Hard Cover, 144 Pages, 1935, 5 x 9 In.	24.00
Gerber Recipe Book, 31 Pages, Copyright 1959, 5 ⅜ x 8 ⅜ In.	15.00
In The Kitchen With Love, Sophia Loren, 250 Pages, 1972	40.00
Italian Family Cooking, By Edware Giobbi, Illustrated, 1st Ed., 1971, 252 Pages	145.00
Jell-O Recipe Book, Through The Menu, Copyright 1927	22.00
Jell-O, Bride, Flower Girl, Genesse Pure Food Co., Booklet, 1916, 6 x 4 In.	50.00
Jell-O, Jack & Mary's Jell-O Recipe Book, Jack Benny, Mary Livingston, Comic Strip, 1937	25.00
New London Cookbook, Albion Press, Leather, 634 Pages, 1811, 8 x 5 In.	325.00
Out Of Swedish Kitchens, Spiral Bound, 180 Pages, c.1960, 6 x 8 In.	18.00
Outdoor Cooking With Reynolds Wrap, c.1950, 28 Pages, 5 x 7 In.	7.00

Saucepans & The Single Girl, By Jinx Kragen, Hardcover, Doubleday, 1965, 256 Pages	40.00
Sixty-Five Delicious Dishes Made With Bread, Fleischmann, 1919, 30 Pages	18.00
Spice Islands, Hardcover, Lane Book Co., 1961, 208 Pages	48.00
St. Louis Cookbook, Bicentennial Issue, St. Louis Symphony Women's Assoc., Reprint, 1964	12.00
Trader Vic's Pacific Island Cookbook, Hardbound, 286 Pages, 1968, Doubleday, 6 x 9 In.	15.00
Waltham Grange Woman's Club, Spiral Bound, 51 Pages, 1938, 6 x 9 In.	12.00
Watkins Salad Book, Elaine Ale, 251 Pages, Published 1946 Watkins Co.	12.00
Wear-Ever New Method, 96 Pages, 1953	8.00

COOKIE JARS with brightly painted designs or amusing figural shapes became popular in the mid-1930s. Many companies made them and collectors search for cookie jars either by design or by maker's name. Listed here are examples by the less common makers. Major factories are listed under their own names in other categories of the book, such as Abingdon, Brush, Hull, McCoy, Metlox, Red Wing, and Shawnee. See also the Disneyana category.

Black Mammy, Patterned Dress, Chrysanthemums, Scarf, Japan, c.1950, 11 In.	107.00
Collegiate Owl, Big Eyes, Tassel Cap, Glasses, American Bisque Co., 1958, 11 In.	165.00
Cookies, Leaves, Beige, Bail Handle, Monmouth, Marked, c.1915, 7 ½ In.	62.00
Cookies, Pink Aluminum, Black Plastic, Kromex, 1950s, 8 ½ In.	50.00
Gingerbread Men, Shapes, Embossed, Glass, Pink, Hazel Atlas, 1950s, 10 In.	36.00
Sailor Girl Elephant, Deforest, c.1960, 12 In.	65.00
Strawberry, Red, Green Stem Lid, American Pottery, 10 In.	60.00
Yogi Bear, American Bisque, Hanna-Barbera, 1961, 13 ½ In.	295.00

COPELAND pieces listed here are those that have a mark including the word *Copeland* used between 1847 and 1976. Marks include *Copeland Spode* and *Copeland & Garrett.* See also Copeland Spode, Royal Worcester, and Spode.

Biscuit Jar, Jasperware Design, Silver Frame, England, 8 In.	35.00
Bowl, Sectioned, Spode Towers, Blue, White, Tureen, Ladle, Cover, 4 Dishes, 1900s, 20 In.	212.00
Bust, Alexandra, Parian, Art Union Of London, Mary Thornycroft, c.1863, 14 ¾ In. *Illus*	900.00
Bust, May Queen, White, Art Union Of London, Parian, 1973, 12 ½ In.	127.00
Bust, Princess Alexandra, Signed F.M. Miller, Stepped Black Glass Base, Parian, c.1850, 13 In.	295.00
Centerpiece, 2 Hooved Putti, Eating Grapes, Footed, Multicolor, 15 x 10 In.	575.00
Figurine, Classical Woman, Standing, Holding Urn, Gilt Brass Round Base, Parian, 1875, 24 x 8 In.	184.00
Figurine, Egeria, J.H. Foley R.A., Parian, c.1850, 28 In.	561.00
Oyster Plate, 5 Wells, Crescent Shape, Leaves, Shells, Multicolor, 9 In.	403.00
Pedestal, Etruscan Revival, Ceramic, Fluted, Painted Designs, Marked, c.1840, 35 In. *Illus*	2629.00
Plate Set, Hunt Scenes, Gilt Rim, Lionel Edwards, 10 In., 12 Piece	1541.00
Serving Bowl, Lid, Fig Finial, Tab Handles, Flow Blue Staffordshire Transfer, c.1850, 6 ½ x 9 In.	207.00
Urn, Birds, Flowers, Gilt Rim, Ring Handles, Oval, c.1820, 14 In., Pair	1000.00

COPELAND SPODE appears on some pieces of nineteenth-century English porcelain. Josiah Spode established a pottery at Stoke-on-Trent, England, in 1770. In 1833, the firm was purchased by William Copeland and Thomas Garrett and the mark was changed. In 1847, Copeland became the sole owner and the mark changed again. W.T. Copeland & Sons continued until a 1976 merger when it became Royal Worcester Spode. The company was bought by the Portmeirion Group in 2009. Pieces are listed in this book under the name that appears in the mark. Copeland, Royal Worcester, and Spode have separate listings.

COPELAND SPODE ENGLAND

Bone Dish, Half Moon Shape, Yellow Border, Silver Trim, 8 ¾ In.	22.00
Bowl, Cherubs, Gilt, Turquoise Ribbon Exterior, Scrolled Feet, 1880s, 10 x 5 In.	1850.00
Plate Set, Huntsman, From Drawings By J. F. Herring Sen, 10 ¼ In., 12 Piece	780.00
Plate, Cream Color, Gilt & Rose Design, 1900s, 10 ½ In., 12 Piece *Illus*	1003.00
Plate, Solid Color Border, Gilt Rim, England, 1900, 10 ¾ In., 8 Piece	403.00
Platter, Oriental Landscape, Multicolor, Marked, 19 x 14 ¼ In.	104.00
Tureen, Underplate, Tower, Pink, 10 & 16 In., 2 Piece	450.00

COPPER has been used to make utilitarian items, such as teakettles and cooking pans, since the days of the early American colonists. Copper became a popular metal with the Arts & Crafts makers of the early 1900s, and decorative pieces, like desk sets, were made. Other pieces of copper may be found in Arts & Crafts, Bradley & Hubbard, Kitchen, Roycroft, and other categories.

Basket, Victorian, Repousse Cupids, Flowers, Scrolls, Silvered, c.1850, 18 In.	84.00
Bed Warmer, Pierce Shield, Crown Pattern, Barley Twist Oak Handle, England, c.1820, 39 In.	518.00
Bed Warmer, Wrigglework Bird, c.1805, 39 ½ In.	89.00

Coin-Operated Machine, Vending, Stamps, U.S. Postage, Porcelain, Monro-Matlack Co., Cleveland, Oh., 7 ½ x 16 In. $420.00

Showtime Auction Services

TIP
Wipe glass dry with newspapers for a special shine.

Consolidated, Lamp, Figural, Santa Claus Shade, Pair Of Shoes Base, 9 ½ In. $2,760.00

Early Auction Co.

Consolidated, Syrup, Crisscross, Cranberry Opalescent, Metal Lid, 7 In. $690.00

Early Auction Co.

COPPER

C

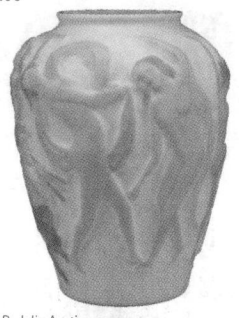

Consolidated, Vase, Art Deco, Dancing Nudes, Scarves, Satyr Playing Instrument, 12 In.
$115.00

James D. Julia Auctioneers

Copeland, Bust, Alexandra, Parian, Art Union Of London, Mary Thornycroft, c.1863, 14 ¾ In.
$900.00

Skinner, Inc.

Copeland, Pedestal, Etruscan Revival, Ceramic, Fluted, Painted Designs, Marked, c.1840, 35 In.
$2,629.00

Neal Auction Co.

Bowl, Hammered, 8 Flutes, 8 Stop Flutes, Radiating From Base, Marked R.R.M., 18 x 7 ¼ In..	71.00
Box, Arts & Crafts, Knot Design, Round, England, c.1910, 3 x 2 In.	427.00
Box, Hammered & Tooled, Animal & Ship Designs, Jewels, Signed, Alfred Daguet, 9 x 11 In. ...	3050.00
Box, Hammered & Tooled, Jewels, Signed, Alfred Daguet, 4 x 10 ½ In.	2440.00
Box, Hammered, Tooled, Stylized Animal, Flowers, Jewels, Enamel, Alfred Daguet, 4 x 9 In. ... *Illus*	3050.00
Box, Kindling, Hammered, Lift Lid, Round Handles, Nailhead Construction, 1916, 14 ½ x 22 In..	6875.00
Brazier, Lid, Etched Flowers, Chased, Pierced, Cranes, Gilding, Swing Handle, Chinese, 7 x 9 In..	518.00
Bucket, Wrought Iron Swing Handle, c.1875, 14 x 26 In.	264.00
Candlestick, Chamber, Hammered, Round Stem, Dish Base, Strap Handle, G. Stickley, 9 In. ..	750.00
Charger, Hammered & Tooled, Eagle, Signed, Alfred Daguet, 19 ½ In.	1830.00
Charger, Hammered, Gustav Stickley, Stamped, 21 In. Diam. ....*Illus*	2750.00
Coffeepot, Brass Mushroom Knob, Gooseneck Spout, F. Clark, 12 ¼ x 12 In.	826.00
Coffeepot, Gooseneck Spout, Dome Lid, Handle, Henry Trottmann, 11 ¾ x 13 In...........*Illus*	130.00
Coffeepot, Lighthouse Shape, Heart Terminal, Wood Handle, 11 In.	295.00
Cuspidor, Tortoise, Step On Head To Lift Shell For Bowl, Patd. Nov. 20, '91, 4 x 14 In.	165.00
Ewer, Brass, Lid, Dragon Designs On Cover, Handle, Spout, India, 24 ½ x 20 In..... 60.00 to 120.00	
Ewer, Flowers, Arabesque, Calligraphy, Ringed Foot, Kashmir, c.1800, 11 In.	472.00
Figurine, Frog, 21 In., Pair.	1007.00
Frame, Hammered, Oval, Tusk Decoration, Curled Feet, Albert Berry, Alaska, 8 ½ In.	2250.00
Jewelry Box, Maiden, Children, Wheat Sheaves, Babies, Chased, Continental, c.1905, 4 ¾ x 12 In..	3600.00
Kettle, Apple Butter, Handles, Stamped J.P. Schaum, Lancaster, Pa., 19 x 27 In.	851.00
Kettle, Apple, Hammered, Iron Bail Handle, 13 x 19 In.	120.00
Kettle, Bail Handle, Impressed D. Benntley, Phila. Pa., 1840, 18 In.	3792.00
Kettle, Dome Lid, Scrolled Knob, Gooseneck, Dovetail, Strap Handle, Stamped, J.A.A., G.B., 8 In..... *Illus*	35.00
Kettle, Flared Side, Iron Swing Handle, 20 x 17 In.	59.00
Kettle, Hammered, Stamped John Lay York, Pa., c.1810, 12 In.	444.00
Kettle, Handle, Stamped W. Heiss, Philadelphia, 11 In.	593.00
Kettle, Hanging, Hot Water, Applied Spout, Iron Bail Handle, Hickman, c.1840, 12 x 12 In.	150.00
Kettle, Lid, Dovetailed, Brass Knob, Handle, Stamped G. Read, c.1790, 11 In...................*Illus*	472.00
Kettle, Stamped W. Wolf, c.1810, 11 ½ In.	533.00
Kettle, Swing Handle, Impressed C. Rabourg, Baltimore, c.1800, 11 ½ In.	1896.00
Kettle, Swing Handle, Stamped J. Kidd, Pa., c.1800, 12 ½ In.	1215.00
Kettle, Swing Handle, Stamped M. Babb, Reading Pa., c.1820, 12 ¾ In.	851.00
Measure, Spout, Handle, 11 ½ x 7 In.	15.00
Molds are listed in the Kitchen category.	
Pitcher, Water, Sailing Ship, Tall Neck, Flared Foot, 15 x 8 x 11 In. ....*Illus*	42.00
Planter, Monteith Form, Painted, Yellow, Country Scenes, Scalloped Rim, 7 x 8 In., Pair	767.00
Planter, Oval, Lobed, Flared, Applied Scroll Handles, c.1820, 7 ¾ x 23 In.	2588.00
Planter, Yacht Shape, Brass, Hexagonal Opening, 1900s, 5 In.	173.00
Pot Set, Lead Lining, Iron Handles, Graduated Sizes, 24, 18, 12 ½, 11 In., 4 Piece	960.00
Pot, Arts & Crafts, Hammered, Hefty Handles, Stamped, 13 ½ x 8 In.	265.00
Pot, Fish, Tray Cover, Brass Handles, Hodgee & Sons, Dublin, 12 ½ x 20 In.	2655.00
Pot, Hammered, Banded, Strap Handles, 17 ½ x 22 In.	154.00
Pot, Lid, Art Nouveau, Embossed Design, Brass Bracket Handles, c.1900, 15 x 12 In.	805.00
Saucepan, Lid, Stamped 28, 7 x 23 In.	130.00
Sculpture, Sound, Harry Bertoia, Rectangular Base, Blades Of Grass Shape, c.1955, 5 ⅜ In..	6250.00
Smoking Set, Hammered, Humidor, Cover, Folded Ashtray, Antler Holder, A. Berry, 19 In........	3625.00
Tankard, Hammered, Arrowheads, Stag Horn Handle, Gold Wash, J. Heinrichs, 9 In.	8750.00
Teakettle, Brass Scroll Handle, Gooseneck Spout, 12 ½ In.	118.00
Teakettle, Dovetail Construction, Swing Handle, Gooseneck Spout, Lancaster, Pa., 15 In.	177.00
Teakettle, Stamped G Wilson, Philadelphia, 1700s, 12 In.	851.00
Teakettle, Stamped M. Babb, Reading, Pa., 11 In.	851.00
Teapot, Repousse, Brass, Pewter Wash Interior, Joseph Maria Olbrich, 1903, 8 x 6 In. ......*Illus*	11250.00
Teapot, Wood, Brass, Footed, Handle, Christopher Dresser, England, c.1885, 9 x 9 In.	1220.00
Tray, Arts & Crafts, Shaped, Rounded Corners, Handles, Scrolled Edges, Stamped, Russia, 22 x 11 In.	267.00
Tray, Hammered, Round, Jugendstil, Germany, c.1905, 25 In.	875.00
Tray, Repousse, Articulated Rim, L.& J.G. Stickley, Stamped Mark, c.1912, 1 ¼ x 18 ¾ In.	1125.00
Trinket Box, Bronze, Pewter, Wood, Cork, Patchwork Design, Hinged Lid, P. Evans, 1970s, 4 x 10 In..	625.00
Tureen, Lid, Tray, Arts & Crafts, Flower Repousse, Scroll Handles, Figural Busts, c.1890, 11 x 13 In. ...	1495.00
Umbrella Stand, Hammered, Bowl Form, Cylindrical Stem, Domed Foot, Arts & Crafts, 30 In.	369.00
Vase, Boot Shape, Repousse Tavern Scene, Maltzeit Prosit, German Toast, 14 x 4 ½ In.	1150.00
Vase, Dried Leaf Design, Flared, 11 In.	79.00
Vase, Flower Repousse, Flared, Embossed, Arts & Craft, Eng., c.1910, 5 x 9 ¾ In., Pair	610.00
Vase, Hammered, Bats, Ring Foot, Cylindrical Neck, Handles, Germany, c.1920, 11 ½ x 7 In...	1625.00
Vase, Hammered, Round Stylized Designs, Green Ground, WMF, 6 x 12 ½ In.	427.00
Warmer, Pierced, Embossed Songbirds, Flowers, Hearts, Octagonal, Bail Handle, Dutch, 10 In.	590.00

COPPER LUSTER *items are listed in the Luster category.*

CORALENE glass was made by firing many small colored beads on the outside of glassware. It was made in many patterns in the United States and Europe in the 1880s. Reproductions are made today. Coralene-decorated Japanese pottery is listed in the Japanese Coralene category.

Biscuit Jar, Lid, Silver Plate, Bail Handle, 19th Century, 6 ¾ x 3 ½ In.	98.00
Fairy Lamp, Mother-Of-Pearl, Diamond Quilted, Pink, Gold Branch Design, 5 In.	259.00
Vase, Blue To Pink, Yellow Flowers, Leaves, Urn Shape, Cylinder Neck, Opaline, 6 In.	115.00
Vase, Pale Blue, Gold Branch, Amber Feet, Foldover Petals, Open Rim, 6 x 4 In.	144.00

CORDEY CHINA COMPANY was founded by Boleslaw Cybis in 1942 in Trenton, New Jersey. The firm produced gift shop items. In 1969 it was acquired by the Lightron Corp. and operated as the Schiller Cordey Co., manufacturers of lamps. About 1950 Boleslaw Cybis began making Cybis porcelains, which are listed in their own category in this book.

Figurine, Buffalo, Marked, 6 ¾ x 11 In.	165.00
Figurine, Gentleman, Holding Hat, Ruffled Shirt, Base, Gilt, 11 In.	125.00
Figurine, Half Woman, Lace Collar & Cuffs, Hat, Bow Draped Over Shoulder, 9 In.	150.00
Figurine, Woman, Applied Flowers, Scrolls, Hat, Base, Gilt, 11 In.	150.00
Figurine, Woman, Pastel Dress, Lace Rim, Flowers, Scrolled Base, Gilt, c.1945, 11 In.	130.00
Lamp, Gentleman, 18th Century Attire, Flower Base, Brass Stand, 25 In.	225.00
Wall Pocket, Woman's Head, Curly Hair, Roses, Red Cheeks, Hat, 8 x 6 x 5 In., Pair	250.00

CORKSCREWS have been needed since the first bottle was sealed with a cork, probably in the seventeenth century. Today collectors search for the early, unusual patented examples or the figural corkscrews of recent years.

Anchor, Brass, Grapes, Rope, King, Embossed, Germany, 5 x 4 In.	65.00
Chrome, Spiral Rings, Worm Screw, Brush, 5 ⅞ x 3 ¾ In.	155.00
Cone Shape, Bakelite Handle, Amber, c.1945.	10.00
Dog, Scottie, Figural, Brass, Art Deco, England, 5 In.	40.00
Knife, Bicycle Scenes, WII Morley & Sons, Germany, 5 In.	395.00
Man, Bowler Hat, Anri, Italy, c.1940, 4 x 2 In.	45.00
Monk, On Barrel, Anri, Italy, c.1950, 6 x 3 In.	115.00
Waiter, Figural, Composition, Painted, Syracuse Ornamental Co., c.1940	185.00
Walrus Tusk, Vines, Leaves, Sterling Cap, Sheffield, 1913, 6 ¼ In.	675.00
Wing Arm, Bottle Opener, Embossed Metalware, Italy, 7 ½ In.	27.00
Wood Handle, Bodeker Drug Co., Williamson Co., c.1898	30.00
Wood Handle, Nubby, France, 6 ½ In.	45.00

CORONATION souvenirs have been made since the 1800s. Pottery, glass, tin, silver, and paper objects with a picture of the monarchs and date have been sold at many coronations. The pieces that mention King Edward VIII, the king who was never crowned, are not rare; collectors should be sure to check values before buying. Related pieces are found in the Commemorative category.

Ashtray, Queen Elizabeth II, Clear Glass, Gilt Trim, Lions, Crown, 1953, 3 x 3 In.	12.00
Cup & Saucer, Queen Elizabeth II, Gilt Design, Blue Ground, Paragon, 1953	125.00
Cup, King George V & Queen Mary, Portraits, Flags, Long May They Live, 1911, 3 In.	70.00
Cup, King George V, Etched Flowers, 2 Handles, Paneled Pedestal Base, Glass, c.1911, 8 In.	390.00
Cup, King George VI, Lid, Clear Glass, Coat Of Arms, Motto Etched, 1937, 12 ½ In.	660.00
Dish, King George V, Ribbed, Scalloped, Portraits, Flags, H.M. Williamson, 1911, 4 ½ In.	24.00
Goblet, Queen Elizabeth II, Gilt Trim, Lions, Crown, Glass, Amber Stem, 1953, 7 In.	50.00
Jug, King Edward VII, Porcelain, Molded, Painted, Lion Handle, 1902, 8 In.	1750.00
Jug, King William IV & Queen Adelaide, Crown On Pillow, Sword, Scepter, Transferware, 1831, 6 In.	695.00
Medallion, Edward VII, Portrait, Bronze, Box, 1902, 2 ¼ In.	93.00
Medallion, Queen Elizabeth II, Brass Color, Portrait, 1953, 3 ½ In.	30.00
Mug, King George V, Coat Of Arms, Lithophane, 1911, 3 ¾ In.	95.00
Pencil, Propelling, Queen Elizabeth, Coat Of Arms, 1953	61.00
Pillow Cover, King George VI, Crown, Banners, Multicolor, Linen, 1937, 35 x 17 In.	55.00
Pin Dish, Queen Elizabeth, Portrait, Gilt Trim, Staffordshire, 4 x 4 In.	57.00
Pin, George VI & Elizabeth, Celluloid, Portraits, Margaret Rose, 1937, 1 ¼ In.	45.00
Plate, Czar Alexander III Coronation, 1882, Eagle, Double Gilt Border, 9 In.	531.00
Plate, Edward VII & Alexandra, Portraits, Flags, Gilt Trim, 1902, 9 ½ In.	150.00
Postcard, Queen Elizabeth II, Portrait, Her Majesty, Glitter, 1953	12.00
Quilt, Queen Victoria, Printed Chintz, Crowning Image, Brown, Blue, Red, 1837, 96 x 92 In.	1003.00

Copeland Spode, Plate, Cream Color, Gilt & Rose Design, 1900s, 10 ½ In., 12 Piece
$1,003.00

Brunk Auctions

Copper, Box, Hammered, Tooled, Stylized Animal, Flowers, Jewels, Enamel, Alfred Daguet, 4 x 9 In.
$3,050.00

Treadway Toomey Galleries

Copper, Charger, Hammered, Gustav Stickley, Stamped, 21 In. Diam.
$2,750.00

Rago Arts & Auction Center

TIP
Furs should be cleaned by experts. Many clean with damp sawdust, then steam and brush the furs.

Copper, Coffeepot, Gooseneck Spout, Dome Lid, Handle, Henry Trottmann, 11 ¾ x 13 In.
$130.00

Conestoga Auction Co., Inc.

Copper, Kettle, Dome Lid, Scrolled Knob, Gooseneck, Dovetail, Strap Handle, Stamped, J.A.A., G.B., 8 In.
$35.00

Conestoga Auction Co., Inc.

Copper, Kettle, Lid, Dovetailed, Brass Knob, Handle, Stamped G. Read, c.1790, 11 In.
$472.00

Brunk Auctions

TIP

Save your wine corks. Cut them in thin slices with a bread knife and slide a piece under a wobbling chair leg.

Shaving Mug, George VI & Queen Elizabeth, Red & Blue Striped Rim, 1937	145.00
Spoon, King George VI, Ridged, Celtic Designs, Saunders & Shepard, Sterling, 1937, 3 ¾ In.	55.00
Tin, King George V & Queen Mary, Prince Of Wales, Lord Mayor, Ground, 1911, 4 x 4 In.	125.00
Tray, Central Handle, King George VI & Queen Elizabeth, Long May They Reign, 1937, 8 In.	85.00
Watch, Queen Elizabeth II, Coat Of Arms, Ingersoll, England, 1953, Pocket	330.00

COSMOS is a pressed milk glass pattern with colored flowers made from 1894 to 1915 by the Consolidated Lamp and Glass Company. Tablewares and lamps were made in this pattern. A few pieces were also made of clear glass with painted decorations. Other glass patterns are listed under Consolidated Lamp and also in various glass categories. In later years, Cosmos was also made by the Westmoreland Glass Company.

Butter, Cover, Stemless Daisy, Pastels, Crosscut Ground, Round	145.00
Butter, Dome Cover, Raised Flowers, c.1894, 5 ¾ x 8 In.	125.00
Lamp, Kerosene, White, Pastel Flowers, 8 ¼ In.	250.00
Pitcher, Syrup, Trellis Pattern, Handle, Tin Hinged Lid, 3 ½ In.	160.00
Pitcher, Water, Textured Lattice Pattern, Daisies, Pastel, Pink Neck, 9 In.	260.00
Shaker, Pink, Metal Lid	40.00
Tumbler, Flowers, Netted Ground, Pink, Yellow, Blue, Pink Rim, 3 ¼ In.	55.00

COVERLETS were made of linen or wool during the nineteenth century. Most of the coverlets date from 1800 to the 1880s. There was a revival of hand weaving in the 1920s and new coverlets, especially geometric patterns, were made. The earliest coverlets were made on narrow looms, so two woven strips were joined together and a seam can be found. The weave structures of coverlets can include summer and winter, double weave, overshot, and others. Jacquard coverlets have elaborate pictorial patterns that are made on a special loom or with the use of a special attachment. Quilts are listed in this book in their own category.

Blue, Red, Green, Cream, Stars & Flowers, Tulips, Starbursts Design, Pa., 1841, 84 x 89 In.	230.00
Blue, White, Central Medallion, Eagle, Deer, Flowers, Double Weave, c.1850, 88 x 82 In.	805.00
Double Weave, Red, Neutral, Blue, Checkerboard, 95 x 78 In.	94.00
Jacquard, 5 Colors, Medallion, Eagle Corners, Wool, Cotton, Holmes County, c.1885 ....*Illus*	211.00
Jacquard, Blue & White Eagle Border, Flowers, Lucretia Holcombe, 1850, 81 x 82 In.	395.00
Jacquard, Blue & White, Eagle, Shield, Prancing Horse, Wool, Cotton, 1836, 74 x 78 In.	940.00
Jacquard, Blue & White, Oak Leaves, Grapevine Border, Wool, Cotton, U.S.A., 72 x 89 In.	206.00
Jacquard, Blue, Red, Emanuel Grube Warwick, T.L., A.C.P.M. Groff, 1837, 91 x 102 In.	207.00
Jacquard, Blue, Red, Green, Inscribed P. Rassweiler, Ohio, 1851, 94 x 81 In.	119.00
Jacquard, Blue, Red, Star, Flower Center, Building, Fence Border, Wool, Cotton, c.1850, 83 x 93 In.	206.00
Jacquard, Blue, Red, White, Inscribed Anna Keim, 1847, 100 x 90 In.	504.00
Jacquard, Blue, Red, White, T. Marsteller, Northampton County, Pa., 1855, 80 x 95 In.	415.00
Jacquard, Blue, Red, White, Urns, Fruit, Birds, Buildings, Fringe, c.1820, 77 x 86 In.	403.00
Jacquard, Blue, Rose, Grapevine Borders, Floral Edge, Chesterville, Ohio, 1852, 70 x 91 In.	176.00
Jacquard, Blue, White, Flower Medallion, Stag, Tree Border, Signed Archd. Davidson, N.Y.	575.00
Jacquard, Blue, White, Nesting Birds, Fringe, c.1855	237.00
Jacquard, Cream, Olive Green, Star, Vines, 8-Point Star Border, Fringe, c.1845, 80 x 89 In.	353.00
Jacquard, Double Woven, Blue, White, Buildings, Pheasants, Flowers, c.1845, 82 x 76 In.	575.00
Jacquard, Indigo Blue & White, Liberty, Eagle, Roses, House, Wool, Cotton, c.1845, 86 x 74 In.	690.00
Jacquard, Memorial Hall, Centennial, Wool, Cotton, Flowers, Fringe, c.1876, 72 x 80 In....*Illus*	235.00
Jacquard, Peacocks, Fruit, Flowers, Star, Wool, Cotton, John Kirst, 1847, 80 x 95 In.	294.00
Jacquard, Red, Blue Stripes, Inscribed G. Baer Antietam Factory, Pa., 1856, 73 x 72 In.	61.00
Jacquard, Red, Blue, Green, Medallion, Eagle, William Ney, Pa., 1800s, 81 x 85 In.	529.00
Jacquard, Red, Blue, Green, Wool, Cotton, Fringe, John Hamelton Machenoy, 1837, 96 x 78 In.	531.00
Jacquard, Red, Cream, Eagle Borders, Inscribed Martin Breneman, Pa., 95 x 82 In.	474.00
Jacquard, Red, Green, Tan, Inscribed Manufactured By A.T. Fehr, Pa., c.1840, 91 x 78 In.	296.00
Jacquard, Red, Green, White, Initialed MBK, c.1850, 85 x 82 In.	298.00
Jacquard, Red, White, Stars, Flowers, Double Cloth, Signed H.A. Griffith, 1846, 95 x 87 In.	1150.00
Overshot, Repeating Stars, Flowers, Wool, Red, Blue, Green, White Cotton, 94 x 86 In.	325.00
Wool, Blue, Gold, Mustard, Red, Leaves, Scrolls, Fringe, c.1790, 72 x 59 In.	1150.00
Wool, Brown, Blue, Checkerboard, Pine Tree Border, Fringe, c.1855, 86 x 93 In.	518.00

COWAN POTTERY made art pottery and wares for florists. Guy Cowan made pottery in Rocky River, Ohio, a suburb of Cleveland, from 1913 to 1931. A stylized mark with the word *Cowan* was used on most pieces. A commercial, mass-produced line was marked *Lakeware*. Collectors today search for the Art Deco pieces by Guy Cowan, Viktor Schreckengost, Waylande Gregory, or Thelma Frazier Winter.

Bookends, Boy, Girl, Cream, 6 ½ In., Pair	127.00
Bookends, Sunbonnet Girl, Ivory Glaze, Impressed Logo, 7 ¼ In., Pair	485.00

Bowl, Jazz, Glazed, Viktor Schreckengost, Signed, Stamped, 1929, 11 ½ x 16 In. ....*Illus*	100000.00
Bowl, Oriental Red Glaze, Relief Flowers, Octagonal, Impressed Mark, c.1930, 9 ¾ x 3 ½ In...	121.00
Bust, Woman, Head In Hand, Black Matte Glaze, Square Base, A.D. Jacobsen, 6 x 11 ¼ In.......	5625.00
Charger, Yellow Glaze, Hound, Impressed, 15 ¼ In. Diam.	92.00
Figurine, Stylized Bird, Blue, Art Deco, 12 In.	81.00
Flower Frog, Mushrooms, Cream, 4 ½ In., Pair	104.00
Paperweight, Elephant, Red, 4 ¾ In.	276.00
Planter, Brown, Flared, 5 ¼ In.	12.00
Plate, Blue, Allover Winged Creatures, Embossed, Marked, 15 ¼ In.	219.00
Plate, Danse Moderne, Glazed, Jazz Series, Viktor Schreckengost, Stamped, 1929, 11 ¼ In.... *Illus*	13750.00
Vase, Blue, Impressed, Scrolls, Lines, 11 ¼ In.	161.00
Vase, Chinese Bird, Flared, Round Base, Marked, 11 ¼ In.	127.00
Vase, Dusty Rose Mottled Glaze, Peach High Gloss Glaze, Cylindrical, Flared Lip, Footed, 6 x 4 In..	29.00
Vase, Green, Sculpted Shoulder, Tapered, 5 ½ In.	81.00
Vase, Iridescent Blue, Cylindrical, 9 ¾ In.	63.00
Vase, Plum Matrix Glaze, Squirrel, Round, Ring Foot, Rolled Rim, Marked, 8 ¼ In.................	172.00

CRACKER JACK, the molasses-flavored popcorn mixture, was first made in 1896 in Chicago, Illinois. A prize was added to each box in 1912. Collectors search for the old boxes, toys, and advertising materials. Many of the toys are unmarked.

Bookmark, Tin Lithograph, Scottie	14.00
Bookmark, Tin, Bulldog, c.1930	28.00
Card, Slide, Ocean, Fish	8.00
Magnifier, Clear, Straight-Sided, Curved Top & Bottom	5.00
Magnifier, Clear, Triangle..	5.00
Sticker, Lick-Em & Stick-Em	10.00
Toy, American Flag Stand-Up, Tin Lithograph, Blue Rim, Oval, 2 ⅜ In., 3 Piece	52.00
Toy, Ax, Metal, Silvertone..	7.00
Toy, Bear, On Roller Skates, Aqua, Plastic	10.00
Toy, Bird, Metal, Metallic Gold	22.00
Toy, Book, Bird, Flicker, Baltimore, Oriole, 1941, 2 ¾ x 2 ¼ In...	40.00
Toy, Book, Famous Explorers, Volume 3	6.00
Toy, Chair, Metal, Green, Blue	15.00
Toy, Clicker, Frog, Metal, Green, 2 In. Diam.	35.00
Toy, Clown Tilter, Face Changes	12.00
Toy, Funny Viewer, Blue, Square, 4-Footed	6.00
Toy, Girl Riding Ostrich, Dark Yellow	12.00
Toy, Hippo, Plastic, Melon	10.00
Toy, Lift To Erase, 3 In A Row	8.00
Toy, Lift To Erase, Girl...	8.00
Toy, Magnifier, Clear, Round, Petal Edge	6.00
Toy, Magnifier, Round, Red	6.00
Toy, Ocarina, Red, Plastic	10.00
Toy, Paint Set, Mysticolor, Stop Sign	10.00
Toy, Pinball Game, Humpty Dumpty, 1960s	9.00
Toy, Rooster, Metal	15.00
Toy, Scoop, Red, Marbleized	10.00
Toy, Top, Blow On It, Blue, Plastic, Scallop Edge	9.00
Toy, Top, Red, Yellow, Blue, Metal, ⅞ In.	12.00
Toy, Top, Stars, Red	10.00
Whistle, Metal	20.00

CRACKLE GLASS was originally made by the Venetians, but most of the wares found today were made since the 1800s. The glass was heated, cooled, and refired so that many small lines appeared inside the glass. Most was made from about 1930 to 1980, although some is made today. The glass is found in many colors, but collectors today pay the highest prices for amberina, cranberry, or ruby red. Cobalt blue is also popular. More crackle glass may be listed in those categories in this book.

Atomizer, Lavender, 5-Sided, Silver Rim, Marcel Franck, 6 In.	95.00
Bowl, Clear, Brass Cherub Stand, 8 In. Diam..	35.00
Candleholder, Red, Pinched, 5 ⅞ In.	45.00
Compote, Verde Green, Label, 1950s, 9 x 7 In.	65.00
Decanter, Ruby, Footed, Clear Stopper, 9 In.	50.00
Dresser Jar, Cover, Mustard Yellow, Black Rim, Egg Shape, Footed, 8 In.	32.00

TIP

Dust the backs of your framed pictures once a year.

C

Copper, Pitcher, Water, Sailing Ship, Tall Neck, Flared Foot, 15 x 8 x 11 In. $42.00

DuMouchelles Art Gallery

Copper, Teapot, Repousse, Brass, Pewter Wash Interior, Joseph Maria Olbrich, 1903, 8 x 6 In. $11,250.00

Los Angeles Modern Auctions (LAMA)

TIP

Copper pans must have tinned interiors to be safe to use for cooking. Always use a wooden spoon. Always have some liquid in the pan when you start cooking. Don't scour the pan; it will damage the layer of tin and expose some copper. To clean up after using the pan, soak it in water then dry it with a soft cloth.

C

TIP

Hold textiles to the light to find the holes.

Coverlet, Jacquard, 5 Colors, Medallion, Eagle Corners, Wool, Cotton, Holmes County, c.1885
$211.00

Garth's Auctioneers & Appraisers

Coverlet, Jacquard, Memorial Hall, Centennial, Wool, Cotton, Flowers, Fringe, c.1876, 72 x 80 In.
$235.00

Garth's Auctioneers & Appraisers

TIP

If you plan to go away on a long trip, put a vase filled with artificial flowers near a lamp where they can be seen from the street. Live flowers only last a few days, so if you can fool a burglar into thinking your flowers are fresh, he will probably pass by and go to a house that appears unoccupied.

Lampshade, Dark Amber, Beehive Style, 4 ¾ x 5 In., Pair	35.00
Pitcher, Bulbous, Cobalt, Applied Handle, 5 ¼ In.	65.00
Pitcher, Ewer Style, Amberina, Attached Handle, 12 In.	55.00
Tumbler, Diagonal Swirl, Smoke, 1950s, 4 ¾ In.	12.00
Vase, 3 Crystal Curled Feet, Flared, 7 In.	75.00
Vase, Bottle, Pinched, Emerald Green, 12 ½ In.	99.00
Vase, Dark Amberina, Applied Snake, Hourglass Shape, 11 ½ In.	60.00
Vase, Hat Shape, Amberina, Ruby To Yellow, 5 ½ In.	65.00
Vase, Light Green, Flared, Footed, 10 In.	40.00

CRANBERRY GLASS is an almost transparent yellow-red glass. It resembles the color of cranberry juice. The glass has been made in Europe and America since the Civil War. It is still being made, and reproductions can fool the unwary. Related glass items may be listed in other categories, such as Rubina Verde.

Bride's Bowl, Hobbs, Swirling Design, Ruffled Opalescent Rim, Silver Plate Holder, 14 x 8 ½ In...	127.00
Dresser Jar, Twist Pattern, 6 In.	93.00
Jar, Silver Dome Lid, Victorian, 6 In.	34.00
Lamp, Hanging, Opalescent Swirl, Metal Cap, 18 x 9 In.	127.00
Perfume Bottle, Gilt Metal Caddy, Thatched Hut Shape, Embossed Flowers, Bees, 5 ¼ In.	604.00
Pitcher, Buttons & Braids Pattern, Baluster, Crimped Rim, Looped Handle, Ring Foot, 10 In..	489.00
Pitcher, Leaf Bracket, Bulbous, Wide Spout, Clear Loop Handle, Ring Foot, 9 In.	173.00
Pitcher, Ribbed Optic Lattice, Opalescent, Tankard Shape, 10 In.	633.00
Salt & Pepper, Crisscross, Opalescent, 3 ½ In., Pair	575.00
Shaker, Angus Swirl, Pressed, 2 ½ In.	23.00
Shaker, Optic Ribbed, Gold Deer, 4 In., Pair	748.00
Sugar Shaker, Textured Bark Body, Enameled Blossoms, Metal Lid, 2 ¾ In.	173.00
Toothpick Holder, Reverse Swirl Pattern, Opalescent, Cylindrical, Ring Bottom, 2 ½ In.	374.00

CREAMWARE, or queensware, was developed by Josiah Wedgwood about 1765. It is a cream-colored earthenware that has been copied by many factories. Similar wares may be listed under Pearlware and Wedgwood.

Basket, Pierced, Strap Handles, Rope Twisted Foot, c.1780, 4 ⅞ x 6 In.	259.00
Figurine, Cradle, Green, c.1805, 3 ½ x 5 In.	456.00
Jug, Black Transfer, Commodore Preble, Fame, Indian, Flags, Banner, Aug. 3, 1804, 9 In.	708.00
Mold, Food, Fish Shape	59.00
Platter, Tortoiseshell Glaze, Green & Yellow Spotted, Manganese Brown, Staffordshire, 16 In.	354.00
Stirrup Cup, Bull's Head, Painted, Yellow, Green, Brown Dotted Stripe, Staffordshire, c.1760, 5 In.	1003.00
Teapot, Lid, Cockpit Hill, Globular, Painted, Exotic Bird, Flowers, Bird Knop, c.1770, 5 ½ In...	826.00
Tureen, Lid, Acorn Finial, Medusa Mask, Lion Ring Handle, 1800s, 10 x 15 In.	1063.00

CROWN DERBY is the name given to porcelain made in Derby, England, from the 1770s to 1935. Andrew Planche and William Duesbury established Crown Derby as the first china-making factory in Derby. Pieces are marked with a crown and the letter *D* or the word *Derby*. The earliest pieces were made by the original Derby factory, while later pieces were made by the King Street Partnerships (1848–1935) or the Derby Crown Porcelain Co. (1876–90). Derby Crown Porcelain Co. became Royal Crown Derby Co. Ltd. in 1890. It is now part of Royal Doulton Tableware Ltd.

Bowl, Bouquet, Scalloped Gilt Trim, Blue, Orange, c.1870	795.00
Bowl, Red Aves, Octagon, 11 In.	210.00
Plate, Tree, Partridge, Blue, Orange, c.1820, 8 ¾ In.	125.00
Tea Set, Imari, Teapot, Creamer, Covered Sugar, 2 Cups & Saucers, 7 Piece	600.00
Tray, Pierced Handle, Roses, Gilt Leaves, c.1800, 8 ¾ x 7 ½ In.	349.00
Urn, Garlands, Scroll, Leaves, Red, Gilt, Lion Feet, c.1810, 4 x 2 ¾ In.	395.00

CROWN DUCAL is the name used on some pieces of porcelain made by A.G. Richardson and Co., Ltd., of Tunstall and Cobridge, England. The name has been used since 1916. Crown Ducal is a well-known maker of chintz pattern dishes. The company was bought by Wedgwood in 1974.

Bowl, Fruit, Flowers, Gilt Trim, Glendale, 5 ⅛ In.	21.00
Bowl, Vegetable, Flowered Teal Border, Fair Oak, 9 In.	42.00
Bowl, Vegetable, Fruits, Citrus, Oval, 8 In.	16.00
Charger, Central Bouquet, Blue Rim, 10 ½ In.	32.00
Plate, Alpine, 10 ⅛ In.	23.00
Platter, Central Flower Basket, Cambridge, Teal, 14 ¼ In.	64.00
Soup, Dish, Underplate, Cobalt Blue & Gold Bands On Border, 2 Handles, 12 Piece	180.00

CROWN MILANO glass was made by the Mt. Washington Glass Works about 1890. It was a plain biscuit color with a satin finish decorated with flowers and often had large gold scrolls. Not all pieces are marked.

Biscuit Jar, Cream Shaded To Rose, Pointillist Stylized Flowers, Oval, 7 ½ In.	403.00
Biscuit Jar, Opal, Arab Scene Of Bedouin, Camels, Pyramids, Marked, 8 In. ....*Illus*	4888.00
Biscuit Jar, Yellow, Oak Leaves, Acorns, Embossed Metal Lid, Turtle Finial, 6 In. ....*Illus*	461.00
Creamer, Pansies, Oriental Style, Bulbous Melon Form, Metal Spout, 3 ½ In.	527.00
Cup & Saucer, Demitasse, Scalloped, Flowers, Applied Loop Handle, CM, Crown	460.00
Dish, Sweetmeat, Melon Ribbed, Stemmed Mums, Stamped CM, 5 In.	374.00
Dresser Box, Lid, Flowers, Bulbous Melon Form, Metal Collar & Handle, 5 In.	702.00
Ewer, Cream Color, Gold Scrolling, Scenic Medallion, Cottage, Rope Twist Handle, 11 In.	3335.00
Ewer, Opal Glass, Cream To Green, Bell Flowers, Rope Twist Handle, Bulbous, Ruffled Spout, 10 ½ In.	748.00
Jar, Lid, Flowers & Medallions, Squatty Bulbous, Shell Finial, Marked, 6 ¾ In.	1035.00
Jardiniere, Pansies, Oriental Decoration, Round, 6 ¾ x 9 ½ In.	567.00
Lamp, Bulbous Base, Mottled Blue, Pink, White Flowers, Leaves, Domed Shade, 14 In.....*Illus*	5175.00
Perfume Bottle, Lid, Gold Finial, Enameled Maidenhead Fern Design, Opal, 6 In.	805.00
Salt, Chick Shape, Pink Enamel, Flowers, Metal Chick Head, 2 x 2 ½ In.	1287.00
Sugar & Creamer, Opal Glass, Blossoms, Gold Scrolling, Shell Handles, Lid, 4 ½ In.	1840.00
Sugar & Creamer, Yellow Flowers, Rounded Rectangle, Reeded Loop Handles	1755.00
Sugar Shaker, Cream Color, Autumn Leaves, Figural Silver Plate Holder, Egg Shape, 9 In.	633.00
Sugar Shaker, Yellow Shaded To Rose, Blue Flower Clusters, 4 ½ In.	201.00
Syrup, Flowers, Gold Lattice, Melon Form, Metal Lid, Twisted Handle, 5 ½ In.	761.00
Syrup, Melon Ribbed, Gold Lattice, Opal Flower Sprays, Marked, 6 In.	575.00
Syrup, Oak Leaves, Bulbous Melon Form, Silver Plate Lid & Handle, 3 ¾ In.	527.00
Vase, Cream Color, Ginko Leaves, Scrolling, Double Gourd, Bulbous, 6 ½ In.	403.00
Vase, Ducks In Flight, Cylindrical, Reeded & Curled Handles, 11 x 5 In.	7605.00
Vase, Enameled Oak Leaves & Acorns, Bulbous, Applied Handles, 8 In.	748.00
Vase, Garden Flower Bouquets, Gold Scrolls, Tapered Urn Shape, 8 ¼ In.	316.00
Vase, Guba Ducks, Blazing Sun, Round, Bird Beak Rim, Handles At Neck, 7 In.	4025.00
Vase, Opal Glass, Gold Scrolling Medallions, Flowers, Gray Mottled Ground, 7 In. ....*Illus*	460.00
Vase, Pansies, Gilt Lattice, Triangular Stick, Acanthus Leaves At Base Of Neck, 8 In.	690.00
Vase, Rose Blooms, Branches, Opalescent, Irregular Cut Rim, Signed, 7 ½ In. ....*Illus*	978.00
Vase, Scrolling Flowers, Pointillist Style, Globe Shape, Scalloped Rim, 4 ¾ In.	288.00

CROWN TUSCAN *pattern is included in the Cambridge glass category.*

CRUETS of glass or porcelain were made to hold vinegar, oil, and other condiments. They were especially popular during Victorian times and have been made in a variety of styles since the eighteenth century. Additional cruets may be found in the Castor Set category and also in various glass categories.

Cameo, Red Satin Glass, Leafy Mums, Camphor Handle, Stopper, Metal Spout, 5 ½ In.	690.00
Canary, Cranberry, Leaf Mold, Faceted Stopper, Northwood, 7 In.	748.00
Cut Glass, Topaz Cut To Clear, Crosscut Diamond, Strawberry Diamond & Fan, 6 ½ In.	100.00
Melon Ribbed, Blueberries, Oak Leaves, Loop Handle, Stopper With Finial, Mt. Washington, 7 In.	805.00
Peach To Yellow, Squat, Ribbed, Stick Neck, Loop Handle, Stopper, Mt. Washington, 7 In.	316.00
Ribbed Pillar Pattern, Blue Stippled Berries, Leaves, Stopper, Mt. Washington, 7 In.	546.00

CT GERMANY was first part of a mark used by a company in Altwasser, Germany (now part of Walbrzych, Poland), in 1845. The initials stand for C. Tielsch, a partner in the firm. The Hutschenreuther firm took over the company in 1918 and continued to use the *CT*.

C. T.

Bowl, Pink & Magenta Roses, Mint Green Rim, Open Handles, 13 ½ In.	115.00
Charger, Blue & White Flowers, Bas-Relief, c.1900, 13 ½ In.	189.00
Dish, Lobster, Miniature Roses, Pink, 2 Sections, Handle, 14 In.	75.00
Plate, Oyster, 7 Wells, Gilt Trim, Green Ribbons, c.1800, 9 ¼ In.	399.00
Relish, Flowers, Leaves, Reticulated Border, 12 In.	80.00
Shaving Mug, Pink Roses, Gilt	38.00

CUP PLATES are small glass or china plates that held the cup while a diner of the mid-nineteenth century drank coffee or tea from the saucer. The most famous cup plates were made of glass at the Boston and Sandwich factory located in Sandwich, Massachusetts. There have been many new glass cup plates made in recent years for sale to gift shops or collectors of limited editions. These are similar to the old plates but can be recognized as new.

Clear, Bull's-Eye Scallops, c.1835, 3 ½ In.	150.00
Glass, Clear, Fleur-De-Lis, Trefoils, Scallops, Center Dot, 3 ¼ In.	100.00

C

Cowan, Bowl, Jazz, Glazed, Viktor Schreckengost, Signed, Stamped, 1929, 11 ½ x 16 In. $100,000.00

Rago Arts & Auction Center

Cowan, Plate, Danse Moderne, Glazed, Jazz Series, Viktor Schreckengost, Stamped, 1929, 11 ¼ In. $13,750.00

Rago Arts & Auction Center

Crown Milano, Biscuit Jar, Opal, Arab Scene Of Bedouin, Camels, Pyramids, Marked, 8 In. $4,888.00

Early Auction Co.

Crown Milano, Biscuit Jar, Yellow, Oak Leaves, Acorns, Embossed Metal Lid, Turtle Finial, 6 In. $461.00

Early Auction Co.

Crown Milano, Lamp, Bulbous Base, Mottled Blue, Pink, White Flowers, Leaves, Domed Shade, 14 In. $5,175.00

Early Auction Co.

Crown Milano, Vase, Opal Glass, Gold Scrolling Medallions, Flowers, Gray Mottled Ground, 7 In. $460.00

Early Auction Co.

Crown Milano, Vase, Rose Blooms, Branches, Opalescent, Irregular Cut Rim, Signed, 7 ½ In. $978.00

Early Auction Co.

Glass, Clear, Rope Rim, Star, 12 Points, Bull's-Eye, Daisies, 3 ½ In.	175.00
Glass, Clear, Ship, Scrolls, Shields, Stars, Scalloped Rim, c.1800, 3 ½ In.	65.00
Pearlware, Dark Blue, Flowers & Vases, c.1825, 3 ¾ In.	200.00
Porcelain, Blue & White, Monastery, On Hill, Farmer, Cow, c.1840, 3 ⅜ In.	100.00
Porcelain, Blue, White, Figures, In Boat, Landscape, Walker & Co., 1875, 4 In.	109.00
Pottery, English Luster, Girl, Holding Basket, Garden, c.1820, 3 ¾ In.	95.00
Pottery, Flowers, Multicolor, Embossed, Staffordshire, 1800s, 4 ⅛ In.	55.00
Pottery, Pearlware, Dark Blue, Fruit, Stippled Ground, c.1825, 3 ½ In.	225.00
Pottery, Pearlware, Winged Cherubs, Holding Roses, c.1825, 3 ⅞ In.	85.00
Pottery, White, Black, Boy Reading, Raised Daisy Border, c.1870, 3 ½ In.	70.00

CURRIER & IVES made the famous American lithographs marked with their name from 1857 to 1907. The mark used on the print included the street address in New York City, and it is possible to date the year of the original issue from this information. Earlier prints were made by N. Currier and use that name from 1835 to 1847. Many reprints of the Currier or Currier & Ives prints have been made. Some collectors buy the insurance calendars that were based on the old prints. The words *large*, *small*, or *medium folio* refer to size. The original print sizes were very small (up to about 7 x 9 in.), small (8.8 x 12.8 in.), medium (9 x 14 in. to 14 x 20 in.), large (larger than 14 x 20 in.). Other sizes are probably later copies. Other prints by Currier & Ives may be listed in the Card category under Advertising and in the Sheet Music category. Currier & Ives dinnerware patterns may be found in the Adams or Dinnerware categories.

American Express Train, Steam Engine, Landscape, Frame, 20th Century, 25 x 34 In.	288.00
American Farm Scenes No. 2, Woman, Children Feeding Animals, Frame, 20 ¾ x 26 ½ In.	531.00
American Farm Scenes No. 3, Barnyard, Frame, 21 ½ x 26 ¾ In.	472.00
American Farm Yard, Evening, Livestock, Maple Frame, 24 ¾ x 31 ¾ In.	588.00
American Homestead, 4 Seasons, Folio, Burl Frame, 16 x 20 In., 4 Piece	1880.00
American Winter Scenes, Morning, Lithograph, Frame, 1854, 22 x 29 In. ....*Illus*	2520.00
Celebrated Horse, Champion Of The Turf, George M. Patchen, Frame, 1860, 23 x 31 ¾ In.... *Illus*	540.00
Darktown Fire Brigade, Investigating A Smoke, Frame, 17 x 13 In.	300.00
Darktown Hook & Ladder Corp, Going To The Front, Frame, 1884, 16 ½ x 12 ½ In.	240.00
Death Of John Quincy Adams, Lithograph, Frame, N. Currier, 1848, 9 ½ x 13 In.	71.00
Entrance To The Highlands, Hudson River, Looking South, Frame, 1864, 11 x 30 ½ In.	1770.00
Futurity Race At Sheepshead Bay, Frame, 20 x 34 In.	547.00
Grazing Farm, Frame, 1865	472.00
Great West, Train, Town, Mountains, Mat, Frame, 1870, 9 x 13 In. ....*Illus*	889.00
Home From The War, Civil War Soldier Embracing Wife, Color Lithograph, 1861, 14 x 10 In.	71.00
James K. Polk, People's Choice, Portrait, Beveled Wood Frame, N. Currier, 1844, 9 ⅝ x 14 In.	370.00
John Wesley Preaching On His Father's Grave, Lithograph, 1742, 12 x 14 In.	71.00
Landscape, Fruit, Flowers, 1862, 20 x 27 In.	120.00
Major Genl. W.T. Sherman, March Through Georgia, Lithograph, Tinted, Frame, 13 x 9 In.	71.00
Midnight Race On The Mississippi, Steamboats, 11 x 14 In.	235.00
Obdurate Mule, Going Back On The Parson, Frame, 1890, 11 x 15 In.	259.00
Prairie Fires Of The Great West, 1800s, Frame, 11 ½ x 15 ½ In.	851.00
Rally Round The Flag Boys, Victory At Last, Frame, 1861, 16 x 20 In. ....*Illus*	382.00
Salvator, Horse, Grass, Reeded Walnut Frame, 1890, 13 x 17 ½ In.	213.00
The King Of The Road, Horse, Man In Buggy, 22 x 30 In.	764.00
Trolling For Blue Fish, Sailboats, Carved Walnut Frame, 1866, 22 ¾ x 29 ⅞ In. ....*Illus*	10200.00
Washington, N. Currier, Wood Frame, 13 x 19 In.	162.00

CUSTARD GLASS is a slightly yellow opaque glass. It was made in England in the 1880s and was first made in the United States in the 1890s. It has been reproduced. Additional pieces may be found in the Cambridge, Fenton, and Heisey categories. Custard glass is called *Ivorina Verde* by Heisey and other companies.

Maize is its own category in this book.

Mug, Paneled Bottom, c.1880	45.00
Vase, Cornucopia, Pink, 9 In.	35.00

CUT GLASS has been made since ancient times, but the large majority of the pieces now for sale date from the American Brilliant period of glass design, 1880 to 1905. These pieces have elaborate geometric designs with a deep miter cut. Modern cut glass with a similar appearance is being made in England, Ireland, Poland, and the Czech and Slovak republics. Chips and scratches are often difficult to notice but lower the value dramatically. A signature on the glass adds significantly to the value. Other cut glass pieces are listed under factory names, like Hawkes, Libbey, and Sinclaire.

Banana Bowl, Hobstar, Nailhead Diamond, Vesica & Harvard, 4 ¼ x 10 ¾ In.	80.00

Banana Bowl, Hobstar, Strawberry Diamond, Cane & Fan, 4 x 9 ½ In.	40.00
Basket, Hobstar, Vesica, Strawberry Diamond & Fan, Crosshatched Handle, 9 x 10 In.	375.00
Bell, Hobstar, Star & Fan, 4 ½ In.	200.00
Bell, Pluto, J. Hoare, 5 ½ In.	150.00
Berry Set, Orleans, Egginton, 3 ¾ x 8-In. Master, 7 Piece	125.00
Bonbon, Hobstar & Long Thumbprint, Notched & Scalloped Pedestal, 10 x 9 In.	150.00
Bookends, Intaglio Flower Branch, 7 ½ x 7 In.	125.00
Bowl, Acorns & Branches, Scalloped Edge, Hobstar Foot, 5 x 6 ½ In.	500.00
Bowl, Alhambra, Oval, Meriden, 3 x 11 In.	1500.00
Bowl, Alhambra, Round, Meriden, 4 ¼ x 9 In.	1000.00
Bowl, Amethyst, Overlay, Clear, Boat Shape, Brass Stand, Bead Rim, Austria, c.1890, 5 ½ x 6 In., Pair.	207.00
Bowl, Assyrian Style, Flat Hobstars, 2 ½ x 10 In.	125.00
Bowl, Blue, Red & Green Swirl, Clear Diamond Windows, Crosscut Fan Border, 4 x 8 In.	2200.00
Bowl, Bolo, J. Hoare, Marked, 4 x 8 In.	60.00
Bowl, Cane, Vesica, Zipper, Intaglio Flowers, 6-Sided, 3 ¾ x 8 ¾ In.	100.00
Bowl, Carolyn, Notched Stem, Pedestal Base, J. Hoare, 8 x 10 In.	175.00
Bowl, Crosscut Diamond, Strawberry Diamond & Fan, Hobstar Center, 3 ½ x 9 In.	148.00
Bowl, Elmira, 4 ½ x 9 In.	260.00
Bowl, Expanding Star, Elite, Gorham Silver Rim, Intaglio Greek Symbols, 4 x 9 In.	125.00
Bowl, Flared, Hobstar Chain, Strawberry Diamond, Hob Button, Prism, 4 x 11 ½ In.	384.00
Bowl, Flared, Hobstar, Nailhead Diamond, Vesica, Zipper, 3 x 12 In.	148.00
Bowl, Florence, J. Hoare, 3 ½ x 8 In.	100.00
Bowl, Fruit, Hobstar, Strawberry Diamond & Prism, Pedestal, 9 ½ x 8 In.	90.00
Bowl, Garland, 4 x 9 In.	200.00
Bowl, Hobstar & Feather, Crimped, Egginton, Marked, 6 ¾ In.	60.00
Bowl, Hobstar, Vesica & Nailhead Diamond, Clark, Signed, 4 x 9 In.	125.00
Bowl, Imperial, 2 x 9 In.	475.00
Bowl, Intaglio Rose Garland, Sinclaire, 4 x 10 In.	50.00
Bowl, Louis XVI Style, Oval, Clear, Gilt Bronze Dolphin Feet, Scrolled Caryatid Handles, 11 x 20 In.	750.00
Bowl, Low, Alhambra, Sterling Rim, Meriden, 1 ¾ x 7 In.	531.00
Bowl, Marcela, Tricorner Shape, Libbey, 2 x 10 In.	3840.00
Bowl, Montrose, Green, Cranberry & Amethyst Cut To Clear, Dorflinger, 4 x 9 In.	65000.00
Bowl, Nailhead Diamond, Prism & Long Thumbprint, Cranberry Cut To Clear, 4 x 9 In.	3300.00
Bowl, Oval, Snowflake & Holly, Sinclaire, 12 In.	2600.00
Bowl, Planeta, Blown Mold, Straus, 3 x 10 In.	325.00
Bowl, Planeta, Napoleon Hat Shape, Straus, 4 ¼ x 12 ¼ In.	300.00
Bowl, Prima Donna, Clark, 2 ¼ x 8 ¾ In.	200.00
Bowl, Propeller, 4 ¼ x 8 ½ In.	150.00
Bowl, Rex, Bishop's Hat Shape, 2 ½ x 10 ¾ In.	1000.00
Bowl, Seneca, 3 ¾ x 9 In.	175.00
Bowl, Success, 8-Sided, Empire, 2 x 8 In.	300.00
Bowl, Sultana, 3 ¼ x 8 In.	175.00
Bowl, Venice, J. Hoare, Marked, 3 ½ x 8 In.	75.00
Bowl, Wild Rose, 4 x 9 In.	1000.00
Bowl, Yale, Pentagon Shape, 3 x 9 In.	175.00
Box, Glove, 3 Flashed Hobstars, Crosshatch & Double Thumbprint, Hinged Lid, 11 In.	350.00
Bread Tray, Hobstar, Nailhead Diamond, Round Hobstars, 13 ¾ x 6 ¾ In.	175.00
Butter, Cover, Hobstar & Hobstar Chain, Fan Highlights, 5 ½ x 8 In.	75.00
Butter, Cover, Hobstar, Prism & Fan, Faceted Knob, 6 x 8 ½ In.	100.00
Butter, Cover, Hobstar, Strawberry Diamond & Fan, 6 x 8 In.	50.00
Candlestick, 6-Sided Stem, Rayed Base, 14 In., Pair	450.00
Carafe, Hobstar, Strawberry Diamond, Vesica & Fan, Step Cut Neck, 8 In.	75.00
Carafe, Lotus, Egginton, 8 In.	75.00
Carafe, Water, Hob Diamond, Ball Shape, Cut Handle, Dorflinger, 9 ¼ In.	300.00
Carafe, Water, Monarch, J. Hoare, 8 ¼ In.	75.00
Card Tray, Flashed Hobstar, Strawberry Diamond & 8-Point Star Border, 7 In.	200.00
Celery Dish, Lotus, Egginton, 10 ¾ In.	50.00
Celery Dish, Venice, J. Hoare, Signed, 11 In.	25.00
Celery Vase, Strawberry Diamonds, Fans, Flashed Vesicas, Knop Stem, Footed, Pa., c.1825, 8 x 4 ⅝ In.	207.00
Chalice, Cut Overlay, Blue, Colorless, Stars, Diamonds, Fan, c.1890, 12 ¼ x 5 In.	3220.00
Chalice, Engraved, Cut Overlay, Ruby, Colorless, Draped Rim, Flowers, Ivy, Round Foot, c.1900, 8 In.	575.00
Chalice, Tapered Bowl, Fan, Chair Bottom Design, Faceted Stem, Round Foot, 11 ½ In.	120.00
Champagne, Hob Button, Gold, Hobstar Foot, Union Glass Co., 5 In.	1050.00
Champagne, Prism Cut, Double Notched Handle, Rayed Base, 13 In.	250.00
Cheese Dish, Lid, Hobstar, Wreath, Nailhead Diamond & Fan, Pinwheel Knob, 7 x 10 In.	500.00
Claret Jug, Silver Mounts, Bacchus Mask, Lid, Horace Woodward & Co., London, 1896, 11 In. *Illus*	2749.00

Currier & Ives, American Winter Scenes, Morning, Lithograph, Frame, 1854, 22 x 29 In.
$2,520.00

Skinner, Inc.

Currier & Ives, Celebrated Horse, Champion Of The Turf, George M. Patchen, Frame, 1860, 23 x 31 ¾ In.
$540.00

Skinner, Inc.

Currier & Ives, Great West, Train, Town, Mountains, Mat, Frame, 1870, 9 x 13 In.
$889.00

Skinner, Inc.

Currier & Ives, Rally Round The Flag Boys, Victory At Last, Frame, 1861, 16 x 20 In.
$382.00

Cowan's Auctions

Currier & Ives, Trolling For Blue Fish, Sailboats, Carved Walnut Frame, 1866, 22 ¾ x 29 ⅞ In. $10,200.00

Skinner, Inc.

Cut Glass, Claret Jug, Star, Silver Mounts, Lid, Horace Woodward & Co., London, 1896, 11 In. $2,749.00

Neal Auction Co.

What Is "Brilliant Period"?

The American "Brilliant Period" of cut glass lasted from 1876, the year of the Philadelphia Centennial Exhibition, until about 1910. Leaded glass used was thick, heavy, deeply cut, and highly polished—hence the name *brilliant*.

Brilliant colored cut glass was made for a shorter period, from the 1880s until 1900. The most popular type was "colored cut to clear" glass: The glassblower created a shape, then the glass was dipped into salts or oxides to give it a coat of color. The blower then finished the blank before the cutter went to work.

Cologne Bottle, Diamond, Arch & Star, Royal Blue Cut To Clear, Ball Shape, 6 In.	350.00
Cologne Bottle, Marlboro, Dorflinger, Bulbous, Faceted Stopper, 7 In.	150.00
Compote, Clear, Blown, Ellipse, Fan, Flute Band, Button Stem, Stepped Foot, c.1840, 8 x 9 ½ In.	196.00
Compote, Crestwick, Notched Teardrop Stem, Egginton, 9 x 9 In.	100.00
Compote, Cylindrical Bowl, Scattered Cut Stars, Round Foot, 8 ½ x 6 ½ In., Pair	492.00
Compote, Diamond, Sawtooth Rim, Diamond Shaped Foot, 1800s, 9 ¾ x 13 ¼ In.	180.00
Compote, Harvard, Oval, 2 Sections, Pattern Cut Pedestal Base, 8 x 12 In.	400.00
Compote, Hobstar & Cane, Notched Stem, 10 x 8 In., Pair	200.00
Compote, Hobstar & Vesica, Hobstar Foot, 9 ½ x 7 ¼ In.	147.00
Compote, Hobstar, Strawberry Diamond & Cane, 8 ½ x 6 In.	60.00
Compote, Hobstar, Strawberry Diamond, Button & Fan, J. Hoare, 11 ¾ x 6 In.	100.00
Compote, Imperial, Star Cut Stem, Faceted Standard, 9 ½ In.	230.00
Compote, No. 100, Rolled Rim Sides, Scalloped Hobstar Base, Elmira, 12 x 9 In.	450.00
Compote, Nubian Black, Intaglio Flowers, Pearl White Edge, Sinclaire, 6 In., Pair	100.00
Compote, Pear & Vintage, Cut Foot, 3 ½ x 8 In.	280.00
Compote, Strawberry Diamond, Notched Teardrop Stem, 9 x 4 ½ In.	80.00
Compote, Tapering Faceted Stem, Stepped Foot, Wide Bowl, Swirled Cutting, 10 x 15 In.	738.00
Cordial, Hobstar, Strawberry Diamond, Vesica & Fan, 3 ¾ In.	40.00
Decanter, Cobalt Blue To Clear, Fans, Bulbous, Fluted, Narrow Neck, Clear Ball Stopper, 9 ¼ In.	92.00
Decanter, Hob Button, Amber, Ball Shape, Clear Handle, Pattern Cut Stopper, 9 In.	1800.00
Decanter, Hobstar & Cane, 3 Neck Rings, 11 ½ In.	100.00
Decanter, Hobstar, Long Thumbprint, Zipper & Kite, J. Hoard, Marked, 8 In.	60.00
Decanter, Lotus, Egginton, 12 ½ In.	40.00
Decanter, Lotus, Snake Handle, Facet Cut Neck Ring, Egginton, 12 In.	75.00
Decanter, Pinwheel & Fan, Step Cut Neck, 12 In.	50.00
Decanter, Regency, Cylindrical, Cut Banding, Faceted Neck, Mushroom Stopper, c.1835, 9 ½ In., Pair	246.00
Decanter, Russian, Crosscut Diamond, Vesica, Zipper, Fan & Tusk, Flip Lid, 10 In.	550.00
Decanter, Ship's, Heart, Cut Spout, Triple Notched Handle, Pitkin & Brooks, 9 ½ In.	400.00
Decanter, Stopper, 11 ¾ x 6 In., Pair	1652.00
Decanter, Stopper, Thousand Eye, 8 ½ In.	250.00
Decanter, Strawberry Diamond, Concave Diamond, Cut Stopper, 12 In., Pair	250.00
Decanter, Water, Bristol Rose, Mt. Washington, 8 ¼ In.	175.00
Dish, Hobstar & Fan, Center Stick Handle, Faceted Knob, 5 ½ x 7 In.	75.00
Dish, Mayonnaise, Hobstar, Nailhead Diamond & Fan, Tusk Shape, J. Hoare, 7 ½ In.	335.00
Dish, Sweetmeat, Lid, Pedestal Base, Thumbprint Cuts, Flint, 13 ½ x 7 In., Pair	805.00
Dish, Witch's Hat Shape, Hobstar & Fan, 6 ½ x 8 In.	75.00
Ewer, Water, Hobstar Chain, Vesica & Fan, Intaglio, Triple Notched Handle, 12 In.	175.00
Ferner, Hobstar, Geometric & Fan, 3-Footed, J. Hoare, 3 ¾ x 7 ¼ In.	60.00
Finger Bowl, Hobstar Center, Geometric Hobstars, Diamond & Fan, 5 In., 6 Piece	50.00
Finger Bowl, Wheat, J. Hoare	800.00
Flask, Crosscut Diamond, Strawberry Diamond, Star & Bar, Heart Shape, Woman's, 4 In.	200.00
Flask, Cut Glass, Diamonds, Yellow To Clear, Silver Cap, Woman's, 5 In.	150.00
Flask, Hobstar On Each Side, Silver Lid, Woman's, 5 ½ In.	100.00
Goblet, Crosscut Diamond & Fan, Notched Stem, Rayed Base, 6 ¼ In.	160.00
Goblet, Middlesex, 6 In.	80.00
Goblet, Parisian, Cranberry Cut To Clear, Hobstar Foot, Dorflinger, 4 ⅝ In.	1450.00
Goblet, Star & Swirled Feather, Green Cut To Yellow, Clear Stem & Foot, 5 In.	300.00
Goblet, Water, Hobstar, Cane, Strawberry Diamond & Fan, Facet Cut Knob, 6 In., 12 Piece	650.00
Goblet, Wine, Eleanor, Cranberry Cut To Clear, Hobstar Foot, J. Hoare, 4 ⅝ In.	2500.00
Goblet, Wine, Hob Button, Punty Border, Cranberry Cut To Clear, 5 In., Pair	600.00
Goblet, Wine, Russian, Star Cut Buttons, Blue Cut To Clear, 4 ⅝ In.	650.00
Goblet, Wine, Russian, Star Cut Buttons, Faceted Knop, Aqua Cut To Clear, 4 ½ In.	4500.00
Hair Receiver, Hobstar Chain, Intaglio Flower Highlights, Signed, Hunt, 3 ½ x 4 ½ In.	200.00
Humidor, Glenwood, Hobstar Cut Lid, Bergen, 7 In.	200.00
Humidor, Hobstar, Vesica, Strawberry Diamond & Fan, 6 ½ In.	225.00
Ice Bucket, Crosscut Diamond, Strawberry Diamond, Block, Star & Fan, Pedestal, Handles, 5 x 10 In.	150.00
Ice Bucket, Hobstar, Strawberry Diamond, Cane & Fan, Blue To Clear, 5 ¾ In.	225.00
Ice Tub, 2 Handles, Parisian, Pattern Cut Handles, Dorflinger, 5 ¼ x 8 In.	354.00
Ice Tub, Acme, 2 Handles, J. Hoare, 4 ½ x 8 ½ In.	500.00
Jam Jar, Vintage, Sterling Lid & Spoon, 3 ½ x 6 In.	125.00
Jar, Glue, Lid, Hobstar, Cane, Strawberry Diamond, Flashed Star, Pinched Waist, 5 In.	300.00
Jar, Wilbur, Bulbous, Dome Lid, Faceted Knob, Quaker City, 8 ½ In.	500.00
Jewelry Box, Strawberry Cutting, Anthemion Escutcheon, Paw Feet, Molded Border, Gilt, Lid, 5 x 4 In.	922.00
Jug, Demi-John, Monarch, J. Hoare, ½ Gal., 14 In.	1000.00
Jug, Hobstar, Vesica & Fan, Triple Notched Handle, Rayed Base, 9 ½ In.	100.00

C

Jug, Rum, Flute, Blue Cut To Clear, Faceted Ring Neck, Notched Handle, Clark, 8 In.	500.00
Jug, Rum, Heart, Hobstar, Strawberry Diamond & Prism, Ball Shape, 7 In.	525.00
Jug, Water, Hobstar, Vesica, Cane & Fan, Hobstar Base, 8 ½ In.	425.00
Knife Rest, Hobstar, Nailhead Diamond, Strawberry Diamond, 5 ½ In.	150.00
Ladle Rest, Hobstar, Strawberry Diamond & Fan, Club Shape, 6 ¾ In.	75.00
Mug, Beer, Notched Handle, No. 50, Dorflinger, 5 In.	300.00
Nappy, Hobstar Cluster, Cane, Vesica, Strawberry Diamond, Gold, 6 In.	944.00
Perfume Bottle, Bull's-Eye & Prism, Green Cut To Clear, Embossed Silver Stopper, 4 In.	200.00
Pitcher, Cider, Lotus, Signed, Egginton, 6 In.	150.00
Pitcher, Cut Flutes, Barrel Shape, Hollow Handle, Wheeling, Va., c.1835, 7 ⅜ x 4 In., Qt.	1035.00
Pitcher, Marquis, Triple Notched Handle, Rayed Base, Egginton, 10 ½ x 8 ½ In.	500.00
Pitcher, Russian Cut, c.1900, 11 In.	240.00
Pitcher, Venetian, Milk, Straus, 6 In.	175.00
Pitcher, Water, Genoa, Hobstar Base, Clark, 9 ¾ In.	200.00
Pitcher, Water, Lotus, Triple Notched Handle, Egginton, Marked, 9 ½ In.	275.00
Pitcher, Water, Zipper, Pinched Waist, Notched Handle, Rayed Base, Silver Spout, 11 In.	175.00
Plate, Festoon, Signed, 7 In.	450.00
Plate, Stars & Pillars, Sinclaire, 7 In.	250.00
Plate, Trellis, Triple Miter, Rayed Center, 6 In.	125.00
Punch Bowl, Clifton, 6 ¾ x 12 In.	260.00
Punch Bowl, Hobstar, Cane, Strawberry Diamond, Harvard, Banana Shape, 11 ½ x 13 In.	826.00
Punch Bowl, Hobstars, Crosshatch, Flaring Base, Spread Foot, Stand, c.1915, 12 ¾ x 14 In.	615.00
Punch Bowl, Marleboro & Fan, Dorflinger, 7 x 14 In.	531.00
Punch Bowl, Palmetto, Deep Notched Edge, Flared Foot, Clark, 13 x 14 In.	750.00
Punch Bowl, Pluto, Notched Edge, J. Hoare, 7 ¾ x 14 ½ In.	650.00
Punch Bowl, Stand, Pinwheel & Dahlia, c.1900, 9 ½ x 10 In.	150.00
Punch Set, Pineapple, Hobstar Panels, Bowl, Liner Plate, 12 Cups, Germany, 9, 11, 3 x 2 ¾ In.	299.00
Rose Bowl, Hobstar, Ground, Polished Rim, 6 x 7 In.	42.00
Rose Bowl, Hobstar, Strawberry Diamond, Star & Fan, Notched Petticoat Base, 7 In.	90.00
Rose Bowl, Middlesex, New England Glass Co., 5 ¼ x 6 ½ In.	150.00
Salt, Trellis, Scalloped Hobstar Foot, Egginton, Master, 2 ¾ x 3 ¼ In.	300.00
Sandwich Tray, Beverly, Handles, Meriden, 5 ½ x 10 In.	130.00
Shrimp Cocktail, Hobstar, Button & Fan, Liner, 5 ½ In.	50.00
Sugar & Creamer, Alhambra, Triple Notched Handles, Meriden	1150.00
Sugar & Creamer, Hobstar & Fan, Petticoat Hobstar Scalloped Base, 4 ¼ In.	325.00
Sugar & Creamer, Hobstar Chain, Long Thumbprint & Prism	175.00
Sugar & Creamer, Royal, Hunt	75.00
Sugar, Lid, Clear, 9 Horizontal Ribs, Rayed Foot, Finial, c.1860, 4 ½ x 4 ¾ In.	104.00
Tankard, Intaglio, Lemon Branch & Leaf, 14 ¼ In.	649.00
Tantalus, Renaissance Bottles, Square, Faceted Stoppers, Oak, Brass, Dorflinger, 12 x 11 In.	550.00
Tazza, Hobstar & Cane, Cut Knob, Hobstar Foot, 6 x 9 In. ....*Illus*	525.00
Tazza, Hobstar, Vesica, Pinwheel & Notched Fan, Footed, Tricorn Rim, 9 x 12 In.	125.00
Tazza, Open Flower, Vesica Petals, Hobstars, Sawtooth Rim, Pedestal, Step Cut Stem, 10 ½ In.	1380.00
Teapot, Russian, Star Cut Buttons, Hobstar Lid, Faceted Knob, 6 x 8 In.	1100.00
Torte Plate, Wafer Base, Butterfly & Daisy, Hobstar Center, Pairpoint, 10 In.	295.00
Toupee Stand, Hobstar, Cane & Fan, 3 ½ x 6 In.	590.00
Tray, Baker's Gothic, Clark, 14 x 8 In.	80.00
Tray, Cheese & Cracker, Aberdeen, Wafer Base, Jewel, 3 x 10 In.	900.00
Tray, Hobstar, Strawberry Diamond & Arch, Tab Handles, 13 ½ x 8 In.	350.00
Tray, Ice Cream, Hobstar, Crosscut Diamond, Nailhead Diamond, Notched Fan, 16 In.	1100.00
Tray, Oval, Planeta, Straus, 11 ½ x 7 ¾ In.	350.00
Tray, Oval, Stars & Prism, Sinclaire, 8 ¾ x 6 ½ In.	250.00
Tray, Quarter Diamond, 8 x 12 In.	100.00
Tray, Round, Alhambra, 12 In.	3850.00
Tray, Success, Handle, Empire, 7 x 10 In.	100.00
Tumbler, Diamonds, Fans, Flutes, c.1830, 3 ¼ In.	138.00
Tumbler, Stars, Fans, Pa, c.1830, 3 ⅛ In.	104.00
Tumbler, Strawberry Diamonds, Fans, Flashed Vesicas, Pa., c.1830, 3 ⅜ In.	104.00
Urn, Tapering Faceted Stems, Stepped Foot, Swirled Design, 12 x 8 In., Pair	738.00
Vase, Bowling Pin, Hobstar, Crosscut Diamond, Strawberry Diamond & Fan, Handles, 14 In.	600.00
Vase, Bud, Tulip, Hobstar, Clear Block & Cross, Rayed Foot, Egginton, 4 ¾ In.	125.00
Vase, Canary Cut, Starburst, 7 ¼ In.	130.00
Vase, Creswick, Pedestal, Egginton, 13 ½ In.	225.00
Vase, Cut & Wheel Intaglio, Etched Flowers, Flared Rim, Paneled, Baluster, 15 x 9 ½ In.	1380.00
Vase, Diamond & Silver Threads, Floral Medallions, Corset Shape, Sinclaire, 14 In.	450.00

Cut Glass, Tazza, Hobstar & Cane, Cut Knob, Hobstar Foot, 6 x 9 In. **$525.00**

Cut Glass, Vase, Hobstars, Vertical Bars, Hobstar Buttons, Fans, Step Cut Neck, Scalloped Edge, 18 In. **$4,025.00**

Humler & Nolan

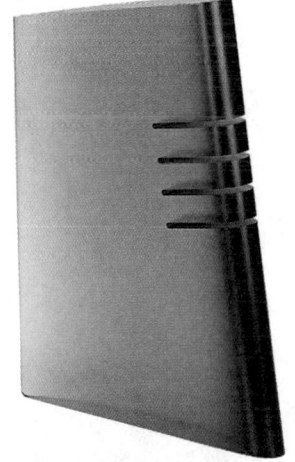

Czechoslovakia Glass, Sculpture, Cast, Cut, Polished, Blue, Petr Hora, 2000, 16 ½ x 12 In. **$3,250.00**

Rago Arts & Auction Center

TIP
Never put anything hot in a cut glass bowl. It was not made to withstand heat and will crack.

143

D'Argental, Vase, Bulbous, Cherry Branches, Cameo, 1900s, 12 x 6 ½ In. $875.00

Rago Arts & Auction Center

Daum, Dish, Frog, On Lily Pad, Pate-De-Verre, Brown & Green, Signed, 6 ½ x 6 ¼ In. $415.00

Skinner, Inc.

Daum, Ewer, Iris, Enameled, Pewter Mounted, Marked, 1895, 11 In. $444.00

Skinner, Inc.

TIP

To loosen a perfume bottle stopper, put the bottle upside down in alcohol for a few days. It may help.

Vase, Electra, Straus, 5 x 6 In.	150.00
Vase, Fan, Flashed Hobstar, Hobstar & Fan Highlights, Footed, Meriden, 8 x 10 In.	400.00
Vase, Hobstar & Wheat Sheaf, Bowling Pin Shape, Step Cut Neck, 9 ¾ In.	100.00
Vase, Hobstar, Cane & Notched Fan, Baluster, Ruffled Rim, Scalloped Foot, 14 In.	400.00
Vase, Hobstar, Crosscut Diamond & Fan, Step Cut Neck, Squat, 6 x 8 In.	175.00
Vase, Hobstar, Double Diamond, Fans, Bowling Pin Shaped, 14 In.	2530.00
Vase, Hobstar, Vesica, Strawberry Diamond, Cane & Fan, Pedestal Fan, 12 In.	200.00
Vase, Hobstars, Tusk & Fan Highlights, Bulbous Top, Reversible, 9 In.	200.00
Vase, Hobstars, Vertical Bars, Hobstar Buttons, Fans, Step Cut Neck, Scalloped Edge, 18 In. *Illus*	4025.00
Vase, Pedestal, Wheel Cut Hobstar, Diamond, Cut Star Base, 13 ½ x 6 In.	630.00
Vase, Red To Crystal Vertical Ribs, Square Foot, 13 x 7 In.	480.00
Vase, Sunflowers, Hobstars, Baluster, Notched Loop Handles At Neck, Scalloped Rim, 15 ½ In.	2875.00
Vase, Thumbprint, Pulled Rim Top Shape Loop Handles, Bulbous, Blue, 10 ½ x 8 ½ In.	115.00
Vase, Trumpet, Pedestal, Vaseline, Diamond Band, Split Arch, Pairpoint, 10 ¼ In.	325.00
Vase, Trumpet, Queens, Hobstar Foot, Hawks, 14 In.	944.00
Vase, Trumpet, Wild Rose, 12 In.	2100.00
Vase, Tulip Shape, Viola, Empire, Scalloped Hobstar Foot, 14 In.	800.00
Vase, Versailles, Intaglio, Corset Shape, Flared Rim, Sinclaire, 12 ¼ In.	225.00
Vase, Wild Rose, 16 In.	1200.00
Water Carafe, Carolyn, Hobstar Base, J. Hoare, 8 In.	147.00
Water Set, Alhambra, Hobstar Base, Triple Notched Handle, Meriden, 7 Piece	2000.00
Wine Set, Fern, Ohio Cut Glass, 4 ⅛ In., 8 Piece	266.00
Wine, Star Block, Faceted Cut Stem, 5 In.	50.00
Wine, Venetian, Cranberry To Clear, 4 ¾ In.	600.00

CYBIS porcelain is a twentieth-century product. Boleslaw Cybis came to the United States from Poland in 1939. He started making porcelains in Long Island, New York, in 1940. He moved to Trenton, New Jersey, in 1942 as one of the founders of Cordey China Co. and started his own company, Cybis Porcelains, about 1950. The firm is still working. See also Cordey.

CYBIS

Bust, Madonna, Bluebird, Signed, 1957, 11 ½ In.	700.00
Figurine, Girl, Seated, Book, Sewing Basket, Bisque, 8 In.	72.00
Figurine, Snowball Bunny, 3 ½ x 4 In.	120.00
Figurine, Thoroughbred, 17 In.	330.00
Figurine, Wild Turkey, c.1975, 11 ½ In.	210.00

CZECHOSLOVAKIA is a popular term with collectors. The name, first used as a mark after the country was formed in 1918, appears on glass and porcelain and other decorative items. Although Czechoslovakia split into Slovakia and the Czech Republic on January 1, 1993, the name continues to be used in some trademarks.

CZECHOSLOVAKIA GLASS

Centerpiece, Cut Crystal, Queen Anne's Lace, 6 x 11 In.	96.00
Perfume Bottle, Art Deco, Pink Iridescent, Intaglio Nude Stopper, J. Pesnicak, 7 ½ In.	265.00
Perfume Bottle, Green Partially Frosted, Intaglio, Classical Figure, Hoffmann, 5 ½ In.	184.00
Pitcher, Queen Anne's Lace, 10 x 7 In.	90.00
Plate, Serving, Cranberry Cut To Clear, 11 In.	96.00
Platter, Queen Anne's Lace, Round, 12 In.	180.00
Sculpture, Cast, Cut, Polished, Blue, Petr Hora, 2000, 16 ½ x 12 In. *Illus*	3250.00

CZECHOSLOVAKIA POTTERY

Bookends, Horse Head, White, Art Deco, 6 ¼ x 6 In.	180.00
Box, Dome Lid, Orange, Green, Yellow, Black Design, Handle, Ditmar-Urbach, 6 x 8 In.	224.00
Canister Set, Silhouettes Of Dancers, 6 Large, 4 Small, 2 Cruets, 7 & 9 In., 12 Piece	150.00
Vase, Frosted To Clear, Nudes In Relief, Cylindrical, 10 In.	210.00

DANIEL BOONE, a pre–Revolutionary War folk hero, was a surveyor, trapper, and frontiersman. A television series, which ran from 1964 to 1970, was based on his life and starred Fess Parker. All types of Daniel Boone memorabilia are collected.

Button, Mingo Ashland, Wear Me & See, Indian, Feathers, Black, White, Red, 1966, 2 ¼ In.	155.00
Cap Gun, Flintlock Rifle, Marx, 42 In.	275.00
Comic Book, Great Adventure, No. 11, Gold Key, 1967	9.00
Figure, Holding Rifle, Base, Plastic, Marx, 3 In.	15.00
Indian Canoe, Inflatable, Indian Head, Multiple International Toy Maker, 1965	20.00
Jigsaw Puzzle, Danger Rapids, Milton Bradley, 1964, 200 Piece	26.00
Lunch Box, Fighting Indians, Metal, 1955	90.00

Lunch Box, Fort, Indians, Fighting, Metal, 1965	18.00
Patch, Patriot Days, Homestead, Leaning Against Rock, 1974	12.00
PEZ Dispenser, Green Body, Coonskin Cap, Made In Austria	56.00
Pocket Knife, Folding, Single Blade, Holding Gun, 3 ½ In.	9.00
Ring, Raised Goldtone Head, Red Plastic, 1960s	14.00
View-Master, 3 Reels, Four Leaf Clover, Fess Parker, 1965	14.00

D'ARGENTAL is a mark used in France by the Compagnie des Cristalleries de St. Louis. The firm made multilayered, acid-cut cameo glass in the late nineteenth and twentieth centuries. D'Argental is the French name for the city of Munzthal, home of the glassworks. Later the company made enameled etched glass.

Vase, Bulbous, Cherry Branches, Cameo, 1900s, 12 x 6 ½ In. ....*Illus*	875.00
Vase, Flowering Vines, Burnt Amber To Yellow Orange, Oval, Signed, 8 In.	531.00
Vase, Landscape, Trees, Cameo Glass, Yellow, Orange, Red, Black, 1900s, 5 x 2 ½ In.	420.00
Vase, Red Flowers, Orange Ground, Tapered, Narrow Flared Neck, Cameo, 6 ¼ In.	780.00
Vase, Ruby Bougainvillea Flowers, & Leaves On Amber Ground, 1910s, 8 ⅞ In.	765.00
Vase, Tapered, Trumpet Flowers, Cameo, Red Over Yellow, 10 In.	900.00
Vase, Trumpet Flowers, Red, Yellow Ground, Cameo Cut, 4 x 10 In.	1098.00

DAUM, a glassworks in Nancy, France, was started by Jean Daum in 1875. The company, now called *Cristalleries de Nancy*, is still working. The *Daum Nancy* mark has been used in many variations. The name of the city and the artist are usually both included. The term *martele* is used to describe applied decorations that are carved or etched in the cameo process.

Atomizer, Fuchsia, Gilt Highlights, Thistles, Scrolling, Cylindrical, Metal Pump Cap, Signed, 3 ½ In.	431.00
Bottle, Decanter Form, Mushrooms, Red, Brown & Green Mottled Amber Round, 6 In.	5165.00
Bottle, Enameled, Mushrooms, Red, Brown, Green, Mottled Amber, Cameo Stopper, c.1910, 6 In.	5164.00
Bowl, Green To Yellow, Olive Branch, Tapered, Rounded Shoulder, Wide Rim, 1900s, 5 x 7 ½ In.	1750.00
Bowl, Pulegoso, Light Green, Paperweight Base, 3-Sided, Engraved Mark, 7 x 4 ¼ In.	300.00
Bowl, Smoky Glass, Tapered, Lobed, Footed, 8 x 10 ¼ In.	296.00
Bowl, Water Lilies, Blue, Gold Trim, Enamel, Verre Parlant, Leaf Shape, Cameo, c.1900, 6 ½ In.	3500.00
Box, Lake Scene, Amber & Brown, Rounded Corners, Round Lid, Signed, 4 x 4 In.	4760.00
Cologne Bottle, Red, Textured, Cameo, Fleur-De-Lis, Enameled Collar, Stopper, Signed, 9 ½ In.	1265.00
Creamer, Flower, Stems, Leaves, Enamel, Gold Trim, Round Foot, Loop Handle, Opalescent, 3 ½ In.	1495.00
Cup, Columbine Flowers, Stems, Textured Yellow To Brown, Footed, Signed, 4 ½ In.	2588.00
Decanter, Mushrooms, Reds, Brown & Green, Mottled Amber, Marked, 6 ½ In.	5165.00
Dish, Frog, On Lily Pad, Pate-De-Verre, Brown & Green, Signed, 6 ½ x 6 ¼ In. ....*Illus*	415.00
Ewer, Flower, Stalk, Pearl To Pink Ground, Gold Trim, Enamel, Etched, 1910, 2 ¼ In.	1250.00
Ewer, Iris, Enameled, Pewter Mounted, Marked, 1895, 11 In. ....*Illus*	444.00
Figurine, Car, Jaguar Type E, Clear, 3 ¼ x 13 In.	1121.00
Figurine, Horse Head, Clear, Signed, France, 8 ½ In.	180.00
Figurine, Horse Head, Stylized, Signed, 5 ½ In.	161.00
Figurine, Raccoon, Polished, Matte Finish, Frosted Tail Accents, 6 ¼ x 8 In.	138.00
Figurine, Stylized Sailboat, Clear Glass, 9 ½ x 7 ½ In.	60.00
Jug, Winter Scene, Mottled Orange Glass, Barren Trees, Snow, Oval, Loop Handle, Spout, 6 In.	3450.00
Lamp, Amber Glass, Etched, Art Deco Squares Design, Domed Shade, c.1930, 25 In.	4375.00
Lamp, Boudoir, Fruiting Trees, Baluster Stem, Domed Foot, Tapered Shade, Cameo, 15 x 5 In.	3375.00
Lamp, Figural, Kneeling Vestal, Offering Domed Shade, Bronze, Marble, c.1930, 12 x 20 In.	5000.00
Lamp, Yellow Ground Shade, Cameo, Plum Cut To Frosted White Base, Marked, 13 In.	1668.00
Plate Set, 4 Seasons, Women & Putti, Purple, Green, Amber, Blue, 10 ½ In., 4 Piece	600.00
Scent Bottle, Stopper, Mottled Blue, Purple, White, Green, c.1910, 10 In.	1375.00
Scent Bottle, Wildflower Stalk, Peach, Blue Ground, Gold Trim Enamel, Etched, Cameo, c.1910, 3 In.	2250.00
Sculpture, Nude, Reclining, Peacock Blue, Cast, Signed, 9 ½ x 9 ½ In.	253.00
Syrup, Cameo, Gilt Thistle, Vines, Silver Lid, Handle, Foot, c.1900, 4 ½ x 4 ½ In.	1680.00
Tumbler, Fuchsia, Gilt Mistletoe, Cameo, Barrel Shape, Signed, 3 ½ In.	230.00
Vase, Applied Blue & Green Leaf, Oval, Swollen Bottom, 6 ⅝ In.	127.00
Vase, Art Deco, Sculpted, Etched, Chevron Geometric Panels, c.1930, 22 ¼ In.	4800.00
Vase, Art Deco, Transparent Green Glass, Geometrics, Cameo Etched, 11 ½ In.	1778.00
Vase, Autumn Leaves, Orange, Yellow, Brown, Mottled, Bulbous, Long Narrow Neck, Flat Rim, 11 In.	8625.00
Vase, Autumn Scene, Trees, Creek, Square, c.1900, 4 ¾ x 2 ¼ In.	3900.00
Vase, Birds, Shells, Brown, To White, Etched, Enamel, Tapered, c.1910, 8 In.	4750.00
Vase, Blue Wildflowers, Frost Ground, Enamel, Marked, 1910, 7 ¼ In.	6000.00
Vase, Brown Leaves, Thorns, Mottled Green Ground, Swollen Collar, Footed, 6 In.	1150.00
Vase, Bud, Bottle Shaped, Round Foot, Scrolling Leaves, Amber, Green, 1900s, 5 ¾ x 2 ½ In.	1750.00

Daum, Vase, Frosted, Cross Of Lorraine Pattern, Gold, Signed, 7 ¼ In.
$748.00

Early Auction Co.

Daum, Vase, Pink Flowers, Mottled Gray & Orange To Pink, Cameo, Signed, 14 In.
$8,165.00

Early Auction Co.

De Vez, Chalice, Owl On Branch, Pine Needles & Cones, Lime Green, Cameo, Signed, 10 In.
$690.00

Early Auction Co.

TIP

Turn a telephone insulator upside down and you can plant a small cactus in the top hole. Use quake wax or the wax used by orthodontists to prevent braces from rubbing to hold the insulator on a saucer or jelly jar cover.

DAUM

Decoy, Black Duck, Sleeping, Charles Bryan, Baltimore, Maryland, c.1900, 6 ½ x 15 x 7 ½ In. $180.00

Gray's Auctioneers LLC

Decoy, Mallard Drake, Hayes Factory, Joliet, Illinois, c.1900, 6 ½ x 16 x 5 ½ In. $221.00

Gray's Auctioneers LLC

Decoy, Mallard Drake, Painted, c.1910, 12 ½ In. $71.00

Conestoga Auction Co., Inc.

TIP

Several modern designers are taking pieces of old machinery or buildings and transforming them into new lamps or tables. The colors and textures of the "found" materials go well with a modern décor. You can find furniture made from railroad ties, iron bowls from construction sites, tin ceilings, repurposed marble, and iron gears. Be sure you are not taking on problems like creosote, asbestos, or lead and that there are no sharp edges or loose pieces to endanger young children.

Vase, Bud, Crow, Fox, Landscape, Gilt Leaves, Frosted Green, Tapered, c.1900, 8 In.	2125.00
Vase, Bulbous Stick, Opalescent, Gray Dutch Scene, Windmill, Sailing Ships, Cameo, Signed, 8 In.	2415.00
Vase, Butterflies, Blue Ground, Pate-De-Verre, Cameo, Marked, c.1910, 6 ½ In.	4750.00
Vase, Clear, Pan, 2 Nude Women Dancers, Cobalt, Orange, Frosted, Pate-De-Cristal, 9 ¾ In.	375.00
Vase, Cobalt Blue, Foil Mottling, Handles At Rim, Bulbous, 5 ⅛ In.	316.00
Vase, Coreopsis, Etched, Enamel, Yellow, Pink, Purple, Flared, Footed, Cameo, 13 x 4 In.	3625.00
Vase, Cotton Plants, Frosted, Brown, Bulbous, Cameo, Art Nouveau, 5 ⅓ x 17 In.	3625.00
Vase, Diamond Shape, Fringed Tulips, Mottled Ground, Gold Trim, Signed, 7 In.	508.00
Vase, Embossed Iris, Pink To Green, Silver Mounts, Cameo, c.1910, 3 ¾ In.	1000.00
Vase, Enameled Purple Violets, Green Leaves, Frosted White, Cameo, Rounded, Signed, 5 x 4 In.	3375.00
Vase, Enameled Red Wildflowers, Frosted Orange, Yellow, Cameo, Cylindrical, 4 ½ x 12 In.	3250.00
Vase, Flowers & Leaves, Deep Cinnamon, Mottled Yellow, Waisted, Saucer Foot, 9 ¾ In.	1035.00
Vase, Flowers, Berries, Yellow To Red Ground, Silver Mounts, Handles, Cameo, c.1910	2750.00
Vase, Flowers, Embossed, Yellow Amber, Rectangular, Squared Rim, Cameo, 4 ¾ In.	600.00
Vase, Flowers, Pink Frosted, Texted, Ground, Flared, Footed, c.1905, 10 ⅞ x 6 In.	2400.00
Vase, Flowers, Purple Ground, Bulbous, Cameo, Marked, 1910, 4 ¾ In.	1500.00
Vase, Frosted, Cross Of Lorraine Pattern, Gold, Signed, 7 ¼ In. ....*Illus*	748.00
Vase, Grapevine, Green, Brown, Purple, Frosted, Scalloped Rim, Signed, Cameo, 6 x 11 In.	2000.00
Vase, Green, Yellow Enamel Flowers, Flies, Mottled Blue, Purple, Carved Foot, 5 x 10 In.	28750.00
Vase, Landscape, Black, Green Trees, Red, Orange Ground, Signed, Cameo, 6 ½ x 22 In.	5000.00
Vase, Landscape, Red, Green, Mottled Frosted Ground, Tapered, Bulbous, Cameo, Signed, 6 x 5 In.	1586.00
Vase, Landscape, Wooded Lake, Mottled Ground, Cameo, Signed, 1900s, 5 ¾ x 3 In.	570.00
Vase, Magenta Ground, Flower Silver Mounts, Round, Tapered, c.1910, 4 In.	1250.00
Vase, Mottled Amber, Orange, Brown Leaves, Acorns, Bugs, Bulbous, Footed, c.1900, 5 ¾ In.	2500.00
Vase, Mottled Citron, Green, Red, Yellow Overlay, Translucent Gray Ground, c.1900, 15 In.	2040.00
Vase, Mottled Frosted Pink, Landscape, Bulbous, Cameo, 6 x 5 In.	1300.00
Vase, Mottled Glass, Orange & Yellow To Purple, Gold Foil Splash, Footed Urn, Signed, 9 In.	173.00
Vase, Mottled Opal, Turquoise Flowers, Pods, Leaves, Rounded Square Shape, Signed, 9 ½ In.	575.00
Vase, Mottled Yellow, Orange, Grapes, Leafy Vines, Tapering Barrel Shape, Snail Handles, 7 In.	5175.00
Vase, Pate-De-Verre, Crystal, Dancing Nude Woman, Marked, 10 x 5 In.	660.00
Vase, Pate-De-Verre, Crystal, Light Blue Graduated To Purple, Vines, Flowers, 8 In.	420.00
Vase, Pillow, Oval, Square Rim, Landscape, Trees, Orange, Red, Amber, Cameo, 1900s, 4 x 6 In.	1063.00
Vase, Pink Flowers, Mottled Gray & Orange To Pink, Cameo, Signed, 14 In. ....*Illus*	8165.00
Vase, Poppies, Orange To Yellow, Mottled, Flattened Square, Round Foot, Cameo, 8 In.	2300.00
Vase, Rain Scene, Windblown Trees, Stick Neck, Bulbous, 3 In.	2070.00
Vase, Red, Purple Flowers, Gray Leaves, Frosted To Blue, Cylindrical, c.1900, 5 In.	2000.00
Vase, Roses, Green Base, Tapered, Footed, Gray Box, c.1950, 13 In.	1612.00
Vase, Rust To Green Ground, Stick Neck, Short Bulbous Base, Mark, c.1955, 24 In.	750.00
Vase, Snow Scene, Trees, Orange & Yellow Mottled, Square Shape, Cameo, Signed, 4 ½ In.	2185.00
Vase, Stems, Insect, Enameled, Gilded, Pale Green, Amber, Cylindrical, Signed, 1880s, 3 In.	2125.00
Vase, Summer Scene, Lake, Trees, Frosted Blue Ground, Signed, 5 In.	2990.00
Vase, Swaying Trees, Clear Falling Glass Rain, Pink, Green, Gray, Tapered, Signed, 6 In.	10350.00
Vase, Textured, Indented Sides, Flower, Dragonflies, Bulbous, Gold Enamel, Pink, 3 x 5 In.	1875.00
Vase, Tulip, Leaves, Mottled Frosted Pink, Orange Ground, Footed, 7 ½ x 25 In.	7500.00
Vase, Winter Landscape, Black, Yellow, Orange, Cylindrical, Enamel, Cameo, Signed, 5 x 13 In.	8750.00
Vase, Winter Scene, Trumpet Shape, Orange, Yellow Mottled, Cameo, Footed, 21 In.	14375.00
Vase, Yellow Iris, Leaves, White Dimpled Ground, Enamel, Footed, Cameo, c.1910, 22 In.	3750.00

DAVENPORT pottery and porcelain were made at the Davenport factory in Longport, Staffordshire, England, from 1793 to 1887. Earthenwares, creamwares, porcelains, ironstone, and other ceramics were made. Most of the pieces are marked with a form of the word *Davenport*.

DAVENPORT LONGPORT STAFFORDSHRE

Cake Plate, Witches, Imari Colors, Gilt, Molded, Square, Rounded Corners, Handles, 9 x 10 In.	75.00
Plate, Green Feather Edge, Sprig, Impressed, England, c.1830, 8 In.	60.00
Plate, Liner, Imari Color Flowers, Blue Ground, Gilt Tracery, Rim, 10 x 8 ⅜ In.	58.00
Tureen, Lid, Underplate, Long Tail Bird Pattern, Lion Mask Handles, c.1825, 14 In.	443.00
Vase, Orange Ground, Green, Blue Geometric Band, Transfer, Marked, c.1895, 9 ½ x 7 ½ In.	120.00

DAVY CROCKETT, the American frontiersman, was born in 1786 and died in 1836. The historical character gained new fame in 1954 when the Walt Disney television show ran a series of episodes featuring Fess Parker as Davy Crockett. Coonskin caps and buckskins became popular and hundreds of different Davy Crockett items were made.

Bowl, Davy, Kneeling, Bee, c.1955, 4 ¾ x 2 In.	30.00
Cap Gun, Pistol, Flintlock Frontier, Plastic, Metal, c.1955, 10 ½ In.	186.00
Cookie Jar, Young Davy, Holding Gun, Brush Pottery, 1956, 10 ½ In.	435.00

D

Doll, Hard Plastic, Coonskin Cap, Fringed Outfit, Sleep Eyes, 1950s, 8 In.	125.00
Flashlight, Compass, Cavalry Scene, Tin Lithograph, Brite-Lite, c.1955, 7 In.	115.00
Frontier Play Suit, Hat, Simulated Cloth Fur, Suede-Like Fringe, Box, 1950s, 12 ½ x 14 In.	173.00
Guitar, 4 Keys & Strings, Strap, Case, Peter Puppet Playthings Inc., 1955, 24 ½ In.	270.00
Lunch Box, At The Alamo, Tin, Adco, c.1955	210.00
Mug, Davy, Covered Wagon, Milk Glass, Brown, Fire-King, 3 ½ In.	14.00
Playset, Davy Crockett At The Alamo, Doll, Paper, Booklet, Marx, 1955, 14 x 24 In.	250.00
Playsuit, Frontiersman, Logo On Shirt, Lace-Up Neck, Collar, Cotton, Leather Fringe	106.00
Ring, Frontier Club, Red, Adjustable, Box, Mid 1950s, 1 ⅜ In.	168.00
Shirt, Davy, Bear, Short Sleeve, Bobby Jr., Size 12	75.00
Toy, Rifle, Repeating, Wild Stallions, Scrollwork, Plastic, Metal, Marx, Box, 33 In.	159.00
Wallet, Plastic, Davy, Coonskin Cap, Coin Pocket, Child's	40.00
Wristwatch, Liberty Bell, Leather Straps, Jeweled Davy Crocket, Box, 1954, 5 In.	230.00

DE VEZ was a signature used on cameo glass after 1910. E. S. Monot founded the glass company near Paris in 1851. The company changed names many times. Mt. Joye, another glass by this factory, is listed in its own category.

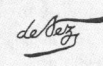

Chalice, Owl On Branch, Pine Needles & Cones, Lime Green, Cameo, Signed, 10 In. ......*Illus*	690.00
Perfumer, Mountainous Lake Scene, Gourd Shape, Yellow, Brown, Orange, Signed, 6 In.	1350.00
Vase, Art Nouveau, Ocean Front Scene, Orange, Purple, Classical Building, Tapered, 7 In.	426.00
Vase, Bulbous, Stick Neck, Pink Flowers, White Ground, Signed, c.1851, 6 ½ In.	1800.00
Vase, Yellow, Crimson Cascading Flowers, Butterflies, Lake Scene, Sailing Ship, 14 In.	1150.00

DECORATED TUMBLERS *may be listed by maker or design or in Advertising, Coca-Cola, Pepsi-Cola, Sports, and other categories.*

DECOYS are carved or turned wooden copies of birds, fish, or animals. The decoy was placed in the water or propped on the shore to lure flying birds to the pond for hunters. Some decoys are handmade; some are commercial products. Today there is a group of artists making modern decoys for display, not for use in a pond. Many sell for high prices.

Black Duck, Carved, Painted, Stamped Handcrafted By Micha, Michigan, 15 In.	502.00
Black Duck, Gunning Bird, Painted, Carved, A. Elmer Crowell, 15 ½ In.	2938.00
Black Duck, Hollow Carved, Paint, Weighted, Barnegat Bay, N.J., 14 In.	104.00
Black Duck, Sleeping, Charles Bryan, Baltimore, Maryland, c.1900, 6 ½ x 15 x 7 ½ In. .*Illus*	180.00
Black Duck, Snuggled Head, Wood, Cork, Paint, N.Y., 18 In.	70.00
Black Duck, Wood, Head Turned Back, Painted, Glass Eyes, c.1900, 16 In.	118.00
Blue Heron, Base, 8 ½ In.	31050.00
Bluebill Drake, Glass Eyes, Swing Neck, Hamilton Bay, Ontario, 12 In.	104.00
Bluebill, Hen, Hollow Carved, Paint, Ontario, 12 ½ In.	377.00
Blue-Winged Teal Drake, Carved, Painted, Mark McNair, 12 In.	1921.00
Butter Ball Drake, Signed Tom Schroeder 1962, 4 ½ In.	904.00
Canada Goose, Back Preening Position, Hollow Carved, Paint, N.J. 19 In.	52.00
Canada Goose, Carved, Black Paint, c.1910, 27 In.	770.00
Canada Goose, George Boyd, Carved, Painted, Seabrook, N.H., c.1920, 18 x 28 In.	18960.00
Canada Goose, Painted, Feather Detail, Black, White, Gray, 22 ½ In.	531.00
Canada Goose, Reaching Position, Hollow Carved, Paint, N.J., 25 In.	58.00
Canada Goose, Wood, Canvas, Black, White Painted Head, 12 ½ x 27 In.	201.00
Canada Goose, Wood, Carved, Paint, Glass Eyes, H.A. Ackerman, c.1965, 18 In.	173.00
Canvasback Drake, Carved, Painted, Herman Rietgraf, 16 In.	1243.00
Canvasback Drake, Painted, Carved, Ralph Johnson, 15 ½ In.	79.00
Canvasback Drake, Red Glass Eyes, c.1880, 15 In.	75.00
Canvasback, Black, Paint, c.1920, 10 ¾ x 17 ½ In.	533.00
Canvasback, Brown, Black Paint, Stamped, W.D. Radford, c.1940, 11 ½ x 18 In.	889.00
Canvasback, Carved, Painted, c.1910, 7 x 15 In.	144.00
Canvasback, Cast Iron, Sink Box, Painted, c.1900, 5 ¼ x 14 In.	1080.00
Canvasback, Glass Eyes, Black & White Paint, Black Bay, c.1900, 19 In.	201.00
Canvasback, Wood, Black, Gray Paint, Black Base, 22 x 28 In.	230.00
Cinnamon Teal, Drake & Hen, Signed, c.1972, 5 x 11 ½ In., Pair	288.00
Coot, Wood, Paint, Carved, Hollow, Mid-Western, 16 In.	1130.00
Crow, Wood, Paint, Warren Scott, c.1870, 14 x 17 In.	1541.00
Curlew, Shorebird, Carved, Painted, Black Vase, 4 x 15 In.	1126.00
Curlew, Shorebird, Carved, Painted, Pole Mount, Round Base, c.1900, 10 x 15 In.	3081.00
Fish, Brook Trout, Spearing, Signed Jim Foote, 1998, 8 ¼ In.	904.00
Fish, Brown Trout, Spearing, Bill Feasel, 7 In.	5900.00

Dedham, Elephant, Cup & Saucer, Blue & White, Stamped
$750.00

Ruby Lane, Inc.

Dedham, Horse Chestnut, Plate, Blue & White, c.1929-43, 8 ½ In.
$180.00

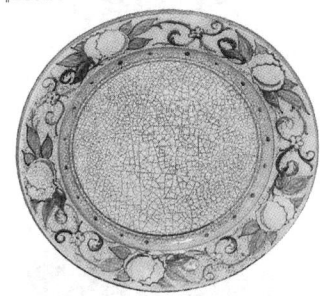

Ruby Lane, Inc.

Dedham, Night & Morning, Pitcher, Embossed Owl & Rooster, Marked, c.1900, 5 x 5 ¾ In.
$525.00

Ruby Lane, Inc.

TIP

Your cell phone's camera is a magnifying glass. Focus on the marking you want to read and go in for a close-up. It is great for ceramics or prints, but a little difficult for metal because of glare. No need for a ruler and a magnifier anymore. Now you can go to a show with a dollar bill (a 6-inch ruler) and a phone.

Dedham, Poppy, Plate, Blue & White,
8 ½ In.
$214.00

Rago Arts & Auction Center

Dedham, Rabbit, Paperweight,
Blue & White, Blue Stamp, c.1929-43
$350.00

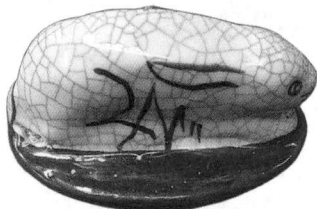

Ruby Lane, Inc.

Dedham, Scottie Dogs, Plate, Crackle
Glaze, Blue Ink Mark, 8 ½ In.
$1,422.00

Skinner, Inc.

Dedham, Scottie Dog, Vase, Portrait,
Blue Rabbit Stamp, 7 x 4 In., Pair
$2,074.00

Rago Arts & Auction Center

Fish, Pike, Spearing, Oscar Peterson, 5 In.	1582.00
Fish, Rainbow Trout, Spearing, Oscar Peterson, 8 ½ In.	4520.00
Fish, Sucker, Spearing, Oscar Peterson, 9 In.	4800.00
Fish, Trout, Spearing, Signed Jim Foote, 1998, 8 ¼ In.	904.00
Goldeneye Drake, Jess Urie, Signed, 6 ¼ In.	28.00
Goldeneye Drake, Worn Paint, Cape Cod, c.1910, 17 In.	162.00
Goose, Hollow, Carved, Painted, Black, Brown, White, Gray Feathers, New Jersey, 12 ¼ x 24 ½ In.	259.00
Goose, White Paint, Wood, 22 x 19 In.	431.00
Goose, Wood, Canvas, c.1930, 12 x 23 In.	830.00
Mallard Drake, Hayes Factory, Joliet, Illinois, c.1900, 6 ½ x 16 x 5 ½ In. ....*Illus*	221.00
Mallard Drake, Painted, c.1910, 12 ½ In. ....*Illus*	71.00
Merganser Duck, Carved, Painted, c.1900, 7 ⅞ x 15 In.	652.00
Merganser Duck, Carved, Painted, New England, c.1900, 19 ½ In.	889.00
Mute Swan, Carved, White Paint, Marked, Horace Graham, c.1960, 33 In.	1062.00
Nodding Bird, Speckled Breast, Carved, Painted, c.1910, 5 In.	1067.00
Owl, Carved, Painted, 20th Century, 18 ½ In.	4503.00
Owl, Carved, Painted, Articulated Wings, Russ Allen, 16 In.	1185.00
Owl, Wood, Carved, Recessed Eyes, Crackled Paint, Gray, Brown, c.1940, 18 ½ In.	920.00
Pintail Drake, Carved, Painted, Delbert Hudson, Chincoteague, Va., c.1930, 22 ½ In.	7703.00
Pintail Drake, Painted, Carved, R. Madison Mitchell, Paint, 1940, 13 In.	1074.00
Pintail Drake, Serpentine Neck, Joseph A. Ferreira, c.1935, 14 In.	255.00
Red Breasted Merganser, Glass Eyes, Carved Wings, Hurley Conklin	189.00
Red-Throated Loon, Signed, Bob Biddle, 20 In., Pair	748.00
Robin Snipe, Carved, Pole Base, H.V. Shourds, New Jersey, c.1910, 9 In.	6250.00
Ruddy Head Drake, Signed Tom Schroeder 1962, 4 ½ In.	961.00
Sandpiper, White Rump, Upswept Wing, Clamshell Base, Jas. Lapham, Mass., c.1960, 8 ¼ In.	224.00
Shorebird, Carved, Gray & White Paint, Tack Eyes, Wooden Stand, Long Beak, c.1900, 15 ½ In.	472.00
Shorebird, Green Paint, Outstretched Neck, Elongated Beak, Glass Bead Eyes, 16 ½ x 13 ½ In., Pair	460.00
Shorebird, Wood, Carved, De Lancey Nicoll Jr., 10 ¼ In.	944.00
Snow Goose, Wood, Paint, Capt. Harry Jobes, c.1980, 21 In.	259.00
Swan, Carved, Painted White, Black Beak, Glass Eyes, Monogram RF, Chincoteague, Va., 24 x 32 In.	295.00
Swan, Carved, Painted, c.1910, 19 ½ In.	415.00
Swan, Sleeper Position, Tack Eyes, Cream Color, Reggie Birch, 23 In.	590.00
Swan, Turned Head, Glass Eyes, Hollow, Painted, 1900s, 20 x 24 In.	690.00
White-Winged Scoter, Black Paint, Cecil Smith, Maine	295.00
Widgeon Drake, Jack Sweet, Erie, Pa., 17 In.	128.00
Widgeon Hen, Jack Sweet, Erie, Pa., 17 In.	174.00

DEDHAM POTTERY was started in 1895. Chelsea Keramic Art Works was established in 1872 in Chelsea, Massachusetts, by members of the Robertson family. The factory closed in 1889 and was reorganized as the Chelsea Pottery U.S. in 1891. The firm used the marks *CKAW* and *CPUS*. It became the Dedham Pottery of Dedham, Massachusetts. The factory closed in 1943. It was famous for its crackleware dishes, which picture blue outlines of animals, flowers, and other natural motifs. Pottery by Chelsea Keramic Art Works and Dedham Pottery is listed here.

Azalea, Plate, Rabbit, Mark, 8 ¼ In.	177.00
Duck, Plate, Blue & White, 8 ½ In.	72.00
Elephant, Tile, Round Band, Blue & White, 5 ½ In.	1007.00
Elephant, Cup & Saucer, Blue & White, Stamped ....*Illus*	750.00
Grape, Plate, Blue & White, 8 ½ In.	23.00
Horse Chestnut, Plate, Blue & White, c.1929-43, 8 ½ In. ....*Illus*	180.00
Iris, Plate, Blue & White Glaze Ground, Blue Ink Mark, 8 ½ In., Pair	237.00
Moth, Candleholder, Blue & White, Blue Ink Mark, 1 ½ In., Pair	326.00
Moth, Plate, Blue & White, 8 ⅜ In.	246.00
Moth, Plate, Rabbit Mark, 8 ½ In.	295.00
Night & Morning, Pitcher, Embossed Owl & Rooster, Marked, c.1900, 5 x 5 ¾ In. ....*Illus*	525.00
Oak Leaves, Pitcher, Oak Block, Handle, Blue & White, Mark, 5 ¾ In.	245.00
Polar Bear, Plate, Blue & White, 8 ½ In.	219.00
Pond Lily, Plate, Rabbit Mark, 8 ½ In., Pair	295.00
Poppy, Plate, Blue & White, 8 ½ In. ....*Illus*	214.00
Rabbit, Coffeepot, Bands, Bulbous Base, Elongated Neck, 9 In.	331.00
Rabbit, Paperweight, Blue & White, Blue Stamp, c.1929-43 ....*Illus*	350.00
Rabbit, Plate, 8 ½ In., 4 Piece	374.00
Rabbit, Platter, Rounded Corners, Blue Ink Mark, 17 x 10 ½ In.	1094.00
Scottie Dog, Vase, Portrait, Blue Rabbit Stamp, 7 x 4 In., Pair ....*Illus*	2074.00
Scottie Dogs, Plate, Crackle Glaze, Blue Ink Mark, 8 ½ In. ....*Illus*	1422.00
Swan, Plate, 8 ¼ In.	92.00

DEGUE is a signature acid-etched on pieces of French glass made by the Cristalleries de Compiegne in the early 1900s. Cameo, mold blown, and smooth glass with contrasting colored rims are the types most often found.

Lamp, Mottled Orange, Red Ground, Black Flowers, 3 Metal Arms, Cameo Signed, 5 x 12 In...	122.00
Vase, Bulbous, Green, Black Leaves, Brown Ground, Acid Etched, Mark, Cameo, c.1930, 18 ½ In..	1750.00

DELDARE, *see Buffalo Pottery Deldare.*

DELFT is a special type of tin-glazed pottery. Early delft was made in Holland and England during the seventeenth century. It was usually decorated with blue on a white surface, but some was polychrome, decorated with green, yellow, and other colors. Most delftware pieces were dishes needed for everyday living. Figures were made from about 1750 to 1800, and are rare. Although the soft tin-glazed pottery was well-known, it was not named delft until after 1840, when it was named for the city in Holland where much of it was made. Porcelain became more popular because it was more durable and Holland gradually stopped making the old delft. In 1876 De Porceleyne Fles factory in Delft introduced a porcelain ware that was decorated with blue and white scenes of Holland that reminded many of old delft. It became popular with the Dutch and tourists. By 1990 all of the blue and white porcelain with Dutch scenes was made in Asia, although it was marked *Delft.* Only one Dutch company remains that makes the traditional old-style delft with blue on white or with colored decorations. Most of the pieces sold today were made after 1891, and the name *Holland* usually appears with the Delft factory marks. The word *Delft* appears alone on some inexpensive twentieth- and twenty-first-century pottery from Asia and Germany that is also listed here.

Bottle, Flowers, Blue & White, Ribbed Neck, Loop Handle, c.1715, 7 In..................	499.00
Bowl, Blue, Flowers, Branches, Manganese, England, c.1790, 8 ¾ In................	531.00
Bowl, Flowers, Faience, c.1820, 6 x 10 In..........................	444.00
Bowl, Tulip, Vines, Yellow, Blue, Melon Ribbed, 12 ¼ In..................	354.00
Bowl, Wading Bird, Peasant Figure, Birds, Leafy Branches, 1700s, 10 ½ In. Diam.	429.00
Candlestick, Windmill, Flowers, Blue & White, Square Cup, Contoured Square Shaft, Base, 7 x 3 In..	180.00
Charger, Blue, Green, Yellow, Red, Flowers, Leaves, Bird, c.1770, 13 ½ In.................	826.00
Charger, Central Floret, Geometric Flower Design, Blue & White, 12 ½ In. Diam.	486.00
Charger, Flowering Tree, Blue & White, Scalloped Edge, Porcelain Claw Factory, 1700s, 14 In. Diam.	588.00
Charger, Flowers & Palm Trees, Blue & White, 14 In..................	575.00
Charger, Green, Blue, Rust Red, Flowers, c.1780, 13 ¼ In.................	649.00
Charger, King William III, Multicolor, Scalloped Edge, c.1695, 13 ¼ In.	2844.00
Charger, Presentation, Inscribed Richard & Sarah Howes Harwich, c.1780, 13 ¾ In.	1304.00
Charger, Putto, Dolphin, Puce & Yellow Enamel, 1700s, 13 ½ In..........	563.00
Charger, Tulip, Multicolor, c.1720, 13 ¾ In.................	3081.00
Clock, Ceramic, Porcelain Dial, Bombe Case, Blue & White, Grandfather Clock Shape, 1800s, 22 In. .	345.00
Figurine, Lion, Shield, 1 Leg Resting On Crest, Mouth Open, Square Base, 1800s, 10 x 8 ½ In., Pair...	1560.00
Flower Brick, Harbor Views, Flower Panels, Blue & White, 3 ½ x 6 ½ In.....................	527.00
Inkwell, Phoenix, Flowers, Cube Shape, Cone Shape, Well, 8 Ball Feet, 5 x 4 In............	84.00
Jar, Mercury Holding Cadusis, Ship, Tobacco Bale, Oval, Hammered Copper Lid, 12 x 9 In......	826.00
Jug, Puzzle, Blue & White, Inscribed, Brave Boys, Come Try Your Skill, c.1770, 7 ¼ In............	944.00
Lamp, Porcelain Base, Milk Glass Ball Shade, Blue Angels, Brass Base, Kosmos Burner, 12 In. .... *Illus*	144.00
Pitcher, Flowers, Baskets, Scrolls, Blue & White, Bulbous, Lobed, 10 ½ In......................	264.00
Plaque, Cattle Drover With Herd, Blue & White, Scrolling Shape, Signed, c.1900	472.00
Plate, Blue, Green, Red, Peafowl, c.1780, 9 In.................	1003.00
Plate, Blue, Red, Green Flower & Dot Panels, Bristol, c.1730, 8 ½ In...................	266.00
Plate, Chinoiserie Figural Scenes, Blue & White, 9 In.................	153.00
Plate, Manganese Ground, Reserves, Square Panels, Insects, Chinese Figure In Garden, 8 ¾ In., Pair	2360.00
Plate, Painted, Green, Blue, Flower Filled Urn, Meandering Sprig Border, Dutch, c.1765, 9 In., Pair....	266.00
Plate, Portrait, Catherine Of Braganza, Dutch, c.1695, 12 In. Diam.........................	431.00
Platter, Flower Basket, Floral Border, Blue & White, Octagonal, c.1970, 15 x 10 In.	180.00
Porringer, Flowers, Blue & White, Handles, c.1800, 2 ½ x 9 ¼ In.	767.00
Punch Bowl, 3 Fish, Blue & Manganese, c.1750, 9 ¼ In...........................	4838.00
Tankard, Stag In Landscape, Monogrammed Pewter Lid, 1776, 9 ½ In........................	1265.00
Tankard, Stylized Tulips, Hinged Pewter Lid, Base, Knop Handle, 5 x 3 In......................	1035.00
Tile, Arts & Crafts, Stag, Chased By Dog, Winter, Multicolor, L.E.F. Bodart, De Porceleyne Fles, 4 x 17 In.	395.00
Tile, De Porceleyne Fles, Ceramic, Cuenca, Peacock Facing Left, 1920s, 17 x 4 ⅝ In...............	449.00
Tile, Jack Rabbit Leaping, Fruiting Tree Branches, Low Relief, Rectangular, 8 ¼ In.................	246.00
Tile, Syndics Of The Drapers Guild, Sepia Colors, Marked, c.1900, 11 ¾ x 19 ¾ In. ....*Illus*	960.00
Tobacco Jar, Indian, Seated, Smoking Pipe, Brass Top, De Vergulde Bloempot, c.1780, 14 In......	1888.00
Vase, Blue & White, Bird, Insect, Dolphin Panels, England, 9 In............................	354.00
Vase, Flowers, Brown, Blue, Yellow, Mark, De Porceleyne Klaauw, 6 ½ In., Pair......................	207.00

TIP

Do not store rhinestone jewelry in airtight plastic bags or wrap.

D

Delft, Lamp, Porcelain Base, Milk Glass Ball Shade, Blue Angels, Brass Base, Kosmos Burner, 12 In. $144.00

James D. Julia Auctioneers

Delft, Tile, Syndics Of The Drapers Guild, Sepia Colors, Marked, c.1900, 11 ¾ x 19 ¾ In. $960.00

Skinner, Inc.

The edited listings of the current prices in this *Kovels' Antiques & Collectibles Price Guide* aren't available on any website. Readers can visit **Kovels.com** to check thousands of past prices and sign up for free information on trends, tips, reproductions, marks, and more.

DENTAL

Denver, Vase, Leafy Plant, Stamped Denaure, 1903-05, 5 ¼ x 6 In. $1,375.00

Rago Arts & Auction Center

Depression Glass, American Sweetheart, Cup & Saucer, Opaque White $8.00

Ruby Lane, Inc.

Depression Glass, Block Optic, Sandwich Server, Handle, Amber, 12 ¾ In. $25.00

Ruby Lane, Inc.

TIP

To ship small pieces of glass, try this trick: Put the glass in a Styrofoam cup, then wrap in bubble wrap or several layers of paper. Stuff sides and bottom of a large box with Styrofoam trays. Then put the antiques on the trays. Pack more Styrofoam around them. Maybe you can get extra trays at your grocery store.

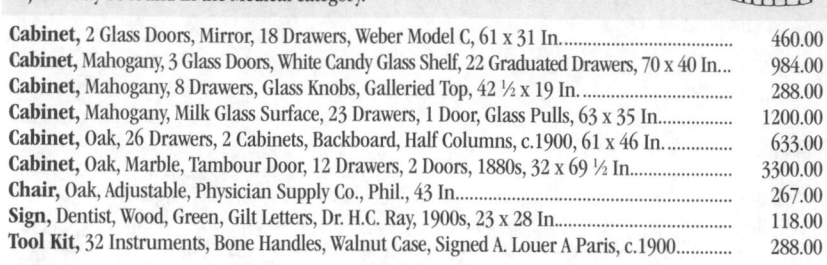

DENTAL cabinets, chairs, equipment, and other related items are listed here. Other objects may be found in the Medical category.

Cabinet, 2 Glass Doors, Mirror, 18 Drawers, Weber Model C, 61 x 31 In.	460.00
Cabinet, Mahogany, 3 Glass Doors, White Candy Glass Shelf, 22 Graduated Drawers, 70 x 40 In.	984.00
Cabinet, Mahogany, 8 Drawers, Glass Knobs, Galleried Top, 42 ½ x 19 In.	288.00
Cabinet, Mahogany, Milk Glass Surface, 23 Drawers, 1 Door, Glass Pulls, 63 x 35 In.	1200.00
Cabinet, Oak, 26 Drawers, 2 Cabinets, Backboard, Half Columns, c.1900, 61 x 46 In.	633.00
Cabinet, Oak, Marble, Tambour Door, 12 Drawers, 2 Doors, 1880s, 32 x 69 ½ In.	3300.00
Chair, Oak, Adjustable, Physician Supply Co., Phil., 43 In.	267.00
Sign, Dentist, Wood, Green, Gilt Letters, Dr. H.C. Ray, 1900s, 23 x 28 In.	118.00
Tool Kit, 32 Instruments, Bone Handles, Walnut Case, Signed A. Louer A Paris, c.1900	288.00

DENVER is part of the mark on an American art pottery. William Long of Steubenville, Ohio, founded the Lonhuda Pottery Company in 1892. In 1900 he moved to Denver, Colorado, and organized the Denver China and Pottery Company. This pottery, which used the mark *Denver*, worked until 1905, when Long moved to New Jersey and founded the Clifton Pottery. Long also worked for Weller Pottery, Roseville Pottery, and American Encaustic Tiling Company. Do not confuse this pottery with the Denver White Pottery, which worked from 1894 to 1955 in Denver.

DENVER C T & P T Co

Vase, Leafy Plant, Stamped Denaure, 1903-05, 5 ¼ x 6 In. ....*Illus*	1375.00

DEPRESSION GLASS is an inexpensive glass that was manufactured in large quantities during the 1920s and early 1930s. It was made in many colors and patterns by dozens of factories in the United States. Most patterns were also made in clear glass, which the factories called *crystal*. If no color is listed here, it is clear. The name *Depression glass* is a modern one and also refers to machine-made glass of the 1940s through 1970s. For more prices, go to kovels.com. Sets missing a few pieces can be completed through the help of one of the many matching services listed on our website.

Adam, Bowl, Cereal, Pink, 5 ¾ In.	10.00
Adam, Bowl, Lid, Pink, 9 In.	40.00
Adam, Bowl, Pink, 4 ¾ In.	25.00
Adam, Bowl, Pink, 8 In.	40.00
Adam, Butter, Cover, Pink	95.00
Adam, Butter, Pink	70.00
Adam, Cake Plate, Green, Footed, 9 ⅞ In.	38.00
Adam, Candlestick, Pink, 4 In., Pair	45.00
Adam, Candy Dish, Lid, Green	125.00
Adam, Candy Jar, Lid, Pink	70.00
Adam, Grill Plate, Green, 7 ½ In.	28.00
Adam, Grill Plate, Green, Square, 9 ½ In.	21.00
Adam, Pitcher, Pink, 32 Oz.	109.00
Adam, Plate, Pink, 6 In.	10.00
Adam, Plate, Square, Pink, 7 In.	26.00
Adam, Relish, 2 Sections, Pink, 8 In.	25.00
Adam, Salt & Pepper, Pink, 4 In.	45.00
Adam, Salt & Pepper, Pink, Footed, 4 In.	45.00
Adam, Tumbler, Footed, 7 Oz.	31.00
Adam, Tumbler, Green, Footed, 9 Oz., 5 ½ In.	79.00
Adam, Tumbler, Pink, Footed, 9 Oz.	119.00
Adam, Vase, Green, 7 ½ In.	150.00
Adam's Rib, Compote, Pink, 8 In.	18.00
Adam's Rib, Compote, Pink, Oval	18.00
Adam's Rib, Cup & Saucer, Green	9.00
American Pioneer, Plate, Pink, 8 In.	12.00
American Sweetheart, Berry Bowl, Pink, 8 ½ In.	65.00
American Sweetheart, Berry Bowl, Pink, Flat, 3 ¾ In.	20.00 to 35.00
American Sweetheart, Chop Plate, Monax, 11 In.	20.00
American Sweetheart, Creamer, Monax	11.00
American Sweetheart, Cup & Saucer	18.00
American Sweetheart, Cup & Saucer, Monax	10.00 to 12.00
American Sweetheart, Cup & Saucer, Opaque White ....*Illus*	8.00
American Sweetheart, Cup & Saucer, Red	80.00
American Sweetheart, Pitcher, Pink, 60 Oz.	1049.00
American Sweetheart, Pitcher, Pink, 70 Oz.	1199.00
American Sweetheart, Plate, Dinner, Monax, 10 In.	28.00
American Sweetheart, Plate, Pink, 8 In.	15.00

American Sweetheart, Plate, Salad, Monax, 8 In.	12.00
American Sweetheart, Platter, Pink, Oval, 13 In.	25.00
American Sweetheart, Salver, Monax, 12 In.	22.00 to 25.00
American Sweetheart, Salver, Pink, 12 In.	18.00 to 22.00
American Sweetheart, Sherbet, Pink, Footed, 4 ¼ In.	22.00
American Sweetheart, Soup, Dish, Flat, Monax, 9 ½ In.	35.00
American Sweetheart, Soup, Dish, Flat, Pink, 9 ½ In.	40.00
American Sweetheart, Soup, Dish, Monax, 4 ¾ In.	100.00
American Sweetheart, Tumbler, Pink, 5 Oz.	129.00
American Sweetheart, Tumbler, Pink, 10 Oz.	179.00
Apple Blossom pattern is listed here as Dogwood.	
Aramis, Tumbler, Cobalt Blue, 12 Oz., 5 In.	18.00 to 20.00
Artura, Server, Yellow, Center Handle	50.00
Atomic Flower, Snack Set, White & Pink, Yellow, Turquoise, Black Flowers, 1950s, 8 Piece	50.00
Aunt Polly, Berry Bowl, Blue, 4 In.	12.00
Aunt Polly, Dish, Pickle, Green, 2 Handles, Oval, 7 ¼ In.	20.00
Aunt Polly, Serving Bowl, Blue, 8 In.	40.00
Aurora, Bowl, Cereal, Pink, 5 ⅜ In.	10.00
Aurora, Bowl, Cobalt Blue, 4 ½ In.	25.00
Avocado, Bowl, Handles, Oval, 8 In.	11.00
Ballerina pattern is listed here as Cameo.	
Banded Rib pattern is listed here as Coronation.	
Basket pattern is listed here as No. 615.	
Block pattern is listed here as Block Optic.	
Block Optic, Candy Jar, Green	25.00
Block Optic, Goblet, Clear, 9 Oz., 5 ¾ In.	15.00
Block Optic, Pitcher, Green, 54 Oz., 8 ½ In.	65.00 to 119.00
Block Optic, Pitcher, Green, Footed, Flared, 4 ¼ In.	15.00
Block Optic, Plate, Salad, Green, 8 In.	8.00
Block Optic, Saltshaker, Green, Round	45.00
Block Optic, Sandwich Server, Handle, Amber, 12 ¾ In. ......*Illus*	25.00
Block Optic, Sugar & Creamer, Footed	56.00
Block Optic, Tumbler, Green, Footed, 9 Oz.	16.00 to 25.00
Boopie, Goblet, Emerald Green, Anchor Hocking, 6 In., 4 Piece	60.00
Bowknot, Cup, Green	10.00
Bubble, Cake Salver, Square Top, Indiana Glass Co., c.1935, 10 ½ x 7 In.	95.00
Bullseye pattern is listed here as Bubble.	
Cabbage Rose pattern is listed here as Sharon.	
Cameo, Bowl, Vegetable, Green, Oval, 10 In.	30.00
Cameo, Butter Tub, Green	229.00
Cameo, Butter, Cover, Round	249.00
Cameo, Cake Plate, Green, 3-Footed, 10 In.	40.00
Cameo, Candlestick, Green 4 In., Pair	60.00
Cameo, Candlestick, Green, 6 In., Pair	95.00
Cameo, Cookie Jar, Lid, Green	60.00
Cameo, Cup & Saucer, Scroll Handle, Green	20.00
Cameo, Dish, Mayonnaise, Green	47.00
Cameo, Grill Plate, Yellow, Spoke Handles, 10 ½ In.	9.00 to 12.00
Cameo, Pitcher, Green, 36 Oz.	94.00
Cameo, Plate, Dinner, Yellow, 9 ⅜ In.	14.00
Cameo, Platter, Green, 13 In.	26.00
Cameo, Sherbet, Yellow, 4 ⅞ In.	98.00
Cameo, Tumbler, Green, Footed, 11 Oz.	41.00 to
74.00 **Cameo,** Tumbler, Yellow, Footed, 9 Oz., 4 ¾ In.	20.00
Candlewick pattern is listed in the Imperial Glass category.	
Caprice pattern is included in the Cambridge Glass category.	
Catalonian, Bowl, Green, 8 ½ In.	40.00
Catalonian, Candlestick, Green	35.00
Catalonian, Vase, Green, Flared, 5 ½ In.	45.00
Cherry Blossom, Berry Bowl, Pink, 4 ¾ In.	18.00
Cherry Blossom, Bowl, 3-Footed, Pink	100.00
Cherry Blossom, Bowl, Cereal, Pink	65.00
Cherry Blossom, Bowl, Fruit, Green, 4 ¾ In.	25.00
Cherry Blossom, Butter, Cover, Pink, Round	140.00
Cherry Blossom, Cake Plate, Pink, Footed	65.00
Cherry Blossom, Cup & Saucer, Delphite	26.00
Cherry Blossom, Cup & Saucer, Green	23.00
Cherry Blossom, Cup & Saucer, Pink	26.00

Depression Glass, Cubist, Tumbler, Pink, Jeannette Glass, c.1930, 3 ⅞ In. $55.00

Ruby Lane, Inc.

Depression Glass, Diamond Optic, Pitcher, Ice Lip, Cobalt Blue, 1930s, 7 In. $65.00

Ruby Lane, Inc.

Depression Glass, Imperial Plain Octagon, Dish, Mayonnaise, Ladle, Underplate, Pink $45.00

Ruby Lane, Inc.

Depression Glass, Refrigerator Dish, Lid, Green, 4 ¼ x 5 ⅜ In. $35.00

Ruby Lane, Inc.

TIP
Never stack cut glass bowls.

D

Depression Glass, Sharon, Plate, Dinner, Amber, 9 ¼ In., Pair
$15.00

Ruby Lane, Inc.

Depression Glass, Sportsman Series, Bowl, Ice, Cobalt Blue, White Ship, 1930s, 4 ¼ In.
$25.00

Ruby Lane, Inc.

Iris

The design of Iris is unusually bold for Depression glass. Molded representations of stalks of iris fill the center of a ribbed plate. Other pieces in the pattern show fewer irises, but the flower is predominant. Edges of pieces may be ruffled or beaded. It was made by Jeannette Glass Company, Jeannette, Pennsylvania, from 1928 to 1932 and then again in the 1950s and 1970s. Early pieces were made in Crystal, Green, Iridescent, and Pink. Later, Crystal and White pieces were decorated with Blue-Green and Red-Yellow two-tone stains. Solid Red-stained after-dinner cups and saucers can be found. The pattern is also called Iris & Herringbone. Reproduction candy vases and coasters have been made in a variety of colors since 1977.

Cherry Blossom, Grill Plate, Green, 9 In.	30.00
Cherry Blossom, Grill Plate, Pink, 9 In.	26.00
Cherry Blossom, Plate, Dinner, Delphite, 9 ⅛ In.	31.00
Cherry Blossom, Plate, Dinner, Green, 9 ⅛ In.	37.00
Cherry Blossom, Platter, Green, 13 In.	79.00
Cherry Blossom, Tray, Handles, Pink	35.00
Cherry Blossom, Tumbler, Footed, Pink, 4 Oz.	14.00
Cherry Blossom, Tumbler, Pink, 4 Oz.	24.00
Cherry Blossom, Tumbler, Pink, 12 Oz.	85.00
Cherry Blossom, Tumbler, Scalloped Foot, Green, 8 Oz.	43.00
Cherryberry, Plate, Green, 6 In.	10.00
Cherryberry, Sherbet, Green, Footed	10.00
Chevron, Pitcher, Milk, Blue, 4 ¼ In.	24.00
Cloverleaf, Bowl, Cereal, Green, 5 In.	69.00
Cloverleaf, Creamer, Green, Footed, 3 ⅝ In.	21.00
Cloverleaf, Cup & Saucer, Green	15.00
Cloverleaf, Sherbet, Green, 3 In.	12.00
Colonial Block, Candy Dish, Green, Lid	50.00
Colonial Block, Sugar, Green, Handles, 3 ¾ In.	15.00
Colonial, Pitcher, Green, 7 ¾ In.	40.00
Colonial, Spoon Holder, Green	25.00
Coronation, Berry Bowl, Royal Ruby, 4 ½ In.	8.00
Coronation, Bowl, Royal Ruby, 8 In.	20.00
Cremax, Cup & Saucer, Delphite Blue	12.00
Cremax, Sugar, Delphite Blue	10.00
Cube pattern is listed here as Cubist.	
Cubist, Berry Bowl, Green, Toothed Edge, 8 In.	24.00
Cubist, Bowl, Pink, Toothed Edge, 4 ½ In.	10.00
Cubist, Butter, Cover, Pink	85.00
Cubist, Candy Jar, Green, Footed	15.00
Cubist, Candy Jar, Lid, Pink, Footed	38.00
Cubist, Cup, Green	12.00
Cubist, Plate, Green, 8 In.	12.00
Cubist, Salt & Pepper, Green	45.00
Cubist, Tumbler, Pink, Jeannette Glass, c.1930, 3 ⅞ In. ......*Illus*	55.00
Dancing Girl pattern is listed here as Cameo.	
Della Robbia, Bowl, Red Flashed, Footed, 12 In.	125.00
Diamond pattern is listed here as Miss America.	
Diamond Line, Pitcher, Pink, 60 Oz.	48.00
Diamond Line, Tumbler, Pink, 9 Oz., 4 In.	12.00
Diamond Optic, Pitcher, Ice Lip, Cobalt Blue, 1930s, 7 In. ....*Illus*	65.00
Diamond Quilted, Bowl, Black, Crimped Edge	20.00
Diamond Quilted, Nappy, Black, Handle	18.00
Diana, Cup, Pink	20.00
Diana, Sherbet, Amber, Footed Cone	12.00
Dogwood, Cake Plate, Pink, 10 In.	80.00
Dogwood, Cup & Saucer, Pink	12.00
Dogwood, Pitcher, Pink, 80 Oz.	329.00
Dogwood, Tumbler, Band, Pink	23.00
Doric & Pansy, Butter, Cover, Teal	270.00
Doric, Soup, Cream, Green, 5 In.	65.00
Dresser Set, Pink, 6 Bottles, Molded Design Of Draped Nude, 3-Footed, 3 x 6 In.	475.00
English Hobnail, Bonbon, Hexagonal, Handle, 6 In.	15.00
English Hobnail, Candlestick, Amber, 9 In.	20.00
English Hobnail, Candlestick, Green, 3 ½ In.	19.00
English Hobnail, Console, Amber, Rolled, 11 In.	30.00
English Hobnail, Nappy, Amber, Square, 6 In.	11.00
Fire-King, Mixing Bowl Set, Modern Tulip Pattern, Red & Black, 4 In., 6 In., & 9 ½ In., 3 Piece	195.00
Fire-King, Mug, White, Red, Couple Dancing, 1950s, 3 ½ In.	40.00
Floral, Candlestick, Green, 4 In.	49.00
Floral, Cup & Saucer, Green	19.00
Floral, Cup & Saucer, Pink	17.00
Floral, Pitcher, Cone Shape, Footed, Pink, 32 Oz.	49.00
Floral, Plate, Dinner, Green, 9 In.	22.00
Floral, Plate, Dinner, Pink, 9 In.	15.00

Floral, Platter, Green, Oval, 10 ¾ In.	30.00
Floral, Sherbet, Green, 2 ⅞ In.	17.00
Florentine No. 1, Cup & Saucer, Green, Footed	19.00
Florentine No. 1, Pitcher, Green, Footed, 36 Oz., 6 ¾ In.	59.00
Florentine No. 1, Plate, Dinner, Green, 9 ¾ In.	36.00
Florentine No. 1, Sugar & Creamer, Pink	25.00
Florentine No. 2, Bowl, Cereal, Yellow, 6 In.	49.00
Florentine No. 2, Bowl, Nut, Yellow, Handle, Footed	60.00
Florentine No. 2, Pitcher, Yellow, Footed	40.00
Florentine No. 2, Plate, Dinner, Yellow, 10 In.	13.00
Florentine No. 2, Saucer, Yellow, 5 ½ In.	3.00
Florentine No. 2, Tumbler, Juice, Yellow	22.00
Flower Rim pattern is listed here as Vitrock.	
Fruits, Cup & Saucer, Pink	17.00
Georgian, Bowl, Cereal, Green	23.00
Georgian, Bowl, Nut, Handle, Footed, Green	35.00
Georgian, Creamer, Green, 3 ½ In.	17.00
Georgian, Cup & Saucer, Footed, Green	11.00
Georgian, Sherbet, Green, 3 In.	13.00
Georgian, Tumbler, Green, 12 Oz.	149.00
Green Parrot, Platter, Oblong, 11 ¼ In.	35.00
Green Parrot, Tumbler, 12 Oz.	110.00
Imperial Plain Octagon, Dish, Mayonnaise, Ladle, Underplate, Pink ....*Illus*	45.00
Iris & Herringbone pattern is listed here as Iris.	
Iris, Bowl, Fruit, Ruffled, Jeannette Glass, 11 In.	20.00
Iris, Bowl, Nut, Metal Base, Jeannette Glass, 11 In.	150.00
Iris, Butter, Iridescent, Lid	20.00
Iris, Candy Dish, Tab Handles, Footed, Jeannette Glass, 3 In.	30.00
Iris, Coaster	86.00
Iris, Cup & Saucer, Demitasse	180.00
Iris, Pitcher, Footed, Jeannette Glass, 56 Oz.	32.00
Iris, Plate, Jeannette Glass, 12 In.	42.00
Iris, Plate, Luncheon, Crystal	60.00
Iris, Tumbler, Flat, Jeannette Glass, 8 Oz.	139.00
Iris, Tumbler, Footed, Jeannette Glass, 12 Oz.	130.00
Jennyware, Bowl, Ultramarine, 8 ¼ In.	45.00
Jennyware, Bowl, Ultramarine, 10 ½ In.	55.00
Jennyware, Mixing Bowl, Pink, 8 ¼ In.	30.00
Jennyware, Mixing Bowl, Pink, 10 ½ In.	40.00
Jubilee, Creamer, Yellow, 6 Oz., 3 ¼ In.	23.00
Jubilee, Cup & Saucer, Yellow	19.00
Jubilee, Saucer, Yellow	6.00
Jubilee, Tumbler, Yellow, Footed, 10 Oz.	35.00
Knife & Fork pattern is listed here as Colonial.	
Lancaster, Bowl, Yellow, Footed, 11 ½ In.	150.00
Lorain pattern is listed here as No. 615.	
Lovebirds pattern is listed here as Georgian.	
Madrid, Bowl, Vegetable, Oval, Amber, 10 In.	20.00
Madrid, Candlestick, Amber, 2 In.	17.00
Madrid, Cup & Saucer, Amber	9.00
Madrid, Cup & Saucer, Green	19.00
Madrid, Grill Plate, Amber, 10 In.	14.00
Madrid, Pitcher, Blue, 60 Oz.	239.00
Madrid, Pitcher, Shouldered, Amber, 36 Oz.	49.00
Madrid, Plate, Dinner, Blue, 10 ½ In.	84.00
Madrid, Plate, Green, 7 ½ In.	23.00
Madrid, Platter, Oval, Blue, 11 ½ In.	47.00
Madrid, Salt & Pepper, Amber, Metal Lids	129.00
Madrid, Sherbet, Blue, Cone Shape, 2 ⅞ In.	16.00
Madrid, Sherbet, Green, Cone Shape, 2 ⅞ In.	12.00
Madrid, Tumbler, Footed, Amber, 5 Oz.	42.00
Madrid, Tumbler, Footed, Amber, 10 Oz.	37.00
Mayfair Open Rose, Bowl, Cereal, Pink	23.00
Mayfair Open Rose, Bowl, Vegetable, Lid, Handles, Pink, 10 In.	138.00
Mayfair Open Rose, Celery Dish, Divided, Pink, 10 In.	249.00

D

Disneyana, Display, Mickey & Minnie Mouse, Mechanical, Old King Cole, c.1935, 32 & 30 In.
$18,785.00

Hake's Americana & Collectibles

Disneyana, Display, Mickey Mouse, Molded, Composition, High Relief, Old King Cole Inc., c.1935, 23 x 42 In.
$4,934.00

Hake's Americana & Collectibles

Disneyana, Doll, Jiminy Cricket, Wood Jointed, Felt, Fabric Tie, Decal, Ideal, 1940s, 8 ½ In.
$171.00

Hake's Americana & Collectibles

TIP

Do not light a cabinet filled with glass with lightbulbs over 25 watts. Stronger bulbs generate too much heat. Some new types of bulbs are brighter and give off less heat.

Disneyana, Doll, Mickey Mouse, Velvet, Felt Ears, Names Stitched On Hands, Steiff, Paper Tag, 7 In. $472.00

James D. Julia Auctioneers

Disneyana, Figurine, Mickey Mouse, Wire Tail, Holding Umbrella, Metal, Germany, c.1932, 3 In. $759.00

Hake's Americana & Collectibles

Disneyana, Pin, Mickey Mouse, Rubies, Sapphires, Full Cut Diamonds, Black Onyx, Mother-Of-Pearl, 2 In. $4,740.00

Skinner, Inc.

Mayfair Open Rose, Cookie Jar, Lid, Pink	74.00
Mayfair Open Rose, Decanter, Bulbous, Pink	239.00
Mayfair Open Rose, Grill Plate, Pink	36.00
Mayfair Open Rose, Pitcher, Shouldered, Pink, 37 Oz.	55.00
Mayfair Open Rose, Saltshaker, Metal Lid, Pink	49.00
Mayfair Open Rose, Tumbler, Footed, Pink, 10 Oz.	43.00
Miss America, Bowl, Curved, 8 In.	50.00
Miss America, Butter, Cover, Round, Pink	879.00
Miss America, Candy Dish, Lid, Footed, Pink, 9 In.	169.00
Miss America, Cup & Saucer	22.00
Miss America, Grill Plate, Pink	26.00
Miss America, Pitcher, Water, Pink, 65 Oz.	100.00
Miss America, Platter, Pink, 13 In.	49.00
Miss America, Relish, 4 Sections, Pink	24.00
Miss America, Tumbler, Pink, 10 Oz.	43.00
Moderntone, Bowl, Nut, 2 Handles, Cobalt Blue	98.00
Moderntone, Creamer, Cobalt Blue	14.00
Moderntone, Cup & Saucer, Cobalt Blue	9.00
Moderntone, Tumbler, Cobalt Blue, 9 Oz.	43.00
Mt. Vernon pattern is included in the Cambridge Glass category.	
No. 615, Berry Bowl, Green, 8 In.	40.00
No. 615, Bowl, Deep, Green, 8 In.	55.00
No. 615, Bowl, Salad, Yellow, 7 1/4 In.	30.00
No. 615, Sugar & Creamer, Yellow, Footed	40.00
Old Florentine pattern is listed here as Florentine No. 1.	
Open Rose pattern is listed here as Mayfair Open Rose.	
Patrician, Bowl, Pink, 8 1/2 In.	25.00
Patrician, Bowl, Vegetable, Oval, Amber, 10 In.	32.00
Patrician, Butter, Cover, Round, Amber	79.00
Patrician, Butter, Pink	75.00
Patrician, Cup & Saucer, Amber	16.00
Patrician, Cup, Amber	9.00
Patrician, Pitcher, Amber, 75 Oz.	109.00
Patrician, Tumbler, Amber, 5 Oz.	33.00
Petal Swirl pattern is listed here as Swirl.	
Pinwheel pattern is listed here as Sierra.	
Poinsettia pattern is listed here as Floral.	
Poppy No. 1 pattern is listed here as Florentine No. 1.	
Poppy No. 2 pattern is listed here as Florentine No. 2.	
Prescut, Cake Stand, Anchor Hocking, 7 1/2 x 13 1/2 In.	18.00
Pretty Polly Party Dishes, see also the related pattern Doric & Pansy.	
Princess, Bowl, Hat, Pink, 9 1/2 In.	30.00
Princess, Cookie Jar, Lid, Green	70.00
Princess, Tumbler, Footed, 10 Oz.	41.00
Princess, Vase, Green, 8 In.	45.00
Prismatic Line pattern is listed here as Queen Mary.	
Provincial pattern is listed here as Bubble.	
Queen Mary, Bowl, Fruit, Pink, Handle, 6 1/8 In.	8.00
Queen Mary, Bowl, Nut, Pink, Handle, Footed	39.00
Queen Mary, Cup, Pink, Pointed Handle	16.00
Queen Mary, Sherbet, Pink, 2 1/8 In.	8.00
Refrigerator Dish, Lid, Green, 4 1/4 x 5 3/8 In. ....*Illus*	35.00
Rose Of Sharon, Plate, Amber, 9 In.	12.00
Royal Lace, Berry Bowl, 10 In.	20.00
Royal Lace, Bowl, Pink, 10 In.	40.00
Royal Lace, Bowl, Rolled Edge, 3-Footed, Cobalt Blue, 10 In.	1199.00
Royal Lace, Bowl, Vegetable, Green, 11 In.	35.00
Royal Lace, Cookie Jar, Lid, Cobalt Blue	419.00
Royal Lace, Cup & Saucer, Cobalt Blue	36.00
Royal Lace, Cup, Cobalt Blue	31.00
Royal Lace, Pitcher, Cobalt Blue, 48 Oz.	189.00
Royal Lace, Sugar & Creamer, Green	15.00
Royal Lace, Sugar & Creamer, Lid, Cobalt Blue	120.00
Royal Lace, Tumbler, Cobalt Blue, 5 Oz.	47.00
Royal Lace, Tumbler, Cobalt Blue, 10 Oz.	179.00
Royal Ruby, Cruet, Lid, 5 In.	16.00

D

Royal Ruby, Tumbler, 20 Oz. 40.00
Royal Ruby, Vase, Crimped, Bud, 3 In. 14.00
Royal Ruby, Vase, Crimped, Flared, 9 In. 49.00
Sailboat pattern is listed here as Sportsman Series.
Saxon pattern is listed here as Coronation.
Sereno, Ashtray, Blue Anchor Hocking, 6 ¼ In. 18.00
Sharon, Bowl, Cereal, Pink. 27.00
Sharon, Bowl, Fruit, Amber, 5 In. 9.00
Sharon, Bowl, Vegetable, Oval, Amber, 9 ½ In. 15.00
Sharon, Cup & Saucer, Amber. 10.00
Sharon, Dinner, Amber, 9 In. 12.00
Sharon, Pitcher, Pink, 80 Oz. 269.00
Sharon, Plate, Dinner, Amber, 9 ¼ In., Pair *Illus* 15.00
Sharon, Platter, Oval, Amber, 12 ½ In. 13.00
Sharon, Salt & Pepper, Pink, Metal Lids 89.00
Sharon, Tumbler, Amber, 12 Oz. 84.00
Sharon, Tumbler, Pink, Footed, 15 Oz. 49.00
Sierra, Berry Bowl, Green, 8 ½ In. 25.00
Sierra, Bowl, Vegetable, Oval, Green, 9 ¼ In. 55.00
Sierra, Platter, Oval, Pink, 11 In. 15.00
Sierra, Salt & Pepper, Pink 25.00
Spiral Flutes pattern is listed in the Duncan & Miller category as Swirl.
Spoke pattern is listed here as Patrician.
Sportsman Series, Bowl, Ice, Cobalt Blue, White Ship, 1930s, 4 ¼ In. *Illus* 25.00
Swirl, Candy Dish, Lid, Ultramarine 35.00 to 40.00
Swirl, Cup, Ultramarine, 6 Piece 20.00
Tea Room, Pitcher, Green 230.00
Tea Room, Sugar & Creamer, Green, Oblong, 3 ½ In. 80.00
Vertical Ribbed pattern is listed here as Queen Mary.
Vitrock, Range Set, Red Tulips, White Ground, Anchor Hocking, 4 Piece 60.00
White Ship pattern is listed here as Sportsman Series.
Wild Rose pattern is listed here as Dogwood.
Windmill pattern is listed here as Sportsman Series.
Windsor, Bowl, 3-Footed, Pink, 7 ⅜ In. 40.00
Windsor, Bowl, Dessert, Pointed Edge, Pink, 8 In. 119.00
Windsor, Bowl, Fruit, Pink, 4 ¾ In. 10.00
Windsor, Pitcher, Pink, 52 Oz., 6 ⅜ In. 40.00
Windsor, Plate, Dinner, Pink, 9 In. 24.00

DERBY has been marked on porcelain made in the city of Derby, England, since about 1748. The original Derby factory closed in 1848, but others opened there and continued to produce quality porcelain. The Crown Derby mark began appearing on Derby wares in the 1770s.

Box, William IV, Silver Gilt, Porcelain Mounted, Flower & Fruit Basket, Chased, Engraved, 3 In. 1416.00
Dish, Heart Shape, Gilded Trim, Martagon Lily, Botanical Design, Marked, c.1815, 9 ¾ In. 148.00 to 688.00
Mug, Orange & Blue Flowers, Gilt Scrollwork, c.1835, 6 ¾ In. 184.00
Plate, Gold Floral Rim, Gilt Sprig In Center, c.1790, 8 ⅜ In. 24.00
Platter, Dessert, Purple Bindweed, Painted, Gilt Fluted Rim, Wm. Pegg, c.1800, 12 In. 531.00
Stirrup Cup, Hound's Head, Stevensen & Hancock, Painted, Sponged, Yellow, Black, c.1865, 3 ¾ In. 767.00
Tile, Glazed, Hand Painted, Fishing Scenes, Wood & Composition Frame, 1800s, 4 ½ x 5 ½ In., Pair 826.00
Tureen, Lid, Flowers, Multicolor, Garland, Gilt, Shell Scroll Handles, Loop Finial, Oval, 7 ⅜ x 4 ½ In. 426.00
Urn, Campana Shape, Cobalt Blue, Gilt, Scrolls, Latticework, Flowers, Marked, 1800s, 5 x 4/12 In., Pair 375.00
Urn, Dome Lid, Ball Finial, Ferns, Leaves, Yellow Ground, Gilt, 15 ½ In. 938.00

DICK TRACY, the comic strip, started in 1931. Tracy was also the hero of movies from 1937 to 1947 and again in 1990, and starred in a radio series in the 1940s and a television series in the 1950s. Memorabilia from all these activities are collected.

Badge, Lieutenant, Cereal Token, Silvered Brass, 1938, 1 ¾ x 2 In. 40.00
Pistol & Targets, Rubber Band, Punch-Out, Miller Bros. Hat Co. Premium, c.1944, 8 x 17 In. 173.00
Toy, Car, Passengers, Marx, 1930s, 20 ½ In. 425.00
Toy, Detective Set, Ink, Magnifying Glass, Roller, Powder, Brush, Box, c.1930, 9 x 15 In. 171.00
Toy, Pop Pistol, Sparkling, Metal, Paint, Decal, Box, 1934, 8 In. 158.00
Toy, Water Gun, Sub-Machine, Plastic, Red, Box, 1950s, 12 In. 231.00
Ukette, Islander, Sparkle Plenty, Plastic, French American Reed Co., 1950, 14 ½ In. 440.00
Wristwatch, New Haven, Box, 1948 360.00

DICKENS WARE *pieces are listed in the Weller category.*

Disneyana, Shovel, Donald Duck, Nephews, Tin Litho Shovel Blade, Ohio Art, 1939, 6 ½ x 7 x 23 In.
$370.00

Hake's Americana & Collectibles

Disneyana, Toy, Donald Duck, Jointed, Composition, Painted, Head Tilts Back, Knickerbocker, 11 ½ In.
$288.00

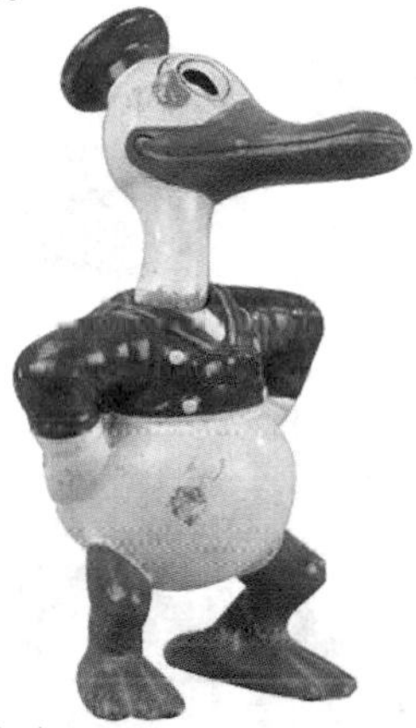

Bertoia Auctions

Disneyana, Toy, Mickey & Minnie Mouse, Handcar, Composition, Steel, Clockwork, Track, Lionel, 8 In.
$402.00

James D. Julia Auctioneers

TIP

Don't put pottery or porcelain with crazed glaze in the dishwasher. It will crack even more.

D

DINNERWARE

D

Disneyana, Toy, Mickey Mouse Washer, Mickey Mouse, Minnie Mouse, Tin Litho, Ohio Art, 1930s, 7 ½ In. $230.00

Hake's Americana & Collectibles

Disneyana, Toy, Mickey Mouse, Cowboy, Riding Pluto, Celluloid, Windup, Japan, 1930s, 8 x 7 In. $1,708.00

Hake's Americana & Collectibles

Disneyana, Toy, Minnie Mouse Knitter, Minnie In Rocking Chair, Tin Lithograph, Linemar, Japan, 6 ½ In. $266.00

Bertoia Auctions

DINNERWARE used in the United States from the 1930s through the 1950s is listed here. Most was made in potteries in southern Ohio, West Virginia, and California. A few patterns were made in Japan, England, and other countries. Dishes were sold in gift shops and department stores, or were given away as premiums. Many of these patterns are listed in this book in their own categories, such as Autumn Leaf, Azalea, Fiesta, Franciscan, Hall, Harker, Harlequin, Red Wing, Riviera, Russel Wright, Vernon Kilns, Watt, and Willow. For more prices, go to kovels.com. Sets missing a few pieces can be completed through the help of one of the many matching services listed on our website, www.kovels.com.

Acacia, Creamer, Harmony House, 2 ½ In.	16.00
Acacia, Cup & Saucer, Harmony House, 2 ½ In.	8.00
Acacia, Sugar, Lid, Harmony House	16.00
Amelia, Bowl, Vegetable, Round, Blue Ridge, 9 In.	44.00
Amelia, Platter, Blue Ridge, 11 ¾ In.	46.00
Amsterdam, Creamer, Homer Laughlin, 10 Oz., 2 ½ In.	18.00
Amsterdam, Cup & Saucer, Footed, Homer Laughlin, 2 ¾ In.	10.00
Amsterdam, Plate, Dinner, Homer Laughlin, 10 ¼ In.	16.00
Amsterdam, Saucer, Homer Laughlin	4.00
Amsterdam, Soup, Dish, Rim, Homer Laughlin, 8 In.	8.00
Apple Blossom, Platter, Johnson Brothers, 12 ¼ In.	21.00
Apple Jack, Bowl, Vegetable, Blue Ridge, 9 In.	36.00
Apple Jack, Plate, Blue Ridge, 6 In.	12.00
Apple Jack, Plate, Blue Ridge, 9 ½ In.	17.00
Apple Trio, Bowl, Fruit, Blue Ridge, 5 ⅜ In.	12.00
Apple Trio, Bread & Butter, Blue Ridge, 6 ¼ In.	11.00
Apple Trio, Creamer, Blue Ridge, 8 Oz., 2 ⅞ In.	32.00
Apple Trio, Cup & Saucer, Footed, Blue Ridge, 2 ⅜ In.	15.00
Apple Trio, Plate, Blue Ridge, 6 ¼ In.	9.00
Arcadia, Cup & Saucer, Homer Laughlin	9.00
Arcadia, Plate, Dinner, Homer Laughlin, 10 ¼ In.	10.00
Arcadia, Plate, Homer Laughlin, 6 In.	6.00
Arcadia, Platter, Oval, Homer Laughlin, 13 In.	26.00
Autumn Apple, Creamer, Blue Ridge, 8 Oz., 2 ⅞ In.	16.00
Autumn Apple, Cup & Saucer, Footed, Blue Ridge, 2 ¼ In.	18.00
Autumn Apple, Cup, Blue Ridge	8.00
Autumn Apple, Plate, Blue Ridge, 7 ¼ In.	14.00
Autumn Apple, Plate, Blue Ridge, 8 ½ In.	15.00
Autumn Apple, Sugar, Lid, Blue Ridge	25.00
Autumn Berry, Plate, Dinner, Blue Ridge, 9 ¼ In.	17.00
Autumn Leaves, Bowl, Fruit, Salem China, 5 In.	9.00
Autumn Leaves, Cup & Saucer, Salem China	8.00
Azalea, Creamer, Crooksville, 8 Oz., 2 ⅜ In.	22.00
Aztec, Casserole, Lid, Iroquois, 2 Qt.	110.00
Aztec, Creamer, Iroquois	15.00
Aztec, Cup & Saucer, Iroquois	9.00
Aztec, Sugar, Lid, Iroquois	16.00
Bayberry, Bowl, Cereal, Lugged Handles, Homer Laughlin, 7 In.	8.00
Bayberry, Cup & Saucer, Homer Laughlin	9.00
Bayberry, Pepper Shaker, 6 Holes, Homer Laughlin	12.00
Beaded Apple, Cup, Blue Ridge	15.00
Beaded Apple, Plate, Dinner, Blue Ridge, 10 ¼ In.	16.00
Becky, Bowl, Vegetable, Oval, Blue Ridge, 9 In.	30.00
Becky, Creamer, Blue Ridge, 8 Oz., 2 ¾ In.	24.00
Becky, Gravy Boat, Blue Ridge	35.00
Becky, Platter, Oval, Blue Ridge, 13 ¼ In.	50.00
Big Apple, Bowl, Fruit, Blue Ridge, 5 ¼ In.	10.00
Big Apple, Creamer, Blue Ridge	15.00
Big Apple, Plate, Dinner, Blue Ridge, 9 ⅞ In.	21.00
Bittersweet, Bowl, Vegetable, Round, Lid, Crooksville, 10 ⅝ In.	40.00
Bittersweet, Cup & Saucer, Crooksville	27.00
Bittersweet, Gravy Boat, Crooksville	23.00
Bittersweet, Plate, Dinner, Crooksville, 10 In.	8.00
Bittersweet, Relish, Crooksville, 9 ½ In.	16.00
Blossomtime, Spoon Holder, Salem China	22.00
Blue Bonnet, Chop Plate, Harmony House, 12 In.	18.00

Blue Bonnet, Creamer, Harmony House, 8 Oz., 3 ¾ In.	18.00
Blue Bonnet, Cup & Saucer, Round Handle, Harmony House	15.00
Blue Laurel, Bowl, Vegetable, Harmony House, 10 ½ In.	28.00
Blue Laurel, Cup & Saucer, Footed, Harmony House	9.00
Blue Laurel, Plate, Dinner, Harmony House, 10 ¼ In.	10.00
Blue Laurel, Relish, 3 Sections, Harmony House	33.00
Bramble, Cup & Saucer, Blue Ridge	12.00
Bramble, Plate, Dinner, Blue Ridge, 10 ⅛ In.	12.00
Briarcliff, Bowl, Cereal, Salem China, 6 ¼ In.	8.00
Briarcliff, Relish, 3 Sections, Salem China	33.00
Briarcliff, Spoon Rest, Salem China	20.00
Carol's Roses, Platter, Blue Ridge, 11 ⅞ In.	65.00
Celeste, Creamer, Homer Laughlin, 8 Oz., 4 In.	17.00
Celeste, Cup & Saucer, Footed, Homer Laughlin	9.00
Celeste, Plate, Dinner, Homer Laughlin, 10 In.	9.00
Cheerio, Platter, Blue Ridge, 12 ½ In.	24.00
Chintz, Candy Dish, Lid, Blue Ridge, 6 In.	125.00
Chintz, Plate, Bread & Butter, Blue Ridge, 6 ¼ In.	8.00
Chintz, Plate, Dinner, Blue Ridge, 10 In.	12.00
Chrysanthemum, Plate, Salad, Blue Ridge, 7 ⅛ In.	12.00
Country Fair, Plate, Salad, Grapes, Blue Ridge, 8 ½ In.	12.00
Country Fair, Plate, Salad, Peaches, Blue Ridge, 8 ½ In.	12.00
Country Fair, Plate, Salad, Pear, Blue Ridge, 8 ½ In.	12.00
Country Road, Bowl, Fruit, Blue Ridge, 5 ¼ In.	8.00
Country Road, Bowl, Vegetable, 9 ¼ In.	21.00
Country Road, Creamer, Blue Ridge	14.00
Country Road, Cup & Saucer, Blue Ridge	12.00
Country Road, Gravy Boat, Blue Ridge	25.00
Country Road, Plate, Dinner, Blue Ridge, 10 ⅜ In.	21.00
Country Road, Plate, Salad, Blue Ridge, 7 ⅛ In.	10.00
Country Strawberry, Plate, Dinner, Homer Laughlin, 10 In.	12.00
Crab Apple, Bowl, Blue Ridge, 7 In.	21.00
Crab Apple, Plate, Dinner, Blue Ridge, 10 ¼ In.	25.00
Crab Apple, Sugar, Handles, Blue Ridge	10.00
Dairy Maid, Bowl, Fruit, Crooksville, 5 ⅜ In.	11.00
Dairy Maid, Cup & Saucer, Crooksville	21.00
Dairy Maid, Plate, Bread & Butter, Crooksville, 6 In.	10.00
Dairy Maid, Plate, Dinner, Crooksville, 10 ¼ In.	15.00
Dazzle, Plate, Bread & Butter, Blue Ridge, 6 In.	8.00
Del Ray, Platter, Harmony House, 13 In.	43.00
Del Ray, Sugar, Lid, Harmony House	16.00
Delicious, Plate, Dinner, Blue Ridge, 10 In.	8.00
Delmar Diana, Bowl, Vegetable, Lid, 2 Handles, Crooksville, c.1960, 7 In.	43.00
Delmar Diana, Sugar & Creamer, Crooksville, c.1950	18.00
Delta Daisy, Bowl, Fruit, Blue Ridge	9.00
Delta Daisy, Cup & Saucer, Blue Ridge	12.00
Delta Daisy, Plate, Dinner, Blue Ridge, 10 ¼ In.	16.00
Delta Daisy, Soup, Dish, Blue Ridge, 5 ¼ In.	10.00
Desert Sand, Plate, Bread & Butter, Johnson Brothers, 6 ½ In.	10.00
Desert Sand, Plate, Dinner, Johnson Brothers, 10 ½ In.	13.00
Desert Sand, Saucer, Johnson Brothers	2.00
Doe Eyes, Creamer, Blue Ridge	20.00
Double Apple, Bread & Butter, Blue Ridge	8.00
Double Apple, Plate, Salad, Blue Ridge, 7 ¼ In.	12.00
Ebonette, Bowl, Fruit, Edwin Knowles, 5 ¾ In.	8.00
Ebonette, Plate, Bread & Butter, Edwin Knowles, 6 ¼ In.	5.00
Ebonette, Plate, Dinner, Edwin Knowles, 10 ½ In.	15.00
Ebonette, Platter, Edwin Knowles, 9 ⅛ In.	25.00
Falling Leaves, Cup, Blue Ridge	5.00
Falling Leaves, Gravy Boat, Blue Ridge	35.00
Falling Leaves, Soup, Dish, Blue Ridge, 8 In.	15.00
Forest Fruit, Plate, Bread & Butter, Blue Ridge, 6 ¼ In.	6.00
Forest Fruit, Plate, Dinner, Blue Ridge, 10 ¼ In.	15.00
Frageria, Plate, Dinner, Blue Ridge, 10 ¼ In.	14.00

D

Disneyana, Wristwatch, Mickey Mouse, Metal Band, Ingersoll, Box, 1930s
$360.00

DuMouchelles Art Gallery

Doll, A.M., 323, Bisque Socket Head, Googly Glass Eyes, Mohair Wig, Composition Body, c.1920, 10 In.
$952.00

Theriault's

Doll, Automaton, Maiden, Bisque, Mohair Wig, Silk Dress, Lorgnette & Fan, Jumeau, 18 In.
$6,325.00

James D. Julia Auctioneers

Doll, Dressel, Man, Bisque Socket Head, Glass Eyes, Mohair Wig, Beard, Jointed, c.1890, 17 In.
$3,080.00

Theriault's

Doll, French, Woman, Wax, Painted Face, Blond Mohair Wig, Label, Hat Boxes, 1915, 12 In.
$3,640.00

Theriault's

Doll, German, Bisque Head & Shoulders, Sculpted Hair, Muslin Body, C.F. Kling Co., c.1870, 17 In.
$1,904.00

Theriault's

French Peasant, Soup, Dish, Blue Ridge, 8 In.	40.00
Friendly Village, Bowl, Cereal, Square, Johnson Brothers, 6 ⅛ In.	10.00
Friendly Village, Cup & Saucer, Johnson Brothers	8.00
Friendly Village, Plate, Bread & Butter, Johnson Brothers, 6 In.	5.00
Friendly Village, Plate, Dinner, Autumn Mist, Johnson Brothers, 10 ½ In.	21.00
Friendly Village, Plate, Dinner, Covered Bridge, Johnson Brothers, 10 ½ In.	25.00
Friendly Village, Plate, Dinner, School House, Johnson Brothers, 9 ⅞ In.	12.00
Friendly Village, Plate, Dinner, Sugar Maples, Johnson Brothers, 10 ½ In.	25.00
Friendly Village, Plate, Dinner, The Well, Johnson Brothers, 10 ½ In.	25.00
Friendly Village, Plate, Johnson Brothers, 7 ¾ In.	13.00
Fruit Fantasy, Saucer, Blue Ridge	4.00
Fruit Fantasy, Sugar, Blue Ridge	6.00
Game Birds, Mug, Partridges, Johnson Brothers	25.00
Golden Apple, Plate, Dinner, Johnson Brothers, 10 In.	16.00
Golden Wheat, Bowl, Fruit, Edwin Knowles, 5 ⅜ In.	7.00
Golden Wheat, Bowl, Fruit, Homer Laughlin, 5 ½ In.	4.00
Golden Wheat, Creamer, Edwin Knowles	21.00
Golden Wheat, Cup & Saucer, Edwin Knowles	12.00
Golden Wheat, Cup & Saucer, Homer Laughlin	9.00
Golden Wheat, Plate, Bread & Butter, Edwin Knowles, 6 In.	4.00
Golden Wheat, Plate, Bread & Butter, Homer Laughlin, 6 In.	4.00
Golden Wheat, Plate, Dinner, Edwin Knowles, 10 ¼ In.	10.00
Golden Wheat, Soup, Dish, Edwin Knowles, 7 ⅝ In.	11.00
Golden Wheat, Soup, Dish, Homer Laughlin, 7 ½ In.	5.00
Golden Willow, Cup & Saucer, Crooksville	9.00
Golden Willow, Plate, Bread & Butter, Crooksville, 6 In.	7.00
Gray Dawn, Plate, Homer Laughlin, 6 ¼ In.	5.00
Gray Dawn, Platter, Homer Laughlin, 13 In.	30.00
Gray Dawn, Relish, 3 Sections, Homer Laughlin	36.00
Green Briar, Bowl, Fruit, Blue Ridge, 5 ⅜ In.	10.00
Green Briar, Plate, Dinner, Blue Ridge, 9 ⅜ In.	16.00
Greydawn, Bowl, Blue, Johnson Brothers, 6 ⅛ In.	14.00
Greydawn, Bowl, Fruit, Blue, Johnson Brothers, 5 In.	8.00
Greydawn, Bowl, Fruit, Green, Johnson Brothers, 5 ⅛ In.	8.00
Greydawn, Bowl, Vegetable, Green, 8 ¼ In.	21.00
Greydawn, Creamer, Blue, Johnson Brothers, 3 In.	18.00
Greydawn, Creamer, Green, Johnson Brothers	18.00
Greydawn, Plate, Bread & Butter, Green, Johnson Brothers, 6 ⅜ In.	6.00
Greydawn, Platter, Green, Johnson Brothers, 13 ¾ In.	25.00
Hanover, Bowl, Vegetable, Harmony House, 10 In.	60.00
Hanover, Cup & Saucer, Footed, Harmony House	14.00
Hanover, Gravy Boat, Underplate, Harmony House	89.00
Hanover, Platter, Harmony House, 14 In.	80.00
Heritage, Bowl, Cereal, Johnson Brothers, 6 In.	10.00
Heritage, Plate, Bread & Butter, Johnson Brothers, 6 ¾ In.	8.00
Heritage, Saucer, Johnson Brothers	5.00
Heritage, Sugar, Lid, Johnson Brothers	30.00
Hibiscus, Cup & Saucer, Salem China	17.00
Hibiscus, Plate, Bread & Butter, Salem China	6.00
His Majesty, Soup, Dish, Johnson Brothers, 8 ⅝ In.	10.00
His Majesty, Tidbit, Johnson Brothers, 2 Tiers	42.00
Hostess, Cup, Edwin Knowles	12.00
Hostess, Plate, Bread & Butter, Edwin Knowles, 6 ⅛ In.	10.00
Indies, Plate, Bread & Butter, Johnson Brothers, 6 ¼ In.	4.00
Indies, Plate, Dinner, Johnson Brothers, 9 ⅞ In.	14.00
Kate, Creamer, Blue Ridge	14.00
Kate, Cup & Saucer, Blue Ridge	21.00
Lazy Daisy, Bowl, Vegetable, Divided, Iroquois, 11 In.	16.00
Lazy Daisy, Casserole, Lid, Iroquois, 2 Qt., 10 ½ In.	85.00
Lazy Daisy, Creamer, Iroquois, 8 Oz., 4 ¼ In.	14.00
Lazy Daisy, Cup & Saucer, Iroquois	10.00
Lazy Daisy, Gravy Boat, Attached Underplate, Iroquois	38.00
Lazy Daisy, Platter, Oval, Iroquois, 15 In.	21.00
Malvern, Soup, Dish, Johnson Brothers, 8 In.	21.00
Margaret Rose, Soup, Dish, Rim, Johnson Brothers, 8 In.	28.00

Melody, Bowl, Cereal, Square, Johnson Brothers, 6 ⅛ In.	6.00
Melody, Bowl, Vegetable, Round, Johnson Brothers, 8 ⅛ In.	18.00
Melody, Plate, Bread & Butter, Johnson Brothers, 6 ⅛ In.	6.00
Mexicana, Baking Dish, Homer Laughlin, 9 ½ In.	42.00
Mexicana, Plate, Square, Homer Laughlin, 10 ½ In.	2.25
Mirror Image, Bowl, Fruit, Blue Ridge	7.00
Mount Vernon, Creamer, Harmony House	17.00
Mountain Ivy, Cup, Blue Ridge	15.00
Mountain Ivy, Saucer, Blue Ridge	4.00
Nola, Chop Plate, Harmony House, 11 In.	22.00
Nola, Cup & Saucer, Footed, Harmony House	8.00
Nola, Plate, Dinner, Harmony House, 10 In.	14.00
Norma, Plate, Salad, Blue Ridge, 7 ⅛ In.	12.00
Oakleaf, Cup & Saucer, Footed, Homer Laughlin	14.00
Oakleaf, Plate, Dinner, Homer Laughlin, 10 In.	16.00
Oakleaf, Soup, Dish, Homer Laughlin, 8 In.	10.00
Old English Countryside, Bowl, Cereal, Johnson Brothers, 6 ¼ In.	12.00
Old English Countryside, Plate, Bread & Butter, Johnson Brothers, 6 ¼ In.	5.00
Opposites, Bowl, Vegetable, Blue Ridge, 9 ¼ In.	24.00
Orchard, Bowl, Vegetable, Oval, Homer Laughlin, 9 In.	43.00
Orchard, Plate, Dinner, Homer Laughlin, 10 In.	8.00
Orchard, Plate, Homer Laughlin, 6 ⅛ In.	7.00
Orchard, Platter, Oval, Homer Laughlin, 11 ¾ In.	50.00
Poinsettia, Bowl, Fruit, Blue Ridge, 5 ¼ In.	15.00
Poinsettia, Cup & Saucer, Blue Ridge	12.00
Poinsettia, Plate, Salad, Blue Ridge, 7 ¼ In.	12.00
Poinsettia, Platter, Blue Ridge, 15 ¾ In.	80.00
Pristine, Plate, Dinner, Blue Ridge, 10 ¼ In.	14.00
Quaker Apple, Bowl, Cereal, Blue Ridge, 6 In.	12.00
Quaker Apple, Plate, Bread & Butter, Blue Ridge, 6 ⅛ In.	10.00
Quaker Apple, Saucer, Blue Ridge	8.00
Red Apple, Plate, Dinner, Blue Ridge, 10 ¼ In.	22.00
Ridge Daisy, Bowl, Fruit, Blue Ridge, 5 ⅜ In.	8.00
Ridge Daisy, Eggcup, Blue Ridge	20.00
Ridge Daisy, Sugar & Creamer, Blue Ridge	50.00
Ridge Harvest, Plate, Dinner, Blue Ridge, 9 ⅜ In.	12.00
Rochelle, Cup & Saucer, Footed, Homer Laughlin	17.00
Rochelle, Plate, Dinner, Homer Laughlin, 9 ⅞	16.00
Rochelle, Plate, Homer Laughlin, 6 In.	6.00
Rochelle, Soup, Dish, Homer Laughlin, 8 In.	8.00
Rocky Plaid, Plate, Bread & Butter, Blue Ridge, 6 ⅜ In.	6.00
Rosemary, Bowl, Vegetable, Divided, Iroquois, 11 In.	30.00
Rosemary, Creamer, Iroquois, 8 Oz., 4 In.	14.00
Rosemary, Cup & Saucer, Iroquois	8.00
Rosemary, Platter, Oval, Iroquois, 15 In.	38.00
Rosewood, Saucer, Homer Laughlin	11.00
Rustic Plaid, Butter, Cover, Blue Ridge	20.00
Rustic Plaid, Cup & Saucer, Blue Ridge	16.00
Rustic Plaid, Plate, Dinner, 9 ½ In.	13.00
Sarasota, Bowl, Blue Ridge, 8 In.	21.00
Silhouette, Jug, Crooksville, 4 In.	28.00
Skytone, Cup & Saucer, Homer Laughlin	12.00
South Wood, Bowl, Vegetable, Homer Laughlin, 9 In.	36.00
South Wood, Cup & Saucer, Homer Laughlin	8.00
South Wood, Plate, Homer Laughlin, 6 ¼ In.	8.00
South Wood, Platter, Oval, Homer Laughlin, 13 In.	16.00
South Wood, Saucer, Homer Laughlin	3.00
Splatter-Blue, Bowl, Cereal, Homer Laughlin, 7 ¼ In.	12.00
Splatter-Blue, Bowl, Vegetable, Homer Laughlin, 9 ¼ In.	35.00
Splatter-Blue, Creamer, Homer Laughlin	25.00
Splatter-Blue, Plate, Dinner, Homer Laughlin, 10 ⅝ In.	21.00
Spray, Bowl, Fruit, Blue Ridge, 5 ½ In.	12.00
Spray, Cup & Saucer, Blue Ridge	13.00
Spring Rose, Bowl, Vegetable, Round, Homer Laughlin, 8 ½ In.	15.00
Spring Rose, Cup & Saucer, Flared, Homer Laughlin	9.00

Doll, Handwerck, Uncle Sam, Bisque Head, Googly Eyes, Composition, Wood, c.1918, 12 In.
$2,363.00

Theriault's

Doll, Hertel & Schwab, 173-9, Bisque Head, Googly Sleep Eyes, Mohair Wig, Toddler, 18 In.
$5,175.00

James D. Julia Auctioneers

Doll, Hertel & Schwab, Bisque, Googly Glass Eyes, Wood & Composition, Boy, 13 In.
$3,835.00

James D. Julia Auctioneers

Doll, Hertel & Schwab, Googly Glass Eyes, Molded Hair, Fully Jointed, Wood & Composition, 16 In. $7,080.00

James D. Julia Auctioneers

Doll, Ideal, Miss Revlon, Vinyl Socket Head, Sleep Eyes, Hair, Swivel Waist, Jointed, c.1956, 20 In. $196.00

Theriault's

TIP

When storing dolls (old or new), be sure to remove any sticky tape that might have been used to hold bows, etc., in place. The glue from the tape will eventually discolor the fabric. If dolls are to be stored a long time, put tissue between the clothing and the doll to keep bright colors from "bleeding" onto the doll. Remove metal that might rust. Save the box and all tags.

Spring Rose, Pepper Shaker, 7 Holes, Homer Laughlin	8.00
Spring Rose, Sugar, Lid, Homer Laughlin, 4 In.	16.00
Star Glow, Cake Plate, Royal China, 10 In.	23.00
Sweet Pea, Bowl, Cereal, Lug Handle, Blue Ridge, 7 In.	12.00
Sweet Pea, Plate, Dinner, Blue Ridge, 10 ¼ In.	22.00
Sweetie Pie, Cup & Saucer, Blue Ridge	20.00
Trotter, Creamer, Crooksville	15.00
Trotter, Cup & Saucer, Crooksville	9.00
Tulip Time, Saucer, Blue Ridge	5.00
Tulip, Bowl, Fruit, Eggshell Nautilus, Homer Laughlin, 5 ⅜ In.	6.00
Tulip, Bowl, Vegetable, Eggshell Nautilus, Homer Laughlin, 8 ½ In.	42.00
Tulip, Cup & Saucer, Eggshell Nautilus, Homer Laughlin	15.00
Tulip, Plate, Bread & Butter, Eggshell Nautilus, Homer Laughlin, 6 ¼ In.	4.00
Tulip, Plate, Dinner, Eggshell Nautilus, Homer Laughlin, 9 ⅞ In.	12.00
Tulip, Platter, Eggshell Nautilus, Homer Laughlin, 11 In.	30.00
Verona, Bone Dish, Half Moon, Johnson Brothers, 6 x 3 ¼ In.	15.00
Wild Rose, Bowl, Vegetable, Iroquois, 9 ⅞ In.	26.00
Wild Rose, Casserole, Lid, Iroquois, 2 Qt., 9 In.	109.00
Wild Rose, Cup & Saucer, Iroquois	8.00
Wild Rose, Plate, Iroquois, 6 ⅝ In.	5.00
Wild Rose, Platter, Oval, Crooksville, c.1970, 11 ½ x 9 In.	25.00
Wild Rose, Salt & Pepper, Iroquois	17.00
Wild Strawberry, Plate, Dinner, Blue Ridge, 10 ¼ In.	12.00
Wild Strawberry, Saucer, Blue Ridge	3.00
Windsor, Plate, White Center, Gilt, Claret Border, Aynsley, 10 ⅜ In., 12 Piece	438.00
Yorktown, Bowl, Fruit, Edwin Knowles, 5 ½ In.	8.00
Yorktown, Bowl, Vegetable, Edwin Knowles, 8 ½ In.	15.00
Yorktown, Bread & Butter, Edwin Knowles, 6 ½ In.	6.00
Yorktown, Plate, Dinner, Edwin Knowles, 10 In.	10.00
Yorktown, Soup, Dish, Edwin Knowles, 8 In.	12.00
Yorktown, Sugar, Lid, Edwin Knowles	41.00

DIONNE QUINTUPLETS were born in Canada on May 28, 1934. The publicity about their birth and their special status as wards of the Canadian government made them famous throughout the world. Visitors could watch the girls play; reporters interviewed the girls and the staff. Thousands of special dolls and souvenirs were made picturing the quints at different ages. Emilie died in 1954, Marie in 1970, Yvonne in 2001. Annette and Cecile still live in Canada.

Dolls, Composition, Madame Alexander, Diapers, Bibs, Wood Bed, Blanket, 7 In., 6 Piece	238.00
Dolls, Composition, Madame Alexander, Dress, Bib, Green Seesaw, 8 In., 6 Piece	290.00
Dolls, Composition, Madame Alexander, Jointed, Wood Bed, Bedding, Clothing, 7 In., 5 Piece	246.00
Dolls, Composition, Madame Alexander, Suits, Bonnets, Name Tags, Playpen, Doll, 8 In., 5 Piece	377.00
Dolls, Composition, Madame Alexander, Toddler Bodies, Dress, 8 In., 5 Piece	377.00
Ribbon Button, We've Seen The Famous Five, Dafoe Hospital, Callander, 1936, 1 ¼ In.	95.00
Sign, Rexall Cod Liver Oil, Quints In Sailor Suits, Puretest Rexall, 1942, 24 x 27 In.	250.00

DIRK VAN ERP was born in 1860 and died in 1933. He opened his own studio in 1908 in Oakland, California. He moved his studio to San Francisco in 1909 and the studio remained under the direction of his son until 1977. Van Erp made hammered copper accessories, including vases, desk sets, bookends, candlesticks, jardinieres, and trays, but he is best known for his lamps. The hammered copper lamps often had shades with mica panels.

Bowl, Copper, Hammered, Inverted Scalloped Leaf Rim, Marked, 3 x 13 In.	750.00
Bowl, Copper, Hand Wrought, Footed, Impressed, 9 x 4 In.	775.00
Centerpiece, Copper, Hammered, Oval, Flared Rim, Recessed Stepped Foot, 3 x 16 In.	984.00
Charger, Copper, Hammered, Impressed Mark, 18 In.	519.00
Charger, Copper, Hammered, Impressed, Open Box Mark, 18 In.	425.00
Charger, Copper, Hammered, Raised Tab Handles, Windmill Stamp, 1920s, 16 x 14 In.	688.00
Charger, Copper, Silver Plated, 12 In.	336.00
Jardiniere, Copper, Hammered, Rolled Rim, Marked, 10 x 8 In.	2000.00
Jardiniere, Copper, Hammered, Round, Folded In Sides, Windmill Stamp, 6 x 8 In.	1250.00
Jardiniere, Copper, Hammered, Round, Rolled Rim, Signed, 10 x 8 In.	2440.00
Lamp, Copper, Hammered, Baluster, Domed Shade, 4-Panel Mica Shade, 23 x 22 In.	16250.00
Lamp, Copper, Hammered, Bulbous, Squat, 4-Panel Mica Shade, 18 x 19 In.	11250.00
Lamp, Copper, Hammered, Bulbous, Tapered, 4-Panel Mica Shade, 20 x 18 In.	8750.00
Lamp, Copper, Hammered, Pear Shape, 4 Panel Mica Shade, c.1911, 21 x 19 In.	22500.00

Tray, D'Arcy Gaw, Copper, Hammered, Handles, 21 In. 2318.00
Vase, Copper, Hammered, Shouldered, 3 x 5 ½ In. 531.00
Vase, Rounded Square, Shouldered, Copper, Hammered, c.1915, 5 ¾ x 4 ½ In. 3125.00

DISNEYANA is a collectors' term. Walt Disney and his company introduced many comic characters to the world. Collectors search for examples of the work of the Disney Studios and the many commercial products modeled after his characters, including Mickey Mouse and Donald Duck, and recent films, like *Beauty and the Beast* and *The Little Mermaid.*

Baby Rattle, Mickey Mouse, Pie-Eyed, Celluloid Head, Wood Handle, 1934, 7 ½ In. 210.00
Badge, Jiminy Cricket, Round, Flower Rim, c.1940, 1 ½ In. 139.00
Bisque Set, Mickey & Minnie, At Table, Seated, Tea Set, Wood & Reed Furniture, 1930s, 2 ¾ In. 173.00
Blackboard, Desk, Mickey Mouse, Wood, Easel, Mickey, Minnie, Pluto, c.1934, 41 ½ In. 421.00
Book & Record, Mickey Mouse Brave Little Tailor, 24 Page, 33 ⅓ Rpm, 1968, 7 x 7 In. 5.00
Book, Bambi, Big Little Book, No. 1469, 1942 120.00
Book, Davy Crockett, Punch-Out, Character Figures, Whitman, 1955, 10 x 14 ¾ In., 6 Pages. 215.00
Book, Pinocchio, Hardcover, Spiral Binding, 96/100, 1939, 10 x 12 In. 548.00
Box, Donald Duck & Mickey Mouse Crayons, Tin, Walt Disney Productions, 1950, 4 ½ x 5 In. 65.00
Bracelet, Minnie Mouse, Brass Link, Enamel, Minnie Looking In Mirror, 1932, 1 ¼ x 6 ½ In. 357.00
Bracelet, Zorro, 6 Charms, Fortress, Gun, Zorro With Whip, Whip, Celluloid Fan, Photo, 1957. 86.00
Card, Mickey Mouse In Santa Suit, Disney Characters, Walt Disney, c.1948, 7 ½ x 8 In. 153.00
Cel, see Animation Art category.
Countertop Standee, Donald Duck, 1st Hardcover Book, Die Cut Cardboard, 1936, 9 x 13 ¾ In. 4807.00
Creamer, Donald Duck, Painted, Arms Handle, Sailor Hat, Long Billed Spout, Lid, c.1930, 4 In. 230.00
Display, Mickey Mouse, Cardboard, Easel Back, Slip-Overs For Boys & Girls, 1920s, 20 x 12 In. 630.00
Display, Mickey & Minnie Mouse, Mechanical, Old King Cole, c.1935, 32 & 30 In. *Illus* 18785.00
Display, Mickey Mouse, Molded, Composition, High Relief, Old King Cole Inc., c.1935, 23 x 42 In. *Illus* 4934.00
Doll, Donald Duck, Musical, Oilcloth, Windup, 1938, 14 In. 840.00
Doll, Jiminy Cricket, Wood Jointed, Felt, Fabric Tie, Decal, Ideal, 1940s, 8 ½ In. *Illus* 171.00
Doll, Mickey Mouse Jazzer, Mount To Record Player, Dances, Velveteen Stuffed, Felt, Box, 1930s, 6 In. 1265.00
Doll, Mickey Mouse, Rubber Tail, Mother-Of-Pearl Pants Buttons, Steiff, Tag, 1930s, 9 ¼ In. 891.00
Doll, Mickey Mouse, Velvet, Felt Ears, Names Stitched On Hands, Steiff, Paper Tag, 7 In. *Illus* 472.00
Doll, Mickey Mouse, Wood, Composition, Red Pants, 1930s, 9 In. 380.00
Figurine, Cinderella, In Ball Gown, Shaw Pottery, 7 ¼ In. 60.00
Figurine, Cinderella, In Rags, Ceramic, Shaw Pottery, 7 In. 120.00
Figurine, Donald Duck, Standing, Head Tilts, Composition, Painted, Knickerbocker, 11 In. 288.00
Figurine, Flip The Frog, Movable Arms, Hat & Bowtie, Celluloid, c.1930, 6 ½ In. 511.00
Figurine, Jiminy Cricket, Animation, Suspended In Bubble, Celluloid, 2 Piece, Frame, 6 x 7 In. 1955.00
Figurine, Mickey Mouse, Beswick, 3 ⅞ In. 96.00
Figurine, Mickey Mouse, Seated In Chair, Metal, Multicolor, Germany, c.1932, 3 ½ x 4 In. 1438.00
Figurine, Mickey Mouse, Wire Tail, Holding Umbrella, Metal, Germany, c.1932, 3 In. *Illus* 759.00
Figurine, Minnie Mouse, Easter Parade Outfit, Knickerbocker, Felt, Composition, 1930s, 12 In. 2998.00
Figurine, Sneezy, Beswick, 3 ½ In. 96.00
Game, Mickey Mouse, Circus, Cardboard Pieces, Box, c.1934, 9 ½ x 20 In. 633.00
Hand Puppet, Dopey, Rubber Head, Felt Hands, Red & White Shirt, Stamped W.D.P., 1940s, 9 In. 45.00
Handbook, Studio Employee, The Ropes At Disney, Illustrated, Map, 1943, 4 x 6 In., 44 Pages. 753.00
Knife, Pocket Mickey Mouse, Single Blade, 1930s, 2 ¾ In. 115.00
Lunch Box, School Bus, Dome Lid, Disney Characters Look Out Windows, Metal, Aladdin, 1960s. 40.00
Magazine, Mickey Mouse, Donald Duck For President, Vol. 1, No. 10, July 1936, 8 x 11 ½ In. 430.00
Magazine, Mickey Mouse, Thanks His Lucky Stars, Mailing Envelope, Vol. 1, Sept. 1933 835.00
Nurse Kit, Minnie Mouse, Nurse's Hat, Walt Disney Productions, Hasbro, c.1970 35.00
Pail, Mickey Mouse, Tin, Lithograph, Surfing, Atlantic City, Ohio Art, 6 In. 570.00
Paint Book, Whitman Book No. 2080, 1937, 11 x 13 ¾ In., 224 Pages 640.00
Paper Doll Book, Mickey & Minnie Mouse, 4 Pages Of Clothes, Saalfield, 1933, 11 ½ In. 200.00
Paper Doll Book, Pinocchio, Cat & Jiminy Cricket On Back, Whitman, 1939, 13 ½ In. 75.00
Paperweight, Mickey & Minnie Mouse, Painted, c.1930, 3 x 2 ¼ In. 1083.00
Patch, Donald Duck, Bending Lightning, Meteorological Squadron, Round, c.1945, 5 x 6 In. 239.00
Pencil Box, Mickey Mouse, Dixon Student Set, Cardboard, Snap Closure, Drawers, 1930s, 5 x 11 In. 115.00
Pencil Sharpener, Donald Duck, Red Bakelite, Donald Dressed As Cowboy, 1950, 1 ½ x 1 ½ In. 65.00
Pencil Sharpener, Donald Duck, Vinyl, Cast Metal, Yellow, Desk Top, 1960s 40.00
Pencil Sharpener, Donald Duck's Home, Mickey Mouse, Moving Eyes, 1950s, 5 x 4 ½ In. 175.00
Pin, Donald Duck Bread, Blue & White, Lithograph, 1950s, 1 ⅛ In. 167.00
Pin, Donald Duck, Jams Jellies, Portrait, 1 ⅛ In. 213.00
Pin, Donald Duck's Nephews, Class Of June, 1942, Oval, Yellow, 2 ¾ In. 223.00
Pin, Honey Bee, Newsboy, Holding Up Newspaper, c.1950, 1 ¾ In. 158.00

Doll, K * R, 114, Gretchen, Bisque Head, Painted, Mohair Wig, Composition, Wooden, 18 In.
$3,024.00

Theriault's

Doll, K * R, Bisque Head, Sleep Eyes, Open Mouth, Wool Wig, Composition Body, Baby, 12 ½ In.
$345.00

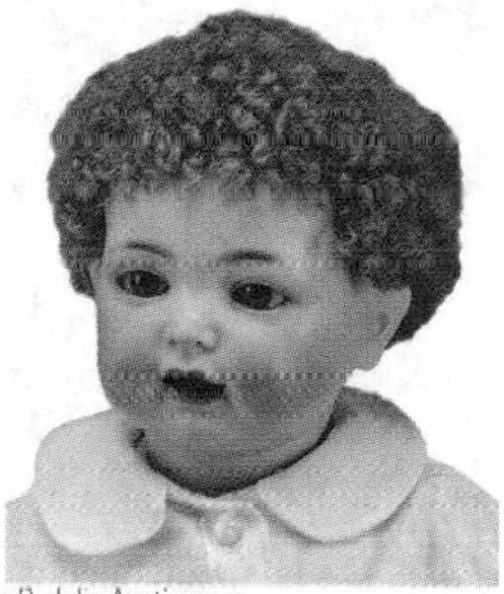

James D. Julia Auctioneers

Doll, Kallus, Composition, Wooden Neck Peg, Molded Body & Dress, Label, 1930s, 18 In.
$1,232.00

Theriault's

Doll, Kathe Kruse, Cloth, Oil-Painted Face, Pouty Mouth, Human Hair Wig, Jointed, c.1920, 17 In. $11,200.00

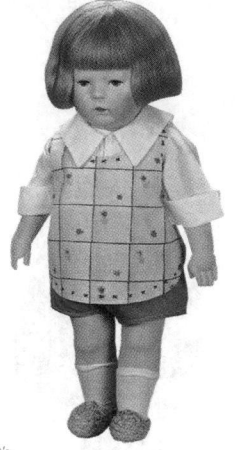

Theriault's

Doll, Kestner, Character, 4 Interchangeable Heads, 1 With Sleep Eyes, Mohair Wigs, 11 In. $4,025.00

James D. Julia Auctioneers

Doll, Lenci, Felt Swivel Head, Pressed & Painted Face, Jointed Shoulders & Hips, Box, c.1935, 9 In. $619.00

Theriault's

Pin, Mickey Mouse Club, Officer, Sergt.-At-Arms, Celluloid, 1928-1930, 2 ¼ In.	460.00
Pin, Mickey Mouse Club, Uptown Red, White, Black, c.1930, 1 ¼ In.	115.00
Pin, Mickey Mouse For Better Health, Milk Promotion, Mickey With Bottle, Celluloid, 1 ¼ In.	271.00
Pin, Mickey Mouse Soap, You're Telling Me, Bastian Bros., Celluloid, 1930s, 1 ¼ In.	3450.00
Pin, Mickey Mouse, Rubies, Sapphires, Full Cut Diamonds, Black Onyx, Mother-Of-Pearl, 2 In. ...*Illus*	4740.00
Pin, Pinocchio, Red, White, Black, 1940, ⅞ In.	115.00
Radio, Snow White, 7 Dwarfs, Wood, Paint, Cottage Window, Dress Lights Up, 1939, 5 ½ x 7 In.	835.00
Raincoat & Hat, Christopher Robin, R.J. Wright, Walt Disney Co., 18 In.	522.00
Roller Skates, Mickey Mouse, Metal, Yellow, Leather Straps, Box, c.1950, 3 x 9 x 4 ½ In.	180.00
Sand Pail, Mickey Mouse, Minnie, Beverage Stand, Pluto, Tin Lithograph, Paint, 1930s, 3 In.	230.00
Shovel, Donald Duck, Nephews, Tin Litho Shovel Blade, Ohio Art, 1939, 6 ½ x 7 x 23 In. ...*Illus*	370.00
Sign, Donald Duck, Sunoco Oil, Keeps Motors Knockless, Donald Jumping Up, Frame, 23 x 35 In.	664.00
Sprinkling Can, Snow White & 7 Dwarfs, Flowers, Fawn, Rabbits, Tin Litho, 1938, 6 ½ In.	173.00
Studio Christmas Card, Envelope, Pinocchio, Signed, 1939, 6 x 7 ½ In., 8 Pages	597.00
Toy Chest, Characters, Cardboard, Wood Frame, 1930s, 14 x 26 x 12 In.	121.00
Toy, Donald & Donna Duck, Drumsticks, Sombrero, Pull Toy, Fisher-Price, No. 160, 1937, 14 In.	3575.00
Toy, Donald Duck, Cart, Dog Pulling Duck In Cart, Wood, Multicolor, Pull Toy, c.1936, 4 x 15 In.	460.00
Toy, Donald Duck, Donald In Rocking Chair, Dumbo, Pluto, Tin Lithograph Box, 1950s, 4 x 5 In.	978.00
Toy, Donald Duck, Driving Car, Plastic, Tin, Lithograph, Windup, Marx, Box, 6 ½ In.	390.00
Toy, Donald Duck, Jointed, Composition, Painted, Head Tilts Back, Knickerbocker, 11 ½ In. ...*Illus*	288.00
Toy, Donald Duck, Phone, With Ice Cream Cone, Wood, Metal, Candlestick Shape, Green, c.1938, 7 In.	575.00
Toy, Donald Duck, Pluto, Doughboy, Pull Toy, No. 744, Fisher-Price, 1942, 14 ½ In.	840.00
Toy, Donald Duck, Pulling Cart, Pull Toy, Fisher-Price, No. 741, 1937, 19 ½ In.	1140.00
Toy, Donald Duck, Riding On Cart, Vibrator Voice, Pull Toy, Fisher-Price, No. 715, 1942, 10 ½ In.	300.00
Toy, Donald Duck, Xylophone, Wood, Paper Label, Pull Toy, 1946, 11 x 13 In.	13 9.00
Toy, Mickey & Minnie Mouse, Handcar, Composition, Steel, Clockwork, Track, Lionel, 8 In. ...*Illus*	402.00
Toy, Mickey & Minnie Mouse, On Motorcycle, Tin, Windup, Tipp Logo, 1930, 9 ½ x 6 ½ In.	28750.00
Toy, Mickey & Minnie Mouse, Seesaw, Fun-E-Flex & Tin Bell, 9 In.	1020.00
Toy, Mickey Mouse Washer, Mickey Mouse, Minnie Mouse, Tin Litho, Ohio Art, 1930s, 7 ½ In. ...*Illus*	230.00
Toy, Mickey Mouse Washer, Tin Litho, Crank Handle, Plunger, 1930s, 8 In.	290.00 to 310.00
Toy, Mickey Mouse, Band, Cymbal On Pluto's Tail, Drum, Wood, Metal, Push Toy, c.1935, 12 In.	411.00
Toy, Mickey Mouse, Car, Tin, Windup, Marx, 11 In.	195.00
Toy, Mickey Mouse, Colorforms, No. 465, Box, 1970	13.00
Toy, Mickey Mouse, Cowboy, Riding Pluto, Celluloid, Windup, Japan, 1930s, 8 x 7 In. ...*Illus*	1708.00
Toy, Mickey Mouse, Drummer, Paper Lithograph, Wood, Pull Toy, Fisher-Price, 7 ½ In.	41.00
Toy, Mickey Mouse, No. 2 Paddleboat, Windup, Wood, Metal, Tin Lithograph, Box, 1930s, 12 In.	4175.00
Toy, Mickey Mouse, Saxophone Player, Moves, Germany, c.1930, 6 In.	633.00
Toy, Mickey Mouse, Sewing Cards, No. 950C, Colorforms, 1970s	10.00
Toy, Mickey Mouse, Sparkler, c.1929, 5 ½ In.	900.00
Toy, Mickey Mouse, Spinning Top, Tin Lithograph, J. Chein, 9 In.	59.00
Toy, Mickey, Minnie, Snow Shovel, Donald, Skating, 26 ½ In.	200.00
Toy, Minnie Mouse Knitter, Minnie In Rocking Chair, Tin Lithograph, Linemar, Japan, 6 ½ In. ...*Illus*	266.00
Toy, Minnie Mouse, Figurine, Fun-E-Flex, Painted, 6 In.	349.00
Toy, Minnie Mouse, Knitting, Rocking Chair, Tin Lithograph, Key Wind, Linemar, Japan, 6 In.	201.00
Toy, Pinocchio, Figaro At Feet, Ceramic, Paint, Multicolor, 1940s, 4 ¼ In.	173.00
Toy, Pinocchio, Riding Delivery Cart, Tin Lithograph, Windup, Marx, 9 ½ In.	489.00
Toy, Pinocchio, Walker, Pronounced Nose, Tin Lithograph, Windup, Marx, 8 ½ In.	316.00
Toy, Pluto, Figurine, Fun-E-Flex, Blue Collar, Pup, Wooden Body, Possible, 1930s, 7 ½ In.	115.00
Toy, Professor Von Drake, Walker, Pointer In Hand, Tin Litho, Clockwork, Linemar, 6 ½ In.	201.00
Toy, Tool Chest, Mickey Mouse, Pluto, Tin Lithograph	450.00
Toy, Top, Spinning, Mickey, Pluto, Minnie, 11 x 9 ½ In.	200.00
Watch, Donald Duck, In Sailor Suit, Back Mickey Decal, c.1939, Pocket	270.00
Watch, Mickey Mouse, Lapel Cord, Box, Ingersoll, 1937, Pocket	720.00
Watch, Mickey Mouse, Mickey's Hands Point, c.1938, 2 In., Pocket.	380.00
Wristwatch, 3 Little Pigs, Leather Band, Box, Ingersoll, 1934	780.00
Wristwatch, Donald Duck, Goldtone Bezal, Vinylite Band, Box, U.S., Time Ingersoll, 1947	300.00
Wristwatch, Mickey Mouse, Ingersoll, Box, 1935, 7 In.	465.00
Wristwatch, Mickey Mouse, Ingersoll, Box, 1947	330.00
Wristwatch, Mickey Mouse, Metal Band, Ingersoll, Box, 1930s	360.00
Wristwatch, Mickey Mouse, Mickey's Hands Point, Celluloid, Metal, Leather Strap, c.1933	1531.00
Wristwatch, Mickey Mouse, Running Mickey Second Hand, Top Hat, Cane Box, Ingersoll, 1937..	2040.00
Wristwatch, Snow White, Cloth Strap & Buckle, U.S. Time, 1939	110.00

DOCTOR, *see Dental and Medical categories.*

D

DOLL entries are listed by marks printed or incised on the doll, if possible. If there are no marks, the doll is listed by the name of the subject or country or maker. Notice that Barbie is listed under Mattel. G.I. Joe figures are listed in the Toy section. Eskimo dolls are listed in the Eskimo section and Indian dolls are listed in the Indian section. Doll clothes and accessories are listed at the end of this section. The twentieth-century clothes listed here are in mint condition.

A.M., 11, Queen Louise, Bisque Head, 4 Teeth, Glass Eyes, Composition, Ball Joints, 29 In........	121.00
A.M., 14, Bisque Socket Head, Sleep Eyes, Open Mouth, Composition, Jointed, 32 In.................	377.00
A.M., 251, Bisque Head, Brown Sleep Eyes, Open Mouth, Cream Lace Dress, Baby, 12 In.	169.00
A.M., 253, Bisque Socket Head, Blue Set Eyes, Composition, Hat, Dress, Nobbi Kid, 7 In.	226.00
A.M., 323, Bisque Head, Blue Googly Eyes, Composition, Marked Germany, 12 In.	367.00
A.M., 323, Bisque Socket Head, Googly Glass Eyes, Mohair Wig, Composition Body, c.1920, 10 In. ...*Illus*	952.00
A.M., 351, Bisque Head, Sleep Eyes, Open Mouth, Composition, Jointed, Blue Suit, Boy Toddler, 25 In.	203.00
A.M., 390, Bisque Head, Blue Set Eyes, Composition, Burgundy Dress, Ribbon Hat, 10 In.........	79.00
A.M., 390, Bisque Head, Blue Set Eyes, Open Mouth Composition, Turquoise Dress, Cap, 27 In.	68.00
A.M., 390, Bisque Head, Brown Sleep Eyes, Jointed, Composition, Yellow Dress, 21 In.............	102.00
A.M., 390, Bisque Head, Brown Sleep Eyes, Open Mouth, Teeth, Jointed, Marked Germany, 30 ½ In.	160.00
A.M., 390, Bisque Head, Sleep Blue Eyes, Open Mouth, Blond Wig, Jointed, Composition, 22 In.	118.00
A.M., 390, Bisque Head, Sleep Eyes, Open Mouth, Mohair Wig, Composition, Jointed, Dress, 34 In.	551.00
A.M., 810, Indian, Bisque Socket Head, Glass Eyes, Open Mouth, Composition Body, 7 ½ In. ...	93.00
A.M., 985, Bisque Head, Blue Sleep Eyes, Dimpled Cheeks, Blond Wig, Composition, Baby, 13 In..	198.00
A.M., Baby Gloria, Bisque Dome, Sleep Eyes, Open Mouth, Teeth, Cloth Body, Long Dress, Germany...	104.00
A.M., Bisque Head, Blue Sleep Eyes, Jointed, Composition, 18 In..................	141.00
A.M., Bisque Head, Brown Set Eyes, Jointed, Composition, Brown Curled Wig, Lace, Hat, Cuffs, 32 In.	396.00
A.M., Bisque Head, Sleep Eyes, Long Brown Wig, Jointed, Composition, 26 In....................	118.00
A.M., Bisque Socket Head, Googly Eyes, Mohair Wig, Papier-Mache Body, c.1928, 13 In.	2800.00
A.M., Bisque, Jointed, Brown Sleep Eyes, Open Mouth, Marked On Head, 30 ½ In.	160.00
A.M., Molded Head, Hair, Googly Eyes, Dress, Baby, 10 In.	960.00
Acme Toy Co., Honey, Composition, Molded Hair, Sleep Eyes, Baby, c.1928, 26 In.	295.00
Advertising, Buddy L, Composition, Baseball Uniform, Cap, c.1910, 12 In............................	180.00
Advertising, Buster Brown Shoes, Anita Flapper, Purple Body, Elongated Arms & Legs, 1930s, 28 In. .	125.00
Advertising, Dole Banana Man, Inflatable Plastic, Long Red Legs, Product Premium, Sealed, 8 x 8 In.	65.00
Advertising, Macy's, Composition, Window Display, Green Victorian Dress, Fur Accessories, 34 In.	476.00
Advertising, Swiss Miss, Cloth, Painted Features, Braided Yellow Yarn Hair, 1978, 17 In.........	35.00
Advertising, Uneeda Dollikin, Vinyl Head, Jointed, Orange Jumpsuit, 1950s, 19 In.	95.00
Alabama Baby, Boy, Cloth, Oil-Painted Face, Applied Ears, White Coat, Shoes, 12 In.	1469.00
Alabama Baby, Painted Hair, Face, Blue Shoes, 14 In................................	290.00
Alexander dolls are listed in this category under Madame Alexander.	
Alt, Beck & Gottschalk, 630, Bisque Socket Head, Closed Mouth, Mohair Wig, Composition, 24 In.	1160.00
American Character, Betsy McCall, Hard Plastic, Chemise, Socks, Shoes, 8 In.	99.00
American Character, Betsy McCall, Hard Plastic, Woven Hat, Organdy Dress, Shoes, Socks, 8 In.	75.00
American Character, Betsy McCall, Vinyl, Flirty Sleep Eyes, Dotted Tulle Dress, 19 In.	145.00
American Character, Suzie The Snoozie, Whimsy, Vinyl, Closed Eyes, c.1960, 14 In.	68.00
American Character, Sweet Sue, Hard Plastic, Dress, Straw Hat, Holding Box, 17 In..............	52.00
Armand Marseille dolls are listed in this category under A.M.	
Arranbee, Cinderella, Hard Plastic, Blond Hair, Headband, Cream Dress, Stars, 17 In.	64.00
Arranbee, Dream, Bisque Head, Set Eyes, Jointed, Cloth, Celluloid Hands, Dress, Germany, 10 In.	55.00
Arranbee, Nancy Lee, Hard Plastic, Brown Mohair Wig, Purple, White Dress, Marked R & B, 18 In. ...	145.00
Automaton, Bakery Boy, Composition Head, Molded Plastic Hands, Cloth Apron, Hat, 33 In...	1243.00
Automaton, Black Dancer, Perry & Co., London, 10 x 6 ½ In...	480.00
Automaton, Black Man, Red Cape, Sign, Free Cigars, Nodder, 28 In..................	3080.00
Automaton, Black Porter, Red Uniform, Crispin's Boot Store Sign, 30 x 30 In........................	1180.00
Automaton, Buffalo Bill, Smoking, Holding Gun, Articulated Mouth, Eyelids, Vichy, c.1890, 28 In.....	26206.00
Automaton, Clown, Playing Lute, Bisque, Papier-Mache Head, Painted, Lambert, Paris, c.1900, 23 In.	9239.00
Automaton, Clown, Playing Lute, Seated On Chair, Articulated Eyelids, Crosses Legs, Vichy, c.1900 ..	10014.00
Automaton, Easter Hare, Seated, Glass Eyes, Turns Head, Lays Eggs, Belgium, c.1930, 27 x 19 ½ In.	5260.00
Automaton, Girl Sitting On Rock, Gold & Purple Dress, Jumeau	3920.00
Automaton, Maiden, Bisque, Mohair Wig, Silk Dress, Lorgnette & Fan, Jumeau, 18 In. ...*Illus*	6325.00
Automaton, Musician, Strums Guitar, Dancer, Bisque Heads, Wind-Up, Germany, c.1900, 15 In..	2858.00
Automaton, Nightingale, Cage, Gold Paint, Wood, Metal, Windup, Bontems, France, c.1880, 19 In.	1200.00
Averill, Bonnie Babe, Bisque Head, Composition Body, White Lace Dress, Marked, 21 ½ In......	242.00
Bahr & Proschild, 320, Bisque Head, Blue Sleep Eyes, Jointed, Composition, Yellow Cape, Dress, 37 In.	2091.00
Barbie dolls are listed in this category under Mattel.	
Bergmann, 1916, Bisque Head, Blue Sleep Eyes, Jointed, Composition, Blue Gown, 25 In.......	170.00
Bergmann, Brown Sleep Eyes, Jointed, Composition, Pink & White Dress, Hat, 25 In.	141.00

Doll, Lenci, Girl, Felt Head, Painted Face, Googly Eyes, Mohair Wig, Jointed, Series III, c.1925, 13 In.
$2,128.00

Theriault's

Doll, Lenci, Hockey Player, Felt Swivel Head, Blond Mohair Wig, Jointed, Paper Label, c.1936, 14 In.
$6,720.00

Theriault's

Doll, Lenci, Opium Smoker, Felt Swivel Head, Painted Face, Closed Eyes, Yarn Hair, c.1920, 12 In.
$1,344.00

Theriault's

Doll, Lenci, Salon Lady, Felt Head, Painted Face, Googly Eyes, Mohair Wig, Jointed, c.1925, 25 In.
$4,480.00

Theriault's

Doll, Madame Alexander, Bride, Margaret, Plastic, Socket Head, Sleep Eyes, 1950, 14 In.
$672.00

Theriault's

Doll, Madame Alexander, Bride, Victorian, Plastic, Socket Head, Sleep Eyes, 1951, 21 In.
$3,920.00

Theriault's

Bergner, Bisque, 3 Faces, Head Knob, Blue Set Eyes, Cloth, Composition, Gown, 12 In.............	565.00
Bergner, Bisque, 3 Faces, Head Knob, Muslin Body, Composition Limbs, Hood, c.1892, 12 In..	1456.00
Bisque Head, Blue Set Eyes, Closed Mouth, Jointed, Composition, White, Yellow Dress, Hat, 18 In.	226.00
Bisque Head, Googly, Composition, Green Lace Dress, Shoes, Pink Bow, 7 ½ In........................	113.00
Bisque Head, Open Mouth, Blue Sleep Eyes, Jointed, Composition, Brown Wig, Lace Dress, 24 In.	1074.00
Bisque, Cup & Saucer Swivel Neck, Glass Set Eyes, Painted Hair, Cloth Body, 18 In.	2552.00
Bisque, Oriental Boy, Swivel Head, Yellow Tint, Glass Eyes, Jointed, 5 ½ In............................	696.00
Bisque, Painted Eyes, Socks, Shoes, Lace Dress, 7 In..	62.00
Black dolls are also included in the Black category.	
Blampoix, Fashion, Bisque Shoulder Head, Kid Body, Blue Set Eyes, Lace Dress, Cap, BS Mark, 16 In.	1102.00
Blossom, Boudoir, Cloth, Painted Silk Face, Eyelashes, Jointed, Dress, Jacket, Hat, c.1930, 25 In.....	210.00
Bonzo, Composition, Wood, Segmented Tail, Name On Bone-Shape Decal, 1930s, 6 ⅜ In.	1202.00
Bye-Lo, Bisque Head, Blue Sleep Eyes, Cloth Body, Celluloid Hands, White Gown, 10 In...........	62.00
Bye-Lo, Bisque, Blue Sleep Eyes, Blond Wig, Germany, Baby, 5 In.......................................	254.00
Bye-Lo, Bisque, Blue Sleep Eyes, Marked Putnam, 5 In...	283.00
Bye-Lo, Bisque, Brown Sleep Eyes, Wig, Baby, 5 In..	367.00
Cage, Jointed Torso, Paint, Iron Slat Base, France, c.1950, 31 In.	604.00
China Head, Flat Top, Cloth Body, Kid Arms, Civil War Black Lace Dress, 26 In.	464.00
China Head, Flat Top, Cloth Body, Leather Arms, White Dress, 27 In.	203.00
China Head, Flat Top, Cloth Legs, Umbrella, Beaded Bag, Floral Dress, Wide Brim Hat, 18 In. ...	254.00
Cloth, Black Woman, Embroidered, Stockinet, Cotton Hair, Articulated Fingers, Clothing, 22 In.	1541.00
Cloth, Organ Grinder, Musical Hurdy-Gurdy, Painted Face, Papier-Mache Hands, Italy, 16 In.	102.00
Cloth, Woman, Stockinet Head, Shoulders, Painted, Muslin Body, Clothing, Bonnet, c.1890, 18 In.	830.00
Conta & Boehme, China Head, Pink Tint, Kid Body, Blacked, Red Dress, 24 ½ In.....................	1682.00
Cosmopolitan, Girl Scout, Hard Plastic, Terri Lee Fashions, Green Uniform, Walker, Box, 8 In.	87.00
Cosmopolitan, Miss Ginger, Vinyl Head, Blond Hair, Sleep Eyes, Red High Heels, 1950s, 23 In..	400.00
Cosmopolitan, Miss Ginger, Vinyl, Sleep Eyes, Plaid Pedal Pushers, High Heels, Late 1950s, 10 In..	185.00
Dolly Darling, John & His Pets, Dogs, Cats, Duck, Fence, Case, 1960s, 4 In. Doll......................	65.00
Dressel, Bisque Head, Painted Eyes, Wig, Composition, Pink, White Dress, Ribbons, Child, 11 In...	904.00
Dressel, Boy, Composition Head, Limbs, Straw Body, Glass Eyes, Scottish Clothes, Holz-Masse, 11 In..	174.00
Dressel, Fashion, Porcelain Swivel Head, Blue Downcast Eyes, Human Hair, Bonnet, c.1910, 14 In....	2576.00
Dressel, Man, Bisque Socket Head, Glass Eyes, Mohair Wig, Beard, Jointed, c.1890, 17 In. .... *Illus*	3080.00
Effanbee, Honey, Hard Plastic, Blond Mohair Wig, Braids, Multicolor Outfit, 14 In..................	40.00
Effanbee, Little Lady, Brown Yarn Hair, Brown Eyes, Blue Gown, Red Plaid Trim, c.1944	200.00
Effanbee, Pat-O-Pat, Cloth, Press Stomach She Claps, Blue Dotted Dress, Pink Trim, 1939, 19 In.	85.00
Effanbee, Patsy Ann, Composition, Blue Sleep Eyes, Short Flower Dress, White Shoes, 19 In...	52.00
Effanbee, Patsy Joan, Composition, Green Sleep Eyes, Heart Bracelet, Blue Check Outfit, 16 In.....	145.00
Effanbee, Patsy, Composition, Painted Eyes, Dress, Red Felt Coat, Purse, Roller Skates, 13 In.	64.00
Effanbee, Patsy, Pajamas, Blue Flowers, Heart Bracelet, 14 In.	29.00
Effanbee, Skippy, Composition Head, Limbs, Cloth Body, Khaki Uniform, Cap, 14 In...............	232.00
Effanbee, Sweetie Pie, Cloth Body, Caracul Wig, Brown Sleep Eyes, Composition Limbs, Box, 20 In....	70.00
Effanbee, Wee Patsy, Closed Mouth, Molded Hair, Yellow Dress, 5 ½ In..................................	440.00
Emmett Kelly, Willie The Clown, Stuffed, Baby Barry Toy Co., N.Y., 1950s, 21 In.	259.00
Fashion, Bisque Socket Head, Blue Glass Eyes, Blond Mohair Wig, Kid Body, Straw Hat, France, 14 In..	2243.00
Fashion, Bisque Socket Head, Bulging Glass Eyes, Leather Body, Wood Legs, France, 17 In.	4600.00
Fashion, Bisque Swivel Neck, Cloth Body, Leather Arms, Cobalt Blue Eyes, 19 In.....................	1534.00
Fashion, Papier-Mache, Shoulder Head, Black Eyes, Closed Mouth, Kid Body, France, c.1850, 21 In.	1904.00
Fashion, Swivel Neck, Bulbous Paperweight Eyes, Leather Kid Body, Blond Mohair, 11 ¾ In...	748.00
Florodora, Sleep Eyes, Brown Wig, Jointed, Composition Body, Pink Dress, Germany, 27 In.....	177.00
Franz Schmidt, Character Toddler, Socket Head, Flirty Eyes, Tongue, Jointed, Composition, 16 In.	367.00
French, Bisque Head, Blue Set Eyes, Open Mouth, Jointed, Composition, Dress, Hat, Mon Cheri, 12 In..	424.00
French, Bisque Head, Brown Set Eyes, Composition, Cork Pate, Walker, 22 In.............................	480.00
French, Bisque Socket Head, Blond, Closed Mouth, Brown Set Eyes, Dress, Marked J.O., Bebe, 16 ½ In..	4900.00
French, Bisque Socket Head, Glass Eyes, Closed Mouth, Dimple, Wig, Bebe, c.1892, 21 In........	4760.00
French, Blue Glass Stationary Eyes, Bee-Stung Lips, Human Hair, Composition Body, c.1900, 16 ½ In.	633.00
French, Cloth, Enamel Eyes, Taufling-Shape Body, Kid Arms, Gown, Lace Trim, c.1785, 5 In..	14560.00
French, Woman, Wax, Painted Face, Blond Mohair Wig, Label, Hat Boxes, 1915, 12 In. ...*Illus*	3640.00
G.I. Joe figures are listed in the Toy category.	
Gaultier, Bisque Socket Head, Paperweight Eyes, Closed Mouth, Leather Body, Human Hair, 19 In.	1770.00
German, Bellhop, Bisque Socket Head, Sculpted Hair, Googly Eyes, Composition Body, c.1920, 11 In.	2576.00
German, Bisque Head & Shoulders, Sculpted Hair, Muslin Body, C.F. Kling Co., c.1870, 17 In. ...*Illus*	1904.00
German, Bisque Head, Intaglio Eyes, Composition, Brown Fur Suit, 7 In.................................	79.00
German, Bisque Head, Molded Hair, Intaglio Eyes, Composition, Blue Dress, Character Baby, 8 In.	254.00
German, Bisque Head, Sleep Eyes, Moving Tongue, Molded Curl, Composition, Dress, Baby, 23 In.	226.00
German, Bisque Socket Head & Shoulders, Closed Mouth, Brown Set Eyes, Hair Wig, Lace Dress, 20 In.	580.00

D

German, Bisque Socket Head, Sleep Eyes, Teeth, Human Hair, Spanish Outfit, Boy, c.1915, 15 In.		616.00
German, Bisque, Glass Brown Set Eyes, Jointed, Crocheted Dress, Hat, 4 ½ In.		102.00
German, Bisque, Open Eyes, Composition Body, Ball-Jointed, Dress, Bonnet, Impressed F. G.		1404.00
German, Bisque, Smiling Mouth, Intaglio Googly Eyes, Composition, 5 ½ In.		375.00
German, Bisque, Swivel Neck, Brown Sleep Eyes, Jointed, Lace Dress, 5 In.		254.00
German, China Head, Flat Top, Red, Black Dress, 37 In.		170.00
German, Domed Composition Head, Googly Eyes, c.1920, 12 In.		1456.00
German, Infantryman, Pressed Felt Head, Glass Eyes, Stuffed Body, Field Uniform, c.1916, 13 In.		7280.00
German, Papier-Mache, Sculpted Beehive Hairdo, Painted Facial Features, Kid Body, c.1840, 15 In.		3584.00
Gladdie, Flange Biscaloid Head, Molded Hair, Glass Eyes, Cloth Body, Composition Arms, Legs, 19 In.		283.00
Greiner, Papier-Mache, Shoulder Head, Black Sculpted Hair, Closed Mouth, Muslin Body, 19 In.		560.00
Gund, Shmoo, Plush Body, Fabric Head, Felt Hat, Pearl Accents, Bow, c.1948, 11 ½ In.		422.00
Halbig, Bisque Socket Head, Sleep Eyes, Open Mouth, Composition Body, Jointed, 22 In.		232.00
Half Dolls are listed in the Pincushion Doll category.		
Handwerck, 79, Bisque Head, Blue Sleep Eyes, Jointed Composition, Wool Red Sailor Dress, 21 In.		396.00
Handwerck, 79, Bisque Head, Brown Sleep Eyes, Jointed Composition, 37 In.		1469.00
Handwerck, 99, Bisque Head, Blue Set Eyes, Jointed, Composition, Dress, Flower Hat, 32 In.		904.00
Handwerck, 109, Bisque Head, Blue Set Eyes, Jointed, Composition, 30 In.		225.00
Handwerck, 109, Bisque, Sleep Eyes, Open Mouth, Hair Wig, Composition, Jointed, 28 In.		261.00
Handwerck, Bisque Head, Blue Set Eyes, Jointed, Composition, Lace Gown, Cap, 29 In.		311.00
Handwerck, Bisque Head, Blue Sleep Eyes, Jointed, Composition, 23 In.		424.00
Handwerck, Bisque Head, Brown Sleep Eyes, Blond Wig, Jointed, Composition, Dress, 26 In.		283.00
Handwerck, Bisque Socket Head, Sleep Eyes, Ball-Jointed, Coat, Cape, Lace Dress, Bonnet, 28 In.		290.00
Handwerck, Uncle Sam, Bisque Head, Googly Eyes, Composition, Wood, c.1918, 12 In. ....*Illus*		2363.00
Hasbro, Dolly Darling, John & His Pets, Blue Shirt, Red Bowtie, Carrying Case, 1960s, 4 In.		65.00
Hertel & Schwab, 152, Bisque Head, Gray Sleep Eyes, Composition, Check Dress, Baby, 18 In.		79.00
Hertel & Schwab, 173-9, Bisque Head, Googly Sleep Eyes, Mohair Wig, Toddler, 18 In. ...*Illus*		5175.00
Hertel & Schwab, Bisque Head, Googly, Toddler, 9 ½ In.		1752.00
Hertel & Schwab, Bisque, Googly Glass Eyes, Wood & Composition, Boy, 13 In. ....*Illus*		3835.00
Hertel & Schwab, Googly Glass Eyes, Molded Hair, Fully Jointed, Wood & Composition, 16 In. ....*Illus*		7080.00
Heubach Koppelsdorf, Black Bisque Head, Brown Set Eyes, Jointed, Composition, c.1900, 11 ½ In.		367.00
Heubach Koppelsdorf, Bug-On-Nose, Molded Hair, Composition, Striped Jumpsuit, Child, 7 In.		2147.00
Heubach, 463, Black Bisque Head, Googly, Composition, Grass Skirt, Baby, 7 In.		565.00
Heubach, 7602, Bisque Head, Pouty Intaglio Eyes, Composition, 12 In.		141.00
Heubach, 7763, Coquette, Bisque Head, Intaglio Eyes, Painted Hair, Jointed, Wood, Composition.		480.00
Heubach, 7977, Baby Stuart, Bisque Head, Molded Bonnet, Painted Eyes, Composition, 7 In.		311.00
Heubach, 8192, Bisque Head, Blue Sleep Eyes, Jointed, Composition, Pink Low-Waisted Dress, 9 ½ In.		102.00
Heubach, 9573, Bisque Head, Brown Sleep Eyes, Composition, Skirt & Blouse, 7 ½ In.		678.00
Heubach, Bisque Head, Blond Molded Hair, Composition, Lace Gown, Slip, Baby, 14 In.		367.00
Heubach, Bisque Head, Blue Sleep Eyes, Jointed, Composition, Burgundy Dress, 11 In.		113.00
Horsman, Poor Pitiful Pearl, Vinyl, Blue Eyes, Blond Hair, Blue & White Polka Dot Dress, 1958, 17 In.		125.00
Horsman, Poor Pitiful Pearl, Vinyl, Sleep Eyes, Rooted Hair, c.1958, 17 In.		125.00
Ideal, Captain Action, Blue Outfit & Hat, Decal On Chest, Gun & Sword, Box, 1966, 12 In.		235.00
Ideal, Miss Curity, Nurse Outfit, Cape, Cap, Marked, 14 In.		232.00
Ideal, Miss Revlon, Vinyl Socket Head, Sleep Eyes, Hair, Swivel Waist, Jointed, c.1956, 20 In. ....*Illus*		196.00
Ideal, Miss Revlon, Vinyl, Head, Sleep Eyes, Plastic Body, Blue Dress, Heels, 18 In.		40.00
Ideal, Mr. Magoo, Vinyl & Cloth, Stuffed Body, 1960s, 8 In.		60.00
Ideal, Patti, Rooted Long Blond Hair, Red Dress, Black Shoes, 18 In.		104.00
Ideal, Penny Brite, Navy Blue & White Checked Rain Outfit, 8 ½ In.		65.00
Ideal, Pinocchio, Composition Head, Wood Body, Felt Bowtie, 7 ½ In.		115.00
Ideal, Shirley Temple, Composition, Sailor Outfit, 15 In.		460.00
Ideal, Shirley Temple, Painted Blue Eyes, Teeth, Original Dress, 1934, 18 In.		55.00
Ideal, Tiny Kissy, Pucker Up, Vinyl, Brown Pixie Haircut, Green Eyes, Jointed At Wrist, 1960s, 16 In.		45.00
Indian dolls are listed in the Indian category.		
Jolly Green Giant, Little Sprout, Rubber, Mailing Wrapper, 1970s, 6 ½ In.		45.00
Jumeau, Auburn Wig, Paperweight Eyes, Open Mouth, Teeth, Wood & Composition Body, 33 In.		805.00
Jumeau, Bisque Head, Blue Eyes, Open Mouth, Jointed Composition, Germany, 21 In.		509.00
Jumeau, Bisque Head, Blue Paperweight Eyes, Closed Mouth, Pink Dress, Hat, Bebe, 15 In.		1469.00
Jumeau, Bisque Head, Blue Sleep Eyes, Jointed Composition, Pull String Crier, Bebe, 16 In.		1413.00
Jumeau, Bisque Head, Glass Eyes, Closed Mouth, Human Hair, Composition, c.1890, 27 In.		3080.00
Jumeau, Bisque Head, Painted Red Lips, Dark Brown Human Hair, Wood & Composition Body, 17 In.		2301.00
Jumeau, Bisque Socket Head, Blue Gray Threaded Eyes, Leather Body, Blond Mohair Wig, 17 In.		2588.00
Jumeau, Bisque Socket Head, Blue Paperweight Eyes, Jointed, Pink, Hat, Dress, Tete, 22 In.		1582.00
Jumeau, Bisque Socket Head, Blue Paperweight Eyes, Jointed, Tete, Bebe, 26 In.		1130.00
Jumeau, Bisque Socket Head, Glass Eyes, Mohair Wig, Composition, Jointed Body, Bebe, c.1890, 11 In.		8400.00

Doll, Madame Alexander, Cheri, Dressed For Opera, Socket Head, Sleep Eyes, Plastic, 1954, 17 In.
$560.00

Theriault's

Doll, Madame Alexander, Cissy, Hard Plastic, Socket Head, Jointed, Sleep Eyes, 1958, 20 In.
$840.00

Theriault's

Doll, Madame Alexander, Cissy, Hard Plastic, Socket Head, Jointed, Sleep Eyes, c.1956, 20 In.
$616.00

Theriault's

D

Doll, Madame Alexander, Edith, Lonely Doll, Vinyl Head, Sleep Eyes, Rooted Hair, 1963, 16 In.
$224.00

Theriault's

Doll, Madame Alexander, Elise, Ballerina, Plastic, Socket Head, Sleep Eyes, Tutu, 1957, 16 In.
$616.00

Theriault's

Doll, Martha Chase, Youth, Sanitary, Stockinet Body, Oil Painted, Articulated, Label, c.1913, 42 In.
$356.00

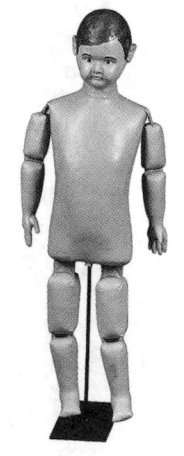

Skinner, Inc.

166

Jumeau, Blue Paperweight Eyes, Closed Mouth, Wood, Composition Body, Blond, 19 In.	1093.00
Jumeau, Fashion, Bisque Head, Cork Wig, Blue Threaded Eyes, Wood Body, Portrait, 21 In.	12995.00
Jumeau, Fashion, Bisque Shoulder Head, Paperweight Eyes, Kidskin, Wood, Dress, 15 In.	3164.00
Jumeau, Fashion, Bisque Socket Head, Paperweight Blue Eyes, Kid Body, Rose Gown, 20 In.	734.00
Jumeau, Fashion, Bisque Swivel Head, Blue Paperweight Eyes, Kid Body, Gray Gown, 14 In.	2147.00
Jumeau, Fashion, Bisque Swivel Head, Blue Paperweight Eyes, Kid Body, Lace Dress, Shoes 20 In.	1469.00
Jumeau, Paperweight Eyes, Open Mouth, Hair, Wood, Composition Body, Jointed, 1907, 26 In.	805.00
Jumeau, Socket Head, Blue Sleep Eyes, Jointed Composition, Pink Dress, Hat, Child, c.1907, 32 In.	1243.00
K * R, 80, Bisque Socket Head, Set Eyes, Open Mouth, Brunette Hair Wig, Composition, Jointed, 31 In.	406.00
K * R, 101, Bisque Head, Blue Painted Eyes, Braids, Jointed Composition, Red Cap, 15 In.	1356.00
K * R, 101, Bisque Head, Blue Painted Eyes, Jointed, Composition, White Dress, 8 In.	452.00
K * R, 114, Bisque Head, Painted Eyes, Closed Mouth, Human Hair, Composition Body, c.1910, 24 In.	4480.00
K * R, 114, Gretchen, Bisque Head, Painted, Mohair Wig, Composition, Wooden, 18 In. ..*Illus*	3024.00
K * R, 115, Bisque Head, Closed Mouth, Molded, Painted Hair, Set Glass Eyes, Composition, 12 In.	1044.00
K * R, 115 A, Bisque Socket Head, Sleep Eyes, Pouty, Dimple, Mohair Wig, c.1914, Toddler, 19 In.	4200.00
K * R, 116, Bisque Head, Blue Flirty Eyes, Moving Tongue, Composition, Coat, Hat, Toddler, 19 In.	396.00
K * R, 117N, Bisque Head, Blue Flirty Eyes, Jointed, Composition, White Pinafore, 16 In.	678.00
K * R, 126, Bisque Head, Flirty Eyes, Open Mouth, Composition, 20 In.	198.00
K * R, 126, Bisque Socket Head, Blue Flirty Eyes, Open Mouth, Composition, Cap, Toddler, 18 In.	261.00
K * R, 128, Bisque Socket Head, Sleep Eyes, Teeth, Mohair Wig, Composition Baby Body, c.1915, 17 In.	728.00
K * R, 191, Bisque Socket Head, Sleep Eyes, Open Mouth, Long Human Hair, Voile Print Dress, 27 In.	348.00
K * R, 192, Bisque Head, Blue Set Eyes, Jointed Composition, Lace Collar, Cuffs, 34 In.	622.00
K * R, Bisque Head, Brown Sleep Eyes, Jointed Composition, Lace Dress, Shoes & Socks, 8 In.	375.00
K * R, Bisque Head, Glass Sleep Eyes, Silk Lashes, Teeth, Human Hair, Wood, Composition, 37 In.	978.00
K * R, Bisque Head, Sleep Eyes, Open Mouth, Wool Wig, Composition Body, Baby, 12 ½ In. ... *Illus*	345.00
K * R, Bisque Socket Head, Glass Sleep Eyes, Pouty, Mohair Wig, Composition Body, c.1912, 23 In.	9520.00
K * R, Kaiser Baby, Bisque Head, Composition Body, Blue Eyes, Painted Lashes, Open Mouth, 15 In.	170.00
Kallus, Composition, Wooden Neck Peg, Molded Body & Dress, Label, 1930s, 18 In. ....*Illus*	1232.00
Kathe Kruse, Blond Hair, Brown Eyes, Jointed Legs, Red Shorts, White Shirt, Vest, Boy, 1950s, 14 In.	450.00
Kathe Kruse, Cloth, Oil-Painted Face, Pouty Mouth, Human Hair Wig, Jointed, c.1920, 17 In. ...*Illus*	11200.00
Kathe Kruse, Cloth, Painted, Wide Jointed Hips, Black Jacket, 14 In.	986.00
Kathe Kruse, Composition Head, Cloth Body, Braided Wig, U.S. Zone Germany, Box, 18 In.	551.00
Kathe Kruse, Plastic Swivel Head, Cloth Body, Hip Joints, Blond Wig, c.1960, 19 In.	173.00
Kestner 211, Bisque, Human Hair Wig, Blue Eyes, Peach Dress & Bonnet, 13 In.	425.00
Kestner, 5, Bisque On Socket Head, Closed Mouth, Sleep Eyes, Composition, Jointed Body, 13 In.	1102.00
Kestner, 143, Bisque Head, Sleep Eyes, Blond Mohair, Open Mouth, Wood, Composition, Bonnet, 13 In.	460.00
Kestner, 146, Bisque Head, Sleep Eyes, Open Mouth, Curly Wig, Composition, Jointed Body, 24 In.	203.00
Kestner, 155, Bisque Head, Blue Sleep Eyes, Jointed Composition, 7 In.	226.00
Kestner, 164, Bisque Head, Blue Sleep Eyes, Jointed Composition, White Gown, Bonnet, 31 In.	452.00
Kestner, 164, Bisque Head, Brown Sleep Eyes, Wig, Composition, Blue Dress, 23 In.	198.00
Kestner, 164, Bisque Socket Head, Blue Sleep Eyes, Jointed Composition, Long Dress, 28 In.	226.00
Kestner, 167, Bisque Head, Brown Set Eyes, Brown Bob Wig, Jointed, Composition, 14 In.	509.00
Kestner, 168, Bisque Head, Blue Sleep Eyes, Open Mouth, 20 In.	311.00
Kestner, 171, Bisque Head, Blue Sleep Eyes, Jointed, Composition, Lacy Peach Dress, 23 In.	254.00
Kestner, 171, Bisque Head, Blue Sleep Eyes, Open Mouth, Jointed, Composition, White Gown, 31 In.	622.00
Kestner, 171, Bisque Head, Brown Sleep Eyes, Brown Wig, Jointed, Composition, Lace Dress, 30 In.	509.00
Kestner, 172, Gibson Girl, Bisque Shoulder Head, Glass Sleep Eyes, Leather Body, Bisque Arms, 16 In.	767.00
Kestner, 192, Bisque Head, Brown Sleep Eyes, Open Mouth, Jointed Composition, Gray Dress, 24 In.	424.00
Kestner, 195, Bisque Head, Brown Sleep Eyes, Kid Body, Composition Arms, Green Dress, 20 In.	141.00
Kestner, 208, Bisque Head, Blue Sleep Eyes, Pouty, Auburn Wig, Mariner's Outfit, c.1910, 19 In.	28000.00
Kestner, 235, Baby, Open Dome, Wig, Sleep Eyes, Open Mouth, Kid, Composition Body, 14 In.	261.00
Kestner, 247, Baby Jean, Bisque Socket Head, Glass Sleep Eyes, Upper Teeth, Mohair Wig, c.1915, 14 In.	560.00
Kestner, 257, Bisque Head, Sleep Eyes, Open Mouth, Tongue, Mohair Wig, Composition, Gown, 18 In.	283.00
Kestner, 260, Bisque Head, Composition, Gray Bonnet, Cream Pinafore, 21 In.	339.00
Kestner, Bisque Head, Bald, Brown Sleep Eyes, Bowed Mouth, 2 Teeth, Composition, 17 In.	537.00
Kestner, Bisque Head, Brown Sleep Eyes, Brown Wig, Jointed Composition, Lace Dress, 30 In.	593.00
Kestner, Bisque Head, Glass Sleep Eyes, Pouty, Blond Mohair Wig, Wood & Composition Body, 16 In.	2128.00
Kestner, Bisque Shoulder Head, Brown Set Eyes, Kid Body, Print Dress, 18 In.	254.00
Kestner, Bisque Shoulder Head, Brown Set Eyes, Molded Teeth, Kid Body, China Arms, 17 In.	367.00
Kestner, Bisque Shoulder Head, Glass Sleep Eyes, Closed Mouth, Mohair Wig, Kid Bod, c.1890, 20 In.	504.00
Kestner, Bisque Socket Head, Sleep Eyes, Open Mouth, Composition Body, Lace Dress, Germany, 40 In.	1624.00
Kestner, Bisque Turned Shoulder Head, Blue Set Eyes, Kid Body, Pink Print Dress, 21 In.	311.00
Kestner, Character, 4 Interchangeable Heads, 1 With Sleep Eyes, Mohair Wigs, 11 In. .....*Illus*	4025.00
Kestner, Sammy, Bisque, Blond Human Hair, Blue Eyes, Peach Dress, Bonnet, 13 In.	425.00
Kewpie dolls are listed in the Kewpie category.	

Kley & Hahn, Walklure, Bisque Head, Brown Eyes, Jointed, Composition, Dress, Hat, 27 In.....	283.00
Koppelsdorf, Bisque Socket Head, Open Mouth, Composition Body, Curly Wig, Toddler, 17 In. .	174.00
Lanternier, Bisque Head, Blue Set Eyes, Jointed, Composition, Cream, Pink Dress, Cap, 18 In. .	226.00
Lenci, Dutch Boy, Felt Swivel Head, Googly Eyes, Mohair Curly Wig, c.1935, 16 In....................	2352.00
Lenci, Equestrian, Molded Pressed Felt, Green Googly Eyes, Yellow Mohair Wig, Riding Crop, 27 ½ In.	5750.00
Lenci, Felt Swivel Head, Googly Eyes, Mohair Wig, Closed Mouth, c.1930, 18 In.......................	6160.00
Lenci, Felt Swivel Head, Pressed & Painted Face, Jointed Shoulders & Hips, Box, c.1935, 9 In. ...*Illus*	619.00
Lenci, Felt, Embroidered Brown & Orange Costume, Blue Glass Eyes, Black Wig, 1930s, 22 In. .	995.00
Lenci, Felt, Painted Face, Hair Wig, Pink, Red, White Dress, Shoes, Red Hat, 16 In....................	116.00
Lenci, Girl, Felt Head, Painted Face, Googly Eyes, Mohair Wig, Jointed, Series III, c.1925, 13 In. *Illus*	2128.00
Lenci, Girl, Felt, Painted Eyes, Blond Wig, Embroidered Dress, Blue Hat, 18 In.	565.00
Lenci, Hockey Player, Felt Swivel Head, Blond Mohair Wig, Jointed, Paper Label, c.1936, 14 In. .*Illus*	6720.00
Lenci, Loretta, Felt, Molded, Painted Face, Hair Wig, Peach Dress, Shoes, 13 In.	116.00
Lenci, Opium Smoker, Felt Swivel Head, Painted Face, Closed Eyes, Yarn Hair, c.1920, 12 In. *Illus*	1344.00
Lenci, Salon Lady, Felt Head, Painted Face, Googly Eyes, Mohair Wig, Jointed, c.1925, 25 In. *Illus*	4480.00
Little Lulu, Vinyl, Fabric Outfit, Earle Pullan, Canada, c.1944, 14 In.	417.00
Lucy Peck, Wax, Shoulder Head, Glass Eyes, Human Hair, Closed Mouth, Muslin, c.1880, 20 In.	1456.00
Madame Alexander, Alexander-Kins, Blond Hair, Christening Gown, Bonnet, Roses, Box, 8 In.	261.00
Madame Alexander, Alexander-Kins, Blond Wig, Tam, Coat, Plaid Buttons, Purse, Shoes, 8 In.	522.00
Madame Alexander, Alexander-Kins, Blond, Wendy Dress, Pinafore, Box, 1970s, 8 In.............	1276.00
Madame Alexander, Alexander-Kins, Blue Cotton Outfit, Straw Hat, 8 In...............................	232.00
Madame Alexander, Alexander-Kins, Blue Felt Skating Outfit, Hat, Skates, Box, 8 In.............	290.00
Madame Alexander, Alexander-Kins, Hard Plastic, Red Hair, Blue Tutu, Ribboned Shoes, 8 In.	93.00
Madame Alexander, Alexander-Kins, Hot Morning, Green, Pink Dress, Straw Hat, c.1956, 8 In.	812.00
Madame Alexander, Alexander-Kins, Maypole Dance, Organdy, Marked, c.1954, 8 In.............	2668.00
Madame Alexander, Alexander-Kins, Painted Eyelashes, Pink Taffeta Jumper, Hat, Box, 1954.	1160.00
Madame Alexander, Alexander-Kins, Pink Cotton Romper, Bonnet, Yellow Apron, 8 In.........	290.00
Madame Alexander, Alexander-Kins, Pink Organdy Dress, Hat, Flowers, Box	290.00
Madame Alexander, Alexander-Kins, Pink, Organdy Dress, Blue Apron, Straw Bonnet, 8 In...	1450.00
Madame Alexander, Alexander-Kins, Red Hair, Box, 1970s, 8 In.	1044.00
Madame Alexander, Alexander-Kins, Red Hair, Pigtails, Blue Stripe Dress, Pinafore, Lace Hat, 1950s	464.00
Madame Alexander, Alexander-Kins, Yellow Dress, Navy Flower Pinafore, Green Straw Hat, Box	174.00
Madame Alexander, Alice In Wonderland, Hard Plastic, Mohair Wig, Blue Dress, c.1951, 14 In.	174.00
Madame Alexander, Babs Skater, Hard Plastic, Fur-Trimmed Dress, Margaret Face, c.1950, 15 In.	81.00
Madame Alexander, Beth, Walker, Bent Knee, Sleep Eyes, c.1967, 8 In.	50.00
Madame Alexander, Brenda Starr Bride, Pierced Ears, Jointed, Yolanda Dress, Flowers, 1964, 12 In.	41.00
Madame Alexander, Bride, Margaret, Plastic, Socket Head, Sleep Eyes, 1950, 14 In. ....*Illus*	672.00
Madame Alexander, Bride, Victorian, Plastic, Socket Head, Sleep Eyes, 1951, 21 In. ....*Illus*	3920.00
Madame Alexander, Carmen Miranda, Composition, Wendy Face, Black Hair, Box, 1942, 15 In.	493.00
Madame Alexander, Chatterbox, Vinyl Head, Pigtails, Sleep Eyes, Talk Button, 1961, 24 In. ..	55.00
Madame Alexander, Cherl, Dressed For Opera, Socket Head, Sleep Eyes, Plastic, 1954, 17 In...*Illus*	560.00
Madame Alexander, Cinderella, Blond Hair, Crown, Margaret Face, Dress, c.1950, 14 In.	81.00
Madame Alexander, Cinderella, Blond Wig, Braid On Top, White Satin Dress, c.1950, 14 In..	145.00
Madame Alexander, Cissette, Ballerina, Gold Net Skirt, Toe Shoes, Tiara, c.1959, 9 In.	70.00
Madame Alexander, Cissette, Blue Dress, Coat, 9 In.	145.00
Madame Alexander, Cissette, Queen, Gold Dress, Crown, Bracelet, Sash, Heels, 1958, 10 In...	203.00
Madame Alexander, Cissette, Queen, Metallic Brocade Dress, Sash, Drop Earrings, c.1960, 9 In.	81.00
Madame Alexander, Cissy, Brown Wig, Taffeta Dress, Hat Box, High Heels, c.1955, 20 In........	493.00
Madame Alexander, Cissy, Hard Plastic, Socket Head, Jointed, Sleep Eyes, 1958, 20 In. ...*Illus*	840.00
Madame Alexander, Cissy, Hard Plastic, Socket Head, Jointed, Sleep Eyes, c.1956, 20 In. ..*Illus*	616.00
Madame Alexander, Cissy, Queen, Gold Brocade Dress, Crown, Gloves, Heels, Snood, 20 In. ..	406.00
Madame Alexander, Cissy, Vinyl Arms, Reddish Brown Wig, Navy Dress, White Stole, Heels, 20 In.	435.00
Madame Alexander, Coco, Melanie, Vinyl, Blond Braided Hair, Blue, Dress, Slippers, 20 In. ..	638.00
Madame Alexander, Composition, Blond Wig, Molded Hair, Tagged Dress, 8 ½ In.	254.00
Madame Alexander, Cynthia, Hard Plastic, Margaret Face, Dress, Tag, 1952, 14 In................	435.00
Madame Alexander, Edith, Lonely Doll, Vinyl Head, Sleep Eyes, Rooted Hair, 1963, 16 In. ..*Illus*	224.00
Madame Alexander, Elise, Ballerina, Plastic, Socket Head, Sleep Eyes, Tutu, 1957, 16 In. ...*Illus*	616.00
Madame Alexander, Elise, Ballerina, Marybel Vinyl Head, Jointed, Blue Outfit, c.1963, 16 In.	145.00
Madame Alexander, Elise, Bride, Jointed, Satin & Tulle Wedding Dress, c.1957, 15 In.	116.00
Madame Alexander, Godey Lady, Plastic Socket Head, Sleep Eyes, Blond Hair, Gown, 1950s, 14 In.	952.00
Madame Alexander, Hard Plastic, Satin Gown, Tagged, Silver Shoes, 21 In.............................	1017.00
Madame Alexander, Jane Withers, Open Mouth, 6 Teeth, Brown Hair, 1930s, 20 In.	595.00
Madame Alexander, Kelly, Hard Plastic, Pierced Ears, Gingham Dress, Pink Pinafore, 11 In.	75.00
Madame Alexander, Lissy, Bride, Jointed, Tulle Dress, Lace Bodice, Veil, Silver Sandals, 12 In.	116.00
Madame Alexander, Lissy, Bride, Jointed, White Dress, Veil, Bouquet, c.1957, 11 In.	104.00

Doll, Mattel, Barbie, American Girl, Blond, Benefit Performance Ensemble $311.00

McMasters Harris Auction Co.

Doll, Mattel, Barbie, Blond Swirl Ponytail, Poodle Parade Ensemble $339.00

McMasters Harris Auction Co.

Doll, Mattel, Barbie, Brunette Ponytail, Senior Prom Ensemble, Wire Stand $339.00

McMasters Harris Auction Co.

Doll, Mattel, Barbie, Brunette Ponytail, Solo In The Spotlight Ensemble, 1961, 11 In.
$112.00

Theriault's

Doll, Mattel, Barbie, Color Magic, Golden Blond Hair, Swimsuit, Headband, 1966, 11 In.
$336.00

Theriault's

Doll, Mattel, Barbie, No. 3, Blond Ponytail, Booklet, Original Box
$565.00

McMasters Harris Auction Co.

Madame Alexander, Lissy, Bride, Tag, High Heels	81.00
Madame Alexander, Little Genius, Cloth, Blond Wig, Sleep Eyes, Composition Limbs, 20 In.	174.00
Madame Alexander, Little Genius, Plastic, Sleep Eyes, Painted Mouth, Cloth, Marked, 1940s, 11 In.	35.00
Madame Alexander, Margaret O'Brien, Hard Plastic, Mohair Wig, Braids, Blue Pinafore, 18 In.	261.00
Madame Alexander, Margot Ballerina, Brown Wig, Dress, Headband, 14 In.	58.00
Madame Alexander, Margot Ballerina, Hard Plastic, Pink Tutu, Hat Box, Marked, c.1954, 18 In.	145.00
Madame Alexander, McGuffey Ana, Composition, Blond Braid Wig, Dress, Straw Hat, 19 In.	70.00
Madame Alexander, Nina Ballerina, Margaret Face, Blue Dress, c.1950, 14 In.	81.00
Madame Alexander, Plastic Socket Head, Sleep Eyes, Brunette, Satin Gown, 1950s, 20 In.	2576.00
Madame Alexander, Poor Cinderella, Hard Plastic, Margaret Face, Tagged Outfit, Wrist Tag, 14 In.	678.00
Madame Alexander, Prince Charming, Hard Plastic, Poodle Wig, Brocade Outfit, c.1950, 14 In.	565.00
Madame Alexander, Prince, White Satin Outfit, Headgear, Plume, Marked Alex, Box, 14 In.	203.00
Madame Alexander, Princess Elizabeth, Silvertone Shoes, Satin Bag, Box, 13 In.	319.00
Madame Alexander, Scarlett O'Hara, Composition, Wendy Ann Face, Dress, Hat, c.1937, 14 In.	203.00
Madame Alexander, Sonja Henie, Composition, Blond Wig, White Outfit, c.1939, 21 In.	145.00
Madame Alexander, Sonja Henie, Composition, Mohair Wig, Clear Eyes, 18 In.	79.00
Madame Alexander, Tiny Betty, Bo Peep, Composition, Tagged Outfit, 7 In.	96.00
Madame Alexander, Train Journey Outfit, Tam, Plaid Skirt, Marked, c.1955	145.00
Madame Alexander, Wendy Bride, Hard Plastic, Stockings, Satin Shoes, c.1952, 14 In.	174.00
Madame Alexander, Winnie, Hard Plastic, Green Sleep Eyes, Braids, Dress, 14 In.	290.00
Martha Chase, Molded Stockinet Head, Painted Hair, Face, Pink Dress, Bonnet, 17 In.	203.00
Martha Chase, Painted Head, Hair, Sateen Body, Blue Dress, 20 In.	339.00
Martha Chase, Youth, Sanitary, Stockinet Body, Oil Painted, Articulated, Label, c.1913, 42 In. .... *Illus*	356.00
Mary Hoyer, Hard Plastic, Green Sleep Eyes, Closed Mouth, Marked On Back, 1950s, 14 In. ...	75.00
Mascotte, Bisque Head, Brown Paperweight Eyes, Jointed, Composition, France, Bebe, c.1900, 13 In.	2599.00
Mattel, Barbie, American Girl, Blond, Benefit Performance Ensemble ....*Illus*	311.00
Mattel, Barbie, Blond Swirl Ponytail, Poodle Parade Ensemble ....*Illus*	339.00
Mattel, Barbie, Brunette Ponytail, Senior Prom Ensemble, Wire Stand ....*Illus*	339.00
Mattel, Barbie, Brunette Ponytail, Solo In The Spotlight Ensemble, 1961, 11 In. ....*Illus*	112.00
Mattel, Barbie, Color Magic, Golden Blond Hair, Swimsuit, Headband, 1966, 11 In. ....*Illus*	336.00
Mattel, Barbie, International Parisian Series, Red Hair, Green Eyes, Pink Halter, Pink Heels, 1979	75.00
Mattel, Barbie, No. 3, Blond Ponytail, Booklet, Original Box ....*Illus*	565.00
Mattel, Barbie, No. 3, Blond Ponytail, Striped Swimsuit, Hoop Earring, Pumps, Box, 11 ½ In.	1130.00
Mattel, Barbie, Twist 'n Turn, Blond, Riding In The Park Ensemble ....*Illus*	339.00
Mattel, Dog, Poodle, Barbie's Dog 'n Duds, Dog Outfits, Accessories, 1964	75.00
Mattel, Ken, Brown Flocked Hair, Summer Sport Shorts, Carrying Case, 1962	220.00
Mattel, Ken, Brunette Flocked Hair, Flannel Blazer, White Pants, 1961, 12 In. ....*Illus*	112.00
Mattel, Midge, Beau Time, Red Hair, Flip Curls, Taffeta Dress, Drop Waist, c.1963, 11 In. ..*Illus*	168.00
Mattel, Twiggy, Shaggy Blond Hair, Open Mouth, Orange & Yellow Dress, Knit Top, Scarf, 1967, 11 In.	165.00
Mattel, Wednesday Addams, Addams Family, Cloth, Yarn Hair, F.A.O. Schwarz, 1962, 19 In.	253.00
Max Oscar Arnold, 200, Bisque Head, Blue Set Eyes, Open Mouth, Teeth, Jointed, Composition, 27 In.	141.00
Max Rader, Bisque Head, Blue Set Eyes, Brown Wig, Composition, White Gown, 13 In.	113.00
Mengersgereuth, 914, Bisque Head, Blue Sleep Eyes, Composition, White Gown, Baby, 18 In.	226.00
Milliner's Model, Papier-Mache, Sculpted Hair, Painted Eyes, Kid Body, Germany, c.1850, 13 In. .	2016.00
Morrell, Wax, Poured, Glass Eyes, Inserted Hair, White Lace Dress, Wood Box England, c.1860, 18 In.	464.00
Nancy Ann Storybook, Goldilocks & Baby Bear, Bisque, Blond Hair, Marked, 1938, 7 In.	1195.00
Nancy Ann Storybook, Pudgy Tummy, Bisque, Jointed, Painted, Red Hair, 5 ½ In.	81.00
Nancy Ann Storybook, Topsy, Fairy Tale Series, Plastic, Black, Painted, Red Check Dress, Pail, Box.	174.00
Nora Wellings, Sailor, Cloth, Painted Face, Brown Suit, White Cap, 12 In.	71.00
Ohlhaver, Bisque Head, Blue Sleep Eyes, Jointed Composition, Blue Velvet Suit, Hat, Lace Cuffs, 25 In.	311.00
Orsini, Bisque, Open Mouth, Pinafore Dress, c.1938, 5 In.	848.00
Orsini, Bisque, Painted Eyes, Bonnet, Crocheted Dress, c.1935, 5 In.	622.00
Paper dolls are listed in their own category.	
Papier-Mache, Molded Head, Wood Limbs, Germany, 19th Century, 14 ¾ In.	415.00
Parian, Blond Molded, Painted Hair, Blue Dress, 26 In.	203.00
Parian, Empress Eugenie, Cloth Body, Green & Black Silk Gown, Pink Luster Hat & Snood, 14 In.	254.00
Pincushion dolls are listed in their own category.	
Playboy, Bunny, Stuffed, Wearing Tuxedo, White, Black, 1960s, 24 In.	86.00
Policeman, Felt, Long Torso, Oversized Feet, Long Jointed Arms & Legs, 18 In.	805.00
Puppet Set, Dennis, Menace, Alice, Henry, Margaret, Mr. Wilson, Vinyl Head, 10 In., 5 Piece.	242.00
Puppet, Alligator, Cloth, Steiff, 9 ½ In., Pair	180.00
Puppet, Green Hornet, Holding Gun & Flashlight, Hat, 1966, 10 ½ In.	185.00
Puppet, Jerry Mahoney, Walter Winchell Show, 1958, 25 In.	125.00
Puppet, Policeman, Smiling, Hat, Bowtie, Fabric Body, c.1905, 23 In.	444.00
Puppet, Polichinelle, Papier-Mache, Horsehair Stuffing, Painted Face, France, 18 In. ....*Illus*	575.00

Raggedy Ann, Painted Face, Red Yarn Hair, Cloth Body, Original Clothes, Molly-'Es, 18 In. ...*Illus*	460.00
Rohmer, Bisque Socket Head, Glass Eyes, Leather Torso, Knee Joints, Mohair Wig, 18 ½ In. ...*Illus*	3450.00
S & H dolls are also listed here as Bergmann and Simon & Halbig.	
S.F.B.J., 60, Bisque Head, Blue Set Eyes, Blond Wig, Walker, Key Windup, White Dress, 15 In. ..	2823.00
S.F.B.J., 233, Bisque Dome Socket Head, Pouty, Sculpted Hair, Blue Squinting Eyes, Boy, c.1912, 23 In.	3360.00
S.F.B.J., 236, Bisque Head, Sleep Eyes, Open Mouth, Jointed, Composition, Lace Gown, Toddler, 27 In.	424.00
S.F.B.J., 236, Bisque Socket Head, Child, Character, Composition, Sleep Eyes, Jointed, 12 In.	290.00
S.F.B.J., 245, Bisque Socket Head, Composition Body, Closed Mouth, Clown Attire, 12 In..........	2088.00
S.F.B.J., 250, Bisque Head, Brown Eyes, Jointed Composition, Blue Suit, 20 In.	283.00
S.F.B.J., 251, Bisque Head, Blue Sleep Eyes, Moving Tongue, Jointed, Composition, 14 In.....	480.00
S.F.B.J., 301, Bisque Head, Brown Sleep Eyes, Jointed Composition, White Gown, 23 In............	141.00
Sasha, Blond Wig, Tan Sweater, Cord Skirt, Belt, Shoes, 18 In.	174.00
Sasha, Brunette Wig, Blue Dancing Dress, Headband, Shoes, Box, 16 In.	145.00
Sasha, Gregor, Jeans, Belt, Navy Sweater, Gold Wrist Tag, 16 In.	464.00
Sasha, Honey Blond Wig, White Silk Dress, Box, 16 In.	116.00
Sasha, Marina, Brunette Wig, Blue, White Sailor Outfit, Box, 16 In.	145.00
Sasha, Serie, Blond Wig, Bangs, Blue Cord Overall, Red Duffle Coat, Marshall Field Tag, 16 In.	754.00
Sasha, Serie, Brunette Wig, Bangs, Navy, White Check Viyella Dress, Marked, 17 In............	464.00
Schoenau & Hoffmeister, 1909, Bisque Head, Blue Set Eyes, Jointed, Composition Eyes, 24 In....	141.00
Schoenau & Hoffmeister, Boy, Bisque Head, Sleep Eyes, Jointed, Composition, Sailor Suit, 17 In.	170.00
Schoenhut, 102, Carved, Painted Braided Hair, Pink Check Dress, White Blouse, Red Shoes, 14 In.	791.00
Schoenhut, 405, Boy, Carved, Painted, Red Jacket, Black Cap, Green Boots, 19 In....................	678.00
Schoenhut, Boy, Wood, Applied Brown Hair, Painted Eyes, Linen Sailor Suit, 16 In. ....*Illus*	826.00
Schoenhut, Boy, Wood, Painted Blue Eyes, Blond Hair, White Linen Sailor Suit, Pond Boat, 16 In..	1003.00
Schoenhut, Carved Hair, Intaglio Eyes, Jointed, Green, Red Dress, 15 In.................................	283.00
Schoenhut, Carved Socket Head, Painted Eyes, Closed Mouth, Mohair Wig, Striped Outfit, Box, c.1912	7840.00
Schoenhut, Girl, Carved Hair, Intaglio Eyes, Blue Dress, Headband, Incised, 15 In.	406.00
Schoenhut, Girl, Painted Face, Jointed, Curly Mohair Wig, c.1935, 14 In.................................	551.00
Schoenhut, Intaglio Eyes, Tacked Wig, Pink Hat, Print Ruffled Dress, 19 In............................	424.00
Schoenhut, Miss Dolly, Painted Face, Blond Wig, Cranberry Union Suit, Shoes, Socks, Incised, 17 In.	348.00
Shirley Temple dolls are included in the Shirley Temple category.	
Simon & Halbig, 122, Bisque Head, Blue Flirty Eyes, Jointed, Composition, Blue Coat & Hat, 23 In.....	480.00
Simon & Halbig, 739, Black Bisque Head, Brown Set Eyes, Composition, Jointed, Sailor Suit, 16 In...	1300.00
Simon & Halbig, 739, Brown Bisque, Open Mouth, Wood, Composition, Jointed, Mohair Wig, 22 In..	1265.00
Simon & Halbig, 939, Socket Head, Set Eyes, Pierced Ears, Jointed, Composition, Wood, Dress, 17 In.	1413.00
Simon & Halbig, 1078, Bisque Head, Blue Sleep Eyes, Composition, Scottish Costume, 8 In.................	141.00
Simon & Halbig, 1078, Bisque Head, Brown Sleep Eyes, Dark Wig, Jointed, Composition, Dress, 22 In.	367.00
Simon & Halbig, 1078, Bisque Head, Glass Sleep Eyes, Teeth, Human Hair Wig, Composition, 21 In..	784.00
Simon & Halbig, 1079, Bisque Head, Blue Set Eyes, Composition, 17 In...................................	367.00
Simon & Halbig, 1079, Bisque Head, Blue Sleep Eyes, Jointed Composition, White Dress, Hat, 32 In...	565.00
Simon & Halbig, 1079, Bisque Head, Blue Sleep Eyes, Open Mouth, Composition, White Gown, 22 In.	198.00
Simon & Halbig, 1079, Bisque Head, Brown Set Eyes, Jointed, Composition, White Lace Gown, 28 In.	396.00
Simon & Halbig, 1079, Incised Head, Blue Glass Sleep Eyes, Mohair Wig, Wood & Composition, 13 In.	403.00
Simon & Halbig, 1159, Bisque Socket Head, Blue Glass Sleep Eyes, Wood & Composition, 24 In.	403.00
Simon & Halbig, 1249, Bisque Head, Brown Sleep Eyes, Open Mouth, Jointed, Composition, 28 In......	1130.00
Simon & Halbig, 1329, Oriental Child, Bisque Head, Glass Sleep Eyes, Composition Body, Wig, 15 In.	1035.00
Simon & Halbig, Bisque Head, 2 Faces, Crying, Smiling Child, Glass Eyes, Wood Body, c.1890, 13 In..	3920.00
Simon & Halbig, Bisque Head, Blue Sleep Eyes, Open Mouth, Composition Jointed Body, 13 ½ In.	225.00
Simon & Halbig, Bisque Head, Blue Sleep Eyes, Wig Pulls, Jointed Composition, Lace Dress, 31 In.	565.00
Sonneberg, Bisque Head, Blue Set Eyes, Jointed, Composition, 14 In...................................	396.00
Sonneberg, Bisque Head, Brown Set Eyes, Jointed, Composition, Wood, Pink Shoes, Lace Gown, 19 In.	480.00
Stan Laurel, Bobbin Head, Painted Composition, Hat In Left Hand, Germany, 1930s, 7 ½ In.	493.00
Steiff, Der Wanderer, Swivel Head, Elongated Nose & Chin, Amber Glass Eyes, Felt Body, c.1928, 16 In.	8120.00
Steiner, Bisque Head, Blue Eyes, Composition Body, Bonnet, Dress, Bebe, 24 In..................	3051.00
Steiner, Bisque Head, Blue Set Eyes, Original Wig, Cream Lace & Pink Dress, Bebe, 16 In.	2825.00
Steiner, Bisque Head, Paperweight Eyes, Auburn Mohair, Wood & Composition, French Body, 18 In....	3738.00
Steiner, Bisque Socket Head, Glass Eyes, Closed Mouth, Mohair Wig, Composition Body, c.1888, 14 In.	3640.00
Steiner, Bisque Socket Head, Sleep Eyes, Open Mouth, Nurser, Composition, Cap, Dress, 11 In.	319.00
Steiner, Blue Glass Stationary Eyes, Fully Jointed Body, Blond Mohair Wig, 11 ½ In..................	3738.00
Steiner, Blue Gray Paperweight Eyes, Brown Human Hair Wig, 27 In.................................	2588.00
Swaine & Co., Bisque Head, Blue Set Eyes, Jointed Composition, Striped Suit, Hat, 11 In.	311.00
Terri Lee, Cowgirl, Hard Plastic, Painted Eyes, Felt Hat, Holster, 16 In..........................	93.00
Terri Lee, Hard Plastic, Blond Wig, Painted Eyes, Red Check Outfit, Straw Hat, Box, 16 In.	145.00
Terri Lee, Hard Plastic, Blond Wig, Red Striped Outfit, Straw Hat, Box, 16 In.	145.00
Topsy Turvy, Red Riding Hood, 3 Dolls In 1, Red, Wolf & Grandmother, 1973, 20 In.	48.00

Doll, Mattel, Barbie, Twist 'n Turn, Blond, Riding In The Park Ensemble
$339.00

McMasters Harris Auction Co.

Doll, Mattel, Ken, Brunette Flocked Hair, Flannel Blazer, White Pants, 1961, 12 In.
$112.00

Theriault's

Doll, Mattel, Midge, Beau Time, Red Hair, Flip Curls, Taffeta Dress, Drop Waist, c.1963, 11 In.
$168.00

Theriault's

Doll, Puppet, Polichinelle, Papier-Mache, Horsehair Stuffing, Painted Face, France, 18 In.
$575.00

James D. Julia Auctioneers

Doll, Raggedy Ann, Painted Face, Red Yarn Hair, Cloth Body, Original Clothes, Molly-'Es, 18 In.
$460.00

James D. Julia Auctioneers

Doll, Rohmer, Bisque Socket Head, Glass Eyes, Leather Torso, Knee Joints, Mohair Wig, 18 ½ In.
$3,450.00

James D. Julia Auctioneers

Uncle Sam, Hat, Playing Drum, Gold, Red Striped Pants, Blue Coat, Key, Windup, Stand, 19 In....	1870.00
Uneeda, Brown Hair, Vinyl Head, Jointed Orange Strapless Jumpsuit, Navy Flats, 1950s, 19 In. .	95.00
Unis, 310, Bisque Head, Blue Set Eyes, Jointed, Composition, Green Dress, France, 24 In.	170.00
Vogue, Betty Jane, Open & Close Green Eyes, Open Mouth, 4 Teeth, Pink Ruffled Dress, 16 In.	155.00
Vogue, Bride, Christening Gown, Poodle Wig, c.1950	203.00
Vogue, Ginger, Socket Head, Sleep Eyes, 5-Piece Strung Body, Box, 1953, 8 In. ....*Illus*	392.00
Vogue, Ginny, Alice In Wonderland, Blue Dress, Blond, Blue Eyes, Box, c.1952, 8 In.	174.00
Vogue, Ginny, Ballerina, Brunette Wig, Headband, Silver Tie Shoes, 8 In.	58.00
Vogue, Ginny, Ballet, Blond, Painted Lashes, Flowers, Headband, Pink Shoes, Gadabout Series, 1953.	203.00
Vogue, Ginny, Bride, Headpiece, White Plastic Shoes, Tag, 1956	52.00
Vogue, Ginny, Fairy Godmother, Original Dress, Painted Blue Eyes, 1949	130.00
Vogue, Ginny, Formal Series, Painted Lashes, Salmon Pink & Black Dress, 1956	52.00
Vogue, Ginny, Hard Plastic, Painted Eyes, Blond Wig, Tyrolean Outfit, Bells, Box	93.00
Vogue, Ginny, Painted Lashes, Bathing Suit, Purse	64.00
Vogue, Ginny, Painted Lashes, Blond Mohair Braids, Red, Blue Plaid Dress, Plastic Belt, c.1952...........	81.00
Vogue, Ginny, Painted Lashes, Check Shirt, Glasses, Walker, c.1953	70.00
Vogue, Ginny, Painted Lashes, Poodle Wig, Pink Dress, 8 In.	46.00
Vogue, Ginny, Painted Lashes, Red Braids, Yellow Pique Dress, 8 In........	70.00
Vogue, Ginny, Playtime, Cowgirl, Painted Lashes, Sleep Eyes, Outfit, Boots, Hat, c.1956, 8 In.	81.00
Vogue, Ginny, Rain Or Shine Group, Blond, Wig, Pink Outfit, Hat, c.1954	81.00
Vogue, Ginny, Red Braided Hair, Painted Lashes, Riding Outfit, Hat	104.00
Vogue, Ginny, Red Riding Hood, Hard Plastic, Painted Lashes, Marked, 1950-51, 8 In. ....*Illus*	102.00
Vogue, Jill, Dark Hair, Marked, 1957, 10 In.	97.00
Vogue, Toddles, Composition, Alice In Wonderland, Dress, Bloomers, Socks, Shoes, Box........	75.00
Vogue, Toddles, Composition, Mohair Wig, White Organdy Dress, Flowers	70.00
Vogue, Toddles, Mohair Wig, Pink Organdy Dress, Matching Bonnet, Marked, Box	203.00
Vogue, Wee Imp, Freckle Face, Red Straight Hair, Aqua Polka Dot Dress, White Apron, 8 In.	58.00
Wax Head, Blue Glass Eyes, Blond Wig, Gauze Covered Sawdust Body, 17 ½ In. ....*Illus*	130.00
Wax Over Composition, Glass Sleep Eyes, Hair Wig, Baby Clothes, England, 27 In................	261.00
Wax Over Composition, Molded Hair, Glass Eyes, Boater Attire, Carton Hat, Squeaker, Boy, 9 In.	928.00
Wax Over Papier-Mache, Cucumber, 8 Wax Dolls Inside, Different Sizes, c.1910, 5 In.	448.00
Wax, Swivel Head, Blue Glass Eyes, Carton, Wood Jointed Body, 15 In.	319.00
Wislizenus, My Sweetheart, Brown Mohair Wig, Blue Eyes, Red Checked Pinafore, Toddler 16 In.	280.00
Wood, Carved, Human Hair Wig, Stuffed Body, Greenland Costume, c.1910, 17 In. ....*Illus*	616.00
Wood, Carved, Jointed, Boy, c.1880, 19 ½ In........	1495.00

DOLL CLOTHES

Boots, Leather, Lace-Up, Pompom, Marked R.S........	57.00
Boots, Leather, Lace-Up, Red Rosettes, 2 ½ In........	226.00
Cape, Wool, Ivory, Embroidery........	40.00
Purse, Leather, Chain Handle, Metal Studs, France, 1 ½ In........	232.00
Shoes, Brown Leather, Light Brown Silk Ribbon, Gold Bead Closures, Marked 3, Bebe Jumeau .	261.00

DONALD DUCK *items are included in the Disneyana category.*

DOORSTOPS have been made in all types of designs. The vast majority of the doorstops sold today are cast iron and were made from about 1890 to 1930. Most of them are shaped like people, animals, flowers, or ships. Reproductions and newly designed examples are sold in gift shops.

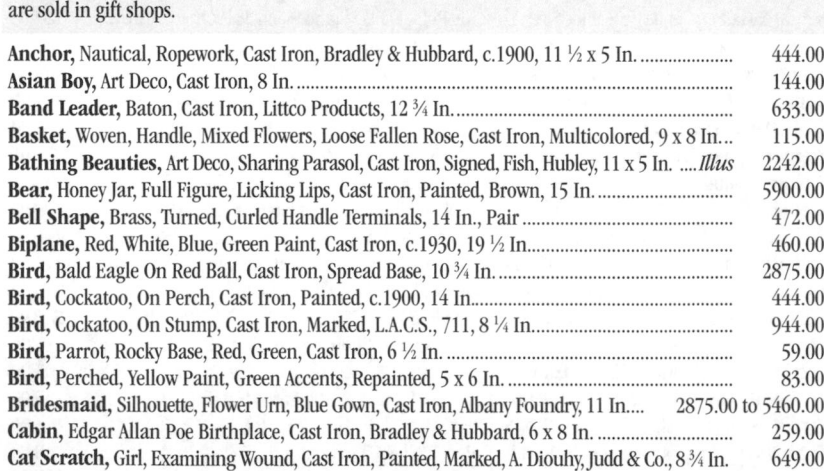

Anchor, Nautical, Ropework, Cast Iron, Bradley & Hubbard, c.1900, 11 ½ x 5 In.	444.00
Asian Boy, Art Deco, Cast Iron, 8 In........	144.00
Band Leader, Baton, Cast Iron, Littco Products, 12 ¾ In........	633.00
Basket, Woven, Handle, Mixed Flowers, Loose Fallen Rose, Cast Iron, Multicolored, 9 x 8 In...	115.00
Bathing Beauties, Art Deco, Sharing Parasol, Cast Iron, Signed, Fish, Hubley, 11 x 5 In. ....*Illus*	2242.00
Bear, Honey Jar, Full Figure, Licking Lips, Cast Iron, Painted, Brown, 15 In.	5900.00
Bell Shape, Brass, Turned, Curled Handle Terminals, 14 In., Pair	472.00
Biplane, Red, White, Blue, Green Paint, Cast Iron, c.1930, 19 ½ In........	460.00
Bird, Bald Eagle On Red Ball, Cast Iron, Spread Base, 10 ¾ In.	2875.00
Bird, Cockatoo, On Perch, Cast Iron, Painted, c.1900, 14 In........	444.00
Bird, Cockatoo, On Stump, Cast Iron, Marked, L.A.C.S., 711, 8 ¼ In........	944.00
Bird, Parrot, Rocky Base, Red, Green, Cast Iron, 6 ½ In.	59.00
Bird, Perched, Yellow Paint, Green Accents, Repainted, 5 x 6 In.	83.00
Bridesmaid, Silhouette, Flower Urn, Blue Gown, Cast Iron, Albany Foundry, 11 In....	2875.00 to 5460.00
Cabin, Edgar Allan Poe Birthplace, Cast Iron, Bradley & Hubbard, 6 x 8 In.	259.00
Cat Scratch, Girl, Examining Wound, Cast Iron, Painted, Marked, A. Diouhy & Judd & Co., 8 ¾ In.	649.00

Cat, Painted, White, Blue Eyes, Cast Iron, Marked, Hubley, 9 x 6 In.	123.00
Cat, Reclining, Cast Iron, U.S.A., c.1800, 2 ⅞ x 4 ¾ In.	1541.00
Cat, Seated, Black Paint, Cast Iron, c.1910, 12 In.	590.00
Cat, Seated, Cast Stone, Painted, 8 ½ x 5 ½ In.	1035.00
Cats, 2, Standing, Painted, Cast Iron, Hubley, c.1910, 7 In.	354.00
Cats, 3, In Basket, Painted, Cast Iron, 8 x 7 In.	144.00
Charleston Dancers, Cast Iron, Fish, Hubley, 8 ¾ In.	2875.00
Clown, Old Tom, Don't You Tell, Cast Iron, 16 ¾ In.	1800.00
Colonial Woman, Hat, Purse, Painted, Cast Iron, 10 x 6 In.	138.00
Conestoga Wagon, Oxen, Cast Iron, Multicolor, c.1910, 7 ¼ x 14 In.	201.00
Cottage Door, Flowers, Stone Steps, Leave Grouch Behind, Sarah Symonds, 6 ¼ x 4 ½ In.	1770.00
Cottage, Cape Cod, Picket Fence, Flowers Over Door, National Foundry, 8 In. ....*Illus*	207.00
Cottage, Flowers, Cast Iron, Hubley, 5 ½ x 8 In.	86.00
Cottage, Thatched Roof, Picket Fence, Flowers, Trees, Iron, Crenier Novelties, 6 x 7 In.	1495.00
Covered Wagon, Oxen, Cast Aluminum, Headford Bros. & Hitchins Foundry, 16 ½ x 7 In.	375.00
Covered Wagon, Painted, Orange & Blue, Canvas Cover, Cast Iron, Hubley, 1930, 8 x 11 In.	201.00
Dapper Dan, Tuxedo, Top Hat, Cane, Hubley, 7 ⅝ x 4 ⅜ In. ....*Illus*	531.00
Dog, Boston Terrier, Cast Metal, Painted, Black, Cream, Green Cloth, Butch, 9 ⅜ x 10 In.	161.00
Dog, Boston Terrier, Standing, Facing Left, Cast Iron, c.1940, 9 ½ x 12 In.	104.00
Dog, Doberman Pinscher, Black, Tan, Hubley, 8 x 7 ¾ In.	748.00
Dog, English Bulldog, Standing, Painted, Cast Iron, 4 x 6 In.	212.00
Dog, German Shepherd, Cast Iron, 9 ½ In.	94.00
Dog, Howling, On Hind Legs, White Paint, Concrete, 11 In.	90.00
Dog, Reclining, Wood, Carved, Brown Paint, Block Base, Folk Art, c.1900, 7 ½ In.	201.00
Dog, Terrier, Cast Iron, 5 ½ x 6 ½ In.	104.00
Dog, Terrier, Cast Iron, Bradley & Hubbard, c.1900, 10 ¼ In.	71.00 to 81.00
Dog, Terrier, Cast Iron, c.1880, 9 x 10 In.	210.00
Dog, Terrier, Seated, Cast Iron, Painted, c.1910, 14 ¾ In.	633.00
Dog, Terrier, Standing, Tail Up, Cast Iron, c.1900, 8 ¼ In.	118.00
Dogwood, Flower With Berries, Wicker Basket, Trellis Handle, Vine, Cast Iron, 12 In.	374.00
Dogwood, Flower, In Basket, Tall Handle, Cast Iron, Painted, Marked No. 1260, Judd Co., 16 x 8 In.	113.00
Drum Major, Cast Iron, Maroon Hat & Coat, White Pants, Baton, 1910, 13 x 4 In.	495.00
Drum Major, Cast Iron, Painted, Creations Co., Lancaster, Pennsylvania, c.1930, 13 In.	444.00
Drum Major, Posing With Baton, Cast Iron, Littco Products, 12 ¾ In.	633.00
Duck, Rainy Day, Cast Iron, Painted, c.1925, 8 In.	374.00
Duck, Walking, Wings Back, Top Hat, Blue Pants, Cast Iron, 4 ¼ x 7 ¾ In. ....*Illus*	944.00
Eagle, God Bless America, Cast Iron, Yellow Paint, 10 ¾ x 7 In.	185.00
Eagle, Spread Wings, Brass, c.1876, 13 In.	1250.00
Elephant & Palm Tree, National Foundry, New York, c.1925, 14 In.	504.00
Elephant, Hokus, Nickel Plated Brass, Lead, Russel Wright, 1930s, 11 ¾ x 5 In. ....*Illus*	7500.00
Elephant, On Barrel, Green, Yellow, Cast Iron, Marked, Taylor Cook, 1930, 8 In.	173.00
Fireplace, Woman Spinning, Embossed, Eastern Specialty Co., 6 x 8 In.	316.00
Fisherman, Yellow Raincoat, Cast Iron, 20 In.	420.00
Flags, 3, Eagle On Ball, Cast Iron, Signed, Sarah W. Symonds, 9 x 6 ⅝ In.	4600.00
Flapper Girl, Fur Coat, Yellow Dress, Hand On Hip, Pointed Finger, 2-Sided, CJO, Judd Co., 8 x 5 In.	2242.00
Flapper Girl, Tiered Dress, Umbrella, Cast Iron, Compliments, Toledo Stove Co., 9 In.	633.00
Flower Basket, Dahlias, Multicolor, Cast Iron, Hubley, 9 ½ x 7 In.	144.00
Flower Basket, Multicolor, Wicker Basket, Cast Iron, Waverly Studio, 1925, 10 In.	201.00
Flower Basket, Tulips, Tiered Basket, Blue Bow, Cast Iron, 13 In.	518.00
Flower Urn, Mixed Bouquet, Black Footed Vase, Cast Iron, Bradley & Hubbard, 12 In.	259.00
Flower Urn, Mixed Flowers, Daisies, White Striped Urn, Cast Iron, 6 ¼ x 4 In.	230.00
Flower Urn, Poppies, Red, Cream Urn, Cast Iron, Hubley, 10 ½ x 8 In.	173.00
Flower Vase, 3 Roses, Red, Orange, Yellow, Gold Vase, Cast Iron, Wedge Back, 11 In.	431.00
Flower Vase, Modernistic Style, Blue & Green, Cast Iron, Hubley, 7 ⅜ x 5 In.	144.00
Flowerpot, Modernistic Style, Blue & White, Orange Dotted Pot, Cast Iron, 10 In.	920.00
Flowerpot, Tulips, Pink, Clay Pot, Cast Iron, Creations Co., 9 x 8 In.	316.00
Flowers, Art Deco Style, Blue, Red, Yellow, White, Wedge Black, Cast Iron, 10 ½ x 6 In.	489.00
Flowers, Art Deco, Daisies, Cast Iron, 6 ⅜ x 5 ¼ In.	115.00
Flowers, Black & White Art Deco Vase, Wedge Back, 8 x 8 In. ....*Illus*	748.00
Flowers, Blue & White, Polka Dotted Pot, Cast Iron, 10 x 9 ½ In. ....*Illus*	920.00
Foo Dog, Full Figure, Painted, Yellow, Red, 6 ¾ x 8 In.	118.00
Footman, Double, Cast Iron, Painted, Signed, Fish, Hubley, 13 In.	633.00
Footmen, 2, Red & Black Uniforms, Cast Iron, Hubley, No. 248, 12 In.	633.00
Fox, Brass Over Iron, England, 10 ½ In.	180.00
French Girl, Curtsey, In Green Dress, CJO, No. 1279, Judd Co., 8 ¾ x 4 ⅜ In.	413.00
French Girl, Yellow & Cream Dress, Cast Iron, No. 23, Hubley, 9 In.	144.00

Doll, Schoenhut, Boy, Wood, Applied Brown Hair, Painted Eyes, Linen Sailor Suit, 16 In.
$826.00

Conestoga Auction Co., Inc.

Doll, Vogue, Ginger, Socket Head, Sleep Eyes, 5-Piece Strung Body, Box, 1953, 8 In.
$392.00

Theriault's

Doll, Vogue, Ginny, Red Riding Hood, Hard Plastic, Painted Lashes, Marked, 1950-51, 8 In.
$102.00

McMasters Harris Auction Co.

Doll, Wax Head, Blue Glass Eyes, Blond Wig, Gauze Covered Sawdust Body, 17 ½ In.
$130.00

Conestoga Auction Co., Inc.

Doll, Wood, Carved, Human Hair Wig, Stuffed Body, Greenland Costume, c.1910, 17 In.
$616.00

Theriault's

Doorstop, Bathing Beauties, Art Deco, Sharing Parasol, Cast Iron, Signed, Fish, Hubley, 11 x 5 In.
$2,242.00

Bertoia Auctions

Frog, Painted, Cast Iron, c.1895, 5 In.	71.00
Fruit & Birds, Marked, Connecticut Foundry, 1929, 6 ½ x 5 ½ In. ....*Illus*	148.00
Fruit Basket, Arched Handle, Cast Iron, Albany Foundry, 11 x 8 In.	316.00
Fruit Basket, Cream French Basket, Cast Iron, Judd Co., 9 ½ x 6 In.	201.00
Geisha On Flowered Cushion, Cast Iron, Hubley, 7 ⅝ In.	288.00
Geometric, Arched, Cast Iron, Bradley & Hubbard, 7 ½ x 4 ½ In.	431.00
Girl Holding Bonnet, Standing On Braided Rug, Cast Iron, Waverly Studios, 8 x 5 In. ..*Illus*	767.00
Girl, Flapper, Brown Dress, Hat, Cast Iron, E.O.M. Co., Toledo, 12 In.	978.00
Gnome, Red & Green Paint, 12 In.	150.00
Golfer, Putting, Painted, Cast Iron, Hubley, c.1900, 8 ½ x 7 ⅛ In.	711.00
Harvest Elf, Cornucopia Hat, Grape Clusters, Leaves, Painted, Cast Iron, c.1925, 11 ⅝ In.	770.00
Horse, Prancing, Red & White Paint, Striped Stepped Base, Cast Iron, c.1910, 11 ½ x 13 In.	1007.00
House, Hancock-Clark House 1698, Brown, Gray, Cast Iron, 4 ⅝ x 6 In.	1725.00
House, Monroe Tavern, Lexington, Mass., Cast Iron, 5 ⅜ x 8 ⅝ In.	2588.00
House, Monticello, Cast Iron, Albany Foundry, 5 ½ x 8 ¾ In.	1495.00
House, Paint, Cast Iron, Greenblatt Studio, 6 x 7 ⅜ In.	59.00
House, Saltbox, Red & White Paint, Cast Iron, 5 ⅞ x 9 ¼ In. ....*Illus*	5750.00
Huckleberry Finn, Cast Iron, Littco, 12 ⅜ In.	805.00
Indian Days, Figure, Headdress, Deer, Campfire, Horseshoe Frame, Cast Iron, c.1931, 13 x 11 ¾ In.	345.00
Jonquils, Yellow Flowers, Cast Iron, Hubley, 7 x 6 In.	316.00
Lighthouse, Cottage, National Foundry, Whitman, Massachusetts, c.1900, x 8 In.	563.00
Lighthouse, Highland Light Cape Cod, 2 Cottages, Embossed, Cast Iron, c.1900, 8 x 9 x 3 In..	2370.00
Lighthouse, Keeper's Cottage, Landscaped Shoreline, Cast Iron, 6 In.	230.00
Lighthouse, Rocky Base, Waves, Cast Iron, c.1900, 10 x 7 In.	1126.00
Lighthouse, Rocky Shoreline, 8 ¼ x 7 In.	978.00
Lion, Cast Iron, Gold Paint, c.1910, 9 x 10 ¾ In.	415.00
Lion, Reclining, Sideward Glancing, Black Paint, Oval Base, Cast Iron, c.1900, 6 In.	2370.00
Lion's Paw, Brass, Elongated, Feathered Handle, Georgian, 15 ½ x 4 In., Pair	1304.00
Little Black Sambo, Umbrella, Iron, Blodgett Studios, Lake Geneva, Wis., 8 ½ In. ....*Illus*	2242.00
Little Red Riding Hood, Wolf, Embossed On Reverse, 7 ½ x 9 ¾ In. ....*Illus*	403.00
Lobster, Red, Green Base, Cast Iron, 12 ½ x 6 ½ In.	1840.00
Mammy, Hands On Hips, Red Dress, White Apron, Cast Iron, Hubley, 8 ¾ In.	115.00
Mary Queen Of Scots, Cast Iron, Painted, Stone Base, House Of Parliament, 1941, 7 ½ x 6 ½ In.	2006.00
Mary Quite Contrary, Child Watering Flowers, Cast Iron, Littco, 12 In.	1093.00
Messenger Boy, Holding Bouquet, Cast Iron, Hubley, Fish, 10 x 5 ¼ In. ....*Illus*	2875.00
Mexican Guitarist, Half Moon Base, Cast Iron, Littco, 11 ¾ In.	4312.00
Mill, Stream, 2-Story House, Cast Iron, Crenier Novelties, 6 ¼ x 8 ¼ In.	978.00
Monkey, On Barrel, Green & Yellow, Cast Iron, Taylor Cook, c.1930, 8 ½ x 5 In. ....*Illus*	748.00
Monkey, Seated, Curling Tail, Cast Iron, Hubley, 8 ⅞ x 4 ⅝ In.	431.00
Monroe Tavern, Lexington, Mass, 1695, Gray, 2-Story Building, Green Grass, Tree, 5 ¼ x 8 ½ In.	2124.00
Old Salt, New England Fisherman, Yellow Rain Gear, Boots, Hat, c.1910, 14 ¾ In...................	1265.00
Olive Picker, Donkey, Baskets, Cast Iron, Hubley, 7 ¾ In.	259.00
Owl, On Books, Cast Iron, Painted, Black, Yellow, Eastern Specialty Mfg., 9 In.	805.00
Parlor Maid, Serving Cocktails, Cast Iron, Fish, Hubley, 9 ¼ In..	5463.00
Parrot, Cast Iron, Painted, 8 In., Pair..	295.00
Parrot, Green, Yellow Shirt, Cast Iron, Taylor Cook, 1930, 10 ½ In.	1495.00
Peacock, On Fence, Trees, A.M. Greenblatt Studios, c.1925, 15 ¼ x 7 ⅛ In. ....*Illus*	472.00
Peacock, Spread Tail, Painted Blue, Green, Brown, 6 ½ x 6 ½ In.	354.00
Pelican, 2-Sided, Cast Iron, Spencer Co., 14 ½ In.	3540.00
Penguin, Turned Head, Cast Iron, 7 ¾ x 4 ⅜ In...	805.00
Penguin, Tuxedo, Top Hat, Hollow, 2-Piece Casting, Hubley, 10 ½ x 4 In.	590.00
Penguin, Yellow & Red, Taylor Cook, 1930, 9 ¼ In.	3738.00
Pheasant, Ringneck, Standing, Leaf Base, Painted, Cast Iron, 8 In..	354.00
Pirate, With Sack, Green Base, Cast Iron, 12 x 9 ¾ In.	1121.00
Poinsettia, Red, Cast Iron, Marked, Judd Co., 10 In. ....*Illus*	649.00
Rabbit, At Fence, Multicolor Pastel Paint, Cast Iron, 8 ½ In.	124.00
Rabbit, Seated, Cast Iron, Black Paint, 11 ½ In.	142.00
Rabbit, Seated, Ears Up, Painted, White & Pink, Cast Iron, U.S.A., c.1900, 11 ⅜ In...................	237.00
Rhumba Dancer, Ruffled Dress, Painted, Cast Iron, 11 ⅛ x 6 ⅜ In. ....*Illus*	2242.00
Rooster, Cast Iron, Painted Black, c.1900, 6 ½ x 6 ½ In..	374.00
Sailboat, Cast Iron, Ocean Base, 2-Piece Casting, Hubley, 17 In..	1955.00
Sailor, Cast Iron, Littco Products, Littlestown, Pennsylvania, c.1930, 11 ⅞ In.........................	711.00
Sailor, Hands On Hips, Bell-Bottom Pants, White Shirt, Littco Products, 11 ½ In.	1610.00
Sheep, Cast Iron, Painted Black, 10 ¼ In., Pair..	502.00
Ship, 3-Masted, Cast Iron, c.1900, 21 x 18 In.	502.00

Doorstop, Cottage, Cape Cod, Picket Fence, Flowers Over Door, National Foundry, 8 In.
$207.00

Bertoia Auctions

Doorstop, Dapper Dan, Tuxedo, Top Hat, Cane, Hubley, 7 ⅝ x 4 ⅜ In.
$531.00

Bertoia Auctions

Doorstop, Duck, Walking, Wings Back, Top Hat, Blue Pants, Cast Iron, 4 ¼ x 7 ¾ In.
$944.00

Bertoia Auctions

Doorstop, Elephant, Hokus, Nickel Plated Brass, Lead, Russel Wright, 1930s, 11 ¾ x 5 In.
$7,500.00

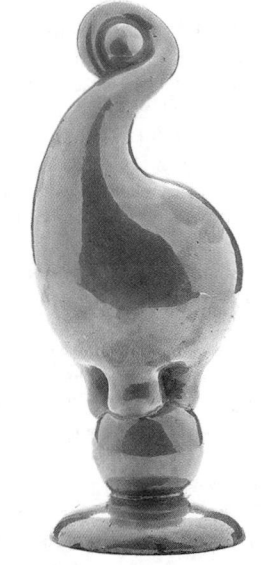

Rago Arts & Auction Center

Doorstop, Flowers, Black & White Art Deco Vase, Wedge Back, 8 x 8 In.
$748.00

Bertoia Auctions

Doorstop, Flowers, Blue & White, Polka Dotted Pot, Cast Iron, 10 x 9 ½ In.
$920.00

Bertoia Auctions

Doorstop, Fruit & Birds, Marked, Connecticut Foundry, 1929, 6 ½ x 5 ½ In.
$148.00

Bertoia Auctions

Doorstop, Girl Holding Bonnet, Standing On Braided Rug, Cast Iron, Waverly Studios, 8 x 5 In.
$767.00

Bertoia Auctions

Doorstop, House, Saltbox, Red & White Paint, Cast Iron, 5 ⅞ x 9 ¼ In.
$5,750.00

Bertoia Auctions

Doorstop, Little Black Sambo, Umbrella, Iron, Blodgett Studios, Lake Geneva, Wis., 8 ½ In.
$2,242.00

Bertoia Auctions

Doorstop, Little Red Riding Hood, Wolf, Embossed On Reverse, 7 ½ x 9 ¾ In.
$403.00

Bertoia Auctions

Doorstop, Messenger Boy, Holding Bouquet, Cast Iron, Hubley, Fish, 10 x 5 ¼ In.
$2,875.00

Bertoia Auctions

Doorstop, Monkey, On Barrel, Green & Yellow, Cast Iron, Taylor Cook, c.1930, 8 ½ x 5 In.
$748.00

Bertoia Auctions

Skier, Woman Posing With Skis, Blue, Red Scarf & Belt, Cast Iron, 12 In.	2588.00
Soldier, Marching, Flower In Gun Barrel, Cast Iron, 12 ⅞ x 7 ⅛ In. ....*Illus*	4600.00
Southern Belle, Flowered Dress, Holding Hat, Cast Iron, 11 ¼ x 6 In. ....*Illus*	173.00
Spanish Dancer, Open Fan, Cast Iron, Waverly Studios, 9 ½ x 5 ¼ In.	345.00
Squirrel, Black Paint, Cast Iron, 8 In.	189.00
Squirrel, On Log, Eating Nut, Cast Iron, Bradley & Hubbard, c.1900, 11 x 9 In.	1185.00
Squirrel, Seated On Log, Eating Nut, Painted, Cast Iron, c.1900, 12 x 10 ¼ In.	4029.00
Stylized Flowers, Pot, Painted, Cast Iron, 10 In.	944.00
Sunbonnet Girl, Cast Iron, 9 x 5 ¾ In.	230.00
Swan, Curled Neck, Leafy Base, Cast Iron, Stamped W.B. & Co., c.1910, 15 ¾ In.	189.00
Tall Ship, Brown, Peach, Red Paint, Cast Iron, 12 In.	28.00
Tiger, Man In Yellow Jacket, Black Top Hat, Fish, No. 269, Hubley, 9 ½ In.	3738.00
Troubadour With Guitar, Black Suit & Hat, Green Shirt, Cast Iron, 11 x 6 In.	374.00
Turkey, Painted, Cast Iron, Robinson, 12 ½ x 11 ½ In.	4130.00
Turkey, Rubber Knobs, Cast Iron, Embossed Base, Bradley & Hubbard, 12 ½ In.	4600.00
Twin Kittens, White In Dress, Black In Jumper, Side-Glancing Eyes, G. Drayton, Hubley, 8 x 5 In.	295.00
Uncle Sam, Hands Behind Back, Bronze, 12 ¼ In.	1495.00
Whistling Jim, Hands In Pockets, Painted, Cast Iron, Bradley & Hubbard, 16 ¼ In.	7080.00
Willow Tree, Resting Sheep, Cast Iron, 7 ¼ In.	1093.00
Windmill, Red Roof, Water Wheel, Water, Ship, Birds, Cast Iron, 9 x 11 In.	2185.00
Woman, Anne Radcliffe, First Woman Donor To Harvard, 1643, Cast Iron, 1927, 14 In.	863.00
Woman, Old Fashioned Pink Dress, Cast Iron, Hubley, 7 ¾ In.	575.00
Woman, Pink Hoop Skirt, Ruffles, Hat, Holding Flowers, Cast Iron, 11 In.	575.00
Woman, With Flower Basket & Parasol, Cast Iron, Bradley & Hubbard, 11 In.	978.00
Woodpecker, On Branch, Cast Iron, Round Base, U.S.A., c.1800, 8 ⅜ In.	1422.00

DOULTON pottery and porcelain were made by Doulton and Co. of Burslem, England, after 1882. The name *Royal Doulton* appeared on the company's wares after 1902. Other pottery by Doulton is listed under Royal Doulton.

Bottle, Ink, Figural, Man's Face, Open Mouth, Forehead Opening, Glazed, c.1880, 1 ⅞ In. *Illus*	173.00
Mug, Handles, Raised Figures, 2-Tone Brown, 5 ½ In.	47.00
Pitcher, Autumn Leaves, Orange, Green, Lambeth, 6 ¾ x 6 ½ In.	150.00
Pitcher, Basin, Black Transfer Floral, Gilt Accents, Stamped, Burslem, c.1890, 11 x 15 ½ In.	120.00
Pitcher, Basin, Flowers, Stripes, Brown Transfer, Burslem, 1880, 10 ½-In. Pitcher	180.00
Pitcher, Raised Classical Scenes, Motto, 2-Tone Brown, 7 In.	83.00
Pitcher, Raised Heraldic Medallions, Motto, 2-Tone Brown, 7 In.	71.00
Platter, Spray Flow Blue, Shaped Rim, Gilt, Oval, Impressed, c.1890, 16 x 21 ½ In.	288.00
Punch Bowl, Blue, Gold, Cream, Gilt Rim, Marked, c.1890, 8 x 14 ¼ In.	94.00
Tankard, Raised Figures, Animals, 2-Tone Brown, 5 ¼ In.	41.00
Tobacco Jar, Stoneware, Raised Apostle Panels, 2-Tone Brown Glaze, Lid, 8 ½ In.	71.00
Urn, Terra-Cotta, Blue, Red, White, Raised Leaves, Garlands, Spigot, Lid, Footed, 14 ½ In.	212.00
Vase, Arts & Crafts, Trees, Green Ground, Gold Accents, Squeeze Bag, Wood Stand, 13 x 24 In.	1830.00
Vase, Brown Flowers, 2 Blue Bands, Lambeth, Bigelow Kennard, 24 x 12 In.	118.00
Vase, Deer Scene In Band, Hannah Barlowe, Impressed Logo, 11 In. ....*Illus*	978.00
Vase, Luscian Ware, Multicolor Flowers, Narrow Opening, Signed Louis Bilton, 13 In.	473.00
Vase, White Daisies, Blue Ground, Dragon Wrapped, Incised JWT, Lambeth, 1878, 14 In. *Illus*	1725.00

DRESDEN china is any china made in the town of Dresden, Germany. The most famous factory in Dresden is the Meissen factory. Figurines of eighteenth-century ladies and gentlemen, animal groups, or cherubs and other mythological subjects were popular. One special type of figurine was made with skirts of porcelain-dipped lace. Do not make the mistake of thinking that all pieces marked *Dresden* are from the Meissen factory. The Meissen pieces usually have crossed swords marks, and are listed under Meissen. Some recent porcelain from Ireland, called *Irish Dresden,* is not included in this book.

Box, Flower Bouquet, Gilt Trim, Oval, 3 ¾ x 7 ½ x 5 ½ In.	295.00
Box, Parcel Gilt, Louis XVI Scenes, Painted, Faux Book Shape, Padded Interior, c.1865, 2 ¾ x 5 ¾ In.	2760.00
Candelabrum, 3-Lights, Figural, Tree Trunk, Cherubs, 10 x 8 ½ In., Pair	96.00
Chocolate Pot, Lid, Pink, Purple & Yellow Flowers, Pinched Waist, c.1920, 10 In.	96.00
Figurine, Wine Maker, Signed, 5 ½ In.	115.00
Figurine, Woman, Orientalist, Standing Over Camel, Hand On Head, c.1920, 6 ½ In.	96.00
Group, 3 Figures, Watching, Playing Backgammon, Period Attire, c.1960, 9 ½ In.	180.00
Group, Children Of King George I, Dogs, Flowers, 8 ½ In.	374.00
Group, Couple Dancing, Red, Green, Gilt, 19th Century, 8 In.	118.00
Plate, Allegorical Scenes On Border, Gilt Trim, 10 ½ In., 12 Piece	3738.00
Soup, Cream, Saucer, Interior Courting Scenes, Fired Gold Lattice, Rim, c.1940, 6 Sets	540.00

Urn, Figures, Landscape Painted Scene, Applied Flowers, Girls, Holding Baskets, c.1910, 19 ½ In..		1200.00
Urn, Lid, Napoleon Portrait, Gilt Crown Verso, Yellow, Handles, Rings, Carl Thieme, c.1901, 15 In.		185.00
Vase, Classical Scenes, Pink Geometric Ground, Gilt Details, Double Gourd, c.1910, 8 In., Pair.		354.00
Vase, Portrait, Lieschen, Preciosa, Gilt, Ruffled Rim, Signed Cop. Hempel, 9 In., Pair		1170.00

DUNCAN & MILLER is a term used by collectors when referring to glass made by the George A. Duncan and Sons Company or the Duncan and Miller Glass Company. These companies worked from 1893 to 1955, when the use of the name *Duncan* was discontinued and the firm became part of the United States Glass Company. Early patterns may be listed under Pressed Glass.

Button Arches, Pitcher, Ruby Stain, Clear Handle, 1900, 12 In.		235.00
Canterbury, Candy Dish, Pink Opalescent, Covered, 1940s, 8 In.		65.00
Cathay, Cocktail, 4 ⅛ In.		9.00
Cathay, Goblet, 6 ½ In.		9.00
Chantilly, Cordial, 4 In.		52.00
Chantilly, Goblet, 7 ¼ In.		23.00
Devon Spray, Goblet, 5 ¾ In.		18.00
First Love, Relish, 5 Sections, 10 In.		65.00
Garland, Cordial, 4 In.		32.00
Garland, Goblet, 7 ¼ In.		24.00
Grape, Relish, Milk Glass, 7 ½ In.		40.00
Grape, Tumbler, Milk Glass, 9 Oz., 4 In.		13.00
Indian Tree, Bowl, 2 Handles, 6 ¼ In.		35.00
Indian Tree, Bowl, Crimped, 11 In.		60.00
Juno, Cocktail, 4 In.		13.00
Juno, Goblet, 6 ¼ In.		19.00
Juno, Plate, Salad, 7 In.		8.00
Juno, Tumbler, 4 ¼ In.		15.00
Mesa, Champagne, 4 ⅞ In.		14.00
Mesa, Wine, 5 In.		23.00
Nobility, Goblet, 5 ⅝ In.		19.00
Nobility, Wine, 4 ¾ In.		17.00
Pharaoh, Console, Art Deco, Green, Footed, 12 ½ In.		75.00
Queen's Lace, Champagne, 5 ⅜ In.		21.00
Queen's Lace, Goblet, 7 ¼ In.		15.00
Queen's Lace, Plate, Salad, 7 ½ In.		13.00
Queen's Lace, Tumbler, Iced Tea, 6 ⅝ In.		11.00
Radiance, Pitcher, 76 Oz., 8 In.		43.00
Radiance, Plate, Serving, 18 ¾ In.		45.00
Ripple, Sherbet, Knobbed Stem, Amber, 4 In.		8.00
Starlight, Goblet, 7 In.		28.00
Starlight, Sherbet, 3 ½ In.		29.00
Starlight, Tumbler, Iced Tea, 6 ⅜ In.		35.00
Tiara, Champagne, 6 In.		8.00
Tiara, Cocktail, 5 ½ In.		12.00
Willow, Cocktail, 4 ½ In.		9.00
Willow, Goblet, 6 ¼ In.		21.00
Willow, Plate, Salad, 7 ½ In.		14.00
Willow, Tumbler, 12 Oz., 5 ⅛ In.		33.00
Willow, Wine, 5 ¼ In.		14.00

DURAND art glass was made from 1924 to 1931. The Vineland Flint Glass Works was established by Victor Durand and Victor Durand Jr. in 1897. In 1924 Martin Bach Jr. and other artisans from the Quezal glassworks joined them at the Vineland, New Jersey, plant to make Durand art glass. They called their gold iridescent glass Gold Luster.

Bowl, Clear, Flared, 14 In.		29.00
Compote, Gold Iridescent, Signed, 6 x 7 ¾ In.		474.00
Compote, Gold, Blue Stripe Bands, Pulled Feather, Blue Lip Wrap, Yellow Luster Stem, 4 ½ x 7 In.		1495.00
Goblet, Optic Ribbed, Red, Reeded Spanish Yellow Standard, 9 In.		115.00
Goblet, Wine, Optic Ribbed Red White, Reeded Spanish Yellow Standard, 9 In.		58.00
Ice Bucket, Red To Clear, Slight Taper, Etched Flower, Leafy Branch, 5 In.		518.00
Jar, Lid, Gold Luster Glass, Applied Shell Shape Finial, Signed, c.1964, 9 ½ In.		1265.00
Jar, Lid, Gold Luster, Marigold, Blue Hearts, Vines, Raspberry Amber Prunt Finial, Oval, 8 In..		1840.00
Vase, Ambergris, Cut, Bulbous, Yellow Luster, Blue Hooked Feather, Cut Flowers, Wheat Stocks, 6 In....		325.00
Vase, Blue & Green Luster, Bulbous, Flared Out Rim, 1920s, 8 x 8 In.		1000.00

Doorstop, Peacock, On Fence, Trees, A.M. Greenblatt Studios, c.1925, 15 ¼ x 7 ⅛ In.
$472.00

Bertoia Auctions

Doorstop, Poinsettia, Red, Cast Iron, Marked, Judd Co., 10 In.
$649.00

Bertoia Auctions

Doorstop, Rhumba Dancer, Ruffled Dress, Painted, Cast Iron, 11 ⅛ x 6 ⅜ In.
$2,242.00

Bertoia Auctions

The edited listings of the current prices in this *Kovels' Antiques & Collectibles Price Guide* aren't available on any website. Readers can visit **Kovels.com** to check thousands of past prices and sign up for free information on trends, tips, reproductions, marks, and more.

Doorstop, Soldier, Marching, Flower In Gun Barrel, Cast Iron, 12 ⅞ x 7 ⅛ In.
$4,600.00

Bertoia Auctions

Doorstop, Southern Belle, Flowered Dress, Holding Hat, Cast Iron, 11 ¼ x 6 In.
$173.00

Bertoia Auctions

Doulton, Bottle, Ink, Figural, Man's Face, Open Mouth, Forehead Opening, Glazed, c.1880, 1 ⅞ In.
$173.00

Glass Works Auctions

Doulton, Vase, Deer Scene In Band, Hannah Barlowe, Impressed Logo, 11 In.
$978.00

Humler & Nolan

Vase, Blue Aurene, Pulled Leaves, Platinum, 3 ½ x 9 In.	688.00
Vase, Blue Aurene, Turquoise To Cobalt Blue, Iridescent, Urn Shape, 6 In.	374.00
Vase, Blue Iridescent, Green, Platinum & Gold Coil, King Tut, Shouldered, Round Foot, 7 In.	1208.00
Vase, Blue Iridescent, Heart & Vine, Cylindrical, Swollen Collar, Flared, 12 ½ In.	1668.00
Vase, Blue Iridescent, White Hearts & Vines, Shouldered, Round Foot, Pinched Neck, Flared, 8 In.	230.00
Vase, Blue Iridescent, White Hearts & Vines, Tapered, Gold Foot, c.1924, 12 In.	1320.00
Vase, Cranberry, Pulled Feather, Cut Flowers, 9 ¾ In.	345.00
Vase, Gold Iridescent, Blue Hearts, Vines, Cylindrical, Flared Rim, 7 In.	403.00
Vase, Gold Iridescent, Elongated, Shouldered, Round Foot, Flared Rim, Signed, 10 ⅛ In.	500.00
Vase, Gold Luster, Pink Highlights, Elongated Urn, Round Foot, Flat Rim, Signed, 10 In.	345.00
Vase, Green, Blue Iridescent, Platinum, King Tut Design, Elongated, Pedestal Foot, Flared Rim, 12 In.	1150.00
Vase, King Tut, Blue, Gold Coils, Opal Ground, 10 In.	978.00
Vase, King Tut, Gold Color, Shouldered, Tapered, Round Foot, Flared Rim, 8 In.	748.00
Vase, King Tut, Gold, Green Coil Design, Double Handles, Luminous Interior, 12 In. .... *Illus*	1265.00
Vase, King Tut, Iridescent Gold & Pink Swirl, 1920s, 11 x 7 In. .... *Illus*	1375.00
Vase, King Tut, Lady Gay Rose, Baluster, Flared Rim, 1920s, 10 x 5 In.	2875.00
Vase, Moorish Crackle, Blue & White, Marigold Interior, 7 ¼ In. .... *Illus*	2250.00
Vase, Pulled Feather, Shouldered, Gold Iridescent, White Pulled Feathers, Blue Iridescent Tips, 6 ½ In.	805.00
Vase, Ribbed, Red Iridescent, Marigold Interior, 8 ½ In. .... *Illus*	2530.00
Vase, White Flowers, Green Ground, Cameo, Signed, 1941, 10 ½ In. .... *Illus*	6900.00

DURANT KILNS was founded by Jean Durant Rice in 1910 in Bedford Village, New York. He hired Leon Volkmar to oversee production. The pottery made both tableware and artware. Rice died in 1919, leaving Leon Volkmar to run the business. After 1930 the name Durant Kilns was changed and only the Volkmar mark was used.

Bowl, Flower Shape, Teal, Eggplant Glaze, Gilt Stand, Incised Leon Volkmar, 1919, 5 x 6 In.	189.00
Vase, Aubergine Glaze, Leon Volkmar, 1921, 15 In. .... *Illus*	115.00
Vase, Experimental, Purple Glaze, Drip, Baluster Shape, Flared Rim, High Shoulder, 1913, 9 ¼ In.	461.00

ELVIS PRESLEY, the well-known singer, lived from 1935 to 1977. He became famous by 1956. Elvis appeared on television, starred in twenty-seven movies, and performed in Las Vegas. Memorabilia from any of the Presley shows, his records, and even memorials made after his death are collected.

Belt, Vinyl, Gold Metal Buckle, 3 Images, Musical Notes, 1956, 2 x 31 In.	299.00
Bracelet, Charm, Goldtone, Guitar, Dog, Framed Picture, Heart, 1950s, 7 In.	85.00
Button, Photo, National Fan Club, Member, Black & White, 1956, ¹⁵⁄₁₆ In. Diam.	155.00
Music Box, Guitar Shape, Transparent Black Plastic, Love Me Tender, 11 x 4 In.	15.00
Pinback, You're Nothin' But A Houn' Dog, Red, White Ground, Green Duck Co., 1956, ⅞ In.	28.00
Plate, Elvis Remembered, Center Profile, Hamilton Collection, 1989, 10 In.	75.00
Record, 45 RPM, 1 Side My Baby Left Me, Flip Side, I Want You, I Need You, I Love You	5.00
Record, Elvis Sings Christmas Songs, RCA Victor, LP, 1951	10.00
Skirt, Sock Hop, Navy, Felt Applique Of Elvis With Guitar, c.1956, 17 x 32 In.	563.00
Ticket, Concert, Market Square Arena, Indianapolis, Indiana, June 26, 1977	125.00

ENAMELS listed here are made of glass particles and other materials heated and fused to metal. In the eighteenth and nineteenth centuries, workmen from Russia, France, England, and other countries made small boxes and table pieces of enamel on metal. One form of English enamel is called *Battersea* and is listed under that name. There was a revival of interest in enameling in the 1930s and a new style evolved. There is now renewed interest in the artistic enameled plaques, vases, ashtrays, and jewelry. Enamels made since the 1930s are usually on copper or steel, although silver was often used for jewelry. Graniteware is a separate category, and enameled metal kitchen pieces may be included in the Kitchen category.

Ashtray, Black & White, Triangular, Annemarie Davidson, California, 6 x 5 In. .... *Illus*	100.00
Ashtray, Chess Pieces, Orange & White, Brown Mottled Ground, 6 x 5 In. .... *Illus*	75.00
Bookmark, Eastern Star, Gold Rope, Clip, c.1950, 5 In.	14.00
Bowl, Lid, Ship, Copper, Rebecca Cauman, Boston, c.1905, 3 ¼ x 5 ½ In. .... *Illus*	1875.00
Bowl, Pedestal, Blue, Multicolor Accents, Miguel Pineda, c.1940, 3 x 5 In.	150.00
Bowl, Underplate, Pink, Green & Lavender Roses & Leaves, Gold Band, Clear Stem, 3 ¼ In.	175.00
Box, Art Nouveau, Flowers & Scrolls, Blue Stone Border, Silver Gilt, Russia, 4 x 3 In.	1304.00
Box, Bonboniere, Bird Shape, Red, Black, Bilston, c.1790, 2 ½ In.	1007.00
Box, Guilloche, Hexagonal, Hinged, Plum, Blue, Carved Ivory Cameo Inset, 2 ⅜ x 2 ⅜ In.	299.00
Box, Lid, Brass Rim, White Interior, Flowers, Blue Ground, Chrysanthemums, Round, 5 x 8 In.	127.00
Box, Necessaire, Courting Scene, Gilt Scrolls, Continental, 1800s, 2 ¾ x 2 ¾ In.	444.00
Box, Portrait, Aristocratic Woman, 1700s Attire, Limoges, c.1920, 2 ¼ x 4 ¼ In.	375.00

Box, Purple Guilloche, Concentric Wavy Rings, Diamond Basket, Edwardian, 3 ½ In.	960.00
Box, Russian Silver, Filigree, Scrollwork, Flower Heads, Turquoise, Amber, Lid, Marked, 1 ¾ x 2 In.	460.00
Box, Silver, Hinged Lid, Woman, Unicorn, Lion, Austria, c.1910, 1 ¾ In. ....*Illus*	600.00
Brushpot, Canted Corners, Mother & Child Scenes, Bracket Feet, Chinese, c.1900, 6 ¼ In. ...... *Illus*	550.00
Creamer, Silver, Round Foot, Loop Handle, Square Spout, Gilt Interior, c.1900, 2 In.	1554.00
Dish, Green Border, Pink, Figure With Bow & Arrow, Ames, 7 ½ In.	750.00
Dish, Green, Flared Rim, Lion, Flowers, Grass, Clouds, Swirls, Yoshida, Japan, c.1850, 8 ¾ In. Diam...	178.00
Dish, Turtle, Geometric Designs, Arthur & Jean Ames, Frame, c.1950, 8 x 7 In.	525.00
Dresser Box, Copper, Red, Country Scene Medallion, Oval, White Scrolling, France, 5 ½ In. ..	518.00
Ewer, Bulbous, Cylindrical Neck, Stylized Lotus Scrolls, Dragon Handle, Chinese, 1800s, 8 ¾ In..	3524.00
Jewelry Box, Harpsichord Shape, Ocean Reserves, Pink, Gilt, Vienna, c.1860, 14 In.	900.00
Kovsh, Applied Blue Stones, Gold Washed, Flared Foot, Russia, 3 ⅛ x 6 In.	1968.00
Needle Case, 18K Gold, Blue, France, 1840s, 3 ⅛ In.	1995.00
Patch Box, Bilston, Mirror, Blue, Cream Interior, Motto, Trifles Shew Respect, 1 ½ x 1 In.	58.00
Pill Box, Pink & White Flowers, Black Ground, Piano Hinge, 1 x ⅞ x ½ In.	50.00
Pin Tray, Fish, Seaweed, Art Deco, Blue, David Anderson, c.1930	380.00
Plaque, Branches, Abstract Ground, Frame, Edward Winter, 1940s, 20 x 31 ½ In. ....*Illus*	5938.00
Plate, Rooster, Under Tree, Raised, Japan, c.1951, 8 In.	27.00
Plate, Woman With Children, Flower Shaped Cartouche, Scrolling Flowers, Fruits, c.1900, 10 ⅛ In.	395.00
Salt & Spoon, Deep Red, Sterling Silver, Meka, c.1950	95.00
Salt Cellar, Chair Shape, Hinged Seat, Gold Washed Interior, Russia, 1888, 3 In.	1599.00
Salt, Sapphire Blue Band, Silver Foot, Rim, Footed, Round, St. Petersburg, c.1915, 1 ½ In.	1680.00
Spoon Set, Floral Back, Impressed Marks, Box, Russia, 4 ½ In.	1920.00
Spoon, Flowers, Scrolls, Gold Wash Bowl, Russia, 6 ¼ In.	345.00
Teapot, Figures In Landscape, Scrolling Flowers, Peking, Chinese, 1700s, 5 In. ....*Illus*	660.00
Tray, Painted, Courting Scene, Scalloped Rim, Flowers, Geometrics, Persia, 10 x 14 In.	390.00
Tray, Rococo Style, Brass, Mirror Center, France, c.1935, 9 ¼ x 14 ¼ In.	246.00
Trinket Box, Copper, Casket Shaped, Scrolling Leaf Legs, Dome Lid, 4 ⅜ In.	349.00
Trinket Box, Lid, Bouquet, Yellow Ground, Copper Trim, Kingsley, 1 ¾ In.	75.00
Urn, Lid, Branches, Birds, Blue Mottled Champleve, Brass Mounts, Handles, c.1850, 10 In., Pair...	325.00
Vase, Bud, Lavender, Yellow Flowers, Flared, Copper, Limoges, 7 In. ....*Illus*	330.00
Vase, Flowers, Blue, Green, White, Gilt Highlights, Signed, Brocard & Fils, 1882, 6 x 4 In.	1250.00
Vase, Geisha, River, Trees, Shouldered, Cylindrical Neck, Chinese, 14 In.	295.00
Vase, Gilt, Ruffled Rim, Etched, c.1945, 6 ½ In.	35.00
Vase, Mallet Shape, Floating Round Flowers, White, Iron Red, Chinese, c.1890, 7 ¼ In.	2066.00
Vase, Red, Silver Foil, Bamboo Design, Granulated Ground, Japan, c.1920, 14 x 8 In.	1020.00
Vinaigrette, Art Deco, Butterflies, Flower, Diamond Border, Gold, Cartier, c.1925, 1 ½ In.	12390.00
Vinaigrette, Art Nouveau, Silver Gilt, Red, Portraits, Egg Shape, Ludwig Politzer, c.1890, 4 In..	531.00
Vinaigrette, Pin, Lady Bug, Pink Jeweled, Pearls, Pierced Grille, Silver Gilt, Germany, c.1910, 1 ½ In.	1416.00

ERPHILA is a mark found on Czechoslovakian and other pottery and porcelain made after 1920. This mark was used on items imported by Ebeling & Reuss, Philadelphia, a giftware firm that was founded in 1866 and out of business sometime after 2002. The mark is a combination of the letters *E* and *R* (Ebeling & Reuss) and the first letters of the city, Phila(delphia). Many whimsical figural pitchers and creamers, figurines, platters, and other giftwares carry this mark.

ERPHILA — Handpainted Czechoslovakia

Dish, 3 Sections, Warwick Pattern, Flowers, Multicolor, Czechoslovakia, 8 In.	45.00
Dresser Doll, Madame Pompadour, Holding Fan, Green Dress, 1920s, 5 ½ In.	110.00
Figurine, Bagpipe Player, Seated, Germany, c.1930, 6 In.	65.00
Figurine, Dog, Terrier, Black, White, Reclining, Marked, Germany, 3 x 1 ¾ In.	35.00
Figurine, Dogs, Borzoi, Running, Base, c.1925, 7 x 5 In.	195.00
Pitcher, Figural, Toucan, Made In Czechoslovakia, 9 x 7 ½ In. ....*Illus*	100.00
Soup, Dish, Plate, 2 Handles, Roses, Multicolor, Cream Ground, Marked	295.00
Teapot, Figural, Woman, Upswept Hair, Tendrils, Hoop Skirt, Marked, Germany	85.00
Vase, Female Nude Panels, Flared Rim, Brick Red, 10 ¼ In.	46.00

ES GERMANY porcelain was made at the factory of Erdmann Schlegelmilch from 1861 to 1937 in Suhl, Germany. The porcelain, marked *ES Germany* or *ES Suhl*, was sold decorated or undecorated. Other pieces were made at a factory in Saxony, Prussia, and are marked *ES Prussia*. Reinhold Schlegelmilch made the famous wares marked *RS Germany*.

1861 E.S. Germany

Bowl, Square, Bird On Branch, 2 Handles, c.1902, 6 ¾ In.	78.00
Dish, Trinket, Mother-Of-Pearl Finish, Gilt, Marked, 4 x 1 ½ In.	48.00
Ewer, Shouldered, Ruffled Rim, Pierced, Dragon Handle, Marked, 7 ¾ In.	250.00
Vase, Oval, Monk, Drinking, Marked, c.1910, 12 In.	87.00
Vase, Sea Goddess, Gold Scrolls, Beaded, Art Nouveau Handles, Marked, 5 In.	275.00

Doulton, Vase, White Daisies, Blue Ground, Dragon Wrapped, Incised JWT, Lambeth, 1878, 14 In.
$1,725.00

Humler & Nolan

Durand, Vase, King Tut, Gold, Green Coil Design, Double Handles, Luminous Interior, 12 In.
$1,265.00

Early Auction Co.

Durand, Vase, King Tut, Iridescent Gold & Pink Swirl, 1920s, 11 x 7 In.
$1,375.00

Rago Arts & Auction Center

Durand, Vase, Moorish Crackle, Blue & White, Marigold Interior, 7 ¼ In.
$2,250.00

Early Auction Co.

E

Durand, Vase, Ribbed, Red Iridescent, Marigold Interior, 8 ½ In.
$2,530.00

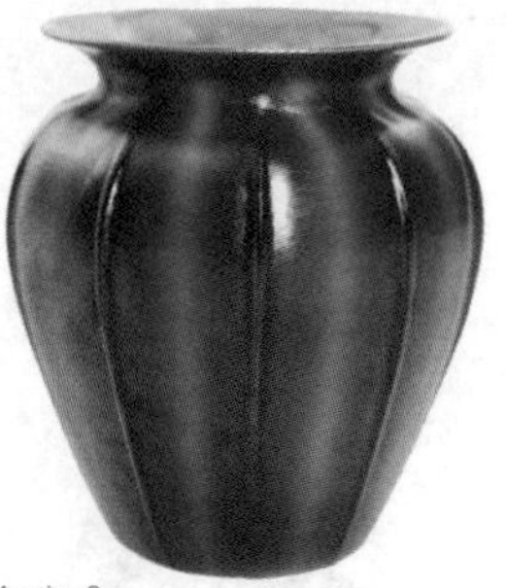

Early Auction Co.

Durand, Vase, White Flowers, Green Ground, Cameo, Signed, 1941, 10 ½ In.
$6,900.00

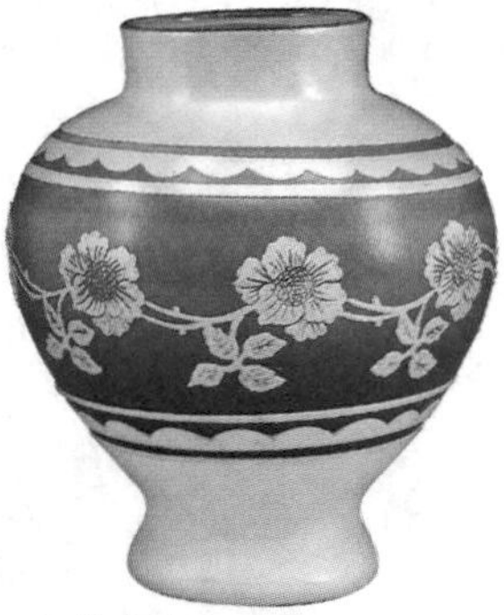

James D. Julia Auctioneers

Durant Kilns, Vase, Aubergine Glaze, Leon Volkmar, 1921, 15 In.
$115.00

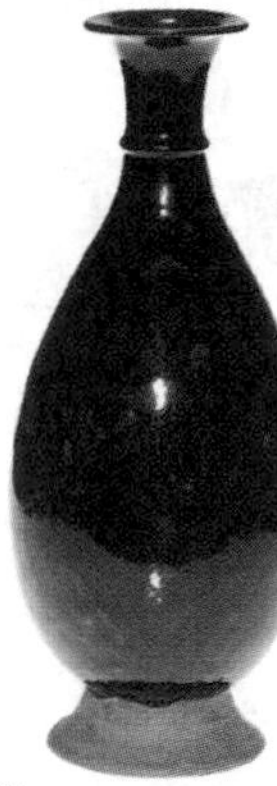

Humler & Nolan

Enamel, Ashtray, Black & White, Triangular, Annemarie Davidson, California, 6 x 5 In.
$100.00

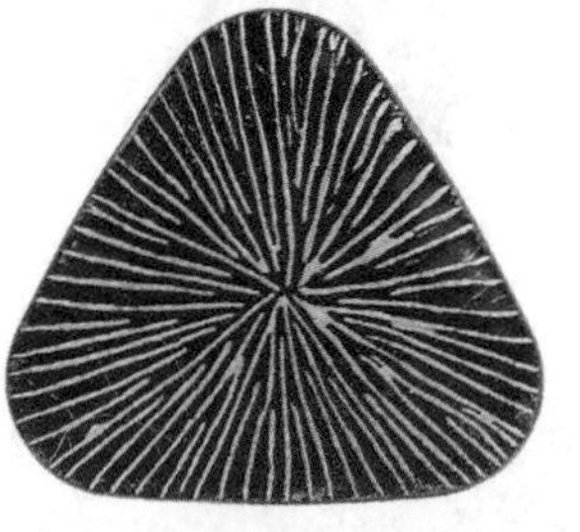

ESKIMO artifacts of all types are collected. Carvings of whale or walrus teeth are listed under Scrimshaw. Baskets are in the Basket category. All other types of Eskimo art are listed here. In Canada and some other areas, the term *Inuit* is used instead of Eskimo.

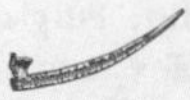

Boots, Basketry, Open Weave, Bootie Form, Early 1900s, 10 1/12 In.	374.00
Bowl, Basketry, Fine Weave, Multicolor Trees, Maltese Tube Crosses, 1940s, 3 x 6 In.	259.00
Charger, Argillite, Dogfish, Whales, Octopus, c.1900, 11 ¼ In.	3231.00
Cribbage Board, Eagle, Relief Walruses, c.1900, 13 In.	237.00
Doll, Fur Parka, Felt Gloves, Boots, Alaska, 8 In.	145.00
Doll, Muskrat Parka, Seal Trim, Caribou Strip, 10 x 13 In.	81.00
Doll, Wood, Carved Painted Face Mask, Fur Costume, Inuit Tribe, c.1910, 23 In. *Illus*	448.00
Earrings, Basketry, Caribou Hair, Round, c.1950, 2 ¾ In.	58.00
Figurine, Bird, Ivory, Inked Beak & Eyes, 1980s, 3 x 3 In.	196.00
Figurine, Bowhead Whale, Hunting Scene, Baleen Eyes, c.1875, 4 ¾ In.	3318.00
Figurine, Eskimo Holding Fish, Soapstone, 1980s, 5 x 7 x 3 In.	127.00
Figurine, Hunter, Polished Stone, Carved, 7 ½ In.	147.00
Figurine, Inuit, Fisherman, Leg Up, Holding Fish, Carved, Stone, 13 x 8 In.	263.00
Figurine, Inuit, Whaler, Kneeling, Hunted Seal, Stone, Signed, 6 x 6 In.	380.00
Figurine, Inuit, Wolf, Seated, Carved, Stone, Signed Etilu Stidlui, 5 x 6 In.	410.00
Figurine, Man Riding Sea Lion, Carved Stone, 1900s, 9 ½ x 4 ½ In. *Illus*	184.00
Hairpin, Bone, Horse Head, Carved, 6 ⅝ In.	110.00
Ice Scratcher, 19th Century, 11 ½ In.	588.00
Ladle, Carved, Human Figure, Inuit, c.1910, 15 ½ In.	119.00
Mask, Sealskin, Fur Trim, c.1950, 10 x 6 In.	259.00
Mask, Stone, Carved, 4 ¼ x 3 ¾ In. *Illus*	248.00
Needle Case, Bone, c.1900, 9 In.	411.00
Pipe, Carved & Etched, Ivory, Camp Scenes, c.1880, 9 In.	2015.00
Rattle, Seal Shape, Wood, Bone Toggles, c.1875, 5 ½ In.	6756.00
Retrieval Hook, Wood, Ivory, Human Head Handle, Bead Labret, 19th Century, 10 In.	8888.00
Seal, Lying On Back, Carved, Soapstone, Inuit, Signed	178.00
Tusk, Walruses, Seals, Bears, Etched, Red, Black, Nunivak Island, 19 In.	5629.00

ETLING glass pieces are very similar in design to those made by Lalique and Phoenix. They were made in France for Etling, a retail shop. They date from the 1920s and 1930s.

ETLING
FRANCE

Bowl, Sea Anemones, Frosted, Marked, c.1925, 12 x 3 In.	395.00
Bowl, Sunflower, Frosted, Footed, 1930s, 8 x 3 In.	428.00
Figurine, Madonna & Child, Opalescent, c.1910, 12 ¾ In.	695.00
Figurine, Madonna, Opalescent, Bowed Head, Open Arms, Oval Base, Frosted, No. 702, 4 In.	200.00

FABERGE was a firm of jewelers and goldsmiths founded in St. Petersburg, Russia, in 1842, by Gustav Faberge. Peter Carl Faberge, his son, was jeweler to the Russian Imperial Court from about 1870 to 1917. The rare Imperial Easter eggs, jewelry, and decorative items are very expensive today.

ФАБЕРЖЕ
КФ

Brooch, Guilloche Enamel, Diamond, Lozenge Shape, Feather Design, c.1910, 1 ¾ In.	4560.00
Cigarette Case, Enamel Guilloche, Moonstone Cabochon Thumbpiece, c.1900, 3 ½ In.	9000.00
Cigarette Case, Silver, Gold, Moire Silk Design, Banding, Diamond Thumbpiece, c.1900, 3 ½ In.	4320.00
Spoon, Serving, Silver, Flat Shape Handle, Enamel, Blue, Geometric Design Bowl, c.1910, 5 ¾ In.	2640.00
Tray, Silver, 6-Sided, Flared Rim, Leaf Border, Silk Lined Case, Marked, c.1910, 5 In.	5040.00

FAIENCE refers to tin-glazed earthenware, especially the wares made in France, Germany, and Scandinavia. It is also correct to say that faience is the same as majolica or Delft, although usually the term refers only to the tin-glazed pottery of the three regions mentioned.

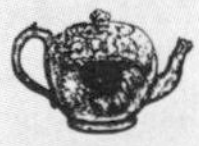

Bookends, Sunflower Shaped, Ladybug, Yellow, Green, Red, Poem, Marked, 1936, 4 ½ x 5 ¼ In.	3000.00
Bowl, Bird In Flight, Copper Luster, Cream Ground, Flared, 17th Century, 13 In.	767.00
Bowl, Dessert, Man, Donkey, Middle East Views, Yellow, Black, Creil, c.1825, 5 In., 6 Piece	236.00
Bowl, Luster Tapestry Scenes, Squat, Louis-Etienne Desmant, c.1900, 9 ⅜ In.	1180.00
Bowl, Yellow, Blue, Green, Red, Brown, Tulips, Leaves, c.1820, 9 In.	130.00
Bulb Pot, Hanging, Blue & White Glaze, Burnt Orange, Flared Sides, Scalloped Edge, 4 ½ x 9 In.	86.00
Candleholder, Figural, Feline Shape, Tails Forms Handle, Happy Face, Painted, France, 1906, 9 ¼ In.	86.00
Charger, Blue, White, Flowers, Leafy Border, Dutch, 12 In.	84.00
Charger, Blue, White, Scalloped Rim, Flower Border, Bird, Insect, c.1790, 13 ¾ In., Pair	1380.00
Figurine, Cat, Sitting, Looking Up, Flowers, 10 In.	165.00

Figurine, Lion, Opposing, Yellow & Black Textured Mane, Tail, Green Plinth Base, 4 x 4 In., Pair	2360.00
Figurine, Parrot, Teal Glaze, Yellow Beak, Feet, Perched, Chinese, 1900s, 9 In., Pair	167.00
Figurine, Roman Warrior, Painted, Continental, 1800s, 17 In.	300.00
Garniture Set, Urn, Vases, Yellow, Green, Apricot, Blue, White, Lion, Ball Finial, 14 x 9 In., 3 Piece	201.00
Jar, Lid, Asian Figure Finial, Signed Base, Dutch, 14 x 6 ½ In.	259.00
Jar, Olive Oil, Oval, Scrollwork, Hunter Killing Deer, Olio De Ifrati, Loop Handles, c.1705, 27 x 21 In.	492.00
Jardiniere, Blue, White Tulips, Stems, Squat, Shouldered, Loop Handles, Inverted Rim, 12 In.	1150.00
Jardiniere, Molded Arches, Scrollwork, Turquoise Ground, Signed, 5 x 6 ¾ In.	215.00
Pitcher, Brown, Green Glaze, Flowers, Faux Spout, 6 ¼ In.	443.00
Pitcher, Figural, Snuff Taker, Tricorn Hat, Buckle Shoes, Plaid Britches, Tree Trunk Handle, 11 In.	426.00
Plaque, Flowers, Leaves, Persia, 14 ¾ x 9 ½ In.	390.00
Plaque, Lion Attacking Deer, Floral Border, Persia, 9 x 14 In.	420.00
Plate, Armorial, Malicorne, Crest Of Brittany, Shaped Rim, Blue, Green Leaves, 9 ⅝ In.	265.00
Plate, Dinner, Multicolor Flowers, Scalloped Rim, Game Cock Mark, 9 ½ In., 10 Piece	976.00
Plate, Man, Dutch Style Hat, Broad Collar, Stylized Flower Border, H. Rhead, Foley, 13 ½ In.	242.00
Plate, Woman, Dutch Style Hat, Stylized Flower Border, Black Ink, H. Rhead, Foley, 13 ½ In.	150.00
Platter, Blue Ground, White Dragons, Gold Center, Continental, 17 In.	300.00
Sculpture, Wall Hanging, Face, Blue Green Glaze, California, 8 x 10 In.	366.00
Tureen, Duck Shape, White, Yellow, Signed Louis Et Felix Kiel, France, 10 x 14 In.	1035.00
Tureen, Lid, Terra-Cotta, Multicolor Enamel, Tin Glaze, Oval, Swags, 11 x 9 In., Pair	190.00
Tureen, Lid, Underplate, Scalloped Edge, Scrolled Handles, Vegetable, Leaf Cluster, 13 In. & 19 In.	575.00
Tureen, Underplate, Rococo, Molded Vegetable, Scrolls, Painted, Strasbourg, 1700s, 23 In.	3438.00
Vase, Art Nouveau, Golden Brown, Relief Mermaids, Marine Life, Marked Vance, 10 In.	123.00
Vase, Crest & Banner, Blue Leaves, White Ground, Italy, 13 ¾ In.	188.00
Vase, Squat, Bulbous, Scrolling Flowers, Mythical Mask, Buff Ground, Blue, 8 ¾ x 9 ¼ In.	345.00
Vase, Wall, Blue, Yellow, Green, Flowers, Geometrics, c.1750, 5 x 8 In.	443.00
Water Jug, Oval, Palm & Scrolled Leaf Pattern, Blue, Orange, Yellow, White Glaze, Italy, c.1950, 12 In.	575.00

FAIRINGS are small souvenir boxes and figurines that were sold at country fairs during the nineteenth century. Most were made in Germany. Reproductions of fairings are being made, especially of the famous *Twelve Months after Marriage* series.

Box, Girl, Sitting On Dresser, Staffordshire, c.1860, 4 In.	85.00
Box, Woman, In Rowboat, Staffordshire, 4 x 3 In.	120.00
Figurine, 3 Pigs, On Log, 4 ½ x 3 In.	59.00
Figurine, Boy, Hugging, Spaniel, Staffordshire, c.1860, 3 x 3 x 2 In.	175.00
Figurine, Cats, In Carriage, 3 ¼ x 2 In.	45.00
Figurine, Kittens, Mama, Germany, 3 ¼ x 2 ½ In.	35.00
Figurine, Last One To Bed, 3 x 3 In.	50.00
Figurine, Pink Pigs, In Basket, Merry Squealers, Germany, 3 ¼ x 2 ¾ x 1 ¾ In.	79.00
Figurine, Pug Dog, Puppies, Germany, 3 x 2 ¾ In.	35.00
Trinket Box, Dresser Mirror, Clock, Ring, c.1890	69.00

FAIRYLAND LUSTER *pieces are included in the Wedgwood category.*

FAMILLE ROSE, *see Chinese Export category.*

FANS have been used for cooling since the days of the ancients. By the eighteenth century, the fan was an accessory for the lady of fashion and very elaborate and expensive fans were made. Sticks were made of ivory or wood, set with jewels or carved. The fans were made of painted silk or paper. Inexpensive paper fans printed with advertising were giveaways in the late nineteenth and early twentieth centuries. Electric fans were introduced in 1882.

Advertising, Shady Lawn Creamery, Mother, Child, Ice Cream, 2-Sided, Cardboard, 1920s, 14 x 8 In.	22.00
Advertising, U.S. Tires, Cars, Open Book, Cardboard, Die Cut, 1920s, 9 x 8 In.	55.00
Bone Sticks, Pastoral Lithograph Scene, Gouache Highlights, Painted, Engraved, Frame, 16 x 23 In.	140.00
Bone, Polished Cotton, Reticulated Sticks, Scroll & Flowers, c.1890, 14 x 8 In.	18.00
Cafe Martin, New York, Folding Wood, Paper, Woman, Sitting, 9 x 17 In.	88.00
Celluloid, Red, White, Blue, c.1935, 4 x 7 In.	45.00
Electric, Airplane, Fuselage Shape, Propeller, Ceiling, Sheet Metal, Aluminum, 27 In.	1475.00
Electric, Brass, 4 Blades, Cage, Western Electric, 16 ½ In.	230.00
Electric, Cast Iron & Metal, Airplane Shape, 2 Blade Propeller, Hanging, 1930s	3300.00
Electric, Emerson, Type 2250, Oscillator, Cast Iron, Spread Base, Box, 1930s, 10 In.	308.00
Electric, Funeral Parlor, Leaf & Vine Framework, Cast Iron, Cutout Scroll Feet, Luminaire, 57 In.	472.00
Electric, General Electric, Oscillating, 1920s, 16 ½ In.	53.00

F

Enamel, Ashtray, Chess Pieces, Orange & White, Brown Mottled Ground, 6 x 5 In.
$75.00

Enamel, Bowl, Lid, Ship, Copper, Rebecca Cauman, Boston, c.1905, 3 ¼ x 5 ½ In.
$1,875.00

Rago Arts & Auction Center

Enamel, Box, Silver, Hinged Lid, Woman, Unicorn, Lion, Austria, c.1910, 1 ¾ In.
$600.00

DuMouchelles Art Gallery

Enamel, Brushpot, Canted Corners, Mother & Child Scenes, Bracket Feet, Chinese, c.1900, 6 ¼ In.
$550.00

Skinner, Inc.

179

Enamel, Plaque, Branches, Abstract Ground, Frame, Edward Winter, 1940s, 20 x 31 ½ In.
$5,938.00

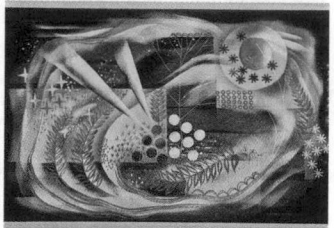

Rago Arts & Auction Center

Enamel, Teapot, Figures In Landscape, Scrolling Flowers, Peking, Chinese, 1700s, 5 In.
$660.00

Cowan's Auctions

Enamel, Vase, Bud, Lavender, Yellow Flowers, Flared, Copper, Limoges, 7 In.
$330.00

DuMouchelles Art Gallery

Erphila Pitcher, Figural, Toucan, Made In Czechoslovakia, 9 x 7 ½ In.
$100.00

Electric, Metal, Spider Web Screen, Bullet Back, Eskimo, USA, 13 x 11 x 9 In.	145.00
Electric, Parlor, 2 Lights, Cast Iron, Ornate Scrolling, Scrolled Tripod Base, 2 Shades, 70 In.	1792.00
Electric, Westinghouse, Mobilaire, 2-Speed, Teal, Floor Model	100.00
Electric, Whiz, Tin Blades, Enameled Base, Black Cage, General Electric, 12 ¼ In.	59.00
Electric, Zephair, 4 Blades, Window, 1950s	85.00
Fly, Clockwork, Cast Iron Base, 2 Oval Blades, 41 In.	1320.00
Ivory Posts, Silk, Flowering Branch, Birds, Peach Shade, Shadowbox Frame, Chinese	908.00
Ivory, Classical Landscape, Riverscape, Paint, Case, c.1860, 13 x 16 In.	266.00
Ivory, Paper, Figures, Landscape, Flowers, Pierced, Watercolor, Chinese, Red Case, c.1660, 12 x 19 In.	885.00
Ivory, Pierced, Carved, Women, Flowers, Duck, Peacock Feathers, Gilt Frame, 12 x 20 In. ..*Illus*	173.00
Mother-Of-Pearl, 17 Sticks, Painted, Courting Scene, Pierced, Gilt, 1800s, 10 x 20 In.	600.00
Mother-Of-Pearl, Paper, Paint, Couples, Garden, Carved Sticks, Signed Lasellar, c.1880, 22 In.	236.00
Mother-Of-Pearl, Silk, Lace, Paint, Boat, Figures, Silvered Sticks, Cozot, Frame, c.1880, 18 In.	354.00
Needlepoint, Ivory, Courting Scene, Flowers, Scrolling, Sticks, Shadowbox Frame, 1800s, 8 x 11 In.	148.00
Paper, Ink, Man Boating, Calligraphy On Reverse, Inscribed, Signed, Wang Tingjue, 1942 ... *Illus*	403.00
Paperboard, Blue Silk Trim, Watercolor Scenes, Girl With Flowers, Girl Sleeping, c.1890, 11 x 8 In.	237.00
Tortoiseshell, Red Sequins, 13 In.	12.00
Wood, Mother-Of-Pearl, Flower Shape, Woman, Exotic, Turned Handle, c.1850, 17 x 9 In., Pair	460.00

FAST FOOD COLLECTIBLES *may be included in several categories, such as Advertising, Coca-Cola, Toy, etc.*

FEDERZEICHNUNG, *see Loetz category.*

FENTON ART GLASS COMPANY was founded in 1905 in Martins Ferry, Ohio, by Frank L. Fenton and his brother, John W. Fenton. They painted decorations on glass blanks made by other manufacturers. In 1907 they opened a factory in Williamstown, West Virginia, and began making glass. The company is still in business, led by Fenton family members, but the company no longer makes art glass. Fenton is noted for early carnival glass produced between 1907 and 1920. Some of these pieces are listed in the Carnival Glass category. Many other types of glass were also made.

Aqua Crest, Pitcher, 1353, Ruffled & Crimped Rim, c.1942	250.00
Ashtray, Flower Form, Black, 3 Legs	18.00
Burmese, Basket, Crimped, Red, Yellow Swirls, 7 In.	125.00
Burmese, Epergne, Flowers, Blue, 9 ½ In., 2 Pieces	150.00
Burmese, Vase, Birds On Branch, Flared, 8 ¼ In.	475.00
Candlestick, Black, Flower Form, 3 Legs, Pair	20.00
Candlestick, Panels, Celestial Blue, 6-Sided Domed Base, Stretch Glass, c.1920, 8 In., Pair	113.00
Candy Jar, Lid, Blue, Urn Shape, Footed, 9 ½ In.	60.00
Coin Dot, Basket, Cranberry, Footed, Clear Handle, 8 In.	45.00
Coin Dot, Jug, Blue, Globular, 7 In.	45.00
Coin Dot, Perfume Bottle, White Opalescent, King's Crown Top, 4 ½ In.	200.00
Daisy & Fern, Cruet, Stopper, Topaz, 6 In.	200.00
Daisy & Fern, Jug, Cranberry Opalescent, 80 Oz.	200.00
Diamond & Rib, Vase, Green, Lime Green Inside, c.1913, 10 ¾ x 3 ½ In.	105.00
Dolphin, Bowl, Aqua Blue, Rolled Edge	35.00
Dolphin, Candy Jar, Cover, Amethyst, Footed, Handles	35.00
Dolphin, Vase, Fan, Jade Green, Footed	65.00
Draped, Pitcher, Cranberry, Ruffled Rim, Footed, Clear Handle, 6 In.	38.00
Elizabeth, Jug, Jade Green, Footed, 48 Oz., 6 ⅜ In.	125.00
Elizabeth, Sherbet, Ruby Red, 5 Oz., 3 ¼ In.	20.00
Elizabeth, Tumbler, Ruby Red, Footed, 9 Oz., 5 ⅜ In.	24.00
Figurine, Bear, Pink, Waving, 4 In.	28.00
Figurine, Happiness Bird, Violets In The Snow, 5 x 4 In.	40.00
Figurine, Luv Bug, Gold, Heart, Robin Spindler, 3 In.	375.00
Figurine, Rooster, Blue, Transparent, 5 In.	25.00
Figurine, Swan, Crystal Velvet, 4 In.	32.00
Florentine Green, Bowl, Flared, Cupped, Stretch Glass, c.1920, 6 x 3 In.	30.00
Florentine Green, Bowl, Open Basket Weave, Stretch Glass, Footed, c.1920, 6 ¾ In.	125.00
Florentine, Vase, Fan, Yellow, 5 ¼ In. ....*Illus*	48.00
Georgian, Creamer, Amber, c.1932	4.00
Hobnail, Bonbon, Milk Glass, Handle, Square, Crimped	18.00
Hobnail, Cake Stand, Milk Glass, Ruffled Rim, 12 ¾ In.	100.00
Hobnail, Decanter, Stopper, Clear	65.00
Hobnail, Jug, Milk Glass, 54 Oz., 8 ½ In.	70.00
Hobnail, Perfume Bottle, Molded, White Over Clear, Blue Stopper, 4 ¼ In., Pair	98.00

Hobnail, Vase, Ruby, Ruffled Rim, 1940s, 3 In.	35.00
Karnak Red, Vase, Hanging Hearts, Cobalt Blue Stem & Foot, 14 In.	10000.00
Peach Crest, Tulip Vase, 1950s, 5 ½ In.	52.00
Pekin Blue, Bowl, Dancing Ladies, Footed, Handles, c.1932, 10 ½ x 4 ½ In.	432.00
Plymouth, Tumbler, Red, 8 Oz., 5 In.	25.00
Poppy, Lamp, Lime Green, Lime Green, 22 In.	157.00
Radiance, Night-Light, Tulips	35.00
Silver Turquoise, Compote, Square Foot, 8 ¼ In.	100.00
Silver Turquoise, Relish, Heart Shape, Crystal Loop Handle, 7 In.	45.00
Stretch Glass, Candy Jar, Lid, Florentine Green, Footed, ½ Lb.	48.00
Stretch Glass, Jug, Green, 7 In.	95.00
Toothpick Holder, Top Hat, Pink, Ruffled Rim, Diamond Body, Pink, 1930s, 3 In.	24.00
Top Hat, Hobnail, Opalescent White, 2 ½ In.	20.00
Twilight Blue, Basket, Tulips, 10 ½ In.	55.00
Twilight Blue, Lamp, Tulips, 21 In.	200.00
Valencia, Candy Dish, Lid, Vivid Orange, 1960s, 6 ¾ x 5 ½ In.	30.00
Vase, Amberina, Tapered, Footed, Ruffled Rim, 8 In.	85.00
Vase, Fan, Paneled Foot, Marigold Iridescent, Stretch Glass, 1930s, 6 In.	40.00
Vase, Mosaic, Orange, Red, Blue, Green, Spun Threading, Purple Iridescent Inside, c.1925, 5 ¼ In.	2370.00
Wisteria, Ashtray, No. 556, 1920s, 5 In.	425.00

FIESTA, the colorful dinnerware, was introduced in 1936 by the Homer Laughlin China Co., redesigned in 1969, and withdrawn in 1973. It was reissued again in 1986 in different colors and is still being made. New colors, including some that are similar to old colors, are introduced regularly. The simple design was characterized by a band of concentric circles beginning at the rim. Cups had full-circle handles until 1969, when partial-circle handles were made. Harlequin and Riviera were related wares. For more prices, go to kovels.com.

fiesta

Apricot, Bowl, Cereal, 6 ⅛ In.	12.00
Apricot, Cup	7.00
Apricot, Plate, Dinner, 10 ½ In.	15.00
Apricot, Plate, Salad, 7 ¼ In.	12.00
Apricot, Platter, 11 ½ In.	25.00
Apricot, Sauceboat	35.00
Apricot, Saucer	4.00
Black, Bowl, Cereal, 6 ½ In.	5.00
Black, Creamer, Disk, 3 ¼ In.	25.00
Chartreuse, Ashtray, 5 ½ In.	37.00
Cobalt Blue, Bowl, Cereal, 6 ⅞ In.	5.00
Cobalt Blue, Plate, Dinner, 10 ½ In.	8.00
Cobalt Blue, Plate, Salad, 7 ¼ In.	5.00
Cobalt Blue, Salt & Pepper	9.00
Cobalt Blue, Saucer	2.00
Gray, Bowl, Cereal, 6 ⅞ In.	15.00
Gray, Creamer, Disk, 3 ¼ In.	62.00
Gray, Plate, Salad, 7 ¼ In.	13.00
Ivory, Mustard	128.00
Red, Mixing Bowl, No. 4, c.1940	300.00
Rose, Bowl, Cereal, 6 ⅞ In.	47.00
Rose, Cup & Saucer	8.00
Rose, Eggcup	48.00
Rose, Plate, Dinner, 10 ½ In.	65.00
Shamrock, Bowl, Cereal, 6 ⅞ In.	23.00
Shamrock, Plate, Dinner, 10 ½ In.	35.00
Shamrock, Snack Plate & Cup	21.00
Turquoise, Bowl, Cereal, 6 ⅞ In.	5.00
Turquoise, Cup & Saucer	7.00
Turquoise, Mixing Bowl, No. 4, c.1936	104.00
Turquoise, Plate, Dinner, 10 ½ In.	6.00
Turquoise, Plate, Salad, 7 ¼ In.	5.00
Yellow, Bowl, Cereal, 6 ⅞ In.	18.00
Yellow, Cup & Saucer	12.00
Yellow, Pitcher, Disk, 6 In.	18.00
Yellow, Plate, Dinner, 10 ½ In.	15.00
Yellow, Plate, Salad, 7 ¼ In.	6.00
Yellow, Saucer	2.00
Yellow, Sugar, Lid	10.00

Eskimo, Doll, Wood, Carved Painted Face Mask, Fur Costume, Inuit Tribe, c.1910, 23 In.
$448.00

Theriault's

Eskimo, Figurine, Man Riding Sea Lion, Carved Stone, 1900s, 9 ½ x 4 ½ In.
$184.00

Allard Auctions

Eskimo, Mask, Stone, Carved, 4 ¼ x 3 ¾ In.
$248.00

Old Barn Auction

Fan, Ivory, Pierced, Carved, Women, Flowers, Duck, Peacock Feathers, Gilt Frame, 12 x 20 In.
$173.00

James D. Julia Auctioneers

Fan, Paper, Ink, Man Boating, Calligraphy On Reverse, Inscribed, Signed, Wang Tingjue, 1942
$403.00

James D. Julia Auctioneers

Fenton, Florentine, Vase, Fan, Yellow, 5 ¼ In.
$48.00

Ruby Lane, Inc.

Findlay, Celery Vase, Onyx, Opal Glass, Copper Leafy Flower, 4 In.
$1,553.00

Early Auction Co.

Findlay, Mustard, Floradine, Frosted Red, White Flowers & Leaves, 4 In.
$1,725.00

Early Auction Co.

FINCH *see Kay Finch category.*

FINDLAY ONYX AND FLORADINE are two similar types of glass made by Dalzell, Gilmore and Leighton Co. of Findlay, Ohio, about 1889. Onyx is a patented yellowish white opaque glass with raised silver daisy decorations. A few rare pieces were made of rose, amber, orange, or purple glass. Floradine is made of cranberry-colored glass with an opalescent white raised floral pattern and a satin finish. The same molds were used for both types of glass.

Celery Vase, Onyx, Opal Glass, Copper Leafy Flower, 4 In. ....*Illus*	1553.00
Celery Vase, Onyx, Silver Highlights, Flowers & Stems, Bulbous, Cylindrical Neck, 6 In.	115.00
Celery Vase, Red Raspberry Flowers, Leaves, Ball Shape, Neck, Shaped Rim, 6 In.	1150.00
Creamer, Onyx, Opal Glass, Silver Flowers & Stems, Opalescent Handle, 4 ½ In.	259.00
Creamer, Onyx, Orange Cream, Orange Flowers, Fluted Neck, Clear Handle, 4 In.	1638.00
Creamer, Onyx, Raspberry Flowers, Pink Onyx Ground, Amber Handle, 5 In.	4025.00
Muffineer, Floradine, Cranberry Flowers, Pink Ground, 5 ½ In.	6900.00
Muffineer, Onyx, Opalescent, Platinum Luster Flowers, Bulbous, Fluted Neck, 5 In.	199.00
Mustard, Floradine, Frosted Red, White Flowers & Leaves, 4 In. ....*Illus*	1725.00
Mustard, Onyx, Red Raspberry, Opal Flowers, 3 ½ In. ....*Illus*	2300.00
Mustard, Onyx, White, Ruby Purple Flowers & Leaves, Bulbous, Metal Lid, 3 ½ In.	3510.00
Pitcher, Onyx, Raised Silver Flowers, Applied Opalescent Handle, 4 ½ In. ....*Illus*	201.00
Saltshaker, Floradine, Opal Body, Cranberry Flowers, 3 In.	5750.00
Saltshaker, Onyx, Copper & Amber Flowers & Leaves, Trailing Stems, Oval, Metal Cap	1495.00
Spooner, Floradine, Frosted Cranberry, White Flowers, 4 ½ In.	1265.00
Spooner, Floradine, Satin Red Glass, White Flower Inclusions, 4 ½ In.	460.00
Spooner, Onyx, Opal Glass, Silver Design, Flowers, Stems, Ribbed Neck, 4 ¼ In.	115.00
Spooner, Onyx, Silver Flowers, 3 ¾ In. ....*Illus*	259.00
Spooner, Opal Glass, Copper Leafy Flowers, Bulbous, Shaped Rim, 4 In.	1380.00
Sugar Shaker, Onyx, Opal Glass, Silver Inclusions, Ribbed Neck, Swollen Lip, 5 ½ In.	230.00
Sugar Shaker, Raspberry, Pink Opal, Flowers, Bulbous, Lobed Neck, Swollen Rim, 5 ½ In.	11500.00
Sugar, Floradine, Satin Red, White Flowers, Leaves, Trailing Stems, Bulbous, Cover, Ball Finial, 6 In..	633.00
Sugar, Lid, Cranberry & White, Scrolling Stems, Blossoms, Ball Finial, 6 In.	748.00
Sugar, Onyx, Opal Glass, Silver Inclusions, 6 In.	173.00
Sugar, Onyx, Opal, Copper Color, Flowers, Trailing Stems, Bulbous, Lid, 6 In.	1725.00
Syrup, Onyx, Opalescent, Platinum Luster Flowers, Fluted Metal Lid, 6 ¾ In.	234.00
Syrup, Opal Glass, Silver Design, Loop Handle, Flip Lid, 7 In.	230.00
Toothpick Holder, Floradine, Stain Red Glass, White Leafy Stems, 2 ½ In.	2070.00
Toothpick Holder, Onyx, Oval, Scalloped Rim, 2 ½ In.	316.00
Tumbler, Floradine, Barrel Shape, Red, White Flowers, 3 ¾ In. ....*Illus*	978.00
Tumbler, Onyx, Barrel Shaped, Copper Flower Design, 3 ¾ In.	1610.00
Tumbler, Onyx, Yellow, Harvest Gold & Orange Flowers, Barrel Shape, 5 In.	1170.00
Tumbler, Peach, Orange, Copper, Flowers, Stems, Wheat, Barrel Shape, 3 ¾ In.	3335.00
Vase, Translucent Red, White Flowers, Bulbous, Shaped Neck, 4 ½ In.	690.00

FIREFIGHTING equipment of all types is wanted, from fire marks to uniforms to toy fire trucks. It is said that every little boy wanted to be a fireman or a train engineer 75 years ago and the collectors today reflect this interest.

Alarm, Telephone, Utica Fire Alarm Co.	450.00
Ax Head, Viking Style, Cast Iron, 11 ¾ In.	180.00
Ax, Parade, Viking Style, 35 ½ In.	840.00
Ax, Wood Handle, Warren Maker, 22 In. ....*Illus*	40.00
Badge, Laurel, 1, S.F.E. Co., Silvered Brass, Embossed, Black Accents, c.1900, 2 ⅕ In.	75.00
Banner, Crossed Helmet, Trumpet, Ax, Ladder, Pike Pole, Linen, 26 x 35 In.	2310.00
Banner, Welcome Brave Boys, Fireman, Saving Child From Fire, Linen, 23 ½ x 36 In.	83.00
Bell, Fire Truck, Brass, 11 ½ x 15 In.	550.00
Bell, Fire Truck, Nickel Plated, Brass Eagle Finial, Mounting Bracket	715.00
Bell, Fire Truck, Nickel Plated, Brass Finial	715.00
Bell, Muffin, Fire Alarm, Wood Turned Handle, 8 ½ In.	358.00
Bell, Truck, Nickel Plated Brass, Eagle Finial, Brass Base, 22 x 12 In. ....*Illus*	990.00
Belt Buckle, Parade, Erie, Pa., Nickel Over Brass, Embossed Torch, Ax	55.00
Belt, Parade, Leather, Embossed Flowers, Active Company, Relief Crossed Trumpets, Ax, Torch..	220.00
Belt, Parade, Leather, William Penn Lettering, Red, Gold, c.1850, 42 In.	178.00
Box, Fire Alarm, Cast Iron, Applied Instructions, 17 x 23 In.	605.00
Box, Fire Alarm, Cast Iron, Break Glass Pull Down Hook Sign, Key, 1889, 18 ¼ In.	330.00
Box, Fire Alarm, Cast Iron, Door Key, 1889, 18 ¼ In. ....*Illus*	330.00
Box, Fire Alarm, Cast Iron, Red, Black Paint, 17 x 23 In.	605.00

Box, Fire Alarm, Red, Pedestal Base, 2-Sided, Gamewell 1584, 124 In.	1440.00
Box, Fire Alarm, The Carl, No. 5, Aluminum, Carl Signal Co., Akron, Ohio, 15 ¾ In. ....*Illus*	413.00
Box, Fire Alarm, Wood, Key, Red Paint, Gold Stenciled Letters, 1888, 9 x 13 ¾ In.	220.00
Bucket, Blue Leather, Gold Stenciled Hotel Block, No. 4, Handle, 13 ½ In.	424.00
Bucket, Chemical Fire, Worcester, Metal, Glass Insert, 11 In.	60.00
Bucket, Fire, Industrial, Galvanized, Red Paint, Rounded Bottom, 13 In., Pair	330.00
Bucket, Fire, Industrial, Metal, Cone Shape, Embossed B & O, Hanging Ring, 16 In.	193.00
Bucket, Flat Swing Handle, Buckminster Family, 1811, 12 In., Pair	1416.00
Bucket, Leather, B.M.C. No. 19, Painted, Handle, 1825, 12 ½ In. ....*Illus*	440.00
Bucket, Leather, Brown, Cone Shape, Thos. Kinne, No. 2, Gold Paint Scrolls, 12 ½ In.	649.00
Bucket, Leather, Cone Shape, Handle, Iron Rings, Gilt, Scrolling Leaves, J.S. Carter, 1827, 12 x 8 In.	805.00
Bucket, Leather, Decorated, Painted Green, N.D. Appleton, New England, 1822, 11 ½ In.	3422.00
Bucket, Leather, Eagle, Shield, Marked Joshua Staples, 1836, 12 In.	7080.00
Bucket, Leather, Gold Painted W.B., Wood Staved, Rawhide Handles, 13 In.	248.00
Bucket, Leather, Paint, Conical, Swing Handle, A. Wendell, New Hampshire, c.1825, 13 x 19 In., Pair	17700.00
Bucket, Leather, Painted, Green, Red, Gilt, No. 1, No. 2, J. Emerson, 1833, 12 In., Pair	7110.00
Bucket, Leather, Red Interior, 1800s, 19 x 9 ½ In.	316.00
Bucket, Leather, Red Paint, Handle, c.1800, 17 In., Pair	826.00
Bucket, Leather, Red, Black, Painted Vines, E.N.C. Monogram, 1830, 13 In.	1000.00
Bucket, Leather, Stencil, Painted Abraham Wendell 1825, Handle, 12 ½ x 18 ¾ In.	2360.00
Bucket, Leather, Vines, Painted, 1830, 13 In.	1100.00
Bucket, Leather, Yellow Medallion, Marked John Cornelius, No. 1 & 2, 1851, 12 In., Pair	3792.00
Bucket, Red Leather, Armorial Crest, Stamped N, 15 ½ In., Pair	661.00
Cannon, Brass, Nickel Plate, Deluge Water Cannon, Wood Base, Salesman's Sample, 21 In.	12100.00
Cart, Hose, Hand Drawn, Wood Spoke Wheels, Red Paint, 53 x 56 x 91 In.	390.00
Clock, Fire Alarm, Cherry Cabinet, Electrical, Marked Gamewell, c.1870, 11 ½ x 24 In.	9900.00
Clock, Fire Alarm, Cherry, Electrical, 110/220/500 Volts, 24 x 11 x 5 In.	9900.00
Dress Uniform, Hook & Ladder Co. No. 1, Hat, Blue Wool, Blazer, Vest, Pants, Phil., c.1900	94.00
Extinguisher, Blue Jay, Tin Tube, Redwood Chemical Co., Newburg, N.Y., 22 In. ....*Illus*	85.00
Extinguisher, Chemical, Embossed Glass Bottle, Lid, Top, Ajax, 12 ½ In.	303.00
Extinguisher, Copper, Holloway, July 9, 1878.	990.00
Extinguisher, Excelsior Dry Compound, Tin Tube, Patriotic, 22 In. ....*Illus*	150.00
Extinguisher, Glass, Contains Chemical, Stopper, Central & Northwest Railway, 17 ½ In.	1020.00
Extinguisher, Minimax, Wall Mount, Bracket, 32 ½ In. ....*Illus*	270.00
Extinguisher, Nickel, Over Brass, Strap Hanger, Pirsch-Standard	270.00
Extinguisher, On Wheels, Red Paint, Metal Tank, Foamite Chemical, 34 x 63 In.	360.00
Extinguisher, Rockford's Kalamazoo, Hand, Cobalt Blue Glass, 10 ½ In. ....*Illus*	480.00
Extinguisher, Utica No. 4, Brass, Hose, Nozzle	270.00
Fire Escape, Davy Automatic Safety, Syracuse, N.Y., 6 ¼ In. Diam.	220.00
Fire Mark, Clasp Hands, Cast Iron, 9 ¼ x 4 ¾ In.	360.00
Fire Mark, Clasp Hands, Germantown Mutual Fire, Cast Iron, 1843, 11 x 8 In.	60.00
Fire Mark, Germantown Mutual Fire 1843, Cast Iron, 11 ⅛ x 8 In.	60.00
Gas Mask, Acme, All Purpose, Case, 12 ½ x 14 ½ In.	55.00
Globe, Fire Lantern, Popcorn, Checker Pattern	165.00
Grenade Set, Paneled, Embossed, Cobalt Blue, Wire Rack, S.F. Hayward, Pat. 1871, 6 ½ In., 3 Piece	960.00
Grenade, Cobalt Blue Glass, Diamond Embossed, 7 ¼ In.	358.00
Grenade, Globular, Vertical Ribbing, Green Glass, 5 ½ In.	440.00
Grenade, Hazelton's High Pressure Chemical Fire Keg, Amber, Brass Neck Ring, c.1890, 11 In. .. *Illus*	489.00
Grenade, Healy's Hand, Yellow Amber, Applied Mouth, c.1885, 11 In. ....*Illus*	1265.00
Helmet, Aluminum, Leather Front, Charleston F.D., 1930s, Size 7 ¼	295.00
Helmet, Atlantic Hose 1, Painted 1780, Lion Finial, Migeod Leather, Cloth Liner	1430.00
Helmet, Cairn's Aluminum Senator, Ladder 1, Anthony CFD, Leather Front ....*Illus*	150.00
Helmet, Chief, High Eagle, Steam Fire Engine, Presentation Plaque, Wilson, N.Y.F.D., 1894 .. *Illus*	5100.00
Helmet, Cortlandt 1 PFD, Running Fireman Finial, White Leather	825.00
Helmet, Leather, Beaver Finial, Leather Front Shield, Lucerne No. 1	6050.00
Helmet, Leather, Bobbie Chief Engineer GFD	1320.00
Helmet, Leather, Boston Fire Volunteer's Pin, c.1810	1540.00
Helmet, Leather, Brass Eagle, Wilson, c.1930	295.00
Helmet, Leather, Dog Finial, Foreman 4 N.F.E., On Shield, Gratacap, 1850s	4675.00
Helmet, Leather, Eagle Finial, Poor Boy Style, Empire 1 F.H.W. Shield, Wilson, c.1835	1430.00
Helmet, Leather, Fox Finial, Franklin 1 Fire Co., Shield 1867, Cloth Liner, Cairns	4400.00
Helmet, Leather, Greyhound Finial, Zhilman, 5 J.H. Cairins Tag	3300.00
Helmet, Leather, Lion Finial, Atlantic Hose 1 Shield, Cloth Liner, Migeod	1430.00
Helmet, Leather, Painted, Lion Finial, Metal Shield, Fairmount 2 Fire Co., 1852 ....*Illus*	2200.00
Helmet, Leather, Seahorse Finial, Leather Shield Enterprise 1 Engine, Gratacap	6050.00
Helmet, Lucerne No. 1 Quebec, Beaver Finial, Leather Front Shield	6050.00

Findlay, Mustard, Onyx, Red Raspberry, Opal Flowers, 3 ½ In.
$2,300.00

Early Auction Co.

Findlay, Pitcher, Onyx, Raised Silver Flowers, Applied Opalescent Handle, 4 ½ In.
$201.00

Early Auction Co.

Findlay, Spooner, Onyx, Silver Flowers, 3 ¾ In.
$259.00

Early Auction Co.

Findlay, Tumbler, Floradine, Barrel Shape, Red, White Flowers, 3 ¾ In.
$978.00

Early Auction Co.

F

Firefighting, Ax, Wood Handle, Warren Maker, 22 In.
$40.00

Showtime Auction Sevices

Firefighting, Bell, Truck, Nickel Plated Brass, Eagle Finial, Brass Base, 22 x 12 In.
$990.00

Showtime Auction Sevices

Firefighting, Box, Fire Alarm, Cast Iron, Door Key, 1889, 18 ¼ In.
$330.00

Showtime Auction Sevices

Firefighting, Box, Fire Alarm, The Carl, No. 5, Aluminum, Carl Signal Co., Akron, Ohio, 15 ¾ In.
$413.00

Showtime Auction Sevices

Helmet, Parade, Metal, Top Spike, Active A Hook & Ladder, Cobleskill, McLilley & Co., c.1890.	1680.00
Helmet, Portland 1891, High Eagle Finial, Parade Torch Topper, Leather, Cloth Liner	725.00
Helmet, Red Leather, High Eagle Finial, Foreman 1 P.G.F.D. Shield, California, Cairns	650.00
Helmet, Red Leather, Lion Finial, Fairmont 2 Fire Co. Shield, Cairns, 1852	2310.00
Helmet, White Leather, Running Fireman Finial, Cortlandt 1 PFD	825.00
Helmet, White Leather, Serpent Finial, 64 Comb Design, Foreman 4 W.F. Co.	11000.00
Hook, Fireman's, Iron, Hand Forged, 10 ½ In.	330.00
Hose Wagon, Horse Drawn, Gleason, Type 610, Plymouth, Mass., 1898, 72 x 72 x 127 In.	24750.00
Hose Washer, Steel, 39 x 35 In.	303.00
Hose, Leather, Riveted, Male, Female Couplers, c.1850, 9 ½ Ft.	715.00
Hydrant, Aluminum, Metal, Fluted Column, Salesman's Sample, 15 In.	1430.00
Kit, Shur Stop For Fire, Metal Case, 6 Extinguishers, International Fire Equipment Corp., 12 x 8 In.	165.00
Ladder, Trussed, Outside Pinstripe, Salesman's Sample, Seagrave & Co, Ohio, 47 In.	1430.00
Lantern, Brass, Blown Glass, Handle, 18 In.	325.00
Lantern, Brass, Cobalt, Clear Globe, Etched Union 3, Pa., c.1874, 13 In.	2252.00
Lantern, Brass, Embossed Dietz, Seagrave Co., Columbus, Ohio, c.1907, 18 ½ x 7 ¼ In.	266.00
Lantern, Brass, Hot Blast, Clear Globe, Wind Guard, Bail Handle, Hook, Dietz King, c.1925, 19 x 6 In.	403.00
Lantern, Brass, Hot Blast, Red Globe, Wind Guard, Bail Handle, Dietz Queen, c.1920, 18 x 6 In.	518.00
Lantern, Chief's, Brass, Green, Over Clear Glass, C.T. Ham Mfg. Co.	780.00
Lantern, Copper, Blue Glass Globe, Wristlet Handle, 18 In.	780.00
Lantern, DeVoursney, Williams, W.M.W., Etched Glass, Eagle Finial, 18 ½ In. .... *Illus*	1440.00
Lantern, Eclipse, Brass, Ruby Glass, Fire Extinguisher Co., Chicago, Pat. Sept. 21, 1886, 20 In. ...... *Illus*	935.00
Lantern, Iron, Hot Blast, Tubular, Clear Globe, Wire Guard, Bail Handle, Dietz King, c.1925, 19 x 6 In.	173.00
Lantern, Metal, Etched Glass Globe, Engraved Kingsford Fire Co., Frame J.H. Kelly	717.00
Lantern, Nickel Plated, Water Shield Embossed White, Patent Aug. 27.1907, Dietz King	540.00
Lantern, Steel, Copper, Red Globe, Embossed Seagrave Co., Patent March 21, 1893, Dietz King	660.00
Nozzle, Adjustable, 2 Outlets, Handle, Wonder Spray Nozzle, Pat. July 31, 1894, 7 In.	440.00
Nozzle, Brass, Colt, Shutoff, Rubberized Handles, Tip, Engraved N.F.D., 19 ½ In.	270.00
Nozzle, Brass, Double Handled Cord, Wrapped, Foamite Trade Mark, 40 ½ In.	193.00
Nozzle, Brass, Handles, Shutoff, Stamped M.F.D. 33 & 8TPI, 35 In.	275.00
Nozzle, Brass, Leather Handles & Shutoff, Eastern Coupling Co., Patent May 1897, 20 In.	390.00
Nozzle, Brass, Leather Handles, Fabric Covered Shaft, S.F. Hayward & Co., c.1860, 31 ½ In. .... *Illus*	120.00
Nozzle, Brass, Leather, Handles, C. Callahan Co., Boston, 21 ½ In.	990.00
Nozzle, Brass, Lift Handle, Valve, 7 ½ In.	550.00
Nozzle, Brass, Nickel, Shutoff Marked Reliance Pat April 21, 1898, 8 ¾ In.	385.00
Nozzle, Brass, Rotating Collar, Stamped Elkhart, 7 In.	300.00
Nozzle, Brass, Shutoff, Base Marked Fireboat 2, c.1880, 26 In.	420.00
Nozzle, Brass, Shutoff, Rubberized Handles, Tip, Engraved N.F.D., Colt, 19 ½ In.	270.00
Nozzle, Handles, Shutoff, Stamped M.F.D. 33, 8TPI, 35 In.	275.00
Nozzle, Nickel, Steamer, Leather Shaft, Samuel Eastman & Co., Coupling Co. Pat. April 7, 1874, 31 In.	1870.00
Nozzle, Nickel, Steamer, Riveted Leather Shaft, R.I. Coupling Co., c.1874, 30 ½ In.	1870.00
Paperweight, Fire Hose Wagon, Franklin Fire Co., Pa., Photograph, Glass, 4 x 2 ½ In.	240.00
Poster, Midnight Alarm, Fireman, In Fire, New York Fire Dept., Lithograph, Frame, c.1950, 27 x 21 In.	1121.00
Pumper, Handle, Triumph Hand Tub, Embossed Seaver & Deming Mfg., Salem, Oh., 36 x 78 In. .	2200.00
Register, Fire Alarm, Reel, Muffin Bell, Punch Style, Gamewell, Pat. 1902, 49 In.	300.00
Sign, Fireman's Top Hat, Pine, Red, Leather Band, Bowery Fireman's Supply, c.1890, 31 x 25 In.	2588.00
Sign, National Fire Of Hartford Insurance, Tin Lithograph, Liberty, Flag, Eagle, 24 x 21 In.	1659.00
Siren, Hand Crank, Sterling Silver, Inter-State Machine Products Co.	720.00
Street Lamp, Ruby Glass Lens, Aluminum Case, Gamewell, 15 In.	550.00
Take-Up Reel, Alarm Register, Brass, Winding Mechanism, Gamewell, 7 ½ In.	210.00
Torch, Engineer's, Brass, 15 In.	240.00
Torch, Hand-Lathed Brass, Cast Iron Spike, 1810-30, 30 In.	468.00
Torch, Parade, Brass, c.1825, 29 In.	495.00
Torch, Parade, Brass, Cast Iron Spike, c.1820, 30 In.	468.00
Torch, Parade, Brass, Pair	715.00
Truck, American LaFrance Pumper, Red, No. 75-3786, Lake Placid, N.Y., 1922, 80 x 96 x 240 In.	38500.00
Truck, Pumper, Seagrave, Canopy Cab, Model 66ES, Liberty Fire Co., 1939, 105 x 280 In.	5100.00
Trumpet, Collapsible, Tin, 17 In.	162.00
Trumpet, Corrugated Bell, Fred Miller Style, 18 In. .... *Illus*	540.00
Trumpet, Presentation, Nickel Plate, Geometrics, Flowers, Fluted Bell, Franklin Fire Co. No. 10, 22 In.	1440.00
Trumpet, Presentation, Silver Plate, Embossed Woman, Eagle Tassel Ring, Union Hose Co., 2, 21 In..	6050.00
Trumpet, Presentation, Silver Plate, Engraved, Inscription, Pennsylvania 1899, 21 In. .... *Illus*	1200.00
Trumpet, Red Paint, Gilt Stencil, 18 ½ In.	649.00
Trumpet, Silver Plate, Union Fire Co., 1869, 20 ½ x 8 In.	2844.00
Trumpet, Silver, Chased Designs, E.D. Mountney, Victorian, 21 ½ In.	1044.00
Trumpet, Tin, Folded Seam, 17 ½ In.	220.00

FIREPLACES were used to cook food and to heat the American home in past centuries. Many types of tools and equipment were used. Andirons held the logs in place, firebacks reflected the heat into the room, and tongs were used to move either fuel or food. Many types of spits and roasting jacks were made and may be listed in the Kitchen category.

Andirons, Bell Metal, Chippendale, Double Urn Top, 18 ¾ x 18 ½ In.	472.00
Andirons, Bell Metal, Lemon Finial, Slipper Feet, 17 In.	384.00
Andirons, Brass, Arts & Crafts, Pierced Sunflower Roundel, c.1910, 28 x 23 In.	460.00
Andirons, Brass, Cannonball Finials, Raised Cabriole Legs, 21 ½ x 22 In.	431.00
Andirons, Brass, Cast, Turned, Cabriole Legs, Spurs, Ball Feet, 12 ½ x 14 ¾ In.	24.00
Andirons, Brass, Chippendale Style, Ribbed Oval Finial, Arch Legs, Claw Feet, c.1950, 21 x 24 In.	189.00
Andirons, Brass, Corrugated Arch Front, Lobed Onion Finials, Tiffany, c.1915, 23 x 8 ½ In.	31250.00
Andirons, Brass, Double Lemon Top, Spurred Cabriole Legs, Ball Feet, Faceted Base, c.1815, 24 ½ In.	338.00
Andirons, Brass, Faceted Ball Standards, Scrolled Legs, Button Feet, Iron Billet Bars, c.1850, 19 In.	239.00
Andirons, Brass, Faceted Urn Finial, Columnar Standard, Square Base, c.1800, 21 In.	299.00
Andirons, Brass, Federal, Acorn Finial, c.1820, 17 ½ In.	813.00
Andirons, Brass, Federal, Turned Shaft, Spurs, Arched Legs, Ball Feet, c.1800, 18 x 9 In.	549.00
Andirons, Brass, Federal, Urn Top, Slipper Feet, New York, 26 x 22 In.	1416.00
Andirons, Brass, Iron, Ball Top, Tapered Goose Neck Shaft, Arched Legs, c.1700, 29 x 14 In.	540.00
Andirons, Brass, Iron, Cabriole Legs, Paw Feet, Satyr Mask, Ring Pull, Acorn Finial, c.1900, 21 x 22 In.	307.00
Andirons, Brass, Iron, Knife Blade, Urn Finials, Penny Feet, 21 x 16 In.	1062.00
Andirons, Brass, Iron, Knife Blade, Urn Top, Medallion, Curved Legs, Penny Feet, 21 x 10 In.	431.00
Andirons, Brass, Iron, Lion Mask Finial, Ribbed Ball & Baluster Shaft, Scroll Base, 1800s, 24 ¾ In.	615.00
Andirons, Brass, Iron, Queen Anne, Urn Tip, Brass, Iron, c.1760, 16 ¼ In.	237.00
Andirons, Brass, Iron, Urn Top, Acorn Finials, Scallop Border, Arched Legs, c.1785, 23 In.	533.00
Andirons, Brass, Lemon Finials, Early 19th Century, 19 In.	181.00
Andirons, Brass, Lighthouse Shape, c.1925, 13 ½ In.	266.00
Andirons, Brass, Rampant Lion, Scrolling Base, Cast Iron Legs, 13 x 17 ½ In.	408.00
Andirons, Brass, Strapwork Base, Pierced, Tassel Shape Skirt, Vase Shape, Bun Feet, c.1900, 25 In.	1168.00
Andirons, Brass, Stylized Dog, c.1900, 18 In.	700.00
Andirons, Brass, Turned Column, Bulbous, Stirrup Leg, Ball Foot, Federal Style, 14 x 8 In.	71.00
Andirons, Brass, Urn Finial, 23 x 13 In.	59.00
Andirons, Brass, Urn Top, Figure Eight Scroll Feet, c.1810, 26 In.	153.00
Andirons, Brass, Woman's Head Finial, Woman & Tree Of Life, Arched Base, Belgium, 20 ½ In.	115.00
Andirons, Bronze, Animal Paw Feet, Acanthus, Curved Finials, 21 x 11 In.	127.00
Andirons, Bronze, Columnar, Gadrooned Capital, Fluted Shaft, Pine Needles, Leaves, c.1900, 29 ½ In.	889.00
Andirons, Bronze, Crowned Woman, Dragons, Flame Finial, c.1900, 17 ½ x 12 In.	173.00
Andirons, Bronze, Federal, Lion Bust, 27 ½ In.	115.00
Andirons, Bronze, Horned Owls, Entwined Snakes, Blocked Base, c.1925, 20 x 14 x 4 In.	5975.00
Andirons, Cast Iron, Aesthetic Movement, Parcel Gilt Leaves, Embossed, Painted, c.1870, 23 ½ In.	750.00
Andirons, Cast Iron, Anchor Shape, 22 ½ x 29 In.	767.00
Andirons, Cast Iron, Ball Finial, Bradley & Hubbard, 24 In.	92.00
Andirons, Cast Iron, Baseball Players, 19 ½ In.	2530.00
Andirons, Cast Iron, Black Man, Waistcoat, Hands On Knees, c.1900, 16 ½ In.	889.00
Andirons, Cast Iron, Black Man, Woman, Seated Position, Painted Black, 16 x 16 ½ In.	295.00
Andirons, Cast Iron, Black Musicians Playing Banjo, 18 x 20 In.	767.00
Andirons, Cast Iron, Bulldog Shaped, Arched Legs, 24 ½ In.	826.00
Andirons, Cast Iron, Duck, 14 x 32 In.	384.00
Andirons, Cast Iron, Fiddlehead Top, Black Paint, 17 ¼ x 16 ⅝ In.	356.00
Andirons, Cast Iron, Figural, Hessian Soldiers, Marching, Multicolor, 19 In.	410.00
Andirons, Cast Iron, Hessian Soldier, Paint, 20 x 19 In.	489.00
Andirons, Cast Iron, Hessian Soldiers, 19 In.	417.00
Andirons, Cast Iron, Hessian Soldiers, Marked M. Bibi, c.1900, 19 ½ x 18 In.	295.00
Andirons, Cast Iron, Hessian, Marching, 20 x 18 In.	83.00
Andirons, Cast Iron, Indian Warrior, c.1900, 18 ¼ In.	1778.00
Andirons, Cast Iron, Indians, Standing, c.1910, 20 In.	345.00
Andirons, Cast Iron, Leg Billet Bar Cast, Curved Legs, Tapered Vertical Shaft, Ring Finial, 11 x 9 ¾ In.	59.00
Andirons, Cast Iron, Owls, Perched On Gnarled Limb, Glass Eyes, Stamped, 14 ¾ x 9 ¼ In.	430.00
Andirons, Cast Iron, Santa Claus, 14 ¾ In.	330.00
Andirons, Cast Iron, Shell Shape, White Paint, c.1920, 12 x 8 ½ In.	660.00
Andirons, Cast Iron, Snake Shape, Tall, Serpentine, Arched Legs, c.1900, 23 ¾ x 17 In.	2328.00
Andirons, Cast Iron, Sun Face, Marked, Raised B&H, Bradley & Hubbard, 16 ¾ x 9 ½ In. ... *Illus*	504.00
Andirons, Cast Iron, Trout, 12 x 15 In.	460.00
Andirons, Cast Iron, Turquoise Enamel Front Square Plates, c.1950, 9 ¾ x 18 ½ In.	1098.00
Andirons, Cat, Seated, Paw On Ball, 7 x 23 In.	590.00
Andirons, Fire Deer, Cast Iron, Signed, Russel Wright, 1930, 15 x 21 In. ... *Illus*	9375.00
Andirons, Gilt Metal, Eagle Head Handles, Plume Finial, Scroll Tripod Base, 23 x 13 ½ In.	936.00

Firefighting, Bucket, Leather, B.M.C. No. 19, Painted, Handle, 1825, 12 ½ In. $440.00

Showtime Auction Sevices

Firefighting, Extinguisher, Blue Jay, Tin Tube, Redwood Chemical Co., Newburg, N.Y., 22 In. $85.00

Showtime Auction Sevices

TIP

Don't overclean hardware, andirons, or other old brass objects. Clean off the worst, but don't try to make them look brand new.

F

FIREPLACE

F

Firefighting, Extinguisher, Excelsior Dry Compound, Tin Tube, Patriotic, 22 In. $150.00

Showtime Auction Sevices

Firefighting, Extinguisher, Minimax, Wall Mount, Bracket, 32 ½ In. $270.00

Showtime Auction Sevices

TIP

Andirons get tarnished and covered with resin from the smoke so they should be cleaned with liquid metal polish and 0000-grade steel wool.

Andirons, Iron, Baroque, Scroll Swing Arms, France, c.1890, 41 ½ In.	118.00
Andirons, Iron, Brass, Art Deco, Swollen U-Shape, Brass Center Sphere, 11 ½ x 17 In.	444.00
Andirons, Iron, Pumpkin Head, Iron, c.1945, 16 x 15 ¾ In.	310.00
Andirons, Iron, Serpent Shape, Screw Finial, 12 ½ x 26 In.	915.00
Andirons, Metal, Acorn Top, Ball Finials, Columnar Shaft, Cabriole Legs, Ball Feet, c.1800, 21 x 21 In.	504.00
Andirons, Metal, Belted Ball Finials, Columnar, Cabriole Legs, Spurred Knees, Slipper Feet, 21 x 11 In.	660.00
Andirons, Metal, Federal, Lemon Top, Columnar, Square Pedestal, Slipper Feet, c.1800, 20 In., Pair	385.00
Andirons, Wrought Iron, Applied Serpent, Head & Ear Finial, Incised Highlights, 22 x 36 In.	518.00
Andirons, Wrought Iron, Arched Base, Paw Feet, Basket Style Tops, Tapered Shaft, Blossoms, 41 In.	590.00
Andirons, Wrought Iron, Arched Legs, New England, 1700s, 17 x 12 In.	207.00
Andirons, Wrought Iron, Arts & Crafts, Spiral Finial, Scrolls & Leaves, Arched Feet, c.1900, 26 ½ In.	3660.00
Andirons, Wrought Iron, Baluster Guard, Stirrup Leg, Penny Foot, Brass Lemon Finial, 14 In.	295.00
Andirons, Wrought Iron, Baroque Style, Griffins, Rings, Ball Finial, Arched Legs, c.1860, 30 x 18 In.	3162.00
Andirons, Wrought Iron, Brass Sunflower, Double Spit Hooks, Tripod Cabriole Legs, 27 x 23 In.	1888.00
Andirons, Wrought Iron, Brass Urn Finials, Baluster Shape, Knife Blade Type, Penny Feet, 21 x 15 In.	130.00
Andirons, Wrought Iron, Brass, Knife Blade, Pa., c.1780, 24 In.	415.00
Andirons, Wrought Iron, Crosspiece, Honey Dipper Top, Spiral Twist Bails, 1850s, 42 x 17 & 48 In.	316.00
Andirons, Wrought Iron, Dog, Spaniel, Seated, Leaf Base, 12 ¾ x 10 ¼ In.	144.00
Andirons, Wrought Iron, Flat Shaft, Stirrup Leg, Penny Foot, Curved Ball Finials, 20 In.	106.00
Andirons, Wrought Iron, Gooseneck Style, Swan & Heart Shape, Arched Legs, c.1910, 25 x 18 In.	480.00
Andirons, Wrought Iron, Gooseneck, Open Hearts, Ball Finials, New England, c.1760, 22 ½ In.	21330.00
Andirons, Wrought Iron, Knife Blade, Brass Finial, Penny Feet, c.1800, 19 In.	288.00
Andirons, Wrought Iron, Knife Blade, Brass Finials, c.1730, 14 x 10 ½ In.	288.00
Andirons, Wrought Iron, Longhorn Bull, Spain, 18 x 31 In.	2300.00
Andirons, Wrought Iron, Pierced Brass, 19 ½ x 18 In.	354.00
Andirons, Wrought Iron, Serpents, Samuel Yellin Style, 12 x 26 x 28 In.	750.00
Andirons, Wrought Iron, Spiral Shafts, Open Spiral Finials, Scrolled Feet, 1800s, 30 In.	413.00
Andirons, Wrought Iron, Twisted & Curled, Ball Finial, Arts & Craft, 16 x 25 x 28 In.	225.00
Andirons, Wrought Iron, Twisted, Curls, Loops, 17 x 36 In.	219.00
Bellows, Carved Oak, Man's Face, Leaves, England, 1800s, 44 x 12 In.	374.00
Bellows, Flowers, Yellow Ground, Paint, New England, c.1860, 17 ½ In.	58.00
Bellows, Fruit Design, Red Paint, c.1830, 16 ½ In.	444.00
Bellows, Giltwood, Oval Putti Panel, Scroll, Flower, Cherub, Lion Mask, Italy, c.1750, 26 x 13 In.	4025.00
Bellows, Leather, Cornucopia, Leaf Design, 18 In.	136.00
Bellows, Painted Tortoiseshell, Gilt, Brass Nozzle, Eckstein & Richardson, 1800s, 16 ½ In.	504.00
Bellows, Painted, Red, Peaches, Leaves, Green Edging, Sunburst, Leather, Cowling, 18 In.	177.00
Bellows, Regency, Brass, Mahogany, England, 24 In.	237.00
Bellows, Relief Carved Mask Handles, Eagle, Bronze Nozzle, Baroque, 30 In.	590.00
Box, Firewood, Open, Blue Paint, Shaped Base, New England, 27 ½ x 25 ¾ In.	690.00
Chenets, Andirons, Brass, Asian Couple, Each On Voluted Scroll, 9 ¼ x 11 ¼ In., Pair	1121.00
Chenets, Andirons, Brass, Louis XVI, Cast Flame Finial, Swag Draped Urns, 14 x 14 In.	118.00
Chenets, Andirons, Brass, Pierced Spire Tops, Bird, Lion Carved, Paw Feet, c.1945, 22 x 22 In.	83.00
Chenets, Andirons, Brass, Seated Man & Woman, Paw Feet, c.1885, 17 x 15 In.	984.00
Chenets, Andirons, Bronze, Cherubs, 19th Century, 16 x 21 In.	1000.00
Chenets, Andirons, Bronze, Cherubs, Leafy Scroll Standards, Napoleon, c.1870, 21 x 52 x 6 In.	1314.00
Chenets, Andirons, Bronze, Cupid, Holding Shells & Garland, c.1800, 18 x 18 In.	900.00
Chenets, Andirons, Bronze, Dog, Resting, Patinated, France, c.1970, 10 ½ In.	375.00
Chenets, Andirons, Bronze, God & Goddess, Staff, Quiver, Mask, Dolphins, Turtles, c.1885, 27 x 14 In.	492.00
Chenets, Andirons, Bronze, Louis XV Style, Cherub, Seated, 11 ½ In., Pair	688.00
Chenets, Andirons, Bronze, Rococo, Curving Leaf Shape, Flame Finial, 18 x 10 x 23 ½ In.	150.00
Chenets, Andirons, Bronze, Stag, Trees, Gilt, Patinated, Stamped C M, 22 ¼ x 14 ½ In.	2160.00
Chenets, Andirons, Gilt Bronze, Empire Style, Winged Sphinx, Woman, Recumbent, 8 ¾ In., Pair	1188.00
Chenets, Andirons, Gilt Bronze, Louis XV Style, River God, On Rock, 30 x 21 In.	1638.00
Chenets, Andirons, Gilt Bronze, Louis XV Style, Scrolling Rococo Shape, 19 In., Pair	188.00
Chenets, Andirons, Gilt Bronze, Louis XVI Style, Acorn Finial, Laurel Branches, 14 In.	813.00
Chenets, Andirons, Gilt Bonze, Louis XVI Style, Garland Urn, Torch Finial, Bourbon, 17 x 17 In.	3125.00
Chenets, Andirons, Gilt Bronze, Man, Woman, Hunting Poses, France, 16 x 21 In.	7475.00
Chenets, Andirons, Gilt Bronze, Mythical Creature, c.1965, 18 ½ x 14 ½ In., Pair	1000.00
Chenets, Andirons, Gilt Bronze, Urn, Pineapple Finials, France, c.1850, 17 In.	625.00
Chenets, Andirons, Gilt Bronze, Urns, Lion Masks, Swags, Garland, 14 x 12 In.	414.00 to 667.00
Chenets, Andirons, Gilt Metal, Fluted Base, Lion's Head, Flame Finial, c.1900, 15 x 17 In.	676.00
Chenets, Andirons, Gilt Metal, Louis XV Style, Acanthus Leaves, Scrolls, c.1890, 17 x 12 In.	944.00
Chenets, Andirons, Gilt Metal, Louis XV Style, Scrolled Leaves, 17 In.	406.00
Chenets, Andirons, Gilt, Bronze, Urn, Ram's Head Masks, Shaped Base, Reticulated Fender, 34 x 17 In.	390.00
Coal Scuttle, Mahogany, Brass Handle, Tin Liner, Shovel Receptacle, 23 x 15 In.	47.00
Coal Scuttle, Portrait, Tole, Black, Gold, Lithograph, 12 x 23 In.	170.00

Coal Scuttle, Tin, Pottery Handle, Reverse Painted Old Man, Dog Scene, c.1850, 13 ½ x 13 ½ In..	130.00
Coal Scuttle, Walnut, Slant Front, Carved Panel, Brass Handle, England, 13 x 16 In.	85.00
Coal Scuttle, Wood, Blue Paint, 20 x 16 In.	259.00
Coal Scuttle, Wood, Carved, Tulips, Stippled Ground, Tin Liner, Hinged Door, c.1890, 12 x 12 ½ In.	69.00
Fan, Victorian Style, Brass, Scrolls, Garlands, Medallions, Palm Leaves, Finial, Pierced, 27 x 38 In..	150.00
Fender, Brass & Gilt, George III Style, Serpentine, Ball Finial, Hairy Paw Feet, 15 ¾ x 49 In.	200.00
Fender, Brass, Club, Leather Upholstered Railing, Balusters, Molded Base, 1900s, 63 x 21 In.	960.00
Fender, Brass, Cove Molded Base, Rail, Turned Supports, Whippets, Adjustable, c.1835, 5 ¾ 3 ¼ In.	1230.00
Fender, Brass, Federal Style, Fenestrated, 11 ½ x 52 In.	130.00
Fender, Brass, Federal, Wire, Curved, c.1830, 12 In.	356.00
Fender, Brass, Federal, Wire, Scroll Design, c.1820, 15 ½ x 56 In.	1185.00
Fender, Brass, George III, Serpentine, Pierced, c.1760, 6 ½ x 33 ½ In.	533.00
Fender, Brass, Green Leather Seats, Nail Heads, England, 21 x 72 In.	819.00
Fender, Brass, Iron, George III, Pierced, Shaped, Swags, Bows, Beaded Border, c.1785, 4 ¾ x 40 In..	215.00
Fender, Brass, Louis XVI Style, Pierced, Central Mask, 4 Urn Finials, 14 x 60 In.	344.00
Fender, Brass, Reticulated Scrolled Panels, Sculpted Claw Feet, Tool Rests, Victorian, 120 In.	150.00
Fender, Brass, Turned Standards, Brass Rods, Turned End Cups, c.1885, 10 x 40 In.	214.00
Fender, Brass, Wire, Knopped Ball Finials, Serpentine, 41 ½ In.	1180.00
Fender, Brass, Wire, Serpentine Front, Brass Rails, Finials, 21 x 50 In.	1888.00
Fender, Brass, Wirework, Demilune, Scrolling, 8 x 32 ¾ In.	180.00
Fender, Gilt Bronze, Acanthus Decorated Urns, Lion's Head Pull, Gadrooning, Paw Feet, 19 x 58 In.	615.00
Fender, Gilt Bronze, Louis XV, Swirling Leaves, Scrolls, c.1900, 17 ½ x 36 ½ In.	960.00
Fender, Gilt Metal, Empire Style, Grotesques, Scrolls, 12 x 67 In.	500.00
Fender, Iron, William IV, Pierced Grape Design, Brass Paw Feet, c.1835, 8 ¼ x 40 In.	492.00
Fender, Wire, Brass Top Rail, c.1850, 40 x 14 In.	181.00
Fender, Wire, Brass, Lemon Finials, Paw Feet, 50 ½ In.	590.00
Fender, Wirework, George III Style, Brass Gallery, Wire Latticework, c.1885, 10 ½ x 36 In.	184.00
Fender, Wirework, Serpentine, Iron Frame, Brass Rail, Turned Finials, Eng., 15 ¾ x 60 In.	443.00
Fire Box, Brass, Relief Courting Scene, Dutch, 17 x 26 x 16 In.	270.00
Fireback, Cast Iron, Draped Woman, Holding Bird, Anchor, Putto, 31 x 20 In.	118.00
Fireback, Cast Iron, Figures, Scrolls, England, 23 x 23 In.	472.00
Fireback, Central Potted Flower, Arched Shape, Cast Iron, c.1750, 29 ½ x 23 ¾ In.	2133.00
Fireboard, Painted, Scenic, Men, Cattle, Farm, Farmhouse, 31 x 41 In.	1180.00
Firestarter, Iron, Removable Flint, George Nelson, Marked, Howard Miller, 12 In.	500.00
Firewood Box, Tole, Hinged Lid, Side Brackets, Brass Fireplace Tools, England, 1800s, 25 x 11 In..	150.00
Footman, Brass, Shaped Apron, Animal Front Legs, Paw Feet, England, 1800s, 12 x 18 In.	59.00
Grate, Brass, Pierced, Bowed, Engraved, Regency, England, 29 ½ x 32 In.	1416.00
Grate, Fender, Brass, Steel, Neoclassical, Anthemia, Urn Shape Finials, Scrolling Vines, 23 x 19 In.	554.00
Guard, Bronze, Satyrs, Blowing Flaming Urn, Shell Plinths, c.1900, 10 x 36 In.	1098.00
Kindling Basket, Hammered Copper, Arts & Crafts, Double Handles, Iron Scrolled Feet, 19 x 15 In.	150.00
Log Holder, Cast Iron, Classical Woman's Head, 5 ¼ x 11 In., Pair	380.00
Log Holder, Wood, Black Forest, Box, Hinged Lid, Kindling, Handle, c.1880, 19 x 21 In.	3738.00
Log Holder, Wood, V Shape, Tacked Copper Lining, Scroll Base, C. Rohlfs, 1902, 21 In.	9375.00
Mantel is listed in the Architectural category.	
Screens are also listed in the Architectural and Furniture categories.	
Screen, Aesthetic Revival, Stained Glass, Brass, Leafy Repousse Frieze, Bird Panel, 36 x 23 In.	1140.00
Screen, Asian Style, Shaped Ebonized Frame, Silk Panel Inset, Flowers, Boxes, Multicolor, 27 x 56 In..	98.00
Screen, Brass & Iron, Wirework, Scrolls, c.1800s, 24 x 32 ½ In.	948.00
Screen, Brass Rail, Vertical Wirework, Swag Border, c.1800, 24 In.	2400.00
Screen, Brass, Fan Shape, Filigree Scallop Rim, 26 ½ In.	88.00
Screen, Bronze, Art Nouveau Style, Panel, Woman In Tree, Embossed, 27 x 24 In.	150.00
Screen, Bronze, Eagle, Spread Wings, 1800s, 34 x 24 In.	2640.00
Screen, Canvas, Painted, Birds, Flowers, Gilt Frame, 61 x 25 In.	230.00
Screen, Copper, Wrought Iron, Hammered, Border, Mythical, Sea Creatures, c.1900, 26 x 22 In.	1500.00
Screen, Courting Couple, Needlepoint, Shaped, Ball & Claw Tripod Base, c.1760, 53 In.	633.00
Screen, Faux Rosewood, Gilt, Silk, Stencil Leaves, Houses, Hugh & John Finlay, c.1825, 16 In.	6613.00
Screen, Federal, Mahogany, Adjustable, D-Shape Table, Turned Standard, Cabriole Legs, 53 In.	2006.00
Screen, Gilt Bronze, Louis XVI Style, Dolphin Feet, Scrolls, Strapwork, Tassels, c.1900, 26 x 34 In.	2214.00
Screen, Gilt Bronze, Louis XVI Style, Folding Fan Shape, Flame Finial, 28 x 41 ½ In.	1750.00
Screen, Gilt Bronze, Napoleon II, Folding, Fan Shape, Mask, Scrolled Base, 1800s, 26 x 26 In.	359.00
Screen, Gilt Bronze, Rocaille Shape Frame, Scrolling, Hanging Putto, Torch, Scrolled Feet, 36 x 29 In.	1046.00
Screen, Gilt, Crested, Leaf Carved Frame, Red, Blue, Gray Tapestry, George Jacob, 1775	2500.00
Screen, Gilt, Lacquer, Courtyard Scene, Shaped, c.1865, 50 In.	130.00
Screen, Giltwood, Leaf, Flower, Shield, Lion, Crown Crest, Pedestal Base, Glass Back, 58 x 28 In.	4025.00
Screen, Hammered Copper, Swags, Panel, Repousse, Wrought Iron Frame, 21 ¾ x 5 ½ In.	531.00
Screen, Lacquer, Painted, Pearl, Folding, Converts To Side Table, c.1890, 32 x 30 In. ...*Illus*	118.00

Firefighting, Extinguisher, Rockford's Kalamazoo, Hand, Cobalt Blue Glass, 10 ½ In.
$480.00

Showtime Auction Sevices

Firefighting, Grenade, Hazelton's High Pressure Chemical Fire Keg, Amber, Brass Neck Ring, c.1890, 11 In.
$489.00

Glass Works Auctions

Firefighting, Grenade, Healy's Hand, Yellow Amber, Applied Mouth, c.1885, 11 In.
$1,265.00

Glass Works Auctions

Firefighting, Helmet, Cairn's Aluminum Senator, Ladder 1, Anthony CFD, Leather Front
$150.00

Showtime Auction Sevices

Firefighting, Helmet, Chief, High Eagle, Steam Fire Engine, Presentation Plaque, Wilson, N.Y.F.D., 1894
$5,100.00

Showtime Auction Sevices

Firefighting, Helmet, Leather, Painted, Lion Finial, Metal Shield, Fairmount 2 Fire Co., 1852
$2,200.00

Showtime Auction Sevices

Firefighting, Lantern, DeVoursney, Williams, W.M.W., Etched Glass, Eagle Finial, 18 ½ In.
$1,440.00

Showtime Auction Sevices

Screen, Mahogany, Arts & Crafts, Leaded Glass, Copper, Tall Ship, England, c.1905, 39 x 30 In.	1875.00
Screen, Mahogany, Bead & Needlework, Flowers, Geometric Designs, c.1835, 58 In. ....*Illus*	584.00
Screen, Mahogany, Bronze Mounted, Columns, Needlework Screen, France, 1800s, 42 x 30 In.	413.00
Screen, Mahogany, Carved, Pierced Leaves, Turned Finials, Cut Velvet, Silk, 47 x 25 In.	311.00
Screen, Mahogany, Silk Embroidery, Carved Ribbon Crest, Round, Sunflower, c.1890, 54 x 38 In.	294.00
Screen, Needlepoint, Moses & Followers, Walnut Tripod Stand, 52 x 24 In.	359.00
Screen, Needlework, Gothic Revival, Gentleman, Rosewood, American, c.1850, 64 x 33 In. ....*Illus*	2032.00
Screen, Oak Stick & Ball Frame, Fabric Panel, Cats By Fireside, Printed, 24 x 35 In.	158.00
Screen, Papier-Mache, Telescoping Brass Stand, Tripod Base, 56 In.	472.00
Screen, Plaque, Wood, Edge Strips, Painted, Cottage Dinner Scene, 17 x 16 ½ In.	403.00
Screen, Pole, Chippendale, Red Toile Indian Scene, Oval Screen, Mahogany, Ma., c.1760, 54 In.	2480.00
Screen, Pole, Edwardian, Mahogany, Oval Frame, Adjustable, Silk, Tripod Base, 61 x 17 In.	215.00
Screen, Pole, George III, Mahogany, Flowers, Urn, Needlework, 18th Century, 59 x 22 x 17 In.	3382.00
Screen, Pole, George III, Scalloped Edge, Bronze Rod, Ring-Turned Stem, 1700s, 63 In., Pair .....*Illus*	836.00
Screen, Pole, Mahogany, Shepherd, Women, Needlepoint Scene, 58 x 20 In.	89.00
Screen, Pole, Needlework Panel, Sleeping Shepherd, Flock, Woman, Parasol, Green Paint, 44 x 15 In.	177.00
Screen, Pole, Neoclassical, Mahogany, Needlepoint, Man, Woman Playing Checkers, 58 x 15 In.	118.00
Screen, Pole, Queen Anne, Mahogany, Needlepoint Panel, Flower Basket, 59 x 19 In.	1180.00
Screen, Pole, Queen Anne, Mahogany, Needlework Panel, Urn & Flowers, 58 In.	920.00
Screen, Pole, Rosewood, Carved, Floral Pettipoint, Rococo, Adjustable, 61 x 18 In.	288.00
Screen, Pole, Victorian, Carved, Adjustable, Tripod Base, Needlepoint, 58 x 19 In.	127.00
Screen, Renaissance Revival, Walnut, Mirror, Metal Spider Web, 48 ½ x 31 In.	575.00
Screen, Tin, Dog Shape, Painted, England, 1800s, 24 ½ In.	563.00
Screen, Tin, Dog Shape, Red Tassel, England, 19 ¼ In.	915.00
Screen, Victorian, Oak, Gilt Metal, Lacquer, Insects, Leaves, Columns, Trestle Base, 40 x 24 In.	878.00
Screen, Wire, Brass, Scrolls, Federal, 30 x 45 ¼ In.	1062.00
Screen, Wirework, Brass Rail, Cast Iron Base, England, 1800s, 16 x 36 In.	575.00
Screen, Wrought Cast Iron, Arts & Crafts Style, 3 Panels, S-Scroll, Sun Bursts, c.1890, 27 x 41 In.	518.00
Screen, Wrought Iron, Art Deco, Hammered, Riveted, c.1905, 36 x 44 In.	378.00
Screen, Wrought Iron, Italian Baroque Style, Ducks, Pierced, Reticulated, 30 x 44 In.	2875.00
Tinder Box, Tinned Iron, Socket On Lid, c.1800, 3 ½ x 4 In.	441.00
Tongs, Ember, Iron, c.1800, 17 ¼ In.	830.00
Tool Rest, Square Bar, Stirrup Legs, Turned-Out Feet, Iron, 16 x 50 x 12 In.	295.00
Tool Set, Brass, Steel, Victorian, Shovel, Fork, Tongs, Rests With Turned Supports, c.1885, 36 In.	276.00
Tool Set, Bronze Pedestal, Windmill, Village Engraved Hood, 5 Hooks & Utensils, c.1860, 41 x 15 In.	690.00
Tool Set, Wrought Iron, Teardrop Handles, T-Shape Holder, Gustav Stickley, 4 Piece	6875.00
Trammel, Double Twist, Ratchet Mechanism, Brass Anvil, Hammer, George Dixon, 50 In. ...*Illus*	472.00
Trammel, Stylized Bird Head, Adjustable Arm, Iron, Pa., 1812, 29 In.	2976.00
Trammel, Whale-Shaped Handle, Wrought Iron Connector, 1800s, 54 In.	115.00

FISCHER porcelain was made in Herend, Hungary, by Moritz Fischer. The factory was founded in 1839 and is still in business. The wares are sometimes referred to as Herend porcelain.   **MF**

Bowl, Vegetable, Cover, Fruits & Flowers, Lemon Finial, 9 ½ In.	600.00
Bowl, Vegetable, Rothschild, Birds, Butterflies, Insects, Gilt, Basket Weave Rim, 10 x 10 In.	247.00
Candelabrum, 5-Light, Queen Victoria, Upper Branches Lift From Base, 17 x 14 In., Pair	210.00
Dish, Chinese Bouquet, Red Flowers, Free-Form Gilt Rim, 11 ½ x 10 In.	179.00
Dish, Multicolor Birds, Black Ground, Shell Shape, Gilt Rim, 9 x 8 In.	298.00
Ewer, Multicolor, Reticulated, Double Spout, 6 In.	120.00
Figurine, Elephant, Upturned Trunk, Green Fishnet, 10 x 15 In.	1131.00
Figurine, Jay, Perched On Branch, Fruit Stem, Buds, Leaves, Multicolor Gloss Glaze, 13 ½ In.	207.00
Figurine, Man, Folk Dancer, Traditional Clothes, 7 ½ In.	60.00
Figurine, Man, Folk Dancer, Traditional Clothes, 12 In.	210.00
Figurine, Man, Nude, Holding Flute, White, Soft Color, Oval Base, 10 ½ In.	299.00
Figurine, Man, Peasant, Leaning On Staff, 11 In.	120.00
Figurine, Rooster, Multicolor, Impressed Mark, 1915-1930, 16 x 13 In.	1001.00
Plate, Dinner, Rothschild Bird, 10 ½ In., 12 Piece	1680.00
Platter, Chinese Bouquet, Embossed Gold Rim, Green, White, Footed, 3 x 10 In., 12 Piece	177.00
Platter, Fish, Rothschild, Birds, Butterflies, Insects, Basket Weave Molded Rim, 20 x 9 ½ In.	345.00
Platter, Rothschild Bird, Shaped Gilt Edge, 16 ¼ In.	189.00
Tea Set, Tray, Open Handles, Pitcher, 2 Covered Bowls, Creamer	590.00
Tray, Painted Green Flowers, Round, Rim, 14 In.	82.00
Tureen, Lid, Underplate, Bird On Branch, Bird Finial, 13 x 17 In.	1180.00
Tureen, Lid, Underplate, Rothschild Bird, Green Handles, Lemon Finial, 14-In. Tureen	1560.00
Tureen, Lid, Underplate, Rothschild Bird, Twig Handles, Lemon Knop, 9 ¾ x 13 In.	761.00
Tureen, Underplate, Printemps, Flowers, Leaf Handles, Lemon Finial, 12 ¾ x 18 In.	708.00
Vase, Regency Style, White, Gilt Accents, Footed, Square Base, 7 ½ x 6 In.	150.00

FISHING reels of brass or nickel were made in the United States by 1810. Bamboo fly rods were sold by 1860, often marked with the maker's name. Lures made of metal, or metal and wood, were made in the nineteenth century. Plastic lures were made by the 1930s. All fishing material is collected today and even equipment of the past thirty years is of interest if in good condition with original box.

Bait Bucket, Copper, Wire Mesh Lid, Wood Grasp Handle, Oval, 16 x 7 ½ x 7 In.	120.00
Bobber, Ferax, Red, Green, Metal, 7 In.	300.00
Bobber, Pike, Green & White, Red Ball Stop, 10 ½ In.	50.00
Bobber, Red, White, Wood Bead, Sinker, Cork, 1950s, 3 x 1 ½ In.	25.00
Creel, Mousel, Wicker, Screw Eye Closure, 19 x 7 x 10 In.	80.00
Creel, Mousel, Wickerwork, Green, Paint, Screw Eye Lid Clasp, 14 x 6 x 8 In.	110.00
Creel, Salmon, Basketry, Strapped On Wood Lid, Blue Paint, Rawhide, Wood Latch, Vt., 10 x 17 In.	531.00
Creel, W.H. McMonies, Fine Weave, Leather Bound, Buckle Strap, Model 61-5, Zippered Pouch ... *Illus*	489.00
Creel, Wing Tip, Woven, Leather Trim, Snap Closure, 15 x 6 x 10 In.	950.00
Fly, Charles Chute, Popham, Salmon	130.00
Fly, Godfrey, Salmon	20.00
Fly, John Dunne, Trout, 1920s	10.00
Fly, MacPherson, Salmon, Popham Pattern, 1914	70.00
Fly, Schmookler, Trout, Wringer Pattern	30.00
Hook, Job Johnson, Sockdologer, c.1847, 4 ¼ In.	110.00
Lure, Creek Chub, Brown Hair Wings & Tail, Fly Rod	110.00
Lure, Creek Chub, Fly Rod, Hum-Bird, Yellow Body & Tail, No. F302 ... *Illus*	184.00
Lure, Creek Chub, Minnow, Silver Doctor, Feather, Floating, Wood, c.1924	100.00
Lure, Heddon, Musky Surfusser, White Strawberry Spot, Glass Eyes, No. 350S ... *Illus*	288.00
Lure, Jamison, Fly Rod, Box, 1 ¼ In.	550.00
Lure, Jamison, Wiggler, White, Gill Marks, Double Hook, 1 ¼ In.	1100.00
Lure, Plastic, Red, White, 2 Triple Hooks, Mustache, 2 ¾ In.	9.00
Lure, Shakespeare, Frog, Double Belly Hook, Rubber, Lead Weight, Mechanical, Rhodes ..*Illus*	92.00
Lure, Shakespeare, Kingfish, White, Red Stripes, c.1940	80.00
Lure, Shakespeare, Minnow, Evolution, Rubber, 1910, 4 In.	384.00
Lure, Turner, Spider, Box, Paper, c.1949	443.00
Minnow Bucket, Ferris & Will, Square, Angle End, 19 ½ x 8 ½ In.	90.00
Minnow Bucket, Swan Floating, Painted, Stencil, Oval, 12 ¼ x 9 x 9 ¾ In. ... *Illus*	219.00
Minnow Bucket, Torpedo Shape, Stenciled Finish, c.1900, 26 In.	550.00
Minnow Cage, Archer Wakeman, Skeleton, Revolving, Nickel Plate, 1880s, 3 In.	266.00
Minnow Trap, Copper, Brass, Tin, Bucket, Latches, 40 x 9 In.	400.00
Minnow Trap, Hinged Lid, Ring, c.1910, 15 x 9 In.	135.00
Minnow Trap, Pyramid, Folding, Metal Mesh Cones, Wellington Metal Products, 14 x 10 In. ..*Illus*	460.00
Reel, B.C. Milam, No. 3, Dog-Leg Handle	600.00
Reel, Bogdan, Model 400, Salmon, Fly, Suede Bag, 4 In.	4100.00
Reel, C.M. Clinton, Sidemount, Trout, Silver, 2 ⅝ In.	3500.00
Reel, Fin-Nor, No. 3, Anti-Reverse, Left-Hand Wind, 3 ⅝ In.	225.00
Reel, Jack Luke, Trout, Ribbed Brass Foot, 3 ⅛ In.	200.00
Reel, Spool, P.H. Walker, Boston, Salmon, Silver, Fred Curtis, Germany, 4 ½ x 1 ⅞ In. ...*Illus*	431.00
Reel, Stan Bogdan, Fly, Salmon, Gold Frame, Model 2, 3 ¾ In.	1600.00
Reel, Stan Bogdan, Model 1, Tail-Plate Click Adjustment, Drag Setting, 3 ¾ In.	1200.00
Reel, Ted Juracsik, Tibor Gulfstream, Saltwater, Gold Finish	350.00
Reel, Ted Williams, Model No. 31231140, Sears Roebuck Co., 1960s	35.00
Rod Case, Leather, Brass Buckle, Aluminum Inside Tube, 49 In.	130.00
Rod, H.L. Leonard, Fly, Bag, 8 Ft.	650.00
Rod, Monterey Model, Split Bamboo 2-Piece, Turned Oak Grips, Montague Rod Co.	175.00
Rod, Pinky Gillum, Flamed Bamboo, Salmon, Stamped, 9 Ft. 6 In.	1400.00
Rod, R.L. Winston, 4-Piece, Green, Graphite, Spey, 13 Ft.	200.00
Rod, Thomas & Thomas, Bamboo Mottled Frame, Catskill Legend, Fly, 8 Ft. 6 In.	1500.00
Rod, Thomas, Salmon, Bamboo, 3-Piece, 2 Tips, 14 Ft.	110.00
Spear, Eel, Iron, Painted, Six Prongs, Blade, Hook Ends, Straight Handle, 1800s, 13 ½ x 8 In.	52.00
Tackle Box, Copper, Hinged Lid, 2 Trays, Slide Latch Compartment, 10 x 9 x 7 In.	70.00
Tackle Box, Wood, Painted, 20 Metal Fishing Lures, c.1930, 6 ½ x 21 ¾ In.	474.00

FLAGS *are included in the Textile category.*

FLASH GORDON appeared in the Sunday comics in 1934. The daily strip started in 1940. The hero was also in comic books from 1930 to 1970, in books from 1936, in movies from 1938, on the radio in the 1930s and 1940s, and on television from 1953 to 1954. All sorts of memorabilia are collected, but the ray guns and rocket ships are the most popular.

Click Ray Pistol, Tin Lithograph, Futuristic Design, Box, Marx, 1950s, 4 ½ x 10 In.	307.00

Firefighting, Lantern, Eclipse, Brass, Ruby Glass, Fire Extinguisher Co., Chicago, Pat. Sept. 21, 1886, 20 In. $935.00

Showtime Auction Sevices

Firefighting, Nozzle, Brass, Leather Handles, Fabric Covered Shaft, S.F. Hayward & Co., c.1860, 31 ½ In. $120.00

Showtime Auction Sevices

Firefighting, Trumpet, Corrugated Bell, Fred Miller Style, 18 In. $540.00

Showtime Auction Sevices

Firefighting, Trumpet, Presentation, Silver Plate, Engraved, Inscription, Pennsylvania 1899, 21 In.
$1,200.00

Showtime Auction Sevices

Fireplace, Andirons, Cast Iron, Sun Face, Marked, Raised B&H, Bradley & Hubbard, 16 ¾ x 9 ½ In.
$504.00

Skinner, Inc.

Fireplace, Andirons, Fire Deer, Cast Iron, Signed, Russel Wright, 1930, 15 x 21 In.
$9,375.00

Rago Arts & Auction Center

TIP
The peridot, a yellowish green stone, is said to protect you from nightmares, ward off evil, bring clarity of thought, and "release negativity."

Figure, Wood Composition, Painted, King Features, 1944, 4 ¾ In.	230.00
Kite, Punch Out, Cardboard, 1950s, 17 ½ x 22 ½ In.	60.00
Rocket Fighter Ship, Sparkling, Windup, Tin Lithograph, Built In Key, c.1935, 12 In.	429.00
Space Outfit, Goggles, Belt, Wrist Compass, Esquire Novelty Co., Display Card, 1951	171.00

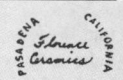

FLORENCE CERAMICS were made in Pasadena, California, from World War II to 1977. Florence Ward created many colorful figurines, boxes, candleholders, and other items for the gift shop trade. Each piece was marked with an ink stamp that included the name *Florence Ceramics Co.* The company was sold in 1964 and although the name remained the same, the products were very different. Mugs, cups, and trays were made.

Figurine, Abigail, Green Dress, 8 ½ In.	120.00
Figurine, Amelia, Ruffled, Low Cut, 8 ¾ In.	127.00
Figurine, Clarissa, Gray Dress, Green Hat & Muff, Gilt Trim, 7 ½ In.	120.00
Figurine, Ethel, Blue Dress & Hat, White Cape, 7 ¼ In.	176.00
Figurine, Matilda, Blue Dress, 8 ½ In.	95.00
Figurine, Matilda, Red Dress, 8 ½ In.	75.00
Figurine, Melanie, Blond, Gray Dress, Pink Hat, 7 ¾ In.	45.00
Figurine, Parakeet, On Stump, Multicolor, 7 ¼ In.	245.00
Figurine, Rita, Beige Dress, Flowers, 9 ½ In.	135.00
Figurine, Sarah, Gray, Green Hat & Purse, 7 ½ In.	84.00
Figurine, Victoria, Seated, White Sofa, Red Dress, 7 x 8 ½ In.	175.00
Planter, Girl, White, Pink, Brown Accents, 6 In.	45.00
Plaque, Woman, Muffler, Umbrella, Mauve, Green, 9 x 6 x 2 In., Pair	135.00

FLOW BLUE was made in England and other countries about 1830 to 1900. The dishes were printed with designs using a cobalt blue coloring. The color flowed from the design to the white body so that the finished piece has a smeared blue design. The dishes were usually made of ironstone china. More Flow Blue may be found under the name of the manufacturer.

Bowl, Vegetable, Ironstone, Octagonal Rim, Marked Cashmere, R&M, 9 ¾ x 8 In.	266.00
Plate, Ironstone, 12-Sided Rim, Marked Cashmere, F.M. & Co., 10 ½ In.	153.00
Plate, Patrick Henry At Virginia Assembly, 1765, Ye Old Historical Pottery, 9 ½ In., Pair	23.00
Plate, Shell Pattern, Flowers, Scrolls, 9 ½ In., 12 Piece	354.00
Plate, Soup, Ironstone, Oriental Theme, 12-Sided Rim, Marked Chapoo, 8 ⅜ In.	35.00
Sugar, Ironstone, Cover, Oriental Theme, 12 Panels, Flared Rim, Loop Handles, Footed, 76 x 7 ¾ In.	153.00
Toothbrush Holder, Molded Relief Flowers, Scroll Border, 4 In.	45.00
Tureen, Lid, Seaweed Pattern, Hexagonal, 11 In.	75.00
Vase, Flowers, Gold Trim, Ruffled Rim, George Jones & Sons, 1924-1951, 22 In.	210.00

Flying Phoenix, *see Phoenix Bird category.*

FOLK ART is also listed in many categories of this book under the actual name of the object. See categories such as Box, Cigar Store Figure, Paper, Weather Vane, Wooden, etc.

Bank, Book, Trick, Mixed Hardwoods, Inlaid Spine Slides To Release Cover, 3 ¾ x 2 ⅝ In.	94.00
Bar Scene, Painted, Mahogany Display Case, Jailhouse Carver, c.1910, 11 ½ x 18 In.	5925.00
Barn, Pine, Green, White Paint, c.1900, 36 x 34 In.	1067.00
Bears, Poplar, Carved, Mother & Cub, Trees, Rocks, c.1950, 9 ½ x 18 In.	206.00
Biplane, Wood, Paint, Tin Wings, Tail & Pilot Silhouette, Stand, c.1900, 23 x 23 In.	558.00
Bird Tree, 3 Birds, Wood, White With Red, Blue With Yellow, Red With Green, Strawser, 1976, 24 In.	354.00
Bird Tree, Softwood, 8 Carved Birds On Wire, Fluted Post, Bead Eyes, c.1900, 25 x 18 In.	705.00
Bird Tree, Wood, Tree Shape Mount, 18 Carved Birds, c.1930, 14 ¼ x 22 In.	47.00
Bird, Canada Geese, Flying, Driftwood Base, Stamped Russ Burr, Mass., Miniature	590.00
Bird, Godwit, Wood, Carved, Paint, Round Base, George Boyd, New Hampshire, Miniature	1770.00
Bird, On Stump, Carved Painted, Schtockschnitzler Simmons, Pa., c.1900, 6 ¼ In.	10665.00
Bird, On Stump, Carved, Yellow, Black, Painted, Schtockschnitzler Simmons, c.1900, 5 ¼ In.	1337.00
Birdhouse, Martin, Pine, Shingled Roof, Paint, c.1910, 26 x 21 In.	267.00
Black Butler, Holding Tray, Wood, Carved, Painted, c.1910, 33 In.	107.00
Bottle, Whimsy, Saloon Scene, Wood, Paper, Foil, Bartender, Patrons, Carl Worner, c.1910, 12 In. *Illus*	1230.00
Bust, American Indian, Headband, Sandstone, Ohio, Ernest Reed, 1900s, 8 In.	151.00
Bust, Man's Head, Carved, Black Paint, Character, Glass Bead Eyes, Cap, c.1900, 7 In.	356.00
Candleholder, Red Clay, 7 Figures Surrounding Holder, c.1950, 7 x 10 In.	60.00
Canister, Tea, Tin, Red & Yellow Flowers, Yellow 8-Point Star, Black Ground, Cup Lid, 6 In.	106.00
Carriage, Horses, Abraham Lincoln, Black Driver, Wood, Felt, Cloth, Base, 28 In.	2607.00
Cat Face, Sheet Iron, Marble Eyes, Paint, 8 ½ x 8 ½ In.	201.00
Catfish, Driftwood Base, Glass Eyes, Metal Whiskers, Paint, Sherman Hensal, c.1950, 13 ½ In.	235.00

F

Church, Wood, Glass, Cutout Windows, Chimney, Paint, U.S.A., 1900s, 11 x 10 In.	118.00
Circus Trainer, Hat, Holding Whip, Wood, Carved, Painted, c.1930, 22 In.	1185.00
Clock, Shelf, Fireplace & Chimney Shape, George Griggs, Faux Bricks, Wood, c.1900, 32 In. . *Illus*	118.00
Cowboy, Wood, Carved, Exaggerated Torso, Glass Marble Eyes, 39 In.	360.00
Cup, Tin, Painted Red & Yellow, James Deems, Apr. 22nd 1889, 4 In.	295.00
Cupboard, Gilt Lettering, National Stores Of Ventnor, Isle Of Wright, England, Grain Paint, 80 x 31 In.	5843.00
Deer, Twig Antler, Carved, Painted, c.1880, 13 ¾ x 11 In.	2607.00
Doll, Hardwood, Carved From Bedpost, Stylized Face, 1800s, 13 ¼ In.	121.00
Eagle, Spread Wings, Liberty Shield, Cast Metal, 40 In.	165.00
Eagle, Spread Wings, Shield Plaque, Wood, Carved, Painted, Maine, c.1910, 25 ½ In.	1652.00
Eagle, Wood, Carved, Perched On Globe, Painted, Square Base, U.S.A., 1900s, 16 In.	147.00
Eagle, Wood, Carved, White Paint, Harold B. Simmons, Maine, 34 ¾ In.	1770.00
Easel, Twig Design Top & Base, Dot Painted, c.1900, 66 In.	345.00
Fish, Wood, Carved, Green, Yellow Painted, Stand, 49 x 15 In.	431.00
Fisherman, Carved Post, Applied Hat, Arms, Paint, c.1990, 40 ¾ In.	354.00
Giraffe, Pine, Carved, Paint, Standing, Rectangular Base, U.S.A., 1900s, 10 ½ In.	211.00
Goat, Curved Horns, Curly Coat, White, Composition, 36 x 42 In.	480.00
Grasshopper, Wood, Carved, Green Paint, c.1950, 26 ¼ In.	1337.00
Holstein Cow, Standing, Black, White Paint, 28 In.	197.00
Horse & Rider, Wood, Painted, 19th Century, 10 x 9 x 5 In.	5664.00
Horse, Prancing, Wood, Paint, 16 ½ x 10 In.	604.00
Horse, Wood, Carved, Dappled, Wood Plank Base, 4 Wheels, 19th Century, 33 x 28 In.	1093.00
Indian, Bow, Arrow, Profile, Paint, Sheet Iron, c.1875, 26 x 14 In.	682.00
Lion, Reclining, Wood, Carved, Painted, Half Open Mouth, Pa., 3 ¾ x 6 ¼ In.	633.00
Locomotive & Track, Wood, Mechanical, 1889, 26 x 14 In.	403.00
Man, Cycling, Tin, Iron, c.1930, 19 In.	504.00
Man, Pipe In Mouth, Beard, Green Hat, Gesturing, 1940s, 15 ½ In.	120.00
Mirror, Carved, Figure Holding Up 7 Fingers, 7 Years Bad Luck, 1800s, 17 ½ x 11 In. .....*Illus*	5700.00
Model, Butcher Shop, Waving Man, Hanging Beef, Cleavers, Wood Case, England, c.1865, 18 x 20 In.	9920.00
Model, Horse Stable, Gabled Roof, Columns, Stalls, Red, Gray, Green Paint, c.1900, 14 x 30 ¼ In..	236.00
Noah's Ark, 80 Animals, Figures, Carved, Painted, Germany, 10 x 20 In.	2108.00
Panel, Eagle, Seed Pods, Leaves, Frame, Lois Devlin, Louisville, Ky., 1967, 14 x 18 In. ....*Illus*	147.00
Parrot, Hardwood, Perched On Swing, Glass Eyes, Painted, On Stand, c.1930, 24 In.	294.00
Pen Wiper, Figural, Teddy Bear, Sitting On Pitcher, Goblet, Pinked Edge Felt, 3 ½ x 3 ½ In. ...	130.00
Pen Wiper, Pugs, Felt, Red Blossom Base, c.1890, 4 ½ In.	1121.00
Pig, Cast Iron, Standing, Curled Tail, Paint, c.1890, 17 ¼ In.	1610.00
Pig, Standing, Wood, Black, Pink Paint, 25 x 15 In.	1495.00
Plaque, Adam & Eve, Carved Sandstone, Fig Leaves, Bust, 2 Snakes, c.1955, 27 x 16 In.	1175.00
Plaque, Homestead, Fields, Animals, Wood, Carved, Paint, Signed, Elijah Pierce, c.1978, 16 x 33 In..	4700.00
Plaque, Inlaid Wood, Octagonal, American Flag, 13 Stars, Fans, Geometric Shapes, 21 ¾ x 22 ¾ In. .	1140.00
Plaque, Rocking Horse, Wood, Gray, Red Paint, 31 ½ In.	531.00
Plaque, The Ascension, Carved, Paint, Cardboard, Glitter, Jesus, Figures, Elijah Pierce, 38 x 24 In.	9400.00
Retablo, Oil On Tin, Christ Child, Red Heart, Flowers, Inscription, c.1875, 14 x 9 ¾ In. ..*Illus*	392.00
Rooster, Paint, Wood, Tin, Iron, c.1850, 22 x 25 In.	4340.00
Root Head Crane, Paint, Black Base, 53 In.	79.00
Shield, American Flag, Painted, Carved Relief Stars, c.1950, 31 x 22 ½ In. ....*Illus*	470.00
Shield, Liberty, Wood, Stars & Stripes, Red, White, Blue, Barnboard Mount, 25 x 10 In.	590.00
Sparrows, Carved, Wood, Paint, Perched On Fungus Base, Bead Eyes, U.S.A., 1900s, 9 ½ x 12 In..	529.00
Sphinx, Seated, Wood, Carved, Painted, Stephen W. Polaha, c.1950, 13 ½ In.	415.00
Stand, Demilune Shape, Crossed Twig Base, Green Paint, Textured Gold Painted, c.1900, 48 x 26 In.	201.00
Theater, Black Men, Dancing, Box, Painted, Crank, Carpet Background, c.1900, 18 x 18 In....	1998.00
Uncle Sam, Riding High-Wheel Bicycle, Wood, Wrought Iron, Signed, R. Tate, 33 In.	241.00
Ventriloquist Head, Pine, Carved, Painted, Mounted, c.1850, 12 ½ In.	486.00
Walking Stick, Evangelist Devil Chaser, Black, Red, Bells, Cymbals, Banjo, Drum, c.1910, 74 In.	173.00
Whimsy, Bird, Red, Pinhead Eyes, Applied Fan-Fold Wings, Tail, Lancaster Country, 6 ½ x 7 In. ...	24.00
Whirligig, 2 Black Men, Articulated, Dancer, Banjo Player, Painted, 18 ½ x 23 In.	663.00
Whirligig, Drummer, Wood, Blue Red, Yellow Paint, 1900s, 25 In.	148.00
Whirligig, Fatty Arbuckle, Pine, Full Body, Front On Both Sides, 1920s, 19 In. ....*Illus*	920.00
Whirligig, Man, Aluminum, Jointed, Tin Blades, Cast Iron Base, Star Sprinkler Corp., c.1910	1205.00
Whirligig, Man, Bowtie, Boutonniere, Tin Hatband, Paddles, Carved, Painted, c.1910, 33 In. ...*Illus*	14220.00
Whirligig, Man, Cap, Paddle In Hand, Stick In Other, Wood, c.1865, 22 x 9 In.	18960.00
Whirligig, Man Sawing Wood, Green, Red, White Paint, c.1915, 21 In.	94.00
Whirligig, Man Sawing Wood, Red, Black, Blue Paint, 17 ¼ In.	356.00
Whirligig, Man, Wearing Hard Hat, Stylized Face, Holding Round Fans, Painted Green, 66 x 20 In.	1180.00
Whirligig, Man, Wearing Top Hat, Carved & Painted, Raising Pennant, 1800s, 17 ¾ x 26 ¼ In....	3910.00
Whirligig, Man, Wood, Iron, Clothespin Form, Painted, Paddle Arms, Tin Hat, 30 In.	1888.00
Whirligig, Nantucket Sailor, Carved, Painted, 16 ½ In.	590.00

TIP

If you take a nail out of the wall and leave a small hole, fill it with spackling paste. Wipe the spackle-filled hole with a damp cloth before it dries to get a smooth finish. If the hole is still showing, use more spackle.

F

Fireplace, Screen, Lacquer, Painted, Pearl, Folding, Converts To Side Table, c.1890, 32 x 30 In.
$118.00

Garth's Auctioneers & Appraisers

Fireplace, Screen, Mahogany, Bead & Needlework, Flowers, Geometric Designs, c.1835, 58 In.
$584.00

New Orleans Auction Galleries, Inc.

Fireplace, Screen, Needlework, Gothic Revival, Gentleman, Rosewood, American, c.1850, 64 x 33 In. $2,032.00

Neal Auction Co.

Fireplace, Screen, Pole, George III, Scalloped Edge, Bronze Rod, Ring-Turned Stem, 1700s, 63 In., Pair $836.00

Neal Auction Co.

Fireplace, Trammel, Double Twist, Ratchet Mechanism, Brass Anvil, Hammer, George Dixon, 50 In. $472.00

Brunk Auctions

Whirligig, Sailor, Stovepipe Hat, Ivory, Wood, Paint, 14 x 18 In.	6844.00
Whirligig, Woman Doing Laundry, Wood, Red, Green, Yellow Paint, 17 In.	119.00
Woman, Blue Dress, Foot On Bracket, Ship's Prow Shape, Wood, Florida, c.1855, 64 In.	1293.00
Woman, With Knapsack, Holding Red Bag, Blue Dress, Wood, Paint, Glitter, Elijah Pierce, 11 In.	5875.00

FOOT WARMERS solved the problem of cold feet in past generations. Some warmers held charcoal, others held hot water. Pottery, tin, and soapstone were the favored materials to conduct the heat. The warmer was kept under the feet, then the legs and feet were tucked into a blanket, providing welcome warmth in a cold carriage or church.

Brass, Octagonal, Pierced, Engraved, Tulips, Sunflowers, Scrolls, Swing Handle, c.1850, 11 x 8 In.	215.00
Buggy, Sheet Metal, Pierced Sides, Embossed Lions, Bail Handle, Lid, 9 x 5 ½ x 4 ¾ In.	160.00

FOOTBALL *collectibles may be found in the Card and the Sports categories.*

FOSTORIA glass was made in Fostoria, Ohio, from 1887 to 1891. The factory was moved to Moundsville, West Virginia, and most of the glass seen in shops today is a twentieth-century product. The company was sold in 1983; new items will be easily identifiable, according to the new owner, Lancaster Colony Corporation. Additional Fostoria items may be listed in the Milk Glass category.

American, Ashtray, Crystal, Square, 2 ⅞ In.	7.00
American, Bowl, Vegetable, 2 Sections, 10 x 7 In.	40.00
American, Goblet, Crystal, 5 Oz.	9.00
American, Pitcher, Water, Straight-Sided, 8 ½ In.	145.00
American, Rose Bowl	10.00
Arcady, Sugar & Creamer	65.00
Arlington, Candleholder, Milk Glass, Paper Label, 4 ¼ In., Pair	35.00
Baroque, Compote, Shirley Etching, 5 In.	40.00
Baroque, Creamer, Blue, Footed, 3 ½ In.	27.00
Baroque, Vase, Yellow, Flared, Flame Handles, 7 ¾ In.	125.00
Beacon, Torte Plate, Scalloped Edge	35.00
Betsy Ross, Basket, Peach, 11 ½ In.	54.00
Buttercup, Sherbet, Footed, 5 ⅝ In., 6 Oz.	13.00
Celestial, Bowl, Fluted, 9 In.	24.00
Chintz, Bowl, Crystal, Flared, 12 In.	55.00
Coin Glass, Ashtray, Blue, 4 Coins, 7 ½ In.	35.00
Coin, Bowl, Amber, 8 ¾ x 5 ½ x 3 In.	65.00
Coin, Bowl, Vegetable, Round, Ruby Red, 8 In.	45.00
Coin, Bowl, Vegetable, Scalloped Rim, Label, c.1970, 8 In.	45.00
Coin, Candy Dish, Amber, 8 ½ In.	55.00
Coin, Creamer, Ruby Red, 3 ½ In.	28.00
Coin, Dish, Jelly, Ruby Red, Footed, 3 ½ In.	22.00
Coin, Nappy, Handle, Ruby Red, 5 ¼ In.	34.00
Coin, Pitcher, Ruby Red, 32 Oz., 6 ½ In.	175.00
Coin, Salt & Pepper, Clear	32.00
Coin, Sugar & Creamer, Olive Green	50.00
Coin, Sugar, Lid, Ruby Red, 5 ¼ In.	44.00
Coin, Vase, Footed, Octagonal, Bud, Ruby Red, c.1970, 8 In.	42.00
Colonial Prisms, Toothpick Holder	10.00
Colony, Butter, Cover, 9 x 3 In.	68.00
Colony, Relish, 3 Sections, Handles, 10 ¾ In.	36.00
Coronet, Bowl, Crystal, Flared, 12 In.	150.00
Coronet, Bowl, Flared, 12 In.	65.00
Coronet, Dish, Mayonnaise, Ladle, 3 x 5 In.	50.00
Coronet, Sugar & Creamer	40.00
Coronet, Sugar & Creamer, Lid, Regal	150.00
Crystal Manor, Tumbler, Wisteria Base, 13 Oz., 5 ½ In.	98.00
Diadem, Candy Dish, Cover, Ebony	56.00
Fairfax, Cup, After Dinner, Green	15.00
Fairfax, Ice Bowl, Green, Liner	32.00
Fairfax, Plate, Azure Blue, 7 ½ In.	12.00
Fairfax, Saucer, Pink	4.00
Fairfax, Sugar & Creamer, Blue	24.00
Fairfax, Sugar & Creamer, Topaz	22.00
Fairfax, Tumbler, Pink, Footed, 5 Oz., 4 ½ In.	16.00
Fascination, Sherbet, Lilac, 7 Oz., 4 ¾ In.	15.00
Fascination, Tumbler, Lilac, Footed, 5 Oz., 4 ¼ In.	9.00

F

Figurine, Duck, Apricot, Satin, 3 ¾ In.	20.00
Figurine, Squirrel, Sitting, Green Mist, 3 In.	20.00
Heather, Tumbler, Footed, 5 Oz., 4 ⅞ In.	18.00
Heather, Vase, Handles, 6 ¼ In.	55.00
Heirloom, Bowl, Blue Opalescent, 10 In.	65.00
Heirloom, Bowl, Blue Opalescent, Oval, 13 In.	70.00
Heirloom, Bowl, Oval, Red, 8 In.	30.00
Heirloom, Bowl, Red, 7 In.	35.00
Heirloom, Bowl, Red, Crimped, 11 In.	65.00
Heirloom, Centerpiece, Pink Opalescent, 12 x 5 In.	115.00
Heirloom, Vase, Stick, Blue Opalescent, 13 ½ In.	55.00
Hermitage, Tumbler, Blue, 4 Oz., 3 In.	18.00
Jamestown, Tumbler, Blue, Footed, 11 Oz., 6 In.	18.00
Jenny Lind, Flask, Cologne, 10 ¾ In.	125.00
Kashmir, Plate, Azure Blue, 9 In.	30.00
Lafayette, Plate, 7 ½ In.	22.00
Lafayette, Sugar & Creamer, Regal Blue	55.00
Lamp, Opal Iridescent, Mushroom Shade, Gold Threading, Green, Gold Hearts, Vines, 13 In. ...*Illus*	2530.00
Lamp, Peg, Florette, Pink Satin Glass, Clear Shade, Consolidated, 18 In.	173.00
Laurel, Candlestick, 6 ¼ In.	33.00
Lotus, Tray, Center Handle, 11 ½ In. Diam.	30.00
Mayfair, Sugar & Creamer, Green, 2 ¾ & 3 ¼ In. ...*Illus*	35.00
Mayfair, Syrup, Topaz, Unturned Edge, 1930s	100.00
Meadow Rose, Dish, Sweetmeat, Handles, 8 x 6 In.	80.00
Midnight Rose, Celery Dish, 11 ¾ x 5 In.	45.00
Monet, Wine Glass, Stemmed, Smoke Gray, 1985, 8 Piece	95.00
Navarre, Nappy, Handle, 6 ¼ x 2 In.	30.00
Navarre, Relish, Oval, 11 In.	40.00
Needlepoint, Tumbler, Teal Blue, 5 ½ In., 16 Oz.	40.00
Romance, Cup & Saucer	24.00
Vase, Art Nouveau, Heart & Vine, Green & Gold Iridescent, Rolled Rim, 11 ½ In. ...*Illus*	920.00
Vase, Gold Iridescent, Free-Form, Pinched Sides, Prunt Corners, 4 ½ In.	316.00
Vase, Green Iridescent, Gold Hearts, Vines, Cylindrical, Square Mouth, 9 ½ In.	1380.00
Versailles, Cup & Saucer, Azure Blue	38.00
Vesper, Ice Bucket, Swing Handle, Amber, 6 In.	60.00
Willowmere, Goblet, Footed, 5 ⅝ In., 12 Oz.	20.00
Wistar, Candlestick, Milk Glass, Pink, 3 x 4 ¾ In.	45.00

FOVAL, *see Fry category.*

FRAMES *are included in the Furniture category under Frame.*

FRANCISCAN is a trademark that appears on pottery. Gladding, McBean and Company started in 1875. The company grew and acquired other potteries. It made sewer pipes, floor tiles, dinnerware, and art pottery with a variety of trademarks. It began using the trade name *Franciscan* in 1934. In 1936, dinnerware and art pottery were sold under the name *Franciscan Ware.* The company made china and cream-colored, decorated earthenware. Desert Rose, Apple, El Patio, and Coronado were best-sellers. The company became Interpace Corporation and in 1979 was purchased by Josiah Wedgwood & Sons. The plant was closed in 1984, but a few of the patterns are still being made. For more prices, go to kovels.com.

FRANCISCAN CHINA
MADE IN CALIFORNIA

Acacia, Chop Plate, 13 In.	70.00
Acacia, Plate, Bread & Butter, 6 In.	9.00
Antique Green, Plate, Bread & Butter, 6 ¼ In.	14.00
Antique Green, Plate, Dinner, 10 ½ In.	40.00
Antique Green, Platter, Oval, 13 In.	80.00
Arabesque, Creamer	56.00
Arabesque, Cup & Saucer, Footed, 2 ¼ In.	32.00
Arabesque, Plate, Dinner, 10 ¾ In.	40.00
Arden, Chop Plate, 13 In.	95.00
Arden, Plate, Bread & Butter, 6 ⅜ In.	10.00
Arden, Plate, Dinner, 10 ⅝ In.	18.00
Blanc, Bowl, 9 In.	50.00
Blanc, Creamer, 2 ½ In.	16.00
Brentwood, Creamer, 2 ½ In.	20.00
Brentwood, Plate, Dinner, 10 In.	24.00
Canton, Bowl, Vegetable, Oval, 8 ⅞ In.	36.00
Canton, Plate, Dinner, 10 ½ In.	42.00

Fishing, Creel, W.H. McMonies, Fine Weave, Leather Bound, Buckle Strap, Model 61-5, Zippered Pouch
$489.00

Lang's Auction, Inc.

Fishing, Lure, Creek Chub, Fly Rod, Hum-Bird, Yellow Body & Tail, No. F302
$184.00

Lang's Auction, Inc.

Fishing, Lure, Heddon, Musky Surfusser, White Strawberry Spot, Glass Eyes, No. 350S
$288.00

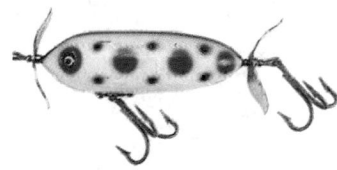

Lang's Auction, Inc.

Fishing, Lure, Shakespeare, Frog, Double Belly Hook, Rubber, Lead Weight, Mechanical, Rhodes
$92.00

Lang's Auction, Inc.

Fishing, Minnow Bucket, Swan Floating, Painted, Stencil, Oval, 12 ¼ x 9 x 9 ¾ In. $219.00

Lang's Auction, Inc.

Fishing, Minnow Trap, Pyramid, Folding, Metal Mesh Cones, Wellington Metal Products, 14 x 10 In. $460.00

Lang's Auction, Inc.

Fishing, Reel, Spool, P.H. Walker, Boston, Salmon, Silver, Fred Curtis, Germany, 4 ½ x 1 ⅞ In. $431.00

Lang's Auction, Inc.

Folk Art, Bottle, Whimsy, Saloon Scene, Wood, Paper, Foil, Bartender, Patrons, Carl Worner, c.1910, 12 In. $1,230.00

Skinner, Inc.

Canton, Plate, Salad, 8 ¼ In.		12.00
Canton, Platter, Oval, 12 ½ In.		70.00
Chelan, Gravy Boat, Underplate Attached		130.00
Chelan, Plate, Bread & Butter, 6 ⅜ In.		9.00
Chelan, Teapot, Lid, 3 Cup, 5 ¼ In.		160.00
Concord, Bowl, Vegetable, Oval, 9 In.		100.00
Concord, Cup & Saucer, Footed		9.00
Concord, Plate, Dinner, 10 ⅝ In.		38.00
Desert Rose, Coffeepot, Lid, 9 In.		56.00
Duet, Bowl, Vegetable, Divided, Round, Lid		75.00
Duet, Cup & Saucer		10.00
Duet, Plate, Dinner, 10 ⅞ In.		12.00
Encore, Cup & Saucer		28.00
Encore, Plate, Bread & Butter, 6 In.		8.00
Encore, Plate, Dinner, 10 ½ In.		18.00
Garland, Bowl, Vegetable, Round, 9 In.		46.00
Garland, Gravy Boat, Attached Underplate		22.00
Garland, Platter, Serving, Oval, 13 In.		20.00
Garland, Salt & Pepper		16.00
Heritage, Bowl, Vegetable, Divider, 10 In.		22.00
Heritage, Cup & Saucer		8.00
Heritage, Plate, Dinner, 10 In.		15.00
Huntington, Bowl, Vegetable, Oval, 9 In.		85.00
Huntington, Chop Plate, 13 In.		140.00
Huntington, Creamer, 5 ¼ In.		50.00
Huntington, Cup & Saucer, Footed		14.00
Huntington, Plate, Dinner, 10 ⅝ In.		30.00
Ivy, Sauceboat, Attached Underplate, 9 In.		24.00
Lucerne, Bowl, Vegetable, Oval, 9 In.		44.00
Lucerne, Cup & Saucer		8.00
Mariposa, Cup & Saucer		38.00
Mariposa, Plate, Bread & Butter, 6 ⅜ In.		14.00
Mariposa, Plate, Dinner, 10 ⅝ In.		60.00
Mariposa, Teapot, Lid, 3 Cup, 5 ¼ In.		360.00
Oasis, Plate, Dinner, 10 ⅞ In.		22.00
Oasis, Platter, Oval, 15 In.		42.00
Sonora, Chop Plate, 13 In.		130.00
Sonora, Cup & Saucer		28.00
Sonora, Plate, Dinner, 10 ⅝ In.		28.00
Sonora, Salt & Pepper		52.00
Sunset, Cup & Saucer		12.00
Sunset, Relish, 3 Sections		110.00
Teak, Plate, Bread & Butter, 6 In.		9.00
Teak, Platter, Oval, 16 In.		160.00
Trio, Cup & Saucer		10.00
Trio, Plate, Dinner, 9 ¾ In.		15.00
Trio, Relish, 3 Sections		100.00
Valencia, Creamer, 3 ¼ In.		24.00
Valencia, Gravy Boat, Underplate		70.00
Valencia, Plate, Dinner, 10 ⅜ In.		12.00
Vase, Conch Shell, Catalina Island, Coral & Ivory Matte, 1940s, 9 x 7 In.		95.00
Westwood, Plate, Bread & Butter, 6 ⅜ In.		10.00
Westwood, Plate, Dinner, 10 ½ In.		26.00
Wildflower, Creamer, 3 ⅝ In.		170.00
Wildflower, Cup & Saucer		90.00
Wildflower, Plate, Dinner, 10 ⅝ In.		115.00
Woodside, Chop Plate, 13 In.		90.00
Woodside, Cup & Saucer		23.00
Woodside, Plate, Salad, 8 ⅜ In.		10.00
Woodside, Platter, Oval, 16 In.		75.00
Woodside, Teapot, Lid, 3 Cup, 5 ¼ In.		160.00

FRANKART INC., New York, New York, mass-produced nude "dancing lady" lamps, ashtrays, and other decorative Art Deco items in the 1920s and 1930s. They were made of white lead composition and spray-painted. *Frankart Inc.* and the patent number and year were stamped on the base.

Ashtray, Nude, Holding Tray, Standing On Orb, Patinated, Marked, 1920s, 24 In.		200.00

Bookends, Nude, On Book, Lead, Painted, 10 In.	750.00
Lamp, 2 Nudes, Green Glass Tube, Marked, 1928, 13 In.	2800.00
Lamp, Nude, 3 Shades, Crackled White, Stepped Base, Marked, c.1930, 12 In.	1375.00
Lamp, Nude, Frosted Glass Panel, Stepped Base, Marked, Pat. 76612, c.1930, 11 In.	2000.00
Lamp, Nude, Holding Globe, Green Crackled Glass, Fluted Pedestal, Marked, c.1930, 8 ½ In. ..*Illus*	2125.00
Lamp, Nude, Holding Tray, Electrified, c.1930	425.00
Lamp, Nude, Kneeling, Crackled Amber Glass Globe, Stepped Base, c.1930, 8 In.	719.00
Lamp, Nudes, Crackled Rose Glass Globe, Stepped Base, Marked, c.1930, 9 In.	594.00
Vase, Nude, Holding Glass Vase, Painted, Green, c.1930, 12 In.	1050.00

FRANKOMA POTTERY was originally known as The Frank Potteries when John F. Frank opened shop in 1933. The factory is now working in Sapulpa, Oklahoma. Early wares were made from a light cream-colored clay from Ada, Oklahoma, but in 1956 the company switched to a red clay from Sapulpa. The firm made dinnerware, utilitarian and decorative kitchenwares, figurines, flowerpots, and limited edition and commemorative pieces. John Frank died in 1973 and his daughter, Joniece, inherited the business. Frankoma went bankrupt in 1990. The pottery operated under various owners for a few years and was bought by Joe Ragosta in 2008. It closed in 2010. The buildings, assets, name, and molds were sold at an auction in 2011.

Ashtray, Oklahoma, Green, Brown, 4 ⅝ x 2 ⅝ In.	14.00
Bowl, Sun Valley, Central Smiling Sun, 6 ⅞ In.	55.00
Bread Warmer, Plainsman, Warm Bread For Your Table, 1950s	13.00
Butter, Cover, Mayan Aztec	36.00
Canteen, Thunderbird, Cork, Leather Strap, 7 x 7 x 2 In.	65.00
Casserole, Wagon Wheel, Desert Gold, Brown, Handles, 10 x 3 In.	35.00
Cookie Jar, Ribbed, Brown, Marked, 8 ¼ In.	18.00
Dish, Dogwood, Desert Gold, 3 ¾ x 3 In.	6.00
Figurine, Cowboy Boot, Prairie Green, 3 ½ In., Pair	44.00
Figurine, Weeping Woman, 5 ½ In.	69.00
Honey Pot, Lid, Bee, Yellow To Rust, 4 ¾ In.	65.00
Mug, Flame, Pedestal	6.00
Mug, Flame, Ribbed Handle	8.00
Mug, Mayan Aztec, Prairie Green Glaze, 3 ⅝ In.	15.00
Mug, Pedestal, Westwind White Sand, 4 ¼ In.	20.00
Mug, Uncle Sam, Red, 1976, 4 ⅛ In.	28.00
Pitcher, Plainsman, Woodland Moss, Qt.	37.00
Planter, Fluted, Yellow, 3 x 7 In.	16.00
Plate, Bread & Butter, Lazybones, Prairie Green, 5 ⅞ In.	3.50
Plate, Christmas, Laid In A Manger, 1969, 8 In.	15.00
Plate, Christmas, The Annunciation, Marked, 1973, 8 ½ In.	18.00
Plate, Easter, He Is Risen, 1972, 7 ½ In.	20.00
Platter, Plainsman, Cinnamon, Oval, 9 ¾ x 6 In.	15.00
Salt & Pepper, Brown, Beige, Handle, 1950s, 5 In.	20.00
Salt & Pepper, Flame, Red, Stoppers, 4 ½ In.	12.00
Saucer, Wagon Wheel, Prairie Wheel, 5 ½ In.	4.00
Sugar & Creamer, Wagon Wheel, Prairie Green	34.00
Trivet, Arrows To Atoms, Dessert Gold, Round, c.1957, 6 In.	40.00
Trivet, Cherokee, Alphabet, 6 In.	24.00
Trivet, Fleur-De-Lis, Red To Yellow, 6 x 6 In.	30.00
Trivet, Indians In Oklahoma, Tan, Round, 6 ⅜ In.	20.00
Trivet, Iowa, Hawkeye State, White Glaze, 6 In.	25.00
Trivet, Liberty Bell, Bicentennial, Desert Gold, Round, 6 ¼ In.	24.00
Tureen, Lazy Bones, Prairie Green, Cover, Ladle, 3 Qt.	125.00
Vase, Black, Ringed, Cylindrical, 10 In.	65.00
Vase, Brown Satin Glaze, Octagonal, Footed, 6 In.	12.00
Vase, Bud, Flame, 4 ⅝ In.	28.00
Vase, Bud, Snail, Black, 6 ¼ In.	22.00
Vase, Praying Hands, White Sand, Marked, 6 ½ x 5 ¼ In.	48.00
Vase, Ram's Head, Desert Gold, Footed, 6 In.	39.00
Wall Pocket, Peach Glow, Acorn Shape, Satin Matte Glaze, 6 x 4 x 2 In.	68.00

FRATERNAL objects that are related to the many different fraternal organizations in the United States are listed in this category. The Elks, Masons, Odd Fellows, and others are included. Also included are service organizations, like the American Legion, Kiwanis, and Lions Club. Furniture is listed in the Furniture category. Shaving mugs decorated with fraternal crests are included in the Shaving Mug category.

Eastern Star, Planter, Star Shape, Symbols Of Biblical Heroines, Green, 6 ½ x 6 ½ In.	32.00

Folk Art, Clock, Shelf, Fireplace & Chimney Shape, George Griggs, Faux Bricks, Wood, c.1900, 32 In.
$118.00

Garth's Auctioneers & Appraisers

Folk Art, Mirror, Carved, Figure Holding Up 7 Fingers, 7 Years Bad Luck, 1800s, 17 ½ x 11 In.
$5,700.00

Cowan's Auctions

Folk Art, Panel, Eagle, Seed Pods, Leaves, Frame, Lois Devlin, Louisville, Ky., 1967, 14 x 18 In.
$147.00

Garth's Auctioneers & Appraisers

TIP
Coffee or tea stains can be removed from a cup by scrubbing with salt on a sponge.

Folk Art, Retablo, Oil On Tin, Christ Child, Red Heart, Flowers, Inscription, c.1875, 14 x 9 ¾ In.
$392.00

Garth's Auctioneers & Appraisers

Folk Art, Shield, American Flag, Painted, Carved Relief Stars, c.1950, 31 x 22 ½ In.
$470.00

Garth's Auctioneers & Appraisers

Folk Art, Whirligig, Fatty Arbuckle, Pine, Full Body, Front On Both Sides, 1920s, 19 In.
$920.00

James D. Julia Auctioneers

Folk Art, Whirligig, Man, Bowtie, Boutonniere, Tin Hatband, Paddles, Carved, Painted, c.1910, 33 In.
$14,220.00

Skinner, Inc.

Elks, Badge, Celluloid, Die-Cut Elk's Head, Purple Ribbon, Syracuse Lodge No. 31, 1904, 3 ¼ In.	81.00
Elks, Landscape, Sepia, Wood, c.1890, 15 ⅓ x 15 In.	55.00
Elks, Tankard, Brown, Full-Length Handle, Warwick, 11 In.	153.00
Elks, Watch Fob, Elk Tooth, 14K White Gold, Elk Head, Clock Striking 11, 1 x ⅝ In.	115.00
Knights Of Pythias, Ceremonial Sword, Scabbard, Wire Wrapped Handle, Clam Shell Guard, 39 In.	48.00
Masonic, 32nd Degree, Pendant, Double Eagle, Gold, 19-In. Chain	1015.00
Masonic, Apron, Cream Ground, Blue Trim, Symbols, Cotton, Silk, 18 x 17 ½ In.	325.00
Masonic, Apron, Emblems, Cream, Silver Trim, Flap Eye Symbol, c.1810, 16 x 14 In.	354.00
Masonic, Apron, Painted Star, Temple, Inscribed Daniel Woodworth, Frame, c.1820, 16 ¾ x 14 ¾ In.	2006.00
Masonic, Apron, Silk, Painted, Rainbow, Figures, Symbols, Hasselkuse, Frame, 1796, 14 In.	826.00
Masonic, Ax, Carved, Painted, No. 8 Berks County Degree Lodge, Heart In Hand, 1800s, 31 In.	1007.00
Masonic, Badge, 14K Gold, Symbols, King Hill Lodge, St. Joseph Missouri, 2 ½ In.	700.00
Masonic, Cane, Maple, Bakelite, Spyglass Handle, Carved, Snake, Anchor, Ivy, Script, c.1910, 38 In.	920.00
Masonic, Cloth, Red Arch, Symbols, Cream Ground, Inscribed John Leland, Frame, 22 x 24 ¾ In.	295.00
Masonic, Column, Fluted, Metal, Side Symbols, Corinthian Caps, Globe Finial, 112 In., Pair	4130.00
Masonic, Goblet, Engraved Symbols, Clear Blown Glass, 5 ½ In.	123.00
Masonic, Gravel, Wood, Racket River Lodge Placard, Frame, 7 ½ In.	142.00
Masonic, Pedestal, Walnut, Inlaid Exotic Woods, Columns, Symbols, c.1876, 34 x 36 In. ....*Illus*	1968.00
Masonic, Pendant, Applied, Painted Symbols, Gold Tone Frame, 1700s, 1 ⅞ In.	840.00
Masonic, Pendant, Emblem, 9K Yellow Gold, Diamonds, 1 In.	349.00
Masonic, Pendant, Symbols, Seed Pearls, Gold Filigree, Blue, Glass Back, Sunburst Frame, 3 ⁵⁄₁₆ In.	1200.00
Masonic, Preceptor's Badge, Enamel, Blue Buckle, Red Dragon, 18K Gold, Eng., c.1890, 3 In.	1180.00
Masonic, Punch Bowl, Gateway, Pulsanti Aperietur, Gilt, c.1770, 14 In.	25000.00
Masonic, Punch Bowl, Symbols, Perfect Ashlar, Serpent, Paddle, c.1790, 20 ¼ In.	32500.00
Masonic, Razor, Symbol-Engraved Blade, Horn Handle, 6 ½ In.	354.00
Masonic, Shaving Mug, A. Riggs, F.L.T., Tent, Crossed Swords, 3 ¾ In.	84.00
Masonic, Shaving Mug, Foye, O.U.A.M., Flags, Arm & Hammer, Ironstone, 3 ½ x 3 ⅜ In. ....*Illus*	94.00
Masonic, Shaving Mug, H.L. Grebinger, Gilt, c.1880, 3 ¾ In.	90.00
Masonic, Shaving Mug, Symbols, Gilt, C.F. Kien, Stamped Germany, 3 ¾ In.	48.00
Masonic, Sign, Hall Lodge, Sand Paint, Arched, 1800s, 49 ¼ x 72 In.	770.00
Masonic, Table, Maple, Inlaid Masonic Symbol, Tripod Base, 29 x 18 In.	240.00
Masonic, Tumbler, Paneled, Etched Symbols, Enclosed Dice, England, c.1780, 2 x 2 In.	330.00
Masonic, Watch Chain, Fob, Sterling, Oval Links, Round Synthetic Ruby, England, 1800s, 14 In.	253.00
Masonic, Watch Fob, Metal Disc, Emblem, Gold Inlaid, 1 ½ In.	48.00
Masonic, Wine, Gilt Etched Symbols & Rims, Tapered Glass, 8 In.	118.00
Masonic, Winking Moon, Tassel Cap, Plaster Supreme Forrest Convention, Baltimore, 16 In.	1062.00
Odd Fellows, Game Board, Checkers, FLT, U.S. Flags, Square, c.1890, 17 ½ In. ....*Illus*	2760.00
Odd Fellows, Jug, Hexagonal, Symbols, Text, Staffordshire, c.1850, 7 ½ x 2 In.	431.00
Order Of The Moose, Shaving Mug, Moose Head, George W. Kuhlman, Bavaria Stamp, 3 ¾ In.	60.00
Royal Ancient Order Of Foresters, Cupboard, 2 Doors, Mirror, Crest, c.1840, 46 x 30 In.	1364.00

FRY GLASS was made by the H.C. Fry Glass Company of Rochester, Pennsylvania. The company, founded in 1901, first made cut glass and other types of fine glasswares. In 1922 it patented a heat-resistant glass called Pearl Ovenglass. For two years, 1926–1927, the company made Fry Foval, an opal ware decorated with colored trim. Reproductions of this glass have been made. Depression glass patterns made by Fry may be listed in the Depression Glass category. Some pieces of cut glass may also be included in the Cut Glass category.

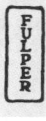

FRY GLASS

Bowl, Hobstar, Strawberry Diamond, Button & Fan, Notched Scalloped Edge, 3 x 10 In.	100.00
Candlestick, Opalescent Turquoise & Cobalt Blue, Twist Stems, Saucer Foot, 11 In., Pair	81.00
Vase, Magnolia Pattern, Baluster, Elongated Flared Rim, 14 ¼ In.	400.00

FRY FOVAL

Candlestick, Opal, Blue Threaded Wrap, Wafers, Opalescent Disc Feet, Cup, 10 ¾ In., Pair	58.00
Vase, Bud, Jack-In-The-Pulpit, Opalescent, Green Lip Wrap, Footed, 10 In.	35.00

FULPER POTTERY COMPANY was incorporated in 1899 in Flemington, New Jersey. It made art pottery from 1909 to 1929. The firm had been making bottles, jugs, and housewares from 1805. Doll heads were made about 1928. The firm became Stangl Pottery in 1929. Stangl Pottery is listed in its own category in this book.

Basket, Flower Lid, Handle, Multicolor, 9 In.	98.00
Bowl, Blue, Brown Glaze, Marked, 14 In.	142.00
Bowl, Flared, Footed, Blue, Yellow, 10 In.	58.00
Bowl, Green Mottled Glaze, Green To Cream Inside, Rounded, Splayed Foot, 11 ½ x 4 In.	230.00
Bowl, Green, 8 ¼ In.	35.00

Bowl, Mirrored Black, Purple Flambe Interior, Wide Rim, Round Foot, 3 ½ x 10 In.	81.00
Bowl, Round, Scalloped, Blue, Crystalline Glaze, Signed, 15 x 3 In.	313.00
Candleholder, Rounded Cone Shape, Gray, Brown, Flambe, Inset Green, Yellow Glass, 5 x 11 In.	625.00
Cat, Resting, Tan, Brown, Blue Glaze, Marked, 9 ½ x 6 In.	1250.00
Cat, Sleeping, Curled Up, Blue Matte Glaze, 9 x 3 In.	750.00
Crock, Stoneware, Flared Rim, Slip Trailed Cobalt Blue Schuster Bro's., c.1880, 1 Gal.	115.00
Dresser Box, Figural Woman, Seated, Hand On Head, Blue Dress, Yellow Base, Marked, 8 In.	81.00
Dresser Box, Figural, Woman, Purple Dress, Polka Dot Base, Marked, 6 ½ In.	63.00
Lamp, Cockatoo, Orange & Yellow, Black Stump, Signed, 13 In. ....*Illus*	604.00
Lamp, Figural, Yellow Parrot, Orange Stump, 11 In.	518.00
Lamp, Mushroom, Leaded Slag Glass, Cucumber Matte Glaze, Marked, c.1910, 21 ½ x 17 In. ..*Illus*	11250.00
Lamp, Perfume, Figural, Parrot, Orange, Yellow, Tree Trunk Base, Signed, 10 In.	518.00
Perfume Lid, Ballerina, 5 In.	23.00
Vase, 3 Handles, Blue, Round, 7 ¼ In.	63.00
Vase, 3 Handles, Round, Dusty Black, 6 ½ In.	127.00
Vase, 4-Buttress Shape, Flemington Green Drip Glaze, Signed, 10 In.	2300.00
Vase, 4-Buttress Shape, Green, Brown, Blue, Flambe Glaze, Marked, 6 x 8 In.	344.00
Vase, Ashes Of Roses, Baluster, Narrow Neck, Spread Foot, Marked, 11 ⅞ In.	345.00
Vase, Baluster, Striated Earth Tones, Oval, c.1915, 11 ½ In.	295.00
Vase, Black & Beige Flambe Glaze, Squat, Smokestack, Flat Rim, 4 ½ x 7 In.	173.00
Vase, Black Drip Over Green Flambe, Foolscap, Trumpet Rim, Spread Foot, Marked, 7 ¼ In.	184.00
Vase, Black, Green Drip Glaze, 4-Buttress Shape, Round Base, Signed, 11 x 14 In.	2806.00
Vase, Blue Flambe Glaze, Buttressed, Marked, 8 ¼ In.	575.00
Vase, Blue Glaze, 2 Handles, c.1920, 6 x 6 ½ In.	148.00
Vase, Blue, Gold, Red Streak Design, 4 Buttress, Smokestack, Marked, 8 In.	230.00
Vase, Blue, Green Leopard Skin Glaze, Flared, Pinched Top, Signed, 6 x 10 ¼ In.	366.00
Vase, Blue, Green, Purple Glaze, Shouldered, Rolled Rim, Marked, 6 ⅝ In.	431.00
Vase, Blue, Snowflake Crystals Design, Handles From Rim To Shoulder, Marked, 7 ⅜ In.	431.00
Vase, Bottle, Moss To Rose Flambe Glaze, Squat Bottom, c.1920, 10 x 9 ½ In.	313.00
Vase, Brown Glaze, Turning Marks, Oval, 2 Loop Handles, 9 In.	59.00
Vase, Brown, Cream, Blue Glaze, Compressed Globular, Stick Neck, Marked, 5 ½ In.	173.00
Vase, Brown, Marked, 9 ½ In.	242.00
Vase, Brown, Tan, Blue Flambe Glaze, 3 Handles, Tapered, 4 ¼ x 6 In.	281.00
Vase, Brown, Tan, Green Flambe Glaze, Cylinder, 2 ¾ x 8 ¼ In.	344.00
Vase, Bulb, Green To Blue, Pinched Waist, Marked, 4 ¼ In.	46.00
Vase, Bulbous, Blue & Gray Flambe Glaze, Marked, 8 In.	325.00
Vase, Bulbous, Blue Flambe, Marked, 5 ½ In.	150.00
Vase, Bulbous, Blue, Brown, Tan, Crystalline Flambe Glaze, Footed, Handles, 9 x 9 In.	688.00
Vase, Bulbous, Cucumber Green, Matte Glaze, Handles, Incised, Paper Label, 12 x 12 In.	563.00
Vase, Bulbous, Green, Crystalline Glaze, Handles, 12 x 12 In.	625.00
Vase, Bulbous, Green, Runny, Brown, Crystalline, Flambe Glaze, 5 ½ x 8 ¼ In.	594.00
Vase, Bulbous, Yellow, Blue, Brown, Flambe Glaze, 3 Handles, Marked, 6 ½ x 6 ½ In.	313.00
Vase, Cafe Au Lait Glaze, Cylindrical, 4 Buttresses, Cutout Triangles, c.1920, 13 ½ In.	4688.00
Vase, Chinese Blue Flambe Glaze, Round, 5 Looped Handles, 10 x 11 In., Pair	1063.00
Vase, Cobalt Blue To Green Flambe Glaze, Bulbous Bottom, Trumpet Neck, c.1915, 15 ¼ x 7 ¾ In.	563.00
Vase, Coppertone, Green, Brown, Mottled, Textured Glaze, 12 ¼ In.	767.00
Vase, Cream To Brown, Lug Handles, Marked, 12 ½ In.	345.00
Vase, Double Handles Shape, Blue, Green, Brown Flambe Glaze, Crystalline, Marked, 6 x 4 ¼ In.	275.00
Vase, Flared Ruffled Rim, Leopard Skin Glaze, 6 x 10 ¼ In.	300.00
Vase, Globular, 5 Loop Handles, Turquoise Glaze, Crystalline Highlights, 10 x 10 In.	325.00
Vase, Gray & Black Glaze, Dripped Over Green, Shouldered, 8 In.	518.00
Vase, Green & Turquoise Over Pink, Bullet Shape, 3 Handles At Neck, Flare Rim, Marked, 6 ¼ In.	288.00
Vase, Green & Yellow Flambe Glaze, Streaked Design, Handles At Rim, Ring Foot, 6 ½ x 9 In.	173.00
Vase, Green Drip Over Fuchsia Glaze, Ring Foot, Cylindrical Neck, Rolled Rim, c.1910, 10 ⅜ In.	230.00
Vase, Green Flambe Glaze, Squat Bottom, Tapered Top, 4 Buttresses, 1910s, 13 x 10 In.	2000.00
Vase, Green Mottled Glaze, Bulbous, Marked, 9 ½ In.	413.00
Vase, Green Variegated Glaze, Crystalline Effect, Cylindrical, Marked, 10 ¾ In.	316.00
Vase, Green, Blue & Pink Glaze, Genie Bottle Shaped, Marked, 8 In.	150.00
Vase, Green, Leopard Skin, Bulbous, Ring Foot, 3 Loop Handles At Shoulder, Stamped, 6 ⅜ In.	1840.00
Vase, Mirror Black & Brown Glaze, Bulbous, Ring Foot, Rolled Rim, Ribbed, 1920s, 11 ½ In., Pair	1625.00
Vase, Mirror Black Glaze, Amphora Shape, 2 Handles, Footed, 13 x 7 ½ In.	531.00
Vase, Mirrored Black Drip Over Blue, Rose, Swollen Shouldered, Marked, 7 ½ In.	207.00
Vase, Mottled Green Crystalline Glaze, Bulbous, 2 Arched Handles, c.1920, 12 x 10 In.	1188.00
Vase, Purple Glaze, Blue Accents, Squat, Squared Handles At Rim, 6 ¼ x 8 In.	196.00
Vase, Speckled Brown Over Green, Oval, 12 x 7 In.	250.00

Fostoria, Lamp, Opal Iridescent, Mushroom Shade, Gold Threading, Green, Gold Hearts, Vines, 13 In.
$2,530.00

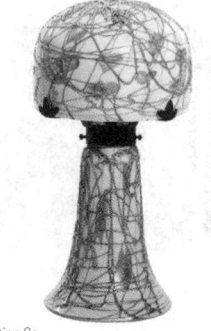

Early Auction Co.

Fostoria, Mayfair, Sugar & Creamer, Green, 2 ¾ & 3 ¼ In.
$35.00

Huby Lane, Inc.

Fostoria, Vase, Art Nouveau, Heart & Vine, Green & Gold Iridescent, Rolled Rim, 11 ½ In.
$920.00

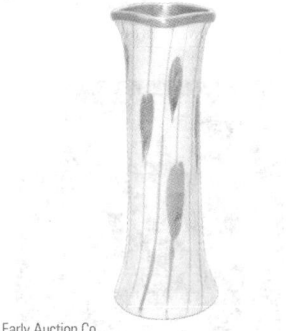

Early Auction Co.

Frankart, Lamp, Nude, Holding Globe, Green Crackled Glass, Fluted Pedestal, Marked, c.1930, 8 ½ In.
$2,125.00

Heritage Auctions

Fraternal, Masonic, Pedestal, Walnut, Inlaid Exotic Woods, Columns, Symbols, c.1876, 34 x 36 In.
$1,968.00

Neal Auction Co.

Fraternal, Masonic, Shaving Mug, Foye, O.U.A.M., Flags, Arm & Hammer, Ironstone, 3 ½ x 3 ⅜ In.
$94.00

Conestoga Auction Co., Inc.

Fraternal, Odd Fellows, Game Board, Checkers, FLT, U.S. Flags, Square, c.1890, 17 ½ In.
$2,760.00

Skinner, Inc.

Fulper, Lamp, Cockatoo, Orange & Yellow, Black Stump, Signed, 13 In.
$604.00

Early Auction Co.

F

Vase, Stick Neck, Green To Deep Magenta, 8 ½ In.	138.00
Vase, Streaky Blue Glaze, Green, Shouldered, Tapered, Spread Foot, Rolled Rim, Marked, 11 ¾ In.	196.00
Vase, Turquoise Glaze, Crystalline Accents, 5 Handles, Globular, 10 ½ x 10 In.	397.00
Vase, Yellow To Brown Flambe Glaze, Shouldered, Tapered, Rolled Rim, 6 ¾ In.	184.00
Vase, Yellow, Brown, Blue Flambe Glaze, Tapered, Flat Border Shoulder, Rolled Rim, c.1920, 10 In.	316.00

FURNITURE of all types is listed in this category. Examples dating from the seventeenth century to the 1970s are included. Prices for furniture vary in different parts of the country. Oak furniture is most expensive in the West; large pieces over eight feet high are sold for the most money in the South, where high ceilings are found in the old homes. Condition is very important when determining prices. These are NOT average prices but rather reports of unique sales. If the description includes the word *style*, the piece resembles the old furniture style but was made at a later time. It is not a period piece. Garden furniture is listed in the Garden Furnishings category. Related items may be found in the Architectural, Brass, and Store categories.

Altar, Teak, 2 Recessed Doors, Pierced, Carved Panels, Skirt, 30 x 38 ½ In.	518.00
Armchairs are listed under Chair in this category.	
Armoire, Art Deco, Mahogany, Inlay, Mirror, 2 Side Doors, Cupid Plaques, Belgium, 86 x 86 In.	938.00
Armoire, Art Deco, Mixed Wood, Mother-Of-Pearl Inlay, Arched Mirror Door, c.1925, 81 x 60 In.	500.00
Armoire, Baroque Style, Parcel Gilt, 2 Panel Doors, Painted, Italy, 5 x 7 ½ Ft.	936.00
Armoire, Biedermeier, Book Matched Doors, Arches, Arrows, Pilasters, Block Feet, 1800s, 76 x 47 In.	1896.00
Armoire, Cypress, Molded Cornice, 2 2-Panel Doors, Shelves, 81 x 51 In.	4183.00
Armoire, French Provincial, Oak, Demilune, Courting Couple, Bun Feet, c.1900, 84 x 36 In.	522.00
Armoire, Gothic Revival, Rosewood, Paneled Doors, Drawers, Demilune, c.1850, 94 x 73 In.	6573.00
Armoire, Ivory, Fruitwood, Hunt Scene, 2 Mirror Doors, 2 Drawers, Italy, c.1790, 88 x 53 In.	5400.00
Armoire, Karges, Mahogany, 2 Doors, Curved Crest, Medallion, Flowers, Swags, Columns, 89 x 53 In.	3094.00
Armoire, Louis XV Style, Gray & Cream Paint, Paneled Doors, Drawers, Cabriole Legs, 76 x 48 In.	492.00
Armoire, Louis XV Style, Kingwood, 3 Parts, Leaf Crest, Molded Cornice, Mirror, 105 x 82 In.	1270.00
Armoire, Louis XV Style, Oak, Flower Basket, Shaped Panel Doors, 1900s, 81 x 47 In.	1353.00
Armoire, Louis XV, Fruitwood, Parquetry, Brass Escutcheon Plates, Cornice, c.1800, 92 x 59 In.	2124.00
Armoire, Louis XV, Pine, Arched Cornice, Raised Panel Doors, Reeded Stile, Hoof Feet, 89 x 57 In.	861.00
Armoire, Louis XV, Walnut, Arched Cornice, 2 Doors, Scalloped Apron, 96 x 23 In.	819.00
Armoire, Louis XVI Style, Parquetry, Bronze Mounts, 3 Doors, Mirror, c.1885, 88 x 74 In.	708.00
Armoire, Mahogany, Double Ogee Cornice, Framed Panel Doors, c.1835, 94 x 72 In.	1107.00
Armoire, Mahogany, Projecting Cornice, Paneled Doors, Vase Shaped Legs, c.1835, 89 x 51 In.	2214.00
Armoire, Oak, Flowers, Urn, Carved, 2 Doors, France, 90 x 59 In.	720.00
Armoire, Paneled Doors, Cabriole Legs, Hoof Feet, West Indies, 1800s, 79 x 56 In.	6765.00
Armoire, Pine, Molded Cornice, Paneled Doors, Fluted Columns, Octagonal Feet, 1800s, 88 x 53 In.	492.00
Armoire, Pine, Painted Flowers, Door, Shelves, Bavaria, 1800s, 69 x 44 In.	237.00
Armoire, Provincial, Painted, 2 Paneled Doors, C-Scroll & Leaf Design, 91 x 68 In.	2952.00
Armoire, Purpleheart Mahogany, 2 Shaped Panel Doors, Turned Feet, 67 x 48 In.	4183.00
Armoire, Renaissance Revival, Oak, Ogee Cornice, Door, Drawer, Masks, Putti, Pilasters, 76 x 45 In.	1188.00
Armoire, Renaissance Revival, Walnut, Carved Crest, 2 Doors, 2 Base Drawers, c.1875, 58 x 20 In.	767.00
Armoire, Rococo Revival, Mahogany, Fruit, Nut Crest, Panel Doors, c.1850, 108 x 73 In.	7170.00
Armoire, Rosewood, Burl, Arched Cornice, Urn Finials, Fluted Columns, 1800s, 102 x 69 In.	2700.00
Armoire, Rosewood, Cornice, Paneled Doors, Molded Feet, Beaded, 1800s, 99 x 62 In.	10158.00
Armoire, Secessionist Style, Wood, Mother-Of-Pearl, Brass, Mirror, Drawer, c.1890, 87 x 44 In.	420.00
Armoire, Walnut, Carved Flower Cornice, Door, Carved Columns, Low Drawer, c.1890, 112 x 54 In.	805.00
Armoire, Walnut, Molded Cornice, Tombstone Shaped Panel Doors, Bracket Feet, c.1835, 87 x 56 In.	338.00
Armoire, Walnut, Ogee Cornice, Molded Doors, Bracket Feet, c.1850, 94 x 73 In.	2749.00
Bar Cart, Bruksbo, Rosewood, Brass, 2 Doors, Square Legs, Casters, Denmark, 1960s, 36 x 30 In.	1250.00
Bar Cart, Burl Walnut, Drawer, Wheels, Base Shelf, c.1955, 29 x 40 In.	500.00
Bar Cart, Lucite, Mirror Glass Shelves, Metal Handles, 1960s, 24 ½ x 16 In.	500.00
Bar Cart, Modern, Brass, 2 Tiers, Glass Shelves, Downswept Legs, c.1980, 27 x 32 In.	720.00
Bar, 2 Barstools, Natural Fiber, Simulated Fabric, Diamond Shape Metalwork, 39 x 47 In., 3 Piece	474.00
Bar, Oak, Granite Top, Curved Panels, c.1900, 44 x 65 In.	1200.00
Bar, Saloon, Oak, Mirror, Columns, San Domingo Model, Brunswick, 1908, 18 Ft. x 9 ½ Ft.	22000.00
Barstool, Industrial Design, Aluminum, Plastic, Square, Seat, Stretcher, 30 x 12 In., Pair	296.00
Bed Steps, 3 Steps, Inset Leather, Hinged, Bulbous Turned Legs, c.1815, 26 x 29 In.	1476.00
Bed Steps, George III Style, Mahogany, 3 Steps, Gilt Inset, Hinged, Bun Feet, c.1875, 25 x 25 In.	1353.00
Bed Steps, Regency, Mahogany, 3 Treads, Potty Chamber, 26 x 32 In.	590.00
Bed Steps, William IV, Mahogany, 3 Steps, Potty Chamber, c.1835, 26 x 19 In.	518.00
Bed, Brass, Column Supports, Scrolled Flowers, Urn Finials, 60 x 56 In.	120.00
Bed, Brass, Polished, Frosted Brass Flower & Scroll Panels, 70 x 58 In.	118.00
Bed, Campaign, Gilt, Brush Metal, c.1850, 39 x 76 In.	1500.00

Bed, Campaign, Nickel Plated Brass, Steel, France, 1960s, 38 x 86 In.	938.00
Bed, Cannonball, Mahogany, Turned Head & Footboard, Leaf Carved, c.1830, 49 x 58 In.	708.00
Bed, Canopy, Jacobean Style, Oak, Panel Headboard, Column Footboard, c.1920, 83 x 89 In.	978.00
Bed, Canopy, Lacquer, Red, Gold, Birds, Flowers, Figures, Chinese, 1800s, 117 x 83 In. ....Illus	3690.00
Bed, Canopy, Sheraton Style, Curly Maple, Eldred Wheeler, 82 x 82 In.	1659.00
Bed, Canopy, Sheraton, Curly Maple, Turned Posts, c.1825, 94 x 60 x 89 In. ....Illus	844.00
Bed, Empire Style, Mahogany, Paneled, Cornice, Fluted Uprights, Top Shape Feet, c.1900, 64 x 83 In.	861.00
Bed, Federal, Mahogany, Leaf & Garland Carved Posts, 1800s, 68 x 53 ½ In.	633.00
Bed, Footboard & Headboard Putti Carved, Ivory Inlay, Italy, Headboard 71 In., Footboard 46 In.	590.00
Bed, Four-Poster, Cannonball, Cherry, Turnings, Rope, 19th Century, 61 x 57 x 82 In.	176.00
Bed, Four-Poster, Colonial Revival, Arch Crest, Carved Flowers, Columns, c.1890, 84 x 43 In., Pair	938.00
Bed, Four-Poster, Federal, Mahogany, Carved, Reeded, Acanthus, Flower Basket, 89 x 77 In.	1534.00
Bed, Four-Poster, Gothic Revival, Figured Mahogany, New Orleans, 88 In.	1298.00
Bed, Four-Poster, Mahogany, Scrolled Headboard, Reeded, Leaf Carved, c.1840, 93 x 81 In.	708.00
Bed, Four-Poster, Molded Canopy, Mahogany, Tapered Columns, Fluted Urns, c.1900, 89 x 65 In.	923.00
Bed, Four-Poster, Sheraton, Mahogany, Arched, Reeded, Legs, New England, 85 x 77 In.	2596.00
Bed, Four-Poster, Sheraton, Softwood, Vase Shape Posts, Rail, Panel Headboard, 83 x 61 In.	354.00
Bed, Four-Poster, Sheraton, Tiger Maple, Turned, Shaped Boards, c.1845, 85 x 80 In.	288.00
Bed, French Empire Style, Mahogany, Bronze Ormolu, Torch Posts, Leaves, c.1910, 37 x 54 In.	660.00
Bed, Gothic Revival, Bird's-Eye Maple, Carved, 3-Panel Headboard, c.1850, 73 x 59 In.	1093.00
Bed, Hired Man's, Plank Legs, Gray Paint, Single, 17 x 77 x 20 In.	325.00
Bed, Louis XV Style, Mahogany, Pierced & Carved Floral Headboard, 1930s, 67 x 57 In.	307.00
Bed, Louis XV Style, Parcel Gilt, Courting Scene, Shell & Flower Crest, c.1910, 53 x 55 x 84 In. ..Illus	615.00
Bed, Mahogany, Gilt Bronze Mounts, Applied Mythical Figures, France, c.1890, 58 x 70 In.	3000.00
Bed, Mahogany, Walnut, Gilt, Fluted Posts, Foot & Headboards, King, 57 x 84 In.	1416.00
Bed, Murphy, Oak, Carved Crest, Mirror, Shelves, Springs, c.1905, 80 x 54 ½ In.	1265.00
Bed, Napoleon III, Mahogany, Molded Cornice, Ormolu Leaves, Uprights, c.1885, 56 x 74 In.	399.00
Bed, Sleigh, Charles X, Mahogany, Marquetry, Flowers, Eagles, Single, Pair	2988.00
Bed, Sleigh, Mahogany, Tubular Crests, Paneled Headboard, Footboard, Scroll Rails, c.1850	956.00
Bed, Victorian, Walnut, Fruit, Leaf, Crest, Finials, Curved Footboard, Carved, Queen, 82 x 81 In.	1770.00
Bench, Alexander Loge, Upholstered, X-Shape Bronze Base, 18 x 22 x 17 In., Pair	3645.00
Bench, Baroque Style, Oak, Dark Stain, Black Needlepoint, Square Legs, 17 x 39 In.	375.00
Bench, Black Forest, Bear Cubs, Standing, Holding Plank, Glass Eyes, c.1880, 26 x 38 In.	2415.00
Bench, Black Forest, Bears, Basswood, Glass Eyes, c.1890, 26 ½ x 45 In. ....Illus	755.00
Bench, Bootjack Ends, Green Paint, 62 ½ In.	173.00
Bench, Bucket, 3 Steps, Blue Paint, Straight Sides, Open Back, 1800s, 43 x 37 In.	590.00
Bench, Bucket, Pine, Backsplash, Drawer, Blue Paint, c.1835, 36 x 40 In.	1033.00
Bench, Bucket, Pine, Cutout Sides, Red Stain, Pa., c.1890, 46 x 37 In.	444.00
Bench, Bucket, Pine, Painted, Pennsylvania, 1800s, 33 x 37 ½ In.	533.00
Bench, Bucket, Pine, Painted, Red Surface, 2 Lower Cupboard Doors, c.1850, 36 ½ x 38 In.	1778.00
Bench, Bucket, Pine, Plank Top, Angled Sides, Open Shelf, 23 x 44 In.	374.00
Bench, Bucket, Pine, Shelf Stretcher, Gray, Red Paint, Pa., c.1800, 30 ½ x 38 ½ In.	1659.00
Bench, Bucket, Poplar, Painted, Blue & Green, 19th Century, 18 x 74 In.	472.00
Bench, Bucket, Poplar, Red Stain, Pa., c.1850, 53 x 44 In.	10665.00
Bench, Bucket, Shaker, Pine, Blue Gray Paint, Shaped Frieze, Arched Ends, c.1900, 18 x 85 x 12 In.	460.00
Bench, Bucket, Softwood, Green, Trough Top, Gallery, Diagonal Brace, Cutout Feet, 34 x 50 In.	266.00
Bench, Chippendale Style, 6 Legs, Ball & Claw Feet, Upholstered, Gold Paint, c.1860, 19 x 45 In.	60.00
Bench, Chrome, Slanted Top, Signed Design Institute Of America, 60 x 16 ½ In.	854.00
Bench, Church Meeting, Plank, Painted, Angled Book Boards, 141 x 33 In., Pair	47.00
Bench, Cobbler's, Pine, Drawer, Turned Legs, 20 x 43 In.	69.00
Bench, Curule, Rosewood, Peaches & Leaves, Bamboo Shaped Stretchers, 1800s, 21 x 29 In.	369.00
Bench, Deacon's, Pine, Poplar, Turned Legs, Stretchers, Plank Seat, Arms, c.1835, 33 x 15 In.	461.00
Bench, Deacon's, Wood, Slat Back, Arms, c.1850, 61 In.	144.00
Bench, Directoire Style, Mahogany, Swan Neck Arms, Gilt, c.1900, 29 x 26 In.	1955.00
Bench, Empire Style, Out-Turned Legs, Upholstered, Bronze Animal Paw Feet, 18 x 17 In.	472.00
Bench, G. Nelson, Birch, Ebonized, Platform Slatted Seat, Box Legs, c.1947, 14 x 48 In.	1000.00
Bench, G. Nelson, Birch, Slats, Ebonized Wood Squared Legs, 1950s, 18 x 103 In.	1500.00
Bench, G. Nelson, Lacquered Wood, Slatted Seat, Square Frame Legs, c.1946, 15 x 73 In.	1875.00
Bench, G. Stickley, Leather Seat, Back, Sides, Shelf Stretcher, 57 x 21 In.	1952.00
Bench, George III Style, Mahogany, Rectangular, Fluted Legs, Spade Feet, c.1900, 17 x 36 In.	98.00
Bench, Gilt Metal, Curved, 4 Ball Finials, France, c.1940, 20 x 31 In., Pair	1875.00
Bench, Gilt, Carved, Scrolled Openwork Frieze, Rosette Blocks, Paw Feet, 20 x 31 In.	1107.00
Bench, Gothic Style, Oak, Arched Back, Knight, Hinge Seat, Lion Support Arms, 61 x 61 In.	625.00
Bench, H. Bertoia, Rosewood, Slatted Seat, Steel Chrome Base, 15 ½ x 78 ¾ In.	2640.00
Bench, Hall, Gilt, High Flared Sides, Carved, Silk Upholstery, Vincent Wolf, 52 x 18 In.	354.00

Fulper, Lamp, Mushroom, Leaded Slag Glass, Cucumber Matte Glaze, Marked, c.1910, 21 ½ x 17 In.
$11,250.00

Rago Arts & Auction Center

F

Furniture, Bed, Canopy, Lacquer, Red, Gold, Birds, Flowers, Figures, Chinese, 1800s, 117 x 83 In.
$3,690.00

New Orleans Auction Galleries, Inc.

Furniture, Bed, Canopy, Sheraton, Curly Maple, Turned Posts, c.1825, 94 x 60 x 89 In.
$844.00

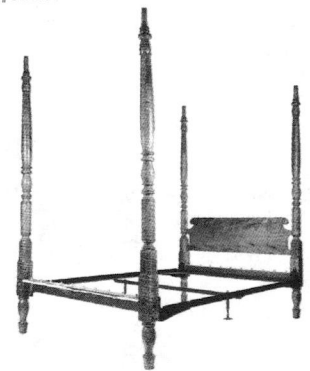

Garth's Auctioneers & Appraisers

The edited listings of the current prices in this *Kovels' Antiques & Collectibles Price Guide* aren't available on any website. Readers can visit **Kovels.com** to check thousands of past prices and sign up for free information on trends, tips, reproductions, marks, and more.

Furniture, Bed, Louis XV Style, Parcel Gilt, Courting Scene, Shell & Flower Crest, c.1910, 53 x 55 x 84 In. $615.00

New Orleans Auction Galleries, Inc.

Furniture, Bench, Black Forest, Bears, Basswood, Glass Eyes, c.1890, 26 ½ x 45 In. $755.00

The Stein Auction Co.

Furniture, Bench, Rocker, Mammy's, Mixed Wood, Green & Gold Stenciling, c.1830, 32 x 71 In. $529.00

Garth's Auctioneers & Appraisers

Furniture, Bench, Window, Chippendale Style, Mahogany, Gilt, Leaf Carved, c.1900, 29 x 42 In. $1,003.00

Brunk Auctions

TIP

Store parasols and umbrellas closed.

Bench, Hepplewhite Style, Mahogany, Upholstered Seat, Spindle Back, 37 x 48 In.	300.00
Bench, Herman Miller, Birch, Slatted, Chrome Steel Round Legs, 1950s, 19 x 73 In.	1625.00
Bench, Leaf Carved Armrest, Cushion, Fluted Legs, Gilt, Painted, Italy, c.1800, 68 In., Pair	4063.00
Bench, Louis XIV, Gilt, Scrolling Legs, Urn Center Stretcher, Paw Feet, 22 x 28 In., Pair	4920.00
Bench, Louis XV Style, Walnut, Cane Seat, Shell Apron, Cabriole Legs, 23 x 34 In.	448.00
Bench, Louis XVI Style, Beech, Painted, Faux Needlepoint Upholstery, 19 x 55 In.	2880.00
Bench, Mahogany, Leather Seat, c.1940, 16 x 4 In., Pair	1140.00
Bench, Mammy's, Hitchcock Style, 12 Spindles, Stenciled, Crest Rail, Arms, c.1890, 30 x 51 In.	805.00
Bench, Milo Baughman, Bronzed Finish, Upholstered, 60 x 24 In.	610.00
Bench, Mixed Wood, Banister Back, Box Compartment, Painted, Johan Werner, c.1901, 35 x 76 In.	189.00
Bench, Neoclassical Style, Mahogany, Carved, Winged Paw Feet, Scroll Arms, 31 x 67 In.	553.00
Bench, Neoclassical, Painted, Carved, Gilt, Verte Frieze, Fluted Legs, c.1800, 18 x 20 In., Pair	1434.00
Bench, Oak, Rosewood, Leopard Shaped Sides, Curved Back, Robert Whitley, 45 x 58 In.	2500.00
Bench, Parzinger, Ebonized Wood, Upholstered, 1960s, 19 x 49 In.	3000.00
Bench, Perriand, Oak, Tokyo, Slatted, France, c.1955, 11 x 89 In.	37500.00
Bench, Pine, Black Paint, Plank Top, Tapered Legs, American, 1800s, 21 x 15 In.	499.00
Bench, Pine, Green Paint, Scalloped Side, Bootjack Ends, 3 Shelves, 1800s, 42 x 36 In.	259.00
Bench, Pine, Mortised, Painted, 1800s, 17 ½ x 48 In.	415.00
Bench, Pine, Painted, Box Shape, Shaped Splats, Fluted Frieze, Tapered Legs, c.1890, 30 x 118 In.	984.00
Bench, Pine, Painted, Faux Grain, Squared Crest Rail, Openwork Back, Upholstered, 30 x 78 In.	3250.00
Bench, Pine, Painted, Molded Edge, Scratch Beaded Rail, Demilune Cutout Ends, c.1800, 18 x 98 In.	889.00
Bench, Pine, Rectangular Shape Seat, Shaped Apron, Scroll Cut Legs, 1800s, 18 x 48 In.	121.00
Bench, Pine, Scrolled Ends, Red Paint, 1800s, 18 ½ x 76 In.	118.00
Bench, Pine, Shaped Panel Back, Curved Arms, Shaped Square Legs, 1800s, 20 x 72 In.	705.00
Bench, Prayer, Victorian, Carved Leaves, Whorl Feet, Needlepoint Cushion, c.1850, 11 x 46 In.	472.00
Bench, Quaker, Meeting, Red Paint, c.1850, 36 x 72 In.	2844.00
Bench, Restoration Style, Bleached Walnut, Velvet Upholstery, 6 Scrolled Legs, c.1900, 19 x 75 In.	2875.00
Bench, Rocker, Mammy's, Mixed Wood, Green & Gold Stenciling, c.1830, 32 x 71 In. .... *Illus*	529.00
Bench, Rocker, Mammy's, Mixed Wood, Painted, Arrow Splats, Scroll Arms, Guard, 35 x 37 In.	1880.00
Bench, Rocker, Mammy's, Windsor, 12 Spindles, Rectangular Crest, 44 x 41 In.	575.00
Bench, Rod Back, Grain Painted, Arms, c.1835, 97 In.	590.00
Bench, Rosewood, Ebonized, Slatted Back, Dragons, Columnar Legs, c.1900, 33 x 43 In.	738.00
Bench, Roycroft, Rectangular Seat, Rounded Sides, Arched Feet, c.1905, 25 x 40 In.	3750.00
Bench, Rush Seat, Wood Frame, Reverse Tapered Legs, 72 x 80 In.	1708.00
Bench, Saber Legs, Paw Feet, Rolled Upholstered Arms, c.1960, 30 x 49 In.	120.00
Bench, Shaker, Meeting House, Pine, Brown Paint, c.1850, 54 ½ In.	594.00
Bench, Shaker, Rounded Front, Half Moon Cutout Supports, c.1855, 114 x 18 In.	652.00
Bench, Table, Walnut, Adjustable, Drawer, Bootjack Feet, c.1870, 20 x 31 In., Child's	1541.00
Bench, Teak, Afdal Bruksbo, 3 Square Supports, 1960s, 14 x 99 In.	1875.00
Bench, V. Kagen, Chenille Upholstery, Curved Kidney Shape, 1950s, 48 x 26 In.	2125.00
Bench, Walnut, Carved, Upholstered, Plain Side Rails, Italy, 90 x 32 In.	1521.00
Bench, Walnut, Crested Back, Velvet Upholstery, Open Arms, c.1890, 35 x 38 In.	165.00
Bench, Walnut, Silk Upholstery, Square, Upcurved Sides, Curvy Legs, 1950s, 16 x 33 In.	2750.00
Bench, Watchmaker's, Oak, Parts, Tools, 12 Drawers, Retractable Work Surface, 1910, 41 x 41 In.	2559.00
Bench, Watchmaker's, Walnut, Gallery Top, Inset Marble Square, 2 Doors, 7 Drawers, 38 In.	657.00
Bench, Wegner, Teak, Slatted, Round Legs, Denmark, 1950s, 13 x 56 In.	8125.00
Bench, Window, Chippendale Style, Mahogany, 43 ½ In.	354.00
Bench, Window, Chippendale Style, Mahogany, Gilt, Leaf Carved, c.1900, 29 x 42 In. .... *Illus*	1003.00
Bench, Window, Limbert, No. 243, Extended Sides, 4 Square Cutouts, 24 x 24 In.	3750.00
Bench, Window, Regency, Faux Bamboo, Black Paint, Raised Cane Ends, Cushion, 52 In.	354.00
Bench, Window, Sheraton, Walnut, Overstuffed Seat, Turned Legs, X-Stretchers, 1800s, 20 x 36 In.	448.00
Bench, Window, Square Sides, Leather Seat, Plank Stretcher, Square Legs, c.1901, 26 x 25 In.	7500.00
Bench, Wormley, Mahogany, Cane Seat, Brass Stretcher, Dunbar, 21 x 17 ½ In., Pair	2806.00
Bench, Wrought Iron, Brass, Velvet Upholstery, Fringe, Curule Sides, c.1940, 18 x 36 In.	450.00
Bookcase, Aesthetic Revival, Walnut, 2 Doors, Interior Shelves, Low Drawers, 59 x 54 In.	944.00
Bookcase, Arts & Crafts, 2 Glass Doors, Overlaid Grid, 7 Shelves, c.1910, 55 x 46 In.	1375.00
Bookcase, Arts & Crafts, Oak, Corner Posts, Through Tenon, Glass Front Doors, Label, 55 x 42 In.	1778.00
Bookcase, Arts & Crafts, Oak, Glass Doors, Lattice Upper Section, c.1910, 59 x 38 In.	533.00
Bookcase, Arts & Crafts, Open, 4 Shelves, Slab Sides, Through Tenon, 21 x 48 In.	275.00
Bookcase, Barrister, Globe-Wernicke, Mahogany, 3 Tiers, 1930s, 56 x 34 In.	360.00
Bookcase, Barrister, Globe-Wernicke, Oak, Glass, 7 Sections, Drawer, 34 x 79 In.	812.00
Bookcase, Barrister, Oak, Top Glass Door, 6 Glass Compartments, 34 x 58 In.	1808.00
Bookcase, Berkey & Gay, Jacobean Style, Oak, Glass Doors, 72 x 49 In.	356.00
Bookcase, Block & Shell, Arched Pediment, Finials, Desk, Dovetailed Drawers, 1900s, 101 x 45 In.	6490.00
Bookcase, Chippendale Style, Mahogany, Desk, Slant Front, Glass Doors, 1900s, 84 x 42 In.	767.00
Bookcase, Chippendale, Walnut, 2 Parts, Slant Front, 4 Drawers, Bun Feet, 1700s, 89 x 47 In.	2233.00

Bookcase, Compass Inlay, Blind Doors, Drop Front, Oxbow Drawers, Bun Feet, 1700s, 84 x 48 In......	546.00
Bookcase, Cypress, Flared Cornice, 5 Shelves, Base Molding, 1800s, 69 x 54 In.	1195.00
Bookcase, Edwardian, Mahogany, Satinwood, 2 Glass Doors, 55 x 49 In..	1125.00
Bookcase, Federal, Mahogany, Shaped Gallery, Brass Ball Finials, Doors, c.1810, 75 x 42 In...............	2015.00
Bookcase, Federal, Tiger, Bird's-Eye Maple, Astragal Glazed, Paneled Door, 72 x 32 In......................	2875.00
Bookcase, G. Magnusson Grossman, Walnut, 3 Tiers, Shelves, Round Legs, c.1955, 29 x 48 In...........	1750.00
Bookcase, G. Stickley, 2 Doors, Paneled Sides, No. 508, 38 ½ x 10 ½ In.	9375.00
Bookcase, G. Stickley, Harvey Ellis, Oak, Inlay, Glass Pane Doors, Decal, 1903, 55 x 55 In. ....*Illus*	18750.00
Bookcase, G. Stickley, No. 542, 2 Doors, Mitered Mullions, Through Tenon, 56 x 36 In....................	10000.00
Bookcase, G. Stickley, No. 702, 2 Mullioned Doors, Overhanging Top, 58 x 47 In............................	7500.00
Bookcase, G. Stickley, Oak, 4 Shelves, Through Tenon Joints, Open D Handles, 40 In.......................	840.00
Bookcase, George II, Gilt, Walnut, Double Dome Mirror Doors, Drop Front, 4 Drawers, 80 x 37 In.	3750.00
Bookcase, George III Style, Mahogany, Astragal Glazed Doors, Slant Front, 88 x 39 In.	2337.00
Bookcase, George III Style, Mahogany, Broken-Arch Pediment, Glass Doors, 78 In............................	1875.00
Bookcase, George III, Mahogany, Gothic Arched Doors, Slide-Out Writing Surface, 88 x 42 In.	3313.00
Bookcase, George III, Mahogany, Pierced Cornice, Finial, Glass Doors, 5 Drawers, 95 x 47 In.	1875.00
Bookcase, George IV, Rosewood, Carved, Column Supports, 3 Open Shelves, 74 x 49 In.	1170.00
Bookcase, Georgian III Style, Mahogany, Inlay, Glass Doors, Pullout Slides, 90 x 94 In. ....*Illus*	3444.00
Bookcase, Georgian Style, Mahogany, 2 Doors, Panels, Rope Turned Columns, c.1895, 82 x 46 In.	588.00
Bookcase, Gilt Mounts, Stepped Cornice, Glass Doors, Grill Doors, Pilasters, 66 In............................	2390.00
Bookcase, Golden Oak, 5 Open Shelves, 2 Doors, Fitted, England, c.1880, 78 x 40 In.	978.00
Bookcase, Gothic Revival, Rosewood, Crest, Tracery Glazed Doors, Drawer, c.1850, 71 x 34 In.	5378.00
Bookcase, Jacobean Style, Oak, Adjustable Shelves, Painted Flower, Ohio, 55 x 19 In. ....*Illus*	294.00
Bookcase, Kittinger, Empire Style, Mahogany, 2 Parts, Inset Grill Doors, Drawers, 85 x 45 In.	469.00
Bookcase, Limbert, Wood, 2 Doors, Glass, Side Shelves, Cutout Board, c.1905, 48 x 51 In.................	13750.00
Bookcase, Louis XVI Style, Mahogany, Gilt, Molded Cornice, Glass Doors, 1800s, 73 x 44 In.............	1722.00
Bookcase, Louis XVI, Mahogany, Brass, Glass Doors, Turned Feet, c.1785, 85 x 48 In.	3227.00
Bookcase, Mahogany, 2 Parts, Molding, Drop Front, Bracket Feet, c.1800, 87 x 44 In......................	1500.00
Bookcase, Mahogany, 3 Glass Doors, Cutout Design, Columns, Ball Feet, c.1890, 61 x 72 In.............	732.00
Bookcase, Mahogany, Astragal Glazed Doors, Drop Front, c.1815, 83 x 43 In..................................	1107.00
Bookcase, Mahogany, Bronze Mounts, 3 Open Shelves, 2-Panel Doors, c.1840, 58 x 36 In.................	2280.00
Bookcase, Mahogany, Cove Cornice, Mullioned Glass Doors, Columns, c.1835, 90 x 50 In.	1476.00
Bookcase, Mahogany, Crossbanded Cornice, Glass Doors, Ivory Pulls, c.1765, 78 x 37 In...................	3437.00
Bookcase, Mahogany, Desk, Glass Doors, Drawers, Column Supports, c.1835, 90 x 50 In.	4270.00
Bookcase, Mahogany, Flared Cornice, Glass Doors, Drop Front, Turned Feet, c.1830, 96 x 47 In.........	4183.00
Bookcase, Mahogany, Glass Doors, Gothic Crest, Glass Knobs, Paw Feet, c.1850, 90 x 45 In.	940.00
Bookcase, Mahogany, Molded Cornice, 2 Glass Paneled Doors, Turned Feet, 1800s, 81 x 48 In.........	2074.00
Bookcase, Mahogany, Mother-Of-Pearl Inlay, Glass Doors, Slatted Sides, 1901, 70 x 35 In..............	9375.00
Bookcase, Mahogany, Overhanging Cornice, Grillwork Doors, Obelisk Columns, c.1835, 55 x 54 In. ...	984.00
Bookcase, Mahogany, Slant Front, Glass Doors, Drawers, Bracket Feet, 1700s, 86 x 42 In.................	472.00
Bookcase, Mixed Wood, Inlay, Glass Mullioned Doors, 2 Drawers, Panel Doors, c.1800, 83 x 50 In.	4688.00
Bookcase, Neoclassical, Mahogany, Columns, Carved Capitals, 2 Doors, 60 x 41 In., Pair ....*Illus*	885.00
Bookcase, Oak, 2 Parts, Broken Pediment, Urn Finial, Glass Doors, 1700s, 94 x 46 In.......................	550.00
Bookcase, Pedestal, Edwardian, Mahogany, Inlay, 5 Drawers, 89 ½ x 17 In., Pair ....*Illus*	3050.00
Bookcase, Poul Hundevad, Rosewood, Shelves, Cupboard Doors, c.1965, 77 x 55 In., Pair.................	3125.00
Bookcase, Queen Anne Style, Walnut, Doors, Lower Slant Front, c.1785, 87 x 41 In.	2214.00
Bookcase, Regency Style, Mahogany, 4 Shelves, Arched Crest, 2 Drawers, 46 x 36 In.........................	702.00
Bookcase, Regency Style, Mahogany, Marble Top, Shelves, Ormolu Columns, 1800s, 37 x 64 In........	2460.00
Bookcase, Regency Style, Mahogany, Molded Cornice, Shelves, Pilasters, Maiden Heads, 79 x 53 In. . .	1353.00
Bookcase, Regency Style, Mahogany, Partitioned Medial Open Shelf, 34 x 34 In.	216.00
Bookcase, Regency, Faux Rosewood, 3 Shelves, Casters, 1800s, 36 x 20 In. ....*Illus*	375.00
Bookcase, Regency, Mahogany, Stepped, Molded Top, 8 Grill Inset Doors, 89 x 210 In.	8125.00
Bookcase, Renaissance Revival, Oak, Dentillated Cornice, Leaves, Ball Feet, c.1865, 67 x 62 In.........	984.00
Bookcase, Revolving, Edwardian Style, Mahogany, Inlay, Pierced, Casters, c.1900, 33 x 20 In. ....*Illus*	1554.00
Bookcase, Revolving, V. Kagan, Rosewood, Travertine, Fabric, 1960s, 74 x 22 In.............................	3000.00
Bookcase, Rohde, Paldao, Birch, Brush Metal, 3 Parts, Shelves, 2 Doors, Drawers, 1930s, 32 x 41 In. ..	5313.00
Bookcase, Sheraton, Mahogany, 2 Parts, 2 Doors, Arched Glass, Desk, Columns, c.1820, 71 x 40 In. . .	940.00
Bookcase, Sheraton, Poplar, Desk, Dovetailed Drawers, Glass Doors, c.1810, 72 x 36 In.	944.00
Bookcase, Walnut, Crest, Mirrored Doors, Serpentine Case, Inlay, Bracket Feet, c.1800, 95 x 43 In......	2390.00
Bookcase, Walnut, Molded Top, Glass Doors, Columns, Lower Drawers, c.1890, 65 x 53 In.	732.00
Bookcase, Walnut, Ogee Molded Cornice, 3 Arched Glass Doors, c.1850, 98 x 74 In........................	1673.00
Bookcase, William IV, Mahogany, 4 Glass Doors, 4 Panel, c.1830, 86 x 89 In..............................	5313.00
Bookrack, Revolving, Mahogany, Dish Top, Ribbed Support, Splayed Legs, c.1900, 40 x 21 In..........	123.00
Bookrack, Stickley Bros., No. 4704, 3 V-Shaped Shelves, Cut Corners, 30 x 29 In.	1375.00
Bookstand, Arts & Crafts, Oak, 4 Open Shelves, Square Posts, c.1912, 40 x 32 In.............................	148.00
Bookstand, Bronze, Altar, Gilt, Enamels, 4 Evangelist Medallions, France, 1800s, 5 ½ x 10 ¾ In......	1210.00

Furniture, Bookcase, G. Stickley, Harvey Ellis, Oak, Inlay, Glass Pane Doors, Decal, 1903, 55 x 55 In.
$18,750.00

Los Angeles Modern Auctions (LAMA)

Furniture, Bookcase, Georgian III Style, Mahogany, Inlay, Glass Doors, Pullout Slides, 90 x 94 In.
$3,444.00

New Orleans Auction Galleries, Inc.

Furniture, Bookcase, Jacobean Style, Oak, Adjustable Shelves, Painted Flower, Ohio, 55 x 19 In.
$294.00

Garth's Auctioneers & Appraisers

F

Furniture, Bookcase, Pedestal, Edwardian, Mahogany, Inlay, 5 Drawers, 89 ½ x 17 In., Pair
$3,050.00

Neal Auction Co.

Furniture, Bookcase, Regency, Faux Rosewood, 3 Shelves, Casters, 1800s, 36 x 20 In.
$375.00

Bonhams

Furniture, Bookcase, Revolving, Edwardian Style, Mahogany, Inlay, Pierced, Casters, c.1900, 33 x 20 In.
$1,554.00

Neal Auction Co.

Bookstand, Dictionary, Cast Iron, Oak Book Holders, Adjustable, c.1895, 36 x 19 In.	336.00
Bookstand, Edwardian, Revolving, Mahogany, Brass, Curved Base, 29 x 15 In.	439.00
Bookstand, Federal, Mahogany, Angled Top, Tripod Base, New England, 32 x 23 In.	708.00
Bookstand, Louis XVI Style, Wood, Parcel Gilt, Adjustable Reticulated Support, c.1845, 12 x 16 In.	660.00
Bookstand, Sheraton, Mahogany, Satinwood, Adjustable, 3 Open Shelves, Drawer, 48 x 21 In.	2832.00
Breakfront, Arts & Crafts, Copper Lights, Mirror Back, Panel Doors, Drawers, 93 x 70 In.	1037.00
Breakfront, Federal Style, Mahogany, 4 Glass Doors, Drawers, Cupboards, c.1965, 84 x 79 In.	999.00
Breakfront, George II Style, Mahogany, 2 Parts, Broken Arch, Fretwork, Doors, Drawers, 94 x 76 In.	2091.00
Breakfront, George III, Mahogany, Drawers, Whippet Pulls, Glass Doors, 1800s, 89 x 108 In.	6490.00
Breakfront, Georgian Style, Mahogany, Dentil Cornice, 3 Geometric Glass Doors, 1800s, 84 x 59 In.	603.00
Breakfront, Mahogany, 4 Doors, 3 Interior Shelves, 2 Drawers, Drop Front, Saginaw, 82 x 71 In.	1080.00
Breakfront, Mahogany, Domed Cornice, Mask, 2 Doors, Fluted Columns, c.1900, 113 x 81 In.	2706.00
Breakfront, Mahogany, Flower Crest, Broken-Arch Pediment, 3 Glass Doors, c.1890, 34 x 45 In.	5658.00
Breakfront, Marquetry, Mirrors, Shelves, Drawers, Doors, Austria, c.1900, 88 x 60 In.	1298.00
Breakfront, Regency, Mahogany, Cock-Beaded Cornice, Glass Doors, c.1810, 85 x 94 In.	3318.00
Buffet, French Provincial Style, Fruitwood, 2 Doors, Dovetailed Drawers, 1900s, 37 x 67 x 21 In.	1770.00
Buffet, Fruitwood, Canted Corners, Cupboard Doors, Scalloped Apron, c.1790, 40 x 59 In.	1845.00
Buffet, Fruitwood, Cornice, Flower Basket, 4 Doors, Shaped Apron, Scroll Toes, c.1850, 83 x 57 In..	2214.00
Buffet, Fruitwood, Upper & Lower Doors, Chevron, Pewter, Carved Skirt, 1800s, 88 x 53 In.	608.00
Buffet, Henri III Style, Oak, Mythical Creatures, Masks, Arched Doors, Fish, 1900s, 106 x 99 In.	3600.00
Buffet, Louis XV Style, Mahogany, Glass Doors, Pierced Leaf Crest, c.1900, 107 x 65 In.	1230.00
Buffet, Louis XV Style, Oak, Shaped Edge, Paneled Cupboard Doors, 1900s, 40 x 97 In.	2214.00
Buffet, Louis XV, Fruitwood, Paneled Doors, Dovetailed Drawers, France, 1800s, 42 x 53 In.	2478.00
Buffet, Oak, Arched Crest, 3 Mirrors, 2 Shelves, 2 Drawers, 2 Doors, Carved, c.1890, 96 x 66 In.	750.00
Buffet, Oak, Leaded Glass, Leaf & Cabochon Carved Crest, Drawer, Paw Feet, c.1900, 72 x 48 In.	1107.00
Buffet, Sam Maloof, Walnut, 2 Drawers, 2 Lower Doors, Block Feet, 33 x 52 In.	7500.00
Bureau, Biedermeier, Burl, 4 Drawers, Black Columns, c.1800, 30 ¾ x 43 In.	474.00
Bureau, Bowfront, White Paint, 4 Beaded Drawers, Splayed Feet, c.1790, 36 x 41 In.	708.00
Bureau, Cherry, Cock-Beaded Drawers, Reeded Columns, Brass Pulls, c.1790, 38 x 39 In. .... *Illus*	5629.00
Bureau, Cherry, Serpentine, String Inlay, Drawers, Columns, Ogee Feet, c.1795, 36 x 37 In.	13035.00
Bureau, Chippendale, Curly Maple, Bowfront, 4 Graduated Drawers, c.1780, 36 x 40 In.	2596.00
Bureau, Chippendale, Mahogany, 5 Drawers, Cock-Beaded, Fluted Columns, c.1780, 33 x 21 In.	2360.00
Bureau, Chippendale, Maple, Cherry, 4 Drawers, Flat Bracket Base, 34 x 37 ½ In.	472.00
Bureau, Chippendale, Walnut, Board Top, 4 Drawers, Fluted Columns, Ogee Feet, c.1885, 34 x 39 In.	1599.00
Bureau, Empire Style, Mahogany, Leather Top, Drawers, Maiden's Heads, Paw Feet, 31 x 57 In.	1107.00
Bureau, Empire Style, Mahogany, Leather Top, Winged Lion Supports, Paw Feet, 33 x 65 In.	3690.00
Bureau, Empire, Mahogany, 4 Drawers, Scroll Supports, Miniature, c.1850, 11 x 11 ¾ In.	237.00
Bureau, Empire, Mahogany, Gray Marble Top, 4 Drawers, Half-Turn Columns, 36 x 51 In.	325.00
Bureau, Federal, Bowfront, Mahogany, Inlay, 4 Drawers, Ogee Feet, Conn., c.1795, 41 x 33 In.	1896.00
Bureau, Federal, Scrolled Backboard, Ring-Turned Columns, c.1820, 44 x 40 x 21 In.	2252.00
Bureau, George I, Burl Walnut, Feather, Crossbanded, Slant Front, Bracket Feet, 1700s, 40 x 36 In.	1216.00
Bureau, George III, Mahogany, Drop Front, Writing Surface, Drawers, Cupboard, c.1800, 38 x 30 In..	984.00
Bureau, Hepplewhite, Mahogany, Bowfront, 4 Cock-Beaded Drawers, c.1790, 40 x 23 In.	708.00
Bureau, Hepplewhite, Mahogany, Inlay, Brass Pulls, 3 Drawers, c.1810, 35 x 35 In.	384.00
Bureau, Louis XV Style, Ebonized, Brass Banding, Cabriole Legs, Sabot Feet, c.1900, 30 x 54 In.	2091.00
Bureau, Louis XV Style, Gilt Edge, Ormolu Corners, Rocaille Mounts, Cabriole Legs, 30 x 59 In.	1126.00
Bureau, Mahogany, Doors, Ivory Figures, Birds, Flowers, Turned Columns, 1800s, 34 x 55 In.	5750.00
Bureau, Mahogany, Mirror, Turned Columns, Scroll Supports, Roses, Claw Feet, c.1825, 67 x 43 In.	4444.00
Bureau, Mahogany, S-Scroll Supports, Graduated Drawers, Paw Feet, 1800s, 66 x 50 In.	720.00
Bureau, Neoclassical, Birch, Painted, Turned Wood Pulls, New England, c.1825, 37 x 38 In.	7110.00
Bureau, Neoclassical, Walnut, Tiger Maple, Drawers, Arrows, Hearts, c.1830, 45 x 40 x 20 In.	533.00
Bureau, Oak, Tombstone Doors, Slant Front, Molded Pediment, Bracket Feet, Eng., 1700s, 79 x 40 In.	1896.00
Bureau, Sheraton, Birch, 4 Drawers, Columns, Ribbed Legs, c.1820, 40 x 43 In.	266.00
Bureau, Sheraton, Cherry, Bowfront, 4 Drawers, Ribbed Legs, c.1820, 40 x 44 In.	295.00
Cabinet, 2 Doors, Carved, Women, Oval Panels, Blue, Red Paint, Italy, c.1860, 41 x 36 In.	1500.00
Cabinet, 4 Looped Glass Doors, 2 Frieze Drawers, Cavendish, Eng., c.1900, 41 x 42 In.	2400.00
Cabinet, Adam Style, Satinwood, Demilune, Fan & Oval Inlay, Banded, 4 Doors, Legs, 35 x 52 In.	2460.00
Cabinet, Architect's, George III Style, Mahogany, 6 Drawers, Bracket Feet, 36 x 54 In.	1230.00
Cabinet, Arne Vodder, Rosewood, Elm, Tambour Doors, Denmark, 1960s, 35 x 89 In.	3251.00
Cabinet, Art Deco, Bar, White Oak, Birch, Marquetry, City Skyline, 1920s, 40 x 34 In.	2250.00
Cabinet, Art Deco, Burl Walnut, Grid Pattern, 5 Drawers, 2 Doors, c.1940, 50 x 69 In.	1560.00
Cabinet, Art Deco, Burl, Mirror Top, 3 Central Drawers, Gilt, c.1930, 23 x 22 In.	1020.00
Cabinet, Art Deco, Lacquered Metal, Steel, Black, Beige, 20 Drawers, 50 x 40 In.	213.00
Cabinet, Art Deco, Oak, 2 Flat Doors, Platform Base, c.1940, 77 x 78 In.	2880.00
Cabinet, Art Deco, Walnut, Rosewood, 2-Panel Doors, 2 Sliding Doors, Italy, c.1955, 92 x 92 In.	1416.00
Cabinet, Arts & Crafts, Mirror, Overhang Top, Shelf, Cutouts, Doors, Drawers, c.1915, 76 x 38 In.	1625.00

Cabinet, Bar, P. Heltborg, Rosewood, Steel Legs, Sliding Doors, Denmark, 1960s, 42 x 45 In.	1625.00
Cabinet, Biedermeier, Walnut, Drawer, Shelf, Hinged Doors, Ebonized Columns, 39 x 38 In.	1064.00
Cabinet, Bowed, Oak, Mirror Gallery, Lion Heads, Glass Door, 3 Shelves, c.1900, 36 x 70 In.	708.00
Cabinet, China, Arts & Crafts, Oak, 12-Pane Door, Glass Side Panels, Square Legs, c.1912, 62 In.	1185.00
Cabinet, China, Arts & Crafts, Oak, Back Rail, Single Door, 12 Panels, Square Legs, 1912	1185.00
Cabinet, China, Breakfront, George III Style, Walnut, Fretwork, Glass Doors, 87 x 72 In.	1016.00
Cabinet, China, G. Stickley, 2 Glass Pane Doors, Iron Hardware, Decal, 40 x 64 In.	5490.00
Cabinet, China, G. Stickley, 12-Pane Door, Shelves, Red Decal, 62 ½ x 36 In. ....*Illus*	3294.00
Cabinet, China, G. Stickley, Glass Pane Door, Iron Hardware, Decal, 36 x 62 In.	1220.00
Cabinet, China, L. & J.G. Stickley, No. 729, 2 12-Pane Doors Over 2 Doors, 70 x 50 In.	12500.00
Cabinet, China, Louis XVI Style, Semicircular, 2 Glass Doors, Fruit, Flowers, 1900s, 89 x 45 In.	830.00
Cabinet, China, Quartersawn Oak, Bowfront, Carved, Plate Grooves, Paw Feet, 73 x 47 In. .....*Illus*	944.00
Cabinet, Compound, Hardwood, 2 Parts, Doors, Burl Inlay, Chinese, c.1800, 105 x 35 In.	948.00
Cabinet, Console, Charles II, Oak, Frieze Drawer, Paneled Doors, Block Feet, 1600s, 35 x 39 In.	1250.00
Cabinet, Corner, Aesthetic Revival, Ebonized Wood, Glass Panel Door, Spindles, 1870s, 69 x 25 In. .*Illus*	625.00
Cabinet, Corner, Chippendale, Butternut, Panel Doors, Shaped Skirt, c.1800, 84 x 44 In.	7080.00
Cabinet, Corner, Federal Style, Mahogany, Glass Door Over Panel Door, c.1900, 92 In.	1003.00
Cabinet, Corner, Federal, Mahogany, 2 Curved Inlaid Panel Doors, c.1805, 49 x 30 ½ In.	900.00
Cabinet, Corner, Federal, Oak, 2 Glass Pane Doors, 2 Drawers, 2 Panel Doors, 83 x 60 In.	1521.00
Cabinet, Corner, George III, Oak, Carved, Glass Door, Fluted Panels, c.1800, 42 x 31 In.	660.00
Cabinet, Corner, Georgian Style, Domed Pierced Cornice, Doors, Bracket Feet, 1900s, 73 In.	553.00
Cabinet, Corner, Georgian Style, Maple, Walnut, Burl Inlay, 2 Glass Doors, 2 Doors, 75 In.	780.00
Cabinet, Corner, Hanging, Bowfront, 2-Panel Doors, Drawers, Green Paint, Gilt, 47 x 20 In.	2875.00
Cabinet, Corner, Hepplewhite, Mahogany, Bowfront, String Inlay, Flowers, c.1800, 45 x 28 In.	615.00
Cabinet, Corner, Lacquer, Bowfront, Carved Gallery, Block Feet, c.1800, 43 x 28 In.	550.00
Cabinet, Corner, Louis XV, Kingwood, Gilt Bronze, Marble Top, Cabriole Legs, 1700s, 34 x 19 In.	425.00
Cabinet, Corner, Mahogany, Dentil Molded Cornice, Glass Doors, Bracket Feet, 1800s, 91 x 40 In.	1912.00
Cabinet, Corner, Mahogany, Shelves, Glass Framed Upper Door, 2 Paneled Doors, 74 x 38 In.	150.00
Cabinet, Display, Biedermeier, Burl, Gilt, Domed Cornice, Urn Finials, Glass Door, 84 x 33 In.	813.00
Cabinet, Display, Canopy Cornice, Glass Door, Fluted Columns, Jesters, c.1900, 90 x 40 In.	900.00
Cabinet, Display, Crescent Shape, Carved, Dragon Base, 24 In. ....*Illus*	1610.00
Cabinet, Display, Edwardian, Burl Walnut, Gilt, 2 Glass Doors, Cabriole Legs, 1800s, 48 x 36 In.	920.00
Cabinet, Display, Edwardian, Mahogany, Leaf Carved Edge, Glass Doors, c.1895, 49 x 44 In.	369.00
Cabinet, Display, Elm, Open Shelves, Scroll Edges, Drawers, Chinese, c.1890, 54 x 82 In.	121.00
Cabinet, Display, Galled, Walnut, Carved, Glass Door, Lake, Weeping Willow, 61 x 28 In.	47200.00
Cabinet, Display, Hardwood, Glass Panels, 2 Parts, Shelves, Doors, Openwork, c.1800, 60 x 41 In.	7898.00
Cabinet, Display, Louis XIV Style, Walnut, Ormolu, Glass Door, Curved, Landscape, 28 x 13 ½ In.	649.00
Cabinet, Display, Louis XVI Style, Walnut, Inlay, Glass Door, Porcelain Plaque, 60 x 21 In.	531.00
Cabinet, Display, Louis XVII Style, Green Paint, Beveled Glass Sides, Door, 1900s, 74 x 29 In.	1422.00
Cabinet, Display, Rosewood, Glass Door, Mirrored, Stepped Shelves, Chinese, 1800s, 47 x 36 In.	690.00
Cabinet, Display, Walnut, Gilt, Crest, Glass Doors, Wavy Skirt, Tapered Legs, c.1902, 77 x 66 In.	5000.00
Cabinet, Eames, Walnut, Metal, Sonic Speaker, Square Legs, Aluminum Frame, c.1956, 28 x 30 In.	3750.00
Cabinet, Ebonized, Gilt, Inlay, Gallery, Drawer, Door, Fluted Pilasters, c.1865, 48 x 30 In.	984.00
Cabinet, Ebonized, Paneled Front, 4 Doors, Figures, Flowers, Block Feet, Tibet, 44 x 49 In.	276.00
Cabinet, Edwardian, Mahogany, 2 Glass & Panel Doors, c.1890, 69 x 44 In.	805.00
Cabinet, Edwardian, Mahogany, Inlay, Shelf, Sliding Door, Ropes, c.1885, 43 x 44 In.	369.00
Cabinet, Edwardian, Satinwood, Bowed, Banding, Flowers, Door, Pilasters, c.1900, 36 x 33 In.	1476.00
Cabinet, Elm, 2 Doors, Drawers, Figures In Garden, Curved Feet, Chinese, c.1865, 44 x 33 In.	693.00
Cabinet, Empire Style, Mahogany, Marble Top, 3 Frieze Drawers, 3 Doors, 42 x 70 In.	1625.00
Cabinet, Empire Style, Mahogany, Palmetto Cornice, Display, Hinged Ebonized Pilasters, 73 x 67 In.	1722.00
Cabinet, Empire Style, Wood, Ormolu, Marble Top, 2 Drawers, 2 Doors, Painted Flowers, 43 x 47 In.	590.00
Cabinet, Empire, Mahogany, Marble Top, Door, Columns, Gilt Banded, 31 ¾ x 17 ½ In.	380.00
Cabinet, Federal, Cherry, Gallery Back, Doors, Columns, Bulbous Feet, c.1830, 55 x 48 In.	1830.00
Cabinet, Filing, Oak, 6 Drawers, 32 ½ x 39 ¼ In.	585.00
Cabinet, Florence Knoll, Rosewood, Marble Top, 6 Drawers, Steel Legs, 1960s, 26 x 37 In.	4375.00
Cabinet, Florence Knoll, Rosewood, Marble Top, Steel Legs, 1960s, 26 x 75 In.	2625.00
Cabinet, Florence Knoll, Walnut, Birch, Leather, Sliding Doors, Metal Legs, 1950s, 31 x 72 In.	3250.00
Cabinet, Food Storage, Poplar, Walnut, Doors, Screen Panels, Drawers, c.1865, 81 In. ....*Illus*	922.00
Cabinet, Fruitwood, 2 Over 2 Doors, Inlaid Diamond & Star Design, Splay Feet, 54 x 44 In.	1230.00
Cabinet, G. Nakashima, Cherry, 2 Sliding Doors, Pandanus Cloth, 4 Oak Shelves, 42 x 12 In.	3750.00
Cabinet, G. Nakashima, Kornblut, Walnut, Burl, 2 Doors, X-Shape Base, c.1970, 22 x 18 In.	16250.00
Cabinet, G. Nakashima, Walnut, 8-Drawers, Raised Supports, 1967, 40 x 30 In.	22500.00
Cabinet, G. Nakashima, Walnut, Overhang Top, Pullout, Plank Legs, 1957, 32 x 104 In.	11815.00
Cabinet, G. Nelson, Basic Series, Walnut, 5 Drawers, Herman Miller, 40 x 40 In., Pair	1037.00
Cabinet, G. Nelson, Oak, Pickled, 4 Drawers, Curved Metal Handles, Herman Miller, 34 x 10 In.	563.00
Cabinet, G. Nelson, Walnut, 8 Drawers, Porcelain Pulls, Tapered Feet, 1950s, 33 x 67 In.	4375.00

Furniture, Bureau, Cherry, Cock-Beaded Drawers, Reeded Columns, Brass Pulls, c.1790, 38 x 39 In.
$5,629.00

Skinner, Inc.

Furniture, Cabinet, China, G. Stickley, 12-Pane Door, Shelves, Red Decal, 62 ½ x 36 In.
$3,294.00

Treadway Toomey Galleries

Furniture, Cabinet, China, Quartersawn Oak, Bowfront, Carved, Plate Grooves, Paw Feet, 73 x 47 In.
$944.00

Conestoga Auction Co., Inc.

F

Furniture, Cabinet, Corner, Aesthetic Revival, Ebonized Wood, Glass Panel Door, Spindles, 1870s, 69 x 25 In. $625.00

Rago Arts & Auction Center

Furniture, Cabinet, Display, Crescent Shape, Carved, Dragon Base, 24 In. $1,610.00

Cottone Auctions

Furniture, Cabinet, Food Storage, Poplar, Walnut, Doors, Screen Panels, Drawers, c.1865, 81 In. $922.00

New Orleans Auction Galleries, Inc.

Cabinet, George I, Burl Walnut, Bone Pulls, Cock-Beaded Doors, Flat Bun Feet, 1700s, 14 x 17 In.		875.00
Cabinet, George III, Mahogany, Bowfront, Lift Top, Tambour Door, Drawer, 34 x 18 In.		236.00
Cabinet, George III, Satinwood, Demilune, 2 Doors, Drawer, Bowed, c.1910, 40 x 42 In.		900.00
Cabinet, Georgian Style, Wood, Door, Fluted Columns, Allover Flowers, Painted, c.1900, 36 x 22 In.		300.00
Cabinet, Gothic Revival, Mahogany, Crenelated Cornice, Carved Door, Footed, c.1850, 57 x 33 In.		1195.00
Cabinet, Gun, Roycroft, Glass Door, Crest, Drawer, Block Feet, c.1905, 62 x 29 In.		6875.00
Cabinet, H. Probber, Oak, Ebonized, 8 Drawers, 14 x 15 In.		2250.00
Cabinet, H. Wegner, Teak, Oak, Brass, 6 Drawers, Sliding Doors, X-Supports, 1950s, 50 x 66 In.		6875.00
Cabinet, H. Wegner, Teak, Oak, Square, Sliding Doors, Shelves, Drawers, Peg Door, 1960s, 53 x 62 In.		3750.00
Cabinet, Hanging, Pine, Painted, Crest, 3 Shelves, Mirrored Door, Towel Rod, 1800s, 23 x 22 In.		148.00
Cabinet, Hanging, Walnut, Poplar, Black Stain, Panel Doors, 4 Drawers, 1800s, 22 x 19 ½ In.		529.00
Cabinet, Hardwood, Dragon, Shelves, Ivory, Beveled Glass, Chinese, c.1900, 68 x 27 In.	*Illus*	3220.00
Cabinet, Hat Chest, Huanghuali, Panel Doors, Chinese, 1900s, 87 x 49 In.	*Illus*	56288.00
Cabinet, Hi-Fi, Walnut, Lacquer, Plank Supports, Sliding Doors, 1950s, 32 x 72 In.		1250.00
Cabinet, Jacobean, Oak, Arched Panel Door, Pilasters, c.1790, 23 x 27 In.		2066.00
Cabinet, James Mont, Lacquered Wood, Gilt Design, Cornice, 4 Doors, Shelves, 1950s, 79 x 80 In.		2500.00
Cabinet, Jewelry, Regency, Mahogany, Inlay, 2 Doors, 4 Drawers, 18 x 13 In.		1180.00
Cabinet, John Stewart, Ebonized, Brass Trimmed, Drawer, 2 Doors, 23 x 26 In., Pair		360.00
Cabinet, Kingwood, Marble Top, 3 Doors Over 4 Tambour Doors, Slide Shelf, 1800s, 61 x 40 In.		360.00
Cabinet, Lacquer, 2 Doors, Birds, Leaves, Greek Key Carved Feet, 1800s, 50 x 39 In.		861.00
Cabinet, Lacquer, Chinoiserie, Gilt Stand, Pierced Apron, Cabriole Legs, 1800s, 48 x 28 In.		570.00
Cabinet, Lacquer, Molded Cornice, Paneled Doors, Vines, Pagodas, c.1790, 82 x 42 In.		1195.00
Cabinet, Lacquer, Paneled Doors, Shelf, Figures, Dragon, Chinese, c.1900, 35 ½ x 24 In.	*Illus*	177.00
Cabinet, Leather, Trunk Shape, Barrel Top, Scrolling Bosses, Iron Handles, 1800s, 20 x 46 In.		1440.00
Cabinet, Letter, Walnut, Glass Door, Shelves, Molded Cornice, Brass Inlay, 17 In.		138.00
Cabinet, Limbert, No. 452, Glass Door & Sides, 4 Shelves, Casters, 59 x 44 In.		4688.00
Cabinet, Liquor, Arts & Crafts, Humidor, Quartersawn Oak, Hammered Copper, 50 In.		1495.00
Cabinet, Louis XV Style, Oak, Cornice, 2 Glass Doors, Scalloped Frieze, c.1850, 97 x 58 In.		2214.00
Cabinet, Louis XV, Burl, Paneled Doors, Cornice, Scroll Feet, France, c.1800, 94 x 57 In.		1416.00
Cabinet, Louis XV, Parquetry, Marble Top, Ormolu Mounts, 4 Drawers, c.1890, 33 x 39 In.		395.00
Cabinet, Louis XVI Style, Gilt, 2-Panel Doors, Rounded, Musical Trophies, Shelf, 49 x 51 In.		1143.00
Cabinet, Louis XVI Style, Mahogany, Bowed Marble Top, Drawer, c.1890, 39 x 38 In.		1168.00
Cabinet, Louis XVI Style, Mahogany, Cornice, Ormolu Frieze, Top Shape Feet, c.1900, 58 x 53 In.		1845.00
Cabinet, Louis XVI Style, Mahogany, Marble, Metal Gallery, Tambour Doors, c.1890, 31 x 28 In.		1150.00
Cabinet, Louis XVI Style, Walnut, Carved Crest, Skirt, Glass Doors, Shelves, c.1900, 104 x 84 In.		885.00
Cabinet, Louis XVI Style, Walnut, Marble Top, Doors, Gilt, Flowers, Tapered Feet, 54 x 31 In.		1800.00
Cabinet, Louis XVI, Mahogany, Brass Gallery, Marble Top, Tambour Door, c.1800, 29 x 20 In.		2125.00
Cabinet, M. Nakashima, Walnut, Pandanus Cloth, Sliding Doors, Striped, c.1947, 32 x 60 In.		6875.00
Cabinet, Mahogany, Marble Top, Ogee Frieze Drawer, Mirror Door, Bracket Feet, c.1840, 39 x 28 In.		5975.00
Cabinet, Marble Top, Frieze Drawers, Panel Doors, Pylon Columns, Block Feet, c.1800, 42 x 70 In.		3884.00
Cabinet, Marquetry, Mullioned Glass Doors, Barley Twist Legs, Pear Shape Feet, c.1895, 62 x 36 In.		1185.00
Cabinet, Millet, Louis XV Style, Mixed Wood, Marble Top, 2 Doors, Gilt Bronze, 35 x 51 In.		4375.00
Cabinet, Mixed Wood, Lacquer, 2 Doors, Apron, Black, Gold Flowers, Mongolia, c.1900, 36 x 55 In.		529.00
Cabinet, Modern, Metal, 10 Drawers, 2 Doors, Open Shelf, Painted, c.1940, 42 x 59 In.		360.00
Cabinet, Moroccan, Painted, 2 Doors, Geometric & Flower Accents, Footed, c.1900, 56 x 27 In.		492.00
Cabinet, Mounted, Chippendale Style, Mahogany, Finials, Pierced, 2 Doors, c.1905, 23 x 14 In.		295.00
Cabinet, Music, Mahogany, 2 Doors, Carved Putti, Grapes, Faces, Italy, c.1910, 61 x 33 In.		1416.00
Cabinet, Music, Mahogany, Hourglass Shape, 2 Doors, Claw Feet, 34 x 24 In.		3540.00
Cabinet, Music, Oak, Bowfront, Claw Feet, Door, 35 x 21 In.		531.00
Cabinet, Nanna Ditzel, Teak, Oak, 2 Cupboard Tops, Doors, Cutout Legs, 1960s, 40 x 48 In.		3125.00
Cabinet, Napoleon III, Ebonized, Boulle, Brass Gallery Top, Doors, Drawers, c.1865, 53 x 29 In.		738.00
Cabinet, Napoleon III, Ebonized, Bronze, Serpentine Marble Top, Door, Disc Feet, c.1890, 43 x 45 In.		359.00
Cabinet, Napoleon III, Ebonized, Door, Millwork, Ormolu Mounts, c.1865, 44 x 32 ¼ In.		1476.00
Cabinet, Napoleon III, Ebonized, Gilt, Marble Top, Stiles, Caryatids, Disc Feet, 1800s, 42 x 39 In.		478.00
Cabinet, Napoleon III, Kingwood, Outset Corners, Flower Inlaid Door, c.1890, 42 x 26 In.		657.00
Cabinet, Napoleon III, Marble Top, Door, Pilaster, Leaves, Bracket Feet, c.1865, 42 x 28 In.		522.00
Cabinet, Neoclassical, Mahogany, 2 Doors, 2 Drawers, Overhang Top, 85 x 50 In.		826.00
Cabinet, Neoclassical, Mahogany, Round, Marble Top, Door, 29 x 14 In.		531.00
Cabinet, Oak, Tartan Design, Paneled & Dovetailed Doors, Painted Highlights, 1800s, 36 x 48 In.		1298.00
Cabinet, Oak, Triple Bowfront, Mirror, Door, Columns, Carved, 68 x 50 In.		2242.00
Cabinet, Olive Burl, Chrome Steel, Drawers, Doors, Square Legs, Switzerland, 1970s, 27 x 48 In.		1750.00
Cabinet, P. Evans, Bronze, Composite, Sculptured Metal Doors, Signed, 1968, 18 x 50 In.	*Illus*	10000.00
Cabinet, P. Evans, Steel, Chrome, Brass, Shelves, Doors, Geometrics, Cityscape, 1970s, 84 x 48 In.		5000.00
Cabinet, Parlor, George III Style, Ebonized, Bowed Center, Door, Landscape, c.1900, 55 x 52 In.		553.00
Cabinet, Parzinger, Maple, Lacquered Wood, Brass, 6 Drawers, Footed, 1950s, 33 x 70 In.		5000.00
Cabinet, Pine, Double Door, Panel Doors, Pilasters, Applied Ornaments, Ball Feet, c.1860, 25 x 36 In.		58.00

Cabinet, Post Office, Walnut, Poplar, Cutout Pediment, Cubbyhole, Fitted, c.1885, 22 x 30 In.	316.00
Cabinet, Printer's, Oak, 20 Narrow Drawers, Hamilton Mfg. Co., 31 x 43 In.	1904.00
Cabinet, Queen Anne Style, Mahogany, 2 Divided Pane Doors, Stand, c.1850, 50 x 37 In.	575.00
Cabinet, Queen Anne Style, Mahogany, Gallery Top, Drawers, Cabriole Legs, c.1900, 50 x 37 In.	374.00
Cabinet, Regency Style, Mahogany, Fabric-Lined Doors, Metalwork, 33 x 30 In., Pair ....*Illus*	4063.00
Cabinet, Regency Style, Oak, Marble Top, Arched Cupboard Doors, c.1790, 36 x 56 In.	2091.00
Cabinet, Regency, Gilt Brass, Inlay, Rosewood, Marble Top, Grillwork Doors, c.1815, 34 x 47 In.	8125.00
Cabinet, Regency, Rosewood, Brass, 4 Pleated Green Silk Doors, Wire Panels, 37 x 68 In.	4095.00
Cabinet, Regency, Satinwood, Lift Top, Turned Feet, Drawer, 2 Doors, Miniature, 15 ¾ x 11 ½ In.	708.00
Cabinet, Removable Door Panels, Interior Shelves, Drawers, Chinese, 1900s, 64 x 38 In. ....*Illus*	600.00
Cabinet, Renaissance Revival, Oak, Carved, Glass Doors, Chamfered Sides, c.1850, 68 In. ....*Illus*	6871.00
Cabinet, Renaissance Revival, Walnut, Carved, Panel Doors, Lion Masks, Italy, c.1600, 31 x 44 In.	2950.00
Cabinet, Renaissance Style, Mahogany, Marble Top, Panel Doors, Maiden, Block Feet, 62 x 36 In.	1722.00
Cabinet, Robsjohn-Gibbings, Ebonized, Door, Cube Shape, Widdicomb, c.1940, 33 x 18 In., Pair........	2375.00
Cabinet, Rosewood, Compartments, Storage, Lotus Scrolls, Chinese, 1800s, 51 x 20 In.	4740.00
Cabinet, Rosewood, Enameled Steel Legs, Sliding Doors, Drawers, Italy, 1960s, 32 x 83 In.	4688.00
Cabinet, Rosewood, Gilt, Demilune, Panel Center Door, Side Glass Doors, 1800s, 40 x 59 In.	598.00
Cabinet, Rosewood, Sliding Doors, Round Feet, Omann Jun, Denmark, 1960s, 33 x 79 In.	2000.00
Cabinet, Sam Maloof, Walnut, Masonite, Open Lower Shelves, Sliding Doors, 1954, 32 x 72 In.	6875.00
Cabinet, Sam Maloof, Walnut, Open Shelf, 2 Drawers, 2 Doors, Cylindrical Legs, 1966, 79 x 37 In.	9375.00
Cabinet, Sewing, Stand, Rosewood, Pearl Inlay, Hinged Top, Fitted Interior, c.1890, 43 x 16 In.	563.00
Cabinet, Sheet Music, Arts & Crafts, 2-Panel Doors, 12 Interior Shelves, 34 ½ x 17 In.	610.00
Cabinet, Shibayama Style, Wood, Openwork, Flowers, Dragons, Ivory, Gold, 1800s, 83 x 51 In.	7110.00
Cabinet, Side, Elm, Carved & Scrolled Apron, Brackets, Chinese, c.1895, 34 x 42 In.	118.00
Cabinet, Side, Rosewood, Gilt, Breakfront, Marble Top, Door, String Inlay, c.1850, 36 x 53 In.	1659.00
Cabinet, Side, Rosewood, Inlaid Frieze, Musical Trophy, Conforming Sides, c.1850, 49 x 60 In.	3585.00
Cabinet, Speaker, G. Nelson, Birch, Tambour Top, Square Feet, c.1946, 23 x 34 In.	813.00
Cabinet, Specimen, Hardwood, 24 Drawers, Cabriole Legs, Ball Feet, 24 x 25 In.	345.00
Cabinet, Spice, 7 Drawers, Tramp Art, Carved, c.1900, 12 x 7 In.	243.00
Cabinet, Spice, Chippendale, Door, Drawer, Fitted Interior, 29 ¼ x 20 ½ In.	1003.00
Cabinet, Spice, Pine, Ocher Paint, 11 Drawers, 1800s, 13 ¼ x 26 ½ In.	1304.00
Cabinet, Spice, Walnut, Arched, 2 Doors, Inlaid Panels, England, 23 x 20 x 9 In.	1265.00
Cabinet, Spice, Walnut, Crest, Parquetry, Pa., c.1860, 21 x 18 ½ In.	2252.00
Cabinet, Spice, Walnut, Pediment, Feet, 9 Drawers, Porcelain Pulls, 19th Century, 28 x 23 In.	708.00
Cabinet, Tabletop, Hinged Top, Drawers, Silver Mounts, Chinese, c.1750, 12 x 16 ½ In.	7670.00
Cabinet, Tabletop, Lacquer, Doors, Landscape Design, Outscrolled Feet, Chinese, 1800s, 26 x 19 In.	288.00
Cabinet, Tambour, Walnut, Mirror, Columns, Drawer, Door, Inlay, Italy, 1700s, 38 x 18 In.	1725.00
Cabinet, Teak, 2 Tambour Doors, Fitted Interior, Stamped Denmark, 62 x 30 In.	976.00
Cabinet, Tulipwood, Gilt Bronze, Cornice, Latticework, Sabot Feet, 1700s, 85 x 34 In.	2900.00
Cabinet, Vamo Sonderborg, Teak, Rounded Sliding Doors, 4 Drawers, Denmark, 94 x 20 In.	1250.00
Cabinet, Victorian, Walnut, Glass Doors, Drawers, Secret Compartment, L Shape, 91 x 77 In.	960.00
Cabinet, Victorian, Walnut, Incised Flower Backsplash, 2 Doors, 2 Open Shelves, c.1875, 29 x 24 In.	259.00
Cabinet, Walnut, 4 Drawers, Wood Pull, Scroll Base, c.1890, 16 x 18 In.	153.00
Cabinet, Walnut, Cupboard Doors, Drawers, Stepped Base, France, c.1930, 67 x 49 In.	8000.00
Cabinet, Walnut, Drawer, Open Shelf, Carved Grotesques, Bun Feet, c.1900, 44 x 51 In.	474.00
Cabinet, Walnut, Poplar, Panel & Glass Doors, Heart Pierced, Stepped Cornice, 1800s, 79 x 45 In.	4956.00
Cabinet, Walnut, Wall Mount, Double Glass Doors, Shelf, Curved Mullions, Brass Finials, 27 x 24 In.	311.00
Cabinet, Widdicomb, Mahogany, 2 Doors, Painted Panel Doors, Stretcher Base, 41 x 61 In.	537.00
Cabinet, William Spratling, Mahogany, 2 Square Panel Doors, Stamped, 1950s, 40 x 31 In.	748.00
Cabinet, Wine, Oak, Top Glass Door, Drawer, Low Door, Carvings, Horner & Co., c.1890, 65 x 31 In.	2588.00
Cabinet, Wood, Painted, Panel Door, Asian Tiger, Block Legs, Square, Chinese, c.1930, 33 x 31 In.	450.00
Cabinet, Wormley, Inset Ceramic Tiles, 11 Drawers, Dunbar, 1956, 29 x 48 x 20 In. ....*Illus*	11250.00
Cabinet, Wormley, Walnut, Brass Doorknocker Handles, Doors, Drawers, Casters, 1940s, 30 x 70 In.	3125.00
Cabinet-On-Stand, Chinoiserie, Chippendale Style, Japanned, Black, Doors, Drawers, 68 x 47 In.	460.00
Cabinet-On-Stand, Ebonized, Lapis Lazuli Inlay, Doors, Shaped Apron, Hoof Feet, 1800s, 48 x 25 In.	2689.00
Cabinet-On-Stand, George III Style, Swan Neck, Urn Finials, Cluster Columns, c.1900, 41 x 20 In..	984.00
Cabinet-On-Stand, Hardwood, Faux Bamboo, Pierced, Dovetailed, Chinese, 1800s, 68 x 32 In. *Illus*	3186.00
Cabinet-On-Stand, Louis XVI Style, Ebonized, Gilt, Urn, Flowers, Fluted Legs, c.1900, 61 x 46 In.	3250.00
Cabinet-On-Stand, Specimen, Mahogany, Drawers, 1800s, 38 x 26 In.	474.00
Cabinet-On-Stand, Tortoiseshell, Mahogany, Burl Maple, 2 Doors, Platform Stretcher, 55 x 24 In.	750.00
Candlestand, Adjustable, 2 Candle Sockets, Urn Finial, 3 Scrolled Feet, Iron, 1700s, 65 In.	531.00
Candlestand, Adjustable, Tapered Shaft, 2 Arms, 4 Scrolled Feet, 18th Century, 32 ¼ In.	413.00
Candlestand, Alligatored Finish, Tilt Top, Tripod Legs, Turned Column, c.1835, 26 x 17 In.	294.00
Candlestand, Carved Standard, Gilt Paint, Italy, 1700s, 42 In.	540.00
Candlestand, Chippendale Style, Mahogany, Round, Tilt Top, Ball & Claw Feet, 23 x 13 In.	247.00
Candlestand, Chippendale, Cherry, Applied Beading, 3 Cabriole Legs, Conn., c.1785, 26 x 14 In.	173.00

Furniture, Cabinet, Hardwood, Dragon, Shelves, Ivory, Beveled Glass, Chinese, c.1900, 68 x 27 In.
$3,220.00

Cottone Auctions

Furniture, Cabinet, Hat Chest, Huanghuali, Panel Doors, Chinese, 1900s, 87 x 49 In.
$56,288.00

Skinner, Inc.

Furniture, Cabinet, Lacquer, Paneled Doors, Shelf, Figures, Dragon, Chinese, c.1900, 35 ½ x 24 In.
$177.00

Brunk Auctions

Furniture, Cabinet, P. Evans, Bronze, Composite, Sculptured Metal Doors, Signed, 1968, 18 x 50 In. $10,000.00

Rago Arts & Auction Center

Furniture, Cabinet, Regency Style, Mahogany, Fabric-Lined Doors, Metalwork, 33 x 30 In., Pair $4,063.00

Doyle New York

Furniture, Cabinet, Removable Door Panels, Interior Shelves, Drawers, Chinese, 1900s, 64 x 38 In. $600.00

Skinner, Inc.

Furniture, Cabinet, Renaissance Revival, Oak, Carved, Glass Doors, Chamfered Sides, c.1850, 68 In. $6,871.00

Neal Auction Co.

Candlestand, Chippendale, Cherry, Tilt Top, Scalloped, c.1780, 27 x 18 In.	1612.00
Candlestand, Chippendale, Dish Tilt Top, Line Inlay, Turned Column, Snake Feet, c.1800, 29 x 19 In.	482.00
Candlestand, Chippendale, Mahogany, Tilt Top, Round, 3 Cabriole Legs, c.1810, 38 x 28 In.	1150.00
Candlestand, Chippendale, Mahogany, Tilt Top, Turned Column, Snake Feet, c.1795, 29 In.	1763.00
Candlestand, Chippendale, Maple, Dish Top, Turned Shaft, Snake Feet, c.1795, 28 x 17 In.	542.00
Candlestand, Chippendale, Walnut, Dish Top, Pa., 27 ½ x 19 ½ In.	385.00
Candlestand, Curly Maple, Walnut Tilt Top, Turned Column, Spider Legs, c.1800, 29 x 18 In.	411.00
Candlestand, Ebonized, Gilt Leaves, Faux Marble, 3-Footed, Continental, c.1900, 29 x 16 In.	296.00
Candlestand, Federal, Birch, Square Top, Tripod Base, New England, c.1810, 26 ½ x 16 ½ In.	119.00
Candlestand, Federal, Cherry, Inlay, Octagonal Top, Reeded Post, Spade Feet, c.1815, 28 x 24 In.	8295.00
Candlestand, Federal, Cherry, Round Top, Urn & Ring Support, Tripod Base, 1800s, 27 x 20 In.	118.00
Candlestand, Federal, Cherry, Scalloped Top, Urn Standard, New England, c.1805, 27 x 14 In.	1185.00
Candlestand, Federal, Mahogany, Tilt Top, Oval, Mass., c.1780, 24 x 25 In.	1860.00
Candlestand, Federal, Mahogany, Tilt Top, Tiger Maple Inlay, Snake Feet, c.1785, 29 x 24 In. ..*Illus*	540.00
Candlestand, Federal, Maple, Pine, Shaped Top, Baluster Shaft, c.1800, 28 x 17 In.	323.00
Candlestand, Federal, Tiger Maple, Tilt Top, Ring & Baluster Standard, Spider Legs, 28 x 21 In.	403.00
Candlestand, George II, Mahogany, Round, Tripod Base, c.1760, 25 ½ x 23 ½ In.	178.00
Candlestand, George II, Mahogany, Round, Tripod Splayed Legs, c.1760, 27 ¾ x 21 In.	273.00
Candlestand, George II, Mahogany, Tilt Top, Urn Standard, c.1765, 27 x 18 ¾ In.	911.00
Candlestand, George III, Mahogany, Piecrust Top, Tripod Base, c.1800, 25 x 19 In.	500.00
Candlestand, George III, Mahogany, Turned Standard, Tripod Base, c.1780, 29 x 24 In.	296.00
Candlestand, Hepplewhite, Mahogany, Inlay, Oval Tilt Top, Tripod Base, Ma., 29 x 16 In.	354.00
Candlestand, Hepplewhite, Tiger Maple, Square Top, 3 Spider Legs, c.1790, 27 x 16 In.	384.00
Candlestand, Mahogany, Beaded Edge, Twist Baluster, Turned Base, c.1850, 27 In.	246.00
Candlestand, Mahogany, Reticulated Frieze, Columnar Stem, Tripod, c.1850, 35 In.	1076.00
Candlestand, Mahogany, Ring & Baluster Stem, Arched Legs, Victorian, 29 x 17 In. ....*Illus*	717.00
Candlestand, Mahogany, Square, Fluted & Reeded Post, Tripod Legs, c.1790, 26 x 16 In.	4800.00
Candlestand, Mahogany, Tilt Top, Reeded Urn Shaft, Cabriole Legs, Spade Feet, c.1800, 35 x 25 In.	301.00
Candlestand, Mahogany, Tilt Top, Rounded, Vase Shaft, Spider Legs, c.1800, 30 x 26 In.	369.00
Candlestand, Mahogany, Turned Standard, Tripod Base, Snake Feet, c.1750, 26 x 16 In.	2070.00
Candlestand, Mahogany, Vase & Ring Post, Tripod Base, Pad Feet, c.1795, 26 x 16 In.	889.00
Candlestand, Maple, Adjustable, Tripod Base, Painted, New Hampshire, c.1810, 24 x 13 In.	2066.00
Candlestand, Maple, Birch, Tapered Shaft, Tripod Base, N.Y., c.1830, 24 x 16 In.	504.00
Candlestand, Maple, Double Molded Edge, Turned Pedestal, 3 Legs, c.1780, 25 x 16 In.	472.00
Candlestand, Maple, Square Top, Turned Standard, Tripod Base, New England, 1810, 25 x 14 In.	296.00
Candlestand, Mixed Wood, Adjustable, Threaded Bar, Drip Tray, Wool Winder, 1800s, 42 In. ....*Illus*	153.00
Candlestand, Pine, Painted, Baluster Standard, Tripod Base, c.1800, 28 x 19 In.	296.00
Candlestand, Queen Anne Style, Maple, Cherry, Dish Tilt Top, Birdcage, 30 x 20 In.	325.00
Candlestand, Queen Anne, Cherry, Dish Tilt Top, Turned Standard, Tripod Leg Base	4012.00
Candlestand, Queen Anne, Cherry, Maple, Square Top, Urn Standard, New Eng., 28 x 17 In.	472.00
Candlestand, Queen Anne, Dish Tilt Top, Birdcage, 29 x 19 In.	1003.00
Candlestand, Queen Anne, Mahogany, Dish Top, Vase Shape Standard, 27 x 18 In.	118.00
Candlestand, Queen Anne, Mahogany, Molded Edge, Cabriole Legs, 28 x 18 In.	83.00
Candlestand, Queen Anne, Mahogany, Scalloped Dish Tilt Top, Tripod Base, 26 x 21 In.	826.00
Candlestand, Queen Anne, Mahogany, Tilt Top, Ball Standard, Tripod Base, c.1760, 28 x 20 In.	2844.00
Candlestand, Queen Anne, Mahogany, Tilt Top, Turned Column, Tripod Legs, c.1800, 29 In.	176.00
Candlestand, Queen Anne, Maple, Round Top, Painted, c.1760, 25 ½ x 20 In.	472.00
Candlestand, Queen Anne, Square Top, Urn Standard, Cabriole Legs, 27 x 17 ¾ In.	177.00
Candlestand, Queen Anne, Walnut, Dish Tilt Top, Ball Standard, c.1760, 28 x 21 In.	3555.00
Candlestand, Queen Anne, Walnut, Dish Top, Ball Standard, Pa., c.1765, 28 x 17 In.	3555.00
Candlestand, Queen Anne, Walnut, Dish Top, Round, Tripod Base, c.1760, 27 x 19 In.	6518.00
Candlestand, Queen Anne, Walnut, Drawer, Turned Pedestal, Tripod Base, Pa., c.1780, 27 x 14 In.	2844.00
Candlestand, Queen Anne, Walnut, Tilt Dish Top, Birdcage Support, c.1775, 29 x 20 In. ....*Illus*	7800.00
Candlestand, Queen Anne, Wood, Baluster Support, Stain, Delaware, c.1790, 27 x 18 In.	1778.00
Candlestand, Ratchet, Maple, Pennsylvania, Late 1700s, 33 ½ In.	6683.00
Candlestand, Regency, Mahogany, Tripod Feet, c.1820, 29 x 23 In.	237.00
Candlestand, Round, Vase & Ring Post, Tripod, Cabriole Legs, Pad Feet, c.1800, 27 x 18 In.	178.00
Candlestand, Tiger Maple, Octagonal Top, Applied Edge, Tripod Base, 1700s, 27 x 13 In.	443.00
Candlestand, Tiger Maple, Oval Corners, Tripod Cabriole Legs, c.1795, 30 x 18 x 13 In.	1304.00
Candlestand, Tiger Maple, Rectangular Tilt Top, Splayed Tripod Base, c.1820, 28 x 18 In.	690.00
Candlestand, Tiger Maple, Shaped Top, Vase & Ring Post, Tripod Base, c.1800, 29 x 21 In.	960.00
Candlestand, Tilt Top, Game Board, Painted, New England, c.1815, 37 x 28 In.	8060.00
Candlestand, Tilt Top, Round, Urn & Ring Support, Tripod Legs, c.1810, 28 x 19 In.	345.00
Candlestand, Walnut, Pine, Square Top, 4 Downswept Feet, Carved, c.1920, 30 x 13 In.	184.00
Candlestand, Walnut, Square Top, Line Inlay, 3 Downswept Legs, c.1810, 28 x 16 In.	633.00
Candlestand, Walnut, Turned Standard, Crackled Finish, Pa., c.1815, 29 x 13 In.	178.00

Candlestand, William & Mary, Pine, Maple, Cross Stretcher, Painted, Pa., c.1760, 26 x 17 In. 770.00
Candlestand, Windsor, Maple, Ash, Dish Top, Turned Shaft, Tripod, c.1800, 26 x 14 In...................... 411.00
Candlestand, Wood, Adjustable, 2 Sheet Tin Holders, Stool Base, c.1800, 31 ½ In. 316.00
Candlestand, Wrought Iron, Brass, Adjustable, 2 Candle Cups, Claw Feet, 15 ¼ In. 1185.00
Candlestand, Wrought Iron, Candle Cup, Rush Holder, Arrow Feet, 1700s, 47 In.............................. 1541.00
Canterbury, George III, Mahogany, 4 Compartments, Drawer, Casters, c.1800, 19 x 18 In. 956.00
Canterbury, George III, Mahogany, 4 Open Shelves, Drawer, Casters, c.1820, 22 x 17 In. 523.00
Canterbury, George III, Mahogany, Drawer, Square Legs, c.1790, 20 x 20 x 13 In.................... 1553.00
Canterbury, Mahogany, 4 Open Shelves, Scroll Carved, Drawer, c.1920, 27 x 16 In.................. 118.00
Canterbury, Neoclassical, Mahogany, Drawer, Casters, c.1810, 18 x 15 In. ....*Illus* 800.00
Canterbury, Regency, Mahogany, 2 Drawers, England, c.1830, 21 x 24 In. 1116.00
Canterbury, Regency, Rosewood, Carved & Pierced, Drawer, England, 19 x 19 In. 978.00
Canterbury, Regency, Rosewood, X-Shape, 4 Compartments, Dividers, Shelf, c.1815, 20 x 16 In... 1304.00
Canterbury, Rosewood, 4 Lyre Dividers, Spindle Sides, Drawer, 17 x 19 In................................ 984.00
Canterbury, Rosewood, Pierced Gallery, Finials, Barley Twist Uprights, Turned Feet, 40 x 22 In. 1195.00
Canterbury, Sheraton, Mahogany, Drawer, Carved Spindle, 18 x 14 In. 1180.00
Canterbury, Victorian, Mahogany, Scroll Dividers, Feathers, Drawer, 1800s, 22 x 20 In........... 1125.00
Canterbury, Walnut, 3 Sections, Drawer Below, Wood Pulls, Legs, Casters, 18 x 20 In............. 414.00
Canterbury, Walnut, Pierced, Carved, Rod Divided, Drawer, c.1860, 25 x 25 In. 94.00
Card Holder, Black Forest, Figural, Bear, Holding Plant Holder, Shell Shape Dish, 48 In........ 3163.00
Cart, Danish Modern, Rosewood, Veneer, Laminate, Edge Lip, Shaped Frame, 23 x 47 In........ 365.00
Cart, Serving, Walnut, Laminate, X-Shape Supports, Tray Shelf, 1950s, 28 x 36 In.................... 1125.00
Cellarette, George III, Hexagonal, Hinged Lid, Handles, Squat Legs, c.1795, 25 x 19 In........... 889.00
Cellarette, George III, Mahogany, Brass Handles, Stand, Square Legs, c.1800, 26 x 19 In........ 1107.00
Cellarette, George III, Mahogany, Fret Carved Brackets, Rectangular, 25 ½ x 18 In................. 1180.00
Cellarette, George III, Mahogany, Hexagonal, Brass Banding, Hinged Top, c.1800, 28 x 19 In. . 246.00
Cellarette, George III, Mahogany, Octagonal, Brass Banding, Stand, c.1800, 27 x 20 In. 615.00
Cellarette, Georgian, Mahogany, Brass Bound, Square Legs, 27 x 17 In. 1062.00
Cellarette, L. & J.G. Stickley, Doors, Copper Pullout Shelf, Square Legs, c.1912, 34 x 32 In...... 6250.00
Cellarette, Limbert, 2 Doors, Drawer, Glass Pullout Shelf, Bottle Holder, c.1910, 38 x 31 In. ... 4063.00
Cellarette, Mahogany, Banded, Geometric Inlay, Brass Handles, Octagonal, c.1850, 14 x 12 In. 767.00
Cellarette, Mahogany, Hinged Lid, Fitted Interior, Stand, Spindle Legs, 28 x 21 In. 1320.00
Cellarette, Neoclassical, Mahogany, Carved, Bulbous Standard, Reeded Legs, Casters, 32 x 17 In.. 1180.00
Cellarette, Regency, Mahogany, Greek Key Banding, Pedestal, Outcurved Feet, 1800s, 29 x 19 In.. 590.00
Cellarette, Square Top, Open Shelf, Door, Bun Feet, Wood Hardware, 22 x 22 In. 1464.00
Cellarette, William IV, Mahogany, Sarcophagus, Leaves, Scrolled Feet, c.1835, 23 x 34 In....... 492.00
Cellarette, William IV, Oak, Sarcophagus Shape, Scroll Feet, 1800s, 22 x 46 x 24 In............... 1553.00
Cellarette, William IV, Rosewood, Cylindrical, Domed, Finial, Lotus Feet, c.1835, 36 In........... 4182.00
Cellarette, William IV, Rosewood, Dome Lid, Bottle Case, Decanters, Lotus Feet, 1835, 36 x 20 In. 4180.00
Chair Set, Adirondack Style, Willow, 5 Vertical Slats, Arched Back, 35 x 18 In., 7 .... 864.00
Chair Set, Arched Back, Open Arms, Upholstered, c.1930, 36 x 20 In., 4.................................... 660.00
Chair Set, Balloon Back, Painted, Free Hand & Stenciled Design, c.1850, 33 ¼ In., 6 .....*Illus* 999.00
Chair Set, Bootjack, Pine, Fruit Basket Crest, Salmon Paint, Pa., c.1830, 4............................... 1007.00
Chair Set, Chippendale Style, Mahogany, Pierced Splat, Upholstered Seat, Henkel Harris, 8 ... 4029.00
Chair Set, Chippendale, Mahogany, Carved, Openwork, Owl's Eye Splat, Upholstered Seat, 6.. 7965.00
Chair Set, Chrome, Enamel Frame, Striped Upholstery, Herman Miller, 23 x 27 In., 4............. 488.00
Chair Set, Chrome, Grid Back, Faux Bamboo Frame, Upholstered, c.1960, 32 x 16 In., 4........ 960.00
Chair Set, Erno Fabry, Mahogany, Vinyl Upholster, 1957, 27 x 19 In., 6.................................. 4375.00
Chair Set, Fauteuil, Louis XVI Style, Gilt, Medallion Back, Carved, Upholstered, Arms, 36 In., 6 1476.00
Chair Set, George III Style, Mahogany, Shaped Splat, Padded Seat, 1 Armchair, 6.................... 296.00
Chair Set, Hepplewhite, Mahogany, Shieldback, Serpentine Sides, Upholstered, 38 In., 8 .... 2070.00
Chair Set, Hepplewhite, Mahogany, Shieldback, Vertical Spines, 2 Arm Chairs, 12.................. 7375.00
Chair Set, Knoll, Life, Padded Seat, 5-Prong Stationary Base, c.1950, 6 .... 1800.00
Chair Set, L. & J.G. Stickley, 3-Slat Back, Padded Seat, 38 x 26 In., 10 .... 4063.00
Chair Set, L. & J.G. Stickley, Ladder Back, No. 1350, 3 Horizontal Slats, 34 In., 6.................... 1875.00
Chair Set, Metal, Slat Back, Seat, Tube Frame, France, c.1960, 31 x 15 In., 6 .... 1080.00
Chair Set, Neoclassical Style, Windsor, Fanback, Oak, 2 Armchairs, Upholstered Seat, 6.......... 236.00
Chair Set, Oak, Flared Back, Upholstered Seat, France, c.1940, 33 x 18 In., 6.......................... 1200.00
Chair Set, Queen Anne Style, Mahogany, Pierced Vase Shape Splat, 2 Armchairs, 8 .... 1652.00
Chair Set, Queen Anne Style, Walnut, 2 Armchairs, Padded Seat, 6 .... 4029.00
Chair Set, Queen Anne, Maple, Vase Shape Splat, Rush Seat, Spanish Foot, c.1720, 42 In., 4.. 6325.00
Chair Set, Regency Style, Parcel Gilt, Painted, Scroll Arms, Splayed Legs, Upholstered, 8 .... 3438.00
Chair Set, Regency, Mahogany, Tablet Crest, Reeded, Twist Splat, 1800s, 33 In., 6.................. 345.00
Chair Set, Swivel, Burke, Dallas, Multicolor Seats, 4.. 360.00
Chair Set, Teak, Horizontal Back Rail, Faux Leather Seat, Svegards Markaryd, 30 In., 8......... 729.00
Chair Set, Thonet, Bentwood, Upholstered Seat, Back, 1950s, 33 In., 4.................................. 695.00

Furniture, Cabinet, Wormley, Inset Ceramic Tiles, 11 Drawers, Dunbar, 1956, 29 x 48 x 20 In.
$11,250.00

Los Angeles Modern Auctions (LAMA)

F

Furniture, Cabinet-On-Stand, Hardwood, Faux Bamboo, Pierced, Dovetailed, Chinese, 1800s, 68 x 32 In.
$3,186.00

Brunk Auctions

Furniture, Candlestand, Federal, Mahogany, Tilt Top, Tiger Maple Inlay, Snake Feet, c.1785, 29 x 24 In.
$540.00

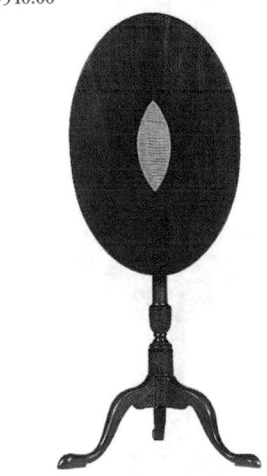

Cowan's Auctions

207

Furniture, Candlestand, Mahogany, Ring & Baluster Stem, Arched Legs, Victorian, 29 x 17 In.
$717.00

Neal Auction Co.

Furniture, Candlestand, Mixed Wood, Adjustable, Threaded Bar, Drip Tray, Wool Winder, 1800s, 42 In.
$153.00

Conestoga Auction Co., Inc.

Furniture, Candlestand, Queen Anne, Walnut, Tilt Dish Top, Birdcage Support, c.1775, 29 x 20 In.
$7,800.00

Skinner, Inc.

Chair Set, Windsor, Arrow Back, Mixed Wood, Mustard Paint, Stencil, c.1840, 17 In., 6	823.00
Chair Set, Windsor, Bent Rodback, Flower Crest, Yellow Paint, c.1810, 6	5688.00
Chair Set, Windsor, Bow Back, Green Paint, 1 Armchair, New England, 4	649.00
Chair Set, Windsor, Mixed Wood, Bamboo Turnings, H-Stretcher, c.1830, 35 In., 6	764.00
Chair Set, Windsor, Sack Back, Black Paint, Arms, c.1795, 37 In., 6	9920.00
Chair Set, Windsor, Square Back, Red, New England, c.1810, 34 In., 6	9480.00
Chair, Aalto, Birch, L-Shape Leg, Round Seat, Squared Open Back, c.1933, 31 In.	219.00
Chair, Aalto, Birch, Square Curved Arms & Legs, Finland, 1950s, 30 x 33 In.	3250.00
Chair, Aalto, Birch, S-Shape Seat & Back, Curved Arms & Legs, Finland, 1930s, 24 x 31 In.	3375.00
Chair, Apostle, Oak, High Back, Carved, Tiered Figures, 13 Figures, Multicolor, 59 In.	480.00
Chair, Arbus Style, Rounded Back, Open Arms, Upholstered, Nailheads, c.1940, 35 In., Pair	960.00
Chair, Arbus Style, Upholstered, Curved Arms, Saber Legs, France, c.1940, 32 In., Pair	480.00
Chair, Arched Back, Downswept Arms, Tufted Upholstery, France, 30 x 31 In., Pair	960.00
Chair, Arrow Back, Black Paint, Pa., c.1805, 20 ¼ In., Child's	356.00
Chair, Arrow Back, Painted, Arms, c.1805, 17 ½ In.	59.00
Chair, Art Deco Style, Jean-Louis Godivier, Leather, Black Metal, c.1980, 27 x 26 In.	300.00
Chair, Art Deco, Mahogany, Square Padded Back & Arms, Tapered Legs, c.1905, 41 In., Pair	4674.00
Chair, Art Deco, Oscar Bach, Gilt Brass, Wrought Iron, Mask, Trestle Base, 36 x 20 In. ....*Illus*	590.00
Chair, Art Deco, Parquetry Top, Scrolled Tapered Legs, c.1930, 30 x 47 In.	1440.00
Chair, Art Nouveau, Barrel Back, Rosewood, Mahogany, Cloth, G. Feure, c.1900, 35 In.	2596.00
Chair, Art Nouveau, Edouard Diot, Walnut Frame, Upholstered, c.1960	236.00
Chair, Arts & Crafts, High Back, Heart Cutout, Slat Sides, Leather Seat, Eng., 27 x 24 In.	366.00
Chair, Arts & Crafts, Mahogany, Curved Back, Slats, Saddle Seat, Arms, c.1900, 49 In., Pair	430.00
Chair, Arts & Crafts, Oak, Dowel Back, Seat, Open Arms, Organic Shape, 24 x 31 In.	813.00
Chair, Arts & Crafts, Tall Back, Wide Slat, Carved, Upholstered Seat, England, 54. In.	1625.00
Chair, Ballroom, Louis XVI Style, Oval Cane Back, Seat, Fluted Legs, Cushion, 1890	240.00
Chair, Bamboo, Japanned, Woven Reed Seat, c.1880, 25 In., Child's	395.00
Chair, Banister Back, Carved, Turned, Pierced, Prince Of Wales Crest, c.1755, 45 In.	1778.00
Chair, Banister Back, Maple, Turned Legs, Stretchers, Splint Seat, Painted, 42 In., Pair	521.00
Chair, Banister Back, Oak, Rush Seat, Spindle Back, Turned Rails, Stretcher, New Eng., c.1780	207.00
Chair, Banister Back, Painted, Gilt, Pinwheel Carved Scroll Arms, Turned Legs, 1700s, 48 In.	5036.00
Chair, Banister Back, Shaped Crest, Carved Star, Black Paint, 43 x 17 In.	770.00
Chair, Barcelona, Mies Van Der Rohe, Steel X-Shape Legs, 1960s, 30 x 30 In., Pair	5000.00
Chair, Baroque Style, Carved, Scroll Arms, Legs, Apron, Stretcher, Upholstered, 51 x 28 In., Pair	1006.00
Chair, Baroque Style, High Back, Cane Seat, Scroll Arms, Carved Stretcher, 53 In.	123.00
Chair, Baroque Style, Walnut, Carved Leaves, Leather Upholstery, c.1720, 41 x 19 In., Pair	720.00
Chair, Baroque Style, Walnut, Carved, Lion Masks, Upholstered, Italy, c.1900, 43 In. ....*Illus*	295.00
Chair, Barrel Back, Padded, Square Tapered Legs, Brass Castor, Arms, 1800s, 42 x 29 In.	375.00
Chair, Beach, Curved Legs, Open Arms, Ball Finial Rests, Italy, c.1750, 35 x 21 In., Pair	4313.00
Chair, Bentwood, J. Hoffmann, Barrel Back, Austria, c.1910, 28 x 22 In., Pair	750.00
Chair, Bentwood, Otto Wagner, Openwork Back, Saddle Seat, Brass Cap Feet, 22 x 21 In.	793.00
Chair, Bergere, Carved, Painted, Upholstered, Arms, England, c.1900, 36 x 30 In.	1840.00
Chair, Bergere, Empire, Mahogany, Gilt, Arms, Maiden Busts, Paw Feet, c.1890, 39 In.	3690.00
Chair, Bergere, Empire, Mahogany, Gilt, Crest, Swans, Paw Feet, Closed Arms, c.1815, 37 In.	3444.00
Chair, Bergere, George III, Cane Back, Sides, Gilt, Cushion, Closed Arms, c.1775, 37 In. ...*Illus*	2400.00
Chair, Bergere, George IV, Mahogany, Bellflower, Fluted Uprights, Closed Arms, c.1825	896.00
Chair, Bergere, Hardwood, Inlay, Shaped Crest, Closed Arms, c.1900, 40 In., Pair	2337.00
Chair, Bergere, Louis XV Style, Fruitwood, Domed Back, Closed Arms, Flowers, c.1890, 42 In.	861.00
Chair, Bergere, Louis XV Style, Fruitwood, Domed Back, Leaf Crest, Closed Arms, Ottoman, 37 In.	2337.00
Chair, Bergere, Louis XV Style, Fruitwood, Flower Crest, Carved Legs, Closed Arms, 38 In., Pair	922.00
Chair, Bergere, Louis XV Style, Fruitwood, Shaped Back, Closed Arms, 1900s, 38 In., Pair	885.00
Chair, Bergere, Louis XV Style, Walnut, Cane Seat, Back, Cushion, Closed Arms, c.1890, 33 In.	1955.00
Chair, Bergere, Louis XV Style, White Paint, Shell Carved, Closed Arms, 39 In., Pair	2375.00
Chair, Bergere, Louis XV, Painted, Arched, Upholstered, Closed Arms, Meunnier, c.1775, 32 In.	5700.00
Chair, Bergere, Louis XV, Upholstered, Painted, Closed Arms, Nadal Laine, 1786, Pair	6250.00
Chair, Bergere, Louis XVI Style, Carved, Upholstered, Closed Arms, c.1940, 41 In., Pair	390.00
Chair, Bergere, Louis XVI Style, Chestnut, Upholstered, Closed Arms, c.1920, 39 In.	575.00
Chair, Bergere, Louis XVI Style, Domed Back, Closed Arms, 1900s, 37 In., Pair	1599.00
Chair, Bergere, Louis XVI Style, Domed Back, Leaf Carved, Closed Arms, 1700s, 37 In.	1599.00
Chair, Bergere, Louis XVI Style, Domed Back, Molded Frame, Closed Arms, c.1890, 35 In., Pair.	1722.00
Chair, Bergere, Louis XVI Style, Fruitwood, Fluted, Closed Arms, c.1900, 34 In.	369.00
Chair, Bergere, Louis XVI Style, Gilt, Rounded Back, Closed Arms, c.1900, 41 In.	649.00
Chair, Bergere, Louis XVI Style, Gilt, Wreath & Torchere Crest, Closed Arms, c.1890, 38 In. ... *Illus*	615.00
Chair, Bergere, Louis XVI, Carved, Painted, Upholstered, Closed Arms, 1760, 35 x 25 In.	4000.00
Chair, Bergere, Mahogany, Domed Back, Scrolled Legs, Closed Arms, c.1950, 51 In., Pair	2337.00
Chair, Bergere, Mahogany, Padded Back, Leaf Carved Frame, Closed Arms, 1900s, 41 In.	553.00

F

Chair, Bergere, Napoleon III, Gilt, Upholstered, Closed Arms, c.1850, 30 x 26 In., Pair............	1250.00
Chair, Bergere, Napoleon III, Upholstered, Closed Arms, c.1880, 34 x 31 In., Pair.................	1440.00
Chair, Bergere, Regency Style, Gilt, Carved Crest, Closed Arms, 1800, 34 x 38 In., Pair............	720.00
Chair, Bergere, Regency Style, Mahogany, Reeded Legs, Closed Arms, 1800s, 38 In..................	603.00
Chair, Bergere, Regency Style, Mahogany, Reeded Legs, Upholstered, Closed Arms, 38 In........	181.00
Chair, Bergere, Rococo Revival, Mahogany, Arched Barrel Back, Lion Masks, Closed Arms, c.1861	837.00
Chair, Bidet, Mahogany, Shaped Back, Flip Seat, Leather Upholstery, Brass, 33 x 15 In.	1035.00
Chair, Biedermeier, Birch, Gilt Oval Splat, Shaped Arm Supports, Scroll Rail, 35 x 21 In........	219.00
Chair, Biedermeier, Birch, Saber Legs, Shaped Backrest, Upholstered, 33 x 18 In., Pair..........	184.00
Chair, Biedermeier, Fruitwood, Flared Padded Back, Crest, Scroll Arms, c.1850, 30 In.............	984.00
Chair, Biedermeier, Walnut, Pierced Lyre Shape Splat, 1800s, 35 x 18 In..............................	299.00
Chair, Black Forest, Inlaid Wood, Plays Music When You Sit On It ....*Illus*	3360.00
Chair, Blackwood, Kashmiri Carved, Pierced, Curved Back, c.1850, 39 x 33 In.	2000.00
Chair, Brass, Tube Frame, Upholstered, Mastercraft, 24 x 19 ½ In., Pair..............................	938.00
Chair, Bugatti, Oak, Pewter Inlay, Silk, Square Back Circle Center, Arms, c.1900, 45 In...........	3800.00
Chair, Burl, Carved, Orange & Green Patina, Swivels, 34 In..	504.00
Chair, C. Pollock, Chrome Steel, Black Leather Sling, Knoll, 25 x 24 In., Pair	1875.00
Chair, Campeachy, Walnut, Arched Crest, Scroll Arms, Curule Supports, c.1810, 35 In. ...*Illus*	5185.00
Chair, Campeachy, Walnut, Scroll Arms, Turned Stretcher, Upholstered, 1800s, 25 In. ....*Illus*	235.00
Chair, Campeachy, Walnut, Upholstered, Arms, Sloping Back, Trestle Base, 34 x 29 In., Pair...	1035.00
Chair, Carved Cabriole Legs, Painted, Upholstered, Italy, 1700s, 44 x 28 In.	1610.00
Chair, Cast Iron, Scrolled, Pierced Seat & Back, Black Paint, 35 ½ x 18 In., Pair..................	88.00
Chair, Cathedral Crest, Padded Back Seat & Arms, Needlepoint Upholstery, c.1850..................	3884.00
Chair, Cedar, Banister Back, Shaped Crest, Turned Stiles & Stretchers, c.1800, 40 In..............	1476.00
Chair, Charles II Style, Oak, Carved Crest, Panel Back, Arms, Turned Legs, Stretcher, Pair.......	1416.00
Chair, Charles II, Walnut, Oval Cane Back, Mask, Dolphin Carved, Twist Supports, Pad Seat, c.1750 .	1250.00
Chair, Chinese, Rosewood, Carved, Lacquered, Dragon Shape Arms, Pierced Back, 32 In.........	189.00
Chair, Chippendale Style, Curly Maple, Shaped Crest, Pierced Splat, Arms, Eldred Wheeler, Pair....	1422.00
Chair, Chippendale Style, Hardwood, Carved Crest, Plank Seat, Gadrooned, 1700s, 37 In., Pair.	575.00
Chair, Chippendale Style, Mahogany, Carved, Scroll Armrests, Supports, Pierced Back, 44 In..	426.00
Chair, Chippendale Style, Mahogany, Pierced Splat, Ball & Claw Feet, 1800s, 42 In., Pair	1920.00
Chair, Chippendale Style, Rolled Arms, Upholstered, Ball & Claw Feet, 1900s, 44 In.................	264.00
Chair, Chippendale Style, Walnut, Rush Seat, Pierced Splat, Curved Crest, Stretcher, 41 In., Pair...	357.00
Chair, Chippendale, Black Lacquer, Leather Seat, Chinese, c.1730, Pair	23600.00
Chair, Chippendale, Cherry, Arched Crest, Molded Ears, Openwork Splat, c.1750, 38 In.	115.00
Chair, Chippendale, Cherry, Pierced Vase Splat, Square Legs, Stretcher, c.1795, 38 In.	235.00
Chair, Chippendale, Cherry, Shaped Crest, Carved, Pierced Splat, Square Legs, 39 In.	326.00
Chair, Chippendale, Mahogany, Carved, Pierced Splat, Serpentine Crest Rail, Pair..................	590.00
Chair, Chippendale, Mahogany, Carved, Upholstered Seat, Stretcher, Pair...........................	1180.00
Chair, Chippendale, Mahogany, Pierced Fret, Carved Arms, 1700s, 38 In., Pair	20000.00
Chair, Chippendale, Mahogany, Pierced Splat, Cabriole Legs, Ball & Claw Feet, c.1700, 38 In..	294.00
Chair, Chippendale, Mahogany, Reticulated Splat, Carved, Pad Seat, Open Arms, 41 In., Pair .	600.00
Chair, Chippendale, Mahogany, Serpentine Crest, Openwork Splat, c.1780, Pair......................	2500.00
Chair, Chippendale, Mahogany, Serpentine Crest, Scrolled Pierced Splat, Carved, Pair	4248.00
Chair, Chippendale, Mahogany, Shaped Back, Fleur-De-Lis Splat, H-Stretcher, c.1790	259.00
Chair, Chippendale, Mahogany, Shaped Crest Rail, Owl's Eye Splat, Upholstered Seat, Pair.....	8260.00
Chair, Chippendale, Mahogany, Vase Shape Splat, Shaped Crest, Cabriole Legs, 1700s, 39 In. .	603.00
Chair, Chippendale, Mahogany, Wing, Upholstered, New England, c.1780............................	2844.00
Chair, Chippendale, Pierced Slat, Slip Seat, Valanced Skirt, England, c.1780, 39 In.................	575.00
Chair, Chippendale, Rush Seat, Open Arms, New England, c.1760, 17 x 43 In........................	633.00
Chair, Chippendale, Shell, Ball & Claw Feet, Tulip, Bowknot Crest, Volute Ears, c.1790, 39 In.	3444.00
Chair, Chippendale, Walnut, Pierced Splat, Ball & Claw Feet, c.1770, 40 In. ....*Illus*	9600.00
Chair, Chippendale, Walnut, Serpentine Crest Rail, Shaped Ears, Pierced Splat, c.1750	5015.00
Chair, Chippendale, Walnut, Shell & Volute Carved Crest, Pierced Splat, Arms, c.1770	35550.00
Chair, Chippendale, Wing, Upholstered, Rolled Arms, Fluted Legs, c.1795, 47 In.....................	150.00
Chair, Choir, Gothic Revival, Walnut, Molded Pediment, Crowned Man, Spiral Stiles, France, 80 In...	1422.00
Chair, Chrome Frame, D-Shape, Brown, White Cowhide Cushions, c.1950, 28 x 32 In.	671.00
Chair, Chrome Frame, Tuft Leather Seat, Flexible Back, Italy, 1960s, 25 x 25 In., Pair.............	1188.00
Chair, Club, Art Deco, Leather, c.1930, 33 x 32 In., Pair	1800.00
Chair, Club, Art Deco, Rhulman Style, Leather, Barrel Back, c.1930, 32 x 23 In., Pair..............	2280.00
Chair, Club, Art Deco, Triangle Arch Back, Upholstered, France, c.1940, 37 ½ x 26 In.............	1920.00
Chair, Club, Barrel Back, Column Supports, Upholstered, France, c.1950, 29 x 28 In., Pair.....	1200.00
Chair, Club, Curved, Tapered Wood Feet, Linen Upholstery, Italy, c.1950, 35 x 32 In., Pair.......	1000.00
Chair, Club, Kem Weber, Chrome Steel, Ebonized Wood, Lloyd Mfg. Co., 1930s, 29 x 33 In., Pair .*Illus*	5000.00
Chair, Club, Leather, Arched Back, Rolled Arms, c.1960, 30 x 36 In...................................	240.00
Chair, Club, Leather, Rolled Arms, France, c.1890, 36 x 30 In., Pair.................................	1200.00

Furniture, Canterbury, Neoclassical, Mahogany, Drawer, Casters, c.1810, 18 x 15 In.
$800.00

Neal Auction Co.

Furniture, Chair Set, Balloon Back, Painted, Free Hand & Stenciled Design, c.1850, 33 ¼ In., 6
$999.00

Garth's Auctioneers & Appraisers

Furniture, Chair, Art Deco, Oscar Bach, Gilt Brass, Wrought Iron, Mask, Trestle Base, 36 x 20 In.
$590.00

Brunk Auctions

TIP
A fresh ink stain on wood can be removed by washing it with water and then applying lemon juice.

Furniture, Chair, Baroque Style, Walnut, Carved, Lion Masks, Upholstered, Italy, c.1900, 43 In.
$295.00

Brunk Auctions

Furniture, Chair, Bergere, George III, Cane Back, Sides, Gilt, Cushion, Closed Arms, c.1775, 37 In.
$2,400.00

Skinner, Inc.

Furniture, Chair, Bergere, Louis XVI Style, Gilt, Wreath & Torchere Crest, Closed Arms, c.1890, 38 In.
$615.00

New Orleans Auction Galleries, Inc.

Chair, Club, Louis Philippe, Arch Back, Downswept Arms, France, c.1880, 33 x 30 In., Pair.....	1020.00
Chair, Club, Maple, Gray Leather, Arms, Norman Bel Geddes, c.1945, 34 x 29 In.	125.00
Chair, Club, Modern, Maple, Open Arms, Splayed Legs, Upholstered, c.1950, 31 x 26 In.	300.00
Chair, Club, Walnut, Spindle Arms, Cushions, France, c.1955, 31 x 28 In., Pair	5000.00
Chair, Cock Fighting, Victorian, Mahogany, Pierced, Carved, Drawer, Leather Seat, 32 x 22 In. .	430.00
Chair, Convenience, Shaker, Pine, Red Stain, Breadboard Sides, Porcelain Pot, c.1845	1404.00
Chair, Corner, Bugatti, Walnut, Curved Crest Rail, Bone, Brass & Pewter Inlay, 28 In. .....*Illus*	5080.00
Chair, Corner, Carved, Gilt, Silk Embroidered Upholstery, c.1890, 31 x 27 In. .....*Illus*	885.00
Chair, Corner, Cherry, Vase & Ring-Turned Post, Heart Cutout Slats, Shaped Arms, 29 x 18 In. .	948.00
Chair, Corner, Chippendale Style, Mahogany, Ball & Claw Feet, Arms, Pad Seat, 32 x 32 In.	316.00
Chair, Corner, Chippendale Style, Mahogany, Pierced Carved Splat, Arms, Cabriole Legs	288.00
Chair, Corner, Chippendale, Cherry, Knuckle Carved Handholds, c.1795, 30 In.	1126.00
Chair, Corner, Chippendale, Maple, Vase Shape Splat, Stretcher, Upholstered Seat.....	236.00
Chair, Corner, George II Style, Mahogany, Pierced Splats, Ball & Claw Feet, 31 In. .....*Illus*	531.00
Chair, Corner, George III, Fruitwood, Stepped Crest, Vase Shape Splats, c.1795, 31 In.	861.00
Chair, Corner, George III, Mahogany, Low Back, Curved Seat, Reeded Legs, c.1780, Pair.....	3125.00
Chair, Corner, Mahogany, Carved, Pierced Splats, c.1880, 32 In. .....*Illus*	359.00
Chair, Corner, Maple, Rush Seat, Ladder Back, Double Stretcher, Ball Finial, 1700s	115.00
Chair, Corner, Maple, Rush Seat, Porringer Arms, c.1765	443.00
Chair, Corner, Maple, Scroll Arms, Pierced Vase Shape Splat, c.1795, 31 In.	1185.00
Chair, Corner, Marquetry, Flowers, Birds, Cabriole Legs, Ball & Claw Feet, c.1900, 31 In.	356.00
Chair, Corner, Pierced Splats, Mother-Of-Pearl Inlay, Chinese, 1900, 33 In., Pair .....*Illus*	225.00
Chair, Corner, Queen Anne, Mahogany, Pierced Splats, Scalloped Rails, 1700s, 32 x 27 In. ... *Illus*	944.00
Chair, Corner, Queen Anne, Maple, Pine, Turned Arms, Cabriole Legs, Pad Feet, 29 In.	1995.00
Chair, Corner, Queen Anne, Shaped Crest, Pierced Splats, Slip Seat, c.1750, 32 ½ In.	3680.00
Chair, Corner, Queen Anne, Walnut, Stepped Crest, 2 Splats, 3 Stiles, Cabriole Legs, c.1775	4063.00
Chair, Corner, Queen Anne, Walnut, Urn-Shape Splats, Upholstered, 1700s, 43 In. .....*Illus*	1062.00
Chair, Corner, Yew, Pierced Slats, Carved, Turned, Slip Seat, 1750	413.00
Chair, Country Queen Anne, Maple, Chestnut, Vase Splat, Rush Seat, c.1760, 17 In.	705.00
Chair, Cow Horn, Purple Silk Headrest & Seat, c.1900, 35 x 38 In.	295.00
Chair, Cow Horn, Wegner, Teak, Hardwood, Shaped Rail, Woven Seat, 29 x 23 In.	2370.00
Chair, Curly Maple, Lyre Back, Tapered Legs, Ohio, c.1845, 35 In.	211.00
Chair, Curule, Fruitwood, Cushion Seat, Italy, 1800s, Pair.....	972.00
Chair, Curule, Renaissance Revival, Iron, Bronze, Finials, Upholstered Seat, c.1800, 32 In. .. *Illus*	2750.00
Chair, Curved Back, Gilt Metal, Open Arms, Greek Key Details, Upholstered, c.1960, 29 x 24 In., Pair .	3250.00
Chair, Curved Back, Mahogany, Upholstered, c.1940, 26 ½ In., Pair	1375.00
Chair, Desk, Mahogany, Slat Back, Swivel, Spoke Caster Legs .....*Illus*	42.00
Chair, Desk, Wood, Carved Splat, Upholstered Seat, Rollers	480.00
Chair, Directoire Style, Gilt, Painted, Carved Crest, Reticulated Back, Arms, Griffins, Paw Feet	1076.00
Chair, Directoire, Fruitwood, Carved, Lyre Splat, H-Stretcher, c.1800, Pair	1016.00
Chair, Dutch Style, Carved, Upholstered, Paw Feet, Arms, 1900s, 49 In. .....*Illus*	118.00
Chair, E. Carpenter, Black Walnut, Ebony, Straight Back, Leather, 1980s, 34 In. .....*Illus*	7500.00
Chair, Eames, DKR-2, Wire Mesh, Naugahyde, H. Miller, c.1952, 32 In., Pair .....*Illus*	1125.00
Chair, Eames, LCM, Oak, Black Seat, Aniline Dyed, 1945, 29 x 19 In.....	1125.00
Chair, Eames, Lounge, Ottoman, Leather, Laminated Rosewood Armrest, 40 x 34 In.	650.00
Chair, Eames, Swivel, Aluminum Frame, Wool, Herman Miller, 25 x 28 In., Pair.....	1188.00
Chair, Ebonized, Gilt, Mother-Of-Pearl, Cabriole Legs, Arms, c.1850, 38 In., Pair.....	944.00
Chair, Ebonized, Painted, Gilt, Carved, Pierced Back, Seat, Open Arms, Chinese, c.1900, 37 x 25 In.	270.00
Chair, Edwardian, Slatted Back, Medallion, Feathers, Downswept Arms, c.1900, 36 In.	430.00
Chair, Egg, Arne Jacobsen, Ottoman, Chrome Plated Frame, Cowhide Upholstered, c.1967, 42 In.	6250.00
Chair, Egg, Arne Jacobsen, Wool Upholstered, Aluminum Base, F. Hansen, Denmark, 36 In.....	2928.00
Chair, Egyptian Revival, Painted, Carved, Scrolled Back, Upholstered Seat, 28 In., Pair.....	1541.00
Chair, Elm, Yoke Back, Arched Crest, Carved, Outscrolled Arms, Chinese, 1800s, 46 In., Pair...	805.00
Chair, Elm, Yoke Back, Serpentine Crest, S-Scroll Splat, Curved Arms, 1800s, 47 In., Pair	400.00
Chair, Empire Style, Mahogany, Ormolu, Figural Arms, Paw Feet, 1800s, 38 In., Pair	1320.00
Chair, Empire Style, Mahogany, Padded Back, Ormolu Mounted Crest, c.1900, 38 In.	430.00
Chair, Empire Style, Parcel Gilt, Downswept Scroll Arms, Fluted, c.1900, 21 In., Pair.....	1659.00
Chair, Empire, Wood, Upholstered, Open Arms, Carved Legs, c.1860, 35 x 23 In., Pair.....	660.00
Chair, Fauteuil, Cartouche Back, Carved Crest, Apron, Upholstered, Arms, c.1795, 36 In., Pair	474.00
Chair, Fauteuil, Carved Crest Rail, Apron, Cabriole Legs, Padded Back, Seat, Arms, c.1740	1625.00
Chair, Fauteuil, Carved Crest, Shaped Back, Upholstered, Arms, Cabriole Legs, c.1760.....	406.00
Chair, Fauteuil, Egyptian Revival, Walnut, Bronze, Wing Back, Upholstered, Arms, Pair.....	5079.00
Chair, Fauteuil, Gilt, Carved Back, Leather Upholstery, Padded Arms, c.1920, 35 In.	500.00
Chair, Fauteuil, Louis XIV Style, Fruitwood, Upholstered, Arms, c.1900, 41 In.	1107.00
Chair, Fauteuil, Louis XV Style, Fruitwood, Domed Cane Back, Arms, c.1800, 35 In.....	338.00
Chair, Fauteuil, Louis XV Style, Fruitwood, Flower Crest, Upholstered, Arms, 37 In., Pair.....	738.00

F

Chair, Fauteuil, Louis XV Style, Fruitwood, Shaped, Crest, Upholstered, Arms, c.1850, 35 In., Pair .	1968.00
Chair, Fauteuil, Louis XV Style, Fruitwood, Spiral Uprights, Upholstered, Arms, c.1850, 39 In.	461.00
Chair, Fauteuil, Louis XV Style, Fruitwood, Upholstered, Arms, c.1900, 35 In.	369.00
Chair, Fauteuil, Louis XV Style, Oak, Cane Back, Shaped Crest, Scroll Arms, c.1790, 33 In.	676.00
Chair, Fauteuil, Louis XV Style, Walnut, Arched Crest, Padded Arms, c.1890, Pair	610.00
Chair, Fauteuil, Louis XV Style, Walnut, Carved, Scrolling Leaves, Needlepoint, Arms, 1800s, 40 In.	1896.00
Chair, Fauteuil, Louis XV, Carved, Arched Crest, Upholstered, Arms, c.1750, 35 In., Pair	2700.00
Chair, Fauteuil, Louis XV, Fruitwood, Carved Crest, Upholstered, Arms, c.1750, 15 In., Pair	2350.00
Chair, Fauteuil, Louis XV, Gilt, Cartouche Back, Upholstered, Carved, Cabriole Legs, c.1750	6250.00
Chair, Fauteuil, Louis XV, Painted, Arch Crest, Upholstered, Arms, c.1750, 35 In., Pair	3600.00
Chair, Fauteuil, Louis XV, Parcel Gilt, Serpentine Apron, Upholstered, Arms, c.1795, 34 In., Pair	3107.00
Chair, Fauteuil, Louis XV, Walnut, Molded Skirt, Cabriole Legs, Padded Arms, c.1750	1076.00
Chair, Fauteuil, Louis XV, White, Green Paint, Upholstered, Arms, c.1750, 38 x 27 In., Pair	2500.00
Chair, Fauteuil, Louis XVI Style, Arms, H-Stretcher, Upholstered, Arms, 43 In.	799.00
Chair, Fauteuil, Louis XVI Style, Domed Back, Ribbon Crest, Scroll Arms, c.1890, 39 In.	861.00
Chair, Fauteuil, Louis XVI Style, Gilt, Carved Crest, Upholstered, Arms, 1900s, 39 In., Pair	900.00
Chair, Fauteuil, Louis XVI Style, Medallion Back, Scroll Arms, 38 In., Pair	922.00
Chair, Fauteuil, Louis XVI Style, Ribbon Crest, Upholstered, Scroll Arms, c.1890, 39 In., Pair	615.00
Chair, Fauteuil, Louis XVI Style, Walnut, Ribbon Crest, Upholstered, Arms, c.1900, 43 In., Pair .	584.00
Chair, Fauteuil, Louis XVI, Carved Flowers, Round Tapered Legs, Arms, 1700s, Pair	1067.00
Chair, Fauteuil, Louis XVI, Walnut, Padded Back, Seat, Carved Frame, Arms, c.1780	1375.00
Chair, Fauteuil, Mahogany, Padded Back, Leather, Scroll Arms, H-Stretcher, c.1900, 45 In.	3444.00
Chair, Fauteuil, Napoleon III, Rosewood, Domed Back, Leaf Crest, Padded Arms, 38 In., Pair .	1230.00
Chair, Fauteuil, Neoclassical, Shaped Crest, Wreath, Upholstered, Arms, 1800s, Pair	1195.00
Chair, Fauteuil, Regency Style, Gilt, Leaf Crest, Upholstered, Arms, 1900s, 43 In., Pair	2337.00
Chair, Fauteuil, Restauration, Mahogany, Curved Back, Pad Seat, Upholstered, Arms, c.1820 .	2125.00
Chair, Fauteuil, Restauration, Mahogany, Upholstered, France, c.1845, 36 In., Pair	1750.00
Chair, Fauteuil, Ribbon Crest, Oval Back, Carved, Upholstered, Arms, 39 In., Pair	800.00
Chair, Fauteuil, Scrolled Crest, Baluster Uprights, Upholstered, Padded Arms, 1800s, 34 In.	799.00
Chair, Fauteuil, Walnut, Shell & Mask Crest, Cabriole Legs, Upholstered, Arms, Italy, c.1800, 50 In.	1599.00
Chair, Fauteuil, Wood, Scroll Back, Mask Crest, Upholstered, Arms, Ball & Claw Feet, 45 In.	2214.00
Chair, Faux Bamboo, Curved Back, Arms, Painted, Upholstered, c.1950, 26 x 27 In., Pair	1500.00
Chair, Federal Style, Mahogany, Arched Back, Shaped Arms, H-Stretcher, c.1900	717.00
Chair, Federal, Cherry, Urn Carved, Rush Seats, c.1790, 39 In., Pair	2108.00
Chair, Federal, Inlaid Mahogany, Shieldback, Fruit Carved Crest Rail, Samuel McIntire	354.00
Chair, Federal, Mahogany, Arched Crest, Carved Slats, Upholstered Seat, N.Y., c.1820, Pair	625.00
Chair, Federal, Mahogany, Arms, Pierced Horizontal Slats, Upholstered Seat, c.1810	593.00
Chair, Federal, Mahogany, Shieldback, Pierced Splat, Carved, Serpentine Front, c.1800, 38 In. .	356.00
Chair, Federal, Mahogany, Urn Back, Arched Crest, Shaped Stiles, Scroll Splat, 38 In.	474.00
Chair, Federal, Serpentine Crest, Wings, Scroll Arms, c.1825, 48 ¾ In.	2370.00
Chair, Federal, Shieldback, Tapered Legs, Pad Feet, Arms, New England, c.1800, Pair	830.00
Chair, Fiberglass, Lacquered, Rocket Back, Wing Arms, Steel Cage Base, c.1960, 50 x 46 In.	3438.00
Chair, Folding, Brass, Steel Frame, Sling Armrests, Maison Jansen, France, 1960s, 25 x 35 In.	1125.00
Chair, French Empire Style, Metal, Painted, Eagle, Scroll Arms, 34 x 20 In., Pair	1495.00
Chair, Fruitwood, Cutout Crest, 3 Shaped Slats, Turned Legs, Stretcher, 1700s, 36 x 15 In.	460.00
Chair, Fruitwood, Shaped Crest, Inlaid Flower Splat, Cabriole Legs, c.1900, 38 In., Pair	110.00
Chair, Fruitwood, Shell Shape Seat, Tripod Base, Gilt, Carved, France, c.1890, 22 In.	443.00
Chair, Fruitwood, Square Back, Scroll Arms, Cabriole Legs, Pad Feet, c.1900, 36 In., Pair	861.00
Chair, G. Nakashima, Walnut, Square Slat Back, Arm, Peg Legs, Cushion, 1980s, 30 In., Pair .	8125.00
Chair, G. Nelson, Birch, Cane, Enameled Steel Legs, Frame, c.1955, 29 x 21 In.	1375.00
Chair, G. Stickley, 3-Slat Back, Pad Seat, Arched Rail, Open Arms, 25 x 22 In.	7320.00
Chair, G. Stickley, No. 324, Fixed Back, Slatted Sides, 2 Cushions, c.1907, 39 x 29 In.	2000.00
Chair, G. Stickley, No. 390, Fixed Back, Spindle Sides, 2 Cushions, 38 x 29 In.	4375.00
Chair, G. Stickley, Oak, Leather Seat, 3 Horizontal Slats, Stretchers, 26 In.	86.00
Chair, G. Stickley, Oak, Pewter, Inlay, Arms, Red Decal, H. Ellis, c.1903, 47 x 22 In. ....*Illus*	17500.00
Chair, G. Stickley, Tall Spindle Back, Corbel Supports, Leather Seat, Arms, 27 x 23 In.	4270.00
Chair, Gainsborough, Mahogany, Curved Back, Arms, Leather, 1800s, 37 x 26 In.	805.00
Chair, Gazelle, Walnut, Cane Seat, Brass, Dan Johnson, 1950s, 32 ½ x 20 In., Pair ....*Illus*	10625.00
Chair, George II Style, Fruitwood, Round Interlacing Back, Scroll Arms, Bellflowers, 35 In.	276.00
Chair, George II Style, Mahogany, Leaf Carved, Padded Back, Seats, Arms, 41 x 29 In.	2106.00
Chair, George II, Mahogany, Scroll Openwork Back, Slip Seat, c.1765, 39 In., Pair	3720.00
Chair, George II, Mahogany, Shaped Splat, Upholstered Seat, c.1760, Pair	395.00
Chair, George III Style, Mahogany, Carved Splat, Flat Arms, Square Legs, 1900s, 37 In., Pair ..	461.00
Chair, George III Style, Mahogany, Domed Back, Scroll Arms, Fluted Legs, c.1900, 46 In.	307.00
Chair, George III Style, Mahogany, Earred Crest, Pierced Splat, Scroll Arms, c.1890, 39 In.	215.00
Chair, George III Style, Mahogany, Pagoda Crest, Pierced Splat, Reeded Arms, c.1900, 41 In., Pair	984.00

Furniture, Chair, Black Forest, Inlaid Wood, Plays Music When You Sit On It
$3,360.00

Victorian Casino Antiques

Furniture, Chair, Campeachy, Walnut, Arched Crest, Scroll Arms, Curule Supports, c.1810, 35 In.
$5,185.00

Neal Auction Co.

Furniture, Chair, Campeachy, Walnut, Scroll Arms, Turned Stretcher, Upholstered, 1800s, 25 In.
$235.00

Garth's Auctioneers & Appraisers

Furniture, Chair, Chippendale, Walnut, Pierced Splat, Ball & Claw Feet, c.1770, 40 In.
$9,600.00

Skinner, Inc.

Furniture, Chair, Club, Kem Weber, Chrome Steel, Ebonized Wood, Lloyd Mfg. Co., 1930s, 29 x 33 In., Pair
$5,000.00

Rago Arts & Auction Center

Furniture, Chair, Corner, Bugatti, Walnut, Curved Crest Rail, Bone, Brass & Pewter Inlay, 28 In.
$5,080.00

Leslie Hindman Auctioneers

TIP
Wash aluminum furniture with a mixture of liquid detergent and water. Use aluminum paste wax.

Chair, George III Style, Pierced Barrel Back, Upholstered, Arms, Kittinger, 33 x 28 In., Pair	480.00
Chair, George III Style, Spider Back, Carved, Gadrooned, Scroll Feet, Arms, 37 In.	356.00
Chair, George III Style, Wing, U-Shape Back, Scroll Arms, 1800s, 39 x 33 In.	1000.00
Chair, George III, Leaf Top Rail, Vase Splat, Serpentine Seat & Arms, 1700s, 37 In., Pair	5000.00
Chair, George III, Mahogany, Curved Back, Carved Splat, Reeded, c.1780, 37 In., Pair	504.00
Chair, George III, Mahogany, Pierced Splat, Shaped Arms, c.1800, 41 In., Pair	522.00
Chair, George III, Mahogany, Pierced Vase Splat, Open Arms, c.1780	750.00
Chair, George III, Mahogany, Scroll Carved Top Rail, Pierced Splat, 1700s, 40 In., Pair	850.00
Chair, George III, Mahogany, Shaped Crest, Ladder Splat, Scroll Arms, c.1815, 37 In.	246.00
Chair, George III, Mahogany, Square Seat & Back, Arms, Turned Feet, 40 x 27 In.	805.00
Chair, George IV, Rosewood, Mahogany, Leather, Padded, Recliner, Robert Daws, c.1840	2375.00
Chair, Georgian Style, Cabriole Legs, Ball & Claw Feet, Flared Armrests, 1800s, 37 In., Pair	1778.00
Chair, Georgian Style, Gilt, Serpentine Crest, Upholstered, Carved Arms, 42 In., Pair	4888.00
Chair, Georgian Style, Mahogany, Upholstered, Cabriole Legs, 1890s, 40 x 26 In.	2500.00
Chair, Georgian Style, Walnut, Carved, Upholstered, Scroll Arms, Cabriole Legs, 42 In., Pair...	720.00
Chair, Gerrit Thomas Rietveld, Rood Blauwe Stoel, Red, Blue, Wood, c.1960, 35 In.	21250.00
Chair, Giraffe, Arne Jacobsen, Laminated Beech, Ash, Upholstered, F. Hansen, c.1957, 41 x 24 In. .	3750.00
Chair, Gondola, Mahogany, Curved Back, Painted, E. Boiceau, c.1925, 30 x 19 In., Pair	16250.00
Chair, Gothic Revival, Ebony Inlay, Carved Leaves, Pierced Quatrefoil, Casters, 1800s, 37 In., Pair	948.00
Chair, Gothic Revival, Mahogany, Arched Crest Rail, Padded Back, Cabriole Legs, c.1850	2271.00
Chair, Gothic Revival, Mahogany, Lancet Back, Tracery Carvings, c.1845, Pair	4575.00
Chair, Gothic Revival, Mahogany, Rosewood, Cathedral Back, c.1850, Child's	359.00
Chair, Gothic Revival, Mahogany, Upholstered, Open Arms, Saber Legs, 35 x 22 In., Pair	1140.00
Chair, Gothic Revival, Oak, Carved, Arms & Legs, Upholstered, c.1860, 41 x 24 In.	1000.00
Chair, Gothic Revival, Oak, Pierced Back, Carved Legs, Square Seat, c.1850	1076.00
Chair, Gothic Revival, Rosewood, Arched Back, Peak Crest, Turned Legs, 1800s, 45 In.	236.00
Chair, Gothic Revival, Rosewood, Cathedral Back, Conforming Seat, Tapered Legs, c.1850	538.00
Chair, Gothic Revival, Rosewood, Cathedral Crest, Upholstered Arms & Seat, c.1850 ......*Illus*	2988.00
Chair, Gothic Revival, Walnut, Cathedral Back, Arms, Upholstered Seat, c.1850 ......*Illus*	8365.00
Chair, Gothic Revival, Walnut, Chevron Carved Back, Reeded Frieze, Paw Feet, c.1850	1793.00
Chair, Gothic Revival, Walnut, Upholstered Cathedral Back, Turned Legs, c.1850, 34 In.	793.00
Chair, H. Bertoia, Diamond, Coated Steel Wire, Rod Sleigh Feet, Oatmeal Fabric, 31 In.	270.00
Chair, Hall, Gothic Revival, Mahogany, Carved, Lancet Back, Saber Legs, c.1840, Pair	2629.00
Chair, Hall, Gothic Revival, Mahogany, Cathedral Back, Turned Legs, c.1850	1016.00
Chair, Hall, Gothic Revival, Oak, Lancet Cathedral Back, Tracery Brackets, c.1845, 41 In.	2271.00
Chair, Hall, Gothic Revival, Rosewood, Cathedral Back, Carved, Tracery Legs, c.1850	598.00
Chair, Hall, Gothic Revival, Walnut, Cathedral Back, Chamfered Legs, Brackets, c.1845, 47 In..	3466.00
Chair, Hall, Gothic Revival, Walnut, Cathedral Back, Pointed Stiles, Carved Legs, c.1850	1195.00
Chair, Hall, Renaissance Revival, Pierced Back, Leaf Crest, Phoenixes, Arms, Putti, 56 In.	889.00
Chair, Hall, Rococo Revival, Walnut, Carved Crest, Hound's Heads, Masks, c.1850, 50 In.	3444.00
Chair, Hall, Rohlfs, Oak, Reticulated Back, c.1905, 50 x 17 ¾ In. .....*Illus*	8125.00
Chair, Hall, Rohlfs, Quartersawn Oak, Buffalo, N.Y., 1902, 57 In. .....*Illus*	34500.00
Chair, Hall, Walnut, Shaped Back, Stylized Tracery, Crocket Finial, Lift Seat, c.1850	2271.00
Chair, Hardwood, Bone Inlay, Star & Crescent Crest, Pierced Back, Scroll Feet, Pair	369.00
Chair, Hardwood, Carved, Pierced Splat, Open Arms, Chinese, 42 x 22 In. .....*Illus*	4956.00
Chair, Harlow, Mirak, Art Deco Style, Lacquered, Upholstered, A. Soudavar, 29 x 36 In.	719.00
Chair, Hepplewhite, Mahogany, Curved Back, Upholstered, Carved Arms, 52 In.	708.00
Chair, Hepplewhite, Mahogany, Shieldback, Curved Vertical Splats, c.1800	443.00
Chair, Hickory, Barrel Shape, Woven Seat & Back, Arms, c.1900	118.00
Chair, High Back, Leaf Carved, Painted, Upholstered, Open Arms, Italy, 44 x 29 In.	6900.00
Chair, Horseback, Bamboo, Lattice Splat, Cane Seat, Chinese, 37 In., Pair .....*Illus*	5500.00
Chair, Huanghuali, Folding, Dragon Medallion, Rattan Seat, Arms, Chinese, 1700s, 42 In. ....*Illus*	14220.00
Chair, Hunter, Carved, Sit Down, Rest Thy Weary Bones, Crest, c.1905, 51 In. .....*Illus*	46875.00
Chair, Hunzinger, Aesthetic Revival, Swivel, Walnut, Woven Wire, c.1880, 38 In. .....*Illus*	1080.00
Chair, Invalid's, Louis XVI, Cane Back, Padded Arms, Pullout Footrest, Painted, 44 x 26 In.	1404.00
Chair, Iron, Red Velvet, Column Back, Finials, Arch Legs, Arms, 1920s, 47 In., Pair	4375.00
Chair, Italian Renaissance, Barrel Back, Walnut, Carved, Plank Seat, Arms, 1500s, 33 x 25 In. ..*Illus*	2124.00
Chair, Italian Renaissance, Walnut, Gilt, Carved Finials, Arms, Upholstered, c.1790, 52 In., Pair...	3450.00
Chair, Italian Renaissance, Walnut, Upholstered, Carved, Arms, c.1670, 38 x 23 In., Pair	4600.00
Chair, J. Quistgaard, Rosewood, Swivel Back, Tubular Frame, c.1960, 29 x 26 In., Pair	3250.00
Chair, Jacobean Style, Oak, Carved Flower Back, Cane Seat, Barley Legs, c.1900, 41 In., Pair ..	72.00
Chair, Jacobean, Oak, Scrolled Crest, Turned Stiles & Legs, Scroll Feet, c.1690, 19 In.	563.00
Chair, Jacobean, Walnut, Barley Twist Stiles, Stretchers, Upholstered Seat, Cushion, Pair	325.00
Chair, Jean Prouve, Anthony, Oak Seat, Enamel, Metal, c.1954, 34 ½ In.	4000.00
Chair, Juror's, Walnut, Slatted Backrest, Turned Legs, Contoured Arms, Stretcher	120.00
Chair, Knoll Brno, Chrome Frame, Black, Upholstered Back, 32 x 22 In., Pair	360.00

F

Chair, Ladder Back, Arms, Acorn Finials, c.1800, 22 In., Child's	58.00
Chair, Ladder Back, Maple, Arched Slats, Turned Front Legs, Stretcher, c.1800, 16 In.	301.00
Chair, Ladder Back, Maple, Arms, Double Block Stretchers, Finials, Woven Seat, c.1800, 39 In.	413.00
Chair, Ladder Back, Maple, Ball Finials, Woven Seat, c.1860, 22 In.	230.00
Chair, Ladder Back, Mixed Wood, Urn Finials, Stretcher, c.1900, 45 In., Pair	499.00
Chair, Ladder Back, Red Paint, Sausage Turnings, New England, Pair	443.00
Chair, Ladder Back, Rush & Leather Seat, Red Paint, Arms	767.00
Chair, Ladder Back, Rush Seat, Open Arms, Black Paint, Delaware Valley, 17 x 44 In.	374.00
Chair, Ladder Back, Rush Seat, Turned Supports, Box Stretcher, Painted, c.1800, 44 x 23 In.	246.00
Chair, Ladder Back, Stretcher, Green Paint, Woven Seat, c.1790, 23 In., Child's	711.00
Chair, Le Corbusier, LC1 Basculant, Leather, Chrome Steel, Swivel, Italy, 25 x 24 In.	1003.00
Chair, Leather, Foam, Baseball Mitt Shaped, Italy, 1970s, 33 x 63 In.	4063.00
Chair, Leather, Rectangular Back, Straight Arms, c.1950, 34 x 27 In., Pair	1599.00
Chair, Limbert, No. 605, Cane Seat & Back, Wide Arms, Slat Sides, c.1910, 40 In.	6250.00
Chair, Lolling, Chippendale, Mahogany, Serpentine Crest, Arms, Beaded Legs, c.1795, 39 In.	1422.00
Chair, Lolling, Federal Style, Mahogany, Upholstered, Curved Arms, 1900s, 41 x 29 In., Pair	1121.00
Chair, Lolling, Federal, Cherry, Arched Back, Open Arms, Upholstered, c.1800, 42 x 16 In.	546.00
Chair, Lolling, Federal, Mahogany, Arched Crest, Square Legs, 1810, 43 x 27 In.	530.00
Chair, Lolling, Federal, Mahogany, Bellflower Carved Arm, Upholstered, c.1800, 30 x 13 In.	5890.00
Chair, Lolling, Federal, Mahogany, Serpentine Crest Rail, Upholstered, Arms, 46 x 27 In.	1093.00
Chair, Louis XIII Style, Oak, Carved, Domed Back, Barley Twist Uprights, 44 In.	492.00
Chair, Louis XV Style, Carved, Cabriole Legs, Upholstered, Arms, c.1960, 39 x 26 In.	210.00
Chair, Louis XV Style, Fruitwood, Carved, Gilt, Cabriole Legs, Arms, c.1950, 18 In.	470.00
Chair, Louis XV Style, Tapestry, Carved Beech, Painted, Open Arms, 1800s, 43 x 27 In.	590.00
Chair, Louis XV, Provincial, Carved Crest, Padded Back, Seat, Cabriole Legs, c.1750, Pair	688.00
Chair, Louis XV, Walnut, Arched Back, Serpentine Arms, Cabriole Legs, 1700s, 41 In.	1062.00
Chair, Louis XVI Style, Carved Back & Legs, Arms, Upholstered, c.1920, 38 x 25 In., Pair	660.00
Chair, Louis XVI Style, Fruitwood, Carved Back, Arms, Turned Legs, Stretcher, 1900s, 39 In.	236.00
Chair, Louis XVI Style, Low Sides, Ring-Turned Legs, Peg Feet, 1900s, 41 In.	3444.00
Chair, Louis XVI, Arched Back, Carved, Upholstered, Fluted Legs, c.1820, 35 In., Pair	720.00
Chair, Louis XVI, Beech, Domed Back, Fluted Legs, Top Shape Feet, c.1790, 34 In.	861.00
Chair, Louis XVI, Carved, Painted, Open Arms, Padded Seat & Back, c.1930, 35 In.	600.00
Chair, Louis XVI, Carved, Parcel Gilt, Open Arms, Pair	6490.00
Chair, Lounge, Adjustable, Aluminum, c.1960, 33 x 27 In., Pair	720.00
Chair, Lounge, Beech, Laminated, S-Shape, Square Curved Feet & Back, Italy, c.1933, 20 x 24 In.	2500.00
Chair, Lounge, Cane Seat & Back, Adjustable, c.1910, 40 x 56 In., Pair	720.00
Chair, Lounge, Chrome Metal, Woven String, Curved Frame, Arms, c.1930, 31 x 25 In., Pair	4000.00
Chair, Lounge, Chrome Steel Frame, Brown Leather, Scandinavian, 25 x 32 In.	549.00
Chair, Lounge, Flared Headrest, Straight Arms, Leather Upholstery, Denmark, 27 x 40 In.	793.00
Chair, Lounge, George Eknes, Rosewood, Steel, Leather Cushion, Swivel, 26 x 30 In.	1215.00
Chair, Lounge, Kem Weber, Chrome Steel, Leatherette, Maple Arms, c.1934, 31 x 28 In., Pair .. *Illus*	15000.00
Chair, Lounge, Maurice Villency, White Leather, c.1950, 60 In.	1093.00
Chair, Lounge, Modern, Wood Frame, Upholstered, Italy, 28 x 31 In., Pair	3120.00
Chair, Lounge, Ottoman, Eames Style, Leather, Laminated Rosewood, Selig, 40 In.	650.00
Chair, Lounge, Paulin, Steel Frame, Wool Upholstery, Artifort, c.1973, 25 ½ x 32 In.	1125.00
Chair, Lounge, Robsjohn-Gibbings, Walnut, Spindles, Cushions, Widdicomb, 26 x 32 In., Pair .	4270.00
Chair, Lounge, Sycamore, Open Arms, Velvet Upholstery, c.1940, 37 x 27 In., Pair	450.00
Chair, Lounge, W. Hoffman, Chrome, Steel, Armrests, Upholstered, Howell, 1930s, 24 x 29 In.	375.00
Chair, Lounge, Ward Bennett, Barrel, Tufted, Wood Frame, Brickel, 1970s, 32 x 28 In., Pair	598.00
Chair, Lounge, Wegner, Oak, Weaved Cord Seat & Back, Arms, 1950s, 28 In., Pair	300.00
Chair, Lounge, Wilma Salotto, Leather, Wood, Steel Frame, c.1980, 31 x 55 In., Pair	720.00
Chair, Lounge, Wood, Upholstered, Open Arms, France, c.1960, 32 x 27 In., Pair	2640.00
Chair, Mahogany, Arched Back, Tapered Legs, Upholstered, c.1810, 44 x 32 In.	486.00
Chair, Mahogany, Arched Crest, Square Legs, Padded Arms, H-Stretcher, c.1890, 37 In., Pair ..	2074.00
Chair, Mahogany, Barrel Back, Closed Arms, Serpentine Seat Rail, Casters, c.1890, 35 In.	246.00
Chair, Mahogany, Carved, Brass Nail Trim, Upholstered, Open Arms, c.1880, 41 x 27 In.	805.00
Chair, Mahogany, Carved, Vine, Flower, Frame, Upholstered, Cabriole Legs, c.1890, 35 x 26 In.	633.00
Chair, Mahogany, Domed Back, Fret Carved Arms & Legs, H-Stretcher, 1800s, 42 In.	215.00
Chair, Mahogany, Domed Back, Scroll Arms, Ball & Claw Feet, 1800s, 42 In., Pair	738.00
Chair, Mahogany, Domed Back, Scroll Arms, Scroll Toes, c.1900, 36 In., Pair	369.00
Chair, Mahogany, Flower Carved Oval Back, Upholstered, Arms, c.1950, 38 x 24 In., Pair	944.00
Chair, Mahogany, Leather, Adjustable, Brass Fittings, c.1958, 29 x 24 In.	840.00
Chair, Mahogany, Leather, Brass, Scroll Open Arms, England, c.1910, 41 x 23 In.	500.00
Chair, Mahogany, Leather, Scrolled Crest & Arms, Padded Back, c.1830	1076.00
Chair, Mahogany, Scrolled Seat & Back, Padded Arms, Curule Supports, c.1850	478.00
Chair, Mahogany, Shaped Crest, Pierced Splat, Ball & Claw Feet, c.1900, 39 In., Pair	338.00

Furniture, Chair, Corner, Carved, Gilt, Silk Embroidered Upholstery, c.1890, 31 x 27 In.
$885.00

Brunk Auctions

Furniture, Chair, Corner, George II Style, Mahogany, Pierced Splats, Ball & Claw Feet, 31 In.
$531.00

Leslie Hindman Auctioneers

Furniture, Chair, Corner, Mahogany, Carved, Pierced Splats, c.1880, 32 In.
$359.00

Neal Auction Co.

Furniture, Chair, Corner, Pierced Splats, Mother-Of-Pearl Inlay, Chinese, 1900, 33 In., Pair
$225.00

Skinner, Inc.

Furniture, Chair, Corner, Queen Anne, Mahogany, Pierced Splats, Scalloped Rails, 1700s, 32 x 27 In.
$944.00

Brunk Auctions

Furniture, Chair, Corner, Queen Anne, Walnut, Urn-Shape Splats, Upholstered, 1700s, 43 In.
$1,062.00

Brunk Auctions

TIP
Use a credit card to scrape hardened candle wax from a table.

Chair, Mahogany, Shepherd's Crook Arms, Upholstered, England, 38 In. ......*Illus*	270.00
Chair, Mahogany, Square Back, Padded Arms, Leaf Carved, Scroll Feet, 1800s, 39 In.	720.00
Chair, Mahogany, Tufted Leather, Arms, Casters, England, c.1970, 40 x 27 In.	1125.00
Chair, Mahogany, Volute Crest, Scroll Slat, Rounded Rail, Arms, Saber Legs, c.1835, 30 In.	738.00
Chair, Maple, Banister Back, Arched Crest, Shaped Arms, Turned, Stretchers, c.1755, 56 In.	1067.00
Chair, Maple, Banister Back, Curved Crest, Turned Legs & Stretcher, Arms, c.1795, 45 In.	512.00
Chair, Maple, Slat Back, Arms, Painted, New England, c.1710, 43 x 17 In. ......*Illus*	1599.00
Chair, Marc Du Plantier, Oak, Upholstered, Pad Feet, Arms, c.1940, 34 In., Pair	12500.00
Chair, Marcel Breuer, Beech, Cane Back & Seat, Chromed Tubular Steel, 1930s, 34 In.	6875.00
Chair, Marco Zanuso, Fabric, Metal Cylindrical Legs, Arms, Square Back, 1950s, 32 In., Pair..	3750.00
Chair, Marquetry Splat, Bone Inset, Shell Crest, Cabriole Legs, Stretcher, c.1800, 44 In., Pair..	1003.00
Chair, Marquise, Gilt, Needlepoint Upholstery, Italy, c.1845, 40 x 35 In., Pair...	3750.00
Chair, Mategot, Lounge, Copacabana, Iron, Enamel, Leather, 1950s, 30 x 25 In., Pair ....*Illus*	8750.00
Chair, McCobb, Walnut, Vertical Rods, Shaped Crest, Drop-In Upholstered Seat, Arms, 37 In. .	115.00
Chair, Merklen Brothers, Mahogany, Wheel Back, Upholstered Seat, c.1890, 34 In.	950.00
Chair, Milo Baughman, Chrome, Padded Arms, Tuft Faux Fur, Thayer-Coggin, 30 x 32 In.	531.00
Chair, Milo Baughman, Lounge, Metal Frame, Brass Finish, Upholstered, 29 x 31 In.	427.00
Chair, Mixed Wood, Marquetry, Bird, Flowers, Shaped Crest, Curved Arms, c.1900, 46 In.	235.00
Chair, Molar, Wendell Castle, White, c.1969, 25 x 29 In., Pair...	2500.00
Chair, Morgan Colt Style, Sling Seat & Back, Iron Scroll Legs & Arms, c.1940, 46 x 21 In.	540.00
Chair, Morris, Arts & Crafts, Oak, Carved Mask Armrests, Lion Paw Feet, c.1910	326.00
Chair, Morris, Arts & Crafts, Oak, Leather, Arms, Vertical Slats, Adjustable Back, 32 x 32 In.	1422.00
Chair, Morris, G. Stickley, Leather Cushions, Sling Seat, Arms, Red Decal, 1902, 37 x 30 In. ...*Illus*	17080.00
Chair, Morris, L. & J.G. Stickley, No. 798, Onandaga Shops, 37 x 32 In.	3750.00
Chair, Morris, Neoclassical, Mahogany, Leather, Slat Arms, Adjustable Back, Child's	295.00
Chair, Morris, Oak, Slats, Carved Orb & Cross, Roycroft, N.Y., c.1905, 44 x 37 In. .....*Illus*	5938.00
Chair, Mr. & Mrs., Carved Frame & Crest, Upholstered, 1 Armchair, 23 x 36 In., Pair	253.00
Chair, Nanna Ditzel, Teak, Upholstered, Curved, Soren Willadsen, Denmark, 28 x 26 In.	1500.00
Chair, Necessary, Federal, Wing, Upholstered, Removable Slip Seat, c.1820, 45 x 32 In.	460.00
Chair, Necessary, William & Mary, Painted, Dome Shape Crest, c.1720	2133.00
Chair, Neoclassical, Fruitwood, Scrolled Crest, Figure, Garland, Italy, c.1700, 17 In.	1659.00
Chair, Neoclassical, India Trade, Ebonized Hardwood, Carved, Rattan Back, Arms, Cushion ...	1416.00
Chair, Neoclassical, Mahogany, Upholstered, Arched Crest, Reeded Legs, c.1820, 49 In.	2015.00
Chair, Neoclassical, Parcel Gilt, Carved Frame, Pad Seat, Tapered Legs, Italy, Pair, c.1790	875.00
Chair, Neoclassical, Rosewood, Arched Crest, Padded Arms, Saber Legs, Casters, c.1850	717.00
Chair, Neoclassical, Walnut, Barrel Shape, Peaked Crest, Leaf Carved Legs, Italy, 18 In., Pair..	1067.00
Chair, Nutting, Windsor, Fanback, Mixed Wood, Writing Arm, Drawers, 1900s, 42 In. .....*Illus*	531.00
Chair, Oak, Carved, Peacocks, Spindle Back, Shaped Crest, Arms, Victorian, 44 In.	431.00
Chair, Oak, Carved, Turned Legs & Supports, Upholstered, Arms, c.1900, 47 In., Pair	295.00
Chair, Office, Aluminum, Tilts, Swivel, Upholstered, Fine Rest, 1930s, 26 x 23 In.	397.00
Chair, Office, Oak, Swivel, Slat Back, Open Arms, c.1910, 33 x 23 In.	30.00
Chair, Openwork, Dragon, Chilong, Gourd, Arms, Chinese, 1700s, 42 In., Pair	8295.00
Chair, Ottoman, Gehry, Laminated Corrugated Cardboard, Masonite, c.1970, 29 In.	4375.00
Chair, P. Laszlo, Stained Wood, Upholstered, Slat Back, Curved Arms, c.1952, 32 In.	8800.00
Chair, Painted, Yellow Striped, Gilt, Tablet Back, Scroll Crest, Plank Seat, c.1830, 18 In.	2133.00
Chair, Parcel Gilt, Faux Grained, Cane, Open Arms, Upholstered, c.1850, 33 x 21 In.	1500.00
Chair, Parcel Gilt, Ribbon Crest, Oval Back, Fluted Legs, Stretcher, 40 In., Pair	163.00
Chair, Piano, William IV, Rosewood, Brass Inlaid Rails, Lyre Panel, c.1835, 31 x 15 In.	805.00
Chair, Pine, Green Paint, Cutout Bird Crest, Pa., 1800s, 18 ½ In.	237.00
Chair, Pine, Rush Seat, Painted Stencil, c.1850, 16 In., Child's	296.00
Chair, Plank Seat, Painted, Shaped Splat, Lancaster County, Pa., 1800s, Pair	770.00
Chair, Plank, Cherry, Cutout Heart, Chamfered Legs, Ohio, 1800s, 17 x 35 In.	470.00
Chair, Planter's, Anglo-Colonial, Hardwood, Carved, Crest, Boot Rests, 1800s, 40 x 50 ½ In. ...*Illus*	2271.00
Chair, Plywood, Wrought Iron Frame, Legs, c.1960, 31 x 18 In.	420.00
Chair, Poul Kjaerholm, Chromed Steel Frame, Cane Seat, c.1957, 28 ½ In., Pair	9375.00
Chair, Prayer, Oak, Cushion Top Back Frame, Shelf, Turned Legs, Stretcher, 40 In.	300.00
Chair, Queen Anne Style, Mahogany, Shaped Splat, Shell Carved, 1900s, 39 x 22 In., Pair	118.00
Chair, Queen Anne Style, Marquetry, Arched Crest Rail, Serpentine Front, c.1850, 18 In.	264.00
Chair, Queen Anne, Bow Rail Crest, Carved Ears, Cabriole Legs, c.1780, 39 x 18 In.	863.00
Chair, Queen Anne, Carved, Brown Paint, Rush Seat, Arms, c.1750, 45 ½ In. ......*Illus*	10665.00
Chair, Queen Anne, Cherry, Arched, Pierced Crest Rail, Slip Seat, 1700s, 38 x 22 In.	489.00
Chair, Queen Anne, Cherry, Scrolled Handholds, Rush Seat, Delaware Valley, c.1755	2370.00
Chair, Queen Anne, Mahogany, Oak, Arms, Shell Carved Knees, Trifid Feet, 1700s, 44 In.	176.00
Chair, Queen Anne, Maple, Carved Crest, Vase Splat, Spanish Foot, c.1765, 41 In.	375.00
Chair, Queen Anne, Maple, Red Leather Splat & Seat, Painted, Gilt, Boston, c.1790, Pair	4740.00
Chair, Queen Anne, Maple, Spoon Crest, Vase Splat, Cabriole Legs, c.1750, 41 In.	1126.00

Chair, Queen Anne, Maple, Vase Splat, Carved Crest, Turned Legs, Arms, 1700s, 42 In., Pair....	529.00
Chair, Queen Anne, Shaped Seat Rails, Black Vase Stretchers, Arms, c.1750, 40 In.	5925.00
Chair, Queen Anne, Shaped Splat, Scalloped Crest Rail, Padded Seat, c.1750	504.00
Chair, Queen Anne, Shaped, Splat, Pad Seat, Cabriole Legs, New Jersey, 1700s, 40 x 21 In.	649.00
Chair, Queen Anne, Spoon Crest, Vase Splat, Beaded Legs, Needlework Seat, c.1755, 41 In.......	652.00
Chair, Queen Anne, Tiger Maple, Splat Back, Upholstered, Balloon Seat, 1700s, 39 In. ....*Illus*	590.00
Chair, Queen Anne, Vase Shape Splat, Shaped Skirt, Cabriole Legs, c.1750...........................	1534.00
Chair, Queen Anne, Walnut, Arched Crest, Cabriole Legs, Upholstered, c.1750, 46 In................	7110.00
Chair, Queen Anne, Walnut, Baluster Turned Arm Supports, Shaped Skirt, 42 x 23 In.	944.00
Chair, Queen Anne, Walnut, Shaped Back, Cabriole Legs, Paw Feet, c.1750, 39 In., Pair	1180.00
Chair, Queen Anne, Walnut, Shaped Splat, Slipper Feet, New England, c.1760	474.00
Chair, Queen Anne, Walnut, Spoon Crest, Compass Seat, Vase Splat, c.1750, 41 In.	1164.00
Chair, Queen Anne, Walnut, Upholstered, Carved Cabriole Legs, Crook Arms, c.1710, 40 ½ In. ..*Illus*	2489.00
Chair, Queen Anne, Walnut, Vase Shape Splat, Cabriole Legs, Pad Feet, c.1770, Pair..............	790.00
Chair, Reclining, Hardwood, Shaped Arms, Flowers, Serpent Entwined Legs, c.1800, 41 x 29 In.	1434.00
Chair, Reclining, Louis XV Style, Square Studded Back, Arms, Turned Legs, 1800s	850.00
Chair, Red Leather, Curved Channel Back, Walnut Legs, Arms, c.1900, 46 In.	431.00
Chair, Red Paint, Turned, Joined, Low Back, Wood Plank Seat, c.1790, 35 In.	1185.00
Chair, Regency Style, Bamboo Pattern Upholstered, Blue & White, 1950, 30 In.	195.00
Chair, Regency Style, Cane, Mahogany, Upholstered Arms, Casters, 41 x 28 In. ....*Illus*	875.00
Chair, Regency Style, Mahogany, Curved Crest, Lyre Splat, Arms, c.1900, 35 In., Pair..............	984.00
Chair, Regency Style, Mahogany, Mother-Of-Pearl Inlay, Arms, c.1910, 30 In.	235.00
Chair, Regency Style, Shell Carved Back, Upholstered, Saber Legs, 36 In., Pair ....*Illus*	1000.00
Chair, Regency, Mahogany, Crest Rail, Turned Splat, Upholstered, Scroll Arms, 33 In. ....*Illus*	688.00
Chair, Regency, Mahogany, Domed Crest, Spiral Ribbed Splat, c.1815, 34 In., Pair..................	430.00
Chair, Regency, Mahogany, Upholstered, Lion's Head Arm Supports, 40 x 28 In., Pair.............	16380.00
Chair, Renaissance Revival, Burl Walnut, Carved, Shieldback, Padded Arms, c.1850 ....*Illus*	777.00
Chair, Renaissance Revival, Peaked Crest, Pierce Carved Splat, Trapezoid Seat, 48 In.............	250.00
Chair, Rock-A-Feller, Seat Rocks, Side Stationary, Leather, L. Loom, 1930s, 29 x 35 In., Pair...	7930.00
Chair, Rococo Revival, Rosewood, Pierced Crest, Oval Back, Cabriole Legs, c.1860, 40 In., Pair.	420.00
Chair, Rococo Revival, Rosewood, Pierced Crest, Oval Panel, Cabriole Legs, c.1865, 40 In.......	553.00
Chair, Rococo Revival, Rosewood, Pierced Crest, Scrolls, Grapes, Cabriole Legs, c.1865, 36 In.	1045.00
Chair, Rococo, Wood, Armorial Crest, Pad Seat, Cabriole Legs, Painted, Parcel Gilt, Pair.........	1125.00
Chair, Rosewood, Carved, Lacquered, Pierced, Dragon Arms, Chinese, c.1900, 34 ½ In. ..*Illus*	200.00
Chair, Rosewood, Dragon Carved Arms, Back, Legs, Chinese, 1800s, 43 x 25 In.	978.00
Chair, Rosewood, Official's Hat, Plank Back, Arms, Dragon Medallion, 1800s, Pair..................	3705.00
Chair, Rosewood, Pierced Back, Dragon, Clouds, Carved Apron, Asia, c.1900, 40 In..................	922.00
Chair, Rosewood, Pierced, Carved, Clouds, Fish, Dragon Arms, Chinese, 1800s, 37 In................	4888.00
Chair, Rosewood, Stepped Crest, Pierced, Carved Splat, Vines, Pierced Arms, 1800s, 36 In........	345.00
Chair, Rosewood, Turned Finials, Pierced Back, Leaves, X-Stretcher, c.1880, Pair..................	5975.00
Chair, Roycroft, Meditation, Leather Upholstery, Marked, c.1905, 34 ½ x 24 In.	1375.00
Chair, Roycroft, Square Back & Legs, Plank Splat, Stretcher, GPI On Splat, c.1905, 41 x 26 In...	2625.00
Chair, Roycroft, Vertical Slat Back, Leather Seat, 25 x 17 In.	1875.00
Chair, Salon, Round Back, Tufted Upholstery, Carved Frame, c.1930, 35 x 20 In.	89.00
Chair, Savonarola, Fruitwood, Carved Rosettes, Collapsible, Italy, c.1800, 34 x 26 In.	374.00
Chair, Savonarola, Walnut, Carved Lion's & Cherub's Heads, England, 46 In...........................	690.00
Chair, Sedan, Vitrine, Wood, Gilt Scrolls, Courting Scenes, Door, Glass Shelves, 1700s, 72 x 21 In..	1495.00
Chair, Shaker, Convenience, Ladder Back, Mixed Wood, Hinged Seat, 1800s, 42 In. ....*Illus*	3240.00
Chair, Shaker, Ladder Back, Curly Maple, Splint Seat, Finials, c.1850, 42 In.	115.00
Chair, Shaker, Ladder Back, Woven Seat, Crackle Finish, New England, c.1850	119.00
Chair, Shaker, Yellow Paint, Slat Back, c.1850, 39 In., Pair..	356.00
Chair, Sheraton, Mahogany, Turned Legs & Posts, Upholstered, 1800s, 46 In.	2585.00
Chair, Sitzmaschine, J. Hoffmann, Beech, Mixed Metals, Upholstered, c.1905, 42 In................	26250.00
Chair, Slat Back, Oak, Heart Cutout, Square Legs & Stretcher, c.1900, 46 In.	2125.00
Chair, Slat Back, Turned, Painted, Vase & Ring-Turned Stiles, Scroll Arms, c.1790, 48 In.	889.00
Chair, Slipper, Belter, Walnut, Pierced, Carved, Molded, Flowers, Leaves, c.1850, 38 In...........	201.00
Chair, Slipper, Edwardian, Mahogany, Carved, Arms, Legs, Upholstered, c.1880, 27 x 20 In.	690.00
Chair, Slipper, Renaissance Revival, Walnut, Carved & Pierced Crest, Arms, c.1880, Pair.........	590.00
Chair, Slipper, Renaissance Style, Arch Crest, Finials, Carved, c.1870, 49 x 19 In., Pair	708.00
Chair, Slipper, Sheraton Style, Ring-Turned Legs, Painted, Tuft Upholstered, c.1905, 30 x 24 In. ...	518.00
Chair, Slipper, Victorian, Walnut, Carved, Velvet Upholstery, 26 x 22 In., Pair......................	209.00
Chair, Slipper, Victorian, Walnut, Tuft Upholstered, Round, Scroll Support, 30 In.	60.00
Chair, Steer Horn Stiles, Padded Arms, Outswept Horn Legs, Leather, c.1890........................	2091.00
Chair, Swan, Arne Jacobsen, Red Wood, Upholstery, Fritz Hansen, 30 x 30 In.	915.00
Chair, Swivel, Leather, Brass Studs, Peaked Back, Italy, 27 x 32 In., Pair	411.00
Chair, Swivel, Oak, Shaped Spindles, Sculpted Seat, Arms, c.1915, 18 x 23 In.	395.00

Furniture, Chair, Curule, Renaissance Revival, Iron, Bronze, Finials, Upholstered Seat, c.1800, 32 In.
$2,750.00

Leslie Hindman Auctioneers

Furniture, Chair, Desk, Mahogany, Slat Back, Swivel, Spoke Caster Legs
$42.00

DuMouchelles Art Gallery

Furniture, Chair, Dutch Style, Carved, Upholstered, Paw Feet, Arms, 1900s, 49 In.
$118.00

Garth's Auctioneers & Appraisers

Furniture, Chair, E. Carpenter, Black Walnut, Ebony, Straight Back, Leather, 1980s, 34 In. $7,500.00

Rago Arts & Auction Center

Furniture, Chair, Eames, DKR-2, Wire Mesh, Naugahyde, H. Miller, c.1952, 32 In., Pair $1,125.00

Los Angeles Modern Auctions (LAMA)

Furniture, Chair, G. Stickley, Oak, Pewter, Inlay, Arms, Red Decal, H. Ellis, c.1903, 47 x 22 In. $17,500.00

Los Angeles Modern Auctions (LAMA)

Chair, Swivel, Wegner, Steel, Oak Back, Leather Upholstery, J. Hansen, c.1960, 29 x 22 In.	17500.00
Chair, Swivel, Wegner, Teak, Leather, Chrome Steel, J. Hansen, 1950s, 27 x 29 In. ....*Illus*	17500.00
Chair, Throne, Ebonized, Parcel Gilt, Greek Key, Pierced Crest, Posts, c.1900, 43 x 34 In.	3198.00
Chair, Tiger Maple, Carved Splat, Rush Seat, Saber Legs, c.1855, 33 x 17 In., Pair	300.00
Chair, Tub, Empire, Mahogany, Domed Crest, Ormolu Accents, Lyre Splat, Arms, 30 In.	2091.00
Chair, Tulip, Paulin, Upholstered, Artifort, 28 x 23 In.	458.00
Chair, Vanity, Louis XVI Style, Cane Back, Shaped Seat, Round Legs, c.1900, 36 In.	236.00
Chair, Vanity, Lucite, Frame, Pad Seat, Reflectone Corp., Signed 1948, 17 x 17 In.	488.00
Chair, Vanity, Rococo Style, Walnut, Carved Back, Arms, Upholstered, c.1855, 28 x 26 In.	472.00
Chair, Victorian, Ebonized, Shaped Crest, Domed Splat, Mother-Of-Pearl Inlay, c.1885, 38 In.	215.00
Chair, Victorian, Fruit, Flower Carved, Upholstered, 39 x 20 In., Pair	413.00
Chair, Victorian, Japanned Bamboo, Woven Reeded Seat, c.1880, 25 In., Child's	450.00
Chair, Victorian, Mahogany, Carved Shieldback, Plank Seat, c.1875, Pair	688.00
Chair, Victorian, Mahogany, Carved, Crest, Tuft Upholstery, 43 x 26 In., Pair	920.00
Chair, Victorian, Maple, Leather, Brass Nails, Shaped Back, Arms, 35 x 23 In.	2223.00
Chair, Victorian, Walnut, Carved Crest, Arms, Legs, Upholstered, c.1855	144.00
Chair, Victorian, Walnut, Loop Back, Slats, Shield Carved Knees, Cushion, 35 x 18 In., Pair	71.00
Chair, Voltaire, Late Classical, Mahogany, Scrolled Crest Padded Back, Seat & Arms	1464.00
Chair, Voltaire, William IV, Mahogany, Closed Arms, Scroll Supports, Carved Legs, c.1835, 43 In.	2091.00
Chair, W. Platner, Nickel Wire Base, Wool Upholstery, Knoll, 27 x 22 In., Pair	2625.00
Chair, Walnut, Carved North Wind Design, c.1890, 47 x 20 In.	440.00
Chair, Walnut, Carved Satyr Crest, Pentagram Shape Plank Seat, Arms, 1800s, 43 In., Pair	2530.00
Chair, Walnut, Carved Stile, Pierced Valance, Upholstered, Spain, c.1850, 51 x 24 In., Pair	431.00
Chair, Walnut, Cruciform Legs, Upholstered, Arms, Brass Finials, Italy, c.1890, 58 x 29 In.	1035.00
Chair, Walnut, Faux Bamboo Openwork, Medallion Back, Hunzinger, c.1869, 32 In.	444.00
Chair, Walnut, Flared Crest, Pierced Splat, Urn, Square Legs, Spade Feet, 36 In., Pair	375.00
Chair, Walnut, Masks, Caryatids, Ornately Carved, c.1890, 46 x 22 In., Pair	1012.00
Chair, Walnut, Square Curved Back, Swirl Arms, Shaped Skirt, Cabriole Legs, 37 x 25 In.	345.00
Chair, Walnut, Square Scrolled Back & Sides, Arms, Carved Apron, 1800s, 44 In.	2700.00
Chair, Walnut, Twist Arms & Uprights, Stretchers, Upholstered, c.1600	492.00
Chair, Wassily, M. Breuer, Leather Strips, Tubular Steel Chromed Frame, Knoll, 31 x 28 In., Pair	490.00
Chair, Wave, Iron Frame, Woven Cane, Danny Ho Frog, c.1970, 50 x 45 In.	236.00
Chair, Wegner, Ash, Teak, Peacock Back, Crest, Arms, Round Legs, 1960s, 42 x 30 In.	2500.00
Chair, Wegner, Teak, Cane Seat, Arms, Marked, Johannes Hansen, 30 x 25 In. ....*Illus*	1250.00
Chair, Wegner, Teak, Cane Seat, Curved Back, Arms, Denmark, 1960s, 30 x 25 In., Pair	6250.00
Chair, Wegner, Teak, Rosewood, Cow Horn Back, Curved Seat, Denmark, 1950s, 30 In., Pair	8125.00
Chair, Wegner, Wishbone, Teak, Natural Fiber, Curved Slat, Tapered Legs, 29 In.	385.00
Chair, Wicker, Cattail Back, Round Seat, 33 x 24 In.	660.00
Chair, William & Mary Style, Carved, Pierced Back, Arms, Upholstered Seat, 55 x 30 In.	184.00
Chair, William & Mary, Banister Back, Carved Crest, Spanish Feet, Mass., c.1730	4740.00
Chair, William & Mary, Maple, Upholstered Seat & Back, Boston	1298.00
Chair, William IV, Mahogany, Leather, Arms, Bulbous Turned Feet, c.1835, 42 In.	861.00
Chair, William IV, Mahogany, Shieldback, Compass Seat, H-Stretcher, c.1835, 42 In.	153.00
Chair, William IV, Walnut, Scroll Rail, Scallop Shell, Arms, Fluted Legs, 43 In., Pair	1100.00
Chair, Windsor, 6 Spindles, Bow Back, Elm, Medial Rail, Shaped Arms, 1800s, 39 In., Pair	288.00
Chair, Windsor, 6 Spindles, Bow Back, Turned Legs, Painted, New England	1534.00
Chair, Windsor, 7 Spindles, Sack Back, Fanned, Painted, c.1800, 40 ½ In. ....*Illus*	16590.00
Chair, Windsor, 7 Spindles, Sack Back, Painted, Carved Saddle Seat, 35 x 17 In.	948.00
Chair, Windsor, 7 Spindles, Saddle Seat, Black Paint, c.1820, 36 In.	144.00
Chair, Windsor, 9 Spindles, Bowed Stretcher Base, Green Paint, Seaver & Frost	885.00
Chair, Windsor, 9 Spindles, Fanback, Bulbous Base, Black Paint, c.1790	295.00
Chair, Windsor, 13 Spindles, White Paint, Angled Arms, c.1810, 35 In.	345.00
Chair, Windsor, Bow Back, Black Paint, R.I., c.1790	9480.00
Chair, Windsor, Bow Back, Braced, Brown Paint, E. Dyer, Rhode Island, c.1800, 38 In., Pair	4230.00
Chair, Windsor, Bow Back, Pine, Ash, Dark Stain, New England, 39 x 21 In.	146.00
Chair, Windsor, Bow Back, Pine, Ash, Turned Spindles, Continuous Arm, c.1790, 39 In.	492.00
Chair, Windsor, Braced, Comb Back, Plant Seat, Turned Legs, Label, Nutting, 1920s	415.00
Chair, Windsor, Cage Back, Carved Seat, Medallion, Arms, Bamboo Turned Base, c.1820	150.00
Chair, Windsor, Colonial Revival, Bow Back, Pine, Bulb Turned Legs, Arms, c.1900	1076.00
Chair, Windsor, Comb Back, Carved Ears, Knuckled Arms, Turned Legs, Phil., c.1770	1896.00
Chair, Windsor, Comb Back, Mixed Wood, Painted, Gold Turnings, Arms, 1900s, 18 x 44 In.	999.00
Chair, Windsor, Comb Back, Slats, Writing Arm, Drawer, Black Paint, New England	1770.00
Chair, Windsor, Comb Back, Turned Legs, Arms, New England	826.00
Chair, Windsor, Continuous Arm, James Bertine, New York, c.1790, 38 In.	1304.00
Chair, Windsor, Elm, Arched Crest, Plank Seat, Carved, c.1820, 35 x 22 In., Pair	1800.00
Chair, Windsor, Fanback, Pine, Cherry, Ash, Scrolled Ears, Arms, c.1800	590.00

F

Chair, Windsor, Fanback, Spindles, Mixed Wood, Gray Paint, Turned, 35 In., Pair	823.00
Chair, Windsor, Fanback, Vase & Ring Turnings, Saddle Seat, Painted, c.1795, 37 In.	1304.00
Chair, Windsor, Fanback, Vase & Ring Turnings, Shaped Saddle Seat, Arms, c.1795, 45 In.	1007.00
Chair, Windsor, Fanback, Wide Ears, Saddle Seat, Spanish Brown Stain, Phil., c.1780	593.00
Chair, Windsor, Hoop Back, c.1820, 17 x 36 In.	115.00
Chair, Windsor, Hoop Back, Painted, Arms, 1800s, 23 ½ In., Child's	267.00
Chair, Windsor, Hoop Back, Saddle Seat, Splayed Legs, Black Paint, Arms	1298.00
Chair, Windsor, Low Back, Black Paint, Oval Tablet, Schooner, Gold Highlights, 32 x 24 In.	59.00
Chair, Windsor, Mixed Wood, Arched Crest, Bamboo Turned Spindles & Legs, c.1805, 36 In.	353.00
Chair, Windsor, Mixed Wood, Painted, Bamboo Turned Legs, c.1820, 33 In., Pair	176.00
Chair, Windsor, Mixed Wood, Red Paint, Plank Seat, Scroll Arms, 33 x 22 In.	354.00
Chair, Windsor, Pine, Cherry, Ash, Scrolled Ears, Flared Back, Saddle Seat, c.1800	590.00
Chair, Windsor, Sack Back, Arms, Black Paint, New Eng., c.1800, 44 x 25 In.	5580.00
Chair, Windsor, Sack Back, Arms, Splayed Legs, Black Paint, c.1850	1150.00
Chair, Windsor, Sack Back, Bulbous Stretchers, Arms, Painted, New Eng., c.1770	2844.00
Chair, Windsor, Sack Back, Green Paint, Henzey, Philadelphia, c.1790	5451.00
Chair, Windsor, Sack Back, Mixed Wood, Baluster Arm Supports, c.1790, 39 In.	823.00
Chair, Windsor, Sack Back, Mixed Wood, Baluster Legs, Arms, Painted, c.1790, 16 In.	441.00
Chair, Windsor, Sack Back, Mixed Wood, Baluster Legs, Painted, Arms, c.1790, 17 In.	499.00
Chair, Windsor, Sack Back, Plank Seat, Turned Arm Support, Red Paint, Phil., c.1775	2607.00
Chair, Windsor, Sack Back, Red Paint, Pa., c.1790	2133.00
Chair, Windsor, Sack Back, Red Paint, Yellow Pinstripes, Pa., c.1800, 25 In., Child's	711.00
Chair, Windsor, Sack Back, Scroll Arms, Baluster Turned Legs, Arms, Phil., c.1780	3318.00
Chair, Windsor, Sack Back, Scroll Arms, Baluster Turned Legs, Philadelphia, c.1770	7700.00
Chair, Windsor, Sack Back, Vase & Ring Turnings, Saddle Seat, Painted, c.1795, 41 In.	2573.00
Chair, Windsor, Writing Arm, Flower Crest, Green Paint, Pa., c.1825	1778.00
Chair, Wing, Biedermeier, Bleached Mahogany, Checkered Bands, 42 x 23 In., Pair	1872.00
Chair, Wing, Cane, High Back, Lacquered Wood, Upholstered Seat, 44 x 23 In.	552.00
Chair, Wing, Carved, Shaped Legs, Upholstered, 46 x 33 In.	173.00
Chair, Wing, Chippendale, Mahogany, Canted Back, Serpentine Crest, Arms, Stretcher	4484.00
Chair, Wing, Chippendale, Mahogany, Scroll Arms, Square Legs, Upholstered	1770.00
Chair, Wing, Chippendale, Mahogany, Upholstered, c.1780	1298.00
Chair, Wing, Chippendale, Mid-Atlantic, c.1780	668.00
Chair, Wing, Edwardian, Mahogany, Domed Back, Square Legs, c.1900, 47 In.	246.00
Chair, Wing, George II Style, Mahogany, Fluted Legs, Outscrolled Arms, c.1900, 46 In.	369.00
Chair, Wing, George III Style, Mahogany, Domed Back, Arms, Square Legs, c.1890, 35 In.	553.00
Chair, Wing, George III Style, Mahogany, Padded Back, Arms, Ball & Claw Feet, 1800s, 46 In.	922.00
Chair, Wing, George III, Mahogany, Barrel Back, Damask Upholstery, Marlboro Feet	1298.00
Chair, Wing, George III, Mahogany, Leather, Brass Trim, Barrel Back, c.1790, 46 x 35 In.	4025.00
Chair, Wing, George III, Mahogany, Serpentine Crest, Arms, Upholstered, Stretcher	3068.00
Chair, Wing, George III, Mahogany, Stretcher, Upholstered, c.1780	356.00
Chair, Wing, Kittinger, Chippendale Style, Upholstered, Stretcher Base	590.00
Chair, Wing, Kittinger, Leather Upholstery, Brass Studded	2360.00
Chair, Wing, Mahogany, Serpentine Back, Scroll Arms, Cabriole Legs, Ball & Claw Feet	1722.00
Chair, Wing, Orientalist Revival Shape, Mahogany, Cabriole Legs, Damask, c.1890, 48 x 32 In.	4600.00
Chair, Wing, Queen Anne Style, Mahogany, Arched Crest, Scroll Arms, Apron, 49 In.	1195.00
Chair, Wing, Queen Anne Style, Mahogany, Shaped Arms, H-Stretcher, c.1850, 47 In.	738.00
Chair, Wing, Queen Anne, High Back, Arms, Cabriole Legs, Upholstered, c.1770, 50 In.	1093.00
Chair, Wing, Sheep Shearer, Pine, High Back, Drawer, England, 26 x 55 In.	316.00
Chair, Wing, Sheraton, Mahogany, Scroll Arms, Loose Cushion, Ring-Turned Legs	1534.00
Chair, Womb, Eero Saarinen, Ottoman, Wrought Iron, Wool Upholstery, 36 x 38 ½ In.	1800.00
Chair, Womb, Eero Saarinen, Steel Frame, Cushion Seat, Basket Weave, c.1950, 34 In.	553.00
Chair, Wood Laminate, Wool Upholstery, Curved Frame, Knoll, c.1977, 29 x 30 In.	960.00
Chair, Wood, Brass, Folding, Horseshoe Back, Curved Crest, Arms, 1900s, 43 In., Pair	2271.00
Chair, Wood, Mother-Of-Pearl Inlay, Shaped Openwork Scroll Crest, Syria, 44 x 16 In.	269.00
Chair, Wood, Padded Slip Seat, Open Arms, Belgium, c.1940, 39 x 25 In., Pair	360.00
Chair, Wormley, Alexandria, Mahogany, Walnut, Shaped Crest, Leather, Arms, c.1960, 32 In. ..*Illus*	1920.00
Chair, Writing Arm, 6 Spindle Back, Plank Seat, Stretchers, Pa., c.1835	516.00
Chair, Yew, Brown Paint, Back Panel Heart Cutout, Arms, 3 Legs, Norway, c.1800, 40 x 25 In.	345.00
Chair, Yew, Shaped Divided Splat, Spindle Arm Supports, England, c.1790	325.00
Chair, Yoruba Tribe, Beaded Ground, Multicolor, Arms, Nigeria, 38 In., Pair	2337.00
Chair, Zephyr, Wendell Castle, Walnut, Signed, 1979, 28 x 25 ½ In. ....*Illus*	16675.00
Chair, Zitan, Bats, Peaches, Openwork Back, Stretcher, Arms, c.1900, 39 x 25 In.	570.00
Chair, Zitan, Openwork Crest, Carved Birds, Peonies, Dragons, Bone Spindles, 38 In.	861.00
Chair, Rocker, is listed under Rocker in this category.	
Chair-Table, Blue Paint, Square Top, Arched Ends, Medial Shelf, New England, 30 x 58 In.	177.00

Furniture, Chair, Gazelle, Walnut, Cane Seat, Brass, Dan Johnson, 1950s, 32 ½ x 20 In., Pair
$10,625.00

Rago Arts & Auction Center

Furniture, Chair, Gothic Revival, Rosewood, Cathedral Crest, Upholstered Arms & Seat, c.1850
$2,988.00

Neal Auction Co.

Furniture, Chair, Gothic Revival, Walnut, Cathedral Back, Arms, Upholstered Seat, c.1850
$8,365.00

Neal Auction Co.

Furniture, Chair, Hall, Rohlfs, Oak, Reticulated Back, c.1905, 50 x 17 ¾ In.
$8,125.00

Rago Arts & Auction Center

Furniture, Chair, Hall, Rohlfs, Quartersawn Oak, Buffalo, N.Y., 1902, 57 In.
$34,500.00

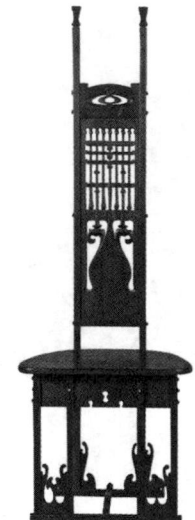

Cottone Auctions

Furniture, Chair, Hardwood, Carved, Pierced Splat, Open Arms, Chinese, 42 x 22 In.
$4,956.00

Brunk Auctions

Chair-Table, Drawer, Oval Top, Red Paint, 28 x 60 In.	4484.00
Chair-Table, Mixed Wood, Pine, Green Paint, Drawer, 1800s, 26 x 57 x 36 In.	823.00
Chair-Table, Pine, 2-Board Top, Beadboard Ends, 29 x 91 In.	413.00
Chair-Table, Pine, 3-Board Top, Bun Feet, 1700s, 30 x 45 In. ....*Illus*	1293.00
Chair-Table, Pine, Drawer, Shoefoot Base, New England, c.1780, 28 x 41 ½ In.	830.00
Chair-Table, Pine, Maple, Overhang Top, Oval Corners, Hinged, c.1800, 27 x 51 In.	10073.00
Chair-Table, Pine, Red Paint, New England, c.1800, 28 ½ x 45 In.	948.00
Chair-Table, Red Stain, Round, New England, c.1810, 27 ½ x 43 ½ In.	474.00
Chair-Table, Round Top, Hung Drawer, Box Base, 2 Drawers, Turned Feet, 28 x 48 In.	944.00
Chair-Table, Wood, Green Paint, Round Top, Shelf, Stretcher, c.1800, 28 x 40 In.	2337.00
Chair-Table, Wood, Painted, Turned Posts, Stretcher, 29 x 53 In.	267.00
Chaise Longue, Bouloum, Olivier Mourgue, Tubular Steel, Upholstered, 25 x 58 In.	660.00
Chaise Longue, Egyptian Revival, Mahogany, Inlay, Scenic, Lion's Head, Tail Legs, 85 In.	40625.00
Chaise Longue, Louis XV, Beech, Flowers, Round Back, Arms, 1700s, 42 x 75 In.	1900.00
Chaise Longue, Louis XV, Beech, Molded Crest, Cushions, Padded Arms, 1700s, 33 In.	360.00
Chaise Longue, Louis XV, Beech, Serpentine Crest, Padded Arms, 1700s, 34 x 60 In.	359.00
Chaise Longue, Louis XVI Style, Cane Back & Foot, Painted, 59 In. ....*Illus*	500.00
Chaise Longue, Louis XVI, Carved Walnut, Upholstered, Square Arms, c.1790, 39 x 60 In.	767.00
Chaise Longue, Louis XVI, Molded Back, Padded Arms, Scrolls, Fluted Legs, 41 x 73 In.	1434.00
Chaise Longue, Milo Baughman, Mohair S-Shape Seat, Chromed Metal, 1970s, 35 x 68 In.	2625.00
Chaise Longue, Perriand, Chrome Frame, Canvas, Le Corbusier, Jeanneret, 1930s, 25 x 21 In.	20000.00
Chaise Longue, Regency Style, Ebonized Frame, Upholstered, 1950s, 33 x 27 In.	144.00
Chaise Longue, Regency, Ebonized, Cane, Stenciled, 71 ½ In. ....*Illus*	2000.00
Chaise Longue, V. Kagan, Walnut, Upholstered, c.1950, 35 x 56 In.	5625.00
Chaise Longue, Warren McArthur, Aluminum, Cotton Cushions, Armrests, 1930s, 25 x 52 In.	2750.00
Chaise Longue, Wicker, Black Paint, c.1920, 42 x 51 In.	150.00
Chest, Anglo-Indian, Camphorwood, Brass Bail, Corners, c.1845, 24 x 37 ¾ In.	180.00
Chest, Art Deco, Veneered, Figured Calamander, Brass Mounted, c.1950, 34 x 39 In. ...*Illus*	1230.00
Chest, Ash, Black Stain, White Lacquer, Brushed Steel, 18 Drawers, 1970, 67 x 25 In.	7110.00
Chest, Bachelor's, Chippendale, Mahogany, Dovetailed Drawers, c.1800, 35 x 37 In.	1770.00
Chest, Bachelor's, Federal, Mahogany, Drawers, Brass Handles, Bulbous Legs, c.1820, 48 x 23 In.	837.00
Chest, Bachelor's, George I, Walnut, Hinged Top, 5 Drawers, Shaped Base, 30 x 30 In.	4425.00
Chest, Bachelor's, George III Style, Mahogany, Bowfront, 4 Drawers, 30 ½ x 23 ½ In.	356.00
Chest, Bachelor's, George III, Mahogany, 2 Beaded Drawers, Shaped Base, 33 x 41 In.	1298.00
Chest, Bachelor's, George III, Mahogany, 3 Drawers, Bracket Feet, c.1785, 36 x 34 In.	1845.00
Chest, Bachelor's, George III, Mahogany, 5 Drawers, Bracket Feet, 30 x 26 ½ In.	1458.00
Chest, Bachelor's, George III, Mahogany, Graduated Drawers, 1700s, 31 x 30 In.	1500.00
Chest, Bachelor's, George III, Mahogany, Molded Edge, Shaped Bracket Feet, c.1800, 29 x 27 In.	553.00
Chest, Bachelor's, Georgian, Mahogany, Pine, 3 Drawers, Dressing Slide, c.1800, 35 x 38 In.	575.00
Chest, Bachelor's, Widdicomb, Mahogany, Line Inlay, Drawers, Linen Slide, 29 x 22 In.	577.00
Chest, Basswood, Dovetailed, Wrought Iron Handles, Painted Design, 1820-50, 11 x 28 In.	470.00
Chest, Biedermeier, 3 Parquetry Drawers, Ebonized Trim, 30 x 40 In.	476.00
Chest, Biedermeier, Birch, Parcel Ebonized, 3 Drawers, c.1845, 34 x 49 In.	2125.00
Chest, Biedermeier, Mahogany, Overhang, 6 Drawers, Block Feet, c.1835, 59 x 39 In.	1185.00
Chest, Black Enamel, Drawers, Brass Pulls, Gold Paint, Spain, c.1950, 32 In., Pair ....*Illus*	1046.00
Chest, Blanket, 2 Faux, 2 Drawers, Lift Top, Bracket Base, c.1860, 40 x 38 In.	266.00
Chest, Blanket, American Indian, Newspaper Lining, Mass., 1850s, Miniature, 5 x 11 In.	384.00
Chest, Blanket, Arts & Crafts, Lift Top, Bentwood Supports, Cushion, 39 x 16 In.	488.00
Chest, Blanket, Brown, 6-Board, Lift Top, Delaware Valley, c.1810, 21 x 51 In.	266.00
Chest, Blanket, Butternut, Poplar, Paneled, Painted, American, 1800s, 19 x 30 In.	235.00
Chest, Blanket, Carved Frieze & Diamond Panel, Lift Top, 1800s, 30 x 33 In.	210.00
Chest, Blanket, Carved Roundel, Hinged Top, Handles, Flowers, Scrolls, France, c.1795, 24 x 46 In.	608.00
Chest, Blanket, Cherry, Lift Top, 2 Drawers, c.1804, 28 x 48 In.	267.00
Chest, Blanket, Chippendale, Cherry, Iron Strap Hinges, Ogee Feet, c.1835, 27 x 50 In.	323.00
Chest, Blanket, Chippendale, Pine, Dovetailed, Iron Strap Hinges, Till, c.1800, 28 x 50 In.	1652.00
Chest, Blanket, Chippendale, Pine, Poplar, Painted Flowers, Columns, Pa., 25 x 50 In. ...*Illus*	9400.00
Chest, Blanket, Chippendale, Walnut, Dovetailed, Brass Handles, c.1800, 28 x 50 In.	823.00
Chest, Blanket, Chippendale, Walnut, Pa., c.1785, 28 ½ x 51 In.	830.00
Chest, Blanket, Chippendale, Walnut, Rosewood, Drawers, Iron Rails, c.1790, 29 x 50 In.	826.00
Chest, Blanket, Curly Maple, Snipe Hinges, Bracket Base, c.1800, 27 x 46 In.	472.00
Chest, Blanket, Dome Lid, Leather, Brass, Continental, Marked, 1879, 29 x 44 In.	750.00
Chest, Blanket, English Oak, Carved Panels, Square Legs, 26 x 49 In.	443.00
Chest, Blanket, Federal, Cherry, Flowerpot & Tulip Inlay, Shaped Skirt, 1800s, 19 x 41 In.	1180.00
Chest, Blanket, Federal, Drawer, Arched Apron, Grain Painted, 31 ½ x 43 ½ In.	413.00
Chest, Blanket, Federal, Grain Painted, Lift Top, 4 Lower Drawers, c.1830, 43 x 41 In.	16120.00
Chest, Blanket, Federal, Painted, Vinegar Decorated, 2 Drawers, New England, 40 x 44 In.	7670.00
Chest, Blanket, Federal, Walnut, Pine, String Inlay, Dovetailed, French Feet, 27 x 50 In.	441.00

F

Chest, Blanket, Flowers, Red, Green Stars, Painted, Pa., c.1795, 23 x 51 In.	9480.00
Chest, Blanket, Flowers, Urn, Painted, Scroll, New York, 19 x 46 In.	2480.00
Chest, Blanket, Grain Painted, 6-Board, Hinged, Molded Top, c.1825, 25 x 47 In.	889.00
Chest, Blanket, Green Paint, Arched Bracket Base, New England, 21 x 47 In.	325.00
Chest, Blanket, Green Paint, Lift Top, Drawer, Bootjack Ends, New England, 21 x 22 In.	767.00
Chest, Blanket, Hard Pine, Lift Top, 2 Low Drawers, c.1800, 24 ½ x 48 In.	178.00
Chest, Blanket, Hepplewhite, Walnut, Dovetailed, Till, American, c.1820, 24 x 41 In.	441.00
Chest, Blanket, Jacobean, Oak, Carved, Floral Scrolling, 1600s, 24 x 45 In.	504.00
Chest, Blanket, Mixed Wood, Inlay, Dovetailed, Drawers, Bone Knobs, c.1835, 9 x 16 In.	1293.00
Chest, Blanket, Oak, Paneled, Hinged Top, Iron Handles, Stile Feet, c.1800, 37 x 48 In.	400.00
Chest, Blanket, Oak, Poplar, Painted, Virginia, c.1860, 22 x 30 In.	575.00
Chest, Blanket, Ocher, Orange Geometric Top, Painted, Tulips, Pa., 26 x 38 ½ In.	23700.00
Chest, Blanket, Painted Sunflowers, Vase, Joel Palmer, Mid 1800s, 19 x 32 In.	14950.00
Chest, Blanket, Painted, 2 Drawers, Blue, Inscribed Hanaden Bitsch, 1795, 27 x 49 In.	1007.00
Chest, Blanket, Painted, Hinged Lid, Till, Scalloped Apron, Bracket Feet, c.1800, 15 x 32 In.	1003.00
Chest, Blanket, Painted, Hinged, Drawer, Cutout Ends, c.1775, 34 x 42 x 19 In.	2252.00
Chest, Blanket, Painted, Lift Top, Bracket Feet, York Co., Pa., c.1810, 23 ½ x 45 In.	770.00
Chest, Blanket, Pennsylvania Dutch, Blue Paint, Birds, Flowers, c.1820, 40 x 24 In.	575.00
Chest, Blanket, Pine, 6-Board, Gray Paint, Demilune Ends, c.1805, 22 x 44 In.	705.00
Chest, Blanket, Pine, Black Flower Swag, Blue Ground, BW, 1800s, 5 x 8 In.	3081.00
Chest, Blanket, Pine, Blue Paint, c.1850, 24 x 39 In.	356.00
Chest, Blanket, Pine, Bootjack Ends, Alligatored Black Paint, c.1800, 21 x 45 In.	499.00
Chest, Blanket, Pine, Bootjack Ends, Red & Black, Grain Painted, c.1845, 23 ½ x 40 ½ In.	266.00
Chest, Blanket, Pine, Carved, Red Paint, Reeded Molding, c.1800, 25 x 44 In.	1304.00
Chest, Blanket, Pine, Dovetailed Case, Strap Hinges, Turned Feet, 1800s, 27 x 50 In.	499.00
Chest, Blanket, Pine, Dovetailed, Stenciled, Drawers, Bracket Feet, c.1865, 31 x 49 In.	663.00
Chest, Blanket, Pine, Dovetailed, Till, Bracket Feet, c.1850, 27 x 48 In.	382.00
Chest, Blanket, Pine, Faux Curly Maple Paint, c.1850, 24 x 42 In.	2115.00
Chest, Blanket, Pine, Faux Graining, Dovetailed Case, Till, Turned Feet, 1800s, 27 x 44 In.	118.00
Chest, Blanket, Pine, Figured Maple, Orange Red Borders, Initials, Till, 1800s, 20 x 39 In.	422.00
Chest, Blanket, Pine, Grain Painted, Bracket Feet, Pa., c.1850, 11 x 17 ½ In.	296.00
Chest, Blanket, Pine, Graining, Scrollwork, Dovetailed, Till, Bracket Feet, c.1815, 14 x 13 In.	881.00
Chest, Blanket, Pine, Hinged Lid, Cutout Feet, Shell Sponge Paint, Va., c.1825, 14 x 27 In.	489.00
Chest, Blanket, Pine, Hinged Lid, Molded Edges, Painted, Whaling Ship, c.1800, 28 x 51 In.	460.00
Chest, Blanket, Pine, Hinged Lid, Painted, Virginia, c.1830, 13 x 26 In.	173.00
Chest, Blanket, Pine, Lift Top, Drawer, Bracket Base, c.1860, 36 x 43 ½ In.	118.00
Chest, Blanket, Pine, Lift Top, Scalloped Apron, Blue Paint, Delaware, c.1780, 22 x 43 In.	1007.00
Chest, Blanket, Pine, Lift Top, Snipe Hinges, Drawer, c.1770, 35 x 39 In.	130.00
Chest, Blanket, Pine, Mahogany Grain Painted, Till, Ball Feet, c.1865, 38 x 17 In.	259.00
Chest, Blanket, Pine, Oak Graining, Wallpaper Lined, Strap Hinges, 1800s, 16 x 38 In.	646.00
Chest, Blanket, Pine, Ocher Ground, Potted Tulips, Strap Hinges, Pa., c.1800, 5 x 12 In.	2607.00
Chest, Blanket, Pine, Olive Green Paint, c.1800, 17 x 36 ½ In.	3318.00
Chest, Blanket, Pine, Painted, 2 Hinged Lids, Turned Feet, 1800s, 20 x 66 In.	593.00
Chest, Blanket, Pine, Painted, Blue Ground, Urn, Fruit, Delaware, c.1810, 18 x 36 In.	11850.00
Chest, Blanket, Pine, Painted, Bracket Feet, New England, c.1800, 23 x 38 In.	2066.00
Chest, Blanket, Pine, Painted, c.1805, Miniature, 12 ½ x 19 ¾ In.	119.00
Chest, Blanket, Pine, Painted, Flowers, Ethnic Decoration, c.1810, 21 x 39 In.	356.00
Chest, Blanket, Pine, Painted, Nest, Bluebirds, Hearts, Leaves, Figures, 1900s, 16 x 44 In.	767.00
Chest, Blanket, Pine, Painted, Ocher Sponged, Pa., 1800s, 11 ¼ x 16 In.	1541.00
Chest, Blanket, Pine, Painted, Salmon Swirls, Pa., c.1815, 26 x 44 In.	504.00
Chest, Blanket, Pine, Painted, Salmon Swirls, Pa., c.1815, 26 x 46 In.	1007.00
Chest, Blanket, Pine, Painted, Swag, Spread Eagle, c.1850, 5 ¾ x 12 In.	1778.00
Chest, Blanket, Pine, Paneled, Graining, Turned Feet, c.1850, 25 x 43 In.	2115.00
Chest, Blanket, Pine, Poplar, Dovetailed, Turned Feet, c.1830, 24 x 43 x 19 In.	444.00
Chest, Blanket, Pine, Poplar, Painted, Dovetailed, 3 Drawers, Strap Hinges, 1789, 27 x 50 In.	1410.00
Chest, Blanket, Pine, Red & Brown, Grain Painted, Ball Feet, c.1850, 48 x 26 In.	86.00
Chest, Blanket, Pine, Red Grain Painted, Pa., c.1840, 7 ¾ x 8 ¾ In.	356.00
Chest, Blanket, Pine, Red Paint, c.1850, 23 x 42 In.	207.00
Chest, Blanket, Pine, Red Paint, Dovetailed, Till, Bracket Feet, c.1830, 27 x 48 In.	392.00
Chest, Blanket, Pine, Red Paint, Lift Top, Figures, Animals, Bootjack Ends, 19 x 38 In.	207.00
Chest, Blanket, Pine, Red, Yellow Grain Paint, Pa., c.1850, 23 x 36 In.	444.00
Chest, Blanket, Pine, Rosewood Grain Painted, New England, c.1850, 15 x 39 In.	267.00
Chest, Blanket, Pine, Till, Iron Hinges, c.1850, 11 ½ x 25 ½ In., Child's	259.00
Chest, Blanket, Pine, Till, Painted Inscription, Md., c.1860, 47 x 19 ½ In.	230.00
Chest, Blanket, Pine, Walnut, Red Grain, Black Trim, Corner Drawer, c.1855, 21 x 43 In.	734.00
Chest, Blanket, Pine, Yellow Grain Painted, Drawer, Scalloped Apron, c.1820, 30 ½ x 42 In.	1422.00
Chest, Blanket, Poplar, 2 Drawers, Brass Hardware, Mid Atlantic, 1700s, 33 x 50 In.	415.00

Furniture, Chair, Horseback, Bamboo, Lattice Splat, Cane Seat, Chinese, 37 In., Pair
$5,500.00

Skinner, Inc.

Furniture, Chair, Huanghuali, Folding, Dragon Medallion, Rattan Seat, Arms, Chinese, 1700s, 42 In.
$14,220.00

Skinner, Inc.

Furniture, Chair, Hunter, Carved, Sit Down, Rest Thy Weary Bones, Crest, c.1905, 51 In.
$46,875.00

Rago Arts & Auction Center

Furniture, Chair, Hunzinger, Aesthetic Revival, Swivel, Walnut, Woven Wire, c.1880, 38 In.
$1,080.00

Cowan's Auctions

Furniture, Chair, Italian Renaissance, Barrel Back, Walnut, Carved, Plank Seat, Arms, 1500s, 33 x 25 In. $2,124.00

Brunk Auctions

Furniture, Chair, Lounge, Kem Weber, Chrome Steel, Leatherette, Maple Arms, c.1934, 31 x 28 In., Pair $15,000.00

Rago Arts & Auction Center

Furniture, Chair, Mahogany, Shepherd's Crook Arms, Upholstered, England, 38 In. $270.00

Cowan's Auctions

TIP

To get rid of mildew on wooden furniture, wipe the wood with a cloth dipped in this mixture: a cup of water mixed with one tablespoon of bleach and one tablespoon of liquid dishwashing detergent. Then wipe the wood dry.

Chest, Blanket, Poplar, Dovetailed, Black Over Red Paint, Bracket Feet, c.1850, 20 x 39 In.	3290.00
Chest, Blanket, Poplar, Dovetailed, Brown Over Cream Grain, Turned Feet, c.1875, 24 x 44 In. *Illus*	1058.00
Chest, Blanket, Poplar, Dovetailed, Painted Design, Cutout Feet, c.1835, 24 x 35 In.	646.00
Chest, Blanket, Poplar, Dovetailed, Red Stain, Interior Till, American, 1800s, 21 x 32 In.	264.00
Chest, Blanket, Poplar, Grain Painted, Dovetailed, Molded Edge, Pa., 1800s, 24 x 50 In.	235.00
Chest, Blanket, Poplar, Grain Painted, Green, Bracket Base, c.1885, 19 In.	59.00
Chest, Blanket, Poplar, Ocher Grain Painted, Pa., 1800s, 20 1/4 x 25 1/2 In.	563.00
Chest, Blanket, Poplar, Painted, 6-Board, Till, Turned Feet, W. Va., c.1835, 19 x 32 In.	441.00
Chest, Blanket, Poplar, Painted, Dovetailed, Molded Edge, Turned Feet, c.1865, 17 x 31 In.	558.00
Chest, Blanket, Poplar, Painted, Joseph Lehn, Miniature, 7 x 10 x 6 In. *Illus*	1652.00
Chest, Blanket, Poplar, Paneled, 2 Drawers, Turned Feet, American, c.1855, 25 x 37 In.	176.00
Chest, Blanket, Poplar, Red Flame Graining, Paneled, Till, 1800s, 27 x 36 In.	558.00
Chest, Blanket, Poplar, Red Grain Painted, Raised Ball Feet, Pa., c.1850, 23 x 38 In.	326.00
Chest, Blanket, Red Gray Paint, Lift Top, Scalloped Skirt, c.1830, 15 x 32 In.	434.00
Chest, Blanket, Red Paint, 6-Board, Hinged Top, Bootjack Ends, c.1815, 25 x 52 In.	360.00
Chest, Blanket, Renaissance Revival, Oak, Carved Panels, England, 29 x 39 x 23 In.	295.00
Chest, Blanket, Sheraton, Walnut, Low Drawer, Turned Feet, Pa., c.1830, 24 x 38 In.	267.00
Chest, Blanket, Smoky Black Paint, Yellow Ground, Pa., c.1820, 17 x 37 In.	2133.00
Chest, Blanket, Stenciled Stylized Design, Blue Paint, c.1935, 20 x 38 In.	4340.00
Chest, Blanket, Strap Hinges, 3 Drawers, Till, Turned Feet, c.1800, 29 x 49 x 23 In.	1320.00
Chest, Blanket, Sycamore, Base Drawer, Bracket Feet, New York, c.1770, 28 x 40 In.	365.00
Chest, Blanket, Tiger Maple, 2 Drawers, Pa., c.1895, 19 x 26 In.	770.00
Chest, Blanket, Tulips, Yellow, 2 Drawers, Catharina Reichner, Pa., 1789, 29 x 47 In.	28440.00
Chest, Blanket, Walnut, Bracket Feet, Pa., c.1800, Miniature, 11 x 21 In.	237.00
Chest, Blanket, Walnut, Diamond Inlay, Dovetailed, Strap Hinges, c.1800, 25 x 47 In.	147.00
Chest, Blanket, Walnut, Dovetailed, Overhang, Bootjack Ends, c.1800, 8 x 14 In.	881.00
Chest, Blanket, Walnut, Dovetailed, Till, Bracket Feet, c.1850, 21 x 45 In.	176.00
Chest, Blanket, Walnut, Line Inlay, Mid Atlantic, c.1820, 24 x 40 In.	267.00
Chest, Blanket, Walnut, Painted, Dovetailed, Strap Hinges, Turned Feet, c.1815, 25 x 51 In.	235.00
Chest, Blanket, Walnut, Pennsylvania, c.1800, 26 x 47 1/2 In.	237.00
Chest, Blanket, Walnut, Poplar, Stained, Mortised, Molding, Spool Feet, c.1835, 12 x 18 In.	558.00
Chest, Blanket, Walnut, Strap Hinges, Covered Till, Bracket Base, c.1790, 26 x 52 In.	561.00
Chest, Blanket, Walnut, Sulfur Inlay, Inscribed Elisabeth Bruain, 1776, 26 x 49 In.	3081.00
Chest, Blanket, William & Mary, Painted, Drawers, Arch Molding, 44 x 39 In.	1003.00
Chest, Blanket, Wood, Blue Paint, c.1865, 37 x 17 In.	201.00
Chest, Blanket, Wood, Painted Wreath, 6-Board, Lift Top, Bracket Feet, c.1800, 21 x 38 In.	2963.00
Chest, Blanket, Wood, Painted, Dovetailed, Reeded, Bracket Feet, c.1835, 28 x 48 In.	940.00
Chest, Blanket, Yellow, Red Grain Painted, Pa., c.1830, 15 x 25 In., Child's	2108.00
Chest, Bombay, Lacquered, Gilt, Bulbous Drawers, Wavy Apron, 1900s, 33 x 36 In.	300.00
Chest, British Colonial, Mahogany, 6 Drawers, Cabriole Legs, c.1910, 29 x 40 In.	354.00
Chest, Burl Walnut, 7 Drawers, Molded Edge, Italy, 1700s, 57 x 29 In.	1408.00
Chest, Burl Walnut, Shaped Top, Crossbanded, Molded, 1700s, 33 x 39 In.	1125.00
Chest, Butler's, Federal, Mahogany, 4 Drawers, 44 x 42 In.	456.00
Chest, Butler's, George III, Mahogany, 5 Drawers, Bracket Feet, 35 1/2 x 28 In.	356.00
Chest, Butler's, Pine, Grain Painted, 4 Drawers, England, 37 x 22 In.	254.00
Chest, Butler's, Regency, Mahogany, Drop Front, Splayed Feet, c.1815, 45 x 48 In.	1107.00
Chest, Campaign, Anglo-Indian, Rosewood, Carved Sunburst, 45 x 40 In.	920.00
Chest, Campaign, Anglo-Indian, Teak, 4 Drawers, c.1850, 41 x 38 In.	1380.00
Chest, Campaign, Mahogany, 5 Drawers, Inset Brass Handles, 39 x 39 In.	660.00
Chest, Campaign, Mahogany, Brass Bound, 2 Parts, 4 Drawers, 37 x 28 In.	2124.00
Chest, Campaign, Mahogany, Brass Bound, 4 Drawers, 18 x 12 3/4 In., Child's	885.00
Chest, Campaign, Mahogany, Brass Bound, Drawers, Turnip Feet, c.1820, 43 x 36 In.	1380.00
Chest, Campaign, Mahogany, Pine, 7 Drawers, Bun Feet, England, 61 x 42 In.	1495.00
Chest, Campaign, Victorian, Mahogany, Brass, 4 Drawers, c.1865, 36 x 37 In.	676.00
Chest, Camphorwood, Brass Bound, Carved, Scenes, Chinese, c.1860, 15 x 16 In.	118.00
Chest, Camphorwood, Brass Bound, Scenes, Spread Eagle, Chinese, 1800s, 15 x 38 In.	236.00
Chest, Camphorwood, Carved Birds, Flowers, Paneled, Chinese, 23 x 39 x 20 In.	180.00
Chest, Carved, Painted, Eagle, Banner, Slogan, c.1900, 20 x 50 In.	1612.00
Chest, Carved, Painted, Landscape, Urn, Flowers, c.1875, 29 x 58 x 24 In.	470.00
Chest, Carved, Shaped Backsplash, Columns, 5 Drawers, Mass., c.1810, 19 x 16 In.	12400.00
Chest, Charles II, Oak, Graduated Drawers, Flattened Ball Feet, 40 x 39 In.	6875.00
Chest, Cherry, 4 Drawers, Beading, Bun Feet, Virginia, c.1820, 29 x 37 1/2 In.	460.00
Chest, Cherry, 4 Drawers, Grain Painted, Shaped Apron, Pa., c.1830, 25 x 22 In., Child's	889.00
Chest, Cherry, Maple, Backsplash, Glove Drawers, Columns, c.1835, 58 x 49 In.	470.00
Chest, Cherry, Mushroom Knobs, Overhang, 3 Drawers, c.1840, 44 x 41 In.	1695.00
Chest, Cherry, Outset Crossbanded Drawer, Turned Columns, c.1850, 46 x 44 In.	554.00
Chest, Cherry, Pine, 4 Drawers, Split Columns, Scrolled Feet, c.1830, 23 x 19 In.	382.00

F

Chest, Cherry, Pine, Columns, Biscuit Corners, 4 Drawers, c.1820, 41 x 46 In.	542.00
Chest, Chippendale Style, Mahogany, 9 Drawers, Bracket Feet, c.1740, 46 x 38 In.	2280.00
Chest, Chippendale Style, Mahogany, Carved, 4 Drawers, 1800s, 39 x 37 In.	1200.00
Chest, Chippendale Style, Tiger Maple, Sunburst, Drawers, E. Wheeler, 54 x 37 In.	2242.00
Chest, Chippendale, Beaded Drawers, Columns, Ogee Feet, c.1775, 31 x 40 In.	813.00
Chest, Chippendale, Birch, Bowfront, Red Finish, Portsmouth, N.H., 32 x 38 In.	1298.00
Chest, Chippendale, Birch, Stained, 6 Drawers, New Hampshire, c.1800, 62 x 36 In.	4340.00
Chest, Chippendale, Bird's-Eye Maple, 4 Drawers, 41 x 45 In.	354.00
Chest, Chippendale, Cherry, 2 Short Doors, 4 Graduated Drawers, Pa., 61 In.	1652.00
Chest, Chippendale, Cherry, 4 Drawers, Bracket Feet, c.1795, 37 x 40 In.	1058.00
Chest, Chippendale, Cherry, 4 Graduated Drawers, Bracket Feet, 36 x 40 ½ In.	1770.00
Chest, Chippendale, Cherry, 9 Drawers, New England, c.1790, 76 x 39 In.	3658.00
Chest, Chippendale, Cherry, 9 Drawers, Quarter Columns, c.1790, 68 x 40 In.	1610.00
Chest, Chippendale, Cherry, 10 Drawers, Carved Columns, Scalloped Feet, c.1780, 69 x 24 In.	1495.00
Chest, Chippendale, Cherry, Maple, 6 Drawers, Levi Webster, N.H., c.1790, 58 x 36 In.	13035.00
Chest, Chippendale, Cherry, Molded Cornice, 7 Drawers, Bucks County, Pa., 1700s, 73 x 41 In.	4063.00
Chest, Chippendale, Cherry, Molded Cornice, Drawers, Bracket Feet, c.1795, 53 x 36 In.	2015.00
Chest, Chippendale, Cherry, Molded Crest, Beaded, French Feet, c.1800, 69 x 42 In.	1763.00
Chest, Chippendale, Cherry, Molded Top, Beaded, Ogee Feet, c.1795, 35 x 37 In.	2940.00
Chest, Chippendale, Cherry, Oxbow, Ball & Claw Feet, c.1755, 42 x 21 In.	2214.00
Chest, Chippendale, Cherry, Pine, 6 Drawers, Spurred Feet, c.1810, 54 x 39 In.	1998.00
Chest, Chippendale, Cherry, Pine, Columns, Beaded, Ogee Feet, c.1795, 64 x 44 In.	3819.00
Chest, Chippendale, Cherry, Pine, Serpentine, Brass Pulls, Bracket Feet, c.1790, 33 x 41 In.	2360.00
Chest, Chippendale, Cherry, Pullout Slide, Painted Flower Baskets, c.1790, 35 x 35 In. ...*Illus*	3000.00
Chest, Chippendale, Cherry, Reeded Columns, Drawers, Pa., 1790, 33 x 37 In.	1094.00
Chest, Chippendale, Cherry, Serpentine, Molded, Scratch-Beaded Drawers, 33 x 36 In.	5819.00
Chest, Chippendale, Mahogany, 4 Drawers, Molded Edge, Eng., 37 x 38 In.	1121.00
Chest, Chippendale, Mahogany, 5 Drawers, Bracket Feet, 40 x 38 In.	590.00
Chest, Chippendale, Mahogany, 5 Drawers, Carved Brackets, England, 45 x 44 In.	502.00
Chest, Chippendale, Mahogany, 6 Drawers, Shaped Bracket Feet, c.1800, 43 x 21 In.	489.00
Chest, Chippendale, Mahogany, Block Front, Cock-Beaded, Brass Pulls, c.1770, 30 x 33 In. ...*Illus*	17775.00
Chest, Chippendale, Mahogany, Drawers, Fluted Columns, Bracket Feet, 33 x 42 In.	649.00
Chest, Chippendale, Mahogany, Lift Top, Inside Mirror, 6 Drawers, England, 30 x 31 In.	1180.00
Chest, Chippendale, Mahogany, Serpentine, 4 Drawers, Bracket Feet, 36 x 43 In.	1652.00
Chest, Chippendale, Mahogany, Serpentine, 4 Drawers, Mass., c.1780, 33 x 36 In.	1054.00
Chest, Chippendale, Mahogany, Serpentine, Cock-Beaded, Ogee Feet, c.1795, 34 x 40 In.	8888.00
Chest, Chippendale, Maple, 5 Drawers, Bracket Feet, New Eng., 48 x 36 In.	1298.00
Chest, Chippendale, Maple, Fan, Dentil Cornice, Ball & Claw, c.1795, 80 x 41 In.	16450.00
Chest, Chippendale, Maple, Fan, Drop Pendant, Bracket Base, c.1795, 60 x 35 In.	2015.00
Chest, Chippendale, Maple, Molded Cornice, 5 Drawers, c.1760, 44 x 39 In.	1416.00
Chest, Chippendale, Maple, Molded Cornice, Drawers, New Eng., c.1790, 49 x 36 In.	748.00
Chest, Chippendale, Maple, Pine, 4 Drawers, New Eng., c.1790, 32 x 38 In.	1416.00
Chest, Chippendale, Oak, Pine, 5 Beaded Drawers, England, c.1780s, 38 x 20 In.	1265.00
Chest, Chippendale, Tiger Maple, 5 Drawers, Bracket Base, c.1780, 46 x 39 In.	2124.00
Chest, Chippendale, Tiger Maple, 6 Drawers, Bracket Feet, New Eng., 50 x 38 In.	3068.00
Chest, Chippendale, Tiger Maple, 6 Drawers, Fan Drop, New Eng., 56 x 41 In.	2596.00
Chest, Chippendale, Tiger Maple, 6 Drawers, Fan, Bracket Feet, 40 x 21 In.	3245.00
Chest, Chippendale, Tiger Maple, Stepped Edge, Scratch-Beaded, 57 x 35 In.	7110.00
Chest, Chippendale, Walnut, 4 Beaded Drawers, Virginia, c.1805, 38 x 44 In.	1380.00
Chest, Chippendale, Walnut, 4 Cock-Beaded Drawers, c.1820, 40 x 36 In.	863.00
Chest, Chippendale, Walnut, 5 Drawers, Beading, Va., c.1790, 39 x 36 In.	1093.00
Chest, Chippendale, Walnut, 6 Drawers, Bracket Feet, Reeded, c.1770, 65 x 41 In.	3081.00
Chest, Chippendale, Walnut, 7 Drawers, Ogee Padded Feet, Pa., c.1770, 54 x 37 In.	11850.00
Chest, Chippendale, Walnut, Columns, Cabriole Legs, Phila., c.1775, 32 x 26 In.	7703.00
Chest, Chippendale, Walnut, Columns, Dentil Cornice, Ogee Feet, c.1795, 65 x 38 In.	5423.00
Chest, Chippendale, Walnut, Fluted, Pegged Backboard, Ogee Feet, c.1775, 67 x 48 x 25 In.	10030.00
Chest, Chippendale, Walnut, Greek Key, Scalloped Frieze, Pa., c.1770, 70 x 39 In.	7703.00
Chest, Chippendale, Walnut, Inlay, Carved, 4 Drawers, Pa., 20 x 22 In.	5850.00
Chest, Chippendale, Walnut, Line Inlay, 5 Drawers, Pa., c.1795, 38 x 36 In.	593.00
Chest, Chippendale, Walnut, Reeded Columns, Ogee Feet, c.1790, 34 x 41 In.	3227.00
Chest, Chippendale, Walnut, Reeded Columns, Ogee Feet, c.1795, 65 x 41 In.	3200.00
Chest, Chippendale, Walnut, Reeded Corners, 4 Drawers, Pa., c.1770, 36 x 38 In.	1304.00
Chest, Dorothy Draper, Commode, Painted, Henredon, c.1960, 28 x 39 In., Pair	4750.00
Chest, Dower, Arched Panels, Tulips, Hearts, Stippled Red, Dated 1808, 29 x 48 In.	5451.00
Chest, Dower, Arts & Crafts, Canted Sides, Carved Handles, Brass Balls, 34 x 21 In.	563.00
Chest, Dower, Baroque, Walnut, Carved, Fleur-De-Lis, Paw Feet, 1700s, 22 x 43 In.	2360.00
Chest, Dower, Chippendale, Pine, Fish, Leopard, Strap Hinges, c.1775, 27 x 51 In.	1180.00

Furniture, Chair, Maple, Slat Back, Arms, Painted, New England, c.1710, 43 x 17 In.
$1,599.00

Skinner, Inc.

Furniture, Chair, Mategot, Lounge, Copacabana, Iron, Enamel, Leather, 1950s, 30 x 25 In., Pair
$8,750.00

Rago Arts & Auction Center

Furniture, Chair, Morris, G. Stickley, Leather Cushions, Sling Seat, Arms, Red Decal, 1902, 37 x 30 In.
$17,080.00

Treadway Toomey Galleries

FURNITURE

Furniture, Chair, Morris, Oak, Slats, Carved Orb & Cross, Roycroft, N.Y., c.1905, 44 x 37 In.
$5,938.00

Rago Arts & Auction Center

Furniture, Chair, Nutting, Windsor, Fanback, Mixed Wood, Writing Arm, Drawers, 1900s, 42 In.
$531.00

Brunk Auctions

Furniture, Chair, Planter's, Anglo-Colonial, Hardwood, Carved, Crest, Boot Rests, 1800s, 40 x 50 ½ In.
$2,271.00

Neal Auction Co.

TIP

To cover a scratch in wooden furniture, mix a paste of instant coffee and water and rub it into the scratch. Another quick fix is to color the scratch with the proper color crayon.

Chest, Dower, Diamond Border, Ocher Sponge Paint, Pa., c.1800, 24 x 50 In.	3555.00
Chest, Dower, Flowers, Bracket Feet, Painted, Lancaster, Pa., c.1780, 25 x 48 In.	1701.00
Chest, Dower, Heart, Birds, Potted Flowers, Fish, Bracket Feet, Pa., 1780, 22 x 46 In.	42660.00
Chest, Dower, Painted, Elizabeth Hollinger, Pa., 1808, 21 x 48 ½ In.	948.00
Chest, Dower, Painted, Flowers, Urn, Half Drawers, Pa., c.1790, 25 x 48 In. ...*Illus*	4444.00
Chest, Dower, Pine, Drawers, Scalloped Apron, Hex, Star Design, c.1815, 31 x 49 In.	45030.00
Chest, Dower, Pine, Painted, Tulips, Flowers, Blue Ground, Pa., c.1800, 30 x 48 In.	20145.00
Chest, Dower, Pine, Painted, Tulips, Red Ground, c.1838, 21 ¾ x 42 ½ In.	5688.00
Chest, Dower, Pine, Salmon Swirl Paint, Handles, Pa., c.1800, 24 x 41 In.	3555.00
Chest, Dower, Pine, Tulips, Polka Dots, Painted, Marked WW, 1838, 25 x 36 In.	20145.00
Chest, Dower, Pine, Tulips, Unicorns, Green, David Ellinger, Pa., c.1800, 33 x 47 In.	4029.00
Chest, Dower, Poplar, Painted, Ocher Sponged, Green Panels, c.1800, 28 x 51 In.	6518.00
Chest, Dower, Poplar, Painted, Scrolls, Mustard, Red, Blue, Pa., c.1770, 26 x 51 In.	2844.00
Chest, Dower, Poplar, Tulips, Birds, Drawers, Inscribed P. Zerbe, c.1800, 28 x 48 In.	14220.00
Chest, Dower, Potted Flowers Panels, Columns, Hearts, Pa., c.1785, 28 x 47 ½ In.	7703.00
Chest, Dower, Red, Yellow Paint, Bracket Feet, 22 x 50 In.	4960.00
Chest, Dower, Renaissance Revival, Walnut, Iron Handles, Germany, 1700s, 28 x 60 In.	1955.00
Chest, Dower, Stenciled Tulips, Yutzi-Shockey Family, Pa., 1838, 29 x 41 In.	14160.00
Chest, Dower, Tan Flowers, Blue, Inscribed Cadarina Haffern, 1793, Pa., 24 x 47 In.	1896.00
Chest, Dower, Tulip, Clover Panels, Inscribed JCBR, 1777, 23 x 48 ½ In.	1185.00
Chest, Dower, Walnut, Carved, Hinged Lid, Rosettes, Leaves, Scallops, Paw Feet, 1700s, 20 x 41 In.	575.00
Chest, Dower, Walnut, Carved, Molded Edge, Raised Panel, Italy, c.1700, 23 x 63 In.	518.00
Chest, Drawers, Metal Mounts, Side Handles, Japan, c.1900, 35 x 17 x 46 In. ...*Illus*	150.00
Chest, Dresser, Gothic Revival, Mahogany, Marble, Mirror, c.1835, 94 x 44 In.	2151.00
Chest, Edwardian Style, Mahogany, Doors, 4 Drawers, Painted Cupids, 60 x 38 In.	594.00
Chest, Elm, 9 Drawers, Blue Finish, Chinese, 1900s, 71 x 26 In.	646.00
Chest, Empire Style, Mahogany Veneers, Twist Columns, Backsplash, 44 x 40 In.	265.00
Chest, Empire Style, Mahogany, 4 Drawers, Ormolu Pilaster, c.1890, 49 x 51 In., Pair	3198.00
Chest, Empire Style, Mahogany, 5 Drawers, Chinese Chippendale Brass, 62 x 56 In.	826.00
Chest, Empire Style, Wood, 7 Drawers, Marble Top, Gilt Bronze, c.1850, 64 x 44 In.	1375.00
Chest, Empire, Cherry, Bird's-Eye Maple, 4 Drawers, Scrolled Stiles, 44 x 42 In.	266.00
Chest, Empire, Mahogany, 7 Drawers, Stenciled, Columns, Pa., c.1840, 44 x 41 In.	395.00
Chest, Empire, Poplar, Grain Painted, 4 Drawers, Glass Knobs, J. Rupp, 47 x 43 In.	295.00
Chest, Empire, Tiger Maple, Drawers, Glass Knobs, Chimney Backsplash, 65 x 47 In.	575.00
Chest, Federal Style, 4 Drawers, Inlaid Edge, Apron, Bracket Feet, 45 x 43 In.	403.00
Chest, Federal Style, Mahogany, Carved, Tilt Mirror, Convex Drawers, 46 x 72 In.	354.00
Chest, Federal Style, Walnut, Inlay, 4 Drawers, Kite Escutcheons, 1900s, 40 x 35 In.	472.00
Chest, Federal, 4 Drawers, Blue Paint, c.1860, 39 ½ x 39 In.	1380.00
Chest, Federal, Birch, Bowfront, Line Inlay, 4 Drawers, 37 ½ x 40 In.	770.00
Chest, Federal, Bowfront, 4 Drawers, New England, c.1855, 38 x 37 In.	547.00
Chest, Federal, Cherry, 6 Drawers, Bracket Feet, c.1810, 51 ¾ x 36 ¾ In.	1126.00
Chest, Federal, Cherry, Bowfront, 4 Drawers, French Feet, c.1800, 38 x 42 In.	837.00
Chest, Federal, Cherry, Bowfront, 4 Drawers, Pa., c.1805, 39 ½ x 37 ½ In.	711.00
Chest, Federal, Cherry, Bowfront, 4 Graduated Drawers, c.1810, 36 ½ x 37 In.	652.00
Chest, Federal, Cherry, Bowfront, 4 Graduated Drawers, Turned Legs, 40 x 45 In.	3705.00
Chest, Federal, Cherry, Bowfront, Line Inlay, 4 Drawers, c.1805, 35 x 39 ½ In.	1304.00
Chest, Federal, Cherry, Bowfront, Reeded Pilasters, 4 Drawers, Pa., 37 ½ x 39 In.	911.00
Chest, Federal, Cherry, Cock-Beaded, Barber Pole Inlay, c.1800, 41 x 41 In.	1476.00
Chest, Federal, Cherry, Inlay, Dovetailed, Square Feet, 1800s, 43 x 40 In.	1062.00
Chest, Federal, Cherry, Ivory Inlay, Turned Legs, Ball Feet, c.1800, 42 x 41 In.	956.00
Chest, Federal, Cherry, Mahogany, Line Inlay, 4 Drawers, c.1805, 36 x 40 In.	533.00
Chest, Federal, Cherry, Serpentine Top, Drawers, c.1810, 36 x 36 In. ...*Illus*	14400.00
Chest, Federal, Cherry, Tiger Maple, Ebony Stringing, Drawers, c.1810, 40 x 42 In.	3450.00
Chest, Federal, Mahogany, 4 Beaded Drawers, Flared Feet, c.1810, 39 x 20 ½ In.	1610.00
Chest, Federal, Mahogany, 4 Drawers, Cock-Beaded, c.1804, 41 x 43 In.	633.00
Chest, Federal, Mahogany, Bird's-Eye Maple, Bowfront, 4 Drawers, 41 x 41 In.	3450.00
Chest, Federal, Mahogany, Bowfront, 4 Beaded Drawers, c.1830, 37 x 41 In.	1250.00
Chest, Federal, Mahogany, Bowfront, 4 Drawers, Phila., c.1805, 37 x 41 In.	1823.00
Chest, Federal, Mahogany, Bowfront, 4 Drawers, Reeded Columns, 1800s, 44 x 44 In.	780.00
Chest, Federal, Mahogany, Bowfront, 4 Drawers, Reeded Columns, c.1810, 43 x 45 In.	2629.00
Chest, Federal, Mahogany, Bowfront, 4 Drawers, Shaped Apron, 38 x 42 In.	563.00
Chest, Federal, Mahogany, Bowfront, 4 Drawers, Skirt, French Feet, 40 x 43 In.	1003.00
Chest, Federal, Mahogany, Cherry, Bowfront, 4 Drawers, Shaped Apron, 37 x 43 In.	1652.00
Chest, Federal, Mahogany, Cock-Beaded, Reeded Sides, Bail Pulls, 1800s, 38 x 44 In.	538.00
Chest, Federal, Mahogany, Inlaid Cornice, Bowfront Drawer, c.1805, 27 x 18 In.	3081.00
Chest, Federal, Mahogany, Inlay, Bowfront, 4 Drawers, 32 ¾ x 36 In.	3422.00

Chest, Federal, Mahogany, Inlay, Serpentine, 4 Beaded Drawers, c.1805, 35 x 40 In.	1000.00
Chest, Federal, Mahogany, Inlay, Serpentine, 4 Drawers, Va., c.1800, 43 x 48 In.	3100.00
Chest, Federal, Mahogany, Inlay, Shaped Skirt, French Feet, c.1820, 48 x 44 In.	1320.00
Chest, Federal, Mahogany, Inlay, Shaped Top, Brass Pulls, c.1810, 36 x 39 In.	2015.00
Chest, Federal, Mahogany, Maple, Bowfront, Brass Pulls, Curved Skirt, c.1810, 38 x 40 In.......	1845.00
Chest, Federal, Mahogany, Pine, Bowfront, Shaped Skirt, French Feet, c.1800, 40 x 43 In.......	1003.00
Chest, Federal, Mahogany, Rosewood Veneer, Bowfront, French Feet, c.1810, 38 x 41 In.	3081.00
Chest, Federal, Mahogany, Tiger Maple, Bowfront, 4 Drawers, 35 x 43 In.	1035.00
Chest, Federal, Maple, 4 Drawers, New England, 34 x 37 In.	594.00
Chest, Federal, Maple, Bowfront, Inlaid Banding, Beaded, c.1810, 37 x 39 In........................	1007.00
Chest, Federal, Maple, Tiger Maple, Spiral Posts, Brass Pulls, c.1825, 42 x 40 In. ....*Illus*	1541.00
Chest, Federal, Mixed Wood, Bowfront, 4 Beaded Drawers, c.1905, 37 x 44 In.	920.00
Chest, Federal, Tiger Maple, Backsplash, 3 Drawers, Serpentine Apron, 43 x 38 In.	384.00
Chest, Federal, Walnut, 4 Drawers, Inlaid Eagle Skirt, 39 ½ x 36 In.......................................	1541.00
Chest, Federal, Walnut, Bird's-Eye Maple, Columns, Block Front, 43 x 54 In.	271.00
Chest, Federal, Walnut, Crotch Veneer, Line Inlay, 4 Drawers, Pa., c.1800, 37 x 37 In.	7703.00
Chest, Federal, Walnut, Inlay, 5 Graduated Drawers, Bracket Feet, 44 x 39 In.	1534.00
Chest, Federal, Walnut, Line Inlay, 4 Drawers, Pa., c.1800, 36 ¾ x 38 In..............................	770.00
Chest, Federal, Walnut, Line Inlay, 5 Drawers, Pa., c.1805, 63 ½ x 39 ¼ In.	2844.00
Chest, Federal, Walnut, Line Inlay, Bowfront, 3 Drawers, Pa., c.1810, 36 x 42 In..................	563.00
Chest, Federal, Walnut, Poplar, Barber Pole Inlay, Drawers, Pa., c.1810, 44 x 39 In.	1175.00
Chest, Federal, Walnut, Reeded Pilasters, 4 Drawers, Va., c.1820, 42 x 42 In.......................	1380.00
Chest, Figured Wood, Sliding Panel Doors, Drawers, Japan, c.1900, 62 x 33 In.	920.00
Chest, Flame Mahogany, Step Back, Drawers, Serpentine, Bracket Feet, 41 x 43 In.	150.00
Chest, French Empire, Mahogany, Brass Knobs, Ormolu Mounts, c.1815, 17 x 13 In...............	403.00
Chest, French Provincial, Oak, String Inlay, Molded Edge, c.1815, 30 x 36 In.	2252.00
Chest, Fruitwood, 3 Drawers, France, 1700s, 34 ¾ x 50 In.	1815.00
Chest, G. Nakashima, Walnut, 5 Drawers, Recessed Handholds, 1967, 53 x 36 In.	9800.00
Chest, G. Stickley, 5 Drawers, Paneled Sides, Wood Knobs, 37 x 19 ½ In.	2875.00
Chest, George I, Oak, 8 Drawers, Front Ball Feet, c.1700, 31 ¾ x 30 In..................................	1094.00
Chest, George II, Mahogany, Brass, 8 Graduated Drawers, c.1760, 69 x 39 In..........................	2640.00
Chest, George II, Mahogany, Serpentine, Brass Pulls, C-Scroll Feet, c.1790, 39 x 46 In.........	3068.00
Chest, George II, Mahogany, Serpentine, Drawers, Scroll Skirt, 1800s, 34 x 40 In.	1586.00
Chest, George II, Walnut, 2 Shell-Carved Drawers, Cabriole Legs, c.1750, 37 x 38 In.	1000.00
Chest, George II, Walnut, 5 Drawers, Bracket Feet, 1700s, 36 x 38 In.	1250.00
Chest, George III Style, Mahogany, 2 Parts, Stepped Cornice, Fluted, 82 x 48 In....................	1200.00
Chest, George III Style, Mahogany, 4 Drawers, Bracket Feet, 32 x 29 In.	1500.00
Chest, George III Style, Mahogany, 7 Graduated Drawers, Brass, 60 x 28 In.	2160.00
Chest, George III Style, Oak, Diamond Inlay, 5 Drawers, c.1795, 38 x 40 In.	738.00
Chest, George III, Mahogany, 4 Drawers, Bracket Feet, c.1815, 36 x 37 In.	800.00
Chest, George III, Mahogany, 4 Graduated Drawers, c.1790, 39 x 19 In.	813.00
Chest, George III, Mahogany, 8 Drawers, 84 x 44 In.	1755.00
Chest, George III, Mahogany, Banded, 5 Drawers, Bracket Feet, 1785, 36 x 39 In.	1107.00
Chest, George III, Mahogany, Bowfront, 4 Drawers, c.1790, 39 x 40 In.	474.00
Chest, George III, Mahogany, Dentil Molded Cornice, Drawers, 1800s, 66 x 37 In....................	750.00
Chest, George III, Mahogany, Dressing Slide, 4 Drawers, Bracket Feet, c.1790, 33 x 37 In. ...*Illus*	1554.00
Chest, George III, Mahogany, Inlay, Bowfront, 4 Drawers, c.1790, 32 x 41 In.	889.00
Chest, George III, Mahogany, Molded Cornice, Frieze, 7 Drawers, 74 x 43 ½ In......................	6726.00
Chest, George III, Mahogany, Molded Edge, Pilasters, Ogee Feet, c.1800, 39 x 43 In.	676.00
Chest, George III, Mahogany, Oak, 4 Drawers, Cutout Feet, Eng., c.1800, 34 x 35 In.	470.00
Chest, George III, Mahogany, Serpentine Top, Ogee Feet, 1800s, 34 x 30 In.	625.00
Chest, George III, Mahogany, Serpentine, 4 Drawers, Brass Bail Handles, 40 x 43 In..............	3159.00
Chest, George III, Mahogany, Slide, 4 Drawers, 28 ¾ x 31 ½ In...	1250.00
Chest, George III, Mahogany, Slide, Hinged Mirror, French Feet, 34 x 36 In.	1150.00
Chest, George III, Walnut, 5 Drawers, Shaped Apron, Grain Painted, c.1780, 37 x 42 In.	182.00
Chest, George III, Walnut, Banded, 5 Drawers, Herringbone, c.1790, 39 x 36 In.	2337.00
Chest, Georgian, Mahogany, Graduated Drawers, Ivory Pulls, Flared Feet, 21 x 17 In..............	748.00
Chest, Georgian, Mahogany, Serpentine, String Inlay, Ivory Pulls, 1700s, 38 x 49 In..............	2573.00
Chest, Georgian, Walnut, 10 Drawers, Cabriole Legs, c.1750, 53 ½ x 40 In.	2640.00
Chest, Georgian, Walnut, Figured Top, Herringbone Inlay, 1700s, 35 x 38 In.	984.00
Chest, Gothic Revival, Oak, Linenfold Paneling, Dragon Hinge, 1800s, 30 x 62 In....................	474.00
Chest, Grain Painted, 4 Drawers, Knob Pulls, Shaped Bracket Feet, 42 x 39 In......................	5428.00
Chest, Henkel Harris, Mahogany, 5 Drawers, 34 ½ x 40 In., Pair	395.00
Chest, Henredon, Mahogany, Bowfront, 4 Graduated Drawers, 37 x 39 In.	1778.00
Chest, Hepplewhite Style, Burl, Veneers, Dovetailed Drawers, c.1990, 39 x 38 In.	590.00
Chest, Hepplewhite Style, Mahogany, 5 Drawers, String Inlay, 1900s, 48 x 35 In.....................	92.00

Furniture, Chair, Queen Anne, Carved, Brown Paint, Rush Seat, Arms, c.1750, 45 ½ In.
$10,665.00

Skinner, Inc.

Furniture, Chair, Queen Anne, Tiger Maple, Splat Back, Upholstered, Balloon Seat, 1700s, 39 In.
$590.00

Brunk Auctions

Furniture, Chair, Queen Anne, Walnut, Upholstered, Carved Cabriole Legs, Crook Arms, c.1710, 40 ½ In.
$2,489.00

Skinner, Inc.

F

Furniture, Chair, Regency Style, Cane, Mahogany, Upholstered Arms, Casters, 41 x 28 In.
$875.00

Bonhams

Furniture, Chair, Regency Style, Mahogany, Mother-Of-Pearl Inlay, Arms, c.1910, 30 In.
$235.00

Garth's Auctioneers & Appraisers

Furniture, Chair, Regency Style, Shell Carved Back, Upholstered, Saber Legs, 36 In., Pair
$1,000.00

Leslie Hindman Auctioneers

Chest, Hepplewhite Style, Tiger Maple, 4 Drawers, c.1850, 14 x 13 In.		944.00
Chest, Hepplewhite, Birch, 4 Drawers, Bracket Feet, c.1790, 36 x 40 In.		236.00
Chest, Hepplewhite, Birch, Pine, Drawers, Brass, New England, c.1800, 39 x 41 In.	*Illus*	1116.00
Chest, Hepplewhite, Cherry Inlay, 4 Graduated Drawers, Shaped Apron, 39 x 40 In.		767.00
Chest, Hepplewhite, Cherry, 5 Dovetailed Drawers, American, c.1800, 43 x 39 In.		323.00
Chest, Hepplewhite, Cherry, 9 Drawers, Scalloped Apron, Pa., c.1810, 62 x 38 In.		1304.00
Chest, Hepplewhite, Cherry, Bowfront, 4 Drawers, Pa., c.1810, 38 ½ x 41 In.		608.00
Chest, Hepplewhite, Cherry, Line Inlay, 5 Drawers, Pa., c.1810, 40 x 39 ½ In.		889.00
Chest, Hepplewhite, Cherry, Pine, Inlay, 4 Drawers, French Feet, c.1820, 41 x 39 In.		646.00
Chest, Hepplewhite, Cherry, Serpentine, 4 Drawers, Splayed Feet, c.1810, 42 x 39 In.		770.00
Chest, Hepplewhite, Mahogany, 5 Drawers, England, c.1795, 40 ¾ x 41 ¾ In.		296.00
Chest, Hepplewhite, Mahogany, 5 Drawers, Flared Feet, c.1800, 41 x 41 In.		334.00
Chest, Hepplewhite, Mahogany, Bowfront, 3 Drawers, French Feet, 35 x 40 In.		944.00
Chest, Hepplewhite, Mahogany, Bowfront, 4 Drawers, New England, 37 x 42 In.		590.00
Chest, Hepplewhite, Mahogany, Eagle, Star Inlay, 4 Drawers, N.Y., 44 x 21 In.		4012.00
Chest, Hepplewhite, Mahogany, Figured, Bowfront, Dovetailed, 1800s, 36 x 36 In.		1062.00
Chest, Hepplewhite, Mahogany, Inlay, Bowfront, 4 Drawers, 37 x 42 In.		1062.00
Chest, Hepplewhite, Mahogany, Maple, Bowfront, Beaded, c.1790, 40 x 40 In.		1121.00
Chest, Hepplewhite, Mahogany, Poplar, Bowfront, 5 Drawers, c.1810, 37 x 39 In.		362.00
Chest, Hepplewhite, Walnut, Dovetailed, Beading, Shaped Apron, c.1800, 60 x 43 In.		1808.00
Chest, Ivory, Ebony, Satinwood, Marble Top, Courting Figures, 1800s, 35 x 22 In.	*Illus*	5750.00
Chest, Jacobean Style, Oak, Graduated Drawers, Panel Fronts, Bun Feet, 38 x 38 In.		2607.00
Chest, Lid, Camphor, Dragons, Flowers, Geometric Designs, Foo Dog, Block Feet, 21 x 39 x 20 In.	*Illus*	130.00
Chest, Lingerie, Parquetry, Ormolu Mounts, 7 Drawers, c.1900, 55 x 24 In.		652.00
Chest, Liquor, Oak, Iron Mounted, Sponged, Swing Handles, c.1800, 11 x 15 In.		521.00
Chest, Louis XV Style, Marble, 6 Drawers, Inlay, Bronze, France, c.1910, 46 x 25 In.		720.00
Chest, Louis XVI Style, Walnut Inlay, Gilt Bronze, Marble, 8 Drawers, 65 x 27 In.		5313.00
Chest, Mahogany, 4 Drawers, Pullout Leather Writing Surface, 1800s, 37 x 27 In.		1300.00
Chest, Mahogany, 6 Drawers, Columns, Paw Feet, c.1800, 52 x 47 In.		732.00
Chest, Mahogany, Banded Inlay, 5 Drawers, French Feet, Eng., c.1803, 50 x 49 In.		978.00
Chest, Mahogany, Beaded Moldings, 5 Drawers, c.1850, 21 x 19 In.		267.00
Chest, Mahogany, Bombe, 4 Drawers, Figured, Splayed Legs, c.1800, 32 x 35 In.		615.00
Chest, Mahogany, Bombe, Graduated Drawers, Ball & Claw Feet, c.1900, 11 x 14 In.		344.00
Chest, Mahogany, Bowfront, 2 Half Drawers Over Drawers, c.1810, 36 x 35 In.		502.00
Chest, Mahogany, Canted Corners, Paneled Door, Writing Surface, 1800s, 51 x 42 In.		444.00
Chest, Mahogany, Frieze, 2 Inset Drawers, Ring-Turned Feet, c.1850, 14 x 15 In.		531.00
Chest, Mahogany, Inlay, Crossbanded, Drawers, Post & Ball Pulls, Bracket Feet, c.1715, 42 x 38 In.		984.00
Chest, Mahogany, Inlay, Step Back, Cherub Medallions, Urns, Peg Feet, c.1930, 60 x 38 In.		952.00
Chest, Mahogany, Multicolor Panels, Horse Head, Urn, Drape, Scroll, Pinstripes, c.1890, 16 x 9 In.		83.00
Chest, Mahogany, Projecting Drawer, Scroll Column, Scroll Feet, c.1850, 45 x 42 In.		215.00
Chest, Mahogany, Shell Carved, 4 Drawers, 35 x 36 In.		236.00
Chest, Mahogany, String Inlay, Molded Diamond, 3 Drawers, England, c.1860, 31 x 29 In.		325.00
Chest, Maple, 6 Drawers, Ball Feet, Rhode Island, c.1760, 45 x 38 In.		472.00
Chest, Maple, Pine, Door, 6 Interior Doors, New England, c.1700, 20 x 19 In.		1736.00
Chest, Maple, Red Paint, Drawers, Molded Cornice, Wood Pulls, c.1800, 51 x 36 In.		9480.00
Chest, Marquetry, Rectangular Top, 2 Drawers, Square Tapered Legs, 33 x 18 In.		1625.00
Chest, Mixed Wood, Drawers, Molded Cornice, Brass Pulls, 1800s, 15 ½ x 12 In.	*Illus*	325.00
Chest, Mixed Wood, Overhung Top Drawer, 3 Lower Drawers, c.1850, 49 x 43 In.		1495.00
Chest, Mule, Cherry, Poplar, Lift Top, 2 Dovetailed Drawers, 1800s, 40 x 37 In.		294.00
Chest, Mule, Chippendale, Curly Maple, 2 Dovetailed Drawers, c.1800, 39 x 37 In.		764.00
Chest, Mule, George III, Mahogany, Oak, Drawers, Fluted Columns, c.1790, 36 x 64 In.		441.00
Chest, Mule, Pine, Drawer, Red Paint, Iron Hardware, c.1845, 8 x 7 ¾ In.		2252.00
Chest, Mule, Pine, Hinged Top, Dovetailed Drawers, Faux Drawers, c.1715, 44 x 38 In.		2410.00
Chest, Mule, Pine, Lift Top, Paneled, Lower Drawer, England, 28 x 41 In.		369.00
Chest, Mule, Pine, Paint Decorated, Drawers, Bracket Feet, c.1800, 42 x 39 ½ In.		2468.00
Chest, Mule, Pine, Red Paint, Drawer, Half Moon Ends, c.1800, 26 x 38 In.		705.00
Chest, Mule, Pine, Red Paint, New England, c.1800, 40 x 36 ¼ In.		415.00
Chest, Mule, Pine, Rosewood Grain, Stenciled, Flowers, New England, c.1800, 39 x 41 In.		529.00
Chest, Mule, White Pine, Red Paint, Graduated Drawers, Bracket Feet, c.1790, 52 x 37 In.		510.00
Chest, Neoclassical, Carved, Painted Garlands, 4 Drawers, Raised Legs, Italy, 28 x 27 In.		720.00
Chest, Neoclassical, Mahogany, Ormolu Mounted, 3 Drawers, Continental, 39 x 48 In.		944.00
Chest, Neoclassical, Painted, Stencil Decoration, Drawers, Mirror, New York, 64 x 37 In.		1770.00
Chest, Neoclassical, Walnut, Checkered Inlay, 3 Drawers, Italy, 12 x 18 ½ In.		380.00
Chest, Norman Bel Geddes, Enamel, Steel, Simmons, c.1930, 44 x 39 In.	*Illus*	750.00
Chest, Oak, Carved, Geometric Design, 4 Brackets, England, 1700s, 46 x 39 In.		1722.00
Chest, Oak, Carved, Hinged Top, Interior Compartments, Drawer, Handles, 29 x 47 In.		570.00

Chest, Oak, Hinged Lid, Dentil Molded, Inlay, Paneled Reserves, c.1700, 30 x 55 In.................. 1968.00
Chest, P. Evans, Cityscape Samples, Chrome, Brass, Lift Top, Compartments, 1970s, 36 x 15 In. 9480.00
Chest, Parquetry, Rounded Corners, Slide, Drawers, Cabriole Legs, 27 x 17 In. 500.00
Chest, Parzinger, Black Japanned, Red Leather, 4 Drawers, Charak, c.1960, 34 x 44 In. 2000.00
Chest, Pilgrim, Paneled Oak, Drawer, Knob Pulls, Escutcheon, 34 x 47 x 23 In....................... 3776.00
Chest, Pine, 4 Drawers, 4 Turned Legs, c.1820, 33 x 33 In... 240.00
Chest, Pine, 6-Board, Bootjack Ends, 19th Century, 23 x 35 x 17 In. 1422.00
Chest, Pine, Blue Ground, 3 Potted Tulip Panels, Bracket Feet, c.1790, 22 x 50 In. 15405.00
Chest, Pine, Grain Painted, Crossbanded, 4 Drawers, c.1850, 10 x 9 In. 542.00
Chest, Pine, Oak, Ebonized Columns, Turned Ball Front Feet, Drawers, c.1700, 36 x 39 In. 6518.00
Chest, Pine, Painted, 6-Board, Fan Design, c.1800, 24 ½ x 41 x 17 In. 2370.00
Chest, Pine, Painted, Lift Top, Drawer, Cutout Ends, c.1790, 36 x 37 In. 296.00
Chest, Pine, Painted, Molded Lift Top, Arch Molded Case, Round Knobs, c.1745, 40 x 36 In..... 2607.00
Chest, Pine, Red Paint, Drawers, Hinged Top, Cutout Base, Molding, c.1790, 36 x 19 In. 5333.00
Chest, Pine, Red Paint, Hinged Lift Top, Arch Molded Case, Drawers, c.1700, 39 x 39 In. 2370.00
Chest, Pine, Red, Yellow Sunburst Design, Blatt, Pa., c.1820, 25 ¾ x 48 In. 3792.00
Chest, Pine, Salmon Red Paint, Chest Over Drawers, Lift Top, Bun Feet, Vt., c.1710, 50 x 36 In.. 3437.00
Chest, Pine, Shaped Apron, 3 Drawers, Southern, c.1850, 30 x 36 In...................................... 403.00
Chest, Pine, Stenciled Designs, Grain Painted, 3 Drawers, New York, c.1840, 41 x 45 In. 1725.00
Chest, Pine, Yellow Paint, 2 Drawers, Lift Top, Turned Knobs, c.1790, 39 x 37 In. 1422.00
Chest, Poplar, 6 Drawers, Scrolled Stiles & Feet, Mahogany Grain Painted, c.1850, 49 x 43 In. 663.00
Chest, Poplar, Brown Paint, 4 Drawers, Brass Pulls, Turned Feet, c.1710, 39 x 34 In. 3555.00
Chest, Poplar, Green Sponge Hearts, Red Ground, 1802, 14 ½ x 24 In. 6518.00
Chest, Poplar, Hinged Lid, Urn & Flower Painted Panels, c.1805, 22 x 52 In. 1093.00
Chest, Poplar, Lift Top, 2 Drawers, Mid Atlantic, 1700s, 32 ½ x 50 In. 415.00
Chest, Poplar, Ocher Grain Painted, 5 Drawers, Inscribed J. Gastle, 38 ½ x 18 ¾ In. 2370.00
Chest, Poplar, Orange, Ocher Grain Painted, Pa., c.1830, 16 x 31 In..................................... 3792.00
Chest, Poplar, Red Paint, 6-Board, New England, c.1810, 16 ½ x 28 In., Child's 356.00
Chest, Queen Anne, 6 Drawers, New England, c.1760, 50 x 36 In. 1308.00
Chest, Queen Anne, Black Paint, 4 Drawers, Ball Feet, Conn., c.1750, 37 ½ x 36 In. 1185.00
Chest, Queen Anne, Cherry, Fan Carvings, 11 Drawers, c.1770, 77 x 39 ¼ In.......................... 8888.00
Chest, Queen Anne, Cherry, Fan Carvings, Stepped Cornice, c.1780, 76 x 38 In........................ 4740.00
Chest, Queen Anne, Cherry, Shell Carving, c.1750, 72 x 37 ½ In. ....*Illus* 2963.00
Chest, Queen Anne, Maple, 5 Drawers, Red Paint, New England, c.1770, 44 x 37 In. 5451.00
Chest, Queen Anne, Maple, 9 Drawers, Shaped Apron, c.1765, 73 x 38 In. 4740.00
Chest, Queen Anne, Maple, Black Paint, 8 Drawers, Peter Bartlett, N.H., c.1790, 75 x 38 In. 35550.00
Chest, Queen Anne, Maple, Fan Carved Molded Cornice, Pad Feet, c.1765, 73 x 40 In. 5170.00
Chest, Queen Anne, Maple, Pine, 2 Sections, 10 Drawers, c.1750, 74 x 41 In. 2531.00
Chest, Queen Anne, Maple, Pine, Molded Cornice, Scroll Apron, c.1765, 72 In. 6933.00
Chest, Queen Anne, Maple, Scroll Apron, Acorn Drops, Dovetailed, Pad Feet, c.1755, 71 x 41 In..... 5053.00
Chest, Queen Anne, Pine, 2 Parts, 10 Drawers, Shaped Skirt, Pad Feet, c.1765, 71 x 37 In. 2233.00
Chest, Queen Anne, Poplar, 2 Parts, Dovetailed Drawers, Ohio, 1900s, 76 x 43 In. 1998.00
Chest, Queen Anne, Tiger Maple, Drawers, Brass Hardware, New England, c.1790, 69 x 36 In. ..*Illus* 10800.00
Chest, Queen Anne, Walnut, 7 Drawers, Scalloped Skirt, c.1765, 75 x 41 In........................... 14220.00
Chest, Queen Anne, Walnut, Fan Carved, 4 Drawers, New England, c.1765, 30 x 34 ¾ In......... 2844.00
Chest, Queen Anne, Walnut, Line Inlay, 9 Drawers, Delaware Valley, c.1765, 62 x 38 In. 3555.00
Chest, Queen Anne, Walnut, Red Stain, 9 Drawers, Red Stain, Pa., c.1765, 66 x 38 ¾ In. 5214.00
Chest, R.J. Horner, Faux Bamboo, Maple, Mirror, 5 Drawers, c.1898, 74 x 31 In. 2032.00
Chest, Red, Yellow Cat's-Eye Design, Berks County, Pa., c.1810, 26 ¾ x 48 In. 8888.00
Chest, Regency Style, Mahogany, Bowed Top, Molded Edge, 5 Drawers, c.1815, 40 x 36 In....... 1045.00
Chest, Regency, Mahogany, 5 Drawers, Lockside, 18 ½ x 15 In. 584.00
Chest, Regency, Mixed Wood, Inlay, 5 Drawers, Splayed Feet, c.1805, 41 x 40 In. 3600.00
Chest, Regency, Parquetry, Marquetry, 6 Drawers, Scrolling Leaves, 58 x 39 In. 633.00
Chest, Rhode, Mahogany, Leather, Herman Miller, c.1940, 35 x 44 In. 750.00
Chest, Roycroft, Chestnut, 3 Drawers, Square Backsplash, Overhang, c.1905, 38 x 44 In. 1875.00
Chest, Salmon Red Paint, 4 Drawers, Oval Embossed Brass Pulls, c.1790, 37 x 20 In. 2844.00
Chest, Salmon Swirl Paint, 3 Drawers, Bracket Feet, Pa., c.1810, 29 x 48 In........................... 1185.00
Chest, Sea, Pine, Blue Gray Paint, Hinged Lid, Interior Till, Chalk, 17 x 43 In. 403.00
Chest, Sea, Pine, Painted Ship Scene, Maid Of The Loch, Green, 1800s, 12 x 38 In. 764.00
Chest, Seed, Pine, Bird's-Eye Maple Paint, Glass Door, 20 Interior Drawers, Pa., 23 x 16 In. 1185.00
Chest, Shaker, Dovetailed, Chamfered Edge, 3 Drawers, Turned Pulls, c.1840, 36 x 37 In. 474.00
Chest, Sheraton Style, Cherry, Tiger Maple, Carved Backsplash, 4 Drawers, c.1850, 57 x 20 In. . 354.00
Chest, Sheraton, Birch, Crossbanded, Reeded Columns, 4 Drawers, c.1800, 42 x 43 In............. 1116.00
Chest, Sheraton, Birch, Half Columns, Turned Legs, 4 Drawers, New England, c.1840, 45 x 42 In. 267.00
Chest, Sheraton, Cherry, 4 Dovetailed Drawers, American, c.1850, 45 x 43 In. 676.00
Chest, Sheraton, Cherry, 4 Drawers, Shaped Apron, c.1810, 43 ½ x 40 In. 326.00

Furniture, Chair, Regency, Mahogany, Crest Rail, Turned Splat, Upholstered, Scroll Arms, 33 In.
$688.00

Leslie Hindman Auctioneers

Furniture, Chair, Renaissance Revival, Burl Walnut, Carved, Shieldback, Padded Arms, c.1850
$777.00

Neal Auction Co.

Furniture, Chair, Rosewood, Carved, Lacquered, Pierced, Dragon Arms, Chinese, c.1900, 34 ½ In.
$200.00

Conestoga Auction Co., Inc.

The edited listings of the current prices in this *Kovels' Antiques & Collectibles Price Guide* aren't available on any website. Readers can visit **Kovels.com** to check thousands of past prices and sign up for free information on trends, tips, reproductions, marks, and more.

Furniture, Chair, Shaker, Convenience, Ladder Back, Mixed Wood, Hinged Seat, 1800s, 42 In.
$3,240.00

Cowan's Auctions

Furniture, Chair, Swivel, Wegner, Teak, Leather, Chrome Steel, J. Hansen, 1950s, 27 x 29 In.
$17,500.00

Rago Arts & Auction Center

Furniture, Chair, Wegner, Teak, Cane Seat, Arms, Marked, Johannes Hansen, 30 x 25 In.
$1,250.00

Los Angeles Modern Auctions (LAMA)

Chest, Sheraton, Cherry, Bird's-Eye Maple, Bowfront, Mass., 38 x 43 In.	4956.00
Chest, Sheraton, Cherry, Pine, Dovetailed Drawers, Hinged Top, c.1835, 51 x 40 In.	1116.00
Chest, Sheraton, Cherry, Poplar, 4 Drawers, Southern, c.1845, 45 ½ x 40 ½ In.	374.00
Chest, Sheraton, Cherry, String Inlay, 4 Drawers, Turned Legs, c.1810, 46 x 39 ½ In.	385.00
Chest, Sheraton, Cherry, Turned Columns, 4 Drawers, c.1815, 46 x 41 In.	304.00
Chest, Sheraton, Curly Maple, Carved, 5 Drawers, Pa., c.1830, 48 ½ x 40 In.	533.00
Chest, Sheraton, Hardwood, Bowfront, 4 Bird's-Eye Maple Drawers, c.1820, 38 x 41 In.	1534.00
Chest, Sheraton, Inlaid Mahogany, Bowfront, 4 Drawers, New England, 41 x 45 In.	2832.00
Chest, Sheraton, Mahogany, 4 Graduated Drawers, Turned Feet, 43 x 42 ½ In.	472.00
Chest, Sheraton, Mahogany, Bowfront, Scrolled Apron, Drawers, c.1820, 38 x 42 In.	323.00
Chest, Sheraton, Mahogany, Bowfront, Turret Corners, 4 Drawers, Mass., 41 x 48 In.	1265.00
Chest, Sheraton, Mahogany, D-Shape, Reeded Columns, Turned Feet, c.1800, 42 x 41 In.	323.00
Chest, Sheraton, Mahogany, Shaped Backsplash, Drawers, Rope Turned, Pineapple, 56 x 46 In.	207.00
Chest, Sheraton, Mahogany, Tiger Maple, Backsplash, New England, 47 x 44 In.	531.00
Chest, Sheraton, Painted, 4 Graduated Drawers, Turned Legs, c.1870, 45 x 39 In.	1200.00
Chest, Sheraton, Walnut, 4 Drawers, Paneled Sides, Turned Legs, c.1810, 46 x 40 ½ In.	425.00
Chest, Sheraton, Walnut, 5 Drawers, Pennsylvania, c.1810, 46 x 43 ½ In.	456.00
Chest, Sheraton, Walnut, 5 Drawers, Reeded Pilasters, Cannon, Bugle Brasses, 39 x 19 In.	220.00
Chest, Specimen, 7 Drawers, Pa., c.1950, 23 ¼ x 15 In.	178.00
Chest, Spice, Mahogany, 12 Drawers Inside, Pa., 1800s, 16 ¾ x 12 ½ In.	1896.00
Chest, Spice, Oak, Hinged Door, Painted Circles, England, c.1790, 14 x 13 ½ In.	533.00
Chest, Sugar, Cherry, Hinged Lid, Dovetailed Drawers, Turned Legs, 1800s, 32 x 37 In.	3776.00
Chest, Sugar, Cherry, Hinged Lid, Drawer, Tapered Legs, c.1800, 35 x 22 In.	4465.00
Chest, Sugar, Federal, Cherry, Lift Top, Hinged Lid, Inlaid Escutcheon, 1800s, 31 x 37 In.	1180.00
Chest, Sugar, Sheraton, Cherry, Lift Top, Turned Legs, c.1800, 37 x 40 In.	2880.00
Chest, Tansu, Figured Wood, Sliding Panel Doors, Drawers, Japan, c.1900, 62 x 33 In.	575.00
Chest, Tiger & Curly Maple, 4 Drawers, Carved Columns, 40 ¾ x 53 In.	805.00
Chest, Tiger Maple, 6 Graduated Drawers, Brass, c.1775, 61 ½ x 36 x 18 In.	4740.00
Chest, Tiger Maple, Cherry, 7 Drawers, Brass Bail Pulls, Moses Osborn, c.1790, 63 In. ......*Illus*	17775.00
Chest, Tool, Pine, Painted, Jacob Kahler N.W.O., 1895, 18 x 31 In.	529.00
Chest, Victorian, Faux Bamboo, Marble Top, Drawers, Diamond Pattern, c.1890, 39 x 22 In., Pair	2706.00
Chest, Victorian, Walnut, 3 Drawers, Incised Scrolls, c.1885, 32 x 42 In.	173.00
Chest, Victorian, Walnut, Marble Top, Carved Pulls, 3 Drawers, Secret Drawer, c.1865, 49 x 24 In.	531.00
Chest, Victorian, Wood, Marble Top, Beveled, Shaped Backsplash, c.1890, 38 x 32 In.	201.00
Chest, Walnut, 3 Drawers, France, c.1830, 33 x 38 In.	1000.00
Chest, Walnut, 4 Drawers, Ball Feet, c.1825, 42 ½ x 41 ½ In.	489.00
Chest, Walnut, 4 Drawers, Bracket Feet, 35 x 41 ½ In.	688.00
Chest, Walnut, 5 Drawers, Applied Moldings, Bracket Feet, Va., c.1800, 43 x 42 In.	4313.00
Chest, Walnut, Flower Carved, Lid, Wrought Iron Detail, Spain, 1600, 32 x 64 In.	1725.00
Chest, Walnut, Hinged Lid, Applied Moldings, Fitted Interior, Va., 1875, 22 x 38 In.	489.00
Chest, Walnut, Ivory Inlay, Vines, Flowers, Brass Bail Handles, Stepped, Drawers, Italy, 33 x 28 In.	1323.00
Chest, Walnut, Molded Top, 5 Drawers, Columns, French Feet, Pa., c.1800, 47 x 32 In., Pair ...	18960.00
Chest, Walnut, Poplar, 5 Dovetailed Drawers, Shaped Skirt, French Feet, c.1850, 40 x 42 In.	1770.00
Chest, William & Mary, 2 Short & 5 Long Drawers, Red Paint, 1757, 54 x 40 In.	5664.00
Chest, William & Mary, 5 Drawers, Red Paint, Ball Feet, c.1730, 42 x 36 In.	1304.00
Chest, William & Mary, 5 Drawers, Red Paint, Ball Feet, New England, 38 x 37 In.	1770.00
Chest, William & Mary, Circassion Walnut, Inlay, Drawers, c.1710, 66 x 62 In. ....*Illus*	4182.00
Chest, William & Mary, Maple, 5 Drawers, Applied Edge, Bun Feet, 36 x 36 ¾ In.	1888.00
Chest, William & Mary, Maple, Pine, 2 Parts, Drawers, Cabriole Legs, 1700s, 66 x 36 In.	2703.00
Chest, William & Mary, Oak, 3 Drawers, Ball Feet, England, c.1690, 38 x 23 In.	633.00
Chest, William & Mary, Oak, 4 Drawers, Brass Acorn Pulls, Block Feet, 1600s, 36 x 38 In.	1541.00
Chest, William & Mary, Oak, Carved, Lift Top, 4 Drawers, Painted Flower Rondels, 17 x 19 In.	380.00
Chest, William & Mary, Oak, Drawers, Applied Molding, Ball Feet, 37 x 41 In.	24780.00
Chest, William & Mary, Walnut, Bone, Brass Mounts, 4 Drawers, Arched Recess, 44 In.	3159.00
Chest, William IV, Mahogany, Bowfront, Drawers, Reeded Pilaster, c.1835, 44 x 42 In.	861.00
Chest, Wormley, Walnut, Brass, Inset Ceramic Tile, 4 Drawers, 1950s, 33 x 34 In.	2000.00
Chest, Yellow Pine, Grain Painted, Dovetailed Construction, Pa., c.1810, 21 x 42 In.	652.00
Chest-On-Chest, Chippendale Style, Mahogany, Broken-Arch Pediment, c.1900, 81 x 38 In.	805.00
Chest-On-Chest, Chippendale, Cherry, Fan, Broken Pediment, c.1795, 89 x 40 In.	10073.00
Chest-On-Chest, Chippendale, Maple, 8 Drawers, Shell, Fan Carved, c.1800, 83 x 39 In.	35550.00
Chest-On-Chest, Chippendale, Maple, Molded Cornice, Beaded Drawers, c.1795, 71 x 37 In.	2370.00
Chest-On-Chest, Chippendale, Maple, Stepped Cornice, Shaped Apron, c.1795, 73 x 38 In.	9480.00
Chest-On-Chest, Chippendale, Tiger Maple, Molded Cornice, Bracket Feet, 78 x 40 In.	5079.00
Chest-On-Chest, Chippendale, Tiger Maple, Swan Neck Crest, 7 Drawers, 79 x 41 In.	7552.00
Chest-On-Chest, Chippendale, Walnut, 8 Drawers Over 5 Drawers, Pa., c.1770, 76 ½ x 43 In.	7898.00
Chest-On-Chest, George II, Mahogany, Dentil Cornice, Bracket Feet, 1700s, 73 x 42 In.	738.00

Chest-On-Chest, George III Style, Mahogany, Round Pulls, 7 Drawers, 73 x 44 ½ In.	1896.00
Chest-On-Chest, George III, Mahogany, Boxwood Inlay, 8 Drawers, c.1770, 74 x 44 ½ In.......	1304.00
Chest-On-Chest, George III, Mahogany, Dentil Cornice, Pilasters, c.1790, 74 In.....................	4182.00
Chest-On-Chest, George III, Mahogany, Dovetailed Drawers, c.1800, 72 x 46 In.....................	1528.00
Chest-On-Chest, George III, Mahogany, Line Inlay, 8 Drawers, c.1770, 70 x 42 In..................	1304.00
Chest-On-Chest, George III, Mahogany, Molded Cornice, Bail Handles, c.1750, 69 x 40 In.....	823.00
Chest-On-Chest, George III, Mahogany, Molded Cornice, Bracket Feet, c.1785, 73 x 41 In......	1722.00
Chest-On-Chest, George III, Walnut, Molded Cornice, Banded, Bracket Feet, c.1790, 66 x 41 In.	1230.00
Chest-On-Chest, George III, Walnut, Oak, Molded Cornice, Banded, c.1790, 66 x 43 In.	1722.00
Chest-On-Chest, Georgian, Mahogany, Dentil Cornice, Bracket Feet, c.1800, 72 x 45 In.	2629.00
Chest-On-Chest, Georgian, Mahogany, Projected Cornice, Bail Handles, 1700s, 76 x 44 In. ...	1076.00
Chest-On-Chest, Walnut, Stained Beech, Drawers, Sliding Doors, 1950s, 47 x 45 In.	3500.00
Chest-On-Frame, Dunlap, Maple, Molded Cornice, 5 Drawers, Scroll & Fan, 52 x 46 In.	1610.00
Chest-On-Frame, Queen Anne Style, Walnut, 8 Drawers, 72 x 38 In.	770.00
Chest-On-Frame, Queen Anne, Cherry, Grain Painted, Drawers, N.H., c.1790, 60 x 36 In.	5036.00
Chest-On-Frame, Queen Anne, Oak, Paneled, Slant Front, Shaped Stand, 1700s, 38 x 40 In..	1076.00
Chest-On-Frame, Queen Anne, Shaped Apron, Cabriole Legs, Pa., c.1770, 70 x 39 In.	1944.00
Chest-On-Frame, Walnut, Gadrooning, 3 Doors, Carved Panel Back, 1800s, 52 x 51 In...........	1200.00
Chest-On-Frame, William & Mary Style, Japanned, Drawers, X-Stretcher, 62 x 41 In. ....*Illus*	1541.00
Chest-On-Frame, William & Mary Style, Maple, Lift Top, 2 Drawers, c.1945, 47 x 39 In.	1298.00
Chiffonier, Louis XVI Style, Kingwood, Chamfered Corners, Cabriole Legs, c.1890, 52 In.	610.00
Chiffonier, Regency, Mahogany, Brass, Drawer, 2 Arch Doors, Scroll Supports, 44 x 45 In.......	702.00
Chiffonier, Regency, Mahogany, Open Shelf, Drawer, 2 Doors, Columns, 47 x 35 In.................	2223.00
Chiffonier, Regency, Rosewood, Brass Pierced Gallery, Scrolling Leaves, c.1815, 49 x 38 In. ...	2091.00
Chiffonier, Roycroft, Chestnut, Drawers, Door, Carved Mark, c.1907, 55 ½ x 42 In. ....*Illus*	15000.00
Chiffonier, William IV, Rosewood, Pierced Brass Gallery, Barley Twist, Door, c.1835, 56 x 27 In.....	538.00
Chifforobe, Art Deco, Waterfall, Drawers, 1930s, 68 x 37 In.	59.00
Clothes Rack, G. Stickley, 2 Tapered Posts, Iron Hooks, Shoefoot, Decal, 13 ½ 22 In.	3660.00
Clothespress, Hepplewhite, Mahogany, Cock-Beaded, c.1775, 82 x 48 x 21 In.	1175.00
Coat Rack, Costumer, G. Stickley, Double, No. 53, 2 Posts, 6 Double Hooks, 72 x 22 In.	2000.00
Coat Rack, Federal, Brown Stain, 3 Iron Hooks, Baluster Column, Tripod Legs, 1800s, 73 In..	2489.00
Coat Rack, Victorian, Walnut, Hanging, Star Shape, Collapsible, 41 In.....................................	819.00
Coffer, Georgian, Oak, Paneled Sides, Lid, Staple Hinges, c.1800, 22 x 40 x 19 In.	206.00
Coffer, Mahogany, Oak, Dovetailed Case, Figured Veneer, Stand, c.1800, 33 x 45 In.	940.00
Coffer, Renaissance Revival, Walnut, Carved, Recessed Panels, Raised Frame, c.1900, 70 x 22 In..	120.00
Commode Chair, Louis XV, Leather, Brass Tacks, Faience Basin, c.1775, 32 x 13 x 20 In.	236.00
Commode, 2 Drawers, Canted Fluted Corners, Square Tapered Legs, c.1800, 36 x 46 In.............	2091.00
Commode, 3 Drawers, Molded Hardware, Shaped Feet, Scroll Toes, 1800s, 34 x 38 In...............	2091.00
Commode, Baroque Style, Inlay, Book Matched, Serpentine, Bracket Feet, c.1900, 35 x 43 In. ...	1659.00
Commode, Bedside, Gallery Top, Handles, Drawer, Cupboard, Square Legs, 30 x 20 In.	1062.00
Commode, Bedside, George III Style, Mahogany, Hinged Top, Cupboard Doors, 28 x 23 In.......	215.00
Commode, Bedside, Mahogany, Gallery, Pierced Handles, c.1785, 31 x 22 In.	430.00
Commode, Biedermeier, Walnut, Stepped Top, Rounded Corners, Drawers, c.1850, 33 x 34 In.	984.00
Commode, Black Marble Top, Wood, Crossbanded, Gilt Mounts, 3 Drawers, 35 x 45 In..............	738.00
Commode, Bombe, Butternut, Drawers, Ball & Claw Feet, Canada, 1700s, 30 x 31 In. ....*Illus*	77025.00
Commode, Bombe, Drawers, Painted Flowers, Italy, c.1900, 23 x 21 In., Pair ....*Illus*	1107.00
Commode, Bombe, Louis XV Style, Walnut Veneer, Marble Top, c.1950, 34 x 51 x 25 In.	354.00
Commode, Bombe, Louis XV Style, Walnut, Flower Inlay, Rouge Marble Top, 34 x 31 In.............	472.00
Commode, Bombe, Multicolor, Court Figures, Panel Door, Cabriole Legs, 1800s, 34 x 24 In., Pair	3286.00
Commode, Bombe, Venetian Painted, 2 Drawers, Molded Sides, 1800s, 34 x 49 In. ....*Illus*	2988.00
Commode, Bookmatch Veneer, Gilt, Serpentine, Marble Top, Splayed Legs, 35 x 49 In.	1000.00
Commode, Chinoiserie, Pagodas, Trees Blossoms, 3 Drawers, 35 x 45 ¾ In.	5625.00
Commode, Ebonized, Bronze, Marble Top, 3 Drawers, Fluted Columns, c.1940, 33 x 35 In.	1020.00
Commode, Ebonized, Marble Top, Gesso Designs, Splayed Legs, c.1800, 36 x 34 In...................	2952.00
Commode, Empire Style, Mahogany, Marble Top, Ormolu, Columns, 1800s, 40 x 49 In.	1920.00
Commode, Empire, Mahogany, Drawer, 2 Doors, Hidden Drawer, c.1860, 33 x 25 In...................	59.00
Commode, Empire, Mahogany, Gilt Bronze, Marble, 3 Drawers, Paw Feet, c.1850, 34 x 51 In. ...	2250.00
Commode, Empire, Marble Top, Drawers, Columns, Ball Feet, Brass Handles, 1800s, 40 x 50 In. ...	1180.00
Commode, Empire, Wood, Marble Top, 3 Drawers, Columns, Bronze, France, c.1840, 36 x 51 In. ...	2040.00
Commode, French Provincial, Walnut, 4 Drawers, c.1750, 32 x 46 In.	3680.00
Commode, French Provincial, Walnut, Serpentine Top, Apron, Scroll Feet, 1700s, 34 x 52 In.	4025.00
Commode, Fruitwood, Bronze Ormolu Accents, Masks, Marble Top, 2 Drawers, 31 x 40 In.	2700.00
Commode, Fruitwood, Bronze, Dovetailed Drawers, Serpentine Top, 1900s, 32 x 55 In.............	826.00
Commode, Fruitwood, Inlaid 8-Point Star, Diamond Shape Legs, Italy, c.1700, 31 x 19 In.	2133.00
Commode, Fruitwood, Parquetry, 2 Drawers, Flowers, Square Legs, c.1800, 29 x 21 In.	2151.00
Commode, Fruitwood, Rosewood, Marble Top, Bombe, Banded, Apron, Shield, 1700s, 36 x 42 In........	4182.00

Furniture, Chair, Windsor, 7 Spindles, Sack Back, Fanned, Painted, c.1800, 40 ½ In.
$16,590.00

Skinner, Inc.

Furniture, Chair, Wormley, Alexandria, Mahogany, Walnut, Shaped Crest, Leather, Arms, c.1960, 32 In.
$1,920.00

Skinner, Inc.

Furniture, Chair, Zephyr, Wendell Castle, Walnut, Signed, 1979, 28 x 25 ½ In.
$16,675.00

Cottone Auctions

Furniture, Chair-Table, Pine, 3-Board Top, Bun Feet, 1700s, 30 x 45 In.
$1,293.00

Garth's Auctioneers & Appraisers

TIP

Never buy a repainted chair if you can buy one with original paint. Never strip all the paint from a chair if you can restore the original paint.

F

Furniture, Chaise Longue, Louis XVI Style, Cane Back & Foot, Painted, 59 In. $500.00

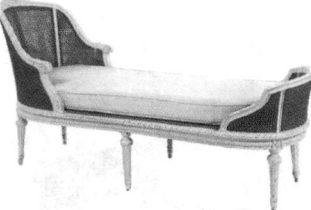

Leslie Hindman Auctioneers

Furniture, Chaise Longue, Regency, Ebonized, Cane, Stenciled, 71 ½ In. $2,000.00

Bonhams

Iron Hardware

The iron hardware used on platform rockers is often referred to as Lowentraut for Peter Lowentraut, who owned half the patent rights given to George Hall in 1887 for his invention of a swing mechanism at the base of a glider-rocker. Although the patent applied only to the hardware, not the chair, it was copied by many, and the name Lowentraut is sometimes used for any glider-rocker. The hardware design is still in use and replacements can be bought today.

Commode, Fruitwood, Serpentine Top, Chamfered Stiles, Cabriole Legs, c.1760, 30 x 36 In.	4183.00
Commode, George III, Mahogany, Leather Insets, 2 Steps, 25 ½ x 18 ½ In.	273.00
Commode, Gothic Revival, Molded Marble Top, Drawer, Door, Columns, c.1845, 30 x 17 In.	956.00
Commode, Hepplewhite, Mahogany, Demilune, Line Inlay, Drawers, c.1800, 36 x 37 In.	2006.00
Commode, Kingwood, Marble Top, Drawers, Inlay, Diamond Design, Italy, c.1900, 35 x 40 In.	553.00
Commode, Kingwood, Marble Top, Serpentine Top, Banding, Drawers, c.1795, 33 x 39 In.	3444.00
Commode, Louis XV Style, Kingwood, Marble Top, Flower Lattice, c.1900, 36 x 46 In.	2214.00
Commode, Louis XV Style, Marble Top, Flower Inlay, Cabriole Legs, 34 x 50 In.	922.00
Commode, Louis XV Style, Marble Top, Gilt, Parquetry, Skirt, c.1900, 35 x 41 In.	1534.00
Commode, Louis XV Style, Marquetry, Jasperware, Marble Top, Inlay, Square Legs, 30 x 24 In., Pair	625.00
Commode, Louis XV Style, Mixed Wood, Marble Top, Leaf Mounts, 3 Drawers, 36 x 48 In.	1875.00
Commode, Louis XV Style, Parquetry, Bombe, Drawers, Curved Legs, 29 x 25 In. .... *Illus*	594.00
Commode, Louis XV Style, Walnut, Gilt, Marquetry, Bombe Shaped, Marble Top, 31 x 34 In.	239.00
Commode, Louis XV, Bookmatch Veneer, Breakfront Marble Top, Shaped Skirt, 36 x 48 In.	469.00
Commode, Louis XV, Fruitwood, 3 Drawers, 38 x 50 In.	3186.00
Commode, Louis XV, Fruitwood, Serpentine Top, 2 Drawers, Cabriole Legs, Apron, 34 x 60 In.	2360.00
Commode, Louis XV, Marquetry, Walnut, Marble Top, 3 Drawers, Cabriole Legs, 35 x 45 In.	938.00
Commode, Louis XV, Walnut, Bombe, Serpentine Top, Drawers, Cabriole Legs, c.1750, 34 x 47 In.	7170.00
Commode, Louis XV, Walnut, Serpentine Top, 4 Drawers, Flower Apron, Stile Feet, 35 x 52 In.	1900.00
Commode, Louis XVI Style, Bronze Mounts, Shaped Marble, Cabriole Legs, c.1900, 29 x 19 In., Pair	549.00
Commode, Louis XVI Style, Fruitwood, Marble Top, Inlay, Square Legs, c.1850, 33 x 36 In.	3444.00
Commode, Louis XVI Style, Mahogany, Marble Top, Doors, Brass Banding, Pegs, c.1900, 34 x 51 In.	1845.00
Commode, Louis XVI Style, Parquetry, Marble Top, Drawers, Doors, Demilune, c.1965, 34 x 31 In.	480.00
Commode, Louis XVI, Fruitwood, Demilune, Marble Top, Rounded Doors, Inlay, c.1790, 35 x 33 In.	7500.00
Commode, Louis XVI, Kingwood, Marble, Serpentine, Scalloped Skirt, Cabriole Legs, 34 x 50 In.	1076.00
Commode, Louis XVI, Mahogany, Marble Top, 3 Drawers, c.1790, 33 x 38 In.	2500.00
Commode, Louis XVI, Marquetry, Mixed Wood, Marble Top, 3 Drawers, Ribbons, 31 x 38 In.	438.00
Commode, Louis XVI, Mixed Wood, Marble Top, Gilt Mounts, 2 Drawers, c.1900, 29 x 29 In., Pair	1800.00
Commode, Mahogany, 3 Step, Leather Inset, Turned Front Legs, England, 1800s, 27 x 18 In.	490.00
Commode, Mahogany, Gallery, Shelves, Square Legs, c.1885, 30 x 22 In.	184.00
Commode, Mahogany, Galley Top, Drawer, Cupboard Door, Reeded Legs, Casters, c.1800	359.00
Commode, Mahogany, Inlay, Foldover Top, 2 Drawers, 2 Doors, England, c.1790, 21 x 18 In.	201.00
Commode, Mahogany, Marble Top, 2 Drawers, Doors, Fitted Interior, c.1905, 38 x 72 In.	8750.00
Commode, Mahogany, Marble Top, 3 Drawers, Bowed Front, Splayed Legs, c.1890, 26 x 22 In.	984.00
Commode, Mahogany, Marble Top, 3 Graduated Drawers, Fluted Stiles, c.1860, 35 x 52 In.	1875.00
Commode, Mahogany, Marble Top, Fluted Columns, Door, Octagonal Base, c.1850, 30 x 15 In.	598.00
Commode, Mahogany, Square Top, Raised Gallery, Cupboard Doors, c.1795, 31 x 21 In.	676.00
Commode, Marble Top, 3 Drawers, String Inlay, Flared Bottom, Baltic, c.1790, 38 x 71 In. .... *Illus*	1200.00
Commode, Marble Top, 4 Drawers, Bracket Feet, France, c.1850, 35 x 52 In.	840.00
Commode, Marble Top, Walnut Veneer, Bronze, Shaped Skirt, 1900s, 27 x 46 In.	531.00
Commode, Marquetry, Marble Top, 3 Graduated Drawers, Square Tapered Legs, 37 x 45 In.	3500.00
Commode, Marquetry, Mixed Wood, Bombe, 3 Drawers, Inlaid Urn, Ribbon, c.1760, 34 x 52 In.	6875.00
Commode, Marquetry, Mixed Wood, Marble Top, 3 Drawers, Metal Mounts, 34 x 44 In.	531.00
Commode, Neoclassical, Mahogany, Brass Edge, String Inlay, Drawers, Russia, 37 x 39 In.	4797.00
Commode, Neoclassical, Mahogany, Marble Top, Philadelphia, c.1830, 32 x 35 In.	1541.00
Commode, Neoclassical, Marble Top, Diamond Inlay, Drawers, Square Feet, c.1800, 34 x 23 In., Pair	2832.00
Commode, Neoclassical, Marquetry Urn Panels, Marble Top, Tapered Legs, c.1800, 35 x 49 In.	8850.00
Commode, Neoclassical, Oak, Marble Top, 3 Drawers, Turned Legs, c.1800, 31 x 55 In.	1000.00
Commode, Neoclassical, Walnut, 2 Drawers, Scroll Design, Fluted Legs, c.1800, 33 x 35 In.	3690.00
Commode, Neoclassical, Walnut, Marble Top, Parquetry Drawers, Fluted Legs, France, 33 x 35 In.	2875.00
Commode, Oak, Rounded Top, Drawers, Cabriole Legs, Scrolled Toes, 1900s, 29 x 41 In.	492.00
Commode, Regency Style, Kingwood, Marble Top, Frieze Drawer, Splayed Feet, c.1900, 36 x 49 In.	1230.00
Commode, Regency Style, Mahogany, Brass Bands, Strapwork, Serpentine, Bracket Feet, 37 x 52 In.	2460.00
Commode, Rococo, Walnut, Banded Top, 2 Drawers, Raised Legs, Italy, c.1760, 32 x 27 In.	1500.00
Commode, Rococo, Wood, Flowers, Green, 3 Drawers, 1700s, 38 x 49 In.	4738.00
Commode, Rococo, Wood, Painted, Flowers, 4 Drawers, 1700s, 14 x 18 In.	2415.00
Commode, Rosewood, Ebonized Top, 4 Drawers, Raised Stepped Base, 39 x 61 In.	780.00
Commode, Rosewood, Marble Top, Drawer, Door, Pendant Brackets, c.1850, 31 x 20 In.	2510.00
Commode, Rosewood, Marble Top, Drawers, Inlaid Flowers, c.1900, 29 x 26 In., Pair	984.00
Commode, Tulipwood, Parquetry, Marble Top, 4 Drawers, Italy, 36 x 48 ¾ In.	644.00
Commode, Walnut, Gilt, 3 Panel Drawers, Short Legs, c.1750. 41 x 51 In.	4688.00
Commode, Walnut, Inlay, Marble Top, 3 Drawers, Gilt Mounts, Cabriole Legs, 33 x 30 In.	219.00
Commode, Walnut, Inlay, Serpentine, Conforming Drawers, Scrolled Apron, 1700s, 33 x 58 In.	6325.00
Commode, Walnut, Marble Top, Drawers, Paneled Sides, Cabriole Legs, 1800s, 39 x 49 In.	3286.00
Commode, Walnut, Neoclassical, Canted Corners, 3 Long Drawers, c.1825, 34 x 50 In.	3750.00
Commode, Walnut, Parquetry, Concave Top, Drawers, Bun Feet, Germany, 1700s, 33 x 50 In.	4025.00

Commode, Walnut, Parquetry, Marquetry, Germany, c.1790, 33 x 50 In.	5000.00
Commode, Walnut, Serpentine Top, Bombe Shape, Inlay, Apron, Italy, 1700s, 38 x 49 In.	4200.00
Commode, Walnut, Serpentine, 4 Drawers, Scroll Inlay, Base Molding, Italy, 1700s, 32 x 24 In.	2645.00
Commode, Wood, Marble Top, Gilt Metal Mounts, Painted, 2 Drawers, Bombe, c.1960, 33 x 28 In.	625.00
Counter, Shaker, Pine, Hinged Doors, 4 Graduated Drawers, c.1820, 31 x 29 In.	5925.00
Counter, Store, Walnut, Fruitwood, 2 Drawers, Short Turned Legs, c.1920, 28 x 78 In.	625.00
Cradle, Curly Maple, Dovetailed, Heart Cutouts, Ohio, 1800s, 18 x 41 In.	118.00
Cradle, Pine, Hardwood, Green Paint, Scroll Detail, Dovetailed, Rocking, 1800s, 25 x 41 In.	235.00
Cradle, Poplar, Cutout End, Cheese Cutter Rockers, Mustard Paint, c.1845, 22 ½ x 39 In.	92.00
Cradle, Poplar, Double Arch Ends, Cutout Handles, Cheese Cutter Rockers, c.1850, 21 x 39 In.	92.00
Cradle, Tiger Maple, Hooded, Pa., 19th Century	213.00
Cradle, Tiger Maple, Shaped Cutout Headboard, Footboard, Cutter Rockers, 25 x 44 In.	142.00
Cradle, Walnut, Dovetailed, Heart Cutouts, Blanket Bar, c.1830, 25 x 17 x 40 In.	176.00
Cradle, Walnut, Poplar, Dovetailed, Heart Cutouts, Stenciling, 1849, 23 x 43 In.	121.00
Cradle, Walnut, Scalloped Head, Footboards, Dovetailed, Shenandoah Valley, 40 In.	179.00
Cradle, Windsor, Rocking, c.1800, 25 x 39 ½ In.	444.00
Cradle, Windsor, Rod Back, Splayed Legs, Pa., 33 ¾ x 28 In.	1185.00
Cradle, Wood, Turned & Carved Posts, Raised Panel Headboard, Open Crest, Italy, 1700s, 45 x 43 In.	575.00
Credenza, Burl Walnut, Marble Top, Putti, Door, Strapwork, 1800s, 45 x 36 In.	1000.00
Credenza, Chinese Style, Black Lacquer, Bowfront, 3 Drawers, 3 Doors, c.1950, 32 x 53 In.	450.00
Credenza, Danish Modern, Rosewood Veneer, 3 Compartments, 2 Sliding Doors, 32 x 65 In.	1337.00
Credenza, G. Nelson, Walnut, Black Laminate Door, Metal, File Drawer, Herman Miller, 80 x 19 In.	1304.00
Credenza, Mid Century, Mixed Wood Inlay, Shoreline Scene, Johnson Furniture Co., 30 x 36 In.	590.00
Credenza, Oak, Curved Ends, 8 Drawers, Metal Handles, Knoll, 81 x 20 In.	2196.00
Credenza, Oxblood, 4 Doors, Rounded, Chrome Base, c.1980, 29 x 72 In.	960.00
Credenza, P. Evans, Cityscape, Chrome, Brass, Geometric, 3 Double Doors, 1970s, 32 x 90 In. *Illus*	11258.00
Credenza, Regency, Rosewood, Marble, Doors, Pilasters, Maiden's Heads, Gilt, c.1815, 33 x 46 In.	1045.00
Credenza, Regency, Rosewood, Pierced Brass Gallery, Mirror, Cupboard Doors, c.1815, 62 x 72 In.	1353.00
Credenza, Scandinavian Design, Teak Veneer, 3 Compartments, Sliding Doors, Drawers, 80 x 18 In.	729.00
Credenza, Wrought Iron, Mirror, Scrolling, Flowers, Wood Top, c.1900, 65 x 31 In.	180.00
Crib, Neoclassical, Curly Maple, Acorn Finials, Cane Sides, Drop Front, c.1850, 29 x 47 In.	235.00
Crib, Sheraton, Mahogany, Ring-Turned Posts, Acorn Finial, Spindled Sides, c.1810, 32 x 52 In.	253.00
Cupboard, 2 Glass Doors Over 2 Panel Doors, Drawers, Painted, 1800s, 44 x 78 In.	2185.00
Cupboard, 2 Glass Doors, 2-Panel Doors, Drawers, Carved, Faux Paint, c.1830, 84 x 50 In.	20145.00
Cupboard, 2-Panel Doors, Yellow, Green Paint, 1800s, 50 ½ x 84 In.	173.00
Cupboard, 4 Paneled Doors, Cast Iron Spring Latches, Dovetailed Case, 41 x 55 In.	83.00
Cupboard, 4-Panel Doors, Yellow, Red, Painted, 78 x 33 In.	9300.00
Cupboard, Baroque, Removable Cornice, Paneled Doors, Brass Hardware, c.1800, 85 x 64 In.	767.00
Cupboard, Blind, 2 Doors, Shell, Flowers, Barley Twist Leg, 6-Footed, 1930s, 60 x 38 In.	518.00
Cupboard, Bonnetiere, Louis XV Style, Oak, Panel Door, Flower Basket, Crest, 1900s, 71 x 31 In.	472.00
Cupboard, Bookcase, Gothic Style, 2 Sections, Tenons, Drop Front Desk, c.1900, 89 x 42 In.	294.00
Cupboard, Burl, Double Pedestal, Green, Marble Top, Mirror Crest, Shelves, Door, 73 x 80 In.	2645.00
Cupboard, Campaign Style, Mahogany, 2 Doors, 5 Drawers, c.1870, 88 x 56 In.	826.99
Cupboard, Cherry, Walnut, Poplar Shelves, 2 Sections, Panel Doors, Shelves, 91 x 45 In.	1410.00
Cupboard, Cherry, Walnut, Stepped Cornice, Arched Doors, Matchstick Trim, c.1825, 36 x 30 In.	1998.00
Cupboard, Chimney, Pine, Paneled Door, Shelves, Pullout Bins, 1800s, 69 x 26 In.	470.00
Cupboard, Chimney, Pine, Poplar, Red & Yellow Paint, Door, Stepped Cornice, 61 x 25 In.	482.00
Cupboard, Chimney, Poplar, Raised Panel Door, 3 Shelves, Red Over Blue Paint, 67 x 21 In.	323.00
Cupboard, Chimney, Shaker, Pine, 2 Paneled Doors, White Pulls, c.1800, 76 x 25 In.	582.00
Cupboard, Chimney, Walnut, 2 Paneled Doors, Shaped Bracket Base, c.1815, 81 x 24 In.	1175.00
Cupboard, Chippendale, Step Back, Walnut, Pine, Glass Panes, c.1800, 88 x 70 In. *Illus*	4994.00
Cupboard, Chippendale, Walnut, Pewter, Shelves, Paneled Doors, c.1800, 77 x 51 x 18 In.	4248.00
Cupboard, Corner, 2 Sections, Molded Top, Glass Door, Drawers, Bracket Feet, 1700s, 77 x 34 In.	1125.00
Cupboard, Corner, Arched, Softwood, Panel Doors, Recessed Panel Lower Doors, 105 x 56 In.	826.00
Cupboard, Corner, Cherry, 2 Arched Glass Doors, 2 Flat Doors, Applied Designs, c.1810, 91 x 55 In.	668.00
Cupboard, Corner, Cherry, 2 Sections, Butterfly Shelves, Panel Doors, Bracket Feet, 99 In.	460.00
Cupboard, Corner, Cherry, 2 Sections, Scrolled Swan Neck Crest, Pinwheels, c.1800s, 85 In.	6518.00
Cupboard, Corner, Cherry, Glass Doors, 2-Panel Doors, Bracket Feet, Red Stain, c.1820, 89 x 40 In.	3792.00
Cupboard, Corner, Cherry, Glazed Panel Door, 8 Panes, Lower Cupboard Doors, c.1835, 29 x 28 In.	316.00
Cupboard, Corner, Cherry, Palladium Glass Doors, 3 Drawers, 2 Low Doors, c.1930, 108 x 53 In.	1150.00
Cupboard, Corner, Cherry, Poplar, 2 Sections, 12-Pane Door, Panel Door, c.1820, 41 x 23 In.	3525.00
Cupboard, Corner, Cherry, Poplar, 4 Blind Doors, Drawers, Bracket Feet, 1800s, 83 x 45 In.	1116.00
Cupboard, Corner, Cherry, Poplar, Glass Doors, Panel Doors, Apron, 1800s, 86 x 51 In.	940.00
Cupboard, Corner, Cherry, Scrolled Pediment, Upper & Lower Doors, 1800s, 94 x 42 In.	708.00
Cupboard, Corner, Chippendale Style, Inlaid Oak, Shaped Shelves, Glass Door, c.1900, 78 x 34 In.	413.00
Cupboard, Corner, Chippendale, Walnut, Carved Crest, Glass Doors, 2 Panel Doors, 94 x 46 In.	1180.00

Furniture, Chest, Art Deco, Veneered, Figured Calamander, Brass Mounted, c.1950, 34 x 39 In.
$1,230.00

New Orleans Auction Galleries, Inc.

Furniture, Chest, Black Enamel, Drawers, Brass Pulls, Gold Paint, Spain, c.1950, 32 In., Pair
$1,046.00

Skinner, Inc

Furniture, Chest, Blanket, Chippendale, Pine, Poplar, Painted Flowers, Columns, Pa., 25 x 50 In.
$9,400.00

Garth's Auctioneers & Appraisers

Furniture, Chest, Blanket, Poplar, Dovetailed, Brown Over Cream Grain, Turned Feet, c.1875, 24 x 44 In.
$1,058.00

Garth's Auctioneers & Appraisers

Furniture, Chest, Blanket, Poplar, Painted, Joseph Lehn, Miniature, 7 x 10 x 6 In.
$1,652.00

Conestoga Auction Co., Inc.

Furniture, Chest, Chippendale, Cherry, Pullout Slide, Painted Flower Baskets, c.1790, 35 x 35 In.
$3,000.00

Skinner, Inc.

Furniture, Chest, Chippendale, Mahogany, Block Front, Cock-Beaded, Brass Pulls, c.1770, 30 x 33 In.
$17,775.00

Skinner, Inc.

Furniture, Chest, Dower, Painted, Flowers, Urn, Half Drawers, Pa., c.1790, 25 x 48 In.
$4,444.00

Skinner, Inc.

Cupboard, Corner, Curly Walnut, Panel Doors, Mortise & Peg, Scalloped Apron, c.1835, 80 x 36 In.		764.00
Cupboard, Corner, Federal, Barrel Back, 3 Open Shelves, Panel Door, Gray Paint, 80 x 39 In. ...		1300.00
Cupboard, Corner, Federal, Cherry, Arched Glass Doors, 3 Shelves, Shaped Apron, 81 x 51 In....		236.00
Cupboard, Corner, Federal, Cherry, Barber Pole Inlay, 12-Pane Door, 85 x 49 In.		5900.00
Cupboard, Corner, Federal, Walnut, 20 Panes, Glazed Doors, Lower Doors, 1800s, 99 x 52 In. .. *Illus*		1534.00
Cupboard, Corner, Federal, Walnut, Rope & Tassel Inlay, Paneled Doors, c.1800, 82 x 51 In. ...		1534.00
Cupboard, Corner, George II, Oak, 2 Panel Doors, Black Paint, Gilt Trim, Carved, 74 x 32 In....		468.00
Cupboard, Corner, Glass Door, 2 Panel Doors, 2 Drawers, c.1820, 85 x 50 ½ In.		474.00
Cupboard, Corner, Glass Door, 2 Panel Doors, c.1815, 87 x 50 ½ In.		5563.00
Cupboard, Corner, Glass Door, 2 Panel Doors, Scalloped Apron, Painted, Pa., c.1920, 87 x 42 In.		5103.00
Cupboard, Corner, Grain Painted, 2 Sections, 9-Pane Door, Pa., 84 x 50 In....		1840.00
Cupboard, Corner, Hanging, Chippendale, Poplar, Pediment, Carved, Painted, c.1780, 43 x 27 In.		6325.00
Cupboard, Corner, Hanging, George III, Mahogany, Inlay, 2 Panel Doors, 41 x 36 In.....		354.00
Cupboard, Corner, Hanging, Pine, Graining, Door, Shaped Panel, Beaded Trim, c.1885, 33 x 30 In.		441.00
Cupboard, Corner, Hanging, Pine, Scalloped Sides, Red Paint, Pa., c.1800, 37 x 26 In.		3555.00
Cupboard, Corner, Hanging, Walnut, Beaded Crest, Door, c.1800, 28 x 26 In.....		533.00
Cupboard, Corner, Hard Pine, Upper Glass Door, Low Panel Doors, Painted, c.1810, 87 x 38 In.		3792.00
Cupboard, Corner, Mahogany, Maple, 12-Pane Door, American, c.1815, 44 x 32 In.....		603.00
Cupboard, Corner, Mahogany, Ogee Drawer, Panel Door, Fitted Interior, Russia, c.1850, 55 x 36 In.		633.00
Cupboard, Corner, Mahogany, Pine, Door, Geometric Panes, Hanging, c.1800, 42 x 30 In.		911.00
Cupboard, Corner, Mahogany, Pine, Shell Crested, Shaped Shelves, 2 Doors, 78 x 16 In.		885.00
Cupboard, Corner, Maple, Glass Door, Drawer, 2 Panel Doors, 58 x 30 In., Child's		334.00
Cupboard, Corner, Mixed Wood, Inlay, 2 Glass Doors, 2 Panel Doors, Tenn., c.1800, 88 x 48 In.		2990.00
Cupboard, Corner, Old Blue Paint, Stepped Cornice, 4 Paneled Doors, 76 x 54 In.....		896.00
Cupboard, Corner, Pine, 2 Doors, Red, Painted, Pa., c.1820, 76 ¼ x 38 In.		1778.00
Cupboard, Corner, Pine, 2 Sections, 12 Panes, Shelves, Lower Panel Doors, c.1810, 86 x 49 In.		7931.00
Cupboard, Corner, Pine, 2 Sections, Doors, Arched Panes, Cutout Feet, c.1835, 82 x 68 In.......		1645.00
Cupboard, Corner, Pine, 2 Sections, Paneled Doors, Blue Paint, Pa., 1800s, 84 x 52 In.		1007.00
Cupboard, Corner, Pine, Arched Glass Door, 2 Arched Panel Doors, Pa., c.1780, 94 x 50 In.....		2844.00
Cupboard, Corner, Pine, Cornice, Glass Doors, 3 Shelves, 3 Lower Drawers, c.1800, 84 x 45 In.		1067.00
Cupboard, Corner, Pine, Flame Grained, 12-Pane Door, Drawer, Panel Doors, c.1840, 89 x 46 In.		7110.00
Cupboard, Corner, Pine, Flame Grained, Fluted Pilasters, Arched Panel Doors, c.1850, 76 x 61 In.......		3819.00
Cupboard, Corner, Pine, Glass Door, Drawer, 2 Panel Doors, c.1815, 86 x 45 In.		444.00
Cupboard, Corner, Pine, Gray Paint, Beaded Door, Bracket Feet, 1800s, 60 x 43 In.....		734.00
Cupboard, Corner, Pine, Painted, Barrel Back, Door, Cornice, Bracket Feet, 1700s, 80 x 50 In.....		2703.00
Cupboard, Corner, Pine, Poplar, 2 Sections, Cornice, Panel Door, Bracket Feet, c.1815, 94 x 46 In.		738.00
Cupboard, Corner, Pine, Projecting Cornice, Arched Mullion Glazed Doors, c.1790, 99 x 59 In.		2337.00
Cupboard, Corner, Pine, Steeple Clock, 4 Panel Doors, 2 Glass Doors, 3 Drawers, 83 In......		708.00
Cupboard, Corner, Pine, Stepped, Blocked, 2 Arched Panel Doors, 2 Square Doors, c.1770, 94 x 58 In.		3318.00
Cupboard, Corner, Poplar, Panel Doors, Molded Cornice, Drawer, c.1850, 81 x 54 In.....		1645.00
Cupboard, Corner, Poplar, Raised Panel Doors, Blue Over Red Paint, c.1820, 78 x 45 In.....		5875.00
Cupboard, Corner, Poplar, Spool Turnings, Glass Panel Doors, Crest, c.1850, 87 x 48 In.		3525.00
Cupboard, Corner, Sheraton, Curly Maple, Walnut, Glass Panes, Dovetailed, c.1835, 87 In. .... *Illus*		2115.00
Cupboard, Corner, Softwood, Cornice, Paneled Blind Door, Shelves, Red Paint, 41 x 35 In......		649.00
Cupboard, Corner, Tiger Maple, 2 Sections, Dentil Cornice, 12-Pane Door, 1900s, 90 x 40 In.		2916.00
Cupboard, Corner, Tiger Maple, Curved Glass Doors, Drawer, Panel Doors, c.1860, 39 x 22 ½ In.......		2645.00
Cupboard, Corner, Walnut, 2 Glass Doors, 2 Panel Doors, Flared Feet, Va., c.1805, 90 x 51 In.		5463.00
Cupboard, Corner, Walnut, Cutout Pediment, Finials, Glass Door, 2 Panel Doors, c.1845, 37 x 17 In....		4600.00
Cupboard, Corner, Walnut, Raised Panel Doors, Cock-Beaded, c.1860, 86 x 50 In.....		2410.00
Cupboard, Corner, Yellow Paint, Glazed Door, Cupboard Doors, Shaped Apron, c.1845, 79 x 43 In.		1778.00
Cupboard, Corner, Yellow Pine, Glazed Doors, 2 Sections, c.1890, 89 x 51 In. .... *Illus*		2252.00
Cupboard, Country, Maple, Pine, Step Back, 2 Panel Doors, 2 Shelves, 72 x 44 ½ In.....		531.00
Cupboard, Country, Pine, Step Back, Scalloped Cornice, Sides, Paneled Doors, 75 x 42 In.		325.00
Cupboard, Dutch, Chippendale, Cherry, 2 Glass Doors, Drawers, 2 Panel Doors, Pa., 64 x 27 In.		1276.00
Cupboard, Dutch, Federal, Cherry, 2 Glass Doors, Drawers, Pa., c.1820, 86 x 50 In.....		3792.00
Cupboard, Dutch, Softwood, Cove Cornice, Open Shelves, 3 Drawers, 2 Doors, Pa., c.1800, 80 x 37 In.		403.00
Cupboard, Dutch, Walnut, 2 Panel Doors, Open Shelf, 2 Base Doors, c.1830, 82 x 48 In.		633.00
Cupboard, Dutch, Walnut, 2 Sections, 2 Glass Doors, 2 Drawers, 2 Panel Doors, c.1850, 82 x 49 In.		770.00
Cupboard, Dutch, Walnut, 2 Sections, Raised Panel Doors, Candle Drawers, c.1810, 84 x 50 In.		2844.00
Cupboard, Dutch, Walnut, Grain Painted, 2 Glass Doors, Drawers, Panel Doors, c.1800, 83 x 48 In.....		16590.00
Cupboard, Federal, Cherry, Inlay, Glass & Panel Doors, Drawer, Lancaster Co., c.1820, 97 x 45 In.....		54.00
Cupboard, Federal, Cherry, Vine & Flower Inlay, Broken Pediment, Finial, 1800s, 93 x 47 In......		3068.00
Cupboard, Federal, Pine, Wall, 3-Panel Frieze, Pilasters, Glass Door, Shelves, c.1800, 43 x 25 In......		830.00
Cupboard, Flame Finial Crest, Carved, Glass Doors, 2 Drawers, 2 Panel Doors, 97 x 55 In......		1180.00
Cupboard, George III, Mahogany, Scroll Gallery, Tambour Door, Square Legs, c.1780, 30 x 14 In......		474.00
Cupboard, George III, Pine, Door, Carved, Pedestal Shape, Plinth, c.1790, 17 x 17 In., Pair		4063.00

Cupboard, Grain Painted, 3 Drawers, Molded Edge, Shaped Sides, Square Feet, c.1900, 18 In.	115.00
Cupboard, Gumwood, 2 Panel Doors, Low Panel Drawers, Hudson Valley, c.1790, 68 x 55 ½ In.	7703.00
Cupboard, Hanging, 2 Doors, 3 Drawers, Pa., c.1815, 19 ½ x 33 In.	1944.00
Cupboard, Hanging, Chippendale, Pine, Panel Door, Fluted Columns, Pa., c.1780, 27 x 19 In.	3792.00
Cupboard, Hanging, Livery, White Pine, 3 Doors, Vertical Open Slats, New Eng., c.1800, 31 x 48 In.	3100.00
Cupboard, Hanging, Oak, Broken Swan Crest, 2 Glass Doors, Drawer, c.1790, 35 ½ x 31 ½ In.	711.00
Cupboard, Hanging, Pine, Door, 6 Glass Panels, Shelves, American, 1800s, 35 x 21 In.	793.00
Cupboard, Hanging, Pine, Painted, Cornice, Canted Edge, Hinged Doors, Shelves, c.1800, 21 x 22 In.	1541.00
Cupboard, Hanging, Pine, Painted, Glazed Door, Cock-Beaded, Chamfered Border, 1800s, 34 x 31 In.	1185.00
Cupboard, Hanging, Pine, Panel Door, Cornice, Continental, c.1790, 29 x 19 In.	385.00
Cupboard, Hanging, Pine, Plank Doors, Pilasters, 3 Shelves, Red Paint, 1800s, 37 x 29 In.	294.00
Cupboard, Hanging, Pine, Red Paint, Glass Paned Door, Molded Cornice, Shelf, 29 x 24 In.	885.00
Cupboard, Hanging, Poplar, Cove Cornice, 6-Pane Door, Faux Graining, American, 1800s, 35 x 32 In.	646.00
Cupboard, Hanging, Queen Anne, Walnut, Door, 2 Drawers, Scalloped Shelf, c.1760, 36 x 24 In.	5925.00
Cupboard, Hanging, Shaker, Pine, Panel Door, Dovetailed, Latch, c.1845, 24 x 24 In.	1778.00
Cupboard, Hanging, Shaker, Pine, Panel Door, Dovetailed, Molded Cornice, c.1845, 24 x 24 In.	593.00
Cupboard, Hanging, Walnut, Panel Door, Iron Hinges, Pa., c.1750, 34 x 36 In.	15405.00
Cupboard, Hanging, Walnut, Raised Panel Door, Fitted Interior, Pa., c.1755, 32 x 23 In.	10073.00
Cupboard, Hanging, Walnut, Shaped Pierced Crest, Hinged Door, Glass Panel, c.1850, 34 x 31 In.	593.00
Cupboard, Hymnal, Shaker, Pine, Glazed, 2 Glass Paned Doors, 3 Drawers, c.1850, 85 x 54 In.	2370.00
Cupboard, Jelly, 5 Hightop Drawers Over 3 Drawers, 3 Doors, 1800s, 52 x 53 ½ In.	356.00
Cupboard, Jelly, Cherry, Gallery Top, 2 Drawers, Doors, Ivory Escutcheon, c.1815, 46 x 43 In.	633.00
Cupboard, Jelly, Empire, Mahogany, Columns, Backsplash, 2 Doors, 2 Drawers, c.1840, 46 x 46 In.	729.00
Cupboard, Jelly, Federal, Cherry, Walnut, Dovetailed Drawers, Panel Doors, 1800s, 58 x 44 In.	1003.00
Cupboard, Jelly, Pine, Blue Paint, Raised Panel Door & Ends, American, 1800s, 55 x 29 In.	1175.00
Cupboard, Jelly, Pine, Flame Grain Painted, Ohio, c.1850, 46 ½ x 43 In.	1007.00
Cupboard, Jelly, Pine, Poplar, 2 Raised Panel Doors, Red Paint, Pa., c.1820, 53 x 37 In.	8888.00
Cupboard, Jelly, Poplar, Ocher Grain Painted, Pa., c.1830, 50 x 49 ½ In.	1033.00
Cupboard, Jelly, Poplar, Ocher Swirl Painted, Pa., c.1850, 48 x 36 In.	1007.00
Cupboard, Jelly, Softwood, 2 Drawers, Panel Doors, Bracket Feet, 3-Board Gallery, 52 x 41 In.	295.00
Cupboard, Jelly, Softwoods, Cutout Gallery, 2 Drawers, Over 2 Panel Doors, c.1850, 53 x 48 In.	431.00
Cupboard, Jelly, Walnut, 2 Panel Doors, Mid 1800s, 52 ½ x 37 In.	415.00
Cupboard, Jelly, Walnut, Poplar, Green Paint, 2 Panel Doors, Block Feet, 1800s, 50 x 37 In.	512.00
Cupboard, Louis XV, Fruitwood, Step Back, Molded Cornice, Shelves, Panel Doors, 90 x 54 In.	2124.00
Cupboard, Louis XV, Oak, Pewter, Upper Shelf, Dovetailed Drawers, Doors, c.1800, 92 x 74 In.	2596.00
Cupboard, Maple, Pine, 3 Parts, Removable Cornice, 3 Doors, Drawers, 1800s, 85 x 80 In.	823.00
Cupboard, Marble Top, Ormolu Mounted Panels, 2 Doors, France, c.1930, 39 x 49 In.	2124.00
Cupboard, Oak, Carved, Overhanging Hood, Doors, Drawers, Bun Feet, 18th Century, 71 x 59 In.	796.00
Cupboard, Oak, Top Gallery, Glass Door, 4 Panel Doors, 2 Drawers, Carved, Belgium, 94 x 61 In.	1416.00
Cupboard, Oak, Tracery, Doors, Projecting Crockets, Finials, Arches, Tapestries, 81 x 46 In.	2430.00
Cupboard, Oak, Upper Shelves, 2 Lower Panel Doors, Drawer, Carved, c.1800, 76 x 65 In.	830.00
Cupboard, Painted, Chip Carved Ends, Hinged Door, Block Turned Supports, c.1700, 49 x 36 In.	2844.00
Cupboard, Pennsylvania Dutch, Cherry, Glass Pane Doors, Drawers, 2 Panel Doors, 61 x 86 In.	3900.00
Cupboard, Pennsylvania Dutch, Pine, 2 Sections, Glass Doors, Panel Doors, c.1820, 84 x 56 In.	1541.00
Cupboard, Pennsylvania Dutch, Pine, 6-Pane Doors, Drawers, c.1840, 84 x 52 In.	16590.00
Cupboard, Pewter, Oak, 3 Open Upper Shelves, Lower Drawers, 2 Doors, 1800s, 61 x 79 In.	960.00
Cupboard, Pewter, Pine, 2 Sections, Shelves, Hooks, Drawers, Kneehole Shelf, 1800s, 84 x 62 In.	823.00
Cupboard, Pewter, Pine, Brown Paint, Shelves, Square Feet, 1800s, 75 x 50 In.	823.00
Cupboard, Pewter, Pine, Open Scalloped Top, 2 Drawers, 2 Doors, Rattail Hinges, 80 x 50 In.	3792.00
Cupboard, Pewter, Pine, Poplar, Scalloped, 2 Shelves, 2 Doors, Planked, Pa., c.1820, 75 x 44 In.	504.00
Cupboard, Pewter, Walnut, 3 Open Shelves, 3 Drawers, 2 Doors, c.1770, 89 x 57 In.	2133.00
Cupboard, Pewter, Walnut, Open Step Back Top, 2 Shelves, Panel Doors, c.1800, 80 x 57 In.	1185.00
Cupboard, Pine, 2 Doors, 2 Drawers, Grain Painted, New England, 60 x 36 In.	3555.00
Cupboard, Pine, 2 Shelves, Plank Door, Cutout Feet, Va., c.1820, 75 x 28 In.	920.00
Cupboard, Pine, 3 Drawers, 2 Doors, 2 Open Shelves, c.1805, 81 x 48 In.	593.00
Cupboard, Pine, 4 Doors, Red Stain, Pa., c.1850, 66 ¾ x 41 ½ In.	948.00
Cupboard, Pine, 4 Panel Doors, Red Paint, Pa., c.1820, 78 x 36 In.	6518.00
Cupboard, Pine, 6 Open Shelves, 2 Low Doors, Wide Planks, c.1850, 78 x 84 In.	729.00
Cupboard, Pine, Cornice, 4 Panel Doors, Scalloped Skirt, Grain Painted, N.J., c.1820, 73 x 46 In.	6518.00
Cupboard, Pine, Dentil, Glass Pane & Raised Panel Doors, Drawers, c.1810, 87 x 64 In. .... Illus	6025.00
Cupboard, Pine, Flame & Tiger Grain Painted, Panel Doors, c.1820, 70 x 40 In.	3555.00
Cupboard, Pine, Hanging, 2 Pane Glass Doors, Overhang Cornice, 1800s, 39 x 34 In.	411.00
Cupboard, Pine, Painted, Hanging, Door, 19th Century, 22 x 16 In.	296.00
Cupboard, Pine, Painted, Hanging, Scandinavia, c.1816, 19 ½ x 14 In.	395.00
Cupboard, Pine, Panel Door, Scalloped Apron, Painted, Pa., 59 x 35 In.	851.00
Cupboard, Pine, Paneled Door, 9-Pane Over 2 Doors, Bracket Feet, Va., c.1800, 74 x 37 In.	8888.00

Furniture, Chest, Drawers, Metal Mounts, Side Handles, Japan, c.1900, 35 x 17 x 46 In.
$150.00

Skinner, Inc.

F

Furniture, Chest, Federal, Cherry, Serpentine Top, Drawers, c.1810, 36 x 36 In.
$14,400.00

Skinner, Inc.

Furniture, Chest, Federal, Maple, Tiger Maple, Spiral Posts, Brass Pulls, c.1825, 42 x 40 In.
$1,541.00

Skinner, Inc.

Furniture, Chest, George III, Mahogany, Dressing Slide, 4 Drawers, Bracket Feet, c.1790, 33 x 37 In.
$1,554.00

Neal Auction Co.

Furniture, Chest, Hepplewhite, Birch, Pine, Drawers, Brass, New England, c.1800, 39 x 41 In. $1,116.00

Garth's Auctioneers & Appraisers

Furniture, Chest, Ivory, Ebony, Satinwood, Marble Top, Courting Figures, 1800s, 35 x 22 In. $5,750.00

Cottone Auctions

Furniture, Chest, Lid, Camphor, Dragons, Flowers, Geometric Designs, Foo Dog, Block Feet, 21 x 39 x 20 In. $130.00

Conestoga Auction Co., Inc.

Furniture, Chest, Mixed Wood, Drawers, Molded Cornice, Brass Pulls, 1800s, 15 ½ x 12 In. $325.00

Conestoga Auction Co., Inc.

Cupboard, Pine, Poplar, 4 Doors, Paneled, Molded Cornice, Fixed Shelves, c.1850, 72 x 47 In.	460.00
Cupboard, Pine, Poplar, Applied Columns, 2 Sections, Pennsylvania, 92 x 46 In.	805.00
Cupboard, Pine, Poplar, Ogee Cornice, Panel Doors, Open Shelf, 4 Drawers, c.1840, 78 x 45 In.	546.00
Cupboard, Pine, Poplar, Step Back, Panel Doors, c.1800, 74 ½ x 52 In.	1422.00
Cupboard, Pine, Recessed Panel Door, Red Paint, Pa., c.1820, 36 x 22 In.	5832.00
Cupboard, Pine, Red Paint, Flat-Molded Cornice, Hinged Doors, Cutout Feet, c.1795, 50 x 39 In.	1541.00
Cupboard, Pine, Red Paint, Glass Doors, 2 Doors, Panel Doors, 1800s, 89 x 58 In.	2500.00
Cupboard, Pine, Red Stain, 2 Drawers, 2 Doors, Pa., c.1850, 42 x 45 ½ In.	770.00
Cupboard, Pine, Scalloped Shelves, Door, Red Stain, c.1820, 72 ½ x 36 In.	948.00
Cupboard, Pine, Step Back, 2 Shelves, 2 Drawers, Over Door, c.1830, 73 x 43 In.	1180.00
Cupboard, Pine, Step Back, Raised Panel Doors, Blue Gray Paint Over Red, c.1810, 71 x 33 In.	2350.00
Cupboard, Poplar, Grain Painted, 2 Sections, Panel Doors, Dutch, Pa., c.1850, 84 x 51 In.	6518.00
Cupboard, Poplar, Plank Door, Blue Paint, American, 1800s, 48 x 31 In.	588.00
Cupboard, Raised Panel Doors, Painted, Overhang Top, Bracket Feet, Canada, 74 x 57 In.	1888.00
Cupboard, Regency, Mahogany, Brass, Arched Doors, Drawer, Low Doors, c.1825, 88 x 43 In.	3750.00
Cupboard, Renaissance Style, Stepped Cornice, Panel Door, Turned Supports, Knights, 95 x 59 In.	625.00
Cupboard, Rococo, Mahogany, Marquetry, Arched Doors, 3 Drawers, c.1830, 91 x 65 In.	12000.00
Cupboard, Shaker, 14 Drawers, Brown, Salmon Paint, Canterbury, N.H., c.1860, 40 x 19 In.	22515.00
Cupboard, Shaker, Infirmary, Pine, Red Finish, Canted Foot, Turned Pulls, 86 x 34 In.	111150.00
Cupboard, Shaker, Pine, Cupboard Doors, 6 Drawers, Turned Pulls, c.1800, 91 x 42 In.	3555.00
Cupboard, Shaker, Pine, Door, 5 Drawers, Turned Cherry Knobs, c.1835, 83 x 33 In.	3437.00
Cupboard, Shaker, Pine, Door, 10 Drawers, White Porcelain Knobs, c.1875, 69 x 39 In.	2252.00
Cupboard, Shaker, Sister's, Pine, 2 Doors, 6 Drawers, Dovetailed, 62 x 42 In. .... *Illus*	122850.00
Cupboard, Shaker, Sister's, Top Doors, 10 Drawers, Mt. Lebanon, c.1850, 66 x 53 In. .... *Illus*	4740.00
Cupboard, Softwood, Painted, 2 Doors, Molded Cornice, Panel Doors, 74 x 52 In.	1121.00
Cupboard, Softwoods, 2 Panel Doors, Over 2 Short Doors, Painted, Va., c.1855, 67 x 31 In.	2760.00
Cupboard, Southern Walnut, Paneled Doors, Latch Closure, Bracket Feet, 59 x 38 In.	620.00
Cupboard, Step Back, 3 Open Shelves, 3 Plate Rails, 2 Panel Doors, Red Paint, 83 x 48 In.	4366.00
Cupboard, Step Back, Cherry, Green Paint, 4 Panel Doors, Bracket Feet, 1800s, 82 x 43 In.	1058.00
Cupboard, Step Back, Grain Painted, Scalloped Molding, Glass Doors, c.1890, 19 x 34 In.	345.00
Cupboard, Step Back, Mixed Wood, 2 Glass Doors, 2 Raised Panel Doors, c.1850, 80 x 46 In.	1035.00
Cupboard, Step Back, Pine, 2 Open Shelves, Panel Door, Blue Paint, c.1960, 77 ½ x 39 ½ In.	708.00
Cupboard, Step Back, Pine, Poplar, Grain Painted, Glazed Doors, Ohio, c.1850, 83 In. .... *Illus*	588.00
Cupboard, Step Back, Pine, Poplar, Open Top, 2 Shelves, Plank Door, 1800s, 74 x 32 In.	2468.00
Cupboard, Step Back, Poplar, 2 Sections, 6-Pane Doors, Drawers, c.1850, 85 x 51 In.	5288.00
Cupboard, Step Back, Walnut, 2 Glass Doors, 2 Panel Doors, Va., c.1845, 72 x 44 In.	8050.00
Cupboard, Step Back, Walnut, 2 Sections, Paneled Doors, Drawers, Cornice, c.1850, 87 x 51 In.	1175.00
Cupboard, Step Back, Wood, 2 Panel Doors, Red Paint, Pa., c.1820, 78 ½ x 40 In.	5688.00
Cupboard, Victorian, Oak, Stepped Cornice, Glazed & Paneled Doors, Drawers, Footed, 85 x 40 In.	300.00
Cupboard, Victorian, Walnut, Hanging, Blind Door, Shaped Back Board, Gallery Cornice, 35 x 26 In.	177.00
Cupboard, Wall, Grain Painted, Molded Cornice, Glazed Hinged Doors, Drawer, c.1800, 39 x 30 In.	889.00
Cupboard, Wall, Grained Paint, Door, Over 4 Drawers, Bleached Case, Ohio, c.1840, 82 x 37 In.	593.00
Cupboard, Wall, Pine, 2 Panel Doors, Green Paint, N.J., c.1830, 77 x 59 ¼ In.	9480.00
Cupboard, Wall, Pine, Painted, Green, Black, Blue, 1800s, 58 x 36 In.	2252.00
Cupboard, Walnut, 2 Glass Doors, 2 Doors, 2 Panel Doors, Pa., c.1810, 87 x 52 In.	2015.00
Cupboard, Walnut, 3 Open Shelves, Scalloped, 3 Drawers, 2 Doors, Pa., c.1775, 78 x 55 In.	8888.00
Cupboard, Walnut, 4 Panel Doors, Yellow Paint, Chillicothe, Ohio, c.1800, 95 x 64 x 20 In.	705.00
Cupboard, Walnut, Fluted Sides, Open Shelf, Over 2 Panel Doors, 69 x 47 In.	295.00
Cupboard, Walnut, Pine, Crotch Doors, Columns, 2 Drawers, Block Feet, c.1840, 39 x 26 In.	3995.00
Cupboard, Walnut, Raised Panel Doors, Shaped Bracket Base, c.1820, 71 x 20 In.	499.00
Cupboard, Walnut, Step Back, 12 Glass Panes Over 2 Doors, Shelves, c.1830, 73 x 44 In. .... *Illus*	8050.00
Cupboard, Walnut, Winged Putti Heads, Doors, Drawers, Bun Feet, 1800s, 83 x 46 In.	1337.00
Cupboard, Welsh, Oak, Shelves, Drawers, Doors, Bracket Feet, 80 x 67 In. .... *Illus*	4500.00
Cupboard, Welsh, Pine, 3 Open Shelves, Flanking Cabinets, 3 Drawers, 1800s, 72 x 73 In.	793.00
Cupboard, Welsh, Yew, Open Top, Scalloped Cornice, c.1750, 92 x 78 In.	3318.00
Daybed, Arts & Crafts, Oak, Leather Upholstery, Lifetime, c.1910, 23 ½ x 79 ½ In.	267.00
Daybed, B. Mathsson, Birch, Cotton Webbing, Upcurved Headrest, Sweden, c.1936, 21 x 90 In.	7500.00
Daybed, Bamboo Style, Brass Frame, Upholstered, Tufted Seat, Pillow Rolls, 1900s, 30 x 78 In.	316.00
Daybed, Bentwood Twig Base, Woven Seat, Old Hickory, Marked, 74 x 29 x 18 In.	900.00
Daybed, Black Slats, Slanted, Cushion, J.M. Young, 75 ½ x 28 ½ In.	1220.00
Daybed, CiteOak, Fabric, Blue Lacquered Steel, c.1949, 21 x 98 In.	37500.00
Daybed, Empire, Mahogany, Bronze Mounted Columns, France, c.1840, 41 x 77 In.	900.00
Daybed, Folding, Campaign Style, Tufted Red Leather, Brass, Steel Frame, 40 x 36 ½ In.	2337.00
Daybed, J. Adnet, Brass, Spindled Frame, Curved, Leather, France, 1940s, 86 x 35 In.	9375.00
Daybed, Louis Philippe, Mahogany, Head, Footboard, Turned Finials, c.1875, 39 x 77 In.	738.00
Daybed, Louis XV Style, Walnut, Carved, Molded Rails, Cabriole Legs, c.1900, 37 x 78 In.	922.00

Daybed, Wood, White Paint, Curved Swan Head Terminals, c.1900, 25 x 83 In. 500.00
Daybed, Woven Seat, Bentwood Twig Base, Marked Old Hickory, 74 x 29 In. 1098.00
Desk & Chair, Frankl, Mahogany, Cork, Leather, Brass, Aluminum, Johnson, 1950s, 59 In. .. *Illus* 5000.00
Desk Inset, Hardwood, 3 Drawers, Cubbyholes, Dividers, Chinese, 7 ¼ x 19 In. 295.00
Desk, Aalto, Birch, 5 Drawers, Square Legs, Casters, Rolling Cabinet, c.1948, 29 x 45 In. 1250.00
Desk, Aluminum, Bakelite Pulls, P.B. Cow & Co., Hunting Aviation Ltd., c.1945, 30 x 46 In. .. *Illus* 1320.00
Desk, Anglo-Indian, Rosewood, Leaves, Flowers, Carved, 2 Drawers, c.1805, 31 x 48 In. 1800.00
Desk, Architect, George III, Mahogany, Ratchet Top, 2 Drawers, 31 x 36 In. 1188.00
Desk, Art Deco Style, Lacquered, T-Shape, Geometric, Drawers, 29 x 45 In. .... *Illus* 1000.00
Desk, Art Deco, Burl, Rounded Corners, Drawers, Door, Pedestals, Square Legs, 31 x 63 In. 813.00
Desk, Art Deco, Drop Front, Mahogany, Arched Gallery, Columnar Legs, 1920s, 46 x 19 ½ In. 250.00
Desk, Arts & Crafts, Drop Front, Quartersawn Oak, England, c.1910, 48 x 29 In. .... *Illus* 250.00
Desk, Arts & Crafts, Oak, Oak Veneer, Drawer, Hammered Pulls, Shelf, c.1912, 30 x 36 x 24 In....... 385.00
Desk, Arts & Crafts, Oak, Stepped Top, 5 Kneehole Flanked Drawers, c.1925, 50 x 32 In. 500.00
Desk, Biedermeier, Cylinder Roll Top, Veneers, Leather Inset Surface, Drawers, 44 x 49 In............. 1208.00
Desk, Burl Walnut, 2 Wells, Lift Top, Bronze Mounts, c.1880, 15 x 10 In. 354.00
Desk, Burl Walnut, Drawer, Trestle Legs, Spindle Supports, England, 30 x 34 In............................. 840.00
Desk, Butler's, Drop Front, Fitted Interior, 3 Doors, Shelves, Mahogany, England, c.1890. .... 1770.00
Desk, Campaign, Mahogany, Folding, Leatherette Fitted Interior, Inkwell, 38 x 22 In. 587.00
Desk, Campaign, Mahogany, Leather, Fitted Well, 13 Drawers, Brassbound, Eng., 59 x 30 In. 7552.00
Desk, Captain's, Mahogany Veneers, Fold-Out Top, Fitted Interior, 2 Drawers, c.1850, 34 x 32 In... 295.00
Desk, Captain's, Sheraton, Mahogany, Hinged Top, Side & Front Drawer, 37 x 30 In....................... 1062.00
Desk, Cherry, Drawer, Fitted Interior, Pa., 33 ½ x 29 In.. 182.00
Desk, Chippendale Style, Mahogany, Leather, Shaped Apron, Bail Handles, c.1900, 31 x 54 In. 598.00
Desk, Chippendale Style, Slant Front, Mahogany, Ball & Claw Feet, Brass Pulls, 42 x 36 In............. 161.00
Desk, Chippendale, Drop Front, Fitted Interior, Drawers, Ormolu Brass, c.1770, 45 x 41 In. 37200.00
Desk, Chippendale, Drop Front, Mahogany, Doors, Fitted Interior, 4 Drawers, c.1765, 95 x 40 In. .. 1896.00
Desk, Chippendale, Drop Front, Mahogany, Serpentine, Ball & Claw Feet, c.1765, 45 x 42 In......... 8750.00
Desk, Chippendale, Drop Front, Oxbow, 4 Graduated Drawers, Claw Feet, 42 x 41 In...................... 1150.00
Desk, Chippendale, Drop Front, Walnut, Fitted Interior, Drawers, Pa., c.1780, 45 x 41 In. 2607.00
Desk, Chippendale, Slant Front, Cherry, Fitted Interior, Drawers, 21 x 22 ½ In., Child's................. 1770.00
Desk, Chippendale, Slant Front, Cherry, Fitted Interior, Drawers, Mass., c.1770, 43 x 40 In........... 4740.00
Desk, Chippendale, Slant Front, Cherry, Fitted Interior, Inlay, Drawers, Columns, 44 x 38 In......... 3776.00
Desk, Chippendale, Slant Front, Cherry, Reeded Quarter Columns, Bracket Feet, c.1795, 44 x 36 In. 711.00
Desk, Chippendale, Slant Front, Cherry, Thumb-Molded Drawers, Bracket Feet, c.1795, 42 x 40 In.. 593.00
Desk, Chippendale, Slant Front, Curly Maple, Hinged, Dovetailed, Bracket Feet, c.1760, 41 x 36 In.. 4818.00
Desk, Chippendale, Slant Front, Fitted Interior, 4 Drawers, Brass Handles, Ogee Feet, 41 x 36 In.... 2574.00
Desk, Chippendale, Slant Front, Fitted Interior, 4 Graduated Drawers, 39 x 45 In............................ 431.00
Desk, Chippendale, Slant Front, Mahogany, Block Front, Cock-Beaded Drawers, c.1770, 42 x 39 In. 4740.00
Desk, Chippendale, Slant Front, Mahogany, Fitted Interior, 4 Drawers, Ma., 43 x 37 In................... 1062.00
Desk, Chippendale, Slant Front, Mahogany, Fitted Interior, 4 Graduated Drawers, 41 x 41 In......... 649.00
Desk, Chippendale, Slant Front, Mahogany, Pine, Drawers, Fitted Interior, c.1860, 42 x 31 In........ 999.00
Desk, Chippendale, Slant Front, Maple, Cubbyholes, 4 Graduated Drawers, c.1780, 42 x 36 In....... 1150.00
Desk, Chippendale, Slant Front, Maple, Fitted Interior, 4 Drawers, c.1790, 42 x 37 ¾ In................. 826.00
Desk, Chippendale, Slant Front, Maple, Fitted Interior, 4 Graduated Drawers, Apron, 44 x 38 In.... 354.00
Desk, Chippendale, Slant Front, Maple, Fitted Interior, Drawers, c.1790, 41 x 41 In. .... *Illus* 2596.00
Desk, Chippendale, Slant Front, Maple, Pine, Drawers, Bracket Feet, c.1800, 41 x 36 In............... 823.00
Desk, Chippendale, Slant Front, Maple, Thumb-Molded, Fitted Interior, Drawers, 40 x 37 In......... 590.00
Desk, Chippendale, Slant Front, Mixed Wood, Fitted Interior, 5 Drawers, c.1790, 43 x 40 In......... 1610.00
Desk, Chippendale, Slant Front, Pine, Fitted Interior, New England, 5 Drawers, 38 x 35 In. 767.00
Desk, Chippendale, Slant Front, Walnut, 4 Drawers, Pa., c.1800, 42 x 46 In. 770.00
Desk, Chippendale, Slant Front, Walnut, Fitted Interior, 4 Drawers, Pa., c.1730, 41 x 38 In............. 21015.00
Desk, Chippendale, Slant Front, Walnut, Inlay, Fitted Interior, Drawers, c.1800, 40 x 38 In........... 593.00
Desk, Chippendale, Slant Front, Walnut, Inside Drawers, Compartments, c.1770, 43 x 37 In...*Illus* 3000.00
Desk, Chippendale, Slant Front, Walnut, Maple, Stepped Interior, Boston, 43 x 36 In................... 1180.00
Desk, Chippendale, Slant Front, Walnut, Pinwheel, Fans, Wooden Pulls, c.1790, 42 x 36 In......... 3555.00
Desk, Clerk's, Federal, Slant Front, Walnut, Drawer, Fitted, Turned Legs, 44 x 40 In. 1230.00
Desk, Clerk's, Slant Front, Mahogany, Balustrade Gallery, 2 Drawers, Doors, c.1880, 54 x 36 In. 600.00
Desk, Clerk's, Walnut, Foldover Lid, Fitted Interior, Drawers, Turned Legs, c.1800, 48 x 34 In......... 1135.00
Desk, Counting House, Slant Front, 2 Lids, Mahogany, 2 Drawers, Turned Legs, c.1860, 51 x 49 In. 2596.00
Desk, Davenport, Slant Front, Gothic Revival, Mahogany, Tracery, Arched Panels, c.1850, 31 x 19 In. 492.00
Desk, Davenport, Slant Front, Victorian, Walnut, Gallery, Fitted Interior, Drawers, 33 x 23 In......... 406.00
Desk, Drop Front, Kimbel & Cabus, Oak, Brass Enamel, Felt, 1870s, 54 x 36 In. .... *Illus* 1500.00
Desk, Drop Front, Tabletop, Walnut, Flower Decoupage Tablets, Oval, Drawers, c.1800, 9 x 18 In.. 920.00
Desk, Drop Leaf, Mahogany, Leather, 2 Drawers, Turned Stretcher, Henredon, 36 x 24 In................ 232.00
Desk, Dutch Style, Bombe, Marquetry, Mahogany Veneer, Blister Front, c.1910, 37 x 45 In. 1323.00

Furniture, Chest, Norman Bel Geddes, Enamel, Steel, Simmons, c.1930, 44 x 39 In.
$750.00

Los Angeles Modern Auctions (LAMA)

Furniture, Chest, Queen Anne, Cherry, Shell Carving, c.1750, 72 x 37 ½ In.
$2,963.00

Skinner, Inc.

Furniture, Chest, Queen Anne, Tiger Maple, Drawers, Brass Hardware, New England, c.1790, 69 x 36 In.
$10,800.00

Skinner, Inc.

F

Furniture, Chest, Tiger Maple, Cherry, 7 Drawers, Brass Bail Pulls, Moses Osborn, c.1790, 63 In.
$17,775.00

Skinner, Inc.

Furniture, Chest, William & Mary, Circassion Walnut, Inlay, Drawers, c.1710, 66 x 42 In.
$4,182.00

New Orleans Auction Galleries, Inc.

Furniture, Chest-On-Frame, William & Mary Style, Japanned, Drawers, X-Stretcher, 62 x 41 In.
$1,541.00

Skinner, Inc.

Desk, Eames, Birch Plywood, Masonite, Open Shelf, Drawers, Steel Legs, c.1950, 29 x 60 In.	2800.00
Desk, Ebonized, Drawers, Cupboard Doors, Legs, Geometric & Leaf Design, c.1900, 32 x 54 In.	2952.00
Desk, Edwardian, Burl Walnut, Kidney Shape, Cabriole Legs, c.1900, 32 x 49 x 26 In.	2151.00
Desk, Edwardian, Drop Front, Satinwood, Brass, Fitted Interior, Drawer, 44 x 26 In.	234.00
Desk, Edwardian, Drop Front, Wood, Brass Gallery, Inlay, 2 Drawers, c.1910, 42 x 30 In.	120.00
Desk, Edwardian, Mixed Wood, Leather Inset, Kneehole, Drawers, England, 29 x 42 In.	1093.00
Desk, Edwardian, Satinwood, Leather Surface, U-Shape, Apron, 1800s, 37 x 42 In.	2800.00
Desk, Elm, 2 Pedestals, Shelves, Drawers, Puddingstone Top, Chinese, c.1890, 34 x 49 In. .... *Illus*	235.00
Desk, Empire Style, Ebonized Mahogany, Inset, Marble Top, Tapered Legs, c.1860, 34 x 47 In.	1250.00
Desk, Empire Style, Mahogany, Ebonized, Leather Top, Curule Supports, Frieze Drawers, 30 x 44 In. .	1046.00
Desk, Empire Style, Marble, Mahogany, Gilt, Lyre Supports, France, c.1905, 30 x 59 In.	1610.00
Desk, Empire, Drop Front, Marble Top, Fitted Interior, 4 Drawers, France, c.1840, 56 x 40 In.	1080.00
Desk, Federal, Drop Front, Mahogany, Drawers, Bracket Feet, c.1800, 43 x 43 In.	1195.00
Desk, Federal, Drop Front, Walnut, Panel Doors, Molding, Bracket Feet, c.1850, 56 x 31 In.	598.00
Desk, Federal, Mahogany, Arch Glass Doors, Over 4 Drawers, c.1820, 52 x 40 In.	1265.00
Desk, Federal, Slant Front, Fitted Interior, 4 Drawers, Brass Hardware, 43 ½ x 38 In.	649.00
Desk, Federal, Slant Front, Pine, Red Wash, Frieze Drawer, Square Legs, c.1800, 40 x 22 In.	896.00
Desk, Federal, Slant Front, Walnut, Fitted Interior, Drawers, Inlay, Pa., c.1805, 41 x 40 In.	504.00
Desk, Federal, Slant Front, Walnut, Fitted Interior, Slides, Drawers, Apron, 45 x 40 In.	431.00
Desk, G. Nakashima, Walnut, Pedestal, Drawers, X-Shape Support Feet, 1967, 29 x 60 In.	8125.00
Desk, G. Nelson, Drawer, Mesh Basket, Sliding Doors, Metal Legs, 1946, 41 x 55 In.	4375.00
Desk, G. Stickley, Drop Front, Fitted Interior, Copper Strap Hardware, Decal, 26 x 12 In.	10980.00
Desk, George II Style, Black Lacquer, Fisherman, Lake, Pagoda, Bun Feet, 1800s, 30 x 42 In.	750.00
Desk, George III Style, Mahogany, Pierced Fretwork, Drawers, Ball & Claw Feet, 31 x 50 In.	1107.00
Desk, George III Style, Mahogany, Serpentine Front, Frieze Drawer, Tapered Legs, 29 x 34 In.	1250.00
Desk, George III Style, Walnut, Canted Corners, Drawers, Cabriole Legs, Shell, c.1900, 31 x 53 In.	615.00
Desk, George III, Burl Walnut, Tambour, Cock-Beaded Drawer, c.1805, 6 ½ x 14 In.	354.00
Desk, George III, Kneehole, Crossbanded, Molded Edge, Apron, Cupboard, c.1800, 28 x 32 In.	438.00
Desk, George III, Slant Front, Mahogany, Fitted Interior, 4 Drawers, c.1770, 40 ½ x 42 In.	395.00
Desk, George III, Slant Front, Mahogany, Fitted Interior, 5 Drawers, c.1800, 43 x 41 In.	750.00
Desk, George III, Slant Front, Mixed Wood, Opposing Lids, Banded, c.1800, 35 x 21 In.	1375.00
Desk, Georgian, Slant Front, Mahogany, Fitted Interior, 4 Drawers, c.1810, 41 x 40 In.	633.00
Desk, Georgian, Slant Front, Mahogany, Shaped Gallery, Cupboard, Trestle Base, 1800s, 36 x 24 In.	369.00
Desk, Gerald McCabe, Orange Crate Modern, Eon Furniture, c.1970, 29 x 60 In.	313.00
Desk, Gilt Leather Top, Ebonized Frame, 5 Drawers, Tapered Legs, Jansen, c.1940, 31 x 59 In.	2280.00
Desk, Gothic Revival, Slant Front, Ebonized, Lift Top, Scrolled Back, c.1850, 58 x 51 In.	5676.00
Desk, Hardwood, Open Fitted Top, Folding Writing Surface, 7 Drawers, 40 x 34 ½ In.	5192.00
Desk, Helge Vestergaard Jensen, Rosewood, Teak, Square Legs, c.1950, 31 x 59 In.	12500.00
Desk, Hepplewhite, Drop Front, Cherry, Fitted Interior, 4 Drawers, c.1800, 48 x 39 In.	767.00
Desk, Hepplewhite, Mahogany, Inlaid Banding, Mass., c.1800, 48 x 39 In.	444.00
Desk, Hepplewhite, Slant Front, Cherry, Fitted Interior, 4 Drawers, Flared Feet, New Eng., 45 x 44 In.	413.00
Desk, Hepplewhite, Slant Front, Mahogany, 4 Drawers, c.1790, 44 x 42 In.	738.00
Desk, Hepplewhite, Slant Front, Walnut, 3 Graduated Drawers, Fitted Interior, 42 x 41 In.	767.00
Desk, Hepplewhite, Slant Front, Walnut, Stand-Up, Fitted Interior, Drawer, c.1820, 44 In.	316.00
Desk, Jacaranda, Gianfranco Frattini, Brass, Tambour Top, Y Legs, Stretcher, 1950s, 38 x 51 In.	2500.00
Desk, Jean Prouve, Oak, Lacquered Steel, 8 Drawers, c.1943, 30 x 79 In.	56250.00
Desk, Jeanneret, Teak, Side Skirt, Squared V Legs, Stretchers, c.1960, 28 x 32 In.	1875.00
Desk, Kai Kristiansen, Teak, Floating Top, Openwork Frame, Denmark, 1960s, 60 x 32 In. ... *Illus*	1067.00
Desk, Karl Springer, Leather, Chrome Steel, Rounded Corners, Drawer, 1970s, 29 x 59 In.	6563.00
Desk, Kneehole, English Oak, 9 Drawers, Black Leather Top, Gold Tooled Edge, 1800s, 42 x 23 In.	1700.00
Desk, Kneehole, Mahogany, 7 Drawers, Door, c.1750, 28 ¾ x 28 ½ In.	711.00
Desk, Kneehole, Mahogany, Bookcase, Carved, Glass Doors, Scroll Panes, c.1830, 89 x 25 In.	3000.00
Desk, Kneehole, Mahogany, Recessed Door, Bail Handles, Bracket Feet, c.1750, 31 x 34 In.	711.00
Desk, Kneehole, Mahogany, Serpentine Top, 3 Drawers, Carved Eagle Supports, c.1900, 32 x 52 In.	738.00
Desk, L. & J.G. Stickley, No. 401, 2 Drawers, Shaped Backsplash, 34 x 34 x 20 In.	1500.00
Desk, Lady's, Drop Front, Walnut, Compartments, Open Shelf, c.1890, 60 x 29 In.	374.00
Desk, Lady's, Rosewood, Pierced Crest, Cupboard Door, Peg Feet, Chinese, c.1890, 48 x 36 In.	4182.00
Desk, Louis XV Style, Ebonized, Bronze, Drawers, Shaped Skirt, Cabriole Legs, 31 x 47 In.	885.00
Desk, Louis XV Style, Inlay, Bronze, Leather Top, Flaming Urn Appliques, 1900s, 32 x 60 In.	2832.00
Desk, Louis XV Style, Ormolu Mounts, Fitted Interior, Medial Shelf, 28 x 24 In.	395.00
Desk, Louis XV Style, Tulipwood, Marquetry, Gilt, Hinged Top, 4 Drawers, c.1890, 30 x 34 In.	406.00
Desk, Louis XV Style, Walnut Veneer, Arch Crest, Cabriole Legs, c.1900, 47 x 36 In.	472.00
Desk, Louis XV, Tulipwood, Ormolu, 3 Drawers, c.1740, 30 x 52 In.	5625.00
Desk, Louis XV, Walnut, Drawers, Central Recess, Cabriole Legs, c.1755, 31 x 62 In.	650.00
Desk, Louis XVI Style, Satinwood, Ormolu, Kidney Shape, Letter Boxes, 1900s, 39 In.	270.00
Desk, Louis XVI Style, Wood, Leather, Bronze Mounts, Reeded Legs, c.1900, 30 x 39 In.	2640.00
Desk, Lovig, Rosewood, Flip Top, Gallery, Square Legs, Denmark, 1960s, 34 x 64 In.	3750.00

Desk, Mahogany, Maple, Inlay, 2 Setback Arched Doors, 2 Drawers, c.1800, 41 x 39 In.	3410.00
Desk, Mahogany, Ormolu, Inset Leather Top, 3 Drawers, France, c.1900, 32 x 51 In.	952.00
Desk, Mahogany, Pine, Slant Front, Drawers, Bracket Feet, c.1815, 48 x 38 In.	940.00
Desk, Marquetry Scrolls, Mahogany, Satinwood, Leather, S&H Jewell, c.1910, 30 x 54 In.	875.00
Desk, Marquetry, Inset Leather Top, Apron Drawer, Cabriole Legs, France, 29 x 44 In.	489.00
Desk, Mixed Wood, Drawers, Openwork Stretcher, Chinese, c.1800, 32 x 47 x 26 In.	590.00
Desk, Mother-Of-Pearl, Lacquer, Slanted Hinged Lid, Church, Compartments, c.1850, 11 ¾ x 16 In.	243.00
Desk, Nanna Ditzel, Teak, Drawers, 1950s, 28 ¾ x 57 x 29 ½ In.	3750.00
Desk, Napoleon III, Amboyna, Ebonized, Gilt, Gallery, Leather, Drawers, Oval, 38 x 46 In.	2000.00
Desk, Neoclassical Style, Leather Top, Ormolu, Garland Handles, 1800s, 31 x 73 In.	1320.00
Desk, Neoclassical Style, Mahogany, Inlay, 3 Drawers, Faux Ivory Supports, 35 x 70 In.	2124.00
Desk, Oak, Rocaille Carved, Kidney Shape, Kneehole, 6 Drawers, Paw Feet, 31 x 48 In.	861.00
Desk, On Frame, Lift Lid, Stretcher, Pa., 19th Century, 40 x 22 In.	504.00
Desk, On Frame, Pine, Divided Interior, Tapered Leg Base, Stretchers, c.1850, 47 x 48 In.	353.00
Desk, On Frame, Slant Front, Pine, Butterfly Hinges, Turned Legs, Shelves, c.1700, 38 x 37 In.	649.00
Desk, On Frame, William & Mary, Slant Front, Hard Pine, Baluster Turned Legs, 35 x 34 In.	1416.00
Desk, Partners, Edwardian, Shaped, Slanted Top, 6 Side Drawers, c.1880, 34 x 66 In.	480.00
Desk, Partners, Flip Top, Teak, Pigeonholes, Drawers, Block Legs, Lovig, 1960s, 34 x 64 In.	2875.00
Desk, Partners, George III Style, Mahogany, Frieze Drawers, Cupboard, c.1900, 31 x 60 In.	738.00
Desk, Partners, George III Style, Mahogany, Leather, 6 Drawers, Reverse Door, 30 x 59 In.	702.00
Desk, Partners, Pedestals, George III Style, Mahogany, Drawers, Cupboard, 1900s, 30 x 60 In.	1845.00
Desk, Partners, Pedestals, Tooled Leather Top, 3 Drawers In Each, England, 31 x 66 In.	2242.00
Desk, Partners, Regency, Mahogany, Pine, Drawers, Turned Legs, Leather, 1800s, 31 x 71 In.	2233.00
Desk, Partners, William IV, Mahogany, Leather Top, Tapered Reeded Legs, 29 x 54 In. .... *Illus*	953.00
Desk, Partners, Wormley, Leather, 5 Drawers, Tapered Legs, 1940s, 30 x 56 In.	2750.00
Desk, Pearwood, 2 Drawers, Side Cartonnier, c.1940, 37 x 45 In.	2000.00
Desk, Plantation, Pine, 2 Panel Doors, Fitted Interior, Slides, Drawer, 61 x 44 In.	575.00
Desk, Plantation, Poplar, 2 Sections, 2 Blind Doors, Slotted Interior, Drawers, c.1850, 86 x 41 In. .	588.00
Desk, Plantation, Sheraton, Slant Front, Walnut, Turned Legs, Ball Feet, c.1850, 41 x 73 In.	3444.00
Desk, Plantation, Slant Front, Cherry, Letter Slots, Scroll Gallery, 2 Drawers, 39 x 61 In.	1195.00
Desk, Plantation, Slant Front, Walnut, Case Top, 2 Fitted Cabinets, 57 x 43 In.	1793.00
Desk, Queen Anne, Drop Front, Mahogany, Fitted Interior, 4 Drawers, Pa., c.1740, 40 x 36 In.	2133.00
Desk, Queen Anne, Slant Front, Cherry, Fitted Interior, 4 Drawers, 42 x 36 In.	770.00
Desk, Queen Anne, Slant Front, Figured Walnut, Storage Compartment, 4 Drawers, 37 x 28 In.	1534.00
Desk, Queen Anne, Slant Front, Maple, Fitted Interior, 3 Drawers, c.1750, 39 x 33 In.	938.00
Desk, Queen Anne, Slant Front, Tiger Maple, Fitted Interior, Drawers, New Eng., c.1770, 41 x 36 In.	770.00
Desk, Queen Anne, Slant Front, Walnut, 4 Drawers, Brass Pulls, 40 x 36 In.	1495.00
Desk, Queen Anne, Slant Front, Walnut, Pa., c.1760, 41 x 36 In.	1126.00
Desk, Queen Anne, Slant Front, Walnut, Pine, Drawers, Ogee Feet, c.1760, 44 x 40 In.	9640.00
Desk, Regency Style, Leather Top, Slides, 2 Drawers, c.1940, 30 ½ x 39 ½ In.	960.00
Desk, Regency, Slant Front, Mahogany, Shaped Apron, Square Feet, c.1800, 44 x 39 In.	850.00
Desk, Rohde, Paldao, Rosewood, Brass, 2 Pedestals, Drawers, Kidney Shape Top, 1930s, 30 x 57 In.	3250.00
Desk, Roll Top, C Roll, French Regency Style, Rosewood, Trestle, E. Bleu, 44 x 44 In.	1440.00
Desk, Roll Top, C Roll, Neoclassical, Marquetry, Shell, Flower Swags, Dutch, 43 x 33 In.	1265.00
Desk, Roll Top, C Roll, Neoclassical, Walnut, Inlay, Fitted Interior, 3 Drawers, 40 x 45 In.	2125.00
Desk, Roll Top, C Roll, Walnut, Serrated Edge, Carved Frieze, Paneled Lid, c.1890, 48 x 43 In.	295.00
Desk, Roll Top, C Roll, Walnut, Spindle Gallery, Doors, Drawers, Molded, c.1898, 63 x 35 In.	777.00
Desk, Roll Top, Herman Miller, Tambour, Fitted Interior, Metal Base, c.1970, 33 x 49 In.	840.00
Desk, Roll Top, Mahogany, Brass Gallery, Marble, Fitted Interior, 4 Drawers, 27 x 2 In.	1250.00
Desk, Roll Top, Mahogany, Pierced Brass Gallery, Mirror, Fitted Interior, Drawers, 59 x 32 In.	625.00
Desk, Roll Top, Oak, Drawers, Kneehole, 12 Pigeonholes, Cross Support, 42 x 60 In. .... *Illus*	330.00
Desk, Roll Top, Rococo, Mahogany, Fitted Interior, Figural Panels, Drawers, T. Rang, Dutch	3240.00
Desk, Rosewood, 7 Drawers, Ole Wanscher, Denmark, c.1950, 29 x 66 In.	2500.00
Desk, Rosewood, Fretwork Crest, Shelves, Drawers, Cupboard, Pierced Apron, c.1890, 48 x 36 In.	1968.00
Desk, Rosewood, Glass Top, 2 Drawers, Tapered Legs, c.1960, 32 x 51 In.	480.00
Desk, Roycroft, Drop Front, Drawer, Bail Handles, Tapered Legs, c.1905, 44 x 39 In.	4063.00
Desk, Roycroft, Mahogany, 5 Drawers, Block Legs, Casters, c.1905, 30 x 60 In.	4375.00
Desk, Ruhlmann, Oak, Canvas, Drawer, Round Tapered Legs, France, c.1933, 30 x 47 In.	8100.00
Desk, S. Hedges, Mahogany, Drawer, Hinged, Opens To Chair, c.1854, 29 x 35 In.	4481.00
Desk, School, Lift Top, Pine, Double, Shoe Feet, Pa., c.1810, 27 x 46 In.	356.00
Desk, School, Oak, Attached Chair, Child's .... *Illus*	84.00
Desk, School, Oak, Iron Frame, Painted, Fold Down Seat, Inkwell Hole, c.1872, 29 x 22 In., Pair ..	108.00
Desk, School, Wood, Push Top, Attached Chair, Child's	660.00
Desk, Schoolmaster's, Drop Front, Pine, Maple, Fan Carved Interior, Drawer, 37 x 30 In.	295.00
Desk, Schoolmaster's, Slant Front, Green Paint, Signed S. Cohen, Pa., 36 x 26 In.	243.00
Desk, Schoolmaster's, Slant Front, Pine, Pa., c.1810, 39 x 34 ½ In.	207.00
Desk, Sewing, Shaker, Pine, Yellow Stain, Walnut Pulls, 2-Board Back, c.1820, 37 x 26 x 17 In.	5265.00

Furniture, Chiffonier, Roycroft, Chestnut, Drawers, Door, Carved Mark, c.1907, 55 ½ x 42 In.
$15,000.00

Rago Arts & Auction Center

Furniture, Commode, Bombe, Butternut, Drawers, Ball & Claw Feet, Canada, 1700s, 30 x 31 In.
$77,025.00

Skinner, Inc.

Furniture, Commode, Bombe, Drawers, Painted Flowers, Italy, c.1900, 23 x 21 In., Pair
$1,107.00

New Orleans Auction Galleries, Inc.

Furniture, Commode, Bombe, Venetian Painted, 2 Drawers, Molded Sides, 1800s, 34 x 49 In.
$2,988.00

Neal Auction Co.

Furniture, Commode, Louis XV Style, Parquetry, Bombe, Drawers, Curved Legs, 29 x 25 In.
$594.00

Leslie Hindman Auctioneers

Furniture, Commode, Marble Top, 3 Drawers, String Inlay, Flared Bottom, Baltic, c.1790, 38 x 71 In.
$1,200.00

Skinner, Inc.

Furniture, Credenza, P. Evans, Cityscape, Chrome, Brass, Geometric, 3 Double Doors, 1970s, 32 x 90 In.
$11,258.00

Skinner, Inc.

Furniture, Cupboard, Chippendale, Step Back, Walnut, Pine, Glass Panes, c.1800, 88 x 70 In.
$4,994.00

Garth's Auctioneers & Appraisers

Desk, Shaker, Pine, Maple, Red Stain, Cupboard Doors, 3 Drawers, Turned Pulls, c.1810, 55 x 39 In.....	2133.00
Desk, Shaker, Sewing, Maple, Red Stain, Flower, Pullout Slide, c.1845, 39 x 30 In.............	42120.00
Desk, Shaker, Sewing, Pine, 24 Drawers, Fold-Out, Painted, c.1890, 64 x 43 In..............	5000.00
Desk, Shaker, Sister's, Sewing, Maple, Drawers, Pullout Slide, Sabbathday Lake, c.1845, 39 In. ...... *Illus*	42120.00
Desk, Shaker, Slant Front, Pine, Maple, Alfred Merrick Collier, 1861, 48 x 31 In. .... *Illus*	37440.00
Desk, Shaker, Table Top, Pine, Red Washed, Lid, 3 Interior Drawers, Brass Pulls, c.1820, 11 x 30 In.	356.00
Desk, Sheraton, Lady's, Birch, Cock-Beaded Drawers, Hinged Shelf, Doors, c.1800, 52 x 40 In.......	646.00
Desk, Sheraton, Mahogany, Broken-Arch Pediment, 2 Doors, Fitted Interior, c.1830, 37 x 18 In.....	460.00
Desk, Sheraton, Mahogany, Inlay, 6 Drawers, Arched Doors, New Eng., 61 x 44 In................	708.00
Desk, Slant Front, Birch, Fitted Interior, 4 Drawers, c.1780, 42 x 38 In.	295.00
Desk, Slant Front, Cherry, 4 Drawers, Shaped Skirt, Bail Handles, 1800s, 43 x 42 In.	767.00
Desk, Slant Front, Cherry, Line Inlay, Slides, 2 Drawer Base, c.1810, 20 x 24 In.	504.00
Desk, Slant Front, Cherry, String Inlay, Carved Fan, Compartments, c.1790, 42 x 37 In. .... *Illus*	8295.00
Desk, Slant Front, Drawers, Brackets, Medial Door, Base Molding, Bracket Feet, Italy, 40 x 27 In. ..	1470.00
Desk, Slant Front, Fitted Interior, 3 Drawers, Bracket Feet, Painted, New Eng., c.1800, 42 x 30 In..	7110.00
Desk, Slant Front, Mahogany, Inlay, 4 Drawers, Splayed Bracket Feet, c.1805, 42 x 39 In.	2280.00
Desk, Slant Front, Maple, Well Interior, 3 Graduated Drawers, New England, 37 x 36 In.	708.00
Desk, Slant Front, Oak, House Of Representatives, Federal Crest, c.1856, 36 x 29 In. .... *Illus*	12548.00
Desk, Slant Front, Oak, Pedestal, Egg & Dart Molding, Balustrade Gallery, c.1850, 48 x 60 In........	717.00
Desk, Slant Front, Pine, Applied Gallery, Drawer, Cross Stretcher, c.1845, 35 x 37 In.	259.00
Desk, Slant Front, Pine, Cherry, Drawer, Stand, Red Wash, c.1820, 40 x 21 In..........	207.00
Desk, Slant Front, Walnut, Burl, Turned Block Uprights, Disc Feet, c.1850, 30 x 22 In.	598.00
Desk, Slant Front, Walnut, Fitted Interior, 4 Drawers, Bracket Feet, c.1780, 41 x 30 In.	649.00
Desk, Spinet, Mahogany, Flip Top, Fitted Interior, Slide Writing Leaf, c.1920, 32 x 36 In.	92.00
Desk, Stickley Bros., Drop Front, Fitted Interior, Drawer, 30 x 15 In................	671.00
Desk, Stickley Bros., Shaped Gallery, Cubbies, Square Legs, Slats, c.1905, 37 x 36 In.	1063.00
Desk, Table Top, Pine, Grain Painted, New England, c.1810, 12 x 24 ½ In.............	563.00
Desk, Table Top, Slant Front, Walnut, Poplar, 2 Interior Drawers, 9 x 25 x 12 ½ In.	323.00
Desk, Tambour, Federal, Inlaid Mahogany, 2 Sections, Center Door, Panels, Drawer, 48 x 40 In.....	4720.00
Desk, Tambour, Mahogany, Inlay, Sliding Door, Fitted Interior, Drawers, c.1920, 46 x 38 In.	375.00
Desk, Tambour, Metal, Cylinder Shape, Brass Pulls, Stock Legs, c.1920, 63 x 25 In............	1560.00
Desk, Teak Ebonized Frame, Rounded Corners, Legs, Side Drawers, Roma, c.1960, 29 x 71 In.......	1440.00
Desk, Teak, Pigeonhole Backsplash, Straight Legs, Stretchers, Denmark, 29 x 64 In...........	1016.00
Desk, Vargueno, Drop Front, Inlay, Carved Dancer Panel, 16 Drawers, Spain, 55 x 34 In.	4425.00
Desk, Veneer, Drawers, Compartments Behind Book Bindings, Inlays, 1700s, 37 x 33 In. ...... *Illus*	3250.00
Desk, Walnut, Leather Top, Drawers, Shaped Skirt, Cabriole Legs, c.1915, 31 x 50 In........	92.00
Desk, Walnut, Leather, Chrome Legs, Half Round Top, Drawer, 1950s, 79 x 46 In..........	1159.00
Desk, William IV, Mahogany, Fitted Gallery Shelf, Hinged Top, Leather, c.1835, 44 x 54 In. ... *Illus*	984.00
Desk, Wood, Inlay, Pullout Surface, Geometric Design, Tapered Legs, Italy, 1700s, 31 x 39 In.........	5175.00
Desk, Wooton, Walnut, Burl, Oilcloth Top, Rotary Storage Base, 31 x 60 In. .... *Illus*	2271.00
Desk, Wormley, Mahogany, Lacquered, Drawers, Cupboard Door, 1940s, 30 x 60 In..........	3125.00
Desk-Bookcase, Baroque, Bombe, Inlay, Fitted Interior, Glazed Doors, 1700s, 92 x 45 In. ..... *Illus*	3540.00
Dining Set, Danish Modern, Rosewood, Drop Center, 6 Chairs, Leather Seat, 40 x 19 In., 7 Piece..	3200.00
Dining Set, Horner, Round Table, Griffin Supports, Serpentine Cabinet, c.1900, 12 Piece	16675.00
Dining Set, Oval Medallion Back, Leather Seat, Dunbar, 1950s, 40-In. Diam. Table, 5 Piece..........	270.00
Dining Set, Roche Bobois, Walnut, Ebony, Inlay, Table, 8 Chairs, Credenza, Cabinets, Mirror ...*Illus*	2187.00
Dresser, Arne Vodder, Rosewood, Curved Drawers, Round Feet, 1960s, 32 x 39 In., Pair..........	4063.00
Dresser, Arts & Crafts, Pewter Trim, Mirror, Square Columns, Shelves, c.1900, 63 x 45 In.	813.00
Dresser, Campaign Style, 4 Drawers, Bail Handles, Block Feet, 1900s, 32 x 38 In.	357.00
Dresser, Chinese Style, Teak, Mirror, 4 Drawers, Carved Fretwork, Painted, c.1920, 45 x 35 In...	805.00
Dresser, Eastlake Style, Walnut, Marble Top, Flowers, Mirror, Drawers, c.1880, 81 x 48 In.......	413.00
Dresser, Eastlake, Walnut, 4 Drawers, Mirror, Carved Crest, c.1880, 82 In.	207.00
Dresser, Eastlake, Wood Panel Inserts, Marble Top, 3 Drawers, Brass Pulls, 33 x 41 In.	330.00
Dresser, Empire, Mahogany, Marble Top, Drawers, Ball & Spindle Feet, 1800s, 45 x 43 In.......	148.00
Dresser, Federal, Mahogany, Marble Top, Mirror, Drawers, 2 Doors, c.1820, 68 x 45 In............	1652.00
Dresser, Frankl, Mahogany, 8 Drawers, Mirror, Station Wagon Design, 1940s, 32 x 66 x 23 In..	6875.00
Dresser, G. Nakashima, Walnut, Drawers, Plank Supports, Cutout Handles, 1962, 53 x 36 In.	8125.00
Dresser, G. Nelson, Walnut, Brushed Aluminum Knobs, Graduated Drawers, 1950s, 41 x 40 In.....	3125.00
Dresser, G. Stickley, Graduated Drawers, Backsplash, Tapered, Bail Handles, c.1905, 53 x 40 In. ...	9375.00
Dresser, Gentleman's, G. Nakashima, Walnut, Elm, Brass Knobs, Cabinet, 1950s, 50 x 56 In..	3750.00
Dresser, Mahogany, Carved, Arched Doors, Drawers, 2 Doors, Chinese, 68 x 32 ½ In. .....*Illus*	177.00
Dresser, Mahogany, Drawers, Flower Stiles, Wreaths, Ring Pulls, Twist Legs, 32 x 48 In...........	1547.00
Dresser, McCobb, 4 Drawers, Brass Knobs, 41 x 36 In..................	212.00
Dresser, McCobb, Walnut Veneer, Metal Trim, Short & Long Drawers, Label, 45 x 38 In..........	770.00
Dresser, Mirror, 3 Drawers, Pine, Green Smoke Paint, New England, c.1890, 24 x 14 In.	356.00
Dresser, Oak, Ebonized, Projected Demilune, Doors, Drawers, Plinth Base, 29 x 72 In............	777.00

F

Dresser, Oak, Mahogany, Drawers, Zigzag Inlay, V Legs, L. Paolozzi, 1950s, 34 x 49 In.............	1875.00
Dresser, Parzinger, Mahogany, Tooled Leather, Brass Knobs, Block Legs, 1950s, 48 x 36 In.	2500.00
Dresser, Parzinger, Mahogany, Tooled Leather, Gilt, 4 Drawers, 1950s, 34 x 44 In.	2250.00
Dresser, Pewter, Pine, Shelves, Ogee-Molded Cornice, 2 Parts, New Eng., c.1885, 78 x 69 In. ....*Illus*	1045.00
Dresser, Pine, Fiddle Front, Cove Molded Cornice, Heart Reticulated Stiles, Shelves, 101 x 75 In. ..	956.00
Dresser, Pine, Molded Cornice, Shelves, Bowed, Drawers, Columnar Supports, 1890, 99 x 127 In.	1230.00
Dresser, Pine, Stained, Cornice, Scalloped Frieze, Shelves, Top Shape Feet, c.1850, 84 x 60 In........	799.00
Dresser, Queen Anne, Oak, Molded Top, 3 Drawers, Scalloped Apron, Pad Feet, 1700s, 34 x 77 In.	2629.00
Dresser, Rosewood, Lacquered Wood, 8 Drawers, Plank Base, 1960s, 32 x 84 In.	4375.00
Dresser, Sheraton, Mahogany, Scroll Backsplash, Carved Posts, Columns, c.1840, 60 x 23 In.	189.00
Dresser, Svend Langkilde, Rosewood, 4 Drawers, X-Shape Supports, Denmark, 1960s, 26 x 40 In.	1875.00
Dresser, Teak, Lift Top, Drawers, Carved Handles, Square Legs, Stretcher, Denmark, 48 x 48 In.....	777.00
Dresser, Victorian, Burl Walnut, 5 Drawers, Brass Bail Handles, c.1885, 34 x 58 In.	575.00
Dresser, Victorian, Rosewood, Marble Top, Tilt Mirror, Serpentine Front, c.1850, 82 x 44 In. ..	374.00
Dresser, Victorian, Walnut, 8 Drawers, Mirror, S-Shape Brackets, c.1880, 75 x 42 In..............	182.00
Dresser, Victorian, Walnut, Carved Crest, 3 Panel Drawers, Mirror, Candlestands, 78 x 42 In..	240.00
Dresser, Walnut, Stained Beech, Stenciled, Curved, Round Legs, Sweden, 1950s, 34 x 79 In.......	5313.00
Dresser, Welsh, Elm, Upper Open Shelves, Lower, Drawers, Paneled Doors, 1800s, 75 x 55 In..	1495.00
Dry Sink, Center Panel Door, Sponge Painted, c.1880, 20 ½ x 22 ½ x 11 In..........................	1495.00
Dry Sink, Cherry, Copper Lined, Drawer, 2 Doors, Bracket Feet, 1800s, 49 x 41 In.	460.00
Dry Sink, Drawer, 2 Cupboard Doors, Grain Painted, Pa., 36 x 37 ½ In.	7110.00
Dry Sink, Federal, Figured Mahogany, Hinged, 2 Drawers, T. Seymour, Boston, 33 x 37 In......	3944.00
Dry Sink, George III, Mahogany, Satinwood Inlay, Top Opens, Basins, Shelves, 9 x 10 In.	2124.00
Dry Sink, Pine, Open Shelf, 2 Doors, Brown, Yellow Stippled, Pa., c.1850, 39 x 41 In.............	711.00
Dry Sink, Poplar, Lift Top, 2 Drawers, 2 Doors, c.1840, 38 x 44 In...	224.00
Dry Sink, Shaker, Cherry, Cock-Beaded, Cupboard Doors, Hinged Top, c.1830, 33 x 38 In.......	1422.00
Dry Sink, Shelf, 2 Drawers, Over Well, 2 Doors, Drawers, Grain Painted, Pa., c.1850, 49 x 60 In...	770.00
Dry Sink, Softwood, Grain Painted, Hooded, Upper Shelf, Drawers, Panel Doors, 57 x 46 In.........	708.00
Dry Sink, Softwood, Gray Paint, Cut Corner Splashback, Hinged Lift Top, Drawers, 35 x 37 In......	708.00
Dry Sink, Softwood, Slant Front, 2 Lower Panel Doors, Turned Feet, 49 x 31 In.	266.00
Dry Sink, Walnut, Poplar, Painted, Drawers, Doors, Bracket Feet, Drain Board, 1800s, 34 x 48 In.	1145.00
Dry Sink, Wood, Well, 3 Doors, Bracket Feet, Green Paint, Pa., 1800s, 32 x 60 ½ In..................	4740.00
Dumbwaiter, George III Style, Mahogany, Dished, Vase Shape Stem, c.1900, 32 x 24 In.........	430.00
Dumbwaiter, George III, Mahogany, 2 Tiers, Dish Edge, Revolving, c.1780, 34 x 15 In........	121.00
Dumbwaiter, George III, Mahogany, 3 Revolving Graduated Shelves, Tripod Base, 47 In........	1725.00
Dumbwaiter, George III, Mahogany, Turned Pedestal, Rotating Top, c.1800, 35 x 24 In.......	382.00
Dumbwaiter, Victorian, Walnut, Applied Roundels, 3 Shelves, Paw Feet, 1880s, 35 x 42 In.	875.00
Dumbwaiter, Walnut, 2 Tiers, Round, Splayed Legs, 15 ½ x 31 In.	460.00
Dumbwaiter, William IV, Oak, Telescopic, 3 Tiers, Scrolled Trestle Base, c.1800, 31 x 42 In. ...	837.00
Easel, Bamboo, Fan Shaped Crest, Finials, Shelf, End Arrows, Hinged, c.1890, 66 x 30 In.	307.00
Easel, Renaissance Revival, Walnut, Gilt Incised, Adjustable, 84 x 28 ½ In................................	644.00
Easel, Walnut, Ebonized, Metal Wolf Bust, Adjustable, c.1865, 80 x 36 In. ....*Illus*	5227.00
Etagere, Edwardian, Mahogany, Brass, 3 Tiers, Oval, 29 x 23 In..	702.00
Etagere, Federal, Mahogany, 4 Tiers, Turned Uprights, Drawer, c.1800, 52 x 19 In.	3050.00
Etagere, Hanging, Corner, Rosewood, Pierced Scrollwork, Mirror, Shelves, c.1850, 58 x 22 In.	1793.00
Etagere, Louis XVI Style, Mahogany, Acorn Finials, Brass Stringing, c.1900, 38 x 20 In.	430.00
Etagere, Lucite, Brass, Arch Top, 5 Glass Shelves, c.1970, 92 x 47 In...	1140.00
Etagere, Lucite, Chrome, Brass, 3 Shelves, c.1970, 32 x 31 ½ In...	900.00
Etagere, Mahogany, 2 Tiers, Reticulated Gallery, Ring-Turned Support, c.1850, 39 x 20 In.....	1708.00
Etagere, Mahogany, 4 Tiers, Drawer, Barley Twist Supports, Spire Finials, 59 x 21 In..............	1220.00
Etagere, Mahogany, 5 Open Shelves, 3 Drawers, Turned Legs, Urn Finials, 66 x 18 In...........	863.00
Etagere, Mahogany, Gallery, Marble Top, Frieze Drawer, Tapered Supports, 3 Shelves, 41 x 26 In..	875.00
Etagere, Mahogany, Gilt Metal, Gallery Top, X-Shape Supports, Mirror Back, 24 x 41 In........	469.00
Etagere, Mahogany, Marble Top, 4 Tiers, Frieze Drawer, Shaped Apron, 1800s, 38 x 21 In........	237.00
Etagere, Mahogany, Mirrors, Grotesques, Leaves, Flowers, Shelves, 2 Doors, c.1860, 72 x 48 In.	438.00
Etagere, Mahogany, Shelves, Gallery, Turned Supports & Legs, Casters, c.1820, 37 x 18 In......	563.00
Etagere, Regency Style, Ebonized, Gilt, 3 Open Shelves, 2 Drawers, Brass Casters, 54 x 44 In..	1169.00
Etagere, Regency, Mahogany, Carved, 3 Tiers, Adjustable Trestles, 43 x 54 In.........................	1872.00
Etagere, Regency, Mahogany, Drawer, 2 Shelves, Turned Spindles, Casters, c.1825, 55 x 16 In...	533.00
Etagere, Regency, Rosewood, 4 Corner Brass Acorn Finials, Turreted Feet, 67 x 26 In.	461.00
Etagere, Rococo Revival, Rosewood, Carved, Mirror Back, American, c.1850, 64 x 40 In. ...*Illus*	3585.00
Etagere, Rococo Revival, Rosewood, Urn Finials, Mirror, Pierced, Marble Top, c.1850, 102 x 55 In.	3286.00
Etagere, Sheraton, Mahogany, Oak, 5 Tiers, 2 Drawers, Spindle Supports, Eng., 75 x 17 In.....	2242.00
Etagere, Sheraton, Rosewood, 3 Tiers, Acorn Finial, Ring-Turned Legs, c.1800, 56 x 16 In.......	2032.00
Etagere, Steel, Brushed, 7 Shelves, Brass Accents, Black Leatherette Shelves, 1900s, 89 x 48 In.	690.00
Etagere, Victorian, Bamboo, Mirror, Chinoiserie Top, Door, 4 Shelves, Embossed, c.1875, 61 x 29 In.	1444.00

Furniture, Cupboard, Corner, Federal, Walnut, 20 Panes, Glazed Doors, Lower Doors, 1800s, 99 x 52 In.
$1,534.00

Brunk Auctions

Furniture, Cupboard, Corner, Sheraton, Curly Maple, Walnut, Glass Panes, Dovetailed, c.1835, 87 In.
$2,115.00

Garth's Auctioneers & Appraisers

Spot the Copy
The original Barcelona Chair designed in 1929 by Mies van der Rohe has often been copied. The early chair had chrome sections joined by lap joints fastened by chromed screws. Look carefully at the corners of the top of the back of the chair for this type of joint.

F

Furniture, Cupboard, Corner, Yellow Pine, Glazed Doors, 2 Sections, c.1890, 89 x 51 In. **$2,252.00**

Skinner, Inc.

Furniture, Cupboard, Pine, Dentil, Glass Pane & Raised Panel Doors, Drawers, c.1810, 87 x 64 In. **$6,025.00**

Garth's Auctioneers & Appraisers

Furniture, Cupboard, Shaker, Sister's, Pine, 2 Doors, 6 Drawers, Dovetailed, 62 x 42 In. **$122,850.00**

Willis Henry Auctions, Inc.

Etagere, Victorian, Mahogany, 2 Tiers, Mushroom Knops, 34 x 38 In.	410.00
Etagere, Victorian, Mahogany, Carved, Gallery, 3 Tiers, Turned Legs, 47 x 48 In.	1053.00
Etagere, William IV, Mahogany, Gallery, 3 Shelves, Turned Backsplash, Finials, 44 In.	896.00
Etagere, William IV, Mahogany, Gallery, 3 Tiers, Reeded Uprights, Casters, c.1800, 42 x 47 In.	1554.00
Footrest, Mahogany, Flower Needlepoint Cover, 1800s, 20 ½ x 19 ¾ In.	281.00
Footstool, Chippendale Style, Walnut, Shell Carved Knees, Upholstered, c.1890, 19 x 21 In.	944.00
Footstool, Curly Maple, Bandy Legs, Ohio, c.1850, 7 x 15 In.	588.00
Footstool, Federal, Walnut, Carved Skirt, Upholstered, c.1825, 10 x 10 ½ In.	748.00
Footstool, G. Stickley, Spindled Sides, Square Legs, Upholstered Seat, c.1905, 15 x 20 x 16 In.	1750.00
Footstool, Gothic Revival, Mahogany, Carved, Casters, c.1850, 19 x 24 In. *Illus*	861.00
Footstool, Jacobean Style, Walnut, Upholstered, Shaped Skirt, Wavy X-Stretcher, 20 x 22 In.	345.00
Footstool, Louis XVI Style, Beech, Fluted Frieze, Tapered Legs, Turned Feet, c.1850, 7 x 14 In.	215.00
Footstool, Louis XVI Style, Fruitwood, Ribbon Carved, Top Shape Feet, c.1900, 9 x 16 In.	215.00
Footstool, Louis XVI Style, Gilt, Leaf Corner Blocks, Tapered Fluted Legs, c.1900, 9 x 10 In.	307.00
Footstool, Mahogany, Needlework Upholstery, Turned Legs, American, c.1890, 15 x 22 In.	176.00
Footstool, Painted, Carved, Needlepoint Upholstery, 1800s, 18 x 19 In., Pair	1035.00
Footstool, Pine, Bottom Step, Concord School Of Philosophy, c.1900, 5 x 15 In.	705.00
Footstool, Pine, Grain Painted, Bird, Branch, Shaped Skirt, Bootjack Ends, 1800s, 7 x 14 In.	151.00
Footstool, Pine, Painted, Blue, Scroll Apron, Heart Shape Splayed Legs, Maine, c.1820, 7 x 15 In.	690.00
Footstool, Regency, Rosewood, Upholstered, Scrolled Sides, c.1820, 7 x 15 In., Pair	830.00
Footstool, Salmon Paint, Incised Compass Star, Keyhole Cutout Feet, Shaped Skirt, 7 x 14 In.	35.00
Footstool, Shaker, Pine, Turned Legs, Mt. Lebanon, N.Y., 12 x 11 In.	162.00
Footstool, Sheraton, Mahogany, Upholstered, Turned Legs, New York, 7 ½ x 12 In., Pair	354.00
Footstool, Victorian, Oval Leather Top, Nailhead Trim, Turned Feet, c.1850, Pair	538.00
Footstool, Walnut, Needlepoint, Oval, Round, Turned Feet, c.1888, 5 x 11 ½ In.	35.00
Footstool, Walnut, Needlepoint, Reclining Cat, Olive Ground, Roses, Skirt, Ball Feet, 7 x 16 In.	83.00
Frame, Alfred Daguet, Wood, Inlaid Designs, Applied Brass, Repousse, Enamel, 15 x 23 In. *Illus*	1098.00
Frame, Baroque Style, Leaf & Fruit Twisted Ribbon, Acanthus Leaf, c.1775, 65 x 54 In.	3540.00
Frame, Bugatti, Mahogany, Brass, Pewter Inlay, Glass Front, Suede Back, c.1900, 9 x 6 In.	5625.00
Frame, Cherry, Turned Half Columns, Blocked Corners, Carved, Pa., 1800s, 17 x 13 In.	267.00
Frame, Chip Carved, Painted, 1892, 15 ½ x 5 In.	472.00
Frame, Giltwood, Carved, Fruit, Acorns, Gadrooned, 23 x 20 In.	472.00
Frame, Giltwood, Openwork Shells, Flourishes, 31 x 27 x 3 ½ In.	826.00
Frame, Giltwood, Plaster, Paper Label, Durure Encadrement, Paris, 24 x 20 x 2 In.	1652.00
Frame, Giltwood, Scrolling, Leaves, 31 x 26 In.	72.00
Frame, Half Turned Columns, Block Columns, Gilt Stencil, Painted, Pa., 15 x 12 In.	356.00
Frame, Heart & Arrow Appliques, Lollipop Ends, New Eng., c.1910, 21 x 16 In.	830.00
Frame, Mahogany, Beaded Edge, Fan Carved, c.1850, 14 x 12 ¾ In.	711.00
Frame, Neoclassical, Gilt Bronze, Mother-Of-Pearl Inset, Guilloche, Laurel, France, 14 x 10 In. *Illus*	1397.00
Frame, Pine, Dot, Leaf, Stripe Design, Red, Black, Yellow Paint, Pa., c.1850, 17 x 15 In.	2844.00
Frame, Poplar, Reeded Quarter Columns, Blocked Corners, Carved, Red Paint, 18 x 16 In.	504.00
Frame, Regency Style, Oak, Carved, 40 x 28 In.	410.00
Frame, Rococo, Giltwood, Carved, Mirror, Italy, 33 In.	590.00
Frame, Stepped Molding, Yellow, Grain Painted, 1800s, 19 x 16 ¾ In., Pair	2187.00
Frame, Stylized Flowers, Gold, Red Stripe, Black, Painted, 1800s, Pa., 15 ¾ x 14 In.	1541.00
Frame, Tiger Maple, Blocked Corners, Carved, Pa., 17 ⅜ x 15 ½ In.	533.00
Frame, Walnut, Oval, Applied Chain Design, c.1880, 18 x 13 In.	259.00
Frame, Wood, Cutouts, Applied Brass, Repousse, Green Jewel, A. Daguet, 19 x 25 In.	1098.00
Frame, Wood, Flower Blocked Corners, 18 ½ x 15 In., Pair	972.00
Hall Seat, Oak, Beveled Mirror, Scroll Cut Top Edge, Applied Ribbon, Flowers, 4 Hooks, 91 x 55 In.	1652.00
Hall Seat, Quartersawn Oak, Mirror, Half Columns, Fan Top, Hinged Seat, Hooks, 84 x 32 In. *Illus*	708.00
Hall Stand, Black Forest, Bear, Baby Bear Climbing Tree, Mirror, c.1880, 80 x 27 In.	2588.00
Hall Stand, Black Forest, Bear, Standing, Glass Eyes, Cub, Seated In Tree, Mirror, c.1940, 83 x 31 In.	2160.00
Hall Stand, Black Forest, Walnut, Mother Bear, Cub, Mirror, Branch Shape Frame, 1800s, 77 In.	1888.00
Hall Stand, French Provincial Style, Oak, Mirror, Hooks, Umbrella Stand, 84 x 51 In.	615.00
Hall Stand, Mirror, Coat Hooks, Umbrella Stand, Cast Iron, Victorian, c.1880, 85 x 24 In.	450.00
Hall Stand, Oak, Beveled Mirror, Glove Box, Lid, Iron Hardware, England, 1905, 79 x 36 In. *Illus*	1020.00
Hall Stand, Renaissance Revival, Walnut, Marble Top, Mirror, Umbrella Holders, 1800s, 79 In.	600.00
Hall Stand, Victorian, Mahogany, Oval Mirror, Scrolls, Pierced, 88 x 29 In.	1521.00
Hall Stand, Victorian, Oak, Lift Seat, Mirror Back, Cast Iron Hooks, c.1890, 80 x 28 In.	690.00
Hall Stand, Victorian, Oak, Mirror, Mask Crest, Hinged Seat, Winged Griffins, c.1885, 95 x 61 In.	1476.00
Hall Stand, Wrought Iron, Hooks, Mirror, Flower Basket, Shields, Figures, Eng., 1800s, 83 x 33 In.	840.00
Hall Tree, Black Forest, Bear, Standing Beside Tree, c.1890, 77 In.	3220.00
Hall Tree, Iron, Tree Shape, Stylized Leaves, Branches, Root Base, Shell Tray, c.1910, 71 x 24 In.	840.00
Hall Tree, Victorian, Wood, 12 Curved Arms, Eagle Finial, Carved, Splayed Legs, 82 x 23 In.	354.00
Hat Tree, Nickeled Cast Iron Hooks, Wood Pole, Porcelain Base, Koken, 75 In.	1232.00

Highboy, Cherry, Molded Hinged Top, Scalloped Apron, Curved Legs, c.1790, 43 x 39 In......... 3081.00
Highboy, Cherry, William & Mary, 5 Drawers, Turned Base, Stretcher, 64 x 38 ½ In. 330.00
Highboy, Chippendale Style, Mahogany, 2 Sections, Ball & Claw Feet, c.1910, 88 x 40 In. ... *Illus* 767.00
Highboy, Chippendale, Walnut, Swan Neck Crest, Rosettes, Shell, c.1795, 90 x 45 In................. 7768.00
Highboy, George II Style, Burl, Pitched Pediment, Carved Knees, 1900s, 81 x 45 In............... 885.00
Highboy, Queen Anne Style, Curly Maple, Eldred Wheeler, 87 x 37 In. 5214.00
Highboy, Queen Anne Style, Mahogany, Broken Arch Crest, Urn Finials, Fan, 1800s, 88 x 40 In..... 625.00
Highboy, Queen Anne, Burl Walnut, 9 Drawers, Cabriole Legs, Mass., 66 x 37 In. 10030.00
Highboy, Queen Anne, Cherry, 9 Drawers, Raised Cabriole Legs, c.1750, 74 x 43 In. 5400.00
Highboy, Queen Anne, Cherry, Birch, 2 Sections, Drawers, Shaped Apron, 76 x 39 In.............. 9440.00
Highboy, Queen Anne, Cherry, Fan, Brass Handles, Curved Legs, Pad Feet, c.1795, 74 x 37 In.. 3851.00
Highboy, Queen Anne, Maple, 10 Drawers, Acorn Drops, New Eng., 73 x 40 In........................ 5605.00
Highboy, Queen Anne, Maple, 2 Fan Carvings, 10 Drawers, Cabriole Legs, 82 x 28 In.............. 4029.00
Highboy, Queen Anne, Maple, 5 Top Drawers, Over 4 Drawers, Carved Fan, 70 x 39 In............ 1046.00
Highboy, Queen Anne, Maple, 9 Drawers, Shaped Apron, Cabriole Legs, Ma., 71 x 39 In........... 4720.00
Highboy, Queen Anne, Maple, Curly Maple, 5 Upper, 4 Lower Drawers, c.1760, 69 x 39 In. 944.00
Highboy, Queen Anne, Red Stain, 6 Drawers, Shaped Apron, Cabriole Legs, 66 x 41 In............. 3540.00
Highboy, Victorian, Oak, 5 Drawers, Scalloped Backsplash, Bail Handles, c.1900, 54 x 32 In.... 270.00
Highchair, Buggy, Convertible, Lever, Cane Seat, Back, Buggy, 31 x 16 In. 177.00
Highchair, Chippendale, Maple, Ash, Painted, Rope Tied Seat Frame, c.1780, 32 x 15 In......... 1840.00
Highchair, George III, Mahogany, Shaped & Pierced Splat, Stretchers, c.1760........................ 889.00
Highchair, Hickory, Woven Seat, No. Carolina, c.1850, 35 In... 119.00
Highchair, Ladder Back, Mixed Wood, Black Paint, Rush Seat, 1700s, 32 In.......................... 206.00
Highchair, Ladder Back, Woven Seat, 2 Stretchers, Arms, Blue Paint, c.1790........................... 2370.00
Highchair, Mahogany, Metamorphic, Needlepoint Seat, Open Sloped Arms 865.00
Highchair, Mixed Wood, Red Paint, Ladder Back, Splint Seat, 1800s, 35 In............................ 235.00
Highchair, Windsor, Bow Back, Brown Paint, Arms, Pa., c.1790, 36 In. 1541.00
Highchair, Windsor, Bow Back, Plank Seat, Continuous Arm, 33 x 14 In. 6490.00
Highchair, Windsor, Bow Back, Spindles, Arms, Seat, Vase & Ring-Turned Legs, Pa., Child's ... 6490.00
Highchair, Zig-Zig Kinderstoel, Oak, Gerrit T. Rietveld, c.1963, 34 x 17 ¾ In....................... 25000.00
Huntboard, Federal, Walnut, Cherry, 2 Doors, Cellarette Drawer, 1800s, 38 x 51 In. ....*Illus* 9440.00
Huntboard, Federal, Walnut, Inlay, 3 Drawers, Square Tapered Legs, 36 x 41 In..................... 3884.00
Huntboard, Federal, Walnut, Line Inlay, Tapered Legs, Banded Cuffs, Va., c.1790, 41 x 62 In.. 7110.00
Huntboard, Federal, Walnut, Yellow Pine, Door, Drawer, Tapered Legs, c.1810, 43 x 54 In. 8837.00
Huntboard, Hepplewhite, Pine, 4 Drawers, Square Tapered Legs, 42 x 49 In. 3776.00
Huntboard, Hepplewhite, Walnut, Inlay, 5 Drawers, Virginia, 40 x 66 In. 1304.00
Huntboard, Kittinger, Mahogany, 3 Drawers, Tall Tapered Legs, c.1960, 41 x 57 In............... 774.00
Huntboard, Poplar, Drawer, Raised Legs, c.1820, 36 x 44 In. 431.00
Huntboard, Rococo, Walnut, Bowfront Case, Molded Edge, Drawers, Mirrors, 76 x 73 In....... 1035.00
Huntboard, Walnut, Door, 4 Drawers, Breadboard Ends, Georgia, c.1840, 46 x 74 In............. 9775.00
Hutch, Oak, Carved, Marble, Drawer, Doors, Beveled Glass Doors, c.1900, 83 x 55 In. 1440.00
Hutch, Provincial, Mahogany, 2 Parts, Fretwork, Fluted Stiles, Molded Pediment, c.1900, 84 x 60 In.. 356.00
Jardiniere, Mahogany, Urn Shape, Copper Insert, Beaded Festoons, Gilt Paw Feet, 16 In......... 450.00
Jardiniere, Napoleon III, Walnut, Gilt Gallery, Oval, Ribbon Knot Handles, Liner, 7 x 16 In.... 875.00
Jardiniere, Rosewood, Gilt, Round, 3 Scroll Legs, Maitland Smith, 50 x 19 In., Pair.............. 1440.00
Kas, Gumwood, 2 Raised Panel Doors, 2 Drawers, Old Red Paint, 71 x 63 In............................. 1035.00
Kas, William & Mary, Gumwood, Raised Panel Doors, Front Ball Feet, 73 x 64 In................... 4425.00
Kneeler, Prie-Dieu, Gilt, Scrolled, Pierced, Upholstered, Cabriole Legs, c.1830, 36 x 19 In. 1265.00
Kneeler, Prie-Dieu, Louis XV, Walnut, Carved, Padded Armrest, Upholstered, c.1790, 34 x 22 In. ... 420.00
Kneeler, Prie-Dieu, Oak, 3 Panels, c.1930, 33 x 60 In... 324.00
Kneeler, Prie-Dieu, Oak, Paneled, Shelf, Leather Knee Rest, c.1930, 33 x 60 In., Pair............. 270.00
Kneeler, Prie-Dieu, Walnut, Carved, Needlepoint, Lobed, Fluted Stiles, Cross, c.1910 ....*Illus* 478.00
Kneeler, Prie-Dieu, Wrought Iron, Burgundy Velvet Kneeler, Armrest, c.1920, 36 x 23 In........ 354.00
Lap Desk, Anglo-Indian, Quill, Sandalwood, Ivory Penwork, Fitted Interior, c.1850, 7 x 14 In. . 1063.00
Lap Desk, Burl Walnut, Shaped Brass Corners, Hinges & Lock, Victorian, England, 5 x 19 x 9 In. . 960.00
Lap Desk, Calamander Wood, Slant Lid, Gilt Tooled Leather, 3 Secret Drawers, 15 x 10 In. 717.00
Lap Desk, Roll Top, Oak, Brass, Fitted Interior, Drawer, England, c.1885, 16 x 18 In.............. 461.00
Lap Desk, Victorian, Mahogany, Slant Front, Divided Interior, c.1830, 16 In............................ 210.00
Library Ladder, Maple, 5 Steps, Tiger Graining, Collapsible, c.1900, 62 In............................. 144.00
Library Ladder, Regency Style, Mahogany, Brass Edges, Beaded, Handles, Folding, 58 In. 1230.00
Library Ladder, Silvered Metal Rope, c.1975, 70 In., Pair 1000.00
Library Ladder, Walnut Stain, 4 Steps, Removable Turned Pole, Hinges, 38 x 66 In............... 702.00
Library Steps, Directoire Style, Mahogany, Foldover Seat, Needlepoint, 21 x 24 x 18 In. 2031.00
Library Steps, Mahogany, Leather, Hinged Case, England, 82 In... 1722.00
Library Steps, Mahogany, Pierced Tracery Back, Down Curved Arms, c.1850, 26 x 24 In........ 1315.00
Library Steps, Mahogany, Tooled Leather, Lift Top, England, 24 x 18 x 30 In........................ 542.00

Furniture, Cupboard, Shaker, Sister's, Top Doors, 10 Drawers, Mt. Lebanon, c.1850, 66 x 53 In. $4,740.00

Skinner, Inc.

Furniture, Cupboard, Step Back, Pine, Poplar, Grain Painted, Glazed Doors, Ohio, c.1850, 83 In. $588.00

Garth's Auctioneers & Appraisers

Furniture, Cupboard, Walnut, Step Back, 12 Glass Panes Over 2 Doors, Shelves, c.1830, 73 x 44 In. $8,050.00

Jeffrey S. Evans & Assoc.

Furniture, Cupboard, Welsh, Oak, Shelves, Drawers, Doors, Bracket Feet, 80 x 67 In.
$4,500.00

Leslie Hindman Auctioneers

Furniture, Desk & Chair, Frankl, Mahogany, Cork, Leather, Brass, Aluminum, Johnson, 1950s, 59 In.
$5,000.00

Rago Arts & Auction Center

Furniture, Desk, Aluminum, Bakelite Pulls, P.B. Cow & Co., Hunting Aviation Ltd., c.1945, 30 x 46 In.
$1,320.00

Skinner, Inc.

Furniture, Desk, Art Deco Style, Lacquered, T-Shape, Geometric, Drawers, 29 x 45 In.
$1,000.00

Leslie Hindman Auctioneers

Library Steps, Oak, Railing, Arm Supports, England, c.1850, 83 x 48 In.	6820.00
Library Steps, Regency Style, Mahogany, 4 Spiraling Rungs, Inset Leather, 66 In.	461.00
Library Steps, Regency Style, Mahogany, Central Pole, Kittinger, 1900s, 59 x 30 In. *Illus*	558.00
Library Steps, Regency Style, Mahogany, Spiral Rungs, Block & Ball Feet, 66 In.	492.00
Library Steps, Regency Style, Mahogany, Table, Leather, Turned Legs, 28 x 28 In.	738.00
Library Steps, Regency Style, Wood, Spiral, Turned Bannister, 4 Steps, 1900s, 20 x 45 In.	450.00
Library Steps, Sheraton, Mahogany, Upholstered, Risers, Turned Supports, c.1925, 22 x 20 In.	826.00
Library Steps, Turned Post, Conforming Base, 4 Steps, Smith & Watson, 65 x 20 x 20 In.	717.00
Library Steps, Victorian, Mahogany, Spiral, 4 Steps, Leather Treads, c.1890, 60 In.	153.00
Linen Press, Chippendale, Cherry, Inlay, 2 Flat Doors, 3 Drawers, 80 x 49 In.	944.00
Linen Press, Chippendale, Cherry, Paneled Doors, Inlaid Pilasters, c.1775, 74 x 46 x 18 In.	10665.00
Linen Press, Chippendale, Gumwood, Doors, Fitted Interior, Drawers, c.1780, 74 x 44 In.	16590.00
Linen Press, Chippendale, Mahogany, Molded Cornice, Paneled Doors, Drawers, 92 x 53 In.	2091.00
Linen Press, Chippendale, Red Paint, Tombstone Doors, Reeded Stiles, Doors, 77 x 49 In.	2360.00
Linen Press, Chippendale, Rosewood, Arch Top, Panel Doors, Drawers, N.Y., 75 x 53 In.	1180.00
Linen Press, Federal Mahogany, 2 Raised Panel Doors, Drawers, Sample, 24 x 15 In.	944.00
Linen Press, Federal, Inlaid Mahogany, 2 Doors, 2 Drawers, c.1795, 48 x 49 x 22 In.	1770.00
Linen Press, Federal, Poplar, 2 Panel Doors, 6 Drawers, New York, 75 x 49 In.	1121.00
Linen Press, George III Style, Mahogany, 2 Parts, Coffered Doors, Drawers, 71 x 52 In.	2250.00
Linen Press, George III Style, Mahogany, Molded Cornice, Paneled Doors, Drawers, 87 x 48 In.	1230.00
Linen Press, George III, Mahogany, Inlay, Stepped Cornice, Paneled Doors, c.1790, 75 In.	717.00
Linen Press, George III, Mahogany, Shell Inlay, Doors, Oval Panels, c.1790, 81 x 50 In.	4270.00
Linen Press, George III, Mahogany, Swan Neck Pediment, Doors, Drawers, 80 x 45 In., Pair	4680.00
Linen Press, Neoclassical, Mahogany, Drawer, Paneled Doors, Columns, Paw Feet, 40 x 41 In.	1888.00
Linen Press, Pine, 2 Doors, 4 Drawers, England, c.1750, 74 x 48 In.	444.00
Linen Press, Regency Style, Mahogany, Paneled Doors, Drawers, 1800s, 83 x 49 In.	2360.00
Love Seat, Barcelona, Modern, Chromed Frame, Leather Cushions, 1920s, 30 x 59 In.	1535.00
Love Seat, Federal Style, Mahogany, Flower, Carved Rail, Arms, Upholstered, 55 In.	413.00
Love Seat, Kittinger, Mahogany, Rolled Arms, Upholstered, 33 x 61 In., Pair	444.00
Love Seat, Majorelle, Walnut, Flared Frame, Velvet Upholstery, c.1970, 52 ½ In.	1888.00
Love Seat, Paolo Buffa, Upholstered, Fan Back, Curved Arms, Italy, 1950, 35 x 60 In.	3125.00
Love Seat, Wormley, Mahogany, Leather, Dunbar, 55 x 34 In.	1464.00
Lowboy, Chippendale Style, Walnut, Overhanging Top, Shell Carved, 29 x 33 In.	1135.00
Lowboy, E. Wheeler, Tiger Maple, Slate Top, Drawers, Fan, Drop Finials, c.1985, 32 x 32 In.	944.00
Lowboy, George I, Burl Walnut, Featherband Top, Drawers, Shaped Apron, 30 x 28 In.	3508.00
Lowboy, George I, Oak, Central Drawer, 2 Side Drawers, Apron, Cabriole Legs, 28 x 32 In.	3250.00
Lowboy, George II, Mahogany, Apron, Drawers, Cabriole Legs, England, 29 x 30 In.	460.00
Lowboy, George II, Oak, Molded, Shaped Frieze, Pad & Ball Feet, 1700s, 30 x 73 In.	837.00
Lowboy, George II, Walnut, Dish Top, Beaded Drawer, Brass Pulls, Duck Pad Feet, 29 x 27 In.	1006.00
Lowboy, Queen Anne Style, Cherry, Cabriole Legs, Early 1900s, 32 x 32 In.	474.00
Lowboy, Queen Anne Style, Cherry, Drawers, Shell Carved, Council Craftsmen, 22 x 34 In.	472.00
Lowboy, Queen Anne Style, Mahogany, Drawers, Overhung Top, Cabriole Legs, 30 x 34 In.	720.00
Lowboy, Queen Anne Style, Maple, Drawers, Cabriole Legs, Brass Pulls, 33 x 36 In.	58.00
Lowboy, Queen Anne, Curly Maple, 4 Drawers, Fan, Cabriole Legs, 32 x 33 In.	1180.00
Lowboy, Queen Anne, Mahogany, Molded, Shell, Acorn Pendants, Cabriole Legs, 30 x 33 In.	1722.00
Lowboy, Queen Anne, Walnut, 3 Drawers, Apron, Cabriole Legs, Pa., 29 x 35 In.	3304.00
Lowboy, Queen Anne, Walnut, 4 Drawers, Fan Carving, Cabriole Legs, c.1760, 31 x 33 In.	4305.00
Lowboy, Queen Anne, Walnut, Drawers, Cabriole Legs, c.1750, 30 x 35 In.	1725.00
Lowboy, Queen Anne, Walnut, Drawers, Drop Finials, Cabriole Legs, New Eng., 31 x 36 In.	2950.00
Lowboy, Queen Anne, Walnut, Lobed Corners, Cabriole Legs, England, c.1710, 29 x 30 In.	889.00
Mirror, Acorn Shape Frame, Carved Oak Leaf Crest, c.1870, 37 x 23 In., Pair	6325.00
Mirror, Adam Style, Faux Marble, Column, Arched, Landscape Painted, c.1920, 46 x 22 In.	177.00
Mirror, Adam Style, Gilt Composition, Urn Crest, Leaves, Openwork, c.1900, 55 x 50 In.	767.00
Mirror, Adam Style, Giltwood, Shield Shape, Urn, Swags, Crest, Candleholders, c.1800, 46 In.	316.00
Mirror, Adam Style, Giltwood, Urn & Scroll Crest, Oval, 1900s, 43 x 25 In.	354.00
Mirror, Adam Style, Phoenix Carved Wood Frame, 53 x 30 In.	295.00
Mirror, Armorial, Table Top, Metal, Pierced Brass Urn, Acanthus Stand, 20 In.	354.00
Mirror, Art Deco, Sandblasted, 3-D Flowers, Impalas, Goldtone, c.1930, 46 x 18 In.	600.00
Mirror, Art Deco, Wrought Iron, Enameled, Pierced Leaves, Scrolls, Tassels, c.1930, 23 x 33 In.	375.00
Mirror, Arts & Crafts, Copper, Cabochon, Flower, Leaves, England, c.1900, 21 x 34 In.	2500.00
Mirror, Baroque Style, Burl, Scrolled Crest, Coat Of Arms, Brass Mounts, 56 x 36 In.	1554.00
Mirror, Baroque Style, Ebonized, Scalloped Top, Shell Crest, Flower Garland, 50 x 27 In.	615.00
Mirror, Baroque Style, Metal, Arched Crest, Repousse Fruit Basket, Grapes, 33 x 19 In.	125.00
Mirror, Baroque, Parcel Gilt, Carved, Pierced Applique, Gesso, c.1700, 26 x 21 In.	944.00
Mirror, Biedermeier, Cherry, Ebonized, Peaked Crest, c.1805, 61 x 31 In.	875.00
Mirror, Biedermeier, Giltwood, Ebonized Columns, Cast Relief, c.1810, 63 x 29 In. *Illus*	805.00

Mirror, Biedermeier, Mahogany, Pyramid Crest, Ormolu Star, Maidens' Heads, c.1890, 41 x 47 In.	492.00
Mirror, Biedermeier, Pier, Fruitwood, Double Eagle, Arrow, Torch, Columns, 65 x 31 In.	920.00
Mirror, Black Forest, Beech, Gilt Slip, Oak Leaves, Acorns, Swag Pediment, c.1890, 39 x 29 In.	1150.00
Mirror, Brass Rods, Clear Plastic Flowers, Round, 1950s, 17 x 3 ½ In.	671.00
Mirror, Bronze, 2-Tone, Pierced Scrolls, Classical Symbols, c.1930, 33 x 24 In.	600.00
Mirror, Bull's-Eye, Federal Style, Giltwood, Gesso, Acanthus, Beads, Eagle, 39 In.	390.00
Mirror, Burl Walnut, Giltwood, Acanthus Carved Crest, Broken Pediment, 1700s, 67 x 34 In.	1400.00
Mirror, C. Jere, Raindrops, Patinated Copper, Brass, Signed, 1968, 34 x 5 ¾ In. *Illus*	6250.00
Mirror, Cast Iron Frame, Scrolling, Leaf Crest, Reticulated, c.1890, 17 x 13 In.	90.00
Mirror, Cheval, Empire Style, Mahogany, Broken Swan Neck Crest, Brass Feet, c.1900, 74 x 29 In.	237.00
Mirror, Cheval, Empire Style, Mahogany, Shaped Crest, Splayed Legs, c.1900, 77 x 32 In.	1845.00
Mirror, Cheval, Empire, Mahogany, Ormolu, Pediment Top, Flowers, Wreath, 1800s, 73 x 35 In.	1006.00
Mirror, Cheval, Faux Bamboo, Pierced Crest, Ball Finial Supports, c.1890, 77 x 29 In.	2032.00
Mirror, Cheval, George II, Mahogany, Brass Finials, Line Inlay, c.1820, 67 x 28 In.	237.00
Mirror, Cheval, Gothic Revival, Mahogany, Giltwood, Spiral Twist Supports, 72 x 50 In.	2125.00
Mirror, Cheval, Neoclassical, Mahogany Veneer, Paneled Back, Casters, c.1825, 96 x 50 In. *Illus*	1888.00
Mirror, Cheval, Neoclassical, Mahogany, Pedimented Crest, Square Supports, 1800s, 74 x 35 In.	1075.00
Mirror, Cheval, Oak, Carved, Pierced Crest, Fold-Out Shelf, c.1850, 75 x 32 In. *Illus*	4183.00
Mirror, Cheval, Victorian, Openwork, Rope Twist Border, Corner Design, c.1890, 71 x 28 In.	398.00
Mirror, Chippendale Style, Giltwood, Pierced Shell Work Crest, Flowers & Leaves, 58 x 35 In., Pair.	1230.00
Mirror, Chippendale Style, Mahogany, Eagle Crest, Molded, Carved Frame, c.1800, 35 x 20 In.	374.00
Mirror, Chippendale Style, Mahogany, Giltwood, Eagle Crest, Garlands, c.1890, 40 x 20 In.	206.00
Mirror, Chippendale Style, Mahogany, Prince Of Wales Crest, Gilt Garlands, 1900s, 41 x 19 In.	147.00
Mirror, Chippendale Style, Tiger Maple, Shaped Crest, Pendant, 33 x 17 In.	189.00
Mirror, Chippendale Style, Veneer, Giltwood, Phoenix, Continental, 1900s, 55 x 26 In. *Illus*	353.00
Mirror, Chippendale Style, Walnut, Parcel Gilt, Frieze Set, Leaves, Phoenix Heads, 1800s, 39 x 26 In.	531.00
Mirror, Chippendale, Giltwood, Pierced Pagoda Crest, Reverse Painted, Chinese, 28 x 16 In. *Illus*	18750.00
Mirror, Chippendale, Mahogany Inlay, Parcel Gilt, Applied Phoenix Crest, Carved, 29 In.	118.00
Mirror, Chippendale, Mahogany Veneer, String Inlay, Oval Patera, Crest, c.1750, 37 x 20 In.	705.00
Mirror, Chippendale, Mahogany, Flower Basket, 44 In.	383.00
Mirror, Chippendale, Mahogany, Fretwork, Phoenix Bird Crest, c.1790, 47 x 19 In.	185.00
Mirror, Chippendale, Mahogany, Gilt Gesso, Scrolled Frame, Phoenix Crest, c.1795, 38 x 22 In.	385.00
Mirror, Chippendale, Mahogany, Giltwood, Scroll Crest, Carved Eagle, c.1790, 38 x 20 In.	478.00
Mirror, Chippendale, Mahogany, Inlay, Carved Scroll Crest, c.1805, 21 ½ x 13 In.	177.00
Mirror, Chippendale, Mahogany, Parcel Gilt, Broken Pediment, Phoenix Crest	4248.00
Mirror, Chippendale, Mahogany, Parcel Gilt, Pierced & Gilt Phoenix, 34 In.	531.00
Mirror, Chippendale, Mahogany, Parcel Gilt, Scrolled Crest, Pediment, 26 In.	236.00
Mirror, Chippendale, Mahogany, Phoenix Crest, Giltwood, Openwork Carved, c.1760, 34 In.	295.00
Mirror, Chippendale, Mahogany, Phoenix Crest, Parcel Gilt, c.1790, 37 In.	243.00
Mirror, Chippendale, Urn, Flower Crest, Giltwood, Carved, 22 x 48 In.	805.00
Mirror, Chippendale, Walnut, Gilt Gesso, Carved Scrolling Design, c.1795, 28 x 18 In.	2726.00
Mirror, Chippendale, Walnut, Gilt Gesso, Scrolled Frame, Leaves, England, c.1795, 36 x 20 In.	415.00
Mirror, Chippendale, Walnut, Giltwood, Carved Crest, Phoenix, Molded Border, c.1795, 22 x 14 In.	889.00
Mirror, Chippendale, Walnut, Parcel Gilt, Scalloped Crest Rail, Urn, Flowers, c.1785, 43 x 19 In.	522.00
Mirror, Colonial Revival, Mahogany, Giltwood, Broken Swan Neck, Finials, Eagle, 61 x 24 In.	246.00
Mirror, Convex, Giltwood, 2 Candle Arms, Eagle Crest, c.1780, 40 In.	1778.00
Mirror, Convex, Giltwood, Composition, Eagle, Swags, Carved, Round, c.1890, 45 x 24 In.	1250.00
Mirror, Convex, Giltwood, Eagle Crest, Leaves, Shell Carved, 39 x 25 In.	531.00
Mirror, Convex, Giltwood, High Crest, Applied Leaf Mounts, c.1800, 36 ½ In.	325.00
Mirror, Convex, Regency, Gilt, Leaves, Scrolls, Dragons, Round, Candle Branches, Painted, 50 x 28 In.	3510.00
Mirror, Convex, Regency, Giltwood, Gilt Composition, Eagle Crest, Swags, Round, c.1810, 45 x 24 In.	1250.00
Mirror, Convex, Regency, Giltwood, Reeded, Carved, Round, 26 In.	1287.00
Mirror, Convex, Sunburst, Giltwood, c.1950, 34 x 27 In.	840.00
Mirror, Convex, William IV, Giltwood, Eagle Crest, Scrolls, c.1830, 38 x 25 In.	1250.00
Mirror, Copper, Repousse Designs, Oval, Liberty & Co., Paper Label, c.1905, 25 x 21 In.	1000.00
Mirror, Courting, Baltic Walnut, Parcel Gilt, Reverse Painted Panel, Woman In Hat, 29 In.	561.00
Mirror, Courting, Baltic Walnut, Parcel Gilt, Shaped Crest, Garland, Fruit Basket, 30 In.	354.00
Mirror, Courting, Molded Frame, Reverse Painted Glass, Wood Case, 1700s, 9 x 7 In. *Illus*	2760.00
Mirror, Courting, Painted Flowers On Crest & Side Panels, c.1795, 12 x 8 In.	711.00
Mirror, Courting, Queen Anne, Walnut, Peaked Carved Crest, 18 ½ x 10 In.	266.00
Mirror, Courting, Reverse Glass Painted Panels, Crest, Box, Red Paint, c.1900, 16 ½ In.	441.00
Mirror, Dressing, Federal, Mahogany, Pine, Inlay, Drawer, Brass Knobs, c.1840, 16 x 14 In.	161.00
Mirror, Dressing, Giltwood, Plumed Crest, Leafy Scrolls, Cabriole Legs, Italy, 1800s, 30 x 23 In.	1750.00
Mirror, Dressing, Hepplewhite, Mahogany, Bowfront, Acorn Finials, c.1800, 20 x 19 In.	87.00
Mirror, Dressing, Mahogany, Swivel, Acorn Finials, Ribbed Columns, Drawers, c.1800, 20 x 21 In.	715.00
Mirror, Dressing, Triptych, Beveled Glass, Adjustable, Embossed Iris, 3 Legs, 57 In.	474.00

Furniture, Desk, Arts & Crafts, Drop Front, Quartersawn Oak, England, c.1910, 48 x 29 In.
$250.00

Rago Arts & Auction Center

Furniture, Desk, Chippendale, Slant Front, Maple, Fitted Interior, Drawers, c.1790, 41 x 41 In.
$2,596.00

Brunk Auctions

Furniture, Desk, Chippendale, Slant Front, Walnut, Inside Drawers, Compartments, c.1770, 43 x 37 In.
$3,000.00

Skinner, Inc.

Furniture, Desk, Drop Front, Kimbel & Cabus, Oak, Brass Enamel, Felt, 1870s, 54 x 36 In. $1,500.00

Rago Arts & Auction Center

Furniture, Desk, Elm, 2 Pedestals, Shelves, Drawers, Puddingstone Top, Chinese, c.1890, 34 x 49 In. $235.00

Garth's Auctioneers & Appraisers

Furniture, Desk, Kai Kristiansen, Teak, Floating Top, Openwork Frame, Denmark, 1960s, 60 x 32 In. $1,067.00

Skinner, Inc.

Furniture, Desk, Partners, William IV, Mahogany, Leather Top, Tapered Reeded Legs, 29 x 54 In. $953.00

Leslie Hindman Auctioneers

Mirror, Eastlake, Walnut, Carved, Black Accents, 23 x 50 In.	147.00
Mirror, Empire Style, Gilt, Painted, Shield, Flowers, Leaves, Beveled Plate, 1800s, 47 x 56 In. ....*Illus*	236.00
Mirror, Empire Style, Mahogany, Gilt Bronze Mounted Panel, c.1850, 73 x 48 ½ In.	900.00
Mirror, Empire Style, Wood, Half-Turned Columns, Gilt Figural Plaque, Chariot, Putti, 51 x 23 In.	184.00
Mirror, Empire, Ebonized, Parcel Gilt Stylized Leaves, 51 x 31 In.	944.00
Mirror, Empire, Mahogany, Grain Painted, 26 ½ x 20 ½ In.	58.00
Mirror, Empire, Mahogany, Ogee Molded Frame, c.1850, 50 x 26 In.	173.00
Mirror, Federal Style, Burl, Cut Silhouette, Carved, Giltwood, Shell, Fan, 46 x 24 ½ In.	150.00
Mirror, Federal Style, Giltwood, Swan Crest, Cornucopia, Flowers, Oval, 33 x 32 In.	760.00
Mirror, Federal Style, Mahogany, Parcel Gilt, Eagle, Garland Crest, c.1870, 32 x 49 In.	840.00
Mirror, Federal Style, Reverse Painted, Inlay, Scrollwork, Urn, Flowers, c.1890, 54 x 24 In.	1062.00
Mirror, Federal, Convex, Gold Balls, Eagle Pediment, Gilt, c.1820, 39 In.	2360.00
Mirror, Federal, Gilt Gesso, Painted, Stencil, Horse, Wagon, Cottage, Columns, c.1800, 29 In.	415.00
Mirror, Federal, Giltwood, Carved, Molded Cornice, Bas-Relief Panel, Women, 49 x 30 In.	2242.00
Mirror, Federal, Giltwood, Columns, House & Bridge Scene Panel, c.1820, 26 ½ x 13 In.	89.00
Mirror, Federal, Giltwood, Convex, Carved Eagle Crest, 2 Candleholders, Prisms, 42 In.	2832.00
Mirror, Federal, Giltwood, Cove & Rope Molding, Columns, Applied Leaves, 44 In.	472.00
Mirror, Federal, Giltwood, Eagle Crest, 13 Carved Stars, Oval, Baltimore, 42 x 28 In.	1304.00
Mirror, Federal, Giltwood, Fruit Basket, Half Columns, Rosettes, 1800-25, 30 x 14 In. .... *Illus*	276.00
Mirror, Federal, Giltwood, Gesso, Rope Twist, Shell & Leaf Spray, c.1810, 32 x 19 In. .... *Illus*	356.00
Mirror, Federal, Giltwood, Molded Crest, Rope Twist, Reverse Painted, c.1810, 28 x 17 In. .... *Illus*	236.00
Mirror, Federal, Giltwood, Overhung Carved Cornice, Reverse Painted Flowers, 44 x 26 In.	590.00
Mirror, Federal, Giltwood, Reverse Painted Panel, Church, Landscape, 34 x 19 In.	295.00
Mirror, Federal, Giltwood, Reverse Painted Panel, Rope Twist Columns, 38 ½ In.	236.00
Mirror, Federal, Giltwood, Reverse Painted, Bridge, Waterfall Scene, c.1830, 27 ½ x 15 In.	122.00
Mirror, Federal, Giltwood, Reverse Painted, Eagle, Urn Finials, 43 x 22 In.	281.00
Mirror, Federal, Giltwood, Spiral Column, Cornucopia Crest, Cornice, c.1815, 31 x 16 In.	89.00
Mirror, Federal, Giltwood, Tablet, Turned Half Columns, Blocks & Rosettes, c.1835, 63 x 34 In.	369.00
Mirror, Federal, Inlaid Mahogany, Swan Neck Crest, Eagle Finial, 44 ½ In.	1180.00
Mirror, Federal, Mahogany, Crest, Reeded Columns, Reverse Paint Tablet, c.1820, 41 x 19 In........	1410.00
Mirror, Federal, Mahogany, Divided Pane, Turned Columns, Brass Rosettes, c.1830, 49 x 25 In.	575.00
Mirror, Federal, Mahogany, Giltwood, Constitution, Phoenix Crest, Carved, c.1800, 64 In.	2916.00
Mirror, Federal, Mahogany, Inlay, Oval, Turned Supports, Splayed Legs, c.1850, 24 x 28 In.	240.00
Mirror, Federal, Mahogany, Landscape & Houses Panel, Reverse Painted, c.1830, 23 In.	415.00
Mirror, Federal, Mahogany, Reeded Columns, Sailing Ship Panels, Painted, c.1820, 36 x 17 In.....	385.00
Mirror, Federal, Mahogany, Scrolling Crest, Conforming Apron, c.1800, 42 x 22 In.	478.00
Mirror, Federal, Pine, Mahogany, Reverse Painted Ship, Reeded Half Columns, c.1820, 37 x 22 In.	470.00
Mirror, Federal, Pine, Stepped Architectural Cornice, Reverse Paint, Columns, c.1800, 22 x 13 In.	646.00
Mirror, Federal, Reverse Painted Naval Battle Scene, c.1825, 32 x 16 In.	563.00
Mirror, Federal, Shaving, Adjustable, c.1805, 18 x 15 In.	91.00
Mirror, Federal, Split-Spindle, Giltwood, Reverse Painted Landscape Panel, New Eng., 40 In.	708.00
Mirror, Folk Art, Oyster Shells, Green Paint, Double Arched Top, Square Shape, 1900s, 28 x 25 In.	180.00
Mirror, French Provincial, Walnut, Molded Shell, Leaf Frame, Beaded Slip, c.1850, 44 x 44 In.	615.00
Mirror, George II Style, Giltwood, Rectangle, Pierced, Scroll Carved Frame, 49 x 28 In.	454.00
Mirror, George II Style, Mahogany, Openwork, Prince Of Wales Crest, c.1915, 39 x 9 In.	147.00
Mirror, George II Style, Walnut, Parcel Gilt, Eagle Rondel, 41 ½ x 23 ¾ In.	351.00
Mirror, George II, Giltwood, Chimney Glass, Floral Etched Panels, 64 x 25 In.	1416.00
Mirror, George II, Giltwood, Flower, Scrolls, Shaped Crest & Apron, 46 x 22 In.	3510.00
Mirror, George II, Parcel Gilt, Swan Neck Pediment, c.1760, 37 In.	1659.00
Mirror, George II, Walnut Veneer, Swan Neck Pediment, Gilt Masks, Shell, c.1765, 51 x 27 In........	4674.00
Mirror, George II, Walnut, Parcel Gilt, Scalloped Leaf Band, Swan Neck Crest, Eagle, 52 x 26 In. ..	1404.00
Mirror, George III Style, Giltwood, Carved, Oval, Diagonal Gadrooned Frame, 54 x 44 In..............	1989.00
Mirror, George III Style, Giltwood, Pierced Branches, Pagoda Shape Crest, Swan, 62 x 34 In., Pair.	3690.00
Mirror, George III Style, Mahogany, Giltwood, Flower Basket Crest, Carved, 1800s, 51 x 27 In.	920.00
Mirror, George III Style, Wood, Flowers, Scrolls Over Pane, Gold Paint, 44 x 28 In.	563.00
Mirror, George III, Giltwood, Eagle, Chains, Scrolling Flowers, Reeded Columns, c.1800..............	3884.00
Mirror, George III, Giltwood, Shaped Plate, Scrolls, Flowers, Leaves, Swags, 1700s, 44 x 28 In........	950.00
Mirror, George III, Giltwood, Shell & Leaf Crest, Pierced Flowers Pendant, c.1785, 56 x 24 In........	1353.00
Mirror, George III, Parcel Gilt, Reticulated, Scrolled, Pierced, c.1775, 55 x 31 In.	3600.00
Mirror, George IV, Giltwood, Eagle Crest, Round Convex Mirror, Reeded Border, 37 x 25 In..........	1200.00
Mirror, Georgian, Mahogany, Giltwood, Carved Crest, Ears, Shaped Pane, c.1755, 51 ½ In...........	1778.00
Mirror, Gilt Gesso, Carved, Reticulated Arched Crest, Square, Italy, 1700s, 51 x 26 In.	3105.00
Mirror, Gilt Gesso, Reverse Painted, Fruit Basket, Split Baluster, c.1830, 30 x 15 In.	356.00
Mirror, Gilt Gesso, Spread Wing Eagle, Rocks, Leafy Scrolls, Bellflower Pendant, c.1800, 42 In......	2370.00
Mirror, Gilt Iron, Sun Shape, Leafy & Pointed Rays, Round Center, France, 1940s, 20 In. Diam.	1875.00
Mirror, Gilt Metal, Layered Rectangle, Jean Philippe, c.1970, 37 x 26 In........................	2250.00

Mirror, Gilt Wrought Iron, Pointed Crest, Pierced, P. Kiss, 1920s, 1920s, 35 x 12 In.	1875.00
Mirror, Giltwood, Acanthus Crest, Oval Shaped, Scrolled Brackets, c.1800, 35 x 49 In.	717.00
Mirror, Giltwood, Arched Cornice, Flowers, Women Holding Garland, c.1900, 101 x 56 In., Pair	13200.00
Mirror, Giltwood, Arched Openwork Crest, 3 Plumes, Multicolor, Continental, 1700s, 29 x 16 In.	800.00
Mirror, Giltwood, Arched Upper Panel, Acanthus Frame, Urn Finial, 1800s, 55 x 25 In.	1200.00
Mirror, Giltwood, Basket, Flower Carved Crest, c.1850, 13 ½ x 20 ½ In.	115.00
Mirror, Giltwood, Carved Urn, Flower Crest, Swag Frame, Continental, c.1940, 58 x 30 In.	330.00
Mirror, Giltwood, Carved, Cherub Head & Angel Wing Crest, Scrolling, Italy, 20 ¼ In.	366.00
Mirror, Giltwood, Carved, Flower Basket Crest, 1800s, 58 x 42 In.	178.00
Mirror, Giltwood, Carved, Split Baluster Surround, Leaf Blocks, c.1830, 53 x 29 In.	1098.00
Mirror, Giltwood, Carved, Split Baluster, Rosettes, Caleb P. Wayne, 1800s, 25 x 19 In.	657.00
Mirror, Giltwood, Columnar, Acorn Drops, Painted Tablet, Riverscape, c.1830, 38 x 23 In.	196.00
Mirror, Giltwood, Composition, Pierced Crest, Scroll Carved, Lapis Blue Border, c.1865, 54 x 32 In.	600.00
Mirror, Giltwood, Convex, 12 Balls, Eagle, Olive Branches, Shield, Arrows, c.1900, 36 x 27 In.	461.00
Mirror, Giltwood, Convex, Molded Frame, Spherules Design, c.1825, 27 In. Diam.	1793.00
Mirror, Giltwood, Convex, Round, Shadowbox Frame, Balls Design, c.1885, 16 In. Diam.	492.00
Mirror, Giltwood, Eagle Crest, Rays, England, c.1855, 45 ½ x 30 In.	2125.00
Mirror, Giltwood, Engraved Classical Figures, Curved Crest, Italy, c.1750, 28 x 15 In., Pair	972.00
Mirror, Giltwood, Flower Basket Crest, Lobed Plate, Pendant Fan Carving, 50 x 20 In.	415.00
Mirror, Giltwood, Flowers, Scrolls, LaBarge, 41 x 37 In.	268.00
Mirror, Giltwood, Gesso, Flower Border, Arched, c.1905, 64 x 37 In.	472.00
Mirror, Giltwood, Gesso, Leaf, Ribbon, Flower Carved Crest, c.1900, 45 x 29 In.	450.00
Mirror, Giltwood, Guilloche Molded Frame, France, 60 x 24 In.	984.00
Mirror, Giltwood, Half Column, Reverse Painted Riverscape Panel, c.1830, 32 x 16 In.	236.00
Mirror, Giltwood, Harvest Mask, Swan Crest, Scrolls, Divided Panes, c.1850, 63 x 34 In.	625.00
Mirror, Giltwood, Leaf & Ventilated Slip, Flower Carved Molded Frame, France, 55 x 44 In.	676.00
Mirror, Giltwood, Lyre, Scrolls, Shields, Leaves, Molded Frame, Italy, c.1890, 46 x 21 In. .... *Illus*	2952.00
Mirror, Giltwood, Molded Frame, Flower Bouquet, Scrolling Leaves, c.1890, 62 x 40 In.	1599.00
Mirror, Giltwood, Neoclassical Style, Bird Crest, Wreath, Anthemion Corners, 74 x 64 In.	738.00
Mirror, Giltwood, Oval, Leaf Pierced Crest, Putto, Candle Cups, France, 78 In.	313.00
Mirror, Giltwood, Oval, Pierced, Urn Finial, Fell Flowers, Pendants, 1900s, 48 x 27 In., Pair	2160.00
Mirror, Giltwood, Painted, Mirrored Glass, Square, Wavy Interior Border, Italy, 1940s, 31 In.	2250.00
Mirror, Giltwood, Pierce Carved Leaves & Shell, Egg & Dart Border, Italy, 35 x 39 In.	1375.00
Mirror, Giltwood, Pierced & Scrolling Crest, Leaves & Shells, c.1890, 60 x 31 In.	984.00
Mirror, Giltwood, Pierced, Scrolled, Carved, Venetian, 105 x 68 In.	4720.00
Mirror, Giltwood, Rectangular, Split Baluster, Molded Surround, Rosettes, c.1890, 44 x 77 In.	2629.00
Mirror, Giltwood, Reticulated Frame, Putti, Scrollwork, 1700s, 27 x 23 In.	5819.00
Mirror, Giltwood, Reticulated Frame, Putti, Scrollwork, Continental, 1700s, 26 ½ x 23 In.	1722.00
Mirror, Giltwood, Reverse Painted, Cornice, Suspended Balls, Maiden, Child, c.1810, 30 x 16 In.	184.00
Mirror, Giltwood, Ring-Turned Split Baluster Frame, Rosette Blocks, c.1830, 25 x 42 In.	598.00
Mirror, Giltwood, Scrolls, Flowers, Leaves, Crosshatching, c.1885, 46 x 32 In.	1107.00
Mirror, Giltwood, Shaped, Pierced, Acanthus Scrolls, Birds, Flowers, 1800s, 56 x 29 In.	1900.00
Mirror, Giltwood, Spindle Gallery Crest, Bellflowers, Columns, c.1885, 79 x 46 In.	1476.00
Mirror, Giltwood, Stepped Cornice, Continental, c.1790, 13 x 22 In.	230.00
Mirror, Giltwood, Stepped Leaf Carved Frame, Italy, c.1700, 18 x 15 In.	500.00
Mirror, Giltwood, Sunburst, Oval, c.1960, 35 x 28 In.	720.00
Mirror, Giltwood, Sunburst, Round Center, Pointed Rays, Leaf Molded, 24 In. Diam.	461.00
Mirror, Giltwood, Swirling Leaf Scrolls, Oval Plate, c.1900, 10 x 8 In.	184.00
Mirror, Girandole, Gilt Gesso, Eagle On Rocks Crest, Leaves, c.1800, 41 x 23 In.	4444.00
Mirror, Girandole, Giltwood, Carved Eagle Finial, Leaf Crest, Round, c.1815, 34 x 16 In.	12400.00
Mirror, Girandole, Giltwood, Eagle Finial, Dolphin Appliques, 58 x 46 In.	4977.00
Mirror, Girandole, Giltwood, Eagle, Ball & Chain In Beak, Candle Sconces, c.1800, 28 x 26 In.	1422.00
Mirror, Girandole, Giltwood, Eagle, Grapevines, Scrolled Candle Supports, 48 x 29 In.	4063.00
Mirror, Girandole, Giltwood, Eagle, Leaf Carved, Ball Embellishments, Round, 18 x 41 In.	1180.00
Mirror, Glass, Brass, Copper, Round, Leafy Branch Border, C. Jere, 1982, 31 In. Diam.	2000.00
Mirror, Glass, Repeating Rocaille Design, Parcel Gilt, Etched Leaves, Italy, 35 x 24 In.	469.00
Mirror, Gothic Revival, Venetian, Gilt Decorated, Carved, Flowers, Scrolling Leaves, 25 x 16 In.	115.00
Mirror, Gothic Revival, Walnut, Cathedral Crest, Shaped Plate, Carved, c.1850, 81 x 35 In.	1912.00
Mirror, Grotto Style, Bull's-Eye, Beveled Plate, Molded Frame, Abalone Shells, 37 In. Diam.	676.00
Mirror, Hall, Louis XV Style, Giltwood, Cherubs, Leaves, Panes, France, c.1870, 56 x 71 In.	4425.00
Mirror, Hepplewhite, Giltwood, Classical Figures, Symbols, 1795, 46 x 24 In.	830.00
Mirror, Infinity, Gilt Metal, c.1970, 36 x 20 In.	1875.00
Mirror, Italian Style, Sunburst, Beveled Plate, 8 Canted Rays, 37 In. Diam.	399.00
Mirror, Jacobean Style, Giltwood, Scalloped, Beaded, Lunette Sections, Chain, 27 x 23 In.	738.00
Mirror, Karl Springer, Domed & Beveled Glass, Arched Top, 1970s, 48 x 30 In.	2750.00
Mirror, Louis Philippe, Giltwood, Painted, Beaded Border, c.1860, 39 x 28 In., Pair	720.00

Furniture, Desk, Roll Top, Oak, Drawers, Kneehole, 12 Pigeonholes, Cross Support, 42 x 60 In.
$330.00

DuMouchelles Art Gallery

F

Furniture, Desk, School, Oak, Attached Chair, Child's
$84.00

Victorian Casino Antiques

Furniture, Desk, Shaker, Sister's, Sewing, Maple, Drawers, Pullout Slide, Sabbathday Lake, c.1845, 39 In.
$42,120.00

Willis Henry Auctions, Inc.

TIP
Large mirrors should not be taken down to be cleaned. Get an assistant to hold the mirror steady while it is being wiped.

Furniture, Desk, Shaker, Slant Front, Pine, Maple, Alfred Merrick Collier, 1861, 48 x 31 In.
$37,440.00

Willis Henry Auctions, Inc.

Furniture, Desk, Slant Front, Cherry, String Inlay, Carved Fan, Compartments, c.1790, 42 x 37 In.
$8,295.00

Skinner, Inc.

Furniture, Desk, Slant Front, Oak, House Of Representatives, Federal Crest, c.1856, 36 x 29 In.
$12,548.00

Neal Auction Co.

Furniture, Desk, Veneer, Drawers, Compartments Behind Book Bindings, Inlays, 1700s, 37 x 33 In.
$3,250.00

Skinner, Inc.

Mirror, Louis Philippe, Pierced Crest, Putti, Urn Finials, Garland, 1800s, 37 x 14 In.	1770.00
Mirror, Louis XV Style, Angled Crest, Scrolling Leave & Flowers, c.1850, 75 x 35 In.	799.00
Mirror, Louis XV Style, Gilt, Flowers, Music Trophy Crest, Pierced, 67 x 39 In.	2340.00
Mirror, Louis XV Style, Giltwood, Domed, C-Scroll Leaf & Flower Crest, c.1890, 81 x 49 In.	1599.00
Mirror, Louis XV Style, Giltwood, Rectangular, Acanthine Frame, Corner Accents, 48 x 57 In.	338.00
Mirror, Louis XV Style, Metal, Scrolls, Shells, Cherubs, Flower Terminal, Gold Paint, Oval, 22 In.	625.00
Mirror, Louis XV, Giltwood, Arched Crest, Fleur-De-Lis, Divided Pane, 35 x 22 In.	5313.00
Mirror, Louis XVI Style, Giltwood, Arched, Woman, Putto, Lyre, Painted, Pane, 70 x 50 In.	2500.00
Mirror, Louis XVI Style, Giltwood, Cabochons, Beaded, Flowers, Mask, c.1900, 68 In.	2435.00
Mirror, Louis XVI Style, Giltwood, Carved Garlands, Ribbons, c.1860, 39 x 29 In.	875.00
Mirror, Louis XVI Style, Giltwood, Flower Wreath, Torch, Ribbon Frame, c.1900, 68 x 41 In.	1353.00
Mirror, Louis XVI Style, Giltwood, Flowers, Leaves, Divided Panes, Octagonal, c.1860, 76 In.	3125.00
Mirror, Louis XVI Style, Giltwood, Openwork Crest, Cabochon, Cherubs, Cushion Shape, 53 x 40 In.	1845.00
Mirror, Louis XVI Style, Giltwood, Oval, Beaded, Woman Profile, Acanthus Pendant, 47 x 32 In.	793.00
Mirror, Louis XVI Style, Giltwood, Oval, Pierced Borders, Scrolls, Fruit, c.1885, 27 x 17 In., Pair	922.00
Mirror, Louis XVI Style, Giltwood, Reeded, Canted Corners, Shield, Flowers, c.1900, 77 x 61 In.	461.00
Mirror, Louis XVI Style, Giltwood, Reeded, Scrolled Corbels, Pierced Crest, 51 In.	738.00
Mirror, Louis XVI Style, Giltwood, Scrolls, Torchere, Molded Leaf Frame, 1800s, 54 x 31 In.	799.00
Mirror, Louis XVI Style, Giltwood, Shield, Cherubs, Flowers, Leaves, c.1890, 79 x 49 In.	3444.00
Mirror, Louis XVI Style, Giltwood, Wreath Crest, Flowers, Brass Rosettes, c.1900, 59 x 60 In.	1476.00
Mirror, Louis XVI Style, Ormolu, Shaped Pediment, Acanthus Crest, Guilloche, c.1890, 51 x 29 In.	2214.00
Mirror, Louis XVI Style, Painted Panel, Shell, Scroll, Molded Frame, c.1850, 60 x 33 In. .... *Illus*	1845.00
Mirror, Louis XVI, Walnut, Giltwood, Painted, Flowers, Woman's Portrait, Roundel, 28 x 17 In.	450.00
Mirror, Mahogany, Carved, Parcel Gilt Eagle Crest, c.1750, 43 x 23 In.	875.00
Mirror, Mahogany, Crocketed Cathedral, Stylized Leaves, Tracery, c.1845, 60 x 32 In.	2091.00
Mirror, Mahogany, Giltwood, Broken-Arch Pediment, Shell Crest, Wm. Sprinks, 47 x 28 In.	590.00
Mirror, Mahogany, Giltwood, Cornucopia, Fruit & Nuts On Crest, Beribboned Base, 1800s	610.00
Mirror, Mahogany, Giltwood, Reverse Painted, Blue, Gilt Flowers, Eagle, 1900s, 45 x 10 In.	30.00
Mirror, Mahogany, Intertwined Oak Leaves Border, Pierced, Carved, Oval, 27 x 25 In.	354.00
Mirror, Mahogany, Parcel Gilt, Carved, Pierced, 2 Swans Crest, Dolphin Base, 58 x 45 In.	590.00
Mirror, Mahogany, Split Baluster, Bull's-Eye Corner Blocks, Gilding, 1800s, 9 x 7 In.	2252.00
Mirror, Napoleon III, Argente, Shaped Crest, Molded Frame, c.1865, 61 x 38 In.	1722.00
Mirror, Napoleon III, Giltwood, Beaded, Leaves, Ogee Molding, Ribbons, c.1890, 43 x 37 In.	246.00
Mirror, Napoleon III, Giltwood, Ogee Molding, Leaves, Stippled, Ribbons, 39 x 33 In.	553.00
Mirror, Napoleon III, Giltwood, Oval, Molded, Beaded, Leaf Pierced, Putti, c.1885, 74 x 55 In.	3444.00
Mirror, Napoleon III, Giltwood, Oval, Molded, Lovebirds, Torch, Beaded, c.1865, 41 x 24 In.	1045.00
Mirror, Napoleon III, Giltwood, Oval, Molded, Scroll, Pierced, Putti, Grapes, c.1850, 64 x 41 In.	3198.00
Mirror, Napoleon III, Giltwood, Painted, Molded Leaves, Flowers, Ribbon, c.1885, 48 x 31 In.	615.00
Mirror, Napoleon III, Giltwood, Rounded, Flower Basket, Leaf, Scrolls, c.1865, 91 x 54 In.	3444.00
Mirror, Neoclassical Style, Giltwood, Guilloche, Carved Frieze, Reeded Pilasters, 1900s, 37 x 56 In.	676.00
Mirror, Neoclassical Style, Giltwood, Scrolls, Swags, Urn Crest, Carved, 39 x 26 In., Pair	380.00
Mirror, Neoclassical Style, Wood, Urn Crest, Scrolled Frame, Swans, Leaves, 52 x 22 In., Pair	938.00
Mirror, Neoclassical, Gilt Gesso, Brass Flower Medallion Corners, c.1830, 26 x 17 In.	770.00
Mirror, Neoclassical, Gilt Gesso, Tablet, Gazebo, Man, Sailboat, c.1800, 33 x 18 In.	474.00
Mirror, Neoclassical, Gilt Gesso, Torch, Arrow Quiver, Vines, Gilt, Painted, c.1790, 36 In.	770.00
Mirror, Neoclassical, Giltwood, Carved, Bowknot, Arrows, Flowers, Oval, 1800s, 28 x 15 In.	593.00
Mirror, Neoclassical, Giltwood, Marble, Scrolls, Urn, Flowers, Drop Finials, c.1810, 39 x 17 In.	1495.00
Mirror, Neoclassical, Giltwood, Painted, Carved, Lyre & Griffins, Leaf Pendants, 73 x 39 In.	1722.00
Mirror, Neoclassical, Medallion Corners, Pierced Crest, Bowknot, c.1785, 45 x 12 In.	2091.00
Mirror, Neoclassical, Projected Crown, Scrolling Leaves, Columns, 1700s, 64 x 50 In.	299.00
Mirror, Oscar Bach, Bronze, Pierced Crest, Virgo, Aries Designs, c.1925, 41 x 22 In.	4140.00
Mirror, P. Evans, Chrome Plated Steel, Brass, Rectangular, Cityscape, 1970s, 70 x 20 In.	5000.00
Mirror, Painted, Gilt, Beaded Oval Frame, Leaf Cartouche, Bracket Base, c.1850, 47 x 60 In.	1315.00
Mirror, Parcel Gilt, Columns, Griffins, Arrows, Painted, Italy, c.1850, 47 x 54 In., Pair	4000.00
Mirror, Parcel Gilt, Mahogany, Arched, Cabochon, Flowers, Leaves, Brackets, c.1885, 91 x 60 In.	276.00
Mirror, Patinated Bronze, Jean Charles, France, c.1970, 45 x 39 In.	2750.00
Mirror, Pier, Black Forest, Walnut, Bird's Nest Crest, Grapes, Candle Shelf, c.1890, 109 x 42 In.	575.00
Mirror, Pier, Blocked Cornice, Swag & Medallions, Columns, c.1810, 45 x 24 In.	1016.00
Mirror, Pier, Empire, Gilt Bronze, Molded, Urn, Rosettes, Palmette Border, 50 x 30 In.	750.00
Mirror, Pier, French Empire, Painted, Leaf Wreath, Swan, Medallions, c.1900, 43 In.	2952.00
Mirror, Pier, George I, Walnut, Parcel Gilt, Shaped Crest, Leaf Medallion, 51 x 19 In.	2750.00
Mirror, Pier, George II, Mahogany, Parcel Gilt, c.1775, 41 x 18 In.	500.00
Mirror, Pier, George III Style, Gilt, Painted, Broken-Arch Crest, Plume, Ruins, c.1890, 64 x 55 In.	3585.00
Mirror, Pier, Georgian Style, Giltwood, Broken-Arch Crest, Flowers, Crosshatch Border, 78 x 43 In.	1185.00
Mirror, Pier, Giltwood, Block Cornice, Shell, Pilasters, Victorian, 51 x 28 In. .... *Illus*	281.00
Mirror, Pier, Giltwood, Carved Crest, Divided Pane, 1800s, 47 x 24 In.	2000.00

Mirror, Pier, Giltwood, Divided Plate, Molded Frame, Carved, 1800s, 34 x 18 In.	777.00
Mirror, Pier, Giltwood, Leaf, Urn, Flowers, Swags, Satyrs, Italy, c.1850, 70 x 49 In.	4888.00
Mirror, Pier, Giltwood, Molded Cornice, Spherules, Gothic Tracery, Columns, c.1800, 42 x 25 In.	837.00
Mirror, Pier, Mahogany, Stepped Cornice, Giltwood, Leaves, Masks, c.1835, 71 x 35 In.	2214.00
Mirror, Pier, Neoclassical, Birch, Parcel Gilt, Molded Projecting Cornice, 45 x 24 In.	938.00
Mirror, Pier, Neoclassical, Ebonized, Giltwood, Columns, Fleur-De-Lis Corners, 55 x 28 In.	1968.00
Mirror, Pier, Neoclassical, Gilt Gesso, Carved, c.1810, 64 x 37 In.	1541.00
Mirror, Pier, Neoclassical, Giltwood, Painted, Classical Soldier, 47 x 15 In., Pair .... *Illus*	188.00
Mirror, Pier, Regency, Giltwood, Projected Crest, Turned Columns, 1800s, 45 x 26 In.	598.00
Mirror, Pier, Regency, Giltwood, Urn Crest, Scrolls, Banded, 1800s, 57 x 27 In.	1016.00
Mirror, Pier, Renaissance Revival, Giltwood, Molded Frame, Scrolls, Wreath, 102 In.	345.00
Mirror, Pier, Renaissance Revival, Walnut, Giltwood, Marble Shelf, c.1890, 101 x 35 In.	938.00
Mirror, Pier, Rococo Revival, Giltwood, Pierced Crest, Carved Scrolls, 1800s, 84 x 36 In.	300.00
Mirror, Pier, Rococo Style, Painted, Flowers, Peak Crest, Shaped Frame, c.1890, 107 x 41 In.	840.00
Mirror, Pier, Sleeping Maiden, Pierced Flowers, Gilt Gesso Frame, c.1895, 83 x 37 In.	633.00
Mirror, Pine, Gilt, Carved Leaf Frame, Scrolls, Openwork, 1900s, 62 x 33 In.	881.00
Mirror, Pine, Mahogany, Mortise & Tenon, Pierced, Painted, c.1825, 19 x 10 In.	1778.00
Mirror, Pine, Reverse Glass, Landscape, Stenciled Leaves, 1800s, 26 x 14 In.	235.00
Mirror, Pine, Scrolled Crest, Molded Frame, Brown Stain, c.1790, 19 x 11 In.	1440.00
Mirror, Pine, Urn Crest, Leafy Garland, 1800s, 31 x 17 In., Pair	705.00
Mirror, Poplar, Stained, Applied Cherub On Crest, 1800s, 20 ½ x 12 ½ In.	30.00
Mirror, Porcelain, Painted, Oval, Shield, Flowers, Meissen Style, 1900s, 16 x 12 In.	420.00
Mirror, Queen Anne, Mahogany Veneer, Scrolling Crest, Beveled, c.1775, 23 ½ x 12 In.	563.00
Mirror, Queen Anne, Mahogany, Giltwood, Stepped Mirror Plates, c.1750, 33 x 14 ½ In.	1422.00
Mirror, Queen Anne, Mahogany, Scalloped Crest, Gilt Bezel, 28 x 17 In.	504.00
Mirror, Queen Anne, Mahogany, Scrolled Crest, c.1780, 22 ½ x 11 ½ In.	237.00
Mirror, Queen Anne, Walnut, Parcel Gilt, Pierced Crest, Leaves, Molded, c.1795, 36 In.	582.00
Mirror, Queen Anne, Walnut, Pine, Cutout Crest, Carved, 2 Plates, c.1760, 48 x 17 ½ In.	460.00
Mirror, Queen Anne, Walnut, Scrolled Crest, Molded Frame, Beveled Glass, 15 x 10 In.	563.00
Mirror, Queen Anne, Walnut, Shaped Crest, c.1740, 32 x 19 In.	2133.00
Mirror, Regency, Giltwood, Bull's Eye, Dolphins Crest, Eagle, c.1815, 37 x 23 In.	2952.00
Mirror, Regency, Giltwood, Column Supports, Carved Capitals, c.1815, 41 x 15 In.	531.00
Mirror, Regency, Giltwood, Gadrooned Cornice, Fluted Pilaster, c.1815, 28 x 61 In.	338.00
Mirror, Regency, Giltwood, Rectilinear Shape, Beveled, Reeded Frame, c.1835, 42 x 32 In.	676.00
Mirror, Regency, Giltwood, Reverse Painted, Landscape, Columns, c.1800, 30 x 57 In.	1020.00
Mirror, Regency, Giltwood, Round, Eagle, Leaves, Pineapple Pendant, 1800s, 49 x 29 In.	4920.00
Mirror, Regency, Giltwood, Stag, Leaf Crest, Candle Arms, Eng., c.1810, 41 x 26 In.	4720.00
Mirror, Renaissance Revival, Cartouche, Molded, Ornamental Corners, c.1860, 73 x 52 In.	2460.00
Mirror, Renaissance Revival, Giltwood, Central Cartouche, Brackets, c.1865, 73 x 52 In.	553.00
Mirror, Reverse Painted Landscape, Ruins, Wood, Composition, c.1800, 40 x 21 In.	295.00
Mirror, Reverse Painted, Flowers, Mahogany, c.1830, 21 x 12 In.	176.00
Mirror, Rococo Revival, Giltwood, Arched Top, Carved Cupid, 2 Birds, c.1850, 65 x 42 In.	1800.00
Mirror, Rococo Revival, Giltwood, Pierced Crest, Fruit, Corn, Leaves, Beaded, c.1850, 95 x 43 In.	1342.00
Mirror, Rococo Revival, Giltwood, Shaped Surround, Scrolled Acanthus, c.1890, 34 x 39 In.	478.00
Mirror, Rococo Revival, Molded Composition, Beveled Mirror, 1800s, 45 x 28 ½ In. .... *Illus*	1062.00
Mirror, Rococo Revival, Shaped Carved Frame, Giltwood, c.1800, 46 x 31 In.	353.00
Mirror, Rococo Style, Giltwood, Flowers, Scrolls, Carved, Arched Crest, c.1975	360.00
Mirror, Rococo Style, Giltwood, Interlocking C-Scrolls, Leaves, Pierced, c.1885, 51 x 29 In.	861.00
Mirror, Rococo Style, Giltwood, Mahogany, Pierced, Shell, Scrolls, Scalloped, 73 x 33 In.	657.00
Mirror, Rococo Style, Giltwood, Oval, Pierced, Scrolls, 52 ½ x 29 In.	1063.00
Mirror, Rococo Style, Giltwood, Pierced, Flower, Shield Shape, 49 x 28 In., Pair	1500.00
Mirror, Rococo Style, Giltwood, Rocaille Crest, Vines, Leafy Scrolls, 58 x 41 In.	1250.00
Mirror, Rococo Style, Giltwood, Shaped Frame, Scrolling Rocaille, Flowers, Putti, 68 In.	593.00
Mirror, Rococo Style, Giltwood, Shield, Scrolls, Carved Crest, Wing Mask, 30 x 17 In.	1375.00
Mirror, Rococo, Giltwood, Carved Scrolling Leaves, Openwork, c.1800, 36 x 21 In.	295.00
Mirror, Rococo, Giltwood, Carved, Openwork, Scrolling Leaves, Leaf Tips, 55 x 38 In.	980.00
Mirror, Rococo, Giltwood, Molded, Rounded Crest, France, 1800s, 49 x 33 In.	472.00
Mirror, Rococo, Giltwood, Pierced Scrollwork, Flowers, Shell Finial, 35 x 25 In.	399.00
Mirror, Rococo, Giltwood, Rocaille, Cartouche, Divided Pane, Scrolls, Leaves, c.1800, 104 x 71 In.	1750.00
Mirror, Shaving, Black Lacquer, Oval, Giltwood, Chinoiserie Paint, Victorian, 53 x 12 In.	600.00
Mirror, Shaving, Door, Swing Candleholders, Brass, France, 32 x 18 In.	236.00
Mirror, Shaving, Federal, Mahogany, Brass Finials, 3 Drawers, c.1850, 22 ½ x 15 In.	326.00
Mirror, Shaving, George II, Mahogany, Drawer, c.1760, 23 x 14 In.	237.00
Mirror, Shaving, George III, Mahogany, c.1790, 24 ¾ x 18 ½ In.	267.00
Mirror, Shaving, Georgian, Mahogany Veneer, Pine, Scroll Crest, Gold Liner, Stand, c.1795, 19 In.	235.00
Mirror, Shaving, Hepplewhite, Mahogany, 3 Drawers, c.1810, 22 x 22 ½ In.	273.00

Furniture, Desk, William IV, Mahogany, Fitted Gallery Shelf, Hinged Top, Leather, c.1835, 44 x 54 In.
$984.00

New Orleans Auction Galleries, Inc.

F

Furniture, Desk, Wooton, Walnut, Burl, Oilcloth Top, Rotary Storage Base, 31 x 60 In.
$2,271.00

Neal Auction Co.

Furniture, Desk-Bookcase, Baroque, Bombe, Inlay, Fluted Interior, Glazed Doors, 1700s, 92 x 45 In.
$3,540.00

Brunk Auctions

Furniture, Dining Set, Roche Bobois, Walnut, Ebony, Inlay, Table, 8 Chairs, Credenza, Cabinets, Mirror
$2,187.00

Skinner, Inc.

Furniture, Dresser, Mahogany, Carved, Arched Doors, Drawers, 2 Doors, Chinese, 68 x 32 ½ In. $177.00

Conestoga Auction Co., Inc.

Furniture, Dresser, Pewter, Pine, Shelves, Ogee-Molded Cornice, 2 Parts, New Eng., c.1885, 78 x 69 In. $1,045.00

New Orleans Auction Galleries, Inc.

Furniture, Easel, Walnut, Ebonized, Metal Wolf Bust, Adjustable, c.1865, 80 x 36 In. $5,227.00

Neal Auction Co.

Mirror, Shaving, Sheraton, Mahogany, c.1825, 29 x 25 ½ In.	119.00
Mirror, Sheraton, Grain Painted, Reverse Painted Landscape Panel, 33 ½ In.	236.00
Mirror, Square Corners, Leaves, Strapwork, Beading, Morning Glories, c.1885, 34 x 79 In.	584.00
Mirror, Stepped Cornice, Star Carved Cartouche, 2 Finials, Syria, c.1900, 66 x 41 In.	1680.00
Mirror, Tabernacle, Federal, Giltwood, Shaped Crest, Banding, Reverse Painted, 47 x 30 In.	3750.00
Mirror, Tabernacle, Giltwood, Fruit Basket Panel, Carved, c.1870, 32 x 20 In.	71.00
Mirror, Tabernacle, Giltwood, Rounded, Gilt Leaves, Gadrooned, 1880s, 56 x 26 In.	1107.00
Mirror, Tabernacle, Neoclassical, Mahogany, Grooved, Ribbon, Balusters, 42 x 22 In.	127.00
Mirror, Tabernacle, Renaissance Style, Pine, Shaped Crest, Columns, Shelf, c.1800, 44 x 32 In.	732.00
Mirror, Tramp Art, Chip Carved Frame, 1908, 22 x 13 ¾ In.	267.00
Mirror, Tramp Art, Crest Arch, c.1850, 21 x 17 ¾ In.	91.00
Mirror, Trifold, Tole, Applied Flowers, Branches, c.1910, 28 x 38 In.	750.00
Mirror, Urn, Garland Finial, Frame, c.1890, 34 x 21 In.	130.00
Mirror, Venetian Style, Leaf Design, Shaped Crest, Beveled Glass, Oval, 34 x 19 In.	117.00
Mirror, Venetian, Shaped & Domed, Pierced Frame, Italy, 1900s, 49 x 33 In.	1045.00
Mirror, Victorian, Giltwood, Mask Crest, Arched, Columns, c.1865, 78 x 63 In.	885.00
Mirror, Victorian, Giltwood, Shield Crest, Shaped, Scrolled, 24 In.	119.00
Mirror, Victorian, Walnut, Side Stands, Leaf, Fluted Carvings, 58 x 105 In.	932.00
Mirror, Walnut Veneer, Gilt Gesso, Shaped Crest, Flowers, Beaded, c.1775, 25 In.	356.00
Mirror, Walnut Veneer, Rococo, Scrolled, Pierced Crest, Bracket, c.1790, 29 x 12 In.	711.00
Mirror, Walnut, Carved, Oval, Beveled, Scrolling Vines, Grapes, 1800s, 24 x 21 In.	1955.00
Mirror, Walnut, Gilt Gesso, Arched, Candle Shelves, Drop Finials, c.1860, 30 x 22 In.	711.00
Mirror, Walnut, Mahogany, Photograph, Man, Woman, Columns, c.1850, 39 x 22 In.	120.00
Mirror, Walnut, Projecting Cornice, Leaves, Berries, Vines, Pilasters, c.1890, 58 x 41 In.	307.00
Mirror, Wendell Castle, Walnut, Hanging, Free-Form, Signed, 1976, 16 x 14 In.	8625.00
Mirror, William & Mary, Walnut Frame, 18 ½ In.	1180.00
Mirror, Wood, Black Paint, Carved, Dragons & Pearls, Elongated, 72 x 37 In.	1230.00
Mirror, Wood, Carved, Dolphins, Beading, Continental, 1800s, 47 x 33 In.	764.00
Mirror, Wood, Garlands, Ribbons, Flowers, Cupid, Shaped, Painted, France, c.1890, 31 x 24 In.	840.00
Mirror, Wood, White Wash, Flower Filled Urn Scene, Painted, c.1780, 50 x 18 In.	690.00
Mirror, Wrought Iron, Tole, Leaf & Flower Surround, Rope Molded, c.1900, Pair	732.00
Ottoman, Brown Leather, Nailhead, Bun Feet, Century Furniture, 20 x 25 x 15 In.	207.00
Ottoman, Frank Lloyd Wright, Hexagonal, Taliesin Design, Henredon, 28 x 31 x 19 In.	950.00
Ottoman, Victorian Style, Needlework Upholstery, Tassels, 17 x 23 In.	527.00
Ottoman, Walnut, Shell Knees, Cabriole Legs, Grotesque Masks, 19 x 24 In.	330.00
Overmantel mirror, see Architectural category.	
Parlor Set, Limbert, Oak, Curved Crest, Cane Splat, Ebony Inlay, 38-In. Chair, 3 Piece	900.00
Pedestal, Blackamoor Presenting Basket, Multicolor, Majolica, 20 In.	1195.00
Pedestal, Blackamoor, Woman, Holding Torch, Sarong, Turban, Gilt, c.1890, 48 In.	2460.00
Pedestal, Blackamoors, Rectangular Top, Multicolor Paint, c.1730, 28 x 20 In.	5580.00
Pedestal, Boulle Style, Marquetry, Gilt Bronze, Tapered, Masks, 51 x 18 In.	3500.00
Pedestal, Brass, Steel, Round Glass Top, Triangular Stretcher, c.1970, 32 x 14 In., Pair	600.00
Pedestal, Cherry, Gilt Bronze, Revolving Top, Palmetto, Masks, Griffin, c.1865, 49 In.	984.00
Pedestal, Column, Black Marble, Gilt Mounts, Octagonal Base & Top, 51 x 12 In.	506.00
Pedestal, Ebonized Wood, Fretwork, Medial Shelf, Chinese, c.1910, 29 ½ x 20 ½ In.	420.00
Pedestal, Ebonized, Parcel Gilt, Figural, Black Man, Standing, Sphere, Tray, 80 In.	2125.00
Pedestal, Edwardian, Mahogany, Satinwood Inlay, Square Top, Tapered, c.1900, 45 x 12 In.	153.00
Pedestal, Egyptian Revival, Marble, Bronze, Stepped Swivel Top, Lotus, c.1850, 43 In.	5378.00
Pedestal, Elizabethan Style, Oak, Turned Legs, Box Stretcher, Carved, c.1920, 16 x 12 In.	60.00
Pedestal, Georgian, Wood, Ebonized, Barley Twist Carved, 48 ½ x 15 ½ In.	201.00
Pedestal, Gilt Bronze, Marble Top, Figural Standard, c.1965, 41 x 16 In., Pair	750.00
Pedestal, Gilt Bronze, Marble, Column, Scroll Leaves, Rosettes, 1800s, 50 In.	1680.00
Pedestal, Gilt, Flowers, Swags, Ram's Heads, Carved, 3 Legs, c.1900, 44 x 19 In.	660.00
Pedestal, Gilt, Round Top, Kneeling Black Man Support, Leaf Crown, Square Base, 20 In., Pair	4500.00
Pedestal, Gilt, Round Top, Tiered Petal Shape Frieze, Chrysanthemum Base, 1900s, 29 In., Pair	4920.00
Pedestal, Green Marble, Carved, Swirled, Fluted Shaft, c.1900, 38 In.	575.00
Pedestal, Green Marble, Gilt Bronze Mount, Classical Detail, 48 x 12 In., Pair	805.00
Pedestal, Louis XV Style, Gilt, Gesso Round Marble Top, Shelf, Tripod, 47 x 12 In.	413.00
Pedestal, Louis XVI Style, Gilt, Fluted Column, Flower Swags, c.1900, 47 x 16 In.	1722.00
Pedestal, Mahogany, Rope Twist, Tripod Legs, Ball & Claw Feet, c.1950, 59 In., Pair	326.00
Pedestal, Marble, Round Top, Fluted Column, Faceted Base, 35 In.	183.00
Pedestal, Marble, Round Top, Leaf Carved Frieze, Fluted Standard, Octagonal Base, Italy, 42 In.	415.00
Pedestal, Marble, Twist Carved Standard, 8-Sided Base, Continental, 41 In. ....*Illus*	191.00
Pedestal, Narra Wood, Kneeling Man, Holding Top, Carved, 27 x 19 In., Pair	288.00
Pedestal, Neapolitan, Copper, Silvered Bronze, Column Stem, Athena, Sphinx, 30 x 12 In.	5938.00
Pedestal, Neoclassical Style, Gilt, Faux Marble, Fluted Column, Bellflowers, 46 In., Pair	1230.00

Pedestal, Neoclassical Style, Mahogany, Fluted, Stepped Base, 43 x 15 In., Pair......	720.00
Pedestal, Neoclassical Style, Marble, Brass, Square, Corinthian Capital, 40 x 11 In.	676.00
Pedestal, Neoclassical, Marble, White, Square Top & Columns, c.1900, 43 x 17 In., Pair......	1315.00
Pedestal, Neo-Grec, Swivel Top, Rosettes, Turned Stem, c.1875, 39 x 15 In.	1553.00
Pedestal, Oak, Carved Leaves, Bear Claw Feet, 20 x 18 In.	3300.00
Pedestal, Oak, Rectangular Marble Top, Rounded Front, Garland Border, 28 x 18 In.	406.00
Pedestal, Onyx, Gilt Bronze, Square Top, Cylindrical, Paw Feet, France, 1800s, 38 In.	568.00
Pedestal, Onyx, Green & Brown Veins, Square Top, Octagonal, 43 x 14 In.	960.00
Pedestal, Onyx, Square Top, Rounded Corners, Spiral Twist Column, 41 x 14 In......	553.00
Pedestal, Pine, Poplar, Crossed Torches, Ax, Stepped Base, c.1850, 30 x 19 In.	911.00
Pedestal, Renaissance Revival, Onyx, Brass Bands, Scrollwork, Putti, c.1890, 43 In......	734.00
Pedestal, Satinwood, Ribbon Mahogany, Square Top, Banded, Tapered, c.1900, 46 In.	184.00
Pedestal, Stickley Bros., Square Top, Cane Inserts On Sides, c.1915, 34 x 14 In.	1250.00
Pedestal, Victorian, Cherry, Swirled Tapered Column, Carved Apron., c.1880, 17 x 14 In.	443.00
Pedestal, Victorian, Marble, Brass, Column, Rotating Top, c.1800, 31 x 14 In.	1045.00
Pedestal, Victorian, Round Top, Turned Post, Black, Gold Paint, Tripod, 11 x 38 In.	180.00
Pedestal, White Marble, Column Shape, c.1890, 39 x 11 In.	236.00
Pew, Church, Wood, Plank Seat & Back, Shaped Legs, Square Arms, 45 x 32 In.	329.00
Pew, Gothic Revival, Oak, Leaf Carved, Plank Seat, 52 In.	413.00
Pew, Pine, Adjustable Back Rail, England, 68 x 12 In.	209.00
Pie Safe, 2 Doors, Punched Tin Panels, Painted, N. Carolina, c.1850, 50 x 40 In.	1093.00
Pie Safe, Cherry, 12 Pinwheel Panels, 2 Drawers, 41 x 18 In.	1392.00
Pie Safe, Cherry, Punched Flowers, 2 Doors, Dovetailed Drawers, c.1815, 59 In......	431.00
Pie Safe, Cherry, Punched Tin Panels, Mid-Atlantic, c.1830, 45 x 41 In.	1458.00
Pie Safe, Hanging, Tin Panels, Farmhouse, Pinwheel, Door, Pa., c.1840, 32 x 28 In......	2015.00
Pie Safe, Iron, Walnut, Slant Top, Hinged, Geometric Stars, c.1725, 20 x 13 In.	597.00
Pie Safe, Pine, 12 Punched Tin Panels, Flowers, Gallery, Doors, Painted, Va., c.1855, 55 x 43 In..	374.00
Pie Safe, Pine, Mortise & Pegged, Punched Tin Panels, Geometric, 56 x 43 In......	999.00
Pie Safe, Pine, Poplar, 8 Tin Panels, Pinwheels, Painted, Tapered Legs, 48 x 45 In. ....*Illus*	1567.00
Pie Safe, Pine, Poplar, Doors, Drawer, Punched Tin Panels, Stars, Painted, 1800s, 59 x 40 In.	1145.00
Pie Safe, Pine, Poplar, Gallery, Doors, 16 Punched Tin Panels, Va., c.1850, 51 x 54 In.	1265.00
Pie Safe, Pine, Well Top, Drawer, 2 Paneled Doors, Painted, c.1820, 53 x 43 In.	431.00
Pie Safe, Poplar, Diamond Pattern, c.1850, 42 x 54 In.	1145.00
Pie Safe, Poplar, Drawers, Doors, Tin Diamonds, Turned Feet, c.1850, 42 x 54 In.	1145.00
Pie Safe, Punched Tin Panels, Cutout Gallery, Drawers, Panel Doors, Va., c.1850, 43 x 46 In..	288.00
Pie Safe, Softwood, 6 Punched Tin Panels, Gallery, Drawers, Doors, Painted, c.1855, 54 x 44 In. ..	920.00
Pie Safe, Walnut, 6 Punched Tin Panels, Drawers, 2 Doors, Va., c.1870, 58 x 43 In.	1840.00
Pie Safe, Walnut, 8 Punched Tin Panels, Drawers, Doors, Va., c.1835, 54 x 44 In.	1610.00
Pie Safe, Walnut, 12 Arched Tin Panels, Drawer, Doors, Va., c.1850, 54 x 42 In.	1725.00
Pie Safe, Walnut, Punched Tin Panels, Dovetailed Backsplash, 2 Doors, 57 In.	1885.00
Pie Safe, Walnut, Punched Tin Panels, Drawers, Dovetails, 1800s, 56 x 39 In. ....*Illus*	37760.00
Pie Safe, Walnut, Punched Tin Panels, Horse, Figures, 1800s, 46 x 17 In......	4956.00
Planter, Burl, Marquetry, Bronze Ormolu Gallery, Metal Well, 1800s, 30 x 32 In.	210.00
Planter, Napoleon III, Boullework, Casket Shape, Serpentine Sides, Scroll Feet, c.1865, 9 x 15 In.	1107.00
Planter, Neoclassical Style, Tapering Square Shape, Paw Feet, Wood, Metal, 23 x 16 In., Pair.	553.00
Planter, Neoclassical, Center Roundel, Draped Garland, Fluted Base, 20 x 48 In......	1080.00
Planter, Victorian, Papier-Mache, Globe Shape, Painted, Gilt, Flowers, Metal Liners, 44 x 17 In. ....*Illus*	2142.00
Plate Warmer, Sheet, Tinned, Dome Lid, Cabriole Legs, Iron, England, c.1790......	142.00
Podium, Arts & Crafts, Slant Front, Wood, Paneled, Shelves, Carved Text, 15 x 50 In.	793.00
Rack, Baking, Brass, Bronze Wheat, Shelves, Arabesque Brackets, 1900s, 93 x 36 In.	237.00
Rack, Baking, Iron, Brass, Lines & Scrolls, 3 Shelves, 4 Partitions, France, 95 x 98 In.	2651.00
Rack, Baking, Wrought Iron, Shelves, Openwork, Brass Frame, c.1930, 84 x 73 In.	900.00
Rack, Bread, Louis XV Style, Oak, Glazed Door, Hinges, Carved Frieze, 1900s, 38 x 24 In.	885.00
Rack, Bread, Walnut, Carved, Spires, Finials, Turned Posts, France, c.1825, 43 x 30 In.	1067.00
Rack, Drying, Country, 3 Folding Sections, Blue Paint, Tin Hinges, 1800s, 50 x 26 In.	88.00
Rack, Drying, Folding, Pegged, Mortise & Tenon, 1800s, 71 x 41 In.	90.00
Rack, Hanging, Painted, Lower Shelf, L-Shape Hanging Hooks, 40 x 51 In.	201.00
Rack, Hanging, Wood, Tulip Design, 12 Hooks, Drawers, Painted, c.1850, 36 x 6 In.	144.00
Rack, Luggage, Roycroft, Chestnut, Slatted Top, Square Legs, c.1905, 25 x 30 In.	1063.00
Rack, Magazine, Flowers, Gilt, Scalloped, Painted, Cutout Handle, Mass., c.1900, 19 x 15 In...	365.00
Rack, Magazine, G. Stickley, Oak, Open, Half Moon Cutouts, c.1904, 40 x 14 In.	1750.00
Rack, Magazine, Stickley Bros., Wood, Shelves, Cutout Heart, c.1905, 44 x 14 In.	1875.00
Rack, Magazine, Walnut, Bellflowers, Turned Stretcher, Shelf, c.1890, 46 In.	1230.00
Rack, Magazine, Walnut, Mahogany, 5 Graduated Tiers, H-Stretcher, c.1950, 25 x 28 In......	8750.00
Rack, Magazine, Wormley, Mahogany, Brass, Tray Top, Shelf, 1950s, 24 x 34 In.	1750.00
Rack, Magazine, Wormley, Walnut, Birch, 5 Tiers, Arched Feet, 1947, 25 x 24 In.	875.00

Furniture, Etagere, Rococo Revival, Rosewood, Carved, Mirror Back, American, c.1850, 64 x 40 In.
$3,585.00

Neal Auction Co.

Furniture, Footstool, Gothic Revival, Mahogany, Carved, Casters, c.1850, 19 x 24 In.
$861.00

Neal Auction Co.

Furniture, Frame, Alfred Daguet, Wood, Inlaid Designs, Applied Brass, Repousse, Enamel, 15 x 23 In.
$1,098.00

Treadway Toomey Galleries

Furniture, Frame, Neoclassical, Gilt Bronze, Mother-Of-Pearl Inset, Guilloche, Laurel, France, 14 x 10 In.
$1,397.00

Leslie Hindman Auctioneers

Furniture, Hall Seat, Quartersawn Oak, Mirror, Half Columns, Fan Top, Hinged Seat, Hooks, 84 x 32 In. $708.00

Conestoga Auction Co., Inc.

Furniture, Hall Stand, Oak, Beveled Mirror, Glove Box, Lid, Iron Hardware, England, 1905, 79 x 36 In. $1,020.00

Skinner, Inc.

Furniture, Highboy, Chippendale Style, Mahogany, 2 Sections, Ball & Claw Feet, c.1910, 88 x 40 In. $767.00

Conestoga Auction Co., Inc.

Rack, Magazine, Wrought Iron, Metal, Handle, Shield Shape Ends, 17 x 12 In.	42.00
Rack, Plate, Green, Dovetail & Pin, Shelves, Rails, Continental, c.1850, 33 x 49 x 6 In.	270.00
Rack, Plate, Hanging, Walnut, Marquetry, Scalloped Frieze, Shelves, c.1870, 36 x 59 In.	690.00
Rack, Quilt, Mahogany, String Inlay, 34 ½ x 8 ½ x 27 In.	60.00
Rack, Quilt, Red Stain, c.1850, 40 x 34 ¼ In.	178.00
Rack, Quilt, Wood, 3 Horizontal Bars, Grain Painted, Pa., 36 x 22 ½ In.	1185.00
Rack, Wine, Wood, 2-Sided, Wire Loop Holders, Wheels, France, c.1900, 103 x 84 In.	900.00
Recamier, Empire Style, Downswept Back, Shaped Legs, Painted, c.1940, 32 x 48 In.	600.00
Recamier, Empire Style, Mahogany, Gilt Mounts, Scrolls, Carved, c.1910, 32 x 76 In.	2070.00
Recamier, Empire, Mahogany, Flared Sides, Upholstered, 83 x 30 In.	472.00
Recamier, Empire, Walnut, Canted, Rolled Crest, Serpentine Frame, Leather, 34 x 63 In.	1770.00
Rocker, Adirondack Style, Bentwood, Double Arms, Slat Seat, Stretcher, 42 x 23 x 35 In.	59.00
Rocker, Arrow Back, Writing Arm, Grain Painted, Flowers, New England, 46 In.	173.00
Rocker, Arts & Crafts, Oak, Upholstered, c.1920, 35 x 26 ½ In.	375.00
Rocker, Arts & Crafts, Vertical Back Rails, Arms, Cushion, c.1912, 37 x 20 In.	148.00
Rocker, Barrel Back, Vertical Slats, Cushion, 24 ½ x 31 ½ In.	1875.00
Rocker, Bent Twig, Ivory Paint, c.1890, 46 In.	24.00
Rocker, Boston, Mixed Wood, Stenciled Crest, Grain Painted Seat, c.1830, 14 In.	88.00
Rocker, Double, Shaker, Maple, Tape Seat & Back, New Lebanon, N.Y., 35 x 37 In. ....*Illus*	18720.00
Rocker, Eames, Fiberglass, Molded Arms, Gray, c.1965, 16 x 27 In.	1725.00
Rocker, G. Nakashima, Walnut, Hickory, Single Arm, Spindle Back, 1960s, 35 In.	8750.00
Rocker, G. Stickley, 3 Back Slats, Leather Seat, Red Decal, 18 x 19 In., Child's	427.00
Rocker, G. Stickley, No. 323, Slatted Sides, 2 Cushions, Red Decal, 41 x 29 In.	1875.00
Rocker, G. Stickley, Oak, 3 Horizontal Back Rails, Rush Seat, 32 In.	120.00
Rocker, G. Stickley, Spindle Back, Leather Seat, Red Decal, 26 x 30 In., Pair	3660.00
Rocker, George IV, Mahogany, Leather, Arms, Swan Neck Supports, 37 x 22 In.	410.00
Rocker, Glider, Victorian, Oak, Wood Wheels, Spokes, Honeycomb Cloth, 48 x 24 In.	58.00
Rocker, Iron Frame, Tufted Leather, c.1970, 38 x 28 In.	450.00
Rocker, L. & J.G. Stickley, Oak, Vertical Slats, Flat Arms, Cushion, c.1912, 34 x 26 In.	395.00
Rocker, Ladder Back, 3 Slats, Arms, Woven Seat, Virginia, 35 ½ x 16 In.	230.00
Rocker, Ladder Back, Oval Finials, Red Paint, c.1800, 26 In., Child's	119.00
Rocker, Ladder Back, Shaker, 4 Slats, Woven Seat, Arms, Mt. Lebanon, c.1860, 14 x 41 In.	173.00
Rocker, Limbert, Leather Cushions, Flat Arm, Branded, 32 x 37 In.	2440.00
Rocker, Maple, Acorn Finials, Graduated Slats, Tape Seat, c.1835, 42 In.	2340.00
Rocker, Mixed Wood, Spindle Back, Splayed Arms, Splint Seat, Painted, 1800s, 41 In.	90.00
Rocker, Oak, Cane Seat, Horizontal Splats, Carved Wind Design, 49 x 22 In.	226.00
Rocker, Oak, Shaped Back, Spindle Arm Supports, c.1900, 39 x 27 In.	118.00
Rocker, Officer's, Mixed Wood, Union Shield Crest, Fabric, Fringe, Folding, 1860s, 35 In.	177.00
Rocker, Pine, Settle Back, Blue Paint, New England, c.1760, 24 x 12 In., Child's	5925.00
Rocker, Plank Bottom, Brown, Gold, Red Flowers, Painted, Pa., c.1850, Child's	119.00
Rocker, Platform, Wicker, Partial Label, Ordway Brothers, c.1900, 50 In. ....*Illus*	422.00
Rocker, Potty, Walnut, Stained, Red Paint, Pa., c.1790, Child's	444.00
Rocker, Red Paint, Gilt, Shell, Leaves, Flowers, 31 In.	2015.00
Rocker, Shaker, 5 Slats, Splint Seat, Flat Arms, New Lebanon, N.Y., c.1825, 48 ½ In. ......*Illus*	5265.00
Rocker, Shaker, Ladder Back, 3 Arch Slats, Ball Finials, Woven Ash Seat, c.1880, 38 x 16 In.	92.00
Rocker, Shaker, Shawl Back, Taped Seat, 1800s, 27 In., Child's ....*Illus*	115.00
Rocker, Shaker, Woven Back, Seat, Open Arms, Label, Mt. Lebanon, 16 x 41 In.	431.00
Rocker, Shaped Splat, Black, Gold Leaves, Geometrics, Woven Seat, c.1830, 35 In.	201.00
Rocker, Slat Back, Red Paint, Scroll Arms, Woven Grass Seat, c.1750, 43 In.	830.00
Rocker, Softwood, Painted, Gold, Bronze, Stencil, Vase Splat, Scroll Seat, 46 x 23 In.	118.00
Rocker, Stickley Bros., 5 Slats, Hip Rail Sides, Open Arms, 31 x 34 In.	397.00
Rocker, T. Day, Mahogany, Scrolled, Fleur-De-Lis Arm Supports, c.1850, 39 x 23 In.	863.00
Rocker, Victorian, Oak, Carved Crest & Splat, Arms, Leather Pad Seat, 45 x 24 In.	144.00
Rocker, Victorian, Oak, Carved Crest, 7 Spindles, Rolled Seat, 39 x 23 In.	96.00
Rocker, Wicker, Heart Back, Red, Brown Paint.	165.00
Rocker, Windsor, Adjustable Writing Arm, Flower, Red Stain, New Eng., c.1830	296.00
Rocker, Windsor, Arrow Back, Grain Painted, Arms, c.1835, 36 x 17 In.	92.00
Rocker, Windsor, Bow Back, Incised, Spindles, Faux Bamboo Legs, Stretcher, 36 In.	230.00
Rocker, Windsor, Comb Back, Double, Spindles, Arms, 1800s	615.00
Rocker, Windsor, Comb Back, Green Paint, New England, c.1800	1304.00
Rocker, Windsor, Sack Back, Turned Legs, Arms, Pa., c.1800	89.00
Rocker, Windsor, Spindles, Writing Arm, Drawer, Blue Paint	236.00
Schrank, Federal, Walnut, Ogee Cornice, Inlay, Panel Doors, Drawers, c.1800, 83 x 57 In.	13035.00
Schrank, Poplar, Blue Paint, 2 Doors, 3 Drawers, Pa., c.1760, 82 ½ In.	1541.00
Schrank, Walnut, Arched Panel Doors, Fluted Columns, Drawers, c.1770, 83 x 57 In.	28440.00
Schrank, Walnut, Cornice, Panel Doors, Drawers, Bracket Feet, c.1790, 86 x 69 In.	28440.00

F

Screens are also listed in the Architectural and Fireplace categories.

Screen, 2-Panel, Hardwood, Shaped Crest, Pierced, Flowers, Leaves, Birds, c.1900, 74 x 70 In.	399.00
Screen, 2-Panel, Pierced Crest, Birds, Branches, Painted Landscape, c.1950, 71 x 62 In.	338.00
Screen, 3-Panel, 9 Sketches, Gunfights, Signed, Francisco Toledo, 43 x 54 In...............	4012.00
Screen, 3-Panel, Arched Tops, Landscape, Flamingos, 66 x 66 In................................	625.00
Screen, 3-Panel, Arched, Embossed Leather, Gilt, Brass Trim, c.1910, 60 x 70 In...................	575.00
Screen, 3-Panel, Bamboo, Geometric, c.1950, 67 ½ x 66 In.	360.00
Screen, 3-Panel, Baroque Style, Oil On Canvas, Scene, Gilt Frame, c.1900, 73 x 56 In. ...*Illus*	1652.00
Screen, 3-Panel, Beech, Fruitwood, Austria, c.1910, 67 x 63 In.	375.00
Screen, 3-Panel, Black Lacquer, Gilt, Flowers, Birds, Bronze Mounts, c.1910, 40 x 40 In.	460.00
Screen, 3-Panel, Curved Wood Frame, Country Fair, France, c.1850, 66 x 60 In.	2185.00
Screen, 3-Panel, Glass, Fabric, Carved Leaf & Scroll Frame, France, 67 x 55 In...................	298.00
Screen, 3-Panel, Neoclassical, Flowers, Urns, Putti, Scrolls, Painted, c.1860, 68 x 32 In.	1000.00
Screen, 3-Panel, Oak, Tulip Panels, c.1905, 68 In.	207.00
Screen, 3-Panel, Place De La Bastille Scene, Rainy Day, Trompe L'Oeil, 1900s, 68 x 57 In........	307.00
Screen, 3-Panel, Regency Style, Painted, Tan, Urn, Swag, 72 x 54 In.	84.00
Screen, 3-Panel, Shaped Arch Crest, Carved Design, Mashrabiyya, Syria, 76 x 72 In.	448.00
Screen, 3-Panel, Silk, Gilt, 3 Mirrors, c.1910, 70 x 50 In.	720.00
Screen, 3-Panel, Tapered Posts, Spindles, Carved Trim, Leather, Arts & Crafts, 87 x 72 In........	700.00
Screen, 4-Panel, Fabric, Embroidery, Wood, Hinged, Dogwood, Eagle, 66 x 89 In.	71.00
Screen, 4-Panel, Flowers, Domestic Scenes, Painted, 1800s, 76 In.	540.00
Screen, 4-Panel, Hardwood, Bird, Animal, Carved, Chinese, 92 x 85 In.	2832.00
Screen, 4-Panel, Jade Plaque, Lotus, Chain Woven, Bats, Flowers, 1700s, 11 x 13 In.	1304.00
Screen, 4-Panel, Neoclassical Style, Decoupage, Gods, Leaves, Marbleized, 78 x 96 In.	644.00
Screen, 4-Panel, Painted Leather, Scrolling Leaves, Gilt Ground, 1800s, 77 x 96 In...................	3750.00
Screen, 4-Panel, Painted Wood, Landscape, Castle, Flowers, c.1890, 56 x 124 In.	1416.00
Screen, 4-Panel, Red Lacquer, Garden Landscape, Geisha, c.1900, 75 x 77 In........................	4920.00
Screen, 4-Panel, Stone Inset, Figures, Animals, Lacquered, c.1875, 74 x 80 In.	1121.00
Screen, 4-Panel, Tooled, Painted Leather, Rosewood, Gilt Flowers, Leaves, c.1800, 71 x 120 In.	1270.00
Screen, 4-Panel, Wood, Birds, Branches, Painted, Peach, Green, Yellow, 70 x 64 In.................	4600.00
Screen, 4-Panel, Wood, Courtesans, Garden, Red & Gold Lacquer, Chinese, 68 x 64 In.	978.00
Screen, 4-Panel, Wood, Hardstone, Landscape, Courtyard, Bird, c.1900, 34 x 30 In...................	1541.00
Screen, 4-Panel, Wood, Pierced, Scrolled Flowers, India, c.1950, 76 x 80 In............................	431.00
Screen, 4-Panel, Wood, Reticulated, Pierced, Arched Crests, Indian, c.1910, 73 x 80 In.	354.00
Screen, 4-Panel, Woven Wool, Walnut Frame, Square Legs, c.1950, 72 x 96 In.	1750.00
Screen, 6-Panel, Coromandel Style, Folding, Oriental Images, Black, Gold Foil, 79 x 96 In.....	299.00
Screen, 6-Panel, Painted Landscape, Reeded Square Columns, Geometric, 1900s, 19 x 35 In.	127.00
Screen, 8-Panel, Landscape, Lake, Figures, Paint On Paper, Wood, Chinese, 92 x 124 In.......*Illus*	780.00
Screen, 10-Panel, Folding, Continuous Scene, Figures, Mountains, Chinese, 83 x 165 In.	55200.00
Screen, 12-Panel, Village Scene, Flower Border, 107 In....................	4688.00
Screen, Ebonized Wood, Painted Symbols, Carved, Foo Dog, c.1900, 55 x 32 In.	236.00
Screen, Gilt Metal Frame, Painted, Stylized Shells, Grotesque Mask, Swags, 33 In.	800.00
Screen, Lacquer, Black & Gold, Figures, Landscape, Chinese, c.1985, 68 x 54 In......................	2500.00
Screen, Rosewood, Needlework, Bead & Stump Work, Pedestal, c.1850, 84 x 39 In. ....*Illus*	2700.00
Screen, Rosewood, Reticulated, Rosette, Leaves, Trestle Base, 53 x 26 In.	2390.00
Screen, Table, Hardwood, Marble, Deer, Peach Tree Panel, 1939, 19 x 13 In.	420.00
Screen, Table, Jade, Carved, God Of Longevity, Round, Openwork Scrolls, Stand, 20 x 11 In....	590.00
Screen, Table, Round, Marble Stone Inset, Landscape, Openwork, Chinese, c.1990, 18 In.	411.00
Screen, Table, Sandalwood, Pierced Scroll Border, Inlaid Ivory Palace, 1800s, 32 x 24 In.	518.00
Screen, Table, Wood, Horn, Dragons, Clouds, Chinese, 12 In. ....*Illus*	300.00
Secretary, Butler's, Empire, Mahogany, Paneled Sides, Ogee, 47 x 42 ½ In.	201.00
Secretary, Butler's, Georgian, Mahogany, Drop Front, Urn Inlay, Drawers, 46 x 49 In..............	360.00
Secretary, Butler's, Mahogany, Fold-Out Top Drawer, Lower Drawers, c.1850, 39 x 43 In.	236.00
Secretary, Chippendale Style, Mahogany, Oval Inlay, Glass Doors, Feather Crest, c.1910, 81 x 42 In.	729.00
Secretary, Chippendale, Walnut, Broken Arch, Panel Doors, c.1755, 99 x 38 In.......................	37920.00
Secretary, Drop Front, 4 Paneled Doors, Painted, Fitted, Sweden, c.1900, 92 x 52 In.	6000.00
Secretary, Drop Front, Biedermeier, Mahogany, Mirror, Inlaid Burl, c.1850, 78 In. ....*Illus*	1722.00
Secretary, Drop Front, Biedermeier, Walnut, Crown, Columns, Doors, 1800s, 63 x 33 In.	418.00
Secretary, Drop Front, Biedermeier, Wood, Marble, Fitted Interior, Columns, 60 x 39 In.	813.00
Secretary, Drop Front, Chippendale, Cherry, Pierced Crest, Doors, c.1775, 111 x 43 In.	5451.00
Secretary, Drop Front, Chippendale, Mahogany Veneer, Inlay, Oxbow, c.1790, 83 x 42 In. ... *Illus*	7800.00
Secretary, Drop Front, Directoire Style, Stepped, Drawers, Block Feet, 1800s, 55 x 51 In.	3444.00
Secretary, Drop Front, Directoire, Mahogany, 2 Parts, Cupboard Doors, 1800s, 57 x 36 In......	633.00
Secretary, Drop Front, Empire, Fruitwood, Canted, Paneled Doors, c.1850, 58 x 38 In.	1476.00
Secretary, Drop Front, Empire, Mahogany, Gilt Metal Mounted, 53 x 38 In.	1180.00
Secretary, Drop Front, Empire, Mahogany, Gilt Metal Mounted, 59 x 37 In.	1534.00

Furniture, Huntboard, Federal, Walnut, Cherry, 2 Doors, Cellarette Drawer, 1800s, 38 x 51 In.
$9,440.00

Brunk Auctions

Furniture, Kneeler, Prie-Dieu, Walnut, Carved, Needlepoint, Lobed, Fluted Stiles, Cross, c.1910
$478.00

Neal Auction Co.

Furniture, Library Steps, Regency Style, Mahogany, Central Pole, Kittinger, 1900s, 59 x 30 In.
$558.00

Garth's Auctioneers & Appraisers

The edited listings of the current prices in this *Kovels' Antiques & Collectibles Price Guide* aren't available on any website. Readers can visit **Kovels.com** to check thousands of past prices and sign up for free information on trends, tips, reproductions, marks, and more.

Furniture, Mirror, Biedermeier, Giltwood, Ebonized Columns, Cast Relief, c.1810, 63 x 29 In. $805.00

Cottone Auctions

Furniture, Mirror, C. Jere, Raindrops, Patinated Copper, Brass, Signed, 1968, 34 x 5 ¾ In. $6,250.00

Rago Arts & Auction Center

Furniture, Mirror, Cheval, Neoclassical, Mahogany Veneer, Paneled Back, Casters, c.1825, 96 x 50 In. $1,888.00

Brunk Auctions

Secretary, Drop Front, Federal, Mahogany, Eagle, Glass Doors, Drawers, 81 x 43 In.	3304.00
Secretary, Drop Front, Federal, Mahogany, Glass Doors, Drawers, 1700s, 88 x 42 In.	1007.00
Secretary, Drop Front, George III, Mahogany, Pierced, 2 Doors, Drawers, c.1790, 93 x 42 In.	3450.00
Secretary, Drop Front, Hepplewhite, Mahogany, Glass Doors, Drawers, c.1820, 76 x 43 In.	2714.00
Secretary, Drop Front, Louis XVI, Fruitwood, Marble, Reeded Columns, Peg Feet, c.1790, 57 x 37 In.	896.00
Secretary, Drop Front, Mahogany, Carved, Glass Doors, Drawers, Fitted, c.1800, 102 x 44 In.	13800.00
Secretary, Drop Front, Mahogany, Rosewood, Marble, Cupboard Doors, c.1800, 60 x 41 In.	1076.00
Secretary, Drop Front, Mahogany, Rosewood, Marble, Ivory Pulls, c.1865, 63 x 39 In.	840.00
Secretary, Drop Front, Marble Top, Inlay, Fitted Interior, Gilt Bronze, 55 x 35 In. ....*Illus*	1625.00
Secretary, Drop Front, Mirrored Top, 3 Drawers, Cupboard, c.1880, 72 x 39 In.	444.00
Secretary, Drop Front, Mixed Wood, 2 Pierced Glass Doors, Panel Doors, c.1840, 84 x 40 In.	1150.00
Secretary, Drop Front, Walnut, Arched Crest, Mirrored Doors, c.1800, 94 x 42 x 21 In.	3107.00
Secretary, Drop Front, Walnut, Gilt Finials, Arched Doors, Drawers, Eng., 91 x 39 In.	3422.00
Secretary, Drop Front, Walnut, Interior Slots & Drawers, Stretcher, 5 Legs, c.1930, 45 x 37 In. ..*Illus*	540.00
Secretary, E. Wheeler, Drop Front, Queen Anne Style, Cherry, Panel Doors, 79 x 35 In.	2370.00
Secretary, E. Wheeler, Slant Front, Cherry, Acorn Finial, 2 Doors, Fitted, 89 x 38 In.	5192.00
Secretary, Edwardian, Painted Classical Figures, Elliptical Glazed Door, 85 x 36 In.	3585.00
Secretary, Empire, Mahogany, Glass Doors, 3 Drawers, c.1840, 88 x 44 In.	444.00
Secretary, Federal, Figured Mahogany, Eagle, Reverse Painted Panels, 73 x 42 In.	3540.00
Secretary, Federal, Mahogany, Glass Doors, Tambour Doors, Fitted Interior, 77 x 34 In.	1625.00
Secretary, Federal, Mahogany, Inlaid, Setback, 2 Doors, 2 Drawers, c.1860, 39 x 46 In.	1093.00
Secretary, Federal, Mahogany, Inlay, 2 Tambour Doors, 2 Drawers, 45 x 37 In.	708.00
Secretary, Federal, Mahogany, Inlay, Finials, Arched Glass Doors, c.1810, 87 x 42 In.	2133.00
Secretary, Federal, Mahogany, Inlay, Glass Doors, Drawers, Eagle Finials, Mass., 94 x 42 In.	7080.00
Secretary, Federal, Mahogany, Maple, Inlay, 2 Arched Panel Doors, 2 Drawers, 78 In.	2304.00
Secretary, George II, Mahogany, Dentiled Cornice, Glass Doors, Drawers, 90 x 49 In.	1230.00
Secretary, Hepplewhite, Cherry, Urn Finials, 2 Glass Doors, Drawers, c.1800, 90 x 43 In.	1180.00
Secretary, Hepplewhite, Mahogany, Maple Veneer, c.1800, 77 ½ x 37 ½ In.	1422.00
Secretary, Mixed Wood, 2 Tambour Doors, Drawers, Felt Surface, 1800s, 46 x 35 In.	1438.00
Secretary, Regency, Mahogany, 2 Glass Doors, Fitted Drawer, 106 x 48 In.	2925.00
Secretary, Regency, Mahogany, Ivory Inlay, 2 Doors, Fitted Interior, 4 Drawers, c.1825, 89 x 43 In.	1440.00
Secretary, Rohde, Drop Front, Laurel, 3 Drawers, Door, Signed, H. Miller, 1930s, 32 x 41 In.	4575.00
Secretary, Roll Top, Burl Walnut, Molded Cornice, Shaped Doors, Drawer, c.1885, 94 x 48 In.	1722.00
Secretary, Sheraton, Drop Front, Mahogany, Carved Crest, Flat Doors, Drawer, 65 x 31 In.	354.00
Secretary, Sheraton, Mahogany, 2 Doors, Hinged Writing Surface, Drawers, Ma., 60 x 44 In.	1180.00
Secretary, Slant Front, Burl Walnut, 3 Parts, Broken Arch, 2 Doors, 1700s, 78 x 38 In.	2760.00
Secretary, Slant Front, Chippendale, Glass Doors, Drawers, Fitted, England, 86 x 40 In.	1416.00
Secretary, Slant Front, George I, Walnut, Shaped Cornice, Glazed Door, 77 x 28 In.	7500.00
Secretary, Slant Front, George III Style, Walnut, Glass Doors, Fitted, Drawers, 80 x 35 In.	1020.00
Secretary, Slant Front, George III, Mahogany, 2 Panel Doors, Beaded Drawers, c.1790, 81 x 46 In.	3450.00
Secretary, Slant Front, Mahogany, Fitted Interior, Drawers, England, c.1775, 91 ½ In. ...*Illus*	1880.00
Secretary, Slant Front, Walnut, Mirror Doors, 4 Drawers, Dutch, c.1750, 90 x 48 In.	6875.00
Secretary, Slide-Out, Painted, Flowers, Gold Designs, Brass Knobs, France, c.1910, 51 In.	1650.00
Secretary, Victorian, Slant Front, Burl Walnut, Molded, Glazed Door, 103 x 41 In.	502.00
Secretary, Walnut, Leather, 2 Glass Doors, Shelves, Drawers, c.1900, 44 x 50 In.	510.00
Semainier, Louis XVI Style, Kingwood, Marble Top, Demilune, Drawers, 52 x 26 In.	329.00
Semainier, Louis XVI Style, Mahogany, Brass, Marble Top, 7 Drawers, 64 x 38 In.	3125.00
Semainier, Mahogany, Marble Top, Gilt, Drawers, Flowers, 1800s, 61 x 40 In.	1500.00
Semainier, Walnut, Bowfront, 7 Drawers, Brass Banded, Columns, 1800s, 42 x 21 In.	800.00
Server, 2 Drawers, 2 Panel Doors, Carved Apron, Cabriole Legs, France, c.1750, 41 x 54 In.	840.00
Server, Bowfront, Mahogany, 6 Tapered Legs, England, c.1820, 36 x 82 In.	590.00
Server, British Colonial, Mahogany, Arched Back, Spindle Side Gallery, 2 Drawers, 54 x 40 ½ In.	738.00
Server, Drop Leaf, Mahogany, Lyre Supports, Maitland-Smith, c.1990, 30 x 44 In.	1012.00
Server, E. Wheeler, Chippendale Style, Curly Maple, 31 x 51 ½ In.	948.00
Server, Empire, Mahogany, 2 Drawers, Over 2 Doors, Carved, 37 x 45 In.	295.00
Server, Empire, Oak, Mirror Backsplash, Drawers, Open Shelves, Glass Door, 55 x 46 In.	504.00
Server, Federal, Cherry, 6 Drawers, Cellarette Doors, Columns, Bun Feet, 1800s, 42 x 50 In.	720.00
Server, Federal, Mahogany, 2 Drawers, Turned Harp Supports, c.1855, 34 x 34 In.	115.00
Server, Federal, Mahogany, Scrolled Backsplash, Drawers, Reeded Legs, c.1820, 34 x 32 In.	593.00
Server, French Provincial, Cherry, Ebony & Ivory Inlay, Panel Doors, 1800s, 46 x 53 In.	521.00
Server, G. Stickley, 2 Drawers, Copper Hardware, Shelf Stretcher, 42 x 18 In.	2196.00
Server, G. Stickley, 2 Drawers, Iron Pulls, Low Shelf, Red Decal, 42 x 20 In.	9150.00
Server, G. Stickley, 2 Drawers, Square Gallery, Shaped Apron, Shelf, c.1905, 39 x 39 In.	2125.00
Server, G. Stickley, Mirrored Backsplash, Drawers, Overhang Top, c.1915, 50 x 52 In.	1750.00
Server, George III Style, Ebonized, Flowers, 3 Drawers, Faux Bamboo Legs, c.1880, 30 x 36 In.	375.00
Server, Hepplewhite Style, Mahogany, 2 Dovetailed Drawers, c.1900, 33 x 38 In.	826.00

F

Server, Hepplewhite Style, Mahogany, Inlay, 2 Drawers, Shaped Apron, 29 x 42 In.	326.00
Server, Hepplewhite, Mahogany, 2 Drawers, England, c.1890, 37 x 31 In.	156.00
Server, L. & J.G. Stickley, Drawers, Medial Shelf, c.1912, 39 x 48 In.	2375.00
Server, Limbert, 2 Drawers, Open Shelf, Square Legs, 3 Stretchers, 36 x 39 In.	1250.00
Server, Louis XV Style, Marble, Fruitwood, Cabinet Door, Hinged Drawers, c.1900, 34 x 48 In.	1416.00
Server, Louis XV, Walnut, Dovetailed Drawers, Panel Doors, Scroll Feet, c.1800, 38 x 51 In.	1298.00
Server, Louis XVI Style, Mahogany, Marble, Lattice Door, Curved Sides, 38 x 52 In.	2749.00
Server, Mahogany, 2 Tiers, Doors, Spiral Spindles, 1800s, 44 x 48 x 19 In.	1003.00
Server, Mahogany, 3 Drawers, Reeded Edge, Columns, Shelf Stretcher, c.1825, 35 x 37 In.	5313.00
Server, Mahogany, Marble Top, Beaded Drawers, Shelf, Bun Feet, c.1825, 37 x 36 In.	1045.00
Server, Mid Century Modern, 4 Drawers, Glass Shelf, Johnson Furniture Co., 30 x 59 In.	177.00
Server, Oak, Marble Top, Gilt, Cupboard Doors, Ormolu, Drawers, c.1890, 43 x 72 In.	5166.00
Server, Pine, Gallery, 2 Panel Doors, Over 2 Drawers, England, 26 x 37 In.	354.00
Server, Pine, Poplar, Gallery, 2 Drawers, 2 Doors, Southern, c.1845, 38 x 36 In.	316.00
Server, Pine, Red Paint, 2 Dovetailed Drawers, Doors, c.1855, 55 x 50 In.	1087.00
Server, Regency Style, Black, 3 Open Shelves, 2 Grill Panel Doors, c.1940, 64 x 45 In.	840.00
Server, Regency, Mahogany, Bowfront, 3 Drawers, Turned Legs, c.1820, 32 x 35 ½ In.	593.00
Server, Regency, Mahogany, Drawer, Rope Twist Insets, Reeded Legs, c.1835, 67 x 30 In.	3198.00
Server, Renaissance Revival, Oak, Openwork, Putti, Shelf, Griffins, Marble Top, c.1890 ...*Illus*	5676.00
Server, Rococo, Rosewood, Marble, Mirrored Doors, Frieze Drawer, c.1850, 41 x 45 In.	1599.00
Server, Rohde, Mahogany, Birch, 3 Drawers, Cupboard Door, c.1930, 34 x 48 In.	1250.00
Server, Rohde, Oak, Straight Supports, Herman Miller, 1939, 35 x 18 In.	610.00
Server, Rosewood, Scrolled Backsplash, Reticulated, Shelves, c.1840, 50 x 45 In.	837.00
Server, Roycroft, Drawer, Bail Handles, Plate Rack, Shelf, c.1905, 43 x 44 In.	5938.00
Server, Sheraton Style, Inlaid Mahogany, Drawer, Shelf, 1900s, 41 x 38 In.	326.00
Server, Sheraton, Cherry, Shaped Gallery, Drawers, Paneled Doors, c.1850, 43 x 40 In.	588.00
Server, Sheraton, Mahogany Veneer, Drawers, Shelf, Opalescent Pulls, 36 x 35 In.	617.00
Server, Shop Of The Crafters, Oak, Inlay, Glass Tile, Door, 1904-20, 40 x 42 In. ....*Illus*	2625.00
Server, Walnut, 3 Open Shelves, Turned Columns, England, 42 x 46 In.	295.00
Server, Walnut, Marble Top, Scrolled Backsplash, Bust, Doors, c.1850, 66 x 72 In.	488.00
Settee, 3-Arch Back, Open Arms, Pierced, Ebonized, Burma, c.1890, 48 x 56 In.	1416.00
Settee, Adirondack Style, Twig Design, Blue Paint, c.1855, 41 x 21 In.	288.00
Settee, Anglo-Indian, Hardwood, Cane, Swag, Acanthus Carved, Turned Legs, 69 In.	708.00
Settee, Arrow Back Slats, Ivory Paint, Pa., c.1850, 33 x 51 In.	652.00
Settee, Art Deco, Carved Back, Reeded Arm Supports, Upholstered, 32 x 49 In.	780.00
Settee, Arts & Crafts, Oak, Slat Back, Arms, Upholstered, c.1915, 38 x 65 In.	480.00
Settee, Biedermeier, Birch, Shaped Back, Arms, Splayed Legs, Moire, 36 x 62 In.	1150.00
Settee, Biedermeier, Walnut, Straight Back, Scroll Arms, Carved, 82 In.	2125.00
Settee, Chippendale Style, Mahogany, Pierced Double Chairback, Carved, c.1930	266.00
Settee, Chippendale Style, Mahogany, Pierced Splat, Shaped Arms, 39 x 48 In.	460.00
Settee, Directoire, Mahogany, 4-Shield Back, Lyre Splats, Shaped Arms, 35 x 67 In.	708.00
Settee, Eastlake, Walnut, Carved, Upholstered, c.1855, 34 In.	173.00
Settee, Edwardian, Satinwood, Arched Crest, Winged Arms, Tapered Legs, 35 x 44 In.	837.00
Settee, Empire Style, Mahogany, Gilt Metal, Straight Back, Padded Rest, 46 In.	406.00
Settee, Federal Style, Rosewood, Stenciled, Roll Over, Armrests, Upholstered, 36 x 84 In.	878.00
Settee, Federal, Mahogany, Arched Spindle Back, Open Arms, Upholstered, 43 In.	767.00
Settee, Federal, Mahogany, Inlay, Square Back, Carved Arm, Legs, Upholstered, 52 In.	531.00
Settee, Flowers, Apple Green Ground, Shaped Back, Arms, Pa., c.1840, 37 x 78 In.	911.00
Settee, G. Nakashima, Walnut, Upholstered, Bench Seat, Peg Legs, 1966, 31 x 48 In.	5313.00
Settee, G. Stickley, Slat Back & Sides, Even Arm, Cushion Seat, 29 x 72 In.	4375.00
Settee, George III Style, Mahogany, Downswept Arms, Chamfered Legs, c.1900, 37 x 80 In.	984.00
Settee, George III, Flowers, Downswept Arms, Feather Splat, Serpentine Seat, 1700s, 41 x 96 In.	1800.00
Settee, George III, Mahogany, Fluted Arms, Ring-Turned Splayed Legs, 34 x 64 In.	650.00
Settee, George III, Wood, Carved Stiles, Finials, Arms, Cushion, Italy, c.1750, 39 x 94 In.	3738.00
Settee, Hepplewhite Style, Mahogany, Double Shieldback, Open Arms, 43 In.	212.00
Settee, Hepplewhite Style, Triple Chairback, Pierced Splat, Upholstered Seat	652.00
Settee, J. Hoffmann, Beech, Curved Spindles, Arms, J. & J. Kohn, Austria, c.1905, 30 x 48 In.	1750.00
Settee, Kittinger, Chippendale Style, Mahogany, Serpentine Arms, 1900s, 38 x 45 In.	1410.00
Settee, L. & J.G. Stickley, Oak, 7-Splat Back, Leather Upholstery, 72 x 36 In.	1180.00
Settee, Ladder Back, Mahogany, Domed, Bulbous Finials, Arms, Stretcher, 33 x 57 In.	338.00
Settee, Limbert, Double Back, Seat, Vertical Slats, Leather, Open Arms, 41 x 19 In.	610.00
Settee, Louis Philippe, Slung Back, Open Arms, Upholstered, c.1880, 27 x 60 In.	600.00
Settee, Louis XVI Style, Beech, Arched Crest, Curved Arms, c.1800, 40 x 76 In.	590.00
Settee, Louis XVI Style, Domed Back, Leaf Finials, Pad Arms, Fluted Legs, 38 x 64 In.	922.00
Settee, Louis XVI Style, Downswept Arms, Fluted Legs, 1800s, 38 x 41 In.	1599.00
Settee, Louis XVI Style, Fruitwood, Curved, Guilloche Carved, Reeded Arms, 40 x 48 In.	799.00

Furniture, Mirror, Cheval, Oak, Carved, Pierced Crest, Fold-Out Shelf, c.1850, 75 x 32 In.
$4,183.00

Neal Auction Co.

Furniture, Mirror, Chippendale Style, Veneer, Giltwood, Phoenix, Continental, 1900s, 55 x 26 In.
$353.00

Garth's Auctioneers & Appraisers

Furniture, Mirror, Chippendale, Giltwood, Pierced Pagoda Crest, Reverse Painted, Chinese, 28 x 16 In.
$18,750.00

Leslie Hindman Auctioneers

Furniture, Mirror, Courting, Molded Frame, Reverse Painted Glass, Wood Case, 1700s, 9 x 7 In.
$2,760.00

Skinner, Inc.

Furniture, Mirror, Empire Style, Gilt, Painted, Shield, Flowers, Leaves, Beveled Plate, 1800s, 47 x 56 In.
$236.00

Brunk Auctions

Furniture, Mirror, Federal, Giltwood, Fruit Basket, Half Columns, Rosettes, 1800-25, 30 x 14 In.
$276.00

New Orleans Auction Galleries, Inc.

Furniture, Mirror, Federal, Giltwood, Gesso, Rope Twist, Shell & Leaf Spray, c.1810, 32 x 19 In.
$356.00

Skinner, Inc.

Furniture, Mirror, Federal, Giltwood, Molded Crest, Rope Twist, Reverse Painted, c.1810, 28 x 17 In.
$236.00

James D. Julia Auctioneers

Furniture, Mirror, Giltwood, Lyre, Scrolls, Shields, Leaves, Molded Frame, Italy, c.1890, 46 x 21 In.
$2,952.00

New Orleans Auction Galleries, Inc.

Furniture, Mirror, Louis XVI Style, Painted Panel, Shell, Scroll, Molded Frame, c.1850, 60 x 33 In.
$1,845.00

New Orleans Auction Galleries, Inc.

Furniture, Mirror, Pier, Giltwood, Block Cornice, Shell, Pilasters, Victorian, 51 x 28 In.
$281.00

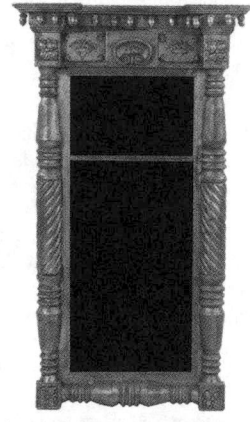

Leslie Hindman Auctioneers

Furniture, Mirror, Pier, Neoclassical, Giltwood, Painted, Classical Soldier, 47 x 15 In., Pair
$188.00

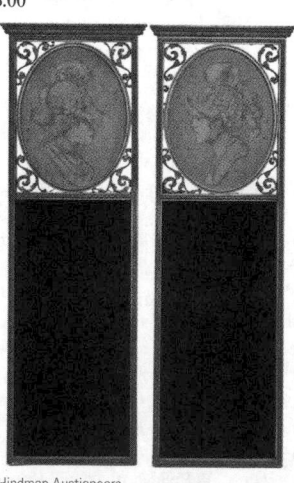

Leslie Hindman Auctioneers

Settee, Louis XVI Style, Garland Carved Frame, Upholstered, Jansen, 75 In.	1625.00
Settee, Louis XVI Style, Gilt, Oval Back, Rope Carved, Fluted Legs, c.1890, 40 x 49 In.	799.00
Settee, Louis XVI Style, Gilt, Upholstered Back, Padded Arms, Fluted Legs, 38 x 48 In.	780.00
Settee, Louis XVI, Curved, Carved Back, Upholstered, Round, 8 Fluted Legs, c.1780, 71 In.	1875.00
Settee, Mahogany, Cane, Triple Back, Scroll Arms, Square Legs, c.1900, 38 In.	922.00
Settee, Mahogany, Mother-Of-Pearl, Serpentine Crest, Pierced, Arms, c.1910, 49 In.	344.00
Settee, Mahogany, Multicolor Needlepoint, Shell Carved Legs, 1700s, 42 x 55 In.	266.00
Settee, Mission, Oak, Vertical Slat Back, Shaped Crest, Flat Arms, c.1910, 39 x 59 In.	547.00
Settee, Mixed Wood, Downswept Arms, Flowers, Painted, Pa., c.1850, 35 x 74 In.	243.00
Settee, Napoleon III, Fringe Upholstery, c.1880, 30 x 53 In.	900.00
Settee, Neoclassical, 3-Part Back, Carved Leaf, Swag, Open Arms, c.1850, 62 In.	1000.00
Settee, Neoclassical, Fruitwood, Lyre Shape Armrests, c.1700, 34 x 83 In.	1067.00
Settee, Neoclassical, Walnut, Triple Chairback, Pierced, Arms, Italy, c.1850, 61 In.	469.00
Settee, Regency Style, Cane Back, Sunflower, Bowed Seat, Scroll Arms, 35 x 83 In.	2280.00
Settee, Rococo Revival, Rosewood, Rosalie, Attributed To Belter, c.1850, 38 x 40 In. ..... *Illus*	6100.00
Settee, Rococo Revival, Walnut, Pierced Flower Crest, Grapes, c.1885, 41 x 73 In.	553.00
Settee, Sam Maloof, Walnut, Square Back, Shaped Arms, 1966, 37 x 50 In.	9375.00
Settee, Shaped Back, Gilt Finials, 2-Section Seat, Upholstered, 37 x 53 In.	413.00
Settee, Slipper, Neoclassical, Mahogany, Serpentine Back, Tufted Silk, 29 x 42 In.	369.00
Settee, Stickley Bros., Slat Back, Square Legs & Stretcher, Drop Arms, c.1910, 38 x 61 In.	938.00
Settee, Triple Arch Back, Cushion Seat, Cane, Turned Legs, c.1830, 45 x 67 In.	1140.00
Settee, Victorian, Japanned, Cane Back, Curved Arms, Cushion, c.1890, 29 x 68 In.	3250.00
Settee, W. Platner, Steel Cage Base, Round Back, Oval Seat, 1960s, 32 x 67 In.	6875.00
Settee, Walnut, Serpentine Back, Carved Flower Crest & Apron, 1800s, 35 x 45 In.	115.00
Settee, Wendell Castle, Fiberglass, Rubber, Molar Shaped, White, 1960s, 26 x 48 In.	2625.00
Settee, Windsor Style, Wood, Continuous Arm, Shaped Plank Seat, 40 x 51 In.	1180.00
Settee, Windsor, Bamboo Turned, Square Back, Painted, Yellow Stripes, 34 x 74 In.	4444.00
Settee, Windsor, Bow Back, 33 Spindles, Plank Seat, Downswept, Arms, c.1790, 36 x 16 In.	2070.00
Settee, Windsor, Bow Back, Writing Arm, Turned Legs, Delaware Valley, c.1790	4503.00
Settee, Windsor, Mixed Wood, Painted, Stenciled Flowers, Scroll Arms, c.1820, 35 x 74 In.	1175.00
Settee, Windsor, Oak, Pine, Spindle Back & Arms, Plank Seat, c.1820, 15 x 33 In.	1055.00
Settee, Windsor, Rod Back, Black Paint, 8 Splayed Legs, Pa., c.1820, 33 x 73 In.	889.00
Settee, Windsor, Rod Back, Plank Seat, Painted, Pa., 1790, 30 ½ x 36 In.	3318.00
Settee, Windsor, Wood, Curved Spindle Back, Painted, W. Wallick, 39 x 82 In.	1823.00
Settee, Wood, Chinoiserie, Slat Back, Turned Uprights, Rush Seat, c.1800, 32 x 36 In.	1230.00
Settee, Wood, Half Spindle Back, Shaped Carved Rail, Pa., c.1840, 33 x 72 In.	207.00
Settle, Colonial Revival, Pine, Hinged Lid Seat, Pierced Wings, Paneled, 61 x 52 In.	546.00
Settle, Fir, High Concave Back, Drawers, Beaded Boards, Scroll Arms, c.1795, 69 x 74 In.	889.00
Settle, G. Stickley, No. 208, Even Arm, Wide Slats All Round, 29 x 76 In.	5000.00
Settle, G. Stickley, Oak, No. 286, Upholstered, Red Decal, 1904-12, 49 x 48 In.	5675.00
Settle, Georgian, Elm, Curved, Planked Back, Handgrips, Cushion, 59 x 42 In.	978.00
Settle, Oak, Raised Panel, Seat Compartment, Square Back, Arms, 1700s, 19 x 47 In.	1998.00
Settle, Painted, Green, Paneled Back, Lift Up Seat, Turned Arms, 43 x 42 In.	708.00
Settle, Queen Anne Style, Oak, 4 Panel Back, Upholstered, 3 Front Legs, 41 x 72 In.	805.00
Settle, Queen Anne, Oak, Arched Back, Scroll Arms, Cabriole Legs, c.1790, 41 x 72 In.	1434.00
Settle, Roycroft, Slat Back & Sides, Square Feet, Cushions Seat, c.1905, 38 x 77 In.	3750.00
Settle, Shop Of The Crafters, Quartersawn Oak, Inlay, Paul Horti, c.1906, 71 In. ....*Illus*	6250.00
Settle, Stickley Bros., Wood Slat Back, Flaring Arms, Foam Seat, c.1909, 36 x 84 In.	5938.00
Settle, Wide Plank Flat Back, Open Arms, Ocher Paint, England, c.1750, 48 x 81 In.	237.00
Shelf, 3 Tiers, Spool Turned Supports, c.1850, 33 x 30 ½ In.	71.00
Shelf, Anglo-Indian, Teak, 2 Shelves, Turned Supports, 1800s, 47 x 46 In.	173.00
Shelf, Corner, Gilt, Carved, Mirrored Back, 1800s, 62 x 21 In.	978.00
Shelf, Corner, Pine, 3 Open Shelves, Blue Paint, c.1904, 35 x 30 In.	345.00
Shelf, Hanging, Cherry, Scalloped Crest, Cutouts, Pa., c.1850, 30 ½ x 15 ¾ In.	1778.00
Shelf, Hanging, Mahogany, 3 Graduated Tiers, Demilune Ends, c.1800, 34 x 25 In.	1960.00
Shelf, Hanging, Mahogany, Gilt, Pagoda Roof, Pierced Gallery, c.1900, 38 x 30 In.	2700.00
Shelf, Hanging, Mahogany, Jigsaw Cut Sides, Dovetailed, Shaped Crest, c.1870, 22 x 21 In.	264.00
Shelf, Hanging, Mahogany, Scrolled Ends, American, 1800s, 34 x 29 In.	558.00
Shelf, Hanging, Pine, Painted, 3 Shelves, c.1910, 31 x 29 ¼ In.	304.00
Shelf, Hanging, Poplar, Tulip Shape, Carved, c.1905, 22 x 17 In.	356.00
Shelf, Hanging, Raised Carving, Curved Arms, Tramp Art, c.1900, 15 ⅝ x 15 In.	144.00
Shelf, Hanging, Regency, Mahogany, Open Ends, Drawers, Eng., c.1820, 30 x 24 In.	805.00
Shelf, Hanging, Shaker, Maple, Red Wash, 3 Drawers, c.1835, 38 x 36 In.	2489.00
Shelf, Hanging, Softwood, Faux Grained, Shaped Base, Lancaster County, 11 x 32 In.	83.00
Shelf, Hanging, Softwood, Whale End, Red Paint, American, 1900s, 36 x 28 In.	118.00
Shelf, Hanging, Walnut, 3 Open Tiers, 2 Doors, Inlay, Dutch, c.1790, 36 ½ x 20 In.	178.00

Furniture, Mirror, Rococo Revival, Molded Composition, Beveled Mirror, 1800s, 45 x 28 ½ In.
$1,062.00

Brunk Auctions

Furniture, Pedestal, Marble, Twist Carved Standard, 8-Sided Base, Continental, 41 In.
$191.00

Leslie Hindman Auctioneers

Furniture, Pie Safe, Pine, Poplar, 8 Tin Panels, Pinwheels, Painted, Tapered Legs, 48 x 45 In.
$1,567.00

Garth's Auctioneers & Appraisers

Furniture, Pie Safe, Walnut, Punched Tin Panels, Drawers, Dovetails, 1800s, 56 x 39 In.
$37,760.00

Brunk Auctions

Furniture, Planter, Victorian, Papier-Mache, Globe Shape, Painted, Gilt, Flowers, Metal Liners, 44 x 17 In.
$2,142.00

New Orleans Auction Galleries, Inc.

Furniture, Rocker, Double, Shaker, Maple, Tape Seat & Back, New Lebanon, N.Y., 35 x 37 In.
$18,720.00

Willis Henry Auctions, Inc.

Shelf, Louis XVI Style, Gilt Bronze, Marble, Leaf Supports, c.1935, 22 In.	72.00
Shelf, Oak, Grain Painted, Hanging, Molded Drawers, Pot Bar, Hooks, France, 15 x 51 In.	115.00
Shelf, Oak, Hanging, 7 Shelves, Spindle Gallery, Drawers, Wales, c.1790, 55 x 43 In.	474.00
Shelf, Rosewood, Ormolu, Porcelain Mounts, Shaped, France, 35 x 15 In., Pair	356.00
Shelf, Smoke Decorated, Open Shelves, Yoke Front, Painted, c.1850, 28 x 20 In.	236.00
Shelf, Wood, Carved, Cherub Support, Fern Scroll, Applied Stain, 14 x 13 ½ In.	109.00
Shelf, Wood, Shelves, Center Divider, Tombstone Ends, Open Sides, Painted, 41 x 36 In.	141.00
Sideboard, Art Deco, Burl, Nickel Panel, Stepped Top, Curved Doors, c.1930, 38 x 57 In.	650.00
Sideboard, Art Deco, Macassar, Basket Weave Top, Doors, Cabinet, France, 91 x 22 In.	2530.00
Sideboard, Art Deco, Oak, Marble, 2 Doors, Viking Panels, France, c.1940, 43 x 79 In.	960.00
Sideboard, Art Nouveau, Mahogany, Carved, Molded Mirror Back, 63 x 77 In.	106.00
Sideboard, Arts & Crafts, Glass Doors, 3 Drawers, 2 Glass, 2 Panel Doors, 54 x 24 In.	1342.00
Sideboard, Arts & Crafts, Oak, Shelf, Drawers, Copper Hardware, England, c.1910, 37 x 54 In. ... *Illus*	813.00
Sideboard, Chippendale Style, Mahogany, Bowfront, Panel Doors, c.1900, 51 x 72 In.	646.00
Sideboard, Edwardian, Rosewood, Marquetry, Shelves, Doors, Drawers, 42 x 54 In. .... *Illus*	500.00
Sideboard, Federal Style, Mahogany Inlay, Drawers, Doors, 40 x 66 In. .... *Illus*	1625.00
Sideboard, Federal Style, Mahogany, c.1930, 41 ¾ x 60 In.	296.00
Sideboard, Federal, Inlaid Mahogany, Crossbanded, Bowfront, c.1810, 40 x 66 In.	4313.00
Sideboard, Federal, Mahogany, Bellflower Inlay, Bowfront, Drawers, Doors, 42 x 67 In.	3792.00
Sideboard, Federal, Mahogany, Bowfront, Drawer, Doors, Brass Pulls, c.1800, 41 x 72 In.	2689.00
Sideboard, Federal, Mahogany, Drawers, Brass Rope Twist Handles, c.1800, 36 x 33 In.	1755.00
Sideboard, Federal, Mahogany, Fruit, Flower, Basket, Acanthus, c.1820, 42 x 69 x 21 In.	2370.00
Sideboard, Federal, Mahogany, Husk Inlay, 4 Cupboard Doors, c.1800, 41 x 71 In.	4720.00
Sideboard, Federal, Mahogany, Inlay, 3 Drawers, 2 Doors, N.Y., c.1800, 40 x 72 In.	6612.00
Sideboard, Federal, Mahogany, Inlay, Bowfront, Banded, Drawers, c.1810, 39 x 71 In.	948.00
Sideboard, Federal, Mahogany, Inlay, Checkered Frieze, Recessed Doors, 41 x 72 In.	3510.00
Sideboard, Federal, Mahogany, Inlay, Shaped Front, 2 Doors, 7 Drawers, 49 x 68 In.	384.00
Sideboard, Federal, Mahogany, Spiral, Reeded Legs, Mass., c.1815, 37 x 80 In.	972.00
Sideboard, Federal, Mahogany, Veneer, Serpentine, String Inlay, Doors, c.1805, 40 x 63 In.	2083.00
Sideboard, Federal, Mahogany, Veneers, Inlay, Brass Pulls, c.1810, 43 x 72 In. .... *Illus*	5664.00
Sideboard, Federal, Mixed Wood, Line Inlay, Serpentine Drawers, c.1810, 39 x 72 In.	8050.00
Sideboard, Federal, Tiger Maple, Mahogany Inlay, Drawers, c.1810, 38 x 51 In. .... *Illus*	2875.00
Sideboard, G. Stickley, 2 Cupboards, 4 Drawers, Plate Rack, c.1908, 48 x 56 x 21 In.	6250.00
Sideboard, G. Stickley, 3 Drawers, 2 Doors, Through Tenons, Decal, 1902, 44 x 60 In. .... *Illus*	35380.00
Sideboard, G. Stickley, Oak, Plate Rack, Doors, Drawers, Strap Hardware, c.1910, 48 x 66 In. ...*Illus*	2875.00
Sideboard, G. Stickley, Plate Rail, 4 Drawers, Doors, Iron Pulls, Red Decal, 56 x 21 In.	5937.00
Sideboard, G. Stickley, Wood, Cupboard Doors, Plate Rack, Marked, c.1912, 49 x 56 In.	3500.00
Sideboard, George III Style, Mahogany, Satinwood Banding, Brass Rail, 2 Doors, 57 x 60 In.	1476.00
Sideboard, George III, Mahogany, Bowed, Cutlery Drawer, Spade Feet, c.1790, 35 x 43 In.	799.00
Sideboard, George III, Mahogany, Bowfront, Cupboard, Cellarette, c.1800, 37 x 67 In.	1722.00
Sideboard, George III, Mahogany, Brass Rail, Serpentine Drawers, c.1800, 36 x 70 In.	2460.00
Sideboard, George III, Mahogany, Brass, Inlay, Drawers, Reeded Legs, c.1860, 39 x 81 In.	6250.00
Sideboard, George III, Mahogany, Drawers, Inlaid Backsplash, Scotland, c.1800, 43 x 72 In.	2400.00
Sideboard, George III, Mahogany, Inlaid Backsplash, Brass Rail, c.1800, 58 x 107 In.	1888.00
Sideboard, George III, Mahogany, Marquetry, Stringing, Demilune, c.1790, 38 x 72 In.	2214.00
Sideboard, George III, Marquetry, Mixed Wood, Bowed, 3 Drawers, c.1790, 35 x 60 In.	4063.00
Sideboard, George III, Rosewood, Serpentine, Stringing, Doors, Bellflower, 34 x 45 In.	2706.00
Sideboard, George IV, Mahogany, Serpentine Front, Line Inlay, c.1800, 37 x 69 In.	593.00
Sideboard, Hepplewhite Style, Demilune, Drawers, Cabinet Doors, 1900s, 35 x 47 In.	531.00
Sideboard, Hepplewhite Style, Inlaid Mahogany, 4 Doors, Drawers, 41 x 62 In.	295.00
Sideboard, Hepplewhite Style, Inlaid Tambour Door, Figured Veneers, 1900s, 43 x 66 In.	1062.00
Sideboard, Hepplewhite Style, Mahogany, Banding, Drawers, Cabinet Doors, 36 x 73 In.	1888.00
Sideboard, Hepplewhite Style, Mahogany, Bowfront, Banding, Inlay, c.1990, 40 x 66 In. ...... *Illus*	1293.00
Sideboard, Hepplewhite Style, Mahogany, Inlay, 3 Drawers, 2 Doors, Mersman, 72 x 40 In.	780.00
Sideboard, Hepplewhite Style, Mahogany, Inlay, Gallery, Drawer, 2 Doors, 37 x 66 In.	590.00
Sideboard, Hepplewhite Style, Mahogany, Poplar, Inlay, Drawers, 4 Doors, c.1900, 36 x 64 In.	999.00
Sideboard, Hepplewhite, Figured Mahogany, Inlay, Serpentine, New York, 42 x 70 In.	6325.00
Sideboard, Hepplewhite, Mahogany, Inlay, Bowfront, Bottle Drawers, 39 x 62 In.	2360.00
Sideboard, Hepplewhite, Mahogany, Inlay, Drawers, c.1800, 36 x 78 x 26 In.	1180.00
Sideboard, Hepplewhite, Mahogany, Inlay, Gallery, Stepped Back, England, 59 x 96 In.	1888.00
Sideboard, Hepplewhite, Mahogany, Line Inlay, 3 Drawers, 2 Doors, c.1795, 40 x 67 In.	4029.00
Sideboard, Hepplewhite, Mahogany, Pine, Drawers, Doors, Sawtooth Trim, 42 x 76 In.	5288.00
Sideboard, Hepplewhite, Mahogany, Satinwood, Shaped, Tambour Doors, 36 x 67 In.	2390.00
Sideboard, Hepplewhite, Mahogany, Tambour, Banded Top, Cellarette Drawer, 1800s, 37 x 72 In.	1180.00
Sideboard, Hepplewhite, Mahogany, Teardrop Inlaid Capitals, Banding, c.1800, 39 x 69 In.	8295.00
Sideboard, Hepplewhite, Pine, Drawers, Turned Pulls, Tapered Legs, c.1820, 43 x 52 In.	3290.00

Sideboard, Hepplewhite, Serpentine Front, Mahogany, Sawtooth Trim, c.1795, 41 x 75 In..............	5287.00
Sideboard, Jacobean Style, Oak, 2 Drawers Between 2 Doors, Rorimer Brooks, 73 In.......................	588.00
Sideboard, L. & J.G. Stickley, No. 731, Plate Rack, Drawers, 2 Doors, 49 x 72 In.	5313.00
Sideboard, L. & J.G. Stickley, Oak, Copper, Backsplash, 5 Drawers, 2 Doors, 47 x 56 In....................	1250.00
Sideboard, L. & J.G. Stickley, Plate Rack, Strap Hardware, 2 Doors, Drawers, c.1907, 48 x 54 In....	6250.00
Sideboard, Limbert, 5 Drawers, 2 Doors, Mirror Top, c.1905, 59 x 60 In.	6875.00
Sideboard, Limbert, Mirror Back, 3 Drawers, 2 Doors, 45 x 19 In.	1464.00
Sideboard, Louis XV Style, Walnut, Marble Top, Drawer, Carved Apron, c.1900, 39 x 88 In.............	3444.00
Sideboard, Louis XVI Style, Kingwood, Walnut, Metal, 2 Drawers, Demilune, 30 x 27 In.	406.00
Sideboard, Louis XVI Style, Oak, D-Shape, 2 Carved Doors, Shelves, 1900s, 44 x 64 In.....................	1778.00
Sideboard, Louis XVI, Birch, Burl, Ebonized, Oval Plaque, c.1900, 39 x 60 In.	600.00
Sideboard, Mahogany, 2 Frieze Drawers, 2 Arched Doors, c.1860, 17 x 19 In., Child's................	354.00
Sideboard, Mahogany, Backsplash, Capitals, 6 Drawers, Doors, Carved, c.1830, 51 x 65 In.............	826.00
Sideboard, Mahogany, Black Forest, Carved Backsplash, Drawer, 2 Doors, 68 x 74 In................	649.00
Sideboard, Mahogany, Bowfront, Cupboard, Columns, Ball Feet, c.1825, 40 x 51 In....................	1067.00
Sideboard, Mahogany, Gallery, Cupboard Doors, Columns, c.1815, 43 x 75 In.......................	1968.00
Sideboard, Mahogany, Marble, Bowed, 3 Drawers, Columns, Mirrors, c.1845, 33 x 78 In.	6875.00
Sideboard, Mahogany, Mirror Backsplash, Cornucopia, Columns, c.1825, 67 x 72 In..............	7170.00
Sideboard, Mahogany, Mirror Backsplash, Pedestal Base, Door, c.1800, 54 x 76 In.	717.00
Sideboard, Mahogany, Pediment Backsplash, 2 Doors, Scroll Feet, c.1840, 42 x 47 In.	2032.00
Sideboard, Marble Top, Oak, Chinoiserie, Asian Symbols, Jansen, c.1910, 41 x 73 In......................	4080.00
Sideboard, Mixed Wood, 3 Drawers, 3 Panel Doors, Straight Legs, c.1835, 49 x 59 In.	748.00
Sideboard, Neoclassical, Mahogany, Drawers, Doors, Columns, c.1825, 39 x 50 In. .... *Illus*	492.00
Sideboard, Oak, H. Schwartz, 2 Doors, 5 Drawers, Curved Feet, RomWeber, 38 x 84 In...................	738.00
Sideboard, Parzinger, Gilt Metal, Leather, 4 Doors, X-Design, Charak Modern, c.1946, 33 x 65 In.	6875.00
Sideboard, Regency Style, Mahogany, Drawer, Pedestals, Paw Feet, c.1900, 45 x 85 In.	950.00
Sideboard, Regency Style, Mahogany, Inlay, Serpentine Front, Cabinets, 1900s, 36 x 76 In.....	1058.00
Sideboard, Regency, Mahogany, 5 Drawers, Raised Legs, c.1805, 36 x 52 In.	2125.00
Sideboard, Regency, Mahogany, Brass Rail, 2 Drawers, 2 Doors, 6 Legs, 49 x 54 In.................	2340.00
Sideboard, Regency, Mahogany, Bronze, Brass, 2 Drawers, 2 Doors, c.1810, 38 x 73 In.	8125.00
Sideboard, Regency, Mahogany, Inlay, Bowfront, Drawers, Turned Legs, c.1800, 37 x 55 In....	734.00
Sideboard, Renaissance Revival, Burl Walnut, Glass Doors, Cupboards, c.1890, 91 x 66 In......	1434.00
Sideboard, Robsjohn Gibbings, Mahogany, Widdicomb, c.1950, 34 In.............................	2750.00
Sideboard, Roycroft, Mirror, Drawers, Doors, Leaded Glass, c.1905, 52 x 60 In. ....*Illus*	8750.00
Sideboard, Shapland & Petter, Inlaid Doors, Medallion, Square Legs, c.1900, 47 x 55 In.	3125.00
Sideboard, Sheraton, Mahogany, Bowfront, Kneehole, Spade Feet, 36 x 60 In.........................	2375.00
Sideboard, Sheraton, Mahogany, Flame Birch, D-Shape, Bowed, Drawers, 43 x 63 In.	7080.00
Sideboard, Sheraton, Mahogany, Inlay, Bowed, 5 Drawers, 2 Doors, Ma., c.1800, 43 x 72 In...	5015.00
Sideboard, Sheraton, Mahogany, Shaped Top, Doors, Drawers, Reeded, c.1815, 51 x 74 In.....	1116.00
Sideboard, Shop Of The Crafters, Quartersawn Oak, Wood Inlays, Mirror, Label, 56 x 54 In....*Illus*	4830.00
Sideboard, Stickley Bros., Plate Rail, 4 Drawers, 2 Doors, 54 x 21 In..	2196.00
Sideboard, Stickley Bros., Quaint, Oak, 4 Drawers, 2 Doors, 1910, 44 x 60 In...........................	4500.00
Sideboard, Walnut, Nude Supports, Carved, 5 Doors, 2 Drawers, Germany, c.1900, 72 x 59 In.	450.00
Sideboard, Walnut, Pine, 6 Drawers, 2 Doors, Column Sides, c.1850, 41 x 58 In.....................	575.00
Sideboard, William IV, Mahogany, Drawers, Sheraton Legs, Ball Feet, c.1835, 38 x 73 In........	1230.00
Sideboard, Wormley, Mahogany, Marble, Drawers, Tambour Door, Dunbar, 40 x 72 In. .*Illus*	9840.00
Sofa, Adam Style, Beech Frame, Upholstered, Arched, c.1890, 41 x 89 In.................................	5750.00
Sofa, Biedermeier, Walnut, Carved, Serpentine Crest, Upholstered, Scroll Legs, Arms, 90 In.....	1000.00
Sofa, Camelback, Mahogany, Outscrolled Arms, Cabriole Legs, Scrolled Toes, c.1900, 33 x 82 In...	922.00
Sofa, Camelback, Poplar, Turned Legs, Faux Flamestitch Upholstery, 1900s, 19 x 64 In.	441.00
Sofa, Chippendale Style, Camelback, Mahogany, Ball & Claw Feet, Shell Knees, 84 x 35 In......	368.00
Sofa, Chippendale Style, Camelback, Single Cushion, Upholstered, c.1900, 81 x 36 In.............	1895.00
Sofa, Chippendale Style, Camelback, Straight Legs, Upholstered, 1900s, 36 x 64 In..................	382.00
Sofa, Chippendale Style, Mahogany, Shaped Back, Arms, H-Stretcher, c.1980, 20 x 34 In.........	331.00
Sofa, Chippendale, Camelback, Upholstered, Carved Wood Legs, 33 ¾ x 81 ½ In......................	920.00
Sofa, Chippendale, Mahogany, Camelback, Arms, Shell Carved Legs, 1700s, 35 x 74 In............	2596.00
Sofa, Chippendale, Mahogany, Camelback, Upholstered, c.1790, 39 x 85 In...........................	1458.00
Sofa, Chippendale, Walnut, Arched Back, Flared Arms, Upholstered, 37 x 78 In........................	2133.00
Sofa, Classical Empire, Mahogany, Padded Back, Rolled Crest, Arms, Scroll Ears, 39 x 83 In....	460.00
Sofa, Country, Turned Legs, Red Paint, Faux Flamestitch Upholstery, 1900s, 36 x 73 In..........	723.00
Sofa, Edwardian Style, Leather, Curved Back, Tufted, Double Seat, Brass Tacks, 30 x 75 In......	799.00
Sofa, Federal, Camelback, Mahogany, Upholstered, Signed Collins Allen, c.1810, 90 In............	2750.00
Sofa, Federal, Claw Feet, Scroll Arms, Silk Upholstery, c.1810, 34 x 77 In. ....*Illus*	1495.00
Sofa, Federal, Mahogany Inlay, Horsehair Upholstery, Brass Tack Design, 1800, 34 x 76 In.	2600.00
Sofa, Federal, Mahogany, Arched Back, Scroll Arms, Upholstered, 73 In.	826.00
Sofa, Federal, Mahogany, Birch Inlay, Arched Back, Reed Handholds, c.1810, 37 x 77 In.........	919.00

Furniture, Rocker, Platform, Wicker, Partial Label, Ordway Brothers, c.1900, 50 In.
$422.00

Garth's Auctioneers & Appraisers

Furniture, Rocker, Shaker, 5 Slats, Splint Seat, Flat Arms, New Lebanon, N.Y., c.1825, 48 ½ In.
$5,265.00

Willis Henry Auctions, Inc.

Furniture, Rocker, Shaker, Shawl Back, Taped Seat, 1800s, 27 In., Child's
$115.00

Cottone Auctions

F

TIP

To clean tortoiseshell, rub it with a mixture of jeweler's rouge and olive oil.

Furniture, Screen, 3-Panel, Baroque Style, Oil On Canvas, Scene, Gilt Frame, c.1900, 73 x 56 In.
$1,652.00

Brunk Auctions

Furniture, Screen, 8-Panel, Landscape, Lake, Figures, Paint On Paper, Wood, Chinese, 92 x 124 In.
$780.00

DuMouchelles Art Gallery

Furniture, Screen, Rosewood, Needlework, Bead & Stump Work, Pedestal, c.1850, 84 x 39 In.
$2,700.00

DuMouchelles Art Gallery

Sofa, Federal, Mahogany, Inlay, Upholstered, Turned Armrests, Legs, c.1810, 36 x 59 In.	3720.00
Sofa, Federal, Mahogany, Reeded Arms, Legs, Upholstered, New England, c.1800, 35 x 78 In.	4266.00
Sofa, Federal, Mahogany, Reeded Rail, Upholstered, Brass Rail Trim, c.1820, 35 x 84 In.	1610.00
Sofa, Flemish Style, Triple Camelback, Turned Legs, Stretchers, Upholstered, 38 x 78 In.	920.00
Sofa, George III Style, Mahogany, Upholstered, Domed Back, Outscrolled Arms, 1900s, 37 In.	738.00
Sofa, Georgian, Chippendale Base, Upholstered, c.1790, 86 In.	1062.00
Sofa, Gothic Revival, Mahogany, Crocketed Back, Scroll Arms, Quatrefoil Feet, c.1855, 91 In.	2749.00
Sofa, Hepplewhite, Camelback, Mahogany, Carved Arms, Legs, Upholstered, 80 x 35 In.	246.00
Sofa, Hepplewhite, Mahogany, Carved Frame, Upholstered, c.1810, 79 In.	1534.00
Sofa, Knoll, Leather Cushions, Wood Base, c.1970, 32 x 63 In.	1020.00
Sofa, Louis XVI Style, Gilt, Beaded Crest, Curved Arms, Fluted Uprights, 34 x 46 In.	956.00
Sofa, Louis XVI Style, Gilt, Rounded Crest Rail, Upholstered, Cabriole Legs, Carved Apron, 48 In.	572.00
Sofa, Louis XVI Style, Wood, High Back, Carved, Painted, Upholstered, c.1960, 34 x 150, 2 Piece	840.00
Sofa, Mahogany, Bronze Mounts, Cylinder Crest Rail, Columnar Supports, c.1800, 33 x 79 In.	8664.00
Sofa, Mahogany, Carved Back, Legs, Outscrolled Arms, Velvet Upholstery, c.1830, 35 x 74 In.	444.00
Sofa, Mahogany, Carved Crest, Eagles, Leaves, Scroll Arms, Shaped Apron, 1800s, 34 x 94 In.	738.00
Sofa, Mahogany, Carved, Birds, Leaves, Cornucopia, Shaped Back, Rolled Arms, 1800s, 78 In.	331.00
Sofa, Mahogany, Leaf Carved, Downswept Back, Eagle's Heads, Paw Feet, c.1885, 44 x 88 In.	1968.00
Sofa, Mahogany, Paneled Crest Rail, Scroll Arms, Reeding, Rosettes, Paw Feet, c.1825, 33 x 88 In.	522.00
Sofa, Mahogany, Scrolled Crest, S-Curve Uprights, Ogee Seat Rail, Scroll Feet, c.1835, 32 x 79 In.	837.00
Sofa, Mahogany, Serpentine Back, Brass Mounts, Gothic Arm Supports, c.1820, 38 x 84 In.	353.00
Sofa, Milo Baughman, Curved Bronzed Frame, Wool Upholstery, 61 x 34 In.	1830.00
Sofa, Neoclassical, Mahogany, Bronze Mounts, Shaped Feet, Casters, 1800s, 89 In. ....*Illus*	11352.00
Sofa, Neoclassical, Mahogany, Carved Crest, Arms, Samuel Field McIntire, Mass., 84 In.	1180.00
Sofa, Neoclassical, Mahogany, Carved, Cornucopia, Flowers, Paw Feet, 89 In.	826.00
Sofa, Neoclassical, Mahogany, Carved, Paw Feet, Upholstered, c.1820, 33 x 84 In. ....*Illus*	649.00
Sofa, Neoclassical, Mahogany, Carved, Pillar, Scroll Crest Rail, Upholstered, 89 In.	354.00
Sofa, Neoclassical, Mahogany, Carved, Upholstered, Paw Feet, Casters, c.1810, 34 x 88 In. ..... *Illus*	2153.00
Sofa, Neoclassical, Mahogany, Flame Veneers, Ogee Crest Rail, c.1840, 87 x 36 In. ....*Illus*	837.00
Sofa, Neoclassical, Mahogany, Ormolu Mounted, Box Shape, High Arms, New York, 81 In.	2124.00
Sofa, Neoclassical, Mahogany, Scroll Arms, Crest Rail, Turned Legs, Upholstered, 87 In.	354.00
Sofa, P. Evans, Patchwork Chrome Squares, Wool Upholstery, Directional, 108 x 36 In.	15860.00
Sofa, Renaissance Revival, Ebonized, Bronze Roundel, Padded Arms, Putti, Hoof Feet, c.1865, 76 In.	3286.00
Sofa, Risom, Walnut, Upholstered, 6 Cushions, c.1950, 33 x 81 In.	625.00
Sofa, Robsjohn-Gibbings, Mahogany, Cane Seat & Back, Square Arms, 1950s, 29 x 65 In.	2500.00
Sofa, Rococo Style, Hardwood, Arched Crest, Outcurved Arms, Stretcher, 1900s, 16 x 88 In.	2468.00
Sofa, Rosewood, Brass, 3 Inset Drawers, Square Back & Arms, Vinyl Upholstery, c.1970, 81 x 30 In.	2000.00
Sofa, Sectional, McCobb, Ranch Oak Frame, Cushions, E. Brandt, 30 x 172 In., 4 Piece	576.00
Sofa, Sectional, Milo Baughman, Walnut, Vinyl, Thayer-Coggin, c.1960, 78 & 66 In.	3438.00
Sofa, Sheraton Style, Cherry, Curved Back, Shaped Arms, Inlaid Banding, Reeded Legs, 36 x 78 In.	353.00
Sofa, Sheraton Style, Mahogany, Inlaid Crest & Apron, Reeded Arms & Legs, c.1935, 39 x 42 In.	264.00
Sofa, Sheraton, Mahogany, Maple, Arched Back, Sides, Carved Arms, Upholstered, 76 In.	944.00
Sofa, Sheraton, Square Back, Arms, Carved Arms, Legs, Black Leather, 78 In.	236.00
Sofa, Teak, Cane Back, Wool Seat, Curved Arms, Hvidt & Nielsen, 1960s, 34 x 66 In.	5313.00
Sofa, V. Kagan, Walnut, Upholstered, Floating Seat & Back, 3 Arch Support, 1950s, 27 x 99 In.	8125.00
Sofa, Victorian, Walnut, Pierced Top Rail, Upholstered, Cabriole Legs, c.1875, 70 In.	605.00
Sofa, W. Haines, Quilted Upholstery, c.1960, 31 x 91 In.	5000.00
Sofa, Walnut, Arched Serpentine Crest, Scroll Arms, Bowfront Apron, Italy, 1700, 50 x 93 In.	1912.00
Sofa, Walnut, Canted Support, Wood Spindles, Upholstered Seat, Denmark, 28 x 73 In.	582.00
Sofa, Wegner, Oak, Upholstered, Getama, 1954, 31 ½ x 82 x 30 In., Pair	5938.00
Sofa, Wormley, Curved, Tufted Velvet Upholstery, Rounded Arms, Dunbar, c.1950	8750.00
Sofa, Wormley, Floating Back, Mahogany, Upholstered, Curved Arms, Dunbar, 88 x 30 In.	2750.00
Stand, Arts & Crafts, Quartersawn Oak, Gallery Top, 26 ½ x 14 In.	106.00
Stand, Asian Style, Softwood, Stained, Carved, Dragons, Round Mid Shelf, 30 x 23 In.	130.00
Stand, Bamboo, 4 Shelves, Open Back & Sides, Wood Burned, 41 x 14 In. ....*Illus*	83.00
Stand, Bamboo, Lacquer, Domed Back, Cupboard, Shelves, Stretcher, Splayed Feet, c.1900, 44 x 18 In.	246.00
Stand, Baroque, Giltwood, Shaped Top, Pierced Flowers, Scrolls, Italy, 9 x 15 ¾ In.	936.00
Stand, Basin, Corner, Federal, Mahogany, Bird's-Eye Maple Veneer, c.1810, 42 x 23 In. ...*Illus*	600.00
Stand, Bell Hop Figure, Holding Tray, Wood, Painted, 48 In.	1093.00
Stand, Biedermeier, Marble Top, 3 Flat Legs, Gilt Acanthus Leaf Columns, 38 x 14 In.	173.00
Stand, Birch, Pine, Black Paint, Yellow, Drawer, Scalloped Stretchers, c.1800, 26 x 20 In.	1800.00
Stand, Birch, Tiger Maple, Drawer, Vase & Ring-Turned Legs, Spiral Carved, c.1825, 29 x 18 In.	415.00
Stand, Bottle, Mahogany, Molded Dish Top, Shaped Apron, Saber Legs, c.1795, 12 In.	359.00
Stand, Butler's, Mahogany, Tray, Cutout Handles, X-Shape Legs, Woven Supports, 1800s, 30 x 40 In.	646.00
Stand, Butler's, Oak, Carved, Cabriole Table Leg, Claw Foot, Applied Bust, Round Top, 27 x 13 In.	83.00
Stand, Casket, Walnut, Turned Legs, Pennsylvania, 1800s, 24 x 70 x 26 In.	122.00

Stand, Chamber, Mahogany, Gallery Top, Tambour Door, Concealed Pot, c.1790, 31 x 21 In...		720.00
Stand, Cherry, Drawer, Overhang Top, Banded Edge, String Inlay, c.1810, 28 x 18 In...		1103.00
Stand, Cherry, Drawer, Wavy Fan Inlay, Oval & Icicle Inlaid Legs, c.1800, 28 x 20 In. ...		2726.00
Stand, Cherry, Geometric Inlay, Drawer, Presentation Label, 1810, 27 x 20 In. ...		4029.00
Stand, Cherry, Inlaid Checkerboard Top, Drawer, Turned Legs, 28 x 19 In. ...		295.00
Stand, Cherry, Molded Edge, Drawer, Tapered String Inlaid Legs, 1815, 28 x 18 In. ...		230.00
Stand, Cherry, Oval Inlay, Stringing, Icicle Inlaid Legs, Drawer, c.1805, 27 x 19 In. ...		4288.00
Stand, Cherry, Red Wash, 2 Drawers, Wooden Pulls, Turned Legs, 30 x 19 In...		353.00
Stand, Chinese, Mahogany, Carved, Pierced, Marble Inset Top, 24 x 13 In...		196.00
Stand, Directoire Style, Ebonized, Bronze Gallery, 2 Drawers, c.1940, 26 x 20 In., Pair ...		1200.00
Stand, Display, Mahogany, Fretwork, Glass Shelf, Low Shelf, c.1770, 30 ½ x 12 ½ In...		267.00
Stand, Display, Mahogany, Square Top, Carved Supports, Outswept Feet, c.1900, 50 x 12 In...		1200.00
Stand, Donald Deskey, Primavera Wood, Streamline Shape, 3 Drawers, Widdicomb, 15 x 18 In. ...		4270.00
Stand, Dressing, Federal, Mahogany, Mirror, 4 Drawers, Marble Top, Scroll Legs, 30 x 74 In. ...		390.00
Stand, Dressing, Lacquered, Mirrors, Birds, Foo Dogs, Dragons, Chinese, c.1875, 70 x 22 In. ....*Illus*		1239.00
Stand, Dressing, Mahogany, Brass Gallery, String Inlay, Bowfront Drawer, Shelf, 28 x 22 In...		354.00
Stand, Drink, Stickley Bros., Copper Top, Arched Apron, Splayed Legs, 18 x 28 In...		2625.00
Stand, Empire, Mahogany, Shaped Backsplash, Scrolled Front Legs, Lower Shelf, c.1840, 35 x 22 In..		182.00
Stand, Federal Style, Mahogany, Pierced Brass Gallery, Drawer, Open Shelf, 1900s, 29 x 16 In. ...		176.00
Stand, Federal, Birch, Drawer, Shaped Top, Oval Corners, Cock-Beaded, Reeded Legs, c.1825, 29 In.		980.00
Stand, Federal, Birch, Maple, Serpentine Top, Square Tapered Legs, New Eng., c.1810, 29 x 21 In....		972.00
Stand, Federal, Birch, Red Stain, Drawer, Beaded & Chamfered Edge, c.1800, 29 x 20 In...		356.00
Stand, Federal, Cherry, Carved, Drawer, Red Paint, Chamfered Top, Straight Apron, 28 x 16 In. ...		4444.00
Stand, Federal, Cherry, Inlay, Drawers, Bookend Panels, Icicles, c.1800, 29 x 18 In...		1560.00
Stand, Federal, Maple, Dish Top, Tripod Base, New England, c.1820, 25 x 12 In. ...		938.00
Stand, Federal, Mixed Wood, Grain & Stippled Paint, Drawer, Turned Legs, 28 x 24 In...		94.00
Stand, Federal, Sponge Grain Painted Top, Drawer, Tapered Legs, c.1815, 28 x 19 In. ...		3450.00
Stand, Fern, Bronze, Ram's Head Mounts, Grapevines, Hoof Feet, Robert Adam, 1800s, 39 In. ..*Illus*		1320.00
Stand, Fern, Contemporary, Marble Top, 38 In., Pair...		176.00
Stand, Fern, Hardwood, Carved Apron, Lower Shelf, Chinese, 32 In...		105.00
Stand, Fern, Onyx Top, Reticulated, Curved Legs, Medial Shelf, 29 x 18 In...		374.00
Stand, Fern, Westlake, Carved, Elk Jumping Fence, Marble Top, c.1900, 36 In. ...		330.00
Stand, Figural Pedestal, Tumbling Jester, Octagonal Leather Top, Continental, 1900s, 35 In. ....*Illus*		705.00
Stand, Folio, Walnut, Ebonized, Roundel, Mask, Beaded Base, Ball & Claw Feet, c.1865, 49 x 30 In..		3444.00
Stand, George III Style, Inlay, Yew, Fruitwood, Round Top, Outcurved Feet, Stretcher, 29 x 17 In...		118.00
Stand, George III, Mahogany, Marble Top, Carved Corners, Square Fluted Legs, c.1780, 14 x 17 In..		711.00
Stand, Gothic Revival, Hexagonal, Inset White Marble Top, Scrolled Feet, 30 x 30 In. ...		2360.00
Stand, Hall, Renaissance Revival, Burl Walnut, Fish Scale Blocks, Lion's Masks, c.1880, 98 x 58 In.		2689.00
Stand, Hardwood, Carved, Famille Rose Inset Top, Warriors, Pierced Apron, c.1890, 16 x 14 In...		1416.00
Stand, Hardwood, Carved, Flowers, Cabriole Legs, Lower Shelf, 29 x 22 In. ...		150.00
Stand, Hardwood, Marble Top, Carved, Chinese, c.1890, 35 ½ x 12 In., Pair ...		668.00
Stand, Hardwood, Marble Top, Stylized Foo Dog Heads, Claw Feet, Chinese, 22 x 21 In. ..*Illus*		575.00
Stand, Hardwood, Round Marble Top, Carved, Pierced Frieze, Cabriole Legs, c.1900, 24 In.		243.00
Stand, Hepplewhite, Cherry, Square Top, Drawer, Square Tapered Legs, 1800s, 25 x 20 In. ...		264.00
Stand, Hepplewhite, Drawer, Walnut, Drawer, Overhang Top, Tapered Legs, 1800s, 29 x 20 In...		206.00
Stand, Hepplewhite, Hardwood, Overhanging Top, Drawer, Splayed Legs, 1800s, 27 x 24 In. ...		374.00
Stand, Hepplewhite, Inlaid Mahogany, Turtle Top, Drawer, Newburyport, 29 x 18 In...		1180.00
Stand, Hepplewhite, Mixed Wood, Overhung Top, Drawer, Tapered Legs, c.1820, 28 x 20 In...		633.00
Stand, Hepplewhite, Pine, Green Paint, Drawers, Overhang Top, 29 x 17 In...		590.00
Stand, Hung Mu Wood, Pierced, Leaf, Berry Carved, Chinese, c.1910, 17 x 13 ½ In...		189.00
Stand, Jacobean Style, Oak, Drawer, Chip Carved Frieze, Ring-Turned Legs, 1900s, 27 x 20 In. .		119.00
Stand, Jardiniere, Neoclassical Style, Bronze, Lions, Garlands, Flowers, 3-Part Base, 42 In...		956.00
Stand, Kettle, Mahogany, Inlay, Scalloped Gallery, Drawer, Round, Tapered Legs, 29 x 13 In...		875.00
Stand, Lavabo, Musical Instruments, Flower Painted, Green Ground, Drawer, Shaped Apron, 68 In...		153.00
Stand, Lectern, Wood, Carved, Twist Column, Wavy Tray Top, Tripod Base, 1900s, 55 x 19 In..		210.00
Stand, Limbert, Magazine, 4 Shelves, Demilune Cutouts, Tapered, c.1905, 37 x 16 In. ...		1500.00
Stand, Limbert, Plant, 8-Sided Top, 4-Sided Base, Rectangular Cutouts, 28 x 18 In. ...		2625.00
Stand, Little Journeys, Rectangular Top, 2 Shelves, Shoefoot Base, 26 x 14 In...		610.00
Stand, Louis XVI Style, Round Marble Top, Painted, Fluted Legs, France, 1900s, 31 x 18 In...		177.00
Stand, Low Tiles, Flowers, Brown Glaze, 12 Tiles, Wrought Iron, Marked, 27 x 6 In. ...*Illus*		1422.00
Stand, M. Nakashima, Black Walnut, Rosewood, Drawer, Door, X-Base, c.1964, 24 x 30 In., Pair...		8125.00
Stand, Magazine, G. Stickley, 3 Shelves, Arched Slab Sides, Signed Decal, 22 x 13 In. ...		1830.00
Stand, Magazine, G. Stickley, Overhang Top, Shelves, Arched Sides, Square Legs, c.1907, 42 x 22 In.		2000.00
Stand, Magazine, L. & J.G. Stickley, No. 47, Tapered, 4 Shelves, 42 x 20 In. ...		2500.00
Stand, Magazine, Renaissance Revival, Walnut, Cheval Base, Turned Feet, 5 Positions, 48 x 33 In...		1107.00
Stand, Magazine, Robsjohn-Gibbings, Widdicomb, Mahogany, Birch, 1950s, 30 x 24 In...		732.00

Furniture, Screen, Table, Wood, Horn, Dragons, Clouds, Chinese, 12 In.
$300.00

Skinner, Inc.

F

Furniture, Secretary, Drop Front, Biedermeier, Mahogany, Mirror, Inlaid Burl, c.1850, 78 In.
$1,722.00

New Orleans Auction Galleries, Inc.

Furniture, Secretary, Drop Front, Chippendale, Mahogany Veneer, Inlay, Oxbow, c.1790, 83 x 42 In.
$7,800.00

Skinner, Inc.

Furniture, Secretary, Drop Front, Marble Top, Inlay, Fitted Interior, Gilt Bronze, 55 x 35 In.
$1,625.00

Leslie Hindman Auctioneers

Furniture, Secretary, Drop Front, Walnut, Interior Slots & Drawers, Stretcher, 5 Legs, c.1930, 45 x 37 In.
$540.00

DuMouchelles Art Gallery

Furniture, Secretary, Slant Front, Mahogany, Fitted Interior, Drawers, England, c.1775, 91 ½ In.
$1,880.00

Garth's Auctioneers & Appraisers

Stand, Magazine, Roycroft, 3 Tiers, Shaped Crest, Tapered, Arched Square Feet, c.1905, 37 x 16 In..	2000.00
Stand, Mahogany, Drop Leaf, Square Turned Legs, 2 Drawers, Alligator Molding, c.1830, 29 In........	259.00
Stand, Mahogany, Maple Inlay, Octagonal Top, Square Legs, X-Stretcher, 1800s, 27 x 12 In.	390.00
Stand, Mahogany, Revolving, 3 Tiers, Spindled Galleries, c.1900, 38 x 23 In.	1230.00
Stand, Mahogany, Satinwood, Brass Gallery, Low Shelf, 3 Drawers, Leather, c.1950, 28 x 23 In........	149.00
Stand, Maid, Full Profile, Cutout, Black, White Paint, c.1935, 30 ½ In.	84.00
Stand, Maple, Painted, Turned Splayed Legs, New England, 19th Century, 25 x 17 In......................	119.00
Stand, Marquetry, Flowers, Urn, 2 Drawers, Square Tapered Legs, c.1920, 16 x 19 In.	266.00
Stand, McCobb, Walnut Frame, Metal Trim, Shelf, Drawer, Calvin, 21 x 21 In., Pair	1375.00
Stand, Music, Adjustable, Gilt, Carved, Brass Arms, Puppy Painting, Black, c.1910, 40 In.	1725.00
Stand, Music, Empire Style, Mahogany, 19th Century, 47 x 20 In.	920.00
Stand, Music, George III, Mahogany, Hinged Adjustable Surface, Drawer, Pedestal Base, 28 x 21 In.	633.00
Stand, Music, Neoclassical, Mahogany, Octagonal Lift Top, Twist Standard, Tripod Base, 29 x 20 In.	472.00
Stand, Music, Victorian, Fruitwood, 2-Sided Top, Pierced, Scrolling Leaves, Rotating, c.1890, 52 In.	553.00
Stand, Music, Victorian, Walnut, 2 Hinged Pockets, Black, Gold Spoon Carved, 22 x 51 In.	565.00
Stand, Music, Wrought Iron, Scrolling 3-Part Base, 1800s, 60 In.	230.00
Stand, Neoclassical, Mahogany, Drop Leaves, 2 Drawers, Square Base, c.1835, 29 ½ x 18 In.	148.00
Stand, Parlor, Eastlake, Walnut, Marble Top, Victorian, 29 x 27 In.	153.00
Stand, Parquetry, Tilt Top, Gadrooned Edge, Acanthus Carved, Square Base, c.1890, 29 x 21 In.	546.00
Stand, Parzinger, Wood, Lacquered, Square, Studded, Milk Glass, Brass Handles, 1950s, 22 x 24 In.	4375.00
Stand, Pine, Cherry, Black Paint, Gilt, Stenciled, Drawer, Beaded, Square Legs, c.1800, 26 x 20 In....	711.00
Stand, Pine, Cherry, Slant Front, Scalloped Apron, Block Legs, c.1805, 36 x 23 In.	236.00
Stand, Pine, Drawer, Red & Black Smoke Paint, Pa., c.1810, 31 x 19 In.	563.00
Stand, Pine, Drop Leaf, 2 Drawers, Turned Legs, 28 x 16 In.	71.00
Stand, Pine, Green Paint, Square Top, Shaped Apron, Square Splayed Legs, c.1795, 25 x 19 In.	840.00
Stand, Pine, Poplar, Overhung Top, Red Brown Paint, Drawer, Splayed Legs, Pa., c.1830, 28 x 17 In.	326.00
Stand, Pine, Red Stain, Drawer, Spool Turned Legs, Wood Pulls, c.1890, 29 x 15 In.	58.00
Stand, Plant, 4 Graduated Tiers, Wrought Iron, c.1920, 48 x 77 In.	420.00
Stand, Plant, Arts & Crafts, Mahogany, Hexagonal Top, Cutout Base, 13 ½ x 18 In., Pair	275.00
Stand, Plant, Arts & Crafts, Steel, Square, England, c.1910, 29 ¾ x 14 In. ....*Illus*	250.00
Stand, Plant, Ceramic, Elephant Shape, Blue, Platform On Back, Harness, c.1900, 22 In., Pair	633.00
Stand, Plant, Flower Top, Spiral Stem, Tripod Base, Iron, c.1890, 48 ½ In.	224.00
Stand, Plant, G. Stickley, Chestnut, Indigo Grueby Tile, Square Legs, c.1901, 30 x 13 In.	6250.00
Stand, Plant, Mahogany, Fretwork Gallery, Lower Shelf, Shaped Shelves, c.1900, 44 x 22 In.	215.00
Stand, Plant, Mahogany, Reeded Rim, Medial Shelf, New York, c.1810, 31 x 13 ½ In.	2232.00
Stand, Plant, Mahogany, Square Top, Carved Support, 4 Splayed Legs, 42 x 14 In.	148.00
Stand, Plant, Pine, Wire, Looped Fence Design, Green Paint, c.1900, 7 x 13 ½ In.	178.00
Stand, Plant, Regency, Rosewood, Bronze, Round Top, Columns, Scroll Feet, c.1820, 38 In.	657.00
Stand, Plant, Rosewood, Porcelain Quatrefoil, Apron, Cabriole Legs, Chinese, 1800s, 33 x 19 In..	1912.00
Stand, Plant, Victorian Style, Cast Iron, 3 Tiers, Round, 3 Reticulated Shelves, 37 x 37 In.	615.00
Stand, Plant, Wrought Iron, Copper, Scroll Tripod Base, Turnings, Hammered Bowl, 43 x 12 In., Pair	299.00
Stand, Portfolio, Ebonized, Brass Legs, Metamorphic, Trestle Base, c.1898, 38 x 30 In.	359.00
Stand, Portfolio, George IV, Satinwood, Rosewood, Walnut, Adjustable, Trestle Support, 44 x 29 In.	3744.00
Stand, Portfolio, Walnut, Serpentine Frame, Trestle Base, Arched Scroll Legs, 48 In.	1554.00
Stand, Reading, Hepplewhite, Pine, Hinged, Angled Top, 2 Drawers, Tapered Legs, c.1805, 31 x 23 In.	920.00
Stand, Regency, Mahogany, Drawer, Cross Stretcher, c.1815, 29 x 16 In.	296.00
Stand, Rosewood, Beaded Caved Skirt, Square Legs, Shade Stretcher, Chinese, 1800s, 33 x 17 In.	777.00
Stand, Rosewood, Brass, Square Top, Drawer, Shelf, Y-Shape, France, 1930s, 25 x 18 In., Pair......	2375.00
Stand, Rosewood, Carved Scrolled Brackets, Square Legs, Shaped Box Stretcher, 1900s, 25 x 13 In.	590.00
Stand, Rosewood, Lobed Marble Top, Cock-Beaded, Pierced, Ball & Claw Feet, 1900s, 36 In..........	304.00
Stand, Rosewood, Marble Inset, Plaque, Carved Dragon & Scrolls, Paw Feet, 1800s, 32 x 16 In......	1659.00
Stand, Rosewood, Marble Top, Mother-Of-Pearl Inlay, Pierced Skirt, 1800s, 31 x 16 In., Pair	598.00
Stand, Rosewood, Marble Top, Pierced Apron, Shelf, Ball & Claw Feet, Chinese, c.1890, 32 x 17 In.	461.00
Stand, Rosewood, Marble, Square Top, Scrolling Lotus, Shelf, Ball & Claw Feet, 1800s, 33 x 9 In., Pair	2963.00
Stand, Rosewood, Openwork Apron & Shelf, Square Legs, Chinese, 1800s, 33 x 17 In.	478.00
Stand, Rosewood, Satinwood Line & Fan Inlay, 2 Tiers, Shaped Frieze, c.1900, 27 x 21 In.	472.00
Stand, Shaker, Pine, Cherry, Drawer, Overhanging Top, Square Tapered Legs, c.1825, 27 x 29 In.	1126.00
Stand, Shaker, Walnut, 1-Board Round Top, Arched Tripod Base, American, c.1850, 28 x 14 In. ...	940.00
Stand, Shaving, Brass, Mahogany, Candle Arms, c.1890, 58 In.	207.00
Stand, Shaving, Eastlake, Wood, Marble, Mirror, Crested Door, 3 Drawers, Carved, 45 x 13 In.	384.00
Stand, Shaving, George I Style, Japanned, Green, Mirror, Slant Front, Fitted, Drawer, 38 In..........	688.00
Stand, Sheraton, Cherry, 2 Drawers, Drop Leaf, Turned Legs, c.1815, 29 x 20 In.	142.00
Stand, Sheraton, Cherry, Curly Maple, 1-Board Top, Dovetailed Drawers, Beading, c.1860, 30 x 20 In.	147.00
Stand, Sheraton, Cherry, Drawer, Turned Legs, c.1830	148.00
Stand, Sheraton, Cherry, Drop Leaf, Drawer, c.1815, 28 x 21 In.	91.00
Stand, Sheraton, Cherry, Mahogany, Drawer, c.1830, 27 x 15 ¾ In.	130.00

Stand, Sheraton, Cherry, Poplar, 2 Drawers, Scratch Beading, Turned Legs, 27 x 21 In.	411.00
Stand, Sheraton, Curly Maple, Drop Leaf, 2 Drawers, Opalescent Pulls, 29 x 16 In.	881.00
Stand, Sheraton, Curly Maple, Poplar, Dovetailed Drawer, 2-Board Top, 1800s, 29 x 18 In.	529.00
Stand, Sheraton, Curly Maple, Poplar, Drawer, Turned Legs, American, c.1815, 28 x 18 In.	512.00
Stand, Sheraton, Curly Maple, Poplar, Turned Legs, 2 Drawers, Glass Pulls, c.1850, 29 x 22 In. ...	3173.00
Stand, Sheraton, Drawer, Walnut & Maple, Bowed Drawer, c.1820, 29 x 18 ¾ In.	410.00
Stand, Sheraton, Mahogany, 2 Drawers, Brass Handles, Turned Legs, c.1800, 29 x 17 In.	71.00
Stand, Sheraton, Mahogany, 2 Drawers, Glass Pulls, Rope Turned Legs, c.1820, 31 x 19 In.	502.00
Stand, Sheraton, Mahogany, Medial Shelf, 2 Drawers, Turned Legs, 28 x 22 In.	472.00
Stand, Sheraton, Maple, 3 Drawers, Reeded, Turned Legs, 26 x 19 In.	1180.00
Stand, Sheraton, Maple, Drop Leaf, 2 Drawers, Reeded, Turned Legs, 29 ½ x 20 In.	767.00
Stand, Sheraton, Pine, 2 Drawers, Turned Legs, c.1805, 28 x 21 In.	148.00
Stand, Sheraton, Poplar, Dovetailed Drawer, Red & Gray Paint, American, c.1800, 31 x 19 In.	264.00
Stand, Sheraton, Tiger Maple, 2 Drawers, c.1830, 27 ½ x 19 In.	504.00
Stand, Sheraton, Tiger Maple, 2 Drawers, Turned Legs, 29 x 20 In.	590.00
Stand, Sheraton, Tiger Maple, Drawer, Overhang Top, Splayed Turned Legs, 30 x 20 In.	1416.00
Stand, Sheraton, Walnut, 2 Drawers, Acanthus Carved Legs, Glass Knobs, 30 x 24 In.	345.00
Stand, Sheraton, Walnut, Projecting 2-Board Top, Drawer, Turned Legs, c.1835, 29 x 21 In.	246.00
Stand, Smoking, Black Butler, Red Coat, Long Legs, Brass Trim, Iron, 35 In.	249.00
Stand, Smoking, Butler, Ashtray, Match Holder, Painted, Iron, 33 In.	390.00
Stand, Smoking, Electric, Accessories, Ivory Accent Marble At Base, Top, 28 In.	86.00
Stand, Smoking, Figural, Butler, Gray Hair, Cast Iron, 37 In. ....*Illus*	420.00
Stand, Smoking, Rohlfs, Octagonal Top, Cutout Sides, 2 Shelves, 24 x 24 In.	6100.00
Stand, Smoking, Stickley Bros., Copper Ashtray, Drawer, Shelf, 13 x 13 In.	281.00
Stand, Softwood, Red, Square Top, Reeded Skirt, Beaded Tapered Splayed Legs, Pa., 1800s, 7 In.	2596.00
Stand, Stickley Bros., Drinks, Copper Top, Round, Arched Skirt, 28 x 18 In.	2500.00
Stand, Stickley Bros., No. 131, Square Top, Arched Skirt, X-Shape Base, 34 x 14 In.	1625.00
Stand, Table Top, Mahogany Satinwood, Shield Mirror, c.1860, 33 x 25 In.	236.00
Stand, Teak, Square Marble Top, Shelf, Carved Pierced Apron, Shelf, Square Legs, 32 x 17 In.	317.00
Stand, Television, Swivel, 4 Legs, Upholstered Grill, Universal Woodcrafters, 1950s, 15 x 24 In.	300.00
Stand, Tiger Maple, Oval Top, 3 Curved Outswept Legs, c.1820, 28 ½ x 19 ¼ In.	1150.00
Stand, Urn, Georgian, Mahogany, Piecrust Top, Tripod Base, Scroll Feet, c.1800, 37 x 17 In., Pair....	590.00
Stand, Victorian, Iron, White Onyx, Cream & Gold Paint, Scrolls, Flowers, Shelf, c.1900, 30 In.	207.00
Stand, Walnut, Octagonal, Turned Pedestal Base, Italy, 1700, 27 x 17 In.	345.00
Stand, Wood, Fluted Column, Carved, Square Base, Baker Furniture, 36 x 17 In.	276.00
Stand, Wood, Pierced Fret Design, Square Legs, Humpback Stretchers, China, 47 x 15 In. ....*Illus*	1320.00
Stand, Work, Federal, Mahogany, 5 Drawers, Tripod Feet, c.1830, 33 x 24 ½ In.	516.00
Stand, Work, Sheraton, Mahogany, 2 Drawers, Reeded Legs, Ma., c.1810, 27 x 18 In.	593.00
Stand, Writing, Neoclassical, Mahogany, Lyre Pedestal, Footed, Pa., c.1840, 28 x 23 In.	273.00
Stand, Writing, Sheraton, Mahogany, 2 Drawers, Pa., c.1810, 30 x 18 In.	889.00
Stool, A. Girard, Aluminum Frame, Upholstered, Herman Miller, 1960s, 16 x 17 ½ In.	4063.00
Stool, Anglo-Indian, Bamboo, Cushion, Canterbury Compartment, Leather, c.1890, 21 x 24 In. ...	676.00
Stool, Ash, Pine, Red Paint, Chamfered Top, Splayed Legs, Turned Stretchers, 1800s, 26 In.	563.00
Stool, Baroque, Walnut, Egg & Dart Edge, Trestle Supports, Turned Stretcher, Italy, 19 x 24 In.	351.00
Stool, Butterfly, Sori Yanagi, Laminated Rosewood, Brass, Tendo, 1954, 16 x 16 ½ In. ....*Illus*	1875.00
Stool, Cricket, Limbert, Leather Seat, Cutout Base, Key & Tenon, 20 x 15 x 19 In.	325.00
Stool, Cricket, Limbert, Leather Seat, Cutout Supports, Shelf Stretcher, 20 ½ x 19 ½ In.	397.00
Stool, David Gilhooly, Elephant Foot, Whiteware, Fabric, 1966, 12 x 16 x 17 In. ....*Illus*	3525.00
Stool, Eero Saarinen, Tulip, Aluminum, Enameled, Brown Fabric Seat, Label, 18 x 13 In.	300.00
Stool, Egyptian Revival, Wood, Dog Heads Front Legs, Tail Back Legs, Gilt Paw Feet, c.1910, 29 In..	3163.00
Stool, Empire, Figured Mahogany, Padded Top, 16 x 18 x 17 In., Pair	575.00
Stool, G. Nakashima, Walnut, Upholstered, Square Seat, Plank X-Base, c.1977, 16 x 21 In.	3750.00
Stool, George II, Mahogany, Pad Seat, Leaf Carved Cabriole Legs, Ball Feet, c.1760, 17 x 22 In.	2500.00
Stool, George II, Mahogany, Upholstered, Carved Cabriole Legs, Paw Feet, 17 x 22 In.	250.00
Stool, George III, Mahogany, Dipped Seat, Tapered, 23 ¾ x 15 In.	351.00
Stool, Heywood-Wakefield, Wicker, Needlepoint Top, c.1900, 9 ¾ x 14 ½ x 11 ½ In. ....*Illus*	48.00
Stool, Horseshoe, Rest Your Foot Here, Iron, c.1900, 12 x 10 In.	144.00
Stool, Huanghuali, Square, Openwork Ladder Frieze, Cylindrical Legs, 21 x 19 In., Pair	5975.00
Stool, I. Noguchi, Teak, Steel, Rocking, Round Top & Bottom, Crossing Rods, 1950s, 11 x 14 In.	5000.00
Stool, Ice Cream Parlor, Floor Mounted, Black Base, Red Leather Seat, 1930s, 19 In., 5 Piece	500.00
Stool, L. & J.G. Stickley, No. 398, Arched Skirt, Leather Top, Studs, 17 x 19 In.	813.00
Stool, Lacquer, Gilt, Scroll Top, Apron, S-Curved Legs, Scroll Feet, Dragons, Pearl, c.1700, 14 x 20 In.	2390.00
Stool, Louis XV Style, Fruitwood, Suede Rectangular Top, Carved Frieze, Scroll Toes, 18 x 20 In.	799.00
Stool, Louis XV Style, Rosewood, Needlework Top, Cabriole Legs, Scroll Toes, c.1890, 17 x 22 In.	430.00
Stool, Louis XV Style, Shaped Apron, Molded Cabriole Legs, Scroll Toes, c.1890, 10 x 36 In.	799.00
Stool, Mahogany, Curule Base, Boss, Turned Stretcher, Upholstered, c.1800, 15 x 15 In.	598.00

Furniture, Server, Renaissance Revival, Oak, Openwork, Putti, Shelf, Griffins, Marble Top, c.1890
$5,676.00

Neal Auction Co.

Furniture, Server, Shop Of The Crafters, Oak, Inlay, Glass Tile, Door, 1904-20, 40 x 42 In.
$2,625.00

Rago Arts & Auction Center

Furniture, Settee, Rococo Revival, Rosewood, Rosalie, Attributed To Belter, c.1850, 38 x 40 In.
$6,100.00

Neal Auction Co.

Furniture, Settle, Shop Of The Crafters, Quartersawn Oak, Inlay, Paul Horti, c.1906, 71 In.
$6,250.00

Los Angeles Modern Auctions (LAMA)

Furniture, Sideboard, Arts & Crafts, Oak, Shelf, Drawers, Copper Hardware, England, c.1910, 37 x 54 In. $813.00

Rago Arts & Auction Center

Furniture, Sideboard, Edwardian, Rosewood, Marquetry, Shelves, Doors, Drawers, 42 x 54 In. $500.00

Leslie Hindman Auctioneers

Furniture, Sideboard, Federal Style, Mahogany Inlay, Drawers, Doors, 40 x 66 In. $1,625.00

Leslie Hindman Auctioneers

Furniture, Sideboard, Federal, Mahogany, Veneers, Inlay, Brass Pulls, c.1810, 43 x 72 In. $5,664.00

Brunk Auctions

> **TIP**
> Stained marble tabletops can be touched up by using paste wax and steel wool.

Stool, Mahogany, Cyma Molded Frame, Ogee Bracket Feet, Cushion Seat, c.1850, 10 x 17 In.	184.00
Stool, Mahogany, Needlepoint, Cabriole Legs, Pad Feet, Ireland, 1800s, 18 x 22 ½ In. ....*Illus*	1680.00
Stool, Mahogany, Octagonal Top, Fluted Column, Serpentine Base, Bun Feet, c.1835, 21 x 15 In.	246.00
Stool, Maple, Scroll Arms, Legs, Carved, Quilt Pad Seat, New York, c.1835, 20 x 25 In., Pair	2480.00
Stool, Neoclassical Style, Brass, Curule Shape, X-Shape Base, Arms, 1900s, 28 x 26 In.	1045.00
Stool, Neoclassical Style, Gilt, Curule Shape, Flowers, Peg Feet, Fluted Arms, c.1890, 26 x 29 In.	307.00
Stool, Oak, Duck Shape, Turned Legs, Stretcher, c.1900, 28 ½ x 15 In.	1265.00
Stool, Oak, Joined, Pegged, Apron, Baluster Turned Legs, Block Bases, Stretchers, 17 x 18 In.	380.00
Stool, Oak, Padded Top, Storage, Shaped Frieze, Cabriole Legs, Pointed Toes, 1800s, 19 x 19 In.	338.00
Stool, Oak, Square, Pinched Waist Support, France, c.1955, 18 x 11 In.	325.00
Stool, Pad Seat, Adjustable, Iron, Green Paint, c.1920, 26 x 15 In., Pair	660.00
Stool, Painted, Fruit, Black Ground, Pa., c.1850, 6 x 12 In.	3081.00
Stool, Piano, Gothic Revival, Cast Iron, Pierced Skirt, Tapered Stem, Casters, c.1850, 21 x 17 In.	478.00
Stool, Piano, Mahogany, Adjustable, Upholstered Seat, Carved Dolphins, Leaves, Paw Feet, 22 In.	500.00
Stool, Piano, Neoclassical, Mahogany, Gilt, Swivel Seat, Acanthus Base, Paw Feet, c.1800	488.00
Stool, Piano, Sheraton, Mahogany, Adjustable, Reeded Legs, 19 x 24 In.	325.00
Stool, Piano, Victorian, Walnut, Turned Legs, Glass Ball & Iron Claw Feet, Adjustable, 19 x 15 In.	60.00
Stool, Regency, Mahogany, Upholstered, Reeded Legs, 1800s, 18 ½ x 19 In. ....*Illus*	250.00
Stool, Regency, Upholstered, Painted, c.1810, 20 x 12 ½ In., Pair	563.00
Stool, Robsjohn-Gibbings, Bleached Walnut, Pad Seat, Widdicomb, 21 x 17 ½ In., Pair	1875.00
Stool, Shaker, Maple, Ash, Red Wash, Swivel, c.1895, 26 x 17 In.	2015.00
Stool, Shaker, Revolving, Spindle Back, Mount Lebanon, N.Y., c.1860, 28 In.	7552.00
Stool, Sheraton, Mahogany, Serpentine, Upholstered, 16 x 14 ½ In.	472.00
Stool, Vertical Lucite Rods, Lucite Base, Vinyl Seat, 1940s, 16 x 20 In., Pair	1300.00
Stool, Walnut, Curule Shape, Carved Leaves, Roundels, Turned Stretchers, c.1835, 28 x 20 In.	461.00
Stool, William & Mary, Oak, Jointed, Ring-Turned Legs, Box Stretcher, 1700s, 18 x 12 In.	944.00
Stool, William & Mary, Oak, Turned Legs, Base Stretcher, c.1710, 20 ½ x 18 ¾ In.	711.00
Stool, Windsor, Walnut, Dish Top, Turned Legs, Pa., c.1770, 25 x 18 ½ In.	6518.00
Stool, Wrought Iron, Leather Woven Strapping, Swift & Monell, 18 x 16 In.	351.00
Stool, X-Frame, Carved Scroll Feet, Blue Tassel Cushion, c.1950, 26 x 30 In., Pair	2500.00
Storage Unit, Eames, Plywood, Metal, 2 Sliding Doors, 2 Shelves, 11 Drawers, c.1952, 58 x 47 In.	8250.00
Storage Unit, Eames, Plywood, Metal, 3 Drawers, Shelf, 2 Sliding Doors, c.1952, 32 x 47 In.	5040.00
Sugar Chest, Sheraton, Walnut, Turned Legs, c.1825, 29 x 35 In.	711.00
Sugar Chest, Walnut, Batten Edge, Fitted Interior, Raised Legs, c.1840, 31 x 20 In.	4025.00
Table, Aalto, Birch, Square Top, Upcurved Sides, Shelf, Box Frame Legs, c.1930, 24 x 24 In.	4063.00
Table, Adam Style, Marble Top, Urn & Ram's Head Frame, Stretcher Base, Urn Finial, 30 x 56 In.	472.00
Table, Adam Style, Mixed Wood, Inlay, Carved Rosettes, Leaves, c.1940, 30 x 68 In.	413.00
Table, Adjustable To Bench, Pine, Red Paint, Pa., 1800s, 28 ½ x 55 In.	2844.00
Table, Aesthetic Revival, Walnut, Carved, Drawer, Shelves, Gallery, Turned Legs, c.1890, 30 x 22 In.	236.00
Table, Aesthetic Revival, Walnut, Stick & Ball Design, Shelf Stretcher, Brass Feet, 26 x 17 In.	750.00
Table, African Drum, Skin Top, Round, 3 Figural Supports, c.1900, 25 x 20 In.	5463.00
Table, Aldo Tura, Gilt Bronze, Lacquered Goatskin, Curled Edges, Splayed Legs, c.1950, 19 x 40 In.	3000.00
Table, Altar, 2 Frieze Drawers, Carved Flowers, Pierced Brackets, Chinese, c.1910, 34 x 60 In.	472.00
Table, Altar, Cedar, Arched Apron, Square Legs, Geometric Panels, Chinese, 1700s, 36 x 79 In.	1900.00
Table, Altar, Downswept Scroll Ends, Pierced Frieze, Octagonal Side Stretchers, c.1900, 43 In.	1458.00
Table, Altar, Elm, Molded Apron, Pierced Carved Brackets, Chinese, c.1900, 33 x 97 In.	411.00
Table, Altar, Elm, Square Scrolled Ends, Carved Apron, Chinese, 1800s, 33 x 54 In.	657.00
Table, Altar, Figured, Carved Wood, Dark Purple, Figured Top, 34 x 76 x 16 In.	20060.00
Table, Altar, Ironwood, Weathered Surface, Chinese, 1800s, 34 x 96 In.	861.00
Table, Altar, Wood, Banded Top, Shaped Apron, Columnar Supports, Shelf, 28 ¾ x 28 In.	522.00
Table, Altar, Wood, Carved Openwork, Demilune End Panel Legs, Leaves, Scroll, c.1900, 13 x 41 In.	180.00
Table, Altar, Wood, Incurvate, Openwork Skirt, Square Legs, Scroll Toes, c.1900, 34 x 37 In.	11950.00
Table, Altar, Wood, Lacquer, Coastal Scene, Flowers, Pedestal Legs, Openwork, Chinese, 32 x 49 In.	360.00
Table, Altar, Wood, Mother-Of-Pearl Inlay, Dragon, Flowers, Openwork, c.1950, 36 x 49 In.	180.00
Table, Aluminum, Copper, Leaf Design Apron, Karl Bock, P.A. Fiebiger, c.1935	1250.00
Table, Anglo-Indian, Rosewood, Marquetry, Lovers, Seated, Carved Pedestal, 26 x 21 In.	388.00
Table, Art Deco, Wrought Iron, Marble, Tapered, Tapered Support, c.1940, 36 x 46 In.	900.00
Table, Art Nouveau, Majorelle Cathay, Round Top, Curvate Legs, Wrought Iron, 24 x 29 In.	472.00
Table, Arts & Crafts, 2 Drawers, Slat Sides, Low Shelf, Imperial, c.1905, 49 x 32 In.	180.00
Table, Arts & Crafts, Ash, Octagonal, Cross Stretcher, Cutout Sides, 32 x 32 x 29 In.	225.00
Table, Asian Figures, Reverse Gilding, Landscape, France, c.1970, 18 x 47 In.	625.00
Table, Baker's, Downswept, Scrolled Base, Iron, 30 x 38 In.	600.00
Table, Bamboo, Demilune, Chinese, 19th Century, 34 ½ x 37 ½ In. ....*Illus*	369.00
Table, Baroque Style, Oak, Carved Apron, Retractable Leaves, Ring-Turned Legs, 30 x 57 In.	344.00
Table, Baroque Style, Walnut, Carved Apron, Octagonal, Italy, 29 x 35 In.	500.00
Table, Baroque Style, Walnut, Marble Top, Flower Carved Trestle Supports, 20 x 27 In.	219.00

F

Table, Baroque Style, Walnut, Needlepoint Flower Top, Carved Apron, Base Stretcher, 27 x 34 In......	375.00
Table, Baroque Style, Walnut, Scrolled Trestle Supports, S-Scroll Iron Stretcher, Italy, 30 x 45 In.	920.00
Table, Bench, Pine, Oak, Green Paint, Pa., c.1860, 29 x 96 In..	1896.00
Table, Bench, Pine, Trestle Base, Painted, 1900s, 28 ½ x 71 x 38 ½ In...	326.00
Table, Bench, Poplar, Trestle Base, Pennsylvania, c.1880, 30 x 77 x 42 In....................................	415.00
Table, Bentwood, 2-Tier Top, Round, c.1960, 22 ½ x 24 ½ In..	330.00
Table, Biedermeier, Tilt Top, Satinwood, Medallion, Panels, 3 Splayed Legs, c.1850, 29 x 46 In.........	2337.00
Table, Biedermeier, Veneered Inlay Top, Splayed Legs, Drawer, Pullout Writing Surface, 19 x 27 In..	207.00
Table, Biedermeier, Walnut Veneer, Drop Leaf, Drawer, Lyre Shape Base, c.1860, 31 x 41 In..............	368.00
Table, Billy Baldwin, Glass, Metal, American, c.1970, 16 x 40 x 22 In. ....*Illus*	2280.00
Table, Bird's-Eye Maple, Triangle Carved Apron, 3 Splayed Legs, Schott Furniture, 24 x 22 In., Pair.	984.00
Table, Black Lacquered, Round Top, Columnar Stem, Tripod Splayed Legs, c.1865, 29 In..................	615.00
Table, Black Marble Top, Round, Gilt, Mosaic, Inlay, Carved Pedestal, 1800s, 30 x 28 In................	27600.00
Table, Blue Paint, Drawer, Cabriole Legs, England, c.1855, 39 ½ x 29 In.....................................	1380.00
Table, Blue, Green Paint, Deep Apron, Turned Legs, c.1880, 33 x 73 In..	600.00
Table, Bouillotte, Parquetry, Marquetry, Round Top, Candle Slide, Skirt, 27 x 15 In...........................	1673.00
Table, Boulle Turtle Top, Ormolu Mounts, Drawer, Cabriole Legs, c.1900, 31 x 40 In.......................	590.00
Table, Brass Tray, Engraved, Impressed Red, Black Designs, Round, 6-Leg Base, India, 22 x 30 In....	59.00
Table, Brass Tray, Hammered, Pierced, Scalloped Shoulder, 6-Leg Teak Base, 20 x 36 In..................	71.00
Table, Brass, Faux Marble, Drum Shape, Stamped, France, c.1940, 21 ½ x 16 In.	625.00
Table, Bronze, Brass Frame, Cast Openwork Apron, Flowers, Shelves, Fluted Legs, 26 x 19 In...........	242.00
Table, Bronze, Green Marble Top, Round, Curved Supports, Paw Feet, 27 x 24 In., Pair	5000.00
Table, Burl Walnut, Canted Corners, Frieze Drawer, Tripod Base, 31 x 20 In...................................	58.00
Table, Burl, Leaf Inlay, Molded Edge, Cabriole Legs, Pad Feet, 28 In..	313.00
Table, Butcher Block, Painted, Round, Pa., c.1865, 25 x 33 In..	444.00
Table, Butler's Tray, Mahogany, Brass Hinges, Square Legs, 18 x 27 In..	531.00
Table, Card, Chippendale, Cherry, Cock-Beaded Half Drawers, Gadroon Skirt, c.1775, 29 x 33 In.	4148.00
Table, Card, Chippendale, Mahogany, Serpentine Top, Claw Feet, c.1770, 27 x 34 In.......................	26070.00
Table, Card, Empire, Mahogany, Burl Veneer, Lyre Base, Swivel, c.1840, 28 x 36 In. 153.00 to 266.00	
Table, Card, Federal, Birch, Mahogany, Serpentine, Foldover, Ma., 28 x 36 In.................................	826.00
Table, Card, Federal, Cherry, Mahogany, Diamond & Leaf Inlay, c.1800, 30 x 35 In.	1541.00
Table, Card, Federal, Cherry, String & Leaf Inlay, D-Shape, Hinged Top, Swing Leg, 30 x 36 In.........	4700.00
Table, Card, Federal, Curly Maple, Pine, Striping, Molded, Tapered Legs, Pierced, 28 x 34 In............	617.00
Table, Card, Federal, Inlay, Mahogany, Pine, Curved Corners, Tapered Legs, c.1810, 29 x 36 In........	723.00
Table, Card, Federal, Mahogany, Flame Birch Veneer Inlay, Checkered Bands, c.1810, 30 x 37 In.	1920.00
Table, Card, Federal, Mahogany, Foldover, Reeded, Tapered Legs, Phil., 29 x 36 In., Pair.................	2124.00
Table, Card, Federal, Mahogany, Inlay, Serpentine Ends, Checkered Bands, c.1800, 30 x 36 In.........	1304.00
Table, Card, Federal, Mahogany, Rosette Corners, Leaf Pedestal, Carved, Paw Feet, 29 x 36 In.........	354.00
Table, Card, Federal, Mahogany, Rosewood Inlay, Demilune, Hinged Top, 29 x 36 In.........................	1475.00
Table, Card, Federal, Mahogany, Splayed Legs, New England, c.1820, 29 x 37 In.............................	237.00
Table, Card, Federal, Maple, Red Paint, Drawer, Hinged Top, Breadboard Ends, 28 x 38 In.	2844.00
Table, Card, Flame Birch, Mahogany, Serpentine, Seymour School, Boston, c.1800, 37 In.................	3680.00
Table, Card, George III, Mahogany, Hinged Top, Flower Heads, Fretwork, Marlboro Legs, 29 x 36 In.	1422.00
Table, Card, Hepplewhite Style, Mixed Wood, Inlaid Fan & Banding, Demilune, 1900s, 30 x 36 In.....	353.00
Table, Card, Hepplewhite, Drawer, Brown Paint, New England, 29 x 36 In..	531.00
Table, Card, Hepplewhite, Mahogany, Foldover Top, Line & Checker Inlay, c.1795, 30 x 36 In.	1067.00
Table, Card, Hepplewhite, Mahogany, Foldover, Demilune, Pa., c.1800, 28 ½ x 36 In.......................	152.00
Table, Card, Hepplewhite, Mahogany, Inlay, c.1800, 29 x 35 In.	889.00
Table, Card, Hepplewhite, Mahogany, Inlay, Demilune, 30 ½ x 36 In.	472.00
Table, Card, Hepplewhite, Mahogany, Inlay, Foldover Top, Drawer, 30 x 38 In.................................	177.00
Table, Card, Hepplewhite, Mahogany, Inlay, Foldover Top, Ma., c.1795, 29 x 36 In.	1541.00
Table, Card, Hepplewhite, Mahogany, Inlay, Foldover, Shaped Corners, Ma., 29 x 35 In.	826.00
Table, Card, Hepplewhite, Mahogany, Inlay, Hinged Top, Shaped Corners, Tapered Legs, 32 x 36 In.	1062.00
Table, Card, Hepplewhite, Mahogany, Inlay, Hinged Top, Tapered Legs, Ma., 30 x 36 In......................	2360.00
Table, Card, Hepplewhite, Mahogany, Inlay, Thistle, Leaf & Line Inlay, c.1800, 30 x 36 In.	805.00
Table, Card, Hepplewhite, Maple, Drawer, 31 x 36 x 16 In..	207.00
Table, Card, Hepplewhite, Tiger Maple, Birch, Inlaid Mahogany, Mass., 30 x 36 In...........................	767.00
Table, Card, Mahogany, Ebony Inlay, Lift Top, Shaped Apron, Square Legs, c.1902, 30 x 25 In.	750.00
Table, Card, Mahogany, Fan & String Inlay, Demilune, Tapered Legs, c.1795, 30 x 35 In. *Illus*	1440.00
Table, Card, Mahogany, Foldover, Brass Mounts, c.1820, 29 x 37 In...	1375.00
Table, Card, Mahogany, Shaped Top, Line Inlay, Light Wood Panels, c.1900, 30 x 36 In.	354.00
Table, Card, Mahogany, Shaped Top, Urn Shaft, Outcurved Claw Feet, 1900s, 30 x 30 In....................	46.00
Table, Card, Mahogany, String Inlay, Folding Top, Serpentine, Square Legs, c.1795, 30 x 36 In.........	130.00
Table, Card, Mahogany, Veneer, Reeded Edge, Cock-Beaded, Oval Corners, c.1820, 30 x 38 In.........	474.00
Table, Card, Neoclassical, Mahogany, Carved, Gilt Stenciled, Duncan Phyfe, 30 x 18 x 36 In.	1003.00
Table, Card, Neoclassical, Mahogany, Serpentine Front, Oval Corner, Ball Feet, c.1820, 29 x 36 In....	948.00

Furniture, Sideboard, Federal, Tiger Maple, Mahogany Inlay, Drawers, c.1810, 38 x 51 In.
$2,875.00

James D. Julia Auctioneers

Furniture, Sideboard, G. Stickley, 3 Drawers, 2 Doors, Through Tenons, Decal, 1902, 44 x 60 In.
$35,380.00

Treadway Toomey Galleries

Furniture, Sideboard, G. Stickley, Oak, Plate Rack, Doors, Drawers, Strap Hardware, c.1910, 48 x 66 In.
$2,875.00

Rago Arts & Auction Center

Furniture, Sideboard, Hepplewhite Style, Mahogany, Bowfront, Banding, Inlay, c.1990, 40 x 66 In.
$1,293.00

Garth's Auctioneers & Appraisers

Furniture, Sideboard, Neoclassical, Mahogany, Drawers, Doors, Columns, c.1825, 39 x 50 In.
$492.00

New Orleans Auction Galleries, Inc.

Furniture, Sideboard, Roycroft, Mirror, Drawers, Doors, Leaded Glass, c.1905, 52 x 60 In.
$8,750.00

Rago Arts & Auction Center

Furniture, Sideboard, Shop Of The Crafters, Quartersawn Oak, Wood Inlays, Mirror, Label, 56 x 54 In.
$4,830.00

Cottone Auctions

Furniture, Sideboard, Wormley, Mahogany, Marble, Drawers, Tambour Door, Dunbar, 40 x 72 In.
$9,840.00

Skinner, Inc.

Table, Card, Queen Anne, Mahogany, Square Top, Shaped Apron, Carved, 30 x 30 In.	560.00
Table, Card, Regency, Mahogany, Demilune, Trick Leg, Banded, 28 x 36 In.	885.00
Table, Card, Sheraton, Birch, Mahogany Veneer, Inlaid Medallion, Hinged Top, 35 x 17 In. .....*Illus*	1528.00
Table, Card, Sheraton, Mahogany, Birch, Flip Top, Serpentine, Tapered Legs, New Eng., 30 x 35 In..	2242.00
Table, Card, Sheraton, Mahogany, Birch, String Inlay, Turned & Reeded Legs, c.1815, 30 x 36 In.	3995.00
Table, Card, Sheraton, Mahogany, Flame Birch, String Inlay, Cartouche, 30 x 36 In.	1180.00
Table, Card, Sheraton, Mahogany, Flip Top, Gateleg, Reeded Legs, c.1820, 27 x 36 In.	270.00
Table, Card, Sheraton, Mahogany, Foldover Top, Reeded, Pa., 36 x 17 In.	472.00
Table, Card, Sheraton, Mahogany, Inlay, Foldover, Reeded Legs, 35 x 17 In.	259.00
Table, Card, Sheraton, Mahogany, String Inlay, c.1815, 30 x 36 In.	3995.00
Table, Card, Sheraton, Maple, Foldover Top, Carved Molding, c.1825, 28 ½ x 35 In.	590.00
Table, Cast Iron, Marble Dish Top, Pierced Skirt, Scroll Legs, De Patisserie, 1800s, 31 x 48 In.	3884.00
Table, Center, Aesthetic Revival, Mahogany, Brass Inlay, Drawers, Shelf, c.1890, 30 x 38 In. .....*Illus*	1195.00
Table, Center, Art Nouveau, Mahogany, Female Nude Supports, c.1910, 29 x 40 In. ....*Illus*	1645.00
Table, Center, Baroque Style, Walnut, Spool Turned Legs, Double Scroll Iron Stretcher, 32 x 36 In..	1265.00
Table, Center, Biedermeier, Black Stencil, Lower Shelf, Bronze Mounts, 1900s, 37 x 32 In. ....*Illus*	413.00
Table, Center, Biedermeier, Blond Wood, Round Banded Top, Stenciled, Bun Feet, 31 x 37 In.	307.00
Table, Center, Chippendale Style, Mahogany, Carved Flowers, Ball & Claw Feet, c.1900, 31 x 56 In..	944.00
Table, Center, Empire Style, Mahogany, Marble Top, Square Legs, Stretcher, c.1890, 32 x 49 In.	3444.00
Table, Center, Empire, Mahogany, Round Top, Column Support, Tripod Base, 30 x 45 In.	420.00
Table, Center, Gothic Revival, Walnut, Octagonal Marble Top, Chamfered Stem, c.1845, 30 x 35 In.	9840.00
Table, Center, Gray Marble Top, Urn Pedestal Base, Paw Feet, Round, c.1880, 29 ½ x 39 In.	1920.00
Table, Center, Louis XVI Style, Gilt, Marble Top, Flowers, Medallion, c.1890, 36 x 49 In.	5412.00
Table, Center, Louis XVI Style, Mahogany, Marble Top, Brass Bands, Inlay, c.1885, 29 x 21 In.	584.00
Table, Center, Louis XVI Style, Mahogany, Ormolu, Glass Top, Tiers, Hexagon Base, 34 x 33 In.	1968.00
Table, Center, Louis XVI Style, Oval Marble Top, Gold Paint, Cane Stretcher, 1900s, 32 x 30 In.	117.00
Table, Center, Mahogany, Marble Top, Cyma Frieze, Octagonal Columns, c.1935, 31 x 30 In.	738.00
Table, Center, Mahogany, Marble Top, Molded Frieze, Scrolled Legs, c.1833, 30 x 35 In.	5975.00
Table, Center, Mahogany, Segmented Round Top, Tapered Chamfered Support, 1800s, 29 In.	538.00
Table, Center, Mahogany, Serpentine Marble Top, Outswept Feet, 1800s, 30 x 43 In.	1135.00
Table, Center, Mahogany, Square Top, Pedestal, Ribbon Moldings, Ogee Feet, c.1835, 28 x 33 In.	246.00
Table, Center, Mahogany, String Inlay, Interlacing Geometric Design, c.1785, 31 x 54 In.	738.00
Table, Center, Mahogany, Tilt Top, Compass Star Inlay, Carved, c.1850, 30 x 41 ½ In. ....*Illus*	2988.00
Table, Center, Marble Top, Carved Pedestal, Tripod Base, Paw Feet, c.1860, 30 x 36 In.	1680.00
Table, Center, Neoclassical, Walnut, Marble Top, Columnar Legs, Concave Stretcher, c.1850, 32 In..	1599.00
Table, Center, Oak, Veneer Of Various Wood Discs, Revolving, Continental, c.1850, 29 x 36 In. .... *Illus*	3444.00
Table, Center, P. Evans, Bronzed Steel, Welded, Glass Top, 1960s, 26 x 48 In. ....*Illus*	7500.00
Table, Center, Papier-Mache, Round, Spread Wing Eagle Supports, France, c.1900, 29 x 34 In.	1434.00
Table, Center, Pedestal, Mahogany, Marble Top, Frieze, Ormolu, Block Feet, c.1825, 35 x 12 In.	430.00
Table, Center, Regency Style, Mahogany, Radial Extension Leaves, c.1910, 29 ½ x 50 In.	2015.00
Table, Center, Regency, Mahogany, Tilt Top, Molded Edge, Columnar Standard, c.1815, 29 x 36 In.	430.00
Table, Center, Renaissance Revival, Burl Walnut, Rosewood, Inlay, c.1875, 30 x 48 In. ....*Illus*	6210.00
Table, Center, Rohlfs, Cutout Base, Door, Marked, c.1904, 25 ½ x 31 ½ In. ....*Illus*	2000.00
Table, Center, Rosewood, Mahogany, Brass Inlay, Round, Scrolling Leaves, c.1950, 31 x 24 In.	338.00
Table, Center, Teak, Marble Top, Birdcage, Carved Pedestal, Dragon Feet, 35 x 54 In.	10350.00
Table, Center, Tortoise Shape Marble Top, Carved Fruit, Cabriole Legs, c.1865, 30 x 48 In.	2706.00
Table, Center, Walnut, Burl, Marble Top, Gilt Incised Details, Turned Spindles, c.1885, 30 x 33 In.	307.00
Table, Center, Walnut, Burl, Marble Top, Turned Stand, Outstretched Legs, c.1865, 30 x 34 In.	984.00
Table, Center, Walnut, Carved, Inset Marble Top, Wreath Frieze, Tapered Legs, c.1900, 30 x 28 In.	780.00
Table, Ceramic, Faux Bamboo Octagonal Top & Legs, c.1960, 23 x 31 In.	720.00
Table, Chair, Pine, Round Scrubbed Top, Square Base, Plank Seat, New England, c.1810, 25 x 43 In.	230.00
Table, Charles II, Oak, Turned Legs, Base Stretcher, Drawer, c.1690, 27 x 32 In.	978.00
Table, Charles X, Mahogany, Marble Top, Brass Inlay, Base Shelf, c.1825, 35 x 36 In.	1500.00
Table, Cherry, Cypress, Overhanging Plank Top, Drawer, Square Legs, c.1800, 30 x 58 In.	8365.00
Table, Chess, Rosewood, Marble & Blackwood Checkerboard, Carved Dragon, 31 x 20 In.	2370.00
Table, Chippendale Style, Hardwood, Carved Apron, Shelf, Chinese, 28 x 16 In.	295.00
Table, Chippendale, Cherry, Dish Top, Tripodal Base, Turned Pedestal, Snake Feet, 1700s, 27 x 21 In.	338.00
Table, Chippendale, Mahogany, Ball Standard, Tripod Feet, Pa., 1770, 28 ½ x 34 ¾ In.	1033.00
Table, Chippendale, Mahogany, Mixed Wood, 3 Drawers, Ball & Claw Feet, c.1775, 28 x 36 In.	4340.00
Table, Chippendale, Mahogany, Tilt Top, Bulbous Standard, Tripod Base, 28 x 30 ¼ In.	356.00
Table, Chippendale, Mahogany, Tilt Top, Piecrust, 3 Claw Feet, 30 x 36 In.	354.00
Table, Chippendale, Mahogany, Tilt Top, Round Top, Tripod Base, c.1850, 29 x 22 In.	1000.00
Table, Chippendale, Mahogany, Tilt Top, Serpentine Edge, Ball & Claw Feet, 27 x 32 In.	767.00
Table, Chippendale, Piecrust Top, Tilt, Birdcage Support, Mahogany, c.1775, 28 x 27 In.	4977.00
Table, Chippendale, Walnut, Drawer, Scalloped Apron, Cabriole Legs, Pa., c.1780, 29 x 36 In.	7703.00

Furniture, Sofa, Federal, Claw Feet, Scroll Arms, Silk Upholstery, c.1810, 34 x 77 In.
$1,495.00

Cottone Auctions

Furniture, Sofa, Neoclassical, Mahogany, Bronze Mounts, Shaped Feet, Casters, 1800s, 89 In.
$11,352.00

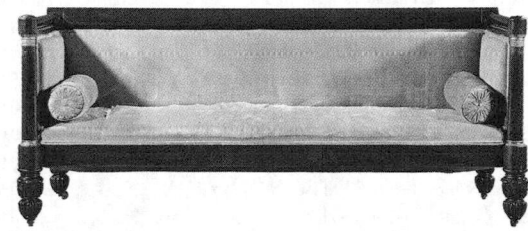

Neal Auction Co.

Furniture, Sofa, Neoclassical, Mahogany, Carved, Paw Feet, Upholstered, c.1820, 33 x 84 In.
$649.00

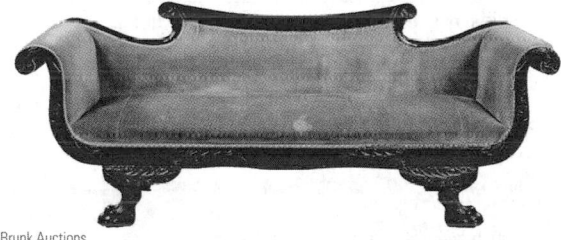

Brunk Auctions

Furniture, Sofa, Neoclassical, Mahogany, Carved, Upholstered, Paw Feet, Casters, c.1810, 34 x 88 In.
$2,153.00

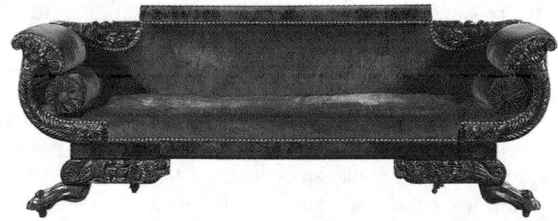

Neal Auction Co.

Furniture, Sofa, Neoclassical, Mahogany, Flame Veneers, Ogee Crest Rail, c.1840, 87 x 36 In.
$837.00

Neal Auction Co.

Furniture, Stand, Bamboo, 4 Shelves, Open Back & Sides, Wood Burned, 41 x 14 In.
$83.00

Conestoga Auction Co., Inc.

Furniture, Stand, Basin, Corner, Federal, Mahogany, Bird's-Eye Maple Veneer, c.1810, 42 x 23 In.
$600.00

Skinner, Inc.

Furniture, Stand, Dressing, Lacquered, Mirrors, Birds, Foo Dogs, Dragons, Chinese, c.1875, 70 x 22 In.
$1,239.00

James D. Julia Auctioneers

Furniture, Stand, Fern, Bronze, Ram's Head Mounts, Grapevines, Hoof Feet, Robert Adam, 1800s, 39 In.
$1,320.00

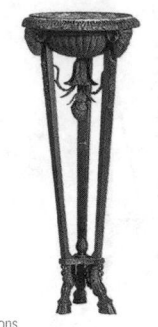

Cowan's Auctions

Furniture, Stand, Figural Pedestal, Tumbling Jester, Octagonal Leather Top, Continental, 1900s, 35 In.
$705.00

Garth's Auctioneers & Appraisers

Furniture, Stand, Hardwood, Marble Top, Stylized Foo Dog Heads, Claw Feet, Chinese, 22 x 21 In.
$575.00

Cottone Auctions

TIP

If cane or rush chair seats seem dry, spray them with water using a mister. A cane or rush seat that is used lasts only about 10 to 12 years. Keeping it from drying out extends its life.

Table, Chippendale, Walnut, Molded Edge, 5 Drawers, Scalloped Apron, c.1770, 32 x 32 In.	4503.00
Table, Chrome Plated Steel, Ring Base, Round Glass Top, 1970s, 42 x 5 In. Top.	575.00
Table, Cobalt Blue Glass Top, Steel Frame, Gilt Metal, Maison Jansen, France, c.1940, 17 x 42 In.	2000.00
Table, Coffee, Aldo Tura, Lacquered Goatskin Over Wood, Round Top, 24 x 39 ½ In.	3500.00
Table, Coffee, Arts & Crafts, Round, Cross Stretcher Base, 43 ½ x 18 ½ In.	732.00
Table, Coffee, Brass, Glass, Molded Border, Coral Lacquer, Square Legs, 1980s, 15 x 56 In.	492.00
Table, Coffee, Bronze, Bamboo Design, Glass Top, Gilt Shelf, 17 x 39 In.	780.00
Table, Coffee, Bronze, Glass Top, Beveled, Square, c.1970, 14 x 47 In.	1560.00
Table, Coffee, Bronze, Glass Top, Reeded Legs, Shaped Stretcher, c.1960, 19 x 31 In.	900.00
Table, Coffee, Bronze, Shaped Glass Top, Figural Base, Nude Woman, Gege, 1959, 17 x 46 In.	8125.00
Table, Coffee, Brushed Nickel, Brass, Glass, Ram's Head Masks, Hoof Feet, 39 x 39 In.	483.00
Table, Coffee, Chrome Frame, Glass Top, Square Legs, c.1970, 16 x 36 In.	420.00
Table, Coffee, Directoire, Style, Bronze, Gilt, Leather Top, c.1940, 17 ½ x 36 In.	1200.00
Table, Coffee, Eames, Calico Ash Plywood, Dish Top, Round Steel Legs, c.1946, 15 x 34 In.	6250.00
Table, Coffee, Eames, Surfboard, Black Laminate Top, Wire Base, Herman Miller, 1950s, 89 x 29 In.	2196.00
Table, Coffee, Ebonized, Bone, Mother-Of-Pearl Branches, Carved Border, c.1950, 19 x 56 In.	522.00
Table, Coffee, F. Henningsen, Rosewood, Drawers, Brass Handles, Denmark, 1930s, 21 x 52 In.	938.00
Table, Coffee, Federico Armijo, Pine, Laminated, Brass, Glass, Signed, 1970s, 18 x 32 In. *Illus*	2250.00
Table, Coffee, Frankl, Lacquered Cork, Mahogany, Angled Plank Legs, c.1948, 14 x 48 In.	1250.00
Table, Coffee, Frankl, Lacquered Cork, Mahogany, Johnson Furniture, c.1948, 44 x 43 In.	4375.00
Table, Coffee, Frankl, Lacquered Cork, Mahogany, Shaped Top, Round Corners, c.1953, 15 x 75 In.	8750.00
Table, Coffee, Frankl, Lacquered Cork, Mahogany, Square U-Shape Legs, Tray Top, 1940, 13 x 72 In.	5000.00
Table, Coffee, G. Nakashima, Black Walnut, Round, Tapered Legs, c.1955, 13 x 48 In.	8750.00
Table, Coffee, G. Nakashima, Black Walnut, Square, Greenrock, c.1965, 15 x 24 x 24 In.	8750.00
Table, Coffee, G. Nakashima, Minguren I, Walnut, Free-Form Slab Top, 1987, 48 x 34 In.	1830.00
Table, Coffee, G. Nakashima, Slab, Plank Leg, Round Legs, Shaped End, 1980s, 13 x 83 In.	9375.00
Table, Coffee, G. Nakashima, Walnut, Minguren II, Elongated, Plank Base, 1980, 13 x 65 In.	11875.00
Table, Coffee, G. Nakashima, Walnut, Rosewood, Bench, Shaped Plank Top, 1973, 13 x 76 In.	8750.00
Table, Coffee, G. Nakashima, Walnut, Rosewood, Cone Shape, Plank Support, 1966, 59 In.	10625.00
Table, Coffee, G. Nakashima, Walnut, Slab, Plank Support, Angled Block Leg, 1970, 13 x 48 In.	6875.00
Table, Coffee, Gilt, Glass Top, Rounded Corners, Tree Shape Base, France, c.1960, 16 x 48 In.	6875.00
Table, Coffee, Glass Top, Bronze Horse Supports, Ebonized Wood Base, c.1950, 49 x 23 ½ In.	1080.00
Table, Coffee, H. Probber, Terrazzo, Wood, Elongated Oval Top, Cube Base, c.1968, 18 x 72 In.	1125.00
Table, Coffee, I. Noguchi, Asymmetrical Glass Top, 2 Interlocking Wood Legs, 1970s, 16 x 50 In.	830.00
Table, Coffee, I. Noguchi, Green Glass Top, Free-Form, Ebonized Curvilinear Legs, 49 In.	900.00
Table, Coffee, J. Adnet, Mahogany, Iron, Plank Top, Horn Legs, France, 1940s, 44 x 21 In.	2875.00
Table, Coffee, James Mont, Lacquer, Mahogany, Brass, Tray Top, Scroll Legs, 1960s, 36 In.	1500.00
Table, Coffee, Jeaneret, Teak, Rectangle Top, Splayed Legs, c.1955, 36 x 17 ½ In.	3250.00
Table, Coffee, Louis XVI Style, Onyx, Ormolu, Inlaid Pietra Dura Border, 18 x 48 In.	307.00
Table, Coffee, Onyx, Book Matched, Bronze, Tapered Legs, Italy, 1950s, 39 x 24 In.	3750.00
Table, Coffee, Oval Top, Shelf, Turned Legs, Green Paint, David T. Smith, Ohio, 1900s, 24 x 36 In.	382.00
Table, Coffee, P. Evans, Bronze, Copper, Slate Top, Patchwork Design, Block Legs, 1970s, 48 x 36 In.	3750.00
Table, Coffee, P. Evans, Glass, 4 Pyramids, Welded, Lacquer, Signed, c.1973, 36 x 16 In. *Illus*	5333.00
Table, Coffee, P. Guariche, Leather Top, Steel H-Supports, Brass Stretcher, 1950s, 15 x 44 In.	1625.00
Table, Coffee, Peter Hvidt, Teak, Chrome Steel, France & Sons, Denmark, 1960s, 17 x 51 In. *Illus*	3750.00
Table, Coffee, Philip & Kelvin LaVerne, Bronze, Pewter, Enamel, Sleigh Top, 1974, 57 x 22 In.	12500.00
Table, Coffee, Philip & Kelvin LaVerne, Bronze, Pewter, Etruscan, Round, 1960s, 17 x 36 In.	8750.00
Table, Coffee, Philip & Kelvin LaVerne, Bronze, Pewter, Shaped Top, 1960s, 16 x 44 In.	7500.00
Table, Coffee, Philip & Kelvin LaVerne, Bronze, Riverbank, c.1965, 52 x 22 In. *Illus*	21600.00
Table, Coffee, Philip & Kelvin LaVerne, Bronze, Round Top, Chinoiserie Scene, 18 x 48 In.	3302.00
Table, Coffee, Philip & Kelvin LaVerne, Odyssey, Bronze, Pewter, Enamel, 1960s, 17 x 48 In. *Illus*	6250.00
Table, Coffee, Pine, Drawers, Plank Top, Shaped Skirt, Turned Feet, 1800s, 18 x 45 In.	115.00
Table, Coffee, Regency Style, Smoke Glass Top, Brass Frame, X-Stretcher, c.1980, 16 x 39 ½ In.	480.00
Table, Coffee, Reverse Painted, Gilt Scrolled Base, Round Marble Top, c.1940, 16 x 27 ½ In.	330.00
Table, Coffee, Richard Schultz, Orange Enamel Top, Tapered White Legs, 15 ½ x 47 ¾ In.	660.00
Table, Coffee, Rosewood, Aluminum, Round Top, Tripod Base, Fritz Hansen, 1950s, 36 In.	1000.00
Table, Coffee, Rosewood, Green Stone Inset Top, Carved Apron, Beaded Legs, 1800s, 18 x 37 In.	657.00
Table, Coffee, Rosewood, Tapered Legs, Hiorth Ostlyngen, Norway, 20 x 30 In.	178.00
Table, Coffee, Sam Maloof, Brown Oak, 2 Frieze Drawers, Lower Shelf, Signed, 1972, 20 x 48 In.	8750.00
Table, Coffee, Silas Seandel, Bronze, Glass, Welded, Cylindrical Legs, Inscribed, 1980s, 33 x 60 In.	2625.00
Table, Coffee, Steel, Glass, Square Top, Cylindrical Legs, Crisscross, A. Scarpa, 1967, 45 x 45 In.	1250.00
Table, Coffee, Stone Tile Top, Wood Frame, Roger Capron Sho-Gun, France, 1971, 39 x 27 In.	1464.00
Table, Coffee, V. Kagan, Glass Tiles, Walnut M-Shape Base, Crescent Top, 14 x 56 In.	11875.00
Table, Coffee, Walnut, Travertine Sculpted Top, Boomerang Shaped, 1950s, 14 x 51 In.	3125.00
Table, Coffee, Wolfgang Hoffman, Chrome, Glass Top, Howell, 32 x 26 ¾ In.	2440.00

Table, Coffee, Wood, Carved, Pierced Skirt, Scroll Legs, Chinese, c.1900, 10 x 20 In.	236.00
Table, Coffee, Wood, Craved Apron, Cabriole Legs, Gilt, Painted, c.1940, 18 x 43 In.	480.00
Table, Coffee, Wood, Recessed Top, Door, Panels, Iron Mounts, Turned Legs, c.1800s, 20 x 57 In.	305.00
Table, Coffee, Wood, Resin, Enamel, Round, 12 Block Legs, F. Dresse, 1970s, 40 In.	15000.00
Table, Coffee, Wormley, Mahogany, Travertine, Round Top, Square Legs, c.1957, 49 In. Diam.	5938.00
Table, Coffee, Yellow Toleware, Figures, Trees, Folding Metal Stand, 1900s, 23 x 46 ½ In.	2415.00
Table, Console, Adam Style, Painted, Inlaid Mahogany, c.1800, 31 x 36 In., Pair	4029.00
Table, Console, Aluminum, O-Shape Pedestal, c.1950, 72 x 20 x 36 In.	4200.00
Table, Console, Art Deco, Mixed Wood, Curved Base Support, c.1925, 30 x 54 In.	250.00
Table, Console, Baroque Style, Gilt, Marble Top, Shaped Skirt, Shells & Flowers, 1800s, 29 x 47 In.	531.00
Table, Console, Burl, Bronze, Etched, Drawers, Round Legs, 1970s, 28 x 72 In.	2250.00
Table, Console, Chippendale Style, Burl Walnut, Demilune, 3 Legs, 1920s, 30 x 33 In.	720.00
Table, Console, Demilune, Art Deco, Iron, Feather Pattern, c.1940, 30 x 34 ½ In.	3120.00
Table, Console, Demilune, Federal, Cherry, Flower & String Inlay, c.1795, 29 x 45 In.	613.00
Table, Console, Demilune, Gilt, Painted, Marble Top, Leaf Carved Frieze, Fluted Legs, Italy, 36 x 47 In.	750.00
Table, Console, Demilune, Shaped Apron, Green Ground, Painted Flowers, Shelf, c.1920, 38 x 35 In.	180.00
Table, Console, Donald Deskey, Mahogany, Arched Base Support, c.1930, 29 ½ x 20 In.	12500.00
Table, Console, Empire Style, Mahogany, Marble Top, 19th Century, 33 x 44 In.	432.00
Table, Console, Empire, Column Front, Gilt Bronze Capitals, Platform Base, c.1800, 32 x 29 In.	374.00
Table, Console, George II Style, Marble Top, Carved & Pierced Skirt, Cabriole Legs, 35 x 56 In.	2500.00
Table, Console, George II, Mahogany, Line Inlay, 2 Drawers, c.1790, 32 In.	296.00
Table, Console, Gilt, Carved, Composition, Onyx Top, France, c.1945, 26 x 33 In.	500.00
Table, Console, Gilt, Marble Top, Bowed, Pierced Frieze, Mask, Scroll Toes, c.1885, 37 x 42 In.	1722.00
Table, Console, Gilt, Marble Top, Gilt Apron, 4 Drawers, Fluted Legs, Italy, c.1960, 34 x 99 In.	840.00
Table, Console, Iron, Marble Top, Gilt, Leaf & Berry Scrolling, Openwork, France, c.1900, 36 x 55 In.	944.00
Table, Console, James Mont, Marble Top, Gilt, Demilune, Leaves, 1960s, 31 x 36 In.	3250.00
Table, Console, Karl Springer, Lacquer, Goatskin, 2 Drawers, c.1970, 28 x 80 In.	3250.00
Table, Console, Louis XV Style, Gilt, Marble Top, Pierced Frieze, Scroll Legs, 1800s, 39 x 48 In.	1168.00
Table, Console, Louis XV Style, Gilt, Marble Top, Pierced Frieze, X-Stretcher, c.1900, 34 x 41 In.	922.00
Table, Console, Louis XV Style, Gilt, Serpentine Marble Top, C-Scroll Frieze, 38 x 56 In.	1400.00
Table, Console, Louis XV Style, Mahogany, Shell Carved Corners, Rocaille Apron, Painted, 32 x 56 In.	1500.00
Table, Console, Louis XV Style, Marquetry, Mixed Wood, Gilt, Marble, Drawer, Scrolls, 35 x 48 In.	11875.00
Table, Console, Louis XVI Revival, Rosewood, Ebonized, Marble Top, Mirror, c.1885, 38 x 66 In. ..Illus	2214.00
Table, Console, Louis XVI Style, Bronze, Marble Top, Emmanuel Beurdeley, c.1880, 35 x 33 In. ..Illus	17500.00
Table, Console, Louis XVI Style, Carved, Parcel Gilt Swag, Marble Top, 3 Legs, c.1910, 31 x 58 In.	1440.00
Table, Console, Louis XVI Style, Demilune Marble Top, Drawers, Leaf Inlay, 33 x 25 In., Pair	688.00
Table, Console, Louis XVI Style, Fruitwood, Marble Top, D-Shape, Fluted Legs, 1900s, 38 x 82 In.	1185.00
Table, Console, Louis XVI Style, Gilt, Marble Top, Demilune, France, c.1910, 34 x 36 In.	354.00
Table, Console, Louis XVI Style, Mahogany, Shaped Marble Top, Pierced Scroll, 39 x 90 In.	2032.00
Table, Console, Louis XVI, Brass Gallery, Marble Top, Stretcher, Drawers, c.1800, 34 x 51 In.	5000.00
Table, Console, Louis XVI, Wood, Marble, Demilune, Carved, Painted, c.1800, 35 x 52 In., Pair	15000.00
Table, Console, Mahogany, Bronze, Shaped Leather Top, Drawer, 29 ½ x 45 In.	960.00
Table, Console, Mahogany, Concave Corners, S-Scroll Supports, Stretchers, 34 x 60 In.	1000.00
Table, Console, Mahogany, Drawer, Mirror Back, Columnar Legs, Incurved Shelf, 1800s, 39 x 44 In.	420.00
Table, Console, Mahogany, Inlay, Rope Border, Flowers, Pilasters, Paw Feet, 1800s, 42 x 59 In.	668.00
Table, Console, Mahogany, Marble Top, Shaped & Carved Apron, Long Legs, 38 x 35 In.	345.00
Table, Console, Neoclassical Style, Carved, Blond Mahogany, Marble Top, 37 x 48 In.	960.00
Table, Console, Neoclassical Style, Gilt, Ebonized, Marble Top, Rosettes, Italy, 38 x 91 In.	488.00
Table, Console, Neoclassical, Gilt, Marble Top, Carved Leaves, Masks, Italy, c.1800, 37 x 45 In.	2000.00
Table, Console, Neoclassical, Gilt, Marble Top, Scrolling Leaf Inlay, Ball Feet, 36 x 59 In.	500.00
Table, Console, Neoclassical, Parcel Gilt, Marble Top, Carved Frieze, Painted, c.1810, 52 x 25 In.	4375.00
Table, Console, Oak, Marble Top, Reeded Legs, Pierced Shell Stretcher, c.1795, 30 x 37 In.	1968.00
Table, Console, Oak, Plaster, White Wash, Carved Legs, Maison Jansen, 1960s, 32 x 60 In.	1875.00
Table, Console, Regency Style, Bronze, Nickel, Glass Top, X-Shape Sides, c.1950, 34 x 52 In.	1140.00
Table, Console, Regency Style, Mahogany, String Banding, Drop Leaf, c.1890, 28 x 25 In.	738.00
Table, Console, Regency, Mahogany, Demilune, Scalloped Skirt, Tapered Legs, 25 x 50 In.	8125.00
Table, Console, Renaissance Revival, Oak, Scrolling Leaves, Mask, Dragons, 1800s, 32 x 55 In.	972.00
Table, Console, Rococo, Mirror, Arched, Pierced, Serpentine Top, Cabriole Legs, 32 x 39 In.	8963.00
Table, Console, Rohde, Chrome Plated Steel, Wood, Troy Sunshade Co., 1930, 27 x 42 In.	1250.00
Table, Console, Rosewood, Marble Demilune Top, Pierced Apron, Serpentine, Dragon, 1800s, 52 In.	18400.00
Table, Console, Rosewood, Serpentine Marble Top, Carved Flowers, Shelf, c.1850, 40 x 58 In., Pair .	6274.00
Table, Console, Roycroft, Half Moon, Block Backsplash, Square Legs, c.1905, 36 x 48 In.	3375.00
Table, Console, Shellwork, Crescent Top, Bowfront, Cabriole Legs, 1900s, 32 x 43 In.	230.00
Table, Console, Stainless Steel, Z-Shape, Gabriella Crespi, Italy, 1970s, 32 x 48 In.	7500.00
Table, Console, Walnut, Molded Marble Top, Quatrefoil Frieze Drawer, c.1850, 29 x 39 In.	2271.00

Furniture, Stand, Low Tiles, Flowers, Brown Glaze, 12 Tiles, Wrought Iron, Marked, 27 x 6 In.
$1,422.00

Skinner, Inc.

Furniture, Stand, Plant, Arts & Crafts, Steel, Square, England, c.1910, 29 ¾ x 14 In.
$250.00

Rago Arts & Auction Center

Furniture, Stand, Smoking, Figural, Butler, Gray Hair, Cast Iron, 37 In.
$420.00

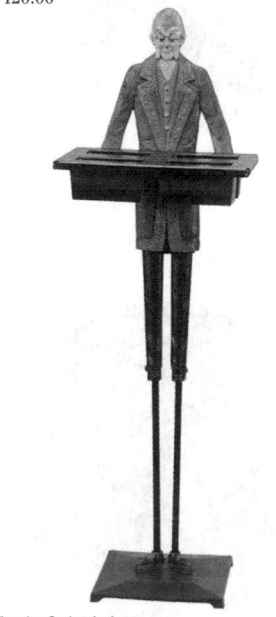

Victorian Casino Antiques

TIP
To move small pieces of furniture put the legs on a blanket or throw rug then drag it.

Furniture, Stand, Wood, Pierced Fret Design, Square Legs, Humpback Stretchers, China, 47 x 15 In. $1,320.00

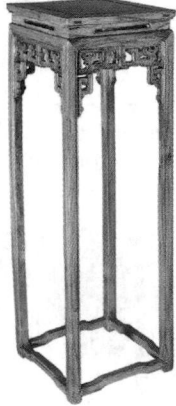

Skinner, Inc.

Furniture, Stool, Butterfly, Sori Yanagi, Laminated Rosewood, Brass, Tendo, 1954, 16 x 16 ½ In. $1,875.00

Los Angeles Modern Auctions (LAMA)

Furniture, Stool, David Gilhooly, Elephant Foot, Whiteware, Fabric, 1966, 12 x 16 x 17 In. $3,525.00

Cowans + Clark + DelVecchio

Table, Curio, Mahogany, Satinwood, Heart Shape, Hinged Top, Mirror, 3 Legs, c.1930, 29 x 20 In. *Illus*	1080.00
Table, Curved Legs, Brass, Red Leather, Pierre Cardin, c.1970, 30 x 53 In.	3750.00
Table, Curved Top Edges, Carved, Painted, Chinese, c.1940, 30 x 33 In.	563.00
Table, Cypress, 2-Board, Overhanging Top, Square Legs, c.1890, 29 x 46 In.	1434.00
Table, Cypress, Plank Top, Overhanging, Square Tapered Legs, c.1890, 29 x 55 In.	359.00
Table, Dairy, George III, Pine, Plank Top, Breadboard Ends, Drawers, Scalloped Apron, 33 x 71 In.	1725.00
Table, Demilune, George III, Mahogany, Inlay, Crossbanded Top, 2 Swivel Drawers, 30 x 30 In.	995.00
Table, Demilune, Mahogany, Maple Inlay, Ribbed, Turned Legs, c.1870, 28 x 48 In.	295.00
Table, Dining, Aalto, Birch, Laminated, Curved Top Rectangular Legs, c.1932, 28 x 72 In.	3750.00
Table, Dining, Cherry, Oval Top, Square Tapered Legs, Leaf Inserts, Thomas Moser, 30 x 73 In.	3750.00
Table, Dining, Cherry, Plank Top, Shaped Apron, Drawer & Slide, Hoof Feet, c.1800, 30 x 79 In.	3690.00
Table, Dining, Chippendale Style, Mahogany, Henkel Harris, 6 In. Leaves, 44 x 68 In.	1541.00
Table, Dining, Crossbanded, Ball & Claw Feet, 2 Leaves, Henredon, 76 x 30 In.	430.00
Table, Dining, Drop Leaf, Baroque Style, Oak, Geometric Inlay, H-Stretcher, 31 x 71 In.	118.00
Table, Dining, Drop Leaf, Chippendale, Mahogany, Ball & Claw Feet, c.1770, 16 ¾ x 44 In.	1541.00
Table, Dining, Drop Leaf, Chippendale, Mahogany, Cabriole Legs, Cutout Apron, c.1770, 28 x 48 In.	1422.00
Table, Dining, Drop Leaf, Chippendale, Mahogany, Oval, Double Swing Legs, Ireland, 29 x 63 In.	1725.00
Table, Dining, Drop Leaf, Federal, Mahogany, Inlay, Demilune Top, Swivel Leg, c.1800, 48 x 22 In.	1035.00
Table, Dining, Drop Leaf, Federal, Walnut, 2 Swivel Legs, Tidewater, Virginia, c.1800, 41 x 55 In.	431.00
Table, Dining, Drop Leaf, Gateleg, William & Mary Style, Oak, Plank Top, 1900s, 30 x 79 In.	826.00
Table, Dining, Drop Leaf, George II, Mahogany, Pad Feet, c.1760, 27 ½ x 38 In.	415.00
Table, Dining, Drop Leaf, George III Style, Mahogany, Demilune, Square Fluted Legs, 31 x 55 In.	2091.00
Table, Dining, Drop Leaf, George III, Mahogany, Cabriole Legs, c.1760, 28 x 41 In.	911.00
Table, Dining, Drop Leaf, Mahogany, Oak, Scroll & Leaf Carved Pedestal, c.1830, 29 x 40 In.	411.00
Table, Dining, Drop Leaf, Mahogany, Swing Leg, Single-Board Top, Square Legs, c.1900, 29 x 52 In.	369.00
Table, Dining, Drop Leaf, McCobb, Hardwood, Square Legs, Round Stretcher, c.1950, 30 x 53 In.	1107.00
Table, Dining, Drop Leaf, Oak, Round, Trestle Base Butterfly Supports, c.1700, 29 x 56 In.	708.00
Table, Dining, Drop Leaf, Queen Anne Style, Mahogany, Oval, D-Ends, Tapered Legs, 1700s, 129 In.	928.00
Table, Dining, Drop Leaf, Queen Anne, Maple, Red Paint, c.1750, 28 x 48 In.	8888.00
Table, Dining, Drop Leaf, Queen Anne, Maple, Turned Legs, New England, 27 x 43 In.	4130.00
Table, Dining, Drop Leaf, Sheraton, Cherry, 2 Swivel Legs, c.1850, 29 ½ x 20 In.	161.00
Table, Dining, Eero Saarinen, Rosewood, Tulip, Black Metal Base, 29 x 60 In.	1920.00
Table, Dining, Empire Style, Round, Shaped Pedestal Base, Scroll Feet, Leaves, 30 x 54 In.	316.00
Table, Dining, Empire Style, Walnut, Oak Inlay, Round Top, Pedestal, Round Feet, 30 x 48 In.	538.00
Table, Dining, Federal Style, Mahogany, 3 Pedestals, Brass Paw Casters, 1900s, 30 x 168 In.	1645.00
Table, Dining, Federal Style, Mahogany, Double Pedestal, Splayed Legs, c.1905, 29 x 67 In.	885.00
Table, Dining, Federal, Cherry, Birch, Pegged, 3 Sections, Tapered Legs, Casters, 30 x 92 In.	708.00
Table, Dining, Flip Top, Curule Base, Italy, c.1960, 31 x 47 ½ In.	720.00
Table, Dining, G. Stickley, Square Plank Top, 5 Square Legs, X-Stretcher, c.1902, 31 x 54 In.	6875.00
Table, Dining, G. Stickley, Square Top, 5 Legs, 2 Leaves, c.1912, 28 x 44 In.	1500.00
Table, Dining, George III Style, Mahogany, 2 Pedestal, Baluster, Outswept Legs, 29 x 100 In.	750.00
Table, Dining, George III Style, Mahogany, Double Pedestal, Reeded Edge, Saber Legs, 29 x 65 In.	813.00
Table, Dining, George III Style, Mahogany, Double Pedestal, Rounded Corners, 1800s, 76 In.	625.00
Table, Dining, George III Style, Mahogany, Turned Pedestals, Reeded Legs, 1800s, 30 x 67 In.	956.00
Table, Dining, George III, Mahogany, 2 Pedestal, Oval, Reeded, Paw Feet, c.1790, 29 x 87 x 46 In.	2509.00
Table, Dining, Georgian Style, Gadrooned Oval Top, Eagle Carved Legs, Crank, 29 x 94 In.	1434.00
Table, Dining, Georgian Style, Mahogany, Rounded Corners, Double Tripod, 30 x 73 In.	612.00
Table, Dining, Hepplewhite, Mahogany, Demilune, 2 Ends, String Inlay, c.1800s, 29 x 51 In.	353.00
Table, Dining, Jacobean Style, Oak, Breadboard Ends, Turned Legs, Trestle Base, 31 x 102 In.	885.00
Table, Dining, Karl Springer, Parchment, Round Top, Steel & Brass Base, 1970s, 72 In. Diam.	2375.00
Table, Dining, L. & J.G. Stickley, Overhang Top, Mousehole Legs, Stretcher, c.1906, 30 x 84 In.	8125.00
Table, Dining, Limbert, Pedestal, 4 Leaves, Marked, c.1910, 28 ½ x 54 In. *Illus*	2500.00
Table, Dining, Limbert, Round, Block Legs, 6 Leaves, 29 x 60 In.	6250.00
Table, Dining, Louis XV Style, Fruitwood, Carved Serpentine Apron, Cabriole Legs, 30 x 83 In.	478.00
Table, Dining, Louis XVI Style, Gilt, Bronze, Glass Top, Rosettes, Fluted Tapered Legs, 29 x 76 In.	2500.00
Table, Dining, Louis XVI Style, Mahogany, Gilt, Oval Top, Tapered Fluted Legs, c.1950, 30 x 41 In.	738.00
Table, Dining, Louis XVI, Mahogany, Brass Mounts, 3 Leaves, 74 x 44 ½ In.	2478.00
Table, Dining, M. Nakashima, Walnut, Root Burl, Rosewood, Signed, 1994, 28 ½ x 48 In. *Illus*	4375.00
Table, Dining, Mahogany, Bronze, Round Top, Cluster Column Supports, 1800s, 30 x 46 In.	1434.00
Table, Dining, Mahogany, Crossbanded Edge, Turned Support, Eng., 1800s, 28 ½ x 57 In.	523.00
Table, Dining, Mahogany, Shaped Top, 9 Dished Roundels, Rosettes, Turned Stem, 28 x 32 In.	3965.00
Table, Dining, Maple, Ebonized, Round Top, Parquetry, Drum Base, 29 x 66 In.	1315.00
Table, Dining, Milo Baughman, Mahogany, Rosewood, Ash, Walnut, Planks, 1970s, 39 x 72 In.	1875.00
Table, Dining, Oak, Double Pedestal, 2 Stepped Plinth Bases, c.1940, 30 x 72 In.	1080.00
Table, Dining, P. Evans, Bronze, Branch-Like Metal Base, Textured, Glass Top, 1970, 96 x 48 In.	8125.00
Table, Dining, P. Evans, Chrome Steel, Brass, Octagonal Glass Top, Base, 1970s, 29 x 40 In.	3125.00

F

Table, Dining, P. Evans, Cityscape, Burl, Metal, Glass, Offset Pattern, 1970s, 96 x 48 In.		6518.00
Table, Dining, P. Evans, Walnut, Maple, Brass Center Tile Design, Rounded, c.1970, 30 x 96 In.		8000.00
Table, Dining, Parzinger, Mahogany, Satinwood, Brass, Charak Modern, 1940s, 30 x 68 x 38 In. *Illus*		3375.00
Table, Dining, Parzinger, Mahogany, Square Top, Curved Legs, X-Stretcher, 23 x 29 In.		2500.00
Table, Dining, Queen Anne Style, Curly Maple, Overhang Top, H-Stretcher, c.1990, 30 x 72 In.		1998.00
Table, Dining, Queen Anne Style, Mahogany, Double Pedestal, Cabriole Legs, 1900s, 29 x 66 In.		441.00
Table, Dining, Raphael, Lacquered Wood, Brass, Round Top, Glass Legs, c.1959, 44 In Diam.		12500.00
Table, Dining, Regency, Mahogany, 3 Sections, c.1815, 29 ½ x 47 ¾ In.		304.00
Table, Dining, Regency, Mahogany, Rectangular Tilt Top, Reeded Legs, c.1815, 27 x 49 In.		837.00
Table, Dining, Regency, Mahogany, Tilt Top, Platform Pedestal, Incurving Legs, 65 x 44 In.		259.00
Table, Dining, Regency, Mahogany, Tilt Top, Reeded Edge, Splayed Legs, 1800s, 29 x 50 In.		360.00
Table, Dining, Renaissance Revival, Oak, Carved, Molded, 6 Leaves, c.1890, 32 x 32 In. *Illus*		4920.00
Table, Dining, Rococo Revival, Walnut, Oval Top, Carved Pedestal, Scrolling Feet, 1800s, 28 x 55 In.		299.99
Table, Dining, RomWeber, Oak, Carved Wood Base, Leaves, Harry Schwartz, 73 x 38 In.		1875.00
Table, Dining, Roycroft, Round Top, Block Supports, X-Base, Casters, c.1905, 30 x 54 In.		8750.00
Table, Dining, S. Rodrigues, Jacaranda, Rounded, Ladder Style Legs, 1950s, 39 x 78 In.		2250.00
Table, Dining, Stickley Bros., Round, Pedestal Base, Quaint Tag, 4 Leaves, 48 x 30 In.		2196.00
Table, Dining, W. Platner, Walnut Veneer Top, Round, Bronzed Steel, 1960s, 29 x 54 In.		3500.00
Table, Dining, William IV, Rosewood, Round Top, Faceted Stem, 3 Legs, 32 x 54 In.		6250.00
Table, Dining, Wolfgang Hoffman, Black Lacquer Top, Cross Stretcher, Howell, 20 x 20 In.		1464.00
Table, Dining, Wolfgang Hoffman, Round Black Top, Bakelite, Chrome Base, Howell, 36 x 31 In.		1464.00
Table, Dining, Wood, Round, X-Stretcher, Ambrose Heal, c.1915, 48 x 29 ½ In.		575.00
Table, Dining, Wood, Slated End Supports, Slab Top, c.1950, 36 x 7 In.		201.00
Table, Dining, Wormley, Mahogany, Tawi, Brass, Overhang Top, Plank Supports, 1950s, 30 x 84 In.		8125.00
Table, Donald Deskey, Art Deco, Rosewood, Drawer, Door, Open Shelf, 17 x 29 In., Pair		984.00
Table, Dore Bronze, Black Granite Top, Round, Molded Edge, X-Supports, 25 x 16 In., Pair		5535.00
Table, Drafting, Chippendale, Mahogany, Molded Edge, Fitted Interior, 31 x 32 In.		826.00
Table, Drafting, George III, Mahogany, Adjustable, 30 x 37 In.		2457.00
Table, Drafting, Mahogany, 2 Writing Boards, Column Support, Crank, 1800s, 30 x 37 In.		767.00
Table, Drafting, Marble Top, Chrome Legs, Large Casters, c.1950, 33 x 84 In.		1800.00
Table, Drafting, Plank Top, Cantilevered Adjustable Base, c.1910, 32 x 55 In.		180.00
Table, Drafting, Regency, Mahogany, Brass, Adjustable, 2 Candle Slides, Trestle Base, 27 x 40 In.		4212.00
Table, Dressing, Cherry, 2 Tiers, Crossbanded, Vase & Ring-Turned Legs, c.1825, 37 x 32 In.		415.00
Table, Dressing, Chippendale Style, Mahogany, 2 Drawers, Curved Legs, 30 x 18 ¾ In.		189.00
Table, Dressing, Chippendale, Mahogany, Shell Carved Knees, Slipper Feet, c.1740, 28 x 34 In.		2124.00
Table, Dressing, Empire Style, Mahogany, Gilt, Mirror, Columns, Drawers, 1800s, 59 x 37 In.		610.00
Table, Dressing, Empire Style, Mahogany, Round Mirror, Concave Shelf, c.1900, 55 In.		492.00
Table, Dressing, Empire, Mahogany, Marble Top, Drawer, Arched Mirror, 1800s, 62 x 32 In.		767.00
Table, Dressing, Federal, Birch, Mahogany, Shaped Back, 2 Drawers, N.H., c.1810, 36 x 35 In.		3500.00
Table, Dressing, Federal, Tiger Maple, Drawer, 2 Tiers, Box, c.1810-15, 37 x 36 In. *Illus*		10200.00
Table, Dressing, George II, Mahogany, 2 Drawers, Overhung Top, Tapered Legs, c.1760, 28 x 32 In.		518.00
Table, Dressing, George II, Walnut, 4 Drawers, Cabriole Legs, 28 x 30 In.		1125.00
Table, Dressing, George III, Mahogany, 3 Drawers, Square Tapered Legs, Hinged Leaves, 36 x 33 In.		500.00
Table, Dressing, George III, Oak, Overhang Top, 3 Drawers, Shaped Apron, c.1770, 29 x 30 In.		207.00
Table, Dressing, Georgian, Oak, Molded Top, 3 Drawers, Turned Legs, Pad Feet, 1700s, 29 x 31 In.		1007.00
Table, Dressing, Gothic Revival, Maple, Mirror, Marble Top, Carved Frieze, c.1850, 63 x 33 In.		1195.00
Table, Dressing, Louis XV Style, Fruitwood, Drawers, Shaped Front, Drawers, 31 x 34 In.		472.00
Table, Dressing, Mahogany, Inlaid Lift Top, Mirror, Band Of Drawers, c.1930, 30 x 31 In.		240.00
Table, Dressing, Mahogany, Mirror, 3 Drawers, Raised Turned Legs, c.1845, 71 x 36 In.		375.00
Table, Dressing, Mahogany, Mirror, Tapered Supports, Columns, Curved Shelf, c.1840, 67 x 33 In.		359.00
Table, Dressing, Mahogany, Oval Mirror, Scrolling, Flower Basket, Marble Top, c.1850, 66 x 42 In.		1599.00
Table, Dressing, Mahogany, Stepped Top, Drawers, Shaped Backsplash, c.1880, 39 x 33 In.		259.00
Table, Dressing, Mahogany, String Inlay, 4 Drawers, c.1800, 32 x 38 ½ In.		649.00
Table, Dressing, Maple, Molded Edge, Drawer, Tapered Legs, Pad Feet, c.1915, 29 x 37 In.		461.00
Table, Dressing, Mirror, Sheraton, Mahogany, Scroll Support, 3 Drawers, Shelf, 58 x 37 In.		944.00
Table, Dressing, Napoleon III, Mahogany, Ormolu Putti, Medallion Crest, Cabriole Legs, 56 x 32 In.		584.00
Table, Dressing, Neoclassical, Ormolu Mounted, Attached Mirror, Urn Finials, 53 x 30 In.		1534.00
Table, Dressing, Pine, Grain Painted, Shaped Crest, New England, c.1825, 33 x 31 ½ In.		122.00
Table, Dressing, Queen Anne, Burl, Drawers, Leaf Carved Knees, Slipper Feet, 1700s, 29 x 28 In.		944.00
Table, Dressing, Queen Anne, Burl, Veneers, Dovetailed Drawers, Shaped Skirt, 1700s, 29 x 30 In.		1770.00
Table, Dressing, Queen Anne, Mahogany, 4 Drawers, Fan Carved, Conn., c.1765, 31 x 30 In.		972.00
Table, Dressing, Queen Anne, Poplar, Dovetailed, Brass, c.1745, 28 x 33 x 21 In.		4248.00
Table, Dressing, Queen Anne, Walnut, 2 Drawers, Cabriole Legs, c.1750, 29 x 30 In.		1722.00
Table, Dressing, Queen Anne, Walnut, 3 Drawers, Scalloped Apron, c.1750, 27 x 34 In.		978.00
Table, Dressing, Queen Anne, Walnut, Inlaid Sunburst Design, Notched Apron, c.1700, 26 x 23 In.		1778.00
Table, Dressing, Queen Anne, Walnut, Inlay, 4 Drawers, Carved, Mass., c.1750, 29 x 34 In.		14880.00

F

Furniture, Stool, Heywood-Wakefield, Wicker, Needlepoint Top, c.1900, 9 ¾ x 14 ½ x 11 ½ In. $48.00

Gray's Auctioneers LLC

Furniture, Stool, Mahogany, Needlepoint, Cabriole Legs, Pad Feet, Ireland, 1800s, 18 x 22 ½ In. $1,680.00

Cowan's Auctions

Furniture, Stool, Regency, Mahogany, Upholstered, Reeded Legs, 1800s, 18 ½ x 19 In. $250.00

Bonhams

Furniture, Table, Bamboo, Demilune, Chinese, 19th Century, 34 ½ x 37 ½ In. $369.00

New Orleans Auction Galleries, Inc.

Furniture, Table, Billy Baldwin, Glass, Metal, American, c.1970, 16 x 40 x 22 In. $2,280.00

Palm Beach Modern Auctions

Furniture, Table, Card, Mahogany, Fan & String Inlay, Demilune, Tapered Legs, Spade Feet, c.1795, 30 x 35 In. $1,440.00

Skinner, Inc.

Furniture, Table, Card, Sheraton, Birch, Mahogany Veneer, Inlaid Medallion, Hinged Top, 35 x 17 In. $1,528.00

Garth's Auctioneers & Appraisers

Furniture, Table, Center, Aesthetic Revival, Mahogany, Brass Inlay, Drawers, Shelf, c.1890, 30 x 38 In. $1,195.00

Neal Auction Co.

Table, Dressing, Rosewood, Serpentine Mirror, Marble Top, Urn Finial, c.1850, 67 x 47 In.	3286.00
Table, Dressing, Rosewood, Shaped Mirror, Serpentine Marble Top, c.1850, 73 x 44 In.	1793.00
Table, Dressing, Sheraton, Cherry, Scrolled Backsplash, Opalescent Pulls, c.1830, 36 x 34 In.	470.00
Table, Dressing, Sheraton, Stencil Decorated, Raised Deck, Drawers, Maine, c.1850, 36 x 31 In.	863.00
Table, Drop Leaf, Chippendale, Bird's-Eye Maple, c.1800, 37 x 36 In.	385.00
Table, Drop Leaf, Chippendale, Cherry, Molded Legs, c.1780, 28 x 43 ½ In.	177.00
Table, Drop Leaf, Chippendale, Mahogany, 6 Legs, Carved Knees, Ireland, 28 x 18 ½ In.	8888.00
Table, Drop Leaf, Chippendale, Mahogany, Linenfold Legs, c.1780, 28 x 48 In.	413.00
Table, Drop Leaf, Chippendale, Mahogany, Rectangular, Cabriole Legs, 27 ½ x 47 In.	1888.00
Table, Drop Leaf, Chippendale, Mahogany, Tapered Legs, Ball & Claw Feet, 29 x 37 In.	1475.00
Table, Drop Leaf, Chippendale, Serpentine Stretcher, Chamfered Legs, Drawer, c.1795, 27 x 28 In.	230.00
Table, Drop Leaf, Chippendale, Tiger Maple, c.1790, 29 x 47 In.	356.00
Table, Drop Leaf, Chippendale, Walnut, Ball & Claw Feet, Pa., c.1770, 29 x 17 In.	474.00
Table, Drop Leaf, Chippendale, Walnut, Pa., c.1790, 28 x 57 x 45 In.	148.00
Table, Drop Leaf, Eldred Wheeler, Queen Anne Style, Rounded Leaves, Pad Feet, 28 x 28 In.	502.00
Table, Drop Leaf, Elizabethan Style, Oak, Fluted Cup & Cover Supports, Stretcher, 31 x 73 In.	2300.00
Table, Drop Leaf, Empire, Mahogany, Drawer, Column Support, Gilt Mounts, 30 x 36 In.	240.00
Table, Drop Leaf, Federal, Mahogany, Drawer, Carved Base, Brass Paw Casters, c.1815, 28 x 24 In.	356.00
Table, Drop Leaf, Federal, Mahogany, Gilt, Medial Shelf, Carved, Ebonized, c.1815, 27 x 26 In.	593.00
Table, Drop Leaf, Federal, Mahogany, String Banding, Frieze Drawer, c.1800, 29 x 31 In.	6765.00
Table, Drop Leaf, Federal, Walnut, 3 Parts, Elliptical Ends, Inlaid Apron, 1800s, 30 x 104 In.	1320.00
Table, Drop Leaf, Federal, Walnut, Inlay, Frieze Drawer, Square Tapered Legs, c.1800, 28 x 39 In.	657.00
Table, Drop Leaf, Fruitwood, Square Fluted Legs, Carved Patera, X-Shape Base, c.1790, 30 x 36 In.	1722.00
Table, Drop Leaf, Gateleg, Cherry, Maple, Turned Base, Drawer, c.1700, 25 x 44 In.	948.00
Table, Drop Leaf, Gateleg, Cherry, Turned Legs, c.1915, 29 x 73 In.	590.00
Table, Drop Leaf, Gateleg, Danish Style, Wood, c.1960, 28 ½ x 72 In.	780.00
Table, Drop Leaf, Gateleg, George III, Mahogany, Slender Turned Legs, Stretcher, 1700s, 27 x 10 In.	375.00
Table, Drop Leaf, Gateleg, Oak, Rounded Ends, C-Shaped Leaves, Frieze Drawer, 27 x 39 In.	594.00
Table, Drop Leaf, Gateleg, Top Geometric Carvings, Drawer, Oval Leaves, c.1850, 29 x 47 In.	649.00
Table, Drop Leaf, George II, Mahogany, Gateleg, Rounded Leaf, c.1750, 29 ¾ x 55 In.	1625.00
Table, Drop Leaf, George II, Oak, Gateleg, Demilune, Straight Legs, Pad Feet, 1700s, 29 x 54 In.	688.00
Table, Drop Leaf, George III, Mahogany, Demilune, Tapered Legs, Hoof Feet, 1800s, 29 x 66 In.	1000.00
Table, Drop Leaf, George III, Mahogany, Drawer, Turned Column, Outswept Legs, 29 x 49 In.	400.00
Table, Drop Leaf, George III, Mahogany, D-Shape Leaves, Frieze Drawers, 1700s, 29 x 36 In.	1000.00
Table, Drop Leaf, George III, Mahogany, Round, Fly Leg, Cabriole Legs, c.1865, 28 x 65 In.	615.00
Table, Drop Leaf, George III, Mahogany, Square Tapered Legs, Spade Feet, c.1800, 29 x 42 In.	369.00
Table, Drop Leaf, George III, Satinwood, Crossbanded, Drawer, Tapered Legs, c.1785, 28 x 32 In.	4000.00
Table, Drop Leaf, Harvest, Pine, Maple, 6 Legs, New England, c.1920, 29 x 143.00	4503.00
Table, Drop Leaf, Hepplewhite, Birch, Drawer, Tapered Legs, 29 x 36 In.	104.00
Table, Drop Leaf, Louis XV Style, Marquetry, D-Shape Leaves, Leafy Scrolls, Cabriole Legs, 30 x 35 In.	563.00
Table, Drop Leaf, Louis XVI Style, Figural, Flower Inlay, Drawer, c.1910, 29 x 25 In.	1121.00
Table, Drop Leaf, Mahogany, Board Top, Shaped Leaves, Drawer, c.1815, 29 x 38 In.	861.00
Table, Drop Leaf, Mahogany, D-Shape Leaves, Banded Top, Turned Legs, Casters, 28 x 36 In.	500.00
Table, Drop Leaf, Mahogany, Frieze Drawer, Fluted Column Supports, Carved, 29 x 32 In.	1180.00
Table, Drop Leaf, Mahogany, Maple, Drawer, Twist-Turned Legs, 29 x 22 In.	266.00
Table, Drop Leaf, Mahogany, Mixed Wood, Shaped Leaves, Turned Legs, c.1835, 29 x 38 In.	118.00
Table, Drop Leaf, Mahogany, Pad Legs, England, c.1750, 28 x 47 In.	295.00
Table, Drop Leaf, Mahogany, Reeded Edge, Frieze Drawer, Turned Pedestal, c.1825, 29 x 56 In.	522.00
Table, Drop Leaf, Mahogany, Rounded Leaves, Drawer, 29 x 48 In.	266.00
Table, Drop Leaf, Mahogany, Vase Shape Support, Hinged Leaves, Scroll Feet, c.1825, 28 x 39 In.	711.00
Table, Drop Leaf, Maple, Paint Design, Turned Legs, c.1815, 28 x 36 In.	382.00
Table, Drop Leaf, Maple, Pine, Red Wash, Tapered Legs, 2 Swing Legs, c.1800, 30 x 46 In.	558.00
Table, Drop Leaf, Neoclassical, Mahogany, 2 Drawers, New England, 29 x 18 In.	826.00
Table, Drop Leaf, Neoclassical, Mahogany, Pedestal Base, New England, c.1935, 29 x 42 In.	178.00
Table, Drop Leaf, Oak, Frieze Drawer, Gateleg, Box Stretcher, England, c.1795, 28 x 49 In.	584.00
Table, Drop Leaf, Oak, Gateleg, Spindle Legs, c.1750, 30 x 48 In.	177.00
Table, Drop Leaf, Pine, Maple, Gateleg, 27 x 41 x 45 In. ....*Illus*	575.00
Table, Drop Leaf, Queen Anne Style, Cherry, Cabriole Legs, Pad Feet, Eldred Wheeler, 28 x 43 In.	230.00
Table, Drop Leaf, Queen Anne, Birch, Cabriole Legs, Pad Feet, 18th Century, 27 x 47 In.	353.00
Table, Drop Leaf, Queen Anne, Cherry, Cabriole Legs, 29 x 48 In.	384.00
Table, Drop Leaf, Queen Anne, Cherry, Round Top, Cabriole Legs, Rolled Apron, c.1775, 29 x 47 In.	889.00
Table, Drop Leaf, Queen Anne, Mahogany, Oak, Demilune, Turned Legs, Pad Feet, 28 x 42 In.	235.00
Table, Drop Leaf, Queen Anne, Mahogany, Round Ends, Demilune, Turned Legs, c.1765, 29 x 47 In.	235.00
Table, Drop Leaf, Queen Anne, Mahogany, Tapered Cabriole Legs, Ma., 28 x 17 In.	2478.00
Table, Drop Leaf, Queen Anne, Maple, Red Stain, Oblong, New Hampshire, c.1800, 27 x 17 In.	6200.00
Table, Drop Leaf, Queen Anne, Maple, Round Top, Cutout Apron, Cabriole Legs, c.1750, 28 x 42 In.	711.00

F

Table, Drop Leaf, Queen Anne, Oak, Swing Leg, Oval Top, Cabriole Legs, 1700s, 27 x 46 In.	300.00
Table, Drop Leaf, Queen Anne, Oval Top, Plain Frieze, c.1760, 28 x 43 In.	780.00
Table, Drop Leaf, Queen Anne, Rectangular, Straight Skirt, Cabriole Legs, c.1795, 27 x 36 In.	1845.00
Table, Drop Leaf, Queen Anne, Tiger Maple, Raised Cabriole Legs, New Eng., 27 x 48 In.	1534.00
Table, Drop Leaf, Queen Anne, Tiger Maple, Straight Legs, c.1760, 27 ½ x 36 In.	2242.00
Table, Drop Leaf, Queen Anne, Walnut, Oval Top, Tapered Legs, c.1775, 27 ½ x 61 In.	660.00
Table, Drop Leaf, R. J. Horner, Maple, Faux Bamboo, Gatelegs, Sunderland, 27 x 29 In.	478.00
Table, Drop Leaf, Regency Style, Mahogany, Turned Stretcher, 28 ½ x 56 In. ....Illus	375.00
Table, Drop Leaf, Regency Style, Mahogany, Turned Supports, 28 x 43 In. ....Illus	1000.00
Table, Drop Leaf, Regency, Mahogany, Brass, Turned Stretcher, Drawers, c.1810, 28 x 38 In.	750.00
Table, Drop Leaf, Regency, Mahogany, Rounded Ends, Drawer, c.1815, 30 x 39 In.	522.00
Table, Drop Leaf, Shaker, Drawer, Tapered Leg, Signed, Brother James Phelps, 19 x 36 In.	920.00
Table, Drop Leaf, Sheraton Style, Oak Grain Painted, Turned Legs, Drawer, c.1890, 24 x 24 In.	115.00
Table, Drop Leaf, Sheraton, Curly Maple, 6 Legs, Rectangular Top, 1820, Opens To 63 In.	810.00
Table, Drop Leaf, Sheraton, Mahogany, 2 Drawers, Turned Legs, c.1840, 26 x 13 In.	374.00
Table, Drop Leaf, Sheraton, Mahogany, C-Shape Leaves, Frieze Drawer, Casters, 28 x 28 In.	1750.00
Table, Drop Leaf, Sheraton, Mahogany, Drawer, c.1830, 25 x 16 In., Child's	92.00
Table, Drop Leaf, Sheraton, Mahogany, Tapered Reeded Legs, c.1810, 30 x 48 In.	150.00
Table, Drop Leaf, Sheraton, Mahogany, Turned, Reeded Legs, Drawer, 1800s, 29 x 34 In.	588.00
Table, Drop Leaf, Sheraton, Walnut, Drawer, Turned Legs, 18 x 14 In.	162.00
Table, Drop Leaf, Tiger Maple, 2 Drawers, Turned Legs, c.1820, 28 x 16 In.	944.00
Table, Drop Leaf, Tiger Maple, Hinged Leaves, Breadboard Ends, c.1850, 24 x 50 In.	472.00
Table, Drop Leaf, Tiger Maple, Turned Table, c.1840, 16 x 36 ½ In.	115.00
Table, Drop Leaf, Walnut, Tapered Legs, North Carolina, c.1805, 28 ½ x 41 ½ In.	460.00
Table, Drop Leaf, Walnut, Triangular Top, 3 Leaves, 3 Carved Legs, Swivel, c.1890, 27 x 26 In.	2185.00
Table, Drop Leaf, William & Mary, Gateleg, Cherry, Drawer, New England, c.1740, 28 x 18 In.	652.00
Table, Drop Leaf, William & Mary, Maple, Gateleg, Drawer, Demilune, 27 x 36 In.	3776.00
Table, Drop Leaf, William & Mary, Oak, Carved, Gateleg, Drawer, Block Legs, 30 x 48 In.	2691.00
Table, Drop Leaf, William & Mary, Oak, Gateleg, 2 Drawers, Shoe Feet, c.1700, 29 x 38 In.	415.00
Table, Drop Leaf, William & Mary, Oak, Gateleg, Block & Ring-Turned Legs, 23 x 33 In.	385.00
Table, Drop Leaf, William IV Style, Mahogany, Molded Top, Arched Legs, c.1890, 29 x 47 In.	244.00
Table, Drum, Federal Style, Mahogany, Round Lobed Top, Leather, Drawer, c.1950, 28 x 32 In.	230.00
Table, Drum, Glass Covered Leather Top, Painted American Eagle, Legs, c.1935, 18 x 25 In.	147.00
Table, Drum, Regency, Mahogany, Round Leather Top, Banded Edge, Drawer, c.1815, 28 In.	1792.00
Table, Drum, Regency, Mahogany, Walnut, Ormolu, Carvings, Brass Ram Feet, c.1825, 30 x 38 In.	12500.00
Table, Drum, Regency, Mixed Wood, Octagonal, Leather, Drawers, Saber Legs, c.1810, 32 x 45 In.	3750.00
Table, Duncan Phyfe Style, Drop Leaf, Drawer, Brass Pulls, 32 x 29 In.	403.00
Table, E. Fickett, Plywood, Biomorphic, Top, Angled Plank Legs, c.1950, 18 x 55 In.	1063.00
Table, Eames, Laminate, Steel, Aluminum, Round White Top, Black Post, Herman Miller, 29 x 48 In.	123.00
Table, Eastlake, Walnut, Marble Top, Carved Pendant Finials, 22 x 29 In.	170.00
Table, Ebonized, Marble Top, Medial Shelf, Splayed Legs, c.1940, 25 x 20 In.	1680.00
Table, Edwardian Style, Mahogany, Pierced Gallery, Square Top, Flower Spray, 27 x 16 In., Pair	399.00
Table, Edwardian Style, Octagonal Top, Spiral Legs, Cross Stretchers, Carved, Pierced, 29 x 36 In.	150.00
Table, Edwardian, Mahogany, Inlay, Conch Shell Frieze, Tapered Legs, 32 x 37 In.	1035.00
Table, Edwardian, Mahogany, Openwork Gallery, Fret Carved Frieze, c.1900, 28 x 33 In.	582.00
Table, Edwardian, Mahogany, Satinwood Inlay, Flowers, Swags, Frieze Drawer, 29 x 23 In.	1375.00
Table, Edwardian, Satinwood, 5 Drawers Gallery, Pullout Surface, Drawer, Painted, 49 x 25 In.	1287.00
Table, Edwardian, Satinwood, Inlay, Medallion, Frieze Drawer, Tapered Legs, c.1900, 29 x 23 In.	1200.00
Table, Eero Saarinen, Enameled Metal, Formica, Round Top & Base, 1957, 20 In., Pair	1500.00
Table, Empire Style, Berkey & Gay, Mahogany, Mirror, Carved Petticoat Legs, c.1900, 36 x 41 In.	708.00
Table, Empire Style, Gilt Bronze, Marble Top, Ram's Heads, Hoof Feet, 32 In. Diam., Pair	5904.00
Table, Empire Style, Mahogany, Marquetry, Caryatid, Triangular Base, c.1955, 29 x 32 In.	2125.00
Table, Empire Style, White Marble Top, Gallery & Swan Supports, Gilt Metal, 19 x 40 In.	1375.00
Table, Empire, Mahogany, 4-Column Base, Lion's Paw Feet, 30 ½ x 48 In.	649.00
Table, Empire, Mahogany, Swivel Top, Tapered Support, Ribbon Carved, c.1830, 29 x 36 In.	920.00
Table, Farm, Oak, Banded Edge, Shaped Frieze, Cabriole Legs, 30 x 81 In.	861.00
Table, Farm, Pine, 2 Drawers, Turned Legs, Continental, c.1850, 31 x 72 In.	236.00
Table, Farm, Pine, Frieze Drawers, Slatted Shelf Stretcher, Square Legs, c.1900, 32 x 105 In.	799.00
Table, Federal, Birch, Tiger Maple, 2 Drawers, New England, c.1810, 30 x 19 In.	1541.00
Table, Federal, Cherry, Drawer, Tray Top, Splayed Legs, c.1790, 27 x 15 In.	1007.00
Table, Federal, Fruitwood, Overhung Top, Drawer, Tapered Legs, 27 x 22 In.	188.00
Table, Federal, Mahogany, Cock-Beaded, Double Lyre Supports, Casters, c.1820, 30 x 36 x 19 In.	889.00
Table, Federal, Mahogany, Inlay, 2 Drawers, 2 Leaves, Splayed Legs, Boston, c.1815, 28 x 38 In.	25300.00
Table, Federal, Mahogany, Inlay, Fly Leaf, Cabriole Legs, Paw Feet, c.1825, 31 x 34 In.	295.00
Table, Federal, Mahogany, Pine, Drawer, Tapered Legs, Arched X-Stretchers, c.1790, 39 x 21 In.	1058.00
Table, Federal, Mahogany, Serrated Banding, Inlay, c.1795, 29 x 35 In.	3000.00

Furniture, Table, Center, Art Nouveau, Mahogany, Female Nude Supports, c.1910, 29 x 40 In.
$1,645.00

Garth's Auctioneers & Appraisers

Furniture, Table, Center, Biedermeier, Black Stencil, Lower Shelf, Bronze Mounts, 1900s, 37 x 32 In.
$413.00

Brunk Auctions

Furniture, Table, Center, Mahogany, Tilt Top, Compass Star Inlay, Carved, c.1850, 30 x 41 ½ In.
$2,988.00

Neal Auction Co.

TIP

Don't lean back on your bed's headboard if you have wet or oily hair. You will damage the finish on the bed.

Furniture, Table, Center, Oak, Veneer Of Various Wood Discs, Revolving, Continental, c.1850, 29 x 36 In. $3,444.00

New Orleans Auction Galleries, Inc.

Furniture, Table, Center, P. Evans, Bronzed Steel, Welded, Glass Top, 1960s, 26 x 48 In. $7,500.00

Rago Arts & Auction Center

Furniture, Table, Center, Renaissance Revival, Burl Walnut, Rosewood, Inlay, c.1875, 30 x 48 In. $6,210.00

James D. Julia Auctioneers

Furniture, Table, Center, Rohlfs, Cutout Base, Door, Marked, c.1904, 25 ½ x 31 ½ In. $2,000.00

Rago Arts & Auction Center

Table, Federal, Mahogany, Tiger Maple Inlay, Demilune, Square Legs, c.1800, 30 x 36 In.	5428.00
Table, Federal, Maple, Cherry, 2 Drawers, Raised, Turned Legs, Ball Feet, c.1820, 28 ½ x 21 In.	660.00
Table, Federal, Walnut, 1-Board Round Top, Drawer, Square Splayed Legs, c.1800, 29 x 26 In.	9440.00
Table, Federal, Walnut, Drawer, Overhung Top, Va., c.1800, 30 x 42 In.	1380.00
Table, Federal, Walnut, Inlay, 3 Drawers, Tapered Legs, c.1820, 39 x 21 In.	500.00
Table, Federal, Walnut, Overhanging Top, Pa., c.1800, 29 x 29 In.	444.00
Table, Florence Knoll, Walnut, Chrome Steel Base, Round, 48 x 28 In.	793.00
Table, Florence Knoll, Walnut, White Laminate Top, Drawer, 1950s, 20 x 20 In., Pair	488.00
Table, Florence Knoll, White Laminate Top, Chrome Base, Round, 29 ½ x 96 In.	1320.00
Table, Folding, Eames, Walnut Top, Square, Chrome Legs, Herman Miller, 1950s, 34 x 34 In.	854.00
Table, Folding, Wormley, Mahogany, Rectangle, Tapered Leg, Dunbar, 54 x 34 In.	875.00
Table, Frank Lloyd Wright, Copper Taliesin Design, 2 Leaves, Heritage Henredon, 48 x 29 In.	1830.00
Table, French Empire Style, Gilt Bronze, Mahogany, Marble Top, Fluted Legs, c.1900, 30 x 32 In.	1434.00
Table, French Empire Style, Wood, Marble Top, Bronze Mounts, Base Shelf, Round, c.1960, 25 x 21 In.	207.00
Table, French Empire, Mahogany, Gray Marble Top, Round, 3 Column Legs, c.1890, 28 x 33 In.	590.00
Table, French Provincial, Fruitwood, Drawer, Carved Apron, 28 x 27 In.	594.00
Table, French Provincial, Fruitwood, Drawer, Scalloped Apron, 27 x 14 ½ In.	527.00
Table, Fruitwood, Tapered Legs, Overhanging Top, France, c.1830, 30 x 64 In.	2066.00
Table, G. Nakashima, Madrona Wood, Rounded Triangle Top, 3 Round Legs, c.1941, 12 x 20 In.	2500.00
Table, G. Nakashima, Rosewood, Cross-Legged Support, 1964, 18 ¾ x 46 In.	18750.00
Table, G. Nakashima, Walnut, Hickory Legs, c.1987, 23 x 28 In., Pair	7320.00
Table, G. Stickley, No. 439, Round, Square Legs, X-Stretcher, 26 x 26 In.	6875.00
Table, Game, Anglo-Portuguese, Checkerboard, Drawers, Barley Twist Legs, 1800s, 41 x 28 In.	2390.00
Table, Game, Art Deco, Mahogany, Round, Octagonal Pedestal, Round Base, 31 x 47 In.	2500.00
Table, Game, Art Nouveau, Fruitwood, Mother-Of-Pearl Inlay, Handkerchief, c.1900, 30 x 21 In.	356.00
Table, Game, Chippendale Style, Burl, Carved Knees, Drawer, Ball & Claw Feet, 1900s, 31 x 34 In.	826.00
Table, Game, Directoire, Wood, Bronze, Flip Top, Demilune, c.1840, 31 x 44 In.	780.00
Table, Game, Drop Leaf, Marquetry, D-Shape, Fluted Legs, Cross Stretcher, 1800s, 30 x 21 In.	1265.00
Table, Game, Edwardian Style, Mahogany, Flip Top, Shaped Top, Inlay, c.1950, 30 x 36 In.	615.00
Table, Game, Edwardian, Mahogany, Handkerchief, Square Top, Drawer, c.1900, 31 x 20 In.	369.00
Table, Game, Empire, Flame Mahogany, Swivel Top, Lyre Support, Scroll Legs, c.1840, 29 x 17 In.	480.00
Table, Game, Federal, Birch, Flip Top, Inlay, Bowfront, Reeded Legs, Ma., c.1820, 30 x 43 In.	1188.00
Table, Game, Federal, Inlaid Mahogany, Flip Top, Square Tapered Legs, 1800s, 28 x 23 In.	2806.00
Table, Game, Federal, Inlaid Maple, Flip Top, Square Tapered Legs, c.1800, 29 x 35 In.	1076.00
Table, Game, Federal, Mahogany, Flip Top, Inlay, Demilune, Swivel Leg, c.1820, 29 x 18 In.	546.00
Table, Game, Federal, Mahogany, Flip Top, Inlay, Square Tapered Legs, England, 1800s, 28 x 35 In.	2032.00
Table, Game, Federal, Mahogany, Husk Inlay, Demilune, Tapered Legs, c.1805, 29 x 36 In.	1375.00
Table, Game, Federal, Mahogany, Line Inlay, Flip Top, c.1810, 29 x 17 In.	885.00
Table, Game, Federal, Mahogany, Reeded, Turned & Leaf Carved Legs, c.1810, 28 x 36 x 18 In.	1003.00
Table, Game, Federal, Mahogany, Shaped Top, Reeded Edges & Legs, c.1810, 29 x 36 In.	1916.00
Table, Game, Flip Top, 4 Ring-Turned Columns, Trestle Base, Turned Feet, c.1835, 30 x 36 In.	676.00
Table, Game, French Directoire, Flip Top, Wood, Bronze Mounts, Tapered, c.1900, 29 x 27 ½ In.	720.00
Table, Game, Fruitwood, Rounded, Frieze Drawers, Cabriole Legs, c.1900, 30 x 33 In.	738.00
Table, Game, George II Style, Mahogany, Flip Top, Cabriole Legs, c.1890, 31 x 34 In.	1265.00
Table, Game, George II Style, Mahogany, Outset Corners, Drawer, Cabriole Legs, 1800s, 29 x 31 In..	1778.00
Table, Game, George II, Mahogany, Flip Top, Drawer, Leaf Carved Cabriole Legs, 30 x 36 In.	2457.00
Table, Game, George II, Mahogany, Quadruple Top, Carved, c.1750, 29 ½ x 33 ½ In.	2916.00
Table, Game, George III, Mahogany, Flip Top, Drawer, Tapered Legs, 29 x 40 In.	1250.00
Table, Game, George III, Mahogany, Flip Top, Serpentine, Gadrooned Apron, Scroll Feet, 29 x 35 In.	1225.00
Table, Game, George III, Mahogany, Inlay, Flip Top, Tapered Legs, 28 x 36 In.	938.00
Table, Game, George III, Satinwood, Flip Top, Demilune Top, String Inlay, Sunburst, 30 x 37 In.	2706.00
Table, Game, Georgian, Mahogany, Flip Top, Frieze Drawer, Cabriole Legs, 1700s, 29 x 31 In.	610.00
Table, Game, Hardwood, Square Top, Beaded Skirt & Legs, Chinese, 1800s, 31 x 31 In.	1434.00
Table, Game, Hepplewhite, Mahogany, Flame Birch Panels, New England, 29 x 36 In.	486.00
Table, Game, Hepplewhite, Mahogany, Flip Top, Shell Inlay, Tapered Legs, Ma., 30 x 36 In.	708.00
Table, Game, Hepplewhite, Maple, Flip Top, Drawer, 32 x 29 In.	328.00
Table, Game, Louis XV Style, Kingwood, Banding, Frieze Drawers, Cabriole Legs, c.1865, 28 x 29 In.	1107.00
Table, Game, Mahogany, Brass Inlay, Flip Top, Stringing, Turned Columns, c.1815, 30 x 38 In.	2460.00
Table, Game, Mahogany, Flip Top, Carved, Ring-Turned Legs., c.1830, 30 x 36 In.	633.00
Table, Game, Mahogany, Flip Top, Concave Apron, Flaring Square Pedestal, c.1855, 29 x 35 In.	420.00
Table, Game, Mahogany, Flip Top, D-Shape, Columnar Supports, Paw Feet, c.1850, 29 x 36 In.	492.00
Table, Game, Mahogany, Flip Top, Gilt Stencil, Trestle Support, Paw Feet, c.1825, 30 x 36 In.	3286.00
Table, Game, Mahogany, Flip Top, Lyre Support, Reeded Saber Legs, c.1820, 29 x 36 In.	1076.00
Table, Game, Mahogany, Flip Top, Tapered Column, Reeded Paw Feet, c.1825, 32 x 36 In.	430.00
Table, Game, Mahogany, Green Felt, Cup Holders, Tripod Base, Cabriole Legs, 1900s, 28 x 28 In.	588.00
Table, Game, Mahogany, Porringer Top, Carved Knees, Ball & Claw Feet, 1900s, 29 x 34 In.	382.00

Table, Game, Mahogany, Swivel Top, Columnar Shaft, Acanthus Carved, c.1800, 30 x 36 In.	1586.00
Table, Game, Napoleon III, Flip Top, Gilt Metal, Cabriole Legs, Sabots, 31 x 35 In.	1000.00
Table, Game, Neoclassical, Fruitwood, Flip Top, Walnut Inlay, Tapered Legs, Italy, 29 x 33 In.	1170.00
Table, Game, Neoclassical, Mahogany, Carved Fruit Basket, Spiral Twist Legs, 30 x 40 In.	1135.00
Table, Game, Neoclassical, Walnut, Inlay, Flip Top, 2 Drawers, Italy, 31 x 32 In.	234.00
Table, Game, Oak, Mahogany, Flip Top, Square Tapered Legs, England, 1800s, 29 x 36 In.	299.00
Table, Game, Parquetry, Chariot, Chess, Backgammon, Roulette Boards, Wheel, Italy, 30 x 30 In.....	690.00
Table, Game, Poker, Fold-Out Backgammon Board, Mahogany, Felt, Compartments, 32 x 43 In......	325.00
Table, Game, Queen Anne, Mahogany, Flip Top, Triple Top, Tapered Legs, 1700s, 39 x 31 In.	1599.00
Table, Game, Queen Anne, Walnut, Beaded, Turned Legs, 29 x 40 x 17 In.	382.00
Table, Game, Regency, Chinoiserie, Drawer, Shaped Square, Bulbous Shaft, c.1830, 32 x 28 In.	1845.00
Table, Game, Regency, Mahogany, Board Inlay, Trestle Base, Saber Legs, Drawers, Eng., 28 x 28 In..	2360.00
Table, Game, Renaissance Revival, Burl Walnut, Flip Top, Demilune, Casters, 31 x 36 In.	359.00
Table, Game, Rosewood, Gadrooned Swivel Top, Pierced Leaves, Carved, Lions, c.1850, 33 x 35 In...	3107.00
Table, Game, Round, Pedestal Base, Brass Guard, Berkey For Widdicomb, 25 x 48 In...................	72.00
Table, Game, Sheraton Style, Mahogany, Rounded Corners, Frieze Drawer, 31 x 25 In.	406.00
Table, Game, Victorian, Mahogany, Flip Top, Green Felt, Ivory Ball, 2 Cues, 34 x 30 In.	443.00
Table, Game, Victorian, Walnut, Carved, Reverse Painted Checkerboard, Mirror, Shelf, 28 x 26 In...	878.00
Table, Game, Victorian, Walnut, Flip Top, 2 Panel Drawers, Trestle Base, 31 x 22 In.	84.00
Table, Game, Walnut, Flip Top, Carved Cabriole Legs, c.1890, 30 x 33 In.	590.00
Table, Gateleg, Oak, Oval Top, Ring-Turned Supports, Ball Feet, Eng., 1800s, 27 x 35 In.	237.00
Table, Gateleg, Stickley Bros., Oak, Drawers, H-Stretcher, Quaint, 30 In...............................	660.00
Table, George II, Mahogany, Tilt Top, Tripod Base, c.1765, 28 ½ x 30 ¼ In.	152.00
Table, George III Style, Japanned Red, Gilt Chinoiserie, Scrolled Stretcher, 19 x 36 In.	4375.00
Table, George III Style, Mahogany, Double Pedestal, Curved, Reeded, 4 Leaves, 31 x 72 In.	1000.00
Table, George III Style, Mahogany, Hexagonal Gallery Tilt Top, Tripod Legs, 30 x 29 In.	1404.00
Table, George III Style, Mahogany, Round Tilt Top, Birdcage Support, 1800s, 28 In..................	307.00
Table, George III Style, Mahogany, Tilt, Crossbanded, Inlay, Pedestal, Reeded Legs, 29 In. Diam......	1722.00
Table, George III, Mahogany, Gallery Top, Tapered Legs, 30 x 34 In.	2691.00
Table, George III, Mahogany, Inlay, Drawer, Brass Drop Handles, Tapered Legs, 27 x 18 In.	556.00
Table, George III, Mahogany, Line Inlay, Drawer, c.1780, 28 ½ In..	385.00
Table, George III, Mahogany, Round Revolving Top, Frieze Drawers, c.1800, 30 x 41 In...............	2829.00
Table, George III, Mahogany, Satinwood Band, Foldover, Spade Feet, 29 x 38 In.	688.00
Table, George III, Mahogany, Serpentine, Tapered Legs, Spade Feet, c.1770, 32 x 55 In.	1625.00
Table, George III, Mahogany, Tilt Top, 3-Board, Turned Pedestal, Cabriole Legs, c.1790, 30 In.........	399.00
Table, George III, Mahogany, Tilt Top, Reeded Edge, Columnar Standards, 1800s, 28 x 54 In.........	676.00
Table, George III, Satinwood, Mahogany, Leather Top, Tilt Top, Tripod Base, 28 x 42 In.	1750.00
Table, George III, Scroll Legs, Round, Paw Caps, 3 Leaves, 30 x 52 In.	531.00
Table, George IV Style, Mahogany, Octagonal Faux Marble Top, Fluted Column, 1900s, 29 x 33 In. ..	750.00
Table, George IV, Brass, Oak, Parcel Gilt, Leather Top, Footrest, Leaf Carved, Trestle Sides, 29 x 44 In.	1638.00
Table, George IV, Mahogany, Leather Top, 3 Drawers, Trestle Supports, Saber Legs, 29 x 36 In.	2500.00
Table, George IV, Mahogany, Round Top, X-Shape Supports, England, c.1820, 25 x 25 In.	241.00
Table, Georgian Style, Mahogany, Marble Top, Carved Frieze & Knees, 1800s, 30 x 39 In.	441.00
Table, Georgian, Mahogany, Yew, Tilt Top, Marquetry, Tripod Base, 30 x 39 In............................	648.00
Table, Gilt Bronze, Onyx Round Top, 3 Nude Females Supports, Antelope Legs, c.1900, 30 x 13 In. ...	1200.00
Table, Glass Top, Polished Steel Frame, Stacked Discs, Enamel Stretcher, Directional, 47 x 31 In.	244.00
Table, Glass Top, Round, Gilt Steel Frame & X-Shape Stretcher, c.1960, 19 x 46 In.	240.00
Table, Glass Top, Wrought Iron Stylized Gilt Base, Round, c.1950, 21 x 36 In.	2640.00
Table, Gothic Revival, Mahogany, Marble Top, Shaped Skirt, Turned Legs, c.1845	1464.00
Table, Grosfield House, Wood, Dark Stain, Carved Feather Supports, Platform Base, 40 x 22 In........	1098.00
Table, Hardwood, Marble Top, Scalloped, Pierced, Carved, Chinese, c.1890, 32 In........................	3125.00
Table, Harvest, Cherry, Drawer, Pullout Extension Slide, Turned Legs, c.1890, 30 x 69 In..............	944.00
Table, Harvest, Drop Leaf, Federal, Cherry, Swing Turned Legs, Straight Apron, c.1800, 30 x 73 In. ..	4148.00
Table, Harvest, Drop Leaf, Pine, Turned Legs, c.1800, 29 x 110 In...	2242.00
Table, Harvest, Drop Leaf, Sheraton, Green Paint, Turned Legs, 29 x 72 In.	2242.00
Table, Harvest, Drop Leaf, Sheraton, Pine, Poplar, Backsplash, 2 Drawers, 32 x 66 In.	948.00
Table, Harvest, Drop Leaf, Wood, Turned Legs, c.1855, 17 ½ x 60 In.	1380.00
Table, Harvest, Pine, Maple, Stained, New England, c.1820, 28 ½ x 142 ½ In................................	3081.00
Table, Harvest, Pine, Trestle Foot, Breadboard Top, Mortise & Tenon, Stretcher, c.1810, 34 x 107 In.	4148.00
Table, Harvest, Roycroft, Rectangular, Block Legs, Ball Feet, Marked, c.1905, 30 x 120 In.	7500.00
Table, Harvest, Sheraton, Birch, Pine, 1-Board Top, Drop Leaf, c.1815, 30 x 96 In..........................	1998.00
Table, Hepplewhite Style, Quartersawn Oak, Cloverleaf Top, Shelf, 3 Legs, Victorian, 30 x 25 In........	750.00
Table, Hepplewhite, Drawer, Tapered Legs, Pa., c.1810, 27 x 20 In.	1304.00
Table, Hepplewhite, Tiger Maple, Inlay, Drawer, Pa., c.1810, 28 x 21 ¾ In.	2015.00
Table, Huanghuali, Panel Top, Painted, Turned Legs, Cylindrical Stretchers, c.1900, 35 x 83 In.	11070.00
Table, Huanghuali, Panel Top, Reverse S-Curve Feet, Leaf, Chinese, 1700s, 13 x 37 In.	2607.00

Furniture, Table, Coffee, Federico Armijo, Pine, Laminated, Brass, Glass, Signed, 1970s, 18 x 32 In.
$2,250.00

Rago Arts & Auction Center

F

Furniture, Table, Coffee, P. Evans, Glass, 4 Pyramids, Welded, Lacquer, Signed, c.1973, 36 x 16 In.
$5,333.00

Skinner, Inc.

Furniture, Table, Coffee, Peter Hvidt, Teak, Chrome Steel, France & Sons, Denmark, 1960s, 17 x 51 In.
$3,750.00

Rago Arts & Auction Center

> **TIP**
> *Worcestershire sauce is a good brass polish.*

Furniture, Table, Coffee, Philip & Kelvin LaVerne, Bronze, Riverbank, c.1965, 52 x 22 In.
$21,600.00

Skinner, Inc.

Furniture, Table, Coffee, Philip & Kelvin LaVerne, Odyssey, Bronze, Pewter, Enamel, 1960s, 17 x 48 In. $6,250.00

Rago Arts & Auction Center

Furniture, Table, Console, Louis XVI Revival, Rosewood, Ebonized, Marble Top, Mirror, c.1885, 38 x 66 In. $2,214.00

New Orleans Auction Galleries, Inc.

Furniture, Table, Console, Louis XVI Style, Gilt, Marble Top, Emmanuel Beurdeley, c.1880, 35 x 33 In. $17,500.00

Leslie Hindman Auctioneers

Furniture, Table, Curio, Mahogany, Satinwood, Heart Shape, Hinged Top, Mirror, 3 Legs, c.1930, 29 x 20 In. $1,080.00

DuMouchelles Art Gallery

Table, I. Noguchi, Chess, Bird's-Eye Maple, Acrylic, Aluminum, Herman Miller, c.1945, 19 x 26 In. *Illus*	187500.00
Table, Ice Cream, Marble Top, Brass Standard, 30 ½ x 30 In.	98.00
Table, Inlaid Bird Top, Triangular, Dutch, c.1850, 42 x 21 In.	546.00
Table, Iron, Inlaid Stone Top, Tripod Base, France, c.1955, 18 x 36 In.	1750.00
Table, J. Hoffmann, Spindle Legs, Round, Ball Detail, 23 ½ x 29 In.	732.00
Table, Jacobean Style, Oak, Draw Leaf, Frieze, Baluster Legs, Curved Stretcher, 30 x 72 In.	826.00
Table, Jacobean Style, Oak, Skirt, Fitted Drawer, Turned Legs, Stretcher Base, 31 x 39 In.	1265.00
Table, Jacobean, Oak, Recessed Panels, Carved, Spool Feet, Eng., 23 x 38 In.	2065.00
Table, Jacobean, Walnut, Drawer, Bobbin Turned Legs, Serpentine Stretcher, Eng., 28 x 30 ½ In.	3540.00
Table, Jean Prouve, Oak Seat, Lacquered Steel Legs, c.1950, 26 ½ x 31 In.	37500.00
Table, Kingwood, Marble Top, Gilt Metal Mounts, Germany, c.1750, 28 ½ x 24 In.	3750.00
Table, Kurt Ostervig, Teak, Pullout Leaves, Round Legs, Arched Apron, c.1965, 70 x 41 In.	486.00
Table, LaVerne, Bronze, Pewter, Etched, Round, Shelf, Cylindrical Legs, 1960s, 23 x 24 In.	2750.00
Table, Leather, Nail Trim, Octagon Top & Base, Block Legs, c.1940, 27 x 24 In.	480.00
Table, Library, Art Deco, Mahogany, Leather Top, Base Stretcher, c.1930, 30 x 79 In.	4000.00
Table, Library, Arts & Crafts, Oak, Drawer, Side Shelves, Square Stretcher, c.1915, 30 x 42 In.	600.00
Table, Library, Arts & Crafts, Walnut, Carved Legs, Gordon Russell, 84 x 36 In.	4600.00
Table, Library, Empire Style, Mahogany, Column, Shelf, Cowan Furniture Co., c.1914, 30 x 34 In.	460.00
Table, Library, Empire Style, Mahogany, Gilt Bronze, Leather, Supports, 3 Drawers, 30 x 63 In.	2000.00
Table, Library, Frank Lloyd Wright, Pine, Medial Shelf, c.1952, 30 x 60 In.	10625.00
Table, Library, G. Stickley, 2 Drawers, Lower Shelf, Block Legs, c.1906, 30 x 48 In.	1625.00
Table, Library, G. Stickley, Arched Skirt, X-Stretcher, 29 ½ x 44 In.	2000.00
Table, Library, G. Stickley, Hexagonal Top, 6 Plank Legs, Cross Stretchers, c.1902, 31 x 50 In.	4375.00
Table, Library, G. Stickley, Leather Top, Splayed Legs, Apron, Round, 45 x 29 In.	2300.00
Table, Library, G. Stickley, Wood, Overhung Top, Shelf Stretcher, c.1906, 30 x 48 In.	1250.00
Table, Library, George II Style, Walnut, Writing Surface, Cabriole Legs, Pad Feet, c.1900, 30 x 96 In.	1168.00
Table, Library, Jacobean Style, Inlay, Canted Corner Shape, England, c.1850, 30 x 66 In.	1416.00
Table, Library, L. & J.G. Stickley, Oak, 2 Drawers, Hammered Pulls, 29 x 54 In.	1560.00
Table, Library, Limbert, Drawer, Overhung Top, Shelf Stretcher, Block Legs, c.1908, 29 x 40 In.	1375.00
Table, Library, Limbert, Oak, Side Drawers, Lower Shelf, Marked, c.1910, 48 x 34 In. *Illus*	5312.00
Table, Library, Limbert, Oval, Square A-Shape Legs, Shelf Stretcher, c.1907, 30 x 45 In.	1875.00
Table, Library, Oak, Swag Carved Supports, Trestle Base, c.1890, 30 x 174 In.	2375.00
Table, Library, Renaissance Revival, Pine, Gadrooned, Leaves, Caryatid Legs, 32 x 71 In.	2750.00
Table, Library, Renaissance Revival, Pine, Leaf Frieze, Pierced Apron, Shell, X-Stretcher, 33 x 55 In.	1875.00
Table, Library, Renaissance Revival, Walnut, Marble Top, Demilune Ends, Drawer, Trestle, 29 x 53 In.	1845.00
Table, Library, Rosewood, Brass Stringing, Spindles, Incurved Legs, Paw Feet, c.1885, 30 x 38 In.	1353.00
Table, Library, Walnut, Carved Apron, Drawer, Scrolled Supports, Stretcher, Spain, 1700s, 33 x 36 In.	1610.00
Table, Library, Walnut, Marble Top, Carved Apron, Drawer, Tapered Legs, France, 1800s, 30 x 45 In.	460.00
Table, Library, Walnut, Parquetry, Banded Design, Gilt Accents, Scroll Legs, Dolphin Feet, Italy	1912.00
Table, Library, Walnut, Sunflower Border, Apron, Square Legs, Ivy, Shelf, Feet, c.1895, 29 x 47 In.	1020.00
Table, Lift Top, Federal, Mahogany, Adjustable Felt Pad, Fitted Interior, c.1810, 31 x 26 In.	5925.00
Table, Limbert, Drawer, Low Stretcher, Tapered Legs, Rectangular, 36 x 24 In.	688.00
Table, Limbert, Oak, Oval, Corbel Supports, Cutout Sides, Lower Shelf, c.1910, 30 x 45 In. *Illus*	1126.00
Table, Limbert, Round Top, Square Shelf, Tapered Legs, Signed, 22 x 26 In.	1063.00
Table, Linden, Figural, Grizzly, Hinged Head, Arm Holding Tray, Black Forest, 1900, 37 In.	5313.00
Table, Louis Philippe, Mahogany, Round, Bulbous Standard, Triangular Base, 30 x 32 In.	531.00
Table, Louis Philippe, Marble Top, Drawer, Scroll Front Legs, Paw Feet, 43 x 39 In.	594.00
Table, Louis Philippe, Wood, Marble Top, Pedestal Base, Tripod Base, Casters, c.1860, 29 x 41 In.	1680.00
Table, Louis XIV Style, Marquetry, Bronze Mounts, Drawers, Marble Top, c.1930, 30 x 21 In.	120.00
Table, Louis XV Style, Black Lacquer, Drawers, Bronze, Cabriole Legs, 1900s, 31 x 51 In.	738.00
Table, Louis XV Style, Mahogany, Drawers, Ormolu Band, Shields, Maiden Head, c.1900, 31 x 49 In.	1168.00
Table, Louis XV Style, Rosewood, Bronze, 3 Bombay Drawers, Saber Legs, c.1900, 30 x 19 In.	150.00
Table, Louis XV Style, Round Marble Top, Brass Gallery, Drawer, 29 x 26 In.	649.00
Table, Louis XV Style, Walnut, Carved Hunt Scene, Shaped Apron, Cabriole Legs, c.1900, 20 x 37 In.	1035.00
Table, Louis XV, Ebonized, Brass, Gilt Bronze, Leather, Drawer, Cabriole Legs, 31 x 64 In.	11250.00
Table, Louis XVI Style, Beech, Parcel Gilt, Needlepoint Top, 9-Sided Top, 31 x 36 In.	813.00
Table, Louis XVI Style, Fruitwood, Marble Gallery Top, Drawer, Fluted Legs, 30 x 26 In.	875.00
Table, Louis XVI Style, Fruitwood, Parquetry, Gilt Metal, Leather Top, 2 Drawers, 31 x 51 In.	1875.00
Table, Louis XVI Style, Gilt Bronze, Round Marble Top, Cabriole Legs, c.1890, 30 x 27 In.	350.00
Table, Louis XVI Style, Gilt, Carved, Onyx Oval Top, Cane Low Shelf, c.1920, 31 x 35 In.	210.00
Table, Louis XVI Style, Gilt, Marble Top, Arched Stretcher, 17 x 42 In.	406.00
Table, Louis XVI Style, Gilt, White Onyx Top, Leaf, Berry Frieze, Fluted Legs, Stretcher, 30 x 54 In.	1188.00
Table, Louis XVI Style, Kingwood, Gilt, Musical Trophy, Leaves, Fluted Legs, 31 x 55 In.	1500.00
Table, Louis XVI Style, Mahogany, Brass Gallery, 2 Drawers, Square Legs, 31 x 27 In.	1000.00
Table, Louis XVI Style, Mahogany, Brassbound, 2 Drawers, c.1860, 28 x 36 In.	688.00
Table, Louis XVI Style, Mahogany, Drawers, Fluted Legs, Shaped Feet, c.1850, 30 x 51 In.	1230.00

Table, Louis XVI Style, Mahogany, Lift-Off Top, Planter, Pierced Brass Gallery, c.1900, 32 x 25 In.	1168.00
Table, Louis XVI Style, Mahogany, Marble Top, Gilt Metal Mounts, Stretcher, Paw Feet, 33 x 33 In....	1375.00
Table, Louis XVI Style, Mahogany, Mixed Wood, Inlay, Bronze, Saber Legs, 18 x 28 In.	3600.00
Table, Louis XVI Style, Mahogany, Shaped Marble Top, Cabriole Legs, France, 1800s, 30 x 25 In.......	240.00
Table, Louis XVI Style, Marble Top, Leaf Carved Apron, Fluted Legs, Painted, 17 x 42 In.....................	1750.00
Table, Louis XVI Style, Mixed Wood, Marble Top, Drawer, Shelf, Round, 30 x 22 In., Pair	1625.00
Table, Louis XVI Style, Oak, Oval Marble Top, Fluted Frieze, Wreaths, Stretcher, 1900s, 30 x 55 In.	1126.00
Table, Louis XVI Style, Rosewood, Flower Inlay, Drawer, Cabriole Legs, 1800s, 30 x 39 In..................	1020.00
Table, Louis XVI Style, Tulipwood, Marble Top, Brass Gallery, Drawer, Round, Shelf, 31 x 19 In.	531.00
Table, Louis XVI, Mixed Wood, Marble Top, Reeded, Round, c.1790, 30 x 24 In................................	3000.00
Table, Low, Mahogany, Marble Top, Faceted Stem, Scrolled Feet, 21 x 31 In.	366.00
Table, Mahogany, Arched Bowfront, S-Curve Pilasters, Cupboard Doors, c.1835, 42 x 44 In.	1476.00
Table, Mahogany, Arched Frieze, Paneled Door, Slide, Scroll Columns, Paw Feet, c.1835, 34 In.........	1476.00
Table, Mahogany, Brass Moldings Drawer, Tapered Legs, 30 x 36 In.	246.00
Table, Mahogany, Bronze, Marble Top, Frieze Drawer, Sphinx & Mask Legs, 31 x 34 In.	7500.00
Table, Mahogany, Faux Zebrawood, Clustered Columns, Curved Base, c.1950, 29 x 130 In.	657.00
Table, Mahogany, Figured Round Top, Tapered Pedestal, Base, Scroll Feet, c.1835, 28 In.	1476.00
Table, Mahogany, Inlay, 3 Leaves, Tripod Pedestal Base, c.1830, 29 x 110 In.	2596.00
Table, Mahogany, Leather Top, 2 Frieze Drawers, Gillows-Lancaster, c.1825, 31 x 36 In.	2587.00
Table, Mahogany, Marble Top, Round, Urn Standard, Tripod Base, Paw Feet, c.1860, 31 x 33 In.	1125.00
Table, Mahogany, Marquetry, Foldover, Tapered Legs, Carved Shells, c.1800, 29 x 36 In.	594.00
Table, Mahogany, Round Marble Top, Frieze, Caryatid Supports, Bun Feet, 1800s, 27 x 17 In.	3944.00
Table, Mahogany, Round, Gilt Metal Mount, Tripod Base, France, c.1920, 30 x 37 In.....................	1625.00
Table, Mahogany, Shaped Top, Apron, Carved Molding, Leaves, 62 x 42 In..................................	177.00
Table, Mahogany, Shaped Top, Clover Shape, Fluted Urn Base, Grand Rapids, 15 x 25 In.	75.00
Table, Maple, Overhanging Top, Drawer, Painted, New England, c.1850, 30 x 39 In.........................	1701.00
Table, Maple, Overhanging Top, Drawer, Stain, New England, c.1770, 26 x 40 In.	1778.00
Table, Marble Top, Cast Iron Trestle Base, Toulouse, France, c.1920, 28 ½ x 63 In........................	840.00
Table, Marble Top, Drum, Openwork Apron, Turned Pedestal, Tripod Feet, 1900s, 29 x 21 In.	316.00
Table, Marble Top, Ebonized, Brass Mounts, Maison Jansen, France, c.1960, 25 x 19 In., Pair..........	4750.00
Table, Marble Top, Figural Whippet Dog Support, Iron, 31 x 16 In., Pair ....*Illus*	3198.00
Table, Marble Top, Gilt Mounts, Round, Tripod Base, c.1830, 29 x 36 In..	5625.00
Table, Marquetry, Fruitwood, Marble Top, Gilt Metal, 2 Drawers, Cabriole Legs, 29 x 24 In., Pair......	1250.00
Table, McCobb, Maple, Drawer, Turned Legs, 24 x 22 In., Pair..	325.00
Table, Metal, Adjustable, Cast Iron Wheel, c.1930, 32 x 68 In.	2280.00
Table, Metal, Petal Shape Top, Star Splayed Base, Richard Schultz, 19 x 16 In.	1020.00
Table, Mixed Wood, Marble Top, Round, Shelf, France, c.1890, 30 x 21 In.	875.00
Table, Mixed Wood, Walnut, 3-Board Top, Drawer, Tapered Legs, 1800s, 57 x 37 In.......................	470.00
Table, Napoleon III, Ebonized, Brass Banding, Drawer, Cabriole Legs, c.1865, 28 x 25 In.	492.00
Table, Napoleon III, Marquetry, Animals, Swag, Leaves, Gilt Mounts, Oval, c.1880, 31 x 60 In..........	7500.00
Table, Neoclassical Style, Marble Top, Stretcher, Gesso Frame, Rectangular, c.1900, 32 x 57 In.......	2478.00
Table, Neoclassical, Figured Mahogany, Tilt Top, Oval, Ring-Turned Support, c.1800, 50 x 37 In.......	1150.00
Table, Neoclassical, Mahogany, 4 Drawers, Curved Base Shelf, Casters, c.1825, 31 x 29 In.	2006.00
Table, Neoclassical, Mahogany, Brass Inlay, Round, 4 Scroll Legs, Base Marble, Russia, 31 x 30 In. ...	2340.00
Table, Neoclassical, Mahogany, Round Marble Top, Tapered Pedestal, Melon Feet, 40 x 30 In.	2950.00
Table, Neoclassical, Mahogany, Wavy Veneer, Marble Top, Candle Slides, c.1800, 29 x 32 In.	6000.00
Table, Neoclassical, Mixed Wood, Metal Gallery, 2 Drawers, Shelf, France, c.1890, 31 x 21 In.	4313.00
Table, Nesting, Projecting Corners, Applied Print, c.1910, 22 x 23 In., 3 Piece ....*Illus*	1230.00
Table, Nesting, Regency Style, Mahogany, 21 x 20 In., 3 Piece ....*Illus*	594.00
Table, Nesting, V. Kagan, Walnut, Mosaic Glass, Kagan-Dreyfuss, 1950s, 21 x 28 In., 3 Piece ......*Illus*	9375.00
Table, Niels Vodder, Teak, Beech, Kidney Shape, 2 Tiers, Round H-Support Legs, 1940s, 22 x 39 In...	1125.00
Table, Oak, 2 Leaves, Triangular Stem, Ebonized Sides, Roundels, 3 Scroll Feet, 1800s, 29 In...........	608.00
Table, Oak, Bleached, Open Shelf Support, Tapered Legs, c.1940, 26 x 17 In., Pair.........................	660.00
Table, Oak, Carved Flowers, Spiral Column Legs, Base Shelf, c.1910, 30 x 45 In.	177.00
Table, Oak, Carved, Fluted Frieze, Leaf Scrolls, Turned Stretcher, Column, c.1950, 25 x 48 In.	608.00
Table, Oak, Glass Claw Feet, Carved Shelf, 29 x 26 In..	440.00
Table, Oak, Oval Beaded Skirt, Twisted Legs, England, 19 x 18 x 11 In..	1200.00
Table, Oak, Pine, Overhanging Top, Drawer, New England, 24 x 25 ½ In.......................................	4503.00
Table, P. Buffa, Mahogany, Brass, Rounded Triangular Top, Italy, 1950s, 17 x 24 In.	5313.00
Table, P. Evans, Chromed Metal, c.1970, 15 x 55 x 43 In., 3 Piece ....*Illus*	3075.00
Table, P. Evans, Cityscape, Glass, Burl, Brass, Directional, c.1970, 16 ½ x 38 In. ....*Illus*	1320.00
Table, Parquetry, Copper Trim, Metal Cage Base, 28 x 36 In...	1440.00
Table, Parquetry, Mixed Wood, Leather Insert, 2 Drawers, 2 Faux Drawers, 29 x 43 In.....................	1375.00
Table, Parquetry, Walnut, Drawer, Shaped Legs, c.1870, 31 x 36 In...	767.00
Table, Parsons Style, Ostrich Textured Vinyl, Brass Nailhead Trim, 14 x 14 In., Pair	69.00
Table, Parsons, Parquetry Top, Francis Company, 21 x 22 In., Pair..	360.00

Furniture, Table, Dining, Limbert, Pedestal, 4 Leaves, Marked, c.1910, 28 ½ x 54 In.
$2,500.00

Rago Arts & Auction Center

Furniture, Table, Dining, M. Nakashima, Walnut, Root Burl, Rosewood, Signed, 1994, 28 ½ x 48 In.
$4,375.00

Rago Arts & Auction Center

Furniture, Table, Dining, Parzinger, Mahogany, Satinwood, Brass, Charak Modern, 1940s, 30 x 68 x 38 In.
$3,375.00

Rago Arts & Auction Center

Furniture, Table, Dining, Renaissance Revival, Oak, Carved, Molded, 6 Leaves, c.1890, 32 x 32 In.
$4,920.00

Neal Auction Co.

TIP
Never try to dry a piece of marble with a hair dryer.

Furniture, Table, Dressing, Federal, Tiger Maple, Drawer, 2 Tiers, Box, c.1810-15, 37 x 36 In.
$10,200.00

Skinner, Inc.

Furniture, Table, Drop Leaf, Pine, Maple, Gateleg, 27 x 41 x 45 In.
$575.00

Cottone Auctions

Furniture, Table, Drop Leaf, Regency Style, Mahogany, Turned Stretcher, 28 ½ x 56 In.
$375.00

Doyle New York

The Bed Is a Status Symbol

In the seventeenth and eighteenth centuries the bed was a status symbol. The head of the house and his wife used the bed, which had curtains that gave privacy. Others often slept in one room on small mats on the floor. The more people in the room, the warmer it was.

Table, Parzinger, Leather, Mahogany, Round, Charak Modern, c.1955, 16 x 34 In.	1500.00
Table, Parzinger, Maple, Ebonized, Inlay, Leaves, Charak Modern, c.1970, 29 In.	3250.00
Table, Pedestal, Marquetry, Fruitwood Inlay, Floral, Leaves, Bronze Gallery, c.1880, 28 x 14 In.	180.00
Table, Pembroke Style, Mahogany, Shaped Top, Drawer, Molded Legs, 1900s, 28 x 19 In., Pair	323.00
Table, Pembroke, Chippendale, Mahogany, Pa., c.1790, 28 ½ x 19 ½ In.	207.00
Table, Pembroke, Chippendale, Mahogany, Serpentine Leaves, c.1780, 28 x 20 In.	425.00
Table, Pembroke, Federal, Burl, Inlay, Tapered Legs, Leaf Supports, 29 x 32 In.	649.00
Table, Pembroke, Federal, Cherry, Drawer, Tapered Legs, c.1800, 29 x 21 In.	374.00
Table, Pembroke, Federal, Cherry, Skirt, Faux Drawers, c.1800, 29 x 36 x 19 In.	237.00
Table, Pembroke, Federal, Inlay, Oval Leaves, c.1790, 28 ½ x 21 In.	474.00
Table, Pembroke, Federal, Mahogany, Drawer, Casters, Pa., c.1800, 29 x 21 x 32 In.	851.00
Table, Pembroke, Federal, Mahogany, Drawer, Tapered Legs, c.1800, 27 x 41 ½ In.	360.00
Table, Pembroke, Federal, Mahogany, Feather Inlay, Drawer, Brass Pull, c.1800, 28 x 32 In.	1180.00
Table, Pembroke, Federal, Mahogany, Shell Inlay, Drawer, c.1800, 29 x 20 In.	9920.00
Table, Pembroke, Federal, Mahogany, Star Inlay Top, c.1790, 29 x 30 In.	4340.00
Table, Pembroke, Federal, Mahogany, Veneer, Reeded Legs, Casters, c.1805, 28 x 34 In. ....*Illus*	649.00
Table, Pembroke, George III Style, Mahogany, Frieze Drawer, Square Legs, Casters, 29 x 37 In.	399.00
Table, Pembroke, George III, Inlay, Mahogany, Drawer, Inlay, Tapered Legs, 27 x 17 In.	748.00
Table, Pembroke, George III, Mahogany, Drawer, Tapered Legs, Brass Box Casters, 28 x 30 In.	644.00
Table, Pembroke, George III, Mahogany, Inlay, Leaves, Drawer, c.1790, 29 x 21 In.	575.00
Table, Pembroke, George III, Mahogany, Marquetry Top, c.1750, 28 x 22 In.	1000.00
Table, Pembroke, George III, Mahogany, Rectangular Leaves, Pierced Stretcher, c.1800, 28 x 25 In.	813.00
Table, Pembroke, George III, Mahogany, String Inlay, Drawer, 29 x 20 In.	369.00
Table, Pembroke, Georgian, Mahogany, Inlay, Drawer, Rounded Leaves, 27 x 35 In.	826.00
Table, Pembroke, Hepplewhite, Cherry, Line Inlay, c.1805, 28 x 21 ½ In.	474.00
Table, Pembroke, Hepplewhite, Curly Maple, Serpentine Leaves, Beading, 29 x 36 In.	3068.00
Table, Pembroke, Hepplewhite, Inlaid Mahogany, Drawer, N.Y., 28 x 31 In.	7552.00
Table, Pembroke, Hepplewhite, Mahogany, Dovetailed Drawers, 1800s, 27 x 35 In.	354.00
Table, Pembroke, Hepplewhite, Mahogany, Drawer, England, c.1800, 28 x 20 In.	415.00
Table, Pembroke, Hepplewhite, Mahogany, Drawer, Tapered Legs, N.Y., 28 x 32 In.	649.00
Table, Pembroke, Mahogany, Bird's-Eye Maple, Inlay, Hinged Leaves, c.1810, 29 x 36 In.	1150.00
Table, Pembroke, Mahogany, Demilune Leaves, Tapered Legs, England, c.1800, 29 x 30 In.	593.00
Table, Pembroke, Mahogany, Drawer, Cross Stretcher Base, c.1790, 29 x 32 In.	1062.00
Table, Pembroke, Sheraton, Curly Maple, Turned Legs, c.1825, 27 x 22 In.	652.00
Table, Pembroke, Sheraton, Mahogany, Shaped Leaves, Drawer, Reeded Legs, N.Y., 36 x 21 In.	354.00
Table, Pier, Charles X, Mahogany, Marble Top, Swan Head, Serpentine Tier, c.1830, 36 x 44 In.	896.00
Table, Pier, Chippendale, Mahogany, Drawer, Carved Border, Phila., c.1775, 27 x 35 In.	326.00
Table, Pier, Empire, Mahogany, Marble Top, Mirror, Curl Supports, c.1845, 37 x 42 In.	972.00
Table, Pier, Empire, Mahogany, Marble Top, Recessed Mirror, Scrolled Supports, 36 x 40 In.	649.00
Table, Pier, Empire, Marble, Caryatid Front Supports, Carved Legs, 1800s, 37 x 68 In.	7080.00
Table, Pier, French Empire, Mahogany, Gilt Metal Mount, Slate Top, Shelf, 38 x 53 In.	826.00
Table, Pier, George III, Inlaid Demilune Top, Wave Pattern Border, c.1790, 31 x 40 In.	1200.00
Table, Pier, George III, Mahogany, Crossbanded, Inlaid Urn, Square Inlaid Legs, c.1790, 34 x 48 In.	3081.00
Table, Pier, George III, Marble Top, Gadrooned Skirt, Ball & Claw Feet, c.1750, 30 x 49 In.	33750.00
Table, Pier, Gilt, Marble Top, Demilune, Pierced Skirt, Stretcher, Artichoke Finial, c.1800, 34 x 44 In.	1298.00
Table, Pier, Louis XVI Style, Fruitwood, Painted, Marble Top, Urn, Flowers, 1800s, 34 x 364 In.	1652.00
Table, Pier, Mahogany, Banded Crest, Columns, Shaped Shelf, Mirror, Bun Feet, c.1835, 36 x 39 In.	1168.00
Table, Pier, Mahogany, Egyptian Marble Top, Bronze, Mirror, c.1810, 36 x 36 In. ....*Illus*	2988.00
Table, Pier, Mahogany, Gilt, Marble Top, Columns, Corinthian Capitals, 36 x 37 In.	1722.00
Table, Pier, Mahogany, Marble Top, Ogee Frieze, Scrolled Supports, Mirror Back, 37 x 42 In.	1434.00
Table, Pier, Mahogany, Marble Top, Scroll Columns, Vines, Paw Feet, Shelf, c.1835, 44 x 46 In.	2706.00
Table, Pier, Mahogany, Mirror, Marble Top, Carved Columns, c.1830, 37 x 41 In.	326.00
Table, Pier, Mahogany, Mirrored Back, Shaped Legs, c.1830, 36 x 43 ½ In.	1422.00
Table, Pier, Mahogany, Molded Frieze, Scrolls, Columns, Serpentine Shelf, c.1835, 37 x 39 In.	984.00
Table, Pier, Mahogany, Stenciled Gilt Frieze, Marble Top, Mirror, c.1825, 37 x 46 In.	1875.00
Table, Pier, Mahogany, Stenciled, Marble Top, Columns, Pilasters, Gilt Feet, c.1800, 38 x 40 In.	4183.00
Table, Pier, Neoclassical Style, Carved, Lion's Head, Rosette, Medallion, Italy, 37 x 55 In.	885.00
Table, Pier, Neoclassical, Mahogany, Black & Gold Marble Top, 32 x 39 In.	7080.00
Table, Pier, Rococo, Oak, Marble Top, Diamond Design, Carved Knees, Italy, 1700s, 29 x 51 In.	1659.00
Table, Pier, Wood, White Paint, Marble Top, Shell Support, c.1965, 32 x 38 In.	944.00
Table, Pine, Maple, Drawer, Overhang, New England, c.1805, 27 ½ x 42 In.	178.00
Table, Pine, Maple, Red Paint, Base Stretcher, New England, c.1790, 27 x 27 ½ In.	889.00
Table, Pine, Overhang, Drawer, Brown Paint, Tapered Legs, c.1810, 28 x 42 In.	236.00
Table, Pine, Plank Top, Cut Corners, Tapered Legs, Oval, England, 29 ½ x 102 In.	1062.00
Table, Pine, Red Paint, Splayed Tapered Legs, Pa., c.1810, 28 ½ x 16 ½ In.	770.00
Table, Plank Top, Shaped Legs, Curved Wrought Iron Stretcher, 30 x 71 In.	780.00

Table, Plank Top, X-Shape Iron Base, 71 x 35 ½ In.	840.00
Table, Queen Anne Style, Ebonized, Bird & Leaf Design, Rounded Leaves, 27 In.	246.00
Table, Queen Anne Style, Mahogany, Silver, 2 Candle Slides, c.1950, 26 x 30 In.	276.00
Table, Queen Anne Style, Oak, Gateleg, Rounded Leaves, 24 x 27 In.	499.00
Table, Queen Anne Style, Pine, Green Paint, Porringer Top, c.1990, 26 x 35 In.	211.00
Table, Queen Anne, Black Paint, Breadboard Ends, Drawer, 28 x 36 In.	207.00
Table, Queen Anne, Cherry, Tilt Top, Cabriole Legs, E. Chapin, Hartford, Conn., 27 x 40 In.	236.00
Table, Queen Anne, Cherry, Tilt Top, Round, Carved Knees, c.1785, 27 x 33 In.	504.00
Table, Queen Anne, Cherry, Walnut, 3 Drawers, Serpentine Apron, 29 x 31 In.	938.00
Table, Queen Anne, Mahogany, Square, Tilt Top, Tripod, 28 x 35 In.	295.00
Table, Queen Anne, Mahogany, Tilt Top, Tripod Base, 28 x 32 In.	118.00
Table, Queen Anne, Maple, Cherry, Drawer, Wavy Apron, c.1750, 29 x 25 In.	1770.00
Table, Queen Anne, Maple, Overhang Oval, Painted, 24 x 29 In.	7110.00
Table, Queen Anne, Maple, Pine, Oval Top, New England, 26 ½ x 36 ½ In.	944.00
Table, Queen Anne, Maple, Round, Tilt Top, New England, c.1780, 28 x 35 In.	207.00
Table, Queen Anne, Maple, Tilt Top, Tapered Pedestal, Snake Feet, 28 x 30 In.	118.00
Table, Queen Anne, Tilt Top, Red Paint, Candle Slides, Carved Apron, 27 ½ x 26 ½ In.	649.00
Table, Queen Anne, Walnut, 5 Drawers, Scalloped, Delaware Valley, c.1765, 29 x 31 In.	3792.00
Table, Queen Anne, Walnut, Lift Top, 2 Drawers, Scalloped Apron, Turned Legs, 30 x 32 ½ In.	7703.00
Table, Queen Anne, Walnut, Scalloped Corner, Drawer, Pa., c.1765, 29 x 32 In.	770.00
Table, Queen Anne, Walnut, Tilt Dish Top, Column Support, Pa., 28 ½ x 34 In.	805.00
Table, Queen Anne, Walnut, Tilt Top, Tripod Feet, Pa., c.1790, 30 ½ x 35 In.	356.00
Table, R. Capron, Walnut, Stoneware, Flower, Rounded Corners, 1960s, 11 x 39 In., Pair	3625.00
Table, Reading, George IV, Oak, Gilt, Leaf Cast Edge, Trestles, Footrest, 29 x 44 In.	16380.00
Table, Reading, Mahogany, Iron, Dish Top, Paw Feet, 1800s, 29 In.	533.00
Table, Refectory, Carved Apron, Flowers, Drawers, Turned Legs, Spain, c.1890, 33 x 77 In.	489.00
Table, Refectory, Chestnut, Flip Top, Pullout Supports, Dutch, 30 x 78 In.	8625.00
Table, Refectory, Draw Leaf, Stretcher, Turned Legs, Bun Feet, Dutch, 71 x 33 In.	652.00
Table, Refectory, Hardwood, Brown Finish, Barley Twist Legs, 1800s, 30 x 56 In.	323.00
Table, Refectory, Mahogany, Fruitwood, Banded, Runner Feet, Stretcher, c.1900, 29 x 33 In.	1722.00
Table, Refectory, Oak, Baluster Supports, Plank Stretcher, Runner Feet, 1800s, 29 x 79 In.	1722.00
Table, Refectory, Oak, Baluster Supports, Stretcher, Shaped Feet, France, 29 x 118 In.	7500.00
Table, Refectory, Oak, Bulbous Urn, Trestle Base, England, 1800s, 30 x 66 In.	1380.00
Table, Refectory, Oak, Carved, Plank Top, Trestle Support, 1600s, 31 x 87 In.	2868.00
Table, Refectory, Oak, Plank Top, Pegged, Stretcher, Block Feet, France, 1900s, 30 x 78 In.	826.00
Table, Refectory, Oak, Rectangular Top, Turned Bulbous Legs, Box Stretcher, 1700s, 30 x 73 In.	1353.00
Table, Refectory, Renaissance Revival, Walnut, Inlay, Shaped Stretcher, Italy, 1600s, 32 x 70 In.	1955.00
Table, Refectory, Rorimer Brooks, Jacobean Style, Oak, Carved Grapevine Skirt, 72 In.	1175.00
Table, Refectory, Walnut, Carved Top, Trestle, 19th Century, 32 x 108 In.	3205.00
Table, Regency Style, Mahogany, Dish Top, Spiral Pedestal, Tripod Base, 21 x 18 In.	1265.00
Table, Regency Style, Mahogany, Inlaid Banding, Carved Leaves, 29 x 187 In.	4920.00
Table, Regency Style, Mahogany, Oval, Reeded Edge, String Inlay, Pedestal, 28 x 72 In.	984.00
Table, Regency Style, Mahogany, Round, 4 Drawers, Rotating Pedestal, 1800s, 31 x 42 In.	3776.00
Table, Regency Style, Mahogany, Round, Frieze Drawers, Pedestal, Casters, 1800s, 30 x 47 In.	3068.00
Table, Regency, Mahogany, Carved, Leather Top, Drawer, Turned Legs, 31 x 34 In.	1287.00
Table, Regency, Mahogany, Double Gateleg, Block Turned Legs, 1800s, 28 x 30 In.	230.00
Table, Regency, Mahogany, Drawer, 3 Splayed Legs, England, c.1820, 28 x 27 In.	178.00
Table, Regency, Mahogany, Gallery, Banded Door, Turned Legs, 31 x 15 In.	585.00
Table, Regency, Mahogany, Inlay, Round, Tilt Top, Splayed Legs, Casters, 29 x 49 In.	2691.00
Table, Regency, Mahogany, Oval Tilt Top, 28 ½ x 66 In.	590.00
Table, Regency, Mahogany, Oval Tilt Top, Reeded Edge, Pedestal, c.1815, 30 x 57 In.	522.00
Table, Regency, Mahogany, Tilt Top, Pedestal, Brass Paw Feet, 65 x 44 In.	259.00
Table, Regency, Rosewood, Brass, Leather Top, 2 Drawers, Trestle, c.1820, 30 x 36 In.	4063.00
Table, Regency, Rosewood, Inlay, Brass, 2 Drawers, Shaped Stretcher, 29 x 37 In.	1121.00
Table, Regency, Round Tilt Top, Mixed Wood, Turned Standard, 29 x 50 In.	2070.00
Table, Renaissance Revival, Alexander Roux, Rosewood, Hinged Leaves, 53 x 26 In.	575.00
Table, Renaissance Revival, Marble Flower Inlay, Greek Key Trim, Round, c.1855, 31 x 31 In.	5451.00
Table, Renaissance Revival, Walnut, Carved Pedestals & Stretcher, c.1920, 30 x 86 In.	2040.00
Table, Renaissance Revival, Walnut, Carved, Brown Marble Top, 32 x 29 In.	961.00
Table, Renaissance Revival, Walnut, Carved, Masks, Trestle, Paw Feet, c.1700, 30 x 96 In.	2813.00
Table, Renaissance Revival, Walnut, Carved, Oval Marble Top, 37 x 30 In.	960.00
Table, Renaissance Revival, Walnut, Egg & Dart Trim, Carved Panel & Legs, c.1900, 60 x 25 In.	780.00
Table, Rent, Mahogany, Round, Lidded Slot, 8 Drawers, Pedestal, Cupboard, c.1900, 61 In.	2460.00
Table, Restauration, Walnut, Round Marble Top, Curved Triangular Stem, 31 x 39 In.	1725.00
Table, Robsjohn-Gibbings, Mahogany, 2 Tiers, Widdicomb, c.1951, 27 ½ x 36 ½ In.	625.00
Table, Robsjohn-Gibbings, Tufted Upholstery, Dunbar, 1940s, 96 x 33 In.	1875.00

TIP

Wicker should not be left outside in the yard. If the wicker is painted, it may survive a few seasons on a porch. Unimportant wicker furniture can be repainted about every three years. The paint will preserve it. Use two coats of paint and a coat of marine varnish; or for a natural finish, use a single coat of marine varnish.

Furniture, Table, Drop Leaf, Regency Style, Mahogany, Turned Supports, 28 x 43 In.
$1,000.00

Doyle New York

Furniture, Table, I. Noguchi, Chess, Bird's-Eye Maple, Acrylic, Aluminum, Herman Miller, c.1945, 19 x 26 In.
$187,500.00

Los Angeles Modern Auctions (LAMA)

The edited listings of the current prices in this *Kovels' Antiques & Collectibles Price Guide* aren't available on any website. Readers can visit Kovels.com to check thousands of past prices and sign up for free information on trends, tips, reproductions, marks, and more.

FURNITURE

F

Furniture, Table, Library, Limbert, Oak, Side Drawers, Lower Shelf, Marked, c.1910, 48 x 34 In.
$5,312.00

Rago Arts & Auction Center

Furniture, Table, Limbert, Oak, Oval, Corbel Supports, Cutout Sides, Lower Shelf, c.1910, 30 x 45 In.
$1,126.00

Skinner, Inc.

Furniture, Table, Marble Top, Figural Whippet Dog Support, Iron, 31 x 16 In., Pair
$3,198.00

New Orleans Auction Galleries, Inc.

Furniture, Table, Nesting, Projecting Corners, Applied Print, c.1910, 22 x 23 In., 3 Piece
$1,230.00

New Orleans Auction Galleries, Inc.

Table, Robsjohn-Gibbings, Walnut, Cylindrical Apron, Outcurved Feet, c.1960, 15 x 66 In.	625.00
Table, Rococo Revival, Carved, Gilt, Marble Top, Leaf, Ribbon, Round, 3 Legs, c.1880, 19 x 21 In.	2588.00
Table, Rococo Revival, Mahogany, Marble Top, Cabriole Legs, Finial, 1800s, 29 x 32 In.	239.00
Table, Rococo Revival, Marquetry, Splayed Legs, c.1890, 30 x 23 In.	411.00
Table, RomWeber, Oak, Trestle, Splayed Legs, 2 Leaves, H. Schwartz, 30 x 78 In.	738.00
Table, Rosewood, Inlaid Octagonal Marble Top, Gilt, 3-Part Base, England, c.1980, 28 ¾ In.	1000.00
Table, Rosewood, Marble Top, Mother-Of-Pearl Inlay, Chinese, c.1900, 48 x 30 In.	472.00
Table, Rosewood, Ormolu, Octagonal Tilt Top, Gilt Vines, Tripod, 1800s, 42 x 23 In.	889.00
Table, Rosewood, Round Marble Top, Pierced Frieze, Pedestal, Ball & Claw Feet, c.1900, 32 In.	547.00
Table, Rosewood, Rounded Rectangular Top, Flowers, Pendant, Round Legs, c.1890, 12 x 18 In.	369.00
Table, Rosewood, Walnut, Brass Mounts, Arched Base, 2 Leaves, c.1940, 30 x 90 In.	3500.00
Table, Roycroft, Black Walnut, Overhang, 2 Drawers, Lower Shelf, Square Legs, c.1905, 30 x 49 In.	5313.00
Table, Roycroft, Drawer, Slatted Sides, Shelf, Square Legs, Mackmurdo Feet, c.1905, 30 x 48 In.	2750.00
Table, Roycroft, Mahogany, 8-Sided, Drawers, Shelf, Orb & Cross, c.1905, 30 x 45 In. ....*Illus*	5312.00
Table, S. Marx, Faux Parchment, Round, Quigley, c.1950, 14 x 33 In., Pair	2750.00
Table, Sawbuck, 3-Board Scrub Top, Breadboard Ends, 19th Century, 30 x 33 x 75 In.	2289.00
Table, Sawbuck, Brown Paint, Diagonal Cross Stretchers, X-Support Legs, c.1855, 29 x 33 In.	1541.00
Table, Sawbuck, Pine, 3-Board Top, Breadboard Ends, Red Finish, 30 x 75 In.	2290.00
Table, Sawbuck, Pine, Breadboard Ends, X-Supports, 1800s, 30 x 82 In.	750.00
Table, Sawbuck, Pine, Red Paint, American, 1800s, 28 x 29 In.	558.00
Table, Sawbuck, Pine, Red Paint, Rectangular, X-Shape Legs, Plank Stretcher, c.1825, 28 x 37 In.	1169.00
Table, Sawbuck, Pine, Yellow Paint, Concave, Rounded Corners, Shelf, c.1800, 29 x 83 In.	14220.00
Table, Serving, Arts & Crafts, Tray Top, X-Shape Supports, Trestle Feet, c.1900, 33 x 36 In.	478.00
Table, Serving, Pine, Linen Slide, Drawer, Painted, New England, c.1805, 31 x 28 In.	652.00
Table, Serving, Sheraton, Mahogany, 2 Frieze Drawers, Turned Legs, 28 x 31 In.	460.00
Table, Sewing, Burl Walnut, Tapered, Overhanging Lift Top, 3 Arched Legs, England, 26 x 19 In.	418.00
Table, Sewing, Charles X, Ivory Inlaid Drawer, X-Shape Legs, France, 30 x 23 In.	444.00
Table, Sewing, Chinoiserie, Lift Top, Baluster Supports, Stretcher, Paw Feet, c.1800, 28 x 24 In.	1169.00
Table, Sewing, Ebonized, Gilt Metalwork, Porcelain Roundel, Bust Mounts, c.1865, 31 x 14 In.	359.00
Table, Sewing, Federal Style, Mahogany, 3 Drawers, Hinged Center, Oval, 29 x 24 In.	119.00
Table, Sewing, Federal, Bird's-Eye Maple, Drawer, c.1805, 28 ½ x 26 In.	868.00
Table, Sewing, Federal, Cherry, Overhang, Drawer, Tapered Legs, 1800s, 29 x 22 In.	359.00
Table, Sewing, Federal, Curly Maple, 2 Drawers, Painted, Boston, c.1805, 29 x 20 In.	19840.00
Table, Sewing, Federal, Mahogany, Bird's-Eye Maple, Drawer, c.1810, 30 x 20 x 15 In.	4444.00
Table, Sewing, Federal, Mahogany, Octagonal Lift Top, Silk Bag, c.1790, 29 x 21 In.	385.00
Table, Sewing, Federal, Mahogany, Oval Corners, Reeded Edge, Drawer, Bag, c.1810, 29 x 20 In.	3600.00
Table, Sewing, Federal, Mahogany, Rounded Leaves, 3 Drawers, Bag, Lion Pulls, Mass., 29 x 18 In.	1062.00
Table, Sewing, Fruitwood, Acanthus Carved, Cabriole Legs, Scroll Feet, 29 x 17 In.	413.00
Table, Sewing, Fruitwood, Ribs, Checkerboard Inlay, 2 Lids, Silk Basket, France, 28 x 19 In.	748.00
Table, Sewing, George III, Mahogany, Drop Leaf, Brass Inlay, Ball Feet, c.1805, 30 x 37 In.	478.00
Table, Sewing, George III, Rosewood, Line Inlay, Brass Gallery, Silk Basket, c.1810, 31 x 20 In.	1725.00
Table, Sewing, Hepplewhite, Mixed Wood, Breadboard Top, Drawer, c.1830, 39 x 30 In.	294.00
Table, Sewing, Hepplewhite, Poplar, Pine Breadboard Top, Drawer, 1800s, 31 x 42 In.	646.00
Table, Sewing, Lacquered, Gilt Scene, Pedestal, Ball & Claw Feet, Chinese, 1800s, 33 x 20 In.	241.00
Table, Sewing, Mahogany, 2 Drawers, Carved Stem, Arched Legs, Paw Feet, c.1830, 31 x 21 In.	732.00
Table, Sewing, Mahogany, Concave Drawer, Flaring Column, Bun Feet, c.1835, 30 x 25 In.	399.00
Table, Sewing, Mahogany, Demilune Lift Top, Pendants, Reeded Pedestal, c.1800, 29 x 27 In.	2706.00
Table, Sewing, Mahogany, Drop Leaf, 3 Drawers, Pedestal, Paw Feet, c.1835, 32 x 41 In.	118.00
Table, Sewing, Mahogany, Drop Leaf, Pedestal, Serpentine Base, Bun Feet, c.1835, 29 x 19 In.	338.00
Table, Sewing, Mahogany, Drop Leaf, Yoke Support, Outswept Legs, c.1825, 29 x 16 In.	478.00
Table, Sewing, Mahogany, Lift Top, Drawers, Baluster, Saber Legs, Paw Feet, c.1800, 32 x 24 In.	2032.00
Table, Sewing, Mahogany, Star Inlay, 2 Hinged Lids, Drawer, Tapered Legs, 29 x 26 In.	500.00
Table, Sewing, Mahogany, String Inlay, Bag, Lyre Supports, Stretcher, c.1810, 28 x 23 In.	300.00
Table, Sewing, Martha Washington, Federal Style, Mahogany, Banded, c.1925, 28 x 29 In.	219.00
Table, Sewing, Martha Washington, Neoclassical, Mahogany, Bag, New York, 24 x 25 In.	590.00
Table, Sewing, Mother-Of-Pearl, Round Removable Inlaid Top, 1800s, 30 x 21 In.	700.00
Table, Sewing, Neoclassical, Cherry, Carved, Flame Inlay, Drawers, Casters, c.1850, 29 x 20 In.	588.00
Table, Sewing, Neoclassical, Mahogany, Column Supports, Shaped Base, 29 x 21 In.	472.00
Table, Sewing, Neoclassical, Mahogany, Drop Leaf, Drawers, c.1810, 29 x 21 In. ....*Illus*	1220.00
Table, Sewing, Neoclassical, Satinwood Inlay, Half Round, Tambour Door, c.1815, 31 x 25 In. ... *Illus*	20913.00
Table, Sewing, Papier-Mache, Black Lacquer, Mother-Of-Pearl, Lift Top, Lyre, c.1870, 31 x 18 In.	600.00
Table, Sewing, Pine, Beveled Edge, Square Tapered Legs, Splayed Feet, c.1900, 27 x 29 In.	615.00
Table, Sewing, Pine, Maple, Scrub Top, Rounded Corners, Red Wash, c.1800, 29 x 39 In.	147.00
Table, Sewing, Queen Anne, Walnut, Painted Drawers, Stretcher Base, Baluster Legs, 30 x 52 In.	1998.00
Table, Sewing, Regency, Japanned, Abalone, Gilt, Hinged, Scalloped Edges, 28 x 19 In.	115.00
Table, Sewing, Regency, Mahogany, Silk Basket, Lyre Base, Brass Paw Feet, c.1810, 28 x 24 In.	3750.00

Table, Sewing, Rietveld, Wood, Red, Black Paint, Dutch, c.1965, 23 ¾ In.	16250.00
Table, Sewing, Rococo Revival, Rosewood, Hinged Top, Basket, c.1850, 32 x 21 In.	896.00
Table, Sewing, Shaker, Birch, Maple, Drawer, Overhang, Tapered Legs, c.1830, 28 x 42 In.	1007.00
Table, Sewing, Shaker, Overhang, Drawer, c.1870, 30 ½ x 29 In.	1725.00
Table, Sewing, Sheraton Style, Mahogany, Inlay, Drawers, Reeded Legs, 1900s, 29 In., Pair	529.00
Table, Sewing, Sheraton, Cherry, 2 Drawers, Ring-Turned Legs, 29 x 22 x 20 In.	708.00
Table, Sewing, Sheraton, Mahogany, 2 Drawers, Bag Slide, Tapered Legs, Mass., 29 x 18 In.	2655.00
Table, Sewing, Sheraton, Mahogany, 2 Drawers, Brass Pulls, Tapered Legs, 1800s, 28 x 18 In.	448.00
Table, Sewing, Sheraton, Mahogany, 2 Drawers, Round Drop Leaf, New England, 29 x 16 In.	708.00
Table, Sewing, Sheraton, Mahogany, Astragal Top, Mass., c.1810, 33 x 27 ½ In.	267.00
Table, Sewing, Sheraton, Mahogany, Astragal Top, Mass., c.1815, 28 ½ x 23 ½ In.	178.00
Table, Sewing, Sheraton, Mahogany, Bag Drawer, Boston, 31 x 21 In.	708.00
Table, Sewing, Sheraton, Mahogany, Bird's-Eye Maple, Leaves, Drawers, Fabric Bag, 29 x 19 In.	1323.00
Table, Sewing, Sheraton, Mahogany, Maple Banding, 2 Drawers, Pullout Bag, Mass., 23 x 17 In.	2360.00
Table, Sewing, Sheraton, Mahogany, Oval, Stepped Front, Fitted Interior, Drawer, 28 ½ In.	738.00
Table, Sewing, Softwood, Painted, 2 Tiers, Pincushion Top, 1800s, 13 x 8 In.	354.00
Table, Sewing, Softwood, Red Finish, Gold, 4 Drawers, Molded, Chinese, c.1880, 34 x 77 In.	301.00
Table, Sewing, Victorian, Bird's-Eye Maple, Carved, Molded, Hinged, Mirror, Drawer, 31 x 24 In.	236.00
Table, Sewing, Walnut, Drawer, Sliding Basket, G.E. Fuller, c.1870, 24 x 16 x 24 In.	1495.00
Table, Sewing, Walnut, Overhang, Hinged, Drawer, Dovetailed, c.1850, 31 x 25 x 19 In.	1265.00
Table, Sewing, Walnut, Turtle Top, Storage Well, Bulbous Legs, Stretcher, c.1865, 29 x 28 In.	369.00
Table, Sewing, Wegner, Teak, Oak, Drop Leaf, Drawer, Basket, Denmark, 1960s, 24 x 26 In.	875.00
Table, Sewing, Wood, Bird's-Eye Maple Veneer, Hinged Lid, Mirror, Lyre Shape, c.1910, 26 x 17 In.	410.00
Table, Shaker, Birch, 1-Board Top, Front Drawer, 2 Drawers On End, c.1835, 26 x 32 In. *Illus*	14040.00
Table, Shaker, Pine, Maple, Red Wash, Shaped Apron, Round Legs, c.1820, 30 x 29 In.	3629.00
Table, Sheraton, Cherry, 2 Drawers, Carved Legs, 21 x 20 In.	147.00
Table, Sheraton, Cherry, Curly Maple, Drawer, New England, c.1820, 28 x 19 In.	296.00
Table, Sheraton, Cherry, Drawer, Turned Legs, New England, 30 x 18 ½ In.	472.00
Table, Sheraton, Drawer, Turned Baluster Legs, c.1850, 29 x 17 ¾ In.	219.00
Table, Sheraton, Mahogany, 2 Drawers, Ring-Turned & Tapered Legs, 28 x 10 In.	546.00
Table, Sheraton, Mahogany, Curly Maple, Drawer, Mass., c.1815, 28 ¾ x 26 ½ In.	1094.00
Table, Sheraton, Mahogany, Drawer, Turned Legs, c.1820, 31 x 36 In.	474.00
Table, Sheraton, Mixed Wood, 2 Drawers, Pa., c.1835, 29 ½ x 19 In.	119.00
Table, Sheraton, Pine, Overhang, Drawer, Red Stain, Pa., c.1830, 29 ½ x 45 ½ In.	415.00
Table, Sheraton, Walnut, Square Top, Drawer, Turned Legs, c.1850, 30 x 23 In.	127.00
Table, Side, Art Deco, Mahogany, Lacquered Wood, Round, 2 Tiers, 1930s, 26 x 18 In., Pair	938.00
Table, Side, Bamboo, Lacquered, Flowers, Bracketed Legs, Shelf, England, c.1900, 30 x 23 In.	239.00
Table, Side, Banded, Shelf Stretcher, Square Legs, Fret Carved Feet, c.1900, 32 x 17 In., Pair	1107.00
Table, Side, Biedermeier, Fruitwood, Inlay, Round Top, Drawer, Lyre Support, 29 In.	1265.00
Table, Side, Cherry, Square Top, Drawer, Turned Tapered Legs, c.1830, 29 x 20 In.	538.00
Table, Side, Federal Style, Mahogany, Inlay, Drop Sides, Drawer, Bail Handle, 27 x 20 In., Pair	590.00
Table, Side, Federal, Cherry, Poplar, 2 Drawers, Square Overhang, Round Legs, 1800s, 30 x 22 In.	354.00
Table, Side, Federal, Mahogany, Inlay, Drawer, Door, Round Legs, 1800s, 38 x 18 In.	590.00
Table, Side, Federal, Mahogany, Oak, Drawer, Side Drop Leaf, X-Stretcher, 28 x 30 In.	767.00
Table, Side, Federal, Tiger Maple, 1-Board Top, Dovetailed Drawer, 1800s, 29 x 22 In.	885.00
Table, Side, Florence Knoll, Green Marble Top, Chrome Frame, 17 ½ x 27 In.	450.00
Table, Side, French Provincial, Fruitwood, Shaped Gallery Top, Pierced Sides, 31 x 18 In.	1464.00
Table, Side, Fruitwood, Guilloche Frieze, Curved Shelf Stretcher, Fluted Legs, 1800s, 29 x 25 In.	956.00
Table, Side, G. Nakashima, Walnut, Cut Tree Design, 3 Cylindrical Legs, 38 x 17 In.	2500.00
Table, Side, G. Stickley, Round, Square Cutout Legs, Round Shelf, c.1905, 29 x 30 In.	5625.00
Table, Side, George III Style, Mahogany, Marble Top, Drawer, Bellflower, c.1900, 30 In., Pair	1968.00
Table, Side, George III Style, Mahogany, Satinwood, Demilune, Leaves, Bellflowers, 35 x 56 In.	553.00
Table, Side, George III, Mahogany, Bowfront, Dentil Frieze, Swing-Out Drawers, c.1790, 29 In.	861.00
Table, Side, George III, Mahogany, Marble Top, Molded Edge, Cabriole Legs, c.1790, 34 x 53 In.	2214.00
Table, Side, George III, Mahogany, String Banding Inlay, Frieze Drawers, c.1815, 33 x 32 In.	461.00
Table, Side, George III, Oval, Mahogany, Drawer, Frieze, Square Legs, c.1775, 31 x 60 x 25 In.	1968.00
Table, Side, George III, Satinwood, Demilune, Fluted Inlay, Fruit Garland, c.1790, 30 x 42 In.	738.00
Table, Side, Georgian, Oak, Molded Top, Frieze Drawer, Turned Stretcher, c.1750, 26 x 31 In.	1195.00
Table, Side, Glass Octagonal Top, Snake Around Tapered Stem, A. Redmile, 23 x 28 In.	1375.00
Table, Side, Gothic Revival, Rosewood, Frieze Drawers, Carved Quatrefoils, c.1845, 28 x 32 In.	1076.00
Table, Side, Hardwood, Round Marble Top, Cabriole Legs, Shelf, c.1898, 32 In., Pair	2706.00
Table, Side, Hepplewhite, Tiger Maple, Overhang Top, Square Legs, 28 ½ x 18 ½ In.	295.00
Table, Side, J. Dickinson, Plaster, Enameled, Round Top, 3 Footed Legs, Incised, 1970s, 21 x 18 In.	7500.00
Table, Side, Jean Royere, Enameled Wrought Iron, Hexagonal Marble Top, 25 x 20 In.	2250.00
Table, Side, Kingwood, Ormolu, Turtle Shape Top, Cherubs, Shaped Base, c.1900, 30 x 22 In.	2214.00
Table, Side, Louis XV, Fruitwood, Molded Top, Shaped Frieze, Cabriole Legs, c.1800, 27 x 30 In.	896.00

Furniture, Table, Nesting, Regency Style, Mahogany, 21 x 20 In., 3 Piece
$594.00

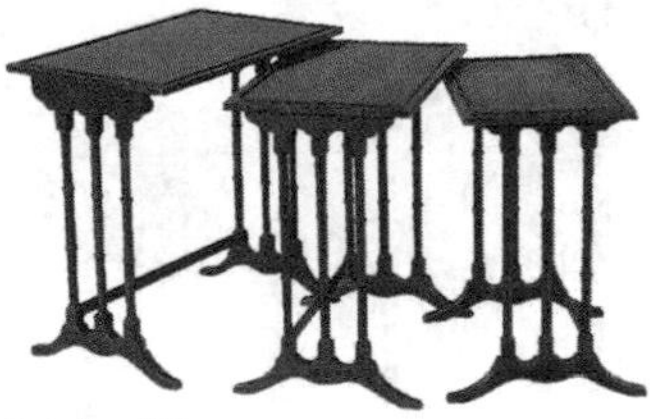

Doyle New York

Furniture, Table, Nesting, V. Kagan, Walnut, Mosaic Glass, Kagan-Dreyfuss, 1950s, 21 x 28 In., 3 Piece
$9,375.00

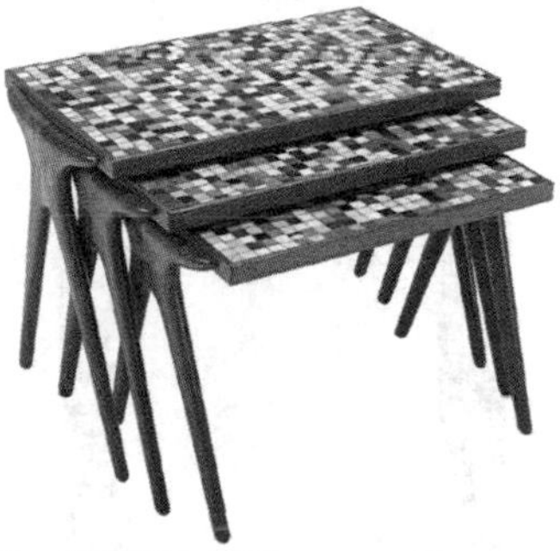

Rago Arts & Auction Center

Furniture, Table, P. Evans, Chromed Metal, c.1970, 15 x 55 x 43 In., 3 Piece
$3,075.00

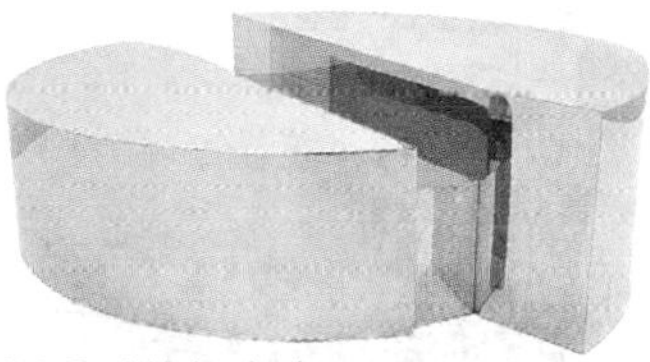

Palm Beach Modern Auctions

Furniture, Table, P. Evans, Cityscape, Glass, Burl, Brass, Directional, c.1970, 16 ½ x 38 In.
$1,320.00

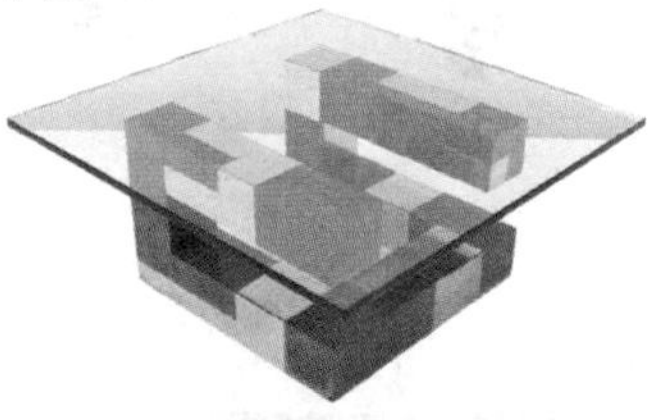

Palm Beach Modern Auctions

Names are the Same

Craftsman, Arts & Crafts, Roycroft, and finally *Crafts-style* are all alternative names for Mission style furniture first popular from 1900 to 1920, then revived in the 1980s.

F

Furniture, Table, Pembroke, Federal, Mahogany, Veneer, Reeded Legs, Casters, c.1805, 28 x 34 In.
$649.00

Brunk Auctions

Furniture, Table, Pier, Mahogany, Egyptian Marble Top, Bronze, Mirror, c.1810, 36 x 36 In.
$2,988.00

Neal Auction Co.

Furniture, Table, Roycroft, Mahogany, 8-Sided, Drawers, Shelf, Orb & Cross, c.1905, 30 x 45 In.
$5,312.00

Rago Arts & Auction Center

Furniture, Table, Sewing, Neoclassical, Mahogany, Drop Leaf, Drawers, c.1810, 29 x 21 In.
$1,220.00

Neal Auction Co.

Table, Side, Louis XVI Style, Mahogany, Demilune, Guilloche Apron, Pinecone, 31 x 43 In., Pair	984.00
Table, Side, Louis XVI Style, Mahogany, Gilt, Gallery, Marble Top, Sabots, c.1900, 28 x 20 In.	2600.00
Table, Side, Louis XVI Style, Walnut, Marble, Drawers, Door, Fluted Legs, c.1900, 35 x 16 In.	120.00
Table, Side, Mahogany, Marble Top, Round, Brass Gallery, Fitted Candlesticks, c.1900, 29 In., Pair	922.00
Table, Side, Mahogany, Mother-Of-Pearl Inlay, Round Top, Shelf Stretcher, c.1900, 27 x 24 In.	1625.00
Table, Side, Mahogany, Ormolu, Round, Drawer, Fluted Legs, Sabots, 1900s, 31 x 30 In.	3600.00
Table, Side, Marble Top, Gold Scrolling, Demilune, Doors, Italy, c.1800, 33 x 23 In., Pair	4250.00
Table, Side, Neoclassical Style, Bronze, Granite, Splayed Lion's Paw Feet, 20 x 21 In., Pair	2160.00
Table, Side, Neoclassical Style, Mahogany, Fluted Supports, Shelf, c.1875, 38 x 50 x 22 In.	430.00
Table, Side, Neoclassical, Faux Marble Top, Scrolling Leaf Design, c.1890, 35 x 41 In.	1107.00
Table, Side, Neoclassical, Faux Marble, Demilune, Pendant Scrolls, c.1800, 29 x 36 In.	984.00
Table, Side, Neoclassical, Mahogany, Faux Marble, Carved Griffins, Urn, c.1950, 33 x 49 In.	1722.00
Table, Side, Neoclassical, Walnut, Pedestal, Shaped Base, Italy, 1800s, 33 x 35 In.	1315.00
Table, Side, Oak, Frieze Drawers, Molding, Vase Shape Legs, Box Stretcher, c.1900, 29 x 48 In.	461.00
Table, Side, P. Evans, Bronze, Rosewood Top, Round, Metal Sides, Swirl Design, 16 x 20 In.	5000.00
Table, Side, Pine, Demilune, Figured Top, Banded Frieze, c.1835, 30 x 46 In., Pair	1107.00
Table, Side, Pine, Maple, Red Paint, Drop Leaf, 2 Drawers, Octagonal Legs, c.1800s, 27 x 23 In.	2963.00
Table, Side, Pine, Painted, Reeded Edge, Beaded Skirt, Demilune Cutout Ends, c.1800, 31 x 35 In.	770.00
Table, Side, Regency, Mahogany, 3 Frieze Drawers, Tapered Legs, c.1805, 32 x 48 In.	875.00
Table, Side, Regency, Mahogany, Drawer, Brass Banding, Reeded Legs, Paw Feet, c.1815, 28 In.	861.00
Table, Side, Resin, Round Top, 3 Y-Shape Supports, White, J. Dickinson, 1970s, 22 x 20 In.	3250.00
Table, Side, Rohlfs, Wood, Flower Shape Top, Cutouts, Shaped Legs, Stretcher, c.1910, 26 x 26 In.	8125.00
Table, Side, Rosewood, Bamboo Molded Edge, Square Legs, Box Stretcher, 1800s, 34 x 36 In.	920.00
Table, Side, Rosewood, Inset Marble, Drawers, Pierced, Scrolls, Square Legs, 1800s, 52 x 36 In.	837.00
Table, Side, Rosewood, Marble Top, Lotus, Leaves, Pierced Apron, Paw Feet, c.1890, 18 x 16 In.	676.00
Table, Side, Rosewood, Marble Top, Pierced Frieze, Shelf, Mother-Of-Pearl Vine, 1800s, 31 x 16 In.	460.00
Table, Side, Rosewood, Round, Famille Verte, Flowers, Masks, Shelf, Frieze, 1800s, 32 x 27 In.	3680.00
Table, Side, Roycroft, Mahogany, Round, Square Legs, Mackmurdo Feet, c.1905, 30 x 36 In.	4063.00
Table, Side, Roycroft, Round, Rolled Rim Apron, Square Outcurved Legs, Marked, 30 x 36 In.	4375.00
Table, Side, Sheraton, Cherry, Pine, Drawer, Split Columns, Turned Legs, c.1835, 26 x 20 In.	382.00
Table, Side, Stickley Bros., 2 Drawers, Drop Leaves, Slats, Shelf Stretcher, c.1910, 28 x 18 In.	1875.00
Table, Side, Walnut, Cherry, Octagonal, Drawers, Acorn Drops, Baluster Shaft, c.1830, 29 x 24 In.	441.00
Table, Side, Walnut, Oval Marble Top, Column, Incised Line, 4 Feet, c.1865, 30 x 29 In.	246.00
Table, Side, Walnut, Turned Block Supports, Tapered Stem, Outswept Legs, c.1890, 29 x 32 In.	305.00
Table, Side, Walnut, White Paint, Round, Turned Legs, American, 1800s, 27 x 26 In.	1116.00
Table, Side, William & Mary, Walnut, Plank Top, Box Stretcher, Turned Legs, 1700s, 26 x 18 In.	518.00
Table, Steel, Ceramic Top, Crossed Legs, France, c.1970, 11 ¾ x 49 In.	375.00
Table, Steel, Gilt Metal, Glass Top, Jansen, France, c.1940, 17 ½ x 37 In.	2000.00
Table, Steel, Slate Top, c.1970, 16 x 41 In.	375.00
Table, Steel, Tile Inset, Italy, c.1970, 13 x 49 ½ In.	1375.00
Table, Stickley Bros., Octagonal, Low Shelf, Cross Stretcher, 26 x 26 In.	610.00
Table, Stickley Bros., Round, Square Legs, X-Stretcher, Disc Shelf, c.1910, 30 x 25 In.	2125.00
Table, Storage Basket Base, Woven Cane, Lid, Acrylic Inlay, Footed, Philippines, 1900s, 23 x 21 In.	180.00
Table, Storage Basket, Woven Cane, Round Lid, Acrylic Inlay, Philippines, 1900s, 23 x 21 In.	240.00
Table, Sugar Pine, 1-Board, Turned Legs, 1800s, 28 x 54 ½ In.	499.00
Table, Tailor's, Shaker, Birch, Pine, Red Wash, Overhanging Top, Drawers, 1830s, 33 x 99 In.	2000.00
Table, Tavern, Cherry, Overhang, Drawer, Vase & Ring-Turned Legs, c.1750, 27 x 29 In.	14220.00
Table, Tavern, Cherry, Overhang, Square Legs, Cutout Apron, c.1800, 26 x 35 In.	4700.00
Table, Tavern, Chippendale, Pine, Maple, 1-Board Oval Top, Ring & Baluster Frame, 25 x 28 In.	590.00
Table, Tavern, Maple, Demilune Leaves, Canted Apron, Splayed Legs, 1700s, 25 x 28 In.	470.00
Table, Tavern, Maple, Pine, Drawer, Overhang, Breadboard Ends, c.1750, 26 x 43 In.	1896.00
Table, Tavern, Maple, Pine, Overhang, Drawer, Turned Legs, Box Stretcher, c.1750, 26 x 42 In.	1320.00
Table, Tavern, Overhang, 2 Drawers, c.1810, 30 x 60 In.	1107.00
Table, Tavern, Pine, Breadboard Ends, Turned Legs, Stretcher Base, 24 x 37 In.	165.00
Table, Tavern, Pine, Breadboard Top, Drawer, c.1800, 30 x 30 In.	266.00
Table, Tavern, Pine, Maple, New England, c.1800, 25 ¼ x 45 In.	415.00
Table, Tavern, Pine, Maple, Overhang, Quarter Round Edge, Stretcher Base, 29 x 37 In.	3835.00
Table, Tavern, Pine, Maple, Red Paint, Overhanging Top, Turned Legs, Box Stretcher, 27 x 40 In.	1080.00
Table, Tavern, Pine, Overhang, Drawer, Beaded Skirt, Turned Legs, c.1750, 25 x 28 In.	9184.00
Table, Tavern, Pine, Round Top, Triangle Shelf, Tripod Base, England, 32 x 30 In.	348.00
Table, Tavern, Poplar, Overhang Top, Stretcher, Pa., 18th Century, 30 x 67 x 33 In.	948.00
Table, Tavern, Queen Anne Style, Drawer, Breadboard Top, Turned Legs, Box Stretcher, 27 x 33 In.	294.00
Table, Tavern, Queen Anne, Birch, Pine, Dovetailed Drawer, Breadboard Top, 1700s, 28 x 33 In.	558.00
Table, Tavern, Queen Anne, Maple, Cherry, Oval, Straight Legs, c.1760, 26 x 35 In.	590.00
Table, Tavern, Renaissance Style, Walnut, Plank Top, Baluster Columns, 1900s, 33 x 94 In.	1680.00
Table, Tavern, Teak, 2-Board Overhang, Dovetailed Drawer, Turned Legs, 1700s, 29 x 64 In.	472.00

Table, Tavern, Tilt Top, Round, 2-Pedestal Base, 4 Scroll Legs, c.1820, 43 x 38 In.	270.00
Table, Tavern, Walnut, Lift Top, Drawer, Splayed Legs, Button Feet, 29 x 34 In.	1185.00
Table, Tavern, William & Mary Style, Curly Maple, Turned Stretcher, 1900s, 28 x 30 In.	1058.00
Table, Tavern, William & Mary, Breadboard Ends, Turned Legs, Box Stretcher, 24 x 29 In.	1062.00
Table, Tavern, William & Mary, Maple, Scalloped Skirt, Splayed Legs, c.1780, 24 x 31 In.	2990.00
Table, Tavern, William & Mary, Walnut, 2-Board, Wood Pins, Drawers, Box Stretcher, 79 x 42 In.	2006.00
Table, Tea, Chippendale Style, Mahogany, Pierced Brass Gallery, Cabriole Legs, c.1935, 28 x 30 In.	353.00
Table, Tea, Chippendale Style, Ribbon Mahogany Veneer, Pinch Corners, Scrolled Feet, 42 x 31 In.	460.00
Table, Tea, Chippendale Style, Tilt Top, Carved, Round, Scrolls, Shells, Pedestal Base, 31 x 32 In.	357.00
Table, Tea, Chippendale Style, Tilt Top, Piecrust Edge, Carved, Tripod, 31 x 29 In.	178.00
Table, Tea, Chippendale, Mahogany, 1-Board, Round, Tripod Base, Carved Knees, 1700s, 29 x 29 In.	708.00
Table, Tea, Chippendale, Mahogany, Box Support, 3 Cabriole Legs, Pad Feet, c.1760, 27 In.	1920.00
Table, Tea, Chippendale, Mahogany, Dish Top, Leaf Carved, Tripod Feet, c.1765, 29 x 32 In.	1778.00
Table, Tea, Chippendale, Mahogany, Tilt Top, 1-Board, Baluster Shaft, Cabriole Legs, 1700s, 28 x 30 In.	241.00
Table, Tea, Chippendale, Mahogany, Tilt Top, 3 Cabriole Legs, c.1780, 46 x 28 In.	863.00
Table, Tea, Chippendale, Mahogany, Tilt Top, Tripod Base, Column, Birdcage, 1700s, 29 x 40 In.	382.00
Table, Tea, Chippendale, Mahogany, Tilt Top, Urn Shaft, Cabriole Legs, c.1790, 28 x 35 In.	323.00
Table, Tea, Chippendale, Maple, Tilt Top, Tripod Base, 18th Century, 26 x 29 In.	413.00
Table, Tea, Chippendale, Piecrust Top, Birdcage, Fluted Column, Tripod, 1800s, 47 x 32 In.	480.00
Table, Tea, Chippendale, Tilt Top, Column & Vase Stem, Tripod Legs, 29 x 25 In.	497.00
Table, Tea, Chippendale, Walnut, Tilt Dish Top, Birdcage, Ball, Arched Legs, c.1795, 30 x 34 In.	1315.00
Table, Tea, Federal, Mahogany, Tilt Top, Parquetry, Twisted Reeded Stem, Tripod, c.1825, 29 x 28 In.	660.00
Table, Tea, George II Style, Walnut, Satinwood, Banded, Dish Top, Hoof Feet, 1800s, 31 x 31 In.	750.00
Table, Tea, George II, Mahogany, Gateleg, c.1750, 28 x 33 ½ In.	2500.00
Table, Tea, George III Style, Mahogany, Dish Top, Drawer, Cabriole Legs, Pad Feet, 29 x 31 In.	430.00
Table, Tea, George III Style, Mahogany, Dish Top, Fret Carved, Ball & Claw Feet, 27 x 27 In.	492.00
Table, Tea, George III, Mahogany, Banded, Demilune, Shaped Apron, Spade Feet, c.1800, 30 x 36 In.	500.00
Table, Tea, George III, Mahogany, Round Tilt Top, Vase Stem, Spider Legs, 1700s, 29 x 23 In.	244.00
Table, Tea, George III, Mahogany, Tilt Piecrust Top, Carved Tripod Legs, Urn, 1700s, 28 x 30 In.	2000.00
Table, Tea, George III, Mahogany, Tilt Top, Tripod Legs, Pad Feet, 28 x 33 In.	234.00
Table, Tea, Georgian, Mahogany, Tilt Top, Birdcage, Arched Legs, Pad Feet, 1700s, 38 x 35 In.	1107.00
Table, Tea, Georgian, Walnut, Tilt Top, Round, Tapered Stem, Pad Feet, 1700s, 27 x 32 In.	299.00
Table, Tea, Kingwood, Ormolu, Tray Top, Carved Legs, France, c.1905, 22 x 25 In.	2750.00
Table, Tea, Kittinger, Chippendale, Mahogany, Piecrust Edge, Birdcage, 30 x 37 In.	1725.00
Table, Tea, Maple, Pine, Painted, Beaded Apron, Box Stretchers, Block Legs, 1700s, 27 x 26 In.	3081.00
Table, Tea, Maple, Round Overhanging Top, Ring-Turned Legs, New England, c.1790, 25 x 31 In.	2133.00
Table, Tea, Queen Anne Style, Candle Slides, Shaped Apron, E. Wheeler, c.1985, 28 x 27 In.	944.00
Table, Tea, Queen Anne Style, Curly Maple, Tray Top, Candle Slides, E. Wheeler, c.1980, 27 x 28 In.	844.00
Table, Tea, Queen Anne Style, Mahogany, Arched Frieze, Shells, Cabriole Legs, 1800s, 29 x 32 In.	430.00
Table, Tea, Queen Anne Style, Mahogany, Tilt Top, Tripod Cabriole Legs, 1800s, 10 x 9 In.	582.00
Table, Tea, Queen Anne Style, Mahogany, Tray Top, Candle Slides, Scalloped, c.1950, 27 x 18 In.	783.00
Table, Tea, Queen Anne Style, Mahogany, Tray Top, Scroll Apron, Cabriole Legs, c.1895, 27 x 29 In.	1880.00
Table, Tea, Queen Anne Style, Maple, Tray Top, Drawer, E. Wheeler, 31 x 32 In.	1888.00
Table, Tea, Queen Anne Style, Walnut, Gateleg, Round, Cabriole Legs, 1900s, 27 x 30 ½ In.	360.00
Table, Tea, Queen Anne, Cherry, Round, Tripod Base, c.1770, 28 x 35 In.	237.00
Table, Tea, Queen Anne, Cherry, Tilt Top, Round, Vase & Ring-Turned Support, 1700s, 29 x 36 In.	889.00
Table, Tea, Queen Anne, Drop Leaf, Black Paint, Round, Cabriole Legs, Shaped Apron, 27 x 36 In.	2370.00
Table, Tea, Queen Anne, Mahogany, Scalloped Apron, New England, 27 x 30 In.	2790.00
Table, Tea, Queen Anne, Maple, Oval Top, Drawer, c.1795, 27 x 35 In.	2133.00
Table, Tea, Queen Anne, Maple, Oval, Cutout Apron, Turned Legs, Pad Feet, c.1795, 26 x 32 In.	533.00
Table, Tea, Queen Anne, Porringer Top, Turned Legs, Offset Pad Feet, R.I., 26 x 32 In.	4484.00
Table, Tea, Queen Anne, Tilt Top, Cherry, Round, Birdcage Standard, Cabriole Legs, 27 x 27 In.	118.00
Table, Tea, Queen Anne, Walnut, Round, Birdcage, Tripod, Chester Country, Pa., c.1760, 29 x 35 In.	1304.00
Table, Tea, Rosewood, Carved, Pierced Skirt, Berries & Vines, Cabriole Legs, 20 x 25 In.	177.00
Table, Tea, Roycroft, Round, Square Legs, X-Stretcher, Disc, Marked, c.1905, 24 x 23 In.	3000.00
Table, Tea, Tilt Top, George III, Mahogany, Square, Urn Standard, c.1770, 28 x 29 In.	267.00
Table, Tea, Tilt Top, Mahogany, 2-Board, Round, Turned Pedestal, Tripod, c.1800, 27 x 31 In.	235.00
Table, Tea, Tilt Top, Mahogany, Round, Piecrust Edge, Ring-Turned Post, c.1795, 29 x 30 In.	2015.00
Table, Tea, Tilt Top, Mahogany, Square, Indented Corners, Vase & Ring Support, c.1798, 28 x 33 In.	480.00
Table, Tea, Tilt Top, Walnut, Birdcage, Baluster, Cabriole Legs, Pad Feet, Pa., 1700s, 28 x 33 In.	441.00
Table, Tea, Vinhatico, Tilt Top, Scalloped, Fluted Pedestal, Cabriole Legs, 30 x 27 In.	472.00
Table, Telephone, Tortoiseshell Leather Veneer, Spiral Legs, W. Haines, Stergis, c.1950, 31 x 14 In.	3750.00
Table, Tiger Maple, Cherry, 2 Drawers, Turned Legs, c.1845, 29 x 24 In.	518.00
Table, Tile Top, Blue, Green, Low Stretcher, Charles Volkmar, 34 x 22 In.	458.00
Table, Tile Top, Native American On Horseback, Taylor, California, 1920s, 19 x 25 ½ x 18 In. ...Illus	2375.00

Furniture, Table, Sewing, Neoclassical, Satinwood Inlay, Half Round, Tambour Door, c.1815, 31 x 25 In.
$20,913.00

Neal Auction Co.

Furniture, Table, Shaker, Birch, 1-Board Top, Front Drawer, 2 Drawers On End, c.1835, 26 x 32 In.
$14,040.00

Willis Henry Auctions, Inc.

Furniture, Table, Tile Top, Native American On Horseback, Taylor, California, 1920s, 19 x 25 ½ x 18 In.
$2,375.00

Rago Arts & Auction Center

Furniture, Table, Tray, Stand, Mahogany, Faux Bamboo, Chinoiserie, Folding, 1800s, 20 x 28 In.
$177.00

Brunk Auctions

Furniture, Table, Writing, Renaissance Revival, Mahogany, Drawers, Wreath, Ohio, 1880s, 30 x 42 In. $826.00

Brunk Auctions

Furniture, Tabouret, Roycroft, Oak, Mouse Hole, Carved Orb & Cross, N.Y., c.1905, 20 ½ x 15 In. $3,125.00

Rago Arts & Auction Center

Furniture, Umbrella Stand, Arts & Crafts, Oak, 6-Sided, Cutout Sides, Removable Cover, c.1912, 28 In. $444.00

Skinner, Inc.

Furniture, Umbrella Stand, Fornasetti, Painted, Lithograph Transfer, Brass, 1950s, 22 x 10 In. $1,625.00

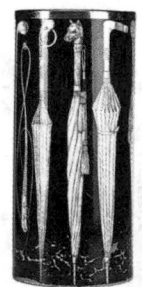

Rago Arts & Auction Center

Table, Tile Top, Round, 12 Zodiac Medallions, Tapered Square Legs, Leaf, 31 In. Diam.	369.00
Table, Tilt Top, Biedermeier, Burl, Ebonized, Tripod, Spayed Legs, 1800s, 28 x 24 In.	399.00
Table, Tilt Top, Chippendale Style, Mahogany, Piecrust Edge, Acanthus Pedestal, 27 In. Diam.	259.00
Table, Tilt Top, Chippendale Style, Mahogany, Piecrust Edge, Birdcage Support, c.1790, 29 x 34 In..	615.00
Table, Tilt Top, Chippendale, Walnut, Tripod Base, Cabriole Legs, Turned Column, 1700s, 29 x 38 In.	5875.00
Table, Tilt Top, Federal, Mahogany, Octagonal Top, Tripod Base, c.1790, 30 x 22 In.	237.00
Table, Tilt Top, Federal, Mahogany, Tripod Legs, c.1810, 28 ¼ x 18 ¼ In.	518.00
Table, Tilt Top, Hepplewhite, Mahogany, Pedestal Standard, Splayed Legs, 27 x 18 In.	130.00
Table, Tilt Top, Louis XVI Style, Mahogany, Marble, Round, Brass Edge, Tripod Base, 28 x 26 In.	1287.00
Table, Tilt Top, Mahogany, Gallery, Rectangle, 3 Cabriole Legs, c.1750, 24 x 30 In.	295.00
Table, Tilt Top, Mahogany, Inlay, Urn Pedestal, Turned Standard, Cabriole Legs, Oval, 29 x 56 In.	944.00
Table, Tilt Top, Mahogany, Piecrust Top, 3 Columns, Tripod Base, England, c.1850, 28 x 36 In.	1062.00
Table, Tilt Top, Mahogany, Round, Turned Pedestal, Tripod Base, Snake Feet, 28 x 36 In.	212.00
Table, Tilt Top, Mahogany, Tripod Base, North Carolina, 1700s, 28 x 36 In.	2070.00
Table, Tilt Top, Mother-Of-Pearl Inlay, Painted Flowers, Gold Scrolling Leaves, 1800s, 40 x 22 In.	243.00
Table, Tilt Top, Oak, Octagonal, Painted Scenic Rondel, Tripod Legs, 26 ½ x 26 In.	644.00
Table, Tilt Top, Papier-Mache, Flowers, Tiered Standard, Domed Foot, Oval, c.1870, 26 x 25 ½ In.	344.00
Table, Tilt Top, Papier-Mache, Mother-Of-Pearl Inlay, Scenes, Painted, Victorian, 41 In.	179.00
Table, Tilt Top, Rosewood, Round, Scroll Feet, c.1875, 28 x 48 In.	3600.00
Table, Tilt Top, Sheraton, Mahogany, Shaped Top, Fluted Shaft, Spider Legs, c.1830, 28 x 23 In.	127.00
Table, Tray Top, Biedermeier, Elm, Canted, Inlaid Star, Tapered Legs, Stretcher, c.1900, 28 x 36 In.	861.00
Table, Tray, Edwardian, Mahogany, Oval, Brass Gallery, Chamfered Legs, 21 x 29 In.	369.00
Table, Tray, Mahogany, Fold Down Sides, 19 x 31 ½ x 21 ½ In.	561.00
Table, Tray, Mahogany, Hinged Top, Molded Edge, X-Shape Legs, Folding, 1800s, 28 x 36 In.	652.00
Table, Tray, Mahogany, Silver Plate, Pierced Gallery, X-Stretcher, Square Legs, c.1950, 22 x 25 In.	922.00
Table, Tray, Stand, Black Lacquer, Flowers, Rope Twist Border, Cabriole Legs, 18 x 34 In.	1500.00
Table, Tray, Stand, Mahogany, Faux Bamboo, Chinoiserie, Folding, 1800s, 20 x 28 In. ....*Illus*	177.00
Table, Tray, Stand, Papier-Mache, Lacquer, Gilt, Pagodas, Phoenix, Turned Legs, c.1860, 32 x 18 In.	480.00
Table, Tray, Stand, Papier-Mache, Shaped Oval, John Bardon & Sons, London, c.1870, 21 x 32 In.	531.00
Table, Trestle, Arts & Crafts, Ash, Low Stretchers, Shoefoot Base, 73 x 45 In.	1830.00
Table, Trestle, Chip Carved Frieze, Scrollwork, Shaped Feet, Italy, 1800s, 35 x 76 In.	851.00
Table, Trestle, Jacobean Style, Oak, Plank Top, Carved Frieze, Turned Legs, Bun Feet, 32 x 72 In.	1216.00
Table, Trestle, Renaissance Style, Walnut, Plank Top, Splayed Scrolls, Iron Stretchers, 30 ½ In.	837.00
Table, Trestle, Walnut, Plank Top, Curved Iron Supports, Italy, 17th Century, 33 x 43 In.	1300.00
Table, V. Kagan, Aluminum, Venetian Glass Tiles, Round, Cylindrical Base, 1950s, 14 x 31 In.	6875.00
Table, V. Kagan, Walnut, Glass Mosaic Tile, Box Shape, Cylindrical Base, 1950s, 19 32 In.	2500.00
Table, Van Keppel & Green, Camel, Double Box Supports, Adjustable, c.1946, 15 x 67 In.	3750.00
Table, Victorian Style, Cast Iron, Scalloped, Pierced, Round, Griffin Tripod, 1900s, 21 x 20 In.	369.00
Table, Victorian, Japanned, Black, Gilt, Stretcher, Carved Legs, c.1850, 30 x 41 In.	1250.00
Table, Victorian, Mahogany, Tilt Top, Carved Edge, Acanthus Pedestal, Scroll Feet, 31 x 52 In.	826.00
Table, Victorian, Oak, Pedestal, Round, Reeded Column, Scroll Legs, Leaves, 30 x 44 In.	316.00
Table, Victorian, Oak, Round, Barley Twist Stem, Tripod, Splayed Scroll Legs, c.1865, 29 In.	553.00
Table, Victorian, Tilt Top, Castle, Riverscape, Painted, Black, Gilt Base, 27 x 22 In.	189.00
Table, Victorian, Turtle Marble Top, Carved Apron, Legs, Base Finial, 30 x 32 In.	560.00
Table, Victorian, Walnut, Burl, Tilt Top, Scalloped Oval, England, c.1850, 36 ½ x 50 In.	403.00
Table, Victorian, Walnut, Marble Top, Carved Scrolls, Urns, Round, 27 x 31 In.	189.00
Table, Victorian, Walnut, Marble Top, Carved, Base Stretcher, 29 x 34 In.	266.00
Table, Victorian, Wood, Carved, Marble Top, Round, 4 Scroll Legs, 30 x 42 In.	200.00
Table, W. Platner, Wood Top, Black Wire Base, Round, Knoll, 18 x 19 In.	244.00
Table, Walnut, 3 Drawers, Carved Barley Twist Legs, Stretcher, 3 Drawers, 47 ½ x 32 ½ In.	510.00
Table, Walnut, 3 Drawers, Scalloped Skirt, Turned Legs, Stretcher, c.1750, 29 x 59 In.	649.00
Table, Walnut, 3 Drawers, Stenciled Knobs, Pa., c.1855, 30 x 22 ½ In.	415.00
Table, Walnut, Berry, Leaf Carved Rim, Round, 3 Fluted Legs, 26 x 20 In.	3163.00
Table, Walnut, Block Inlaid Top, Scalloped Apron, Splayed Legs, Pa., c.1790, 28 x 24 In.	4977.00
Table, Walnut, Gilt Incised Skirt, Base, Carved Legs, c.1875, 30 x 77 In.	148.00
Table, Walnut, Inlay, Leather Top, 3 Frieze Drawers, Gilt Bronze Mounts, 30 x 59 In.	2000.00
Table, Walnut, Inlay, Stringing, Oval Top, Baluster Supports, Finial, c.1850, 28 x 53 In.	1195.00
Table, Walnut, Marble Specimen Top, Round, C-Scroll Supports, Pedestal, 1800s, 24 x 32 In.	3884.00
Table, Walnut, Molded Edge, Shaped Supports, Iron Stretchers, Italy, 22 x 31 In.	575.00
Table, Walnut, Parquetry, Marble Top, Gilt Metal Mounts, 5 Drawers, 32 x 14 In., Pair	2000.00
Table, Walnut, Plank Top, Shaped Skirt, Cabriole Legs, Pad Feet, 1700s, 31 x 34 In.	2271.00
Table, Wicker, Red Paint, Round, Cross Stretcher Base, 21 x 28 In.	136.00
Table, William & Mary Style, Burl Walnut, Gateleg, Oval, Demilune, Trestle, c.1850, 28 x 40 In.	533.00
Table, William & Mary Style, Walnut, Inlay, Frieze Drawer, X-Stretcher, c.1850, 28 x 42 In.	625.00
Table, William & Mary, Pine, Drawer, Turned Legs, Stretcher, c.1750, 28 ½ x 29 In.	486.00

F

Table, William & Mary, Spindle Carved Gateleg, 2 Drawers, c.1730, 28 ½ x 17 ½ In.		3792.00
Table, William & Mary, Walnut, Gateleg, Oval Top, Triangle Base, Pa., c.1700, 28 x 33 In.		14220.00
Table, William IV, Mahogany, Carved, Scroll Terminals, Turned Feet, 1840, 36 x 53 In.		1075.00
Table, Wine, Fruitwood, Round Tilt Top, Block Supports, Trestle Base, 1800s, 30 x 41 In.		896.00
Table, Wine, George III, Mahogany, Tilt Top, Gallery For Wine Bottles, c.1735, 31 In.		922.00
Table, Wolfgang Hoffman, Lacquer, Red Top, Chrome Base, 18 x 20 ½ In.		610.00
Table, Wood Top, Painted, Cast Iron, Serpentine Shell Apron, c.1880, 33 x 47 In.		3840.00
Table, Wood, Carved, Pierced, Marble Inset, Foo Dog Support, Round, Asian, 32 x 22 In.		2006.00
Table, Wood, Marble Top, Drawer, Iron Tubular Legs & Stretcher, 24 x 24 In., Pair		600.00
Table, Wood, Overhang, Red Paint, Drawer, c.1750, 42 ½ x 29 In.		3565.00
Table, Wood, Rectangular Top, Lyre Support, 4 Splayed Legs, 28 x 15 ½ In., Pair		154.00
Table, Wood, Red & Gold Paint, Profile Cut Legs, Stretchers, Chinese, 79 x 32 In.		212.00
Table, Wormley, Ebonized, Round, 2 Tiers, Tripod Base, Dunbar, c.1955, 28 In.		1750.00
Table, Wormley, Patinated Metal, Blue Tile Top, Dunbar, c.1955, 16 x 45 In.		6250.00
Table, Wormley, Walnut, Birch, Brass, Round Top, Tapered Stem, Tripod Base, 1940s, 25 In.		2375.00
Table, Wormley, Walnut, Brass, Rectangular, Shelf, H-Stretcher, Block Legs, c.1952, 15 ½ x 66 In.		875.00
Table, Wormley, Walnut, Marble Top, Sheaf Of Wheat Base, Dunbar, 1960s, 21 x 20 ½ In.		688.00
Table, Writing, Brushed Steel, Veneer, Gilt Leather, Drawers, Block Feet, 31 x 63 In.		3444.00
Table, Writing, Ebonized, Burl, Roundels, Trestle Base, Brass Finial, c.1850, 34 x 48 In.		2460.00
Table, Writing, Elm, 2 Drawers, Molded Apron, Square Legs, Chinese, c.1890, 31 x 40 In.		353.00
Table, Writing, George III Style, Mahogany, Drawers, Cabriole Legs, c.1900, 33 x 63 In.		1353.00
Table, Writing, George III Style, Mahogany, Inset Leather, 3 Drawers, Tapered Legs, 30 x 60 In.		2706.00
Table, Writing, George III Style, Mahogany, Leather, 2 Drawers, Tapered Legs, c.1900, 30 x 46 In.		338.00
Table, Writing, George III, Mahogany, Bowed Top, Frieze Drawer, c.1800, 28 x 30 In.		478.00
Table, Writing, Gothic Revival, Ebonized, Oak, Drop Finials, Arched Legs, c.1850, 30 x 40 In.		7469.00
Table, Writing, Louis XV Style, Burl Satinwood, Bronze, 3 Drawers, Cabriole Legs, 32 x 63 In.		1180.00
Table, Writing, Louis XV, Walnut, Leather, Frieze, Drawer, Hoof Feet, c.1790, 29 x 44 In.		1845.00
Table, Writing, Oak, Crossbanded, Tooled Leather, Square Legs, c.1930, 31 x 79 In.		1800.00
Table, Writing, Queen Anne Style, Oak, Drawer, Overhang Top, Pad Feet, 1900s, 28 x 28 In.		531.00
Table, Writing, Queen Anne, Walnut, 3 Drawers, Cabriole Legs, Slipper Feet, 27 x 30 In.		2750.00
Table, Writing, Renaissance Revival, Mahogany, Drawers, Wreath, Ohio, 1880s, 30 x 42 In.	*Illus*	826.00
Table, Writing, William IV Style, Mahogany, 2 Drawers, Turned Legs, 1900s, 30 x 48 In.		861.00
Table, Writing, William IV Style, Mahogany, Banded, Drawers, Turned Legs, 31 x 60 In.		2091.00
Table, Writing, William IV, Amboyna Veneer, Calamander Band, 3 Drawers, c.1840, 29 x 45 In.		5520.00
Table, Wrought Iron, Marble Top, Scrolled Base, Apron, c.1930, 31 x 68 In.		2600.00
Table, Wrought Iron, Matte Glaze Ceramic Tile Top, Scrolling Base, 24 x 14 In.		299.00
Table, Yew, Plank Top, Trestle, Splayed Legs, Wrought Iron Stretcher, c.1900, 30 x 79 In.		2952.00
Tabouret, G. Stickley, Cut Corners, Grueby Inset Tile, X-Stretcher, 22 x 17 In.		13750.00
Tabouret, G. Stickley, Round Top, Cross Stretcher Base, Signed Decal, 18 x 19 In.		488.00
Tabouret, G. Stickley, Round, Notched Cross Stretcher Base, 18 x 19 In.		400.00
Tabouret, G. Stickley, Wood, Clip Corner, Square Seat, X-Stretcher, c.1902, 22 x 17 In.		6875.00
Tabouret, L. & J.G. Stickley, Octagonal Seat, Square Legs, X-Stretcher, c.1912, 20 x 18 In.		1188.00
Tabouret, Red Lacquered, Round, Dragon, Greek Key Border, Pierced Frieze, Shelf, c.1900, 30 In.		184.00
Tabouret, Regency Style, Mahogany, Upholstered Seat, Shaped Supports, Stretcher, 18 x 21 In.		344.00
Tabouret, Rosewood, Hexagonal, Cloisonne, Fretwork, Bun Feet, c.1950, 19 x 16 In., Pair		1230.00
Tabouret, Rosewood, Marble Inset, Carved, Lobed, Openwork Aprons, Paw Feet, 18 x 17 In.		161.00
Tabouret, Rosewood, Marble Top, Beaded Rim, Pierced Frieze, Ball & Claw Feet, c.1900, 18 In.		273.00
Tabouret, Rosewood, Round Marble Top, Pierced, X-Stretcher, Paw Feet, c.1890, 19 In.		461.00
Tabouret, Roycroft, Oak, Mouse Hole, Carved Orb & Cross, N.Y., c.1905, 20 ½ x 15 In.	*Illus*	3125.00
Tabouret, Roycroft, Overhang, Box Stretcher, Block Legs, Marked, c.1907, 19 x 12 In.		1375.00
Tabouret, Stickley Bros., No. 314, Round, 3 Legs, c.1905, 18 x 15 In.		1500.00
Tabouret, William Haines, Revolving, Upholstered, Prentice, c.1960, 13 x 19 In.		500.00
Tea Cart, Aalto, Birch, Laminate, 2 Tiers, 2 Front Wheels, c.1950, 31 x 34 In.		3750.00
Tea Cart, Aalto, Birch, Laminated, Painted, Wheels, 2 Shelves, Finland, 1930s, 22 x 36 In.		4688.00
Tea Cart, Brass, Glass Shelves, 2 Tiers, Rounded Corners, Beaded Edge, Reeded Handles, 25 x 28 In.		430.00
Tea Cart, Edwardian, Mahogany, Brass Gallery, Shelves, Tambour Door, c.1900, 28 x 35 In.		2706.00
Tea Cart, Mahogany, 3 Tiers, Backsplash, Turned Supports, Casters, 42 x 48 In.		1098.00
Umbrella Stand, Arts & Crafts, Oak, 6-Sided, Cutout Sides, Removable Cover, c.1912, 28 In.	*Illus*	444.00
Umbrella Stand, Arts & Crafts, Wood, Painted Panel, Tiled, Spindles, c.1900, 50 x 29 In.		1250.00
Umbrella Stand, Bear, Fruitwood, c.1910, 37 In.		1250.00
Umbrella Stand, Black Forest, Bear, Holding Branch, c.1880, 32 In.		2243.00
Umbrella Stand, Black Forest, Bear, On Rockwork, c.1880, 32 In.		2243.00
Umbrella Stand, Brass, Squared, Canted Corners, Lion Mask, Ring Handles, 22 x 10 ½ In.		138.00
Umbrella Stand, Cast Iron, Ornate Scrolls, Divided Drip Pans, 31 x 34 In.		960.00
Umbrella Stand, Cast Iron, Sailor, Holding Rope, On Anchor, Dolphins, 1800s, 27 x 15 In.		460.00
Umbrella Stand, Cast Iron, Sailor, On Pedestal, Anchor, Bales, Rope, c.1875, 28 x 18 In.		1298.00

Furniture, Vanity, M. Graves, Briar, Lacquer, Glass, Brass, Upholstery, Memphis Milano, 95 x 55 In. $20,000.00

Rago Arts & Auction Center

Furniture, Vitrine, Adam Style, Satinwood, 4-Sided, Glass Shelf, 2 Doors, Painted, 1900s, 86 x 43 In. $4,956.00

Brunk Auctions

TIP
You can cover up a scratch or ding on a piece of furniture with a felt-tip marker.

Furniture, Vitrine, Louis XV Style, Mahogany, Corner, Inlay, 62 x 28 In. $360.00

DuMouchelles Art Gallery

Furniture, Wagon Seat, Grain, Wood & Iron $392.00

Victorian Casino Antiques

Furniture, Wardian Case, Gothic Revival, Iron, Glazed Panels, Finial, Pierced Base, c.1850, 36 x 18 In. $5,795.00

Neal Auction Co.

Umbrella Stand, Corner, Eastlake, Walnut, Cutouts, Metal Tray, C.B. Blake, 1870, 42 x 18 In...	1150.00
Umbrella Stand, Cow Horn, Brass, Holding Loops, Base Tray, c.1900, 34 In............................	2530.00
Umbrella Stand, Cutout Back, Brass Drip Pan, 10 x 10 x 30 In..	305.00
Umbrella Stand, Fornasetti, Painted, Lithograph Transfer, Brass, 1950s, 22 x 10 In. .....*Illus*	1625.00
Umbrella Stand, Gothic Revival, Oak, Carved, Tracery, Scroll Arms, Inset Metal Pan, c.1850, 36 In.	244.00
Umbrella Stand, Marquetry, Walnut, Tulipwood, Leaf Design, Metal Liner, Galle, c.1900, 27 In.	5313.00
Umbrella Stand, Roycroft, Square, Slatted, c.1905, 30 x 12 In.	2000.00
Vanity, M. Graves, Briar, Lacquer, Glass, Brass, Upholstery, Memphis Milano, 95 x 55 In. .....*Illus*	20000.00
Vanity, Rohde, Rosewood, Glass, 4 Drawers, 4 Lidded Compartments, Herman Miller, 56 x 18 In..	2750.00
Vanity, Roycroft, Mirror, Square Supports & Legs, Drawer, Marked, c.1905, 56 x 39 In.	1875.00
Vitrine, Adam Style, Satinwood, 4-Sided, Glass Shelf, 2 Doors, Painted, 1900s, 86 x 43 In. ... *Illus*	4956.00
Vitrine, Biedermeier, Burl, Peaked Cornice, Glazed Door & Sides, Mirror, 65 x 31 In...............	1625.00
Vitrine, Chrome, Glass, Door, 4 Interior Shelves, Flared Legs, 67 x 21 In...............................	1560.00
Vitrine, Edwardian, Mahogany, Breakfront, Glass Case, Cock-Beaded, c.1900, 71 x 39 In.	3200.00
Vitrine, Edwardian, Mahogany, Pagoda Shaped, Glazed Door, Drawer, Stand, c.1885, 66 x 29 In. .	492.00
Vitrine, Empire Style, Mahogany, Frieze, Glass Doors, Shelves, Brass, Ormolu, 73 x 67 In.	1722.00
Vitrine, Empire Style, Mahogany, Palmetto Cornice, Brass, Glass Doors, Pilasters, 73 x 67 In.	1722.00
Vitrine, French Provincial, Openwork Cornice, Doors, Flower Basket, c.1900, 80 x 58 In.........	3198.00
Vitrine, George III Style, Pagoda Shape Back, Glazed Door, Square Legs, Gilt, 71 x 27 In.	922.00
Vitrine, George III, Mahogany, 4 Shelves, Glass Door, R.J. Horner, c.1900, 66 x 30 In..............	1063.00
Vitrine, Louis XV Style, Mahogany, Bowed, Painted, Courtiers, Drawer, c.1900, 65 x 27 In.	1107.00
Vitrine, Louis XV Style, Mahogany, Brass, Hinged Top, Cabriole Legs, c.1900, 30 x 43 In..........	461.00
Vitrine, Louis XV Style, Mahogany, Corner, Inlay, 62 x 28 In. ....*Illus*	360.00
Vitrine, Louis XV Style, Mahogany, Pierced Brass Gallery, Glass Top, c.1900, 40 x 19 In.	767.00
Vitrine, Louis XV Style, Marble, Parquetry, Shaped Apron, Cabriole Legs, 1900s, 64 x 28 In.....	295.00
Vitrine, Louis XVI Style, Gilt, Demilune, Beaded, Gadrooned, Bellflowers, 54 x 25 In.	1000.00
Vitrine, Louis XVI Style, Gilt, Peak Crest, Carved, Leaves, Shells, Courting Couple, 70 x 32 In.	2000.00
Vitrine, Louis XVI Style, Mahogany, Hinged Glass Panel, Brass Banding, Stretcher, 30 x 31 In...	615.00
Vitrine, Louis XVI Style, Mahogany, Ormolu, Glass Door, Shelves, Tapered Legs, c.1900, 53 x 23 In.	180.00
Vitrine, Louis XVI Style, Parcel Gilt, Carved Frieze, Glazed Doors, Square Legs, 63 x 62 In.......	3750.00
Vitrine, Marble Top, Top Drawer, 2 Door, c.1800, 61 x 36 ½ In.	668.00
Vitrine, Parcel Gilt, Painted, Glazed Door, Carved Bellflowers, Mirrored Interior, 23 In............	191.00
Vitrine, Regency Style, Mahogany, Lift Table Top, Lotus Carved Frieze, 31 x 47 In....................	430.00
Vitrine, Tulipwood, Gilt, Bombe, Arched Crest, Urn Finials, Glazed Door, Spain, 77 x 44 In.	448.00
Vitrine, Vernis Martin, Brass Gallery, Curved Glass Sides, Painted Couples, France, 60 x 39 In. .	978.00
Vitrine, Walnut, 2 Glass Doors, Bombe Base, 4 Drawers, Bracket Feet, c.1975, 79 x 84 In.	3000.00
Vitrine, Walnut, Glazed Top, Tufted Silk Back Panel, Ball & Claw Feet, 37 x 49 In....................	1891.00
Vitrine, Wood, Florentine Carved, Glass Shelves, Turned Legs, c.1880, 58 x 43 In.	8050.00
Wagon Seat, Grain, Wood & Iron ....*Illus*	392.00
Wall Bracket, Oak, Carved, Eagle Shape, Dark Stain, Germany, 18 ¼ x 19 ¼ In.	205.00
Wall Storage, Mid Century Modern, Teak Veneer, Drawers, Double Doors, Shelves, 21 x 32 In..	608.00
Wall Unit, Scandinavian, Teak Veneer, Metal, 3 Piece, Drawers, Cabinet, Shelf, 81 x 44 In.	304.00
Wardian Case, Gothic Revival, Iron, Glazed Panels, Finial, Pierced Base, c.1850, 36 x 18 In. ...*Illus*	5795.00
Wardrobe, 2 Doors, Grain Painted, Pa., c.1850, 82 x 54 In.	267.00
Wardrobe, Edwardian, Mahogany, Dentil Cornice, Paneled Doors, Banding, c.1900, 78 x 59 In.	492.00
Wardrobe, Mahogany, Panel Doors, Drawers, Mirrored Doors, c.1835, 86 x 86 In....................	1250.00
Wardrobe, Pine, 2 Doors, 2 Drawers, Diamond Panels, Pediment, c.1850, 93 x 85 In. .....*Illus*	2892.00
Wardrobe, Schrank, Painted Flowers, Leaves, Blue Ground, Door, 1826, 74 x 41 In.................	3081.00
Wardrobe, Victorian, Burl Walnut, Mirror Door, 2 Side Doors, c.1900, 86 x 90 In.	1638.00
Wash Stand, Shaker, Gallery Top, 2 Drawers, 2 Doors, Turned Legs, c.1850, 31 x 22 In..........	1304.00
Washstand, Cherry, Scalloped Backsplash, Drawer, Shelf, Turned Feet, c.1835, 31 x 18 In.	264.00
Washstand, Corner, Federal, Mahogany, Drawer, 2 False Drawers, 1800s, 44 In. ....*Illus*	360.00
Washstand, Corner, Federal, Mahogany, Gallery, Basin Cutout, Drawer, c.1830, 44 x 22 In.....	160.00
Washstand, Corner, Mahogany, Carved Backsplash, Shelf, Drawer, England, 45 x 29 In..........	185.00
Washstand, Corner, Mahogany, Drawer, Shelf Stretcher, c.1950, 50 x 28 In............................	540.00
Washstand, Empire, Pine, Flame Grain Painted, c.1850, 37 ¼ x 20 In...................................	178.00
Washstand, Federal, Cherry, Gallery, Drawer, Turned Supports, Shelf Stretcher, 31 x 20 In.....	117.00
Washstand, Gothic Revival, Mahogany, Serpentine Marble Top, Paneled Doors, c.1840, 32 x 33 In.	2749.00
Washstand, Mahogany, Marble Top, Cyma Frieze, Cupboards, Mirror, c.1835, 32 x 36 In........	1107.00
Washstand, Mahogany, Marble Top, Drawer, S-Scroll Supports, Shelf, c.1835, 30 x 28 In.	399.00
Washstand, Mahogany, Marble Top, Pewter Bowl, 2 Drawers, England, c.1860, 36 x 36 In.	1140.00
Washstand, Maple, Rolling Pine Backsplash, Cutouts For Glasses, Richmond, Va., 1840s	495.00
Washstand, Pine, Faux Marble Backsplash, Top, Shelf, Drawers, Turned Legs, c.1835, 40 x 36 In.	236.00
Washstand, Sheraton, Gallery, Flowers, Tole & Mustard Paint, 17 x 16 In.	136.00
Washstand, Sheraton, Grain Painted, Splash Guard, Cutout, Shelf, Maine, c.1830, 41 x 20 In.	920.00
Washstand, Sheraton, Mahogany, Drop Leaf, Lift Top, Bowl, Tumbler, Drawer, 29 x 17 In.......	81.00
Washstand, Sheraton, Mahogany, Hinged, Slant Top, Drawer, c.1810, 41 x 24 In....................	617.00

Washstand, Sheraton, Tiger Maple, Backsplash, Drawer, Turned Legs, 1800s, 36 x 17 In.	180.00
Washstand, Victorian, Mahogany, Gallery, Marble, 2 Doors, England, c.1900, 34 x 42 In.	127.00
Wastebasket, G. Stickley, Slatted, Riveted Iron Hoop, Signed Paper Label, 12 x 14 In.	2000.00
Whatnot Shelf, Regency Style, Mahogany, Shelves, Turned Supports, Drawer, 1900s, 42 x 19 In.	590.00
Whatnot Shelf, Regency, Mahogany, 3 Shelves, 6 Drawers, Turned Supports, 1900s, 66 x 20 In.	590.00
Whatnot Shelf, Victorian, Black Lacquer, Brass, Gallery Top, 3 Shelves, Lyre Supports, 46 x 36 In.	1814.00
Window Seat, Empire Style, Gilt Painted, Cane, Pierced Lyre Shape Rolled Ends, 26 x 44 In.	472.00
Window Seat, George III Style, Mahogany, Box Shape, Chamfered Legs, H-Stretcher, 18 x 43 In.	430.00
Window Seat, George IV, Mahogany, Capitals, Upholstered, Legs, c.1810, 28 x 38 In.	889.00
Window Seat, Louis XVI Style, Gilt, Cane Back, Pierced, Scroll Arms, Footed, 29 x 52 In.	522.00
Window Seat, Louis XVI Style, Gilt, Painted, Upholstered Seat, Rolled Arms, Turned Legs, 57 In.	750.00
Window Seat, Louis XVI Style, Mahogany, Leaf Carved Armrest, Fluted Legs, 24 x 26 In.	184.00
Window Seat, Queen Anne Style, Mahogany, Cabriole Legs, Footed, c.1900, 21 x 37 In.	295.00
Window Seat, Regency, Rosewood, Gilt, 1 Side Outscrolled, Carved Uprights, c.1815, 28 x 44 In.	1107.00
Window Seat, Rosewood, Flower & Leaf Carved Armrests, Chinese, c.1890, 24 x 26 In.	110.00
Window Seat, Victorian, Mahogany, Scrolling Sides, Upholstered, Ball & Claw Feet, 39 x 32 In.	552.00
Wine Cooler, Stand, George III, Mahogany, Brass Wreath Handles, c.1850, 20 x 27 In.	1000.00
Wine Cooler, Table, French Provincial, Fruitwood, Metal, Marble, Shelf, 29 x 26 In.	799.00

G. ARGY-ROUSSEAU is the impressed mark used on a variety of glass objects in the Art Deco style. Gabriel Argy-Rousseau, born in 1885, was a French glass artist. In 1921, he formed a partnership that made pate-de-verre and other glass. The partnership ended in 1931 and he opened his own studio. He worked until 1952 and died in 1953.

G-ARGY-ROUSSEAU

Pendant, Pate-De-Verre, Fuchsia Blossoms, Amber & Coral, Silk Tassel, Signed, 2 ⅝ In.	920.00
Vase, Apple Picker, Women Picking Fruit, Pate-De-Verre, Greek Key Base, 9 In.	8750.00
Vase, Faunes Et Nymphes, Cream, Violet, Rose, Pate-De-Verre, c.1925, 8 ¾ In.	10000.00
Vase, Pan Et Satyres, Purple, Red Faces, Dots, Black Outlining, c.1925, 8 ⅞ In.	9375.00
Vase, Primeveres, Cream, Black, Red Ball Design, c.1925, 6 ¾ In.	5625.00
Vase, Rayons De Soleil, Yellow, Red, Black, Lobed, Pate-De-Verre, c.1925, 5 ⅞ In.	9375.00

GALLE was a designer who made glass, pottery, furniture, and other Art Nouveau items. Emile Galle founded his factory in France in 1874. After Galle's death in 1904, the firm continued to make glass and furniture until 1931. The *Galle* signature was used as a mark, but it was often hidden in the design of the object. Galle glass is listed here. Pottery is in the next section. His furniture is listed in the Furniture category.

Galle

Atomizer, Deep Orange Flowers, Peach Ground, Brass Mount, Cameo, Signed, 11 x 2 ¾ In.	798.00
Atomizer, Frosted Blue, Stemmed Flowers, Red Leather Gift Box, Cameo, Signed, 10 In. *Illus*	2415.00
Atomizer, Indigo To Citron, Frosted, Blossoming Stems & Leaves, Tapered, Marked, 9 In.	431.00
Biscuit Jar, Silver Lid, Red, Flowers, Angled, Rounded Square, 1920s, 6 ¼ x 4 In.	406.00
Bottle, Frosted Peach, Green Thistle, Triangular, Cameo, Marked, 4 In.	345.00
Bowl, Frosted Pink, Green Leaves, Seed Pods, Melon Ribs, Undulating Rim, Marked, 8 In.	633.00
Bowl, Green Leaves, Peach Ground, Shaped Rim, Footed, Cameo, 4 ½ x 8 In.	7110.00
Figurine, Duck, White Ground, Blue, Orange, Flowers, Dragonfly, Marked, Galle Nancy, 7 x 8 In.	1265.00
Jug, Dragonfly, Flowers, Clear, Enamel, Melon Lobed, Segmented Handle, Flame Stopper, 8 In.	1125.00
Lamp Base, Flowers, Anemones, Amber, Cameo, 17 ½ In.	322.00
Lamp, Conical Shade, Bulbous Body, Leaves, Flowers, Cameo Glass, c.1900, 12 x 10 ½ In.	5000.00
Lamp, Domed Shade, Yellow, Crimson Flowers, Metal Frame, Bronze Base, Cameo Glass, 18 x 33 In.	9775.00
Lamp, Hanging, Flowers, Orange Red, Amber Glass, Cameo, 3 Chains, c.1910, 5 ½ x 15 ¾ In.	7500.00
Perfume Bottle, Silver Screw Cap, Ribbed, Flower, Tapered, Amber, Red, Marked, 3 ½ In.	1896.00
Plate, Flowering Vine, Purple To Yellow & Frosted Ground, Cameo Glass, Marked, 2 x 8 ½ In.	1108.00
River Landscape, Brown, Yellow & Pink Ground, Cameo Cut, 9 x 19 ½ In.	4375.00
Scent Bottle, Flowers, Gold, Tan Ground, Embossed Silver Mounts, Intaglio Signed, c.1900, 6 ½ In.	3000.00
Vase, Apple Blossoms, Leaves, Cream, Green, Pink, Bulbous, Round Foot, 1890s, 3 ½ x 3 ½ In.	2125.00
Vase, Bottle Shape, Ring Foot, Clematis, Purple & Cream, Cameo, Signed, 11 ¾ In.	1000.00
Vase, Brown, Yellow, Rose Leaves, Green Overlay, Stick Neck, Flared Base, Cameo, c.1920, 25 ¾ In.	3750.00
Vase, Bud, Brown Ground, Tan Overlay, Stick Neck, Cameo, c.1900, 6 ¾ In.	805.00
Vase, Bud, Orange Flowers, Lime Green Shaded Ground, Cameo, c.1925, 5 ½ In.	600.00
Vase, Bulbous, Flowers, Cameo, Yellow, Blue, Green, Marked, 7 x 6 In.	1500.00
Vase, Bulbous, Pedestal, Round Foot, Neck, Enamel, Gilt, Butterflies, Flowers, Web, 1890s, 6 x 4 In.	1875.00
Vase, Chrysanthemum, Cameo Glass, Urn Shape, Foot, Leaves, Amber, Orange, Marked, c.1900, 6 ⅜ In.	7500.00
Vase, Clear Shaded To Green, Marquetry Flower, Wheel Carving, Marked, 10 In. *Illus*	25875.00
Vase, Cylindrical Form, Yellow With Blue Leaves & Green Okra, Marked, 7 ½ In.	5020.00
Vase, Cylindrical, Stick Neck, Cameo Cut Flowers, Orange Over Frosted, 17 In.	1500.00
Vase, Dragonfly, Lily Pond, Flowers, Green, Amber, Frosted, Rounded Square, Flat Rim, Cameo, 10 In.	8625.00
Vase, Flowers, Blue, Green, Yellow, Bulbous, Cameo, Marked, 7 ½ x 6 ½ In.	1830.00
Vase, Flowers, Green & Purple Cut To Pink, Squat, Elongated Neck, Cameo Glass, 9 ½ In.	1298.00

Furniture, Wardrobe, Pine, 2 Doors, 2 Drawers, Diamond Panels, Pediment, c.1850, 93 x 85 In.
$2,892.00

Garth's Auctioneers & Appraisers

Furniture, Washstand, Corner, Federal, Mahogany, Drawer, 2 False Drawers, 1800s, 44 In.
$360.00

Cowan's Auctions

Galle, Atomizer, Frosted Blue, Stemmed Flowers, Red Leather Gift Box, Cameo, Signed, 10 In.
$2,415.00

Early Auction Co.

Galle, Vase, Clear Shaded To Green, Marquetry Flower, Wheel Carving, Marked, 10 In.
$25,875.00

James D. Julia Auctioneers

Galle, Vase, Frosted Crimson, Green Cascading Leaves, Seed Pods, Cameo, Marked, 4 In.
$259.00

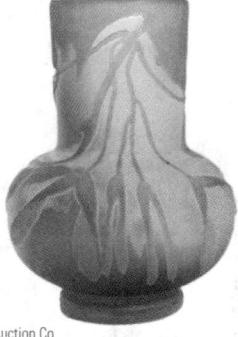

Early Auction Co.

Galle, Vase, Grapevine, Leaves, Clusters, Cameo, Marked, 11 In.
$10,350.00

Early Auction Co.

TIP
Remove pencil marks and other smudges with a Mr. Clean Magic Eraser or a Scotch-Brite Easy Erasing Pad.

Vase, Flowers, Leaves, Red, Burgundy, Frosted, Yellow, Bulbous, Cameo, 2 ½ x 8 In.	1500.00
Vase, Flowers, Leaves, Yellow Ground, Round, Tapered, Cameo, c.1900, 8 ½ In.	3750.00
Vase, French Cameo, Lake Scene, Trees, Green Frosted Background, Marked, 3 ½ In.	575.00
Vase, Frosted Crimson, Green Cascading Leaves, Seed Pods, Cameo, Marked, 4 In. ....*Illus*	259.00
Vase, Frosted Peach, Wisteria, Blue, Green Leaves, Cylindrical, Crimped Top, Cameo, Marked, 8 ½ In.	805.00
Vase, Frosted Yellow & Pink, Branches, Berries, Flat Sided, Bulbous, Handles At Rim, Cameo, 5 ½ In..	1150.00
Vase, Fruit Vine, Green, Clear, Long Neck, Tapered, Intaglio Etched, 11 ¼ In.	3250.00
Vase, Gold Trees, Leaves, Pink, White, Brown, Flared, Cameo, c.1920, 23 ¾ In.	3000.00
Vase, Grapes, Leafy Vines, Mulberry, Caramel, Amber Color, Shouldered, Tapered, 13 ¾ In.	1840.00
Vase, Grapes, Leaves, Orange, White, Urn Shape, Cameo, 2 ⅞ In.	184.00
Vase, Grapevine, Leaves, Clusters, Cameo, Marked, 11 In. ....*Illus*	10350.00
Vase, Gray Leaves, White To Pink, Flared Stick Shape, Cameo, c.1920, 14 In.	1875.00
Vase, Gray, Purple Vines, Leaves, Bulbous, Cylindrical Neck, Ring Foot, Cameo, Marked, 7 In.	345.00
Vase, Green Aquatic Leaves, Orange & Frosted Ground, Oval, Squat, c.1925, 3 x 3 In.	840.00
Vase, Green Flowers, White, Tapered Cylinder, Cameo, c.1920, 14 In.	1500.00
Vase, Green Leaves & Bud Overlay, White, Cylindrical, Cameo, c.1920, 10 ¼ In.	2250.00
Vase, Lake Scene, Citron, Amethyst Cut, Gray Ground, Flat Oval, c.1900, 10 In.	2880.00
Vase, Landscape, Earth Tones, Tapered, Flared Rim, 11 ½ In.	1560.00
Vase, Landscape, Trees, Lake, Autumn Colors, Oval, Pinched Neck, 9 ¼ In.	823.00
Vase, Landscape, Trees, Shades Of Green, Squat, Cameo, 1900s, 4 ½ x 5 In.	1063.00
Vase, Leaf & Berry, Bulbous Bottom, Flared Neck, Olive Green Cut To Pink, Cameo Glass, 4 ⅜ In. .	590.00
Vase, Leaf & Vine, Burnt Orange Cut To Frosted, Squat, Cameo Glass, 2 ⅜ In.	472.00
Vase, Leafy Branches, Green, Yellow Mottled Glass, Brown Foot, Cameo, Marked, 6 ½ x 18 In.	8125.00
Vase, Light Brown Leaves, Blue Ground, Oval, Cameo, c.1920, 9 ¾ In.	1625.00
Vase, Lilac Flowers, Pink Blossoms, Stems, Leaves, Yellow, Flared Rim, Flared Foot, 19 x 10 In..	5750.00
Vase, Marquetry Leaves, Amber, Purple, White, Cream, Lily Pads, Canoe Shape, Marked, 6 ½ In.	6900.00
Vase, Mottled Yellow, Brown & Amber Blossoming Branches, Oval, Flared Mouth, Marked, 6 ½ In.	661.00
Vase, Oak Branches, Beetle, Orange, Brown, Elongated Oval, Footed, Cameo, 1900s, 15 x 4 In. .	4688.00
Vase, Orange Flowers, Frosted, Cylindrical, Bulbous Foot, Cameo Cut, 6 x 17 ½ In.	1830.00
Vase, Orange Flowers, Pale Yellow Ground, Cameo, 11 ½ In.	7110.00
Vase, Oval Shape, Slight Flared Rim, Flowers & Leaves, Brown, Yellow, Marked, 1900s, 6 ½ x 4 ¼ In.	5313.00
Vase, Oval, Flared Ruffle Rim, Iris, Purple, Clear, Fire Polished, Marked, 7 ¾ In.	1250.00
Vase, Oval, Shouldered, Catkins Design, Green & Purple, Cameo, Marked, 6 ¼ In.	625.00
Vase, Pink Frosted, Cameo, Tree Scene, Pond Lily, Bulbous Smokestack, Marked, 6 In.	489.00
Vase, Pink, Lime Green, Thistle Pattern, Cameo, Marked, c.1915, 24 ½ x 10 In.	922.00
Vase, Poppy Pods, Leaves, Green, Frosted, Wavy Rim, Tapered, Cameo, Marked, 6 x 14 In.	2806.00
Vase, Purple Draped Fuchsia, Amethyst Overlay, Translucent Citron, c.1905, 18 ¾ In.	960.00
Vase, Purple Flowers, Frosted Apricot, Bulbous, Flared Neck, Cameo, c.1910, 6 In.	840.00
Vase, Purple Leaves, Frosted, Urn Shape, Flat Rim, Signed, 3 In.	345.00
Vase, Purple Pendant Vine & Flowers, Frosted, Cylindrical, Pinched Rim, 8 ⅜ In.	861.00
Vase, Red Cherry Blossoms, Gold, Leaves, Bulbous, Narrow Neck, Marked, 5 ¼ In.	748.00
Vase, Red Flowers, Burgundy Leaves, Yellow, Swollen, Tapered Foot, 12 In.	3321.00
Vase, Red Pears, Leaves, Yellow, Bulbous, Tapered Base, Cameo, Marked, 11 x 13 In.	10000.00
Vase, Red, Butterscotch, Flowers, Trailing Vines, Bulbous Egg Shaped, Flared Rim, Marked, 6 ¼ In. ..	5463.00
Vase, Rowboat, Lake, Trees, Tapered, Narrow, Smokestack Bottom, Flared Rim, Marked, 24 x 7 ½ In.	3375.00
Vase, Squat, Flared Rim, Round Foot, Enamel, Gilt, Flowers, Stems, Green, 1890s, 2 ¾ x 4 In.	500.00
Vase, Stick, Bleeding Heart, Acid Cut, Spread Base, 13 ½ In.	2760.00
Vase, Stick, Geraniums, Cameo, Marked, 23 ¼ In. ....*Illus*	2000.00
Vase, Swirled Flower, Deep Red, Cinched Waist, Cameo, 3 ½ In.	2252.00
Vase, Tapered, Lobed Rim, Poppy Pods, Leaves, Cameo, Green, Signed, 14 In.	2300.00
Vase, Trees, Landscape, Blue To Green Ground, Enameled, c.1910, 10 In.	5625.00
Vase, Trumpet, Green, Pale Blue, Pink Flowering Vines, Honeysuckles, Cameo, Marked, c.1900, 22 In.	5904.00
Vase, Tulip In Wind, Fire Polished, Brown Shaded To Gold, Cylindrical, Scalloped, 15 x 6 In.	6250.00
Vase, Wisteria, Shaded Cream Ground, Tapered, c.1900, 11 ½ x 4 In.	1125.00
Vase, Yellow, Crimson Pinecones, Round Flared Foot, Narrow Stem, Flared Neck, Marked, 11 ½ In.	403.00

GALLE POTTERY was made by Emile Galle, the famous French designer, after 1874. The pieces were marked with the initials *E. G.* impressed, *Em. Galle Faiencerie de Nancy,* or a version of his signature. Galle is best known for his glass, listed above.

Pitcher, Pansy, Foil, Allover Gilding, Signed, 10 ½ In. ....*Illus*	1725.00
Plate, Peacocks, Flowers, Shell, Scalloped Rim, Marked Editeur Nancy, c.1900, 12 ¾ x 14 In..	178.00

GAME collectors like all types of games. Of special interest are any board games or card games. Transogram and other company names are included in the description when known. Other games may be found listed under Card, Toy, or the name of the character or celebrity featured in the game.

Arcade Target, Carnival, Jockey & Donkey, Cast Iron, U.S.A., c.1900, 16 ½ x 18 ½ In.	474.00

G

Backgammon Set, Corkboard, Oilcloth Case, 22 ½ x 15 In.	86.00
Bazooka Bagatelle Marble Pinball, Marbles, Marx, Box, 12 ½ x 6 ⅜ In.	85.00
Bermuda Triangle, Milton Bradley, Board, 1976, 20 x 12 In.	60.00
Block Puzzle, Father Christmas, Driving Motor Bus, Holly On Head, 7 x 6 ¼ In.	708.00
Blondie's Comic Construction Set, Dagwood, Baby Dumpling, Daisy, King, Copyright 1930-34. *Illus*	201.00
Board, Backgammon, Rosettes, Painted, Eagles & Diamonds On Reverse, c.1890, 18 x 12 In....*Illus*	1778.00
Board, Checkers & Parcheesi, Multicolor, Red Mitered Frame, 17 ¼ x 17 ¼ In.	5175.00
Board, Checkers, Wood, Applied Molding, Yellow, Black, Red, Painted, c.1900, 15 x 15 In.	711.00
Board, Chinese Checkers, Plywood Panel, Pine Frame, Yellow Ground, Multicolor, c.1880, 16 x 16 In.	1495.00
Board, Cribbage, Inlaid Exotic Woods, Drawer, 8 Carved Ivory Pegs, c.1800, 14 ½ In....*Illus*	235.00
Board, Cribbage, Iron, Shaped Sides, Brass Pegs, Original Paint, John Gill, 10 ¾ In.	392.00
Board, Cribbage, Mixed Exotic Woods, Inlaid, Drawer, 8 Carved Ivory Pegs, 15 In.	235.00
Board, Cribbage, Mixed Woods, Parquetry, Drawers At Ends, Stepped Base, 20 In.	588.00
Board, Parcheesi, Paint, Gilt, Incised, Square Panel, Moldings, c.1895, 27 x 27 In.	3437.00
Board, Parcheesi, Pine, Painted, Multicolor, New England, c.1890, 22 x 22 In.	18225.00
Board, Parcheesi, Pine, Red, Black Paint, c.1805, 25 ¼ x 24 In.	2430.00
Board, Parcheesi, Poplar, Multicolor, Blue, Red, Yellow, Blue Field, Black Borders, c.1850, 20 x 20 In.	9488.00
Board, Wood, Painted, Multicolor, Yellow, Black, Green, Maroon, c.1900, 14 ¾ In.	1265.00
Bomber Ball, Cardboard, Marble Or Chalk Bombs, Ship Targets, Game Makers, 1940s, 13 x 19 In.	278.00
Box, Wood, Inlaid, House, Oak Leaves & Acorns, Compartments, Tunbridge Ware, 11 In.	940.00
Capture Hitler, Central V Design, Box, Window On Lid, Marble, 1942, 8 ½ x 8 ½ In.	337.00
Casino Marker Chips, Multi-Denomination, Wood Holder...*Illus*	196.00
Checkerboard, 2-Sided, Black & Green, Mustard & Black Mill Game, c.1810, 11 ¾ x 12 In.	1035.00
Checkerboard, Blackwell Co., S. Durham Tobacco, Men Smoking, 13 x 20 In.	176.00
Checkerboard, Brass, Copper, 4 Notched Copper Feet, Art Deco, 9 ½ In.	240.00
Checkerboard, Incised, Painted, Black, Cream, Initialed AM, U.S.A., 1900s, 22 ½ x 22 ½ In.	118.00
Checkerboard, Pine, Breadboard Ends, Painted, Yellow, Green, Black, c.1910, 20 x 24 ½ In.	783.00
Checkerboard, Pine, Marbleized Border, Paint, 19 x 18 ¾ In.	3792.00
Checkerboard, Pine, Red, Black Paint, 17 ¼ x 21 ½ In.	1007.00
Checkerboard, Pine, Red, Black, Yellow Designs, c.1890, 18 x 29 In....*Illus*	723.00
Checkerboard, Reverse Glass, Red, White, Green Border, Oak Frame, c.1910, 19 x 19 In.	118.00
Checkerboard, Square Panel, Molding, Black & Yellow Paint, Flowers, Leaves, 1800s, 15 x 15 In.	2760.00
Checkerboard, Wood, Grain Painted, Mitered Molding, Black, Red Border, c.1895, 18 ½ x 18 ½ In.	770.00
Checkerboard, Yellow Pine, Red & Black Paint, Numbers, c.1895, 15 ½ x 15 In.	2015.00
Checkerboard, Yellow, Black Squares, Geometric Painted Designs, Slate, Frame, 1920s, 20 In.	358.00
Checkers, Mahogany Board, Scribed Lines, Storage Wells, Turned Wood Checkers, c.1900, 13 x 11 In.	369.00
Checkers, Wood Board, Painted, Playing Pieces, Hand Carved, Signed, J.H. Brown, 9 ½ x 14 ¾ In.	563.00
Chess Set, Marble Board, Gilt Metal Feet, Chess Pieces 4 ½ In., Board 4 x 22 ½ In.	354.00
Cinderella, Backdrop, Wand, Cards, Slipper, Board, Box, 1950, 19 x 9 In.	210.00
Consult The Educated Monkey, Tin, Board, 1916, 6 x 5 ½ In.	120.00
Dextcrity Puzzle, Mechanical Mirror, Photographer, Camera, Reflects Image, Germany, c.1910	280.00
Faro, A. Ball & Co., Chicago, Ill., Case	560.00
Faro, George W. Williams, New York, Case Keeper	1624.00
Gee-Wiz, Horse Race, Metal, Wood, Wolverine Supply & Mfg. Co., Pittsburgh, Board, 1928	224.00
Hee Haw, Wooden Balls, Arcade Style, Milton Bradley, Board, Box, c.1936	23.00
Horse Race, Square Pedestal, Felt Field, 3 Circles, 9 Lead Horses, Lever, 16 x 7 ½ In.	403.00
Horse Race, Windup, 8 Cast Iron Horses & Riders, Round, Bowman, 13 In.	390.00
House That Jack Built, McLoughlin Bros., Card, 1887, 6 ¼ x 4 ½ In.	210.00
Jigsaw Puzzle, Eagle, Wood, Fitted Frame, Removable Bottom, c.1980, 17 x 21 In.	147.00
Jigsaw Puzzle, Fire Engine, Horses, Burning Building, Wood, McLoughlin Bros., 1901, 13 x 18 In.	523.00
Jigsaw Puzzle, Last Supper, Milton Bradley, 1000 Piece, 1965, 26 x 20 In.	25.00
Jigsaw Puzzle, Peter Rabbit, Publisher's Box, 1930s, 8 ½ x 1 ½ In....*Illus*	131.00
Jigsaw Puzzle, Red Riding Hood, Girl, Wolf, Cardboard, Wood Frame, c.1905, 14 x 10 In.	303.00
Jigsaw Puzzle, Scroll, Animal Antics, Parade, Boxed Set, McLoughlin Bros., 10 x 15 & 13 x 25 In.	295.00
Jigsaw Puzzle, Two Friends, Lithographed, Labeled, Wooden Box, Slide Lid, c.1850, 7 x 9 In...*Illus*	280.00
Jigsaw Puzzle, Yellow Kid, Box, 1890s, 13 ¾ x 14 In.	150.00
Junk Yard, Pinball Action, Ideal, Target, Board, Box, 1975	35.00
Keno, Goose Cage, Numbered Wooden Balls, Crank Handle, 12 In....*Illus*	150.00
King Zor The Dinosaur, Cavemen, Dinosaurs, Monster Eggs, Box, Ideal, Board, 1962, 10 x 19 ½ In.	246.00
Mah Lowe, Mahjong Gambling Tile Set, Bakelite, E.S. Lowe, N.Y., Case	81.00
Mahjong, Case, 152 Pieces, Dice, Stand, Bakelite, 4 x 20 ½ In.	83.00
Mahjong, Case, Teak, Brass, 5 Interior Drawers, Bone, Bamboo Pieces, Chinese, c.1950, 8 x 8 In.	2588.00
Mail Express, Train, Snow, People Shoveling, McLoughlin, Board, 1895, 14 x 22 In.	330.00
Man From U.N.C.L.E., Plastic Pistol, Suction Cup Darts, Building Target, Box, 1965, 12 x 17 In.	173.00
Mary Hartman, TV Show Set In Fernwood, Ohio, Reiss Game Co., Board, 1977	30.00
Mather's Parlor Baseball, 10 Steel Balls, Metal Mechanism, Tin Litho, Box, 1909, 23 ½ x 19 In.	1080.00

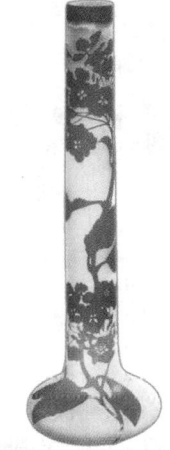

Galle, Vase, Stick, Geraniums, Cameo, Marked, 23 ¼ In.
$2,000.00

Leslie Hindman Auctioneers

Galle Pottery, Pitcher, Pansy, Foil, Allover Gilding, Signed, 10 ½ In.
$1,725.00

James D. Julia Auctioneers

Game, Blondie's Comic Construction Set, Dagwood, Baby Dumpling, Daisy, King, Copyright 1930-34
$201.00

Victorian Casino Antiques

Game, Board, Backgammon, Rosettes, Painted, Eagles & Diamonds On Reverse, c.1890, 18 x 12 In.
$1,778.00

Skinner, Inc.

G

Game, Board, Cribbage, Inlaid Exotic Woods, Drawer, 8 Carved Ivory Pegs, c.1800, 14 ½ In.
$235.00

Garth's Auctioneers & Appraisers

Game, Casino Marker Chips, Multi-Denomination, Wood Holder
$196.00

Victorian Casino Antiques

Game, Checkerboard, Pine, Red, Black, Yellow Designs, c.1890, 18 x 29 In.
$723.00

Garth's Auctioneers & Appraisers

Game, Jigsaw Puzzle, Peter Rabbit, Publisher's Box, 1930s, 8 ½ x 1 ½ In.
$131.00

Bloomsbury House

Old Maid, Whitman Publishing Co., 45 Cards, Box, 1937	60.00
Peter Coddle's Trip, Milton Bradley, 24 Cards, Box, 1930s, 6 x 7 ½ In.	24.00
Pinball, 5 Star Final, Tabletop, Wood, Glass	420.00
Pinball, Push-M-Up, Sports Lithographs, Drinks, Girls, Wood, Glass Top, Electric, 27 x 15 In.	59.00
Poker Set, Chip Caddy, Mahogany, Folding Handle, Pressboard Cover, Chips, 3 ¾ x 8 ¾ In.	59.00
Poker Set, Red Plastic Case, White, Blue, 6 ½ x 3 In.	15.00
Poker Set, Wood, Glass, Drop Front, Compartments, Humidor, Matches, Cards, Chips, 11 x 8 In.	400.00
Psychic Baseball, Game Pieces, Cards, Parker Brothers, Board, 1933	115.00
Puzzle, Aunt Jemima, 2-Piece, Cardboard, Die Cut, Red, Yellow, 4 x 3 In.	385.00
Roulette Wheel, Deluxe, H.C. Evans, Goddess Of Chance Finial, Carved, Wood, 31 In.	4500.00
Roulette Wheel, Table, Wood, Paneled Base, Reeded Edge, B.C. Wills Co., 100 x 49 In.	2185.00
Space Pilot, Rocket Spinner, Space-O-Meter, Wooden Markers, Board, Box, 1951, 10 x 22 ½ In.	115.00
Spiral Drop Tower, Round Wood Base, Painted Numbers, Marble, Multicolor, c.1898, 10 In.	392.00
Squeeze The Juice, O.J. Simpson & Attorneys, Board, Box	25.00
Stanley In Africa, Board, Box, Bliss, 1891, 8 x 18 In. _Illus_	4000.00
Table, Craps, One-Man Tub, Oak, Raised Sides, Turned Stretcher & Legs	780.00
Table, Gambling, Roulette, Inlaid Wood Wheel, Oak Claw Feet	3720.00
Tarzan In The Jungle, Lion Targets, Cardboard, Battery, Joseph Schneider, 1935, 7 x 10 In. _Illus_	209.00
Telegraph Messenger, Board, Spinner, Cardboard, Box, J.H. Singer Co., 7 ⅜ x 7 ¼ In. _Illus_	44.00
Tiddlywinks, Cup, Winks, Milton Bradley, Board, Box, 1920s, 7 x 7 In.	32.00
Time Tunnel, Board, Cards, Spinner, Tokens, Markers, Box, Kent Productions, 1966, 10 x 19 ½ In.	417.00
U.S. Marshal, Pistol, 5 Cent, A.B.T. Mfg. Co., Keys, Target, 1950s _Illus_	360.00
Untouchables, Mechanical, Instruction Sheet, Target, Box, 1959-1963, 8 x 21 In.	374.00
Wheel, Gambling, Cutout Design, Black & Yellow, Wood, Backboard, Reversible, c.1949, 36 In. Diam.	354.00
Wheel, Gambling, Dice, Cast Iron Stand, Tripod Base, H.C. Evans & Co., 32 In.	2280.00
Wheel, Gambling, Horse, Odds Changer, Cast Iron Stand, H.C. Evans & Co., 39 x 20 In. _Illus_	3640.00
Wheel, Gambling, Numbers, Mirrored Spokes, 4-Legged Base, Wood, Glass, c.1920, 71 ½ In. _Illus_	3995.00
Wheel, Gambling, Painted Wood, 3 Rotating Graduated Panels, Numbers, c.1900, 16 In.	1593.00
Wheel, Gambling, Revolving, 4 Shaped Spokes, Multicolor, c.1920, 23 ¼ In.	1093.00
Wheel, Gambling, Wood, Red Paint, Black Numbers, Cast Iron Base, 35 x 20 In.	443.00
Wheel, Gambling, Wood, Yellow Paint, Numbers, 6 Spokes, Metal Pins, 36 ½ In.	266.00
Yacht Race, N.Y. Harbor, Folding Board, Spinner, Rule Sheet, McLoughlin, 8 ½ x 16 ½ In.	575.00

GAME PLATES are plates of any make decorated with pictures of birds, animals, or fish. The game plates usually came in sets consisting of twelve dishes and a serving platter. These sets were most popular during the 1880s.

Birds, Flower Design, A. Klingenberg Carlsbad, 8 ¼ In., 4 Piece	100.00
Birds, Gilt Trim, Lenox, c.1910, 9 ⅛ In., 12 Piece	2900.00
Canvasback In Flight, Acorn Border, Sinclaire, Signed, 9 In.	375.00
Elk, Transfer, Green, Blenheim China, c.1900, 12 In.	110.00
Fish, In Pond, Elite Limoges, c.1905, 9 In., 6 Piece	630.00
Fish, Raised Gilt Scrolls, Scalloped, Haviland, c.1890, 10 In., 4 Piece	949.00
Mallard Duck, Pheasant Border, Porcelain, Paneled, Teal, 8 ½ In.	18.00
Pheasants, Gilt Trim, Limoges, 9 ½ In., c.1900, 12 Piece	846.00
Rabbits, Forest Scene, Rosenthal, c.1900, 7 ½ In., 6 Piece	350.00

GARDEN FURNISHINGS have been popular for centuries. The stone or metal statues, urns and fountains, sundials, small figurines, and wire, iron, or rustic furniture are included in this category. Many of the metal pieces have been made continuously for years.

Armillary, Directionals, Stars, Figures, Round, Bronze, c.1930, 44 In.	3600.00
Bench, Back Flower Roundel, Carved Edge Seat, c.1850, 44 x 80 In.	8100.00
Bench, Colebrookdale Style, Faux Bois, Green Paint, Cast Iron, c.1950, 35 x 52 In., Pair	840.00
Bench, Continuous Back & Arm, Openwork, Cast Iron, Fern Design, Green, 33 x 54 In.	3884.00
Bench, Curved Back, Pierced Seat, Winged Griffin Legs, White Paint, Iron, c.1930, 29 x 38 ½ In.	960.00
Bench, Curved Seats, Baluster Supports, Cast Stone, 17 x 42 In., Pair	480.00
Bench, Curved, Dolphin, Poseidon Back, Arms, Bronze, Iron, Oscar Bach, c.1910, 43 x 57 In.	32400.00
Bench, Curved, Egg & Dart Edges, Dolphin Supports, 17 ½ x 15 In., Pair	540.00
Bench, Demilune Back, Scrolling Strapwork, Leaves, Cabriole Legs, Wrought Iron, 58 x 65 In.	492.00
Bench, Egg & Dart, Scrolled, Fluted Basses, Cast Stone, c.1940, 18 ½ x 59 In., Pair	1200.00
Bench, Flower Design Back, Pierced, Scrolled Arms & Legs, Cast Iron, Paint, c.1900, 33 x 41 In.	617.00
Bench, Gothic Style, Openwork Back, Sides, Cast Iron, 34 x 56 In., Pair	3360.00
Bench, Half Columns, 3 Sections, Sandstone, c.1900, 19 x 40 In.	441.00
Bench, Hammered Finials, Rope Stile, X-Shape Legs, Turned Stretcher, Paw Feet, Iron, 28 x 47 In.	1304.00
Bench, Intertwined Rosettes, Serpentine Seat, Scrolled Arms, Cast Iron, 32 x 44 In., Pair	1476.00
Bench, Openwork Back & Apron, Curved Arms, Cast Iron, Cream Paint, 34 x 55 In., Pair	950.00

Bench, Passion Flowers, Arms, Cast Iron, Marked Hinderer, c.1850 ... 2987.00
Bench, Pierced, Quatrefoils In Diamonds, Spindle Legs, Cast Iron, White Paint, 36 x 76 In. ... 4388.00
Bench, Scroll & Flower Carved Apron, Terra-Cotta, c.1930, 19 ½ x 54 In. ... 840.00
Bench, Scroll & Torch Openwork Sides & Back, Plank Seat, Cast Iron, 39 x 28 In. ... 480.00
Bench, Scrolled, Openwork Back, Arms, White Paint, Cast Iron, 59 ½ x 43 ¾ In. ... 1722.00
Bench, Twig, Leaf Back & Arms, Cast Iron, c.1890, 30 x 49 In. ... 1320.00
Bench, Victorian, Pierced, Cabriole Legs, c.1880, 35 x 27 In. ... 780.00
Bench, White House Rose Garden Design, Flowers, Arches, Cabriole Legs, 38 x 63 ½ In., Pair. 2706.00
Bench, Winged Lion Supports, Paw Feet, Carved Marble, c.1850, 18 ½ x 59 In. ... 1920.00
Bench, Winged Putti, Lyres, Leaves, Hoof Feet, Ram's Heads, Arms, Cast Iron, 31 x 42 In., Pair. 984.00
Birdbath, 2 Perched Birds, Shell Shape, Cast Iron, 11 ½ x 18 ½ In. ... 420.00
Birdbath, 8 Doves, Perched On Rim, White Porcelain, c.1950, 11 x 29 In. ... 390.00
Birdbath, Carved Limestone, Separate Base, William Edmondson, c.1940, 27 ½ x 8 x 16 In.... *Illus* 2832.00
Birdbath, Scalloped Edge, Cast Stone, c.1960, 33 x 33, Pair ... 150.00
Birdbath, Shell Shape, Seahorse Base, Cast Stone, c.1960, 34 ½ x 32 In. ... 360.00
Birdhouse, Clapboard, 2 Porches, Chimneys, Tar Paper Roof, Painted, c.1950, 22 x 27 In.... *Illus* 558.00
Boot Scraper, Cat Shape, With Attitude, Cast Iron, Red Paint, c.1860, 12 x 10 ¼ In. ... 1610.00
Boot Scraper, Iron, Flat Top, Arched Cutouts, 2 Curved Supports, Faceted Ball Finials, 16 x 17 In.. 266.00
Box, Seed, Walnut, Hinged Lid, Fitted Interior, 3 Low Drawers, c.1850, 7 x 16 ½ In. ... 325.00
Chair, Fern Design, Green, Openwork, Continuous Back & Arm, Cast Iron, Pair ... 2390.00
Chair, Lily-Of-The-Valley Openwork, Cast Iron, c.1850, 33 ½ x 26 ½ In., Pair ... 5760.00
Chair, Lily-Of-The-Valley Openwork, Pierced Seat, Cast Iron, c.1870, 33 x 27 In., Pair ... 4800.00
Chair, Lyre & Scroll Pierced, Cabriole Legs, Cast Iron, c.1880, 33 x 21 In., 4 Piece ... 1800.00
Chair, Mategot Style, Fan Back & Arms, Wrought Iron, c.1950, 37 x 24 In., 4 Piece ... 1440.00
Chair, Oval Back, Scrolled Arms, Wirework, c.1950, 34 x 30 In. ... 420.00
Chair, Saucer Shape, Mesh Back & Seat, Wrought Iron, c.1960, 30 x 25 In., 4 Piece ... 1080.00
Chair, Saucer Shape, Spring Base, Woodard, c.1960, 30 ½ x 30 In., Pair ... 840.00
Chair, Scrolled Back, Arms, Pierced Seat, Hair Pin Legs, Wrought Iron, c.1940, 29 x 20 In., 6 Piece ... 1680.00
Chair, Scrolls, Arms, Wrought Iron, White Paint, France, c.1940, 45 x 28 In., Pair ... 390.00
Chair, Stylized Cat Back, Cast Iron, Richard Bawden, 35 In., Pair ... *Illus* 4000.00
Chair, Victorian Style, Dished Seat, Arched Crest, Openwork, Rosettes, Cast Iron, 36 In., Pair.. 399.00
Chair, Wrought Iron, Shaped Back, Scrolling Back, Slatted Seat, Scrolling Arms, 44 In. ... 123.00
Chair, Wrought Iron, Victorian, Rounded Crest, Slatted Seat, Twisted Cluster Legs, 44 ½ In. ... 123.00
Figure, 2 Children, Ladder, 89 x 24 In. ... 1320.00
Figure, Angel, Lyre, Zinc, France, c.1910, 32 x 15 In. ... 390.00
Figure, Boy, Arms Holding Planter, Cast Concrete, 1900s, 46 ¾ In. ... *Illus* 767.00
Figure, Classical Women, Grapes, Flowers, Concrete Or Cast Stone, c.1900, 61 In., Pair... *Illus* 1534.00
Figure, Crane, Bronze, Verdigris, 68 x 21 In., Pair ... 1540.00
Figure, Crouching Aphrodite, Plinth Base, Classical Designs, Cast Iron, 69 In. ... 2510.00
Figure, Deer, Cast Iron, c.1910, 31 x 31 In. ... 1007.00
Figure, Diana, Bronze, Elkington Mason & Co., 1854, 68 x 21 ½ In. ... 22800.00
Figure, Dog, Seated, Holding Flower Basket, Iron, 25 x 16 In., Pair ... 360.00
Figure, Dog, Sitting, Flower Basket In Mouth, Painted, Concrete, 22 In. ... 158.00
Figure, Fish, Cement, c.1955, 14 ½ x 33 ½ In. ... 384.00
Figure, Foo Dog, Seated, Carved, Marble, 25 x 10 In., Pair ... 1200.00
Figure, Gnome, Standing, Finger To Mouth, Pointed Cap, Paint, Iron, 1900s, 26 In., Pair ... 313.00
Figure, Guanyin, Lotus Blossom, Fan, Carved Green Stone, Asia, 1900s, 43 In. ... 353.00
Figure, Kneeling Archer, Seminude, Bronze, c.1900, 44 x 38 In. ... 3444.00
Figure, Lion, Seated, Terra-Cotta, 29 In. ... 356.00
Figure, Lion, Standing, Raised Head, Mane, Plinth, Cast Stone, c.1940, 31 ½ x 12 In., Pair ... 720.00
Figure, Pan, 2 Flutes, Lead, Stone Base, c.1920, 38 x 9 In. ... 480.00
Figure, Pan, Snake Wrapped Leg, Lead, 37 ½ x 12 In. ... 1440.00
Figure, Pixie, Cement, 20 In. ... 150.00
Figure, Puppy, Cast Lead, c.1950, 8 ½ x 4 In. ... 300.00
Figure, Putto, Seated On Orb, Lead, 36 ½ x 18 In., Pair ... 6240.00
Figure, Stork, Carved, Wood, c.1910, 58 In. ... 148.00
Figure, Tortoise, Gray, Head Out & Up, Lead, 5 x 12 In. ... 748.00
Figure, Woman, Cupid, Draped Gown, Limestone, Platinum Based, c.1900, 79 x 30 In. ... 3600.00
Figure, Woman, Draped Gown, Bouquet, Carved Stone, c.1890, 79 x 24 In. ... 5040.00
Figure, Woman, Seated On Flowers, Vines, c.1960, 46 x 19 In. ... 960.00
Finial, Ball Top, Stepped Base, Carved, Marble, c.1850, 31 x 15 In. ... 2640.00
Finial, Pineapple, Stepped Base, Cast Iron, 23 x 10 In., Pair ... 660.00
Fountain, 3 Putti Support, Marble, c.1870, 24 ½ x 23 ½ In. ... 1440.00
Fountain, 3 Tiers, Concrete, Marked Henri Studios, 37 x 56 In. ... 196.00
Fountain, Baroque Style, Cherub, Scrolled Base, Marble, Italy, 35 ½ x 23 In. ... 840.00

Game, Jigsaw Puzzle, Two Friends, Lithographed, Labeled, Wooden Box, Slide Lid, c.1850, 7 x 9 In.
$280.00

Theriault's

Game, Keno, Goose Cage, Numbered Wooden Balls, Crank Handle, 12 In.
$150.00

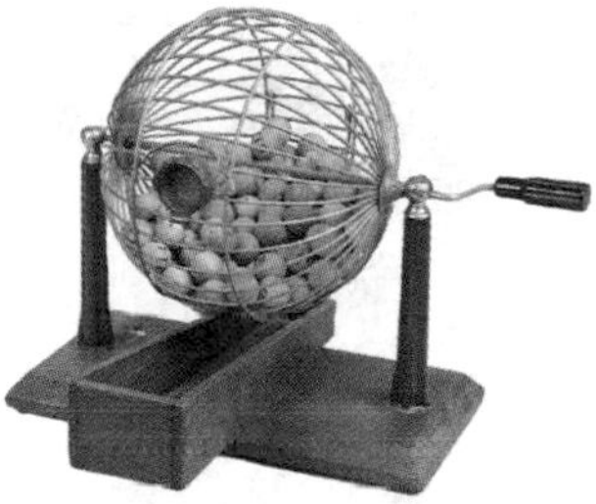

Victorian Casino Antiques

Game, Stanley In Africa, Board, Box, Bliss, 1891, 8 x 18 In.
$4,000.00

Game, Tarzan In The Jungle, Lion Targets, Cardboard, Battery, Joseph Schneider, 1935, 7 x 10 In.
$209.00

Hake's Americana & Collectibles

G

Game, Telegraph Messenger, Board, Spinner, Cardboard, Box, J.H. Singer Co., 7 ⅜ x 7 ¼ In.
$44.00

Wm Morford Antiques

Game, U.S. Marshal, Pistol, 5 Cent, A.B.T. Mfg. Co., Keys, Target, 1950s
$360.00

Victorian Casino Antiques

Game, Wheel, Gambling, Horse, Odds Changer, Cast Iron Stand, H.C. Evans & Co., 39 x 20 In.
$3,640.00

Victorian Casino Antiques

Fountain, Boy, Bronze, 33 In.	424.00
Fountain, Boy, Holding Boot, Rocks, Pond Creatures, Cast Iron, Lead, J.W. Fiske, c.1880, 60 x 58 In.	4977.00
Fountain, Boy, Leaning Against Wall, Pouring Water, Bronze Patina, 47 x 24 x 33 In.	3300.00
Fountain, Boy, Seated, Holding Frog, Fish Fountain Heads, Bronze, 29 x 27 In.	1140.00
Fountain, Cherub, Goose, Zinc, 40 In.	1888.00
Fountain, Classical Style, 3 Tiers, Putti, Dancing, Playing Music, Bronze, 108 x 48 In.	5400.00
Fountain, Dolphin, Bronze, Robert Wyland, Incised 1992, 60 x 24 In.	5015.00
Fountain, Duck Shaped, Spouts Water, Bronze, 15 ½ x 17 In., Pair	492.00
Fountain, Duck, Standing On Sphere, Ducklings, Lead, c.1930, 27 x 15 In.	570.00
Fountain, Fish, Bronze, Verdigris Patina, 18 x 11 In.	480.00
Fountain, Fluted Basin, Wreath, Acanthus Feet, Opposing Frogs, Cast Iron, 1800s, 28 x 28 In.	1599.00
Fountain, Man, Woman, Cherub, Bronze, 80 x 28 In.	1955.00
Fountain, Putto, Holding Dolphin, Fish, Lead, Gray Patina, 23 In.	590.00
Fountain, Putto, Holding Frog, Standing In Leaf Shell Basin, Bronze, 18 x 22 ½ In.	1020.00
Fountain, Renaissance Style, Acanthus, Figures, Dolphin Canopy, Bronze, 103 x 44 In.	6000.00
Fountain, Swan, Uplifted Beak Spout, Long Curved Neck, Zinc, c.1900, 35 ½ x 27 In.	1058.00
Fountain, Upper Petal Bowl, Cherub Support, Leaves, Raised Base, c.1880, 45 x 42 In.	1320.00
Fountain, Water Nymph, Fruit, Tassels, Swags, Leaf Carved, Casket Shape, Stone, 156 x 69 In.	5463.00
Gate, Art Deco, Geometrics, Scrolls, Wrought Iron, c.1910, 53 x 55 In.	330.00
Gate, Scrolled Rows, Wrought Iron, c.1920, 77 x 59 In., Pair	780.00
Gate, Scrolled Top, Oval Panels, Zinc Detail, Wrought Iron, c.1910, 143 x 120 In., Pair	1440.00
Gate, Stanchions, Banded Scrolls, Wrought Iron, 80 ½ x 59 In., Pair	540.00
Gate, Studded Grid Bottom, Scrolled Flower Top, Wrought Iron, c.1880, 81 x 36 In.	840.00
Gnome, 2 Sections, Screw Fasteners, Painted, Cast Iron, 10 ¾ In.	224.00
Gnome, Old Man, Crawling, Iron, 27 x 12 x 12 In.	240.00
Gnome, Painted, Cast Iron, c.1900, 10 x 21 In.	330.00
Hitching Post Cap, Napoleon Bust, Epaulet Rings, Paint, Cast Iron, c.1850, 8 In.	13035.00
Hitching Post, Black, Stable Boy, Cast Iron, c.1955, 43 In.	148.00
Hitching Post, Eagle's Head, Ring, Column Support, Stepped Base, Cast Iron, c.1850, 21 x 46 In.	2990.00
Hitching Post, Horse Head, Black Paint, Iron, 45 ½ In.	489.00
Hitching Post, Horse Head, Fluted Column, Lion Masks, Cast Iron, c.1890, 70 ½ In.	1020.00
Hitching Post, Horse Head, Iron, 1800s, 47 ½ In.	403.00
Hitching Post, Horse Head, Ring, Column Support, Cast Iron, c.1850, 41 In.	2990.00
Hitching Post, Horse Head, Ring, Column Support, Cast Iron, c.1850, 49 In.	1840.00
Hitching Post, Jockey, Black Coat, White Pants, Red Hat, Hand In Pocket, Iron, 24 In.	84.00
Hitching Post, Jockey, Cast Iron, Label, Foundry Union Beach, N.J., 1800s, 47 In. *Illus*	2868.00
Hitching Post, Jockey, Cast Iron, White Oak Foundry, Peapack, N.J., 1800s, 46 ½ In. *Illus*	1464.00
Hitching Post, Jockey, Holding Ring, Red, Black, White Paint, Iron, 48 In.	443.00
Hitching Post, Jockey, Paint, Iron Stamped, McKittrick Foundry, Union Beach, N.J., 47 In.	537.00
Hitching Post, Jockey, Pedestal Base, Plaster, 48 In.	112.00
Hitching Post, Lighthouse Shape, Black, White Stripes, Ring, Metal, Over Wood, 26 In.	210.00
Jardiniere, Louis XVI Style, Musical Instruments, Gilt Bronze Swags, Marble Sides, Insert, 6 x 12 In.	3750.00
Jardiniere, Square, Molded Borders, Waves & Rope Pattern Edge, Lead, c.1750, 27 x 27 In.	805.00
Lavabo, Lion Mask, Relief Details, Painted Red, Cast Aluminum, 30 x 17 In.	207.00
Lavabo, Shaped Back, Painted Red, Cast Iron, 26 x 22 ½ In.	69.00
Lawn Sprinkler, Spinning, Copper, c.1950, 47 In.	59.00
Maiden, Satyr, Holding Instruments, Scrolled Pedestal Base, Limestone, 49 In., 4 Piece	5900.00
Maiden, Seated, Flower Swags, Gown, Feeding Bird, Square Base, Marble, 1800s, 32 x 43 In.	4920.00
Mailbox Holder, Uncle Sam, Figural, Multicolored, Iron, Columbia Iron Foundry, Pa., 57 In.	13640.00
Ornament, 2 Owls, Sitting In Branches, Cast Cement, 15 x 10 In.	109.00
Ornament, Grotesque Mask, Leafy Beard, Head, Cast, Cement, 10 x 10 In.	92.00
Ornament, Sunflower, Tin, Painted, 28 In.	830.00
Pedestal, 3 Caryatid Supports, Hoof Feet, Triangle Base, Zinc, c.1900, 36 ½ x 16 In.	780.00
Pedestal, Fluted Column Shape, Stepped Top, Paw Feet, Marble, c.1910, 43 x 16 In.	420.00
Pedestal, Rolled Rim, Fluted Column, Limestone, c.1860, 43 x 27 ½ In.	1080.00
Pilaster, Art Deco, Scrolled Volutes, Flowers, Terra-Cotta, c.1910, 101 x 21 In., Pair	540.00
Plant Stand, see Furniture, Stand, Plant	
Planter, 3 Tiers, Green Paint, Circular Shelf, Pedestal Base, Cast Iron, Victorian, 36 x 27 In.	3163.00
Planter, Art Deco, Rolled Rim, 3 Handles, Terra-Cotta, Galloway, c.1930, 8 ¾ x 18 In., Pair	960.00
Planter, Baluster Urn Shaped, Swirl Handles, Square Base, Cast Iron, 16 ½ In.	400.00
Planter, Box, Bird, Stripes, Wood, Carved, E. Ackerman, 1973, 9 x 9 ½ In., Pair	500.00
Planter, Eagle, Satyr, Embossed, Bulbous Base, Ring Handles, Copper, c.1890, 27 x 15 In.	570.00
Planter, Earthcells, 4 Connected Pots, Narrow Bottom, Swollen Center, D. Cressey, c.1963, 14 x 26 In.	4375.00
Planter, Flamingo, Figural, Iron, 56 In.	115.00
Planter, Keg, Oak, Herring, Copper Inset, Brass Staves, 24 x 13 ½ In.	1035.00
Planter, Neoclassical Figures, Eagle Feet & Handles, Rectangular, Ebonized, Brass, c.1815	1080.00

Planter, Relief Design, Flat Rim, Leaf Shaped Feet, Cast Iron, c.1900, 15 x 23 In.	531.00
Planter, Ribbed, Rolled Rim, Blue Green Galloway Glaze, c.1930, 20 x 24 ¾ In.	1920.00
Planter, Ring Handles, Cast Iron, France, c.1920, 12 x 26 In.	240.00
Planter, Scrolls & Flowers, Wrought Iron, c.1930, 37 x 31 In.	420.00
Planter, Splayed Base, Paint, Wirework, 30 x 34 In.	88.00
Planter, Swan, White, Iron, 14 ½ x 10 In., Pair	270.00
Sculpture, Abstract, Squared Column Base, Painted Rust, Oxidized, Wrought Iron, 72 x 17 In.	150.00
Sculpture, Flower, Amethyst, Spiral Spring, Stainless Steel, Whitmore Boogaerts, 2003, 71 In. ..*Illus*	1140.00
Sculpture, Lily Pads, 5 Stacked Abstract Forms, Steel Wire Rod, John Risley, 1965, 65 In. .. *Illus*	4800.00
Seat, Barrel Shape, Blue & White, Birds, Flowers, Pierced, Coin Design, Porcelain, 1800s, 21 In., Pair	676.00
Seat, Barrel Shape, Chinese Symbols, Ring Handles, Faux Straw Paint, Pottery, Italy, 16 x 16 In.	127.00
Seat, Barrel Shape, Famille Rose, Phoenix, Cranes Flying, 1800s, 19 x 11 ½ In.	500.00
Seat, Barrel Shape, Famille Rose, Pierced Top, Birds, Butterflies, Flowers, 1800s, 17 ½ x 14 In.	2588.00
Seat, Barrel Shape, Pierced, White & Cobalt Blue, Flowers, Scroll, Staffordshire, c.1885, 19 x 13 In.	461.00
Seat, Blue & White, Flowers & Leaves, Scroll Design, Ceramic, 1892, 20 In.	854.00
Seat, Celadon, Birds, Flowers, Hexagonal, Porcelain, 18th Century, 19 In.	2940.00
Seat, Elephant, Chinese Style, Yellow Glaze, 22 x 12 In.	167.00
Seat, Famille Rose, Barrel Shape, Hexagonal, 1800s, 18 In.	2300.00
Seat, Famille Rose, Birds, Blossoms, Hexagonal, c.1900, 18 ½ x 12 ½ In., Pair	2900.00
Seat, Famille Verte, Hexagonal, Pierced Top, Raised Gilt Bosses, Porcelain, 18 x 11 x 11 In.	235.00
Seat, Famille Verte, Multicolor, Ivory Band, Guardian Lions, Foo Dogs, Chinese, 1800s, 18 ½ x 14 In.	3450.00
Seat, Medallion, Shaped Apron, Scrolled Legs, Round Stretcher, Pad Feet, Majolica, c.1867, 18 ½ In.	2015.00
Seat, Olive Green, Dragons, Raised, Pierced, Pottery, Chinese, 20 x 14 In.	120.00
Seat, Rose Medallion, Barrel Shape, Pierced Cashes, Chinese, 19th Century, 19 In.	2370.00
Seat, Rose Medallion, Imperial Court Scenes, Chinese, 1800s, 11 ½ x 9 ½ In.	12650.00
Seat, Settee, Pierced Crest & Back, Cutout Seat, Scroll Arms, Splayed Legs, Cast Metal, c.1890	1434.00
Seat, Snail Shape, Silver Gilt, Cushion, c.1950, 18 ½ x 24 In.	360.00
Seat, Tree Trunk Shape, Curved Branch Supports, Rope Tied Center, Triangular Base, c.1875, 18 In.	1000.00
Set, Four Seasons, 2 Settees, 4 Chairs, Marble Top Table, Painted, Cast Iron, 7 Piece	5535.00
Set, Openwork, Painted, Cast Iron, Settee, 2 Chairs, Stool, Bench, 1900s, 5 Piece.. *Illus*	767.00
Set, Wrought Iron, White, Ivy, Glass Top Table, Curved Bench, 4 Chairs, 2 End Tables	395.00
Settee & Chair, Lyre Back, Openwork Seat, Iron, c.1910, Settee 32 ½ x 47 In., Chair 33 In. *Illus*	2242.00
Settee, Fern & Blackberry Design, Lattice, Cast Iron, Green Paint, c.1895, 36 x 58 In.	2963.00
Settee, Laurel Design, Green Paint, Pierced, Flowers, Shaped Legs, Arms, Iron, c.1895, 32 x 38 In.	830.00
Settee, Scrollwork, Double Back, Cast Iron, Virginia, c.1890, 29 ½ x 16 ½ In.	489.00
Silhouette, Boy & Dog, Sitting In Flower Vines, Sawmill Blade, Iron, c.1900, 67 x 54 In.	940.00
Silhouette, Figure Playing Flute, Sawmill Blade, Iron, c.1900, 57 x 33 In.	470.00
Sphere, Band Carved, Stone, c.1880, 16 In., Pair	510.00
Stool, Corset Shape Back, Leaf & Scroll, Revolving Seat, Pierced Apron, Cast Iron, c.1890, 33 In.	2091.00
Sundial, Armillary, Art Deco Figure Support, Copper, 30 ½ x 35 In.	1560.00
Sundial, Bronze Dial, Stepped Top, Base, Carved Swags, 43 x 23 In.	660.00
Sundial, Bronze, Engraved Star, Scroll, Lettering, England, 1800s, 14 In.	668.00
Sundial, Cast Metal, Patinated, Inscribed Tyme Thyeth Trothe, 10 x 12 In.	1121.00
Sundial, Column, 6-Sided, Stepped Base, Bronze, Stone, c.1940, 39 x 13 In.	540.00
Sundial, Compass Rose, Arabic Numerals, Octagon, Engraved, c.1800, 10 ⅛ x 10 ⅛ In.	6765.00
Sundial, Diptych, Wood, Printed Paper Dials, Compass, String Gnomon, c.1850, 3 In. .. *Illus*	504.00
Sundial, Flame & Urn, Octagon, Bronze, Stone, Carved, England, 1800s, 43 x 16 ½ In.	1140.00
Sundial, Pedestal, Classical Figures, Zodiac Symbols, Cast Iron, Painted Rust, 63 In.	357.00
Sundial, Pedestal, Fluted Column, Flared Base, Bronze, Cast Iron, Victorian, 45 x 17 In.	1599.00
Sundial, Pedestal, Tapered, Paneled, Bronze, Stone, 43 ½ x 12 ¾ In.	1380.00
Sundial, Verdigris Bronze, Stone Column, Stepped Base, Signed J. Myers, c.1900, 44 x 15 ½ In.	1140.00
Table, Console, Flowers, Scrolls, Wrought Iron, France, c.1930, 32 x 36 In.	480.00
Table, Curved Front & Base, Turtle Design, 30 x 33 ½ In.	480.00
Table, Flower & Vine Open Column, Swirl Base, Wrought Iron, Marble Top, Round, 30 x 21 In.	780.00
Table, Onyx Top, Round, Wrought Iron Legs, Spider Shape Stretcher, c.1940, 30 x 36 In.	600.00
Table, Pierced Design, Triangular Pedestal, Platform Base, Round, Cast Iron, 28 x 24 In.	492.00
Table, Pierced Round Top, Medial Shelf, Cast Iron, Colebrookdale, 28 x 24 In.	390.00
Table, Potting, Wood Plank Top, Metal Medial Shelf, 6 Legs, c.1930, 34 x 80 In.	840.00
Table, Potting, Zinc Top, Wrought Iron Base, 32 x 61 In.	510.00
Table, Scrolled Apron, Glass Top, Wrought Iron, Round, c.1950, 28 x 42 In.	510.00
Urn, 2 Parts, Removable Handles, White Paint, Cast Iron, Marked, Kramer Bros., c.1900, 33 In., Pair	783.00
Urn, American Shield, Lincoln, Square Pedestal Base, 2 Loop Handles, Cast Iron, c.1850, 22 x 15 In.	323.00
Urn, Baroque Style, Cupid, Mask Rim, Bronze, Patina, 1900s, 39 x 17 ½ In. .. *Illus*	3068.00
Urn, Bell Shape, Handles, Cream Paint, Cast Iron, c.1910, 31 x 26 In., Pair	750.00
Urn, Black Paint, Cast Iron, Stand, c.1960, 43 In., Pair	750.00
Urn, Campana, Fluted, Reeded Socle, Square Base, Cast Iron, 31 ½ x 25 ½ In., Pair	375.00

Game, Wheel, Gambling, Numbers, Mirrored Spokes, 4-Legged Base, Wood, Glass, c.1920, 71 ½ In.
$3,995.00

Garth's Auctioneers & Appraisers

G

Garden, Birdbath, Carved Limestone, Separate Base, William Edmondson, c.1940, 27 ½ x 8 x 16 In.
$2,832.00

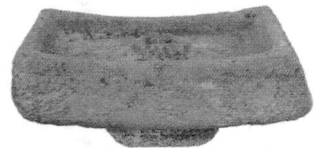

Brunk Auctions

Garden, Birdhouse, Clapboard, 2 Porches, Chimneys, Tar Paper Roof, Painted, c.1950, 22 x 27 In.
$558.00

Garth's Auctioneers & Appraisers

Garden, Chair, Stylized Cat Back, Cast Iron, Richard Bawden, 35 In., Pair
$4,000.00

Leslie Hindman Auctioneers

Garden, Figure, Boy, Arms Holding Planter, Cast Concrete, 1900s, 46 ¾ In. $767.00

Brunk Auctions

Garden, Figure, Classical Women, Grapes, Flowers, Concrete Or Cast Stone, c.1900, 61 In., Pair $1,534.00

Brunk Auctions

Garden, Hitching Post, Jockey, Cast Iron, Label, Foundry Union Beach, N.J., 1800s, 47 In. $2,868.00

Neal Auction Co.

TIP

Some old locks must have the key turned twice to open.

Urn, Campana, Gadroon Lip, Ribbed Body, Waisted, Square Base, Cast Iron, c.1900, 18 x 21 In.....	215.00
Urn, Campana, Ribbed Body, Molded Lip, 2 Handles, Pedestal Foot, Square Base, Iron, 24 In., Pair	492.00
Urn, Campana, Rolled Rim, Melon Carved Bowl, Socle, Stepped Base, Cast Stone, 26 x 20 In., Pair	1020.00
Urn, Campana, Round Pedestal Foot, Square Base, Ribbed Body, Flare Rim, Cast Iron, 20 In., Pair	123.00
Urn, Campana, Shell Rim, Fluted, Square Pedestal, Stepped Base, Cast Iron, c.1900, 34 x 19 In.	922.00
Urn, Carved Rim, Scrolled Handles, Raised Tapered Plinth, 36 In.	2400.00
Urn, Cast Iron, Victorian, Tazza Shape, Scalloped Rim, Fluted Body, 12 ¾ In.	215.00
Urn, Egg & Dart Rim, Star & Scroll Handles, Leaves, Stepped Base, Cast Iron, c.1880, 33 x 38 In...	1920.00
Urn, Fluted Bowl, Stepped Base, Cast Iron, France, c.1900, 13 x 16 In., Pair	500.00
Urn, Fluted, Molded Egg & Dart Rim, Plinth Base, Cast Iron, 18 x 24 In., Pair	1673.00
Urn, Gadrooned Rim, Dragon Handles, Cast Iron, Label Corneau Alfred, France, c.1880, 20 ½ x 18 In..	480.00
Urn, Handles, Bulbous Bowl, Applied Wreath, Raised Socle, Plinth, Cast Iron, c.1870, 45 x 36 In...	1140.00
Urn, Iron, Watering Trough, c.1850, 21 x 46 In.	2185.00
Urn, Neoclassical Style, Campana, Egg & Dart Rim, Fluted & Lobed, Cast Iron, 30 ½ In., Pair	922.00
Urn, Neoclassical, Campana Shape, Cast Iron, Laurel Wreath, Mask Handles, 56 In., Pair.......	2829.00
Urn, Palmette Molded Rim, Lobed Body, Square Base, Cast Iron, c.1900, 18 ½ x 20 ½ In., Pair .	922.00
Urn, Pierced Flower Design, Classical Base, Cast Iron, 43 ½ x 18 In., Pair	960.00
Urn, Pineapple, Square Base, Cast Iron, 24 In., Pair	300.00
Urn, Poseidon Face, Snake Handles, Cast Iron, 38 ½ x 30 In., Pair	960.00
Urn, Putti Handles, Basket Weave Rim, Lions, Rings, Stepped Plinth, 37 x 31 In., Pair	1080.00
Urn, Regency Style, Curled Leaf Shape, Carved, Marble, 30 ½ x 19 In., Pair	3840.00
Urn, Relief Wreaths, Black Paint, Pedestal Base, Stand, Cast Iron, c.1900, 33 x 19 ½ In...*Illus*	944.00
Urn, Renaissance Style, Acanthus, Lion's Mask & Ring Handles, Bronze, 41 x 43 In.	1320.00
Urn, Satyr Handles, Flower Garland, Fluted Base, Terra-Cotta, England, 18 ½ x 18 ½ In.	510.00
Urn, Scalloped Rim, Cast Iron, 24 x 24 In., Pair.	1200.00
Urn, Scroll Handles, Round Foot, Square Stepped Base, Flared Rim, Cast Iron, c.1900, 34 x 30 In.	353.00
Urn, Shallow Bowl, Scalloped Rim, Iron, Kramer Brothers, Dayton, c.1900, 31 In., Pair..*Illus*	1116.00
Urn, Shallow Lobed Bowl, Fluted Base, Cast Iron, c.1880, 19 ½ x 30 In., Pair	1020.00
Urn, Shaped Rim, Melon Bowl, Lion Handles, Rings, Cast Iron, Woodbury, 1800s, 12 x 16 In., Pair	2280.00
Urn, Speckled Oatmeal Glaze, Banded, Pottery, Stamped, Galloway, U.S.A., 1920s, 20 In., Pair	1250.00
Urn, Stepped, Rolled Rim, Lobed Bowl, Plinth Base, c.1860, 26 x 28 In.	1440.00
Urn, Victorian, Figural Handles, Iron, 23 ¾ In., Pair .....*Illus*	1250.00
Urn, White Paint, Removable Handles, Iron, Kramer Bros., Ohio, c.1900, 33 In., Pair......*Illus*	646.00
Well Head, Rope Twist Border, Leaves, Shields, Carved, Stone, Italy, c.1650, 34 x 46 In.	22800.00

GARDNER PORCELAIN WORKS was founded in Verbiki, outside Moscow, by the English-born Francis Gardner in 1766. The Gardner family retained ownership of the factory until 1891 and produced porcelain tablewares, figurines, and faience.

ГАРДНЕРЪ

Figurine, Balalaika Player, Painted, c.1900, 8 ½ In.	805.00
Figurine, Dancing Peasant, Blue Dress, Pink Apron, c.1900, 7 ½ In.	690.00

GAUDY DUTCH pottery was made in England for the American market from about 1810 to 1820. It is a white earthenware with Imari-style decorations of red, blue, green, yellow, and black. Only sixteen patterns of Gaudy Dutch were made: Butterfly, Carnation, Dahlia, Double Rose, Dove, Grape, Leaf, Oyster, Primrose, Single Rose, Strawflower, Sunflower, Urn, War Bonnet, Zinnia, and No Name. Other similar wares are called Gaudy Ironstone and Gaudy Welsh.

Bowl, Single Rose, c.1850, 9 ⅞ In.	385.00
Bowl, War Bonnet, Flower Border, c.1850, 8 In.	178.00
Coffeepot, Single Rose, 1800s, 12 In.	1659.00
Coffeepot, Single Rose, c.1850, 11 ¾ In.	2844.00
Cup & Saucer, Butterfly, c.1850	415.00
Cup & Saucer, Dahlia, c.1850	4029.00
Cup & Saucer, Primrose, c.1820	2133.00
Plate, Butterfly, Multicolor, 1800s, 8 In.	533.00
Plate, Single Rose, c.1850, 9 ¾ In.	267.00
Saucer, Double Rose, Blue, Green, Yellow Leaves, Blue Band, Red Rim, 5 ½ In., Pair	118.00
Tea Set, Teapot, Creamer, Sugar, Lid, War Bonnet, c.1850, 3 Piece	415.00
Waste Bowl, Single Rose, c.1850, 3 ⅛ x 6 ⅛ In.	178.00

GAUDY IRONSTONE is the collector's name for the ironstone wares with the bright patterns similar to Gaudy Dutch. It was made in England for the American market after 1850. There may be other examples found in the listing for Ironstone or under the name of the ceramic factory.

Basin, Footbath, Painted, 1800s, 8 x 20 In.	213.00
Plate, Ashworth's Real Ironstone China, Co., c.1840, 10 In., 12 Piece	590.00

G

GAUDY WELSH is an Imari-decorated earthenware with red, blue, green, and gold decorations. Most Gaudy Welsh was made in England for the American market. It was made from 1820 to about 1860.

Mug, Straight-Sided, Applied Loop Handle, Tar Baby, Copper Luster Accent, 3 x 3 In.	59.00
Pitcher, Pagoda Shape, Cobalt Blue, Orange & Green Flowers, Double Curve Handle, 6 ½ In. *Illus*	59.00

GEISHA GIRL porcelain was made for export in the late nineteenth century in Japan. It was an inexpensive porcelain often sold in dime stores or used as free premiums. Pieces are sometimes marked with the name of a store. Japanese ladies in kimonos are pictured on the dishes. There are over 125 recorded patterns. Borders of red, blue, green, gold, brown, or several of these colors were used. Modern reproductions are being made.

Bowl, Geisha, Mountains, Flowers, 8 Sections, Scalloped, Orange Rim, c.1920, 7 In.	55.00
Chocolate Cup & Saucer, 3 Geisha, River, 24K Gold Accents, Red Trim, 1920s	40.00
Condensed Milk Holder, Lid, Geisha, Loop Handles, Blue Scalloped Trim	85.00
Cup & Saucer, Geisha, Sitting By Lake, Birds, Green Trim	25.00
Dresser Box, Geisha, Pink, Orange, Green Trim, 1950s, 2 x 3 ½ In.	26.00
Hair Receiver, 2 Geisha, Flowers, Hut, 1930s, 3 ½ In.	19.00
Hair Receiver, 2 Geisha, Flowers, Red Trim, 1930s, 3 ½ In. Diam	19.00
Match Holder, 2 Geisha, Flowers, Lanterns, 4 ½ x 2 ½ In.	42.00
Plate, Geisha, House By Lake, Birds, Trees, Octagonal, c.1950, 6 ½ In.	38.00
Plate, Geisha, Village, Bridge, Red Trim, c.1925, 7 In.	49.00
Plate, Moriage & Pierced Handles, Geisha, In Boat, Trees, Mountain, 9 ⅝ In.	69.00
Tray, 3 Geisha, Gate, Red Flowers & Trim, 5 ⅜ x 3 ⅜ In.	19.00

GENE AUTRY was born in 1907. He began his career as the "Singing Cowboy" in 1928. His first movie appearance was in 1934, his last in 1958. His likeness and that of the Wonder Horse, Champion, were used on toys, books, lunch boxes, and advertisements.

Button, Pinback, Official Club, Portrait, 1 ¼ In. Diam	38.00
Cutouts, Camp Scenes, Chuck Wagon, 1940s	35.00
Record, South Of The Border, 78 RPM, 10 In.	12.00
Suspenders, Pistol Adjustments, Child's, 1950s	25.00
Wristwatch, Champion, Horseshoe, Red, Cream, Wilane, 1948	270.00
Wristwatch, Smiling Cowboy, Holding Gun, Metal Band	46.00

GIBSON GIRL black-and-blue decorated plates were made in the early 1900s. Twenty-four different 10 ½-inch plates were made by the Royal Doulton pottery at Lambeth, England. These pictured scenes from the book *A Widow and Her Friends* by Charles Dana Gibson. Another set of twelve 9-inch plates featuring pictures of the heads of Gibson Girls had all-blue decoration. Many other items also pictured the famous Gibson Girl.

Illustration, Birds Of A Feather, 2 Women Talking Intimately, Zoo Cages, Ink & Pencil, 15 x 14 In.	575.00
Illustration, Conversation, Man & Woman Talking, Older Couple Watching, Pen & Ink, 23 x 29 In.	575.00
Illustration, Dapper Gentleman, Leaning On Table, Pen & Pencil, Signed, 23 x 14 ½ In.	230.00
Illustration, Girl At Fence, Man Leaning On Railing Sketch On Reverse, 23 x 12 ½ In.	345.00
Illustration, Girl On Chair, Ink & Pencil, Signed, Unpublished, 15 x 21 In.	288.00
Picture, Automaton, Woman, Brown Hair, Eyes, Mouth & Head Move, 1890s, 27 In.	2128.00
Plate, A Message From The Outside World, 10 ½ In.	50.00
Plate, A Quiet Dinner With Dr. Bottles, 10 ½ In.	85.00
Plate, Mr. Waddles Arrives Late & Finds Her Card Filled, 10 ½ In.	125.00
Plate, She Becomes A Trained Nurse, 10 ½ In.	140.00
Plate, She Goes To The Fancy Dress Ball As Juliet, 10 ½ In.	155.00
Plate, They Go Fishing, 10 ½ In.	130.00
Washbasin, Tole, Blue, Holding Opera Glasses, Gilt, France, 1800s, 29 x 31 x 27 ½ In. *Illus*	108.00

GIRL SCOUT collectors search for anything pertaining to the Girl Scouts, including uniforms, publications, and old cookie boxes. The Girl Scout movement started in 1912, two years after the Boy Scouts. It began under Juliette Gordon Low of Savannah, Georgia. The first Girl Scout cookies were sold in 1928.

Barrette, Plastic, Symbol Shape, Yellow, 1 ½ x 1 ¼ In.	10.00
Beanie, Brown, Emblem, 1950s	18.00
Book, Becky & Tatters A Brownie Scout Story, Hardcover, c.1940, 100 Pages, 6 x 8 In.	10.00
Button, I Am Needed, Trefoil Pin, Black & White, Celluloid, 1 ¾ In.	10.00
Cookbook, Soft Cover, Cooking With A Purpose, 15 Pages, 5 ½ x 7 ½ In.	10.00
Doll, Black Girl, Vinyl, Sleep Eyes, Effanbee, Fluffy, Girl, Box, 1964, 8 In.	165.00

Garden, Hitching Post, Jockey, Cast Iron, White Oak Foundry, Peapack, N.J., 1800s, 46 ½ In.
$1,464.00

Neal Auction Co.

G

Garden, Sculpture, Flower, Amethyst, Spiral Spring, Stainless Steel, Whitmore Boogaerts, 2003, 71 In.
$1,140.00

Skinner, Inc.

Garden, Sculpture, Lily Pads, 5 Stacked Abstract Forms, Steel Wire Rod, John Risley, 1965, 65 In.
$4,800.00

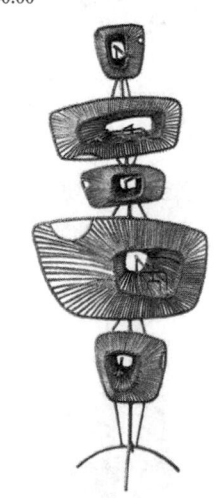

Skinner, Inc.

Garden, Set, Openwork, Painted, Cast Iron, Settee, 2 Chairs, Stool, Bench, 1900s, 5 Piece
$767.00

Brunk Auctions

Garden, Settee & Chair, Lyre Back, Openwork Seat, Iron, c.1910, Settee 32 ½ x 47 In., Chair 33 In.
$2,242.00

Brunk Auctions

Garden, Sundial, Diptych, Wood, Printed Paper Dials, Compass, String Gnomon, c.1850, 3 In.
$504.00

Skinner, Inc.

Garden, Urn, Baroque Style, Cupid, Mask Rim, Bronze, Patina, 1900s, 39 x 17 ½ In.
$3,068.00

Brunk Auctions

Doll, Uniform, Green, Jointed, Box, Effanbee, Fluffy, 8 In.	65.00
Handbook, Hard Cover, 1932, 404 Pages	5.00
Jack Knife, Green, Emblem, Can Opener, Screwdriver, Duty Master, Utica, N.Y., 3 ½ In.	45.00
Keychain, Eagle, 1970s, ⅞ In.	7.50
Mess Kit, Pan, Dish, Bowl, Emblem, 1940s	20.00
Mug, Green Logo, Santa Fe Trail Council, c.1965	6.00
Paper Dolls, Foreign Nations, Uniforms, Dejournette Of Atlanta, Box, 1950s	45.00
Ring, Bezeled, Insignia, Green Stone, Faceted, 10K Gold Filled, Size 6 ½ In.	125.00
Uniform, Junior, Hat, Belt, Purse, Sash, Tie, Green, Yellow, 1960, Size 10	69.00

GLASS factories that are well known are listed in this book under the factory name. This category lists pieces made by less well-known factories. Additional pieces of glass are listed in this book under the type of glass, in the categories Glass-Art, Glass-Blown, Glass-Bohemian, Glass-Contemporary, Glass-Midcentury, Glass-Venetian, and under the factory name.

Bowl, Center, Sapphire Blue, Twisted Body Optic, Square Flared Rim, Scrolling Arms, 9 x 22 In.	47.00
Cruet, Stopper, Amber, Blue, Victorian, 9 In.	28.00
Cruet, Stopper, Blue Lobed Sides, Amber Handle, Victorian, 8 In.	34.00
Pitcher, Rainbow Swirl, Baluster, Loop Handle, Victorian, 8 ½ In.	230.00
Pitcher, Topaz, Coin Dot, Flowers, Leaves, Gold Accents, Rope Twist Loop Handle, Ruffle Rim, 8 In.	201.00
Punch Cup, Green Opaque, Blue Metallic Band, Gold Outline, New England Glass, 2 ¾ In... *Illus*	201.00
Sugar, Dome Lid, Clear, Globe Bowl, Daisy Engraved, Stepped Standard, Bakewell, c.1825, 7 x 4 ⅜ In.	8625.00
Vase, Cranberry, Gold Fan Cartouches, Flowers, Elongated Body, 5-Point Rim, Footed, 12 In...	173.00
Vase, Gray, Opalescent, Ribbed, Scalloped Rim, Rough Pontil, c.1860, 9 ½ x 5 In.	633.00
Vase, Opal, Blue & Gold Coil Pattern, Gold Inside, Swollen Neck, Vineland Flint, 10 In.	527.00
Vase, Portrait, Green, St. Bernard's Head, Shouldered, Cylindrical Neck, 14 In.	230.00

GLASS-ART. Art glass means any of the many forms of glassware made during the late nineteenth or early twentieth century. These wares were expensive when they were first made and production was limited. Art glass is not the typical commercial glass that was made in large quantities, and most of the art glass was produced by hand methods. Later twentieth-century glass is listed under Glass-Contemporary, Glass-Midcentury, or Glass-Venetian. Even more art glass may be found in categories such as Burmese, Cameo Glass, Tiffany, and other factory names.

Bowl, Pulled Feather Design, Silvery Gold, Orange, Trumpet, 4 ⅞ x 13 ⅛ In.	173.00
Butter, Cover, Green Opaque, Satin, Purple Staining, Undulating Gold Band, Oval, 6 ¼ In.	1265.00
Cross, Slag, Copper Frame, Green Patina, c.1920, 36 x 24 In.	390.00
Ornament, Dragonfly, Mosaic, Metal Overlay, Purple Wings, Blue Body, Red Eyes, 10 x 14 In.	3081.00
Plate, Tulips, Roses, Carved, Vienna, J & L Lobmeyr, 1880s, 9 ½ In. *Illus*	1125.00
Tantalus, Napoleon III Style, Satinwood, Rosewood, Decanters, Glasses, Gilt Mounts, 11 x 14 In.	750.00
Vase, Amber, Opalescent Turquoise Stripes, Pinched Waist, Ruffle Rim, 8 In.	316.00
Vase, Art Nouveau Style, Green Iridescent, Metal Frame, 12 In.	387.00
Vase, Blue & Gold Iridescent, Pulled Feather, Silver Thread Overlay, Shouldered, c.1978, 7 ⅞ In.	295.00
Vase, Blue Irises On Black, Green Stems, Moon, Stars, Tapered, Signed, 10 ½ In.	633.00
Vase, Blue, Gold Aurene Feathers, Swirl Design, Bulbous, Flared Rim, 7 ¼ In.	690.00
Vase, Bud, Art Nouveau, Blue Iridescent, Shaded To Green, Gold, Silver Overlay, c.1900, 3 In.	540.00
Vase, Clear, Emerald Lines, Peaked, 12 ¼ In.	652.00
Vase, Emerald Green Pulled Feathers, Gold, Rippled, Shouldered, Ring Neck, Flared Rim, 7 ¾ In.	259.00
Vase, Emerald Green, Silver Overlay, Ruffled Top, Footed, 8 In.	1121.00
Vase, Flambe, Silver Overlay, 14 In.	1007.00
Vase, Flask Shape, Wavy Pink, White Latticinio, 8 ½ In.	265.00
Vase, Flint, Green Cut To Clear, Circles, Rectangles, Roses, Flared, Scalloped Rim, 7 ¼ x 5 In.	48.00
Vase, Foil Patches, Layered, Blue, Green, Purple, Iridescent, Elongated Oval, Signed, 10 ½ In.	460.00
Vase, Fuchsia, Flowering Branches, Gilded, Shouldered, Rolled Rim, B. Schverer, c.1890, 5 x 2 In.	3250.00
Vase, Fuchsia, Sweat Pea Flowers, Silvery Green Leaves, Shouldered, Flared Rim, 7 In.	230.00
Vase, Gold Iridescent, Heart Shape Leaves, Stems, 7 ¼ In.	153.00
Vase, Golden Feathers, Peacock Blue Design, Iridescent, Trumpet, Round Foot, 10 In.	460.00
Vase, Green Iridescent, Tapered, Cone Shape, Bronze Footed Tripod Base, c.1900, 13 In.	590.00
Vase, Green, Purple Iridescent, Threaded, c.1900, 5 ½ In.	215.00
Vase, Green, Urn Shape, Gilt Key Fret, Flowers, Footed, c.1890, 9 ½ In.	165.00
Vase, Iridescent Pulled Feathers, 10 Trailing Gold Iridescent Prunts, Martin Bach, 13 In. *Illus*	7475.00
Vase, Iridescent, Blue Green, Purple, Ruby Highlights, Silver Strands, Swelled Base, Dome Top, 8 ⅛ In.	224.00
Vase, Iridescent, Raised Design, Pewter Mount & Handles, Van Hauten, c.1900, 7 ⅞ In. *Illus*	854.00
Vase, Molded Fruit, Frosted Ground, Tapered, 7 In.	2000.00
Vase, Opal, Enameled Pink Flowers, Shouldered, Amber Rigaree Handles, 9 In.	115.00
Vase, Orange Iridescent, Platinum Oil Spot, Pulled Collar, Foldover Rim, Round Foot, 8 ¼ In.	259.00
Vase, Orange, Iridescent, Opal Interior, Ruffled Rim, Ring Foot, 6 ¾ In.	58.00

Vase, Orchids, Purple, Squat, Rolled Rim, B. Schverer, c.1890, 3 x 3 In.	625.00
Vase, Pink Flowers On Orange Ground, Green Leaves, Bulbous, Turned Down Rim, 9 ½ In.	1265.00
Vase, Pulled Arches, Zipper Design, Urn Shape, Yellow, Blue, Green, 6 ½ In.	403.00
Vase, Pulled Drape Design, Blue, Green, Purple, Gold Iridescent, Beaker, Flared Rim, 9 In.	127.00
Vase, Pulled Honey Gold Feathers, Maroon Threads, Shouldered, 1978, 8 ¼ In.	345.00
Vase, Purple Hearts, Silvery Blue Vines, Gold, Bulbous, Ring Foot, 2 ½ In.	316.00
Vase, Rainbow Pastels, Tartan Pattern, Bulbous, Flared Rim, Signed, 6 In.	633.00
Vase, Red, Gold, Blue Pulled Feather Design, Shouldered, Flat Rim, 11 ¾ In.	431.00
Vase, Silver Overlay, Yellow Iridescent, c.1910, 4 In.	531.00
Vase, Sinuous Feathers, Gold Iridescent, Red, Gourd Shape, Flattened, 1979, 6 ½ In.	460.00
Vase, Spattered Leaves, Cobalt Blue Swirling Vines, Iridescent Rainbow, Swollen Rim, 1986, 6 In.	219.00
Vase, Tapered, Trees In Landscape, Blue Cut To Colorless, Frosted, c.1900, 10 ¼ In., Pair...*Illus*	237.00
Vase, Trumpet Shape, Green To Clear, Swirling Lilies & Leaves Pattern, c.1915, 11 ½ In.	338.00

GLASS-BLOWN. Blown glass was formed by forcing air through a rod into molten glass. Early glass and some forms of art glass were hand blown. Other types of glass were molded or pressed.

Bell, Garden, Green Aqua, Flared, Knob, 15 ½ x 17 In.	590.00
Bottle, Chestnut, Dark Yellow Olive, Rounded Collar, Pontil, 9 In.	2691.00
Bottle, Chestnut, Green, Irregular String Lip, 4 ⅜ x 3 ¼ In.	2340.00
Bottle, Storage, Golden Amber, Cylindrical, Wide Neck, Squared Collar, 8 ¾ In.	896.00
Bottle, Storage, Sea Green, Cylindrical, Shouldered, Wide Neck, Ring Collar, 11 In.	269.00
Bowl, Amber, Flared, Folded Rim, Rough Pontil, c.1835, 3 ¾ x 8 ½ In.	805.00
Bowl, Amber, Swirled Ribs, Foldover Rim, Ohio, c.1835, 6 In.	470.00
Bowl, Blue, Green, Olive Inclusions, Rolled Over Rim, Rough Pontil, c.1850, 2 ½ x 11 ¾ In.	219.00
Bowl, Green, Crystal Pinched Handles, Flared Rim, Tooled Scallops, 6 ½ x 11 In.	24.00
Bowl, Leech, Topaz, Ribs, Swirled To Left, Globular, Squat, Flattened Rim, c.1870, 2 In.	840.00
Cake Stand, Beaded Rim, Banded Hourglass Pedestal, Domed Base, 8 x 12 In.	189.00
Cheese Dome, Plate, Red Amber, Bubbles, Finial, c.1860, 6 ½ x 8 In.	115.00
Claret, Clear, Amber Ovals, Blown, Engraved Flowers, Swags, Grapes, Raised Stem, c.1875, 5 In.	259.00
Compote, Amber, Short Standard, Rough Pontil, c.1850, 3 ¾ x 6 In.	2070.00
Compote, Lily Pad, Aquamarine, Applied Base, Tooled Rim, Redford Glass Works, c.1840, 3 ½ In.*Illus*	1115.00
Compote, Round, Fluted Border, Knopped Stem, Disk Base, 1800s, 9 x 10 ¾ In.	780.00
Creamer, Aqua, Threaded Neck, Globular, Flared Foot, c.1860, 3 ⅞ In.	1495.00
Creamer, Black, Low Skirted, Applied Solid Handle, c.1840, 4 ½ x 2 ¼ In.	69.00
Creamer, Cobalt Blue, Bulbous, Wide Cylindrical Neck, Pinched Spout, Footed, 4 In.	146.00
Creamer, Cobalt Blue, Bull's-Eye, Diamond Diaper, Flared Rim, Clear Handle, 4 In.	308.00
Creamer, Green, Lily Pad, Pinched Spout, Flared Rim, Parallel Lines, Scroll Handle, c.1850, 4 In.	5060.00
Decanter, Clear, Zoomorphic, Applied Limbs, Rough Pontil, c.1900, 7 ¾ x 8 ¾ In.	259.00
Decanter, Oranges, Red, White, Blue Swirls, Narrow Neck, Cylindrical, Spherical Stopper, 12 x 5 In.	60.00
Dish, Baluster Stem, Ribbed, Ruffled Rim, Footed, c.1800, 4 ⅜ x 5 ¼ In.	235.00
Fish, Crystal, Amber Eyes, Pectoral Fins, Italy, 11 ¾ x 17 In.	24.00
Flycatcher, Etched Bamboo Decoration, Applied Feet, Ball Stopper, 9 x 8 In.	598.00
Goblet, Blue Opalescence, White Stem, 6 ½ In., 12 Piece	345.00
Jar, Clear, Applied Cobalt Rings, Lid, American, c.1850, 12 ½ x 6 In.	441.00
Jug, 32 Vertical Ribs, Aqua, Spherical, Crimped Loop Handle, Footed, c.1835, 5 In.	3360.00
Jug, Amber, Bell Form, Cinched Waist, Flared Base, Ear Handle, Leaf Rigaree, 8 ½ In.	728.00
Jug, Aqua, Oval, Wafer Base, Curled Loop Handle, Outward Folded Mouth, 3 ¼ In.	168.00
Jug, Golden Amber, Oval, Elongated Neck, Curled Handle, Sloping Collar, 6 ⅜ In.	168.00
Jug, Honey Yellow, Tapered, Ear Handle, Rigaree, Double Collar, Pinched Spout, 8 In.	280.00
Milk Pan, Golden Amber, Flared Sides, Outward Rolled Rim, 4 x 8 ¾ In.	702.00
Milk Pan, Lockport Blue, Tapering Sides, Outward Rolled Rim, 3 ¾ x 9 In.	3218.00
Pitcher Set, Spherical, Amber, Applied Blue Loop Handle, Coin Spot, 4 Mugs, 8 & 4 ½ In.	35.00
Pitcher, Baluster, Medial Band, Rigaree Terminal, Disk Base, 4 ½ In.	270.00
Pitcher, Barrel Form, Wide Flared Neck, Crimped Strap Handle, 8 In.	280.00
Pitcher, Clear, Medial Shoulder, Hollow Handle, c.1860, 8 ¾ x 5 ¾ In., ½ Gal.	230.00
Pitcher, Daniel Crawford Scotch Whiskey, Ruby, White, 7 In.	118.00
Pitcher, Marbrie Loops, Clear, Frosted, Applied Solid Handle, Pa., c.1860, 6 x 2 ¾ In.	288.00
Pitcher, Sea Green, Sheared Mouth, Pour Spout, Applied Handle, 3-Piece Mold, c.1830, 4 ½ In... *Illus*	1404.00
Pitcher, Tumbler Set, Amber, Tapered, Loop Handle, Dogwood, Bittersweet, 9 & 3 ¾ In., 5 Piece	47.00
Serving Dish, Green, White Cased Underside, Scalloped, Rippled Rim, Gold Dust Swirls, 3 ½ x 14 In.	47.00
Stein, Clear Over Internal Drapery Threads, Red, White, Black, Figural Thumblift, 1 Liter.... *Illus*	690.00
Sugar, Amber, Flared, Footed, Sheared Rim, 6 ⅜ x 9 In.	585.00
Sugar, Cobalt Blue, 11 Diamond Pattern, Stiegel Type, Dome Lid, Ribbed Finial	7020.00
Sugar, Cobalt Blue, Fluted, Ribbed Base, c.1830, 3 ⅛ x 4 ½ In.	690.00

G

Garden, Urn, Relief Wreaths, Black Paint, Pedestal Base, Stand, Cast Iron, c.1900, 33 x 19 ½ In. $944.00

Brunk Auctions

Garden, Urn, Shallow Bowl, Scalloped Rim, Iron, Kramer Brothers, Dayton, c.1900, 31 In., Pair $1,116.00

Garth's Auctioneers & Appraisers

Garden, Urn, Victorian, Figural Handles, Iron, 23 ¾ In., Pair $1,250.00

Leslie Hindman Auctioneers

Garden, Urn, White Paint, Removable Handles, Iron, Kramer Bros., Ohio, c.1900, 33 In., Pair $646.00

Garth's Auctioneers & Appraisers

Gaudy Welsh, Pitcher, Pagoda Shape, Cobalt Blue, Orange & Green Flowers, Double Curve Handle, 6 ½ In.
$59.00

Conestoga Auction Co., Inc.

G

Gibson Girl, Washbasin, Tole, Blue, Holding Opera Glasses, Gilt, France, 1800s, 29 x 31 x 27 ½ In.
$108.00

Gray's Auctioneers LLC

Glass, Punch Cup, Green Opaque, Blue Metallic Band, Gold Outline, New England Glass, 2 ¾ In.
$201.00

Early Auction Co.

Glass-Art, Plate, Tulips, Roses, Carved, Vienna, J & L Lobmeyr, 1880s, 9 ½ In.
$1,125.00

Rago Arts & Auction Center

Sugar, Globular, Gallery Rim, Bell-Shaped Lid, Pedestal Foot, 7 ¼ In.	308.00
Vase, Flattened Shape, Flared Neck, Applied Zigzag Collar, Ribbed Knop, Dome Foot, 13 In., Pair	118.00
Vase, Globe Shaped, Textured, Ruffle Rim, Blue & Red Swirling Design, Chaos Series, 7 ½ In.	430.00
Vase, Marbrie Loops, Clear, Frosted, Applied Neck Rings, c.1870, 9 ½ x 3 ⅜ In., Pair	431.00
Vase, Mottled Blue Green, Long Stick Neck, 7 ¾ In.	575.00
Vase, Red Lip Wrap, William Morris, 1980, 11 ½ x 6 In. ....*Illus*	1875.00
Vase, Teardrop, Green, Purple & White Variegated Petals, 8 In.	71.00
Vase, Trumpet, Green & Lavender Base, Swirling Seaweed Design, France, 13 ½ In.	522.00
Wedding Cup, Amber Glass, Ribbed Gilded Overlay, 10 ½ In. ....*Illus*	1656.00
Whimsy, Beaver Hat, Folded Brim, Sunburst, Geometrics, 2 ¼ In.	168.00
Whimsy, Top Hat, Clear, Blue Tint, Turned Up Brim, Foldover Lip, 4 ½ x 6 ¾ In.	35.00
Witch's Ball, Clear End Of Day, 1820, 5 ½ In.	35.00
Witch's Ball, Cranberry Opalescent, Crisscross, Oriental Reticulated Wood Stand, 8 In.	1323.00
Witch's Ball, Rose & White Looping, Sheared Mouth, 1840-70, 6 ½ In. ....*Illus*	556.00
Witch's Ball, Sea Green, Opaque Loopings, Sheared Mouth, 5 ½ In.	2106.00
Witch's Ball, Stand, Pale Green, 4 Draping Line Panels, Flared Mouth, 7 & 5 ½ In.	189.00

GLASS-BOHEMIAN. Bohemian glass is an ornate overlay or flashed glass made during the Victorian era. It has been reproduced in Bohemia, which is now a part of the Czech Republic. Glass made from 1875 to 1900 is preferred by collectors.

Beaker, White To Cranberry, Footed, 5 ¾ In.	258.00
Biscuit Jar, Lid, Green, Oil Spots Design, Molded Raindrops, 7 In.	269.99
Bottle, White Cut To Ruby, Gilt, Teardrop Shape Stopper, Flared Rim, c.1880, 7 ½ In., Pair	720.00
Bowl, Frosted, Raised Gold & Blue Enamel, Undertray, c.1900, 8 ⅝ In. Diam.	148.00
Compote, Gilt, Cut, Ruby Glass, 5 x 4 In.	180.00
Compote, Painted, Gilt Accents, 6 ⅜ In., Pair	375.00
Compote, Round, Cut Rim, Gold & Platinum Leaves, Molded Silver Base, c.1900, 8 ¼ In. Diam.	207.00
Compote, Ruby Red, Drapery Pattern, Footed, 17 ½ x 11 ¾ In.	472.00
Cordial Set, Malachite, Flying Birds, 6-Sided, 12-In. Decanter, 5 Piece	215.00
Cruet, Green, Gold Moorish Medallions, Spots, Scrolling Flowers, Lobmeyr Mark, 9 ½ In., Pair	920.00
Decanter, Amethyst, Gilding At Neck, Stopper, Signed 9, 10 x 4 ½ In.	92.00
Decanter, Blue Opaline, Qajar Monarch Medallion, Flowers, Bottle Shape, 22 In.	3750.00
Decanter, Cut Clear, Ruby Red, Bottle Shape, c.1915, 13 x 7 In.	118.00
Decanter, Enameled Scrolls, Flowers, Cobalt Blue, Spire Stopper, c.1915, 15 ½ In.	2337.00
Decanter, Green, Enameled Flowers & Scrolls, Spear Point Stopper, c.1915, 15 ¾ x 3 ½ In.	1599.00
Decanter, Spire Stopper, Banded Neck, Bulbous, Enamel Flowers, Gilt, Spheres, 22 ¼ In., Pair.	3081.00
Decanter, Stopper, Clear To Ruby Red, c.1900, 14 ½ In.	518.00
Decanter, Stopper, Cut, Faceted Body, Enamel Flower Panels, Gilt, Blue Handle, 10 ½ In.	201.00
Dresser Box, Hinged Lid, Metal Flowers, Leaves, Cranberry Stylized Waves, 1800s, 6 In.	330.00
Ewer, Enameled, Triple Globe Shape, Stylized Design, Multicolor, Stopper, Bird Finial, 14 In.	531.00
Figurine, Bird, Spread Wings, Iridescent Gray Blue & Gold, 1920s-30s, 4 x 5 ½ In.	185.00
Goblet, Crackle, Red, Gold Snake Encircling Stem, 8 In.	472.00
Jar, Lid, Cranberry Cutback, Round, 6 ½ In.	57.00
Lamp, Crystal, Enamel Overlay, Clear To Ruby Flash, Brass Base, 20 In.	48.00
Lusters, Painted Flowers, Green, Gilt, 2 Clear Prism Rows, Electric, 14 In., Pair	298.00
Perfume Bottle, Flask, White Cut To Ruby, Waisted, Gilt Metal Collar, Hinged Lid, 3 ½ In.	86.00
Perfume Bottle, Stopper, Blue Over White, Millefiori Flowers, 7 In.	345.00
Tumbler, Ruby Stained, 3 Figure Engraved Panels, c.1870, 4 ½ x 3 In.	288.00
Urn, Green, Rainbow Iridescent, Handles, Kralik, 12 In. ....*Illus*	460.00
Urn, Lid, Green, Greek Key Design, Trumpet Foot, Flowers, Spear Knop, c.1885, 15 In., Pair	1845.00
Vase, Amethyst Black, Raindrops, Swollen Bottom, Garlic Mouth, Ruffle Rim, Rindskopf, 11 In.	299.00
Vase, Blue, Iridescent, Pulled, Ruffled Rim, Rindskopf, 9 ¼ In.	443.00
Vase, Cobalt Blue, Clear Foot, Snowflake Design, 16 x 8 In.	295.00
Vase, Cranberry, Flared, Footed, 10 In.	62.00
Vase, Cranberry, Portrait, Woman, White Medallion, 9 ¾ In.	510.00
Vase, Enameled Swallows In Flight, Cylindrical, Spread Foot, Ruffle Rim, Herrach, 6 In.	374.00
Vase, Enameled, Cranberry To Clear, Gilt Accents, Flowers, Swags, c.1930, 14 x 5 ½ In.	150.00
Vase, Gold Iridescent, Purple Splatter, Mottled Shell Shape, Starfish Base, W. Kralik, 8 In.	86.00
Vase, Gold Iridescent, Royal Blue Swirl, Squat, Pinched Neck, Trifold Rim, W. Kralik, 6 In.	316.00
Vase, Green Pulled Iridescent, Rolled Neck, Kralik Siberband, 6 x 14 ¼ In.	488.00
Vase, Green, Clear Foot, Cinched Waist, 13 ½ x 7 In., Pair.	354.00
Vase, Iridescent, Multicolor Enamel Flowering Plant, Butterfly, Fritz Heckert, 7 ¾ In.	115.00
Vase, Lime Green, Maroon Confetti Design, Twisted Shape, Smokestack, Rindskopf, 12 ½ In.	219.00
Vase, Mottled Burgundy, Leaves, Bottle Shape, Twisted, Dimpled, Wide Ruffle Rim, Rindskopf, 11 ¼ In.	299.00
Vase, Multicolor Flowers, Bulbous, Ruffle Rim, Red Interior, 8 In.	288.00

Glass-Art, Vase, Iridescent Pulled Feathers, 10 Trailing Gold Iridescent Prunts, Martin Bach, 13 In.
$7,475.00

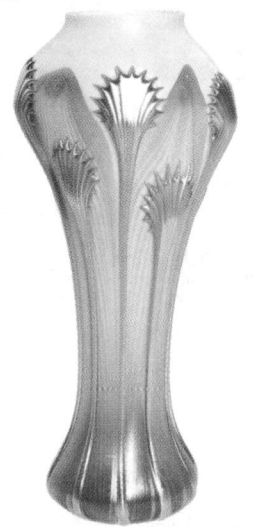

Early Auction Co.

Glass-Art, Vase, Iridescent, Raised Design, Pewter Mount & Handles, Van Hauten, c.1900, 7 ⅞ In.
$854.00

Neal Auction Co.

Glass-Art, Vase, Tapered, Trees In Landscape, Blue Cut To Colorless, Frosted, c.1900, 10 ¼ In., Pair
$237.00

Skinner, Inc.

Glass-Blown, Compote, Lily Pad, Aquamarine, Applied Base, Tooled Rim, Redford Glass Works, c.1840, 3 ½ In.
$1,115.00

Norman C. Heckler & Company

Glass-Blown, Pitcher, Sea Green, Sheared Mouth, Pour Spout, Applied Handle, 3-Piece Mold, c.1830, 4 ½ In.
$1,404.00

Norman C. Heckler & Company

Glass-Blown, Stein, Clear Over Internal Drapery Threads, Red, White, Black, Figural Thumblift, 1 Liter
$690.00

Fox Auctions

Glass-Blown, Vase, Red Lip Wrap, William Morris, 1980, 11 ½ x 6 In.
$1,875.00

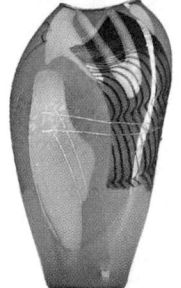

Rago Arts & Auction Center

Glass-Blown, Wedding Cup, Amber Glass, Ribbed Gilded Overlay, 10 ½ In.
$1,656.00

The Stein Auction Co.

Glass-Blown, Witch's Ball, Rose & White Looping, Sheared Mouth, 1840-70, 6 ½ In.
$556.00

Norman C. Heckler & Company

Glass-Bohemian, Urn, Green, Rainbow Iridescent, Handles, Kralik, 12 In.
$460.00

Humler & Nolan

Glass-Contemporary, Sculpture, Pastel, Dominick Labino, 1972, 8 ¼ x 3 In. $1,125.00

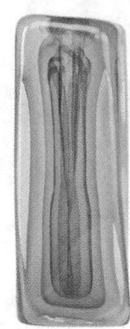

Rago Arts & Auction Center

Glass-Contemporary, Sculpture, Seaform, Ball In Bowl, Orange, Red, Turquoise Lip, Signed, Dale Chihuly, 4 x 8 In. $3,525.00

Garth's Auctioneers & Appraisers

Glass-Contemporary, Vase, Blown, Multicolor, Handles, Ettore Sottsass, Memphis, Italy, 1982, 16 ½ x 8 ½ In. $1,875.00

Los Angeles Modern Auctions (LAMA)

Glass-Contemporary, Vase, Cased, Pink, White Flowers, Green Leaves, Silver, Vines, Charles Lotton, 1989, 9 In. $920.00

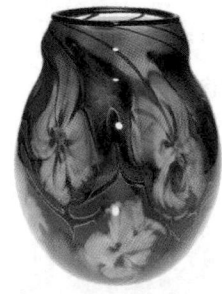

Humler & Nolan

Vase, Pink To Fuchsia, Gold Enamel Leaves & Branches, Blue Plums, Oval, Narrow Neck, 6 ½ In.	230.00
Vase, Pink To Green Iridescent, Wide Flared Rim, Rindskopf, c.1905, 12 In.	660.00
Vase, Portrait, Cranberry, Bell Shape Vase, c.1890, 11 In., Pair	840.00
Vase, Purple Iridescent, Squat Base, Long Neck, Folded & Ruffled Rim, 13 In.	353.00
Vase, Rose Color, Ribbed, Blossoming Branches, White Cameo, Crimped Rim, 8 In.	58.00
Vase, Ruby Flashed, Etched Stag, Doe, Running In Forest, c.1890, 12 ¾ In., Pair	443.00
Vase, Trumpet, Blue To Clear, Stag Scenes, 30 ¾ In., Pair	4250.00

GLASS-CONTEMPORARY includes pieces by glass artists working after 1970. Many of these pieces are free-form, one-of-a-kind sculptures. Paperweights by contemporary artists are listed in the Paperweight category. Earlier studio glass may be found listed under Glass-Midcentury or Glass-Venetian.

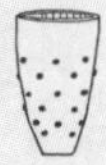

Bowl, Butterfly, Amethyst Cutback, Studio Art, Dated 1993, 7 ½ In.	45.00
Bowl, Iridescent Amber, Green, Lines, Free-Form, Signed Susie Von Trotha, 1986, 14 ½ In.	469.00
Compote, Blue Bowl, Clear Stem, Steuben Shape, Dominick Labino, 6 ¾ x 6 In., Pair	69.00
Egg, Blue & Gold Iridescent Coils, King Tut Pattern, Signed, C. Lotton, 1981, 2 ½ In.	288.00
Guitar, Leaded, Stained Glass, Copper, Wood Feet, 40 In.	540.00
Perfume Bottle, Pinched Waist, Gold Iridescent, Teardrop Stopper, Lundberg, 6 In.	86.00
Perfume Bottle, Purple, Clear, Heart Shape, Dabber, 5 In.	40.00
Perfume Bottle, Stopper, Bubbles, Green, Yellow, Clear, Iridescent, R. Eickholt, 1987, 5 In.	73.00
Sculpture, Abstract Torso, Signed Karen Ehart, 25 In.	385.00
Sculpture, Abstract, Signed Gilles Payette, 33 ½ In.	237.00
Sculpture, Open Flower Shape, Red To Amber, Paradise Persian, Signed, D. Chihuly, 11 x 17 In.	4700.00
Sculpture, Pastel, Dominick Labino, 1972, 8 ¼ x 3 In. *Illus*	1125.00
Sculpture, Rounded Top, Cylindrical Bottom, Pink, White, Swirls, D. Labino, 1974, 8 ¼ x 4 In.	2125.00
Sculpture, Seaform, Ball In Bowl, Orange, Red, Turquoise Lip, Signed, Dale Chihuly, 4 x 8 In. *Illus*	3525.00
Spooner, Green Opaque Satin Finish, Amethyst, Gold Staining, New England, 3 ½ In.	29.00
Vase, Blown, Multicolor, Handles, Ettore Sottsass, Memphis, Italy, 1982, 16 ½ x 8 ½ In. *Illus*	1875.00
Vase, Blown, Red, White Stylized Flowers, Green Leaves, Signed Lotton, 1900s, 9 x 5 ½ In.	1845.00
Vase, Blue Body, Orange Foot, Green Birds, On Black Handles, David Levi, 1997, 26 ½ In.	649.00
Vase, Blue Iridescent, Cypriot, Dripped Lava, Signed, Charles Lotton, 1981, 6 ¼ In.	374.00
Vase, Blue Iridescent, Dripped Lava, Cypriot, Rounded, C. Lotton, 1981, 4 ¼ In.	345.00
Vase, Blue Iridescent, Gold Tipped Pulled Feather Design, Oval, Flare Rim, Signed, Strini, 5 In.	115.00
Vase, Blue Iridescent, Wave Pattern, Bulbous, Pinched Neck, Charles Lotton, 1982, 5 In.	345.00
Vase, Blue, Gold Iridescent Pulled Feather Design, Oval, Signed, Charles Lotton, 1981, 5 ¼ In.	316.00
Vase, Blue, Pink Flowers, Leaves, Cylindrical, Swollen Rim, C. Lotton, 11 ⅞ In.	805.00
Vase, Cased, Pink, White Flowers, Green Leaves, Silver, Vines, Charles Lotton, 1989, 9 In. *Illus*	920.00
Vase, Cobalt Blue, Red Strawberries, Green Vines, Bulbous Urn Shape, Orient & Flume, 5 ¼ In.	184.00
Vase, Cypriot Design, Blue Iridescent Lava Drip, Textured, Copper Color, C. Lotton, 1981, 6 In.	518.00
Vase, Flattened Square Shape, Stonehenge Multicolor Glass, Signed, 1984, 12 ¼ x 11 ¼ In.	6875.00
Vase, Flower Shape, Petal Rim, Amber, Horizontal Stripes, Red Lip Wrap, D. Chihuly, 9 ¾ x 10 In.	3819.00
Vase, Fuchsia, Red, Yellow Iridescent, Elongated Oval, Handles Below Oval Rim, D. Labino, 7 In.	431.00
Vase, Gold Iridescent, Dimpled Base, 5 In.	28.00
Vase, Gold Iridescent, Pulled Blue Leaves, Stems, Blue Rim, Signed Lotton, 1986, 7 x 4 In.	604.00
Vase, Gold Iridescent, Red Pulled Feather, Bulbous, Stick Neck, Round Foot, Lundberg, 7 ½ In.	201.00
Vase, Gold Iridescent, Threaded Spiral Neck, Applied Dots, Genie Bottle Shape, 1978, 4 In.	115.00
Vase, Gold Iridescent, Triangular, Pinched Sides, Ring Foot, Rolled Rim, 4 ¾ In.	144.00
Vase, Iridescent Blue, Signed A. Allison, 5 ½ In.	107.00
Vase, Iridescent Gold, Clear, Cone Shaped, J. Barrett Studio, 1976, 12 ½ In.	11.00
Vase, Iridescent Red, Lava Design, Signed, Charles Lotton, 1979, 4 ½ In. *Illus*	316.00
Vase, Iridescent Swirl, Dated 1991, 6 ½ In.	73.00
Vase, Lava Cypriot, Green, Gold, Pink Iridescent, Pear Shape, Signed, C. Lotton, 1983, 3 ⅞ In.	345.00
Vase, Lava Glass, Mottled, Blue Drip, Signed Charles Lotton, 1982, 5 ½ x 4 ½ In.	277.00
Vase, Mirror Blue, Brown Swags, Oval, Signed Lotton, 1973, 3 ½ In.	403.00
Vase, Opal, Turquoise Pulled, Golden Wings, Elongated Oval, Rolled Rim, C. Lotton, 10 In.	546.00
Vase, Opaque Red, Applied Black Glass Handles, Base Knop, Dante Marioni, c.1970, 34 In.	1180.00
Vase, Orange Flowers, Green Leaves, Red, Bulbous, Swollen Neck, Signed, C. Lotton, 9 In.	805.00
Vase, Orange Flowers, Green Leaves, Round, Peiser Studios, 5 In.	173.00
Vase, Peacock Feathers, Swollen Neck, Flared Rim, Orient & Flume, 1973, 10 ½ In.	460.00
Vase, Pulled Gold, Blue Feather, Iridescent, Tapered, Flared, Cobalt, Lundberg Studios, 10 ½ In.	500.00
Vase, Ruby Calla Lilies, Ivory Yellow, Shouldered, Tapered, Signed, Satava, 12 ½ In.	575.00
Vase, Sunset Verre-De-Soie, Black Vines, Green Leaves, Orange, Squat, C. Lotton, 7 ¼ In.	460.00
Vase, Turquoise Iridescent, Silver Overlay, Blown, Steven Lundberg, 1975, 3 ½ x 2 ¾ In.	129.00
Vase, Vase, Bottle Shaped, Green & Blue Eruptions, D. Labino, 1969, 12 ⅞ In.	316.00
Vase, Vines, Silvered Leaves, Blue, Purple, Pink, Squat, Turned Down Rim, C. Lotton, 1987, 5 ½ In.	748.00

GLASS-CUT, *see Cut Glass category.*

GLASS-DEPRESSION, *see Depression Glass category.*

GLASS-MIDCENTURY refers to art glass made from the 1940s to the early 1970s. Some glass factories, such as Baccarat or Orrefors, are listed under their own categories. Earlier glass may be listed in the Glass-Art and Glass-Contemporary categories. Italian glass may be found in Glass-Venetian.

Bowl, Green, Blue Threading, Purple Ground, Higgins, 4 ¼ x 12 In.	91.00
Decanter, Scandinavian Style, Square Glass Stopper & Base, 9 x 4 In. ....*Illus*	48.00
Dish, Leaf Shape, Round, Tapio Wirkkala, 1950s, 2 ¼ x 9 ¾ In.	1875.00
Vase, Fan Shape, Fused Glass Threads, Orange, Red, Yellow, Black, Signed Z, c.1951, 11 x 8 In.	7500.00
Vase, Intarsia, Red, White, Blue, Barovier & Toso, Italy, 1960s, 6 x 7 x 5 ½ In. ....*Illus*	2500.00

GLASS-PRESSED, *see Pressed Glass category.*

GLASS-VENETIAN. Venetian glass has been made near Venice, Italy, since the thirteenth century. Thin, colored glass with applied decoration is favored, although many other types have been made. Collectors have recently become interested in the Art Deco and fifties designs. Glass was made on the Venetian island of Murano from 1291. The output dwindled in the late seventeenth century but began to flourish again in the 1850s. Some of the old techniques of glassmaking were revived, and firms today make traditional designs and original modern glass. Since 1981, the name *Murano* may be used only on glass made on Murano Island. Other pieces of Italian glass may be found in the Glass-Contemporary and Glass-Midcentury categories of this book.

Aquarium, Glass Block, Jellyfish, Cuttlefish, Seaweed, Attributed To Cenedese & Co., 1950, 6 ½ x 4 In.	940.00
Basket, Sapphire Blue, Turquoise, Murano, 8 ½ x 5 ½ In.	68.00
Bird, Teal, Applied Murrine Eyes, Copper Wire Feet, Alessandro Pianon Pulcini, 1960s, 12 In. *Illus*	2963.00
Bonbon, Lid, Latticinio, Pedestal, Blue, White, Clear, Gold Flecks, Flower Finial, 6 x 4 In.	127.00
Bookends, Paperweight, Apple, Pear, Murano, 6 ½ In.	205.00
Bowl, Basket Weave, Amber Rectangles, Violet Edges, Bulbous, Barovier, 6 x 8 In.	2214.00
Bowl, Blown, Enamel, Painted, Murano, c.1920, 3 x 5 In.	60.00
Bowl, Centerpiece, Clear Plum Flared Rim, Signed Barbini, 18 In.	127.00
Bowl, Clear, Gold Flecks, Swirled Ribbed, Lavender Glass Blooms, Murano, 10 ½ x 8 ½ In.	86.00
Bowl, Fruit, Lid, Ladle, Figural Pears & Leaves, Rigaree Trim, Ball Stem, Pedestal, Lilac, 7 ½ In.	127.00
Bowl, Laguna, Fused Burst Gold Foil, Red, Tommaso Buzzi, 1930s, 12 In. Diam.	1875.00
Bowl, Ribbon & Lattice Detail, Pink, Green, Blue, Copper, Dino Martens, Italy, 1900s, 5 x 6 In.	115.00
Bowl, Rings Of Interior Bubbles, Gilt Flecked, Signed, Murano, 5 ½ x 11 ¼ In.	276.00
Bowl, Shell Shape, Deep Scallop Rim, Bump Texture, White, Murano, 1940s, 6 ¾ x 15 In.	4375.00
Candelabrum, Blue Glass, Base Classical Figures, Swag Cups, 16 x 14 In., Pair	208.00
Candlestick, Blown, Green Iridescent, Blue Accents, Bobeches, 25 x 8 In.	720.00
Candlestick, Ruby Glass, Gold Flecks, Crystal Dolphin, Flared Foot, Ruffled Rim, 8 ¾ x 4 ½ In.	293.00
Candlestick, Yellow, Cobalt Blue Rim, Raised Detail, Broad Foot, Ribbed, Murano, 15 ½ In., Pair	460.00
Chandelier, 8-Light, Murano, Multicolor Flowers, 36 x 38 In.	2400.00
Compote, Speckled Gold, Flared Rim, Footed, Murano, c.1970, 13 ½ x 18 ½ In.	413.00
Decanter, Clown Shape, Orange End Of Day, Applied Hair, Eyes, Mouth, Hat, Stopper Head, 15 x 8 In.	83.00
Decanter, Stopper, Flowers, Fruit, Strapwork Etched, Signed, 1882, 10 ½ In., Pair	2875.00
Dresser Bottle, Pale Green, Multicolor Flower & Leaf Stopper, 8 In.	288.00
Figurine, Bird, Black Beak, Swollen Body, Purple, White Bands, Gilt Legs, Murano, 1985, 37 In.	948.00
Figurine, Cockatoo, Perched On Branch, Turquoise, Gold Foil, 14 ¼ In.	316.00
Figurine, Elephant, Josef Marcolin, Murano, 10 x 10 In.	300.00
Figurine, Female, Gold & Turquoise, Murano, 1960s, 12 ¾ x 3 ¼ In.	625.00
Figurine, Lady's Bonnet, Slag, White, Tan & Clear, Black Trim, White Bow, Murano, 1950s, 10 x 5 In.	200.00
Figurine, Person, Arms Up, Gold & Red, Murano, 1960s, 15 x 4 ½ In.	1875.00
Figurine, Poodle, Red, Vaseline, Murano, 10 In.	151.00
Figurine, Pulcini Bird, Copper Legs, Patina, Vistosi, Murano, 1960s, 8 ½ x 5 In. ....*Illus*	4375.00
Figurine, Rooster, Red, White & Blue Swirl, Gold Foil Inclusions, Cupped Base, 10 In.	345.00
Figurine, Split Oval Shape, Linear Design, Black, Orange, Italy, 1983, 7 ½ In.	1651.00
Figurine, Woman, Clutches Vase, Blackamoor, Hand Blown, 1940s, 10 x 4 ½ In.	575.00
Goblet, Pink, Gold Flecks, Twist Stem, Leaf Shape Base, 5 ⅝ In., 6 Piece	575.00
Hourglass Timer, 2 Ovals, Teal, Blue, Venini, c.1950, 7 ½ In.	554.00
Lamp, Spherical, Orange, Metal, Single Socket, Alfredo Barbini, 1970s, 17 In. Diam.	2000.00
Man & Woman, Peasant Attire, Green Opaque, Barovier & Toso, Murano, 16 In. & 17 In.	863.00
Mirror, Girandole, 5 Rectangular Sections, Wells, Applied Leaves, Shelves, Electric, Murano, 65 In.	1500.00
Pitcher, Figural, Dog, Clear, Blue Accents, 1900s, 9 In.	690.00
Pitcher, Murrine, Fratelli Toso, c.1910, 15 x 6 ½ In. ....*Illus*	2750.00

Glass-Contemporary, Vase, Iridescent Red, Lava Design, Signed, Charles Lotton, 1979, 4 ½ In.
$316.00

Early Auction Co.

G

Glass-Midcentury, Decanter, Scandinavian Style, Square Glass Stopper & Base, 9 x 4 In.
$48.00

Glass-Midcentury, Vase, Intarsia, Red, White, Blue, Barovier & Toso, Italy, 1960s, 6 x 7 x 5 ½ In.
$2,500.00

Rago Arts & Auction Center

Glass-Venetian, Bird, Teal, Applied Murrine Eyes, Copper Wire Feet, Alessandro Pianon Pulcini, 1960s, 12 In.
$2,963.00

Skinner, Inc.

Glass-Venetian, Figurine, Pulcini Bird, Copper Legs, Patina, Vistosi, Murano, 1960s, 8 ½ x 5 In.
$4,375.00

Rago Arts & Auction Center

Glass-Venetian, Pitcher, Murrine, Fratelli Toso, c.1910, 15 x 6 ½ In.
$2,750.00

Wright

Glass-Venetian, Urn, Black, Blue & Red Swirl Interior, Rolled Collar, Lino Tagliapietra, Murano, 1981, 12 ¼ In.
$2,415.00

Humler & Nolan

Glass-Venetian, Vase, Canne Glass, Murano, Lino Tagliapietra, 1988, 20 ½ x 14 ¼ In.
$11,250.00

Rago Arts & Auction Center

Glass-Venetian, Vase, Misshapen Oval Mouth, 5 Layers, Grid, Lino Tagliapietra, Murano, 1987, 13 In.
$2,460.00

Skinner, Inc.

Glass-Venetian, Vase, Occhi, Eyes, Tobia Scarpa, Incised Venini Italia, c.1960-70, 8 ¼ In.
$5,000.00

Wright

Glass-Venetian, Vase, Sommerso, Flavio Poli, Valva, Valve, Seguso, 1952-53, 10 ½ In.
$11,875.00

Wright

Glass-Venetian, Vase, Tapered, Vertical Bands, Mottled, Signed, Cenedese, Murano, Italy, 1900s, 14 In.
$510.00

Skinner, Inc.

G

Plate, Fish, Green Border, Marked, c.1913, 10 ¼ In.	22500.00
Platter, Blown, Teal Green, Gold Flecks, Controlled Bubbles, Murano, 12 ½ In.	109.00
Tray, Rounded Rectangular, Red, White U-Design, Alfredo Barbini, 1970s, 9 ½ x 6 ½ In.	1875.00
Urn, Black, Blue & Red Swirl Interior, Rolled Collar, Lino Tagliapietra, Murano, 1981, 12 ¼ In..*Illus*	2415.00
Vase, Amethyst, Ribbed, Rippled Rim, Seguso, 5 ½ x 5 In.	115.00
Vase, Bottle Shaped, Blue & Green Streak Design, Murano, 1950s, 14 ½ x 5 ½ In.	8750.00
Vase, Canne Glass, Murano, Lino Tagliapietra, 1988, 20 ½ x 14 ¼ In.*Illus*	11250.00
Vase, Clear, Blue & Green Murrines, Cylinder, Vistosi, Italy, 1976, 7 ¼ x 7 ¾ In.	94.00
Vase, Clear, Gold Flecks, Open Flower Shape, Pinched Rim, Reversed Base, Murano, 20 In.	259.00
Vase, Globular, Lavender, Red, Seguso, c.1952, 10 ½ In.	11875.00
Vase, Handkerchief, Clear, Pink & White Lines, Marked, 7 x 5 ½ In.	425.00
Vase, Handkerchief, Pink, White Stripes, Signed Venini, Murano, 7 x 5 ½ In.	519.00
Vase, Hat Shape, Multicolor, Wavy Rim, Dino Martens, 1950s, 6 ¾ x 10 ¾ In.	4063.00
Vase, Jack-In-The-Pulpit, Green, Shaded, Gold Flowers, c.1900, 17 In.	270.00
Vase, Millefiori, Mottled Blue, Tapered Cylinder, Label, 11 ¾ x 6 In.	173.00
Vase, Misshape Oval Mouth, 5 Layers, Grid, Lino Tagliapietra, Murano, 1987, 13 In.*Illus*	2460.00
Vase, Multicolor Patches, Oval, Giuliano Tosi, Murano, 23 x 11 In.	767.00
Vase, Occhi, Eyes, Tobia Scarpa, Incised Venini Italia, c.1960-70, 8 ¼ In.*Illus*	5000.00
Vase, Orange, White Interior, Bulbous, Ribbed, Lobbed Lip, Seguso, 7 ¼ x 6 ¼ In.	69.00
Vase, Peach, Flared Scalloped Rim, Waisted, Gold Accents, Murano, c.1950, 11 x 8 In.	288.00
Vase, Rounded Square, Cylindrical Neck, Cobalt Blue, Turquoise, Silver Stripes, c.1965, 7 ½ x 7 In.	1875.00
Vase, Shouldered, Chiacchiera, Green, Black, Stringing Design, Murano, 1986, 12 ¼ x 7 In.	2125.00
Vase, Sommerso, Flavio Poli, Valva, Valve, Seguso, 1952-53, 10 ½ In.*Illus*	11875.00
Vase, Sommerso, Olive Green To Blue, Suspended Bubble, Cylindrical, 22 In.	492.00
Vase, Stick Neck, Amber To Clear, Blossoms, Paper Label, A.Ve.M, c.1960, 18 In.	7500.00
Vase, Tapered, Vertical Bands, Mottled, Signed, Cenedese, Murano, Italy, 1900s, 14 In.*Illus*	510.00
Vase, Trumpet Rim, Loop Handle, Swollen, Flared Foot, Green, Yellow, White, Signed, 1980s, 17 x 9 In.	2000.00
Vase, Tutti-Frutti, Red Cased, Rods & Canes, Millefiori, Bronze Aventurine, 15 In.	1046.00
Vase, White To Clear Spatter, Murano, Signed, 14 In.	600.00
Vase, Wide Wavy Rim, Circles Design, Clear, Ercole Barovier, c.1966, 8 x 6 ¼ In.	813.00
Vase, Yellow Over Mottled White & Clear, Caned Grid, Ruffled, L. Tagliapietra, 12 In.	2214.00

GLASSES for the eyes, or spectacles, were mentioned in a manuscript in 1289 and have been used ever since. The first eyeglasses with rigid side pieces were made in London in 1727. Bifocals were invented by Benjamin Franklin in 1785. Lorgnettes were popular in late Victorian times. Opera Glasses are listed in the Opera Glass category.

14K Yellow Gold, Round Brilliant Cut Diamonds, Peach Lenses, Brass Hinge, Signed Cazal, 5 ½ In.	5175.00
Lorgnette, Flower & Scroll Border, 14K Gold, Trace Link Chain, Krementz & Co., 4 In.	1440.00
Lorgnette, Platinum, Onyx, Ribbed Frame, Diamond Melee Handle, Garlands, Art Deco	1422.00
Lorgnette, Silver, Mask, Tiger Lilies, Art Nouveau, 7 In.	356.00
Magnifying, Artist's Palette, Leaves, Gold Washed Silver, Art Nouveau, France, 5 In.	652.00
Sunglasses, Aviator, Cartier	420.00
Sunglasses, By Designer Anthony Martin, Blue Design, Marked Madeline, 1970s	25.00

GLIDDEN POTTERY worked in Alfred, New York, from 1940 to 1957. The pottery made stoneware, dinnerware, and art objects.

Casserole, Lid, Boston Spice, Handles, 8 ¼ x 5 ½ In.	225.00
Planter, Brown & Black Speckled Glaze, 4 x 4 x 3 In.	28.00
Plate, Clown, Weight Lifter, Abstract, Marked, 5 ½ x 5 ½ In., Pair	25.00
Tray, Turquoise, 5 Sections, 14 ¾ x 11 ¼ In.	95.00
Vase, Serpentine Shape, Mottled Turquoise, 7 ½ x 3 In.	65.00
Vase, Squat, Pillow, Speckled Turquoise Glaze, 9 x 6 x 5 In.	75.00

GOEBEL is the mark used by W. Goebel Porzellanfabrik of Oeslau, Germany, now Rodental, Germany. The company was founded by Franz Detleff Goebel and his son, William Goebel, in 1871. It was known as F&W Goebel. Slates, slate pencils, and marbles were made. Soon the company began making porcelain tableware and figurines. Hummel figurines were first made by Goebel in 1935 and are now being made by another company. Goebel is still in business. Old pieces marked *Goebel Hummel* are listed under Hummel in this book.

Figurine, 2 Titmouse Birds In Tree, 5 In.	28.00
Figurine, Robin, On Branch, 3 ½ In.	17.00
Figurine, Woman, Baby, Rock-A-Bye Baby, 6 In.	45.00
Stein, Monk, Pewter Lid, ½ Liter.*Illus*	130.00

TIP
Dry good glassware with a towel that has not been washed with fabric softener. The chemicals in the softener will leave a film.

Goebel, Stein, Monk, Pewter Lid, ½ Liter
$130.00

Fox Auctions

Goldscheider, Bust, Woman, Brown Skin, Yellow Headdress, Green Curls, Stamped, 1930s, 15 x 17 In.
$1,250.00

Rago Arts & Auction Center

Goldscheider, Bust, Woman, Light Skin, Golden Curls, Stamped, 1940s-50s, 12 x 4 ¾ In.
$938.00

Rago Arts & Auction Center

Goldscheider, Masks, Black & White, Held By White Hand, Orange Curls, Stamped, 1930s, 14 x 7 ¼ In. $1,125.00

Rago Arts & Auction Center

G

Gouda, Charger, Advertising, Plateelbakkery Zuid-Holland, Marked, 12 ¼ In. $173.00

Humler & Nolan

Gouda, Charger, Pudora Pattern, Dragon, Orange Ground, Scale Design On Rim, 1931, 16 ¾ In. $551.00

Skinner, Inc.

Gouda, Charger, White Chrysanthemums, Dark Blue, Orange Rim, Zuid, Marked, c.1910, 16 ¾ In. $474.00

Skinner, Inc.

GOLDSCHEIDER was founded by Friedrich Goldscheider in Vienna in 1885. The family left Vienna in 1938 and the factory was taken over by the Germans. Goldscheider started factories in England and in Trenton, New Jersey. The New Jersey factory started in 1940 as Goldscheider-U.S.A. In 1941 it became Goldscheider-Everlast Corporation. From 1947 to 1953 it was Goldcrest Ceramics Corporation. In 1950 the Vienna plant was returned to Mr. Goldscheider and the company continues in business. The Trenton, New Jersey, business, called Goldscheider of Vienna, imports all of the pieces.

Bust, Black Skin, Light Blue Curls, Wood Stand, Brass Tag, Austria, 1930s, 13 ½ In.	750.00
Bust, Brown Skin, Blue Curls, Marked, Austria, 1930s, 12 ½ In.	1000.00
Bust, Woman, Brown Skin, Yellow Headdress, Green Curls, Stamped, 1930s, 15 x 17 In...*Illus*	1250.00
Bust, Woman, Light Skin, Golden Curls, Stamped, 1940s-50s, 12 x 4 ¾ In. ...*Illus*	938.00
Compote, Sculpted Head, Woman, Yellow & Green Glaze, 5 x 7 In.	650.00
Figurine, Boy Holding 2 Puppies, 9 ½ x 3 ½ In.	216.00
Figurine, Rose, Art Deco Dancer, Blue Skirt, Shaped Base, Viennese, 14 ½ In.	960.00
Masks, Black & White, Held By White Hand, Orange Curls, Stamped, 1930s, 14 x 7 ¼ In...*Illus*	1125.00

GOLF*, see Sports category.*

GOOFUS GLASS was made from about 1900 to 1920 by many American factories. It was originally painted gold, red, green, bronze, pink, purple, or other bright colors. Many pieces are found today with flaking paint, and this lowers the value.

Bowl, Footed Base, Grapes, Leaves, Dugan Glass, 10 In.	18.00
Bowl, Red Grapes, Gold Leaves, Scalloped, 7 In.	18.00
Bowl, Roses, Red, Gold, 9 ¼ In.	13.00
Plate, Labella Rose, Leaves, 1910, 10 ¼ In.	40.00
Rose Bowl, Milk Glass, Puffy Rose, Leaves, 5 ½ In.	38.00
Vase, Raised Flowers, Gold, Red, Green, 12 ¼ In.	125.00

GOUDA, Holland, has been a pottery center since the seventeenth century. Two firms, the Zenith pottery, established in the eighteenth century, and the Zuid-Hollandsche pottery, made the brightly colored art pottery marked *Gouda* from 1898 to about 1964. Other factories followed. Many pieces featured Art Nouveau or Art Deco designs. Pattern names in Dutch, listed here, seem strange to English-speaking collectors.

Barrel, Stand, Top Stopper, Green, Yellow Flowers, Black Ground, 11 ½ In.	86.00
Bowl, Stylized Flowers, Handles, Brown, 10 ¾ In.	52.00
Charger, Advertising, Plateelbakkery Zuid-Holland, Marked, 12 ¼ In. ...*Illus*	173.00
Charger, Prinsenhof Pattern, Orange & Yellow Flowers, Matte Glaze, Scrolling Vines, c.1900, 16 ½ In.	368.00
Charger, Pudora Pattern, Dragon, Orange Ground, Scale Design On Rim, 1931, 16 ¾ In...*Illus*	551.00
Charger, Rosalie, Bird On Branch, Blossoming Branches, Olive Green Border, c.1900, 14 ¼ In...	830.00
Charger, Stylized Bird In Tree, Wave Border, 1929, 3 x 18 ¾ In.	500.00
Charger, White Chrysanthemums, Dark Blue, Orange Rim, Zuid, Marked, c.1910, 16 ¾ In....*Illus*	474.00
Compote, Stylized Flowers, Blue, White, Red, 2 ½ In.	46.00
Jardiniere, Laric, Blue, Yellow, Green, Shouldered, 1930, 9 ½ x 13 In.	156.00
Lamp Base, Persian Style Decoration, Blue, Green, Yellow, White, Baluster, c.1930, 19 In.	188.00
Plate, Bird, Branches, Berries, Jo Bennis, 1929, 2 ¼ x 14 ¼ In...*Illus*	313.00
Poppy, Butterfly, Orange, Green, Blue, Gourd Shape, Ring Foot, 4 ¾ In.	127.00
Saucer, Brown, Orange, Yellow, Green, Handle, 7 In.	17.00
Vase, 3 Owls, Baluster, Spread Foot, Cream, Blue, Brown, Matte Glaze, 1900s, 25 ¾ In.	4444.00
Vase, Bellflowers, Swirls, Red, Blue, Green, Spread Foot, Tapered, Shouldered, Handles, Marked, 9 In.	431.00
Vase, Bird, Flowering Branches, Abstract Designs, Marked, 1923, 10 ¼ In.	504.00
Vase, Butterflies, Sunflowers, Brown & Yellow, Rozenburg, Incised, V.W., c.1910, 19 ½ In...*Illus*	4444.00
Vase, Dragon, White, Brown, Orange Ground, Bulbous, 1931, 7 ½ x 8 ½ In.	531.00
Vase, Flowers, Multicolor, Noda Pattern, c.1920, 7 ¾ In., Pair	180.00
Vase, Green Birds, Perched On Branch, Pear Shape, Pinched Neck, Handles, c.1900, 9 ¾ In., Pair	1701.00
Vase, Madeleine Pattern, Matte Glaze, Tapered, Flower Banding, Marked, c.1930, 7 ⅝ In.	474.00
Vase, Mary, Stylized Flowers, Stained Glass Effect, Bulbous, 1923, 17 x 9 ½ In.	500.00
Vase, Stork, High Glaze, Geometric Flower Accents, Marked, c.1930, 12 In. ...*Illus*	338.00
Vase, Stylized Flowers, Gold, Red, Blue, Bulbous, Stick Neck, Ring Foot, Rolled Rim, 24 In.	920.00
Vase, Woman, Apron, Carrying Basket, Elongated Oval, Ring Foot, Smokestack Rim, Marked, 10 In..	184.00

GRANITEWARE is enameled tin or iron used to make kitchenware since the 1870s. Earlier graniteware was green or turquoise blue, with white spatters. The later ware was gray with white spatters. Reproductions are being made in all colors. There is a second definition of the word *graniteware* meaning a blue speckled pottery. Only the metal graniteware is listed here.

Chamber Pot, Blue & White Swirl, Black Handle & Rim, 5 x 9 In.	38.00

Coffeepot, Blue Speckled, Bail Handle, Handled Lid, 11 In.	35.00
Coffeepot, White, Red Trim, Hinged Lid, Glass Knob, 8 ¾ In.	42.00
Colander, Gray, Footed, Handles, 10 ½ In. Diam.	30.00
Cream Skimmer, Loop Handle, White, 6 In.	22.00
Dustpan, Black & Gray, c.1930, 12 ¾ x 9 ¾ In.	55.00
Funnel, Blue & White, Handle, 3 ½ In.	25.00
Ladle, Gray, 1800s, 16 x 4 ¾ In.	20.00
Ladle, White, Red Trim, 14 In.	18.00
Lid Holder, Gray Speckled, 25 In.	125.00
Milk Can, Blue Speckled, Wire Handle, Lid, 9 ½ In.	84.00
Milk Pail, Gray, Bail Handle, Lid, 10 x 6 ⅝ In.	24.00
Mold, Turk's Head, Robin's Egg Blue, Spouted, c.1890, 4 x 9 In.	35.00
Mug, Chicken Wire Design, White, Blue Rim, 4 In.	100.00
Pitcher, Cobalt Blue & White Swirl, Black Handle & Trim, 4 ¼ In.	135.00
Platter, Elongated Octagonal, White, Red Trim, 14 ½ x 10 In.	28.00
Pudding Pan, Blue & White Swirl, Black Rim, 7 x 1 ¾ In.	40.00
Teakettle, Gray, Mottled, Swing Handle, Wood Grip, 2 Attached Handles, Lid, 11 In.	94.00
Washstand, White, Black Trim, Label, Lisk Flintstone Porcelain, 12 In. Diam.	42.00
Water Bucket, Blue Mottled, Wood Handle, 11 In.	295.00

GRUEBY FAIENCE COMPANY of Boston, Massachusetts, was founded in 1894 by William H. Grueby. Grueby Pottery Company was incorporated in 1907. In 1909, Grueby Faience went bankrupt. Then William Grueby founded the Grueby Faience and Tile Company. Grueby Pottery closed about 1911. The tile company worked until 1920. Garden statuary, art pottery, and architectural tiles were made until 1920. The company developed a green matte glaze that was so popular it was copied by many other factories making a less expensive type of pottery. This eventually led to the financial problems of the pottery. Cuerda seca and cuenca are techniques explained in the Tile category. The company name was often used as the mark, and slight changes in the form help date a piece.

Bowl, Folded-In Rim, Cone Shape Body, Green Matte Glaze, Light Green Glossy Interior, 4 x 9 ½ In.	652.00
Bowl, Green Matte Glaze, Scalloped Rim, Buds, Stamped, c.1910, 3 ½ x 7 In.	1000.00
Bowl, Ivory, Green Inside, Lobed, Folded-In Sides, Wilhelmina Post, 2 x 5 In.	344.00
Bowl, Leaves, Green Matte Glaze, Squat, 3 x 5 ½ In.	1750.00
Bowl, Overlapping Leaves, Green Matte Glaze, Folded-In Sides, 3 x 9 In.	1875.00
Bowl, Overlapping Leaves, Green Matte Glaze, Round, 4 x 10 In.	1875.00
Bowl, Overlapping Leaves, Green Matte Glaze, Square, 3 x 6 In.	1875.00
Bowl, Vertical Leaf Design, Suspended Green Matte Glaze, Marked, 6 x 3 ½ In.	750.00
Bowl, Vertical Leaves, Carved, Suspended Green Matte Glaze, Round, 6 x 3 ½ In.	915.00
Frieze, 3 Tiles, Geometric, Greek Key, Green, Ivory, Frame, c.1910, 7 x 22 In.	563.00
Frieze, Tile, Green, Yellow, Geometric Shapes, 2 Tiles Joined, Oak Frame, 17 ½ x 10 ½ In.	732.00
Frieze, Water Lilies & Lily Pads, 11 6-In. Tiles, c.1905, 66 In.	9375.00
Lamp, Yellow Flowers, Green Matte, Melon Lobed, Domed Slag Glass Acorn Shade, 18 In.	15000.00
Paperweight, Scarab, Blue Matte Glaze, Impressed Logo, Sticker, 1 ⅜ x 3 ⅞ In. ......*Illus*	403.00
Paperweight, Scarab, Green Glaze, Marked, 3 ¾ In.	1000.00
Paperweight, Scarab, Green Matte Glaze, Oval, 3 ¾ In.	1200.00
Tile, Tall Ship, Waves, Green, c.1900, 7 ¾ In.	1188.00
Tile, Trees, Plants, Square, 1910s, 12 In. ....*Illus*	9375.00
Trivet, Pewter, Tile, Ship, 3 Speckled Oatmeal Sails, Green Ground, Square, 6 In.	1063.00
Vase, Applied Vertical Line, Mottled Green Matte Glaze, Flared Shape, 6 x 3 ½ In.	875.00
Vase, Blue Matte Glaze, Ribbed, Flared, 9 x 12 In.	793.00
Vase, Brown Matte Glaze, Cylinder, Impressed, 5 ½ x 11 In.	2875.00
Vase, Carved & Applied Leaves, Speckled Oatmeal Glaze, Swollen Cylinder, 7 ¾ In.	3000.00
Vase, Dark Green Matte Glaze, Flared Base, 5 x 5 ½ In.	671.00
Vase, Drippy Brown, Tan Glaze, Marked Atwood Grueby, 8 x 14 In.	750.00
Vase, Embossed Leaves, Green Matte Glaze, Impressed Ruth Erickson, 5 x 7 In.	2000.00
Vase, Flared Rim, Tapered, Green Glaze, Tooled Leaves, Yellow Buds, Impressed, c.1904, 10 In.	29625.00
Vase, Flared, Ribbed, Mottled Blue Matte Glaze, Marked, 12 In.	650.00
Vase, Green Matte Glass, Applied Leaves, Blossoms, Bulbous, Flared Rim, Marked, c.1900, 22 In.	20400.00
Vase, Green Matte Glaze, Applied & Carved Leaves, Stamped, c.1905, 6 ½ x 4 ½ In. .....*Illus*	3750.00
Vase, Green Matte Glaze, Inverted Cone Shape, 4 ⅞ In.	460.00
Vase, Green Matte Glaze, Leaf & Bud, Bulbous, Impressed, 4 ½ x 5 ¼ In.	594.00
Vase, Green Matte Glaze, Leaves, Marked, c.1900, 12 ½ In. ....*Illus*	6518.00
Vase, Green Matte Glaze, Linear Leaves, Cylindrical, Stamped, 15 ½ In.	3186.00
Vase, Green Matte Glaze, Lobed, Tapered, 7 ½ x 5 In.	1000.00
Vase, Green Matte Glaze, Ribbed Design, Bulbous, Pinched Neck, Marked, 9 ¼ In.	2875.00

Gouda, Plate, Bird, Branches, Berries, Jo Bennis, 1929, 2 ¼ x 14 ¼ In.
$313.00

Rago Arts & Auction Center

Art Deco Pottery Prices Up
Art Deco pieces by Boch Freres and Gouda pottery from the early twentieth century have returned to popularity. Prices are up at antiques shows.

Gouda, Vase, Butterflies, Sunflowers, Brown & Yellow, Rozenburg, Incised, V.W., c.1910, 19 ½ In.
$4,444.00

Skinner, Inc.

Gouda, Vase, Stork, High Glaze, Geometric Flower Accents, Marked, c.1930, 12 In.
$338.00

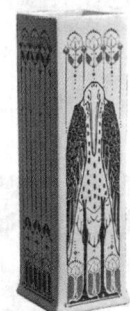

Skinner, Inc.

The edited listings of the current prices in this *Kovels' Antiques & Collectibles Price Guide* aren't available on any website. Readers can visit Kovels.com to check thousands of past prices and sign up for free information on trends, tips, reproductions, marks, and more.

G

Grueby, Paperweight, Scarab, Blue Matte Glaze, Impressed Logo, Sticker, 1 3/8 x 3 7/8 In.
$403.00

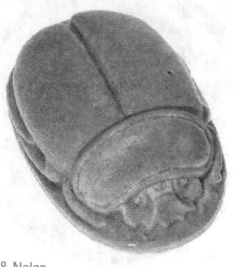

Humler & Nolan

Grueby, Tile, Trees, Plants, Square, 1910s, 12 In.
$9,375.00

Rago Arts & Auction Center

Grueby, Vase, Green Matte Glaze, Applied & Carved Leaves, Stamped, c.1905, 6 1/2 x 4 1/2 In.
$3,750.00

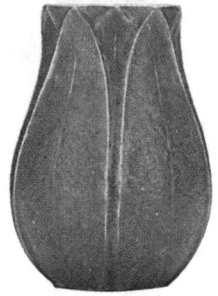

Rago Arts & Auction Center

Grueby, Vase, Green Matte Glaze, Leaves, Marked, c.1900, 12 1/2 In.
$6,518.00

Skinner, Inc.

Vase, Green Matte Glaze, Ribbed Neck, Low, Round, 5 1/2 x 3 In.	580.00
Vase, Green Matte Glaze, Silver Overlay, Stylized Flowers, Tapered, 6 3/4 x 3 1/2 In.	2500.00
Vase, Leaves & Buds, Mauve Matte Glaze, Bulbous Bottom, Flared Neck, 7 x 5 In.	2375.00
Vase, Light Green Matte Glaze, Raised Geometric Band, Wide Mouth, Tapered, 4 1/2 In.	474.00
Vase, Overlapping Leaves, Green Matte Glaze, Cylindrical, Double Lobed Rim, 8 x 5 In.	864.00
Vase, Ribs, Brown Matte Glaze, Bulbous Bottom, Flared Neck, c.1905, 6 3/4 x 4 1/2 In.	938.00
Vase, Squat, Rolled Rim, Green Matte Glaze, Impressed Mark, 5 x 3 In.	475.00
Vase, Stylized Leaves, Blue Matte Glaze, Pear Shape, 5 1/2 x 6 1/2 In.	3000.00
Vase, Vertical Leaves, Green Matte Glaze, Shouldered, Carved, Marked JE, 5 x 9 1/2 In.	1342.00
Vase, Vertical Ribs, Yellow Matte Glaze, Squat, c.1900, 6 x 9 In.	3000.00
Vase, Yellow Trefoils, Rounded Leaves, Stamped, c.1905, 13 x 8 In. ....*Illus*	6875.00

GUN, *see Toy.*

GUSTAVSBERG ceramics factory was founded in 1827 near Stockholm, Sweden. It is best known to collectors for its twentieth-century artwares, especially Argenta, a green stoneware with silver inlay. The company was sold in the 1990s.

Gustafsberg

Bowl, Aquamarine Mottled Glaze, Icicle Rim, Splayed Feet, Argenta, 1900s, 3 1/4 x 7 1/2 In.	316.00
Jar, Lid, Art Deco, Canteen Shape, Nude Woman, Ribbed, Stamped, c.1910, 9 1/2 x 9 1/2 In. ...*Illus*	59.00
Jardiniere, Tin Glaze, Cobalt Blue, Twist Handles, Marked, 1926, 13 1/2 x 18 In.	920.00

HAEGER POTTERIES, INC, Dundee, Illinois, started making commercial artwares in 1914. Early pieces were marked with the name *Haeger* written over an *H*. About 1938, the mark *Royal Haeger* was used in honor of Royal Hickman, a designer at the factory. The firm is still making florist wares and lamp bases.

Bowl, Brown, Black Speckles, Tab Handles, 15 x 11 3/4 x 3 7/8 In.	25.00
Bowl, Celtic-Like Central Design, 11 1/2 In.	36.00
Bread Tray, Whole Wheat, 15 3/4 x 6 3/4 x 3 In.	32.00
Figurine, Bear, Seated, Reddish Brown, White, 4 In.	34.00
Figurine, Gazelle, Blue, Paper Label, 21 1/2 In.	60.00
Jardiniere, Basket Weave, Off-White, 5 x 6 7/8 In.	38.00
Mixing Bowl, Yellow Brown, Scalloped Trim, Mottled Bumpy Texture, 7 5/8 In.	25.00
Planter, Madonna & Child, White, 11 1/2 In.	30.00
Planter, Ribbed, Green, 8 x 3 1/4 In.	23.00
Planter, Salmon, Fluted, Marked, 9 x 3 1/2 In.	20.00
Planter, Untied Shoe, White, 5 x 3 1/2 In.	19.00
Planter, Woman, Seated, Holding Bowl, White, Mint Green, Marked, 12 x 8 1/2 In.	35.00
Vase, Abstract Shape, Earth Tones, Tall Pedestal, Stamped, 12 x 8 In. ...*Illus*	18.00
Vase, Green, 7 In.	12.00

HALF-DOLL, *see Pincushion Doll category.*

HALL CHINA COMPANY started in East Liverpool, Ohio, in 1903. The firm made many types of wares. Collectors search for the Hall teapots made from the 1920s to the 1950s. The dinnerware of the same period, especially Autumn Leaf pattern, is also popular. The Hall China Company merged with Homer Laughlin China Company in 2010. Autumn Leaf pattern dishes are listed in their own category in this book.

HALL'S
SUPERIOR
QUALITY
KITCHENWARE

Baker, Westinghouse, Yellow, Ridged, 5 3/8 In.	126.00
Ball Jug, Black	75.00
Cream Jug, Helmet Shape, Pink, Blue, Green Flowers, Swags, 4 In.	63.00
Dish, Lid, Westinghouse, Blue, 6 x 4 x 4 In.	36.00
Dish, V-Shape Lid, Montgomery Ward, Scalloped Foot, White, 1940s, 8 x 5 x 4 In.	26.00
Leftover, Delphinium Blue, Rectangular, Lid, 6 1/4 In.	24.00
Morning Glory, Custard Cup, 3 1/2 x 2 1/4 In., 4 Piece	27.00
Refrigerator Ware, Casserole, Lid, General Electric, Tab Handles, Yellow & Gray, 9 3/4 In.	37.00
Spiral Fluting, Saucer, Painted, Roses, Bouquets, Swags, 7 3/4 In.	23.00
Teapot, Brown, Hollywood Style, Lid, 5 Cups	22.00
Teapot, Chrysler, Dodecagon, Metal Lid, 3 Cup	76.00
Teapot, Cobalt, Gold, Pedestal, Fluted, Lid, 7 1/4 In., 6 Cup	65.00
Teapot, French Flower Gold, Lid, 6 Cup	89.00
Teapot, Game Bird, Quail, English Setter, Lid, 2 Cup	210.00
Teapot, Lipton, Green, Lid, 6 Cup	100.00
Teapot, Lipton, Yellow, Lid, 4 Cup	96.00
Teapot, Rhythm, Pink, Lid, 6 In.	55.00

Teapot, Silver Shaped, Painted, Multicolor Enamel, Flower Basket, 6 x 9 x 4 ½ In.	299.00
Teapot, Tan, Ribbed, Football Shape, 6 ¾ In.	195.00
Tom & Jerry, Punch Bowl Set, Bowl, Lid, Cups, 10 Piece	75.00
Waste Bowl, Footed, Painted, Roses, Bouquets, Swags, 4 ¾ x 2 ⅜ In.	81.00

HALLOWEEN is an ancient holiday that has changed in the last 200 years. The jack-o'-lantern, witches on broomsticks, and orange decorations seem to be twentieth-century creations. Collectors started to become serious about collecting Halloween-related items in the late 1970s. The papier-mache decorations, now replaced by plastic, and old costumes are in demand.

Ashtray, Skeleton, Porcelain, Bobbing, Legs On Springs, Japan, 1920s, 3 ¼ x 2 ¼ In.	90.00
Basket, Jack-O'-Lantern, Orange, Green, Germany, Squat, 9 ½ In.	300.00
Bat, Red Devil, Cardboard, 6 ½ In.	900.00
Black Cat, Papier-Mache, Arch Back, 11 ½ x 10 ½ In.	826.00
Blower, Witch Head, 6 In. ......*Illus*	175.00
Box, Candy, Butterfinger, Be Good To Your Goblins, 1950s, 9 ¾ x 4 ¼ In.	55.00
Centerpiece, Winking Cat, Die Cut, Seated Atop A Honeycomb Base, 1940s-50s, 12 x 6 In.	30.00
Costume, Captain Nemo Diver, Complete, Marked Ben Cooper, Box, 1950s	95.00
Costume, Gypsy Girl, Mask, Headpiece, 2-Piece Outfit, Box, 1940s, Size Medium	65.00
Costume, Masquerade Gypsy Girl, Box, 1940s, Size Medium	65.00
Costume, Pebbles & Bamm Bamm, Molded Plastic, Rayon, Ben Cooper, Box, 1962, Size Medium, Pair	144.00
Costume, Phantom, Molded Plastic Mask, Cloth Head Piece, Collegeville, c.1958, 9 x 11 In.	417.00
Costume, Wild West, Gun, Khaki Pants, Black & Orange Shirt, Wyandotte, 1930s	185.00
Costume, Wilma Flintstone, Molded Plastic, Rayon, Ben Cooper, Box, 1960s, Size Medium	86.00
Decoration, Walking Witch, Embossed, Holding Broom, Germany, 1930s, 15 ¾ x 6 In.	115.00
Figure, Masquerade, Composition Face, Jester Outfit, Holding Noisemaker, c.1900, 5 ¾ In.	345.00
Figure, Pumpkin Head, Feet, Windup, 5 ¾ In.	360.00
Fortune Card, Pumpkin, Owl, Lift Me Off Pumpkin Shell & Your Fortune I Will Tell, 1911, 4 In.	45.00
Hat, Witch, Painted Face, Black, Orange, Black, Gold, 16 In.	570.00
Jack-O'-Lantern, Candleholder, Hanging, Electrified, Tin, Orange Paint, 6 ½ In.	452.00
Jack-O'-Lantern, Pressed, Formed Paperboard, Happy Face, Extended Accordion Base, 14 In.	472.00
Jack-O'-Lantern, Red Cat Head, Cardboard, 5 In.	660.00
Jack-O'-Lantern, Yellow, Composition, Metal Handle, 4 In.	360.00
Lantern, Cat, Papier-Mache, Orange, Handle, 8 In.	40.00
Lantern, Goblin, Pressed Cardboard, Large Eyes & Mouth, Germany, 1930s, 7 x 3 In.	125.00
Lantern, Man-In-The-Moon, Composition, Grinning Half Moon Face, Hanger, c.1900, 2 ¾ x 3 ¾ In.	765.00
Lantern, Pumpkin, Globe, Jack-O'-Lantern, Tin, Orange & Black, 6 ¾ In.	835.00
Lantern, Punch, Composition, Wire Handle, Crown, Filigree, Paper Insert Eyes, c.1910, 4 ½ In..*Illus*	460.00
Lantern, Segmented Cardboard Frame, Hanging, Illustrated, 1930s, 8 ½ x 7 ½ In.	159.00
Marionette, Pumpkin Head, 6 In. ......*Illus*	2200.00
Mask, Witch Head, Fangs, Paint, Rubber, 12 In.	270.00
Napkin, Cloth, Fringed, Orange & Brown, 6 x 6 In., 4 Piece	25.00
Napkin, Witch Riding Jack-O'-Lantern, Orange & Black, Beach Products, 1940s, 36 Piece	55.00
Paper Doll, Dolly Dingle, Orange & Black Dress, Grace Drayton, October 1927, Uncut	50.00
Pin, Jack-O'-Lantern, Goldtone, Witch's Hat, C-Clasp, Jonette Jewelry Co., Late 1980s, 2 x 1 ¾ In.	25.00
Postcard, Boy With Jack-O'-Lantern, Embossed, Clapsaddle, Postmarked 1907	35.00
Postcard, Skeletons Playing Poker, Smoking & Drinking, Copyright 1906 By H.H. Tammen	10.00
Postcard, Young Boy & Girl Startled By Black Cat, Don't Say Scat, Raphael Tuck, 1912	40.00
Toy, Pumpkin Head, Felt, Orange, Black, 1930s, 20 ½ In.	6000.00

HAMPSHIRE pottery was made in Keene, New Hampshire, between 1871 and 1923. Hampshire developed a line of colored glazed wares as early as 1883, including a Royal Worcester–type pink, olive green, blue, and mahogany. Pieces are marked with the printed mark or the impressed name *Hampshire Pottery* or *J.S.T. & Co., Keene, N.H.* Many pieces were marked with city names and sold as souvenirs.

Bowl, Mauve Snakeskin Glaze, Green Highlights, Marked, 1904-14, 3 x 5 In.	275.00
Ewer, Green Matte Glaze, Handle, Impressed, J.S.T. & Co., c.1910, 9 ¼ In.	533.00
Lamp Base, Green Matte Glaze, Lotus, Incised, Bulbous, Squat, 16 In.	1320.00
Lamp, Green Matte Glaze, Lined, Flared Base, 15 x 7 ½ In.	550.00
Mug, Green Matte Glaze, Round Bottom, Tapered Waist, 3 Loop Handles, 4 ¾ In.	230.00
Vase, Blue Matte Glaze, Green Mottling, Bulbous, Rounded Shoulder, Marked, 4 ⅛ In.	219.00
Vase, Blue Matte Glaze, Overlapping Leaves, Tapered, Shouldered, 6 ⅝ In.	259.00
Vase, Blue Peacock Glaze, Mottled, Cylindrical, 2 Arched Handles, Flat Rim, 7 ⅞ In.	489.00
Vase, Green Matte Glaze, Applied Leaves, Tall Neck, Marked, c.1910, 9 ⅜ In. ......*Illus*	830.00
Vase, Green Matte Glaze, Arrowroot Leaves, Bulbous, Narrow Rim, Marked, 3 ⅝ In.	230.00

Grueby, Vase, Yellow Trefoils, Rounded Leaves, Stamped, c.1905, 13 x 8 In.
$6,875.00

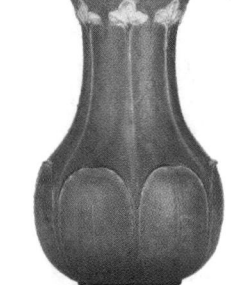

Rago Arts & Auction Center

Gustavsberg, Jar, Lid, Art Deco, Canteen Shape, Nude Woman, Ribbed, Stamped, c.1910, 9 ½ x 9 ½ In.
$59.00

Brunk Auctions

Haeger, Vase, Abstract Shape, Earth Tones, Tall Pedestal, Stamped, 12 x 8 In.
$18.00

DuMouchelles Art Gallery

Halloween, Blower, Witch Head, 6 In.
$175.00

H

303

Halloween, Lantern, Punch, Composition, Wire Handle, Crown, Filigree, Paper Insert Eyes, c.1910, 4 ½ In.
$460.00

Hake's Americana & Collectibles

Halloween, Marionette, Pumpkin Head, 6 In.
$2,200.00

Hampshire, Vase, Green Matte Glaze, Applied Leaves, Tall Neck, Marked, c.1910, 9 ⅜ In.
$830.00

Skinner, Inc.

Hampshire, Vase, Green Matte Glaze, Dandelions, Raised, Glaze, M In Circle Mark, 6 In.
$518.00

Humler & Nolan

Vase, Green Matte Glaze, Cylindrical, 7 In.	275.00
Vase, Green Matte Glaze, Dandelions, Raised, Glaze, M In Circle Mark, 6 In. ....*Illus*	518.00
Vase, Green Matte Glaze, Ear Of Corn, Husk, Squat, Ring Foot, Flared Rim, Marked, 5 ½ In....	460.00
Vase, Green Matte Glaze, Greek Key, Bulbous, 2 Reticulated Handles, Signed, 10 x 14 ½ In......	1500.00
Vase, Green Matte Glaze, Leaves, Buds, 4 x 6 ½ In.	580.00
Vase, Green Matte Glaze, Molded Cabbage Rose Leaves, Squat, Marked, c.1916, 2 ½ x 4 ½ In..	374.00
Vase, Green Matte Glaze, Oval Design, Squat, Ribbed Cylindrical Neck, Marked, 6 ¾ In.	575.00
Vase, Green Matte Glaze, Shouldered, 4 x 7 In.	336.00
Vase, Green Matte Glaze, Shouldered, Vertical Leaves, Buds, 6 ¼ In.	475.00
Vase, Green Matte Glaze, Smokestack, Tubular Neck, 2 Curved Handles, Marked, 4 ½ In........	189.00
Vase, Green Matte Glaze, Tapered Neck, Organic Handles, Marked, 6 x 6 In.	375.00
Vase, Green Matte Glaze, Wide Mouth, Bulbous Shape, Marked, 5 In.	327.00
Vase, Green, Molded Flowers & Leaves, Shouldered, 6 ⅞ In.	460.00

HANDEL glass was made by Philip Handel working in Meriden, Connecticut, from 1885 and in New York City from 1893 to 1933. The firm made art glass and other types of lamps. Handel shades were made not only of leaded glass in a style reminiscent of Tiffany but also of reverse painted glass. Handel also made vases and other glass objects.

Lamp, Adjustable, Bronze, Pulled Opalescent Green Shade, Signed, 18 ½ x 10 ¼ In...............	1380.00
Lamp, Base, 3-Light, Aztec, Bronze, Patina, Cap, Finial, Signed, 23 ¼ In.	460.00
Lamp, Chipped Ice Shade, Daisies, Multicolored, Bronze Stick Base, 14 In.	2760.00
Lamp, Chipped Ice Shade, Goldenrod, Ferns, Red Sky, 3-Socket Brass Base, 18 x 24 In.	8125.00
Lamp, Chipped Ice Shade, Leaves & Berries, Bulbous Bronze Base, 22 In.	5289.00
Lamp, Chipped Ice Shade, Poppy Tam-O'-Shanter, Flower Brass Base, Signed, 12 x 19 In........	1500.00
Lamp, Chipped Ice Shade, Winter Landscape, Tree Trunk Base, Boudoir, 14 In.	1840.00
Lamp, Cone Shade, Painted, Bridge, River, Trees, Patinated Metal Baluster Base, 27 In.	3690.00
Lamp, Cone Shape Skirted Shade, Stylized Leaves & Berries, Square Base, 1920s, 24 In.	3750.00
Lamp, Domed Shade, Desert Landscape, Orange Ground, Bronze Base, Greek Key, 23 In.	2460.00
Lamp, Domed Shade, Landscape, Reverse Painted, Brass Base, c.1905, 24 x 17 ¾ In.	1534.00
Lamp, Domed Shade, Patinated Metal, Ocher, Textured Band, 3 Sockets, Ribbed Standard, 17 x 21 In.	1304.00
Lamp, Domed Shade, Pink Roses, Leaves, Yellow Ground, Ribbed Bronze Standard, c.1920, 25 x 16 In.	1125.00
Lamp, Etched & Reverse Painted Shade, Evergreen Trees, Bronze Spread Base, 21 x 14 In.	3500.00
Lamp, Faceted Slag Glass Shade, Enamel Overlay, Leaves, 3 Sockets, c.1910s, 23 x 16 In....*Illus*	2750.00
Lamp, Floor, Pyramid Glass Shade, Metal Overlay, Base, Adjustable Arm, 16 x 61 In.	1464.00
Lamp, Glass Shade, Beaded Edge, Pat'd 07, 27 ¾ x 18 In.	1320.00
Lamp, Hanging, Forest Scene, Obverse Painted, Globular, Chain, 10 x 42 In.	2196.00
Lamp, Hanging, Obverse Painted Shade, Parrots, 9 ½ In.	1422.00
Lamp, Leaded Glass Shade, Apple Blossom, Leaf Embossed Metal Base, 33 x 18 In.	5605.00
Lamp, Octagonal Shade, Ginko Leaves, Mottled Yellow To Peach, Tapered Base, 22 In.	1968.00
Lamp, Octagonal Slag Shade, Molded Flower Base, 24 In.	1920.00
Lamp, Paneled Shade, Cattails, Slag Glass, Bronze Adjustable Base, c.1915, 80 x 22 In.	15000.00
Lamp, Paneled Slag Shade, Caramel, Bronze Tapered Base, Spread Foot, 23 x 16 In.	3250.00
Lamp, Piano, Domed, Mosaic Slag Shade, Green, Fluted Arm, Weighted Base, 6 ¾ In.......*Illus*	2400.00
Lamp, Piano, Pine Needle Overlay, Slag Glass, Cylindrical, Adjustable, 12 x 13 In.	2375.00
Lamp, Shade, Sunset Landscape & Palm Trees, Green, Orange, Metal Overlay, Base, 19 x 21 In. ...	1708.00
Lamp, Slag Glass, Faceted, Applied Geometric Overlay, Enamel, 4 Sockets, 1910s, 65 ½ x 22 In... *Illus*	5000.00
Lamp, Student, Reverse Painted Nordic Landscape, Bronze Fluted Base, Arched Arm, 10 In. ...	2625.00
Lamp, Teardrop Shape, Painted, Flowers, Parrots, Chipped Ice, Signed, 5 x 7 In.	334.00
Shade, Leaded, Arts & Crafts, Cloth Tag, 57 In.	850.00
Shade, Reverse Painted, Landscape, Blue, Orange, White, Black, Metal Overlay, 20 x 24 In. ...	935.00
Shade, Slag Glass, Stylized Leaves & Berries, Patinated Metal Frame, Square, 6 x 4 In., Pair...	875.00
Vase, Teroma, Dutch Lake Scene, Windmills, Sailboat, Gray Glass, 7 ¼ In........*Illus*	403.00
Vase, Teroma, Mountains, Trees, Stream, Ink Stamp, John Bailey, 10 In........*Illus*	920.00

HARDWARE, *see Architectural category.*

HARKER POTTERY COMPANY was incorporated in 1890 in East Liverpool, Ohio. The Harker family had been making pottery in the area since 1840. The company made many types of pottery but by the Civil War was making quantities of yellowware from native clays. It also made Rockingham-type brown-glazed pottery and whiteware. The plant was moved to Chester, West Virginia, in 1931. Dinnerware was made and sold nationally. In 1971 the company was sold to Jeannette Glass Company, and all operations ceased in 1972. For more prices, go to kovels.com.

Alpine, Bowl, Vegetable, Round, 8 In.	16.00
Alpine, Chop Plate, 11 In.	15.00

Alpine, Platter, Oval, 13 In.	28.00
Alpine, Salt & Pepper	18.00
Blue Dane, Cup & Saucer, Footed	8.00
Blue Dane, Plate, Bread & Butter, 6 ⅜ In.	5.00
Blue Mist, Bowl, Fruit	8.00
Blue Mist, Creamer, 3 ½ In.	10.00
Blue Mist, Cup & Saucer	7.00
Blue Mist, Sugar, Lid	16.00
Bouquet, Gravy Boat, Underplate	42.00
Bouquet, Plate, Bread & Butter, 6 ¼ In.	5.00
Bouquet, Plate, Dinner, 10 ¼ In.	16.00
Bouquet, Platter, Oval, 13 In.	18.00
Chesterton, Bowl, Fruit, Blue	7.00
Chesterton, Bowl, Vegetable, Oval, Blue, 9 In.	30.00
Chesterton, Bowl, Vegetable, Round, Blue, 8 In.	27.00
Chesterton, Creamer, Celadon, 2 ¼ In.	16.00
Chesterton, Cup & Saucer, Blue	8.00
Chesterton, Plate, Bread & Butter, Blue, 6 ¼ In.	8.00
Chesterton, Plate, Bread & Butter, Celadon, 6 In.	6.00
Chesterton, Plate, Bread & Butter, Cocoa, 6 ¼ In.	6.00
Chesterton, Platter, Oval, 11 In.	41.00
Chesterton, Sugar, Lid, Cocoa	24.00
Cock O'Morn, Butter, Cover, Coral, ¼ Lb.	22.00
Cock O'Morn, Cream & Sugar, Coral	32.00
Cock O'Morn, Cup & Saucer, Coral	8.00
Cock O'Morn, Cup & Saucer, Yellow	8.00
Cock O'Morn, Plate, Dinner, Coral, 10 In.	8.00
Cock O'Morn, Platter, Oval, Coral, 11 In.	28.00
Cock O'Morn, Platter, Oval, Yellow, 11 In.	28.00
Cock O'Morn, Soup, Dish, Lug Handles, Yellow, 7 In.	9.00
Coronet, Bowl, Vegetable, Round, 8 In.	16.00
Coronet, Casserole, Lid, Round, 2 Qt., 9 In.	43.00
Coronet, Cup & Saucer	7.00
Coronet, Plate, Bread & Butter, 6 In.	8.00
Coronet, Salt & Pepper	18.00
Country Charm, Plate, Dinner, 11 In.	15.00
Daisy Lane, Plate, Bread & Butter, 6 In.	8.00
Dresden Duchess, Cup & Saucer, Footed	12.00
Dresden Duchess, Plate, Bread & Butter, 6 In.	8.00
Early Morn, Cup & Saucer	8.00
Early Morn, Plate, Dinner, 10 In.	8.00
Early Morn, Platter, Oval, 13 In.	20.00
Everglades, Plate, Salad, 7 In.	8.00
Everglades, Platter, Serving, Oval, 13 In.	36.00
Forest Flower, Bowl, Fruit, 5 In.	7.00
Forest Flower, Cup & Saucer	8.00
Forest Flower, Plate, Dinner, 10 In.	8.00
Forest Flower, Platter, Serving, Oval, 13 In.	20.00
Forest Flower, Salt & Pepper	16.00
Garden Trail, Coaster, 4 ¾ In.	6.00
Garden Trail, Creamer	16.00
Garden Trail, Plate, Bread & Butter, 6 In.	6.00
Godey, Bowl, Vegetable, Round, 8 In.	22.00
Godey, Plate, Bread & Butter, 6 In.	6.00
Godey, Plate, Dinner, 10 In.	8.00
Godey, Platter, Serving, Oval, 11 In.	18.00
Golden Dawn, Casserole, Lid, Round, 1 ½ Qt., 7 In.	47.00
Golden Dawn, Cup & Saucer	7.00
Golden Dawn, Sugar & Creamer	28.00
Lemon Tree, Bowl, Vegetable, Round, 8 In.	16.00
Lemon Tree, Creamer, 3 In.	14.00
Lemon Tree, Cup & Saucer	8.00
Lemon Tree, Platter, Oval, 13 In.	20.00
Magnolia, Bowl, Vegetable, Round, 8 In.	21.00
Magnolia, Plate, Bread & Butter, 6 In.	7.00
Magnolia, Platter, Serving, Oval, 13 In.	42.00

Handel, Lamp, Faceted Slag Glass Shade, Enamel Overlay, Leaves, 3 Sockets, c.1910s, 23 x 16 In.
$2,750.00

Rago Arts & Auction Center

Handel, Lamp, Piano, Domed, Mosaic Slag Shade, Green, Fluted Arm, Weighted Base, 6 ¾ In.
$2,400.00

Skinner, Inc.

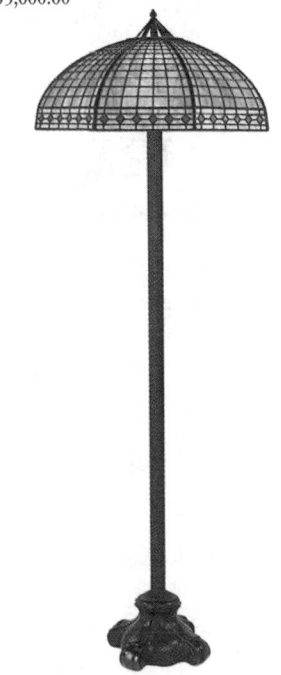

Handel, Lamp, Slag Glass, Faceted, Applied Geometric Overlay, Enamel, 4 Sockets, 1910s, 65 ½ x 22 In.
$5,000.00

Rago Arts & Auction Center

Handel, Vase, Teroma, Dutch Lake Scene, Windmills, Sailboat, Gray Glass, 7 ¼ In.
$403.00

Early Auction Co.

Handel, Vase, Teroma, Mountains, Trees, Stream, Ink Stamp, John Bailey, 10 In.
$920.00

Humler & Nolan

Haviland, Centerpiece, 2 Women Supports, Gilt Trim, Panels, Limoges, c.1850, 12 x 16 In.
$1,599.00

New Orleans Auction Galleries, Inc.

Author and Inventor

Lewis Carroll, who wrote *Alice in Wonderland*, invented the Wonderland Postage-Stamp Case in 1889. It was a folder with 12 slots marked to hold the most common stamps. He also invented a writing tablet called the Nyctograph that could be used at night to take notes in the dark.

Modern Tulip, Casserole, Lid, Round, Qt., 7 In.	65.00
Peacock Alley, Bowl, Vegetable, Oval, Divided, 10 In.	45.00
Peacock Alley, Cup & Saucer	6.00
Peacock Alley, Plate, Bread & Butter, 5 In.	8.00
Peacock Alley, Plate, Salad, 7 In.	7.00
Pepper White, Cup & Saucer	9.00
Pepper White, Plate, Dinner, 10 In.	10.00
Persian Key, Bowl, Vegetable, Oval, 9 In.	21.00
Persian Key, Cup & Saucer	8.00
Persian Key, Gravy Boat	23.00
Persian Key, Mug, 3 ½ In.	8.00
Persian Key, Plate, Dinner, 10 In.	10.00
Persian Key, Platter, Oval, 13 In.	16.00
Rosebud, Bowl, Vegetable, Oval, Divided, 10 In.	20.00
Rosebud, Saucer	7.00
Sea Fare, Plate, Bread & Butter, 5 In.	11.00
Shell Pink, Gravy Boat	24.00
Shell Pink, Platter, Serving, Oval, Round, 8 In.	23.00
Shell Pink, Saucer	1.00
Snowleaf, Cup & Saucer	8.00
Snowleaf, Platter, Serving, Oval, 11 In.	15.00
Snowleaf, Saucer	3.00
Sun Glow, Bowl, Vegetable, Round, 8 In.	16.00
Sun Glow, Creamer	16.00
Sun Glow, Cup & Saucer	8.00
Sun Glow, Soup, Dish, Lug Handles, 7 In.	9.00
Sun Valley, Bowl, Fruit, Rim, 5 ½ In.	8.00
Sun Valley, Cup & Saucer	8.00
Vine Lace, Chop Plate, 11 In.	23.00
Vintage, Plate, Salad, 7 In.	18.00
Vintage, Platter, Serving, Oval, 11 In.	24.00
Vintage, Saucer	5.00
Vintage, Sugar, Lid, 2 ⅜ In.	20.00
Violet, Creamer	27.00
Violet, Plate, Bread & Butter, 6 In.	7.00
Violet, Saucer	4.00
Violet, Vegetable, Round, 8 In.	76.00
White Cap, Bowl, Vegetable, Oval, Divided, 10 In.	16.00
White Cap, Creamer, 3 ⅝ In.	16.00
White Cap, Cup & Saucer	8.00

HARLEQUIN dinnerware was produced by the Homer Laughlin Company from 1938 to 1964, and sold without trademark by the F. W. Woolworth Co. It has a concentric ring design like Fiesta, but the rings are separated from the rim by a plain margin. Cup handles are triangular in shape. Seven different novelty animal figurines were introduced in 1939. For more prices, go to kovels.com.

Chartreuse, Bowl, Salad, 7 ⅜ In.	42.00
Chartreuse, Gravy Boat	42.00
Chartreuse, Nut Dish, Handle, Footed	55.00
Forest Green, Teapot, Lid, 3 Cup, 4 ⅞ In.	198.00
Gray, Cup & Saucer	12.00
Gray, Nut Dish, Handle, Footed	30.00
Gray, Plate, 9 ¼ In.	12.00
Light Green, Bowl, Nut, Round, Basket Weave, 3 In.	149.00
Light Green, Bowl, Vegetable, Round, 8 In.	65.00
Light Green, Cup, After Dinner	98.00
Light Green, Plate, Bread & Butter, 6 ¼ In.	8.00
Light Green, Plate, Dinner, 10 In.	38.00
Maroon, Bowl, Fruit, 5 ⅝ In.	12.00
Maroon, Figurine, Cat	200.00
Maroon, Figurine, Duck	200.00
Maroon, Figurine, Fish	200.00
Maroon, Plate, Bread & Butter, 6 ¼ In.	9.00
Mauve Blue, Ashtray, Basket Weave, 4 ½ In.	48.00
Mauve Blue, Creamer, 2 ⅝ In.	26.00

Mauve Blue, Cup & Saucer	15.00
Mauve Blue, Figurine, Cat	230.00
Mauve Blue, Figurine, Fish	190.00
Mauve Blue, Figurine, Penguin	168.00
Mauve Blue, Plate, 9 ¼ In.	20.00
Medium Green, Bowl, Fruit	48.00
Medium Green, Cup & Saucer	16.00
Medium Green, Relish, 3 Sections	148.00
Medium Green, Teapot, Lid, 3 Cup, 4 ⅞ In.	2499.00
Red, Eggcup, Double, 3 ¾ In.	28.00
Red, Plate, Bread & Butter, 6 ¼ In.	8.00
Red, Plate, Luncheon, 9 In.	15.00
Red, Tumbler, 4 ¼ In.	38.00
Rose, Butter, Cover, ½ Lb.	160.00
Rose, Cup & Saucer	10.00
Rose, Gravy Boat	27.00
Rose, Pitcher, Tankard, 4 ⅞ In.	74.00
Rose, Plate, Bread & Butter, 6 ¼ In.	6.00
Rose, Plate, Dinner, 10 In.	34.00
Rose, Plate, Salad, 7 ¼ In.	9.00
Spruce Green, Cup	15.00
Spruce Green, Figurine, Duck	199.00
Spruce Green, Figurine, Lamb	180.00
Spruce Green, Figurine, Penguin	199.00
Spruce Green, Plate, Bread & Butter, 6 ¼ In.	8.00
Spruce Green, Plate, Dinner, 10 In.	40.00
Turquoise, Bowl, Fruit, 5 ⅝ In.	9.00
Turquoise, Cup & Saucer	10.00
Turquoise, Gravy Boat	18.00
Turquoise, Plate, Bread & Butter, 6 ¼ In.	7.00
Turquoise, Plate, Dinner, 10 In.	24.00
Turquoise, Salt & Pepper	24.00
Turquoise, Sugar, Lid, Open Finial, 2 ¾ In.	30.00
Yellow, Ashtray, 4 ½ In.	42.00
Yellow, Creamer	18.00
Yellow, Figurine, Donkey	200.00
Yellow, Figurine, Fish	150.00
Yellow, Figurine, Penguin	180.00
Yellow, Gravy Boat, Underplate	22.00
Yellow, Pitcher, Ball, 7 In.	46.00
Yellow, Pitcher, Tankard, 4 ⅞ In.	43.00
Yellow, Plate, Dinner, Homer Laughlin, 1950s, 10 In.	50.00

HATPIN collectors search for pins popular from 1860 to 1920. The long pin, often over four inches, was used to hold the hat in place on the hair. The tops of the pins were made of all materials, from solid gold and real gemstones to ceramics and glass. Be careful to buy original hatpins and not recent pieces made by altering old buttons.

14K Yellow Gold, Balloon Shape, Filigree, Etruscan Revival, 9 In.	175.00
14K Yellow Gold, Umbrella Shape, Silver Colored Shaft, c.1900, 6 ¼ In.	125.00
Bakelite, Yellow, Rhinestones, Incised Leaves, c.1930, 5 In.	65.00
Brass, Filigree, Star Of David, Paste Stones, Victorian, 11 In.	125.00
Celluloid, Rhinestone, Beige Swirl, 1920s, 2 ½ In.	29.00
Clear Lucite, Brass Rose, c.1900, 8 In.	65.00
Copper, Filigree, Spherical, 9 In.	100.00
Glass, Amber & Brown, Rhinestone Band, 6 In.	48.00
Gold Plate, Amethyst, Heart Shape, c.1900, 6 In.	120.00
Gunmetal, Mourning, Egg Shape, Victorian, 11 In.	125.00
Jet Stones, Sphere, Victorian, 7 In.	42.00
Lead Crystal, Sterling Silver, Repousse, Daisies, c.1905, 7 ⅝ In.	130.00
Malachite, Ball, 16K Yellow Gold Stem, 3 ¼ In.	39.00
Porcelain, Bavarian, Pink Roses, Blue Border, 5 ⅛ In.	78.00
Repousse, Art Nouveau, Lady, Flowing Hair, 6 ¾ In.	128.00
Rock Crystal Navette, Platinum & Diamond Mount, Cartier, c.1915, Pair	17775.00
Sterling Silver, Golf Club Shape, Birmingham, 1908, 10 In.	195.00

TIP
Store glass right side up to protect the rims.

Hawkes, Vase, Trumpet, Easter, Teutonic, Scalloped Hobstar Cut Foot, 14 In.
$595.00

H

Head Vase, Jackie Kennedy, Black Gloved Hand, Scarf Draped On Head, Inarco, Japan, 6 ¼ In.
$230.00

Hake's Americana & Collectibles

Holly Amber, Compote, Lid, Footed, Greentown, 8 In.
$690.00

Early Auction Co.

Holly Amber, Toothpick Holder, Greentown, 2 ½ In. $316.00

Early Auction Co.

Horn, Cup, Libation, Rhinoceros, Carved, Friends Of Winter, Bamboo, Bats Inside, 1700s, 11 In. $10,413.00

Skinner, Inc.

Horn, Cup, Libation, Rhinoceros, Lotus Shape, Blossom, Leaf Base, Stand, Chinese, 1800s, 2 ⅝ x 3 In. $14,220.00

Skinner, Inc.

Howdy Doody, Baseball Mitt, Howdy Portrait, Leather-Like, Vinyl Piping, Metal Rivets, Kagran, 1950s, 7 In. $104.00

Hake's Americana & Collectibles

HATPIN HOLDERS were needed when hatpins were fashionable from 1860 to 1920. The large, heavy hat required special long-shanked pins to hold it in place. The hatpin holder resembles a large saltshaker, but it often has no opening at the bottom as a shaker does. Hatpin holders were made of all types of ceramics and metal. Look for other pieces under the names of specific manufacturers.

Carnival Glass, Purple Grape, 3-Footed	250.00
Elfinware, Flowers, 3 Sections, Germany, c.1900, 4 In.	125.00
Limoges, Flower Shape, Gilded Stem, Mottled Purple Blossom, 4 ¼ In.	210.00
Nippon, Fluted Flared Ribbing, Berries, Leaves, Ribbon, 1930s, 4 ¼ In.	58.00
Nippon, Lotus, Raised Moriage Dots, Blue Ground, 5 In.	118.00
Pheasants, Multicolor, Green Band, Spode, c.1891, 3 ⅝ x 3 ½ In.	88.00
Porcelain, Clown, Dog, Black, White, Yellow Base, Art Deco, Germany, 1920s, 7 In.	480.00
Porcelain, Leaves, Flowers, Multicolor, Saucer Base, 5 ¼ In.	39.00
Porcelain, Pink Roses, Leaves, Scalloped Gilt Trim, 5 In.	35.00
Silver Over Porcelain, Lavender, Flowers, Stems, c.1910, 4 In.	155.00

HAVILAND china has been made in Limoges, France, since 1842. The factory was started by the Haviland Brothers of New York City. Pieces are marked *H & Co., Haviland & Co.,* or *Theodore Haviland.* It is possible to match existing sets of dishes through dealers who specialize in Haviland china. Other factories worked in the town of Limoges making a similar chinaware. These porcelains are listed in this book under Limoges.

HAVILAND & CO.

Centerpiece, 2 Women Supports, Gilt Trim, Panels, Limoges, c.1850, 12 x 16 In. ....*Illus*	1599.00
Charger, Painted Roses, Gilt Trim, Limoges, 1904-20, 14 ¾ In.	36.00
Cup & Saucer, Autumn Leaf, Green, Orange, Yellow, Pink, Gold Trim	25.00
Cup & Saucer, Pink Geometric Border, Footed	65.00
Cup & Saucer, Transfer Flowers, Mauve, Brown, Square, Folded Corners, Embossed, 2 ½ x 4 ⅛ In.	110.00
Plate Set, Floral, Gold Border, Pastel Ground, 6 Different Flowers, Oval, c.1890, 8 ½ In., 6 Piece	375.00
Plate, Bobwhite Quail, Wheat Field, Pink Border, Gold Scalloped Trim, c.1870, 9 ½ In.	159.00
Plate, Camellia, 6 ½ In., 4 Piece	37.00
Plate, Dessert, Autumn Leaf, Green, Orange, Yellow, Pink, 7 ½ In.	25.00
Plate, Dorset, Scalloped Edge, Gold Trim, Pink, Yellow Roses, Spoon Rest, 11 ¾ x 9 In.	35.00
Platter, Chippendale Regency, Peach & Yellow Roses, White Ground, Gold Trim, 15 x 10 In.	48.00
Platter, Dorset, Scalloped Edge, Gold Trim, Pink, Yellow Roses, Spoon Rest, 16 ⅜ x 13 In.	75.00
Platter, Rosebud, Scalloped Edge, Gold Trim, c.1950, 15 x 11 In.	30.00
Saucer, Gainsborough, Gold Trim, 8 ¼ In., Pair	10.00
Saucer, White, Flower Border, Pink, Blue, White, c.1970, 6 In.	6.00
Serving Bowl, White, Leaves, Vines, Ranson, c.1890, 10 x 7 ½ In.	70.00
Vase, Medieval Night Street Scene, Purple, Black, Cylinder, Signed L. Saquet, 15 ¼ Ix 7 In.	1180.00

HAVILAND POTTERY began in 1872, when Charles Haviland decided to make art pottery. He worked with the famous artists of the day and made pottery with slip glazed decorations. Production stopped in 1885. Haviland Pottery is marked with the letters *H & Co.* The Haviland name is better known today for its porcelain.

HAVILAND & CO.

Cachepot, Relief Flowers, Brown Ground, c.1870, 6 x 14 In.	3800.00

HAWKES cut glass was made by T. G. Hawkes & Company of Corning, New York, founded in 1880. The firm cut glass blanks made at other glassworks until 1962. Many pieces are marked with the trademark, a trefoil ring enclosing a fleur-de-lis and two hawks. Cut glass by other manufacturers is listed under either the factory name or in the general Cut Glass category.

Bowl, Brazilian Variation, Hobstar & Strawberry Diamond, 2 ½ x 9 In.	80.00
Bowl, Festoon, Notched Scalloped Rim, 2 ½ x 9 ½ In.	400.00
Bowl, Gravic, 6 Tusks, 6 Hearts, Engraved Leaves & Flowers, 5 x 10 In.	250.00
Bowl, Hobstar With Strawberry Diamond Highlights, Marked, 3 ¼ x 8 In.	100.00
Bowl, Low, Victor, Marked, 8 In.	175.00
Bowl, North Star, 3 ¾ x 8 In.	75.00
Candlestick, Diamond Cut Band, Punty Highlights, Marked, 14 In., Pair	125.00
Carafe, Water, Chrysanthemum Pattern, Pattern Cut Neck Ring, 9 ¼ In.	950.00
Carafe, Water, Queen's Pattern, Pinched Neck, 7 In.	350.00
Cordial, Flute & Greek Key, Marked, 6 In., 3 Piece	100.00
Cruet, Hobstar & Crosscut Diamond, Handle, Marked, 7 In.	15.00
Decanter, Intaglio Cut Flowers, Silver Cap, Collar, Marked, 9 ½ x 3 ¼ In.	805.00
Decanter, Ship's, Engraved Flowers & Leaves, Squat, Cut Handle & Stopper, 7 In.	250.00
Dresser Box, Iris, Round, Hinged, Cut Base, Marked, 3 x 6 In.	300.00

Goblet, Engraved, Iris, 7 ¾ In., 4 Piece	150.00
Goblet, White Wine, Flute Pattern, Green Cased, Clear Stem, Monogram, 6 ¾ In., Pair	300.00
Jewelry Box, Heart Shape, Hobstar Chain, Engraved Flowers, 3 x 6 In.	300.00
Perfume Bottle, Clear, Thumblift, Bulbous, Dabber, Silver Collar, Handle, c.1905, 4 ¾ In., Pair	600.00
Pitcher, Water, Marquis, Squat, Marked, 8 In.	500.00
Plate, Holland Pattern, 7 In., 6 Piece	200.00
Plate, Rayed Center, Greek Key Border, Marked, 10 ½ In.	50.00
Punch Cup, Brunswick, Pedestal, Marked, 4 Piece	350.00
Rose Bowl, Constance, 3-Footed, Marked, 6 x 8 In.	375.00
Rose Bowl, Kensington, Scalloped Foot, 8 ¼ x 6 ½ In.	2000.00
Rose Bowl, Navarre, 5 ¾ x 6 ½ In.	250.00
Salt & Pepper, Brunswick, Sterling Silver Lids, Embossed, Marked, 3 In.	200.00
Salt & Pepper, Navarre, Sterling Silver Lids, Embossed, Marked, 3 In.	50.00
Serving Dish, Prism & Ray, Clear Blank, 3 Sections, Handles, 5 x 8 ½ In.	60.00
Serving Set, Platter, 4 Plates, Arched Rims, Stars, Fan & Strawberry Panels, c.1920, Platter 14 In.	1680.00
Tazza, Vesica, Strawberry Diamond & Cane, Hobstar Foot, Rolled Rim, Marked, 7 ½ In.	300.00
Tray, Chrysanthemum, Square Tab Handle, 6 In.	350.00
Tray, Festoon Pattern, Round, 8 Scallops, Notched Edge, 10 In.	600.00
Tray, Hobstar Center, Geometric Boarder, Clear Blank, Acorn Shape, 8 x 10 In.	1100.00
Tray, Ice Cream, Aberdeen, Oval, 15 ¾ x 10 ½ In.	1000.00
Tray, Round, Napoleon Pattern, 10 In.	650.00
Tray, Round, Queen's Pattern, 10 In.	600.00
Vase, Amethyst, Optic Ribbed, Cut Flowers, Sterling Base, 10 In.	115.00
Vase, Brunswick, Trumpet, Marked, 16 In.	400.00
Vase, Cut Glass, Silver, Trumpet, Phoenix, Flowering Branches, Diamond Point Cut, c.1935, 14 In.	615.00
Vase, Etched Flowers & Leaves, Internal Decoration, Flared, Silver Stepped Foot, 14 In.	540.00
Vase, Flowers, Vines, Clear, 8 ¼ In.	35.00
Vase, Green Crystal, Gold Etched Band, Flared Neck, Marked, 11 In.	180.00
Vase, Navarre, Cylindrical, Marked, 9 ¾ In.	240.00
Vase, Navarre, Hobstar Foot, Pedestal, Cylindrical, Marked, 10 In.	100.00
Vase, Navarre, Hobstar Foot, Trumpet Shape, Marked, 10 In.	110.00
Vase, Trumpet, Apple Green, Crosscut Diamond & Vertical Notch, 3 Sections, 18 In.	600.00
Vase, Trumpet, Easter, Teutonic, Scalloped Hobstar Cut Foot, 14 In. ......Illus	595.00
Water Set, Brunswick Pattern, 8 ¾-In. Pitcher, 7 Piece	500.00

HEAD VASES, generally showing a woman from the shoulders up, were used by florists primarily in the 1950s and 1960s. Made in a variety of sizes and often decorated with imitation jewelry and other lifelike accessories, the vases were manufactured in Japan and the U.S.A. Less elaborate examples were made as early as the 1930s. Religious themes, babies, and animals are also common subjects. Other head vases are listed under manufacturers' names and can be located through the index in the back of this book.

Baby, Blue Eyes, 4 In.	25.00
Baby, Girl, Pink Bonnet, Ucagco, c.1950, 6 In.	60.00
Cameo Girl, Eve Dressed For Success, Black Hair, On Phone, Striped Jacket, 6 In.	32.00
Girl, Blond, Graduate, Cap, Diploma, Napco, 1950s, 5 ½ In.	45.00
Girl, Hat, Braids, Blond, Checkered Blouse, Japan, 5 In.	30.00
Girl, Pink Hat, Blue Hat, Bow Mouth, 7 ½ In., Pair	345.00
Girl, Ponytail, Blond Hair, Hat, Cape, c.1955, 5 In.	45.00
Glamour Girl, Red Hair, Pink Hat, Blue Necklace, 7 ¼ In.	37.00
Jackie Kennedy, Black Gloved Hand, Scarf Draped On Head, Inarco, Japan, 6 ¼ In. ......Illus	230.00
Woman, Blond, Green Hooded Cape, Fur Edge, Holly, Red Glove, 7 ¼ In.	95.00
Woman, Demure, Blond, Flower In Hair, Long Lashes, Enesco, 4 ½ In.	125.00
Woman, Flipped Hair, Blue Eyes, Pink Lips, Lego, 6 In.	125.00
Woman, Ivory, Tilted Beret, Hair Curls, 1940s, 8 In.	88.00
Woman, Poinsettia Collar & Hat, Pearls, Inarco, c.1961, 5 ½ In.	68.00
Woman, Ruffled Hat, Long Lashes, Blond Curly Hair, Hand On Check, 7 ½ In.	225.00
Woman, Spanish, Juanita, Hat, Scarf, 6 ¼ In.	75.00

HEDI SCHOOP Art Creations, North Hollywood, California, started about 1945 and was working until 1954. Schoop made ceramic figurines, lamps, planters, and tablewares.

Figurine, French Peasants, Man, Woman, Holding Baskets, 13 ½ In.	220.00
Figurine, Spanish Senorita, Hands On Hips, 2 Baskets, Blue Skirt, 12 ¾ In.	157.00
Planter, Open Book Shape, Flower Names, 7 ½ x 10 In.	156.00
Plaque, Cat, Face, 7 ½ x 7 ½ In.	89.00
Plaque, Cat, Sitting, Stripes, 7 ½ x 7 ½ In.	89.00

Howdy Doody, Doll, Clown, Clarabell, Vinyl Head, Cloth Stuffed Body, Felt Feet & Hands, Ideal, 1950s, 17 ½ In. $115.00

Hake's Americana & Collectibles

Howdy Doody, Statue, Papier-Mache, Blue Jeans, Plaid Shirt, Hat, Lunch Box, 40 x 17 In. $252.00

Victorian Casino Antiques

Hull, Little Red Riding Hood, Cookie Jar $200.00

309

Hummel, Clock, No. 442, Chapel Time, Open Windows, Missing Bee, 11 ½ In. $330.00

DuMouchelles Art Gallery

H

Hummel, Figurine, No. 43, March Winds, Crown Mark, 5 In. $35.00

Conestoga Auction Co., Inc.

Hummel, Figurine, No. 46/3, Madonna, Without Halo, Missing Bee, 16 In. $33.00

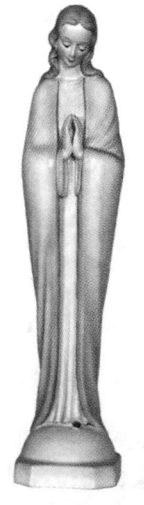

Woody Auction

HEINTZ ART METAL SHOP used the letters *HAMS* in a diamond as a mark. In 1902, Otto Heintz designed and manufactured copper items with colored enamel decorations under the name Art Crafts Shop. He took over the Arts & Crafts Company in Buffalo, New York, in 1903. By 1906 it had become the Heintz Art Metal Shop. It remained in business until 1930. The company made ashtrays, bookends, boxes, bowls, desk sets, vases, trophies, and smoking sets. The best-known pieces are made of copper, brass, and bronze with silver overlay. Similar pieces were made by Smith Metal Arts and were marked *Silver Crest*. Some pieces by both companies are unmarked.

Bowl, Applied Flowers Design, Sterling On Bronze, 9 x 3 In.	219.00
Bowl, Flower, Sterling On Copper, Pat. Aug. 27, 1912, 8 x 3 ½ In.	403.00
Lamp, Cameo Inset, Helmet Shape, Sterling On Bronze, 8 x 10 In.	875.00
Lamp, Poppies, Cutout Shade, Mica Lined, Sterling On Bronze, Patina, 8 x 10 In.	610.00
Trophy, Cylindrical, Sterling On Bronze, Angular Handles, Applied Detail, c.1915, 10 x 9 ½ In.	300.00
Vase, Applied Leaf Vine, Sterling On Bronze, Slender, 5 x 17 ½ In.	500.00
Vase, Applied Organic Design, Sterling On Bronze, Tapered, Impressed Mark, 10 In.	275.00
Vase, Applied Windmill, Sterling On Bronze, Cylindrical, 5 x 12 In.	550.00
Vase, Bud, Applied Leaf & Berries, Sterling On Bronze, Spread Base, Narrow Neck, 9 ½ x 3 ⅜ In.	173.00
Vase, Organic Design, Sterling On Bronze, Tapered, Impressed, 4 ½ x 10 In.	336.00

HEISEY glass was made from 1896 to 1957 in Newark, Ohio, by A. H. Heisey and Co., Inc. The Imperial Glass Company of Bellaire, Ohio, bought some of the molds and the rights to the trademark. Some Heisey patterns have been made by Imperial since 1960. After 1968, they stopped using the *H* trademark. Heisey used romantic names for colors, such as Sahara. Do not confuse color and pattern names. The Custard Glass and Ruby Glass categories may also include some Heisey pieces.

Animal, Dog, Scottie	115.00
Animal, Giraffe Head	110.00
Animal, Goose, Wings Up	90.00
Aristocrat, Candlestick, 7 ½ In.	20.00
Banded Flute, Jug, Lip, 3 Qt.	40.00
Beaded Panel & Sunburst, Salt	40.00
Beehive, Plate, Flamingo, 14 In.	45.00
Charger, Slender Man, Pulled By 2 Greyhounds, Sand Blasted, c.1935, 14 ¼ In.	259.00
Classic, Candlestick, 9 ½ In.	30.00
Colonial Panel, Salt	12.50
Colonial, Compote, Scalloped Top, 8 In.	45.00
Columbia, Candlestick, Pair	25.00
Crystolite, Relish, Round, 5 Sections, 10 In.	12.50
Duquesne, Wine, Sahara Bowl, 3 Oz.	40.00
Empress, Ashtray	10.00
Empress, Cruet, Flamingo	35.00
Empress, Nappy, Flamingo, 4 ½ In.	5.00
Fancy Loop, Celery Vase, 6 In.	75.00
Fancy Loop, Toothpick Holder	15.00
Fancy Loop, Tumbler	10.00
Fandango, Sugar & Creamer	30.00
Four Arch, Sugar & Creamer, Lid	280.00
Greek Key, Cruet, 6 Oz.	40.00
Groove & Slash, Compote, 9 In.	125.00
Lariat, Bowl, Gardenia, 13 In.	10.00
Lariat, Nappy, 5 In.	8.00
Lariat, Plate, 14 In.	10.00
New Era, Goblet, Cobalt Bowl	85.00
Oak Leaf, Coaster, Hawthorne	55.00
Octagon, Bowl, 6 In.	17.50
Old Williamsburg, Wine	45.00
Patrician, Candlestick, 7 ½ In., Pair	25.00
Pillows, Rose Bowl, Clear, 1901-12, 3 ¾ x 4 In.	195.00
Pillows, Rose Bowl, Footed	60.00
Pillows, Syrup, Handle, 7 Oz.	70.00
Pineapple & Fan, Sugar	30.00
Pineapple & Fan, Toothpick Holder, Clear With Gold	65.00
Pineapple & Fan, Toothpick Holder, Green	165.00
Pineapple & Fan, Vase, 8 In.	15.00
Plantation, Candlestick, 3-Light	70.00
Pleat & Panel, Compote, Lid	25.00
Prince Of Wales, Toothpick Holder, Plumes	45.00

Priscilla, Ale, 4 Oz.	2.00
Priscilla, Mustard, Lid, c.1904, 4 In.	45.00
Provincial, Plate, Limelight, 8 In.	45.00
Punty & Diamond Point, Toothpick Holder	60.00
Punty & Diamond Point, Vase, 8 In.	55.00
Puritan, Bowl, Crimped, 9 ½ In.	30.00
Puritan, Butter, Cover	45.00
Raised Loop, Celery Vase, 12 In.	17.50
Ribbon Octagon, Sugar & Creamer, Moongleam	45.00
Ridgeleigh, Candlestick, Pair	20.00
Ridgeleigh, Ice Bucket, Clear, Vertical Fluting, Marked, 1935, 4 ½ x 6 ½ In.	85.00
Satellite, Vase, Crimped, 8 ½ In.	140.00
Saturn, Cruet, Silver Stopper	30.00
Spanish, Champagne, Cobalt Bowl	70.00
Spanish, Cocktail, Cobalt Bowl	65.00
Spanish, Cordial, Cobalt Bowl	110.00
Star, Relish, 5 Sections	20.00
Sunburst, Celery Dish	55.00
Sunburst, Compote, 8 ½ In.	105.00
Sunburst, Nappy, Crimped, 8 ½ In.	20.00
Sunburst, Toothpick Holder	150.00
Tudor, Sugar & Creamer, Lid, Hawthorne	165.00
Twist, Cruet, Stopper, 4 Oz.	15.00
Twist, Nappy, 8 In.	25.00
Twist, Plate, Marigold, 7 In.	65.00
Wampum, Candlestick, Pair	10.00
Waverly, Candlestick, 3-Light	30.00
Waverly, Vase, Fan, Orchid Etch, 7 In.	40.00

HEREND, *see Fischer category.*

HEUBACH is the collector's name for Gebruder Heubach, a firm working in Lichten, Germany, from 1840 to 1925. It is best known for bisque dolls and doll heads, the principal products. The company also manufactured bisque figurines, including piano babies, beginning in the 1880s, and glazed figurines in the 1900s. Piano Babies are listed in their own category. Dolls are included in the Doll category under Gebruder Heubach and Heubach. Another factory, Ernst Heubach, working in Koppelsdorf, Germany, also made porcelain and dolls. These will also be found in the Doll category under Heubach Koppelsdorf.

Figurine, Boy, Juggling Apples, 1900s, 7 ¼ In.	449.00
Figurine, Bunny Boy & Girl, 9 In., Pair	695.00
Figurine, Girl, Holding Shell To Ear, Marked, 13 ½ In.	192.00

HISTORIC BLUE, *see factory names, such as Adams, Ridgway, and Staffordshire.*

HOBNAIL glass is a style of glass with bumps all over. Dozens of hobnail patterns and variants have been made. Clear, colored, and opalescent hobnail have been made and are being reproduced. Other pieces of hobnail may also be listed in the Duncan & Miller and Fenton categories.

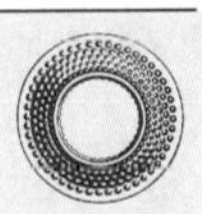

Bowl, Yellow Rim, Hobbs, Brockunier & Co., c.1880, 4 x 4 In.	95.00
Compote, Clear, Columbia Glass Co., c.1875, 9 ¼ In.	175.00
Cruet, Olive Green, Applied Handle, Stopper, Pontil, 1800s, 5 ½ In.	145.00
Pitcher, Sapphire, Applied Handle, Hobbs, Brockunier & Co., 7 ¼ In.	345.00
Tumbler, Cranberry, Opalescent, Hobbs, Brockunier & Co., 4 In.	35.00
Vase, Jack-In-The-Pulpit, Amberina, Kanawha Glass Co., 1950s, 9 ½ In.	35.00

HOLLY AMBER, or golden agate, glass was made by the Indiana Tumbler and Goblet Company of Greentown, Indiana, from January 1, 1903, to June 13, 1903. It is a pressed glass pattern featuring holly leaves in the amber-shaded glass. The glass was made with shadings that range from creamy opalescent to brown-amber.

Butter, Cover, Golden Agate, Ruffle Rim, 7 ¼ In.	863.00
Butter, Domed Cover, Beaded, Scalloped Edge, Greentown, 7 In.	805.00
Compote, Beaded, Pedestal, Flared Dome Foot, Square Bowl, Greentown, 6 ½ In.	633.00
Compote, Lid, Footed, Greentown, 8 In. ....*Illus*	690.00
Compote, Pedestal, Conical, Beaded Rim, Golden Agate, 6 In.	518.00
Creamer, Beaded, Ring Foot, Wavy Spout, Horizontal Bands, Greentown, 4 ½ In.	575.00
Cruet, Amber, Opalescent, Stopper, Greentown, 6 ¾ In.	1035.00

Hummel, Figurine, No. 152/A, Umbrella Boy, Missing Bee, 5 In.
$118.00

Conestoga Auction Co., Inc.

Hummel, Figurine, No. 154/0, Waiter, Full Bee, 6 In.
$110.00

Woody Auction

Hummel, Figurine, No. 196, Telling Her Secret, Full Bee, 6 ¾ In.
$110.00

Woody Auction

TIP
Cheesecloth is a good polishing cloth.

Hummel, Figurine, No. 200/0, Little Goat Herder, Full Bee, 5 In. $96.00

The Stein Auction Co.

Hummel, Figurine, No. 340, Letter To Santa Claus, Missing Bee, 7 In. $59.00

Conestoga Auction Co., Inc.

Hummel, Figurine, No. 353/1, Spring Dance, Three Line Mark, 6 ¾ In. $540.00

The Stein Auction Co.

Hummel, Figurine, No. 369, Follow The Leader, Three Line Mark, 7 In. $480.00

DuMouchelles Art Gallery

Shaker, Early American Pressed Glass, Greentown, 3 ¼ In., Pair	403.00
Spooner, Early American Pressed Glass, Greentown, 4 In.	460.00
Toothpick Holder, Greentown, 2 ½ In. ....*Illus*	316.00
Vase, Beaded Rings, Cylindrical, Slight Taper, Round Foot, Greentown, 6 In.	288.00
Vase, Cylindrical, Round Foot, Beaded Rim, Waisted, 6 In.	403.00

HOLT-HOWARD was an importer that started working in New York City in 1949 and moved to Stamford, Connecticut, in 1955. The company sold many types of table accessories, such as condiment jars, decanters, spoon holders, and saltshakers. Its figural pieces have a cartoon-like quality. The company was bought out by General Housewares Corporation in 1969. Holt-Howard pieces are often marked with the name and the year or *HH* and the year stamped in black. The *HH* mark was used until 1974. The company also used a black and silver paper label. Holt-Howard production ceased in 1990. Similar pieces are being made today by Grant Holt, one of the founders, and are marked *GHA*.

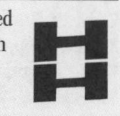

Candle Climbers, Angel, Gilt Accents, 4 In., Pair	24.00
Candleholder, Angel, Petting Deer, 1959, 4 ⅜ x 2 ⅝ In.	75.00
Candleholder, Madonna, Baby Jesus, 1959, 5 ½ x 4 ½ x 1 ½ In.	38.00
Candleholder, Santa Claus, Japan, 3 In., Pair	22.00
Cookie Jar, Santa Claus, 3 Parts, 1964, 8 ½ In.	60.00 to 75.00
Cruet, French Dressing, Pixie, Paper Sticker, 6 In.	105.00
Cruet, Italian Dress, Pixie, Hat, Mustache, c. 1959, 6 ½ In.	105.00
Decanter, Bourbon, Cowboy Hat, Hands On Hips, 10 In.	125.00
Dish, Cottage Cheese, Cover, Kissing Kittens, Bow Rim, 1959	68.00
Eggcup, Chef Man, Red Nose, Blue Scarf, Paper Label, 3 ¾ In., Pair	40.00
Eggcup, Red Rooster, Coq Rouge, 1961	8.00
Jam 'N Jelly, Lemons, Spoons, 4 x 7 ¼ In.	165.00
Nut Dish, Jeeves, 1960, 6 ¾ In.	52.00
Planter, Candy Cane Family, Smiling Faces, 1950s, 6 ½ In.	245.00
Planter, Duck, Mallard, 1959, 5 ¾ x 9 In.	25.00
Salt & Pepper, Man, Old West Style, Beard & Cowboy Hat, Terra-Cotta, Glazed, 6 In.	20.00
Salt & Pepper, Roosters, 4 ½ In.	30.00
Salt & Pepper, Santa Claus, Winking, 4 ¾ In.	19.00
Salt & Pepper, Telephone Operator, Blue Dress, Eyeglasses, 3 In.	95.00
Shaker, Santa Claus, Winking, Nutmeg, c.1960, 4 ½ In.	40.00
Spoon Holder, Birds, Blue, Green, Black, Paper Sticker, 1960, 4 ¼ In., 4 Piece	24.00
Stringholder, Smiling Dog, Glancing Eyes, 5 x 4 ½ In.	75.00
Vase, Rooster Shape, 1960s, 6 In.	43.00

HOPALONG CASSIDY was a character in a series of twenty-eight books written by Clarence E. Milford, first published in 1907. Movies and television shows were made based on the character. The best-known actor playing Hopalong Cassidy was William Lawrence Boyd. His first movie appearance was in 1919, but the first Hopalong Cassidy film was not made until 1934. Sixty-six films were made. In 1948, William Boyd purchased the television rights to the movies, then later made fifty-two new programs. In the 1950s, Hopalong Cassidy and his horse, named Topper, were seen in comics, records, toys, and other products. Boyd died in 1972.

Bottle, Hoppy's Favorite Kuhl's Milk, Clear, Cowboy Image, 9 ¾ In.	12.00
Cowboy Outfit, Vest, Chaps, Faux Suede, Oilcloth, Herman Iskin, Box, 1950, 11 x 14 In.	277.00
Doll, Stuffed Fabric Body, Rubber Head & Hands, Metal Gun, Sheriff, c.1950, 9 x 25 In.	424.00
Flashlight, Cactus, Siren Lite, Tin, Lithograph, 6 ¾ In.	72.00
Game, Board, Spinner, Money, 8 Playing Pieces, Copyright, c.1950	80.00
Gun & Holster, Wyandotte, Box	550.00
Radio, Metal, Red, Cowboy Riding Horse, Cactus, Arvin, c.1950, 4 x 8 x 5 In.	285.00
Ring, Black Metal Cowboy Hat, Compass, Brass, HC, Adjustable, 1952	474.00
Sign, Portrait Image, Embossed Tin, Die Cut, 35 x 34 In.	201.00
Wristwatch, Chrome Case, Black Leather Band, Saddle Shape Display, Box, 1950s	253.00

HORN was used to make many types of boxes, furniture inlays, jewelry, and whimsies.

Back Scratcher, Carved, Left Hand Shape, Faux Bamboo Staff, Gold Over White Paint, 34 In.	384.00
Beaker, Carved, Incised, Exeter Mail Coach, Drivers, Passenger, Lion, Horse, c.1816, 3 ¾ In.	236.00
Bowl, Figures, Flowers Carved, Tapered Oval, Chinese, c.1945, 1 ¼ x 3 In.	540.00
Card Case, Gold Lacquered, Crane, Swamp, Japan, 4 x 2 ½ In.	420.00
Cup, Cutout Heart Handle, Inscribed, Marked Eaton Fuller, Mass., 1792, 3 x 2 In.	1364.00
Cup, Cutout Heart, Crosshatch Design, Inscribed William Faulks Anno 1775 Dom, Penn., 4 In.	3555.00
Cup, Figures, In Boat, Mountains, Tree Handle, Chinese, 4 ½ In.	446.00
Cup, Libation, Animals, Elephant Trunk Handle, 6 In.	357.00

H

Cup, Libation, Carved, Crouching Hydra, Taotie Masks, Leaf Borders, Hydra Handle, 5 ½ x 3 ¾ In..	276.00
Cup, Libation, Carved, Pagoda, Immortal, Mountain Landscape, Chinese, 8 In.	263.00
Cup, Libation, Pagoda, Mountains, Immortal Scenes, Chinese, 8 In.	268.00
Cup, Libation, Relief Carving, Flowers, Cone Shape, Leafy Handle, Round Foot, 3 ½ x 4 ⅜ In.	708.00
Cup, Libation, Rhinoceros, Carved Ducks, Water Lilies, Marked, 4 In.	1840.00
Cup, Libation, Rhinoceros, Carved, Chinese, c.1780, 6 ½ In.	15340.00
Cup, Libation, Rhinoceros, Carved, Friends Of Winter, Bamboo, Bats Inside, 1700s, 11 In. .... *Illus*	10413.00
Cup, Libation, Rhinoceros, Lotus Shape, Carved, Leaf Base, Stand, 1800s, 2 ⅝ x 3 In.. *Illus*	14220.00
Cup, Libation, Scrolling Dragons, Sphere, Pearl, Chinese, c.1900, 2 ½ x 4 In.	1154.00
Figurine, Guanyin, Lotus, Hands Folded Inside Robes, Carved Wood Stand, Chinese, 1800s, 5 ½ In. ..	1337.00
Figurine, Immortal Shou, Holding Staff, Peach, Chinese, 9 In.	208.00
Ladle, Carved Figures On Handle, Abalone Inlay, Northwest Coast, 15 x 4 ½ In.	805.00
Ornament, Carved, Flowers, Leaves, 2 Chinese Men, 12 In.	649.00
Powder Horn, Engraved, Captain John Sutton, Yorktown Camp, Chesapeake Bay Map, 1773, 13 In.	3600.00
Seal, Carved, Scholar Holding Section Of Bamboo, Chinese, 1800s, 3 ½ In.	356.00
Snuff Mull, Applied Silver Thistle, Inscribed Time Is On The Wing, Scotland, c.1800, 2 ¼ In.	356.00
Snuff Mull, Silver Mounts, Hinged Cover, Inset Cairngorm Stone, Engraved, Scotland, 1800s, 2 In....	649.00
Snuff Mull, Silver Mounts, Medallion Cover, Inverted Heart, Flower, Scrolling, Hinged, 1750, 2 In....	2124.00
Vase, Rounded Square, Narrow Neck, Rings, Flared Rim, Red, Chinese, 4 ½ In.	1434.00

HOWARD PIERCE began working in Southern California in 1936. In 1945, he opened a pottery in Claremont. He moved to Joshua Tree in 1968 and continued making pottery until 1991. His contemporary-looking figurines are popular with collectors. Though most pieces are marked with his name, smaller items from his sets often were not marked.

Howard Pierce

Figurine, Angel, Holding Bird, Green, Marked, 5 ¾ In.	110.00
Figurine, Duck, Stretched Neck, 8 ½ In.	32.00
Figurine, Girl, Hands On Chin, Marked, 5 In.	105.00
Figurine, Jack Rabbit, Impressed Mark, 10 ½ In.	225.00
Figurine, Owl, Black Eyes, Shades Of Brown, Stamped, 5 In.	65.00
Figurine, Pig, Brown, Marked, 6 x 3 ½ In.	425.00
Figurine, Quail, Mama, 2 Babies, 3 Piece, 5 ½, 3 ¾, 2 In.	45.00
Vase, Birds Sitting On Tree Stump, White, Stamped, 1960s, 9 In.	75.00
Vase, Double, Open Center, Horse, Tree Figures, Burgundy, Marked, 7 x 9 In.	395.00

HOWDY DOODY and Buffalo Bob were the main characters in a children's series televised from 1947 to 1960. Howdy was a redheaded puppet. The series became popular with college students in the late 1970s when Buffalo Bob began to lecture on campuses.

Baseball Mitt, Howdy Portrait, Leather-Like, Vinyl Piping, Metal Rivets, Kagran, 1950s, 7 In....*Illus*	104.00
Box, Royal Butterscotch Flavor Pudding, Howdy Doody's Favorite, Unopened, 1950s	95.00
Cookie Jar, Howdy's Head, Ceramic, 9 ¼ In.	270.00
Doll, Clown, Clarabell, Vinyl Head, Cloth Stuffed Body, Felt Feet & Hands, Ideal, 1950s, 17 ½ In....*Illus*	115.00
Fun Book, Games, Jokes, Puzzles, Pictures To Color, Whitman, 1950s, 11 x 9 In.	15.00
Jar, Peanut Butter, Flub-A-Dub On Lid, 1950s, 4 ½ In.	95.00
Marionette, Cloth, Wood, Composition, Instructions, Peter Puppet Playthings, c.1950, 6 x 16 In..	158.00
Music Box, Clarabell, Figural, Easel Back, Laminated Cardboard, Windup, 1950s, 7 x 7 In.....	385.00
Pencil Topper, Plastic, Leadworks, Taiwan, 1988, 1 x 1 In.	8.50
Statue, Papier-Mache, Blue Jeans, Plaid Shirt, Hat, Lunch Box, 40 x 17 In....................*Illus*	252.00
Toy, Clarabell, Tin, Windup, Hand Stands, Linemar	350.00
Toy, Howdy Doody, Buffalo Bob, Piano, Tin Lithograph, Windup, 6 ½ In.	540.00
Toy, Zip The Monkey, Hat, Overalls, Original, 20 In.	12.00
Tub Toy, Bubble Pipe, Clarabell The Clown, Plastic, c.1950, 3 ¾ x 5 ¾ In.	115.00
TV Viewer, 5 Films, Colgate Palmolive Peet Co., Cardboard Sealing Strip, Mailer, 5 x 5 In.	127.00
Wristwatch, Boy's, Howdy's Portrait, Metal Case, Green Vinyl Band, c.1950, 3 ¾ x 6 ¾ In.	411.00

HULL pottery was made in Crooksville, Ohio, from 1905. Addis E. Hull bought the Acme Pottery Company and started making ceramic wares. In 1917, A. E. Hull Pottery began making art pottery as well as the commercial wares. For a short time, 1921 to 1929, the firm also sold pottery imported from Europe. The dinnerware of the 1940s (including the Little Red Riding Hood line), the matte wares of the 1940s, and the high gloss artwares of the 1950s are all popular with collectors. The firm officially closed in March 1986.

Hull U.S.A.

Apple, Cookie Jar, Red, Yellow, Green Leaves, 1940s, 8 ½ In.	35.00
Apple, Grease Jar, 1950s	39.00
Apple, Salt & Pepper	19.00
Bird Of Paradise, Vase, Yellow, Green, 10 ¾ In., Pair	17.00
Blossom Flite, Basket, Ruffled Rim, 1955, 9 x 5 ¾ In.	22.00
Blossom Flite, Console, Footed, Ring Handles, 16 ½ x 5 x 6 In.	125.00

TIP

Clean ivory beads and jewelry with denatured alcohol, not water.

Hummel, Figurine, No. 431, The Surprise, Members Gift No. 12, Missing Bee, 5 ½ In.
$55.00

Woody Auction

Hummel, Figurine, No. 640, Authorized Retailer Plaque, U.S. Version, Missing Bee, 5 In.
$110.00

Woody Auction

Hummel, Plate, No. 264, 100th Anniversary, 1971, Heavenly Angel, Three Line Mark, 7 ½ In.
$59.00

Conestoga Auction Co., Inc.

Icon, Mother Of God, Jesus Center, 8-Point Star Frame, Russia, 1800s, 13 ½ x 14 In. $1,320.00

Skinner, Inc.

Icon, St. Alexis, Holding Bible, Punched Pattern, Hinged Glass Door, c.1900, 13 x 11 In. $4,500.00

Skinner, Inc.

Imari, Charger, Dragon Rosettes, Gilt, Birds, Flowers, Figures & Landscape, Marked, 24 ¾ In. $1,888.00

Brunk Auctions

TIP
Keep art, paintings, prints, and textiles away from sunny windows.

Blossom Flite, Creamer, 4 ½ In.	38.00
Bow Knot, Creamer, 3 ¾ In.	51.00
Bow Knot, Vase, Cream, Green, Flowers, Handles, Footed, Marked, 8 ¾ In.	92.00
Bow Knot, Vase, Oval, Square Base, Scalloped Mouth, c.1949, 6 ½ In.	244.00
Bow Knot, Vase, Pink, Blue, Green, 6 In.	119.00
Bow Knot, Wall Pocket, Iron Shape, Pastels, 6 ¼ In., Pair	325.00
Butterfly, Vase, Flowers, Tripod Base, 1956, 6 x 10 In.	45.00
Dogwood, Vase, Oval, Shouldered, 5 ½ In.	69.00
Ebb Tide, Vase, Figural, Fish, Shell, Burgundy, Green, 14 In.	195.00
Fiesta, Jardiniere, Strawberries, Leaves, Tulip Shape, Scalloped, Square Base, 6 ½ In.	50.00
Iris, Vase, 2 Handles, Scalloped Top, Footed, 7 ½ In.	99.00
Little Red Riding Hood, Cookie Jar	*Illus* 200.00
Little Red Riding Hood, Cookie Jar, Basket, Flowers, Hull Ware, 13 In.	265.00
Little Red Riding Hood, Creamer, 6 Oz., 4 ½ In.	500.00
Little Red Riding Hood, Pitcher, Red Poppy Up, 32 Oz., 8 In.	280.00
Little Red Riding Hood, Salt & Pepper, 5 ⅛ In.	48.00
Little Red Riding Hood, Teapot, Lid, 4 Cup, 4 In.	300.00
Magnolia, Pitcher, Globular, 8 ½ In.	55.00
Magnolia, Pitcher, Yellow Flowers, Matte Finish, 7 In.	35.00
Magnolia, Vase, Double Cornucopia, Taupe Ground, 8 ¼ x 12 ¾ In.	140.00
Magnolia, Vase, Footed, 2 Handles, 1946, 6 ¼ In.	75.00
Mirror Brown, Pitcher, c.1960, 7 In.	20.00
Parchment & Pine, Basket, 5 x 8 ¼ In.	32.00
Parchment & Pine, Basket, Green, Yellow, Curved Handle, 16 ½ In.	29.00
Parchment & Pine, Candleholder, Green, Gray, c.1952, 5 In., Pair	25.00
Planter, Dancing Lady, Pink Pleated Skirt, 7 ½ In.	35.00
Planter, Flying Mallard, 3-Sided, Cattails, Green, Gold, 9 ½ x 7 In.	75.00
Planter, Kitten, Plumed Hat, Gilt Trim, Spool, 1950s, 8 x 6 x 3 In.	38.00
Planter, Lady & Basket, Red, Hat, Bow On Waist, 8 ½ In.	19.00
Planter, Poodle, Pink, Green, 1950s, 6 In.	65.00
Serenade, Teapot, Pink, Embossed Bough & Chickadee, 1957	157.00
Sunglow, Bell, Yellow, Loop Handle, 6 ¼ In.	195.00
Sunglow, Salt & Pepper, 3 ⅝ In.	35.00
Sunglow, Wall Pocket, Whiskbroom Shape, Pink, 1952, 8 ¼ In.	50.00
Tokay, Basket, Moon Shape, Twig Handle, 10 ½ In.	50.00
Tokay, Pitcher, Bulbous, 8 In.	22.00
Tokay, Vase, Grapes, Vine Handle, c.1960	29.00
Water Lily, Vase, 2 Handles, Footed, Green, Yellow, Cream, Rose, 9 ½ In.	150.00
Wildflower, Ewer, Dusty Pink, Soft Peach & Green, 1946, 4 ½ In.	95.00
Wildflower, Vase, Blue, Pink, Low Handles, 9 ½ In.	45.00
Wildflower, Vase, Pink Mouth, Flowers, Footed, 6 ½ In.	41.00
Woodland, Console, Cornucopia Shape, Green & Rose Gloss, 6 x 11 In.	80.00
Woodland, Console, Peach To Ivory To Rose, Ribbed, 14 x 4 ½ x 5 ½ In.	185.00
Woodland, Ewer, Twig Handle, Peach Flower, Gloss Finish, 13 ½ In.	325.00

HUMMEL figurines, based on the drawings of the nun M.I. Hummel (Berta Hummel), were made by the W. Goebel Porzellanfabrik of Oeslau, Germany, now Rodental, Germany. They were first made in 1935. The *Crown* mark was used from 1935 to 1949. The company added the *bee* marks in 1950. The *full bee* with variations, was used from 1950 to 1959; *stylized bee,* 1957 to 1972; *three line mark,* 1964 to 1972; *last bee,* sometimes called *vee over gee,* 1972 to 1979. In 1979 the V bee symbol was removed from the mark. *U.S. Zone* was part of the mark from 1946 to 1948; *W. Germany* was part of the mark from 1960 to 1990. The Goebel *W. Germany* mark, called the *missing bee* mark, was used from 1979 to 1990; *Goebel, Germany,* with the crown and *WG,* originally called the *new mark,* was used from 1991 through part of 1999. A new version of the bee mark with the word *Goebel* was used from 1999 to 2008. A special *Year 2000* backstamp was also introduced. Porcelain figures inspired by Berta Hummel's drawings were introduced in 1997. These are marked *BH* followed by a number. They were made in the Far East, not Germany. Goebel discontinued making Hummel figurines in 2008 and Manufaktur Rodental took over the factory in Germany and began making new Hummel figurines. Hummel figurines made by Rodental are marked with a yellow and black bee on the edge of an oval line surrounding the words *Original M.I. Hummel Germany.* The words *Manufaktur Rodental* are printed beneath the oval. Other decorative items and plates that feature Hummel drawings have been made by Schmid Brothers, Inc., since 1971.

Bookends, Bookworm, Boy & Girl, Sitting, Reading Book, 5 ½ In.	96.00
Clock, No. 442, Chapel Time, Open Windows, Missing Bee, 11 ½ In.	*Illus* 330.00
Figurine, No. 11/0, Merry Wanderer, Crown Mark, 5 In.	113.00
Figurine, No. 12/1, Chimney Sweep, Full Bee, 6 ½ In.	58.00
Figurine, No. 16, Little Hiker, Crown Mark, Stamped U.S. Zone, Germany, 6 In.	90.00

Figurine, No. 16/2, Little Hiker, Full Bee, 4 ¼ In.	35.00
Figurine, No. 17/0, Congratulations, Crown Mark, 5 ¾ In.	79.00
Figurine, No. 21, Heavenly Angel, Crown Mark, Full Bee, 4 ½ In.	73.00
Figurine, No. 32/0, Little Gabriel, Stylized Bee, 5 In.	29.00
Figurine, No. 43, March Winds, Crown Mark, 5 In. ....*Illus*	35.00
Figurine, No. 46/3, Madonna, Without Halo, Missing Bee, 16 In. ....*Illus*	33.00
Figurine, No. 47/11, Goose Girl, Last Bee, 8 In.	70.00
Figurine, No. 57/0, Chick Girl, First Mark, U.S. Zone, 3 ½ In.	73.00
Figurine, No. 58/0, Playmates, Stylized Bee, 4 ½ In.	35.00
Figurine, No. 68, Lost Sheep, Crown Mark, Full Bee, 6 In.	124.00
Figurine, No. 72, Spring Cheer, Crown Mark, U.S. Zone Germany, 5 ¼ In.	62.00
Figurine, No. 73, Little Gardener, Crown Mark, U.S. Zone Germany, 4 ¼ In.	62.00
Figurine, No. 86, Happiness, Crown Mark, 5 In.	73.00
Figurine, No. 87, For Father, Full Bee, Box, 5 ¾ In.	305.00
Figurine, No. 94 3/0, Surprise, Last Bee, 4 In.	99.00
Figurine, No. 96 2, Little Shopper, Double Bee, Mark, 5 In.	62.00
Figurine, No. 96, Little Shopper, Double Bee, 5 In.	62.00
Figurine, No. 96, Little Shopper, Full Bee, 5 In.	41.00
Figurine, No. 98, Sister, Full Bee, 5 ½ In.	51.00
Figurine, No. 112/1, Just Resting, Full Bee, 5 In.	64.00
Figurine, No. 128, Baker, Open Eyes, Crown Mark, 5 In.	181.00
Figurine, No. 130/0, Meditation, Full Bee, Made In Germany, 5 ¼ In.	113.00
Figurine, No. 131/2, Street Singer, Full Bee, 5 In.	34.00
Figurine, No. 136/V, Friends, Missing Bee, 11 In.	244.00
Figurine, No. 141/1, Apple Tree Girl, Last Bee, 6 In.	41.00
Figurine, No. 152/A, Umbrella Boy, Missing Bee, 5 In. ....*Illus*	118.00
Figurine, No. 154/0, Waiter, Full Bee, 6 In. ....*Illus*	110.00
Figurine, No. 196, Telling Her Secret, Full Bee, 6 ¾ In. ....*Illus*	110.00
Figurine, No. 196/0, Telling Her Secret, Last Bee, 5 ½ In.	46.00
Figurine, No. 200/0, Little Goat Herder, Full Bee, 5 In. ....*Illus*	96.00
Figurine, No. 217/2 Boy With Toothache, Missing Bee, 5 ½ In.	52.00
Figurine, No. 340, Letter To Santa Claus, Missing Bee, 7 In. ....*Illus*	59.00
Figurine, No. 347, Adventure Bound, Stylized Bee, 7 ½ In.	750.00
Figurine, No. 353/1, Spring Dance, Three Line Mark, 6 ¾ In. ....*Illus*	540.00
Figurine, No. 369, Follow The Leader, Three Line Mark, 7 In. ....*Illus*	480.00
Figurine, No. 399, Valentine Joy, Missing Bee, 6 In.	35.00
Figurine, No. 431, The Surprise, Members Gift No. 12, Missing Bee, 5 ½ In. ...*Illus*	55.00
Figurine, No. 476, Winter Song, Missing Bee, 4 ½ In.	29.00
Figurine, No. 640, Authorized Retailer Plaque, U.S. Version, Missing Bee, 5 In. ......*Illus*	110.00
Plate, No. 264, 100th Anniversary, 1971, Heavenly Angel, Three Line Mark, 7 ½ In. ....*Illus*	59.00

HUTSCHENREUTHER PORCELAIN FACTORY was founded by Carolus Magnus in Hohenburg, Bavaria, in 1814. A second factory was established in Selb, Germany, in 1857. The company made fine quality porcelain dinnerware and figurines. The mark changed through the years, but the name and the lion insignia appear in most versions. Hutschenreuther became part of the Rosenthal division of the Waterford Wedgwood Group in 2000. Rosenthal was bought by Sambonet Paderno Industries, headquartered in Orfento, Novaro, Italy, in 2009.

Bowl, Flowers, Gold Scalloped Rim, Footed, 3 x 13 In.	89.00
Figurine, 3 White Ducks, Walking In Row, Mound Base, Glazed, Label, 9 ¼ x 16 ½ In.	633.00
Figurine, Donkey, Stacked Dog, Cat, Rooster On Back, Marked Lorenz, 7 ½ In.	144.00
Figurine, Elephant, Head Raised, High Black Glass, 8 ½ x 10 In.	70.00
Figurine, Family Affair, Woodcocks, 6 ½ In.	396.00
Figurine, Nude, Sitting On Leopard, Marked, 21 x 13 x 8 In.	3700.00
Figurine, Sparrowhawk, Impressed Label G. Granget, 9 In.	189.00
Group, 3 Dancing Girls Holding Hands, Gilt Flower, 10 x 9 In.	330.00
Plaque, Diane, Huntress, Dogs, Stag, Horse, Jasperware, Pate-Sur-Pate, Frame, c.1905, 5 x 8 ½ In.	60.00
Plate, Dinner, Pink Flowers, Cobalt & Gold Bands, c.1930, 10 ⅝ In., 12 Piece	840.00
Plate, Green Band, Gilt & Textured Border, White Reserve, Royal Bavarian, 9 ½ In., 12 Piece	234.00

ICONS, special, revered pictures of Jesus, Mary, or a saint, are usually Russian or Byzantine. The small icons collected today are made of wood and tin or precious metals. Many modern copies have been made in the old style and are being sold to tourists in Russia and Europe and at shops in the United States. Rare, old icons have sold for over $50,000. The riza is the metal cover protecting the icon. It is often made of silver or gold.

Angel, Carved Wood, Outstretched Arms, Flowing Robes, c.1886, 29 x 22 In.	1476.00
Angel, Painted & Gilded, Wearing Robes, Wings, Outstretched Hands, c.1835, 14 x 8 ½ In., Pair	6457.00

Imari, Dish, Courtesans, Garden, Blue Underglaze, Enamel, Cartouches On Rim, 1700s, 12 In.
$474.00

Skinner, Inc.

Imari, Punch Bowl, Birds, Flowers, Brocade Patterns, 1800s, 18 ½ In.
$584.00

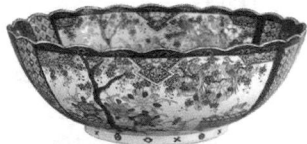

New Orleans Auction Galleries, Inc.

Imperial Glass, Art Glass, Bowl, Yellow, Flared, Scalloped Rim, Variegated Blue Hearts & Vines, 9 In.
$805.00

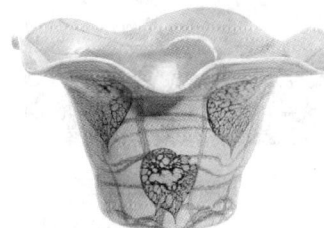

Early Auction Co.

Imperial Glass, Vase, Iridescent, Hearts & Vines, 1920s, 10 x 3 ¾ In.
$1,000.00

Rago Arts & Auction Center

Indian, Bag, Arapaho, Beaded, Leather, Sinew Sewn, Lazy Stitch, c.1900, 10 x 6 In.
$316.00

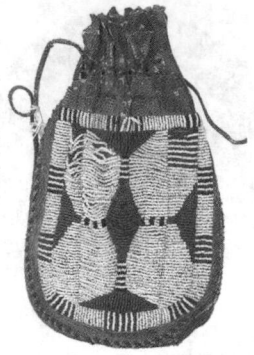

Allard Auctions

Indian, Bag, Plateau, Cloth, Hide, Beaded, Reverse Side Deer, Tree, Hide Strap, c.1900, 13 x 11 ½ In.
$738.00

Skinner, Inc.

Indian, Bag, Sioux, Beaded, Buckskin, Canvas Back, Lazy Stitch, Fringe, c.1910, 12 ½ In.
$690.00

Allard Auctions

Christ, Birth Of Christ, Joseph, Mary, Gilt Repousse, Enamel, Frame, c.1890, 11 x 9 In.	2280.00
Christ, Blessing, Holding Open Bible, Silver Repousse, Engraved, Moscow, 1896, 10 ¾ x 9 In.	1560.00
Christ, Holding Open Book Of Gospels, Silver Gilt Repousse, Cloisonne Halo, 1800s, 12 x 10 ¾ In.	4560.00
Christ, Life Scenes, 4 Panels, Hinged, Russia, 7 x 17 ½ In.	590.00
Christ, Mahogany, Flared Ribbed Base, Carved Torso, Painted, Portugal, 1700s, 17 In.	230.00
Christ, Mary, Disciples, Parcel Gilt Silver, Giltwood Frame, Moscow, 1854, 16 x 13 ½ In.	1416.00
Christ, On Cross, Ivory, Carved, Wood Crucifix, 1800s, 20 x 16 In.	1080.00
Christ, St. John The Baptist, St. Anne, Virgin, Oil On Board, c.1885, 17 x 13 ½ In.	430.00
Crucifix, Rosewood & Silver, Carved, Rococo Cartouches, Marked, Mexico, c.1700, 24 x 18 In. .	1168.00
Elijah, Raising The Widow's Son, Long Hair Robe, Frame, Russia, 13 ¼ x 10 ¼ In.	1200.00
Gabriel, Archangel, Heralding Day Of Judgment, Wall Hanging, Oil On Canvas, 1800s, 19 ¾ x 15 In.	492.00
Guardian Angel, Oval, Silver Gilt, Greek Key Border, Engraved Verse, c.1890, 4 In.	6600.00
John The Baptist, Head Platter, Embroidered Cloth, Gold Leaf Halo, c.1860, 14 x 12 In.	1560.00
Kazan Mother Of God, Infant Jesus Blessing, Silver, Gilt, Enamel, Russia, 1800s, 12 x 10 In.	7200.00
Life Of Christ, Wood Plaque, Painted, 18th Century, Russia, 12 ¼ x 10 ½ In.	575.00
Madonna & Child, Carved Wood, Child Delivering Blessing, Sacred Heart, 1800s, 48 In.	720.00
Madonna & Child, Kneeling Saint, Silver, Enamel, Moscow, 1961, 12 ½ x 10 ½ In.	1180.00
Madonna & Child, Oil On Wood, Gilt Carved Shadowbox, Glass Door, Italy, 1700s, 13 x 9 In.	2415.00
Madonna & Child, Tempera On Wood, Repousse Copper Riza, Cloisonne, 19th Century, 12 x 10 In.	478.00
Madonna & Child, Wood, Painted, Covered With Silver Riza, Russia, 7 x 5 ¾ In.	331.00
Madonna Of The Lemons, Seated, Holding Baby Jesus, Robes, N. Barabino, Italy, c.1850, 17 x 9 In.	2706.00
Mary Magdalene, Jar, Arched, Leaf Tip, Beaded Border, Silver Riza, Russia, c.1910, 4 x 3 In. .	4800.00
Mary Magdalene, Plaque, Porcelain, Gilt Frame, 5 ¾ x 4 In.	359.00
Mary, Holding Baby Jesus, John Standing, Carved Group, Square Base, 1700s, 11 ½ In.	546.00
Mary, Saints, Baby Christ Held Above, Russia, 1800s, 5 ¼ x 4 ¼ In.	201.00
Mother Of God, Jesus Center, 8-Point Star Frame, Russia, 1800s, 13 ½ x 14 In. ....*Illus*	1320.00
Mother Of God, Virgin's Presentation In The Temple, Frame, Russia, 1800s, 7 x 5 ½ In.	3600.00
Santos, St. Francis Of Assisi, Holding Skull & Cross, Crown, Spain, c.1790, 11 In.	1725.00
Santos, Statue, Bearded Saint, Flowing Gown, Gilt, Black & Red Flowers, Wood Base, c.1815, 39 In.	1845.00
Sophia, God The Father, Christ, Angels, Mary, John The Baptist, 1800s, 12 x 10 In.	1920.00
St. Alexis, Holding Bible, Punched Pattern, Hinged Glass Door, c.1900, 13 x 11 In. ....*Illus*	4500.00
St. Barbara, St. Peter, St. John The Evangelist, Multicolor, Gilt, Greece, 18 x 13 In.	1560.00
St. Cosmos, Damian, Tempera & Gilt On Panel, Label, 17th Century, 8 ½ x 6 ⅞ In.	2726.00
St. George, Slaying Dragon, Silver Gilt, Niello, 12 ½ x 10 ½ In.	2640.00
St. John The Baptist, Wings, Holding Disc Of Infant Jesus, Frame, Russia, c.1800, 12 x 10 In. .	1140.00
St. Mary Of Egypt, Wood, Silver, Gilt, Life Scenes, Paint, c.1860, 12 ¾ x 11 In.	1625.00
St. Nicholas, Blessing, Silver Gilt Repousse, Enamel Halo, Book, Russia, c.1915, 10 ¾ x 8 ¾ In.	4800.00
St. Nicholas, Painted, Gold Leaf, Incised Christ, Mother Of God, Russia, c.1880, 14 x 12 In.	2640.00
St. Nicholas, Panel, Tempera, Silver, Gold Gilding, Russia, 1800s, 14 x 12 ¼ In.	413.00
St. Seraphim Of Sarov, Silver Repousse Riza, c.1908, 5 ¼ x 4 ½ In.	570.00
St. Seraphim, Paint, Gold Leaf, Russia, c.1890, 10 ½ x 8 ¾ In.	1164.00
St. Yvgeny, St. Katerina, Silver, Painted, Enamel, Oklad, Hallmark, 7 x 5 ½ In.	1955.00
Virgin Mary, Holding Christ, His Hand Help Up In Blessing, Russia, c.1700, 9 x 7 In.	700.00
Virgin Of Guadalupe, Outstretched Hands, Wood, J. Silva, Mexico, 36 x 13 x 5 In.	345.00

IMARI porcelain was made in Japan and China beginning in the seventeenth century. In the eighteenth century and later, it was copied by porcelain factories in Germany, France, England, and the United States. It was especially popular in the nineteenth century and is still being made. Imari is characteristically decorated with stylized bamboo, floral, and geometric designs in orange, red, green, and blue. The name comes from the Japanese port of Imari, which exported the ware made nearby in a factory at Arita. Imari is now a general term for any pattern of this type.

Bowl, Alternating Patterns, Cobalt Blue, Iron Red, Orange, Green, Chinese, c.1920, 12 In., Pair	210.00
Bowl, Fishing Boat, Dragonfly, Tapestry Design, Footed, Japan, c.1890, 3 ½ x 10 ½ In.	330.00
Bowl, Melon Shape, Ribbed Sides, Multicolor, c.1850, 7 x 15 In.	173.00
Bowl, Panels, Flowers, Feathers, Banded Striped Foot, c.1925, 4 x 10 In.	153.00
Charger, 7 Gods Of Luck, Red Ground, Japan, 18 In.	240.00
Charger, Dragon Rosettes, Gilt, Birds, Flowers, Figures & Landscape, Marked, 24 ¾ In....*Illus*	1888.00
Charger, Flowers, Birds, Iron Red, Blue, White, 18 ¼ In., Pair.	837.00
Charger, Foo Dog, Flower Medallion, Spiraling Panels, Geometric, Leaves, Gilt Accents, c.1890, 18 In.	338.00
Charger, Hexagonal, Flower Arrangements, Multicolor, 1800s, 13 In., Pair	489.00
Charger, Panels, Birds In Trees, Horses, Beehives, Orange Crackle Ice Design, 1800s, 18 ⅛ In. Diam..	615.00
Charger, Phoenix, Leaf Medallion, Women In Garden, Foo Dogs, c.1900, 54 In. Diam.	1045.00
Charger, Scalloped Edge, Flowers, Panels, Blossoms, Landscapes, Leaves, 18 In. Diam., Pair ..	1968.00
Charger, Scalloped Rim, Flower, Mythical Animal Reserves, Blue, Orange, Japan, 2 x 17 ½ In..	489.00
Charger, Shaped Panels, Women In Flowering Landscape, 1900s, 21 ½ In. Diam.	676.00

Dish, Courtesans, Garden, Blue Underglaze, Enamel, Cartouches On Rim, 1700s, 12 In. ....*Illus*   474.00
Dish, Lid, Red, Yellow, Orange, Flowers, c.1825, 13 x 6 In... 295.00
Dish, Rose, Provinces, Friesland Arms, Cobalt Blue Diaper Rim, Paneled, 18 ¾ In. 25850.00
Ginger Jar, Dome Lid, Foo Dog Finial, Ribbed Body, Gilt, Dragons, Flowers, c.1900, 18 In., Pair   1968.00
Jar, Lid, Flower, Figure Reserves, Cobalt Blue, Ribbed, Japan, c.1880, 20 In. 546.00
Mug, Paint, Gilt, Flowers, Birds, Butterfly, Chinese, c.1750, 4 ½ In. 325.00
Platter, Mums, Butterflies, Cranes, Willows, Oval, Japan, c.1900, 14 x 11 ½ In. 259.00
Punch Bowl, Birds, Flowers, Brocade Patterns, 1800s, 18 ½ In...............................*Illus*   584.00
Umbrella Stand, Bamboo, Geometrics, Iron Red, Underglaze Blue, Japan, 24 x 8 ¼ In........ 420.00
Umbrella Stand, Bird, Flowers, Trees, Blue Underglaze, Red Molded Bands, Japan, 1800s, 24 x 9 In.   660.00
Umbrella Stand, Cylindrical, Blue, Iron Red, Garden Scenes, Flowers, 1900s, 24 In................ 307.00
Umbrella Stand, Cylindrical, Flat Lip, Flowers, Cherry Trees, 24 x 8 ½ In............................. 540.00
Umbrella Stand, Flowers, Orange, Blue, White, Japan, c.1900, 24 In................................... 153.00
Umbrella Stand, Landscape Panels, Flower Ground, Japan, c.1850, 27 ½ In. 240.00
Vase, Bottle Shape, Ring Foot, Children, Flower, Dragons, Phoenix, Red, Gilt Accents, 1800s, 18 In. 237.00
Vase, Double Gourd, Scrolling Flowers, Leaves, Phoenix, Bamboo, Gilt, c.1890, 14 ¾ In......... 178.00
Vase, Figural Panels, Butterfly Medallions, Flowers, Flared, Scalloped Rim, Japan, c.1850, 27 In... 570.00
Vase, Oval Body, Waisted Neck, Flaring Fluted Rim, Dragons, Bird, Leaves, Multicolor, c.1890, 48 In... 4738.00
Vase, Painted, Enameled, Stylized Flowers, Birds, Woman Holding Teapot, Flared Rim, 21 In.   354.00

IMPERIAL GLASS CORPORATION was founded in Bellaire, Ohio, in 1901. It became a subsidiary of Lenox, Inc., in 1973 and was sold to Arthur R. Lorch in 1981. It was sold again in 1982, and went bankrupt in 1984. In 1985, the molds and some assets were sold. The Imperial glass preferred by the collector is freehand art glass, carnival glass, slag glass, stretch glass, and other top-quality tablewares. Tablewares and animals are listed here. The others may be found in the appropriate sections.

Art Glass, Bowl, Yellow, Flared, Scalloped Rim, Variegated Blue Hearts & Vines, 9 In.......*Illus*   805.00
Beaded Block, Pitcher, Water, 1930s, 6 In. 300.00
Candlewick, Cake Plate, Pedestal, 5 x 11 In. 85.00
Candlewick, Nappy, Heart Shape, 3 x 6 x 6 In.. 20.00
Cosmos, Punch Bowl, Flowers, Clear, 1913, 9 ¼ x 12 In. 250.00
Mayflower, Pitcher, Marigold, 9 In. 30.00
Provincial, Goblet, Olive Green, Stemmed, 1960s-70s, 6 Piece.. 50.00
Tray, Gray Iridescent, Stretch Glass, Handle, c.1920, 10 ⅝ In.. 45.00
Vase, Amber Iridescent, Red Drape Design, Footed Urn Shape, Trumpet Rim, 9 In.................. 805.00
Vase, Blue & White Marbled, Cylindrical, Rounded Shoulder, Cobalt Blue Interior, 11 In......... 288.00
Vase, Blue & White Marbled, Wide Rim, Cobalt Blue Interior, 8 In. 144.00
Vase, Bottle Shape, Blue, Incised Lines, Gilt Base, Pierced, Beaded Edge, 30 In...................... 399.00
Vase, Cobalt Blue, White Heart Vines, Bulbous, Trumpet Neck, 2 Handles At Waist, Signed, 10 In... 690.00
Vase, Cobalt Blue, White, Black, Marbled Design, Orange Interior, 8 ¼ In. 345.00
Vase, Iridescent, Hearts & Vines, 1920s, 10 x 3 ¾ In..*Illus*   1000.00
Vase, Jack-In-The-Pulpit, Translucent Glass, Blue Draped Swag Design, 10 In........................ 920.00
Vase, Peach, Blue Pulled Feather, Orange Interior, Bulbous, S-Shape Handles At Rim, 6 ½ In.   403.00
Waffle Block, Basket, Yellow Cast, Twisted Rope Handle, 10 In. 22.00

INDIAN art from North and South America has attracted the collector for many years. Each tribe has its own distinctive designs and techniques. Baskets, jewelry, pottery, and leatherwork are of greatest collector interest. Eskimo art is listed under Eskimo in this book.

Amulet, Tlingit, Bone, Alligator Shape, 19th Century, 5 In. 4406.00
Baby Carrier, Dayak, Multicolor, Beaded Panel, Shell Discs, Boar Tusks, Wood, 14 ½ In......... 711.00
Bag, Apache, Hide, Beaded, Crescents, Crosses, Lazy Stitch, 3-Sided Tabs, 1940s, 9 x 5 In........ 633.00
Bag, Arapaho, Beaded, Leather, Sinew Sewn, Lazy Stitch, c.1900, 10 x 6 In.....................*Illus*   316.00
Bag, Cree, Pipe, Beaded, Flowers, Buckskin, Tabbed Top, Fringe, c.1880, 19 x 7 In................. 431.00
Bag, Nez Perce, Corn Husk, Arrows, Geometric Forms, Hop String, 1950, 15 x 20 In. 1150.00
Bag, Plateau, Beaded, Deer, 2 Hunters Carrying Deer, 2-Sided, Woman's, 1930s, 8 x 9 In........ 633.00
Bag, Plateau, Beaded, Eagle, Flowers, c.1950s, 13 ¾ x 11 ½ In. 431.00
Bag, Plateau, Beaded, Flowers, Buffalo, 2-Sided, 1930s, 9 x 7 ½ In....................................... 748.00
Bag, Plateau, Beaded, Horse, Child's, 1950, 8 ½ x 7 In.. 431.00
Bag, Plateau, Cloth, Hide, Beaded, Reverse Side Deer, Tree, Hide Strap, c.1900, 13 x 11 ½ In.. *Illus*   738.00
Bag, Plateau, Hide, Beaded, Deer, Horses, Multicolor, c.1900, 8 ½ x 7 ¼ In............................ 1410.00
Bag, Root, Plateau, Woven, Jute, Cotton String, Stacked Triangles, 1930s, 15 x 10 In. 531.00
Bag, Sioux, Beaded, Buckskin, Canvas Back, Lazy Stitch, Fringe, c.1910, 12 ½ In............*Illus*   690.00
Bag, Sioux, Possible, Teepee, Buffalo Hide, Quill Work, Sinew, Horsehair Suspensions, 19 In..... 1610.00
Bag, Wasco, Sally, Woven, Human Figures, Symbols, Cylindrical, Buckskin Trim, 1940, 7 In. ... 2300.00
Bandolier, Iroquois, Beaded, Blue Horses, Flowers, c.1880, 16 x 13 x 5 In............................. 1725.00

Indian, Bandolier, Iroquois, Beaded, Flowers, Panel, Wide Strap, c.1900, 41 x 14 In.
$1,035.00

Allard Auctions

Indian, Basket, Hupa, Fine Woven, Overlapping, Openwork, Braided & Flared Rim, 9 x 6 ½ In.
$230.00

Allard Auctions

Indian, Bowl, Salado, Gila, Abstract Parrots, 3 ½ x 7 ¾ In.
$288.00

Allard Auctions

Indian, Bracelet, Navajo, 3 Bands, 3 Turquoise Stones, Old Pawn Silver, 1950s, 6 ⅝ x 1 ⅛ In.
$161.00

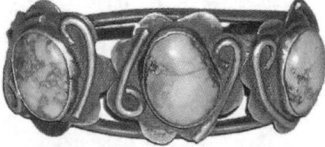

Allard Auctions

Indian, Coat, Navajo, Hide, Wool, Embroidered, Hand Painted, Fringe, Woman's, 44 In.
$165.00

Old Barn Auction

Indian, Dispatch, Case, Sioux, Beaded, Cornaline D'Aleppo Crosses, Sinew Sewn, 10 x 12 In.
$1,265.00

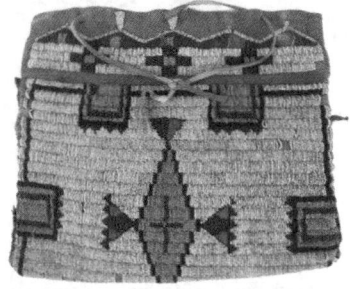

Allard Auctions

Indian, Doctor's Bag, Sioux, Beaded Hide, c.1900, 12 ½ x 5 In.
$2,640.00

Cowan's Auctions

TIP
Never oil a basket. It will attract dirt.

Indian, Dress, Hopi, Woman's, Wool, Black, Red & Green Trim & Fringe, c.1950, 36 x 24 In.
$92.00

Allard Auctions

Indian, Dress, Plains, Girl's, Cowrie Shells, Striped Ribbons, c.1910, 30 ½ In.
$720.00

Skinner, Inc.

Indian, Dress, Umatilla, Purple & Red Trade Cloth, Beaded Roses, Ribbon Trim, 38 x 47 In.
$633.00

Allard Auctions

Indian, Gloves, Cree, Men's, Gauntlets, Moose Hide, Beads, Fur Trim, Fringe, c.1950s, Small-Medium
$403.00

Allard Auctions

Indian, Jar, Acoma, Piecrust Rim, Geometric & Fineline Designs, 1950s, 6 ½ x 7 In.
$92.00

Allard Auctions

Indian, Jar, Storage, Zuni, 4 Colors, 3 Large Birds, Flowering Plants, 16 ¼ In.
$24,000.00

Skinner, Inc.

Indian, Leggings, Sioux, Buckskin, Beaded, Geometric Symbols, Sinew Sewn, 18 In.
$920.00

Allard Auctions

Bandolier, Iroquois, Beaded, Flowers, Panel, Wide Strap, c.1900, 41 x 14 In..............*Illus*	1035.00
Bandolier, Potowatomie, Beaded, Geometric Patterns, Canvas, Wool Tuff Fringe, 15 In.	978.00
Basket, Apache, Bowl Shape, Standing Figure, Crosses, 1900s, 3 ½ x 13 In.	881.00
Basket, Apache, Figures, c.1900, 13 In. Diam...........................	1560.00
Basket, Apache, Figures, Geometrics, Multicolor, Round, 15 ¼ In........................	2714.00
Basket, Apache, Star, Brown, Tan, Round, 12 ½ In..........................	1298.00
Basket, Apache, Woven, Geometric Lines, Oval, 1930s, 4 x 13 x 9 In.......................	259.00
Basket, Bowl, Yokut, Figures, 24 ½ x 8 ⅜ In..........................	3850.00
Basket, Burden, Pomo, Cone Shape, c.1900, 16 ¼ x 16 In.............................	1293.00
Basket, Chehalis, 2-Color Rhomboid Figures, 3 x 5 ¾ In..........................	138.00
Basket, Cherokee, Shopping, River Cane, Walnut, Yellowroot, 2 Hinged Wood Handles, c.1950, 18 In.	944.00
Basket, Cherokee, Splint, Woven, River Cane, White, Oak, Oval Arched, Handle, c.1900, 12 x 10 In.	207.00
Basket, Choctaw, River Cane, Diamond Pattern, Natural, Orange, Purple, 12 ⅜ In.	120.00
Basket, Double Band Pattern, Pedestal Base, Early 1900s, 4 x 6 ½ In.	138.00
Basket, Hopi, Coiled, Mesa Plaque, Eagle, 1960s, 16 In...........................	288.00
Basket, Hopi, Coiled, Mesa Plaque, Navajo Wedding Basket Pattern, 1970s, 8 In.	115.00
Basket, Hupa, Fine Woven, Overlapping, Openwork, Braided & Flared Rim, 9 x 6 ½ In. ..*Illus*	230.00
Basket, Iroquois, Birch Bark, Porcupine Quill, Arrows & Flowers, Round, c.1950, 3 x 5 In.	259.00
Basket, Klamath, Serrated Diamond Forms, Squared Base, 5 x 8 ½ In.	288.00
Basket, Klamath, Soft Weave, Striking Lightning Figures, Flared, c.1910, 4 x 9 In.....................	230.00
Basket, Lid, Attu, Fine Weave, Embroidered Flowers & Bands, Knot Handle, 4 x 3 In.................	374.00
Basket, Lid, Papago, Coiled, 3-Color Snake Decoration, Oval, 1960s, 9 ½ x 12 In.....................	219.00
Basket, Lid, Penobscot, Birch Bark, c.1900, 9 ½ x 15 In...........................	207.00
Basket, Lid, Tsimshian, Woven, 3 Openwork Bands, Gold Chevrons, 1910, 11 x 17 In.	748.00
Basket, Modoc, Woven, Colored Band, Wide Braided Band, Beaded Rim, 1920s, 6 x 6 In.	230.00
Basket, Papago, 4 Flowers, Coyote Tracks, Tohono O'Odham, 3 x 13 In.	288.00
Basket, Papago, Olla, Standing Figures, Geometric, Braided Rim, 1900s, 8 x 9 In................	206.00
Basket, Pima, Checkered Design, 8 x 5 ¾ In.........................	192.00
Basket, Pima, Decorated, Zigzag, 5 ½ x 20 In.........................	460.00
Basket, Pima, Geometric, White Beads Stitched To Outside, Early 20th Century, 2 ½ x 4 In. ...	512.00
Basket, Pima, Horse, Human Figures & Words, Phoenix, Silver Leaf Lard, 1910, 10 x 13 In.	460.00
Basket, Pomo, Dark Brown, Tan Weave, c.1920, 5 x 2 ½ In........................	575.00
Basket, Puget Sound, Overlapping Checkered Diamonds, Fine Weave, 1910, 8 x 10 x 9 In.......	316.00
Basket, Skokomish, Diamonds, Red Dog Figure Band, Cylindrical, Rim Loops, 9 x 10 In.	1495.00
Basket, Skokomish, Human Figures, Braided Rim, 1930, 7 x 16 x 6 In.	489.00
Basket, Southwest, Bowl Shape, Birds, c.1910, 6 x 10 In.........................	59.00
Basket, Storage, Choctaw, River Cane, Herringbone Pattern, Green & Natural, 23 In...............	657.00
Basket, Tlingit, Cauldron Form, Overlapping Geometrics, Rolled Rim, 3 Legs, c.1920, 5 x 5 In.	489.00
Basket, Tlingit, Multicolored Overlapping Key Pattern, Cylindrical, 1900, 9 x 12 In..............	1610.00
Basket, Tlingit, Multicolored Overlapping, Striped Triangles, Cylindrical, 1900, 4 x 7 In.	230.00
Basket, Tray, Yokuts, Circles, c.1930.........................	2800.00
Basket, Woodland, Splint, Lid, Geometric, Scroll, Heart & Flowers, c.1895, 7 ½ x 6 In.	948.00
Basket, Yokut, Friendship, Bottleneck, Caladium Root, California, c.1900, 6 x 10 In..............	8680.00
Basket, Yurok, Woven, Repeating Arrowhead Band, Raised Stitches, 4 x 7 In..........................	633.00
Belt Buckle, Zuni, Silver, Coral, Turquoise, Cast, Oval, Entwined Snakes, Effie Calavaza, 3 ½ In...	189.00
Belt, Zuni, Concha, Silver, Red Coral Inlaid Cardinals, J. Livingston, 1970s, 36 In.	460.00
Blanket Strip, Cheyenne, Hide, Beaded, Geometric Shapes, Blue, Red, White, c.1880, 32 In...	940.00
Blanket, Navajo, Chief's, 3rd Phase, Red, Black, Ivory, Gray, c.1900, 67 x 50 In.................	4025.00
Blanket, Navajo, Multicolor Stripes, 45 x 61 In.........................	8120.00
Bolo, Mother-Of-Pearl, Square Cut, Channel Work, 14K Gold Tips, N. Lubela, 2 x 2 In.............	633.00
Bolo, Navajo, Silver, Turquoise, Teardrop Finishes, Signed WT, 2 ¼ x 1 ½ In.....................	176.00
Bolo, Zuni, Red Coral, Turquoise Mosaic Inlay, 2 ½ In.........................	59.00
Bolo, Zuni, Silver, Coral, Turquoise, Snakes, Braided Leather, Effie Calavaza, 2 x 3 In............	153.00
Bolo, Zuni, Spiritual Figure, Head Feathers, Turquoise, Coral, 2 x 3 ⅛ In..........................	767.00
Bolo, Zuni, Turquoise, Jet, Mother-Of-Pearl, Shell, Coral, Silver, c.1940, 4 In.	2478.00
Bowl, Acoma, Painted, Bird, Hex, Orange, Black, 7 x 10 ¼ In.	415.00
Bowl, Eastern Woodlands, Burl, Oval, Openwork Handles, c.1790, 5 ¾ x 18 In.	5688.00
Bowl, Great Lakes, Burl, 8 ½ x 4 In.........................	55.00
Bowl, Great Lakes, Maple, Hooked Handles, 19th Century, 5 x 14 x 16 In.	4148.00
Bowl, Hope, Multicolor Katsina, c.1910, 3 ½ x 9 In.........................	301.00
Bowl, Hopi, Avian Design, Nampeyo, c.1950, 3 x 10 In.	978.00
Bowl, Laguna, Thin Walls, Multicolor Decoration, Curled Rim, 1930s, 4 ½ x 9 ½ In..................	230.00
Bowl, Mission, Basketry, Valero Stars, Diamonds, Female Figures, c.1910, 4 x 16 In..............	518.00
Bowl, Mush, Hupa, Dark Brown, Gold Overlapping Triangles, 1900, 5 x 9 In.	230.00
Bowl, Mush, Yurok, Basketry, Stepped Decoration, 2 Rows Raised Stitches, 1930s, 4 x 8 In......	374.00
Bowl, Northwest Coast, Frog Shape, Carved, c.1900, 10 x 4 ¼ In.	1293.00

Indian, Mask, Northwest Coast, Cedar, Eagle, Light Bulb Socket Eyes, Don Lelooska, 1960s, 21 x 14 In.
$748.00

Allard Auctions

Indian, Mask, Northwest Coast, Portrait, Cedar, Carved, Painted, Labrette Lip, Hair, 1960s, 11 ½ x 10 In.
$575.00

Allard Auctions

Indian, Moccasins, Arapaho, Beaded, Buckskin, Parfleche Soles, Hourglass Symbols, c.1910, 10 In.
$977.00

Allard Auctions

Indian, Moccasins, Sioux, Beaded, Hide, c.1935, 10 In.
$720.00

Cowan's Auctions

Indian, Moccasins, Southern Arapaho, Hide, Beaded, Fringe, Geometric Designs, c.1875, 11 In.
$5,535.00

Skinner, Inc.

Indian, Necklace, Navajo, Squash Blossom, Silver, Handwrought Beads, Turquoise Cabochons, 25 In.
$460.00

Allard Auctions

Indian, Rattle, Sioux, Deer Leg Hide, Buckskin-Wrapped Handle, Child's, c.1900, 8 ½ x 2 In.
$259.00

Allard Auctions

TIP

Use shallow boxes to store dolls. They are not to be piled on top of each other.

Bowl, Northwest Coast, Wood, Oval, Carved Frog, Masks, Abalone Insets, 3 ½ x 14 In.	5175.00
Bowl, Pima, Basketry, Stepped Diamonds, Fylfot, Butterflies, 1930s, 4 ¾ x 8 ½ In.	288.00
Bowl, Pueblo, Black, Serpent Design, Mary Cain, c.1950, 7 ½ x 4 ½ In.	240.00
Bowl, Salado, Gila, Abstract Parrots, 3 ½ x 7 ¾ In. ....*Illus*	288.00
Bowl, San Ildefonso, Black On Black, Feathered Wings Design, Helen Gutierrez, 6 x 5 In.	144.00
Bowl, San Ildefonso, Black On Black, Symbol Band, Signed, Marie, 1950s, 3 x 5 ½ In.	489.00
Bowl, San Ildefonso, Black, Polished, Matte Avanyu Pattern, Marie, 1920s, 3 x 6 In.	690.00
Bowl, Santo Domingo, Stylized Leaves, Red Base, Wavy Folded-In Rim, 1950s, 6 x 9 In.	138.00
Bowl, Woodlands, Burl, Flared, Carved Base, c.1890, 6 x 10 In.	207.00
Bowl, Yellowware, 2 Lug Handles, c.1930, 6 ¼ x 11 In.	115.00
Box, Northwest Coast, Cedar, Beaver Design, Concave Sides, Inlaid Bone Discs, 15 x 10 In.	978.00
Bracelet, Navajo, 3 Bands, 3 Turquoise Stones, Old Pawn Silver, 1950s, 6 ⅝ x 1 ⅛ In.....*Illus*	161.00
Bracelet, Navajo, Cuff, Green Turquoise, Silver Discs, Triple Band Supports, 3 ¼ In.	177.00
Bracelet, Navajo, Cuff, Silver, 5 Bands, 2 Fox Turquoise, 5 x 1 x 3 In.	316.00
Bracelet, Navajo, Cuff, Silver, Oxblood Coral Cabochons, Black Matrix, 2 ½ In.	189.00
Bracelet, Navajo, Cuff, Turquoise, Silver, Stamped, Beaded, Ed Begay, 5 ½ x 1 ½ In.	230.00
Bracelet, Zuni, Silver, Rosette, 90 Turquoise, K. & M. Eriacho, 1970s, 5 In.	207.00
Buckle, Navajo, Silver, Oval, Fluted, Repousse, 3 ½ x 3 In.	830.00
Buckle, Zuni, Silver, Turquoise, Jet Mother-Of-Pearl, Cartouche Shape, Central Figure, Owls, 4 In.	2124.00
Buffalo Robe, Ojibwe, Decorated, 18 Scenes, Horses, Weapons, Pageantry, c.1900, 79 x 77 In.	2013.00
Canoe Paddle, Northwest Coast, Carved, Painted, 35 ¾ In.	531.00
Canteen, Papago, Woven Pitch, Coated, c.1900, 8 In.	59.00
Canteen, Polacca, 2 Lobes, Faces, Hats, Earrings, Rain Clouds, Loop Handles, c.1880, 5 x 7 In.	5464.00
Club, Eastern Plains, Ash Handle, Triangular Cutouts, Ball Head, Metal Spike, c.1875, 26 In.	10600.00
Club, Iroquois, Wood, Carved, 22 ½ In.	1652.00
Club, Plains, Skull Cracker, Stone Head, Wood Handle, Horsehair Suspension, c.1875, 33 In.	1185.00
Club, War, Plains, Stone Head, Rawhide-Wrapped & Beaded Handle, c.1930, 17 In.	219.00
Coat, Navajo, Hide, Wool, Embroidered, Hand Painted, Fringe, Woman's, 44 In. ....*Illus*	165.00
Courting Flute, Plains, Wood, c.1875, 22 In.	1528.00
Cradle, Pomo, Basketry, Bent Willow, Woven, U-Shape, 1940s, 19 x 12 x 6 In.	196.00
Cradle, Sioux, Beaded, Symbols, Crosses, Buffalo Hide, Sinew Sewn, c. 1900, 15 x 23 In.	1380.00
Dance Paddle, Northwest Coast, Carved, Wood, Painted, c.1870, 36 In.	1304.00
Dispatch, Case, Sioux, Beaded, Cornaline D'Aleppo Crosses, Sinew Sewn, 10 x 12 In......*Illus*	1265.00
Doctor's Bag, Sioux, Beaded Hide, c.1900, 12 ½ x 5 In. ....*Illus*	2640.00
Doll, Cradle, Kiowa, Beaded Hide, c.1900-30, 20 In. ....*Illus*	1230.00
Doll, Plains, Hide, Beaded Features, Shirt, Moccasins, Black Hair, c.1920, 17 x 10 In.	403.00
Doll, Sioux, White, Red, Turquoise, Black Beads, Cloth, Hide Sewn, c.1910, 17 In.	472.00
Doll, Skookum, Bully Good Indian Girl & Boy, Plastic Heads, Headdresses, Blankets, c.1950, 6 In., Pair	200.00
Dress, Cheyenne, Beaded Yoke & Tabs, Pony Beaded Chest Fringe, c.1950, Small	345.00
Dress, Hopi, Woman's, Wool, Black, Red & Green Trim & Fringe, c.1950, 36 x 24 In........*Illus*	92.00
Dress, Plains, Girl's, Cowrie Shells, Striped Ribbons, c.1910, 30 ½ In. ....*Illus*	720.00
Dress, Umatilla, Purple & Red Trade Cloth, Beaded Roses, Ribbon Trim, 38 x 47 In........*Illus*	633.00
Drum, Taos, Barrel, Cottonwood Log, Rawhide Faces & Lacing, 1950s, 20 x 13 In.	230.00
Drumstick, Hopi, Wood, Buckskin Covered Head & Handle, 24 In.	35.00
Effigy, Bear, Chumash, Standing On All Fours, Shell Inlaid Eyes, Black Stone, c.1850, 4 x 2 In.	3318.00
Figure, Owl, Zuni, Pottery, Wings, Tail, Hooknose, Pocket, 1940s, 9 x 8 In.	374.00
Game, Blackfoot, Stick, Buffalo Ribs, Beadwork Bag & Stand, 1910, 7-In. Sticks, 6 Piece	805.00
Gloves, Blackfoot, Men's, Gauntlets, Buckskin, Beaded Cuffs, Fringe, c.1920, Large	288.00
Gloves, Cree, Men's, Gauntlets, Moose Hide, Beads, Fur Trim, Fringe, c.1950s, Small-Medium...*Illus*	403.00
Halibut Hook, Northwest Coast, Bird Shape, Wood, c.1890, 8 In.	593.00
Hat, Karuk, Basketry, Overlapping Bands, Zigzag Pattern, 1920s, 4 x 7 In.	431.00
Hat, Makah, Basketry, Lines & Dots, Cone Shape, c.1950, 7 ½ x 8 ½ In.	460.00
Hat, Nez Perce, Basketry, Beargrass, Overlapping Color Blocks, Fez Form, 1940s, 7 x 6 In.	1840.00
Hat, Pomo, Basketry, 4 Stepped Bands, c.1920, 4 x 6 ½ In.	345.00
Headdress, Cherokee, Buffalo Hide, Pelvic Bone, Horns, Tin Cones & Feathers, 15 x 11 In.	230.00
Headpiece, Plateau, Crown, Beaded, Red Roses, Leaves, Blue Ground, 1920, 24 x 5 In.	259.00
Hide Scraper, Plains, Elk Antler, Engraved, Geometric Designs, 19th Century, 13 ¼ In.	5037.00
Hook, Halibut, Carved, 2 Sections, Twine, Splint, Iron, Bird Shape, 12 x 5 In.	345.00
Jar, Acoma, Piecrust Rim, Geometric & Fineline Designs, 1950s, 6 ½ x 7 In. ....*Illus*	92.00
Jar, Acoma, Umber Parrot, Geometric Designs, Marked, c.1930, 6 ¾ x 8 ½ In.	470.00
Jar, Cochiti, Effigy Pitcher, Spout Head, Arched Handle, 1940s, 9 ½ x 8 In.	518.00
Jar, Hopi, Migration Pattern, Wide Shoulders, Nampeyo, 1970s, 3 ½ x 7 In.	403.00
Jar, Hopi, Squat, Flared Neck, Diamond Design, c.1940, 5 x 5 ½ In.	460.00
Jar, Maricopa, Black Long Designs, Ling Neck, Flared Rim, B. Johnson, c.1950, 12 x 7 In.	460.00
Jar, San Ildefonso, Black On Black, Feather Pattern On Shoulder, F. Naranjo, 1970s, 6 In.	288.00

I

Jar, San Luis Potosi, Water, Olla, Flowers On Shoulder, c.1910, 9 x 13 In.		403.00
Jar, Santa Clara, Blackware, Eagle Figures, F. Chavarria, 1960s, 6 x 5 In.		316.00
Jar, Santo Domingo, Olla, Curvilinear Pattern, Multicolored, Wide Mouth, 1930s, 9 x 9 In.		259.00
Jar, Storage, Zuni, 4 Colors, 3 Large Birds, Flowering Plants, 16 ¼ In.	*Illus*	24000.00
Jar, Zuni, Stepped Hatched Design, Checkered, Shouldered, 6 ½ In.		415.00
Katsina, Hopi, Cottonwood Root, Mudhead, Protruding Features, Painted, 1950s, 8 In.		230.00
Katsina, Hopi, Cottonwood, Carved, Painted, Signed Darrell Youvella, 12 ¼ x 3 ¼ In.		176.00
Katsina, Hopi, Muzrini Bean, c.1930, 8 In.		646.00
Katsina, Hopi, White Buffalo Dancer, Shell Necklace, Bracelet, 24 In.		374.00
Knife Sheath, Dakota, Beadwork, Multicolor, Knife, 10 In.		518.00
Knife Sheath, Sioux, White, Red, Green, Yellow Geometrics, Sinew Sewn, c.1890, 10 In.		708.00
Knife, Woodlands, Crooked, Fist Shape, Iron, Wood, c.1845, 4 x 10 In.		2232.00
Ladle, Lakota, Buffalo Horn, Loon Handle, 11 ¼ In.		948.00
Ladle, Plains, Horn, Carved, Rawhide Suspension, c.1890, 14 ¾ In.		474.00
Ladle, Woodlands, Hardwood, Pouring Spout, Tabbed Handle, c. 1880, 23 x 3 x 6 In.		115.00
Leggings, Sioux, Buckskin, Beaded, Geometric Symbols, Sinew Sewn, 18 In.	*Illus*	920.00
Mask, Ibibio, Pierced Eyes, Stand, Wood, 7 ½ In.		444.00
Mask, Kwakiutl, Ceremonial, Mosquito, Beak, Carved, Red, Black, Brown, Green, 7 ¼ x 5 ½ In.		863.00
Mask, Northwest Coast, Carved, Multicolor, Smiling Face, Round Frowning Face, c.1900, 20 x 13 In.		460.00
Mask, Northwest Coast, Cedar, Eagle, Light Bulb Socket Eyes, Don Lelooska, 1960s, 21 x 14 In.	*Illus*	748.00
Mask, Northwest Coast, Portrait, Cedar, Carved, Painted, Labrette Lip, Hair, 1960s, 11 ½ x 10 In.	*Illus*	575.00
Medicine Bag, Sioux, Flag Design, c.1920, 5 ¾ x 4 ¼ In.		744.00
Medicine Necklace, Crow, Beads, Elk Teeth, Stones, Pouch, c.1870, 15 In.		1838.00
Moccasins, Arapaho, Beaded, Buckskin, Parfleche Soles, Hourglass Symbols, c.1910, 10 In.	*Illus*	977.00
Moccasins, Arapaho, Geometric Patterns, Beads, Deer Rawhide Soles, c.1970, Woman's		82.00
Moccasins, Arapaho, Smoked Hide, Rawhide Soles, Multicolor Striped Beads, c.1875, 9 In.		1067.00
Moccasins, Blackfoot, Beaded, Crosses, Elk Hide, Sinew Sewn, Ribbon Trim, 1900, 11 In.		431.00
Moccasins, Central Plains, Cloth Cuffs, Glass & Metallic Beads, Geometric, c.1875, 10 In.		1422.00
Moccasins, Cheyenne, Beaded, Quilled, Arrows, Sinew Sewn, Lazy Stitch, 1910, 11 In.		920.00
Moccasins, Cheyenne, Geometric Rectangular Panel, Beaded, Multicolor, c.1875, 9 In.		711.00
Moccasins, Cree, Moose Hide, Beaded, Sinew Sewn, Lazy Stitch Edge, c.1920, 12 In.		633.00
Moccasins, Lakota, Hide, Beaded, Hard Sole, Geometric, Multicolor, 10 In.		1348.00
Moccasins, Shoshoni, Buckskin, Beaded, Flowers, Bootie Style, Child's, 4 ¾ In.		219.00
Moccasins, Sioux, Beaded, Hide, c.1935, 10 In.	*Illus*	720.00
Moccasins, Sioux, Beaded, Multicolor, 3 ⅝ In.		165.00
Moccasins, Sioux, Beaded, Sinew Sewn, Lazy Stitch, Ceremonial, 1900, 9 ½ In.		1725.00
Moccasins, Southern Arapaho, Hide, Beaded, Fringe, Geometric Designs, c.1875, 11 In.	*Illus*	5535.00
Necklace, Navajo, Carved Turquoise Disks, Sterling, Bead Spacers, Silver Clasp, 28 In.		368.00
Necklace, Navajo, Silver, Coral, Turquoise, Teardrop Pendant, Wire Strand, Beads, Marie Kee, 26 In.		212.00
Necklace, Navajo, Squash Blossom, Silver, Handwrought Beads, Turquoise Cabochons, 25 In.	*Illus*	460.00
Necklace, Navajo, Turquoise, Silver, Feather, Berry, Scrolling Black Matrix, Strands, Beads, 17 ½ In.		295.00
Necklace, Santo Domingo, Thunderbird, Turquoise & Red Mosaic, Bone Heshi, 1930s, 22 In.		173.00
Necklace, Zuni, Silver, Double Beaded, 10 Squash Blossoms, Turquoise, 32 In.		759.00
Necklace, Zuni, Squash Blossom, 10 Knifewing Gods, Naja, Turquoise, Spiny Oyster, 29 In.		1093.00
Necklace, Zuni, Squash Blossom, Turquoise Cabochons, Silver, Hook Clasp, 34 In.		414.00
Olla, Acoma, Figures, Flared, Squat, 1930s, 7 ½ x 10 In.		460.00
Olla, Acoma, Heart Geometrics, Gray, Cream, c.1940, 9 In.		920.00
Olla, Santo Domingo, Stylized 4-Leaf Clover, Beige, Black, Orange, 10 In.		652.00
Olla, Southwest, Black & Orange Geometric Decoration, 11 In.		3318.00
Panel, Navajo, Black, White, Red, Geometric, Gray Field, Frame, 16 x 23 In.		336.00
Parfleche, Plateau, Rawhide, Mineral Painted Designs, Buckskin Fringe & Ties, 11 x 4 In.		259.00
Pendant, Navajo, Turquoise, 5 Concentric Circles, Needlepoint, Silver Mount, V. Begay, 6 In.		288.00
Pipe Bag, Lakota, Beaded, Quilled, Geometric Design, Fringe, c.1875, 37 In.		2133.00
Pipe Bowl, Chippewa, Locomotive Style, Lead Inlaid, Geometric Cross, c.1850, 4 x 2 In.		1103.00
Pipe Bowl, Eastern Sioux, Catlinite, Bird's Claw, c.1875, 3 ¼ In.		1007.00
Pipe, Dakota, T-Shape Bowl, Stone & Lead, Wood Stem, 10 ¾ In.		600.00
Pipe, Plains, Catlinite, Squared Shank, Flared Bowl, c.1875, 27 In.		1422.00
Pipe, Plains, Quill Wrapped, Ash Stem, Stone Bowl, c.1900, 24 ½ In.		711.00
Pipe, Woodlands, Presentation, Ax End, Curly Maple Stem, Silver Inlay, Bone Tip, 18 In.		1035.00
Pitcher, Anasazi, Black On Red, Handle, Geometric Design, 4 x 3 ¾ In.		330.00
Pitcher, Anasazi, Black On White, Handle, Geometric Stepped Design, 7 x 7 In.		467.00
Plate, San Ildefonso Pueblo, Feather Pattern, Blackware, Maria & Santana, 6 ¾ In.		1150.00
Plate, Southwestern, Pottery, Blackware, Etched Feather Design, Juanita, 11 In.		470.00
Pot, Zuni, Fetish, Olla, Turquoise Encrusted, Spirit Holes, Antler Fetishes, 1970s, 9 In.		374.00
Pouch, Chippewa, Bandolier, Grapevine Beaded, White Ground, c.1900, 42 In.		1121.00

Indian, Rug, Navajo, Crystal Weaving, Central Lozenge, Red Accents, 1950s, 62 x 39 In.
$805.00

Allard Auctions

Indian, Rug, Navajo, Fish Hooks, S's, Crosses, 1950s, 48 x 24 In.
$184.00

Allard Auctions

Indian, Sash, Dance, Hopi, Woven, Applique Designs, c.1950, 4 ¾ x 120 In.
$138.00

Allard Auctions

I

Indian, Totem Pole Model, Northwest Coast, Cedar, Burl, Marked, Hood River, 1940s, 15 x 8 In.
$138.00

Allard Auctions

Indian, Totem, Northwest Coast, Human, Duck, Whale, Painted, 17 x 10 In.
$770.00

Old Barn Auction

Indian, Toy Cradleboard, Apache, Bent Willow, Beads, Cloth Doll & Body, Early 1900s, 11 x 4 ½ x 4 In.
$403.00

Allard Auctions

Rattle, Blackfoot, Rawhide, Wood, Cloth Wrapped Handle, Red Ocher, Braided, c.1875, 10 In.	593.00
Rattle, Dance, Haida, Raven, c.1890, 12 In.	4960.00
Rattle, Navajo, Wood Handle, Hide, Dew Claws, 10 ½ In.	302.00
Rattle, Northwest Coast, Clapper, Alder Wood, Zoomorphic Figure & Face, 1960s, 12 x 2 In.	316.00
Rattle, Northwest Coast, Knee Dance, Dew Claw, c.1875, 9 In.	411.00
Rattle, Plains, Hide, Red, Green, c.1900, 9 In.	823.00
Rattle, Sioux, Deer Leg Hide, Buckskin-Wrapped Handle, Child's, c.1900, 8 ½ x 2 In. .... *Illus*	259.00
Reins, Crow, Braided, Horsehair, 1902, 53 In.	412.00
Retablo, Southwest, Wood, Carved, Multicolor, Our Lady Of Guadalupe, Frame, c.1860, 19 x 12 In.	8888.00
Rug, Navajo, 2 Gray Hills, Geometric Design, Wool, Gray & Brown, Annie Yazzie, c.1975, 8 x 8 ½ In.	265.00
Rug, Navajo, 2 Yei Holy Figures, Feathers, Basket, Birds, 1920s, 59 x 51 In.	978.00
Rug, Navajo, 5 Rainbow Yei Figures, Black Ground, c.1950, 35 x 48 In.	690.00
Rug, Navajo, Central Double Cross, Stepped Crosses, Stacked Triangles, 91 x 42 In.	1422.00
Rug, Navajo, Crystal Weaving, Central Lozenge, Red Accents, 1950s, 62 x 39 In. .... *Illus*	805.00
Rug, Navajo, Diamonds, Ivory Ground, c.1930, 86 x 55 In.	889.00
Rug, Navajo, Fish Hooks, S's, Crosses, 1950s, 48 x 24 In. .... *Illus*	184.00
Rug, Navajo, Germantown, Serrate X Design, Multicolor, c.1875, 55 x 35 In.	1185.00
Rug, Navajo, Klagetoh, Homespun Wool, X Pattern, Serrated Edges, c.1920, 63 x 42 In.	863.00
Rug, Navajo, Lightning Bands, White Ground, 1940s, 62 x 32 In.	805.00
Rug, Navajo, Multicolor Stepped Diamond Medallion, Beige, Black Border, Wool, 94 x 142 In.	940.00
Rug, Navajo, Optical Geometrics, Gray, Black, White, Soft Weave, 1910, 52 x 78 In.	489.00
Rug, Navajo, Stacked & Stepped Diamonds, Variegated Ground, 1930s, 58 x 34 In.	711.00
Rug, Navajo, Stacked, Serrated Diamonds, c.1940, 102 x 57 In.	948.00
Rug, Navajo, Storm Pattern, Fylfot Crosses, Water Bugs, Symbols, c.1930, 92 x 49 In.	1610.00
Rug, Navajo, Tapestry, Four Corners Reservation Symbols, M. Thompson, 25 x 21 In.	374.00
Rug, Navajo, Tree Of Life, Birds, Multicolor, c.1975, 29 x 22 In.	2938.00
Rug, Navajo, Two Gray Hills, Geometrics, Homespun, 1960s, 44 x 30 In.	316.00
Rug, Navajo, Two Gray Hills, Geometrics, Key Border, Wool, Earth Tone, 1930s, 49 x 30 In.	1265.00
Rug, Navajo, Western Reservation, Homespun, Red & Gold Serrated Border, 50 x 28 In.	374.00
Rug, Navajo, Woven, Yei, Blue Ground, Black & White Stylized C's Border, 34 x 56 In.	316.00
Rug, Navajo, Yei, 7 Figures, Variegated Ground, Wool, c.1950, 53 x 33 In.	504.00
Saddle, Crow, Hide, Beaded, Red, Blue, c.1875, 24 x 11 In.	5288.00
Saddle, Plains, Wood, Rawhide Covered, Incised Decoration, c.1870, 19 In.	1250.00
Sash, Dance, Hopi, Woven, Applique Designs, c.1950, 4 ¾ x 120 In. .... *Illus*	138.00
Sheath, Plains, Rawhide, Copper Rivets, c.1875, 11 In.	1126.00
Snowshoes, Woodlands, Bentwood, Rawhide Lacing, Red Wool Tufts, c.1910, 33 x 10 In.	173.00
Speaker's Staff, Haida, Carved, Frog, Raven, Bear, Man, Wood, c.1875, 54 In.	2233.00
Spoon, Northwest Coast, Carved Horn, Totemic Handle, Inlaid Abalone Eyes, c.1880, 8 In.	1007.00
Spoon, Northwest Coast, Sheep Horn, Totemic Design, 15 In.	415.00
Storage Box, Penobscot, Birch Bark, Decorated, Eagle, Cross, Geometrics, Round, c.1870, 7 ¼ x 6 In.	708.00
Teepee, Plains, Warrior Stripes, Beaded Medallion, Symbols, 1960s, 144 In.	489.00
Tobacco Bag, Blackfoot, Hide, Beaded, Fringe, Geometric, c.1875, 33 In.	8225.00
Token Pouch, Northern Plains, Beaded, Quilled, Multicolor, c.1875, 3 ¾ x 2 ½ In.	940.00
Tomahawk, Missouri River, Iron Pipe, Blade, Bowl, Carved Wood Handle, Brass Tacks, 21 x 8 ½ In.	1035.00
Tomahawk, Plains, Ash, Brass Tacks, Beads, Thimbles, Ribbon, c.1870, 24 ¾ In.	10665.00
Tomahawk, Plains, Pipe, Ash, Brass Tacks, c.1875, 18 ¾ In.	8295.00
Tomahawk, Woodlands, Iron Head, Inlaid Turtle, Maple Haft, Silver Bands, 19 In.	920.00
Totem Pole Model, Northwest Coast, Cedar, Burl, Marked, Hood River, 1940s, 15 x 8 In. ... *Illus*	138.00
Totem Pole, Northwest Coast, Multicolor, Early 20th Century, 36 ¾ In.	2963.00
Totem Pole, Northwest Coast, Raven-Halibut-Beaver, Carved, Painted, Ray Peck, Alaska, 50 In.	1003.00
Totem Pole, Northwest Coast, Walrus Ivory, c.1920, 5 In.	1003.00
Totem Pole, Tlingit, Carved, Painted, c.1920, 54 In.	2607.00
Totem Pole, Tlingit, Cedar, 3 Figures, 1920s, 14 In.	288.00
Totem Pole, Wood, 4 Stacked Figures, Attached Wings, Painted, 51 x 20 In.	59.00
Totem, Northwest Coast, Human, Duck, Whale, Painted, 17 x 10 In. .... *Illus*	770.00
Toy Cradleboard, Apache, Bent Willow, Beads, Cloth Doll & Body, Early 1900s, 11 x 4 ½ x 4 In. *Illus*	403.00
Toy Cradleboard, Choctaw, Doll, Beaded, Pine Backboard, c.1998, 10 x 4 ½ In. .... *Illus*	207.00
Toy Cradleboard, Kiowa, Beaded, Buckskin, Brass Tacks, Shaped Body, 35 x 10 x 9 In.	11500.00
Toy Cradleboard, Northern Plains, Beaded, Vines, Brass Tacked Boards, 34 x 8 x 10 In.	1150.00
Toy Cradleboard, Paiute, Basketry, Cloth, Woven Straps, X's On Sunshade, 1940s, 26 In.	288.00
Toy Cradleboard, Plateau, Wood, White Buckskin Cover, Lacing, Plastic Doll, 1960s, 20 x 8 In.	489.00
Tray, Apache, Basketry, Woven, Radiating Stepped Pattern, 1940s, 4 x 15 In.	374.00
Tray, Choctaw, Basketry, River Cane, Natural, Brown, Green, 5 x 15 x 14 ½ In.	299.00
Tray, Maidu, Basketry, Tight Weave, Redfern Decoration, Early 1900s, 2 ¼ x 11 ½ In.	374.00
Tray, Northwest Coast, Birch, Spruce Root Stitching, c.1880, 14 x 14 x 2 In.	296.00
Tray, Pima, Basketry, Woven, 5-Point Pattern, Black Center, 1940s, 3 x 12 In.	196.00
Trunk, Northwest Coast, Bentwood, Painted Bear Design, c.1950, 14 x 31 x 16 In.	1495.00

I

Vase, Hopi, Smokestack, Drawing Design, Brown, Tan, Nampeyo, c.1900, 4 ½ x 3 ½ In.............	1410.00
Vase, Hopi, Stylized Parrots, Multicolor, Patina, 1930s, 12 x 4 ½ In.................................*Illus*	518.00
Vase, San Ildefonso, Pottery, Black On Black, Scalloped Design, Arrows, 1940s, 6 x 7 In..........	127.00
Vase, Santa Clara, Wedding, Avanyu Serpent, Multicolored, Double Neck, 8 x 5 In....................	230.00
Walking Stick, Chippewa, Wood, Human Torso, Carved, Twisted Shaft, Brass End Cap, 33 ¾ In. ...*Illus*	1920.00
Wallet, Northern Plains, Beaded, Boy & Girl Figures, Leather, 1950s, 7 ½ x 3 In........................	69.00
War Club, Northeast Woodlands, Figured Maple, Curved Handle, Simulated Arrow Detail, 1800s, 24 In.	978.00
Weaving, Navajo, Eyedazzler, Germantown, c.1900, 48 x 32 In. ....*Illus*	1140.00
Weaving, Rio Grande, c.1935, 87 x 52 In. ....*Illus*	1800.00
Yarn Bag, Chippewa, Finger Woven, Geometric Band, Multicolor, c.1850, 9 x 9 In.	593.00

INDIAN TREE is a china pattern that was popular during the last half of the nineteenth century. It was copied from earlier Indian textile patterns that were very similar. The pattern includes the crooked branch of a tree and a partial landscape with exotic flowers and leaves. Green, blue, pink, and orange were the favored colors used in the design. Coalport, Spode, Johnson Brothers, and other firms made this pottery.

Berry Bowl, Warwick, 5 In.	8.00
Bowl, Cereal, Coalport, 6 In.	20.00
Bowl, Cereal, Johnson Brothers, 6 In.	12.00
Bowl, Fruit, Aynsley, 5 ¼ In.	31.00
Bowl, Vegetable, Oval, Coalport, 8 In.	110.00
Bowl, Vegetable, Oval, Spode, 10 In.	120.00
Bowl, Vegetable, Red, Spode, 9 ¼ x 7 In.	125.00
Cake Stand, Myott, Staffordshire	40.00
Coffeepot, Lid, Aynsley, 5 Cup, 7 ⅜ In.	189.00
Creamer, Coalport, 8 Oz., 3 ⅝ In.	32.00
Creamer, Spode, 3 ¼ In.	46.00
Cup & Saucer, Coalport	36.00
Cup & Saucer, Footed, Aynsley	20.00
Cup & Saucer, Footed, Spode	34.00
Cup & Saucer, Johnson Brothers	10.00 to 12.00
Cup & Saucer, Myott, Staffordshire	15.00
Eggcup, Double, Spode, 3 ⅝ In.	60.00
Eggcup, Spode, 2 ¼ In.	50.00
Gravy Boat, Underplate, Myott, Staffordshire	47.00
Plate, Bread & Butter, Johnson Brothers, 6 ¼ In.	6.00
Plate, Bread & Butter, Salem, 6 In.	4.00
Plate, Dinner, Aynsley, 10 ½ In.	45.00
Plate, Dinner, Coalport, 10 In.	55.00
Plate, Dinner, Johnson Brothers, 10 In.	17.00 to 20.00
Plate, Dinner, Spode, 10 In.	60.00
Plate, Salad, Salem, 7 ¼ In.	7.00
Platter, Johnson Brothers, 12 ¼ In.	24.00
Platter, Serving, Oval, Coalport, 11 In.	80.00
Platter, Serving, Oval, Salem, 13 In.	20.00
Salt & Pepper, Spode, 3 ⅝ In.	279.00
Soup, Dish, Johnson Brothers, 8 In.	12.00
Sugar, Aynsley, 2 ⅝ In.	41.00
Sugar, Lid, Spode, 2 ¾ In.	70.00
Tureen, Lid, Coalport, 10 In.	1500.00
Tureen, Lid, Spode, 3 Qt., 9 ¾ In.	1000.00

INKSTANDS were made to be placed on a desk. They held some type of container for ink, and possibly a sander, a pen tray, a pen, a holder for pounce, and even a candle to melt the sealing wax. Inkstands date to the eighteenth century and have been made of silver, copper, ceramics, and glass. Additional inkstands may be found in these and other related categories.

Basalt, Black, Tray, 2 Handles, Center Bottle, 2 Wells, England, 1800s, 6 ¾ x 3 ¾ In.	830.00
Black Napoleon Bust, Empire Style, Gilt Bronze, Marble, 2 Wells, Pen Recess, Bun Feet, 8 x 12 ½ In.	531.00
Brass, Recessed Tray, Winged Sphinxes, Center Reservoir, Pen Holder, c.1900, 4 ½ x 9 In........	215.00
Bronze Dore, Sienna Marble, Pen Rest, 3 Urns, 1 Lid, c.1890, 9 ¾ x 5 In...............................	334.00
Bronze, Amboyna, Ormolu, Ram's Head, Flower Pen Holder, Brass Bun Feet, 6 ¾ x 9 ¾ In.........	384.00
Bronze, Copernicus, Seated Between Globes, Marble Base, Paw Feet, 1800s, 10 ½ x 16 In.	1140.00
Bronze, Scrolled, Pierced Back & Feet, 2 Covered Pots, Putti Masks, c.1860, 9 x 15 In............	357.00
Bronze, Tray, Insert, Lid, Verdigris, Marked, Denmark, 17 ¼ x 9 ½ In.	345.00
Copper, Hammered, Silver, Brass, 2 Bowls, Stamped, J. Heinrichs, c.1910, 4 ¼ x 10 In............	2000.00

Indian, Toy Cradleboard, Choctaw, Doll, Beaded, Pine Backboard, c.1998, 10 x 4 ½ In.
$207.00

Allard Auctions

I

Indian, Toy Cradleboard, Kiowa, Doll, Beaded Hide, c.1900-30, 20 In.
$1,230.00

Cowan's Auctions

Indian, Vase, Hopi, Stylized Parrots, Multicolor, Patina, 1930s, 12 x 4 ½ In.
$518.00

Allard Auctions

Indian, Walking Stick, Chippewa, Wood, Human Torso, Carved, Twisted Shaft, Brass End Cap, 33 ¾ In.
$1,920.00

Skinner, Inc.

Indian, Weaving, Navajo, Eyedazzler, Germantown, c.1900, 48 x 32 In.
$1,140.00

Cowan's Auctions

Indian, Weaving, Rio Grande, c.1935, 87 x 52 In.
$1,800.00

Cowan's Auctions

Inkstand, Porcelain, Baby In Bassinet, Children, Das Jungste Bruder, Inkwell & Sander, 5 ¼ x 6 ½ In.
$270.00

Cowan's Auctions

Gilt Metal Lids, Blue & White Pots, Bowl, Shaped Red Tray, c.1860, 10 In.	563.00
Glass, Blue, 2 Shells, Wells, Nickel Plated Brass Covers, c.1875, 3 ½ x 6 ¾ In.	2875.00
Meissen, Blue Onion Pattern, Clear Glass Insert, Tray, 6 ¾ x 9 ½ In.	110.00
Metal, Shakespeare's House, Musical Movement, 2 Melodies, Wood Base, c.1900	537.00
Porcelain, Baby In Bassinet, Children, Das Jungste Bruder, Inkwell & Sander, 5 ¼ x 6 ½ In. ...._Illus_	270.00
Porcelain, Owl, Red Glass Eyes, Wide Wings, Green Glaze, Clear Well, Austria, c.1910, 7 x 9 In.	375.00
Silver Gilt, Armorial Engraving, Leafy Pots & Candle Holder, Tray, Shell Handles, c.1840, 14 ¾ In. .	8125.00
Silver Gilt, George II, Pen Rest, Ink Pot, Taperstick, Pounce Pot, John Barbe, c.1738, 5 ½ In.	1298.00
Silver, Oval Base, Leaves, Hinged Cover, Mythological Creature, Pierced Feet, c.1900, 6 x 12 In.	418.00
Silver, Pierced Scrolls, Hinged Lids, Footed, Glass Inserts, Candlestick, Snuffer, Wilkinson, c.1852	1920.00
Standish, Mahogany Case, Drawer, Round Feet, Glass Ink & Water Wells, c.1815, 6 ¾ x 11 ½ In.	553.00

INKWELLS, of course, held ink. Ready-made ink was first made about 1836 and was sold in bottles. The desk inkwell had a narrow hole so the pen would not slip inside. Inkwells were made of many materials, such as pottery, glass, pewter, and silver. Look in these categories for more listings of inkwells.

Brass, 2 Horseshoes, Horse's Head, Hinged Jockey Caps, 3 ¼ x 6 ½ In.	360.00
Brass, Malachite Cabochon, 5 Loose Rings, Linked Rings, Continental, c.1870, 3 x 3 ½ In. ... _Illus_	235.00
Bronze Dore, Cupid Reading, Rococo, Hinged Lid, Glass Insert, Agate, 3 ½ x 6 ½ In.	173.00
Bronze, Bull's Head, Figural, Late 19th Century, 4 ¾ In.	411.00
Bronze, Copper, Fox's Head, Painted, Early 1900s, 4 In.	1007.00
Bronze, Dog, Pouncing On Rabbit, Tree Stump, Stepped Base, 3 x 4 ¼ In.	385.00
Bronze, Flower, Bird, Dolphin Quadrants, Dome Lid, Finial, Side Pen Rests, Paw Feet, c.1850, 7 In.	1840.00
Bronze, Hands Holding Urn, Figural, Hinged, Footed Oval Base, c.1900, 5 ½ x 7 In.	382.00
Bronze, Paneled, Zodiac, Tiffany, c.1900, 3 ½ x 6 x 6 In.	413.00
Cut Glass, 6-Sided, Embossed Sterling Silver Lid, Monogram, DEH, 2 ½ In.	250.00
Enamel, Champleve, Domed, Square Base, 4 ½ In.	472.00
Faience, Turquoise, 4 x 5 ½ x 5 ½ In.	152.00
Glass, Cobalt Blue, Sheffield Silver Lid, Round, 1880-1900, 4 ⅛ In.	109.00
Glass, Cut, Swirled Body, Hinged Silver Plated Cover, France, c.1820, 4 In.	72.00
Glass, Iridescent, Banded, Copper Lid, 3-Sided, Kralik, Austria, 3 ½ x 2 ½ In.	488.00
Glass, Iridescent, Banded, Copper Lid, Kralik, Austria, c.1910, 3 ½ x 2 ½ In.	400.00
Green Iridescent, Ribbed, Loetz, Hinged Metal Lid, 4 ¼ x 2 ¾ In.	230.00
Inkcake, Temple, Landscape, Dragons, Relief Carved, Quanlong Mark, Chinese, 5 x 3 In. ..... _Illus_	1195.00
Pewter, Round Tray, 5 Quill Holes, Glass Ink Liner, 2 ¼ x 3 ¾ In.	71.00
Porcelain, Chinese Man, Seated, Yellow Robe, Pot, Pen, Signed, Aladdin, Made In France, 7 ½ In.	460.00
Porcelain, Woman In Chair, Book, Interior Wells, Germany, 5 In. _Illus_	264.00
Redware, Rounded Foot, Tapered Shoulder, Flared Spout, Brown Glaze, c.1853, 2 ½ In.	210.00
Sienna Marble, Glass, Eagle Bronze Corner Mounts, Empire Style, 19th Century, 6 x 7 ½ In.	450.00
Silver Plate, Flowers, Glass Insert, Presentation, 1891, 4 x 3 In.	156.00
Silver, Curling Trophy, Gold Inside, Glass Insert, Edinburgh, Hamilton & Inches, 1800s, 3 In. _Illus_	1800.00
Silver, Waisted Collar, Hinged Lid, Gadroon Rim, Domed Base, Engraved, c.1906, 5 ½ In. Diam.	246.00
Stone, Taotie Mask, Carved, Shang Dynasty Style, Character Inscription, Chinese, 6 In.	117.00
Tortoiseshell, Silver Hinge, Ball & Claw Feet, MBA Hallmarks, Marked, 1912, 3 x 3 ¼ In. .... _Illus_	470.00
Whippet, Reclining, Blue Pillows, Copper Luster, Staffordshire, 5 ½ x 7 ½ In., Pair	35.00
Wood, Black Forest, Dog, Carved, Red Glass Eyes, Switzerland, c.1890, 3 ¼ In. _Illus_	472.00
Wood, Dog's Head, Black Forest Style, Carved, Glass Eyes, 3 x 4 In.	235.00
Wood, Dog's Head, Boxer, Carved, c.1900, 2 ¾ In.	180.00

INSULATORS of glass or pottery have been made for use on telegraph or telephone poles since 1844. Thousands of styles of insulators have been made. Most common are those of clear or aqua glass; most desirable are the threadless types made from 1850 to 1870.

A.U., Light Aqua, 1871	30.00
Am. Tel. & Tel., Hemingray, Blue	25.00
Brookfield, Aqua, Swirl, 3 ½ x 2 ¼ In.	9.00
California, Smoky Clear, Annealing Lines	30.00
California, Smoky Purple	25.00
Canadian Pacific Railway, Ceramic, White, 3 ¾ In.	35.00
Chambers Pat Aug 14 1877, Aqua, Bell Shape, Spread Skirt	532.00
Cobalt Blue, Threaded, Porcelain, 3 ½ In.	16.00
Confederate Egg, Dark Green, Tapered Top & Bottom, 2 Rings, 4 ¼ In.	812.00
Diamond, Straw, Tall	12.00
E.C. & M. Co., S.F., Green Aqua, 4 ¼ In.	392.00
E.C. & M. Co., S.F., Light Aqua, Milky Striations, 4 In.	728.00
H.G. Co., Petticoat, Beehive, Orange Amber, E Mold	1456.00
H.G. Co., Petticoat, Beehive, Yellow Amber, Bubbles, K Mold	896.00

H.G. Co., Petticoat, Clear	50.00
Hemingray 12, 8 ¾ In.	30.00
Hemingray 9, 7-Up Green, 3 ½ In.	28.00
Hemingray, Amber, Sharp Drip Point	75.00
Hemingray, No. 19, Carnival Glass	616.00
Hemingray, No. 19, Light Cobalt Blue, Milky Striations, Notched Edge	840.00
Hemingray, No. 19, Teal Green, Yellow Tones, Notched Edge	420.00
Hemingray, No. D 514, Honey Amber, Squat	308.00
Hemingray, Tramp, Blue	15.00
Lapp, Split Ear Top, Mottled Pumpkin Brown, 1930, 3 ¾ In.	25.00
M.T. Co., Teal Green, Tapered Skirt	952.00
Maydwell, Green, Milk Glass	25.00
McLaughlin, Apple Green	20.00
McLaughlin, Gray, Sharp Drip Points	20.00
McLaughlin, Olive Amber Black Glass, Round Drip Points	20.00
McLaughlin, Teal Black Glass	20.00
Mt. Washington, Ram's Horn, Cobalt Blue	532.00
N.A.T. Co., Patent May 2 1893, Peacock Blue, Hemingray	672.00
No Name, Beehive, Aqua, Threaded	280.00
No Name, Black Glass, Pilgrim Hat	644.00
No Name, Porcelain, Tan, Teapot, 2 Rings, Threadless, 4 ¼ In.	588.00
No Name, Porcelain, White, Paneled Pilgrim Hat	448.00
S. McKee & Co., Aqua Blue Glass, Pittsburgh, 1860s	448.00
San Francisco, Wooden, Tiger Stripe Grain, Cable Top, Side Wire Groove	235.00
Signal, Porcelain, Threaded, White, Incised PP, 3 ½ In.	15.00
Star, Green & Aqua, Amber	25.00
Star, Olive Green	20.00
Threadless, Pilgrim Hat, Olive Black, 1860-72, 4 In. ....*Illus*	527.00
U.P.R.R., Mulford & Biddle, Aqua, 1860s	560.00
W. Brookfield, 45 Cliff St., N.Y., Dark Amethyst, Domed Shape	476.00
W. Brookfield, Cauvet's Patent, Aqua, 1870s	45.00
W.E. Mfg. Co., Patent Dec. 19, 1871, Dark Teal Glass, Hemingray	448.00
Wade, Dot Dash, Aqua, Cylindrical, 6 Rings	476.00
Whitall Tatum Co., No. 1, Aqua, 4 In.	10.00

IRISH BELLEEK, *see Belleek category.*

IRON is a metal that has been used by man since prehistoric times. It is a popular metal for tools and decorative items like doorstops that need as much weight as possible. Items are listed here or under other appropriate headings, such as Bookends, Doorstop, Kitchen, Match Holder, or Tool. The tool that is used for ironing clothes, an iron, is listed in the Kitchen category under Iron and Sadiron.

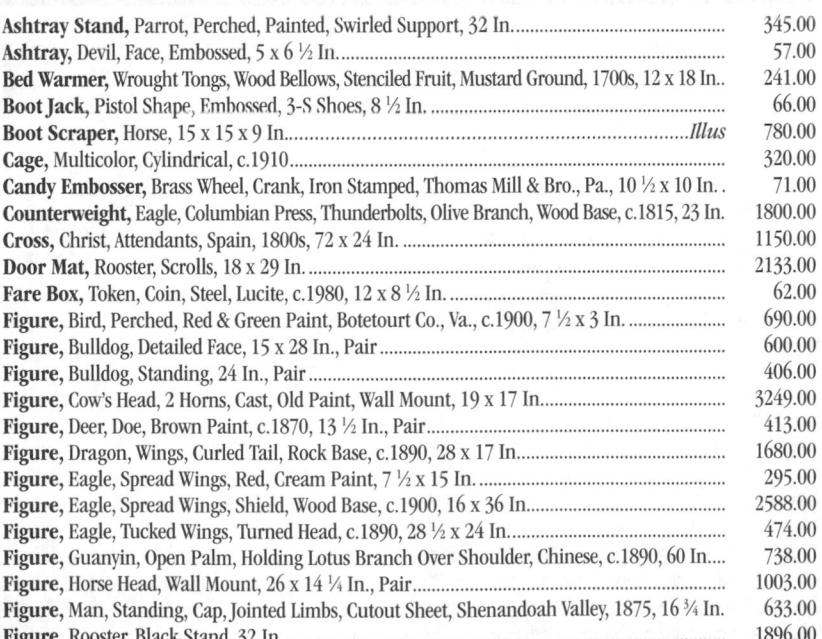

Ashtray Stand, Parrot, Perched, Painted, Swirled Support, 32 In.	345.00
Ashtray, Devil, Face, Embossed, 5 x 6 ½ In.	57.00
Bed Warmer, Wrought Tongs, Wood Bellows, Stenciled Fruit, Mustard Ground, 1700s, 12 x 18 In.	241.00
Boot Jack, Pistol Shape, Embossed, 3-S Shoes, 8 ½ In.	66.00
Boot Scraper, Horse, 15 x 15 x 9 In. ....*Illus*	780.00
Cage, Multicolor, Cylindrical, c.1910	320.00
Candy Embosser, Brass Wheel, Crank, Iron Stamped, Thomas Mill & Bro., Pa., 10 ½ x 10 In.	71.00
Counterweight, Eagle, Columbian Press, Thunderbolts, Olive Branch, Wood Base, c.1815, 23 In.	1800.00
Cross, Christ, Attendants, Spain, 1800s, 72 x 24 In.	1150.00
Door Mat, Rooster, Scrolls, 18 x 29 In.	2133.00
Fare Box, Token, Coin, Steel, Lucite, c.1980, 12 x 8 ½ In.	62.00
Figure, Bird, Perched, Red & Green Paint, Botetourt Co., Va., c.1900, 7 ½ x 3 In.	690.00
Figure, Bulldog, Detailed Face, 15 x 28 In., Pair	600.00
Figure, Bulldog, Standing, 24 In., Pair	406.00
Figure, Cow's Head, 2 Horns, Cast, Old Paint, Wall Mount, 19 x 17 In.	3249.00
Figure, Deer, Doe, Brown Paint, c.1870, 13 ½ In., Pair	413.00
Figure, Dragon, Wings, Curled Tail, Rock Base, c.1890, 28 x 17 In.	1680.00
Figure, Eagle, Spread Wings, Red, Cream Paint, 7 ½ x 15 In.	295.00
Figure, Eagle, Spread Wings, Shield, Wood Base, c.1900, 16 x 36 In.	2588.00
Figure, Eagle, Tucked Wings, Turned Head, c.1890, 28 ½ x 24 In.	474.00
Figure, Guanyin, Open Palm, Holding Lotus Branch Over Shoulder, Chinese, c.1890, 60 In.	738.00
Figure, Horse Head, Wall Mount, 26 x 14 ¼ In., Pair	1003.00
Figure, Man, Standing, Cap, Jointed Limbs, Cutout Sheet, Shenandoah Valley, 1875, 16 ¾ In.	633.00
Figure, Rooster, Black Stand, 32 In.	1896.00

Inkwell, Brass, Malachite Cabochon, 5 Loose Rings, Linked Rings, Continental, c.1870, 3 x 3 ½ In.
$235.00

Cowan's Auctions

Inkwell, Inkcake, Temple, Landscape, Dragons, Relief Carved, Quanlong Mark, Chinese, 5 x 3 In.
$1,195.00

Neal Auction Co.

Inkwell, Porcelain, Woman In Chair, Book, Interior Wells, Germany, 5 In.
$264.00

Cowan's Auctions

The edited listings of the current prices in this *Kovels' Antiques & Collectibles Price Guide* aren't available on any website. Readers can visit **Kovels.com** to check thousands of past prices and sign up for free information on trends, tips, reproductions, marks, and more.

I

Inkwell, Silver, Curling Trophy, Gold Inside, Glass Insert, Edinburgh, Hamilton & Inches, 1800s, 3 In.
$1,800.00

Skinner, Inc.

Inkwell, Tortoiseshell, Silver Hinge, Ball & Claw Feet, MBA Hallmarks, Marked, 1912, 3 x 3 ¼ In.
$470.00

Cowan's Auctions

Inkwell, Wood, Black Forest, Dog, Carved, Red Glass Eyes, Switzerland, c.1890, 3 ¼ In.
$472.00

Brunk Auctions

Insulator, Threadless, Pilgrim Hat, Olive Black, 1860-72, 4 In.
$527.00

Norman C. Heckler & Company

Figure, Snake, Flattened, Head, Looped Body, Tapered Tail, 12 x 4 In.	236.00
Figure, Woman On Horse, 1800s, 16 ½ In.	316.00
Hand Cuffs, Barrel Lock, Chain Lug, Link, Turnbuckle, Screw Key, Wrought, 9 ¼ In.	118.00
Hook, Swivel, Conestoga Wagon, Serpent's Head, Arrow Shaped End, Wrought, 5 ⅝ In.	59.00
Horse Leg, Hoof, 30 In., Pair........*Illus*	825.00
Horseshoe, Upturned Calkins, 6 Holes, c.1780, 5 In.	90.00
Jail Cell, Strap & Rivet Construction, Door, Black Paint, 1800s, 86 x 62 x 86 In. ....*Illus*	3055.00
Manhole Cover, Image Of Asheville City Hall, North Carolina, 23 ½ In.	470.00
Plaque, Eagle & Union Shield, E Pluribus Unum, Banner, Olive Branch, Stand, c.1890, 26 ½ x 20 In.	2040.00
Safe, J. Scott's Patent Asbestos, Phila., Fitted Interior, Loop Handle, Black Paint, c.1850, 30 ½ x 21 In.	1063.00
Safe, Victor, Painted, Combination Lock, Owner's Manual, Geo. A. Scheid. 21 In.	1320.00
Safe, Vulcan, Painted Scene, G.A. Bohnet, 15 In.	1380.00
Seal, Embossing, Buffalo Live Stock Exchange, Lion's Head, Black, Gold Trim, 1887, 11 In.	230.00
Shackles, Eye Terminal, Iron Cross Bar, 18th Century, 15 ½ In.	1125.00
Snow Bird, Eagle, Spread Wings, c.1850, 5 x 9 In., 8 Piece	288.00
Stall Divider, Lattice Work, 85 x 32 ½ In., 2 Piece	212.00
Stand, Missal, Hammered, Eagle & Orb Support, Arched Tripod Base, Spain, c.1750, 60 x 23 ½ In.	9775.00
Stirrups, Ottoman Style, Relief Flowers, Perforated Base, Braided Rope, Tassels, 8 ½ x 5 In.	173.00
Strongbox, Studded Hinged Lid, Hanging Clasps, Painted Flowers & Birds, Steel, c.1700, 18 x 28 In.	3600.00
Target, Rooster, c.1855, 21 x 10 In.	119.00
Tether, Bulldog Head, 14 ½ In.	1320.00
Tether, Feeder, Footed, 19 ½ x 4 ¾ In.	330.00
Tether, Horse, Embossed, Borden's, Round, 6 x 3 ½ In.	440.00
Tinder Lighter, Flintlock, Pistol Grip, Ball Pommel, Wrought, c.1790, 7 ½ In.	1763.00
Vase, Deer, Relief, Oval, Japan, c.1900, 6 ½ In.	58.00
Windmill Weight, Bison, Black Paint, 10 ¾ In.	1080.00
Windmill Weight, Boss Bull, 14 ½ x 13 In.	1560.00
Windmill Weight, Buffalo.	1895.00
Windmill Weight, Buffalo, Painted, Wood Base, Dempster, 17 x 13 In.	390.00
Windmill Weight, Bull, Brown, 12 ½ In.	900.00
Windmill Weight, Bull, Molded, c.1850, 13 x 14 In.	500.00
Windmill Weight, Bull, Painted, Fairbury, Nebr., 24 ½ x 18 In.	840.00
Windmill Weight, Bull, White Paint, 24 ½ In.	150.00
Windmill Weight, Chicken, Cat, Painted Red, White, Elgin, 16 In.	720.00
Windmill Weight, Eclipse, Painted, Wood Stand, 10 ¼ In.	450.00
Windmill Weight, Fish, c.1860, 20 ½ In.	5400.00
Windmill Weight, Horse, Black Paint, 17 ¼ In.	840.00
Windmill Weight, Horse, Black Paint, 19 In.	780.00
Windmill Weight, Horse, Bobtail, Painted, Dempster Mill Mfg., Co., c.1910, 17 In.	588.00
Windmill Weight, Horse, Dempster Mill Mfg., Co., c.1910, 17 x 17 In.	652.00
Windmill Weight, Rooster, 18 x 16 In.	504.00
Windmill Weight, Rooster, Black Paint, 15 x 22 In.	1612.00
Windmill Weight, Rooster, Elgin Wind Power & Pump Co., c.1910, 19 ¼ In.	770.00
Windmill Weight, Rooster, White, Red Paint, 9 In.	210.00
Windmill Weight, Rooster, White, Red Paint, Hummer, 17 ¼ In.	1080.00 to 1440.00
Windmill Weight, Squirrel, Painted Silver, Elgin, 14 x 15 In.	570.00
Windmill Weight, W Shape, Green, 9 x 17 In.	390.00
Wine Rack, Curved, Basket Weave Strips, Salterini, 11 x 17 In.	549.00

IRONSTONE china was first made in 1813. It gained its greatest popularity during the mid-nineteenth century. The heavy, durable, off-white pottery was made in white or was decorated with any of hundreds of patterns. Much flow blue pottery was made of ironstone. Some of the decorations were raised. Many pieces of ironstone are unmarked, but some English and American factories included the word *Ironstone* in their marks. Additional pieces may be listed in other categories, such as Chelsea Grape, Chelsea Sprig, Flow Blue, Gaudy Ironstone, Mason's Ironstone, Moss Rose, Staffordshire, and Tea Leaf Ironstone.

Bowl, Blue Dragon & Clouds, Gilt, Marked, c.1895, 3 ½ x 9 ⅛ In., Pair	478.00
Bowl, Soup, Willow, Orange & Blue, Green Border, Marked, c.1835, 10 ¼ In., Pair	73.00
Cheese Keeper, Blue & White, Flowers, Staffordshire, Stamped, 1800s, 9 ½ x 11 ¼ In.....*Illus*	150.00
Pitcher, Battle Scene, Vulture, Snake, Palm Tree, American Flag, Rifles, White, c.1865, 9 In.	288.00
Plate, Siam, Blue & White, J. Clementson, 1800s, 8 In., 6 Piece	42.00
Platter, Amherst Pattern, Orange, Blue, Flowers, Pagoda, Garden, Marked, c.1835, 17 x 21 ½ In.	184.00
Platter, Wild Turkey, Native American, Johnson Bros., Cut Corners, 15 ½ x 20 In.	150.00
Tureen, Cover, Flowers, Multicolor Transfer, Gilt Finial, 14 In.	23.00
Tureen, Cover, Landscape, Flowers, Cobalt Blue & White, Gilt Handles, Round Foot, 1800s, 9 ¾ x 14 In.	230.00

ISPANKY figurines were designed by Laszlo Ispanky, who began his American career as a designer for Cybis Porcelains. In 1966, he established his own studio in Pennington, New Jersey; since 1976, he has worked for Goebel of North America. He works in stone, wood, or metal, as well as porcelain. The first limited edition figurines were issued in 1966.

Bust, David, Sling Over Shoulder, 11 ½ In.	895.00
Bust, Kanani, Long Black Hair, Flowers In Hair, 5 ½ In.	250.00
Bust, Woman, Hair Up, Blue Bow On Shoulder, 9 In.	300.00
Figurine, Ballerina, 15 In.	375.00
Figurine, Boy Painting, Coveralls, Hand On Head, Hat, 10 In.	250.00
Figurine, Girl, Carrying Wheat & Basket, Bonnet, 9 In.	325.00
Figurine, Girl, Holding Hat, Flowers In Hair, 9 In.	250.00
Figurine, Mr. & Mrs. Otter, True Love, Holding Hands, Signed, 13 In.	1950.00
Figurine, Woman, Nude, Long Blond Hair, Seated, 10 ½ In.	475.00

IVORY from the tusk of an elephant is thought by many to be the only true ivory. To most collectors, the term *ivory* also includes such natural materials as walrus, hippopotamus, or whale teeth or tusks, and some of the vegetable materials that are of similar texture and density. Other ivory items may be found in the Scrimshaw and Netsuke categories. Collectors should be aware of the recent laws limiting the buying and selling of elephant ivory and scrimshaw.

Ball, Carved, Hinged, Interior Scenes, Condamnation De Mort, France, 1700s, 2 In.	518.00
Bouquet Stand, Openwork Roses & Lilies, Urn Shape Standard, Domed Foot, 1800s, 5 ⅜ In.	398.00
Box, Carte-De-Visite, Carved, Figures In Garden Pavilion, Chinese, 1800s, 3 ⅝ x 2 ¼ In.	1823.00
Box, Carved, Relief Lion, Guarding Female Lion, Crouching Tiger On Lid, Japan, 1800s, 3 ½ In.	885.00
Box, Casket Shape, Carved, Battle Scene, Flowers, Animal Mask Feet, Hinged Lid, 1800s, 6 ½ x 5 In.	5629.00
Box, Cylindrical, Domed Cover, Carved Flowers, 1800s, 9 ½ x 5 In.	1701.00
Box, Gourd Shape, Carved Leaves, Flower, Gourd, Bat, Peach, c.1900, 4 ⅜ In.	5925.00
Box, Lid, Cylindrical, Carved Dragons, Clouds, Pierced, Leaf Rim, Elephant Finial, 1900s, 5 ⅛ In.	243.00
Box, Lift-Off Lid, Cylindrical, Rococo Style, Carved, Shepherd, Sheep, 2 Lovers In Garden, 5 ¼ In.	711.00
Box, Mother-Of-Pearl, Bird, Flowers, Leaves, Hinged Lid, Chinese, 2 x 4 In.	120.00
Box, Oval, Carved Lotus Petals, Grasshoppers, Insects Atop Leaves, Lid, Chinese, 1800s, 4 x 2 In.	830.00
Box, Removable Lid, Carved, Flower Basket, Flower Border, Round, 2 ¾ x 1 ¼ In.	299.00
Brushpot, Carved, Scholars, Travelers, Mountain Landscape, 5 ¼ In.	2645.00
Brushpot, Figures, Landscape, c.1830, 9 x 4 In.	2450.00
Brushpot, Lohans, Immortals, Landscape, Inscriptions, Etched, Signed, Chinese, 5 ¼ In.	5142.00
Buddha, Head Model, Cylindrical, Openwork Crown, Serene Face, Wood Stand, 12 ½ In.	550.00
Candlestick, Tapered Cylinder, Bulbous Socket, 9 ¼ In., Pair	330.00
Case, Calling Card, Cover, Shaped Cartouche, Figures, Village, Flowering Branches, 4 ½ x 3 In.	2510.00
Crucifix, Carved, Gilt Inri Script, 6 ½ x 12 ½ In.	489.00
Crucifix, Carved, Rosewood Cross, Silver Inri Plaque, 29 In.	3000.00
Cuff Links, Devil Face, Signed, Asian, 1 In., Pair	110.00
Doctor's Doll, Nude Woman, Reclining, Holding Flower, 1800s, 5 In. ....*Illus*	230.00
Doctor's Doll, Nude, Reclining, Arm Behind Head, Crossed Legs, Wood Stand, Japan, 5 ½ In.	210.00
Doctor's Doll, Nude, Reclining, Holding Peony, Hardwood Stand, Chinese, 11 In.	2040.00
Doctor's Doll, Reclining, Hardwood Stand, Japan, c.1880, 5 ½ In.	252.00
Figurine, African Elephant, Walking, Curved Tusks, White, c.1930, 7 ¾ x 4 ½ In.	863.00
Figurine, Apple, Figures In Village Landscape, Trees, 4 In.	478.00
Figurine, Archbishop, Hinged Robe, Scenes, King & Courtiers, 1800s, 12 In.	2070.00
Figurine, Banana, Half Peeled, Carved, 6 In.	2280.00
Figurine, Banana, Partially Peeled, Japan, 1800s, 5 ½ In.	826.00
Figurine, Barge, Elephant, Peacock, 12 Oarsmen, India, 1800s, 18 ⅜ In.	1845.00
Figurine, Basket Maker, Seated, Showing Wares, Japan, c.1900, 3 ½ In.	1007.00
Figurine, Basket Vendor, Cinnabar Cartouche, 1800s, 5 ¼ In.	1955.00
Figurine, Boat, Barge, Banners & Lanterns, 1800s, 12 In.	1168.00
Figurine, Boat, River, Figures, Flags, Chinese, 8 x 11 In.	823.00
Figurine, Boy, In Pajamas, Holding Lit Candle, Barthelemy, France, Art Deco, 5 ¼ In.	875.00
Figurine, Branch, Kumquat Tree, Budding Fruit, Leaves, Signed, Ryokuzan Saku, 10 ¾ In.	711.00
Figurine, Buddha, Raised Hands, Holding Beads, c.1900, 6 In.	1225.00
Figurine, Buddha, Squatting, Holding Fan, Carved, Signed Base, 4 x 3 In.	374.00
Figurine, Cabbage Leaf, Cricket, Applied Pigments, Carved Wood Base, Chinese, 7 ¾ In.	920.00
Figurine, Cabbage Plant, Grasshopper On Top, Painted, c.1900, 10 ½ In.	799.00
Figurine, Cockatoo, Perched On Rosewood Tree, Red Wing Plumage, 1800s, 4 ½ In.	518.00
Figurine, Daimyo, Woman, Flowing Robe, Basket, Blossoms, Stand, Chinese, 1800s, 7 x 8 In.	633.00
Figurine, Deity, Woman, Standing, Wearing Robes, Bouquets, Phoenix Headdress, 1900s, 10 ⅝ In.	676.00
Figurine, Dragon, Articulated, Hinged Jaw, Painted Eyes, Scales, Spikes, Japan, 1800s, 30 In.	920.00
Figurine, Easkshmi, Holding Musical Instrument, Carved & Pierced, Wood Stand, c.1900, 7 ½ In.	338.00
Figurine, Elder, Seated, Holding Lizard, Painted, 8 ½ x 4 In.	690.00

Iron, Boot Scraper, Horse, 15 x 15 x 9 In.
$780.00

Showtime Auction Sevices

Iron, Horse Leg, Hoof, 30 In., Pair
$825.00

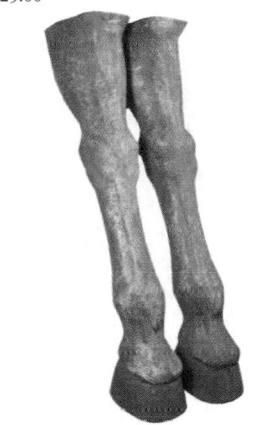

Showtime Auction Sevices

Iron, Jail Cell, Strap & Rivet Construction, Door, Black Paint, 1800s, 86 x 62 x 86 In.
$3,055.00

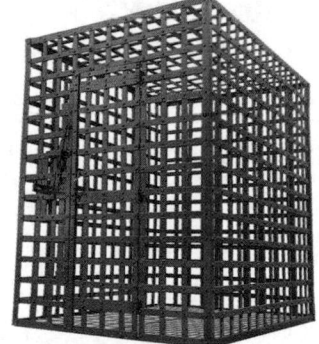

Garth's Auctioneers & Appraisers

Ivory, Doctor's Doll, Nude Woman, Reclining, Holding Flower, 1800s, 5 In.
$230.00

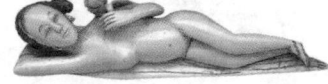

James D. Julia Auctioneers

Ivory, Figurine, Goddesss, Guanyin, Cup, Flowing Robe, Inlays, Stand, 1800s, 7 In. $3,318.00

Skinner, Inc.

Ivory, Figurine, Scholar, Child, Robe, Holding Staff, c.1900, 6 ¾ x 2 ¼ In. $236.00

Brunk Auctions

Ivory, Figurine, Seven Gods Of Good Fortune, Carved From Sphere, Chinese, 1800s, 2 ⅛ In. $243.00

Skinner, Inc.

Ivory, Figurine, Skull, 3 Demons, Signed, Gi Yu Ku Zen, Japan, 7 ½ In. $30,550.00

Garth's Auctioneers & Appraisers

Figurine, Elephants, In Circle, Holding Clear Glass Sphere With Raised Trunks, Chinese, 4 In.	150.00
Figurine, Emperor, Empress, Court Robes, Sword, Scepter, Stand, Wire Inlay, 1900s, 16 In., Pair	3444.00
Figurine, Fisherman, Pole, Basket, Rosewood Stand, Stand, Chinese, 9 In.	708.00
Figurine, Foo Dog, Imperial, On Haunches, Ink Details, Wood Base, Chinese, 1900s, 2 ½ In., Pair	307.00
Figurine, Foo Dog, Oval Base, Cubs, Curled Mane, Feathered Tail, 1900s, 12 ½ In.	1722.00
Figurine, Foo Dog, Seated, Pup Climbing Up Back, Pedestal, 5 ¼ In., Pair	369.00
Figurine, Geisha, Standing, Wearing Kimono, Wood Base, 1900s, 7 ¼ In.	110.00
Figurine, Geisha, Young Waving Boy On Back, Incised Robes, Round Base, Signed, Japan, 7 ½ In.	330.00
Figurine, God Of Longevity, Robe, Bald, Bats, Holding Staff, Peach, Carved In Round, 9 In.	676.00
Figurine, God Of Wisdom, Seated, Fan, God Of Wealth, On Ladder, Rubbing His Head, 1800s, 3 ⅛ In.	304.00
Figurine, God, Multi Head & Arm, Mythological Animal, Wood Stand, 6 ¼ In.	3630.00
Figurine, Goddess, Guanyin, Standing, Hand Raised, c.1910, 9 ½ In.	1680.00
Figurine, Goddess, Lan Tsai Ho, Scattering Basket Of Flowers, Stand, c.1900, 13 ½ In.	1230.00
Figurine, Goddess, Guanyin, Cup, Flowing Robe, Inlays, Stand, 1800s, 7 In. ....*Illus*	3318.00
Figurine, Goddess, Guanyin, On Lion, Holding Ruyi Scepter, Flaming Halo, Stand, 1900s, 15 In.	3444.00
Figurine, Goddess, Guanyin, Standing, Holding Pearl Of Light, Vessel, Lotus Blossom, c.1900, 10 ½ In.	984.00
Figurine, Grape Harvester, Standing, Holding Tool, Sack, Carved Walnut Base, France, 1800s, 6 In.	480.00
Figurine, Horse, Rearing, Onyx Base, 6 x 5 In.	327.00
Figurine, Horse, White, Black Mane, Jewels, Chinese, 1900s, 5 ½ x 5 ½ In., Pair	480.00
Figurine, Immortal, Lu Tung-Pin, Slayer Of Monsters, Wood Stand, 12 In.	3525.00
Figurine, Infant, Wine Cup, Wineskin, Wood Base, France, Signed Clovis Delacour, c.1900, 4 ¾ In.	1200.00
Figurine, Kabuki Holding Drum, Revolving Face, Japan, 3 In.	120.00
Figurine, Lady, Holding Flowers & Fan, Wood Base, c.1925, 12 In.	1102.00
Figurine, Lion, Attacking Snake, Wood Stand, 6 x 6 In.	446.00
Figurine, Lion, Buddhistic, Holding Ribbons In Mouth, Playing With Cub, Lotus Base, 1900s, 7 ½ In.	522.00
Figurine, Lion, Imperial, Seated, Paw On Ball, Wood Base, Male, Female, 1900s, 7 ¾ In., Pair	4674.00
Figurine, Lion, Prowling Stance, Rosewood Stand, Chinese, c.1900, 13 ¾ In.	480.00
Figurine, Lion, Prowling, Rosewood Stand, c.1910, 13 ¾ In.	580.00
Figurine, Lion, Seated, Cub, Male & Female, Foot On Ball, Wood Stands, 1900s, 5 In., Pair	922.00
Figurine, Madonna & Child, Wearing Crowns, Octagonal Wood Stand, Coat Of Arms, 21 In.	9000.00
Figurine, Madonna, Spanish Colonial, Carved, Gilt Trim, c.1750, 7 In.	4025.00
Figurine, Maiden, Immortal, Long Robes, Tiger, Holding Flowers, c.1800, 13 ¼ In.	1888.00
Figurine, Maiden, Long Robe, Holding Flowers, Base, 8 In.	184.00
Figurine, Man With Gourd & Broom, Carved, Inset Red Cartouche, Gi Yo Ko, 7 In.	452.00
Figurine, Man, Reclining, Cup In Hand, Blue, Black Accents, Chinese, c.1905, 10 In.	316.00
Figurine, Man, Robed, Carrying Sticks, Wood Base, Japan, 6 In.	119.00
Figurine, Man, Standing, Wearing Tricorner Hat, Socle Base, 6 ¾ In.	1000.00
Figurine, Marsh Birds, Plants, Pond, Hardwood Stand, Japan, 1800s, 6 In.	403.00
Figurine, Meiren, Standing, Outstretched Arms, Bird Shaped Headdress, Cloisonne Robe, 13 ¼ In.	448.00
Figurine, Monk, Lohan, Staff, Scrolls, Bark, Carved Plinth, c.1895, 9 ¾ In.	540.00
Figurine, Monkey Trainer, Wrestling With Octopus, Wood Plinth, Japan, 1800s, 5 ¼ In.	403.00
Figurine, Musician, Woman, Playing Mandolin, Ruyi Head Peg Box, c.1905, 9 ¾ In., Pair	960.00
Figurine, Napoleon, Standing, Wearing Uniform, Hand In Vest, Rectangular Base, 1800s, 8 In.	708.00
Figurine, Nude, Woman Extending Arms, Armbands, Art Deco, Octagonal Base, 1920s, 3 ⅝ In.	1154.00
Figurine, Orange, Carved, Multicolor, 1 ½ In.	5950.00
Figurine, Our Lady Of Lourdes, Holding Rosary, Embroidered Edge, Rose Petals, 1800s, 10 In.	1200.00
Figurine, Pagoda, 5 Stage, Tassels, Buddhist Figures, Painted, Hardwood Stand, 1800, 14 ¾ In.	1495.00
Figurine, Peacock, Flowering Prunus Trees, Wood Stand, c.1890, 9 ½ In., Pair	1353.00
Figurine, Peddler, Walking, Open Mouth, Wares On Back, In Hands, Japan, c.1900, 6 ¼ In.	1107.00
Figurine, Phoenix, Flowering Peony, Rocks, Square Pierced Wood Stand, Marked, c.1900, 17 ½ In.	2091.00
Figurine, Reclining Apsara, Fan In Hand, Robes, Carved Wood Stand, Chinese, 1800s, 7 In.	2726.00
Figurine, Robed Woman, Standing, Holding Scarf In Outstretched Arms, Pedestal, 18 ½ In.	5250.00
Figurine, Scholar, Child, Robe, Holding Staff, c.1900, 6 ¾ x 2 ¼ In. ....*Illus*	236.00
Figurine, Scholar, Standing With Child, Holding Branch Of Peaches, Stand, c.1900, 10 In.	1230.00
Figurine, Seven Gods Of Good Fortune, Carved From Sphere, Chinese, 1800s, 2 ⅛ In. ......*Illus*	243.00
Figurine, Skull, 3 Demons, Signed, Gi Yu Ku Zen, Japan, 7 ½ In. ....*Illus*	30550.00
Figurine, St. Francis, Christ Child, Padouk Wood Base, c.1900, 3 ½ In.	184.00
Figurine, St. George & The Dragon, Russia, c.1890, 4 In.	1062.00
Figurine, St. George, Slaying Dragon, Carved, c.1850, 5 ¼ In.	588.00
Figurine, St. George, Slaying Dragon, Padouk Wood Stand, 8 In.	799.00
Figurine, Three Graces, Oval Socle, France, c.1890, 8 In.	2880.00
Figurine, Warrior On Horseback, Tiered Base, Sword, c.1900, 14 x 8 ½ In.	2337.00
Figurine, Woman, Dancing, Gilt, Bronze, Marble, Claire Colinet, France, c.1920, 12 ½ In.	2015.00
Figurine, Woman, Holding Bowl, Gilt Apron, Onyx, O. Gladenbeck, Germany, c.1900, 13 ½ In.	3159.00
Figurine, Woman, Phoenix Headdress, Robe, Sashes, Octagonal Base, 20th Century, 23 In.	3444.00
Figurine, Woman, Standing, Holding Book, Hair In Twist, Flowers, Robes, c.1950, 10 x 3 In.	600.00
Figurine, Zodiac Animals, Seated Water Buffalo, Dragon, Serpent, Ram, c.1900, 2 ¼ In.	230.00

I

Group, Krishna With Raddha, Wood Base, c.1900, 7 In.	799.00
Group, Lions, Buddhistic, 2 Adults, 3 Cubs, Playing, Brocade Ball, Wood Base, 1900s, 8 ½ In..	984.00
Incense Burner, Lid, Bulbous, 3 Lion's Head Feet, Strap Handles, Foo Dog Finials, 1900s, 6 In.	861.00
Jar, Men Fighting Octopus, Carved, Inset Eyes, Rectangular, Japan, c.1925, 4 In.	118.00
Letter Opener, Carved, Pierced Handle, 8 Immortals, Trellis Ground, 1800s, 11 ½ In.	563.00
Magnifying Glass, Carved Handle, Ear Of Corn Shape, Brass Surround, 8 ¾ In.	173.00
Okimono, Wood Gatherer, Older Man, Smiling, Japan, c.1910, 9 In.	1320.00
Page Turner, Acanthus Carved Capital, Elephant, India, 10 ½ In.	575.00
Page Turner, Carved & Pierced, 2 Figures, Rocks, Flowers, Diamond Reserve, Chinese, 1800s, 11 ½ In.	652.00
Paper Knife, Curved, Horn Handle, Victorian, c.1890, 16 In.	300.00
Parasol Handle, Carved Figures, Pavilions, Leaves, Puzzle Ball Top, Chinese, c.1900, 13 In..	180.00
Parasol Handle, Carved, Peony Flowers, Mountain Landscape, Japan, 9 ½ In.	288.00
Plaque, Carved, Saint, Continental, 18th Century, 5 x 3 ½ In.	666.00
Plaque, Gallic Wars Scene, Flames, Carts, Oxen, Ebony & Bone Inlaid Frame, 1800s, 6 x 12 In.	11000.00
Puzzle Ball, Stand, Carved Peonies, Woman, Dragon Base, Chinese, 1900s, 16 In. .... *Illus*	1067.00
Rondel, Positions From Karma Sutra, Matted, Rococo Gilt Frame, 1800s, 8 ½ x 8 In., Pair	215.00
Storage Box, Engraved Flowers, Scroll Borders, Landscape Design, Bracket Base, 1700s, 9 x 20 In.	6325.00
Table Screen, Garden, Figures, Calligraphy, Rectangular, Stand, Chinese, 1700s	2722.00
Trinket Box, Gilt Copper, Oval, Carved, Travelers, Trees, Metal Band Base, Ball Feet, Lid, 1700s, 4 In..	2400.00
Trinket Box, Jade Oval, Carved, Casket Shape, Roses, Leaves, Lid, Chinese, 1800s, 6 ½ In.	1440.00
Trinket Box, Rectangular, Stepped Base, Lid, Elephant Finial, 1800s, 4 ½ In.	522.00
Trinket Box, Relief Carved, Elephants, Trees, Lid, Round, 1900s, 5 ¼ In.	330.00
Tusk, African Elephant, Curved, 74 In.	8700.00
Tusk, Carved, 24 Men & Women, Trees, Dragons, Phoenix Birds, Wood Stand, 53 ⅜ x 13 In. .....*Illus*	10925.00
Tusk, Carved, 8 Immortals, Gourds Of Spilled Water, Gilt, Wood Stand, c.1900, 16 ½ In.	2160.00
Tusk, Elephant, Conforming Jichimu Stand, Openwork, Asia, c.1900, 30 In.	1680.00
Tusk, Stand, Horse & Carriage, Village, Mountains, Forest Landscape, Signed, 11 In.	1353.00
Urn, Gilt, Mythological Shape, Handles, Carved, 5 x 3 ¾ In., Pair	384.00
Vase, Carved, Pine Trees, Village Scene, Craftsmen, Builders, Samurai, Farmers, 1800s, 8 In..	1225.00
Vase, Lid, Cylindrical, 3 Claw Feet, Dragon Ring Handles, Foo Dog Finials, Wood Stand, 1900s, 20 In..	4674.00
Wine Ewer, Hexagonal, Dragon Handle & Spout, Beehive Shape Neck, Dome Lid, c.1920, 14 ⅜ In.	1722.00

JACK-IN-THE-PULPIT vases, shaped like trumpets, resemble the wildflower named jack-in-the-pulpit. The design originated in the late Victorian years. Vases in the jack-in-the-pulpit shape were made of ceramic or glass.

Vase, Amethyst Iridescent, 13 In.	186.00
Vase, Green, Pad Base, Flared Neck, End-Of-Day Blown Glass, Ruffled Collar, Victorian, 12 In..	47.00
Vase, Light Green To Clear, Venetian Crystal, Gilt Flowers, Scrolling, c.1900, 17 In.	150.00

JADE is the name for two different minerals, nephrite and jadeite. Nephrite is the mineral used for most early Oriental carvings. Jade is a very tough stone that is found in many colors from dark green to pale lavender. Jade carvings are still being made in the old styles, so collectors must be careful not to be fooled by recent pieces. Jade jewelry is found in this book under Jewelry.

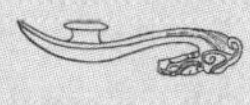

Belt Buckle, Dragon, 14K Gold Mount, 18th Century, 3 ½ In.	4287.00
Belt Buckle, Dragon's Head Hook, Curved Chilong, Pale Green, Chinese, 3 ¾ In.	334.00
Belt Hook, Archaic Style, Relief Carved, Hydra Dragon, Flower Button, Wooden Stand, 5 ¼ In.	2952.00
Blade, Ceremonial, Mountains, Waves, Carved, Brown, Chinese, 6 ¼ In.	4248.00
Boulder, Green, White, Figure, Landscape Scene, Carved, Chinese, c.1945, 4 ½ x 5 In.	3750.00
Bowl, Carved, 3 Dragons, Celadon Color, Stand, 8 In.	4182.00
Bowl, Cover, U-Shape, Waisted Foot, Band Of Ruyi Heads, Phoenix Birds In Flight, Dragons, 3 In.	488.00
Bowl, Octagonal, Flower Carved Panels, Flat Petal Shape Rim, Wood Stand, c.1900, 6 x 9 In..	3250.00
Box, Carved Flowers & Leaves, Shaped Oval, Pale Green, Lid, Chinese, 4 ¼ In.	1541.00
Box, Carved, Hardwood Stand, c.1900, 1 ½ x 4 ¾ In.	354.00
Box, Round, Carved, 4 Bats, Foo Dog, Dark Green Color, ¾ x 3 ⅛ In.	177.00
Box, Round, Flower Shaped Cover, Geometric Banding, Marked, 1900s, 2 ⅛ In. Diam.	107.00
Brush Holder, Carved Crane & Pine Trees, Wood Base, Apple Green, 5 ½ In.	568.00
Brush Washer, Flowers, Free Ring Handles, c.1825, 1 x 9 x 5 In.	17150.00
Brush Washer, Lotus Leaf Shape, Green & Brown, Hardwood Stand, Chinese, 1 ⅞ In.	1840.00
Carving, 2 Children, Branch, White, Green Tint, c.1900, 2 ¼ In.	288.00
Carving, 2 Fish, Leaping Up Waterfall, Marked, Yong Zheng Yu Zhi, 6 In.	7110.00
Carving, Bamboo, Plum Flowers, Gray, Russet Markings, Chinese, 2 ¼ In.	459.00
Carving, Mountain, Pine Trees, House, 3 Figures, 2 Deer, Green, Gray, Russet Markings, Chinese, 5 In..	3038.00
Censer, Lid, Celadon Gray, Globular, Upraised Curved Flange Handles, Scrolling Dragons, 5 ½ x 7 In.	1588.00
Censer, Lid, Lotus Bud, Plants, Frog Shape Finial, Carved, 7 ¾ In. ....*Illus*	956.00
Cup, Dragon Handles, Foot Ring, Green, Brown, Stand, 5 ¼ In.	3645.00
Cup, Nephrite, Carved Plum Design, Engraved Background, China, Late 1800s, 4 In.	2233.00

TIP

Changes in temperature may cause old ivory to crack.

Ivory, Puzzle Ball, Stand, Carved Peonies, Woman, Dragon Base, Chinese, 1900s, 16 In.
$1,067.00

Skinner, Inc.

Ivory, Tusk, Carved, 24 Men & Women, Trees, Dragons, Phoenix Birds, Wood Stand, 53 ⅜ x 13 In.
$10,925.00

Elite Decorative Arts

Jade, Censer, Lid, Lotus Bud, Plants, Frog Shape Finial, Carved, 7 ¾ In.
$956.00

Sloans & Kenyon

J

Jade, Figurine, Buddha, Seated, Double-Lotus Throne, Wood Base, Chinese, c.1900, 10 ⅜ In.
$3,402.00

Skinner, Inc.

Jewelry, Bracelet, Bakelite, Orange, Carved, Flower & Leaf, Spring Hinge, 1930s, 5 In.
$173.00

Hake's Americana & Collectibles

Jewelry, Bracelet, Bangle, Drums, Blue, Enamel, Gold Plated, Stamped, Hermes Paris, Made In Austria
$480.00

DuMouchelles Art Gallery

Jewelry, Bracelet, Cuff, Copper, Bronze, Heart Advances My Pulse, Claire Falkenstein, c.1975, 5 ⅝ x 3 In.
$5,925.00

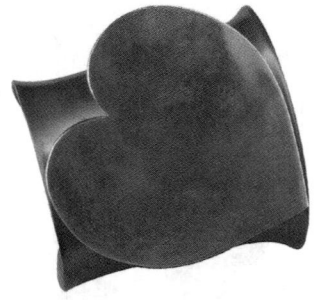

Skinner, Inc.

Cup, Oval, Ruffle Spout, Square Handle, Pierced, White, Gray Spots, Masks, Chinese, c.1900, 3 ¼ In...	1722.00
Figurine, Bird, Tail Plumage, Leafy Sprig In Beak, White, Silk Cord, 1700s, 3 ¾ In...	2214.00
Figurine, Birds, Perched On Flowering Tree, Oval Wood Base, Footed, Green, Amber, 6 ¼ In...	478.00
Figurine, Buddah, Seated, Laughing, Boy, Lavender, Chinese, 6 ½ In...	425.00
Figurine, Buddha, Seated, Double-Lotus Throne, Wood Base, Chinese, c.1900, 10 ⅜ In...*Illus*	3402.00
Figurine, Cat, Butterfly, Black, White, Wood Footed Base, c.1800, 2 In...	2450.00
Figurine, Crane, Hand Carved, Chinese, c.1950, 3 ½ x 4 In., Pair...	173.00
Figurine, Flower Filled Basket, White, Chinese, 5 ¼ In...	359.00
Figurine, Foo Dog, Lavender, Wood Ruyi Head Shape Base, 4 ½ In...	598.00
Figurine, Foo Dog, Seated, Black Striations, Hardwood Stand, 3 ¾ In., Pair...	173.00
Figurine, Goddess, Crane & Deer, Flowing Robes, Wood Stand, 1900s, 7 x 5 ½ In...	676.00
Figurine, Guanyin, Carrying Lotus Flower, White, Chinese, 13 ½ In...	387.00
Figurine, Guanyin, Goddess Of Mercy, Carved, Hardwood Plinth, White, Russet Markings, 7 In....	1955.00
Figurine, Horse, Mottled Green, Russet Accents, c.1910, 2 x 3 ¾ In...	240.00
Figurine, Kylin, Reclining, 2 Horns, Snarling, Wings, Coiled Tail, White & Yellow, c.1755, 6 ¾ In.	2706.00
Figurine, Mandarin Ducks, Lotus, Wood Base, Apple Green, 6 ⅛ In...	329.00
Figurine, Mythical Animal, 2 Reclining Water Buffalo, Green, Gray, Russet Marks, Chinese, 4 In.	948.00
Figurine, Mythical Beast, Green, Seated, Open Mouth, Shaped Wood Stand, Wire Inlay, 1900s, 6 ¾ In.	150.00
Figurine, Phoenix, Standing On Rocky Outcrop, Spinach Green, Wooden Base, c.1915, 20 In.	1353.00
Figurine, Ram, Dragonet, On Hind Quarters, Chinese, c.1960, 3 In.	120.00
Finial, Bird, Sitting, Legs Tucked, Wings Curved Upward, Pierced, Russet, Chinese, 2 In...	1793.00
Finial, Pagoda Shape, Scrolling Clouds, c.1800, 3 ¾ In...	1715.00
Group, 3 Goats, Long Horns, Sphere, Engraved Ying Yang, White, 2 ¼ x 3 In...	522.00
Hook, Carved Dragon's Head, Crouching Chilong, Pale Green, Chinese, 4 In...	972.00
Incense Burner, Masks, Dragon Jump Rings, Lid, Foo Dog Finials, Tripod Feet, c.1900, 10 x 12 In.	1062.00
Incense Holder, Carved Landscape Scene, Scholar, Pine Trees, Bird, Stand, 8 ¼ In...	1185.00
Jar, Cover, Openwork Flowers & Branches, Spinach Green, Carved, Wood Base, 6 In...	9520.00
Jar, Dome Lid, Celadon, Russet Inclusions, Cylindrical, Beaded Panels, Chinese, 7 ¼ x 3 ½ In...	1200.00
Plaque, Bird, Leaves, Openwork, Square, White, Chinese, c.1900, 3 In...	720.00
Plaque, Carved, Dragon Boat, Figures, Openwork, Celadon Color, Chinese, c.1890, 4 ¼ In...	353.00
Plaque, Openwork, Carved Child & Lotus, Chinese, 3 In...	425.00
Scepter, Curved, Russet, Mottled Yellow, Shou Symbol, Chinese, 9 ¾ In...	1452.00
Scepter, Ruyi, Hardwood, Scrolling Shape, Mounted Reticulated Plaques, Chinese, c.1900, 19 ¾ In.	450.00
Sword Handle, Ram's Head, Ruby, Diamond, Emerald, Pearl Inlay, Gilt Trim, Chinese, 6 ½ In....	2795.00
Teapot, Globular, Scrolling Lotus, Curled Leaves, Lotus Bud Finial, 4 Cups, Chinese, 7 In. ...	1304.00
Teapot, Lid, Fish, Lotus, Tendrils, Flowers, Lavender, Apple Green Markings, Frog Finial, 1900s, 5 In..	593.00
Toggle, Monkey, Riding Horse, c.1800, 1 x 2 In.	1960.00
Tray, Sterling Feet & Handles, Flower Studs, Dark Green, Chinese, 1800s, 8 ½ x 12 In...	1968.00
Vase, Arrow, Carved Chilong, Lappet Border, Handles At Neck, Chinese, c.1900, 5 ⅞ In...	5333.00
Vase, Carved Design, Dragon Handles, Loose Rings, Pale Green, Lid With Handles, 8 ½ In. ...	1185.00
Vase, Hu Shape, Carved Scrolling Lotus, Leaves, S-Curve Handles, Dome Lid, Square Finial, 9 In...	6075.00
Vase, Lid, Beast Head Handles, Rings, Dragons, Temple Lion Finial, 1900s, 9 In...	660.00
Vase, Lid, Carved Flowers, Loop Handles, Pale Green, 8 ½ In...	237.00
Vase, Lid, Chrysanthemums, Peaches, Peonies, Birds, Cats, Chinese, 1900s, 8 ½ In...	711.00
Vase, Lid, Flattened Hu Shape, Taotie Design, Chilong Scroll Handles, White, Chinese, 7 ½ In...	4740.00
Vase, Lid, Spinach Green, Handles At Neck, Rings, Round Wood Base, 8 ¼ In...	657.00
Vase, Pink, Russet, Elephant Mask Handles, Dragons, Flattened Pear Shape, 1700s, 3 In...	2070.00
Vase, Scrolling Lotus, Leaves, Splayed Foot, Handles, Dome Lid, Pale Celadon, Wood Stand, 12 In.	4740.00

JAPANESE WOODBLOCK PRINTS *are listed in this book in the Print category under Japanese.*

JASPERWARE can be made in different ways. Some pieces are made from a solid-colored clay with applied raised designs of a contrasting colored clay. Other pieces are made entirely of one color clay with raised decorations that are glazed with a contrasting color. Additional pieces of jasperware may also be listed in the Wedgwood category or under various art potteries.

Shaving Mug, Green Matte, Man Being Shaved & Getting Haircut, 1800s, 3 ¾ x 3 ½ In...	70.00

JEWELRY, whether made from gold and precious gems or plastic and colored glass, is popular with collectors. Values are determined by the intrinsic value of the stones and metal and by the skill of the craftsmen and designers. Victorian and older jewelry has been collected since the 1950s. More recent interests are Art Deco and Edwardian styles, Mexican and Danish silver jewelry, and beads of all kinds. Copies of almost all styles are being made. American Indian jewelry is listed in the Indian category. Tiffany jewelry is listed here.

Belt Buckle, Bronze, Abstract Form, Lawrence Fane, c.1975, 4 ½ In...	711.00
Belt, Gold Logo, Interlocking C's, Oval Links, Chanel, 42 ½ In...	615.00
Bracelet & Earrings, Sphinx Head, Mesh Band, Miriam Haskell, 9 x ¾ In. Bracelet...	149.00

J

Bracelet & Ring, Hoop, 18K Gold, Movable Figural Mouse, Asprey, 8 ½-In. Bracelet	2160.00
Bracelet, 18K Gold, 4 Chains, Oval Faceted Smoky Quartz, Open Oval Links, Nanis, 7 In.	1438.00
Bracelet, 18K Gold, Brushed Finish, Interlocking Links, Nanis, 9 ½ In.	2013.00
Bracelet, 3 Coral Bead Strands, Gold Filled Clasp, Victorian, 6 ½ x ½ In.	215.00
Bracelet, 5 Black Onyx Cabochons, 18K Gold Oval Links, Marzo, 1930s, 9 In.	4148.00
Bracelet, 6 Medallion Plaques, Lava, Classical Women's Faces, Oval, c.1910	206.00
Bracelet, 30 Diamonds, 14K White Gold, c.1960, 7 In.	944.00
Bracelet, Aurora Borealis, Rose Montee, Pearls, 3 Strands, Haskell, c.1950, 6 ¾ In.	395.00
Bracelet, Bakelite Panels, Red, Brass Dots, 1940s, 6 ½ In.	325.00
Bracelet, Bakelite, Orange, Carved, Flower & Leaf, Spring Hinge, 1930s, 5 In. *Illus*	173.00
Bracelet, Bangle, 14K Yellow Gold, Engraved Scrolls, Florentine, Victorian, 2 ½ In.	1869.00
Bracelet, Bangle, Drums, Blue, Enamel, Gold Plated, Stamped, Hermes Paris, Made In Austria... *Illus*	480.00
Bracelet, Bangle, Hinged, 18K Gold, Incised Diamonds, Van Cleef & Arpels, 6 ¾ In.	6518.00
Bracelet, Bangle, Hinged, Horseshoe & Bits, Pearls, 15K Gold, Art Nouveau, 6 ½ In.	948.00
Bracelet, Bangle, Hinged, Tennis Racquet, Engraved Scrolls, Minshull & Latimer, 1884	652.00
Bracelet, Bangle, Hinged, Tortoiseshell Bust Of Maiden, Profile, 6 ⅜ In.	593.00
Bracelet, Bangle, Silver, 2 Pear-Cut Amethysts, Bezel Mounts, Mexico, 2 ⅓ In.	207.00
Bracelet, Bangle, Silver, Amethyst, 18K Gold, Tiffany, 3 ¾ In.	158.00
Bracelet, Bangle, Titanium, 18K Gold Cable Design, David Yurman, 3 In.	276.00
Bracelet, Braided, Pearl, Gem Clusters, Rope Twist Edge, 14K Gold, c.1950, 7 In.	1298.00
Bracelet, Butterfly, Cloisonne, Blue, Red Enamel, c.1990, 8 In.	74.00
Bracelet, Cable, 18K Gold, Leather, Magnetic Clasp, David Yurman, 8 In.	253.00
Bracelet, Cameo Panels, Lava, Hercules, Hebe, 3 Grotesque Masks, 18K Gold, 7 In.	1103.00
Bracelet, Camphor Glass Center, Diamonds, Gold Filigree, Slide-In Clasp, Art Deco, 6 ¾ In.	403.00
Bracelet, Coral Beads, 6 Strands, 14K Gold Abstract Clasp, Arthur King, 7 In.	1440.00
Bracelet, Cuff, 7 Rope Twist Rows, 18K Gold, Van Cleef & Arpels, 6 ½ In.	5225.00
Bracelet, Cuff, Asymmetrical, Silver, Overlaid S Shapes, Wire, Modernist, Marked, RB Sterling, 6 ½ In.	132.00
Bracelet, Cuff, Copper, Bronze, Heart Advances My Pulse, Claire Falkenstein, c.1975, 5 ⅝ x 3 In.. *Illus*	5925.00
Bracelet, Cuff, Double Hinged, Silver, Stylized Flowers, Stamped, Taxco, 2 ⅓ In.	184.00
Bracelet, Cuff, Hinged, 50's Coral Cabochons, 18K Gold, S. Schepps, 6 ½ In.	13025.00
Bracelet, Cuff, Hinged, Applied Rope & Star Designs, Diamonds, G. Montebello, 6 In.	4266.00
Bracelet, Cuff, Hinged, Diamond, Retro	23000.00
Bracelet, Cuff, Hinged, Lion's Head, Sapphire Eyes, Diamonds, 18K Textured Gold, D. Webb...	19973.00
Bracelet, Cuff, Hinged, Silver, Onyx Terminals, Diamonds Border David Yurman, 2 ¼ In.	575.00
Bracelet, Cuff, Hinged, White Daisy, 1960s, 7 x 2 ⅛ In.	46.00
Bracelet, Cuff, Leaves & Berries, Sterling Silver, M. Buccellati, 6 ¼ In.	889.00
Bracelet, Cuff, Mask, Granulated Animals, Beaded Rim, Etruscan Style, 1880s, 8 In.	2489.00
Bracelet, Cuff, Silver, 3 Ridges, Tapered, Stamped, Bayanihan	307.00
Bracelet, Cuff, Silver, Asymmetrical, Checkerboard Design, Basketweave Squares, Yaacov Helle....	615.00
Bracelet, Cuff, Silver, Chased Navajo Pattern, Marked, Darin Bill, 7 x ⅝ In.	150.00
Bracelet, Cuff, Silver, Henry Steig, 6 ¼ In. *Illus*	521.00
Bracelet, Cuff, Silver, Nanna & Jorgen Ditzel, Georg Jensen, No. 107, 6 ¼ In.	1140.00
Bracelet, Cuff, Silver, Raised Vine, B. Goodspeed, Mexico, Men's, 8 x 1 ¾ In.	268.00
Bracelet, Cuff, Silver, Turquoise Cabochons, Leaf Shapes, Marked, Fred Guerro, 2 ½ In.	167.00
Bracelet, Flower, Enamel, Gilt Repousse, 3 Hooked Sections, Slide Clasp, Victorian, 7 In., Pair.	413.00
Bracelet, Gray & Tan, Woven Leather, Stainless Steel Hook & Eye Clasp, Stamped, Hermes, Box, 7 In.	259.00
Bracelet, Line, 16 Synthetic Sapphires, Diamond Spacers, Platinum, Art Deco, 6 ⅝ In.	1778.00
Bracelet, Line, Faceted Onyx Rectangles, Platinum, Beaded, Art Deco, 7 ¼ In.	2370.00
Bracelet, Link, 18K Gold, Oval, Hammered, Walter Schluep, 8 In.	3600.00
Bracelet, Link, 4 Star Sapphires, Diamonds, Platinum, Art Deco, Raymond Yard, 7 In.	15405.00
Bracelet, Link, 8 Silver, Abstract, Amethyst Cabochon, Antonio Pineda, 7 In.	1304.00
Bracelet, Link, Circular, 14K Gold, Tiffany & Co., 1970s, 7 ⅞ In.	3437.00
Bracelet, Link, Copper, Brass, Hourglass Shape, Renoir, Art Deco, 1950s, 6 ½ x 1 In.	74.00
Bracelet, Link, Cushion Shape, Ball Spacers, Silver, William Spratling, c.1940, 8 In.	1140.00
Bracelet, Link, Greek Key, Turquoise Enamel, Sterling Silver, Margot De Taxco, 7 ¼ In.	130.00
Bracelet, Link, Hexagonal & Oval, Diamonds, Platinum, Beaded, Art Deco, Wise, 7 In.	7705.00
Bracelet, Link, Interlocked, 14K Gold, c.1960, 8 In.	960.00
Bracelet, Link, Kite Shape, Bezel Set Round & Square Gems, Slide Clasp, 18K Gold, c.1945, 7 ½ In. ...	840.00
Bracelet, Link, Rectangular, Diamond, Emerald, Onyx, Geometric Design, Art Deco, 7 In.	18290.00
Bracelet, Link, Round, Interlocking, 18K Gold, Toggle Closure, Hermes, 8 In.	7800.00
Bracelet, Link, Round, Oval, Beaded Rims, Silver, Hector Aguilar, 7 ½ In.	385.00
Bracelet, Link, Silver, Arts & Crafts Style, Binder Brothers, Marked, A & C, 1930s, 7 ½ x ⅝ In.	145.00
Bracelet, Link, Stylized Buds, Moonstone Cabochons, Georg Jensen, No. 11, 7 In.	780.00
Bracelet, Link, Stylized Flowers, Sterling Silver, Impressed Marks, Kalo, 7 ½ In. *Illus*	549.00
Bracelet, Love, 18K Gold, Bezel Set Diamonds, A. Cipullo, Cartier, 1970, 5 ¾ In.	3851.00
Bracelet, Love, 18K Gold, Inset Screws, Cartier, 6 In.	3318.00

Jewelry, Bracelet, Cuff, Silver, Henry Steig, 6 ¼ In.
$521.00

Skinner, Inc.

Jewelry, Bracelet, Link, Stylized Flowers, Sterling Silver, Impressed Marks, Kalo, 7 ½ In.
$549.00

Treadway Toomey Galleries

Jewelry, Bracelet, Ram's Heads, Ruby Eyes, Textured, Ribbed, 18K Gold, La Laounis, Greece
$3,068.00

Brunk Auctions

Jewelry, Bracelet, Turquoise Cluster, Enamel, Bead & Rope Twist, 14K Gold, Hinge, Engraved, Victorian
$1,416.00

Brunk Auctions

TIP

If one link in your antique gold chain breaks, be very careful. There are probably other worn links that will soon break.

JEWELRY

Jewelry, Charm, Carousel, 3 Horses, 14K Gold, Rose Gold Horse, Stamped, Beverly Hills, 1 In.
$300.00

DuMouchelles Art Gallery

Jewelry, Charm, Mardi Gras, Mistick Krewe Of Comus, Gods & Goddesses, Gold, 1908
$538.00

Neal Auction Co.

Jewelry, Charm, Mardi Gras, Mistick Krewe Of Comus, Mahabharata, Sterling Silver, Enamel, 1903
$418.00

Neal Auction Co.

Jewelry, Earrings, Button, Pink, Goldtone Logo, Clip-On, Chanel, France, 1 ⅜ In.
$210.00

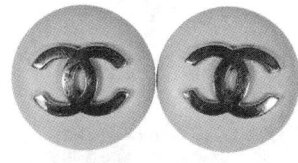

DuMouchelles Art Gallery

TIP
Use an old toothbrush to clean your jewelry.

Bracelet, Lucite, Lavender, Cabochons, Silver Filigree, Century, 1950s, 7 ¼ x 1 ½ In.	68.00
Bracelet, Lucite, Leaf, Moonstone, Lilac, Lavender, Purple, Lisner, 1950s, 7 In.	74.00
Bracelet, Mesh, 9 Octagonal Beads, Brushed Goldtone Metal, 7 x ⅞ In.	30.00
Bracelet, Mossi, 5 Rows Glass Cabochons, Silver, Lalique, 5 ¼ x 2 ⅝ In.	1200.00
Bracelet, Padlock Heart, Gold Filled, Victorian, 1860-80, 6 In., Pair	215.00
Bracelet, Padlock, Heart, Links, 15K Gold, Monogram, Edwardian, 1900, 7 ½ In.	895.00
Bracelet, Pearls, 2 Strands, Sterling Silver Toggle Clasp, Tiffany & Co., 7 ½ In.	235.00
Bracelet, Pearls, Marcasite, Sterling, Retro, 1940s, 7 ¾ x ¾ In.	165.00
Bracelet, Pietra Dura, 5 Oval Panels, Different Flowers, Grape Cluster, 18K Gold	3198.00
Bracelet, Plaques, 7 Moonstones, 18K Gold, Beaded, Rope Twist Trim, H. Haarstick, 7 In.	3555.00
Bracelet, Plaques, Diamonds, 18K White Gold, Jabel	1610.00
Bracelet, Plaques, Oval & Leafy, Sapphire Cabochons, Beaded, Silver, G. Jensen, 7 In.	1541.00
Bracelet, Plaques, Stylized Birds, Silver Pearls, Mohl-Hansen, G. Jensen, 7 ½ In.	652.00
Bracelet, Platinum Strap, Openwork, Arabesques, Diamonds, Emeralds, Art Deco, 7 ¼ In.	29038.00
Bracelet, Ram's Heads, Ruby Eyes, Textured, Ribbed, 18K Gold, La Laounis, Greece......*Illus*	3068.00
Bracelet, Reeded Band, Girl Holding Roses, Octagonal, Enamel, Moscow, c.1890, 2 ½ In.	2040.00
Bracelet, Rhinestone, White, 6 Tiers, Round, 3 Baguettes, c.1950, 7 x 1 In.	55.00
Bracelet, Silver Pearls, Leafy Borders, Large Links, G. Jensen, 7 In.	770.00
Bracelet, Silver, 4 Carved Carnelians, Fold-Over Clasp, Art Deco, 7 In.	161.00
Bracelet, Silver, Flower Links, Silver Pearls, Signed, Georg Jensen, 7 ½ In.	1422.00
Bracelet, Silver, Gold Wash, 8 Oval Faceted Amethysts, Victorian, 8 In.	242.00
Bracelet, Silver, Puffy Reeded Links, Interlocking C Shapes, Hinged Clasp, Bayanihan, 7 In.	219.00
Bracelet, Silver, Shell, Articulated, Vertical Links, Taxco, Mexico, 6 ¾ In.	173.00
Bracelet, Tennis, 25 Diamonds, Sapphires, Platinum, Tiffany & Co.	8855.00
Bracelet, Turquoise Cluster, Enamel, Bead & Rope Twist, 14K Gold, Hinge, Engraved, Victorian...*Illus*	1416.00
Buckle, 2 Hands, Linked At Thumbs, Silver, Tortoiseshell, W. Spratling, 4 In.	2015.00
Buckle, Alligator, Sterling Silver, Kieselstein-Cord, 3 In.	960.00
Buckle, Pastes, Round, Silver & Gilt Metal Mount, Victorian, 2 ⅜ In.	237.00
Chain, Chatelaine Clip & Pin Ball, Silver, Samuel Richards, Philadelphia, c.1800	1033.00
Charm, Carousel, 3 Horses, 14K Gold, Rose Gold Horse, Stamped, Beverly Hills, 1 In......*Illus*	300.00
Charm, Elephant, Coral, Carved, Diamond Stripe, Platinum, Art Deco, 1 In.	2607.00
Charm, Mardi Gras, Mistick Krewe Of Comus, Gods & Goddesses, Gold, 1908...........*Illus*	538.00
Charm, Mardi Gras, Mistick Krewe Of Comus, Mahabharata, Sterling Silver, Enamel, 1903 . *Illus*	418.00
Charm, Open Book, Class Book Committee, 1917, 14K Gold, ¾ x ⅞ In.	235.00
Charm, Round Inset Jewels, 18K Gold, Italy, c.1960, 1 ¼ In.	688.00
Chatelaine, Purse, Scissors, Knife, Pincushion, Pencil, Notepad, Opener, London, c.1850, 20 In.	1200.00
Chatelaine, Shaped Spiral, 3 Graduated Bead Borders, Silver, Tiffany, 2 In.	368.00
Chatelaine, Silver, Scissors, Thimble, Button Hook, Victorian	150.00
Cigarette Case, Ballerina, Diamond Hem, Ribbed Case, 18K Gold, Van Cleef & Arpels, 3 x 2 In.	8295.00
Cigarette Holder, Jade, Platinum Mount, Faceted, Diamonds, Leather Box, F. Gatti, Italy, c.1890, 4 In.	413.00
Clip, Dress, Bakelite, V Shape, Amber, Red & Green Semicircles, E.A. Phinney Co., 1931, 3 In., 4 Piece	115.00
Clip, Dress, Garnets, Spinels, Tourmalines, 14K Bicolor Gold Scroll, 1 ½ In., Pair	1778.00
Clip, Dress, Scallop Shell Shape, 14K Gold, Tiffany & Co., 1 In., Pair	1541.00
Clip, Dress, Stylized Ribbon, Flowers, Diamonds, 14K Gold, J.E. Caldwell, 1 ½ In., Pair	3437.00
Clip, Fibula, Ram's Head, Gold Ropework, Applied Beads, Etruscan Revival, 2 ⅜ In.	1304.00
Clip, Flower, 4 Diamond Petals, 18K Gold, Van Cleef & Arpels, 1 In.	3360.00
Clip, Fur Ruby, Diamond, 18K Gold, Retro, c.1935, 3 x 1 In.	403.00
Clip, Hair, Bow, Diamond Melee, Platinum, Beaded, Art Deco, 1 ⅜ In.	1080.00
Clip, Jester, 18K Gold, Coral Beads, Green Enamel, Diamonds, Van Cleef & Arpels, 2 In.	14400.00
Clip, Lantern, Figural, 18K Gold, Retro, 1 ¾ In.	960.00
Clip, Rock Crystal, Frosted, Diana With Bow, Diamond Surround, Art Deco, 1 ½ In.	2607.00
Clip, Stylized Bird, Diamonds, Platinum, Beaded Trim, Art Deco, Tiffany & Co., 1 In.	711.00
Clip, Sweater, 2 Flowers, 18K Gold, Ruby Melee Center, 3 Box Link Chains, Pair	2328.00
Cuff Links & Tie Tack, Nugget, 14K Gold	380.00
Cuff Links, 14K Bicolor Gold, Sapphire Cabochons, Octagonal, Sigler Bros., ½ In.	483.00
Cuff Links, 14K Gold, Ridged, Square Cut Ruby Stripe, Tiffany & Co.	1896.00
Cuff Links, 14K Gold, Round Rubies, Oval, Grooved Border, Hohenstine Jewelers, ¾ In.	265.00
Cuff Links, 14K White Gold, Round Cut Diamonds, Black Enamel, Rectangular, Halle Bros., ⅝ In.	265.00
Cuff Links, 2 Knots, 14K Gold, Box, Tiffany & Co.	840.00
Cuff Links, 2 Malachite Tablets, Oval, Seed Pearl Bar, Double Link, 14K Gold	830.00
Cuff Links, 2 Man In The Moon Faces, 1 Coral, 1 18K Gold, Round, Carved	1304.00
Cuff Links, Ball, Ribbed, 18K Gold, Sapphire Cabochons, Cartier, Box, c.1990	2252.00
Cuff Links, Black Onyx, Circle Of Diamonds, 18K Gold Double Link, France	1007.00
Cuff Links, Bulldog, Front & Back Linked Together, Silver	652.00
Cuff Links, Cameo, Hardstone, Blackamoor Bust, Gold	2607.00
Cuff Links, Cushion Shape, Scroll & Bead Border, 18K Gold, Arts & Crafts, Tiffany	2760.00

Cuff Links, Devil's Head, Sterling Silver, Diamond Melee Eyes, Sapphire Mouth, ⅞ In.	326.00
Cuff Links, Game Bird Shape, Rectangular Baton, 14K Gold, Shell Case	444.00
Cuff Links, Game Birds, Shorebirds, Reverse Painted Glass, 14K Gold	1560.00
Cuff Links, Glass Ovals, Goldtone Metal, Swank, c.1960, Men's, 1 In.	55.00
Cuff Links, Grid, Oval, 14K Gold, Cartier	444.00
Cuff Links, Grotesque Faces, Dragon, Silver, Henrik Moller, Norway	948.00
Cuff Links, Horse's Head, Glass, Reverse Painted, 14K Gold Disc	652.00
Cuff Links, Lion's Head, 14K Gold, Demantoid Garnet Eyes, Art Nouveau, ⅝ In.	1440.00
Cuff Links, Mercury, Lapis, Intaglio, Oval, Brushed 18K Gold Gadroon Mount, Lebeau, 1 In.	900.00
Cuff Links, Moonstone, Bezel Set, 14K Gold Double Link Mount	385.00
Cuff Links, Moonstone, Heart-Shaped, Sapphire & Diamond Surround, 14K Gold	3081.00
Cuff Links, Mother-Of-Pearl Discs, Diamond Melee, Platinum Over 14K Gold Mount, Howe & Co.	385.00
Cuff Links, Platinum Over Gold, Round Cut Diamond, Engraved, Pair	556.00
Cuff Links, Playing Cards, 4 Aces, 14 K Gold, Black & Red Enamel, Cartier	2640.00
Cuff Links, Poodles, Seated, Silver, Fenwick & Sailors, 1 x 1 In.	84.00
Cuff Links, Rectangle, Ribbed, 14K Gold, Tiffany & Co.	770.00
Cuff Links, Rock Crystal, 2 Octagons, Line Of Diamonds, 14K Double Link Mount	1067.00
Cuff Links, Sardine Can, Half Of Top Rolled Back With Opener, Silver, ⅞ In.	711.00
Cuff Links, Square, Oval, Synthetic Sapphire Bar, Diamond, Platinum Over Gold, Art Deco	948.00
Cuff Links, Stylized Knots, 18K Gold, Black Enamel Accents, Verdura, 1 In.	2100.00
Cuff Links, Turquoise Cabochons, Oval, Platinum, Double Link	490.00
Dress Set, Man's, Iolite, Carved, Diamond Melee, 18K Gold, S. Schepps	2133.00
Dress Set, Man's, Malachite Tablet, Oval, Onyx Frame, Gold Mount, Larter, 5 Piece	593.00
Dress Set, Man's, Mother-Of-Pearl Tablet, Seed Pearl Center, Double Link, 14K Gold, Larter	593.00
Dress Set, Man's, Navette Shape, 18K Gold, Diamond X, Round Studs, 5 Piece	750.00
Dress Set, Man's, Onyx Tablets, Platinum Over Gold Mount, Larter & Sons, 5 Piece	652.00
Dress Set, Man's, Sapphire, Emerald & Diamond Borders, Platinum, Art Deco, 5 Piece	5036.00
Dress Set, Men's, Button, Onyx Disc, 18K Gold Rim, 2 Crossed Stitches, Tiffany, 5 Piece	1800.00
Dress Set, Men's, Onyx Disc, Platinum & Diamond Basket Weave, Edwardian, 4 Piece	1800.00
Earrings, 2 Rectangles, Bubbles, Copper, Brass, H. Harmon, Mexico, 1950s, 1 ½ In.	106.00
Earrings, 2 Shaped Cabochon Peridot, Joined By Diamond, 18K Gold, Donna Vock, 1 ¾ In.	1148.00
Earrings, 5 Flowers Opals, Diamond, Clip-On, Marked, Hardy Bros., ½ In.	480.00
Earrings, 14K Bicolor Gold, Round, Clip-On, Cartier, ¾ In.	472.00
Earrings, 18K Gold, Peridot, Pear Cut, Round Cut Diamonds, Eli Frei, 1 In.	2185.00
Earrings, Amazonite, Kite Shape, 2 Suspended Coral Batons, Marcasite, Art Deco, 2 In.	770.00
Earrings, Amethyst, Snowflake Shape, Pierced, 1980s, ¾ In.	20.00
Earrings, Aquamarine, Diamond Melee, 14K Gold Leafy Mount, S. Schepps, ¾ In.	2133.00
Earrings, Aquamarine, Oval, Sapphire Surround, 18K White Gold, Seaman Schepps, 1 In.	1659.00
Earrings, Baroque Pearls, Rhinestones, Brushed Gold Flower, Miriam Haskell, 2 ½ In.	141.00
Earrings, Blue Topaz Pyramid, 18K Bicolor Gold Square Mount, Bulgari, 1 In.	1541.00
Earrings, Butterfly, Abstract, 18K Gold, Clip-On, Angela Cummings, 1993, 1 In.	2214.00
Earrings, Button, Pink, Goldtone Logo, Clip-On, Chanel, France, 1 ⅜ In. ....*Illus*	210.00
Earrings, Cable, Silver, 14K Gold, Carnelian Cabochon, Turquoise, David Yurman, ¾ x ⅜ In.	230.00
Earrings, Cascade, Sapphires, Square Cut, Diamonds, 18K Gold, Fred Leighton, 1 In.	2252.00
Earrings, Checkerboard, 18K Gold, Inlaid Mother-Of-Pearl, Tiffany & Co., ¾ In.	2280.00
Earrings, Drop, Bohemian Glass, Red, White, Blue Beads, Geometric, Art Deco, Clip-On, 1950s, 2 In.	38.00
Earrings, Doorknocker Shape, 18K Gold, Black Onyx Accent, Tiffany & Co., 1 ⅝ In.	2015.00
Earrings, Double Hoop, Brass, Art Smith, 1 ½ In. ....*Illus*	504.00
Earrings, Drop, 18K White Gold, Silver, Pearls, Diamond Oval Links, Eli Frei, 2 In.	2185.00
Earrings, Drop, Chalcedony, Torpedo-Shape, Gold Garland Frame, c.1830, 3 In.	2370.00
Earrings, Drop, Pearl, Pave Rhinestones, Raised Leaf, Silver Metal, Box, 1960s, 2 x ¾ In.	68.00
Earrings, Emerald, Pearl, 14K Gold, Oval Sections, Wire Hooks, Victorian, 1 ¾ In.	776.00
Earrings, Fan, Fluted, Maroon, Patinated Metal, Clip-On, JAR, 3 In.	5333.00
Earrings, Faux Pearl, Goldtone, Textured Border, Clip-On, Chanel, 1 In. ....*Illus*	180.00
Earrings, Feather Form, 18K Gold, Clip-On, Cartier, 1 In.	1164.00
Earrings, Fireworks, 18K Gold, Pearl Center, Clip-On, Tiffany & Co., 1 ⅛ In.	1020.00
Earrings, Fish Holding Pearl, Round, 18K Textured Gold, F. Scarini, 1 ½ In.	1422.00
Earrings, Fleur-De-Lis, Copper, Clip-On, Renoir, 1950s, 1 ¼ In.	44.00
Earrings, Flower, 8 Petals, Clear & Turquoise Rhinestones, Clip-On, Hobe, 1 In.	55.00
Earrings, Flower, Gold Openwork Medallion, Green Glass Cabochon, 1960s, 2 ¼ x 1 ⅝ In.	37.00
Earrings, Flower, Shaped Petals, 18K Gold, Clip-On, Chaumet, Paris, 1 In.	1007.00
Earrings, Flower, Silver, Pearls, Marked, Georg Jensen, ⅞ In.	267.00
Earrings, Half Hoop, 50's, Coral Cabochons, 18K Gold, S. Schepps, 1 In.	5925.00
Earrings, Half Hoop, H Form, 18K Gold, Hermes, 1 ½ In.	948.00
Earrings, Harley-Davidson, 14K Gold, Red Enamel, Elongated Diamond Shape, c.1985, 2 ½ In.	58.00
Earrings, Hoop, Alhambra, 18K Gold, Clip-On, Van Cleef & Arpels, 1 ⅜ In.	9480.00

Jewelry, Earrings, Double Hoop, Brass, Art Smith, 1 ½ In.
$504.00

Skinner, Inc.

Jewelry, Earrings, Faux Pearl, Goldtone, Textured Border, Clip-On, Chanel, 1 In.
$180.00

DuMouchelles Art Gallery

Jewelry, Earrings, Pearl, Onyx, Coral, Malachite, Diamonds, 18K, Asch Grossbardt, 1 In.
$1,320.00

Skinner, Inc.

Jewelry, Earrings, Teardrop, Blue Jasper, White Classical Figures, Wedgwood, c.1800, 1 ⅛ In.
$660.00

Skinner, Inc.

Jewelry, Earrings, Turbo Shell, Coral & Emerald Terminals, 14K Gold, Clip-On, Seaman Schepps, 1 ½ In.
$1,164.00

Skinner, Inc.

J

Jewelry, Fob, Scarab, Turquoise, Plique-A-Jour Enamel, Diamonds, 18K Gold, Art Nouveau, 4 ¼ In.
$8,888.00

Skinner, Inc.

Jewelry, Necklace, Berlin Ironwork, Gothic Discs, Lacy Designs, c.1810
$1,717.00

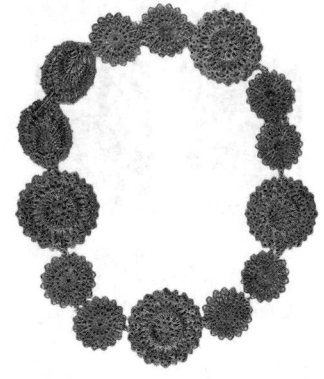

Neal Auction Co.

Jewelry, Necklace, Gardenia Blossoms, 3 Large, 4 Small, Silver, Marked, Buccellati, Italy, Box, 31 In.
$1,845.00

Skinner, Inc.

Earrings, Hoop, Pastel Flowers, Pewter, Embossed, Scrolls, Art Nouveau Style, 1970s, 1 ¾ In..	28.00
Earrings, Huggies, Diamond Insets, 18K Gold, Platinum, Clip-On, Marked, Tiffany & Co........	2530.00
Earrings, Kokeshi Doll, Figural Wood, Painted, Screw Backs, Japan, 1950s, 1 ½ In.................	14.00
Earrings, Lady Bug, 18K Gold, Red & Black Enamel, Cartier, c.1990, ⅝ In.	3851.00
Earrings, Lapis, Oval Cabochon, 18K Gold Cone-Shaped Studs, A. Cummings, 1 In.................	4148.00
Earrings, Leaf, Geranium, Green, Red Veining, Patinated, Clip-On, JAR, 1 ¼ In.	4148.00
Earrings, Leaf, Metal, Bergere, ¾ In.	295.00
Earrings, Leaf, Textured 18K Gold, Diamond Accents, Clip-On, McTeigue, 1 ¼ In.	474.00
Earrings, Mabe Pearl, Double Ring Mount, 18K Gold, Clip-On, Gucci, ⅞ In.	889.00
Earrings, Moonstone Cabochon, Abstract Form, 18K Gold, Clip-On, Trudel, 1 ⅛ In.	652.00
Earrings, Mourning, Heart Drop, Incised, Gold Woven Hair, Netting, c.1860, ½ In.	185.00
Earrings, Oak Leaves, Acorns, Diamonds, 18K Gold, Platinum, Shreve, Crump & Low, 1 In.	1422.00
Earrings, Pearl Center, Diamonds, 18K Gold Clip-On, Schlumberger, ⅞ In..........................	5925.00
Earrings, Pearl, 18K Gold Ribbed Ribbon Mount, Schlumberger, Tiffany & Co., 1 ⅜ In..........	1778.00
Earrings, Pearl, Button Shape, Clip-On, Tiffany, Italy, 1950s...	805.00
Earrings, Pearl, Onyx, Coral, Malachite, Diamonds, 18K, Asch Grossbardt, 1 In.............*Illus*	1320.00
Earrings, Pearl, Rhinestone, Gold Leaf Clusters, Trifari, 1950s, 1 x ¾ In...............................	38.00
Earrings, Pendant, Alhambra, Mother-Of-Pearl, 18K Gold, Van Cleef & Arpels, 2 In.................	5096.00
Earrings, Pendant, Citrine Cluster, 3 Suspended Columns, 18K Gold, M. Cooperman, 3 In.	3555.00
Earrings, Pendant, Gitan, 3 Scroll & Ropework Beads, 18K Gold, C. Bach, 2 ¼ In...................	1067.00
Earrings, Pendant, Hawaii, Cascade, Wirework Rings, 18K Gold, Buccellati, 2 ⅝ In.	4444.00
Earrings, Pendant, Silver, Abstract Open Triangles, Ed Wiener, 3 ¼ In.	1659.00
Earrings, Pillow, Square, 18K Gold, Hammered, Beaded X, Clip-On, E. Locke, ¾ In.	1304.00
Earrings, Pink Cabochon, Rhinestones, Silver Rope Twist Wire Work, Hobe, 1 In.	75.00
Earrings, Rose, 18K Textured Gold, Diamond Melee Accents, Clip-On, Garrard, 1 ⅜ In.	948.00
Earrings, Scroll, S-Shaped, Ribbed, 18K Gold, Tiffany & Co., 1 In.	1164.00
Earrings, Shell, Rock Crystal, Diamond Rim, 18K White Gold, Clip-On, Vhernier, 1 In...........	4148.00
Earrings, Silver, Amethyst Drop, Screwback, Antonia Pineda, Mexico, ¾ x 2 In......................	563.00
Earrings, Silver, Pyramid Top, Oval Hoop Drop, Marked, Hermes	184.00
Earrings, Spray, Diamonds, 7 Cascading Strips, 18K White Gold, R. Coin, 2 In.......................	2370.00
Earrings, Stylized Flower, 5 Petals, Green Melon Glass, Rhinestones, Miriam Haskell, 1 In.....	155.00
Earrings, Stylized Knot, 18K Gold, Hammered, Henry Dunay, 1 ⅜ In.	1715.00
Earrings, Stylized Leaf, 18K Gold, Omega Backs, Marked, Tiffany, ⅞ In.	633.00
Earrings, Stylized Petal, Goldtone, Textured & Polished, Clip-On, JAR, Paris, 1 ¾ In.	1920.00
Earrings, Stylized Ribbon, Curled, Beaded Strip, 18K Gold, Kieselstein-Cord, 1982, 1 In.........	1778.00
Earrings, Teardrop, Blue Jasper, White Classical Figures, Wedgwood, c.1800, 1 ⅛ In........*Illus*	660.00
Earrings, Turbo Shell, 14K Gold, Chalcedony Terminals, Seaman Schepps, 1 ½ In...................	1896.00
Earrings, Turbo Shell, Coral & Emerald Terminals, 14K Gold, Clip-On, Seaman Schepps, 1 ½ In.*Illus*	1164.00
Earrings, Turbo Shell, Turquoise & Coral Terminals, 14K Gold Mount, S. Schepps, 1 In.	1659.00
Earrings, Yellow Sapphire, 18K Gold, Tiffany & Co..	690.00
Fob, Scarab, Turquoise, Plique-A-Jour Enamel, Diamonds, 18K Gold, Art Nouveau, 4 ¼ In.....*Illus*	8888.00
Hairpin, 3 Rows Of Diamonds, Platinum Over Gold Mount, Edwardian..................................	711.00
Hatpins are listed in this book in the Hatpin category.	
Headband, Black Celluloid, Brass, Molded, Filigree Inserts, Edwardian, c.1910, 12 ½ x 5 In...	68.00
Jabot, Moonstone, Fluted, Diamonds, Black Enamel, Platinum Mount, Art Deco, 2 In............	3900.00
Locket, 18K Gold, Woven Design, Van Cleef & Arpels, 1 ½ In..	1185.00
Locket, 18K Matte Gold, Diamond Monogram, 2 Compartments, Tiffany & Co., 1 ½ In.	2015.00
Locket, Art Nouveau, Woman's Profile, Flowing Hair, Silver, Oval, c.1910, 1 ½ x 1 In..............	145.00
Locket, Cameo, Hardstone, Psyche Profile, Bead & Ropework Frame, 18K Gold, 1 ¼ In..........	830.00
Locket, Pierrot Head, 14K Gold, 7 Diamonds, Monogram On Reverse, Art Nouveau, 1 In........	563.00
Necklace & Bracelet, Link, Amethyst, Silver, Scrolls, Beaded, M. De Taxco, 16-In. Necklace ...	1200.00
Necklace & Bracelet, Link, Brickwork, 14K Gold, Faux Buckle, Rubies, Diamonds, Retro	2726.00
Necklace & Bracelet, Link, Domed, Wing Shape, Silver, M. De Taxco, 15 ¼-In. Necklace	770.00
Necklace & Earrings, Bead Clusters, Pink, Yellow, Blue, Green, Miriam Haskell, 29 In...........	106.00
Necklace & Earrings, Beads, Orange Iridescent, Large & Small, 2 Strands, Marvella	25.00
Necklace & Earrings, Leaves, Yellow Green Lucite, Gold Metal, Marvella, 16 In.-Necklace.....	23.00
Necklace, 12 Beads, Silver, Openwork, Black Velvet Cord, Antonio Pinedo, Taxco, 28 In.........	984.00
Necklace, 18K White Gold, Pendant Stamped T & Co., Bezel Set Round Brilliant Cut Diamond, 16 In.	518.00
Necklace, Amethysts, 21 Graduated, Oval Cut, Ruby Beads, Seed Pearls, India, Victorian, 17 In.	649.00
Necklace, Aquamarine, 14K Gold, 3 Sections, Seed Pearl Border, Enamel, Arts & Crafts, 18 In..	2300.00
Necklace, Baroque Pearls, 2 Strands, Cabochon Clasp, Gold Leaves, Robert DeMario, 1950s, 25 In.	195.00
Necklace, Beads, 5 Strands, Dimpled, 18K Gold, Robert Lee Morris, 16 ½ In............................	11258.00
Necklace, Beads, Clear, Faceted, Graduated, 3 Strands, Marvella, 16 In................................	135.00
Necklace, Beads, Glass, Murano, Pink Millefiori Roses, Crystals, 2 Strands, 1950s, 18 ½ In.....	120.00
Necklace, Beads, Ivory, Graduated, c.1900, 30 In..	106.00
Necklace, Beads, Milk Glass, Metal Caps, 6 Strands, Miriam Haskell, 18 In...........................	37.00

Necklace, Berlin Ironwork, Gothic Discs, Lacy Designs, c.1810 ....*Illus*	1717.00
Necklace, Black Velvet, Brass Filigree Band, Victorian, c.1900, 26 In.	115.00
Necklace, Bracelet & Earrings, Link, Double Angel, Beads, Silver, Victoria, Taxco....................	360.00
Necklace, Chain, Brushed Nugget Links, 18K Gold, Marked Marco Bicego, 36 In.	2933.00
Necklace, Choker, Chain Links, Silver, Mexico, 1980s, 7 ¼ x 1 ⅜ In.........................	500.00
Necklace, Choker, Diagonal Links, Brushed Gold Rectangular Panels, Hobe, 14 In...............	75.00
Necklace, Choker, Sterling, Chain Links, Return To Tiffany & Co. Tag, 15 In.	360.00
Necklace, Collar, Silver, Chain Link, Flowers, Marked, Margot De Taxco, c.1960, 15 ¾ In....	1020.00
Necklace, Earrings & Pin, Cameo, Onyx, Split Pearls, Faceted Beads & Drops, Tiffany............	1800.00
Necklace, Fire Opals, Round, Oval & Navette, Beaded Frames, Links, Arts & Crafts, 23 In.......	1896.00
Necklace, Freshwater Pearls, 9 Strands, Abstract Coral & Gold Clasp, A. King, 30 In.	1680.00
Necklace, Gardenia Blossoms, 3 Large, 4 Small, Silver, Marked, Buccellati, Italy, Box, 31 In. .....*Illus*	1845.00
Necklace, Gitan, Scroll & Ropework Beads, 18K Gold, C. Bach, 21 In.	1896.00
Necklace, Half & Half, Free-Form Brass, Art Smith, c.1955, 8 ½ In.	12500.00
Necklace, Jadeite, Emeralds, Round Cut, Double Strand, 14K Gold Wreath Clasp, 28 In.	1179.00
Necklace, Lariat, Silver Wheat Link, Quatrefoil Toggle, Diamonds, David Yurman, 14 In.......	575.00
Necklace, Leaf Shape, Opal, Pearl, 14K Gold, Inlay, Twist Rope Chain, Ray Tracey, 16 In.	449.00
Necklace, Link, 18K White Gold, Brushed Pebble & Diamond, Marco Bicego, 16 In.	1898.00
Necklace, Link, Abstract, 18K Gold, Van Cleef & Arpels, 30 In.	3081.00
Necklace, Link, Barrel, Diamond Melee, Platinum, Van Cleef & Arpels, 23 In.	5036.00
Necklace, Link, Butterfly Shape, Silver, Trifari, Retro Modern, 1950s, 16 In.	95.00
Necklace, Link, Curb, 18K Gold, Dorfman, Germany, 17 ½ In.	9125.00
Necklace, Link, Dogwood Flowers, 14K Bicolor Gold, Aquamarine Drop, Retro, 15 In......	1541.00
Necklace, Link, Leafy, Silver, Georg Jensen, 16 In.	830.00
Necklace, Link, Plain & Etched Zigzags, Silver, Tiffany & Co., 16 In...........................	450.00
Necklace, Link, Round Pendant, Silver, G. Jensen, 16-In. Chain, 2 ½-In. Pendant	1708.00
Necklace, Link, Silver, Scrolls, Amethyst Stones, Margot DeTaxco, 15 In.........................	660.00
Necklace, Link, Square, Black, White & Copper Red Enamel, Silver, M. DeTaxco, 15 In.	679.00
Necklace, Link, Triangular, Interchangeable, Bicolor Gold, J. Fouquet, 9 In.	9480.00
Necklace, Link, Twisted, 18 K Gold, Red Enamel, 11 Charms, Fabor, Italy, 1960s, 27 ½ In.......	2185.00
Necklace, Link, V-Form, Overlapping, Riveted, Beaded, Margot DeTaxco, 15 x 1 In.	525.00
Necklace, Link, X, Double Oval, 18K Gold, Schlumberger, Tiffany & Co., Box, 18 In. ....*Illus*	5688.00
Necklace, Locket, Maiden, Flowing Hair, 14K Gold, 3 Diamonds, Chain, 16 Citrines, 58 In......	2963.00
Necklace, Locket, Mourning, Etruscan Revival, Flying Bird, Bookchain, c.1860, 20 In.	295.00
Necklace, Locket, Puffed Heart, Japanese Engravings, Silver, 1930s, 16 ½ In.	135.00
Necklace, Logo Discs, Faux Pearls, Goldtone, Chanel, France, 74 In.............................*Illus*	780.00
Necklace, Maguey, Stylized Plant, Silver, Hector Aguilar, Taxco, 16 In.......................*Illus*	2607.00
Necklace, Mandarin's Hat Plume Holder, Jade, Double Gourd, Flowers, Beads, 1800s, 36 In....	2415.00
Necklace, Niki Pearls, Baroque Gold, Miriam Haskell, 1950s, 61 In...........................	110.00
Necklace, Pearl Clusters, Goldtone Metal Mount, Marvella, 17 x ½ In...........................	25.00
Necklace, Pearl Tassel, Diamond Caps, Platinum & Pearl Chain, Edwardian, 33 In...............	7703.00
Necklace, Pearls, 2 Strands, Diamond, Ruby, Turquoise, Sapphire Clasp, Erwin Paltscho, 27 In....	1180.00
Necklace, Pearls, 66 Graduated, 18K Gold Clasp, Pearl Accent, Mikimoto, 18 In.	984.00
Necklace, Pearls, 99 Graduated, 14K Gold Clasp, Mikimoto, 29 In.	3120.00
Necklace, Pearls, Freshwater, Graduated, High Luster, Keshi, 17 In............................	276.00
Necklace, Pearls, Gray, Gold Beads, 4 Strands, Platinum, 18K Gold, Tiffany & Co., 17 In.........	7110.00
Necklace, Pegasus, Silver Rhodium, Arched Ribbed Drapes, Coro, 16 In.	85.00
Necklace, Pendant, Abstract, Pink Tourmaline, Arched Tubes, Silver, 18K Gold, Janiye, 17 ½ In.. *Illus*	2963.00
Necklace, Pendant, Cameo, Moonstone, Maiden's Bust, Sapphire Surround, 1920, 25 In.	14220.00
Necklace, Pendant, Cross, 18K Textured Gold, Oval-Link Chain, E. Locke, 16 In......................	1659.00
Necklace, Pendant, Cross, Rhinestones, Elliptical Sections, Paper Clip Chain, Hobe, 2 ½ In.	139.00
Necklace, Pendant, Diamond Knot, 14K Gold Curb Link Chain, Van Cleef & Arpels	2205.00
Necklace, Pendant, Magnifying Glass, Goldtone, Chanel, France, 36 In...........................*Illus*	780.00
Necklace, Pendant, Sunburst Medallion, Copper, Turquoise Teardrop Points, 1950s, 26 In.	70.00
Necklace, Pin & Earrings, Plaques, Black & White Enamel, Silver, M. De Taxco	652.00
Necklace, Pink Coral, Bubble, Beads, 4 Strand, Japan, 1950s, 18 ¼ In...	95.00
Necklace, Plaque, Emeralds, Peridot, Chalcedony, M. Matsukata, Janiye, c.1978, 6 In. ....*Illus*	16590.00
Necklace, Plaques, Links, Leaves & Buds, Silver, Green Onyx Clasp, G. Jensen, 17 In................	1422.00
Necklace, Red Lucite, Faceted, Barrel Shape, Spring Clasp, Art Deco Style, 1950s, 25 In.	58.00
Necklace, Rock Crystal, Graduated, Faceted Beads, Toggle Clasp, 19 In. ....*Illus*	522.00
Necklace, Silver, 8-Chain, 5 Diamond Beads, Lobster Clasp, 18K Gold, David Yurman, 18 In. .	863.00
Necklace, Squash Blossom, Spider Web Turquoise, Silver Beads, Filework Tips, 1950, 24 In....	633.00
Necklace, Tassel, Gold, Thick Braids, Monet, 1950s, 43 In.	120.00
Necklace, Turquoise, Nuggets, Graduated, c.1970, 18 ½ In....................................	288.00
Necklace, Vermeil, Plique-A-Jour, Pastel Floral Geometrics, 3 Chain Tassels, Arts & Crafts, 3 x 16 In.	437.00
Parure, Necklace, Bracelet, Earrings, Coral, Silver, Rebecca Collins, Neiman Marcus, 18-In. Necklace	1012.00

Jewelry, Necklace, Link, X, Double Oval, 18K Gold, Schlumberger, Tiffany & Co., Box, 18 In.
$5,688.00

Skinner, Inc.

Jewelry, Necklace, Logo Discs, Faux Pearls, Goldtone, Chanel, France, 74 In.
$780.00

DuMouchelles Art Gallery

Jewelry, Necklace, Maguey, Stylized Plant, Silver, Hector Aguilar, Taxco, 16 In.
$2607.00

Skinner, Inc.

Jewelry, Necklace, Pendant, Abstract, Pink Tourmaline, Arched Tubes, Silver, 18K Gold, Janiye, 17 ½ In.
$2,963.00

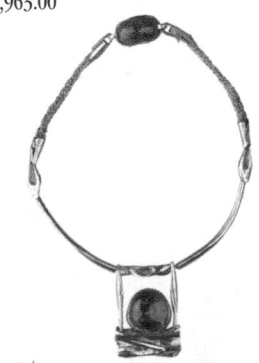

Skinner, Inc.

J

Jewelry, Necklace, Pendant, Magnifying Glass, Goldtone, Chanel, France, 36 In. $780.00

DuMouchelles Art Gallery

Jewelry, Necklace, Plaque, Emeralds, Peridot, Chalcedony, M. Matsukata, Janiye, c.1978, 6 In. $16,590.00

Skinner, Inc.

Jewelry, Necklace, Rock Crystal, Graduated, Faceted Beads, Toggle Clasp, 19 In. $522.00

New Orleans Auction Galleries, Inc.

Pendant, Amethyst, Amazonite & Marcasite Accents, Silver, Jugendstil, T. Fahrner, 2 In.	889.00
Pendant, Amethyst, Garnet, Silver Gilt, Austria-Hungary, 1880-1900, 2 ¼ x 1 ³⁄₁₆ In.	245.00
Pendant, Amethyst, Oval Leafy Frame, 18K Gold, Diamond Accents, 1920s, 2 In.	3437.00
Pendant, Butterfly, Jade, Openwork, 1800s, 2 ½ x 3 ½ In.	796.00
Pendant, Cameo, Moonstone, Maiden, Upswept Hair, 14K Gold Scrolling Mount, 2 ½ In.	1659.00
Pendant, Carved Mask, Jade, Smooth Bottom, 2 ½ x 1 ½ In.	35.00
Pendant, Carved Peach Blossoms, Jade, Green & White, Mounted As Lamp Finial, 2 ½ In.	1100.00
Pendant, Chain, Opalescent Glass, 14K Gold, Art Deco, 16 In.	230.00
Pendant, Cross, Concave Interlocking Circles, Silk Cord, Orlando Orlandini, 4 ½ In.	711.00
Pendant, Cross, Emerald & Ruby Cabochons, Split Pearls, Rose Cut Diamonds, 3 ¼ In...*Illus*	3851.00
Pendant, Cross, Enamel, Leaf & Vine Design, 14K Gold, Victorian, 3 In.	708.00
Pendant, Cross, Pelican Center, Yellow, Green & Clear Pastes, Silver, 4 ½ In. ....*Illus*	563.00
Pendant, Diamond Cutout, Pierced, 18K White Gold, Tapered Bail, Edwardian, c.1890, 1 ¼ x ¼ In.	425.00
Pendant, Face, Abstract, 23K Gold, Pablo Picasso, Box, c.1998. ....*Illus*	16590.00
Pendant, Flower, Abstract, 18K Textured Gold, Slides On Brown Cord, Amalia, 2 ¾ In.	4148.00
Pendant, Flower, Glass, Pate-De-Verre, G. Argy-Rousseau, Cord, Tassel, 2 ½ In.	1560.00
Pendant, Flower, Rhinestones, Blue & Clear Stones, Detachable Chain, Christian Dior, 1969, 3 In.	330.00
Pendant, Heart With Crown, Amethyst, 9K Gold, Birmingham, c.1910, 1 ½ In..............*Illus*	889.00
Pendant, Heart, Arrow, Pink Sapphires, Diamonds, 18K White Gold, T. Fennell, 1 In.	1126.00
Pendant, Heart, Puffed, Suspended From Baton Link Chain, Silver, Georg Jensen, 3 In.	652.00
Pendant, Horse, Monkey, Bee, Jade, White, Chinese, 1700s, 1 ½ In.	1230.00
Pendant, Insect, Glass, Pate-De-Verre, Relief, Brown & Gold, 2 ⅛ In. ....*Illus*	350.00
Pendant, Jade, White, Carved, 2 Fish, Round, Chinese, 2 In.	236.00
Pendant, Jade, White, Ruji Shape, Shou Symbol, Flowers, Green Silk Cord, Chinese, c.1945, 2 x 3 In.	480.00
Pendant, Madonna, White Resin, Plique-A-Jour Frame, Diamonds, Art Nouveau, 2 In.	444.00
Pendant, Mourning, Child's Silhouette, Moth & Shell Verso, Heart Shape Frame, c.1810, 2 ¼ In.	360.00
Pendant, Owl, Ivory, Gem Eyes, Emerald Bow Tie, 14K Gold Glasses, 1960s, 2 ¼ In.	374.00
Pendant, Peacock, Plique-A-Jour, In Loop, 18K Gold, Trace Link Chain, France, 1 ¾ In.	1126.00
Pendant, Pin, Heart, Silver, Brass, Carol Summers, 4 ¾ x 4 ⅛ In. ....*Illus*	1541.00
Pendant, Pin, Silver Over Gold, Open Curvilinear, Diamonds, Emeralds, Edwardian, 1 ¾ x 1 ½ In.	483.00
Pendant, Rabbit, Twisted Wire, 18K Gold, Ruby Eye, Diamonds, Van Cleef & Arpels, 2 In.	1800.00
Pendant, Sapphire, Blue, 2 Diamond Rows, 14K Gold, Oval, c.1980, 1 ⅛ x ⅞ In.	4960.00
Pendant, Scent, Urn, Enamel, Silver, Courting Couple, Egg Shape, Silver Gilt, Austria, c.1890, 1 ⅞ In.	708.00
Pendant, Spider Web, Rose Cut Diamonds, Ruby Spider, Carnelian, 20K Gold, Coomi, 2 In...*Illus*	1440.00
Pendant, St. Christopher, 18K Gold, Cartier, ⅞ In.	770.00
Pendant, Sunburst, 12 Rays, 14K Gold, 49 Diamonds, c.1875, 1 ¼ In.	1416.00
Pendant, Vinaigrette, Cone Shape, Rounded Cap, Engraved Accents, 1 ½ In.	444.00
Pendant, Watch, Split Pearls, Rose Cut Rubies, Ivory Dial, Arabic Numerals, 1 ⅜ In.	2370.00
Pendant, Woman, Staff, Silver, Enamels, Pearls, Gemstones, Renaissance Revival, 2 ¼ x 1 ½ In.	920.00
Pendant, Wreath, Gold, Rubies, Translucent Enamel, Egg Shape, Russia, c.1900, 2 In.	1440.00
Pendant, Zodiac, Cancer, 18K Gold, Reticulated, Stainless, Leather Cord, Marked, Bulgari, 16 ½ In.	437.00
Pin & Earrings, Bow, Pave Turquoise & Pearls, Tassel Earrings, S.J. Phillips, 2-In. Pin	5925.00
Pin & Earrings, Cameo, Coral, Satyr Heads, Grapes, Flowers, Gold Mount, Tiffany	1020.00
Pin & Earrings, Coral, Grape Cluster, Gold, Victorian, 2 ¼-In. Pin, 1 ½-In. Earrings	1298.00
Pin & Earrings, Flower, Sphere, 14K Bicolor Gold, Blue Enamel, Cartier, 1 ½-In. Pin	593.00
Pin & Earrings, Leafy Branch, Zircon & Pearl Clusters, Edward Oakes, 2-In. Pin	2370.00
Pin & Earrings, Lily Of The Valley, Enamel, Pink, Green, Seed Pearls, 14K Gold, Krementz	1225.00
Pin & Earrings, Maison Gripoix Glass, Faux Pearls, Goldtone, Chanel, France, 2-⅝ In. Pin.....*Illus*	420.00
Pin & Earrings, Oak, Gold, Citrine, Black Paint, L. Nevelson, 1965, 7-In, Earring, 4 In. Pin	16250.00
Pin, 2 Flowers, Pink & Violet Rhinestones, Silver Openwork, Hobe, 1940, 2 In.	250.00
Pin, 2 Horse's Heads, Glass, Reverse Painted, Stirrup Mount, 14K Gold, 1 ½ In.	1185.00
Pin, 2 Snowflakes, Engraved, Diamonds, 14K Gold Rectangular Mount, 1950, 1 ⅜ In.	2447.00
Pin, 2 Stylized Buds, Sapphires, Diamond Melee Accent, 18K Gold, Tiffany & Co., 3 In.	1304.00
Pin, 3 Monkeys, 18K Bicolor Gold, Platinum, Chaumet, 1 ¾ In. ....*Illus*	889.00
Pin, Abstract Star, Textured Rods, 18K Gold, Ed Wiener, 3 ½ In. ....*Illus*	1140.00
Pin, Abstract, Blue Geode, Sapphire & Diamond Melee, Granulated Gold, A. King, 3 In.	2880.00
Pin, Abstract, Textured, Gemstone Cluster, Diamonds, 18K Gold, E. Wiener, 16 ½ In........*Illus*	1422.00
Pin, Aquamarine, 14K Gold Leafy Mount, Diamond Melee, S. Schepps, 1 ½ In.	7110.00
Pin, Bakelite, 3 Red Cherries, Green Stem & Leaves, 1930s, 2 ⅜ In.	225.00
Pin, Bakelite, Cherries, Green Leaves, Hanging From Bar, 3 ½ In.	120.00
Pin, Bakelite, Red, Rhinestone, Geometric, Half Discs, Rounded Faceted Frame, 1940s, 2 x 2 ¾ In.	145.00
Pin, Bar, 12 Diamonds, Platinum, 14K Gold, 1920, 2 In.	1984.00
Pin, Bar, 14K Gold, Rubies, Diamond, Star Shapes, Victorian, 2 x ⅝ In.	121.00
Pin, Bar, Flowers, Reticulated, 14K Gold, Blue Sapphire, Art Deco, 2 ½ In.	150.00
Pin, Bar, Medallion Ends, 4 Suspended Coins, Silver, Art Nouveau, G. Shiebler, 3 In.	356.00
Pin, Bar, Oval, 14K Gold, Blue Sapphire, Art Deco, c.1920, 1 ½ In.	150.00

Jewelry, Pendant, Cross, Emerald & Ruby Cabochons, Split Pearls, Rose Cut Diamonds, 3 ¼ In.
$3,851.00

Skinner, Inc.

Jewelry, Pendant, Cross, Pelican Center, Yellow, Green & Clear Pastes, Silver, 4 ½ In.
$563.00

Skinner, Inc.

Jewelry, Pendant, Face, Abstract, 23K Gold, Pablo Picasso, Box, c.1998
$16,590.00

Skinner, Inc.

Jewelry, Pendant, Heart With Crown, Amethyst, 9K Gold, Birmingham, c.1910, 1 ½ In.
$889.00

Skinner, Inc.

Jewelry, Pendant, Insect, Glass, Pate-De-Verre, Relief, Brown & Gold, 2 ⅛ In.
$350.00

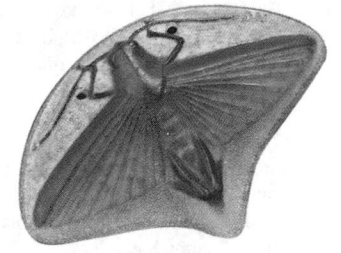

Skinner, Inc.

Jewelry, Pendant, Pin, Heart, Silver, Brass, Carol Summers, 4 ¾ x 4 ⅛ In.
$1,541.00

Skinner, Inc.

Jewelry, Pendant, Spider Web, Rose Cut Diamonds, Ruby Spider, Carnelian, 20K Gold, Coomi, 2 In.
$1,440.00

Skinner, Inc.

Jewelry, Pin & Earrings, Maison Gripoix Glass, Faux Pearls, Goldtone, Chanel, France, 2 ⅝-In. Pin
$420.00

DuMouchelles Art Gallery

Jewelry, Pin, 3 Monkeys, 18K Bicolor Gold, Platinum, Chaumet, 1 ¾ In.
$889.00

Skinner, Inc.

Jewelry, Pin, Abstract Star, Textured Rods, 18K Gold, Ed Wiener, 3 ½ In.
$1,140.00

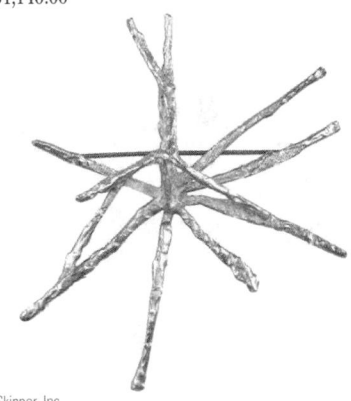

Skinner, Inc.

Jewelry, Pin, Abstract, Textured, Gemstone Cluster, Diamonds, 18K Gold, E. Wiener, 16 ½ In.
$1,422.00

Skinner, Inc.

Jewelry, Pin, Bee, Sapphire, Yellow Enamel Body, Diamond Wings & Accents, Silver, 18K Gold, 1 ¾ In.
$2,844.00

Skinner, Inc.

J

Jewelry, Pin, Bouquet, Hardstone, Nephrite Jade, Ruby & Diamond Accents, 18K Gold, Austria, Hallmarks, 3 In.
$1320.00

Skinner, Inc.

Jewelry, Pin, Cameo, Coral, Maiden, Flowers, Square Cut Garnets, Rose Cut Diamonds, 2 In.
$735.00

Skinner, Inc.

Jewelry, Pin, Cameo, David & Wolf, 14K Gold Frame, c.1910
$382.00

Garth's Auctioneers & Appraisers

Jewelry, Pin, Cameo, Maiden, Hardstone, Upswept Hair, Split Pearls, Gold Mount, 1 ⅜ In.
$593.00

Skinner, Inc.

Pin, Bar, Pierced Serpentine Shape, Platinum, Diamonds, Art Deco, 3 In.	4602.00
Pin, Bar, Platinum, Diamond, Emerald, Art Deco, Tiffany & Co., 2 In.	3798.00
Pin, Bar, Sailboat, Diamond Sails, Garnet Hull, 14K Gold, Edwardian, ¾ In.	770.00
Pin, Baroque Pearl, 3 Emeralds, Diamonds, Abstract Form, 18K Gold, Arthur King, 3 In.	1300.00
Pin, Bear, Holding Turquoise Ball, 18K Textured Gold, Turquoise, Cartier	840.00
Pin, Bear, Walking, 18K Gold, Ruby Eyes, Tiffany, 1 ¾ In.	4140.00
Pin, Bee, 18K Gold, Green Enamel Stripes, Ruby Melee Eyes, Tiffany & Co., 1 In.	840.00
Pin, Bee, 18K Gold, Tiered Body, Granulated Head, Fluted Wings, Hermes, 1 ¾ In.	2880.00
Pin, Bee, Coral Button Body, 18K Gold, Granulated Head, Fluted Wings, Hermes, 1 ⅝ In.	3000.00
Pin, Bee, Sapphire, Yellow Enamel Body, Diamond Wings & Accents, Silver, 18K Gold, 1 ¾ In.. *Illus*	2844.00
Pin, Birds, Nesting, Enamel, Eggs, 18K Gold, Italy, c.1965, 1 ⅞ In.	750.00
Pin, Bouquet, Hardstone, Nephrite Jade, Ruby & Diamond Accents, 18K Gold, Austria, 3 In. ...*Illus*	1320.00
Pin, Bouquet, Leaves, Acorns, Naturalistic, 14K Gold, Buccellati, 1 ½ In.	1304.00
Pin, Bow, 14K Gold, Ruby, Diamond, Acorn Hallmark, Art Deco, 3 In.	420.00
Pin, Bow, Diamond Melee Designs, Platinum, Beaded, Art Deco, 2 In.	2015.00
Pin, Bow, Diamonds, Geometric Shapes, Beaded Platinum Openwork, Art Deco, 3 In.	11850.00
Pin, Bow, Diamonds, Looped, Platinum Over Gold, Diamond Drop Ends, T.B. Starr, 2 In.	2370.00
Pin, Bow, Diamonds, Old European & Single Cut, Platinum, Beaded, Marcus & Co., 2 In.	1778.00
Pin, Bow, Flowers, Diamonds, Platinum Openwork, Edwardian, 1 ½ In.	889.00
Pin, Bow, Platinum, Diamond, Marked, Tiffany & Co., 1 ½ x 1 In.	5175.00
Pin, Bow, Platinum, Gold, Diamond, Belle Epoque, 1 ½ x 1 ½ In.	5265.00
Pin, Bow, Ruby, Pave Diamonds, 18K Gold, Van Cleef & Arpels, 1 In.	1541.00
Pin, Branch, C Shape, Leaves, Goldtone Metal, Sarah Coventry, 1 ¾ x 1 ⅝ In.	6.00
Pin, Branch, Textured, 18K Gold, Bezel Set Mother-Of-Pearl, M. Buccellati, 4 ¾ In.	3308.00
Pin, Bud, Leaves, Sterling Silver, Lapis, Georg Jensen, 3 In.	4444.00
Pin, Butterfly, 22 Multicolor Stones, Prong Set, 18K Gold, W. Weidinger, 1 ½ In.	294.00
Pin, Butterfly, Diamonds, Emeralds, Sapphires, Garnet Head, 18K Gold, Edwardian, 2 In.	5333.00
Pin, Butterfly, Juliana, Aqua, Aurora Borealis, Teal, Peridot, Rhinestone, DeLizza & Elster, 2 x 2 ½ In.	110.00
Pin, Butterfly, Juliana, Ruby Red, Pink Crystals, Goldtone Metal, DeLizza & Elster, 2 x 1 ¾ In.	110.00
Pin, Butterfly, Silver, Hector Aguilera, 2 ¼ In.	170.00
Pin, Calla Lily, Frosted Crystal, Diamond, 18K Gold, Schlumberger, Tiffany, c.1955, 2 ¾ x 1 ¼ In..	978.00
Pin, Cameo, Coral, Maiden, Flowers, Square Cut Garnets, Rose Cut Diamonds, 2 In. ......*Illus*	735.00
Pin, Cameo, David & Wolf, 14K Gold Frame, c.1910	*Illus* 382.00
Pin, Cameo, Flowers, Draped Dress, Diamond Accent, Silver Filigree, 1920s, 1 ⅝ x 1 ½ In.	275.00
Pin, Cameo, Hardstone, Maiden, Curls, Earrings, 18K Greek Key Border, Tiffany, 2 In.	1140.00
Pin, Cameo, Hardstone, Maiden, Jeweled, 14K Gold Mount, Pearl Surround, 1 ½ In.	480.00
Pin, Cameo, Hardstone, Maiden, Upswept Hair, 14K Leaf & Branch Mount, 1 ⅜ In.	533.00
Pin, Cameo, Horn, Court Scene, Oval, Gold Ropework Frame, China, 2 ½ In.	1000.00
Pin, Cameo, Jupiter, Crown Of Oak Leaves, Gold Ropework & Bead Frame, 1 ½ In.	1896.00
Pin, Cameo, Lava, 3 Cherubs, Wreaths, Clouds, 14K Gold Rope Twist Frame, 2 In.	1440.00
Pin, Cameo, Maiden, Hardstone, Upswept Hair, Split Pearls, Gold Mount, 1 ⅜ In............*Illus*	593.00
Pin, Cameo, Onyx, Maiden, Curls, Diadem, Oval, 18K Gold Beaded Mount, 2 In.	510.00
Pin, Cameo, Opal, Cupid & Psyche, South Sea Pearls, Rubies, Diamonds, 18K Gold, 3 x 2 ¾ In..*Illus*	2400.00
Pin, Cameo, Pink Shell, Woman's Profile, 14K Gold Frame, Scrolling, Victorian, 1 ¼ In.	178.00
Pin, Cameo, Shell, 3 Women Reaching For Songbird, 14K Gold Undulating Frame	411.00
Pin, Cameo, Shell, Athena, Helmet, Oval, Gold Mount, c.1910	235.00
Pin, Cameo, Shell, Clipper Ship On Water, Oval Gold Frame, c.1910	235.00
Pin, Cameo, Shell, Dancing Horse, Clock Center, Round, 14K Gold Frame, c.1910	823.00
Pin, Cameo, Shell, Leda & Swan, Classical Image, Oval, Gold Frame, 1920s	294.00
Pin, Cameo, Shell, Oedipus Answers Riddle Of Sphinx, 14K Gold, Pearl Surround, 4 In.	940.00
Pin, Cameo, Shell, Primavera, Figures In Forest, 18K Gold Oval Mount, 3 In.	593.00
Pin, Cameo, Shell, Stylized Butterfly Woman, 3-Sided, 18K Gold Frame, Art Nouveau	353.00
Pin, Cameo, Shell, Victorian Gentleman, Handlebar Moustache, 14K Gold Frame, c.1910	353.00
Pin, Cameo, Shell, Woman, Front View, Hair In Bun, Goldtone Frame, Seed Pearls, 2 In.	264.00
Pin, Cameo, Woman's Profile, Amethyst, Onyx & Diamond Rim, Platinum, Art Deco, 1 ¼ In.	1320.00
Pin, Cameo, Woman's Profile, Bacchante, Grapes, Sterling, Victorian, c.1900, 2 ¼ x 1 ⅛ In.	225.00
Pin, Carnelian Disk, 14K Gold, Black & Green Enamel, Chinese Art Deco, 1 ⅝ In.	253.00
Pin, Charms, Chain, Coin, Pearl, Cameo, Venetian Glass, Citrine, 18K Gold, Elizabeth Locke, 3 In...*Illus*	1960.00
Pin, Chatelaine, Cherub, 3 Venetian Peacock Glass Drops, Gilt Metal, C-Clasp, 1930s, 2 x 2 In. .	120.00
Pin, Chatelaine, Dangling Grape Clusters, Silver, 1930s, 3 ½ x 2 ½ In.	145.00
Pin, Cherry Cluster, Wire Stems, Red, Green Leaves, 1930s, 2 ⅜ In.	224.00
Pin, Chick, 18K Gold, Diamond Wings, Ruby Eye, Van Cleef & Arpels, 1 In.	834.00
Pin, Chinese Man, Under Umbrella, Flower, Figural, Carved Ivory, Ruby, Emerald, 2 x 1 In.	1754.00
Pin, Christmas Tree, Blue, Green, Pink Rhinestones, Hattie Carnegie, 2 ¾ In.	108.00
Pin, Christmas Tree, Gold, Clear & Red Rhinestones, Hobe, 1950s, 1 ⅞ In.	75.00
Pin, Circle, 18 Fluted & Folded Over Curls, Goldtone Metal, Marvella, 2 In.	9.00

J

Pin, Clover, Heart Shape Opals, Diamonds, Silver Over Gold Mount, 1 ½ In. ....*Illus*	1778.00
Pin, Coral, Curved Tube, Twisted Rope Edge, 3 Pendant Drops, Victorian, 2 ½ In.	236.00
Pin, Crop Shape, Horse Head, 14K Gold, Reverse Painted Glass, Sloan & Co., 2 ⅜ In.	356.00
Pin, Deer, Leaping, 14K Gold Openwork, Tiffany & Co., 2 ½ In.	652.00
Pin, Diamond, Blue Sapphire, 14K Gold, Pierced, Art Deco, 2 ⅝ x 1 ⅛ In.	2300.00
Pin, Diamond, Sapphire, 9K Gold, Payton, Pepper & Sons, London, Victorian, 1 ¾ In.	250.00
Pin, Diamonds, Onyx, Platinum, Open Oval, Arrow Ends, Beaded, Art Deco, 3 In.	3081.00
Pin, Diamonds, Silver Pearl, 18K Gold, Scroll Frame, Art Nouveau, 1 ¼ x 1 ⅛ In.	805.00
Pin, Dog, 14K Gold, Tiffany & Co., 2 In. ....*Illus*	600.00
Pin, Dog, Spaniel, Sapphire Melee Eyes, 18K Gold, Tiffany & Co., 1 ⅞ In.	2133.00
Pin, Dog, Terrier, Goldtone Metal, Rhinestones, 1940s, 1 ½ In.	12.00
Pin, Dog, Yorkie, Goldtone Metal, Green Crystal Eyes, Ruby Tongue, BSK, 1960s, 1 ½ x 1 ½ In..	10.00
Pin, Dogwood Blossom, Diamond Center, 18K Textured Gold, Tiffany & Co., 1 ½ In.	1185.00
Pin, Doll Shape, Silver, Blue & White Enamel Dress, Bonnet, Margot De Taxco, 2 In.	129.00
Pin, Dragon, Pearl, Enamel, Diamond, 18K Gold, Tiffany & Co., 1 ½ x 2 ½ In.................*Illus*	8625.00
Pin, Duck, 14K Gold Openwork, Tiffany & Co., 1 ½ In.	652.00
Pin, Earrings, Gold Frame, Leaves, Flowers, Lily Of The Valley, Pietra Dura, Victorian, 2 ¼ x 2 In..	529.00
Pin, Edelweiss, Jade, Diamond, Yellow Stone, Erwin Paltscho, Box, 1 ⅜ In.	944.00
Pin, Egyptian Figure, Kneeling, Harp, Amethyst Scarab, Gold, Enamel, T.B. Starr, 1 In.	10073.00
Pin, Enamel On Copper, Gold Accents, Abstract, Miriam Peck, 1950s, 3 x 2 In.	250.00
Pin, Fan, Open, Textured Goldtone Metal, Miriam Haskell, 2 In.	25.00
Pin, Filigree, White Gold, Diamonds, Pendant Loops, Art Deco, 1 ¼ In.	414.00
Pin, Fish, Articulated, Blue, Green & Orange Enamel, Silver, Margot DeTaxco, 2 In.	133.00
Pin, Flag, Red, White & Blue Swarovski Crystals, 1960s, 2 x 1 ¼ In.	45.00
Pin, Flower Basket, Citrine, Diamonds, 3 Seed Pearls, Greek Key Frame, Edwardian, 2 In.	711.00
Pin, Flower Basket, Emerald, Ruby, Sapphire, Diamonds, Gold, F. Walter Lawrence, 2 In.	3240.00
Pin, Flower Bouquet, Green & Purple Gemstones, 14K Gold Bow, Hobe, 3 In.	250.00
Pin, Flower Spray, 7 Sapphire Cabochons, Diamonds, 18K Gold, Buccellati, 1 ½ In.	2726.00
Pin, Flower Spray, 14K Gold, Diamond, Krementz, 2 ½ In.	374.00
Pin, Flower Spray, 18K Gold, Platinum, Diamonds, Raymond Yard, 2 ½ In.	3629.00
Pin, Flower Spray, Bead Clusters, Sapphires, 18K Gold, Fred, Paris, 2 ¾ In.	1080.00
Pin, Flower, 5 Coral Petals, Diamond Center, 18K Gold, Van Cleef & Arpels, 2 In.	13035.00
Pin, Flower, 14K Gold, Pink & Cream Enamel, Intertwining Leaves, Red Stone, Art Nouveau, 1 x 1 In.	266.00
Pin, Flower, 18K Gold, Ruby Center, Marked, M. Buccellati, Italy, c.1965, 1 ⅛ In.	3220.00
Pin, Flower, Diamond Center, Enamel, 18K Gold, Marked, Tiffany, 1 ⅛ In. ....*Illus*	531.00
Pin, Flower, Florentine Finish Petals, Diamonds, 18K Gold, Cartier, 2 In. ....*Illus*	3851.00
Pin, Flower, Garnet, Pear Shape Moonstones, Gold, Wordley, Allsopp & Bliss, Retro, 4 In.	711.00
Pin, Flower, Rope Work Trim, Trifari, 1960s, 1 ¾ In.	18.00
Pin, Flower, Scrolling Leaves, Stems, Round Cut Diamonds, Silver, 18K Gold, c.1940, 3 ½ In. .	3250.00
Pin, Flower, Silver, Rose Gold Washed, Peridot Stamen, Retro, c.1950, 3 ¼ x 3 In.	125.00
Pin, Flowers, 5 Petal, Gold, Rubies, Watch Drop, Ivory Dial, Retro, Tiffany & Co., 1 ¼ In.	660.00
Pin, Flowers, Gold Washed Silver, Jeweled, Enamel Repousse Granulation, Russia, c.1800, 4 ¾ In.	2185.00
Pin, Flowers, Green Onyx, Silver, Georg Jensen, 2 ⅛ In..............................*Illus*	770.00
Pin, Flowers, Leather, Lavender, Purple, 1980s, 3 ¾ In., 2 Piece	39.00
Pin, Flowers, Openwork, Silver, Amber, Oval Mount, Continental, c.1900, 1 ¼ In.	59.00
Pin, Fruit Salad, Rubies, Emeralds, Diamonds, 14K Gold, Seaman Schepps, 2 In.	7703.00
Pin, Fruit Salad, Tourmalines, Red, Green, Yellow, Amber, Diamonds, Seaman Schepps	9480.00
Pin, Geometric, 14K Gold, Overlaid Circle, Oval, Star, Pearls, Art Deco, 1 ¾ In.	334.00
Pin, Goose Shape, Stylized Feathers, Tiffany Silver, 2 ⅝ In.	690.00
Pin, Grape Cluster, Pearls, Diamond Leaves, Platinum Over Gold Vine, Edwardian, 2 In.	3851.00
Pin, Grape Cluster, Wave & Bead Border, Oval, Silver, Georg Jensen, 2 ⅜ In.	356.00
Pin, Grapes, Leaves, Silver, Harald Nielsen, Georg Jensen, 3 In.	267.00
Pin, Grapevines, Molded Glass, Foiled Ground, Lalique, 2 ¾ In..................*Illus*	1007.00
Pin, Heart, Open, Diamonds, Graduated Platinum Frame, Elsa Peretti, Tiffany, 1 In.	2370.00
Pin, Heart, Silver, Engraved, Anchor Pin, G. Jensen, 14 In.	124.00
Pin, Hematite Cabochon, Silver Mount, Abstract Form, Janiye, 2 ⅜ In.	420.00
Pin, Intertwining Leaves & Vines, 14K Gold Openwork, Arts & Crafts, Germany, 2 In.	504.00
Pin, Jabot, 2 Diamond Rings, Platinum, Beaded, Art Deco, 3 In.	4444.00
Pin, Jade, Baton, Diamond Spiral Scroll & Ends, Art Deco, 2 ¾ In.	3200.00
Pin, Keys, 3 Interlocking Heart-Shaped, 18K Textured Gold, Cartier, 1 ⅝ In.	563.00
Pin, Ladybug, Rubies, Diamond Accents, 18K Gold, Schlumberger, Tiffany, ⅞ In.	2844.00
Pin, Landscape, Bicolor Gold, Victorian, 2 ½ In.	46.00
Pin, Leaf, 18K Gold, 5 Diamonds, Tiffany & Co., 3 In.	940.00
Pin, Leaf, Curved, Platinum, 14K Gold, Diamond, Marked, McTeigue, 1 ¾ In.	1080.00
Pin, Leaf, Lapis Lazuli, Silver, G. Jensen, 1 ¼ In.	260.00
Pin, Leaf, Textured 18K Gold, Polished Vein, Diamond, Tiffany & Co., 2 In.	1107.00

Jewelry, Pin, Cameo, Opal, Cupid & Psyche, South Sea Pearls, Rubies, Diamonds, 18K Gold, 3 x 2 ¾ In. $2400.00

Skinner, Inc.

Jewelry, Pin, Charms, Chain, Coin, Pearl, Cameo, Venetian Glass, Citrine, 18K Gold, Elizabeth Locke, 3 In. $1960.00

Skinner, Inc.

Jewelry, Pin, Clover, Heart Shape Opals, Diamonds, Silver Over Gold Mount, 1 ½ In. $1778.00

Skinner, Inc.

Jewelry, Pin, Dog, 14K Gold, Tiffany & Co., 2 In. $600.00

Skinner, Inc.

J

Jewelry, Pin, Dragon, Pearl, Enamel, Diamond, 18K Gold, Tiffany & Co., 1 ½ x 2 ½ In.
$8625.00

Cottone Auctions

Jewelry, Pin, Flower, Diamond Center, Enamel, 18K Gold, Marked, Tiffany, 1 ⅛ In.
$531.00

Brunk Auctions

Jewelry, Pin, Flower, Florentine Finish Petals, Diamonds, 18K Gold, Cartier, 2 In.
$3851.00

Skinner, Inc.

Jewelry, Pin, Flowers, Green Onyx, Silver, Georg Jensen, 2 ⅛ In.
$770.00

Skinner, Inc.

Clamper Bracelets

"Clamper" bracelets, hinged plastic bracelets that open to be put around a wrist, were originally made from umbrella handles. Albert Weiss & Company made the first bracelets sold under the name *Bon Bon.*

Pin, Lily Of The Valley, 5 Pearls, 18K Gold Wirework, Cartier, 2 ¼ In.	1007.00
Pin, Lizard, Eating Faux Pearl Egg, Enamel & Rhinestone, Coro Craft, Marked, 1942, 2 ¾ In.	1950.00
Pin, Locket, Cameo, Agate, Young Woman, 18K Gold Frame, Victorian, 2 ¼ x 1 ½ In.	776.00
Pin, Lovebirds, Branch, Enamel, Ruby Melee Eyes, Diamond, 18K Gold, Boucheron, Paris, 2 In.... *Illus*	3851.00
Pin, Lover's Eye, 2 Blue Eyes, Gold Frame, Serpent Swallowing Tail, 1 ⅜ In. *Illus*	2337.00
Pin, Lover's Eye, 2 Eyes, Split Pearl Rim, Opaline Glass Surround, Oval Gold Mount, 4 In.	2280.00
Pin, Lover's Eye, Brown Eye, Hair Curl, Gold Oval Frame, Diamond Engraving, 1 In.	1845.00
Pin, Loving Heart, 18K Gold, Paloma Picasso, Tiffany & Co., 1 ¼ In.	444.00
Pin, Man, Sombrero, Blanket Over Shoulder, Silver, Enamel, Margot De Taxco, 2 In.	247.00
Pin, Mask, 18K Gold, Baroque Pearl Drops, Leaf Mounts, Rubies, Tony Duquette, 3 In.	1659.00
Pin, Micro Mosaic, Landscape, Stream, Figures In Boat, 14K Gold Frame, 1 ¾ x 1 ⅜ In.	1080.00
Pin, Micro Mosaic, Pharaoh Head, Gold, Murano Glass Drops, 14K, Venetian, 1800s, 1 ⅛ In... *Illus*	1888.00
Pin, Micro Mosaic, Roman Forum, 14K Gold Mount, Italy, c.1875, 2 In. *Illus*	353.00
Pin, Mobius Strip, Free-Form, Silver, Torun Bulow-Hube, G. Jensen, 2 ½ In.	385.00
Pin, Mourning, 14K Gold, Onyx, Seed Pearls, Diamond, Hair Compartment, Victorian, 1884, 2 In..	387.00
Pin, Mourning, Order Of The Garter, Enamel Belt, Crown Crest, Red, Green Stones, 14K Gold, 1 ½ In.	1920.00
Pin, Nosegay, Sapphires, Rubies, Diamond Melee, 14K Bicolor Gold, Tiffany & Co., 3 ½ In.	1659.00
Pin, Owl, Citrine, Sapphire Eyes, Diamond & Emerald Accents, 18K Gold, Champagnat, 2 In..	2963.00
Pin, Paisley, 10 Turquoise Cabochons, Diamonds, 18K Gold, Tiffany & Co., 1 ½ In.	948.00
Pin, Palm Tree, 18K Gold, Diamond & Coral Accents, Cartier, c.1960, 2 ¼ In.	5500.00
Pin, Pear Shape, 14K Gold, Diamonds, Pearl Drop, Art Nouveau, France, 1 ½ In.	563.00
Pin, Pendant, Locket, Gold, Raised Scroll Border, Open Rectangular Pin, Diamonds, Victorian, 2 In...	311.00
Pin, Pendant, Silver, Grapevine Design, Georg Jensen, 1 ½ In.	94.00
Pin, Pierced Scrollwork, 18K Gold, Art Nouveau, Weiss, ⅞ In.	889.00
Pin, Pietra Dura, Micro Mosaic, Gondola, Birds, Goldstone Glass, Silver Mount, 2 ⅞ In...*Illus*	356.00
Pin, Plaques, Silver, Enamel, Abalone, Gold, 14K Gold, Earl Pardon, c.1989, 2 ⅛ In. ....*Illus*	2015.00
Pin, Platinum, 88 Round & Baguette Diamonds, Art Deco, 2 x 1 In.	1200.00
Pin, Platinum, Plaque, Jadeite, Reticulated, Birds, Flowers, Diamond Accents, Art Deco, 1 ½ x 1 In.	518.00
Pin, Portrait, 18th Century Woman, Diamond & Pearl Edge, Jacques & Marcus, 1 In.	563.00
Pin, Portrait, Woman, Ruffled Collar, Gold Mount, Pearl & Diamond Edge, 1 ¼ In.	1080.00
Pin, Rabbit, 14K Gold Openwork, Tiffany & Co., 1 ¾ In.	563.00
Pin, Rabbit, 18K Gold, Floppy Ears, Onyx Belly, Sapphire Eyes, Kutchinsky, 2 In.	1067.00
Pin, Radio, Suspended, Frame, Metal, Stone, Chris Darway, Contemporary, 2 ½ x 3 In.....*Illus*	300.00
Pin, Rebecca At Well, Enamel, 18K Gold Frame, Lotus, Hieroglyphics, Egyptian Revival, 2 In..	1067.00
Pin, Ribbon Shape, White Gold, Diamond, Art Deco, 1 ¼ In.	420.00
Pin, Ribbon, 18K Gold, Diamonds, Marked, Van Cleef & Arpels, 2 In.	6518.00
Pin, Rope Knot, Cartier, 1 ¾ In.	295.00
Pin, Rose Window, Seed Pearls, Center Diamond, 14K Gold, C Clasp, Victorian, 1 In.	311.00
Pin, Rose, 20K Gold, Hammered Petals, Tiffany & Co., 2 In.	1304.00
Pin, Rosette, Sterling, Teardrop-Shaped Turquoise Stones, Marked, Y & R Charley, 2 ¾ In.	150.00
Pin, Safety Pin, 18K Gold, Shaped Lapis, Tiffany & Co., 2 ¼ In.	504.00
Pin, Safety Pin, Diamonds, 2 Sapphire Cabochons, Beaded Trim, Art Deco, Cartier, 2 In.	6493.00
Pin, Sailboat, Flexible Sail, Trace Link Chain, 2 Figures, 18K Gold, Fred, Paris, 2 In.	1896.00
Pin, Sailor, 18K Gold, Pearl Head, Ruby Hat, Enamel Trim, Diamonds, Fred, 1 In.	1659.00
Pin, Scarab, 18K Gold, Porcelain, Turquoise, Egyptian Revival, 2 In.	949.00
Pin, Scarab, Turquoise, Gold Winged Mount, Pharaoh Heads, Brassler Co., 2 In.	720.00
Pin, Scatter, Bicolor, 14K Gold, Art Deco, 2 In., Pair	944.00
Pin, Scottish Terrier, White Enamel, Ruby Eyes, Pave Diamond Bow, 1940s, 1 ½ In.	1778.00
Pin, Sculpture, Woman, Green Hair, Glass, Wood, Bone, Silver, 14K Gold, Tod Pardon, 1 ½ In....*Illus*	2040.00
Pin, Sea Urchin, 18K Gold, Ruby, 6 Diamonds, Tiffany & Co., 1 ¼ In.	1126.00
Pin, Seahorse, Double, Silver, Patina, Mexico, 1 ½ x 2 ½ In.	51.00
Pin, Serpent, Intertwined, Emerald, Ruby Eyes, 14K Gold. *Illus*	1168.00
Pin, Silver, Amber Cabochon, Chrysoprase, Georg Jensen, 1 ½ In. *Illus*	1659.00
Pin, Silver, Moonstone Cabochon, Marked, Georg Jensen, 1 ¼ In.	474.00
Pin, Sled, Rope Handles, 14K Gold, Marked, J.H. Breakell & Co., 1 ¾ x 1 In.	660.00
Pin, Snake, Demantoid Garnets, Diamonds, Ruby Head, Platinum Over Gold, Edwardian, 2 In.	8100.00
Pin, Sonja Henie, White Metal, Red, White & Blue Rhinestones, Figural, 1930s	56.00
Pin, Spider, Emeralds, Diamond Melee, 18K Gold, Cartier, 1 ¼ In.	1422.00
Pin, Sprig & Spray, Diamonds, Pearls, 14K Gold, c.1955, 3 In.	920.00
Pin, Starburst, Diamonds, European Cut, Silver Over Gold, Tiffany & Co., c.1900, 1 ⅝ In. .... *Illus*	8225.00
Pin, Starfish, 18K Gold, Box, c.1980, 1 ¾ In.	1500.00
Pin, Starfish, Diamonds, Platinum, Tiffany & Co., 1 ¾ In.	2963.00
Pin, Starfish, Gold, 18K Gold, Tiffany & Co., c.1965, 2 x 2 In.	1610.00
Pin, Starfish, Logo Center, Faux Pearls, Goldtone, Chanel, France, 3 ¼ In....*Illus*	450.00
Pin, Stick, Cameo, Jet, Cherub Playing Lyre, Oval, Michaud.	264.00
Pin, Stylized Blossom, Silver, Georg Jensen, No. 63, 1 ½ In.	360.00

Pin, Stylized Figure, 3-Sided Mount, Silver, Ed Weiner, 2 In.	178.00
Pin, Stylized Flowers, Sterling Silver, Impressed Marks, Kalo, 2 ½ In...............*Illus*	244.00
Pin, Stylized Frog, Blue Rock Crystal, Diamond Melee Webbed Feet, Vhernier, 2 In......	6518.00
Pin, Stylized Leaf, 18K Gold, Tiffany & Co., 2 ¼ In.	840.00
Pin, Stylized Lily Of The Valley, Sterling Silver, Impressed Marks, Kalo, 2 ½ In. ....*Illus*	397.00
Pin, Stylized Pansy, 18K Frosted Gold, Pink Sapphires, Diamond Melee, Sonia B., 2 In.	889.00
Pin, Stylized Penguin, 14K Gold, Ribbon Form, Openwork, Tiffany & Co., 1 ¾ In.	1200.00
Pin, Stylized Ribbon, 9 Sapphires, Diamonds, 14K Bicolor Gold, Mauboussin, Retro, 2 In.	1896.00
Pin, Stylized Sunburst, Silver, Carved Mask, Amethyst Quartz, H. Harmon, 7 In.	2200.00
Pin, Stylized W, Silver, Hammered, Alexander Calder, c.1962, 1 ⅜ In x 2 ⁵⁄₁₆ In.	22140.00
Pin, Stylized Woman, Sterling Silver, Ed Wiener, Stamped, 1950s, 3 x 2 In. ....*Illus*	1000.00
Pin, Sunburst, 12 Alternating Rays, Yellow Gold, Diamonds, Diamond Center, c.1950, 1 ⁵⁄₁₆ In..	620.00
Pin, Swirl, 2 Pearls, 14K Gold, 1 ½ In...	339.00
Pin, Swordfish, Pave Diamonds, Ruby Eye, Blue Enamel Fins, Platinum, Cartier, 1 ¼ In........	3555.00
Pin, Textured & Engraved Gold, 24K & 18K, Quartz, Nancy Michel, Janiye, 3 In. ....*Illus*	1244.00
Pin, Whale, Lapis, Rock Crystal Tail, Diamond Melee Spray, Vhernier, 1 ½ In.	1080.00
Pin, Woman, Egyptian Costume, Enamel, Gold, Art Nouveau, 2 In. ....*Illus*	459.00
Pin, Wood Nymph, Diamonds, 14K Gold, c.1960, 2 ¼ In.	540.00
Pin, Wreath, Faux Pearl, Faceted Rhinestones, Eisenberg Ice............................	34.00
Ring, 14K Gold, Silver Alternating Bands, Marked, D. Yurman	322.00
Ring, 18K Gold, 2 Kinetic Layered Perforated Bands, Engraved Gucci Logo, Size 11	690.00
Ring, 18K Gold, Organic Design, Allover Fragments, John Paul Miller, Size 5 ½	3240.00
Ring, 18K Gold, Round Pink Tourmaline, Bezel Mount, Tiffany, Size 5........................	633.00
Ring, 2 Pearls, Diamond Melee Sides, Platinum Mount, Marcus & Co., Size 8........................	652.00
Ring, 2 Rubies, Pear Shape, Diamond Melee Shoulders, 18K Gold, Van Cleef & Arpels	2844.00
Ring, 3 Diamonds, 14K Bicolor Gold, Applied Flowers, Edwardian, c.1910, Size 6........................	495.00
Ring, 3 Rows, Rope Twist, Mark, Schlumberger, Tiffany & Co., Size 5 ¾.	582.00
Ring, Abstract, Textured, 18K Gold, Platinum & Diamond Accents, Size 7 ....*Illus*	1659.00
Ring, Amethyst, 14K White Gold, Filigree, Art Deco, c.1930, Size 3 ¼	165.00
Ring, Amethyst, Oval Cut, Diamond Melee Surround, 14K Gold, J.E. Caldwell, Size 6	3555.00
Ring, Amethyst, Square, 14K White Gold, Engraved Shoulders, Art Deco, Size 8........................	322.00
Ring, Aquamarine, Emerald Cut, 18K White Gold, Round Cut Diamonds, Art Deco Style, Size 7	242.00
Ring, Aquamarine, Emerald Cut, 4 Round Cut Diamonds, 14K White Gold, Art Deco, Size 9 ...	949.00
Ring, Aquamarine, Emerald Cut, Diamonds, 14K Gold, J.E. Caldwell & Co., Size 8	700.00
Ring, Aquamarine, Red Rod Shape Stones, Platinum, Art Deco, 1920-40, Size 5 ....*Illus*	2468.00
Ring, Band, 18K Gold, Diamond Melee Stars, Chaumet, Paris, Size 7 ½	735.00
Ring, Band, Panthere, 18K Gold, Brickwork, Cartier, Size 6 ¾	1778.00
Ring, Banded Agate, Oval, Tablet, Silver, Sam Kramer, 1 In., Size 8 ¼	444.00
Ring, Bank, Kelly, Silver, 18K Gold Purse Drop, Hermes, Size 6 ¾................................	960.00
Ring, Bombe, 14K Gold, Round Brilliant Cut Diamonds, La Rich, Size 5 ½.......................	253.00
Ring, Bombe, 18K Gold, Ribbed, Rope Twist, Marked, Cassis, c.1970, Size 8 ¼	1003.00
Ring, Bombe, Amethyst, Turquoise, 14K Gold, c.1960, Size 9 ½	688.00
Ring, Bombe, Coral, 18K Gold, Cartier, Marked, Size 5	3081.00
Ring, Bombe, Raised Shoulders, 3 Rows Diamonds, 2 Rows Rubies, 14K Rose Gold, Retro, Size 5 ½...	834.00
Ring, Buckle, 14K Gold, Diamond, French Cut Sapphire, Size 6	161.00
Ring, Buckle, Diamonds, Turquoise Enamel Band, 14K Gold, Retro, Size 6 ¼.................	593.00
Ring, Cameo, Hardstone, Nude Male, Holding Lion Skin & Thyrsus, 14K Gold Mount, Size 6 ..	2252.00
Ring, Cameo, Moonstone, Maiden, Sapphire Frame, 14K Gold, Size 6............................*Illus*	2520.00
Ring, Cameo, Profile, Blackamoor, Diamond Collar, Ruby Border, Size, 6 ¾	3555.00
Ring, Cameo, Shell, Young Man, Curly Hair, Classical Robes, Size 6........................	176.00
Ring, Carnelian, Intaglio, Curly Haired Youth, Oval, 10K Gold Mount, Size 8 ½	1541.00
Ring, Cat's Eye Chrysoberyl, Bezel Set, Owl Shoulders, 14K Gold, Bailey, Banks, Biddle............	6518.00
Ring, Cat's Eye Chrysoberyl, Diamond Surround, Platinum, Edwardian, Size 6 ½	2370.00
Ring, Cat's Eye Chrysoberyl, Gold Basket Weave Band, Man's, 1930s, ¾ In., Size 9 ½	5288.00
Ring, Chalcedony, Intaglio, Anchor, Peace Banner, Textured Gold Mount, Size 8 ½..................	948.00
Ring, Citrine, Faceted, Bezel Set, Ribbed 18K Gold Mount, Bulgari, Size 5	1126.00
Ring, Citrine, Oval Cut, Side Diamonds, 14K Gold, c.1960, Size 6 ½	518.00
Ring, Citrine, Oval, 14K Gold, Seed Pearl Border, Flowers, Art Deco, Size 7 ¼	805.00
Ring, Citrine, Pyramid Shape, 18K Gold, Bulgari, Size 7	1659.00
Ring, Cocktail, Sapphires, Sunburst, 14K Gold, 1950s, Size 6 ½	374.00
Ring, Diamond Filigree, Platinum, Bezel, Bead Set, Art Deco, Size 6	1668.00
Ring, Diamond, Brown Orange, Bezel Set, Platinum Ribbed Band, T. St. Clair, Size 6 ¼	4385.00
Ring, Diamond, Center, 18K Gold, Marked, Jabel, Size 8...	2360.00
Ring, Diamond, Channel Set Sapphires, Platinum Filigree, Art Deco, Size 7	3565.00
Ring, Diamond, Curved Baguette, Platinum, c.1950, Size 6 ¼...................................	1208.00
Ring, Diamond, Platinum, Filigree Mount, Art Deco, Size 7 ½....................................	2817.50

Jewelry, Pin, Grapevines, Molded Glass, Foiled Ground, Lalique, 2 ¾ In.
$1007.00

Skinner, Inc.

Jewelry, Pin, Lovebirds, Branch, Enamel, Ruby Melee Eyes, Diamond, 18K Gold, Boucheron, Paris, 2 In.
$3851.00

Skinner, Inc.

TIP

Pearls should be stored in their own silk or cotton pouch.

Jewelry, Pin, Lover's Eye, 2 Blue Eyes, Gold Frame, Serpent Swallowing Tail, 1 ⅜ In.
$2337.00

Skinner, Inc.

Jewelry, Pin, Micro Mosaic, Pharaoh Head, Gold, Murano Glass Bead Drops, 14K, Venetian, 1800s, 1 ⅛ In.
$1888.00

Brunk Auctions

J

Jewelry, Pin, Micro Mosaic, Roman Forum, 14K Gold Mount, Italy, c.1875, 2 In. $353.00

Garth's Auctioneers & Appraisers

Jewelry, Pin, Pietra Dura, Micro Mosaic, Gondola, Birds, Goldstone Glass, Silver Mount, 2 ⅞ In. $356.00

Skinner, Inc.

Jewelry, Pin, Plaques, Silver, Enamel, Abalone, Gold, 14K Gold, Earl Pardon, c.1989, 2 ⅛ In. $2015.00

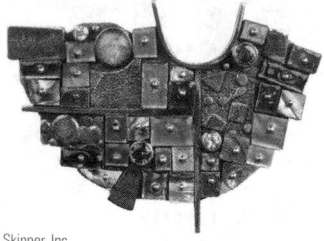

Skinner, Inc.

Jewelry, Pin, Radio, Suspended, Frame, Metal, Stone, Chris Darway, Contemporary, 2 ½ x 3 In. $300.00

Skinner, Inc.

TIP
Rust stains from old pins or hooks and eyes may come out with lemon juice.

Ring, Diamond, Round Cut, Filigree, 14 & 18K Gold, Art Deco, Size 7	690.00
Ring, Diamond, Round, 18K White Gold, Open Shoulder Design, Art Deco, Size 5 ¼	299.00
Ring, Diamond, Round, Brilliant Cut, Open Shoulders, Diamond Melee, Retro, Size 6 ½	426.00
Ring, Diamond, Sapphire Rim, 18K White Gold, Shoulders, Art Deco Style, Size 6 ½	1955.00
Ring, Diamonds, Channel Set, Lucida Cut, 18K Gold, Platinum, Box, Tiffany & Co., Size 9	2607.00
Ring, Diamonds, Round, 18K White Gold, Stepped Mounting, Retro, Size 7	253.00
Ring, Dinner, Emerald Cabochon, Diamond, 14K Gold, Retro, 1960s, Size 8	1425.00
Ring, Emerald, Diamonds, Yellow Gold, Platinum, Tiffany c.1980	2124.00
Ring, Emerald, Full & Baguette Cut Diamonds, Carved, Round, White Gold, Art Deco, Size 9	891.00
Ring, Emerald, Peridot, Abstract Form, 18K Textured Gold Mount, Janiye, 1978, Size 5 ¾	4266.00
Ring, Emerald, Rectangular Cut, Rope Twist Diamond Surround, Platinum, c.1955, Size 7 ¼	1840.00
Ring, Eternal Link, 56 Diamonds, Platinum, Tiffany & Co., Size 6	2844.00
Ring, Eternity Band, Platinum, Alternating Sections, Sapphires, Diamonds, Size 8	2875.00
Ring, Etoile, Inset Diamonds, Platinum, Tiffany & Co., Size 6 ½	1422.00
Ring, Face, From Nose Down, Pave Diamond Melee, 18K Gold, Sonia B., Size 7	2726.00
Ring, Fire Citrine, Diamond, 14K White Gold, Filigree, Art Deco, 1930s, Size 6 ¼	325.00
Ring, Frog, 14K Gold, Emerald Melee Eyes, Van Cleef & Arpels, Size 3	2607.00
Ring, Frog, 18K Gold, Lapis, Carved, Green Enamel, Marked, David Webb, Size 6	2844.00
Ring, Glass, Green, Etched, Center Diamond, 18K White Gold Filigree, Art Deco, 1920s, Size 6	195.00
Ring, Glass, Molded & Impressed Leaves, Blue, Lalique, Size 7 ¼	9480.00
Ring, Gold, Open Shoulders, Silver Pearl, Seed Pearls, Victorian, Size 6	121.00
Ring, Half Band, Coral & Diamond Melee Terminals, 18K Gold, Cartier, 1960s, Size 5	1185.00
Ring, Heart, Beaded Cross, 18K Gold, Kieselstein-Cord, Size 6 ½	1422.00
Ring, Horseshoe, 18K Gold, Diamonds, Rose & Full Cut, Retro, Size 4 ¾	3200.00
Ring, Iridescent Blue & Green Favrile Glass Scarab, 14K Yellow Gold, Tiffany, Size 6	483.00
Ring, Jade, Oval, 14K Gold, Art Deco Revival, Size 7 ½	750.00
Ring, Jadeite Cabochon, Oval, Diamond & Sapphire Accents, Platinum, Beaded, Art Deco	6518.00
Ring, Jadeite, 18K Gold, Chinese, c.1920, Size 6	919.00
Ring, Jadeite, Oval Cabochon, 18K Gold Mount, Verdura, Size 5 ¼	4444.00
Ring, Knot, Citrine Center, 14K Bicolor Gold, Cartier, Retro, Size 5 ¼	889.00
Ring, Lapis, Rectangular Tablet, 18K Gold Geometric Mount, Arne Johansen, Size 6 ¼	1440.00
Ring, Lion & Torch, Heraldic, 14K Gold, Man's, Marked, March 8, 1872, Size 11	518.00
Ring, Lion's Head, 14K Gold, European Cut Diamond In Mouth, Art Nouveau, Size 7 ¼	1778.00
Ring, Love, Squared Band, 18K Gold, Pierced Letters, D. Claflin, Tiffany, 1970s, Size 5 ¼	2963.00
Ring, Maiden, Robe, Enamel, Beaded & Rope Twist Border, Oval, 18K Gold, HV, Size 5 ½ .....*Illus*	1185.00
Ring, Micro Mosaic, Scarab, 18K Gold, Leather Fitted Case, Italy, 1800s, Size 6 ½ ....*Illus*	708.00
Ring, Moonstone Cabochon, 14K Gold, Enamel, 1930s, Size 10 ¼	325.00
Ring, Moonstone, 14K White Gold, Marcus & Co., Size 7	900.00
Ring, Moonstone, Domed Oval, Leafy Shoulders, Tendrils, Edward Oakes, c.1940, Size 4 ½	2489.00
Ring, Mourning, Coffin Shaped Stone, Gold, For R. Hearsey, Age 23, Mass., 1773	1121.00
Ring, Mourning, Gentleman's Portrait, Enamel, 18K Gold, 1780, Size 6 ½	889.00
Ring, Onyx, Oval Tablet, Greek Inscription, Gold Ribbed, Mount, Kieselstein-Cord, 1984	1103.00
Ring, Opal, 14K Gold, 6 Graduated Cabochon Stones, Diamonds, Retro, 1940s, Size 5 ½	385.00
Ring, Opal, 14K White Gold Filigree Mount, Yellow Flower Accents, Art Deco, Size 9	368.00
Ring, Opal, Black, Pearl Strip, Diamond, 14K Gold, Ross Coppelman, c.1990, Size 7	944.00
Ring, Peridot, Oval Cut, Abstract Mount, 18K Gold, Arthur King, Size 6 ½	6667.00
Ring, Platinum Filigree, European Cut Diamond, Diamond Accents, Art Deco, Size 6 ¼	834.00
Ring, Platinum, Diamonds, Round, Stepped Sides, Art Deco, Size 7	288.00
Ring, Platinum, Open Design, Round Cut Diamonds, Bezel Set, Elsa Peretti, Tiffany, Size 6	891.00
Ring, Poison, Moonstone, Oval, 14K Gold Shank, Maiden, Bellflowers, Compartment	2489.00
Ring, Poison, Sapphire, Navette Shape, Bezel Set, Diamond Border, Compartment, 18K Gold	1541.00
Ring, Puzzle, 4 Bands, Silver, 1970s, Size 9 ½	55.00
Ring, Red Spinel, Diamond, Channel Set, 14K Bicolor Gold, 1900s, Size 9 ¾	195.00
Ring, Rubies, Channel Set, Diamond, 18K Rose Gold, Art Deco, Size 7 ¾	495.00
Ring, Ruby, Cabochon, Bezel Set, 18K Gold, Loree Rodkin, 7 ¾	948.00
Ring, Sapphire, Purple, Oval, 18K Gold Leafy Mount, Seed Pearls, Arts & Crafts, Size 8	2370.00
Ring, Sapphire, Round Cut, 14K White Gold, Filigree Mount, Art Deco, Size 5 ½	247.00
Ring, Sapphire, Yellow, Pave Diamonds, 18K Gold, Schlumberger, Tiffany, Size 5	15405.00
Ring, Signet, 14K Gold, Monogram, Marked, Tiffany & Co., Size 9	201.00
Ring, Signet, Swan Feeding Young, 14K Gold, Cartier, Size 7	1541.00
Ring, Silver, Pebble Design, Concave, Marked, John Hardy, Size 7	138.00
Ring, Silver, Raised Circle Design, Square Mount, Round Diamonds, John Hardy, Size 7	230.00
Ring, Smoky Quartz, White Stone, Silver Wire Wrap, Claire Falkenstein, 1980s, Size 9.....*Illus*	600.00
Ring, Spiga, Chevron Link, Flexible, Coiled, 18K Gold, Bulgari, Box, Size 7	1185.00
Ring, Star Sapphire, Domed Oval, 2 Tapered Baguettes, Man's, 20th Century, Size 9 ½	1808.00

Jewelry, Pin, Sculpture, Woman, Green Hair, Glass, Wood, Bone, Silver, 14K Gold, Tod Pardon, 1 ½ In.
$2040.00

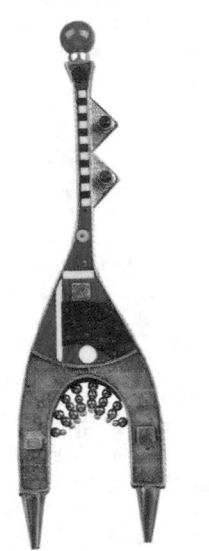

Skinner, Inc.

Jewelry, Pin, Serpent, Intertwined, Emerald, Ruby Eyes, 14K Gold
$1168.00

New Orleans Auction Galleries, Inc.

Jewelry, Pin, Silver, Amber Cabochon, Chrysoprase, Georg Jensen, 1 ½ In.
$1659.00

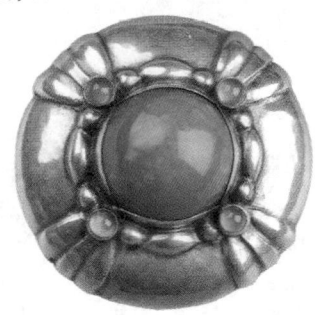

Skinner, Inc.

Jewelry, Pin, Starburst, Diamonds, European Cut, Silver Over Gold, Tiffany & Co., c.1900, 1 ⅝ In.
$8225.00

Garth's Auctioneers & Appraisers

Jewelry, Pin, Starfish, Logo Center, Faux Pearls, Goldtone, Chanel, France, 3 ¼ In.
$450.00

DuMochelles Art Gallery

Jewelry, Pin, Stylized Flowers, Sterling Silver, Impressed Marks, Kalo, 2 ½ In.
$244.00

Treadway Toomey Galleries

Jewelry, Pin, Stylized Lily Of The Valley, Sterling Silver, Impressed Marks, Kalo, 2 ½ In.
$397.00

Treadway Toomey Galleries

Jewelry, Pin, Stylized Woman, Sterling Silver, Ed Wiener, Stamped, 1950s, 3 x 2 In.
$1000.00

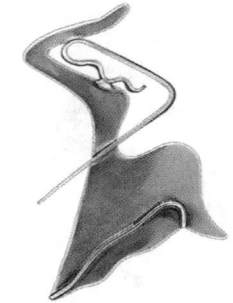

Rago Arts & Auction Center

Jewelry, Pin, Textured & Engraved Gold, 2 4K & 18K, Quartz, Nancy Michel, Janiye, 3 In.
$1244.00

Skinner, Inc.

Jewelry, Pin, Woman, Egyptian Costume, Enamel, Gold, Art Nouveau, 2 In.
$459.00

Skinner, Inc.

Jewelry, Ring, Abstract, Textured, 18K Gold, Platinum & Diamond Accents, Size 7
$1659.00

Skinner, Inc.

Jewelry, Ring, Aquamarine, Red
Rod Shape Stones, Platinum, Art Deco,
1920-40, Size 5
$2468.00

Garth's Auctioneers & Appraisers

Jewelry, Ring, Cameo, Moonstone,
Maiden, Sapphire Frame, 14K Gold, Size 6
$2520.00

Skinner, Inc.

Jewelry, Ring, Maiden, Robe, Enamel,
Beaded & Rope Twist Border, Oval,
18K Gold, HV, Size 5 ½
$1185.00

Skinner, Inc.

Jewelry, Ring, Micro Mosaic, Scarab, 18K
Gold, Leather Fitted Case, Italy, 1800s,
Size 6 ½
$708.00

Brunk Auctions

Ring, Sunburst, Diamonds, 14K Gold, 1950s, Size 5	2500.00
Ring, Tahitian Pearl, Diamond Melee, Platinum, Tiffany & Co., Size 5 ½	1896.00
Ring, Tricolor Gold, Rolling Design, Marked, Cartier, 4 ¾ In.	593.00
Ring, Walrus Head, 18K Gold, Sapphire Cabochon Eyes, Bone Tusks, Tiffany & Co., Size 5	2963.00
Sautoir, Seed Pearls, Woven Strap, Tassel, Platinum & Diamond Cap, Edwardian, 42 In.	6000.00
Stickpin, Coin, Silver, Classical Profile, Gold Ropework Frame, Beaded, Wiese, France	1541.00
Stickpin, Horse & Rider, Stone Fence, 14K Gold, Glass, c.1890, 3 In.	3850.00
Stickpin, Horseshoe, Diamonds, European Cut, Platinum Over Gold Mount, Edwardian	356.00
Stickpin, Jockey's Cap, Moonstone, Oval, 14K Gold, ½ In.	338.00
Stickpin, Maiden's Head, 14K Gold, Enamel, Diamond Bandeau, Split Pearls, Art Nouveau	385.00
Stickpin, Owl, Fire Opal, Diamond Eyes, Gold Branch, Art Nouveau, ¾ In.	1067.00
Stickpin, Woman Playing Flute, 18K Gold, Sapphire, Diamonds, Art Nouveau, ¾ In.	173.00
Tiara, Filigree, 9 Aquamarines, Brite Cut, Peruzzi, Italy, 1 ¾ x 5 ½ In.	1180.00
Tie Pin, Grotesque Face, Labradorite, Diamond Accents, Gold Mount, Victorian, 1 In.	1896.00
Toggle, Agate, Carved, Openwork, Lotus & Crabs, Chinese, 1800s, 1 ¾ In. ....*Illus*	2772.00
Vinaigrette, Walnut Form, Pierced Grille, Goldtone Metal, Victorian, ¾ In.	720.00
Watches are listed in their own category.	

JOHN ROGERS statues were made from 1859 to 1892. The originals were bronze, but the thousands of copies made by the Rogers factory were of painted plaster. Eighty different figures were created. Similar painted plaster figures were produced by some other factories. Rights to the figures were sold in 1893, and the figures were manufactured for several more years by the Rogers Statuette Co. Never repaint a Rogers figure because this lowers the value to collectors.

Group, Rip Van Winkle At Home, c.1871, 19 In.	1295.00
Group, Wounded To The Rear, One More Shot, 2 Civil War Soldiers, 1865, 23 In.	1200.00 to 1808.00

JOSEF ORIGINALS ceramics were designed by Muriel Joseph George. The first pieces were made in California from 1945 to 1962. They were then manufactured in Japan. The company was sold to George Good in 1982 and he continued to make Josef Originals until 1985. The company was then sold to Southland Corporation. The name is now owned by Applause, and the Birthday Girl series is still being made.

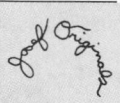

Ashtray, Black Poodle, Flowers, Gilt Trim, Japan, 3 ½ In. Diam.	25.00
Figurine, Birthday Girl, Age 8, Yellow Dress, 5 In.	15.00
Figurine, Birthday Girl, Age 14, Pink Dress, Parasol, 6 ½ In.	18.00
Figurine, Birthstone Girl, October, Blue Dress, Holding Flower, 4 In.	23.00
Figurine, Boy, Graduation Cap & Gown, 4 In.	16.00
Figurine, Heart In Hand, Green Dress, Butterflies, 9 In.	109.00
Figurine, Kitten, Meowing, Foil Label, Japan, 3 x 2 In.	18.00
Figurine, Mama, Blue Dress, Apron, Bottle In Hand, 7 ½ In.	110.00
Figurine, Ostrich, Mother & Baby, 5 ½ In.	30.00
Figurine, Rocking Kangaroo, Joey, c.1955, 5 ½ In.	60.00
Head Vase, Stand-Up Collar With Roses, Eyelashes, 4 ¾ In.	89.00
Music Box, Santa Boy, Playing Mandolin, 8 In.	15.00
Music Box, Santa Boy, Playing Mandolin, Paper Label, 8 In.	24.00
Pie Bird, Yellow, 1950s, 3 ½ In.	54.00
Pin Tray, Girl, Purple Dress, Hands Clasped, 4 In.	125.00
Trinket Box, Praying Nun, Black Habit, Rosary, 5 In.	59.00

JUDAICA is any memorabilia that refers to the Jews or the Jewish religion. Interests range from newspaper clippings that mention eighteenth- and nineteenth-century Jewish Americans to religious objects, such as menorahs or spice boxes. Age, condition, and the intrinsic value of the material, as well as the historic and artistic importance, determine the value.

Challah Knife, Sterling, Engraved, Hebrew Script, Serrated Blade, Stamped Wolpert, 13 In.	247.00
Magilla Scroll, 24 Sheets, Hebrew, Leather Parchment, Wood Spindle, c.1800, 20 x 11 In.	615.00
Menorah, 9-Light, Silver, Bird & Stag Caps, 21 x 15 In.	4800.00
Paperweight, Star Of David, Clear, Steuben, 2 ½ In.	238.00
Scroll Holder, Parcel Gilt, Motto, Flowers, Pierced Base, Rotating Handle, Austria, 1882, 14 ½ In.	8775.00
Scroll Of Esther, Enamel, Blue Ground, Silver Cased, Vermeil, Woman's Head, 1900s, 10 ¼ In.	2400.00
Spice Box, Silver Plate, Ivory Center, 13 In.	327.00
Spice Tower, Silver, Deer Design, Hexagonal, 9 In.	900.00
Torah Finials, Silver, Hallmarks, Vienna, c.1890, 13 In.	3900.00
Torah Pointer, Silver, Cymbal Playing Rabbi, Filigree Dome, Tapered Shaft, Coral Cabochon, 6 ⅜ In.	94.00

Torah Pointer, Silver, Lion Finial, Filigree Grip, Turquoise Cabochons, Russia, 10 ½ In.	*Illus*	106.00
Torah Pointer, Silver, Lion Finial, Filigree, Coral, Turquoise, Spiral Chain, 10 ½ In.	189.00 to	443.00
Torah Pointer, Silver, Round Knop, Tapered, Wirework, Pointing Hand, Chain, 1900s, 6 ½ In.		148.00
Torah Pointer, Silver, Star, Spread Wing Eagle Finial, Onyx Cabochon, Embossed Shell, 11 ¼ In.		201.00

JUGTOWN POTTERY refers to pottery made in North Carolina as far back as the 1750s. In 1915, Juliana and Jacques Busbee set up a training and sales organization for what they named Jugtown Pottery. In 1921, they built a shop at Jugtown, North Carolina, and hired Ben Owen as a potter in 1923. The Busbees moved the village store where the pottery was sold to New York City. Juliana Busbee sold the New York store in 1926 and moved into a log cabin near the Jugtown Pottery. The pottery closed in 1959. It reopened in 1960 and is still working near Seagrove, North Carolina.

Bowl, Dogwood Blossoms, Salt Glaze, c.1910, 3 ¼ x 9 In.	354.00
Bowl, Redware, Orange, Speckled Lead Base Glaze, Brown Brushwork, Handles, 5 ¾ x 10 ¾ In.	86.00
Oil Jar, Mirror Black Glaze, Bulbous, Ridged Sides, Applied Handles, Stamped, 6 x 7 In.	354.00
Vase, Chinese Blue, Purple Mottled Glaze, Unglazed Base, 4 ¼ x 4 ½ In.	575.00
Vase, Egg Shape, Wine Red, Over Gray Glaze, Stamped, 6 In.	148.00
Vase, Gourd, Drippy White Glaze Neck, Impressed Stamp, North Carolina, 7 In.	403.00
Vase, Mirror Black Glaze, Bell Shape, North Carolina, 7 ¼ x 6 ¾ In.	748.00
Vase, Mottled Blue, Green, Tapered, 6 In.	150.00
Vase, Variegated Green, Black, Marked, 7 ½ In.	150.00
Vase, Yellow Slip, Clear Lead Glaze, 3 Applied Pinch Handles, North Carolina, 7 In.	460.00
Vase, Yellow Slip, Oval, Impressed Stamp, North Carolina, 6 ⅝ In.	460.00

JUKEBOXES play records. The first coin-operated phonograph was demonstrated in 1889. In 1906 the Automatic Entertainer appeared, the first coin-operated phonograph to offer several different selections of music. The first electrically powered jukebox was introduced in 1927. Collectors search for jukeboxes of all ages, especially those with flashing lights and unusual design and graphics.

Ami, Model B, Art Deco Style, Front Panel Display, Wood Case, Plexiglas, 78 RPM, c.1948, 64 x 32 In.	600.00
Ami, Model D 80, Music For You, Fluted Bottom, 45 RPM, c.1951	784.00
Mills, Do-Re-Mi, Art Deco Style, Wood Veneer, Green Cloth, Angled Front, 1930s, 51 In.	270.00
Mills, Studio, 5 Cents, Walnut, Art Deco Style, 1930s, 63 x 40 In.	900.00
Packard, Pla-Mor, Model 769, The Manhattan, 78 RPM Records, c.1947	7280.00
Rock-Ola, Tempo 2, Model 1485, Holds 100 Discs, German Version, 1959	4005.00
Seeburg Wall-O-Matic, Metal, 20 Buttons, Flip Selector	210.00
Seeburg, Model 200, Select-O-Matic, 100 Selection, Tail Fins, Brake Lights, c.1958, 58 x 35 In.	900.00
Wurlitzer, Model 71, Light-Up Speaker, Automatic	4480.00
Wurlitzer, Model 78-E, Wagon Wheel, Multi-Selector, 78 RPM Records, c.1941	4480.00
Wurlitzer, Model 81, Mae West Stand, 23 x 57 x 19 In.	18700.00
Wurlitzer, Model 81, Mae West Stand, Coin & Keys, 23 x 57 In.	*Illus*	18700.00
Wurlitzer, Model 750-E, Multi-Selector, 78 RPM Records, Key, c.1941	*Illus*	6720.00
Wurlitzer, Model 850, Peacock, Lights Up, 78 RPM Records, c.1941	12320.00
Wurlitzer, Model 1500, Multi-Select, Keyboard Decoration, 45 & 78 RPM, c.1952	1800.00
Wurlitzer, Model 3210, Americana II, Multi-Selector, 45 RPM, c.1968	336.00
Wurlitzer, Model 7810, Wagon Wheel, c.1941	1150.00

KATE GREENAWAY, who was a famous illustrator of children's books, drew pictures of children in high-waisted Empire dresses. She lived from 1846 to 1901. Her designs appear on china, glass, napkin rings, and other pieces.

Book, Language Of Flowers, 2 Women, Hardcover, 1978, 9 x 7 In., 61 Pages	28.00
Book, Mother Goose, Hardcover, c.1900	125.00
Book, Under The Window, Hardcover	15.00
Bowl, Silver Plate, Ball Feet, Boy, Girl, Reed & Barton, 6 ¾ x 4 In.	165.00
Candlestick, Silver Plate, Girl, Flowers, Bonnet, Purse, James Tufts Co., c.1900, 5 In., Pair	525.00
Drawing, 3 Women Walking On Windy Day, Watercolor, Pen & Ink, 3 ¾ x 5 ¾ In.	561.00
Match Holder, Silver Plate, Girl, James Tufts, c.1885, 4 ¾ In.	580.00
Napkin Ring, Girl, Holding Umbrella, Boy, Rolling Hoop, James Tufts	1975.00
Napkin Ring, Silver Plate, Boy On Stomach, Dog, James W. Tufts	550.00
Plate, Almanac, Aquarius, Royal Doulton, 8 ¼ In.	15.00
Tray, 4 Scenes, Engraved, James Tufts Co., c.1885, 7 In. Diam.	155.00
Trinket Box, Black Ebonized Wood, Girls In Garden, Holding Skirts, 7 x 5 In.	75.00
Washbasin, Children Playing, Divided, Handle, 1900s, 15 x 10 In.	220.00

Jewelry, Ring, Smoky Quartz, White Stone, Silver Wire Wrap, Claire Falkenstein, 1980s, Size 9
$600.00

Skinner, Inc.

Jewelry, Toggle, Agate, Carved, Openwork, Lotus & Crabs, Chinese, 1800s, 1 ¾ In.
$2772.00

Garth's Auctioneers & Appraisers

K

Judaica, Torah Pointer, Silver, Lion Finial, Filigree Grip, Turquoise Cabochons, Russia, 10 ½ In.
$106.00

Conestoga Auction Co., Inc.

TIP
Rings should be cleaned regularly to remove bits of soap and cosmetics and oil. The stones will have more sparkle.

KAY FINCH

Jukebox, Wurlitzer, Model 81, Mae West Stand, Coin & Keys, 23 x 57 In. $18700.00

Showtime Auction Services

Jukebox, Wurlitzer, Model 750-E, Multi-Selector, 78 RPM Records, Key, c.1941 $6720.00

Victorian Casino Antiques

Kenton Hills, Vase, Pastel Flowers, Signed, Alza Stratton, Unica In Black Slip, 10 In. $288.00

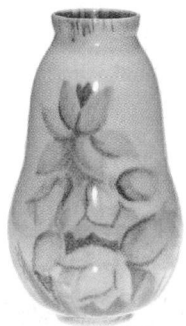

Humler & Nolan

KAY FINCH CERAMICS were made in Corona Del Mar, California, from 1935 to 1963. The hand-decorated pieces often depicted whimsical animals and people. Pastel colors were used.

Kay Finch CALIFORNIA

Figurine, Angel, Hands Crossed, Head Down, Blond, 3 ⅞ In.	48.00
Figurine, Bird, Baby, Chocolate Brown, 4 ½ In.	40.00
Figurine, Cat, Muff, Gray, Blue, 3 In.	65.00
Figurine, Cat, Pink, Purple, Green, Closed Eyes, 3 In.	65.00
Figurine, Couple, Peasant Boy & Girl, Brown, Yellow, Blue	107.00
Figurine, Dog, Skye Terrier, 11 In.	250.00
Figurine, Kangaroo, Apron, Bow, 9 In.	181.00
Figurine, Rooster, Butch, Multicolor, 6 ½ In.	70.00
Figurine, Singing Bird, Stand, Pink, 4 In.	195.00
Figurine, Woman, Flowered Dress, Muff, Cape, 1950s, 7 In.	48.00
Planter, Bear, Alphabet Block, Pink, 5 ¾ In.	45.00

KAYSERZINN, *see Pewter category.*

KELVA glassware was made by the C. F. Monroe Company of Meriden, Connecticut, about 1904. It is a pale, pastel-painted glass decorated with flowers, designs, or scenes. Kelva resembles Nakara and Wave Crest, two other glasswares made by the same company.

KELVA

Box, Faceted Red Mottled, Green Flower, C.F. Monroe, 3 ½ In.	86.00
Dresser Box, Mottled Green, Pink Flowers, Metal Center Banding, Squat, 3 ¾ In.	201.00
Dresser Box, Pink Flowers, Gray Grained Ground, 4 x 6 In.	267.00
Dresser Box, Round, Hinged Lid, Painted Flowers, Stamped, 3 ½ x 8 In.	300.00

KENTON HILLS POTTERY in Erlanger, Kentucky, made artwares, including vases and figurines that resembled Rookwood, probably because so many of the original artists and workmen had worked at the Rookwood plant. Kenton Hills opened in 1939 and closed during World War II.

Bookends, 2 Owls, Perched, Pale Blue High Glaze, 5 ¾ In.	489.00
Sign, Kenton Hills Porcelains, Logo, Spanish Red Glaze, Shaped, 6 x 10 ½ In.	1840.00
Tray, Horse Head, Oxblood Glaze, Marked, 1 ½ x 7 ¼ In.	127.00
Vase, Ivory, Purple & Pink Ring Of Flowers, Blue Rim, c.1941, 6 x 4 ¼ In.	595.00
Vase, Pastel Flowers, Signed, Alza Stratton, Unica In Black Slip, 10 In. *Illus*	288.00
Vase, Unica, Fish Band, Bulbous, Brown, Cream, Signed, Alza Stratton, 7 x 7 In.	375.00

KEW BLAS is the name used by the Union Glass Company of Somerville, Massachusetts. The name refers to an iridescent golden glass made from the 1890s to 1924. The iridescent glass was reminiscent of the Tiffany glass of the period.

KEW-BLAS

Bowl, Sherbet, Iridescent Gold, Footed, Signed, c.1900, 3 In.	212.00
Compote, Iridescent, Flared Ruffled Onionskin Rim, Twisted Stem, Bell Foot, 8 In.	210.00
Finger Bowl, Underplate, Iridescent Gold, Ruffled Scallop Rim, Signed, c.1900, Bowl 2 ½ x 5 In.	354.00
Pitcher, Gold Iridescent, Applied Handle, Signed, 7 ¾ In.	230.00
Pitcher, Iridescent, Opal, Green, Gold, Pulled Feather, Applied Handle, Signed, 4 ½ In. *Illus*	690.00
Vase, Gold Loop Design, Platinum Iridescent, Shouldered, Flare Lip, Signed, 8 In.	460.00
Vase, Iridescent Gold, Green Feathering, Round, Signed, 3 ¼ In.	531.00
Vase, Iridescent, Green Pulled Feather Tipt Iridescent Gold, Signed, 5 ½ In.	575.00
Vase, Pulled Feather, Green, Ivory, Flared Rim, Signed, 20th Century, 5 x 2 ½ In.	480.00
Vase, White Pulled Feather Design, Green & Gold Tipped, Beaker, Ruffled Rim, 8 In.	805.00

KEWPIES, designed by Rose O'Neill, were first pictured in the *Ladies' Home Journal*. The figures, which are similar to pixies, were a success, and Kewpie dolls and figurines started appearing in 1911. Kewpie pictures and other items soon followed. Collectors search for all items that picture the little winged people.

Bell, Porcelain, Bride, Groom, 1970s, 4 In.	65.00
Bisque, Bellhop, Jointed Pinned Arms, Molded Vest & Cap, Marked, O'Neill, 3 ¾ In.	75.00
Bisque, Crying, Crawling, 3 x 2 ½ In.	18.00
Bisque, Doodle Dog, Painted Brown Spots, Side-Glancing Eyes, Wings, 3 In. *Illus*	672.00
Bisque, Molded, Curls, Forelock, Wings, Side-Glancing Eyes, O'Neill Mark, Box, c.1915, 6 In. *Illus*	448.00
Bisque, Pair, Reading Book, Bench, 3 ½ In.	275.00
Bisque, Playing Mandolin, 2 In.	175.00
Bisque, Reclining On Tummy, Winking, Propped On One Arm, Foot Up, Lefton, 4 x 3 In.	37.00
Bisque, Swivel Head, Molded Topknot, Curls, Side-Glancing Eyes, Starfish Hands, c.1912, 18 In.	5880.00
Bowl, Action Kewpies, Rose O'Neill, Prussia Royal Rudolstadt, 1912, 7 ¾ In.	375.00

Calendar, 1977, Kewpie Dolls, Full Pad, Rose O'Neill, 8 ½ x 7 ½ In.	80.00
Celluloid, Wavy Hair, Side-Glancing Eyes, Japan, 9 ½ In.	25.00
Composition, Checked Dress, Flowers, Cameo Doll Co., 1930s, 12 In.	145.00
Composition, Jointed, Flowers, Shorts, Straw Hat, 13 In.	60.00
Composition, Jointed, Side-Glancing Eyes, Cameo Doll Co., 1940s, 13 In.	125.00
Composition, Spring Strung Arms, Blue Base, Side-Glancing Eyes, 1913, 12 In.	250.00
Cup & Saucer, Crawling, Kicking, Playing, Rose O'Neill, Prussia Royal Rudolstadt, 1912	175.00
Inkwell, Bisque, Holding Pen, Sitting On Inkwell, Germany, c.1900, 4 ¼ In.	1200.00
Mask, Molded Cloth, Side-Glancing Eyes, Red Cheeks, 1920s, 3 ½ x 3 In.	125.00
Plaque, Celluloid, Kewpie Carrying Gifts, 7 In.	106.00
Plaque, Etched Glass, Holding Flower, Rose O'Neill, 8 x 6 In.	235.00
Plaque, Playing Violin, Birds, Start The Day On A Happy Note, Jasperware Green, Oval	24.00
Postcard, Our First Flag, 1776-1976 Bicentennial	6.00
Postcard, Pledge Allegiance, Bicentennial 1776-1976	6.00
Tobacco Flannel, Farmer, Hat Filled With Berries, Rake, 1914, 4 ¼ x 5 ½ In.	20.00
Tobacco Flannel, Soldier, Pink & Tan Ground, 1914, 4 ¼ x 5 ½ In.	15.00
Wedding Topper, Celluloid, Holding Bouquet, Wedding Dress, 1930s	55.00

KITCHEN utensils of all types, from eggbeaters to bowls, are collected today. Handmade wooden and metal items, like ladles and apple peelers, were made in the early nineteenth century. Mass-produced pieces, like iron apple peelers and graniteware, were made in the nineteenth century. Also included in this category are utensils used for other household chores, such as laundry and cleaning. Other kitchen wares are listed under manufacturers' names or under Advertising, Iron, Tool, or Wooden.

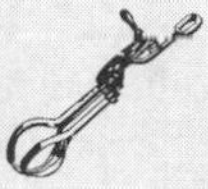

Asparagus Bundler, Cast Iron, Enamel, 2 Half Hoops, End Plate, 10 In.	180.00
Batter Bowl, Yellowware, Concave Flutes, Panels, Scalloped Border, c.1886, 4 x 9 ½ In.	115.00
Board, Cutting, Cherry, Ram's Head Nut, 18 ¾ In.	104.00
Board, Cutting, Pine, Man Shape, c.1855, 21 In.	1007.00
Board, Dough, Cherry, Shaped Handle, Hanging Hole, 26 ½ x 18 ¾ In.	106.00
Bowl, Dough, Pine, Birch, Handle, 1800s, 6 ½ x 20 ½ In., Pair	215.00
Bowl, Wood, Turned, Shallow Foot, Blue Gray Paint, Narrow Rim Band, 7 x 21 In.	153.00
Box, Sugar, Pine, Red Grain Paint, Interior Iron Cutter, c.1820, 10 ½ x 17 ½ In.	711.00
Bread Box, Copper, Removable Lid, 2 Handles, c.1900, 15 ½ In.	173.00
Bread Box, Pine, Hinged, Applied Letters, Vents, Paint, c.1925, 10 x 13 In.	374.00
Bread Box, Wood, Flowers, Gold Stencil, Blue Ground, Paint, c.1920, 16 x 24 In.	148.00
Broiler, Wrought Iron, Revolving, Basting Well Handle, 25 ½ In.	450.00
Butter Mold, look under Mold, Butter in this category.	
Butter Paddle, Burl, Crook Handle, 1800s, 6 In.	588.00
Butter Paddle, Burl, Crook Handle, 19th Century, 11 ½ In.	441.00
Butter Paddle, Carved Handle, c.1800, 7 In.	711.00
Butter Paddle, Maple, Horse Head Handle, Indian Carved, 1800s, 9 ½ In.	415.00
Butter Scoop, Burl, Scalloped Edge Handle, 1800s, 9 ½ In.	969.00
Butter Stamp, Compass Star, Tulip, Wood, Double Sided, 1800s, 4 ¼ In.	181.00
Butter Stamp, Eagle, Carved, Handle, Round, 1800s, 4 ½ In. Diam.	558.00
Butter Stamp, Eagle, Handle, Scrubbed Surface, Round, c.1855, 4 ¼ In.	353.00
Butter Stamp, Fruit, Leaves, Chip Carved Borders, Turned Handle, 1800s, 9 ½ In.	1067.00
Butter Stamp, Geometric, Hardwood, Pa., 1800s, 3 x 2 In.	59.00
Butter Stamp, Hearts & Flowers, Sawtooth Border, Elongated Oval, 1800s, 3 x 5 ½ In.	1410.00
Butter Stamp, Tulip & Star, c.1855, 4 In.	323.00
Butter Stamp, Tulip, Stars, Handle, Scrubbed Surface, 1800s, 5 In.	235.00
Butter Tub, Pottery, Orange & Green, Mottled, Incised Leaves, Rope Twist Handles, 10 In.	767.00
Butter, Cherry, Red Stain, Slide Lid, Stamped, Bucks County, Pa., c.1865, 16 x 16 In.	456.00
Cabbage Cutter, Maple Frame, Sliding Finger Jointed Box, 3 Adjustable Steel Blades, 26 x 9 In.	12.00
Cabbage Cutter, Walnut, Iron Blade, Pierced Handle, Ram's Horn Iron Nut, 17 ½ x 7 In.*....Illus*	24.00
Cake Pan, Heart Shape, Tinned Sheet Iron, Cone Shape Center Vent, 16 x 13 In.	71.00
Canister, Copper, Bulbous, Cylindrical Base, Riveted Heart-Shaped Handle Rings, 8 In.	35.00
Canister, Lid, Milk, Sheet Steel, Blue & White Swirls, Wire Bail Handle, 11 In.	83.00
Cheese Caddy, Mahogany, 2 Compartments, Flowers, Scrolled Edge, Casters, c.1835, 8 ½ x 16 In.	461.00
Cheese Cutter, Mechanical, Full Wheel, Cast Iron, Computing Cheese Cutter, 1905, 10 x 20 In.	201.00
Cheese Cutter, Templeton, Wood Cutting Board, Round, Countertop, Computing Scale Co.	1020.00
Cheese Slicer, Wood Cutting Board, Computing Scale Co., Dayton, Ohio, Pat. 1903*........Illus*	510.00
Cherry Pitter, Cast Iron, Wood Plank Mount, Patent Date 1863 & 1866, 9 x 13 In.	35.00
Chopper, Meat & Vegetable, Revolving, Tin, Mechanical, c.1835, 3 x 16 ½ In.	529.00
Chopper, Red Cast Iron, Crank Handle, Wood Board Base, Metal Bowl, 18 In.	259.00
Chopper, Revolving, Tin, Mechanical, Starrett's, c.1825, 13 In.	529.00
Churn, Barrel Shape, Side Crank, Treen, Tabletop, c.1850, 13 ½ x 6 In.	230.00

Kew Blas, Pitcher, Iridescent, Opal, Green, Gold, Pulled Feather, Applied Handle, Signed, 4 ½ In.
$690.00

Early Auction Co.

Kewpie, Bisque, Doodle Dog, Painted Brown Spots, Side-Glancing Eyes, Wings, 3 In.
$672.00

Theriault's

K

Kewpie, Bisque, Molded, Curls, Forelock, Wings, Side-Glancing Eyes, O'Neill Mark, Box, c.1915, 6 In.
$448.00

Theriault's

Kitchen, Cabbage Cutter, Walnut, Iron Blade, Pierced Handle, Ram's Horn Iron Nut, 17 ½ x 7 In.
$24.00

Conestoga Auction Co., Inc.

Kitchen, Cheese Slicer, Wood Cutting Board, Computing Scale Co., Dayton, Ohio, Pat. 1903
$510.00

Victorian Casino Antiques

Kitchen, Cookie Cutter, Heart In Hand, Tin, 4 ¼ In.
$560.00

Conestoga Auction Co., Inc.

Kitchen, Cookie Cutter, Indian, Standing, Tomahawk, 7 ¾ x 3 ⅝ In.
$1,298.00

Conestoga Auction Co., Inc.

Kitchen, Cookie Cutter, Man's Head, Wavy Hair, Tin, 5 ⅝ x 4 ⅝ In.
$531.00

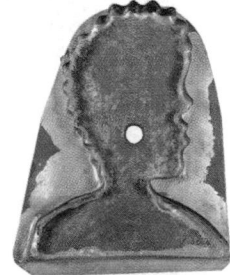

Conestoga Auction Co., Inc.

Churn, Barrel, Brass Strapping, Turned Lid, c.1840, 42 x 9 ½ In.	58.00
Churn, Barrel, Wood, Cast Iron Crank, Wood Grip, Metal Bands, Stave Body, Footed, 15 x 13 In.	59.00
Churn, Bentwood, Gray Paint, c.1850, 22 ½ x 7 In.	127.00
Churn, Bentwood, M. Brown & Co., Wapakoneta, Ohio, 1900, 32 In.	148.00
Churn, Cylinder, White Cedar, 2 Metal Bands, Cast Iron Crank, Shoe Feet, R.C.W., 17 x 15 In.	59.00
Churn, D.F. Haynes & Co., Stenciled Crown, Stripes, Lug Handle, c.1875, 3 Gal., 16 In.	374.00
Churn, Dasher, Staved Wood, Cone Shape, Iron Wire Bands, Knobbed Lid, 20 x 42 In.	83.00
Churn, Dazey, 2 Wheels, Hand Crank, c.1917	210.00
Churn, Dazey, Sheet Metal, Cast Iron Base, Overhead Gear & Crank, Wood Lid, 28 x 15 In.	47.00
Churn, Oak Cabinet, Paddles, Stencil, Model No. 3, Standard Churn Co., Wapakoneta, Oh., 24 x 30 In.	168.00
Churn, Pine, Blue Paint, c.1850, 32 In.	444.00
Churn, Pine, Round Tub, Crank, Blue Paint, c.1855, 19 In.	91.00
Churn, Plunger, Blue Paint, Wood, Barrel, c.1860, 25 In.	130.00
Churn, Tabletop, Blue Paint, Rounded Bottom, Handled Lid, 16 x 13 In.	236.00
Churn, Wood, Painted Blue, 1800s, 40 In.	267.00
Coffee Grinders are listed in the Coffee Mill category.	
Coffee Mills are listed in their own category.	
Coffee Urn, Nickel Plate, Lobed Dome Lid, Finial, Cylindrical, Handles, Cabriole Feet, c.1870, 41 In.	1422.00
Coffeepot, Pewter, Organic Repousse Design, Tudric, Liberty & Co., c.1905, 6 x 4 x 5 In.	1000.00
Coffeepot, Tin, 1800s, 8 ½ x 7 In.	35.00
Coffeepot, Tin, Cone On Cone Shape, Hawk Beak Spout, Dome Cover, Loop Handle, 7 In.	94.00
Colander, Sheet Iron, Bucket Shape, 3 Panels, Rolled Rim, Loop Handles, Tube Feet, 7 x 10 In.	47.00
Colander, Tinned Sheet Iron, Cone Shape, 4 Panels, Strap Handles, 7 x 12 In.	35.00
Colander, Yellowware, Diamond, Embossed, Ovals, c.1930, 11 In. Diam.	125.00
Cookie Board, Hardwood, Impressed Man & Woman, German Costume, 14 x 9 In.	106.00
Cookie Cutter, Angel Head, Stylized, Wings, Tin, 3 ¾ In.	47.00
Cookie Cutter, Angel In Flight, Tin, 4 ¾ In.	47.00
Cookie Cutter, Carpenter's Hand Saw, Tin, 6 ⅛ In.	295.00
Cookie Cutter, Cat, Seated, Tin, Half Round Strap Handle, 4 x 3 ¼ In.	83.00
Cookie Cutter, Fish, Tin, 5 ½ In.	59.00
Cookie Cutter, Heart In Hand, Tin, 4 ¼ In. ....*Illus*	560.00
Cookie Cutter, Indian, Standing, Tomahawk, 7 ¾ x 3 ⅝ In. ....*Illus*	1298.00
Cookie Cutter, Man's Head, Smiling, Large Nose, Wavy Hair, Tin, 4 ¾ In.	165.00
Cookie Cutter, Man's Head, Wavy Hair, Tin, 5 ⅝ x 4 ⅝ In. ....*Illus*	531.00
Cookie Cutter, Mermaid, Tin, 5 ¾ In.	59.00
Cookie Cutter, Monkey On Elephant, Tinned Sheet Iron, 7 ¾ x 7 ¾ In.	415.00
Cookie Cutter, Multiple Shapes, In Circle, Tin, 7 ¼ x ¾ In.	35.00
Cookie Cutter, Soldier Playing Bugle, Tin, Sheet Iron, 1800s, 10 ⅜ In.	304.00
Cookie Cutter, Woman, Holding Basket, 14 In.	259.00
Cookie Jar, Casper, Ceramic, Holding Cookie In Hand, Smiling, c.1960, 13 ½ In.	253.00
Cookie Jar, Flintstones, Fred Swinging Golf Club, Dino Caddy Finial, Lid, c.1960, 6 ½ x 14 In.	633.00
Corn Grinder, Cast Iron, Wood Grip, F. Wilson, Easton, Pa., 1881, 20-In. Wheel, 10 x 10 In.	24.00
Corn Sheller, Cast Iron, Wood Housing, Wedge Shape Hopper, Side Crank	59.00
Corn Sheller, Separator, Dazey, Wood Case, Cast Iron Grinding Gears, Wheels, Crank, 43 x 20 In.	71.00
Cream Separator, Bradley Economy King, Cast Iron, Table Top, Crank, Sears, 12 In.	90.00
Cream Separator, Economy King, Crank, Plated Steel Tank, Screened Funnel, Booklet, 24 x 12 In.	59.00
Deodorizer, Shmoo, Al Capp, Figural, Ceramic, Rubber Cap, Foil Label, Late 1940s, 5 ½ In. ....*Illus*	183.00
Dough Box, Cupboard, Pine, Painted Red, Lift Lid, Lower Doors, New England, c.1810, 32 x 35 In.	911.00
Dough Box, Lid, Pine, Cutout Handles, 23 In.	197.00
Dough Box, Lift Top, Flared Turned Legs, Grain Paint, Pa., c.1820, 29 ¼ x 48 In.	5103.00
Dough Box, Pine, Cover, Splayed Turned Legs, 29 ¾ x 32 In.	236.00
Dough Box, Pine, Overhang Lid, Splayed Legs, Pa., c.1810, 28 x 54 x 30 In.	182.00
Dough Box, Pine, Poplar, Blue, Green Paint, Shenandoah Valley, c.1850, 10 x 28 In.	207.00
Dough Box, Pine, Poplar, Molded Detail, Chip Carving, 1800s, 8 ¾ x 33 In.	646.00
Dough Box, Pine, Stand, Turned Legs, c.1850, 28 ½ x 40 ½ In.	182.00
Dough Box, Pine, Stand, Turned Splayed Legs, Red Paint, Pa., c.1840, 30 x 48 In.	1422.00
Dough Box, Plank Cover, Dovetailed, Canted Sides, Baluster Ring-Turned Legs, c.1860, 30 x 49 In.	115.00
Dough Box, Slide Lid, Splayed Legs, 29 x 27 In.	255.00
Dough Box, Softwood, 1-Board Top, Canted Sides, Turned Legs, Bun Feet, 26 ½ x 29 In. ..*Illus*	59.00
Dough Box, Softwood, Overhung 3-Board Top, Cutout Skirt, Splayed Legs, Pa., c.1820, 29 x 25 In.	345.00
Dough Box, Splayed Legs, Red Paint, c.1890, 20 ½ x 43 In.	115.00
Dough Box, Stand, French Provincial, Walnut, Shaped Skirt, Baluster Supports, 33 x 55 In.	1195.00
Dough Box, Stand, Pine, Hinged Lid, Tapered, Scalloped Apron, Splayed Legs, 1800s, 31 x 33 In.	430.00
Dough Box, Stand, Pine, Kneading Board Top, Rectangular, Turned Legs, c.1850, 28 x 18 In.	489.00
Dough Box, Stand, Poplar, Turned Legs, c.1760, 28 ½ x 54 In.	1541.00
Dough Box, Walnut, Removable Overhung Top, Turned Legs, Stand, Pa., 29 x 53 In.	1422.00

K

Dough Box, Walnut, Splay Leg Stand, Tapered, Pinned 3-Board Top, 30 x 41 In.	1080.00
Dough Scraper, Brass, Iron, Stamped Peter Derr, 1860, 4 In.	948.00
Dough Scraper, Brass, Wrought Iron, Turned Wood Handle, Peter Derr, 1854, 6 ½ In.	1944.00
Dough Scraper, Double Heart Cutout, Punched Pinwheels, Wrought Iron, Pa., c.1830, 2 ½ x 2 In.	4266.00
Dough Scraper, Heart Cutout, Wrought Iron, Pa., c.1830, 2 ¾ x 3 ¼ In.	1422.00
Dough Scraper, Iron Blade, Brass Ferule, Turned Wood Handle, c.1848, 6 In.	723.00
Dutch Oven, Griswold No. 13, Lid	750.00
Egg Timer, Chick, Wooden, Glass Timer Mounted On Side, Marked Germany, 1920, 4 x 3 In.	55.00
Fish Kettle, Cast Iron, Oval, Tripod Legs, England, 26 In.	1298.00
Flue Cover, Glass, Metal Rim, Woman, Seaside Hotel, Red Dress & Hat, c.1910, 9 ½ In.	115.00
Fondue Set, Enamel, Metal Pot, 6 Forks, Ernest Soho Creations, Japan, 1970s, 5 x 7 In.	175.00
Food, Chopper, Platform, Iron Swan's Neck Hinge, Wood Handle, 1800s, 17 ¾ In. *Illus*	94.00
Fork, Flesh & Spatula, Wrought Iron, Copper, Brass Inlays, Wrigglework, Pa., c.1830, 19 In.	1304.00
Fork, Flesh, 3 Tines, Heart-Shaped Center, Wrought Iron, Pa., c.1800, 20 ½ In.	1094.00
Fork, Flesh, Copper, Brass, c.1845, 19 ½ In.	1541.00
Fork, Flesh, Wrought Iron, Brass Inlay, Inscribed 1787, AR, 16 ½ In.	356.00
Fork, Meat, Curled Fiddle Back, Wrought Iron, Stamped Levera A. Zarfoss, c.1920, 14 ½ In.	29.00
Fork, Roasting, Wrought Iron, Signed Frederick Co., c.1900, 21 In.	345.00
Fruit Crusher, Hand Crank, American Wringer Co., 17 ½ x 8 ½ In.	110.00
Fruit Crusher, Universal, Wood, Tapered Bin, Crank, American Wringer Co., 18 x 9 x 15 In.	110.00
Fruit Juice Extractor, Table Top, Sunkist, Metal Label, Aluminum, Electric, 1922, 16 x 8 In.	71.00
Fruit Press, Enterprise, 6-Qt. Canister, Internal Colander, Wheel Driven, Iron, 17 x 12 In.	35.00
Frying Pan, Ram's Horn Top, Long Handle, Iron, 1800s, 42 In.	443.00
Grain Bin, Pine, 2 Slant Front Doors, 2 Interior Compartments, Shoe Feet, 1800s, 34 x 41 In.	403.00
Grater, Hanging, Wood, Handle, c.1860, 12 In.	230.00
Griddle, Griswold No. A 14, Round, Bailed	35.00
Griddle, Heart Design Handle, Tripod Feet, Cast Iron, 1700s, 13 ¾ In.	237.00
Gridiron, Hanging, Curved, Flat Strap Basket, Wrought Iron	94.00
Gridiron, Short Legs, Inline Handle, Hanging Ring Finial, Wrought Iron, 20 x 10 In. *Illus*	59.00
Grinder, Herb, Canoe Shape, Grinding Wheel, Wooden Handle, Angled Feet, Cast Iron, 16 In.	173.00
Grinder, Herb, Cast Iron, Wood, Crescent Shape, 18 In.	738.00
Grinder, Meat, Cast Iron, Sheet Metal Hopper, Wheels, Wood Plank Mounted, 25 x 25 In.	59.00
Ice Bucket, Lid, Metal, Glass Liner, Bakelite Handles, Everlast Metal Co., c.1935, 7 ½ In. *Illus*	36.00
Icebox, Oak, Brass Hardware, White Clad, Simmons Hardware Co., St. Louis, 35 x 41 In.	248.00
Icebox, Oak, Paneled, Lift Top Door, Lower Door, Ice Compartment, c.1900, 41 x 26 In.	108.00
Icebox, Paneled, Porcelain Lining, Salesman's Sample, 8 x 12 In.	2040.00
Icebox, Walnut, Mirrored Back, Rosette Crest, Storage, Zinc Lined, Block Feet, c.1890, 64 x 38 In.	388.00
Iron, Glass, Green Paint, Saunders Model 1038, 9 In.	1140.00
Kettle Stand, Brass, Iron, Cutout Hearts, Pierced Apron, Handles, Cabriole Legs, c.1905, 13 x 13 In.	259.00
Kettle Tilter, Wrought Iron, 7 ½ x 21 ½ In.	189.00
Kettle, Brass, Copper, Hand Forged, Iron Bail Handle, Tom York, Maine, c.1920, 19 In.	173.00
Kettle, Cast Iron, 3-Footed, Shaped Loop Handle, 12 Gal., 22 In.	35.00
Kettle, Cast Iron, Swing Handle, Tripod Feet, c.1750, 13 x 15 In.	510.00
Kettle, Copper, Brass Wood, 3-Footed, Benham & Froud, c.1885, 9 x 9 ½ In.	1000.00
Kettle, Hearth, Bronze, Double Spout, Swivel Ring, Man's Head Supports, c.1780, 12 ½ x 5 In.	288.00
Kettle, Water, Cast Iron, Sphere Shaped, Lid, Gooseneck Spout, Swing Handle, 10 ½ x 8 ½ In.	47.00
Knife Sharpener, Electric, Plastic, Nelson, Carvel Ball & Briddell, 1955, 3 ¼ x 5 In. *Illus*	250.00
Ladle, Punched Flower, Pretzel Finial, Wrought Iron, Copper, Pa., c.1830, 21 ½ In.	2015.00
Ladle, Straining, Wrought Iron, Copper, Brass, c.1830, 22 In.	356.00
Ladle, Tasting, Brass Bowl, Wrought Iron Handle, Signed Berks Co., Penn., c.1850, 10 ¼ In.	690.00
Malt Mixer, Hamilton Beach, Drink Master, Green Porcelain, Chrome, Aluminum Cup, Single	144.00
Malt Mixer, Hamilton, Drinkmaster, No, 30, Porcelain, Electric, 4-Fold Aerator, Cup, Countertop.	96.00
Malt Mixer, Red, Metal, Hamilton Beach, c.1950, 13 x 10 In.	295.00
Mangle, Industrial, Cast Iron, On Wheels, Wood Rollers, Painted, Baadh & Whinthers Efterfolger	531.00
Masher, Maple, Turned Handle, Button End, 11 In.	24.00
Match Holders can be found in their own category.	
Match Safes can be found in their own category.	
Measure, Cone Shape, Wood, Metal Bands, Painted, Amber, Red, Blue, Flowers, Leaves, 14 x 11 In.	71.00
Mixing Bowl, Interior Salt Glazed, Sloped, 3 Manganese Rings, Rolled Rim, Redware, 3 ¾ x 10 In.	94.00
Molds may also be found in the Pewter and Tinware categories.	
Mold, Butter, 2-Sided, Eagle, Spread Wing, Reverse, Goose, Standing, 1800s, 4 ⅛ In.	86.00
Mold, Butter, Flower, Star Shape, Lollipop Handle, Wood, c.1850, 8 ¾ In.	345.00
Mold, Butter, Swan, Notched Border, Maple, Stained, 5 ½ In.	35.00
Mold, Butter, Tulip, Faceted Handle, Scrubbed Surface, Wood, 1800s, 4 In.	470.00
Mold, Cake, Galleried Rim, Orange Lead Glaze, Redware, c.1870, 10 In.	230.00
Mold, Cake, Rounded Sides, Central Funnel, Brown Glaze, Yellow, Redware, 1800s, 9 ¾ In. Diam.	58.00

Kitchen, Deodorizer, Shmoo, Al Capp, Figural, Ceramic, Rubber Cap, Foil Label, Late 1940s, 5 ½ In.
$183.00

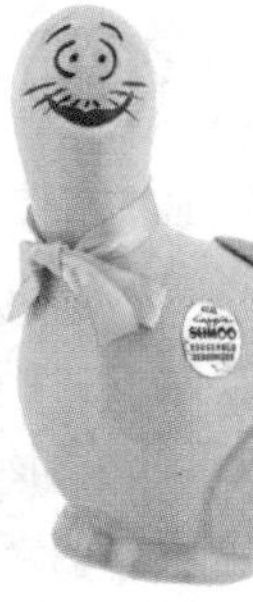

Hake's Americana & Collectibles

Kitchen, Dough Box, Softwood, 1-Board Top, Canted Sides, Turned Legs, Bun Feet, 26 ½ x 29 In.
$59.00

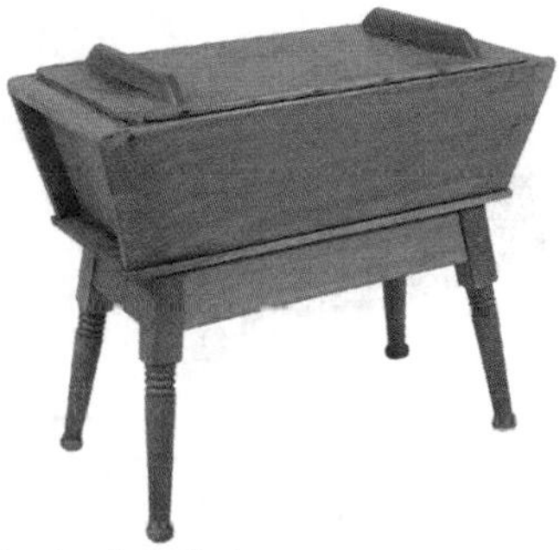

Conestoga Auction Co., Inc.

Kitchen, Food, Chopper, Platform, Iron Swan's Neck Hinge, Wood Handle, 1800s, 17 ¾ In.
$94.00

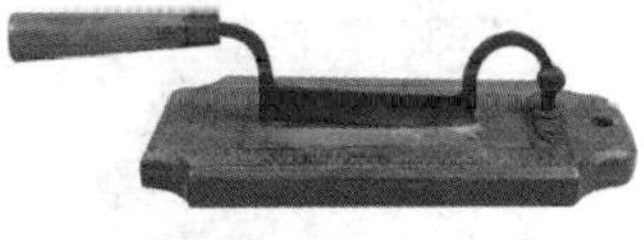

Conestoga Auction Co., Inc.

Kitchen, Gridiron, Short Legs, Inline Handle, Hanging Ring Finial, Wrought Iron, 20 x 10 In.
$59.00

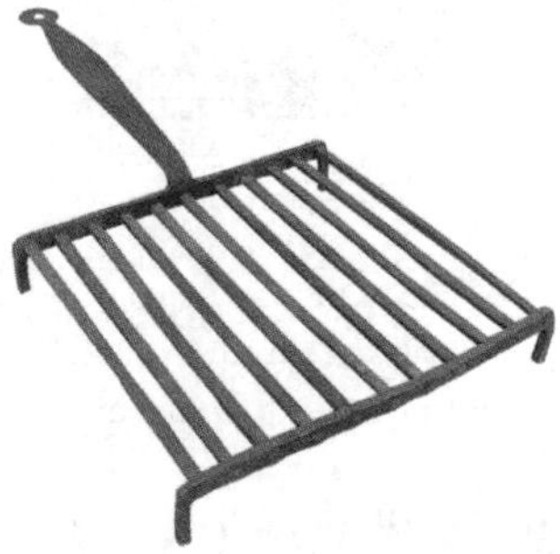

Conestoga Auction Co., Inc.

K

Kitchen, Ice Bucket, Lid, Metal, Glass Liner, Bakelite Handles, Everlast Metal Co., c.1935, 7 ½ In.
$36.00

Heritage Auctions

Kitchen, Knife Sharpener, Electric, Plastic, Nelson, Carvel Ball & Briddell, 1955, 3 x 5 In.
$250.00

Los Angeles Modern Auctions (LAMA)

Kitchen, Mold, Cookie, Maple, Carved, 8 Panels, Pennsylvania, 1800s, 7 ⅜ x 3 ½ In.
$83.00

Conestoga Auction Co., Inc.

Size Matters

Size makes a difference when pricing cast-iron cookware. Very small and very large pieces sell for higher prices than medium-sized pans. A Griswold No. 1 pan can be worth over $3,000.

Mold, Cake, Turk's Head Form, Redware, Manganese Spatter, Lobed Rim & Nose, 9 In.	47.00
Mold, Cake, Turk's Head Form, Yellowware, 16 Spiral Flutes, 10 ¼ In.	35.00
Mold, Candy, Yellow Kid, c.1905, 4 ¾ In.	120.00
Mold, Cheese, Punched Tin, Heart Shape, Applied Tubular Feet, Hanging Ring, 1800s, 3 ¼ In.	295.00
Mold, Cookie, Maple, Carved, 8 Panels, Pennsylvania, 1800s, 7 ⅜ x 3 ½ In. ....*Illus*	83.00
Mold, Corn, Yellowware, Impressed, Oval, Footed, 8 ¼ x 6 In.	48.00
Mold, Fish Shape, Redware, Salt Glaze, Manganese Specks, 14 x 7 In.	59.00
Mold, Fish, Pa., Redware, 1800s, 2 ¾ x 10 ¼ In.	356.00
Mold, Fish, Scaled Body, Manganese Daubs, Clear Glaze, Redware, Pa., c.1860, 12 ¼ In.	403.00
Mold, Food, Heart Shape, Depressions, Manganese, Piecrust Rim, C.N. Foltz, Redware, 1985, 2 x 7 In.	12.00
Mold, Food, Stag's Head, Hunter's Horn, White Enamel, Handles, Cast Iron, Blue Enamel, 10 x 13 In.	118.00
Mold, Ice Cream, Rabbit, Basket On Back, c.1900, 16 In.	41.00
Mold, Jelly, Copper, Tin Lined, Lobed, Victorian, c.1850, 2 ½ In., 6 Piece	207.00
Mold, Lobster Jelly, Copper, Tin Lined, Germany, c.1900, 10 ½ In.	649.00
Mold, Redware, Ruffled Rim, Manganese Splash, Pa., 1800s, 3 ¼ x 10 ¼ In.	119.00
Mold, Redware, Turk's Head, 12 Wide Flutes, Raised Center, 3 ¼ x 11 ½ In.	83.00
Mold, Turk's Head, Yellowware, 9 x 3 In.	125.00
Mold, Woman's Head, Hat, Cast Iron, Mott Iron Works, 16 In.	345.00
Mold, Candle, see Tinware category.	
Mold, Ice Cream, see also Pewter category.	
Mortar & Pestle, Burl, c.1750, 9 ½ In.	385.00
Mortar & Pestle, Burl, Turned, 19th Century, 6 ½ In.	271.00
Mortar & Pestle, Cast Iron, Bell Shape, c.1690, 7 ½ x 8 ¼ In.	403.00
Mortar & Pestle, Cast Iron, Flared Rim, Foot, 4 ½ In.	89.00
Mortar & Pestle, Treen, 7 In.	118.00
Mortar & Pestle, Treen, Mahogany, 7 In.	58.00
Mortar & Pestle, Wood, 22 x 11 ½-In. Mortar, 40 x 2 ¾-In. Pestle	88.00
Mortar & Pestle, Wood, Turned, 1800s, 5 ¼ x 4 ¾ & 6 ¾ In.	94.00
Mortar & Pestle, Wood, Turned, Incised Rings, 1800s, 6 ½ & 9 In.	24.00
Mortar & Pestle, Wood, Turned, Reeded Design Center, Round Foot, Lignum Vitae, 8 In.	46.00
Pan, Baking, Yellowware, Rockingham Glaze, 8-Sided, Banded Rim, 2 x 12 x 9 In.	118.00
Pantry Box, Bentwood, Green Paint, Round, Lid, c.1815, 9 ½ In.	230.00
Pantry Box, Bentwood, Lapped Seams, Round, Red Paint, Soda Label, Murdock & Co., Mass, 2 x 6 In.	264.00
Pantry Box, Bentwood, Round, Blue Paint, Lid, c.1850, 10 x 16 ½ In.	425.00
Pantry Box, Maple, Pine, Painted Flowers, Vines, Red, Salmon, Green, New England, 1840, 3 x 7 In.	748.00
Pantry Box, Painted, Fruit, Flowers, Band Handle, Round, 13 x 11 In.	1534.00
Pantry Box, Pine, Ash, Gray Paint, Round, Stave & Hoop Construction, c.1820, 12 ¼ In.	677.00
Pantry Box, Stenciled Lid, Concentric Circle, Painted Green, 1800s, 2 ⅝ x 4 ½ In.	533.00
Pantry, Conestoga Chuck Wagon, Stenciled, Metal, Patent 1893, 30 x 35 x 11 ½ In.........*Illus*	840.00
Pasta Cutting Mill, 5 Blades, Cast Iron, Wood Grip Crank, Charles P. Giunta, 10 ½ x 12 ½ In..	153.00
Peel, Wrought Iron, Ram's Horn Handle, Stamped John Hill, New England, c.1750, 44 In.	184.00
Peel, Wrought Iron, Ram's Horn Top, 1800s, 45 In.	94.00
Pie Crimper, Star Cutout Spokes & Handle, Fork End, Bone, Sailor Carved, c.1835, 9 ½ In. ...	1778.00
Pitcher, Hearth, Lift-Off Lid, Baluster Shape, Handle, Raised Lettering, Cast Iron, c.1800, 12 ¾ In..	1348.00
Pitcher, Hectoliter, Steel, Polished, 24 In.	236.00
Pizza Cutter, Striding Lion, Front Paws Grasping Blade, Wood Stand, Marked, T. Latane, 7 ½ In..	1888.00
Plate Warmer, Tinned Sheet Iron, Dome Lid, Cabriole Legs, c.1775	141.00
Pot, Hearth, Cast Iron, Swing Handle, Tripod Feet, 2 Qt., c.1895, 8 In.	356.00
Pot, Iron, Globular, Molded Side Handles, 3 Feet, Marked, 10 ½ x 13 ½ In.	177.00
Rack, Meat, 6 Hooks, Iron, 23 x 14 ½ In.	259.00
Rack, Meat, Arch, Scroll Detail, Wrought Iron, France, c.1900, 34 x 105 In.	120.00
Rack, Meat, Hanging, Carved, Painted, Scandinavia, c.1850, 21 x 68 In.	365.00
Rack, Meat, Pine, Wrought Iron, Molded Low Edge, 9 Hooks, Paint, c.1850, 8 ½ x 26 In.	184.00
Rack, Utensil, Scrolls, Tulip Terminals, Iron, c.1830, 12 x 22 In.	2015.00
Rack, Utensil, Walnut, Hooks, Pa., c.1780, 11 ¼ x 33 In.	948.00
Reamers are listed in their own category.	
Refrigerator, Pressed Steel, Water Bottle, Tin Pan, Wyandotte, Salesman's Sample, 5 ¼ x 9 ½ In.	420.00
Roaster, Bird, Wrought Iron, Arched, 2 Hook Levels, Drip Pan, c.1850, 15 ½ x 13 ½ In.	345.00
Roaster, Fish, Hearth, Hinged, Pierced Handle, Wrought Iron, c.1812, 33 x 10 ½ In.	1348.00
Roaster, Griswold No. 9, Oval	350.00
Rolling Pin, Glass, Red Marbrie Loops, Green Ground, Pinched Knob Ends, c.1870, 14 ½ x 2 In.	219.00
Rolling Pin, Lignum Vitae, 19th Century, 15 ¼ In.	948.00
Rolling Pin, Rosewood, c.1850, 19 In.	563.00
Rolling Pin, Wood, Faces, Pinstripes, Geometrics, Carved, Black, Yellow, Red Paint, Pa., c.1900, 19 In.	2607.00
Rotisserie, Wrought Iron, Adjustable, Heart Design, 35 In.	1652.00
Saffron Safe, Wood, Turned, Cone Shape, Ringed, 3 Legs, 12 x 4 ½ In.	142.00

K

Salt & Pepper Shakers are listed in their own category.

Salt Box, Pine, Painted Red, Pa., 1800s, 8 ¾ x 4 ¾ In. 356.00

Salt Box, Pine, Poplar, Slant Lid, Cutout Back, 2 Drawers, Pa., c.1850, 4 ¼ x 11 ¾ In. 243.00

Salt Box, Wall, Cherry, Slant Hinged Lid, Pa., c.1810, 11 ¾ x 12 In. 770.00

Salt Box, Wall, Pine, Slant Lid, Cutout Back, Green Paint, c.1875, 13 x 6 ½ In. 207.00

Salt Box, Wall, Poplar, Painted, Acorn, Lollipop Shape Back, Faux Oak, Pa., c.1850, 11 x 11 ½ In. ... 889.00

Sausage Press, Crank, Iron, National Specialty, 19 In., 4 Qt. 136.00

Scoop, Burl, Long Handle, 14 In. 71.00

Scoop, Coconut, Ivory Details, Abalone Inlay, Curved Handle, 1800s, 12 ½ In. 834.00

Scoop, Ice Cream, Aluminum, Divided Bowl, Bohlig Mfg. Co., No. 12, 1908, 10 In. 275.00

Scoop, Ice Cream, Cold Dog, Silver, Wood, 2 Cylinders, Fisher-Orillia, Pat. 1922, 9 ½ In. 480.00

Scoop, Ice Cream, Cylindrical Dip, Flat Paddle Release, Mosteler Mfg., 8 ½ In. 198.00

Scoop, Ice Cream, Gilchrist, No. 31, Nickel Plate, Wood Handle, Size 20, 1915, 10 ¼ In. 125.00

Scoop, Ice Cream, Metal, Squeeze Handle, 1901, 9 ¾ In. 480.00

Scoop, Ice Cream, Nickel Plated Brass, Wood Handle, Gilchrist Co., No. 31, 1915, 11 ½ In. 330.00

Scoop, Ice Cream, Nickel Plated Brass, Wood Handle, Manos Novelty Co., Ohio, Pat. Nov. 1925... *Illus* 4400.00

Scoop, Ice Cream, Nickel Plated Brass, Wood Handle, Round Bowl, Point Outside, 11 ¼ In. 630.00

Scoop, Icypi, Ice Cream Sandwich, Wood Handle, Automatic Cone Co., 9 ¾ In. ....*Illus* 110.00

Sieve, Wrought Iron Handle, Pierced Copper Bowl, c.1850, 23 In. 374.00

Skillet, Griswold No. 4, Slant Logo, Heat Ring 150.00

Skillet, Griswold No. 6, Chrome, Dome Lettered Lid 55.00

Skillet, Griswold No. 10, c.1937 .... 50.00

Skillet, Griswold No. 14, Iron Mountain 500.00

Skillet, Wapak, No. 6, Cast Iron, 2-Sided Spouts, 13 ⅛ In. 71.00

Skillet, Wrought Iron, 3 Legs, Integral Handle, 8 ¾ x 13 ¼ In. 47.00

Skimmer, Brass, Impressed A.D. Richmond, New England, 21 ½ In. 356.00

Skimmer, Copper Bowl, Wrought Iron Handle, Hanging Curl, c.1855, 6 x 1 ¾ In. 138.00

Slaw Board, Walnut, Carved, Tombstone Shape, Cutout Heart, c.1845, 16 x 7 In. 207.00

Slaw Board, Walnut, Heart Cutout Crest, Pa., c.1805, 18 x 6 ¾ In. 889.00

Spatula, Punched Star, Pa., c.1860, 18 ½ In. 1126.00

Spatula, Wrought Iron, Inlaid Brass, Monogram IB, Pa., 1826, 21 In. 5346.00

Spatula, Wrought Iron, Stamped E.P. Sebasion, Pa., 19th Century, 19 ½ In. 3792.00

Spice Box, Cherry, Wall, 6 Drawers, Shaped Back, Pa., c.1860, 9 ½ x 6 ¼ In. 326.00

Spice Box, Cinnamon, Sheet Iron, Yellow, Black, Lift Lid, Porcelain Knob, Taylor & Staley, 9 x 8 In. ... 94.00

Spice Box, Kaw Chief, Cinnamon, Paper Labels, Indian Image, 12 x 4 ½ x 9 In. 540.00

Spice Box, Multicolor, Removable Lid, Hexagon, Tin Lithograph, c.1875, 34 ½ In. 1955.00

Spice Box, Painted, 9 Drawers, Shaped Back Board, c.1890, 14 ½ x 18 ¼ In. 533.00

Spice Box, Sheet Iron, Japanned, Gold Stripes, Riveted Ring Handle On Lid, 4 x 9 x 6 In. 35.00

Spice Box, Walnut, Open Top, Drawer, White Porcelain Pull, 1800s, 5 ½ x 12 In. 325.00

Spice Box, Yellow, Sheet Iron, Red, Crown, Lift Lid, Porcelain Knob, Davison & Silvers, 9 x 8 In. ... 71.00

Spoonrest, Figural, Mary Poppins, Wearing Apron, Medicine Spoons, Ceramic, Enesco, 1964, 5 ¾ In. ... 86.00

Sugar Cutter, Chicken Finial, Metal, 1800s, 4 ¼ In. 711.00

Sugar Nippers, Hand Finished, Engraved, Box Hinge, Finger Guard, Wrought Iron, c.1820, 9 ½ In. ... 130.00

Sugar Nippers, Iron, Turned Wood Handle, Iron Cover Wood Base, c.1810, 6 ½ x 14 In. 211.00

Teakettle, Cast Iron, Domed Lid, Brass Finial, Gooseneck, Split Mouth Spout, Ball Handle, 1810 .. 225.00

Teapot, Stepped Round Lid, Bail Handle, Curved Spout, Maker's Name, Cast Iron, c.1840, 10 In. 326.00

Toaster, Openwork Scrolls, Iron, 13 x 17 In. 144.00

Toaster, Openwork Squares, Iron, 14 x 17 ½ In. 81.00

Towel Dispenser, Painted Green, Upper Bin, Hand Hold, Roller, Continental, 23 x 10 In. 24.00

Tray, Cocktail, Reverse Painted Glass, Chrome Frame & Handles, c.1930, 17 x 10 In. ......*Illus* 688.00

Tray, Cutlery, Pine, Paint, Cutout Handle, 18 ¾ In. 177.00

Tray, Utensil, Tiger Maple, Cutout Handle, c.1900, 6 In. 59.00

Trivet, see Trivet category.

Utensil Box, Slant Hinged Lid, Mahogany, Scalloped Handle, 10 x 16 ½ In. 296.00

Utensil Box, Yellow, Green, Orange, Black Geometrics, Paint, New England, c.1820, 6 ¾ x 15 In. 4977.00

Utensils, Spice Of Life Set, Metal, Ekco, 1970s, 5 Piece 45.00

Vacuum Cleaner, Harvey Stone Sales Co., Sheet Metal, Painted Green, Wood Pump Grips, 51 In. 59.00

Vegetable Cutter, Iron, Black, Red, Gold Detail, Hopper, Cutting Wheel, Enterprise, 15 In. 130.00

Waffle Iron, Geometric Designs, 1800s, 23 ½ In. 106.00

Waffle Iron, Griswold No. 18, Heart & Star 100.00

Washboard, Wood, Rippled Glass, Hen, Flowers 35.00

Washing Machine, Maytag, Cast Iron, Lift Lid, Salesman's Sample, 1920s, 4 x 7 ¼ In. ....*Illus* 424.00

Washing Machine, Wonder Washer, Stand, Victor Mfg. Co., Sample, c.1919, 22 x 16 In... *Illus* 5333.00

Washtub, Queen Stencil, Wood, Stave Construction, Cover, Battened Hatch, 3 Legs, 1895, 27 x 25 In. ... 118.00

Wringer, No. 32, Crank Operated, Made By Lowell Of Erie, Pa., Late 1890s 35.00

Kitchen, Pantry, Conestoga Chuck Wagon, Stenciled, Metal, Patent 1893, 30 x 35 x 11 ½ In.
$840.00

Showtime Auction Sevices

Kitchen, Scoop, Ice Cream, Nickel Plated Brass, Wood Handle, Manos Novelty Co., Ohio, Pat. Nov. 1925
$4,400.00

Rich Penn Auctions

K

Kitchen, Scoop, Icypi, Ice Cream Sandwich, Wood Handle, Automatic Cone Co., 9 ¾ In.
$110.00

Rich Penn Auctions

Kitchen, Tray, Cocktail, Reverse Painted Glass, Chrome Frame & Handles, c.1930, 17 x 10 In.
$688.00

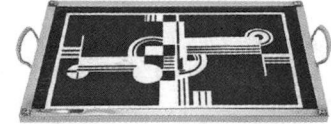

Heritage Auctions

The edited listings of the current prices in this *Kovels' Antiques & Collectibles Price Guide* aren't available on any website. Readers can visit **Kovels.com** to check thousands of past prices and sign up for free information on trends, tips, reproductions, marks, and more.

Kitchen, Washing Machine, Maytag, Cast Iron, Painted, Lift Lid, Salesman's Sample, 1920s, 4 x 7 ¼ In.
$424.00

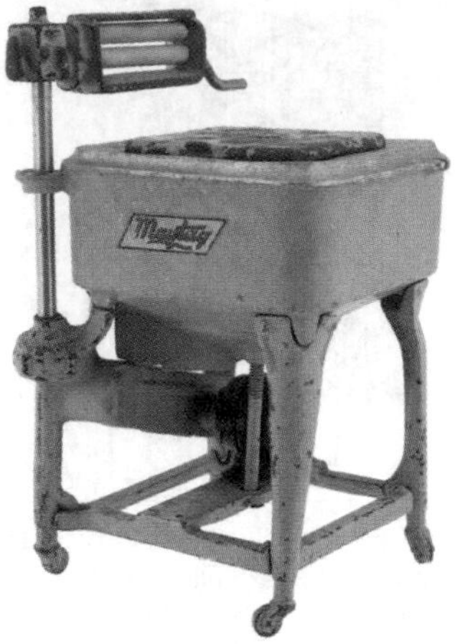

Hake's Americana & Collectibles

Kitchen, Washing Machine, Wonder Washer, Stand, Victor Mfg. Co., Sample, c.1919, 22 x 16 In.
$5,333.00

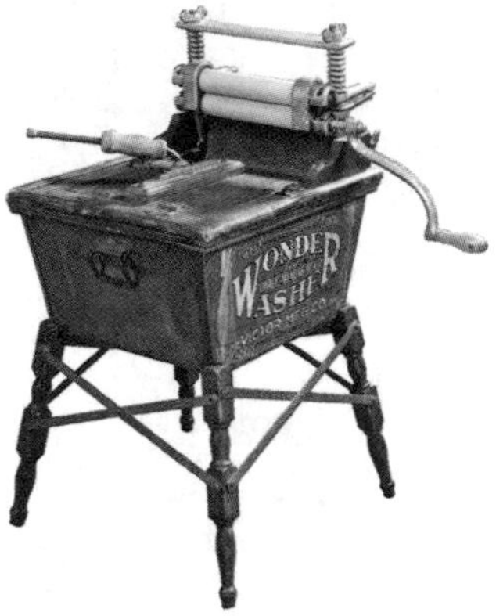

Skinner, Inc.

Knife, Sash, Copper, Brass, Sheath, Asia, 17 ⅜ In.
$325.00

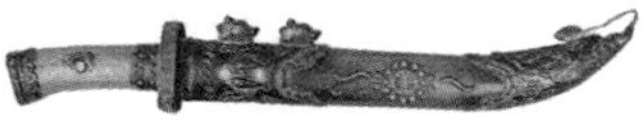

Conestoga Auction Co., Inc.

Kosta, Sculpture, Head Resting, Sand Cast, Etched, Bertil Vallien, Kosta Boda, 1997, 5 x 8 In.
$5,625.00

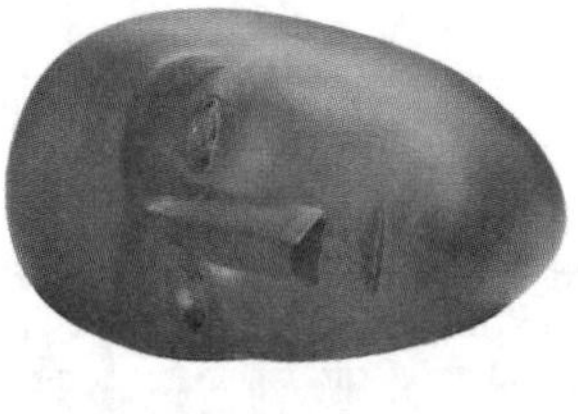

Rago Arts & Auction Center

KNIFE collectors usually specialize in a single type. In the 1960s, the United States government passed a law that required knife manufacturers to mark their knives with the country of origin. This seemed to encourage the collectors, and knife collecting became an interest of a large group of people. All types of knives are collected, from top quality twentieth-century examples to old bone- or pearl-handled knives in excellent condition.

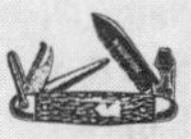

Bone Handle, English, c.1600, 8 In.	350.00
Boot, Spear Point, Ricasso, Ebony Grip, Brass Ferrule, c.1850	275.00
Bowie, Clipped Point, Horn Grip, Marked, c.1850, 6 ½ In.	425.00
Bowie, Double Edge Blade, Nickel Silver Guard, Horn & Ivory Handle, George Wostenholm, 12 1/12 In.	575.00
Bowie, Steel, Wood Handle, Tapered Blade, Guard, Brass Fittings, 13 In.	575.00
Dagger, Curved Blade, Inlaid Panels, Fold Design, 19th Century, 19 In.	250.00
Dagger, Enamel, Flowers, Leaves, Birds, Cartouches, Middle East, 1900s, 14 In.	608.00
Dagger, Malay, Wood Grip, Iron Ferrule, Horn Guard, 19th Century, 4 ¾ In.	110.00
Dagger, Polished Steel, Jade Gilded & Inlaid Rubies Handle, Scabbard, India, c.1900, 12 In.	4594.00
Dagger, Silver, Embossed, Kindjal, Russia, c.1900, 14 In.	2550.00
Dagger, Steel, Lobed Grip, Silver Bands, Scroll Panels, Indo-Persian, 6 In.	235.00
Dagger, Sudanese, Curved Blade, Cross Guard, c.1880, 10 ⅜ In.	385.00
Dagger, Tribal, North African Tuareg, Double Edged Blade, Rawhide Handle, Sheath, 9 In.	106.00
Machete, Carved Wood Handle, Diamond Grip, Brass Hand Guard, Bowie Shape Blade, 23 In.	69.00
Pocket, Brass, Horn, 2-Blade, Etched Deer, Dog, Hunter, 1850s, 9 ½ In.	299.00
Sash, Copper, Brass, Sheath, Asia, 17 ⅜ In. *Illus*	325.00
Stiletto, Carved Wood Handle, Italy Or Spain, 10 ¼-In. Blade, 15 ¼ In.	127.00
Trench, L.F. & C.V.U.S. Model, World War I, Brass Handle, Pointed Knuckles, 6 ¾ In.	518.00

KNOWLES, *Taylor & Knowles items may be found in the KTK and Lotus Ware categories.*

KOREAN WARE, *see Sumida.*

KOSTA, the oldest Swedish glass factory, was founded in 1742. During the 1920s through the 1950s, many pieces of original design were made at the factory. Kosta and Boda merged with Afors in 1964 and created the Afors Group in 1971. In 1976, the name Kosta Boda was adopted. The company merged with Orrefors in 1990 and is still working.

KOSTA

Bowl, Engraved, Lines, Amber Rim, Flared, 9 ½ In.	79.00
Dish, Clear Glass, Square, Flared Sides, Kosta Boda, 4 x 7 ¾ x 7 ¾ In.	48.00
Sculpture, Head Resting, Sand Cast, Etched, Bertil Vallien, Kosta Boda, 1997, 5 x 8 In. *Illus*	5625.00
Sculpture, Sitting Mouse, Cheese, Yellow, Clear Frosted Glass, 3 ½ In.	177.00
Vase, Bronze Iridescent, White Swirls, B. Vallien, 3 In.	50.00
Vase, Purple, Textured, B. Vallien, 2 ¼ In.	55.00

KPM refers to Berlin porcelain, but the same initials were used alone and in combination with other symbols by several German porcelain makers. They include the Konigliche Porzellan Manufaktur of Berlin, initials used in mark, 1823–1847; Meissen, 1723–1724 only; Krister Porzellan Manufaktur in Waldenburg, after 1831; Kranichfelder Porzellan Manufaktur in Kranichfeld, after 1903; and the Krister Porzellan Manufaktur in Scheibe, after 1838.

K.P.M

Bough Pot, Lid, Birds, Perched In Tree, Floral Bouquet, Knop, Flowers, Insects, c.1800, 10 In., Pair	1298.00
Bowl, Lid, Latticed, Wavy, Vine Handles, Reticulated, Footed, Marked, c.1912, 15 ½ In.	210.00
Bowl, Lid, U-Shape, Basket Weave Rim, Birds, Insects, Bacchus Finial, 14 x 11 In.	425.00
Charger, Flowers, White, Ground, Gilt Garland Edge, 14 ½ In.	154.00
Compote, Pink Rose Spray & Gilt Band, 3 Griffin Supports, Round Base, c.1850, 5 ½ x 7 In.	460.00
Compote, Rose Sprays, Reticulated Rim, Swirled Shaft, Foot, Gilt, Marked, c.1850, 7 x 9 ½ In.	690.00
Figural Group, Apollo, Holding Lyre, Minerva, Cupid, Arrow Quiver, Bow, Laurel Leaves, 13 ¼ In.	863.00
Figurine, Blackamoor, Covered Cup, Blanc De Chine, 1800s, 7 ¼ & 7 ½ In., Pair	304.00
Lithophane, see also Lithophane category.	
Plaque, 2 Children Reading Book, L. Eckard, 10 x 12 In.	10350.00
Plaque, Classical Woman, Holding Oil Lamp, Painted, Marked, Jeweled Frame, 19 x 16 In.	10800.00
Plaque, Countess Sophie Potocka, 1700s Attire, Blue Dress, Frame, 11 x 8 ¾ In.	1875.00
Plaque, Diana, Goddess Of The Hunt, Disrobing, Dogs, Arrows, Giltwood Frame, c.1890, 16 x 12 In.	3444.00
Plaque, Girl, Beatrice Cenci, Oval, 5 ¼ In.	236.00
Plaque, Girl, In White Robe, Holding Roses, Turesse Des Roses Landelle, Frame, 1800s, 13 x 8 In.	3450.00
Plaque, Girl, Pink Dress, Coral Necklace, Curly Hair, Giltwood Frame, Marked, 7 ¼ x 5 ½ In.	1778.00
Plaque, Girl, White Dress, Carrying Basket, Frame, Marked, 9 x 6 ⅓ In.	2573.00
Plaque, Gypsy Boy, 19th Century, 8 ½ x 6 In.	1968.00
Plaque, Jan Hus Before The Constance Council, Frame, 27 x 33 In.	14640.00
Plaque, Mary Magdalene, Painted, Frame, 1800s, 9 ¾ x 13 In.	2280.00

Plaque, Monk, Wine Cellar, Tasting Wine, Frame, c.1890, 9 ¼ x 6 ¼ In..................	2500.00
Plaque, Mother, Nude Child, Balcony, White Gown, Red Shawl, Gold Frame, Signed, 10 x 13 In. ..	1150.00
Plaque, Old Woman, White Cap, Fur Collar, After Balthasar Denner, 21 ½ x 19 ¼ In.	1265.00
Plaque, Oval, Painted, Woman, Praying, Flower Bouquet, Frame, 7 x 5 In............................	750.00
Plaque, Peasants, 1809 In Tirol, Vor Dem Aufstand, Manuscript, Franz Defregger, c.1880, 9 ½ x 12 In..	2460.00
Plaque, Romeo, Juliet, Before Friar Lawrence, Porcelain, Frame, F. Till, c.1890, 14 x 16 In.	16250.00
Plaque, Woman, Dress, Red Hair, Tray, Tochter Des Calefen, Signed Ullmann, 1800s, 11 x 9 In.	1955.00
Plaque, Woman, Dress, Seated, Victorian Style, Porcelain, Marked, 1800s, 10 ¾ x 8 ⅞ In........	1185.00
Plaque, Woman, Holding Fruit, Signed M. Von Christoph Deininger, Frame, 15 x 12 In............	9920.00
Plaque, Woman, Revealing Robe, Red Velvet Curtain, Pierced Gilt Frame, c.1900, 9 x 6 ¼ In.	5000.00
Plaque, Woman, Seated, Pink Chair, Looking Into Mirror, Signed, Gold Frame, 5 ½ x 8 ½ In.	10350.00
Plaque, Woman, White Dress, Oval, Carved Leaf, Berry Fruitwood Frame, c.1890, 7 x 5 ½ In..	1680.00
Plaque, Woman, White Dress, Porcelain, Signed Anne, Oval Frame, 1800s, 7 x 5 In.................	668.00
Plate, Embossed Triple Gold Rim, 10 ½ In., 12 Piece	767.00
Plate, Impressed Rocaille, Shaped Rim, Gold Ground, 8 ¾ In., 8 Piece	750.00
Platter, Flowers, Brown, Gray, Gilt, Oval, 17 In.	60.00
Platter, Gilt Flower Design, Floral Edge, Shaped Handles, Oval, 17 In.	59.00
Serving Dish, Double Shell, Handle, Flower Finial, Birds, Insects, Trees, Gilt Border, 11 ¾ In.	125.00
Stein, Altemberg Style, Glazed Relief, Brown, Cream, 1 Liter, c.1870	460.00
Vase, Pansies, Encircling Neck, Orange, Yellow, Squat, Flared Rim, 1910, 3 ⅞ In...............	805.00
Vase, White, Reticulated, Gilt Trim, Scepter Marked, 7 x 5 ½ In...............................	25.00

KUTANI porcelain was made in Japan after the mid-seventeenth century. Most of the pieces found today are nineteenth-century. Collectors often use the term *Kutani* to refer to just the later, colorful pieces decorated with red, gold, and black pictures of warriors, animals, and birds.

Brushpot, Red Ground, Reserves, Transfer Scenes, Multicolor, Gilt, Cylinder Shape, 4 ¾ In....	92.00
Plate, Center Shishi, Geometric Design, Flowering Branches, Buddha Hand, 1800s, 9 ½ In., Pair.	598.00
Vase, Baluster, Animal Shaped Handles, Wood Base, Mythological Scenes, 1800s, 14 In., Pair.	1107.00
Vase, Cylindrical, Molded, Peony Sprays, Iron Red & Gilt Diaper Banding, c.1900, 20 In., Pair..	1554.00
Vase, Thousand Scholars, Performing 4 Accomplishments, Marked, Hyoyu, c.1900, 12 x 11 ½ In.	3125.00

L.G. WRIGHT Glass Company of New Martinsville, West Virginia, started selling glassware in 1937. Founder "Si" Wright contracted with Ohio and West Virginia glass factories to reproduce popular pressed glass patterns like Rose & Snow, Baltimore Pear, and Three Face, and opalescent patterns like Daisy & Fern and Swirl. Collectors can tell the difference between the original glasswares and L.G. Wright reproductions because of colors and differences in production techniques. Some L.G. Wright items are marked with an underlined *W* in a circle. Items that were made from old Northwood molds have an altered Northwood mark—an angled line was added to the *N* to make it look like a *W*. Collectors refer to this mark as "the wobbly W." The L.G. Wright factory was closed and the existing molds sold in 1999.

Beaded Curtain, Pitcher, Blue Glass, 4 In..	42.00
Daisy & Button, Slipper Shoe, Aqua Glass, 4 ¾ In...	10.00
Daisy & Button, Vase, Hat Shape, Yellow, 2 ¼ In...	12.00
Eye Winker, Toothpick Holder, Yellow Glass, 2 ¼ In...	70.00
Moon & Star, Candy Dish, Scalloped Glass, 5 ¾ In.	32.00
Moon & Star, Toothpick Holder, Red Glass, 2 In.	10.00
Moss Rose, Pitcher, Custard Glass, Cylindrical, Applied Handle, 5 ½ In......................	54.00
Moss Rose, Pitcher, Custard Glass, Globular, Crimped Rim, 6 ½ In.	60.00
Moss Rose, Plate, Swirl, Milk Glass, 8 ⅜ In...	20.00
Thumbprint, Vase, Cranberry Glass, Ruffled, Footed, 7 ½ In...................................	95.00

LACQUER is a type of varnish. Collectors are most interested in the Chinese and Japanese lacquer wares made from the Japanese varnish tree. Lacquer wares are made from wood with many coats of lacquer. Sometimes the piece is carved or decorated with ivory or metal inlay.

Box, Lid, Black, Hardstone Inlay, Bird On Flowering Branch, China, 4 x 6 x 10 In..................	2410.00
Box, Hinged Lid, Landscape Scenes, Metal Handles, Tin Caddy, Chinese, 1900s, 13 x 8 ½ In... *Illus*	500.00
Box, Oxcart, Garden, Prunus, Bamboo, Gold, Brown, Japan, c.1900, 12 x 15 In.................... *Illus*	1845.00
Box, Red, Incised Green Branches, Gourd Shape, Black Interior, Chinese, c.1910, 8 x 9 In.......	300.00
Box, Sweetmeat, Abalone, Round, Flattened, Black, Inlaid Leaves Flowers & Instruments, Lid, 16 In..	266.00
Brush Holder, Square Shaped, Children At Play Design, Chinese, 8 ½ In.	418.00
Brushpot, Multicolor Marbleized Surface, Interior Hole, Plug, Oriental, 1900s, 8 ½ x 8 ½ In.	1035.00
Comb, Gold, Landscape, Samurai, Boat, Stylized Animals, c.1910, 3 ½ x 1 ½ In......................	259.00

Lacquer, Box, Hinged Lid, Landscape Scenes, Metal Handles, Tin Caddy, Chinese, 1900s, 13 x 8 ½ In.
$500.00

Skinner, Inc.

Lacquer, Box, Oxcart, Garden, Prunus, Bamboo, Gold, Brown, Japan, c.1900, 12 x 15 In.
$1,845.00

New Orleans Auction Galleries, Inc.

Lacquer, Wall Panel, Carved, Jade, Soapstone, Wood, Mother-Of-Pearl, Chinese, 1800s, 45 x 30 In., Pair
$19,120.00

Neal Auction Co.

TIP

Lacquered wood can be damaged by a sudden change in humidity. Keep lacquer away from heat sources, preferably in a room with high humidity.

L

Lalique, Figurine, Dog, Labrador, Sitting Sam, Marked, Box, 2001, 14 In.
$790.00

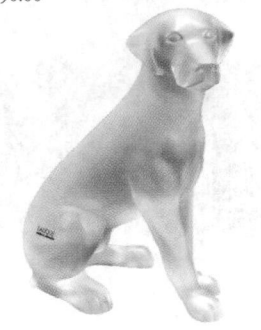

Skinner, Inc.

Lalique, Figurine, Water Buffalo, Molded, Frosted, Signed Lalique, France, 14 ½ In.
$1,080.00

Leslie Hindman Auctioneers

Lalique, Paperweight, Bison, Clear & Frosted, R. Lalique, c.1931, 4 x 5 In.
$1,250.00

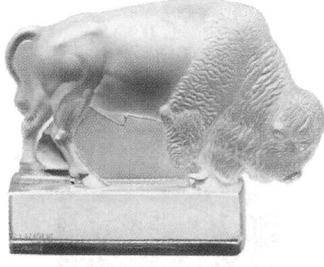

Rago Arts & Auction Center

Lalique, Perfume Bottle, Camille, Frosted Electric Blue, Stopper, Etched, R. Lalique, 2 ¼ x 2 ¼ In.
$1,875.00

Rago Arts & Auction Center

Teapot, Gilt Design, Waisted, Splay Body, Curved Handle, Scroll Spout, Dome Lid, c.1800, 4 x 7 In.	478.00
Trinket Box, Black, Flying Stork, Clouds, Interior Compartments, Carved Feet, Lid, 1800s, 10 x 17 In.	173.00
Trinket Box, Octagonal, Gilt Dragons, Figures, Courtyards, Claw Feet, Lift Lid, Chinese, 6 x 15 In.	413.00
Trinket Box, Rosewood, Mother-Of-Pearl, Sprinkled Lacquer, Leaves, Grapes, Insects, 4 x 6 In.	984.00
Wall Panel, Carved, Jade, Soapstone, Wood, Mother-Of-Pearl, Chinese, 1800s, 45 x 30 In., Pair... *Illus*	19120.00
Writing Box, Gilt, Night Scene, Moon, Stream, Tall Grass, Japan, 2 x 8 x 10 In.	300.00

LADY HEAD VASE, *see Head Vase.*

LALIQUE glass was made by Rene Lalique in Paris, France, between the 1890s and his death in 1945. The glass was molded, pressed, and engraved in Art Nouveau and Art Deco styles. Pieces were marked with the signature *R. Lalique*. Lalique glass is still being made. Pieces made after 1945 bear the mark *Lalique*. After 1980 the registry mark was added and the mark became *Lalique ® France*. In the prices listed here, this is indicated by Lalique (R) France. Some pieces that are advertised as ring dishes or pin dishes were listed as ashtrays in the Lalique factory catalog and are listed as ashtrays here. Jewelry made by Rene Lalique is listed in the Jewelry category.

R. LALIQUE

Bookends, Longchamp, Horse Head, Clear, Frosted, Silver Collar, Black Base, c.1929, 6 x 6 In.	18750.00
Bottle, Scent, Emerald Green, Rectangular, Graduated Stepped Stopper, Marked, 6 ¼ In.	1150.00
Bowl, Calypso, Swirling Sirens, Flared, Frosted, Clear, 14 x 2 ½ In.	1000.00
Bowl, Caviar, Frosted, Dolphin Knop, 3 Dolphin Feet, Domed Lid, 10 x 8 In.	1230.00
Bowl, Caviar, Olga, Round, Frosted, Flat Rim, Sturgeon Head Handles, c.1985, 4 ¾ x 8 ¾ In.	615.00
Bowl, Centerpiece, Champs Elysees, Oak Leaves, Signed, 10 x 18 In.	840.00
Bowl, Champs Elysees, Leaves, Oval, Frosted, Clear, 7 ½ x 18 In.	799.00 to 1063.00
Bowl, Chiens No. 1, Greyhounds, Opalescent, 8 ½ x 9 In.	3275.00
Bowl, Coupe, Martigues, School Of Fish, Clear, Opalescent, c.1935, 14 ⅜ In.	4375.00
Bowl, Elizabeth, Molded Sparrows, Leafy Branches, Frosted, Footed, 1900s, 5 ⅜ x 5 ¾ In.	399.00
Bowl, Epines, Thistle, Flared, Etched, 4 ¾ x 10 In.	196.00
Bowl, Gui No. 2, Mistletoe, Mint Green Opalescent, 1921, 18 ½ In.	5100.00
Bowl, Gui, Mistletoe, Berry Feet, Clear, Opalescent, c.1926, 3 ⅞ x 9 ⅜ In.	480.00
Bowl, Honfleur, Geranium, Leaves, Raised Border, Signed, 10 ¾ x 2 In.	266.00
Bowl, Luxembourg, Band Of Putti, Festoons, Molded, Frosted, R. Lalique, 10 ½ In.	2750.00
Bowl, Nemours, Rosettes, Frosted, 3 ½ x 10 In.	304.00
Box, Daphne, Molded Nude, Crystal, Hinged Lid, Signed, 2 x 3 In.	300.00
Box, Houppes, Pompoms, Opalescent, Round, c.1921, 4 ½ x 5 ½ In.	3450.00
Box, Lid, Seminude Woman, Holding Hourglass, Zodiac Signs, Green, Square, Marked, 2 ½ x 5 In.	472.00
Caviar Set, Igor, Bowl, Liner, Dolphin Feet & Finial, Box, 10 In.	729.00
Ceiling Light, Charmes, Leaves, Amber, Demi-Coupe, Brass Fittings, Silk Cord, 5 x 14 In.	1375.00
Ceiling Light, Dahlias, Frosted, Brown Patina, Brass Sockets, Silk Cord, c.1921, 5 ½ x 12 In.	1375.00
Ceiling Light, Lausanne, Amber, Demi-Coupe, 4 Brass Sockets, c.1929, 5 x 15 In.	1625.00
Ceiling Light, Lausanne, Fruit, Leaves, White Opalescent, Domed, 3 Chains, c.1930, 15 In.	5625.00
Champagne Bucket, Ganymede, Nudes, Grape Leaves, Frosted, Clear, Footed, Handles, c.1970, 9 In.	922.00
Champagne, Angel, Frosted, Clear, 8 ⅛ In., 8 Piece	1625.00
Chandelier, 6-Light, Frosted Leaves, Brass, 4 Tubular Standards, Hexagonal Base, 33 ¼ In.	6250.00
Clock, Iris, Clear, Frosted, Round, White Dial, Domed Foot, 6 ½ x 8 In.	1000.00
Clock, Naiades, Mermaids, Goldtone Dial, Arabic Numbers, Greek Key, Bezel, 4 ½ x 4 ½ In.	4740.00
Decanter, Parme, Circles, Clear, Frosted, 10 ½ In.	360.00
Door Handle, Isere, Fluted, Chrome Fitting, Signed, 7 x 4 In.	344.00
Dresser Box, Band Of Nudes, Cylindrical, Domed Lid, Signed, 4 ½ In.	173.00
Figurine, Ara, Cockatoo, Semi-Spread Wings, Signed, 12 In.	1200.00
Figurine, Bemara, Lion, Seated, Frosted, Signed, 8 x 8 In.	587.00
Figurine, Cat, Frosted, Polished Base, Signed, 1900s, 8 x 3 ½ In.	492.00
Figurine, Coquet, Sparrow, Frosted, 3 In.	82.00
Figurine, Cygnet, Swan, Head Down, Frosted, Clear, Etched Oval Base, c.1990, 24 ½ x 15 In.	4248.00
Figurine, Danseuse, Nude Dancer, Frosted, 9 In.	480.00
Figurine, Deux Poissons, Two Fish, Signed, 11 x 10 In.	1920.00
Figurine, Dog, Labrador, Sitting Sam, Marked, Box, 2001, 14 In. ......*Illus*	790.00
Figurine, Flower, Frosted, Black Enamel Dots, 4 x 4 ¼ In.	120.00
Figurine, Gros Poisson Vagues, Fish, Frosted, Bronze Lighted Base, Etched R. Lalique, c.1922, 15 In.	5175.00
Figurine, Gros Poissons Vagues, Big Fish Waves, 1950s, 12 x 16 In.	1438.00
Figurine, Leopard, Stalking, Frosted, Indented Spots, 4 ¾ x 14 ½ In.	546.00
Figurine, Leopard, Stalking, Frosted, Signed, 15 In.	889.00
Figurine, Madonna, 10 In.	420.00
Figurine, Nude Woman, Huddled Position, Opaque Black, Marked, 2 ½ In.	173.00
Figurine, Ours, Polar Bear, 6 In.	288.00
Figurine, Ours, Polar Bear, Seated, Frosted, Signed, 7 In.	225.00

L

Figurine, Panther, Crouching, Etched R. Lalique, 14 ¼ In., Pair	2500.00
Figurine, Tancrede, Cheetah, Seated, Frosted, Rocky Base, Marked, Box, 10 In.	770.00
Figurine, Tete D'Aigle, Eagle's Head, Clear, Frosted, Etched R. Lalique, 1928, 4 ½ In.	184.00
Figurine, Vuelta Noir, Black Bull, Label, 5 x 5 In.	345.00
Figurine, Water Buffalo, Molded, Frosted, Signed Lalique, France, 14 ½ In. *Illus*	1080.00
Goblet, 6 Figurines, Smoky Topaz, Flared, Etched R. Lalique, 7 ½ x 5 ½ In.	2750.00
Hood Ornament, Coq Nain, Cockerel, Opaline, Blue Edges, 8 ½ x 5 ½ In.	504.00
Hood Ornament, Tete D'Aigle, Eagle's Head, Frosted, Clear, Metal Collar, Black Base, c.1928, 5 ⅜ In.	3750.00
Hood Ornament, Tete D'Aigle, Eagle's Head, Signed, Sticker, c.1928, 4 ½ In.	115.00
Hood Ornament, Victoire, Spirit Of Wind, Frosted, Clear, Molded R. Lalique, c.1928, 6 In.	21250.00
Inkwell, Biches, Does In Forest, Molded, Frosted, Engraved R. Lalique, 1913, 4 x 6 x 6 In.	2468.00
Jar, Trois Figurines, Le Dandy Rachelle, Frosted, Molded R. Lalique, 3 ¾ In.	510.00
Lamp, Camelia, Frosted, Clear, Nickeled Metal Base, Engraved R. Lalique, c.1928, 17 ¾ In.	31250.00
Lamp, Hanging, Charmes, Leaves, Etched Bowl, Clear, Frosted, 4 Chain Supports, c.1924, 21 x 13 In.	3500.00
Lighter, Tokio, Clear, Frosted Flower Medallions, Signed Lalique France, 4 x 2 ⅞ In.	96.00
Mirror, Floride, Flower Shape, Clear, Teal Blue Cabochons & Band, Easel Back, 10 ¼ In.	531.00
Paperweight, Bison, Clear & Frosted, R. Lalique, c.1931, 4 x 5 In. *Illus*	1250.00
Paperweight, Turtle, Amber & Clear, Etched Mark, 1980, 5 ¾ In.	200.00
Perfume Bottle, Camille, Frosted Electric Blue, Etched R. Lalique, 1927, 2 ¼ x 2 ¼ In.	6250.00
Perfume Bottle, Camille, Frosted Electric Blue, Stopper, Etched, R. Lalique, 2 ¼ x 2 ¼ In. *Illus*	1875.00
Perfume Bottle, Dahlia, Embossed Flower Head, Black Enamel Stamen, Signed, 5 In.	690.00
Perfume Bottle, D'Orsay, Black Glass, Squared Column, Flattened Square Stopper, c.1912, 5 In.	750.00
Perfume Bottle, Lily Of The Valley, Bulbous, Flower Stopper, Frosted, 4 ½ In.	173.00
Perfume Bottle, Misti, Etched Butterflies, Frosted, Round, Flattened, Stopper, c.1913, 2 x 3 ¼ In.	2375.00
Perfume Bottle, Myosotis Flacon No. 3, Sepia, Round, Kneeling Nude Woman Finial, c.1928, 9 In.	4375.00
Perfume Bottle, Pavots D'Argent, Radiating Waves, Clear, Round, Flattened, 1930s, 3 x 2 ½ In.	531.00
Perfume Bottle, Requete, Clear, Blue Trim, Flattened, Serrated Edge, Stopper, 3 ½ In.	489.00
Perfume Bottle, Sirenes, Mermaids, Opalescent & Frosted, Rounded Square, Domed Lid, c.1920, 7 In.	2000.00
Perfume Burner, Sirenes, Mermaids, Frosted, Domed Lid, Molded R. Lalique, 7 x 3 ½ In.	3000.00
Perfume Tester, La Renommee D'Orsay, 5 Chamber, Frosted, c.1922, 1 ¾ x 8 ¾ In.	2375.00
Plaque, Masque De Femme, Woman's Face, Fish Border, Frosted, Clear, Square, 12 ½ In.	3125.00
Statue, Grande Nue Socle Lierre, Female Nude, Long Hair, Frosted, Wood Base, 1919, 16 In.	12500.00
Tray, Berbere, Goat & Berries, Frosted & Clear, Round, 15 ¼ In.	151.00
Tumbler, Whiskey, Femme Antiques, Classical Women, Frosted, Clear, Molded, 4 In., 12 Piece	1375.00
Vase, Allover Leaves, Molded, Frosted, Tapered Cylinder, Signed, 9 In.	2250.00
Vase, Bacchantes, Frieze Of Nudes, Tapered Cylinder, 9 ¾ In.	2813.00
Vase, Bacchantes, Nude Women, Inscribed, Box, 9 ½ In. *Illus*	2530.00
Vase, Bagatelle, Birds Nested In Leaves, 7 In.	780.00
Vase, Bagatelle, Birds, Leaves, Frosted, Oval, Clear Flared Rim, 6 ¾ In.	460.00
Vase, Bagheera, Lion's Paw, Frosted, Clear, Footed, 8 ½ x 6 In.	374.00
Vase, Beliers, Ram Handles, Frosted Smoky, Pedestal Foot, c.1925, 7 ½ x 9 ½ In.	2875.00
Vase, Biches, Deer, Leaves, Dark Cobalt, Oval, 6 ¾ In.	438.00
Vase, Borneo, Birds, Leaves, Engraved, 11 ½ In.	891.00
Vase, Chevreuse, Frosted, Green Patina, Tapered, Stepped, c.1930, 6 x 7 In.	2625.00
Vase, Courges, Gourds, Red, Bulbous Teardrop Shape, c.1914, 7 ½ x 7 ½ In.	57000.00
Vase, Danaides, Female Nude, Urn On Shoulder, Pouring Water, Amber, c.1926, 7 ¼ x 5 ½ In.	7500.00
Vase, Domremy, Thistles, Smoky Gray Patina, R. Lalique, France, c.1926, 8 ½ x 8 In. *Illus*	1375.00
Vase, Druide, Mistletoe, Branches, Gray, Signed, c.1932, 6 ⅞ In.	1573.00
Vase, Epis, Leaves, Side By Side, Opalescent, Beaded, Flared, Art Deco, R. Lalique, 6 In.	575.00
Vase, Esterel, Leaves, Etched, Amber, Squat, Tapered, c.1923, 6 ¼ x 6 ½ In.	4688.00
Vase, Female Nude Handles, Bulbous, Rolled Rim, Flowers, Frosted Gray, c.1926, 5 x 6 ½ In.	7500.00
Vase, Formose, Swirling Carp, Green, Round, Footed, Narrow Rim, Swimming Fish, c.1924, 7 x 7 In.	8750.00
Vase, Grenade, Blue, Engraved R. Lalique, c.1930, 4 ½ x 4 ½ In. *Illus*	3500.00
Vase, Gui, Mistletoe & Berries, Opalescent, Globular, c.1935, 6 ½ In.	900.00
Vase, Ingrid, Clear & Frosted, Marked, Late 1900s, 10 ½ In. *Illus*	1180.00
Vase, Ispahan Rose, Roses, Thorny Branches, Signed, 9 ⅜ x 7 ¾ In.	1020.00
Vase, Luxembourg, Cherub Band, Round, Frosted, c.1965, 8 ¼ x 10 In.	2640.00
Vase, Luxembourg, Cherubs, Frosted, 9 x 8 In.	690.00
Vase, Marignane, Leafy Vines, Buttressed Rows, Clear, Frosted, Cylindrical, c.1940, 9 ¼ In.	2040.00
Vase, Martinique, 2 Stylized Wings, Clear To Amber To Gold, Tapered, Marked, c.1990, 12 ½ In.	1416.00
Vase, Moissac, Overlapping Raised Leaves, Frosted Teal Blue, Tapered, Wide Rim, c.1927, 5 x 6 In.	3125.00
Vase, Monaco, 3 Fish Bands, Smoke Gray, Flared, Marked, 7 ¼ In.	719.00
Vase, Ormeaux, Elm Leaves, Amber, Round, Pinched Neck, Flared Lip, c.1926, 6 ½ x 5 In.	2750.00
Vase, Ormeaux, Overlapping Elm Leaves, Amber, Bulbous, 1926, 6 ½ In.	1185.00
Vase, Owl Stem, Frosted, Square Base, Wide Rim, c.1990, 9 ½ In.	472.00
Vase, Raisins, Grapes & Vines, Frosted, Flared, c.1928, Etched R. Lalique, 6 x 3 ½ In.	688.00

Lalique, Vase, Bacchantes, Nude Women, Inscribed, Box, 9 ½ In.
$2,530.00

Cottone Auctions

Lalique, Vase, Domremy, Thistles, Smoky Gray Patina, R. Lalique, France, c.1926, 8 ½ x 8 In.
$1,375.00

Rago Arts & Auction Center

Lalique, Vase, Grenade, Blue, Engraved R. Lalique, c.1930, 4 ½ x 4 ½ In.
$3,500.00

Rago Arts & Auction Center

Lalique, Vase, Ingrid, Clear & Frosted, Marked, Late 1900s, 10 ½ In.
$1,180.00

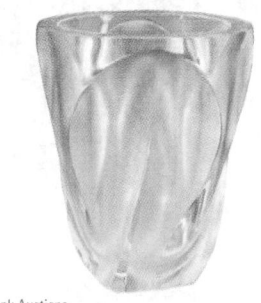

Brunk Auctions

L

Lamp, Bouillotte, 4-Light, Hanging, Tole Shade, Glass Chimneys, Drip Pans, Electrified, 26 In.
$896.00

Neal Auction Co.

Lamp, Chandelier, 1-Light, Aalto, Enameled, Painted Metal, Brass, Plastic, 1950s, 12 x 6 In.
$2,375.00

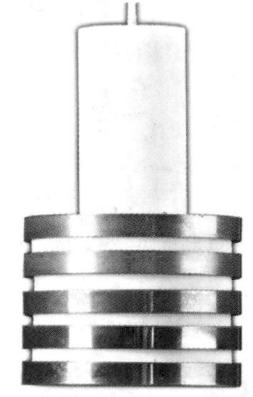

Rago Arts & Auction Center

Lamp, Chandelier, 8-Tier, Cased Glass, Drops, Painted, Stamped, Venini Murano, 1960s, 21 x 24 In.
$1,875.00

Rago Arts & Auction Center

Vase, Royat, Interlocking Chevrons, Ridges, Frosted & Clear, Protruding Disc Rim, Signed, 6 In....	288.00
Vase, Satyr, Ivy Swags, Molded, Frosted, Acid Etched Signature, 7 x 6 ½ In.	719.00
Vase, Senlis, Opaque Black, Spherical, Pinched Neck, Bronze Leaf Handles, 1925, 10 In.	3600.00
Vase, Silenes, Satyr Masks, Leafy Branches, Molded, Frosted, Tapered, Cylindrical, Signed, 8 In.	1063.00
Vase, Sylvie, 2 Entwined Doves, Extended Wings, Signed, 8 In.	420.00
Vase, Sylvie, 2 Entwined Doves, Frosted, Signed, 8 x 6 In.	425.00
Vase, Verone, Birds, Scrolls, Clear & Frosted Flared, Ring Foot, 1980s, 7 ½ x 11 In....................	1230.00

LAMPS of every type, from the early oil-burning Betty and Phoebe lamps to the recent electric lamps with glass or beaded shades, interest collectors. Fuels used in lamps changed through the years; whale oil (1800–40), camphene (1828), Argand (1830), lard (1833–63), turpentine and alcohol (1840s), gas (1850–79), kerosene (1860), and electricity (1879) are the most common. Other lamps are listed by manufacturer or type of material.

3-Light, Floor, Wrought Iron, Turned Standard, Scrolled Tripartite Base, Mica Shade, 66 In...	748.00
Advertising, Schlitz, Pure Mark, Gold Woman, Holding Light-Up Globe, c.1976, 45 In............	1920.00
Aladdin, Brass, Relief Flowers, Paneled Sided, Electrified, Mantle Lamp Co., c.1900, 33 In......	60.00
Aladdin, Kerosene, White Milk Glass Shade, Pink Base, 25 In..	209.00
Argand, 2-Light, Silver Plate, Acanthus Collar, Flame Finial, Paw Feet, 23 In., Pair................	1135.00
Betty, Brass, Round Lid, Standing Bird Shape, Bird Finial, Tooled Hanger, c.1810, 4 ¾ x 11 In..	374.00
Betty, Brass, Wrought Iron, Peter Derr, Berks County, Pa., 1859, 5 ¼ In................................	1185.00
Betty, Grease, Copper, Iron, Stamped Peter Derr 1834, Pa., 5 ¾ In..	2844.00
Betty, Ram's Horn, Sheet Iron, Tin Back, Scrolled Ram's Horns, Black Paint, c.1800, 4 ½ x 4 ½ In.	575.00
Betty, Wrought Iron, Round, Swinging Cover, Cutout Rooster, Finial, 5 ⅜ x 12 In.	115.00
Bicycle, Carbide, Nickel Plated, White Star, Brown & Smith, Font Base, Wick Tube, Reflector, 8 In.	165.00
Bouillotte, 4-Light, Hanging, Tole Shade, Glass Chimneys, Drip Pans, Electrified, 26 In. .... *Illus*	896.00
Bradley & Hubbard lamps are included in the Bradley & Hubbard category.	
Ceiling, Leaded Glass, Opal, Geometric, Half Dome Shape, 4-Light, 7 x 17 In.	460.00
Chandelier, 1-Light, Aalto, Enameled, Painted Metal, Brass, Plastic, 1950s, 12 x 6 In.........*Illus*	2375.00
Chandelier, 2-Light, Frosted Glass, Gilt Metal, Tubes, Intersecting, Italy, 1960s, 19 x 19 ¼ In....	375.00
Chandelier, 2-Light, Gilt Brass, Putto, Twisted Flower Branches, France, c.1900, 27 x 19 In......	1722.00
Chandelier, 3-Light, Iron, 3 Prickets, Round, Tiffany, c.1900, 17 In..	237.00
Chandelier, 3-Light, Turned Shaft, Red Paint, Sheet Iron Band, Slotted Cups, Bobeches, 20 In.	3738.00
Chandelier, 3-Light, Wedgwood, Blue Jasper, Gilt Metal, Classical Relief, Pendant Drop, 34 x 16 In.	1062.00
Chandelier, 3-Light, White Opaline Glass, Gilt Bronze Mounts, c.1970, 24 x 12 In.	2500.00
Chandelier, 4-Light, Brass, Baluster Shaft, Scrolled Arms, c.1750, 14 x 11 In.............................	1304.00
Chandelier, 4-Light, Brass, Stag Shaped Mounts, 3 Globe Shades, 14 ¼ In...............................	1375.00
Chandelier, 4-Light, Louis XVI Style, Gilt Bronze, Crystal, Plumes, Drapery, 4 Figures, 33 x 24 In.	1912.00
Chandelier, 4-Light, Louis XVI Style, Gilt Metal, Pierced, Coiled, Candle Shaped, 26 x 16 In......	338.00
Chandelier, 4-Light, Neoclassical Style, Gilt Brass, Ruby Glass, Bowl, Bead Chains, Spears, 21 x 18 In.	584.00
Chandelier, 4-Light, Scrolling Leafy Branches, Porcelain Flower Heads, 33 In.	600.00
Chandelier, 4-Light, Wrought Iron, Drip Pans, c.1775, 17 x 14 In..	1896.00
Chandelier, 5-Light, Antler, Plaid Shades, Drop Light, Cut Glass Shade, U.S.A., 1900s, 32 x 30 In.	767.00
Chandelier, 5-Light, Basket Shape, Spears, Urn Finials, Pinecone Pendants, 1900s, 49 x 38 In., Pair.	6000.00
Chandelier, 5-Light, Empire Style, Bronze, 5 Rope Supports, Dome, Glass Shades, c.1890, 48 x 33 In.	1652.00
Chandelier, 5-Light, Glass, Baluster Standard, Scrolling Arms, Hanging Prisms, Italy, 26 In......	1063.00
Chandelier, 6-Light, Arts & Crafts, Wrought Iron, Scrolling Crown, Mica Inset Frame, 25 In..	375.00
Chandelier, 6-Light, Brass, Opaline Glass, Prism, Scrolling Arms, Medallion, 33 x 19 In.	1722.00
Chandelier, 6-Light, Brass, Renaissance Style, Double Cone Standard, Leaf Finial, Oil, 37 x 17 In.	584.00
Chandelier, 6-Light, Bronze, 6 Chains, Suspended Hub, 3 Arms, Pendant Sockets, Prisms, 48 x 20 In.	2607.00
Chandelier, 6-Light, Bronze, Ball Base, Finials, Scrolling Arms, Virgin Mary Figure, 36 x 35 In.	922.00
Chandelier, 6-Light, Bronze, Rope Twist Standard, Faux Candles, Chains, Wreaths, 37 x 23 In.	1107.00
Chandelier, 6-Light, Cranberry Glass, Beaded Swags, Bobeches, Candles, Clear Shades, c.1900, 40 In.	922.00
Chandelier, 6-Light, Crown Shape Leafy Canopy, Acorn Finial, Glass Pan, Scroll Arms, Chains, 26 In.	1968.00
Chandelier, 6-Light, Cut Glass, Faceted Teardrops, Beaded Swag, Prisms, 1900s, 30 x 21 In......	676.00
Chandelier, 6-Light, Empire Style, Gilt Metal, Black Standard, Scrolled Branches, Chains, 21 x 19 In.	531.00
Chandelier, 6-Light, Georgian Style, Scrolling Arms, Beaded Swag, Pendant Drops, 36 In.........	837.00
Chandelier, 6-Light, Gilt Brass, Basket Shape, Scrolled Arms, Crystal, Swags, c.1900, 26 x 18 In.....	767.00
Chandelier, 6-Light, Gilt Metal, Basket, Swag Column, Masks, Prisms, 40 ½ In............................	563.00
Chandelier, 6-Light, Gilt Metal, Cylindrical Standard, Scrolls, Glass Chains, Prisms, 43 x 19 ½ In.	750.00
Chandelier, 6-Light, Gilt Metal, Urn, Fleur-De-Lis Standard, Scrolled Leaf Branches, 28 x 32 In.....	500.00
Chandelier, 6-Light, Giltwood, Carved, Italy, c.1890, 29 x 24 In.	590.00
Chandelier, 6-Light, Glass, C-Shape, Hanging Prisms, France, 16 In.......................................	750.00
Chandelier, 6-Light, Glass, Spiral Shape Frame, Scrolling Arms, Grape Cluster Drops, Italy, 35 In.	3250.00
Chandelier, 6-Light, Iron, Red, Green Paint, S-Scrolls, Leaves, Italy, c.1900, 43 x 33 In., Pair.	984.00
Chandelier, 6-Light, Louis XV Style, Silvered Metal, Clear Prisms	3803.00

L

Chandelier, 6-Light, Louis XV Style, Walnut, Reeded Standard, Leaf Carved Arms, 44 x 35 ½ In.		1107.00
Chandelier, 6-Light, Patinated Metal, Gilt, Scrolled Arms, Chains, France, c.1890, 25 ¼ x 14 ½ In.		1500.00
Chandelier, 6-Light, Regency Style, Silver Plate, Beads, Prisms, Bell Shape, Waterford, c.1900, 27 In.		1200.00
Chandelier, 6-Light, Rock Crystal, Beaded Swags, Pendants, Gilt Frame, 1900s, 32 x 26 In.		2400.00
Chandelier, 6-Light, Rococo Revival, Gilt Brass, 3 Graces, Art, Industry, Science, c.1850, 70 x 31 In.		9532.00
Chandelier, 6-Light, Russian Neoclassical, Bronze, Egyptian Masks, Prisms, Oil, c.1835, 32 x 18 In.		5313.00
Chandelier, 6-Light, Rustic, Wrought Iron, Chains, Scrolled Arms, Bobeches, Painted, 19 x 25 In..		138.00
Chandelier, 6-Light, Wood, Carved, Painted, Turned Shaft, Tulips, Curved Arms, Tassel, 1800s, 25 In.		948.00
Chandelier, 6-Light, Wrought Iron, Gilt, Pineapple Shape, Leaf & Tassel Base, c.1950, 26 x 23 In..		649.00
Chandelier, 7-Light, Empire Style, Patinated Bronze, Chains, Acorn Knop, Glass Shades, 46 x 30 In..		1750.00
Chandelier, 8-Light, Art Deco, Iron, 4 Rod-Shaped Arms, Round Openwork, Alabaster Shade, 20 In..		830.00
Chandelier, 8-Light, Baltic Neoclassical Style, Cut Glass, Prisms, Curved Arms, Chains, 40 x 32 In.		6250.00
Chandelier, 8-Light, Bow Corona, Star Gallery, Masks, Beaded Chains, Prisms, 36 x 40 In.		7995.00
Chandelier, 8-Light, Brass, Crystal, Scroll Arms, Prism Swags, 39 ¾ In........................		922.00
Chandelier, 8-Light, Brass, Scrolls, Flowers, Swags, Gas, Electrified, c.1900, 44 x 26 In.		3186.00
Chandelier, 8-Light, Bronze, Crystal, Scrolled Arms, Prism Swags, Faux Candles, Shades, 41 In.		1045.00
Chandelier, 8-Light, Cut Glass, Bronze, Scrolled Arms, Hanging Prism Festoons, Sprays, 33 x 27 In.		3936.00
Chandelier, 8-Light, Empire Style, Inverted Bowl, Gilt Bronze, Acanthus, 30 x 25 In.		920.00
Chandelier, 8-Light, Gilt Bronze, 3 Tiers, Pendants, France, 45 In.		1500.00
Chandelier, 8-Light, Gilt Bronze, Crystal, Scrolled Arms, Flower Head Prisms, Spears, 48 x 31 ½ In.		799.00
Chandelier, 8-Light, Glass, Faceted, Crosshatched, S-Shape Arms, Prisms, Draped Beads, 34 In......		615.00
Chandelier, 8-Light, Iron, Hammered, Frosted Glass, Octagonal, Chains, c.1915, 40 x 31 In. .		1080.00
Chandelier, 8-Light, Louis XVI Style, Silvered Bronze, Tiered Standard, Leaves, Reserves, 25 x 34 In.		2250.00
Chandelier, 8-Light, Metal, Glass, Scrolled Frame, Ball & Pendant Prisms, Swags, 1900s, 40 In.		1353.00
Chandelier, 8-Light, Neoclassical Style, Gilt Bronze, Quiver Standard, Pinecone Finial, c.1900, 37 In.		1845.00
Chandelier, 8-Light, P. Evans, Bronze, Sculptured, Jagged, Round, Chains, 1970s, 35 x 47 In...........		15000.00
Chandelier, 8-Light, Pineapple, Painted, Palm Branch Arms, Shades, 33 x 36 In.		259.00
Chandelier, 8-Light, Rococo Style, Gilt Brass, 20th Century, 20 ½ x 24 In........................		120.00
Chandelier, 8-Light, Rococo Style, Scalloped Bowl, Flower Cup Arms, Italy, 16 x 30 ½ In.		1872.00
Chandelier, 8-Light, Tin, Black Paint, c.1820, 26 x 38 In.		6820.00
Chandelier, 8-Light, Venetian Glass, Twisted Arms, Multicolor Flower Pendants, 29 x 31 In. ..		3286.00
Chandelier, 8-Light, Wrought Iron, Pierced Coiled Arms, Faux Candles, Arched Canopy Top, 49 In.		369.00
Chandelier, 9-Light, Bronze, Alabaster, 3 Marble Columns, Putti Supported Arms, c.1915, 40 x 22 In.		1770.00
Chandelier, 9-Light, Empire Style, Bronze, Scrolled Arms, Greek Key, Crystal Drops, c.1900, 29 x 21 In.		885.00
Chandelier, 9-Light, Gilt Bronze, 2 Tiers, Bulbous, Leaves, Stars, Pendants, c.1900, 25 x 26 In........		553.00
Chandelier, 9-Light, Glass, Cage Shape, Baluster Crown, Scrolling Arms, Swags, Prisms, 28 In.......		750.00
Chandelier, 10-Light, Brass, Splayed Arms, Trumpet Glass Shade, c.1940, 13 x 45 In.		720.00
Chandelier, 10-Light, Empire Style, Bronze, Inverted Dome, Painted Black, Gilt, Electrified, 18 x 30 In.		546.00
Chandelier, 10-Light, Empire Style, Gilt Bronze, Green, Leaves, 3 Falcons, Acorn Pendant, 40 x 24 In.		1230.00
Chandelier, 10-Light, Louis XV Style, Gilt Bronze, Leaf Standard, 2 Tiers, Conforming Arms, 21 x 23 In.		313.00
Chandelier, 10-Light, Wood, Metal, Italy, c.1950, 24 x 27 In.		780.00
Chandelier, 12-Light, Baroque Style, Brass, Scrolled Arms, Faux Candles, 28 x 25 ¼ In.		492.00
Chandelier, 12-Light, Beaded Glass Tree, Tiered, Drops, Drip Pans, Sweden, 53 x 40 In....................		4680.00
Chandelier, 12-Light, Bohemian Glass, 3 Tiers, Beaded Ropes, Prisms, c.1900, 52 x 36 In.		3600.00
Chandelier, 12-Light, Brass, Scrolled Arms, 2 Tiers, Faux Candles, 35 x 25 ¼ In..........................		615.00
Chandelier, 12-Light, Bronze, Brass, 2 Tiers, Bulbous Shaft, 1900s, 38 x 36 In.		430.00
Chandelier, 12-Light, Cut Glass, 2 Tiers, Canopy, Scrolled Arms, Bead Swags, Prisms, 47 x 33 In....		1599.00
Chandelier, 12-Light, Empire Style, Bronze, Metal, Leaf Plaque, Pineapple Finial, 30 x 30 In.		2460.00
Chandelier, 12-Light, Giltwood, Carved, c.1890, 33 x 41 ½ In.		2750.00
Chandelier, 12-Light, Louis XV Style, Bronze, Crystal, Scroll Arms, Prisms, Ball Finial, 38 x 25 In..		1476.00
Chandelier, 12-Light, Louis XVI Style, Bronze Dore, Crystal, Teardrop, Draped Strands, 50 x 22 ½ In.		1845.00
Chandelier, 12-Light, Rococo, 2 Tiers, Cut Glass Spires, Canopy, Prisms, c.1790, 44 In.....................		4182.00
Chandelier, 13-Light, Bronze & Crystal, Prism Chains, c.1900, 39 x 29 In..............................		1180.00
Chandelier, 14-Light, Louis XVI Style, Gilt Bronze, Scrolling Arms, Bellflowers, c.1900, 37 x 30 In.		3198.00
Chandelier, 15-Light, Gilt Bronze, Corona, Goat's Head Masks, Snakes, c.1800s, 39 ½ x 28 In..		3355.00
Chandelier, 16 Light, Renaissance Revival, Scrolled, c.1890, 51 In....................................		2250.00
Chandelier, 16-Light, Bag Shape, Stepped Caps, Cut Glass Chain Swags, c.1935, 66 x 37 In.		3936.00
Chandelier, 16-Light, Wood, Iron Cups, Baluster Shaft, Scrolled Arms, c.1810, 37 ½ x 36 In. .		3555.00
Chandelier, 18-Light, 2 Tiers, Iron, Wood, Gilt, Paint, Electrified, c.1850, 33 x 45 In.		10540.00
Chandelier, 18-Light, Gilt Metal, Column Standard, Acanthus Leaf Branches, 32 x 30 In.		2813.00
Chandelier, 18-Light, Louis XVI Style, Gilt Bronze, Brass, Beaded Swags, Prisms, Tiered, 51 x 33 In.		7995.00
Chandelier, 18-Light, Rococo Style, Gilt Bronze, Leaves, Cherubs, Winged Women, c.1900, 41 x 30 In.		2185.00
Chandelier, 18-Light, Tin, Circular Rim, Curved Arms, Draped Chain, 20 ½ In. Diam....................		472.00
Chandelier, 19-Light, Glass Serpentine Arms, 2 Tiers, Prism Swags, Faceted Ball Finial, 32 In.........		1230.00

Lamp, Electric, Angelo Lelli, Cobra, Brass, Chrome, Enameled Steel, Arredoluce, Italy, 1960s, 24 ½ In.
$2,250.00

Rago Arts & Auction Center

Lamp, Electric, Duffner & Kimberly, Colonial Pattern, Leaded Glass Shade, Gilt Bronze, 22 x 18 In.
$6,985.00

Leslie Hindman Auctioneers

Lamp, Electric, Figural, Skeleton Head, Amber Glass Eyes, Porcelain, 8 In.
$230.00

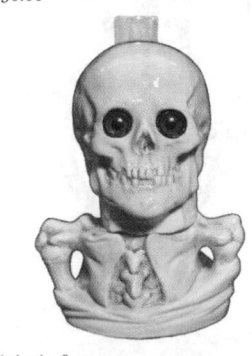

Early Auction Co.

Lamp, Electric, Glass Panels, Bronze Grapevine Overlay, Twisted Beadwork Stem, Riviere Studios, 19 In. $2,415.00

James D. Julia Auctioneers

Lamp, Electric, Glass Panels, Landscape, Bronze Base, NCR Presentation 1923, 19 x 14 In. $1,375.00

Showtime Auction Sevices

Lamp, Electric, Jacque Duval Brasseur, Gilt Iron, Brass, Bronze, Fossil, France, 1960s, 36 x 21 In. $2,500.00

Rago Arts & Auction Center

Chandelier, 20-Light, Crystal, 2 Tiers, Scrolling Arms, Pendant Drops, Ball Finial, 57 In.	1673.00
Chandelier, 20-Light, Gilt Brass, Faceted Crystals, Prisms, Scrolling Arms, c.1990, 42 x 28 In.	2596.00
Chandelier, 20-Light, Gilt Metal, Glass, Acanthus Leaf Branches, Prisms, 37 x 30 In.	2000.00
Chandelier, 20-Light, Glass, Birdcage, 2 Tiers, Prisms, Swags, 1900s, 46 x 41 In.	3300.00
Chandelier, 22-Light, Clear Glass Beading, Bronze Fittings, c.1955, 52 x 36 In.	1062.00
Chandelier, 25-Light, Chrome, Glass, Round, Radiating Bulbs, c.1960	375.00
Chandelier, 31-Light, Crystal, Basket Shape, 2 Tiers, Beads, Pendants, 1900s, 57 x 48 In.	6000.00
Chandelier, 8-Tier, Cased Glass, Drops, Painted, Stamped, Venini Murano, 1960s, 21 x 24 In. *Illus*	1875.00
Chandelier, Art Deco, Wood, Metal, Lacquered, Chinoiserie, Parchment Shades, c.1930, 41 x 39 In.	3125.00
Chandelier, Brass, Crystal, Canopy, Scrolled Arms, Pendants, Prism Swags, 28 x 21 In.	307.00
Chandelier, Crystal, Chrome, Enameled Steel, Round, Rays, Hans Harold Rath, 1960s, 21 In. Diam.	3000.00
Chandelier, Cut Crystal, Round Scalloped Shade, Chains, Faceted Lusters, c.1890, 18 x 16 In.	735.00
Chandelier, Enamel, Aluminum, Steel, Artichoke Shape, Henningsen, Denmark, 1980s, 18 x 24 In.	4375.00
Chandelier, Frosted Glass, Etched Leaves, Bowl Shape, Silk Rope, Lalique, c.1924, 13 ½ In. Diam.	3800.00
Chandelier, Hanging, Cranberry Shade, Brass Accents, 14 In.	396.00
Chandelier, Saloon, Brass, Glass Honeycomb Globes, Crystal Prisms, 54 x 28 In.	3300.00
Cranberry Opalescent Glass, Vertical Striped Base, Shade, 9 In.	1323.00
Double Fairy, Gilt Bronze, Scrolled Grapevine Support, Electrified, Victorian, 10 ¾ In.	150.00
Electric, 2-Light, Arredoluce, Triennial, Cone Shades, Chrome Plated, Black Enamel, 72 In.	2952.00
Electric, 2-Light, Arts & Crafts, Slag Glass Shades, Bronze Plated Hexagonal Base, 20 x 20 In.	449.00
Electric, 2-Light, Boch Freres, Pottery, Elongated Teardrop, Crackle Glaze, Sgraffito, Brass, 24 In.	138.00
Electric, 2-Light, Figural, Boy, Girl, Spelter, Patina, Flower Lights, Faux Marble Base, 14 In., Pair	253.00
Electric, 2-Light, Porcelain, Sang De Boeuf, Teardrop, Elongated Neck, c.1920, 34 In.	357.00
Electric, 3 Bubbles, Pull Chain, Chrome, 1960s, 26 In.	75.00
Electric, 3-Light, E. Burton, Abalone Shell Shades, Curled, Copper Base, Hammered, 9 x 17 In.	2562.00
Electric, 3-Light, E. Burton, Copper, Hammered, Abalone Shell Shades, 16 x 14 In.	20000.00
Electric, 4-Light, Renaissance Style, Alabaster, Gilt Bronze, Cornucopia, Italy, 71 x 13 In.	4973.00
Electric, 5-Light, Victorian, Patinated Bronze, Winged Putto, 5 Lily Stems, 30 ½ In.	720.00
Electric, 6-Light, Palm Tree, Milk Glass Globes, Sahara Hotel & Casino, Las Vegas, 1960s, 78 In.	1020.00
Electric, Angelo Lelli, Cobra, Brass, Chrome, Enameled Steel, Arredoluce, Italy, 1960s, 24 ½ In. *Illus*	2250.00
Electric, Architectural, White Marble Base, Ionic Column, Squared, 29 In., Pair	357.00
Electric, Arredoluce, Brass, Black Enamel, Marble, Adjustable, Italy, c.1960, 62 In.	2125.00
Electric, Art Deco Style, Macassar, Alabaster Torchere Shades, 77 In., Pair	3360.00
Electric, Art Deco Style, Ram, Standing, Grassy Base, Majolica, 1930s, 14 x 17 In.	600.00
Electric, Art Deco, Alabaster, Seminude Woman, Sitting Cross Legged, Glass Globe, 13 x 12 In.	351.00
Electric, Art Deco, Alabaster, Seminude Woman, Seated, Crackle Glass Ball, Round Base, 13 x 12 In.	357.00
Electric, Art Deco, Man & Woman, Standard, Swivel Arm, Stepped Base, Colonial Premier, 49 In.	385.00
Electric, Art Deco, Mica Shade, Geometric Panels, Patinated Metal Base, 2 Cranes, 28 In.	415.00
Electric, Art Deco, Muller Freres Shade, Starburst, Bell Shape, White To Orange, Pink, 9 x 15 In.	267.00
Electric, Art Nouveau, Bronze, 2 Dolphins, Stained Glass Shade, Lit Base, c.1900, 24 x 19 In.	3120.00
Electric, Art Nouveau, Cast Brass, Silver Plate, Branch Buttresses, Frosted Globe Shade, 12 In.	561.00
Electric, Art Nouveau, Gilt Metal, White Opaque & Gold Tile Shade, 15 ¾ In.	177.00
Electric, Art Nouveau, Green & Caramel Slag Glass Shade, Cast Metal Scroll Base, Fluted, 21 x 17 In.	354.00
Electric, Art Nouveau, Nautilus Shell Shade, Bronze, Ribbed Arm, Swirled Base, 13 ½ In.	2520.00
Electric, Art Nouveau, Sleeping Girl, Gilt Bronze, Nautilus Shell Shade, 15 In.	2375.00
Electric, Art Nouveau, Woman Shape, Patinated Metal, Nautilus Shell Shade, 21 In.	1955.00
Electric, Arteluce, Chromed Metal, Adjustable Arm, Black Leather, Spherical Shade, 1960s, 59 In.	385.00
Electric, Artemide, Nesso, Plastic, White, Mushroom Shade, 4 Sockets, Marked, 13 x 20 In.	237.00
Electric, Arts & Crafts, 4-Light, Iron Base, Copper Foil Scaled Glass Shade, c.1945, 63 x 18 In.	443.00
Electric, Arts & Crafts, Copper, Hammered, Strapwork, Mica Shade, Cone Shape, 19 x 19 In.	948.00
Electric, Arts & Crafts, Leaded Glass Shade, Bronze 2-Handled Base, 20 x 25 In.	850.00
Electric, Arts & Crafts, Leaded Glass, Pyramid Shade, Tulips, Column Standard, 14 x 14 In.	397.00
Electric, Arts & Crafts, Oak Shaft & Base, Mica Shade, Mica Lamp Co., 60 x 25 In.	540.00
Electric, Bergman, Peeping Ali, Bronze, Nude Woman In Dome, c.1910, 12 ¼ In.	5053.00
Electric, Black Glass, Domed Shade, Reverse Painted, Lake Scene, c.1910, 21 ¾ x 16 In.	360.00
Electric, Bouillotte, Bronze, Candelabrum Shape, Hammered, Dish Base, Mica Shade, 33 In.	299.00
Electric, Brass Column, Gunmetal Finish, Green Glass Shade, 29 In.	104.00
Electric, Brass, Arched Arm, Wood Base, Tripod Legs, c.1960, 70 In.	540.00
Electric, Brass, F. Barbedienne, Classical Frieze, Paw Feet, Flared Etched Glass Shade, Signed, 22 x 8 In.	180.00
Electric, Brass, Leaf Shade, Stem Standard, Floor Ring, T. Barbi, Italy, 1970s, 17 x 17 In.	2652.00
Electric, Brass, Marble, Black Enamel, Adjustable, Arredoluce, Italy, c.1960, 62 In.	1750.00
Electric, Brass, Overlapping Leaf Shapes, Flared, Stardust Casino & Hotel, Las Vegas	219.00
Electric, Bronze, Bottle Shape, Engine-Turned Texture, Pierced Collar, Hexagonal Shade, 28 In.	104.00
Electric, Bronze, Column, Tapered Lithophane Shade, Catskill Falls, 17 In., Pair	472.00
Electric, Bronze, Green Slag Glass Shade, 3 Ram's Heads, Swag, Bows, Curved Arms, 16 x 7 ½ In.	690.00
Electric, Bronze, Horse Head, Rope Base, 25 x 6 In., Pair	60.00

Electric, Bronze, Spherical Iridescent Shade, Insects, Bronze Plant Life Base, Bird, c. 1910, 16 ¼ In.	5036.00
Electric, Bronze, Swan, Cast, Ebonized Wood Base, Glass Honeycomb Finial, 31 ½ In., Pair	219.00
Electric, Bronze, Woman Reclining, Holding Glass Shell Shade, Signed, Wuyh, 1992, 15 x 20 In.	633.00
Electric, C. Lotton, Millefiori, Pink Flowers, Green Base & Shade, Wavy Rim, 1992, 18 x 25 In.	2196.00
Electric, Caramel Slag Glass Shade, Hexagonal, Metal, Dragon Overlay, 3 Sockets, c.1910, 25 In.	919.00
Electric, Cast Bronze, Serpent, Cone Shaped Mottled Glass Shade, Vincent Garnier, 22 ¼ In.	978.00
Electric, Cast Metal, Basket Of Flowers, Multicolor Paint, 1920s, 22 In.	124.00
Electric, Cast Metal, Oil Lamp Shape, 2 Sockets, Linen Shade, Wood Finial, 32 In.	29.00
Electric, Ceiling, Hall, Cut Glass, Spear & Double Ball Prisms, 9 x 10 In.	246.00
Electric, Cold Painted Bronze, Arab Man On Camel, Palm Frond Shade, Austria, 21 x 9 In.	3680.00
Electric, Copper, Hammered, Cutout Landscape, Glass Panels, Benedict Studios, 13 x 22 In.	4062.00
Electric, Copper, Mixed Metals, Gilt Sea Life, Green Patina, c.1930, 36 x 8 In.............................	840.00
Electric, Cut Glass, Beverly Pattern, Mushroom Shade, Prisms, Meriden, 13 ½ x 7 In.	650.00
Electric, D. Deskey, Chrome, Adjustable, c.1930, 66 ½ In.	3250.00
Electric, Domed Shade, Water Lily, Pink, White, Variegated Green Ground, Tree Trunk Base, 28 x 24 In.	2818.00
Electric, Duffner & Kimberly, Cherry Blossoms, Slag Glass, Sinewy Metal Base, 25 In.	8125.00
Electric, Duffner & Kimberly, Colonial Pattern, Leaded Glass Shade, Gilt Bronze, 22 x 18 In....*Illus*	6985.00
Electric, Egyptian Revival, Bronze, 2 Sphinxes, Column, Oval Base, 9 ¾ x 7 ¼ In............................	585.00
Electric, Emeralite, Green Glass, Adjustable, Embossed Base, H.G. McFadden, 13 x 9 In.	345.00
Electric, Empire Style, Metal, Gueridon Shape, 3 Supports, Tripartite Base, Paper Shade, 30 In.	42.00
Electric, Enamel Pendant Shade, Pulley Weight, Adjustable, Iron, Marked, Saunders, 87 In............	780.00
Electric, F. Gehry, Fish, Copper, Silicone, Wood Base, c.1983, 80 x 36 In........................	122500.00
Electric, Figural, H. Muller, Seminude Woman, Sitting On Rocks, Playing Mandolin, 3-Light, 32 In.	1725.00
Electric, Figural, Nude, Male, Holding Snake, Cast Iron, 26 ½ x 6 In.	2588.00
Electric, Figural, Santa Claus, Climbing Down Chimney, Green, Orange, Black Base, 11 In............	1000.00
Electric, Figural, Skeleton Head, Amber Glass Eyes, Porcelain, 8 In. ....*Illus*	230.00
Electric, G. Grossman, Enameled Metal, Grasshopper, Floor, c.1949, 51 In.	5625.00
Electric, G. Kovacs, White Enamel Base, Shades, Marked, 18 x 29 In., Pair............................	793.00
Electric, G. Magnusson Grossman, Enameled Metal, Tripod Legs, Cone Shade, c.1947, 50 x 15 In.	6875.00
Electric, G. Nelson, Bubble, Steel, White, Translucent Plastic, Howard Miller, 1970s, 26 In.	115.00
Electric, G. Pesce, Fish, Open Sky Series, Polyurethaned Resin, 1995, 25 ¾ x 12 In.	2500.00
Electric, G. Sarfatti, Brass, Adjustable, Enameled Steel, Stamped, Arteluce, 1951, 60 x 15 In.	5938.00
Electric, G. Stickley, Copper, Steer Willow, Silk, Marked, c.1905, 18 ¾ x 16 ¼ In.	1875.00
Electric, Gilt Bronze, Coiled Snake Standard, Gold Glass Shade, France, c.1970, 64 In.	5250.00
Electric, Giltwood, Carved, Black, Gold, Square, c.1940, Pair..	1375.00
Electric, Glass Panels, Bronze Grapevine Overlay, Beadwork Stem, Riviere Studios, 19 In. .....*Illus*	2415.00
Electric, Glass Panels, Landscape, Bronze Base, NCR Presentation 1923, 19 x 14 In. ....*Illus*	1375.00
Electric, Glass, Column, Silver Fittings, Label, Holzheimer's, 37 ½ In.	69.00
Electric, Glass, Frosted, Silver & Gold Coins, c.1955, 32 In., Pair	500.00
Electric, Hanging, Billiards, Double Drop, Black Domed Shades, Score Markers, c.1930, 37 x 55 In.	330.00
Electric, Hanging, Domed Shade, Leaded Glass, Acorn, 14 ¼ In.	5015.00
Electric, Hanging, Etched Baccarat Shade, Scene, Brass Mounts, Lantern Shape, c.1905, 9 x 8 In.	531.00
Electric, Hanging, Leaded Slag Glass, Hexagonal, Flower, Pierced Gilt Metal Frame, 9 x 21 In........	282.00
Electric, Hanging, Slag Glass Panels, Greek Key, White, Caramel, Red, c.1910, 16 x 26 In.	210.00
Electric, Industrial Design, Metal, Accordion Arm, 15 In.	150.00
Electric, J. Adnet, Chrome Plated Steel, Ebonized Wood, Articulated, c.1930, 10 x 11 ¾ In..............	3125.00
Electric, J. Frank, Metal, Brass, Painted, Curved Top, Outswept Tripod Feet, Sweden, c.1935, 48 ½ In...	3100.00
Electric, J. Hoffmann, Brass, Cinched Base, Fabric Shade, Vienna, c.1920, 18 ¼ In........................	10000.00
Electric, J. Martin, Sheet Metal, Yellow, Cone Shaped Base, Vertical Spindle, 2 Candle Sockets, 24 In....	708.00
Electric, J. Perzel, Desk, Chromium Plated, Curved Arm, Glass Base, Blue Shade, c.1930, 14 In.	625.00
Electric, J. Royere, Wrought Iron, Tripod Base, White Shade, France, c.1950, 66 In.	4000.00
Electric, Jacque Duval Brasseur, Gilt, Brass, Bronze, Fossil, France, 1960s, 36 x 21 In......*Illus*	2500.00
Electric, Jefferson, Reverse Painted Shade, Moonlit Landscape, Patinated Metal Base, 23 In............	1625.00
Electric, K. Versen, Chromed Brass, Steel, Glass, Silk & Paper Shade, c.1934, 15 ¾ In.	6875.00
Electric, Leaded Glass Shade, Yellow Tiles, Flower Edge, Bronze Molded Base, 24 x 18 In.	1298.00
Electric, Leaded Glass, Hanging, Leaves & Flowers, Rose, Lavender, Green, Wine, 15 x 28 In.	1680.00
Electric, Leaded Slag Glass, Pink Flowers, Metal Tree Trunk Base, Patina, 25 x 18 In.............*Illus*	660.00
Electric, M. Fantoni, Ceramic, Incised, Multicolor Glaze, Lacquered Wood Base, c.1955, 26 x 10 ½ In.	1375.00
Electric, Marble Obelisk Base, Bronze Figural Swag Mounts, c.1920, 35 x 6 In., Pair	480.00
Electric, Metal Overlay Shade, Grape Leaves, Slag Glass, 3 Sockets, Acorn Pulls, 23 x 16 In......*Illus*	1715.00
Electric, Metal, Industrial Design, Domed Shade, Label, Jielde, France, c.1950, 60 In., Pair	1200.00
Electric, Metal, Weighted Arm, Cantilevered, Tin Shade, Cast Iron Adjustable Base, 65 In................	570.00
Electric, Miller, Leaded Glass, Tulip, Bronze, 1910s, 18 x 15 In....................................*Illus*	1375.00
Electric, Miller, Slag Glass, 6 Curved Panels, Metal Base, Signed, 26 ½ x 20 In....................	212.00
Electric, Moe Bridges, Reverse Painted Shade, Autumn Landscape, Metal Base, c.1920, 24 x 18 In.	1180.00
Electric, Mosaic, Domed Geometric Shade, Green Slag Glass, Patinated Metal, 3 Sockets, 22 x 19 In.	2844.00

Lamp, Electric, Leaded Slag Glass, Pink Flowers, Metal Tree Trunk Base, Patina, 25 x 18 In.
$660.00

DuMouchelles Art Gallery

Lamp, Electric, Metal Overlay Shade, Grape Leaves, Slag Glass, 3 Sockets, Acorn Pulls, 23 x 16 In.
$1,715.00

Skinner, Inc.

Lamp, Electric, Miller, Leaded Glass, Tulip, Bronze, 1910s, 18 x 15 In.
$1,375.00

Rago Arts & Auction Center

L

Lamp, Electric, Prairie School, Oak, Slag Glass, 2 Sockets, c.1910, 25 x 23 In. $2,500.00

Rago Arts & Auction Center

Lamp, Electric, Slag Glass Shade, Scenic, Eiffel Tower Base, Revere Manufacturing, 18 ½ In. $920.00

Humler & Nolan

Lamp, Electric, Tommaso Barbi, Leaf, Brass, Italy, 1970s, 72 x 20 In. $2,125.00

Rago Arts & Auction Center

Lamp, Electric, V. Kagan, Back-Lit, Lacquered Walnut, Brass, Kagan-Dreyfuss, 1950s, 8 ¾ x 17 In., Pair $5,000.00

Rago Arts & Auction Center

Electric, Mosaic, Domed Shade, Green Slag Glass Panels, Stylized Leaf Border, 2 Sockets, 20 x 15 In.	796.00
Electric, Mosaic, Glass, Trellis, Flowers, Octagonal Shade, Bronze Base, 4 Sockets, c.1975, 28 x 24 In....	2066.00
Electric, Murano Glass, Opaque Mushroom Shade, Round Black Metal Base, 18 In.	147.00
Electric, Neoclassical Style, Brass, Urn Shape, Putto Medallions, Handles, Acanthus Feet, 22 In., Pair...	173.00
Electric, Neoclassical Style, Fruitwood, Obelisk, Leaf Base, Shade, Wreath Finial, 33 In., Pair..	676.00
Electric, Neoclassical Style, Gilt, Urn Shape, Husk Garlands, Leaves, c.1860, 15 In., Pair	875.00
Electric, Neoclassical Style, Green Slag Glass Shade, Paneled, Gilt, Cast Metal Base, 22 x 17 In.	328.00
Electric, Oriental Style, Tole, Canister, Figure Smoking Pipe, Figure Carrying Bundle, 24 In., Pair..	575.00
Electric, P. Henningsen, Copper, Red Enamel, 3-Part Shade, Brass Base, c.1927, 62 x 20 In.	22500.00
Electric, Peacock, Bronze, Beaded Feathers, Blue, Green, Clear, Amber, 17 x 15 In.	900.00
Electric, Peacock, Feather Shade, Enameled Glass, 21 x 10 In.	4715.00
Electric, Pewabic Style, Celadon, Fish, Double Dragon's Head Handles, Finial, 24 In.	420.00
Electric, Pink Mother-Of-Pearl Glass, Diamond Quilted, Footed, Oval Base, Ruffled Rim Shade, 6 In.	1093.00
Electric, Pink Pearl Glass, Diamond Quilted, Rectangular, Rigaree Feet, Ruffled Rim, 10 In..	805.00
Electric, Plaster, Figural, Dog, On Rocky Outcrop, Painted, Green Textured Globe, 10 x 14 ½ In.	69.00
Electric, Porcelain, Pate-Sur-Pate, Celadon, White Glaze, Instruments, Flowers, 29 In., Pair	615.00
Electric, Pot Metal, Painted, Slag Glass Shade, Ivory, 6 Panels, 2 Sockets, 21 x 16 In.	95.00
Electric, Prairie School, Oak, Slag Glass, 2 Sockets, c.1910, 25 x 23 In.................*Illus*	2500.00
Electric, R. Sonneman, Chrome, Glass, Cylindrical Standard, Cluster, 9 Spheres, 27 ½ In.	504.00
Electric, Reverse Painted Shade, Lake Scene, Woods, Figures On Path, c.1910, 17 ¾ x 25 In.	
316.00 **Electric,** Rock Crystal, 4 Graduated Globes, Round Marble Base, 1900s, 26 x 6 In., Pair	3600.00
Electric, Sconce, Arts & Crafts, Slag Glass, Metal, Hooded Top, Wood Mounts, 15 In., Pair	351.00
Electric, Sewer Tile, Tree Shape, Grapevines, Animals, Bucket, Ohio, c.1900, 12 In.	176.00
Electric, Sienna Marble, Tapered Column, Ormolu Capital, Anthemion Base, Stamped Austria, 16 In..	460.00
Electric, Silver Plate, Columnar Supports, Square Base, Milk Glass Shade, 22 In., Pair	1300.00
Electric, Slag Glass Shade, Brass-Plated Daylily Base, 2 Sockets, Patinated, 22 x 15 In.	118.00
Electric, Slag Glass Shade, Dolphin Base, Iron, Salem Bros., 25 x 18 ½ In.	944.00
Electric, Slag Glass Shade, Scenic, Eiffel Tower Base, Revere Manufacturing, 18 ½ In.............*Illus*	920.00
Electric, Slag Glass, Green 8-Panel Shade, Cherub Base, Painted Gold, 19 In.	146.00
Electric, Slag Glass, Green Opaque Glass Inserts, Cast Metal Lampshade, 2 Sockets, 29 x 18 In.	178.00
Electric, Spelter, Figural, Seminude Man, Holding Torch, Multicolor, Marble Base, Victorian, 30 In.	146.00
Electric, Student, Brass, 2 Arms, Acorn Reservoir, Green Glass Shades, 22 ¾ In.	235.00
Electric, Student, Brass, Green Glass Shade, Etched Dragons, 24 In.	236.00
Electric, Student, Brass, Green Shade, Electrified, 16 ½ In.	153.00
Electric, Student, Tole, Gilt, 2 Adjustable Candleholders, Cone Shades, Pierced Rim, 20 x 13 In..	1007.00
Electric, T.H. Robsjohn Gibbings, Chrome, Cross Base, Paper Shade, Hansen, 16 ¾ x 56 In., Pair....	3625.00
Electric, Tommaso Barbi, Leaf, Brass, Italy, 1970s, 72 x 20 In.................*Illus*	2125.00
Electric, V. Kagan, Aluminum, 3 Tubes, Varying Heights, Matte Black Interiors, 48 In.	366.00
Electric, V. Kagan, Back-Lit, Lacquered Walnut, Brass, Kagan-Dreyfuss, 1950s, 8 ¾ x 17 In., Pair ..*Illus*	5000.00
Electric, Von Nessen, Brass, Pierced Chrome Plated Steel, Glass, Chase, 1933, 9 In., Pair..........*Illus*	688.00
Electric, W.D. Teague, Bakelite Shade, Brushed Aluminum Cone Stem, Domed Base, 13 In.	510.00
Electric, Wood, Black Forest, Bird, Grape Clusters, Quail Feather Shade, c.1910, 28 x 17 In., Pair....	2300.00
Electric, Wrought Iron, Brass Base, Center Brass Knob, 3 Scrolled Legs	531.00
Electric, Wrought Iron, Tubular Stem, Conical Shade, Glass Beads, Aqua, Coral, Italy, 72 In., Pair..	1722.00
Fairy, Burmese Shade, Tapestry Ware Holder, Creamware Cup, Taylor, Tunnicliffe & Co., 7 ¼ In...	1438.00
Fairy, Glass, Flowers, Pink Shaded To Black, Mottled Yellow Ground, Spade Base, 17 In.	1968.00
Fat, Brass, Iron, Gimbal, Impressed John Derr, Mid 19th Century, 9 ¼ In.	2252.00
Fat, Brass, Wrought Iron, Peter Derr, Berks County, Pa., 1844, 6 In.	4740.00
Fat, Cast Iron, 2 Spouts, Dish Base & Handles, Marble Furnace, 1820, 5 ¾ In.	705.00
Fat, Iron Spiral Twist Wick Pick, Adjustable Sawtooth Trammel, Hanging Candleholder, 8 x 20 In..	826.00
Fat, Wrought Iron, 2-Sided, Teardrop Shades, Tripod Base, Hook Top, c.1800, 17 In.	144.00
Fat, Wrought Iron, Wrigglework Lid, Initialed J.S., Pa., 1844, 5 ¼ In.	2252.00
Fluid, Cut Glass, Cranberry Cut To Clear, White Opalescent Base, 12 In.	288.00
Fluid, Cut Glass, Green To Clear, Opalescent Base, 14 ½ In.	575.00
Fluid, Cut Glass, Thumbprint, Cobalt Blue To Clear, Brass & Marble Base, 12 ½ In.	1035.00
Fluid, Cut Glass, Thumbprint, Cranberry To Clear, Stepped Marble Base, 16 ½ In.	2070.00
Fluid, Finger, Hobbs Coin Spot, Opalescent, Eldorado W.B.G. Comp. Burner, Chimney, c.1900 ..*Illus*	127.00
Fluid, Heart & Waffle, Yellow Encased Font, Pressed Glass Base, Brass Neck Band, c.1900 ...*Illus*	104.00
Fluid, Hobbs Coin Spot, Cranberry, Opalescent, No. 2 Queen Anne Burner, c.1900, 9 ¼ In....*Illus*	207.00
Fluid, Miner's, Cap, Cloth, Leather Visor, Metal Clip, 4 ½ In.	130.00
Fluid, Peg, Pewter Candlestick, Blown Glass, 9 ½ In.	118.00
Fluid, Porcelain, Dresden Style, Applied Cherubs, Raised & Painted Flowers, Scrolling, 1800s, 27 In..	152.00
Fluid, Sawtooth, Flat, Sandwich Glass, Electrified, 10 ¾ In.	71.00
Gas, Metal, Classical Maiden, Dimpled Cut & Etched Shade On Head, Brass Base, 17 In.	984.00
Gasolier, 3-Light, Bronze, Fluted, Winged Goat Masks, Etched Ball Shades, 36 x 24 In.	3050.00
Grease, Earthenware, Albany Slip Glaze, Samuel Routson, Wayne County, Ohio, c.1840, 5 In.	1645.00

Handel lamps are included in the Handel category.

Hanging, Cranberry Hobnail Glass, Clear Pendants, Electrified, c.1890, 14 In.	390.00
Kerosene, Banquet, Gothic Style, Bronze Column, Marble Base, Etched Glass, c.1910, 36 In... *Illus*	359.00
Kerosene, Carriage, Brass, Nickel Plated, 5 Glazed Panels, Pendant, Eagle Finial, Pair	649.00
Kerosene, Carriage, Brass, Tole, Winged Eagle Finial, Beveled Glass, c.1920, 33 x 8 In.	960.00
Kerosene, Cut Glass, Mushroom Shade, Hobstar, Cane, Zipper, Vesica & Fan, Prisms, 20 x 12 In..	1050.00
Kerosene, Cut Glass, Strawberry Dome, Harvard Pattern, Engraved Flowers, Spear Prisms, 23 In.	900.00
Kerosene, Deitz, Beacon, No. 13, Blue Lacquer, Cone Reflector, Bail Handle, Wall Bracket, 20 In.	266.00
Kerosene, Gone With The Wind, Embossed Feather, Frosted Shade, Electrified, Victorian, 26 In.	295.00
Kerosene, Gone With The Wind, Red Glass, Molded Flowers On Body & Globe, c.1860, 27 In..	384.00
Kerosene, Green Opaque Glass Shade, Amethyst & Amber Staining, New England, 10 In... *Illus*	17825.00
Kerosene, Petomax Rapid, Chrome, Glass, Arched Handle	224.00
Oil, Banquet, Copper Shell Font, Round, Metal Stem & Foot, Maroon Cased Globe, 15 In.	230.00
Oil, Bronze, Figural, Infant Water Carrier, 2 Pink Glass Petal Shades, Signed A. Moreau, c.1910, 26 In..	1080.00
Oil, Carriage, Nickeled Brass, 4-Tiered Steeple Form, Bowed Glass, Cowles, 34 In., Pair	1434.00
Oil, Courting Scene, Blue Ground, Sevres, c.1850, 21 In.	334.00
Oil, Cranberry Glass, Cone-Shaped Shade, Cupped Top, 8 In.	130.00
Oil, Cranberry Glass, Ivy, Brass Collar, Threaded Brass Burner, 6 ¾ In.	443.00
Oil, Cut Glass, Prism & Thumbprint, Matching Shade, Landers, Frairy & Clark, 14 In.	900.00
Oil, Cut Glass, Wheeler Pattern, Ball Shape, Oxford Font, Mt. Washington, 9 In.	300.00
Oil, E. Miller, Brass, Double Arm, Orange Shade, c.1890, 21 In.	889.00
Oil, End-Of-Day Glass Shades, 5 Applied Clear Feet, c.1875, 8 In. *Illus*	1093.00
Oil, Finger, Blue Glass, Nutmeg, Cylindrical Base, Wire Finger Ring, Brass Collar & Burner, 6 ¼ In.	47.00
Oil, Gilt Cast Metal, Globe Shade, Electrified, 31 In.	71.00
Oil, Glass Shade, Flowers, Bronze, Figural, Children On Base, Duplex, 40 In.	210.00
Oil, Green Glass, Tin Finger Ring, Embossed, Threaded Tin Pan, Brass Collar, 6 ½ In.	59.00
Oil, Green Opalescent Glass, Paneled, Chimney, Applied Shell Feet, 11 ¼ In. *Illus*	460.00
Oil, Honey Amber Glass, White Spatter, c.1875, 6 In. *Illus*	633.00
Oil, Kettle, Wrought Iron, 4 Curved Legs, Pointed Feet, c.1810, 10 ¼ In.	345.00
Oil, Kettle, Wrought Iron, Turnip Wood Base, c.1810, 10 ¾ In.	115.00
Oil, Little Gem, Green Glass, Adjustable Brass Burner, Loop Handle, Hexagonal Foot, 7 ¼ In.... *Illus*	47.00
Oil, Marriage, Glass, 2 Fonts, Opalescent Robin's-Egg Blue, Clear Shades, Stem & Foot, 19 In.	878.00
Oil, Milk Glass, Amber, Daisy & Button, Dotted Straps, Brass Burner, 8 ¼ In.	71.00
Oil, Milk Glass, Swan, Embossed, Nutmeg Burner, 8 In. *Illus*	518.00
Oil, Milk Glass, Transfer, Cherub, Flowers, 8 ¾ In.	106.00
Oil, Neoclassical Style, Bronze, Ram's Head Spouts, Dolphin, Merman, Scroll Handle, c.1820, 9 In.	390.00
Oil, Owl, Porcelain, Inset Eyes, Gold Highlights, Yellow-Cased Half Shade, 10 In. *Illus*	403.00
Oil, Pottery, Green Matte Glaze, 4 Buttresses, Woven Shade, Wheatley, Marked, 19 In.	1500.00
Oil, Pressed Glass, Amethyst, Gothic Panel, Petal Rim, Domed, Brass, Milk Glass Base, 13 In., Pair	266.00
Oil, Pressed Glass, Blue Translucent, Cylindrical, Swollen Top & Bottom, Finger Ring, 7 In.	47.00
Oil, Pressed Glass, Greek Key Band, Beaded Rim, 8 In.	47.00
Oil, Pressed Glass, Hobnail, Blue Translucent, Brass Pedestal Base, Disc Foot, Brass Collar, 8 In.	47.00
Oil, Pressed Glass, Relief Feathers, Red, Footed, Globe Shade, Brass Collar, 9 In.	295.00
Oil, Pressed Milk Glass, Beaded, Double Drape, Drum Shaped Font, Brass Burner, 8 In.	12.00
Oil, Punty & Oval, White To Clear, Gilt Flower Band, Sandwich Glass, c.1860, 13 x 5 In.	173.00
Oil, Rushlight, Wrought Iron, c.1790, 8 ⅝ In.	207.00
Oil, Skater's, Brass, Cone Shaped Molded Base, Wire Bail Handle, 7 In.	83.00
Oil, Student, Brass, Milk Glass Shade, 12 ¾ x 7 ⅜ In.	153.00
Oil, Student, Milk Glass Shade, Brass Arm, Adjusting Ring, Screw, Knob, Electrified, 21 In.	59.00
Oil, Tin, Elliptical Reflector, Iron, Canister Font, Brass Burner, Chimney, Hook, 13 In., Pair	153.00
Oil, Tin, Hog Scraper, Narrow Tube Shape, Round Foot, 6 ½ In., Pair	150.00
Oil, Wedding, White Opaline Reservoirs, Brass Burners, Ripley, E.F. Jones 1859, 13 ¾ x 9 ½ In..	575.00
Pairpoint lamps are in the Pairpoint category.	
Perfume, Blue Glass Shade, Top Well, Silver Metal Base, Reticulated Border, France, 1930s, 5 In..	296.00
Rushlight, Iron, Twisted, Arched Legs, Flattened Feet, Ball Shaped Counterweight, c.1800, 11 ⅛ In..	489.00
Rushlight, Wrought Iron, Adjustable Shaft, X-Shape Wood Base, c.1800, 35 In.	460.00
Rushlight, Wrought Iron, Tripod Base, Curled Feet, c.1800, 15 In.	259.00
Rushlight, Wrought Iron, Twisted, Octagonal Wood Base, c.1800, 9 ½ In.	316.00
Rushlight, Wrought Iron, Twisted, Round Base, 1800s, 28 In., Pair	235.00
Sconce, 1-Light, Bronze, Cornucopia Shape, Oval Backplate, Fluted Sides, Beaded Edge, 6 ½ x 8 In..	492.00
Sconce, 1-Light, Gilt Metal, Tulip Cups, Vines, Gilt Leaves, Glass Prisms, c.1950, 20 x 4 In., Pair	461.00
Sconce, 1-Light, Sheet Iron, 2 Geese, Horseshoe, Folk Art, 17 ½ x 30 In.	450.00
Sconce, 1-Light, Tin, Candle, Round Pan, Geometric Petal-Shaped Disks, c.1815, 10 x 9 ½ In..	3480.00
Sconce, 1-Light, Tole, Copper, Green & Yellow Paint, France, 1800s, 14 ½ x 5 In., Pair	896.00
Sconce, 1-Light, Walnut Plaque, Scrolled Ends, Needlework, Landscape, 1800s, 12 x 8 In., Pair	2530.00
Sconce, 2-Light, Arts & Crafts Style, Iron, Gilt, Hammered, Tassels, Scrolls, 14 ¼ x 10 ½ In., Pair.	184.00
Sconce, 2-Light, Brass, Bow & Tassel, 20 ½ In., Pair	234.00

Lamp, Electric, Von Nessen, Brass, Pierced Chrome Plated Steel, Glass, Chase, 1933, 9 In., Pair
$688.00

Los Angeles Modern Auctions (LAMA)

Lamp, Fluid, Finger, Hobbs Coin Spot, Opalescent, Eldorado W.B.G. Comp. Burner, Chimney, c.1900
$127.00

Glass Works Auctions

Lamp, Fluid, Heart & Waffle, Yellow Encased Font, Pressed Glass Base, Brass Neck Band, c.1900
$104.00

Glass Works Auctions

The Lamp Shade Is Important

The prices of lamps with painted, blown out, or stained glass shades are based primarily on the shade. A substitute base of the expected quality does not lower the value by much.

L

Lamp, Fluid, Hobbs Coin Spot, Cranberry, Opalescent, No. 2 Queen Anne Burner, c.1900, 9 ¼ In.
$207.00

Glass Works Auctions

Lamp, Kerosene, Banquet, Gothic Style, Bronze Column, Marble Base, Etched Glass, c.1910, 36 In.
$359.00

Neal Auction Co.

Lamp, Kerosene, Green Opaque Glass Shade, Amethyst & Amber Staining, New England, 10 In.
$17,825.00

Early Auction Co.

Sconce, 2-Light, Brass, Eagle Shape, Laurel Wreath Circle, 1900s, 10 In., Pair	92.00
Sconce, 2-Light, Brass, Renaissance Style, Leaves & Berries, Scrolls, Urn Finials, 1800s, 9 In., Pair	236.00
Sconce, 2-Light, Brass, Reticulated Scroll Frame, Bacchus Mask, Mirror, c.1900, 17 In., Pair	295.00
Sconce, 2-Light, Bronze, 3-Leaf Crest, Jansen, c.1940, 19 x 8 In., Pair	540.00
Sconce, 2-Light, Bronze, Empire Style, Winged Blackamoor, Ball, Crown, 14 ½ x 10 ½ In., Pair	492.00
Sconce, 2-Light, Bronze, Gilt, Black Cherub, Fruit Basket, Entwined Arms, c.1910, 28 In., Pair	1416.00
Sconce, 2-Light, Bronze, Grimacing Demons, Pendant Finial, France, 24 In., Pair	1185.00
Sconce, 2-Light, Bronze, Quiver & Arrow, Leaf Molded Scroll Arms, France, c.1900, 17 ½ In., Pair	522.00
Sconce, 2-Light, Bronze, Woman, Shawl, Holding Basket Of Flowers, c.1900, 10 ½ x 7 In., Pair	430.00
Sconce, 2-Light, Cut Glass, Brass, Notched Arms, Swan's Head, Swags, Prisms, c.1885, 21 In., Pair	615.00
Sconce, 2-Light, Empire, Gilt Bronze, Scrolls, Swags, 1870, 44 x 19 In., Pair	3600.00
Sconce, 2-Light, George III Style, Glass, Tapered Stem, S-Scroll Arms, Finial, Prisms, 19 In., Pair	750.00
Sconce, 2-Light, Georgian Style, Glass Shade, Pointed, Pineapple Finial, 1900s, 14 In., Pair	1035.00
Sconce, 2-Light, Gilt Bronze, Backplate, Candle Branches, Beaded Edge, c.1890, 6 x 9 In., Pair	399.00
Sconce, 2-Light, Gilt Bronze, Branch, Silk Shade, Felix Agostini, France, 1960s, 23 x 11 ½ In., Pair	8125.00
Sconce, 2-Light, Gilt Bronze, Drapery & Tassel Back, Curved Arms, 24 ¾ In., Pair	236.00
Sconce, 2-Light, Gilt Metal, Hammered Brass, Medallion, Scroll Border & Arms, c.1890, 18 In., Pair	472.00
Sconce, 2-Light, Gilt Metal, Porcelain Vines, Flowers, Clear Drops, c.1985, 20 In., Pair	750.00
Sconce, 2-Light, Giltwood, Eagle, Spread Wing, c.1950, 22 In., Pair	148.00
Sconce, 2-Light, Giltwood, Mirrored, Scrolling, Pierced Shell Crest, Vines & Leaves, 10 ¼ In., Pair	215.00
Sconce, 2-Light, Gothic Revival, Wrought Iron, c.1895, 24 x 16 In., Pair	590.00
Sconce, 2-Light, Louis XV Style, Gilt Bronze, Cast Leaf Backplate, Scroll Arms, c.1850, 14 ½ In., Pair	625.00
Sconce, 2-Light, Louis XV Style, Gilt Bronze, Torch, Ribbon, Scrolled Arms, Garland, 27 ½ In., Pair	717.00
Sconce, 2-Light, Louis XV, Gilt Bronze, Scrolled Arms, c.1850, 26 In., Pair	2125.00
Sconce, 2-Light, Louis XVI Style, Bronze, Porcelain, Ribbon, Tassels, Basket, Flowers, 21 x 7 In., Pair	922.00
Sconce, 2-Light, Louis XVI Style, Gilt Bronze, Leaf, Ribbon, Putto, Pipes, Arms, 18 In., Pair	1875.00
Sconce, 2-Light, Lyre Shape, Black Paint, Scrolled Arms, Bellflowers, Finials, 1900s, 18 ¾ In., Pair	649.00
Sconce, 2-Light, Metal, Leaves, Scroll Arms, Branches, Prisms, c.1915, 15 x 14 In., Pair	276.00
Sconce, 2-Light, Neoclassical Style, Bronze, Cameo Glass Shades, Leaves, c.1900, 16 ¼ x 12 ¼ In.	1968.00
Sconce, 2-Light, Neoclassical Style, Fluted Column, Bow & Arrow, Black Eagle Top, 31 x 12 In., Pair	500.00
Sconce, 2-Light, Neoclassical Style, Gilt, Carved, Circle, Swag, Scroll Arms, 1900s, 44 In., Pair	1770.00
Sconce, 2-Light, Neoclassical Style, Metal, Round, Scrolled Branches, Leaves, 20 x 10 In., Pair	153.00
Sconce, 2-Light, Regency Style, Gilt Bronze, Arrows, Wreath, Center Ball, 1900s, 12 x 9 In., Pair	369.00
Sconce, 2-Light, Rock Crystal, Rose Quartz, Scrolling Vine, Leaves, Flower, 27 ½ x 17 In., Pair	3050.00
Sconce, 2-Light, Rococo Style, Wood, Silvered, Scrolling Leaf Arms, 18 x 9 In., Pair	299.00
Sconce, 2-Light, S. Yellin, Wrought Iron, Round, Scalloped Edge, 14 In., 6 Piece	8750.00
Sconce, 2-Light, Silver Plate, Oval, Scroll Arms, Urn Cups, Sheffield, 14 In., Pair	2988.00
Sconce, 2-Light, Venetian Glass, Petal Inserts, Vaseline Arms & Cups, Scrolled, 16 x 14 In., Pair	600.00
Sconce, 2-Light, Venetian Style, Gilt Metal, Rope Twist Scroll Arms, c.1900, 18 x 13 In.	236.00
Sconce, 3-Light, Adam Style, Giltwood, Shield, Mirror Back, Flowers, Urn, 1800s, 43 x 18 In., Pair	1020.00
Sconce, 3-Light, Adam Style, Urn, Bellflower, Sheep's Head, Leaf Top, c.1935, 17 x 13 In., Pair	861.00
Sconce, 3-Light, Beading, Prism Swags, Mirror Back, 14 x 12 In., Pair	417.00
Sconce, 3-Light, Brass, Leaf & Scrolls, 24 In., Pair	92.00
Sconce, 3-Light, Brass, Winged Satyr, Flowers, Scrolled Arms, France, 18 x 13 ½ In., Pair	978.00
Sconce, 3-Light, Bronze, C-Scrolls, Leaves, Flowers, Urns, Flame Finial, France, 30 x 14 In., Pair	922.00
Sconce, 3-Light, Bronze, Gilt, Satyr Holding Flower Swags, Winged Griffins, c.1900, 18 x 15 In.	861.00
Sconce, 3-Light, Empire Style, Sand Cast, Lyre Back, Spread Eagle, 15 ½ In., Pair	236.00
Sconce, 3-Light, Gilt Bronze, Torchere, Hunting Horn Arms, Shades, c.1900, 21 x 13 In., Pair	546.00
Sconce, 3-Light, Gilt Metal, Flowers, Urn, Prisms, Maison Bagues, c.1930, 25 x 16 In., Pair	4183.00
Sconce, 3-Light, Gilt, Prince Of Wales Plume, Scrolling Arms, Carved, Italy, 22 x 16 ½ In., Pair	1845.00
Sconce, 3-Light, Gold Iridescent Glass Shades, Venice, 1920, 36 In., Pair	2500.00
Sconce, 3-Light, Louis XVI Style, Bronze Dore, Urn Finial, Ram's Head, Leaves, 19 x 14 In., Pair	837.00
Sconce, 3-Light, Louis XVI Style, Gilt Bronze, Flowers, Bow Crest, Acanthus, 1800s, 19 ½ In., Pair	1400.00
Sconce, 3-Light, Louis XVI Style, Gilt Bronze, Tassel, Backplate, Branch Sockets, 31 x 14 In., Pair	625.00
Sconce, 3-Light, Louis XVI Style, Gilt Metal, Swags, Sheaths, Palladio, Italy, c.1950, 28 x 14 In., Pair	863.00
Sconce, 3-Light, Louis XVI Style, Gilt, Leaf & Branches, Carved Ribbon & Trophy, 39 ¼ x 15 In.	531.00
Sconce, 3-Light, Metal, Brass, Serpentine Shape, Parchment Shades, 1940s, 12 x 54 ½ In., Pair	12500.00
Sconce, 3-Light, Neoclassical, Gilt Bronze, Onyx, Flaming Torch, Scrolled Arms, 18 In., Pair	2750.00
Sconce, 4-Light, Bronze, Acanthus Plume, Flowers, Scrolls, c.1900, 27 ½ x 17 In., Pair	720.00
Sconce, 4-Light, Gilt Bronze, Arrow, Bowknots, Swan, Anthemia, Bellflowers, 25 x 10 In., Pair	922.00
Sconce, 5-Light, Bronze, Tapered, Reeded Flower Arms, c.1920, 6 x 21 In., Pair	240.00
Sconce, 5-Light, Gilt Bronze, Harp Backplate, Hanging Laurel Branches, 36 ¼ x 17 ½ In., Pair	6150.00
Sconce, 5-Light, Gilt Bronze, Shell, Fruit, Flowers, S-Shape Arm, France, 19 x 16 ¾ In., Pair	2460.00
Sconce, 5-Light, Louis Philippe Style, Bronze, Scrolled Palmette Back, Gilt Cups, 12 x 14 In., Pair	738.00
Sconce, 5-Light, Louis XVI Style, Gilt Bronze, Scrolled Arms, Flower Shade, 42 x 16 In., Pair	369.00
Sconce, 7-Light, Gilt, Shaped Mirror Back, Scrolled Leaf Branches, 32 x 19 ½ In., Pair	875.00
Sconce, 9-Light, Brass, 3 Tiers, Calla Lilies, Pussy Willows, Grapes, Leaves, France, 1800s, 27 In.	60.00

Sconce, Arm, Clenched Hand, Giltwood, Carved, c.1820, 16 ¾ x 8 In., Pair	2040.00
Sconce, Brass, Scroll Arm, Leaf, Flower Etched Glass Hurricane Shade, 17 In., Pair	1298.00
Sconce, Bronze, Rectangular, Openwork Scrolls, Stamped, France, 1960s, 22 x 13 In., Pair	4375.00
Sconce, Cast Iron, Torch, Urn Finial, Textured Glass Globe, c.1925, 25 ½ In.	236.00
Sconce, Giltwood, Mirror, Laurel Wreaths, Bowknot Crest, Scroll Arms, Lotus, 18 x 10 In., Pair	461.00
Sconce, Louis XV, Bronze, Cut Glass, Leaves, Flower Petal Prisms, Blossoms, 21 x 12 In., Pair	1045.00
Sconce, Metal, Mirror, Round, 9 ¾ In.	230.00
Sconce, Renaissance Style, Metal, Torch, Shield, Yellow Glass Inserts, 27 x 12 In., Pair	150.00
Sconce, Spanish Colonial, Silver Plate, Cartouche, Putto, Scrolled Arm, 24 x 16 In., Pair	1315.00
Sconce, T. Barbi, Brass, 2 Leaves On Stem, Italy, 1970s, 18 x 23 In., Pair	2000.00
Sconce, Textured Glass, Gold Foil, Barovier & Toso, Italy, c.1950, 23 In., Pair	1500.00
Sconce, Tin, Candle, Embossed, Beaded Panels, Crimped Edges, Demilune Cups, 13 x 3 ¾ In., Pair	780.00
Sconce, Tin, Oak Leaf, Keystone Shape, Crimped Edges, c.1890, 24 In., Pair	863.00
Sconce, Tole, Glass, Domed, 19 x 8 In., Pair	410.00
Sconce, Wood, Mirror, Tin Socket, Paint, Round, c.1850, 11 ½ In., Pair	1888.00
Sconce, Wrought Iron, c.1890, 19 x 10 In., Pair	295.00
Sinumbra, Brass, Column Standard, Vine Etched Glass Shade, Stepped Base, 36 In.	531.00
Solar, Brass, Lacquered, Fluted Column, Marble Base, Etched Glass Shade, Prisms, 24 In.	615.00
Solar, Bronze, Gothic Cathedral Column, Stepped Base, Squat Etched Glass Shade, 25 In.	2390.00
Solar, Bronze, Marble, Green Opaline Standard, Frosted & Etched Shade, Prisms, c.1850, 23 In.... *Illus*	184.00
Tallow, Brass, Drip Pan, Iron Spout Wick Holder, Tubular Column, Cone Base, 12 ¼ x 8 In.	94.00
Terra-Cotta, Figural, Renaissance Style, Gate Keeper, Holding Lighted Tin Lantern, c.1900, 31 In.	300.00
Tiffany lamps are listed in the Tiffany category.	
Torchere, 5-Light, Renaissance Revival, Iron, Tripod Base, 76 In.	4012.00
Torchere, Art Deco, Glass, Silver Plate, Twisted Stem, Frosted Amber Shade, 66 In...........*Illus*	633.00
Torchere, Iron, Black Paint, Flared Rim, Reeded Standard, Paw Feet, c.1910, 53 In.	546.00
Torchere, Iron, Twisted, Scrolled Supports, 36 In., Pair	516.00
Torchere, Metal Shaft, Spiral Twist, 3 Candle Cups, Electrified, c.1905, 79 In., Pair	518.00
Whale Oil, Amethyst, 4-Printie Block, 2 Burners, Boston & Sandwich, c.1845, 11 In., Pair	1475.00
Whale Oil, Peg Lamp, Silver Plate, Sheffield, 10 x 10 ½ In., Pair	148.00
Whale Oil, Pewter, Double Lens, Drum Font, c.1820, 10 ½ In.	593.00
Whale Oil, Pressed Glass, Berry, Vine Engraved Clear Glass, Stepped Base, c.1840, 9 ¾ In., Pair	708.00
Whale, Horn Of Plenty, Double Burners, Sandwich Glass, 10 In., Pair	561.00
Whale, Leaf In Clambroth, Column Brass Stem, Flower Foot, Sandwich Glass, c.1850, 11 In.	266.00

LAMPSHADE

Hurricane, Clear Glass, Cut Stars & Swags, Faceted Base, 24 In., Pair	2832.00

LANTERNS are a special type of lighting device. They have a light source, usually a candle, totally hidden inside the walls of the lantern. Light is seen through holes or glass sections.

Brass, Colored Glass Panels, Trefoil Pierced Frame, Gothic, 10 ⅝ x 6 ⅞ In.	120.00
Brass, Copper, Pierced Door, Ruffled Scroll Cartouche, Acorn Feet, c.1810, 18 In.	1298.00
Brass, Copper, Whale Oil, Red Globe, Wire Guard, 2 Tube Burners, Ring Handle, c.1875, 18 x 6 In.	529.00
Brass, Hurricane, String Burn, Manhattan Brass Co., c.1875, 7 x 3 In.	259.00
Brass, Iron, Kerosene, Pierced, Clear Globe, Bail Handle, Wilmot Burner, c.1875, 17 x 12 In.	230.00
Brass, Iron, Pierced, Sliding Door, Clear Globe, Bail Handle, G.W. Woodward, c.1875, 17 x 6 In.	230.00
Brass, Pierced, Stars, Blown Globe, Tube Burner, Boston & Sandwich Glass Co., c.1875, 18 x 5 In.	920.00
Brass, Pierced, Stars, Diamonds, Etched Globe, Handle, Boston & Sandwich Co., c.1875, 17 x 6 In.	749.00
Brass, Tin, Copper, Stamped SAA, 17 ¼ In., Pair	593.00
Bronze, Crown Shape, Upper & Lower Cage, 43 x 25 In.	2160.00
Bronze, George III Style, Scrolled Body, Acanthine Corona & Finial, 4 Lights, 36 x 14 In., Pair	1830.00
Candle, Cherry, Turned & Molded, Square, Wire Bail Handle, Columnar Corners, c.1800, 20 x 9 In.	889.00
Candle, Sheet Iron, Pierced, Round, 3 Square Lenses, Cone Top, Loop Handle, 10 x 5 In.	590.00
Candle, Tin, Pierced Stars, Cone Top, Cobalt Blue Teardrop Glass, Loop Handle, 17 In.	944.00
Candle, Tinned Sheet Iron, 4 Glass Panels, Pyramid Canopy, Ring Handle, 18 x 6 In.	354.00
Carriage, Brass, Urn Finial, Oval, Beveled Glass Panels, Turned Stem, Pair	1315.00
Carriage, Tin, 3 Clear, 1 Red Round Pane, Embossed Eclipse, c.1905, 14 ½ In., Pair	98.00
Coach, Brass & Iron, Tapered Hexagon, Windows, Crown Finial, Swag Tiers, c.1900, 22 In., Pair	590.00
Coach, Copper, Iron, 2 Swag & Tassel Tiers, Eagle Finial, 22 In., Pair	472.00
Copper, Brass, Label, Bauer Lamp & Reflector Co., San Francisco, c.1890, 19 In. ....*Illus*	147.00
Copper, Sliding Shutter, Cone Top, Strap Handle, c.1850, 12 x 4 ½ In.	127.00
Engine Room, Wedge Burner, Chimney, Beveled Glass, Reflector, Davey & Co., 8 ¼ x 19 In.	184.00
Fire, Metal Frame, Etched Glass Globe, Engraved, Kingsford Fire Co. 5, Hose Co. 2, J.H. Kelly	715.00
Fire, Tin, Red Paint, New England, c.1830, 20 In.	1240.00
Fire, Wristlet Handle, Blue Globe, 18 In.	780.00

Lamp, Oil, End-Of-Day Glass Shades, 5 Applied Clear Feet, c.1875, 8 In. $1,093.00

James D. Julia Auctioneers

Lamp, Oil, Green Opalescent Glass, Paneled, Chimney, Applied Shell Feet, 11 ¼ In. $460.00

James D. Julia Auctioneers

Lamp, Oil, Honey Amber Glass, White Spatter, c.1875, 6 In. $633.00

James D. Julia Auctioneers

Lamp, Oil, Little Gem, Green Glass, Adjustable Brass Burner, Loop Handle, Hexagonal Foot, 7 ¼ In.
$47.00

Conestoga Auction Co., Inc.

Lamp, Oil, Milk Glass, Swan, Embossed, Nutmeg Burner, 8 In.
$518.00

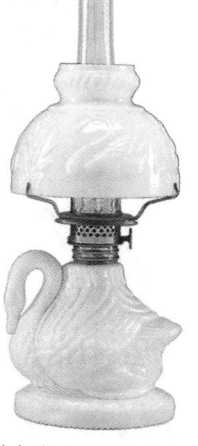

James D. Julia Auctioneers

Lamp, Oil, Owl, Porcelain, Inset Eyes, Gold Highlights, Yellow-Cased Half Shade, 10 In.
$403.00

James D. Julia Auctioneers

Globe, Etched Glass, Tin, Black Paint, Pierced Chimney & Base, c.1815, 13 ½ In.	450.00
Hall, Bronze, Glass Panels, Louis XVI, Leaf Design, France, c.1900, 26 x 14 In.	649.00
Hall, Gilt Bronze, Gothic Revival, Trefoil Pierced, Fretwork, Crenellated Edge, Chains, c.1885, 31 In.	922.00
Hall, Gilt Metal, Frosted Glass, Open Harp, Bell, Globe Shade, Leafy Scroll Frame, c.1850, 33 x 17 In.	837.00
Hall, Glass Panes, Engraved, Hexagonal, Gothic Style, c.1850, 15 ½ x 9 In.	732.00
Hall, Opaline Glass, Green, Tulip Shape Shade, Scroll Drop, c.1885, 9 In.	553.00
Hall, Satin Glass, Blue, Oblong, Faceted, Angel Heads, Flowers, Rondels, c.1885, 24 In.	461.00
Hanging, Chinese Style, Iron, Pierced Flowers, Interior Glass Shade, c.1950, 30 In., Pair	575.00
Hanging, Leaded Glass, Crackle Glass, Brass Frame, Art Deco Style, 29 x 10 x 10 In. ......*Illus*	360.00
Hanging, Metal, Pierced, Dragon Crown, c.1900, 53 x 16 In., Pair	1320.00
Hanging, Pierced Bronze, Champleve, Flowers, Birds, Chinese, 21 ½ In., Pair	3450.00
Hanging, Shells, Lead Frame, Painted Figures, Donkey Cart Scene, Japan, 1800s, 15 ½ x 12 In.	805.00
Hanging, Tin & Glass, Pierced, Ring Handle, c.1815, 14 ½ In.	420.00
Iron, Clear Globe, Double Tube Burner, Bail Handle, White Star, c.1875, 12 x 5 In.	196.00
Iron, Contour Guards, Square, Sliding Door, Bail Handle, Hiram L. Piper Co., c.1875, 15 x 7 In.	138.00
Iron, Pierced, Strap Handle, Sunburst Pattern, Sliding Door, E.F. Parker, c.1855, 18 In.	316.00
Iron, Punched Star, Bars, Dots, Hinged Door, Single Socket Holder, Green Paint, c.1850, 9 x 5 In.	288.00
Iron, Punched, Sunburst, Dot, Strap Handle, c.1850, 17 ½ x 6 ¼ In.	138.00
Iron, Square, Hinged Frame, Reflector, Black Paint, Bail Handle, C.T. Ham No. 6, 7 x 8 ½ In.	288.00
Iron, Triangular, Black Paint, 2 Clear Panes, H.L. Piper, c.1935, 25 x 13 In.	173.00
Iron, Tubular, Globe Mounted, Dietz Pioneer, c.1925, 24 x 11 ½ In.	460.00
Kerosene, Brass, Interior Font, Wick Holder, Wire Cage, Wire Handle, National, 10 x 6 In.	165.00
Kerosene, Brass, Pierced, Globe, Wire Guard, Sliding Door, Bail Handle, Sargent, c.1875, 17 x 6 In.	196.00
Oil Font, Copper, Glass Panes, Marked Viking, Mid 19th Century, 11 In.	118.00
Oil, Iron, Bail Handle, Concave Sides, Sliding Pane, E.F. Haskell, c.1880, 15 x 8 In.	219.00
Porcelain, Enameled, Figural Scenes, Leaf Sprigs, Yellow Ground, Chinese, 1800s, 11 In.	850.00
Porcelain, Famille Rose, Hexagonal Oval, Waisted Neck & Foot, Pierced, Flowers, 18 ¾ In.	366.00
Reading Railroad, Tinned Sheet Iron, Wire Guards, Bail Handle, Clear Globe, 9 ⅜ In.	59.00
Ship, Copper & Glass, Anchor, Cylindrical, Narrow Top, Bail Handle	252.00
Ship's, Oil, Brass, Cylindrical, Rounded Top, Handle, Marked, Stern, 19 In.	295.00
Street Lamp, Iron, Mounted, Tubular, Clear Globe, Bail Handle, Dietz Pioneer, c.1920, 24 x 11 ½ In.	460.00
Street, Dome Lid, Copper, Tapered, Corner Trim, Acorn Finial, Foster & Pullen, c.1950, 48 x 17 In.	2214.00
Street, Galvanized Steel, Hinged Door, Oil Lamp, Finger Hole, Marked Perko, 11 x 19 In.	115.00
Tin, Glass Panes, Black Paint, U.S.A., c.1880, 15 In.	176.00
Tole, Iron, Rococo Style, Hexagonal, Leaves, Glass Panels, Scrolled Brackets, 53 x 16 In., Pair	956.00
Wall, Sheet Iron, 3 Lenses, Hinged Door, Domed Lid, Wire Handle, Mounting Clip, 13 In.	413.00
Whale Oil, Iron, Brass, Pierced, Globe, Wire Guard, Double Tube Burner, Handle, c.1875, 13 x 6 In.	207.00
Whale Oil, Iron, Double Tube Burner, Bail Handle, New England Glass Co., c.1875, 19 x 6 In.	1380.00
Whale Oil, Iron, Pierced Star, Diamond, Red Globe, Wire Guard, 2 Tubes, Handle, c.1875, 17 x 6 In.	374.00
Whale Oil, Iron, Pierced Stars, Diamonds, 8-Panel Clear Globe, Strap Ring Handle, c.1850, 12 x 4 In.	259.00
Whale Oil, Iron, Pierced Stars, Diamonds, Clear Globe, Strap Ring Handle, c.1850, 14 ⅜ x 6 ⅜ In.	259.00
Whale Oil, Iron, Pierced, Bail Handle, Tin Tube Burner, New England Glass Co., c.1855, 19 x 6 In.	1380.00
Whale Oil, Iron, Pierced, Clear Blown Globe, Double Tube Burner, Strap Handle, c.1850, 16 x 4 In.	316.00
Whale Oil, Iron, Pierced, Clear Globe, Double Tube Burner, Bail Handle, J.D. Brown, c.1875, 19 x 6 In.	196.00
Whale Oil, Iron, Pierced, Clear Globe, Strap Ring Handle, Double Tube Burner, c.1850, 13 x 4 In.	1380.00
Whale Oil, Iron, Pierced, Purple Ribbed Globe, Strap Ring Handle, c.1850, 12 x 4 In.	489.00
Whale Oil, Iron, Pierced, Red Globe, Bail Handle, c.1875, 17 x 5 In.	289.00
Whale Oil, Iron, Punched, Hinged Door, 2 Windows, Strap Handle, c.1850, 17 x 5 ½ In.	374.00
Wood, Snipe Hinge Door, Sheet Iron Vent Cover, Wrought Wire Swing Bail, Tin Socket, 9 ½ x 5 In.	236.00
Wood, Tin Cover, 3 Panes, Bull's Eye, Loop Handle, 13 In.	2478.00

LE VERRE FRANCAIS is one of the many types of cameo glass made by the Schneider Glassworks in France. The glass was made by the C. Schneider factory in Epinay-sur-Seine from 1918 to 1933. It is a mottled glass, usually decorated with floral designs, and bears the incised signature *Le Verre Francais*.

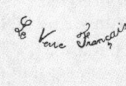

Compote, Black, Orange Swirled, Blue Mottled, Black Stem, Yellow Base, 7 ½ x 9 In.	3949.00
Vase, Azurette, Bulbous, Footed, Cameo, Blue, Aqua Ground, Signed, c.1925, 4 In.	711.00
Vase, Cameo, Blue, Stylized Palm Trees, Mottled White Ground, Signed, 11 In. ......*Illus*	2500.00
Vase, Cardimine, Cameo, Goblet Shape, Orange Mottled Land Cress, c.1927, 12 ¼ In.	1580.00
Vase, Dragonflies, Orange, Green Aquatic Plants, Turquoise Ground, 12 In.	1230.00
Vase, Fuchsia, Blue Shading To Opalescent White, Red Overlay, Signed ......*Illus*	1344.00
Vase, Mirettes Pattern, Orange Flowers, Mottled Yellow, Royal Blue, Cup Shape, 17 In.	1610.00
Vase, Monnaies Du Pape, Cameo Glass, Cylindrical, Branches, Flowers, c.1921, 12 ½ In.	2100.00
Vase, Pavots, Red Flowers, Tapered, Flared Rim, Cushion Foot, 10 In.	2214.00
Vase, Primrolles, Cameo Glass, Trumpet Shape, Flower Petals, Orange, Yellow, 6 ½ In.	948.00
Vase, Raisin Violet, Purple, Orange Ground, 2 Neck Handles, Cameo, 15 In.	3198.00

Vase, Rhododendrons, Cameo Glass, Flared Rim, Purple, White & Orange Ground, c.1927, 4 ½ In. ... 972.00
Vase, Spirale, Red Cameo, Stylized Spiral Rose, Yellow, Green Base, c.1921, 5 ½ In. ... 674.00
Vase, Stylized Flowers, Lavender, Geometric, White Mottled Ground, Signed Charder, 6 In. ... 608.00
Vase, Tortue, Cameo, Orange Red Tortoises, Orange Ground, c.1925, 8 In. ... 1304.00

LEATHER is tanned animal hide and has been used to make decorative and useful objects for centuries. Leather objects must be carefully preserved with proper humidity and oiling or the leather will deteriorate and crack. This damage cannot be repaired.

Basket, Key, Even Rim, Sharkskin Sides, Arched, Rolled Handle, Va., c.1875, 9 x 5 In. ... 1840.00
Basket, Key, Shaped Oblong, Scroll Design, Maroon Interior, S.S. Cottrell & Co., c.1860, 7 x 4 In. ... 1840.00
Figure, Elephant, Trumpeting, 19 ¼ x 22 ¾ In. ... 59.00
Footrest, Pig Shape, Standing, England, 1900s, 17 x 29 ½ In. ... 1062.00
Hat Box, Stitched, Handle, Lock, Black Paint, England, 10 ½ x 13 ½ In. ... 29.00
Powder Flask, Carved, 1841, 9 x 18 In. ... 385.00
Saddle, Kentucky Style, Hand Tooled, c.1930, 17 In. ... 345.00
Saddle, Parade, Tooled, Silver Mounts, Flowers, Leaf Medallions, c.1950 ... *Illus* ... 472.00
Saddle, Park Style, English Lady's Riding, c.1930, 14 In. ... 115.00
Saddle, Western Style, Hand Tooled, c.1930, 16 In. ... 690.00
Saddle, Western, Extra-Wide Fenders, Snap Pockets, Stamped Details, 6-In. Cantle, 16 In. ... *Illus* ... 196.00

LEEDS pottery was made at Leeds, Yorkshire, England, from 1774 to 1878. Most Leeds ware was not marked. Early Leeds pieces had distinctive twisted handles with a greenish glaze on part of the creamy ware. Later ware often had blue borders on the creamy pottery. A Chicago company named Leeds made many Disney-inspired figurines. They are listed in the Disneyana category.

LEEDS POTTERY.

Bowl, White, Cobalt Blue Scene, Garden House, Fence, Flowers, Tin Glaze, Footed, 4 ½ x 9 ½ In. ... 443.00
Charger, Blue Feather Edge, Floral Bouquets, c.1840, 13 In. ... 470.00
Charger, Pagoda & Fence, Pearlware, Blue & White, Shell Edge, Yorkshire, c.1785, 15 In. ... 649.00
Cup, Ale Banner, Frog Inside, Double Handle, Footed, 5 ¼ In. ... *Illus* ... 411.00
Pitcher, Flower Basket Design, Molded Leaf Handle, c.1815, 9 In. ... 353.00
Plate, Blue Feather Edge, Eagle Center, England, c.1840, 8 In. ... 1645.00
Plate, Blue Feather Edge, Flower Urn, 12 In. ... 486.00
Plate, Blue Feather Edge, Flowers, 1800s, 9 ½ In. ... 294.00
Plate, Dessert, Pavilion, Trees, Blue, White, Embossed Edge, c.1800, 8 In. ... 58.00
Plate, Pagoda & Fence, Pearlware, Blue & White, Shell Edge, Yorkshire, c.1785, 8 ¼ In., Pair. ... 502.00
Plate, Pearlware, Blue Asian Man, Umbrella, Feather & Swag Border, 9 ½ In. ... 270.00
Platter, Blue Feather Edge, Gaudy Blue Flowers, c.1830, 11 ½ x 15 In. ... 353.00
Sauceboat, Pearlware, Herring Shape, Borders, Fins, Underglaze Blue, c.1790, 8 ½ In. ... 3776.00
Teapot, Lid, Finial, Delicate Sprig, Loop Handle, S-Spout, Bulbous, England, c.1815, 7 In. ... 118.00

LEFTON is a mark found on pottery, porcelain, glass, and other wares imported by the Geo. Zoltan Lefton Company. The company began in 1941. George Lefton died in 1996 and the company was sold in 2001. The company mark has changed through the years, but because marks have been used for long periods of time, they are of little help in dating an object.

Cookie Jar, Little Miss Dainty, Blond Hair, Flower Hat, c.1957, 7 ½ In. ... 105.00
Figurine, Dog, Poodle, Spaghetti, Gilt, Paper Label, 3 ½ In. ... 35.00
Figurine, Girl, August, Sticker, 5 In. ... 15.00
Figurine, Infant Of Prague, Crown, Flowers, Gilt, 1940s, 8 ½ In. ... 170.00
Figurine, Pink Lady, Ruffled Dress, Gilt Trim, Bonnet, 4 In. ... 28.00
Planter, Girl Carrying Wreath & Christmas Presents, Red & White Dress, 1960s, 4 x 4 x 3 In. ... 18.00
Plate, Fruit, Marked, 8 ¼ In. ... 16.00

LEGRAS was founded in 1864 by Auguste Legras at St. Denis, France. It is best known for cameo glass and enamel-decorated glass with Art Nouveau designs. Legras merged with Pantin in 1920 and became the Verreries et Cristalleries de St. Denis et de Pantin Reunies.

Vase, Art Deco, Oval, Chartreuse Green, Cased To Brown & White Mottled, Etched, Fruit, 14 In. ... 334.00
Vase, Black, Gray, Pulled, Radiating Art Deco Design, Etched Stamp, c.1930, 21 In. ... 2500.00
Vase, Cherry Blossoms, Painted, Light Green, Blue Ground, Gilt Rim, 4 x 18 In. ... 1464.00
Vase, Columns Burgundy Sunflowers, Pale Pink Chipped Backdrop, Swollen, Cameo, 8 In. ... 230.00
Vase, Cylindrical, Enameled Cameo, Cherry Blossoms, Green To Blue Ground, Gilt Rim, 18 In. ... 1000.00
Vase, Forest, Lake Scene, Square, Pinched Neck, Green, Rose Sky, Cameo, c.1920, 5 ½ In. ... 633.00
Vase, Lake Scene, Trees, Mottled, Orange, Red, Blue, Rounded Square Shape, Square Mouth, 4 In. ... 1840.00
Vase, Leaf Pattern, Amethyst, Frost Peach, Bottle Shape, Narrow Neck, Flare Lip, Signed, 8 ½ In. ... 633.00
Vase, Leaves, Branches, Raspberries, Triangular, Tugged Rim, Cameo, 13 In. ... 920.00
Vase, Mauve Vines & Fruit, Lavender, Teardrop Shape, Etched, Cameo, c.1915, 6 ¾ x 4 ½ In. ... 615.00
Vase, Orange Poppies, Mottled Orange Shaded To Green, Cylindrical, Swollen, 12 In. ... 360.00

Lamp, Solar, Bronze, Marble, Green Opaline Standard, Frosted & Etched Shade, Prisms, c.1850, 23 In.
$184.00

New Orleans Auction Galleries, Inc.

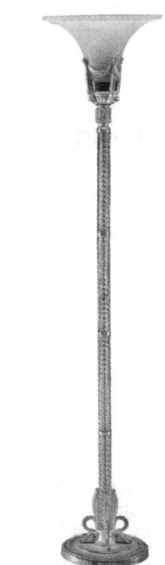

Lamp, Torchere, Art Deco, Glass, Silver Plate, Twisted Stem, Frosted Amber Shade, 66 In.
$633.00

James D. Julia Auctioneers

Lantern, Copper, Brass, Label, Bauer Lamp & Reflector Co., San Francisco, c.1890, 19 In.
$147.00

Garth's Auctioneers & Appraisers

Lantern, Hanging, Leaded Glass, Crackle Glass, Brass Frame, Art Deco Style, 29 x 10 x 10 In.
$360.00

DuMouchelles Art Gallery

Le Verre Francais, Vase, Cameo, Blue, Stylized Palm Trees, Mottled White Ground, Signed, 11 In.
$2,500.00

Skinner, Inc.

Le Verre Francais, Vase, Fuchsia, Blue Shading To Opalescent White, Red Overlay, Signed
$1,344.00

Victorian Casino Antiques

Leather, Saddle, Parade, Tooled, Silver Mounts, Flowers, Leaf Medallions, c.1950
$472.00

Brunk Auctions

Vase, Purple, Olive Cut Flowers, Branches, Translucent Mottled Ground, Cameo, c.1910, 19 In.	780.00
Vase, Stick Shape, Frosted Purple Glass, Stemmed Fuchsia, Cameo Carved, 4 ½ x 13 In.	1000.00
Vase, Tassel Design, Swags, Diamond Pattern, White, Yellow, Cameo, Enamel, Elongated Oval, 12 In.	259.00
Vase, Trees In Field, Orange, Yellow, Brown, Cameo, Cylindrical, Hatched Egg Rim, 5 In.	431.00
Vase, Yellow, Green Ivy, Cameo, Signed, 6 ½ In. ....*Illus*	288.00

LENOX porcelain is well-known in the United States. Walter Scott Lenox and Jonathan Coxon founded the Ceramic Art Company in Trenton, New Jersey, in 1889. In 1896 Lenox bought out Coxon's interest, and in 1906 the company was renamed Lenox, Inc. The company makes porcelain that is similar to Irish Belleek. In 2009, after a series of mergers, Lenox became part of Clarion Capital Partners. The marks used by the firm have changed through the years, so collectors can date the ceramics. Related pieces may also be listed in the Ceramic Art Co. category.

Bowl, Patriots, Transfer Portraits, Founding Fathers, 24K Gold Trim, 1776-1976, 4 x 9 In.	54.00
Charger, Art Nouveau Maiden, Porcelain, Round, Green Belleek Mark, A.I Toye, 14 In.	688.00
Demitasse Set, Art Nouveau, Cream, Silver Overlay, Pot, Sugar, Lid, Creamer, Demitasse Pot, 7 ½ In.	345.00
Figurine, Ballerina, Pink Tutu, Green Mark, 6 In.	446.00
Plate, Dessert, Cobalt Blue & Gold Bands On Border, c.1920, 7 ¼ In., 12 Piece	270.00
Plate, Dinner, White, Ivory Border, Gold Laurel Leaf Edge, 10 ½ In., 12 Piece	150.00
Plate, Painted, Cupid, Wearing Armor, Pink Border, Gilt Detail, Signed H. Nosek, 10 ¼ In.	360.00
Stein, Man Begins Golf Swing, Sterling Lid, Print Under Glaze, ½ Liter ....*Illus*	1093.00
Stein, Native American, Chief, Headdress, Black & White Grisaille Illustration, c.1900, 7 ¼ In.	413.00
Tea Service, Art Deco, Teapot, Sugar, Creamer, Stamped, 3 To 7 In.	84.00
Tea Set, Architects', Teapot, Sugar, Creamer, 6 Plates, 6 Cups, 6 Saucers, Waste Bowl, 1933	96.00
Tea Set, George Washington, Teapot, Sugar, Creamer, Cup, Saucer, 4 To 6 In.	96.00
Tea Set, Hawthorne, Teapot, Sugar, Creamer, Limited Edition, 4 To 6 In.	48.00
Tea Set, Porcelain With Vines & Flowers, Silver Overlay, Glass Trivet, 8-Cup Teapot	475.00
Tea Set, Shell Shape Body, Pink, White Handle, Spout, Footed, Teapot, Sugar, Creamer, 4 To 6 In.	84.00
Vase, Enameled, Scenic, Vanity, Cherub Surrounded By Roses, Gilt Detail Reserve, 10 ¼ x 8 In.	660.00
Vase, Kate Sears, Embossed Flower Sprig, Ragged Gilt Edge Rim, 9 ¾ x 6 ½ In.	270.00
Vase, Walter Scott, Child Seated On Nautilus Shell, White, Glass Dome, 8 x 7 ½ In.	300.00

LETTER OPENERS have been used since the eighteenth century. Ivory and silver were favored by the well-to-do. In the late nineteenth century, the letter opener was popular as an advertising giveaway and many were made of metal or celluloid. Brass openers with figural handles were also popular.

Alligator, Treen, c.1875, 9 In.	275.00
Billiken, Ivory, Carved, 7 In.	45.00
Black Man, Cigar Pencil In Mouth, Germany, 8 ¼ In.	285.00
Dagger, Hilt, Brass, 7 ½ In.	14.00
Duck, Wood, Amber Glass Eyes, Painted, 1950s, 7 ½ In.	15.00
Elephant, Pierced Flowers, Plastic, 7 In.	20.00
George Washington Bust, Celluloid, Japan, 1920s, 7 ½ In.	90.00
Indian Chief Head, Celluloid, Niagara Falls, 7 ¾ In.	95.00
Marching Elephants, Celluloid, Openwork, 7 x 1 In.	10.00
Miraculous Mary, Rhodium Plated Silver, 3 ⅝ In.	44.00
Mother-Of-Pearl, Sterling Silver, Tassel, 19th Century, 3 In.	115.00
Ostrich Feather, Claw, Brass, Belgium, 7 ¾ In.	75.00
Porcelain, Pink Flowers, Marked, Aubril 159 Palais-Royal, 9 In.	59.00
Ram's Head, Brass, c.1950, 11 In.	55.00
Shield Shape, Pennant, University Of Illinois, Metal, 4 ⅞ In.	28.00
Shoe Shape, Cuba, Flag, Treen, 7 ⅝ In.	40.00
Sterling Silver, Green Carved Stone, Tribal Figure, Mexico, 1940s, 5 ½ In.	78.00
Totem Pole, Bird Mask, Bone, 6 In.	35.00
Wood, Geometric Design, Victorian, 1880s, 11 In.	65.00
Wrought Iron, Scrolled, 9 In.	25.00

LIBBEY Glass Company has made many types of glass since 1888, including the cut glass and tablewares that are collected today. The stemwares of the 1930s and 1940s are once again in style. The Toledo, Ohio, firm was purchased by Owens-Illinois in 1935 and is still working under the name Libbey Inc. Maize is listed in its own category.

Bowl, Colonna Pattern, Notched Scalloped Rim, Cut Glass, 3 ½ x 9 In.	95.00
Bowl, Flowers, Greek Key & Vesica, Oval, Cut Glass, Signed, 11 ½ x 7 ½ In.	100.00
Bowl, Morello, Draped Sides, Scalloped Edge, 4 x 9 In.	5500.00
Bowl, Neola, Marked, 3 ½ x 8 In.	175.00
Butter, Cover, Gloria, Hobstar Finial, Cut Glass, 5 ½ x 8 In.	150.00

L

Butter, Cover, Harvard, Cut Glass, 7 ½ x 9 ½ In.	300.00
Candlestick, Clear, Opaque Moonstone Figural Camel Stem, Flared Cup, 5 In., Pair	450.00
Celery Dish, Neola, 5 ½ x 12 In.	175.00
Champagne, Wedgemere, Hobstar Scalloped Petticoat Base, Cut Glass, Monogram, 4 In.	1200.00
Cider Jug, Diana, Triple Notched Handle, Hobstar Base, 7 ¼ In.	400.00
Compote, Hobstar & Fan, Cut Glass, Signed, 8 x 7 In.	40.00
Compote, Somerset, Clear Blank, Signed, 11 ¼ x 6 In.	175.00
Compote, Somerset, Tall Stem, 11 x 6 ¼ In.	125.00
Creamer, Pink & White Stripe, Footed, Loop Handle, Wide Rim, Opal Interior, Marked, 5 ½ In.	230.00
Creamer, Pink & White, Ribs, Bulbous, Loop Handle, 3 In.	259.00
Decanter, Corinthian, Scalloped Hobstar Stopper, Notched Snake Handle, Cut Glass, 11 In.	200.00
Decanter, Somerset, Pinched Waist Bell Shape, Flattened Stopper, 13 In.	2100.00
Jug, Waverly, Teardrop Shape, Triple Notched Handle, Pattern Cut Stopper, 8 In.	350.00
Mug, Harvard, Barrel Shape, Triple Notched Handle, Cut Glass, 4 ½ In.	300.00
Pitcher, Cider, Glenda, Triple Notched Handle, Hobstar Base, 7 ½ In.	500.00
Pitcher, Empress, Triple Notched Handle, Cut Glass, Marked, 8 ½ In.	75.00
Pitcher, Sultan, Cut Glass, Marked, 8 ¾ In.	100.00
Pitcher, Water, Spillane, 8 ½ In.	125.00
Rose Bowl, Harvard, Cut Glass, 7 ¹⁄₁₂ In.	100.00
Rose Bowl, Imperial Pattern, 5 ½ x 6 ½ In.	475.00
Rose Bowl, Spillane, Signed, 5 x 6 ½ In.	300.00
Sugar & Creamer, Colonna, Wafer Base, Cut Glass, Marked	200.00
Tazza, Colonna, Scalloped Hobstar Foot, Cut Glass, 5 ½ x 9 ½ In.	200.00
Tray, Flowers, Greek Key & Vesicas, Round, Tab Handles, Cut Glass, 11 ½ In.	600.00
Tray, Ice Cream, Sonora, 17 ½ x 10 ¼ In.	400.00
Tray, Round, Ellsmere, Cut Glass, 11 ½ In.	1100.00
Tray, Sultana, Cut Glass, Signed, 12 ½ x 8 In.	300.00
Tumbler, Maize, Custard Glass, Blue Stocks, 4 In.	40.00
Tumbler, Maize, White, Yellow Stalks, Gilt Highlights, 4 In.	52.00
Vase, Amberina, Bulbous Pinched Sides, Trifold Rim, Amber Rigaree, 6 In.	316.00
Vase, Amberina, Optic Ribbed Coupe, Flared Scalloped Rim, Acid Stamped, 5 ½ In.	316.00
Vase, Empress, Flower Center, Facet Cut Ring Neck, Cut Glass, 5 ¾ x 8 In.	354.00
Vase, Sweet Pea, Engraved Orchid, Ruffled, Footed, Cut Glass, Signed, 5 x 8 In.	125.00
Wine, Silver Leaf Pattern, Stemmed, 6 ¼ In., 8 Piece	40.00

LIGHTERS for cigarettes and cigars are collectible. Cigarettes became popular in the late nineteenth century, and with the cigarette came matches and cigarette lighters. All types of lighters are collected, from solid gold to the first of the recent disposable lighters. Most examples found were made after 1940. Some lighters may be found in the Jewelry category in this book.

Cartier, Reeded, Engraved Polly, Gold Color, Personal Property Polly Bergen, 2 ¾ In.	230.00
Cigar, Laazora, Metal, Oak, 15 ½ In.	420.00
Cigar, Lighter, Lamp Shape, Repousse Flowers & Leaves, Silver, Reed & Barton, c.1900, 2 ¾ In.	184.00
Cigar, Pressed Glass, Daisy & Button Pattern, Round Foot, Scalloped Rim, 8 ¼ x 5 In.	413.00
Cigar, Roman Goddess, Holding Green Globe, 22 In.	358.00
Cigar, Sands Casino, Las Vegas, 14K Gold Plated, Zippo Style, Florentine	150.00
Dunhill, 27 Signal Flags, 14K Gold, Enamel, Cartier, c.1931, 5 ½ In.	14160.00
Dunhill, Goldtone, Textured, 2 ½ In.	150.00
Dunhill, Sheffield Silver Plate, Monogram, c.1920, 4 In.	330.00
Dunhill, Silver Plate, Leafy Monogram, England, c.1920, 4 In.	330.00
Dupont, Lacquered Red, S.T, Tag, Box, France, 2 ¼ x 1 ½ In.	390.00
Gorham, Cigar, Copper, Silver Fan, Figure Smoking Pipe, Squirrel, Dragon Handle, c.1883, 2 ½ In.	384.00
Ideal, Cigar, Countertop, Pull Out Torch Wand, Hole Punch, 4 ¾ x 6 ½ In.	330.00
Park Lighter, Little Miss Sunbeam Bread, Brushed Aluminum, Sunbeam Girl, 1960s, 2 ¼ x 1 ¼ In.	55.00
Ronson, Countertop, Bronze, Figural, Monkey, Ashtray	300.00
Ronson, Silver Chrome Plate, Tempo, c.1955, 3 ½ x 2 x 2 ½ In.	24.00
Ronson, Tortoiseshell, Art Deco, 1930s, 2 x 4 In.	94.00
Silver, Enamel, Embossed Courting Couple, 2 ¼ In.	139.00
Silver, Engraved, Cobalt Blue Inlay, Floral Leaves, Enamel Courting Scene, Woman's, 2 ¼ x 1 ½ In.	108.00
Sunoco, Gas Pump Shape, Chrome, Blue, Yellow, 3 ⅝ x 2 In.	660.00

LIGHTNING RODS AND LIGHTNING ROD BALLS are collected. The glass balls were at the center of the rod that was attached to the roof of a house or barn to avoid lightning damage. The balls were made in many colors and many patterns.

LIGHTNING ROD

Metal Rod, Arrow, Glass Ball, Embossed, Wood Base	*Illus*	168.00

Leather, Saddle, Western, Extra-Wide Fenders, Snap Pockets, Stamped Details, 6-In. Cantle, 16 In.
$196.00

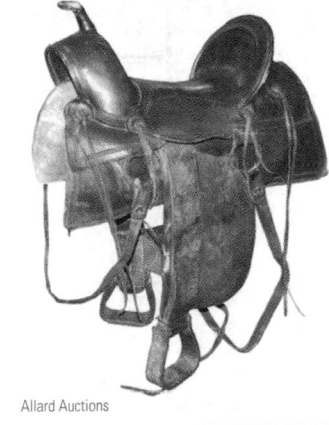

Allard Auctions

Leeds, Cup, Ale Banner, Frog Inside, Double Handle, Footed, 5 ¼ In.
$411.00

Garth's Auctioneers & Appraisers

Legras, Vase, Yellow, Green Ivy, Cameo, Signed, 6 ½ In.
$288.00

Early Auction Co.

Lenox, Stein, Man Begins Golf Swing, Sterling Lid, Print Under Glaze, ½ Liter
$1,093.00

Fox Auctions

Lightning Rod, Glass Ball, Embossed, Metal Rod, Arrow, Wood Base
$168.00

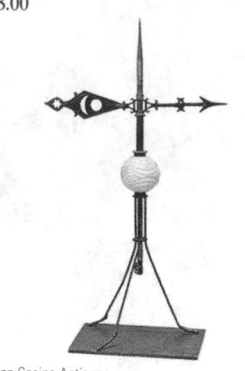

Victorian Casino Antiques

Limoges, Fish Set, Gilt Shell Rim, Fish, Flower Sprig, Salmon Pink Ground, c.1900
$922.00

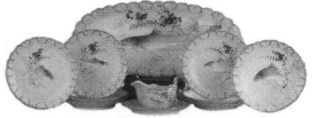

New Orleans Auction Galleries, Inc.

Limoges, Plaque, Copper, Enamel, Woman, Wings, Rose, Brass, Velvet Frame, Signed, c.1890, 5 x 3 In.
$600.00

DuMouchelles Art Gallery

Lindbergh, Button, Portrait, Draped American Flag, Wheeling, W.Va., August 1927, W&H, 2 In.
$695.00

Hake's Americana & Collectibles

LIGHTNING ROD BALL

Milk Glass, Purple, Mid 1800s, 5 x 5 In.	95.00
Moon & Stars, Purple, 4 ¼ In.	125.00

LIMOGES porcelain has been made in Limoges, France, since the mid-nineteenth century. Fine porcelains were made by many factories, including Haviland, Ahrenfeldt, Guerin, Pouyat, Elite, and others. Modern porcelains are being made at Limoges and the word *Limoges* as part of the mark is not an indication of age. Haviland, one of the Limoges factories, is listed as a separate category in this book.

Bowl, Flowers, Scalloped Rim, Gold Handles, Scrolled Feet, 11 In.	34.00
Box, Flowers, White Ground, Gilt Trim, 4 ½ x 3 ½ In.	36.00
Cake Plate, Yellow Flowers, Gold Open Handles, Rim, 10 ½ In.	40.00
Censer, Dove, Enamel, Copper, Gilt, Shaped Wings, Round Base, 8 In.	840.00
Censer, Gilt Copper, Dove Shape, Articulated Wings, Lid, Yellow, Blue, 8 In.	100.00
Fish Set, 2 Gold Fish, Blue Ground, Scalloped, 23-In. Platter, 9-In. Plate, 9 Piece	472.00
Fish Set, Gilt Shell Rim, Fish, Flower Sprig, Salmon Pink Ground, c.1900 ....*Illus*	922.00
Game Set, Plate, Platter, Oval, Game Birds, c.1890, Platter, 18 ½ In.	1000.00
Jardiniere, Painted, Peonies, 8 ¾ x 12 In.	660.00
Jardiniere, Pink & Yellow Roses, Fired-On Gold Trim, Footed, 1905, 11 x 11 In.	1440.00
Plaque, Betrayal Of Christ, Gold Highlights, Signed, Gilt Frame, 5 ½ x 4 In.	1200.00
Plaque, Copper, Enamel, Woman, Wings, Rose, Brass, Velvet Frame, Signed, c.1890, 5 x 3 In... *Illus*	600.00
Plaque, Peasant Woman, Holding Vase, Paint, Frame, c.1900, 7 x 5 In.	413.00
Plaque, Portrait, Rebecca At The Well, Marked T & V, 5 ¾ x 7 ¼ In.	160.00
Plaque, Round, Romani Woman, Green Background, Signed, Frame, 12 ⅛ In.	563.00
Plate, Couple In Garden, Blue & Gilt Border, 1950s, 9 In.	30.00
Plate, Couple, Cupids, Gilt Scalloped Rim, Cabinet, Signed C. Rochette, c.1900, 9 ½ In., Pair .	1652.00
Plate, Flower Border, Center, Wm. Guerin & Co., c.1925, 11 In., 18 Piece	1500.00
Plate, Flower Transfer, Gold, Green, Red Stamp, William Guerin & Co., 8 ½ In., 11 Piece	92.00
Plate, Marie-Ange, Girl Eating Apple, Box, 8 In.	30.00
Plate, Salad, Yellow Daffodils, Lavender Scrolled Border, Marked, 1891-1914, 8 In.	125.00
Platter, Painted, Fish, Signed G. Rosier, Green Coronet Black Stamp, 13 In.	86.00
Platter, Painted, Snipes, Flambeau Mark, 13 In.	58.00
Platter, Transfer, Courting Couple In Wooded Landscape, Scalloped Edge, Oval, 20 In.	59.00
Punch Bowl Set, Grapevines, Enameled, Art Deco Style, Flared, 1920s, 13 Piece	420.00
Tazza, Cobalt Blue Enamel, Knight, Page, Scroll Rim, Short Flared Foot, 1800s, 8 ¾ In.	570.00
Thimble, Victorian Couple, Gilt, 1 In.	12.00
Triptych, Enamel Panels, Crowning, Woman Saint, Bible Scenes, Leather Case, c.1720, 18 ½ In. .	8850.00
Vase, Birds, Branches, Green Ground, Embossed Neck, Jean Pouyat, c.1910, 5 ½ x 6 ½ In.	384.00
Vase, Dragonflies, Leaves, Orange Opalescent Luster Glaze, Bernardaud & Co., 9 ¼ x 5 ¾ In. .	184.00
Vase, Peacock, Round Window, Flowers, Turquoise, Pink, Green, Cylindrical, Foot, Marked, 14 In.	288.00
Vase, Portrait, Woman, Garden Panels, Gilt Handles, Marked Guerin Pouyat Elite Ltd., 21 In.	298.00
Vase, Urn Shape, 3 Handles, Couple, Crossing Brook, Signed, M.A. Allen, 1800s, 10 ¼ In.	398.00

LINDBERGH was a national hero. In 1927, Charles Lindbergh, the aviator, became the first man to make a nonstop solo flight across the Atlantic Ocean. In 1932, his son was kidnapped and murdered, and Lindbergh was again the center of public interest. He died in 1974. All types of Lindbergh memorabilia are collected.

Bookends, Eagle, Airplane, Lindbergh In Hat, Cast Iron, 1928, 6 x 5 In.	155.00
Button, Portrait, Draped American Flag, Wheeling, W.Va., August 1927, W&H, 2 In.........*Illus*	695.00
Button, Welcome Home, Our Ace, Capt. Lindbergh, Flag, 1 ¼ In.	173.00
Charm, Spirit Of St. Louis, Gold Plate, c.1960, 1 In.	20.00
Decanter, Plane Shape, Cork Propeller, 1972, 10 x 8 x 3 In.	65.00
Photograph, Lindbergh In Jumpsuit, 9 ½ x 6 ¼ In.	135.00
Plate, Plane, Statue Of Liberty, Eiffel Tower, Yellow, Poppy Border, USA, 8 In.	35.00
Sheet Music, Lucky Lindy, Abel Baer, L. Wolfe Gilbert, 1927	18.00
Toy, Airplane, Lindy, Blue, Gear On Tail, Cast Iron, Cast Wheels, Hubley, 10 In.	1150.00
Watch, Pocket, New York To Paris, Green Face, Ingraham, Box, 1928	300.00

LITHOPHANES are porcelain pictures made by casting clay in layers of various thicknesses. When a piece is held to the light, a picture of light and shadow is seen through it. Most lithophanes date from the 1825–75 period. A few are still being made. Many lithophanes sold today were originally panels for lampshades.

Candle Screen, Woman, Man Holding Rifle, Dog Drinking Out Of Bucket, Iron, 4 x 6 In.	695.00
Candleholder, Romeo & Juliet, Woman By Window, Metal Frame, c.1860, 6 x 3 In.	1295.00
Lamp, 4 Panels, Classical Scenes, Porcelain, 23 In.	896.00

Panel, 2 Men, Tools, Signed, 5 ¾ x 6 ½ In.	275.00
Panel, Children, Dog, Stone Fence, Mountains, Trapezoidal, c.1880, 5 ½ x 3 ½ x 5 ¼ In.	125.00
Panel, Girl, Dog, Puppies, Signed, 4 ⅞ x 6 In.	295.00
Panel, Gothic Revival, Molded, Woman, Bronze Stand, Marble Base, 1800s, 17 x 9 ½ In.....*Illus*	549.00
Panel, Lovers Escaping Storm, Hanger, 4 ¼ x 5 ³⁄₁₆ In.	200.00
Panel, Maiden Praying, Signed PPM, 5 ¼ x 6 ½ In.	395.00
Panel, Maiden With Angel, Marked, 4 ⅜ x 5 ¼ In.	130.00
Plaque, Bar Scene, Beggars, Child In Window, 19th Century	349.00
Plaque, Little Girl, Praying, German Saying, 5 ¾ x 4 ⅝ In.	249.00
Plaque, Little Girl, Sleeping With Dog, Round, 4 In.	85.00
Plaque, Man, Holding Snuffbox, 19th Century, 8 ⅝ x 7 ¾ In.	275.00

LIVERPOOL, England, has been the site of many pottery and porcelain factories since the eighteenth century. Color-decorated porcelains, transfer-printed earthenware, stoneware, basalt, figurines, and other wares were made. Sadler and Green made print-decorated wares starting in 1756. Many of the pieces were made for the American market and feature patriotic emblems, such as eagles and flags. Liverpool pitchers are called Liverpool jugs by collectors.

Bowl, Multicolor, Building, Tower, Square Border, Interior Bouquet, c.1760, 10 In.	147.00
Jug, American Sailing Ships, Swags, 10 ½ In.	1955.00
Jug, Black Memorial Transfers, George Washington, c.1800, 9 ½ In.	705.00
Jug, Eagle, Success To Independent Boston Fusiliers, July 4 1787, 11 ½ In.	6440.00
Jug, Farm Scenes, Black Transfer, c.1890, 8 In.	189.00
Jug, Gen. Washington, Great Seal, Medallions, Black Transfer, c.1802, 10 ¾ In.	3835.00
Jug, Hope & Trade, Ships, Great Seal Of United States, Enamel, Black Transfer, 1804, 8 In.	885.00
Jug, John Adams, Portrait, Cato, Ship, Marked, James Snow, c.1820, 9 ¾ In.	5625.00
Jug, Man, Masonic Images, Farm, Man & Horse On Reverse, Pink Luster Trim, c.1800, 7 ½ In....*Illus*	210.00
Jug, Ship, Emblem Of America, Reverse Attack On Tripoli, Black Transfer, c.1810, 9 In.	1007.00
Jug, Success To The Crooked But Interesting Town Of Boston, Black Transfer, c.1810, 6 ½ In... *Illus*	5700.00
Jug, Washington, Ascending To Glory, Ship, American Flag, Creamware, c.1800, 12 In.	1067.00
Puzzle Jug, Delft Blue, White, Verse, Pierced Neck, Flowers, c.1765, 7 ¼ In.	944.00

LLADRO is a Spanish porcelain. Juan, Jose, and Vicente Lladro opened a ceramics workshop in Almacera in 1951. They soon began making figurines in a distinctive, elongated style. In 1958 the factory moved to Tabernes Blanques, Spain. The company makes stoneware and porcelain figurines and vases in limited and unlimited editions. Dates given are first and last years of production.

LLADRÓ

Figurine, Afternoon Promenade, Girl, With Parasol, No. 7636, 11 In.	118.00
Figurine, Afternoon Tea, Girl, Arms Out, Wide Brim Hat, No. 1428, 14 In.	141.00
Figurine, Anniversary Dance, Man, Woman, Waltzing, No. 1372, 12 ¼ In.	141.00
Figurine, Baby's Outing, No, 4938, Salvador Debon, c.1976, 14 In.	600.00
Figurine, Bar Mitzvah Day, Boy, Studying Scroll, No. 6004, 8 In.	82.00
Figurine, Belinda With Her Doll, No. 5045G, 11 In.	178.00
Figurine, Can I Play, Boy, Bat, No. 7610, 8 ¼ In.	59.00
Figurine, Cinderella & Fairy Godmother, No. 7553, 9 x 8 In.....*Illus*	390.00
Figurine, Cinderella, Alfredo Ruiz, No. 4828, c.1975, 9 ¾ In.	153.00
Figurine, Clown & Girl, Little Ballerina, Sitting With Clown, No. 5020, 13 In.	382.00
Figurine, Clown's Head, Cone Hat, Hands Under Chin, No. 5129, 13 In.	141.00
Figurine, Daily Chores, Stoneware, No. 2329M, Box, 13 In.	238.00
Figurine, Death Of The Swan, Ballerina, Seated, No. 4855, 5 In.	185.00
Figurine, Destination Big Top, Sad Clown, No. 6245, 8 In.	118.00
Figurine, Dreams Of A Summer Past, Girl, Hands Under Chin, No. 6401, 9 ¾ In.	118.00
Figurine, Fairy Godmother, No. 5791, Stamped, 11 x 8 In.	108.00
Figurine, Girl On Carousel Horse, No. 1469G, 15 ½ In.	266.00
Figurine, Girl With Mother's Shoe, No. 1084, 7 ½ In.	79.00
Figurine, Girl With Pot Of Flowers, No. 5223, 7 In.....*Illus*	47.00
Figurine, Glorious Spring, No. 5284, 12 x 6 In.	270.00
Figurine, Good Night, Mother & Child, Hugging, No. 5449, 8 ¼ In.	165.00
Figurine, Hebrew Scholar, Boy, Carrying Books, No. 6029, 8 In.	94.00
Figurine, Hindu Children, No. 5352, 9 ½ In.	330.00
Figurine, Japanese Elegance, Woman, Fans, Matte, Jose Puche, No. 6966, 20 ½ In.	1180.00
Figurine, Lady Grand Casino, Woman, Hand On Vase, No. 5175, 13 ½ In.	129.00
Figurine, Masquerade Ball, Clown & Girl Dancing, No. 5452, 9 In.	118.00
Figurine, Michiko, Japanese Dancer, No. 1447, 8 ¾ In.	165.00
Figurine, Mile Of Style, Clown, Smelling Flower, No. 6507, 13 ½ In.	153.00
Figurine, Mother's Day, No. 5596, 9 In.	234.00

Lithophane, Panel, Gothic Revival, Molded, Woman, Bronze Stand, Marble Base, 1800s, 17 x 9 ½ In. $549.00

Neal Auction Co.

Liverpool, Jug, Man, Masonic Images, Farm, Man & Horse On Reverse, Pink Luster Trim, c.1800, 7 ½ In. $210.00

Skinner, Inc.

Liverpool, Jug, Success To The Crooked But Interesting Town Of Boston, Black Transfer, c.1810, 6 ½ In. $5,700.00

Skinner, Inc.

L

TIP
Gilt frames can be cleaned with beer.

Lladro, Figurine, Cinderella & Fairy Godmother, No. 7553, 9 x 8 In. $390.00

DuMouchelles Art Gallery

Lladro, Figurine, Girl With Pot Of Flowers, No. 5223, 7 In. $47.00

Conestoga Auction Co., Inc.

Loetz, Centerpiece, Gold Tendrils, Bulb Top, Vertical Threads, c.1915, 15 In. $4,140.00

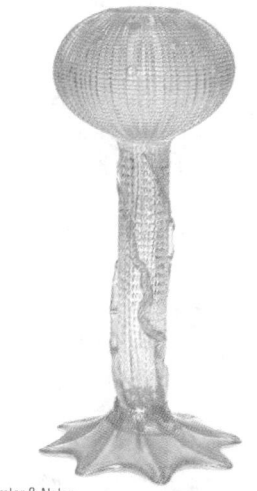

Humler & Nolan

> **TIP**
> *Use a soft-bristle paint brush to dust lampshades.*

Figurine, Naughty Girl, No. 5006, 9 ½ In.	60.00
Figurine, Neglected, Clown, Lying Down, No. 1503, 2 ¼ In.	82.00
Figurine, Oration, Kneeling Shakespearean Actor, Sword, No. 5357, 9 In.	118.00
Figurine, Practice Makes Perfect, Norman Rockwell Series, No. 1408G	266.00
Figurine, Preparing For The Sabbath, Girl Polishing Candlesticks, No. 6183, 7 ¼ In.	129.00
Figurine, Reading The Torah, Rabbi At Lectern, No. 1995, 14 ¼ In.	153.00
Figurine, Scarecrow & The Lady, Girl, Dancing With Man Of Straw, No. 5385, 9 ¾ In.	282.00
Figurine, Sea Captain, No. 4621, 14 ⅝ In.	72.00
Figurine, Sincerity, No. 2422, 17 In.	120.00
Figurine, Spring Dance, Girl, Long Dress, Wide Hat, No. 5663, 8 ¾ In.	141.00
Figurine, Story Time, Boy, Girl Reading On Settee, 1700s Attire, No. 5229, 15 In.	270.00
Figurine, Summer Stock, Norman Rockwell Series, No. 01011407, 10 ¼ In.	224.00
Figurine, Ten & Growing, Girl, Kissing Boy's Cheek, No. 7635, 7 In.	118.00
Figurine, Up & Away, No. 5975G, Santa In Sleigh, 14 ½ x 18 In.	1121.00
Figurine, Wedding, Bride, Groom, No. 4808, 7 ½ In.	129.00
Figurine, Wedding, Groom & Bride, No. 1404, 11 ½ In.	120.00
Group, Ballet Trio, 3 Ballerinas, Column Flowering Urn, No. 5235, 17 x 11 In.	600.00
Group, Gossips, No. 4984, 12 x 8 In.	150.00
Group, Making A Wish, No. 5910, 9 x 9 ½ In.	330.00
Group, New Playmates, No. 5456, 4 ½ x 5 In.	180.00
Group, Reception, Woman & Man, White Rose, Goblet, No. 1504, 14 In.	270.00
Group, Springtime In Japan, 2 Kimono Clad Women, No. 1445, 14 x 6 ½ In.	403.00
Tree Topper Figurine, Angel, Wings, Holding Scroll, 8 ½ In.	150.00

LOCKE ART is a trademark found on glass of the early twentieth century. Joseph Locke worked at many English and American firms. He designed and etched his own glass in Pittsburgh, Pennsylvania, starting in the 1880s. Some pieces were marked *Joe Locke,* but most were marked with the words *Locke Art.* The mark is hidden in the pattern on the glass.

Bonbon, Poppy, c.1910, 4 ½ x 2 ¾ In.	250.00
Sherbet, Daisy & Lines, Optic Ribbing, Footed, c.1910, 3 ½ x 3 ⅝ In., Pair	260.00
Sherbet, Ivy, Optic Ribbing, Signed, c.1910, 3 ¼ x 3 ⅝ In., Pair	260.00

LOETZ glass was made in many varieties. Johann Loetz bought a glassworks in Klostermuhle, Bohemia (now Klastersky Mlyn, Czech Republic), in 1840. He died in 1848 and his widow ran the company; then in 1879, his grandson took over. Most collectors recognize the iridescent gold glass similar to Tiffany, but many other types were made. The firm closed during World War II.

Loetz Austria

Biscuit Jar, Gold, Papillon Pattern, Tapered, Metal Lid, Bail Handle, 8 ¼ In.	418.00
Bottle, Gold Iridescent, Sterling Silver Overlay, Dimpled Sides, 9 In.	2415.00
Bowl, Art Nouveau, Oil Spot, Blue, Green, Purple, White Metal Stand, Stems, Flowers, 9 x 6 In.	1064.00
Bowl, Oil Spot, Iridescent, Pinched Shape, Trefoil Rim, 4 ¾ x 6 ¼ In.	391.00
Bowl, Translucent, Iridized Crystal Canes, Gold Lip Wrap, Applied Cascading Leaves, 8 In.	2415.00
Bride's Basket, Green Iridescent Glass, Silver Plated Frame, 1880-1900, 10 x 10 In.	210.00
Centerpiece, Gold Tendrils, Bulb Top, Vertical Threads, c.1915, 15 In. ....*Illus*	4140.00
Lamp, Iridescent Glass Shade, Bronze, Woman, Peter Tereszczuk, c.1900, 14 ½ x 7 In.....*Illus*	3750.00
Lampshade, Yellow, Ruffled Rim, Blue Hooked Feathers, 4 ½ In.	431.00
Tankard, Green & Blue Iridescent, Loop Handle, Metal Collar, Cloisonne Accents, 12 ¼ In.	431.00
Vase, Amber & Gold Iridescent, Pulled Silver & Blue Trails, Tapered, c.1900, 11 ⅝ In.	5313.00
Vase, Amber, Blue, Orange Pulled Design, Applied Striped Tendrils, Flared Rim, Round, c.1900, 5 In.	5938.00
Vase, Amber, Orange, Gold Drip, Platinum Zipper Design, Waisted Neck, c.1900, 7 ½ In.	17500.00
Vase, Blue & Green Iridescent, Raindrops, Thumbprint Impressions, Ruffle Rim, 4 In.	2510.00
Vase, Blue & Green Iridescent, Ribbed, Zipper, Bulbous Neck, Spread Foot, 9 ½ In.	690.00
Vase, Blue & Green, Ruffled Rim, Art Nouveau Silver Overlay, c.1906, 12 ½ In.	3900.00
Vase, Blue Aurene, Gold, Green Iridescent, Dragged Loop, Squashed, Footed, 6 ½ In.	12650.00
Vase, Blue Iridescent, Gold, Green, Purple, Oil Spots, Drips, Flat Cylinder Shape, c.1900, 7 In.	1063.00
Vase, Blue Iridescent, Melon Ribbed, Silver Overlay, 6 ½ In. ....*Illus*	4600.00
Vase, Blue Iridescent, Oil Spot, Translucent Green, Silver Overlay, Pinched Neck, 5 In.	2875.00
Vase, Blue Iridescent, Pink Highlights, Zipper Pattern, Wave Design, Yellow Ground, 3 ½ In.	1093.00
Vase, Blue Wave, Gold Drips, Iridescent, Incised, Austria, 6 ¼ In.	3400.00
Vase, Blue, Green Pulled Feathers, Plum Ground, Cylindrical, Bulbous Base, c.1900, 11 ¾ In.	5000.00
Vase, Blue, Oil Spot, Squat Base, Elongated Neck, Flared Rim, c.1900, 18 x 8 In.	750.00
Vase, Blue, Pink Iridescent, Flower Silver Overlay, Wavy Mouth, Dimpled Sides, c.1900, 5 ¼ In.	2375.00
Vase, Bud, Amber Iridescent, Flower Silver Overlay, Ruffled Mouth, Oval, c.1900, 5 ½ In.	1063.00
Vase, Cobalt Blue, Gourd, Disk Base, Handles, Scrolled Tips, Flared Rim, 7 In.	1076.00
Vase, Cobalt Blue, Green, Pulled Feather, Poppies, Silver Overlay, 13 x 6 ½ In.	7480.00
Vase, Conch Shell, Blue Iridescent, Seaweed, Golden Diaspora Pattern, Wave Base, 3 ¾ x 5 ½ In.	418.00

L

Vase, Enameled, Stylized White Flowers, Aqua & White Swirled Base, Lady's Leg, 6 In.	1560.00
Vase, Federzeichnung, Brown, Air Trap Octopus, Gold Tracery, Oval, Shouldered, 7 In.	1610.00
Vase, Federzeichnung, Mother-Of-Pearl, Octopus Design, Footed Urn, Marked, 9 In.	2990.00
Vase, Federzeichnung, Octopus, Mother-Of-Pearl, Brown, Gold Tracery, 9 In. *Illus*	1208.00
Vase, Federzeichnung, Octopus, Mother-Of-Pearl, Brown, Gold, 7 ¼ In. *Illus*	1840.00
Vase, Federzeichnung, Quatrefoil Rim, Brown Pearl Satin, Gilt, 1875-1925, 6 ¼ In. *Illus*	1944.00
Vase, Gold Iridescent, Applied Connected Phanomen Bands, Signed, 14 In.	1035.00
Vase, Gold Iridescent, Blue, Platinum, Silver Overlay, Oil Spots, Flowers, Ruffle Rim, 4 ½ In.	2300.00
Vase, Gold Iridescent, Honeycomb Drip Silver Overlay, Flared Cylindrical Rim, 8 In.	15405.00
Vase, Gold Iridescent, Silvery Blue, Astraa, Gathered Ruffle Rim, Impressions At Neck, 7 In.	508.00
Vase, Gold Iridescent, Trifold Rim, Feather Plumes, 7 ⅜ In. *Illus*	575.00
Vase, Gold Oil Spots, Pink, Green Blue Iridescent, Silver Flower Overlay, Flared Rim, c.1900, 3 In.	750.00
Vase, Gold Oil Spots, Silver Swirled Trails, Silver Overlay, Tapered Oval, c.1900, 3 ½ In.	2500.00
Vase, Golden Pulled Design, Green & Blue Iridescent, Smokestack, Cylinder, 4 ¾ In.	239.00
Vase, Green Iridescent, 4 Handles, Footed, 5 ½ x 7 In.	366.00
Vase, Green Iridescent, Blue, Purple, Pink Pulled Trails, Waisted Cylinder, c.1900, 9 ½ In.	5625.00
Vase, Green Iridescent, Melon Ribbed, Cinched, Scalloped Rim, Signed, 5 x 6 ½ In.	431.00
Vase, Green Iridescent, Mother-Of-Pearl, Gold, 4 Handles, 9 ¾ In.	7475.00
Vase, Green Iridescent, Swirled Blue Oil Spots, Silver Flower Overlay, Tapered Baluster, c.1900, 5 In.	1500.00
Vase, Green, Pale Blue Threaded Trails, Shouldered, Flared Rim, 7 ⅛ In.	388.00
Vase, Green, Pale Blue, Papillon, Baluster, Melon Ribbed, 4 ¾ In.	167.00
Vase, Green, Peach Glaze, Applied Silver Flowers, Flared, 3 x 5 In.	563.00
Vase, Honey Color, White, Balloon Shaped, Blue Iridescent Highlights, Raindrop Design, 8 x 7 In.	374.00
Vase, Iridescent Amber, Multicolor Rods, Gold, Pink Wavy Bands, Hexagonal Baluster, c.1900, 8 ⅜ In.	5938.00
Vase, Iridescent Amber, Pulled Orange, Silver, Plum Waves, Trumpet Neck, Squat Base, c.1900, 7 In.	11875.00
Vase, Iridescent Cameo, Orange, Gold Cameo Leaves, Cylindrical, 7 In.	1610.00
Vase, Iridescent Gold, Purple, Green, Blue Oil Spots, Pulled Silver Flower Overlay, c.1900, 7 In.	3125.00
Vase, Iridescent Green, Applied Threading, Ruffled Top, Ground Pontil, 8 ¾ x 5 ¾ In.	299.00
Vase, Iridescent Peach, Blue Wave Design, Silver Flower Overlay, Ruffled Rim, c.1900, 6 ¼ In.	56.00
Vase, Iridescent Pulled Design, Wavy Rim, 6 x 4 ½ In.	519.00
Vase, Mottled Gold Design, Swollen Top, Pinched Waist, Round Foot, 12 In.	388.00
Vase, Mottled Swirled Amber, Cream, Green Splashes, Silver Overlay, Squat, Ring Foot, 4 In.	2875.00
Vase, Oil Spots, Blue, Green, Purple, Dimpled Shoulder, Iridescent, c.1900, 7 ⅛ In.	1750.00
Vase, Oil Spots, Gold, Iridescent, Amber, Globular, Ruffled Mouth, 3 Handles, c.1900, 5 In.	7500.00
Vase, Oil Spots, Gold, Runny Iridescent Ground, Tapered Neck, Flared Rim, Oval, c.1900, 9 ¼ In.	1000.00
Vase, Oil Spots, Green, Purple, Gold Iridescent, Dimpled Sides, Flat Rim, 5 In.	1750.00
Vase, Orange, Platinum, Gold, Plum Pulled Bands, Iridescent, Stepped Body, c.1900, 7 ⅛ In.	17500.00
Vase, Pampas, Blue, Plum, Drip Trails, Gold Iridescent, Twisted Triangle Shape, c.1900, 9 ½ In.	1188.00
Vase, Peach Iridescent, Cobalt Blue, Green, Gold Trails, Silver Iris Overlay, c.1900, 8 ⅛ In.	4688.00
Vase, Pink Iridescent, Oil Spot Bottom, 3 Bulbous Lobes, Footed, 12 In.	1208.00
Vase, Platinum Oil Spots, Blue, Green Raspberry Ground, Wavy Rim, Dimpled Sides, c.1900, 4 ¾ In.	2500.00
Vase, Platinum Pulled Designs, Amber Ground, Iridescent, Globular, c.1900, 5 ⅞ In.	1500.00
Vase, Pulled Feather, Green & Turquoise Iridescent, Flared Rim, c.1900, 9 x 4 In.	1000.00
Vase, Pulled Wavy Iridescent, Pinched, Signed, 4 ½ x 4 ¼ In.	1098.00
Vase, Red To Green Iridescent, Sterling Floral Overlay, 10 ½ In.	4977.00
Vase, Red, Gold, 3 Blown-Out Rings, Dots, Genie Bottle, Round Foot, 12 In.	956.00
Vase, Ruby, Amber, Iridescent, Pulled Design, Side Mouth, Rope Twist Handle, Footed, c.1900, 8 ¼ In.	7500.00
Vase, Rusticana, Green Iridescent, Wavy Lines, 6 ½ x 6 In.	259.00
Vase, Stick, Blue Iridescent, Oil Spot, Spread Base, Flattened Rim, 11 In.	1208.00
Vase, Threading, Optical Ribbing, Green, Trumpet Shape, Round Foot, 12 In.	388.00
Vase, Tobacco Jar, Blue Oil Spots, Gourd Shape, Dome Lid, Silver Flower Overlay, c.1903, 9 In.	4063.00
Vase, Translucent Green, Gold Iridescent Striping, Coin Spot, Undulating Rim, 8 In.	633.00
Vase, Trumpet Shape, Gold Iridescent, Pulled Leaf Design, 11 In.	623.00
Vase, Waisted, Pulled Rim, Dimples, Gold, c.1900, 8 In.	615.00

LONE RANGER, a fictional character, was introduced on the radio in 1932. Over three thousand shows were produced before the series ended in 1954. In 1938, the first Lone Ranger movie was made. Television shows were started in 1949 and are still seen on some stations. The Lone Ranger appears on many products and was even the name of a restaurant chain for several years.

Badge, Lone Ranger Magazine Club, Brass, Black Enamel, 1937, ⅞ In.	612.00
Cheerios Box, Gun & Holster Set Offer, c.1949, 7 ½ x 10 ⅛ In.	209.00
Container, Silver Bullet Pops, Green Orange Label, Round, Handle, 1940, 4 ¾ In.	180.00
Costume Kit, Gun, Mask, Lariat, Hi-Yo Silver, Envelope, 1930s, 6 x 9 In.	230.00
Doll, Tonto, Lone Ranger, Cloth Pants, Top, Box, 20 ¼ In., 2 Pieces	1440.00
Figurine, On Silver, Right Arm In Air, Holding Cowboy Hat, c.1958	271.00
Flashlight, Lone Ranger, Riding Silver, Usalite, Box, 6 ¾ In.	150.00

Loetz, Lamp, Iridescent Glass Shade, Bronze, Woman, Peter Tereszczuk, c.1900, 14 ½ x 7 In.
$3,750.00

Rago Arts & Auction Center

Loetz, Vase, Blue Iridescent, Melon Ribbed, Silver Overlay, 6 ½ In.
$4,600.00

James D. Julia Auctioneers

L

Loetz, Vase, Federzeichnung, Octopus, Mother-Of-Pearl, Brown, Gold Tracery, 9 In.
$1,208.00

Early Auction Co.

Loetz, Vase, Federzeichnung, Octopus, Mother-Of-Pearl, Brown, Gold, 7 ¼ In.
$1,840.00

Early Auction Co.

Loetz, Vase, Federzeichnung, Quatrefoil Rim, Brown Pearl Satin, Gilt, 1875-1925, 6 ¼ In.
$1,944.00

Skinner, Inc.

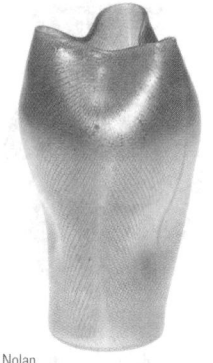

Loetz, Vase, Gold Iridescent, Trifold Rim, Feather Plumes, 7 ⅜ In.
$575.00

Humler & Nolan

Lone Ranger, Ring, 6-Gun, Plastic, Adjustable Brass Band, Kix Cereal Premium, 1947
$115.00

Hake's Americana & Collectibles

Lunch Box, Chuck Wagon, Domed, Metal, Aladdin, 1958, 6 ½ In.
$221.00

Hake's Americana & Collectibles

Game, Target, Pop-Up, Plastic, Dart Revolver, Darts, 1966, 19 x 22 In.	209.00
Gloves, Leather, Cuffs, Metal Studs, Child's, c.1938, 8 ½ In.	139.00
Pilot Radio, Black Case, Decal, 15 In.	1140.00
Pin, Promotion Of Sunday Comic Page, Examiner, White, Red & Blue Lettering, 1938, 1 ¼ In.	316.00
Poster, Kix, Lone Ranger 6-Shooter Ring, 1950s, 14 x 17 In.	150.00
Ring, 6-Gun, Plastic, Adjustable Brass Band, Kix Cereal Premium, 1947......*Illus*	115.00
Ring, Meteorite, Kix Promotion, Celluloid Dome Cover, Rock Pebbles, 1942	2588.00
Script, Radio Pilot Episode, WXYZ Radio, Aired January 20 1933, 8 ½ x 14 In., 14 Sheets	2300.00
Slot Machine Glass, Light-Up Display, Plexiglas Panel, Bally, 7 ½ x 19 In.	153.00
Target Set, Metal Pistol, 2-Sided Targets, Marx, Box	150.00
Toothbrush Holder, Riding Silver, Chalkware, 4 In.	70.00
Toy, Balloon, Famous Riders, Riding Silver, Wood, Cardboard, c.1939, 3 ¾ x 6 ¼ In.	345.00
Toy, Push Puppet, Lone Ranger Riding Silver, Plastic, Wood, 1940s, 5 ¼ In.	221.00
Watch, Lone Ranger, Riding Silver Decal, Lapel Cord, New Haven, 1940, Pocket	120.00

LONGWY WORKSHOP of Longwy, France, first made ceramic wares in 1798. The workshop is still in business. Most of the ceramic pieces found today are glazed with many colors to resemble cloisonne or other enameled metal. Many pieces were made with stylized figures and Art Deco designs. The factory used a variety of marks.

Bowl, Footed, Banded Rim & Base, Blue, 8 x 3 In.	160.00
Box, Octagonal, 3 Storks, Wading, 10 In.	2950.00
Cachepot, White Medallion, Flowers, Multicolor, 5 ¾ x 5 ¾ In.	345.00
Charger, Black & White Horses, Blue, Cobalt Trim, 15 In.	3450.00
Charger, Coat Of Arms, Rising Sun, 3 Flowers, 18 In.	750.00
Charger, Flowers, Birds On Branch, Faience, 1914, 9 In.	280.00
Compote, Flowers, Gold Trim, c.1893, 2 x 9 In.	525.00
Mustard, Stylized Flowers, Leaves, Hinged Lid, 3 ¾ In.	175.00
Plate, Whimsical, People, Bowling, Dancing, c.1885, 8 In.	82.00
Trivet, Art Deco, Flowers, Yellow, Black, Brown, c.1920, 8 x 8 In.	235.00
Vase, Flared, Rim & Base Border, Flowers, 15 In.	3450.00
Vase, Flowers, Multicolor, Blue Ground, Globular, 10 In.	1650.00

LONHUDA POTTERY COMPANY of Steubenville, Ohio, was organized in 1892 by William Long, W. H. Hunter, and Alfred Day. Brown underglaze slip-decorated pottery was made. The firm closed in 1896. The company used many marks; the earliest included the letters *LPCO*.

Vase, Painted Flowers, Gloss Glaze, 3-Footed, Handled, Impressed Mark, Weller, 3 ¾ x 4 ⅛ In.	118.00
Vase, Painted Flowers, Gloss Glaze, Bulbous, Flared Rim, 3-Footed, Signed Weller	83.00
Vase, Standard Glaze, Scalloped Rim, 3-Footed, 4 In.	69.00
Vase, Wheat, 2 Handles, Brown Glaze, c.1895, 8 ½ x 6 ½ In.	327.00

LOSANTI was made by Mary Louise McLaughlin in Cincinnati, Ohio, about 1899. It was a hard paste decorative porcelain. She stopped making it in 1906.

Vase, Leaves, Carved, Celadon Glaze, Bulbous, M.L. McLaughlin, 1901, 3 x 3 ½ In.	5000.00
Vase, Painted, Cream Ground, Blue, Brown Flowers, Bulbous, Carved Neck, 7 x 8 In.	950.00

LOTUS WARE was made by the Knowles, Taylor & Knowles Company of East Liverpool, Ohio, from 1890 to 1900. Lotus Ware, a thin porcelain that resembles Belleek, was sometimes decorated outside the factory. Other types of ceramics that were made by the Knowles, Taylor & Knowles Company are listed under KTK.

Biscuit Jar, Lid, Raised Flowers & Berries, c.1890, 6 ½ In.	350.00
Bowl, Lid, Pink Roses, Gold Trim, Ball Shape, Reticulated Handles, 8 In.	938.00
Dish, Lid, Cabbage Leaf Shape, Applied Flower Finial, Feet, Oval, 6 In.	460.00
Dish, Lid, Melon Ribbed Shape, Pierced Florettes, Oval, 6 ½ In.	1783.00
Ewer, Etruscan, Bulbous, Slender Neck, Scrolled Handle, Spout, Filigree Ribbing, 9 ½ In.	900.00
Tea Set, Venice, Raised Flowers, Ribbed, Notched Rim, Handles, Pot, Sugar, Creamer, c.1890 .	250.00
Vase, Lid, Enamel Painted Roses, Parcel Gilt, Reticulated Handles, 7 ½ x 6 ½ In.	945.00

LOW art tiles were made by the J. and J. G. Low Art Tile Works of Chelsea, Massachusetts, from 1877 to 1902. A variety of art and other tiles were made. Some of the tiles were made by a process called "natural," some were hand-modeled, and some were made mechanically.

Tile, Flowers, Navy, c.1881, 6 x 3 In.	29.00
Tile, Leaves, Flowers, Green, Impressed, 3 x 6 In.	12.00
Tile, Men Playing Backgammon, Mother Holding Baby, Dog, c.1890, 4 ½ x 4 ½ In.	230.00
Tile, Sun Flowers, Black, Impressed, 4 ¼ x 4 ¼ In., Pair	23.00
Tile, Swirl Pattern, Yellow, c.1890, 4 ¼ x 4 ¼ In.	65.00

LOY-NEL-ART, *see McCoy category*.

LUNCH BOXES and lunch pails have been used to carry lunches to school or work since the nineteenth century. Today, most collectors want either early tobacco advertising boxes or children's lunch boxes made since the 1930s. These boxes are made of metal or plastic. Boxes listed here include the original Thermos bottle inside the box unless otherwise indicated. Movie, television, and cartoon characters may be found in their own categories. Tobacco tin pails and lunch boxes are listed in the Advertising category.

Aluminum, Dome, Double Latch, Name Plate, Metal Handle, 10 x 7 x 4 In.	13.00
Annie, Sandy, Metal, Red, Aladdin, 1981	39.00
Astronaut, Dome, Metal, Planet Surface, Spacemen, c.1960	233.00
Boy On Rocket, Vinyl, Hinge Lid, c.1960	173.00
Chuck Wagon, Dome, Metal, Aladdin, 1958, 6 ½ In. ....*Illus*	221.00
Donny & Marie, Vinyl, Aladdin, 1976	71.00
Dutch Cottage, Dome, Metal, American Thermos Co., 1958	425.00
E.T., Metal, Yellow, Blue, Aladdin, 1982	87.00
Evel Knievel, Metal, Image Of Evel Smiling, Jumping Canyon, Aladdin, 1974	55.00
Fireball X15, Thermos, King Seeley Thermos Co., 1964, 7 x 9 In.	306.00
Get Smart, Agent 99 & K-13, Metal, King Seeley Thermos Co., 1966	290.00
Hometown Airport, Tin, Dome, Lithograph, 9 x 6 ½ In.	450.00
Kung Fu, Metal, David Carradine, c.1972	115.00
Pac Man, Metal, Multicolor, Ball Midway Mfg., 1980	65.00
Peanuts, Characters, Tin, King Seeley Thermos Co., 1960s	89.00
Red Plaid, Tin, King Seeley Thermos Co., 1964	37.00
Roy Rogers & Dale Evans, Double R Bar Ranch, Roy On Horse, American Thermos, 8 ½ x 6 In.	175.00
Smokey The Bear, Be Careful With Matches, Vinyl, King Seeley Thermos Co., 1960s, 6 ½ In. ..	316.00
Space Theme, Vinyl, Young Boy Holding Space Helmet, Astronaut, 1960s	115.00
Thermos, Cabbage Patch Kid, Plastic, Yellow, 1983	12.00
Tom Corbett, Space Cadet, Metal, Blue, Aladdin, 1952	173.00
Toppie, Plaid Elephant, Kroger's Grocery Store, Metal, American Thermos Products Co., c.1958 ... *Illus*	2784.00
Traveler, Metal, Ohio Art, 1964	95.00
VW Microbus, Red, White, Metal, Omni Graphics Inc., 1960s, 4 ¾ x 10 ¾ In.	615.00
Wagon Train, Metal, King Seeley Thermos Co., 1964, 6 ½ x 9 In.	153.00
Wrangler, Vinyl, Cowboy Lassoing Calf, Aladdin, c.1962	115.00
LUNCH BOX THERMOS	
Barbie, Midge, Skipper, Plastic, Mattel, 1965, 8 Oz.	19.00
Barbie, Photos Of Ponytail Barbie, Navy Ground, Red Cup, 1962	45.00

LUSTER glaze was meant to resemble copper, silver, or gold. The term *luster* includes any piece with some luster trim. It has been used since the sixteenth century. Some of the luster found today was made during the nineteenth century. The metallic glazes are applied on pottery. The finished color depends on the combination of the clay color and the glaze. Blue, orange, gold, and pearlized luster decorations were used by Japanese and German firms in the early 1900s. Fairyland Luster was made by Wedgwood in the 1900s. Tea Leaf pieces have their own category.

Charger, Three Fish, Yellow Scales, Anemone Ground, England, c.1890, 14 In.	4130.00
Cobalt Blue, Box, Cover, Mottled, Hummingbird, Rectangular, Orange Interior, c.1920, 6 ¾ In. ...	889.00
Fairyland luster is included in the Wedgwood category.	
Mottled Green & Pink, Bowl, Gilded Dragons, Medallion, Mother-Of-Pearl Interior, c.1920, 8 ⅝ In..	889.00
Mottled Orange & Red, Bowl, Gilded Design, Mottled Blue Interior, Octagonal, c.1920, 8 In.	504.00
Mottled Orange, Bowl, Gilded Motifs, Dragons, Flower Medallion, c.1920, 8 ¾ In.	652.00
Purple, Vase, Gilded Dragons, Pearl Interior, Landscapes, Trumpet Shape, c.1920, 11 ⅜ In.....	1422.00
Sunderland luster pieces are in the Sunderland category.	

LUSTRES are mantel decorations or pedestal vases with many hanging glass prisms. The name really refers to the prisms, and it is proper to refer to a single glass prism as a lustre. Either spelling, luster or lustre, is correct.

Bohemian Glass, Cranberry, Cutback, Sphere Prisms, 13 ½ In.	267.00
Bohemian Glass, Cranberry, White Cutback, Ferns, Hobnails, Clear, Gilt, c.1900, 13 ½ In., Pair..	1440.00
Bohemian Glass, Cranberry, White, Inverted Spear Prisms, 13 In., Pair	240.00
Bohemian Glass, Green, Frosted, Flowers, Gilt Sprigs, c.1885, 12 ½ In., Pair ....*Illus*	553.00
Bohemian Glass, Multicolor Flowers, Cobalt Blue, Opaque White, Clear Prisms, 13 In., Pair.	1000.00
Cranberry Glass, Clear Prisms, Flowers, Gilt, 13 ¾ x 6 ¼ In., Pair	546.00
Cranberry Glass, Cutback, Bird, Flower Portraits, Spear Prisms, 13 In., Pair	1695.00

Lunch Box, Toppie, Plaid Elephant, Kroger's Grocery Store, Metal, American Thermos Products Co., c.1958
$2,784.00

Hake's Americana & Collectibles

Lustres, Bohemian Glass, Green, Frosted, Flowers, Gilt Sprigs, c.1885, 12 ½ In., Pair
$553.00

New Orleans Auction Galleries, Inc.

L

Maize, Pitcher, Iridescent, Blue Stalks, Applied Handle, 9 In.
$230.00

Early Auction Co.

Majolica, Bowl, Putti Holding Basket, 3-Way Handle, Marked, 1868, 12 ½ In.
$1,541.00

Skinner, Inc.

Majolica, Centerpiece, Nautilus Shell, Mermaid, Putti, Seaweed, Mermen Supports, 1874, 20 In.
$4,148.00

Skinner, Inc.

Majolica, Charger, Equestrian Battle Scene, Multicolor, French, 16 In.
$480.00

DuMouchelles Art Gallery

Majolica, Clock, Putti, Lion's Head, Marble Dial, Gilded Roman Numerals, Pendulum, Key, c.1870, 17 In.
$711.00

Skinner, Inc.

Cut Glass, Clear, Footed, Sphere Prisms, 11 In., Pair	110.00
Cut Glass, Painted Flowers, Gilt Crown Top & Trim, 10 Spear Prisms, 14 In., Pair	2596.00
Green Opaline, Scalloped Rim, 13 In., Pair	300.00

MACINTYRE, *see Moorcroft category.*

MAIZE glass was made by W.L. Libbey & Son Company of Toledo, Ohio, after 1889. The glass resembled an ear of corn. The leaves were usually green, but some pieces were made with blue or red leaves. The kernels of corn were light yellow, white, or light green.

Bowl, White Kernels, Green Leaves, 8 x 3 ½ In.	85.00
Pitcher, Iridescent, Blue Stalks, Applied Handle, 9 In. ....*Illus*	230.00
Spooner, Custard, 4 ¼ x 3 ¼ In.	70.00
Tumbler, Blue Leaves, 4 In.	110.00
Tumbler, Green Leaves, Brown Tips, 4 In.	145.00
Vase, Ear Of Corn, Green Leaves, c.1890, 6 ½ In.	195.00

MAJOLICA is a general term for any pottery glazed with an opaque tin enamel that conceals the color of the clay body. It has been made since the fourteenth century. Today's collector is most likely to find Victorian majolica. The heavy, colorful ware is rarely marked. Some famous makers include Minton; Griffen, Smith and Hill (marked *Etruscan*); and Chesapeake Pottery (marked *Avalon* or *Clifton*). Majolica made by Wedgwood is listed in the Wedgwood category.

Basket, Bird On Branch, Ribbon, Bamboo Shape Handle, Blue, Yellow Trim, Rectangular, 10 In.	184.00
Basket, Flower Branch, Leaves, Turquoise, Ribbon Tied Handle, 8 In.	173.00
Bowl, Dog, Landscape Green, Blue, Yellow, Round, Spain, c.1810, 12 In.	2124.00
Bowl, Oblong, Lion's Head, Leaves, Maidens, Scroll Feet, Serpentine Base, c.1885, 13 ½ x 19 ½ In.	307.00
Bowl, Putti Holding Basket, 3-Way Handle, Marked, 1868, 12 ½ In. ....*Illus*	1541.00
Bowl, Reticulated Woven Basket, Daisies, Tripod Base, Branches, Pigeons, c.1870, 12 ¾ In.	652.00
Box, Lid, Dog Finial, Rectangular Cushion, Blue, Gold Trim, George Jones, c.1880, 10 In.	1185.00
Bust, Alexander The Great, Hand Painted, Italy, c.1850, 6 ½ In.	345.00
Butter, Cover, Artichoke Shape, Bird	184.00
Butter, Undertray, Rabbits In Cabbage, Green & Brown, 5 ½ In.	403.00
Cake Stand, Maple Leaves, Green, Yellow, Blue On Pink, Brown Stump Pedestal, Ivy, 5 x 9 ½ In.	71.00
Candlestick, Figural, Putto, Round Beaded Base & Border, Leaves, 1864, 10 ⅛ In., Pair	1778.00
Centerpiece, 2 Mermaids, Supporting Shell Shape Bowl, Leaf Garlands, Square Base, 1869, 11 ½ In.	3851.00
Centerpiece, Cherub, Holding Bowl, Riding Dolphin, Shell Dishes, Coral, Wave Feet, c.1870, 15 In.	2370.00
Centerpiece, Nautilus Shell, Mermaid, Putti, Seaweed, Mermen Supports, 1874, 20 In. ...*Illus*	4148.00
Charger, Charity Of St. Martin Of Tours, Multicolor, Masks, Acanthus Border, Italy, 20 In.	1440.00
Charger, Crab, Oysters, Palissy Ware, Portugal, 13 In.	600.00
Charger, En Avant, Joan Of Arc, On Horseback, Multicolor, Scalloped Rim, 12 ¼ In.	40.00
Charger, Equestrian Battle Scene, Multicolor, French, 16 In. ....*Illus*	480.00
Charger, Lobster, On Sand, Oysters, Multicolor	115.00
Charger, Lobster, Oysters, Palissy Ware, 13 In.	720.00
Charger, Regal Woman, On Horseback, 15 In.	208.00
Charger, Woman, Riding Dolphins, Interlocking Masks & Vine Border, Yellow, Blue, 1800s, 20 In.	472.00
Cheese Dish, Cylindrical Lid, Lily Pads, Bud Finial, Cattails, Cobalt Blue, Round Foot, c.1895, 10 In.	2015.00
Cheese Keeper, Dome Lid, Rope & Fern, Cobalt Blue, Yellow, Trees, 12 In.	345.00
Cheese Keeper, Round, Flowers & Leaves, Brown, Green, 7 In.	127.00
Clock, Putti, Lion's Head, Marble Dial, Gilded Roman Numerals, Pendulum, Key, c.1870, 17 In. ..*Illus*	711.00
Compote, Flower Shape Dish, Leaf & Vine Pedestal, Round Base, 8 ½ x 9 ½ In.	259.00
Compote, Oval Bowl, 2 Seated Sphinxes, Ruffled Rim, Lower Finial, Shaped Base, 5 ¾ In.	1185.00
Compote, Pierced Bowl, Robed Child, Figural Pedestal, Cutout Lower Dish, Scroll Feet, c.1895, 23 In.	2370.00
Compote, Stylized Dolphin, Marked, 19th Century, 16 ½ In.	750.00
Dish, 3 Lobed, Leaves, Flowers, Butterfly Perched On Edge, 3 Leaf Shaped Feet, c.1890, 5 x 11 In.	1896.00
Dish, Asparagus, Victorian, Asparagus Nest In Basket Of Grape Leaves, c.1885, 3 ¾ x 15 In.	153.00
Dish, Begonia Leaf Shape, Pink, Yellow, Brown, Green, 7 ½, 7 ¾, 9 In., 3 Piece	94.00
Dish, Game, Lid, Boar's Head, Deer Heads Under Handles, George Jones, c.1890, 12 ¾ In. ...*Illus*	1722.00
Dish, Grape Leaf Shape, Pink, Green, Yellow, Blue, Brown Stem, 11 ½ x 9 ¼ In., 2 Piece	106.00
Dish, Sweetmeat, Figural, Mermaid, Holding Shell Atop Her Head, 8 In.	207.00
Egg Basket, Flowers, Branch Shape Handle, Turquoise, Lavender, 6 Holes For Eggs, 8 In.	138.00
Figurine, Black Boy, Accordion, Shaped Bowl, Multicolor, 4 In.	37.00
Figurine, Cockatoo, Perched On Branch, Green, Yellow, Brown, c.1900, 17 In., Pair	633.00
Figurine, Lion, Reclining, Rectangular Architectural Base, Yellow, Green Vines, Leaves, 5 x 3 In., Pair	115.00
Figurine, Man, Seated, Behind Wheelbarrow, England, c.1920, 10 x 11 ½ In.	189.00
Figurine, Parrot, Green, Blue, Pink Head, Signed, France, c.1910, 11 ½ In., Pair	489.00

L

Majolica, Dish, Game, Lid, Boar's Head, Deer Heads Under Handles, George Jones, c.1890, 12 ¾ In.
$1,722.00

Skinner, Inc.

Majolica, Garden Seat, Flowers, 6-Sided, Multicolor, Minton, c.1870, 19 ¾ In.
$2,040.00

Skinner, Inc.

Majolica, Jardiniere, Stand, Flowers, Leaves, Relief, George Jones, 1800s, 6 ⅜ In.
$780.00

Skinner, Inc.

Majolica, Jug, Fish, Flat Panels, Enamel, Holdcroft, c.1880, 8 ¼ In.
$510.00

Skinner, Inc.

Majolica, Pedestal, Neptune, Italy, 27 In.
$805.00

Cottone Auctions

Majolica, Plaque, Lizards, Snake, Frog, Moss Ground, Palissy Ware, Mafra & Son, Portugal, 1800s, 15 In.
$1,541.00

Skinner, Inc.

Majolica, Toby Jug, Peasant Woman, Man, Hair Forms Handles, Hat Spouts, Minton, c.1890, 11 In., Pair
$660.00

Skinner, Inc.

Majolica, Umbrella Stand, Stork, Bulrushes, Water Lilies, Multicolor Enamel, c.1885, 38 x 17 In.
$3,690.00

New Orleans Auction Galleries, Inc.

Majolica, Vase, 2 Kittens, Playing, Turquoise, Carpet Under Urn, Brownfield, c.1874, 10 In.
$3,851.00

Skinner, Inc.

M

Malachite, Vase, Art Deco, Ingrid, Female Figures, Geometric Ribbing, Schlevogt, 1930s, 9 ⅝ In., Pair
$523.00

Skinner, Inc.

Map, Americas, Hand Colored Engraving, Abraham Ortelius, Antwerp, Frame, 1587, 23 ½ x 28 ½ In.
$2,938.00

Garth's Auctioneers & Appraisers

Map, Dakotas, Sectional, Lithograph, Hand Colored, Engraved, Silas Chapman, 1872, 29 x 21 In.
$1,920.00

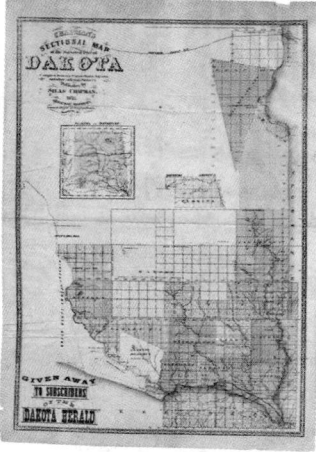

Skinner, Inc.

TIP

Put a dryer sheet inside a stored book to keep it from becoming musty.

Figurine, Rooster, Hen, Mound Base, Multicolor, Italy, 17 x 15 x 10 In.	115.00
Font, Terra-Cotta, Multicolor Enamel, Tin Glaze, Cherubs, Open Top Arch, 15 x 8 In.	351.00
Garden Seat, Corn, Wheat Sheaves, 19th Century, 19 In.	400.00
Garden Seat, Flowers, 6-Sided, Multicolor, Minton, c.1870, 19 ¾ In. ....*Illus*	2040.00
Garden Seat, Round, Faux Thatch, Opening, Cylindrical, Blue, Birds, Lily Pads, c.1870, 17 ½ In.	2963.00
Garniture, Bronze, Bowl, 2 Vases, Quatrefoil Rim, Gilded Feet, Scrollwork, 14 ¼ In., 3 Piece .	551.00
Humidor, Bear, Seated, Wearing Green Coat, Holding Pipe, 6 In.	115.00
Humidor, Cat, Seated, Holding Fish, Scarf Tied Around Head, 6 ¾ In.	207.00
Humidor, Dog, Sitting, Singing, Playing Guitar, Multicolor, 8 ¼ x 6 In.	814.00
Humidor, Indian, Seated On Rocks, Pipe, Traditional Clothing, Multicolor, 9 ½ In.	104.00
Humidor, Pig, Seated, Blue Apron, Holding Broom, Pipe In Mouth, Multicolor, 8 In.	121.00
Jam Jar, Lid, Underplate, Spoon, Orange Shape, Twig & Leaf Handle, Leaf Plate, 4 x 5 In.	52.00
Jardiniere, Cobalt Blue, Putti, Yellow Leaves Border, Round Foot, 8 ½ In.	115.00
Jardiniere, Stand, Flowers, Leaves, Relief, George Jones, 1800s, 6 ⅜ In. ....*Illus*	780.00
Jardiniere, Undertray, Marsh, Birds, Lily Pads, Bulrushes, Dragonflies, Leaves, c.1870, 13 ⅝ In. ..	1185.00
Jug, Fish, Flat Panels, Enamel, Holdcroft, c.1880, 8 ¼ In. ....*Illus*	510.00
Lamp Base, Bulbous, Cobalt Blue Glaze, Applied Fruit Sprig, Leaves, Wood Base, 27 ½ In.	92.00
Lobster Dish, Lid, Oval Shaped, Leaf Borders, Brown, Yellow, Orange, c.1871, 6 ¼ In.	711.00
Oyster Server, 4 Graduated Rows, Holders, 2 Fish Finial, Scalloped Foot, c.1862, 10 In.	7350.00
Pedestal, Green, Gilt, Leaves, Scrolling, Continental, c.1890, 25 ½ In.	210.00
Pedestal, Leaves, Brown, Green, 13 ¾ In.	29.00
Pedestal, Neptune, Italy, 27 In. ....*Illus*	805.00
Pedestal, Square Notched Base, Rope Twist Standard, Cobalt Blue, Gilt Trim, c.1890, 31 x 11 In..	615.00
Pin Dish, Relief Flowers, Leaves, Slatted Ground, Double Twig Handles, Footed, 10 ½ x 8 ¾ In.	63.00
Pitcher, Dahlia Blossom, Cream Diamond Ground, c.1900, 10 ⅞ x 6 In.	81.00
Pitcher, Dog Shape, On Hind Legs, Pouring Lip, Brown Glaze, Green Ears, 7 ¼ In.	142.00
Pitcher, Fish Shape, Open Mouth Spout, Tail Handle, Leaf Base, Multicolor Glaze, 12 In.	98.00
Pitcher, Fish Shape, Open Mouth, Seaweed Base, c.1900, 9 x 3 In.	92.00
Pitcher, Fish Shape, Tail Forms Handle, Mouth Open, Pink Interior, 12 ¾ In.	345.00
Pitcher, Flower, Bird, Branches, Applied Handle, Scrolled Fleur-De-Lis Bands, Marked, 7 In.	81.00
Pitcher, Frog, Hunting, Pouch, Powder Flask, Gun, Holding Snake, Multicolor Glaze, 10 In.	173.00
Pitcher, Insects, Flowers, Multicolor, c.1880, 8 x 6 ½ In.	150.00
Pitcher, Merman, Holding Spiral Shell, Coral Handle, Waves, Round Base, c.1895, 14 In.	2726.00
Pitcher, Owl Shape, Mound Base, Multicolor Glaze, Marked, 8 In.	161.00
Pitcher, Shell & Seaweed, Raised Design, Metal Lid, c.1890, 6 In.	87.00
Planter, Blue, Fruit & Flower Garland, Claw Feet, Minton, 16 x 13 In., Pair	2070.00
Planter, Leaping Stag, Flower Border, Italy, 25 x 24 In., Pair	1380.00
Planter, Stand, Multicolor, Cherub Pedestal, Lion Heads, Swags, Paw Feet, 2 Sections, 40 x 19 In.	288.00
Planter, Tree Shape Base, Overhanging Leaf Rim, Frogs, Clams, Nest, Snake, Footed, 1800s, 11 In.	790.00
Plaque, Crab In Relief, Multicolor, Palissy Ware, 1800s, 12 ½ In.	180.00
Plaque, Group Of Musicians, Glazed, Multicolor, Signed, Borner, 1800s, 5 ¾ x 11 ⅝ In.	237.00
Plaque, Lizards, Snake, Frog, Moss Ground, Palissy Ware, Mafra & Son, Portugal, 1800s, 15 In.. *Illus*	1541.00
Plate, Asparagus, France, 9 In.	106.00
Plate, Asparagus, Green, Pink, Well, Depose, Luneville, France, c.1940, 9 ⅞ In., 6 Piece	196.00
Plate, Basket Weave Relief, Swans, Wings Spread, Footed, Oval, Mark, Morley, 12 ½ x 9 ¾ In..	40.00
Platter, Begonia Leaf On Bark, 2 Green Tab Handles, Oval, c.1900, 9 x 12 ½ In.	81.00
Platter, Grapevine, Pears, Apples, Enameled Glaze, Alfred Renoleau, Palissy Ware, 12 ½ x 17 In..	978.00
Platter, Lizard, Snake, Insects, Mossy Ground, Jose A. Cunha, Palissy Ware, 9 ¼ In.	380.00
Sardine Box, Basket Weave, Turquoise, Yellow, 2 Sardines, Handle, Shell Corners	316.00
Sardine Box, Lid, Overlapping Fish, Flowers, Leaves, Square, Rounded Corners	150.00
Sardine Dish, Tray, Lid, 3 Fish, Leaves, Pink, Green, Yellow Trim, George Jones, c.1890, 4 In.	3185.00
Sugar, Lid, Vines, Leaves, Cobalt Blue Ground, Basket Weave Base, Brown Handles, c.1900, 6 x 5 In.	81.00
Syrup, Pear Shape, Lobed, Loop Handle, Pewter Top, Mottled, 9 In.	196.00
Tazza, Birds, Berries, Flowers, Turquoise, Molded, Pedestal, Signed H, 5 ¾ x 8 ¾ In.	104.00
Tazza, Maple Leaves, Pink Ground, Tree Trunk Standard, Etruscan, Pa., c.1895, 5 x 9 In., Pair.	150.00
Teapot, Dachshund, Sitting Up, Extended Paws Are Spout, Looping Tail Is Handle, 8 In.	109.00
Teapot, Figural, Fish, Swallowing Fish, Tail Forms Handle, Green, Yellow, Brown, 11 ½ In.	259.00
Teapot, Flowers, Leaves, Cat Handle, Flattened Shape, Rose Finial, Blue, Green, White, 6 x 9 In.	748.00
Teapot, Sugar, Lid, Cauliflower, Green Leaf Loop Handle, Etruscan, 4 ¾ x 6 ¾ In.	118.00
Toby Jug, Peasant Woman, Man, Hair Forms Handles, Hat Spouts, Minton, c.1890, 11 In., Pair ..*Illus*	660.00
Tray, Asparagus & Artichoke, Molded Relief Images, Leaves, Animal Profiles, Oval, 14 x 10 ½ In.	35.00
Tray, Blackberry, Cream Ground, Green Handles, Oval, Chesapeake Pottery, 1880, 9 ½ x 13 In.	127.00
Tureen, Lid, Underplate, Ladle, Cauliflower Shape, Floret Handles, Oval, 10 x 7 & 11 x 10 In.	150.00
Umbrella Stand, Cylindrical, Green, Trees, Swollen Rim, 20 In.	161.00
Umbrella Stand, Panels, Molded With Thistles, Turquoise Drip Design, England, c.1885, 25 ½ In.	153.00
Umbrella Stand, Stork, Bulrushes, Water Lilies, Multicolor Enamel, c.1885, 38 x 17 In.... *Illus*	3690.00

Vase, 2 Kittens, Playing, Turquoise, Carpet Under Urn, Brownfield, c.1874, 10 In. ....*Illus*	3851.00
Vase, Bacchus Figural Handles, Footed, Multicolor, 11 In.	104.00
Vase, Bulbous, Raised Corn, Leaves, Corncob Handles, Multicolor, Glaze, 10 ½ x 10 In.	242.00
Vase, Flowering Branches, Shouldered, Cloud Collar, Narrow Neck, Turquoise, c.1890, 14 In.	2205.00
Vase, Flowers & Hummingbird, Branches, Yellow, Square, Trumpet Rim, 10 ½ In.	127.00
Vase, Orange Flowers, Blue Ground, Leaf Handles, 13 In.	113.00
Vase, Rooster, Standing, Cylindrical Wheat Sheaf Shape Container, c.1895, 27 ¾ In.	4740.00
Vase, Spill, Blackamoor Shape Support, c.1855, 27 ½ In.	750.00
Vase, Strawberry Plants, Dome Base, Pink Berries, Green Leaves, Brown Ground, 12 x 7 ½ In.	173.00
Vase, Winged Woman, Harp, Lavender, 8 In.	690.00

MALACHITE is a green stone with unusual layers or rings of darker green shades. It is often polished and used for decorative objects. Most malachite comes from Siberia or Australia.

Box, Bronze, Leafy Handle, Bracket Feet, 7 x 14 ½ x 10 In.	1968.00
Box, Egg Shape, Halves, Silver Metal Lining, 3 Ostrich Legs, c.1950, 9 In.	210.00
Box, Gilt Bronze Overwork, Scrolls, Oval Portrait Medallion, Blue, Casket Shape, 7 x 3 ½ In.	600.00
Group, Women, Rocks, Lantern, Dragon, Carved, Chinese, 13 ¾ In.	3327.00
Vase, Art Deco, Ingrid, Female Figures, Geometric Ribbing, Schlevogt, 1930s, 9 ⅝ In., Pair ...*Illus*	523.00
Vase, Flattened Shape, Relief Dragons, Lion Mask Ring Handles, Foo Dog Finial, 67 In.	368.00

MAPS of all types have been collected for centuries. The earliest known printed maps were made in 1478. The first printed street map showed London in 1559. The first road maps for use by drivers of automobiles were made in 1901. Collectors buy maps that were pages of old books, as well as the multifolded road maps popular in this century.

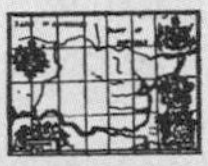

Americas, Hand Colored Engraving, Abraham Ortelius, Antwerp, Frame, 1587, 23 ½ x 28 ½ In.. *Illus*	2938.00
Asia, Arabian Peninsula, East Indies, Scandinavia, Engraved, 2 Page Folio, Homann, 1720, 19 x 23 In.	420.00
Atlas, American, Published By John Reid, New York, 1796	7788.00
Battle Of Monmouth, American Revolution, British Army Main Columns, June 28 1778, 19 x 15 In.	76700.00
Bucks County, Ink, Watercolor, Mr. Murray's School, Frame, c.1820, 12 x 15 In.	415.00
Celestial, Johann Homann, Johann Doppelmayr, Nuremburg, 1740s, 21 x 24 In., Pair	489.00
Dakotas, Sectional, Lithograph, Hand Colored, Engraved, Silas Chapman, 1872, 29 x 21 In. ...*Illus*	1920.00
Fezzae & Morocco, Abraham Ortelius, Theatrum Orbis Terrarum, 1570, Antwerp, 1900s, 15 x 20 In.	338.00
Globe, 12 Copper Engraved Gores, Brass Meridian, Josiah Loring, 18 x 19 In. ....*Illus*	4320.00
Globe, Celestial, Lithograph, Brass Engraved Meridian, Time Dial, Ernst Schottr & Co., 7 ¾ x 8 In.	2015.00
Globe, Celestial, Urn & Tripod Stand, Newton & Son, London, 1818, 40 x 15 In., Pair	12650.00
Globe, Gilman Joslin, Boston, 10 x 18 In.	2950.00
Globe, Library, Paper On Wood, Walnut, W. & A.K. Johnstone, c.1900, 18 x 40 In. ....*Illus*	2252.00
Globe, Light Inside, Wood Base, 17 x 14 x 12 In.	89.00
Globe, Mahogany Base, Political Map Lines, Rand McNally & Co., c.1920, 18 x 39 In.	540.00
Globe, Mahogany Stand, Joslin, 6 x 9 ¾ In.	1062.00
Globe, Plaster, Brass Meridian Ring, Calendar & Zodiac, Cruchley's, London, 1800s, 19 In. ...*Illus*	660.00
Globe, Stand, String Inlaid Frame, Turned Mahogany Legs, Stretchers, England, 1862, 22 ¾ In.	3851.00
Globe, Steel, Paper Horizon, 3-Legged Stand, Gilman Joslin, c.1910, 42 x 16 In.	2125.00
Globe, Terrestrial, Metal, Paper Overlay, Brass, Mahogany Stand, Replogle Globes, 46 x 38 In. ...*Illus*	1150.00
Globe, Turned Wood Pedestal, Weber Costello Co., c.1900, 20 In.	837.00
Hemisphere, Double, Silk, Ink, On Silk, Signed Eliza, Allen, Gilt Frame, 1793, 23 In.	844.00
Holy Land, Hand Colored Engraving, Matted, Frame, Amsterdam, 1659, 28 ¼ x 32 ¾ In.	382.00
Italy, Engraving, Hand Coloring, Giovanni Antonio & Fabio Magini, Frame, c.1600, 17 ¼ x 22 In.	253.00
La Louisaiana Et Du Cours Du Mississipi, Guillaume De L'Isle, Paris, 1718, 19 x 25 In.	13742.00
London To Cambridge, London To Rye, Road, Strip, Hand Colored, Frame, 11 ½ x 16 In.	59.00
Long Island, Courtland Smith, 1925, 25 x 35 In.	900.00
Louisiana & River Mississippi, Copper Plate Engraving, John Senex, London, 1721, 19 x 22 In.	1793.00
Maris Pacifici, Engraved, Color, Abraham Ortelius, 13 ⅝ x 19 ¾ In.	4503.00
Mexico, Florida Territories & Antilles, Guillaume De L'Isle, Paris, 1703, 18 x 23 In.	2988.00
New England, Coast, Engraved, Levinus Hullsius, Frankfurt, 1 Sheet Folio, 13 ¾ x 11 ¾ In.	2460.00
New York City, Pocket, Manhattan Below 34th St., Brooklyn, David H. Burr, c.1840, 22 x 19 In.	236.00
North America, European Settlements, Whatever Else Is Remarkable, West Indies, c.1745, 15 x 19 In.	431.00
Ohio Valley, East Coast States, To Louisiana, Robert De Vaugondy, 1755, 27 ½ x 19 ¼ In.	288.00
Oxonium, College Arms Borders, Double Page, Engraved, Johannes Blaeu, c. 1665, 15 x 20 In. ...*Illus*	240.00
Rhine, Nuremburg, Johann Baptist Homann, Hand Colored, Matted, Frame, c.1730, 31 x 27 In.	294.00
Road, Oklahoma, Mobil Travel Map, 1967	7.00
United States, Eastern, N.Y., Mass., Jan Jansson, 17th Century, 15 ½ x 20 In. ....*Illus*	472.00
United States, West Territories, New England Detail, Nancy B. Phelps, Age 10, Pen & Ink, 17 x 23 In.	1121.00
Virginia & Maryland, John Speed, Double Plate, Copper Plate Engraving, 14 ¾ x 19 ¼ In.	3290.00

Map, Globe, 12 Copper Engraved Gores, Brass Meridian, Josiah Loring, 18 x 19 In. $4,320.00

Gray's Auctioneers LLC

Map, Globe, Library, Paper On Wood, Walnut, W. & A.K. Johnstone, c.1900, 18 x 40 In. $2,252.00

Skinner, Inc.

M

Map, Globe, Plaster, Brass Meridian Ring, Calendar & Zodiac, Cruchley's, London, 1800s, 19 In. $660.00

Skinner, Inc.

The edited listings of the current prices in this *Kovels' Antiques & Collectibles Price Guide* aren't available on any website. Readers can visit **Kovels.com** to check thousands of past prices and sign up for free information on trends, tips, reproductions, marks, and more.

Map, Globe, Terrestrial, Metal, Paper Overlay, Brass, Mahogany Stand, Replogle Globes, 46 x 38 In.
$1,150.00

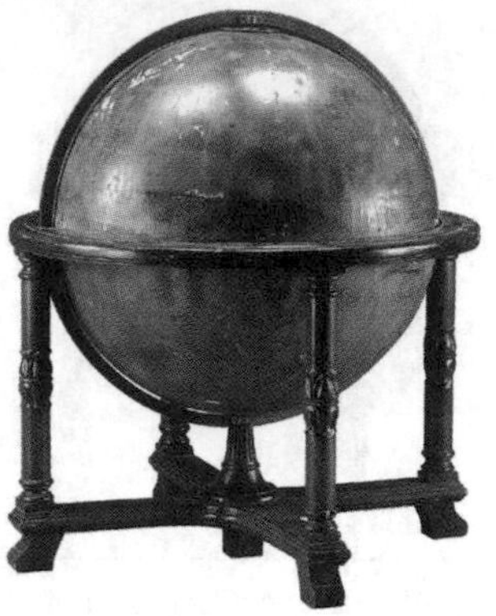

James D. Julia Auctioneers

Map, Oxonium, College Arms Borders, Double Page, Engraved, Johannes Blaeu, c. 1665, 15 x 20 In.
$240.00

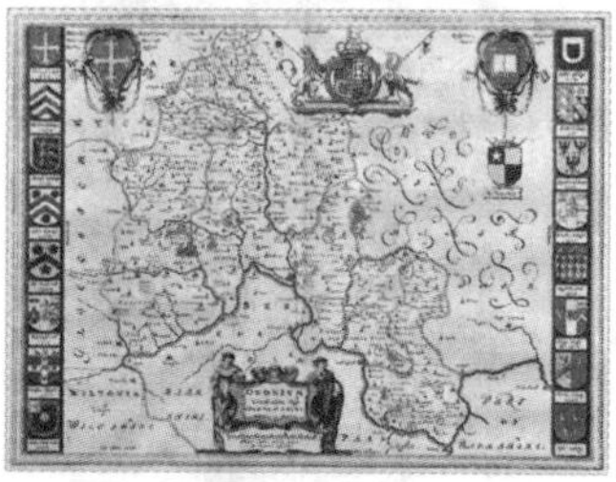

Skinner, Inc.

Map, United States, Eastern, N.Y., Mass., Jan Jansson, 17th Century, 15 1/2 x 20 In.
$472.00

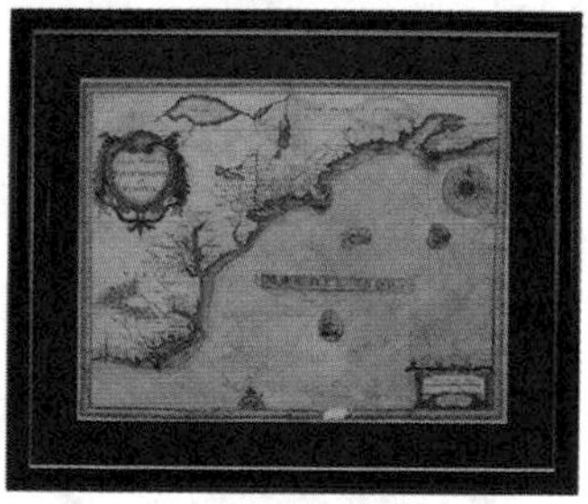

Brunk Auctions

Marble, Lutz, Pink, Green Lines, Opaque, 7/8 In.
$25,800.00

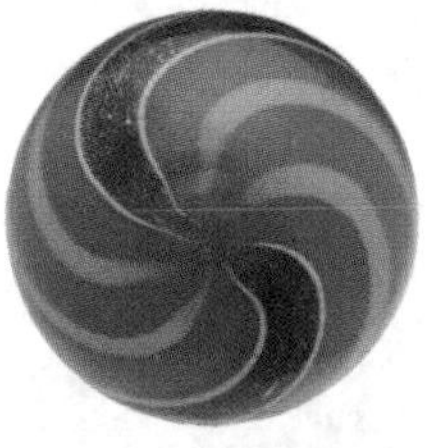

Morphy Auctions

Virginia, Copper Plate Engraving, Laid Paper, Hand Colored, M. Carey & Sons, 1818, 13 1/2 x 20 In.	708.00
Virginia, Seat Of War, Md., Del., Va., D.C., Bird's-Eye View, Civil War, Linen, 22 x 30 In.	1998.00
Virginia, Valley, Civil War, Frame, c.1880, 16 x 7 In.	184.00

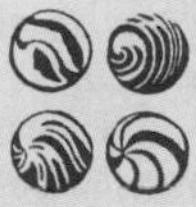

MARBLE collectors pay highest prices for glass and sulphide marbles. The game of marbles has been popular since the days of the ancient Romans. American children were able to buy marbles by the mid-eighteenth century. Dutch glazed clay marbles were least expensive. Glazed pottery marbles, attributed to the Bennington potteries in Vermont, were of a better quality. Marbles made of pink marble were also available by the 1830s. Glass marbles seem to have been made later. By 1880, Samuel C. Dyke of South Akron, Ohio, was making clay marbles and The National Onyx Marble Company was making marbles of onyx. The Navarre Glass Marble Company of Navarre, Ohio, and M. B. Mishler of Ravenna, Ohio, made the glass marbles. Ohio remained the center of the marble industry, and the Akron-made Akro Agate brand became nationally known. Other pieces made by Akro Agate are listed in this book in the Akro Agate category. Sulphides are glass marbles with frosted white figures in the center.

Akro Agate, Corkscrew, Yellow, Orange, 7/16 In.	21.00
Akro Agate, Corkscrew, Yellow, Orange, White, 5/8 In.	29.00
Akro Agate, Corkscrew, Yellow, Raspberry, Blue, Green, 9 1/6 In.	154.00
Akro Agate, Oxblood, Lemonade, 5/8 In.	85.00
Christensen Guinea, Clear, Multicolor, 9/16 In.	300.00
End Of Day, Polished Pontil, 1890s, 3/4 In.	85.00
Fiber Optic, Blue, Pink, Green, 2 In.	18.00
Joseph Swirl, Candy Floss, Pontil, 1890s, 5/8 In.	40.00
Lutz, Pink, Green Lines, Opaque, 7/8 In. ...*Illus*	25800.00
Onionskin, Green, Pontil, Germany, 1800s, 3/4 In.	99.00
Sulphide, Clear, Lamb, Sitting, Jim Davis, Signed, 2 3/16 In.	100.00
Swirl Core, Multicolor, 7/8 In.	37.00
Swirl, Divided Core, Orange, Green, White, 3 In. ...*Illus*	28200.00

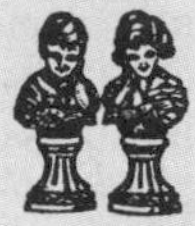

MARBLE CARVINGS, such as large or small figurines, groups of people or animals, and architectural decorations, have been a special art form since the time of the ancient Greeks. Reproductions, especially of large Victorian groups, are being made of a mixture using marble dust. These are very difficult to detect and collectors should be careful. Other carvings are listed under Alabaster.

Bust, Carmen, Emmanuel Villanis, Pedestal, Signed, 39 In. ...*Illus*	1610.00
Bust, Cicero, Gazing Left, 22 x 11 In.	2340.00
Bust, Gentleman, Beard, Incised, Franklin Simmons Sculptor Roma 1871, 28 x 20 In. ...*Illus*	2000.00
Bust, Girl, Jacques Francois Joseph Saly, 18 In.	936.00
Bust, Maiden, Renaissance Style, Signed, Prof. Giuseppe Bessi, Italy, 14 In.	5100.00
Bust, Man, Bearded, White, 33 In.	1968.00
Bust, Man, Flowing Hair, Lace Collar, White, Italy, c.1890, 24 1/2 In.	1375.00
Bust, Man, Sideburns, Signed Joseph Mozier, c.1850, 24 In.	2065.00
Bust, Man, White, Neville Northey Burnard, 21 3/4 In.	750.00
Bust, Marie Antoinette, Head Turned Left, High Hairdo, Flowers, Curls, France, c.1850, 33 In.	5250.00
Bust, Mother, Child, Holding Shoulder, Smiling, White, 23 In.	2500.00
Bust, Napoleon, General's Hat, c.1890, 22 In.	2125.00
Bust, Woman, Aristocrat, White, Signed Mercie, France, 30 1/2 In.	2500.00
Bust, Woman, Cap On Head, Gray, Veined, Marked Cecchini, Italy, c.1900, 13 x 11 In.	266.00
Bust, Woman, Classical, c.1850, 23 1/4 In.	2375.00
Bust, Woman, Gown, Cap, Capital Base, c.1870, 31 x 18 In.	2160.00
Bust, Woman, Gown, Gold Collar, Scarf, Fleur-De-Lis, Octagonal Base, 11 x 11 In.	472.00
Bust, Woman, Lace Cap, Ruffled Bodice, Carrara, c.1890, 22 In.	900.00
Bust, Woman, Noble Bearing, Inscribed Pugi, Continental, c.1890, 27 In.	1500.00
Bust, Woman, Older, Pleated Shirtwaist, Round Socle, White, c.1890, 28 1/2 In.	633.00
Bust, Woman, Ringlets, Green Socle, Cipriani, Italy, c.1900, 5 1/2 In.	325.00
Bust, Woman, Scarf On Head, Wavy Hair, Alabaster Base, Italy, c.1880, 44 1/2 x 17 1/2 In.	1180.00
Bust, Woman, Seminude, Side Swept Hair, 18 x 11 In.	780.00
Bust, Young Woman, Filmy Scarf Over Face, Italy, c.1850, 19 x 14 In.	944.00
Compote, Thessalonian Green, Fluted Shaft, Handles, Stepped Base, 7 1/2 x 11 In., Pair	8050.00
Obelisk, Monument, Inlaid Marble, Pedestal Base, Continental, 21 In., Pair ...*Illus*	1464.00
Pedestal, Cloisonne, Brass Column, Lion's Paw Feet, c.1890, 38 x 9 In.	1003.00
Pedestal, Gray, Tapered, 1800s, 43 1/2 x 12 1/2 In.	875.00
Pedestal, Lotus Leaves, Pear Shape Column, Square Base, White, 40 In.	413.00
Pedestal, Louis XVI Style, Gilt Metal Mounts, Square Top, Column Support, 26 x 15 In.	1625.00
Pedestal, Louis XVI, Rouge, Fluted, Bronze Dore Band, Square Base, 47 In., Pair	2310.00

Pedestal, Red, Rotating Square Top & Base, 41 ½ In. 472.00

Sarcophagus, Roman Soldiers, Animal Scene, 29 x 66 In. 10625.00

Statue, Adriadne & Panther, White, c.1850, 15 1/12 In. 600.00

Statue, Allegory Of Autumn, Alabaster, Bronze, E. Rizec, Stamped Schumacher, 1920s, 14 In. 3000.00

Statue, Crouching Venus, c.1900, 25 ½ In. 2031.00

Statue, David, Sling Shot, Fig Leaf, 72 In. 2337.00

Statue, Elephant, Trunk Down, c.1850, 14 ½ In. 830.00

Statue, Foo Dog, White, Chinese, 36 In., Pair 748.00

Statue, Girl, Slave, Cowering, c.1910, 22 ½ In. 544.00

Statue, Harem Dancer, Patinated Bronze, A. Gory, 28 ¼ In. *Illus* 10030.00

Statue, Lamb, Reclining, Textured Wool, c.1875, 6 In. 558.00

Statue, Maiden, Basket Of Flowers, A. Cipriani, 18 In. 470.00

Statue, Our Lady Of Everlasting Help, Virgin Mary, Christ Child, Carrara, c.1950, 66 In. *Illus* 3198.00

Statue, Owl, On Tree Stump, Painted, Italy, 12 In. 480.00

Statue, Ram, Rearing, Metal Stand, 10 ½ x 11 ¼ In. 4680.00

Statue, Roman Statesman, Rouge, Honey, White, c.1950, 35 In. 720.00

Statue, Seminude Woman, Seated, Holding Flower, Carrara, Alabaster, c.1900, 23 x 13 In. 1800.00

Statue, Standing Child Angel, Crossed Arms, American School, c.1850, 42 ½ In. *Illus* 5079.00

Statue, Three Graces, Oval Base, 20 x 13 In. 540.00

Statue, Venus, Partly Draped, Gray Base, White, c.1890, 54 ¾ In. 8400.00

Statue, Virgin, Child, Cherubs, Italy, c.1850, 31 x 12 ½ In. 210.00

Statue, Woman, Flower Garland, White, Signed A. Piazza, Italy, c.1890, 31 x 14 In. 1020.00

Statue, Woman, Nude, Holding Cloth, Tree Trunk, Round Stand, 26 In. 1680.00

Statue, Woman, Nude, Kneeling, Flowing Hair, White, 1900s, 33 x 19 x 17 In. 3000.00

Statue, Woman, On Barrel, With Wine Glass, Ewer, 21 In. 300.00

Statue, Woman, Standing, Sheer Gown, c.1885, 31 ½ In. 1180.00

Tazza, Black, Rouge Marble Accents, Scroll Support, Flared Rim, Belgium, c.1900, 9 x 7 In. 120.00

Urn, Black, Variegated, Bronze Rim & Pedestal, 20 In., Pair *Illus* 295.00

Urn, Dome Lid, Louis XVI Style, Ram's Head Handles, Bronze Mounts, 14 ¾ In., Pair 750.00

Urn, Lid, French Empire Style, Bronze Mounts, Acorn Finial, Swan Handles, c.1900, 20 In., Pair 570.00

Urn, Lid, Gilt Bronze Mounts, France, 21 ½ x 10 In., Pair *Illus* 2700.00

Urn, Lid, Louis XVI Style, Leaves, Berries, Gilt Mounts, Leaf Handles, c.1900, 27 3/34 In., Pair 5625.00

Urn, Lid, Louis XVI Style, Ram's Head Handles, Hoof Feet, Gilt Bronze Mounts, 24 In., Pair 6875.00

Urn, Louis XVI Style, Gilt Bronze Scrolled Swags, Handles, Drilled For Lamp, 20 In., Pair 1250.00

Urn, Neoclassical, Belted Bell Shape, Square Base, White, 22 x 15 ½ In., Pair 2340.00

MARBLEHEAD POTTERY was founded in 1905 by Dr. J. Hall as a rehabilitative program for the patients of a Marblehead, Massachusetts, sanitarium. Two years later it was separated from the sanitarium and it continued operations until 1936. Many of the pieces were decorated with marine motifs.

Jar, Lid, Geometric Pattern, Oatmeal Glaze, M. Milner, S. Tutt, 5 ½ x 5 In. 13750.00

Tile, Fish, Brown, Blue Whiplash Currents, Green Speckled Matte Ground, c.1920, 6 x 6 In. 3776.00

Tile, Flower Basket, Blue, Yellow, Red Flowers, Green Leaves, Oak Frame, Impressed, 4 ½ In. 288.00

Tile, Ship, Tan, Yellow Ground, Frame, Signed, 17 In. 1750.00

Trivet, Tile, Rooster, Ship Mark, ⅝ x 5 In. 313.00

Vase, 3 Stylized Birds In Medallions, Incised, Green Glaze, Tapered, 1920s, 6 x 4 In. 2000.00

Vase, Blue Matte Glaze, Cylinder Shape, Impressed, 4 x 7 In. 406.00

Vase, Blue Matte Glaze, Stylized Branches, Leaves, Berries, Round, Tapered, 5 x 4 ½ In. 1500.00

Vase, Blueberry Wreath Band, Gray, Bulbous, Squat Shape, Marked, 3 ⅛ x 5 ½ In. 1093.00

Vase, Flowers, Carved, Stone Gray Ground, Squat, Ship Mark, 3 ¾ x 4 ½ In. 625.00

Vase, Fruit Trees, Oatmeal Glaze, Swollen, A. Hennessey, S. Tutt, 7 x 4 In. 5000.00

Vase, Geometric Banding, Cylindrical, Green, Marked, 6 In. 4370.00

Vase, Geometric Design, Green, Rounded Bottom, Bell Shape, Ring Foot, 1920s, 6 x 5 ¼ In. 6250.00

Vase, Green Matte, Tapered, Wide Rim, 3 ⅝ In. 359.00

Vase, Green, Brown, Yellow Mottled Matte Glaze, Tapered, 4 x 6 ¾ In. 469.00

Vase, Indigo Matte Glaze, Ship Mark, 8 ¾ x 6 In. 500.00

Vase, Leaves, Pinecones, Matte Glaze, Cylindrical, Folded In Rim, c.1925, 11 In. 7500.00

Vase, Peaches, Green Glaze, Tapered, Arthur Hennessey, 1920s, 4 x 3 ½ In. 1875.00

Vase, Prairie Flowers, Yellow, Round Square Shape, Marked, 4 ⅜ In. 1093.00

Vase, Stylized Flowers, Incised, Blue Glaze, M. Milner, S. Tutt, 8 ¾ x 4 In. 3125.00

Vase, Stylized Flowers, Incised, Tapered, Squat, Flared Rim, Ship Mark, 4 x 4 In. 1500.00

Vase, Stylized Fruit Trees, Green, Blue, Brown, Tan Ground, Hennessey, Tutt, Paper Label, 7 In. 9145.00

Vase, Stylized Trees, Glazed, 8 ½ x 9 In. *Illus* 5313.00

Vase, Yellow Roses, Blue Glaze, Tapered, 1920s, 3 ¾ x 3 ½ In. 1188.00

Wall Pocket, Green Matte Glaze, Bulbous, Tapered, 5 x 5 In. 219.00

Marble, Swirl, Divided Core, Orange, Green, White, 3 In.
$28,200.00

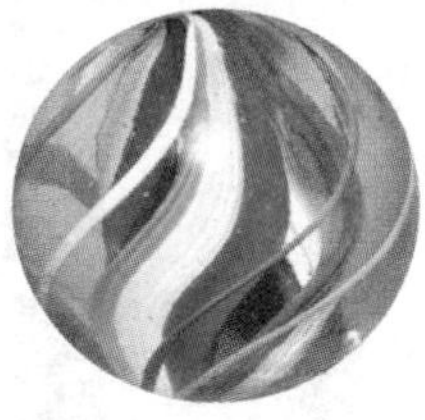

Morphy Auctions

Marble Carving, Bust, Carmen, Emmanuel Villanis, Pedestal, Signed, 39 In.
$1,610.00

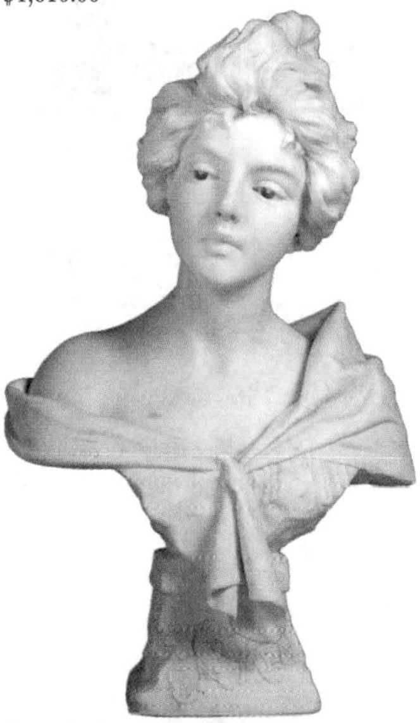

Cottone Auctions

Marble Carving, Bust, Gentleman, Beard, Incised, Franklin Simmons Sculptor Roma 1871, 28 x 20 In.
$2,000.00

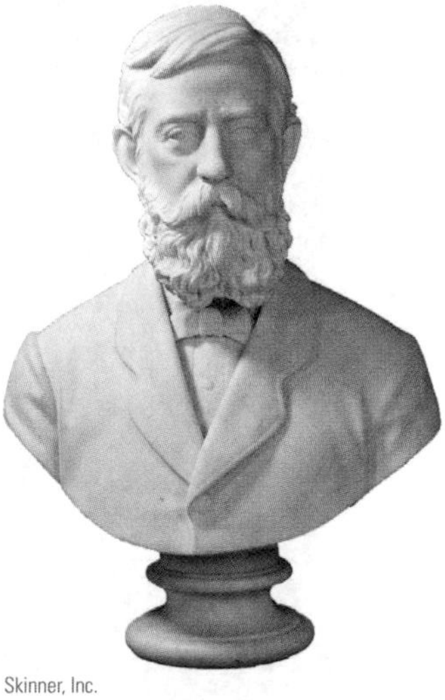

Skinner, Inc.

M

Marble Carving, Obelisk, Monument, Inlaid Marble, Pedestal Base, Continental, 21 In., Pair
$1,464.00

Neal Auction Co.

Marble Carving, Statue, Harem Dancer, Patinated Bronze, A. Gory, 28 ¼ In.
$10,030.00

Brunk Auctions

Marble Carving, Statue, Our Lady Of Everlasting Help, Virgin Mary, Christ Child, Carrara, c.1950, 66 In.
$3,198.00

New Orleans Auction Galleries, Inc.

MARTIN BROTHERS of Middlesex, England, made Martinware, a salt-glazed stoneware, between 1873 and 1915. Many figural jugs and vases were made by the three brothers. Of special interest are the fanciful birds, usually made with removable heads. Most pieces have the incised name of the artists plus other information on the bottom.

Creamer, Starfish, 1872, 3 x 2 ½ In.	189.00
Pitcher, Incised, Slip Leaf, Branch, Blue, Gray, Cream, Cylinder, c.1880, 8 ¾ x 2 ½ In.	240.00
Pitcher, Leaves, Branches, Tall, Modeled, Incised, Slip Glaze, 1800s, 8 ¾ x 2 ½ In.	240.00
Pitcher, Salt Glazed, Cobalt Blue Vines, Old English Letter J, Incised, c.1890, 8 In. ......*Illus*	510.00
Tile, Bird, Stoneware, Unglazed, c.1890, 8 ½ In.	7560.00
Tobacco Jar, Bird, On Stand, Glazed Stoneware, Signed, Dated, 1898, 10 x 4 In.	20160.00
Tobacco Jar, Bird, Salt Glazed, Enameled Wood, Signed, 1913, 9 x 3 ¾ In. ......*Illus*	36250.00
Vase, Birds, On Branches, 3 Chicks In Nest, Carved, Etched, Impressed, c.1885, 7 In.	1750.00
Vase, Butterfly, Flowers, Carved, Etched, Impressed, Marked, 8 ½ In.	1650.00
Vase, Butterfly, Flowers, Incised, 1898, 5 ⅞ In.	605.00
Vase, Demons, Glazed Stoneware, Signed R.W. Martin Bros., 1901, 8 x 4 In.	17640.00
Vase, Organic Shape, Stoneware, Modeled, Incised, Slip Glaze, Signed, 8 ½ x 2 ½ In.	330.00
Vase, Shouldered, Leaves, Flowers, Blue, Green, Footed, Signed, c.1900, 8 ½ x 2 ½ In.	330.00
Vase, Stoneware, Wading Bird, Raised, Brown Glazed Earthenware, 1894, 9 ½ In.	8125.00

MARY GREGORY is the name used for a type of glass that is easily identified. White figures were painted on clear or colored glass as the decoration. The figures chosen were usually children at play. The first glass known as Mary Gregory was made in about 1870. Similar glass is made even today. The traditional story has been that the glass was made at the Boston & Sandwich Glass Company in Sandwich, Massachusetts, by a woman named Mary Gregory. Recent research has shown that none was made at Sandwich. In fact, all early Mary Gregory glass was made in Bohemia. Beginning in 1957, the Westmoreland Glass Co. made the first Mary Gregory–type decorations on American glassware. These pieces had simpler designs, less enamel paint, and more modern shapes. France, Italy, Germany, Switzerland, and England, as well as Bohemia, made this glassware. Children standing, not playing, were pictured after the 1950s.

Bottle, Barber, Girl, Amethyst Glass, c.1900, 7 ¼ In.	120.00
Bottle, Barber, Girl, Cobalt Blue Glass, c.1900, 7 ½ In.	90.00
Bottle, Cologne, Blue, Enameled Children, Rib Optic, c.1895, 8 ½ In., Pair	258.00
Box, Hinged, Blue Ground, Ornate Brass Feet, Round, 6 In.	186.00
Country Basket, Cranberry, Clear Applied Handle, 8 In.	75.00
Decanter, Stopper, Boy, Flowers, Mountains, Enameled Green, Clear Loop Handle, 10 ½ In.	71.00
Decanter, Stopper, Cherub, Flowers, Enameled Blue, Teardrop Body, Flared Mouth, 10 In.	130.00
Pitcher, Boy, Fishing, Amethyst, 6 In.	65.00
Pitcher, Boy, In Knee Britches, Cranberry Glass, 9 In.	235.00
Pitcher, Girl On Swing, Amethyst, 6 In.	66.00
Pitcher, Green, Girl, Boy, Clear Handles, 7 In., Pair	300.00
Powder Box, Lid, Child In White, Green, 3 ¾ x 4 In.	110.00
Scent Box, Bottles, Girl, Flower, Beveled Cobalt Blue Glass, Gilt, 4 ½ x 5 In.	1200.00
Vase, Amber, Square, Tapered, Enameled Winged Fairies, Leaves, Gold Rim, Arched Base, 7 In., Pair	106.00
Vase, Boy, Fishing, Amethyst, 6 In.	60.00
Vase, Cranberry, Victorian Children, Scrolled Gilt Snail Feet, 7 In. ......*Illus*	575.00
Vase, Girl, On Swing, Amethyst, 6 In.	56.00
Vase, Green, Opalescent Figure, Cherub Playing Lyre, White Flowers, 7 x 3 ½ In.	84.00
Vase, Jack-In-The-Pulpit, Boy, Fishing, Cobalt Blue, 8 In.	60.00

MASONIC, *see Fraternal category.*

MASON'S IRONSTONE was made by the English pottery of Charles J. Mason after 1813. Mason, of Lane Delph, was given a patent for this improved earthenware. He usually called it *Mason's Patent Ironstone China.* It resisted chipping and breaking, so it became popular for dinnerware and other table service dishes. Vases and other decorative pieces were also made. The ironstone was decorated with orange, blue, gold, and other colors, often in Japanese-inspired designs. The firm had financial difficulties but the molds and the name *Mason* were used by many owners through the years, including Francis Morley, Taylor Ashworth, George L. Ashworth, and John Shaw. Mason's joined the Wedgwood group in 1973 and the name is still found on dinnerware.

Charger, Watteau, Man, Trees, Flowers, White, Brown Transfer, 15 In.	84.00
Cup & Saucer, Regency, Flowers, Blue, Demitasse	60.00
Pitcher, Luster, Multicolor, Oriental Taste, Flowers, Birds, Insects, 8 ¾ In.	86.00
Pitcher, Milk, Ribbed Rim, Red Willow, c.1900, 5 ½ In.	135.00
Plate, Niagara Falls, Maple Leaf Border, Transfer, Brown, 10 In.	45.00

Platter, Watteau, Brown, 14 In.	110.00
Thimble, Flowers, Blue, White Ground, Gilt, 1 In.	35.00

MASSIER, a French art pottery, was made by brothers Jerome, Delphin, and Clement Massier in Vallauris and Golfe-Juan, France, in the late nineteenth and early twentieth centuries. It has an iridescent metallic luster glaze that resembles the Weller Sicardo pottery glaze. Most pieces are marked J. Massier. Massier may also be listed in the Majolica category.

J.Massier fils

Bowl, Centerpiece, Shaped Rim, 4 Relief Flowers, Handles, Leaves, Scrolled Feet, c.1895, 9 x 18 In.	1304.00
Ewer, Stylized Leaf, Berry Design, Metallic Glaze, Wavy Rim, Delphin, 5 x 9 In.	33937.00
Jardiniere, Shaped Openwork Pedestal, 2 Bacchus Handles, Majolica, c.1884, 41 x 21 In.	1000.00
Vase, 4 Handles, Leaf Design, Metallic Glaze, Signed, 2 x 3 In.	250.00
Vase, Bulbous, Indented, Butterflies, Metallic, 4 In.	600.00
Vase, Butterfly, Deep Red Metallic Glaze, Bulbous, Jerome, 3 ½ x 4 In.	732.00
Vase, Flowers, Gold Iridescent Metallic Glaze, Tapered, c.1900, 5 ½ x 6 In.	1000.00
Vase, Flowers, Multicolor Metallic Glaze, Wing Handles, Round Base, 3 x 4 ½ In.	344.00
Vase, Green & Gold Iridescent Glaze, Tapered, 4 Naturalistic Handles, 10 x 6 In.	1000.00
Vase, Handle, Bulbous, Stylized Leaf & Berry Design, Metallic Glaze, 9 In.	325.00
Vase, Insect Design, Metallic Glaze, Tapered Square, Signed Clement, 3 ½ x 10 ¼ In.	1342.00
Vase, Leaf Designs, Brown Metallic Glaze, 4 Handles, Signed Clement, 2 x 3 In.	305.00
Vase, Leaf Designs, Rust Metallic Glaze, Indented Shape, Signed Clement, 2 ¼ x 2 ½ In.	275.00
Vase, Moorish, Baluster, 2 Handles, c.1900, 13 ¼ x 7 ½ In.	1188.00
Vase, Orchids, Iridescent, Tapered, c.1900, 12 x 6 ½ In.	1125.00
Vase, Stylized Flowers, Shouldered, Metallic Glaze, Signed Clement, 4 ½ x 5 ½ In.	732.00
Vase, Stylized Poppies, Red, Peach, Green Metallic Glaze, Bulbous, 3 ½ x 6 In.	438.00
Vase, Tapered, Underwater Vegetation, Metallic Glaze, 2 x 3 In.	275.00
Vase, Tapering Square Shape, Insect, Metallic Glaze, Signed, 10 ¼ In.	1100.00
Vase, Underwater Vegetation, Metallic Glaze, Tapered, Signed Clement, 2 ¾ x 3 In.	336.00

MATCH HOLDERS were made to hold the large wooden matches that were used in the nineteenth and twentieth centuries for a variety of purposes. The kitchen stove and the fireplace or furnace had to be lit regularly. One type of match holder was made to hang on the wall, another was designed to be kept on a tabletop. Of special interest today are match holders that have advertisements as part of the design.

Beetle, Metal, Striker On Bottom, Bradley & Hubbard, West Meriden, Conn., 2 x 3 ½ In.	392.00
Boot, Base, Metal, Woonsocket Boot Co., 3 x 2 x 1 In.	132.00
Boy, On Log, Yellowware, c.1885, 8 In.	75.00
Boy, Seated, Playing Guitar, Sitting On Stump, Matte Glaze, Johann Maresch, 12 ½ In.	115.00
Boy, Standing Against Hollow Tree Stumps, Oval Base, Ceramic, 5 ⅝ x 5 In.	12.00
Brick, Lime, Cement, Coal, Wood, Olney & Payne Bros., Nickel Plated, 4 x 5 ¼ In.	367.00
Cigar Holder, Pig, Table Top, Brass Cups, White Metal, 4 ¼ x 8 ½ In.	220.00
Colonial Men, Baskets, Trunk, Round Base, 6 x 7 ¼ In.	270.00
Cottage, Brass, 4 ¼ In.	90.00
Devil, Tail, Holding Bowl, On Wheels, Brass, Enamel, 1 ⅞ x 2 ¼ In.	385.00
Devil, Wheelbarrow Shape, Brass, Painted, Enamel Wheel Rims, 1 ⅞ x 2 ¼ x 4 ½ In. *Illus*	385.00
Dispenser, Feed One Match, Nickel Plated Cast Iron, Chain Design, Standard Mfg.	672.00
Dog, Hunting Cigar Well, Cast Iron, 4 ½ x 9 ½ In. *Illus*	270.00
Dog, Retriever, Hunting A Quail, Nickel Plated, Cast Iron, 10 x 3 ½ In.	270.00
Drinking Men, Barrel For Matches, Knapsack, For Corkscrew, Metal, Marble Base, 5 ½ x 6 ½ In.	83.00
Eagle, On Rocks, Match, Cigar, Cigarette Wells, Pot Metal, Paint, 7 x 8 In.	110.00
Farmer's Head, Wheat, Tools, Iron, 6 x 4 In.	154.00
Flowers, Longwy, Faience, 2 ½ In.	135.00
Frog, Embossed, Star Bicycles, Cast Iron, 4 In.	330.00
Gothic Winged Dragon, Brass, 3 x 7 x 7 In.	83.00
Hand Holding Goblet, Embossed, Drink Feigenspans Lager, Cast Iron, 5 x 3 ½ x 2 ¾ In. *Illus*	330.00
Hanging, Tole, Crimped Back, Multicolor, Flowers, Black Ground, Signed Ruth H. Wolf, 7 ½ x 4 In.	178.00
Hiker, Elf Style, Long Nose, Wood, Carved, Metal Holder On Back, Tray Base	56.00
Hyatt Jumbo Roofing, Elephant Shape, Bronze, Matches	230.00
Indian Head, Heart Shape Backboard, Wood, Painted, 12 In.	4063.00
Indian, Standing, Wearing Robe, Tree Stump, Canoe Ashtray, Multicolor, Austria, 8 ¾ In.	104.00
Jenny Lind, Glass, c.1876, 4 ½ In.	65.00
Lighter, Man, In Derby Hat, Cast Iron, 5 ¾ x 6 In.	330.00
Lobster, Yellowware, Striker In Lid, Impressed, 5 ½ In.	135.00
Man, Black, Quadruple Silver Plate, 3 Bowls, 7 ½ x 4 ½ In.	110.00
Man, Top Hat, Holding Well, Pine, Carved, Painted, c.1900, 10 In.	948.00
Man, Woman, Carrying Basket On Back, Tin, Cast Iron Plinth, Paint, c.1870, 13 In., Pair	390.00

Marble Carving, Statue, Standing Child Angel, Crossed Arms, American School, c.1850, 42 ½ In.
$5,079.00

Neal Auction Co.

Marble Carving, Urn, Black, Variegated, Bronze Rim & Pedestal, 20 In., Pair
$295.00

Brunk Auctions

M

Marble Carving, Urn, Lid, Gilt Bronze Mounts, France, 21 ½ x 10 In., Pair
$2,700.00

DuMouchelles Art Gallery

Marblehead, Vase, Stylized Trees, Glazed, 8 ½ x 9 In.
$5,313.00

Rago Arts & Auction Center

Martin Brothers, Pitcher, Salt Glazed, Cobalt Blue Vines, Old English Letter J, Incised, c.1890, 8 In.
$510.00

Cowan's Auctions

Martin Brothers, Tobacco Jar, Bird, Salt Glazed, Enameled Wood, Signed, 1913, 9 x 3 ¾ In.
$36,250.00

Rago Arts & Auction Center

Mary Gregory, Vase, Cranberry, Victorian Children, Scrolled Gilt Snail Feet, 7 In.
$575.00

Early Auction Co.

Match Holder, Devil, Wheelbarrow Shape, Brass, Painted, Enamel Wheel Rims, 1 ⅞ x 2 ¼ x 4 ½ In.
$385.00

Showtime Auction Sevices

Milwaukee Binders & Mowers, Tin Lithograph, Blue, White, 4 x 3 In.	358.00
No Flies On Green, Joyce & Co., Fly, Cast Iron, Hinged Wings, Paint, c.1900, 2 x 4 ½ In.	460.00
Painted, Multicolor, Shaped Back, Pa., c.1880, 15 ¼ x 5 In.	89.00
Shovel & Bucket Shape, Hanging, Metal, 9 x 3 In.	440.00
Striker, Boy, Black, Sitting On Cotton Bale, Jar, Majolica, 7 ½ x 4 ½ In.	119.00
Striker, Olney & Payne Bros., Brick, Lime, Cement, Coal, Wood, Nickel Plate, 4 x 5 ¼ In.	367.00
Turtle, Tailors Trimmings Chicago, Cast Iron, J.H. Lesher, 5 ½ x 3 In.	240.00

MATCH SAFES were designed to be carried in the pocket. Early matches were made with phosphorus and could ignite unexpectedly. The matches were safely stored in the tightly closed container. Match safes were made in sterling silver, plated silver, or other metals. The English call these "vesta boxes."

Bill Dugan Cigars, Man's Portrait, Celluloid, 1 ½ x 2 ¼ In.	248.00
Binder Twine, Viper Brand, Celluloid, Red, Green, White Ground, 2 ⅜ x 1 ½ In.	412.00
California Gold Quartz, 14K Gold, Inlaid, Diamond Pattern, 2 ¼ In.	7638.00
Cast Iron, Wood, Dayton Match Safe, Rectangular, 1890s	420.00
Celluloid, King Albert High Grade Cigars, 1 ½ x 2 ⅜ In. ....*Illus*	570.00
Cherry Brand Fine Chocolates & Bonbons, Celluloid, Gusset N.Y., 1 ½ x 2 ¾ In.	240.00
Christopher Columbus, Silver, 2 ⅝ x 1 ¾ x ⅞ In.	880.00
Elite Shoes, Looking For Your Business, Kitten, Celluloid, 2 ¾ x 1 ½ In.	231.00
Fire Design, Bakelite, Black, Eureka Forges Hose Co., 1 ¼ x 3 In.	193.00
German House Pure Rye Whiskey, Lee Mills Portrait, 1 ⅜ x 2 ¼ In.	220.00
Grants Head, Silvered Brass, 3 In.	306.00
Holland Society Cigars, Fiefer's Union 5 Cent Cigar, Celluloid, 1 ½ x 2 ¾ In.	83.00
Holland Society Cigars, Woman's Portrait, 1800s Attire, Celluloid, 1 ½ x 2 ¾ In.	83.00
Jaynell Co., Overalls, There Is No Match, Celluloid, 2 ⅞ x 1 ½ In.	198.00
Meyers, Hat Store, Lady, Topless, Holding Incense, 2 x 1 In.	231.00
Nelson's High Grade Confections, Baby, Box Of Candy, Reaching, 1 ½ x 2 ¼ In.	231.00
Pioneer White Lead Paint, Miner, Tools, Celluloid, Round, 1 ½ x 2 ¾ In.	825.00
Quick Meal Stoves, Factory, Celluloid, Ringen Stove Co., 1 ½ x 2 ⅝ In.	358.00
Rip Van Winkle, Kitties On Back, Celluloid, 1 ½ x 2 ¾ In. ....*Illus*	420.00
Sauer's Extracts, Celluloid, 2 ⅞ x 1 ½ In.	385.00
Turner, Crosby & Co., Shoe, Cream, 2 ⅝ x 1 ½ In.	303.00
World Injector, Celluloid, American Injector Co., Detroit, Mich., 2 ½ x 1 ⅜ In. ....*Illus*	165.00
Yellow Kid, Ranney Refrigerator Co., c.1905, 6 ½ In.	480.00

MATT MORGAN, an English artist, was making pottery in Cincinnati, Ohio, by 1883. His pieces were decorated to resemble Moorish wares. Incised designs and colors were applied to raised panels on the pottery. Shiny or matte glazes were used. The company lasted less than two years.

Vase, Blue, Black, Genie Bottle, Ring Foot, Marked, 12 ¼ In.	115.00
Vase, Moorish, Indigo Glaze, Gilt Trim, c.1883, 10 x 8 ½ In.	344.00
Vase, Moresque Style, Yellow, Gold, Red, Blue, Scrollwork, Bottle Shape, Marked, 18 ½ In.	489.00

McCOY pottery was made in Roseville, Ohio. Nelson McCoy and J.W. McCoy established the Nelson McCoy Sanitary and Stoneware Company in Roseville, Ohio, in 1910. The firm made art pottery after 1926. In 1933 it became the Nelson McCoy Pottery Company. Pieces marked McCoy were made by the Nelson McCoy Pottery Company. Cookie jars were made from about 1940 until December 1990, when the McCoy factory closed. Since 1991 pottery with the McCoy mark has been made by firms unrelated to the original company. Because there was a company named Brush-McCoy, there is great confusion between Brush and Nelson McCoy pieces. See Brush category for more information.

Bowl, Green, 9 In.	52.00
Cookie Jar, Clown, White, Green, Red, c.1945, 9 In.	64.00
Cookie Jar, Dog With Basket, Paws On Top, 12 ½ In.	23.00
Cookie Jar, Hound Dog, Red Tongue, Glossy Tan Glaze, 10 ½ In.	26.00
Cookie Jar, Log, Squirrel, 11 In.	75.00
Cookie Jar, Mammy, White Dress, Green Trim, Red Scarf, Cookies, Marked, 1948, 11 In.	140.00
Cookie Jar, Mammy, White Dress, Red Head Scarf, c.1920, 12 In.	210.00
Cookie Jar, Snow Bear, c.1965, 11 ½ In.	89.00
Cookie Jar, Spaniel In Doghouse, Cream, Blue Bird On Roof, 9 ½ In.	35.00
Cookie Jar, Teapot Shape, Pewter, Hammered, 9 In.	55.00
Figurine, Frog, Seated, Open Mouth, Green, 8 ½ x 14 In.	230.00
Jardiniere, Green, Round, Marked, 9 In.	69.00

M

Jardiniere, Lion, Lioness, Reclining, Brown Border, Green Ground, 9 ½ In.	431.00
Jardiniere, Pedestal, Brown, Green, Brush, 16 ½ In.	104.00
Jardiniere, Springwood Pattern, Mint Green, White Flowers, 6 ¾ x 8 ½ In.	125.00
Oil Jar, Sponged Maroon, White, Handles, 15 ¼ In.	46.00
Planter, Brown Onyx Glaze, Handles, c.1925, 6 x 8 ½ In.	64.00
Umbrella Stand, Loy-Nel-Art, Brown, Yellow Flower, Scalloped Rim, 21 ½ In.	127.00
Vase, Brown, Lined Handles, Waistband, 8 ¼ In.	17.00
Vase, Jeweled, Piped On Design, Bulbous Bottom, Trumpet Neck, Matte Green, 8 ½ In.	258.00
Vase, Magnolia, Pink, Green, c.1950, 8 In.	181.00
Vase, Vellum, Mottled Blue, Tapered, 8 ¼ In.	23.00
Washstand Set, Pitcher & Bowl, Blue & White, Marked.	165.00

McKEE is a name associated with various glass enterprises in the United States since 1836, including J. & F. McKee (1850), Bryce, McKee & Co. (1850 to 1854), McKee and Brothers (1865), and National Glass Co. (1899). In 1903, the McKee Glass Company was formed in Jeannette, Pennsylvania. It became McKee Division of the Thatcher Glass Co. in 1951 and was bought out by the Jeannette Corporation in 1961. Pressed glass, kitchenwares, and tablewares were produced. Jeannette Corporation closed in the early 1980s. Additional pieces may be included in the Custard Glass and Depression Glass categories.

Compote, Diamond, Vaseline, Wide Scallop, Hexagonal Faceted Stem, c.1880, 9 ½ x 10 In.	138.00
Compote, Feather Pattern, Lid, 1890s, 11 ½ In.	150.00
Cup & Saucer, Rock Crystal, Clear, Clear, Footed.	19.00
Pitcher, Rock Crystal, Clear, Squat, Scalloped Rim, 54 Oz., 7 ⅛ In.	239.00
Pitcher, Water, Orange Swirl, Ruffled Rim, c.1920, 8 ¼ In.	150.00
Plate, Rock Crystal, Clear, Scalloped Edge, 8 ⅜ In.	13.00
Vase, Rock Crystal, Cornucopia, Clear, 8 ½ In.	89.00

MECHANICAL BANKS *are listed in the Bank category.*

MEDICAL office furniture, operating tools, microscopes, thermometers, and other paraphernalia used by doctors are included in this category. Veterinary collectibles are also included here. Medicine bottles are listed in the Bottle category. There are related collectibles listed under Dental.

Apothecary Case, Georgian, Mahogany, Hinged Lid, Bottles, Contents, c.1810, 12 x 14 In.*Illus*	767.00
Bleeder, Brass, Engraved, Flowers, Leaves, Side Trigger, Steel Blade, Spring Pull, 1910, 1 ¾ In.	413.00
Box, Apothecary, Wood, Brass Bail Handles, Fitted Interior, 14 Glass Bottles, 9 ½ x 13 x 9 In.	1434.00
Box, Specimen, Black Forest, Carved, Hinged Lid, Standing Bear, Fitted Interior, c.1890, 14 x 13 In.	978.00
Bracket, Apothecary, Gothic Eagle, Ornate Scrolls, Black Enamel, Cast Iron, 3 x 10 x 15 In.	330.00
Bust, Phrenology, Ceramic, Painted Blue Border, Transferred Characteristics, L.N. Fowler, 12 x 6 In.	196.00
Cabinet, Apothecary, 2 Parts, Arched Panels, Glazed Doors, Pilasters, Drawers, c.1830, 75 x 52 In.	3081.00
Cabinet, Apothecary, 45 Drawers, Chinese, 56 ½ x 44 ½ In.	944.00
Cabinet, Apothecary, Cherry, Pine, 2 Glazed & 2 Paneled Doors, 16 Drawers, 89 In.	4270.00
Cabinet, Apothecary, Door, 24 Drawers, Scalloped Skirt, Green Paint, c.1850, 34 x 98 In.	26070.00
Cabinet, Apothecary, Hanging, 10 Drawers, Ocher, Red Stain, New England, c.1890, 16 x 16 ½ In.	1659.00
Cabinet, Apothecary, Mahogany, 2 Doors, Fitted Interior, 12 Bottles, 9 x 7 ¾ In.	216.00
Cabinet, Apothecary, Mahogany, Brass Handle, Fittings, Drawer, Bottles, Scale, c.1860, 7 x 6 In.	380.00
Cabinet, Apothecary, Mahogany, Hinged, 6 Drawers, 21 Bottles, Scale, c.1850, 8 x 8 x 9 In.	1186.00
Cabinet, Apothecary, Mahogany, Lift Top, Fitted Interior, Handles, c.1750, 13 ¼ x 10 ½ In.	1298.00
Cabinet, Apothecary, Pine, 12 Drawers, c.1920, 29 x 36 In.	148.00
Cabinet, Apothecary, Softwood, 9 Drawers, Porcelain Pulls, Red, Green Paint, c.1890, 19 x 12 In.	230.00
Cabinet, Apothecary, Vertical Hinged Doors, Niches, Drawers, Brass Handles, c.1820, 11 x 11 In.	660.00
Cabinet, Display, Booths Pure Drugs, c.1890, 27 x 25 In.	711.00
Cabinet, Oak, Tambour Door, Over 13 Drawers, Scrolled Supports, 36 x 49 In.	1925.00
Case, Apothecary, Mahogany, String Inlay, Fitted Interior, Bottles, c.1850, 12 ½ x 10 ¼ In.	826.00
Casket, Salesman's Sample, Pine, Fabric, Window, Portland Casket Co., Oregon, c.1925, 8 x 3 In.	825.00
Chest, Apothecary, 16 Small Drawers Over 3 Long Drawers, Porcelain Knobs, c.1890, 52 x 36 In.	660.00
Chest, Apothecary, 32 Drawers, Grain Paint, New Hampshire, c.1825, 78 x 36 In.	14888.00
Chest, Apothecary, 40 Drawers, Black Paint, c.1900, 30 x 30 In.	1116.00
Chest, Jujube Wood, Metal Fittings, Medicine Name Inscribed, Korea, 1900s, 66 x 56 In. *Illus*	1778.00
Chest, Ship's Doctor, Yellow Paint, Stencil, 16 ¼ x 22 ¼ In.	1534.00
Counter, Drug Store, Pharmacist's, Oak, Front Shelving, 18 Drawers, 90 x 52 ¼ In.	2200.00
Dryer, Hand, Face, Porcelain, Sani-Dri, 47 In.	248.00
First Aid Cabinet, Johnson's, Industrial, Sheet Steel Case, Wall Mount, Supplies, 11 ½ x 16 In.	47.00
Homeopathic Chemist's Set, Cased, Label, Joseph Marples, 6 x 11 In.	267.00
Leech Jar, Blown Glass, Green, Applied Base, Folded Rim, Lip, c.1840, 11 In.	1058.00

Match Holder, Dog, Hunting Cigar Well, Cast Iron, 4 ½ x 9 ½ In.
$270.00

Showtime Auction Sevices

Match Holder, Hand Holding Goblet, Embossed, Drink Feigenspans Lager, Cast Iron, 5 x 3 ½ x 2 ¾ In.
$330.00

Wm Morford Antiques

Match Safe, Celluloid, King Albert High Grade Cigars, 1 ½ x 2 ⅜ In.
$570.00

Showtime Auction Sevices

Match Safe, Rip Van Winkle, Kitties On Back, Celluloid, 1 ½ x 2 ¾ In.
$420.00

Showtime Auction Sevices

M

Match Safe, World Injector, Celluloid, American Injector Co., Detroit, Mich., 2 ½ x 1 ⅜ In.
$165.00

Wm Morford Antiques

Medical, Apothecary Case, Georgian, Mahogany, Hinged Lid, Bottles, Contents, c.1810, 12 x 14 In.
$767.00

Brunk Auctions

Medical, Chest, Jujube Wood, Metal Fittings, Medicine Name Inscribed, Korea, 1900s, 66 x 56 In.
$1,778.00

Skinner, Inc.

Model, Anatomic, Opens, Labels, Papier-Mache, Iron Base, Dr. Louis Auzoux, France, c.1883, 49 In.	10540.00
Mortar & Pestle, Pharmacy, Cast Bronze, Ornamented Sides, France, 1500s, 5 ½ In.	245.00
Pirate's Arm, Captain Hook's Hook, Leather, Canvas, Hand Rivets, c.1855	944.00
Poster, La Syphilis, Kissing Couple, Gap Tooth Smile Shadow, Theodoro, Paris, c.1926, 46 x 31 In.	450.00
Poster, Third Red Cross Roll Call, Woman, In Uniform, Haskell Coffin, Paper, Frame, 20 x 30 In.	311.00
Sample Case, Prosthetic Eyes, Dr. Snellen's Reform Eyes, 13 In.	1250.00
Sign, Apothecary, Trade, Ross Johnson Drug Co., Est. 1924, Jeweled, Glass, Electric, 34 x 24 In.	7200.00
Surgeon's Kit, Case, c.1880	862.00
Surgeon's Kit, Fitted Rosewood Case, Joseph Fenton, Columbus, Ohio, c.1860, 16 In.	999.00
Table, Metal, Cushion, Adjustable Base, c.1910, 26 x 58 In.	1560.00
Vampire Slaying Kit, Rosewood Box, Brass Banded, Hinged Lid, Contents, c.1900, 6 ½ x 20 In.	10000.00

MEISSEN is a town in Germany where porcelain has been made since 1710. Any china made in the town can be called Meissen, although the famous Meissen factory made the finest porcelains of the area. The crossed swords mark of the great Meissen factory has been copied by many other firms in Germany and other parts of the world. Pieces of Meissen dinnerware in the Onion pattern are listed in their own category in this book.

Bowl, Flowers, White Ground, Cut Corners, Crossed Swords Mark, c.1850, 8 ½ In.	384.00
Bowl, Fruit, Pierced, Basket Weave Molding, Fruit, Flowers, Gilt Rim, Oval, 12 ¼ x 9 In., Pair	529.00
Bowl, Reticulated, Cartouches, 2 Birds On Branch, Gilt Detail, Marked, 1800s, 12 In. Diam.	296.00
Bowl, Yellow, White, Gilt Flowers, Leaves, 11 In.	268.00
Box, Dome Lid, Finial, Flowers, Puce Accents, Yellow Ground, Scrolled Feet, 7 x 6 In.	313.00
Box, Hinged Top, Branch Shaped Handle, Figural Design, Gilt Highlights, Marked, c.1815, 3 ⅛ In.	127.00
Candelabrum, 7-Light, Seated Putti, Flowers, Trailing Vines, Tripartite Base, Marked, 22 In., Pair.	5080.00
Candlestick, Scrollwork Borders, Squirrel, Nut, Pierced Drip Pan, Gilt, c.1865, 4 ½ In., Pair.	369.00
Centerpiece, Basket, Blue, White, Reticulated, Tree, 1700s Attire, Scrolled Base, 20 x 13 In.	1375.00
Chocolate Pot, Yellow Ground, Pink Toile Scenic Reserves, Gilt Accents, 1800, 10 x 7 In.	270.00
Chop Plate, Rose Design, Marked, 13 ¼ In.	502.00
Clock, Mantel, Winged Scribe, Flowers, Rooster, Enameled Dial, Gilt Brass, 8-Day, c.1890, 12 In.. *Illus*	1094.00
Coffee Set, Demitasse, Painted, Pink Roses, Coffeepot, Sugar, Creamer, 6 Cups & Saucers, 15 Piece	600.00
Coffee Set, Swan Neck Handles, Baluster Shape, Pink Roses, Gilt, Marked, 10, 7 ¼, 5 In., 3 Piece.	173.00
Compote, Blue & White, Lattice Reticulated, Gilt Edges, Onion Design, c.1890, 8 ½ In., Pair.	738.00
Compote, Blue Onion, 2 Tiers, Standing Boy Finial, 16 x 10 ¼ In.	480.00
Compote, Gilt, Oval, Reticulated Basket, Boy, Girl Stem, Domed Foot, c.1935, 13 ¾ x 14 In.	1250.00
Dessert Stand, Blue & White, Blue Onion, Tiered, Lattice, Child, Flower Wreath, 16 x 9 ¾ In., Pair	1045.00
Dish, Condiment, Double Clam Shells, Seated Boy, Stirring Porridge, 6 ¾ x 9 ½ In.	1035.00
Dish, Pierced Lattice Edge, Rocaille Cartouches, Flowers, Round, 8 ½ x 2 ¾ In.	184.00
Figurine, Bacchus, Stag Head Loincloth, Raising Cup, Grape Basket, Multicolor, 5 ½ In.	920.00
Figurine, Bird, Perched On Leafy Stump, Black, Peach, White, Green, 12 ½ In.	649.00
Figurine, Bust, Allegorical, Girl, Summer, Boy, Winter, Symbols, 11 In., Pair	3000.00
Figurine, Cherub Tailor, Cutting Pink Cloth, Marked, 4 ½ In.	767.00
Figurine, Cupid Forging Heart, Anvil, 7 x 3 In.	295.00
Figurine, Cupid, Holding Arms Aloft, Quiver, Multicolor, Gilt, 8 ¼ In.	817.00
Figurine, Emblematic Of Autumn, Women In Dress, Holding Shawl, 1920s, 6 ¾ In.	535.00
Figurine, Girl, Holding Basket, Marked, c.1905, 5 In.	662.00
Figurine, Girl, Lawn Bowling, Flowing Brown Hair, Lavender Robe, c.1900, 11 ¾ In.	920.00
Figurine, Girl, Standing, Holding Plant, Kitten At Feet, Round Base, Marked, 7 ⅞ In.	3810.00
Figurine, Golden Oriole, Tree Trunk, Flowers, Closed Wings, Yellow, Black, c.1900, 10 In., Pair	861.00
Figurine, Harlequin Playing Bagpipes, On Cairn, Tricorner Hat, Breeches, Kaendler, c.1737, 4 ¾ In..	767.00
Figurine, Hound, Reclining, Blanc De Chine, 1800s, 18 In.	948.00
Figurine, Kneeling Miner, Ax, Lantern, Incised P. Berger, 1943, 15 ½ In. *Illus*	1125.00
Figurine, Maidens, With Cupid, Blanc De Chine, 1800s, 12 ½ In., Pair	577.00
Figurine, Man, Dancing, Multicolor, Flower Garland, Crossed Swords Mark, c.1950, 6 ½ In.	590.00
Figurine, Man, Seated At Desk, Period Attire, 7 In.	396.00
Figurine, Man, With Fruit, Woman, With Apron Of Flowers, Crossed Swords, 11 In., Pair	3068.00
Figurine, Military Officer, Green Coast, Pants, Tricolor Hat, c.1860, 7 ¾ In.	403.00
Figurine, Monkey, Seated On Tree Stump, Holding Fruits, 13 x 8 In.	738.00
Figurine, Parrot, Multicolor, Perched On Trunk, Cherry Design, 12 In.	2159.00
Figurine, Putti, Binding 2 Hearts Together, Column, Triangular Base, 5 ½ In.	699.00
Figurine, Seated Woman, Tending To Bird, Emerging From Cage, Senses Series, Marked, 5 ¾ In.	625.00
Figurine, Shot Putter, White, c.1936, 12 ¾ In.	360.00
Figurine, Te Les Punis, You Punish Them, Cherub, Breaking Hearts With Hammer, 5 ⅝ In.	584.00
Figurine, Woman Card Player, Wide Hat, Table, Crossed Swords Mark, 6 ½ In.	1150.00
Figurine, Woman Of Fashion, Holding Bible, Seated, Tabletop Spinning Wheel, Marked, 7 x 7 ½ In.	676.00
Figurine, Woman Of Fashion, Seated, Tatting, Reticulated Base, Marked, c.1840, 5 x 3 In.	522.00

Meissen, Clock, Mantel, Winged Scribe, Flowers, Rooster, Enameled Dial, Gilt Brass, 8-Day, c.1890, 12 In.
$1,094.00

Skinner, Inc.

Meissen, Figurine, Kneeling Miner, Ax, Lantern, Incised P. Berger, 1943, 15 ½ In.
$1,125.00

Leslie Hindman Auctioneers

Meissen, Figurine, Woman, Gathering Flowers, Basket, Sickle, Blue Crossed Swords, c.1890, 7 In.
$540.00

Skinner, Inc.

Meissen, Group, Good Father, Seated Man, Settee, Children, Dog, Enamel, Gilt, 1800s, 7 ⅞ In.
$3,500.00

Skinner, Inc.

Meissen, Group, Maidens, Children, Pulling Net, Porpoises, Shells, Plants, Marked, 12 ¾ In.
$2,040.00

Meissen, Mirror, Putti & Crown Portrait Crest, Applied Flowers, Bird, Marked, 33 x 19 In.
$2,540.00

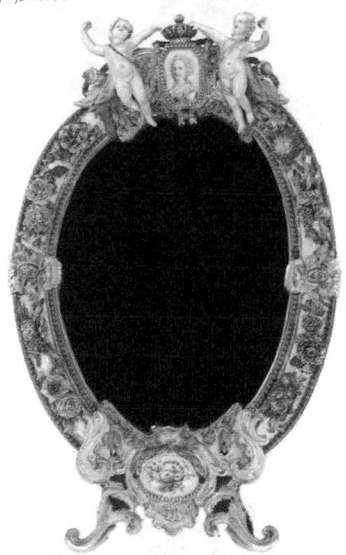

Leslie Hindman Auctioneers

Cowan's Auctions

M

385

Meissen, Tureen, Lid, Grape Cluster, Leaf Undertray, Grape Leaf Handle, Snail Finial, c.1880, 7 In.
$780.00

Cowan's Auctions

Meissen, Vase, Snowball, Applied Fruit, Nuts, Birds, 19th Century, 14 ½ In., Pair
$3,335.00

Cottone Auctions

Merrimac, Vase, Gunmetal Drip Glaze, 3 Handles, Stamped, 3 ½ x 5 In.
$3,000.00

Rago Arts & Auction Center

Merrimac, Vase, Watermelon Rind Glaze, Green, Impressed Sturgeon Pottery Mark, c.1910, 6 ½ In.
$1,304.00

Skinner, Inc.

Figurine, Woman Playing Piano, 18th Century Gown, Lace Headdress, 4 ¾ x 3 ½ In.		1062.00
Figurine, Woman, Gathering Flowers, Basket, Sickle, Blue Crossed Swords, c.1890, 7 In. ....*Illus*		540.00
Figurine, Woman, Seated, Long Dress, Bird In Cage, Shaped Square Base, c.1900, 5 ¾ In.		508.00
Figurine, Woman, Standing, Lace Hat, Reading Letter, 8 In.		424.00
Group, 2 Cherubs, Arrows, Tree, Cupid's Forge, 8 In.		224.00
Group, 2 Gardeners, Vegetables, Flowers, Marked, c.1905, 7 In.		1020.00
Group, 3 Cherubs, Drawing Water From Well, Multicolor, c.1780, 8 ½ x 7 In.		546.00
Group, 3 Classical Muses, Draping Flowers On Cow, Marked, c.1915, 8 ¾ In.		1560.00
Group, 5 Child Musicians, 4 Instruments, Marked, c.1870, 7 ¼ In.		1800.00
Group, Apple Pickers, Mother, 3 Children, 1 In Tree, 11 In.		1320.00
Group, Blackamoor, Rearing Horse, Inscribed, 1900s, 16 ¼ In.		3360.00
Group, Boreas & Oreithyi, 9 ¼ In.		322.00
Group, Broken Bridge, Man Helping Woman Cross Plank, Flowers, Cupid, 9 ¼ x 6 ½ In.		1955.00
Group, Capture Of The Triton, 2 Nymphs, Putto, Fishing Net, Rockwork Base, 11 In.		1800.00
Group, Children Dancing, c.1880, 5 ¾ In.		948.00
Group, Couple Dancing, 18th Century Formal Attire, c.1875, 7 ½ In.		1380.00
Group, Couple, Children, Picking Apples, Marked, c.1900, 10 ½ In.		900.00
Group, Couple, Holding Baby, On Bench, Rococo Style, c.1875, 9 ½ x 6 x 7 In.		1353.00
Group, Courting Couple, Boy, 1700s Attire, Flower Garlands, Rock Pedestal, c.1900, 7 ½ In.		1500.00
Group, Courting Couple, Putti In Tree, Crossed Swords Mark, 7 x 6 ½ In.		978.00
Group, Father Time, Cherubs, On Clouds, Bellows, Peacock, Blue, White, c.1900, 8 ⅞ In.		1375.00
Group, Flora, Classical Woman, Putto, Flower Basket, c.1900, 10 ¾ In.		1080.00
Group, Girl With Goat, Basket Of Fruit, Crossed Swords Mark, 5 ¾ x 4 ½ In.		1035.00
Group, Good Father, Seated Man, Settee, Children, Dog, Enamel, Gilt, 1800s, 7 ⅞ In.......*Illus*		3500.00
Group, Good Mother, Seated, 3 Children, Gilt Details, Marked, c.1850, 9 In.		3645.00
Group, Laendliches Fest, Children, Cherubs, Mandolin, Marked, c.1860, 14 ½ In.		7800.00
Group, Leda, Swan, Seated On Tree Trunk, Purple Cloak, Flowers, Cherub, 6 ¾ In.		1375.00
Group, Maidens, Children, Pulling Net, Porpoises, Shells, Plants, Marked, 12 ¾ In. ....*Illus*		2040.00
Group, Man, Woman, 1700s Attire, 5 x 5 In.		800.00
Group, Satyr Releasing Bird, Girl With Cage, Marked, c.1910, 6 ½ In.		840.00
Group, Satyr Squeezing Grapes, Nymph, 2 Young Satyrs, 9 ½ x 8 In.		978.00
Group, Shepherd & Sheep, Crook, Knitting Needles, Mile Marker, c.1950, 17 In.		1440.00
Group, Unrequited Love, Couple, Garlands, Woman, Spilled Flower Basket, c.1820, 13 x 8 In.		2124.00
Group, Woman Playing Lute, Male Admirers, c.1875, 10 ¼ In.		1380.00
Mirror, Dressing, Putti Finial, Flowers, 13 x 10 In., Pair		1659.00
Mirror, Putti & Crown Portrait Crest, Applied Flowers, Bird, Marked, 33 x 19 In..........*Illus*		2540.00
Plate, Painted Flowers, Gilt, White Ground, Shell Shape, 9 ¾ In., Pair		750.00
Plate, Yellow Dragon, 2 Cocks, Dragon Border, 9 ¼ In., 12 Piece		673.00
Platter, Blue & White, Serpentine Shape, Raised Rim, Flowers & Insects, Marked, c.1800, 15 x 20 In.		522.00
Platter, Tulip, White Ground, Oval, Hausmalerei Mark, 18 ½ In.		590.00
Teapot, Lid, Gilt Edge Harbor Scenes, Yellow Ground, 3 ¼ In.		1003.00
Toothbrush Holder, White, Blue, Cylindrical, Scalloped Top, 4 x 3 In.		25.00
Tray, Pink, Yellow Flowers, Scrolls, Parcel Gilt Handles, Trim, c.1880, 16 x 16 In.		420.00
Tureen, Chicken Shape, Chicks Nestled In Feathers, Multicolor, Marked, 1800s, 6 ½ x 8 ½ In.		1020.00
Tureen, Lid, Grape Cluster, Leaf Undertray, Grape Leaf Handle, Snail Finial, c.1880, 7 In. ....*Illus*		780.00
Urn, Lid, Armorial, Putti Handles, Scrolled Cartouche, Flower Garlands, 16 In.		2588.00
Urn, Lid, Fruit, Flowers, Putti, Floral Finial, Marked, 11 ¼ In., Pair		1534.00
Urn, Potpourri, Country Maid, Cherub, Basket Of Grapes, Basket Weave, Bird Finial, 12 ½ In.		1179.00
Urn, Yellow, Elongated, Double Snake Handles, Fluted Spread Foot, Marked, c.1900, 15 ½ In., Pair		1107.00
Vase, Baluster, Applied Flowers, Marked, 15 In.		1250.00
Vase, Lid, Handle, Cream Ground, Gilt Accents, Multicolor Courting Scenes, 1800s, 5 ⅝ In.		738.00
Vase, Snowball, Applied Fruit, Nuts, Birds, 19th Century, 14 ½ In., Pair ....*Illus*		3335.00
Vase, Stem, Figural, Boy, Holding Dog, Dog Barking Up Tree, Germany, c.1875, 7 ¾ In.		1150.00
Wine Trolley, Rococo Style, Revolving Wheels, Reticulated, Marked, c.1865, 6 ½ x 10 In.		246.00

MERCURY GLASS, or silvered glass, was first made in the 1850s. It lost favor for a while but became popular again about 1910. It looks like a piece of silver.

Ball, Pedestal, Embossed Faux Bois Terra-Cotta, c.1920, 45 x 19 In.		420.00
Dish, Leaf Shape, 10 x 8 ½ In.		111.00
Jar, Diagonal Swirl, Rimmed Lip, 19th Century, 5 ½ In.		220.00
Ornament, Elephant, 1930s, 4 In.		95.00
Tieback Knobs, Drapery Pewter Collar, Screw Base, Etched Grapes, Vines, 44 x 3 In., Pair		23.00
Vase, Bird In Flight, Footed, Flared Rim, c.1850, 12 ¾ In.		275.00
Vase, Engraved Flowers, Cylindrical, 20 x 5 In., Pair		120.00

M

MERRIMAC POTTERY

MERRIMAC POTTERY Company was founded by Thomas Nickerson in Newburyport, Massachusetts, in 1902. The company made art pottery, garden pottery, and reproductions of Roman pottery. The pottery burned to the ground in 1908.

Vase, Gunmetal Drip Glaze, 3 Handles, Stamped, 3 ½ x 5 In.....................*Illus*	3000.00
Vase, Watermelon Rind Glaze, Green, Impressed Sturgeon Pottery Mark, c.1910, 6 ½ In...*Illus*	1304.00
Vase, Yellow, Green Drip Glaze, Bulbous, Impressed, 9 x 9 ¾ In................................	6250.00

METLOX POTTERIES was founded in 1927 in Manhattan Beach, California. Dinnerware was made beginning in 1931. Evan K. Shaw purchased the company in 1946 and expanded the number of patterns. Poppytrail (1946–89) and Vernonware (1958–80) were divisions of Metlox under E.K. Shaw's direction. The factory closed in 1989.

Antique Grape, Bowl, Cereal, 7 ⅜ In................................	13.00
Antique Grape, Gravy Boat, Underplate................................	21.00
Antique Grape, Plate, Dinner, 10 ½ In................................	19.00
Antique Grape, Teapot, Lid, Loop Finial, 4 Cup, 5 ⅜ In................................	50.00
California Ivy, Bowl, Vegetable, Divided, Oval, 11 ¼ In................................	26.00
California Ivy, Celery Dish, 12 In................................	37.00
California Ivy, Cup & Saucer................................	13.00
California Ivy, Mug, Brown Handle, 3 ½ In................................	59.00
California Ivy, Plate, Crescent Shape, 7 ⅛ In................................	43.00
California Ivy, Plate, Dinner, 10 ⅜ In................................	20.00
California Strawberry, Gravy Boat, Underplate................................	16.00
California Strawberry, Pitcher, 8 In................................	30.00
California Strawberry, Plate, Bread & Butter, 6 ½ In................................	11.00
California Strawberry, Salt & Pepper, Green................................	19.00
Cookie Jar, Bear, Sombrero, Fringed Serape, 14 In................................	75.00
Della Robbia, Bowl, Cereal, 7 ¼ In................................	11.00
Della Robbia, Butter, Cover, ¼ Lb................................	28.00
Della Robbia, Plate, Salad, 7 ⅝ In................................	12.00
Fruit Basket, Casserole, Lid, 1 ¼ Qt................................	29.00
Fruit Basket, Jam Dish, Divided, 8 ⅜ In................................	18.00
Fruit Basket, Soup, Dish, 8 ⅛ In................................	14.00
Fruit Basket, Tureen, Soup, Lid, Ladle................................	209.00
Gingham Green, Bowl, Cereal, 5 ¼ In................................	17.00
Gingham Green, Sauceboat, Round................................	16.00
Homespun, Bowl, Cereal, Lug Handles, 7 ½ In................................	19.00
Homespun, Bowl, Pint................................	33.00
Homespun, Chop Plate, 12 ¼ In................................	16.00
Homespun, Cup & Saucer................................	10.00
Homespun, Cup & Saucer, Demitasse................................	26.00
Homespun, Salt & Pepper................................	18.00
Homestead Provincial, Bowl, Vegetable, Divided, Green Handle, Rectangular, 8 ⅝ In.	22.00
Homestead Provincial, Bread Tray, 9 ½ In................................	34.00
Homestead Provincial, Plate, Dinner, 10 In................................	19.00
Homestead Provincial, Platter, Oval, 16 In................................	159.00
Homestead Provincial, Platter, Oval, 22 ½ In................................	356.00
Mayflower, Butter, Cover, ¼ Lb................................	110.00
Mayflower, Chop Plate, 12 In................................	19.00
Mayflower, Creamer, Pointed Handle, 3 ⅞ In.	17.00
Mayflower, Relish, 3 Sections................................	38.00
Mayflower, Saucer................................	5.00
Organdie, Butter Chip, 2 ½ In................................	74.00
Organdie, Chop Plate, 13 ¾ In................................	28.00
Organdie, Mug, 3 ½ In.	29.00
Organdie, Plate, Bread & Butter, 6 ⅜ In................................	4.00
Organdie, Plate, Dinner, 10 ⅜ In................................	24.00
Organdie, Teapot, Lid, 5 Cup, 4 ¾ In................................	59.00
Peach Blossom, Plate, Bread & Butter, 6 In................................	8.00
Peach Blossom, Plate, Dinner, 10 ⅜ In................................	16.00
Peach Blossom, Plate, Dinner, Square, c.1952, 10 ⅜ In................................	21.00
Peach Blossom, Platter, Oval, 9 ⅜ In................................	36.00
Provincial Blue, Bread Tray, 9 ½ In................................	34.00
Provincial Blue, Casserole, Hen on Nest Cover, 7 ⅝ In................................	159.00
Provincial Blue, Creamer, 6 Oz., 3 ¼ In................................	13.00
Provincial Blue, Cup & Saucer................................	7.00

Mettlach, Celery Dish, Lid, Mosaic, Flowers, 8 x 3 In.
$230.00

Fox Auctions

Mettlach, Plaque, No. 148-1044, Neuschwanstein, 14 In.
$144.00

The Stein Auction Co.

Mettlach, Stein, No. 78, Ear Of Corn, 1 Liter
$3,450.00

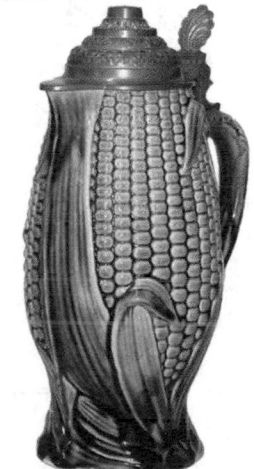

Fox Auctions

M

TIP
Some vintage and antique dishes have overglaze decorations that will eventually wear off. All gold trim is overglaze and could even wipe off a plate hot from the dishwasher.

Mettlach, Stein, No. 1104, Mosaic, Flowers, Inlaid Lid, 2 Liter
$345.00

Fox Auctions

Mettlach, Stein, No. 1530, Man Riding Old Style Bicycle, Print Under Glaze, ½ Liter
$1,955.00

Fox Auctions

Mettlach, Stein, No. 2001C, Scholar Book, Relief, Inlaid Lid, ½ Liter
$420.00

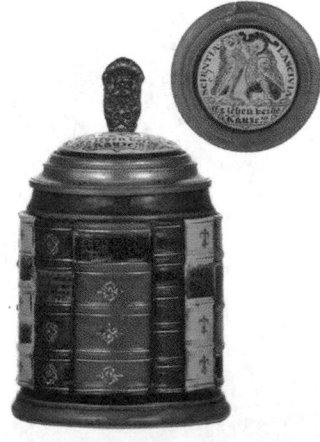

The Stein Auction Co.

Provincial Blue, Plate, Dinner, 10 In.		14.00
Provincial Blue, Tureen, Soup, Hen on Nest Cover, Ladle		799.00
Provincial Fruit, Bread Tray, 9 ½ In.		36.00
Provincial Fruit, Plate, Dinner, Green, 10 ½ In.		10.00
Provincial Fruit, Relish, 3 Sections, 16 In.		22.00
Red Rooster, Chop Plate, 12 ¼ In.		22.00
Red Rooster, Creamer, 3 ⅛ In.		16.00
Red Rooster, Cup & Saucer		20.00
Red Rooster, Dish, Hen On Nest Cover, 5 ⅝ In.		56.00
Red Rooster, Plate, Dinner, 10 In.		18.00
Red Rooster, Platter, Oval, 22 ⅞ In.		379.00
Sculptured Daisy, Creamer, 8 Oz., 3 ¼ In.		7.00
Sculptured Daisy, Cup & Saucer		8.00
Sculptured Daisy, Plate, Dinner, 10 ⅝ In.		15.00
Sculptured Grape, Bowl, Cereal, Rim, 7 ⅜ In.		14.00
Sculptured Grape, Bowl, Fruit, Rim, 6 ⅜ In.		9.00
Sculptured Grape, Cup & Saucer		8.00
Sculptured Grape, Plate, Dinner, 10 ⅝ In.		21.00
Sculptured Grape, Platter, Oval, 9 ½ In.		30.00
Sculptured Zinnia, Bowl, Cereal, 7 ⅜ In.		11.00
Sculptured Zinnia, Bowl, Vegetable, Round, 9 ⅝ In.		27.00
Tickled Pink, Gravy Boat		18.00
Tickled Pink, Platter, Oval, 11 In.		12.00
Tickled Pink, Salt & Pepper		22.00
Vernon Antiqua, Bowl, Nut, Handle		30.00
Vernon Antiqua, Bowl, Vegetable, Divided, Round, 10 ⅝ In.		16.00
Vernon Antiqua, Mug, 3 ¾ In.		50.00
Vineyard, Creamer, 3 ¾ In.		9.00
Vineyard, Plate, Dinner, 10 ⅞ In.		18.00
Vineyard, Saucer		4.00
Woodland Gold, Casserole, Lid, Round, Stick Handle, 1 ½ Qt.		31.00
Woodland Gold, Chop Plate, 13 In.		30.00
Woodland Gold, Cup & Saucer		8.00
Woodland Gold, Pitcher, 5 ⅜ In.		28.00
Woodland Gold, Salt & Pepper		18.00
Woodland Gold, Soup, Dish, 6 ¾ In.		12.00
Woodland Gold, Teapot, Lid, 5 Cup, 5 ½ In.		36.00

METTLACH, Germany, is a city where the Villeroy and Boch factories worked. Steins from the firm are marked with the word *Mettlach* or the castle mark. They date from about 1842. *PUG* means painted under glaze. The steins can be dated from the marks on the bottom, which include a date-number code. Other pieces may be listed in the Villeroy & Boch category.

Beaker, No. 2327-1141, Cavalier, Girl, Schlitt, ¼ Liter		58.00
Beaker, No. 2368-1091, Boy, Serving Tray, ¼ Liter		24.00
Celery Dish, Lid, Mosaic, Flowers, 8 x 3 In.	*Illus*	230.00
Pitcher, No. 2085-15, Sanitary Top, Footed, Green, Cream, Rust Brown, 15 In.		162.00
Plaque, Castles, Cliff, Embossed, c.1900, 17 ½ In., Pair.		480.00
Plaque, No. 134/1044, Bei Odde, 14 In.		132.00
Plaque, No. 148-1044, Neuschwanstein, 14 In.	*Illus*	144.00
Plaque, No. 1044, Cavaliers, Painted, 17 In.		540.00
Plaque, No. 1044-129, Nurnberg Henkersteg, 12 In.		69.00
Plaque, No. 1044-168, Dresden Bruhlsche Terrasse, 12 In.		106.00
Plaque, No. 2013, Prussian Eagle, 27 In.		6000.00
Punch Bowl, Lid, Drinking Gnome Scenes, Scrolled Handles, Gilt, c.1900, 15 In.		300.00
Stein, No. 78, Ear Of Corn, 1 Liter	*Illus*	3450.00
Stein, No. 400, Bavaria, Pewter Lid, 2 ½ Liter		360.00
Stein, No. 621, Hunter, Relief Pewter, PUG, ½ Liter		168.00
Stein, No. 956, Picnic On Grass, PUG, H. Schlitt, 2 Liter		252.00
Stein, No. 966, Children, Horn, PUG, Inlaid Lid, ½ Liter		340.00
Stein, No. 983, PUG, Falstaff, Pewter Lid, ⅓ Liter		480.00
Stein, No. 1104, Mosaic, Flowers, Inlaid Lid, 2 Liter	*Illus*	345.00
Stein, No. 1530, Man Riding Old Style Bicycle, Print Under Glaze, ½ Liter	*Illus*	1955.00
Stein, No. 1724, Fireman, Etched, Inlaid Lid, ½ Liter		1380.00
Stein, No. 1909-1196, Flowers, Art Nouveau, ½ Liter		173.00
Stein, No, 1932, Toasting Cavaliers, Pewter Rim, Thumb Lift, Elf & Beer, Signed Warth, ½ Liter		270.00
Stein, No. 2001C, Scholar Book, Relief, Inlaid Lid, ½ Liter	*Illus*	420.00

Stein, No, 2050, Henpecked Husband, Shell & Mask Thumb Lift, Roy C. De Selms, ½ Liter	1200.00
Stein, No. 2091, St. Florian, Castle Mark, c.1900	450.00
Stein, No. 2106, Monkeys In Cage, Inlaid Lid, ½ Liter ....*Illus*	4320.00
Stein, No. 2140-941, Beer Barometer, Schlitt, ½ Liter	46.00
Stein, No. 2192, Student Joke, Etruscan Style, Etched, Inlaid Pewter Lid, Signed H. Schlitt, 9 ½ In.	325.00
Stein, No. 2235, Barmaid, Raised Glass, Inlaid Lid, ½ Liter	575.00
Stein, No. 2277, Lion, Shield, Inlaid Lid, ½ Liter	1170.00
Stein, No. 2382, Thirsty Knight, Etched, Molded Lid, Signed H. Schlitt, 9 In.	295.00
Stein, No. 2722, Shoemaker, Etched, Glazed, ½ Liter	1560.00
Stein, No. 2889, Etched, Man On Horse, ½ Liter	216.00
Stein, No. 2900, Quilmes, Etched, Inlaid Lid, ½ Liter	240.00
Stein, No. 3043, Munich, Etched, Inlaid Pewter Lid, Marked, 7 In.	266.00
Stein, No. 3089, Socrates, PUG Style, Pewter Rim, Thumblift, Castle Mark, c.1900, 7 In.	390.00
Tureen, No. 5042, Boar's Head, Lid, Red Glaze, 13 x 10 In.	1200.00
Tureen, Undertray, No. 2806, Phanolith, Greek Figures, Handles, Lid, c.1900, 17 In.	201.00
Vase, Betty, Children On Branch, PUG, 12 ½ In. ....*Illus*	342.00
Vase, No. 2667, Flowers, Vines, 13 In.	2880.00
Vase, No. 267/2998, Woman, Print Under Glaze, Hand Painted, 12 ½ In. ....*Illus*	390.00

MILK GLASS was named for its milky white color. It was first made in England during the 1700s. The height of its popularity in the United States was from 1870 to 1880. It is now correct to refer to some colored glass as blue milk glass, black milk glass, etc. Reproductions of milk glass are being made and sold in many stores. Related pieces may be listed in the Cosmos, Vallerysthal, and Westmoreland categories.

Ashtray, Apple Blossom, Hazel Atlas, 1960s, 4 In., 6 Piece	60.00
Berry Bowl, Wild Rose, Indiana Glass, 1970s, 2 x 4 In.	12.00
Biscuit Jar, Embossed Shell, Hand Painted Enamel, Black Handle, Victorian, 11 In.	232.00
Bottle, Barber, Clover Design, Inscribed Toilet Water, c.1900, 9 In.	30.00
Bottle, Barber, Iris, Hand Painted, Inscribed Shampoo, Stopper, 9 ½ In.	90.00
Bottle, Barber, Poppies, Hand Painted, Inscribed Water, Stopper, 9 ½ In.	120.00
Bowl, Grape & Leaves, 8 Panels, Pedestal, Footed, Anchor Hocking, 9 ⅛ x 5 ⅜ In.	22.00
Cake Plate, 6-Sided, Red Arabesques, Red Edge Handles, c.1930, 11 In.	39.00
Candy Dish, Gilt Scalloped Edges, Feathering, Scrollwork, c.1900, 4 ½ x 8 ¾ In.	20.00
Compote, Grape, Pedestal, Scalloped Edge, 7 ⅜ x 10 ⅛ In.	65.00
Dish, Dove In Hand Lid, Marked Patented Aug. 1889 Under Lid, 6 x 8 In.	140.00
Dresser Box, Gold, Blue Highlights, Scrolling, Scalloped, Embossed, Convex Top, 4 ¼ x 2 ¼ In.	20.00
Goblet Set, Grape & Leaves, 5 ¼ x 3 ½ In., 5 Piece	18.00
Lampshade, Sports Figures, Painted, Squat, c.1910, 11 ¾ In.	207.00
Shaker, Grape & Leaves, Pear Shape, Footed, Pewter Top, c.1890, 3 ⅝ In.	40.00
Shaker, Owl Shape, 6 ¼ In.	45.00
Snack Set, Grapes & Leaves, Cup, Footed, Plate, Scalloped Edge, 8 Piece	15.00
Spooner, Moon & Stars, Pedestal, c.1900, 5 ¾ In.	26.00
Sugar & Creamer, Gilt Scroll & Heart, Beading, Oval, 4-Footed, 3 ¾ In.	65.00
Vase, Victorian, Brown Asian Design, 9 In., Pair	79.00
Witch's Ball, Blue & Rose Loopings, Sheared Mouth, 4 ¾ In.	1404.00

MILLEFIORI means, literally, a thousand flowers. Many small pieces of glass resembling flowers are grouped together to form a design. It is a type of glasswork popular in paperweights and some are listed in that category.

Box, Lid, Round, Famille Noire, Flowers, 4 ⅜ In.	179.00

MINTON china has been made in the Staffordshire region of England from 1793 to the present. The firm became part of the Royal Doulton Tableware Group in 1968, but the wares continued to be marked *Minton*. In 2009 the brand was bought by KPS Capital Partners of New York and became part of WWRD Holdings. Many marks have been used. The word *England* was added in 1891. Minton majolica is listed in this book in the Majolica category.

Bowl, Gilt Border, Double Cobalt Rim, Painted Floral Vignettes, Impressed, c.1860, 9 In., Pair	150.00
Compote, Bowl, Pierced Rim, Winged Cherub Supports, Garlands, Doves, c.1895, 8 ½ In.	1593.00
Dessert Service, Green, Painted Birds, Butterflies, Flowers, Gilt Accents, c.1866, 22 Piece	1200.00
Ewer, Squat, Wide Spout, Triton, Mermaid Handle, Pedestal Foot, Cobalt Blue, c.1860, 10 ½ In.	1422.00
Figurine, Bird, Cockatoo, Tree Stump, Blue, Green, Gold, 12 In.	1062.00
Figurine, Miranda, Seated, Green, White Parian, Shell, Wave Base, c.1867, 15 ½ In.	295.00
Group, Babes In The Woods, 2 Sleeping Children, Marked, 1860, 11 ½ In.	1185.00
Jardiniere, Laurel Wreath, Pink Ribbon & Bows, 15 x 13 In.	460.00
Oyster Plate, 6 Wells, Cobalt Blue & Green Mottled, Cracker Well, 9 ¾ In.	690.00

Mettlach, Stein, No. 2106, Monkeys In Cage, Inlaid Lid, ½ Liter
$4,320.00

The Stein Auction Co.

Mettlach, Vase, Betty, Children On Branch, PUG, 12 ½ In.
$342.00

The Stein Auction Co.

Mettlach, Vase, No. 267/2998, Woman, Print Under Glaze, Hand Painted, 12 ½ In.
$390.00

The Stein Auction Co.

M

MINTON

Minton, Vase, Aesthetic Movement, Birds, Flowers, Fish, Butterflies, Vines, Marked, 8 ⅜ In.
$863.00

Humler & Nolan

Mocha, Bowl, Lid, Earthworm, Cat's-Eye, Red Brown Ground, Handles, 1800s, 7 x 9 In.
$8,850.00

Brunk Auctions

Mocha, Pitcher, Earthworm, Applied Handle, 6 ½ In.
$2,250.00

Leslie Hindman Auctioneers

Mocha, Pitcher, Seaweed, Green & Brown Bands, Handle, Spout Tip, c.1810, 6 ½ In.
$863.00

Cottone Auctions

Pilgrim Flask, Dark Green Bowl, Pate-Sur-Pate Salmon Rondel, Trellis Border, 6 x 5 ½ In., Pair	2223.00
Plaque, Woman, Draped, Cherub, Signed China Works Stoke-On-Trent, c.1860, 11 ¾ x 5 In., Pair	210.00
Plate, Drapery, Silhouette Border, Bagley & Co. 10 ¼ In., 12 Pieces	277.00
Plate, Flower Wreath, Raised Turquoise Blue Border, 9 ¾ In., 10 Piece	189.00
Plate, Pate-Sur-Pate, Scalloped Rim, Pierced & Gilded Border, Shell Molded, Cartouche, c.1900, 9 In.	2015.00
Plate, Shaped Rim, Relief Forget-Me-Nots, 3 Flowers Reserves, Medallion, c.1820, 8 ¾ In., Pair	81.00
Plate, Turquoise Border, Gilt Scroll Center, Monogram, 1917, 9 ½ In., 8 Piece	1170.00
Platter, India Tree, Pieced Shell Shape Handles, Footed, Transfer, Gilt, 1889, 15 x 11 In.	75.00
Server, 2 Parts, Pond Lily, Green Leaf Shape Bowls, White Flower Center, 13 In.	127.00
Tureen, Gun Dog, Running Rabbit, Trees, Leaves, Footed, 2 Loop Handles, Turquoise Interior, 12 In.	161.00
Tureen, Lid, Rooster, Branches, Butterflies, Gilt Design, Pierced Scroll Handles, c.1872, 6 x 12 In., Pair	799.00
Vase, Aesthetic Movement, Birds, Flowers, Fish, Butterflies, Vines, Marked, 8 ⅜ In. ....*Illus*	863.00
Vase, Bird Nest Scene, Moon Flask, Shoulder Loop Handles, Impressed, 1917, 13 ¾ In., Pair...	1694.00
Vase, Moon, Pilgrim Flask, Handles, Painted, Cherubs, Blossoms, Cattail Rim, c.1875, 12 x 9 ¾ In.	330.00
Vase, Pampas Grass, Stick Neck, Ball Bottom, Leaf Design, Red, 25 ½ In.	109.00
Vase, Passion Flower Garden, Cylindrical, Slight Flare Bottom, Rolled Rim, Multicolor, 18 In.	1840.00
Vase, Squat, Urn Shape, Latticework Neck, Oval Foot, Turquoise, Yellow, c.1875, 4 ½ In.	306.00
Vase, Urn Shape, Neptune Masks, Cattails, Swan Handles, Cobalt Blue, Footed, c.1895, 11 In., Pair	5629.00
Wall Bracket, Merbaby, Wrapped In Fishing Nets, Mounted On Shaped Wood, c.1881, 19 x 8 In., Pair	885.00

MIRRORS *are listed in the Furniture category under Mirror.*

MOCHA pottery is an English-made product that was sold in America during the early 1800s. It is a heavy pottery with pale coffee-and-cream coloring. Designs of blue, brown, green, orange, black, or white were added to the pottery and given fanciful names, such as Tree, Snail Trail, or Moss. Mocha designs are sometimes found on pearlware. A few pieces of mocha ware were made in France, the United States, and other countries.

Bowl, Earthworm, Cat's-Eye, Yellow Band, 4 ¾ x 9 In., c.1815	235.00
Bowl, Lid, Earthworm, Cat's-Eye, Red Brown Ground, Handles, 1800s, 7 x 9 In..............*Illus*	8850.00
Bowl, Marbleized, Blue, Reeded Green Bands, c.1800, 2 ½ x 5 ¾ In.	518.00
Jardiniere, Stand, Dark Brown Tree, Brush, Tan, Faience, Impressed Creil, c.1810, 7 In., Pair	472.00
Mug, Bands, Ocher, Blue, Brown, Leaf Bundle, 1800s, 5 ⅝ In.	563.00
Mug, Black Seaweed Lines, Blue, Tan Bands, Loop Handle, 5 x 3 ¼ In.	94.00
Mug, Black Seaweed, Lines, Blue Band, Tan Band, Applied Loop Handle, 4 ¾ x 3 ½ In.	106.00
Pepper Pot, Bands, Light Blue, Baluster Shape, Hard Paste, Perforated Crown, Flared Foot, 5 In.	71.00
Pitcher, Black Lines, Blue, Tan Bands, Black Seaweed, Loop Handle, 5 x 3 ¼ In., Qt.	24.00
Pitcher, Earthworm, 2 Bands, Gray & Blue, Loop Handle, Narrow Spout, c.1815, 7 ½ In.	271.00
Pitcher, Earthworm, Applied Handle, 6 ½ In..........*Illus*	2250.00
Pitcher, Earthworm, Blue & Brown Bands, Swollen, Footed, 6 In.	323.00
Pitcher, Earthworm, Flared Foot, Applied Spout, Loop Handle, Black, Blue Bands, 7 In.	384.00
Pitcher, Seaweed, Black Rings, Blue, Olive Band, Concave Body, Footed, 6 x 5 In.	94.00
Pitcher, Seaweed, Blue, Brown & White Bands, Flared Foot, 6 ½ In.	863.00
Pitcher, Seaweed, Green & Brown Bands, Handle, Spout Tip, c.1810, 6 ½ In..........*Illus*	863.00
Pitcher, Twisted Brown Worms, Black, Green Bands, Ocher Ground, 1800s, 7 ¼ In.	885.00
Pitcher, Yellowware, White Band, Brown, Blue Seaweed, Loop Handle, Spout, 5 ¾ x 4 ¾ In.	106.00
Sugar, Lid, Blue & White Seaweed Design, Yellow Trim, 4 x 4 ¾ In.	266.00

MONMOUTH POTTERY COMPANY started working in Monmouth, Illinois, in 1892. The pottery made a variety of utilitarian wares. It became part of Western Stoneware Company in 1906. The maple leaf mark was used until 1930. If *Co.* appears as part of the mark, the piece was made before 1906.

Pitcher, Buttermilk, Orange, Shell Front, 6 In.	45.00
Planter, Turquoise, 5 Openings, 6 ½ In.	95.00
Vase, Fluted, Footed, Blue, 11 In.	125.00
Vase, Rings, Brown, 18 In.	395.00
Vase, Shouldered, Black, 17 In.	990.00

MONT JOYE, *see Mt. Joye category.*

MOORCROFT pottery was first made in Burslem, England, in 1913. William Moorcroft had managed the art pottery department for James Macintyre & Company of England from 1898 to 1913. The Moorcroft pottery continues today, although William Moorcroft died in 1945. The earlier wares are similar to the modern ones, but color and marking will help indicate the age.

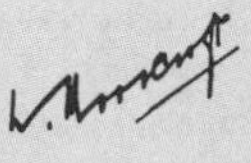

Bowl, Leaf & Blackberry, Green Ground, Flambe Glaze, Footed, 6 In.	250.00

Bowl, Orchids, Multicolor, Impressed, 3 ½ x 4 ½ In.	138.00
Bowl, Pomegranates, Dark Blue Ground, Rolled Rim, 10 ¼ In.	499.00
Box, Lid, Leaf & Berry, Marked, 3 ½ x 5 ½ In.	130.00
Box, Lid, Orchid Pattern, Round, 6 In.	188.00
Jar, Pansy, Cream Ground, Bulbous, Tapered, Macintyre, Florian Ware, 3 ¾ In.	538.00
Lamp Base, Orchid, Blue Ground, 10 x 24 In., Pair	300.00
Plaque, Song Of The Wind, Twin Ruby Poppies, Yellow Dandelions, Marked, 12 x 8 ¾ In.	860.00
Plate, Multiple Sail Ship, Paint, 14 ¼ In.	173.00
Tazza, Pomegranates, Orange, Brown, Rust, Bowl, Hammered Pewter Pedestal, c.1935, 6 x 8 ¾ In.	1125.00
Vase, Bud, Salmon & Green Cornflower, Macintyre, Florian Ware, 12 ½ In.	2689.00
Vase, Cornflowers, Powder Blue, Paper Label, 1928-49, 9 x 4 In. ...Illus	2625.00
Vase, Hibiscus, Yellow Ground, Bulbous, Tapered Neck, 12 ½ In.	250.00
Vase, Iris, Blue Glaze, Baluster Shape, 6 In.	354.00
Vase, Iris, Blue Glaze, Flowers, Leaves, Waisted, Elongated Neck, Round Foot, 6 In.	351.00
Vase, Marinka, Flowers, Multicolor, Shouldered, Tapered, 14 ⅜ In.	633.00
Vase, Orchid, Cobalt Blue Ground, Red Flower, Green Leaves, 6 In.	480.00
Vase, Pansy, Red, Yellow, Cobalt Blue Ground, Impressed, Trumpet Shape, 12 In.	387.00
Vase, Peonies, Green, Purple, Gourd Shape, Ring Foot, Rolled Rim, Signed, 9 ½ In.	374.00
Vase, Pomegranate & Grapes, Blue Ground, Flared, 5 ½ In.	384.00
Vase, Pomegranate, Flared, Footed, Impressed, 7 x 10 In.	531.00
Vase, Poppy, Green Glaze, Tapered Cylinder, Flared Rim, 7 ½ In.	354.00
Vase, Red Poppy, Impressed, 4 ½ x 6 In.	219.00
Vase, Roses & Forget-Me-Nots, Flared, Spread Foot, Macintyre, Florian Ware, 6 ¼ In.	614.00
Vase, Wisteria, Blue Ground, Oval, Tapered, 3 ½ In.	269.00
Vase, Wisteria, Dark Blue Ground, 10 ¼ In.	576.00
Vase, Wisteria, Green Ground, Silver Plated Rim, 3 ½ In.	326.00
Vase, Wisteria, Swollen Cylinder, Folded-In Rim, 7 In.	480.00

MORGANTOWN GLASS WORKS operated in Morgantown, West Virginia, from 1900 to 1974. Some of their wares are marked with an adhesive label that says *Old Morgantown Glass*.

Bell, American Beauty, Pink, 8 In.	40.00
Bowl, Crinkle, Ruby Red, Octagonal, 5 In.	29.00
Candleholder, Peacock Blue, Optic, 4 In., Pair	45.00
Cocktail, Bird Of Paradise, 5 In.	8.00
Cocktail, Fischer, Green, 3 Oz., 4 ⅝ In.	21.00
Cocktail, Rooster, Red, Footed, 3 ⅞ In.	38.00
Cordial, American Modern, Pink, 2 ¼ In.	24.00
Cordial, Eileen, 4 ¾ In.	60.00
Goblet, American Beauty, Pink, 7 ½ In.	33.00
Goblet, Water, Adam, 6 In.	15.00
Goblet, Water, Topaz, 8 ⅛ In.	12.00
Iced Tea, Fairwin, 7 In.	14.00
Juice, Crinkle, Green, 6 Oz., 4 In.	14.00
Juice, Parma, Stem, Red, 4 ⅞ In.	22.00
Parfait, Meadow, Green, Stem, 6 ½ In.	60.00
Pitcher, Crinkle, Tijuana, Amber, 34 Oz., 7 ½ In.	87.00
Pitcher, Crinkle, Tijuana, Amethyst, c.1935, 34 Oz., 7 ½ In.	101.00
Pitcher, Crinkle, Topaz, 54 Oz., 8 ¾ In.	43.00
Plate, Crinkle, Topaz, 6 ½ In.	22.00
Plate, El Mexicano, c.1930, 9 ¼ In.	34.00
Rose Bowl, Peacock Optic, Ruby Red, Globular, 4 In.	45.00
Server, 3 Sections, Ruby Red, Curling Back, 10 x 7 ½ In.	68.00
Sherbet, Crinkle, Peacock Blue, Footed	28.00
Sherbet, Crinkle, Tall, 2 ¾ In.	9.00
Sherbet, Topaz, Tall, 2 ¾ In.	9.00
Tumbler, American Beauty, 4 ¾ In.	55.00
Tumbler, El Mexicano, Ice, c.1932, 5 ½ In.	32.00
Tumbler, Footed, Mayfair, Amber, 10 Oz., 5 ⅝ In.	20.00
Vase, Peacock Optic Blue, c.1940, 3 In.	35.00
Vase, Peacock Optic Blue, Ruffled Rim, c.1950, 3 In.	30.00
Vase, Snowball, c.1930, 7 In.	157.00
Wine, Cathay, c.1925, 3 Oz., 6 In.	18.00
Wine, Monroe, Stiegel Green, Stem, 6 ¼ In.	30.00

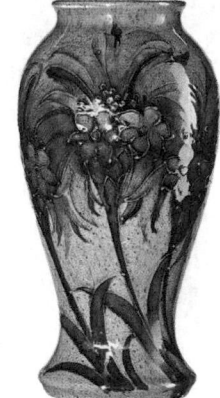

Moorcroft, Vase, Cornflowers, Powder Blue, Paper Label, 1928-49, 9 x 4 In. $2,625.00

Rago Arts & Auction Center

Mosaic Tile Co., Tile, Monk Holding Mug, Happy Grin, Matte Glaze, 2 Tiles, Burled Wood Frame, 17 ¾ In. $575.00

Humler & Nolan

Moser, Cruet, Ruby Glass, Oak Leaves, Enamel Acorns, Faceted Stopper, 7 In. $518.00

Early Auction Co.

M

Moser, Ewer, Birds, Insects, Grapevines, Multicolor, Enamel, Gilt, Applied Scroll Handle & Feet, 13 In.
$2,500.00

Leslie Hindman Auctioneers

Moser, Jug, Claret, Applied Grapevines, Flowers, Parrot, Enamel, Branch Handle, Stopper, Signed, 14 In.
$6,900.00

Early Auction Co.

Moser, Vase, Cranberry, Gold Leaves, Ruffled Rim, Footed, c.1870, 6 In.
$210.00

DuMouchelles Art Gallery

MOSAIC TILE COMPANY of Zanesville, Ohio, was started by Karl Langerbeck and Herman Mueller in 1894. Many types of plain and ornamental tiles were made until 1959. The company closed in 1967. The company also made some ashtrays, bookends, and related giftwares. Most pieces are marked with the entwined MTC monogram.

Figurine, Dog, German Shepherd, Reclining, Tan, Matte Glaze, 6 x 10 In.	85.00
Figurine, Dog, German Shepherd, Sitting, Tan Matte Glaze, 9 In.	125.00
Tile, Monk Holding Mug, Happy Grin, Matte Glaze, 2 Tiles, Burled Wood Frame, 17 ¾ In.....*Illus*	575.00
Tray, Terrier, Brown & White, Tray Base, Green Glaze, 5 x 7 In.	150.00

MOSER glass is made by a Bohemian (Czech) glasshouse founded by Ludwig Moser in 1857. Art Nouveau–type glassware and iridescent glassware were made. The most famous Moser glass is decorated with heavy enameling in gold and bright colors. The firm, Moser Glassworks, is still working in Karlovy Vary, Czech Republic. Few pieces of Moser glass are marked.

Basket, Rubina Verde, Gilt Rigaree Feet, Handle, Insects, Oak Leaf, Enameled, Acorn Jewels, 9 In.	2645.00
Bowl, Pink, Green & Lavender, Clusters Of Roses & Leaves, Gold Band, Underplate, 4 ½ In.	175.00
Cake Stand, Splendid, Hand Cut, Gilded Band, Pedestal, Sticker, Acid Etched, 10 x 5 ¾ In.	104.00
Compote, Cranberry, Enameled, Monogram, 5 ½ x 8 ¼ In.	300.00
Compote, Tree Shape, Bowl, 3 Branch Stem, Enameled Acorns, Insects, Wavy Rim, 12 In.	13800.00
Cordial, Centaur, Pink Glass, Clear Knop, Tapered Stem, Gold Trim, 6 In., Pair	210.00
Creamer, Cranberry, Cut Collar, Overall Silver, Gold Scrolling, Rigaree Handle, Oval, 4 In.	201.00
Cruet, Lid, Jeweled & Enameled, Stopper, Handle, Foot, Gilt Accents, Medallions, Signed, 6 ¾ In.	533.00
Cruet, Ruby Glass, Oak Leaves, Enamel Acorns, Faceted Stopper, 7 In.....*Illus*	518.00
Cup, Topaz, Enameled Leaves, Gold Glass Acorns, Loop Handle, Round Foot, Gilt Highlights, 3 ½ In.	86.00
Decanter, Stopper, Enamel, Fused Grapevine, Insects, Baluster, Amberina, Gilt Handle, c.1885, 14 In.	5192.00
Ewer, Birds, Insects, Grapevines, Multicolor, Enamel, Gilt, Applied Scroll Handle & Feet, 13 In.....*Illus*	2500.00
Ewer, Blue, Flowers, Vines, Birds, Enamel, Gilt, Footed, Twisted Textured Handle, c.1890, 12 x 6 In.	270.00
Ewer, Cranberry, Bird, Branch, Leaves, Jeweled Acorns, Pink, Foot, Stick Neck, Ruffle Rim, 17 In.	6210.00
Finger Bowl, Underplate, Prussian Blue, Gold Scrolling, Multicolor Stylized Flowers, Insects, 6 ¼ In.	115.00
Goblet, Paneled, Enameled Flowers, Amber Pedestal Foot, 6 ¼ In., Pair	345.00
Goblet, Water, Cranberry, Faceted, Multicolor Flowers Medallions, Gold Scrolling, Signed, 7 ¾ In.	115.00
Jar, Lid, Green, Gold Grapevines, Bees, Reeded Domed Foot, Cylindrical, Signed, 14 ¼ In., Pair.	1898.00
Jug, Claret, Applied Grapevines, Flowers, Parrot, Enamel, Branch Handle, Stopper, 14 In.....*Illus*	6900.00
Pitcher, Cranberry Crackle, Pink, Blue Flowers, Leaves, Gold Highlights, Clear Loop Handle, 3 ½ In.	259.00
Pitcher, Cranberry Glass, Gold Grapevines, Enameled Bird, Bulbous, Loop Handle, 6 In.	2875.00
Pitcher, Ruby, Enamel & Gilt Lace, c.1880, 2 ⅓ In.	36.00
Rose Bowl, Ball Shape, Glass, Enameled Flowers & Leaves, Bands, 4 ½ In.	230.00
Rose Bowl, Hummingbirds, Brown, Flared Scalloped Rim, Gold, Silver, 3 Clear Feet, 7 ½ x 7 In.	270.00
Scent Bottle, Cobalt Blue, Flowers & Leaves, Metal Hardware, Flattened Circle, 2 ¼ In.	633.00
Tumbler, Sherry, Clear, Jeweled Gold Accents, 1900, 7 Piece	365.00
Vase, Amber Crackle, 2 Enameled Fish, Seaweed, Swollen, Flat Rim, Footed, 9 ½ In.	230.00
Vase, Amber, Faceted, Gilded Frieze, Warriors, Rounded Square Shape, Lobed, c.1920, 6 x 10 In.	360.00
Vase, Amethyst Color, Bird, Flowering Branch, Gold Bands, Swollen Shoulder, 10 ½ In.	1265.00
Vase, Amethyst To Clear, Butterfly, Acorns, Leaves, Beetle, Gilt, Trumpet, Paperweight Foot, 11 In.	920.00
Vase, Blue, Coralene Flowers, Pillow Shape, Scalloped Rim, Scroll Feet, 8 In.	1323.00
Vase, Blue, Dragonfly, Flowers, Leaves, Stems, Short Neck, Flared Rim, Ring Foot, 5 ¼ In.	863.00
Vase, Blue, Enameled Flowers & Leaves, Gecko, Round Pedestal Foot, Elongated Oval, 8 In.	1093.00
Vase, Clear To Amethyst Color, Enameled Poppies, Bumblebees, Pillow, Scalloped Rim, 7 ¾ In.	1380.00
Vase, Cobalt Blue, Gold Elephants & Giraffes, Cylindrical, Flared Rim, Signed, 14 In.	1035.00
Vase, Cranberry Glass, Pillow, Curled Glass Feet, Pink & Blue Flowers, Scrolls, Gold, 5 In.	518.00
Vase, Cranberry, Cylindrical, Rigaree Feet, Fan Cartouche, Gold Scrolling, Flowers, 14 In.	575.00
Vase, Cranberry, Gold Leaves, Ruffled Rim, Footed, c.1870, 6 In.....*Illus*	210.00
Vase, Cupids, Cream Ground, Bristol, Signed, c.1890, 9 ¼ In.	270.00
Vase, Dragonfly, Purple Flowers, Blue At Neck, Crackle, Signed, 8 In.	600.00
Vase, Enamel Flower Overlays, Gilt, Trumpet Shape, c.1890, 12 x 4 In.	236.00
Vase, Gold, Cranberry, Flowers, Seed Pods, Leaves, Art Nouveau, Signed, 8 ½ In.....*Illus*	374.00
Vase, Green, Enamel, Tree, Blue Lizards, Gold Highlights, Pinched Neck, Flared Rim, 9 In., Pair	1610.00
Vase, Green, Gold Leaf Design, Bees, 3 Handles, Squat, Trumpet Neck, Gold Band, 9 ¼ In.	1150.00
Vase, Green, White Enamel, Nude Fairy, Wings, Tall Grass, Cylindrical, Gold Highlights, 12 ½ In.	345.00
Vase, Hawk, Flying, Marsh Scene, Cattails, Water Lilies, Green To Clear Glass, Cylindrical, 10 In.	2760.00
Vase, Heron By Stream, Enamel, Applied Glass Handles, 20 In.....*Illus*	14375.00
Vase, Iris, Green, Gold, White, Enamel, 11 ½ x 6 In.....*Illus*	840.00
Vase, Iris, Relief Cut, Purple Shaded To Clear, Square, 3 ½ In.	173.00
Vase, Light To Dark Green, Gilt Band, Pinecone Designs, c.1915, 14 x 5 In.	480.00
Vase, Mums, Bumblebees, Clear, Enamel, Pink, Yellow, Gilt, Square, Infolding Scallop Rim, 10 In.	690.00
Vase, Opalescent Pink To Green, Leaves, Jeweled Acorns, Horn Shape Handles, Signed, 7 ½ In.	173.00

Vase, Poppy, Leaves, Cylindrical, Tapered, Gilt Accents, Green, Pink, 1900s, 8 ½ x 3 In.	1063.00
Vase, Portrait, Children At Play, Cranberry, Gilt, Pedestal Foot, Trumpet Mouth, 14 In., Pair	3163.00
Vase, Ruby Red Cartouche Panels, Gold Enamel Overlay, Tapered, 13 ¼ In.	748.00
Vase, Swollen Top, Scalloped Rim, Fruiting Branch, Plum Color To Clear, 1900s, 12 ¼ x 4 ½ In.	469.00
Vase, Topaz Glass, Yellow Sunflowers, Gold Highlights, Trumpet Shape, Saucer Foot, 31 In.	2990.00
Vase, Topaz, Blue Glass, Round Foot, Enameled Blue Bird, Flowers, Cylindrical, Trumpet Rim, 16 In.	3163.00
Vase, Trumpet, Cranberry, Gold Highlights, Enameled Flowers, Pointillist Raised Gold Detail, 14 In.	1438.00
Wine, Clear, Gold Design, Green Reeded Stem, Round Foot, 7 ½ In., Set Of 6	1380.00

MOSS ROSE china was made by many firms from 1808 to 1900. It has a typical moss rose pictured as the design. The plant is not as popular now as it was in Victorian gardens, so the fuzz-covered bud is unfamiliar to most collectors. The dishes were usually decorated with pink and green flowers.

Ashtray Set, Gilt Indent, Edge, Japan, 2 ¾ x 2 ¾ In., 4 Piece	16.00
Bowl, Open Handle, Gilt Trim, Rosenthal, 11 ¼ In. Diam.	75.00
Cake Knife, Stainless Blade, Porcelain, Japan	10.00
Candleholder, Cornucopia Shape, c.1960, 3 ¾ x 4 In., Pair	22.00
Casserole, Lid, Handles, Footed, Glasgow, c.1884, 10 x 6 In.	48.00
Gravy Boat, Attached Underplate, Midcentury Modern Style, Thames China, 9 ½ x 6 ½ In.	54.00
Plate Set, Gilt Undulating Edges, 1950s, 7 In., 6 Piece	30.00
Powder Box, Convex Lid, Square, Gilt Edge, 4 ½ x 1 ½ In.	22.00
Snack Set, Plate, Cup, Scalloped Edge, Shell Shape, 4 ½ x 3 ½ & 8 In., 16 Piece	40.00
Sugar & Creamer, Lid, Gilt Handles, Finial, Edges, Japan, 4 x 6 & 5 In.	35.00
Trinket Box, Gilt Finial Handle, Ruffled Edge, Foil Label, Sutton's Creation, 1950s, 5 x 4 In.	24.00
Vanity Mirror, Porcelain Base, Standard, 2-Sided Swivel Mirror, 11 ¼ In.	16.00
Vase, Bulbous, Gilt Trim, 4 ⅞ In.	45.00

MOTHER-OF-PEARL GLASS, or pearl satin glass, was first made in the 1850s in England and in Massachusetts. It was a special type of mold-blown satin glass with air bubbles in the glass, giving it a pearlized color. It has been reproduced. Mother-of-pearl shell objects are listed under Pearl.

Basket, Rainbow, Folded Down Crimped Rim, Thorn Branch Twisted Handle, 9 ½ In.	748.00
Bowl, Diamond Quilted, Blue To Opal, Blossoms, Crenulated Rim, Silver Plate Stand, 8 ½ In.	460.00
Bowl, Diamond Quilted, Opal To Rose, Crystal Feet, Crimped Foldover Rim, Upswept Edge, 6 ¼ In.	460.00
Bowl, Underplate, Rainbow Shading, Ruffled Rim, 3 In.	575.00
Box, Scent Bottles, Turreted Corners, Lozenge On Lid, c.1850, 3 ¼ x 4 ¼ In.	461.00
Compote, Diamond Quilted, Rainbow Raspberry Prunt, Ruffled Rim, Rigaree Footed, 7 ½ In.	1150.00
Condiment Set, Pink, Raindrop, Kate Greenaway Caddy, Sugar, Salt & Pepper, 11 In.	546.00
Finger Bowl, Diamond Quilted, Blue, Tight Crimped Rim, Ring Foot, 3 In.	144.00
Lamp, Blue, Globe Shape, Crimped Blue Feet, Raindrop, Ruffled Rim Shade, 8 ½ In.	1553.00
Necessaire, Shell Halves, Gilt Bronze, White Marble Plinth, Fitted Interior, Victorian, 6 ½ In.	450.00
Perfume Bottle, Diamond Quilted, Blue Satin Glass, Rigaree Stoppers, 7 ½ In., Pair	316.00
Perfume Bottle, Diamond Quilted, Pink To Fuchsia, Teardrop Shape, Metal Cap, 6 In.	1265.00
Pitcher, Diamond Quilted, Blue Sloping Spout, Camphor Handle, 7 ½ In.	288.00
Pitcher, Diamond Quilted, Yellow Melon Ribbed, Gold Coralene, Reeded Handle, 8 ¾ In.	374.00
Pitcher, Herringbone, Fuchsia To Pink, Melon Ribbed, Trifold Crimp Rim, Branch Handle, 7 In.	81.00
Rose Bowl, Diamond Quilted, Pink Satin Glass, Coralene Applied Seaweed, 3 ½ In.	288.00 *Illus*
Rose Bowl, Pink, 4-Fold, Vertical Ribs, 3 ½ In.	633.00
Saltshaker, Raindrop Pattern, Pink, Peach, Elongated Oval, Silver Plate Caddy, 7 ½ In., Pair	604.00
Spoon, Brass Brad Joiners, 7 ¾ In.	63.00
Sugar Shaker, Diamond Quilted, Blue, 5 ½ In.	288.00
Tumbler, Blue To White, Optic Swirled, Gold Tracery Rim, 3 ¾ In.	230.00
Vase, Blue Satin, Diamond Quilted, 6-Sided, Shouldered, 6 In.	460.00 *Illus*
Vase, Blue, Opal, Moire Pattern, Shouldered, Out-Turned Ruffle Rim, 12 In.	460.00
Vase, Diamond Quilted, Amber, Amethyst Flowers, Bulbous, Cylindrical Neck, Crimped Mouth, 9 In.	1265.00
Vase, Diamond Quilted, Blue To Opalescent Blue, Pinched Waist, Crimped Square Mouth, 9 In.	115.00
Vase, Diamond Quilted, Blue, Ruffled Rim, Camphor Rim, 11 In., Pair	345.00
Vase, Diamond Quilted, Butterscotch To Opal, Spreading Ruffled Rim, Shouldered, 8 In., Pair	201.00
Vase, Diamond Quilted, Fuchsia To Pink, Gold Blossoms, Downfolded Crimped Rim, 7 In.	431.00
Vase, Diamond Quilted, Fuchsia To Pink, Square Crimped Mouth, Ring Foot, 6 In.	92.00
Vase, Diamond Quilted, Moire, Yellow To Opal, Stippled Enamel, 5 ¼ In.	748.00 *Illus*
Vase, Diamond Quilted, Pink, Purple Flowers, Cylindrical, Crown Shape Rim, 9 ½ In., Pair	259.00
Vase, Diamond Quilted, Rainbow, Applied Thorny Branch Handles, Applied Feet, 9 ½ x 10 In.	13225.00 *Illus*
Vase, Diamond Quilted, White Fuchsia Blossoming Branches, Stick Shape, 10 ¼ In.	3105.00
Vase, Golden Yellow, Footed, Raindrop Shape, Crimped Rim, 8 ½ In., Pair	173.00

Moser, Vase, Gold, Cranberry, Flowers, Seed Pods, Leaves, Art Nouveau, Signed, 8 ½ In.
$374.00

James D. Julia Auctioneers

Moser, Vase, Heron By Stream, Enamel, Applied Glass Handles, 20 In.
$14,375.00

James D. Julia Auctioneers

Moser, Vase, Iris, Green, Gold, White, Enamel, 11 ½ x 6 In.
$840.00

DuMouchelles Art Gallery

M

Mother-Of-Pearl, Rose Bowl, Diamond Quilted, Pink Satin Glass, Coralene Applied Seaweed, 3 ½ In.
$288.00

Early Auction Co.

Mother-Of-Pearl, Vase, Blue Satin, Diamond Quilted, 6-Sided, Shouldered, 6 In.
$460.00

Early Auction Co.

Mother-Of-Pearl, Vase, Diamond Quilted, Moire, Yellow To Opal, Stippled Enamel, 5 ¼ In.
$748.00

Early Auction Co.

TIP

Look at your house from the outside and be sure valuable paintings, silver, or other belongings are not visible from the street, especially near doors and windows. It could be an invitation to a burglar.

Vase, Herringbone Pattern, Branch Loop Handles, Thorns, Ring Foot, Bulbous, Wavy Rim, 9 In....	374.00
Vase, Moire, Pink, Ruffled Rim, Sculptured Enamel Bird, Gold Highlights, Bulbous, 6 ½ In....	518.00
Vase, Pink To Opal, Gold Blossoms & Tracery, Bulbous, Narrow Neck, 7 ½ In....	230.00
Vase, Yellow Satin, Ribbed Zipper, Pink Inside, 5 ½ In.....................................*Illus*	776.00
Vase, Yellow, Fleur-De-Lis Design, Enamel Bird, Baluster, Wide Rim, 8 In....	201.00

MOTORCYCLES and motorcycle accessories of all types are being collected today. Examples can be found that date back to the early twentieth century. Toy motorcycles are listed in the Toy category.

Belt Buckle, Gypsy Tour, Enameled, 1950, 1 ¾ x 1 ⅛ In....	75.00
Blotter, Indian Motorcycle, Image Of Scout Cycle, Bath Cycle Co., 1920s, 3 ½ x 5 In....	225.00
Can, Harley-Davidson Pre-Luxe Motorcyle Oil, Round, Metal, Red, White, Blue, Qt....	140.00
Catalog, Indian, 1913 Model, Illustrated Black & White Embossed Cover, 24 Pages, 9 ¾ In....	600.00
Helmet, Corker, Open Face, J. Compton, Sons & Webb, 1960s, Size 7 ½, 8 ¾ x 11 ¾ In....	150.00
Kidney Belt, Black Leather, Rivets, Embossed Harley-Davidson, 1940s....	365.00
License Plate, New Jersey, White, Black Lettering, 1980, 8 x 3 ½ In....	20.00
Matchbox Clip, Indian, Copper Plated, Embossed, Hendee Mfg., 2 ⅜ x 1 ½ In....	130.00
Medal, Art Nouveau, Silver, Illa Regolarita Lodi, Italy, c.1900, 1 ¼ In....	268.00
Miele, Burgundy, Fintel & Sachs Hub Motor, Burgundy, 75 In....	540.00
Miele, Werke K52, Fintel & Sachs Hub Motor, Blue, 1959, 75 In....	780.00
Model, Made From Vaults, Bolts, Springs, Metal, Wood Frame, 11 ½ x 11 ½ In....	49.00
Motorcycle, Honda, Dream, 305cc Engine, Black, Seat, Toaster Style Tank, 1968....	2587.00
Ring, Embossed Leaves, Harley-Davidson, Sterling, Size 10, 1 x 1 In....	99.00
Saddle Bags, Black Leather, Studded, Bolt On, Harley-Davidson, c.1970....	150.00
Sign, Harley-Davidson, Sales, Service, Metal, White Ground, Yellow, Black, Red, 15 ½ x 11 In.	18.00
Sign, Motocyclettes, R. Gillet & Cie, Man, Riding Up Hill, Lightning, Rain, Ribera, 39 x 55 In.	1300.00
Sign, Peugeot, Motorcycle, Speeding Past Moon, Max Ponty, Paris, c.1930, 46 x 30 In....	500.00
Token, Hinkey The Motorcycle Man, Good For 5 Cents In Trade, Aluminum, c.1914, ¹³⁄₁₆ In....	69.00
Watch Fob, Key Ring, Harley-Davidson, Sterling, 1 ½ x 1 ½ In....	95.00
Watch Fob, National Motorcycle Gypsy Tour, Cycle & Sidecar, Bronze Luster, 1921, 1 ½ In....	115.00

MOUNT WASHINGTON, *see Mt. Washington category.*

MOVIE memorabilia of all types are collected. Animation Art, Games, Sheet Music, Toys, and some celebrity items are listed in their own section. A lobby card is usually 11 by 14 inches, but other sizes were also made. A set of lobby cards includes seven scene cards and one title card. An American one sheet, the standard movie poster, is 27 by 41 inches. A three sheet is 40 by 81 inches. A half sheet is 22 by 28 inches. A window card, made of cardboard, is 14 by 22 inches. An insert is 14 by 36 inches. A herald is a promotional item handed out to patrons. Press books, sent to exhibitors to promote a movie, contain ads and lists of what is available for advertising, i.e., posters, lobby cards. Press kits, sent to the media, contain photos and details about the movie, i.e., stars' biographies and interviews.

Action Figure, James Bond 007 Thunderball, Shoots Cap Firing Pistol, Box, 1965, 12 In....	431.00
Button, Employee, Grauman's Chinese Theater, Garbo As Mata Hari, Today's Special Malted Milk, 3 ½ In.	584.00
Button, Sea Hawk, Errol Flynn, Skull & Crossbones, Lithograph, Black, White, 1940, 1 ⅜ In..	230.00
Figure, Jackie Coogan, The Kid, Celluloid, Lithograph Button, 1921, 5 ½ In....	87.00
Glass Set, Monsters, Frankenstein, Mummy, Black Lagoon Creature, Wolfman, c.1960, 6 In....	382.00
Insert, Casablanca, Humphrey Bogart, Warner Bros., 1942, 14 x 36 In....	23000.00
Insert, Creature From The Black Lagoon, Julia Adams, Universal International, 1954, 22 x 28 In.	5850.00
Insert, Dead End, Dead End Kids, United Artists, 1937, 14 x 36 In....	8775.00
Insert, Ebb Tide, Lila Lee, Paramount, 1922, 14 x 36 In....	357.00
Insert, Girl Can't Help It, Jayne Mansfield, 20th Century Fox, 1956, 20 x 28 In....	175.00
Insert, Key Largo, Humphrey Bogart, Warner Bros., 1948, 14 x 36 In....	702.00
Insert, Knockout Reilly, Richard Dix, Paramount, 1927, 14 x 36 In....	292.00
Insert, Padlocked, Louise Dresser, Paramount, 1926, 14 x 36 In....	146.00
Insert, Sea Hawk, Errol Flynn, Warner Bros., 1940, 14 x 36 In....	1755.00
Lobby Card, Abbott & Costello Meet Frankenstein, Universal, 1948, 11 x 14 In....	350.00
Lobby Card, Dr. No, Sean Connery, United Artists, 1962, 11 x 14 In....	936.00
Lobby Card, Gone With The Wind, Clark Gable, MGM, 1939, 11 x 14 In....	1053.00
Lobby Card, Hard Day's Night, The Beatles, United Artists, 1964, 11 x 14 In....	995.00
Lobby Card, I Walked With A Zombie, Tom Conway, RKO, 1943, 11 x 14 In....	936.00
Lobby Card, Lolita, Sue Lyon, MGM, 1962, 11 x 14 In....	643.00
Lobby Card, Some Like It Hot, Monroe, Curtis, Lemmon, 1959, 11 x 14 In., 7 Piece........*Illus*	819.00
Lobby Card, The Monkey's Paw, Aubrey Smith, RKO, 1933, 11 x 14 In....	438.00
Lobby Card, Wizard Of Oz, Judy Garland, 1939, 11 x 14 In., 6 Piece.............*Illus*	1053.00
Mirror, Grace Kelly, Portrait, Color, Celluloid, 1950s, 2 ¼ In....	52.00

M

Pennant, Spider's Web, Green & White, Spider & Web, Felt, 4 Tassels, 1938, 27 ½ In.	459.00
Photograph, Clark Gable, Portrait, Color Tinted, Signed, c.1935, 8 x 10 In.	371.00
Photograph, Jane Russell, The Outlaw, Lying In Hay, Gun, Signed, Color Glossy, c.1941, 8 x 10 In.	127.00
Postcard, Fay Wray, King Kong, Sepia Photo, Ripped Costume, 1930s, 3 ½ x 5 ½ In.	86.00
Poster, Adventures Of Captain Marvel, Tom Tyler, Republic, 1941, 27 x 41 In.	1755.00
Poster, Ah Wilderness, Wallace Berry, MGM, 1935, 27 x 41 In.	292.00
Poster, And Then There Were None, Walter Huston, 20th Century Fox, 1945, 22 x 28 In.	469.00
Poster, Angry Red Planet, Bat Rat Spider Creature, 1960, 22 x 28 In.	253.00
Poster, Arsenic & Old Lace, Cary Grant, Warner Bros., 1944, 27 x 41 In.	1053.00
Poster, Bandit's Baby, Fred Thomson, F.B.O Studio, Silent, 1925, 27 x 41 In.	468.00
Poster, Before The White Man Came, Linen Back, 1 Sheet, Otis Lithograph Co., c.1918, 25 x 39 In.	1265.00
Poster, Bullitt, Steve McQueen, Warner Bros., 1968, 24 x 33 In.	146.00
Poster, Butch Cassidy & The Sundance Kid, 20th Century Fox, 1969, 24 x 34 In.	169.00
Poster, Call It Murder, Humphrey Bogart, Reissue 1934, 27 x 41 In.	70.00
Poster, Cleopatra, Taylor, Harrison, Burton, Linen Back, 1963, 27 x 41 In.	173.00
Poster, Daddy Long Legs, Mary Pickford, First National, 1919, 27 x 41 In.	3510.00
Poster, Dial M For Murder, Grace Kelly, Ray Milland, Hitchcock, Universal, 1954, 27 x 41 In.	2000.00
Poster, Don Winslow Of The Navy, Serial, Linen Back, Universal, 1940, 27 x 41 In.	231.00
Poster, Don't Tell Everything, Gloria Swanson, Paramount, 1921, 27 x 41 In.	819.00
Poster, Easter Parade, Judy Garland, MGM, 1948, 27 x 41 In.	468.00
Poster, Felix The Cat Brings Home The Bacon, Animation, 1924, 27 x 41 In.	2600.00
Poster, From Russia With Love, Sean Connery, United Artists, 1964, 27 x 41 In.	351.00
Poster, Funny Face, Audrey Hepburn, Paramount, 1957, 27 x 41 In.	468.00
Poster, Go West, Buster Keaton, Pathe Studio, 1925, 27 x 41 In.	702.00
Poster, Her Night Of Nights, Marie Prevost, Universal, 1922, 27 x 41 In.	643.00
Poster, High Society, Grace Kelly, MGM, 1956, 27 x 41 In.	351.00
Poster, James Bond Goldfinger, Gosta Aberg, 1965, 39 x 27 In.	650.00
Poster, James Bond, You Only Live Twice, Sean Connery, 1967, 31 x 41 In.	178.00
Poster, Jaws, Roy Scheider, Universal, 1975, 27 x 41 In.	351.00
Poster, Last Of The Mohicans, Harry Carey, Mascot, 1932, 27 x 41 In.	409.00
Poster, Laura, Gene Tierney, Dana Andrews, 20th Century Fox, 1944, 22 x 28 In. ....*Illus*	936.00
Poster, Little Toot, Animation, Disney, 1954, 27 x 41 In.	1755.00
Poster, Lolita, Sue Lyon, MGM, 1962, 27 x 41 In.	468.00
Poster, Mae West, Paramount, 1930s, 20 x 27 In. ....*Illus*	351.00
Poster, Magnificent Seven, United Artists, 1960, 27 x 41 In.	117.00
Poster, North By Northwest, Cary Grant, Hitchcock, MGM, 1958, 27 x 41 In.	555.00
Poster, North By Northwest, Eva Marie Saint, Cary Grant, Hitchcock, MGM, 1959	1100.00
Poster, North West Mounted Police, Gary Cooper, Paramount, 1945, 27 x 41 In.	409.00
Poster, Once Upon A Time In America, Stick Man, Gun, Bottle, Poland, Frame, 1984, 38 x 27 In.	472.00
Poster, Payment On Demand, Bette Davis, 1951, 39 x 24 In.	160.00
Poster, Polly Of The Movies, First National, Silent, 1927, 27 x 41 In.	2760.00
Poster, Pony Soldier, Tyrone Power, 1952, 27 x 41 In.	52.00
Poster, Prizefighter & The Lady, Myrna Loy, MGM, 1933, 22 x 28 In.	468.00
Poster, Psycho, Anthony Perkins, Hitchcock, Paramount, 1960, 27 x 41 In.	1112.00
Poster, Revenge Of The Creature, John Agar, Frame, c.1954, 14 x 36 In.	424.00
Poster, Sabrina, Audrey Hepburn, Paramount, 1954, 27 x 41 In.	263.00
Poster, Seven Year Itch, Marilyn Monroe, 20th Century Fox, 1955, 41 x 81 In.	3276.00
Poster, Shadow Of A Doubt, Hitchcock, Universal, 1943	1400.00
Poster, Society Scandal, Gloria Swanson, Paramount, 1924, 27 x 41 In.	235.00
Poster, Space Master X-7, 1959, 35 x 13 In.	200.00
Poster, Step On It, Hoot Gibson, Universal, 1922, 27 x 41 In.	702.00
Poster, Superman's Peril, George Reeves, 20th Century Fox, 1954, 27 x 41 In.	1053.00
Poster, Swiss Miss, Laurel & Hardy, 1938, 27 x 41 In.	585.00
Poster, Tarzan Finds A Son, Johnny Weissmuller, MGM, 1936, 27 x 41 In.	702.00
Poster, Taxi Driver, Robert De Niro, 1976, 57 x 37 In.	210.00
Poster, The Lone Bandit, Lane Chandler, Linen Back, 1933, 40 x 77 In.	380.00
Poster, Things To Come, H.G. Wells, 1947, 14 x 36 In.	153.00
Poster, Three Godfathers, John Wayne, MGM, 1948, 27 x 41 In.	234.00
Poster, Thunderball, Sean Connery, United Artists, 1965, 27 x 41 In.	702.00
Poster, Why Girls Leave Home, Lola Lane, PRC Studio, 1945, 27 x 41 In.	234.00
Poster, Yearling, Gregory Peck, MGM, 1946, 27 x 41 In.	643.00
Poster, You Can't Cheat An Honest Man, W.C. Fields, Universal, 1939, 22 x 28 In.	585.00
Program, Gone With The Wind, David O. Selznick, MGM, 1939	83.00
Program, The Birth Of A Nation, D.W. Griffith, Epoch Producing Corp., 1916	83.00
Prop, Horse Head, Used In The Godfather, Taxidermy, Styrofoam Mount, 1970s, 34 x 24 In.	11500.00
Theater Turnstile, Lankershim Theater, Admit One 25 Cents, Perey New York	936.00

Mother-Of-Pearl, Vase, Diamond Quilted, Rainbow, Applied Thorny Branch Handles, Applied Feet, 9 ½ x 10 In.

$13,225.00

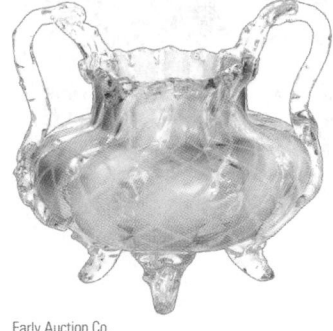

Early Auction Co.

Mother-Of-Pearl, Vase, Yellow Satin, Ribbed Zipper, Pink Inside, 5 ½ In.

$776.00

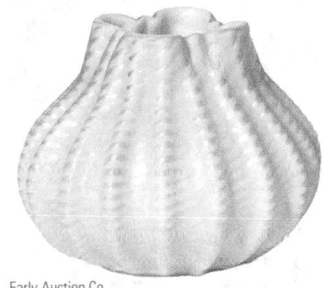

Early Auction Co.

Movie, Lobby Card, Some Like It Hot, Monroe, Curtis, Lemmon, 1959, 11 x 14 In., 7 Piece

$819.00

Hollywood Poster

Movie, Lobby Card, Wizard Of Oz, Judy Garland, 1939, 11 x 14 In., 6 Piece

$1,053.00

Hollywood Poster

M

Movie, Poster, Laura, Gene Tierney, Dana Andrews, 20th Century Fox, 1944, 22 x 28 In.
$936.00

Hollywood Poster

Movie, Poster, Mae West, Paramount, 1930s, 20 x 27 In.
$351.00

Hollywood Poster

Mt. Joye, Rose Bowl, Holly Berry & Leaf, Gilt, Painted, Stamp, 5 ½ x 6 In.
$240.00

DuMouchelles Art Gallery

TIP

Be careful about washing good crystal glasses in the dishwasher. The heat could crack them, especially glasses with cut decorations.

MT. JOYE is an enameled cameo glass made in the late nineteenth and twentieth centuries by Saint-Hilaire Touvier de Varraux and Co. of Pantin, France. This same company made De Vez glass. Pieces were usually decorated with enameling. Most pieces are not marked.

Decanter, Claret, Flowers, Metal Mounts, Hinged Lid, Art Nouveau, c.1900, 9 In.	805.00
Rose Bowl, Holly Berry & Leaf, Gilt, Painted, Stamp, 5 ½ x 6 In. ....*Illus*	240.00
Vase, Cameo, Frosted, Textured, Stylized Enamel Flowers, Signed, 8 In.	403.00
Vase, Cameo, Green, Textured, Urn Shape, Gilt Detail, Red Flowers, 6 In.	115.00
Vase, Cameo, Textured, Gilt, Silver Highlights, Sunflowers, Trumpet Shape, Footed, 10 In.	374.00
Vase, Cameo, Textured, Red Enameled Stemmed Flowers, Bulbous Stick, Bishop Miter Mark, 9 ½ In.	288.00
Vase, Enameled Iris, Dragonflies, Pale Yellow Glass, 5 ½ x 16 In.	1500.00
Vase, Frosted, Indigo To Amethyst, Flowers, Spread Foot, Narrow Stem, Swollen Shoulder, 11 ½ In.	575.00
Vase, Green, Textured, Gold Oak Tree & Acorn Overlay, Marked, 6 In. ....*Illus*	345.00
Vase, Opalescent Aqua, Enamel Pansies, Cylinder, Marked, 15 ¾ x 6 In.	266.00

MT. WASHINGTON Glass Works started in 1837 in South Boston, Massachusetts. In 1870 the company moved to New Bedford, Massachusetts. Many types of art glass were made there until 1894, when the company merged with Pairpoint Manufacturing Co. Amberina, Burmese, Crown Milano, Cut Glass, Peachblow, and Royal Flemish are each listed in their own category.

Atomizer, Daisies, Ribbed, Molded Leaf Feet, 7 In. ....*Illus*	403.00
Biscuit Jar, Mottled Yellow & Tan Leaves, Gilt Branches, Jewel Flowers, Lobed, Lid, 5 ½ In.	748.00
Biscuit Jar, Translucent, 3 Brownies, Mule, Pinch Sided, Lid, 8 In.	4025.00
Bride's Basket, Blue & White, Phoenix, Flowers, Ruffle Rim, Scroll Bail Handle, Pedestal Foot, 10 In.	690.00
Bride's Bowl, Cameo, Pink Cut To Opal, Squared Crimped Top, Griffin, Opal Inside, 8 x 4 In.	518.00
Butter, Cover, Rose Amber, Scalloped Rim, Snail Finial, Coin Spot, 7 In.	12650.00
Cake Plate, Lava, Black Plate, Multicolor Dome Lid, Gold Outlines, 13 ½ In. ....*Illus*	6900.00
Candlestick, Diamond Quilted, Peach, Yellow, Ribbing, Domed Foot, Ball Neck, 7 ¾ In.	230.00
Candlestick, Dolphin, Opaque Blue & White, Pressed, 1845-70, 10 ⅜ In.	354.00
Candlestick, Dolphin, Opaque White, Blue, c.1865, 10 In.	354.00
Candlestick, Enameled Leaf & Berry, Baluster, Ruffled Rim, Spread Foot, 6 In., Pair	2415.00
Candlestick, Petal Hexagonal, Blue, Over Clambroth, c.1860, 8 x 4 In., Pair	748.00
Candlestick, Turquoise, Hexagonal, 2 Knob Stem, Grooved Foot, c.1860, 7 x 4 In., Pair	173.00
Card Tray, Colonial Ware, Shell Shape, Opal Glass, Enamel Pansies, 6 In.	115.00
Container, Bulbous Egg Shape, Yellow To Peach, Daisies, Red Jeweled Flip Lid, 5 In.	431.00
Dish, Sweetmeat, Cream, Scrolling Pansies, Metal Lid, Squat, Lobed, 5 In.	403.00
Ewer, Peach To Yellow, Elongated Egg Shape, Scroll Handle, Upswept Spout, 11 ½ In.	3795.00
Hatpin Holder, Mushroom Shaped, Spread Foot, Tan, Pink, Blue Stippling, Flowers, Leaves, 5 ½ In.	431.00
Perfume Bottle, Egg Shape, Yellow Mums, Pale Blue, 4 In.	920.00
Perfume Bottle, Opal Glass, Enameled Flowers, Metal & Cork Stopper, Egg Shape, 4 In.	460.00
Pitcher, Milk, Newton, Cut Glass, Barrel Shape, Triple Notched Handle, 6 ½ In.	450.00
Powder Box, Flowers, Cream Opaque Ground, Silver Bezel, Lid, Cow Finial, 4 x 6 ¾ In.	140.00
Rose Bowl, Globular, Crimped Rim, Pontil, Blue, 5 In.	58.00
Rose Bowl, Opal Glass, Raspberries, Leaves, Ball Shape, Puckered Rim, 4 In.	144.00
Rose Bowl, White, Yellow Daisies, Satin Glass, Scalloped Rim, Oval, 4 ½ In.	115.00
Salt & Pepper, Cranberry, White & Yellow Mums, Fig Shape, 2 ½ In.	431.00
Salt & Pepper, Cream, Red Flowers, Chick Head Top, 2 ½ In., Pair	690.00
Salt & Pepper, Shell Shape, Pink Flowers, Blue, Green Leaves, 3 In., Pair	834.00
Salt & Pepper, Tomato Shape, Cream Color, Forget-Me-Nots, 1 ¾ In., Pair	173.00
Saltshaker, Chick Head, Seated Egg Shape, Blue, Yellow, Enameled Flowers, 2 ½ In., Pair	489.00
Saltshaker, Fig, Opal, Berries, Peach Finish, c.1890, 2 ½ In.	115.00
Saltshaker, Melon Ribbed, Blue & Opal, Gold Prunus, 2 In.	86.00
Saltshaker, Pink Opaline, White Lilies, Ring Neck, 4 In., Pair	29.00
Sugar & Creamer, Lid, Opaline Glass, Pansies, Red, Blue, Green, Ribbed, 4 In.	144.00
Sugar Shaker, Amber, Blue Flowers, Green Stems, Egg Shape, 4 ¼ In.	144.00
Sugar Shaker, Blue & Purple Pansies, Opal Ground, Blue Ribs, Fig Shape, 4 ¼ In.	920.00
Sugar Shaker, Blue To Opal, Tomato Shape, Daisies, 4 In.	144.00
Sugar Shaker, Chick Head, Beige, Farm Scene, 4 ½ In. ....*Illus*	4255.00
Sugar Shaker, Cockleshell, Opal Glass, Blue & Pink Flowers, 3 In.	201.00
Sugar Shaker, Cream Ground, Blue Berries, Leaves, Metal Lid, Gourd Shape, Lobed, 4 In.	374.00
Sugar Shaker, Egg Shape, Green & Opal, Purple & Red Pansies, 4 In.	230.00
Sugar Shaker, Fig, Tree Bark Texture, Cream, White & Red Flower Clusters, 4 ¼ In.	1035.00
Sugar Shaker, Opal, Blue Flowers, Cream Ground, Egg Shape, Silver Lid, c.1885, 4 ¼ In.	207.00
Sugar Shaker, Opal, Brown, Yellow & White Flowers, Fig Shape, 4 ¼ In.	805.00
Sugar Shaker, Opal, Maiden's Hair Fern, Yellow Ground, Tomato Shape, c.1880, 2 ¾ In.	259.00
Sugar Shaker, Opal, Shasta Daisy, Silver Lid, Embossed c.1970, 4 ¼ In.	161.00

Sugar Shaker, Pale Blue Glass, Elephant Ear Leaves, 4 ¼ In.	173.00
Sugar Shaker, White & Purple Flowers, Leaves, Fig Shape, Metal Top, 4 ¼ In.	575.00
Syrup, Acorns, Leaves, Melon Ribbed, Twisted Rope Handle, Metal Flare Spout, 4 ½ In.	288.00
Toothpick Holder, Diamond Quilted, Glossy, Square Mouth, Shaded, 2 ¾ In.	230.00
Toothpick Holder, Egg Shape, Scalloped Edge, Footed, Yellow, Peach, 3 ½ In.	144.00
Toothpick Holder, Finger Cut Top, Leaves, Blue Berries, Ribbed Pillar, Oval, 2 ½ In.	518.00
Toothpick Holder, Peach, Blueberries, Leaves, Hat Shape, Ruffle Rim, 2 ½ In.	489.00
Tumbler, Lava, Amethyst Glass, Gold, Multicolor, 3 In. ....Illus	1150.00
Tumbler, Pink To White, Cylindrical, Glossy, 3 ¾ In.	460.00
Tumbler, Queens Pattern, Stemmed Daisies, Blue To Pink, Cylindrical, White To Pink, 3 ¾ In.	6900.00
Vase, Bud, Pansies, Leaves, Scrolls, Cream Ground, Stick Neck, Bulbous, 8 In.	375.00
Vase, Dancing Couple, Colonial Ware, Elongated Oval, 2 Handles, 17 ¾ In.	4973.00
Vase, Enameled Flowering Branches, Pale Peach, Egg Shape, Disc Foot, Square Handles, 7 In.	1495.00
Vase, Flowers, Gilt Scrolling, Enamel, Thorn Handles, Colonial Ware, 9 ¼ In. ....Illus	460.00
Vase, Lava, Colored Squares Design, Bulbous, Flared Rim, 2 Reeded Round Handles, 5 In.	2185.00
Vase, Lava, Cone Shape, Pink Opaque, Yellow, Red, Green, Blue, Turquoise Shards, 4 ½ In.	1438.00
Vase, Lava, Shards Of Green, Red, Blue, Gold Accents, Bulbous, Pinched Neck, Flared Rim, 5 In.	1610.00
Vase, Lava, Urn Shape, Black, Gilt, Red, Blue, Yellow, Green, White Shards, Reeded Handles, 4 In.	4025.00
Vase, Opal Glass, Enameled Blackberries & Leaves, Squat, Swollen Stick Neck, 13 In.	1610.00
Vase, Opal Glass, Swirled Bowl Shape, Leaves, Blue Stippled Berries, 4 In.	230.00
Vase, Peach To Gold, Squat, Blueberries, Leaves, 4 ½ In.	173.00
Vase, Pink, Yellow & White Mums, Green Leaves, Double Gourd Shape, 6 ¾ In.	2300.00
Vase, Rose To Amber, Diamond Quilted Body, Squared Mouth, Scalloped Border, 6 In.	144.00
Vase, Storks, Desert Scene, Yellow, Pink, Gold Scroll Handles, Pear Shape, 11 In.	12650.00
Vase, Verona, Rose Amber Wash, Primrose Branches, Bulbous Stick, Trifold Rim, 12 ½ In.	1610.00

MULBERRY ware was made in the Staffordshire district of England from about 1850 to 1860. The dishes were decorated with a reddish brown transfer design, now called mulberry. Many of the patterns are similar to those used for flow blue and other Staffordshire transfer wares.

Coffeepot, Mother, Child, Pond, Bridge, Footed, 11 In.	325.00
Compote, Farming Scene, 1800s, 8 ¾ x 5 In.	73.00
Cup & Saucer, Romantic Scene, Castles, Gardens, Handleless, T. Goodfellow, c.1830	89.00
Plate, Cows, Sheep, Cartouches, 10 In.	115.00
Plate, Palm Trees, Pagoda, Octagonal, 7 In.	75.00
Platter, Corean, Island, Trees, 8-Sided, Podmore, Walker & Co., 17 x 13 In.	600.00
Platter, Washington Vase, Transfer, c.1850, 12 x 15 ¾ In.	104.00
Toothbrush Box, Lid, Castle Scene, c.1860, 8 x 3 x 3 In.	195.00

MULLER FRERES, French for Muller Brothers, made cameo and other glass from about 1895 to 1933. Their factory was first located in Luneville, then in nearby Croismare, France. Pieces were usually marked with the company name.

MULLER FRES
Luneville

Bowl, Light Amber, 5 x 6 ¼ In.	148.00
Chandelier, Dome, 3 Hanging Shades, Grapevine Frame, Wrought Iron, Signed, 25 x 37 In.	2375.00
Vase, Amber Cameo Water Lilies, Leaves, Blue Tones, Shouldered, Round, Signed, 6 ½ In.	144.00
Vase, Cameo, Amber Glass, Orange Mums, Red Stems, Globe Shape, Signed, 12 ¼ In.	2706.00
Vase, Gourd Shape, Bulbous, Orange, Gold Flecks, Diamond Shape Design, 5 In.	431.00
Vase, Gray Glass, Mottled Cobalt Blue, Purple, Green, Signed Luneville, 5 ¼ In.	120.00
Vase, Leaves, Woodbine Vine, Berry Pods, Brown, Orange, Pear Shape, Cameo, 4 In.	345.00
Vase, Mottled Rose, Blue Yellow, Etched, c.1925, 4 ½ In.	633.00
Vase, Rouge Peonies, Leaves, Mottled Yellow Ground, Flared Rim, Round Foot, Signed, 15 In.	1725.00
Vase, Sparrows On Wire, Flying, Mottled Yellow, Crimson & Brown, Cameo, Signed, 13 In. ...Illus	1725.00

MUNCIE Clay Products Company was established by Charles Benham in Muncie, Indiana, in 1922. The company made pottery for the florist and giftshop trade. The company closed by 1939. Pieces are marked with the name *Muncie* or just with a system of numbers and letters, like *1A*.

MUNCIE

Teapot, Lid, Red, Brown Glaze, 6 In.	58.00
Vase, Blue Glaze, 8 In.	6.00
Vase, Blue Glaze, Drippy, Handles, 7 ¾ In.	52.00
Vase, Blue Green, Tapered, Rolled Rim, 9 ½ In.	12.00
Vase, Brown, Green, To Tan, Tapered, 8 ½ In.	35.00
Vase, Pillow, Mauve, Green, 6 In.	81.00

MURANO, *see Glass-Venetian category.*

Mt. Joye, Vase, Green, Textured, Gold Oak Tree & Acorn Overlay, Marked, 6 In. $345.00

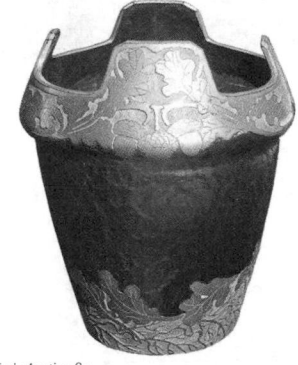

Early Auction Co.

Mt. Washington, Atomizer, Daisies, Ribbed, Molded Leaf Feet, 7 In. $403.00

Early Auction Co.

Mt. Washington, Cake Plate, Lava, Black Plate, Multicolor Dome Lid, Gold Outlines, 13 ½ In. $6,900.00

Early Auction Co.

Mt. Washington, Sugar Shaker, Chick Head, Beige, Farm Scene, 4 ½ In. $4,255.00

Early Auction Co.

M

Mt. Washington, Tumbler, Lava, Amethyst Glass, Gold, Multicolor, 3 In. $1,150.00

Early Auction Co.

Mt. Washington, Vase, Flowers, Gilt Scrolling, Enamel, Thorn Handles, Colonial Ware, 9 ¼ In. $460.00

Early Auction Co.

Muller Freres, Vase, Sparrows On Wire, Flying, Mottled Yellow, Crimson & Brown, Cameo, Signed, 13 In. $1,725.00

Early Auction Co.

MUSIC boxes and musical instruments are listed here. Phonograph records, jukeboxes, phonographs, and sheet music are listed in other categories in this book.	

Accordion, 34 Keys, Black Plastic Case, Italy, 9 x 17 In.	144.00
Accordion, 41 Keys, Black, White, Flowers, Galanti Bros., N.Y. Travel Case, c.1925, 18-In. Keyboard	150.00
Accordion, Solo, Mother-Of-Pearl Accents, Hard Case	102.00
Alto Saxophone, Brass, Yamaha, Case, 26 In.	655.00
Amplifier, 30 Watts, Peavey Delft Blues, Speaker, Tweed Tolex Amplifier, Wheels	236.00
Amplifier, Bass, Fender Musical Instruments, Model Bassman, 1966, 20 In.	840.00
Banjo, 5-String, Lansing, Stamped, 30-Bracket Rim, Case, L.B. Gatcomb, c.1890	450.00
Banjo, Fairbanks Whyte Laydie, Stamped, Branded, Labeled, Vega, c.1895, 10 ¾ In.	3240.00
Banjo, Tenor, 4-String, Model 207, Maple, Inlays, Ebony Fretboard, Slingerland, 11 In.	325.00
Banjo, Tenor, Gibson, 22 Bracket Rim, Stamped, Case, c.1927	420.00
Banjo, Tenor, Resonator, Mother-Of-Pearl Inlay, Peg Board, Hard Shell Case, Vega, c.1927	561.00
Barrel Orchestrion, Weight Driven, 2 8-Air Wood Barrels, Wood Case, J. Klepetar, c.1900, 38 x 90 In.	3988.00
Bow, Violin, French Nickel Mounts, c.1880	240.00
Bow, Violin, Silver Mounts, Johs Monnig.	480.00
Bow, Violin, Silver Mounts, Octagonal Stick, Stamped, W.A. Pfretzschner	240.00
Bow, Violin, Silver Mounts, Round Stick, Stamped, Eury	210.00
Bow, Violoncello, Vuillaume School, Silver Mounts	2040.00
Box, Bee Strikers, Inlaid Horn & Flute, Flowers, Lid, Austria, c.1885, 9 ¼ x 19 In.	1955.00
Box, Burl Veneer, Plays La Paloma, Coming Through The Rye, Swiss, 2 ¾ x 6 In.	69.00
Box, Burled Walnut, Banded, Mother-Of-Pearl Inlays, 6-Tunes, c.1850, 7 x 24 ½ In.	649.00
Box, Calliope, Double Comb, Walnut Case, Border, Stencil, Crank, 12 Discs, 16 x 15 In.	1265.00
Box, Carved Hinged Case, Lift Arm, Comb, Muster Schultz, Celesta, 19 Discs, c.1900, 9 x 15 In.	1188.00
Box, Cylinder, Black, Gilt, Figures In Garden, Phoenix, Flowers, Swiss Organette, c.1900, 9 x 20 In.	4182.00
Box, Cylinder, Mahogany Case, Windup, 6 Tunes, Swiss, St. Croix, 2 ½ x 6 In.	146.00
Box, Cylinder, Mandoline Organcleide, Rosewood, 10 Tunes, 7 Bells, Bremond, Geneva, 36 In. ....*Illus*	4613.00
Box, Cylinder, Rosewood, Inlay, Mask Handle, Ivory Escutcheon, 8 Tunes, c.1890, 6 ½ x 22 ½ In.	717.00
Box, Cylinder, Rosewood, Mahogany, Bells, Drum, Snare Drum, 12 Tunes, Swiss, 12 x 31 In.	4715.00
Box, Cylinder, Snare Drum & 6 Bells, Walnut, Inlay, 8 Tunes, Swiss, 25 ½ x 14 In............*Illus*	3162.00
Box, Cylinder, Victorian, Mahogany Case, 8 Tunes, Swiss, 1800s, 20 In.	330.00
Box, Empress Parlor, Mahogany Case, Claw Feet, c.1900, 59 Discs, 49 x 29 In.	4617.00
Box, Enamel, Metal Frame, Glass, Royal Carriage Shape, Scenes, Austria, c.1910, 7 x 10 ¾ In.	2375.00
Box, Figural, Man In Robes, Ein Feste Burg Islunser Gott, Metal, Painted Silver, Windup, 16 In.	120.00
Box, Melodia, Organ Grinder, Mechanical Orguinette Co., 11 x 12 In.	207.00
Box, Mermod Freres, Lyre Medallion, Rosewood, Single 16-In. Spool, 7 x 27 ¼ In.	1534.00
Box, Miraphone, Parquetry Border, Floral Inlay Panel, Hinged Lid, 7-In. Disc, 13 x 9 In.	321.00
Box, Mr. Christmas, Hanover Style, Wood Case, Glass Sides, Top, 10 Discs, 8 x 14 x 7 In.	210.00
Box, Regina Serpentine No. 50, 8 Discs, c.1890	4760.00
Box, Regina, Changer, Glass Door, Walnut Frame, Scrolled Crest, 26 x 70 In.	9300.00
Box, Regina, Mahogany Case, Casket, Serpentine Lid, Double Comb, Crank, 30 Discs, 29 x 21 In.	8625.00
Box, Regina, Mahogany, Crank, 15 Discs, c.1895, 9 x 14 ½ In.	1000.00
Box, Regina, Mahogany, Double Comb, Sliding Doors, 12 Discs, Pat. May 18, 1897, 84 x 43 In. ....*Illus*	8260.00
Box, Regina, Stepped Mahogany Case, Double Comb, 35 15 ½-In. Discs, 12 x 21 In.	2070.00
Box, Rosewood Inlay, Flowers & Leaves, Birds, Bees, Dragonflies On Chimes, Swiss, 10 x 28 x 13 In.	2400.00
Box, Singing Bird, Beak Opens & Closes, Moves Head, Flaps Wings, Bontems, 1900s, 11 x 22 In. ....*Illus*	805.00
Box, Singing Bird, Brass Box, Key Wind, Germany, 1 ¾ x 4 ⅛ x 2 ⅝ In.	1652.00
Box, Singing Bird, Brass Box, Openwork Scrolling, Key Wind, Germany, 1 ¾ x 4 ⅛ In.	1534.00
Box, Singing Bird, Cage, 2 Birds, France, c.1910, 20 ½ x 11 In. ....*Illus*	1560.00
Box, Singing Bird, Cage, Brass, 3 Animated Feathered Birds, Germany, c.1920, 15 x 10 In.	1205.00
Box, Singing Bird, Cage, Germany, 19th Century, 11 In.	296.00
Box, Singing Bird, Cage, Gesso, Gilt Brass, Windup, Rectangular, Marked KG, c.1930, 10 x 6 In.	345.00
Box, Singing Bird, Cage, Gilded, France, 11 In.	516.00
Box, Singing Bird, Cage, Gilt Brass, Windup, Round, c.1930, 11 ½ In.	374.00
Box, Singing Bird, Enamel, Parcel Gilt, Venetian Scenes, 1800s, 4 ½ x 2 ½ In. ....*Illus*	14160.00
Box, Singing Bird, Flaps Wings, Moves Beak, Black Forest, Spring Driven, Germany, c.1930, 4 x 2 In.	2221.00
Box, Singing Bird, Medallion On Top, Tortoiseshell, 19th Century, 1 ¼ x 4 x 2 ½ In.	2070.00
Box, Singing Bird, Multicolor Feathers, Flaps Wings, Moves Beak, Silver Case, Germany, 9 ½ In.	7620.00
Box, Singing Bird, Perched On Branch, Gilt Metal Cage, Stamped Reuge, Swiss, 11 x 6 ¼ In.	840.00
Box, Singing Bird, Pop-Up Lid, Gilt Silver, Relief Panels, Exotic Birds, Key Wind, 1800s, 4 In. ....*Illus*	2596.00
Box, Singing Bird, Red & Black Plumage, Cloth Flowers, Brass Cage, Clockwork, c.1900, 11 In. ....*Illus*	308.00
Box, Singing Bird, Silver Repousse Case, Cherubs, Scrollwork, 3 ¾ x 2 In. ....*Illus*	2963.00
Box, Singing Bird, Tortoiseshell Case, Engraved Silver Lid, Pop-Up Bird, c.1890, 3 ¾ x 2 ½ In.	3000.00
Box, Singing Bird, Yellow, In Brass Cage, France, c.1910, 11 x 6 ½ In.	600.00
Box, Singing Birds, 3 Birds Singing In Cage, 5 Cent, Key Wind, France	3920.00
Box, Sublime Harmony Piccolo, Cylinder, Oak Case, Drawer, 3 Cylinders, Mermod Freres, 13 x 37 In.	4374.00
Box, Symphonia, Upright, Walnut Veneer, Shelves, Drawers, 40 Discs, Germany, 82 In.....*Illus*	4740.00

M

Music, Box, Cylinder, Mandoline Organcleide, Rosewood, 10 Tunes, 7 Bells, Bremond, Geneva, 36 In.
$4,613.00

Skinner, Inc.

Music, Box, Cylinder, Snare Drum & 6 Bells, Walnut, Inlay, 8 Tunes, Swiss, 25 ½ x 14 In.
$3,162.00

James D. Julia Auctioneers

Music, Box, Regina, Mahogany, Double Comb, Sliding Doors, 12 Discs, Pat. May 18, 1897, 84 x 43 In.
$8,260.00

Conestoga Auction Co., Inc.

Music, Box, Singing Bird, Beak Opens & Closes, Moves Head, Flaps Wings, Bontems, 1900s, 11 x 22 In.
$805.00

Victorian Casino Antiques

Music, Box, Singing Bird, Cage, 2 Birds, France, c.1910, 20 ½ x 11 In.
$1,560.00

DuMouchelles Art Gallery

Music, Box, Singing Bird, Enamel, Parcel Gilt, Venetian Scenes, 1800s, 4 ½ x 2 ½ In.
$14,160.00

Brunk Auctions

Music, Box, Singing Bird, Pop-Up Lid, Gilt Silver, Relief Panels, Exotic Birds, Key Wind, 1800s, 4 In.
$2,596.00

Brunk Auctions

Music, Box, Singing Bird, Red & Black Plumage, Cloth Flowers, Brass Cage, Clockwork, c.1900, 11 In.
$308.00

Skinner, Inc.

Music, Box, Singing Bird, Silver Repousse Case, Cherubs, Scrollwork, 3 ¾ x 2 In.
$2,963.00

Skinner, Inc.

M

Music, Box, Symphonia, Upright, Walnut Veneer, Shelves, Drawers, 40 Discs, Germany, 82 In.
$4,740.00

Skinner, Inc.

Music, Box, Symphonion, Eroica, Triple Disc, Oak, 12 Sets Of Discs, 1889, 28 ½ x 81 x 18 ½ In.
$24,600.00

Showtime Auction Sevices

Music, Guitar, Gibson, Electric, Firebird VII, Case, 1964, 19 In.
$4,920.00

Skinner, Inc.

Box, Symphonia, Walnut, Carved Crest & Columns, Tombstone Door, 4 Discs, 82 In.	5600.00
Box, Symphonion Disc, Tune Plaque No. 10, Painted Winter Scene, 11 x 9 In.	690.00
Box, Symphonion, Eroica, Triple Disc, Oak, 12 Sets Of Discs, 1889, 28 ½ x 81 x 18 ½ In...*Illus*	24600.00
Box, Symphonion, Mahogany, Lion's Head Pull, Children Playing Instruments, Germany, 22 x 18 In.	1659.00
Box, Thorens, Birds, Flowers Engraved, Silvered, Key Wind, 49 Discs, 4 Legs, Swiss, 9 x 17 In.	850.00
Box, Tremolo Zither, Rosewood, Inlaid, Single Roll, 6 Songs, 6 In.	540.00
Box, Walnut, Grain Paint, Inlays, 6 Tunes, Swiss, c.1870, 6 ¼ x 20 In.	443.00
Box, Whip Holder, Scottie Dog, Gun, Overcoat, Whip Activated, Germany, c.1870, 12 In.	1458.00
Box, Whistler, Man, Lamppost, Wood, Carved, Paint, Germany, 21 ½ In.	356.00
Box, Wood, Inlaid Flowers, Black Highlights, Hinged Lid, Glass Door, Swiss, 7 x 23 In.	660.00
Box, Zither-Harmonique, Cylinder, 6 Tunes, Walnut Case, 22 ¼ x 9 In.	1035.00
Bugle, Brass, Copper, 1940s, 11 In.	96.00
Calliope, Chevy Cab Truck, 6 Rolls, Model CA-43, Red, Blue Paint, Tangley, 1925, 184 x 96 In.	7700.00
Chime, Arts & Crafts, Sonora, Oak Case, Brass, Lever Actuated, c.1910, 9 x 9 ½ x 6 In.	184.00
Clarinet, Boxwood, E Flat, Turned, Brass Fittings, 1800s, 16 ¾ In.	295.00
Drum, Snare, Remo, 12 ½ In.	11.00
Flageolet, 1-Key, Firth & Hall, Stamped, c.1830, 17 ½ In.	120.00
Flute, 3-Key, 14 ¾ In.	48.00
Flute, Boxwood, 1-Key, Firth, Pond & Co., 4 Sections, Ivory Keys, Endcap, Brass Key, c.1860, 24 In.	240.00
Flute, Gemeinhardt, E71436	23.00
Flute, Harry Bettoney, Grenadilla Body, Nickel Keys, c.1905, 23 ⅞ In.	270.00
Flute, Rosewood, 6-Key, Nickel Rings & Keys, 23 ⅝ In.	84.00
Gittern, Fruitwood, Gilt Openwork Soundhole, Tortoise Inset Fretboard, 26 ½ x 11 ⅜ In.	649.00
Gong, Figural Stand, Wood, Brass, Temple Guardians, Monkeys, Indonesia, 1900s, 33 x 58 In.	529.00
Guitar, Acoustic, Gibson L-48, Sunburst Arch Top.c.1965, 41 In.	1190.00
Guitar, Acoustic, Gurian J-M Model, Rosewood, Herringbone Rope Purfling, Case, 1978, Jumbo	1416.00
Guitar, Acoustic, Martin HD-28 6-String, Maple, Walnut, Case, 40 ¾ In.	2415.00
Guitar, Baroque, Cerin Marco Anatonio Label, c.1800, 17 ¾ In.	1080.00
Guitar, C.F. Martin, Style, Spruce Top, Ivory, Mother-Of-Pearl, Rosewood, Snowflakes, 1900	4200.00
Guitar, Electric, Bass, Fender Musical Instruments, Style Bass VI, Case, c.1974, 18 ½ In.	3000.00
Guitar, Electric, Bass, Gibson, Model EB-1, 1958, 19 In.	2607.00
Guitar, Electric, C.F. Martin E-28, Mahogany, Hard Shell Case, 1982	1416.00
Guitar, Electric, Fender, 12-String, Model Electric XII, 1965, 18 In.	1659.00
Guitar, Electric, Fender, Jaguar, 1965, 17 In.	3081.00
Guitar, Electric, Fender, Stratocaster, 1963, 15 ¾ In.	10073.00
Guitar, Electric, Fender, Stratocaster, Teal Body, Dot Inserts, Brushed Metal, 1984-88	1320.00
Guitar, Electric, Fender, Stratocaster, Teal Body, Dot Inserts, Metal Tuning Keys, 1984-88	900.00
Guitar, Electric, Fender, Telecaster Custom, 1967, 15 ¾ In.	2963.00
Guitar, Electric, Fullerton, Telecaster, 1953, 15 ¾ In.	38513.00
Guitar, Electric, Gibson, Pete Townshend Signature Model, 2000	4900.00
Guitar, Electric, Ventures Model, Mostrite Of California, Stamped, Case, Strap, 1965, 15 ⅝ In.	2280.00
Guitar, Electric, Washburn, 6-String, Dimebag Darrell Model, Hard Case, 47 In.	124.00
Guitar, Gibson 125 TDC Single Cutaway, P-90 Single Coil Pick Ups, Soft Shell Case, 1963	2950.00
Guitar, Gibson LG-1, 6-String, Sunburst Finish, Mother-Of-Pearl Fret Inlays, Case, c.1950	805.00
Guitar, Gibson, Electric, Firebird VII, Case, 1964, 19 In. ....*Illus*	4920.00
Guitar, Gibson, Electric, Les Paul TV Model, Original Vibrato, Case, 1959, 14 In........*Illus*	5880.00
Guitar, Gibson, Electric, Model ES-350T, 1963.................................*Illus*	5333.00
Guitar, Gibson, Les Paul Ace Frehley, Sunburst, Hard Shell, No, 90198396	2760.00
Guitar, Gibson, Les Paul, Ultima, Custom Shop, Sunburst Quilt Top, Abalone Inlay	6038.00
Guitar, Jazz Base, Fender, Maple, Block Inlays, Sunburst Body, c.1970	2714.00
Guitar, Panormo, Rosewood, Spanish Style, 37 x 11 ⅜ In.	3540.00
Guitar, Parlor, New World, 12 Frets, Slotted Peg Head, George Washburn, 1897, 13 x 9 In.	354.00
Guitar, Tiple, C.F. Martin & Company, Style T-18, Stamped, 1922	600.00
Harmonica, Super Chromonica In C, Hard Case, Hohner, 1 ½ x 6 ½ In.	86.00
Harp, 46-String, Maple, Gilt Flowers, Tuning Key, Cover, Lyon & Healy, Model 15, c.1953, 71 In.	4025.00
Harp, Empire Style, Maple, Parcel Gilt, Classical Figures, Sebastian Erard, London, 67 In.	1195.00
Harp, European, Hand Painted, Putti In Flight, Cream, Black Borders, Ball Feet, 1800s, 36 x 36 In.	300.00
Harp, Gothic Column, Bird's-Eye Maple, Rosewood, 7 Pedal, Sebastian Erard, 1850, 70 x 37 In.	2596.00
Harp, Mixed Woods, Parcel Gilt, 7-Pedal, Dog Feet, S. Erard, Paris, c.1840, 70 x 37 In.	1416.00
Harp, Pedal, Giltwood, Ram's Heads, Dancing Maidens, 42 String, Erard, France, c.1820, 67 In.	3737.00
Harp, Sitka Spruce, Tiger Maple, Rosewood, Lyon & Healy, c.1926, 70 ½ In.	7500.00
Horn, Baritone, Brass, Engraved Carl Fischer Reliable New York, 25 ½ x 14 In.	74.00
Mandolin Banjo, Gibson, MB-2, Resonator Back, Black Hard Case, 1929, 27 In.	708.00
Mandolin, Gagliano, Fabricante Di, Via Sanita 79, Napoki, Case, Label, Naples, c.1880, 12 ⅝ In..*Illus*	420.00
Mandolin, Gibson, Style F-4, Label, 1915, 13 In. ....*Illus*	3555.00

M

Mandolin, Labeled Sistema De Meglio, c.1890, 31 In.	110.00
Mandolin, Vega Company Label, Branded, c.1925, 12 ¾ In.	570.00
Melodeon, Classical, Rosewood Veneer, Foldover Top, Ivory & Wood Keys, Bellows, 1800s, 31 x 29 In.	299.00
Melodeon, Mahogany, Tapered Legs, Carhart's Improved, 30 ½ x 29 In.	236.00
Nickelodeon, Wurlitzer Pianino, Piano, Mandolin, Nickel Drop, Oak Cabinet, 1913, 41 x 61 In.	3600.00
Organ, Fairground, 61 Keys, 25-30 Piece Band, Painted, Belgium Decap, 1935, 162 x 90 In.	21000.00
Organ, Pump, Walnut, Carved, Kimball-Chicago, Victorian, 51 ¾ x 49 ¼ In.	62.00
Organ, Roller, Glass, Wood, Stenciled, Crank, Lift Top, c.1900, 18 x 15 In.	908.00
Organ, Serinette, Crank Barrel, Side Sliding Lever, France, c.1750, 10 ½ x 5 ¾ In.	726.00
Piano, Baby Grand, Brambach, Mahogany Case, Salesman's Sample, 18 x 14 x 22 In.	8250.00
Piano, Baby Grand, Ebonized, Mason & Hamlin, No. A3247A, c.1925, 40 x 59 In.	1140.00
Piano, Baby Grand, Steinway & Sons, Walnut, Model M, Bench, c.1962, 66 x 57 In.	4600.00
Piano, Baby Grand, Steinway, Mahogany, Bench, c.1911, 70 In.	5000.00
Piano, Baby Grand, William Knabe, Mahogany, No. 148424, Bench, 60 In.	600.00
Piano, Concert Grand, Steinway, Model D, Rosewood Case, Marlborough Legs, c.1881, 105 x 59 In.	9200.00
Piano, Console, Steinway, Ebonized Black Case, Bench, 42 x 59 In.	540.00
Piano, Grand, J. Schneider & Neffe, Walnut, String Inlay, Stool, Austria, c.1880, 37 x 73 In.	575.00
Piano, Grand, Rosewood, Leaf Carved, Candle Slides, Collard & Collard, c.1860, 80 x 59 In.	7735.00
Piano, Grand, Rosewood, Square, c.1910, 39 x 74 In.	177.00
Piano, Grand, Square, Steinway, Rosewood, Ornate Carving, Shaped Legs, c.1885	4500.00
Piano, Grand, Steinway, Ebonized, Bench, c.1903, 70 ¾ In.	9375.00
Piano, Grand, Steinway, Ebonized, c.1929, 69 In.	7500.00
Piano, Grand, Steinway, Mahogany, Model M, Ball & Claw Feet, Bench, c.1935, 37 x 56 In.	27000.00
Piano, Grand, Steinway, Model L, Mahogany, Cabriole Legs, Claw Feet, Bench, 56 x 67 In.	12650.00
Piano, Grand, Steinway, Model M, No. 318273, Mahogany, c.1945, 38 ¾ x 67 In.	6195.00
Piano, Grand, United Piano Makers, Rosewood, Square, Cast Iron Sound Board, Stool, 80 x 40 In.	443.00
Piano, Player, Poppers, Oak Parquet Cabinet, 13 Music Rolls, Welt Piano, 1925, 61 x 59 In.	2880.00
Piano, Player, Smith & Barnes, Orchestrion, Mahogany, Gilt, 31 Music Rolls, 63 In.	1800.00
Piano, Player, Stuyvesant Pianola Orchestrion, 33 Music Rolls, c.1900, 80 x 99 In.	2400.00
Piano, Rosewood, Fold-Up Keyboard, Metal Wood, 55 x 47 In.	138.00
Pianoforte, Regency, Mahogany, Hinged Top, Shelf, 68 Keys, Comkinson & Co., 32 x 65 In.	885.00
Polyphone, Walnut Case, Marquetry, Putto, Single Comb, Disc Music Box, 1800s, 13 x 25 In.	480.00
Saxophone, Alto, Bundy II, Brass, Mother-Of-Pearl, Chrome, Black Case, Selmer Co., 28 In.	480.00
Saxophone, French Alto, Henri Seler, Paris, 1935	3430.00
Saxophone, King Voll-True, Hard Case, 25 In.	203.00
Saxophone, Soprano, Brass, Evette Buffet Crampon, Case, 27 In.	357.00
Saxophone, Soprano, Brass, Yanagisawa, Case, 27 In.	952.00
Saxophone, Soprano, Buescher, Elkhart, 1925	521.00
Saxophone, Soprano, Model Mark IV, 1977	2695.00
Saxophone, Tenor, Brass, Haynes Schwelm, Case, 32 In.	238.00
Saxophone, Tenor, Buescher, Elkhart, 1921	425.00
Saxophone, Tenor, French, Model Mark VI, 1961	6518.00
Saxophone, The Indiana, Martin, Hard Case, 24 In.	124.00
Tambourine, Hide, Wood, Red Paint, E.J. Kirschner, Minstrel Show, Philadelphia, 1902, 8 In.	259.00
Trumpet, Brass, F.E. Olds & Sons, No. 381248, Case, 18 ½ In.	186.00
Ukelin, Wood, Stringed, Tuning Crank, Bow, Label Manufactures Advertising Co., 28 x 8 In.	59.00
Ukulele, C.F. Martin & Company, Stamped, c.1930, 9 ⁷⁄₁₆ In.	450.00
Ukulele, Soprano, Mahogany, Martin, Small	153.00
Vignette, Dancing Kittens, Windup, Shadowbox Frame, Gilt, Au Nain Bleu, c.1890, 16 x 12 In. *Illus*	1120.00
Viola, Bow, Nickel Mounted, Octagonal, Stamped Tourte	240.00
Viola, D'Amore, Scroll Carved, Head Of Man With Mustache, Flame Soundholes, 30 ½ x 9 ½ In.	2596.00
Viola, Neapolitan, School Of Vincanzo Sannino, c.1920, 16 ¾ In.	11850.00
Violin, Alfredo Del Lungo Di Giuseppe, Fece In Firenze Nel, 1939	72.00
Violin, Antonious & Hieronymous Fr. Amati Creonen, Bow, Case, c.1700, 23 In.	978.00
Violin, Antono Monzino E. Figli, Label, c.1915	7110.00
Violin, Antonus Gragnann Fecit, Label, 1835	11850.00
Violin, August Eberle, Carrollton, Ohio, 1930, 24 In.	180.00
Violin, Bow, Gold Mounted, Round, Nickel Ferrule	2160.00
Violin, Charles H. Herrick, Winchester, Label, 1912, 14 In.	3000.00
Violin, Chipot-Vuillaume, French, Label, c.1885, 14 In.	2880.00
Violin, Giuseppe Lucci, Label, 1971	13200.00
Violin, John A. Gould, Hamilton, Manuscript Label, 1885, 14 In.	2880.00
Violin, Ludwig Glaser Jr., Markneukirchen, Label, 1925, 14 In.	4613.00
Violin, Oreste Martini, Miantua, 1919	11025.00
Violin, Paolo Casstello, Genoa, c.1775	79625.00

Music, Guitar, Gibson, Electric, Les Paul TV Model, Original Vibrato, Case, 1959, 14 In.
$5,880.00

Skinner, Inc.

Music, Guitar, Gibson, Electric, Model ES-350T, 1963
$5,333.00

Skinner, Inc.

Music, Mandolin, Gagliano, Fabricante Di, Via Sanita 79, Napoki, Case, Label, Naples, c.1880, 12 ⅝ In.
$420.00

Skinner, Inc.

The edited listings of the current prices in this *Kovels' Antiques & Collectibles Price Guide* aren't available on any website. Readers can visit **Kovels.com** to check thousands of past prices and sign up for free information on trends, tips, reproductions, marks, and more.

M

Music, Mandolin, Gibson, Style F-4, Label, 1915, 13 In. $3,555.00

Skinner, Inc.

Music, Vignette, Dancing Kittens, Windup, Shadowbox Frame, Gilt, Au Nain Bleu, c.1890, 16 x 12 In. $1,120.00

Theriault's

Nailsea, Fairy Lamp, Cranberry, Clear Holder, 4 ¾ In. $115.00

Early Auction Co.

Natzler, Bowl, Folded, Yellow, Gertrud & Otto Natzler, c.1956, 5 ¼ x 3 ¼ In. $2,520.00

Cowans + Clark + DelVecchio

Violin, Paul Bailly, France, Label, c.1900, 14 ½ In.	2040.00
Violin, Paul Kaul, Nantes, Chenantais-Kaul Label, No. 42, 1912	10200.00
Violin, Petrus Joannes Mantegazz Fecit Me Label, c.1780, Case	6000.00
Violin, Sewell L. Boyce, Norwich, New York, Label, 1893, 14 In.	3360.00
Violin, Stefanio Scarampella Mantua, c.1910	94800.00
Violin, Tiger Maple, Arno Erwin Hendel, Markneukirchen, Germany, c.1920	800.00
Violin, Trade, Eduard Reichert, Germany, 1908, 14 In.	277.00
Violin, Tyrolean, Kloz Family, Nicolaus Amatus, c.1770	8295.00
Violoncello, August Winderlich, Markneukirchen, Label, c.1900	5100.00
Violoncello, Charles Buthod, France, c.1800	4622.00
Zither, Triola, Mechanical, 25-Note Paper Rolls, Crank Operated, Paul Riessner, 1919	949.00

MUSTACHE CUPS were popular from 1850 to 1900 when the large, flowing mustache was in style. A ledge of china or silver held the hair out of the liquid in the cup. This kept the mustache tidy and also kept the mustache wax from melting. Left-handed mustache cups are rare but are being reproduced.

Bamboo Design, Handle, Geometric Rim, Brownhills	30.00
Brown, Ringed Foot, Finger Grip Handle, Frankoma, 1960s, 4 In.	27.00
Majolica, Butterfly, Multicolor, Fielding	54.00
Man, Handle Bar Mustache, Blue Trim, Multicolor, 3 ¾ In.	23.00
Painted Flowers, Gilt Rim, Scroll Handle, Scalloped Base, Limoges, 3 ½ In.	15.00
Painted Flowers, Gilt Ruffled Rim, Red Mark, R.S. Prussia, 3 ½ x 4 ½ In.	77.00
Painted Flowers, Gilt Scalloped Rim, Scroll Handle, Gold Crown Mark, 3 ½ In.	17.00
Painted Flowers, Lattice, Gilt Scalloped Rim, Scroll Handle, Nippon, 3 ½ In.	17.00
Painted Victorian Scene, Women, Gold Trim, Scroll Handle, Royal Bavarian, 3 In.	15.00
Pink Azaleas, Pitkin & Brooks, c.1910	119.00
Saucer, Majolica, Fishnet, Shells, Multicolor, Fielding	393.00

MZ AUSTRIA is the wording on a mark used by Moritz Zdekauer on porcelains made *MZ Austria* at his works in Altrolau, Austria, from 1884 to 1909. The mark was changed to MZ *Altrolau* in 1909, when the firm was purchased by C.M. Hutschenreuther. The firm operated under the name Altrolau Porcelain Factories from 1909 to 1945. It was nationalized after World War II. The pieces were decorated with lavish floral patterns and overglaze gold decoration. Full sets of dishes were made as well as vases, toilet sets, and other wares.

Bonbon, Pink Roses, Gold Beading, Pearl Luster Interior, Handles, Round, 7 ½ x 2 In.	60.00
Cake Plate, Green Ground, White Center, Poppies, Raised Enamel, Gilt, Open Handles, 10 ½ In.	49.00
Dish, Arts & Crafts, 4 Lobes, Split Handle, White Ground, Multicolor, Signed, 11 x 7 In.	147.00
Dresser Tray, Pink Roses, Green Ground, Cutout Handles, c.1900, 12 ½ x 8 ¼ In.	75.00
Egg Plate, 6 Wells, Salt & Pepper, Blackberries, Multicolor, Luster, 1900s, 9 ½ x 9 In.	199.00
Hair Receiver, Painted, Blue Flowers, Multicolor, Dragon & Crown Mark, 3 ½ x 3 In.	32.00
Plate Set, Dessert, Bluebird, Blooming Branch, Stamped, 7 ¾ In., 4 Piece	65.00
Plate Set, Dessert, White Ground, Pink Rose Swags, Blue Flowers, Gilt Border, 6 In., 4 Piece	180.00
Tea Set, Teapot, Sugar, Creamer, Green, Roses, Gold Handles, Trim, Finials, Diamond Shape, 1930s	65.00
Vase, Arts & Crafts, Iris, Violet, Green, Yellow, Cylindrical, 9 ½ x 2 ¾ In.	597.00

NAILSEA glass was made in the Bristol district in England from 1788 to 1873. The name also applies to glass made by many different factories, not just the Nailsea Glass House. Many pieces were made with loopings of either white or colored glass as decoration.

Bowl, Shouldered, Blue, Clear, c.1875, 3 ¾ x 7 ½ In.	175.00
Bowl, Yellow, White, Ruffled Rim, 3 ⅞ x 5 In.	225.00
Fairy Lamp, Cranberry, Clear Holder, 4 ¾ In. ....*Illus*	115.00
Fairy Lamp, Fuchsia, Clear, Trifold Base, Ruffled Rim, Clear Insert, Footed, 8 In.	259.00
Fairy Lamp, Fuchsia, Crimped Rim, Opaque Swags, Swirl Design, 5 ¾ In.	173.00
Flask, Cranberry To Clear, Looping, 9 In.	154.00
Flask, Pink, White Case, Oval, 7 In.	94.00
Pipe, Whimsy, Blue Opalescent, Bulbous Bowl, Victorian, c.1875, 16 ¾ In.	450.00
Rolling Pin, Red & Blue Splashes, Open Pontil, 19th Century, 14 ¼ x 2 In.	295.00

NAKARA is a trade name for a white glassware made about 1900 by the C. F. Monroe **NAKARA** Company of Meriden, Connecticut. It was decorated in pastel colors. The glass was very similar to another glass, called Wave Crest, made by the company. The company closed in 1916. Boxes for use on a dressing table are the most commonly found Nakara pieces. The mark is not found on every piece.

Biscuit Jar, Blue To Opal, Enameled Blossoms, Gold Accents, Branch, Lid, Marked, 7 ½ In.	748.00

M

Box, Burmese, Enameled Flowers, Gilt Metal Banding, Hinged, Satin Lining, 2 ½ In.	86.00
Dresser Box, Green Stylized Gilt Bands, Pink Flowers, Bishop Miter Shape, 8 In.	431.00
Dresser Box, Yellow, Red Flowers, Bishop Miter Shape, Marked, 6 In.	345.00

NANKING is a type of blue-and-white porcelain made in China from the late 1700s to the early 1900s. It was shipped from the port of Nanking. It is similar to Canton wares listed in that category, but it is of better quality. The blue design was almost the same, a landscape, building, trees, and a bridge. But a person was sometimes on the bridge on a Nanking piece. The "spear and post" border was used, sometimes with gold added. Nanking sells for more than Canton.

Bowl, Scalloped Edge, Lion Armorial, 1800s, 10 ¾ In.	652.00
Gravy Boat, Crimped Edge, Blue, White, Handle, c.1775, 7 ¼ x 3 ¼ In.	450.00
Mug, Twisted Handle, Raised Dot, Blue Flowers, Willow Tree Scene, Floral Border, 5 ½ x 4 In.	236.00
Plate, People On Bridge, Spear Border, c.1800, 7 ½ In.	165.00
Platter, Blue & White, Landscape, Diaper Border, 18th Century, 10 x 6 In.	625.00
Platter, Blue & White, Landscape, Leaf Border, c.1800, 14 ½ x 10 ¾ In.	288.00
Platter, Octagonal, Blue & White, Riverscape, 1700s, 16 ¼ In.	418.00
Salt, Lid, Blue & White, People, Pagoda, Houses, Trees, Boats, 3 x 1 x 2 In., Pair	550.00
Sugar, Lid, Twisted Branch Handles, Strawberry Finial, Landscape, River, 5 ½ In.	325.00
Tureen, Soup, Lid, Blue & White, Undertray, Gilt Trim, c.1800 13 ½ In.	4250.00

NAPKIN RINGS were in fashion from 1869 to about 1900. They were made of silver, porcelain, wood, and other materials. They are still being made today. The most popular rings with collectors are the silver plated figural examples. Small, realistic figures were made to hold the ring. Good and poor reproductions of the more expensive rings are now being made and collectors must be very careful.

Bakelite, Dog, Scottie, Orange, Red, Black Eye, Pair	48.00
Ivory, Carved, 2 In., Pair	24.00
Pewter, Fire Helmet, Embossed, Crossed Nozzle, Trumpet, Ladder, 2 ½ x 2 ¼ In.	210.00
Silver Plate, Dog Pulls Ring, Wheels, Pierced	660.00
Silver Plate, Figural, Bird, On Leaf, Victorian, 3 ½ In.	90.00
Silver Plate, Figural, Bison, 3 ½ In.	132.00
Silver Plate, Figural, Boy Teaching Dog Tricks, Rogers Smith & Co., 3 ½ x 3 ¼ In.	525.00
Silver Plate, Figural, Little Boy, Ruffled Collar, Hat, Meriden, 3 ½ In.	111.00
Silver Plate, Figural, Ring On Turtle's Back, 3 In.	240.00
Silver Plate, Lily Pad, Engraved June 7th, 1884, Meriden Britannia Co., 3 In.	85.00
Sterling Silver, Buttoned Cuff Shape, Floral Scrollwork, Marked, Denmark, 2 In., Pair	90.00
Sterling Silver, Enameled, Turquoise, Blue, Red, White, Scrolls, Geometric, 3 In.	92.00
Sterling Silver, Peter Rabbit, Etched, Flattened Oval, 3 ½ In.	48.00

NASH glass was made in Corona, New York, from about 1928 to 1931. A. Douglas Nash bought the Corona glassworks from Louis C. Tiffany in 1928 and founded the A. Douglas Nash Corporation with support from his father, Arthur J. Nash. Arthur had worked at the Webb factory in England and for the Tiffany Glassworks in Corona.

NASH

Bowl, Gold Iridescent, Drapery, Footed, 8 In.	288.00
Bowl, Gold Iridescent, Flared, Textured Body, Footed, Signed, 3 ¾ In.	316.00
Vase, Amber, Gold, Lower Ribbing, Crimped Rim, Round Foot, Inverted Bell Shape, 4 In.	259.00
Vase, Gold Iridescent, Pink, Blue, Round Foot, Trumpet Shape, Scalloped Rim, Signed, 9 In.	345.00
Vase, Gold Iridescent, Purple, Slender Trees, Ring Foot, Tapered Cylinder, 7 ¼ In.	345.00

NATZLER pottery was made by Gertrud Amon and Otto Natzler. They were born in Vienna, met in 1933, and established a studio in 1935. Gertrud threw thin-walled, simple, classical shapes on the wheel, while Otto developed glazes. A few months after Hitler's regime occupied Austria in 1938, they married and fled to the United States. The Natzlers set up a workshop in Los Angeles. After Gertrud's death in 1971, Otto continued creating pieces decorated with his distinctive glazes. Otto died in 2007.

G + O
NATZLER

Bowl, Cobalt Blue Glaze, Striped Interior, Ring Foot, Wide Rim, 1956, 3 ½ x 9 In.	4063.00
Bowl, Folded, Yellow, Gertrud & Otto Natzler, c.1956, 5 ¼ x 3 ¼ In. ....*Illus*	2520.00
Bowl, Green Tinge, Folded, Earthenware, Gertrud & Otto Natzler, c.1956, 5 ½ In.	4113.00
Bowl, Yellow, Round Foot, Squared, Otto & Gertrud Natzler, Signed, c.1960, 3 x 6 In.	2625.00
Coupe, Ring Foot, Rounded Square, Yellow Gold Glaze, Otto & Gertrud Natzler, 3 ½ x 4 In.	2250.00
Plate, Curdled Design, Green & Brown, Otto & Gertrud Natzler, 1941, 10 ½ In. ....*Illus*	2000.00
Vase, Cube, Protruding, Pierced Top, Verdigris Volcanic Glaze, Signed, 1977, 9 ¼ x 7 In. .. *Illus*	5000.00
Vase, Folded, White & Blue Volcanic Glaze, Signed, Otto & Gertrud, 6 x 9 ½ In. ....*Illus*	21250.00

Natzler, Plate, Curdled Design, Green & Brown, Otto & Gertrud Natzler, 1941, 10 ½ In.
$2,000.00

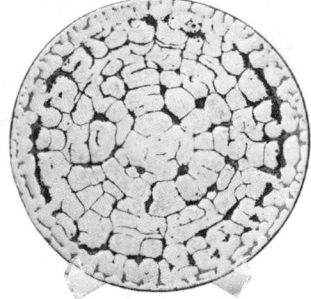

Rago Arts & Auction Center

Natzler, Vase, Cube, Protruding, Pierced Top, Verdigris Volcanic Glaze, Signed, 1977, 9 ¼ x 7 In.
$5,000.00

Rago Arts & Auction Center

Natzler, Vase, Folded, White & Blue Volcanic Glaze, Signed, Otto & Gertrud, 6 x 9 ½ In.
$21,250.00

Rago Arts & Auction Center

Nautical, Ashtray, RMS Lusitania, Red Enamel Pendant, Silver Plate, 5 Cigarette Slots, c.1910, 4 ½ In.
$330.00

DuMouchelles Art Gallery

N

Nautical, Canoe, Birch Bark, 30 Ribs, 5 Thwarts, c.1925, 168 x 39 In.
$4,140.00

Nautical, Sailor's Valentine, Double, Hinged, Shell Mosaic, Seed Shells Form Home Again, 1800s, 9 In.
$2,300.00

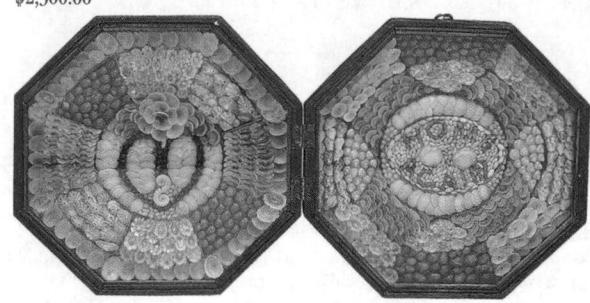

James D. Julia Auctioneers

James D. Julia Auctioneers

Nautical, Lamp, Engine Order, Brass, Glass Window With Inserts, Electrified, 18 In.
$690.00

Nautical, Octant, Spencer Barrett, Ebony, Mahogany, Keystone Box, Chase C. Hutchinson, 11 In.
$830.00

Nautical, Sextant, Brass, Sliding Index Arm, Magnifier, Dollond, London, Case, c.1800, Miniature
$2,880.00

Skinner, Inc.

Skinner, Inc.

Nautical, Pond Boat, SS Marie's, Wood, Painted, Metal Wall Mount, c.1900, 58 x 66 In.
$1,304.00

Bertoia Auctions

Nautical, Model, Frigate, Planks, Baleen & Bone, Napoleonic, Prisoner-Of-War-Made, c.1790, 13 x 16 In.
$2,726.00

Skinner, Inc.

Skinner, Inc.

NAUTICAL antiques are listed in this category. Any of the many objects that were made or used by the seafaring trade, including ship parts, models, and tools, are included. Other pieces may be found listed under Scrimshaw.

Anchor, Wrought Iron, Traditional Shape, With Chain, 1800s, 68 In.	177.00
Ashtray, RMS Lusitania, Red Enamel Pendant, Silver Plate, 5 Cigarette Slots, c.1910, 4 ½ In... *Illus*	330.00
Ax, Boarding, Crosshatch Carved Handle, 15 In.	531.00
Ax, Boarding, Naval, Iron Blade, Ferrel, Pick, Hickory Haggle, 1800s, 16 In.	345.00
Bell, Ship's, Brass, Mounting Bracket, Engraved Ticonderoga, 1900s, 8 ¾ x 9 In.	748.00
Bell, Ship's, Metal, Mounting Bracket, 8 In.	325.00
Binnacle, Brass, Floating Compass, Marked, Newton Bros., England, c.1900, 18 ½ In.	118.00
Binnacle, Brass, Standing, Double Gimbaled Compass, Helmet Shape Lid, Gyro-Compass, 50 x 30 In.	1770.00
Binnacle, Compass, Brass, Round Case, Viewing Window, Wood Plinth, Sestrel, 21 x 13 In.	437.00
Blackjack, Stepped Haft, Egg Shape Lead Head, Wrist Strap, c.1860, 19 In.	265.00
Bosun's Whistle, Sterling, Curving Tube, Ball With Flange, 5 ⅝ In.	178.00
Bottle Holder, Wine, Copper, Brass, SS York, England, 7 ½ x 12 ½ In.	2242.00
Bowl, Scroll Feet, Officers Service, From Imperial Yacht Queen Victoria, Russia, c.1881, 8 ½ In.	2832.00
Box, Lid, Sailor's Valentine, Faux Ivory, Round, Engraved Presentation, Marked M.S. Aftek, 1 ½ In.	238.00
Box, Sailor's, Pine, Compass, Star, Hearts, Painted, New Eng., c.1830, 7 x 12 ½ In.	2252.00
Box, Sailor's, Seaman, Ship Scenes, Eagles, Painted, Oval, c.1860, 13 ¼ In.	4248.00
Box, Ship's Carpenter, Exotic Inlays, 7 ¼ x 6 ½ In.	3068.00
Cannon, Model, Brass Barrel, Walnut Carriage, 9 ¼ In.	24.00
Cannon, Signal, Brass, Wood Carriage, Rectangular Plinth, HMS Swallow, c.1890, 16 In.	1800.00
Cannon, Signal, Bronze, Wrought Iron, 1700s, 8 x 18 In.	356.00
Canoe, Birch Bark, 30 Ribs, 5 Thwarts, c.1925, 168 x 39 In. ....*Illus*	4140.00
Canoe, Wood, Ribbed, Cane Seat, Paddles, Marked Old Towne Canoe, Sample, c.1900, 51 x 10 In.	11500.00
Cap, Officer's, Commander E.H. Cope, U.S. Navy Pay Officer, Leather Case, 1800s, 7 ½ x 18 In.	575.00
Chest, Blue Green Paint, Strap Hinges, Interior Till, Side Handles, c.1860, 17 x 43 In.	472.00
Chest, Interior 3-Masted Ship Scene, New England, 16 ½ x 35 ½ In.	472.00
Chest, Pine, Painted, Thatcher's Twin Lights, Cape Anne Ma., C. Gurshin, 19 x 51 In.	1534.00
Chest, Pine, Slanted Front, Open Interior, Rope Handles, Blue Paint, c.1815, 13 x 38 In.	316.00
Chest, Sea, Camphorwood, Rope Becket Handles, 19 ¾ x 42 In.	1770.00
Chest, Sea, Hardwood, Brass, Plaque Inscribed R.A. Laue, 17 x 39 In.	1298.00
Chest, Sea, Pine, Blue Paint, Large Ring Handles, New England, c.1850, 15 x 39 In.	304.00
Chest, Sea, Pine, Cherry Top, Painted Green, Wrought Hinges, Rope Handles, Lewis McKee, 39 x 17 In.	805.00
Chest, Sea, Pine, Painted, Seascape Panels, New England, 18 x 36 In.	711.00
Chest, Sea, Pine, Red Paint, New England, c.1805, 17 x 48 In.	119.00
Chest, Sea, Whalebone, Oak, 3 Drawers, c.1850, 7 x 7 ¾ In.	708.00
Chest, Ship, 4 Stars Design, 6-Board, Blue Paint, Ditty Box, Drawer Interior, 16 ½ x 44 In.	885.00
Chronometer, Hamilton, Model 22, Deck Watch, Brass Fitting Stamped 8052, 10 ½ x 8 x 8 In.	805.00
Chronometer, Mahogany Case, Brassbound, England, c.1810, 6 ¾ x 6 ¾ In.	2655.00
Chronometer, Swiss Quartz Movement, Brassbound Mahogany Case, Tiffany & Co., 5 ½ In.	384.00
Chronometer, U.S. Navy, Hamilton, Model 21, Wind Indicator, 21 Jewel, 10 x 10 In.	1380.00
Clinometer, U.S. Navy, Phenolic, MK 111 Mod. O, Fee & Stemwedel, 1942, 12 x 8 In.	98.00
Clock, Admiral, Chelsea Rose, Brass, Silvered Dial, Hinged Bezel, Tilden-Thurber, 13 x 13 In.	2013.00
Clock, Ashcroft Mfg. Co., Ship's Bell, Bronze & Brass, Round, 19th Century, 4 x 13 In.	360.00
Clock, Bell, Round, Brass, Kelvin White Co., Seth Thomas, c.1860, 5 ½ In.	236.00
Clock, Chelsea, Ship's Bell, Brass, Made From Aneroid Barometer, 5 ¾ x 3 ½ In.	115.00
Clock, Chelsea, Ship's Bell, Mahogany, 10 x 22 In.	270.00
Clock, Chelsea, Ship's Bell, Mahogany, White Face, Wright Kay & Co., 10 x 22 In.	180.00
Clock, Chelsea, U.S. Navy, Phenolic Case, Black Face, Military Numbers, 7 ½ In.	224.00
Clock, Ship's Bell, Brass, Nickel Plated, Wall Mountable, England, c.1930, 8 In. Diam.	246.00
Clock, Ship's, Brass Case, Round, Arabic Numerals, 2-Key Wind, External Bell, c.1880	270.00
Clock, Ship's, Brass Case, Silver Tone Dial, Arabic Numerals, Chelsea, Key, 5 ¾ x 3 ½ In.	265.00
Clock, Ship's, Brass, Mahogany, Ivory Case, 4 x 6 In.	1298.00
Clock, Ship's, No. 10 Model, Ship's Wheel Bezel, 8-Day Wind, Waterbury, 4 ¼ In.	150.00
Clock, Ship's, Seth Thomas, Brass Case, Hinged Door, Silvertone Dial, 7 x 4 In.	92.00
Clock, Ship's, Shelf, Brass, Quartz, Dolphin Shape Supports, 14 x 14 In.	210.00
Clock, Ship's, U.S. Navy, Chelsea, 12E, Hinged Screw Down Face, 8 ½ x 3 ½ In.	219.00
Clock, Soviet Submarine, Aluminum Case, 12 Jewel Movement, Box, 9 x 4 In.	63.00
Clock, Soviet Submarine, Komandirsky, Aluminum Case, White Dial, Red Star, Key Wind, 9 In.	75.00
Clock, Waterbury, Brass, Jewel Movement, Porcelain Dial, Time & Bell Strike, Round, c.1900, 6 In.	148.00
Compass, Astronomical, Brass, Lithograph Compass Rose, Embossed, Lilley & Son, c.1860, 12 In.	2531.00
Compass, Brass, Gimbal Mount, Oil Lamp, Sestrel, 9 ½ x 9 In.	219.00
Compass, Bronze, Gimbal, Iver C. Weilbach & Co., c.1905, 8 ⅜ In.	326.00
Compass, Dory, Gimbaled, Signed, J.H. Rowe, Box, c.1890, 2 x 4 ¾ In.	307.00

Netsuke, Ivory, Courtier, Holding Gourd, Signed, 1800s, 2 ¼ In.
$173.00

James D. Julia Auctioneers

Netsuke, Ivory, Daikoku, God Of Wealth & Guardian Of Farmers, Coral Branch, 1800s, 1 ¾ In.
$173.00

James D. Julia Auctioneers

Netsuke, Ivory, Demon & Monk, Arm-Wrestling On Tiger Skin, Signed, 1800s, 1 ¼ x 3 In.
$173.00

James D. Julia Auctioneers

Netsuke, Ivory, Masks, Cluster, Signed, Konmin, 1800s, 2 x 1 ⅜ In.
$403.00

James D. Julia Auctioneers

N

Netsuke, Ivory, Octopus, 1800s, 1 In.
$173.00

James D. Julia Auctioneers

Netsuke, Ivory, Tengu, Birdlike Creature, Clam, 1800s, 1 ¾ In.
$920.00

James D. Julia Auctioneers

Newcomb, Candlestick, Flowers, Yellow Buds, Tall Stems, Marie De Hoa Leblanc, 1907, 9 ¼ x 5 ¼ In.
$3,375.00

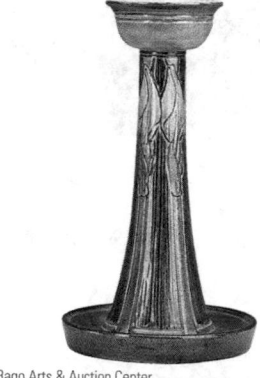

Rago Arts & Auction Center

Newcomb, Jar, Lid, Cherokee Roses, Relief, Matte Glaze, Anna Frances Simpson, 1919, 6 ⅞ In.
$11,353.00

Neal Auction Co.

Compass, Dory, Mahogany, Brass, Eugene H. Sherman, c.1900, 7 x 4 In.	207.00
Compass, Dry Card, Captain's Tell-Tale, Simon Vissiere, France, 4 ¾ In.	885.00
Compass, S Boat, Brass, Cherry Box, 1850s, 4 ½ x 3 ¾ In.	144.00
Compass, Sailor's, Ivory Case, Engraved From Sweetheart Lucy, 1 ½ x 1 ⅞ In.	944.00
Compass, Ship's, U.S. Navy, Brass Gimbal Mount, Oil Lamp, Lionel Co., 10 x 10 In.	265.00
Compass, Whaler's Dory, Hinged Wood Blocks, Paper Face, Hook & Eye, c.1820, 3 ¾ In.	650.00
Desk, Ship Captain's, Sheraton, Mahogany, Folding Lid Writing Surface, Cupboard, 35 x 25 In.	1150.00
Diorama, Brigantine Niagara, Carved Wood, String, Paint, Shadowbox, c.1900, 22 x 27 In.	529.00
Diorama, Clipper Ship, Union, Dimensional Model, Painted Interior, Plaster Frame, 31 x 44 In.	1294.00
Diorama, Schooner, 2-Masted, Wood, Carved, Painted, Dimensional Sea, Frame, 19 x 27 In.	504.00
Diorama, Views Of Narragansett Bay & Block Island, Boat, Excursion View Co., 1878, 13 ¼ In.	944.00
Ditty Bag, Sailmaker's, Canvas, Knotwork, Tools Inside, Inscribed King Vanucie, 14 In.	354.00
Ditty Box, 4-Finger, Oval, Bone, Inlaid Mahogany Abalone Star, New Eng., c.1850, 5 x 10 In.	10665.00
Ditty Box, Sailor's, Maple, Star, Diamond Inlays, Mirror Lid, Fitted Interior, c.1850, 7 x 14 In.	593.00
Eagle, Pilot House, Carved, Gilded, Spread Wings, c.1860, 42 x 66 In.	9113.00
Fid, Whalebone, Spike Shape, 1800s, 13 ¼ In.	345.00
Figurehead, Admiral Collingwood, Torso, Uniform, Wood, Paint, England, c.1835, 44 In.	16520.00
Figurehead, Holding Lamb, Staff, Painted, c.1950, 79 x 72 In.	944.00
Figurehead, Mermaid, Wood, Painted, Continental, c.1860, 56 ¾ In.	2370.00
Figurehead, Native American, Headdress, Outstretched Hand, Wood, Paint, c.1835, 86 In.	15340.00
Figurehead, Woman, Blond Cornucopia Dress, Wood, Base, c.1850, 31 In.	3304.00
Figurehead, Woman, Wood, 4-Masted Bark, Joseph Dollar, Painted, 1902, 103 x 31 In.	165200.00
Flag, Boat, U.S. Navy, 13 Stars, Stamped, Ensign No. 6 Navy Yard, c.1900	649.00
Hat, Cocked, U.S. Navy, Full Dress, Junior Officer, Black & Gold Bullion Lace, c.1900, 7 ¼ In.	253.00
Helm, 8-Spoke Wheel, Teak, Brass, Tapered Column, 1900s, 46 ½ In.	911.00
Helmet, Diving, Copper, Brass, Morse Fisheries, c.1940	4484.00
Kettle, Steamship Utah, Swing Handle, Brass, 12 x 9 ½ In.	224.00
Lamp, Engine Order, Brass, Glass Window With Inserts, Electrified, 18 In. ....*Illus*	690.00
Lamp, Ship's Bell, Hammered Copper, Swings, Pull Chain, Cast Metal Frame, 12 x 11 In.	150.00
Lantern, Brass, Anchor, Blue Lens, Vertical Guards, Bail Handle, E. Miller No. 2, c.1900, 15 x 7 In.	748.00
Lantern, Brass, Blackout, Bail Handle, U.S. Coast Guard, c.1875, 15 x 12 In.	345.00
Lantern, Brass, Bow, Clear Lens, Bail Handle, Robert Findlay Mfg., c.1900, 14 x 6 In.	345.00
Lantern, Brass, Bronze, Clear Lens, Vertical Wire Guard, Bail Handle, c.1910, 19 x 7 In.	345.00
Lantern, Brass, Combination Launch, Red, Clear, Green Lens, Geo. Terry Co., c.1920, 13 x 11 In.	690.00
Lantern, Brass, Combination Launch, Red, Green Lens, Ring Handle, c.1890, 11 x 8 In.	748.00
Lantern, Brass, Combination Launch, Ring Handle, Red, Green, Clear Lens, c.1925, 11 x 7 ½ In.	863.00
Lantern, Brass, Copper, Impressed Figures, Japan, c.1975, 26 x 12 In.	259.00
Lantern, Brass, Copper, Masthead, Bail Handle, A. Ward Hendrickson & Co., c.1925, 25 x 12 In.	547.00
Lantern, Brass, Copper, Triangular, Sliding Door, Bail Handle, Meteorite, c.1925, 26 x 16 In.	288.00
Lantern, Brass, Electric, Masthead, Hooded Lens, Perkins, Brooklyn, c.1940, 15 x 12 In.	196.00
Lantern, Brass, Iron, Flat Back, Bail Handle, Stern, c.1920, 21 x 9 In.	259.00
Lantern, Brass, Iron, Ring Handle, Shubert & Cottingham, c.1910, 15 x 6 ½ In.	161.00
Lantern, Brass, Lifeboat, Pierced Leaf Top, Base, Bail Handle, Perkins, c.1935, 15 ¾ x 5 ¾ In.	184.00
Lantern, Brass, Masthead, Hinged Lid, Bail Handle, F.H. Lovell & Co., c.1920, 25 x 13 In., Pair	345.00
Lantern, Brass, Metal, Electric, Blackout Shroud, Flat Back, Square Handle, c.1935, 18 In.	184.00
Lantern, Brass, Navigation, Handles, Kelvin Bottomley & Maird, Glasgow, c.1920, 11 x 5 In.	316.00
Lantern, Brass, Octagonal, Red, Clear Glass Panels, Kerosene, 19 In.	413.00
Lantern, Brass, Signal, Rotating Yoke, Kokosha Co. Ltd., c.1975, 17 x 8 In.	805.00
Lantern, Bulkhead, Galvanized Painted Steel, Oil Lamp, Brass Font, Reflector, 15 x 6 ½ In.	63.00
Lantern, Copper, Brass, Port, Triangular, Hinged Door, Bail Handle, c.1904, 24 x 14 In.	259.00
Lantern, Fishing Boat, Square, Fitted Sheet Glass, Hinged Burner, Chimney, Davey & Co., 15 x 11 In.	236.00
Lantern, Iron, Anchor, Clear Ribbed Globe, Black Paint, Russell & Watson, c.1890, 21 x 7 ¾ In.	748.00
Lantern, Iron, Black Paint, Wire Guard, Red Lens, c.1910, 18 ¾ x 7 In.	161.00
Lantern, Iron, Brass, Anchor, Purple Globe, Ring Handle, c.1880, 22 x 9 In.	403.00
Lantern, Iron, Brass, Signal, Wire Guard, Ring Hook, Perkins Marine Lamp, c.1945, 22 x 7 In.	431.00
Lantern, Masthead, Galvanized, Fresnel Lens, Sliding Door, Kerosene Lamp, Meteorite, 23 x 12 In.	161.00
Lantern, Nickeled Iron, Brass, Ring Handle, Perkins, Brooklyn, N.Y., c.1935, 20 ¾ In.	489.00
Lantern, Ship's, Brass, Oil Lamp, Glass Chimney, Marked Neptune, 15 ½ In.	178.00
Lantern, Ship's, Painted Onion Globe, Blue Green Glass, 18 ½ In.	1180.00
Light, Candle, Sheffield Silver Plate, Side Bracket, Gimbles, Top Lifts, 1800s, 7 ½ In.	150.00
Light, Masthead Port, Starboard Combination, Copper, Lens Guard Cage, c.1925, 32 In.	173.00
Log, Ship's, Great Lakes Steamship, A.M. Byers, 1953, 1961, 22 x 17 In., 2 Piece	52.00
Model, ½ Ship On Board, Gerome, c.1950, 45 x 9 In.	190.00
Model, Archibald Russel, 4-Masted, Carved, Painted, 27 x 45 In.	472.00
Model, Clipper, Flying Cloud, Wood, Clipper, Rigged Hull, Figurehead, Bell, 28 x 37 In.	354.00

Model, Friendship Of Salem, Rigged, Black, White, Green, Wood Stand, 48 ½ x 64 In.	1416.00
Model, Frigate, Planks, Baleen & Bone, Napoleonic, Prisoner-Of-War-Made, c.1790, 13 x 16 In....*Illus*	2726.00
Model, Merchant Ship, Wood, Painted, 3-Masted, Square Rigged, Bone, Brass, Anchors, 32 x 39 In.	356.00
Model, Normandie, Wood, 3-Level Deck, 3 Smokestacks, Painted, 44 x 13 In.	408.00
Model, Ocean Liner, Carved Wood, Tin, Paint, Moving Rudder, Portholes, 9 x 36 In.	558.00
Model, Pine, Paint, Half Hull, Delmar-Morgan, Stand, 1800s, 6 x 50 In.	411.00
Model, Sailboat, 2-Masted, Cannons, Lifeboat, Anchor, Glass & Wood Case, 1900s, 13 x 19 ½ In.	944.00
Model, Sailing Boat, Steam Packet, Cygnet, 3-Masted, Wirework, c.1875, 15 x 11 In.	656.00
Model, Schooner, Wood, 2-Masted, Ropes, Stand, 25 x 22 In.	161.00
Model, Speedboat, Snipe, Live Steam, Horizontal Boiler, Bowman Models, Eng., c.1930, 22 In.	377.00
Model, SS Presto, Shipyard Built, Museum Cased, Mirrored Back, 72 x 20 In.	1351.00
Model, USS Constitution, Wood, Fully Rigged, 25 x 36 In.	390.00
Model, USS Preston, Hollow Constructed, Painted Gray, No. 327, Wiring, Steam Stacks, 63 x 24 In.	834.00
Model, Whaling Boat, Ivory, Bone, Rigging, Oak Display Case, 14 x 17 In.	3450.00
Model, Whaling Boat, Ivory, Mahogany Plinth, 1800s, 2 ¼ x 12 ¾ In.	1003.00
Oar, Wood, Carved, Polynesia, c.1900, 69 x 5 In.	1200.00
Oars, Wood, Painted, c.1905, 91 In.	207.00
Octant, Brass, Ebony, Ivory, Wood Case, Kleman & Zoon, 19th Century	326.00
Octant, Brass, Vernier Type, Ivory Scale, Ebony Grip, Mahogany Box, G. Heath, 11 x 11 In.	403.00
Octant, Ebony, Ivory, Brass, Wedge Shape Mahogany Box, B.T. Browning & Rust, 13 x 12 In.	460.00
Octant, Spencer Barrett, Ebony, Mahogany, Keystone Box, Chase C. Hutchinson, 11 In....*Illus*	830.00
Picture, Germanic, White Star Royal Mail Steamer, A. Jacobsen, Gilt Gesso Frame, 22 x 36 In.	15405.00
Pike, Ship's, Naval, Iron Blade, Tang, Shoe, Collar, Oak Shaft, c.1810, 12 ¾ In.	1610.00
Plaque, Model, Tugboat, Half Hull, 19th Century, 5 ⅝ x 20 In.	3851.00
Plaque, Oak, Cast Copper, HMS Foudroyant, Salvaged Material, England, 14 x 12 In.	1495.00
Plate, Officers Service, From Imperial Yacht Queen Victoria, Russia, 1871-1881, 10 ½ In., Pair	5074.00
Pond Boat, Cotton Sails, Brass Hardware, Green Trim, c.1900, 97 x 79 In.	1126.00
Pond Boat, Crown, Mahogany, Forward Cabin, Mono Hull Sloop, Bermuda Sails, 17 x 52 In.	767.00
Pond Boat, Sailboat, Carrie Price, 25 x 22 In.	237.00
Pond Boat, Sloop, Plank On Frame, Stand, 27 ¼ x 22 In.	1770.00
Pond Boat, Sloop, Wood, Canvas Sails, Brass, Aluminum Fittings, Ropes, Display Stand, 53 x 70 In.	1006.00
Pond Boat, SS Marie's, Wood, Painted, Metal Wall Mount, c.1900, 58 x 66 In. ....*Illus*	1304.00
Pond Boat, Wood, Base, 1900s, 44 x 37 In.	411.00
Pond Boat, Yacht, J Style, Planked, Painted, 88 x 65 In.	1180.00
Porthole, Brass, 15 In.	120.00
Propeller, Bronze, 19 In.	92.00
Pump, Marine Transfer, Brass, Copper, Iron, Carriage, Handles, Wheels, Belleville, 1800s, 54 x 18 In.	288.00
Quadrant, Brass, Ebony, Ivory, Endersbee & Son, Case, 11 ½ In.	472.00
Quadrant, Davis, Rosewood, Boxwood, Ivory, 25 In.	8260.00
Rope Becket, Cleats, Copper Star, 11 In., Pair	767.00
Sailboat, Pond Sailor, Wood, Cloth Sails, c.1940, 29 In.	230.00
Sailor's Box, Pine, Brass Feet, Encrusted Seashells, Paper Liner, c.1860, 8 x 13 In.	512.00
Sailor's Box, Teak, Ivory, Scrimshaw, 6-Pointed Stars, 3-Finger, Oval, Lid, c.1850, 3 ½ x 8 ¾ In.	4600.00
Sailor's Valentine, Double Shellwork, Velvet, Octangular, Hinged, 8 ¾ In.	4425.00
Sailor's Valentine, Double, Hinged, Shell Mosaic, Seed Shells Form Home Again, 1800s, 9 In. ..*Illus*	2300.00
Sailor's Valentine, Limpets, Seed Shells, Bivalves, Forget Me Not, Octagonal Case, c.1850, 9 x 8 ¾ In.	2714.00
Sailor's Valentine, Shellwork, Double Panel, Octagonal, 1800s, 8 ¾ x 8 ½ In.	2844.00
Sailor's Valentine, Shellwork, Flowers, Octagonal, 14 ¾ In.	5310.00
Sailor's Valentine, Shellwork, Heart, Ever Thine, Octagonal, Hinged, 9 ½ In.	5310.00
Sailor's Valentine, Shellwork, Vase, Flowers, 8 ¾ In.	1180.00
Scale, Gold Coin, Brass, Adjustable, H. Bell, England, Hinged, Brass Box, 5 ¼ In.	460.00
Searchlight, Brass, Neverout, Silvered Reflector, Round, Rose Manufacturing Co., c.1925, 16 x 6 In.	374.00
Searchlight, Ship's, Carbon Arch, Bronze Diamond, 10 x 17 In.	161.00
Sextant, Brass, Ebony, Mahogany Case, Spencer, Browning & Rust, c.1810, 11 x 13 In.	1593.00
Sextant, Brass, Sliding Index Arm, Magnifier, Dollond, London, Case, c.1800, Miniature......*Illus*	2880.00
Sextant, Brass, Wood, Browning & Rust, London, 14 In.	270.00
Sextant, Ivory, Brass, Wood, Inscribed Gardner, Glasgow, 17 ½ In.	236.00
Sextant, Kelvin & Hughes, London, Brass Engraved Case, 1917, 5 x 6 In.	177.00
Sextant, Vernier Type, Eyepieces, Fitted Mahogany Box, Riggs & Bros., c.1900, 9 x 10 In.	414.00
Ship Log, Walker's Excelsior IV, Rotator, Hook, 100-Foot Line, Sinker, Oil, Box, 1950s, 16 x 8 In.	150.00
Ship Manifest, Canova Of Castine, Capt. Henry Whitney, New Orleans To Liverpool, 23 x 18 In.	304.00
Ship Model, see Nautical, Model.	
Ship Stern Board, Carved, Viroqua, Indian Chieftain, War Bonnet, Black Banner, 18 x 31 In.	2415.00
Ship's Wheel, Bronze, Cleveland Ship Building Co., c.1890, 49 ½ x 37 In.	2360.00
Ship's Wheel, Mahogany, Iron Hub, 47 In.	100.00

Newcomb, Mug, Jester Masks, Ribbons, Bells, Marked, Joseph Meyer, 1902, 4 ½ In.

$8,365.00

Neal Auction Co.

Newcomb, Vase, Jasmine, 2 Handles, Mazie Teresa Ryan, Marked, 1905, 4 ½ x 4 ½ In.

$3,500.00

Rago Arts & Auction Center

Newcomb, Vase, Magnolia Blossoms, Sadie Irvine, Marked, 1907, 5 ½ x 3 ¼ In.

$1,375.00

N

Rago Arts & Auction Center

TIP

Some tea and coffee stains on dishes can be removed by rubbing them with damp baking soda.

Nodder, Happy Homer, Homebuilder, Composition, Staggs-Bilt Homes, Phoenix, Arizona, 6 x 2 ⅞ In. $231.00

Wm Morford Antiques

Nodder, Mandarin, Green Floral Gown, Giltwood Base, Parian, Marked, Blue Anchor, c.1885, 18 In. $215.00

New Orleans Auction Galleries, Inc.

Nodder, Theodore Roosevelt, On Elephant, Holding Big Stick, Composition, Painted, 7 x 5 In. $3,173.00

Cowan's Auctions

Ship's Wheel, Protruding Spokes, Round, 44 In.	165.00
Ship's Wheel, Teak, 10 Spokes, Brass Tie-Downs, c.1920, 72 In.	575.00
Ship's Wheel, Teak, Mahogany, Blue Gray Paint Trace, 10 Spokes, Rudder Rope Drum, 68 In.	230.00
Ship's Wheel, Wood & Brass, 60 In.	420.00
Ship's Wheel, Wood, Brass Fittings, 58 In.	460.00
Ship's Wheel, Wood, Brass, Oriental Characters, 48 In.	118.00
Ship's Wheel, Wood, Brass, Scotland, 48 In.	259.00
Ship's Wheel, Wood, Turned Handles, Iron Hub, c.1900, 39 x 2 ½ In.	295.00
Skiff, Mahogany, Oars, Mounts, Chris-Craft, Hudson & Lester Hardware Kit, 1955, 161 x 62 In.	3162.00
Sternboard, Eagle, Wood, Demilune, Paint, 68 ½ In.	590.00
Telegraph Lamp, Ship's, Brass, Bell Sound When Levers Are Moved, 1960s, 19 x 8 In.	236.00
Telescope, Mahogany, Brass, Single Draw, 53 ½ In.	620.00
Transom, Troughton & Simms, London, c.1900, 8 x 4 In.	207.00
Trunk, Seaman's, Camphorwood, Leather, Brass Studs, China, 10 x 26 In.	944.00
Voyage Log, Cadet Edward H. Harrison, Leather Bound Boards, Oct. 1881 To April 1882	190.00
Wall Mounts, Jovial Sailor, Cast Iron, Paint, 14 In., Pair	1121.00
Watch, U.S. Navy, Hamilton, Aluminum Case, Marked Bureau Of Ships, 8 ½ x 9 In.	891.00

NETSUKES are small ivory, wood, metal, or porcelain pieces used as toggles on the end of the cord that held a Japanese money pouch or inro. The earliest date from the sixteenth century. Many are miniature carved works of art. This category also includes the ojime, the slide or string fastener that was used on the inro cord.

Boxwood, Buddha, Laughing, Seated, Open Robe, 19th Century, 2 In.	58.00
Boxwood, Sashi, Elongated, Relief Carved, Lotus Seed Pods, Leaves, Signed, Shimizu, 1800s, 7 ½ In.	1094.00
Boxwood, South Seas Islander, c.1800, 2 ¼ In.	1035.00
Boxwood, Tomotada, Wild Hound, Ivory Eyes, Carved, 1 ¼ In.	6900.00
Boxwood, Wild Hound, Ivory Eyes, Marked, c.1790, 1 ¼ In.	863.00
Ebony, Guardian Lion, Base, 18th Century, 1 ¾ In.	460.00
Ivory, 2 Sumo Wrestlers, One Holding Other On Shoulder, Signed, 2 In.	2023.00
Ivory, 3 Rabbits, Sitting Atop Each Other	210.00
Ivory, 5 Rabbits, Seated In Basket, 1700s, 1 ¼ x 1 ¾ In.	115.00
Ivory, 7 Figures, Dragon Sailing Ship, Gods Of Fortune, Signed, 2 In.	357.00
Ivory, Carved, Large Headed Fish, Open Tooth Filled Mouth, 3 Mice, Signed, 2 In.	357.00
Ivory, Carved, Old Man & Baby	120.00
Ivory, Carver Of Daruma Figures, Image Coming To Life, Signed, 1800s, 1 ¾ x 2 ¼ In.	266.00
Ivory, Courtier, Holding Gourd, Signed, 1800s, 2 ¼ In. *Illus*	173.00
Ivory, Daikoku, God Of Wealth & Guardian Of Farmers, Coral Branch, 1800s, 1 ¾ In. *Illus*	173.00
Ivory, Demon & Monk, Arm-Wrestling On Tiger Skin, Signed, 1800s, 1 ¼ x 3 In. *Illus*	173.00
Ivory, Farmer, Water Buffalo, Sheaves Of Grain, Signed, 1800s, 1 ¼ In.	354.00
Ivory, Farmer, Wife, 2 Children, Digging Up Bell, Marked, 19th Century, 1 ¾ In.	345.00
Ivory, Immortal Set, Each Holding Their Attribute, Wood Stand, Signed, 2 In., 7 Piece	410.00
Ivory, Man, Carrying Lapis Lazuli Mask, 2 In.	125.00
Ivory, Man, Monkey, On Log, Smoking Pipe, 1 ¾ In.	179.00
Ivory, Masks, Cluster, Signed, Konmin, 1800s, 2 x 1 ⅜ In. *Illus*	403.00
Ivory, Mouse, Stealing Pomegranates From Basket, Signed Mitsuhiro, 1800s, 1 ¾ In.	805.00
Ivory, Octopus, 1800s, 1 In. *Illus*	173.00
Ivory, Phoenix Boat, Demon, Playing Board Game, Oni, 2 ¼ In.	655.00
Ivory, Seated Rabbit, Raised Front Leg, Signed, Gyokuzan, 1800s, 1 ½ In.	119.00
Ivory, Shishi, Foo Dogs, Reclining, Open Mouth, Signed, 1800s, ¾ x 1 ¾ In.	236.00
Ivory, Shishi, Hermit Sage With Foo Dog, 1700s, 2 ¼ In.	1610.00
Ivory, Snail, Crawling, Out Of Shell, 1700s, 1 ¼ x 1 ½ In.	316.00
Ivory, Tengu, Birdlike Creature, Clam, 1800s, 1 ¾ In. *Illus*	920.00
Ivory, Treasure Boat, 7 Gods Of Good Fortune, 2 ½ x 3 ½ In.	390.00
Ivory, Wood, Demon, Crying, Severed Arm, 19th Century, 2 ½ In.	403.00
Wood, Ivory, Bucket, Snail, Signed, 19th Century, 1 ¾ In.	403.00
Wood, Man, Standing, Open Mouth, 4 ¼ In.	1112.00
Wood, Mask, Fox, Movable Jaw, Signed Deme Uman, Ten Ka Ichi, 1700s, 1 ¾ In.	374.00

NEW MARTINSVILLE Glass Manufacturing Company was established in 1901 in New Martinsville, West Virginia. It was bought and renamed the Viking Glass Company in 1944. In 1987 Kenneth Dalzell, former president of Fostoria Glass Company, purchased the factory and renamed it Dalzell-Viking. Production ceased in 1998.

Carnation, Powder Jar, Crystal, 4 ½ x 3 In.	34.00
Crystal Eagle, Candlestick, 2-Light, Colonial Blue, Inverted Teardrop Center, c.1936, 5 ¾ In., Pair	125.00

N

Hen, Figurine, Crystal, 5 x 5 ½ In.	125.00
Moondrops, Sugar & Creamer, Ruby, 2 ½ In.	45.00
Moondrops, Sugar, Open, Ruby, Double Handles, 2 ½ In.	22.00
Queen Anne, Creamer, Crystal, 1936, 6 x 2 In.	18.00
Radiance, Bowl, Etched, 3 Dolphin Feet, 11 x 3 ½ In.	35.00
Radiance, Bowl, Mayonnaise, Underplate, Meadow Wreath, 1930s, 5 ½ x 2 ¼ & 7 ¼ In.	21.00
Radiance, Cake Stand, Prelude, Center Threaded Post, Sterling Foot, 3 ¾ x 3 ½ In.	70.00
Radiance, Candleholder, Ruby, 8 In., Pair	245.00
Radiance, Sugar, Meadow Wreath, c.1938, 3 In.	10.00

NEWCOMB POTTERY was founded at Sophie Newcomb College, New Orleans, Louisiana, in 1895. The work continued through the 1940s. Pieces of this art pottery are marked with the printed letters *NC* and often have the incised initials of the artist and potter as well. A date letter code was printed on pieces made from 1901 to 1941. Most pieces have a matte glaze and incised decoration.

Bowl, Narcissus Band, Blue, Green & Pink, Squat, Anna F. Simpson, 4 ½ x 10 In.	777.00
Bowl, Pale Blue Glaze, Low Open Shape, Marked, c.1905, 7 ¼ In. Diam.	478.00
Bowl, Peach Flower, Light Blue, 9 ¼ In.	1380.00
Candlestick, Chamber, Leaves, Berries, Poem, Tray Base, Loop Handle, 1908, 4 ¼ x 5 In.	418.00
Candlestick, Flowers, Yellow Buds, Tall Stems, Marie De Hoa Leblanc, 1907, 9 ¼ x 5 ¼ In. *Illus*	3375.00
Case, Tall Pine & Moon, Blue, Green & Yellow Matte, Tapered, A.F. Simpson, 1921, 7 In.	3660.00
Creamer, Lid, Encircling Irises, Cream, Blue, Green, Bulbous, Loop Handle, c.1909, 4 In.	3680.00
Jar, Blue Matte Glaze, Raised Flowers, Vine & Leaves, Marked Anna Frances Simpson, 1919, 7 In.	4720.00
Jar, Lid, Cherokee Roses, Relief, Matte Glaze, Anna Frances Simpson, 1919, 6 ⅞ In. *Illus*	11353.00
Jardiniere, Pine Needles & Cones, Marie De Hoa Leblanc, 1907, 8 ½ x 10 In.	3198.00
Mug, Jester Masks, Ribbons, Bells, Marked, Joseph Meyer, 1902, 4 ½ In. *Illus*	8365.00
Pitcher, Sarracenia, Cobalt Blue, Green, Cylindrical, Banded Bottom, 1901, 14 ½ In.	6572.00
Pot, Squat, Blue Green Matte Glaze, Mauve Edge, Wild Rice Design, Flower Frog, c.1918, 4 x 6 In.	1353.00
Syrup, Sailboat Band, Green, Blue, White, Tapered, Desiree Roman, 5 x 4 In.	2500.00
Trivet, Oak Tree, Cascading Branches, A.F. Simpson, 1925, 5 ½ In. Diam.	3125.00
Urn, Dome Lid, Lilies Of The Valley, Melon Shape, Round Foot, Blue, Marked, c.1930, 5 ¾ In.	4485.00
Vase, Blue Body, Incised, Trailing Blue Stems, 2 ¾ In.	668.00
Vase, Bulbous, Painted Tulips, Leona Nicholson, 10 x 9 In.	9000.00
Vase, Chocolate & Turquoise Glaze, Ridged, Combed Design, Disc Base, Round, Marked, 6 ½ In.	374.00
Vase, Cypress Trees, Blue, Green, Cream, Shouldered, H. Bailey, 5 ½ x 12 In.	15000.00
Vase, Daffodil, Painted, Bulbous, H. Bailey, 4 ½ x 6 ½ In.	2000.00
Vase, Daffodils, Blue, Green Matte Glaze, Painted, Carved, Alma Mason, 3 x 6 In.	1464.00
Vase, Daffodils, Stylized Stems, Blue Green, Tapered, Swollen Rim, A.F. Simpson, 7 In.	2375.00
Vase, Flowers, Painted, Sadie Irvine, 6 ½ x 9 ½ In.	4375.00
Vase, Freesia, Blue, Pink Matte Glaze, Anna F. Simpson, 1929, 6 In.	2032.00
Vase, Fruiting Vines, Sadie Irvine, 1922, 3 ⅝ In.	976.00
Vase, Iris, Art Deco Style, Blue, Green, Yellow, Pink, Oval, C.M. Chalaron, 1922, 6 In.	1195.00
Vase, Jasmine, 2 Handles, Mazie Teresa Ryan, Marked, 1905, 4 ½ x 4 ½ In. *Illus*	3500.00
Vase, Live Oak Trees, Spanish Moss, Full Moon, Blue, A.F. Simpson, 1926, 6 In.	3375.00
Vase, Live Oaks, Moss, Semimatte, Blue & Green, A.F. Simpson, 1918, 11 In.	6871.00
Vase, Magnolia Blossoms, Sadie Irvine, Marked, 1907, 5 ½ x 3 ¼ In. *Illus*	1375.00
Vase, Moon & Moss, Blue Semimatte Glaze, Cylinder, Sadie Irvine, 1922, 11 ¾ In.	5079.00
Vase, Moon & Moss, Blue Vellum Glaze, Paper Label, Joseph Meyer, 1917, 10 x 6 ¼ In.	1092.00
Vase, Moon & Moss, Blue, Green, Sadie Irvine, 1930, 5 ⅛ In.	3050.00
Vase, Moon & Moss, Landscape, Blue & Green, Urn Shape, Marked, 1929, 5 ⅞ x 6 In.	3660.00
Vase, Moon & Moss, Oak Design, Vellum Glazed, 1928, 6 ¾ In.	2952.00
Vase, Moon Landscape, Blue, Carved, Painted, Round, Sadie Irvine, 6 x 4 In.	1875.00
Vase, Mossy Trees, Tapered, Carved, Painted, Anna Frances Simpson, 4 x 8 In.	4688.00
Vase, Oak Trees, Moss, Blue Matte Glaze, Squat, Marked, Sadie Irvine, 1916, 6 x 8 ¼ In.	7768.00
Vase, Oak Trees, Sadie Irvine, 1919, 4 In.	1952.00
Vase, Pine Tree, Cylindrical, Flared Rim, Turquoise, c.1913, 9 ¾ In.	2952.00
Vase, Pink Blossom Bands, Fluted, Cylindrical, Tapered Rim, A.F. Simpson, 6 x 4 In.	1500.00
Vase, Pink Flower, Blue Matte Glaze, Cylinder, Sadie Irvine, 1926, 6 ¾ x 2 ¾ In.	2151.00
Vase, Poppies, Art Deco Style, Blue, Green, Pink, Yellow, Pinched Waist, S. Irvine, 1924, 9 In.	1673.00
Vase, Scenic, Live Oak Trees, Spanish Moss, Blues & Green, Sadie Irvine, 1917, 8 In.	3250.00
Vase, Shouldered, Grape Clusters, Pale Blue, Green, Pink, 1917, 5 ¾ x 5 In.	1875.00
Vase, Spanish Moss, Oak Trees, Henrietta Bailey, 1931, 12 ½ In.	7500.00
Vase, Stylized White Lilies, Raised Enamel, Blue Ground, Tapered, M. Sheerer, 11 In.	23750.00
Vase, Sweet Peas, High Glaze, Green, White, Tapered, Esther Elliot, 1897, 9 ¼ In.	9375.00
Vase, Tree Landscape, Gray, Cream, Painted, Tapered, Amelie Roman, 6 x 9 ½ In.	22500.00

Noritake, Dresser Doll, Woman, Patterned Dress & Cloak, Art Deco, Red M In Wreath, 9 In.
$1,466.00

A.H. Wilkens

Noritake, Dresser Jar, Indian Maiden, Feather Plumed Hat, 8-Sided Base, Green M In Wreath, 10 ¼ In.
$13,529.00

A.H. Wilkens

Noritake, Dresser Tray, Woman Applying Lipstick, Art Deco, Red M In Wreath, 10 ⅛ In.
$2,255.00

A.H. Wilkens

Noritake, Powder Jar, Woman Holding Feather Puff, Flat, Luster Glaze, Art Deco, Red M In Wreath, 4 In.
$451.00

A.H. Wilkens

TIP

The first place a burglar looks for valuables is in the bedroom. A better choice is in your garage or freezer.

North Dakota School of Mines, Bowl, Fruits, Vegetables, Flora Huckfield, Ink Stamp, Incised, 9 ⅛ In. $316.00

Humler & Nolan

North Dakota School of Mines, Flower Arranger, Bag Shape, Gathered Neck, Pieced, Margaret Pachl, 4 In. $173.00

Humler & Nolan

North Dakota School of Mines, Vase, Angular Designs, Oatmeal Matte Glaze, Impressed, Ferock, State ND Lettering, 12 In. $2,760.00

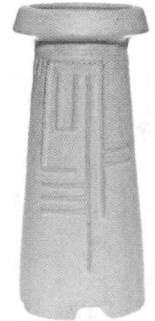

Humler & Nolan

Vase, Trees, Spanish Moss, Blue Green, Marked, 1929, 7 ¾ In.	3738.00
Vase, Trumpet Flowers, 4 Handles, Round, Sadie Irvine, 6 x 4 In.	1375.00
Vase, Tulip Band, Blue, Cream, Bulbous, Painted, Leona Nicholson, 10 x 9 In.	10980.00
Vase, Water Lilies, Long Stems, Incised, Painted Blue, Green, Cobalt Blue, c.1902, 16 In.	29500.00
Vase, Zephyr Lily, Blue, Green, Yellow, Cylindrical, Ring Foot, Flared Rim, 1915, 8 ⅜ In.	3383.00
Water Lilies, Stems, Water, Marked, Harriet Coulter Joor, 15 ¾ In.	29500.00

NILOAK POTTERY (*Kaolin* spelled backward) was made at the Hyten Brothers Pottery in Benton, Arkansas, between 1910 and 1947. Although the factory did make cast and molded wares, collectors are most interested in the marbleized art pottery line made of colored swirls of clay. It was called Mission Ware. By 1931 the company made castware, and many of these pieces were marked with the name *Hywood*.

Ashtray, Football Shape, Crow-Burlingame Co.	125.00
Cornucopia, Dusty Rose, Marked, 9 x 5 ½ In.	39.00
Ewer, Flying Eagle, Stars, Blue Over Rose, Marked, 1940s, 10 ¼ In.	58.00
Pitcher, Ball, Black Gloss, Paper Label, 7 x 8 In.	125.00
Planter, Parrot, White, 1940s, 4 x 6 x 3 In.	39.00
Tulip Bowl, Elf With Pipes, Paper Label, 7 In.	295.00
Vase, Marbleized, 2 Handles, Olive Green, 1930s, 6 In.	45.00
Vase, Marbleized, Brown, Tan, Blue, Marked, 6 x 14 In.	500.00
Vase, Marbleized, Brown, Tan, Blue, Red, Tapered, Marked, 4 ½ x 9 ½ In.	281.00
Vase, Marbleized, Red, Black, Marked, 8 ¼ In.	127.00

NIPPON porcelain was made in Japan from 1891 to 1921. *Nippon* is the Japanese word for "Japan." A few firms continued to use the word *Nippon* on ceramics after 1921 as a part of the company name more than as an identification of the country of origin. More pieces marked *Nippon* will be found in the Dragonware, Moriage, and Noritake categories.

Chocolate Pot, Leaves & Flowers, Scalloped Foot, Narrow Body, Loop Handle, Lid, Finial, 11 In.	46.00
Jug, Scenic, Painted, Ducks, Green, Gray, Moriage Branch Handle, Oval, Green Maple Leaf Mark, 8 In.	230.00
Plaque, Painted, Molded Relief, Bedouin, On Camel, Yellow Sun, Dessert, Greek Key Border, 10 In.	374.00
Plate, Painted, Saint Bernard, Raised Enamel, Jeweled Order, Blue Maple Leaf Mark, 10 In.	173.00
Tobacco Humidor, Egyptian Revival, Square, Coffered Lid, Multicolor Enamel, 4 ¾ x 3 ½ In.	92.00
Vase, Flowers Allover, Green, Gold Luster Ground, Basket Handle, 9 In.	47.00
Vase, Flowers, Leaves, Oriental Border, Gilt Trim, C-Scroll Handles, Oval Rings, Marked, c.1915, 15 In.	922.00
Vase, Painted, Roses, Multicolor, Gilt, Handles, Signed, 11 In.	70.00
Vase, Rose, Gilt Rim, Handles, 7 ½ In.	58.00
Vase, Roses, Gilt Handles, Scalloped Rim, Paint, Signed, 11 In.	119.00

NODDERS, also called nodding figures or pagods, are figures with heads and hands that are attached to wires. Any slight movement causes the parts to move up and down. They were made in many countries during the eighteenth, nineteenth, and twentieth centuries. A few Art Deco designs are also known. Copies are being made. A more recent type of nodder is made of papier-mache or plastic. These often represent sports figures or comic characters. Sports nodders are listed in the Sports category.

Asian Man, Seated, Marked Dresden, 10 In.	208.00
Baby Skeezix, Bisque, 2 ¾ In.	65.00
Black Boy, Praying, White Gown, Alms Box, Wood Frame Box, Sponge Painting, 11 x 5 ½ In.	295.00
Bulldog, Papier-Mache, Brown, Pull, 23 In.	840.00
Cat, Chalkware, Painted, Pennsylvania, 19th Century, 4 x 8 ¼ In.	1659.00
Chinese Man, Seated, Holding Fan, Porcelain, c.1950, 6 In.	295.00
Chinese Man, Seated, White, Pink Pantaloons, Cap, Hinged Head, Hands Pivot, 6 ½ x 5 ½ In.	71.00
Chinese Woman, Laughing, Pigtail, Seated, Yellow Slippers, Meissen, 7 In.	8125.00
Giraffe, Wood, Painted, 1960s, 4 ½ In.	10.00
Happy Homer, Homebuilder, Composition, Staggs-Bilt Homes, Phoenix, Arizona, 6 x 2 ⅞ In. *Illus*	231.00
Japanese Boy & Girl, Kiss Me, Magnet Lips, Papier-Mache, 4 ¾ In., Pair	50.00
Japanese Man, Bisque, Ardalt, 7 In.	60.00
Mandarin, Green Floral Gown, Giltwood Base, Parian, Marked, Blue Anchor, c.1885, 18 In. *Illus*	215.00
Oriental Girl, Winks, Papier-Mache, Kimono, Holding Lantern, 6 In.	45.00
Policeman, Hand On Gun, Mustache, Beard, Porcelain, c.1930, 8 In.	625.00
Salt & Pepper shakers are listed in the Salt & Pepper category.	
Theodore Roosevelt, On Elephant, Holding Big Stick, Composition, Painted, 7 x 5 In. *Illus*	3173.00
Woman, Cloak, Vegetable Basket, Apron, Bonnet, Glasses, Bisque, 7 In.	24.00
Woman, Pink Coat, Fur Trimmed, Cape, Bonnet, Bisque, 7 In.	35.00

N

NORITAKE porcelain was made in Japan after 1904 by Nippon Toki Kaisha. The best-known Noritake pieces are marked with the *M* in a wreath for the Morimura Brothers, a New York City distributing company. This mark was used until the early 1950s. There may be some helpful price information in the Nippon category, since prices are comparable. Noritake Azalea is listed in the Azalea category in this book.

Ashtray, Lime Glaze, Image Of Japanese Pavilion With Trylon & Perisphere, 4 ¾ x 5 ⅜ In.	75.00
Baker, Round, Abilene, 9 ⅜ In.	44.00
Bowl, Fruit, Verona, 5 ⅝ In.	8.00
Bowl, Vegetable, Oval, Arden, 10 In.	20.00
Bowl, Vegetable, Oval, Divided, Colmar, 10 In.	48.00
Bowl, Vegetable, Oval, Norwich, 10 In.	46.00
Bowl, Vegetable, Oval, Peony, 10 In.	42.00
Bowl, Vegetable, Oval, Tuscan, 10 In.	38.00
Cake Plate, Acacia, Handle, 10 ¾ In.	80.00
Cake Stand, Ramsey, 10 x 6 In.	37.00
Chop Plate, Safari	16.00
Coffeepot, Lid, Abilene, 7 Cup, 7 In.	56.00
Coffeepot, Lid, Swan Lake, 6 Cup	40.00
Coffeepot, Lid, Watercress, 7 Cup, 7 In.	130.00
Creamer, Colmar, 6 Oz., 4 In.	16.00
Creamer, Norwich, 10 Oz., 3 ¾ In.	21.00
Creamer, Swan Lake, 8 Oz., 3 ½ In.	22.00
Cup & Saucer, Adrian	15.00
Cup & Saucer, Allure, Footed	30.00
Cup & Saucer, Bamboo	23.00
Cup & Saucer, Blanche, Footed	10.00
Cup & Saucer, Cecily	9.00
Cup & Saucer, Demitasse, Roslyn	13.00
Cup & Saucer, Fontana	10.00
Cup & Saucer, Footed, Darleen	15.00
Cup & Saucer, Footed, Elenor	9.00
Cup & Saucer, Footed, Peony	36.00
Cup & Saucer, Paragon	15.00
Cup & Saucer, Roanoke	7.00
Cup & Saucer, Roslyn	20.00
Cup, Barton, Footed	28.00
Dresser Doll, Woman, Patterned Dress & Cloak, Art Deco, Red M In Wreath, 9 In. ....*Illus*	1466.00
Dresser Jar, Indian Maiden, Feather Plumed Hat, 8-Sided Base, Green M In Wreath, 10 ¼ In. .... *Illus*	13529.00
Dresser Tray, Woman Applying Lipstick, Art Deco, Red M In Wreath, 10 ⅞ In. ....*Illus*	2255.00
Figurine, Woman Dancing, Art Deco, Red Base, Stamped, 8 In.	2142.00
Gravy Boat, Underplate, Bluelace	28.00
Gravy Boat, Underplate, Camden	26.00
Gravy Boat, Underplate, Darleen	36.00
Hair Receiver, 2 Piece, 3-Footed, Blue Flowers, Leaves, Vines, c.1910, 2 ½ In.	14.00
Nut Dish, Handle, Footed, Watercress	40.00
Plaque, Painted, Relief Scene, Moose, Green Forest, Signed, Green M In Wreath, 10 ½ In.	316.00
Plaque, Painted, Sculpted Relief, Squirrel Eating Nuts, Green M In Wreath, 10 ½ In.	201.00
Plate, Bread & Butter, Acacia, 6 In.	8.00
Plate, Bread & Butter, Darleen, 6 ½ In.	9.00
Plate, Bread & Butter, Delnor, 6 ⅜ In.	7.00
Plate, Bread & Butter, Paragon, 6 ½ In.	8.00
Plate, Dinner, Amy, 10 In.	30.00
Plate, Dinner, Delnor, 10 ½ In.	9.00
Plate, Dinner, Goldcrest, 10 In.	28.00
Plate, Dinner, Ramsey, 10 ½ In.	14.00
Plate, Dinner, Safari, 10 ⅝ In.	15.00
Plate, Dinner, Verona, 10 ½ In.	16.00
Plate, Salad, Camden, 8 In.	10.00
Plate, Salad, Orchid, 8 ¼ In.	8.00
Plate, Salad, Tara, 7 ½ In.	9.00
Platter, Oval, Tuscan, 11 ¾ In.	33.00
Platter, Serving, Oval, Acacia, 16 In.	60.00
Platter, Serving, Oval, Adrian, 13 In.	46.00
Platter, Serving, Oval, Blanche, 16 In.	36.00
Platter, Serving, Oval, Fontana, 12 In.	36.00

North Dakota School of Mines, Vase, Apple Blossoms, Flora Huckfield, 9 x 6 In. $22,500.00

Rago Arts & Auction Center

North Dakota School of Mines, Vase, Band Of Riders On Horseback, Mountains, Green Glaze, Incised JY, Marked, 1900s, 7 ½ In. $1,840.00

James D. Julia Auctioneers

N

North Dakota School of Mines, Vase, Coyotes, Carved, Julia Mattson, Indigo Stamp, c.1935, 3 ½ x 3 ¾ In. $3,000.00

Rago Arts & Auction Center

TIP
If you have a lightweight vase that tips easily, fill it with sand.

North Dakota School of Mines

North Dakota School of Mines, Vase, Fish, Up & Down Positions, Tan & Cream Glazes, Margaret Pachl, 6 ⅞ In. $518.00

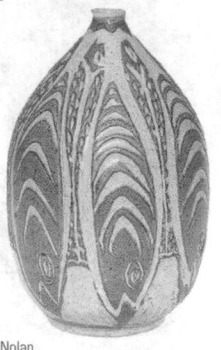

Humler & Nolan

TIP
Check wall-hung and glass shelves regularly to be sure they have not loosened or bent.

North Dakota School of Mines, Vase, Trees, Blue Glossy Glaze, Wanda Wells, 1924, 9 x 5 In. $16,250.00

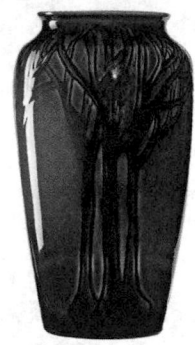

Rago Arts & Auction Center

North Dakota School of Mines, Vase, Yellow Glaze, Ruffled Rim, Dickota Dickinson, 6 In.

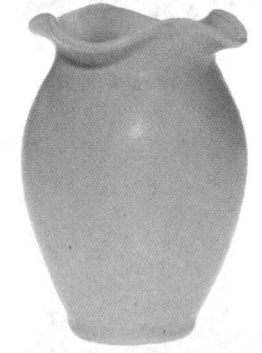

Humler & Nolan

Platter, Serving, Oval, Roanoke, 14 In.	18.00
Powder Jar, Woman Holding Feather Puff, Flat, Luster Glaze, Art Deco, Red M In Wreath, 4 In....*Illus*	451.00
Ramekin, Belmont	18.00
Relish, 3 Sections, Bluelace	33.00
Relish, Belmont, 8 ¼ In.	16.00
Salt & Pepper, Roanoke	26.00
Salt & Pepper, Watercress	18.00
Soup, Dish, Paragon, 7 ⅜ In.	9.00
Sugar & Creamer, Bamboo	48.00
Sugar & Creamer, Tara	23.00
Sugar, Lid, Goldcrest, 3 In.	34.00
Teapot, Lid, Arden, 4 Cup, 4 ⅝ In.	139.00
Vase, Woman In Gown, Headdress, Luster Glaze, Art Deco, 7 ½ In.	1503.00
Wall Pocket, Woman With Headdress, Art Deco, 8 In.	395.00

NORSE POTTERY COMPANY started in Edgerton, Wisconsin, in 1903. In 1904 the company moved to Rockford, Illinois. The company made a black pottery, which resembled early bronze relics of the Scandinavian countries. The firm went out of business in 1913.

Bowl, Lid, Copper Glaze, Incised Geometric Design, Handles, Signed, 8 x 3 ½ In.	368.00
Bowl, Serpent, Copper Glaze, Incised Design, 3-Footed, Signed, 3 In.	207.00
Jardiniere, Mythological Beast Shape Handles, Incised Design, 3 Animal Face Feet, 15 In.	527.00
Vase, Brown Amber Glaze, Geometric Design, Pillar Shape, Flared Base, 9 In.	28.00
Vase, Brown Glaze, Scrolling Design, Slender, Flared Base, Neck, 11 ½ In.	28.00
Vase, Geometric, Black Metallic Glaze, Handles, 12 x 6 In.	375.00

NORTH DAKOTA SCHOOL OF MINES was established in 1898 at the University of North Dakota. A ceramics course was included in the curriculum and pieces were made from the clays found in the region. Students at the university made pieces from 1909 to 1949. Although very early pieces were marked *U.N.D.*, most pieces were stamped with the full name of the university.

Bowl, Fruits, Vegetables, Flora Huckfield, Ink Stamp, Incised, 9 ⅛ In. ......*Illus*	316.00
Box, Indian Chief, Incised, Brown Glaze, Round, 2 x 5 In.	450.00
Case, Cowboy, Lasso, Why Not Minot, Tan, Brown, Swollen, J. Mattson, 6 x 3 In.	2000.00
Flower Arranger, Bag Shape, Gathered Neck, Pieced, Margaret Pachl, 4 In. ......*Illus*	173.00
Plaque, Woman Tennis Player, Blue, Green, Yellow, Julia Mattson, 1934, 6 x 4 In.	1500.00
Tile, Trees, Stylized Landscape, Green, Yellow, Blue, Square, H. Fried, 1926, 7 In.	11250.00
Vase, Angular Designs, Oatmeal Matte Glaze, Impressed, Ferock, State ND Lettering, 12 In.... *Illus*	2760.00
Vase, Apple Blossoms, Flora Huckfield, 9 x 6 In. ......*Illus*	22500.00
Vase, Band Of Riders On Horseback, Mountains, Green Glaze, Incised JY, Marked, 1900s, 7 ½ In..*Illus*	1840.00
Vase, Bare Trees, Interlacing Branches, Dark Green, Amber, Tapered, Rolled Rim, 7 ⅞ In.	4600.00
Vase, Bison, Green, Brown Matte Glaze, M. Cable, 6 ½ x 4 ½ In.	1875.00
Vase, Black, Gray, Red Glaze, Cylinder, 1926, 6 x 11 In.	563.00
Vase, Buffalo, Carved, Brown, White, Bulbous, J. Mattson, 3 ¼ x 4 ½ In.	2375.00
Vase, Cacti, Carved, Tan, Blue Ground, Bulbous, J. Mattson, 1938, 5 x 4 ¾ In.	1000.00
Vase, Carved Designs, Rectangular, Green Matte Glaze, 3 ¾ x 2 ½ In.	250.00
Vase, Covered Wagon, Greens, Tapered, F. Huckfield, F.L. Hammers, 1932, 4 x 5 In.	2125.00
Vase, Coyotes, Carved, Julia Mattson, Indigo Stamp, c.1935, 3 ½ x 3 ¾ In. ......*Illus*	3000.00
Vase, Fish, Up & Down Positions, Tan & Cream Glazes, Margaret Pachl, 6 ⅞ In. ......*Illus*	518.00
Vase, Indian Symbols, Carved, Brown, Oval, Straight Neck, Mrs. J. Conners, 9 x 6 In.	2875.00
Vase, Leaves, Gray, Turquoise, Signed Schnell, 10 ½ In.	322.00
Vase, Meadow, Trees, Rolling Hills, Green, Shoulder Band, Elongated Oval, 1916, 7 ⅞ In.	10350.00
Vase, Palm Trees, Incised, Brown, Tan, Oval, Flared Rim, 6 ¾ x 3 In.	2125.00
Vase, Prairie Dogs, Wheat, Green, Sage, Ring Foot, Pear Shape, 1943, 2 In.	403.00
Vase, Raised Letters, Multicolor Swirl, Mottled Gray, Brown Glaze, 3 ½ x 3 ½ In.	438.00
Vase, Scandinavian Maids, Pyramid Shape, Yellow, Green, Marked, c.1952, 3 ½ In.	575.00
Vase, Stylized Birds, Bentonite, Squat, 1948, 4 ½ x 5 In.	750.00
Vase, Stylized Grapevines, Blue Ground, Bulbous, Tapered, 5 ¾ x 5 In.	2375.00
Vase, Trees, Blue Glossy Glaze, Wanda Wells, 1924, 9 x 5 In. ......*Illus*	16250.00
Vase, Trillium, Flowers, Blue, Gray, Lavender, Shouldered, Tapered, Stamped, 1926, 7 ¼ In.	1725.00
Vase, Tulips, Carved, Yellow, Mottled, Oval, Folded In Rim, Doris Brown, 7 x 3 In.	6250.00
Vase, Wild Carrots, Stripes, White, Blue, Round, M. Thormodsgard, 1932, 7 x 8 In.	2500.00
Vase, Yellow Flowers, Brown Glaze, Cylindrical, 5 x 3 In.	150.00
Vase, Yellow Glaze, Ruffled Rim, Dickota Dickinson, 6 In. ......*Illus*	58.00

NU-ART *see Imperial category.*

NUTCRACKERS of many types have been used through the centuries. At first the nutcracker was probably strong teeth or a hammer. But by the nineteenth century, many elaborate and ingenious types were made. Levers, screws, and hammer adaptations were the most popular. Because nutcrackers are still useful, they are still being made, some in the old styles.

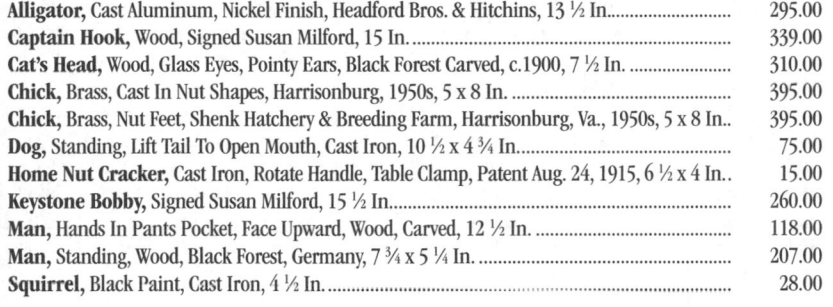

Alligator, Cast Aluminum, Nickel Finish, Headford Bros. & Hitchins, 13 ½ In.	295.00
Captain Hook, Wood, Signed Susan Milford, 15 In.	339.00
Cat's Head, Wood, Glass Eyes, Pointy Ears, Black Forest Carved, c.1900, 7 ½ In.	310.00
Chick, Brass, Cast In Nut Shapes, Harrisonburg, 1950s, 5 x 8 In.	395.00
Chick, Brass, Nut Feet, Shenk Hatchery & Breeding Farm, Harrisonburg, Va., 1950s, 5 x 8 In.	395.00
Dog, Standing, Lift Tail To Open Mouth, Cast Iron, 10 ½ x 4 ¾ In.	75.00
Home Nut Cracker, Cast Iron, Rotate Handle, Table Clamp, Patent Aug. 24, 1915, 6 ½ x 4 In.	15.00
Keystone Bobby, Signed Susan Milford, 15 ½ In.	260.00
Man, Hands In Pants Pocket, Face Upward, Wood, Carved, 12 ½ In.	118.00
Man, Standing, Wood, Black Forest, Germany, 7 ¾ x 5 ¼ In.	207.00
Squirrel, Black Paint, Cast Iron, 4 ½ In.	28.00

NYMPHENBURG, *see Royal Nymphenburg.*

OCCUPIED JAPAN was printed on pottery, porcelain, toys, and other goods made during the American occupation of Japan after World War II, from 1947 to 1952. Collectors now search for these pieces. The items were made for export. Ceramic items are listed here. Toys are listed in the Toy category in this book.

OCCUPIED JAPAN

Creamer, Elephant Shape, Pink Ears, 5 In.	75.00
Cup & Saucer, Pagoda, Gilt Trim.	75.00
Figurine, Clown, Dog, Orange, Green, Polka Dots, Ruffles, Ardalt, 3 ½ x 4 In.	125.00
Figurine, Clown, Riding Donkey, Orange, Green, Stripes, Ruffles, Ardalt, 4 ¾ x 4 In.	125.00
Figurine, Clown, Riding Pig, Orange, Blue, Polka Dots, Ardalt, 5 x 4 ⅛ In.	125.00
Figurine, Colonial Couple, Dancing, 3 ¼ In.	24.00
Figurine, Dutch Girl, Sitting, Flowered Red Dress, 4 ¾ In.	14.00
Figurine, Parrot Sitting On Grape Bunch, Multicolor, 6 In.	28.00
Figurine, Woman Dancing, Holding Lace Shirt, Pink, Green, 6 In.	30.00
Match Safe, Woman, Holding Fan, 3 ½ x 2 ½ x 1 In.	30.00
Plate, Flowers, Ucagco, Red, Pink, 7 ¼ In.	28.00
Salt & Pepper, Roses, Milwaukee Wisconsin Ship	17.00
Soup, Dish, Celebrate, 7 ¼ In.	8.00
Toby Mug, General MacArthur, Merit, c.1950, 4 ⅜ In.	24.00
Toby Mug, Innkeeper, Holding Lantern, 5 In.	35.00
Toothpick Holder, Boy, Playing Guitar, 3 In.	21.00
Toothpick Holder, Girl, Playing Ukulele, 3 ½ In.	15.00
Vase, Figural, Cherub, Playing Accordion, 4 In.	18.00

OFFICE TECHNOLOGY includes office equipment and related products, such as adding machines, calculators, and check-writing machines. Typewriters are in their own category in this book.

Cabinet, Woodruff Improved File Holder, Style B, Oak, 42 Boxes, c.1887, 94 x 43 In.	3696.00
Check Writer, Green Metal, Series 600, Paymaster Corp.	20.00
Check Writer, Protectograph, Todd, c.1915, 16 x 8 x 4 In.	45.00
Check Writer, Safe Guard, Model S, c.1920.	250.00
Copy Machine, Crank Handle, Moistening Attachment, Leonard Bailey, c.1886, 17 x 12 In.	395.00
Copying Press, Hand Driven, c.1880, 15 ¾ x 12 ¼ x 15 In.	844.00
Dictaphone, Columbia, Model T, 10 x 12 ½ In.	236.00
Dictaphone, Model 10, Electric Motor Drive, England, c.1925	338.00
Dictating Machine, Parlograph, Electric, Horn, 3 Cylinders, Carl Lindstrom, Germany, c.1910.	690.00
Drum Calculating Machine, Wood Roller, Schumann & Co., 1910	5829.00
Envelope Sealer, Porcelain, 1940s, 4 ¼ x 3 ½ x 3 ¼ In.	65.00
Postal Chute, United States, Letter Drop, Brass, 8 x 60 In.	113.00
Stenotype Machine, Case, 1940s, 9 x 11 x 6 In.	100.00
Tape Dispenser, Cast Iron, Art Deco, 1930s, 5 ¾ In.	75.00
Time Recorder, Number Buttons, Flowers, Paint, Iron, Oak, Simplex, 17 ¾ x 21 ½ In.	1375.00
Time Stamp Machine, Cast Iron, Automatic Time Stamp Co., No. 36102, 1920s	616.00
Vault Timer, 3 Watch Movements, Key, Porcelain Dials, Diebold, 7 x 4 ½ In.	466.00

Ohr, Inkwell, Burnt Baby, Snake, 1892-94, 3 x 2 ¾ In.
$1,875.00

Rago Arts & Auction Center

Ohr, Inkwell, Cabin, Mottled Olive Green Glaze, Impressed G.E. Ohr, Biloxi, c.1885, 3 In.
$7,475.00

Glass Works Auctions

Ohr, Teapot, Pinched Waist, Glazed, Stamped, 1890s, 6 ¾ x 8 In.
$46,875.00

Rago Arts & Auction Center

Ohr, Vase, Bisque Fired, Irregular Folds, Script Signature, c.1900, 5 x 6 In.
$20,000.00

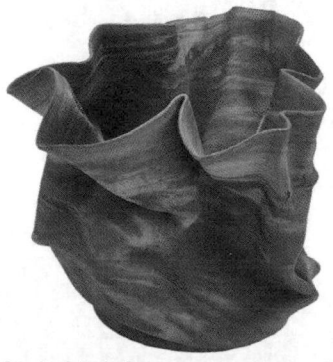

Rago Arts & Auction Center

O

Ohr, Vase, Dimpled, Mottled Brown, Gunmetal Glaze, Stamped, 1890s, 3 x 3 ½ In. $2,125.00

Rago Arts & Auction Center

Ohr, Vase, Folded, Mottled Green Glaze, Stamped, 1890s, 3 ¾ x 5 In. $8,750.00

Rago Arts & Auction Center

Opalescent, Windows, Pitcher, Blue, Ruffled Rim, Applied Handle, 9 In. $201.00

Early Auction Co.

Orrefors, Vase, Ariel, Girl & Dove, Engraved, Gold Paper Label, Edvin Ohrstrom, 7 ¼ x 5 In. $18,750.00

Rago Arts & Auction Center

OHR pottery was made in Biloxi, Mississippi, from 1883 to 1906 by George E. Ohr, a true eccentric. The pottery was made of very thin clay that was twisted, folded, and dented into odd, graceful shapes. Some pieces were lifelike models of hats, animal heads, or even a potato. Others were decorated with folded clay "snakes." Reproductions and reworked pieces are appearing on the market. These have been reglazed, or snakes and other embellishments have been added.

Bowl, Squat, Red Blister Glaze, Flattened Rim, Green Speckled Interior, 1890s, 2 ¼ x 4 In.	2125.00
Chamber Pot, Faux Fecal Matter, Joke Souvenir, Marked, 2 ⅜ In.	369.00
Cup, 3 Loop Handles, Shaped Rim, Matte Red, Green Flambe, Amber Glaze, Signed, 1900s, 4 x 5 In.	8125.00
Dish, Green & Amber Glaze, Boat Shape, Pointed Ends, Folded Out Rim, 2 ¼ x 7 In.	3250.00
Inkwell, Burnt Baby, Snake, 1892-94, 3 x 2 ¾ In...*Illus*	1875.00
Inkwell, Cabin, Mottled Olive Green Glaze, Impressed G.E. Ohr, Biloxi, c.1885, 3 In.........*Illus*	7475.00
Mug, Body Twist Design, Twisted Handle, Round Foot, Brown, Beige, Stamped, 1896, 3 ¼ x 4 ½ In.	2000.00
Mug, Speckled Green, Brown & Amber Glaze, 3 Handles Of Different Shapes, 4 x 6 In..............	4688.00
Pitcher, Sponge Glaze, Bulbous, Ring Foot, Ear Shape Handle, Stamped, 1900s, 5 ½ x 6 In....	4688.00
Pitcher, Sponged Gunmetal Glaze, Cutout Handle, Undulating Rim, Footed, 5 x 6 In..............	15000.00
Pitcher, Sponged Indigo & Amber Glaze, Bulbous, Shaped Ribbon Handle, 6 ½ x 6 In.	32500.00
Teapot, Inverted Lid, Mustard Glaze, Mottled Green, Blue Slip, Stamped, 4 ½ x 8 ½ In.	22705.00
Teapot, Pinched Waist, Glazed, Stamped, 1890s, 6 ¾ x 8 In.................................*Illus*	46875.00
Vase, Bisque Fired, Irregular Folds, Script Signature, c.1900, 5 x 6 In. ....*Illus*	20000.00
Vase, Brown & Green Glaze, Bulbous, Dimples, Crumpled Rim, c.1900, 3 x 3 ½ In..............	8750.00
Vase, Brown Sponge Glaze, In-Body Twist, Bulbous Bottom, Straight Neck, 5 ½ x 4 ½ In........	5000.00
Vase, Brown, Bulbous, In-Body Twist, Raised Rim, 4 ½ x 4 ½ In.	3750.00
Vase, Cylindrical, Rounded Bottom, Folded Rim, Green Speckle, Black Glaze, 1890s, 4 ½ x 3 ¾ In..	1125.00
Vase, Dimpled, Mottled Brown, Gunmetal Glaze, Stamped, 1890s, 3 x 3 ½ In...................*Illus*	2125.00
Vase, Folded, Mottled Green Glaze, Stamped, 1890s, 3 ¾ x 5 In.............................*Illus*	8750.00
Vase, Gunmetal & Amber Speckled Glaze, Ring Foot, Cylindrical Neck, 1900s, 2 ¾ x 3 ¼ In....	1250.00
Vase, Mottled Black Glaze, 4 Dimpled & Folded Sides, 2 ¾ x 3 In............................	3750.00
Vase, Mottled Mauve & Indigo Glaze, In-Body Twist, Footed, 7 x 2 ¾ In.	11875.00
Vase, Mottled Oxblood Glaze, Bulbous, Fold-Out Rim, 1890s, 3 ½ x 4 In.	8750.00
Vase, Mottled Raspberry & Green Glaze, Tapered, Ruffled Rim, c.1900, 4 x 4 In.................	10625.00
Vase, Orange Glaze, Pedestal Foot, Molded Center, Cylindrical Neck, Tortured Design, Signed, 3 In.	1840.00
Vase, Oxblood & Green Glaze, Pinched Baluster Shape, Footed, 1890s, 7 x 2 ¾ In.	5000.00
Vase, Pear Shape, Body Twist Design, Raspberry & Green Speckled Glaze, 1890s, 4 x 3 In........	10000.00
Vase, Raspberry, Gray & Indigo Blister Glaze, Cinched Waist, Pinched Rim, 5 x 2 In.	10625.00
Vase, Sponged Pink, Indigo, Green, Gunmetal & Yellow Glaze, Crimped Rim, 1890s, 5 In.......	10625.00
Vase, Sponged Purple & Green Glaze, Cone Shape Bottom, Flared Top, Crimped, 7 In.............	6875.00

OLD IVORY china was made by the Ohme Porcelain Works in Silesia, Germany, a factory working from 1882 to 1928. The china had an ivory matte background and was usually decorated with flowers or fruit. Dinner sets, fish sets, mustache cups, and souvenir pieces were made. Pieces were marked with a crown, the cipher *OH*, and the word *Silesia*. Some pieces are also marked with the words *Old Ivory*. The pattern numbers appear on the base of many pieces.

Cake Plate, No. 16, 11 In...	125.00
Cake Plate, No. 84, 9 ⅝ In..	59.00
Plate, Black Berries, Purple, Pink, Green, Gilt Trim, Marked, 7 ½ In......................	45.00
Plate, Dessert, Pink Blossoms, Gilt Rim, 6 In., 4 Piece...............................	50.00
Toothpick Holder, No. 16, 2 ¼ In...	195.00

OLD PARIS, *see Paris category.*

OLD SLEEPY EYE, *see Sleepy Eye category.*

ONION PATTERN, originally named bulb pattern, is a white ware decorated with cobalt blue or pink. Although it is commonly associated with Meissen, other companies made the pattern in the late nineteenth and the twentieth centuries. A rare type is called *red bud* because there are added red accents on the blue-and-white dishes.

Bowl, Blue & White, Meissen, 14 In..	225.00
Bowl, Vegetable, Lid, Blue & White, Roune, Meissen, 13 ½ x 8 In.	250.00
Cake Stand, Blue & White, Pedestal, Meissen, 13 x 4 ¾ In.................................	295.00
Coffeepot, Blue & White, Hoop Finial, Meissen, 10 ½ In.	190.00
Funnel, Blue & White, Handle, Meissen, 5 ½ x 4 In.	69.00
Platter, Blue & White, Meissen, 20 ½ x 15 In.	350.00
Platter, Blue & White, Oval, Meissen, 15 ¼ In..	53.00
Rolling Pin, Blue & White, Wood Handles, 14 ½ In.......................................	455.00

O

Soup Tureen, Blue & White, Oval, Rococo Handles, Scrolls, Marked, Meissen, c.1840, 9 ¾ x 14 In.	276.00
Soup, Dish, Blue & White, Underplate, Handles, Blue Crossed Swords, Meissen, 6 Sets	240.00
Warming Plate, Blue & White, Spigot, Handles, Copper, Meissen, 1890s, 9 x 2 In.	125.00

OPALESCENT GLASS is translucent glass that has the tones of the opal gemstone. It originated in England in the 1870s and is often found in pressed glassware made in Victorian times. Opalescent glass was first made in America in 1897 at the Northwood glassworks in Indiana, Pennsylvania. Some dealers use the terms *opaline* and *opalescent* for any of these translucent wares. More opalescent pieces may be listed in Hobnail, Pressed Glass, and other glass categories.

Charleston, Tumbler, 6 Panels, Tapered, Wide Rim Band, c.1870, 3 ⅝ x 3 ⅜ In.	184.00
Coinspot, Pitcher, Blue & Pink Banding, Triangular Mouth, Loop Handle, 10 ½ In.	489.00
Colonial, Goblet, Polished Pontil, c.1860, 6 In.	1380.00
Daisy In Crisscross, Pitcher, Blue, Baluster, Crimped Rim, Loop Handle, 9 In.	546.00
Diamond Quilted, Finger Bowl, Blue, Gold Enamel Blossoming Branch, Crimped Rim, 3 In.	115.00
Epergne, Scalloped Green Trim, 3 Trumpet Vases, Base Bowl, 11 In.	208.00
Honeycomb, Pitcher, Cranberry, Square Mouth, Clear Reeded Handle, 7 In.	460.00
Klondyke, Bowl, Blue, Northwood, 8 x 3 ¾ In.	24.00
Spanish Lace, Celery Vase, Blue, Trifold Ruffled Rim, 6 ½ In.	52.00
Windows, Pitcher, Blue, Ruffled Rim, Applied Handle, 9 In. ....*Illus*	201.00

OPALINE, or opal glass, was made in white, green, and other colors. The glass had a matte surface and a lack of transparency. It was often gilded or painted. It was a popular mid-nineteenth-century European glassware.

Bowl, Napoleon III, Bronze Scroll Pierced Base, Putti & Flowers, Pink, Pierced Rim, c.1865, 6 x 18 In.	1107.00
Centerpiece, French Blue, Bird, Flower, Ormolu Scrolls, Chalice Shape, c.1850, 13 ¾ x 13 ½ In.	2415.00
Salt, Silver Basket, Reticulated Grapevines, Oval, 1800s, 2 x 4 In., Pair	173.00
Shaker, White, Molded Heron, Lighthouse, Pressed Glass, 3 ¼ In.	12.00
Vase, Cherubs, Girls, Signed E.F. Roger, 1800s, 8 In.	115.00
Vase, Enameled Leprechaun & Flower Design, Footed Base, Oval Body, 1800s, 13 In., Pair	374.00
Vase, Flowers, Birds, High Waisted, France, 15 ½ In., Pair	760.00
Vase, Napoleon III, Trumpet Top, Inverted Foot, Greek Key Border, Gilt Swags, c.1865, 15 ½ In.	369.00

OPERA GLASSES are needed because the stage is a long way from some of the seats at a play or an opera. Mother-of-pearl was a popular decoration on many French glasses.

Enamel, Paint, Mother-Of-Pearl Bezels, Gilt Brass Frame, Engraved, France, 2 ½ x 9 In.	553.00
Mother-Of-Pearl, Gilt Metal, O.H. Meder, Leipzig, Leather Case, 3 ¾ In.	117.00
Mother-Of-Pearl, Lemoire, 3 x 4 In.	47.00
Raised Gilt, Bouquet, Enamel, Blue Ground, France, 19th Century, 2 ½ x 4 ½ In.	625.00

ORPHAN ANNIE first appeared in the comics in 1924. The last strip ran in newspapers on June 13, 2010. The redheaded girl, her dog Sandy, and her friends were on the radio from 1930 to 1942. The first movie based on the strip was produced in 1932. A second movie was produced in 1938. A Broadway musical that opened in 1977, a movie based on the musical and produced in 1982, and a made-for-television movie based on the musical produced in 1999 made Annie popular again, and many toys, dishes, and other memorabilia have been made.

Ashtray, Annie & Sandy, Lusterware, 1930s, 3 x 4 In.	75.00
Button, Ovaltine Promotion, Voter's, Multicolor, Round, 1931, 1 ¼ In.	298.00
Code Captain Secrets Folder, Badge, Ovaltine Premium, 1939, 3 ¼ x 6 ½ In.	170.00
Manual, Decoder Badge, Secret Society, 1936	75.00
Nodder, Daddy Warbucks, Hanging Pockets, Bisque, Germany, 3 ⅜ In.	95.00
Ring, March Birthstone, Wisdom, Aquamarine Color, Brass, 1936	230.00
Secret Society Ring, Lead Proof, Burst Lines, 5-Point Star, Robbins Co., 1936, 1 ½ x 3 ¼ In.	1150.00
Toothbrush Holder, Annie & Sandy, On Chair, Bisque, Japan, 3 ¾ In.	125.00
Toy, Sandy, Figures, Metal Base, Wheels, Hobo Bundle, Windup, 1930s, 6 ¾ & 3 In., 2 Piece	2846.00
Water Pistol, Premium, Club Manual Offering, Black, Metal Barrel, 1942, 3 ⅛ x 5 ½ In.	75.00

ORREFORS Glassworks, located in the Swedish province of Smaaland, was established *Orrefors* in 1898. The company is still making glass for use on the table or as decorations. There is renewed interest in the glass made in the modern styles of the 1940s and 1950s. In 1990, the company merged with Kosta Boda. Most vases and decorative pieces are signed with the etched name Orrefors.

Bowl, Center, 8-Sided, Square Base, 10 In.	82.00
Bowl, Cobalt Blue, Clear Banded Rim, Round, Tapered, 7 In.	28.00

Orrefors, Vase, Ariel, Trapped Bubble Circles, Cobalt Blue, Edvin Ohrstrom, 1900s, 6 ½ In.
$2,829.00

Skinner, Inc.

Orrefors, Vase, Fish, Ocean Plants, Blown Glass, Edvard Hald, 5 x 4 ½ In.
$300.00

Gray's Auctioneers LLC

Ott & Brewer, Vase, Orchid, Fired On Gold, Leaves, Stems, Butterflies, Handles, Marked, 14 In.
$1,495.00

Humler & Nolan

Overbeck, Figurine, Dodo Bird, Colorful Outfit, Marked, 3 ¾ In.
$374.00

Humler & Nolan

Overbeck, Figurine, Southern Belle, Grotesque, Hoop Skirt, Hat, Blue, Pink, White, Impressed, 4 ¼ In. $230.00

Humler & Nolan

Overbeck, Flower Arranger, Flower Shape, Blue & Brown, Impressed, 2 ⅞ In. $173.00

Humler & Nolan

Overbeck, Vase, Stylized Trees, Matte Glaze, Stamped OBK, E & F, c.1920, 10 ¾ x 5 In. $13,750.00

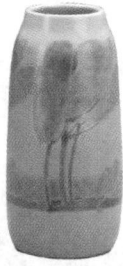

Rago Arts & Auction Center

TIP

If you are searching flea markets and yard sales, don't offer too little for a treasure. Being too cheap will mean that you may not hear about other similar items the dealer has not yet set out for sale. Offer a low but fair price, usually 20 percent off the market price.

Bowl, Engraved, Quilted, 6 In.	51.00
Bowl, Etched, Diamond Pattern, 5 In.	40.00
Bowl, Inverted Bell Shape, Stylized Flower Design, Eva Englund, 6 ⅛ In.	413.00
Bowl, Lattice Design, Sven Palmquist, 8 ¼ In. Diam.	625.00
Bowl, Paneled, Clear, 10 In.	73.00
Bowl, Selena, Pearlized Glass, Sven Palmquist, Marked, c.1950, 9 ¾ x 2 ½ In.	86.00
Champagne Flute, Crystal, 8 ¾ In., 4 Piece	150.00
Figurine, Bear, Seated, Clear, 4 In.	17.00
Goblet Set, Wine, Prelude, 25 Piece	480.00
Vase, Apple Shape, Clear Glass, Sweden, Signed, 1957, 15 x 12 ½ In.	2500.00
Vase, Ariel, Girl & Dove, Engraved, Gold Paper Label, Edvin Ohrstrom, 7 ¼ x 5 In. ...*Illus*	18750.00
Vase, Ariel, Trapped Bubble Circles, Cobalt Blue, Edvin Ohrstrom, 1900s, 6 ½ In. ...*Illus*	2829.00
Vase, Block Pattern, Square, Clear, 6 ½ In.	85.00
Vase, Engraved, Geese, 7 In.	62.00
Vase, Engraved, Girl, Moon, 6 ½ In.	102.00
Vase, Fish, Ocean Plants, Blown Glass, Edvard Hald, 5 x 4 ½ In. ...*Illus*	300.00
Vase, Free-Form Rim, Clear, Tapered, 8 In.	57.00
Vase, Melon, Mouth Blown, Narrow Cylindrical Neck, Ball Shape Body, Blue, 1959, 13 x 12 ½ In.	3125.00
Vase, Panel, Tapered, Triangular, Clear, 11 ½ In.	73.00
Vase, Petal Rim, Shaped Rim, Clear, 5 ½ In.	40.00
Vase, Ribbed, Clear, Round, 8 In.	73.00
Vase, Sven Palmquist, Inscribed, 20th Century, 8 ½ x 5 ½ In.	420.00
Vase, Tulip Shape, Clear, Signed, 8 ¼ x 6 In.	73.00
Vase, Young Woman, Bird, Etched, Clear, Tapered, Oblong, 5 ¼ In.	57.00

OTT & BREWER COMPANY operated the Etruria Pottery at Trenton, New Jersey, from 1871 to 1892. It started making belleek in 1882. The firm used a variety of marks that incorporated the initials O & B.

Charger, Blue Poppies, Fluted, Gilt, 10 In.	78.00
Plate, Blue Poppy Transfer, Gilt Highlights, Fluted Blank, 10 In.	78.00
Soup, Dish, Pink Flowers, Metallic Gold Trim, c.1875, 9 ¼ In.	20.00
Vase, Orchid, Fired On Gold, Leaves, Stems, Butterflies, Handles, Marked, 14 In. ...*Illus*	1495.00

OVERBECK POTTERY was made by four sisters named Overbeck at a pottery in Cambridge City, Indiana. They started in 1911. They made all types of vases, each one-of-a-kind. Small, hand-modeled figurines are the most popular pieces with today's collectors. The factory continued until 1955, when the last of the four sisters died.

Figurine, Choir Singer, Holding Hymnal, Grotesque, Pink, Blue, Brown, Marked, 5 ¼ In.	288.00
Figurine, Dodo Bird, Colorful Outfit, Marked, 3 ¾ In. ...*Illus*	374.00
Figurine, Dog, Wild, Grotesque, Pink, Blue, Green, Black, Marked, 2 ¼ x 3 ½ In.	374.00
Figurine, Featherless Chick, Standing, Grotesque Design, Pale Blue, Cream, Marked OBK, 3 ⅞ In.	207.00
Figurine, Skunk, Arched Back, Tail Curled, Black & White, Marked, 1 ⅝ x 3 ¼ In.	403.00
Figurine, Southern Belle, Grotesque, Hoop Skirt, Hat, Blue, Pink, White, Impressed, 4 ¼ In. ...*Illus*	230.00
Flower Arranger, Flower Shape, Blue & Brown, Impressed, 2 ⅞ In. ...*Illus*	173.00
Vase, Monochromatic, Sage Green, Flowers, Reeded, Bulbous Oval, Flared Rim, Marked, 8 ¼ In.	1840.00
Vase, Organic Design, Carved, Brown Matte Glaze, Tapered, 3 x 5 ½ In.	4375.00
Vase, Stylized Trees, Matte Glaze, Stamped OBK, E & F, c.1920, 10 ¾ x 5 In. ...*Illus*	13750.00
Vase, Yellow Matte Glaze, Carved Geometric Patterns, Square, Ring Foot, Wide Rim, 1914, 3 ⅜ In.	316.00

OWENS POTTERY was made in Zanesville, Ohio, from 1891 to 1928. The first art pottery was made after 1896. Utopian Ware, Cyrano, Navarre, Feroza, and Henri Deux were made. Pieces were usually marked with a form of the name Owens. About 1907, the firm began to make tile and discontinued the art pottery wares.

Bowl, Aboriginal, Round, Brown, Tan Bands, 7 ¼ In.	35.00
Jardiniere, Garlands, Scalloped Rim, Majolica, Green, Brown Glaze, 8 ¾ In.	46.00
Jug, Cherries, Leaves, Opalescent Green Glaze, Handle, Marked, 6 x 7 ½ In.	406.00
Tankard, Utopian, Signed C. Minnie Terry, 13 ¼ In.	92.00
Tile, Grapes, Arts & Crafts, Oval Frame, 12 x 12 In.	225.00
Tile, Grapes, Purple, Green, Orange, Carved, Painted, Oak Frame, 12 In.	275.00
Vase, Aboriginal, Geometric Designs, Flared Base, 5 ⅓ In.	63.00
Vase, Cyrano, Bud, Black Ground, Curly White Design, 6 ½ In.	35.00
Vase, Feroza, Brown Metallic Luster, Gold Color, Ruffle Rim & Foot, Elongated Handles, 8 ¼ In.	275.00
Vase, Flower, Leaves, Brown Ground, Standard Glaze, Impressed, c.1910, 8 In. ...*Illus*	60.00
Vase, Henri Deux, Art Nouveau Maiden, Handles, 10 ½ x 9 ½ In. ...*Illus*	813.00

Vase, Henri Deux, Woman's Face, Black Ground, 6 ½ In.	161.00
Vase, Leaves, Brown, Squared Shoulder, Marked Harry Larzelere, 4 x 3 In.	250.00
Vase, Orange Flowers, Brown Glaze, Long Neck, Marked, 10 ½ In.	161.00
Vase, Red Poppies, 7 In.	141.00
Vase, Soudaneze, Purple Grape & Vine Band, Green Ground, 6 In.	52.00
Vase, Utopian, Chrysanthemums, Blue, White, Cylindrical, Haubrich, 5 x 15 In.	938.00
Vase, Utopian, Flowers, Square, Marked, 10 ½ In.	127.00
Vase, Utopian, Geraniums, Brown, Orange, Yellow, Genie Bottle, Trumpet Mouth, 13 ½ In.	150.00
Vase, Utopian, Heron, Standing On Leg, Marsh, Lotus, Cattail, Mae Timberlake, Marked, 14 In..*Illus*	1495.00
Vase, Utopian, Orange Flowers, Green Leaves, Long Neck, Brown Ground, 10 ½ In.	115.00
Vase, Utopian, White Horse, Brown, Amber Glaze, Ruffled Rim, Loop Handles, Signed, 7 In.	977.00
Vase, Utopian, Yellow Clematis, Orange, Bulbous, Loop Handles At Neck, Wavy Rim, Ring Foot, 3 In.	160.00

OYSTER PLATES were popular from the 1880s. Each course at dinner was served in a special dish. The oyster plate had indentations shaped like oysters. Usually six oysters were held on a plate. There is no greater value to a plate with more oysters, although that myth continues to haunt antiques dealers. There are other plates for shellfish, including cockle plates and whelk plates. The appropriately shaped indentations are part of the design of these dishes.

3 Wells, Wave Design, Flowers, Gray & Brown, Haviland, Limoges, 6 In.	150.00
4 Wells, Flowers, Multicolor, Haviland, c.1880, 8 ½ In.	399.00
4 Wells, Pink & Brown Highlights, Germany, c.1890, 8 ½ In.	95.00
5 Wells, Blue & White, Vignette Reserve, Scalloped Edge, Weimar, 8 In., 8 Piece	1076.00
5 Wells, Cabbage Roses, Gold Trim, Tressemann & Vogt Limoges, c.1900, 9 ½ In.	175.00
5 Wells, Crescent Shape, Yellow, Pink, 19th Century, 9 In.	125.00
5 Wells, Flowers, Leaves, Gilt Accents, Scalloped, Haviland, 8 ½ In.	58.00
5 Wells, Flowers, Scalloped Edge, Gilt Trim, c.1895, 8 ¼ In.	85.00
5 Wells, Hexagon, Flowers, Elite Works Limoges, c.1900, 8 x 8 In.	90.00
5 Wells, Rutherford B. Hayes, White House, Haviland, Limoges, c.1880, 8 ⅝ In. .....*Illus*	16800.00
5 Wells, Scalloped Square Shape, Pink, White, Gold Flower Border, Beehive, 9 In.	161.00
5 Wells, Seaweed Relief, Flowers, Ribbed, Gilt, Germany, 8 In.	75.00
5 Wells, Square, Pink, France, 9 ¾ In.	251.00
6 Wells, Blue, Pink, Etruscan, Majolica, c.1880, 10 In.	225.00
6 Wells, Blue, Yellow Trim, Keller & Guerin St. Clement, c.1900, 10 In.	275.00
6 Wells, Divided, Yellow, Majolica, Gien, c.1940, 9 ½ In.	45.00
6 Wells, Gray, Hall, 10 In.	50.00
6 Wells, Pale Pink, Green, Shell Shape, Haviland, c.1890, 8 ¾ In., 10 Piece	472.00
6 Wells, Shell Shape, Starfish Center, Fouillen, Quimper, c.1925, 9 In.	68.00
6 Wells, Shells, Flowers, Marked, George Jones, 10 In.	275.00
6 Wells, Shells, Gilt, White Ground, Meissen, 9 In.	150.00
6 Wells, White, Gold Trim, Charles Ahrenfeldt, c.1910, 8 In.	78.00

PADEN CITY GLASS MANUFACTURING COMPANY was established in 1916 at Paden City, West Virginia. The company made over twenty different colors of glass. The firm closed in 1951. Paden City Pottery may be listed in Dinnerware.

Ardith, Tray, Center Handle, Yellow, Square, 9 In.	39.00
Cavendish, Cup, Clear	15.00
Chevalier, Goblet, Water, Clear, 5 ⅞ In.	18.00
Crow's Foot, Cup, Footed, Ruby	13.00
Crow's Foot, Plate, Dinner, Amber, 9 In.	13.00
Crow's Foot, Sugar & Creamer, Ruby, 1920s	26.00
Cupid, Bowl, Green, Oval, Scalloped Edge, Footed, 1930s, 8 ½ In.	250.00
Cupid, Bowl, Paneled, Cheriglo, Pink, 10 x 3 In.	169.00
Cupid, Compote, Copen Blue, Flared, 5 ¼ In.	90.00
Eden Rose, Vase, Top Hat Shape, 5 x 3 In.	95.00
Emerald Glo, Condiment Jar, Lid, Emerald Green, 3 ½ In.	16.00
Estelle, Compote, Clear, 6 ⅝ In.	26.00
Figurine, Goose, Clear, 5 ¼ In.	70.00
Figurine, Pelican, Clear, 10 In.	500.00
Figurine, Pouter Pigeon, Clear, 5 ⅝ In.	115.00
Gazebo, Creamer, Clear, 3 ⅜ In.	30.00
Gothic Garden, Compote, Yellow, 6 In.	48.00
Gothic Garden, Plate, Square, Yellow, 8 ½ In.	20.00
Gothic Garden, Sugar, Yellow, 3 In.	25.00
Heather & Primrose, Creamer, Footed, 3 ¼ In.	16.00
Heather & Primrose, Relish, 3 Sections, 10 In.	16.00

Owens, Vase, Flower, Leaves, Brown Ground, Standard Glaze, Impressed, c.1910, 8 In.
$60.00

DuMouchelles Art Gallery

Owens, Vase, Henri Deux, Art Nouveau Maiden, Handles, 10 ½ x 9 ½ In.
$813.00

Rago Arts & Auction Center

Owens, Vase, Utopian, Heron, Standing On Leg, Marsh, Lotus, Cattail, Mae Timberlake, Marked, 14 In.
$1,495.00

Humler & Nolan

P

Oyster Plate, 5 Wells, Rutherford B. Hayes, White House, Haviland, Limoges, c.1880, 8 ⅝ In.
$16,800.00

Skinner, Inc.

TIP

Watercolors and sketches should be kept out of sunlight. Hang framed works on a wall that is shaded.

Painting, On Ivory, Portrait, Woman, Frame, c.1835, 5 x 4 In.
$1,560.00

Cowan's Auctions

Pairpoint, Lamp, Bird Of Paradise, Reverse Painted, Metal Base, Dolphins, Signed, 22 x 17 In.
$4,370.00

Cottone Auctions

Largo, Centerpiece, Blue, 12 ¾ In.		32.00
Largo, Compote, Ruby, Ruffled Rim, 4 ½ In.		65.00
Lucy, Bowl, 3-Footed, Ruby, 10 ¾ In.		56.00
Mrs. B, Creamer, Scalloped, Black, 3 In.		20.00
Mrs. B, Sugar, Black, 3 ⅛ In.		20.00
Party Line, Vase, Fan, Footed, Green, 6 ⅞ In.		36.00
Penny, Cup & Saucer, Ruby		9.00
Penny, Plate, Bread & Butter, Ruby		18.00
Penny, Tumbler, Ruby, 9 Oz., 4 In.		12.00
Spring Orchard, Tray, Center Handle, Clear, 11 In.		48.00

PAINTINGS listed in this book are not works by major artists but rather decorative paintings on ivory, board, or glass that would be of interest to the average collector. Watercolors on paper are listed under Picture. To learn the value of an oil painting by a listed artist, you must contact an expert in that area.

Oil On Board, Allegory Of Spring, France, Giltwood & Stencil Frame, c.1915, 5 ½ x 3 ¾ In....		215.00
Oil On Board, Coastal Scene, George Guaniny, France, Frame, c.1950, 13 x 20 In.		305.00
Oil On Board, Florida Landscape, Willie Daniels, c.1970, 36 x 24 In.		764.00
Oil On Board, Flowers, Still Life, Gilt Frame, c.1890, 9 x 11 In.		593.00
Oil On Board, Horse Cart Under Brooklyn Bridge, Frame, c.1925, 12 x 9 ½ In.		531.00
Oil On Board, January, Winter Street Scene, Antonia Pietro Martino, c.1950, 12 x 18 ½ In. ...		2015.00
Oil On Board, Landscape, Fort, Indian Encampment, American School, Frame, 1800s, 7 x 14 In.		2252.00
Oil On Board, Notre Dame, Jean De La Fontinelle, 7 x 10 In.		210.00
Oil On Board, Orleans River Scene, Ethel Baker Mayo, Frame, c.1960, 16 x 20 In.		295.00
Oil On Board, Portrait Of A Young Girl, Frame, c.1855, 24 x 20 In.		660.00
Oil On Board, Presque Isle Sept. 73, Barn, Field, Junius Brutus Stearns, Frame, 1873, 5 ¾ x 8 In.		590.00
Oil On Board, River, Fisherman, Silo, Frame, 9 ½ x 12 In.		82.00
Oil On Board, Stone Mill, Covered Bridge, Winter Landscape, Dolores Hackenberger, 8 x 24 In. ...		325.00
Oil On Board, The Barnyard, Charles Chapman, Frame, 8 x 10 ½ In.		263.00
Oil On Board, Trees, Pond, Frame, Frederick Sturgis Laurence, 15 x 18 In.		823.00
Oil On Canvas, 7 Miles To Chippenham, Horse & Buggy, Sign, c.1820, 13 ½ x 18 In.		770.00
Oil On Canvas, Abstract Lines, Circles, Thomas Bacher, c.1980, 36 x 54 In.		649.00
Oil On Canvas, Alpine Landscape, Lake, 1900s, 18 x 23 In.		165.00
Oil On Canvas, Arab Man, Traditional Clothes, Holding Out Hand, M. Daryer, 18 x 12 In.		403.00
Oil On Canvas, Aurora Reining In The Clouds, Putti, Giltwood Frame, Italy, 1700s, 28 ½ x 38 In.		3444.00
Oil On Canvas, Benedict In A Stall, J. Quinton 1879, 31 x 36 In.		2457.00
Oil On Canvas, Black Woman, Sitting, Hearth, Gilt Gesso Frame, 22 x 27 ½ In.		593.00
Oil On Canvas, Boy Holding Book, Girl Holding Cat, American School, c.1840, 47 x 30 In.		11850.00
Oil On Canvas, Brighton Coach, Landscape, J.W.F., Gold Frame, c.1900, 20 x 32 In.		1701.00
Oil On Canvas, Bring In The Hay Cottage Scene, Arthur Stark, Frame, c.1850, 15 x 21 In.		1154.00
Oil On Canvas, Bustling Paris Street Scene, Frame, France, Jean Salabet, 26 x 36 In.		1888.00
Oil On Canvas, Charlotte Seymour, Lace Headwear, Collar, New England, Frame, c.1825, 27 x 21 In.		9480.00
Oil On Canvas, Chickens, Barn Scene, Jeanne Davies, Frame, c.1970, 24 x 20 In.		3555.00
Oil On Canvas, Cow, Landscape, Frame, c.1845, 11 x 16 ¼ In.		1007.00
Oil On Canvas, Cows, Landscape, Thos. B. Craig, Embossed Gold Frame, 12 x 16 In.		267.00
Oil On Canvas, Dubious Tale, Men Talking, Louis C. Moeller, Frame, 30 x 48 In.		1170.00
Oil On Canvas, Farm, Barn, Draft Horses, Oleg Ulitskiy, c.1975, 28 ½ x 32 ½ In.		489.00
Oil On Canvas, Fisherman Hauling Nets, Julius F.L. Runge, Germany, Frame, c.1915, 20 x 32 In.		472.00
Oil On Canvas, Fox Hunting, 3 Horses & Riders, Red Jackets, Fence, Pal Fried, Hungary, 36 x 24 In.		1845.00
Oil On Canvas, Fruit & Leaves In Basket, Table, C.T. Metcalf, 1800s, 18 x 21 In.		512.00
Oil On Canvas, Gentleman, Oval, Bow Crested & Beaded Frame, c.1790, 11 ½ x 9 ½ In.		533.00
Oil On Canvas, Girl, Blue Dress, Holding Rose, Frame, Clock, c.1820, 35 ½ x 28 In.		5214.00
Oil On Canvas, Girl, White Dress, Holding Rose, On Shore, Ships, 46 x 36 In.		1534.00
Oil On Canvas, Giza Plateau, Franz Theodor Aerni, c.1900, 17 x 37 In.		9200.00
Oil On Canvas, Horse, Jockey, Cloudy Landscape, Frame, c.1850, 16 x 22 In.		415.00
Oil On Canvas, Hounds On The Scent, George Frederic Rotig, 1903, 42 x 52 In.		3042.00
Oil On Canvas, Kittens At Play, Straw, Plaster Molded Wood Frame, c.1900, 8 x 15 In.		71.00
Oil On Canvas, Landscape, Town Scene, G. Martino, c.1950, 20 x 30 In.		533.00
Oil On Canvas, Lion, S. West, Frame, 1908, 30 x 50 In.		415.00
Oil On Canvas, Madonna, Mexico, 1938, 16 ¾ x 12 ½ In.		708.00
Oil On Canvas, Man-Of-War Signallino, Ships, Sea, c.1850, 12 x 18 ½ In.		474.00
Oil On Canvas, Moon Glow, Alexander Reich-Staffelstein, 26 x 33 In.		936.00
Oil On Canvas, Nautical Scene, B. Voight, Frame, 21 x 18 In.		270.00
Oil On Canvas, Parisian Street Scene, Emilio Carranza, 18 x 23 In.		1140.00
Oil On Canvas, Pier Houses, Sidney Marsh Chase, Frame, c.1945, 20 x 24 In.		384.00

P

Oil On Canvas, Portrait Of A Gentleman, Black Coat, White Shirt, E.E. Finch, 24 x 20 In.	826.00
Oil On Canvas, Portrait Of An Artist, Bernhard Gutmann, c.1910, 42 x 47 In.	936.00
Oil On Canvas, Portrait Of Court Officer, French School, Frame, 66 x 51 In.	2691.00
Oil On Canvas, Portrait Of Girl, Wearing Hat, Burr H. Nicholls, Frame, c.1900, 24 x 19 In.	472.00
Oil On Canvas, Portrait, Lucy Bently Wheeler, Arched Molded Frame, c.1815, 54 x 28 In........	22515.00
Oil On Canvas, Portrait, Woman In White, Holding Music Sheet, Frame, c.1815, 30 x 25 In. .	1968.00
Oil On Canvas, Rural Landscape, Alfred Steinacker, Frame, c.1900, 12 x 24 In......................	531.00
Oil On Canvas, Sailboats, Sea, Clouds, Hank Dekker, 14 ½ x 12 ½ In.	499.00
Oil On Canvas, Seated Child With Dog, Red Dress, Tree, Thomas Gregg, Frame, 1800s, 30 x 25 In.	646.00
Oil On Canvas, Shorebirds In The Rushes, M. Olivier, 1905, 30 x 22 In.	351.00
Oil On Canvas, Spinners, Edward Frere '63, Frame, 20 x 26 In..	819.00
Oil On Canvas, Still Life, Fruit, J, Fairbank, Frame, c.1900, 24 x 36 In................................	881.00
Oil On Canvas, Still Life, Wicker Basket, Cherries, Strawberries, Other Fruit, Frame, 17 x 23 In...	207.00
Oil On Canvas, The Flower Seller, Frame, Arthur Drummond, 1889, 27 ½ x 22 In.	4428.00
Oil On Canvas, The Spinner, Women At Spinning Wheel, John W. Dunsmore, Frame, 34 x 24 In.	118.00
Oil On Canvas, Union Drummer Boy, Winter Campaign, Greatcoat, Tent, 30 x 24 In.............	325.00
Oil On Canvas, Woman, Wearing Kimono, Holding Fan, Frame, G. Campi, Italy, c.1900, 39 x 29 In.	1722.00
Oil On Canvas, Woodland Scene, John Semon, Gilt Frame, c.1890, 15 ½ x 18 ⅜ In...............	518.00
Oil On Glass, Portrait, Betty, Woman, Yellow Dress, Blue Scarf, Pine Frame, c.1860, 11 x 8 In. .	316.00
Oil On Masonite, Landscape, Tree Lined Stream, Woods, House, J. Muth, Frame, 26 x 38 In. .	94.00
Oil On Masonite, Man, Hunting Attire, Val D'Ognes, Frame, 1931, 46 x 26 In......................	2875.00
Oil On Masonite, Rainbow Fleet, Multicolor Sails, Jerome Howes, Frame, c.1970, 9 x 36 In...	1888.00
Oil On Panel, Backyard Trellis, Robert William Vonnoh, Frame, 1890, 10 ½ x 13 ¼ In...........	2875.00
Oil On Panel, Grande Dame, Dog's Head, Woman's Body, Thierry Poncelet, 16 x 12 In..........	518.00
Oil On Panel, Landscape, Waterfall, c.1880, 35 x 15 ¼ In..	89.00
Oil On Panel, Yacht Racing, Fred Daniels, Giltwood Frame, c.1925, 10 x 8 In......................	1416.00
Oil On Paper, Peasants Working In Fields, c.1955, 9 x 12 ½ In..	212.00
Oil On Velvet, Flower Compote Theorem, David Ellinger, Frame, c.1980, 14 x 14 In................	790.00
On Ivory, Portrait, Woman, Frame, c.1835, 5 x 4 In. ....*Illus*	1560.00

PAIRPOINT Manufacturing Company started in 1880 in New Bedford, Massachusetts. It soon joined with the glassworks nearby and made glass, silver-plated pieces, and lamps. Reverse-painted glass shades and molded shades known as "puffies" were part of the production until the 1930s. The company reorganized and changed its name several times but is still working today. Items listed here are glass or glass and metal. Silver-plated pieces are listed under Silver Plate.

Basket, Water Lily, Natural Shape, Twisted Vine Handle, Moriage Blossoms, Green, Gilt, 7 x 10 In.	414.00
Biscuit Jar, Cream Ground, Red Flowers, Metal Lid, Circle Finial, Bail Handle, 9 In................	115.00
Bride's Basket, Pale Pink, Deep Rose Ruffled Bowl, Acorn & Oak Silver Handle, 12 ¼ x 10 In..	207.00
Bride's Bowl, Etched Cranberry Rim, Figural & Deer Stand, Signed, 6 ½ x 8 ¾ In.................	403.00
Candleholder, Coleus, Amber, 15 ¾ In..	375.00
Candleholder, Savoy, 6 In.	300.00
Candlestick, Tapered, Curved Tendrils, Reticulated Base, c.1890, 8 ¼ In.	245.00
Compote, Cobalt Blue & Clear Swirl, Wave Rim, Clear Stem & Foot, 5 x 8 In.	585.00
Compote, Etched Floral Swags, Bulbous Foot, Controlled Bubble, 5 ½ In............................	86.00
Compote, Flambeau, Cherry, Silver Overlay, Clear Bubble Knop, Black Foot, 5 x 8 In.............	761.00
Compote, Rosaria, Diamond Quilted, Clear Bubble Ball, Wafer Foot, 7 x 8 In........................	644.00
Compote, Veneti, Clear, Red & White Twisted Stem, Wafer Base, 6 ½ x 7 In..........................	644.00
Jug, Yellow, Peach, Cylindrical, Shouldered, Narrow Neck, Loop Handle, 5 ½ In.	132.00
Lamp, Bird Of Paradise, Reverse Painted, Metal Base, Dolphins, Signed, 22 x 17 In.........*Illus*	4370.00
Lamp, Chipped Ice Shade, Domed, Reverse Painted Trees, Mahogany Base, 15 In.	633.00
Lamp, Puffy, Butterflies, Blue Flowers, Rounded Corners, Metal, c.1920, 14 x 23 In.	2750.00
Lamp, Puffy, Papillon, Butterfly, Mottled, Green, White, Open Top, Bronze, 14 In. ....*Illus*	2760.00
Lamp, Puffy, Rose Bouquet, Reverse Painted, Brass Base, With Applied Feet, 21 ¼ In.......*Illus*	8625.00
Lamp, Puffy, Rose, Pink Bouquet, Bronze Web Base, 13 x 22 In..	11300.00
Lamp, Puffy, Roses, Frosted Scalloped Shade, 13 x 20 In...	1925.00
Lamp, Puffy, Roses, Lattice, 13 x 20 In..	1925.00
Lamp, Red, Yellow Flowers, Blue, Green Frosted Ground, Candle, 8 In................................	460.00
Lamp, Reverse Painted Floral Shade, Bronze, Marble Base, 1900s, 22 ½ In..........................	1422.00
Lamp, Reverse Painted Shade, Bird Of Paradise, 3-Part Base, 22 x 17 ½ In..........................	2500.00
Lamp, Reverse Painted Shade, Domed, Green Lappets, Pheasant, Flower Border, c.1925, 8 x 20 In.	594.00
Lamp, Reverse Painted Shade, Flowers, Bronze 2 Handle Base, Signed, 21 x 25 In.	1159.00
Lamp, Reverse Painted Shade, Flowers, Pink, Blue, Green, Iron Base, 16 x 22 In......................	1760.00
Lamp, Reverse Painted Shade, Flowers, Signed, 23 x 14 In.............................*Illus*	2300.00
Lamp, Reverse Painted Shade, Parrots, Jungle Plants, Frosted, Brass Base, Signed, 22 In.....*Illus*	2875.00
Lamp, Reverse Painted Shade, Sailboats, Brass Tapered Stem, Openwork Base, 19 In.	5523.00

Pairpoint, Lamp, Puffy, Papillon, Butterfly, Mottled, Green, White, Open Top, Bronze, 14 In.
$2,760.00

Early Auction Co.

Pairpoint, Lamp, Puffy, Rose Bouquet, Reverse Painted, Brass Base, With Applied Feet, 21 ¼ In.
$8,625.00

James D. Julia Auctioneers

Pairpoint, Lamp, Reverse Painted Shade, Flowers, Signed, 23 x 14 In.
$2,300.00

Cottone Auctions

P

Pairpoint, Lamp, Reverse Painted
Shade, Parrots, Jungle Plants, Frosted,
Brass Base, Signed, 22 In.
$2,875.00

Early Auction Co.

Pairpoint, Pickle Castor, Opalware,
Mums, White, Ruby Red, Ribbed Lid,
10 ½ In.
$138.00

Humler & Nolan

Paper, Book, John Audubon, Birds Of
America, 1st Edition, 7 Octavo Volumes,
1840
$33,600.00

Skinner, Inc.

Lamp, Reverse Painted Shade, Scenic Landscape, Bronze Vase Shape Base, 3-Light, 23 x 17 In.	863.00
Lamp, Reverse Painted Shade, Trees, Mountains, 4-Branch Stem, Marble Base	1265.00
Lamp, Reverse Painted Shade, Winter Scene, Copper Paneled Stem, Scalloped Foot, 23 In.	3760.00
Paperweight, Bubbled, Green & White Swirling Strands, Etched Grapevine, Stand, 4 In.	115.00
Pickle Castor, Opalware, Mums, White, Ruby Red, Ribbed Lid, 10 ½ In. ....*Illus*	138.00
Shaker, Pink, Stemmed Flowers, Leaves, Globe Shape, 2 In.	35.00
Sugar & Creamer, White, Flower Enamel, Pink Interior, Opalescent Handles, Stippled Rim, 3 ¼ In..	144.00
Tray, Oval, Silver Leaf Pattern, Cut Glass, 13 x 10 In.	700.00
Vase, Amethyst, Cut Lattice Pattern, Flared, Clear Bubble Ball, Footed, 9 ¼ In.	187.00
Vase, Chipped Ice Finish, Blossoming Flowers, Shouldered, Rolled Rim, Signed, 12 In.	230.00
Vase, Chipped Ice Finish, Grape Clusters, Leaves, Elongated Oval, Pedestal Foot, Flared Lip, 6 In..	374.00
Vase, Cranberry Cut To Clear, Darlington Engraving, Clear Ball, Flared Rim, 11 In.	351.00
Vase, Pink Flowers, Blue & Green Branches, Bulbous, Stick, Opal Glass, 18 In., Pair	604.00

PALMER COX, *Brownies, see Brownies category.*

PAPER collectibles, including almanacs, catalogs, children's books, some greeting cards, stock certificates, and other paper ephemera, are listed here. Paper calendars are listed separately in the Calendar category. Paper items may be found in many other sections, such as Christmas and Movie.

Award Of Merit, Watercolor, Ink, Bird, Flower Tree, Red, Green, Pa., 4 x 3 ¼ In.	356.00
Birth Record, Heart, Script, Green, Black Leaves, Flower, Watercolor, Ink, Pa., 1749, 6 x 7 ½ In.	851.00
Birth Record, Shoennaur Family, Printed, Block Colored, Wood Frame, 14 x 10 ½ In.	35.00
Birth & Baptism, Angels, Birds, Daniel Rauenzahn, Allentown, Pa., 1866, 17 x 12 In.	118.00
Book, Big Little, Dick Tracy Detective, Whitman, No. W-707, c.1933, 4 x 4 ⅜ In., 318 Pages	370.00
Book, Big Little, Little Orphan Annie, Whitman, No. 708, c.1933, 4 x 4 ⅜ In., 318 Pages	115.00
Book, John Audubon, Birds Of America, 1st Edition, 7 Octavo Volumes, 1840..........*Illus*	33600.00
Book, Little Nemo In Slumber-Land, Platinum Age, Buffield & Co., c.1906, 11 x 16 ½ In., 64 Pages	886.00
Book, Pat The Bunny, First Edition, Dorothy Kunhardt, Simon & Schuster, 1940, 4 ⅛ x 5 ⅜ In.. *Illus*	5000.00
Book, Pop-Up, Little Orphan Annie, Circus, Pleasure Books Inc., 1935, 8 x 9 In., 16 Pages	190.00
Book, Pop-Up, Terry & The Pirates, Blue Ribbon Press, Pleasure Books Inc., 1935, 8 x 9 In., 10 Pages	438.00
Book, Pop-Up, Tim Tyler In The Jungle, Pleasure Books Inc., 1935, 8 x 9 In., 16 Pages	247.00
Bookplate, Flower Branch, Watercolor, Ink, In Bible, Elisabetha Funcfin, 1794, 6 ½ x 3 ½ In..	1541.00
Bookplate, Paul Revere, Chippendale, Armorial, Engraved, Gardiner Chandler, 3 ¼ x 2 ¾ In..	1180.00
Broadside, Bounty, Recruiting, $75.00, 9 Months Service, Plattsburgh, N.Y., Nov. 1862, 13 x 9 In.	499.00
Broadside, Carversville & Doylestown Stage Line, Schedule, J. Eisentrager, 1881, 20 x 13 In..	325.00
Broadside, Grand Entertainment At A.O.H. Hall, Social Dance, Gilbertville, Ma., 1897, 25 x 18 In.	83.00
Broadside, Household Goods Sale, Lincoln University, Andrew Ortlip, Frame, 1906, 33 x 25 In..	59.00
Broadside, John Wilkes Booth, Boston Performance, Macbeth, October 7, 1863, 6 x 18 In.	2760.00
Broadside, Map, Moscow, 100 Anniversary War Of 1812 Victory, Frame, c.1913, 27 x 21 In.	2400.00
Broadside, New Line Of Stages, Providence, R.I., To Worcester, Mass., Frame, c.1821, 23 x 17 In..	106.00
Broadside, Ogdensburg, N.Y. Fourth Of July, 1888, Black & White, Frame, 28 ½ x 43 ½ In.	484.00
Broadside, Ship, Albion & Sailor Boy, c.1825, 11 ¼ x 8 ¾ In.	207.00
Broadside, Stereopticon Entertainment, Dec. 29, 1898, Chas. W. Eddy, Ma., 20 x 19 In.	649.00
Broadside, Vrasserie Schneider, Color Lithograph, Ship's Deck, People Drinking, Frame, 23 x 32 In.	115.00
Calligraphy, Doves, Nest, Pen, Ink, Scroll Paper, From Abner Miller Teacher, Frame, c.1902, 6 x 8 In.	86.00
Calligraphy, Plaque, Demilune Ends, Putti, Elianor Wilson, Script Writing, c.1752, 9 x 14 In.	144.00
Certificate, East, West Nottingham Temperance Society Membership, Vignettes, c.1898, 13 x 15 In.	12.00
Coloring Book, Planet Of The Apes, Artcraft, 1974, Uncut	22.00
Contract, Rider, Tom Cruise, Signed, 1987, 8 ½ x 11 In.	115.00
Contract, Rita Hayworth, MCA Artists Ltd., Signed, 1959, 8 ½ x 13 In.	196.00
Cutwork, Scherenschnitte, Hearts, Shields, Flower, Names, Color, Frame, c.1890, 15 x 18 In.....*Illus*	151.00
Deck Plan, Titanic, 1st Class, Dated January 6, 1912, 29 ½ x 40 In.	4294.00
Family Record, Watercolor, Ink, Benjamin & Elisabeth Berge, In Martin Luther Bible, 5 x 4 In. ..	711.00
Fraktur, Award Of Merit, Watercolor, Flowering Tree, Red, Yellow, Pa., 1800s, 3 ⅝ x 2 ½ In..	356.00
Fraktur, Birth & Baptism, Flowers, German Script, Joseph Mac-Wollin, Lancaster County, 1808...	177.00
Fraktur, Birth Certificate, Ink, Watercolor, Flowers, Angels, Joseph Lochbaum, c.1800, 13 x 14 ¾ In.	711.00
Fraktur, Birth Certificate, Watercolor, Hearts, Parrots, Engraved, Lancaster County, 1786, 12 x 15 In.	354.00
Fraktur, Birth Record, Birds, Flower Vines, Anna Maria Dieffendorfer, Frame, 1815, 12 ½ x 16 In.	1094.00
Fraktur, Birth Record, Cutout Arches, Swags, Leaves, Catherine Reszler, 1833, Pa., 7 ½ x 9 ½ In..	1126.00
Fraktur, Birth Record, Ink, Watercolor, Adam & Eve, Mermaids, Name, c.1776, 12 x 16 In.	652.00
Fraktur, Birth Record, Ink, Watercolor, Catherine Mengin, 1795, 13 x 16 In.	2252.00
Fraktur, Birth Record, Multicolor Parrots, Flowers, Women, Angels, Name, 1782, 13 x 16 In..	1062.00
Fraktur, Birth Record, Multicolor, Flowers, Birds, Maria Magdalena, Berks County, 1792, 8 x 13 In.	5015.00
Fraktur, Birth Record, Watercolor, Ink, Anna Maria Kaufmann, Berks County, Pa., 1782, 8 x 13 In.	1185.00

Fraktur, Birth Record, Watercolor, Ink, Engraved Text, Perry Levan, Black Painted Frame, 11 x 17 In.	826.00
Fraktur, Birth Record, Watercolor, Ink, Red Flowers, Script, Matin Brechall, Frame, 1823, 8 x 12 In. ...	652.00
Fraktur, Birth Record, Watercolor, Pinprick, Anna Oberholtzer, Eagle, Tulip, 1816, 7 x 5 ½ In.........	243.00
Fraktur, Birth, Hand Colored, Birth Scene, Birds, Gazebo, Elizabeth Lorah, Pa., 1820, 16 x 13 In....	115.00
Fraktur, Birth, Watercolor, Ink, Flowers, Text, Johan Odenwalder, New Jersey, 1771, 16 x 12 ¾ In.	173.00
Fraktur, Bookplate, Ink, Watercolor, Squirrel, Figures With Baskets, Johannes Mayer, c.1795, 5 x 3 In...	3081.00
Fraktur, Bookplate, Ink, Watercolor, Tulip Vine, Pa., c.1830, 4 x 3 ¾ In.	652.00
Fraktur, Bookplate, Tulip Tree, Ink, Watercolor, Multicolor, Frame, Pa., 1800s, 4 ½ x 4 In...............	3081.00
Fraktur, Bookplate, Tulips, Red, Blue, Yellow, Name, Watercolor, Ink, Phila., c.1840, 7 x 4 In.	563.00
Fraktur, Bookplate, Watercolor, Angel, Trumpet, Birds, Flowers, Johann F. Eyer, c.1800, 3 ⅞ x 6 ¼ In...	711.00
Fraktur, Bookplate, Watercolor, Bird, On Flower, Vine, Pa., c.1820, 3 ⅜ x 4 ¾ In.	1067.00
Fraktur, Bookplate, Watercolor, Script, Heart, Tulip Vines, Phillip Markel, Frame, Pa., 1790, 4 x 6 In.	504.00
Fraktur, Cherub, Angels, Birds, German Verse, Ludwig Family, Watercolor, 20 x 17 In.	106.00
Fraktur, Eagle, Angels, Tablet, German Verse, Watercolor, Blumer & Busch, 1846, 16 x 14 In...........	118.00
Fraktur, Ink, Paper, Watercolor, Red, Yellow, Bird, Tulip Tree, Heart, Frame, Pa., 1810, 4 x 2 In.	1659.00
Fraktur, Ink, Watercolor, Metamorphosis, Stages To Man, Adam & Eve To Death, c.1800, 4 x 3 In. .	4503.00
Fraktur, Ink, Watercolor, Vorschrift, Signed Johannes Henge, Phila., Frame, 1757, 12 x 15 In.........	296.00
Fraktur, Marriage Certificate, Watercolor, Ink, Flowers, Heart, Birds, Pa., 1829, 8 x 6 ¾ In..............	472.00
Fraktur, Military Record, Eagle, 28-Star Flag, Liberty Union, G.G. Eubank, Kentucky, 26 In.............	411.00
Fraktur, Printed, Hand Colored, Heart Shaped Leaf & Flower Border, Jungmann, 12 x 15 ½ In.......	267.00
Fraktur, Putti, Angels, Birds, German Text, Watercolor, Illuminated, 1862, 16 x 13 In......................	106.00
Fraktur, Reward Of Merit, Ink, Watercolor, Warwick, Head, Flag, Bird, Flowers, Frame, 1830, 4 x 6 In.	652.00
Fraktur, Reward Of Merit, Watercolor, Distelfink, Branch, For Sarah Lerch, Frame, c.1800, 3 x 4 In.	456.00
Fraktur, Reward Of Merit, Watercolor, Ink Flowering Tree, Multicolor, Pa., 1800s, 5 x 3 ¼ In.........	356.00
Fraktur, Schwenkfelder, Watercolor, Plumed Bird, Rose Branch, c.1850, 7 x 5 ¼ In....................	444.00
Fraktur, Songbook, Malle Aldorfer, Watercolor, Ink, Mary Hershey, Pa., Frame, 1800, 6 x 3 ¾ In. ...	1007.00
Fraktur, Valentine, Heart, Flower Vine, Watercolor, Ink, Frame, 1814, 4 x 3 In................................	533.00
Fraktur, Watercolor, Cutwork, Trumpets, Angels, Name, Frame, Pa., 1793, 8 x 13 In................	1541.00
Fraktur, Watercolor, Distelfink, Berries, Flowers, Signed David Y. Ellinger, Frame, c.1960, 8 x 6 In..	770.00
Fraktur, Watercolor, Flowers, Script, Trees, Inscribed Sara Weber, Pa., Durs Rudy, 1806, 6 ¼ x 10 In....	2252.00
Fraktur, Watercolor, German Script, Hearts, Tulips, Deer, Birds, Frame, Ephrata, Pa., 13 x 16 In.	236.00
Fraktur, Watercolor, Girl With Sheep, Pa., c.1840, 5 ¼ x 5 ½ In..	2015.00
Fraktur, Watercolor, Ink, 2-Headed Eagle, Tulips, Francis Weisel, Pa., c.1838, 8 ¾ x 7 In..............	3555.00
Fraktur, Watercolor, Ink, Angels, Flowers, Swans, Painted Frame, New Hope, Pa., c.1791, 13 x 15 In....	472.00
Fraktur, Watercolor, Peacock, Tulips, Signed David Y. Ellinger, Frame, c.1960, 10 ½ x 14 ½ In.	1007.00
Fraktur, Watercolor, Saint, Book, Multicolor Painted Frame, Cutout Heart Crest, Pa., 4 ½ x 3 ½ In.	5925.00
Fraktur, Women, Feeding Birds, Lambs, Initials SU, Frame, Pennsylvania, 1838, 9 ½ x 11 ½ In......	770.00
Handbill, Auction, Orphan's Court Sale Of Real Estate, Bucks Co., Pa., 1894, 23 ½ x 19 ¼ In.	356.00
Illustration, Cover, Harper's Bazaar, Watercolor, Woman, Monkey, Bird, 1922, 19 x 14 In.......	960.00
Land Deed, Ephraim Bullen, Sherborn, Mass., To Abraham Cossens, March 28, 1728, 12 x 15 ½ In..	270.00
Magazine, Pinup, Bettie Page, Premiere Issue, 1963, 8 ⅜ x 11 In.	459.00
Magazine, Playboy, 1st Issue, Full Color, Marilyn Monroe Nude, Seated Marilyn, Waving, 1953	2040.00
Menu, Southern Hotel, Bird Cover, Summer Tanger, Audubon, Baltimore 1949, 2 Pages	23.00
Music, Page, Antiphonal Leaf, Illuminated, Vellum, 27 x 19 In.	45.00
Newspaper Page, Lincoln Assassination, New York Herald, April 15, 1865	94.00
Poster, Conservation, Over Fishing, Boy, Man, Maine Dept. Of Inland Fisheries, 1940s, 28 x 22 In.	550.00
Stock Certificate, American Utilities & General Corp., 30 Shares, Class B, 1931, 8 x 11 ¾ In.	10.00
Theorem, Watercolor, Cornucopia Filled With Flowers, Gilt Molded Frame, 17 x 14 ½ In........	325.00
TV Guide, TV Space Men On Cover, Vol. 5, No. 8, NYC, Pre-National, 1952, 5 ¼ x 8 ¼, 40 Pages	86.00
Wallpaper, Gouache & Graphite, Art Deco, Birds, Flowers, Leaves, Frame, 19 x 13 ¼ In...*Illus*	123.00
Wallpaper, Panel, Terpsichore & Euterpe, Frame, Continental, c.1900, 44 x 22 ½ In., Pair... *Illus*	4481.00
Wallpaper, Panel, Garden Of Beaujon, Windmill, Village, Paulot Et Carre, c.1820, 64 x 66 In.	2990.00

PAPER DOLLS were probably inspired by the pantins, or jumping jacks, made in eighteenth-century Europe. By the 1880s, sheets of printed paper dolls and clothes were being made. The first paper doll books were made in the 1920s. Collectors prefer uncut sheets or books or boxed sets of paper dolls. Prices are about half as much if the pages have been cut.

American Soldier, American Doughboy Profile, Outfits, Military Equipment, Saalfield, 1937, 10 In.	100.00
Baby Sparkle Plenty, 2 Dolls, 6 Pages Of Outfits, Accessories & Toys, Saalfield, 1948, 10 In.	50.00
Blondie, Dagwood, Baby Dumpling & Dogs, Whitman, 1941...	250.00
Boots & Her Buddies, Boots & Rod Ruggles, Saalfield, 1943, 10 ½ In.	125.00
Carnation Ice Cream, Betty, 3 Outfits, 9 x 11 ½ In., Uncut...	7.00
Fantasy Dolls, Bride, Bridesmaid, Dixie, Debutante, Box, M. Vestal, c.1948, 20 x 12 In., 4 Piece	47.00
Let's Play With The Baby, Girl, Boy, 2 Babies, 8 Pages Of Outfits, Merrill, 1948	50.00
Life-Size, Rosy Cheeks, Curly Blond Hair, Blue Eyes, Blue Romper, Whitman, 1959, 34 In.......	95.00

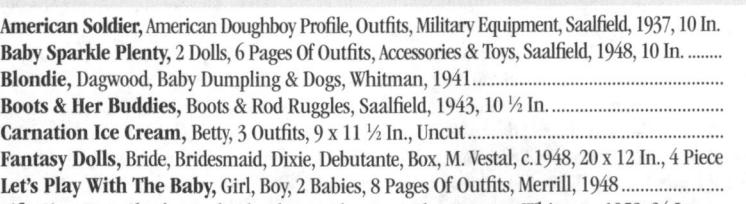

Paper, Book, Pat The Bunny, First Edition, Dorothy Kunhardt, Simon & Schuster, 1940, 4 ⅛ x 5 ⅜ In.
$5,000.00

Aleph-Bet Books

Paper, Cutwork, Scherenschnitte, Hearts, Shields, Flower, Names, Color, Frame, c.1890, 15 x 18 In.
$151.00

Garth's Auctioneers & Appraisers

Paper, Wallpaper, Gouache & Graphite, Art Deco, Birds, Flowers, Leaves, Frame, 19 x 13 ¼ In.
$123.00

Skinner, Inc.

Postal Codes

Zip codes were in use by 1963. Postal zones, one- or two-digit numbers, were used from 1943 to 1963. The nine-digit zip started in 1980.

P

Paper, Wallpaper, Panel, Terpsichore & Euterpe, Frame, Continental, c.1900, 44 x 22 ½ In., Pair
$4,481.00

Neal Auction Co.

Paperweight, Ayotte, Bird, Red Tanager, Branch, Mistletoe Berries, Leaves, Signed, 3 ¼ x 2 In.
$748.00

James D. Julia Auctioneers

Papier-Mache, Clown Head, Painted Face, Red Ball Nose, Hudson's Parade, Detroit, c.1940, 66 x 39 In.
$300.00

DuMouchelles Art Gallery

Little Alice Busy Bee, Doll, Outfits, School Books, 1900s	65.00
Little Bo Peep, Staff, 5 In.	5.00
Margaret O'Brien, Fun On The Farm, 2 Dolls, Cloth By Hedwig Jo Meinner, 5 Pages	175.00
Nancy & Sluggo, Book, Whitman, 1974, Uncut	22.00
Pat Boone, 2 Dolls, Tennis Outfits & Dress Outfits, Copyright Pat Boone, 1959	69.00
Sonja Henie, Queen Of The Ice, 3 Dolls, 27 Outfits, Merrill Publishing Co., 1940, 13 x 11 In., Uncut	195.00
Tillie The Toiler, 2 Dolls, 8 Pages, Whitman Publishing, Copyright 1921, 13 x 10 ½ In.	125.00
Tiny Tots, Bill & Betty, Cardboard, Whitman, 1940s	30.00
Wedding Of The Paper Dolls, Bride, Groom, Maid Of Honor, Bridesmaid, Merrill, 1935, 10 In.	150.00

PAPERWEIGHTS must have first appeared along with paper in ancient Egypt. Today's collectors search for every type, from the very expensive French weights of the nineteenth century to the modern artist weights or advertising pieces. The glass tops of the paperweights sometimes have been nicked or scratched, and this type of damage can be removed by polishing. Some serious collectors think this type of repair is an alteration and will not buy a repolished weight; others think it is an acceptable technique of restoration that does not change the value. Baccarat paperweights are listed separately under Baccarat.

Advertising, Boyertown Casket, Figural, Painted, Cast Metal, c.1930, 1 ¾ x 2 ¼ x 5 In.	138.00
Advertising, Lion Oil Co., Lion, Metal, Bronze Finish, 2 x 3 x 1 In.	99.00
Advertising, Monarch Fire Insurance Co., Lion, Metal, c.1910, 5 x 3 ⅝ In.	115.00
Advertising, Osborne & Co., Harvesting Machinery, Plow, Glass, 2 ½ x 4 In.	154.00
Advertising, Outcault, Yellow Kid, Say Ain't I A Heavy Weight, Figural, Metal, 7 x 3 In.	132.00
Advertising, Railroad Coal Car, Central Coal Mining Co., Copper Plated Metal, c.1920s, 3 x 6 In.	185.00
Advertising, Reda Trailer Service, Tractor Trailer, Glitter, Glove, Plaster Base, 1950s, 2 ¾ x 2 ¾ In.	158.00
Advertising, Sheffield Milk, Dairy Cows, Trees, Glass, Round, 1 ⅜ x 3 In.	143.00
Advertising, Turtle, Bernstein's Fish Grotto, Iron, Celluloid Hinged Lid, Paint, Green, 2 ⅜ In.	95.00
Advertising, Voss Brothers, Ocean Wave Washing Machines, Glass, 2 ⅝ x 4 ⅛ In.	99.00
Advertising, Wistar's Balsam Of Wild Cherry, Cures Coughs, Influenza, Clock, 3 In.	211.00
Ayotte, Bird, Red Tanager, Branch, Mistletoe Berries, Leaves, Signed, 3 ¼ x 2 In. ....*Illus*	748.00
Ayotte, Bluebird, Blossoms, Leafy Branch, Round, Clear Ground, 3 ⅝ In. Diam.	978.00
Ayotte, Round, 2 Finches, Yellow, Green, Branches, Purple Berries, Nest, Eggs, Signed, 3 ¾ x 2 ⅛ In.	978.00
Bronze, Gilt, Napoleon, Cresting Seas Base, Rococo Brass Handle, c.1885, 3 ¾ x 8 In.	1168.00
Bronze, Snail, Silver Finish, Polished Turbo Shell, WMF, c.1915, 1 ½ x 4 ½ In.	922.00
Bust, Sulphide, Charles A. Lindbergh, Crystal, Blue Overlay, Snowflake Base, France, 3 x 1 In.	400.00
Bust, Sulphide, Queen Elizabeth II, Millefiori, Teal Ground, 1953, 3 x 1 ¾ In.	600.00
Caithness, Green, Orange Lines, Cobalt Blue Ground, Bubble, Egg Shape, Scotland, 4 In.	28.00
Ceska, Glass, Aerial, Facet Cut, Polished, 4 ½ In.	115.00
Clichy, Center Rose Cane, Red, Blue, Green, White Cane Circlets, Clear Ground, 1800s, 1 ¼ x 2 In.	502.00
Clichy, Central Green, White Flower, Looped Cane Strands, Turquoise Ground, 1800s, 2 x 3 In.	885.00
Clichy, Morning Glory, Yellow, Pink Blossom, Green Leaves, 2 x 2 ½ In.	5015.00
Clichy, Pansy, Multifaceted, 2 ¼ In.	550.00
Donofrio, Green Frog, Lily Pads, Purple Lily, Signed, 3 ¼ In. Diam.	546.00
Flower Bouquet, Primrose, Blossoms, Leaves, Opaque Black Ground, 6 Faceted Sides, 1980, 2 ¾ In.	144.00
Glass, Crown, White, Blue, Green Twisted Canes, Flowing, 2 ⅝ In.	224.00
Glass, Moving Turtle, Scalloped Border, Reeded, Brown, Tan, 3 In. Diam.	115.00
Glass, Round, Dark Planet, Swirling Patterns, Land, Sea, Heaven, Signed, 1977, 2 ½ In.	92.00
Glass, Scramble, Multicolor, c.1860, 2 ¾ In.	130.00
Hippocampus, Green Crystalline Glaze, Reclining Creature, Rectangular Base, c.1924, 2 ¾ x 4 In.	690.00
Jade, Tortoiseshell Shape, Chocolate Color, 3 ½ In.	239.00
Kaziun, Pink Rope Rose, Green Leaves, Twist Torsade Border, Dark Amethyst Ground, 2 In.	259.00
Kaziun, Rabbit, Cane Clusters, Twist Torsade, Aventurine Blue Ground, Pedestal Foot, 2 ¾ In.	403.00
Manson, 3 Butterflies, Pink & White Flowers, Millefiori Canes, c.1981, 2 ⅞ In. Diam.	230.00
Manson, Underwater, Iridescent Blue Stingray, Green Fish, Sand Ground, c.1980, 2 ¾ In. Diam.	288.00
Millefiori, Butterfly, Concentric Rings, 5 Side Facets, Signed, 1975, 3 In. Diam.	403.00
Millefiori, Concentric Canes, Multicolor, Cobalt Blue Overlay, Faceted, 1975, 3 ⅜ In. Diam.	575.00
Millefiori, Mushroom Center, Double Overlay, Opaque Green To White, 3 In.	472.00
New England Glass Co., 5 Scattered Horses, Eagle Canes, 1800s, 1 ½ x 2 ¼ In.	354.00
New England Glass Co., Apple, Red, Yellow, Round Base, 1800s, 2 ½ x 3 In.	1062.00
New England Glass Co., Blue Flower, Red, Blue, White Cane Circles, 1800s, 2 x 2 ½ In.	885.00
New England Glass Co., Fruit, White Latticinio Ground, c.1860, 2 x 2 ½ In.	288.00
New England Glass Co., Millefiori, 3 Green Leaves, Nosegay, White Latticinio, c.1860, 1 ¾ x 2 ½ In.	403.00
New England Glass Co., Multicolor Dahlia, White Latticinio Ground, 1800s, 2 x 2 ½ In.	3776.00
New England Glass Co., Peach, Yellow Pears, Leaves, Threaded Pink Sides, 1800s, 2 x 3 In.	4425.00
New England Glass Co., Pink Poinsettia, Millefiori Cane Circle, Frosted Ground, 2 x 3 In.	649.00
New England Glass Co., Poinsettia, Controlled Bubbles, White Latticinio, c.1880, 2 x 3 In.	196.00
New England Glass Co., Red, White Cane Garlands, 4 Flower Center., White Latticinio, 2 ⅕ x 3 In.	1003.00
New England, Apple Shape, Crimson, Yellow, Clear Disc Foot, 2 ½ In.	288.00

P

Purple, Yellow Pansy, Green Leaves, French Faceted, Clear Ground, c.1860, 2 ¾ In. 354.00
Richard Olmas, Clematis, Red, Yellow Stamen, 1988, 2 ½ x 3 In. 115.00
Rosenfeld, Blue Central Flower, Pink & Yellow Flowers, Clear Ground, 2 ⅝ In. Diam. 201.00
Salazar, 3 Blue Flower Blossoms, 2 Butterflies, Leaves, Clear Ground, 1986, 3 In. Diam. 144.00
Sandwich Glass, Scramble, Broken Cane, Multicolor, c.1890, 2 ⅝ In. 295.00
St. Louis, Bouquet, Blue Blossom, Red, White Clematis, Side Printies, 1800s, 2 x 3 In. 560.00
St. Louis, Bouquet, Side & Top Facets, Red, White, Signed, 1970, 2 ⅞ In. Diam. 575.00
St. Louis, Flower Bouquet, Heart Shape Millefiori, Amethyst Ground, Round, 1983, 3 In. Diam. .. 259.00
St. Louis, Honeycomb Pattern, Yellow Rose, Red & White, Crystal Pedestal Foot, c.1977, 4 x 5 In. 748.00
St. Louis, Millefiori Rings, Latticinio Basket Foot, Multicolor, Signed, 1972, 3 x 3 In. 978.00
St. Louis, Pink Dahlia, Overlapping Panels, Star Cut Base, 1800s, 2 ¼ x 3 In. 1003.00
St. Louis, Sulphide, Cupid, Amour, Flower Border, Pink, Faceted Sides & Top, 3 x 1 ¾ In. 325.00
St. Louis, White Center Flower, White & Pink Latticinio Tiers, 1 ½ x 3 In. 1062.00
Stankard, Lady Slipper Blossoms, Leaves, Roots, Tapered Rectangle, Black, Pink, 1988, 6 x 3 In.. 6900.00
Stankard, Morning Glory, Leaves, Stems, Clear Ground, Signed, 3 In. Diam. 1035.00
Tarsitano, Blossoms, Leaves, Round, Pulled Out Water Splashes Shape, Clear Ground, 1994, 5 In. 661.00
Tarsitano, Fruit & Flower, Blue Flowers, Yellow Stamen, Berries, Clear Ground, 6-Sided, 3 ⅜ In.. 805.00
Tarsitano, Holly Berries, Green Leaves, White Blossoms, 6-Sided, Faceted, Star Cut Base, 3 ¼ In.. 805.00
Tarsitano, Snake, Brown, Slithering, Muslin Ground, Round, 1994, 3 ½ In. Diam. 345.00
Trabucco, Flower Bouquet, Round, Pink, Blue Blossoms, Blue Ground, Signed, 1987, 3 ¾ In. 863.00
Trabucco, Pink Rose, Buds, Green Leaves, 1985, 3 ¼ In. 236.00
Trabucco, Purple Rose, Buds, Leaves, Clear Ground, Faceted, Signed, 1986, 3 ¼ In. Diam. 345.00
Trabucco, Striped Salamander, Spattered Green, Round, Signed, 3 x 3 In. 690.00

PAPIER-MACHE is made from paper mixed with glue, chalk, and other ingredients, then molded and baked. It becomes very hard and can be painted. Boxes, trays, and furniture were made of papier-mache. Some of the nineteenth-century pieces were decorated with mother-of-pearl. Papier-mache is still being used to make small toys, figures, candy containers, boxes, and other giftwares. Furniture made of papier-mache is listed in the Furniture category.

Bowl, Chinoiserie Asian Figures, Scalloped Rim, Round Bell Foot, c.1860, 13 ¾ In. 240.00
Cigar Case, View Of Baltimore, c.1850, 2 ¾ x 5 ½ In. 2673.00
Cigar Case, View Of The Capitol In Washington, Oval, c.1850, 3 x 5 ¾ In. 3159.00
Clown Head, Painted Face, Red Ball Nose, Hudson's Parade, Detroit, c.1940, 66 x 39 In. ..*Illus* 300.00
Figure, Pig, Painted Hold, Silver Glitter, Pink Ruffled Collar, 40 x 17 In. 201.00
Figure, Woman, Articulated Continental, 28 In. 649.00
Figure, Woman, Tattoo Artist Sample, Inscribed Heart, England, 35 In. 4130.00
Hat Stand, Woman's Head, Flower Top, Gemma Taccogna, Mexico, 10 In. 36.00
Ice Cream Cone, Eat It All, Yellow, White Paint, 20 In. 682.00
Lap Desk, Mother-Of-Pearl Inlay, Lacquer, Gilt, 2 Brass-Mounted Inkwells, 1800s, 18 ½ x 12 In.. *Illus* 354.00
Mask, Parade, Yellow Kid, Large Ears, c.1920, 20 In. 330.00
Milliner's Head, Painted Features, Walnut Stand, c.1840, 36 ¾ In. 1541.00
Milliner's Head, Painted, France, 14 ½ In. 443.00
Parade Head, W.C. Fields, Mardi Gras, 1960s, 48 In. ....*Illus* 504.00
Sculpture, Standing Woman, Seminude, Carved Wood Base, c.1953, 61 x 14 In. 3690.00
Tray, Castle, Coastal Scene, Gilt Flowers, England, c.1830, 14 In. 120.00
Tray, Oval, Coach & Horses, Geometric Gilt Border, Victorian, 24 ½ In. 750.00
Tray, Shaped Crystal Palace Scene, Black Field, Paint, England, c.185017 1/14 x 13 In. 805.00
Writing Box, Black, Painted Flowers, Gilt Scrolling Edge, England, c.1850, 3 x 10 ½ In. 150.00
Writing Box, Regency, Painted Scene, Velvet Surface, Inkwell Slots, Pen Tray, c.1820, 12 x 10 In.. 600.00

PARASOL, *see Umbrella category.*

PARIAN is a fine-grained, hard-paste porcelain named for the marble it resembles. It was first made in England in 1846 and gained in favor in the United States about 1860. Figures, tea sets, vases, and other items were made of Parian at many English and American factories.

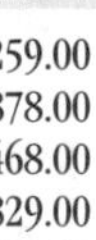

Bust, Girl, Upswept Hair, Closed Eyes, Pedestal, Blue Mark, 19 In. 259.00
Bust, Hera, England, 12 ¾ x 7 ½ In. 878.00
Bust, Julio Claudian Clytie, 11 ½ x 8 In. 468.00
Figurine, Greek Slave, Standing, Nude, Leaning On Pedestal, Round Base, c.1850, 21 In. 2829.00
Figurine, John Milton, Pillar, Scroll, 19th Century, 6 ¼ x 3 ⅞ In. 1121.00
Figurine, Man, Woman, Bouquet, Country Dress, Pastel, c.1890, 19 In., Pair 212.00
Figurine, Napoleon, Standing, Hat In Hand, Hand In Vest, Square Base, 8 ¾ In. 138.00
Figurine, Nora Creena, Copeland, Marked, 1876, 21 ½ In. ....*Illus* 2390.00
Figurine, Putti, Seated On Basket, Grapes & Leaves, Wreath On Head, Signed, c.1915, 19 x 9 In.... 1107.00
Figurine, Wood Nymph Caressing 2 Deer, After C.B. Birch, 19 ½ In. 3286.00
Group, Maidens & Putti, Chest Of Jewelry, Lovebirds, Round Base, 14 x 9 In. 430.00

Papier-Mache, Lap Desk, Mother-Of-Pearl Inlay, Lacquer, Gilt, 2 Brass-Mounted Inkwells, 1800s, 18 ½ x 12 In.
$354.00

Brunk Auctions

Papier-Mache, Parade Head, W.C. Fields, Mardi Gras, 1960s, 48 In.
$504.00

Victorian Casino Antiques

Parian, Figurine, Nora Creena, Copeland, Marked, 1876, 21 ½ In.
$2,390.00

Neal Auction Co.

Parian, Pitcher, Uncle Tom's Cabin Scenes, Relief Molded, Figural Handle, c.1873, 3 x 4 ¼ In.
$1,645.00

Cowan's Auctions

Paris, Apothecary Jar, Lid, c.1825, 10 In.
$854.00

Neal Auction Co.

Paris, Plate, Egyptian Landscape, Mask Heads, Animals, Gilt Edges, Mark, c.1795, 9 ¼ In.
$2,868.00

Neal Auction Co.

Paris, Scent Bottle, Jacob Petit Style, Sultan & Sultana, Jewelry, Enamel, Gilded, c.1850, 10 ½ In., Pair
$3,240.00

Skinner, Inc.

Group, Mother, Seated Next To Infant In Cradle, Oval Base, France, c.1808, 12 ½ In.	598.00
Group, Soldier & Family, Late 19th Century, 19 ¼ In.	59.00
Pitcher, Blue Cast Glaze, Woodland Game Relief, Applied Whippet Handle, 11 In.	59.00
Pitcher, Blue Ground, White Matte Grape & Putti Relief, Molded Loop Handle, 9 ¼ x 7 In.	142.00
Pitcher, Blue, White Branch Handle, Boys Climbing Trees, Lozenge Mark, 7 ½ In.	83.00
Pitcher, Buff, Relief Tavern Scenes, Drinking Men, Scot On Horseback, Witches, c.1835, 9 x 6 In.	59.00
Pitcher, Long Neck, Serpent Handle, White, c.1895, 11 ½ In.	356.00
Pitcher, Neoclassical, White, Goddesses, Cherubs, Handle, Scalloped Rim, Footed, 10 ⅜ In.	59.00
Pitcher, Relief Scenes, Lion Killing Deer, Bear, Dogs, Vines, Berries, Hound Handle, c.1835, 6 In.	94.00
Pitcher, Uncle Tom's Cabin Scenes, Relief Molded, Figural Handle, c.1873, 3 x 4 ¼ In. *Illus*	1645.00
Pitcher, Waterfall, Bennington, Vt., 19th Century, 9 ¼ In.	178.00

PARIS, Vieux Paris, or Old Paris, is porcelain ware that is known to have been made in Paris in the eighteenth or early nineteenth century. These porcelains have no identifying mark but can be recognized by the whiteness of the porcelain and the lines and decorations. Gold decoration is often used.

Apothecary Jar, Lid, c.1825, 10 In. *Illus*	854.00
Basket, Gilt, Flared Paw Feet, 8 ¾ In., Pair	875.00
Candlestick, Rococo Style, Cutout Standard, Applied Blossoms, Red, Blue, Paint, Gilt, Pair, 9 ¾ In.	406.00
Centerpiece, Oval Bowl, Scroll Base, Downturned Leaves, Gilded Edge, c.1850, 13 x 14 In.	369.00
Clock, Round Face, Blue Ground, Gilt Classical Designs, Angel Handles, Square Plinth, c.1820, 13 In.	3750.00
Compote, Molded, Gilded, Raised Paw Feet, Bulbous Stem, 9 ½ In., Pair	625.00
Compote, Pedestal, Cylindrical Body, Square Base, Gothic Tracery, Blue, Gilt, c.1850, 9 x 6 ½ In.	854.00
Fish Platter, Décor De La Reine, Elongated Octagonal, Cornflower Sprays, c.1850, 2 ⅛ x 23 ¼ In.	359.00
Garniture, Classical Ruins, Apple Green Ground, Trumpet Form, Gilt Trim, 9 x 7 In., Pair	915.00
Jardiniere, Blue, Pedestal, Gilt Edge Greek Key Border, 3 Neoclassical Portrait Medallions, 7 ½ In.	118.00
Jardiniere, Flower Reserves, Green Ground, Gilt Rims, Lion's Head Handles, 7 ½ x 8 In., Pair	410.00
Planter, Pierced Lid, Flower Sprays Reserves, Gilt Scroll Border, Raised Feet, c.1800, 6 ¼ In., Pair	3750.00
Plate, Egyptian Landscape, Mask Heads, Animals, Gilt Edges, Mark, c.1795, 9 ¼ In. *Illus*	2868.00
Platter, Small Flowers, White Ground, Oval, c.1850, 2 ½ x 14 ¼ In.	35.00
Scent Bottle, Jacob Petit Style, Sultan & Sultana, Jewelry, Enamel, Gilded, c.1850, 10 ½ In., Pair *Illus*	3240.00
Tray, Dessert, 4 Tiers, Lavender, Gilt, Scalloped Edges, Wreath Finial, c.1850, 22 ¼ In.	861.00
Urn, Figures, Landscapes, Historic Events, Gilt, Handles, c.1810, 17 ½ In., Pair	2006.00
Urn, Flower Painted, Gilt, Swan Handles, 1800s, 11 In., Pair	344.00
Urn, Flowers, Black Ground, Gilt Rims & Medial Handles, c.1890, 11 ¼ In., Pair	406.00
Urn, Garniture, Italian Landscapes, Mother & Child, Swan's Head Handles, c.1835, 13 x 6 ½ In., Pair	738.00
Urn, Landscape, Deer, Applied Gilt Handles, Pedestal, Platform Base, J. Missant, c.1850, 15 x 9 In. *Illus*	354.00
Urn, Lid, Finial, White Ground, Gold Decoration, France, 15 x 7 In.	36.00
Urn, Painted, Gilt, Napoleonic Scene, Shield, Trophies, Apricot Panel, Campana Shape, 8 In., Pair	260.00
Urn, Potpourri, Gilt, Chinoiserie Panels, 3 Figures, Lid, Handles, Square Base, c.1830, 5 ¾ In.	359.00
Vase, Campana Shape, Gilt Bleu-De-Roi, Flowers, Traceries, 1800s, 8 ¼ In.	1793.00
Vase, Classical Female Nudes, Venus & Cupid, Gilt, Laurel Wreath, Handles, c.1850, 25 ½ In. *Illus*	5100.00
Vase, Cornucopia, Flower Garlands, Claret Ground, Gilt Trim, Ruffled Edge, 15 In., Pair	359.00
Vase, Courting Scene, Indian Kneeling, Landscapes, Gilt Handles, Base, Darte, c.1820, 16 ½ In., Pair.	5925.00
Vase, Flowers, Stag, Figural, Multicolor, Flared, 17 ½ In., Pair	717.00
Vase, Garniture, Gothic Arches, Knights, Women, Swan Handles, Gilt Borders, c.1850, 16 In., Pair *Illus*	4780.00
Vase, Gold & Blue, Classical Designs, Term Handles, c.1810, 10 ¼ In. *Illus*	299.00
Vase, Landscape, Figures, Pink Gold Neck, Flared Base, 16 In.	79.00
Vase, Loop Handles At Neck, Round Foot, Flower Band, Gothic Border, c.1850, 9 In., Pair	1315.00
Vase, Neoclassical, Urn Shape, Swan, Handles, Gilt, Reserves, Lake, Mother, Children, 11 ½ In.	92.00
Vase, Paddlewheel, Rowboat, Lighthouse Scene, c.1860, 18 In.	1121.00
Vase, Peafowl On Railing Reserve, Aubergine Ground, Angled Handles, c.1880, 12 In., Pair	590.00
Vase, Purple Matte Ground, Gilt Griffins, Lozenges, Gold Dragon Head Handles, c.1810, 10 ¾ In.	1875.00
Veilleuse, Teapot, Gothic Designs, Lavender, Gilt Accents, 1800s, 8 ¼ In. *Illus*	538.00

PATE-DE-VERRE is an ancient technique in which glass is made by blending and refining powdered glass of different colors into molds. The process was revived by French glassmakers, especially Galle, around the end of the nineteenth century.

Sculpture, Rose, Lavender, Frosted, Variegated, Box, Signed Daum, 4 x 3 ½ In.	161.00

PATENT MODELS were required as part of a patent application for a United States patent until 1880. In 1926 the stored patent models were sold as a group by the U.S. Patent Office and individual models are now appearing in the marketplace.

Animal Trap, Metal Cage, P.E. Wallford, No. 214013, April 8, 1879, 8 ½ x 3 In. *Illus*	460.00
Barometer, Clock Driven, Enamel Clock Dial, Brass Gears, 2 Parts, 18 In.	236.00

Cotton Planter, Globe Cotton Planter, Remington Agl'Co, Barna's, 1879, 18 x 5 x 9 In...*Illus*	7763.00
Fly Trap, Wood, Mesh Screen Receptacles, T.M. Scott, No. 19382, Feb. 16, 1858, 11 ½ x 9 ½ In....*Illus*	632.00
Moldboard Walking Plow, Tin, Hardwood, Adjustable Parts, Pat'd May 6, 1875, 8 ¼ In.	708.00
Railroad Rail, No. 127445, Wood, Metal, Jn. Winslow, June 4, 1872, 4 ½ In.	140.00

PATE-SUR-PATE means paste on paste. The design was made by painting layers of slip on the ceramic piece until a relief decoration was formed. The method was developed at the Sevres factory in France about 1850. It became even more famous at the English Minton factory about 1870. It has since been used by many potters to make both pottery and porcelain wares.

Charger, Maidens, Dancing In Circle, Impressed, c.1910, 13 ½ In.	8125.00
Flask, Pilgrim, Lid, Gilt, Putti Medallion, Minton, Crowned Globe Mark, 1884, 14 In........*Illus*	3227.00
Plaque, Oval, Green Ground, White Slip Design, Boy, Gazing Through Telescope, Frame, c.1875, 6 In.	2133.00
Plaque, Rex, Woman, Altar, Kicking Cupid, White Cameo Relief, Rectangle, Frame, c.1910, 12 x 7 In.	7500.00
Plaque, Woman's Head, Cupid On Her Shoulder, Puce A L'Oreille, Signed, Rousseau, 7 ⅝ In...*Illus*	4140.00
Vase, Apollo, Lyre, Mirror Black Ground, Oval, Lamp Mount, Gilt Metal Base, 11 ½ x 30 In.....	761.00
Vase, Cherub, Letter, Dove, Rose Ground, Blue Pear Shape, Germany, c.1910, 5 In.	150.00
Vase, Flowers, Classical Figures, Blue, Gilt Handles, 12 ¼ In., Pair	106.00
Vase, White Slip, Maidens, Cupid, Cherub On Reverse, Marc-Louis Solon, c.1890, 16 In...*Illus*	39600.00

PAUL REVERE POTTERY was made at several locations in and around Boston, Massachusetts, between 1906 and 1942. The pottery was operated as a settlement house program for teenage girls. Many pieces were signed *S.E.G.* for Saturday Evening Girls. The artists concentrated on children's dishes and tiles. Decorations were outlined in black and filled with color.

Bowl, Band Of Trees, Beige & Yellow Landscape, Marked, Albina Mangini, 1913, 6 In.	575.00
Bowl, Green, Black Brown Lotus Flower Border, Marked, SMB S.E.G., 3 x 6 ½ In. ....*Illus*	480.00
Bowl, Lid, Yellow Daffodils, Cuerda Seca, Green Ground, Round, S.E.G., 3 x 5 In........................	4688.00
Breakfast Set, Louise, Her Plate, Her Bowl, Her Mug, Blue Glaze, Bunny Center, 7 ½, 5 ½, 3 ½ In..	711.00
Cup & Saucer, Plate, Blue Swan Band, White Ground, Albina Mangini, S.E.G., 1914, 3 ¾, 6, 6 ½ In..	652.00
Jug, Milk, Lotus Flower Band, Cuerda Seca, S.E.G., 1911, 3 x 3 ¾ In.	813.00
Pitcher, Cream, Rabbit, Band, Name, Marked, Paper Label, 4 ¼ In......................................*Illus*	432.00
Pitcher, Roosters, This Is The Cock That Crew In The Morn, Yellow, S.E.G., 6 In.	2250.00
Pitcher, Tapered, Loop Handle, Band Of Irises, Black Outline, Yellow, Cream Ground, Marked, 7 ⅜ In.	1150.00
Pitcher, Teal Blue Ground, Brown Drips, 7 ¼ In...	104.00
Plate, Laurence, His Plate, Rabbit In Landscape, Yellow Glaze, S.E.G., 7 ¾ In...........................	360.00
Salt & Pepper, Underplate, Blue, White, Landscape Band, S.E.G., 1913....................................	250.00
Tile, Boston Harbor, Ship, Bay Where Lay The Somerset, Blue, Cream, Green, S.E.G., 6 In.	2460.00
Tile, Hull Street Galloupe House, Signed, Fannie Levine, 1909, 3 ½ In.	375.00
Tumbler, White Lotus Flower Band, Blue Glaze, Cylindrical, S.E.G., 5 ⅜ In...............................	420.00
Vase, Bud, Stylized Trees, Yellow Cuerda Seca, Tapered, F. Levine, S.E.G., 5 x 2 In....................	938.00
Vase, Lotus, Cuerda Seca, S.E.G., c.1925, 6 ½ x 3 ½ In. ....*Illus*	2125.00

PEACHBLOW glass was made by several factories beginning in the 1880s. New England peachblow is a one-layer glass shading from red to white. Mt. Washington peachblow shades from pink to bluish-white. Hobbs, Brockunier and Company of Wheeling, West Virginia, made Coral glass that they marketed as Peach Blow. It shades from yellow to peach and is lined with white glass. Reproductions of all types of peachblow have been made. Related pieces may be listed under Gundersen and Webb Peachblow.

Bowl, Fuchsia To Pink, Squat, Ruffled Rim, 4 x 8 ¼ In.	431.00
Condiment Set, Mustard, Shakers, Ribbed Barrel, White Daisies, Pairpoint Silver Caddy, 7 In..	10350.00
Creamer, Dark Rose To Light Rose, Squat, Ribbed Loop Handle, 3 In......................................	380.00
Creamer, Fuchsia To Amber, Square Ruffled Rim, Loop Handle, Bulbous, 4 ¼ x 4 ½ In.	230.00
Creamer, Square Mouth, Shaded, Applied Reeded Handle, 4 ½ In..	1208.00
Creamer, Square Mouth, Tapered Body, Glossy Finish, Shell Shape Handle, 4 ½ In..................	259.00
Creamer, Squat, Bulbous, Reeded Ring Handle, 3 In.	489.00
Cruet, Amber Faceted Stopper, Reeded Handle, Oval, Hobbs, Brockunier, Wheeling, 7 In.	374.00
Cruet, Mahogany To Yellow, Bulbous, Ruffled Spout, Amber Loop Handle, Faceted Stopper, 7 In...	316.00
Finger Bowl, Fuchsia To Pink, Pinched Ruffled Rim, 5 ½ In.	259.00
Pitcher, Mahogany To Yellow, Amber Loop Handle, Cylindrical, Tapered, 9 In.	2760.00
Pitcher, Mahogany To Yellow, Bulbous, Square Mouth, Amber Loop Handle, 8 In.	863.00
Pitcher, Pheasant On Blossoming Branch, Gold Enamel, Applied Camphor Handle, 8 ¾ In.. *Illus*	230.00
Punch Bowl, Shiny Rouge To Pink, Deep Red, Rigaree Upper Rim, Pedestal, Spread Foot, 12 In.	2300.00
Shaker, Glossy, Ribbed Pillar Shape, Pairpoint Caddy, Mt. Washington, 7 In., Pair..................	3450.00
Sock Darner, Round Head, 4 ½ In.	45.00
Sugar & Creamer, Pink To White, Loop Handles, 3 ¾ In.	1380.00
Tankard, Pitcher, Shaded Blue To Pink, Mt. Washington, 7 ½ In.	1725.00

Paris, Urn, Landscape, Deer, Applied Gilt Handles, Pedestal, Platform Base, J. Missant, c.1850, 15 x 9 In. $354.00

Brunk Auctions

Paris, Vase, Classical Female Nudes, Venus & Cupid, Gilt, Laurel Wreath, Handles, c.1850, 25 ½ In. $5,100.00

Skinner, Inc.

Paris, Vase, Garniture, Gothic Arches, Knights, Women, Swan Handles, Gilt Borders, c.1850, 16 In., Pair $4,780.00

Neal Auction Co.

Paris, Vase, Gold & Blue, Classical Designs, Term Handles, c.1810, 10 ¼ In. $299.00

Neal Auction Co.

Paris, Veilleuse, Teapot, Gothic Designs, Lavender, Gilt Accents, 1800s, 8 ¼ In. $538.00

Neal Auction Co.

Patent Model, Animal Trap, Metal Cage, P.E. Wallford, No. 214013, April 8, 1879, 8 ½ x 3 In. $460.00

James D. Julia Auctioneers

TIP

Never leave a note outside explaining that you are not at home.

Tumbler, Satin Finish, Cylindrical, Hobbs, Brockunier, Wheeling, 5 ¼ In.	184.00
Tumbler, Wild Rose, Shading Opal To Rose, New England, 4 In. ....*Illus*	259.00
Vase, Cherry Red To Butter, Glossy, Stand-Up Rim, Hobbs, Brockunier, 4 ½ x 5 In.	293.00
Vase, Cranberry To Yellow, Griffin Holder Base, Tapered, Shouldered, Stick Neck, 10 In.	920.00
Vase, Footed Lily Shape, Trifold Petal Rim, Pale Blue To Pink, 10 In.	978.00
Vase, Fuchsia To White, Enameled Flowering Branch, Amber Handles, Ruffled Rim, 4 ½ In.	173.00
Vase, Fuchsia To White, Gilt Cascading Gingko Branch, Bulbous, Stick Neck, 9 ½ In.	173.00
Vase, Jack-In-The-Pulpit, Ruffled Rim, Mt. Washington, 8 In. ....*Illus*	575.00
Vase, Lily, Pink To Fuchsia, Round Foot, Ruffled Rim, 9 In.	345.00
Vase, Lily, Wild Rose, Matte, Tricorner Rim, New England Glass, 9 x 4 In.	468.00
Vase, Mahogany To Yellow, Stick Neck, Bulbous, Ring Foot, Glossy, 11 In.	
1265.00 **Vase,** Morgan, Red Shaded To Yellow, Griffin Holder, 10 ¼ In. ....*Illus*	2530.00
Vase, Optic Ribbed, Acid Finish, Flaring, Petal Top, 4 ⅜ In.	1380.00
Vase, Orange Neck, Apricot Base, 12 ¼ In.	148.00
Vase, Pale Pink To Fuchsia, Conical Beehive Shape, Pinched Sides, 7 In.	431.00
Vase, Peach To Red, Footed, c.1870, 5 In., Pair	72.00
Vase, Pinched Sides, Spider In Web, Gold Leaves, Ruffled, Square Mouth, 4 ½ In.	1610.00
Vase, Pink To Amber, White Dogwood Branch, Flowers, Urn Shape, Cylindrical Neck, 8 In.	3105.00
Vase, Pink To Fuchsia, Gold Accents, Spider, Web, Square, Pinched Sides, Square Ruffled Rim, 4 ½ In.	1610.00
Vase, Pink To White, Bulbous, Optic Ribbed, Trifold Mouth, Rigaree Drip, 3 Reeded Feet, 8 In.	9775.00
Vase, Pink, Bulbous Stick, Glossy, Squared Rim, 9 In.	403.00
Vase, Satin, Dark Mahogany To Butter, Gourd Form, 10 ½ In.	439.00
Vase, Stick, Dark To Light Rose, Cup Shape Rim, New England Glass, 9 In.	322.00
Vase, Stick, To Bulbous Base, 10 ⅝ In.	356.00
Vase, Wheeling, Bulbous Stick Shape, Glossy, 9 In.	690.00
Whiskey, Fuchsia To Pink, Square Mouth, 2 ¼ In.	201.00

PEANUTS is the title of a comic strip created by cartoonist Charles M. Schulz (1922–2000). The strip, drawn by Schulz from 1950 to 2000, features a group of children, including Charlie Brown and his sister Sally, Lucy Van Pelt and her brother Linus, Peppermint Patty, and Pig Pen, and an imaginative and independent beagle named Snoopy. The Peanuts gang has also been featured in books, television shows, and a Broadway musical.

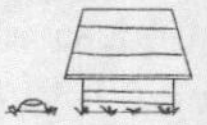

Book, A Golden Celebration, Soft Cover, 255 Pages	18.00
Book, Charlie Brown's All Stars, Hard Cover, 1st Edition, World Publishing, 44 Pages, 1966	7.00
Brush, Charlie Brown Shape, Cowboy Hat, Composition, Avon, c.1971, 6 In.	8.00
Bulletin Board, Burlap, Wood Hanging Pole, Snoopy On Doghouse, 1960s, 33 x 17 In.	55.00
Button, Snoopy, Moon Landing, I'm On The Moon!, Space Helmet, Blue, White, 1969, 1 ¾ In.	115.00
Cake Pan, Aluminum, Charlie Wearing Baseball Attire, Wilton, 1960s, 13 x 11 In.	50.00
Magnet, Snoopy, 1970s, 2 ¾ In.	6.00
Nodder, Snoopy, Santa Suit, Composition, 3 ¾ In.	75.00
Pajama Bag, Lucy, Cotton, 26 In.	40.00
Program, You're A Good Man Charlie Brown, United Features, 1969, 8 x 8 In., 24 Pages	13.00
Spoon, Chef Snoopy, Stainless Steel, Rubber Bowl, c.1965, 5 ½ In.	12.00

PEARLWARE is an earthenware made by Josiah Wedgwood in 1779. It was copied by other potters in England. Pearlware is only slightly different in color from creamware and for many years collectors have confused the terms. Wedgwood pieces are listed in the Wedgwood category in this book. Most pearlware with mocha designs is listed under Mocha.

Pearl

Bough Pot, Enameled, Urn Shape, Medallions, Leaf Border, Scroll Handles, Staffordshire, 9 ½ In..	590.00
Coffeepot, Lid, Blue & White, Pagodas, Trees, Rocks, Handle Terminals, Knop, England, c.1800, 12 In.	502.00
Coffeepot, Lid, Strawberry Pattern, England, c.1810, 11 ¼ In.	2015.00
Creamer, Lid, Cow Shape, Bocage, Charles Tittensor, Staffordshire, c.1820, 7 ¾ In.	1416.00
Figurine, Boy, Sleeping Under Tree, Dog, John Walton, Staffordshire, c.1820, 5 ½ In.	230.00
Figurine, Bull, Painted, Now Captain Lad, Bull Beating, England, c.1810, 9 ½ x 13 ½ In.	948.00
Figurine, Lion, Reclining, Bocage, c.1820, 4 ¾ In., Pair	1652.00
Figurine, Lion, Standing, Paw On Ball, Painted, Staffordshire, c.1800, 9 x 11 ½ In.	1422.00
Figurine, Pitcher, Inscribed James Hardman, Man On Horseback, Motto, England, 1823, 5 ½ In.	486.00
Jug, Miser, Portrait, Pratt Type, c.1800, 5 ¼ In. ....*Illus*	300.00
Jug, Silver Resist Luster, c.1815, 9 In.	944.00
Punch Bowl, Cell, Diaper Pattern, Large Central Fish, Text, Blue, White, Transfer, c.1800, 5 x 11 In.	518.00
Salt, Feather Border, Blue & White, Pedestal, England, c.1845, 2 ⅛ x 3 ⅛ In.	184.00
Tea Caddy, Putti Relief, England, c.1790, 5 In.	2015.00
Teapot, Sugar & Creamer, Strawberry & Leaf, Staffordshire, c.1815, Teapot 6 ¼ In., 3 Piece	590.00
Vase, Columnar, Fluted, Double Ring Bottom, Square Base, Iron Red, c.1800, 12 In., Pair	2133.00

PEKING GLASS is a Chinese cameo glass first made popular in the eighteenth century. The Chinese have continued to make this layered glass in the old manner, and many new pieces are now available that could confuse the average buyer.

Bowl, Amethyst Color, Flower Shape, Petal Rim, Lobed Body, c.1900, 12 ¼ In. Diam.	230.00
Bowl, Dark Pink, Wide Flared Rim, 1800s, 10 ½ In. Diam.	230.00
Bowl, Dark Ruby Red Color, Engrailed Border, Ribbed Body, 1800s, 2 ¼ x 14 In.	403.00
Bowl, Footed, Wide Rim, Flared Lip, Translucent Gold, c.1900, 11 ½ In., Pair	1080.00
Bowl, Jade Green Color, Ring Foot, Wide Ruffled Rim, c.1900, 5 x 11 ¾ In.	89.00
Bowl, Jade Green, Pierced, Engraved Leaf Base, Handles, Carved Hardstone, Pewter, 3 x 9 ¼ In.	81.00
Bowl, Opaque Pink, Oval, Lobed Body, Wavy Rim, 1700s, 2 ¼ x 6 ⅝ In.	177.00
Bowl, Orange Cut To White, Butterflies, Morning Glories, Footed, Flared Lip, 6 ½ x 3 In.	98.00
Bowl, Red, Carved Animals, 18th Century Mark, 2 ¾ x 6 ¼ In., Pair	5750.00
Bowl, Yellow, Cameo Carved, Birds, Vining Flowers, Rosewood Stand, 4 x 6 In.	345.00
Bowl, Yellow, Carved Prunus Branch, Wood Stand, 4 ¼ In., Pair	590.00
Censer, Translucent Green, Squat, Tripod Feet, Round Handles At Rim, c.1860, 2 ¾ x 4 In.	3738.00
Cup, Shaped Green, Gilt Leaf Frame, 4 x 3 ½ In., Pair	130.00
Figurine, Guanyin, Standing, Malachite Green, 1800s, 10 ⅝ In. *Illus*	575.00
Figurine, Guanyin, Standing, Robes, Cobalt Blue, 1800s, 10 ¼ In.	805.00
Ginger Jar, Lid, Honeycomb, Cased White To Turquoise, 1800s, 7 ⅜ In. *Illus*	633.00
Jar, Lid, Mustard Yellow Scrolls, Seals, White Opaque Ground, 5 ¾ In.	2588.00
Scroll Weight, Tubular Shape, Pale Green Ground, Dark Swirls, 1800s, 6 ½ In.	118.00
Vase, Bamboo Design, Red, Orange, Black, Elongated Oval, Copper Tripod Base, c.1800, 6 ¼ In.	3738.00
Vase, Battle Scene, Cameo, Red To Snowflake, Bottle Shape, Marked, c.1750, 9 ¼ In. *Illus*	4600.00
Vase, Blue To Silver, Flecked Turquoise, Birds & Flowers, 1900s, 9 In.	676.00
Vase, Bottle Shape, Ring Foot, Cylindrical Neck, Amber Color, 1700s, 14 ⅜ In.	2473.00
Vase, Bottle Shape, Ring Foot, White, Pink, Carved, Butterfly, Peony Flowers, c.1800, 7 In.	1185.00
Vase, Carved Cranes, Branches, Red, Over Opaque White, c.1960, 8 In.	120.00
Vase, Green Overlay, Opaque White, Lotus Flowers, Leaves, Marked, 1800, 8 In. *Illus*	1215.00
Vase, Green, Long Thin Neck, Bulbous Base, c.1905, 8 ⅝ In.	165.00
Vase, Pink Overlay, Snowflake Ground, Dragons Flying, Scrolling Lotus, c.1800, 8 In.	2370.00
Vase, Pink, Turquoise, Cameo, Flowering Trees, Leaves, Square Shape, c.1800, 7 ¾ In., Pair	3450.00
Vase, Square, Brown Overlay, Yellow, Phoenix, Elephant Handles, Recessed Base, c.1800, 8 In.	1185.00
Vase, Tapered, Shouldered, Red & Orange, Swirled Pattern, c.1800, 6 In.	2415.00
Vase, Yellow, Carved, Historical Scene Design, 10 ¾ In.	492.00

PENS replaced hand-cut quills as writing instruments in 1780, when the first steel pen point was made in England. But it was 100 years before the commercial pen was a common item. The fountain pen was invented in the 1830s but was not made in quantity until the 1880s. All types of old pens are collected. Float pens that feature small objects floating in a liquid as part of the handle are popular with collectors. Advertising pens are listed in the Advertising section of this book.

Dip, Blown Glass, Light Green, Red & Green Bird Finial, 1920s, 6 ½ In.	105.00
Dip, Glass, Nicholas Lutz Style, Colorless, White, Cobalt Blue Striped, c.1860, 6 ⅞ In.	69.00
Dip, Mother-Of-Pearl, Gold Filled Top, Iridescent, c.1870, 6 ½ In.	75.00
Dip, Wood, Carved Leaf Shape Stem, Cuba, Painted Bird, 1950s, 9 ¼ In.	150.00
Dip, Wood, Carved, Tree Branch Shape, Washington, D.C., c.1900, 8 In.	125.00
Eversharp Wahl, Fountain, Coral, Gold Seal, 1930s, 4 ⅝ In.	215.00
Geo. S. Parker Duofold, Jr., Fountain, Deluxe Black	81.00
Geo. S. Parker Duofold, Jr., Fountain, Mandarin Yellow	173.00
Mark Cross, Fountain, Reeded Finish, Engraved, 14K Yellow Gold, 5 ¼ In.	351.00
Montblanc, Fountain, Meister Stuck 146	288.00
Pelikan 120, Fountain	69.00
Sheaffer, Fountain, 14K Gold, Reeded Surface, Twist-Off Cap, Signed, 5 ¼ In.	408.00
Van Cleef & Arpels, 14K Gold, Engraved Flowers, Ruby & Diamond Cap, 4 In.	948.00
Writing Brush, Soapstone, Carved, Animal Hair Brush, Chinese, 1900s, 15 In. *Illus*	173.00

PEN & PENCIL

2 In 1, 14K Yellow Gold, Fountain Pen, Retractable Lead Pencil, 5 ¾ In.	495.00
Cartier, 2 In 1, 14K Yellow Gold, Bamboo, Retractable, Ballpoint, 5 ¼ In.	667.00
Cross, 14K Yellow Gold, Retractable Pencil, Stamped, 5 In., Pair	184.00
Sheaffer, Ballpoint Pen, Mechanical Pencil, Case, Goldtone, 5 In.	55.00
Sheaffer, White Dot, Green Marble, 14K Gold	425.00
Wahl-Eversharp, Fountain, Gray, 14K Gold, Box	149.00

Patent Model, Cotton Planter, Globe Cotton Planter, Remington Agl'Co, Barna's, 1879, 18 x 5 x 9 In.
$7,763.00

James D. Julia Auctioneers

Patent Model, Fly Trap, Wood, Mesh Screen Receptacles, T.M. Scott, No. 19382, Feb. 16, 1858, 11 ½ x 9 ½ In.
$632.00

James D. Julia Auctioneers

Pate-Sur-Pate, Flask, Pilgrim, Lid, Gilt, Putti Medallion, Minton, Crowned Globe Mark, 1884, 14 In.
$3,227.00

Sloans & Kenyon

Pate-Sur-Pate, Plaque, Woman's Head, Cupid On Her Shoulder, Puce A L'Oreille, Signed, Rousseau, 7 ⅝ In.
$4,140.00

Humler & Nolan

The edited listings of the current prices in this *Kovels' Antiques & Collectibles Price Guide* aren't available on any website. Readers can visit **Kovels.com** to check thousands of past prices and sign up for free information on trends, tips, reproductions, marks, and more.

P

Pate-Sur-Pate, Vase, White Slip, Maidens, Cupid, Cherub On Reverse, Marc-Louis Solon, c.1890, 16 In. $39,600.00

Skinner, Inc.

Paul Revere, Bowl, Green, Black Brown Lotus Flower Border, Marked, SMB S.E.G., 3 x 6 ½ In. $480.00

Skinner, Inc.

Paul Revere, Pitcher, Cream, Rabbit, Band, Name, Marked, Paper Label, 4 ¼ In. $432.00

Humler & Nolan

Paul Revere, Vase, Lotus, Cuerda Seca, S.E.G., c.1925, 6 ½ x 3 ½ In. $2,125.00

Ragn Arts & Auction Center

PENCILS were invented, so it is said, in 1565. The eraser was not added to the pencil until 1858. The automatic pencil was invented in 1863. Collectors today want advertising pencils or automatic pencils of unusual design. Boxes and sharpeners for pencils are also collected. Advertising pencils are listed in the Advertising category. Pencil boxes are listed in the Box category.

Cartier, 14K Yellow Gold, Retractable, Engraved, Signed, 6 In.	414.00
Gambling, Rogue's, Sterling & Enamel Case, Bavaria, 3 ¼ In.	265.00
Mechanical, Figural, Head, Jewels, Italy, c.1900, 4 In.	99.00
Mechanical, Red Swirl, Bakelite, 1950s	15.00
Ritepoint, Mechanical, Bakelite, Navy, Amber, 5 ¼ In.	45.00
Sign, Wood Carved, Green Paint, Multicolor, c.1900, 60 In.	3555.00
Tiffany & Co., 14K Gold, 6 ⅛ In.	780.00
Wahl-Eversharp, Mechanical, Gold Filled, Checkered, c.1917, 4 In.	100.00
Wahl-Eversharp, Mechanical, Gold Filled, Grecian Border, Ring Top, c.1924, 3 ½ In.	55.00
Walther League, Mechanical, Plastic, Black & Cream, Brass	30.00

PENCIL SHARPENER

Alarm Clock, Metal, Marked Germany, 1 ½ x 1 In.	42.00
Bakelite, Green, 1930-40, 1 x ¾ x ⅜ In.	12.00
Fireplace Hearth, Pot Metal, Brass Finish, 3 x 2 ⅓ In.	10.00
Giant, Desk Top, 6 Size Holes, Metal, Painted, Removable Barrel, Box, 1950s, 4 x 2 ½ In.	55.00
Globe, Multicolor, Sharpener Base, 1920s, 3 ⅝ x 5 ½ In.	155.00
Happy, From Snow White, Celluloid, Japan, 2 ½ In.	173.00
Jupiter 1, Guhl & Harbeck, Germany, c.1920	285.00
Man, In Lederhosen, Hat, Mustache, Tin, Painted, West Germany	135.00
Mod Space Age, Egg Shape, Orange, Boston	95.00
Pelican, Celluloid, Metal, Painted, Japan, c.1940, 3 ⅛ In.	95.00
Spanky, Our Gang, Plastic, Amber Color, Octagonal, Raised Brass Rim, Catalin, c.1930, 1 ⅛ In.	98.00

PENNSBURY POTTERY worked in Morrisville, Pennsylvania, from 1950 to 1971. Full sets of dinnerware as well as many decorative items were made. Pieces are marked with the name of the factory.

Pennsbury Pottery

Amish, Creamer, Man In Heart, 8 Oz., 4 In.	22.00
Amish, Vinegar & Oil, Head Stoppers, 7 In.	150.00
Ashtray, Shovel Shape, Failess Works, Embossed, 6 ¾ x 5 In.	45.00
Black Rooster, Ashtray, Round, 5 In.	16.00
Black Rooster, Cup & Saucer	26.00
Black Rooster, Salt & Pepper	22.00
Folk Art, Bowl, Vegetable, 9 In.	53.00
Folk Art, Cup & Saucer	21.00
Folk Art, Plate, Bread & Butter, 6 ½ In.	8.00
Folk Art, Salt & Pepper	24.00
Hex, Mug, 3 ⅛ In.	12.00
Hex, Pitcher, 3 ¾ In.	22.00
Hex, Plate, Bread & Butter, 6 ½ In.	12.00
Locomotive, Bowl, 7 ¾ x 5 ¾ In.	24.00
Map, Rotary International, Embossed, Plate, 8 In.	40.00
Red Rooster, Casserole, Lid, Round, 1 Qt., 6 ½ In.	115.00
Red Rooster, Cookie Jar, Lid, 8 In.	140.00
Red Rooster, Cup & Saucer	18.00
Red Rooster, Plate, Dinner, 10 In.	36.00
Red Rooster, Teapot, Lid, 4 Cup, 4 ¼ In.	70.00

PEPSI-COLA, the drink and the name, was invented in 1898 but was not trademarked until 1903. The logo was changed from an elaborate script to the modern block letters in 1963. Several different logos have been used. Until 1951, the words *Pepsi* and *Cola* were separated by 2 dashes. These bottles are called "double dash." In 1951 the modern logo with a single hyphen was introduced. All types of advertising memorabilia are collected, and reproductions are being made.

PEPSI-COLA

Ad, Fashion Is For The Slender, Woman, Dressing, Ladies' Home Journal, 1953, 10 ½ x 13 ⅝ In.	15.00
Ad, Picture Of Poise, Blond Bombshell, Ladies' Home Journal, 1956, 10 ¼ x 14 In.	12.00
Ad, Sitting Pretty, Blond Woman, Iron Spiral Staircase, McCall's, 1958, 10 x 13 ½ In.	15.00
Bank, Vending Machine Shape, 5 Cents, Tin, Painted, Hallmark, c.1983, 3 ¼ x 4 ¾ In.	14.00
Bottle 6-Pack, Glass Swirl, Metal Cap, Cardboard Carrying Case, Early 1960s, 2 ½-In. Bottle	42.00
Bottle Carrier, Aluminum, Embossed Red Painted Label, Adjustable Handles, 8 ⅜ In., Pair	301.00
Bottle Carrier, Metal, Red Logo, Blue Stripes, Holds 6 Bottles, 1950s, 8 x 5 ½ x 7 ½ In.	49.00
Bottle Opener, Wood Handle, Drink Pepsi-Cola, Perfectum Edelstahl Rost Frei, Germany, 6 In.	15.00

Box, Red, Green Paint, Wood, 1940s, 18 ½ x 10 ½ In.	150.00
Cooler, Chest, Aluminum, Red Logo, Crostrom's Mfg. Service, 1950s, 22 x 13 x 13 In.	140.00
Cooler, Script Logo, White, Opener, Split Door, Gullwing, 1940s, 44 x 32 In.	2280.00
Fountain Pen, Metal Bottle Shape Clip, Stripes, Red, White, Blue, Celluloid, Box, c.1930, 4 ⅞ In.	99.00
Glass, Aquaman, Super Series, Multicolor, 1976	25.00
Glass, Wonder Woman, Super Series, Multicolor, 1976	25.00
Lighter, Evervess Sparkling Water, Made By Pepsi, 1950s, 2 ¾ In.	39.00
Paperweight, Glass, Blue, White, Controlled Bubbles, c.1980, 3 x 3 In.	55.00
Pin, Pepsi Quiz Club, Elephant, Giraffe, Koala, Round, Australia, c.1950, 1 ¼ In.	52.00
Salt & Pepper, Tray, Pepsi Glass, Bottle, Ceramic Tray, Box, Miniature	17.00
Sign, America's Biggest Nickel's Worth, 5 Cents, Tin Lithograph, Red, White, Blue, 1940s, 10 x 30 In.	550.00
Sign, Bottle Cap Shape, Drink Pepsi-Cola, Red, White, Blue, Tin, 32 In. Diam.	240.00
Sign, Bottle Cap Shape, More Bounce To The Ounce, Cardboard, Woman, Tray, 1940s, 13 x 29 In.	253.00
Sign, Bottle Cap Shape, Yellow, Navy, Red, Embossed Tin, 1940s, 13 ¼ In.	330.00
Sign, Pepsi-Cola Cops, Pepsi & Pete, 6 Pack, Cardboard, Die Cut, c.1940, 14 ½ x 21 ¼ In...*Illus*	209.00
Strawholder, Tin, Chrome Plated, Double Dash, For Sweetheart Straws, c.1940, 3 ¾ x 4 ½ In.	375.00
Straws, Have A Pepsi, Stripes, Bottle Cap, Box, c.1950s, 10 ¾ x 3 ⅞ In.	99.00
Thermometer, Light Refreshment, Tin Litho, Embossed Dot Logo Bottle Cap At Top, 1955, 7 x 27 In.	154.00
Toy, Truck, 1940 Ford Replica, Die Cast, Premier Edition, Display Stand, Box, 1:18 Scale	25.00
Uniform, Baseball Shirt, Pants, White, Red Piping, 1940s	330.00

PERFUME BOTTLES are made of cut glass, pressed glass, art glass, silver, metal, enamel, and even plastic or porcelain. Although the small bottle to hold perfume was first made before the time of ancient Egypt, it is the nineteenth- and twentieth-century examples that interest today's collector. DeVilbiss Company has made atomizers of all types since 1888 but no longer makes the perfume bottle tops so popular with collectors. These were made from 1920 to 1968. The glass bottle may be by any of many manufacturers even if the atomizer is marked *DeVilbiss*. The word *factice*, which often appears in ads, refers to store display bottles. Glass or porcelain examples may be found under the appropriate name such as Lalique, Czechoslovakia, Glass-Bohemia, etc.

Andre Chenier, Apple Blossom, Pink Blossoms & Lid, Box, 1930s, 5 In.	40.00
Atomizer, Gold Metal, Applied Ornaments, Green Faceted Glass, Stamped E. & J.B., 7 x 2 In.	115.00
Bombi, Black Magic, Ribbed Sides, Black Ball Cap, c.1945, 6 ¼ In.	32.00
Cappi By Cheramy, Horizontal Ribs, Red Bakelite Cap, c.1921, 2 ½ In.	17.00
Chanel, No. 5, 2 ½ In.	85.00
Charles V, Versart, Black Ribbed Cap, c.1950, 1 ½ In.	14.00
Chloe, Narcisse, Frosted Flower Petal Stopper, Factice, 13 x 9 In.	750.00
Christian Dior, Dolce Vita, Globular, Indented Circles, Gold Neck, Factice, 14 x 10 x 30 In.	600.00
Cranberry Glass, Lay Down, Double Ended, Silver Plated Cap, 5 In.	149.00
Crystal, Art Deco Style, 6-Sided Bottle & Stopper, Amber, Blue, West Germany, 1950s, 6 In., Pair	98.00
Cut Glass, Red, Elongated Lay Down Shape, 9 In.	259.00
Cut Glass, Ruby To Clear, Etched Grapevine, Long Neck, Swirled Stopper, 7 ¾ In.	65.00
DeVilbiss, Art Glass, Bronze, Jeweled Mounts, 7 ½ In. *Illus*	1783.00
DeVilbiss, Atomizer, French Blue & Black Enamel, Metal Top, Blue Silk Cord, Bulb, 8 In.	104.00
DeVilbiss, Atomizer, Frosted Blue Glass, Baluster, Spread Foot, 6 ½ In.	53.00
DeVilbiss, Red, Black Swirls, Atomizer, Acid Etched Mark, 7 In.	180.00
Gabella, Compose De Parfum, Paneled, Ribbed, Cork Stopper, 4 In.	65.00
Givenchy, Le De Givenchy, Satin Box, c.1965, 2 ¾ In.	65.00
Glass, Enamel, 3 Classical Women, Fruit, Bellflower & Scroll Borders, Gilt Metal Mount, 3 ½ In.	177.00
Glass, Faceted, Dome Shape, Alternating Amber & Clear Panels, Stopper, 5 ¼ In.	161.00
Glass, Pink, Round, Faceted, Stopper, 5 ¾ In.	288.00
Glass, Ribbed, Alexandrite Blue Interior, Clear Stopper, Round, Vandermark, 5 ¾ In., Pair	81.00
Guerlain, Shalimar, Urn Shape, Pedestal, ½ Moon Cap, 1960s, 4 ⅛ In.	55.00
Hand Shape, Burmese Glass, Queen's Pattern, Dotted Daisies, Stopper, Mt. Washington, 7 In...*Illus*	6613.00
Harriet Hubbard Ayer, Yu, Pink Plastic Cap, 1937, 5 ½ x 2 ⅝ In.	35.00
Jean Paul Gaultier, Chinese Red Door, Figural, Dress, Red, Factice, 6 In.	125.00
Karl Lagerfeld, Sun, Moon & Stars, Ball Shape, Cobalt Blue, Raised Design, Factice, 9 x 24 In.	250.00
Laura Ashley, No. 1, Flowers, Leaves, Glass Stopper, Gold Neck, Factice, 13 In.	750.00
Nina Ricci, Capricci, Lattice Pattern, Lalique, Factice, 6 x 5 In.	385.00
Porcelain, Painted, 2 Geishas, Trees, Silver Metal Cap, Silver Marks, A.B. & Co., 2 ¼ In.	92.00
Silver, Art Nouveau, Melon Shape, Long Neck, Repousse, Schiebler, c.1870, 6 In., Pair	920.00
Silver, Enamel, Painted, Amorous Couples, Landscape, Hermann Bohm, c.1890, 4 ¼ In.	1298.00
Silver, George III, Enameled, Urn & Garlands, Gilt Repousse, Flask, c.1800, 3 ¼ In.	1062.00
T.J. Holmes Co., Champ, Pyramid Shape, Yellow, Atomizer, Box, c.1930, 5 In.	65.00
Vial, Cut Crystal, 14K Gold Hinged Lid, Synthetic Ruby, Glass Stopper, Krementz, 3 ¼ In.	184.00

Peachblow, Pitcher, Pheasant On Blossoming Branch, Gold Enamel, Applied Camphor Handle, 8 ¾ In. $230.00

Early Auction Co.

Peachblow, Tumbler, Wild Rose, Shading Opal To Rose, New England, 4 In. $259.00

Early Auction Co.

Peachblow, Vase, Jack-In-The-Pulpit, Ruffled Rim, Mt. Washington, 8 In. $575.00

Early Auction Co.

P

TIP

Check the supports on wall-hung shelves once a year. Eventually a heavy load will cause "creep," the metal brackets will bend, and the shelf will fall.

Peachblow, Vase, Morgan, Red Shaded To Yellow, Griffin Holder, 10 ¼ In. $2,530.00

Humler & Nolan

Pearlware, Jug, Miser, Portrait, Pratt Type, c.1800, 5 ¼ In. $300.00

Skinner, Inc.

Peking Glass, Figurine, Guanyin, Standing, Malachite Green, 1800s, 10 ⅝ In. $575.00

James D. Julia Auctioneers

PETERS & REED POTTERY COMPANY of Zanesville, Ohio, was founded by John D. Peters and Adam Reed in 1897. Chromal, Landsun, Montene, Pereco, and Persian are some of the art lines that were made. The company, which became Zane Pottery in 1920 and Gonder Pottery in 1941, closed in 1957. Peters & Reed pottery was unmarked.

Bowl, Green, Embossed, 9 In.	23.00
Jug, Brown Glaze, Applied Blue Grapes & Green & Yellow Leaves, 1900s, 5 ¾ In.	150.00
Mug, Brown Glaze, Grapes, 5 ¼ In.	79.00
Planter, Blue Embossed Rim, Flower Band, Cream Ground, 8 In.	12.00
Planter, Moss Aztec, Triangular Designs, Green, Brown, Rectangular, 12 ¼ In.	144.00
Sprinkler, Frog, Green, 6 ½ In.	81.00
Sprinkler, Frog, Seated, 12 In.	63.00
Vase, Aztec, Red, Green, 8 In.	69.00
Vase, Bud, Double, Flowers, 6 ¼ x 2 x 6 ¼ In.	85.00
Vase, Butterfly, Tan, Round, 6 ¼ In.	5.50
Vase, Chromal, Scenic, Mountains, Trees, High Glaze, Round, Ring Foot, 6 ⅛ In.	287.00
Vase, Daisies, Green, 6 In.	60.00
Vase, Double Bud, Decorated Ivory, Flowers, Red, Blue, Yellow & Green, 1899, 6 ½ In.	95.00
Vase, Double Bud, Red, Blue, Yellow & Green On Ivory, 1920s, 6 ¼ x 6 ¼ In.	95.00
Vase, Landsun, Mottled Blue To Brown, 6 In.	23.00
Vase, Marbleized, Brown, Green, Tan Veining, Tapered, 7 ½ In.	23.00
Vase, Marbleized, Brown, Tan Veining, 4 In.	9.00
Vase, Marbleized, Green, Red, Brown, Handles, 11 In.	104.00
Vase, Moss Aztec, Vestal Virgins, 6 ¾ In.	35.00
Vase, Shadow Ware, Drippy Brown Glaze, 6 ¾ In.	40.00
Vase, Shadow Ware, Green, Orange Streak, 8 ¾ In.	29.00
Wall Pocket, Daisy, Brown Glaze, Triangle, 7 ¾ In.	35.00
Wall Pocket, Moss Aztec, Embossed Berries, Brown, Green, Triangle, Signed, Ferrell, 7 ½ In.	29.00

PETRUS REGOUT, *see Maastricht category.*

PEWABIC POTTERY was founded by Mary Chase Perry Stratton in 1903 in Detroit, Michigan. The company made many types of art pottery, including pieces with matte green glaze and an iridescent crystalline glaze. The company continued working until the death of Mary Stratton in 1961. It was reactivated by Michigan State University in 1968.

PEWABIC

Bowl, Copper Luster Glaze, Turquoise, Pedestal, Wide Rim, Domed Round Foot, 1 ½ x 3 In.	127.00
Bowl, Green Iridescent Glaze, Mark, 2 ½ x 5 ¾ In.	180.00
Candlestick, Green Iridescent, Gray Glaze, Round Spread Foot, Rolled Rim, Mich., c.1900, 6 In.	118.00
Plaque, Ohio State University, Logo, Arched, Pink Over Green, Marked, 7 ¾ x 7 ⅝ In.	403.00
Plate, 5 Panels, Black Rook On Branch, Paper Label, 10 In.	748.00
Plate, Rabbit & Tree Border, Yellow & Green, M.C. Perry, c.1905, 9 In. Diam.	938.00
Tile, Boy On Fish, Green, 4 x 4 In.	60.00
Tile, Sailboat, In Circle, Brown, To Tan, 4 x 4 In.	35.00
Trivet, Globe, North & South America, Teal Matte Glaze, Round, 6 ¾ In.	180.00
Vase, Black, Turquoise Blotches, c.1920, 8 ½ x 8 In. ....*Illus*	1920.00
Vase, Blue Iridescent, Luster Glaze, Shouldered, Tapered, Rolled Rim, Marked, 11 ¼ In.	863.00
Vase, Blue Luster Glaze, 10 ½ x 7 ¾ In.	875.00
Vase, Blue, Flared Rim, 1995, 5 ¾ In.	40.00
Vase, Bronze Metallic Glaze, Bulbous, Impressed Mark, 6 x 7 ½ In.	1586.00
Vase, Bulbous, Bronze Glaze, 6 x 7 ½ In.	1300.00
Vase, Bulbous, Horizontal Striations, Shaded Blue Iridescent Glaze, 5 ½ x 5 In.	1200.00
Vase, Cream, Green, Brown Glaze, Shouldered, Marked, 5 x 5 In.	366.00
Vase, Gray Matte Glaze, Impressed Logo, 4 ¾ In. ....*Illus*	230.00
Vase, Green Matte Glaze, Stylized Leaves, Purple Rim, Marked, 5 In.	240.00
Vase, Green Metallic Glaze, Bronze Accents, Shouldered, Impressed, 7 x 6 In.	1586.00
Vase, Metallic Luster, Blue, Green & Tan, Marked, Shouldered, 6 In.	518.00
Vase, Red, Brown, Green Metallic Glaze, Blue Crystalline Highlights, Round, 4 ½ x 4 In.	2562.00
Vase, Round, Red & Green Metallic Glaze, Blue Highlights, Marked, 4 x 4 In.	2100.00
Vase, Shouldered, Cream, Green & Brown Glaze, Marked, 5 x 5 In.	300.00
Vase, Shouldered, Green Glaze, Bronze Accents, Marked, 7 x 6 In.	1300.00
Vase, Squat, Shouldered, Green, Brown & Blue Iridescent Glaze, 5 ½ In.	454.00
Vase, Tan, Brown Matte Glaze, Shouldered, 4 ½ x 7 In.	938.00

PEWTER is a metal alloy of tin and lead. Some of the pewter made after 1840 has a slightly different composition and is called Britannia metal. This later type of pewter was worked by machine; the earlier pieces were made by hand. In the 1920s pewter came back into fashion and pieces were often marked *Genuine Pewter.* Eighteenth-, nineteenth-, and twentieth-century examples are listed here.

Ashtray, Nude, Figural, Gold Plated, 3 Legs, Leaves, 31 In.................................. 450.00
Baptismal Bowl, Leonard, Reed & Barton, Ribbed Stem & Foot, Mass., c.1840, 6 x 7 ¾ In. 593.00
Basin, Blakeslee Barns Inside Well, c.1815, 1 ¾ x 6 ⅝ In. 652.00
Basin, Blakeslee Barns, c.1815, 2 ¼ x 9 In................................... 237.00 to 474.00
Basin, Love, c.1790, 2 x 11 ⅜ In. 1067.00
Basin, Lovebird, Love Touchmark, 3 x 11 ½ In. 353.00
Basin, Molded Rim, London Mark, England, 3 x 11 ¾ In. 71.00
Basin, Thomas Badger, Wide Rim, c.1800, 2 x 8 In............................ 148.00
Basin, Thomas Boardman, Ribbed Rim, Conn., c.1840, 1 ⅞ x 6 ½ In. 182.00
Basin, Thomas Danforth III, Philadelphia, c.1800, 3 x 12 In........... 356.00
Beaker, Boardman & Hart, New York, c.1840, 5 ¼ In. 504.00
Beaker, Inverted Bell Shape, Spread Foot, Flared Lip, Incised Lines, c.1840, 2 ½ In. ... 85.00
Beaker, J.B. Woodbury, Cylinder, Ribbed, New England, c.1830, 3 In. 178.00
Beaker, Peter Derr, Cylindrical, c.1850, 3 In. 365.00
Beaker, Thomas D. Boardman, Lucius Hart, Mark, 1700s, 4 x 3 In., Pair 2124.00
Beaker, Thomas Danforth II, Cylinder, Conn., c.1770, 5 ¼ In............... 1007.00
Bedpan, Boardman & Co., Round, Handle, c.1840, 10 ½ In. 326.00
Biscuit Jar, Liberty & Co., Hammered, Repousse Flowers, 5 ½ x 5 ½ In........ 427.00
Biscuit Jar, Liberty & Co., Hammered, Tudric, Stylized Repousse Flowers, 5 x 5 In.......... 350.00
Bowl, Charcoal, Shaped Cup, Lobed Rim, Gem Flowers, Carved Stone Handle, Chinese, 2 x 6 In... 575.00
Bowl, Crossman, West & Leonard, Lobed, Footed, Mass., c.1830, 3 ⅝ x 6 ½ In........ 444.00
Bowl, David Melville, Flared Rim, Inscribed S, Touchmark, 1700s, 2 x 8 In............ 353.00
Bowl, Robert Graham, James Wardrop, Stamped, Glasgow, Scotland, 16 In............. 472.00
Bucket, Cone Shape, Drop Ring Handles, Flared Rim, Beaded Foot, English, Zinn, 7 ¼ x 7 ⅜ In.. 94.00
Butter, Liberty & Co., Tudric, Green Glass Liner, Archibald Knox, England, c.1905, 7 In.   900.00 to 1098.00
Candlestick, Chamber, Roswell Gleason, Ring Handles, Touchmark, Dorchester, 3 ½ In., Pair. 529.00
Candlestick, Flagg & Homan, Baluster, Cincinnati, c.1850, 5 ¼ In., Pair................. 1645.00
Candlestick, Freeman Porter, Flared Base, Maine, c.1850, 6 ¼ In., Pair........... 711.00
Candlestick, Fuller & Smith, Tapered Standard, Conn., c.1850, 8 ½ In. 415.00
Candlestick, Henry Hopper, Attached Holder & Saucer, New York, c.1845, 5 In., Pair.............. 1067.00
Candlestick, Removable Boheche, Tapered Shafts, Domed Base, c.1820, 10 In., Pair............. 178.00
Candlestick, Sellew & Co., Baluster, Bobeches, Cincinnati, 1830-60, 8 In., Pair........... 588.00
Chalice, George III, Acorn Knop, Engraved Bow, Scotland, Marked 1794, 8 ¾ In., Pair........... 885.00
Chalice, J.C. Heyne, Ribbed, Banded, Lancaster, Pa., c.1760, 8 ¾ In. 11258.00
Chalice, Johann Christoph Heyne, Lancaster, c.1760, 8 ¾ In. 5925.00
Chalice, Leonard, Reed & Barton, Mass., c.1835, 7 ¼ In., Pair 356.00
Chalice, Peter Young, Maker's Mark, New York, Late 1700s, 8 ½ x 2 ½ In....... 3540.00
Chalice, Peter Young, Turned Stem, Stepped Base, New York, c.1785, 8 ⅜ In. 5451.00
Chalice, Raised, Molded Base, Concave Stem, Wedding Band Knop, Tulip Cup, Flared Rim, 9 x 4 In. 94.00
Chalice, Roger, Smith & Co., Stepped Base, Embossed, Touchmark, New Haven, c.1850, 7 In.. 121.00
Chalice, Tapered, Knopped Stem, Dome Foot, 10 In., Pair 590.00
Chalice, Thomas Danforth Boardman, Shaped Pedestal, Conn., 7 ¼ In., Pair.. 147.00
Chalice, Timothy Brigden, Stepped Base, Albany, c.1810, 8 ¾ In., Pair 7110.00
Chalice, William Calder, Rhode Island, c.1835, 6 In., Pair 948.00
Charger, Gershom Jones, Round, c.1800, 13 ½ In. 288.00
Charger, John Skinner, Mass., c.1775, 15 In............................ 1185.00
Charger, Nathaniel Austin, Mass., c.1780, 15 In.......................... 711.00
Charger, Tho. Leapidge, Recessed Center, Engraved Rim, Bird, Vine, London, c.1690, 21 ¾ In.. 4130.00
Charger, Townsend & Crompton, Molded Rim, England, 15 In. 207.00
Chocolate Pot, Lid, Sailboat, Church, Red, Gilt Painted, Brass Stand, Dutch, 17 ½ In............ 177.00
Coffeepot, Allen Porter, Gooseneck Spout, Dome Lid, Scroll Handle, Touchmark, 11 ½ In. 147.00
Coffeepot, Ashbil Griswold, 10 In.. 266.00
Coffeepot, Boardman & Hart, New York, c.1840, 11 ½ In. 119.00
Coffeepot, Bulbous, Flared Pedestal, Applied Gooseneck Spout, Cast Handle, 10 ½ In............. 59.00
Coffeepot, I. Trask, Lighthouse Shape, Dome Lid, Engraved Borders, Serpentine Spout, c.1830, 12 In. 770.00
Coffeepot, Liberty & Co., Tudric, Organic Repousse, Signed Archibald Knox, 1905, 6 x 4 In.... 625.00
Coffeepot, Liberty & Co., Tudric, Repousse Design, Archibald Knox, c.1905, 6 x 4 In............. 1220.00
Coffeepot, R. Gleason, Baluster Shape, Hinged Lid, Molded Base, Painted Handle, c.1850, 10 ¾ In. .. 237.00
Coffeepot, R. Gleason, Wood Handle, 11 In. 75.00
Coffeepot, Roswell Gleason, Footed, Black Finial & Handle, c.1840, 9 ½ In. 119.00
Coffeepot, Rufus Dunham, Reeded Bands, Black Angle Handle, Footed, Marked, c.1845, 11 ¾ In. 296.00
Coffeepot, W. Calder, Black Scroll Handle, Tapered, Rhode Island, c.1835, 11 In............... 326.00
Coffeepot, Wrigglework, Tulips, Distelfinks, Inscribed Sarah Gargas, Willoughby, Pa., c.1840, 11 In. 2607.00
Compote, Art Nouveau, Figural, Nymph, Blossoming Lily Pads, Dove, WMF, 1900, 8 ¼ x 11 ¾ In.. 360.00
Creamer, Parks Boyd, Beaded Rim, Philadelphia, c.1805, 5 ⅜ In............ 5451.00
Creamer, Scalloped Spout, Shaped Handle, Footed, c.1770, 4 In............... 2370.00

Peking Glass, Ginger Jar, Lid,
Honeycomb, Cased White To Turquoise,
1800s, 7 ⅜ In.
$633.00

James D. Julia Auctioneers

Peking Glass, Vase, Battle Scene, Cameo,
Red To Snowflake, Bottle Shape, Marked,
c.1750, 9 ¼ In.
$4,600.00

James D. Julia Auctioneers

Peking Glass, Vase, Green Overlay,
Opaque White, Lotus Flowers, Leaves,
Marked, 1800, 8 In.
$1,215.00

P

Skinner, Inc.

TIP
An old pewter cleaner is a mixture of mild scouring powder and olive oil. This is okay for everyday pieces, but too harsh for top quality collector's pieces.

Pen, Writing Brush, Soapstone, Carved, Animal Hair Brush, Chinese, 1900s, 15 In. $173.00

James D. Julia Auctioneers

Pepsi-Cola, Sign, Pepsi-Cola Cops, Pepsi & Pete, 6 Pack, Cardboard, Die Cut, c.1940, 14 ½ x 21 ¼ In. $209.00

Hake's Americana & Collectibles

Perfume Bottle, DeVilbiss, Art Glass, Bronze, Jeweled Mounts, 7 ½ In. $1,783.00

Cottone Auctions

Creamer, William Will, Footed, Philadelphia, c.1780, 4 ¾ In.	8295.00
Crumb Tray, Tudric, Hammered, Organic Design, Blue Enamel, Repousse, Marked, 10 x 4 In.	425.00
Cup, Thomas Boardman, Footed, Ribbed Base, 2 Handles, c.1840, 6 ¼ In.	652.00
Dish, Art Nouveau, Divided, Flowers, Irregular Leaf Rim, Stamped Silberzinn, Germany, c.1900, 9 In.	60.00
Dish, Deep, James Porter, c.1800, 13 ⅛ In.	3402.00
Dish, Deep, Wide Rim, Joseph Leddell, c.1740, 13 ½ In.	593.00
Dish, Hiram Yale & Co., Banded Rim, Conn., c.1825, 11 ⅛ In.	326.00
Dish, Thomas Danforth III, Philadelphia, c.1800, 11 ½ In.	668.00
Eggcup, Banded Rim, Peter Derr, c.1830, 3 In.	3318.00
Ewer, Bulbous Body, Pedestal, Raised Foot, Applied Loop Handle, Graduated Beaded Handle, 8 ½ In.	35.00
Ewer, Lid, Flared Foot, Bulbous, Flared Mouth, Applied Loop Handle, Hinge Base, Thumbpiece, 8 In.	295.00
Flagon, Communion, Lid, Boardman & Co., Hartford, 14 In.	1410.00
Flagon, George II, Tapered, Molded Rim, S Scroll Thumbpiece, Scotland, 1742, 13 In., Pair	2360.00
Flagon, Hinged Lid, Double Acorn, S-Strap Handle, Ringed Stirrup Handle, 1800s, 27 In.	153.00
Flagon, Hinged Lid, Scroll Handle, Boardman & Co., 12 ¼ In.	711.00
Flagon, Lighthouse Shape, Domed Lid, Fillet, Scrolled Handle, Thumbpiece, c.1825, 10 In.	356.00
Flagon, Lighthouse Shape, Double Scroll Handle, Molded Thumbpiece, O. Trask, c.1830, 11 ¾ In.	711.00
Flagon, Presentation, Engraved, Thomas Danforth Boardman, Hartford, Conn., c.1825, 11 ½ In.	502.00
Flagon, Ribbed, Banded, Smith & Feltman, New York, c.1850, 10 ½ In.	122.00
Flagon, Ribbed, Boardman & Hart, New York, c.1835, 8 In.	2430.00
Flagon, Scroll Thumbpiece, Engraved Wick Chapel 1799, Robert Kinnieburgh, Scotland, 10 ½ In.	649.00
Flagon, Scrolled Handle, Ribbed, Banded, Samuel Danforth, Conn., c.1805, 13 ¼ In.	11258.00
Flask, Concentric Banding, John Bassett, New York, c.1750, 4 ¾ In.	889.00
Flask, J.C. Heyne, Lancaster, Pa., c.1760, 4 ⅝ In.	1778.00
Flask, Lid, Concentric Line Embossed, c.1750, 4 ¼ In.	326.00
Flask, Lid, James Weekes, New York, c.1830, 6 ¾ In.	356.00
Funnel, Reeded, Frederick Bassett, New York, 1775, 5 ¾ In.	608.00
Hot Water Urn, 3 Spouts, Cabriole Legs, Gilt Sprigs, Figure On Horse, Cow, c.1785, 18 In.	338.00
Humidor, Relief Zodiac Symbols, Finial, Woman's Profile, Cedar Lined, Oscar B. Bach, 7 x 4 ¼ In.	173.00
Knife, Butter, Liberty & Co., Tudric, c.1905, 1 x 5 ¾ In.	350.00
Ladle, Sellew & Co., Engraved Initials, Cincinnati, 1830-60, 11 In.	676.00
Ladle, William Will, c.1775, 11 ¾ In.	1896.00
Lamp, Roswell Gleason, Fluid, Bulbous Rim, Stepped Base, Mass., c.1840, 8 In., Pair	563.00
Lamp, Single Lens, Drum Shaped Font, Camphene Burners, c.1850, 8 ¼ In.	593.00
Measure, Boardman & Hart, Reeded Bands, Handle, New York, 1829, 5 In., Pair	830.00
Measure, Side Spout, Scroll Handles, c.1850, 7 In., Qt., Pair	118.00
Measure, Thomas Boardman, Ribbed, Handle, New York, 1826, 6 ⅞ In.	1007.00
Mold, Candle, 18 Tubes, Pine, Pa., 1800s, 19 x 19 ¼ In.	1067.00
Mold, Candle, 24 Tubes, Wood Frame, c.1810, 17 ½ x 21 ¾ x 6 ¼ In. ....*Illus*	649.00
Mold, Candle, 24 Tubes, Wood, 16 x 21 In.	708.00
Mold, Candle, 24 Tubes, Wood, Metal, Stamped J. Calverley, 18 x 21 In.	1659.00
Mold, Ice Cream, Ship, 2 Sections, 4 Pt., 1898, 13 In.	470.00
Mug, Boardman & Hart, c.1840, 3 ¾ In.	1840.00
Mug, Boardman & Hart, Medial Band, Scrolled Handle, c.1835, Half Pint, 3 ¾ In.	652.00
Mug, Frederick Bassett, Ribbed Bands, New York, c.1775, 6 ⅛ In.	20145.00
Mug, Hammered, Double Scroll Handle, Rim Band, c.1795, 5 ⅝ In.	356.00
Mug, Joseph Austen & Son, Cork Ireland, Pt., 4 ½ In.	236.00
Mug, Nathaniel Austin, Banded, Mass., c.1780, 6 In.	2607.00
Mug, Parks Boyd, Philadelphia, c.1805, 4 ¼ In.	3555.00
Mug, Samuel Hamlin, Banded Base, Rhode Island, c.1820, 4 ⅜ In.	3555.00
Mug, Samuel Hamlin, Scroll Handle, Providence, R.I., 1767-1856, 4 ½ In.	411.00
Mug, Thomas & Sherman Boardman, Conn., c.1835, 5 ⅞ In.	770.00
Mug, Thomas Boardman, Conn., c.1830, 4 ⅝ In.	356.00
Picture Frame, J. Strongwater, Enamel, Crystal, Orchids, 5 x 3 ¾ In.	246.00
Pitcher, Cider, Scroll Handle, England, 9 ½ In.	266.00
Pitcher, David Curtiss, Banded Base, c.1830, 7 ¾ In.	474.00
Pitcher, George Richardson, Rhode Island, c.1830, 7 ½ In.	182.00
Pitcher, Hinged Lid, Handle, 1800s, 12 ½ x 7 In.	288.00
Pitcher, Hinged Lid, Henry Hopper, Reeded Bands, New York, c.1845, 9 In.	1007.00
Pitcher, Rufus Dunham, Westbrook, Maine, c.1850, 6 ¾ In.	178.00
Pitcher, Thomas Boardman, Conn., c.1840, 10 In.	444.00
Pitcher, Woman Shape, Flemish, c.1890, 15 x 6 In.	2185.00
Plate Set, Bush & Perkins, c.1780, 6 ¾ In., 4 Piece	118.00
Plate, Francis Bassett, Wide Border, New York, c.1750, 8 ⅜ In.	1896.00
Plate, Gershom Jones, Rhode Island, c.1790, 8 ¼ In.	356.00
Plate, London, Rim Has Engraved Crowned B, England, 1700s, 9 ¾ In., 6 Piece	294.00

P

Plate, Marked Cornelius Bradford, Flat Rim, c.1755, 9 ⅞ In.	1896.00
Plate, Peter Young, Wide Rim, New York, c.1785, 8 ⅞ In.	1422.00
Plate, Robert Palethorp, Jr., 7 ¾ In., Pair	474.00
Plate, Samuel Kilbourn, Baltimore, c.1825, 7 ¾ In.	296.00
Plate, Thomas & Sherman Boardman, Conn., c.1840, 6 ½ In.	326.00
Plate, Thomas Badger, 8 In.	264.00
Plate, Thomas Badger, Boston, c.1805, 12 ⅛ In.	504.00
Plate, Thomas Byles, Philadelphia, c.1755, 9 ¼ In.	504.00
Plate, William Billings, Stepped Rim, Rhode Island, c.1800, 8 ¼ In.	444.00
Porringer, Bulbous, Boss Bottom, Pierced Flowered Handle, c.1825, 4 ¾ In.	770.00
Porringer, David Melville, Tab Handle, Rhode Island, c.1770, 5 In.	1304.00
Porringer, Elisha Kirk, Tab Handle, York, Penn., c.1785, 5 ¼ In.	999.00
Porringer, Frederick Bassett, Openwork Handle, New York, c.1775, 5 In.	1778.00
Porringer, John Will, Cutout Handle, New York, c.1760, 5 ⅛ In.	2607.00
Porringer, Richard Lee, Pierced Handle, c.1800, 2 ¼ In.	181.00
Porringer, Samuel Danforth, Openwork Handle, Conn., c.1805, 5 In.	1185.00
Porringer, Samuel Hamlin, Jr., Rhode Island, 8 In.	354.00
Porringer, Short Openwork Handle, Marked R.G., c.1800, 4 ¼ In.	486.00
Porringer, Thomas & Sherman Boardman, Openwork Scrolled Handle, Conn., c.1830, 5 In.	207.00
Porringer, William Billings, Openwork Handle, Rhode Island, c.1800, 5 ½ In.	3318.00
Porringer, William Calder, Openwork Handle, Rhode Island, c.1830, 5 ¼ In.	119.00
Porringer, William Will, Pierced Handle, Philadelphia, 1764-1798, 1 ¼ x 7 ½ In.	2596.00
Punch Bowl, Presentation, To President Alvan Macauley, By Packard-Boston Org., c.1910, 8 x 14 In.	147.00
Salt, William Will, Footed, Philadelphia, c.1790, 2 ¼ In.	711.00
Sugar, Lid, George Richardson, Rhode Island, c.1835, 5 ¼ In.	652.00
Sugar, Lid, Johann Christoph Heyne, Lobed, Lancaster, Pa., c.1765, 5 ¼ In.	23700.00
Sugar, Lid, Thomas Danforth II, Banded, Footed, Conn., c.1770, 5 In.	2370.00
Sugar, Lid, William Will, Beaded Rim, Philadelphia, c.1775, 5 ½ In.	21330.00
Sugar, Lid, William Will, Ribbed Finial, Footed, Philadelphia, c.1775, 4 ¾ In.	3555.00
Tankard, Banded, Dome Lid, Scroll Handle, England, 11 ¼ In.	2006.00
Tankard, Banded, Flared, Scroll Thumbpiece, Engraved Kirk Musselburgh 1786, Scotland, 10 In.	1062.00
Tankard, Eagle, Oak Leaves, Judgenstil, Germany, Stamped, 13 ½ In.	203.00
Tankard, Hinged Lid, Henry Will, Dragon Handle, New York, c.1775, 7 In.	11850.00
Tankard, Hinged Lid, Love, Scrolled Handle, c.1790, 7 ½ In.	2844.00
Tankard, Hinged Lid, William Will, Philadelphia, c.1775, 7 ⅞ In.	15405.00
Tankard, Kayserzinn, Stylized Leaves, Jugendstil, Germany, 15 In. ....Illus	203.00
Tankard, Love, Banded, Philadelphia, c.1790, 7 ½ In.	5214.00
Tankard, Watts & Harton, England, 7 In.	266.00
Tea & Coffee Set, Peter Behrens, Nickel Plated, Stamped, Eduard Hueck, c.1904, 4 Piece.... Illus	813.00
Teapot, Ashbil Griswold, Ribbed, Black Handle, Conn., c.1810, 6 ½ In.	178.00
Teapot, Dome Lid, Bulbous, Reeded Spread Foot, Scroll Handle & Spout, Black Paint, c.1830, 7 In.	59.00
Teapot, Israel Trask, Federal, Oval, Engraved Shield Shape Monogram, Touchmark, 8 In.	2115.00
Teapot, Josiah Danforth, Banded, Black Squared Handle, Conn., c.1830, 7 ¾ In.	296.00
Teapot, Pear Shape, Dome Lid, Painted Handle, Marked, c.1825, 7 ¼ In.	1007.00
Teapot, Samuel Danforth, Beaded Lid Rim, Conn., c.1805, 7 In.	1185.00
Teapot, Samuel Danforth, Conn., c.1805, 8 ¾ In.	395.00
Teapot, Thomas Boardman, Engraved, Marked, XX, 8 In. ....Illus	964.00
Teapot, Thomas Boardman, New York, c.1840, 7 ¼ In.	385.00
Teapot, William Will, Wood Handle, Philadelphia, c.1770, 6 ½ In.	37920.00
Teapot, William Will, Wood Handle, Philadelphia, c.1780, 6 In.	41310.00
Tureen, Lid, Duck Shape, Gem Set, Koi On Back Handle, Chinese, c.1910, 9 x 12 In.	1150.00
Urn, Greek Revival, Relief Frieze, Horse Drawn Chariot, Anthemion, Swan Handles, 18 x 9 In., Pair...	943.00
Vase, Liberty & Co., Tudric, Tapered, Charles Annesly Voysey, 1905, 3 ¼ x 9 In.	793.00
Wine Pot, Moon Shape, Engraved Poem, Jade Handle Spout & Finial, Chinese, c.1900, 8 ½ x 6 ½ In.	5015.00

PHOENIX BIRD, or Flying Phoenix, is the name given to a blue-and-white dinnerware popular between 1900 and World War II. A variant is known as Flying Turkey. Most of this dinnerware was made in Japan for sale in the dime stores in America. It is still being made.

Chocolate Pot, Flying Birds, 6-Sided, Finial, 27 Oz., 9 In.	58.00
Cup & Saucer, Flying Birds, Marked	21.00
Gravy Boat, Underplate, Birds, Japan, 7 In.	39.00
Salt & Pepper, Birds, Globular, Japan	16.00
Sugar & Creamer, Flying Birds, Japan	25.00
Tureen, Lid, Flying Birds, Handles, Round, 7 ½ In.	69.00

PHOENIX BIRD

Perfume Bottle, Hand Shape, Burmese Glass, Queen's Pattern, Dotted Daisies, Stopper, Mt. Washington, 7 In.
$6,613.00

Early Auction Co.

Pewabic, Vase, Black, Turquoise Blotches, c.1920, 8 ½ x 8 In.
$1,920.00

DuMouchelles Art Gallery

Pewabic, Vase, Gray Matte Glaze, Impressed Logo, 4 ¾ In.
$230.00

Humler & Nolan

Pewter, Mold, Candle, 24 Tubes, Wood Frame, c.1810, 17 ½ x 21 ¾ x 6 ¼ In.
$649.00

Conestoga Auction Co., Inc.

Pewter, Tankard, Kayserzinn, Stylized
Leaves, Jugendstil, Germany, 15 In.
$203.00

Leslie Hindman Auctioneers

Pewter, Tea & Coffee Set, Peter Behrens,
Nickel Plated, Stamped, Eduard Hueck,
c.1904, 4 Piece
$813.00

Rago Arts & Auction Center

Pewter, Teapot, Thomas Boardman,
Engraved, Marked, XX, 8 In.
$964.00

Garth's Auctioneers & Appraisers

P

TIP

*Wear gloves when
handling valuable
photographs. The
oils and salts in your
skin can damage the
photos.*

PHOENIX GLASS Company was founded in 1880 in Pennsylvania. The firm made commercial products, such as lampshades, bottles, and glassware. Collectors today are interested in the "Sculptured Artware" made by the company from the 1930s until the mid-1950s. Some pieces of Phoenix glass are very similar to those made by the Consolidated Lamp and Glass Company. Phoenix made Reuben Blue, lavender, and yellow pieces. These colors were not used by Consolidated. In 1970 Phoenix became a division of Anchor Hocking, which was sold to the Newell Group in 1987. The factory is still working.

Vase, Berry & Leaf Design, Custard Yellow Ground, Cylinder, 18 In.	266.00
Vase, Bittersweet Pattern, Raised Purple Grapes, Leaves, Stem, 9 ½ x 5 In.	66.00
Vase, Nude Women, Veil Dancing, Pan Playing Syrinx, Panpipes, Peach & Blue, Urn, 11 ¾ In.	230.00
Vase, Wild Rose Design, Blooms & Buds, Coral Pin Wash Over Satin Crystal, 1934, 10 In.	250.00
Vase, Wild Rose, Blooms & Buds, Coral Pink Wash Over Satin Glass, 1933, 10 In.	250.00

PHONOGRAPHS, invented by Thomas Edison in 1877, have been made by many firms. This category also includes other items associated with the phonograph. Jukeboxes and Records are listed in their own categories.

Brunswick, Ultona, Oak Case, Disc, Slide-Out Trays, Floor Model, c.1918, 47 x 22 In.	472.00
Capitol, Lamp, Shade Lifts To Reveal Player, Burns-Pollock Electric Mfg. Co., 28 In. ... *Illus*	1020.00
Columbia, BK, Cylinder, Lyre Reproducer, Crank, Lid	400.00
Columbia, Graphophone B1, Sterling, Red 8-Panel Horn	600.00
Columbia, Graphophone BII, Improved Sterling, Oak Spear Tip, Rear Horn	1300.00
Columbia, Graphophone Q, Cylinder, Reproducer, Lid	300.00
Columbia, Graphophone, Cylinder, Crank	472.00
Columbia, Model AZ, Cylinder, Lyre Reproducer, Crank, Red Morning Glory 8-Panel Horn	600.00
Decca, Cowboy, Horses, Suitcase Model	70.00
Doll, Edison, Talking Machine, Glass Eye, Open Mouth, Tin Torso, Bahr & Proschild, 22 In.	7260.00
Edison, Amberola, Cylinder, Oak Case, 17 ½ x 22 In.	531.00
Edison, Amberola, Model 30, Oak Case, Floor Cylinder, 44 x 16 In.	620.00
Edison, Disc, Record Player, Leather Case, 1928	189.00
Edison, Fireside, Model A, Cylinder, Black Cygnet Horn	944.00
Edison, Fireside, Model A, Cylinder, C Reproducer, Black Cone Horn, Gold Band	325.00
Edison, Gem, Cylinder, Black Cone Horn, Gold Band & Lid	425.00
Edison, Gem, Model B, Model C Reproducer, Brass Horn, Oak Case, 2-Minute Cylinder, 1905..	635.00
Edison, Home, Metal Horn, Brass Tip, 16 x 12 In.	840.00
Edison, Model A, Opera, Cylinder, Cygnet Horn, 21 x 36 In.	4130.00
Edison, Standard, Cylinder, Horn	531.00
Edison, Standard, Dome Lid, Handle, Crank	420.00
Edison, Standard, Model C Reproducer, Oak, 18-In. Morning Glory Horn, Records, 13 x 12 In... *Illus*	460.00
Edison, Standard, Model S Soundbox, Crane, Wood Horn, 4-Minute Cylinder	2859.00
Edison, Standard, Suitcase Model, Brass Horn, Handle, Crank	450.00
Edison, Triumph, Cylinder, Hand Painted Flower Oak Case, Crank	649.00
Hand Crank, The Graphophone, Hammered Tin Horn, c.1900	720.00
Paillard, Oak Case, Disc, Blue Painted Horn, Swiss, c.1910, 18-In. Brass Bell Horn	885.00
Pathe, Diffuser, Mahogany Case, Disc, Crank, France, 14 x 20 ½ In.	472.00
Pathe, Grain Oak, Lid Horn, Disc, France, 15 x 18 In.	3776.00
Pathe, Gramophone, Horn, Metal Arm, 8-In. Disc, Speed Control, Box, France, c.1900, 10 ¾ In... *Illus*	800.00
Premier, Mahogany, Disc, Record Player, Floor Model, 58 x 27 In.	767.00
RCA, His Master's Voice, Disc, Mahogany Horn, England, 15 In.	767.00
Regina, Style 140, Horn, Plays 15 ½-In. Discs, 40 x 20 ½ In. ... *Illus*	4800.00
Standard, Model A, Standard Talking Machine Co., 12 x 11 ½ In. ... *Illus*	420.00
Stromberg Carlson, Cabinet, AM-FM Radio, Turntable, Wood, c.1947	120.00
Victrola, No. 300, Sound Box, 2 Side Cabinets, c.1920, 37 x 38 In.	150.00
Victor III, Disc, Painted Flowers, Exhibition Reproducer, 9-Panel Horn	900.00
Victor M, Disc, Concert Reproducer, Record Screw, Brass Bell Horn, Crank	900.00
Victor Victrola, Oak, Crank, 41 In.	180.00
Victor, Eldridge R. Johnson, Brass Horn, Concert Reproducer	2300.00
Victor, Monarch Special, Music Master Wood Horn, 11 x 12 ¼ In. ... *Illus*	3300.00
Victor, V, Talking Machine, Oak, Disc, Horn, 16 x 21 In.	2655.00
Victor, VV-VI, Oak Case, Disc, 11 x 15 In.	148.00
Victor, VV-VXA, Victrola, Record Player, Mahogany Case, 14 ½ x 17 In.	413.00
Victor, VV-XL, Mahogany Case, Exhibition Reproducer, 1915, 44 x 22 ¾ In.	403.00
Zenith, Model J880R, Cobra-Matic, Console, Radio, Multi-Speed Turntable, 1950s	270.00

PHOTOGRAPHY items are listed here. The first photograph was a view from a window in France taken in 1826. The commercially successful photograph started with the daguerreotype introduced in 1839. Today all sorts of photographs and photographic equipment are collected. Albums were popular in Victorian times. Cartes de visite, popular after 1854, were mounted on 2 ½-by-4-inch cardboard. Cabinet cards were introduced in 1866. These were mounted on 4 ¼-by-6 ½-inch cards. Stereo views are listed under Stereo Card. Stereoscopes are listed in their own section.

Album, Tintype, Leather Cover, Gold Embossed, Hinged Brass Clasp, Gem Size	153.00
Albumen Print, Abraham Lincoln Funeral, Monument Square, Cleveland, Sweeney, 11 x 14 In.	1528.00
Albumen Print, Abraham Lincoln, Oval Mat, Frame, G.B. Ayres, 1860, 12 In.	1293.00
Albumen Print, African American Union Recruits Joining Up, 7 x 9 ½ In.	780.00
Albumen Print, Blackfoot Brave & Pony, Rifle, W. Notman, 7 ½ x 9 ½ In.	2640.00
Albumen Print, Good Buffalo, Peace Medal, Hair Feather, A. Gardner, c.1870, 11 In.	1410.00
Albumen Print, Indian Squaws, Blackfoot Camp, Notman & Son, 7 x 9 In.	646.00
Albumen Print, Lone Wolf, Silver Cross, 2 Hair Feathers, A. Gardner, c.1870, 10 In.	1763.00
Albumen Print, Pvt. George Warner, Gettysburg Amputee, 1863	823.00
Albumen Print, R. Linn With Stereoview Camera, Lookout Mountain, 1863, 11 In.	22325.00
Albumen Print, Two Whistles, Indian Prisoner, O.S. Goff, 7 ½ x 9 ¼ In.	999.00
Albumen Print, U.S. Customs House, Richmond, Va., 1865, 8 x 10 In.	499.00
Ambrotype, Butcher & Son, About To Slaughter Sheep, Case, ¼ Plate....Illus	881.00
Ambrotype, Confederate 2nd Lieutenant, Drawing His Sword, c.1861, ⅙ Plate....Illus	4700.00
Ambrotype, Outing At Niagara Falls, Platt D. Babbit, c.1860, 7 x 9 In.	4025.00
Ambrotype, Street Scene, Stagecoach, Figures, Buildings, Embossed Paper Case, ¼ Plate	5333.00
Ambrotype, Street Scene, Thayers Inn, c.1850, ¼ Plate	5333.00
Ambrotype, Texas Confederate Soldier With Star Belt, Frame, ⅙ Plate	4500.00
Ambrotype, Virginia Militiaman, Mount Vernon Guards, Civil War, Frame, ⅑ Plate	240.00
Button, Streetcar, Pink Tint, c.1910, 2 ¾ In. ....Illus	69.00
Cabinet Card, American Horse Sioux Chief, J.N. Choate, Carlisle, Pa.	499.00
Cabinet Card, Arapaho Indian Camp Family, Buffalo Skin Teepee, Will Soule, 1870	600.00
Cabinet Card, Columbia Light Roadster, 3 Riders, Nesbit, Bloomsburg, Pa., c.1885	144.00
Cabinet Card, High Wheeler, Rider, Taylor, Rochester, N.Y., 1883	115.00
Cabinet Card, Kiowa Indian Camp Family, Buffalo Skin, Teepee, Will Soule, 1870	420.00
Cabinet Card, Red Cloud, Young Spotted Tail & C.P. Jordan, c.1882	1293.00
Cabinet Card, Shaker Elder, Henry Blinn, Signed, Canterbury, New Hampshire, 4 ⅛ x 2 ½ In.	293.00
Camera, Daguerreotype, Brass Handle, Sliding Box Focus, France, 1940s, Whole Plate, 11 x 8 In.	1880.00
Camera, Kodak, Brownie, c.1935	35.00
Camera, Kodak, Leather Bound, Lacquered Metal Box, Walter Teague, 1930, 9 In....Illus	1000.00
Camera, Nikon S2 Chrome, 50 mm, c.1955	830.00
Camera, Rochester Optical & Camera Co., King, Mahogany, Brass Case, Bakelite Plate, c.1900..Illus	444.00
Camera, Zeiss, Ikon, Folding, Roll Film, Compur Rapid Shutter, Kodak Case, 1930s, 4 ¾ x 3 ½ In.	123.00
Carte De Visite, Little Brave, Arikara Scout, 7th Cavalry, c.1870	4113.00
Carte De Visite, Log Cabin, Painted Stippled Wood Frame, 7 ½ x 8 ¾ In.	71.00
Carte De Visite, Lt. Col. George A. Custer, S. Wing, March 1873	823.00
Carte De Visite, Lt. Thomas Tarbell, Civil War Soldier, Sitting, 1860s	480.00
Carte De Visite, Major General Benjamin Cheatham, Autograph, M. Brady, 1865	1175.00
Daguerreotype, 2 Children, Brother, Sister, Case, J. Vannerson, Double ⅙ Plate	176.00
Daguerreotype, Baby, Postmortem, Tinted, Stamped Anson, Full Case, ⅙ Plate	470.00
Daguerreotype, Brigadier General, Persifor F. Smith, Post Mexican War, c.1855, Whole Plate	4700.00
Daguerreotype, Coal Miner, Frame, c.1850, ½ Plate, 4 ½ x 3 ¼ In.	5925.00
Daguerreotype, George Washington, Portrait, Hinged Leather Case, ¼ Plate	652.00
Daguerreotype, James Whitcomb, Indiana Governor, Case, 1851, ⅙ Plate	2938.00
Daguerreotype, Man With Colorful Cravat & Pocket Watch, 2 ¼ x 3 In.	382.00
Daguerreotype, Man With Tabletop Cutting Tool, ½ Case, ¼ Plate	4994.00
Daguerreotype, Sarah T. Bolton, Poet, Sitting, Crossed Arms, Case, 1850, ¼ Plate	3055.00
Daguerreotype, Trapper, Wool Jacket, Fur Cap, Rifle, Axe, Powder Horn, ⅙ Plate	14100.00
Graphotrope, Carte De Visite, 27 Photographs, William Walker, Patd. June 12th 1866, 8 In.. Illus	2133.00
Magic Lantern, Gun Metal Tin Burner Housing, Brass Mounts, Pat. 1861, Marcy Sciopticon, 19 In.	272.00
Photograph, 2 Men With Cart Of Chianti, Sepia, Oak Frame, 14 x 19 In.	118.00
Photograph, A. Lincoln Funeral Train, Harrisburg, Pa., Silver Gelatin, 12 x 14 In.	764.00
Photograph, Abraham Lincoln, Profile, Silver Print, A. Hesler, G. Ayres, 1860, 25 ¾ x 19 ½ In.	1700.00
Photograph, Airship, U.S.S. Akron, Dock, M. Bourke-White, 1931, 17 x 23 In.	2160.00
Photograph, Apache Reaper, Platinum, Signed, Edward Curtis, 1906, 5 ¾ x 7 ¾ In.	1410.00
Photograph, Armed Gun Boat Commodore Perry, Mathew Brady, c.1864, 7 ¾ x 5 ¾ In.	1020.00
Photograph, Bus Story, Man Out, 2 Children In, Bus, Silver Print, E. Bubley, 1947, 8 ½ x 13 In.	1700.00
Photograph, Chief Rain-In-The-Face & Wife, Wedding Day, Silver Gelatin, 6 x 8 In.	588.00
Photograph, Child Pea Picker, Silver Print, Dorothea Lange, 1935, 7 ½ x 9 ½ In.	4200.00
Photograph, Cincinnati League Park, Opening Game, Panorama, 1912, 50 In.	13200.00

Phonograph, Capitol, Lamp, Shade Lifts To Reveal Player, Burns-Pollock Electric Mfg. Co., 28 In.
$1,020.00

Morphy Auctions

Phonograph, Edison, Standard, Model C Reproducer, Oak, 18-In. Morning Glory Horn, Records, 13 x 12 In.
$460.00

James D. Julia Auctioneers

Phonograph, Pathe, Gramophone, Horn, Metal Arm, 8-In. Disc, Speed Control, Box, France, c.1900, 10 ¾ In.
$800.00

Skinner, Inc.

Phonograph, Regina, Style 140, Horn, Plays 15 ½-In. Discs, 40 x 20 ½ In. $4,800.00

Morphy Auctions

Phonograph, Standard, Model A, Standard Talking Machine Co., 12 x 11 ½ In. $420.00

Morphy Auctions

Phonograph, Victor, Monarch Special, Music Master Wood Horn, 11 x 12 ¼ In. $3,300.00

Morphy Auctions

Photograph, Civil War Veterans, Mauch Chunk, Welcome Home Celebration, Frame, 1919, 9 x 15 In.	118.00
Photograph, Civil War Veterans, Shaking Hands Over Angle War, 50th Anniversary, 1913, 17 x 20 In.	153.00
Photograph, Comanche Indians, Panorama, That Man Stone, Chickasha, Ok., 29 In.	382.00
Photograph, Electric Train, Electrification Of New York Extension, 15 x 19 In.	295.00
Photograph, Fifth Avenue, Horse, Photogravure, Tissue, Frame, Stieglitz, 1896, 9 x 12 In.	57500.00
Photograph, Gertrude Stein, Silver Print, Signed, Imogen Cunningham, 1937, 8 x 6 ½ In.	3600.00
Photograph, House Where Jesse James Was Killed, Silver Gelatin, April 3, 1882, 3 ¾ x 5 In.	588.00
Photograph, New York City, Third Ave. El Train View, Silver Print, Signed E. Erwitt, 1955, 17 x 12 In.	4200.00
Photograph, Organ Grinder, Street Singer, Silver Print, E. Atget, c.1899, 8 ½ x 6 ½ In.	2000.00
Photograph, Pauline De Rothschild, Signed Horst, Silver Print, 1940s, 9 ½ x 7 ½ In.	4600.00
Photograph, Pine Ridge Sioux Indians, Hot Springs, S.D., W.R. Cross, 1890, 5 x 7 In.	558.00
Photograph, Sanitary Dept., Mule Team Wagons, Black Workers, Managers, Frame, 11 x 57 In.	153.00
Photograph, Sepia, Girl, Toy Lamb, Fringed Chair, J. Loeffler, Tomkinsville, N.Y., Frame, 8 x 6 In.	35.00
Photograph, Sepia, President Lincoln, Son Tad, Oval Frame, Signed O. Kobler, 1865, 13 x 11 In.	142.00
Photograph, Sioux Indian Chiefs On Horseback, W.R. Cross, 1896, 7 ¼ x 9 In.	300.00
Photograph, Sioux Indians At Frontier Day, Cheyenne, Wyo., Panorama, 1924, 10 x 36 In.	480.00
Photograph, Sitting Bull, Silver Gelatin, D.F. Barry, Cardstock Mount, 7 x 9 In.	764.00
Photograph, Tree Lined Canal, Holland, Silver Print, A. Eisenstaedt, c.1978, 16 x 10 ¾ In.	5000.00
Photograph, Warren G. Harding Funeral Procession, Band, Caisson, Dignitaries, Frame, 11 x 40 In.	106.00
Photograph, World War I Cavalry, Dress Parade, 150 Mounted Troopers, Colors, Frame, 11 x 19 In.	83.00
Tintype, Confederate Bandsman, Charleston Grays, Holding Saxhorn, 1861	382.00
Tintype, Confederate First Sergeant, Civil War, Frame, ⅙ Plate	900.00
Tintype, Mounted Cavalry Trooper, Civil War, Frame, ⅙ Plate	1293.00

PIANO BABY is a collector's term. About 1880, the well-decorated home had a shawl on the piano. Bisque figures of babies were designed to help hold the shawl in place. They range in size from 6 to 18 inches. Most of the figures were made in Germany. Reproductions are being made. Other piano babies may be listed under manufacturers' names.

Baby, Crawling, 7 ¼ x 4 ⅝ In.	150.00
Baby, In Shoe, Bisque, Sculpted Hair, Beaded Teeth, Dimples, Heubach, c.1910, 12 In. ...... *Illus*	2250.00
Baby, Lying On Side, Holding Bunny, Kitten On Top, 6 ¼ x 2 ⅜ In.	135.00
Baby, Lying, Hand To Chin, 6 ⅛ x 3 ¼ In.	120.00
Baby, Playful Hands & Feet, 10 ½ In.	375.00
Baby, Playing With Toes, 7 x 4 ½ In.	85.00
Boy, In Bamboo High Chair, Clapping Hands, 9 In.	280.00
Boy, In Wood Tub, Pouring Water Over Head, 6 x 4 ¾ In.	135.00
Boy, Sitting, Hands On Feet, 8 x 8 In.	175.00
Boy, Wearing Nightshirt, Holding Toy, 4 ½ x 4 In.	135.00
Girl, Crawling, Blond, Green Dress, 6 In.	75.00
Girl, Nude, Reaching, Pigtails, 8 In.	65.00
Girl, Playing With Toes, On Pillow, 5 ¼ In.	225.00
Girl, Sitting, Holding Cup, 8 ¼ x 5 In.	155.00
Girls, Twins, Playing, Pink, Green, 5 In.	140.00

PICKARD China Company was started in 1893 by Wilder Pickard. Hand-painted designs were used on china purchased from other sources. In the 1930s, the company began to make its own china wares in Chicago, Illinois. The company now makes many types of porcelains, including a successful line of limited edition collector plates.

Ashtray, Round, Floral Chintz, 3 In.	16.00
Bowl, Vegetable, Oval, Avena, 9 In.	47.00
Bowl, Vegetable, Oval, Gossamer, 9 In.	65.00
Coffeepot, Lid, Avena, 5 Cup, 5 ¾ In.	180.00
Creamer, Crescent, 8 Oz., 3 In.	52.00
Cup & Saucer, Footed, Brocade	18.00
Cup & Saucer, Footed, Floral Chintz	22.00
Cup & Saucer, Footed, Geneva	40.00
Cup & Saucer, Footed, Greenbriar	23.00
Cup & Saucer, Footed, Rose & Daisy	70.00
Cup & Saucer, Footed, Windsor	10.00
Gravy Boat, Underplate, Crescent	100.00
Gravy Boat, Underplate, Windsor	139.00
Pitcher, Gilt, Porcelain, c.1960, 7 ½ In.	47.00
Plate, Bread & Butter, Cameo, 6 ½ In.	16.00
Plate, Dinner, Floral Chintz, 10 ⅝ In.	10.00
Plate, Dinner, Geneva, 10 In.	50.00
Plate, Dinner, Greenbriar, 10 ¾ In.	26.00

P

Photography, Ambrotype, Butcher & Son, About To Slaughter Sheep, Case, ¼ Plate
$881.00

Cowan's Auctions

Photography, Ambrotype, Confederate 2nd Lieutenant, Drawing His Sword, c.1861, ⅙ Plate
$4,700.00

Cowan's Auctions

Photography, Button, Streetcar, Pink Tint, c.1910, 2 ¾ In.
$69.00

Hake's Americana & Collectibles

Photography, Camera, Kodak, Leather Bound, Lacquered Metal Box, Walter Teague, 1930, 9 In.
$1,000.00

Los Angeles Modern Auctions (LAMA)

Photography, Camera, Rochester Optical & Camera Co., King, Mahogany, Brass Case, Bakelite Plate, c.1900
$444.00

Skinner, Inc.

Photography, Graphotrope, Carte De Visite, 27 Photographs, William Walker, Patd. June 12th 1866, 8 In.
$2,133.00

Skinner, Inc.

Piano Baby, Baby, In Shoe, Bisque, Sculpted Hair, Beaded Teeth, Dimples, Heubach, c.1910, 12 In. $2,250.00

Theriault's

Picture, Calligraphy, Ink On Paper, Leaping Stag, Frame, 1800s, 21 x 28 In. $1,541.00

Skinner, Inc.

Picture, Diorama, Roach Fish, Mounted, Underwater Scene, Wood Case, c.1903, 12 ⅝ x 18 x 5 ½ In. $1,062.00

Brunk Auctions

Picture, Engraving, Cincinnati, Bird's-Eye View, Illustrated News, Charles Fries, 1886, 22 x 40 In. $3,900.00

Cowan's Auctions

Platter, Serving, Oval, Brocade, 12 In.	100.00
Platter, Serving, Oval, Crescent, 15 In.	260.00
Platter, Serving, Oval, Laurel, 15 In.	90.00
Relish, 4 Sections, Rose & Daisy	160.00
Soup, Dish, Fantasy, 7 ⅞ In.	28.00
Soup, Dish, Garland, 7 In.	33.00
Sugar, Lid, Cameo	90.00
Sugar, Lid, Fantasy	32.00
Teapot, Lid, Geneva, 4 Cup, 8 ¼ In.	230.00
Vase, Red, Pink Roses, Yellow Ground, Gilt Handles, Signed M. Rost. Leroy, Limoges, c.1905, 16 In.	4800.00

PICTURES, silhouettes, and other small decorative objects framed to hang on the wall are listed here. Some other types of pictures are listed in the Print and Painting categories.

Aquatint, Pencil, Railroad Avenue, Clarence Holbrook Carter, Signed, Dated '31, Mat, 7 x 9 In.	242.00
Calligraphy, Ink On Paper, Leaping Stag, Frame, 1800s, 21 x 28 In. *Illus*	1541.00
Calligraphy, Ink On Paper, Nesting Birds, Within Wreath Of Birds, 27 x 21 In.	189.00
Campbell's Soup Shopping Bag, Paper, Screen Print, Day-Glo Paint, Andy Warhol, 20 x 17 In.	1725.00
Cut Paper, Armorial, Motto, Fortuna Sequatur, Garlands, Gilt Round Frame, c.1780, 20 ½ In.	1416.00
Cut Paper, Bear, In Forest, Blue Ground, Frame, c.1785, 7 ½ x 8 ¾ In.	7316.00
Diorama, Roach Fish, Mounted, Underwater Scene, Wood Case, c.1903, 12 ⅝ x 18 x 5 ½ In. *Illus*	1062.00
Drawing, Pen & Ink, Spenserian Verse, Heart Shape, Rachel Arnold 1841, Frame, 9 ½ x 11 ½ In.	176.00
Embroidery, Japanese Panels, Crane, Ducks, Silk, 39 ½ x 18 ½ In., Pair	900.00
Embroidery, Settlers, House, Shore, Ship, Flowers, Vines, Silk, Walnut Frame, 20 x 14 In.	230.00
Enamel On Copper, Thomas Jefferson, W.R. Birch, Miniature, 1 ½ x 1 In., Frame Case	11750.00
Engraving, Cincinnati, Bird's-Eye View, Illustrated News, Charles Fries, 1886, 22 x 40 In. *Illus*	3900.00
Fabric, Beadwork, Owl In Tree, Dragonfly, Snail, Moon, Star, Gilt Molded Frame, 17 x 12 ½ In.	35.00
Feltwork, Basket, Fruit, Black Ground, Frame, England, 11 ¾ x 14 In.	944.00
Feltwork, George III, Basket Of Strawberries, Black Ground, Frame, Oval, England, 10 ¼ x 12 In.	1062.00
Gouache On Paper, Ship Sooloo Salem, Domenico Gavarrone, Frame, 1848, 18 x 25 In. *Illus*	5925.00
Ink & Color On Paper, Armored Warrior, Halo, Caparisoned Horse, India, 1900s, 14 x 11 ¼ In. *Illus*	425.00
Ink On Paper, Scroll, Hanging, Pavilions, Mountains, Rivers, 8 Seals, Wang Yuanqi, 36 x 16 In. *Illus*	24150.00
Micro Mosaic, St. Peter's Square, Vatican, Blue, Pink Flower Border, Italy, 1800s, 3 ¾ x 4 ¾ In. *Illus*	738.00
Needlepoint, Memorial, Flying Eagle, Flag, My Country Tis Of Thee, Photograph, Frame, 18 x 18 In.	94.00
Needlework, 2 Stags At Rest, Stylized Trees, 19th Century, 15 x 20 In.	288.00
Needlework, Castle, Couple, Flowers, Trees, Birds, Animals, Silk, Metallic Braid, c.1650, 14 x 17 In.	3318.00
Needlework, Cornucopia, Brown Ground, Blue, Pick, Ivory Flowers, Panel, Frame, 1700s, 23 x 20 In.	122.00
Needlework, Cottagers, On Silk, Reverse Painted Glass, Gilt Frame, Initials, c.1810, 14 x 10 In. *Illus*	949.00
Needlework, Dog, St. Bernard, Lying On Rug, Hooked & Sheared Wool, Glass Eyes, 25 In.	2360.00
Needlework, Eagle, 13 Stars, Stripes, Shield, Flags, Frame, c.1876, 28 x 31 In.	1314.00
Needlework, Eagle, Spread Wings, Flag, Shield, Philippines-China-Siberia, Wood, 26 x 21 In.	86.00
Needlework, Family, Thatched Roof Cottage, Silk, Gilt Frame, Early 19th Century, 24 In.	531.00
Needlework, Floral Bouquets, Strawberry Vine Border, Catharine Bertolet, 1857, 24 x 25 ½ In.	296.00
Needlework, Heart In Hand, Yellow & Blue Border, Marbleized Mat, 1800s, 6 ¾ x 5 ⅞ In.	354.00
Needlework, Linen, Cow, Dog, Tree, Initialed M.A.T., c.1818, 15 ¼ x 13 ¼ In.	142.00
Needlework, Man, Seated By Water, Doves Bringing Offerings, Biblical, Frame, c.1800, 16 x 14 In.	153.00
Needlework, Memorial, Monument, Silk, Jason Gay, Age 18, 1792, By Abigail Gay, 1803, 18 x 18 In.	978.00
Needlework, Memorial, Silk, Watercolor, Ink, Monument, Mary Lamson, c.1803, 19 x 15 In. *Illus*	4444.00
Needlework, Memorial, Silk, Willow, Urn On Stand, Mrs S Adams, Frame, 1802, 11 x 8 ½ In. *Illus*	531.00
Needlework, Memorial, Willow, Urn, For Rev'd Timothy Fuller, Age 66, 1805, Frame, 10 x 15 In.	518.00
Needlework, Parrot, Floral Wreath, Black Ground, Green Painted Plaster Molded Frame, 16 x 15 In.	83.00
Needlework, Pastoral Scene, Lovers Cymon & Iphigenia, Ivory Face, Hands, Silk, Frame, 14 x 9 ½ In.	118.00
Needlework, Pastoral, Man, Woman Under Tree, Frame, Signed, E. Bradley, 1771, 23 x 16 In.	3304.00
Needlework, Rebecca At The Well, Tent Stitch, Eleanor Peterman, Frame, 1844, 26 ½ x 27 In.	266.00
Needlework, Roosters, Landscape, Ellen Hartman, Reading, Pa., 1858, 10 x 9 ½ In.	237.00
Needlework, Shepherdess, Pastoral Scene, Sheep, Mary Hartman, Reading, Pa., c.1860, 26 x 21 In.	119.00
Needlework, Silk On Silk, Lord Nelson's Manton Place, c.1810, 22 ¼ x 28 ¼ In.	235.00
Needlework, Silk, Chenille, Mother, Children, Animals, Cottage, Frame, Name, 1804, 35 x 42 In.	3068.00
Needlework, Silk, Chenille, Painted, Woman, Seated, Tree, Flower Basket, Frame, c.1800, 11 x 10 In.	235.00
Needlework, Silk, Chenille, Satin, Medallion, Woman, Holding Flowers, In Garden, 1600s, 8 x 7 In.	2478.00
Needlework, Silk, Satin, Painted, Map, Mary Russell, Pleasant Valley, N.Y., 21 x 29 In.	1298.00
Needlework, Silk, Woman In Garden, Holding Flower & Shears, Pond, Frame, c.1815, 10 ¼ x 13 In.	307.00
Needlework, Spring Flower Bouquet Center, Bouquet Spandrels, Mahogany Frame, 16 x 16 In.	83.00
Needlework, Street Scene, Family, Carriage, Animals, Rosewood Frame, 27 x 27 In.	1035.00
Needlework, Stumpwork, Cockatoo, On Beaded Branch, Flowers, Grapes, Frame, 23 x 21 In.	288.00
Needlework, Verse, Flowers, Berries, Eliza Hammond Rock Run Female Seminary, 1824, 16 x 21 In.	3555.00

Oil On Tin, Views Of Buildings, Berks Country Almshouse, C.C. Hofmann, 1879, 33 x 40 In....	11275.00
Panel, Deer, Landscape, Lacquer, Gilt, Signed De Con, France, 28 x 51 In.................................	395.00
Pastel, Charcoal, On Canvas, Muses, Wings, Eric Pape, 127 x 79 In.	1495.00
Pastel, On Paper, Deer, Lying Down, Woods, Gilt Frame, 1800s, 15 ½ x 20 In.	1778.00
Pastel, On Paper, Frame House, Blue Sky, Marilyn Propp, 1973, 23 x 20 In.	275.00
Pastel, On Sandpaper, Niagara Falls, Grisaille View, Steamboat, c.1870, 28 x 37 In.	1410.00
Pencil, Paper, Reuben Lowell House, Richmondville, Schoharie Cty, Fritz Vogt, 1890, 16 x 22 In...	10620.00
Pinprick, Memorial, Angels, Doves, Watercolor Wreath, Embossed Shells, Pen, Ink Verse, 10 x 7 ½ In..	88.00
Plaque, Pietra Dura, Chickens, Rooster, Hardstone Specimens, Continental, c.1880, 5 ¼ x 7 ½ In.	660.00
Plaque, Pietra Dura, Parrot, Branch, Fruit, Berries, Inlaid Design, Italy, 1900s, 33 ¾ x 22 In. ...*Illus*	360.00
Plaque, Pietra Dura, Peasants Dancing, Black Slate Ground, 8 ⅝ x 12 ¼ In.	540.00
Portrait, Wax Relief, Lord William Campbell, Frame, Anne Damer, Label, 1775, 2 x 1 In......*Illus*	30680.00
Portrait, Painted, Embossed Silk, Charles I, Twisted Wire & Seed Pearl Surround, Frame, 20 x 11 In.	2714.00
Print, Ted Williams, Splendid Splinter, At Bat, Serigraph, L. Neiman, Frame, 38 x 46 In.	3000.00
Reverse Painted Glass, Patriotic, Flags, Eagle, Shield, Foil, Mother-Of-Pearl, c.1890, 19 x 13 In...*Illus*	1080.00
Shellwork, Pavilion, Tropical, Reclining Figure, Shadowbox Frame, Victorian, England, 14 x 17 In..	413.00
Shellwork, Urn, Floral Bouquet, Shadowbox Frame, England, c.1780, 7 ½ x 10 ¼ In.	1180.00
Silhouette, Cut, Man, Top Hat, Gold Accents, Frame, c.1830, 4 ½ x 3 ¾ In.	224.00
Silhouette, Girl, Rooster, Gilt Frame, Phil., c.1890, 6 x 4 In.	504.00
Silhouette, Hollow Cut, Watercolor, Puffy Sleeve Artist, Man, Woman, Frame, 1830, 3 x 2 In., Pair	3792.00
Silhouette, Lady, Blue Dress, Puffy Sleeve, Hollow Cut, Watercolor, Black Pine Frame, 3 ½ x 3 In.	1240.00
Silhouette, Man, Hollow Cut, Embossed Peale Museum Stamp, Gilt Frame, c.1810, 6 ¼ x 5 ¼ In..	90.00
Silhouette, Man, Jabot, Blue, Gilt, Cut Paper, c.1840, 4 ½ x 3 ¾ In.	62.00
Silhouette, Man, Profile, Cut Paper, Gilt, Blue Highlights, Frame, c.1850, 4 x 3 In.	111.00
Silhouette, Man, Profile, Jabot, Jacket, Cut Paper, Gilt Inset Frame, c.1840, 6 ½ x 4 ½ In.............	98.00
Silhouette, Man, Woman, Double Hollow Cut, Reverse Painted Glass, New England, 1800s, 5 x 8 In.	1422.00
Silhouette, Mrs. Warden Pope, Oval, Frame, Kentucky, 1808, 4 x 3 In.	259.00
Silhouette, Portrait, Young Girl, Playing With Top, Frame, 19th Century, 7 ¼ x 4 ½ In.	533.00
Silhouette, Sea Captain, 3-Masted Whaler, 2 Whales, Paper, Wood & Nye Co., Frame, 15 x 13 In....	118.00
Silhouette, Watercolor, Woman, Standing, Frame, 7 x 4 ¼ In.	266.00
Silhouette, Woman, Bust, Black Paper, Under Glass, Ebonized, Gilt Metal, c.1810, 3 ½ x 3 In...*Illus*	96.00
Silhouette, Woman, Hollow Cut, Watercolor, Dress, Reverse Painted Glass, c.1830, 5 x 4 In. ...	1580.00
Silhouette, Woman, Puffy Sleeve, Watercolor, Hollow Cut, New England, c.1810, 3 ¼ x 2 ½ In.......	948.00
Silhouette, Woman, Standing, Cut & Pasted, Bronze Detail, Tiger Maple Frame, c.1850, 10 x 9 In.	345.00
Stumpwork, Eglomise, Silk, Woman, Flower Crown, Classical Scene, Gilt Frame, 1800s, 9 x 6 In.	240.00
Theorem, Oil, On Velvet, Compote Of Fruit, Green Ground, Multicolor, Frame, 17 x 21 ½ In............	2596.00
Theorem, Oil, On Velvet, Compote Of Fruit, William Rank, 22 ½ x 24 ½ In.	395.00
Theorem, Oil, On Velvet, Farm Scene, Sulky Rider, Signed William Rank, c.1950, 18 x 20 In.........	178.00
Theorem, Oil, On Velvet, Flower Bouquet, Peach, Blue, Gold, Wood Frame, 1850, 16 ½ x 17 In......	770.00
Theorem, Oil, On Velvet, Fruit In Bowl, Multicolor, Giltwood Frame, 14 ½ x 19 In.	2645.00
Theorem, Oil, On Velvet, Fruit, Slab Table, New England, 1800s, 17 x 22 ½ In.	1422.00
Theorem, Oil, On Velvet, Memorial, Church, Trees, Monuments, Mourners, c.1830, 21 x 23 In. ...	474.00
Theorem, Oil, On Velvet, Rooster, Tulips, Domed Perch, Red Painted Frame, G.B. French, 18 x 17 In.	94.00
Theorem, Oil, On Velvet, Strawberry Basket, Signed David Y. Ellinger, 11 x 14 In.........................	1896.00
Theorem, Oil, On Velvet, Tole Coffeepot, Signed Wm. Rank, Frame, c.1950, 7 ½ x 5 In.	119.00
Theorem, Watercolor, Flowering Tree, Red, Green, Signed Martha Balek, c.1890, 14 ½ x 13 ½ In...	356.00
Theorem, Watercolor, On Paper, Bowl Tilted, Spilled Fruit, Branch, Gilt Frame, c.1810, 18 x 26 In.	4503.00
Theorem, Watercolor, On Paper, Flowers, Decorated Vase, Gold Frame, c.1820, 12 ½ x 11 ½ In.	7703.00
Theorem, Watercolor, On Velvet, Basket, Strawberries, Bird, Garnet French, c.1945, 16 x 20 In.	354.00
Tinsel, Woman, Standing, Music Book, Curtains, Mirror, Label, Frame, c.1825, 8 x 6 ½ In......*Illus*	390.00
Wall Sculpture, Patinated Metal, Sailboats, Rods Form Waves, Curtis Jere, c.1967, 25 x 62 In...*Illus*	711.00
Watercolor, Baby, White Gown, Holding Roses, Oval, Gold Frame, c.1850, 2 ⅜ x 1 ⅞ In.	889.00
Watercolor, Blue Hollyhocks, Blue Painted Frame, Signed, Laura Coombs Hills, 7 x 4 ½ In.	633.00
Watercolor, Child, Riding Dog, Nathan Eldridge, 6 ¾ x 8 ½ In.	533.00
Watercolor, Colored Pencil, Patriotic, Eagle On Drum, Crossed Flags, Muskets, Frame, 13 x 14 In.	230.00
Watercolor, Early Morning Hialeah, Horse, Rider, Signed Menasco, c.1950, 15 ½ x 22 ¾ In......	248.00
Watercolor, Fabric, Portrait, Gentleman, Lock Of Hair, Hinged Case, Miniature, 2 In. ....*Illus*	6000.00
Watercolor, Fisherman At Sea, Signed, Georges Haquette, 17 x 21 In.....................................	353.00
Watercolor, Flowering Tree, From Heart, Deep, Dot Painted Frame, Sarah Kriebel, c.1875, 10 x 8 In.	889.00
Watercolor, Fresh From The Garden, Jean Georges Vibert, Frame, c.1880, 13 ½ x 10 In.............	1580.00
Watercolor, Gouache & Pencil On Board, Cuckoo, Magnolia, Roger Tory Peterson, 25 x 21 In...*Illus*	5036.00
Watercolor, Gouache On Ivory, Portrait, Woman, Gilt Brass, Signed, R.M. 1780, 1 ⅞ x 1 ½ In....*Illus*	1304.00
Watercolor, Gouache, Landscape, Estate On Hill, c.1860, 11 ½ x 15 ½ In.	395.00
Watercolor, Gouache, Summer Park View, Francis Hopkinson Smith, Frame, 13 x 24 In...........	575.00
Watercolor, Graphite On Paper, Gentleman, Side View, Wood Frame, Da Lee, 2 ¾ x 2 In. ......*Illus*	1541.00
Watercolor, Ink On Paper, Hart Family Record, 1880, Roses, Hearts, Peacocks, Flags, 17 x 22 In.	830.00
Watercolor, Ink On Paper, Paxson Family Record, Vines Flowers, Birds, Frame, 1800s, 6 ¾ x 7 In.	889.00

Picture, Gouache On Paper, Ship Sooloo Salem, Domenico Gavarrone, Frame, 1848, 18 x 25 In.
$5,925.00

Skinner, Inc.

Picture, Ink & Color On Paper, Armored Warrior, Halo, Caparisoned Horse, India, 1900s, 14 x 11 ¼ In.
$425.00

Skinner, Inc.

Picture, Ink On Paper, Scroll, Hanging, Pavilions, Mountains, Rivers, 8 Seals, Wang Yuanqi, 36 x 16 In.
$24,150.00

James D. Julia Auctioneers

TIP

Don't forget to dust the backs and tops of framed pictures several times a year.

Picture, Micro Mosaic, St. Peter's Square, Vatican, Blue, Pink Flower Border, Italy, 1800s, 3 ¾ x 4 ¾ In. $738.00

Skinner, Inc.

Picture, Needlework, Cottagers, On Silk, Reverse Painted Glass, Gilt Frame, Initials, c.1810, 14 x 10 In. $949.00

Cottone Auctions

Picture, Needlework, Memorial, Silk, Watercolor, Ink, Monument, Mary Lamson, c.1803, 19 x 15 In. $4,444.00

Skinner, Inc.

Watercolor, Ink, Dolly Dingle Paper Dolls, Gwennie & Denny, G. Drayton, 1920, 30 x 22 In.	542.00
Watercolor, Ink, Flowering Tree, Multicolor, Francis Weisel, c.1840, 9 x 7 ½ In.	770.00
Watercolor, Ink, Heart, Script, Tulip Trees, Birds, For Maria Brieanin 1783, Johann Eyer, 8 x 6 In.	3081.00
Watercolor, Landscape, Covered Bridge, Frame, Signed Ranulph Bye, c.1970, 12 ½ x 20 ½ In.	267.00
Watercolor, Marseilles Streets, Signed Eugene Galien-Laloue, Frame, 1909, 8 ½ x 12 ½ In.	1755.00
Watercolor, Mosque Courtyard, N.E. Williams, Frame, 26 x 20 In.	234.00
Watercolor, On Board, House In Bermuda, Charles Ziegler, Frame, c.1926, 6 x 7 ¼ In.	826.00
Watercolor, On Ivory, George Washington, 1800s, 3 x 2 ½ In.	1304.00
Watercolor, On Ivory, Man, Seated, Holding Clarinet, Oval, Wood Frame, 3 x 2 ½ In.	1778.00
Watercolor, On Ivory, Portrait, Woman, Oval Frame, c.1900, 2 ¼ x 2 In.	119.00
Watercolor, On Paper, Child, Whip, Thomas Hill Wroughton Age 4 ½, Frame, c.1860, 7 x 6 In.	518.00
Watercolor, On Paper, Cutout, Soldier, Riding Horse, Holding Pistol, c.1835, 6 x 7 In.	248.00
Watercolor, On Paper, Ducks Flying Over The Dunes, Roy Martell Mason, Frame, c.1960, 14 x 20 In.	590.00
Watercolor, On Paper, Farm Scene, Yellow House, N.J, c.1805, 8 x 10 In.	2607.00
Watercolor, On Paper, Heading Out, Sailboat, Fred Pansing, c.1900, 6 x 9 ½ In.	1003.00
Watercolor, On Paper, Memorial, Tree, Covered Urn, Curl Maple Veneer Frame, c.1850, 14 x 14 ½ In.	353.00
Watercolor, On Paper, Pennsylvania Folk Art Birds, Yellow, Green, Dubiel, Frame, c.1945, 6 x 4 ½ In.	345.00
Watercolor, On Paper, Sunset Over Marshland, Ornate Giltwood Frame, 10 ½ x 14 In.	590.00
Watercolor, On Paper, Theorem Of A Cornucopia, Flowers, Gilt Frame, 16 ¾ x 14 ½ In.	324.00
Watercolor, On Paper, Woman, Blue Dress, Standing By Chair, Oval Frame, 8 x 6 In.	153.00
Watercolor, On Paper, Woman, Blue Dress, With Boy, Frame, c.1890, 15 x 11 In.	384.00
Watercolor, On Paper, Woman's Profile, White Bonnet, Yellow Dress, Gold Frame, c.1850, 5 x 3 ½ In.	1107.00
Watercolor, On Silk, Mourning, To The Memory Of Caroline Sawyer, Aged 6 Years, 1818, 24 x 31 In.	177.00
Watercolor, Portrait, Gentleman In Black Suit, ¾ Length, 1800s, 6 x 4 ¼ In.	354.00
Watercolor, Portrait, Girl, Brown Hair, Blue Dress, Holding Doll, Mat, Gilt Frame, c.1850, 8 x 6 ½ In.	969.00
Watercolor, Portrait, Older Woman, Long Dress, Shawl, Bonnet, Frame, Wybrants, c.1855, 10 x 8 In.	165.00
Watercolor, Portrait, William Thompson, Seated, Pa., c.1800, 8 ¾ x 6 ½ In.	533.00
Watercolor, Portrait, Woman, Blue Dress, Elisabeth Tyson, Aged 34, Frame, 1842, 13 x 8 In.	295.00
Watercolor, Portrait, Young Woman, Bust, Under Glass, Gold Frame, c.1810, 3 x 2 ½ In. *Illus*	300.00
Watercolor, Purple, Red Bird, Flower Branch, Inscribed B. Ebersole, 1891, 3 x 5 In.	948.00
Watercolor, Rooster, Frame, Wood Frame, Pa., c.1840, 6 ¾ x 6 In.	334.00
Watercolor, View Of Hudson From Garrison, West Point, Signed R.F. Kemble, Frame, 5 ½ x 7 In.	504.00
Watercolor, Woman Reading, Lace Bonnet, Shawl, Black Dress, Apron, c.1830, 9 ½ x 7 ½ In.	345.00
Watercolor, Woman, In Yellow Dress, Holding Small Animal, Primitive, Pa., Mid 1800s, 9 x 7 In.	911.00
Watercolor, Woman, Seated In Windsor Chair, Pa., 1800s, 7 x 5 ½ In.	296.00
Watercolor, Yellow Bird, Black Wings, Frame, 1800s, 4 ½ x 3 ½ In.	395.00
Wax Relief, Sir Walter Raleigh, Red Ground, Gilt Frame, 1800s, 5 x 4 In.	108.00
Wool, Woven, British Ship, Fishing Trawler, Mountainous Coast, Frame, 14 x 18 In.	472.00

PICTURE FRAMES *are listed in this book in the Furniture category under Frame.*

PIERCE, *see Howard Pierce category.*

PIGEON FORGE POTTERY was started in Pigeon Forge, Tennessee, in 1946. Red clay found near the pottery was used to make the pieces. Molded or thrown pottery with matte glaze and slip decoration was made. The pottery closed in 2000.

The Pigeon Forge Pottery Pigeon Forge Tenn

Bowl, Beige, Blue Interior, 2 ¾ In.	6.00

PILKINGTON TILE AND POTTERY COMPANY was established in 1892 in England. The company made small pottery wares, like buttons and hatpins, but soon started decorating vases purchased from other potteries. By 1903, the company had discovered an opalescent glaze that became popular on the Lancastrian pottery line. The manufacture of pottery ended in 1937. Pilkington's Tiles Ltd. has worked from 1938 to the present.

Charger, Lancasterian, St. George & Dragon, Blue, Red, Copper Luster, Richard Joyce, 19 In. *Illus*	15340.00
Tile, Lighthouse, Sea Gulls, Water, 6 x 6 In.	48.00
Tile, Toro, Bullfight, 6 In.	75.00
Vase, 6-Sided, Stick Neck, Marked, c.1906, 10 ½ In.	235.00
Vase, Flowers, Scrolled Luster Plants, Bottle Shape, Royal Lancastrian, c.1909, 6 ½ In. *Illus*	600.00
Vase, Gilt Fish, Underwater Plants, Royal Lancastrian, c.1907, 4 ¾ In. *Illus*	720.00
Vase, Jade, Grapes, Leaves, Marked, c.1907, 13 In.	450.00

PILLIN pottery was made by Polia (1909–1992) and William (1910–1985) Pillin, who set up a pottery in Los Angeles in 1948. William shaped, glazed, and fired the clay, and Polia painted the pieces, often with elongated figures of women, children, flowers, birds, fish, and other animals. Pieces are marked with a stylized Pillin signature.

W + P
Pillin

Plaque, Square, White, Gray & Black, 3 Ballerinas, Signed, 9 ⅛ In.	403.00

Picture, Needlework, Memorial, Silk, Willow, Urn On Stand, Mrs S Adams, Frame, 1802, 11 x 8 ½ In.
$531.00

Brunk Auctions

Picture, Plaque, Pietra Dura, Parrot, Branch, Fruit, Berries, Inlaid Design, Italy, 1900s, 33 ¾ x 22 In.
$360.00

Cowan's Auctions

Picture, Portrait, Wax Relief, Lord William Campbell, Frame, Anne Damer, Label, 1775, 2 x 1 In.
$30,680.00

Brunk Auctions

Picture, Reverse Painted Glass, Patriotic, Flags, Eagle, Shield, Foil, Mother-Of-Pearl, c.1890, 19 x 13 In.
$1,080.00

Skinner, Inc.

Picture, Silhouette, Woman, Bust, Black Paper, Under Glass, Ebonized, Gilt Metal, c.1810, 3 ½ x 3 In.
$96.00

DuMouchelles Art Gallery

Picture, Tinsel, Woman, Standing, Music Book, Curtains, Mirror, Label, Frame, c.1825, 8 x 6 ½ In.
$390.00

Skinner, Inc.

Picture, Wall Sculpture, Patinated Metal, Sailboats, Rods Form Waves, Curtis Jere, c.1967, 25 x 62 In.
$711.00

Skinner, Inc.

Picture, Watercolor, Fabric, Portrait, Gentleman, Lock Of Hair, Hinged Case, Miniature, 2 In.
$6,000.00

Skinner, Inc.

Picture, Watercolor, Gouache & Pencil On Board, Cuckoo, Magnolia, Roger Tory Peterson, 25 x 21 In.
$5,036.00

Skinner, Inc.

P

441

Picture, Watercolor, Gouache On Ivory, Portrait, Woman, Gilt Brass, Signed, R.M. 1780, 1 ⅞ x 1 ½ In.
$1,304.00

Skinner, Inc.

Picture, Watercolor, Graphite On Paper, Gentleman, Side View, Wood Frame, Da Lee, 2 ¾ x 2 In.
$1,541.00

Skinner, Inc.

Picture, Watercolor, Portrait, Young Woman, Bust, Under Glass, Gold Frame, c.1810, 3 x 2 ½ In.
$300.00

DuMouchelles Art Gallery

Tile, Girl, With Bird On Shoulder, Painted, Glazed, Signed Polia Pillin, 5 ⅝ x 5 ⅝ In.	265.00
Tile, Girl, With Penguin, Painted, Glazed, Multicolor, Signed Polia Pillin, 5 ⅝ x 5 ⅝ In.	357.00
Vase, 3 Women, Bird, Tree, Cylinder, Blue, Gold, Rust, Signed, 10 ¼ In.	1035.00
Vase, Brown, Woman's Face, Blue Headdress, Signed, Polia Pillin, 5 ¼ x 5 ¼ In.	523.00
Vase, Bud, Woman, Brown, Blue, Stick Neck, Marked, 7 ¼ In.	345.00
Vase, Globular, Woman, Birds, Green Glaze, Marked, 4 ½ In.	375.00
Vase, Long Neck, Tapered, 15 ¼ In.	196.00
Vase, Mottled Red, Dripped Blue & Yellow Glaze, Cylindrical, Signed, 13 ¼ In.	575.00
Vase, Portraits Of Women, Smokestack Bottom, Bell Shape, Pinched Neck, Flared Lip, Signed, 10 ⅜ In.	1265.00
Vase, Stick Neck, Dark Blue, 9 ½ In.	104.00
Vase, Wavy Green, Blue, Cylinder, 14 ¾ In.	115.00
Vase, Woman, Holding Bird, Dancing Woman, Cream, Yellow, Red, Bottle Shape, Signed, 8 ⅝ In.	374.00
Vase, Woman, Bird On Her Wrist, Woman & Horse Obverse, Signed, 7 In. .... *Illus*	690.00
Vase, Woman, Cat In Lap, Moon, Sun, Blue, Green, Pink, Flattened Circle, Stick Neck, Rolled Lip, 9 In.	1150.00
Vase, Woman, Dancing, Green Ground, Flared, Signed Polia Pillin, 6 x 5 ¼ In.	550.00
Vase, Woman, Horses, Blue Ground, Marked, 6 In.	375.00
Vase, Women, Deer, Blue, Green, Black, Cylinder, 3 ½ x 10 In.	500.00
Vase, Women, Guitar, 4-Sided, 11 ¾ x 4 ¼ In.	938.00
Vase, Women, Horses, Blue Ground, Cylindrical, Signed, 2 ¾ x 6 In.	458.00

PINCUSHION DOLLS are not really dolls and often were not even pincushions. Some collectors use the term "half-doll." The top half of each doll was made of porcelain. The edge of the half-doll was made with several small holes for thread, and the doll was stitched to a fabric body with a voluminous skirt. The finished figure was used to cover a hot pot of tea, powder box, pincushion, whiskbroom, or lamp. They were made in sizes from less than an inch to over 9 inches high. Most date from the early 1900s to the 1950s. Collectors often find just the porcelain doll without the fabric skirt.

Anna Pavlova, Ballerina, Cream Dress, Flowers, Purple Ribbons, Stand, Germany, 10 In.	435.00
Bisque Head, Brown Set Eyes, Fabric Hair, Pins, 5 ½ In.	35.00
Blond Coiled Braided Hair, Arms Outstretched, Molded Painted Bodice, Blue Dress, 12 In.	81.00
Camargo Dancer, Arms Outstretched, Striated Brown Hair, Applied Flowers, Dress, 11 In.	145.00
Court Woman, Pink, Molded Gray Hair, Arms Holding Letters, Blue Velvet Dress, 12 In.	145.00
Dancer With Gauffered Cap, Arms Away, Pink Tutu, Cloth Lower Body, 10 In.	203.00
Egyptian Woman, Necklace, Tassels, Turban, Dressel & Kister, Germany, c.1910, 4 ½ In. ...... *Illus*	7840.00
Fanny Elssler, Molded Hair, Flowers, Arms Away, Black, Gold Dress, Seated, Cushioned Chair, 11 In.	290.00
Flapper, Hand On Hip, Blue, Green Dress, Wood Stand, Marked Germany, 9 ½ In.	203.00
Flower Dancer, Ballerina, Arms Outstretched, Pink Tint, Yellow Petal Dress, Germany, 10 In.	186.00
French Court Girl, Arms Out, Green Hat, Dress, 7 ½ In.	93.00
French Court Woman, Pink Tint, Arms To Buttons, Gray, Blue Dress, Hat, Germany, 12 In.	104.00
French Court Woman, Pink, Hands Outward, Gray Hair, Applied Flowers, Net Dress, 11 In.	116.00
Girl, Extended Arms, Intertwined Fingers, Incised, Germany, c.1900, 10 In. ...... *Illus*	1680.00
Jenny Lind, Pink Tint, Molded Brown Hair, Hands Up, Marked Goebel, 12 In.	174.00
Madonna, Child In Arms, Molded Hair, Painted Face, Red Dress, Gold Shawl, Veil, Germany, 14 In.	174.00
Medieval Dancer, Pink Tint, Net Dress, Gold Headband, 9 ½ In.	174.00
Nude Woman, Pink Tint, Short Brown Hair, Dressel & Kister, Germany, 5 ½ In. .... *Illus*	896.00
Pierrot, Lying On Side, Porcelain, Marked, Germany, c.1920, 8 In. .... *Illus*	616.00
Swinger, Bisque, Painted, Jointed, Gray Hair, Period Net Dress, Hat, Applied Flowers, 10 In.	319.00
Woman, Basket Of Fish, Bisque, Dressel & Kister, Germany, c.1920, 5 In. .... *Illus*	3136.00
Woman, Colorful Bonnet, Holding Letter, Germany, c.1900, 5 ½ In. .... *Illus*	616.00
Woman, Holding Wreath, Lace Ruffles, Dresden Flowers, Rudolstadt, Germany, c.1900, 5 In. *Illus*	2352.00

PINK SLAG *pieces are listed in this book in the Slag Glass category.*

PIPES have been popular since tobacco was introduced to Europe by Sir Walter Raleigh. Carved wooden, porcelain, ivory, and glass pipes and accessories may be listed here.

Box, Chippendale, Cherry, Pine, Red Paint, Open Top, Shaped Crest, c.1775, 17 x 5 In.	2070.00
Box, Mahogany, Wall, England, c.1805, 20 In.	119.00
Box, Pine, Brown Paint, Shaped Pierced Hanger, Drawer, U.S.A., c.1800, 21 In.	356.00
Box, Wall, Walnut, Carved, France, Early 19th Century, 21 x 8 ¼ In.	213.00
Burl, Carved Devil, Leather Case, 2 x 3 x 7 ½ In.	110.00
Burl, Devil, Hand Carved, Lucite Tip, Leather Case, 2 x 3 x 7 ½ In.	110.00
Meerschaum, Carved, Cherub, Nude Woman, Leaves, Turkey, 14K Gold Band, Case, 4 ½ x 9 In.	1126.00
Meerschaum, Figural, Monarch, Crown, 7 In.	193.00
Meerschaum, Horse, Owned By Porfirio Diaz, Mexican Leader, 7 In.	3850.00
Meerschaum, Silver & Gold Arched Trim, Tortoise Stem, Leather Case	220.00

Meerschaum, Silver, Lidded Cap, Soldiers On Bowl, Swords, Rifles, Horn Mouthpiece, 1800s, 12 In.	149.00
Meerschaum, Skull & Bones, Leather Case, 6 ½ In.	935.00
Meerschaum, Skull, Franz Heiss & Sohne, Case, 3 x 2 ½ In.	220.00
Meerschaum, Woman Seated, Holding Basket, Case, 3 ½ In.	45.00
Opium, Cast, Engraved, Phoenix, Seated Man, Poem On Reverse, Chinese, 10 In.	150.00
Opium, Wood, Brass Mounts, Jade Mouthpiece Stopper & Removable Bowl, 1900s, 19 ¾ In.	338.00
Pipe Bowl, Jasperware, Classical Figures, Wedgwood, 2 ½ In. ....*Illus*	330.00
Rack, Pine, Peaked Roof, Paint, 13 ¾ x 7 ½ In.	119.00
Tamper, Fruitwood, Hound & Hare Shape, Articulated Ribs, Curled Tail, c.1790, 3 ¼ In.	354.00
Tobacco Box, Brass, Chased Scene, Smoking, Drinking, Sailboat, Lid, Engraved, Dutch, 6 x 2 In.	120.00
Tobacco Box, Brass, Engraved, Archer, Hanged Doors, Compartments, 5 ⅛ x 1 ⅞ In.	119.00
Tobacco Box, Copper, Brass, Frederick The Great, Shield, Eagle, Johann Heinrich Giese, c.1756, 6 ½ In.	885.00
Tobacco Box, Honesty, Brass, Turned Wood Handle, Coin-Operated, England, 1800s, 5 x 9 In.	230.00
Tobacco Box, Marble, Shaped Lid, Gilt Metal Mounted, France, c.1750, 8 x 13 In.	1625.00
Tobacco Box, Regency, Ghoulish Vision Scene, Wigglework Line, Hinged Lid, c.1800, 3 ⅜ In.	593.00
Tobacco Box, Wood, Ship Shape, Buxom Figure, 1784	950.00
Wood, Bear Claw, Carved, Leather Case, Marked Jones No. 4, 5 ½ In.	120.00

PIRKENHAMMER is a porcelain manufactory started in 1802 by Friedrich Holke and J. G. Lilst. It was located in Bohemia, now Brezova, Czechoslovakia. The company made tablewares usually decorated with views and flowers. Lithophanes were also made. The mark of the crossed hammers is easy to remember as the Pirkenhammer symbol.

Bowl, Vegetable, Lid, Handles, Flowers, Yellow Band	140.00
Cake Plate, White, Embossed, Scalloped, Rose, Handles, 10 ⅞ In.	70.00
Cup & Saucer, Birds, Butterflies, Gilt Trim, Demitasse	125.00
Plate, Bouquets, Aladdin, 10 In.	24.00
Plate, Flowers, Center Spray, c.1949, 7 ⅜ In.	38.00
Sign, Green Mark, Gilt Trim, 1 ⅞ In.	40.00

PISGAH FOREST POTTERY was made in North Carolina beginning in 1926. The pottery was started by Walter B. Stephen, who had been making pottery in that location since 1914. The pottery continued in operation after his death in 1961. The most famous kinds of Pisgah Forest ware are the cameo type with designs made of raised glaze and the turquoise crackle glaze wares.

Teapot, Lid, Covered Wagon, Oxen, Cameo, Green Matte, Glossy Blue, W.B. Stephen, 5 ½ In.	944.00
Urn, Dancing Couples, Green Matte Glaze, Impressed, Longpine, Arden, N.C., c.1953, 8 In. ... *Illus*	708.00
Vase, Dark Aubergine Glaze, Impressed, 1924, 10 ¼ In.	316.00
Vase, Green Over Yellow Crystalline Glaze, Baluster, 1935, 7 ½ x 6 In.	469.00
Vase, Mottled Brown, Green, Stepped Shoulder, Marked, 6 In.	92.00
Vase, Pate-Sur-Pate Castle Scene, Blue Matte Ground, Gloss Green, W.B. Stephen, 1949, 13 In.	1534.00
Vase, Red, Rolled Rim, Molded Mark, 7 ¾ x 6 In.	176.00
Vase, Variegated Green, Brown Glaze, 6 ½ In.	46.00
Vase, Westward Ho, Olive Matte Glaze, Glossy Turquoise, Eggplant, W.B. Stephen, 6 ¼ In. ... *Illus*	826.00

PLANTERS PEANUTS memorabilia are collected. Planters Nut and Chocolate Company was started in Wilkes-Barre, Pennsylvania, in 1906. The Mr. Peanut figure was adopted as a trademark in 1916. National advertising for Planters Peanuts started in 1918. The company was acquired by Standard Brands, Inc., in 1961. Standard Brands merged with Nabisco in 1981. Some of the Mr. Peanut jars and other memorabilia have been reproduced and, of course, new items are being made.

Box, 24 Pack, Planters 5 Cent Salted Peanuts, Die Cut Cardboard, c.1935, 8 x 8 ½ In.	300.00
Box, The World Goes Nuts For Planters Chocolate Peanuts, 1930s, 8 ¾ x 5 In.	270.00
Cocktail Glass, Mr. Peanut Figural Stem, Red Flared Top, 1950s, 5 In., 4 Piece	126.00
Container, Figural, Mr. Peanut, Papier-Mache, Removable Hat, 1930s, 12 ½ In. ....*Illus*	308.00
Container, Mr. Peanut, Top Hat, Cane, Souvenir Of Norfolk, Paint, Papier-Mache, 1930s, 12 ½ In.	210.00
Costume, Mr. Peanut, Molded Vinyl, Peanut Body, Top Hat, 1960s, 46 In.	505.00
Costume, Mr. Peanut, Peanut Shop, Toothy Grin, Black Hat, Papier-Mache, 1920s, 49 In.	1320.00
Costume, Parade, Mr. Peanut Torso, Pince Nez, Orange, Black, Papier-Mache, c.1935, 49 In.	1020.00
Display Case, Mr. Peanut, 5 Cents, Hot, Metal, Glass, Peaked Top, Light-Up, Warms	360.00
Display, Mr. Peanut, Leaning On Cane, Peanuts At Feet, Painted, Cast Metal, 1930s, 7 ½ In.	639.00
Display, Planters Best Peanut, 5 Cent Bars, Good Food, Always Crisp, Cardboard, 1930s, 12 In.	1560.00
Display, Rack, Mr. Peanut, 2-Sided, Tin, 8 x 15 In.	30.00
Doll, Mr. Peanut, Jointed, Wood, Schoenhut Toy Co., 8 ¼ x 4 ½ In. ....*Illus*	154.00
Glass, Circus, Mr. Peanut Stilt Walker, Juggler, Trapeze Artist, Leopard Trainer, 1950s, 5 x 3 In.	85.00
Glass, Cocktail, Red Glass On Top, Mr. Peanut Leaning On Cane Base, 1950s, 4 Piece	125.00

Pilkington, Charger, Lancasterian, St. George & Dragon, Blue, Red, Copper Luster, Richard Joyce, 19 In. $15,340.00

Brunk Auctions

Pilkington, Vase, Flowers, Scrolled Luster Plants, Bottle Shape, Royal Lancastrian, c.1909, 6 ½ In. $600.00

Skinner, Inc.

Pilkington, Vase, Gilt Fish, Underwater Plants, Royal Lancastrian, c.1907, 4 ¾ In. $720.00

Skinner, Inc.

Pillin, Vase, Woman, Bird On Her Wrist, Woman & Horse Obverse, Signed, 7 In. $690.00

Humler & Nolan

Pincushion Doll, Egyptian Woman, Necklace, Tassels, Turban, Dressel & Kister, Germany, c.1910, 4 ½ In. $7,840.00

Theriault's

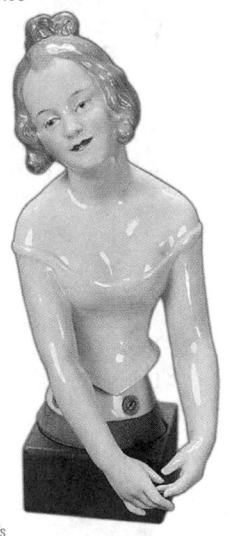

Pincushion Doll, Girl, Extended Arms, Intertwined Fingers, Incised, Germany, c.1900, 10 In. $1,680.00

Theriault's

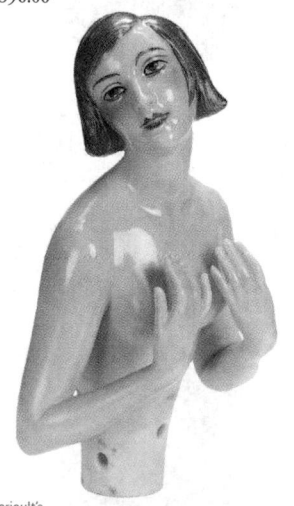

Pincushion Doll, Nude Woman, Pink Tint, Short Brown Hair, Dressel & Kister, Germany, 5 ½ In. $896.00

Theriault's

Goblet, Wine, Mr. Peanut Stem, Green, 5 In.	270.00
Hand Puppet, Mr. Peanut, Hands Out, Yellow, Black, Rubber, 6 ½ In.	390.00
Jar, Display, Red & Blue, White, Mr. Peanut, Lid, c.1960, 10 x 7 In., Pair	135.00
Jar, Embossed, Pennant, 5 Cent Salted Peanuts, Relief Image On Lid, c.1926, 8 x 12 ¾ In.	153.00
Jar, Knopped Lid, Peanuts, 4 Corners, Embossed Planters, 1930s, 14 In.	180.00
Jar, Knopped Lid, Planters Salted Peanuts, Clear Glass, Rounded, 1930s, 13 In.	270.00
Jar, Only Peanut Bar For Summer, Label, 5 Cents, Glass, Litho Lid, c.1937, 8 ½ x 10 In.	411.00
Jar, Relief Name, Images, Peanut Finial, Square, c.1932, 7 ½ x 13 ¾ In.	144.00
Jar, Salted, 5 Cent, Glass, Round Body, Red, Gold Decal, Embossed, Lid, Peanut Knob, 13 x 9 In.	118.00
Jar, Streamline, Green Tin Lid, Woman Emptying Package, Paper Label, 1930s, 9 ¾ In.	360.00
Lighter, Figural, Peanut Shape, Molded Composition, Textured, 1930s, 2 ⅝ In.	57.00
Nut Dish, Figural, Bisque, Nutshell Holding Cane, Top Hat, 1930s, 3 x 4 In.	146.00
Pin, Mr. Peanut, Leaning On Cane, Yellow Ground, Black, Red, 1940s, 1 ¼ In.	8.00
Pin, Mr. Peanut, World War II, V For Victory, Tin Litho Tab, Yellow Plastic Figure, 2 In.	97.00
Pin, Wear A Lucky Mr. Peanut, Wood, New York World's Fair, 1939, 1 ½ x 3 ½ In.	101.00
Racer, Mr. Peanut Driver, Red, Blue Wheels, Plastic, Box, 1950s, 5 In.	240.00
Salt & Pepper, Mr. Peanut, Pink, Plastic, 3 In.	18.00
Sign, Rack, Mr. Peanut Suggests, Planters To-Day, Yellow, Blue, Tin, c.1950, 12 x 23 In.	150.00
Tin, Planters Peanut Butter, Orange Paint, White, Blue, Red, Gold Label, Handle, 4 In.	6600.00
Tin, Planters Peanut Butter, Yellow Paint, Handle, Lid, Wilkes-Barre, Pa., 1910, 4 In., 1 Lb.	1020.00
Toy, Mr. Peanut, Walking, Windup, Plastic, Built-In Key, 1950s, 8 ½ In.	270.00 to 286.00
Toy, Tapper, Electric, Mr. Peanut, Right Arm & Cane Moves, 1930s, 28 In.	15600.00
Tumbler, Mr. Peanut Image, Enameled, Top Hat & Cane, 1950s, 5 In., 3 Piece	198.00
Vending Machine, Planters Peanut, Arachides, 10 Cent, Blue, Canada, 1960s, 28 x 12 ½ In.	180.00

PLASTIC objects of all types are being collected. Some pieces are listed in other categories; gutta-percha cases are listed in the Photography category. Celluloid is in its own category.

Bookmark, March Of Dimes, Figural, Blue, 3 Dimes At Top, 1940s, 3 In.	20.00
Bottle Stopper, Bird, Off White, Molded, Early 1920s, 3 x 1 ¼ In.	10.00
Coaster Set, Western Scenes, Rodeo Cowboys, Broncos, Yellow, Green, Blue, Red, Molded, 8 Piece	38.00
Keychain Fob, Puzzle Ball, Orange, Navy, Green, Yellow & White, 1950s, 1 In.	15.00
Manicure Set, Bullet Shape Case, Painted Salmon, Enamel Flowers, 4 Tools, Stainless Steel, 3 ¼ In.	65.00
Plaque, Madonna & Child, Pink Translucent, Molded, Wire Hanger, c.1970, 9 ½ x 6 In.	20.00
Trumpet Ware, Melmac Melamine, Box, 1960s, 4 Piece Setting, 20 Piece	30.00
Wall Pocket, Pot Holder Hook, Cats, Pink & Black, Black & Yellow, c.1960, 5 x 3 ¼ In.	28.00

PLATED AMBERINA was patented June 15, 1886, by Joseph Locke and made by the New England Glass Company. It is similar in color to amberina, but is characterized by a cream colored or chartreuse lining (never white) and small ridges or ribs on the outside.

Bowl, Ribbed, Yellow To Rose, New England, 5 In. *Illus*	4600.00
Cruet, Ribbed, Applied Amber Handle, Stopper, New England, 6 ½ In. *Illus*	2703.00
Saltshaker, Ribbed, Corset Shape, Yellow To Rose, New England, 4 In. *Illus*	3163.00
Vase, Lily, Ribbed, Disc Foot, 9 ¼ In. *Illus*	4600.00

PLIQUE-A-JOUR is an enameling process. The enamel is laid between thin raised metal lines and heated. The finished piece has transparent enamel held between the thin metal wires. It is different from cloisonne because it is translucent.

Bowl, Blue Ground, Purple, Green, Flowers, Footed, 2 ½ x 4 In.	98.00
Bowl, Dragon, 5 Toes, Pearl, Phoenix, Rose Ground, Chinese, Box, c.1900, 3 ⅜ x 7 ½ In., Pair.	207.00
Plate, Pink Ground, Green, Yellow, Blue, Orange, White, Flowers, 6 In.	84.00
Spoon, Flower Medallion Bowl, Cloisonne Handle, Scandinavia, c.1900, 7 ½ In.	780.00

POLITICAL memorabilia of all types, from buttons to banners, are collected. Items related to presidential candidates are the most popular, but collectors also search for material related to state and local offices. Memorabilia related to social causes, minor political parties, and protest movements are also included here. Many reproductions have been made. A jugate is a button with photographs of both the presidential and vice presidential candidates. In this list a button is round, usually with a straight pin or metal tab to secure it to a shirt. A pin is brass, often figural, sometimes attached to a ribbon.

Ashtray, General Chester Arthur, Portrait, Pottery, Rolled Rim, 4 In.	152.00
Auto Bumper Tag, Landon, Metal, Round, Reflective Light, Red, Blue, White, 1936, 4 ½ x 3 ½ In.	242.00
Badge, Delegate, Republican Convention, Eagle, Ribbon, 1924, 4 ¾ In.	84.00
Badge, Federal Protective Service Police, Inaugural, Reagan, Brass, Blue, 1981, 2 ⁵⁄₁₆ In.	181.00

Badge, George Washington, White Metal, Sunburst Medallion, Braxmar, 1789-1889, 2 ½ In... 95.00

Badge, Harrison, Brass, Round Photo, Ribbon Shape, Hanging Circle Frame, c.1892, 2 x 2 ¾ In.. 17.00

Badge, Janitor, Chicago GOP Convention, Eagle, Spread Wings, Wreath Frame, 1904, 3 ½ In. 221.00

Badge, O'K Ike Club, Sunflower, Shield Shape, 1 ¼ In. 169.00

Badge, Ribbon, McKinley, Roosevelt, Round Portrait, Jugate, 1900, 3 ½ In. 348.00

Badge, Shield Shape, McKinley, Honest Money & Protection Hanging Circle, Portrait, Leather, 4 In.... 103.00

Badge, William B. Allison, For President, Photo, Flag Ribbon, Allison Iowa Club, 4 ¾ In. 222.00

Ballot Box, Walnut, Octagonal, Molded Top, Hinged Door, Brass Latch, c.1800, 16 ½ x 11 In. 359.00

Bandanna, Blaine For President, James G. Blaine Of Maine, 1884, 16 ½ x 16 ½ In. 177.00

Bandanna, Cleveland, Jugate, Public Office A Public Trust, G.A.R., Cotton, 1888, 22 x 22 ¾ In. 158.00

Bandanna, Cleveland, Public Office A Public Trust, Picture, 1888, 21 x 25 In. 159.00

Bandanna, Garfield, Arthur, Red Cloth, 17 x 21 In. 322.00

Bandanna, James Garfield, Chester Arthur, Red & White Cloth, Jugate, 18 x 20 In. 213.00

Bandanna, Roosevelt Battle Flag, Progressive Party, Red, White, 1912, 22 x 24 In. 190.00

Bandanna, Theodore Roosevelt, Protection To American Industries, Jugate, 22 x 24 In. 316.00

Bandanna, Win With Ike For President, Printed Cotton, Square, 25 In. *Illus* 75.00

Bank, Bear, Figural, Embossed Teddy, Metal, 2 ½ x 3 ¾ In. 374.00

Bank, Still, McKinley & Teddy, Prosperity, Cast Iron, Embossed Portraits, c.1900, 2 ½ x 3 ½ In. 999.00

Bank, Taft & Sherman, Jugate, Milk Glass, Uncle Sam Top Hat, Painted, 1908, 2 ½ In. 588.00

Banner, Clay & Frelinghuysen, Grand Nation, 1844, 12 x 16 In. 278.00

Banner, Franklin D. Roosevelt, Our Gallant Leader, Felt, Dowel, Hanger String, c.1936, 8 ½ x 12 In... 69.00

Bobbin' Head Doll, Lyndon Johnson, 1964, Box, 7 ½ In. 38.00

Bookends, Franklin D. Roosevelt, Name Across Bust, White Metal, c.1933, 3 ¼ x 4 ¼ In. 85.00

Bookmark, Taft, Sherman, Teddy Bear Shape, Heart Shape Cutout, Aluminum, 2 ¾ In. 238.00

Bookmark, Winston Spencer Churchill, Full Body Profile, Metal, England, 4 ¼ In. 84.00

Boot Jack, Roosevelt IV, Donkey Shape, Elongated Ears, Iron, 11 In. 127.00

Bottle, McKinley, Full Dinner Pail, Wire Handle, Wood Grip, Inverted Tin Cup Lid, c.1900, 4 In. 728.00

Bottle, Pig, A Delegate To The National Convention At Chicago, Pottery, c.1884, 7 In. 5175.00

Bottle, Whiskey, Nixon, Watergate, Portrait, Humorous Labels, Olive Green, c.1973, 12 x 3 In... 92.00

Box, James A. Garfield, Portrait Under Glass, Wood, 2 ¾ In. 114.00

Broadside, Funeral Of President Lincoln, Waterville, Maine, Frame, 13 x 12 In. 1200.00

Bust, George Washington, Plaster, 19th Century, 26 In. 700.00

Bust, Patrick Henry, Patinated Zinc, Inscribed, Warner Miskey Merrill, Phila., c.1860, 12 ¾ In.. *Illus* 956.00

Button, 2 Times Is Enough For Any Man, Willkie, Blue, Celluloid, 1 ¼ In. 31.00

Button, ABJ For President, Anybody But Johnson, White, Blue Letters, 1 ¼ In. 19.00

Button, Above The Clouds, Mount Wilson, Illustration Profile, Black & White, c.1912, 1 ½ In... 253.00

Button, Alf Landon, Frank Knox, Sunflower, Jugate, 1936, 1 ¼ In. 4760.00

Button, Alice Roosevelt, Portrait, Hat, Scrolling, Shield, Flag, 1904, 1 ¼ In. 173.00

Button, All The Way With Adlai, Red White, Blue, Celluloid, 6 In. 38.00

Button, Alton Parker, Henry Davis, Portrait, Sepia Tone, Jugate, 3 ½ In. 374.00

Button, Another Member Of The Vast Right Wing Conspiracy, Round, Red & White, c.1970, 3 In. 63.00

Button, Banner, Cleveland, Stevenson, Portraits, Brass Banner Shell, Eagle, Tassels, 1 ¼ In. 258.00

Button, Blinker, Reagan In 80, Portrait, Cardboard, 3 ½ In. 23.00

Button, Blinker, Reagan, Bush, People's Choice, U.S. Map, Stripes, Jugate, 1985, 2 ¼ In. 37.00

Button, Bring Our Men Home From Viet-Nam Now, Blue, Celluloid, 1 ½ In. 52.00

Button, Bryan, American Flag, Celluloid, 1 ¼ In. 626.00

Button, Bryan, In Sunflower, Democratic National Convention, Kansas City, 1900, 1 ¼ In. 162.00

Button, Bryan, Portrait, Ribbon, Bryan & Kern Club, 1908, 3 ½ In. 460.00

Button, Bryan, Stevenson, Flag, Celluloid, W&H Paper, Jugate, 1900, 1 ¾ In. *Illus* 138.00

Button, Bryan, Wishbone, Celluloid, Whitehead & Hoag, 1 ¼ In. 62.00

Button, Bull Moose, Moose Head, White & Brown, Celluloid, 1912, 1 ⅔ In. 364.00

Button, Bush, Quayle, 1988, Elephant Ears, GOP, Jugate, 2 ¼ In. 22.00

Button, Bush, Quayle, Celluloid, Jugate, 1988, 1 ¾ In. *Illus* 7.00

Button, Camelot, Teddy, Robert & John Kennedy, Profiles, Celluloid, 6 In. 28.00

Button, Carter, Mondale, Democratic 1976, Celluloid, Jugate, 9 In. *Illus* 19.00

Button, Carter, Mondale, Donkey, People's Choice, '76, Caricatures, 3 In. 103.00

Button, Carter, Peanut Days, Go Jimmy Go, McCook, Neb., Peanut, Celluloid, 1977, 3 In. 190.00

Button, Clinton For President, Train, 21st Century Express, Green, 1996, 2 ¼ In.. 44.00 to 49.00

Button, Clinton, Gore, Arkansas Legislators, Celluloid, 1992, 2 ¼ In. *Illus* 223.00

Button, Clinton, Gore, Oval Office, Multicolor, Oval, Roy Lichtenstein, Celluloid, 4 In. 39.00

Button, Coolidge, Our President, Deeds Not Words, Easel Back, 1924, 4 In. 2764.00

Button, Cox, For President, 1920, ⅞ In. 1064.00

Button, Crow, Don't Croak, Rooster, James M. Cox, Democratic, Celluloid, 1920, 1 ½ In. 345.00

Button, Democratic Lawyers, Vote Straight, Committee, Blue & White, c.1932, 2 ⅛ In. 3922.00

Button, Democratic Worker, McGovern, Oval, Red, White, Blue, 2 13/16 In. 97.00

Button, Dewey Will Do It, Black & White, c.1944, 1 ½ In. 147.00

Pincushion Doll, Pierrot, Lying On Side, Porcelain, Marked, Germany, c.1920, 8 In.
$616.00

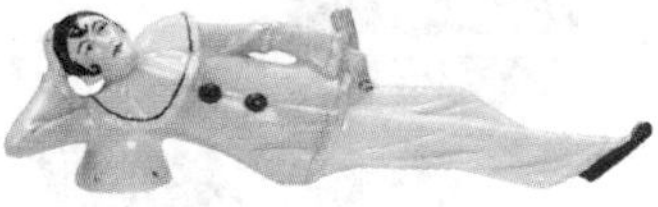

Theriault's

Pincushion Doll, Woman, Basket Of Fish, Bisque, Dressel & Kister, Germany, c.1920, 5 In.
$3,136.00

Theriault's

Pincushion Doll, Woman, Colorful Bonnet, Holding Letter, Germany, c.1900, 5 ½ In.
$616.00

Theriault's

Pincushion Doll, Woman, Holding Wreath, Lace Ruffles, Dresden Flowers, Rudolstadt, Germany, c.1900, 5 In.
$2,352.00

Theriault's

P

Pipe, Pipe Bowl, Jasperware, Classical Figures, Wedgwood, 2 ½ In.
$330.00

DuMouchelles Art Gallery

Pisgah Forest, Urn, Dancing Couples, Green Matte Glaze, Impressed, Longpine, Arden, N.C., c.1953, 8 In.
$708.00

Brunk Auctions

Pisgah Forest, Vase, Westward Ho, Olive Matte Glaze, Glossy Turquoise, Eggplant, W.B. Stephen, 6 ¼ In.
$826.00

Brunk Auctions

"On the Curl"

For a political collector, "on the curl" has a special meaning. It indicates that the name of the maker is printed on the curled edge of a celluloid or tin campaign button.

Button,	Dick Gregory For President, Photo, Cream Ground, 1968, ⅞ In.	10.00
Button,	Draft Beer Not Students, Blue, White, Celluloid, 1 ½ In.	36.00
Button,	Eisenhower, Caricature By David Levine, Celluloid, 6 In.	120.00
Button,	Eisenhower, Nixon, I Like Ike, Vote Republican, Jugate, Celluloid, 3 ½ In.	104.00
Button,	Eleanor Start Packing, Willkies Are Coming, 1 ¼ In.	7.00
Button,	Eugene Debs, Job Harriman, Social Democratic Party, Jugate, Celluloid, ⅞ In.	1680.00
Button,	Eugene V. Debs, Photograph, Celluloid, 1 ¼ In.	403.00
Button,	Fist Holding Dog Tags, SOS, Blue, White, Anti Vietnam, 1 ½ In.	52.00
Button,	Flasher, Be Happy, No Rocky, In '64, Nelson Rockefeller, 2 ½ In.	21.00
Button,	Flicker, Eisenhower Inauguration, Welcome Mr. President, 1953, 7 ½ In.	45.00
Button,	For Freedom, 4FR, Re-Elect Roosevelt, Red, White, Blue, 1 ¼ In.	171.00
Button,	For President, Alfred E. Smith, Button Portrait, Ribbon, Brown Derby Hat, 2 ¾ In.	101.00
Button,	Franklin D. Roosevelt, For President, Portrait, Ribbon, Blue, 1936, 1 ¼ In.	173.00
Button,	Franklin Roosevelt, Portrait, Color, Celluloid, 9 In.	69.00
Button,	G. Washington, 6-Point Star, Shield, Eagle, Arrows, Talons, Branch, 1789, 1 ⅜ In.	4200.00
Button,	Garfield, Arthur, Jugate, Brass Frame, 1 ⅛ In.	338.00
Button,	Garner For President, Photo, 1932, ⅝ In.	20.00
Button,	George Washington, Long Live The President, Brass, Round, 1789, 1 ⅜ In. Diam.	3240.00
Button,	Goldwaters, Indiana's Favorite Family, Yellow, Litho, 3 In.	269.00
Button,	GOP Victory 1932, Elephant, Trunk Up, Blue & White, Celluloid, Republican, 1932, ⅞ In.	148.00
Button,	Harding, Coolidge, Penrose, Trigate, Ribbon, Women's First Vote, 1920, 1 ¼ In.	4773.00
Button,	Harding, Red, White, Blue, Celluloid, Robert Johns Back Paper, 1 ¼ In. ....*Illus*	160.00
Button,	Hitler Hanging, Let's Pull Together, Mechanical, Tin Litho, Evans Novelty, 1 ⅝ In. ....*Illus*	190.00
Button,	Hughes, Fairbanks, Jugate, 1916, 1 ¾ In.	470.00
Button,	Humphrey, Eyes Have It, Green Stylized Sun, Wobbly Eyes, 3 ½ In.	46.00
Button,	Humphrey, Muskie, Eagle, Crossed Flags, Celluloid, 3 ½ In.	268.00
Button,	I Like Ike, Red, White, Blue, Tin Lithograph, 1952, 4 In. ....*Illus*	10.00
Button,	I Wouldn't Buy A Used Car From Either Johnson Or Nixon, Green, Orange, 1 ¼ In.	28.00
Button,	Ike, Dwight D. Eisenhower For President, Photo, Celluloid, 1 ¼ In.	20.00
Button,	Ike, New York State Shape, Blue, Gold, Celluloid, 1 ¼ In.	52.00
Button,	I'm An Arkansas Traveler For Bill Clinton, 1992, 2 ¼ In.	1456.00
Button,	In Gold We Trust, Blue, White, McKinley, Celluloid, ⅞ In.	20.00
Button,	In Your Gut You Know He's Nuts, Anti-Goldwater, Celluloid, 1 ¾ In.	131.00
Button,	Inauguration Day, I Like Ike & Dick, Red, White, Blue, Jugate, 1957, 3 ½ In.	75.00
Button,	Indochina, America, Peace, Amnesty, Black & White, Celluloid, 6 In.	69.00
Button,	Jackie Kennedy, Portrait, Color Photo, Orchid Background, David Russell, 2 ⁵⁄₁₆ In.	52.00
Button,	James Madison, Presidential Centenary, Portrait, White Ground, Floral Rim, c.1909, 1 ¼ In.	111.00
Button,	JFK, Photo, Vote Democratic, Red, White, 1 In.	52.00
Button,	Johnson, Humphrey, Celluloid, Democratic National Committee, Jugate, 1964, 6 In. ...*Illus*	34.00
Button,	Kick Out Depression With A Democratic Vote, Roosevelt, Tin Litho, 1932, 2 ¼ In. ....*Illus*	273.00
Button,	Landon Knox, GOP Elephant, Felt Flower Border, Yellow, Blue, Celluloid, 1 ¾ In.	101.00
Button,	Landon Knox, Red, White, Blue, Lithograph, Tab, 1 In.	11.00
Button,	Landon, Victory, Sunflower, 1 In.	11.00
Button,	McGovern As Robin Hood, Black & White, Green Hat, Celluloid, 2 ¼ In.	34.00
Button,	McGovern, Behind You 1000 Percent, Celluloid, 1 ¼ In.	41.00
Button,	McGovern, It's MCG For Me, 1 ¼ In.	9.00
Button,	McGovern, Peter Max Style, Green Ground, Smiling Face, Star, 1972, 1 ½ In.	278.00
Button,	McGovern, Portrait, Black & Red Spiral Striped Border, 1 ¼ In.	10.00
Button,	McGovern, Shriver, October 27, 1972, White, Blue Letters, Celluloid, 2 ½ In.	43.00
Button,	McKinley, Do You Smoke? Yes-Since 1896, Smoking Factory, W&H Backpaper, 2 ⅛ In. .*Illus*	2087.00
Button,	McKinley, Roosevelt, Celluloid, Ribbon, Jugate, 3 ½ In.	345.00
Button,	McKinley, Roosevelt, Full Dinner Pail, Brown, Celluloid, 1 ¼ In.	117.00
Button,	McKinley, Roosevelt, Full Dinner Pail, Sound Money, Sepia, Jugate, 1 In.	1708.00
Button,	Meredith Mississippi March For Freedom, June, 1966, Alabama Outline, 2 ¼ In.	161.00
Button,	Mondale, Ferraro, Stars & Stripes U.S. Map, Celluloid, Jugate, 1984, 6 In.	29.00
Button,	Mondale, Ferraro, South Dakota, Blue, Red, Jugate, 1984, 3 ½ In.	86.00
Button,	Nader For President, Buffalo, American Reform Party, Celluloid, 2 ¼ In.	29.00
Button,	New York State Citizens For Eisenhower, Blue & White, Celluloid, 3 ½ In.	92.00
Button,	Nixon, I Told You So, Portrait, Capitol Dome, Celluloid, 3 ½ In.	454.00
Button,	Nixon, Pandas, Let Me Make Myself Perfectly Clear, We Did Not Do Anything, 2 ½ In.	40.00
Button,	Pair Of Glasses, Black, Pro Goldwater, Clutchback, Tab, 1 In.	12.00
Button,	Parker, Davis, Flags, Celluloid, Jugate, Whitehead & Hoag Back Paper, 1 ¾ In. ....*Illus*	1165.00
Button,	Parker, Davis, Flags, Wreaths, Jugate, 1904, ⅞ In.	45.00
Button,	Peace Now, Nov. 15, March On Washington, Bring GIs Home Now, 3 ½ In.	840.00
Button,	Peace Sign, Peter Max, Doves, Yellow, Blue, Red, White, 2 ½ In.	87.00
Button,	Peace, Yellow & Red Celluloid, Peace Signs, 1971, 2 ½ In.	182.00

P

Button, Peanut, Smiling, Put A Peanut In Every Pot, Jimmy Carter, 2 ¼ In.	32.00
Button, Perot 96, Leadership For American, Portrait Of Perot, 1996, 2 ½ In.	33.00
Button, Pet Power Loves McGovern, 72, Please Vote, Heart, Blue & White, 2 ½ In.	25.00
Button, Pet Power Loves Nixon, 72, Please Vote, Heart, Red & White, 2 ½ In.	39.00
Button, Photo, Profile, Black & White, Theodore Herzl, Founder Of Zionism, c.1904, ⅞ In.	127.00
Button, Power To The People, Black Panther, Orange Ground, Celluloid, 3 ½ In.	21.00
Button, Reagan Hates Us, Celluloid, 1 ¼ In.	228.00
Button, Reagan, Blue, White Letters, Celluloid, 1 ¼ In.	12.00
Button, Reagan, Bush, Blue, Lime Green Border, Celluloid, 2 ¼ In.	27.00
Button, Retain President Carter, White House, No Vacancy Sign, Celluloid, 1980, 2 ¼ In.	23.00
Button, Robert F. Kennedy Vice President, Cream, Blue, Celluloid, 1 ½ In.	9.00
Button, Ronald Reagan For President, 1980, Sketch Of Reagan, Celluloid, 2 ¼ In.	34.00
Button, Ronald Reagan, For President, Celluloid, 1980, 1 ¾ In. ....*Illus*	8.00
Button, Roosevelt, Booker T. Washington, Equality, Multicolor, c.1901, 1 ¼ In.	4480.00
Button, Roosevelt, Fairbanks, Rope Frame, Twisted Flag, Celluloid, Jugate, 1 ¼ In.	146.00
Button, Roosevelt, Fairbanks, Lady Liberty, Jugate, Celluloid, 1 ¼ In.	144.00
Button, Roosevelt, Fairbanks, Rope Frame, Reading, Pa., Jugate, 2 ¼ In.	374.00
Button, Roosevelt, Governor, Rabbit's Foot, Explanatory Backpaper, 1 ¾ In.	383.00
Button, Roosevelt, Johnson, Progressive Party, Bull Moose, Jugate, 1912, 1 ¾ In.	3080.00
Button, Roosevelt, Portrait, Bust, Rough Rider, Celluloid, 1 ¼ In.	162.00
Button, Roosevelt, Portrait, Stars & Stripes Border, St. Louis Button Co., c.1916, 1 ¼ In.	123.00
Button, Roosevelt, Stand Pat, Hand Holding Cards, Portrait On One Card, 1 ¼ In.	247.00
Button, Rooseveltism, Uncle Sam's White Elephant, Anti-Roosevelt, 1 ¼ In.	392.00
Button, Rooster, New Frontier, Vote Democratic, Kennedy, 1960, 1 ¼ In.	62.00
Button, Rose, Velt On 4 Leaves, Celluloid, 1 ¼ In.	114.00
Button, Sad Face, SAD, Students Against The Draft, Yellow, Celluloid, 1 ½ In.	81.00
Button, Scarlett O'Hara Loves Jimmy Carter, Heart Over Confederate Flag, 2 ¼ In.	20.00
Button, Shield, Eagle, Spread Wings, Gold Wreath, Parker's Portrait In Shield, 1 ¼ In.	253.00
Button, Sign Language For I K E, Celluloid, 1 ¼ In. ....*Illus*	374.00
Button, Sit Tight With Ike, White, Blue, 1 ¼ In.	95.00
Button, Skinny Cats For McGovern, Cat, Standing, Leaning On Words, Celluloid, 1972, 2 In.	336.00
Button, Smith, Guiding Star Of Our Nation, Blue Star, Portrait, ⅞ In.	179.00
Button, Solidarnosc Lives, Solidarity Lives, Fist, Stars, Celluloid, 2 ½ In.	8.00
Button, Stevenson, Hooray For Adlai, 1950s, 1 ¼ In.	560.00
Button, Stevenson, Sparkman, 1952, 3 ½ In.	207.00
Button, Stevenson, Vote Democratic, Don't Let Them Take It Away, Celluloid, 2 ¼ In.	518.00
Button, Sunflower, Landon, Knox, Elephant, Yellow Cloth, Celluloid Center, 3 In.	206.00
Button, Sunflower, Landon's Notification, Topeka, July 23, 1936, Felt, Trapp Print Shop, 2 ¼ In. *Illus*	348.00
Button, Taft, Clothiers' Legion, Our Craft Is For Taft, Portrait, Celluloid, 3 ½ In.	259.00
Button, Teddy Roosevelt, Photo, Sepia Background, 1 ¼ In.	58.00
Button, Thomas Eagleton, Mental Illness Is No Disgrace, Celluloid, 1 In.	18.00
Button, Truman, All 48 In '48, Young Democrats, Tin Lithograph, Red, White, Blue, Tab, 1 In.	84.00
Button, Truman, I'm Just Wild About Harry, Inauguration, 1949, 2 ¼ In.	316.00
Button, Truman, Inauguration, Jan. 20, 1949, Stars & Stripes Border, Celluloid, 1 ¼ In.	167.00
Button, Truman, Stars On Top, Stripes On Bottom, Celluloid, 1 ¼ In.	196.00
Button, Truman, True To Truman Democratic Club Of Wash., Inc., 1948, 1 ¼ In.	1344.00
Button, Van Buren, Democracy, Sulfide, Beveled Glass, Brass Frame, Profile, 1 x 1 ⅛ In.	9323.00
Button, Viva Kennedy, Sombrero Shape, 1960, 1 ¼ In.	6.00
Button, Votes For Women, New York, 1915, Green, Maroon, Celluloid, 1 ¼ In.	805.00
Button, We Can't Eat Sunflowers, Let's Lose With Landon, Celluloid, 2 ¼ In.	1568.00
Button, Welcome From Elba, T.R. In Safari Outfit, Uncle Sam, c.1910, 1 ¼ In.	835.00
Button, Welcome Our Boys Home, Flag, Wilson, Pershing, Jugate, 1919, 1 ½ In.	218.00
Button, Westminster College, Harry Truman, Winston Churchill, Fulton, Red, White, Blue, 1946, 2 In.	696.00
Button, What's Wrong With Being Right, Goldwater, Red, White, Celluloid, 1964, 1 ¾ In.	87.00
Button, William H. Taft, For President, Celluloid, Ribbon, Pin Top, 3 ½ In. ....*Illus*	345.00
Button, William Jennings Bryan, Hobby Horse, My Hobby, Winner, 1900, 2 ⅛ In.	6038.00
Button, William McKinley, Garret Hobart, Flag Border, Celluloid, Jugate, c.1890, 1 ¼ In.	420.00
Button, Willkie For President, Photo, Cream Ground, Celluloid, 1 In.	14.00
Button, Willkie, McNary, Star, Stripes, Key Shape, Lithograph, Tab, ¾ In.	20.00
Button, Willkie, Red & Blue Stripes, Celluloid, 1940, 6 In.	34.00
Button, Women For Reagan, Bush, '84, Celluloid, 2 ¼ In.	8.00
Button, Women Should Vote, Shield, Blue, Red & White Stripes, Celluloid, ⅞ In.	489.00
Button, Women Strike For Peace, Stop The War In Vietnam Now, Celluloid, c.1960s, 3 ½ In. *Illus*	84.00
Button, Youth For Kennedy, John F. Kennedy, Portrait, Celluloid, c.1960, 2 ¼ In.	336.00
Calendar Plate, T. Roosevelt, Months Border, Tin Lithograph, A. Baumler & Co., 1905, 10 In. *Illus*	660.00
Calendar, Franklin Roosevelt Portrait, Past Presidents On Side, 1935, 44 x 21 In.	200.00

TIP

You should not regild, resilver, or repaint political buttons or badges. It lowers the value.

Planters Peanuts, Container, Figural, Mr. Peanut, Papier-Mache, Removable Hat, 1930s, 12 ½ In.
$308.00

Hake's Americana & Collectibles

Planters Peanuts, Doll, Mr. Peanut, Jointed, Wood, Schoenhut Toy Co., 8 ¼ x 4 ½ In.
$154.00

Wm Morford Antiques

Plated Amberina, Bowl, Ribbed, Yellow To Rose, New England, 5 In.
$4,600.00

Early Auction Co.

P

Plated Amberina, Cruet, Ribbed, Applied Amber Handle, Stopper, New England, 6 ½ In.
$2,703.00

Early Auction Co.

Plated Amberina, Saltshaker, Ribbed, Corset Shape, Yellow To Rose, New England, 4 In.
$3,163.00

Early Auction Co.

Plated Amberina, Vase, Lily, Ribbed, Disc Foot, 9 ¼ In.
$4,600.00

Early Auction Co.

Campaign Card, James M. Cox, Portrait, Eagle, Fold-Out, Scorecard, 3 x 5 ½ In.	56.00
Campaign Torch, Tin, Barrel Shape, 3 Burner, Carrying Rod, Mouthpiece, c.1880, 37 In.	518.00
Cane, McKinley Bust Handle, Eagle With Shield, Protection 1896, 34 In.	122.00
Carte De Visite, Abraham Lincoln's Dog Fido, Backstamp, Springfield, Ill.	1763.00
Carte De Visite, Lincoln, Oval, 1864, 2 ¾ x 4 In.	185.00
Cartoon, Jimmy Carter Re-Election Hopes, Charles Werner, 13 x 10 ¾ In.	138.00
Charm Bracelet, Music Box, Nixon, Lodge, Battle Hymn Of The Republic, Brass, 1960, 5 In. . *Illus*	95.00
Charm, Dustpan, He'll Raise The Dust In 1901, McKinley, Metal.	27.00
Charm, Full Dinner Pail, Four Years More, McKinley, Metal, Bail Handle, ⅝ In.	55.00
Check, Signed, Harry Truman, Columbia National Bank, 1964, 2 ¾ x 6 In.	337.00
Cigar Box Label, Lady Cleveland, 1886, 4 x 4 ¼ In.	44.00
Cigar Box, Square Deal, Teddy Roosevelt Portrait, Wood, 14 In.	118.00
Cigar, Light One Up For Woodrow, Wilson Photo On Label, Wrapped, 8 ½ In.	69.00
Cigar, Wrapper, Al Smith On Label, 1928, 9 In.	62.00
Cigar, Wrapper, Calvin Coolidge On Label, Light One Up For Silent Cal, 8 ½ In.	69.00
Clock, Lux, End Of Prohibition, Drink Old Reading Beer, 2 Happy Men, Wood, c.1933, 3 x 5 In.	278.00
Clothing Button, Harrison's Log Cabin, ¾ In.	84.00
Coffee Mill, Old Glory, T. Roosevelt, Chromolitho Tin, Iron, Bronson-Walton Co., 10 In. .... *Illus*	705.00
Dinner Pail, McKinley & Roosevelt, Wood, Printed Portraits, Vote For Full Dinner Pail, c.1900	646.00
Doll, Bull Moose, Teddy, Composition Head, Velour Body, E.I. Horsman Co., c.1912, 11 In.	1880.00
Dress, Fabric, Robert Kennedy, Image Of Bobby, Black & White, 1968, 18 x 33 In.	115.00
Dress, Hubert Humphrey, Portrait, Stars, Stripes, Smock, Paper, 36 In.	48.00
Elephant, Cast Iron, GOP, Wm. H. Taft For President, Photo In Center, 6 ½ x 4 ½ In.	287.00
Envelope, Bell, Everett, Vertical Red Accent Text, All Up With Bell, Patriot, 1860, 3 x 5 ½ In.	143.00
Figure, Theodore Roosevelt, Rough Rider Uniform, Syroco Great American Series, c.1941, 6 In.	155.00
Flask, Admiral Dewey, Our Hero, Label Under Glass, Portrait, Flags, Glass, Canteen, 5 In.	1093.00
Fob, Warren G. Harding For President, Portrait, Celluloid, Leather Band, 1 ½ In.	476.00
Frame, Shield Shape, Stars & Stripes, Abraham Lincoln Portrait, Lithograph, c.1890, 23 x 18 In.*Illus*	420.00
Game, Election '68, Candidate Cards, Crisis Cards, Gameboards, Box, 1968, 9 x 18 In.	129.00
Handkerchief, Presidential Victims Of Assassins, McKinley, Garfield, Lincoln, c.1901, 15 x 16 In. *Illus*	330.00
Handkerchief, Tariff Reform, Red, Silk, 1892, 19 x 19 In.	118.00
Handkerchief, U.S. Flag, W. McKinley Of Ohio, Star Shaped Star Field, Silk, 17 In.	64.00
Hat, Kennedy Will Win, Boater, Plastic, 3 JFK Portraits On Hatband, 12 In.	116.00
Hat, Kennedy, Our Next President, Skimmer, Plastic Faux Straw, Red, 1960, 13 In.	48.00
Horn, Vote Straight Democratic, Nov. 2, 1948, Cardboard, Wood Mouthpiece, 8 In.	112.00
Horseshoe, James A. Garfield Bust Inside, Goldtone Metal, 4 ½ In.	212.00
Impeachment Ticket, Andrew Johnson, Cardboard, 1868, 3 x 5 ½ In.	809.00
Iron Grill, Horace Greeley, Fan Shape, Wood Handle, Embossed, 1800s, 29 ¾ In.	288.00
Jack-In-The-Box, Thank You Teddy, Wood, Rotate Top & Roosevelt Pops Up, Wood, 2 In.	160.00
Jug, T. Roosevelt, Elephant Head Handle, Edward Penfield, Toby Potteries, 7 x 5 In. .... *Illus*	600.00
Knife, Jugate, McKinley, T.R., Celluloid, Pocket, 3 In.	56.00
Lamp, F.D.R. Man Of The Hour, At Ship's Wheel, Bronze Luster, White Metal, Globe, 10 x 5 In.	146.00
Lantern, Paper, Grant, Wilson, Candle Holder, Cylindrical, 1872, 9 In. Diam.	380.00
Lapel Stud, Prohibition Party, Figural, Camel, Cast Aluminum, Brass Rim	57.00
License Plate Attachment, 50th American Presidential Inaugural, Reagan, 1985, 12 In.	106.00
License Plate Attachment, America Needs Roosevelt, Portrait, Red, White, Blue, 4 x 9 ⅞ In.	91.00
License Plate Attachment, Coolidge, Blue & White Metal, 1924, 12 In.	272.00
License Plate Attachment, Forward With Roosevelt, Metal, Gray, White, Blue, 9 ½ In.	69.00
License Plate Attachment, I Like Ike, Metal, Arched, 10 In.	184.00
License Plate Attachment, I'm For Stevenson, Metal, Reflective, 1950s, 10 ½ In.	64.00
License Plate Attachment, Inaugural, Eisenhower, Nixon, Jugate, Dist. Of Col., 1957, 12 In.	433.00
License Plate Attachment, Kennedy For President, Metal, White, Green Letters, 1960, 12 In.	317.00
License Plate Attachment, National Recovery Act, Trucking Industry, Metal, Tan, Blue, 1934, 12 In.	106.00
License Plate Attachment, Ride With Wallace, Caricature, Wallace On Donkey, Metal, 1968, 12 In.	46.00
License Plate Attachment, Roosevelt, Art Deco Letters, Cast Aluminum, c.1932, 5 x 10 ½ In. .	221.00
License Plate Attachment, Win With Dewey & Warren, Tin Litho, Jugate, 1948, 5 x 10 In....*Illus*	209.00
License Plate, Repeal Means The Saloon, Uphold 18th Amendment, c.1932, 2 ⅝ x 12 In., 2 Piece.	133.00
License, Carry On Roosevelt I'll Help, Embossed Letters, Painted, Attachment Holes, 5 ½ x 10 In... *Illus*	140.00
Magic Souvenir, Mystery Of The Year, Pull Tab, Truman Becomes Dewey, 1948, 8 In.	104.00
Mask, Lyndon B. Johnson, Exaggerated Features, Plastic, 10 ½ In.	41.00
Match Holder, Roosevelt, Churchill, Stalin, Color Photographs, Metal, 1 x 2 In.	69.00
Match Safe, Benjamin Harrison Profile, Figural, Bronze Tone Metal, 2 ¾ In.	190.00
Match Safe, Grover Cleveland Profile, Figural, Silvertone Metal, 2 ¾ In.	374.00
Match Safe, McKinley Bust, Figural, Goldtone Metal, 2 ⅝ In.	178.00
Medal, Franklin Pierce, Relief Bust, Indian Peace, Settler & Indian, Silver, 1853, 3 In.	6463.00

Political, Bandanna, Win With Ike For President, Printed Cotton, Square, 25 In.
$75.00

Hake's Americana & Collectibles

Political, Bust, Patrick Henry, Patinated Zinc, Inscribed, Warner Miskey Merrill, Phila., c.1860, 12 ¾ In.
$956.00

Neal Auction Co.

Political, Button, Bryan, Stevenson, Flag, Celluloid, W&H Paper, Jugate, 1900, 1 ¾ In.
$138.00

Hake's Americana & Collectibles

Political, Button, Bush, Quayle, Celluloid, Jugate, 1988, 1 ¾ In.
$7.00

Anderson Americana

Political, Button, Carter, Mondale, Democratic 1976, Celluloid, Jugate, 9 In.
$19.00

Anderson Americana

Political, Button, Clinton, Gore, Arkansas Legislators, Celluloid, 1992, 2 ¼ In.
$223.00

Anderson Americana

Political, Button, Harding, Red, White, Blue, Celluloid, Robert Johns Back Paper, 1 ¼ In.
$160.00

Anderson Americana

Political, Button, Hitler Hanging, Let's Pull Together, Mechanical, Tin Litho, Evans Novelty, 1 ⅝ In.
$190.00

Hake's Americana & Collectibles

Political, Button, I Like Ike, Red, White, Blue, Tin Lithograph, 1952, 4 In.
$10.00

Anderson Americana

Political, Button, Johnson, Humphrey, Celluloid, Democratic National Committee, Jugate, 1964, 6 In. $34.00

Anderson Americana

Political, Button, Kick Out Depression With A Democratic Vote, Roosevelt, Tin Litho, 1932, 2 ¼ In. $273.00

Anderson Americana

Political, Button, McKinley, Do You Smoke? Yes-Since 1896, Smoking Factory, W&H Backpaper, 2 ⅛ In. $2,087.00

Hake's Americana & Collectibles

Political, Button, Parker, Davis, Flags, Celluloid, Jugate, Whitehead & Hoag Back Paper, 1 ¾ In. $1,165.00

Anderson Americana

Medal, Henry Clay, Memorial, High Relief Portrait, Angel With Wreath, Grave Marker, c.1852, 1 ¾ In.	94.00
Medal, Herbert Hoover, Bust, Inaugural March 4 1929, Eagle Reverse, Bronze, 3 In.	881.00
Mirror, Pocket, Wm. H. Murray For President, He Wins Our Battles, Portrait, Round, c.1932, 2 ⅛ In.	276.00
Mug, Abraham Lincoln, Transfer, 3 ⅜ In.	1226.00
Mug, Franklin Roosevelt, Happy Days Are Here Again, Brown, Mottled Glaze, 4 In.	144.00
Mug, Republican-Democratic Campaign, Palmer House, Chicago, Plastic, Donkey, 1952, 3 x 5 In.	75.00
Mug, Tilden, Hendricks, Noggin, Redware, Incised, Barrel Shape, 1876, 5 ¾ In.	1989.00
Mug, William McKinley, Gold & Our Country's Honor, American Eagle, Shield, c.1897, 5 x 5 In.	323.00
Music Box, Nixon & Agnew, Dancing Cancan, Silver Flashed Plastic, c.1972, 6 ½ x 7 In., Pair	127.00
Necktie, For President Roosevelt & Prosperity, 48 In.	88.00
Necktie, Franklin Roosevelt, Fala, Repeating Design, Blue Nylon	55.00
Necktie, I Like Ike, Eisenhower Portrait, Black	61.00
Necktie, We Want Truman, 4 x 52 In. *Illus*	278.00
Necktie, Win With Kennedy, Johnson, Black, Orange, 1960	152.00
Paperweight, Theodore Roosevelt, Charles Fairbanks, Glass, Stars, Stripes, Jugate, 3 In.	690.00
Paperweight, W.J. Bryan Photo, Original Metal Easel, 1896, 3 ½ In.	109.00
Paperweight, William H. Taft, Billy Possum, Metal, Cold Painted, 2 ¾ x 3 ½ In.	323.00
Paperweight, Woodrow Wilson, Portrait In Wreath, Flag, Glass, 4 x 2 ½ In.	52.00
Pennant, Ku Klux Klan, Man On Horseback, Cross, Black, Red, White, 3-Sided, 1920s, 28 In.	863.00
Pennant, Robert E. Kennedy, Destined To Become President, Torch, Blue, 1968, 13 In.	52.00
Photograph, Brigadier Gen. James Garfield, Salted Paper, Matthew Brady, c.1862, 16 ¾ x 19 ¾ In.	7050.00
Photograph, Carrie Nation, Hatchet, Bible, Nichols & Davidson, c.1901, 4 x 5 ½ In.	139.00
Picture, President Grover Cleveland, At Desk, Princeton, Watercolor, Penfield, 1904, 12 x 13 In.	2124.00
Picture, Wood Portrait, Franklin D. Roosevelt, 10 ¼ x 14 In.	230.00
Pin, Ben Tilman, Pitchfork, Impaled Gold Bugs, Embossed, Long Clasp, 1896, 2 In.	474.00
Pin, Big Stick, Figural, Teddy On Side, Metal, 1 ⅛ In.	161.00
Pin, Broom, Portrait, Bryan Broom, Clean Sweep, Brass, ¾ In.	51.00 to 57.00
Pin, Bryan, Photo, Sepia Background, 1 ¼ In.	39.00
Pin, Charles Evans Hughes, Attached Whiskbroom Signifying Clean Sweep, 1916, 1 ¼ x 1 ¾ In.	255.00
Pin, Coffin, Friend Of Trusts & British Gold, McKinley, Metal, Hinged, 1 ¼ In.	217.00
Pin, Donkey, Al Smith, Metal, White Enamel	43.00
Pin, Eagle, Rutherford B. Hayes, Portrait, Ferrotype, 1 In.	784.00
Pin, Elephant, Hobart, Metal, Mechanical, Blanket Flips Up To Reveal Photo, 1 ¼ In.	71.00
Pin, Elephant, Wm. H. Taft For President, Photo, Cast Iron, Gold Paint, 6 ½ x 4 ½ In.	287.00
Pin, Eugene McCarthy, Photo, Red, Cream, Celluloid, 1972, 1 In.	12.00
Pin, FDR, Portrait, Figural, Liberty Bell, Hammered Copper, c.1940, 1 ⅝ In.	76.00
Pin, Figural, Nixon, Metal, Clear Rhinestones, 1968, 1 ½ In.	10.00
Pin, Flag Shape, McKinley, Hobart, Brass, Hinged, Hand, Round Portraits, Jugate, 1896, 1 ¼ In.	281.00
Pin, Flag, Votes For Women, Metal, White Enamel, ⅞ In.	345.00
Pin, G, 64, Figural, Goldwater, Metal, Clear & Blue Rhinestones, 1964, 1 ⅛ In.	23.00
Pin, Garfield, Arthur, Brass Shell, Shield Shape, Anchor, 2 Ovals, Jugate, c.1880, 1 ¼ In.	863.00
Pin, Gen. U.S. Grant, Portrait, 6 Star Point Circle, 1868, ¹³⁄₁₆ In.	380.00
Pin, Gold Bug, Goldtone Metal, RH Co., 5 ¼ In.	815.00
Pin, Gold Bug, Metal, McKinley, Hobart Photos On Wings, Mechanical, 1896, 1 ½ In.	173.00
Pin, Grant, Portrait, Ferrotype, Geometric Brass Frame, c.1868, ¹⁵⁄₁₆ In.	171.00
Pin, Hatchet, Carry A Nation, Mother-Of-Pearl Blade, Rhinestone Accent, Inscription, 2 In.	80.00
Pin, Hoover, GOP, Elephant, Enamel, ⅞ In.	10.00
Pin, Ike, Dick, Sample, A.G. Trimble Co., Jugate, 1 In.	828.00
Pin, In Memoriam, McKinley, Mourning Bow With Round Photo, Portrait, 2 ¾ In.	136.00
Pin, James Garfield, Flags, Eagle, Brass, 1 ¼ In.	1064.00
Pin, Lapel, Railroad & Religion, Christian Endeavor, Round, 1893, ⅞ In.	40.00
Pin, Lapel, Viva '96 Clinton	7.50
Pin, Lincoln, Johnson, Flag, Shield Shape, Brass, Jugate, 1864, 1 ¼ In.	7280.00
Pin, McKinley & Hobart, Gold Bug, Mechanical, Wings Fly Open, c.1896, 1 ¼ x 1 ½ In.	144.00
Pin, McKinley Gold Bug, Goldtone Metal, 5 ¾ In.	184.00
Pin, McKinley, Photo, Gold Background, 1 ¼ In.	23.00
Pin, Navy Man, Anchor, Pearl, Heavy Metal, 2 ½ In.	177.00
Pin, Roosevelt, Dem., Donkey, Double Red Heart Shape, Wood, On Card, 1944, 2 ¾ x 3 ½ In.	86.00
Pin, Shield, Lincoln, Portrait, Cardboard, Metal Frame, ¹⁵⁄₁₆ In.	2352.00
Pin, Stud, Bull Moose, Theodore Roosevelt, Metal, 1 ¼ In.	28.00
Pin, Stud, Landon, Figural, Covered Wagon, 1 ¼ In.	40.00
Pin, Stud, Rough Rider Hat, Theodore Roosevelt, Metal, 1 In.	42.00
Pin, Swastika, Ancient Good Luck Symbol, William Jennings Bryan, Brass, 1908, 1 ¼ In.	137.00
Pin, Taft, Roosevelt, Rehearsing His Stunt, Cartoon, T.R. Training Elephant Taft, 1 ¼ In.	5463.00
Pitcher, Garfield, Portrait, Pottery, Ball Shape, Straight Neck, Gold Trim, 8 In.	374.00

Pitcher, George Washington, Transfer, Creamware, c.1795, 10 ½ In.	6160.00
Pitcher, McKinley, Hobart, Pottery, Bulbous, Fluted, Footed, Jugate, England, 8 In.	492.00
Pitcher, McKinley, In Profile, 2 Leafy Bands, Pottery, White Glaze, Bulbous, 7 In.	117.00
Pitcher, Roosevelt Bears, Scenes, Quotations, Transfer Print, Buffalo Pottery, c.1907, 7 ¾ In... *Illus*	705.00
Pitcher, Theodore Roosevelt, Teddy Bear Shape, Seated, Holding Big Stick, Arm Handle, 8 In.	823.00
Plaque, F.D. Roosevelt, With Eleanor & British Royalty, Color, Celluloid, 9 In.	137.00
Plaque, John A. Logan, Profile, Gold Luster Over White Metal, Oval, 1884, 5 ¾ In.	86.00
Plate, Benjamin Harrison, Whitelaw Reid, Dresden China, 1892, 8 In.	172.00
Plate, Grover Cleveland, Adlai Stevenson, Dresden China, 1892, 8 In.	230.00
Plate, Hancock, Portrait, Civilian Suit, Star Border, Pressed Glass, 6 In.	444.00
Platter, Teddy Roosevelt, Profile, Eagle, Bears, Knife, Gun, Glass, Frosted, 10 x 7 In.	195.00
Pocket Knife, Hoover, Curtis, 2 Portraits, 3 ½ In.	163.00
Portrait, Abraham Lincoln, By Matthew Brady, Oval, Walnut Frame, 1864, 13 ½ x 16 In.	369.00
Postcard, Eugene V. Debs, For President, Socialist Party, Photograph, 1920, 5 ½ In.	392.00
Postcard, McKinley, Roosevelt, Eagle, Flag, Jugate, 5 ½ In.	45.00
Postcard, McKinley's Canton, Ohio, Residence, Covered Wagon, 5 ½ In.	40.00
Postcard, Mechanical, Taft, Next President, Pull My Tail & See, 1908, 5 ½ In.	29.00
Postcard, Roosevelt, Manipulating Russian & Japanese Puppets For Peace, 3 ½ x 5 ½ In.	44.00
Postcard, Taft, Uncle Sam, Pointing & Saying 1912, Nebraska Postmark, 5 ½ In.	32.00
Postcard, Theodore Roosevelt, Portrait On 46-Star U.S. Flag, 5 ½ In.	48.00
Postcard, We Are All For Taft, Caricature Of Taft, Ohio, 5 ½ In.	23.00
Postcard, Wilson, Man Who Put I Can In The American, Portrait, Flags, 1917, 5 ½ In.	62.00
Postcard, Wilson, Washington, Lincoln, Eagle, Flags, America We Love You, 5 ½ In.	45.00
Poster, Alfred E. Smith, Joe T. Robinson, Democratic Nominations, 1928, 27 In.	160.00
Poster, Chicago Welcomes President Ford, Daley, Mayor, Red, White & Blue, 22 x 28 In.	168.00
Poster, Come On Dad, Going To Vote Liberal, Girls, Man, Grafton Arts, London, 1929, 30 x 20 In.	2800.00
Poster, Cox, Roosevelt, Their Election Means Peace, Progress, Prosperity, 1920, 16 In.	179.00
Poster, Elect Kennedy, Time For Greatness, Portrait, 28 x 42 In.	444.00
Poster, Everett C. Benton For Governor, Massachusetts, Cardboard, 1912, 22 x 18 In.	65.00
Poster, FDR, Churchill, United For Victory, Liberty For All, Color, Jugate, 16 x 20 In.	58.00
Poster, George Romney, Portrait, Cardboard, A.G. Trimble Co., 1968, 22 x 14 In.	45.00
Poster, Hoover, Curtis, President, Vice President, Jugate, Frame, 1928, 20 ½ x 26 In.	201.00
Poster, Kennedy, Leadership For The 60s, JFK, Red, White, Blue, 21 x 18 ½ In.	531.00
Poster, Landon & Knox, For U.S., Deeds Not Deficits, Stars & Stripes, 21 x 14 In.	50.00
Poster, Let's Back The Team Of Kennedy, Johnson, 1960, 22 x 14 In.	288.00
Poster, Let's Put Robert Kennedy To Work For New York, Photograph, 33 x 21 In.	240.00
Poster, Lincoln, Johnson, Defenders Of Our Union, Washington, War Heroes, c.1865, 24 x 29 In.	460.00
Poster, McGovern Rally, James Taylor, Tom Rush, Sun., Nov. 5, 1972, 22 x 14 In.	405.00
Poster, Prevent Forced Busing With Wallace On Nov. 7th, School Children, 17 x 11 In.	110.00
Poster, Re-Elect Roosevelt, Vote American Labor, New Deal, 1940, Portrait, 27 x 21 In.	4210.00
Poster, Roosevelt, Fairbanks, Portraits, Black & White, Jugate, Frame, 1904, 28 x 38 In.	591.00
Poster, Roosevelt, Our Friend, Figures, Ben Shahn, 1944, 30 x 39 ¾ In.	3000.00
Poster, Roosevelt, Truman, Missouri Democrats, Vote The Democratic Ticket, 15 x 12 In.	104.00
Poster, Truman, Dewey, Good Man Is Hard To Find, 2 Men, Piano, Ben Shahn, 1948, 45 x 30 In..	5000.00
Print Block, Images Of Grover Cleveland & Charles Hendricks, 1884, 1 ⅝ x 3 In.	63.00
Print, Jefferson Davis, President In Petticoats, Currier & Ives, 1865, 12 x 16 In.	172.00
Print, Polk, Speaker Of The House Of Representatives, U.S.A., Frame, 1838, 19 x 22 In.	135.00
Print, Ronald Reagan, 4 Portraits, Norman Rockwell, 1968, 31 x 22 In.	52.00
Purse, Portrait, W.H. Harrison, Leather, Glass, Horseshoe Shape, Brass Edge, 1840, 2 x 3 In.	1328.00
Record, Ronald Reagan, Speaks Out Against Socialized Medicine, Portrait, 12 ¼ In.	68.00
Record, Speeches Of John F. Kennedy & Franklin D. Roosevelt, 33 ⅓ RPM, Cover	26.00
Ribbon Badge, McKinley's Ward, Canton, Ohio, White, Flag, Fringe, 1896, 9 ½ In.	172.00
Ribbon, Bryan, Tammany Hall, Photo Button, Black Star, Button 1 ¾ In.	246.00
Ribbon, Cleveland Democracy, Erie Co., N.Y., Blue Bar Pin, 1892, 7 In.	478.00
Ribbon, Delegate, National Negro Democratic Convention, August, 1894, Brown, 6 In.	150.00
Ribbon, Democratic Convention, For President, Grover Cleveland, Chicago, 1892, 8 In.	74.00
Ribbon, FDR, Democratic State Convention, Syracuse, 1936, Pin, Tammany, Portrait, 4 In.	178.00
Ribbon, Grand Old Party Still Lives, Protection, Sound Money, T.R. Roosevelt, Paper, 10 In.	76.00
Ribbon, Grant, By Stevens, Tassel, 1868, 5 x 7 In.	126.00
Ribbon, Harding, Parade, Paper Trade, 1920, Portrait In Shell Pendant, 4 ¼ In.	242.00
Ribbon, Harrison, Smiling Cartoon Face, 1888, 2 ¾ x 8 ¼ In.	114.00
Ribbon, Henry Clay, Pride Of America, People's Choice, Portrait, 7 ½ In.	224.00
Ribbon, James A. Garfield, Memorial, Died Sept. 19th, 1881, Portrait, Black Border, 6 In.	96.00
Ribbon, James, 1876, Republican Nomination For President, 1 ½ x 5 ½ In.	126.00
Ribbon, Lincoln, Portrait, Silk, 7 ¾ In.	4144.00

TIP

It is important to have proper lighting for a picture or print that is on display.

Political, Button, Ronald Reagan, For President, Celluloid, 1980, 1 ¾ In. $8.00

Anderson Americana

Political, Button, Sign Language For I K E, Celluloid, 1 ¼ In. $374.00

Anderson Americana

Political, Button, Sunflower, Landon's Notification, Topeka, July 23, 1936, Felt, Trapp Print Shop, 2 ¼ In. $348.00

Hake's Americana & Collectibles

The edited listings of the current prices in this *Kovels' Antiques & Collectibles Price Guide* aren't available on any website. Readers can visit **Kovels.com** to check thousands of past prices and sign up for free information on trends, tips, reproductions, marks, and more.

P

Political, Button, William H. Taft, For President, Celluloid, Ribbon, Pin Top, 3 ½ In.
$345.00

Anderson Americana

Political, Button, Women Strike For Peace, Stop The War In Vietnam Now, Celluloid, c.1960s, 3 ½ In.
$84.00

Anderson Americana

Political, Calendar Plate, T. Roosevelt, Months Border, Tin Litho, A. Baumler & Co., 1905, 10 In.
$660.00

Cowan's Auctions

Political, Coffee Mill, Old Glory, T. Roosevelt, Chromolitho Tin, Iron, Bronson-Walton Co., 10 In.
$705.00

Cowan's Auctions

Ribbon, McKinley, Photo, Chicago Day, Oct. 9th 1896, 2 ½ x 5 ¼ In.	86.00
Ribbon, McKinley, Tanner, Canton Clipper Club, Gold Fabric, Brass Cord Tassels, 1896, 2 ¾ x 2 ½ In.	304.00
Ribbon, Millard Fillmore, For President, For Vice-President, Andrew J. Donelson, 7 In.	432.00
Ribbon, Plumed Knight, Blaine, Logan, Brass Shell Shape, Medieval Knight, Jugate, 4 ¼ In.	2800.00
Ribbon, Portrait, Winfield Scott, Silk, 1852, 3 x 6 In.	316.00
Ribbon, Press, Tammany Hall Ratification Meeting, Oct. 13, 1904, Alton Parker, 6 ¾ In.	286.00
Ribbon, Progressive Party Founders Day, Look Up Not Down, 1912, 2 x 6 In.	97.00
Ribbon, Progressive, Bull Moose Logo, Union Bug, 1912, 1 ⅞ x 10 ¼ In.	158.00
Ribbon, Prohibition, Fish, Brooks, Jugate, Drawn Portraits, 6 ¼ In.	276.00
Ribbon, R.B. Hayes, W.A. Wheeler, Republican Nomination, Woven, 1876, 1 ½ x 5 ½ In.	126.00
Ribbon, Republican Party, 2 Flags, Portrait, T.R. Roosevelt, 1904, 10 In.	146.00
Ribbon, Societatea, Romana De Ajutor, Woodrow Wilson, Flag, Portrait, Pin, c.1917, 8 In.	308.00
Ribbon, Sons Of The Boys In Blue, W.A. McKinley, H.A. Hobart, Red, Jugate, 5 ¾ In.	98.00
Ribbon, Taft, Grand Old Party, Brass Chain, 1908, 2 ⅞ x 1 ¾ In.	316.00
Ribbon, Tammany Hall, Smith, Walker, Coler & Victory, Star, Metal Pin, Captain, 6 ½ In.	364.00
Ribbon, Tammany Society, Columbian Order, July 4th, 1868, Cardboard Back, Fringe, 5 In.	172.00
Ribbon, Tammany, 1932 Democratic National Convention, Chicago, Indian Drop, 4 In.	264.00
Ribbon, Tammany, Columbian Order, July 4th, 1789-1904, N.Y. Daily News, 10 In.	138.00
Ribbon, Tammany, Saratoga, New York, Sept. 11, 1900, Celluloid Indian, 4 ¾ In.	96.00
Ribbon, Tammy Hall, Cleveland, Stevenson, Tiger, Indian, Flag, Fringe, c.1893, 11 ½ In.	345.00
Ribbon, Theodore Roosevelt, 1912 Nebraska Progressive Convention, 2 ½ x 7 ½ In.	114.00
Ribbon, William Henry Harrison, Memorial, Eagle, Banner, Flags, 1841, 7 ¼ In.	95.00
Ribbon, Winfield Scott, Portrait, Silk, Hero Of Many Battles, Lundy's Lane Chippewa, 1852, 3 x 6 In.	316.00
Salt & Pepper, President & Mrs. John F. Kennedy, Portraits, Bell Shape, 2 ¾ In.	35.00
Scale, Cleveland, Harrison, Bisque Figures, Wooden Bar, Metal, c.1890, 5 In. ....*Illus*	764.00
Sheet Music, Cleveland's Grand March, Portrait Of Cleveland, 6 Pages, 14 x 10 ¾ In.	38.00
Sheet Music, Hello, Jimmy, Jimmy Carter Portrait, U.S. Flag, 4 Pages, 1976, 11 x 8 ½ In.	33.00
Sheet Music, National Whig Song, William Henry Harrison, 4 Pages, 1840	139.00
Sheet Music, New Deal March, Uncle Sam & FDR On Cover, 6 Pages, 12 ¼ x 9 In.	84.00
Sheet Music, Wigwam Grand March, Portrait Of Lincoln, 16 x 12 In.	1843.00
Sheet Music, Wilson Campaign, We'll Link His Name With Lincoln, 6 Pages, 12 x 9 In.	46.00
Shoe Brush, Pig Shape, Grover's Head On Pig, Bristles At Top, 1884, 3 x 5 In.	1410.00
Shot Glass, Roosevelt, Fairbanks, Custard Glass, Transfer Portraits, Jugate, 2 ½ In.	353.00
Sign, Humphrey For Florida, Orange, 14 In.	41.00
Sign, Judge Taft, Universal Favorite, 5 Cent Cigar, Portrait, Tin Lithograph, 13 x 19 In. ......*Illus*	470.00
Sign, No Parking, Presidential Inauguration, January 19 To January 20, Frame, 1949, 17 x 11 In.	480.00
Sign, Play, Father Daniel Berrigan, Trial Of The Catonsville Nine, Cardboard, 1971, 14 x 22 In.	115.00
Sign, This House Sold On Goldwater, Orange, Black Letters, 1964, 12 x 17 In.	23.00
Sign, T-R Cigars, Roosevelt Portrait, Tin Litho, Cardboard, American Art Works, 6 x 13 In....*Illus*	1645.00
Smock, Alf Landon, Frank Knox, Sunflowers, Paper, 1936, 46 In.	316.00
Sock, Bryan, Free Stocking, Silver Purse, Cloth, Latch Top, Bastian Brothers, 31 In.	247.00
Stein, President McKinley, Pewter Lid, Pottery, ½ Liter	156.00
Stickpin, Bryan, Mechanical, Caricature, Lower Jaw Opens, 16 To 1, 1 ⅞ In.	920.00
Stickpin, Harrison, Cardboard Photo, Brass Shell, Geometric Design, 1 In.	75.00
Stickpin, Hoover, Elephant, Brown, 1 In.	8.00
Stud, Abraham Lincoln, Photograph, Domed, Mother-Of-Pearl, Brass, 1890s, ¹³⁄₁₆ In.	63.00
Ticket, Convention, Franklin Roosevelt, Attached Stub, 1936, 6 In. ....*Illus*	17.00
Ticket, Democratic National Convention, Chicago, July 7th, 1896, 5 ¾ In.	22.00
Ticket, Democratic National Convention, Kansas City, Guest, 1900, 6 ⅜ In.	40.00
Ticket, Democratic National Convention, Philadelphia, Guest, 1948, 6 ¼ In.	29.00
Ticket, Harrison Inauguration, 1806, 4 In.	153.00
Ticket, Republican National Convention, Philadelphia, Delegate, 1900, 4 ½ In.	25.00
Ticket, Seymour, Blair 1868 Ballot, Democratic, Paper, 2 ¾ x 8 In.	120.00
Tie Clip, Donkey, FDR, 2 ½ In.	66.00
Tin, Simon's Roosevelt Cigars, T.R. Portrait, Tobacco Leaves, 5 In.	106.00
Toothpick Holder, William McKinley, Etched Glass, Fluted Rim, 3 ½ In.	44.00
Torch, Pinecone, James G. Blaine, Wood, F.C. Goodwin, Chelsea, Mass., 1884, 3 ¼ x 9 ¾ In.	764.00
Toy, Theodore Roosevelt, Safari Clothing, Helmet, American Flag, Wood Jointed, Schoenhut, 8 In...*Illus*	1410.00
Toy, William Taft, Celluloid, Weighted Figure, Metal Wheels, 2 ¼ In. & 1 ½ In., 2 Piece ....*Illus*	235.00
Tray, Theodore Roosevelt, Portrait, Vignettes, Raised Rim, Multicolor, Oval, 13 ¾ x 16 ½ In.	354.00
Tray, Theodore Roosevelt, Roses, Cowboy, Metal, Meek & Beach Co., 14 x 16 In. ....*Illus*	158.00
Watch Fob, Charles E. Hughes, Portrait, Horseshoe Design, Leather Strap, 2 In.	115.00
Watch Fob, Cox, Roosevelt, Silvered Brass, Eagle, Oak & Olive Sprays, Leather Strap, 1920	150.00
Watch Fob, Harding, Coolidge, Silvered Brass, Eagle, Oak & Olive Sprays, Leather, Strap, 1920	100.00
Watch Fob, Taft, Round Portrait Button, Black Leather, 1 ¼ In.	86.00
Whistle, McKinley & Hobart, Tin, Painted, 1896, 4 In.	58.00

P

Political, Frame, Shield Shape, Stars & Stripes, Abraham Lincoln Portrait, Lithograph, c.1890, 23 x 18 In.
$420.00

Skinner, Inc.

Political, Handkerchief, Presidential Victims Of Assassins, McKinley, Garfield, Lincoln, c.1901, 15 x 16 In.
$330.00

Skinner, Inc.

Political, Jug, T. Roosevelt, Elephant Head Handle, Edward Penfield, Toby Potteries, 7 x 5 In.
$600.00

Cowan's Auctions

Political, License Plate Attachment, Win With Dewey & Warren, Tin Litho, Jugate, 1948, 5 x 10 In.
$209.00

Hake's Americana & Collectibles

Political, License, Carry On Roosevelt I'll Help, Embossed Letters, Painted, Attachment Holes, 5 ½ x 10 In.
$140.00

Hake's Americana & Collectibles

Political, Charm Bracelet, Music Box, Nixon, Lodge, Battle Hymn Of The Republic, Brass, 1960, 5 In.
$95.00

Hake's Americana & Collectibles

Political, Necktie, We Want Truman, 4 x 52 In.
$278.00

Hake's Americana & Collectibles

Political, Pitcher, Roosevelt Bears, Scenes, Quotations, Transfer Print, Buffalo Pottery, c.1907, 7 ¾ In.
$705.00

Cowan's Auctions

Political, Scale, Cleveland, Harrison, Bisque Figures, Wooden Bar, Metal, c.1890, 5 In.
$764.00

Cowan's Auctions

Political, Sign, Judge Taft, Universal Favorite, 5 Cent Cigar, Portrait, Tin Lithograph, 13 x 19 In.
$470.00

Cowan's Auctions

P

Political, Sign, T-R Cigars, Roosevelt Portrait, Tin Litho, Cardboard, American Art Works, 6 x 13 In. $1,645.00

Cowan's Auctions

Political, Ticket, Convention, Franklin Roosevelt, Attached Stub, 1936, 6 In. $17.00

Anderson Americana

Political, Toy, Theodore Roosevelt, Safari Clothing, Helmet, American Flag, Wood Jointed, Schoenhut, 8 In. $1,410.00

Cowan's Auctions

Political, Toy, William Taft, Celluloid, Weighted Figure, Metal Wheels, 2 ¼ In. & 1 ½ In., 2 Piece $235.00

Cowan's Auctions

POMONA glass is a clear glass with a soft amber border decorated with pale blue or rose-colored flowers and leaves. The colors are very, very pale. The background of the glass is covered with a network of fine lines. It was made from 1885 to 1888 by the New England Glass Company. First grind was made from April 1885 to June 1886. It was made by cutting a wax surface on the glass, then dipping it in acid. Second grind was a less expensive method of acid etching that was developed later.

Bowl, Frosted, Gold Accents, Bulbous, Footed, Undulated Rim, 3 In.	86.00
Candy Jar, Blue Cornflower, Amber Highlights, Egg Shape, Footed, Lid, Ball Finial, 10 In.	230.00
Finger Bowl, Frosted, Gold Trim, Trifold Rim, Squat, 5 In.	58.00
Pitcher, Tankard, Etched Cornflower, Applied Clear Handle, 2 Tumblers, New England, 12 In.	863.00
Shaker, Etched Cornflower, New England, 3 ¾ In., Pair	374.00
Tumbler, Cornflower, Blossom & Butterfly, 3 ¾ In., Pair	144.00
Water Set, Frosted, Pitcher, 2 Tumblers, 8 In., 3 Piece	144.00

PONTYPOOL, *see Tole category.*

POOLE POTTERY was founded by Jesse Carter in 1873 in Poole, England, and has operated under various names since then. The pottery operated as Carter & Co. for several years and established Carter, Stabler & Adams as a subsidiary in 1921. The company specialized in tiles, architectural ceramics, and garden ornaments. Tableware, bookends, candelabra, figures, vases, and other items have also been made. The name *Poole Pottery Ltd.* was taken in 1963. The company went bankrupt in 2003, but is in business today with new owners.

Candlestick, Leaves, Blue, 8 In.	30.00
Nut Dish, White, Ribbed, Footed, Center Handle	27.00
Pin Dish, Delphis, Orange, c.1960, 7 x 4 In.	33.00
Pin Dish, Delphis, Red, c.1960, 7 x 4 In.	28.00
Plate, Grapes, Blue, 10 ¾ In.	40.00
Plate, Leaf Border, Blue, 10 ¾ In.	80.00

POPEYE was introduced to the Thimble Theatre comic strip in 1929. The character became a favorite of readers. In 1932, an animated cartoon featuring Popeye was made by Paramount Studios. The cartoon series continued and became even more popular when it was shown on television starting in the 1950s. The full-length movie with Robin Williams as Popeye was made in 1980. KFS stands for King Features Syndicate, the distributor of the comic strip.

Bank, Daily Dime, Popeye Juggling Coins, Tin, Square	150.00
Belt, Popeye, Olive Oyl & Wimpy, Store Card, Leather, Boy's, 1929, 5 ¼ x 12 In.	127.00
Bubble Set, 2 Pipes, King Features, Box, 1936	135.00
Clock, Alarm, Popeye, Kneeling, Arm Clock Hands, Tin Litho, New Haven Clock Co., c.1930, 4 x 4 In.	1093.00
Cookie Jar, Popeye, Winking, American Bisque, 8 In.	425.00
Costume, Popeye, Mask, Pipe, Sailor's Hat, Tan, Glow In The Dark, Blue Pants, Box, Size Large	38.00
Display, Popeye & Wimpy Sawing Logs, Simonds Saws, Are The Best Wood, Paint, 1930s, 24 x 22 In.	3163.00
Display, Popeye, Wood Carved, Keith Keonis, 1960s, 64 In.	1650.00
Figure, Eugene The Jeep, Composition, Jointed, Painted, Tail, Decal, 1935, 13 In.	383.00 to 675.00
Lunch Box, Popeye, Olive Oyl, Brutus, Metal, Aladdin, 1980	60.00
Pencil Box Set, Crayons, Ruler, Erasers, Sharpener, King Features, 1934	65.00
Phonograph, Popeye, Dynamatic Music Machine, Emerson, Model BSR-M100	35.00
Record Player, Popeye, Olive Oyl, Dance Party, Emerson	250.00
Toothbrush Holder, Popeye, Candy In Wrap, Painted, Chein, 1932, 5 In.	230.00
Toy, Motorcycle Patrol, Popeye Driver, Pulling Spinach, Cast Iron, Red, Hubley, c.1938, 6 In.	431.00
Toy, Motorcycle Patrol, Popeye, Driving, Pulling Spinach, Iron, King, Hubley, 1928, 8 In.	19550.00
Toy, Popeye & Baggage, Wheelbarrow, Tin, Windup, Box, Louis Marx, 1932, 3 x 8 In.	1560.00
Toy, Popeye & Baggage, Wheelbarrow, Trunk, Parrot, Tin Lithograph, Key Wind, King Features, 8 In.	489.00
Toy, Popeye On Tricycle, Tin, Bell On Back, Key Wind, Linemar, Japan, 4 In.	316.00
Toy, Popeye Riding Tricycle, Tin Lithograph, Bell On Rear, Windup, Linemar, Japan, 4 ¼ In. *Illus*	259.00
Toy, Popeye, Barrel Walker, Tin Lithograph, Windup, Chein, Box, 1932, 6 ¾ In.	1080.00
Toy, Popeye, Champ, Tin, Boxing Ring, Celluloid Figures, Box, Marx, 6 ½ x 7 In.	1760.00
Toy, Popeye, Heavy Hitter, Key Wind, Tin Lithograph, Chein, c.1932, 11 ¾ In.	3835.00
Toy, Popeye, Olive Oyl, Dancing On Roof, Jiggers, Box, Tin, Windup, Louis Marx, 1934, 5 x 9 ½ In.	1780.00
Toy, Popeye, Parrot Cages, Carrying, Walking, Black Shirt, Lithograph, Tin, Clockwork, Marx, 8 In.	303.00
Toy, Popeye, Roller Skater, Holding Platter, Tin Lithograph, Cloth Pants, Linemar, Box, 6 ½ In.	690.00
Toy, Popeye, Spinach Eater, Moveable Arms, Wheeled Cart, Pull, Fisher-Price, 1939, 9 In.	770.00
Toy, Popeye, Swee'Pea, Steering Wheel, Lithograph, Pull, Fisher-Price, 1936, 12 In.	660.00
Toy, Popeye, Walker, Moves Back & Forth, Tin Lithograph, Chein, 1932, 6 In.	253.00
Toy, Popeye's Face, Sparkler, Tin Lithograph, Push Lever, Chein, 5 ½ In.	144.00

P

Toy, Rowboat, Popeye, Rowing, Tin Lithograph, Clockwork, Hoge, 1935, 15 In.	4800.00
Toy, Tank, Popeye Shooting Gun, Olive Oyl, Tin Lithograph, Windup, c.1950, 2 ¼ x 4 In.	127.00
Toy, Tugboat, SS Popeye, Pull Toy, Wood, Eating Spinach, Swee'Pea, Olive Oyl, 1940s, 15 ½ In.	190.00
Watch, Popeye, Comic Characters Hands, King Features, New Haven, c.1934, Pocket	1680.00
Watch, Popeye, Thimble Theatre Characters On Dial, Wimpy, Hamburger, New Haven, 1934, Pocket	180.00
Watch, Popeye, Wimpy Chasing Hamburger, New Haven, Box, 1935, Pocket	840.00

PORCELAIN factories that are well known are listed in this book under the factory name. This category lists pieces made by the less well-known factories. Additional pieces of porcelain are listed in this book in the categories Porcelain-Contemporary, Porcelain-Midcentury, and under the factory name.

Basket, Pierced Woven Bowl, Pedestal Shape, White, Gilt, Tucker, c.1825, 9 ½ x 9 ½ In.	3555.00
Bough Pot, Castle Shape, Shrewsbury Castle, Exotic Birds, Flower Stems, c.1825, 4 ¼ x 6 ¾ In.	1298.00
Bowl, Blue Kangxi, Blue Ground, Floral Vignette Panels, Endless Knot Mark, 3 ½ x 7 ½ In.	184.00
Bowl, Brig Oak Of Whitby, Ship, Gilt, England, c.1855, 5 ¼ x 11 In.	474.00
Box, Lid, Round, Blue & White, Flowers, Vines, Dragon, Bird Of Paradise, Ring Foot, c.1900, 8 In.	518.00
Bust, Diana, White, Blue Glaze, Pink & Blue Circlet In Hair, Glazed, Scheibe Alsbach, 12 In.	173.00
Cachepot, Sevres Style, Flowers, Figures, Cylindrical, Beaded Rim, Scroll Feet, Handles, 1800s, 11 In.	1500.00
Censer, Loop Handles, Rings, Pierced Lid, Lion Finial, Turquoise & Gold, c.1900, 4 ½ x 4 ½ In.	1495.00
Centerpiece, Reticulated Bowl, Cherubs Wings, Flowers, Fruit, Schierholz & Sohn, 12 x 12 In.	472.00
Centerpiece, Vase, Round Stepped Base, Seated Cherubs, Shield Shape Holders, c.1850, 14 In.	2868.00
Charger, Battle Scene, Classical Figures, Enamel, Emile Lessore, France, c.1850, 16 ⅞ In. *Illus*	889.00
Charger, Blue & White, Oriental, Bird, Flowers, Floral Reserve Edge, 1800s, 13 ½ In.	144.00
Charger, Blue & White, Pagodas, Bridges, Rocks, Palms, Birds, Flowers, Hanger, Iran, 21 In.	5000.00
Charger, Sevres Style, Battle Scene, Gilt, Blue, Chateau Des Tuileries, Rocroy, 19 ¾ In. *Illus*	4500.00
Compote, 3 Cherubs, Reticulated Bowl, Flowers, Sitzendorf, c.1887, 13 x 11 In.	173.00
Compote, Reticulated Bowl, Cobalt Blue, Gilt, Pedestal, Square Base, 1800s, 8 x 10 ¼ In.	1464.00
Compote, Reticulated Bowl, Scalloped, Pedestal, 3 Cherubs, Flowers, Sitzendorf, c.1887, 13 In.	173.00
Compote, Sweetmeat, 3 Tiers, Flowers, White, Pink, Gilt Accents, Ring Handle, Foot, 16 In., Pair.	489.00
Container, Stacking, Lid, Butterfly Shape, 4 Sections, Multicolor Floral Enamel, Yellow, 8 x 8 In.	98.00
Cup & Saucer, Military, Gott Schutze Deutschland, God Protect Germany *Illus*	60.00
Cup & Saucer, Portrait, Major General, N.P. Banks, April 14, 1863, Rudolph T. Lux, 9 In. Saucer *Illus*	9261.00
Ewer, Flowers, Acanthus Leaves, Blue Underglaze, Gray, Flared Rim, S-Scroll Handle, 5 In.	288.00
Ewer, Turquoise, Scrolled Spout, Ormolu Dragon Handle, Rim, Base, France, c.1890, 26 In.	4375.00
Figurine, Art Deco, Woman Dancing, Long Blue Dress, Metalware Base, c.1930, 12 In.	146.00
Figurine, Blue & White, Man, Woman, In Period Dress, 1800s, 7 In., Pair	108.00
Figurine, Buddha, With 5 Children, Multicolor Glaze, 1900s, 12 ½ x 10 In.	178.00
Figurine, Cat, Seated, Mottled Brown Glaze, 1800s, 11 x 8 ½ In.	403.00
Figurine, Chinese Man, Standing, Hands On Hip, Multicolor, Gilt, Conta & Bohme, 11 In.	115.00
Figurine, Daffodil Seller, Charles Vyse, 1923, 10 ½ In.	1575.00
Figurine, Frog With Umbrella, Marked, Schierholz, 6 ½ In. *Illus*	240.00
Figurine, Guanyin, Lotus Throne, Giving Fearlessness Mudra, Crown, Blanc De Chine, 1800s, 23 In.	1778.00
Figurine, Hungarian Shepherd, Seated On Ground, Staff, Hollohaza, 8 ½ In.	72.00
Figurine, Lipizzaner Horse, Rider, Blue Dress, Keramos, Austria, 17 ½ In.	203.00
Figurine, Lipizzaner Horse, Rider, Marked Wien, 11 ½ x 8 In.	387.00
Figurine, Phoenix Head, Incised, Light Ground, Lotus Flowers, 12 x 6 In.	330.00
Figurine, Robert Burns, Holding Book, Leaning On Tree, Multicolor, Gilt, Oval Base, 13 x 7 In.	115.00
Figurine, Rococo, 1700s Attire, Germany, c.1930, 6 ¼ In., Pair	154.00
Figurine, Soldier, Woman, Antonio Borsato, Italy, 12 In.	223.00
Figurine, Woman, Holding Out Blue Skirt, Art Deco, c.1930, 12 In.	149.00
Figurine, Woman, Standing, Nude, Hands Above Head, Trailing Leaves, 14 ½ In.	325.00
Group, 1700s Style Figures, Man Giving Bouquet To Woman, Germany, c.1930, 12 x 11 In.	210.00
Group, Courtly Woman, Primping At Dressing Table, Gentleman, Sitzendorf, 17 x 17 In.	460.00
Group, George & Eliza Harris, Holding Eva, Inscribed Title, Multicolor, Gilt, 14 x 7 ½ In.	184.00
Group, Horse, 2 Winged Putti, Nude Woman, Flowers, Scroll Base, c.1885, 5 x 6 In.	984.00
Head Rest, Cat Shape, Beige Ground, Brown Flowers On Cat's Back, 5 ½ x 10 In.	36.00
Humidor, Turkey, Wearing Suit, Spectacles, Multicolor Matte Glaze, 7 ¾ x 5 ½ In.	81.00
Jar, Lid, Double Happiness, Underglaze Blue, Flowers, c.1890, 17 In.	345.00
Jar, Lid, Maitland Smith, Blue & White, Figural Scene, Foil Label, 16 In.	80.00
Jar, Lid, Pierced Bronze Collar, Acorn Finial, Flowers, c.1900, 19 ½ x 10 ½ In., Pair	4500.00
Jardiniere, Napoleon III Style, Peach Blossoms, Turquoise, Gilt Bronze, Handles, Rim, 10 x 16 In.	438.00
Jardiniere, Oval, Winged Putti, Bed Of Roses, Figures, Tooled Gilt, France, c.1900, 4 ¼ x 12 ½ In.	676.00
Jardiniere, White, Flowers, Birds, Famille Rose Style, Lion Crest, Cast Metal Rim, Handles, 28 x 16 In.	1121.00
Letter Holder, Green On White, Flowers, Gilt, Shaped, Austria, c.1900, 5 ⅜ x 4 ⅜ In.	35.00
Letter Stand, Louis XV Style, 3 Panels, Scroll Shape, Gilt Flared Feet, Germany, c.1890, 10 x 10 In.	531.00

Political, Tray, Theodore Roosevelt, Roses, Cowboy, Metal, Meek & Beach Co., 14 x 16 In.
$158.00

Hake's Americana & Collectibles

Senior Shooter
Annie Oakley, the famous star of Buffalo Bill's Wild West Show, kept performing her amazing sharpshooting act until she was in her 60s. She quit because of injuries from a car accident.

Popeye, Toy, Popeye Riding Tricycle, Tin Lithograph, Bell On Rear, Windup, Linemar, Japan, 4 ¼ In.
$259.00

Bertoia Auctions

Porcelain, Charger, Battle Scene, Classical Figures, Enamel, Emile Lessore, France, c.1850, 16 ⅞ In.
$889.00

Skinner, Inc.

PORCELAIN

Porcelain, Charger, Sevres Style, Battle Scene, Gilt, Blue, Chateau Des Tuileries, Rocroy, 19 ¾ In.
$4,500.00

Leslie Hindman Auctioneers

Porcelain, Cup & Saucer, Military, Gott Schutze Deutschland, God Protect Germany
$60.00

The Stein Auction Co.

Porcelain, Cup & Saucer, Portrait, Major General, N.P. Banks, April 14, 1863, Rudolph T. Lux, 9 In. Saucer
$9,261.00

Neal Auction Co.

Porcelain, Figurine, Frog With Umbrella, Marked, Schierholz, 6 ½ In.
$240.00

The Stein Auction Co.

Loving Cup, Painted, Grape Clusters, Signed Bischoff, Stamped, c.1900	1440.00
Pastille Burner, Church, Mound Base, Bocage, Applied Flowers, Painted, Gilt, c.1820, 7 x 5 In.	92.00
Pitcher, Flowers, Swirled Blue Glaze, Pewter Base, Hinged Lid, Bayreuth, Germany, c.1750, 15 x 7 In.	3163.00
Place Setting, Roy Lichtenstein, Black, White, Jackson China For Durable Dish, 1966, 5 Piece ...*Illus*	3125.00
Plaque, 2 Cupids, Along Edge Of Pool, Reaching For Quiver, Signed, Germany, 1898, 6 x 8 In.	307.00
Plaque, Courtly Garden Scene, Troubadour, Seated Women, Painted, 9 x 19 ½ In.	2091.00
Plaque, Famille Rose, Scenes Of Old Men Playing Chess, Rosewood & Burl Frame, 1800s	230.00
Plaque, Round, Marguerite, Daisies In Hair, Scroll Frame, Germany, c.1900, 9 In.	215.00 to 861.00
Plate, Cherub, Reclining, Basket, Landscape, Purple, White, Gilt Rim, Vincennes, c.1752	1500.00
Plate, Floral Center, Green Banded Border, Gilt, George Jones & Sons, 10 In., 12 Piece	263.00
Plate, Flowers, Grape & Gilt Border, France, c.1800, 8 ¾ In.	165.00
Plate, Flowers, Leaves, Geometrics, Cyrillic Seal, Imperial Porcelain Factory, c.1900, 8 ¾ In.	2370.00
Plate, Gothic Revival Style, Multicolor Flowers, Cobalt Blue & Gilt Border, France, c.1850, 8 ½ In.	538.00
Plate, Monk, Drinking From Stein, Mounted, Giltwood Frame, Shadowbox, 9 ½ In.	188.00
Plate, Propaganda, Flowers, Leaves, Gilt Rim, Multicolor, Russia, 1921, 9 ½ In.	1007.00
Plate, Sevres Style, Aristocratic Woman, Rose Garland In Hair, Cobalt Border, Reserves, 10 ½ In.	875.00
Plate, St. Petersburg, Arabesque, Imperial Crests, 9 ½ In.	2832.00
Plate, Yellow Border, Gilt Design, Higgens & Seiter, Austria, 9 ½ In., 12 Piece	325.00
Platter, Orange, Eagle In Sepia, Ribbon E Pluribus Unum, Gilt, c.1800, 17 In.	17500.00
Platter, Sea Run Brown Trout, Grass, Cobalt Blue Transfer, Oval, Cauldon, c.1890, 24 In.	325.00
Pot, Lid, Blue & White, Canton Style, Leaf Edge, Pinecone Finial, 1800s, 7 x 9 In.	50.00
Punch Bowl, Grapes, Vines, Gilt Ground, White Rim, c.1890, 16 In.	106.00
Tea Jar, Lid, Blue & White, Cylindrical, Bamboo Design Ribbing, 18 x 10 In., Pair	540.00
Tea Set, Little May & Her Dog, Transferware, Teapot, Sugar, Creamer, 3 Cups & Saucers, Child's	276.00
Teapot, Gilt, Scenes, Mother & Child, France, 8 ¾ In.	203.00
Teapot, Landscape, Bird Design, England, 6 ¼ In.	224.00
Teapot, Melon Shape, Fruit Finial, Painted, Bird, Bamboo, Flowers, Wood Stand, c.1790, 4 x 6 In.	180.00
Tobacco Jar, Asian Child, Red & Yellow Coat, Red & Black Hat, Conta & Bohme, 8 ¼ In.	52.00
Tobacco Jar, Chinese Man, Kneeling, Floral Clothes, Hat, Multicolor, Gilt, Conta & Bohme, 9 ½ In.	115.00
Tobacco Jar, Kaiser Wilhelm I, Seated, Holding Staff, Document, Orb, Conta & Bohme, 10 x 5 ½ In.	115.00
Trinket Box, Blue & White, Flowers, Squat, Round, Lid, 3 ¼ In., Pair	359.00
Trinket Box, Louis XV Style, Serpentine, Blue Ground, Gilt Leaves, Lid, Flower Swags, 5 x 11 In.	307.00
Trinket Box, Medallion, Quails, Grasses, Flowers, Rocks, Lid, Round, Lotus, c.1900, 6 In.	1154.00
Trinket Box, Shield Shape, Man With Flute, Woman, Boy, Scrolled Gilt, Raised Jewels, c.1890, 7 In.	1651.00
Tureen, Lavender, White, Artichoke Knop, Flowers, Scroll Legs, Paint, Hochst, c.1780, 14 ½ In.	4688.00
Umbrella Stand, Blue & White, Water Bird Design, 34 In.	90.00
Urn, Blue, Garniture, Leaf Molded Corners, Gilt Bronze Rope Twists, Bellflowers, c.1900, 24 In.	1230.00
Urn, Bronze, Gilt, Elongated Oval, Lid, Finial, Mask Handles, White, Putti, Woman, Round Foot, 28 In.	3810.00
Urn, Bronze, Satyr Mask Handles, Girl & Putti, Cobalt Blue, Ivory, 20 In.	1250.00
Urn, Flower Bouquets, Green Glaze, Gilt Swan Handles, France, 13 In., Pair	288.00
Urn, Lid, Birds, Bushes, Insects, Blue, Green, Gilt, Handles, France, 1800s, 16 In., Pair	1380.00
Urn, Metallic Glaze, Baluster, Square Gilt Handles At Shoulder, Austria, 9 ¾ In.	200.00
Urn, Peasant Girls, Landscapes, Housed, Flowers, Reverse Panels, Swan Handles, 22 ½ In., Pair	1168.00
Urn, Portraits, Louis XVI, Marie Antoinette, Bronze Ring Handles, c.1885, 27 In., Pair *Illus*	2214.00
Urn, Sevres Style, Flowers, Birds, Gilt, Swan's Neck Handles, France, 20th Century, 27 In., Pair ... *Illus*	1298.00
Urn, Sevres Style, Gilt Bronze, Maiden, Putti, Landscape, Applied Female Mask Handles, 28 In. *Illus*	7500.00
Urn, Upturned Handles, Woman Playing Instrument, Red Ground, Gilt, Square Base, 15 In.	2413.00
Urn, Vienna Style, Eurydice, Orpheus, Transfer Print, Pedestal Base, Scroll Leaf Handles, 33 In.	1000.00
Urn, White, Grid Lattice, Flowers, Floral Medallion, Gilt Edge, Fitz & Floyd, 8 x 8 In.	36.00
Urn, White, Pedestal Base, Griffin Handles, 1800s, 18 ¾ In.	345.00
Urn, Woman, Arm At Neck, Lid, Finial, Square Bronze Pierced Base, Gilt, 1800s, 22 In.	8750.00
Vase, Art Deco, Black Stylized Berry Rows, Yellow, Thomas Bavaria, c.1925, 5 In.	219.00
Vase, Blue Flowers, Divided Rim, Flared Base, Curled Handles, Royal Habsburg, Austria, 14 In.	51.00
Vase, Blue, Purple Flowers, Hexagonal Lobed, Gilt Edged, Vincennes, 1753, 6 ½ In.	6250.00
Vase, Bottle Shape, Flared Rim, Dragon & Pearl, Clouds, Waves, Aubergine, 1800s, 7 ½ In.	1422.00
Vase, Celadon Crystalline Glaze, Bulbous, Squat, Tapered Neck, Adelaide Robineau, 4 In.	15000.00
Vase, Coral Red, Gilt Scrolling Lotus, Leaves, Flowers, Blue S-Scroll Handles, 1800s, 11 In.	3318.00
Vase, Dragon, Chasing Pearl, Crackled Ground, Underglaze Blue, Scrolling, c.1890, 22 ½ In.	1265.00
Vase, Enamel Figural Scenes, Seal Mark, Chinese, Early 20th Century, 14 In.	140.00
Vase, Enamel, Pierced Body, Flared Rim, Scrolling Lotus, Dragons, Blue, Gold, 1900s, 15 In.	2370.00
Vase, Enameled, Pear Shape, Nine Peaches Symbol Of Eternity, Rock, Flowers, 1900s, 13 ⅜ In.	356.00
Vase, Famille Noir, Long Tailed Birds, Flowering Trees, Baluster, 14 In., Pair	2700.00
Vase, Flattened Baluster, Cloud, 1800s, 9 ½ In.	345.00
Vase, Flowers, Yellow, White, Heinrich, Germany, 21 In.	96.00
Vase, Gilt Metal, Paint, Landscape Scene, Picnic, Scroll Handles, Finial, Footed Base, c.1900, 20 ¼ In.	1195.00
Vase, Gourd Shape, Double Handles, Mustard Yellow, Blue, Green, Phoenix Birds, Lotus, 11 x 7 In.	450.00

Vase, Handles, Painted, Boy & Girl, Signed L. Schantz, Ceramic Art Co., 18 ½ x 8 In.	390.00
Vase, Lid, Blue & White, Plum Blossoms, Crackled Ice, Knob Finial, c.1800, 17 ¼ In.	474.00
Vase, Lid, Enameled, Yellow, Flowers, Butterflies, Wisteria, Chinese, 14 ½ x 10 In.	840.00
Vase, Lid, Painted, Flowers, Raised Flowers, Fired Gold Accents, Germany, 1800s, 10 x 7 In.	60.00
Vase, Lid, White, Face, Urn Shape, Spread Foot, Fornasetti, Italy, 1900s, 12 In.	676.00
Vase, Lobed Bottle Shape, Handles At Neck, Turquoise, Scrolled Gilt Base, 1800s, 17 In., Pair.	3750.00
Vase, Painted, Irises, Green, Gilt Rim, Handles, Signed Reury, Early 1900s, 15 ½ x 9 In.	270.00
Vase, Pearled Gilt Border, Tracery Arches, Lion Masks, Paw Feet, Cylindrical, c.1835, 5 ¾ In., Pair	1315.00
Vase, Red Underglaze Blue Seal Mark, 10 In., Pair.	472.00
Vase, Trumpet Neck, Lions, Brocade Balls, Clouds, Flowers, Blue, Red, 1900s, 17 ⅜ In.	4148.00
Vase, Urn Finial, Female Mask Handles, Woman, Putti, By The Sea, Sevres Style, 10 In.	1080.00
Water Urn, Louis XVI, Pansies, Gilt Sprays, Loop Handles, Round Pedestal, Scroll Feet, c.1798, 15 In.	6710.00
Wine Cup, Ming Style, Blue, Green, Flowers, 5 x 2 ¼ In.	115.00

PORCELAIN-ASIAN includes pieces made in China, Japan, Korea, and other Asian countries. Asian porcelain is also listed in Canton, Chinese Export, Imari, Japanese Coralene, Moriage, Nanking, Occupied Japan, Satsuma, Sumida, and other categories.

Basin, Birds, Flowering Branches, Blue & White Glaze, 1800s, 16 In. Diam.	276.00
Bowl, 100 Boys, Turquoise Ground, Gilt Rim, Red Seal, Chinese, 3 ½ x 7 In.	840.00
Bowl, 18 Louhan Scene, Poem, Multicolor, 3 Seals, 23 In. Diam.	1168.00
Bowl, 4 Medallions, Fruits, Lemon Yellow, Marked, Chinese, 1800s, 5 ⅜ In. Diam.	1659.00
Bowl, Alms, Rosewood Lid, Blue & White, Landscape, Marked, Chinese, 5 ½ In. _Illus_	325.00
Bowl, Blue & White, Squirrels, Peach Tree, Chinese, c.1900, 9 In.	1020.00
Bowl, Blue Glaze, Gilt Accents, Banding, Wide Rim, Ring Foot, c.1800s, 2 ½ x 6 ¼ In.	295.00
Bowl, Blue, White, Flared, Doucai, Chinese, 3 x 6 ¼ In.	826.00
Bowl, Bone, Fish Shape, Blue, White, Chinese, 5 In., 12 Piece	384.00
Bowl, Brown, Blue Glazed Interior, Dragons & Clouds Relief Design, 6 In. Diam.	338.00
Bowl, Celadon Crackle Glaze, Koi, Scalloped Rim, Chinese, 20 In.	660.00
Bowl, Fish, Blue, White, Flowers, Pastel Accents, Round, 1900s, 22 In.	252.00
Bowl, Lobed, Copper Red Color, c.1890, 6 ¾ In.	472.00
Bowl, Lotus Flowers, Scrolling Plants, Yellow, Marked, Chinese, 4 ½ In. _Illus_	100.00
Bowl, Lotus Shape, Peach Bloom, 1 ½ x 6 ½ In.	4661.00
Bowl, Louis XV Style, Gilt Bronze, Leaf Handles, Pierced Stand, Scroll Feet, Flowers, 5 x 11 In., Pair	2196.00
Bowl, Mountain Landscape, Silver Gilt, Magenta Glaze Interior, Ring Foot, 1800s, 2 x 4 In.	575.00
Bowl, Mountain Scene, Calligraphy, Paint, Chinese, 1900s, 5 ½ In.	365.00
Bowl, Offering, White Glaze, Dragons, Flaming Pearls, Clouds, Marked, c.1930, 6 In. Diam.	492.00
Bowl, Pale Lavender, Flower Rondels, Scrolling, Wide Rim, Ring Foot, Marked, 8 In. Diam.	345.00
Bowl, Square, Flared Rim, Blue & White, Waves, Clouds, Dragon, Marked, 1900s, 3 x 5 In.	288.00
Bowl, Squirrels, Peach Tree, Blue & White, Round Foot, Chinese, c.1900, 9 In. Diam.	840.00
Bowl, Yellow Ground, Flowers, Vining Leaves, Blue Inside, 3 ½ x 10 In.	600.00
Bowl, Yellow, Aubergine Dragons, Marked, 6 In. Diam.	4182.00
Bowl, Yellow, Green, Children At Play, Wide Rim, Ring Foot, 1900s, 2 ¾ x 6 In.	891.00
Box, Frog Shape, Blue & White, Circles Design, Almond Shape Eyes, 1900s, 11 In., Pair.	2214.00
Box, Lid, Drum Shape, Blue & White, Waves, Clouds, Lotus Blossoms, 1900s, 3 x 5 In.	119.00
Brush Holder, Vase Shape, Squat, Cylindrical Neck, Spur Feet, Peach Bloom Glaze, 1800s, 2 ½ In.	1968.00
Brushpot, Cylindrical, Blue & White, Hunt Scene, Trees, Landscape, c.1800, 6 In.	615.00
Brushpot, Square Shape, Indented Corners, Blue & White, Birds, Flowering Tree, 1900s, 7 In.	615.00
Cachepot, Chien Lung Style, Blue & White, Figural Scenes, Gilded Rim, Mark, Chinese, 7 In.	94.00
Candlestand, Blue & White, Columnar, Bowls, Splayed Foot, Dragon Design, 11 ½ In.	122.00
Censer, Tripod Base, Flanges, Edge Fritting, 4 x 6 In.	584.00
Charger, Blue & White, Birds, Flowering Trees, Scrolling Flower Borders, Japan, 1800s, 27 In.	1185.00
Charger, Blue & White, Flower Garden, Geometric Bands, Chinese, c.1810, 15 In.	92.00
Charger, Famille Rose, Pink & White, Flowers, 1700s, 12 ½ In. Diam., Pair.	598.00
Charger, Kraak, Flaring Rim, Deer, Rocks, Trees, Flowers, Butterflies, Japan, 1700s, 15 In. Diam.	858.00
Charger, White Ground, Pomegranates, Chinese, 3 x 16 In.	1020.00
Cup, Bell Shape Stem, Blue & White, Flowers, Chinese, 3 ½ In.	598.00
Dish, Blue & White, Lobed, 2 Dragons, Flaming Pearl, Clouds, Waves, 17th Century, 14 In. Diam.	2252.00
Dish, Butterflies, Flowers, Sky Blue, Footed, c.1900, 2 x 10 In.	403.00
Dish, Dragon, Chasing Pearl Of Wisdom, Iron Red, Gold, Chinese, 8 ½ In. Diam.	956.00
Dish, Dragon, Flaming Pearl, Green Enamel, Chinese, c.1930, 7 ⅜ In. _Illus_	861.00
Dish, Peaches & Branches, Blue Underglaze, 6 Character Yung-Cheng Mark, 11 x 2 In. _Illus_	3738.00
Dish, Ring Foot, Wide Rim, Blue & White, Stylized Lotus Scrolls, 1900s, 3 x 9 In.	633.00
Dish, Yellow Glaze, Green Design, Peaches, Scrolling Leaves, Incised, 1900s, 11 ⅞ In.	184.00
Ewer, Blue & White, Dragon Shaped Spout & Handle, Riverscape, Japan, 11 In.	179.00
Figurine, Blue & White, Ginger Jar, Lid, Chinese, 1800s, 9 In., Pair	900.00

Porcelain, Place Setting, Roy Lichtenstein, Black, White, Jackson China For Durable Dish, 1966, 5 Piece
$3,125.00

Los Angeles Modern Auctions (LAMA)

Porcelain, Urn, Sevres Style, Flowers, Birds, Gilt, Swan's Neck Handles, France, 20th Century, 27 In., Pair
$1,298.00

Brunk Auctions

Porcelain, Urn, Sevres Style, Gilt Bronze, Maiden, Putti, Landscape, Applied Female Mask Handles, 28 In.
$7,500.00

Leslie Hindman Auctioneers

> **TIP**
> When stacking dinner plates, put a piece of felt or paper between each plate. Never put more than 24 in one stack.

P

Porcelain, Urn, Portraits, Louis XVI, Marie Antoinette, Bronze Ring Handles, c.1885, 27 In., Pair
$2,214.00

New Orleans Auction Galleries, Inc.

Porcelain-Asian, Bowl, Alms, Rosewood Lid, Blue & White, Landscape, Marked, Chinese, 5 ½ In.
$325.00

Skinner, Inc.

Porcelain-Asian, Bowl, Lotus Flowers, Scrolling Plants, Yellow, Marked, Chinese, 4 ½ In.
$100.00

Skinner, Inc.

Porcelain-Asian, Dish, Dragon, Flaming Pearl, Green Enamel, Chinese, c.1930, 7 ⅜ In.
$861.00

New Orleans Auction Galleries, Inc.

Porcelain-Asian, Dish, Peaches & Branches, Blue Underglaze, 6 Character Yung-Cheng Mark, 11 x 2 In.
$3,738.00

James D. Julia Auctioneers

Porcelain-Asian, Flask, Blue, White, Flattened, Figures, Garden, Dragon Handles, Chinese, 1900s, 17 ⅜ In.
$1,722.00

New Orleans Auction Galleries, Inc.

Porcelain-Asian, Jar, Lid, Famille Verte, Chinese Warriors, 1800s, 18 In.
$861.00

New Orleans Auction Galleries, Inc.

Porcelain-Asian, Moonpot Rattle, Toshiko Takaezu, Signed, 7 ½ x 7 In.
$3,750.00

Rago Arts & Auction Center

Porcelain-Asian, Plate, Butterflies, Multicolor, Hand Painted, 1800s, 8 ½ In.
$90.00

DuMouchelles Art Gallery

Porcelain-Asian, Ginger Jar, Blue & White, Antiques, Flowers, Crackle, Cheong Kee & Co., 8 x 7 In.
$1,840.00

James D. Julia Auctioneers

Figurine, Dove, White Glaze, Black Eyes, Chinese, 9 ¼ In.	443.00
Figurine, Dove, Yellow Glaze, Chinese, c.1910, 6 In., Pair	266.00
Figurine, Elephant, Kneeling, Butterfly, Flowers, Blanc De Chine, c.1900, 6 In., Pair	649.00
Figurine, Foo Dog, Blue, Green, Tan, Chinese, 19 ½ In., Pair	978.00
Figurine, Ho Ho Birds, Blue & White Glaze, Feng, Huang, 19 In., Pair	173.00
Figurine, Guanyin, Thousand Arm, Lotus Blossom, Wood Stand, Blanc De Chine, c.1900, 19 In.	3555.00
Figurine, Robed Geisha, Painted, Pink, Red, Turquoise, Flowers, 20 ¼ In.	531.00
Figurine, Rooster, Green, Gold Base, Chinese, 12 ¼ In.	110.00
Figurine, Water Bird, Famille Verte, 16 In., Pair	179.00
Fish Bowl, Turned In Rim, Blue & White, Dragons, Flaming Pearls, 1800s, 19 In. Diam.	1045.00
Flask, Blue, White, Flattened, Figures, Garden, Dragon Handles, Chinese, 1900s, 17 ⅜ In. ..*Illus*	1722.00
Flask, Moon Shape, Handles At Neck, Flowers, Round Foot, 1800s, 10 ½ x 8 In.	2124.00
Flask, Moon, Interlocking Flowers, Blue & White, Chinese, 14 In., Pair	570.00
Ginger Jar, Blue & White, Antiques, Flowers, Crackle, Cheong Kee & Co., 8 x 7 In. ....*Illus*	1840.00
Ginger Jar, Blue & White, Fishing Scene, 7 In.	153.00
Ginger Jar, Blue & White, Pomegranates, Trailing Vines, 1800s, 30 In., Pair	1722.00
Ginger Jar, Dome Lid, Gilt Design, Blue, Ball Finial, Bulbous Shoulder, c.1800s, 8 In., Pair....	1770.00
Ginger Jar, Mandarin Design, Green & Pink Borders, c.1890, 16 ½ In.	73.00
Group, Man & Woman, Standing, Famille Rose, Sexual Embrace, Marked, c.1920, 13 ⅞ In.	478.00
Hat Stand, Blue, White, Mountains, 8-Sided, Quatrefoil Pierced, Chinese, 1800s, 10 ¾ In.	288.00
Hat Stand, Octagonal, Quatrefoil Piercings, Mountain Scene, Blue, White, 1800s, 11 In., Pair .	240.00
Hot Water Dish, Lid, Acorn, Oak Leaf Spray, Green, Yellow, Frog Finial, Chinese, c.1820, 14 In.	590.00
Jar, Bulbous, Blue & White, Flowering Prunus, c.1900, 9 ½ In.	115.00
Jar, Dome Lid, Baluster, Waisted Neck, Splayed, Foot, Scholars, Leaves, Blossoms, 16 ½ In.	3645.00
Jar, Dome Lid, Gourd Shape, Blue & White, Flowers, Chinese, 1800s, 12 In., Pair	1673.00
Jar, Famille Rose, Oval, Bird & Flower Design, Figures, Calligraphy, c.1900, 10 ¾ In., Pair	1037.00
Jar, Lid, Ball Finial, Bulbous, Cobalt Blue Glaze, Gilt Design, c.1800, 8 ½ In.	295.00
Jar, Lid, Cylindrical, Famille Rose Design, c.1900, 6 ½ x 5 ¼ In.	338.00
Jar, Lid, Famille Rose, Figures, Palace, Flowers, Gilt Dragon Handles, Foo Dog Finial, c.1735, 18 In.	1353.00
Jar, Lid, Famille Verte, Chinese Warriors, 1800s, 18 In. ....*Illus*	861.00
Jar, Lid, Flat Rim, Blue & White, Flowers, Scrolling Leaves, 1800s, 17 In.	956.00
Jar, Lid, Hexagonal, Birds, Flowers, Borders, Bats, Lotus Finial, c.1900, 6 ¾ In.	1845.00
Jar, Lid, Red, Green, White, Round, Doucai, Chinese, 4 x 2 ½ In.	1298.00
Jar, Oval, Scrolling Dragon, Flaming Pearl, Clouds, Korea, 1800s, 13 In.	1422.00
Jar, Oval, Splayed Foot, Sinuous Dragon, Flaming Pearl, 11 Figures, 13 ¾ In.	478.00
Jar, Wine, Brown Glaze, Molded Flowers, Geometric, 1800s, 9 ½ In.	119.00
Jardiniere, Carp Shape, Cream, Brown Glaze, 17 ½ In.	531.00
Moonpot Rattle, Toshiko Takaezu, Signed, 7 ½ x 7 In. ....*Illus*	3750.00
Pen Pot, Famille Rose, Seated Figure Under Pine Tree, Smoke Rising, Chinese, 4 ¾ In.	121.00
Planter, Blue & White, Paneled Landscapes, Inset Corners, Footed, Chinese, c.1780, 7 ¾ In.	201.00
Planter, Squat, Ring Foot, Green Dragon, Iron Red Pearls, Chinese, 1800s, 3 x 8 In.	472.00
Plaque, Enameled, Monk Carrying Ax On Shoulder, Hat, Signed, Frame, Chinese, 24 x 15 ½ In.	711.00
Plaque, Painted, Rooster, 2 Chickens, Wood Frame, c.1900, 26 x 18 In.	1304.00
Plate, Black & Green, Dragon, Flaming Pearl, Clouds, Flowers, Marked, c.1900, 7 ⅞ In.	1126.00
Plate, Butterflies, Multicolor, Hand Painted, 1800s, 8 ½ In. ....*Illus*	90.00
Plate, Famille Rose, Lotus Scrolls, Bats, Yellow Borders, c.1900, 12 In. Diam.	221.00
Plate, Flower Panels, Enamel, Famille Verte, Artemesia Leaf Mark, c.1700, 11 ⅜ In. ....*Illus*	5060.00
Plate, Millefleur, Allover Flowers, Chinese, c.1850, 9 ¾ In., 6 Piece	780.00
Plate, Peaches, Bats, White, Marked, c.1950, 7 ¾ In.	400.00
Plate, Pierced Latticework Border, Flowers, Basketweave Design, c.1795, 9 In. Diam.	615.00
Plate, Turquoise Ground, Woman & Children, Ice Borders, Scrolling Lotus, c.1900, 12 In.	492.00
Punch Bowl, Famille Rose, Flower Sprigs & Borders, Landscapes, c.1890, 15 ¾ In. Diam.	1168.00
Punch Bowl, Famille Rose, Flower Sprigs, Blue Borders, 1700s, 10 ¼ In. Diam.	861.00
Punch Bowl, Famille Rose, Hunt Scenes, Orange Ground, Armor Pattern, Gilt, 1700s, 16 In. Diam.	6765.00
Teapot, Iron Red, Gilt, Loop Handle, Scroll Spout, Domed Finial Lid, 4 ⅝ x 7 ¼ In. ....*Illus*	399.00
Teapot, Lid, Flattened Round Shape, Handle, Brown, Engraved Calligraphy, Chinese, 1900s, 8 In.	615.00
Tureen, Lid, Blue, White, Flowers, Pomegranate Handle, Chinese, c.1850, 12 ½ In.	720.00
Tureen, Lid, Octagonal, Blue & White, Boar's Head Finial, Leaf Handle, 1700s, 9 x 14 In.	799.00
Tureen, Lid, Octagonal, Blue & White, Oxen, Flower Border, Handles, Finial, 1700s, 9 x 14 In.	861.00
Tureen, Lid, Oval, Twisted Handles, Sunflower Knop, Undertray, c.1835, 6 x 8 In.	676.00
Umbrella Stand, Blue & White, Birds, Aquatic Plants, Japan, c.1890, 24 In. ....*Illus*	861.00
Urn, Green, Crackle Finish, Brass Mounts, People Republic Of China Label, 16 In., Pair	268.00
Vase, Animal Mask Handles, Faux Jump Rings, Millefleur, c.1900, 12 In., Pair	922.00
Vase, Blue & White, Archaic Style Dragon Handles, Acanthus, Ju-Borders, Chinese, 1800s, 24 In., Pair	1610.00
Vase, Blue & White, Birds, Flowers, Beaker Shape, Trumpet Rim, 1800s, 16 x 7 ½ In., Pair	1093.00
Vase, Blue & White, Immortals, Figures, Horse, Bottle Shape, Chinese, 1800s, 8 ¼ In.	180.00

Porcelain-Asian, Plate, Flower Panels, Enamel, Famille Verte, Artemesia Leaf Mark, c.1700, 11 ⅜ In.
$5,060.00

Elite Decorative Arts

Porcelain-Asian, Teapot, Iron Red, Gilt, Loop Handle, Scroll Spout, Domed Finial Lid, 4 ⅝ x 7 ¼ In.
$399.00

Neal Auction Co.

Porcelain-Asian, Umbrella Stand, Blue & White, Birds, Aquatic Plants, Japan, c.1890, 24 In.
$861.00

New Orleans Auction Galleries, Inc.

Porcelain-Asian, Vase, Bottle Shape, San Duo, 3 Fruits, Acanthus Leaves, c.1910, 12 In.
$5,658.00

New Orleans Auction Galleries, Inc.

P

Porcelain-Asian, Vase, Gourd Shape, Scrolled Flowers, Draped Cloth, Enamel, Famille Rose, c.1750, 5 In. $6,038.00

Elite Decorative Arts

Porcelain-Asian, Vase, Hundred Antiques, Relief, Famille Rose, Ju-Borders, 1800s, 17 ½ In. $984.00

New Orleans Auction Galleries, Inc.

Porcelain-Asian, Vase, Purple & Blue, Flambe Glaze, Relief Pearls, Lug Handles, Chien Lung Mark, c.1910, 12 In. $430.00

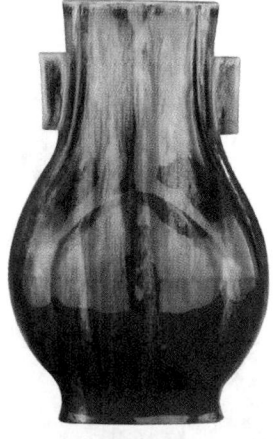

New Orleans Auction Galleries, Inc.

460

Vase, Blue & White, Meandering Foo Dogs, Clouds, Red Ribbons, Chinese, 1900s, 25 In.	146.00
Vase, Blue & White, Peacocks, Flowers, Shouldered, Tapered, Trumpet Rim, c.1900, 30 ½ In.	799.00
Vase, Blue & White, Waves, Acanthus Leaves, Ju-Border, Scrolling Flowers, 16 In.	2415.00
Vase, Blue Glaze, Chinese, c.1800, 15 ¾ In.	780.00
Vase, Blue, Applied Neck Handles, Ring Foot, Chinese, 11 In.	1380.00
Vase, Blue, Green Flowers, Long Neck, Qing Dynasty Marks, 14 ½ In.	208.00
Vase, Bottle Shape, Cobalt Blue & White, Acanthus Leaves, Flower Scrolls, 1800s, 10 ½ In.	690.00
Vase, Bottle Shape, Flowering Peach Tree, Coral Red, Marked, Chinese, 1900s, 8 In.	215.00
Vase, Bottle Shape, Long Neck, Dark Red Glaze, Chinese, 9 ½ In.	98.00
Vase, Bottle Shape, San Duo, 3 Fruits, Acanthus Leaves, c.1910, 12 In. ....*Illus*	5658.00
Vase, Bottle Shape, Stick Neck, Warrior Drawing Sword, Demon, Flowers, c.1900, 8 In.	460.00
Vase, Bottle, Pear Shape, Flared Mouth, Ring Foot, Ivory Glaze, Scroll Leaves Banding, 7 In.	1195.00
Vase, Cobalt Blue Glaze, Bottle Shape, Rolled Rim, Ring Foot, c.1800, 14 In.	885.00
Vase, Cobalt Blue, Gilt Plum Blossoms, Roundels, Square, Cylindrical Neck, 1800s, 18 In.	2844.00
Vase, Compressed Bottle Shape, Dragon, Clouds, Green & White, c.1900, 12 In.	533.00
Vase, Cylindrical, Flared Rim & Foot, Blue & White, 1700s, 9 ½ In., Pair	837.00
Vase, Cylindrical, Flaring Mouth, Man, Water Buffalo, Flowering Tree, 8 ¾ In.	345.00
Vase, Double Gourd, Blue & White, Foo Lions, Lotus, Scrolling Leaves, Phoenix, 1900s, 12 In.	237.00
Vase, Dragon, Red, Green, Clouds, Chinese, 9 In., Pair	476.00
Vase, Dragons At Shoulder, Foo Dog Handles, Flowering Vines, 1800s, 24 In., Pair	307.00
Vase, Dragons, Leaves, Trumpet Rim, Carved Wood Base, c.1700, 17 ½ In.	7380.00
Vase, Earth Tone Vertical Striations, Silver Dragon, Shaped Handles, Chinese, 16 x 10 In.	108.00
Vase, Elephant Shape, Vase On Back, Standing, Blue Glaze, Chinese, 1800s, 8 In.	115.00
Vase, Famille Noire, Pheasants, Flowering Trees, 1800s, 30 In.	115.00
Vase, Famille Rose, Baluster, Scroll Handles, Turquoise, Flowering Trees, 1900s, 14 In., Pair	4920.00
Vase, Famille Rose, Double Gourd, Squirrels & Grapes, Chinese, 1900s, 9 In.	369.00
Vase, Famille Rose, Palace, Armor Pattern, Dragon Handles, Foo Dog Finial, c.1800, 14 In., Pair	1722.00
Vase, Famille Rose, Trumpet Neck, Flared Rim, Flowering Trees, Birds, Rocks, c.1900, 15 In., Pair	1353.00
Vase, Famille Verte, Applied Neck Dragon, Bottle Shape, 14 In.	238.00
Vase, Fish Shape, Open Mouthed Carp, Cresting Wave, Lotus Blossoms, Leaves, 16 In., Pair	1076.00
Vase, Flared Rim, Figures, Flowers, Pale Green, White, Chinese, 24 ¾ In.	1434.00
Vase, Flask Shape, Flower Scrolling, 2 Handles At Neck, 1800s, 10 ¾ In., Pair	5904.00
Vase, Garden, Women, Ho-Ho Bird, Chinese, c.1890, 16 ¾ In., Pair	1440.00
Vase, Gourd Shape, Red Ground, Blue & White, Immortals, 1800s, 11 ½ In., Pair	1599.00
Vase, Gourd Shape, Scrolled Flowers, Draped Cloth, Enamel, Famille Rose, c.1750, 5 In.*Illus*	6038.00
Vase, Hexagonal, Figures, Palace Gardens, Diaper Borders, Gilt, Foo Dog Finial, c.1735, 22 In., Pair	8610.00
Vase, Hexagonal, Figures, Trees, Calligraphy, 1800s, 16 In.	1016.00
Vase, Hexagonal, Flat Flared Rim, Pale Green Ground, Blue Flowers, 1800s, 23 In.	1076.00
Vase, Hundred Antiques, Relief, Famille Rose, Ju-Borders, 1800s, 17 ½ In. ....*Illus*	984.00
Vase, Iron Red Bats, Blue Swirls, White Ground, Double Gourd, Chinese, 7 x 4 In.	472.00
Vase, Iron Red, Dragons, Chasing Pearl, Cloud Bands, Bottle Shape, Ring Foot, 1800s, 15 In.	3450.00
Vase, Multicolor, Mother & Child Scenes, Calligraphy, Chinese, c.1950, 5 ½ In., Pair	115.00
Vase, Oval, Round Cartouches, Turtle, Phoenix, Ruyi Head Banding, Korea, c.1900, 11 ½ In.	711.00
Vase, Pale Green, Incised, Chinese, 13 x 6 ½ In.	720.00
Vase, Parasol Shape Lip, Octagonal Foot, Chinese Man, Peony, Plant, Gilt Scrollwork, 13 In., Pair	1230.00
Vase, Pear Shape, Flared Rim, Grapes, Squirrels, c.1895, 9 In.	649.00
Vase, Purple & Blue, Flambe Glaze, Relief Pearls, Lug Handles, Chien Lung Mark, c.1910, 12 In.*Illus*	430.00
Vase, Red Copper Oxide Glaze, Chinese, c.1804, 15 In.	1888.00
Vase, Rocky Landscape, Water, Blue & White, Chinese, 1800s, 31 ¼ In. ....*Illus*	6628.00
Vase, Rounded Square, Cylindrical Neck, Court Scenes, Landscapes, River, 1800s, 18 In.	1180.00
Vase, Scholar, Students, Flowers, Kutani, Hexagonal, Japan, 6 ¼ In., Pair	177.00
Vase, Square Shape, Ring Foot, Elephant Mask Handles, Cobalt Blue Glaze, 1800s, 11 ½ In.	3450.00
Vase, Square, Red & White, Flowers, Clouds, Bats, Birds, Scrolls, 8 ¼ In.	2596.00
Vase, Trefoil Shape, Famille Rose, Flowers, Birds, Butterflies, 1800s, 12 In.	861.00
Vase, Trumpet Neck, Flared Lip, Blue & White, Peonies & Butterflies, Phoenix, c.1900, 16 In.	296.00
Vase, Trumpet Rim, Famille Noir, Birds, Rocks, Prunus, Green-Black Glaze, 1800s, 17 ½ In.	920.00
Vase, White Ground, Multicolor Flowers, Leaves, Pear Shape, Round Foot, 5 ½ In.	413.00
Vase, White Ground, Red, Green, Dragons, Chinese, 15 x 9 ½ In.	480.00
Vase, Yellow Enamel, 5-Toed Dragons, Leaves, K'and Hse Rain Mark, 9 In., Pair	1093.00
Vase, Yongzheng Style, Red Dragon, Gilt Waves, Interior, Key Fret Design On Foot, 5 x 3 In.	207.00
Water Dropper, Foo Dog Shape, White, Standing, Head Turned To Side	896.00
Water Pot, Blue, Globe, Applied Spout, Knobs, Pine & Prunus Painted, Chinese, 1800s, 10 x 9 In.	173.00
Wine Cup, Blue, White, Red, Waves, Fish, Marked, c.1890, 2 ¾ x 3 ¼ In.	177.00
Wine Pot, Lobed, Bulbous, S-Spout, Loop Handle, Ring Foot, Blue, White, Dragon, 1900s, 5 In.	369.00
Wine Pot, Warmer, Hexagonal, Blue & White, Aquatic Landscapes, Flowers, Lid, c.1900, 7 x 6 In.	920.00

PORCELAIN-CONTEMPORARY lists pieces made by artists working after 1975.

Bowl, Winged, Elsa Rady, 1979, 5 ¾ x 12 In.........................*Illus*	720.00
Figurine, Connoisseur Of Malvern, Freedom, Signed Richard Sefton, 1985, 11 x 9 In. .....*Illus*	210.00
Figurine, Foot, Strap Sandal, Black & Gold Glazes, Fornasetti, 3 ½ x 9 In......................*Illus*	374.00
Frog Sandwich, Smiling Frog, Between Bread Pieces, David Gilhooly, 1982, 6 In.	443.00

PORCELAIN-MIDCENTURY includes pieces made from the 1940s to about 1975.

Bowl, Oxblood Red Glaze, Squat, Signed Laura Anderson, 1951, 2 ¾ x 5 ½ In.	1000.00
Vase, Brown Iron Crystal Glaze, Ring Foot, Bulbous, Signed Laura Anderson, c.1961, 7 x 6 In...	1750.00

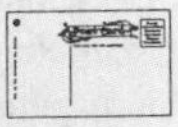

POSTCARDS were first legally permitted in Austria on October 1, 1869. The United States passed postal regulations allowing the card in 1872. Most of the picture postcards collected today date after 1910. The amount of postage can help to date a card. The rates are: 1872 (1 cent), 1917 (2 cents), 1919 (1 cent), 1925 (2 cents), 1928 (1 cent), 1952 (2 cents), 1958 (3 cents), 1963 (4 cents), 1968 (5 cents), 1971 (6 cents), 1973 (8 cents), 1975 (7 cents), 1976 (9 cents), 1978 (10 cents), March 1981 (12 cents), November 1981 (13 cents), 1985 (14 cents), 1988 (15 cents), 1991 (19 cents), 1995 (20 cents), 2001 (21 cents), 2002 (23 cents), 2006 (24 cents), 2007 (26 cents), 2008 (27 cents), 2009 (28 cents), 2011 (29 cents), 2012 (32 cents), 2013 (33 cents). While most postcards sell for low prices, a small number bring high prices. Some of these are listed here.

Arabian Cemetery, 2 Girls Mourning, Signed Fabby, Color, c.1920	16.00
Aragon Wonder Ballroom Stairway, 1100 Lawrence Ave., Chicago, 1933......................	8.00
Arizona, Saguaro, Southwest, Tourist, Botanical, Roadside, 1940s	8.00
Birthday, View Through Porthole, Sailboat, Forget-Me-Nots, Gilt, 1910	7.00
Cemetery, Havana, Interior, Gate, Statues, Color, Linen...............................	5.00
George Bernard Shaw, Autographed, To Mrs. Margaret Houslander, Frame, 1935, 5 ½ x 3 ½ In.	270.00
July 4th, Hurrah The Glorious 4th July, Girl Waving Flag, 1908......................	10.00
July 4th, Patriotic Fireworks Picture, I'll Be Busted On The 4th, 1909 Postmark......................	10.00
Mary Duncan, Movie Star, Sepia Photograph, 1920s, 4 x 5 In.	28.00
Mount Wilson Hotel, Snowbound, San Gabriel Mountains, Chloride Print Glossy, 1930s	10.00
New Orleans, Orange Picking, 1947	8.00
New Year's, Art Deco, Embossed, Woman In Yellow Ball Gown, Natchitoches, La.	5.00
North Carolina, Dogwood Branch, 2 Cardinals, 5 ½ x 3 ¼ In.	8.00
Parker Gun, Old Reliable, Hunter Aiming Rifle At Birds, c.1907, 5 ½ x 3 ½ In. ....*Illus*	420.00
Redwood Highway, Shrine Tree, Drive-Thru, Black & White, 1930s	9.00
Risque, Woman, Naked, Photograph, Early 1900s	60.00
Santa Claus, Baby On Lap, Gilt Scallops, 5 ½ x 3 ½ In.	10.00
Saratoga Race Track, Crowd Near Grandstand, 1906	15.00
Thanksgiving, Blessed, 2 Children In Colonial Dress, Ellen Clapsaddle, Early 1900s............	25.00
Thomas Wolfe Memorial, Asheville, N.C., Chrome, Color King Natural Color	5.00
To My Love, 2 Cupids Playing Tennis, Hearts, Printed In Germany, c.1910, 3 ½ x 5 ½ In.*Illus*	115.00
Venal Falls, Yosemite Valley, 1907......................................	6.00
Venice, Bridge Of Sighs, Young Woman & Child, Color Lithograph, c.1900	28.00
Walter Pidgeon's Home, California, Hand Colored Linen, 1950s...............................	7.00

POSTERS have informed the public about news and entertainment events since ancient times. Nineteenth-century advertising and theatrical posters and twentieth-century movie and war posters are of special interest today. The price is determined by the artist, the condition, and the rarity. Other posters may be listed under Movie, Political, and World War I and II.

A La Place Clichy Toiletted D'Ete, Woman, Dress, Frame, LEM, Chaix, Paris, c.1901, 48 x 34 In.	1300.00
American Music Festival, N.Y. City Ballet, Exhibition, Signed Keith Haring, c.1988, 24 x 36 In. ..	472.00
Antibes, Sunbathers, Beach, Umbrellas, Roger Broders, c.1928, 42 x 30 In.	10000.00
Are We Next?, Be Aware, Swastika, On U.S. Flag, 1965, 34 x 19 In.................................	300.00
Aspen Winter Jazz, Color Silkscreen, Roy Lichtenstein, Chiron Press, Frame, 40 x 26 In........	1094.00
Au Grand Pasteur Meubles Decoration, Man, Furniture, Lithograph, c.1935, 66 ¾ x 51 In.	793.00
Bermuda, 2 Cyclists, Evening Attire, A. Treidler, 1950s, 40 x 24 In.	1500.01
Bermuda, By Air Or Sea, Couple, Boat Rail, c.1940, 41 x 22 In.	1700.00
Bermuda, Fly Pan Am, 2 Sailboats, E. McKnight Kauffer, c.1950, 41 x 28 In...........................	650.00
Bermuda, Ocean, Beach, Loweree, 38 x 23 In..	1000.00
Bicycle, Hurricane, C'Est Un, 'Tis Een, Lithograph, c.1930, 32 ¾ x 23 In..............................	338.00
Bluffers Bluff Only Themselves, Stallers Can't Last, Boy Pretending To Study, 1924, 48 x 36 In.	1300.00
Bob Dylan, Lithograph, Color, Milton Glaser, 33 x 22 In..	236.00
Campbell Soup Box, Silkscreen On Paper, Andy Warhol, 1985, 31 x 20 In............................	767.00
Chang & Fak-Hong, United Magicians Presents Hara-Kiri, Lithograph, Multicolor, 1920s, 17 x 25 In..	123.00

Porcelain-Asian, Vase, Rocky Landscape, Water, Blue & White, Chinese, 1800s, 31 ¼ In.
$6,628.00

Garth's Auctioneers & Appraisers

Porcelain-Contemporary, Bowl, Winged, Elsa Rady, 1979, 5 ¾ x 12 In.
$720.00

Cowans + Clark + DelVecchio

Porcelain-Contemporary, Figurine, Connoisseur Of Malvern, Freedom, Signed Richard Sefton, 1985, 11 x 9 In.
$210.00

DuMouchelles Art Gallery

Porcelain-Contemporary, Figurine, Foot, Strap Sandal, Black & Gold Glazes, Fornasetti, 3 ½ x 9 In.
$374.00

Humler & Nolan

Postcard, Parker Gun, Old Reliable, Hunter Aiming Rifle At Birds, c.1907, 5 ½ x 3 ½ In.
$420.00

Past Tyme Pleasures

Postcard, To My Love, 2 Cupids Playing Tennis, Hearts, Printed In Germany, c.1910, 3 ½ x 5 ½ In.
$115.00

Hake's Americana & Collectibles

Poster, Circus, Banner, Side Show, Ella Wales, 300 Lbs. Of Feminine Charm, Canvas, c.1935, 94 x 90 In.
$588.00

Garth's Auctioneers & Appraisers

Poster, Circus, Ringling Bros. Barnum & Bailey, Clown, Elephant, 6-Piece Lithograph, 194 x 116 In.
$112.00

Victorian Casino Antiques

Children On Diving Board, Paper, Rene Vincent, c.1925, 14 x 13 In.	650.00
Cie Francaise Des Cycles, Couple, On Cycles, Paris, c.1900, 34 x 24 In.	900.00
Circus, Al G. Barnes, Truly Big Show, Tiger On Top Of Elephant, Multicolor, 38 ¾ x 26 In.	460.00
Circus, Banner, Side Show, Ella Wales, 300 Lbs. Of Feminine Charm, Canvas, c.1935, 94 x 90 In.. *Illus*	588.00
Circus, Beatty Cole, Roaring Lion, Paper, On Wood, c.1955, 42 ½ x 28 In.	48.00
Circus, Figuier France, Linen, Frame, Paris, 1920, 53 x 67 In.	531.00
Circus, Great Victorina Troupe, 24 Reserves, Multicolor, 27 ½ x 41 In.	272.00
Circus, Happy Crowd, Willsons Show Printers, Leicester, England, Frame 1950s, 35 x 45 In.	266.00
Circus, Parker & Watts, 35 x 40 In.	128.00
Circus, Pinder, Clown, Smiling, Pointing, France, c.1925, 64 x 48 In.	708.00
Circus, Ringling Bros. & Barnum & Bailey, Dainty Miss Leeitzel, Coy Dancer, 1918, 42 x 28 In.	1000.00
Circus, Ringling Bros. & Barnum & Bailey, World's Biggest Menagerie, 2 Hippos, 1916, 20 x 28 In.	500.00
Circus, Ringling Bros. Barnum & Bailey, Clown, Elephant, 6-Piece Lithograph, 194 x 116 In.. *Illus*	112.00
Circus, Rudy Bros. Circus, Frame, c.1930, 18 ½ x 32 In.	89.00
Circus, The Great Sells Floto Circus, 31 x 23 In.	354.00
Circus, Zellman Bros. Wild Animal Shows, Erie Litho Co., Frame, c.1957, 43 x 16 In.	148.00
Cleopatra, Andy Warhol, Blue, 39 x 26 In.	120.00
Colt Firearms, Cowboy, Horse, Spanish Text, Linen, Frank Schoonover, Frame, 37 ½ x 24 In.	1200.00
Concert, Bill Graham, Fillmore, Jim Kweskin Jug Band, Psychedelic Woman, 1967, 14 x 23 In.	115.00
Concert, Carousel Ballroom, Grateful Dead, Country Joe, Fish, St. Valentine's Day, 1968, 11 x 11 In.	665.00
Concert, Isle Of Wight Music Festival, Day Glo Pink, Dylan, Moody Blues, Who, Aug. 1969, 16 x 30 In.	223.00
Concert, Rock Garden, Big Brother & The Holding Co., Love, CIA, Diamond Shape, 1968, 18 x 18 In.	588.00
Concert, Straight Theater, Grateful Dead, Psychedelic, Red, Orange, San Fran., 1967, 14 x 20 In.	834.00
Concert, Straight Theater, Steve Miller Band, Sopwith Camel, Mystical Images, 1967, 14 x 20 In.	259.00
Cordial Medoc, Color Lithograph, Mounted On Linen, Henri Lemonier, 1900s, 62 x 45 In.	403.00
Cosulich Line, Saturnia-Vulvania, Harry Heugger, Milan, 1933, 36 x 26 In.	900.00
Cuba, Holiday Isles Of The Tropics, Woman, Flying, Sun Hat, Julius Seyler, c.1950, 38 x 22 In.	1100.00
Cusenier, Peach Brandy, Pal, Jean De Paleologue, c.1920, 50 x 35 In.	476.00
Dodgers Are Never Leaders, Don't Pass The Buck, Man, Ducking, Chicago, 1924, 48 x 36 In.	1000.00
Egypt, Sailboats, Ruins, H. Hashim, c.1935, 39 x 28 In.	700.00
Florida, Fly TWA, Sunglasses, Sun, Coastal City, David Klein, 1960s, 40 x 24 In.	1000.00
Fly To South Sea Isles, Via Pan American, Mountain, Sea, Girl, Paul G. Lawler, c.1938, 41 x 27 In.	6000.00
Gismonda Maitres De L'Affiche, Sarah Bernhardt, Paper, A. Mucha, 1896, 15 x 11 In.	1700.00
Harpers, Christmas, Woman, Reading On Red Settee, Edward Penfield, 1894, 18 x 12 In.	950.00
Harpers, July, Woman Lighting Firecrackers, While Reading, Edward Penfield, 1894, 18 x 12 In.	1300.00
Harpers, June, Graduate, Pipe In Mouth, Reading, Edward Penfield, 1895, 18 x 12 In.	750.00
Harpers, March, Farmer, Plow, Horse, Rooster, Edward Penfield, 1899, 15 ½ x 10 ½ In.	425.00
Hunterdon County Flemington Fair, Sept'r '85, Color, Crow, Horses, Band, Frame, 32 x 45 In.	2057.00
India, Air France, Elephant Head Man, Paper, Jean Carlu, c.1950, 38 x 24 In.	450.00
Jacqueline Elsane, Stylized Woman Dancer, Paper, Tito Livio De Madrazo, c.1932, 48 x 28 In.	400.00
Jazz Concert, Benny Goodman, Louis Armstrong, Rochester, Cardboard, 1953, 14 x 22 In.	215.00
Jeanne D'Arc Bernhardt, Woman, Banner, Eugene Grasset, A. Arnould, Paris, 1894, 45 x 30 In.	750.00
Jim Morrison, Promo, Marked Pandora Prod., D. Hordah, Photo By Barich, 33 x 21 ¾ In.	106.00
Jimi Hendrix, Record Shop Promo, Track Records, Marked Platt Poster Co., 1967, 33 x 21 ¾ In.	189.00
John Dillinger, Wanted In 5 States, Public Enemy Number 1, Frame, c.1930, 21 x 16 In.	708.00
Kandahar Lodge Manchester Vermont, Flexible Flyer Splitkein, Downhill Skier, 36 ½ x 23 ½ In.	1121.00
Kar-Mi, Swallows Gun Barrel, Blindfolded Man, National Ptg. & Eng., 1914, 27 x 40 In.. *Illus*	288.00
Keystone Cops, Peter Max, Photo, Police Patrol, Vehicle, Motorcycle, 1967, 24 x 26 In. .. *Illus*	115.00
Kickapoo Indian Remedies, Indian Princess, Liebler & Maass Lith., N.Y., 27 x 38 In.....*Illus*	26450.00
La Divorcee, Operette En 3 Actes, Linen Back, Frame, France, c.1911, 34 x 46 In.	236.00
La Revue Blanche, Woman, Coat, Hat, Henri De Toulouse-Lautrec, Frame, 1895, 50 x 35 In.	8500.00
Lefrevre-Utile, Bernhardt, Woman, Scarf, A. Mucha, Champenois, Paris, 1904, 26 x 19 In.	4800.00
Les Boules De Neiges, Woman, Picking Flowers, Frame, Paul Berthon, 1900, 16 x 22 In.	1000.00
Les Girondins, 4 Acts Et Tableaux, Crowd Scene, Linen, France, c.1910, 43 x 59 In.	354.00
Let's Clear The Air, Forest, Rainbow, Mountain, 1929, 43 x 36 In.	425.00
Lippincotts, March, Woman, Dropping Leaflet, Will Carqueville, 1895, 19 x 12 In.	350.00
London, Soldier, On Horseback, Frank Newbould, 1939, 38 x 25 In.	750.00
Long Live The Red Sun In The People's Heart All Over The World, Mongolia, 1969, 21 x 29 In.	425.00
Lorenzaccio, Starring Sarah Bernhardt, Dagger, Book, Alphonse Mucha, 1896, 81 x 29 In.. *Illus*	4440.00
Los Angeles Olympic Games, 1932, Reaching Athlete, Julio Kileny, Union Litho Co., 38 x 23 In..	3600.00
Love, Peter Max, Psychedelic Colors, Paper, Series D, 1968, 24 x 36 In. ...*Illus*	316.00
Marilyn Monroe, Life Magazine Cover, April 7, Philippe Halsman, 1952, 34 x 26 In.	2006.00
Miles To Hell To Tokyo, Lithograph, Multicolor, Government Printing Office, 1945, 26 x 18 In.	25.00
Monster Beery Exhibition, Western Show, Dayton, Everybody's Going, 1913, 24 x 36 In.	191.00
New Generation Of Leadership, Exhibition, Signed, Roy Lichtenstein, c.1992, 34 x 38 In.	805.00
New York Par La Transat, Ships, New York City Skyline, Albert Brenet, 38 x 25 In.	650.00

P

Poster, Kar-Mi, Swallows Gun Barrel, Blindfolded Man, National Ptg. & Eng., 1914, 27 x 40 In.
$288.00

Hake's Americana & Collectibles

Poster, Keystone Cops, Peter Max, Photo, Police Patrol, Vehicle, Motorcycle, 1967, 24 x 26 In.
$115.00

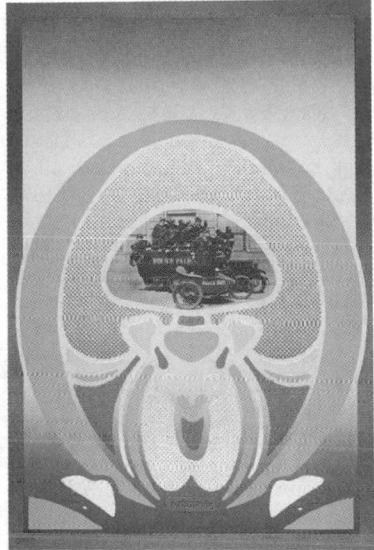

Hake's Americana & Collectibles

Poster, Kickapoo Indian Remedies, Indian Princess, Liebler & Maass Lith., N.Y., 27 x 38 In.
$26,450.00

James D. Julia Auctioneers

Poster, Lorenzaccio, Starring Sarah Bernhardt, Dagger, Book, Alphonse Mucha, 1896, 81 x 29 In.
$4,440.00

Skinner, Inc.

Poster, Love, Peter Max, Psychedelic Colors, Paper, Series D, 1968, 24 x 36 In.
$316.00

Hake's Americana & Collectibles

Poster, Parker's, Perfect Pleasure Producer, Jumping Horse, Carousel, Riverside Print Co., 29 x 22 In.
$1,320.00

Victorian Casino Antiques

Poster, Pierce Cycles, Tried & True, Woman On Bicycle, Bull, Niagara Lith. Co., N.Y., 1800s, 81 x 41 In.
$9,200.00

Copako

Poster, Victory Liberty Loan, For Home & Country, WWI Soldier, Wife, Child, Orr, 40 x 30 In.
$59.00

Conestoga Auction Co., Inc.

Pottery, Bowl, Dragons, Clouds, Ring Bands, Red, Blue Underglaze, 6 Character Mark, c.1890, 5 x 13 In.
$413.00

Brunk Auctions

Pottery, Bowl, Turkey Shape, Red On Yellow, 4 ½ x 3 In.
$248.00

Old Barn Auction

Pottery, Brushpot, Green, Warriors, Deer, Trees, Low Relief, Marked, Chinese, 1800s, 7 x 6 ⅝ In.
$1,033.00

Skinner, Inc.

Pottery, Figurine, Foo Dog, Blue Glaze, Chinese, Missing Tip Of Foot, 6 In.
$42.00

DuMouchelles Art Gallery

TIP

All types of light—sunlight, fluorescent light, and electric lights—will eventually harm paper.

Normandie, Liner, Ocean, Lithograph, Frame, Paris, 1930s, 11 ¼ x 18 ¼ In.		732.00
North Cascades, Mountains, Bold Colors, Ivan Chermayeff, 1972, 42 x 28 In.		900.00
Northern Ireland, Mountains, Sea, Norman Wilkinson, R.B. MacMillan Ltd., Derby, 38 x 24 In.		800.00
Northern Pacific Yellowstone Park, Geyser, Edward Brener, c.1930, 40 x 29 In.		2600.00
Out Of The Running, Late Start Puts You Behind, Horse, Jockey, Racing, Beatty, 1929, 43 ¾ x 36 In.		2000.00
Outer Space, Planets, Peter Max, 1969, 36 x 23 In.		700.00
Palais De Glace, Chaix, Paris, Lithograph, Jules Cheret, Gilt Frame, c.1894, 50 ½ x 36 In.		173.00
Paris Pret A Porter Feminin, Woman, Black Coat, Razzia, c.1990, 35 x 24 In.		106.00
Parker's, Perfect Pleasure Producer, Jumping Horse, Carousel, Riverside Print Co., 29 x 22 In...*Illus*		1320.00
Peacocks, Fruit, Frame, A. Muller, 1901, 22 x 58 In.		1400.00
Pierce Cycles, Tried & True, Woman On Bicycle, Bull, Niagara Lith. Co., N.Y., 1800s, 81 x 41 In...*Illus*		9200.00
Primavera Siciliana, Dabatino Mirabella, Italy, 1931, 36 x 26 In.		800.00
Psychologies Du Militaire Professionel, Horseman, M. Luce, Paris, c.1890, 37 x 25 In.		500.00
Pyramid Of Capitalist System, International Pub., Co., Cleveland, 1911, 19 x 15 In.		4400.00
Royal Mail, Atlantis, Morocco Village Scene, Daphne Padden, 1936, 37 x 24 In.		500.00
Russian Woman Worker, Black, Red, Gray, Black Metal Frame, c.1920, 24 x 17 In.		75.00
Saturday Night Opera, Woman, Headdress, Blue Gown, Paper, Frame, 1887, 45 x 33 In.		150.00
Scarborough, Tonic Holiday, Banner, Pavilion, Umbrellas, Ban, 30 x 20 In.		950.00
Schribners, For September, Couple In Canoe, John Edwin Jackson, 22 x 14 In.		1300.00
Scotland, Highlands & Islands, Royal Route, Hills, Sheep, Tom Gilfillan, Glasgow, c.1945, 40 x 25 In.		500.00
Sidewheel, Mammoth Palace Steamer Bristol, Chromolithograph, Frame, 28 ½ x 40 In.		708.00
Societe Des Artistes Decorateurs, Lithograph, Eugene Grasset, c.1900, 54 x 35 In.		891.00
St. Honore Les Bains, Tennis Players, On Hill, Resort, Roger Broders, c.1928, 39 x 24 In.		2400.00
Sun Valley, Summer Holiday, Horseback Riders, Mountains, Willmarth, 1939, 38 x 24 In.		1800.00
Terrot, Motorcycle, Art Deco, Multicolor, Signed, After B. Lancy, Black Frame, 23 x 36 In.		270.00
Theater, My Partner, Flag, Eagle, Louis Aldrich, 13 x 30 In.		1440.00
Thurston's Greatest Mystery, Vanishing Whippet, Cardboard, Otis Litho Co., 14 x 22 In.		316.00
Torrini The Magician, No Handcuff Or Shackle Prison Cell Or Lock Can Hold Me, 1920s, 21 x 28 In.		560.00
Troupe De Mlle., Eglantine, Lithograph, Dancers, Yellow, Orange, Gray Green, Frame, 13 x 16 In.		71.00
U.S. Army Recruitment, Join The Cavalry, Color Litho, Horses, Soldiers, Frame, 26 x 19 In.		130.00
Victory Liberty Loan, For Home & Country, WWI Soldier, Wife, Child, Orr, 40 x 30 In. ...*Illus*		59.00
Ville De Paris, Les Peintres Temoins De Leur Temps, Lithograph, Chagall, 1963, 30 x 21 ½ In.		351.00
Wilson 6 Horse Hitch Pulling For Victory, Meat Packers Of Chicago, Frame, 18 x 37 ½ In.		35.00
Wispo, 2 Tan Women Sunbathers, Walter Hofmann, c.1955, 67 x 47 In.		1400.00

POTTERY and porcelain are different. Pottery is opaque; you can't see through it. Porcelain is translucent. If you hold a porcelain dish in front of a strong light, you will see the light through the dish. Porcelain is colder to the touch. Pottery is softer and easier to break and will stain more easily because it is porous. Porcelain is thinner, lighter, and more durable. Majolica, faience, and stoneware are all pottery. Additional pieces of pottery are listed in this book in the categories Pottery-Art, Pottery-Contemporary, Pottery-Midcentury, and under the factory name. For information about pottery makers and marks, see *Kovels' Dictionary of Marks—Pottery & Porcelain: 1650–1850* and *Kovels' New Dictionary of Marks—Pottery & Porcelain: 1850 to the Present.*

Bowl, Blue & Green, Border Of Goats & Trees, Seated Child, Middle East, 1 ½ x 9 ½ In.		922.00
Bowl, Conical, Molded Dragons, Roundel, Flower Sprays, Yellow, Chinese, 7 In. Diam.		610.00
Bowl, Demi Lid, Octagonal, Scrolls, Arcaded Top, Figure Smoking A Hookah, Persia, 8 ¾ In. Diam.		369.00
Bowl, Dragons, Clouds, Ring Bands, Red, Blue Underglaze, 6 Character Mark, c.1890, 5 x 13 In...*Illus*		413.00
Bowl, Flared, Green, Tan, Jack Pharo, Kansas, 1972, 3 x 6 In.		132.00
Bowl, Turkey Shape, Red On Yellow, 4 ½ x 3 In.	*Illus*	248.00
Bowl, Turquoise Glaze, Sgraffito Design, Islamic Script, Flower Sprigs, Middle East, 8 In. Diam.		492.00
Brushpot, Green, Warriors, Deer, Trees, Low Relief, Marked, Chinese, 1800s, 7 x 6 ⅝ In..*Illus*		1033.00
Charger, Landscape, Roman Guards, Blue, Yellow, Green, Marked 1168 Italy, 20 In.		480.00
Ewer, White, Black Rondels, Zigzag Design, Chicken Head & Neck Shape, S-Handle, 12 In.		1230.00
Figurine, Dog, Spaniel, Seated, Manganese Glaze, Oval Base, 6 ⅝ In.		83.00
Figurine, Foo Dog, Blue Glaze, Chinese, Missing Tip Of Foot, 6 In.	*Illus*	42.00
Figurine, Foo Dog, Purple Glaze, Striations, Chinese, 1900s, 14 ½ x 8 In., Pair	*Illus*	1888.00
Figurine, Horse, Standing, Head Lowered, Russet Color, Saddle, Harness, Base, Chinese, 17 ½ x 23 In.		615.00
Hat Stand, Stylized Woman's Head, Elongated Neck, Rounded Head & Bust, Italy, 15 In.		390.00
Humidor, Cavalier, Seated, Books, Gun, Matte Glaze, Multicolor, Bernard Bloch, 8 ½ In.		69.00
Humidor, Gnome, On Log, Tall Hat, Multicolor Glaze, Bernard Bloch, 13 In.		403.00
Humidor, Kitty, Seated, Wearing Frilly Dress, Bonnet, Holding Fan, Johann Maresch, 7 In.		173.00
Jar, Drug, Crowned Crest, Lion Head, Shield, Round Foot, Waisted, Italy, 1700s, 8 In.		633.00
Jar, Lid, Sang De Boeuf Glaze, Ball Shape, Stepped Foot, 8 x 9 In., Pair		420.00
Jardiniere, Chinoiserie, Scalloped Apron, Cabriole Legs, Painted, Figures, 23 ½ x 32 In., Pair		2271.00
Jardiniere, Painted, Mountain Village Scenes, Signed, Japan, 11 ½ x 15 In.		60.00

P

Pottery, Figurine, Foo Dog, Purple Glaze, Striations, Chinese, 1900s, 14 ½ x 8 In., Pair
$1,888.00

Brunk Auctions

Pottery, Plant Stand, Chinese Man, Sancai, 3 Intermingled Colors, Glazed, c.1900, 33 In., Pair
$1,840.00

Cottone Auctions

Pottery, Vase, Birds In Flight, Willow Boughs, High Glaze, Kyle Kreigh, Impressed, Door Pottery, 15 In.
$546.00

Humler & Nolan

Pottery, Vase, Blue Faience, Animal & Plant Design, Carl Walters, 1930, 7 ½ x 6 In.
$1,625.00

Rago Arts & Auction Center

Pottery, Vase, Bottle Shape, Line Pattern, Glazed, Marked, Harrison McIntosh, Paper Label, 12 ¾ x 5 In.
$4,063.00

Rago Arts & Auction Center

Pottery, Vase, Picnic Scene, Maija Grotell, Incised MG, 1920s, 4 ½ x 4 ¾ In.
$3,125.00

Rago Arts & Auction Center

Pottery, Vase, Speckled Glaze, Incised, CFB 08, Charles Binns, 1908, 8 ½ x 4 ½ In.
$6,875.00

Rago Arts & Auction Center

Pottery-Art, Bowl, Celadon Crackle Glaze, Signed, Glen Lukens, c.1940, 3 ½ x 4 ¾ In.
$4,688.00

Rago Arts & Auction Center

Pottery-Art, Bowl, Glazed, Maija Grotell, New York, 1930s, 5 x 10 ¼ In.
$1,375.00

Rago Arts & Auction Center

Pottery-Art, Ewer, Multicolor Flowers, Gold Accents, Handle, Cincinnati Faience, Incised, 12 In.
$259.00

Humler & Nolan

POTTERY

Pottery-Art, Figurine, Giraffe, Vally Wieselthier, General Ceramic, 11 ½ In.
$161.00

Humler & Nolan

Pottery-Art, Figurine, Horse, Rearing, Vally Wieselthier, General Ceramic, 8 ¾ In.
$207.00

Humler & Nolan

Pottery-Art, Jardinere, Pedestal, Roses, Squeezebag, Motto, Frederick Rhead, Avon Pottery, 1903, 23 x 12 In.
$5,625.00

Rago Arts & Auction Center

Pottery-Art, Pitcher, Flowers, Luster Glaze, Marked, Bursley Ware Charlotte Rhead England, 9 ⅜ In.
$288.00

Humler & Nolan

Pottery-Art, Potpourri Jar, Reticulated Lid & Body, Slip Accents, Alfred Ceramic Guild, 4 In.
$288.00

Humler & Nolan

Pottery-Art, Vase, 3 Panels, Man Sowing, Harvesting, Baking Bread, Relief, Mougin, France, 1920s, 14 ½ In.
$2,520.00

Skinner, Inc.

Pottery-Art, Vase, Band, Multicolored Vegetables, Marked, California Faience, 2 ½ x 4 In.
$432.00

Humler & Nolan

Pottery-Art, Vase, Bats, Crescent Moon, Clouds, Stars, Apple Trees, Slip Trail, Marked, Wardle
$978.00

Humler & Nolan

Jardiniere, Pedestal, Globe Bowl, Old Men, Offerings, Ruffled Rim, Banko, 13 x 17 In.		2000.00
Jug, Oak Leaf, Acorn, Raised Design, Bearded Man, Bulbous, Brown Glaze, Pewter Lid, Handle, 7 In...		115.00
Loving Cup, Cylindrical, Flared Base & Rim, 3 Loop Handles, Green, Spotted Glaze, c.1905, 2 In..		115.00
Pitcher, Oval, Loop Handle, Albany Slip Glaze, Stripes, Flowers, Tanware, c.1875, 5 ½ In		518.00
Plant Stand, Chinese Man, Sancai, 3 Intermingled Colors, Glazed, c.1900, 33 In., Pair *Illus*		1840.00
Planter, D. Cressey, Brown Glaze, Smokestack Bottom, c.1965, 25 x 23 In		1875.00
Planter, D. Cressey, Ribbed Texture, Copper Glaze, Cylindrical Foot, Cup Shape, c.1963, 25 x 17 In......		2375.00
Planter, Orange Glaze, Manganese Spots, Half Sphere Shape, 3 Hanging Holes, 6 x 8 In.........		212.00
Plate Set, Luncheon, Rooster, Blue, White, Yellow, Mauve, Italy, Marked PV, 8 In., 6 Piece.......		42.00
Tobacco Jar, American Indian Head, Feather Headdress, Multicolor, Karl Bodner, 6 ½ In.		40.00
Tobacco Jar, Lid, Fighting Monks, Turnip Pile, Incised, Multicolor, 8 In.		92.00
Umbrella Stand, Abstract Flower Design, Cylindrical, Ring Foot, Cobalt Blue, Yellow, 22 ¼ In.		633.00
Umbrella Stand, Flambe Style, Glazed, Raised Dragon, Chinese, 24 x 9 In.		150.00
Umbrella Stand, Iridescent Pink, Off White Glaze, Cylindrical, Irregular Rim, Signed, 20 x 9 In.		180.00
Urn, Agateware, Marbled Clay, Scroll Handles, Base, Brown, Tan, White, c.1850, 22 In.............		6518.00
Urn, Turquoise Glaze, Baluster, 2 Angular Handles, Galloway, 1920s, 32 x 14 In., Pair.............		2375.00
Vase, Birds In Flight, Willow Boughs, High Glaze, Kyle Kreigh, Impressed, Door Pottery, 15 In. ....*Illus*		546.00
Vase, Blue Faience, Animal & Plant Design, Carl Walters, 1930, 7 ½ x 6 In......................*Illus*		1625.00
Vase, Bottle Shape, Line Pattern, Glazed, Marked, Harrison McIntosh, Paper Label, 12 ¾ x 5 In..*Illus*		4063.00
Vase, Brown Drip Glaze, Tapered Sides, Scroll Footed, Japan, 10 ¼ x 12 ¼ In..........................		48.00
Vase, Brown, Red, Green, Cylinder, Crown Devon, England, 7 ¼ In.		81.00
Vase, Classical Figures, Greek Key Band, Brown, Red, Footed, Upturned Handles, c.1800, 13 In.		956.00
Vase, Encircling Nude Women, Arms Up, Elongated Oval, Flared Rim, Marked, Mougin, 13 In..		1610.00
Vase, Indian Group Line, Bulbous, Star Pattern, Orange Glaze, Marked, 1935, 5 ½ x 5 ¼ In. ...		150.00
Vase, Mottled Blue & Gray, Squat, 2 Loop Handles At Neck, Rolled Rim, Stamped, 5 ¼ x 8 In..		625.00
Vase, Picnic Scene, Maija Grotell, Incised MG, 1920s, 4 ½ x 4 ¾ In.............................*Illus*		3125.00
Vase, Sang De Boef Glaze, Bottle Shape, Squat Bottom, Stepped Base, 14 ½ x 9 In....................		1560.00
Vase, Speckled Glaze, Incised, CFB 08, Charles Binns, 1908, 8 ½ x 4 ½ In. ....*Illus*		6875.00

POTTERY-ART Art pottery was first made in America in Cincinnati, Ohio, during the 1870s. The pieces were hand thrown and hand decorated. The art pottery tradition continued until the 1930s when studio potters began making the more artistic wares. American, English, and Continental art pottery by less well-known makers is listed here. Most makers listed in *Kovels' American Art Pottery,* such as Arequipa, Ohr, Rookwood, Roseville, and Weller, are listed in their own categories in this book. More recent pottery is listed under the name of the maker or in another pottery category.

Bowl, Blue, Orange Drips, Flared, Harding Black, 1945, 2 ¾ x 9 ¼ In..		688.00
Bowl, Celadon Crackle Glaze, Signed, Glen Lukens, c.1940, 3 ½ x 4 ¾ In......................*Illus*		4688.00
Bowl, Encircling Stylized Serpent, Squat, Smokestack, Black & Gray, San Ildefonso, 6 x 7 ½ In.....		863.00
Bowl, Glazed, Maija Grotell, New York, 1930s, 5 x 10 ¼ In..*Illus*		1375.00
Bowl, Grapes, Vines, Gray & Blue Glaze, 3 Cylindrical Feet, Signed C. Poillon, 1905, 7 x 13 In....		3250.00
Bowl, Gray, Incised Lines, Harding Black, 1959, 2 ¼ x 8 In..		495.00
Bowl, Green Carved Designs, Concave Band, Blue Ground, R. Canfield, 1919, 3 x 6 In.............		1250.00
Bowl, Green Frog, Brown Arched Leaf, Boat Shape, Impressed Freiwald Art Pottery, 12 In.		604.00
Bowl, Lavender Mottled, Glossy Souffle Glaze, Opalescent, Curved Sides, Ruskin, 11 ¼ x 3 ¼ In....		150.00
Bowl, Liner, Red Glaze, Robertson Hollywood, c.1950, 4 ⅞ x 7 ¾ In.......................................		266.00
Bowl, Roosters, Barbotine, Gray, Straight Sides, 4-Footed, C. Virion, France, 1880s, 5 x 9 In....		750.00
Bowl, Round, Flat Rim, Sitting Mouse, Green Blue Glaze, 1900s, 5 ¼ In.		119.00
Bowl, Trees, Red Clay Colored Body, Squat, Wide Rim, Saucer Shape, Marked Rhead, 2 x 5 ½ In....		1955.00
Charger, Joan Of Arc, Fleur-De-Lis, Viva La Bevr, Keller & Guerin, Signed Marchal, 11 In. Diam.....		316.00
Creamer, Smoky Blue, Art Nouveau Design, Cylindrical, Square Handle, Rhead, 4 ¼ In.		144.00
Crock, Round, Green, Black Band, Footed, Marked Avon, 6 ¼ In...		115.00
Ewer, Blue, Brown, Arched Handle, North State Pottery, 12 In.		86.00
Ewer, Multicolor Flowers, Gold Accents, Handle, Cincinnati Faience, Incised, 12 In.........*Illus*		259.00
Figurine, Dog, Begging, Robinson Ransbottom, Brown, 6 ½ In.		75.00
Figurine, Dog, Spaniel, Seated, Freestanding Front Legs, Tooled, Paint, G. Bagnall, c.1870, 10 In.		529.00
Figurine, Fireplace, Chimneys, Kiln, Dark Brown Glaze, Ohio, c.1890, 6 x 7 In.		118.00
Figurine, Giraffe, Vally Wieselthier, General Ceramic, 11 ½ In.............................*Illus*		161.00
Figurine, Horse, Rearing, Vally Wieselthier, General Ceramic, 8 ¾ In..............................*Illus*		207.00
Figurine, Reclining Lion, Oval Base, Amber Running Glaze, Ohio, c.1870, 14 In.		411.00
Figurine, Woman Volleyball Player, Ball, Schau Bach Kunst, 9 ⅜ In.................................		219.00
Group, Barroom Trio, Nattily Dressed Singers, Incised, Brayton, Laguna Pottery, 8 x 6 In.......		132.00
Heron, Molded Flower, Green Moss Mottled Glaze, Round, 7 ½ In......................................		142.00
Jar, Arts & Crafts, Copper, Hammered, Black, Handles, Stamped, Russia, c.1910, 20 In.............		460.00
Jardiniere, 3 Handles, Yellow Flowers, Magenta Base, 10 ¾ In.......................................		65.00
Jardiniere, Majolica, Spongeware, Green, Brown, Yellow, c.1900, 10 In............................		150.00
Jardiniere, Pedestal, Roses, Squeezebag, Motto, Frederick Rhead, Avon Pottery, 1903, 23 x 12 In..*Illus*		5625.00

Pottery-Art, Vase, Birds, Grasses, Gold Accents, Tan & Green, Impressed, Matt Morgan, 12 ¼ In. $533.00

Skinner, Inc.

Pottery-Art, Vase, Blue-Gray Hare's Fur Glaze, Incised, Berndt Friberg, Sweden, 1960s, 7 ½ x 6 ½ In. $1,500.00

Rago Arts & Auction Center

Pottery-Art, Vase, Daffodils, Incised, Jervis, c.1906, 5 ¾ x 4 In. $1,750.00

Rago Arts & Auction Center

Pottery-Art, Vase, Daisies, Blue, Yellow, Mary L. Yancey, Iowa State College, 1920s, 9 x 5 In. $45,000.00

Rago Arts & Auction Center

P

Pottery-Art, Vase, Freesia, Modeled, San Diego, Marked, Valentien, 1911-14, 8 x 3 In. $1,625.00

Rago Arts & Auction Center

Pottery-Art, Vase, Gourd Shape, Masks, Pate-Sur-Pate, Taxile Doat, Signed, 1929, 3 ½ x 3 ½ In. $8,750.00

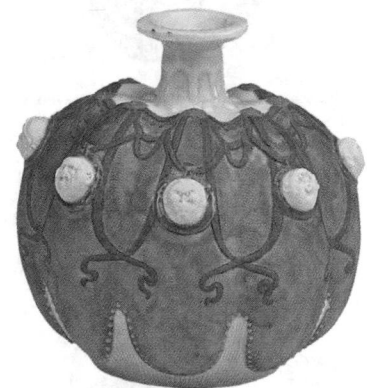

Rago Arts & Auction Center

Pottery-Art, Vase, Iridescent, Deco Spiral Designs, Copper Luster Glaze, Jean Barol, 7 ⅝ In. $403.00

Humler & Nolan

Pottery-Art, Vase, Brown & Green Matte Glaze, Stamped, W.J. Walley, c.1900, 6 ½ x 3 ½ In. $1,000.00

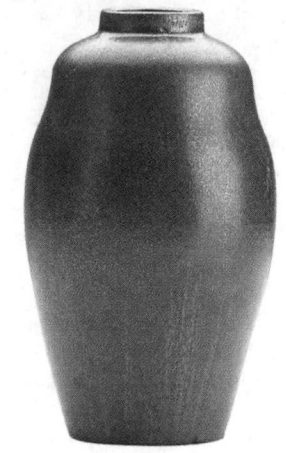

Rago Arts & Auction Center

Pottery-Art, Vase, Green Matte, Handicraft Guild Of Minneapolis, Impressed Mark, 13 ¼ x 5 ¾ In. $1,000.00

Rago Arts & Auction Center

Pottery-Art, Vase, Mottled Lavender & Green Glaze, Reticulated Foot, Cats, Plants, Marked, E. Klabena, 13 In. $2,160.00

Skinner, Inc.

Pottery-Art, Vase, Mottled Yellow Glaze, Slender Neck, Whalebone Mark, Brouwer, 7 In. $633.00

Humler & Nolan

Pottery-Art, Vase, Neutral, Cobalt Blue, Diamond Design, Glazed, Signed Kaneko 67, 13 ½ x 6 In. $2,813.00

Los Angeles Modern Auctions (LAMA)

Pottery-Art, Vase, Pine Trees, Saw Beyond The Fiery Forges Flame, Stamped, Jervis, 1913, 8 x 3 In. $6,250.00

Rago Arts & Auction Center

Pottery-Art, Vase, Ruby Luster, Dragons, William De Morgan, 1870s, 10 x 7 ½ In. $6,875.00

Rago Arts & Auction Center

P

Jardiniere, Squeezebag, Glorious Summer Symphony, Green, Orange, Avon, 7 ¾ In. 489.00
Oil Jar, Green Glaze, Tapered, Pacific Pottery, 13 x 23 ½ In. 366.00
Pitcher, Flowers, Luster Glaze, Marked, Bursley Ware, Charlotte Rhead, England, 9 ⅜ In. .... *Illus* 288.00
Pitcher, Large Pink Flowers, Green, Signed Suzanne Tormey, Santa Barbara Ceramic, 7 ½ In. ... 150.00
Pitcher, Runny Brown Glaze, North Star Pottery Co., 6 ¼ In. 17.00
Pitcher, Stylized Tulips, Pink & White, Brown Ground, Jervis, 6 ½ x 8 ½ In. 625.00
Planter, Kemp Style, Flared Rim, Bulbous, Abstract Flowers, Brown, Green, 1900s, 9 x 10 In. .. 210.00
Plate, Red Day Lilies, Green Ground, Signed Anne Collinson, Santa Barbara Ceramic, 7 ¾ In. .. 58.00
Potpourri Jar, Reticulated Lid & Body, Slip Accents, Alfred Ceramic Guild, 4 In. .... *Illus* 288.00
Tankard, Laughing Pig, Pewter Collar, Hinged Thumbpiece, Musterschultz, 7 ¾ In. 325.00
Teapot, Blue Leaves, Silver Line Trunks, Black Ground, Avon, 4 ½ In. 834.00
Umbrella Stand, Green Glaze, Molded Flowers, c.1900, 20 ¼ x 10 ½ In. 359.00
Vase, 3 Panels, Man Sowing, Harvesting, Baking Bread, Relief, Mougin, France, 1920s, 14 ½ In.. *Illus* 2520.00
Vase, Bachelor's Buttons, Turquoise, Mary Yancey, Iowa, 1930, 6 In. 3750.00
Vase, Band, Multicolored Vegetables, Marked, California Faience, 2 ½ x 4 In. .... *Illus* 432.00
Vase, Bats, Crescent Moon, Clouds, Stars, Apple Trees, Slip Trail, Marked, Wardle .... *Illus* 978.00
Vase, Birds, Grasses, Gold Accents, Tan & Green, Impressed, Matt Morgan, 12 ¼ In. .... *Illus* 533.00
Vase, Blue & White, Leaves Flowers, Bottle Shape, Turkey, c.1890, 10 ¾ In., Pair 590.00
Vase, Blue, 8-Sided, Stepped Architectural Design, Buttresses, Mougin, c.1930, 14 x 8 In. 375.00
Vase, Blue-Gray Hare's Fur Glaze, Incised, Berndt Friberg, Sweden, 1960s, 7 ½ x 6 ½ In.. *Illus* 1500.00
Vase, Bottle, Yellow Crystalline Glaze, University City, Mo., 1912, 10 x 2 ½ In. 10625.00
Vase, Brown & Green Matte Glaze, Stamped, W.J. Walley, c.1900, 6 ½ x 3 ½ In. .... *Illus* 1000.00
Vase, Brown Glaze, Swirled Tan Overlay, Applied Gems, Loop Handles, Bretby, 8 x 13 In. 915.00
Vase, Burnt Sienna Glaze, Flared, Signed G & O Natzler, 5 ¾ x 3 In. 3537.00
Vase, Cobalt Blue, Yellow Flowers, Vines, Tapered, Flared Rim, H. Wilcox, c.1921, 8 In. 3220.00
Vase, Daffodils, Incised, Jervis, c.1906, 5 ¾ x 4 In. .... *Illus* 1750.00
Vase, Daisies, Blue, Yellow, Mary L. Yancey, Iowa State College, 1920s, 9 x 5 In. .... *Illus* 45000.00
Vase, Dark Green, Red & Orange Flowers, Stems, Baluster, Swollen Shoulders, Kezonta, 9 ⅞ In. 374.00
Vase, Flared Rim, Extended Neck, Bulbous, Abstract Flowers, Brown, Kemp, 1900s, 23 x 9 In.. 330.00
Vase, Flask Shape, Square Handles At Rim, Footed, Flowers, Gold, Hungarian Style, 11 ¼ In. . 288.00
Vase, Flowers Around Rim, Matte Green, Red, Yellow, Bulbous, Squat, Sara Sax, c.1923, 6 In.. 4025.00
Vase, Flowers, Green Glaze, Tapered, 3 Pinched Sides, D. Zumbo, Frejus, c.1900, 25 x 6 In. 750.00
Vase, Freesia, Modeled, San Diego, Marked, Valentien, 1911-14, 8 x 3 In. .... *Illus* 1625.00
Vase, Frosted Green, Black Glaze, Handles, Tapered, 9 ¼ In. 86.00
Vase, Gourd Shape, Masks, Pate-Sur-Pate, Taxile Doat, Signed, 1929, 3 ½ x 3 ½ In. .... *Illus* 8750.00
Vase, Grand Feu, Yellow Crystalline Glaze, Squat Bottom, Bottle Neck, 6 x 3 In 1000.00
Vase, Green & Blue Crystalline Glaze, Baluster, Charles Binns, 1929, 8 x 5 In. 11875.00
Vase, Green & Raspberry Flambe Glaze, Shouldered, W. Jervis, Rose Valley, 8 In. 2125.00
Vase, Green Crystalline Glaze, Tapered, Bulbous Bottom, Norweta, 9 ¾ In. 938.00
Vase, Green Matte Glaze, 3 Pinched Handles, Cylindrical, R. Radcliffe, c.1915, 8 In. 875.00
Vase, Green Matte, Handicraft Guild Of Minneapolis, Impressed Mark, 13 ¼ x 5 ¾ In. ..... *Illus* 1000.00
Vase, Green Mottled Malachite Glaze, Flared Rim, Tapered, North Carolina, c.1940 .... 316.00
Vase, Green, Brown Glaze, Twisted Handles, 4 Wells, Organic Shape, Vance & Co., 9 x 10 In. 458.00
Vase, Hazy Branches, Leaves, Long Neck, Francis Joseph Vontury, 13 ¼ In. 46.00
Vase, Horned Devil Head Handles, Long Tongue, Signed, c.1900, 12 In. 5462.00
Vase, Incised Stripes, Blue Vertical, Green Horizontal, Arthur Baggs, 5 x 5 In. 750.00
Vase, Incised, Flared Rim, Green, Blue, Black Glaze, Chelsea Keramic Art Works, c.1889, 11 x 6 In. 533.00
Vase, Iridescent, Deco Spiral Designs, Copper Luster Glaze, Jean Barol, 7 ⅝ In. .... *Illus* 403.00
Vase, Lid, Horizontal Bands, Green, Tan, Betty Fres, c.1850, 11 In. 1265.00
Vase, Lid, Red Glaze, Harding Black, 1956, 6 ¾ x 5 ½ In. 220.00
Vase, Lion Head, Handles, Pale Green, Marked, Burley Winter, 18 ½ In. 431.00
Vase, Mottled Blue, Ivory Glaze, Flared, Footed, Signed G & O Natzler, 5 ½ x 2 ½ In. 2440.00
Vase, Mottled Lavender & Green Glaze, Reticulated Foot, Cats, Plants, Marked, E. Klabena, 13 In.. *Illus* 2160.00
Vase, Mottled Pink Glaze, Blue Highlights, Tapered, Lug Handles, N. Carolina, 21 In. 316.00
Vase, Mottled Plum Glaze, Bulbous Bottom, Slight Taper, Paul Cox, 6 ½ x 6 In. 594.00
Vase, Mottled Yellow Glaze, Slender Neck, Whalebone Mark, Brouwer, 7 In. .... *Illus* 633.00
Vase, Neutral, Cobalt Blue, Diamond Design, Glazed, Signed Kaneko 67, 13 ½ x 6 In. ...... *Illus* 2813.00
Vase, Orange To Brown Glaze, Paneled, Ogontz, Lakeside, Ohio, 6 ½ In. 127.00
Vase, Owl, Moon, Mottled Green, Signed Richard, Freiwald, 9 ¾ In. 230.00
Vase, Oxblood Glaze, Flared & Flattened Rim, Catalina, 11 x 9 ½ In. 375.00
Vase, Oxblood Glaze, Round, White Flare Rim, Narrow Neck, Brother Bezanson, 3 ½ x 5 ½ In.. 368.00
Vase, Pine Trees, Saw Beyond The Fiery Forges Flame, Stamped, Jervis, 1913, 8 x 3 In. ..... *Illus* 6250.00
Vase, Purple Matte Glaze, Blue Green Accents, Zanesville, Ohio, c.1920, 20 In. 270.00
Vase, Red, Brown, Tan Matte Glaze, Ribbed, Arthur Braggs, 8 x 8 In. 3750.00
Vase, Red, White Flowers, Blue Ground, Tapered Cylinder, Santa Barbara Ceramic, 7 ¼ In. 46.00
Vase, Round, Squat Stepped Design, Stick Neck, 2 Handles, C. Dresser, Ault, 7 x 8 In. 313.00

Pottery-Art, Vase, Skyscrapers, Impressed, Stonelain Pottery, Signed, Schreiber, 16 ½ x 6 ½ In.
$469.00

Rago Arts & Auction Center

Pottery-Art, Vase, Stick, Swirl Ribs, Avocado Glaze, Speckled, Chicago Crucible Co., 8 In.
$316.00

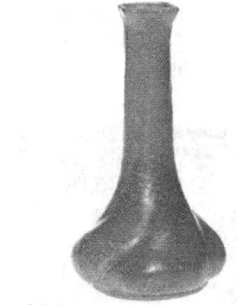

Humler & Nolan

Pottery-Art, Vase, Thistles, Squeeze Bag, Blue Ground, Albert Cusick, Avon Faience, 8 ⅛ In.
$1,265.00

Humler & Nolan

Pottery-Art, Vase, Trees, Signed, California Faience, 6 ½ x 4 In.
$4,063.00

Rago Arts & Auction Center

P

Pottery-Art, Water Jug, Flower Band, Faience, Handle, Signed, Byrdcliffe, 10 x 8 In.
$3,125.00

Rago Arts & Auction Center

Pottery-Contemporary, Bowl, Orange Pink Speckled Matte Glaze, Brown, Vivika & Otto Heino, 11 ¾ x 10 In.
$1,046.00

Skinner, Inc.

Pottery-Contemporary, Bowl, Raku, Canyon, Wayne Higby, 1987, 12 ¾ x 19 ¾ In.
$4,200.00

Cowans + Clark + DelVecchio

> **TIP**
> *Don't use a repaired plate for food. It could be a health hazard.*

Pottery-Contemporary, Bowl, Ribbed, Lavender, Gray Accents, Stoneware, Incised, Otto Heino, 2000s, 11 In.
$800.00

Skinner, Inc.

Pottery-Contemporary, Jug, Picasso, Stylized Face, Brushed Glaze, Madoura, 1969, 12 ¼ In.
$4,375.00

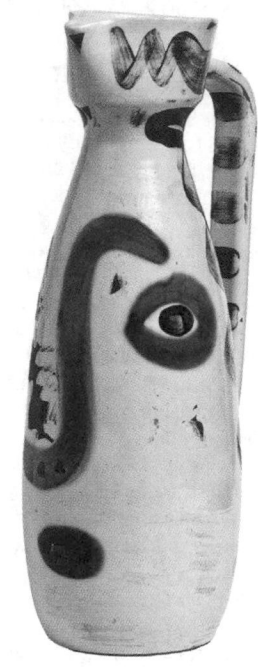

Los Angeles Modern Auctions (LAMA)

Pottery-Contemporary, Moonpot, Rattle, Monochrome Drip Glaze, Toshiko Takaezu, Signed, 9 x 8 ½ In.
$4,688.00

Rago Arts & Auction Center

Pottery-Contemporary, Platter, Nude Drawing, Stoneware, Ken Ferguson, 1983, 4 x 23 ½ In.
$1,080.00

Cowans + Clark + DelVecchio

Pottery-Contemporary, Sculpture, Abstract, Ash Glazed, Stoneware, A. Zimmerman, 1988, 45 x 17 In.
$1,560.00

Cowans + Clark + DelVecchio

Pottery-Contemporary, Teapot, Nuclear Nuts, Stoneware, Richard Notkin, 1991, 5 x 8 In.
$6,600.00

Cowans + Clark + DelVecchio

P

Vase, Ruby Luster, Dragons, William De Morgan, 1870s, 10 x 7 ½ In. ....*Illus*	6875.00
Vase, Salamander, Flowers, Bulbous, Brown, Green Matte Glaze, 6 ¼ In.	378.00
Vase, Skyscrapers, Impressed, Stonelain Pottery, Signed, Schreiber, 16 ½ x 6 ½ In. ....*Illus*	469.00
Vase, Speckled Blue Gloss, Flowers, Dentil Molding, Tapered, Shouldered, Auburn, c.1940, 8 In.	196.00
Vase, Squeezebag Decoration, Squat Double Gourd Shape, Avon, F.H. Rhead, 5 x 5 ½ In.	594.00
Vase, Stick, Swirl Ribs, Avocado Glaze, Speckled, Chicago Crucible Co., 8 In. ....*Illus*	316.00
Vase, Striated Red Chrome Glaze, Oval, Ring & Loop Handles, c.1930, 17 In.	1035.00
Vase, Stylized Blossoms, Leaves, Arrows, Tan, Green, Gold Trim, E. & H. Overbeck, 6 In.	11250.00
Vase, Stylized Flowers, Yellow, Green, Brown, Clews Chameleon, England, 8 ¼ In.	184.00
Vase, Thistles, Squeeze Bag, Blue Ground, Albert Cusick, Avon Faience, 8 ⅛ In. ....*Illus*	1265.00
Vase, Threshold, Violet Crackle Glaze, Squeezebag Decoration, 6 ½ x 4 In.	500.00
Vase, Trees, Signed, California Faience, 6 ½ x 4 In. ....*Illus*	4063.00
Vase, Violets, Incised, Enameled, Ovoid, Linna Irelan, Roblin, 1898-1906, 5 In.	2375.00
Vase, Yellow, Red, Blue, Shouldered, Swollen Neck, Wiener Werkstatte, Marked, 8 In.	690.00
Wall Pocket, Green Matte Glaze, Carved Designs, Oakwood, 8 x 5 In.	610.00
Water Jug, Flower Band, Faience, Handle, Signed, Byrdcliffe, 10 x 8 In. ....*Illus*	3125.00

POTTERY-CONTEMPORARY lists pieces made by artists working about 1975 and later.

Ashtray, Bird Under The Sun, Oiseau Au Soleil, Pablo Picasso, 1952, 6 ¼ In.	1107.00
Basket, Tortoise & Hare, Stoneware, Ken Ferguson, c.2007, 13 x 16 In.	5876.00
Bowl, Albert Green, c.1990, 8 ½ In.	60.00
Bowl, Folded Flower Form, Mottled Lavender & White Glaze, 17 In.	150.00
Bowl, Orange Pink Speckled Matte Glaze, Brown, Vivika & Otto Heino, 11 ¾ x 10 In. ....*Illus*	1046.00
Bowl, Raku, Canyon, Wayne Higby, 1987, 12 ¾ x 19 ¾ In. ....*Illus*	4200.00
Bowl, Ribbed, Lavender, Gray Accents, Stoneware, Incised, Otto Heino, 2000s, 11 In. ....*Illus*	800.00
Bowl, Sage Green, Wide Rim, Round Foot, Reeded, Stoneware, Salto, 1960s, 3 x 7 In.	625.00
Bowl, Squat, Ring Foot, Reeded Interior, Etched, Cream, Blue, Stoneware, Heino, 1988, 5 x 14 In.	438.00
Bowl, Surface & Void, Earthenware, Martin Smith, c.1999, 9 x 13 ½ In.	1560.00
Bowl, Tea, White Glaze, 3-Dimple Sides, Ruth Duckworth, 5 x 4 In.	519.00
Charger, Roofscape, Earthenware, Lidya Buzio, 1988, 16 In.	2820.00
Charger, Square, Stoneware, Albert Green, 18 ¼ In.	90.00
Figure, Elysian Fields, Stoneware, Glazed, Rudy Autio, c.1988, 30 ½ x 21 In.	12044.00
Figure, Rock Head, Whiteware, Jack Earl, c.1978, 17 x 6 ½ In.	5100.00
Figurine, Elf & Puppy, Ceramic, Wool, Yarn, M. Lucero, c.2003, 33 x 26 In.	11750.00
Ice Bucket, Smudge Design, Shaped Body, Wavy Foot, Stoneware, P. Voulkos, 1978, 8 x 10 In.	6250.00
Jug, Picasso, Stylized Face, Brushed Glaze, Madoura, 1969, 12 ¼ In. ....*Illus*	4375.00
Moonpot, Brown, Green, Speckled Glaze, Oval, Stoneware, T. Takaezu, 7 ½ x 5 In.	3000.00
Moonpot, Rattle, Bulbous, White, Brown, Glazed, Stoneware, Toshiko Takaezu, 6 x 6 In.	2250.00
Moonpot, Rattle, Monochrome Drip Glaze, Toshiko Takaezu, Signed, 9 x 8 ½ In. ....*Illus*	4688.00
Oil Jar, Green Glaze, Pacific Pottery, 23 In.	300.00
Pitcher, Pillow Shape, Loop Handle, Faience, Drip Design, B. Woodman, 1980s, 17 x 21 In.	4688.00
Planter, Brown Glaze, Flared Sides, Hangs, Stoneware, Toshiko Takaezu, 6 x 8 In.	1250.00
Platter, Nude Drawing, Stoneware, Ken Ferguson, 1983, 4 x 23 ½ In. ....*Illus*	1080.00
Sake Pot, Whiteware, Green, Purple, Peter Shire, 1981, 5 ¾ x 8 In.	764.00
Sculpture, Abstract, Ash Glazed, Stoneware, A. Zimmerman, 1988, 45 x 17 In. ....*Illus*	1560.00
Teapot, Nuclear Nuts, Stoneware, Richard Notkin, 1991, 5 x 8 In. ....*Illus*	6600.00
Teapot, Teddy Roosevelt, Silver Glaze, Anthony Bennett, c.1986, 9 ½ x 3 ½ In.	2468.00
Vase, Black Glaze Lip, Sphere Shape, Brown, Black Speckles, Foot, Heino, 8 ½ In.	1007.00
Vase, Black, Handles, David Shaner, Stoneware, 1980, 13 ½ x 14 In. ....*Illus*	4080.00
Vase, Bottle, Double Handles, Earthenware, Beatrice Wood, c.1978, 4 ½ x 4 In.	1680.00
Vase, Bud, Olive Green Drip Glaze Over Mirrored Auburn, Stoneware, F. Wildenhain, 6 x 5 In....*Illus*	500.00
Vase, Bulbous, Cylindrical Lip, Brown, White, Etched, C. Conover, 1970s, 13 x 15 In.	4063.00
Vase, Canyon De Chelly, Slips, Stoneware, R. Turner, c.1984, 9 ½ x 9 ½ In. ....*Illus*	3600.00
Vase, Gray, Cream Drip Glaze, Round, Narrow Neck, Stoneware, T. Takaezu, c.1970, 9 In.	3750.00
Vase, Lid, Blue & White, Porcelain, Ralph Bacerra, c.1980, 6 x 6 In.	1200.00
Vase, Lid, Brown Matte Glaze, Black Designs, Signed Harrison McIntosh, 7 ½ x 9 In.	2684.00
Vase, Oval, Uneven Rim, Beige, Pink Matte Glaze, Richard Devore, 14 x 10 In. ....*Illus*	2880.00
Vase, Pinecone Design, Red Glaze, Turquoise Interior, Signed, Fantoni, 1950s, 3 x 8 In.	488.00
Vase, Stylized Flowers, Leaves, Green, Marked Jesse Wolf, Ephraim, c.1998, 7 In.	115.00
Vase, Woman, Holding Bird, Yellow Glaze, Guido Gambone, Italy, 4 x 11 In.	976.00

POTTERY-MIDCENTURY includes pieces made from the 1940s to about 1975.

Bottle, Green Crystalline Glaze, Lip, Signed, Natzler, 1962, 11 ¼ In. ....*Illus*	3125.00
Bowl, Blue, Cream, Curvy Shapes, Ring Foot, Flat Rim, Stoneware, Jun Kaneko, 1965, 8 x 10 In...	2813.00
Bowl, Crackleware, Blue Bands, Dots On Rim, Glen Lukens, 7 ¼ In.	500.00

Pottery-Contemporary, Vase, Black, Handles, David Shaner, Stoneware, 1980, 13 ½ x 14 In.
$4,080.00

Cowans + Clark + DelVecchio

Pottery-Contemporary, Vase, Bud, Olive Green Drip Glaze Over Mirrored Auburn, Stoneware, F. Wildenhain, 6 x 5 In.
$500.00

Rago Arts & Auction Center

Pottery-Contemporary, Vase, Canyon De Chelly, Slips, Stoneware, R. Turner, c.1984, 9 ½ x 9 ½ In.
$3,600.00

Cowans + Clark + DelVecchio

Pottery-Contemporary, Vase, Oval, Uneven Rim, Beige, Pink Matte Glaze, Richard Devore, 14 x 10 In.
$2,880.00

Skinner, Inc.

P

Pottery-Midcentury, Bottle, Green Crystalline Glaze, Lip, Signed, Natzler, 1962, 11 ¼ In. $3,125.00

Los Angeles Modern Auctions (LAMA)

Pottery-Midcentury, Bowl, Flared, Swirls, Wax Resist, Glazed, Signed, Antonio Prieto, 3 ½ x 14 In. $1,375.00

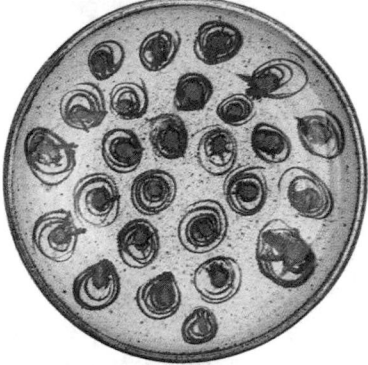

Rago Arts & Auction Center

Pottery-Midcentury, Chalice, Mother & Child Medallions, Luster Glaze, 4 Handles, Beatrice Wood, 11 x 6 In. $4,063.00

Rago Arts & Auction Center

Pottery-Midcentury, Figurine, Cubist, Glazed, Marcello Fantoni, Signed, 1950s, 15 x 7 ½ In., Pair $4,375.00

Rago Arts & Auction Center

Pottery-Midcentury, Plate, 2 Bulls, Edition Picasso Madoura, 7 ⅞ In. $2,070.00

Humler & Nolan

Pottery-Midcentury, Plate, Face, Black, Green, Blue Glaze, Applied Features, Picasso, 15 ¾ x 12 ¾ In. $5,900.00

Brunk Auctions

Pottery-Midcentury, Plate, Face, White Clay, Pablo Picasso, 1963, 9 ¾ In. $5,000.00

Los Angeles Modern Auctions (LAMA)

Pottery-Midcentury, Plate, Woman, Glazed, Signed, Beatrice Wood, 1940s, 8 ½ In. $1,625.00

Rago Arts & Auction Center

Pottery-Midcentury, Plate, Woman's Face, White Clay, Marked, Picasso, 1953, 15 x 12 ⅝ In. $9,840.00

New Orleans Auction Galleries, Inc.

TIP

The surface of Niloak marbleized pottery is porous. Oil from your skin, glue residue from sticky labels, and any other type of oil will make permanent marks.

P

Bowl, Flared, Swirls, Wax Resist, Glazed, Signed, Antonio Prieto, 3 ½ x 14 In..................*Illus*	1375.00
Bowl, Mottled Oxblood Luster, Flared, Short Foot, Natzler, 2 x 5 In.	438.00
Bowl, Ring Foot, Leaves, Blue, Green, Cream Glaze, Stoneware, H. McIntosh, 3 x 6 In..............	1125.00
Bowl, Sky Blue Glaze, Footed, Gertrud & Otto Natzler, Signed, 3 ½ x 7 ½ In............................	4375.00
Bowl, Vertical Stripes, Gray, White, Speckled, Flared, Stoneware, Harrison McIntosh, 3 x 6 In.	469.00
Bowl, White, Copper Rim, Stoneware, Lucie Rie, c.1970, 2 ¾ x 5 ¾ In...................................	3120.00
Canister, Tea, Horizontal Bands, Stoneware, Marguerite Wildenhain, Pond Farm, c.1950, 6 x 3 In.	625.00
Chalice, Mother & Child Medallions, Luster Glaze, 4 Handles, Beatrice Wood, 11 x 6 In. .*Illus*	4063.00
Charger, Black Glaze, Multicolor Dots, Incised, Stoneware, Jun Kaneko, U.S.A., 1991, 4 x 25 In.	3625.00
Charger, Brown, Pink Glaze, Swirls, Flat Rim, Stoneware, P. Voulkos, 1950s, 12 In. Diam.	1875.00
Dish, Footed, Brown & Cream, Scribble, Swirls, Stoneware, P. Voulkos, 1950s, 7 In. Diam........	1500.00
Figurine, Cubist, Glazed, Marcello Fantoni, Signed, 1950s, 15 x 7 ½ In., Pair..................*Illus*	4375.00
Pitcher, Woman's Face, Yellow, Pink Fruit, White, Loop Handle, B. Wiinblad, c.1955, 6 In......	92.00
Planter, Squat, Flat Rim, Scroll Feet, Lug Handles, Stoneware, D. Reitz, c.1950, 16 x 24 In.....	1125.00
Plaque, Heart, Brown, Blue, Tray Edges, Slab, Stoneware, P. Voulkos, c.1961, 10 ½ x 8 In.	2500.00
Plate, 2 Bulls, Edition Picasso Madoura, 7 ⅞ In. ....*Illus*	2070.00
Plate, Face, Black, Green, Blue Glaze, Applied Features, Picasso, 15 ¾ x 12 ¾ In..............*Illus*	5900.00
Plate, Face, White Clay, Pablo Picasso, 1963, 9 ¾ In. ....*Illus*	5000.00
Plate, Sunflower, Green & Beige Glaze, Stoneware, McIntosh, 1976, 7 ¾ In. Diam.	1125.00
Plate, Woman, Glazed, Signed, Beatrice Wood, 1940s, 8 ½ In.................................*Illus*	1625.00
Plate, Woman's Face, White Clay, Marked, Picasso, 1953, 15 x 12 ⅝ In...........................*Illus*	9840.00
Sculpture, Earthenware, Frog Pizza, Pie Crust Border, Signed, D. Gilhooly, 1977, 2 x 11 In....	625.00
Teapot, Square Body & Spout, Circle Design, Lid, Disc Finial, P. Shire, 1981, 5 ½ x 8 In...........	625.00
Tile, Tower Building, Iowa State College, Cream, Brown, M. Yancey, 4 In.....................	938.00
Tureen, Underplate, Cabbage Form, Lettuce Ware, Dodie Thayer, 6 x 11 In., Pair.............	2950.00
Vase, Ball Shape, Round Foot, Drip Design, Brown, White, Stoneware, P. Voulkos, 1961, 4 x 3 In. ..	2750.00
Vase, Bell Shape, Black, White, Line Banding, Stoneware, L. Rie, 1950s, 12 ½ x 7 In.	3250.00
Vase, Bottle Shape, Flared Rim, Glazed, Earth Tones, Lucie Rie, London, 1970s, 12 x 5 In..... *Illus*	3750.00
Vase, Bud, Dandelions, Blue, Green, Red Ground, Tapered, M. Yancey, 7 In.	3750.00
Vase, Bulbous Balloon Shape, Narrow Mouth, Drip Glaze, Turquoise, Green, Rose, 5 In.........	500.00
Vase, Cylindrical, Swollen Stick Neck, Brown, Stoneware, P. Soldner, c.1962, 51 x 10 In...........	6250.00
Vase, Glazed, Vertical Lines, Stoneware, H. McIntosh, 1955-59, 19 x 7 In.....................*Illus*	4375.00
Vase, Herringbone Pattern, Signed, Voulkos, 1950s, 10 ½ In..............................*Illus*	2125.00
Vase, Katap, Glazed, Plastic Insert, Signed, Claude Conover, c.1961, 14 ½ x 16 In.............*Illus*	5938.00
Vase, Mottled Iridescent Oxblood Glaze, Cone Shape, Beatrice Wood, 5 In.	750.00
Vase, Stoneware, Bernard Leach, c.1969, 4 ½ In.	470.00
Vase, Stylized Leaves & Buds, Blue, Green, Bulbous, M. Yancey, Iowa, 5 x 5 In.....................	5625.00
Vase, Yantra, X & Diamond Design, White Glaze, E. Sottsass, 6 x 11 In.............................	438.00

POWDER FLASKS AND POWDER HORNS were made to hold the gunpowder used in antique firearms. The early examples were made of horn or wood; later ones were of copper or brass.

POWDER FLASK

Copper, Embossed, Brass Luster Finish, Eagle, Shield, Pistols, Motto Banner, 1860s, 4 ⅝ In.	231.00

POWDER HORN

Bone, Incised Flowers, Vines, Tulips, Initialed LPH, 5 ¼ In.	474.00
Bone, Incised Hunters, Heart, Animals, Suns, Birds, Flowers...	444.00
Bone, Iron Mounts, Silk Fringe, Etched Boar, Stag, Spain, 1500s, 22 In............................	4888.00
Carved Tip, Wood Stoppers, Brass Brads, Fred Benlehr, 1860s, 11 ½ In.	240.00
Carved, Cottage, Horse, Birds, Heart, Hex Sign, Flowers, Turned Wood Cap, Pa., 1800s, 11 In..	413.00
Carved, Ship, Birds, Tree, Pine Plug, Pewter Pull, 1800s, 11 In...	147.00
Carved, Snake Head Spout, Dog, Bear Head Strap Hook, Banner, 1877, 9 ½ In........................	470.00
Hell Horse, Engraved William Steel Peekskill August Y 1777, Houses, Dragon, Wood Spout, 13 In..	3450.00
Hunter, Dogs, Deer, Long Tailed Bird, Trees, Engraved, Baltis Crewell 1805, 12 In...........*Illus*	1880.00
Silver, Bone, Faux Horn, Etched, Beading, Flowers, 10 In.	90.00

PRATT ware means two different things. It was an early Staffordshire pottery, cream-colored with colored decorations, made by Felix Pratt during the late eighteenth century. There was also Pratt ware made with transfer designs during the mid-nineteenth century in Fenton, England. Reproductions of the transfer-printed Pratt are being made.

PRATT FENTON

Creamer, Cow With Milkmaid Shape, Green Stepped Base, c.1800, 5 x 6 ½ In.	690.00
Creamer, Cow, Milkmaid, Stool, Black, Manganese Enamel Splotches, c.1810, 5 ⅜ x 6 ¼ In...	403.00
Creamer, Fox Head Shape, Swan Handle, c.1840, 5 In.	531.00
Cup, Pope & Devil, Double Faced, Pearlware, Painted, Green, Ocher, Black, c.1800, 6 ¼ In......	826.00
Mug, Cylindrical, Leaves, Green, Blue, Brown, Orange, c.1800, 3 ¾ In............................	120.00
Pitcher, Blue Ground, Brown Overlay Hunt Scene, Marked, 1850s, 7 ¾ x 7 In.........................	45.00

Pottery-Midcentury, Vase, Bottle Shape, Flared Rim, Glazed, Earth Tones, Lucie Rie, London, 1970s, 12 x 5 In.
$3,750.00

Rago Arts & Auction Center

Pottery-Midcentury, Vase, Glazed, Vertical Lines, Stoneware, H. McIntosh, 1955-59, 19 x 7 In.
$4,375.00

Los Angeles Modern Auctions (LAMA)

Pottery-Midcentury, Vase, Herringbone Pattern, Signed, Voulkos, 1950s, 10 ½ In.
$2,125.00

Rago Arts & Auction Center

Pottery-Midcentury, Vase, Katap, Glazed, Plastic Insert, Signed, Claude Conover, c.1961, 14 ½ x 16 In.
$5,938.00

Los Angeles Modern Auctions (LAMA)

Powder Horn, Hunter, Dogs, Deer, Long Tailed Bird, Trees, Engraved, Baltis Crewell 1805, 12 In.
$1,880.00

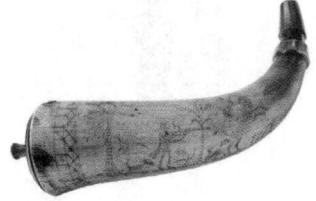

Garth's Auctioneers & Appraisers

Pressed Glass, Block & Fan, Carafe, 8 ½ In.
$95.00

Ruby Lane, Inc.

Pressed Glass, Heart Plume, Pitcher, 7 ⅛ In.
$165.00

Ruby Lane, Inc.

Pressed Glass, Honeycomb, Spooner, 4 ⅞ In.
$65.00

Ruby Lane, Inc.

Plaque, Relief Hunting Scene, England, c.1800, 6 x 12 ¾ In.	608.00
Stirrup Cup, Fox Mask, Molded Wavy Coat, Ocher Glaze, Blue Eyes, Long Lashes, c.1800, 6 In.	1534.00
Sugar Box, Lid, Pearlware, Molded Medallion, Painted Ocher, Blue, Green, c.1800, 5 In.	1121.00
Teapot, Lid, Figural, Woman, Seated, Brown Tub Chair, Blue, Orange Paint, c.1815, 8 ¼ In.	1298.00

PRESSED GLASS, or pattern glass, was first made in the United States in the 1820s after the invention of glass pressing machines. Hundreds of patterns of pressed glass were made in complete table settings. Although the Boston and Sandwich Works was the most famous of the pressed glass factories, there were about sixteen other factories making pressed glass from 1830 to 1850, and still more from 1850 to 1900, when pressed glass reached its greatest popularity. It is now being widely reproduced. The pattern names used in this listing are based on the information in the book *Pressed Glass in America* by John and Elizabeth Welker. There may be pieces of pressed glass listed in this book in other categories, such as Lamp, Ruby, Sandwich, and Souvenir.

Acorn, Shaker, Pink, Hobbs, 2 ½ In.	29.00
Ada, Shaker, Ruby, 3 In.	23.00
Alaska, Shaker, Green, White Enameled Flowers, 3 In., Pair	46.00
Beaded Shell, Butter, French Opalescent, 6 ½ In.	25.00
Bellflower Double Vine, Jug, Molasses, Opaque White, Applied Handle, c.1860, 6 x 4 ½ In.	1265.00
Block & Fan, Carafe, 8 ½ In. ....*Illus*	95.00
Blue Opaque, Bulging Petal, 2 In., Pair	29.00
Cable, Goblet, 6 In.	32.00

Candlewick as a pressed glass pattern is properly named Banded Raindrop. There is also a pattern called Candlewick, which has been made by Imperial Glass Corporation since 1936. It is listed in this book in the Imperial Glass category.

Cherry & Cable, Biscuit Jar, Amethyst, 3 ¾ In.	25.00
Cherry & Cable, Biscuit Jar, Green Opalescent, 2 Handles, 8 In.	48.00
Cherry & Cable, Bowl, Crystal, Hand Painted Ruby Cherries With Gold Leaves, 9 ½ In.	53.00
Cherry & Cable, Bowl, Green Opalescent, Hand Painted Cherries With Gold Leaves, 9 ½ In.	55.00
Cherry & Cable, Bowl, Vaseline Opalescent, Flared, 6 x 9 In.	50.00 to 53.00
Cherry & Cable, Butter, Crystal, Hand Painted Ruby Cherries, Gold Leaves, 6 In.	41.00
Cherry & Cable, Butter, Green Opalescent, 6 In.	24.00
Cherry & Cable, Butter, Red, 6 In.	39.00
Cherry & Cable, Pitcher, Green Opalescent, 60 Oz., 8 ¼ In.	48.00
Cherry & Cable, Spoon Holder, Crystal, 2 ¼ In.	11.00
Cherry & Cable, Water Set, Black Amethyst, 60 Oz. Pitcher, 8 Oz. Tumbler, 7 Piece	130.00
Cord & Tassel, Salt & Pepper, Pink Opaque, 2 In., Pair	29.00
Curtain, Jug, Molasses, Clear, 6 Vertical Panels, Hollow Handle, Hinged Tin Lid, c.1860, 7 In.	104.00
Daisy In Crisscross, Syrup, White Opalescent, 6 In.	59.00
Dolphin, Candlestick, Double Step, Starch Blue, 6-Petal Socket, Square Base, c.1850, 10 x 10 In., Pair	219.00
Dolphin, Candlestick, Hexagonal, Translucent Soft Blue, Urn Shape Socket, c.1860, 6 x 4 In.	690.00
Double Circles, Spooner, Canary Yellow, 6-Sided Bowl, 6-Petal Rim, Footed, c.1860, 6 x 3 In.	184.00
Elizabeth, Pitcher, Passion Pink, 72 Oz.	65.00
Elizabeth, Water Set, Passion Pink, 72 Oz. Pitcher, 4 Oz. Tumbler, 5 Piece	130.00
Eyewinker, Candy Dish, Blue Opalescent, 5 ¼ In.	30.00
Eyewinker, Jam Jar, Blue Opalescent, 5 In.	25.00
Eyewinker, Pitcher, Blue Opalescent, 8 In.	30.00
Eyewinker, Saltcellar, Green Opalescent, 1 ½ In.	6.00
Eyewinker, Spoon Holder, Green Opalescent, 5 ¾ In.	30.00
Eyewinker, Toothpick Holder, Blue Opalescent, 2 ¼ In.	8.00
Fern & Daisy, Lamp, Oil, Green Opalescent, 14 In.	75.00
Heart Plume, Pitcher, 7 ⅛ In. ....*Illus*	165.00
Hexagonal, Candlestick, Deep Violet, Urn Shape, Knop Stem, Hexagonal Stem, c.1860, 9 x 5 In.	345.00
Hexagonal, Candlestick, Translucent Blue, Over Clambroth, Flat Top, Tapered, c.1850, 8 x 4 In.	288.00
Holly, Sugar & Creamer	198.00
Honeycomb, Spooner, 4 ⅞ In. ....*Illus*	65.00
Honeycomb, Spooner, Opalescent, 5 Rows, Round Foot, c.1855, 5 ⅜ x 3 ¼ In.	259.00
Horn Of Plenty, Spooner, Clambroth, Polished Pontil, c.1860, 4 ½ x 3 ½ In.	633.00
Horseshoe, Cake Stand, 10 x 7 ¼ In. ....*Illus*	120.00
Inverted Fan & Feather, Water Set, Pink Slag, Pitcher, 4 Tumblers, Dugan, 8 In.	748.00
Inverted Thistle, Berry Bowl, Pink, Inverted, 2 x 5 In.	12.00
Inverted Thistle, Bowl, Red, 9 In.	40.00
Inverted Thistle, Breakfast Set, Cobalt Blue, 4 ½ In.	40.00
Inverted Thistle, Cake Plate, Red, 4 ½ x 8 ½ In.	40.00
Inverted Thistle, Compote, Clear, 7 ½ In.	35.00
Inverted Thistle, Egg Plate, Pink, 11 ½ In.	30.00
Inverted Thistle, Juice Set, Cobalt Blue, 72 Oz. Pitcher, 12 Oz. Tumblers, 7 Piece	100.00

Inverted Thistle, Pitcher, Red, 24 Oz.	40.00
Inverted Thistle, Salt & Pepper, Cobalt Blue, 3 ¼ In.	20.00
Inverted Thistle, Syrup, Cobalt Blue, 4 ½ In.	25.00
Inverted Thistle, Syrup, Red, 4 ½ In.	30.00
Jeweled Moon & Star pattern is listed here as Moon & Star.	
Late Thistle pattern is listed here as Inverted Thistle.	
Loop, Cake Stand, Colorless, 9 Loops & Rims, Hexagonal Stem, Round Foot, c.1860, 4 x 9 In.	161.00
Lyre, Salt, Opaque Violet Blue, 4 Scrolled Feet, c.1840, 1 ⅞ x 3 ⅛ In.	259.00
Moon & Star, Sugar & Creamer, Vaseline, 3 In.	50.00
New York Honeycomb, Bowl, Medium Green, Hemispherical, New England Glass, c.1865, 4 ⅝ In.	104.00
Oblong, Salt, Deep Cobalt Blue, Flat Top, Base, c.1860, 1 ½ x 2 ⅛ In.	748.00
Oblong, Salt, Shaped Flat Top, c.1860, 1 ½ x 2 ⅛ In.	219.00
O'Hara Loop, Bowl, Turquoise Blue, Wavy Rim, c.1865, 3 x 9 ¼ In.	431.00
Oval Pedestal, Salt, Cobalt Blue, France, c.1840, 2 x 2 In.	184.00
Paneled Grape, Punch Set, Vaseline Opalescent, Red Hooks, 11 In. Bowl, Ladle, 8 Cups	250.00
Paneled Swan With Fish, Creamer, Colorless, c.1885, 5 ⅞ In.	35.00
Pigeon Blood, Shaker, Gaudy, 3 In., Pair	23.00
Pineapple & Fan, Butter, Dome Lid, Saw-tooth Edge, 8 x 4 In. ....*Illus*	45.00
Pittsburgh, Salt, Steamboat Shape, Rope Ring, Stourbridge Flint Glass, c.1840, 1 ⅞ x 3 ⅝ In.	460.00
Queen, Compote, Cobalt Blue, 7 ¾ In.	45.00
Queen, Sugar & Creamer, Vaseline, 7 ½ In.	55.00
Question Mark, Candlestick, c.1891, 2 x 5 ½ In. ....*Illus*	45.00
Royal Oak, Condiment Set, Royal Oak, Creamer, Sugar, Waste, Northwood, 6 ½ In.	201.00
Sawtooth, Compote, Opaque White, Hexagonal Knop, High Stem, Round Foot, c.1860, 10 x 9 In.	230.00
Sawtooth, Compote, Vaseline, Hexagonal Stem, Round Foot, c.1870, 6 x 8 In.	81.00
Shaker, Green, Aster & Leaf, 3 In., Pair	40.00
Shaker, Stippled Acanthus, Blue, Gilt Highlights, 3 In.	23.00
Shell & Scroll, Inkstand, Receiver, 2 Holes, Opalescent, Blue, c.1870, 5 ⅜ x 8 ⅞ In.	184.00
Shell & Star, Salt, Deep Cobalt Blue, Diamond Point Base, c.1840, 2 x 3 ⅛ In.	1150.00
Stars & Fan, Ashtray, Double, Anchor Hocking, 1960s, 7 ¾ In. ....*Illus*	17.00
Strawberry Diamond, Salt, Medium Bottle Green, Scallop Rim, c.1835, 2 x 2 ⅛ In.	259.00
Strawholder, 2 Piece, 8-Sided, Clear, 12 x 4 In.	495.00
Vase, Yellow, 8 Ribs, 8-Petal Flared Rim, Square Base, Pillar Molded, c.1850, 11 ¾ x 5 In.	1265.00
Westward Ho, Compote, Lid, Clear & Frosted, Pedestal Base, 14 ¾ x 8 In.	84.00
Zipper, Vase, Passion Pink, 9 ½ In.	35.00

PRINT, in this listing, means any of many printed images produced on paper by one of the more common methods, such as lithography. The prints listed here are of interest primarily to the antiques collector, not the fine arts collector. Many of these prints were originally part of books. Other prints will be found in the Advertising, Currier & Ives, Movie, and Poster categories.

Allier, Paul, Exotic Dancers, Art Deco, Choir, Signed, Numbers, Mat, Frame, 22 ½ x 17 ½ In., Pair	288.00

Audubon bird prints were originally issued as part of books printed from 1826 to 1854. They were issued in two sheet sizes, 26 ½ inches by 39 ½ inches and 11 inches by 7 inches. The quadrupeds were issued in 28-by-22-inch prints. Later editions of the Audubon books were done in many sizes, and reprints of the books in the original sizes were also made. The words *After John James Audubon* appear on all of the prints, including the originals, because the pictures were made as copies of Audubon's original oil paintings. The bird pictures have been so popular they have been copied in myriad sizes using both old and new printing methods. This list includes originals and later copies because Audubon prints of all ages are sold in antiques shops.

J.W. Audubon

Audubon, American Crossbill, Aquatint, Havell, 30 x 24 In.	1434.00
Audubon, American Flamingo, G. Such & Zone, 39 ½ x 26 ³¹⁄₂ In.	2806.00
Audubon, American Red Fox, J.T. Bowen, Frame, 1846, 22 x 27 In.	944.00
Audubon, American Redstart, Birds Of America, Aquatint, Copper Plate Engraved, c.1838, 25 x 34 In.	660.00
Audubon, American Robin, Engraved, Aquatint, Havell, 37 x 25 In.	11950.00
Audubon, Barn Owl, Birds Of America, Chromolithograph, J. Bien, c.1860, 39 x 26 In.	649.00
Audubon, Black-Throated Diver, Engraved, Aquatint, Havell, 26 x 39 In.	7170.00
Audubon, Blue-Winged Teal, Birds Of North America, Royal Octavo Edition, 5 ⅝ x 8 ⅞ In.	107.00
Audubon, Bullock's Oriole, Mexican Goldfinch, Water Thrush, Aquatint, 39 ½ x 26 ½ In.	1722.00
Audubon, Canada Otter, Lithograph, Imperial Folio, J.T. Bowen, 1844, 22 x 28 In.	649.00
Audubon, Canvas Back, Duck, Birds Of America, J. Bien, New York, Frame, 1860, 37 ½ x 49 In.	2596.00
Audubon, Cat Bird, Birds Of America, Aquatint, Copper Plate Engraving, c.1838, 17 ½ x 22 ½ In.	1020.00
Audubon, Cayenne Tern, Birds Of America, Engraved, Havell, Frame, 1835, 17 x 22 In.	472.00
Audubon, Chipping Squirrel, Viviparous Quadrupeds, J.T. Bowen, Frame, c.1845, 30 x 24 In.	1180.00
Audubon, Columbia Magpie Or Jay, Colored Lithograph, J.T. Bowen, Frame, 9 x 5 ⅜ In.	150.00
Audubon, Evening Grosbeak, Plate 373, J. Whatman, 1837, 39 ½ x 26 ½ In.	2091.00
Audubon, Flamingo, Chromolithograph, 38 x 26 In.	19120.00

Pressed Glass, Horseshoe, Cake Stand, 10 x 7 ¼ In.
$120.00

Ruby Lane, Inc.

Pressed Glass, Pineapple & Fan, Butter, Dome Lid, Saw-tooth Edge, 8 x 4 In.
$45.00

Ruby Lane, Inc.

Pressed Glass, Question Mark, Candlestick, c.1891, 2 x 5 ½ In.
$45.00

Ruby Lane, Inc.

Pressed Glass, Stars & Fan, Ashtray, Double, Anchor Hocking, 1960s, 7 ¾ In.
$17.00

Ruby Lane, Inc.

The edited listings of the current prices in this *Kovels' Antiques & Collectibles Price Guide* aren't available on any website. Readers can visit **Kovels.com** to check thousands of past prices and sign up for free information on trends, tips, reproductions, marks, and more.

P

Print, Audubon, Le Petit Caporal, R. Havell, J. Whatman, Frame, 1833, 29 ¾ x 21 ½ In. $1,265.00

James D. Julia Auctioneers

Print, Audubon, Maryland Marmot, Woodchuck & Groundhog, Bowen, Frame, 1842, 32 ½ x 37 In. $1,265.00

James D. Julia Auctioneers

Print, Calder, Alexander, Lithograph On Paper, Signed, 20 ¼ x 28 ½ In. $1,080.00

Gray's Auctioneers LLC

> ### TIP
> *Don't frame a good print in a clip frame. There should be air space between the paper and the glass.*

Audubon, Florida Cormorant, Birds Of North America, Lithograph, Royal Octavo, 5 ⅝ x 8 ½ In.	58.00
Audubon, Flying, Osprey, Holding Fish, Chromolithograph, 1860, 39 ½ x 26 ½ In.	4780.00
Audubon, Le Petit Caporal, R. Havell, J. Whatman, Frame, 1833, 29 ¾ x 21 ½ In. ....*Illus*	1265.00
Audubon, Mallard Duck, Birds Of America, J. Bien, New York, Frame, 1860, 37 ½ x 49 ¼ In.	2596.00
Audubon, Maryland Marmot, Woodchuck & Groundhog, Bowen, Frame, 1842, 32 ½ x 37 In...*Illus*	1265.00
Audubon, Red Bellied Squirrel, Lithograph, J.T. Bowen, 28 x 22 In.	837.00
Audubon, White Headed Eagle, Havell, Aquatint, 37 x 24 In.	4780.00
Audubon, White Ibis, Havell, Engraved, c.1836, 25 x 38 In.	8962.00
Audubon, Yellow-Crowned Heron, Birds Of America, Chromolithograph, 1860, 37 x 24 In.	1800.00
Bachelder, Jonathan Badger, National Soldier's Home, Maine, Lithograph, 1872, 24 x 33 In.	460.00
Baillie, J., Washington, Romanesque Pose, Lithograph, Watercolor, Frame, 14 x 10 In.	83.00
Barralet, John James, Lithograph, First Philadelphia Water Works, Mat, France, 6 ¾ x 12 In.	35.00
Benson, W., Dusk, Etching, On Paper, Signed, c.1910, 9 ½ x 10 ½ In.	944.00
Benson, W., Moonlight, Etching, Drypoint, Signed, c.1910, 7 x 9 In.	2596.00
Berwald, L., Boy & Dog, Chromolithographic, Diptych, Raphael Tuck & Sons, 34 x 14 In.	12.00
Beyer, F.J., 20 Mule Team, Hauling Borax From Death Valley, Lithograph, Color, Cardstock, 15 x 41 In.	24.00
Braque, Georges, Deux Oiseaux, Lithograph, Mat, Frame, 9 x 3 ½ In.	1680.00
Calder, Alexander, Beastie, Lithograph, Signed, Frame, c.1968, 20 x 26 In.	240.00
Calder, Alexander, Lithograph On Paper, Signed, 20 ¼ x 28 ½ In. ....*Illus*	1080.00
Catesby, Mark, Brown Curley, White Arrow Arum, Monogram, Giltwood Frame, 14 x 10 In...*Illus*	3304.00
Civil War Veterans, Chromolithograph, Confederate In Gray, Union, Blue, Children, Frame, 21 x 17 In.	189.00
Currier & Ives prints are listed in the Currier & Ives category.	
Ernst, Max, Dechet D'Atelier, Lithograph, Color, Mat, Frame, 1968, 18 ½ x 15 ⅜ In.	840.00
Erte, Aries, Serigraph, Pencil Signed, 17 x 12 In.	176.00
Erte, Hindu Princess, Serigraph, Hotstamping, Embossing, Frame, 27 x 33 In.	540.00
Erte, Salon, Serigraph, Frame, 1989, 16 ¼ x 24 In.	420.00
Erte, Symphony In Black, Serigraph, Pencil Signed, Certificate, 17 x 17 In.	439.00
Gilbert, Albert Earl, American Bald Eagle, Photolithograph, Colored, Signed, Frame, 22 x 16 In.	12.00
Gould & Richter, Hummingbirds, Lithograph, Color, Frame, 20 x 14 In.	30.00
Gould & Richter, John, Eagle Owl, Rabbit, Lithograph, Mat, Frame, 13 ¼ x 22 In...........*Illus*	360.00
Hogarth, William, Credulity, Superstition & Fanaticism, Engraving, Frame, c.1762, 21 x 17 In.	235.00
Hull, William, Washington Receiving Salute, Trenton, Steel Engraving, c.1860, 27 x 35 In.	118.00

Icart prints were made by Louis Icart, who worked in Paris from 1907 as an employee of a postcard company. He then started printing magazines and fashion brochures. About 1910 he created a series of etchings of fashionably dressed women and he continued to make similar etchings until he died in 1950. He is well known as a printmaker, painter, and illustrator. Original etchings are much more expensive than the later photographic copies.

Icart, Cigarette Memories, Woman On Pillows, Smoking, Signed, Frame, 39 x 29 In.	1350.00
Icart, Erotic Scene, Woman Under Cushions, Signed, Frame, 18 x 20 In.	1000.00
Icart, French Lady, Dog On Lap, Frame, 31 x 23 In.	195.00
Icart, Lady Of The Camellias, Etching, Aquatint, Signed, Frame, 19 ¾ x 23 ¾ In.	375.00
Icart, Spanish Dance, Etching, Signed, 20 ⅜ x 13 ⅜ In...............................*Illus*	805.00
Icart, Sweet Mystery, Woman & Black Cat, Dry Point & Etching, Oval, Frame, 20 x 16 In.	1680.00
Inamn, Henry, William Penn, Mezzotint, Colored, Mat, Frame, c.1835, 21 x 16 In.	295.00

Jacoulet prints were designed by Paul Jacoulet (1902–1960), a Frenchman who spent most of his life in Japan. He was a master of Japanese woodblock print technique. Subjects included life in Japan, the South Seas, Korea, and China. His prints were sold by subscription and issued in series. Each series had a distinctive seal, such as a sparrow or butterfly. Most Jacoulet prints are approximately 15 x 10 inches.

Jacoulet, Daikoku, Japanese Woman, Mouse, Frame, c.1952, 15 ½ x 12 In.	540.00
Jacoulet, Ebisu, Japanese Man With Carp, Frame, c.1952, 15 ½ x 12 In.	780.00
Jacoulet, Old Man, White Flowing Beard & Hair, Black & White Robe, 18 ½ x 14 In.	531.00
Jacoulet, Tahitian Couple On A Beach, Frame, c.1941, 12 x 15 ¼ In.	1440.00

Japanese woodblock prints are listed as follows: Print, Japanese, name of artist, title or description, type, and size. Dealers use the following terms: Tate-e is a vertical composition. Yoko-e is a horizontal composition. The words Aiban (13 by 9 inches), Chuban (10 by 7 ½ inches), Hosoban (13 by 6 inches), Koban (7 by 4 inches), Nagaban (20 by 9 inches), Oban (15 by 10 inches), Shikishiban (8 by 9 inches), and Tanzaku (15 by 5 inches) denote approximate size. Modern versions of some of these prints have been made. Other woodblock prints that are not Japanese are listed under Print, Woodblock.

Japanese, F. Fujita, Winter Scene, Pencil Signed 1972, Woodblock, Frame, 12 x 16 In.	124.00
Japanese, Hasui, Kawase, Snowfall Over Lake With Pagoda, 14 x 9 ½ In.	2091.00

P

Print, Catesby, Mark, Brown Curley, White Arrow Arum, Laid Paper, Monogram, Frame, 14 x 10 In.
$3,304.00

Brunk Auctions

Print, Gould & Richter, John, Eagle Owl, Rabbit, Chicks, Lithograph, Mat, Frame, 13 ¼ x 22 In.
$360.00

Skinner, Inc.

Print, Icart, Spanish Dance, Etching, Signed, 20 ⅜ x 13 ⅜ In.
$805.00

Cottone Auctions

Print, Professor Low, Cattle, Breeds, Lithograph, London, Frame, 1840, 12 x 16 In., 4 Piece
$799.00

New Orleans Auction Galleries, Inc.

Print, Woodblock, Baumann, Gustave, From Hillside Gardens, Aluminum Leaf, 12 ½ x 12 ½ In.
$5,625.00

Rago Arts & Auction Center

Print, Woodblock, Esherick, Wharton, Riding, Rice Paper, Signed, 6 x 4 In.
$2,625.00

Rago Arts & Auction Center

Print, Woodblock, Nicholson, William, E For Executioner, Signed, Mat, Frame, 1898, 12 ¾ x 9 In.
$418.00

Neal Auction Co.

Print, Woodblock, Rice, William, Eucalyptus Greentree, Signed, Frame, 7 ¾ x 3 ½ In.
$1,875.00

Rago Arts & Auction Center

P

Print, Yardlong, Alfred Everitt Orr, Woman In Yellow Dress, Frame, 1914, 8 x 35 In.
$180.00

Victorian Casino Antiques

TIP

Fabrics decorated with metal threads should not be washed. Wipe with a cotton swab and ammonia.

Japanese, Hasui, Kawase, Yagumo Bridge, Nagata Shrine, Frame, 13 x 9 ½ In.	554.00
Japanese, Hasui, Shrine In Snowy Landscape, Signed, 9 ⅜ x 14 In.	806.00
Japanese, Hasui, Spring Evening At Kintaikyo Bridge, 14 ¼ x 9 ½ In.	210.00
Japanese, Hiroshige, Moonlit Harbor Scene, Azechi, 14 ¼ x 10 In.	48.00
Japanese, Hiroshige, Sanuki Province, Mt. Shoto View, Frame, 14 x 8 ½ In.	316.00
Japanese, Hiroshige, Suhou Province, Kintai Bridge, Mountains, Frame, 14 x 9 In.	316.00
Japanese, Hiroshige, Tokokawa Bridge, Yoshida, 8 ¾ x 13 ½ In.	360.00
Japanese, Hiroshige, Utagawa, Kilns By The Hashiba Ferry On Sumida River, Frame, 13 ½ x 8 ¾ In.	178.00
Japanese, Hiroshige, Utagawa, Port Scene, Frame, 13 x 9 In.	393.00
Japanese, Hiroshige, Woman, Child, Hand Colored, Woodblock, Frame, 10 x 14 In.	45.00
Japanese, Hoshi, Joshi, Red Tree, Signed, Numbered, Mat, Frame, 1973, 16 ¼ x 22 In.	2358.00
Japanese, Kawase, Cherry Blossoms & Moon At Matsuyama Castle, 14 x 9 In.	331.00
Japanese, Kawase, Moon At Magome, 1930, 14 ½ x 9 ½ In.	422.00
Japanese, Kunisada, 2 Actors Fighting, Frame, 19th Century, 13 ½ x 9 ¼ In.	325.00
Japanese, Kuniyoshi, Kabuki Actor, Sword, Frame, 12 ½ x 9 In.	60.00
Japanese, Kuniyoshi, Utagawa, Girl, Kimono Blowing In Breeze, c.1845, 13 In.	400.00
Japanese, Nakayama, Abstract Butterfly & Horse, Signed, 1964, 35 x 23 ½ In.	992.00
Japanese, Saito, Chickens, 17 ½ x 12 ¾ In.	600.00
Japanese, Saito, Kiyoshi, Black & White Cats, Woodblock, Frame, c.1975, 10 ½ x 16 In.	678.00
Japanese, Saito, Kiyoshi, Kyoto Village Scene, Apple Tree, Children, 23 x 17 In.	273.00
Japanese, Shima, Tamami, Bell Tower, Color, Signed, Frame, 1960, 23 ¾ x 17 In.	144.00
Japanese, Shiro, Owl On Branch With Moon, 16 x 10 ¾ In.	240.00
Japanese, Shoes On, Women With Umbrellas, 14 x 9 ½ In.	1476.00
Japanese, Shoson, 2 Ducks, Frame, 15 x 10 ¼ In.	212.00
Japanese, Shunga, 5 Amorous Adventures, Watercolor On Rice Paper, Frame, 6 x 13 ¼ In.	173.00
Japanese, Toyokuni III, Diptych, Seven Gods Of Good Fortune, 1800s, 14 x 20 In.	150.00
Japanese, Toyokuni, Triptych, 3 Kabuki Actors, Blossoming Trees, Frame, 1800s, 14 x 28 In.	150.00
Japanese, Utamaro, 4 Geisha, 14 ¾ x 10 ¼ In.	388.00
Japanese, Winter Scene, Woman, Umbrella, Woodblock, Frame, 8 x 11 In.	28.00
Japanese, Yoshida, Toshi, 2 Owls, Tree Branch, Pencil Signed, Woodblock, Frame, 21 x 13 In.	170.00
Kellogg & Comstock, Lithograph, Colored, Shakers, Mode Of Worship Dance, Frame, 9 ¾ x 13 ¾ In.	189.00
Knigin, Michael, Sambaso, Lithograph, Pencil Signed, 25 x 19 In.	59.90
Kurz & Allison, General George Crook, Lithograph, Black & White, 28 x 22 In.	47.00
Mottram, C., Boston, Panoramic, City, Boats, People, Lithograph, Color, 1857, 35 x 48 In.	690.00

Nutting prints are popular with collectors. Wallace Nutting is known for his pictures, furniture, and books. Collectors call his pictures Nutting prints although they are actually hand-colored photographs issued from 1900 to 1941. There are over 10,000 different titles. Wallace Nutting furniture is listed in the Furniture category.

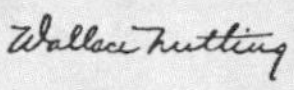

Wallace Nutting

Nutting, Affectionately Yours, Girl Writing Near Fire, Signed, Frame, c.1920, 20 x 16 In.	250.00
Nutting, An April Freshet, Trees, Blossoms, Flooded River, Signed, Frame, c.1920, 16 x 10 In.	135.00
Nutting, Birch-Lined Country Road, Signed, Frame, c.1920, 10 x 12 In.	125.00
Nutting, Chair For John, Girl At Table, Fireside, Signed, Frame, c.1920, 20 x 16 In.	225.00
Nutting, Cold Day, Girl, Coring Apples, Fireplace, Signed, Frame, c.1920, 14 x 12 In.	150.00
Nutting, Country Road, Oak Tree, Wayside Inn, Signed, Frame, c.1920, 22 x 18 In.	275.00
Nutting, Farewell, Women On Porch, Signed, Frame, 11 x 14 In.	175.00
Nutting, Farm Path, Stone Wall, Apple Blossoms, Signed, Frame, 12 x 10 In.	135.00
Nutting, Flowering Time, Flowering Trees, Frame, 21 x 41 In.	30.00
Nutting, Girl, Coring Apples, Fire, Signed, Frame, 7 x 5 In.	65.00
Nutting, Girl, Drinking Tea By Fire, Signed, Frame, c.1920, 14 x 11 In.	165.00
Nutting, Girl, Embroidering By Fire, Signed, Frame, c.1920, 14 x 11 In.	175.00
Nutting, Girl, Inspecting Lines, Highboy, Signed, Frame, 15 x 13 In.	165.00
Nutting, Girl, Playing Harp, Fire, Signed, Frame, c.1920, 16 x 12 In.	165.00
Nutting, Honeymoon Shore, Signed, Frame, c.1930, 5 x 4 In.	50.00
Nutting, Little River With Mt. Washington, Signed, Frame, c.1920, 17 x 11 In.	145.00
Nutting, Little River, Country Road, Stream, Signed, Frame, c.1930, 5 x 4 In.	45.00
Nutting, Meeting Branches, Pink Apple Blossoms, Blue Stream, Signed, Frame, c.1920, 12 x 10 In.	125.00
Nutting, Morning Duties, Signed, Frame, c.1920, 14 x 11 In.	150.00
Nutting, Quilting Party, 3 Girls In Bedroom, Quilting, Signed, Frame, c.1920, 20 x 16 In.	250.00
Nutting, Quilting Party, Signed, Frame, 10 x 12 In.	50.00
Nutting, Rain Of Gold, Signed, Frame, c.1920, 16 x 12 In.	135.00
Nutting, Silhouette, Children Caroling, Snow On Steps, Frame, c.1927, 5 x 6 In.	35.00
Nutting, Silhouette, Girl, Flowers In Urn, c.1927, 4 x 4 In.	28.00
Nutting, Silhouette, Girl, In Front Of Vanity, Holding Necklace, Frame, c.1927, 4 x 4 In.	28.00
Nutting, Spanish Mission, Ivy Draped Columns, Signed, Frame, c.1920, 17 x 14 In.	235.00
Nutting, Sunshine & Music, Signed, Frame, c.1920, 12 x 8 In.	75.00
Nutting, Thatch Roof House, Flower Garden, Signed, Frame, 16 x 13 In.	250.00

P

Nutting, Tree Lined Lake, Mountain, Frame, c.1930, 20 x 16 In.	150.00
Palmer, F., View Of New York From Brooklyn Heights, Lithograph, Hand Colored, Currier, 1849, Folio	1180.00

Parrish prints are wanted by collectors. Maxfield Frederick Parrish was an illustrator who lived from 1870 to 1966. He is best known as a designer of magazine covers, posters, calendars, and advertisements. His prints have been copied in recent years.

Maxfield Parrish

Parrish, Air Castles, 1910, Frame, 13 x 17 In.	395.00
Parrish, Calendar Of Sunshine, 1916, 8 x 6 In.	300.00
Parrish, Circes Palace, Woman, Pot, 1908, 9 ¼ x 11 In.	275.00
Parrish, Garden Of Allah, Frame, 1918, 21 x 13 In.	225.00
Parrish, Girl In Canyon, Frame, 10 x 6 In.	105.00
Parrish, King Presented With Tarts, 1925, 10 x 12 In.	95.00
Parrish, Pied Piper, Lithograph, Frame, 6 ½ x 20 ½ In.	243.00
Parrish, Stars, Girl On Rock, Frame, c.1927, 12 x 20 In.	250.00
Parrish, The Characters, 1925, 10 x 12 In.	55.00
Professor Low, Cattle, Breeds, Lithograph, London, Frame, 1840, 12 x 16 In., 4 Piece ....*Illus*	799.00
Schreckengost, Viktor, Ying's First Litter, Color Serigraph, Signed, Numbered, Frame, 12 x 16 In.	207.00
Scott, E.T., Red Lion Camp Meeting, Colored Lithograph, 1853, Frame, 12 x 16 In.	325.00
Tudor, Tasha, 2 Children, Dog, Birds, Barn Door, Watercolor, Frame, c.1970, 6 ½ x 8 In.	2607.00
Van Geel, Pierre Coneille, Lithograph, Hibiscus Palustris, Aster Novae Aniliae, c.1828, 21 x 17 In.	109.00
Vargas, Alberto, Opening Night, Woman, Seminude, Continuous Tone, 1996, 22 x 15 ½ In.	300.00
Warhol, Andy, Castelli Galleries Invitation, Silkscreen, Color, Signed, Frame, 1981, 11 ¾ x 11 ¾ In.	7475.00
Wessel, John, Portrait, Bay Colt, Eagle, Brother To Spread Eagle, Colored, 1805, 24 x 28 In.	177.00

Woodblock prints that are not in the Japanese tradition are listed here. Most were made in England and the United States during the Arts and Crafts period. Japanese woodblock prints are listed under Print, Japanese.

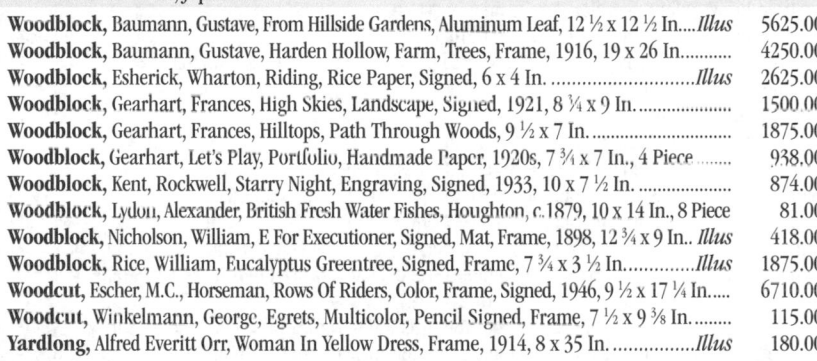

Woodblock, Baumann, Gustave, From Hillside Gardens, Aluminum Leaf, 12 ½ x 12 ½ In....*Illus*	5625.00
Woodblock, Baumann, Gustave, Harden Hollow, Farm, Trees, Frame, 1916, 19 x 26 In.	4250.00
Woodblock, Esherick, Wharton, Riding, Rice Paper, Signed, 6 x 4 In. ....*Illus*	2625.00
Woodblock, Gearhart, Frances, High Skies, Landscape, Signed, 1921, 8 ¼ x 9 In.	1500.00
Woodblock, Gearhart, Frances, Hilltops, Path Through Woods, 9 ½ x 7 In.	1875.00
Woodblock, Gearhart, Let's Play, Portfolio, Handmade Paper, 1920s, 7 ¾ x 7 In., 4 Piece	938.00
Woodblock, Kent, Rockwell, Starry Night, Engraving, Signed, 1933, 10 x 7 ½ In.	874.00
Woodblock, Lydon, Alexander, British Fresh Water Fishes, Houghton, c.1879, 10 x 14 In., 8 Piece	81.00
Woodblock, Nicholson, William, E For Executioner, Signed, Mat, Frame, 1898, 12 ¾ x 9 In.. *Illus*	418.00
Woodblock, Rice, William, Eucalyptus Greentree, Signed, Frame, 7 ¾ x 3 ½ In..............*Illus*	1875.00
Woodcut, Escher, M.C., Horseman, Rows Of Riders, Color, Frame, Signed, 1946, 9 ½ x 17 ¼ In.....	6710.00
Woodcut, Winkelmann, George, Egrets, Multicolor, Pencil Signed, Frame, 7 ½ x 9 ⅜ In.	115.00
Yardlong, Alfred Everitt Orr, Woman In Yellow Dress, Frame, 1914, 8 x 35 In. ....*Illus*	180.00

PURINTON POTTERY COMPANY was incorporated in Wellsville, Ohio, in 1936. The company moved to Shippenville, Pennsylvania, in 1941 and made a variety of hand painted ceramic wares. By the 1950s Purinton was making dinnerware, souvenirs, cookie jars, and florist wares. The pottery closed in 1959.

Purinton Pottery

Apple, Chop Plate, 11 In.	34.00
Apple, Cup & Saucer	12.00
Apple, Dish, Pickle, 6 ⅛ In.	120.00
Fruit, Creamer, 14 Oz., 4 ½ In.	21.00
Fruit, Salt & Pepper, 3 In.	30.00
Intaglio, Butter, Brown	16.00
Intaglio, Jam Dish, Brown	16.00
Intaglio, Relish, Brown, 3 Section, 9 ⅜ In.	18.00
Ivy, Jug, Dutch, Red Blossom, 5 In.	34.00
Normandy Plaid, Bowl, Cereal, 5 ½ In.	8.00
Normandy Plaid, Relish, 3 Sections	33.00
Shooting Star, Vase, Bulbous, Handles, 5 In.	20.00

PURSES have been recognizable since the eighteenth century, when leather and needlework purses were preferred. Beaded purses became popular in the nineteenth century, went out of style, but are again in use. Mesh purses date from the 1880s and are still being made. How to carry a handkerchief and lipstick is a problem today for every woman, including the Queen of England.

Alligator, Brown, Lucite Top Frame, Brass, Coin Purse, Mirror, 11 x 7 In. ....*Illus*	148.00
Alligator, Clutch, Flap Closure, Gold, Rhinestone & Enamel Tiger, Coin Purse, Judith Leiber, 5 x 9 In.	1968.00
Alligator, Clutch, Plum, Amethyst, Rose Quartz Cube Closure, Judith Leiber, c.1993, 6 x 9 In.	2706.00

Quilters Get Sunday Off
Tradition says you never quilt on Sunday.

Purse, Alligator, Brown, Lucite Top Frame, Brass, Coin Purse, Mirror, 11 x 7 In.
$148.00

Ivey-Selkirk Auctioneers

Purse, Basket, Nantucket, Hinged Lid, Scrimshaw Panel, Swing Handle, 12 x 9 ½ In.
$600.00

DuMouchelles Art Gallery

Purse, Beaded, Peacocks, Silver Plate Frame, Beaded Fringe, Chain Handle, 7 In.
$60.00

P

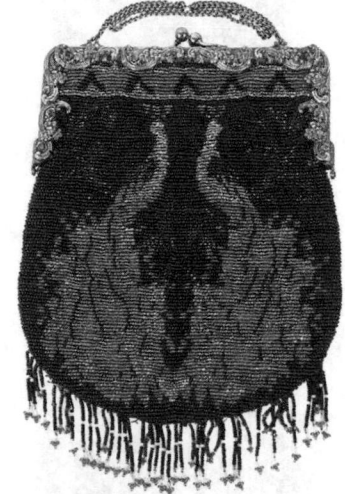

DuMochelle Art Gallery

TIP
Don't store a leather purse or jacket in a damp space. Leather could become moldy. Keep in a spot with fresh dry air. If you store the purse in a plastic bag, be sure to put holes in the bag for air circulation.

Purse, Beaded, White, Pink Flowers, Chain Handle, Label, Handmade, Made In France
$23.00

Copake

Purse, Mesh, 14K Gold, Sapphire Clasps, 4 ½ x 5 In.
$5,290.00

Cottone Auctions

Purse, Minaudiere, Mouse, Multicolored Crystals, Judith Leiber, 5 ½ In.
$1,560.00

DuMouchelles Art Gallery

Basket, Nantucket, Hinged Lid, Scrimshaw Panel, Swing Handle, 12 x 9 ½ In.............*Illus*	600.00
Beaded, Crystal, Pearl, Frances Hirsch, Label, Belgium..............................	180.00
Beaded, Flower Basket, Pink, Cranberry, Foldover, c.1840, 4 ½ x 4 In............	326.00
Beaded, Flowers, Fringe, Sapphire, Cabochon Clasp, 14K Frame, Tiffany & Co., 5 x 6 In.........	948.00
Beaded, Peacocks, Silver Plate Frame, Beaded Fringe, Chain Handle, 7 In. ....*Illus*	60.00
Beaded, White, Pink Flowers, Chain Handle, Label, Handmade, Made In France ....*Illus*	23.00
Box, Bird Design, Faux Pearl Flowers, White Plastic Handle, Enid Collins, 1960s, 11 x 6 In.	85.00
Canvas, Cowhide Trim, 2 Zippers, Padlock, Leather Handles, Monogram, Louis Vuitton, 9 x 12 ½ In.	676.00
Canvas, Monogram, Shoulder Strap, Draw String Close, Louis Vuitton, 10 ½ x 14 In..............	660.00
Cherry Blossom, Burgundy, Flowers, Faux Jewels, Top Handle, Takashi Murakami, 12 x 8 In.	1250.00
Cherry Blossom, Gilt Brass Corners, Takashi Murakami, Louis Vuitton, 6 x 9 In.....................	813.00
Cloth, Clutch, Tan, Brown, Logo, Red & Green Twill Tape, Strap Handle, Brass Stirrup, Gucci, 9 x 5 In.	201.00
Deerskin, Hobo, Tan, Rope Handle, Silver Rings, Interior Logo Fabric, Embossed, Prada, 15 x 15 In.	861.00
Faille, Black, 14K Gold Basketweave Frame, Green Tourmaline, Chain, Cartier, 1955, 7 In......	3555.00
Figural, Bird, Long Bill, Bulbous, Silver, Wrist Chain, Stamped................................	345.00
Lambskin, Camera Bag, Beige, Quilted, Interlocking Cs, Flap Pocket, Gold Chain, Chanel, 7 x 9 In. ..	1599.00
Lambskin, Foldover, Brown, Quilted, Interlocking Cs, Laced Chain Strap, Chanel, 6 ½ x 9 In.	1845.00
Lambskin, Gold Quilted, Slip Pocket, Removable Gilt Chain, Stamped, Chanel, Box, 4 ¼ x 6 ½ In.	1168.00
Leather, Alma, Epi, Yellow, 2 Zippers, Padlock & Keys, Purple Interior, Louis Vuitton, 9 x 12 In.	1353.00
Leather, Belt, Buckle, Silvertone Metal Flap Closure, Impressed Ferragamo, 17 x 9 ½ In.........	529.00
Leather, Birkin, Black, Goldtone Hardware, Dust Cover, Hermes, 13 ¾ In.	9600.00
Leather, Birkin, Blue Jean, Palladium Hardware, Hermes, Paris, Box, Rain Cover, 14 x 7 In. ..	14400.00
Leather, Black Quilted, Goldtone Quilted Chain Shoulder Strap, Chanel, 5 x 7 ¼ In............	920.00
Leather, Black, Adjustable Strap, Brass Closure, Louis Vuitton, 10 ¼ x 10 In.	978.00
Leather, Black, Clutch, Triangular, Foldover Flap, Louis Vuitton, 14 ½ x 8 ½ In..........	460.00
Leather, Brown, Hobo, Fendi, 17 x 23 In...	179.00
Leather, Brown, Mailbag, Shoulder Straps, Stamped, Louis Vuitton, France, 17 In..............	1652.00
Leather, Brown, White, Salvatore Ferragamo, 11 x 16 In............................	208.00
Leather, Brown, Wood Handles, Gucci, 7 x 17 In....................................	149.00
Leather, Epi, Flap Front, Logo, Purple Suede Lining, Shoulder Strap, Stamped, Vuitton, 7 x 8 In.	518.00
Leather, Garden Party, Black, Negona, Pebbled, Beige Chevron Canvas Lining, Hermes, 14 x 10 In.	2990.00
Leather, Green, Shoulder, Christian Dior	238.00
Leather, Kelly, Black, Brass Lock, Keys, Stamped, Hermes Paris, c.1950, 9 x 11 In.	3540.00
Leather, Kelly, Black, Removable Jewelry Case, Hermes, c.1968, 13 x 13 In..............	3540.00
Leather, Kelly, Burgundy, Red, Tan, Hermes, Paris, 9 ½ x 13 In......................	3332.00
Leather, Kelly, Navy, Brass Lock, Keys, Stamped, Hermes Paris, c.1950, 9 x 11 In................	3540.00
Leather, Pebbled, Shoulder, Bone, Belt Strap, Zipper, Dust Cover, Dooney & Bourke, 9 ½ x 6 In.	178.00
Leather, Quilted, Bronze Metallic, Oval, Double C Logo, Chain, Tassel, Chanel, 5 ½ x 7 ¼ In..	575.00
Leather, Red, Gilt Metal Mounts, Label, Hermes, Paris, 1930s, 9 ½ In...............	885.00
Leather, Reptile Skin, Hobo, Shoulder, Metal Grommets, Studs, Lobster Clasp, Prada, 11 x 13 In.	311.00
Leather, Sac Plat GM Tote, Epi, Logo, 2 Handles, Cotton Interior, Louis Vuitton, 12 x 11 In.....	679.00
Leather, Shoulder, Strap Handle, Silver Metal Rings, Antler Mount, Yves St. Laurent, 12 x 14 In.	414.00
Leather, Stylized Flowers, Snap Closure, Lace Handle, c.1915, 11 x 6 In......................	150.00
Lizard, Constance, Black, Goldtone H Clasp, Shoulder Strap, Dust Cover, Hermes, 7 In..........	3120.00
Lizard, Satin, Pearlized, Scalloped, Cabochon Cluster, Giuseppe Zanotti, Italy, 9 x 9 In......	492.00
Lucite, Hand Shaped Clasp, Goldtone Trim, Chain, Leiber, 5 x 6 In....................	208.00
Mesh, 14K Gold, Sapphire Clasps, 4 ½ x 5 In..................................*Illus*	5290.00
Mesh, Flower Design, Chain, Art Deco, c.1930, 7 x 5 In............................	50.00
Mesh, Gold Leafy Frame, Sapphire Thumbpiece, Link Chain, Tiffany & Co., 5 In..........	4248.00
Mesh, Gold, Zipper, Whiting & Davis, 7 ½ x 5 ½ In.................................	45.00
Mesh, Goldtone, Chain, Signed, Whiting & Davis, c.1925, 6 x 5 In.....................	50.00
Mesh, Silver, 14K Gold, Cabochon Clasp, Whiting & Davis, 1921, 6 x 5 In.............	446.00
Mesh, Silver, Attached Coin Purse, Tassel, Germany, 9 x 4 ½ In......................	362.00
Mesh, Silver, Openwork Frame, Monogram, c.1900, 6 x 6 ½ In.	354.00
Mesh, Silver, Rectangular, Diamond, Sapphire Frame, c.1920, 14 ½ In................	313.00
Mesh, Silver, Sapphire, Serrated Base, Chain, Whiting & Davis, c.1910, 6 x 4 In.	150.00
Micro Beaded, Gold, Tan, Blue, Red Orange, Mirror, Pin Purse, Marked, Sterling, 1920s, 6 ¾ x 8 In..	395.00
Microfiber, Pebbled Leather, Black, Shoulder, Silver Ornaments, Side Pockets, Prada, 8 x 13 In. ..	656.00
Minaudiere, Brass, Etched Elephants, Stags, Coral & Lapis Thumbpiece, Cartier, 15 In.	563.00
Minaudiere, Butterflies, Silver Washed Gold Openwork, Rubies, Boucheron, c.1945, 12 In.....	1541.00
Minaudiere, Mouse, Multicolored Crystals, Judith Leiber, 5 ½ In. ....*Illus*	1560.00
Minaudiere, Silver, Diapered, Gold & Diamond Monogram Clasp, P. Flato, 6 In......	3794.00
Needlework, Flame Stitch, Initialed AM, 1775, Pennsylvania, 4 x 6 ¾ In................	770.00
Needlework, Flamestitch Cover, Silk, Folded, 1700s, 4 x 5 ½ In......................	362.00
Needlework, Flowers, Geometric, Tan, Green, Rose, Inscribed Huldah H Line, 1829, 7 x 5 In..	805.00
Nylon, Black, Prada, Italy, 10 x 12 In..	100.00
Ostrich, White, Shoulder Bag, Gathered, Ivory, Cut Stone, Gusseted, Judith Leiber, 1979, 5 ¾ x 6 ¼ In.	676.00

P

Patent Leather, Quilted, Black, Shoulder Strap, Chanel, 9 x 10 ½ In.	688.00
Pocket, Pieced, Appliqued, Chintz, Stars, Squares, Silk Roses, Linen Straps, c.1800, 10 x 13 In.	3105.00
Silk Satin, Leather Edge, Baguette, Gathered, Silvertone Chain, Emilio Pucci, Dust Bag, 5 x 9 In.	338.00
Snakeskin, Black, Curved Frame, Gem Bows, Judith Leiber, 8 ½ x 6 ¾ In.	325.00
Snakeskin, Black, Pleated, Silvered Frame, Semiprecious Stones, Judith Leiber 7 ½ x 11 ½ In.	345.00
Snakeskin, Cream, Goldtone Frame, Semiprecious Stones, Chain, Judith Leiber 9 x 9 ½ In.	115.00
Snakeskin, Cream, Multi-Gem Closure, Judith Leiber, 10 x 7 In.	325.00
Snakeskin, Lizard, Disco Pouch, Drawstring, Rhinestone Tab, Strap, Judith Leiber, Box, 5 x 9 In.	307.00
Steel, Gold Cut, Hairband Shaped Frame, Painted Photos, 1920s, 9 x 6 In.	1200.00
Suede, Black Tutti Frutti Clasp, Rubies, Emeralds, 18K Gold, Envelope, Art Deco, 5 x 8 In.	13035.00
Suede, Braided Leather Handle, Closure, Burberry, 6 x 13 In.	149.00
Suede, Leather, Black, Satchel, Double Handle, Silvertone Studs, Ferragamo, 14 x 5 ½ x 7 In.	299.00
Suede, Leather, Silvertone Fittings, Cloth Interior, Pocket, Black, Cole Haan, 13 x 9 In.	63.00
Suede, Quilted, Kidskin Lining, Drawstring, Zippered Side Pocket, Chanel, 9 x 10 In.	675.00
Vermeil, Clutch, Oval, Ribbed, Sodalite Tablet, Mirror Inside, Bulgari, 6 ½ x 3 ½ In.	1845.00
Vinyl, Black, Grained, Double Swing Handle, Verdi, 1950s, 5 x 10 In.	50.00
Vinyl, Screen Print, Tote, Campbell's Soup Can, Zipper, Straps, Cylindrical, 1960s, 9 x 15 In.	183.00
Wool, Hot Pink, Multicolor Flecks, Quilted, Leather Trim, Shoulder, Impressed CD, Dior, 8 x 9 ½ In.	489.00

QUEZAL glass was made from 1901 to 1924 at the Queens, New York, company started by Martin Bach, Sr. Other glassware by other firms, such as Loetz, Steuben, and Tiffany, resembles this gold-colored iridescent glass. Martin Bach died in 1921. His son-in-law, Conrad Vahlsing Jr., went to work at the Lustre Art Company about 1920. Bach's son, Martin Bach Jr., worked at the Durand Art Glass division of the Vineland Flint Glass Works after 1924.

Quezal

Bowl, Gold Iridescent, Melon Ribs, Squat, Flared Rim, Signed, 2 x 6 ¼ In.	201.00
Bowl, Gold Iridescent, Ribbed, Flared Rim, Signed, 10 In. Diam.	230.00
Candlestick, Cobalt, Amber, Tapered Column, Wide Flat Rim, c.1922, 9 ¾ In., Pair.	531.00
Chandelier, Inverted Dome, Gold Iridescent, Metal Tassel, 3 Chain Support, 17 ½ x 32 In.	2300.00
Compote, Opal Glass, Green & Gold Iridescent Leaves, Round Pedestal Foot, Signed, 13 ¾ In.	1150.00
Lamp, Gilt Metal, 4 Scrolling Foot Base, Signed, c.1900, 19 x 16 In.	360.00
Lampshade, Iridescent, Green Swirls, Gold Pulled Feather & Coil, Signed, 9 ¾ x 2 ¼ In...*Illus*	1610.00
Lampshade, Lily, Bell Shape, Gold Pulled Feather, Signed, 5 ¼ In. ...*Illus*	402.00
Lampshade, Opal Glass, Green Pulled Feathers, Gold Tips, Cone Shape, Ruffled Rim, Signed, 5 ½ In.	115.00
Sherbet, White, Green & Gold Chain & Pulled Feather, Spread Foot, 4 x 3 In., 6 Piece	3220.00
Vase, Blue Iridescent, Swollen Shoulder, Pinched Neck, Spread Foot, Flared Lip, 10 ¼ In.	374.00
Vase, Blue King Tut, Marigold Iridescent, Double Gourd, Footed, 7 ½ In.	748.00
Vase, Bud, Blue Iridescent, Stick, Teardrop Shape Bottom, Figural Bronze Base, 12 ¾ In.	863.00
Vase, Flower Shape, Opal, Green, Gold Pulled Feathers, Trifold Gold Rim, Footed, Signed, 6 In.	920.00
Vase, Gold Iridescent Foot, Ruffled Rim Compote, Signed, 8 ½ In.	104.00
Vase, Gold Iridescent, Silver Overlay Flowers & Leaves, 5 In.	492.00
Vase, Gold, Green, Pulled Feather, Corset, 5 Pointed Star Rim, Threaded, Reeded Teardrops, 6 In.	4600.00
Vase, Gold, White Feathers, Purple Iridescent, Wavy Mouth, Tapered, Signed, c.1900, 6 ½ In.	945.00
Vase, Green & Gold Iridescent, Pulled Feathers, Squat Base, Elongated Neck, 8 ¼ In.	3525.00
Vase, Green Pulled Feather, Iridescent, Flared Rim, Marked, 6 In. ...*Illus*	4500.00
Vase, Green, Gold Pulled Feather, Onionskin, Rounded Foot, Flower Shape, Ruffle Rim, Signed, 6 In.	2760.00
Vase, Green, Pulled Feather, Gold Iridescent Leaves, Swollen Neck, Waisted, Spread Foot, 4 ½ In.	1495.00
Vase, Green, Pulled Feather, Platinum, Ivory, Gold, Trumpet Shape, Stretched Ruffle Rim, 6 ½ In.	1035.00
Vase, Jack-In-The-Pulpit, Green, Pulled Feather, Gold & Platinum, 9 In.	2588.00
Vase, Jack-In-The-Pulpit, Round Swollen Foot, Green, Pink & Blue Pulled Feather, c.1915, 13 In.	5600.00
Vase, Lily, Flower Shape, Opal, Gold Iridescent, Green Pulled Feathers, Trifold Rim, 6 In.	2128.00
Vase, Purple & Blue Iridescent, Silver Overlay, Squat, Bulbous, Bottle Neck, Flared Lip, 8 In.	1725.00
Vase, Trumpet, Pulled Feather Design, 7 In.	881.00

QUILTS have been made since the seventeenth century. Early textiles were very precious and every scrap was saved to be reused. A quilt is a combination of fabrics joined to a filler and a backing by small stitched designs known as quilting. An appliqued quilt has pieces stitched to the top of a large piece of background fabric. A patchwork, or pieced, quilt is made of many small pieces stitched together. Embroidery can be added to either type.

Amish, Bars, Chrome Yellow, Red, Royal Blue, Indiana, c.1920, 77 x 79 In.	267.00
Amish, Bars, Red, Beige, Gray, Green Basket Border, c.1910, 77 x 77 In.	593.00
Amish, Diamonds, Stars & Feathers, Navy, Red & Pink, Brown Border, Cotton, 1925, 75 x 89 In.	1280.00
Amish, Patchwork, Diamond Blocked, Purple, Pink, Lancaster Co., c.1920, 43 x 43 In.	4029.00
Amish, Patchwork, Double Nine Patch, Diamond Shape, Blue, Tan, Purple, Pa., c.1920, 86 x 70 ½ In.	1541.00
Amish, Patchwork, Irish Chain Variation, Navy Blue, Violet, Green Backing, Initials, 1940, 62 x 74 In.	1567.00
Amish, Patchwork, Log Cabin, Maroon, Black, Alternating Stripe Border, c.1900, 73 x 69 In.	356.00

Quezal, Lamp Shade, Iridescent, Green Swirls, Gold Pulled Feather & Coil, Signed, 9 ¾ x 2 ¼ In.
$1,610.00

Early Auction Co.

Quezal, Lamp Shade, Lily, Bell Shape, Gold Pulled Feather, Signed, 5 ¼ In.
$402.00

Early Auction Co

Quezal, Vase, Green Pulled Feather, Iridescent, Flared Rim, Marked, 6 In.
$4,500.00

Skinner, Inc.

Quilt, Patchwork, Crazy, Double Sided, 13-Patch Blocks, Mixed Shapes & Fabrics, Calico, 70 x 70 In.
$165.00

Conestoga Auction Co., Inc.

Quilt, Patchwork, Lone Star, Cotton, Printed Back, c.1890, 83 ½ x 83 ½ In. $764.00

Garth's Auctioneers & Appraisers

Quilt, Patchwork, Stars, 8-Point, Grid, Orange Peel, Circles, Flowers On Reverse, 1875-90, 94 x 96 In. $470.00

Garth's Auctioneers & Appraisers

Quimper, Inkstand, Flowers, Man, 2 Inserts, Lids, Marked, Henriot Quimper France, c.1900, 7 x 4 In. $633.00

Glass Works Auctions

Quimper, Platter, Oval, Man & Woman, Leafy Border, Marked, HB, c.1885, 11 ½ x 14 ½ In. $206.00

Garth's Auctioneers & Appraisers

482

Amish, Patchwork, Maroon, Blue, White, Early 20th Century, 80 x 67 In.	243.00
Amish, Patchwork, Rainbow Bar, Yellow, Blue, Brown, Red, Purple, Teal, 1900s, 80 x 72 In.	243.00
Amish, Pierced Bar, Red, Blue, Orange, Pa., c.1930, 77 x 76 In.	1422.00
Amish, Purple, Black Border, Wool Center, Iowa, Crib, 43 x 38 In.	444.00
Amish, Sunshine & Shadow, 4 Corner Blocks, Feather Stitching, 60 x 60 In.	177.00
Appliqued, 17 Circles, Trailing Vine Border, White, Signed Nancy Hoover, 1843, Pa., 82 x 92 In.	2370.00
Appliqued, Abstract, Green, Maroon, Border, Mustard Yellow Ground, 1800s, 78 In.	144.00
Appliqued, Bars, Multicolor Red Ground, Pa., c.1920, 74 x 72 In.	2015.00
Appliqued, Carolina Lily, Tulip Vine Border, Red, Green, Pa., c.1900, 70 x 88 In.	948.00
Appliqued, Center Pierced Star, Flowers, Birds, Trees, Oak Leaf Border, c.1850, 111 x 110 In.	11850.00
Appliqued, Cherry Trees, Black, Yellow Birds, Vine Border, Sawtooth Edge, 1800s, 82 x 82 In.	4503.00
Appliqued, Cross Tulip, Red, Green, Yellow, c.1890, 80 x 82 In.	729.00
Appliqued, Eagle, Red, Green, Orange, White Ground, c.1885, 76 x 76 In.	1185.00
Appliqued, Eagle, Spread Wings, White Ground, Green & Yellow Floral Calico, 93 ½ x 81 In.	826.00
Appliqued, Eagle, Tulips, Red, Green, c.1895, 76 x 76 In.	1458.00
Appliqued, Eagles, Triple Color Border, c.1915, 84 x 86 In.	1541.00
Appliqued, Elephant, 28 Black Images, Orange, Cotton, Chambray Backing, c.1930, 80 x 90 In.	764.00
Appliqued, Flowers & Leaves, Blocks, Wavy Stems, Pink & Green, White Ground, 1900s, 80 x 74 ½ In.	104.00
Appliqued, Flowers, Red, Green, Yellow, Scalloped Edge, Sampler, Pa., c.1890, 86 x 88 In.	3081.00
Appliqued, Flowers, Vines, Multicolor, c.1910, 84 x 65 In.	148.00
Appliqued, Hawaiian, Leafy Pinwheel, Pineapples, Leaves, Flowerpots, Red & White, 74 x 66 In.	944.00
Appliqued, Indian Pinwheel, Red, Green, Navy Blue, Lancaster Co., Pa., c.1900, 76 x 92 In.	444.00
Appliqued, Irish Broderie, Flowers, Geometrics, Butterflies, Birds, Frame, c.1850, 86 x 87 In.	3840.00
Appliqued, Lone Star, Rainbow, Sawtooth Border, Blue, Cotton, Berks County, c.1900, 88 x 94 In.	3318.00
Appliqued, Mariner's Compass, Chips, Whetstone, Red, Green, Yellow, Pa., c.1890, 84 x 100 In.	1304.00
Appliqued, Mariner's Compass, Leaf, Animal Diamonds, Red, Green, Gold, 1800s, 87 x 94 In.	1007.00
Appliqued, Oak Leaf & Acorn, Sawtooth Border, White, Red, Green, Pa., 1800s, 80 x 94 In.	711.00
Appliqued, Pink Flowers, Green Leaves, Pink Swag Border, c.1910, 99 x 85 In.	61.00
Appliqued, Postage Stamp Bowmansville Star, Multicolor, Pa., c.1885, 80 x 80 In.	3555.00
Appliqued, President's Wreath, Green, Red, White, Beaver Falls, Pa., c.1870, 96 x 96 In.	1304.00
Appliqued, Rose, Holly Berry, Green, Red Pattern, Blue Ground, Lancaster, Pa., c.1890, 92 x 92 In.	2370.00
Appliqued, Spiral Flowers, Red, White, Pennsylvania, c.1840, 80 x 88 In.	6875.00
Appliqued, Starflower, Red, Green, Va., c.1850, 96 x 114 In.	2300.00
Appliqued, Stars, Blue, White, Band Border, Cotton, Calico, c.1890, 72 x 72 In.	575.00
Appliqued, Stylized 4-Leaf Buds, Trapunto Diamonds, Olive, Gold, Burgundy, Cream, 80 x 65 In.	646.00
Appliqued, Sunburst, 30 Circles, Mary Loman, c.1850, 90 x 104 In.	2015.00
Appliqued, Trapunto, Rose Wreath, Red, Green, White, Pa., c.1860, 87 x 87 In.	770.00
Appliqued, Triangles, Sawtooth Border, Blue, White, Calico Squares, c.1870, 95 x 92 In.	1713.00
Appliqued, Tulips, Red, Green & White, Red & Green Leaf Border, 1880s, 84 x 78 In.	550.00
Appliqued, Tulips, Red, Green, Blue, White, Leaf & Vine Border, 1800s, 84 x 78 In.	550.00
Appliqued, Whig Rose, Red, Green Calico, Flowers, Birds, Vine Border, Crib, 34 x 34 ½ In.	502.00
Appliqued, Whig Rose, Yellow Ground, Pa., c.1900, 92 x 92 In.	889.00
Campaign, William Henry Harrison, Flying Geese, White & Pink Flowers, Wreath, 101 x 92 In.	1035.00
Crazy, Fan Corners, Multicolor, Hudson Ladies Social & Benevolent Circle, c.1905, 62 x 74 In.	1416.00
Crazy, Random Shapes, Embroidery, Center Strip Fan Block, Multicolor, Satin, Velvet, 68 x 66 In.	708.00
Crazy, Vine, Flower Border, Signed, My Mother 1886, 63 x 63 In.	2023.00
Mennonite, Appliqued, Flower Blocks, Stripe Border, Rose, Red, Green, Pa., c.1890, 92 x 94 In.	4503.00
Mennonite, Appliqued, Oak Leaves, Squares, Orange, Green, Pa., c.1890, 90 x 92 In.	577.00
Mennonite, Patchwork, Lone Star, Brown Field, Triple Border, Cotton, c.1915, 74 x 76 In.	354.00
Mennonite, Patchwork, Lone Star, Satellite Stars, Red, Cotton Prints, c.1930, 84 x 88 In.	211.00
Mennonite, Patchwork, Pine Tree, Sawtooth Diamond, In Diamond, Red, Brown Back, 81 x 82 In.	181.00
Mennonite, Patchwork, Serrated Diamond, In Square, Gray, Red, Crib, c.1900, 43 x 43 In.	1659.00
Moravian, Appliqued, Flower Wreaths, Squares, Purple, Orange, Green, c.1900, 82 x 82 In.	486.00
Moravian, Appliqued, Reverse, Hearts, Birds, Tulips, Pumpkin, Brown, c.1900, 86 x 84 In.	4029.00
Patchwork & Appliqued, 4 American Flags, Eagle Holding Flag, Mid 20th Century, 87 x 88 In.	4975.00
Patchwork, 4 Patch, Red, White, Yellow, c.1955, 72 x 75 In.	431.00
Patchwork, 9 Patch Variation, Blue & White, c.1880, 75 x 83 In.	356.00
Patchwork, 9 Patch, Trapunto Star, Pink, Red, Yellow, c.1860, 75 x 77 In.	1215.00
Patchwork, American Star, 8-Point, Multicolor, Blue Ground, c.1910, 73 x 68 In.	115.00
Patchwork, Appliqued, 9 Patch, Flowers, Red, Blue, Brown, Wool, Lancaster, Pa., c.1890, 70 x 77 In.	504.00
Patchwork, Appliqued, Compass Variation, Yellow, White, Green, Pa., 1800s, 74 x 84 In.	972.00
Patchwork, Appliqued, Indian Head, Buffalo Horns, Red, White, Blue, Cotton, 1940s, 88 x 82 In.	1541.00
Patchwork, Bars, Pink Sawtooth Border, Green, Pink, Calico, Black Calico Back, 82 x 81 In.	236.00

Patchwork, Basket Pattern, Red, Green, Blue, Yellow Ground, Pa., c.1880, 86 x 78 In.		2133.00
Patchwork, Bear Paw, Lilac & Black, Cream, Cotton, c.1900, 59 x 83 ½ In.		553.00
Patchwork, Bear's Paw Variation, Green, White, Red Print, Pa., 19th Century, 94 x 94 In.		711.00
Patchwork, Bear's Paw, White, Alternating Calico Blocks, 1860s, 76 x 80 In.		935.00
Patchwork, Birds Flying, Pink, Brown Border, Cotton Prints, Muslin, c.1880, 78 x 89 In.		118.00
Patchwork, Blazing Star, Diagonal, Cotton Prints, Blue, Pink, Blue Border, c.1870, 77 x 79 In.		362.00
Patchwork, Blue, Green, White, Pa., c.1890, 98 x 101 In.		148.00
Patchwork, Bowtie, Multicolor Dress & Shirting Prints, Border, Cotton, Flannel, 80 x 84 In.		382.00
Patchwork, Broken Star, Multicolor, White Field, Pink Border, Backing, Cotton, c.1950, 86 x 84 In.		59.00
Patchwork, Bull's Eye, Chips, Whetstones, c.1890, Berks County, Pa., 84 x 84 In.		15405.00
Patchwork, Center Star, Brown, Beige, Blue, Inscribed Twila Swan, Lancaster, Pa., 1800s, 24 x 24 In.		326.00
Patchwork, Checkerboard, Brown Black, White, c.1860, 80 x 80 In.		316.00
Patchwork, Chimney Sweep, Green Lattice, Red Connector Blocks, c.1900, 75 x 91 In.		115.00
Patchwork, Cotton, Multicolor Strips, Ella Pettaway, Gees Bend, Alabama, 74 x 85 In.		1062.00
Patchwork, Crazy, Double Sided, 13-Patch Blocks, Mixed Shapes & Fabrics, Calico, 70 x 70 In.. *Illus*		165.00
Patchwork, Crazy, Flowers, Birds, Butterfly, Fan, From Grandma To Addie 1894, 69 ½ x 84 In.		288.00
Patchwork, Diamond Star, White, Red, Yellow, c.1850, 88 ½ x 91 In.		546.00
Patchwork, Double Irish Chain, Brown, Tan, Rust, c.1955, 72 x 85 In.		161.00
Patchwork, Double Irish Chain, White Ground, Yellow, Green, c.1880, 75 x 86 In.		711.00
Patchwork, Dresden Plate, 12 Blocks, Pink, Green, Blue, 84 x 104 In.		83.00
Patchwork, Dresden Plate, Crazy, Thistle Corners, c.1900, 66 x 60 In.		444.00
Patchwork, Drunkard's Path, Rocky Road To Dublin, Blue, White, Va., c.1860, 64 x 80 In.		259.00
Patchwork, Farmer's Delight, White, Red, Va., c.1850, 76 x 88 In.		978.00
Patchwork, Flower Wreath, Sawtooth Border, Blue Ground, Crib, c.1900, 39 x 37 In.		415.00
Patchwork, Flowers, Leaves, Yellow Border, Plume Quilting, Kathryn Shelly Geesey, Pa., 84 x 85 In.		443.00
Patchwork, Flying Geese, Red, White, 1800s, 63 ½ x 80 In.		374.00
Patchwork, Geometric, Iris, Lotus Flowers, Black Field, Yellow Border, Cotton, Sateen, 66 x 85 In.		1541.00
Patchwork, Geometrics, Pink, Cream Ground, c.1990, 84 x 84 In.		384.00
Patchwork, Irish Chain, Sawtooth Border, Rust, Green, White, Cotton, c.1850, 93 x 65 In.		288.00
Patchwork, Irish Chain, Yellow, Maroon, Green, Lebanon Co., Pa., c.1900, 88 x 84 In.		889.00
Patchwork, Log Cabin, Barn Raising, Blue, Red, Black, Gray Squares, Pa., c.1890, 86 x 88 In..		474.00
Patchwork, Log Cabin, Barn Raising, Diamond Overlay, Pa., c.1890, 82 x 82 In.		1304.00
Patchwork, Log Cabin, Pineapple, Red, Black, Yellow, Pink, White, Pa., 78 x 78 In.		1778.00
Patchwork, Lone Star, Brown Ground, Triple Border, c.1915, 74 x 76 In.		354.00
Patchwork, Lone Star, Cotton, Printed Back, c.1890, 83 ½ x 83 ½ In. *Illus*		764.00
Patchwork, Lone Star, Eagle, Red, White Diamonds, c.1890, 85 x 87 In.		3555.00
Patchwork, Lone Star, Mosaic, Felt, Red, White, Black, 94 x 95 In.		5451.00
Patchwork, North Carolina Lily, Alternating Green & Red Borders, Muslin Back, c.1900, 80 x 83 In.		264.00
Patchwork, Ocean Waves, White Triangles, Muted Red, Blue Ground, c.1850, 73 x 95 In.		173.00
Patchwork, Orange, Blue & Yellow Calico, Orange Border, 75 x 57 In.		59.00
Patchwork, Pineapple Log Cabin, c.1850, 80 x 80 In.		460.00
Patchwork, Pinwheel, 9 Blocks, Red, Tan, White, Latticework, 1800s		504.00
Patchwork, Pinwheel, Bird & Flower Border, Stars, Flowering Vines, Daisy, c.1855, 92 x 92 In..		1150.00
Patchwork, Pinwheels, Floral Chintz Border, Maker Inscribed, Little Britain, 1845, 106 x 106 In.		2370.00
Patchwork, Pyramid, Inverted, Red, Blue, c.1905, 64 x 78 In.		431.00
Patchwork, Radiating Square Postage Stamp, Multicolor, c.1910, 72 x 84 In.		326.00
Patchwork, Radiating Star, Multicolor, c.1860, 82 x 82 In.		593.00
Patchwork, Roman Bars, Yellow, Red Stripes, Blue Border, Pa., c.1890, 72 x 90 In.		201.00
Patchwork, Sawtooth Hollow Square, Red, White Ground, Bound Edges, 75 x 74 In.		944.00
Patchwork, Schoolhouse, Multicolor Prints, Shirting Weaves, Yellow Ground, Cotton, 91 x 72 In.		411.00
Patchwork, Square In Square, Red, Green, Pa., 19th Century, 82 x 81 In.		356.00
Patchwork, Star Of Bethlehem, 8 Small Stars, Blue, White, Red, Yellow, c.1855, 103 x 103 In...		431.00
Patchwork, Star, 8-Point, Multicolor, Calico, Stretcher Frame, 36 x 36 In.		531.00
Patchwork, Star, Diamond Patches, Red, Green Border, Prints, Print Backing, c.1910, 77 x 90 In.		1121.00
Patchwork, Star, Pinwheel Design, Red, White, Red Stripe Border, c.1945, 77 x 75 In.		518.00
Patchwork, Stars, 8-Point, Grid, Orange Peel, Circles, Flowers On Reverse, 1875-90, 94 x 96 In.. *Illus*		470.00
Patchwork, String Crazy, Multicolor, Scalloped Edge, 19th Century, 72 x 59 In.		6518.00
Patchwork, Sunbonnet, Friendship, Multicolor, Orange Lattice, c.1940, 68 x 85 In.		30.00
Patchwork, Touching Stars, 4 Patch, Border, Cotton, c.1940, 80 x 84 In.		177.00
Patchwork, Tree Of Life, Black, Purple, 20th Century, 78 x 81 In.		1185.00
Patchwork, Wedding Ring, Multicolor, Scalloped Edge, c.1910, 76 x 95 In.		119.00
Patchwork, Wild Goose Chase, Lattice, Variable Star, Va., c.1850, 82 x 106 In.		920.00
Trapunto, Stylized Flowers, Pinks, Purples, 20th Century, 90 x 81 In.		382.00

Radio, Fada, Art Deco Style, Bakelite, Mottled Butterscotch, Red Knobs, 11 x 7 ½ In.
$316.00

James D. Julia Auctioneers

Radio, Mike Radio, Station KBKC, 1480 KC, White Plastic, Decal, 14 In.
$144.00

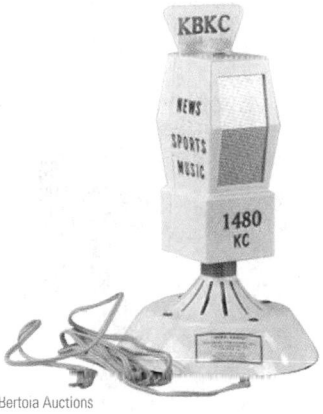

Bertoia Auctions

Red Wing, Vase, Amphora Shape, Handles, Stamped, 9 x 10 In.
$500.00

Rago Arts & Auction Center

Redware, Bowl, Utility, Straight-Sided, Rolled Over Rim, Glazed Interior, 4 x 9 ¾ In.
$59.00

Conestoga Auction Co., Inc.

Q

Redware, Dish, Yellow Slip, Twisted
Lines, Coggled Rim, 10 ¾ In.
$295.00

Conestoga Auction Co., Inc.

Redware, Jar, Runny Blue Green Glaze,
4 Lug Handles, Impressed, J.H. Owen,
9 ½ In.
$767.00

Brunk Auctions

Redware, Pitcher, Manganese Glaze,
Pulled Spout, Applied Handle,
7 ½ x 5 ¼ In.
$47.00

Conestoga Auction Co., Inc.

Richard, Vase, Lake Scene, Tall Trees,
Cabin, Bridge, Mountains, Cameo,
Signed, 10 ¼ In.
$403.00

Early Auction Co.

QUIMPER pottery has a long history. Tin-glazed, hand-painted pottery has been made in Quimper, France, since the late seventeenth century. The earliest firm was founded in 1708 by Pierre Bousquet. In 1782, Antoine de la Hubaudiere became the manager of the factory and the factory became known as the HB Factory (for Hubaudiere-Bousquet), de la Hubaudiere, or Grande Maison. Another firm, founded in 1772 by Francois Eloury, was known as Porquier. The third firm, founded by Guillaume Dumaine in 1778, was known as HR or Henriot Quimper. All three firms made similar pottery decorated with designs of Breton peasants and sea and flower motifs. The Eloury (Porquier) and Dumaine (Henriot) firms merged in 1913. Bousquet (HB) merged with the others in 1968. The group was sold to an American holding company in 1984. More changes followed, and in 2011 Jean-Pierre Le Goff became the owner and the name was changed to Henriot-Quimper.

HR Quimper

Bonbon, Faience, Swan Shape Finial, Breton Musician, Bretonne With Spindle, 5 ½ x 4 ¾ In. .	196.00
Bowl, Man, Seated, Blue & Leafy Bands, Fluted Sides, c.1875, 5 x 13 In.	235.00
Cruet, Double, Men & Women, Oil & Vinegar, Arched Center Handle, 2 Spouts, 7 In.	235.00
Inkstand, Flowers, Man, 2 Inserts, Lids, Marked, Henriot Quimper France, c.1900, 7 x 4 In. . *Illus*	633.00
Jardinere, Dancers, Breton Costumes, Notched Rim, 4-Footed, 6 x 10 In.	235.00
Jardiniere, Malicorne Fishermen, Flower, Rectangular, Notched, 4-Footed, E. Dessier, 10 In...	235.00
Jardiniere, Man & Woman In Costume, Flowers, Fan Shape, Notched Edge, 6 x 11 In.	235.00
Knife Rest, Breton Man, 3 ½ In.	48.00
Plate, Fish, Plat De Poisson, Faience, Leaf Designs, Bretons In Landscape, Henriot, 18 ½ x 8 In.	207.00
Plate, Portrait, Breton, Bretonne, Paul Foullien, Henriot, 6 ¾ x 6 ¾ In., Pair	161.00
Plate, Woman Spinning Yarn, Blue & White Border, Signed, Penhars, 9 ¼ In.	206.00
Platter, Oval, Man & Woman, Leafy Border, Marked, HB, c.1885, 11 ½ x 14 ½ In. *Illus*	206.00
Trivet, Painted, Roosters, Flower Border, 8 x 8 In., Pair	72.00
Vase, Bagpipe Shape, Painted, Peasants, Woman With Yarn, Man Playing Pipe, 5 ¾ In., Pair .	138.00
Vase, Bottle Form, 2 Couples, Feathered Designs, 4 Lug Handles, c.1875, 10 In.	90.00

RADIO broadcast receiving sets were first sold in New York City in 1910. They were used to pick up the experimental broadcasts of the day. The first commercial radios were made by Westinghouse Company for listeners of the experimental shows on KDKA Pittsburgh in 1920. Collectors today are interested in all early radios, especially those made of Bakelite plastic or decorated with blue mirrors. Figural advertising radios and transistor radios are also collected.

Fada, Art Deco Style, Bakelite, Mottled Butterscotch, Red Knobs, 11 x 7 ½ In. *Illus*	316.00
Lone Ranger, Silver, Horse Lights, Red Dials, Veined Plastic, Beetle Majestic, Not Working, 7 In....	5610.00
Microphone, Velocity, Black Enameled Metal, Chromium Plated Brass, Square Base, c.1938, 13 ⅜ In.	6200.00
Mike Radio, Station KBKC, 1480 KC, White Plastic, Decal, 14 In. *Illus*	144.00

RAILROAD enthusiasts collect any train memorabilia. Everything is wanted, from oilcans to whole train cars. The Chessie system has a store that sells many reproductions of its old dinnerware and uniforms.

Ashtray, Pennsylvania Railroad, Logo, White, Red, 5 ¼ In.	50.00
Ashtray, Pullman, Brass Base, Flower Embossed, Marked, 25 x 11 In.	181.00
Badge, Ribbon, Veteran Employee Assoc. Of Milwaukee Road Reunion, Cardboard, 1946, 6 In.	75.00
Bell, Locomotive, Brass, Iron Yoke, Stamped, 16 ½ x 15 In.	325.00
Bell, Railroad Crossing, Brass, Black Paint, Indiana, c.1850, 9 x 14 In.	176.00
Blanket, Pullman, Sleeping Car, 72 x 56 In.	79.00
Bowl, Great Northern Railroad, Glory Of The West, Footed, 9 ½ In.	351.00
Bowl, Steamship, Alaska Line Steamship, Shenango China, 7 ½ In.	40.00
Boxcar, New York Central, Salesman's Sample, 38 x 8 In.	440.00
Broadside, W. Ross's Express, Graphic Train, Crowd Of People, Wood Frame, 13 x 20 In.	295.00
Button, Big Railroad Strike 1922, Steam Locomotive, Phila. Badge, 1 ¼ In.	82.00
Button, Chessie Cat, 24th Annual Meeting, Greenbrier Valley Fair Grounds, W. Va., 1940, 1 ¼ In...	86.00
Button, Photo, P.H.M.A.A., Freight Car, Baltimore Badge Back Paper, c.1904, 1 ¼ In.	69.00
Carafe, Union Pacific, Glass, Silver Frame, International Silver Co., 10 x 7 In.	480.00
Casserole, Lid, Western Pacific, Feather River, Oval, 7 ½ In.	234.00
Chair, Pullman Passenger Car, Brass Seat Number, 34 x 27 ½ x 27 In., Pair	176.00
Chair, Pullman, Padded Seat, Turned Legs, Centavilla, 1920s, 33 x 16 In.	113.00
Clock, Western Union Denver Station, Oak Case, 8-Day, Paper Label, Gilbert, c.1900, 67 x 21 In....	354.00
Compote, Maine Central Railroad, 4 ½ x 8 ¾ In.	409.00
Cup & Saucer, Baltimore & Ohio, Centenary, 6 ¼ In., 12 Sets.	187.00
Cup & Saucer, Milwaukee Road, Traveler, Demitasse, 6 Sets	410.00
Cup & Saucer, Santa Fe, California Poppy, 10 Sets.	105.00
Cuspidor, Pullman, Nickel Silver, Round, 7 In.	113.00
Desk, Rock Island Station, Cubbyhole Shelves, 2 Drawers, Turned Legs, 55 x 66 In.	325.00

Eggcup, Double, Baltimore & Ohio, Centenary, 3 ¼ In., 9 Piece	117.00
Eggcup, Milwaukee Road, Traveler, 2 ½ In., 5 Piece	211.00
Hand Cart, 2 Man, Wood, Iron, Salesman's Sample, 10 x 6 x 8 In.	3300.00
Jug, Deodorizer, Pullman, Earthenware, Cork Stopper, 9 ¼ x 5 ½ In.	85.00
Lamp, Marker, Black Paint, Wire Handle, 4 Lenses, Adlake, 8 ½ x 10 In.	226.00
Lantern, Brass, Clear Globe, Bail Handle, Conductor's, Kelly Lamp Works, c.1875, 16 x 6 In.	489.00
Lantern, Brass, Clear Globe, Wire Guard, Bail Handle, John Irwin, c.1875, 14 x 6 In.	316.00
Lantern, Brass, Clear Globe, Wire Guard, Wick Burner, Conductor's, S.B. Underhill, c.1875, 16 x 5 In.	460.00
Lantern, Brass, Iron, Clear Globe, Wire Guard, Hinged, J. Sangster, c.1870, 16 ½ x 6 ½ In.	230.00
Lantern, Brass, Iron, Red Globe, Wire Guard, Bail Handle, Steam Gauge & Lantern, c.1890, 17 x 6 In.	460.00
Lantern, Brass, Nickel, Blue Globe, Wire Guard, Conductor's, Wm. Porter & Sons, c.1850, 16 x 6 In.	575.00
Lantern, Burlington Route Railroad, Globe, c.1922, 10 ½ x 6 ½ In.	158.00
Lantern, Canadian National Railroad, Burner, 3 Blue, 1 Red Lens, Marked HL Piper, 16 x 9 In.	173.00
Lantern, Clear Panes, Silvered Reflector, Strap Handle, Iron, Dietz, No. 2, c.1900, 23 x 10 In.	316.00
Lantern, Copper, 3 Clear Panes, Square, Hinged, Station, Peter Gray & Sons, c.1910, 17 x 9 In.	207.00
Lantern, Gasoline, 3 Color, White, Red, Green, Metal, c.1900, 12 ¼ In.	190.00
Lantern, Iron, 3 Clear Panes, Mercury Glass Reflector, United States Supply, c.1910, 10 x 10 In.	288.00
Lantern, Iron, Hinged Shutter, Bail Handle, Gilt, Black Paint, Peter Gray, Boston, c.1890, 13 x 8 In.	173.00
Lantern, Iron, Red, Clear, Blue Bull's-Eye Lens, Hinged, Black Paint, Signal, Peter Gray, c.1900, 15 In.	184.00
Lantern, Iron, Signal, Blue Lens, Bail Handle, Armspear Manufacturing, Co., c.1900, 15 x 7 ½ In.	374.00
Lantern, Kansas City Southern Railway, Wire Handle, Clear Globe, Adlake, c.1915, 10 ½ x 6 In.	283.00
Lantern, New York Central, Iron, Brass, Clear Globe, Bail, Conductor's, C.T. Ham, c.1890, 16 x 4 In.	1150.00
Lantern, Station, Copper, Brass, G. Adroite, England, 22 x 9 In.	585.00
Menu Holder, Milwaukee Road, Sterling Silver, Stamped, 4 ¾ In., 3 Piece	351.00
Place Setting, Baltimore & Ohio, Centenary, 5 Piece	70.00
Place Setting, Southern Pacific, Prairie Mountain Wildflowers, 5 Piece	152.00
Plate, Baltimore & Ohio Railroad, Blue Transfer, Staffordshire, c.1850, 10 ⅛ In.	652.00
Plate, Baltimore & Ohio Railroad, Shell Border, Blue Transfer, Enoch Wood & Sons, c.1825, 11 In.	590.00
Plate, C & O, George Washington, Gold Rim, Central Portrait, 10 ½ In.	28.00
Plate, Great Northern Railroad, Glory Of The West, 9 ¾ In.	80.00
Plate, Soup, C & O, George Washington, Gold Rim, 9 In.	17.00
Platter, Great Northern Railroad, Glory Of The West, Oval, 10 In.	95.00
Platter, New York Central, Dewitt Clinton, Oval, 11 ½ In.	70.00
Platter, Southern Pacific, Harriman Blue Top, Oval, 14 ¾ In.	94.00
Platter, Western Pacific, Oval, 11 ¼ In.	90.00
Poster, Aroostook Flyer, General Motors Diesel Locomotives, Mountains, B. Hill, 1950s, 23 x 17 In.	700.00
Poster, New York Central System, Century In The Highlands Of The Hudson, c.1938, 32 x 16 In.	425.00
Sconce, Pullman, Berth, Gold Paint, Tinted, Clear Globes, 10 x 5 In., Pair	215.00
Sign, B & O Railroad, Baltimore Station Scene, Round, Paint, Cast Iron, c.1910, 16 ½ In.	144.00
Sign, Barber Logo, Metal, Art Deco, c.1940, 23 x 14 ½ In.	311.00
Sign, Employees Must Not Cross Tracks, Porcelain, 12 x 24 In.	295.00
Sign, Railway Crossing, R X R, Round, Yellow, Black, Porcelain, 1950s, 24 In.	330.00
Sign, Railway Express Agency, Porcelain, Black & Yellow, 72 x 11 In.	448.00
Sign, Railway Express Agency, Porcelain, Black, Yellow, 120 x 11 In.	585.00
Sign, Railway Express Agency, Red, Porcelain, Diamond Shape, 36 x 36 In.	280.00
Sign, Railway Express, Century Of Service, 1839-1939, Celluloid, Carl Burger, 28 ½ x 11 ¾ In.	1100.00
Sign, Rock Island Railroad, Train, Landscape, Reverse Glass, Paint, Frame, 1907, 89 ¾ x 26 ¾ In.	7200.00
Sign, Train Station, Old Betsy Run, Yakima & Tacoma, Steam Engine, Landscape, 50 x 99 In.	2300.00
Sign, Warning, Structure Will Not Clear Man On Side Of Car, Cast Iron, Pedestal, 30 x 47 In.	280.00
Step Stool, Pullman, Rag Holder Underside, Cross Textured Top, Footed, Marked, 10 x 16 In.	509.00
Teapot, Lid, Pullman, Green, Gold Trim, Logo, 6 In., Pair	215.00
Teapot, Union Pacific, International Silver, 10 x 7 ½ In.	203.00
Teapot, Western Pacific, Cobalt Blue, Paneled, 4 ½ In., Pair	351.00
Telegraph, Receiver, Transmitter, Wall Bracket	325.00
Whistle, Bronze, Crosby Steam Gage & Valve, Boston, Walnut Base, 19th Century, 12 x 7 In.	58.00

RAZORS were used in ancient Egypt and subsequently wherever shaving was in fashion. The metal razor used in America until about 1870 was made in Sheffield, England. After 1870, machine-made hollow-ground razors were made in Germany or America. Plastic or bone handles were popular. The razor was often sold in a set of seven, one for each day of the week. The set was often kept by the barber who shaved the well-to-do man each day in the shop.

Case, Fitted, Basket Weave Pattern, Flip Lid, Bengall Razors, 1 ½ x 7 In.	104.00
Display, Barrel Brand, Barbers King, Peres Plant Scene, D. Peres, c.1900, 24 In.	14400.00
Straight, Barber Pole Shape, Yellow, Blue, Red Celluloid, Koken, Closed, 5 ½ In.	4950.00
Strop, Golden Gate, Will & Finck, Barbers' Supplies & Toilet Requisites, 17 ½ In.	193.00

TIP
Figurines are often damaged. Examine the fingers, toes, and other protruding parts for damage or repairs.

Rookwood, Bookends, Blackbird, Light Brown Matte Glaze, Shirayamadani, 1929, 5 ½ In.
$489.00

Humler & Nolan

Rookwood, Bookends, Dog, Collie, Chestnut Matte Glaze, W. McDonald, 1929, 6 In.
$431.00

Humler & Nolan

Rookwood, Bookends, Penguins, Brown & Gray Glaze, 1924, 5 ¾ In.
$1,320.00

Skinner, Inc.

R

Rookwood, Bowl, Fern, Yellow Matte Glaze, Impressed, 1910, 7 ½ x 2 ¾ In.
$316.00

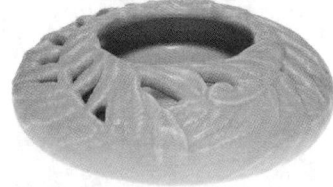

Humler & Nolan

Rookwood, Mug, Lion, Standard Glaze, E.T. Hurley, 1898, 4 ⅝ In.
$1,093.00

Humler & Nolan

Rookwood, Paperweight, Monkey, Chestnut Matte Glaze, Shirayamadani, 1930, 3 ⅞ In.
$316.00

Humler & Nolan

Rookwood, Pitcher, Birds Flying, Lacy Clouds, Oriental Grasses, Albert Valentien, 1885, 9 ½ In.
$460.00

Humler & Nolan

TIP
Early plates often have no rim on the bottom.

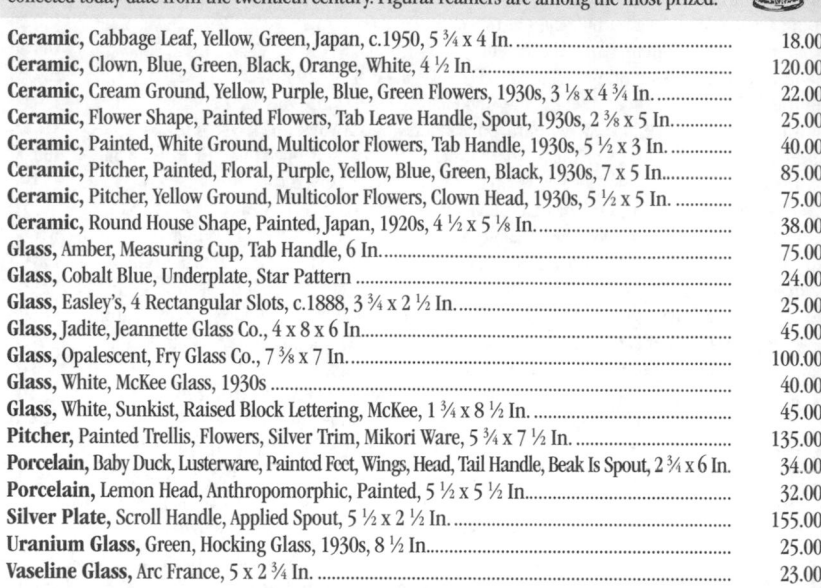

REAMERS, or juice squeezers, have been known since 1767, although most of those collected today date from the twentieth century. Figural reamers are among the most prized.

Ceramic, Cabbage Leaf, Yellow, Green, Japan, c.1950, 5 ¾ x 4 In.	18.00
Ceramic, Clown, Blue, Green, Black, Orange, White, 4 ½ In.	120.00
Ceramic, Cream Ground, Yellow, Purple, Blue, Green Flowers, 1930s, 3 ⅛ x 4 ¾ In.	22.00
Ceramic, Flower Shape, Painted Flowers, Tab Leave Handle, Spout, 1930s, 2 ⅜ x 5 In.	25.00
Ceramic, Painted, White Ground, Multicolor Flowers, Tab Handle, 1930s, 5 ½ x 3 In.	40.00
Ceramic, Pitcher, Painted, Floral, Purple, Yellow, Blue, Green, Black, 1930s, 7 x 5 In.	85.00
Ceramic, Pitcher, Yellow Ground, Multicolor Flowers, Clown Head, 1930s, 5 ½ x 5 In.	75.00
Ceramic, Round House Shape, Painted, Japan, 1920s, 4 ½ x 5 ⅛ In.	38.00
Glass, Amber, Measuring Cup, Tab Handle, 6 In.	75.00
Glass, Cobalt Blue, Underplate, Star Pattern	24.00
Glass, Easley's, 4 Rectangular Slots, c.1888, 3 ¾ x 2 ½ In.	25.00
Glass, Jadite, Jeannette Glass Co., 4 x 8 x 6 In.	45.00
Glass, Opalescent, Fry Glass Co., 7 ⅜ x 7 In.	100.00
Glass, White, McKee Glass, 1930s	40.00
Glass, White, Sunkist, Raised Block Lettering, McKee, 1 ¾ x 8 ½ In.	45.00
Pitcher, Painted Trellis, Flowers, Silver Trim, Mikori Ware, 5 ¾ x 7 ½ In.	135.00
Porcelain, Baby Duck, Lusterware, Painted Foot, Wings, Head, Tail Handle, Beak Is Spout, 2 ¾ x 6 In.	34.00
Porcelain, Lemon Head, Anthropomorphic, Painted, 5 ½ x 5 ½ In.	32.00
Silver Plate, Scroll Handle, Applied Spout, 5 ½ x 2 ½ In.	155.00
Uranium Glass, Green, Hocking Glass, 1930s, 8 ½ In.	25.00
Vaseline Glass, Arc France, 5 x 2 ¾ In.	23.00

RECORDS have changed size and shape through the years. The cylinder-shaped phonograph record for use with the early Edison models was made about 1889. Disc records were first made by 1894, the double-sided disc by 1904. High-fidelity records were first issued in 1944, the first vinyl disc in 1946, the first stereo record in 1958. The 78 RPM became the standard in 1926 but was discontinued in 1957. In 1932, the first 33 ⅓ RPM was made but was not sold commercially until 1948. In 1949, the 45 RPM was introduced. Compact discs became available in the U.S. in 1982 and many companies began phasing out the production of phonograph records.

Frank Sinatra, Sinatra & Strings, Reprise, Stereophonic LP, 1961	5.00
Grease, Original Soundtrack, Bee Gees, RSO Records, 33 ⅓ LP Stereo, 1978	25.00
Guy Lombardo, This Is Guy Lombardo & His Orchestra, RCA Victor, 45 RPM, 1954	15.00
Isaac Hayes, Let's Stay Together, Soulsville, 45 RPM, Enterprise, 1972	8.00
Lani McIntyre & His Aloha Islanders, Songs Of Hawaii, Varsity, LP, 1940s	16.00
Little Red Riding Hood, Narrated By David Allen, 78 RPM, Columbia, 1947	75.00
Michael Jackson, Thriller, Epic, Stereo, LP, 1982	55.00
Patty Duke, Patty, Cover, 33 ⅓ RPM, United Artists, 1966	10.00
Ray Bradbury, Martian Chronicles, Mark 56 Records, LP, 1976	24.00
Richie Valens, La Bamba, Del-Fi Label, 45 RPM, 1950s	43.00
Vincent Edwards, Vincent Edwards Sings, Decca, LP, 1960s	15.00

RED WING POTTERY of Red Wing, Minnesota, was a firm started in 1878. The company first made utilitarian pottery, including stoneware jugs and canning jars. In the 1920s art pottery was introduced. Many dinner sets and vases were made before the company closed in 1967. Rumrill pottery made by the Red Wing Pottery for George Rumrill is listed in its own category. For more prices, go to kovels.com.

Bob White, Bread Tray, 23 ¾ In.	120.00
Bob White, Casserole, Lid, 4 Qt., 9 In.	140.00
Bowl, Yellow, Low, Lid, Round, 8 In.	90.00
Capistrano, Plate, Dinner, 1950s, 11 In.	18.00
Dish, Feeding, Clown, Blue, Hankscraft, 1940s	52.00
Flower Frog, Ivory Seashore On Top Of Coral Base, 1942, 8 ½ x 4 ½ In.	150.00
Lexington, Creamer	16.00
Lexington, Gravy Boat, Rectangular Liner, Roses	19.00
Lexington, Platter, Oval, 13 In.	30.00
Magnolia Chartreuse, Plate, Salad, 7 ¼ In., 6 Piece	30.00
Provincial Ware, Casserole, Lid, Cinnamon, Unglazed, Handle, Spout, 3 ¼ x 4 ½ In.	10.00
Roundup, Plate, Dinner, Wagon, 10 ⅞ In.	180.00
Smart Set, Platter, c.1955, 14 In.	97.00
Spongeware, Bowl, White Ground, Blue, Dark Red, Paneled, 8 ½ x 4 ¾ In.	160.00
Vase, 2 Lions, Green, Brown Matte Glaze, Bulbous, Marked, 6 x 7 ½ In.	125.00
Vase, 4 Panels, Woodland Scenes, Tapered, Round Foot, Square Handles, Marked, c.1920, 12 In.	184.00

R

Vase, Amphora Shape, Handles, Stamped, 9 x 10 In.............................*Illus*	500.00
Vase, Chartreuse, Wing Shape, Layered Leaves At Base, Black Matte Interior, 10 x 5 ½ In.	195.00
Vase, Gladiola Fan, Pink, Lobed, 12 ¼ In.	12.00
Vase, Green Glossy Glaze, Vertical Ribs, Handles, 9 ½ In.	71.00
Vase, Impressed Flowers, Mint Green, Cylinder, Marked, 7 ¾ In.	17.00
Violin, Plaque, Pink, Black Speckles, 4 Strings, 1950s, 13 x 1 ½ In.	25.00

REDWARE is a hard, red stoneware that originated in the late 1600s and continues to be made. The term is also used to describe any common clay pottery that is reddish in color.

Bank, Blue, Brown Dripped Glaze, Bottle Shape, c.1850, 8 In.	326.00
Bank, Globular, Manganese Splotching, Dog Finial, Dated 1862, 5 ½ In.	4266.00
Bank, Lead Glaze, Dark Orange Ground, Finial, Rounded, Carved Slot, Pa., c.1850, 5 ½ In.....	210.00
Bank, Oval, Coggle Wheel Shoulder Decoration, Unglazed, 3 ½ In.	144.00
Bank, Pitcher Shape, Handle, c.1850, 4 ½ In.	1652.00
Bank, Red Brown Glaze, Flecks, Pointed Finial, Oval, Diagonal Slot, Tooled Bands, c.1860, 2 ¾ In.	58.00
Bank, Wagon, Conestoga Shape, 1800s, 5 ¾ In.	4977.00
Bowl, 3-Color Slip, Cream, Brown, Green, Tapered, Flared Rim, N.C., 1800s, 13 In..................	403.00
Bowl, Green, Cream Slip Dots, Banded, Rounded Rim, c.1850, 3 ¾ x 7 In.............	3450.00
Bowl, Green, Cream Slip Star, Bands, Snow Hill Society, Pa., 2 ¾ x 11 In.............	8888.00
Bowl, Green, Red Slip, Flower, 1819, 10 ¼ In.	652.00
Bowl, Iron Flecks, Pocket Rim, Flared Rim, c.1830, 5 ¾ x 12 In.	86.00
Bowl, Lid, Star & Tulip Slip, Pa., c.1800, 5 x 8 ½ In.	5214.00
Bowl, Lid, Yellow, Black Slip, Bucks County, Pa., 1800s, 5 ½ x 8 ½ In.	4740.00
Bowl, Manganese Design, Pa., c.1850, 3 ½ x 8 In..	148.00
Bowl, Manganese Splash, Line & Dot Rim, 3 x 7 ½ In.......................................	652.00
Bowl, Milk, Mottled Glaze, Molded Rim, Flared Side, Coggled Band, Pa., 1800s, 4 ½ x 11 In....	212.00
Bowl, Moravian, Brown, Yellow Slip, c.1810, 15 In.	770.00
Bowl, Multicolor, Mocha Seaweed, Round Foot, Tooled Rim, 1800s, 2 x 4 ¾ In........	1323.00
Bowl, Parrot, Flowers, Yellow, Green Slip, Ned Foltz, Reinholds, Pa., 1974, 2 ¼ x 8 ¼ In.	106.00
Bowl, Pinwheel Slip, Pa., 13 ¼ In...	504.00
Bowl, Slip Design, England, c.1855, 3 x 11 ¾ In...	148.00
Bowl, Slip Trail Lines, Tulips, Triple Beaded Rim, Peter Bell, Hagerstown Md., c.1815, 12 In. ..	3163.00
Bowl, Speckled Light Brown Glaze, Stamped Heart & Croft, Chambersburg, Va., c.1870, 4 ¼ In.	575.00
Bowl, Star Center, German Script, Dated 1827, 11 ¼ In.....................................	237.00
Bowl, Utility, Straight-Sided, Rolled Over Rim, Glazed Interior, 4 x 9 ¾ In. ....*Illus*	59.00
Bowl, Yellow Slip X, 1800s, 7 ¾ In..	296.00
Bowl, Yellow, Green Slip, Marked Willoughby Smith, c.1880, 8 ½ In.....................	1778.00
Butter Tub, Impressed John Bell, Waynesboro, Pa., 5 ¾ x 8 ½ In.........................	3555.00
Charger, 2-Line Yellow Slip, c.1845, 13 In..	310.00
Charger, Coggled Rim, Yellow Slip, Initials GL, 1800s, 12 ¼ In...........................	805.00
Charger, Green Tulip, Yellow Slip Ground, Sgraffito, Bucks County, Pa., c.1805, 12 ⅜ In........	3555.00
Charger, Knight Riding Rearing Horse, Marked Dondolo, 23 In.............................	345.00
Charger, Orange Glaze, Yellow Slip Squiggles, Coggled Rim, Round, Greg Shooner, 21 In.......	189.00
Charger, Slip Decorated, Shoulder Firelock, Sgraffito Red Coated Soldiers, Lester Breininger, 13 In.	130.00
Charger, Trotting Horse, Coggled Rim, Lester Breininger, 1974, 12 ¼ In.................	83.00
Charger, Tulip, Pinwheel, Sgraffito, Red, Yellow Ground, C. Mumbauer, c.1810, 11 ¾ In.........	11258.00
Charger, Yellow Crossed Circles, Wavy Border, Coggled Rim, Huntington, N.Y., c.1845, 14 In. .	2990.00
Charger, Yellow Curly Edge Pinwheel, Coggled Rim, Huntington, N.Y., c.1840, 12 ⅜ In...........	4140.00
Charger, Yellow Slip Bands, Red Ground, Coggled Rim, c.1830, 12 ⅛ In.	201.00
Charger, Yellow Slip Lines, Coggled Rim, c.1850, 12 In....................................	230.00
Charger, Yellow Slip, 4-Line Squiggle & Dot, Pa., 1800s, 15 ¼ In........................	2015.00
Charger, Yellow Slip, c.1850, 14 ½ In.	1304.00
Charger, Yellow Slip, Simon Singer, Bucks Co., 1894, 12 ¾ In............................	1778.00
Charger, Yellow, Green Slip, Conn., 1800s, 13 ¾ In..	2015.00
Charger, Yellow, Green Slip, Dated 1807, Line & Dot Bands, 13 ⅝ In.	4740.00
Colander, Green, Orange Glaze, Pa., c.1845, 6 In..	444.00
Colander, Slip Band, Zigzag Design, c.1810, 3 ¾ x 8 ¾ In.................................	2607.00
Creamer, Green, Brown Slip, Over Orange Ground, Oval, Footed, Strap Handle, Pa., c.1860, 3 In..	1035.00
Creamer, Manganese Streaks, Dark Red Ground, New England, c.1845, 3 ⅞ In.	518.00
Crock, Coggled Border, Incised, Sarah Lee, July 14, 1837	708.00
Crock, Manganese Bands, Oval, 1800s, 6 ¼ In.	415.00
Crock, Manganese Splash, Lug Handles, New England, c.1850, 10 In.	296.00
Crock, Manganese Tulip, Incised Banding, Rolled Rim, Stamped John Bell, c.1860, 3 Gal.......	403.00
Crock, Rotund, Center Bulge, Tapered, Flared Collar, Oval, John W. Bell, Waynesboro, c.1880, 14 In. ..	144.00
Crock, Stamped John Bell, Waynesboro, Molded Collar, Oval, 6 x 4 ¾ In.	129.00

Rookwood, Pitcher, Crabs, Waves, Crushed Shape, Loop Handle, Maria Longworth Nichols, 1883, 8 In. $1,495.00

Humler & Nolan

Rookwood, Pitcher, Incised Clouds, Flowers, Smear Glaze, Chaplet Style, Albert Valentien, 1884, 8 In. $805.00

Humler & Nolan

Rookwood, Plaque, Landscape, Vellum Glaze, Trees, Stream, C. Schmidt, 1917, 9 ⅜ In. $2,990.00

Humler & Nolan

R

Rookwood, Sign, Rook On Branch, Dark Blue, Green Leaves, 1915, 4 x 8 ½ In. $6,038.00

Humler & Nolan

Rookwood, Tile, Fish, Swirling Waters, Oak Arts & Crafts Frame, E.T. Hurley, 9 x 12 ⅜ In. $1,035.00

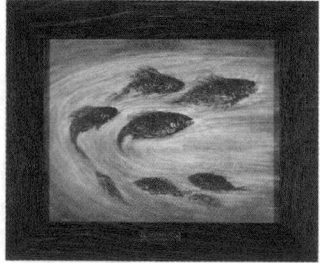

Humler & Nolan

Rookwood, Trivet, Dutch Mother & Children, Harbor, Square, Impressed, 1927, 5 ¾ In. $173.00

Humler & Nolan

Rookwood, Trivet, Flower Basket, Butterflies, Blue, Impressed Logo, 1930, 5 ½ x 5 ½ In. $120.00

DuMouchelles Art Gallery

Crock, Stamped Upton M. Bell, Waynesboro, Pa., Oval, Molded Collar, Salt Glazed Interior, 7 x 8 In.	189.00
Crock, Storage, Interior & Upper ⅓ Exterior Glaze, Bulbous, Molded Rim, Ear Handles, 20 In..	130.00
Crock, Terra-Cotta Glaze, Manganese Splotches, Crescent Handles, Incised, Bulbous, 11 x 9 In.....	460.00
Crock, W. Smith, Williamsport, Tapered, Wide Rim, Loop Handle, 8 x 8 In................	212.00
Crock, Yellow, Green Glaze, Incised Collar, Flared Rim, 1800s, 9 x 6 ¾ In.............	167.00
Crock, Yellow, Green Slip Flowers, Loop Handles, Bucks Co., Pa., c.1805, 7 In.	4266.00
Cuspidor, Coggled Moldings To Shoulder, Tooled Base, Cream Glaze, c.1865, 6 In. Diam........	288.00
Dish, Eagle, Spread Wing, Sgraffito, Jacob Medinger, 7 ¾ In................	948.00
Dish, Green Splashes, White Serpentine Slip Lines, Amber Over Glaze, Coggled Rim, 7 ⅝ In...	354.00
Dish, Rabbit Silhouette, Eggs, Yellow Slip, Coggled Rim, L. Breininger, Pa., Rainy Day, 1989, 10 In.	35.00
Dish, Rippled Spiral Line, 12 In....................	422.00
Dish, Yellow Slip, Green, Impressed Leaf Silhouettes, Coggled Rim, L. Breininger, Pa., 1979, 11 In..	12.00
Dish, Yellow Slip, Incised Cat, Followed By Mouse, Coggled Rim, Lester Breininger, Pa., 1975, 7 In.	50.00
Dish, Yellow Slip, Incised Flowers, Heart, Green Accents, L&B Breininger, Pa., 1975, 8 In........	106.00
Dish, Yellow Slip, Incised, Yea!, Scouts!, Manganese Spatter, Green, Lester Breininger, 7 ¾ In.	118.00
Dish, Yellow Slip, Twisted Lines, Coggled Rim, 10 ¾ In. ....*Illus*	295.00
Doorstop, Block, Lion's Head Relief, Square, Hollow, Marked M, 4 ⅜ In........	47.00
Figurine, Dog, Seated, Holding Basket Of Fruit, Brown Glaze, Pa., c.1845, 5 ½ In.	2015.00
Figurine, Dog, Seated, Holding Basket, With Jug, Dark Brown Glaze, 5 In...............	563.00
Figurine, Dog, Seated, Red Glaze, c.1865, 5 In.............	889.00
Figurine, Dog, Seated, Sponged Manganese Glaze, Red Ground, c.1850, 2 ¼ In........	201.00
Figurine, Dog, Spaniel, Yellow Glaze, Red Splotches, Pa., 1800s, 6 ½ In............	1185.00
Figurine, Dog, Standing, Cream Sponge Cold Painted, Oval Base, 9 ½ In..........	460.00
Figurine, Fallen Indian, Molded, Multicolor Glaze, Slab Base, 6 In............	165.00
Figurine, Hen, On Nest, Cream, Blue, c.1860, 6 ¼ In..........	356.00
Figurine, Lion, Standing, Green, Brown, Cold Painted, c.1890, 8 In.	29.00
Figurine, Monkey Head, Leaf Hat, Opening At Base, Speckled Manganese Glaze, c.1890, 5 ½ In....	1265.00
Figurine, Rooster, Painted, 20th Century, 14 ½ In...........	89.00
Figurine, Seated Dog, Holding Fruit Basket, Pa., 1800s, 4 ¼ In.	4029.00
Flask, Manganese Bird, Flowers, Pa., c.1860, 6 In............	3402.00
Flask, Orange Glaze, Manganese Splotches, Molded Rim, 1800s, 7 ¼ In........	288.00
Flask, Ring, Manganese Splotches, Clear Glaze, Pa., c.1860, 8 ½ In..........	1955.00
Flask, Rings, Squared Edges, D. Kellogg, Ohio, c.1850, 8 ⅞ In.............	230.00
Flowerpot, 5 Yellow Slip Bands, Manganese Brush Strokes, Tapered, Neck Holes, 7 In...........	47.00
Flowerpot, Attached Saucer, Brown Streak Glaze, Orange, Flared Rim, Bell Shape, c.1880, 5 ¼ In.	259.00
Flowerpot, Attached Undertray, Brown, Green Mottled Glaze, Cream Ground, 9 In..............	830.00
Flowerpot, Attached Undertray, Mottled Green, Brown Glaze, 7 ¾ In.	178.00
Flowerpot, Double Coggled Rim, Attached Saucer Base, Green, Brown Mottled Glaze, c.1870, 9 In.	1024.00
Flowerpot, Glazed, Manganese Sponging, Orange Ground, Oval, John Bell, c.1880, 5 ½ x 6 In.	575.00
Flowerpot, Glazed, Tapered, Tooled Shoulder, Crimped Rim, Baecher, c.1860, 6 In..............	201.00
Flowerpot, Green & Brown, Coggled Rim & Saucer, Splash Design, c.1890, 9 In.	460.00
Flowerpot, Saucer, Coggled, Rounded Rim, Rudolph, Shippensburg, Pa., c.1870, 8 ½ In........	1150.00
Flowerpot, Saucer, Cream, Brown Splotches, Orange Ground, Flared, Pa., c.1850, 3 ⅝ In........	316.00
Flowerpot, Saucer, Green, Brown, Cream Slip c.1860, 4 ½ In..........	460.00
Flowerpot, Undertray, Green Slip Wavy Band, Cream Splotches, c.1850, 6 ½ In.	237.00
Flowerpot, Yellow Slip Dots, Scrolls, Basket Shape, Twist Handle, Saucer, 1824, 8 ½ x 5 In.....	235.00
Jar, Apple Butter, Henry Gast, Lancaster, 1840-80, 4 ¼ x 4 In.	94.00
Jar, Canning, Brown Manganese Glaze, Coggled Shoulder, c.1850, 3 ½ In........	201.00
Jar, Canning, Cylindrical, Wax Sealer Rim, Stamped John Bell, c.1860................	518.00
Jar, Cream, Oval, Tooled Shoulder, Glazed Interior, Rolled Rim, c.1885, 4 ¼ In.........	173.00
Jar, Cream, Tooled Shoulder, Squared Rim, Lead & Manganese Glaze, John Bell, c.1880, 9 In.	173.00
Jar, Glazed, Manganese Vertical Daubs, Flared Rim, Tooled, 1800s, 6 ⅜ In.........	144.00
Jar, Green Brown, Over Cream Slip, Oval, Bell & Sons, Virginia, c.1890, 8 ⅝ In........	489.00
Jar, Lid, Green Copper Slashes, Yellow Ground, Acorn Finial, Handle, c.1800, 7 In............	1035.00
Jar, Lid, Manganese Splash, New England, 1800s, 12 ¾ In.	415.00
Jar, Lid, Splashed Manganese, Oval, Flared Rim, Lug Handles, New England, c.1835, 8 ¾ In...	201.00
Jar, Lid, Yellow, Cream Flower Slip, Green, Manganese Brown, Bucks Co., Pa., c.1800, 8 In.......	10620.00
Jar, Manganese Glaze, Straight Sides, Beveled Shoulder, Cupped Mouth, 8 In., Pair	47.00
Jar, Manganese Splashes, Orange Ground, Ribbed Lug Handles, c.1835, 8 ½ In.................	29.00
Jar, Manganese Splotch, Bulbous, Rolled Rim, Ear Handles, New York, 9 ½ In............	1840.00
Jar, Manganese Tulip, Rounded Rim, Hand Signed J. Bell, Pa., c.1860, 10 ½ In............	834.00
Jar, Manganese X Slashes, Incised, Banded, Flared Rim, c.1820, 4 ⅜ In.................	1265.00
Jar, Manganese, Banded, Bulbous, Tapered Neck, Phil., c.1800, 10 In.	633.00
Jar, Runny Blue Green Glaze, 4 Lug Handles, Impressed, J.H. Owen, 9 ½ In.................*Illus*	767.00
Jar, Rust Glaze, Applied Lizard, Berries, Cold Paint, c.1890, 6 ¾ In...........	173.00
Jar, Shenandoah Valley, Lead Glaze, Green Mottled, Orange, Tooled Rim, Schweinfurt, 8 ⅝ In..	288.00

R

Jar, Shenandoah Valley, Oval, Footed Base, Red-Brown Lead & Manganese Glaze, 7 In.	58.00
Jar, Storage, Straight-Sided, Flared Collar, Rim, Manganese Mottled, Glaze, 6 ¾ x 5 In.	71.00
Jug, Batter, Spout, Brown Glaze, Yellow Slip Sprig, 5 In.	403.00
Jug, Bulbous, Flared Collar Spout, Manganese Glaze, Pa., 1800s, 9 ¾ In.	118.00
Jug, Bulbous, Flared Foot, Brown, Black Glaze, 5 ¾ In.	167.00
Jug, Cream, Brown Glaze, Ribbed Handle, Maine, 1800s, 8 ¼ In.	1185.00
Jug, Flat Ribbed Handle, Manganese Splotches, 1800s, 7 ½ In., Qt.	863.00
Jug, Green Speckle Glaze, Oval, Bristol County, c.1820, 10 ½ In.	1180.00
Jug, Harvest, Oval, Flattened Top, Tooled Shoulder, Spout, Green & Orange Glaze, c.1855, 11 ½ In.	920.00
Jug, Manganese Slashes, Olive Glazed Ground, Rounded Spout, Applied Handle, c.1860, 8 In.	115.00
Jug, Manganese Splash, Handle, 1800s, Pa., 13 ¼ In.	237.00
Jug, Manganese, Brown Glaze, Spout, Flared Rim, 1800s, 10 In.	259.00
Jug, Mottled Green, Orange, Ribbed Spout, Small Strap Handle, Galena, Illinois, c.1850, 10 ½ In.	3105.00
Jug, Orange, Green Mottled Glaze, Oval, Loop Handle, New England, c.1820, 9 ¾ In.	830.00
Jug, Oval Shape, Reeded Handle, Manganese Splotch Design, Yellow Glaze, c.1800, 11 In.	5925.00
Jug, Oval, Incised Line On Shoulder, Reeded Handle, Mottled Orange, Brown Glaze, c.1815, 8 ⅜ In.	780.00
Jug, Oval, Round Foot, Ribbed Strap Handle, Flattened Spout, Manganese Sponging, c.1855, 8 ½ In.	2300.00
Jug, Raised Gold Paint, Stick Neck, Handle, Stamped Speese & Son, Gettysburg, c.1890, 9 In.	633.00
Jug, Sgraffito, Yellow Glaze, Double Fish Design, Bulbous, Wisconsin, Stamped E.A., 10 In.	106.00
Jug, Terra-Cotta Glaze, Green, Red, Brown Splotches, Bulbous, Shenandoah Valley, 1800s, 11 In.	288.00
Loaf Pan, 3-Line Yellow Slip, Coggled Rim, Octagonal, Pa., c.1800, 7 ¾ x 6 ⅞ In.	2185.00
Loaf Pan, 3-Line Clef Slip, Oval, Pa., 14 x 21 In.	1126.00
Loaf Pan, Coggled Rim, Wavy Lines, Leaves, c.1800, 3 x 11 x 15 In.	918.00
Loaf Pan, Oval, Coggled Rim, Divider, Brown, Cream Color Trails Design, c.1890, 10 ½ In.	115.00
Loaf Pan, Yellow & Green Slip Stripes, Combing, Signed, L. Breininger, Pa., 1977, 1 ½ x 9 ½ In.	83.00
Loaf Pan, Yellow Slip Crosses, Squiggles, L. Breininger, Robesonia, Pa., 1972, 13 ¼ In.	118.00
Loaf Pan, Yellow Slip Lines, Philadelphia, c.1950, 15 In.	690.00
Loaf Pan, Yellow Slip, Coggled Rim, S-Scroll Squiggle, Dots, 1800s, 16 x 11 In.	1180.00
Mug, Manganese Splotches, Cylindrical, Footed, Strap Handle, Pa., c.1850, 2 ⅝ In.	173.00
Mug, Oval, Loop Handle, Green & Brown, c.1890, 4 In.	1035.00
Mug, Yellow & Green Tulip, Yellow Slip Heart, Bulbous, c.1862, 5 ¼ In.	1035.00
Mug, Yellow, Green Slip Dash, Pa., 1800s, 2 ⅝ In.	1778.00
Pie Plate, 2 Boys, Playing Fife, Drum, Sgraffito, Jacob Medinger, c.1900, 8 ⅝ In.	1067.00
Pie Plate, Brown, Yellow Slip, c.1860, 9 In.	474.00
Pie Plate, Green Slip Tulip, Pa., 1800s, 8 In.	1896.00 to 2370.00
Pie Plate, Green, Brown Slip, Diehl Pottery, Pa., c.1800s, 6 ¾ In.	1126.00
Pie Plate, Green, Yellow Combed Slip, Pa., 6 ½ In.	21330.00
Pie Plate, Peafowl Design, Pa., 1800s, 6 ⅜ In.	1067.00
Pie Plate, Slip Concentric Circle, Pa., 1800s, 9 ¼ In.	563.00
Pie Plate, Wavy Line, Yellow Slip, Pa., c.1850, 3 ⅞ In.	652.00
Pie Plate, Wavy Yellow Slip, 1800s, 9 In.	395.00
Pie Plate, Yellow Green Slip Ramona Singer, Bucks Co., Pa., c.1890, 8 ¼ In.	1541.00
Pie Plate, Yellow Slip Clef, Miniature, Pa., 1800s, 4 ⅜ In.	1007.00
Pie Plate, Yellow Slip Fern, 9 ¾ In.	1422.00
Pie Plate, Yellow Slip Star, Fern Sprigs, Pa., 1800s, 9 ¾ In.	504.00
Pie Plate, Yellow Slip, Green Splash, Pa., 1800s, 8 ¾ In.	889.00
Pie Plate, Yellow Slip, Pa., 9 In.	444.00 to 770.00
Pie Plate, Yellow, Brown Slip, Tulip Design, Dryville, Pa., 19th Century, 8 In.	1422.00
Pie Plate, Yellow, Brown Wavy Slip, Pa., 6 ⅞ In., Pair	1541.00
Pie Plate, Yellow, Green Slip Tulip, Diehl Pottery, 1800s, 8 ½ In.	11258.00
Pie Plate, Yellow, Green, Brown Tree, Stylized, Diehl Pottery, Pa., 1800s, 7 ⅞ In.	20145.00
Pie Plate, Yellow, Green, Brown Tulip Slip, Diehl Pottery, Pa., 1800s, 7 ¾ In.	17775.00
Pitcher, Batter, Lid, Manganese, Pa., 1800s, 8 ¼ In.	356.00
Pitcher, Batter, Manganese Flower Design, Squat, Oval, Coggled Shoulder, Handle, c.1865, 7 In.	1035.00
Pitcher, Bulbous, Applied Loop Handle, Manganese Glaze, Pa., 1800s, 2 In.	118.00
Pitcher, Green Copper Glaze, Reeded Bands, Lid, c.1800, 11 In.	9480.00
Pitcher, Green, Orange Mottled Glaze, Oval, Applied Ribbed Handle, New Eng., c.1835, 7 In.	431.00
Pitcher, Incised Eagle, Spread Wing, Jacob Medinger, 5 ¼ In.	1007.00
Pitcher, Lid, Splashed Manganese, Orange Ground, Loop Handle, New England, c.1820, 6 ½ In.	
115.00 **Pitcher,** Manganese Glaze, Pulled Spout, Applied Handle, 7 ½ x 5 ¼ In. ....*Illus*	47.00
Pitcher, Manganese Splatter, c.1850, 10 In.	365.00
Pitcher, Manganese Splotches, Round, Rolled Rim, Loop Handle, Foot Bead, 7 ¼ In.	47.00
Pitcher, Milk, Brown Glaze, C-Scroll Handle, Pinched Spout, 4 ¼ In.	144.00
Pitcher, Milk, Manganese Glaze, Ribbed Handle, 1800s, 5 In.	518.00
Pitcher, Mottled Tan, Green & Brown Splash Decoration, 6 ½ In.	2070.00
Pitcher, Oval, Applied Handle, Orange & Green Mottled Glaze, Green Slip, c.1870, 10 ½ In.	470.00

Rookwood, Vase, American Indian, Portrait, Standard Glaze, Governor Of The San Juan Pueblo, 9 In.
$5,175.00

Humler & Nolan

Rookwood, Vase, Deer, Ivory Jewel, Jens Jensen, 1934, 7 x 3 ¾ In.
$1,500.00

Rago Arts & Auction Center

Rookwood, Vase, Fish, Crabs, Gold Netting, Limoges Glaze, M.L. Nichols, Stand, 1882, 13 In.
$6,613.00

R

Humler & Nolan

Rookwood, Vase, Fish, Swimming, Green, Turquoise, Rose Fechheimer, 1905, 12 In.
$8,338.00

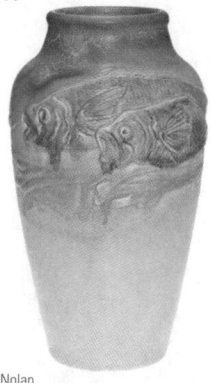

Humler & Nolan

TIP

Put foam or paper plates between the china plates stacked for storage.

Rookwood, Vase, Flowers, Diamond Grid, Mat Moderne, W. Rehm, 1931, 6 ⅞ In.
$748.00

Humler & Nolan

Rookwood, Vase, Flowers, Leaves, Black Opal Glaze, Sara Sax, Shirayamadani, 1927, 6 ¾ In.
$4,715.00

Humler & Nolan

Pitcher, Tapered Oval, Reeded Handle, Stippled Banding, Mottled, Streaked Flecks, c.1815, 10 In.	780.00
Plate, 3-Line Yellow Slip, Coggled Rim, Pa., c.1860, 11 ½ In.	288.00
Plate, Green, Brown Slip, Tulip, Dryville, Berks County Pa., c.1860, 8 In.	4888.00
Plate, Marriage, Sgraffito, Multicolor, Doves, Overlapping Heart, Tulips, Stahl Pottery, c.1948, 10 In.	403.00
Plate, Slip Tulip, Dryville, 1800s, 11 In.	563.00
Plate, Wavy Yellow Slip, Spotted, Striped Design, Coggled Rim, Pa., c.1830, 10 In.	345.00
Plate, Yellow & Green Slip Tulip, Flowers, Southeastern Pa., c.1810, 11 In.	14220.00
Plate, Yellow Clef Slips, Wavy Lines, c.1850, 9 In.	345.00
Plate, Yellow Slip, Pa., c.1830, 8 In.	236.00
Plate, Yellow Trails Coggled Rim, Sponge Border, Pa., c.1870, 9 ¾ In.	1725.00
Plate, Yellow Wavy Slip Trails, Clefs, Coggled Edge, c.1850, 9 ⅞ In.	1150.00
Plate, Yellow, Black Slip, c.1820, 8 ½ In.	189.00
Plate, Yellow, Brown Wavy Slip, Coggled Rim, Berks County, Pa., c.1870, 6 ⅞ In.	1035.00
Platter, Loaf, Slip Squiggle Lines, Oval, Stamped J. McCully, 16 ¾ x 11 In.	1458.00
Platter, Manganese Glaze, Border, Green Slip Fish, Scalloped Edge, 16 ½ x 14 In.	12.00
Pot Stand, Daniel In The Den Relief, Black, Stamped John Bell Waynesboro, Pa., c.1860, 9 ¾ In..	652.00
Puzzle Jug, Cylindrical, Loop Handle, 7 Shaped Holes, 8 ¾ In.	83.00
Rattle, Bird, Pa., 1800s, 3 In.	1007.00 to 1778.00
Serving Bowl, Slab Dividers, Salt Glazed, 3 x 12 x 7 ⅜ In.	83.00
Shaving Mug, Manganese Glaze, Divided Soap Compartment, Loop Handle, 4 In.	83.00
Stein, Pewter Lid, Ball Thumbpiece, Strap Handle, Narrow Neck, 7 Figures, Shields, c.1671, 10 In..	1094.00
Sugar, Glazed, Stepped Shoulder, Orange Ground, Signed Isaac Boyer, Pa., 1848, 3 ¾ In.	1150.00
Sugar, Green Glaze, Bird Finial, Anthony Baecher, Winchester, Va., c.1880, 4 ⅜ In.	47150.00
Sugar, Lid, Manganese Splash, Berks Co., Pa., c.1850, 3 ½ x 4 ½ In.	593.00
Sugar, Lid, Oval, Handles, Flared Rim, Yellow, Green Copper Sponging, Finial, c.1815, 4 ¾ In. .	1035.00
Sugar, Olive & Spotted Orange, Lead Glaze, Flat Rim, Tab Handles, Footed, c.1870, 3 x 4 In. ..	201.00
Tart Plate, Yellow, Green Wavy Lines, Grid, Dot Pattern, Pa., c.1850, 4 ½ In.	18960.00
Tart Plate, Yellow, Green, Manganese Slip, Wavy Lines, Stars, Pa., c.1870, 4 ⅞ In.	6518.00
Tray, Match Holder, Dog Finial, Manganese Splash, c.1800, 3 ½ x 6 ½ In.	1185.00
Trencher, Combed Yellow Slip Decoration, Coggled Rim, 3 x 16 x 11 In.	708.00
Urn, Coggled Rim, Manganese, Brown Glaze, 2 Ribbed Handles, 1800s, 11 In.	805.00
Vase, Applied Heart, Glazed, Flared Rim, Open Handles, Signed, W.W. Cline, Indiana, 1904, 6 ¼ In.	920.00
Vase, Cylindrical, Flared Base, Rim, Impressed, John Bell, c.1880, 7 ½ In.	317.00
Vase, Green Glaze, Thumbprint Rim, Shenandoah Valley, c.1890, 3 In.	273.00
Wall Pocket, Mask, Yellow Glaze, Green, Brown, D.P. Shenfelder, Reading, 10 ¾ x 9 In.	16590.00

REGOUT, *see Maastricht category.*

RICHARD was the mark used on acid-etched cameo glass vases, bowls, night-lights, and lamps made by the Austrian company Loetz after 1918. The pieces were very similar to the French cameo glasswares made by Daum, Galle, and others.

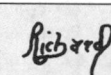

Vase, Lake Scene, Tall Trees, Cabin, Bridge, Mountains, Cameo, Signed, 10 ¼ In. *Illus*	403.00

RIDGWAY pottery has been made in the Staffordshire district in England since 1808 by a series of companies with the name Ridgway. Ridgway became part of Royal Doulton in the 1960s. The transfer-design dinner sets are the most widely known product. Other pieces of Ridgway may be listed under Flow Blue.

Bowl, Oriental Pattern, Gold Rim, Blue Transfer, Man, Camel, Buildings, 8 x 6 In.	55.00
Dish, Dessert, Pierced Handles, Scalloped Border, Castle, Yellow, 19th Century, 10 x 10 In., Pair	650.00
Gravy Boat, Attached Underplate, Willow, England, c.1920, 9 x 6 In.	275.00
Jug, Bulrushes Pattern, Blue Gray Salt Glaze, Black Metal Lid, c.1848, 8 ¾ In.	285.00
Jug, Bundle Of Bamboo, Green Gray, c.1835, 7 ½ In.	174.00
Jug, Tan, Salt Glazed, Robert Burns Tam-O'-Shanter, 1835, 9 ¼ x 7 ½ In.	120.00
Mug, Racing The Mail, Black, Tan, 4 In., Pair	45.00
Pitcher, Jousting Knights, Grape & Leaf Design On Base, Pewter Hinged Lid, c.1840, 6 In.	595.00
Pitcher, Milk, Willow, Blue & White Transfer, 7 ¾ In.	65.00
Plate, Child's, Temple Pattern, Blue, 3 ⅞ In.	55.00
Plate, Grecian Pattern, Green, Transfer, 9 ½ In.	100.00
Plate, Nankin Jar Pattern, Blue Gray, Transfer, c.1840, 10 ½ In.	75.00
Platter, Oxford Views, Wadham College, Flower Border, Blue & White, Octagonal, c.1835, 17 In.	486.00
Toast Rack, Leaf Knob, 6 x 2 ¾ x 3 In.	50.00

RIFLES *that are firearms are not listed in this book. BB guns and air rifles are listed in the Toy category.*

RIVIERA dinnerware was made by the Homer Laughlin Co. of Newell, West Virginia, from 1938 to 1950. The pattern was similar in coloring and in mood to Fiesta and Harlequin. The Riviera plates and cup handles were square. For more prices, go to kovels.com.

Green, Bowl, Vegetable, Lid, Rectangular	104.00
Green, Creamer	15.00 to 16.00
Green, Gravy Boat	39.00
Green, Pepper	11.00
Green, Sugar	10.00
Ivory, Creamer	20.00
Ivory, Plate, Bread & Butter, 6 ¼ In.	9.00
Ivory, Platter, Oval, 13 In.	45.00
Mauve Blue, Cup, Footed	22.00
Mauve Blue, Plate, 9 In.	139.00
Mauve Blue, Platter, Oval, 13 In.	49.00
Mauve Blue, Sugar, Lid	29.00
Orange, Salt & Pepper	11.00
Red, Baker, 9 x 6 In.	24.00
Red, Creamer	22.00
Red, Pepper	20.00
Red, Sugar	28.00
Turquoise, Butter, Cover	95.00
Yellow, Bowl, Vegetable, Lid, Rectangular	159.00
Yellow, Creamer	16.00
Yellow, Cup, Footed	19.00
Yellow, Gravy Boat	54.00
Yellow, Plate, 9 In.	110.00
Yellow, Platter, Oval	44.00
Yellow, Shaker, Pepper	17.00

ROCKINGHAM, in the United States, is a pottery with a brown glaze that resembles tortoiseshell. It was made from 1840 to 1900 by many American potteries. Mottled brown Rockingham wares were first made in England at the Rockingham factory. Other types of ceramics were also made by the English firm. Related pieces may be listed in the Bennington category.

Cup, Cylindrical, Applied Lizard, Leaf, Acorns, Moth, Brown Glaze, c.1890, 3 ½ In.	144.00
Figurine, Dog, Spaniel, Red Brown Glaze, c.1890, 10 ½ In.	106.00
Figurine, Spaniel, Seated, 10 ¾ In.	325.00
Flask, Book Shape, Mottled Brown Glaze, c.1870, 5 ½ x 2 In., Pt.	150.00
Flask, Fruit Basket Shape, Footed Base, Streaky Brown Glaze, 1800s, 7 In.	201.00
Milk Pan, Yellowware, Glazed, 12 In.	47.00
Mixing Bowl, Mottled Brown Glaze, Flared, Rolled Rim, 19th Century, 4 ½ x 9 In.	90.00
Pitcher, 6-Sided, Streaky Brown Glaze, Ornate Handle, E. Bennett, c.1850	29.00
Pitcher, Firemen, Fire Engine, Grapevines, Hound Handle, 1800s, 9 In.	748.00
Pitcher, Hunting Scene, Hound Chasing Deer, Brown Over Cream Glaze, c.1860, 6 ½ In.	86.00
Pitcher, Peacock & Tree, Tankard Shape, Mottled Brown Over Yellow Glaze, Loop Handle, 8 In.	29.00
Pitcher, Presentation, Anchor, Leaf, Frog, Brown Glaze, Smokestack, Hand Signed, 1886	1495.00
Shaving Mug, Portly Man, Streaky Brown Glaze, Twig Handle, Signed, E. Bennett, c.1850, 4 In.	173.00
Sugar, Dome Lid, Rebekah At The Well, Streaky Brown, E. Bennett, Baltimore, c.1850, 6 In.	144.00

ROGERS, *see John Rogers category.*

ROOKWOOD pottery was made in Cincinnati, Ohio, from 1880 to 1960. All of this art pottery is marked, most with the famous flame mark. The *R* is reversed and placed back to back with the letter *P*. Flames surround the letters. After 1900, a Roman numeral was added to the mark to indicate the year. The company went bankrupt in 1941. For several years various owners tried to revive the pottery, but by 1967 it was out of business. The name and some of the molds were bought by a collector in 1984. In 2005, Christopher Rose and his brother, Patrick, bought the company and 3,700 original molds, the name, and trademark. Today they make architectural tile, art pottery, and special commissions.

Ashtray, Bronze, Round, Fish, Swirling Water, Blue Eye, Marked, E.T. Hurley, ½ x 3 ¾ In.	633.00
Ashtray, Fish Shape, Cream, 1945, 9 ¼ In.	40.00
Ashtray, Green Glaze, Reclining German Shepherd On Rim, 6 ½ In.	104.00
Ashtray, Pelican Shape, Blue & Tan Matte Glaze, c.1930, 4 x 6 In.	403.00
Bookends, Blackbird, Light Brown Matte Glaze, Shirayamadani, 1929, 5 ½ In. ....*Illus*	489.00
Bookends, Dog, Collie, Chestnut Matte Glaze, W. McDonald, 1929, 6 In. ....*Illus*	431.00

Rookwood, Vase, Flowers, Long Stems, Shaded Blue Ground, Shirayamadani, 1945, 7 ¾ In.
$1,560.00

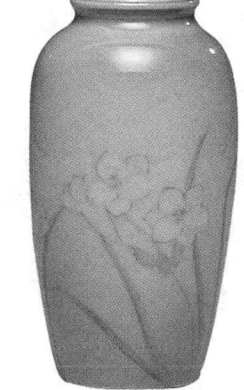

Cowan's Auctions

Rookwood, Vase, Plants, Flowers, Limoges Style, Handles, Maria Nichols, Marked 1882 MLN, 10 ½ x 6 ¾ In.
$1,750.00

Rago Arts & Auction Center

Rorstrand, Bowl, Pink Flowers, Green Stems, Reticulated Rim, Marked, 2 ⅞ x 5 ⅛ In.
$518.00

Humler & Nolan

R

Rookwood Ink Stamp Mark
Henry Farny, who is now best-known for his western paintings, designed the ink stamp mark first used by Rookwood in 1881.

ROOKWOOD

Rose Mandarin, Pitcher, Palace Scenes, Ivory Glaze, Butterflies, Flowers, Gilt Highlights, c.1850, 9 ½ In. $2,645.00

James D. Julia Auctioneers

Rose Medallion, Bottle, Figures, Flowers, 19th Century, 12 ¼ In. $448.00

Sloans & Kenyon

Rose Medallion, Dish, Lid, Hot Water, Figures, Flowers, 19th Century, 17 In. $1,673.00

Sloans & Kenyon

TIP

When storing dishes, glassware, and especially textiles, don't use old newspapers for wrapping. The ink will come off and may leave permanent stains.

Bookends, Eagle, Spread Wings, Sideward Glancing, Black Glaze, Rectangular Base, c.1931, 7 In..	748.00
Bookends, Girl Leaning On Bench, Holding Book, Blue Glaze, 1927, 5 ½ In.	360.00
Bookends, Penguins, Brown & Gray Glaze, 1924, 5 ¾ In. ....*Illus*	1320.00
Bookends, Rook, Blue Glaze, 5 ⅜ In.	213.00
Bookends, Rooks, Green Matte Glaze, William McDonald, 1921, 6 ¼ In.	1003.00
Bookends, Union Terminal, Ivory Matte Glaze, Arthur Conant, 1933, 4 ½ x 7 In.	7188.00
Bookends, Water Lily, Turquoise High Glaze, Tray Base, Marked, c.1945, 3 ⅝ In.	81.00
Bowl, Blue Glaze, 1925, 10 In.	107.00
Bowl, Brown, Tan, 1922, 6 ¾ In.	35.00
Bowl, Fern, Yellow Matte Glaze, Impressed, 1910, 7 ½ x 2 ¾ In. ....*Illus*	316.00
Bowl, Green Matte Glaze, Red Berries, Leaves, Squat, Wide Rim, c.1907, 1 ½ x 7 ½ In.	288.00
Bowl, Green Vellum Glaze, Lotus Blooms, Yellow Squat, Rounded, c.1909, 1 ⅝ x 6 In.	748.00
Bowl, Pansies, Handles, Sallie Toohey, 1888, 7 x 2 In.	406.00
Bust, Woman, Downward Cast Eyes, Ivory Glaze, 1929, 8 In.	240.00
Candleholder, Water Lily, Mustard Yellow, 1924, 5 ¼ In.	115.00
Candlestick, Bronze, Seahorse, Round Tray Base, Rolled Rim, c.1905, 6 ¾ In.	431.00
Candlestick, Runny Green Glaze, Flared Base, 6 ¾ In., Pair	122.00
Candlestick, Seahorse Supports, Ivory Glaze, 3-Sided, 1930, 4 In., Pair	270.00
Ewer, Bird, Leafy Trees, Bulbous, Ruffled Rim, Ring Foot, Scroll Handle, 1884, 11 ⅜ In.	575.00
Ewer, Irises, Blue, Brown, Green, S-Handle, Ruffled Spout, 1902, 15 In.	575.00
Ewer, Pansy, Standard Glaze, Constance Baker, 1896, 10 ¾ In.	885.00
Ewer, Wild Roses, Brown & Amber Glaze, Globular, Squat, Ruffled Rim, c.1895, 6 In.	138.00
Humidor, Lid, Deep Brown Glaze, Ball Finial, 1955, 7 In.	138.00
Humidor, Pipes, Matches, Holly, Standard Glaze, Cylindrical, Round Knob, c.1898, 7 In.	431.00
Jardiniere, Green Matte Glaze, Shouldered, Rolled Rim, 1905, 16 x 12 In.	488.00
Jug, Portrait, Man, Standard Glaze, Sturgis Laurence, 1896, 5 x 4 ¾ In.	500.00
Jug, Whiskey, Green Matte Glaze, Bulbous, Handle, Flame Stopper, 1906, 7 ⅞ In.	460.00
Mug, Lion, Standard Glaze, E.T. Hurley, 1898, 4 ⅝ In. ....*Illus*	1093.00
Mug, Stars Come Out, Oglala Sioux, Standard Glaze, 3 Handles, G. Young, 8 x 9 In.	1375.00
Paperweight, Cat, Seated, Wine Madder Glaze, 1945, 6 ⅝ In.	345.00
Paperweight, Clowns, Elephant, Black Over Blue Glaze, Rectangular Base, Marked, c.1923, 3 ½ In..	518.00
Paperweight, Duck, Marbled Green Glaze, 1929, 3 ½ In.	240.00
Paperweight, Elephant, Blue & Green Matte Glaze, 1945, 3 ¾ x 4 In.	356.00
Paperweight, Elephant, Standing, Blue Matte Glaze, Rectangular Base, 1926, 3 ⅞ In.	403.00
Paperweight, Female Nude, Sitting, Ivory Glaze, 1930, 4 ¼ x 4 In.	330.00
Paperweight, Foo Dog, Seated, Pink Matte Glaze, Rectangular Base, Marked, c.1924, 3 ¾ x 4 ⅝ In.	460.00
Paperweight, Impressed Verse, Red, Black, Round Green Base, 1937, 3 ½ x 3 ¼ In.	1750.00
Paperweight, Monkey, Chestnut Matte Glaze, Shirayamadani, 1930, 3 ⅞ In. ....*Illus*	316.00
Paperweight, Pelican, Standing, Ivory Matte Glaze, Square Base, 1936, 4 ¾ In.	633.00
Paperweight, Tulip, Leaves, Rectangular, Molded, Green Matte Glaze, 1904, 4 ⅝ x 2 ⅜ In.	748.00
Pin Tray, Female Nude On Rim, Ivory Glaze, 1947, 4 ½ In.	330.00
Pitcher, Birds Flying, Lacy Clouds, Oriental Grasses, Albert Valentien, 1885, 9 ½ In. ....*Illus*	460.00
Pitcher, Butterflies, Bulbous, Angular Handle, A. Valentien, 1883, 7 ¾ In.	281.00
Pitcher, Crabs, Waves, Crushed Shape, Loop Handle, Maria Longworth Nichols, 1883, 8 In.....*Illus*	1495.00
Pitcher, Crucible, Hops, Standard Glaze, Tapered, Wide Rim, 3 Spouts, c.1907, 5 ⅝ In.	359.00
Pitcher, Flowers, Peach, Black Glaze, Silver Overlay, 6 ¾ In.	1896.00
Pitcher, Incised Clouds, Flowers, Smear Glaze, Chaplet Style, Albert Valentien, 1884, 8 In. ....*Illus*	805.00
Pitcher, Iris, Brown, Blue, Ball Shape, S-Handle, Ruffled Rim, 1891, 11 ½ x 6 In.	3375.00
Pitcher, Swallows, Leaves, Albert Valentien, 1882, 7 ¼ In.	705.00
Planter, Olive Green Glaze, Rectangular, Geometric Border, Loop Handles, 1926, 4 x 11 ⅞ In.	316.00
Plaque, Autumn Landscape, Vellum Glaze, Fred Rothenbusch, Frame, 1914, 16 x 14 In.	4000.00
Plaque, Autumn, Vellum Glaze, Fred Rothenbusch, Frame, 1914, 11 x 8 In.	4880.00
Plaque, Lake In Landscape, Vellum Glaze, Sara Sax, Frame, c.1915, 12 x 17 ½ In.	5313.00
Plaque, Landscape, Stream, Wooded Banks, Trees, Pale Blue, Green, Vellum Glaze, 1919, 9 x 13 In.	5750.00
Plaque, Landscape, Vellum Glaze, E.T. Hurley, Frame, 1942, 15 x 17 ½ In.	4270.00
Plaque, Landscape, Vellum Glaze, Trees, Stream, C. Schmidt, 1917, 9 ⅜ In. ....*Illus*	2990.00
Plaque, Quiet Reflections, Venice, Vellum Glaze, Carl Schmidt, 1921, 10 x 13 In.	2500.00
Plaque, The Hillside, Vellum Glaze, Lenore Asbury, 1913, 4 ½ x 8 ½ In.	1062.00
Sign, Rook On Branch, Dark Blue, Green Leaves, 1915, 4 x 8 ½ In. ....*Illus*	6038.00
Tile, Fish, Swirling Waters, Oak Arts & Crafts Frame, E.T. Hurley, 9 x 12 ⅜ In. ....*Illus*	1035.00
Tile, Flowers, Faience, Oak Frame, 9 x 9 In.	275.00
Tile, Peacocks, Sipping From Fountain, Green, Turquoise, Square, Faience, 11 ¾ x 11 ⅗ In. ..	748.00
Tile, Rook, Poppy, Faience, Matte Glaze, Sallie Toohey, 10 ½ x 8 ½ In.	3250.00
Tile, Rooster, Gold, Turquoise, Red, Square, Frame, c.1924, 5 ⅝ x 5 ⅝ In.	575.00
Tile, Rose, Green, Brown, Pink, Tan Matte Glaze, Faience, Oak Frame, 10 x 10 In.	281.00
Tile, Seahorse, Gray, Purple, Tan Matte Glaze, Faience, Oak Frame, 7 x 7 In.	594.00

R

Tile, Ship, Faience, Round, 12 In.	875.00
Tile, Stork, Wings Up, Pink Matte, Lavender, Yellow, Green, Square, Marked, c.1930, 5 ½ In.	173.00
Tile, Swan, On Water, Faience, Frame, 8 ½ x 10 ½ In.	4600.00
Tile, Tea, Dove, Latticework, Roses, Pink, Blue, Yellow, 1924, 5 ⅝ In.	230.00
Trinket Box, Lid, Reclining Nude On Lid, Rounded Square, Blue Matte Glaze, 3 ½ In.	316.00
Trivet, Dutch Mother & Children, Harbor, Square, Impressed, 1927, 5 ¾ In. ....*Illus*	173.00
Trivet, Dutch Mother & Children, Windmill, Boat On Sea, Multicolor, 1930, 5 ½ x 5 ½ In.	84.00
Trivet, Flower Basket, Butterflies, Blue, Impressed Logo, 1930, 5 ½ x 5 ½ In. ....*Illus*	120.00
Tyg, Bats, Gold Plating, Pink Poppies, Iris Glaze, Cylindrical, Swollen, c.1899, 9 ⅜ In.	9200.00
Vase, 3 Ducks, Strutting, Spiky Flower Stalks, Blue & Cream, c.1931, 5 ½ In.	1150.00
Vase, 4 Flowers, 8-Petal, Embossed, Mottled Green Glaze, Buttressed Rim, 1929, 6 In.	180.00
Vase, American Indian, Portrait, Standard Glaze, Governor Of The San Juan Pueblo, 9 In..... *Illus*	5175.00
Vase, Band Of Swirls, Green Matte Glaze, Z Line, Bulbous, Marked, 1903, 5 ⅛ In.	489.00
Vase, Bengal Brown Glaze, Handkerchief Shape, 1959, 8 In.	173.00
Vase, Black Iris Glaze, Bulbous, Carl Schmidt, 1907, 5 x 8 ½ In.	10625.00
Vase, Black Opal, Cylindrical, 11 ½ In.	265.00
Vase, Black Opal, White Roses, Beaker, Flared Foot, c.1924, 5 ¾ In.	690.00
Vase, Black Ruby Tulips, Green Leaves, Matte Glaze, Shouldered, Rolled Rim, 1925, 11 In.	3105.00
Vase, Blue Green Butter Fat Glaze, Wax Matte, Kathrine Jones, 1929, 9 ¼ In.	449.00
Vase, Blue Matte Glaze, Geometric, Squat, Footed, c.1910, 3 ½ x 6 In.	288.00
Vase, Blue Matte Glaze, Green, Red, Oval, Swollen Shoulder, Rolled Rim, 1921, 6 In.	420.00
Vase, Blue Matte Glaze, Rose Hip Band At Neck, Flared Lip, c.1936, 4 ½ In.	108.00
Vase, Bluebird, Berry Branches, Orange, Gray, Vellum Glaze, Elongated Oval, 1917, 11 In.	1554.00
Vase, Branches, Bands, Turquoise & Cobalt Blue, Urn Shape, Round Foot, c.1928, 6 ¼ In.	863.00
Vase, Brown Glaze, Embossed Design, 1915, 5 ¾ In.	196.00
Vase, Brown Leaves, Scrolling, Green Matte Ground, Tapered, 1921, 12 ¼ x 6 In.	938.00
Vase, Brown, Frosted Overlay, High Shoulder, 5 ¾ In.	253.00
Vase, Brown, Green, Vertical Lines, 6 ½ In.	276.00
Vase, Bud, Gray, Red, Squat, Tapered, 1912, 3 ¼ In.	150.00
Vase, California Poppies, Yellow, Blue, Jewel Porcelain, K. Shirayamadani, 1922, 9 In.	3375.00
Vase, Calla Lily, Molded, Mottled Brown Glaze, Flared, 1922, 14 In.	275.00
Vase, Calla Lily, Molded, Mottled Brown Matte Glaze, Flared, 1922, 5 x 14 ½ In.	336.00
Vase, Calla Lily, White, Green, Yellow, Elongated Oval, Rolled Rim, c.1903, 5 ½ In.	633.00
Vase, Cherry Blossom Sprigs, Vellum Glaze, Tapered, Swollen Neck, E. Hurley, 8 In.	375.00
Vase, Cherry Blossoms, White, Yellow Vellum, Elongated Oval, Rolled Rim, c.1926, 6 ½ In.	920.00
Vase, Clematis, Blue, White, Purple, Smokestack, Flared Rim, c.1925	3565.00
Vase, Clematis, Leaves, Vines, Turquoise, Tapered, Swollen Neck, Ring Foot, c.1928, 5 ½ x 7 In.	575.00
Vase, Clover, Brown Standard Glaze, Clara Lindeman, 1914, 7 ½ In.	472.00
Vase, Clover, Vellum Glaze, Cylindrical, Folded In Rim, Lorinda Epply, 1906, 6 x 3 In.	531.00
Vase, Crocus, Iris Glaze, Bulbous, Carl Schmidt, 1908, 9 ½ In.	1800.00
Vase, Crocus, Multicolor, Iris Glaze, Bulbous, Carl Schmidt, 1908, 5 x 9 ½ In.	2196.00
Vase, Dark Green Glaze, Tapered, 1923, 7 ¼ In.	130.00
Vase, Dark Purple Matte Glaze, Cylindrical, Banding, c.1922, 6 ½ In.	345.00
Vase, Deer, Ivory Jewel, Jens Jensen, 1934, 7 x 3 ¾ In. ....*Illus*	1500.00
Vase, Deer, Leaping, Crystalline Matte Glaze, Blue, Green, Elongated Oval, 1927, 16 ¾ In.	2300.00
Vase, Diamonds, Triangles, Overlapping, Purple, Jewel Porcelain, Shirayamadani, 12 In.	5000.00
Vase, Dogwood Blossoms, Gold Trim, Round, Stand-Up Rim, H. Peachey, 1882, 7 In.	625.00
Vase, Dogwood, White, Pink, Blue, Vellum Glaze, Swollen, Flared Rim, Ring Foot, 1945, 6 ⅜ In.	1093.00
Vase, Dragon, Standard Glaze, Long Neck, Bulbous Base, Sturgis Laurence, c.1900, 9 ¼ In.	975.00
Vase, Dragonflies, Vellum Glaze, Cylindrical, Carl Schmidt, 1904, 4 x 8 ½ In. ....*Illus*	1375.00
Vase, Dragonfly, Berry Branches, Mahogany Glaze, Tapered, c.1884, 11 ⅝ In.	2300.00
Vase, Eagle Owl, Iris Glaze, Bulbous, Grace Young, 1904, 5 x 9 In.	2000.00
Vase, Fish, Blue Green Glaze, Rose Fechheimer, 1904, 4 ½ x 4 ½ In.	1298.00
Vase, Fish, Crabs, Gold Netting, Limoges Glaze, M.L. Nichols, Stand, 1882, 13 In. ....*Illus*	6613.00
Vase, Fish, Swimming, Green, Turquoise, Rose Fechheimer, 1905, 12 In. ....*Illus*	8338.00
Vase, Flower Band, Blue & Green, Purple Ground, Matte Glaze, Vera Tischler, 1924, 8 ½ In.	480.00
Vase, Flower Band, Turquoise Matte Glaze, Oval, M.H. McDonald, 1924, 9 In.	688.00
Vase, Flower, Blue Matte Glaze, Tapered, 1928, 6 ¼ In.	277.00
Vase, Flower, Embossed, Art Deco Style, Mottled Teal Green Glaze, Oval, 1928, 5 ¾ In.	270.00
Vase, Flowers, Blue, Brown, Green, Copper High Gloss Glaze, Lorinda Epply, 1926, 11 ½ In.	1955.00
Vase, Flowers, Blue, Gray Ground, Round, 5 ½ In.	167.00
Vase, Flowers, Brown Ground, Charles Jasper McLaughlin, 7 In.	403.00
Vase, Flowers, Brown Rose Ground, Blue Mottled Glaze, c.1925, 10 In.	805.00
Vase, Flowers, Diamond Grid, Mat Moderne, W. Rehm, 1931, 6 ⅞ In. ....*Illus*	748.00
Vase, Flowers, Green Matte Glaze, 1912, 6 ½ x 15 ½ In.	2196.00
Vase, Flowers, Leaves, Amber, Yellow, Blue, Square, Shouldered, Ring Foot, c.1914, 8 ½ In.	1495.00

Rose Medallion, Teapot, Scenic Panels, Wicker Wrapped Handles, Fitted Woven Carrier, Silk Lined, c.1900, 7 In. $84.00

DuMouchelles Art Gallery

Roseville, Baneda, Vase, Pink, Handles, 10 ½ x 8 In. $563.00

Rago Arts & Auction Center

Roseville, Della Robbia, Vase, Fish, Incised, Rozane, c.1910, 10 ½ x 3 ½ In. $3,125.00

Rago Arts & Auction Center

R

Roseville, Della Robbia, Vase, Grapes & Vines, Marked, Rozane, 10 ¼ In. $1,955.00

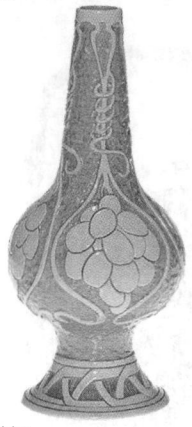

Humler & Nolan

Roseville, Della Robbia, Vase, Poppies, Carved Flowers, Seed Pods, Marked, 14 ¼ In. $11,213.00

Humler & Nolan

Roseville, Della Robbia, Vase, Wild Roses, Cutout Rim, Marked, Rozane, c.1910, 15 ½ x 6 In. $43,750.00

Rago Arts & Auction Center

Vase, Flowers, Leaves, Black Opal Glaze, Sara Sax, Shirayamadani, 1927, 6 ¾ In.............*Illus*	4715.00
Vase, Flowers, Leaves, Black, Green Glaze, Rectangular, Rounded Corners, c.1925, 4 ¾ In.......	518.00
Vase, Flowers, Leaves, Brown, Yellow Matte Glaze, 1927, 3 ½ x 9 In.......	406.00
Vase, Flowers, Leaves, Pale Pink, Blue, White, Pear Shape, Sara Sax, 1927, 5 x 3 In.	1375.00
Vase, Flowers, Leaves, Pink, Lavender, Wax Matte Glaze, Bulbous, Janet Harris, 1930, 5 ½ x 7 In.	688.00
Vase, Flowers, Leaves, Spiraling Tendrils, Green, Blue, Purple, Squat, Ring Foot, c.1922, 5 ⅛ In. ...	230.00
Vase, Flowers, Long Stems, Shaded Blue Ground, Shirayamadani, 1945, 7 ¾ In.............*Illus*	1560.00
Vase, Flowers, Mahogany Glaze, Bottle Form, Grace Hall, 1903, 6 x 3 ¼ In........	127.00
Vase, Flowers, Molded, Blue Green Glaze, Cylindrical, c.1924, 11 ¾ In........	142.00
Vase, Flowers, Pierced, Pale Green Glaze, Z Line, Squat, 1901, 4 x 6 In........	938.00
Vase, Flowers, Pink, Blue, Cream Ground, Flared Mouth, 1944, 5 ¾ In........	265.00
Vase, Flowers, Snow Drops, Purple, Shouldered, Rolled Rim, 1924, 5 ½ x 3 In........	750.00
Vase, Flowers, Wax Matte Glaze, Tapered, Elizabeth Lincoln, 1929, 4 x 8 ¼ In........	938.00
Vase, Flowers, Yellow Matte Glaze, Urn Shape, Rolled Rim, c.1940, 5 In........	207.00
Vase, Fruit & Flowers, Molded, Green Crystalline Glaze, Oval, 1924, 4 ¼ In........	94.00
Vase, Geisha, Holding Fan, Standard Glaze, Cylindrical, G. Young, 1900, 10 ¼ In........	8913.00
Vase, Geometric, Green & Tan Rectangles, Vellum Glaze, Waisted, E. Hurley, 1913, 6 In.........	1000.00
Vase, Geometric, Green Over Pink Matte Glaze, Tapered Neck, c.1905, 5 ⅜ In........	288.00
Vase, Green, Brown, Tapered, 1885, 11 ¼ In........	1035.00
Vase, Green, Embossed, 1929, 4 ½ In........	150.00
Vase, Green, Pink Matte Glaze, Impressed Art Nouveau Decoration, Pinched Neck, 5 ¾ In.	83.00
Vase, Hops, Brown, Green, Jug Shape, Flattened Flared Rim, Handles, c.1890, 15 x 12 ½ In. ...	1495.00
Vase, Horses, Rider, Red, Dark Blue, Mottling, Urn Shape, 1934, 5 ¼ x 4 ½ In........	1375.00
Vase, Irises, Carved, Ombroso, Swollen Neck, 1913, 6 ⅛ In.	403.00
Vase, Jack-In-The-Pulpit, Blue & Green Frogskin Glaze, c.1922, 14 ½ In.	316.00
Vase, Landscape, Autumn Trees, Buildings, Vellum Glaze, Ed Diers, 1922, 8 x 17 ½ In.	1875.00
Vase, Landscape, Blue, Tan, Vellum Glaze, Edith Wildman, 1911, 3 x 8 In.	1098.00
Vase, Landscape, Kataro Shirayamadani, 1909, 7 x 14 ¼ In.	2625.00
Vase, Landscape, Lake, Trees, Grass, Vellum Glaze, Green, Blue, Elongated Oval, 1919, 9 x 4 In.	1375.00
Vase, Landscape, Seacoast, Vellum Glaze, Oval, E. Hurley, 1906, 8 ½ x 4 ½ In.	1125.00
Vase, Landscape, Shore, Swirling Water, Vellum, Edward T. Hurley, 1906, 9 ½ In.	1725.00
Vase, Landscape, Vellum Glaze, Carl Schmidt, c.1920, 10 ¼ In.	1000.00
Vase, Landscape, Vellum Glaze, Green, Blue, Cream Matte, Crackle, Cylindrical, 1914, 6 ¾ In.	708.00
Vase, Landscape, Water Reflection, Blue, Green, Vellum Glaze, Carl Schmidt, 1920, 4 x 10 In..	1220.00
Vase, Leaf Sprigs, Light Blue Ground, Mat Moderne, Swollen, 1931, 10 ½ In.	438.00
Vase, Leaves & Berries, Black Opal Glaze, Tapered, Kataro Shirayamadani, 1922, 7 ¾ In........	1464.00
Vase, Leaves, Green, Red Ground, Lobed, Tapered, 1930, 4 ¾ In.	345.00
Vase, Leaves, Pointed, Vertical, Green Matte Glaze, Arts & Crafts, 1912, 15 In.	1700.00
Vase, Leaves, Vertical, Green Matte Glaze, 1912, 6 ½ x 15 ½ In........	2074.00
Vase, Lily Of Valley, Blue, Vellum Glaze, Caroline Steinle, 1912, 7 ½ In.	177.00
Vase, Luna Moths, Green, Blue, Purple, Shouldered, Tapered, Rolled Rim, c.1905, 10 In........	3450.00
Vase, Magenta, Flared To Base, 7 In.	276.00
Vase, Mat Moderne, Incised Designs, Swollen, Flared Rim, E. Barrett, 1929, 8 In.	563.00
Vase, Meadow Scene, Vellum Glaze, Fred Rothenbusch, 1920, 9 ½ In........	1300.00
Vase, Monk Tending Garden, Aerial Blue Glaze, Bruce Horsfall, 1894, 4 x 7 In........	6250.00
Vase, Mottled Gray Glaze, Paneled, Cinched Waist, Buttressed Handles, 6 In........	118.00
Vase, Mustard, Flared, 4 Handles, Footed, 4 In........	144.00
Vase, Nasturtium, Iris Glaze, Cylindrical, Fred Rothenbusch, 1902, 8 x 3 ½ In........	1125.00
Vase, Orchids, Blue, White, Yellow, Pink, Vellum Glaze, Shouldered, 1930, 10 ¾ In........	2990.00
Vase, Oxblood Glaze, Oval, Tapered, 1951, 3 ¾ In.	180.00
Vase, Peacock Feathers, Green, Amber, Shouldered, Tapered, c.1895, 14 In.	4945.00
Vase, Peacock Feathers, Incised, Green Matte, Cinched Waist, Z Line, S. Toohey, 10 In.............	1063.00
Vase, Peacock Feathers, Mottled Blue, Green, Rounded Square, Pedestal Foot, c.1921, 6 ⅝ In.	161.00
Vase, Peonies, Iris Glaze, Olga Reed, 1903, 5 ½ x 14 In.	4270.00
Vase, Plants, Flowers, Limoges Style, Handles, Maria Nichols, Marked 1882 MLN, 10 ½ x 6 ¾ In... *Illus*	1750.00
Vase, Portrait, Beggar Woman, Brick Wall, Yellow, Amber Glaze, Square, Tapered, Pinched Neck, 7 In.	3335.00
Vase, Purple, Pink, Glossy Glaze, Squat, Upturned Square Handles, Rolled Rim, c.1935, 4 x 5 ½ In.....	219.00
Vase, Red Glaze, Tapered, 1915, 9 ¼ In.	81.00
Vase, Red, Glaze, Black Drip, Flare Rim, c.1932, 6 ¾ In........	431.00
Vase, Rooster, Pink Flowers, Blue, Gray High Glaze, Shouldered, c.1920, 14 ½ In.	3220.00
Vase, Rose, Embossed, Cylindrical, 1920, 11 ½ In.	339.00
Vase, Rose, Yellow, Iris Glaze, Shouldered, Cylindrical Neck, J. Zettel, 1902, 6 In.	5594.00
Vase, Roses, Yellow, Buff Ground, Rose Fechheimer, 1903, 9 ¾ In........	350.00
Vase, Scenic, Forest, Vellum Glaze, Swollen Shape, E.T. Hurley, 1913, 11 ¾ In.	1763.00
Vase, Scenic, Mountains, Trees, Yellow Ground, 10 ½ In.	1955.00
Vase, Scenic, Summer Trees, Lake, Vellum, Tapered, E.T. Hurley, 1938, 11 ½ In.	2185.00

Vase, Sea Foam Glaze, Double Handles, c.1930, 4 x 5 In.	108.00
Vase, Sheep, Shepherdess, Pale Blue, White, Swollen Center, 1894, 5 ½ x 3 In.	2000.00
Vase, Stylized Arches, Carved, Brown Matte Glaze, Swollen, 1922, 10 ½ In.	400.00
Vase, Stylized Design, Dark Brown Matte Glaze, 1922, 7 x 10 ½ In.	488.00
Vase, Stylized Flower, Red Matte Glaze, Cylindrical, Swollen Neck, c.1922, 6 ½ In.	259.00
Vase, Stylized Flowers, Blue & Tan, Bulbous, 1945, 6 ½ x 7 In.	313.00
Vase, Thistles, Brown, Green Glaze, Katherine Hickman, c.1900, 11 ¾ In.	295.00
Vase, Triangles, Incised, Green, Tapered, 1921, 7 In.	184.00
Vase, Tulip, Ivory, Carved, Sea Green Glaze, Matt Daly, 1899, 5 x 5 ½ In.	5000.00
Vase, Tulips, Lavender, Blue Ground, White At Neck, Vellum Glaze, c.1915, 11 In.	161.00
Vase, Tulips, Oval, Neck Band, K. Shirayamadani, 7 ¼ In.	1410.00
Vase, Venetian Boat Scene, Iris Glaze, Carl Schmidt, 1902, 4 x 8 ½ In.	5938.00
Vase, Virginia Creeper, Brown & Amber Glaze, Globular, Squat, Flared Rim, c.1891, 7 ¼ In.	345.00
Vase, Wild Rose, Mahogany Glaze, Tiger Eye Shouldered, Tapered, c.1890, 5 ¾ In.	920.00
Vase, Wisteria, Blue, Green, Iris Glaze, Bulbous, Caroline Steinle, 1909, 4 x 6 ½ In.	875.00
Vase, Woodlands, Black, Green, Tapered, Spread Foot, Inverted Rim, 1909, 13 ½ x 6 In.	3625.00

RORSTRAND was established near Stockholm, Sweden, in 1726. By the nineteenth century Rorstrand was making English-style earthenware, bone china, porcelain, ironstone china, and majolica. The company is still working and is now owned by Fiskars Sweden. The three crown-mark has been used since 1884.

Bowl, Pink Flowers, Green Stems, Reticulated Rim, Marked, 2 ⅞ x 5 ⅛ In. ....*Illus*	518.00
Bowl, Vegetable, Blue Fire, Round, 1 ½ Qt.	150.00
Bust, Girl, Blond Hair, Blue Eyes, 3 ¾ In.	315.00
Cake Plate, Flora, 11 ¾ In.	70.00
Creamer, Lotta	20.00
Cup & Saucer, After Dinner, Blanca	12.00
Cup & Saucer, Elisabeth	36.00
Pitcher, Lid, Satyr Playing Music, Woman In Cart, Cupids, Birds, 13 ¾ In.	750.00
Plate, Bread & Butter, Brilliant, 6 ¾ In.	8.00
Plate, Christmas, Fisherman Holding Net, Boat, North Star, Box, 1969, 8 x 8 In.	85.00
Plate, Salad, Blanca, 9 ⅝ In.	8.00
Platter, Hunter, On Horse, Spearing Beast, Snowy Mountains, Flow Blue, c.1900, 9 In.	35.00
Platter, Majolica, Flowers, Oval, Crimped, 13 x 9 In.	55.00
Relish, Lotus, 3 Sections	54.00
Thimble, Crown, Stylized Snowflakes, Gilt, 1 In.	45.00
Umbrella Stand, Green, Brown Leaves, Flowers, Ivory Ground, Lobed, Marked, 26 ½ In.	354.00
Vase, Art Nouveau Style, Multicolor, Faience, 14 ¼ In.	395.00
Vase, Pillow, Wildflowers, Narrow Neck, 8 x 5 In.	95.00

ROSALINE, *see Steuben category.*

ROSE BOWLS were popular during the 1880s. Rose petals were kept in the open bowl to add fragrance to a room, a popular idea in a time of limited personal hygiene. The glass bowls were made with crimped tops, which kept the petals inside. Many types of Victorian art glass were made into rose bowls.

Amethyst, Flowers, Applied Blue Branches, Crimped Top, Victorian, 5 In.	47.00
Aqua, Opal Mottle, 1960s, 3 ½ In.	36.00
Blue Satin Glass, Flowers, 4 In.	125.00
Blue, Twisted, Bubbles, 5 ½ In.	41.00
Butterflies, Flowers, Raised Enameling, Gilt Trim, Footed, 5 In.	125.00
Cranberry, Swirl, North American Art Glass, 9 In.	122.00
Crimped Rim, Daisy & Fern, Northwood Glass, c.1890, 4 In.	141.00
Emerald Green, Applied Green Rigaree, Diamond Quilted, 1960s, 5 In.	60.00
Grape Clusters, Leaves, Fluted Curled Lip, 6-Footed, 4 ½ In.	49.00
Pink, Mother-of-Pearl Glass, Herringbone Pattern, c.1875, 3 In.	150.00
Pinwheels, Stars, Poland, 1900s	75.00
Ribbed, Melon Shape, Clear Pressed Glass, c.1940, 6 ½ In.	65.00
Yellow To White Satin Glass, c.1880, 3 In.	55.00

ROSE CANTON china is similar to Rose Mandarin and Rose Medallion, except that no people or birds are pictured in the decoration. It was made in China during the nineteenth and twentieth centuries in greens, pinks, and other colors.

Charger, Peonies, Butterflies, Green Scrollwork, Pink Lotus Flowers, c.1900, 15 In.	307.00

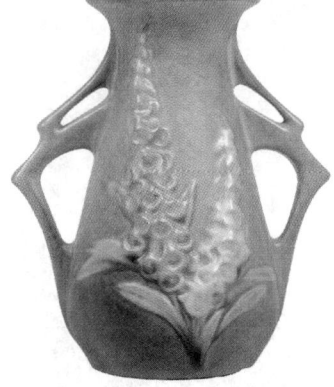

Roseville, Foxglove, Vase, Blue Green, Tapered, Angular Handles, 6 ¼ In. $71.00

Conestoga Auction Co., Inc.

Roseville, Fuchsia, Vase, Green, Pink, Flowers, Green Leaves, 2 Handles, 15 ½ In. $161.00

Humler & Nolan

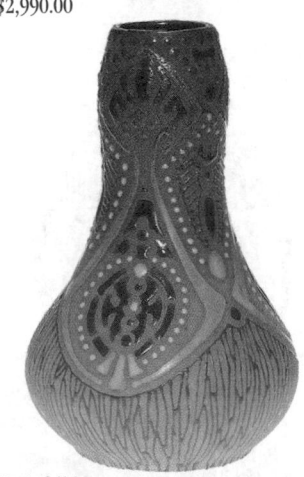

Roseville, Fudji, Vase, Blue & Green, Art Nouveau Decoration, 7 ¾ In. $2,990.00

Humler & Nolan

Roseville, Iris, Ewer, Green To Blue, Stepped Handle, 10 ½ In. $330.00

DuMouchelles Art Gallery

Roseville, Rozane Royal, Vase, 2 Kittens, Signed, C.L. Leffler, 19 ¾ In. $3,795.00

Humler & Nolan

R

Roseville, Sunflower, Vase, Green & Blue, Handles, 5 ¼ In. $266.00

Conestoga Auction Co., Inc.

ROSE MANDARIN china is similar to Rose Canton and Rose Medallion. If the panels in the design picture only people and not birds, it is Rose Mandarin.
v

Bowl, Handled Porringer, c.1830, 7 ½ In.	676.00
Bowl, Painted, Fox Hunt Scenes, 6 ½ x 16 In.	10073.00
Bowl, Palette, Flower Sprays, Butterflies, c.1785, 10 ¼ In.	1180.00
Bowl, Palette, Gilt Metal Mounted, Painted, Domestic Scenes, c.1784, 10 x 16 In.	1652.00
Bowl, Reserves, Flowers, Iron Red, Gilt, Wood Stand, 4 ⅜ x 10 In.	288.00
Bowl, Vegetable, Lid, Top & Side Handles, Figures, Palace Scenes, c.1870, 6 ½ x 12 In.	1495.00
Box, Fitted Lid, Blue Bats, Cash Coins, Floral Sprigs, 1800s, 3 ¼ x 8 ½ In.	518.00
Cider Jug, Lid, Finial, Swollen, Twist Loop Handle, Historical Scene, Figures, c.1830, 11 In.	799.00
Figurine, Dignitary, c.1820, 14 ¼ In.	3068.00
Jar, Lid, Foo Dog Finial, Gilt Mythical Creature Handles, 1785, 11 ¼ In., Pair	2360.00
Pen Box, Lid, Court Scene, 1800s, 6 ¾ x 3 ½ In.	896.00
Pitcher, Palace Scenes, Ivory Glaze, Butterflies, Flowers, Gilt Highlights, c.1850, 9 ½ In.*Illus*	2645.00
Plate, 8 ¾ In., 12 Piece	502.00
Plate, Birds, Butterfly Reserves, Allegorical Scene, Chinese, 1800s, 8 ½ In., 4 Piece	518.00
Plate, Flower Basket, Blue Vine Border, Octangular, c.1785, 9 In., Pair	826.00
Plate, Interior Scenes, Bird & Flower Border, 8 ½ In., 12 Piece	2478.00
Plate, Romances At The 3 Kingdoms, Butterfly, Flower Border, Gilt, Chinese, 1800s, 8 In., 5 Piece.	1955.00
Platter, Dome Lid, White Ground, c.1805, 8 x 15 ¾ In.	1840.00
Platter, Fish, Oval, Figures, Pavilion, Bird, Flower Border, 23 ½ x 10 In.	1610.00
Platter, Landscape Scenes, Oblong, Orange, Blue, 1800s, 9 ½ x 13 In., 4 Piece	2066.00
Punch Bowl, Figures, c.1830, 6 ½ x 16 In.	4025.00
Teapot, Figures, Pavilion, Garden, c.1830, 6 ¼ In.	720.00
Teapot, Flowers, Figures, Gilt, 2 Handles, 5 x 6 In.	84.00
Tray, Oval, Pavilion, Cover, Pinecone Knop, c.1850, 3 ½ x 11 In.	1150.00
Umbrella Stand, White, Painted, Palace Scenes, Flowers, Birds, Butterflies, c.1890, 24 x 9 In.	863.00
Vase, Dome Lid, Hexagonal Shape, Foo Dog Finial, 1900s, 17 In.	2300.00
Washbasin, Roses & Scroll Rim, Garden, c.1865, 5 x 16 In.	461.00

ROSE MEDALLION china was made in China during the nineteenth and twentieth centuries. It is a distinctive design with four or more panels of decoration around a central medallion that includes a bird or a peony. The panels show birds and people. The background is a design of tree peonies and leaves. Pieces are colored in greens, pinks, and other colors. It is similar to Rose Canton and Rose Mandarin.

Bottle, Figures, Flowers, 19th Century, 12 ¼ In. *Illus*	448.00
Bottle, Water, Gooseneck Shape, Lid, c.1840, 14 In.	978.00
Bowl, Butterflies, Flowers, Symbols, Round, Tapered, c.1905, 5 x 11 ½ In.	240.00
Bowl, Flowers, Figures, Gilt Rim, 1800s, 6 x 14 ⅜ In.	830.00
Bowl, Panels, Figures Conversing, Flowers, Birds, Insects, Wide Rim, Ring Foot, c.1890, 8 ¾ In.	173.00
Bowl, White Center, Flowers, Birds, Porcelain, 9 In.	120.00
Bowl, Wide Rim, Alternating Reserves, 4 ½ x 14 ½ In.	690.00
Chamber Pot, Famille Rose, Gilt Accents, Dome Lid, Loop Handle, 8 ⅝ In.	338.00
Charger, Radiating Figural, Bird, Flower Panels, c.1870, 14 ½ In.	189.00
Creamer, Famille Rose, Scalloped Rim, c.1900, 5 ⅜ In.	98.00
Dish, Lid, Hot Water, Figures, Flowers, 19th Century, 17 In. *Illus*	1673.00
Garden Seat, Barrel Shaped, Pierced, Faux Nail Heads, c.1885, 19 x 13 In.	676.00
Jar, Lid, Molded Gilt Dragons At Shoulder, Foo Dog Finial, c.1898, 25 ½ In.	1495.00
Jar, Lid, Panels, Garden, Flowers, 19th Century, 4 ¾ In.	86.00
Pitcher, Interior Scene Cartouche, Scalloped Rim, c.1850, 5 In.	325.00
Planter, Figures, Courtyard, 19th Century, 8 ¼ x 13 In.	531.00
Plate, Painted, B. Altman & Co., 8 In., 8 Piece	48.00
Platter, Oval, Mandarin Figures, Roses, Peony Rondel, c.1900, 14 ¼ x 17 In.	338.00
Punch Bowl, Figures, Birds, c.1900, 6 x 16 In.	1320.00
Punch Bowl, Figures, Flowers, 1800s, 13 ¼ In.	430.00
Punch Bowl, Figures, Flowers, c.1840, 16 In.	1888.00
Punch Bowl, Panels, Figures, Peonies, Ho Ho Birds, c.1885, 6 x 14 ½ In.	799.00
Serving Dish, Famille Rose, Saucer Shape, Flowers, Figures, 1800s, 14 ⅞ In. Diam.	430.00
Teapot, Scenic Panels, Wicker Wrapped Handles, Fitted Woven Carrier, Silk Lined, c.1900, 7 In. *Illus*	84.00
Tureen, Lid, Mandarin Panels, Peonies, Gilt Pinecone Knop, c.1885, 5 ½ x 9 ½ In.	338.00
Umbrella Stand, 1800s, 23 ½ In.	1541.00
Umbrella Stand, Cylindrical, 20th Century, 24 In.	330.00
Umbrella Stand, Flowers, c.1950, 21 In.	210.00
Vase, Applied Gilt Mythical Creatures, Flared Rim, c.1850, c.1850, 17 ½ In.	885.00

Vase, Bottle Shaped, Painted, Reserve Court Scenes, Figures, c.1880, 13 In.		63.00
Vase, Fan Shaped Panels, Flowers, Moths, Birds, Bats, Baluster, Trumpet Rim, c.1860, 25 In.		345.00
Vase, Figures, Roses, Butterflies, Gilt Foo Dog Handles, Molded Lip, c.1865, 32 In., Pair		2767.00
Vase, Shoulder Dragons, Foo Dog Handles, 24 x 9 In., Pair		1755.00
Vase, Tapering Cylindrical Shape, Gilt Foo Dog Handles, Figures, Stand, 1800s, 9 ½ In., Pair		430.00
Vase, Waisted, Scalloped Rim, c.1860, 37 In., Pair		4130.00

ROSE O'NEILL, *see Kewpie category.*

ROSE TAPESTRY porcelain was made by the Royal Bayreuth factory of Tettau, Germany, during the late nineteenth century. The surface of the porcelain was pressed against a coarse fabric while it was still damp, and the impressions remained on the finished porcelain. It looks and feels like a textured cloth. Very skillful reproductions are being made that even include a variation of the Royal Bayreuth mark, so be careful when buying.

Creamer, Flowers, Pinch Sided, Gold Enamel Handle & Rim, 3 ½ In.		92.00
Pin Tray, Clover Leaf Shape, Arched Ring Handle, Gold Edge, c.1890, 4 ½ x 5 In.		160.00

ROSEMEADE POTTERY of Wahpeton, North Dakota, worked from 1940 to 1961. The pottery was operated by Laura A. Taylor and her husband, R.I. Hughes. The company was also known as the Wahpeton Pottery Company. Art pottery and commercial wares were made.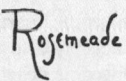

Bank, Elephant, Seated, Trunk Up, Pink, Dakota		475.00
Bowl, Aqua Shaded, Rose Matte Glaze, 7 ½ x 5 x 2 ¾ In.		49.00
Figurine, Goldfinch, ¾ x 1 ½ In., Pair		425.00
Figurine, Nude Woman, Chalk, Gold, Pink, Yellow, Signed, 5 x 3 ¾ In.		49.00
Figurine, Prairie Dog, Seated, 1 ¼ x 1 In.		50.00
Salt & Pepper, Chow Dog, Red Glaze, Black Ear Tips, Nose, Base, Dakota		139.00
Salt & Pepper, Pelican, Natural Color, Gloss Glaze, Dakota, 3 x 2 ½ In.		125.00
Salt & Pepper, Pheasants, Male & Female, 3 x 4 & 3 x 2 In., Pair		28.00
Salt & Pepper, Skunk, Dakota, 2 ½ x 3 In., Pair		48.00
Spoon Rest, Tulip Shape, Pink, Green, 5 ½ In.		80.00
Tea Bell, Tulip Shape, Painted, 3 ¾ In.		100.00
Vase, Tulip Shape, Blue Satin Matte Glaze, Each Petal Has Hole For Flower, 3 x 3 ½ In.		29.00

ROSENTHAL porcelain was made at the factory established in Selb, Bavaria, in 1880. The factory is still making fine-quality tablewares and figurines. A series of Christmas plates was made from 1910. Other limited edition plates have been made since 1971. In 1998 Rosenthal was acquired by the Waterford Wedgwood Group. Rosenthal was bought by Sambonet Paderno Industries, headquartered in Orfento, Novaro, Italy, in 2009. Rosenthal china is still being produced in Bavaria.

MARKE
Rosenthal

Bone Dish, Purple, Yellow Flowers, Stems, Bavaria, c.1910		9.00
Champagne Flute, Cut Crystal, Signed, 7 In., 9 Piece		150.00
Figurine, Dancer, Korean, Knee Up, Ornate Costume, Constantin H. Defanti, c.1919, 16 In.		1610.00
Figurine, Dove, White, Signed Fritz Heidenreich, 6 In.		92.00
Figurine, Girl, Asian Attire, Gilt Highlights, Flower Frog Base, 13 ½ In.		920.00
Figurine, Monkey, Seated By Pond, Painted, Signed Ferdinand Liebermann, 4 ½ x 8 x 5 ¾ In.		598.00
Figurine, Sleeping Fauns, 2 Seated Figures, Stamped, c.1912, 9 ½ x 4 ¾ In.		413.00
Figurine, Turtledove, White, Green Base, Impressed F. Heidenreich, 6 In., Pair		179.00
Fish Set, Platter, Serving Plates, Blue Fish, White Rims, 10 x 24 In. Platter, 13 Piece		403.00
Jar, Dome Lid, Bird, Flowers, Ball Finial, Black, Silver, Red, 12 ¼ In.		230.00
Pitcher, Berries, Leaves, Blue, Green, Yellow, Purple, Stylized 2-Loop Handle, c.1910, 12 x 7 In.		108.00
Tea Set, Flash Pattern, Dorothy Hafner, c.1980, 3 Piece		210.00
Vase, 2 Abstract Figures, Multicolor, Cylindrical, Bjorn Wiinblad, 7 ½ x 4 ¾ In.		150.00
Vase, Art Deco Style, White Matte Finish, Glazed Interior, Oval, 8 & 9 In., 2 Piece		70.00
Vase, Modern Design, Multicolor, Signed, 9 x 8 In.		117.00
Vase, Vega, Op Art, Gold, Black, Satin Finish, Studio Line, Victor Vasarely, 11 x 10 In.		1080.00

ROSEVILLE POTTERY COMPANY was organized in Roseville, Ohio, in 1890. Another plant was opened in Zanesville, Ohio, in 1898. Many types of pottery were made until 1954. Early wares include Sgraffito, Olympic, and Rozane. Later lines were often made with molded decorations, especially flowers and fruit. Most pieces are marked *Roseville*. Many reproductions made in China have been offered for sale the past few years.

Apple Blossom, Bowl, Green, Handles, 10 ¾ In.		40.00
Artware, Mug, Multicolor Squares, Black, 5 In.		23.00

Royal Bayreuth, Cracker Jar, Tomato, Blue Mark, 9 ¼ In.
$550.00

Woody Auction

Royal Bayreuth, Humidor, Female Clown, Yellow, Blue Mark, 5 In.
$550.00

Woody Auction

Royal Bayreuth, Mustard, Orange, Spoon, Blue Mark, 3 ½ In.
$50.00

Woody Auction

R

Royal Bayreuth, Pitcher, Clown, Red, Blue Mark, 6 ½ x 9 In.
$400.00

Woody Auction

Royal Bayreuth, Teapot, Apple, Yellow, Blue Mark, 4 ½ In.
$150.00

Woody Auction

Royal Bonn, Stein, Men Riding Bicycles, Print Over Glaze, Pottery, 3 Liter
$1,035.00

Fox Auctions

TIP

Bring a price guide book to an auction. It isn't possible to remember everything, but it is possible to look most items up. We think Kovels' Antiques & Collectibles Price Guide *is the best resource.*

Azurean, Vase, Houses, River Bank, Impressed Mark, 10 x 11 In.	1725.00
Baneda, Vase, Bud, Olive Green, Orange Buds, 3-Sided, Handles, Marked, 4 In.	299.00
Baneda, Vase, Green, Iridescent Orange, Blue Drip, Handles, Footed, Marked, 10 ¼ In.	1006.00
Baneda, Vase, Green, Orange Berries, Blue Drip, Base Handles, 8 ½ In.	604.00
Baneda, Vase, Green, Orange Berries, Blue Drip, Handles, Footed, Marked, 6 In.	390.00
Baneda, Vase, Green, Orange Flowers, Small Neck Handles, Tapered, 4 ½ In.	265.00
Baneda, Vase, Green, Orange, Bulbous, Handles, 6 In.	374.00
Baneda, Vase, Green, Orange, Tapered, Handles, Foil Label, 15 ½ In.	2530.00
Baneda, Vase, Green, Urn Shape, Handles At Rim, 4 In.	149.00
Baneda, Vase, Green, Yellow Berries, Blue Drip, Shoulder Handles, 7 ¼ In.	368.00
Baneda, Vase, Mauve, Blue & Green Band, Shoulder Handles, Footed, 6 ¼ In.	230.00
Baneda, Vase, Mauve, Flower Band, Handles, 10 ¼ In.	345.00
Baneda, Vase, Pink, Handles, 10 ½ x 8 In. ....*Illus*	563.00
Baneda, Vase, Purple, Flower Band, Handles, 9 ⅓ In.	316.00
Baneda, Vase, Trumpet, Mauve, Blue & Green Band, Base Handles, 8 ¼ In.	460.00
Bittersweet, Basket, Pink, Brown Handle, Marked, 11 In.	115.00
Bittersweet, Vase, Green, Red Flowers, Triangular Rim, Brown Handles, 8 ¼ In.	104.00
Blackberry, Jardiniere, Green, Brown Leaves, Round, Marked, 4 In.	230.00
Bleeding Heart, Basket, Blue, Green, Round Foot, Circle Handle, 9 ⅝ x 9 ½ In.	207.00
Bleeding Heart, Basket, Marked, 10 In., Pair	180.00
Bleeding Heart, Jardiniere, Blue, Green, Pink, Marked, 6 In.	82.00
Bleeding Heart, Jardiniere, Pedestal, Blue, 32 x 17 In.	1063.00
Bleeding Heart, Vase, Blue, Green, Pink, 6-Point Rim, Low Handles, 8 ½ In.	150.00
Bleeding Heart, Vase, Flared Rim, Handles, 10 x 18 In.	458.00
Bleeding Heart, Vase, Green, Pink, Flared, Shaped Rim, Handles, 8 x 15 In.	275.00
Bushberry, Bowl, Green, Orange, Boat Shape, Brown Handles, 10 In.	173.00
Bushberry, Bowl, Leaves, Brown, Green, Branch Handles, 13 ¼ In.	23.00
Bushberry, Jardiniere, Orange Berry, Leaf Band, Green, Round, Marked, 5 In.	161.00
Bushberry, Pitcher, Ice Lip, Blue, Pink, Green Flowers, Marked, 9 In.	115.00
Bushberry, Vase, Bud, Burnt Orange, Green, 7 ⅜ In.	24.00
Bushberry, Vase, Green, Pink & Yellow Flowers, Low Handles, Marked, 6 ¼ In.	115.00
Bushberry, Vase, Orange, Green, Angular Handles, 18 ½ In.	288.00
Carnelian, Vase, Blue, Green, Tapered, Scroll Handles, Marked, 8 In.	80.00
Carnelian, Vase, Brown, Rusty Red, 12 In.	334.00
Carnelian, Vase, Green, 6 In.	104.00
Carnelian, Vase, Rose Pink, Yellow, Green Streaks, Squat, Trumpet Neck, Scroll Handles, 10 ¼ In..	259.00
Cherry Blossom, Vase, Blue, Pink, Handles, 5 ¼ In.	150.00 to 230.00
Cherry Blossom, Vase, Green, Pink, Handles, 4 In.	173.00
Cherry Blossom, Vase, Green, Pink, Handles, 8 ¼ In.	518.00
Chloron, Umbrella Stand, Fish, Lizards, Snakes, Underwater Foliage, Green Glaze, 21 In.	977.00
Chloron, Vase, Mottled Green Glaze, Tapered, Stamped, 10 ¾ In.	2185.00
Clematis, Candlestick, Green, Yellow Flowers One Side, Pink On Other, 1950s, Pair	125.00
Clematis, Candlestick, Pink Flowers, Green, Handles, 2 ¼ In., Pair	23.00
Clematis, Flower Frog, Blue, White, Yellow Center, Holes, 4 x 4 ½ In., 2 Piece	35.00
Clematis, Green, Yellow Flower, Angular Handles, 7 In.	92.00
Clematis, Jardiniere, Pedestal, Yellow Flowers, Brown, 25 In.	518.00
Columbine, Bowl, Blue, Yellow Flowers, Lug Handles, 9 ½ In.	29.00
Columbine, Jardiniere, Red, Pink Flowers, Scalloped Rim, Handles, 7 In.	35.00
Columbine, Vase, Blue Flowers, Orange To Green, Low Handles, Footed, 8 ½ In.	115.00
Columbine, Vase, Pink, Handles, 7 x 17 In.	335.00
Columbine, Vase, Pink, Handles, 9 x 14 ½ In.	366.00
Cosmos, Vase, Pink & White Flowers, Blue, Tapered, Wavy Rim, Handles, 12 ½ In.	92.00
Cremona, Vase, Swirled Flowers, Pale Green, 12 ¼ In.	196.00
Dahlrose, Vase, Yellow Daisy, Brown, Bulbous, 11 In.	518.00
Dahlrose, Vase, Yellow Flower, Brown, Tapered, 10 ¼ In.	242.00
Dahlrose, Vase, Yellow Flowers, 12 ½ In.	316.00
Dahlrose, Wall Pocket, Cone Shape, Double Opening, Pink, Branch Handle, 8 ¼ In.	161.00
Della Robbia, Vase, Fish, Incised, Rozane, c.1910, 10 ½ x 3 ½ In. ....*Illus*	3125.00
Della Robbia, Vase, Grapes & Vines, Marked, Rozane, 10 ¼ In. ....*Illus*	1955.00
Della Robbia, Vase, Poppies, Carved Flowers, Seed Pods, Marked, 14 ¼ In. ....*Illus*	11213.00
Della Robbia, Vase, Wild Roses, Cutout Rim, Marked, Rozane, c.1910, 15 ½ x 6 In. ....*Illus*	43750.00
Dogwood, Jardiniere, White Blossoms, Green, 13 In.	115.00
Dogwood, Vase, Raised Flowers, Marked, 8 ¼ In.	287.00
Dogwood, Vase, White Blossoms, Green, c.1925, 6 In.	60.00
Donatello, Bowl, White Cherubs, Seated, Green, Blue, Ribbed Rim, 6 ½ In.	207.00
Donatello, Candlestick, Cherub Band, Green, Brown, 8 In.	23.00
Donatello, Jardiniere, Pedestal, Relief Cherub Band, Ribbed, Cream, Green Glaze, 20 In.	296.00

Earlam, Vase, Mottled Green, Round, Handles, 4 In.	127.00 to 173.00
Earlam, Vase, Orange Speckled, Handles, 5 ¾ In.	35.00
Egypto, Lamp Oil, Lid, Green, Squat, Handle, Marked, 4 ½ In.	460.00
Egypto, Pitcher, Curdled Green Glaze, Scrollwork, Rozane, 7 ¼ x 4 ½ In.	469.00
Falline, Bowl, Pea Pods, Brown, Green, Handles, 11 In.	69.00
Falline, Vase, Brown, Green Leaves, Handles, Marked, 7 ¼ In.	390.00
Ferella, Candlestick, Brown, Green, Pink, Drip Cup, Footed, 4 In., Pair	184.00
Ferella, Vase, Pink, Splotches, Oval, Shell Neck & Foot, 2 Handles, 8 x 8 In.	500.00
Fish, Jardiniere, Pink, Green, Blue Majolica Glaze, 9 ½ x 11 In.	330.00
Florentine, Basket, Hanging, 7 In.	46.00
Florentine, Jardiniere, Mottled Brown Panels, Handles, Marked, 8 ¼ In.	58.00
Foxglove, Bookends, Green Leaves, Rusty Red Glaze, Stepped Base, 5 ¾ In.	173.00
Foxglove, Bowl, Pink Flowers, Green Leaves, Wavy Rim, Handles, 15 ½ In.	46.00
Foxglove, Jardiniere, Pedestal, Green, 2 Angular Handles, 30 In.	499.00
Foxglove, Vase, Blue Green, Tapered, Angular Handles, 6 ¼ In. ....*Illus*	71.00
Foxglove, Vase, Flowers, Pink, Blue, Handles, c.1945, 12 ¼ In.	180.00
Foxglove, Vase, Yellow & Pink Flowers, Blue, Long Handles, 4 ¼ In.	52.00
Freesia, Vase, Blue, Marked, 8 In.	180.00
Freesia, Vase, Green, White & Purple Flowers, Handles, 9 ½ In.	58.00
Fuchsia, Jardiniere, Blue, Footed, Handles, 5 ¼ In.	104.00
Fuchsia, Jardiniere, Mustard Yellow, Green, Pink, Rim Handles, Footed, 9 ½ In.	414.00
Fuchsia, Pitcher, Ice Lip, Green, Brown, 8 In.	288.00
Fuchsia, Vase, Green & Pink Flowers, Brown, Handles, Footed, 6 ¼ In.	104.00
Fuchsia, Vase, Green Leaves, Brown, Handles, 10 ½ In.	161.00
Fuchsia, Vase, Green, Pink, Flowers, Green Leaves, 2 Handles, 15 ½ In. ....*Illus*	161.00
Fudji, Vase, Blue & Green, Art Nouveau Decoration, 7 ¾ In. ....*Illus*	2990.00
Fujiyama, Vase, Stylized Flowers, Swollen, Rounded Square Mouth, Rozane, 10 ⅛ In.	518.00
Futura, Vase, Arches, Faceted Neck, Brown, Tan, Buttressed Handles, 14 x 6 In.	1875.00
Futura, Vase, Brown, Green, Angular Handles, Footed, 9 In.	604.00
Futura, Vase, Flowers, Brown, Green Glaze, Handles, c.1920, 6 In.	177.00
Futura, Vase, Pleated Star Shape, Green, Pink, Footed, Label, 8 ¼ In.	196.00
Futura, Vase, Sea Gull, Brown, Gray, 10 ¼ In.	863.00
Futura, Vase, Shaded Green Glaze, Horizontal Lobes, Tapered, Footed, 10 ¼ In.	2645.00
Futura, Vase, Shooting Star, Blue, Green, Tapered Round Base, 10 ¼ In.	230.00 to 316.00
Gardenia, Bowl, White, Green, Gray, Scalloped Rim, Handles, 11 In.	46.00
Geometric, Vase, Blue & Green, 3-Sided, Round Foot, 9 In.	230.00
Geometric, Vase, Enamel, Swirls, Aladdin's Lamp Shape, Swollen Rim, 1906, 7 ¾ x 5 In.	2625.00
Holly, Bowl, Creamware, Red, Green, Handles, 10 ¼ In.	115.00
Imperial I, Vase, Mottled Brown, Green, Flared Base, Handles, c.1920, 11 ½ x 7 ½ In.	154.00
Imperial II, Bowl, Rose, Green, Tapered, 8 In.	127.00
Imperial II, Vase, Golden Ochre Over Frothy Blue, 11 x 6 ¾ In.	688.00
Iris, Ewer, Green To Blue, Stepped Handle, 10 ½ In. ....*Illus*	330.00
Iris, Vase, Pink, Handles, 9 x 15 In.	305.00
Iris, Vase, White, Turquoise, Handles, 5 In.	92.00
Ivory, Humidor, Lid, Lions, Flowers, Green, Cream, 6 ¼ In.	92.00
Ixia, Vase, Orange Shaded To Yellow Glaze, Lavender Flowers, Oval, Pad Foot, 7 ½ In.	106.00
Ixia, Vase, Pink Flowers, Green Ground, Handles, 9 ½ In.	52.00
Ixia, Vase, Pink Flowers, Yellow Ground, Buttressed Handles, Marked, 7 ¾ In.	46.00
Ixia, Vase, Pink Flowers, Yellow Ground, Cylindrical, Buttressed Handles, Marked, 10 ¾ In.	86.00
Laurel, Bowl, Green, Orange, 6 ¾ In.	104.00
Luffa, Bowl, Leaves, Horizontal Lines, Blue, Tan, Brown, Small Neck Handles, 6 ¼ In.	161.00
Magnolia, Ashtray, White, Blue, Handles, Marked, 7 ½ In.	23.00
Magnolia, Bowl, White, Yellow, Pink, Brown, Handles, Marked, 11 In.	23.00
Magnolia, Cookie Jar, Lid, Yellow Flowers, Blue Ground, Handles, 11 In.	207.00
Magnolia, Vase, Brown, Yellow, White, Low Handles, Footed, 6 ¼ In.	86.00
Magnolia, Vase, White, Green, Handles, 10 ¼ In.	115.00
Mara, Vase, Green Iridescent, Pink, Yellow, Pear Shape, Loop Handles At Rim, 5 ⅜ In.	1093.00
Matte Green, Jardiniere, 8 ½ In.	81.00
Matte Green, Jardiniere, Spherical, 3-Footed, 10 x 8 In.	225.00
Matte Green, Umbrella Stand, Storks, 21 In.	632.00
Matte Green, Wall Pocket, Green, 3-Sided, 11 In.	115.00
Ming Tree, Basket, Blue, White, Branch Handle, Marked, 8 ¼ In.	86.00
Ming Tree, Bookend, Green, Brown, Tan, Marked, 5 ½ In.	35.00
Ming Tree, Vase, Green, Peach Flowers, Branch Handle, Footed, 6 In.	92.00
Mongol, Vase, Blue & White Organic Decoration, Marked, 3 ¾ In.	632.00
Moss, Vase, Green, Orange, Handles, 8 x 12 ½ In.	458.00
Moss, Vase, Pink, Green, Flared Rim, Handles, Footed, Marked, 10 ¾ In.	104.00

Royal Copenhagen, Figurine, Faun, Kneeling Holding Parrot, Green Stamp, 7 In.
$540.00

DuMouchelles Art Gallery

Royal Copenhagen, Vase, Bats, Pine Boughs, Stamped, 1889-1922, 8 ¾ x 5 In.
$1,625.00

Rago Arts & Auction Center

Royal Copenhagen, Vase, Budding, Relief, Glazed, Axel Salto, Signed, 5 x 3 ½ In.
$3,250.00

Rago Arts & Auction Center

R

Royal Crown Derby, Vase, Lid, Flowers, Raised Gilt Work, Medallions, Strapwork, Marked, 1886-87, 12 ¾ In. $1,230.00

New Orleans Auction Galleries, Inc.

Royal Doulton, Animal, Buffalo, Red, Flambe, C.J. Noke, Marked, 1900s, 10 ½ In. $2,607.00

Skinner, Inc.

Royal Doulton, Character Jug, John Peel, D 5612, 1936-60, 6 ½ In. $120.00

DuMouchelles Art Gallery

Gold Notes
24-karat gold is pure gold; 18-karat is 75 percent gold mixed with another metal like nickel or copper; 14-karat is 58.5 percent gold.

Mostique, Jardiniere, Flower, Green, Peach, 8 ½ In.	127.00
Mostique, Vase, Green, Orange, Tapered, 6 In.	46.00
Mostique, Wall Pocket, Green, Red, Yellow, 3-Sided, 12 ½ In.	81.00
Pauleo, Vase, Gold Glaze, Bulbous, Footed, 5 In.	331.00
Pauleo, Vase, Red Metallic Luster Glaze, Swollen, Rolled Rim, Foot Ring, Marked, 14 In.	575.00
Peony, Basin, Yellow, Green Leaves, Open Handles, 2 ¾ x 6 ¾ In.	71.00
Peony, Tea Set, Pink, Turquoise, Grooved, Round Lid, Flared Spout, Lug Handle, 3 Piece	71.00
Peony, Vase, Flowers, Yellow, Green, Angular Handles, 9 In.	144.00
Pine Cone, Bowl, Console, Brown, Impressed Logo, 4 x 13 In.	149.00
Pine Cone, Flowerpot, 5 In.	63.00
Pine Cone, Vase, Blue, Impressed Logo, 7 ¼ In.	207.00
Pine Cone, Vase, Brown, Impressed Logo, 8 In.	85.00 to 218.00
Pine Cone, Vase, Brown, Impressed Logo, 14 ½ In.	460.00
Pine Cone, Vase, Bud, Brown, Marked, 8 ⅜ In.	172.00
Pine Cone, Vase, Burst Glaze Bubbles, Marked, 8 ⅜ In.	218.00
Pine Cone, Vase, Green, Yellow Brown, Marked, 7 ¼ In.	242.00
Pine Cone, Vase, Orange, Green, Base Handles, 10 In.	374.00
Poppy, Ewer, Pink Matte, Green Leaves, Flowers, Shaped Spout, Loop Handle, Spread Foot, 18 ¼ In.	374.00
Poppy, Vase, Pink, Green, Handles, Footed, Signed, 9 ½ x 6 ½ In.	110.00
Primrose, Vase, White Blossoms, Blue Ground, Shoulder Angled Handles, 6 ½ In.	46.00
Rhead, Umbrella Stand, Stylized Trees, Cranes, Squeezebag, Gray, 3 Handles, 21 In.	1375.00
Rosecraft, Bowl, Brown, Tan Grapes, Leaves, 4 x 6 ¼ In.	71.00
Rosecraft, Vase, Bud, Double, Gate, Brown, Marked, 4 ¾ In.	69.00
Royal Capri, Vase, Gold Stippled Finish, Swollen Collar, Rolled Rim, Bell Foot, 7 ⅜ In.	219.00
Rozane Royal, Umbrella Stand, Orange, Green Fronds, Brown, 22 In.	265.00
Rozane Royal, Vase, 2 Kittens, Signed, C.L. Leffler, 19 ¾ In. *Illus*	3795.00
Rozane Royal, Vase, Flared Rim, Signed W.H., 15 In.	288.00
Rozane Royal, Vase, Virginia Creeper, Berries, Leaves, Green, Gray, Tapered, Garlic Mouth, 10 ⅝ In.	345.00
Rozane, Bowl, Green, Rectangular, Marked, 7 ½ In.	23.00
Rozane, Jardiniere, Pedestal, Standard Glaze, Green, Brown, Gold Flower, Tapered, 21 In.	173.00
Rozane, Umbrella Stand, Cream, Pastel Flowers, Cylindrical, 19 In.	207.00
Rozane, Vase, Green, Sage, Cream, Red Clover, Stems, Squared Neck & Rim, Footed, Marked, 11 In.	230.00
Rozane, Vase, Man's Face, Dark Brown, Bulbous, Flared Rim, Marked, 21 In.	1840.00
Rozane, Vase, Multicolor Flowers, Speckled Gray, Footed, 10 In.	52.00
Rozane, Vase, Pastel Flowers, Gray Ground, Marked, 7 ¾ In.	58.00
Rozane, Vase, Portrait, Hound, Signed, Claude Leffler, 21 ½ In.	960.00
Rozane, Vase, Portrait, Indian, Brown Glaze, Dunlavy, 20 In.	4500.00
Rozane, Vase, Red & Orange Flowers, Brown Glossy Glaze, Oval, 9 ¼ In.	264.00
Rozane, Vase, Roses, Swollen Collar, Trumpet Foot, Flat Flared Rim, 3 Elongated Handles, 13 In.	316.00
Silhouette, Vase, Cornucopia, Leaves, Turquoise, Green, Marked, 6 ½ x 8 ½ In., Pair	59.00
Silhouette, Vase, White, Green, 6 ¼ In.	18.00
Snowberry, Bowl, Green, Handles, Footed, 12 ¼ In.	46.00
Snowberry, Console Set, Sticker, 16-In. Bowl, 5-In. Candlestick, 3 Piece	60.00
Snowberry, Vase, Green, Handles, 8 In.	92.00
Sunflower, Bowl, Green, Yellow, Round, 4 ½ In.	190.00
Sunflower, Vase, Green & Blue, Handles, 5 ¼ In. *Illus*	266.00
Sunflower, Vase, Green, Orange Flowers, Cylindrical, 10 ¾ In.	661.00
Sunflower, Vase, Green, Yellow, Handles, 10 ½ In.	546.00
Sunflower, Vase, Green, Yellow, Orange, Cylindrical Neck, Handles At Neck, 9 In.	1035.00
Sunflower, Wall Pocket, Double Arch Top, 7 ⅜ x 6 In.	688.00
Teasel, Vase, Blue, Incised, Marked, 7 ¼ In.	92.00
Thorn Apple, Pot, Green, Pink, White, Cylindrical, 5 ¼ In.	29.00
Vista, Vase, Stylized Trees, Greens, Cylindrical, 2 Handles, 12 x 6 ½ In.	625.00
Vista, Wall Pocket, Green, 9 ¼ In.	460.00
Water Lily, Bowl, Blue, Scalloped Rim, 10 ¾ x 3 ½ In.	104.00
Water Lily, Bowl, Brown, Yellow, Globe Shape, Handles, 6 ¼ In.	63.00
Water Lily, Conch Shell, Brown, Yellow, 4 ¾ In.	52.00
Water Lily, Vase, Handles, Marked, 7 ¼ In.	40.00
Water Lily, Vase, Pink, Green, 6 ¼ In.	47.00
White Rose, Vase, Blue, 15 In.	234.00
White Rose, Vase, Blue, Handles, 8 ½ In.	238.00
White Rose, Vase, Pillow, Pink, Handles, 8 ½ In.	104.00
White Rose, Vase, Pink, To Green, Handles, 19 In.	345.00
Wincraft, Vase, Fan, Green, Pink, 6 ½ In.	52.00
Wincraft, Vase, Panther, Orange, Black Figure, 20th Century, 10 ½ x 6 ¼ In.	360.00
Wincraft, Wall Pocket, Green, Brown, Mustard Yellow, Shield Shape, 6 ¼ In.	104.00

Windsor, Vase, Ferns, Green & Gold, Blue Mottled Glaze, c.1931, 7 ¼ x 7 ½ In.	650.00
Windsor, Vase, Ferns, Spherical, Blue Mottled Glaze, 1931, 7 ¼ In.	650.00
Wisteria, Vase, Leafy Stem, Flowers, Angular Handles, 6 ½ x 8 ½ In.	690.00
Wisteria, Vase, Pink Flowers, Embossed Green Leaves, Base Handles, Marked, 8 ¼ In.	288.00
Wisteria, Vase, Pink Flowers, Green Leaves, Small Rim Handles, 4 In.	104.00
Zephyr Lily, Bowl, Yellow Flowers, Green & Brown, Handles, 6 ¼ In.	81.00
Zephyr Lily, Vase, Green Matte Glaze, 2 Handles, 5 ½ x 10 ½ In.	122.00
Zephyr Lily, Vase, Green, 2 Handles, Marked, 10 ½ In.	100.00

ROWLAND & MARSELLUS COMPANY is part of a mark that appears on historical Staffordshire dating from the late nineteenth and early twentieth centuries. *Rowland & Marsellus* is the mark used by an American importing company in New York City. The company worked from 1893 to about 1937. Some of the pieces may have been made by the British Anchor Pottery Co. of Longton, England, for export to a New York firm. Many American views were made. Of special interest to collectors are the plates with rolled edges, usually blue and white.

Bowl, Courtship Scene, Swag & Scroll Border, Blue & White, 7 ½ In.	80.00
Plate, Albany, New York, Blue & White, 10 In.	98.00
Plate, Allegheny County Court House, Pittsburgh, Pa., Flow Blue, 10 In.	135.00
Plate, American Poets, Blue Transfer, 10 In.	85.00
Plate, Bridgeport, Conn., Flow Blue, 10 In.	125.00
Plate, Bridgeport, Connecticut, Flow Blue, 1893-1938, 10 ¼ In.	120.00
Plate, Buffalo, N.Y., Flow Blue	130.00
Plate, Capitol, Washington, D.C., Blue & White, 10 In.	50.00
Plate, Faneuil Hall, Historical Boston, Blue & White, Rolled Edge, 10 In.	50.00
Plate, Garfield Monument, Cleveland, Oh., Flow Blue, 10 In.	125.00
Plate, Independence Hall, Flow Blue, 9 ¾ In.	85.00
Plate, Landing Of Hendrick Hudson, Blue & White, Rolled Edge, 10 In.	150.00
Plate, Myles Standish, Flow Blue, Rolled Edge, 10 In.	145.00
Plate, Pilgrim Hall, Blue & White, 1800s, 10 In.	35.00
Plate, Poet Longfellow, Flow Blue, 10 In.	100.00
Plate, Providence, R.I., Flow Blue, Blue & White, 10 In.	135.00
Plate, Robert Burns, Flow Blue, Rolled Edge, 10 In.	108.00
Plate, Souvenir Of Cleveland, Ohio, Blue & White, Rolled Edge, 10 In.	125.00
Plate, St. Paul's Union Church, Blue & White, Rolled Edge, 1924	95.00
Plate, Teddy Roosevelt, Blue & White, Rolled Edge, 10 In.	250.00
Plate, Thousand Islands, Flow Blue, 10 In.	120.00
Plate, Topeka, Kansas, Flow Blue, 1893-1938, 10 In.	129.00
Plate, View Of Denver, Blue & White, 10 In.	100.00

ROY ROGERS was born in 1911 in Cincinnati, Ohio. In the 1930s, he made a living as a singer; in 1935, his group started work at a Los Angeles radio station. He appeared in his first movie in 1937. From 1952 to 1957, he made 101 television shows. The other stars in the show were his wife, Dale Evans, his horse, Trigger, and his dog, Bullet. Roy Rogers memorabilia, including items from the Roy Rogers restaurants, are collected.

Badge, Deputy Sheriff, Star Shape, Whistle, Goldtone, 1950s, 2 ½ x 2 ¾ In.	75.00
Bobble Head, Hand On Gun, Hip, Signature Decal, Japan, 1962, 6 ½ In.	153.00
Button Set, Post Grape Nuts Flakes Premiums, Lithograph, 1953, ⅞ & 1 ⅛ In., 18 Piece	910.00
Button, Member Roy Rogers Riders Club, Photo, Cowboy Hat, 1950s, 1 ¼ In.	69.00
Button, Portrait, Hanger, Red Fabric, White Metal Horseshoe, 1950s, 1 ¼ In.	52.00
Button, Riders Club, Blue Ground, Roy & Trigger, 1 ¾ In.	86.00
Camera, Flash, Trigger, Black, Box, c.1950, 4 x 5 x 9 In.	168.00
Coin, Good Luck Forever, Trigger, Horseshoe, 1 ⅛ In.	35.00
Comic Book Rack, Tin Lithograph, Roy Rogers, Trigger, 2 Sections, 12 x 9 x 8 In.	175.00
Cup, Figural, King Of Cowboys, Cowboy Hat, F & F Mold & Die Works, 4 ½ In.	51.00
Figures, Roy & Dale, Waving, Shelf Sitters, Rubber, 3 In., Pair	35.00
Flashlight, Roy, Riding Trigger, Tin, Lithograph, Usalite, Box, 6 ¾ In.	120.00
Guitar, Range Rhythm, Wood, Box, 30 ½ In.	125.00
Gun Holster Set, 2 Guns, Pewter Finish Grips, Flash Draw, Box	1375.00
Gun Holster Set, Double, Leather, Metal, 1950s	100.00
Harmonica, Roy Rogers Riders, Plastic, Metal, 1940-1950, 4 In.	15.00
Horseshoe Set, Box	185.00
Jewelry Set, Official, Brass Cuff Links As Boots, Tie Clip Is Trigger's Saddle, 1950s	28.00
Lantern, Tin Lithograph, Ohio Art, Bail Handle, Battery, 1950s, 7 ¼ In.	145.00
Life Magazine Cover, Trigger, Signed Happy Trails, July 12, 1943, 10 ⅜ x 14 In.	949.00
Mug, Figural, Head, Porcelain, 4 In.	75.00

Royal Doulton, Figurine, The Boatman, HN 2417, 7 In.
$240.00

DuMouchelles Art Gallery

Royal Doulton, Pitcher, Battle Of Hastings, Battle Scenes, Black Rim, 7 ½ x 4 ¾ In.
$240.00

DuMouchelles Art Gallery

Royal Doulton, Plate, Landscape Scene, Raised Gold Leafy Border, P. Curnock, 1900s, 10 ⅝ In., 12 Piece
$3,555.00

Skinner, Inc.

Royal Doulton, Vase, Slip Colors, Green, Yellow, Red, White, Black, Blue, Drip Glaze, Marked, 10 ¼ In. $6,038.00

Humler & Nolan

Royal Dux, Centerpiece, 3 Dancing Maidens, Pedestal, Multicolor Flowers, Gold Rim, 20 In. $720.00

DuMouchelles Art Gallery

R

TIP

If you are uncomfortable when trying to buy an antique, either because of the attitude of the dealer or some of the information you are given, walk away. There are other shops and other antiques.

Paper Dolls, Roy & Dale Evans, Trigger, 6 Pages, Accessories, Uncut, 1950	105.00
Pitcher, Plastic, Roy Written In Front Of Hat, Made By F & F Mold & Die Works, 4 ¼ In.	85.00
Pitcher, White Hat, King Of The Cowboys, Plastic, F & F Mold & Die Works, Dayton, Ohio, 4 ¼ x 4 In.	85.00
Record, Dale Evans, Riders, Suzy Snowflake, 32 Feet 8 Little Tails, Little Nipper, 78 RPM, c.1950	12.00
Ring, Microscope, Quaker Cereals, Brass, Roy, Trigger, Hinged Red Plastic, 1949	104.00
Sheet Music, Bible Tells Me So, Roy & Dale Evans, Paramount, 1950	20.00
Shirt, White, Needlework, Trigger, Roy, Boys, Size 12	120.00
Stopwatch, Trigger, Silver Luster Case, Box, 1959, 2 ⅛ In.	288.00
Toy, Dale Evans, On Buttermilk, Queen Of Cowgirls, Hat, Vinyl Reins, Hartland, 1950s	135.00
Toy, Roy, Trigger, Lasso, Oval Base, Tin Lithograph, Clockwork, Marx, 11 In.	230.00
View-Master, Viewer, 1950s	45.00
Watch, Roy, Trigger, Chrome Case, Bradley, Box, c.1959, Pocket	240.00
Wristwatch, Bandanna, Brushed Silver Case, Tooled Leather Band, Limited Edition, Fossil, 1993	150.00
Wristwatch, Dale Evans, Horse Buttermilk, Brown Ground, Leather Band, Ingraham, 1955	210.00
Yo-Yo, Roy Rogers & Trigger, King Of Cowboys, National Roundup, All Western Plastics	28.00

ROYAL BAYREUTH is the name of a factory that was founded in Tettau, Bavaria, in 1794. It has continued to modern times. The marks have changed through the years. A stylized crest, the name Royal Bayreuth, and the word *Bavaria* appear in slightly different forms from 1870 to about 1919. Later dishes may include the words *U.S. Zone,* the year of the issue, or the word *Germany* instead of *Bavaria*. Related pieces may be found listed in the Rose Tapestry, Snow Babies, and Sunbonnet Babies categories.

Bowl, Poppy, Blue Mark, c.1910, 9 ½ x 5 In.	115.00
Bowl, Roses, Openwork Handles, 10 In.	34.00
Cracker Jar, Tomato, Blue Mark, 9 ¼ In. ....*Illus*	550.00
Creamer, Devil & Cards, Underglaze Blue Mark, c.1900	165.00
Creamer, Lobster, 3 ¾ In.	41.00
Creamer, Lobster, Claw Spout, c.1900, 4 x 5 In.	113.00
Creamer, Parrot, Multicolor, 3 ½ In.	175.00
Creamer, Rose Tapestry, 1902, 3 ½ In.	89.00
Cup & Saucer, Apple, On Leaf Saucer, Stem Handle, Demitasse	85.00
Dish, Trinket, Pierrot, Orange Cloak, White Collar, Black Hat, Buttons, Shoes, 7 x 6 ¼ In.	165.00
Figure, High Top Boot, Left Foot, Man's, Orange Tan, Glossy Interior	320.00
Hatpin Holder, Coachman, Blue Mark, 4 ¼ In.	225.00
Hatpin Holder, Hunting Scene, Green To Blue Ground, c.1902, 4 ⅝ x 2 In., Pair	625.00
Humidor, Female Clown, Yellow, Blue Mark, 5 In. ....*Illus*	550.00
Match Holder, Red Clown, 5 x 3 ½ In.	165.00
Mustard, Orange, Spoon, Blue Mark, 3 ½ In. ....*Illus*	50.00
Pitcher, Banded, Black, Orange, Applied Transfer, Greek Designs, Shield Wreath, Figures, 5 In.	24.00
Pitcher, Clown, Red, Blue Mark, 6 ½ x 9 In. ....*Illus*	400.00
Pitcher, Devil & Cards, Overlapping Playing Cards Shape Body, Devil Handle, 7 ½ In.	316.00
Pitcher, Maple Leaf, Oranges, Greens, Blue Mark, 5 ¾ In.	400.00
Pitcher, Mouse, Gray, Brown Eyes, 5 ¼ In.	1600.00
Pitcher, Pansy, Lavender Rim, Blue Mark, 6 ½ In.	500.00
Pitcher, Strawberry, 6 ¾ In.	400.00
Pitcher, Tomato Shape, Red, Green, 8 In.	102.00
Pitcher, Tomato, 4 ¾ x 3 ¼ In.	85.00
Plate, Luncheon, Tulip Border, Bouquet Center, Scalloped Rim, Gold Rim, 9 ½ In., 8 Piece	245.00
Plate, Shepherdess, Flock Of Sheep, Holding Lamb, Gold Rim, 9 In.	85.00
Stringholder, Rooster, Multicolor, Marked 2B, c.1900, 6 ½ x 3 In.	295.00
Sugar & Creamer, Hunting Dogs, Fishing, c.1900, 3 x 4 & 3 x 4 ½ In.	115.00
Sugar & Creamer, Pansy, Multicolor, Green Mark, c.1910, 4 x 5 & 4 x 5 In.	295.00
Teapot, Apple, Yellow, Blue Mark, 4 ½ In. ....*Illus*	150.00
Teapot, Sugar, Grapes, Iridescent, Pink, Purple, 7 ½ x 4 & 5 ½ x 3 In.	125.00
Toothpick Holder, Shell, Figural, Spiky, White Satin Finish, Footed, 3 In.	149.00

ROYAL BONN is the nineteenth- and twentieth-century trade name used by Franz Anton Mehlem, who had a pottery in Bonn, Germany, from 1836 to 1931. Porcelain and earthenware were made. The factory was purchased by Villeroy & Boch in 1921 and closed in 1931. Many marks were used, most including the name Bonn, the initials FM, and a crown.

Clock, Ansonia, La Corsica, Painted Flowers, Blue Edges, Pendulum, 13 ½ In.	330.00
Clock, Ansonia, La Tesle, Porcelain, Spiral Gong Strike, Pendulum, 10 x 8 In.	184.00
Clock, Ansonia, Maroon, Enameled Flowers, Scrolled Shape, 12 ¼ In.	382.00
Stein, Men Riding Bicycles, Print Over Glaze, Pottery, 3 Liter ....*Illus*	1035.00

Urn, Leaves, Gilt, Scroll Finial, Handles, c.1900, 30 x 16 x 11 In..................... 478.00
Vase, Portrait, Half Clad Woman, Woodland Background, Gilt Ribbon Rim, Base, Signed, 17 In.... 554.00
Vase, Portrait, Soldier, Young Cavalier, Brown Ground, Signed H. Hopp, 10 In. 123.00

ROYAL COPENHAGEN porcelain and pottery have been made in Denmark since 1775. The Christmas plate series started in 1908. The figurines with pale blue and gray glazes have remained popular in this century and are still being made. Many other old and new style porcelains are made today.

Bowl, Incised Wavy Lines, Glazed Stoneware, Denmark, 1960s, 6 x 10 In. 2000.00
Candelabrum, 6-Light, Blue, White, Snails, Mythical Figures, 1900, 22 In. 944.00
Compote, Reticulated Bowl, 3 Putti, On Turtle Base, 16 x 11 ½ In......................... 649.00
Figurine, 2 Children With Black Dog, 5 x 5 ½ In......................... 108.00
Figurine, Amager Girl, Woman Seated, Dahl Jensen, 9 In........................ 348.00
Figurine, Faun, Kneeling Holding Parrot, Green Stamp, 7 In........................*Illus* 540.00
Figurine, Faun, Seated, With Frog On Knees, High Gloss, Marked, 4 ¾ In. 178.00
Figurine, Girl, Goose, Marked, 7 ½ In........................ 195.00
Figurine, Heron, 11 In........................ 203.00
Figurine, Heron, Standing In Reeds, Pierced, Glazed, Marked, 11 ½ In........................ 299.00
Figurine, Mythological Man Kissing Maiden, Sea Foam, 18 In........................ 590.00
Figurine, Refugees, No. 1284, Dahl Jensen, 9 ½ In........................ 406.00
Figurine, Satyr, Seated, Column Capital, Holding Aladdin's Lamp, 5 ¾ In. 322.00
Figurine, Young Hercules, Sleeping, Shield, Sword, Bisque, 7 ½ x 5 ½ In........................ 150.00
Plate, Dinner, Fruit Center, Beige Border, Gilt Edge, 1900s, 9 In., 12 Piece........................ 89.00
Plate, Luncheon, Flora Danica, 8 ¾ In., 4 Piece 2588.00
Plate, Windjammer, Nautical Scenes, Open Lattice Border, 11 In., 6 Piece 120.00
Platter, Flora Danica, Oval, 16 ¼ In x 13 In........................ 1185.00
Platter, Flora Danica, Round, 13 ¼ In........................ 729.00
Sauceboat, Flora Danica, Alpine Willowherb Design, 7 In........................ 375.00
Tray, Flora Danica, Oval Shape, Vine Handle, Wood Sorrels Accents, 9 ½ In........................ 750.00
Tureen, Lid, Undertray, Flora Danica, Branch Shape Handle, 1900s, 16 x 13 In........................ 9200.00
Vase, Bats, Pine Boughs, Stamped, 1889-1922, 8 ¾ x 5 In........................*Illus* 1625.00
Vase, Blue Faience Glaze, Round Top, Squared Body, 9 In........................ 181.00
Vase, Boat, Harbor, Blue, Cylindrical, Signed, c.1910, 9 x 7 In. 89.00
Vase, Budding, Relief, Glazed, Axel Salto, Signed, 5 x 3 ½ In........................*Illus* 3250.00
Vase, Gray Roses, White Ground, Silver Snakes On Rim & Handles, 6 x 5 In. 3125.00
Vase, Roses, Lavender To White Ground, 9 In........................ 120.00
Vase, Spherical, Celadon Glaze, Impressed Flowers, Frog Relief, Hans Henrik Hansen, 1937, 5 ¾ In. 304.00
Vase, Straight Neck, Swollen Body, Brown Glaze, Geometric, Nils Thorsson, 9 ½ In........................ 356.00
Vase, Tapered, Orange, Gray Crackle Neck, Foot, Gold Band, 7 In........................ 120.00
Wine Cooler, Flora Danica, Tapered, Gilt Rim, Handles, c.1955, 6 ⅜ x 10 In........................ 4000.00

ROYAL COPLEY china was made by the Spaulding China Company of Sebring, Ohio, from 1939 to 1960. The figural planters and the small figurines, especially those with Art Deco designs, are of great collector interest.

Wall Pocket, Apple Shape, Red, Green, Leaves, 1950s, 5 ½ In........................ 28.00
Wall Pocket, Oriental Girl, Black Hair, Yellow Hat, Green Shirt, Marked, 7 ¾ In. 45.00
Wall Pocket, Pirate Head, Dark Hair, Gray Head Scarf, Green Shirt, 1950s, 8 In........................ 55.00

ROYAL CROWN DERBY COMPANY, LTD., is a name used on porcelain beginning in 1890. There is a complex family tree that includes the Derby, Crown Derby, and Royal Crown Derby porcelains. The Royal Crown Derby mark includes the name and a crown. The words *Made in England* were used after 1921. The company became part of Allied English Potteries Group in 1964. It was bought in 2000 and is now privately owned.

Candlestick, Old Imari Pattern, Tapered, Square Foot, 10 ¾ In., Pair 847.00
Compote, Imari Design, c.1950, 5 x 9 ½ In., Pair........................ 165.00
Ewer, Old Imari, Gilt Handle, Spout & Base, 10 In........................ 403.00
Jar, Avas, Lid, Red Design, 9 In........................ 52.00
Paperweight, Bengal Tiger, Multicolor Decoration, Gold Trim, Box 115.00
Paperweight, Bird, Chaffinch, Nesting, Multicolor Decoration, Gold Trim, 2 ½ In. 77.00
Paperweight, Bird, Nuthatch, Blue, White, Red, Gold Trim, Box, 4 ½ In........................ 58.00
Paperweight, Fawn, Multicolor Decoration, Gold Trim, Box, 5 ½ In........................ 115.00
Plate, Gold, Flowers, 10 In., 12 Piece 226.00
Plate, Molded White Basket Weave Border, Gilt Center Medallion & Rim, 9 ¼ In., 12 Piece 94.00
Plate, Raspberry Border, Center Flower, 8 ¾ In., Pair........................ 84.00

Royal Flemish, Jug, Shouldered, Shields, Flowers, Bull's-Eye Designs, Gold Applied Rope Twist Handle, 9 In. $7,475.00

Early Auction Co.

Royal Flemish, Pitcher, Fish, Shells, Coral, Seaweed, Gold Highlights, Rope Twist Handle, 8 In. $9,200.00

Early Auction Co.

Royal Flemish, Sugar Shaker, Fig Shape, Yellow Bark, Blue Raspberry Clusters, 4 ¼ In. $2,185.00

Early Auction Co.

The edited listings of the current prices in this *Kovels' Antiques & Collectibles Price Guide* aren't available on any website. Readers can visit **Kovels.com** to check thousands of past prices and sign up for free information on trends, tips, reproductions, marks, and more.

R

Royal Flemish, Vase, Frosted Gray, Gold Stippled Medallions, Multicolor Pansies, 2 Handles, 6 In.
$1,495.00

Early Auction Co.

Royal Flemish, Vase, Seagulls, Flying, Sunset, Cranberry, Gold, Signed, 12 ½ In.
$11,500.00

James D. Julia Auctioneers

Royal Doulton Figurines

Figurines were made at the end of the nineteenth century. From 1909 to 1914 small figurines were made. Royal Doulton figurines have been made every year since. They were realistic models of people, like the Old Balloon Seller or Top o' the Hill. Royal Doulton artists were making more contemporary figurines by 1978, and figurines like the Images line of streamlined white figures were created.

Tray, Tea, Serpentine Sides, Gilt Handles, Marked, c.1885, 18 x 14 In.	123.00
Vase, Dome Lid, Gilt Ferns, Bamboo Shoots, Cobalt Blue Ground, c.1900, 15 In.	875.00
Vase, Gilt Flowers, Butterflies, Red Ground, Garlic Mouth, Oval, Scrolled Handles, c.1880, 5 ¼ In.	106.00
Vase, Gilt Garlands, Double Loop Handles, Green Ground, Tiffany & Co., 9 In.	132.00
Vase, Lid, Flowers, Raised Gilt Work, Medallions, Strapwork, Marked, 1886-87, 12 ¾ In. *Illus*	1230.00
Vase, Yellow Glaze, Gold, Flower, Leafy Stem, Handles At Rim, 7 ½ In., Pair	230.00

ROYAL DOULTON is the name used on Doulton and Company pottery made from 1902 to the present. Doulton and Company of England was founded in 1853. Pieces made before 1902 are listed in this book under Doulton. Royal Doulton collectors search for the out-of-production figurines, character jugs, vases, and series wares. Some vases and animal figurines were made with a special red glaze called flambe. Sung and Chang glazed pieces are rare. The multicolored glaze is very thick and looks as if it were dropped on the clay. In 2005 Royal Doulton was acquired by the Waterford Wedgwood Group, which was bought by KPS Capital Partners of New York in 2009 and became part of WWRD Holdings.

Animal, Bulldog, Seated, DA 222	48.00
Animal, Greyhound, HN 1066	211.00
Animal, Monkeys, Cuddling, Flambe	288.00
Animal, Peruvian Penguin, On Rocks, Flambe, Signed, Noke, 9 In.	653.00
Animal, Spaniel, With Pheasant, HN 1001	134.00
Bowl, Cottage, Stream, Scalloped, Flared Rim, Black Underglaze, Flambe, 10 In.	180.00
Bowl, Dickens Scene, Yellow, Green, 8 In.	62.00

Royal Doulton character jugs depict the head and shoulders of the subject. They are made in four sizes: large, 5 ¼ to 7 inches; small, 3 ¼ to 4 inches; miniature, 2 ¼ to 2 ½ inches; and tiny, 1 ¼ inches. Toby jugs portray a seated, full figure.

Character Jug Set, Beatles, D 6724, D 6725, D 6726, D 6727, 6 In., 4 Piece	415.00
Character Jug, Albert Einstein, D 7023, 7 In.	122.00
Character Jug, Bacchus, D 6499, 7 In.	20.00
Character Jug, Beethoven, D 7201, 7 In.	77.00
Character Jug, Bill Sykes, D 6981, 7 In.	134.00
Character Jug, Buddy Holly, D 7100, 8 In.	211.00
Character Jug, Captain Henry Morgan, D 6469, c.1957, 3 ½ x 4 In.	35.00
Character Jug, Charlie Chaplin, D 6949, 7 ¼ In.	192.00
Character Jug, Chopin, D 7030, 7 In.	140.00
Character Jug, Clown, D 6834, 7 In.	96.00
Character Jug, Davy Crockett & Santa Ana, 2 Faces, D 6729, 7 In.	115.00
Character Jug, Elgar, D 7118, 7 In.	288.00
Character Jug, Fortune Teller, D 6523, 2 ½ In.	95.00
Character Jug, George Stephenson, D 7093, 7 In.	345.00
Character Jug, H.G. Wells, D 7095, 6 ¾ In.	154.00
Character Jug, Handel, D 7080, 7 In.	96.00
Character Jug, Happy John, D 6070, 5 ¼ In.	23.00
Character Jug, Jane Eyre & Mr. Rochester, Double Headed, D 7115, 4 ¾ In.	77.00
Character Jug, John Peel, D 5612, 1936-60, 6 ½ In. *Illus*	120.00
Character Jug, Lord Nelson & Lady Hamilton, Double Headed, D 7092, 4 In.	116.00
Character Jug, Mozart, D 7031, 7 In.	124.00
Character Jug, Mr. Micawber, D 7047, 7 ½ In.	124.00
Character Jug, Mr. Pickwick, D 6959, 7 In.	116.00
Character Jug, Paul McCartney, D 6724, 5 ½ In.	86.00
Character Jug, Phantom Of The Opera, D 7017, 7 In.	562.00
Character Jug, Punch & Judy Man, D 6590, 7 In.	151.00
Character Jug, Quasimodo, D 7108, 7 In.	134.00
Character Jug, Sairey Gamp, D 5528, 3 ¼ In.	11.00
Character Jug, Santa Claus, No. D 6668, Large	51.00
Character Jug, Scaramouche, D 6564, 2 ½ In.	122.00
Character Jug, Schubert, D 7056, 6 ¾ In.	86.00
Character Jug, Sir Francis Drake, D 6660, Square, Twist Handle, Signed, 11 In.	480.00
Character Jug, St. George, D 7129, 7 ½ In.	232.00
Character Jug, Tchaikovsky, D 7022, 7 In.	140.00
Character Jug, Ugly Duchess, D 6607, 2 ½ In.	113.00
Charger, Itch Yer On, Guvnor, Automobile Series, 13 ¾ In.	180.00
Coffeepot, Lid, English Renaissance, Gilt, c.1970, 9 ½ In.	202.00
Cup & Plate, Bunnykins, Playing, Hook & Ladder Fire Truck, 3 In.	32.00
Cup & Plate, Bunnykins, Winter Scene, Camping, 1968-75, 3 In.	28.00
Cup & Saucer, Blue Mottled Ground, Gilt Embossed Borders, Demitasse	225.00

R

Cup & Saucer, Ivory Ground, Raised Gilt Design, c.1920	120.00
Cup & Saucer, Pickwick Papers, Sam Weller, Fat Boy, Mr. Pickwick & Mrs. Cluppins	95.00
Cup & Saucer, Vanity Fair, c.1970	7.00
Dish, Entree, Lid, Gaythorne, V1480, Tan Leaf, Brown Scroll, 11 ¼ In.	49.00
Dish, Lid, Art Deco, Violets, Black Scrolling, 5 ¼ In.	50.00
Figurine, A Child From Williamsburg, HN 2154	28.00
Figurine, A Good Catch, HN 2258, 7 ¼ In.	85.00
Figurine, A Penny's Worth, HN 2408	100.00
Figurine, Abdullah, HN 2104	192.00
Figurine, Alexandra, HN 2398, Margaret Davies, 1970-76, 8 ¼ In.	75.00
Figurine, All Aboard, HN 2940	134.00
Figurine, Apple Maid, HN 2160	116.00
Figurine, Ascot, Sporting Heritage Series, HN 3471	125.00
Figurine, Bachelor, HN 2319	96.00
Figurine, Balloon Man, HN 1954	116.00
Figurine, Bedtime Story, HN 2059	77.00
Figurine, Belle Of The Ball, HN 1997	134.00
Figurine, Bess, HN 2002	77.00
Figurine, Biddy, HN 1513	58.00
Figurine, Blacksmith, HN 2782	53.00 to 116.00
Figurine, Boatman, HN 2417, 7 In.	*Illus* 240.00
Figurine, Bonnie Lassie, HN 1626, Leslie Harradine, 1934-53, 5 ¾ x 5 ½ In.	163.00 to 395.00
Figurine, Bridget, HN 2070	96.00
Figurine, Buffalo, Red, Flambe, C.J. Noke, Marked, 1900s, 10 ½ In.	*Illus* 2607.00
Figurine, Bunnykins, Autumn Days, DB 5, c.1980, 4 ¼ In.	165.00
Figurine, Bunnykins, Beefeater, DB 163	173.00
Figurine, Bunnykins, Drum Major, DB 27, Golden Jubilee Stamp	86.00
Figurine, Bunnykins, Drummer, White, DB 26	154.00
Figurine, Bunnykins, Family Photograph, DB 67	154.00
Figurine, Bunnykins, Jester, DB 161	140.00
Figurine, Bunnykins, Mountie, DB 135	376.00
Figurine, Bunnykins, Olympic, DB 28B	232.00
Figurine, Bunnykins, Playtime, DB 80	134.00
Figurine, Bunnykins, Playtime, Woman Bunny With Girl, DB 8, c.1990, 4 In.	85.00
Figurine, Bunnykins, Tally Ho, DB 12, Signed K, 4 ¾ x 2 In.	35.00
Figurine, Carpenter, HN 2678	124.00
Figurine, Carpet Seller, HN 1464	103.00 to 116.00
Figurine, Chief, HN 2892	106.00
Figurine, China Repairer, HN 2943	95.00 to 116.00
Figurine, Christmas Morn, HN 1992, 7 In.	48.00 to 150.00
Figurine, Christmas Parcels, HN 3493, c.1994, 6 In.	50.00
Figurine, Christmas Time, HN 2110	86.00
Figurine, Christopher Columbus, HN 3392, 12 In.	270.00
Figurine, Clarissa, HN 2345, 7 In.	46.00
Figurine, Clemency, HN 1643	388.00
Figurine, Clockmaker, HN 2279	140.00 to 150.00
Figurine, Clown, HN 2890, 9 In.	35.00 to 106.00
Figurine, Cobbler, HN 1706	116.00
Figurine, Columbine, HN 1439	538.00
Figurine, Coralie, HN 230, 7 ¼ In.	57.00
Figurine, Countess Spencer, HN 3320	96.00
Figurine, Country Lass, HN 1991	77.00
Figurine, Cradle Song, HN 2246	116.00
Figurine, Daisy, HN 1575	232.00
Figurine, Daydreams, HN 1731	45.00
Figurine, Debutante, HN 2213, 5 In.	83.00
Figurine, Delight, HN 1772	163.00
Figurine, Doctor, HN 2858	96.00
Figurine, Elegance, HN 2264, 7 ½ In.	46.00
Figurine, Elizabeth, HN 4426, 8 ½ In.	71.00
Figurine, Ermine Coat, HN 1981	77.00 to 95.00
Figurine, Family Album, HN 2321	96.00
Figurine, Farmer's Wife, HN 3164	116.00
Figurine, Fisherman, HN 4511	77.00
Figurine, Flora, HN 2349	96.00
Figurine, Florence Nightingale, HN 3144	142.00 to 173.00
Figurine, Flower Seller's Children, HN 1342	173.00

Royal Worcester, Figurine, Bob-White Quail, Signed, Ronald Van Ruychevelt, 1969, 5 ½ In.
$330.00

DuMouchelles Art Gallery

Royal Worcester, Figurine, Bull, British Friesian, Signed, Inscribed, Doris Lindner, 1964, 7 ½ x 10 In.
$600.00

DuMouchelles Art Gallery

TIP

If you ever loan anything to a museum or historical society, be sure to check on the museum's insurance coverage and the value it placed on your piece. We loaned a county fair sign for a centennial celebration and it was displayed in a sunny window. The printing faded until it was too light to read. Turns out there was no insurance coverage on the sign and we were not paid for the loss.

R

Roycroft, Chandelier, Copper & Iron, Hammered, Milk Glass Globe, Victor Toothaker, 1920s, 28 x 14 In. $8,125.00

Rago Arts & Auction Center

Roycroft, Planter, Fernery, Karl Kipp, Copper, Hammered, Nickel Silver, Orb & Cross, KK, c.1913, 6 x 7 In. $33,750.00

Rago Arts & Auction Center

Roycroft, Vase, American Beauty, Copper, Hammered, Grove Park Inn, Marked, c.1913, 22 x 8 In. $2,625.00

Rago Arts & Auction Center

Figurine, Foaming Quart, HN 2162	77.00
Figurine, Forty Winks, HN 1974	76.00
Figurine, Fragrance, HN 2334, 7 ½ In.	60.00
Figurine, Friar Tuck, HN 2143	100.00
Figurine, Game Keeper, HN 2879	288.00
Figurine, Gemma, HN 3661, 8 In.	81.00
Figurine, General Robert E. Lee, HN 3404	768.00
Figurine, Golliwog, HN 2040	192.00
Figurine, Good King Wenceslas, HN 2118	163.00
Figurine, Good King Wenceslas, HN 3262, 9 In.	60.00
Figurine, Goody Two Shoes, HN 2037, 5 ¼ In.	23.00
Figurine, Graduate Female, HN 3016	96.00
Figurine, Graduate Male, HN 3017	96.00
Figurine, Grandpa's Story, HN 3456	115.00
Figurine, Granny's Heritage, HN 2031	173.00
Figurine, Harlequin, HN 2737	480.00
Figurine, Helmsman, HN 2499, 1973, 9 In.	390.00
Figurine, Hilary, HN 2335, 7 In.	36.00
Figurine, Hold Tight, HN 3298	182.00
Figurine, Hornpipe, HN 2161	328.00
Figurine, Huntsman, HN 2492	120.00
Figurine, Huntsman, On Horse, Horn, HN 1408, 1930, 9 In.	1645.00
Figurine, Jack, HN 2060, Jill, HN 2061, Pair	116.00
Figurine, Jean, HN 2032	96.00
Figurine, Jersey Milk Maid, HN 2057, 7 In.	58.00
Figurine, Jester, HN 2016	103.00
Figurine, Jolly Sailor, HN 2172	288.00
Figurine, Jovial Monk, HN 2144	96.00
Figurine, Kathleen, HN 1252	365.00
Figurine, Lady Charmaine, HN 1948	66.00
Figurine, Laird, HN 2361	47.00
Figurine, Last Waltz, HN 1215, 8 In.	48.00
Figurine, Last Waltz, HN 2315, 7 ½ In.	46.00
Figurine, Lido Lady, HN 4247	66.00
Figurine, Lights Out, HN 2262	86.00
Figurine, Lisa, HN 2310, 7 In.	81.00
Figurine, Long John Silver, HN 2204	192.00
Figurine, Lunchtime, HN 2485, 8 In.	250.00
Figurine, Margaret, HN 2397, 7 ¾ In.	79.00
Figurine, Marguerite, HN 1928	77.00
Figurine, Marie, HN 1370, 5 In.	23.00 to 24.00
Figurine, Mary Jane, HN 1990, 7 ⅝ In.	98.00
Figurine, Mask Seller, HN 2104	106.00
Figurine, Master Sweep, HN 2205	173.00
Figurine, Mayor, HN 2280	124.00
Figurine, Maytime, HN 2113	76.00
Figurine, Mendicant, HN 1365	95.00 to 134.00
Figurine, Mid-Summer Noon, HN 2033	142.00
Figurine, My Love, HN 2339, 6 In.	48.00
Figurine, Napoleon, HN 3429	768.00
Figurine, News Vendor, HN 2891	100.00
Figurine, Nicola, HN 2839, 7 In.	83.00
Figurine, Old Balloon Seller, HN 1315	77.00 to 84.00
Figurine, Old Ben, HN 3190	77.00
Figurine, Old Mother Hubbard, HN 2314	124.00
Figurine, Oliver Hardy, HN 2775	144.00
Figurine, Omar Khayyam, HN 2247	59.00 to 96.00
Figurine, Owl, HN 2042	124.00
Figurine, Paisley Shawl, M 4, c.1940, Miniature	76.00
Figurine, Parisian, Matte Finish, HN 2445	58.00
Figurine, Partners, HN 3119	106.00
Figurine, Patricia, M 25, Miniature	116.00
Figurine, Penelope, HN 1901	96.00
Figurine, Pied Piper, HN 2102	106.00
Figurine, Pillow Fight, HN 2270	96.00
Figurine, Piper, HN 2907, Michael Abberley	71.00
Figurine, Potter, HN 1493, 7 In.	65.00

Figurine, Pretty Polly, HN 2768, 6 ½ In.	42.00
Figurine, Pride & Joy, HN 2945	116.00
Figurine, Priscilla, HN 1340	154.00
Figurine, Promenade, HN 3072, Reflections Collection, Box, 13 In.	113.00
Figurine, Punch & Judy Man, HN 2765	140.00
Figurine, Puppetmaker, HN 2253	163.00
Figurine, Queen Elizabeth, Queen Mother, HN 3189	106.00
Figurine, Rest A While, HN 2728	85.00
Figurine, Richard The Lionheart, HN 3675	168.00
Figurine, Robin, M 38, Miniature	173.00
Figurine, Roseanna, HN 1926	96.00
Figurine, Sailor's Holiday, HN 2442	96.00
Figurine, Saint George, HN 2051	118.00
Figurine, Sandra, HN 2275, 8 ¼ In.	62.00
Figurine, Santa Claus, HN 4175	106.00
Figurine, Sea Harvest, HN 2257	76.00 to 106.00
Figurine, Shepherd, HN 751	461.00
Figurine, Shepherd, HN 1975	96.00
Figurine, Shore Leave, HN 2254	95.00 to 106.00
Figurine, Silks & Ribbons, HN 2017	76.00 to 77.00
Figurine, Sonia, HN 1738	557.00
Figurine, Sorcerer, HN 4252, Box	153.00
Figurine, Sorceress, HN 4253, Box	118.00
Figurine, Southern Belle, HN 2425, Signed M. Davies, 1958-97, 7 ½ In.	295.00
Figurine, Spring Flowers, HN 1807	116.00
Figurine, Spring Morning, HN 1922, 7 ½ In.	58.00 to 77.00
Figurine, Stop Press, HN 2683	86.00
Figurine, Suitor, HN 2132	122.00
Figurine, Sunshine Girl, HN 4245	288.00
Figurine, Suzette, HN 2026	86.00
Figurine, Sweet Anne, HN 1496, Leslie Harradine, 1932-67, 7 In.	275.00
Figurine, Sweet Dreams, HN 2380	42.00 to 100.00
Figurine, Sweet Lavender, HN 1373	372.00
Figurine, Swimmer, HN 4246	134.00
Figurine, Tailor, HN 2174	244.00
Figurine, Taking Things Easy, Cream Jacket, HN 2620	103.00
Figurine, Taking Things Easy, White, HN 2680	106.00
Figurine, Tall Story, HN 2248	77.00
Figurine, Thank You, HN 2732	76.00
Figurine, Thanks, Doc, HN 2731	124.00
Figurine, Thanksgiving, Matte Glaze, HN 2446	55.00
Figurine, Tinker Bell, HN 1677	28.00
Figurine, Tiptoes, HN 3293	134.00
Figurine, Tom Bombadil, HN 2924, 5 ½ In.	192.00
Figurine, Top Of The Hill, HN 1834, 7 ⅜ In.	95.00
Figurine, Town Crier, HN 2119	120.00
Figurine, Tumbling, HN 3283, 9 In.	116.00 to 208.00
Figurine, Two Bed, HN 1805	66.00
Figurine, Vice Admiral Lord Nelson, HN 3489	768.00
Figurine, Victoria, HN 2471, Signed M. Davies, 1976, 6 ½ In.	295.00
Figurine, Victorian Lady, HN 728	106.00
Figurine, Vivienne, HN 2073	96.00
Figurine, Wayfarer, HN 2362	77.00
Figurine, Will He, Won't He, HN 3275	95.00 to 116.00
Figurine, Winston S. Churchill, HN 3433	672.00
Figurine, Wintertime, HN 3060	47.00
Figurine, Wizard, HN 2877	77.00
Figurine, Yeoman Of The Guard, HN 2122	232.00
Jug, Desert Scenes, D 3192, Nomads, Camels, Palm Trees, 1909-26, 5 x 8 In.	175.00
Jug, Eglington Tournament, Jousting Scene, Green, Blue, White, 7 x 8 In.	140.00
Jug, Tunis, D 3538, Moorish Gateway, 1912-45, 5 ½ In.	375.00
Liquor Container, William Grant, Large, 7 ½ In.	183.00
Mask, Greta Garbo, HN 1593	365.00
Mask, Madame Pompadour, HN 1824, Small	192.00
Mask, Marlene Dietrich, HN 1541	173.00
Mask, Sweet Anne, HN 1590	173.00

Roycroft, Vase, Bud, Copper, 3 Handles, Leaf Design, Orb & Cross, c.1919, 7 ¼ x 4 ¼ In.
$3,375.00

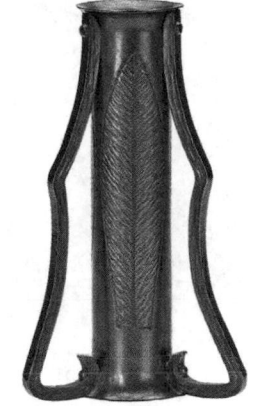

Rago Arts & Auction Center

Roycroft Vase, Copper, Hammered, American Beauty, Marked, 1906-10, 12 x 6 In.
$625.00

Rago Arts & Auction Center

Roycroft, Vase, Copper, Hammered, Green Paint, Walter Jennings, Orb & Cross Mark, c.1912, 7 x 3 In.
$10,000.00

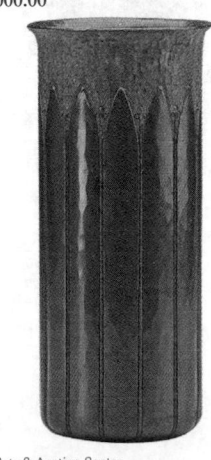

Rago Arts & Auction Center

R

TIP

Don't like to haggle over prices? Just write the price you will offer on a small card and give it to the dealer to consider. Or ask the dealer to write down the lowest acceptable price. Probably a good ploy for very expensive antiques or art.

Rozenburg, Vase, Owls, Hague, Netherlands, Signed, Samuel Schellink, 1897, 17 ¾ x 11 ½ In.
$11,250.00

Rago Arts & Auction Center

RRP, Jardiniere, Pedestal, Purple Glaze, Geometric Designs, 31 x 15 In.
$750.00

Rago Arts & Auction Center

Match Stand, Stoneware, Playing Card Suits, Green, Orange Sponging, England, 3 x 3 In.	35.00
Money Box, Bunnykins, Brambly Hedge Store Stump, DBH 18	77.00
Mug, Bunnykins, Hug A Mug, Albion Shape, Double Handles, c.1980	25.00
Pitcher, Battle Of Hastings, Battle Scenes, Black Rim, 7 ½ x 4 ¾ In. *Illus*	240.00
Pitcher, Jolly Toby, 6 In.	28.00
Pitcher, Pickwick Papers, Square, Press Molded, Multicolor, White Hart Inn, 5 ⅜ In.	24.00
Plate, Artful Dodger, 10 ¼ In.	80.00
Plate, Bread & Butter, Chatham, H 5141, c.1980, 6 ½ In.	10.00
Plate, Center Reserve, Yellow Roses, Floral Rim Reserves, 12 Edges, J. Price, 10 ⅜ In.	695.00
Plate, Dessert, Pink Ground, Raised Gilt Gadrooned Edge, Medallion, c.1920, 8 ¾ In.	150.00
Plate, Dessert, Vanity Fair, 6 ⅜ In.	7.00
Plate, Dinner, Cobalt Blue, Gilt, Gadrooned Edge, Raised Pattern, c.1920, 12 Piece	3600.00
Plate, Dinner, Vanity Fair, 10 ½ In.	12.00
Plate, Don Quixote, Blanket Tossing, Painted Over Transfer, 1906-28, 10 ¼ In.	99.00
Plate, Festival Children Of The World, Magdalena, Brenda Burke, 1984, 8 ½ In.	45.00
Plate, Fish, James Birbeck, Sr., 9 In., 4 Piece	1495.00
Plate, Hudson Valley Town Scenes, Blue Transfer, 10 ½ In., c.1920, 10 Piece	142.00
Plate, Kingswood, Floral Bouquet Center, Turquoise Scalloped Border, Luncheon	35.00
Plate, Landscape Scene, Raised Gold Leafy Border, P. Curnock, 1900s, 10 ⅝ In., 12 Piece *Illus*	3555.00
Plate, New Cavaliers, D 3051, Lion & Shield Border, C.J. Noke, c.1909, 9 ½ In.	125.00
Plate, Salad, Vanity Fair, 7 ⅞ In.	7.00
Plate, Spanish Ware, Pastel Flowers, Ivory Ground, Raised Gilt, Reticulated Border, c.1890, 10 In.	195.00
Plate, Zunday Zmocks Series, Scene 9, 1936-50, 7 ¾ In.	150.00
Platter, Turkey, Shell & Scrolling Leaf Border, D 5962, 1900s, 21 x 17 In.	600.00
Serving Dish, Chelsea Rose, Oval, c.1943	16.00
Tea Set, Harrow, Teapot, Creamer, Sugar, c.1977, 7 & 4 ¾ & 4 In., 3 Piece	110.00
Tea Set, Series Ware, Monks In The Cellar, c.1910, 3 Piece	84.00
Toby Jug, Celsius & Fahrenheit, D 7143, 1999, 4 ¾ In.	140.00
Toby Jug, Lewis Carroll, D 7078, 1997, 6 ½ In.	77.00
Toby Jug, Old Father Time, D 7609, 6 ½ In.	127.00
Toby Jug, Winston Churchill, D 6171, 9 In.	56.00
Urn, Lid, Gilt Berry Finial, Rim, Painted Rose, Signed H. Piper, 26 In.	523.00
Vase, Blue Chrysanthemums, Cream Ground, Tapered Foot, Marked, 1918, 11 ½ In.	165.00
Vase, Blue Enamel Daisies, Bronze Color Ground, Impressed Mark, c.1900, 3 ¾ In.	95.00
Vase, Flambe, Country Scene, Narrow Neck, 8 ¼ In.	280.00
Vase, Foliage Ware, Gourd Shape, Textured Leaf Relief, Brown, Taupe, Blue Mottled Glaze, 1928, 8 In.	109.00
Vase, Pastoral Scene, Flambe, 8 x 3 ½ In.	144.00
Vase, Shakespeare, Juliet, Footed, 1912-28, 3 ⅛ In.	125.00
Vase, Slip Colors, Green, Yellow, Red, White, Black, Blue, Drip Glaze, Marked, 10 ¼ In. *Illus*	6038.00
Vase, Stoneware, Cobalt Blue, Gilt, White Designs, 1902-22, 11 ¼ In., Pair	375.00
Washbasin & Pitcher, Art Nouveau, Aubrey R & N, c.1900, 13 ½ x 7 ⅜ In.	1500.00

ROYAL DUX is the more common name for the Duxer Porzellanmanufaktur, which was founded by E. Eichler in Dux, Bohemia (now Duchov, Czech Republic), in 1860. By the turn of the twentieth century, the firm specialized in porcelain statuary and busts of Art Nouveau-style maidens, large porcelain figures, and ornate vases with three-dimensional figures climbing on the sides. The firm is still in business.

Bust, Maiden, Hands Clasped To Face, 1905, 18 ¼ In.	750.00
Centerpiece, 3 Dancing Maidens, Pedestal, Multicolor Flowers, Gold Rim, 20 In. *Illus*	720.00
Centerpiece, Art Nouveau, Parcel Gilt, 2 Women, c.1930, 21 x 15 In.	325.00
Centerpiece, Nymph, Putti, Supporting Oval Bowl, Rocaille Base, 20 In.	406.00
Centerpiece, Woman, 2 Putti, Supporting Bowl, Flower Design, Blue Glaze, 20 x 16 In.	230.00
Figurine, Water Bird, Black, White, 11 ½ In.	40.00
Urn, White, Painted, Blue Flowers, Gilt Detail, Handles, 25 x 13 In.	420.00
Vase, Blue & Green Iridescent, Purple, Ribbon Handles & Rim, Bell Shape, 5 ½ In.	575.00
Vase, Cobalt Blue Iridescent, Smokestack, Ribbon Handles, Wrapped Around Body, 8 ½ In.	460.00
Vase, Cream Engraved Berries, Leaves, Gold Handles, Wood Base, 20 In., Pair	85.00
Vase, Figural, 2 Green Nymphs, Pink Irises, Luster Glazed, Marked, c.1900, 15 ½ In.	1007.00

ROYAL FLEMISH glass was made during the late 1880s in New Bedford, Massachusetts, by the Mt. Washington Glass Works. It is a colored satin glass decorated with dark colors and raised gold designs. The glass was patented in 1894. It was supposed to resemble stained glass windows.

Biscuit Jar, Barrel Shape, Flower Collar, Silver Plate Lid, Collar & Handle, 8 In.	1610.00
Biscuit Jar, Raised Gold Tone Panels, Black, Green Shield, Rampant Lion, 7 In.	1495.00
Bottle, Butterflies, Leaves, Scroll Band Around Neck, Bulbous, Stopper, 5 ½ In.	3163.00

Ewer, Bulbous Stick Shape, Raised Gold Panels, Coat Of Arms, Lions, Twisted Handle, 12 ½ In.	2300.00
Jug, Shouldered, Shields, Flowers, Bull's-Eye Designs, Gold Applied Rope Twist Handle, 9 In. .... *Illus*	7475.00
Perfume Bottle, Blue White Flowers, Green Leaves, Egg Shape, 4 In..................................	1380.00
Perfume Bottle, Lid, Frosted, Enameled Butterflies, Jewel Accents, Bulbous, 5 ¾ In...............	1610.00
Pitcher, Fish, Shells, Coral, Seaweed, Gold Highlights, Rope Twist Handle, 8 In. ....*Illus*	9200.00
Pitcher, Water, Fish & Shells, Enamel Over Raised Gilt Grids, Rope Twist Handle, 8 In.	19550.00
Sugar Shaker, Fig Shape, Yellow Bark, Blue Raspberry Clusters, 4 ¼ In.........................*Illus*	2185.00
Vase, Frosted Gray, Gold Stippled Medallions, Multicolor Pansies, 2 Handles, 6 In. ....*Illus*	1495.00
Vase, Scrolling Medallions, Pansies, White Ground, Squat, Swollen Stick Neck, 12 ½ In.	2300.00
Vase, Seagulls, Flying, Sunset, Cranberry, Gold, Signed, 12 ½ In......................................*Illus*	11500.00

ROYAL HAEGER, *see Haeger category.*

ROYAL HICKMAN designed pottery, glass, silver, aluminum, furniture, lamps, and other items. From 1938 to 1944 and again from the 1950s to 1969, he worked for Haeger Potteries. Mr. Hickman operated his own pottery in Tampa, Florida, during the 1940s. He moved to California and worked for Vernon Potteries. During the last years of his life he lived in Guadalajara, Mexico, and continued designing for Royal Haeger. Pieces made in his pottery listed here are marked *Royal Hickman or Hickman.*

Lamp Base, 2 Greyhound Dogs, Black, c.1938..	300.00
Vase, Gladiola, Ruffled, Chartreuse, Yellow Drip Glaze, c.1949, 11 x 9 In..................	150.00
Vase, Horse Head, Blue, Plum Mottled Glaze, 9 x 11 ½ In., Pair..............................	81.00
Vase, Horse On Wave, Agate Green, 1940s, 8 In..	125.00
Vase, Ocean Blue, Bow Base, c.1940, 11 In..	40.00
Vase, Peacock, Mauve, Blue, 13 x 7 In..	85.00
Vase, Pierced Gladiola, Brown, Chartreuse Drip Glaze, c.1949, 14 x 11 In.	150.00
Vase, Swan, Sky Blue, 1940s, 10 ½ In..	60.00

ROYAL NYMPHENBURG is the modern name for the Nymphenburg porcelain factory, which was established at Neudeck-ob-der-Au, Germany, in 1753 and moved to Nymphenburg in 1761. The company is still in existence. Marks include a checkered shield topped by a crown, a crowned *CT* with the year, and a contemporary shield mark on reproductions of eighteenth-century porcelain.

Figurine, Bird, On Branch, Blue, Yellow, Germany, 8 ½ In..	266.00
Figurine, Parrot, Multicolor, Marked, 8 In., Pair	823.00
Group, Putti, Around Stump, Marked, 8 ¾ In.	300.00

ROYAL RUDOLSTADT, *see Rudolstadt category.*

ROYAL VIENNA, *see Beehive category.*

ROYAL WORCESTER is a name used by collectors. Worcester porcelains were made in Worcester, England, from about 1751. The firm went through many different periods and name changes. It became the Worcester Royal Porcelain Company, Ltd., in 1862. Today collectors call the porcelains made after 1862 "Royal Worcester." In 1976, the firm merged with W.T. Copeland to become Royal Worcester Spode. The company was bought by the Portmeirion Group in 2009. Some early products of the factory are listed under Worcester. Related pieces may be listed under Copeland, Copeland Spode, and Spode.

Biscuit Jar, Roses, Yellow Ground, Silver Rim, Handle, c.1904, 6 ½ In.	180.00
Bowl, Lily Pad, Ivory, Veining, Crinkled Edge, Frog & Flower Base, 7 x 11 In.	590.00
Candlestick, Floral, Scrolling, Bulb Shape Base, Scrolling Leaf Tips, Flower Bud Cup, 6 ¾ In., Pair ...	86.00
Figurine, Allegorical, Sorrow, Peach Garment, Gold Leaf, Dead Dove, 16 x 5 In.	240.00
Figurine, Bob-White Quail, Signed, Ronald Van Ruychevelt, 1969, 5 ½ In.....................*Illus*	330.00
Figurine, Bull, British Friesian, Signed, Inscribed, Doris Lindner, 1964, 7 ½ x 10 In. ......*Illus*	600.00
Figurine, Punch, Bust, Blue Strip Hat, Yellow Shirt..	23.00
Figurine, Sailor, Holding Rope, 1882, 17 ¼ In..	472.00
Pitcher, Multicolor Flowers, White Ground, Stepped Spout, Gilt, 6 ½ In.	58.00
Plate, Blind Earl, Branches, Leaves, Butterflies, Scalloped Rim, Cream, Gilt, 1800s, 9 ¼ In. Diam.	239.00
Plate, Cobalt Blue & Gold Border, c.1899, 9 ¾ In., 12 Piece	472.00
Plate, Embassy, Gold Design On Green Border, 8 In., 12 Piece	120.00
Plate, Village Houses, Signed, 10 ¾ In., 4 Piece...	588.00
Tea Set, Footed Platter, Willow, 1881, 7 Piece	1200.00
Toothpick Holder, Figural, Putti & Goat, Basket, Round Base, 4 ¾ In.	207.00
Vase, Basket Weave, Flowering Branches, Branch Shape Feet, Ear Handles, Multicolor, 8 In....	431.00
Vase, Floral Relief Panels, Bamboo Trim & Feet, Rectangular, 11 In.	460.00

Rug, Caucasian Shirvan, Geometric, Red, Navy Blue, Beige, Cream, Multiple Borders, 3 Ft. 9 In. x 6 Ft.
$1,107.00

New Orleans Auction Galleries, Inc.

Rug, Caucasian, Medallions, Blue, Green, Red, Animals, People, 3 Ft. 10 In. x 6 Ft. 9 In.
$1,770.00

Brunk Auctions

R

TIP

If the border of a rug is badly frayed or missing, it dramatically lowers the value. A rug with a good fringe could be worth $1,500; without a border, the same rug could be worth only $100.

Rug, Chinese, 8 Mullahs, Standing In
Clouds, Blue Ground,
4 Ft. 2 In. x 2 Ft. 5 In.
$531.00

Brunk Auctions

Rug, Chinese, Flower Bouquets, Hanging
Lanterns, Rose, Blue Borders, 1900s,
9 Ft. x 11 Ft. 4 In.
$354.00

Brunk Auctions

Rug, Gabbeh, Contemporary, Squares,
Jewel Tones, 8 Ft. x 9 Ft. 10 In.
$2,500.00

Rago Arts & Auction Centera

Rug, Hooked, Deer, Pine Trees, Sawtooth
Borders, Wool, Cotton, Knit, c.1910,
19 x 38 In.
$470.00

Garth's Auctioneers & Appraisers

ROYCROFT products were made by the Roycrofter community of East Aurora, New York, in the late nineteenth and early twentieth centuries. The community was founded by Elbert Hubbard, famous philosopher, writer, and artist. The workshops owned by the community made furniture, metalware, leatherwork, embroidery, and jewelry. A printshop produced many signs, books, and the magazines that promoted the sayings of Elbert Hubbard. Furniture by the Roycroft community is listed in the Furniture category.

Andirons, Iron, Scrolling, Rings & Chain, c.1900, 25 ½ x 12 ½ In.	1125.00
Andirons, Iron, Twisted, Stacked Curls, Marked, 13 x 30 ½ In.	7930.00
Andirons, Twisted & Curled, c.1901, 13 x 21 x 30 In.	6500.00
Ashtray, Armchair, Copper, Tooled Leather Strap, Cat Design, Weights, 12 x 2 ½ In.	214.00
Bowl, Copper, Hammered, Round, Marked 11 x 3 In.	480.00
Bowl, W. Jennings Attributed, Impressed, c.1915, 19 ¾ x 6 ⅛ In.	17500.00
Candlestick, Copper, Hammered, Squared Column, 4 Penny Feet, 11 x 4 In., Pair	2875.00
Candlestick, Copper, Hammered, Strap, Square Stem, Footed, c.1910, 11 ¾ In., Pair	2000.00
Candlestick, Copper, Hammered, Tooled, Double Rod Standard, Flat Base, 3 ¼ x 8 In., Pair	366.00
Chandelier, 4-Light, Copper, Round, Heart Cutouts, Chains, Hanging Sockets, c.1910, 32 x 16 ¼ In.	2125.00
Chandelier, Copper & Iron, Hammered, Milk Glass Globe, Victor Toothaker, 1920s, 28 x 14 In.....*Illus*	8125.00
Jardiniere, Copper, Hammered, Footed, Cylindrical, Rounded Bottom, Banding, c.1915, 11 x 10 ¼ In.	3750.00
Lamp, Copper, Hammered, Mica Helmet Shade, Paneled, Brass Rivets, 12 ½ In.	690.00
Planter, Fernery, Karl Kipp, Copper, Hammered, Nickel Silver, Orb & Cross, KK, c.1913, 6 x 7 In. .... *Illus*	33750.00
Sign, Build Strong, Carved Oak, Orb & Cross Mark, c.1920, 5 x 19 ½ In.	1625.00
Vase, American Beauty, Copper, Hammered, Grove Park Inn, Marked, c.1913, 22 x 8 In...*Illus*	2625.00
Vase, American Beauty, Copper, Hammered, Rivets, Long Neck, Signed, 8 x 18 In.	2250.00
Vase, Bud, Copper, 3 Handles, Leaf Design, Orb & Cross, c.1919, 7 ¼ x 4 ¼ In. ....*Illus*	3375.00
Vase, Copper, Hammered, American Beauty, Marked, 1906-10, 12 x 6 In....................*Illus*	625.00
Vase, Copper, Hammered, Applied Organic Design, Cylinder, 3 x 6 ½ In.	1188.00
Vase, Copper, Hammered, Green Paint, Walter Jennings, Orb & Cross Mark, c.1912, 7 x 3 In.. *Illus*	10000.00
Vase, Copper, Hammered, Smokestack Bottom, Stick Neck, Flared Lip, Round Foot, c.1910, 7 x 3 ¼ In.	1000.00
Vase, Copper, Hammered, Smokestack, Cylindrical Neck, Trumpet Rim, c.1910, 18 x 7 In.	2625.00
Vase, Copper, Hammered, Squat, Marked, 6 ½ x 4 ½ In.	275.00 to 336.00

ROZANE, *see Roseville category.*

ROZENBURG worked at The Hague, Holland, from 1890 to 1914. The most important pieces were earthenware made in the early twentieth century with pale-colored Art Nouveau designs.

Charger, Flower Bouquet, Yellow, Green, Cobalt Blue, Marked, c.1900, 17 ½ In.	1007.00
Tile, 2 Dairy Cows, Farmer, Heading Homeward, Hilly Pasture, Frame, 1887, 6 ½ x 6 ½ In.	546.00
Vase, Owls, Hague, Netherlands, Signed, Samuel Schellink, 1897, 17 ¾ x 11 ½ In...........*Illus*	11250.00
Vase, Parrot, Tulips, Turquoise, Red, Blue, Green, Bulbous Genie Bottle, Flared Rim, 4 ½ In...	184.00
Vase, Spread Wing Bird, Flowers, Multicolor, Squat, Narrow Rim, Marked, 6 x 8 ½ In.	374.00

RRP, or RRP Roseville, is the mark used by the firm of Robinson-Ransbottom. It is not a mark of the more famous Roseville Pottery. The Ransbottom brothers started a pottery in 1900 in Ironspot, Ohio. In 1920, they merged with the Robinson Clay Product Company of Akron, Ohio, to become Robinson-Ransbottom. The factory closed in 2005.

Jardiniere, Pedestal, Purple Glaze, Geometric Designs, 31 x 15 In. ....*Illus*	750.00
Jardiniere, Pedestal, Rufftone, Blue, White Speckled Glaze, Pedestal Base, 34 In.	230.00

RS GERMANY is part of the wording in marks used by the Tillowitz, Germany, factory of Reinhold Schlegelmilch from 1914 until about 1945. The porcelain was sold decorated and undecorated. The Schlegelmilch families made porcelains marked in many ways. See also ES Germany, RS Poland, RS Prussia, RS Silesia, RS Suhl, and RS Tillowitz.

Hatpin Holder, Hatpins, Pink, Green, 7 In.	40.00
Plate, Black Swans, Pond, Open Handles, 1900s, 9 ¾ In.	1250.00
Toothbrush Holder, Roses, Flowers, Pink, 3 ½ In.	52.00

RS POLAND (German) is a mark used by the Reinhold Schlegelmilch factory at Tillowitz from about 1946 to 1956. After 1956, the factory made porcelain marked *PT Poland*. This is one of many of the RS marks used. See also ES Germany, RS Germany, RS Prussia, RS Silesia, RS Suhl, and RS Tillowitz.

Bowl, Center, Poland's Countess Potocka, Gold Stencil, Lily Mold, Footed, c.1900, 10 x 3 ½ In...	1495.00
Plate, Pink, Orange Roses, White Ground, Cut Out Handles, Molded Edges, c.1950, 10 In.	135.00
Vase, Black Geese, Green Ground, Silhouette Leaves, Grass, Pear Shape, Marked, 4 ½ In.	225.00
Vase, Pheasants, Woodland Scene, Bulbous, Gold Rim, 4 ½ x 4 In.	195.00

RS PRUSSIA appears in several marks used on porcelain before 1917. Reinhold Schlegelmilch started his porcelain works in Suhl, Germany, in 1869. See also ES Germany, RS Germany, RS Poland, RS Silesia, RS Suhl, and RS Tillowitz.

Berry Bowl, Embossed Flowers, 10 In.	62.00
Biscuit Jar, Swans In Lake, Scroll Handles, 6 x 7 ½ In.	425.00
Bowl, Rose Clusters, Silver Rim, Iridescent Glaze, Red Star Mark, c.1900, 10 In.	84.00
Celery Dish, Pierced Handles, 4 Relief Irises, Iridescent Molded Border, Pink Roses, c.1900, 12 In..	210.00
Cup & Saucer, Child, Lion Scene, 2 ⅜ In.	225.00
Dresser Tray, Center Bouquet, Art Nouveau, Gilt, 11 x 7 In.	600.00
Hatpin Holder, Glass Bead Hatpins, Red Mark, c.1900, 4 ¾ x 3 ¾ In.	90.00
Plate, Portrait, Melon Eaters, Pearl Cartouche, Green Scalloped Rim, Footed, Wreath Mark, 10 In.	690.00
Toothbrush Holder, Green Leaves, Blue & Red Flowers, 9 ¼ In.	175.00
Tray, Dresser, Swans In Lake, Open Handles, 12 x 7 ½ In.	652.00
Vase, Woman, With Dove, Cameo Handles, Enameled Flowers, 4 x 6 In.	950.00

RS SILESIA appears on porcelain made at the Reinhold Schlegelmilch factory in Tillowitz, Germany, from the 1920s to the 1940s. The Schlegelmilch families made porcelains marked in many ways. See also ES Germany, RS Germany, RS Poland, RS Prussia, RS Suhl, and RS Tillowitz.

Bowl, Ivory, Leaves & Grapes, Gold Trim, Ruffled Rim, c.1900, 9 ½ x 5 In.	60.00
Bowl, Orange Poppies, Gold Rim, Oval, Cut In Handles, Blue Mark, c.1915, 10 ¼ x 6 ¾ In.	85.00
Bowl, Peach Roses, Ruffled Edge, Footed, c.1868, 9 ½ x 4 ½ In.	90.00
Cake Plate, White Roses, Gold Filigree, Green Ground, 3 Handles, 1905-45, 7 ¾ In.	24.00
Jam Jar, Lid, Underplate, Rose, Violet, 5 ½ x 4 ¾ In.	90.00
Pitcher, Arts & Crafts Iris, Signed M. Church, c.1929, 5 ½ x 9 In.	295.00
Plate, Art Nouveau, Springtime, Mucha Woman, Signed Yvette Raymond Oubrem, 1904-38, 12 ¼ In.	995.00
Plate, Serving, Arts & Crafts Flowers, Tiered, Signed A.B. Elliff, c.1926, 3 x 9 ½ In.	145.00
Sugar & Creamer, Pansies, Purple, Yellow, Gilt Highlighting, c.1904-38, 3 ½ x 6 In.	89.00
Syrup, Underplate, Lily Of The Valley, c.1910, 5 ½ & 3 ½ x 5 In.	95.00

RS SUHL is a mark used by the Reinhold Schlegelmilch factory in Suhl, Germany, between 1900 and 1917. The Schlegelmilch families made porcelains in many places. See also ES Germany, RS Germany, RS Poland, RS Prussia, RS Silesia, and RS Tillowitz.

Plaque, Tavern Scene, 9 In.	75.00
Plate, Melon Boy, Cobalt Blue Border, 6 In.	128.00
Vase, White Roses, Black To White Ground, Double Handle, Green Mark, 14 ½ In.	126.00

RS TILLOWITZ was marked on porcelain by the Reinhold Schlegelmilch factory at Tillowitz from the 1920s to the 1940s. Table services and ornamental pieces were made. See also ES Germany, RS Germany, RS Poland, RS Prussia, RS Silesia, and RS Suhl.

Console, Art Deco, Green Luster, Dogwood Flowers, Leaves, Gold Rim, 10 In.	38.00
Tea Set, Teapot, Sugar, Creamer, Pink Rose Clusters, Gold Trim, M.E. Clemens, c.1919	263.00
Vase, Art Deco Iris, Gold Luster, 1904-38, 9 x 5 In.	165.00

RUBINA is a glassware that shades from red to clear. It was first made by George Duncan and Sons of Pittsburgh, Pennsylvania, in about 1885. This coloring was used on many types of glassware.

Pitcher, Coin Spot, Fuchsia To Yellow, Squared Mouth, Loop Handle, 7 ½ In.	230.00
Pitcher, Water, Lincoln Drape, Clear To Red, Opalescent, Urn Shape, Ruffled Rim, 9 In.	288.00
Vase, Iris, Leaves, Gold & Yellow Enamel, Optic Ribbing, Flared Bottom & Rim, 13 In.	403.00

RUBINA VERDE is a Victorian glassware that was shaded from red to green. It was first made by Hobbs, Brockunier and Company of Wheeling, West Virginia, about 1890.

Creamer, Coin Spot, Baluster, Loop Handle, Square Ruffled Rim, Amber To Pink, 4 ½ In.	115.00
Lamp, Hanging, Citrus To Cranberry, Opalescent Swags, Ruffled Edge Shade, 10 In.	546.00

RUBY GLASS is the dark red color of a ruby, the precious gemstone. It was a popular Victorian color that never went completely out of style. The glass was shaped by many different processes to make many different types of ruby glass. There was a revival of interest in the 1940s when modern-shaped ruby table glassware became fashionable. Sometimes the red color is added to clear glass by a process called flashing or staining. Flashed glass is clear glass dipped in a colored glass, then pressed or cut. Stained glass has color painted on a clear glass. Then it is refired so the stain fuses with the glass. Pieces of glass colored in this way are indicated by the word *stained* in the description. Related items may be found in other categories, such as Cranberry Glass, Pressed Glass, and Souvenir.

Epergne, Top Wavy Bowl, 2 Bulb Shapes, Silver Mounts, Marble Base, Tufts, Boston, c.1880	2375.00

Rug, Hooked, Dog Sled Scene, Figures, Grenfell, Newfoundland, Labrador, 1900s, 33 ½ x 45 ½ In.
$554.00

Skinner, Inc.

Rug, Karabagh, Medallions, c.1890, 15 Ft. 6 In. x 3 Ft. 6 In.
$750.00

Skinner, Inc.

Rug, Kazak, Star, Red, Blue, Gray Ground, Geometric Border, c.1810, 8 Ft. 6 In. x 4 Ft. 7 In.
$24,000.00

Skinner, Inc.

R

Rug, Kerman, Center Medallion, Palm
Leaves, Multiple Borders, Flowers,
8 Ft. 10 In. x 11 Ft.
$738.00

New Orleans Auction Galleries, Inc.

Rug, Marasali, Pictorial, Mother & Child,
Man & Woman, Borders, c.1885,
5 Ft. 6 In. x 4 Ft. 3 In.
$3,900.00

Skinner, Inc.

Rug, Modernist, Verner Panton,
Squares, Rust To Orange, Wool, Label,
England, c.1950, 8 Ft.
$1,215.00

Skinner, Inc.

> **TIP**
> *Store a rug by rolling
> it; never fold it.*

Mustard, Silver Rope Twist Overlay, Monogram Spoon, 3 x 3 In.	193.00
Pitcher, Press Molded, Canister Shape, Loop Handle, Raised Dots, 8 x 5 In.	35.00
Whimsy, Hat, 6 In.	46.00

RUGS have been used in the American home since the seventeenth century. The oriental rug of that time was often used on a table, not on the floor. Rag rugs, hooked rugs, and braided rugs were made by housewives from scraps of material. American Indian rugs are listed in the Indian category.

Afghan, Prayer, English, Arabic Inscriptions, 20th Century, 4 Ft. 10 In. x 2 Ft. 9 In.	107.00
Aubusson, Green, Pink, Bone, Elongated Lozenge, Flowers, Panel Border, Wool, 6 Ft. 4 In. x 3 Ft. 11 In..	178.00
Aubusson, Oval Flower Medallion, Russet, Flowers, Tan Border, France, c.1875, 13 Ft. x 10 Ft. 8 In.	1250.00
Avar, Transcaucasus, Red On Blue & Vice Versa, c.1910, Runner, 17 Ft. 9 In. x 5 Ft. 4 In.	236.00
Bakhtiari, Repeating Flowers & Scrolls, Blue Ground, Persian, Runner, 7 Ft. 5 In. x 16 Ft.	767.00
Balouch, Indigo Blue, Red Ground, 3 Diamond Shapes, Zag Bolts, Flower Border, 4 Ft. 8 In. x 2 Ft. 9 In.	184.00
Balouch, Pictorial, Cityscape, Cars, Red, Tan, Navy Ground, Geometric Border, 2 Ft. 6 In. x 4 Ft. 4 In.	63.00
Balouch, Stylized Geometrics, Orange, Tan, Black Border, Fringe, c.1905, 5 Ft. 5 In. x 3 Ft.	207.00
Bessarabian, Ivory Fields, Flower Sprays, Vine Border, Balkans, 1866, 13 Ft. 8 In. x 10 Ft. 4 In.	3448.00
Bidjar, Allover Flower Medallions, Blue Field, Leaf Border, Persia, c.1910, 16 x 12 Ft.	10625.00
Bidjar, Blue Ground, Camel Border, c.1920, Runner, 4 Ft. 3 In. x 16 Ft. 3 In.	362.00
Bidjar, Blue, Red, Cream Stylized Flowers, Scrolls, Black Field, c.1910, 7 Ft. x 4 Ft. 6 In.	2607.00
Bidjar, Herati Pattern, Red, Blue, Cream Border, c.1910, 17 Ft. 6 In. x 11 Ft. 2 In.	2430.00
Bidjar, Lattice, Blue, Ivory, Red, Blue Flowers, Border, Wool, Cotton, Runner, 10 Ft. 6 In. x 3 Ft. 8 In.	265.00
Bidjar, Palmettes, Flowers, 3 Borders, Blue Field, Persia, c.1880, 18 Ft. x 11 Ft. 5 In.	16120.00
Boteh, Red Field, Geometric, Multiple Borders, Persia, 6 Ft. 2 In. x 3 Ft. 9 In.	219.00
Braided, 9 Mats Joined, Multicolor, 6 Ft. 10 In. x 6 Ft. 8 In.	71.00
Braided, Flower Medallions, Red, Gray, Yellow, Scalloped, Round, c.1850, 2 Ft. 7 In.	230.00
Cabistan, Wool, Blue Ground, Medallions, Red Birds, Geometrics, 3 Borders, 72 x 46 In.	540.00
Caucasian, 3 Pendant Medallions, Red, Blue, Geometric Border, 4 Ft. 8 In. x 6 Ft. 8 In.	295.00
Caucasian, Diamond Pattern Center, Blue, Burgundy, Tan, c.1900, 9 Ft. 2 In. x 5 Ft.	326.00
Caucasian, Elongated Lozenges, Blue, Geometrics, Animals, Wool, On Wool, 5 Ft. 2 In. x 3 Ft. 9 In.	546.00
Caucasian, Medallions, Blue, Green, Red, Animals, People, 3 Ft. 10 In. x 6 Ft. 9 In. ....*Illus*	1770.00
Caucasian, Prayer, Octagons, Blue Ground, Stepped Border, 4 Ft. 9 In. x 3 Ft. 8 ½ In.	1872.00
Caucasian, Shirvan, Geometric, Red, Navy Blue, Beige, Cream, Multiple Borders, 3 Ft. 9 In. x 6 Ft. .*Illus*	1107.00
Chinese, 8 Mullahs, Standing In Clouds, Blue Ground, 4 Ft. 2 In. x 2 Ft. 5 In............*Illus*	531.00
Chinese, 9 Imperial Dragons, Cloud, Ivory Ground, Blue Green Wave Border, Silk, 8 x 5 Ft.	1250.00
Chinese, Allover Flowers, Butterflies, Blue, Cream, c.1875, 13 Ft. 4 In. x 10 Ft.	2813.00
Chinese, Art Deco, Border, Multicolor Flowers, Rust Ground, Wool, Nichols, 7 Ft. 9 In. x 9 Ft. 6 In.	1778.00
Chinese, Flower Bouquets, Hanging Lanterns, Rose, Blue Borders, 1900s, 9 Ft. x 11 Ft. 4 In.......*Illus*	354.00
Chinese, Tan & Pink Foo Dog Panels, Fretwork, Butterfly Borders, 13 Ft. x 12 Ft. 6 ½ In.	12890.00
Chinese, Tree Of Life, Birds & Flowers, Floral Border, Silk, 5 x 3 Ft.	1135.00
Gabbeh, Contemporary, Squares, Jewel Tones, 8 Ft. x 9 Ft. 10 In.......................*Illus*	2500.00
Hamadan, Gold, Navy Medallion, Serrated Arabesque Edge, Red Ground, 3 Ft. 5 In. x 5 Ft. 5 In.	295.00
Hamadan, Leaves, Flowers, Ivory Medallions, Red, Blue Ground, 2 Ft. 3 In. x 3 Ft. 9 In.	83.00
Heriz, Gabled Medallions, Salmon, Green, Aqua, Red, Stylized, Blue Ground, 2 Ft. 9 In. x 4 Ft. 1 In.	189.00
Heriz, 5 Serrated Medallions, Amber, Blue, Brick Red Ground, Runner, 3 x 10 Ft.	1416.00
Heriz, Abrash Spandrels, Flower Border, Blue, Red, Pale Green, Tan, c.1925, 10 x 12 Ft.	3055.00
Heriz, Center Medallion, Brown, Tan, Black, c.1940, 12 Ft. 6 In. x 9 Ft. 9 In.	365.00
Heriz, Center Medallion, Ivory, Blue, Red Brown Ground, Ivory Cornerwork, 10 x 13 Ft.	5428.00
Heriz, Gabled Medallion, Blue Pendants, Red Ground, 8 Ft. 3 In. x 11 Ft. 10 In.	1121.00
Heriz, Geometric Medallion, Spandrels, Leaf, Vine Border, Red Field, Persia, c.1880, 12 x 9 ½ Ft.	10000.00
Heriz, Hexagonal Medallion, Blue Spandrels, Leaf, Vine Border, Persia, c.1900, 14 Ft. 6 In. x 10 Ft. 1 In..	4063.00
Heriz, Indigo Medallion, Red, Ivory Spandrels, Multicolor Floral Vining, Border, 8 Ft. x 9 Ft. 10 In.	805.00
Heriz, Red Field, Center Medallion, Multiple Borders, 14 Ft. 4 In. x 9 Ft. 10 In.	978.00
Heriz, Stylized Flowers, Serrated Blue Geometric Border, Red Field, c.1920, 12 Ft. 8 In. x 9 Ft. 10 In.	948.00
Hooked, 2 Chickens, 2 Chicks, Red, Blue, Brown, c.1910, 25 ½ x 43 In.	830.00
Hooked, 2 Chickens, Facing Each Other, Multicolor Striped Ground, Rag, 37 x 21 In.	384.00
Hooked, 2 Deer With Antlers, Brown, Multicolor Mixed Rag Rug Ground, Wood Frame, 28 x 51 In.	826.00
Hooked, 2 Doves, Spade Center, Gray, Blue, Red, c.1910, 18 ½ x 35 ½ In.	2607.00
Hooked, 2 Lions, Under Tree, Diamond Border, Peach, Red, Blue, Brown, c.1945, 23 x 39 In.	10007.00
Hooked, 2 Roosters, Facing, Black, Red, c.1925, 30 x 52 In.	1541.00
Hooked, 3 Hummingbirds, Gray, Red, Blue Tan, c.1910, 31 x 46 In.	608.00
Hooked, 15 Squares, Kitchen Utensil & Food Images, Brown Ground, Multicolor, c.1910, 54 x 34 In.	243.00
Hooked, Black & White Cow, Green Ground, Black & Red Checkered Border, Frame, 16 x 25 ½ In..	71.00
Hooked, Black Scottie Dog, Flower Border, 30 x 90 In.	267.00
Hooked, Brown Scottie Dog, Red Ground, Gray Border, 1920, 23 x 36 In.	400.00

Hooked, Cat, Surrounded By Animals, 1936, 26 x 36 In.	2844.00
Hooked, Cat, Window, Flowers, Butterflies, Stretcher Frame, 25 ½ x 36 In.	531.00
Hooked, Center Flower, Birds On Branch, Rabbits In Corners, 1800s, 37 x 38 In.	805.00
Hooked, Center Tablet, 3 Red Tulips, Blue Field, Beige Border, Bound, 26 x 20 In.	94.00
Hooked, Chicken, Flanked By 2 Cats, Block Border, Red, Gray, Black, 35 x 52 In.	2370.00
Hooked, Deer, Pine Trees, Sawtooth Borders, Wool, Cotton, Knit, c.1910, 19 x 38 In. ....Illus	470.00
Hooked, Diamonds, Blue Nosegay & Flower, Gray & Beige Ground, Braided Wool, 1920s, 30 x 50 In.	245.00
Hooked, Dog Sled Scene, Figures, Grenfell, Newfoundland, Labrador, 1900s, 33 ½ x 45 ½ In. ...Illus	554.00
Hooked, Dog, Crouching On Cushion, Black Ground, Multicolor Flowers, c.1910, 21 x 37 In.	474.00
Hooked, Dog, King Charles Spaniel, Green Field, Multicolor Borders, Wool, c.1900, 24 x 44 In.	353.00
Hooked, Dog, Poodle, Cave Canem, Floral Border, Leaf Wreaths, God Be Wi Ye, HVC, 1932, 40 x 54 In.	830.00
Hooked, Dog, Reclining, Oval Leaf Surround, Fringe, Multicolor, 28 x 46 In.	472.00
Hooked, Dog, Seated, On Multicolor Diamond Patterned Rug, Leaf Oval Surround, 28 x 46 In.	472.00
Hooked, Dog, Spaniel, On Multicolor Pillow, Oval Reserve, 20th Century, 25 ½ x 43 In.	326.00
Hooked, Dog, Striated Ground, Floral Wreath Border, Wool, On Burlap, c.1890, 20 x 37 In.	1058.00
Hooked, Domestic Zoo, Hearts, Geometrics, Magdalena Briner Eby, Pa., 72 x 24 In.	531.00
Hooked, Duck Family, Blue, Green, Yellow, Black Border, Frame, 24 x 33 ¾ In.	472.00
Hooked, Faces, Clovers, Central Star, Wool, Cotton, 1923, 37 x 38 ½ In.	11258.00
Hooked, Flower Basket, Black Ground, Scalloped Edge, Frame, 19 ½ x 30 In.	413.00
Hooked, Flower Basket, Block Pattern Border, 1800s, 34 x 49 In.	2015.00
Hooked, Flowering Branches, Red, Wool, Frame, c.1875, 34 x 65 In.	1067.00
Hooked, Geometric, Stripes, Shapes, Red, Navy, Black, Gray, Wool, Wood Frame, c.1970, 26 x 46 In.	237.00
Hooked, Green, Red, Pink, Beige, Tan Horizontal Stripes, Rag, 113 x 164 In.	237.00
Hooked, High Relief, Flower Panels, c.1910, 25 x 71 In.	504.00
Hooked, Horse Drawn Conestoga Wagon, Pa., 1900s, 24 x 47 In.	148.00
Hooked, Horse, Galloping, Chickens, 1902, 24 x 66 In.	3888.00
Hooked, Horse, Running, White, Blue Field, Red Flowers, Wool, On Burlap, 1927, 30 x 46 In.	499.00
Hooked, Horse, Tan, Red Flowers, Tan & Gray Ground, Dark Gray Border, 19 x 33 In.	118.00
Hooked, Horse, Trotting, Red Rose, Scalloped Border, 23 x 39 In.	1062.00
Hooked, House, Abstract Border, Wool, Cotton, Velvet, c.1900, 30 x 41 In.	1126.00
Hooked, House, Trees, Multicolor, 20th Century, 26 ½ x 38 In.	178.00
Hooked, Jute, Cat, Sitting, Hearth, Checkerboard Border, Wool, c.1900, 22 x 37 In.	1126.00
Hooked, Landscape, House, Gray Border, c.1910, 17 x 35 In.	213.00
Hooked, Leaf, Flower, Black Ground, c.1840, 31 ½ x 47 In.	608.00
Hooked, Log Cabin In Woods, Family Surrounding, Barbara Evelyn Merry, 1900s, 24 x 34 In.	474.00
Hooked, Log Cabin, Gray Ground, c.1915, 20 ½ x 37 In.	668.00
Hooked, Mallard Ducks, Multicolor, 1900s, 35 x 39 In.	30.00
Hooked, Ms. Hen, House, Flag, Laura H. Loeffler, c.1925, 35 x 26 In.	2232.00
Hooked, Palm Trees, Candles, Flowers, Rooster, Fish, Hourglass, Maker's Names, c.1950, 126 x 105 In.	1150.00
Hooked, Peacock, Big Tail, Crown, Flying Birds, Fabric, On Burlap, c.1930, 24 x 36 In.	482.00
Hooked, Pinwheels, Multicolor, Philphlots, Pa., 20th Century, 28 x 44 In.	770.00
Hooked, Ram, Black Ground, Checkered Border, c.1910, 24 ½ x 40 In.	267.00
Hooked, Red Apple, Branches, Leaves, Yellow Background, Green Border, Frame, 26 x 34 In.	12.00
Hooked, Red Roses, Flowerpot, Stretcher Frame, 36 ½ x 34 ¾ In.	649.00
Hooked, Repeating Rectangles, Multicolor, c.1910, 32 x 22 In.	201.00
Hooked, Rooster, Flowerpots, Initials J & L, Tan Ground, 19 x 32 In.	575.00
Hooked, Sheep, White, Light Blue Ground, Salted Dark Blue Border, Rag, 38 x 20 In.	201.00
Hooked, Spotted Pig & 8 Piglets, White, Brown Ground, Rag, 38 x 21 In.	413.00
Hooked, Spotted Pig, Black, White, Gray, Red Nose, Initials A.L., 37 x 21 In.	266.00
Hooked, Street Scene, Multicolor, Pa., 1909, 38 x 53 In.	148.00
Hooked, Striped Diamond Pattern, Black Ground, 25 x 39 In.	296.00
Hooked, Town Scene, Automobile, c.1910, 18 x 38 In.	356.00
Hooked, Winter Scene, Horse Pulling Sled, Barrel Of Sap, Cabin, Quebec, c.1900, 19 ½ x 14 In.	325.00
Indo-Kashan, Rose, Allover Flowers, Sprays, Blue Leaf Borders, India, c.1935, 21 Ft. 9 In. x 11 Ft. 2 In.	1375.00
Isfahan, Allover Flowers, Ivory Ground, Red Palmette Border, Persia, c.1955, 12 Ft. x 8 Ft. 2 In.	500.00
Isfahan, Star Medallion, Birds, Vines, Buff Ground, Flower Border, Iran, c.1980, 5 Ft. 7 In. x 3 Ft. 6 In.	1375.00
Karabagh, Medallions, c.1890, 15 Ft. 6 In. x 3 Ft. 6 In. ....Illus	750.00
Kashan, Animals, Trees, Vases, Rose Field, Persia, c.1920, 20 Ft. x 12 Ft. 11 In.	5000.00
Kashan, Blue, Yellow Flowers, Red Ground, 3 Medallions, c.1910, 6 Ft. 8 In. x 4 In.	1458.00
Kashan, Flower Medallion, Ivory Field, Palmette Border, Silk, Persia, c.1925, 11 ½ Ft. x 7 Ft. 10 In.	4063.00
Kashan, Flowers, Burgundy, Camel Spandrels, c.1935, 10 Ft. 4 In. x 14 Ft.	3055.00
Kashan, Repeating Flowers & Vines, Brick Red Ground, Ivory Borders, Silk, 6 x 9 Ft.	2360.00
Kazak, 2 Eagle Medallions, Multiple Borders, Red Fields, 6 Ft. 8 In x 4 Ft. 1 In.	5346.00
Kazak, 3 Serrated Diamonds In Medallion, Coral, Blue Ground, 3 Ft. 10 In. x 6 Ft.	1180.00
Kazak, 4 Geometric Medallions, Red, Ivory, Green, Peach, Ivory Border, 5 Ft. 10 In. x 7 Ft. 3 In.	885.00
Kazak, Dark Blue, Peach Geometric Center Medallion, Red Ground, 3 Ft. 10 In. x 5 Ft. 5 In.	384.00
Kazak, Gold, Blue, Green, Tan Latchhook Medallions, Red Ground, 2 Ft. 5 In. x 8 Ft. 6 In.	472.00

Rug, William Morris Style, Stylized Flowers, Teal Ground, 8 Ft. 10 In. x 12 Ft. 3 In.
$1,250.00

Rago Arts & Auction Center

Rug, Wool, Abstract Design, Embroidered Signature, P. Klcc, 1970s, 6 Ft. 5 In. x 5 Ft.
$1,063.00

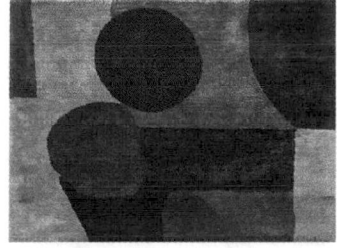

Rago Arts & Auction Center

Ruskin, Jar, Lid, Purple Crystalline Glaze, Silver Overlay, Flowers, Vines, Marked, 1908, 6 ½ In.
$5,036.00

Skinner, Inc.

R

Ruskin, Vase, On Stand, Flared, Oxblood Flambe Glaze, Stamped, Paper Labels, 1906, 10 x 4 In.
$1,500.00

Rago Arts & Auction Center

Russel Wright, Wood, Oceana, Box, Lid, Cherry, Branded, Klise Wood Working, 1930s, 3 x 9 x 6 In.
$2,000.00

Rago Arts & Auction Center

TIP

Wear a short-sleeved shirt when cleaning shelves of collectibles like glasses or small porcelain figurines or even large breakables. Long sleeves may brush the items off the shelf. Put a towel in the sink, dip the pieces in soapy water, rinse, and air dry. Clean and dry the shelves before putting the clean collectibles back.

Kazak, Prayer Rug, Brown, Tan, Black, Serrated Border, Blue Geometric, c.1900, 4 Ft. 2 In. x 3 Ft. 2 In.	1126.00
Kazak, Star, Red, Blue, Gray Ground, Geometric Border, c.1810, 8 Ft. 6 In. x 4 Ft. 7 In............*Illus*	24000.00
Kerman, Center Flower Medallion, Ivory Ground, Red Border, Persia, c.1920, 16 Ft. x 11 Ft. 5 In.....	1250.00
Kerman, Center Medallion, Palm Leaves, Multiple Borders, Flowers, 8 Ft. 10 In. x 11 Ft. ....*Illus*	738.00
Kerman, Center Medallion, Red, Blue Corner Ornaments, Navy Border, 10 Ft. 2 In. x 13 Ft. 6 In.	345.00
Kerman, Central Ivory Medallion, Flower Border, c.1900, 12 Ft. x 9 Ft. 6 In.	5925.00
Kerman, Flower Medallion, Burgundy Field, Indigo Border, Persia, c.1925, 25 Ft. 3 In. x 14 Ft. 4 In..	1875.00
Kerman, Hunters, Wildlife, Tan, Brown Border, Silk Highlights, Persia, c.1955, 18 Ft. 9 In. x 12 Ft. 2 In.	5625.00
Kerman, Rose, Red, Ivory, Blue, Elongated Medallion, Palmettes, Wool, Cotton Weft, 4 Ft. x 2 Ft. 1 In..	81.00
Kerman, Vase Of Flowers, 2 Trees, Ivory Ground, Persian, 6 Ft. 10 In. x 9 Ft. 11 In.	1180.00
Kurdish, 5 Octagonal Medallions, Brick Red Ground, Ivory Hook Border, 3 x 6 Ft.	413.00
Lesghi, Star Medallion, Hexagonal Lattice, Saffron Field, Caucasus, c.1890, 5 Ft. 7 In. x 3 Ft. 10 In.	1500.00
Lillihan, Multicolor Flowers, Red Field, Floral Latticework Border, Guard Borders, c.1900, 9 x 12 Ft.	805.00
Mahal, Allover Vine Pattern, Buff Field, Flower Border, Persia, c.1925, 17 Ft. 4 In. x 13 Ft. 2 In.........	4063.00
Mahal, Gold, Rust, Beige Flowers, Dark Blue Ground, 12 Ft. x 8 Ft. 10 In.	502.00
Mahal, Pendant Medallion, Open Red Field, Spandrels, Vine Border, Persia, c.1880, 18 Ft. 5 In. x 10 Ft.	4063.00
Malayer, Diamond Medallions, Pink Flower Heads, Trellis, Runner, c.1900, 2 Ft. 11 In. x 20 Ft. 1 In......	863.00
Malayer, Multiple Vine, Flower Borders, Central Geometric Rows, Red Field, c.1910, 19 Ft. 2 In............	1094.00
Marasali, Pictorial, Mother & Child, Man & Woman, Borders, c.1885, 5 Ft. 6 In. x 4 Ft. 3 In. .....*Illus*	3900.00
Mashad, Red Field, Medallion, Extending Palmettes, Vines, Ivory Border, 10 Ft. 11 In. x 7 Ft. 10 In.	702.00
Modernist, Edward McKnight Kauffer, Machine Woven, Tibetan Wool, 2000, 12 Ft. 2 In. x 9 Ft. 1 In.	2250.00
Modernist, Verner Panton, Squares, Rust To Orange, Wool, Label, England, c.1950, 8 Ft. .....*Illus*	1215.00
Needlepoint, Dog, Spotted & Striped, Olive Carpet, Flower Border, Wool, 3 Ft. x 1 Ft. 10 In...............	2242.00
Oushak, Allover Trees, Flowers, Red Ground, 15 x 11 Ft.	3510.00
Oushak, Orange & Tan, Band Border, Fringe, Wool, Cotton, India, c.1965, 15 Ft. 9 In. x 12 Ft...........	1200.00
Penny, Multicolor, Black Ground, Gold Stars, 1 Ft. 6 In. x 2 Ft. 8 In.	978.00
Persian, Hand Knotted, Blue, Green, Ivory, Red Ground, Iran, Runner, 10 Ft. 2 In. x 2 Ft. 9 In.	117.00
Persian, Northwest, Trees, Leaves, Hexagonal Lattice, Cream Ground, Brown, Blue, 3 Ft. 3 ½ In. x 4 Ft.	760.00
Persian, Repeating Medallions, Geometrics, Dark Blue Ground, 4 Ft. 3 In. x 9 Ft.	1342.00
Qashqai, Boteh Pattern, Blue Field, Wool, Cotton Weft, 8 Ft. 2 In. x 3 Ft. 4 In.	598.00
Qum, Allover Flowers, Vines, Buff Ground, Vine Border, Iran, c.1955, 6 Ft. 10 In. x 4 Ft. 8 In.	750.00
Sarouk, 7 Rows Floral Scrolling Medallions, Blue Ground, Red Border, 4 Ft. 7 In. x 6 Ft. 3 In...........	345.00
Sarouk, Central Medallion, Allover Leaves, Flowers, Red, Blue, Green, 8 x 10 Ft.	1638.00
Sarouk, Feraghan, Central Medallion, Ivory Field, Rosette Border, Persia, c.1900, 6 Ft. 3 In. x 4 Ft..	1625.00
Sarouk, Flower Clusters, Red Field, Black Border, Lotus Blossoms, 21 Ft. 6 In. x 10 Ft. 7 In...........	1093.00
Sarouk, Flower Medallion, Palmettes, Borders, Wool, Cotton, 11 Ft. 8 In. x 18 Ft. 4 In.	380.00
Sarouk, Flowers, Brick Red Ground, Persian, 3 Ft. 3 In. x 4 Ft. 9 In.	472.00
Sarouk, Flowers, Red Ground, Blue Palm, Vine Border, North Persia, c.1945, 15 Ft. 7 In. x 11 Ft. 11 In.	1500.00
Sarouk, Flowers, Vines, Medallions, Dark Blue Border, North Persia, c.1925, 16 Ft. 5 In. x 10 Ft. 4 In. ...	1500.00
Sarouk, Stylized Flowers, Red Ground, Runner, 6 Ft. 9 In. x 2 Ft. 1 In.	785.00
Serapi, Blue Central Medallion, Red, Blue, Cream, c.1900, 12 Ft. 2 In. x 8 Ft. 7 In.	10073.00
Serapi, Central Medallion, Flowers, Gold, Green, Red, Blue, 9 x 12 Ft.	1298.00
Serapi, Central Medallion, Red Field, Ivory Corner, Geometric, Blue Field Border, 12 Ft. x 9 Ft. 2 In.	5832.00
Serapi, Gabled Central Medallion, Ivory, Red, Blue Designs, 9 Ft. 4 In. x 12 Ft. 10 In......................	1298.00
Serapi, Red, Green, Blue Medallion, Ivory Arches, Gray Blue, Red Spandrels, 6 Ft. x 8 Ft. 9 In.......	767.00
Shirvan, Conjoined Stepped Red Medallions, Tree Shape, Blue Field, Borders, 4 Ft. 3 In. x 6 Ft.......	403.00
Sultanabad, Green Gold Arabesque Vine, Flowers, Red Ground, 8 Ft. 2 In. x 9 Ft. 10 In.	885.00
Tabriz, Abrash Design, Flowers, Turquoise Blue, Tan, Border, Fringe, c.1930, 9 Ft. 6 In. x 12 Ft.......	1175.00
Tabriz, Center Medallion, Red Ground, Leaf Borders, Blue Ground, 9 Ft. 10 In. x 12 Ft. 9 In.	546.00
Tabriz, Concentric Triangles, Flower Border, Brown, Tan, 10 Ft. 3 In. x 15 Ft........................	11115.00
Tabriz, Flowers, Branches, Tan Ground, Brown Palmette Border, Persia, c.1955, 11 Ft. 6 In. x 8 Ft. 2 In..	1250.00
Tabriz, Pendant Medallion, Rust Ground, Blue Rosette, Leaf Border, Persia, c.1900, 13 Ft. x 9 Ft. 7 In...	5313.00
Tribal, Garden Panels, Geometric Border, Flowers, Wool, 6 Ft. 4 In. x 4 Ft. 3 In.	150.00
Turkoman, Red Field, 3 Rows Of 9 Guls, Geometric Border, 6 Ft. 5 In. x 3 Ft. 11 In.	620.00
William Morris Style, Stylized Flowers, Teal Ground, 8 Ft. 10 In. x 12 Ft. 3 In. ....*Illus*	1250.00
Wool, Abstract Design, Embroidered Signature, P. Klee, 1970s, 6 Ft. 5 In. x 5 Ft........................*Illus*	1063.00
Wool, Horsehair, Woven, Purple, Orange Red, Signed, 1973, 5 Ft. 1 In. x 4 Ft. 9 In.	4318.00

RUMRILL POTTERY was designed by George Rumrill of Little Rock, Arkansas. From 1933 to 1938, it was produced by the Red Wing Pottery of Red Wing, Minnesota. In January 1938, production was transferred to the Shawnee Pottery in Zanesville, Ohio. It was moved again in December of 1938 to Florence Pottery Company in Mt. Gilead, Ohio, where Rumrill ware continued to be manufactured until the pottery burned in 1941. It was then produced by Gonder Ceramic Arts in South Zanesville until early 1943.

RumRill

Console, Looping Scroll Handles, Pink Matte Glaze, Green Overspray, No. 303, 6 x 11 ½ In.	95.00
Pitcher, Pastel Green, 9 x 6 ½ In..	86.00

Vase, Blue, Spiral Lobed, Low Handles, Marked, 9 ½ In.	17.00
Vase, Florentine, Pink Glaze, Green, Tapered Neck, Flaring Rim, Scroll Handle, 10 x 7 ¾ In.	70.00
Vase, Goldenrod, Long Neck, Applied Shoulder Scroll, 10 In.	40.00
Vase, Green Matte Glaze, 2 Handles, Ruffled Rim, Tapered, 6 ¾ x 4 ¼ In.	25.00
Vase, Indian Group, Star Pattern, Mottled Orange & Bay, 1935, 5 ½ In.	150.00
Vase, Manhattan, Silver, Blue Tone Metallic Geometric Lines, Cream Ground, 10 In.	250.00
Vase, Pastel Blue, Scalloped Rim, Scrolled Handles, Fluted Neck, Bulbous Base, 7 ½ x 4 ½ In.	49.00

RUSKIN is a British art pottery of the twentieth century. The Ruskin Pottery was started by William Howson Taylor, and his name was used as the mark until about 1899. The factory, at West Smethwick, Birmingham, England, stopped making new pieces in 1933 but continued to glaze and sell the remaining wares until 1935. The art pottery is noted for its exceptional glazes.

Jar, Lid, Purple Crystalline Glaze, Silver Overlay, Flowers, Vines, Marked, 1908, 6 ½ In. *...Illus*	5036.00
Vase, On Stand, Flared, Oxblood Flambe Glaze, Stamped, Paper Labels, 1906, 10 x 4 In. *..Illus*	1500.00
Vase, Pinched Neck, Turquoise Glaze, Paper Label, 1914, 9 In.	275.00
Vase, Purple Glaze, Green Crystalline, Silver Overlay, Flared, 1905, 6 x 7 In.	1625.00
Vase, Turquoise Glaze, Iridescence, Marked, 1914, 3 ¼ x 9 In.	336.00

RUSSEL WRIGHT designed dinnerware in modern shapes for many companies. Iroquois China Company, Harker China Company, Steubenville Pottery, and Justin Tharaud and Sons made dishes marked *Russel Wright*. The Steubenville wares, first made in 1938, are the most common today. Wright was a designer of domestic and industrial wares, including furniture, aluminum, radios, interiors, and glassware. A new company, Bauer Pottery Company of Los Angeles, is making Russel Wright's American Modern dishes using molds made from original pieces. The pottery is made in Highland, California. Pieces are marked *Russel Wright by Bauer Pottery California USA.* Russel Wright Dinnerware and other original pieces by Wright are listed here. For more prices, go to kovels.com.

Aluminum, Bowl, Walnut Lid, Stamped, 4 x 8 In.	473.00
Aluminum, Bun Warmer, Swivel Lid, Sphere Shape, Rattan Bail Handle, 10 In.	225.00
Aluminum, Cheese Server, Lid, Inset Maple Disc Knob, 16 In.	800.00
Aluminum, Cocktail Set, Decanter, Strainer, Lid, 6 Cups, Tray, Cork, c.1930, Tray 13 In., 10 Piece	9600.00
Aluminum, Cocktail Shaker, Tumblers, Spun, Shaker, 11 In., Tumbler, 2 ½ In., 7 Piece	2016.00
Aluminum, Lamp, Oak, Stoneware Base, Paper Shade, Bauer Pottery, 1941, 23 ¼ In.	6250.00
Aluminum, Server, 2-Tier, Rattan Handle, 12 x 8 In.	300.00
Aluminum, Tankard, Spun, c.1960, 7 ¾ In.	80.00
Aluminum, Tray, Canape, Round, Loop Handle, Wood Ball, 13 ¾ In.	300.00
Aluminum, Tray, Snack, Round, Wood Handle, Stamped, 10 ¾ In., 3 Piece	438.00
Aluminum, Vase, Spun, Satin Finish, c.1930, 7 In.	6120.00
American Modern, Bowl, Divided, Black Chutney, 13 In.	135.00
American Modern, Bowl, Salad, Oval, Gray Granite, 10 In.	29.00
American Modern, Bowl, Soup, Lug Handles, Seafoam, 7 In., 10 Piece	85.00
American Modern, Coaster, Black Chutney, 4 Piece	50.00
American Modern, Coaster, Gray Granite, 1930s, 3 ½ In., Pair	44.00
American Modern, Compote, Seafoam Green, 4 In.	20.00
American Modern, Cup & Saucer, After Dinner, Black Chutney, 3 ¾ In.	20.00
American Modern, Cup & Saucer, Seafoam Green, Demitasse, 6 Piece	25.00
American Modern, Gravy Boat, Chartreuse, 10 ½ x 2 In.	35.00
American Modern, Pitcher, Granite Gray, 10 ½ In.	69.00
American Modern, Pitcher, Seafoam Green, 10 ¾ In.	95.00
American Modern, Plate, Bread & Butter, Coral, 6 In., 4 Piece	17.00
American Modern, Plate, Hostess, Oval, Handle, Cup Well, Coral, 11 ½ In.	50.00
American Modern, Plate, Salad, Granite Gray, 8 In., 4 Piece	61.00
American Modern, Salad Servers, Seafoam Green	10.00
American Modern, Salt & Pepper, Chartreuse	15.00
American Modern, Shaker, 5-Hole, Granite Gray, 2 In.	10.00
American Modern, Soup, Dish, Lug Handle, Cedar Green, 5 ¼ In.	15.00
American Modern, Soup, Dish, Lug Handle, Coral, 6 ⅛ In.	15.00
American Modern, Sugar, Lid, Squat, Loop Handle, Cedar Green, 4 ½ In.	25.00
American Modern, Teapot, Lemon Yellow, 6 Cup, 11 ½ In.	48.00
American Modern, Teapot, Lid, Seafoam Green, 10 In.	45.00
Eclipse, Tumbler, Oklahoma Shape, 2 Green, 2 Orange, 1 Blue, 1 Purple, 3 ⅜ In.	120.00
Harold's Club & Casino, Plate, Western Style, c.1965, 11 In.	88.00
Iroquois Casual, Bowl, Cereal, Ripe Apricot, 5 ¼ In.	15.00
Iroquois Casual, Bowl, Divided, Coral, 14 In.	78.00

TIP
Only a professional should clean a coin.

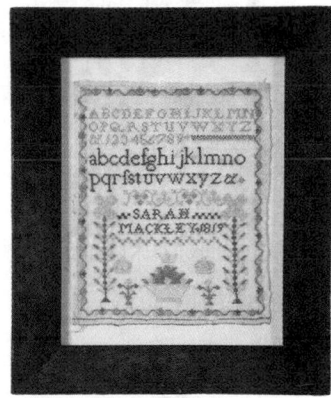

Sampler, Alphabet, Potted Flowers, Crowns, Sarah Mackle 1819, Silk On Wool, Frame, 11 ½ x 9 ½ In. $499.00

Garth's Auctioneers & Appraisers

Sampler, Verse, Flower Basket, Boy, Woman, Dog, Horse, Birds, Name, 1848, Linen, 23 x 18 In. $382.00

Garth's Auctioneers & Appraisers

Samson, Fishbowl, Chinese Style Designs, Multicolor, Mask Handles, 15 ¾ x 22 In. $3,000.00

Leslie Hindman Auctioneers

R

515

RUSSEL WRIGHT

Samson, Group, Woman, Draped Dress, Cherub, Putti, c.1810, 28 ½ In.
$690.00

Cottone Auctions

Satin Glass, Potpourri, Acorn Pattern, Blue, Gold, Enamel, Metal Lid & Base, England, 7 ½ In.
$1,840.00

Early Auction Co.

Satsuma, Bowl, Dragons, Porcelain, Signed, 1800s, 2 ½ x 6 In.
$403.00

Cottone Auctions

TIP
Periodically check your jewelry for loose stones.

Iroquois Casual, Bowl, Vegetable, Nutmeg Brown, Round, 8 In.	20.00
Iroquois Casual, Butter, Cover, Pink Sherbet, 8 In.	85.00
Iroquois Casual, Casserole, Avocado Yellow, 4 Qt.	265.00
Iroquois Casual, Casserole, Lid, Nutmeg Brown, 2 Qt., 8 ½ In.	55.00
Iroquois Casual, Casserole, Pinch Handle, Pink Sherbet, c.1946, 8 ¼ In.	59.00
Iroquois Casual, Cup & Saucer, Oyster, 1949-60	20.00
Iroquois Casual, Pitcher, Lid, Sugar White, 10 ½ In.	17.00
Iroquois Casual, Plate, Dinner, Aqua, 10 In.	65.00
Iroquois Casual, Plate, Dinner, Ice Blue, 10 In.	30.00
Iroquois Casual, Plate, Dinner, Lemon Yellow, 10 In., 6 Piece	20.00
Iroquois Casual, Plate, Dinner, Pink Sherbet, 10 In.	18.00
Iroquois Casual, Plate, Luncheon, Pink Sherbet, 9 In., Pair	30.00
Iroquois Casual, Plate, Salad, Avocado Yellow, 7 ⅜ In.	20.00
Iroquois Casual, Platter, Pink Sherbet, Oval, 12 ½ In.	24.00
Iroquois Casual, Platter, Ripe Apricot, 12 ⅝ In.	45.00
Iroquois Casual, Sauceboat, Lid, Ripe Apricot, 6 In.	245.00
Iroquois Casual, Soup, Dish, Cantaloupe, 5 ¼ In., Pair	12.50
Iroquois Casual, Sugar & Creamer, Stacking, Pink Sherbet, 4 ¾ In.	38.00
Restaurant Ware, Soup, Dish, Ivory Green, 6 ½ In.	17.00
Wood, Bowl, Salad, Oval, Branded Studio Mark, 9 ¾ In., 4 Piece	1000.00
Wood, Oceana, Bowl, Starfish, Biomorphic Shape, Klise, 13 ½ In.	1037.00
Wood, Oceana, Box, Lid, Cherry, Branded, Klise Wood Working, 1930s, 3 x 9 x 6 In. ....*Illus*	2000.00

SABINO glass was made in the 1920s and 1930s in Paris, France. Founded by Marius-Ernest Sabino (1878–1961), the firm was noted for Art Deco lamps, vases, figurines, and animals in clear, colored, and opalescent glass. Production stopped during World War II but resumed in the 1960s with the manufacture of nude figurines and small opalescent glass animals. Pieces made in recent years are a slightly different color and can be recognized. Only vintage pieces are listed here.

Sabino France

Bowl, Birds In Flight, Brass Trim, Porcelain Oval, Lovers In Garden, c.1920, 4 In.	295.00
Figurine, Fox, Sitting, 2 In.	45.00
Figurine, Rabbit, Paper Label, 2 In.	64.00
Figurine, Rooster, Paper Label, 3 ½ In.	49.00
Figurine, Sea Turtle, Signed, 2 In.	66.00
Figurine, Shivering Bird, Marked, 2 ½ In.	140.00
Figurine, Sitting Madonna, Paper Mark, 3 x 4 In.	120.00
Figurine, Snail, 3 ½ In.	260.00
Knife Rest, 2 Level, Geometric, 3 ¼ In., Pair	125.00
Perfume Bottle, Nudes, Vines, Box, 6 In.	175.00
Perfume Bottle, Stopper, Frivolites, Opalescent, 6 ¼ In.	210.00
Plate, Opalescent, Henri IV, Art Deco Border, 8 In.	200.00
Vase, Manta Ray Fish, Art Deco, 8 ¾ In.	590.00
Vase, Seashells, Flared, Opalescent, Signed, 8 In.	2490.00
Vase, Spherical, Stylized Flowers, Pedestal Base, Amber, 15 In.	550.00

SALOPIAN ware was made by the Caughley factory of England during the eighteenth century. The early pieces were blue and white with some colored decorations. Another ware referred to as Salopian is a late nineteenth-century tableware decorated with color transfers.

Salopian

Cup & Saucer, Gray, Green Transfer, Buildings	100.00
Plate, Fisherman, Transfer, Marked, 9 In.	395.00

SALT AND PEPPER SHAKERS in matched sets were first used in the nineteenth century. Collectors are primarily interested in figural examples made after World War I. Huggers are pairs of shakers that appear to embrace each other. Many salt and pepper shakers are listed in other categories and can be located through the index at the back of this book.

Birds, Multicolor, Japan, 1940s, 3 In.	11.00
Blue Quail, Porcelain, Flared Bottom, c.1920, 2 ¾ In.	45.00
Cherry Blossoms, Moriage, Nippon, c.1900	35.00
Crank Telephone Shape, Plastic, Pink, Black, 4 ¾ In.	15.00
Dragon, Ivory, Carved, Black Eyes, 2 In.	57.00
Dutch Boy & Girl, Hugger, Van Tellingen	28.00
Eggs, Bakelite, Red, 1 ½ In.	95.00
Elephant, Polka Dot Hat & Skirt, 3 ¾ In.	31.00
Flowers, Etched, Glass, Green, Metal Top, Stand	25.00
Kewpie Babies, Naked, Flower Hats, Japan, 3 ¼ In.	45.00

Mammy & Chef, Glass, c.1935, 2 ⅞ In.	85.00
Mammy, Nude, Eating Watermelon, Japan, c.1940, 3 ½ In.	265.00
March Flower Girl, Daffodil, Napco, 1950s, 3 ¾ In.	36.00
Matador, Bull, Nodder, Japan, c.1940	195.00
Niagara Falls, Milk Glass, Square, Hazel Atlas, 3 In.	59.00
Pig, Bride & Groom, Japan, c.1945	225.00
Rabbit, Victorian, Gilt Silver, Marked W.H., Box, Miniature............	2309.00
Ribbed, Platonite, Red, White, Hazel Atlas Glass, 1940s, 4 ½ In. ..	38.00
Rooster, White, Colored Feathers, 1940s....................................	49.00
Santa & Mrs. Claus, 3 In...	28.00
Santa Claus, Silver Plate, Godinger, Box....................................	17.00
Shafford Cat, Black, Red Collar, Japan, 1950s, 4 In.	30.00
Sterling, Footed, Ribbed Base, Mauser Co., c.1875.....................	189.00
Swirls, Jadite, Horizontal Ribbed..	80.00
Thanksgiving Turkeys, Chase, Japan, 1950s, 3 ½ x 2 ¼ In.	25.00
Umbrella Shape, Sterling Silver, c.1950, 2 ¾ In.	199.00

SAMPLERS were made in America from the early 1700s. The best examples were made from 1790 to 1840. Long, narrow samplers are usually older than square ones. Early samplers just had stitching or alphabets. The later examples had numerals, borders, and pictorial decorations. Those with mottoes are mid-Victorian. A revival of interest in the 1930s produced simpler samplers, usually with mottoes.

ABCDE

Alphabet, Amanda Widenhammer, Maiden Creek Quaker School, Pa., 1835, Silk On Linen, 16 x 17 In.	504.00
Alphabet, Birds, Essex, Sarah Coker, 1796, Silk On Linen, 14 ¼ x 11 In.	3555.00
Alphabet, Couples, Landscape, Flowers, Silk On Linen, Rebecca Abbot Wilton, 1795, Frame, 15 x 12 In.	593.00
Alphabet, Double Blue Border, Eunice Wells, June 16, 1787, Frame, 11 ⅓ x 9 ¼ In.	1062.00
Alphabet, Flower, Geometric Designs, Anna Hodskins, Frame, 1810, 13 x 12 In.	266.00
Alphabet, Flowers, Border Designs, Tasseled Corners, Sides, Frame, c.1818, 36 ½ x 24 ¼ In............	148.00
Alphabet, Flowers, Catherine Macintyre, Hilltown 1831, Wool On Linen, Pa., Frame, 16 x 17 In.	4503.00
Alphabet, Flowers, Geometric Designs, Silk, Linen, Dolly Woodis, c.1800, 8 x 7 In.	889.00
Alphabet, Hearts, Palm Trees, Verse, Ann Norman 1821, Frame, 18 ½ x 9 ¾ In.	518.00
Alphabet, House, Trees, Scrolled Border, Jenet McCormick, Silk Threads, Linen, c.1815, 17 x 12 In.	1020.00
Alphabet, Numbers, Birds, Flowers, Ann Palmer, 1856, Silk On Linen, Stenciled Frame, 11 x 13 In.	652.00
Alphabet, Numbers, Esther B. Roninson, Frame, 1820, 7 ½ x 15 ½ In...........	236.00
Alphabet, Numbers, Flower Baskets, House, Cats, Bird, Silk On Linen, 1830, 16 ½ x 16 ½ In.	147.00
Alphabet, Numbers, Flowers, Basket, Willow, House, Amanda Hamblin, Age 9, 1827, 18 ½ x 19 In.	209.00
Alphabet, Numbers, Flowers, Frame, 1840, 13 x 15 In.	83.00
Alphabet, Numbers, Flowers, Frame, Catharine Petty, 1782, 10 ¼ x 12 ½ In...........	230.00
Alphabet, Numbers, House, Tree, Deer, Name, Aged 8 Years, 1828, Silk, Linen, Frame, 21 x 15 In.	529.00
Alphabet, Numbers, Motto, Birds, Insect, Plants, Name, Aged 9 Years, Wood Frame, 17 x 13 In.	236.00
Alphabet, Numbers, Red, Green, 1825, Linen, Scotland, 16 x 16 In...........	280.00
Alphabet, Numbers, Roses, Palm Trees, Memorial, Urn, Silk Ribbon, L. Miam, c.1835, 9 x 16 In.	235.00
Alphabet, Numbers, Verse, 1844, Green & Red Linen, Wool & Silk Threads, 16 x 16 In.	280.00
Alphabet, Numbers, Verse, Book & Needle Is All My Delight, Susan A. Stebbins, Age 11, 1782, 21 x 21 In.	1770.00
Alphabet, Numbers, Verse, Mary Boadle, July 6, 1824, Frame, England, 19 ½ x 15 ½ In.	472.00
Alphabet, Potted Flowers, Crowns, Sarah Mackle, 1819, Silk On Wool, Frame, 11 ⅓ x 9 ½ In. .... *Illus*	499.00
Alphabet, Verse, Flowers, Ester Ritter, Reading, Pa., 1832, Silk On Linen, 17 ½ x 17 In.	830.00
Alphabet, Verse, Flowers, Trees, House, Vine Border, Mary Fawcetts, 1806, Frame, 18 x 17 ½ In.......	590.00
Alphabet, Verse, Portico, Lucy Phippen Fuller, 1823, Gilt Wood Frame, 15 ¾ x 16 ¼ In.	122.00
Alphabet, Verse, Sawtooth Border, Rebeckah Parrott, Aged 12, Lynn, Mass., 1812, Frame, 16 x 16 ¼ In.	748.00
Alphabet, Verse, Vines, Shrubs, Butterflies, Basket, Flowers, 1840, Silk, Linen, Frame, 20 x 23 In.	3173.00
Birds, Mammals, Flowers, Insects, Devil, People, Multicolor, 1878, Wood Frame, 22 x 24 In....	106.00
Family Record, Alphabet, Names, 7 Children, c.1834, Silk, Linen, Frame, 17 x 18 In.	499.00
Flowers, Repeat Pattern, Pulled Thread Borders, 21 x 20 In...........	47.00
Flowers, Vase, Miama H. Stauffer, 1878, Wool, Wood Frame, 24 ½ x 26 In.	356.00
House, Birds, Hearts, Miss Elizabeth Hitchcock, 1835, Ohio, Silk On Linen, Frame, 9 ½ x 19 ½ In.	964.00
House, Trees, Rachel Ann Kelly, 1830, Silk On Linen, 10 x 12 In...........	415.00
Map, England, Wales, Mary Walker, 1804, York, Silk, Frame, 19 x 15 ½ In.	711.00
Verse, 4 Seasons, Flowers, Urn, Vines, Trees, Butterflies, Geometric Bands, Name, c.1809, 14 x 12 In.	780.00
Verse, Angels, Buildings, Pink, Blue, Betty Scholes, 1836, Wood Frame, 16 x 15 In.	182.00
Verse, Diamonds, Cornucopias, Basket, Flower Border, Elizabeth Jane Pettit, 13, 1827, 18 x 19 In.	470.00
Verse, Elizabeth Brown, 17—, Silk On Linen, 18th Century, 17 x 12 ¾ In...............	122.00
Verse, Elizabeth Davis, Dated 1817, Quaker, Pa., Frame, 11 x 13 ¼ In.	652.00
Verse, Flower Basket, Boy, Woman, Dog, Horse, Birds, Name, 1848, Linen, 23 x 18 In.......*Illus*	382.00
Verse, Flowers, Figures, Birds, Name, Teacher, 1835, Silk, Linen, 17 x 16 ½ In...........	770.00
Verse, Flowers, Gathered Ribbon Border, Floral Corners, Susannah Beninshove, 1791, 21 x 20 In.	2714.00

Satsuma, Incense Burner, Geishas, Samurai, Shishi Finial, Dragon Handles, c.1890, 25 In.
$1,722.00

New Orleans Auction Galleries, Inc.

Satsuma, Incense Burner, Lid, Samurai, Landscapes, Flowering Peonies, Shishi Lions, 1800s, 18 In.
$790.00

Skinner, Inc.

Satsuma, Jar, Lid, Figures & Landscape Panels, Wood Stand, Signed, 4 ½ x 6 In.
$450.00

DuMouchelles Art Gallery

S

Satsuma, Teapot, Buddhist Figures, Chilong Dragon Spout & Handle, Marked, 7 ⅜ In.
$175.00

Skinner, Inc.

TIP

If possible, remove silverware from the dishwasher before the drying cycle begins.

Satsuma, Teapot, Wisteria, Scrolling Leaves, Gold Trim, Signed, Yabu Meizan, Japan, c.1900, 5 In.
$1,320.00

Skinner, Inc.

Satsuma, Vase, Cream Crackle Ground, Raised Peony & Mu, Fired Gold, Enamel, 1800s, 5 In.
$540.00

DuMouchelles Art Gallery

Verse, Flowers, House, Margaret Nice, 1832, Silk On Linen, Hamburg, 16 ½ x 17 In.	668.00
Verse, House, Couple, Flowers, Birds, Name, 1836, Silk, Linen, Frame, Pa., 17 x 18 In.	2673.00
Verse, House, Flower Bouquets, Baskets, Catherine Kepheart, Silk, On Linen, Pa., 1800s, 18 x 22 In.	425.00
Verse, Kitchen Prayer, Bless My Cozy Kitchen, Linen, Embroidered Frame, 14 x 10 ½ In.	65.00
Verse, Lambs, Deer, Birds, Landscape, Elizabeth Batchelder, 1763, 15 x 17 In.	413.00
Verse, Trees, Stags, Leaf, Flower Border, Elizabeth Barringer 1839, Petit Point, Frame, 12 x 12 In.	767.00
Verse, Zigzag Border, Maria Stine, Mrs. Meguier's School, 1817, Frame, 22 x 24 In.	826.00

SAMSON and Company, a French firm specializing in the reproduction of collectible wares of many countries and periods, was founded in Paris in the early nineteenth century. Chelsea, Meissen, Famille Verte, and Chinese Export porcelain are some of the wares that have been reproduced by the company. The firm used a variety of marks on the reproductions. It closed in 1969.

Bough Pot, Armorial, Iron Red Enamel Mark, 11 ¼ In., Pair	295.00
Bowl, Centerpiece, Cobalt Glaze, Gilt Bronze Leaf Mounts, Round, Footed, France, c.1850, 12 In.	1250.00
Figurine, Dancing Shepherd & Shepherdess, Chelsea Style Gold Anchor Mark, 10 & 10 ¼ In., Pair	354.00
Fishbowl, Chinese Style Designs, Multicolor, Mask Handles, 15 ¾ x 22 In. ....*Illus*	3000.00
Ginger Jar, Lid, Armorial, Flower Sprays, Purple, Pink, Yellow, Signed, 11 ½ In.	160.00
Group, Putto, Garlands, Grapes, Riding, Feeding Goat, France, 7 ½ x 7 In.	236.00
Group, Woman, Draped Dress, Cherub, Putti, c.1810, 28 ½ In. ....*Illus*	690.00
Plate, Armorial, Shield, Gilt, Lion, Horse, Crown, Spearhead Border, Motto, 1800s, 9 In., Pair.	132.00
Plate, Flowers, Armorial, Gilt, 8 In., 12 Piece	205.00
Plate, Fruit Basket Center, Gilt Band, Rim, c.1900, 9 ¼ In., 18 Piece	243.00
Plate, Japanese Kakiemon Style, Courtyard Figures, Wavy Rim, 8 ½ In., Pair	375.00
Teapot, Lid, Pink, Purple Flowers, Gilt, Enamel, Miniature, c.1870, 3 In.	35.00
Urn, Armorial, White Ground, Raised Flowers, Vines, Moriage Enamel, c.1910, 21 x 10 In.	288.00
Urn, Dome Lid, Armorial, Baluster, c.1890, 15 In., Pair	708.00
Urn, Lid, Chelsea Style, Spiral Writhen Shape, Painted, Exotic Birds, Landscape, 14 ¼ In., Pair	1062.00
Vase, Chickens, Flowers, Rose Ground, Double Gourd Shape, Ormolu Mounts, c.1850, 22 In., Pair.	16100.00

SANDWICH GLASS is any of the myriad types of glass made by the Boston & Sandwich Glass Company of Sandwich, Massachusetts, between 1825 and 1888. It is often very difficult to be sure whether a piece was really made at the Sandwich factory because so many types were made there and similar pieces were made at other glass factories. Additional pieces may be listed under Pressed Glass and in other related categories.

Bowl, Fiery Opalescent Blue, Sawtooth Rim, Raised Prism Trumpet Foot, c.1860, 4 x 6 In.	69.00
Candlestick, Chamber, 8-Lobe, Nickel Chimney Gallery, Engraved Vine, c.1870, 7 x 3 In.	288.00
Candlestick, Dolphin Hexagonal Base, Canary Yellow, c.1860, 6 ¾ x 4 In., Pair	518.00
Candlestick, Dolphin, Pressed, Double Step, Canary Yellow, 1845-70, 10 In., Pair	1062.00
Candlestick, Electric Blue, Tulip Mouth, Square Base, c.1850, 9 ½ In.	767.00
Candlestick, Opaque Blue, Over Clambroth, Column Shape, Petal Sockets, c.1860, 9 In., Pair .	1062.00
Candlestick, Petal & Columnar, Canary Yellow, Double Step Base, c.1860, 9 x 3 ⅝ In., Pair	1093.00
Castor, Pepper, Cobalt Blue, 8 Panels, Double Neck Rings, Pewter Lid, c.1840, 5 ¼ In.	115.00
Cologne Bottle, Amethyst, Waisted, 8-Panel Shape, c.1850, 6 ¾ x 2 ½ In.	518.00
Cologne Bottle, Canary Yellow, Ovals, Hexagonal Shape, Cut Air Trap Stopper, c.1860, 5 In.	92.00
Cologne Bottle, Canary Yellow, Thumbprint, Polished Pontil, Finial, c.1850, 7 In.	184.00
Cologne Bottle, Cranberry To Clear, Honeycomb, Etched Flowers, Stopper, 9 ½ In.	106.00
Cologne Bottle, Figural, Bunker Hill Monument, Cobalt Blue, Flared Mouth, 9 In.	819.00
Cologne Bottle, Figural, Fountain, Cobalt Blue, Flared & Flattened Mouth, 4 ½ In.	2106.00
Cologne Bottle, Indians Dancing, Opalescent Milk Glass, Diamond Shape, 5 In.	1872.00
Cologne Bottle, Sapphire Blue, Corset Shape, Palmette & Scrolled Acanthus, 5 ½ In.	995.00
Cologne Bottle, Star & Block, Cranberry Cut To Clear, Pattern Cut Stopper, 7 In.	350.00
Creamer, Cobalt Blue, Waisted Neck, Tooled Rim, Applied Handle, c.1830, 4 ½ x 2 ⅞ In.	3738.00
Cruet, Cobalt Blue, 12 Panels, Plain Lip, Neck Ring, Tam-O'-Shanter Stopper, 7 ¼ In.	115.00
Decanter, Bull's-Eye Sunburst, Diamonds, Clear, Barrel Form, Qt.	134.00
Decanter, Sapphire Blue, 16 Ribs, Plain Lip, Stopper, c.1830, 11 x 9 In., Qt.	3450.00
Lamp, Cut Glass, Punty, Blue Cut To Clear, Brass Standard, Marble Base, 8 In.	336.00
Lamp, Hand, Moon & Star, Colorless, Bell Shape, Extinguisher Sleeve, c.1870, 3 x 2 ½ In.	161.00
Match Tray, Onion, Sapphire Blue, Pressed, Ribbed Gallery, Well, c.1875, 1 ½ x 3 ⅝ In.	259.00
Paperweight, Fruit, White Latticinio Ground, 2 ⅕ x 3 In.	502.00
Paperweight, White Overlapping Petals, Green Stem, White Latticinio Ground, 2 x 2 ½ In.	767.00
Salt Chariot, Pressed, Silvery Opaque Blue, Mottled Scalloped Rim, c.1840, 1 ¾ x 2 ⅛ In.	127.00
Salt, Boat Pressed, Deep Purple, Plain Rim, c.1835, 2 x 4 In.	1495.00
Salt, Boat Pressed, Fiery Opalescent, Plain Rim, Base, c.1835, 2 x 4 In.	316.00
Salt, Capstan Style, Electric Blue, 6-Sided, Grooved Rim, Scalloped Foot, c.1860, 3 x 3 ⅜ In.	288.00

Salt, Lafayet Steamboat, Fiery Opalescent Blue, Marked, c.1840, 1 ⅝ x 1 ⅞ In.	92.00
Salt, Pressed Beaded Strawberry Diamond Oval, Opaque Mottled Blue, c.1830, 1 x 2 ½ In.	374.00
Salt, Pressed Beaded Strawberry Diamond, Fiery Opalescent, Oval, c.1840, 1 ¾ x 2 ¼ In.	431.00
Salt, Pressed Eagle & Shield, Colorless, 4-Footed, c.1835, 2 x 3 ¼ In.	127.00
Salt, Pressed Octagon Oblong, Pale Amethyst, c.1860, 2 ½ x 3 ¼ In.	127.00
Salt, Round Floral, Opaque Powder, Medium Blue, Flower Top, Scallop Foot, c.1840, 2 x 3 In.	1610.00
Saucer, Colorless, Plain Rope Rim, c.1830, 3 ¹¹⁄₁₆ In.	345.00
Spooner, Amethyst, Inverted Diamond & Thumbprint, Stepped Foot, c.1855, 4 ½ x 3 ⅛ In.	748.00
Spooner, Grapevine, Climbing Ivy, Colorless, Green, Brown Stain, c.1860, 5 In.	115.00
Spooner, Snowflake, Opalescent, Plain Rim, Round Foot, 24 Rays, c.1865, 4 ⅞ x 3 ¼ In.	138.00
Spooner, Star & Punty, Cobalt Blue, 6-Sided, Low Foot, c.1860, 4 ¾ x 3 ¾ In.	1955.00
Spooner, Star, Canary Yellow, Hexagonal, Polished Pontil, c.1850, 5 x 3 ⅝ In.	374.00
Spooner, Star, Electric Blue, Hexagonal, Polished Pontil, c.1850, 5 x 3 ¾ In.	518.00
Sugar, Cover, Colorless, Cranberry, Facet Cut Finial, c.1885, 5 ½ In.	259.00
Toothpick Holder, Translucent Blue, Ribbed, Knopped Finial, c.1860, 4 x 2 In.	374.00
Tumbler, Peacock Green, Pressed Lacy, Pointed, 10-Petal Base, c.1845, 1 ¾ x 1 ⅝ In.	230.00
Undertray, Horn Of Plenty, Diamond Point Center, c.1855, 4 ½ x 7 ⅛ In.	3738.00
Undertray, Pressed Lacy Heart, Colorless, Scallop & Point Rim, Rope Ring, c.1840, 4 x 7 In.	150.00
Vase, Blue Pressed, Gauffered Rim, Hexagonal Stem, Round Base, Bigler, c.1850, 10 In.	1422.00
Vase, Hobnail, Leaf, Translucent Starch Blue, Oval, Waisted, Flared Rim, Gilt, c.1860	160.00
Vase, Purple, Clear Dripping Icicles, Oval, Ring Foot, 6 ¼ In.	633.00
Vase, Tulip, Amethyst, Pressed, Octagonal Base, 10 In., Pair	3422.00
Vase, Turquoise, Pressed Loop, Gauffered Rim, Hexagonal Stem, Round Base, c.1850, 10 In.	1541.00

SARREGUEMINES is the name of a French town that is used as part of a china mark. Utzschneider and Company, a porcelain factory, made ceramics in Sarreguemines, Lorraine, France, from about 1775. Transfer-printed wares and majolica were made in the nineteenth century. The nineteenth-century pieces, most often found today, usually have colorful transfer-printed decorations showing peasants in local costumes.

Character Jug, Man With Moustache & Beard, Majolica, 8 ¾ In.	76.00
Pitcher, Green, Knight On Horseback, Man On Donkey, Mask Spout, Majolica, c.1890, 7 In.	240.00
Plate, Fruit, Raised, 2 Apples, Green, Gold, Red, 7 ½ In.	56.00

SASCHA BRASTOFF made decorative accessories, ceramics, enamels on copper, and plastics of his own design. He headed a factory, Sascha Brastoff of California, Inc., in West Los Angeles, from 1953 until about 1973. He died in 1993. Pieces signed with the signature *Sascha Brastoff* were his work and are the most expensive. Other pieces marked *Sascha B.* or with a stamped mark were made by others in his company. Pieces made by Matt Adams after he left the factory are listed here with his name.

Ashtray, Walrus, Mountain, Hemispherical, 5 ¼ In.	50.00
Ashtray, Whimsical Horse, White, Green Brown, Gray Ground, c.1950, 8 x 5 x 1 In.	49.00
Bowl, Pagodas, Trees, Oval, 3 Footed, 1950s, 9 x 7 In.	60.00
Box, Lid, Round, Bands, Blue, Green, Marked, 5 ½ In.	55.00
Card Box, Gold Ground, Green, Blue, Turquoise, Black Base, 1950s, 6 x 5 In.	68.00
Compote, Green, Flowers, 1970s, 3 ½ x 8 In.	28.00
Dish, Dancing Horse, 3-Footed, 10 x 8 x 2 In.	78.00
Dish, Enamel, Green, Gold, Orange, Scalloped Rim, c.1952, 5 ¼ In.	24.00
Dish, Lid, Rooftops, Gray Border, 5 ½ In.	95.00
Dish, Lid, Sultan, Asymmetrical, 10 x 6 x 2 In.	95.00
Figurine, Seal, Green, Resin, 6 x 8 In.	400.00
Mug, Eskimo, Squared Handle, Marked, 5 In.	30.00
Plate, Salad, Surf Ballet, 8 ¼ In.	15.00
Plate, Seal, Teal Blue, 7 ½ x 7 ½ In.	29.00
Vase, Horse Head, Turquoise Ground, Pink, Green, White, Signed, Square, 6 x 3 In.	60.00

SATIN GLASS is a late nineteenth-century art glass. It has a dull finish that is caused by hydrofluoric acid vapor treatment. Satin glass was made in many colors and sometimes has applied decorations. Satin glass is also listed by factory name, such as Webb, or in the Mother-of-Pearl category in this book.

Biscuit Jar, Blue To White, Peacock Eye Design, Enamel Flowers, Silver Lid, Handle, 5 x 9 In.	345.00
Biscuit Jar, Pink, Quilted, Silver Plate Cover, Handle, Collar, Pierced, Flowers, c.1880, 8 x 11 In.	150.00
Potpourri, Acorn Pattern, Blue, Gold, Enamel, Metal Lid & Base, England, 7 ½ In. *Illus*	1840.00
Vase, Peach To Yellow, Tapered, Swollen Collar, 9 ¾ In.	345.00
Vase, Pink, Ruffled Rim, Enameled Flowers, 11 ½ In.	45.00
Vase, Rose Color, Coralene Flowers, Herringbone Pattern, Bulbous, Narrow Neck, 8 ½ In.	288.00

Scale, Balance, Dayton, Style 121, Brass Tray, Scoop, Cast Iron, Computing Scale Co.
$1,344.00

Victorian Casino Antiques

Scale, Balance, John Chatillon & Sons, Iron, Gold Paint, Dial, Nickel Plated, Brass Pan, 12 x 19 In.
$94.00

Conestoga Auction Co., Inc.

Scale, Candy, Dayton, Model 166, Red Paint, Brass Castings, Pinstriped
$900.00

Victorian Casino Antiques

Scale, Candy, Dayton, Model 167, Chrome Scoop, International Business Machines Corp., 3 Lb.
$472.00

Victorian Casino Antiques

S

SATSUMA

Scale, Postal, Toledo, Drum, Style No. 3150 DD, Glass Tray, Iron, 33 In. $720.00

Victorian Casino Antiques

Scale, Weighing, Talking, I Speak Your Weight, 5 Cent, Cast Iron, 1904, 20 x 76 x 32 In. $9,600.00

Showtime Auction Sevices

SATSUMA is a Japanese pottery with a distinctive creamy beige crackled glaze. Most of the pieces were decorated with blue, red, green, orange, or gold. Almost all Satsuma found today was made after 1860, especially during the Meiji Period, 1868–1912. During World War I, Americans could not buy undecorated European porcelains. Women who liked to make hand-painted porcelains at home began to decorate plain Satsuma. These pieces are known today as "American Satsuma."

Bowl, Dragons, Porcelain, Signed, 1800s, 2 ½ x 6 In.......................................*Illus*	403.00
Bowl, Flowers, Gilt Accents, Scenic Design, Wavy Rim, Ring Foot, 1900s, 6 x 13 In...................	264.00
Bowl, Oval, Landscape Panels, Gilt Borders, Blue Ground, Japan, c.1890, 5 ¾ In...................	1815.00
Box, Lid, Chrysanthemum Shape Lid, Court Scenes, Brocade Patterns, Signed, 1800s, 10 In. Diam.	460.00
Box, Lid, Stand, Round, Swirling Bands Of Flowers, Orchids, Crackle Glaze, c.1900, 2 ⅜ In......	267.00
Charger, Samurai, Court Women, Landscape, Scalloped, c.1875, 12 ⅞ In................................	354.00
Ewer, Baluster, Flower Petal Rim, Twist Handle, Samurai, 12 In.	175.00
Ewer, Earthenware, Double Gourd, Flower Baskets, Signed, Late 19th Century, 3 ¾ In.	60.00
Incense Burner, Dome Lid, Flowers, Scholars, L-Shape Handles, Shishi Lion Feet, 1800s, 13 In...	851.00
Incense Burner, Geishas, Samurai, Shishi Finial, Dragon Handles, c.1890, 25 In..........*Illus*	1722.00
Incense Burner, Lid, Samurai, Landscapes, Flowering Peonies, Shishi Lions, 1800s, 18 In.... *Illus*	790.00
Jar, Dome Lid, Gold Enamel, Brocade Pattern Kannon, Arhats, Attendants, c.1900, 10 In.	213.00
Jar, Lid, Figures & Landscape Panels, Wood Stand, Signed, 4 ½ x 6 In............................*Illus*	450.00
Jar, Lid, Figures, Gilt Enamel, Japan, 10 In.	330.00
Jardiniere, Depicting Masked Figures, Butterflies, Flowers, Fans, Japan, 1800s, 10 x 15 In......	146.00
Koro, Silver Lid, Oatmeal Crackle Ground, Figures, Landscape, Character Marks, 1800s, 3 ½ x 4 In.	3000.00
Pin, 6 Figures, Some With Halos, Elaborate Robes, Gold Highlights, Round, Japan, 1 ¾ In......	826.00
Punch Bowl, Figures & Landscapes, Maple Leaves, Multicolor, Gilding, c.1900, 13 ¾ In.........	276.00
Punch Bowl, U-Shape, Gilt Dragon, Deities, Shimazu Mark, c.1940, 9 x 15 In........................	350.00
Teapot, Buddhist Figures, Chilong Dragon Spout & Handle, Marked, 7 ⅜ In....................*Illus*	175.00
Teapot, Wisteria, Scrolling Leaves, Gold Trim, Signed, Yabu Meizan, Japan, c.1900, 5 In. *Illus*	1320.00
Temple Jar, Foo Dog Finial, Figures, Symbols, Footed Base, 18 In....................................	208.00
Urn, Dome Lid, Gilt, Enamel, Court Figures, Warriors, Handles, Japan, c.1910, 23 ¾ In..........	625.00
Vase, Arhats & Kannon, Gold, Marked, 1800s, 9 ⅝ In.	306.00
Vase, Cream Crackle Ground, Raised Peony & Mu, Fired Gold, Enamel, 1800s, 5 In.........*Illus*	540.00
Vase, Double Gourd, Crackled Glaze, Figural, Flowers, Wood Base, Handle, c.1890, 19 In.	98.00
Vase, Doughnut Center, Round, Footed, Gilt, Japan, c.1945, 5 In.	1000.00
Vase, Dragon Handles, Flared Lip, Wood Base, Gilded, Figures, c.1940, 18 In.	600.00
Vase, Enameled, Gilt, Japanese Maple Tree, Square, Rounded Edge, Footed Base, 4 ½ In.	132.00
Vase, Enameled, Painted, Gilt, Figures, Lohans, Warriors, Baluster, Dome Foot, c.1900, 18 ½ In.	210.00
Vase, Flowers, Brown, Tan, White, Applied Ram, Lion's Head Mounts, 21 ½ In.	118.00
Vase, Immortals, Dragons, Raised Scales, Signed, Japan, c.1870, 12 ¼ In.........................	1694.00
Vase, Maple Trees, Ducks, Water, Crackle Glaze, c.1850, 7 ½ In., Pair..........................	575.00
Vase, Moon, Man's Face, Figures, Gilt, 13 ½ In.	345.00
Vase, Phoenix, Scrolling Clouds, Key Fret Border, Pierced Wood Cover, 1800s, 9 ¾ In..............	551.00
Vase, Thousand Faces Design, Women, Gold Kimonos, Elephant Head Handles, Japan, 6 In., Pair	230.00
Vase, Warrior, Mountain Scene, Applied Bow, Gilt, 24 ½ In.......................................	1610.00
Vase, Wisteria, White Ground, Pink, Purple, Green, Gilt Detail, Japan, 6 ¼ In., Pair	108.00

SATURDAY EVENING GIRLS, *see Paul Revere Pottery category.*

SCALES have been made to weigh everything from babies to gold. Collectors search for all types. Most popular are small gold dust scales and special grocery scales.

Balance, Brass, Attached Electric Lamp, Adjustable, Wood Base, Peacock Measure, 24 x 19 In..	89.00
Balance, Brass, Copper, c.1850, 23 ½ In..	59.00
Balance, Brass, Stamped J.A.L., Portugal, 23 In.	119.00
Balance, Brass, Wood Base, 21 x 18 In..	180.00
Balance, Brass, Wood Base, c.1900, 15 In..	120.00
Balance, Butcher's, Brass, Bull's Head Post, 12 Weights, c.1900, 61 ½ In.	431.00
Balance, Christian Becker, Double, Mahogany Case, Drawer, Level, Weights, 18 x 20 In.	420.00
Balance, Country Store, Cast Iron, c.1880, 13 x 22 In..	30.00
Balance, Dayton, Style 121, Brass Tray, Scoop, Cast Iron, Computing Scale Co. ....*Illus*	1344.00
Balance, Fairbanks, Cast Iron, Wood Box, c.1878, Counter..	448.00
Balance, Fan Shape, Stimpson, No. 698930, 10 Lb., Cast Iron, Red, Gold Trim, Glass Plate	784.00
Balance, Gold, Short Beam, Paul Bunge, Mahogany Case, Marble Base, Germany, c.1920	553.00
Balance, Hardware, Dolphins, Brass, National Computing Scale Co., Weights, Tray, c.1897	3000.00

Balance, Henry Troemner, Cased, 1800s, 9 x 11 ¾ In.	296.00
Balance, Henry Troemner, Oak Case, Cast Iron, 2 Aluminum Trays, Labeled, 8 ½ x 18 ¾ In.	71.00
Balance, Howe, Model 13, Sliding Weight Bar, Rutland, Vt.	209.00
Balance, Howe, No. 5, 5 Lb., Brass Scoop	1140.00
Balance, Hunt & Co., Brass, Arms, 2 Bowls, Wood Base, England, 24 ⅗ x 24 ¼ In.	148.00
Balance, Iron, Counterweight, Brass Pan, c.1900, 32 In.	58.00
Balance, John Chatillon & Sons, Iron, Gold Paint, Dial, Nickel Plated, Brass Pan, 12 x 19 In. *Illus*	94.00
Balance, Jones Of Binghamton, Platform, Double Brass Balance Arms, Adjustable, Iron, 24 x 19 In.	59.00
Balance, Perfection, Size 4, 20 Lb., Cast Iron, Large Brass Scoop, American Machine, Pat. 1885	672.00
Balance, Platform, Iron, Wood, 4 Wheels, Housing, Beam, Sliding Weight, Howe, 1867, 46 x 27 In.	59.00
Balance, Seedere Kohlbusch, Mahogany Case, 15 ¾ x 16 ½ In.	177.00
Balance, Toledo, No. 77, 10 Lb., Computing Scale Company, Toledo, Ohio, c.1902	720.00
Balance, W. & T. Avery, Curled Support, Wrought Iron, Brass, Marked, 1894, 45 ½ x 31 In.	308.00
Candy, Angledile, Grocery Store, Orange & Cream, Brass Trim, Glass Tray	2016.00
Candy, Cast Iron, Painted Black, Radius Sweep Dial Indicator, Spirit Level, Aluminum Scoop	24.00
Candy, Dayton, Model 166, Red Paint, Brass Castings, Pinstriped *Illus*	900.00
Candy, Dayton, Model 167, Chrome Scoop, International Business Machines Corp., 3 Lb. *Illus*	472.00
Candy, E.J. Hoadley Co., Mechanical, Cast Iron, Embossed, 6 x 4 x 4 In.	242.00
Candy, National Store Specialty Co., Footed, Scrolling, Brass Scoop	840.00
Candy, Stimpson, Leaner, Orange & Cream Paint, Brass Trim	1120.00
Carnival, Tripod, Armchair, Oak, Silvered Brass, Mad Genius, c.1925	5036.00
Character Readings & Your Future, American Scale Mfg. Co., c.1910, 52 x 27 In.	531.00
Counterbalance, Cheese, Iron Bound Tray, Backboard, Painted, Cheeses, 33 x 34 In.	1265.00
Counterweight, Fish, Cast Iron, c.1860, 20 ½ In.	5400.00
Floor, Doctors Health, No Springs, Porcelain, Cast Iron	288.00
Hanging, Great Western, Basket Tray, Pale Green, Round, 30 Lb.	480.00
Hanging, Iron, 2 Brass Bowls, Italy, 1800s, 60 In.	575.00
Letter, J. & E. Ratcliff, Cast Bronze, Iron Base, Sliding Weight, England, 1800s, 7 ½ In.	411.00
Pharmaceutical, Henry Troemner, Mahogany, Beveled Glass Case, Weights, c.1900, 13 x 19 In.	213.00
Postal, Brass, Stacking & Hanging Weights, Wood Base, 15 x 9 ¼ In.	385.00
Postal, Toledo, Drum, Style No. 3150 DD, Glass Tray, Iron, 33 In. *Illus*	720.00
Postal, Triner Scale & Mfg. Co., Chicago, Ill., Rectangular	112.00
Powder, Husbands & Clarke, Lacquered Brass, Signed, Bristol, England, c.1880, 7 ¾ In.	632.00
Salter's, Brass, Round, England, 1000 Lb., 18 In.	59.00
Store, Pennsylvania, 4 Lb., Red, White & Blue Shield, National Store Specialty Co.	690.00
Weighing, Angldile, Model 303R, Elkhart, Indiana, USA, Top Lights Up, Honest Weight, 29 In.	3900.00
Weighing, Automatic, Kansas City Scale Supply Co., No. A2270, Red, Gold Trim, Glass Plate	4480.00
Weighing, Card Printer, Mechanical, Electric Light, c.1925, 80 In.	613.00
Weighing, Cast Iron, Brass, Lyre Shaped Support, Quadripartite Base, England, c.1895, 30 x 22 In.	209.00
Weighing, Cast Iron, Toledo, 500 Lb., 70 In.	107.00
Weighing, Computing, Barrel, Paint, Pale Blue, Round Glass Tray	1440.00
Weighing, Dayton, No. 146, Cast Iron, Light-Up Marquee, Computing Scale Co.	1232.00
Weighing, Fairbanks Standard, No. 11, 4 Beams, 500 Lb., Wood Posts, Iron, c.1900, Floor	207.00
Weighing, Lollipop Shape, Do You Know Your Exact Weight, White, Blue Stripes, Floor Model	1020.00
Weighing, Pennies, 1 Cent, Displays Dollar Amount, c.1900, 6 x 14 x 12 In.	84.00
Weighing, Talking, I Speak Your Weight, 5 Cent, Cast Iron, 1904, 20 x 76 x 32 In. *Illus*	9600.00
Weighing, Toledo Scale Co., White Porcelain, Honest Weight, No Springs, 6 Lb.	210.00
Weight Set, Cast Bronze, Signed W. & T. Avery, England, c.1890, 100, 300, 400, 500 Oz., 4 Piece	1027.00

SCHAFER & VATER, makers of small ceramic items, are best known for their amusing figurals. The factory was located in Volkstedt-Rudolstadt, Germany, from 1890 to 1962. Some pieces are marked with the crown and *R* mark, but many are unmarked.

Bottle, 10 Different Faces, Relief, Stopper, Handle, 6 In. *Illus*	253.00
Bottle, Woman Sits In Large Goblet, Stopper, Handle *Illus*	115.00
Figurine, Scotsman, Bench, Kilt, Bulging Eyes, Waiting For The Tide, 4 ¾ In.	225.00
Figurine, Singer, Mr. Tenor, Whimsy, 7 ½ In.	385.00
Figurine, Uncle Sam, What You Want, Seated, Legs Apart, Marked, 4 ¼ In. *Illus*	300.00
Flask, Man, Sitting On Stool, One Of The Boys, c.1900, 7 In.	165.00
Hatpin Holder, Cameo, Green Tassels, Red Dots, Gilt, 5 In.	182.00
Match Holder, Police Gnome, Blue Uniform, Mustache	235.00
Match Holder, Scotsman, Kilt, Long Legs, Big Ears & Feet, 7 x 2 ½ In.	185.00
Pitcher, Figural, Bear, Muff, Robe, Open Mouth, 5 ¼ In.	139.00
Pitcher, Woman, Cape, Coned Hat, Fan, Kneeling, Blue & White, 4 In.	150.00
Vase, Figural, Jockey, Google Eyes, Laurel Leaf Wreath On Hat, 5 ¾ In.	125.00

Schafer & Vater, Bottle, 10 Different Faces, Relief, Stopper, Handle, 6 In. $253.00

Fox Auctions

Schafer & Vater, Bottle, Woman Sits In Large Goblet, Stopper, Handle $115.00

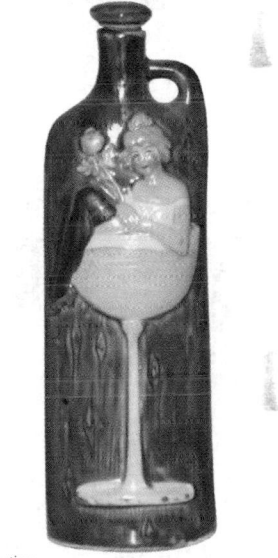

Fox Auctions

Schafer & Vater, Figurine, Uncle Sam, What You Want, Seated, Legs Apart, Marked, 4 ¼ In. $300.00

The Stein Auction Co.

S

Scheier, Bowl, Sgraffito Band, Abstract Figures, Semimatte Glaze, Incised, Edwin & Mary, 7 ⅜ x 12 In.
$1,800.00

Skinner, Inc.

Scheier, Bowl, Sgraffito Figures, Red Brown, Tan & Green Glossy Glaze, Footed, 6 x 7 ¼ In.
$1,304.00

Skinner, Inc.

Scheier, Vase, 6 Repeating Panels, Nude Torso & Head Inside Fish, Green Glaze, Incised, 9 ½ In.
$2,300.00

Humler & Nolan

Scheier, Vase, Mothers & Children, Glazed, Incised, 1990, 13 ⅓ x 10 In.
$3,750.00

Rago Arts & Auction Center

SCHEIER POTTERY was made by Edwin Scheier (1910–2008) and his wife, Mary (1908–2007). They met while they both worked for the WPA, and married in 1937. In 1939, they established their studio, Hillcrock Pottery, in Glade Spring, Virginia. From 1940 to 1968, Edwin taught at the University of New Hampshire and Mary was artist-in-residence. They moved to Oaxaca, Mexico, in 1968 to study the arts and crafts of the Zapotec Indians. When the Scheiers moved to Green Valley, Arizona, in 1978, Ed returned to pottery, making some of his biggest and best-known pieces.

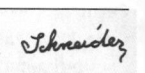

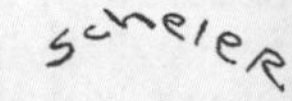

Bowl, Gray Exterior, Green Interior, Signed, 12 x 3 In.	313.00
Bowl, Sgraffito Band, Abstract Figures, Semimatte Glaze, Incised, Edwin & Mary, 7 ⅜ x 12 In...*Illus*	1800.00
Bowl, Sgraffito Figures, Red Brown, Tan & Green Glossy Glaze, Footed, 6 x 7 ¼ In...........*Illus*	1304.00
Bowl, Stylized Faces & Fish, Glossy Brown, Bulbous, 5 x 7 In.	531.00
Charger, Swirling Lines, Yellow Glaze, Stoneware, Signed, 1960s, 16 In. Diam.	1750.00
Group, Square Dancing Couple, Redware, Orange Glaze, Mary Scheier, 5 In.	5000.00
Vase, 6 Repeating Panels, Nude Torso & Head Inside Fish, Green Glaze, Incised, 9 ½ In...*Illus*	2300.00
Vase, Figures, Carved, Rusty Glaze, Charcoal Accents, Signed, 8 ½ x 8 ¼ In.	1586.00
Vase, Figures, Faces, Rounded Bottom, Ring Foot, Signed, 1984, 13 ¼ x 11 In.	1875.00
Vase, Mothers & Children, Glazed, Incised, 1990, 13 ¼ x 10 In...*Illus*	3750.00
Vase, Oak Leaves, Yellow, Blue, Impressed Hillcrock Pottery Logo, c. 1939, 5 ⅛ In...*Illus*	1035.00
Vase, White Glaze, Round, Footed, Stoneware, 1957, 14 ½ In.	1250.00

SCHNEIDER GLASSWORKS was founded in 1917 at Epinay-sur-Seine, France, by Charles and Ernest Schneider. Art glass was made between 1917 and 1930. The company still produces clear crystal glass. See also the Le Verre Francais category.

Bowl, Etched Waves, Dots, Green, Black Foot, c.1920, 13 In.	1375.00
Bowl, Orange Rim, Blue Mottled Patches, Yellow, 3 ⅞ x 13 ½ In.	259.00
Centerpiece, Red Bowl, Grape & Leaf Frame, Wrought Iron, 21 x 12 In.	1000.00
Compote, Purple To Orange, Rounded Rim, Ringed Stem, Signed Foot, 8 x 13 In.	375.00
Lamp, Pheasant, Bronze, Leaded Glass Body, Signed, 16 ½ In...*Illus*	2300.00
Tazza, Mottled Burgundy, Orange, Pedestal, Round Foot, Flat Rim Bowl, 7 ½ In.	863.00
Vase, Line & Circle Design, Enamel, 13 In.	889.00
Vase, Mottled Amber Glass, Lobed, Metal Frame, Vertical Lines & Circles, 7 x 6 In.	432.00
Vase, Mottled Blue To Purple To Orange, Bulbous, Tapered To Padded Foot, Signed, France, 7 In.	230.00
Vase, Mottled Orange & Yellow, Bowl Shape, Metal Cage Frame, Wide Rim, France, 4 In.	230.00
Vase, Pitcher Plants, Mottled Yellow, Cameo, c.1900, 46 In.	676.00
Vase, Red Cased, Mottled, Splotched, Ball Shape, 1920s, 10 x 10 In.	750.00
Vase, White, Amethyst Blossoms, Vines, Handles, Cylindrical, Swollen Neck, Footed, Signed, 13 In.	805.00

SCIENTIFIC INSTRUMENTS of all kinds are included in this category. Other categories such as Barometer, Binoculars, Dental, Medical, Nautical, and Thermometer may also price scientific apparatus.

Barograph, F.G. Schmidt, Mahogany, Beveled Glass, Drawer, 14 ¾ In.	504.00
Barometer, Mahogany, Brass, Mother-Of-Pearl Inlay, Gimbal, England, 38 In.	5900.00
Cable Box, Telegraph, Gamewell, Leaf Finial, Cast Iron, Aluminum, Key, 31 In.	358.00
Calculator, Thatcher, Keuffel & Esser, Inner Cylinder, Outer Scales, Mahogany, Pat. 1881, 23 In. *Illus*	1020.00
Chronometer, Chelsea, Quartz, Chrome Case, Aneroid Barometer, 1900s, 5 ½ In.	230.00
Chronometer, Hamilton Watch Co., Fitted Case, Window, 6 x 5 In.	413.00
Chronometer, Hamilton, 2-Day, Mahogany, Brass, 4 ½ In.	2252.00
Chronometer, Porthouse & French, 2-Day, Brass, Gimbal, Mahogany Box, c.1875, 9 x 10 In.	6325.00
Chronometer, Waltham Watch Co., Mahogany Box, Brass Bound, 5 In.	590.00
Compass, Mining, Cail, Mounted, Wood Tripod, Marked, 1800s, 40 x 7 In.	180.00
Compass, Surveyor's, Folding, Vertical Sight, 3 In.	118.00
Compass, Surveyor's, Richard Patten, N.Y., Engraved Silvered Dial, 14 In...*Illus*	830.00
Level, Surveyor's, B. Pike, Compass, Chest, Signed, N.Y., Mahogany Box, 6 x 14 In.	460.00
Level, Surveyor's, B.K. Elliot Co., Brass, Wood & Brass Tripod, 14 x 15 ½ In.	449.00
Level, Surveyor's, L. Black & Co., Brass, Mahogany Box, Marked, 14 x 7 ½ In.	115.00
Magnifier, Clear Glass, Cast Iron Base, Black, c.1875, 12 ½ In.	499.00
Magnifier, Tabletop, Figural, Nude Girl, Kneeling, Reflecting Pool, Bronze, 3 x 5 ¾ In.	523.00
Magnifying Glass, Ebony, Fruitwood, Gilt Bronze, Round Handle, Vines, Dragon, c.1900, 11 In.	307.00
Magnifying Glass, Gold-Plated Cane Handle, Leaf Relief Designs, Engraved, 1909, 8 ¾ In.	190.00
Magnifying Glass, Tapered Tortoiseshell Handle, Silver Scroll, Flowers, c.1927, 8 In.	215.00
Magnifying Glass, Tortoiseshell Handle, Turned Brass Collar, 4 x 12 ½ In.	799.00
Magnifying Glass, Tortoiseshell, Silver Mounted, Swivels Out Of Case, c.1780, 3 ½ In.	885.00
Microscope, Bausch & Lomb, U.S. Navy Spencer Buffalo, Case, Brass Handle, 10 x 15 ½ In.	118.00

S

Microscope, Binocular, R. & J. Beck, Brass, Wood Case, c.1870 ....*Illus*	600.00
Microscope, Carl Zeiss, Gena, 5 Lenses, Fitted Wood Case, 15 In.	944.00
Microscope, Compound, Cary Type, Lacquered Brass, Concave Mirror, Box Base, 11 In.	443.00
Octant, Ebony, Painted Compass Star, Initials, Brass Sliding Index Arm, 1800s, 5 x 14 In.	1067.00
Signal Horn, Siebe Gorman & Co., Air Supply, Bellows Operated, 26 x 21 In.	460.00
Slide Rule, Spiral, Logarithmic Drum, Wood Handle, Professor Fuller, 1889, 11 ¾ In.	997.00
Spectometer, Adam Hilger, Constant Deviation Type, Brass, Iron Base, c.1920, 14 x 22 In.	210.00
Spyglass, Mahogany Barrel, 2 Draw, Signed Wilson London Day/Night, c.1820, 35 In.	299.00
Spyglass, U.S. Navy, 16 Power, Quartermaster Mark II, Maple Case, c.1942, 31 x 3 ½ In.	633.00
Steam Engine, Salesman's Sample, 1907, 23 x 16 In.	4125.00
Steam Engine, Working Beam, Stuart, Cast Iron, Steel, Brass, Flywheel, c.1930, 1 ½ x 7 In. ..	1082.00
Tattooing Machine, Foot Pedal Power, Flywheel, Belt Drive, Wood Base, Brass, c.1880, 67 In...	285.00
Telescope, A. Bardou, Brass, Ebonized Metal, Mahogany Tripod, France, 52 x 47 In............	4388.00
Telescope, A. Bardou, Brass, Oak & Brass Tapered Tripod Stand, Paris	1722.00
Telescope, Brass & Wood, Floor, Concentric Rings, Adjustable Legs, 55 In............................	615.00
Telescope, Brass, 4 Draw, Leather Cover, c.1890, 10 In.	94.00
Telescope, Canvas Wrapped Barrel, Brass Mounts, Single Draw, c.1860, 20 ¾ In...................	153.00
Telescope, Clarkson & Co., Brass, 3 Draw Eyepiece, Oak Tripod, Broadhurst, 77 x 74 In.........	3000.00
Telescope, Dollond, Brass, Mahogany, Parallel Barrel, Signed, London, c.1800, 19 ¾ In.	130.00
Telescope, Dollond, Draw Tube, Cylindrical, Mahogany Tripod, 37 In................................	1126.00
Telescope, Reflecting, Brass, Rack & Pinion, Folding Tripod, Ramsden, c.1775, 15 In.	1823.00
Telescope, Sam Yeates, Brass, Label, Wood Case, Dublin, Ireland, 29 ½ In...........................	326.00
Telescope, Stand, Brass, Box, 74 x 54 In...	1298.00
Telescope, Van Cort, Brass, Oak Folding Tripod Base, Engraved Name, 36 x 65 In....................	799.00
Telescope, Widdifield & Co., Mahogany, Brass, Folding Tripod Base, Marked, 45 x 62 In..........	1770.00
Telescope, Wood, Leather Covered, Brass Lens Bezels, Eyepiece, 10-Sided, 25 In.	59.00
Transit, Surveyor's, Adjustable Wood Tripod Base, Metal Points, Level, 65 In.	230.00
Transit, Surveyor's, Brass, Marked, Gurley Surveyors, c.1890, 18 In.	165.00
Transit, Surveyor's, Buff & Buff Mfg. Co., 1916, 12 In.	288.00
Transit, Surveyor's, Stanley, Brass, Dual Magnifiers & Bubble Levels, 1800s.....................*Illus*	1320.00
Windmill, Bear Mfg., Model M, Indiana, Salesman's Sample, 19 ½ In...........................	1020.00

SCRIMSHAW is bone or ivory or whale's teeth carved by sailors and others for entertainment during the sailing-ship days. Some scrimshaw was carved as early as 1800. There are modern scrimshanders making pieces today on bone, ivory, or plastic. Other pieces may be found in the Ivory and Nautical categories.

Ball, Walrus, Rabbit, Wolf, Seal, Whales, Black Pedestal Base, New England, c.1850, 2 ½ In.....	2133.00
Basket, Crossed Notched Sticks, Round, Pine Base, 4 ½ x 6 In..	1416.00
Basket, Whalebone, Interlocking Circles, Wood Base, Oval, 3 x 7 In................................	4838.00
Basket, Whalebone, Pierced Trellis Sides, Wood Base, Oval, Swing Handle, 5 ¼ x 5 ¼ In.	2006.00
Belt Buckle, Sailing Ship, White Metal, Initials, 2 ¼ x 1 ¼ In...	115.00
Bodkin, Whalebone, Baleen, Snake Shape, Bead Eyes, 3 ¾ In.	944.00
Bodkin, Whalebone, Carved Arm, Hand On Book, 5 ½ In...	1888.00
Box, Sailor's, Whale Panbone, Engraved, Eagle, Patriotic Seal, Stars, c.1850, 10 ¼ x 7 In........	3163.00
Busk, Baleen, Woman's Figure, Checkerboard, Potted Flowers, Side-Wheeler, 1800s, 14 ¾ In..	415.00
Busk, Panbone, 2-Masted Ship, Eagle, Shield, Rose Bush, 10 ½ In......................................	1180.00
Busk, Vertical Panels, Engraved, Plants, Heart, Checkerboard, c.1875, 11 x 2 In.....................	1007.00
Busk, Whalebone, Potted Flowers, Heart, Star, Geometrics, c.1820, 12 ½ In.	1541.00
Busk, Whalebone, Potted Flowers, Tree, Flag, Clock Designs, Paint, c.1850, 13 In....................	2133.00
Carpenter's Plane, Whalebone, Ship's, Scroll Tip Edge, Steel Blade, 8 ½ In..........................	2596.00
Carpenter's Square, Whalebone, Ship's, Stamped CCV, 15 ¾ In..	1534.00
Cribbage Board, Ivory, Carved, Polar Bear Mask End, 3 Pegged Legs, c.1860, 19 In.	518.00
Ditty Box, Lid, Engraved, Building, Flowers, Wood Base, Oval, 3 x 5 ¼ In.	6372.00
Fid, Whalebone, Ebony, Clenched Fist End, 5 ½ In...	1180.00
Pie Crimper, Whalebone, Carved, Single, Turned Wood Handle, c.1850, 6 ¼ In.	561.00
Pie Crimper, Whalebone, Double Wheels, 3-Tined Fork, 7 In...	2124.00
Rolling Pin, Whalebone, Mahogany, Stand, 18 ¾ In..	502.00
Scrimshander Saw, Whalebone, Carved Head, Steel Blade, 6 x 5 ¾ In.	2124.00
Stave, Corset, Whalebone, Rebel Soldier, Cannon, Flag, Tree, 1800s, 7 ¾ In.	177.00
Tooth, Lady Liberty, U.S. Seal, Liberty Banner, Laurel Wreath, 1800s, 5 ½ In........................	518.00
Tusk, Depicting Ship Mercury, Eagle, 20th Century, 10 In..	1422.00
Tusk, Ship, Sea Captain & Wife, 20th Century, 28 In..	729.00
Walrus Tusk, Black, Red Liberty, Shield, Eagle, Ship, Engraved Allegorical Figures, 17 ½ In. .	6136.00
Whalebone, Carved, Mother-Of-Pearl Inlay, Marble Base, 12 ½ In.......................................	1888.00

Scheier, Vase, Oak Leaves, Yellow, Blue, Impressed Hillcrock Pottery Logo, c. 1939, 5 ⅛ In.
$1,035.00

Humler & Nolan

Schneider, Lamp, Pheasant, Bronze, Leaded Glass Body, Signed, 16 ½ In.
$2,300.00

Humler & Nolan

Scientific Instrument, Calculator, Thatcher, Keuffel & Esser, Inner Cylinder, Outer Scales, Mahogany, Pat. 1881, 23 In.
$1,020.00

Skinner, Inc.

Scientific Instrument, Compass, Surveyor's, Richard Patten, N.Y., Engraved Silvered Dial, 14 In.
$830.00

S

Skinner, Inc.

Scientific Instrument, Microscope, Binocular, R. & J. Beck, Brass, Wood Case, c.1870
$600.00

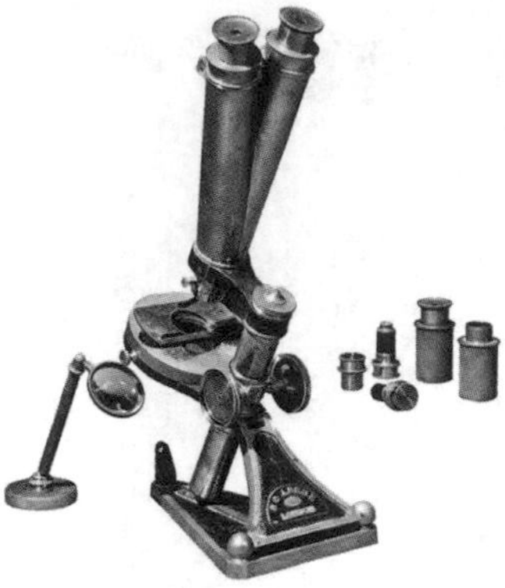

Skinner, Inc.

Scientific Instrument, Transit, Surveyor's, Stanley, Brass, Dual Magnifiers & Bubble Levels, 1800s
$1,320.00

Skinner, Inc.

Determined Artists

Some silhouette artists were born without arms or were otherwise disabled and cut silhouettes with scissors held by their toes or lips. Silhouettes cut in the nineteenth century by Martha Ann Honeywell or Saunders Nellis, both disabled, can be found in museums.

Whalebone, Seam Rubber, Chamfered Cube Head, 4 ¾ In.	1003.00
Whale's Tooth, Battle, USS Constitution & Guerriere, Verso, Open Bible, Flowers, 1800s, 6 ¾ In.	4720.00
Whale's Tooth, Birds, Multicolor, Rosewood Stand, 5 ¾ x 4 ¾ In., Pair	460.00
Whale's Tooth, Compass Rose, 7 In.	1298.00
Whale's Tooth, Engraved, Columbia, Standing, Shield, Eagle, 6 ½ In.	2950.00
Whale's Tooth, Engraved, Couple, 2 Children, Forest, Urn, Leaf & Berry Border, 6 ¼ In.	4248.00
Whale's Tooth, Engraved, Inset Tintype Woman's Portrait, Sawtooth Border, 5 In.	5664.00
Whale's Tooth, Engraved, Man, Rescuing Inca Baby, 6 In.	1416.00
Whale's Tooth, Engraved, Man, Woman, Holding Flags, Painted, 5 ¾ In., Pair	11564.00
Whale's Tooth, Engraved, Pheasant, On Branch, Eagle, Stars, Banner, Black, Red Paint, 6 In.	2006.00
Whale's Tooth, Engraved, Riverbank, Ship, Sawtooth Border, 6 ½ In.	1770.00
Whale's Tooth, Engraved, Sailing Ship, Union Jack Flag, Red Ink, 8 ¼ In.	6018.00
Whale's Tooth, Engraved, Ships, Lighthouse, 5 ¾ In.	2360.00
Whale's Tooth, Engraved, St. Bart's Scene, Ship, Lighthouse, 7 In.	5310.00
Whale's Tooth, Engraved, War Of 1812 Scene, 5 ½ In.	4484.00
Whale's Tooth, Engraved, Woman, Hat, Bustle Dress, Parasol, Black, Red Ink, 6 ½ In.	3540.00
Whale's Tooth, Engraved, Woman, Sawtooth Oval Border, Leaf Rim, 6 In.	15930.00
Whale's Tooth, Engraved, Woman, Standing, Petting Spaniel, On Pedestal, 6 ½ In.	3540.00
Whale's Tooth, Hope, 1800s Attire, Ship, Flying Flag, Anchor, 6 ¾ In.	3422.00
Whale's Tooth, Inscription, Lycka Til, Good Luck, Sweden, 6 In.	219.00
Whale's Tooth, Maltese Crosses, Crown, Letter R, Ribbon, 7 ½ In.	635.00
Whale's Tooth, Plain, 1800s, 6 In.	295.00
Whale's Tooth, Sailing Ship, Flag, Eagle, Woman, Sailor, Flowers, c.1840, 6 ¼ In.	88875.00
Whale's Tooth, Ship Designs, Inscribed, c.1850, 6 In., Pair	1652.00
Whale's Tooth, Woman's Portrait, Rose, Handkerchief, Black Base, Mass., c.1830, 6 ¼ In.	3792.00

SEG, *see Paul Revere Pottery category.*

SEVRES porcelain has been made in Sevres, France, since 1769. Many copies of the famous ware have been made. The name originally referred to the works of the Royal Porcelain factory. The name now includes any of the wares made in the town of Sevres, France. The entwined lines with a center letter used as the mark is one of the most forged marks in antiques. Be very careful to identify Sevres by quality, not just by mark.

Bowl, Centerpiece, Blue Celeste, Courting Couple Reserve, Gilt Bronze Mounts, Handles, 10 x 14 In.	1140.00
Bowl, Centerpiece, Putti, Turquoise Ground, Gilt Trim, Shaped Handles & Feet, 7 x 15 In.	413.00
Bowl, Floral Reserves, Sprays, Gilt Leafy Borders, Flared Rim, 1846, 4 ¼ x 11 ¼ In.	58.00
Bowl, Monteith, Wavy Rim, Painted Flowers, Scroll Handles, Blue Line, Gilt Banding, 5 ⅜ In.	6250.00
Box, Blue Enamel, Gilt, Classical Woman Picking Flowers, Swags, Oval, 2 x 5 In.	748.00
Box, Painted, Peacock Blue Ground, Gilt Scrolling, Flowers, Mark, 1800s, 4 ½ x 6 ½ In.	210.00
Card Tray, Oval Tray, Scroll, Flute, Garden, Swags, Bronze Stand, c.1847, 5 x 12 x 6 In.	984.00
Figure Group, Putti, Riding Goats, Parian, 8 ¼ In., Pair	326.00
Lamp, Porcelain, Putti, Lilac, Green, White, Frosted Globe, Metal, E. Drouet, 1897, 19 x 32 In.	2000.00
Plaque, Courting Couple, Oval Mat, Frame, 3 ½ x 4 ¾ In.	186.00
Plate, Assiette A Palms, Flower Garlands, Cobalt Blue Lobed Border, Gilt Edge, Scrolls, 1773, 9 ¾ In.	2125.00
Plate, Courting Scene, Painted, Celeste Blue Border, Flowers, Fired Gold, Signed E. Cury, c.1841, 9 In.	1020.00
Plate, Mother & Child At Well, Painted, Cobalt Blue Border, Fired Gold Scrolls, Branches, 9 ¼ In.	96.00
Plate, Napoleonic Shield, Bees, Cobalt Blue Ground Border, 9 ½ In., 10 Piece	688.00
Plate, Portrait Centers, Chateau De St. Cloud, Blue Ground, 9 ½ In., 2 Piece	360.00
Pot A Jus, Green Interlaced Loops, Flowers, Gilt Rim, Handle Maria-Theresa, 1758, 2 ¼ In.	7500.00
Salt Cellar, Triple, Blue Celeste, Bird, Landscape, Turquoise Ground, Gilt, 3-Part Handle, 3 ⅜ x 4 In.	7500.00
Sugar, Lid, Alternating Spiral Panels, Cobalt Blue, Flowering Vines, Gilt, c.1758, 4 In.	576.00
Sugar, Lid, Laurel Scroll, Jewel & Flower Head Bands, Gilt Trim & Finial, c.1784, 4 In.	1152.00
Urn, Lid, Multicolor Flowers, Gilt Scroll Leaves, Banding, Ring Handles, Marked, c.1800, 13 ½ In.	239.00
Urn, Lid, Woman, Pink Gown, Orchids, Sun, Scroll Handles, Pineapple Finial, Pedestal Foot, 17 ½ In.	1725.00
Urn, Mantel, Swirled Flower Ribs, Blue, Gilt Neck, Base, Brass Mounts, Marked, c.1950, 21 In., Pair	413.00
Urn, Oval Portrait Medallion, Marie Antoinette, Celeste Blue Ground, Gilt Bronze, 25 In.	2700.00
Urn, Pierced Lid, Oval, Flower Cartouches, Blue, Nude Handles, E. Renard, c.1850, 16 x 13 In.	3163.00
Urn, Portrait, Rustic Woman, Painted, Cobalt Blue Border, Lamp Base, Signed, c.1900, 29 In.	540.00
Vase, 4 Lobes, Musical Trophies, Flowers Painted, Gilt Rims, 1759, 6 ¼ In.	4375.00
Vase, Cherub, Holding Flower, Garland, Rose Pompadour Ground, Baluster, 1853, 12 In., Pair	369.00
Vase, Cobalt Blue, Bronze Ormolu, Allegorical Reserve, Mask Handles, Poitevin, c.1890, 29 x 17 In.	4800.00
Vase, Courting Scene, Cobalt Blue, Bronze Ormolu, c.1900, 30 In. *Illus*	4200.00
Vase, Courting Scene, Flowers In Cartouche, Cobalt Blue, Bronze Ormolu, 30 In.	3300.00
Vase, Lid, Cherubs, Maiden, Arrow, Ormolu Mounts, Urn Shape, Footed, c.1820, 34 In.	3081.00
Vase, Lid, Gilt Bronze Mounts, Woman Face Handles, Yellow, Flowers, Marked, 1700s, 13 ½ In.	720.00

SEWER TILE figures were made by workers at the sewer tile and pipe factories in the Ohio area during the late nineteenth and early twentieth centuries. Figurines, small vases, and cemetery vases were favored. Often the finished vase was a piece of the original pipe with added decorations and markings. All types of sewer tile work are now considered folk art by collectors.

Bank, Boy's Head, Figural, Brown, Ohio, c.1900, 5 In.	118.00
Birdhouse, Bark Design Roof Top, Mushroom Cap Shape Top, Cylindrical, c.1900, 8 ½ x 8 In.	235.00
Figure, Baseball Player, Boy Holding Bat, Seated On A Baseball, Round Foot, Ohio, c.1900, 7 In. ..	176.00
Figure, Cat, Elongated, Seated, Inscribed, c.1900, 13 In.	353.00
Figure, Cat, Sitting, White Under Glaze Feet, Ears, Face & Spots, 7 ¼ In.	118.00
Figure, Crow, Seated On Stump, Dark Glaze, Incised, EJE, c.1900, 9 In.	1175.00
Figure, Dog, Seated, Freestanding Legs, Tooled Detail, Glazed, Ohio, c.1900, 9 In.	211.00
Figure, Dog, Spaniel, Seated, Incised, Inscribed OO, c.1910, 10 In...........................*Illus*	181.00
Figure, Eagle, Standing, Incised Feathers, Ohio, c.1900, 7 In.	705.00
Figure, Frog, Mottled Brown, 8 In.	35.00
Figure, Groundhog, Sitting, Metallic Flecked Glaze, c.1900, 8 ½ In.	1293.00
Figure, Lion, Reclining, c.1900, 6 ½ x 9 In.	181.00
Figure, Owl, Seated On Stump, Metallic Flecked Glaze, Ohio, c.1900, 7 In.	529.00
Figure, Owl, Seated, Slightly Turned Head, Multicolor, Square Base, c.1900, 8 ½ In.	59.00
Lamp Base, Figural, Growling Bear, Circling A Tree, c.1900, 12 ½ In.	323.00
Lamp Base, Tree Trunk Shape, Grapevine, Fungus, Bucket, c.1900, 10 x 10 In.	147.00
Mug, Smoking Indians Design, Headdresses, Cylindrical, Spurred Handle, c.1900, 4 ¼ In.	58.00
Pitcher, Fish, Open Mouth, Tail Forms Handle, Initialed WMF, 10 In.	121.00
Planter, Log Shape, Applied Leaves & Vines, c.1900, 8 x 16 ½ In.	88.00
Planter, Log Shape, Incised Flowers, Bertha Bricker, Tappan, Ohio, c.1910, 9 x 25 x 8 ¾ In. .... *Illus*	588.00
Urn, Garland Rim, Swirl Bowl, Jester Handles, Matte, c.1870, 19 ½ x 27 In.	360.00

SEWING equipment of all types is collected, from sewing birds that held the cloth to tape measures, needle books, and old wooden spools. Sewing machines are included here. Needlework pictures are listed in the Picture category.

Basket, Double Lid, Handle, Pa., c.1890, 6 ½ x 8 ½ In.	504.00
Bird, Brass, Square Clamp, Raised Flowers, 1800s, 5 x 3 ¾ In.	59.00
Bird, Heart Cutout, Pincushion Bird, Clamp, Iron, Inscribed A. Jerould & Co. Patent, c.1860, 4 ¾ In. .	395.00
Box, Anglo-Indian, Ivory, Sandalwood, Penwork, Domed, Fitted Interior, c.1890, 6 ½ x 13 ½ In. ...	2000.00
Box, Anglo-Indian, Wood, Carved, Ivory Inlays, Fitted Interior, Brass Ball Feet, 5 x 13 ⅓ In.	531.00
Box, Bird's-Eye Maple, Lift Ray Top Lid, Flowers, Fruits, Painted, Fitted Interior, c.1830, 6 x 12 ½ In.	3318.00
Box, Burl Veneer, Fitted Interior, Accoutrements, Needle Cases, Spools, c.1850, 4 x 10 ½ In.	385.00
Box, Carved Flowers, Red, Green, Pin Cushion Top, Hinged Lid, c.1860, 6 x 11 x 7 In.	891.00
Box, Chinoiserie, Lacquer, Gilt, Landscape, Figures, Fitted Interior, Paw Feet, Octagonal, 7 x 15 In.	1955.00
Box, Curly Maple, Mahogany, Sarcophagus Shape Lid, Mirror, Removable Tray, c.1835, 9 x 14 In.	844.00
Box, Gilt Lacquer, Hinged Lid, Brass Handles, Carved Paw Feet, Chinese, c.1840, 6 x 14 In.	720.00
Box, Hinged Lid, Chinoiserie, Gilt, Canted Corners, Flowers, Dragon Feet, 1800s, 6 ½ x 14 In. .	720.00
Box, Lacquer, Gilt, On Black Chinese Symbols, Lift Top, Octagonal, Drawer, c.1935, 6 ½ x 14 In. ...	295.00
Box, Lacquer, Landscape Scenes, Ivory Fitted Interior, Octagonal, Chinese, 12 ½ In.	384.00
Box, Lid, Pine, Graining, Flowers, Drawer, Ball Feet, Octagonal, c.1850, 7 x 16 In.	206.00
Box, Mahogany Veneer, Bone Finials, Thread Holes, Velvet Pincushion, Drawer, 1800s, 7 x 7 In... *Illus*	121.00
Box, Mahogany, Geometric Inlay, Lift Top, Drawers, Canted Sides, Platform Base, c.1895, 13 x 14 In..	2133.00
Box, Mahogany, Ivory Inlay, Piano Shape, Keyboard, Lid, Turned Legs, England, 1800s, 6 ½ x 11 In...	295.00
Box, Mahogany, Paint, Ship, Banner, Spread Eagle, Recessed Brass Handles, c.1850, 6 ½ x 17 ½ In. ...	705.00
Box, Pine, Slant Lid, Pincushion, Blue, Green Stippled Paint, Strap Handles, 6 ¾ x 14 ½ In.....	2133.00
Box, Softwood, Red Paint, Fabric, Cross Stitch, House, Willow, Verse, Elizabeth Dorr, 1827, 6 x 3 In.	130.00
Box, Wall, Pine, Embroidery Pincushion, c.1895, 17 In.	504.00
Box, Wallpaper Cover, Pin Cushion Top, c.1850, 3 x 5 In.	326.00
Box, Wood, Panels, Interior Compartments, Gold Ball Feet, Octagonal, c.1815, 6 ¾ x 12 ¾ In...	173.00
Cabinet, Lace Display, Revolving, Round, 4 Sections, Wood, Cast Iron Base, 24 x 35 In....*Illus*	1020.00
Cabinet, Spool, see also the Advertising category under Cabinet, Spool.	
Case, Display, Butterick Patterns, Oak, 20 Glass Fronts, Decals, Floor Model, 32 x 57 x 22 In. *Illus*	8400.00
Dress Form, Wheels, Fiberglass Figure, Woman's, 56 In.	74.00
Hem Marker, Wood & Iron, Marked Boco Patent Pending, 1930s	30.00
Knitting Sheath, Boxwood, Chip Carved Borders, Relief Heart, Clover, Geometrics, c.1740, 7 In.	325.00
Machine, Crane Knitter, Cast Iron, Walnut Desk Case, Cast Iron Trestle Base, 1869, 30 x 32 In.	354.00
Machine, Leather, Treadle, Walking Beam, Iron, Flying Bobbin Deck, Brass Label, 44 x 28 In.	83.00
Machine, Singer, Crank, Painted, Cast Iron, c.1890, 9 x 13 ½ In.	593.00
Measure, Silver, Portrait Design, Unger Bros., 4 ¼ In.	87.00
Needle Case, Umbrella Shape, Ivory, c.1875, 3 ¾ In.	100.00
Needle Pack, Elsie The Cow, Cardboard, Foil Needle Pack Inside, 1950s	20.00

Sevres, Vase, Courting Scene, Cobalt Blue, Bronze Ormolu, c.1900, 30 In. $4,200.00

DuMouchelles Art Gallery

Sewer Tile, Figure, Dog, Spaniel, Seated, Incised, Inscribed OO, c.1910, 10 In. $181.00

Garth's Auctioneers & Appraisers

Sewer Tile, Planter, Log Shape, Incised Flowers, Bertha Bricker, Tappan, Ohio, c.1910, 9 x 25 x 8 ¾ In. $588.00

Garth's Auctioneers & Appraisers

S

Sewing, Box, Mahogany Veneer, Bone Finials, Thread Holes, Velvet Pincushion, Drawer, 1800s, 7 x 7 In. $121.00

Garth's Auctioneers & Appraisers

Sewing, Cabinet, Lace Display, Revolving, Round, 4 Sections, Wood, Cast Iron Base, 24 x 35 In. $1,020.00

Showtime Auction Sevices

Sewing, Case, Display, Butterick Patterns, Oak, 20 Glass Fronts, Decals, Floor Model, 32 x 57 x 22 In. $8,400.00

Showtime Auction Sevices

Pattern, Simplicity Pattern No. 4914, Costume, Female Pirate, Adult, 15 Piece, Uncut	10.00
Pincushion Dolls are listed in their own category.	
Pincushion, Satinwood, Drawer, Tulip Inlay, Carved, Pa., c.1810, 6 x 6 ½ In.	356.00
Pincushion, Umbrella Shape, Grosgrain Cover, Victorian, c.1875, 8 x 4 In.	47.00
Scissors, Brass, Shields, King, Sheath, c.1880, 7 ½ In.	145.00
Sewing Kit, Singer Manufacturing Co., Rubber Mannequin, Jointed, 1949, 12 ½ In.	75.00
Spinning Jenny, Whalebone, Ivory, Prisoner Of War Carved, 5 ⅞ In.	2360.00
Spool Cabinets are listed here or in the Advertising category under Cabinet, Spool.	
Spool Caddy, Tin, Indian Chief Shape Pedestal, Painted, c.1900, 14 In.	118.00
Spool Caddy, Walnut, Interior Holders, Thread Holes, Pedestal Base, Finial, Round, 1867, 8 ½ In.	118.00
Spool Holder, Turned Wood, Pincushion Top, Compartments, C-Clamp Base, Pa., 1800s, 10 In. ...*Illus*	1062.00
Swift, Green Flowers, Yellow Ground, New England, c.1830, 24 In.	474.00
Swift, Single Cage, Fist Clamp, Tortoiseshell, Abalone Diamond Panel, 17 In.	6785.00
Swift, Whalebone, Ivory, Needle Cup, Barrel Shape Fastening Base, c.1850, 18 ¼ In.	1265.00
Tape Loom, Pine, Fishtail Handle, Primitive, 18 ¼ In.	531.00
Tape Loom, Shaped Handle, Wood, 1794, 3 x 6 In.	695.00
Tape Loom, Wood, Heart Cutouts, Painted Love Birds, Red, Yellow, Initialed NL, Pa, 1826, 15 x 14 In.	9480.00
Tape Measure, Bonzo, Dog, Celluloid, Pull Tongue For Tape, Germany, c.1920s, 1 ¼ In.	385.00
Tape Measure, Edison Mazda Lamps, GE, Celluloid, Parrish Design, 1 ½ x ½ In. ....*Illus*	187.00
Tape Measure, Lydia Pinkham, Celluloid, Lydia On Front, Remedies On Back, 1 ¾ In.	125.00
Tape Measure, Pig, White, Pink, Yellow, Japan, 2 In.	49.00
Wool Winder, Brass, Wood, c.1860, 26 x 24 In.	496.00
Yarn Winder, Maple, Shaker Style	175.00
Yarn Winder, Red Paint, Wood Gear, Ring-Turned Post, Tripod Base, 1700s, 36 In.	123.00
Yarn Winder, Wood, c.1845, 54 ½ In.	59.00
Yarn Winder, Wood, Turned, Painted, Leaves, Stars, 7 ⅞ In.	207.00

SHAKER items are characterized by simplicity, functionalism, and orderliness. There were many Shaker communities in America from the eighteenth century to the present day. The religious order made furniture, small wooden pieces, and packaged medicines, herbs, and jellies to sell to "outsiders." Other useful objects were made for use by members of the community. Shaker furniture is listed in this book in the Furniture category.

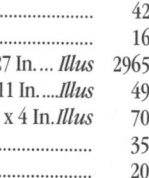

Basket Set, Oval, Lapped Ends, Graduated Sizes, Mt. Lebanon, Largest 13 ½ In., 6 Piece	3650.00
Basket, Apple, Wood Slatted, Wire Stave, c.1890, 18 ½ In. Diam.	420.00
Basket, Round Rim, Square Base, Splint Handles, c.1870, 12 ½ In.	165.00
Bin, Storage, Pine, Maple, Hinged Top, Breadboard Ends, Mt. Lebanon, c.1840, 32 x 27 In. .... *Illus*	29655.00
Bonnet, Sister's, Woven Straw, Palm Leaf, Paper Lining, Cape, Wooden Mold, c.1850, 11 In. .....*Illus*	497.00
Bowl, Maple, Red Stain, Varnished, Lathe Turned, Raised Rim, Footed Base, 15 ¼ x 4 In.*Illus*	702.00
Box, 3-Finger, Lid, 19th Century, 3 x 7 ¼ In.	356.00
Box, 3-Finger, Oval, Copper Tacks, c.1880, 2 x 3 In.	207.00
Box, 3-Finger, Oval, Copper Tacks, Yellow Paint, c.1870, 1 ⅝ x 2 ⅞ In.	431.00
Box, 3-Finger, Oval, Lid, 3 x 6 In.	267.00
Box, 3-Finger, Oval, Lid, Cheese, Green Paint, Branded C. Whitney, c.1890, 6 ¾ x 13 In.	1380.00
Box, 3-Finger, Oval, Lid, Handle, Brown, 1800s, 4 x 10 ¼ In.	94.00
Box, 3-Finger, Oval, Pine, Maple, Orange Finish, c.1840, 2 ½ x 7 x 5 In.	4797.00
Box, 4-Finger, Oval, Lid, 4 x 10 In.	711.00
Box, 4-Finger, Oval, Lid, Rotten Stone Label, 4 x 9 In.	830.00
Box, 4-Finger, Oval, Lid, Tamara Paper Label, New Lebanon, 5 ½ x 13 ½ In.	1304.00
Box, 4-Finger, Oval, Oak, Pine, Yellow Paint, c.1850, 4 ¼ x 11 ½ x 8 ¾ In.	5499.00
Box, 4-Finger, Oval, Pine, Maple, Red Paint, Copper Tacks, 1907, 3 x 8 x 5 In.	6435.00
Box, 4-Finger, Pine, Maple, Bittersweet Painted, Lapped Seams, Lid, Oval, 4 ⅞ x 11 ⅞ In.	1304.00
Box, 4-Finger, Round, Lid, Painted Green, Pine, Maple, Copper Tacks, 4 ⅝ x 12 ¼ In.	770.00
Box, 5-Finger, Maple, Pine, Oval, Copper Tacks, 6 ½ x 10 ½ x 7 ¼ In.	8190.00
Box, 5-Finger, Pine, Maple, Yellow Paint, 4 ½ x 10 x 7 In.	3978.00
Box, Church Collection, Maple, Dovetailed, Turned Handle, 1800s, 3 x 14 In.	474.00
Box, Document, Molded Lid, Pine, Hinged, 9 x 17 In.	351.00
Box, Document, Red Stain, Hinge Lid, Brass Drawer, Ceramic Pull, 1800s, 6 ½ x 13 ¾ In.	1164.00
Box, Glove, Butternut, Brass Hinge, Dovetailed, Nails, New Lebanon, c.1845, 13 ½ x 5 ½ In... *Illus*	2925.00
Box, Handkerchief, Butternut, Dovetailed, Canted Edges, Hinged Lid, c.1900, 4 ⅛ x 8 ⅜ In.	770.00
Box, Hat, Lid, Hinged, 4 Spindle Interior, Hancock, Ma., 19 x 25 In.	293.00
Box, Lid, Oval, Pine & Maple, Fingers, Copper Tacks, Red Stain, c.1890, 3 x 6 In.	300.00
Box, Oval, Grain Painted, c.1850, 4 x 10 ½ In.	972.00
Box, Oval, Lid, Black Milk Paint, Maine, c.1845, 16 x 7 In.	288.00
Box, Storage, Cardboard, Paper Covered, Leaf & Diamond Design, c.1900, 7 x 7 x 4 In.	351.00
Broadside, Black Ink On Card Stock, c.1925, 14 ¼ x 19 ¼ In. ....*Illus*	995.00
Bucket, Applesauce, Wood, Handle, J.S. Kaime, New Hampshire, c.1860, 7 ½ In.	356.00

S

Bucket, Pine, Metal Bands, Bentwood Swing Handle, Paint, Stenciled, 1915, c.1840, 7 In....*Illus* 2457.00
Bucket, Pine, Red Stain, Wire Swing Bail, Turned Wood Grip, Shaped Lid, 15 x 12 In. 4095.00
Bucket, Pine, Yellow Paint, Turned Wood Handle, Iron Bail, 7 ¾ x 10 In. 2691.00
Bucket, Pine, Yellow Paint, Wire Swing Handle, Diamond Bail Plates, J.J.B., 15 x 12 In. 17550.00
Bucket, Sap, Yellow Paint, Inscribed Middle Hall, Canterbury, New Hampshire, 11 ½ x 12 ½ In. 293.00
Carrier, 3-Finger, Maple, Ash Handle, Pine Bottom, Copper Tacks, Inscribed, 7 x 8 x 11 In.... *Illus* 20000.00
Carrier, 3-Finger, Maple, Ash, Fixed Hoop Handle, Beveled, Copper Tacks, 9 x 10 x 7 In. 2047.00
Carrier, 4-Finger, Maple, Pine, Yellow Paint, Copper Tacks, Hickory Handle, 9 x 11 In.....*Illus* 63180.00
Carrier, Pine, Bentwood Handle, Red Paint, Dovetail, c.1835, 8 x 14 x 10 In. 7254.00
Cloak, Wool, Maroon, Silk Lined Hood, Ribbon Ties, 54 In. 1053.00
Dipper, Bentwood, 1800s, 3 ¼ x 6 In. 119.00
Fabric, Raw Silk, Purple, 36 x 36 In. 1404.00
File Box, Pine, Drawer, Molded Lid, Turned Pull, Diamond Shape Escutcheon, c.1845, 6 In. 504.00
Firkin, Blue Paint, Stamped Ephraim Murdoch, c.1866, 11 ¾ In. 1007.00
Firkin, Red Paint, Pine, c.1866, 9 ½ In. 652.00
Firkin, Round, Mustard Paint, Handle, c.1800, 9 ¾ x 9 ½ In. 395.00
Hanger, Bentwood, Curved, String, ¾ x 20 ¼ In. 88.00
Hanger, Pine, Triple Cross Bars, Hanging Hole, c.1850, 24 In. 5031.00
Lap Board, Birch, Red Stain, Rounded Corners, Cutout Waist, Inset Ruler, G.B.C., c.1850, 36 x 18 In. 1521.00
Peg Rail, Maple, Beaded Edge, Turned Pegs, 1800s, 59 In. 294.00
Pincushion, Cherry, Embroidered Satin, Turned Shaft, Spoon, Sister's Steel Thimble, 6 ¾ In....*Illus* 760.00
Pitcher, Tin, Applied Flared Spout, Wire Wrapped & Rolled Rim & Handle, 6 In. 497.00
Press, Wood, Tin, Patina, 14 In. *Illus* 575.00
Rug, Rag, Center Diamond, 19th Century, 40 x 68 In. 178.00
Rug, Rag, Woven, Multicolor, c.1860, 90 x 27 In. 2047.00
Rug, Table, Plush Stripe, Wool Back, Multicolor, 16 ½ x 22 In. 176.00
Scoop, Bird's-Eye Maple, Curved, Raised Handle, Ma., c.1845, Cup, 5 x 3 ¼ In. 1150.00
Sign, Rules For Doing Good, Printed, Later Frame, 8 ⅜ x 6 ¾ In. *Illus* 1007.00
Spitbox, 3-Finger, Oval, Yellow Paint, c.1870, 3 ½ x 12 In. 1185.00
Spitbox, 4-Finger, Maple, Pine, Yellow Paint, Copper Tacks, 5 ¼ x 11 In. 4329.00
Stand, Broom Cutting, Blue Paint, Book Shape, X-Shape Supports, Stretchers, c.1900, 46 x 24 In. 230.00
Work Box, Cherry, Hinged Lid, Ash Handle, Dovetailed, c.1840, 12 x 14 ½ In. 1107.00

SHAVING MUGS were popular from 1860 to 1900. Many types were made, including occupational mugs featuring pictures of men's jobs. There were scuttle mugs, silver-plated mugs, glass-lined mugs, and others.

Bald Eagle, Flags, Flowers, Gilt, Inscribed C. & A. Van Buskirk, 3 ⅝ In. 118.00
Blue Blossoms, Flow Blue, Huttonsteinard, c.1900, 4 In. 269.00
Carriage, Horse Drawn, D.R. Miles, Gilt, Koken Barber Supplics, 4 In. 72.00
Flowers, Gilt Trim, C.C. Cugler, 3 ⅝ In. 40.00
Flowers, W.C. Derby, 3 ½ In. 48.00
Fraternal, Knights Of Pythias, P.R. Watson, 3 ⅞ In. 70.00
Frogs On Unicycle, 4 Frogs, Riding Downhill, F.C. Williams, 3 ⅞ In. 960.00
Gibson Girl, Raised Silhouette, Porcelain, 3 ¾ In. 75.00
Gilt Design, Limoges, c.1915, 3 ½ In. 145.00
Hardware, Rack, Tools, Morse K. Opshaw, Gilt, 4 In. 90.00
Homestead In Winter, Currier & Ives, Blue, White, Japan, 3 ½ In. 15.00
Hunting Dog, C.A. Query, Gilt, Stamped Limoges, France, 3 ¾ In. 48.00
Milk Glass, Footed, Anchor Hocking, Marked, c.1945 9.00
Occupational, Automobile, Green Touring Car, Porter A. Junkins, Stamped China, 3 ½ In. 780.00
Occupational, Automobile, Man In Touring Car, Sportsman Series, 1953, 3 ¾ In. 60.00
Occupational, Automobile, Open Air, C.C. Orth, Gilt, T&V Limoges, France, 3 ¾ In. 1560.00
Occupational, Automobile, Open Air, F.W. Amport, Gilt, Signed G.B.S., T&V Limoges, 3 ½ In.. 330.00
Occupational, Automobile, Open Air, F.W. Rushworth, Gilt, Limoges, Signed JP, 1902, 4 In. 3300.00
Occupational, Automobile, Open Air, Man, Matrin Reich, Felda, Germany, 3 ½ In. 960.00
Occupational, Automobile, Open Air, Man, Penn R. Roberts, Gilt, Germany, 1911, 3 ¾ In. 2400.00
Occupational, Automobile, Red, W.J. Morin, Gilt, T&V Limoges, France, 3 ¾ In. 720.00
Occupational, Bicycler, A.R. Deming, Gilt, Stamped CFH, 3 ½ In. 300.00
Occupational, Blacksmith, Man Pounding Metal, W.F. Rohrbach, 3 ¾ In. 240.00
Occupational, Blacksmith, Man, Working On Horse's Shoe, A.W. Lazro, 3 ¾ In. 60.00
Occupational, Blacksmith, Shoeing Horse, M.J. Tounsburg, 3 ½ In. 71.00
Occupational, Blacksmith, Working On Metal, Xirola Roselli, 1913, 3 ¾ In. 180.00
Occupational, Breeder, E.C. Schneider 193.00
Occupational, Brewer, Toasting With Beer, S. Rochlis, Gilt, 4 In. 3600.00
Occupational, Builder, Arm, Hammer, Symbols, Graney Reich, Marked T & V Limoges 55.00
Occupational, Butcher Shop, L. Montforte, 1923, Blue Wrap, Homer Laughlin, 3 ½ In. 360.00

Sewing, Spool Holder, Turned Wood, Pincushion Top, Compartments, C-Clamp Base, Pa., 1800s, 10 In.
$1,062.00

Conestoga Auction Co., Inc.

Sewing, Tape Measure, Edison Mazda Lamps, GE, Celluloid, Parrish Design, 1 ½ x ½ In.
$187.00

Wm Morford Antiques

Shaker, Bin, Storage, Pine, Maple, Hinged Top, Breadboard Ends, Mt. Lebanon, c.1840, 32 x 27 In.
$29,655.00

Skinner, Inc.

The edited listings of the current prices in this *Kovels' Antiques & Collectibles Price Guide* aren't available on any website. Readers can visit **Kovels.com** to check thousands of past prices and sign up for free information on trends, tips, reproductions, marks, and more.

S

Shaker, Bonnet, Sister's, Woven Straw, Palm Leaf, Paper Lining, Cotton Cape, Wooden Mold, c.1850, 11 In. $497.00

Willis Henry Auctions, Inc.

Shaker, Bowl, Maple, Red Stain, Varnished, Lathe Turned, Raised Rim, Footed Base, 15 ¼ x 4 In. $702.00

Willis Henry Auctions, Inc.

Shaker, Box, Glove, Butternut, Brass Hinge, Dovetailed, Nails, New Lebanon, c.1845, 13 ½ x 5 ½ In. $2,925.00

Willis Henry Auctions, Inc.

Shaker, Broadside, Black Ink On Card Stock, c.1925, 14 ¼ x 19 ¼ In. $995.00

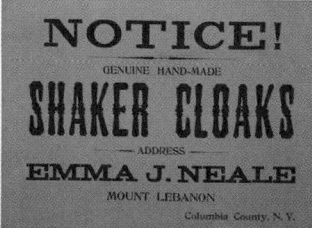

Willis Henry Auctions, Inc.

Occupational, Butcher, C.H. Cleb..*Illus*	138.00
Occupational, Butcher, Man, Killing Cow, 4 In.	120.00
Occupational, Butcher, Preparing Meat, J.F. Loughman, Gilt, Maroon Wrap, 3 ½ In.	210.00
Occupational, Caboose, On Tracks, Black, White, 3 ¾ In.	210.00
Occupational, Caboose, Wm. Simpkins, Marked O. & E.G. Royal Austria	165.00
Occupational, Call, Man On Telephone, Gilt, 3 ½ In.	1080.00
Occupational, Carpenter, Building House, J.F. Reagan, Gilt, T&V Limoges, 3 ½ In.	1440.00
Occupational, Carpenter, Chas. Ashauer Jr., A. Kern Barber Supply, St. Louis	165.00
Occupational, Carpenter, G. Stulkey	110.00
Occupational, Carriage Wheel Repairman, J.P. Wilson, Gilt, T&V Limoges, 3 ½ In.	420.00
Occupational, Carriage, Horse Drawn, Driver, Gilt, C.R. Maize, 4 In.	90.00
Occupational, Carriage, Horse Drawn, Fruit Delivery Wagon, J.R Hadler, Gilt, T&V Limoges, 3 ¾ In.	150.00
Occupational, Carriage, Horse Drawn, G. Shipman	138.00
Occupational, Carriage, Horse Drawn, Livery, C.G. Sheff, Gilt Rim, E. Beminghaus, Ohio, 4 In.	180.00
Occupational, Cart, Horse Drawn, Man, P.H. Crouse, Gilt, C.F.H.D.G.M, 3 ½ In.	150.00
Occupational, Chauffeur, Red Touring Car, E. Van Nostrand, Gilt Rim, T&V Limoges, 3 ½ In.	1140.00
Occupational, Cigar Maker, Rolling Tobacco, G.B. Davis, Gilt, 3 ¾ In.	390.00
Occupational, Clarinet, Patrick J. Kelley	165.00
Occupational, Crane Operator, Western B.S. Co., Felda China, Germany, 3 ¾ In.	10800.00
Occupational, Delivery Wagon, Horse Drawn, Alb. G. Buccholtz, Gilt, Blue Wrap, 4 In.	360.00
Occupational, Dentist, Dentures, Dr. G.F. Hardesty, Gilt, W.C. Heimerdinger, Limoges, 3 ¾ In.	360.00
Occupational, Dentist, With Patient, M.C. Wilbern, Gilt, Stamped Germany, 3 ¾ In.	900.00
Occupational, Dentist, Working On Patient, W.D Dunning, Gilt, 3 ½ In.	240.00
Occupational, Doctor, Bag, Gilt Trim	35.00
Occupational, Eagle, American Flag, Crest, Gilt, G. Mendelson, 1925, 3 ¾ In.	330.00
Occupational, Electrician, Man On Ladder, Leroy G Brower, Gilt, Bavaria, 3 ¾ In.	900.00
Occupational, Engineer, J.G. Smith	248.00
Occupational, Engineer, Jacob Aupperle, Gilt, Stamped A.A. Smith Barber Supplies, 3 ¾ In.	108.00
Occupational, Express Agency Telegraph Operator, Anchor Pottery....................*Illus*	275.00
Occupational, Express Operator, Telegraph, Archer Pottery, N.J.	275.00
Occupational, Fire Wagon, Horse Drawn, Men, Joseph Woburn, Gilt, Chelser H.L. Co., No. 2, 4 In.	1440.00
Occupational, Fireman's Ladder Truck, Wm. A. Woodruff, Gilt, Flower Wrap, 4 In.	210.00
Occupational, Fish, R.C. Baldwing	180.00
Occupational, French Horn, Chas. Forsyth	193.00
Occupational, Grain Wagon, Horse Drawn, Driver, G.F. Morris, Flowers, CFD GDM, 3 ¾ In.	180.00
Occupational, Green Touring Car, G.G. Jenkins, Gilt, 4 In.	1140.00
Occupational, Grocer, Seeley & Co., Gilt, Purple Wrap, 4 In.	180.00
Occupational, Grocer's Wagon, Horse Drawn, W.J. Copter, Purple Wrap, 4 In.	60.00
Occupational, Hearse, Horse Drawn, Clause, Holte	248.00
Occupational, Hearse, Horse Drawn, H. Owens, Marked K.E.	303.00
Occupational, Hearse, Horse Drawn, M.A. Mealey, Gilt, K.F., 4 In.	840.00
Occupational, Horse Trainer, Horse, In Field, c.1880, 4 In.	160.00
Occupational, Ice Wagon, Horse Drawn, J.R. Foster, Vienna, Austria, 3 ¾ In.	30.00
Occupational, Laundry Wagon, Horse Drawn, K.P.M., Germany, 3 ½ In.	240.00
Occupational, Liquor Wagon, Horse Drawn C.G. Neitheimer, Gilt, T&V France, 3 ½ In.	600.00
Occupational, Livery Stable, Chas. F. Rice, Gilt, 3 ¾ In.	270.00
Occupational, Livery Stable, J.D. Slack, Gilt, A.L Undeland, Omaha, 3 ¾ In.	390.00
Occupational, Livery Wagon, Horse Drawn, D.P. Armstrong, Stamped CFH, 3 ¾ In.	150.00
Occupational, Locomotive, Coal Car, A.G. Stevens, Gilt, 4 In.	90.00
Occupational, Locomotive, Gilt, H.A. Hughins, T&V Limoges, 3 ½ In.	120.00
Occupational, Lumber, Wagon, Man, Loading, J. Stewart Thompson, Gilt, 3 ½ In.	270.00
Occupational, Lunch Wagon, Horse Drawn, L. Koonz, Gilt, 3 ¾ In.	1560.00
Occupational, Machinist, Machinery, James Arndt, Gilt, CT Germany, 3 ½ In.	150.00
Occupational, Man Playing Harp, C. Finegan, Gilt, Green Wrap, 3 ½ In.	60.00
Occupational, Man, Working With Metal, Alois Dilliger, Gilt, Koken Barber Supplies, 4 In.	90.00
Occupational, Metal Storage Tank, A.P. Dannelier, Gilt, Blue Wrap, Austria, 4 In.	180.00
Occupational, Milk Delivery Wagon, Horse Drawn, John S. Bunn, Gilt, 3 ½ In.	210.00
Occupational, Milk Wagon, Horse Drawn, C.F. Pomeroy, Gilt Rim, Austria, Maroon Wrap, 4 In.	120.00
Occupational, Plasterer, Working On Room, B.F. Schultz, Stamped T&V Limoges, 3 ¾ In.	180.00
Occupational, Plow, Horse Drawn, Man Behind, D.W. Rose, Gilt, Buckeye Barbers Supply, 4 In.	120.00
Occupational, Plumber, Henry Hess	193.00
Occupational, Plumber, Sink, Tools On Bathroom Floor, J.P. Donahue, France, 3 ½ In.	240.00
Occupational, Police Officer, Standing, B.R. Jones, Limoges, c.1900, 3 ⅝ In..............*Illus*	1265.00
Occupational, Policeman, Billy Club, William Strang, Gilt, T&V Limoges, 3 ½ In.	2160.00
Occupational, Rag Cart, Horse Drawn, Eagle, Gilt, Stamped T&V Limoges, Purple Wrap, 3 ½ In.	4800.00
Occupational, Railroad Accessory Car, H.F. Martin, B.D. Shaw Barber Supply Co., 4 In.	180.00

S

Occupational, Shoemaker, J.A. Murrenbrock, Buckeye Barbers Supply Co., Dayton, Ohio.......	303.00
Occupational, Shoemaker, W.K. Cokin, Gilt, 4 In...............................	60.00
Occupational, Steam Engine, J. Robert Blessing............................	248.00
Occupational, Steam Engine, James Smith, Gilt, Flower Wrap, T&V, 4 In.........	600.00
Occupational, Stone Cutter, Man Carving, Jos. Wostoupal, August Kem St. Louis, 3 ½ In........	300.00
Occupational, Stoneworker, S. Moulton, Gilt, T&V Limoges, 3 ¾ In.........	1320.00
Occupational, Tailor, Man Working With Customer, Gilt, 3 ¾ In............	24.00
Occupational, Tinsmith, G. Williamson, Marked T&V Limoges..................	220.00
Occupational, Trumpeter, Girl Blowing Horn, Blue Dress, W.J. Dorlac.........	248.00
Occupational, Wagon, Horse Drawn, G.G. Splitstoser, Gilt, Koken Barber Supplies, 3 ¾ In.	60.00
Occupational, Wagon, Horse Drawn, Joseph Dielleux, Gilt, France, 3 ¾ In.............	180.00
Occupational, Wagon, Horse Drawn, Wells Fargo Express, Mark Mann, Gilt, 3 ¾ In.	1140.00
Occupational, Watchmaker, Pocket Watch, J.A. Swann, c.1820, 3 ½ In.........	201.00
Occupational, Yellow Trolley, Jas. G. Barclay, Limoges, 3 ¾ In................	120.00
Pink & White Roses, Decal, Semi-Porcelain, c.1900, 3 ⅝ In.................	8.00
Porcelain, Cream, Blue, 3 ¼ In..................	25.00
Porcelain, Flower Spray, Square, c.1920, 4 In...............	150.00
Porcelain, Flowers, 1918..................	15.00
Porcelain, For A Little Shaver, Violets, Occupied Japan, 3 In.............	55.00
Porcelain, Multicolor Rose Band, Germany, 3 ½ In..................	45.00
Porcelain, Pig Shaving, Pink, Green, White, c.1925, 4 In.	67.00
Rooster, Tail Up, Honey & Raspberry Luster, Germany, 4 In.............	45.00
Silver Plate, Leaf, Glass Insert, St. Louis Silver Co., 3 In.............	60.00
Silver Plate, Pierced, Milk Glass Insert, Brush Holder, 3 ½ In..............	225.00
Violets, Brush Rest, Brandenburg, Germany, 4 x 7 In...........	65.00

SHAWNEE POTTERY was started in Zanesville, Ohio, in 1937. The company made vases, novelty ware, flowerpots, planters, lamps, and cookie jars. Three dinnerware lines were made: Corn, Lobster Ware, and Valencia (a solid color line). White Corn pattern utility pieces were made in 1945. Corn King was made from 1946 to 1954; Corn Queen, with darker green leaves and lighter colored corn, from 1954 to 1961. Shawnee produced pottery for George Rumrill during the late 1930s. The company closed in 1961.

Shawnee USA

Ashtray, Boomerang Shape, Aqua, 1950s, 13 x 9 In................	35.00
Bowl, Corn King, 8 In..................	39.00
Cookie Jar, Muggsy, Dog, Blue Bow On Head, White Ground, 11 ½ In............	75.00
Cookie Jar, Smiley Pig, Chrysanthemums, Scarf	375.00
Cookie Jar, Smiley Pig, Red & Blue Flowers, Leaves, 8 In................	100.00
Creamer, Elephant, Trunk Up, Red Ear, 4 In...............	45.00
Creamer, Smiley Pig, Yellow, Blue Bandanna, Raised Flowers, 1940s, 5 x 4 In........	140.00
Creamer, Sunflower, Ball Shape, 4 ½ In.............	34.00
Creamer, Water Can Shape, Flower, Blue Rim, 4 In............	24.00
Darning Egg, Blue Eyes & Tie, 5 ½ In................	125.00
Figurine, Pekinese Dog, Purple Ears & Nose, Closed Eyes, 2 ½ In............	40.00
Figurine, Puppy, Teal Collar & Eyes, Brown Ears, 3 ¼ In..............	52.00
Figurine, Raccoon, Purple Ears, Nose, Feet, 3 ½ In..................	49.00
Lamp, Clown, Sitting On Drum, 11 In................	28.00
Pitcher, Bo Peep, Hat Spout, Cream, Blue, Orange, Marked, 8 In.	17.00
Pitcher, Bo Peep, Lavender Hat, 1940s, 8 In.............	45.00
Pitcher, Chanticleer, Creamy White, 6 Cups, 48 Oz., 10 In.	95.00
Pitcher, Corn King, 8 ¼ In..................	45.00
Planter, Boy With Fish, Tree Stump, 6 ¼ In...........	25.00
Planter, Bridge, Stairs, Flowers, Stones, Green, 9 ¼ x 5 ¼ x 6 In.........	34.00
Planter, Button Shoe, Sky Blue, 1940s, 4 ½ In............	16.00
Planter, Chinese Man, Umbrella, Basket, 5 ¼ In..............	22.00
Planter, Deer, Grass, 1950s, 8 x 6 In..................	24.00
Planter, Dog On Shoe, Yellow, 7 ¾ x 4 ½ In............	37.00
Planter, Girl & Basket, Blond, Red Bow, 8 In................	18.00
Planter, Hobbyhorse, Maroon Saddle & Wheels, 3 x 4 In.	30.00
Planter, Hound Dog, Yellow, 8 ½ In..............	17.00
Planter, Mill, Water Wheel, Trees, 6 x 4 In................	20.00
Planter, Polynesian Girl Head, 5 ½ In.	60.00
Planter, Squirrel, On Log..................	26.00
Planter, Watering Can, Tulips, Basket Weave, Pink, 7 ½ In..............	24.00
Planter, Wishing Well, Dutch Boy & Girl, Blue, Green, 5 x 8 In............	32.00
Pot, Flowers, Green, Attached Underplate, 3 ¾ In..............	10.00

Shaker, Bucket, Pine, Metal Bands, Bentwood Swing Handle, Paint, Stenciled, 1915, c.1840, 7 In.
$2,457.00

Willis Henry Auctions, Inc.

Shaker, Carrier, 3-Finger, Maple, Ash Handle, Pine Bottom, Copper Tacks, Inscribed, 7 x 8 x 11 In.
$20,000.00

Skinner, Inc.

Shaker, Carrier, 4-Finger, Maple, Pine, Yellow Paint, Copper Tacks, Hickory Handle, 9 x 11 In.
$63,180.00

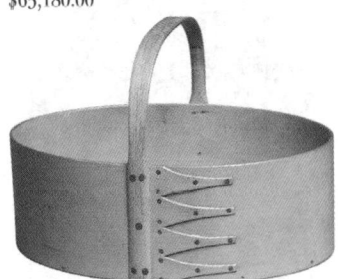

Willis Henry Auctions, Inc.

TIP
Don't buy collectors something for their collection. Buy a book about the collectible or something related to the collection, like a T-shirt picturing a bank for a bank collector.

Shaker, Pincushion, Cherry, Embroidered Satin, Turned Shaft, Spoon, Sister's Steel Thimble, 6 ¾ In. $760.00

Willis Henry Auctions, Inc.

Shaker, Press, Wood, Tin, Patina, 14 In. $575.00

Cottone Auctions

Shaker, Sign, Rules For Doing Good, Printed, Later Frame, 8 ⅜ x 6 ¾ In. $1,007.00

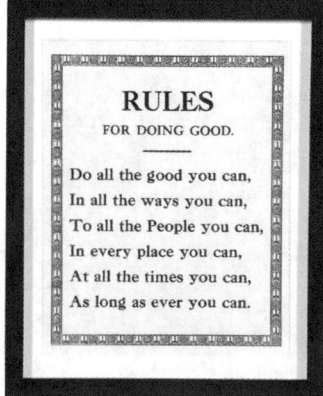

RULES
FOR DOING GOOD.

Do all the good you can,
In all the ways you can,
To all the People you can,
In every place you can,
At all the times you can,
As long as ever you can.

Skinner, Inc.

Salt & Pepper, Owls Winking, Cork Stoppers, 3 In.	30.00
Salt & Pepper, Smiley & Winnie Pig, Pink, c.1945, 3 ¼ In.	48.00
Salt & Pepper, Smiley & Winnie Pig, White, 5 ½ In.	125.00
Shaker, Dutch Girl, Gold Trim, Red Lips, Pig Tails, 5 ¼ In.	60.00
Teapot, Granny Ann, Orange Apron, 8 ½ In.	58.00
Teapot, Granny Ann, Purple Apron, Cape, 8 ½ In.	80.00
Teapot, Piper's Son, 7 In.	89.00
Vase, 2 Handles, Diamond Shapes, Flower Clusters, Gray, 7 ½ In.	45.00
Vase, Bulbous, Ruffled Rim, Green, White Spatter Overlay, c.1955, 8 ½ In.	39.00
Vase, Cone Shape, Boy, Girl, c.1940, 5 In., Pair	25.00
Vase, Double, Window Frame Shape, Yellow Deer, Ivy, Green, 8 x 5 In.	33.00
Vase, Hand, Peach, 10 In.	28.00
Vase, Ivory, Stippled, Bud, 10 In.	10.00
Vase, Ruffled Rim, Cameo, Lavender, 4 ½ In.	9.00
Vase, Swan, Raised Wings, Gray & Burgundy, Bud, 5 In., Pair	45.00

SHEARWATER POTTERY is a family business started by Mr. and Mrs. G.W. Anderson, Sr., and their three sons. The local Ocean Springs, Mississippi, clays were used to make the wares in the 1930s. The company was damaged by Hurricane Katrina in 2005 but was rebuilt and is still in business.

Ashtray, 3 Stylized Fish, Black, White & Brown Slip, Peter Anderson, c.1935, 5 ½ In.	1107.00
Beaker, Stylized Waves & Birds, Blue & Tan, Stamped, 1900s, 4 ¾ x 3 ½ In. ....*Illus*	338.00
Bookends, Pelican, Blue, 10 ¾ x 11 In.	138.00
Bowl, Dockworkers, James McConnell, Mac Anderson, 1974, 5 x 7 In. ....*Illus*	5000.00
Charger, Man & Woman, Nude, Parrot, Flowers, Collage Design, Multicolor, 12 ⅜ In. Diam...	1840.00
Figurine, Don Quixote, Horse, Rider, Sword, 10 In.	138.00
Figurine, Duck, Green Glaze, c.1935, 8 ½ In. ....*Illus*	478.00
Figurine, Horse, Grazing, White, Dapple Gray, 4 ½ x 8 ⅛ In.	546.00
Figurine, Lion, Head Down, Walking Position, Brown Drip Glaze, 5 ½ x 13 In.	492.00
Figurine, Rower, Boat, Oldfield, Marked 89, 8 x 4 ¾ In.	81.00
Figurine, Sancho Panza & Mule, c.1970, 5 x 4 ½ In.	123.00
Figurine, Woman, Basket On Head, Big Feet, Green, Tan Print Dress, 13 ¼ In.	127.00
Mug, Stylized Ducks In Flight, Black & White Slip, Peter Anderson, c.1935, 3 ½ In.	1037.00
Plate, Stylized Birds, Waves, White Slip, Red Rim, P. Anderson, c.1950, 10 ½ In.	9560.00
Sculpture, 3 Fish, Wavy Tails, Ribbed, Green Glaze, Marked, c.1942, 7 ½ In.	366.00
Vase, Alkaline Blue & Green Glaze, Swollen Cylinder, Stand-Up Rim, c.1965, 8 ½ In.	359.00
Vase, Crab & Pelican, Fish, Glazed, Peter Anderson, c.1940, 13 x 6 ½ In. ....*Illus*	38376.00
Vase, Ducks, Black-Necked Stilts, Bulbous, Cloud Rim, J.M. Anderson, 8 ¾ In.	4688.00
Vase, Figures Chopping Wood, Sitting On Steps, Flared, J.M. Anderson, 1977, 8 In.	5625.00
Vase, Lily & Leaves, White, Blue, Red, Green, Pear Shaped, Ring Foot, Flared Rim, c.1950, 6 ⅜ In.	3294.00
Vase, Lotus Blossom, Bronze Glaze, Baluster, Rolled Blue Glaze Rim, c.1940, 8 ½ In.	3286.00
Vase, Nude Woman, Black Hair, Climbing Onto Horse, Cylindrical, Ring Foot, Flared Rim, 9 In. ...	460.00
Vase, Stokesias Design, Mottled Blue & Gray Glaze, Cylindrical, Flat Rim, c.1929, 6 In.	1159.00
Vase, Turquoise Blue, Cylinder, 10 In.	63.00
Vase, Undersea Scene, Aquatic Life, Mottled Blue Glaze, Gilt, Marked, 7 ⅝ In.	185.00
Wall Pocket, Green, Triangular, 7 ½ In.	46.00

SHEET MUSIC from the past centuries is now collected. The favorites are examples with covers featuring artistic or historic pictures. Early sheet music covers were lithographed, but by the 1900s photographic reproductions were used. The early music was larger than more recent sheets, and you must watch out for examples that were trimmed to fit in a twentieth-century piano bench.

Ballad Of Patty Hearst, Red River Dave McEnery, 1974	50.00
Beautiful Hawaiian Love, Leo Feist, 1920s, 11 x 13 In.	34.00
Coney Island, Betty Grable, Cesar Romero, 1930s, 9 ½ x 12 ½ In.	15.00
Cycle March Two-Step, New York & Coney Island, E.T. Paull, c.1880, 13 x 10 In.	58.00
Erros Vanne, Henri De Toulouse-Lautrec, 2 Women, Paper, 1894, 10 x 7 In.	800.00
Faithful Forever, Gulliver's Travel, Glenn Miller, 1939, 9 ½ x 12 In.	12.00
Fiddle Dee Dee, Warner Bros.1958	12.00
Georgy Girl, Lynn Redgrave, Springfield & Dale, 1966, 9 x 12 In.	15.00
Hair, Lyrics By James Rado & Gerome Ragni, 1960s	15.00
I Believe In Music, Mac Davis, Folio Screen Gems-Columbia Music, 1972	8.00
I Love California, State Anthem, A.F. Frankenstein, 1913, 9 ⅜ x 12 ¼ In.	45.00
Les Hirondelles De Mer, Henri De Toulouse-Lautrec, C. Joubert, Paris, c.1895, 14 x 10 In.	600.00

S

My Heart Cries For You, Dinah Shore, 1950	10.00
Peace At Last, M.A. Kidder, Music By H.P. Danks, 1885, 10 x 13 ¾ In.	50.00
Pershing's Crusaders, E.T. Paul, 1918, 11 x 13 In.	25.00
Prize Song, J.H. Warland, Henry Clay Campaign Song, 1844	158.00
Rambling Rose, Joseph McCarthy Jr., Joe Burke, 1948	10.00
Rosalie, Cole Porter, 1937, 12 x 9 In.	5.00
So Tired, Russ Morgan, Decca Records, 1943	6.00
Song Sung Blue, Neil Diamond, 1972	5.00
South Pacific, Rodgers & Hammerstein, 1949	8.00
Sunday, Monday Or Always, Dixie, Bing Crosby, Dorothy Lamour	6.00
That's My Boy, Dean Martin, Jerry Lewis, Edward B. Marks Corp.	7.00
Theme From Love Story, Francis Lai, John Brimhall, 1970	12.00
Turkey In The Straw, Leo Wood, Otto Bonnell, 1920, 12 ½ x 9 ½ In.	10.00
Wait Love Until The War Is Over, T.M. Todd, 1864, 13 In.	115.00
Way Down South In Dixie, E.L. Bolling, 1905, 10 ¾ x 13 ¾ In.	30.00
Whatever You Got, I Want, Michael Jackson, 1974, 11 x 8 ½ In.	25.00
You'll Never Know, Mack Gordon, Harry Warren, 1943	10.00

SHEFFIELD *items are listed in the Silver Plate and Silver-English categories.*

SHELLEY first appeared on English ceramics about 1912. The Foley China Works started in England in 1860. Joseph Ball Shelley joined the company in 1862 and became a partner in 1872. Percy Shelley joined the firm in 1881. The company went through a series of name changes and in 1910 the then Foley China Company became Shelley China. In 1929 it became Shelley Potteries. The company was acquired in 1966 by Allied English Potteries, then merged with the Doulton group in 1971. The name Shelley was put into use again in 1980. A trio is the name for a cup, saucer, and cake plate set.

Bowl, Art Deco, Yellow Fruit, Gray Highlights, 5 In.	72.00
Bowl, Fruit, Blue Dainty, 5 ⅜ In.	45.00
Bowl, Vegetable, Begonia, 9 x 7 In.	79.00
Bowl, Vegetable, Dubarry, 9 x 7 In.	58.00
Butter, Blue Rock, Dainty, Scalloped, 7 ¼ x 4 In.	225.00
Butter, Dome Cover, Rose Spray, Round	150.00
Coffeepot, Blue Rock, 2 Cups, 6 In.	265.00
Creamer, Bridal Rose, Fluted, 2 ½ In.	30.00
Creamer, Cornflower, Scalloped, 3 ½ In.	70.00
Creamer, Freesia, Gilt Trim, Dainty, 2 ¾ In.	60.00
Cup & Saucer, Blossoms, Ludlow Shape	60.00
Cup & Saucer, Blue Dainty	55.00
Cup & Saucer, Blue Dainty, Miniature, 1 ¼ x 2 ½ In.	238.00
Cup & Saucer, Blue Rock	45.00
Cup & Saucer, Blue Rose	39.00
Cup & Saucer, Crabtree, Queen Anne Style	80.00
Cup & Saucer, Crochet	32.00
Cup & Saucer, Green Peony, Demitasse	46.00
Cup & Saucer, Large Fruit With Tendrils	90.00
Cup & Saucer, Lily Of The Valley, Scalloped Rim, Dainty	55.00
Cup & Saucer, Open Rose	50.00
Cup & Saucer, Pink Rose, Henley Shape	40.00
Cup & Saucer, Red Daisy	40.00 to 80.00
Cup & Saucer, Rock Garden	75.00
Cup & Saucer, Rock Garden, Footed	140.00
Cup & Saucer, Rosebud	80.00
Cup & Saucer, Sheraton, Green, Demitasse	45.00
Cup & Saucer, Stocks	48.00
Cup & Saucer, Stocks, Flat Oleander	60.00
Cup & Saucer, Stocks, Pink	40.00
Cup & Saucer, Stocks, Tulip-Like Shape	48.00
Cup & Saucer, Thistle, Dainty	85.00
Cup & Saucer, Turquoise Polka Dots, Stratford Shape	108.00
Cup & Saucer, Wild Anemone	34.00
Cup & Saucer, Woodland	45.00
Dish, Rosebuds, Ruffled Edge, c.1930, 4 ½ In.	40.00
Eggcup, Blue Dainty, 3 ¾ In.	60.00
Gravy Boat, Bridal Rose, 8 In.	75.00

Shaving Mug, Occupational, Butcher, C.H. Cleb.
$138.00

Showtime Auction Sevices

Shaving Mug, Occupational, Express Agency Telegraph Operator, Anchor Pottery
$275.00

Showtime Auction Sevices

Shaving Mug, Occupational, Police Officer, Standing, B.R. Jones, Limoges, c.1900, 3 ⅝ In.
$1,265.00

Glass Works Auctions

Shearwater, Beaker, Stylized Waves & Birds, Blue & Tan, Stamped, 1900s, 4 ¾ x 3 ½ In.
$338.00

New Orleans Auction Galleries, Inc.

TIP
Use your phone camera at a flea market.

Shearwater, Bowl, Dockworkers, James McConnell, Mac Anderson, 1974, 5 x 7 In. $5,000.00

Rago Arts & Auction Center

Shearwater, Figurine, Duck, Green Glaze, c.1935, 8 ½ In. $478.00

Neal Auction Co.

Shearwater, Vase, Crab & Pelican, Fish, Glazed, Peter Anderson, c.1940, 13 x 6 ½ In. $38,376.00

New Orleans Auction Galleries, Inc.

Jam Jar, Bridal Rose, Underplate	60.00
Luncheon Trio, Ashbourne, Plate, Cup, Saucer, Gainsborough Shape, c.1912	165.00
Luncheon Trio, Balls Of Yarn, Plate, Cup, Saucer	99.00
Luncheon Trio, Begonia, Plate, Cup, Saucer	75.00
Luncheon Trio, Melody, Plate, Cup, Saucer	225.00
Luncheon Trio, Wileman, Plate, Cup, Snowdrop Shape	275.00
Luncheon Trio, Yellow Blossom, Oxford Shape, Plate, Cup, Saucer	95.00
Mustard, Bridal Rose, Underplate, Cover	60.00
Nut Dish, Rosebud Fluted, 4 ¼ In.	35.00
Nut Dish, Shamrock, 4 ¼ In.	32.00
Pin Dish, Crocus, Scalloped, 4 ½ x 4 ¼ In.	38.00
Pin Dish, Pink Hibiscus, Tab Handles, Square, 5 x 4 In.	55.00
Plate, Art Deco, Harmony, Blue, Yellow, 1920s, 8 In.	30.00
Plate, Blue Dainty, 10 ¾ In.	65.00
Plate, Dinner, Bridal Rose, 11 In., 6 Piece	380.00
Plate, Old Sevres, 10 ¼ In., 15 Piece	173.00
Platter, Bridal Rose, 14 x 12 In.	155.00
Platter, Dubarry, Oval, 14 ½ In.	78.00
Salt & Pepper, Blue Dainty, 3 ¼ In.	300.00
Soup, Cream, Underplate, Regency, Gilt Handles, 4 Piece	69.00
Soup, Dish, Regency, Gold Trim, Scalloped, Embossed Bands, Dainty, 8 In., 4 Piece	139.00
Sugar & Creamer, Bridal Rose, c.1950	54.00
Sugar & Creamer, Summer Glory, Yellow Chintz	185.00
Sugar, Cape Gooseberry, Regent Shape, 1930s	25.00
Sugar, Violets, 3 ⅜ In.	45.00
Teapot, Blue Dainty, 4 Cup, 5 ½ In.	435.00
Trio, Begonia, Cup, Saucer, Plate	75.00
Trio, Daisy, Cup, Saucer, Plate, Mauve, Dainty	176.00
Trio, My Garden, Cup, Saucer, Plate	120.00
Trio, Pink Harebell, Regent Shape, Cup, Saucer, Plate	60.00
Tureen, Lid, Art Deco, Yellow, Gray, Flowers, 9 ½ x 4 In.	40.00
Vase, Art Deco, Fruit Pattern, Globular, c.1930, 3 ½ x 3 ⅝ In.	116.00
Vase, Deco, Cone Shape, Clarisse Cliff Style, 5 x 4 In.	85.00
Vase, Reddish Orange, Black Border, Fruits, Leaves, Bow, 1920s, 6 ¾ In.	128.00

SHIRLEY TEMPLE, the famous movie star, was born in 1928. She made her first movie in 1932. Thousands of items picturing Shirley have been and still are being made. Shirley Temple dolls were first made in 1934 by Ideal Toy Company. Millions of Shirley Temple cobalt blue glass dishes were made by Hazel Atlas Glass Company and U.S. Glass Company from 1934 to 1942. They were given away as premiums for Wheaties and Bisquick. A bowl, mug, and pitcher were made as a breakfast set. Some pieces were decorated with the picture of a very young Shirley, others used a picture of Shirley in her 1936 *Captain January* costume. Although collectors refer to a cobalt creamer, it is actually the 4 ½-inch-high milk pitcher from the breakfast set. Many of these items are being reproduced today.

Banner, Heidi, Cloth, Hearts, Tugs & Smiles, 20th Century Fox, 1937, 37 x 53 In.	2500.00
Book, Just A Little Girl, 1934, 7 ¾ x 6 ½ In.	47.00
Cards, Bridge, Revenue Stamp, Box, c.1930	165.00
Doll, 3 Outfits, TV Box, Ideal, 1958	345.00
Doll, Blue Party Dress, Pin, Ideal, 1958, 17 In.	135.00
Doll, Composition, Open Mouth, Sleep Eyes, Blond Curly Wig, Ideal, c.1937, 13 In.	158.00
Doll, Composition, Wig, Strung Limbs, Sleep Eyes, Cop Ideal, 1930s, 16 In.	175.00
Doll, Red & White Polka Dot Dress, Ideal, Box, 17 In.	150.00
Doll, Vinyl, Pink Heidi Dress, Ribbon, Ideal, 12 In.	174.00
Paper Doll, Plastic Base, Whitman, Box	15.00
Pen & Pencil, Fountain Pen, Mechanical Pencil, Blue, Box	275.00
Pin, Fan Club, Portrait, Blue On White, 1 ¼ In.	10.00
Pitcher, Milk, Portrait, Signature, Honeycomb, Hazel Atlas, Cobalt Blue, 1930s, 4 ½ In.	28.00
Postcard, Drinking Glass Of Milk, 1930s	28.00
Postcard, Frowning, Tying Hat, 1930s	25.00
Postcard, Sailor Suit, Holding Hat, c.1935	20.00
Sheet Music, Stowaway, 1936	8.00
Soap, Profile Cameos, Cardboard Box, Shirley Photo Top, Kerk Guild, 1930s, 7 ¼ In., 4 Piece	115.00
Watch, Shirley, Holding Her Knees, Marked Paramount, Westclox, 1953, Pocket	270.00

SHRINER, *see Fraternal category.*

SILVER DEPOSIT glass was first made during the late nineteenth century. Solid sterling silver is applied to the glass by a chemical method so that a cutout design of silver metal appears against a clear or colored glass. It is sometimes called silver overlay.

Cocktail Shaker, Red Glass, Applied Sterling Silver Golfer, 1900s, 14 In.............*Illus*	413.00
Decanter, 6 Cups, Repousse Design, Dragons, Clouds, Pearls, c.1900, 9 In., 7 Piece..............	2013.00
Decanter, Flower Heads, Scrolling Vines, Bottle Shape, Loop Handle, Upswept Spout, 8 ½ In..	575.00
Relish, 3 Sections, Georges Briard, 8 x 7 In.............*Illus*	15.00
Vase, Emerald Glass, Baluster Shape, Round Foot, Scrolling, Heart Cartouche, c.1900, 14 ½ In.	1230.00
Vase, Green Glass, Squat, Flared Neck, Art Nouveau Flowers, Alvin, c.1910, 12 In.	538.00
Vase, Overlay, Green Glass, Baluster, Slender, Flowers & Leaves, 14 In..................................	1000.00

SILVER FLATWARE includes many of the current and out-of-production silver and silver-plated flatware patterns made in the past eighty years. Other silver is listed under Silver-American, Silver-English, etc. Most silver flatware sets that are missing a few pieces can be completed through the help of one of the many silver matching services listed on our website, www.kovels.com.

Acorn, Cheese Knife, 8 ¼ In..	120.00
Acorn, Cream Ladle, Marked Georg Jensen, Beaded Oval, 6 ¾ In.	415.00
Acorn, Marmalade Spoon, Georg Jensen, Denmark, 1910-25, 5 ¾ In.......................	84.00
Broad Antique, Fork, Dominick & Haff, 6 ½ In., 12 Piece......................................	330.00
Cactus, Cake Knife, Stainless Steel Blade, Georg Jensen, 10 ¼ In..........................	150.00
Cactus, Date & Olive Fork, Georg Jensen, 4 ½ & 6 ¼ In.......................................	150.00
Chantilly, Salad Spoon, Light Gold Wash, Gorham, c.1895, 8 ¾ In..........................	165.00
Chrysanthemum, Soup Ladle, Shiebler, 1885, 12 In..	239.00
Columbia, Spoon Set, Cream Soup, Monogram, Reed & Barton, 8 Piece..................	150.00
Daisy, Ice Tong, Claw, Monogram, Tiffany & Co., c.1880, 6 In...............................	680.00
Dresden, Nut Spoon, Gilt, Enamel, Whiting, Div. Of Gorham, 6 In...........................	180.00
Francis I, Carving Set, Reed & Barton, 11 & 13 In., 2 Piece..................................	180.00
Francis I, Spoon, Slotted, Reed & Barton, 1907, 8 ¼ In.	215.00
Grape, Berry Spoon, Gilt, Engraved Monogram, Dominick & Haff, 1896, 8 ¼ In.	240.00
Jenny Lind, Fish Set, Coin, J.S. Vancourt, N.Y., Albert Coles, c.1860, Pair..............	239.00
Josephine, Punch Ladle, Double Spout, Frank M. Whiting, c.1895, 13 In.................	173.00
Les Six Fleurs, Serving Fork & Spoon, Reed & Barton, 9 ½ In., 2 Piece	298.00
Mazarin, Punch Ladle, Monogram, Dominick & Haff, 12 ½ In..................................	210.00
Medici, Punch Ladle, Gold Wash Bowl, Monogram, Gorham, 13 In.	293.00
Nellie Custis, Serving Fork & Spoon, Monogram, Lunt, c.1900................................	84.00
No. 41, Spoon, Scallop Bowl, Loop Handle, Georg Jensen, 1920-31, 5 ½ In..............	132.00
No. 81, Salt Spoon, Scroll & Bead Handle, Georg Jensen, 1 ¾ In., 8 Piece..............	330.00
Old English Antique, Salad Set, Monogram, Dominick & Haff, 2 Piece......................	165.00
Old English, Serving Spoon, Towle, c.1797, 12 ½ In., Pair	399.00
Orange Blossom, Tomato Server, William Rogers, 1910, 7 ½ In.	45.00
Repousse, Berry Spoon, S. Kirk & Son, 9 In.	150.00
Repousse, Serving Spoon, Kirk & Son, 9 In...	108.00
Repousse, Steak Knife, Kirk & Son, 12 Piece..	840.00
Royal Danish, Fork & Spoon, International, Child's, 4 ¼ In......................................	96.00
Royal Danish, Seafood Fork, International, 16 Piece...	480.00
St. Cloud, Soup Ladle, Fluted Bowl, Cast Handle, Monogram, Gorham, 13 ½ In.........	415.00
Town & Country, Salad Set, Fork, Spoon, Ebony Handle, A. Adler, 10 ½ & 10 In.	415.00
Turkey, Gravy Ladle, Tiffany & Co., 6 ⅜ In...	308.00
Violet, Soup Ladle, Monogram, R. Wallace & Sons, 12 In......................................	149.00
Virginia, Ice Cream Spoon, Dominick & Haff, 12 Piece...	236.00
Wave Edge, Pastry Server, Monogram, Tiffany & Co., 11 ⅛ In.................................	450.00

SILVER PLATE is not solid silver. It is a ware made of a metal, such as nickel or copper, that is covered with a thin coating of silver. The letters *EPNS* are often found on American and English silver-plated wares. *Sheffield* is a term with two meanings. Sometimes it refers to sterling silver made in the town of Sheffield, England. Sometimes it refers to an old form of plated silver.

Basket, Flowers, Leaves, Hinged Handle, Scalloped Rim, Middletown Plate Co., c.1890, 9 ½ In.	108.00
Basket, Gadroon Edge, Raised Platform, Twist Rim, Handles, Sheffield, 1800s, 6 x 15 ½ x 9 In.	210.00
Biscuit Box, Lobed, U-Shape Handle, Bellflowers, Leafy Scroll Feet, c.1935, 11 x 8 ½ In..........	153.00
Biscuit Box, Ribbed, Lobed Lid, Joseph Ridge & Co., Sheffield, c.1890, 7 In.	142.00
Biscuit Warmer, Shell Shape Opening, Pierced, Branch Supports, Fenton Bros., c.1880, 10 x 8 In.	180.00
Bowl, Allover Octopus Pattern, Repousse, Molded Strap Handle, Egypt, 1 ¾ x 6 ¾ In.	460.00
Bowl, Fruit, Upswept Ends, Squat Waisted Stem, Scroll Feet, Christofle, 1932, 5 ¾ x 12 ½ In...	184.00

Silver Deposit, Cocktail Shaker, Red Glass, Applied Sterling Silver Golfer, 1900s, 14 In.
$413.00

Brunk Auctions

Silver Deposit, Relish, 3 Sections, Georges Briard, 8 x 7 In.
$15.00

Silver Plate, Centerpiece, Palm Trees, Rocky Base, Supporting Ostrich Egg, Elkington & Co., 1873, 14 In.
$399.00

New Orleans Auction Galleries, Inc.

S

SILVER PLATE

Silver Plate, Hot Water Urn, Chased, Repousse, Ivory Spigot Handle, Paw Feet, England, c.1875, 28 In. $764.00

Garth's Auctioneers & Appraisers

Silver Plate, Hot Water Urn, Dome Lid, Applied Reed & Acanthus, William IV, Sheffield, c.1835, 16 ½ x 13 In. $369.00

New Orleans Auction Galleries, Inc.

Silver Plate, Platter, Meat, Dome Lid, Well & Tree, Gadroon Rim, Reservoir, George V, c.1915, 20 x 16 In. $984.00

New Orleans Auction Galleries, Inc.

Bowl, Round, Lobed Flower Shape, X-Shape Block Foot, Italy, 1989, 8 ⅞ In.	203.00
Bowl, Vegetable, Dome Lid, Applied Stirrup Handles, Oval Pedestal Foot, 10 x 13 In.	83.00
Bowl, Vegetable, Ogee Dome Lid, George V, Beaded Rim, Baluster Handle, c.1915, 7 x 18 In.	98.00
Bowl, Viking Ship Shape, Dragon, Glass Liner, Bracket Feet, Oval, Marked Victoria, 15 x 5 In.	1035.00
Cake Basket, Round, Footed, Openwork Swing Handle, Lobed, Flowers, Leaves, 1800s, 11 In.	299.00
Cake Basket, Upswept Ends, Wirework, Curved Rim, Reeded, Twist Handle, c.1815, 4 x 11 In.	246.00
Caviar Dish, Lid, Cut Crystal, Round Foot, Mother-Of-Pearl Spade, 1987, 6 In. Diam.	738.00
Centerpiece, 2 Intertwined Palm Trees, Giraffe, Rock Shape Base, c.1890, 19 ¼ x 16 ¼ In.	885.00
Centerpiece, Arched Scrolling, Wirework, 9 Trumpet Vases, Flower Shape Rims, c.1965, 12 In.	492.00
Centerpiece, Lozenge Shape, Pierced Scroll Gallery, Wirework Legs, c.1950, 14 x 21 In.	153.00
Centerpiece, Palm Trees, Rocky Base, Supporting Ostrich Egg, Elkington & Co., 1873, 14 In....*Illus*	399.00
Centerpiece, Seahorses, Waves, Putto, Shell Shape Dish, Dragons Paw Feet, c.1900, 16 x 37 In.	2800.00
Centerpiece, Victorian, Grapevine Design, Openwork Basket Top, 19 In.	180.00
Chalice, Garlands, Engraved, Tripod Shaft, Eagles, Parker Casper & Co., c.1890, 5 ½ In., Pair	60.00
Champagne Bucket, Stag Mounted, Tapering Cylinder, Greek Key Banding, 10 ½ x 8 In., Pair	956.00
Champagne Cooler, Jugendstil, Pierced Handles, Footed, c.1900, 11 ½ x 11 ½ In.	48.00
Cheese Server, Dome Lid, William IV, Leafy Banding, Leaf Handles, Paw Feet, c.1835, 5 x 12 In.	369.00
Ciborium, Cross Finial, Gilt Interior, 4 In.	24.00
Coaster, Wine, Applied Flower Border, Wood Base, Sheffield, 3 ¼ x 6 In.	345.00
Cocktail Shaker, Apollo, Hammered, Bernard Rice, c.1924, 10 x 7 ½ In.	96.00
Cocktail Shaker, Lid, High Handle, Rogers Bros., 10 ⅜ In.	234.00
Cocktail Shaker, Lighthouse Shape, Meriden Britannia Co., c.1975, 19 In.	4838.00
Cocktail Shaker, Lighthouse Shape, Tapered, Wirework Gallery, Sheffield, 14 In.	861.00
Coffee Biggin, Hinged Dome Lid, Finial, Cylindrical, Beaked Spout, Wood Handle, 10 x 5 In.	276.00
Coffeepot, Dome Lid, Urn Shape, Ear Shape Wooden Handle, Trumpet Foot, 1700s, 11 In.	214.00
Coffeepot, High Foot, Handle, Stand, Gorham, 14 In.	174.00
Compote, Blue Glass Insert, Cupid Support, Flowers, Leaves, Japan, 6 x 5 ½ In., Pair	84.00
Compote, Pedestal, Curled Handles, Incised, Jean Despres, France, c.1935, 6 ½ x 4 ½ In.	1000.00
Cruet Stand, Grapevine Design, Spinning Bottom Panels, Leaf & Shell Feet, 1800s, 21 ½ x 9 In.	770.00
Crumb Catcher, Embossed Winged Devil, Derby Silver Co., 8 ½ x 6 In.	55.00
Crumb Tray, Egyptian Revival Style, Pharaonic Heads, Lotus, Rounded, 8 ½ x 9 In.	239.00
Cup, Allover Scrolls, Strap Handle, Tapered Cylinder, Greece, 4 x 6 In.	518.00
Cup, Ram's Head, Glass Eyes, Stamped Mika, Germany, 3 x 3 In., Liter	109.00
Dish, Entree, Lid, Removable Handle, c.1920, 11 x 8 In.	120.00
Dish, Shell Shape, Scrolling Strawberry Plant, Leaves & Berries Form Handle, c.1890, 7 x 16 In.	215.00
Dish, Stand, Dome Lid, George IV, Molded, Flowers, Banded, Reeded Handles, c.1835, 8 x 15 In.	399.00
Drinking Horn, Oarsman, Holding Antler, Cavalier Finial, 14 In.	480.00
Drinks Cart, 2 Handles, Cabriole Legs, Platform Stretcher, Ball & Claw Feet, c.1935, 36 x 31 In.	2214.00
Egg Frame, Navette Shape, Scroll Rim, Spherical Feet, 4 Egg Spoons, 1885, 6 ½ x 10 In.	184.00
Encrier, Scalloped Shell Bowl, Fish Branch, Lobster Handle, 2 Glass Wells, Cattail Lid, 4 x 12 In.	936.00
Epergne, 4 Branches, 4 Cut Glass Bowls, Scroll Feet, Sheffield, c.1865, 13 x 16 In.	780.00
Epergne, Glass Scalloped Bowl, 4 Scroll Supports Hold Smaller Bowls, c.1965, 15 x 25 In.	1045.00
Epergne, Inverted Bell Shape Base, Trumpet Vase, 6 Scroll Arms, Bowls & Vases, c.1935, 19 In.	522.00
Epergne, Large Cut Glass Bowl, 4 Scrolled Flower Arms, 4 Small Glass Bowls, Victorian, 15 In.	1955.00
Epergne, Lobed Stem, Calyx, Scrolling Arms, Diamond Cut Bowl, c.1835, 19 ½ x 20 ¼ In.	584.00
Epergne, William IV, Glass, Gadroon Bowl, Scrolling, Rocaille Banding, c.1835, 13 x 22 In.	1168.00
Figure, Pheasant, Long Tail, 12 In., Pair	240.00
Fish Server, Fork, Knife, Baluster Handle, Bellflowers, Cabochon, Pierced Scroll Tines, c.1885, 13 In.	123.00
Frame, Crown, Figures, Flowers, Continental, c.1890, 10 ¼ In.	165.00
Fruit Basket, Pierced Trellis Pattern, Pierced Grape Rim, Bail Handle, England, 16 x 11 In.	575.00
Golf Flask, Impressed Mark Evans, Enameled 19th Hole Flag, Man Swinging Club, 8 In.	480.00
Hot Water Urn, Chased, Repousse, Ivory Spigot Handle, Paw Feet, England, c.1875, 28 In.......*Illus*	764.00
Hot Water Urn, Dome Lid, Applied Reed & Acanthus, William IV, Sheffield, c.1835, 16 ½ x 13 In....*Illus*	369.00
Hot Water Urn, Dome Lid, Gadroon, Cavetto Collar, Reeded, Arched Handles, Feet, c.1935, 24 In.	307.00
Hot Water Urn, Lid, Oval, Arched Reeded Handles, Pierced, Urn Finial, Hooved Feet, 22 x 12 In.	399.00
Hot Water Urn, Oval, Steep Arched Handles, Ram's Head Legs, Hooves, c.1785, 21 ½ x 11 In.	676.00
Hot Water Urn, Regency Style, Ribbed, Lion Head Handles, Paw Feet, Medallion, c.1900, 18 In.	353.00
Hot Water Urn, Ribbed Melon Shape, Bun Feet, Treen Spigot, Loop Handles, c.1810, 12 In., Pair	7080.00
Hot Water Urn, Sheffield, Sphinx Finial, Basket Weave Detail, Mask, Ring Handles, 18 x 11 In.	161.00
Jar, Hinged Lid, Embossed, Footed, Victorian, 7 In.	57.00
Jar, Lid, Squat, Lobed Sides, Inlaid Malachite Border, Los Castillo, Taxco, 4 ⅓ x 5 ½ In.	69.00
Jug, Hot Water, Hinged Dome Lid, Oval, Fluted, Beaked Spout, Wood Handle, 11 x 8 In.	338.00
Kettle, Stand, George V, Flattened Circle, Repousse Flower Scrolls, Gooseneck Spout, 13 x 8 In.	215.00
Kettle, Stand, Hinged Dome Lid, Repousse Flowers, Gooseneck Spout, c.1890, 14 x 11 In.	215.00
Lemonade Press, Holds 4 Beakers & 3 Lemons, Lotus Leaf Tray, Ball Feet, c.1885, 14 x 14 In.	2032.00
Loving Cup, Scroll Borders & Feet, Horn Shaped Handles, U.S.A., 1900s, 8 ¾ x 10 ¼ In.	118.00

S

Meat, Lid, Oval, Band Of Patera, Beaded Rim, Ring Handle, Monogram, c.1885, 8 x 14 In......	430.00
Monteith, Barrel Form, Oval, Cutout Wave Border, Reeded Bands, Paw Feet, 9 x 10 In.	3050.00
Pastry Stand, Central Standard, Ring Handle, 3 Graduating Tiers, c.1860, 23 ½ In.	1722.00
Pitcher, Water, Lion, Greek Key Border, Beaded Foot, Baluster, Handle, Gorham, c.1864, 9 ⅞ In.	896.00
Plaque, Cricket Trophy, Shield Shape, Engraved, Merchant Navy Comforts Fund, 1940s, 15 x 13 In...	52.00
Plateau, George V, Round, Ogee Rim, Leafy Scrolls, Shield Cartouches, Mirror Plate, 22 In.	738.00
Plateau, Mirrored, Footed, Stamped Law & Son, England, c.1850, 16 x 50 In.	1580.00
Plateau, Round, Molded Rim, Shaped, Oculus Cut Edge, Mirrored Plate, c.1885, 14 ¼ In. Diam..	153.00
Plateau, Round, Ogee Molded Rim, Leafy Scrolls, Shield, Acanthus Feet, c.1900, 21 In. Diam...	615.00
Platter, Hot Water, Dome Lid, Oval, Engraved Shield, Footed, Handles, Sheffield	413.00
Platter, Hunting Scene, Crimped Edge, Oval, c.1890, 17 ¾ x 23 ¼ In.	5451.00
Platter, Meat, Dome Lid, Well & Tree, Gadroon Rim, Reservoir, George V, c.1915, 20 x 16 In.... *Illus*	984.00
Punch Bowl, Grape Leaf Repousse, Stepped Foot, Bottle Holder, 1900s, 16 In. Diam................	149.00
Salt, Neoclassic, Glass Lined, Oval, Cast Molded, Scroll Legs, 1 ¾ x 2 ½ In., Pair	47.00
Salver, Regency, Oval, Beaded Rim, Shell Feet, Oval Cartouche, Armorial, c.1815, 16 x 12 ½ In.	338.00
Salver, Rounded Square, Gadroon Gallery, Shell & Scroll Corners, Paw Feet, c.1835, 14 In.	153.00
Salver, William IV, Round, Reeded Rim, Flowers, Leaves, Scroll Feet, c.1835, 22 In. Diam.	461.00
Samovar, Inscribed, 25th Anniversary Presentation, c.1897, 18 x 9 In.	300.00
Server, Roll Over Lid, Egyptian Figures, Grapes, Claw Foot, Ivory Handle, 9 x 12 In. ....*Illus*	316.00
Sugar Basket, Oval, Upswept Ends, Gadroon, Flower Band, Beaded Swing Handle, c.1885, 4 In..	153.00
Sugar Basket, Reticulated, Oval Bowl, Leaf Band, Domed Foot, Swing Handle, c.1885, 5 In., Pair	215.00
Supper Set, Water Base, 4 Covered Bowls, Finials, Shakers, T. Bond, 8 x 24 In., 9 Piece...........	1534.00
Table Pheasants, Italy, c.1900, 12 In., Pair	390.00
Tantalus, 3 Decanters, Bottle Frame Tilts Forward, Walker & Hall, Sheffield, c.1915, 13 x 15 In.. *Illus*	430.00
Tea Set, Hammered Leaf, Flower, Fruit, Teapot, Creamer, Sugar, Marked Forbes, 6 ½ x 8 ½ In..	300.00
Teapot, Stop Reed Design, Gadroon Border, Wooden C-Scroll Handle, c.1800, 5 x 10 In..........	531.00
Toast Rack, Oval, Arches, 4 Hoop Dividers, Center Butter Dish, Lid, Scrolled Feet, c.1890, 8 x 8 In.	338.00
Toast Warmer, Shell Shape, Hinged, England, 12 ½ x 12 In.	278.00
Tray, Cartouche Designs, Gadroon Rim, Acanthus Handles, Sheffield, 1850-75, 31 x 19 In.... *Illus*	1107.00
Tray, Figural, Turkey Lid, Flattened Rim, Franco, Italy...	420.00
Tray, Gadroon & Shell Border, Shaped Handles, Rectangular, Tiffany, c.1900, 32 ½ x 6 ¼ In...	649.00
Tray, Galleried Rim, Pierced, Scroll Handles, Monogram, England, c.1860, 36 ¾ x 22 ¼ In.	2337.00
Tray, George V, Shaped Rectangle, Flared Rim, Pierced Gallery, Rocaille Handles, c.1935, 29 In.	307.00
Tray, Grape & Vine Border, Scroll Flowers Handles & Feet, c.1890, 30 ½ x 19 ½ In.	413.00
Tray, Oval Shaped, Regent, Molded Rim, Shell & Scroll Handles, 1938, 18 In.	246.00
Tray, Oval, Chippendale Shaped Rim, Rococo Scrolls, Handles, Flowers, c.1935, 26 x 17 In.....	215.00
Tray, Oval, Pierced Concave Gallery, Serpentine Lobed Rim, Gadroon Handles, c.1935, 28 ½ x 17 In..	246.00
Tray, Oval, Strapwork Border, Chased Center Design, Handles, Scroll Feet, c.1874-80, 32 In....	508.00
Tray, Rectangular, Gallery, Pierced Banding, Serpentine Gadroon Edge, Handles, c.1950, 27 x 17 In..	799.00
Tray, Rectangular, Rounded Reeded Ends, Long Curved Handles, Lurelle Guild, 1940s, 15 In. ...	563.00
Tray, Rounded Rectangular, Wavy Leaf & Berry Rim, Gadroon Handles, England, c.1915, 29 x 18 In.	215.00
Tray, Shell Shape, Flowers, Scrolls, Cabriole Legs, S. Blackinton, 22 x 18 In.............................	420.00
Tray, Victoria Pattern, Oval, Rococo Scroll Edge, Handles & Feet, Rocaille Band, 1956, 28 x 18 ½ In...	492.00
Trivet, Expanding, 3 Parts, Pierced Triangles & Hexagons, c.1950, 7 ½ In.	184.00
Trolley, Sugar, Fluted Bowl, Scalloped Rim, Spoked Wheels, T-Bar Handle, c.1915, 8 ½ x 5 In..	73.00
Trolley, Wine, 2 Coasters, Wagon Style, Gadroon Border, Wood Base & Handle, 1900s, 14 In..	295.00
Tureen, Dome Lid, Cup Shape, Concave Collar, Loop Handles, Legs, Goldfeder, 12 x 14 In.......	35.00
Tureen, Dome Lid, Oval, Acanthus Handle, Blossom Finial, Shield, Footed, 15 In.	354.00
Tureen, Dome Lid, Oval, Chased Flower Band, Square Handles, Beaded Rim, c.1885, 10 x 16 In..	430.00
Tureen, Lid, Oval, Beaded Design, Loop Handles, Octagonal Foot, 8 ⅛ x 12 In.........................	246.00
Tureen, Sauce, Dome Lid, Regency, Gadroon Rim, Reeded Handles, Paw Feet, c.1815, 6 x 9 In.	271.00
Tureen, William IV, Oval, Waisted Neck, Shell & Gadroon Border, c.1835, 11 x 15 ½ In.	984.00
Urn, Lid, Ribbons, Urn Finial, Loop Handles, Pedestal Base, Ball Feet, 1900s, 15 x 11 ½ In., Pair...	826.00
Vase, Golf Bag Shape, Cylindrical, Scroll Handle, Derby Silver Co., c.1920, 10 In.	299.00
Vase, Lobed, Tapering Sides, Spreading Foot, Flowers, Persia, 6 In., Pair	240.00
Vase, Pierced Oak, Acorn, Repousse, Trumpet Shape, Elkington & Co., 1850, 11 In.	144.00
Waiter, Rectangular, Flower Rim, Handles, Walker & Hall, Sheffield, 28 In.............................	189.00
Warming Dome, Copper, Leaf & Shell Handle, Gadroon Band, Engraved Crest, 13 x 10 In......	276.00
Warming Stand, Rococo Dome Lid, Openwork Removable Handle, Scroll Feet, 15 x 27 In......	1554.00
Wine Coaster, Rosebud, Plymouth, 6 In.	70.00
Wine Cooler, Campana Shape, Gadroon Rim, Leaf Handles, Domed Foot, c.1935, 11 x 7 In...	110.00
Wine Cooler, Gadroon, Geometrics, Fruit Engraved Handles, Sheffield, England, 11 x 16 In..	978.00
Wine Cooler, Gadroon, Scallop Border, Reeded Banding, Ring Foot, 1800s, 7 ¼ x 8 In., Pair..	354.00
Wine Cooler, Ruffled Rim & Foot, Campana Shape, Cross Twig Handles, 12 ¼ In.	813.00

Silver Plate, Server, Roll Over Lid, Egyptian Figures, Grapes, Claw Foot, Ivory Handle, 9 x 12 In.
$316.00

James D. Julia Auctioneers

Silver Plate, Tantalus, 3 Decanters, Bottle Frame Tilts Forward, Walker & Hall, Sheffield, c.1915, 13 x 15 In.
$430.00

New Orleans Auction Galleries, Inc.

Silver Plate, Tray, Cartouche Designs, Gadroon Rim, Acanthus Handles, Sheffield, 1850-75, 31 x 19 In.
$1,107.00

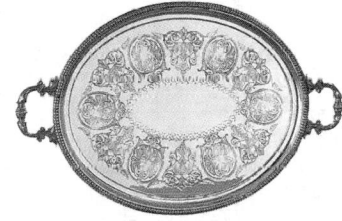

New Orleans Auction Galleries, Inc.

Silver-American, Biscuit Box, Paneled Sides, Swag Design, Bud Finial, Marked, Lunt, c.1980, 7 In.
$708.00

Brunk Auctions

S

Silver-American, Bowl, Classical Medallion, Beaded Loop & Swan Handles, Wood & Hughes, c.1850, 15 In. $1,920.00

Skinner, Inc.

Silver-American, Bowl, Flowers, High Relief Border, Gorham, Hallmarks, 1918, 15 x 11 ¼ In. $649.00

Brunk Auctions

Silver-American, Bowl, Flowers, Repousse, Scroll Border, Monogram, S. Kirk & Son, Hallmarks, c.1880, 5 x 10 In. $1,770.00

Brunk Auctions

Silver-American, Bowl, Openwork, Chrysanthemums, Basket Weave, Acanthus, c.1900, 11 In. $944.00

Brunk Auctions

S

TIP

Clocks should be cleaned and lubricated every five years.

SILVER-AMERICAN. American silver is listed here. Coin and sterling silver are included. Most of the sterling silver listed in this book is subdivided by country. There are also other pieces of silver and silver plate listed under special categories, such as Candelabrum, Napkin Ring, Silver Flatware, Silver Plate, Silver-Sterling, and Tiffany Silver. Silver prices in 2012 became so high many pieces were worth more in meltdown value than as decorative silver. These prices are based on current silver values. For information about makers and marks, see *Kovels' American Silver Marks: 1650 to the Present.*

Aspic Server, Lily, Art Nouveau Style, Silvercraft, 12 In.	144.00
Basket, Lily Pad Shape, Ball Feet, Fixed Handle, Reed & Barton, 1933	595.00
Basket, Openwork, Bail Handle, Pedestal Base, Wavy Rim, U.S.A., 1900s, 7 ¾ x 8 ¼ In.	236.00
Basket, Round, Guilloche Rim, Vine & Berry Handle, Coin, R. & W. Wilson, 12 In.	1434.00
Basket, Splay Foot, Towle, 2 x 8 In.	156.00
Beaker, Cylindrical, Tapered, Flared Rim, Molded Foot Bands, Thauvet Besley, c.1737, 6 In.	2160.00
Berry Serving Set, Medallion, Gold Wash Bowls, Server, 6 Spoons, Gorham, 7 Piece	403.00
Berry Spoon, Empire Pattern, Towle, Patent 1894, 9 In.	180.00
Berry Spoon, Portland Pattern, International, 1913, 9 In.	73.00
Biscuit Box, Paneled Sides, Swag Design, Bud Finial, Marked, Lunt, c.1980, 7 In. ....*Illus*	708.00
Bonbon Spoon, Enamel, Reticulated, Scrollwork & Geometric Design, Gorham, 6 ⅛ In.	296.00
Bowl, 4 Rounded Flared Sides, Pinched Corners, Footed, Arthur Stone, 5 x 9 In.	840.00
Bowl, 8 Wells, Applied Flower Border, Meriden Britannia Co., 9 In.	212.00
Bowl, Allover Chased, Repousse Flowers, Leaves, Black, Starr & Frost, 3 ⅞ x 9 In.	750.00
Bowl, Applied Flower, Scroll Border, Pedestal, William B. Durgin, 6 ½ x 9 In.	767.00
Bowl, Applied Stepped Rim, Pedestal, Shreve & Co., 3 x 14 In.	1003.00
Bowl, Art Nouveau, Repousse, Lilies, Wavy Rim, Bailey Banks & Biddle Co., 3 x 11 In.	413.00
Bowl, Athenic, Gorham, 2 ½ x 5 ⅛ In.	259.00
Bowl, Banded Border, Raised Cypher, Triangle, Round Foot, Arthur Stone, 8 In. Diam.	1265.00
Bowl, Bombe Shape, Hammered, Gilt Grapevines, Handles, Ladle, Gorham, 9 x 18 In.	33600.00
Bowl, Cast, Repousse, Flowers, New York, 8 ½ x 18 In.	2370.00
Bowl, Cereal, Stand, Chased, Engraved, Nursery Rhymes, Monogram, Kerr, c.1910, 4 & 6 In.	354.00
Bowl, Chased Flowers, Blown Out Scalloped Rim, Gorham, 1899, 12 In.	505.00
Bowl, Chased Flowers, Paneled, Flared Lobed Rim, Gorham, Martele, 5 x 11 In.	9840.00
Bowl, Chippendale, Shaped Rim, Reeded Border, Gorham, 1900s, 10 ⅝ x 7 ½ In.	236.00
Bowl, Classical Medallion, Beaded Loop & Swan Handles, Wood & Hughes, c.1850, 15 In.*Illus*	1920.00
Bowl, Classical Raised Rim Band, Footed, Dominick & Haff, 7 x 9 In.	446.00
Bowl, Danish Style Handles, Round, Webster Co., Stamped Logo, 1 ¾ x 11 ½ In.	480.00
Bowl, Engraved Coat Of Arms, Paw Feet, Stamped Zachariah Brigden, 5 In.	944.00
Bowl, Engraved, Wave Edge, Theodore B. Starr, 2 x 8 In.	403.00
Bowl, Flared Rim, Attached Liner, Raised Scrolling Leaves, Gorham, 3 In.	161.00
Bowl, Flower Repousse Border, Monogram, Jacobi & Jenkins, c.1900, 1 ½ x 10 ¼ In.	413.00
Bowl, Flower Shape, Pierced, Leaf Rim, Graff, Washbourne & Dunn, c.1900, 11 In. Diam.	326.00
Bowl, Flowers, High Relief Border, Gorham, Hallmarks, 1918, 15 x 11 ¼ In. ....*Illus*	649.00
Bowl, Flowers, Repousse, Scroll Border, Monogram, S. Kirk & Son, Hallmarks, c.1880, 5 x 10 In. *Illus*	1770.00
Bowl, Footed, Chased Tulip, Monogram, Arthur Stone, Engraved 1915, 3 ½ x 8 In.	3081.00
Bowl, Francis I, Lobed, Fruit & C-Scroll Design, Reed & Barton, 1954, 11 In.	633.00
Bowl, Francis I, Scalloped, Embossed Rim, Reed & Barton, 11 ½ In.	830.00
Bowl, French Pattern, Footed, Flared Rim, Scallop Edged, Repousse, Towle, 1900s, 13 ½ In.	840.00
Bowl, Fruit, Repousse Flowers & Branch Border, S. Kirk & Son, 10 In Diam.	374.00
Bowl, Fruit, Scalloped Rim, Repousse, Flowers, Stamped, Gorham, c.1895, 12 In. Diam.	420.00
Bowl, Grand Baroque, Pierced Rim, Wallace, 12 In.	563.00
Bowl, Grand Baroque, Pierced, Round, Wallace, 10 In.	305.00
Bowl, Lid, Flowers In Relief, Textured Ground, Lapis Knob, H. Petzal, 5 In.	4200.00
Bowl, Lobed Sides, Gadroon Edge, Richard Dimes, 12 In.	565.00
Bowl, Lozenge Shape, Flared Border, Fruit & Leaves, Monogram, Gorham, 1902, 15 x 12 In.	777.00
Bowl, Melon Shape, Shreve, Crump & Low, 8 ¼ In.	153.00
Bowl, Neoclassical, Reeded Rim, Chased Border, Stepped Foot, 6 x 9 In.	1195.00
Bowl, Octagonal Knops, Stepped Domed Foot, Beading, Dominick & Haff, c.1900, 10 In.	1007.00
Bowl, Openwork, Chrysanthemums, Basket Weave, Acanthus, c.1900, 11 In. ....*Illus*	944.00
Bowl, Openwork, Flower Baskets In Corners, Royal Danish, U.S.A., 1900s, 2 ½ x 12 In.	531.00
Bowl, Oval, Scalloped, Cellini Craft, 7 ½ x 5 ½ In.	180.00
Bowl, Petal Design, Footed, Reed & Barton, 4 ¼ x 9 In.	443.00
Bowl, Pierced Handles, 4 Ball Feet, Monogram, Richard Dines Co., 10 ½ In.	443.00
Bowl, Pierced Leaf & Flower Detail, Leaf Shape, Wallace, 11 In., Pair	476.00
Bowl, Pierced Rim, Frank W. Smith Silver Co., 1900s, 10 ½ In.	484.00
Bowl, Pierced Rim, Pedestal Foot, Chased Flowers, Monogram, Whiting Mfg., c.1912, 5 x 11 In.	660.00
Bowl, Prism Shape Sides, Octagonal Foot, Frank Smith, Marked, 2 ¼ x 5 In.	150.00
Bowl, Reeded, Wavy Rim, A.S.A.P., Whiting, c.1900, 3 x 9 ¾ In.	354.00
Bowl, Relief Roses, Undulating Rim, Lobed, Hexagonal, Marked, Whiting, 12 In.	1380.00

Bowl, Repousse Flowers, Branch Border, Footed, Coin, S. Kirk & Son, 5 x 7 In.	649.00
Bowl, Repousse Flowers, Flared Rim, Frank Whiting, 7 x 2 ½ In.	282.00
Bowl, Repousse Hibiscus Border, Monogram, Whiting, 3 ½ x 12 In. .....*Illus*	690.00
Bowl, Repousse, Flowers, Scroll Border, Kirk & Son, 5 ¼ x 9 In.	1298.00
Bowl, Repousse, S. Kirk & Son, 1 ½ x 5 ¾ In., Pair	345.00
Bowl, Reticulated Leaf Rim, Lobed, Oval, Monogram, Gorham, c.1900, 10 x 9 ¼ In.	2070.00
Bowl, Reticulated, Flower Shape, Pierced, Leaves, Undulating Rim Relief, Alvin, 14 In.	719.00
Bowl, Reticulated, Repousse, Footed, Graff, Washbourn & Dunn, 10 ¾ x 10 ¾ In.	554.00
Bowl, Rococo Rim, Leaves, Scrolls, Shells, Pierced, Howard & Co., c.1890, 11 ¼ In.	1121.00
Bowl, Sterling, Repousse, Floral Sprays, Matte Ground, A.G. Schultz & Co., c.1900, 9 In.	384.00
Bowl, Vegetable, Chippendale, Divided, Stamped, Frank Smith Silver Co., 8 x 11 In.	390.00
Bowl, Vegetable, Lid, Repousse Fruit, Birds, Eagle Finial, S. Kirk, 12 In., Pair	7590.00
Bowl, Vegetable, Scrolling Rim, Flower Border, Bailey, Banks & Biddle, Phila., c.1897, 11 In.	1400.00
Bowl, Vertical Panels, Pedestal Base, Reed & Barton, c.1940, 4 x 9 In.	540.00
Bowl, Wavy Gadroon, Flared Flower Rim, Monogram, Gorham, 1892, 2 ½ x 8 In.	461.00
Bowl, Wavy Rim, Domed Round Foot, Chased Roses, Redlich & Co., 6 x 13 ½ In.	2000.00
Bowl, Wavy Rim, Flower Clusters, Gorham, c.1902, 13 In.	885.00
Bowl, Windsor, Rectangular, Fluted Sides, Reed & Barton, 946, 11 ⅜ x 8 In.	406.00
Box, Lid, Carnelian Knob, Fish, Aquatic Plants In Relief, Henry Petzal, 1975, 5 ½ x 5 ½ In.... *Illus*	4800.00
Brandy Warmer, Revere Silversmiths, Inc., 7 In.	72.00
Bread Plate, Embossed Rim, Round, Alvin, 9 In.	192.00
Bread Tray, Monogram, Raised Designs, Rectangular, J.E. Caldwell & Co.	590.00
Bread Tray, Orchid, International, 11 ½ In.	360.00
Bread Tray, Oval, Flower Repousse Border, Jacobi & Jenkins, c.1900, 12 ¼ x 7 In.	354.00
Bread Tray, Reeded, Thread Pattern Rim, Pierced Border, Oval, 11 ½ x 7 ½ In.	518.00
Bread Tray, Reticulated Edge, Flowers, Scrolls, Redlich & Co., c.1890, 2 x 12 ¾ In.	345.00
Bread Tray, Wave Rim, Flower, Leaf Repousse, Whiting, 1 ¾ x 11 ½ In.	585.00
Butter, Beaded Rim, Monogram, Gorham, 1906, 5 ¾ In., 12 Piece	885.00
Butter, Reticulated Insert, Floral Repousse Border, Rim, Marked S. Kirk & Son, 7 In.	236.00
Cake Basket, Chased, Engraved, Hammered, Octagonal, Baltimore, 1903-05, 7 ½ In.	502.00
Cake Basket, Handles Chased, Footed, Thomas Whartenby, Philadelphia, c.1800, 6 x 15 In.	3740.00
Cake Basket, Reticulated Flowers & Handle, Oval, D. Buchanan, Richmond, 14 In.	3585.00
Cake Knife, Server, Flat Server, Cake Breaker, Allan Adler, 4 Piece	770.00
Cake Plate, Flowers, Fixed Handle, International, 11 In.	565.00
Cake Plate, Flowers, Scrolls, Fixed Handle, International, 11 In.	556.00
Cake Plate, Lobed, Oval, Gorham, 10 In.	431.00
Cake Plate, Pierced Design, Fixed Handle, Trademark Logo, W. B. Durgin Co., 9 ½ In.	390.00
Candelabra are listed in the Candelabrum category.	
Candlesticks are listed in their own category.	
Cann, Cup, Molded Rim, Tapered, Incised, Engraved, Samuel Whitney, 1793, 5 In.	16590.00
Cann, Cup, Philip Syng, Jr., Phil., c.1760, 5 ¼ In.	9480.00
Carving Knife, Kirk & Son	42.00
Carving Set, Ram Terminal, Carved Ivory Handles, Steel Blade, Joseph Rogers, Box, 4 Piece	173.00
Centerpiece, Folded Out Lobed Rim, Vines, Footed, Gorham, 1912, 4 x 15 In.	11070.00
Centerpiece, Rectangular Top & Base, Shell Support, Lona P. Schaeffer, 1940s, 4 ½ In.	6875.00
Centerpiece, Reticulated & Repousse Border, Flared Out, J.E. Caldwell, 4 x 15 In.	2300.00
Centerpiece, Ribbed, Openwork Flower Band, Oval, Footed, Whiting, 5 x 11 In.	1180.00
Chalice, Gold Wash Interior, Chaudron & Rasch, Phil., c.1810, 6 ½ In., Pair	4029.00
Chalice, Turned Stem, Bulging Cup, Flared Top, Stodder & Frobisher, c.1820, 6 In.	288.00
Charger, Garland, Lined Border, Marked Black, Starr & Frost, 14 In.	978.00
Charger, Stepped Rim, Kirk & Son, Sold By Shreve, Crump & Low Co., c.1930, 13 ½ In.	780.00
Charger, Tooled Hearts & Flowers, M.C. Knight, Handicraft Shop, c.1910, 13 In.	3240.00
Cheese Scoop, King Style, 19th Century, 11 ¾ In.	295.00
Cheese Scoop, Mouse On Paneled Stem, Beaded Knop, Ball End, Whiting, 8 In.	151.00
Chop Plate, Shaped Flower Edges, Monogram, Gorham, 14 In.	885.00
Cigarette Case, Black Enamel Band, R. Blackinton & Co., 3 x 4 ½ In.	142.00
Cigarette Case, Enamel, Race Car, Driver, Smith & Bartlam, 1935, 5 x 3 In.	1659.00
Cigarette Case, Engine Turned Lines, Monogram, Napier, 3 ¼ In.	90.00
Cigarette Case, Engraved Horizontal Stripe, Monogram, Elgin, 1920, 4 x 3 ¼ In.	293.00
Cigarette Case, Purse Shape, Scrolls, Monogram, Link Handle, c.1900, 3 ½ In.	90.00
Cigarette Case, Rays, Gold Fleur-De-Lis, 4 Sapphires, Thomae Co., Cartier, 3 ½ x 3 In.	189.00
Cocktail Shaker, Hammered, Removable Lid, Cap, Gold Wash Interior, c.1930, 9 ¼ In.	480.00
Cocktail Shaker, Paneled, Angle Handle, Chained Spout, c.1960, 10 ¼ In.	1534.00
Coffeepot, George II, Ebony Handle, Frank Whiting, Co., 9 ¾ In.	443.00
Coffeepot, John McMullin, Philadelphia, c.1800, 10 x 13 In.	1140.00
Coffeepot, Rose Scroll Design, Monogram, Gorham, 1951, 10 x 8 ¾ In.	461.00

Silver-American, Bowl, Repousse Hibiscus Border, Monogram, Whiting, 3 ½ x 12 In.
$690.00

Cottone Auctions

Silver-American, Box, Lid, Carnelian Knob, Fish, Aquatic Plants In Relief, Henry Petzal, 1975, 5 ½ x 5 ½ In.
$4,800.00

Skinner, Inc.

Silver-American, Creamer, Pedestal, Gadroon, Leaves, Scroll Handle, Phila., c.1840, 6 ¼ In.
$840.00

Cowan's Auctions

Silver-American, Creamer, Reeded Collar, Squared Handle, Ball Feet, Monogram, A. Blanchard, 1808-38, 4 ⅞ In.
$4,183.00

Neal Auction Co.

S

Silver-American, Ewer, Chinese Man On Lid, Repousse Flowers, Putti, Castle, S. Kirk, c.1838, 16 In.
$4,920.00

Skinner, Inc.

Silver-American, Fish Set, Lady's Pattern, Hand Clasping Bowl, Wreath, Monogram, Gorham, 13 & 10 In., 2 Piece
$1,560.00

Skinner, Inc.

Silver-American, Julep Cup, Tapered, Bead Borders, Inscribed, Marked, W. Carrington, 1800s, 3 ¾ In.
$1,180.00

Brunk Auctions

Coffeepot, St. James Pattern, M. Fred Hirsch Co., c.1940, 11 ½ In.	657.00
Compote, Chased Swags & Bells, 8-Sided, Dominick & Haff, c.1911, 4 x 10 In.	600.00
Compote, Francis I, Pedestal Base, Reed & Barton, 4 ¼ x 11 ½ In.	1320.00
Compote, Hammered, Tooled, Cutout, Aesthetic Movement, Wm. Durgin, 8 In.	375.00
Compote, Pierced Flower Border, Conforming Domed Foot, Shreve, Crump & Low Co., 4 x 8 In., Pair	875.00
Cordial, Urn Shape, Weighted, Towle, 3 In., 9 Piece	230.00
Cracker Scoop, Francis I, Ribbed Bowl, Embossed Handle, Reed & Barton, c.1907, 9 In.	276.00
Cream Jug, George Aiken, Baltimore, c.1790, 7 ¼ In.	600.00
Creamer, Beaded Rim, Footed, W. Mannerback, c.1820, 6 ⅛ In.	1304.00
Creamer, Bulbous, Squat, Stylized Leaf Band, Footed, Wheelock, Tennessee, 6 In.	3075.00
Creamer, Gadroon, Footed, John David, Phil., c.1775, 5 ¾ In.	3318.00
Creamer, Pedestal, Gadroon, Leaves, Scroll Handle, Phila., c.1840, 6 ¼ In. ......*Illus*	840.00
Creamer, Rectangular, Williamson, c.1810, 6 In.	385.00
Creamer, Reeded Collar, Squared Handle, Ball Feet, Monogram, A. Blanchard, 1808-38, 4 ⅞ In. *Illus*	4183.00
Creamer, Urn Fluted Shape, Square Pedestal Base, Loop Handle, Engraved Flowers, 6 ⅞ In.	502.00
Creamer, Wide Spout, Footed, Ivory Handle, Coin, 5 x 5 In.	148.00
Cup, Aesthetic, Hammered, Marsh Scene, C-Shape Handle, Dominick & Haff, 1882, 4 x 3 In.	1380.00
Cup, Baby, Gadroon Border, Molded Handle, Gorham, c.1899, 2 ¾ In.	246.00
Cup, Cordial, Tankard Shape, Loop Handles, Leatherette Case, Lunt, 1 ⅝ In., 6 Piece	177.00
Cup, Repousse Roses, Buds, Laura K. Field, Jenkins & Jenkins, 1911, 4 ¼ In.	431.00
Cup, Repousse, Rococo, Handle, Coin, Boston, c.1850, 4 In.	219.00
Decanter, Stopper, Scottish Thistle Overlay, Banded Neck, Engraved March 9, Gorham, 9 In.	295.00
Desk Set, Art Deco, Glass, Wood, Inkwell, Pen Tray, Blotter, Monogram, Gorham	207.00
Dipper, Repousse & Engraved Flowers, Scrollwork, Turned Wood Handle, 1800s, 15 In.	1534.00
Dish, 8-Sided, Strainer Insert, Square Handles, Marked, Kalo, 8 x 4 ½ In.	3250.00
Dish, Entree, Lid, Round, Handles, Gorham, 1941, 3 x 9 In.	720.00
Dish, Peacock, Standing, Long Tail, Gorham, 1900s, 4 ¼ x 9 ½ In., Pair	1560.00
Dish, Vegetable, Draped Leaves Rim, Oval, Black, Starr & Frost, 12 In., Pair	1000.00
Dresser Set, Hand Mirror, Brush, Monogram, Alvin, 2 Piece	116.00
Ewer, Chased, Repousse Birds, Grapes, Vines, Kirk & Son, c.1850, 13 ½ In.	2596.00
Ewer, Chinese Man On Lid, Repousse Flowers, Putti, Castle, S. Kirk, c.1838, 16 In. ....*Illus*	4920.00
Ewer, Scrolled Leaf Overlay, Flower, Trellis Diaperwork, Oval Medallion, c.1890, 10 In.	354.00
Figurine, Gazelle, Reclining, Backward Glancing, Signed, Loet Vanderveen, c.1921, 5 x 8 In.	1135.00
Figurine, Swan, Glass Base, Black, Starr & Frost, c.1900, 13 x 14 In.	2400.00
Fish Knife, Wavy Leaf & Berry Handle, George Shiebler & Co., 12 In.	390.00
Fish Server, Scrolling Design, Flowers, Leaves, S. Kirk & Son, c.1850	173.00
Fish Set, Lady's Pattern, Hand Clasping Bowl, Wreath, Monogram, Gorham, 13 & 10 In., 2 Piece *Illus*	1560.00
Flagon, Dome Lid, Palm & Bead Borders, Shield Thumblift, 7 ½ In.	2006.00
Flask, Leather, Gorham, Engraved 1899, 2 Pt., 9 In.	354.00
Flask, Oval, Engraved Monogram, Gorham Mfg., 6 In.	266.00
Fork, Lily, Monogram, Whiting, 1902, 8 In.	153.00
Frame, Green Velvet Back, Lebkuecher & Co., 10 x 12 ½ In.	106.00
Fruit Knife, Japanese Aesthetic Handles, Marked Gorham, 8 In., 12 Piece	1547.00
Ginger Jar, Lid, Oriental Style, Chrysanthemums, Leaves, Birds, Schiebler & Co., 3 ¼ x 3 In.	633.00
Gravy Boat, Scrolled Handle, Monogram, Footed, Bailey Banks & Biddle, c.1900, 4 ⅜ In.	270.00
Hip Flask, Sterling, J.C. Boardman & Co., Connecticut, 1900s, 4 ½ In.	165.00
Hot Water Urn, Stand, Burner, Wavy Rim, S-Spout, Square Handle, Gorham, 1915, 11 In.	1440.00
Ice Cream Fork, Gilt Wash Tines, Engraved Tips, Sterling Silver Mfg., c.1909, 6 Piece	108.00
Ice Cream Server, Bronze Bird & Lizard, Gilt Bowl, Dominick & Haff	2478.00
Ice Pail, Dome Lid, M-Shape Handles, Black, Starr & Gorham, 8 ¾ In.	1000.00
Jam Jar, Silver Lid, Red Enamel Finial, Red Glass, Vines, Rebecca Cauman, 4 In.	420.00
Jar, Canning, Lid, Repousse, Etched Glass, Kirk, 4 ½ x 3 ½ In.	42.00
Jar, Lid, Baluster, Flared Quatrefoil Footed, Raised Scroll & Flower, Reed & Barton, 5 In.	230.00
Jar, Lid, Protruding & Overlapping Scales, Cylindrical, H. Petzal, 1970, 8 In.	3480.00
Jelly Spoon, Tooled Grapes, Blue Enamel, M. C. Knight, Handicraft Shop, 6 In.	540.00
Jewelry Box, Repousse Scrolls & Flowers, Gorham, 2 x 5 In.	390.00
Jug, Maple Syrup, Hammered, Pollywog, Twig Handle, 3-Sided Underplate, 5 In.	2750.00
Julep Cup, Cylindrical, Tapering Sides, Beaded Border, 1800s, 3 ½ In.	826.00
Julep Cup, Molded & Beaded Rim, Coin, Megede, Lexington, Mo., 3 ½ In.	538.00
Julep Cup, Monogram, Baldwin & Miller, Engraved, 4 Piece	420.00
Julep Cup, Slightly Tapered, Molded Rim, Asa Blanchard, Kentucky, 3 ¼ In.	2390.00
Julep Cup, Tapered, Bead Borders, Inscribed, Marked, W. Carrington, 1800s, 3 ¾ In. ......*Illus*	1180.00
Julep Cup, Tapered, Molded Rim, Marked, Wm. M. Sharrard, 1850-80, 3 ⅝ In. ......*Illus*	1554.00
Julep Cup, Tapered, Reed Border, Monogram, c.1850, 3 ¾ In.	413.00
Kettle, Hot Water, Stand, Shaped Wood Handle, Lobed, Scalloped, Gorham, 12 ¼ In.	978.00
Kettle, Stand, Japanesque, Bulbous, Chased, Flower Knop, Marked Gorham, c.1897, 9 In.	2242.00

Ladle, B. Barton Touch, Virginia, 10 ¼ In.	474.00
Ladle, Downturned Tipt Back Fiddle Handle, Pointed Fins, Monogram, 1800s, 13 ¾ In.	1770.00
Ladle, Fiddle & Thread Upturned Handle, Clark & Co., 19th Century, 13 In.	590.00
Ladle, Fiddle Handle, Coin, Chauldron & Rasch, Phil., 13 In.	538.00
Ladle, Fiddleback Terminus, D Monogram, John Curry, Philadelphia, c.1931, 13 In.	237.00
Ladle, George Childs, c.1840, 13 ½ In.	148.00
Ladle, George IV, Flattened Tombstone Handle, W. Bateman, 13 In.	330.00
Ladle, Hammered Bowl, Turned Wood Handle, Franklin Porter Arts & Crafts, 15 ½ In.	207.00
Ladle, Monogram, William Mannerback, Pa., c.1810, 13 ½ In.	593.00
Letter Rack, Art Nouveau, Reticulated North Wind Face, Tuttle, 5 ½ x 9 In.	1035.00
Loving Cup, Art Nouveau, Baluster, Scroll Handles, Monogram, Handles, Gorham, 8 In.	708.00
Loving Cup, Beaded Rim, Applied Floral Handle, Lion Mark, Bailey, 2 x 3 ½ In., 4 Piece	212.00
Macaroni Server, Scroll Pattern, Durgin, c.1886, 10 ½ In.	296.00
Martini Shaker, Underplate, Handle, Gorham, 9 In.	558.00
Muffineer, Perforated Top, Engraved CSC, 6-Sided, Whiting Co., 5 ½ In.	190.00
Mug, Chased Handle, Rim, Foot, Coin, G. Boyce, c.1815, 4 In.	333.00
Mug, Chased, Coin, Pure Silver Co., 2 ¾ In.	71.00
Mug, Leaf Design Foot & Rim, Gorham, 3 ½ In.	354.00
Mug, Repousse, Village Scene, Beaded Border, J.E. Spear & Co., c.1850, 4 In.	944.00
Mug, Trophy, Tapered, Scroll Handle, Engraved Cartouche, Marked, 1800s, 4 x 4 In.	3776.00
Mustard Pot, Repousse Flowers, Kettle Shape, Swing Handle, 3-Footed, Kirk, c.1865, 4 In.	374.00
Napkin Rings are listed in their own category.	
Oyster Fork, Whiting, 8 Piece	130.00
Pan, Brandy Sauce, Wood Handle, Joseph Richardson, c.1790, 3 ½ In.	3792.00
Pepper Pot, Octagonal, Applied Bands, S-Scroll Handle, Herringbone Border, c.1850, 3 In.	502.00
Pie Server, Gilt, Ivory Handle, Stamped, Whiting Mfg. Co., 1890, 10 ¼ In.	780.00
Pitcher, Branch Handle, Repousse, S. Kirk & Son, 6 ½ In.	787.00
Pitcher, Bulbous, Footed, Flowers, Repousse, c.1855, 10 In.	1645.00
Pitcher, Castle Landscape Repousse, Acanthus Scroll Handles, Samuel Kirk, c.1928, 9 ½ In.	4080.00
Pitcher, Chased Handle, Embossed Shoulder Band, Pedestal Foot, Coin, N.Y., c.1830, 11 In.	1422.00
Pitcher, Cream, Aesthetic, Cranes, Embossed Border, Bamboo Style Handle, Whiting, 4 In.	247.00
Pitcher, Georgian Pattern, Tapered, Vines & Scrolls, Handle, Round Foot, Whiting, 10 In.	920.00
Pitcher, Hammered, Gourd Shape, Monogram, M, Kalo, Chicago, 7 ½ x 6 ½ In.	2875.00
Pitcher, Hammered, Kalo, Chicago, c.1910, 10 ¼ x 7 In. ....Illus	2125.00
Pitcher, Hinged Lid, Embossed, Shipwreck, Baluster, Ball Feet, Ear Handle, 1800s, 11 In.	9480.00
Pitcher, Milk, Arts & Crafts, Tapered, Chased, Gothic Panels, John Petty, Ma., c.1907, 5 In.	2596.00
Pitcher, Overall Pierced, Engraved Scalloped Rim, Spout, Gale & Willis, N.Y., 1860, 6 In.	267.00
Pitcher, Paul Revere Style, Applied Loop Handle, Spout, Reed & Barton, 7 ¾ In.	472.00
Pitcher, Repousse Flowers, Leaves, Scroll Handle, Stieff, Baltimore, 9 ½ In.	1205.00
Pitcher, Repousse, Flowers, Pear Shape, Scroll Handle, Coin, S. Kirk & Son, 8 In.	413.00
Pitcher, Ribbed Trim, Scrolled Handle, Bacchante Terminal, Gorham, 15 In.	1750.00
Pitcher, Royal Danish Pattern, C-Shape Handle, International Silver Co., 8 ½ In.	750.00
Pitcher, Stamped Leaf Bands, Monogram, Coin, Ball, Black, & Co., c.1850, 13 x 8 In.	738.00
Pitcher, Talisman Rose, Repousse Flowers, Rose Band, Leafy, Chased, Whiting & Co., 9 In.	805.00
Pitcher, Trophy, St. Andrews Golf Club, To George Clay Hollister, Cartier, 1931, 6 x 8 In.	564.00
Pitcher, Urn Shape, Applied Handle, Pedestal, Shreve & Co., 10 In.	1298.00
Pitcher, Urn Shape, Greek Key Border, Scroll Handle, 14 ¾ In.	1652.00
Pitcher, Vase Shape, Scroll Handle, Stepped Foot, Flowers, Shield, c.1870, 13 In.	1599.00
Pitcher, Water, Angular Handle, Pedestal Foot, Engraved, Reed & Barton, 10 ⅝ In.	920.00
Pitcher, Water, Cat Tails, Water Lilies, Ball Shape, Mauser, c.1903, 7 ½ In.	1265.00
Pitcher, Water, Classical Style, Chased, Gorham Mfg., c.1863-65, 8 ½ In.	1180.00
Pitcher, Water, Engraved Garlands, Ribbed Handle, Thumb Rest, Spaulding & Co., c.1905, 8 In.	690.00
Pitcher, Water, Faceted, Tapered, Monogram, Gorham, 8 ¾ x 10 In.	738.00
Pitcher, Water, Navarre Pattern, Chased, Watson Co., c.1950, 8 ⅞ In.	813.00
Pitcher, Water, Paneled, Pinched Neck, Shaped Handle, Footed, Gorham, 8 In.	900.00
Pitcher, Water, Pear Shape, Ear Shape Handle, Spread Foot, Arthur Stone, 1908-37, 9 In.	948.00
Pitcher, Water, Prelude Pattern, Shaped Handle, International, 9 In.	708.00
Pitcher, Water, Prelude, International, 9 In.	720.00
Pitcher, Water, Prelude, Scroll Handle, Footed, International, 9 In.	660.00
Pitcher, Water, Relief Water Lilies, Bulbous, Footed, Coin, A. Sanborn, 1860s, 11 In.	978.00
Pitcher, Water, Repousse, Flowers & Ferns, Acanthus Leaf Border, c.1900, 8 ½ In.	3304.00
Pitcher, Water, Repousse, Flowers & Ferns, Squared Handle, Ram's Head, 13 In.	2714.00
Pitcher, Water, Scroll Handle, Footed, Monogram, William Gale & Son Co., 1853, 10 In.	497.00
Pitcher, Water, Tapered, Leaf Banding, Reed & Barton, 1936, 8 ¼ In.	533.00
Pitcher, Water, WRS Monogram, Durgin, 7 ⅛ In.	600.00
Pitcher, Winged Lions, Scrolls, Vase Form, Stepped Foot, Gorham, 1897, 10 In.	2318.00

Silver-American, Julep Cup, Tapered, Molded Rim, Marked, Wm. M. Sharrard, 1850-80, 3 ⅝ In.
$1,554.00

Neal Auction Co.

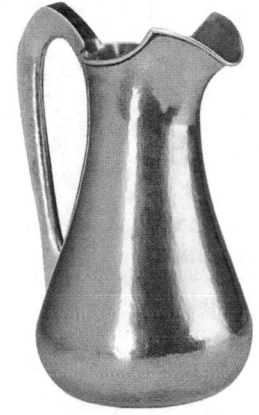

Silver-American, Pitcher, Hammered, Kalo, Chicago, c.1910, 10 ¼ x 7 In.
$2,125.00

Rago Arts & Auction Center

Silver-American, Punch Bowl, Ladle, Hammered, Applied Mixed Metals, Cherry Branch, Gorham, 1881, 10 ½ In.
$31,995.00

Skinner, Inc.

Silver-American, Tankard, Nautical Ropes, Handle, Buoy Finial, Thumblift, Bigelow, Kennard & Co., c.1890, 7 In.
$2,300.00

Fox Auctions

S

Silver-American, Teapot, Hinged Lid, Faceted, Urn Finial, Wood Handle, Marked, William Ball, Jr., 6 In. $1,353.00

Skinner, Inc.

Silver-American, Teapot, Lobed Body, Applied Flower Banding, W.B. North & Co., 8 ½ In. $940.00

Garth's Auctioneers & Appraisers

Silver-American, Vase, Trumpet, Paneled, Engraved, Reeded Borders, Inscribed, Reed & Barton, 1900s, 12 ½ In. $708.00

Brunk Auctions

Silver-Chinese, Tea Strainer, Flower Border, Jadeite Handle, Longevity Symbol, Marked, Box, c.1900, 8 In. $230.00

James D. Julia Auctioneers

Plate, Bread & Butter, Lady Diana Style, Towle, 6 ¼ In., 12 Piece	767.00
Plate, Child's, Flared Border, Wavy Edge, Martele, Gorham, 7 ¾ In.	1180.00
Plate, Gadroon Rim, John McMullin, c.1820, 5 ¾ In., Pair	2607.00
Plate, Maintenon Pattern, Chased Wide Border, Gorham, c.1925, 11 ¼ In., 12 Piece	10000.00
Platter Set, Swedish Modern, Spoon, Fork, Long Handle, Allan Adler, 14 ½ In.	593.00
Platter, Lobed Rim, Round, Randahl, 12 ¼ In.	748.00
Platter, Modern, Hand Hammered, Rectangular, Allan Adler, 17 x 12 In.	3220.00
Platter, Oval, Chevroned Ends, Molded Rim, Monogram, Gorham, 1909, 20 x 13 ½ In.	1476.00
Platter, Oval, Gadroon, F Monogram, Gorham Mfg. Co., 18 In.	1298.00
Platter, Oval, Lobed Border, Flared Pierced Rim, Scrolling Leaves, J.E. Caldwell, 20 In.	1315.00
Platter, Oval, Shaped Rim, Flower Border, Gorham, 18 In.	1180.00
Platter, Raised Rim, Oval, Samuel Kirk & Son, 1925-32, 17 In.	1121.00
Platter, Round, Stepped Rim, Monogram, Shreve & Co., 14 In.	708.00
Platter, Spoon, Mythologique Pattern, Gorham, c.1894, 12 ¾ In.	246.00
Porringer, Etched Children's Figures, Gorham, 2 x 6 ¾ In.	330.00
Porringer, Pierced Scroll Handle, Monogram, 1700s, 7 ¾ In.	444.00
Porringer, Round Bowl, Pierced Scroll Handle, Inscribed, 1831, 8 In.	1126.00
Punch Bowl, Hammered, Bombe Form, Gilt Grapevine Handles, 1881, 18 In.	33600.00
Punch Bowl, Ladle, 12 Cups, Banded Rim, Foot, S. Kirk & Son, 13 ½ In.	4500.00
Punch Bowl, Ladle, Hammered, Applied Mixed Metals, Cherry Branch, Gorham, 1881, 10 ½ In...*Illus*	31995.00
Punch Ladle, Buttercup Pattern, Oval Gold Washed Bowl, Monogram, Gorham, 11 ¾ In.	237.00
Punch Ladle, Hibiscus Flower, Monogram, Double Spout, Art Nouveau, 14 ¾ In.	144.00
Punch Ladle, Imperial Queen, Monogram, Whiting, 1895, 13 In.	246.00
Punch Ladle, Medallion, Silver Gilt, Monogram, Wood & Hughes, New York, c.1865, 15 In.	679.00
Punch Ladle, Oval Bowl, Engraved Leaves, Marked, Andrew Ellicott Warner, c.1850, 13 In.	150.00
Rattle, Figural, Whistle Terminal, 2 Branch Coral Noisemaker Arms, Gorham, 1800s, 4 In.	652.00
Salad Servers, Art Nouveau, Fork, Shell Shape Spoon, Whiplash Flowers, 7 ½ In.	86.00
Salt Server, Aesthetic Revival, Open, Cracked Eggshell Shape, Gorham, 1 x 1 In., 10 Piece	472.00
Salt, Eastlake Style, Scrolled Feet, Leaves, Rim Balls, Marked, 1 ¼ x 2 ¼ In., Pair	130.00
Salt, Master, Shell & Hoof Legs, Anthemion Repousse Rim, Gorham, 2 ½ x 1 ½ In., Pair	299.00
Salt, Oval, Beaded Rim, Lion Marks, Marked Bailey & Co., c.1848, 2 ½ x 4 In.	153.00
Salver, Scalloped Border, 3 Shell & Claw Feet, Dominick & Haff, 12 In.	1020.00
Sauceboat, Bailey & Co., c.1890, Phil., 5 ¾ x 9 ¼ In.	547.00
Sauceboat, Tray, Nautilus Shape, Loop Handle, Wreathes, Ram's Heads, 1700s, 5 ½ x 9 In.	354.00
Sauceboat, Undertray, Oval, Square Handle, Thomas Fletcher, c.1820, 6 x 10 In., Pair	10350.00
Service Plate, Pattern 600, Reed & Barton, c.1932, 10 ¾ In., 12 Piece	10030.00
Serving Bowl, Oval, Cornucopia Repousse, Monogram, Whiting Mfg. Co., 8 x 13 ¾ In.	390.00
Serving Dish, Dome Lid, Scroll Border, Flowers, Handles, Footed, Gorham, 9 ½ x 14 ½ In.	1652.00
Serving Dish, Handle, ELC Monogram, Frank M. Whiting Co., 9 ¾ In.	150.00
Serving Dish, Lobed, Oval, Rocaille Border, Pierced Arabesques, Gorham, 1894, 11 In., Pair	840.00
Serving Dish, Pinecone Relief, J.E. Caldwell, 12 In., Pair	889.00
Serving Pieces, Acorn, Ebony, Sugar Shovel, Knife, Pastry Server, Georg Jensen, c.1945	354.00
Serving Spoon, King, Gold Wash, Pierced Bowl, Monogram, Cased, J.E. Caldwell, 14 x 4 In.	518.00
Shrimp Cocktail, Compote, Reticulated Rim, Hartford Sterling Co., 5 ¼ In., 12 Piece	1320.00
Soup Ladle, Fiddle Handle, Coin, E. Raworth, Nashville, c.1820, 12 ½ In.	1830.00
Spoon Set, Apostles, Cast, Twisted Shaft, Figural Finial, Marked HH, 1690, 4 ½ In., 12 Piece	142.00
Spoon, Oyster, Shell Bowl, Pierced Tine Serration, Coin, Marked Warner, c.1890, 9 ⅞ In.	316.00
Spurs, Link Straps, Buckles, Cartouche, Marked, Bailey, c.1775	5036.00
Sugar & Creamer, Lid, Plymouth, Urn Shape Ebony Finial, Monogram, Gorham, 1912, 6 In.	523.00
Sugar Tongs, William Mannerback, Pa., c.1810, 6 ¼ In.	711.00
Sugar, Lid, Crested, Paneled, Floral Swags, Pendants, Zephern J. Pequignot, c.1850, 7 ¾ In.	389.00
Sugar, Lid, Monogram, R. & W. Wilson, Philadelphia, 1825, 5 ½ In.	600.00
Sugar, Lid, Pineapple Finial, Monogram, John David, Philadelphia, c.1790, 9 In.	1659.00
Sugar, Lid, Royal Danish, Acanthus Design Finial, Handles, International Sterling, 6 In.	265.00
Syrup, Hinge Lid, Underplate, Landscape, S. Kirk & Son Co., c.1900, 4 ½ In.	863.00
Table Swan, Glass, Black, Starr & Frost, c.1900, 13 x 14 In.	2400.00
Tablespoon, Old English Pattern, Bateman Family, c.1792, 9 In., Pair	123.00
Tablespoon, Spread Eagle Mark, Stamped L. Quandale, c.1830, 8 ¾ In., 5 Piece	130.00
Tankard, Cylindrical, Beaded Rims, Hinged, Monogram, Engraved Crest, Motto, c.1853, 6 In.	2040.00
Tankard, Nautical Ropes, Handle, Buoy Finial, Thumblift, Bigelow Kennard & Co., c.1890, 7 In...*Illus*	2300.00
Tazza, Fluted, Cast Shell & Leaf Rim, Domed Foot, William B. Durgin Co., c.1900, 15 In.	1416.00
Tea & Coffee Set, Dome Lid, Oval, Concave Flutes, Boehme, Baltimore, 4 Piece	2868.00
Tea & Coffee Set, Hammered, Tapered, Angular Handles, Lebolt, Chicago, 5 Piece	3125.00
Tea & Coffee Set, Prelude, International Silver, 10 ¾-In. Coffeepot, 7 Piece	1560.00
Tea Set, Beaded Rim & Foot, James E. Spear, Charleston, c.1859, 4 Piece	5975.00
Tea Set, Dome Lids, Corset Neck, Concord Silver Co., 5 Piece	1680.00

Tea Strainer, Repousse, Flowers, S. Kirk & Son, 6 ½ In.	90.00
Tea Urn, Dome Lid, Embossed Flowers, Ram's Head Handles, Gorham Mfg., 18 In.	7080.00
Teakettle, Stand, Vase Shape, Pierced Spread Foot, Wirework, Gorham, c.1916, 11 ½ In.	1126.00
Teapot, Beaded, Chased, Acorn Knop, Leaf Cap Treen Handle, Harvey Lewis, c.1820, 11 In.	1239.00
Teapot, Dome Lid, Bulbous, Lobed, Grape & Vine Rolled Border, Dolphin Finial, 10 In.	9440.00
Teapot, Grand Baroque, Loop Handle, S-Spout, Squat, Wallace, 1941, 9 ¼ x 10 In.	984.00
Teapot, Hinged Lid, Faceted, Urn Finial, Wood Handle, Marked, William Ball, Jr., 6 In. .....*Illus*	1353.00
Teapot, Lighthouse, Turned Finial, Wood Handle, Drop Spout, Monogram, Kirk & Sons, 8 ½ In. ..	510.00
Teapot, Lobed Body, Applied Flower Banding, W.B. North & Co., 8 ½ In. ....*Illus*	940.00
Teapot, Pineapple Finial Monogram, Shield, Wood Handle, Joseph Anthony Jr., c.1795, 6 ¼ In.	7703.00
Teapot, Repousse, Flowers & Leaves, Tapered, Ivory Insulators, Kirk & Son, 6 In.	600.00
Teaspoon Set, Embossed Phoenix, William Haverstick, Philadelphia, c.1780, 6 Piece	458.00
Teaspoon Set, Empire Style, Fiddleback, Mitchell & Tyler, Richmond, Va., c.1866, 6 In., 6 Piece...	165.00
Teaspoon Set, Fiddle, Monogram Handle, Signed J. Lowe, 6 In., 7 Piece	115.00
Teaspoon, Feather Edge, Elliptical Medallion, Sherburne Family, N.H., c.1800, 4 Piece	590.00
Teaspoon, Fiddle Handle, Engraved Jear, Coin, Marked T.W. Brown, North Carolina, 5 ¾ In. ...	300.00
Teaspoon, Fiddle Handle, JSB Monogram, Marked T. Linebach, N. Car., c.1825, 7 ¼ In.	420.00
Tongs, Shell Bowls, Blackberry Vine Engraved Handle, Coin, Marked Foxcroft, c.1830, 6 ¼ In. .	518.00
Tongs, Sugar, Bow Shape, Fiddle Pattern, James Munroe, Barnstable Ma., c.1900, 6 In.	177.00
Tray, Beaded Rim, Engraved, Gratitude, Vines, Leaves, Bigelow Brothers & Kennard, 12 In.	960.00
Tray, Chased Rim, Round, Reed & Barton, 1947, 10 ¾ In.	240.00
Tray, Chased, Repousse Flower, Leaves, Oval, Handles, Frank M. Whiting, c.1938, 30 ¾ In.......	4375.00
Tray, Chased, Scrolled Rim, Monogram, Handles, Theodore Star, N.Y., 19 x 30 ¼ In.................	3318.00
Tray, Chippendale Pattern, Square, Curved Ogee Edges, Frank W. Smith, c.1900, 10 ½ In........	444.00
Tray, Chippendale, Gorham, 1958, 12 In.	600.00
Tray, Coffeepot, Teapot, Kettle, Sugar, Chased, Gorham, c.1941, Coffeepot 10 In., 5 Piece	4688.00
Tray, Cut Corner, Scroll Handles, Engraved Cartouche, Monogram, Reed & Barton, 27 x 16 In. .	2588.00
Tray, Engraved Inscription, Presentation, From Ford Co., Gorham, c.1985, 29 In.	4200.00
Tray, Engraved, Flat Undulating Edge, Oval, International, 16 ¼ x 11 ½ In.	1323.00
Tray, Hampton Court Shield, Scroll Rim, Pierced Handles, Reed & Barton, 17 x 24 In.	2700.00
Tray, Martele, Art Nouveau, Flower Shape, Molded Edge, Scrolling Flowers, c.1900, 16 ½ In. ...	7963.00
Tray, Oval, Center Monogram, Shell & Scroll Border, J.E. Caldwell, 17 In.	2006.00
Tray, Oval, Hammered, Reticulated Handles, BP Monogram, Gorham, 28 x 20 In.	10350.00
Tray, Raised Scalloped Rim, Square, Frank W. Smith Co., 10 ¾ In.	360.00
Tray, Rectangular, Flower Based Handles, 25 In.	3125.00
Tray, Reticulated Edge, Round, Dominick & Haff, c.1906, 12 In.	575.00
Tray, Round, Monogram, Shaped Scroll Rim, Theodore Starr, 12 ½ In.	660.00
Tray, Round, Rolled Rim, Monogram, Gorham, 12 In.	554.00
Tray, Round, Shaped Edge, Monogram, Gorham Mfg., 12 In.	561.00
Tray, Rounded Rectangle, 3 Sections, Hammered, 1900s, 10 ¼ x 12 In.	708.00
Tray, Royal Danish, International, 25 ½ In.	3900.00
Tray, Royal Danish, Oval, International Silver Co., 13 In.	330.00
Tray, Scalloped Border, Hammered Finish, F. Novick, 1900s, 16 In.	1534.00
Tray, Shaped, Stepped Rim, Oval, Monogram, Tuttle Silversmiths, 11 ½ In.	472.00
Tray, Star, Stag's Head, Galleon, Flowers, Stippled Border, Chamfered, Reed & Barton, 17 In...	1112.00
Tray, Windsor, Rounded, Molded Rim, Drinks, Reed & Barton, 1945, 10 ¾ x 7 ½ In.	369.00
Tree Well, Gorham, 14 x 20 In.	1778.00
Trophy Mug, Presented By Judges Of Target Shooting, Gale, Wood & Hughes, c.1843, 4 ¼ In.	472.00
Trophy, Bowl, Silver, Satyr Mask & Scroll Band, Chattahoochee Field Trials, W. Kerr, 9 In.	708.00
Trowel, Presentation, Chased Scrolls, Faux Ivory Handle, Case, Atkin Bros., c.1900, 12 ½ In...	660.00
Tureen, Lid, Stag Handles, Finial, Ball Black & Co., 7 ¾ In..	2252.00
Tureen, Lid, Urn Finial, Repousse Fruit, Scrolls, 16 ½ In.	8962.00
Vase, Baluster Shape, Flower & Bow Cartouche, Monogram, Weighted Base, Gorham, 16 In...	719.00
Vase, Brick Work, Applied Beetle, Stylized Flowers, Oval, Footed, Whiting, 7 In..................	2990.00
Vase, Flared Foot, Raised Scroll, Reeded, Stamped Black, Starr & Frost, Hallmark, 3 In.	207.00
Vase, Grecian Urn Shape, Leaf & Flower Handles, Dominick & Haff, 14 In.	2760.00
Vase, Openwork Swirled Sides, Gorham, c.1890, 12 In...	3500.00
Vase, Pierced Sides, Reeded Panels, Chased, Flowers, Urns, Marked, Gorham, c.1910, 19 In. ...	1652.00
Vase, Reticulated Rim, Repousse Feet, Monogram, Black, Starr & Frost, 6 ½ x 8 ¾ In...........	677.00
Vase, Trumpet, Neoclassical, Monogram, 20 In.	2689.00
Vase, Trumpet, Paneled, Engraved, Reeded Borders, Inscribed, Reed & Barton, 1900s, 12 ½ In....*Illus*	708.00
Vase, Trumpet, Raised Acanthus, Laurel Leaf, Ribbon Swags, Black, Starr & Frost, 7 ¾ In.	299.00
Waiter, Eagle Crest, Oval, Ball & Talon Footed, Marked S. Kirk & Son, 10 In.	531.00
Waste Bowl, Classical, Engraved, Leafy Script, c.1910, 5 ¼ In...................................	531.00
Wine Coaster, Reticulated Rim, Flowers, Scrolls, Redlich & Co., 8 ½ In.........................	230.00
Wine Taster, Round, Danish Style Handle, Stamped, Cartier, 3 ¾ In.............................	120.00

Silver-Continental, Bowl, Fruit, Flowers, Repousse, Bellflower, Scroll Handles, Footed, c.1900, 11 x 22 In. $3,776.00

Brunk Auctions

Silver-Danish, Martini Shaker, Ivory, Cork, Franz Hingelberg, Stamped, Denmark, 1930s, 9 ¾ x 6 ½ In. $8,125.00

Rago Arts & Auction Center

Silver-Dutch, Spoon, Rattail Bowl, Leaf Stem, Hoof To Terminal, Engraved, Marked, c.1650, 6 ⅜ In. $325.00

Skinner, Inc.

Silver-English, Bowl, Monteith, Crenellated Border, Lion Mask & Ring Handles, Sheffield, 14 ¾ x 19 In. $956.00

Neal Auction Co.

Silver-English, Brandy Warmer, Lid, Wood Handle, Finial, Walter Brind, c.1788, 5 ½ In.
$330.00

Cowan's Auctions

Silver-English, Castor, Lighthouse, Pierced Cap, Engraved Crest, Peter Guille, George V, c.1936, 6 In., Pair
$1,599.00

New Orleans Auction Galleries, Inc.

Silver-English, Coffee Set, Coffeepot, Sugar, Creamer, Utensils, Miniature, c.1900, 1 ½-In. Pot
$784.00

Theriault's

Silver-English, Communion Set, Grape Repousse Lid, Edwardian, Gilt Dish, Glass Cup, Traveling, 1934, 5 In.
$2,468.00

Garth's Auctioneers & Appraisers

SILVER-AUSTRIAN

Bowl, Center, Openwork Flower Frame, Masks, Footed, Glass Liner, c.1900, 5 x 8 ¾ In.	649.00
Dresser Box, Repousse, Ivory Napoleonic Lid Portraits, Faux Gem Rim, Round, c.1850	600.00
Ewer, Wine, Spiral Reeded, Pear Shape Bowl, Wisteria Handle, 14 ½ x 7 ½ In., Pair	4388.00
Ladle, Stamped Diana's Head, Lobed Cartouche, Austria-Hungary, 12 In.	150.00

SILVER-AUSTRO-HUNGARIAN

Candlestick, Lion Mask Stepped Base, Handles, 14 ½ In., Pair	1250.00
Plaque, Relief, David & Goliath, Swirls, Oak Frame, 15 x 9 ½ In.	702.00
Platter, Fish, Indented Oval, 23 ⅜ In.	1000.00
Platter, Fish, Ribbed, Scalloped Rim, Oval, 23 In.	1000.00
Sauceboat, Underplate, Square Ear Handles, Tray 9 In.	594.00

SILVER-CAMBODIAN

Censer, Pierced, Repousse, Gods, Warriors, Round, Well, c.1850, 26 In.	7552.00

SILVER-CANADIAN

Chalice, Art Deco Style, Hexagonal, Faceted Stem, Spread Foot, G. Beaugrand, 1900s, 8 In.	533.00
Compote, Shell Shape, Hammered, Open Bud Handle, Grapes, C.P. Petersen, 8 x 9 In.	1190.00
Cup, Sherbet, Semispherical, Flared, Raised Pedestal Base, Hamilton, 3 ½ x 4 In., 6 Piece	266.00

SILVER-CHILEAN

Tray, Anthemion Border, Scrolling Acanthus Handles, 19 ¾ In.	1016.00

SILVER-CHINESE

Bowl, Applied Tree & Birds, Footed, c.1875, 4 x 7 ½ In.	1888.00
Bowl, Repousse, 4 Figures, Praying, Leaftip Rim, 8 ¾ In.	472.00
Bowl, Scrolling Repousse Dragons, 3 Stylized Dragon Shape Feet, c.1900, 10 In. Diam.	3480.00
Cake Plate, Scallop Rim, Openwork, Prunus, Dragons, Pearls, Scroll Handles, Footed, 9 x 13 In.	1528.00
Coffeepot, Dragon Finial & Handle, Warriors, Bamboo, 19th Century, 6 x 10 In.	3675.00
Crumber, Coiled Dragon Handle, Oval Tray, Dragon Gallery, Spider, c.1900, 13 ⅝ In.	593.00
Goblet, Figures, Landscape, Twisted Stem, 1908	2205.00
Mirror, Hand, Ivory, 2 Deer, Landscape, c.1840, 11 In.	3369.00
Mirror, Hand, Jade, Lucky Symbols, Dragon, 19th Century, 10 In.	3369.00
Tankard, Cylindrical, Dragon Handle, Battle Scene, Monogram, 1800s, 5 In.	2370.00
Tea Set, Teapot, Creamer, Open Sugar, Bamboo Reeds, Handle, c.1910, 5 ½ In.	4800.00
Tea Strainer, Flower Border, Jadeite Handle, Longevity Symbol, Marked, Box, c.1900, 8 In. ... *Illus*	230.00
Teapot, Dome Lid, Wood Handle, Repousse Flowers, Chased Lid, c.1850, 8 ¼ In.	805.00
Teapot, Stand, Repousse Dragon Design, Bamboo Shape Handle & Spout, c.1890, 7 ¾ In.	3480.00
Tray, Flower Shape, Openwork Gallery Of Dragons, Fluted Ball Feet, Wang Hing, c.1890, 9 In.	3063.00
Tray, Octagonal, Bamboo Edge, Battle Scenes, Coiled Dragon, c.1890, 19 ¼ In.	5333.00
Vase, Figures In Garden, Tapered, Shouldered, Lion's Mask & Ring Handles, 9 In.	6871.00
Vase, Trumpet Shape, Ruffled Rim, Figural Dragon Support, Round Foot, Wang Hing, c.1900, 9 ½ In.	850.00

SILVER-CONTINENTAL

Beaker, Textured Vertical Bands, Strapwork, Leaves, Monogram, c.1872, 4 ¼ In.	296.00
Bowl, 4 Figural Putti Feet, Ribbed, 3 x 9 In.	450.00
Bowl, 12-Sided, Fluted Swirl Design, Round Pedestal Foot, c.1930, 10 ⅞ In. Diam.	385.00
Bowl, Embossed, Chased Bacchus Face, Grapevines, Scallop Lobes, Footed, c.1960, 10 In.	420.00
Bowl, Fruit, Flowers, Repousse, Bellflower, Scroll Handles, Footed, c.1900, 11 x 22 In. ... *Illus*	3776.00
Bowl, Fruit, Round, Flared Rim, Pierced & Embossed, Fruit Bouquets, c.1900, 9 In. Diam.	307.00
Charger, Knight On Horseback, Repousse Design, Oval, 16 In.	615.00
Dresser Box, Lovers, Sheep, Instruments, Flowers, Inset Gems, 1700s, 3 ½ x 3 In.	2300.00
Figure, Bacchus & Pan, Holding Grapes, 9 ⅝ In.	2135.00
Figure, Cherub, Holding Rose Of Head, Kneeling, Drapery, 6 ¾ In., Pair	1320.00
Frame, Holds 2 Pictures, Leaf Scroll, Ava Gardner Photos, 4 ¼ x 5 ½ In.	650.00
Patch Box, Oval, Cast Flowers, Cornucopia, Geometric Design, Trees, c.1800, 1 x 3 In.	356.00
Punch Bowl, Lobed, Scalloped, Domed Foot, 7 5/7 x 11 ¾ In.	1440.00
Punch Ladle, Wood Spiral Handle, 18 ¼ In.	176.00
Salt Cellar, Ring Handle, 2 Shell Glass Bowl, 2 Dolphin Supports, Oval Base, 7 ½ x 7 In., Pair	500.00
Salt, Shell Dish, Dolphin Base, Master, 2 ½ In., 4 Piece	518.00
Salver, Pierced Scrolled Rim, Etched, Round, c.1830, 12 ¾ In.	711.00
Tea & Coffee Set, Rococo Style, Lampstand, Teapot, Coffeepot, Sugar, Lid, Creamer	3304.00
Tray, Bronze Argente, Rectangular, Flared Rim, Sea Dragon's Heads, Scrollwork, c.1915, 17 In.	399.00
Tray, Flower Rim, Scalloped, Round, 13 In.	813.00
Tray, Irregular Leaf Rim, Round, 13 In.	813.00
Tray, Irregular Leaf Rim, Round, 14 ½ In.	938.00
Urn, Classical Woman Standard, Scroll Handles, c.1890, 11 ½ In.	1580.00

SILVER-DANISH

Asparagus Tongs, Fluted Handles, Scrolled Leaf Terminals, Georg Jensen, 7 ½ In. 3658.00
Bowl, Flared Rim, Open Stem, Berries, Molded Foot, Georg Jensen, c.1919, 4 x 5 ⅞ In. 1476.00
Bowl, Flared Rim, Openwork Band Stem, Leaves, Stepped Base, Evald Nielsen, 4 ¾ x 9 ½ In.... 688.00
Bowl, Footed, Cactus Pattern, Hammered, Round, Marked Georg Jensen, 4 x 7 ¼ In. 1610.00
Bowl, Hammered, Oval, Footed, Ring Handles, Engraved, 1941, 8 x 16 ½ x 3 In. 2358.00
Bowl, Hand Hammered, Reticulated Geometric Foot, Georg Jensen, 5 x 9 In. 649.00
Bowl, Hand Hammered, Wide Rim, Round Flat Foot, Georg Jensen, c.1930, 4 x 8 In. 690.00
Bowl, Lid, Leaf, Ball Finial, Hammered, Tapered, Openwork Stem, G. Jensen, c.1960, 6 x 5 In. ... 938.00
Bowl, Reeded Rim, Round Foot, Georg Jensen, 8 ½ In. Diam. 518.00
Bowl, Round, Hand Hammered, Georg Jensen, c.1960, 9 ½ In. 1125.00
Centerpiece, Reticulated, Footed, Handles, Marked Simon Garth, L. Berth, c.1900, 5 ½ x 17 In. ... 652.00
Cheese Slice, Acorn Pattern, Marked Georg Jensen, 3 x 8 ½ In. 235.00
Coffee Set, Blossom, Coffeepot, Creamer, Sugar, Sugar Nips, Ivory Handles, Georg Jensen, c.1930 5100.00
Coffee Set, Flowers, Ebonized Wood Finials, Jens Sigsgaard, 1934, 3 Piece. 800.00
Compote, Hammered Finish, Leaf & Twig, Tiered Spread Foot, Georg Jensen, c.1920, 4 In. 770.00
Compote, Hammered, Pendant Grape Clusters, Spiral Stem, G. Jensen, c.1955, 5 x 5 In., Pair 2500.00
Demitasse Spoon Set, Sterling, Enamel, Multicolor, Frigast, Case, 6 Piece 240.00
Fork, Spot Hammered, Leaf, Berry Handle, Evald Nielsen, 1924, 10 ¾ In. 250.00
Martini Shaker, Ivory, Cork, Franz Hingelberg, Stamped, Denmark, 1930s, 9 ¾ x 6 ½ In. ..... *Illus* 8125.00
Pitcher, Henning Koppel, Sterling, Stamped, Georg Jensen, c.1948, 11 ½ x 8 ½ In. 13750.00
Platter, Round, Molded Rim, Georg Jensen, c.1935, 14 In. Diam. 3444.00
Poultry Shears, Acorn Pattern, Georg Jensen, c.1945, 10 In. 288.00
Sauce Ladle, Copenhagen, Marked, Georg Jensen, 1912, 7 ¾ In. 276.00
Sauceboat, Hand Hammered, Scrolled Handle, Grape Cluster, Georg Jensen, c.1948, 9 In. 3215.00
Spoon, Medicine, Double Bowl, Hammered, Folding, Georg Jensen, 5 ¾ In. 188.00
Tray, Oval, Stylized Tulip Handles, Beading, Jensen Style, Stamped, 33 x 20 In. 2844.00
Tray, Scalloped Rim, Round, Stamped C.C. Hermann, Denmark, Mid 1960s, 13 In. 780.00

SILVER-DUTCH

Basket, Reticulated, Oval Basket, Boat Shape, Heart Cutouts, 10 x 7 In. 230.00
Bowl, 8 Engraved Acorn Panels, Cherub, Flower Wing Handles, c.1755, 5 ½ In. 295.00
Box, Hinged Lid, Beaded Rim & Base, Amsterdam, 1848, 3 x 6 In. 1659.00
Cake Server, Reticulated Blade, Relief Shepherd Scene, Scrolling, Shells, Animals, 12 ½ x 3 In. ... 230.00
Coffeepot, Hippocampus Knop, Lobed Baluster, Ebonized Handle, Amsterdam, c.1840, 9 In. .. 590.00
Coffeepot, Pear Shape, Flowers & Leaf Repousse, Twig Shape Legs, Horn Handle, c.1850, 7 In. 3200.00
Epergne, Entwined Stem, Leaves, 2-Tiered Glass, Plates, Tulip Finial, Repousse Base, 1853, 22 In. 1020.00
Group, Tavern, Yard Scene, 4 Ball Feet, 3 ¼ x 3 ¼ In. 1380.00
Spoon, Rattail Bowl, Leaf Stem, Hoof To Terminal, Engraved, Marked, c.1650, 6 ⅝ In. ... *Illus* 325.00
Teapot, Flower, Scroll Handle, Winged Cherub Finial, 1837 .... 387.00
Tray, Cartouche Shape, Scrolled Rim, Hallmarks, Minerva Head, 1933, 13 x 17 In. 1080.00

SILVER-ENGLISH. English sterling silver is marked with a series of four or five small hallmarks. The standing lion mark is the most commonly seen sterling quality mark. The other marks indicate the city of origin, the maker, and the year of manufacture. These dates can be verified in many good books on silver. Silver prices in 2012 became so high many pieces were worth more in meltdown value than as decorative silver. These prices are based on current silver values.

Asparagus Tongs, Pierced, Marked, John, Henry, Charles Lias, c.1830, 9 ⅞ In. 356.00
Asparagus Tongs, U Shape, c.1784, 9 ¾ In. 299.00
Bacon Server, Gadroon Edge, Reeded Scrolls, Wooden Handle, 1799, 4 x 13 In. 1180.00
Barber's Bowl, Shears, Quatrefoil, Engraved, Box, Wakely & Wheeler, c.1884, 8 ¾ x 8 ¾ In. ... 391.00
Basket, Classical Figures Band, Oval, Swing Handle, c.1867, 12 ¾ In. 750.00
Basket, Pierced Rim, Embossed, Swing Handle, Crichton Bros., c.1906, 14 In. 8125.00
Beaker, Gilt Ostrich Head, Horseshoe In Mouth, c.1767, 3 ¼ In. 649.00
Berry Spoon, Gold Wash Bowl, Stippled Relief, Fruit, Leaves, T. Wallis II, c.1804, 8 In., Pair .. 115.00
Berry Spoon, Hanoverian Pattern, Chased Flowers, Vines, c.1749, 8 ½ In., Pair 246.00
Biscuit Barrel, Stepped Lid, Cylindrical, Reeded Feet, Ivory Finial, 1937, 6 ½ In. 650.00
Bowl, Chased, Footed, London, c.1811, 3 x 10 ½ In. 900.00
Bowl, Lid, Fluted, Scrolled, Gadroon, Engraved Lion, P. Storr, c.1820, 10 In., Pair 22420.00
Bowl, Gold Wash, Coat Of Arms, Motto, Atkin Brothers, 1892, 10 x 13 In. 2280.00
Bowl, Monteith, Crenellated Border, Lion Mask & Ring Handles, Sheffield, 14 ¾ x 19 In. ... *Illus* 956.00
Bowl, Monteith, Engraved Figures, Crichton Bros., c.1922, 5 x 9 In. 1750.00
Bowl, Monteith, Figure, Dragon, Blossom, Fan Panels, Crichton Bros., c.1922, 9 In. 1750.00
Bowl, Monteith, Wavy Rim, Cherubs, Lion's Head Handles, Domed Foot, 1909, 5 x 7 In. 502.00

Silver-English, Cruet Set, 6 Bottles, Holder, Leaf Handles, Scrolled Feet, Paul Storr, 1810, 9 x 12 In.
$6,000.00

Skinner, Inc.

Silver-English, Kettle, Hot Water, Engraved, Openwork, Feet, Flower Finial, Martin, Hall & Co., c.1880, 14 In.
$2,714.00

Brunk Auctions

Silver-English, Page Turner, Scroll, Flower, Acanthus Handle, Ivory Blade, Henry Wilkinson & Co., 20 In.
$472.00

Brunk Auctions

S

Silver-English, Sauceboat, Engraved Armorial Design, Scrolled Handle, Gadroon, Marked, 1775-76, 9 In., Pair
$4,200.00

Skinner, Inc.

Silver-English, Secretary, Chippendale Style, Drop Front Desk, 3 Drawers, Hallmarks, Miniature, 1800s, 5 In.
$392.00

Theriault's

Silver-English, Tea Set, Gold Washed Interior, Wood Handled Teapot, Monogram, John Emes, 3 Piece
$2,400.00

Skinner, Inc.

Silver-English, Toast Rack, Scroll Handle & Feet, 6 Sections, Handle, John Kilpatrick, 1861, 6 ¼ x 6 In.
$413.00

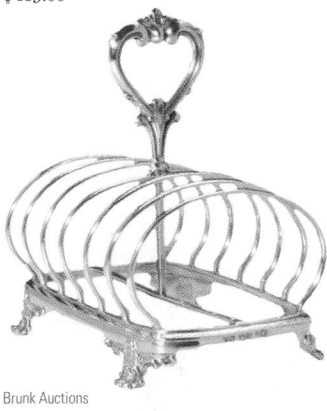

Brunk Auctions

Bowl, Oval, Georgian, Curved Handles, Footed, Engraved, Lion's Head, c.1800, 11 x 19 In.	2300.00
Bowl, Winged Beast Handles, Striated Swirl, Flowers, Repousse, Footed, 1903, 8 In.	823.00
Box, Art Nouveau, Hinged Lid, Scrolling Flowers, Leaves, Vines, William Comyns, 1903, 3 x 3 In.	780.00
Brandy Warmer, Lid, Wood Handle, Finial, Walter Brind, c.1788, 5 ½ In. ....*Illus*	330.00
Bread Basket, William Sumner, London, 1792, 13 ½ In.	1080.00
Cake Basket, Armorial, Engraved, Lobed Sides, Cast Rim, Engraved, c.1810, 14 In.	1416.00
Cake Basket, Engraved Armorial, Burrage Davenport Touch, Reticulated, 4 x 15 In.	4374.00
Cake Basket, Flowers, Pierced Rim, Swing Handle, Repousse, 1803, 14 In.	660.00
Cake Basket, Scalloped, Wheat, Pierced Rim, Stars, Swing Handle, 1769, 3 x 13 In.	1168.00
Cake Basket, Shell Shape, Scalloped, Gadroon, Mermaid Handle, Dolphin Feet, 1929, 7 In.	2963.00
Candelabra are listed in the Candelabrum category.	
Candlesticks are listed in their own category.	
Candy Dish, Glass Lined, Basket, Beading, Arabesque Design, Braided Handle, 1908, 4 In.	533.00
Card Box, Playing Cards In Lid, 4 x 4 In.	1107.00
Castor, Lighthouse, Pierced Cap, Engraved Crest, Peter Guille, George V, c. 1936, 6 In., Pair.....*Illus*	1599.00
Caviar Server, Shell Handles, Dolphin Feet, Fish Finial, Shell Bowl	7800.00
Chalice, Engraved, Plow, Frame, Marked, John, Henry & Charles Lias, c.1830, 7 In.	1003.00
Charger, Crowns, Crests, Gadroon Shell & Leaf Rim, J. Bridge, 11 In., 8 Piece	7920.00
Charger, Gadroon Rim, Flower Engraving, Scrolled Feet, Sebastian Garrard, c.1908, 22 In.	4740.00
Chocolate Pot, Baluster Shape, Molded Round Foot, Treen Handle, c.1758, 12 In.	1652.00
Chocolate Pot, Hinged Lid, Pineapple Finial, Tapered, Ebonized Handle, 1911, 10 In.	431.00
Chocolate Pot, Hinged Lid, Wood Finial, Faceted, Pedestal Base, James Dixon & Sons, c.1913..	300.00
Chocolate Pot, Lid, Engraved, Cylindrical, Wood Scroll Handle, R. Copper, London, c.1705, 9 In..	8260.00
Cigar Tube, Gilt, Hinged, Turned Panels, Sheffield, 1931, 6 ¼ In.	475.00
Cigarette Box, Hinged Dome Lid, Monogram, George V, 1920-21, 2 x 3 ¾ In.	153.00
Cigarette Box, Hinged Lid, Rectangular, Gerard Benney, 1956, 2 x 4 In.	978.00
Coffee Set, Coffeepot, Sugar, Creamer, Utensils, Miniature, c.1900, 1 ½-In. Pot ....*Illus*	784.00
Coffee Urn, Lid, Pineapple Finial, Scroll Handles, William Holmes, c.1795, 20 ¾ x 10 In.	5750.00
Coffeepot, Engraved, Gadroon, Berry Finial, Baluster, Wm. & Jas. Priest, c.1770, 12 In.	3540.00
Coffeepot, Treen Handle, Crest, Richard Gurney & Thomas Cook, c.1762, 9 ½ In.	1750.00
Communion Set, Grape Repousse Lid, Edwardian, Gilt Dish, Glass Cup, Traveling, 1934, 5 In.....*Illus*	2468.00
Container, Egg Shape, 7 Engraved Birds, Hammered Ground, c.1972, 4 ⅜ In.	354.00
Creamer, Helmet Shape, Beaded Rim, Arched Reeded Handle, Footed, 6 ⅜ In.	922.00
Creamer, Helmet Shape, Strap Handles, Domed Foot, Banding, Flowers, c.1793, 5 In.	399.00
Creamer, Oval, Treen, Leaf Banding, c.1797, 11 In.	594.00
Creamer, Pear Shape, Lobed, Leaf Design Spout, C-Scroll Handle, 1835, 7 In.	674.00
Creamer, Repousse Flowers, Leaf Capped Scroll Handle, c.1780, 4 In.	531.00
Cruet Set, 2 Cut Glass Bottles, 3 Pierced Castors, Stand, Crichton Bros., c.1915, 8 ½ In.	3215.00
Cruet Set, 6 Bottles, Holder, Leaf Handles, Scrolled Feet, Paul Storr, 1810, 9 x 12 In........*Illus*	6000.00
Cruet Stand, Boat Shape, Wood Bottom, Hester Bateman Touch, 1790-91, 4 x 6 ¾ In.	356.00
Cruet Stand, Victorian, Seashell Shape, C-Scroll Legs, Dolphin Shape Handle, 1838, 3 x 9 In..	4148.00
Cup, 2 Handles, Engraved, Archer, Heraldic Device, c.1690, 3 x 5 ¾ In.	1722.00
Cup, 2 Scroll Handles, Footed, Repousse Design, c.1731, 6 In.	840.00
Cup, Engraved, Coat Of Arms, Flared, Footed, Thomas Robins, c.1813, 4 x 3 In.	702.00
Cup, Footed, Lily Of The Valley, Handle, 1862, 5 In.	403.00
Cup, Victorian, Repousse, Tapered Cylinder, Scroll Handle, London, 1863, 4 ½ x 3 ⅞ In.	300.00
Dessert Serving Spoon, Bacchanalian, Lias & Wakely, London, c.1885, 9 In., Pair	675.00
Dish, Lid, Rectangular, Ribbed, Twig Handle, Engraved Crest, R. Crossley, 7 x 12 In.	1770.00
Dish, Shell Shape, Scalloped, Scroll Handle, Lions, Shell Feet, 1772, Pair	1185.00
Egg Coddler, 4 Cups, Spoons, Lobed Tray, Crichton Bros., c.1916, 7 ½ In., 9 Piece	1375.00
Egg Coddler, Oval, Scroll Feet, Rooster Finial, Electro Plate Nickel, D. & S.G. Sheffield, 11 In.	150.00
Egg Server, Shell & Leaf Edged, Scroll Heart Shape Handle, Paw Feet, 1825, 9 In.	2726.00
Egg, Easter, Gilt Hippo Inside, Arising From Waves, Oval, c.1955, 3 In.	708.00
Epergne, Domed, Rocaille, 4 Baskets, Caryatid Legs, Leaf Feet, Hutton & Sons, c.1894, 11 x 30 In.	5000.00
Epergne, Edwardian, Trumpet Shape Vase, 2 Scroll Arms, Deakin & Sons, c.1905, 11 x 12 In., Pair	3000.00
Epergne, Trumpet Vase, 2 Scroll Arms & Dishes, Paw Feet, c.1905, 11 x 12 In., Pair.	3000.00
Ewer, Ecclesiastic, Glass, Maltese Cross Finial, Angular Handle, 1925, 7 In., Pair.	270.00
Fish Slice, Fiddle Pattern, Pierced, Trapezoidal, 1809-10, 11 ¾ In.	153.00
Frame, 2 Openings, Enamel, Repousse, Arts & Crafts, 4 ½ x 3 In.	750.00
Goblet, Edwardian, Thistle Shape, Laurel Swags, Knopped Foot, Gilt, c.1901, 5 ⅞ In., Pair....	1230.00
Goblet, Lobed, Gold Wash Interior, HP LP, c.1940, 5 ⅛ In., 18 Piece	6075.00
Grape Scissors, Gilt, Grape Clusters On Handles, 1809, 7 ½ In.	270.00
Hot Water Urn, Armorial, Engraved Lion, Ax, Crown, W. Brind, c.1883, 13 In.	1062.00
Hot Water Urn, Lid, Fluted, Square Base, Craddock & Reid Touch, c.1816, 14 ½ In.	5103.00
Incense Burner, Seal Of Oman, Saucer, Oval Canister, Mappin & Webb, 1963, 6 ½ x 5 ½ In..	403.00
Jug, Hot Water, Engraved Lion Holding Cross, D. Smith Robert Sharp, c.1788, 8 In.	708.00
Kettle, Hot Water, Engraved, Openwork, Feet, Flower Finial, Martin, Hall & Co., c.1880, 14 In.....*Illus*	2714.00

Kettle, Hot Water, Scroll, Shell & Flowers, Wicker Wrapped Handle, Ball Feet, 1903, 14 In. 2478.00

Ladle, Shell Handle, 15 In. 236.00

Liquor Label, Whiskey, 2 Scotch, Repousse, Shells, Leaves, Mask, London, 2 ⅛ x 2 In., 3 Piece. 127.00

Marrow Scoop, Pointed Shoulders, 8 ¾ In. 246.00

Mirror, Easel Back, Rococo Engraved, William Comyns, London, 1898, 17 x 13 In. 750.00

Muffineer, Monogram, Maker's Mark, Jay, Richard Attenborough & Co., 1900s, 9 In. 270.00

Mug, Baluster, Acanthus Crest, Double Scroll Handle, c.1765, 4 x 4 ½ In. 307.00

Mug, Repousse Flowers & Scrolls, Shaped Handle, Fleming, 1720, 4 In. 590.00

Mug, Tapered, Ribbed Bands, Ear Shape Handle, 1810, 3 ¼ In. 563.00

Mustard Pot, Chased Leaves, Shell Thumb Latch, Liner, Bateman Family, 1800, 3 In. 1003.00

Mustard Pot, Cylindrical, Fluted Legs, Ball Feet, C-Scroll Handle, Dome Lid, c.1780, 4 In. 430.00

Mustard Pot, Round, Shell Thumb Latch, Engraved Owl Crest, Marked W. Plummer 236.00

Mustard, Cobalt Glass, Pierced Holder, Gold Wash Spoon, Williamson, 1919, 1 ½ x 2 In. 420.00

Napkin Rings are listed in their own category.

Nutmeg Grater, Hinged Lid, Leaf & Dart Banding, Monogram, c.1799, 1 x 2 In. 799.00

Page Turner, Scroll, Flower, Acanthus Handle, Ivory Blade, Henry Wilkinson & Co., 20 In.... *Illus* 472.00

Page Turner, Thistle Shape, Ivory, Faceted Citrine Handle, Birmingham, c.1909 1007.00

Papboat, Oval, Flared Spout, Alexander Johnston, 4 ½ x 2 ¾ In. 430.00

Pepper, Pierced Top, Pedestal Shape, c.1750, 5 ⅞ In., Pair 325.00

Pheasant, Green Marble Plinth, Asprey, c.1900, 6 ½ In., Pair 360.00

Pitcher, Scalloped Rim, 3 Lion Feet, Scrolled Handle, Marked, c.1898, 7 ½ In. 1337.00

Placecard Holder, Owl Form, Yellow Glass Eyes, Case, 1905, 1 ½ In., 6 Piece 1180.00

Plate, Sterling, Gadroon Rim, Armorial Shields, 1822, 9 ⅝ In., Pair 2160.00

Platter, Meat, Armorial, Molded Rim, Engraved, Oval, Frederick Kandler, 12 In., Pair 1888.00

Platter, Meat, Oval, Shell Cast Edge, Armorial Crest, c.1809, 17 In. 4063.00

Platter, Serpentine Lobed Oval, Gadroon Rim, Coat Of Arms, 1795, 15 x 11 In. 2214.00

Punch Ladle, Baleen Handle, Oval, Side Spout, Stephen Adams Mark, 15 ¾ In. 154.00

Punch Ladle, Fiddle Design, Elliptical Bowl, Barbour Of Stanford Crest, 1822, 14 In. 246.00

Punch Ladle, Fiddle Thread Design, Crest Of Talbot, Paul Storr, c.1811, 13 ¼ In. 861.00

Rattle, Repousse Scrolled Leaves, Flowers, Bells, Coral Tether, c.1885, 4 ¾ In. 403.00

Rattle, Whistle, Coral Handle, Birmingham, c.1820, 5 ¾ In. 296.00

Salad Set, Ivory Handle, Birmingham Mark, Date Letter, B, Lion Rampant, 9 ¾ In. 121.00

Salt, Chased Flowers, Ruffled Rim, 3 Paw Feet, Glass Inserts, E.C. Brown, 2 ¾ In., Pair 153.00

Salt, Cobalt Blue Glass Liner, Pedestal, Oval, Reeded Sides, Footed, 1 ½ x 3 In., Pair 47.00

Salt, Master, Warrior Finial, Masks, Fruit Garlands, Strapwork, c.1910, 19 In. 4063.00

Salt, Spoon, Bulbous, Gold Washed Interior, Marked, WE, c.1890, 2 In., 6 Piece 360.00

Salt, Urn Shape, 2 Handles, Crest, Peter Podie, 2 x 4 ½ In., 4 Piece 885.00

Salver, Gadroon, Beaded Swag, Ball & Claw Feet, 1773, 16 ½ In. 4720.00

Salver, Scalloped Shell Edge, Strapwork Border, Philip Goddard, c.1748, 9 In. 625.00

Salver, Scalloped Shell Edge, Strapwork, Family Crest, Richard Rugg, c.1762, 10 In. 1500.00

Salver, Scalloped, Bracket Feet, c.1718, 10 ½ In. 1888.00

Salver, Shaped Gadroon Rim, Engraved Scrolls, Leaves, R. Rugg, c.1762, 13 ¾ In. 1823.00

Salver, Shaped Gadroon Rim, Engraved Scrolls, Samuel Hennell, c.1815, 11 ¼ In. 948.00

Salver, Shaped Rim, Shells, 3-Footed, 1752, 8 ¾ In. 499.00

Salver, Shell Scalloped Edge, Presentation Text, Engraved, c.1810, 16 In. 2000.00

Salver, Wavy Edge, Applied Shell Border, 3 Hoof Feet, Round, Marked E.C., 6 ¾ In. 212.00

Sauceboat, 3-Footed, C-Shape Handle, Rippled Rim, London, c.1775, 4 x 6 ½ In. 390.00

Sauceboat, Armorial Crests, Gadroon Rim, Shell Pad Feet, William Robertson, c.1749, 9 In.. 1375.00

Sauceboat, Boat Shape, Double Scroll Handle, Leaf, 3 Cabriole Legs, c.1749, 5 ⅝ In. 720.00

Sauceboat, Engraved Armorial Design, Scrolled Handle, Gadroon, Marked, 1775-76, 9 In., Pair .. *Illus* 4200.00

Sauceboat, Georgian Style, 3 Shell Feet, Scroll Handle, 7 In., Pair 413.00

Sauceboat, Scalloped Rim, C-Scroll Handle, Scroll Supports, Samuel Meriton I, 7 In. 413.00

Secretary, Chippendale Style, Drop Front Desk, 3 Drawers, Hallmarks, Miniature, 1800s, 5 In... *Illus* 392.00

Serving Spoon, Dessert, Bacchanalian Pattern, 1884-85, 9 In., Pair 675.00

Serving Spoon, King's Design, Diamond Point Heel, Griffin's Head, c.1832, 12 In. 307.00

Soup Ladle, Hallmarked For London, 1776, 12 ¼ In. 360.00

Spoon, Fiddleback Handle, Scalloped Terminal, George Smith II, Thomas Hayter, 1822, 13 In. 300.00

Spoon, Hanau, Saint With Book, Rooster Crest, J.D, Schleissner & Son, 1902, 7 ½ In. 60.00

Standish, Crest, 4 Sections, Engraved, Ship, Motto, Scroll Feet, Howard Aldridge, 7 In. 590.00

Stuffing Spoon, Alice & George Burrows, London, c.1803, 11 ½ In. 125.00

Stuffing Spoon, Downturned, Engraved Script Initials, 1802, 12 In. 153.00

Stuffing Spoon, Fiddle Pattern, Monogram, 1808-09, 11 ⅞ In. 399.00

Stuffing Spoon, Georgian, Elliptical Bowl, Curved Handle, Thomas Dicks, 12 ¼ In. 190.00

Stuffing Spoon, Half Rib Back Tipt Handle, 1792, 12 In. 130.00

Stuffing Spoon, Hallmarks, Alice & George Burrows, c.1803, 11 ½ In. 123.00

Stuffing Spoon, Shell, Fish Scale, Shield, Gold Wash Bowl, Monogram, Paul Storr, 12 ¼ In.. 1416.00

Silver-English, Trophy, Cup, Lid, Handles, John Newton Mappin, 1888, 19 x 15 ½ In.
$3,300.00

DuMouchelles Art Gallery

Silver-Indonesian, Tea & Coffee Set, Bombe Body Repousse, Delux, c.1950, 7 Piece
$2,390.00

Sloans & Kenyon

Silver-Italian, Watering Can, Gadroon Shoulders, Bands, Flowers, Wood Handle, 1900s, 9 ¾ In.
$900.00

Skinner, Inc.

TIP

Don't wrap silver with rubber bands. The rubber increases tarnish.

Silver-Mexican, Bowl, Obsidian, Marked, Mexico, Tane, Eagle, 3 ¾ x 9 ½ In.
$7,200.00

Skinner, Inc.

Silver-Sterling, Bowl, Lid, Florenz, Repousse, Leaves, Scrolls, Monogram, Cartouches, Pinecone Finial, Gorham, 1925, 13 In.
$2,000.00

Skinner, Inc.

Silver-Sterling, Bowl, Upswept Ends, S-Scroll Wire Foot, Alfredo Sciarotta, c.1965, 10 x 5 In.
$553.00

New Orleans Auction Galleries, Inc.

Silver-Sterling, Fish Serving Set, Moresque, John R. Wendt, Starr & Marcus, c.1875, 11 ½ & 9 ⅞ In., 2 Piece
$475.00

Skinner, Inc.

S

TIP

Cigar ashes, baking soda, and water mix into a paste that is good for cleaning silver.

Stuffing Spoon, Victorian, Fiddle Thread & Shell Pattern, c.1864, 11 ⅞ In.	215.00
Sugar Basket, Flowers & Leaf Design, Wire Frame, Foot, Cobalt Blue, Gold, c.1969, 3 ½ In.	288.00
Sugar Basket, Navette Shape, Lattice, Swing Handle, Oval Foot Ring, 1766, 6 In.	922.00
Sugar Basket, Pierced, Scrolling, Swags, Medallion, Initials, Mountigue, 1784, 7 In.	1180.00
Sugar Tongs, Bow Style, Openwork Handle, Shell Grips, Monogram, c.1790, 5 In.	215.00
Sugar Tongs, Engraved Leaves, Monogram, Nathan Smith & Co., c.1803, 5 ¼ In., Pair	104.00
Sugar, Lid, Inverted Pear Shape, Fluted Cone Knop, Samuel Taylor, c.1765, 6 ½ In.	944.00
Tankard, Dome Lid, Armorial, Tapered, Molded, Humphrey Payne, c.1714, 8 In.	7080.00
Tankard, Dome Lid, Loop Handle, Stepped Ring Foot, c.1735, 8 In.	2760.00
Tankard, Hinged Dome Lid, Tapered Cylinder, c.1743, 7 In.	2070.00
Tankard, Repousse Scrolls, Flowers, Inscribed WPC, c.1748, 5 In.	767.00
Taper Stand, Gadroon Rim, Urn Shape Nozzle, Ring Handle, c.1810, 2 ½ x 4 In.	430.00
Tea & Coffee Set, Hepplewhite Style, Engraved Gothic Initial, Barker Bros., c.1930, 5 Piece	2160.00
Tea Caddy, Dome Lid, Bombe Shape, Top Shape Finial, Openwork Feet, c.1763, 6 In.	1845.00
Tea Set, Edwardian, Georgian, Fluted, Gadroon, Sloped Detail, Ebonized Handle, 3 Piece	776.00
Tea Set, Gold Washed Interior, Wood Handled Teapot, Monogram, John Emes, 3 Piece....*Illus*	2400.00
Tea Set, Ribbed Bottom, Angular Handle, W.W. Harrison, 1900, 4 Piece	1728.00
Tea Set, Teapot, Sugar, Creamer, Wood Handle, 1931, Teapot 7 ¾ In.	748.00
Teapot, Dome Lid, Gadroon Spout, Wood Handle, Banding, c.1783, 5 ¾ x 10 ½ In.	676.00
Teapot, Ebonized Wood Handle & Finial, Martin Hall & Co., c.1904, 5 x 10 In.	1159.00
Teapot, Engraved, Bright Cut Flower Basket, Leaf Borders, George Brasier, c.1794, 5 ½ In.	885.00
Teapot, Lid, Engraved Initials, London, c.1813, 5 ½ In.	590.00
Teapot, Oval, Beaded Edge, Medallions, Cherubs, Wood Handle, 1779, 5 x 9 ½ In.	1659.00
Teapot, Wood Handle & Finial, Bateman, 1801, 6 ½ In.	1116.00
Toast Rack, Leaf Handle, 6 Divided Sleeves, Shell Shape Feet, c.1837, 7 In.	1599.00
Toast Rack, Oval, Beaded Rim, Wirework Dividers, Ring Handle, Ball Feet, 5 ¼ x 7 ½ In.	922.00
Toast Rack, Regency, Shells, Openwork Handle, Arched, Gadroon, Paw Feet, c.1810, 6 x 7 In., Pair	2151.00
Toast Rack, Scroll Handle & Feet, 6 Sections, Handle, John Kilpatrick, 1861, 6 ¼ x 6 In.... *Illus*	413.00
Toddy Ladle, Engraved Oval Bowl, Spout, Carved Wood Handle, Andrew Fogelberg, 1778, 15 In.	219.00
Tray, Armorial, Engraved Crest, Motto, Oval, Handles, c.1780, 27 In.	6136.00
Tray, Concave Lozenge, Footed, Shell & Scroll, Flowers, 1824, 17 ½ In.	5036.00
Tray, Engraved, Crest, Chased Acorn, Oak Leaf, Fruit Vine, Samuel Kirk, c.1830, 13 ½ In.	944.00
Tray, Gallery, Flowers, Strapwork Engraved, Octagonal, Martin Hall & Co., c.1900, 3 x 23 In.	805.00
Tray, Oval, Walker & Hall, Sheffield, c.1914, 15 x 22 In.	1659.00
Tray, Round, Beaded Border, Heraldic Shield, 1785, 16 In.	2950.00
Tray, Scroll & Shell Border, Scroll & Acanthus Feet, Flowers, 1754, 12 ½ In.	1416.00
Tray, Scrolled Edge, Leaves & Strapwork Designs, Round, c.1873, 20 In.	4063.00
Tray, Serving, Rectangular, Gadroon Edge, 2 Leaf Handles, 1932, 24 x 15 In.	2963.00
Tray, Shaped Oval, Monogram, Black, Starr & Gorham, c.1941, 16 ¼ In.	938.00
Trophy, Cup, Lid, Handles, John Newton Mappin, 1888, 19 x 15 ½ In. ....*Illus*	3300.00
Tureen, Lid, Gadroon Border, Shell Feet, Coat Of Arms, c.1771, 11 x 16 In.	7000.00
Tureen, Sauce, Finial, Chased, Pedestal Base, High Handles, H. Chawner, 1790, 9 x 5 In.	403.00
Tureen, Sauce, Oval, Gadroon, Reeded Rim, Arched Handles, c.1796, 7 x 9 ½ In.	1599.00
Tureen, Soup, Dome Lid, George III Style, Chased, Repousse Flowers, Handles, 15 x 21 In.	8400.00
Urn, Dome Lid, Gold Washed, Grapes, Leaves, Scroll Handles, c.1827, 14 ¾ In.	5925.00
Urn, Lid, Georgian, Classical, Oval Finial, Reeded, Flared Foot, Henry Chawner, 8 ½ x 4 In.	677.00
Vase, Bud, Oval, Spool Top, Turned Shaft, Bird & Berry Handles, c.1895, 7 ¼ In.	518.00
Vinaigrette, Hinged Lid, Gold Washed, Grapes Border, Leaves, 1814-15, 1 ½ In.	770.00
Vinaigrette, T. & W.S., Birmingham, 1824, 1 x ¾ In.	270.00
Waiter, Engraved Crest, Gadroon Edge, 3-Footed, E. Cooke, c.1772, 14 In.	2360.00
Waiter, Georgian, Raised Rim, Engraved, Richard Rugg Touch, 1759-60, 7 ⅜ In.	395.00
Waiter, Raised Scalloped Edge, Engraved, J. Smith To J. Smith, 1788, 7 In.	533.00
Waiter, Scalloped, Wolf Crest, Flowers, Monogram, 3, Hoof Feet, J. Carter, c.1770, 9 In.	1770.00
Waiter, Shaped Gadroon Rim, Round, 7 In.	504.00
Water Urn, Urn Shape, Embossed Band, Handles, Shield, Wakelin & Taylor, c.1790, 21 In.	8888.00
Wine Coaster, Pierced Sides, Grapevines, Flowers, Shells, Barnard, c.1843, 6 In., Pair	2950.00
Wine Funnel, Half Ribbed, Wm. Bateman, 5 ½ In.	295.00
Wine Taster, Wirework Scroll Handles, Punchwork, Repousse, Marked, 5 x 1 In.	922.00

SILVER-FINNISH

Dish, Round, Upswept Scrolling Handle, 3 Cone Shape Feet, Finland, 1956, 5 x 5 In.	173.00

SILVER-FRENCH

Bowl, Couple, Lounging, Field, Wavy Rim, Boat Shape, Embossed, E.E. & B., 1800s, 15 In.	3025.00
Bowl, Mirror Plateau, Art Deco, Ebony Handles, Tetard Freres, 16 ½ x 8 In.	14088.00
Case, Cosmetic, Pierced, Gems, 3 Compartments, Marked Boucheron, Paris, c.1950, 5 In.	875.00
Chalice, Rosewood Base, Jean Puiforcat, c.1930, 6 ⅝ In.	9375.00

Coffeepot, Flower Finial, Ebonized Wood Handle, 7 ¾ In.	295.00
Dish, Pierced Rim, Classical Festoons, Marked Lefebvre, 3 x 11 In.	330.00
Jam Jar, Glass Insert, Embossed Women, Griffin Handles, Square Foot, Jean-Pierre Bibron, 8 In.	476.00
Jug, Hot Water, Hinged Lid, Scrolled Leaf Pattern, Reeded Rim, Ebony Handle, c.1825, 9 In.	518.00
Mustard Pot, Lid, Cobalt Blue Glass, Cornucopia, Upscrolled Handle, 1800s, 4 ½ In.	225.00
Plate, First Standard Gilt, Wavy Rope & Flower Rim, Coronet, 2 Shields, Round, 10 ½ In.	767.00
Plate, Laurel Wreath, Floral Swag Border, Gold Washed, Round, c.1860, 10 ¼ In.	420.00
Saucepan, Bracket Spout, Molded Rim, Wood Handle, 2 ½ x 10 ¾ In.	410.00
Tea & Coffee Set, Creamer, Sugar, Lid, Acanthus, Scroll Foot, Emile Puiforcat, c.1910, 4 Piece	4200.00
Tray, Chased Figural Scene, Pierced Border, Oval, 10 ¾ In.	325.00
Tray, Flattened Rim, Repousse Fruits, Vegetables & Nuts, Reims, 10 ½ In.	422.00
Trinket Box, Repousse, Bacchus & Woman Feasting, Scrolling, Hinged Lid, France, 3 x 5 In.	374.00
Urn, Lid, Empire, Cut Crystal, Scroll Handles, Desiree Toussaint Legrand, c.1820, 9 x 7 In.	600.00
Wine Taster, Round, Lobed, Handle, Inscribed, 1903, 3 ¼ In.	230.00

SILVER-GERMAN

Basket, Baroque Style, Repousse Scrolls, Flowers, Pierced Handle, Rectangular, 4 ½ x 8 In.	1080.00
Basket, Glass Handle, Flowers, Sea Scrolls, Lattice, Scalloped Rim, Footed, c.1900, 5 In.	210.00
Basket, Reticulated, Ribbons, Swing Handle, Clear Glass Liner, 9 ¾ In., Pair	938.00
Beaker, Cylindrical, Embossed, Imperial Busts, Fruit Garland, Molded, Ball Feet, c.1900, 4 In.	1230.00
Beaker, Cylindrical, Slight Taper, Reeded Ring Foot, Rolled Rim, Leaves, Acorns, c.1900, 5 In.	885.00
Beaker, Parcel Gilt, Tapering Sides, Wreath & Crown, Spread Foot, 1700s, 5 x 4 ⅜ In.	1770.00
Boat, Putti, Flowers, Scrolling, Hanau Hallmarks, c.1900, 2 ½ x 6 In.	540.00
Bowl, Egyptian Revival, Sphinxes, Medusa Heads, Gilt, Tripod, Paw Feet, 1800s, 6 x 4 In.	510.00
Bowl, Renaissance Style, Young Wood Nymphs, Birds, Flowers, Repousse, Oval, c.1900, 13 In.	780.00
Bowl, Reticulated, Leaves, Flowers, Ram's Head Terminals, Oval, Glass Liner, 11 x 18 In.	3438.00
Bowl, Ribbed Body, 3 Figural Feet, c.1855, 5 ½ In., Pair	153.00
Bowl, Shaped Rim, Irises, Scrolling Leaves, Leaf Handles, Tiered Foot, c.1902, 7 ½ In. Diam.	326.00
Bowl, Urn Shape, 2 C-Scroll Handles, Spread Foot, Stop Reed Body, 7 ¾ x 18 In.	1534.00
Box, Hinged, Repousse, Cherubs, Garden, Oval, Stippled Ground, c.1910, 2 ⅜ x 7 ¾ In.	900.00
Centerpiece, Basket, Eagle Head Handles, Openwork Scroll Leaves, Pedestal, c.1890, 11 ½ In.	720.00
Centerpiece, Reticulated, Ribbons, Masks, Swags, Wheelbarrow Shape, c.1910, 7 x 17 ½ In.	7500.00
Chalice, Jacobean Style, Oval, Embossed Panels, Baluster Stem, Domed Foot, c.1885, 7 ¾ In.	676.00
Chop Plate, Deep Well, Shaped Edge, J. Wagner & Sohn, 1 ¼ x 13 In., Pair	1380.00
Cocktail Shaker, Ogee Dome Lid, Tapered, Cylindrical, Monogram, c.1935, 8 In.	369.00
Creamer, Hinged Lid, Cow Shape, Fly Finial, Flower Rim, J.D. Schleissner Sohne, c.1900, 5 In.	1416.00
Dish, Sweetmeat, Oval, Reticulated, Scrollwork, Leaves, Cherubs, Pierced Foot, c.1900, 4 x 9 In.	415.00
Ewer, Wine, Armorial, Leaf Tip Band, Arched Handle, Marked JG Augsburg, 13 In.	2223.00
Fish Slice, Stamped D Within Triangle, Crescent, Crown, 800, Germany, 11 ½ In.	108.00
Fruit Basket, Repousse, Tapered Oval, Wavy Rim, c.1910, 2 ¼ x 12 ¼ In.	900.00
Jewelry Casket, Hinged Lid, Reticulated, Scroll Feet, Velvet Lined, 3 x 3 ½ x 2 In.	299.00
Platter, Oval, Shaped, H.J. Wilm, Berlin, 23 ¾ x 15 ¾ In.	1495.00
Serving Dish, Arts & Crafts, Oval, Hammered, Louis Werner, c.1910, 12 ¼ In.	420.00
Soup Ladle, Oval Bowl, Tapered, c.1850, 13 ½ In.	178.00
Stirrup Cup, Boar's Head Stand, Over Flared Cup, Inscribed, WIM, 1933, 6 ⅞ x 4 In.	1440.00
Sugar & Creamer, Baluster Shape, Shaped Rococo Rim, Scroll Handles, c.1915, 2 ¾ x 5 In.	307.00
Tea Strainer, Cloisonne, Gilt, Round Pierced Spatulate Handle, 1955, 4 ½ In.	215.00
Teapot, Urn, Leaf Bands, Flowers, Trumpet Foot, Beast Shape Handle, Ivory Tail, c.1800, 8 In.	796.00
Tongs, Beaded Handle, Spade Shape Blade, Quatrefoil Latticework, Scrollwork, c.1885, 11 In.	73.00
Tray, Neoclassical, Pierced Gallery, Scrolled Feet, 11 In.	1000.00
Tray, Repousse, Oval, Reticulated Border, Musical Cherubs, Cornucopia, 17 In.	920.00
Wedding Cup, Sterling, Figural, Woman Wearing Long Dress, Stamped, 5 In.	210.00

SILVER-HUNGARIAN

Box, Hinged Lid, Cushion Shape, Lobed, Rose Blossom Finial, S-Scroll Feet, 4 ½ x 5 In.	415.00
Dish, Lobed, Blossoms, Scrolling Vines, Flower Bracket Feet, c.1900, 14 ¾ x 11 ½ In.	504.00

SILVER-INDIAN

Bowl, High Relief Figures, Dancing, Inverted Rim, Peacock Stamp, 2 ⅓ x 3 ½ In.	98.00
Chocolate Pot, Wood Handle, 3 Paw Feet, 7 In.	420.00

SILVER-INDONESIAN

Tea & Coffee Set, Bombe Body Repousse, Delux, c.1950, 7 Piece ....*Illus*	2390.00

SILVER-IRISH

Coffeepot, Armorial, Engraved, Turned Finial, Leaf Spout, Treen Handle, 1700s, 8 ½ In.	28750.00
Coffeepot, Sterling, Lobed, Repousse Flowers, Scroll Handle, E. Power, c.1830, 9 In.	1080.00
Ladle, Old English Pattern, Mid-Rib Handle, 12 ¼ In.	307.00
Pitcher, Gravy, 3 Hoof Feet, Gadroon Edge, Scroll Handle, Dublin, 8 x 5 In.	563.00

TIP

Don't store alcoholic beverages or perfume in silver containers. It will cause damage.

Silver-Sterling, Pitcher, Water, Tulip Buds, Low Relief, Arthur Stone, Herbert A. Taylor, c.1908-37, 8 ⅞ In. $7,000.00

Skinner, Inc.

Silver-Sterling, Rose Bowl, Openwork Leaves, Monogram, Ferdinand Fuchs & Bros., c.1900, 5 ¾ x 9 In. $708.00

Brunk Auctions

Silver-Sterling, Vase, Flower Petals Extending From Rim, Tapered, Monogram, Gorham, 1900, 7 ¼ In. $800.00

Skinner, Inc.

S

Sleepy Eye, Pitcher, Blue, White, No. 5, 9 In.
$270.00

Showtime Auction Services

Snuffbox, Silver, Hinged Lid, Shell Shape, Repousse Design, Hallmarks, 1 ½ In.
$780.00

DuMouchelles Art Gallery

TIP

Victorian table manners included this rule: Always sip your soup from the side of the spoon, never the tip.

Spatterware, Bowl, Sunburst Flower, Rose & Green, Stamped Blue Blossoms, Leaves, Borders, 15 In.
$94.00

Conestoga Auction Co., Inc.

Punch Bowl, William Thompson, Dublin, 1796, 7 In.	2280.00
Sauceboat, 3 Scroll Supports, C-Scroll Handle, Henry Waldron, c.1755, 8 ½ In.	1121.00
Tea Set, Sterling, Squat, Repousse Flowers, Mask Knees, J. Le Bass, c.1828, 3 Piece	3900.00
Teapot, Sailing Ship, Engraved, Repousse, Squat, Long Neck, Richard Sawyer, 11 In.	1955.00

SILVER-ITALIAN

Bell, Service, Openwork Acanthus & Flowers, 2 ¼ x 3 In.	236.00
Bowl, Chased Leaves, Shells, Lobed, Scroll Flower Handles, Open Stem, Domed Foot, 6 x 18 In.	2500.00
Bowl, Chased, Pierced Rim, Lobed, Stippled, Scroll Leaf Handles, Shell Feet, Florence, 7 x 22 In.	3125.00
Bowl, Chased, Repousse Leaves, Shells, Lobed, Scroll Leaf Handles, Domed Foot, 6 x 18 In.	2500.00
Bowl, Oval, Pierced Rim, Engraved Flowers, Stippled, Lobed, Scroll Leaf Handles, 7 x 22 In.	3125.00
Bowl, Scroll Leaf Handles, Fluted, Oval, c.1970, 5 ½ x 16 In.	1375.00
Box, Chased, Flowers, Leaves, Carnelian Medallion, Hinged Lid, Mask Supports, 1800s, 8 x 9 In.	2400.00
Centerpiece, Octopus, Shell Shape Dish, Footed, Buccellati, c.1985, 16 In.	11900.00
Compote, Grapes, Leaves, Twisted Twig, Nymph, Satyr Standard, 9 x 10 In.	2125.00
Compote, Satyr, Nymph, Grapevines, Twig Shape Standard, Domed Foot, 9 x 10 In.	2125.00
Dish, Leaf Shape, Buccellati, 2 x 7 In.	1440.00
Dish, Round, Radiating Fluted Design, Scalloped Rim, Hammered, Buccellati, 13 In. Diam.	956.00
Salt, Empire Style, Cast, Sheet, Wavy Engraved Rim, Marked, c.1865, 2 ⅛ x 3 ⅜ In., Pair	177.00
Water Font, Oval Medallion, Applied Gilt Figure, Laurel Frame, 5-Arm Scroll, Glass Insert, 12 In.	449.00
Watering Can, Gadroon Shoulders, Bands, Flowers, Wood Handle, 1900s, 9 ¾ In. *Illus*	900.00

SILVER-JAPANESE

Cigarette Case, Velvet Lining, Chased, Engraved, Nagasaki Shipyard & Engine Works, 6 x 3 In.	633.00
Kettle, Sake, Engraved, Diamonds, Cranes, Trees, Bamboo, Swing Handle, 1700s, 9 x 6 ¾ In.	3738.00
Tray, Dresser, Carved Duck, Carnelian, Diamond Shape, Greek Key Border, 1900s, 4 x 3 In.	214.00

SILVER-LATVIAN

Cigarette Case, Samorodok, Blue Glass Inset Cabochon Thumbpiece, c.1900, 4 x 3 In.	489.00

SILVER-MEXICAN

Belt Buckle, Rectangular, Applied Onyx Tube, Marked Antonio Pineda, 1 ½ x 5 ½ In.	660.00
Bowl, Applied Swirl Edge, Paw Feet, Octagonal, Mark, A. Torred Vega, 4 In.	177.00
Bowl, Flower Shape, 3 Ball Feet, Stamped Hecho En Mexico, 3 x 8 In.	240.00
Bowl, Obsidian, Marked, Mexico, Tane, Eagle, 3 ¾ x 9 ½ In. *Illus*	7200.00
Bowl, Oval, Lobed, Flower Design Handles, Undertray, 4 ½ x 17 In.	2875.00
Bowl, Revere, Stepped Foot, Lunt, V Monogram, Inscription, 8 In.	384.00
Bowl, Round Lobed Shape, Hammered, 2 Handles, Flower Rim, Marked, c.1900, 12 ⅕ In.	1080.00
Coffee & Hot Chocolate Set, Sphere Finials, Bulbous Base, William Spratling, 1930s, 4 Piece	1800.00
Goblet, Oval, Flared Rim, Waisted Stem, Domed Foot, 7 ⅜ x 3 ⅛ In., 12 Piece	1968.00
Hors D'Oeuvre Pick Set, Hand Wrought, 12 Mexican Designs, 35 Piece	115.00
Ladle, Sanborn, 10 ½ In.	150.00
Pitcher, Water, Chased, Squat, Sanborn, 8 ¾ In.	885.00
Pitcher, Water, Oval, Rolled Rim, Integral Spout, Strap Handle, Berry Design, c.1965, 8 x 6 In.	399.00
Plate, Serving, Round, Scroll Border, Recessed Plateau, c.1965, 11 In. Diam.	615.00
Platter, Round, Repousse Roses On Rim, c.1950, 15 ½ In. Diam.	984.00 to 1476.00
Punch Bowl, Hammered, Grape Cluster Handles, Footed, Sanborns, 9 x 18 In.	5228.00
Punch Bowl, Impressed Lobe, Stepped Base, 8 ½ x 13 In.	2090.00
Serving Dish, Rectangular, Ribbed Edges & Handles, Open, 1900s, 17 ¼ x 10 ¾ In.	1126.00
Serving Spoon, Flower & Leaf Handle, 11 In.	120.00
Shot Cup, Thimble Shape, Inscribed, Just A Thimbleful, c.1980, 1 ¾ x 1 ⅝ In.	86.00
Sugar & Creamer, Chased Flowers, Birds, Sanborn, Handles, 2 ½ In.	224.00
Tray, Lobed, Scalloped Rim, Round, Marciel, 15 In.	878.00
Tray, Oval, Lobed Border, Scrolling Rim, C-Scroll Handles, 25 In.	1673.00
Tray, Scroll & Flower Border, Handles, c.1900, 19 x 11 In.	1003.00

SILVER-PERUVIAN

Tray, Rectangular, Molded Edge, 18 In.	1003.00

SILVER-RUSSIAN. Russian silver is marked with the Cyrillic, or Russian, alphabet. The numbers 84, 88, or 91 indicate the silver content. Russian silver may be higher or lower than sterling standard. Other marks indicate maker, assayer, or city of manufacture. Many pieces of silver made in Russia are decorated with enamel. Silver prices in 2012 became so high many pieces were worth more in meltdown value than as decorative silver. These prices are based on current silver values. Faberge pieces are listed in their own category.

Asparagus Tongs, Articulated, 19th Century, 9 x 3 ¾ In.	348.00
Box, Cigar, Faux Bois, Cyrillic Inscriptions, Strapwork, Monogram, Russia, c.1895, 2 ¼ x 8 In.	3851.00
Cigarette Case, Hinged Lid, Enamel, Repousse, Scrollwork, Painted, Cabochon, c.1900, 4 ½ In.	5040.00
Cigarette Case, Lid, Enamel, Round Corners, Octagonal Cartouche, Reclining Woman, c.1900, 4 In.	4800.00

Cup & Saucer, Blue & Green, Flowers & Scroll Bead Design, C-Shape Handle, 1895, 4 ⅞ In. ...	4720.00
Cup, Engraved, Imperator's River Yacht Club, Double Eagle, Kokoshnik, 1911, 4 x 2 ¼ In.	1200.00
Cup, Gilt, Enamel, Flared Ring Base, Flowers, Beaded Rim, Geometric Handle, c.1900, 3 In. ...	11400.00
Cup, Vodka, Sterling, Flared Lip, Engraved, Buildings, Leaves, Geometric Borders, 2 x 2 In.	92.00
Egg, Cloisonne, Geometric Center Band, Medallions, Scrolling Leaves, Marked, c.1900, 2 In. ...	2880.00
Figurine, Bulldog, Seated, Gilt Collar, Ruby Stone Eyes, Moscow, c.1920, 4 ½ In.	1625.00
Flaggen, Tapered, Stepped Borders, Loop Handle, Horse Thumbpiece, Bust, c.1875, 8 x 6 In. ...	3775.00
Glasses Case, Niello Enamel, Chased Eye, Moscow, 1857, 2 ½ x 6 In.	546.00
Kovsh, Gilt, Enamel, Hook Handle, Scrolling Leaves, Flowers, Beaded Rim, c.1900, 6 In.	7200.00
Salt, Squat Shape, 3 Ball Feet, Marked, 1 ½ x ½ In., Pair	69.00
Serving Spoon, Gilt, Enamel, Almond Shaped Bowl, Twist Handle, Bell Flowers, Case, c.1900, 7 In.	1800.00
Serving Spoon, Gilt, Enamel, Imperial 2 Headed Eagle, Beading, Twist Handle, c.1900, 7 In. ...	780.00
Spoon, Enamel, Cloisonne Pan Slavic Design, Multicolor, Stamped, c.1892, 5 ¾ x 3 In.	460.00
Tea Glass, Holder, Enamel, Green Ground, Gold Wash Interior, 1800s, 4 x 4 In.	1035.00
Teapot, Gilt, Fluted Lid, Domed Foot, Oval, Grapevines, Snake Handle, Snakeskin, 1813, 8 In.	6600.00
Teapot, Gilt, Hinged Lid, Cloisonne, Flowers, Stippled Ground, Loop Handle, c.1895, 5 In.	5520.00
Tray, Gilt, Champleve Enamel, Elongated Oval, Strapwork Design, Flowers, Banded, 1876, 5 In. ...	1800.00
Warming Pan, Giltwash Interior, Ivory Handle, c.1915, 3 ½ x 8 ¼ In.	550.00

SILVER-SCANDINAVIAN

Beaker, Engraved Flowers, Barrel Shape, Flared Rim, 3 Ball Feet, c.1724, 2 ¾ In.	748.00

SILVER-SCOTTISH

Mustard Ladle, Victorian, Queen's Pattern, Gilt Bowl, Monogram SH, Alexander Coghill, 1851, 6 In.	98.00
Salt & Pepper, Pedestal Shape, 1798, 6 ½ In.	153.00
Teapot, Gadroon Body, Ball Feet, Ebonized Handle, Scrolling, Rosette, 1894, 9 ½ x 9 In.	1064.00
Urn, Flared, Ribbed, Footed, Harlequin Coat Of Arms, 1822, 8 ½ In.	1298.00

SILVER-STERLING. Sterling silver is made with 925 parts silver out of 1,000 parts of metal. The word *sterling* is a quality guarantee used in the United States after about 1860. The word was used much earlier in England and Ireland. Pieces listed here are not identified by country. Silver prices in 2012 became so high many pieces were worth more in meltdown value than as decorative silver. These prices are based on current silver values. Other pieces of sterling quality silver are listed under Silver-American, Silver-English, etc.

Aspic Server, Art Nouveau, Lily Handle, Silvercraft, 12 In.	150.00
Basket, Pierced, Flared, Divided Handle, 8 ½ In., Pair	295.00
Basket, Sweetmeat, Oval, Flowers, Scrolls, Pierced Stars, Swing Handle, 1700s, 1 ¾ x 6 ¼ In.	338.00
Basket, Tapered, Footed, Shaped Handle, 13 ¼ In.	203.00
Beaker, Arts & Crafts, Hammered, Chased Stylized Flower Band, 3 ½ x 2 ¼ In.	121.00
Beaker, Round Stepped Foot, Half Ribs, Alternating Inverted Ribs, c.1767, 8 In.	1150.00
Beaker, Stand, Louis XV, Gilt, Bell Shape, Molded Rim & Foot, c.1739, 2 ¼ x 2 ¼ In.	553.00
Beer Mug, Tapered Cylinder, Molded, Reeded Banding, Scroll Handle, c.1807, 6 In.	1476.00
Bonbon, Oval, Openwork Sides, Embossed Lattice Loops, Scrolls, c.1915, 8 ¼ x 6 ¼ In.	110.00
Bowl, Chrysanthemum Blossoms, Flared Rim, c.1900, 15 In. Diam.	1586.00
Bowl, Flower, Domed Frog Lid, Banding, Leaf & Dart Edge, Cavetto Foot, Finial, c.1910, 4 In.	369.00
Bowl, Flowers & Sailboat, Castles, Bridges, Pedestal, Spread Foot, c.1900, 6 ⅜ x 8 ¾ In.	2360.00
Bowl, Fruit, Lobed Body, Wavy, Flared Rim, Flowers, Leaves, Monogram, 3 x 9 ½ In.	430.00
Bowl, Fruit, Oval, Flared Rim, Openwork Flowers, Leaves, c.1915, 2 ½ x 12 In.	553.00
Bowl, Fruit, Upswept Sides, Rococo Scrolls, Scroll Border, Whiplash Feet, c.1924, 4 x 11 In.	1230.00
Bowl, Gold Wash, Musical Instrument Scenes, Monogram, Medallions, Roses, Footed, 4 x 9 In.	590.00
Bowl, Hexagonal, Shaped Rim, Band Of Hollyhocks, c.1915, 12 In. Diam.	799.00
Bowl, Lid, Engraved, Scrolling Leaves, Vines, Ring Foot, Chrysanthemum Finial, 1700s, 4 x 6 In.	3450.00
Bowl, Lid, Florenz, Leaves, Scrolls, Monogram, Cartouches, Pinecone Finial, Gorham, 1925, 13 In. *Illus*	2000.00
Bowl, Medallion, Leaf Swags, Monogram, Round Foot, Reeded Banding Rim, c.1765, 5 ½ In.	2400.00
Bowl, Molded Rim, Oval Leaf Cartouches, Pierced Handles, Reeded, c.1900, 9 ¾ In.	922.00
Bowl, Openwork Sides, Dancing Cupid, Bellflower & Scroll, Footed, 2 ½ x 14 In.	413.00
Bowl, Oval, Reticulated Border, Openwork Urn Medallions, Square Footed Base, 5 x 17 In.	1495.00
Bowl, Oval, Reticulated, Embossed Fruit & Leaves, Hunting Motif, 1900s, 1 ½ x 10 ⅜ In.	415.00
Bowl, Repousse, Maids, Satyrs, Instruments, Woodland, Footed, Shell Handles, 1800s, 13 In. ...	2070.00
Bowl, Round, Leaf Shape Handles, Twig Gallery, Tiered Spread Foot, 1900s, 9 ¾ In. Diam.	1659.00
Bowl, Shallow, Scalloped, Oval, Cast Flower Handles, 1 ½ x 14 ¾ In.	688.00
Bowl, Shell Decorated, Flared Rim, Round, Hoof Footed Legs, 3 ¼ x 5 ¾ In.	345.00
Bowl, Squat, Shaped Rim, Applied Rococo Style Relief, Monogram, Marked, 5 ¾ x 2 In.	236.00
Bowl, Upswept Ends, S-Scroll Wire Foot, Alfredo Sciarotta, c.1965, 10 x 5 In. ...... *Illus*	553.00
Bowl, Vegetable, Lid, Acanthus Handle, Neoclassical Urns, Garlands, 1914, 11 ½ In.	1140.00
Bowl, Waisted Foot Ring, Lattice Band, Flower Medallion, Molded Rim, 1913, 1 x 7 In.	430.00
Box, Checkered Style, Canted Corners, 1 ¼ x 3 ½ x 5 In.	270.00

Spatterware, Cup & Saucer, Peafowl, Blue, Green, Red, Handleless Cup, 2 ¾ In. & 5 ¾ In.
$142.00

Conestoga Auction Co., Inc.

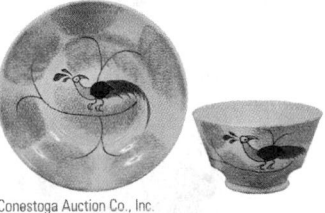

Spatterware, Cup & Saucer, Peafowl, Green, Handleless Cup, 2 ½ x 5 ¾ In.
$266.00

Conestoga Auction Co., Inc.

Spatterware, Cup & Saucer, Rainbow, Red & Blue, 2 ¾ x 5 ¾ In.
$130.00

Conestoga Auction Co., Inc.

Spatterware, Pitcher, Rainbow, Yellow & Purple, Sponge, Wide Spout, Loop Handle, 4 ⅜ In.
$130.00

Conestoga Auction Co., Inc.

S

> **TIP**
> *Don't clean a brass mortar and pestle. It lowers the value.*

Spatterware, Plate, Rabbits Playing Cricket, Virginia Rose, Rabbitware, English Registry Mark, c.1900, 9 ¼ In. $529.00

Garth's Auctioneers & Appraisers

Spelter, Sculpture, Siffleur, Whistler, Charles Vital Cornu, Fabrication Francaise Paris, 26 x 13 ½ In. $826.00

Brunk Auctions

Spinning Wheel, Mixed Woods, Blue Paint, 1800s, 38 In. $118.00

Garth's Auctioneers & Appraisers

Box, Dome Lid, Seated Woman Nude Finial, Putti, At War, Chased, Casket Shape, 6 ½ x 7 In... 1625.00
Brandy Warmer, Round Bowl, Molded Edge & Spout, Spread Foot, Wood Handle, 1900s, 3 In. 444.00
Brandy Warmer, William IV, Bulbous, Domed Lift-Off Lid, Treen Handle, Crest, c.1830, 5 In. 717.00
Bread Basket, Hammered, Pierced Edge, Split Handle, 13 ½ x 6 In. 196.00
Bread Plate, Chased Scroll Border, Flower Sprays, Monogram, 6 ¾ In. Diam. 179.00
Bread Tray, Oval, Flared Rim, Embossed Flowers, Wheat, Scrolls, Shells, c.1965, 12 x 7 In. 276.00
Butter Warmer, Beaker Shape, Flared Lip, Tapered, Reeded Foot, Wood Handle, 1764, 2 ¾ In. 652.00
Candelabra are listed in the Candelabrum category.
Candlesticks are listed in their own category.
Candy Dish, Repousse, Basket, Swing Handle, Flowers, Leaves, Trumpet Foot, c.1900, 4 In. 429.00
Carafe, Flower Overlay, Green Glass, 6 ¾ x 8 In. 1035.00
Celery Dish, Wide Rim, Monogram, J.S. Co., 11 In. 176.00
Claret Jug, Ribbed Crystal Body, Starcut Base, Scroll Handle, Wide Spout, 9 ⅞ In. 598.00
Coaster, Flower Chased Rim, Shallow Center, 6 ⅜ In., 12 Piece. 1875.00
Cocktail Shaker, Tapered, Cylinder, Reeded Banding, Square Handle, c.1900, 10 ¾ x 4 In. 861.00
Coffeepot, Acorn Finial, Scroll & Leaf Spout, Wood Handle, Tiered Foot, c.1950, 9 In. 563.00
Coffeepot, Cone Shape, Hinged Domed Spout, Wooden Handle, 1718, 9 ¾ x 6 ¼ In. 6150.00
Coffeepot, Dome Lid, Tapered, Flower Finial, Beast, Wood Handle, 1733, 9 ½ In. 1007.00
Coffeepot, Dome Lid, Wood Loop Handle, Dragon Spout, c.1800, 7 ½ x 5 In. 450.00
Coffeepot, Octagonal, Long Neck, Scallop Rim, Gooseneck Spout, Scroll Handle, c.1935, 9 In. 430.00
Coffeepot, Tapering Sides, Ring Foot, Scrolled Wood Handle, Stepped Lid, 1700s, 8 In. 1320.00
Coffeepot, Tiered Dome Lid, Baluster, Leaf Finial, Scrolling Leaf Spout, 1765, 10 In. 1126.00
Coffeepot, Wood Square Handle, S-Spout, Reeded Bottom, Narrow Neck, Finial, Gorham, 9 In. 316.00
Compote, Embossed Border, Tall Narrow Stem, Flared Rim, Round Base, c.1900, 5 In., Pair 270.00
Compote, Handles, Leaves, Round Stepped Pedestal Foot, c.1900, 7 In. 240.00
Compote, Lobed Rim, Architectural Scenes, Flowers, Scrolls, Domed Foot, 9 In. 1168.00
Compote, Splayed Foot, Shell & Scroll Rim, 6 ½ x 3 ½ In. 178.00
Compote, Wavy Rim, Embossed Grape Clusters, Vines, Trumpet Foot, c.1885, 6 x 11 In. 461.00
Cordial, Inverted Pear Shape, Raised Foot Pedestal, Marked C EP, 4 In., 6 Piece. 130.00
Creamer, Oval, Reeded Rim, Shoulder Bands, Spout, Monogram, c.1800, 5 In. 148.00
Creamer, Rural Scene, Beaded Rim, Scroll Handle, Domed Foot, 1780-81, 4 x 3 In. 215.00
Cup, Rib Base, J.S. Monogram, c.1710, 3 ⅜ In. 354.00
Decanter, Clear, Swirl Overlay, Square Shape, Monogram, 8 ¼ In. 590.00
Decanter, Glass, Pinched Waist, Pierced Repousse Rococo Style Mounts, Marked, 10 In. 345.00
Decanter, Rooster Shape, Remove Head To Fill, Open Beak Spout, 15 ½ In. 3738.00
Dish, Centerpiece, Boat Shape, Pedestal, Pierced Sides, Leaf Rims, Handles, Roses, 14 x 9 In. 1179.00
Dish, Flowers, Openwork Border, Serpentine Rim, Lobed Well, Pedestal, c.1900, 15 In. Diam. 1554.00
Egg Server, Reeded Handles, 6 Molded Forms, Scalloped Reticulated Border, c.1900, 7 ¼ In. 369.00
Ewer, Lid, Crystal, Rococo Style, Scrollwork, Quatrefoil, Thumbpiece, c.1890, 13 In. 1715.00
Fish Serving Set, Moresque, John R. Wendt, Starr & Marcus, c.1875, 11 ½ In. & 9 ⅞ In., 2 Piece.. *Illus* 475.00
Flask, Leaf Shape, Hammered, Flowers & Leaves, Fingerholds, 6 x 3 ½ In. 1007.00
Frame, Baroque Style, Repousse, Women, Putti, Inscribed, 1700s, 31 x 22 In. 4148.00
Frame, Inman, Oval Frame, Ball Feet, Stamped, 4 x 5 In. 60.00
Frame, Photo, Hinged Book Shape, Engraved, Inscribed 1911, 3 x 2 ⅓ In. 120.00
Fruit Basket, Wirework, Flared Rim, Grapes, Vines, Swing Handle, Footed, c.1834, 4 x 11 In. 3600.00
Fruit Bowl, Band Of Leaves, Beaded Bellflower Rim, Pedestal Gadroon Foot, 1889, 5 x 9 In. 984.00
Gravy Boat, Tray, Gadroon Edges, Leaf Handle, 8 ¾ In. 354.00
Grooming Set, Hand Mirror, Brush, Tortoise Mustache Comb, Faux Alligator Case, 6 x 3 In. 184.00
Horseshoes, Presentation Set, Stamped HH, Harrison & Howson, Fitted Box, 2 x 2 In., Pair. 178.00
Ice Cream Slice, Flat Scroll Handle, Scimitar Shape Blade, Flowers, Ferns, c.1885, 10 ⅜ In. 215.00
Iced Tea Spoon, Shake Style, 12 Piece. 210.00
Jug, Hot Water, Beaked Flat Hinged Lid, Pear Shape, Swags, Wood Handle, 1823-24, 8 x 7 In. 2706.00
Kettle, Stand, Urn Shaped, Flower Baskets, Treen Handle, Shell Feet, c.1900, 12 ¾ In. 1016.00
Knife, Enameled Sheath, Engraved Leaves, Fury, Semiprecious Cabochons, 11 In. 725.00
Ladle, Gilt, Batteau Shape, Flared Spout, Leaves, Baluster Knop, Figural Finial, c.1865, 14 In. 1168.00
Letter Opener, Art Nouveau Style, Mermaid Relief Handle, Marked MMA, 9 ¼ In. 270.00
Loving Cup, Bulbous, Waisted Neck, Domed Base, Reeded Serpentine Scrolls, c.1900, 15 In. 1230.00
Loving Cup, Vase Shape, Cavetto Collar, Square Handles, Round Foot, 1926, 15 In. 861.00
Martini Shaker, Corinthian Yacht Club Race, Maiden, Waves, Seaweed Scrolls, 7 ⅜ In. 1185.00
Mirror, Hand, Fairy, Wearing Gown, Waving Wand, Orchids, Marked, 9 In. 104.00
Napkin Rings are listed in their own category.
Nutmeg Grater, Scrolling Leaf Design, Line & Dot Pattern, c.1800 504.00
Orange Spoon, Old Colonial, Paneled, Beaded Handles, Urn Finial, Flame, 5 ½ In., 7 Piece 130.00
Peppermill, Ebonized Wood, Ball Top, c.1960, 20 ½ In. 813.00
Pitcher, Etched Crystal, Flowers, Silver Rim, 9 ½ In. 120.00
Pitcher, George III Style, C-Scroll Handle, Flared Spout, c.1950, 10 ½ x 10 In. 510.00

Pitcher, Hammered, Bulbous, Wood Handle, Open Peapod Design, Flared Rim, 8 ¼ In...........	1610.00
Pitcher, Oval Reeded Body, Spread Foot, Leaves & Strapwork, c.1900, 9 ½ In...........................	1225.00
Pitcher, Urn Shape, Helmet Spout, Scroll Handle, c.1925, 8 ¾ In.	649.00
Pitcher, Water, Flattened Pear Shape, Shaped Rim, Oval Foot, S-Scroll Handle, c.1915, 10 x 9 ½ In. ..	1476.00
Pitcher, Water, Flowers, Waisted Collar, Crested Handle, Gadroon Banding, c.1950, 11 x 9 In.	615.00
Pitcher, Water, Hexagonal, Squared Handle, Wide Spout, Stepped Foot Ring, c.1914, 7 ½ x 5 ½ In.	1353.00
Pitcher, Water, Repousse Flowers, Baluster, Loop Handle, Spout, Round Foot, c.1886, 7 In......	920.00
Pitcher, Water, Tapered, Stein Shape, Molded Lip, Flat Topped Ear Handle, 1929, 7 ¼ In..........	563.00
Pitcher, Water, Tulip Buds, Low Relief, Arthur Stone, Herbert A. Taylor, c.1908-37, 8 ⅞ In.... *Illus*	7000.00
Pitcher, Water, Urn Shaped, Waisted, Wide Spout, Crested Handle, Domed Foot, 1967, 8 ¾ In.	676.00
Pitcher, Water, Waisted Collar, Integral Spout, Square Leaf Handle, Round Foot, Swags, c.1915, 10 In.	1476.00
Plate, Repousse Dragons, Clouds, Pearls, c.1900, 11 In. Diam..	885.00
Plateau, Round, Beaded Border, Bellflowers, Crest, Eagle, 1800s, 2 x 18 In.	3000.00
Platter Spoon, Victorian, Fiddle Thread & Shell Pattern, Diamond Heel, c.1853, 12 ½ In.	307.00
Platter, Colonial Revival Design, Oval, Serpentine Ends, Molded Rim, 16 x 11 In., Pair..........	1353.00
Porringer, Round, Concave Handle, Engraved Bamboo, Cartouche, C.J. & Co., c.1915, 5 ½ In..	153.00
Potato Fork, Fiddle Pattern, Crest Of Clan MacIver, c.1814, 11 ½ In.	399.00
Punch Bowl, Applied Border, Cast Grapevine, Clusters, Leaves, 5 ½ x 12 In.	1840.00
Punch Bowl, Bucket Shape, Flared Rim, Round Foot Ring, c.1950, 7 ¾ x 16 ½ In.	2214.00
Punch Ladle, Canterbury Pattern, Gold Washed Bowl, Trefoil Shape, Monogram, 12 ¾ In.....	276.00
Punch Ladle, Fiddle Pattern, Elliptical Bowl, Rattail Heel, Monogrammed BFR, c.1846, 14 In.	276.00
Punch Ladle, Napoleon III, Fiddle Thread Design, Round Bowl, Monogram, c.1865, 13 In.	276.00
Punch Ladle, Napoleon III, Violon Filet Design, Round Bowl, Monogram, c.1865, 12 ¾ In.	153.00
Rose Bowl, Openwork Leaves, Monogram, Ferdinand Fuchs & Bros., c.1900, 5 ¾ x 9 In...*Illus*	708.00
Salad Servers, Fork & Spoon, Marked, 7 In., Pair..	190.00
Salt & Pepper, Lion's Heads At Top Of Feet, Marked, 2 Pair, 4 In....................................	360.00
Salt, Master, Navette Shape, Paw Feet, Rope Twist Rim, Eagles, Relief Leaves, 1800s, 3 x 4 In..	184.00
Salt, Swan Shape, Repousse, Swivel Wings, Crystal Body, Cherub Handle Spoon, 3 x 3 In., Pair	265.00
Salver, Georgian, Oval, Scrolling, Flowers, Grapes & Leaf Border, Scroll Feet, 1749, 13 ½ In. Diam.	1840.00
Salver, Round, Monogram, Band Of Bellflowers, Leaves, Talon & Ball Feet, c.1905, 11 ¼ In.	770.00
Salver, Round, Scrolling & Gadroon Border, Lion, Scrolling Flowers, Shell, Footed, 1844, 13 ½ In..	2040.00
Sauceboat, Bateau Shape, Rocaille Rim, Acanthus Handle, Oval Foot, Stand, c.1820, 10 x 10 ½ In.	922.00
Sauceboat, George II, Oval, Reeded, Double C-Scroll Handle, Pad Feet, 1739, 5 ½ x 7 ½ In., Pair.	2015.00
Sauceboat, Repousse Flowers, Acanthus Handle, 3 Scroll & Pad Feet, c.1900, 3 ½ x 5 ¾ In. ...	338.00
Sauceboat, Scalloped Edge, S-Scroll Handle, Shell Shape Pad Feet, 5 x 7 ½ In.	711.00
Serving Dish, Repousse Rim, Neoclassical Flowers, Monogram, Oval, 10 x 8 In.	288.00
Serving Spoon, Bird's Nest Pattern, Gold Wash Bowl, 10 ½ In..	1840.00
Spoon, Oval Bowl, Backward Bent Tip, Engraved Crest, Rampant Lion, 1801, 12 ¼ In............	240.00
Spoon, Souvenir, see Souvenir category.	
Standish, Pierced Wavy Gallery, Laurel Band, Reed & Ribbon Edge, c.1906, 3 ¾ x 10 ½ In.....	1045.00
Straining Spoon, Shell & Thread Design, Engraved, Crest, Chained Griffin, c.1817, 12 ½ In. ..	861.00
Sugar & Creamer, Splayed Foot, Embossed Kylix, Wreaths, 4 ½ x 4 In.	207.00
Sugar & Creamer, Urn Shape, Gadroon Rim, Pedestal Foot, Twig Handles, 1800, 5 ⅛ In.	1541.00
Sugar Basket, Pierced Interlocking Design, Trumpet Foot, Swing Handle, 1900s, 5 ½ In........	330.00
Sugar Tongs, Blossom Pattern, Handles In Heart Shape Frame, c.1945, 5 ¾ In.	296.00
Sugar, Dome Lid, Blossom Shape Knop, Flowers & Leaves, Handles, Footed, c.1873, 5 x 7 In..	504.00
Sugar, Peaked Lid, Urn Shape, Beaded Borders, Splayed Foot, Square Base, c.1800, 10 ¼ In. ..	1320.00
Tankard, Castellated Rim, Shield Cartouche, Strapwork Monogram, Leather, c.1905, 7 In.	478.00
Tazza, Baluster Shape, Pedestal, Shallow Bowl, Relief Rim, Roses, Leaves, Empire, 10 x 4 In..	127.00
Tazza, Chased Flowers, Footed, 2 ½ x 6 ½ In., Pair..	516.00
Tea Strainer, Swinging, Pan, Handle, U.S.A., c.1895, 2 ½ x 7 In.	301.00
Tea Trivet, Octagonal, Molded Rim, Leaf Banding, 4 Spherical Feet, 1 ⅛ x 7 In.	3936.00
Teapot, Hinged Lid, Lobed Melon Shape, Gooseneck Spout, Wood Finial, c.1834, 6 x 10 In......	1599.00
Teapot, Lid, Regency, Swan Neck Spout, Rattan Swing Bail Handle, Hardwood Finial, 1818, 5 In..	800.00
Tobacco Box, Etched, Flowers, Canted Corners, Continental, c.1800, 5 In.	3300.00
Tray, Art Nouveau, Flowers, Shaped Thistle Rim, Oval, c.1900, 17 ¼ x 13 In.	1035.00
Tray, Engraved Arabesque Scrolls, Strapwork, Grotesque Masks, Monogram, 32 x 21 In.	7800.00
Tray, Flower Pattern, Repousse, Monogram, 8 ½ x 6 In.	460.00
Tray, Oval, Segmented Rim, Hammered, Cutout Handles, c.1923, 22 In.	800.00
Tray, Raised Edge, Monogram EWL, 3 x 4 In., 6 Piece..	180.00
Tray, Rectangular, Embossed Designs, Cutout Handles, Wavy Sides, c.1876, 35 x 17 In.	8365.00
Tray, Rectangular, Repousse, Mark J.H. Davis & Co., 11 x 14 In.	652.00
Tray, Repousse Border, Flowers Vines, C-Scrolls, Monogram Center, 10 ¼ x 14 In.	1323.00
Tray, Serving, St. Dunstan, Engraved, Oval, 2 Handles, c.1929, 29 x 18 In.	3450.00
Trophy, Presentation, Chalice Shape, Palm Tree Stem, Grapes, Putti, Golf Bag, 1905, 12 x 8 In.....	1380.00
Trowel, Ceremonial, Engraved, Flower Scrolls, Ivory Handle, Fluted, c.1901, 16 ½ x 5 ¾ In...	553.00

Sports, Baseball, Label, Firecracker, Home Run, 20-Pack, W.L. Stewart Co., Chinese, 3 ½ x 3 In.
$1,200.00

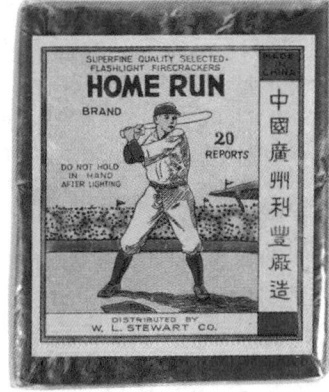

Morphy Auctions

Sports, Baseball, Nodder, Mickey Mantle, New York Yankees, Label, 1960s, 7 In.
$411.00

Hake's Americana & Collectibles

Sports, Baseball, Pendant, Cleveland Indians, A.L. Championship, 10K, Diamond, Chain, 1995, 18 In.
$960.00

Gray's Auctioneers LLC

Sports, Baseball, Trade Stimulator, Miniature Baseball World Champion, Advance Machine Co., 1940s
$1,560.00

Victorian Casino Antiques

Sports, Boxing, Mouthpiece, Muhammad Ali, Rumble In The Jungle, Fight Worn, 1974
$9,560.00

Heritage Auctions

Sports, Football, Jersey, Terry Bradshaw, Pittsburgh Steelers, Game Used, 1977
$21,510.00

Heritage Auctions

Tureen, Bulbous, Oval, Wavy Flutes, Grapevine Band, Scroll Feet, c.1759, 14 ½ In.	2706.00
Tureen, Lid, Urn Shape, Scroll Handles, Beaded, Urn Finial, Spread Foot, c.1900, 9 ½ x 12 In.	649.00
Tussy Mussy, Victorian, Baluster Stem, Cherubs, Flowers, Scrollwork, 5 ¾ In.	385.00
Vase, Conical, Wide Flange, Paneled, 8 ¼ x 9 ¼ In.	403.00
Vase, Flower Petals Extending From Rim, Tapered, Monogram, Gorham, 1900, 7 ¼ In. .....*Illus*	800.00
Vase, Flower Repousse, Engraved Old Elm Beaker, Tapered, c.1910, 7 x 4 ⅞ In.	403.00
Vase, Flowers, Leaves, Chased, Repousse, Handles, 9 ⅜ In.	3438.00
Vase, Trumpet Shape, Annular Band, Wavy Rim, Fluted, Cavetto Foot, 15 ¼ x 6 In.	492.00
Vase, Trumpet, Wavy Rim, Dome Foot, Rococo Swags, Monogram, c.1915, 16 ½ In.	399.00
Waste Bowl, Inverted Pear Shape, Scrolls, Waisted Collar, Domed Foot, 1899, 4 ½ x 5 In.	246.00
Wine Pot, Raised Archaic Design, Jade Knop, Dragon Spout, Arched Handle, c.1900, 6 ½ In.	4600.00

SILVER-SWEDISH

Pitcher, Cream, Classical Shape, Scroll Handle, Pedestal Base, Leaf Band, 1847, 5 ½ In.	180.00

SILVER-TUNESIAN

Basket, Tongs, Pierced, Leaf Vignette Border, Etched, Swing Handle, Monogram, 13 & 8 In.	1200.00

SILVER-TURKISH

Vase, Scroll & Wave, Swirl Base, Openwork Rim, 20th Century, 16 ½ In.	2006.00

SINCLAIRE cut glass was made by H.P. Sinclaire and Company of Corning, New York, between 1904 and 1929. He cut glass made at other factories until 1920. Pieces were made of crystal as well as amber, blue, green, or ruby glass. Only a small percentage of Sinclaire glass is marked with the *S* in a wreath.

Letter Caddy, Rose, Engraved, Marked, 2 ¾ x 6 In.	200.00
Punch Bowl, Hobstar Chain With Cane, Strawberry Diamond & Fan Highlights, 6 x 13 In.	400.00
Vase, Ivy, Engraved, Signed, 15 In.	150.00

SKIING, *see Sports category.*

SLAG GLASS resembles a marble cake. It can be streaked with different colors. There were many types made from about 1880. Caramel slag is the incorrect name for chocolate glass. Pink slag was an American product made by Harry Bastow and Thomas E.A. Dugan at Indiana, Pennsylvania, about 1900. Purple and blue slag were made in American and English factories in the 1880s. Red slag is a very late Victorian and twentieth-century glass. Other colors are known but are of less importance to the collector. New versions of chocolate glass and colored slag glass are being made.

Amethyst & White, Grecian Pony, 5 ½ In.	25.00
Amethyst & White, Hen On Nest Cover, 3 In.	15.00
Amethyst & White, Lion, On Ribbed Base, 5 In.	25.00
Amethyst & White, Saltcellar, Chick Shape, 1 ½ In.	11.00
Amethyst & White, Whiskey Glass & Coaster, Bottoms Up, 3 ¾ In.	25.00
Blue & Red, Cat, On Ribbed Base, 5 In.	25.00
Blue & White, Eyecup, Raised Rib, 2 ¼ In.	10.00
Brown & White, Toby Jar, Owl, 6 ½ In.	40.00
Butterscotch & White, Hen On Nest Cover, Lid, 5 In.	20.00
Pink, Punch Cup, Inverted Fan & Feather, Dugan, 2 ½ In.	86.00
Pink, Salt & Pepper, Reverse Fan & Feather, Dugan, 3 ½ In.	518.00
Red & White, Swan, On Woven Nest, 5 In.	25.00

SLEEPY EYE collectors look for anything bearing the image of the nineteenth-century Indian chief with the drooping eyelid. The Sleepy Eye Milling Co., Sleepy Eye, Minnesota, used his portrait in advertising from 1883 to 1921. It offered many premiums, including stoneware and pottery steins, crocks, bowls, mugs, and pitchers, all decorated with the famous profile of the Indian. The popular pottery was made by Weir Pottery Co. from c.1899-1905. Weir merged with six other potteries and became Western Stoneware in 1906. Western Stoneware Co. made blue and white Sleepy Eye from 1906 until 1937, long after the flour mill went out of business in 1921. Reproductions of the pitchers are being made today. The original pitchers came in only five sizes: 4 inches, 5 ¼ inches, 6 ½ inches, 8 inches, and 9 inches. The Sleepy Eye image was also used by companies unrelated to the flour mill.

Barrel, Sleepy Eye Milling Co., Cream, Wood, Brass, 25 In.	330.00
Crock, Butter, Open Teepee	750.00
Fan, Indian Head, Tassel	190.00
Pitcher, Blue, Gray, Indian, Standing	275.00
Pitcher, Blue, Gray, No. 2, 5 ¼ In.	50.00
Pitcher, Blue, Gray, No. 4, 8 In.	100.00

Pitcher, Blue, White, Blue Rim, No. 1, 3 ½ In.	180.00
Pitcher, Blue, White, No. 2, 5 ¼ In.	170.00 to 320.00
Pitcher, Blue, White, No. 3, 6 ½ In.	75.00 to 390.00
Pitcher, Blue, White, No. 4, 8 In.	90.00 to 280.00
Pitcher, Blue, White, No. 5, 9 In. ....Illus	270.00
Pitcher, Blue, Yellow, Standing Elk	110.00
Pitcher, Lincoln, No. 5	350.00

SLOT MACHINES *are included in the Coin-Operated Machine category.*

SMITH BROTHERS glass was made after 1878. Alfred and Harry Smith had worked for the Mt. Washington Glass Company in New Bedford, Massachusetts, for seven years before going into their own shop. They made many pieces with enamel decoration.

Bowl, Enameled, Water Lilies, Trademark, 6 In.	230.00
Pitcher, Long Spout, Flowers, Yellow, 9 ½ In.	245.00
Powder Jar, Melon, Ribbed, Raised Berries, Ivy, 5 x 3 In.	399.00
Vase, Cylindrical, Enameled, Bird In Flight, 1880s, 4 ½ In.	55.00
Vase, Cylindrical, Pink Ground, Heron, Marsh, Gilt Rim, 4 ¼ In.	75.00

SNOW BABIES, made from bisque and spattered with glitter sand, were first manufactured in 1864 by Hertwig and Company of Thuringia. Other German and Japanese companies copied the Hertwig designs. Originally, Snow Babies were made of candy and used as Christmas decorations. There are also Snow Babies tablewares made by Royal Bayreuth. Copies of the small Snow Babies figurines are being made today and a line called "Snowbabies" was introduced by Department 56 in 1987. Don't confuse these with the original Snow Babies.

Figurine, Boy, Outstretched Arms, Germany, c.1910, 2 In.	48.00
Figurine, Skater, Boy, Girl, Hertwig Co., 1920s, 2 In., Pair	89.00
Figurine, Snow On Tummy On Sled, Germany, 3 In.	139.00
Figurine, Waving, Holding Skis, Flocked Tree, Germany, 2 ¾ In.	184.00
Pitcher, Milk, Girls Sledding, Royal Bayreuth, 1900s, 4 In.	119.00

SNUFF BOTTLES *are listed in the Bottle category.*

SNUFFBOXES held snuff. Taking snuff was popular long before cigarettes became available. The gentleman or lady would take a small pinch of the ground tobacco or snuff in the fingers, then sniff it and sneeze. Snuffboxes were made of many materials, including gold, silver, enameled metal, and wood. Most snuffboxes date from the late eighteenth or early nineteenth centuries.

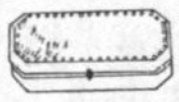

Boxwood, Relief Lid, Carved, Armorial, Tanners, Ram's Head Shape, Initials, c.1710, 3 In.	5015.00
Brass, Arms Of Edinburgh, Scotland, Engraved, 18th Century	150.00
Champleve Enamel, Gold, Vining, Apricot, Blue, Flowers, Gabriel-Raoul Morel, c.1800, 2 ½ In.	5192.00
Coquilla Nut, Carved, Angel Playing Harp, Leaftips, Shoe Base, c.1760, 3 In.	1121.00
Enameled, Tan, Multicolor Flowers, Cupid, Tracery, Hinged Lid, Gilt Brass Rim, Oval, 2 x 2 In.	276.00
Gilt Metal, Agate, Shaped Top, Brown, Yellow, Purple, Scroll, Shells, Flowers, c.1770, 3 In.	2006.00
Horn, Tortoise, Oval, c.1850, 3 ¼ x 1 ¾ In.	84.00
Ivory, Erotic Silver Mounts, c.1900, 2 ¼ x 1 ⅞ In.	415.00
Mahogany, Hinged Lid, Shoe Shape, Carved, Man's Brogan, 2 ⅜ In.	94.00
Maple, Bird Shape, Hinged Lid, c.1820, 2 ¼ x 4 In.	1178.00
Metal, Rectangular, Cut Corners, Gilt Silver Inlay, Cartouche, Calligraphy, Persia, c.1900, 2 ⅛ In.	563.00
Papier-Mache, Andrew Jackson, Black Transfer, Round, 1815, 3 ½ In.	1298.00
Papier-Mache, Duke Of Wellington, Black Transfer, England, c.1905, 3 ¼ In.	325.00
Papier-Mache, Portrait, Woman Wearing Dress, Holding Fan, Ocher, Oval, c.1850, 3 ½ In. Dia.	175.00
Plated Metal, Soldier's Kepi, Square Brim, Hand Cord, Buttons, Flag, 1894, 1 ¼ x 3 In.	212.00
Silver, Chased, Woman's Miniature Portrait, Continental, c.1890, 1 ½ x 2 In.	120.00
Silver, Cloisonne, Gold Washed, Beaded Border, Scrolled Leaves, Hinged Lid, Russia, 1908-17, 2 In.	735.00
Silver, Enamel, Lid, Child Sleeping, 2 Maidens, Green, White, Blue, 1 x 2 ¾ In.	415.00
Silver, Enamel, Oval, Chased Scrollwork, Leaves, 2 Lovers, Blackbird, Italy, 1900s, 1 ¾ x 1 ¼ In.	153.00
Silver, Enamel, Pink Rose, Leaves, Round, c.1850, 2 In.	152.00
Silver, Engraved Bird, Cityscape, Rococo Border, Cartouche, Norway, c.1750, 3 In.	236.00
Silver, Fox Head, Finis Coronet Opus Motto Inside, 2 ⅞ x 2 ⅛ In.	4095.00
Silver, Hinged Dome Lid, Engraved Anthemion, Flowers, Rounded Front, Back, 1 ¾ x 1 ⅜ In.	81.00
Silver, Hinged Lid, Flowers, Leaves, Geometric Border, 1858, ¾ x 2 ¾ In.	250.00
Silver, Hinged Lid, Shell Shape, Repousse Design, Hallmarks, 1 ½ In. ....Illus	780.00
Silver, Lid, Oval, Scrolling Vines, Flowers, Interior Gilt Washed, England, 1902, 2 x 1 In.	230.00

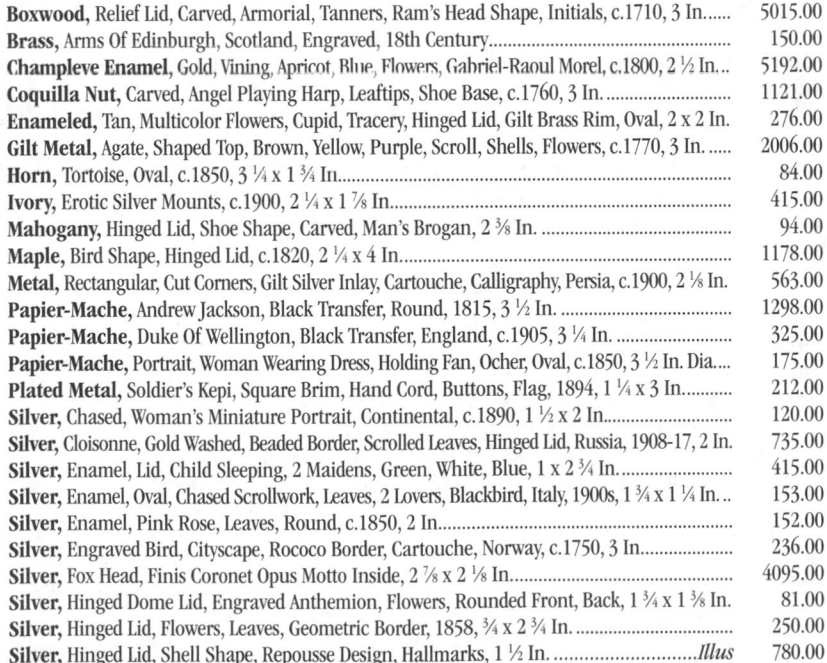

Sports, Football, Label, Firecracker, Touch-Down, 20-Pack, Chinese, 3 ¼ x 2 ¼ In.
$480.00

Morphy Auctions

Sports, Horse Racing, Trade Stimulator, Official Sweepstakes, 1 Cent, Gumball, Rock-Ola Mfg. Co., c.1933
$3,000.00

Victorian Casino Antiques

Staffordshire, Figurine, Cat, 1900s, 7 In., Pair
$48.00

Morphy Auctions

The edited listings of the current prices in this *Kovels' Antiques & Collectibles Price Guide* aren't available on any website. Readers can visit **Kovels.com** to check thousands of past prices and sign up for free information on trends, tips, reproductions, marks, and more.

Staffordshire, Figurine, George Washington, Bust, Incised, Birth & Death Dates, Enoch Wood, 1818, 8 ¾ In. $1,265.00

James D. Julia Auctioneers

Staffordshire, Figurine, Girl, Bonnet, Holding Book, Painted, 19th Century, 2 ½ x 1 In. $10.00

Staffordshire, Figurine, William Gladstone, British Statesman, 1850s, 11 ¾ In. $72.00

Morphy Auctions

Tortoiseshell, Inlaid Niello, Porcelain Mounted, Enamel Portrait Of Woman, 4 In. ....
148.00 Walnut, Burl, Lid, Mr. Liston, Comedian, Painted, Round, England, c.1810, 5 In. 770.00
Walnut, Monkey, Eating Fruit, Wearing Top Coat, Ivory Buttons, Carved, 1845, 5 In. 767.00
Walnut, Pig Shape, Reclining, Hinged Back, c.1900, 4 In. 224.00
Yew, Carved, Hand Shape, Index Finger, Thumb Touching, Pewter Cover, Scotland, 1831, 3 ½ In. .. 2006.00

SOAPSTONE is a mineral that was used for foot warmers or griddles because of its heat-retaining properties. Soapstone was carved into figurines and bowls in many countries in the nineteenth and twentieth centuries. Most of the soapstone seen today is from China or Japan. It is still being carved in the old styles.

Basket, Fruits, Flowers, Carved, Painted, Italy, c.1930, 25 In. 600.00
Bed Warmer, Carved Eagle, Shield, Furled Flags, Wire Swing Handle, c.1800, 7 ½ x 10 In. 2640.00
Brushpot, Carved Mountain, Houses, Trees, Figures, River, Gray, Chinese, 5 In. 304.00
Bust, Boy, Wearing Stocking Cap, Downward Glancing, Shaped Oval Base, c.1900, 5 ¼ In. 180.00
Censer, Dragon Mask Handles, Loose Rings, Cloud Shape Feet, Lotus Finial, Gray, 6 In. 668.00
Censer, Figural, Foo Dogs, Openwork Pedestal, Footed, Pierced Accents, Chinese, 1900s, 12 In.. 150.00
Censer, Foo Dogs, Carved, Openwork Pedestal, Chinese, c.1905, 12 In. 180.00
Centerpiece, Carved Flower Basket, Handle, Fruits, Multicolor, 1900s, 25 In. 150.00
Figurine, Buddha, Seated, Double Lotus Throne, Pearl In Hand, Bell, Celadon Green Color, 12 x 9 In. 5310.00
Figurine, Crab, Milky, Amber, Chinese, 7 ¼ In. 180.00
Figurine, Deity, Olive Green Color, Standing, Chinese, 1700s, 7 In. 230.00
Figurine, Homeless Beggar, Immortal Li Tieguai, Seated On Elephant, Gourd, 1800s, 8 ¾ In. ... 246.00
Figurine, Horse, Standing, Saddle, Square Footed Base, 7 In., Pair 359.00
Figurine, Luohan, Carved, Holding Bird In Upraised Hands, Chinese, 5 In. 948.00
Figurine, Luohan, Seated, Reading Book, Chinese, 1800s, 4 In. 173.00
Figurine, Mi Lo Fu, Seated, Laughing, Butterscotch, Hardwood Stand, 2 ¼ x 3 ½ In. 3450.00
Figurine, Nude, Reclining, Carved, Wood Base, 6 ¼ In. 234.00
Group, 3 Luohans, Smiling Men, Standing, Rockwork Base, Laden Sack, Lion Pup, Scepter, 7 ¾ In... 4302.00
Group, Oval Shape, Figures, Landscape, Orange, Carved, Footed Base, Chinese, 2 ¾ In. 388.00
Group, Scholars & Immortals, Landscape, Pine Trees, Pale Yellow, Russet, 4 In. 456.00
Group, St. George & Dragon, On Horseback, Up On Hind Legs, 1900s, 24 In. 1440.00
Group, Water Buffalos, Waves, Lotus Leaf, Wood Stand, 4 In. 497.00
Screen, Yellow, Figures, Bridge, Mountains, Rocks, Trees, Rosewood Stand, c.1930, 14 x 7 In. ... 3107.00
Seal, 2 Sea Rays, Waves, Rectangular, Chinese, 1800s, 4 In. 246.00
Seal, Bamboo, Script, Characters, Yellow, Red Accents, Chinese, c.1900, 2 In. 122.00
Seal, Carved, Children, Buffalo, Green, Red Markings, White, Chinese, 4 ½ In. 153.00
Seal, Honey & Amber Color, Foo Dog Finial, Square Base, c.1900, 2 In. 345.00
Seal, Landscape, Pine Trees, Child, Orange, Red, Chinese, 9 In. 365.00
Vase, Elongated Oval, Footed Base, Tree, Pine Branches, Flared Rim, Chinese, c.1900, 12 In. ... 120.00
Vase, Pine Branches, Carved, Oval, Chinese, c.1920, 12 In. 144.00

SOUVENIRS of a trip—what could be more fun? Our ancestors enjoyed the same thing and souvenirs were made for almost every location. Most of the souvenir pottery and porcelain pieces of the nineteenth century were made in England or Germany, even if the picture showed a North American scene. In the twentieth century, the souvenir china business seems to have been dominated by the manufacturers in Japan, Taiwan, Hong Kong, England, and the United States. Another popular souvenir item is the souvenir spoon, made of sterling or silver plate. These are usually made in the country pictured on the spoon. Related pieces may be found in the Coronation and World's Fair categories.

Button, Annie Oakley Day, Photo, Riffle, Miami Valley Outdoors, 1946, 1 ¼ In. 557.00
Button, Sacramento, Causeway Celebration, Highway, City, Woman, Wing Accents, 1916, 2 ³⁄₁₆ In. 204.00
Button, Swimming Instructor Ad, Coney Island, Swimming Taught In 6 Lessons, c.1904, 1 ¾ In. 2720.00
Button, Waterloo Street Fair, Girl, Trumpet, Eagle, 1898, 1 ¾ In. 182.00
Compact, Face Powder, West Point, Cadets, Celluloid, 1910, 1 ½ x 2 ¼ In. 75.00
Cup, Asbury Park 1901, Ruby Red Flash Above Clear, Embossed Star, 2 ⅞ In. 40.00
Derby Hat, Los Angeles Olympics, Pressed Felt, Satin Band, 1932, 5 x 6 x 3 ¾ In. 116.00
Handbill, Bob Dylan Concert, 2-Sided, Photo, Playing Harmonica, Norfolk, Va., 1966, 6 x 9 In. 1012.00
Hat, Lititz Bicentennial 1756-1956, Plaited Palm Frond, High Crown, Short Brim, Badge, 5 x 11 In. .. 12.00
Hula Girl, Bare Breasted, Skirt Moves, Lei, Seashell, c.1940s, 11 ½ In. 120.00
Jersey Fish Basket, Basket Weave, Killaloe Crest, Goss, 2 ⅞ x 1 ⅝ x 2 In. 38.00
Jug, Crest, Channel Port Of Newhaven, Ruffled Rim, Goss, 4 In. 105.00
Mug, Cornell Sculling, Team Member Holding Oar, Loop Handle, Gold Trim, c.1910, 5 x 3 ½ In. .. 115.00
Pin, Old Home Week, The Shoe Centre, Buildings, Tools, Roadway, 1907, 1 ¾ In. 75.00
Pin, Olympic Rings, Enamel On Metal, German Inscription, 1936, 1 ¾ In. 75.00
Pin, Panama Pacific Dental Congress, San Francisco, Yellow Poppy, 1915, 1 ½ In. 108.00

Pin, Trolley, Union Horse Railroad Co, Employee Outing, Celluloid, Ribbon, 1913, 1 ¾ x 5 ½ In. ..	222.00
Teapot, Lid, Crest, Hackney, 3 Sabres Of Middlesex, Twisted Handle, Goss, c.1875, 4 ½ In.	125.00
Tray, Charleston Exposition, Black Boy Eating Watermelon, Brass, Raised Rim, 1901-02, 4 In. .	115.00
U.S.N., Air Station, Lakehurst, N.J., Hanger Image, Extended Airship, Aluminum, Embossed, 1 x 2 In.	222.00

SPANGLE GLASS is multicolored glass made from odds and ends of colored glass rods. It includes metallic flakes of mica covered with gold, silver, nickel, or copper. Spangle glass is usually cased with a thin layer of clear glass over the multicolored layer. Similar glass is listed in the Vasa Murrhina category.

Basket, Pink, Ruffled Edge, Vine Handle, 7 ½ In.	85.00
Basket, Yellow, Clear Ruffled Edge, Squared Thorn Handle, 5 In.	80.00
Dresser Box, Pink, Green, Crystal Knob, 4 x 3 In.	150.00
Vase, Fluted Edge, 4-Footed, 10 In.	160.00
Vase, Pinched Waist, Footed, 5 ½ In.	38.00
Vase, Pink, Ruffled & Crimped Rim, Melon Shape, 7 ¾ In.	165.00

SPANISH LACE *is listed in the Opalescent category as Opaline Brocade.*

SPATTER GLASS is a multicolored glass made from many small pieces of different colored glass. It is sometimes called End-of-Day glass. It is still being made.

Bride's Bowl, Ribbon Edge, Squared, 8 ½ x 8 ½ In.	200.00
Lampshade, Hanging, 11 ¾ x 5 In.	95.00
Muffineer, 1880s, 4 ½ In.	141.00
Vase, Swirled, Ribbed, Pulled & Folded Rim, 5 ⅜ x 4 ½ In.	60.00

SPATTERWARE and spongeware are terms that have changed in meaning in recent years, causing much confusion for collectors. Some say that *spatterware* is the term used by Americans, *sponged ware* or *spongeware* by the English. Spatterware is creamware or soft paste dinnerware decorated with colored spatter designs. The earliest pieces were made in the late eighteenth century, but most of the spatterware found today was made from about 1800 to 1850. Early spatterware was made in the Staffordshire district of England for sale in America. Collectors also use the word *spatterware* to refer to kitchen crockery with added spatter made in America during the late nineteenth and early twentieth centuries. Spongeware is very similar to spatterware in appearance. Designs were applied to ceramics by daubing the color on with a sponge or cloth. Many collectors do not differentiate between spongeware and spatterware and use the names interchangeably. Modern pottery is being made to resemble old spongeware, but careful examination will show it is new.

Bowl, Blue, Green, Brown, Yellow Rainbow, 1800s, 4 ½ x 10 ½ In.	474.00
Bowl, Cockscomb, Red, Blue, 1800s, 10 ¾ In.	1778.00
Bowl, Dome Lid, Cobalt Blue, White, c.1890, 4 ¾ x 10 ¼ In.	259.00
Bowl, Rose, Red, Green, 1800s, 2 ½ x 11 In.	444.00
Bowl, Sunburst Flower, Rose & Green, Stamped Blue Blossoms, Leaves, Borders, 15 In. ....*Illus*	94.00
Bowl, Vegetable, Thistle, Red, Yellow, c.1850, 9 ¼ x 6 ¾ In.	1337.00
Charger, Rabbitware, Rabbits Playing Tennis, Virginia Rose Border, c.1890, 13 In.	1116.00
Coffeepot, Rainbow, Red, Blue, Octagonal, Paneled, Flared Rim, Gooseneck Spout, 8 x 9 ½ In.	266.00
Creamer, Purple, Brown Stripe, Staffordshire, 1800s, 3 ¾ x 3 In.	161.00
Creamer, Rainbow, Red, Blue, c.1850, 4 ½ In.	237.00
Creamer, Rainbow, Red, Green, 1800s, 3 ½ In.	304.00
Creamer, Schoolhouse, Red, Green, 1800s, 3 ¾ In.	2370.00
Creamer, Windmill, Blue Rim, 4 ½ In.	1304.00
Crock, Stenciled Butter, Cobalt Blue, White Ground, Cylindrical, c.1890	115.00
Cup & Saucer, Bull's-Eye, Blue, Green, c.1850	3555.00
Cup & Saucer, Deer, Sponge, 19th Century	486.00
Cup & Saucer, Peafowl, Blue, Green, Red, Handleless Cup, 2 ¾ In. & 5 ¾ In. ....*Illus*	142.00
Cup & Saucer, Peafowl, Green, Handleless Cup, 2 ½ x 5 ¾ In. ....*Illus*	266.00
Cup & Saucer, Purple & Black Rainbow, Foot Ring, Bucket Shape, 2 x 4 ½ In.	2124.00
Cup & Saucer, Rainbow, Purple, Green, Yellow, Black, 1800s	1458.00
Cup & Saucer, Rainbow, Red & Blue, 2 ¾ x 5 ¾ In. ....*Illus*	130.00
Doorstop, Dog, Spaniel, Seated, Blue, White, Midwestern, c.1890	1955.00
Jug, Milk, Lid, Cobalt Circles, White Ground, Wide Spout, Applied Handle, c.1890, 17 ¼ In.	460.00
Mug, Rainbow, Yellow, Blue, Orange, Brown, Green, 1800s, 6 In.	593.00
Pitcher, Blue, Red Flowers, Green Leaves, 1800s, 10 ¼ In.	237.00
Pitcher, Cobalt Blue Chainlink, Allover, c.1890, 9 In.	144.00
Pitcher, Rainbow, 5 Colors, 19th Century, 6 ¼ In.	830.00
Pitcher, Rainbow, Blue, Green, Red, c.1850, 6 In.	533.00
Pitcher, Rainbow, Red, Blue, Green, Scalloped Rim, High Handle, 1800s, 7 ¾ In.	3792.00

Staffordshire, Group, Prodigal Returns, Father & Son, Biblical Story, 13 ½ In. $72.00

Morphy Auctions

Staffordshire, Group, Uncle Tom & Eva, Glazed, c.1860, 10 ¾ In. $173.00

Hake's Americana & Collectibles

Staffordshire, Group, Uncle Tom & Eva, Uncle Tom's Cabin, 1850s, 8 ½ In. $270.00

Morphy Auctions

S

Staffordshire, Jug, Cockfighting, Jesters, Harlequin Dancing, Cavalier, Blue Transfer, Sample, 9 ¼ In.
$570.00

Skinner, Inc.

Staffordshire, Jug, Copper Luster, Daniel O'Connel, Portrait, Election Victory, Black Transfer, c.1828, 5 In.
$523.00

Skinner, Inc.

Staffordshire, Plate, Armorial Crest, Verse, Red Transfer, Basket Weave Border, Salt Glaze, 9 ⅛ In.
$3,120.00

Skinner, Inc.

Staffordshire, Plate, Chief Justice Marshall, Side-Wheeler Steamboat, Hudson River, c.1835, 10 In.
$590.00

Conestoga Auction Co., Inc.

Pitcher, Rainbow, Yellow & Purple, Sponge, Wide Spout, Loop Handle, 4 ⅜ In. ....*Illus*	130.00
Pitcher, Tankard, Cobalt Blue & White, Applied Handle, c.1890, 6 ⅞ In.	230.00
Plate, Acorn, Purple, Paneled Rim, Amber, Teal Caps, Black Branch, 7 ¼ In.	384.00
Plate, Acorns, Blue Border, c.1850, 8 ⅓ In.	851.00
Plate, Blue, Peafowl, 1800s, 8 ½ In.	237.00
Plate, Fort, Green & Brown, Blue Rim, 1800s, 9 ½ In.	207.00
Plate, Green Tree, Blue Rim, 1800s, 7 In.	444.00
Plate, Purple, Dahlia, Tricolor, Red, Blue, White, Green Sprigs, 8 ¼ In.	266.00
Plate, Rabbits Playing Cricket, Virginia Rose, Rabbitware, English Registry Mark, c.1900, 9 ¼ In. *Illus*	529.00
Plate, Rabbitware Playing Croquet, c.1890, 9 In.	331.00
Plate, Rabbitware, Blue Transfer Panels, Virginia Rose Border, c.1890, 9 In.	241.00
Plate, Rabbitware, Frog Center, Rose Border, c.1880, 9 In.	176.00
Plate, Rabbitware, Rabbit Center, Bull's-Eye Border, c.1890, 9 In.	147.00
Plate, Rabbitware, Rabbits Riding In Roadster, Virginia Rose Border, c.1890, 9 In.	1928.00
Plate, Rainbow, Red, Blue, 1800s, 8 ½ In.	356.00
Plate, Rainbow, Red, Yellow, Blue, 1800s, 8 ⅝ In.	516.00
Plate, Red Rose Center, Blue, Green, Red Tulip, Scalloped Rim, 9 ¼ In.	141.00
Plate, Schoolhouse, Red, Green Feather Edge, c.1830, 9 ¼ In.	176.00
Plate, Tulip, Red, c.1850, 7 ½ In.	504.00
Plate, Tulip, Red, White, Blue, 1800s, 9 ¼ In.	152.00
Plate, Virginia Rose Center, Rabbit Border, c.1890, 10 ¼ In.	294.00
Platter, Peafowl, Blue, 1800s, 13 ¾ x 17 ¾ In.	1226.00
Platter, Rabbitware, Frog Center, Virginia Rose Border, 10 ½ x 14 ½ In.	353.00
Platter, Rainbow, Blue, Purple, Bull's-Eye, 1800s, 11 x 14 ¼ In.	385.00
Platter, Rainbow, Red, Green, c.1850, 7 ½ x 10 ¼ In.	608.00
Salt & Pepper, Blue, Enameled Underwater Scene, Seaweed, Sculptured Fish, 4 ½ In., Pair ...	690.00
Salt, Rainbow, Red, Green, Pedestal Foot, 1800s, 2 x 3 In.	474.00
Sugar, Lid, Cockscomb, Yellow, Red, c.1850, 3 ¾ x 4 ¾ In.	652.00
Sugar, Lid, Dove, Sprig, Purple Band, c.1850, 4 In.	207.00
Sugar, Lid, Parrot, Blue, c.1850, 6 ¼ In.	296.00
Sugar, Lid, Rainbow, Red, Yellow, Blue Cornflower, Drape Pattern, 1800s, 4 ¼ In.	5214.00
Sugar, Lid, Red Tulip, Blue, Handles, c.1850, 7 ½ In.	296.00
Tea Set, Teapot, Creamer, Sugar, Plates, Cup & Saucers, Red, Child's, c.1840, 21 Piece	470.00
Teapot, Lid, Blue, Fort, Tree, 1800s, 6 ½ In.	237.00
Teapot, Lid, Rooster, Purple, c.1800s, 6 In.	356.00
Teapot, Lid, Schoolhouse, Red, Green, 1800s, 4 ½ In.	3555.00
Waste Bowl, Bull's-Eye Interior, Red, Blue, 1800s, 3 ½ x 6 ½ In.	148.00

SPELTER is a synonym for a zinc alloy. Figurines, candlesticks, and other pieces were made of spelter and given a bronze or painted finish. The metal has been used since about the 1860s to make statues, tablewares, and lamps that resemble bronze. Spelter is soft and breaks easily. To test for spelter, scratch the base of the piece. Bronze is solid; spelter will show a silvery scratch.

Bust, L'Automne, Woman, Leaves & Grapes, Bronze Tone, 12 In.	180.00
Bust, Woman, Art Nouveau, 7 ½ In.	90.00
Horseman, 1700s Spanish Rider, Rectangle Base, 1800s, 10 In.	82.00
Lamp, 3-Light, Fruits D'Automne, Maiden, Classical Dress, Vines, Glass Fruit, Base, c.1910, 40 In.	500.00
Penholder, Desk, Cyclist Shape, 1800s	489.00
Sculpture, Allegorical Figure, Draped Woman, Carrying Irises, Gray Patina, c.1900, 18 In.	150.00
Sculpture, Civil War Army Figure, Gun, 13 In.	330.00
Sculpture, Day, Night, Standing On Eagle's Back, Arm Raised, c.1890, 28 x 12 ½ In., Pair	450.00
Sculpture, Messenger Du Printemps, Woman, Vase, Flowers, 23 ¼ In.	161.00
Sculpture, Porter, Calling Card, Brass Tray, 18th Century Dress, Paint, c.1910, 39 ½ In.	120.00
Sculpture, Renommee, Woman, Warrior Stance, Blowing Horn, France, c.1925, 28 ½ In.	345.00
Sculpture, Richard I, Horse, Drawn Sword, 15 In.	173.00
Sculpture, Siffleur, Whistler, Charles Vital Cornu, Fabrication Francaise Paris, 26 x 13 ½ In. ...*Illus*	826.00
Sculpture, Tiger, Walking, 7 ½ x 21 In.	150.00
Sculpture, Woman, Classical Greek, Holding Bird In Hand, 26 In.	71.00
Sculpture, Woman, Classical, Eagle, 24 In.	158.00

SPINNING WHEELS in the corner have been symbols of earlier times for the past 100 years. Although spinning wheels date back to medieval days, the ones found today are rarely more than 200 years old. Because the style of the spinning wheel changed very little, it is often impossible to place an exact date on a wheel.

Mixed Woods, Blue Paint, 1800s, 38 In. ....*Illus*	118.00
Oak, Carved, 55 x 54 x 8 In.	120.00

S

SPODE pottery, porcelain, and bone china were made by the Stoke-on-Trent factory of England founded by Josiah Spode about 1770. The firm became Copeland and Garrett from 1833 to 1847, then W.T. Copeland or W.T. Copeland and Sons until 1976. It then became Royal Worcester Spode Ltd. The company was bought by the Portmeirion Group in 2009. The word *Spode* appears on many pieces made by the factories. Most collectors include all the wares under the more familiar name of Spode. Porcelains are listed in this book by the name that appears on the piece. Related pieces may be listed under Copeland, Copeland Spode, and Royal Worcester.

Centerpiece, Lying Putti, Fishing Net, Shell, Dog, c.1875, 10 x 11 In.	325.00
Cup & Saucer, Spode's Tower, Flow Blue, Fluted Rim	52.00
Figurine, Canary, On Branch, Yellow, 1940, 5 In.	32.00
Fruit Basket, Underplate, Oval, Reticulated, Transfer, Paint Design, Applied Handles, c.1820, 3 x 9 In.	288.00
Pitcher, Gilt Sparrow Beak Spout, Maroon Ground, Flowers, 1847, 6 In., Pair	395.00
Plate Set, Crimson Border, Fired Gold Edge, 9 In., 20 Piece	210.00
Plate Set, Scenic, Lake, Ruins, Hummingbird & Flower Border, H. Hammersley, 9 ¼ In., 9 Piece	900.00
Plate, Bouquet, Roses, Thistle, Shamrocks, Transfers, c.1825, 9 ½ In.	225.00
Plate, Death Of A Bear, Transfer, 19th Century, 10 In.	285.00
Plate, Westminster Abbey, 900th Anniversary, Gilt, 1965, 10 ½ In.	19.00
Platter, Octagonal, Blue, Green, Burnt Orange, c.1850, 17 x 12 ½ In.	225.00
Platter, Rose Briar, Cream, Scalloped & Fluted Rim, Basket Weave, 14 x 11 In.	120.00
Tazza, Tripartite Base, Entwined Dolphins, Enameled Flowers, Orange, Black, 5 x 9 In.	950.00
Tea Set, Traveling, Blue Willow, Sterling, Leather Case, Silk & Velvet Lining, c.1886, 10 x 13 In.	1200.00
Tureen, Underplate, Tab Handles, Oval, Blue Flower Border, Center Bouquet, c.1810, 9 x 6 In.	110.00
Urn, Flowers, Gilt Vines, Cream Ground, Faux Oval Cabochons, Mask Handles, 11 In., Pair	649.00
Vase, Bird Of Paradise, Peony, Leaves, Chinoiserie, Shouldered, 6 ¼ In.	65.00

SPORTS equipment, sporting goods, brochures, and related items are listed here. Items are listed by sport. Other categories of interest are Bicycle, Card, Fishing, Sword, Toy, and Trap. Kentucky Derby glasses are listed in the Decorated Tumblers category.

Baseball, Badge, Babe Ruth Champions, Quaker Oats Club Premium, 1935, 1 In.	120.00
Baseball, Ball, Autographed, Babe Ruth, 1935	6820.00
Baseball, Ball, Autographed, Babe Ruth, Lou Gehrig, Ty Cobb, Reach Official Ball, c.1926	6820.00
Baseball, Ball, Autographed, Brooklyn Dodgers, 1952, 25 Signatures	565.00
Baseball, Ball, Autographed, Brooklyn Dodgers, 1954, 23 Signatures, Jackie Robinson	500.00
Baseball, Ball, Autographed, Cy Young, 1950	18250.00
Baseball, Ball, Autographed, Honus Wagner, Pittsburgh Pirate Coach, c.1943	10755.00
Baseball, Ball, Autographed, Jim Bottomley, c.1948	14340.00
Baseball, Ball, Autographed, Jimmie Foxx, c.1940	46600.00
Baseball, Ball, Autographed, Leon Day, Baltimore Black Sox, Negro League, c.1890	58.00
Baseball, Ball, Autographed, N.Y. Yankees, 1959, 25 Signatures	1547.00
Baseball, Ball, Thurman Munson, 1979	6700.00
Baseball, Bar Pin, Throwing Award, Suspended Maltese Cross, Initials, 1893, 1 ⅜ In.	75.00
Baseball, Bat, Autographed, Roberto Momen Clemente, Pittsburgh Pirates, 1960 World Series	50190.00
Baseball, Bat, Lou Gehrig, c.1930, 34 ¾ In.	86000.00
Baseball, Belt Buckle, New York Yankees, Tour Of Japan, Brass & Enamel, 1955, 1 ⅝ In.	253.00
Baseball, Button, Babe Ruth, Ask Me, Quaker Oats, For Grocery Clerks, Celluloid, 1934, 3 In.	240.00
Baseball, Button, Bob Wine, Phila. Phillies, Ribbon, Bat & Ball Charm, Photo, 2 ¼ In.	190.00
Baseball, Button, Drink Fan-Taz, A Hit, Round, Ball, Bat, 1 ¼ In.	204.00
Baseball, Button, Mickey Mantle Baseball Special, Phillies Cigars, Glove Giveaway, Mid 1960s, 3 In.	316.00
Baseball, Cap, Babe Ruth, N.Y. Yankees, Game Used, c.1932	239000.00
Baseball, Flip Book, Babe Ruth, Wheaties Giveaway, 1933, 2 ½ x 1 ¾ In.	660.00
Baseball, Glove, Ted Williams, Game Used, 1955	86000.00
Baseball, Jersey, Elston Howard, N.Y. Yankees, Game Used, 1958	14340.00
Baseball, Jersey, Rogers Hornsby, St. Louis Browns, Game Used, 1934	46600.00
Baseball, Label, Firecracker, Home Run, 20-Pack, W.L. Stewart Co., Chinese, 3 ½ x 3 In. *Illus*	1200.00
Baseball, Nodder, Mickey Mantle, New York Yankees, Label, 1960s, 7 In. *Illus*	411.00
Baseball, Pencil Case, Babe Ruth, Base Ball Bat School Companion, Cardboard, Wood, 1930s, 11 In.	288.00
Baseball, Pendant, Cleveland Indians, A.L. Championship, 10K, Diamond, Chain, 1995, 18 In. *Illus*	960.00
Baseball, Photograph, George Herman Babe Ruth, Taking Swing, Black, White, Signed, 8 x 10 In.	3835.00
Baseball, Photograph, Lou Gehrig, Autographed, c.1938	19200.00
Baseball, Photograph, Mickey Mantle, New York Yankee Player, Black & White, Frame, 11 x 9 In.	150.00
Baseball, Photograph, Yankees Legends, Autographed, 1938, 11 x 14 In.	9321.00
Baseball, Radio, Maris, Mantle, Batter, Yankees Uniform, Wood, Plastic, c.1960, 4 x 7 In.	577.00
Baseball, Ring, Babe Ruth, Kellogg's Premium, Plastic, Orange Ground, 1950	60.00
Baseball, Shoes, Joe DiMaggio, Joe In Yankees Uniform Holding Bat, Box, 1950s, 4 x 13 In.	236.00
Baseball, Sign, Baseball At Fair Ground To Day, Tin, Painted, c.1880, 23 ½ x 24 In.	666.00

Stangl, Bird, Red Headed Woodpecker, No. 3725, Glazed, Marked, 7 x 6 ¾ In.
$1,000.00

Rago Arts & Auction Center

Stein, Beaker, Blown Glass, 3rd Reich, Deutschland Erwache, Sieg-Heil, ½ Liter, 8 ¼ In.
$360.00

The Stein Auction Co

Stein, Character, Alligator, Pottery, Marked, Marzi & Remy, ⅓ Liter, 6 In.
$276.00

The Stein Auction Co.

TIP

Always dust from the top down. The dust falls.

Stein, Character, Cat, Painted, Pottery, Inlaid Lid, Marked, RM 575, ½ Liter
$306.00

The Stein Auction Co.

Stein, Character, Fox, Head, Porcelain, Musterschutz, Schierholz, Germany, ½ Liter
$1,950.00

The Stein Auction Co.

Stein, Character, Gentleman Rabbit, Porcelain, Marked, Musterschutz, By Schierholz, ½ Liter
$1,920.00

The Stein Auction Co.

Baseball, Sign, Catcher's Mitt, Ed Bailey Wearing Hat, Rawlings, c.1955, 17 ½ x 23 ¾ In........	173.00
Baseball, Sign, Spalding, National League, Reverse Painted Glass, Chain, 6 x 12 In.	1008.00
Baseball, Trade Stimulator, Miniature Baseball World Champion, Advance Machine Co., 1940s *Illus*	1560.00
Baseball, Uniform, Mickey Mantle, N.Y. Yankees, Game Used, Coach, 1977........................	15540.00
Baseball, Weight Machine, Cast Iron, Steel, Spalding Baseball Logo, 59 x 18 In........................	570.00
Basketball, Jersey, Sheboygan Red Skins, NBA, Game Used, 1949-50	17000.00
Basketball, Jersey, University Of Kansas Jayhawks, Red, Blue, Sleeveless, Game Used, c.1915..	42000.00
Basketball, Program, Harlem Magicians Team, No. 1, Red Cover, 1959, 10 x 8 In....................	55.00
Billiards, Table, Burlwood, Steel, Mother Of Pearl, Plank Legs, Cue Rack, 1980s, 32 x 111 In.	7500.00
Bowling, Ball, Wood, Lignum, c.1880, 8 In.	58.00
Boxing, Bell, Cast Iron, Brass, Round, Pull String	224.00
Boxing, Button, Suspended Metal Boxing Gloves, Gene Tunney, Portrait, 1 ¼ In.	194.00
Boxing, Mouthpiece, Muhammad Ali, Rumble In The Jungle, Fight Worn, 1974.............*Illus*	9560.00
Boxing, Photograph, Muhammad Ali & Sonny Liston, Boxing, May 25, 1965, 24 x 36 In........	126.00
Boxing, Photograph, Muhammad Ali, Color, Letterhead Letter, Signed, Frame, c.1943, 24 x 15 In.	210.00
Boxing, Ring, Joe Louis Face, Boxing Gloves On Each Side, Nickel Plated, Silver Luster, 1940s	2875.00
Boxing, Trunks, Autographed, Muhammad Ali, Thrilla In Manila, Fight Worn, 1975	185300.00
Boxing, Trunks, Sonny Liston, Cassius Clay, Fight Worn, 1964	64000.00
Crew, Scull Exercise Machine, Wood, Iron, A.G. Spalding & Bros., c.1895, 73 x 57 In.	1080.00
Football, Ball, Autographed, Oakland Raiders, First Game, 1960	14000.00
Football, Ball, Autographed, University Of Michigan, National Champions, 1948	3300.00
Football, Button, Ditka For Mayor, Mike Ditka Photo, Kelly's Pub, Orange, Blue, 2 In..............	175.00
Football, Figure, Broadway Joe Namath, Jets Uniform, Tuff Tux Outfit, Stand, c.1970, 12 In...	127.00
Football, Figure, Johnny Unitas, Colts Quarterback, Decal Sheet, Hartland Plastics, 1960s, 8 ¼ In.	384.00
Football, Game, Intercollegiate, Tin Lithograph, Frantz, c.1932, 13 ½ x 9 In.	94.00
Football, Jersey, Aaron Rodgers, Green Bay Packers, Game Used, Unwashed, 2011	25693.00
Football, Jersey, Terry Bradshaw, Pittsburgh Steelers, Game Used, 1977.......................*Illus*	21510.00
Football, Label, Firecracker, Touch-Down, 20-Pack, Chinese, 3 ¼ x 2 ¼ In.....................*Illus*	480.00
Football, Patch, Notre Dame Fighting Irish, Felt, Football Player On Shamrock, 1930s, 6 ½ x 8 In....	130.00
Football, Pennant, Cleveland Browns, Brownie The Elf, Felt, 1960s, 34 In.	125.00
Football, Photograph, Notre Dame Team, Rockne's Last Season, 1929-30, Autograph, Frame, 7 x 23 In.	8126.00
Football, Ring, NFL Championship, Detroit Lions, Pat Harder, MVP Of Game, 14K Gold, 1952	14240.00
Golf, Badge, Masters Tournament, Bobby Jones, Horton Smith, Autographed........................	24000.00
Golf, Bag, Cart, Tiger Woods Model, Buick Logos, Navy, Light Blue, Silver, Double Zipper, Nike	150.00
Golf, Gold Medal, British Open Championship, Walter Hagen, 1922...	80000.00
Golf, Practice Mat, Arnold Palmer, Balls, Vinyl Grass, Plastic, Die Cut, Box, 1960s, 12 x 14 In.	86.00
Golf, Sign, Golfers, Celebrating, Leaf Border, Iron, 2-Sided, c.1960, 31 x 34 In.	300.00
Hockey, Gold Pass, Bill Barilko, Maple Leaf Gardens, Lifetime, 1947.............................*Illus*	4070.00
Hockey, Jersey, Gordie Howe, Hartford Whalers, Game Used, 1979-80	18400.00
Hockey, Jersey, Wayne Gretzky, Los Angeles Kings, Game Used, 1989-90..............................	10635.00
Horse Racing, Stimulator, Official Sweepstakes, 1 Cent, Gumball, Rock-Ola Mfg. Co., c.1933....*Illus*	3000.00
Horseback Riding, Crop, Silver Greyhound Head, Engraved, Braided, Lacquered Stick, 1909, 28 In.	150.00
Hurling, Gaming Stick, Wood, Mushroom Shape Terminal, 18th Century, 53 In.......................	325.00
Juggling, Indian Clubs, Maple, Paint, 24 In., Pair	237.00
NASCAR, Fire Suit, Dale Earnhardt, Daytona 500, 1995	15540.00
Pool, Cabinet, Cue, Wood, Painted, 2 Doors, Rack, Bench Stand, 2 Cues, Chalkboard, Drawers, 86 In.	58.00
Pool, Table, Mahogany, 6 Pockets, Pull-Out Rack, Brunswick-Balke-Collender, c.1915, 45 x 81 In..	4000.00
Pool, Table, Walnut, Aluminum Corners & Leg Bands, c.1940, 62 x 111 In.	6000.00
Rowing, Rowboat, Aluminum, White Painted Wood Hull, Mullins Torpedo, 15 Ft. 10 In..........	767.00
Skating, Ice Skates, Carbon Steel, Clamp On, Winchester Skates, c.1920, 11 ½ In., Pair.........	112.00
Skating, Ice Skates, Oak Soles, Steel Blades, S.C. & S. Winslow, Worcester, Mass., 1860s, 11 ½ x 2 In. ..	46.00
Snowshoes, Salesman's Sample, 19 ¾ In...	440.00
Snowshoes, Wood, Painted, c.1910, 59 In.	119.00
Track, Shoes, Michael Johnson, Gold, Autographed, 1996 Summer Olympics, Atlanta	8485.00
Trap Shooting, Score Card, Winchester, Shotguns & Shells, Excel At The Trap, 1906, 5 x 3 In..	235.00

STAFFORDSHIRE, England, has been a district making pottery and porcelain since the 1700s. Hundreds of kilns are still working in the area. Thousands of types of pottery and porcelain have been made in the many factories that worked and still work in the area. Some of the most famous factories have been listed separately, such as Adams, Davenport, Ridgway, Rowland & Marsellus, Royal Doulton, Royal Worcester, Spode, Wedgwood, and others. Some Staffordshire pieces are listed under categories like Fairing, Flow Blue, Mulberry, Shaving Mug, etc.

Bank, House Shape, Marbleized Glaze, 4 ¾ In.	267.00
Bowl, American Scene, Obelisk, Eagle, c.1815, 6 ¼ In. Diam..	723.00
Bowl, Chestnut, Pierced Canova Pattern, Blue, Stand, 1826..	395.00
Bracket, Horse Head, Horseshoe, Enamel, Gilt, Paint, c.1890, 10 In., Pair...............................	531.00

S

Coffeepot, Dome Lid, Flowers, Dark Blue Transfer, c.1845, 9 ½ x 5 In.	546.00
Coffeepot, Dome Lid, Loop Handle, S-Spout, Blue Transfer, Round Foot, c.1835, 12 In.	1145.00
Decanter, Bear Shape, Standing, c.1750, 11 x 5 In.	575.00
Dish, Hen On Nest Cover, Chick On Back, 1800s, 6 ½ In.	533.00
Ewer & Basin, Classical Scenes, Flowers, Blue Transfer, c.1850, Pitcher 11 In., Basin 5 x 13 In.	46.00
Figurine, Allegorical, British Lion, Standing Over Napoleon, Multicolor, Gilt, 9 x 7 In.	161.00
Figurine, Cat, 1900s, 7 In., Pair. ....*Illus*	48.00
Figurine, Church, White, Red Door, Window Detail, Turrets, 9 In.	60.00
Figurine, Country House, Dog, Arch, Mossy Bocage, Multicolor, Gilt, 5 ½ x 6 In.	52.00
Figurine, Dog, Dalmatian, Elongated Style, Oval Base, 19th Century, 9 In., Pair	780.00
Figurine, Dog, King Charles Spaniel, Black, White, Brown & White Puppy, Blue, Gilt, 6 x 5 In.	63.00
Figurine, Dog, Spaniel, Black & White, Gilt Collar, Chain, c.1900, 9 ¾ In., Pair	354.00
Figurine, Dog, Spaniel, Copper Luster, Brown & White, 10 ¾ In., Pair.	236.00
Figurine, Dog, Spaniel, Copper Luster, On White, 10 In., Pair	224.00
Figurine, Dog, Spaniel, Gilt Collar, Black Chain, Red & White, 1800s, 8 ½ In., Pair	259.00
Figurine, Dog, Spaniel, Green, White, Gold, 13 In., Pair	384.00
Figurine, Dog, Spaniel, Holding Flower Baskets, Rust, White, Chains, 1800s, 7 In., Pair	472.00
Figurine, Dog, Spaniel, Ivory Ground, Brown & Gold Flecks, 15 x 12 In., Pair	72.00
Figurine, Dog, Spaniel, Red, White, Black Collar, 12 In., Pair	325.00
Figurine, Dog, Spaniel, Red, White, Gilt Collar, 9 ½ In., Pair	325.00
Figurine, Dog, Spaniel, Rust & White, Gold Highlights, 13 ½ In., Pair	118.00
Figurine, Dog, Spaniel, White, Basket In Mouth, 9 In., Pair	1003.00
Figurine, Dog, Spaniel, White, c.1875, 12 x 4 In.	104.00
Figurine, Dog, Spaniel, White, Glass Eyes, Gold Highlights, 9 ¾ In., Pair	212.00
Figurine, Dog, Spaniels, Seated, Barrel, Red & White, Chain, Oval Base, 1800s, 8 ½ In.	259.00
Figurine, Dog, Whippet, Brown, Tan, c.1890, 11 x 9 In., Pair	431.00
Figurine, Dog, Whippet, c.1910, 11 In., Pair	354.00
Figurine, Dog, Whippet, Seated, Rabbit, c.1855, 11 ½ In., Pair	588.00
Figurine, Duke Of Wellington, Leaning On Cannon, Military Trophies, 10 ½ x 4 ¾ In.	738.00
Figurine, Eagle, Gilt Crest, Articulated, Perched On Stump, c.1860, 7 In.	354.00
Figurine, Garibaldi, c.1860, 19 ½ In.	69.00
Figurine, George Washington, Bust, Incised, Birth & Death Dates, Enoch Wood, 1818, 8 ¾ In. .. *Illus*	1265.00
Figurine, Girl, Bonnet, Holding Book, Painted, 19th Century, 2 ½ x 1 In. ....*Illus*	10.00
Figurine, Girl, Seated On Dog, Hat, Black, White, c.1885, 5 ½ In., Pair	590.00
Figurine, Girl, Seated, Chair, Bird On Hand, Cat, 8 In.	24.00
Figurine, Horse, Back Vase, Orange, Green, Grass Base, 1800s, 10 ½ In., Pair	944.00
Figurine, Horse, Tree Vase, Green, Brown, Black, c.1850, 10 ¾ In.	354.00
Figurine, Jenny Lind, Seated, Clutching Cross, Opera Banner, 1880s, 13 In.	266.00
Figurine, Lion, Recumbent, Rusty Brown, c.1960, 10 In.	118.00
Figurine, Man Riding A Horse, Oval Base, 8 In.	138.00
Figurine, Monk, Black Robe, Holding Cross, 10 ¼ In.	767.00
Figurine, Parrots, Nest Of Eggs, Multicolor, 1800s, 7 ½ In., Pair	369.00
Figurine, Peking Duck, Orange, Green, Yellow, English Crown, 8 ½ In.	17.00
Figurine, Rooster, Mound Base, Painted, Hollow, Head Is Lid, 8 ¾ In.	230.00
Figurine, Shakespeare, c.1860, 19 ½ In.	35.00
Figurine, Whippet, Standing, Catch In Mouth, Rabbit, 1800s, 11 ½ In., Pair	230.00
Figurine, William Gladstone, British Statesman, 1850s, 11 ¾ In. ....*Illus*	72.00
Garniture, Boy, Girl, On Flower, Festooned Clock, Dogs, Flags, Holding Bowl, Spoon, 11 In., Pair.	118.00
Group, Man, Woman, Dog, Clock Holder, 13 In.	58.00
Group, Prodigal Returns, Father & Son, Biblical Story, 13 ½ In. ....*Illus*	72.00
Group, Tythe Pig, Minister, Man, Holding Pig, Woman, Baby, Tree, c.1850, 6 ½ In.	200.00
Group, Uncle Tom & Eva, Glazed, c.1860, 10 ¾ In. ....*Illus*	173.00
Group, Uncle Tom & Eva, Uncle Tom's Cabin, 1850s, 8 ½ In. ....*Illus*	270.00
Humidor, Woman, Long Dress, Wide Brimmed Hat, Holding Dog, Multicolor, 8 ½ In.	58.00
Jug, Cockfighting, Jesters, Harlequin Dancing, Cavalier, Blue Transfer, Sample, 9 ¼ In...*Illus*	570.00
Jug, Copper Luster, Daniel O'Connel, Portrait, Election Victory, Black Transfer, c.1828, 5 In. .....*Illus*	523.00
Mug, Eagle, Spread Wing, Transferware, Yellow Glaze, c.1845, 2 ⅛ x 2 ⅛ In.	805.00
Mug, Field Sports, Dogs, Rabbit, Black, White Transfer, Francis Morley & Co., c.1850, 3 x 3 In...	104.00
Pill Box, Blue Enamel, Token Of Regard, Painted White Dove, Fence, Round, c.1810, 1 ¼ In..	266.00
Pitcher, Abolitionist's, Uncle Tom's Cabin Scenes, c.1850, 8 In.	770.00
Pitcher, Eagle, Blue Transfer, 1800s, 7 ¼ In.	1701.00
Pitcher, Exotic Animals & Figures, William Guy, Elsmore & Forster, 1860, 9 ¼ In.	948.00
Pitcher, Man, Seated, Holding Glass, Pitcher, Spatter Design, Hat Spout, c.1890, 9 ¾ In.	944.00
Pitcher, Satyr, Canary, 1810, 4 ½ In.	267.00
Plate, Admiral Perry, Iron Red Transfer, Blue Shell Edge Rim, c.1820, 9 ⅞ In.	2060.00
Plate, America & Independence, States Border, Blue Transfer, c.1820, 10 ½ In.	558.00
Plate, Andrew Jackson, Transfer, Pink Luster Border, c.1825, 8 ⅝ In.	593.00
Plate, Armorial Crest, Verse, Red Transfer, Basket Weave Border, Salt Glaze, 9 ⅛ In.........*Illus*	3120.00

Stein, Character, Iron Maiden Torture Chamber, Stoneware, ½ Liter
$219.00

Fox Auctions

Stein, Character, Mother-In-Law, Pottery, Marked, 680, ½ Liter
$193.00

The Stein Auction Co.

Stein, Character, Munich Child, Holding Stein & Radish, Porcelain, ½ Liter
$472.00

Fox Auctions

S

559

Stein, Character, Sad Radish, Porcelain, Figural Leaf Inlay Lid, Schierholz, ⅛ Liter
$225.00

Fox Auctions

Stein, Character, Stahl, Mother-In-Law, Porcelain, ½ Liter
$58.00

Fox Auctions

Stein, Glass, Blown, Flowers, Cased, Cranberry, White On Clear, Inlaid Lid, ½ Liter
$480.00

The Stein Auction Co.

Plate, Bank Of The United States, Philadelphia, c.1840, 10 In.	356.00
Plate, Blue, Landing Of General Lafayette, Marked, Blue Transfer, 1880s, 10 In.	200.00
Plate, Boston State House, Flower Border, Blue Transfer, c.1845, 9 ¾ In.	184.00
Plate, Chief Justice Marshall, Side-Wheeler Steamboat, Hudson River, c.1835, 10 In. ......*Illus*	590.00
Plate, City Of Albany New York, Blue Transfer, Enoch Wood & Sons, c.1825, 10 ½ In.	531.00
Plate, Columbus, Blue Transfer, Oval, James & Ralph Clews, c.1820, 14 ⅜ In.	2950.00
Plate, Dam, Water Works, Boat, Philadelphia, Blue Transfer, Henshall, Williamson & Co., c.1830, 9 In.	472.00
Plate, Detroit, Blue Transfer, James & Ralph Clews, c.1820, 18 ½ In.	2478.00
Plate, Exchange, Baltimore, Fruit, Flowers, Blue Transfer, Henshall, Williamson & Co., c.1820, 10 In.	295.00
Plate, Fair Mount Near Philadelphia, Eagle Border, Blue Transfer, c.1820, 10 In.	259.00
Plate, Hospital Boston, Vine Border, Blue Transfer, Ralph Stevenson, c.1830, 9 ¼ In.	531.00
Plate, Landing Of The Fathers At Plymouth, Blue Transfer, c.1820, 9 ⅞ In.	127.00
Plate, Nahant Hotel Near Boston, Eagle Border, Blue Transfer, c.1845, 9 In.	259.00
Plate, Peace Plenty, Scroll, Flowers, Blue Transfer, c.1835, 10 ¼ In.	147.00
Plate, Pine Orchard House, Mountains, Blue Transfer, Enoch Wood & Sons, c.1820, 11 In.	236.00
Plate, Pittsfield, Massachusetts, Blue Transfer, James & Ralph Clews, c.1820, 10 ½ In.	236.00
Plate, Sandusky, Blue Transfer, Oval, James & Ralph Clews, c.1820, 16 ½ In.	4248.00
Plate, Soup, American & Independence, States Border, Blue Transfer, c.1835, 10 ½ In.	235.00
Plate, Soup, La Grange, Dark Blue Transfer, Impressed E. Woods, c.1825, 10 ¼ In.	295.00
Plate, Spread Wing Eagle, Lafayette & Washington Busts, Scalloped, c.1824, 6 ⅝ In.	1304.00
Plate, Texian Campaign, Purple, White Transfer, c.1860, 8 ¼ In.	230.00
Plate, Upper Ferry Bridge, River Schuylkill, Eagle Border, c.1835, 9 In. Diam.	206.00
Platte, Marmora, Oval, White, Blue Transfer, c.1860, 8 ¾ x 10 ⅝ In.	46.00
Platter, 2 Hunters & Hounds, Flower & Game Bird Border, Oval, 12 x 9 In.	480.00
Platter, Amula Pattern, Flowers, Urn, Blue Border, Canted Oval, E. Challinor & Co., 17 ½ In.	266.00
Platter, Castle Garden Battery, New York, Blue Transfer, Enoch Wood & Sons, c.1820, 21 In.	3304.00
Platter, Conway Castle, Blue & White, Wales, R. Hall, 15 In.	118.00
Platter, Dog, Chasing Bird, Landscape, Blue Transfer, 18 In.	298.00
Platter, Lions & Cubs, Flower Border, Blue Transfer, c.1835, 15 x 19 ½ In.	823.00
Platter, Mendenhall Ferry, Eagle Border, Blue Transfer, Stubbs & Kent, c. 1830, 17 In.	1461.00
Platter, Newburg, Hudson River, Brown Transfer, Jas., & Ralph Clews, c.1822, 16 In.	236.00
Platter, Regent's Street, London, Blue Transfer, 1800s, 13 ½ x 17 ¼ In.	122.00
Platter, Sandusky, Dark Blue Transfer, James & Ralph Clews, 16 ¾ In.	3304.00
Platter, Upper Ferry Bridge, Schuylkill River, Border, Blue Transfer, Joseph Stubbs, c.1835, 19 In.	1770.00
Platter, View Of Dublin, Blue Transfer, Impressed Wood, c.1830, 11 ¾ x 14 ¾ In.	575.00
Platter, Windsor Castle, Clews, Impressed, c.1845, 13 x 17 In.	259.00
Platter, Woodland, Horse, Cart, Black Transfer, Pink & White Border, 15 ½ In.	118.00
Serving Bowl, Lid, Fairy Villas, Blue Transfer, Lug Handles, Adams Flow Blue, c.1900, 6 x 10 In.	69.00
Spill Vase, Cow, Tree Stump, Oval Grassy Base, c.1840, 10 ½ In., Pair	780.00
Stirrup Cup, Fox's Mask, Pink Luster, c.1820, 4 ¼ In.	767.00
Stirrup Cup, Hare's Head, 1810-20, 6 ¾ In.	1534.00
Stirrup Cup, Hound's Head, Mottled Pink Luster, c.1820, 5 ¼ In.	1062.00
Sugar, Lid, House In Landscape, Rose Transfer Print, Flared Collar & Foot, 7 In.	295.00
Sugar, Lid, Washington's Tomb, Blue Transfer, Outcurved Handles, Scalloped Rim, 1800s, 6 In.	115.00
Tea Set, Brown Transferware, Children's, Service For 8.	170.00
Teapot, Lid, Camel, Kneeling, Howdah, Umbrella, Stylized Handle, c.1745, 6 In.	11800.00
Teapot, Lid, Isle Of Man Sailor, Rope, Majolica, Wm. Brownfield, 9 In.	118.00
Teapot, Lid, Red Rose, Brown & Black Spatterware, c.1875, 6 x 6 In.	403.00
Tobacco Jar, English Bobby, Green Uniform, Gilt, 7 ½ In.	23.00
Toby Jugs are listed in their own category.	
Tureen, Hen Shape Lid, Basket Nest Bottom, 1800s, 3 ½ In., Pair	270.00
Vase, Dog, Spaniel, White, Tree Stump Bowl, c.1845, 13 In., Pair.	708.00
Vase, Urn Shape, Drapery, Putti, Wyvern Handles, Shell, Scroll Borders, c.1790, 10 In., Pair.	738.00
Waste Bowl, Lafayette At Franklin's Tomb, Blue Transfer, c.1845, 3 x 5 ⅜ In.	230.00
Watch Holder, 3 Graces, 3 Posing Women, Flowers, Doves, Multicolor, Gilt, 11 ⅝ x 8 In.	98.00

STAINLESS STEEL *items may be listed in the Chrome category.*

STANGL POTTERY traces its history back to the Fulper Pottery of New Jersey. In 1910, Johann Martin Stangl started working at Fulper. He left to work at Haeger Pottery from 1915 to 1920. Stangl returned to Fulper Pottery in 1920, became president in 1926, and changed the company name to Stangl Pottery in 1929. Stangl acquired the firm in 1930. The pottery is known for dinnerware and a line of bird figurines. Martin Stangl died in 1972 and the pottery was sold to Frank Wheaton Jr. of Wheaton Industries. Production continued until 1978, when Pfaltzgraff Pottery purchased the right to the Stangl trademark and the remaining inventory was liquidated. A single bird figurine is identified by a number. Figurines made up of two birds are identified by a number followed by the letter *D* indicating Double.

STANGL

Bird, Audubon Warbler, No. 3740, 7 In.	1063.00
Bird, Crossbill, No. 372B, 5 ¾ In.	1500.00

Bird, Kinglet Family, No. 3853, 5 ¼ In. 98.00
Bird, Magpie Jay, No. 3758, 10 ¾ In. 375.00
Bird, Red Headed Woodpecker, No. 3725, Glazed, Marked, 7 x 6 ¾ In. .... *Illus* 1000.00
Bird, Scissortail Flycatcher, No. 3757, 10 ¾ In. 375.00
Bittersweet, Bowl, Fruit, 5 ½ In. 8.00
Bittersweet, Platter, Oval, 14 ¾ In. 42.00
Blueberry, Casserole, Lid, 3 ¾ In. 36.00
Blueberry, Double Eggcup, 3 ⅜ In. 22.00
Country Garden, Bread Tray, 15 ¼ In. 40.00
Country Garden, Plate, 10 ⅛ In. 26.00
Fruit & Flowers, Mug, 2 ¾ In. 56.00
Fruit & Flowers, Pitcher, 16 Oz., 4 ½ In. 119.00
Fruit & Flowers, Teapot, Lid, 5 Cup, 4 ½ In. 259.00
Fruit, Coffeepot, Lid, 6 Cup, 7 ½ In. 150.00
Fruit, Cup & Saucer 18.00
Fruit, Plate, 10 In. 38.00
Garden Flower, Creamer, 6 Oz., 3 In. 23.00
Garland, Bowl, Vegetable, Divided, Oval, 10 ¾ In. 59.00
Garland, Pitcher, 64 Oz., 6 ¼ In. 64.00
Golden Harvest, Dish, Pickle, 10 ½ In. 30.00
Golden Harvest, Soup, Dish, Lug Handles, 6 ⅛ In. 24.00
Magnolia, Creamer, 8 Oz., 2 ¾ In. 28.00
Magnolia, Double Eggcup, 3 ⅜ In. 18.00
Magnolia, Plate, Dinner, 10 ⅛ In. 23.00
Magnolia, Salt & Pepper 30.00
Provincial, Bowl, Vegetable, Divided, Oval, 10 ⅞ In. 21.00
Provincial, Plate, Dinner, 10 In. 16.00
Town & Country, Candlestick, Blue, 7 ½ In. 49.00
Town & Country, Chop Plate, Blue, 12 ½ In. 44.00
Town & Country, Creamer, Blue, 10 Oz., 3 ½ In. 33.00
Tulip, Pot, Yellow, Marked, 3 ⅝ In. 18.00
Vase, Green, Red, Yellow, Green, Lobed, Footed, 9 ¼ In. 23.00
Vase, Mottled Green, Blue, Lobed, Footed, 6 ¼ In. 23.00
Wild Rose, Gravy Boat 24.00
Wild Rose, Plate, Dinner, 10 ⅛ In. 28.00

STAR TREK AND STAR WARS collectibles are included here. The original *Star Trek* television series ran from 1966 through 1969. The series spawned an animated TV series, three TV sequels, and a TV prequel. The first *Star Trek* movie was released in 1979 and eleven others followed, the most recent in 2013. The movie *Star Wars* opened in 1977. Sequels were released in 1980 and 1983; prequels in 1999, 2002, and 2005. All six episodes are being converted to 3D and will be re-released beginning in 2012. Other science fiction and fantasy collectibles can be found under Batman, Buck Rogers, Captain Marvel, Flash Gordon, Movie, Superman, and Toy.

STAR TREK

Bank Mold, Captain Kirk, Copper, For Vinyl Bank, Play Pal Plastics, 12 ½ In. 177.00
Book & Record, Passage To Moauv, 1979 .... 18.00
Buckle, Metal, Coppertone, Starship Enterprise, 1976, 1 ⅝ x 2 In. 45.00
Coloring Book, Rescue At Raylo, Whitman Publishing Co., 30 Page, 1978 .... 18.00
Game, Pinball, The Next Generation, Electric, Williams, 1994, 77 x 29 In. 2706.00
Lunch Box, Dome, Tin, Aircraft, Lithograph, 9 x 6 ½ In. 270.00
Toy, Astrocopter, Helicopter, Pilot Figure, Soldiers, Box, 1967, 6 ¼ x 12 ¼ In. 466.00

STAR WARS

Bank, Mechanical, Qui-Gon Jinn, Episode 1 .... 42.00
Calendar, 1979, Movie Pictures, Full Pad 22.00
Comic Book, No. 13, Marvel, July 1978 .... 4.00
Cookie Jar, Chewbacca, 16 x 10 In. 130.00
Figure, C3PO, Jointed, 12 In. 45.00
Figure, Han Solo, Camouflaged Trench Coat 12.00
Figure, Princess Leia Organa, Kenner 10.00
Lamp, Darth Vader, Bust, Black Gloss, Multicolor Lights, Ceramic, Figural, c.1977, 14 In. 115.00
Movie Poster, Release, Main Characters, 1977, 27 x 41 In. 253.00
PEZ Dispenser, Luke Skywalker 21.00
Poster, Starfield, Raised Lightsaber, Black & White, 1977, 22 x 28 In. 115.00
Record Tote, R2-D2, C3PO, White Handle, Plastic, 1982, 7 ¾ x 8 In. 120.00
Toy, Chewbacca, Plush, Regal Co., 1970s, 22 In. 40.00
Toy, Imperial Shuttle Vehicle, Opening Cockpit, Wing Cannons, Sounds, Box, 1984, 15 x 17 x 20 In. 209.00

Stein, Occupational, Shoemaker, Eagle Finial, Porcelain, ½ Liter
$189.00

Fox Auctions

Stein, Porcelain, Prinzessen Marianne Von Preussen 1846, Flowers & Cherub Inlaid Lid, Dresden, ½ Liter
$4,560.00

The Stein Auction Co.

Stein, Porcelain, Royal Vienna Style, Motto, Gilding, Beehive Mark, 1 Liter
$870.00

The Stein Auction Co.

Stein, Porcelain, Rugby Game, Inlaid Lid, Lithophane, Transfer By Swaine, Delft, ½ Liter
$450.00

The Stein Auction Co.

Stein, Pottery, Couple, Well Dressed, Strolling, Etched, No. 722, Dumler & Breiden, ½ Liter
$147.00

Fox Auctions

Stein, Pottery, Man & Student, Transfer, Enameled, Pewter Lid, Hauber & Reuther, Marked H.R., 1 Liter
$450.00

The Stein Auction Co.

STEINS have been used by beer and ale drinkers for over 500 years. They have been made of ivory, porcelain, stoneware, faience, silver, pewter, wood, or glass in sizes up to nine gallons. Although some were made by Mettlach, Meissen, Capo-di-Monte, and other famous factories, most were made by less important German potteries. The words *Geschutz* or *Musterschutz* on a stein are the German words for "patented" or "registered design," not company names. Steins are still being made in the old styles. Lithophane steins may be found in the Lithophane category.

Bamboo, Silver Plate Mounts, Jungle Scene, c.1880, 8 ½ In.	3360.00
Beaker, Blown Glass, 3rd Reich, Deutschland Erwache, Sieg-Heil, ½ Liter, 8 ¼ In. ....*Illus*	360.00
Character, Alligator, Pottery, Marked, Marzi & Remy, ½ Liter, 6 In. ....*Illus*	276.00
Character, Artillery Shell, Pewter, Bavarian Crest, Pewter Lid, ½ Liter	360.00
Character, Artillery Shell, Porcelain, Lithophane, ½ Liter	312.00
Character, Barmaid, Porcelain Lid, Pewter Strap, ½ Liter	2760.00
Character, Bustle Woman, Blue, Reinhold Hanke, ½ Liter	2530.00
Character, Cat, Painted, Pottery, Inlaid Lid, Marked, RM 575, ½ Liter ....*Illus*	306.00
Character, Chinaman, Braided Handle, Schierholz, ½ Liter	1035.00
Character, Devil, Porcelain, Bohne & Sohne, ½ Liter	492.00
Character, Fox, Head, Porcelain, Musterschutz, Schierholz, Germany, ½ Liter ....*Illus*	1950.00
Character, Frog, Blue & Purple Salt Glaze, Stoneware, Pewter Rim, ½ Liter	390.00
Character, Gentleman Rabbit, Porcelain, Marked Musterschutz, ½ Liter	360.00
Character, Gentleman Rabbit, Porcelain, Marked, Musterschutz, By Schierholz, ½ Liter.... *Illus*	1920.00
Character, Gnome, Pottery, Diesinger, ½ Liter	300.00
Character, Happy Radish, Porcelain, Schierholz, ⅓ Liter	114.00
Character, Iron Maiden Torture Chamber, Stoneware, ½ Liter. ....*Illus*	219.00
Character, Iron Maiden, Stoneware, Inlaid Lid, Marked, T.W., ½ Liter.	390.00
Character, Man On High Wheel Bicycle, Stoneware, Pewter Lid, ½ Liter	1740.00
Character, Man With Pipe, Hanke Pottery, ½ Liter	142.00
Character, Monk Reading Paper, Stoneware, Kolnische Zeitung, ½ Liter	276.00
Character, Mother-In-Law, Pottery, Marked, 680, ½ Liter. ....*Illus*	193.00
Character, Munich Child, Holding Bible, Lithograph, Martin Pauson, ½ Liter	271.00
Character, Munich Child, Holding Stein & Radish, Porcelain, ½ Liter. ....*Illus*	472.00
Character, Munich Child, Porcelain, ½ Liter	96.00
Character, Munich Child, Porcelain, Lithophane, ½ Liter	505.00
Character, Oriental Man, Pottery, Inlaid Lid, ½ Liter	276.00
Character, Owl, Head & Neck Lift, Pewter Hinge, Round Base, Ceramic, Impressed, 8 In.	121.00
Character, Owl, Porcelain, Inlaid Lid, Bohne & Sohne, ½ Liter	2340.00
Character, Owl, Pottery, Marked M.W.G., ½ Liter	204.00
Character, Pig, Inlaid Lid, Pottery, ½ Liter	204.00
Character, Radish Lady, Porcelain, Marked Musterschutz, Schierholz, ½ Liter.	313.00
Character, Rich Man, Top Hat, Tie, Pottery, Marked, Thewalt, Germany, ½ Liter	288.00
Character, Sad Radish, Loop Handle, Leaf Finial, Dome Lid, Pewter, Musterschutz, ½ Pt., 7 ¼ In.	165.00
Character, Sad Radish, Porcelain, Figural Leaf Inlay Lid, Schierholz, ⅛ Liter ....*Illus*	225.00
Character, Stahl, Mother-In-Law, Porcelain, ½ Liter. ....*Illus*	58.00
Character, Target Girl, Inlaid Lid, Musterschutz, Schierholz, ½ Liter.	276.00
Cross-Eyed Man, Porcelain, Bohne & Sohne, ½ Liter.	1080.00
Enamel On Copper, People Dancing, Village, 7 In., ½ Liter.	3000.00
Faience, Brown Horse, Leaping, Pewter Lid, Bayreuther Walzenkrug, c.1780, 10 In.	480.00
Faience, Figure, Seated, Bugs, Yellow, Blue, Ribbed, Pewter Lid & Footring, Walzenkrug, c.1790, 8 In.	870.00
Faience, Flowers, Blue Glaze, Pewter Lid & Footring, c.1800, 8 ½ In.	390.00
Faience, Flowers, Blue White, Pewter Lid, c.1785, ¼ Liter, 4 ½ In.	172.00
Faience, Flowers, Multicolor, Pewter Lid, Footring, Schrezheimer Walzenkrug, c.1750, 8 ½ In.	600.00
Faience, Jesus, Joseph, Pewter Lid & Footring, Bayreuth Birnkrug, 1816, 11 In.	2220.00
Faience, Man & Bird, Pewter Lid & Footring, 1790, 9 In.	720.00
Faience, Orange, Green Loops, Leaves, Pewter Lid, Footring, Schrezheimer Walzenkrug, c.1800, 8 In.	360.00
Faience, Stag, Trees, Pewter Lid, Schrezheimer Walzenkrug, c.1760, 9 ¼ In.	630.00
Faience, White Horse, Leaping, Pewter Lid, Hannoversch Mundener Waltzenkrug, c.1800, 9 In....	312.00
Glass, Blown, Dog, Hunter, Facet Cut White Enamel, ½ Liter	184.00
Glass, Blown, Flowers, Cased, Cranberry, White On Clear, Inlaid Lid, ½ Liter. ....*Illus*	480.00
Glass, Blown, Purple On White, Brass Counts, ½ Liter.	1680.00
Glass, Clear, Fluted, Blue Insert, Pewter Lid, Bicycle & Rider, 7 ½ In.	100.00
Glass, Clear, Postcard, Painted, Pewter Lid, c.1900, ½ Liter.	96.00
Glass, Coat-Of-Arms, Enameled, White, Cased, Pewter Lid, ½ Liter.	192.00
Glass, Dog, Blue On Clear, Inlaid Lid, c.1850, ½ Liter.	3240.00
Glass, Enamel Overlay, Pink Over Clear, c.1880, ⅛ Liter.	161.00
Glass, Red On Clear Overlay, Jewels, Pewter Lid, c.1880, ½ Liter.	198.00
Glass, Stag, In Forest, Antler Finial & Thumblift, Pewter Lid, ½ Liter.	264.00

Mettlach steins are listed in the Mettlach category.

Military, Erinnerung An Meine, Dienarzeit, Pewter Lid, Helmet, Stoneware, ½ Liter	316.00
Military, Pottery, Komp Kraftfahrabteilung, 1933, ½ Liter	420.00
Occupational, Shoemaker, Eagle Finial, Porcelain, ½ Liter.....................*Illus*	189.00
Pewter, Baluster, Hinged Lid, Stepped Foot, Engraved Inscriptions & Dated 1732, 11 In.	300.00
Porcelain, Flowers, Strawberry Finial, Gilt, c.1875, 1 Liter	1620.00
Porcelain, Prinzessen Marianne Von Preussen 1846, Cherub Inlaid Lid, Dresden, ½ Liter ....*Illus*	4560.00
Porcelain, Royal Vienna Style, Motto, Gilding, Beehive Mark, 1 Liter	870.00
Porcelain, Rugby Game, Inlaid Lid, Lithophane, Transfer By Swaine, Delft, ½ Liter........*Illus*	450.00
Pottery, Couple Dancing, Mandolin Player, Etched, 1 Liter	196.00
Pottery, Couple, Well Dressed, Strolling, Etched, No. 722, Dumler & Breiden, ½ Liter......*Illus*	147.00
Pottery, Man, Student, Transfer, Enameled, Pewter Lid, Hauber & Reuther, Marked, 1 Liter ......*Illus*	450.00
Pottery, Military, Relief, Pewter Lid, Marked 1434, Bavarian, ½ Liter	102.00
Pottery, Statue Of Liberty, Relief, ⅛ Liter	35.00
Regimental, 3 Comp., 67 Inft. Regt., Eagle Thumblift, Friedrich Lindenberg, 1901, ½ Liter, 10 In.	253.00
Regimental, Feld Backer Abthlg., Train Batl. Nr. 13, Gargoyle Thumblift, c.1885, 1 Liter.....*Illus*	1020.00
Regimental, Roster, 2 Comp., Jager Bataillon, St. Hubert Thumblift, 1911-13, ½ Liter, 10 In..	2880.00
Regimental, Roster, 2 Komp, 10 Lothring, Inftr., Regt. Nr. 174, Names, Scenes, 1907, ½ Liter..... *Illus*	19320.00
Regimental, Roster, 3 Battr, Feld Art. Regt No. 17, St. Barbara Thumblift, c.1905, ½ Liter, 9 In.	1110.00
Regimental, Roster, 9 Comp, Bayr. Inft. Regt. No. 18, Lion Thumblift, c.1907, ½ Liter, 11 In..	205.00
Regimental, Roster, 10 Comp., Bayr. Inft, Regt. No. 16, Passau, Lion Thumblift, c.1913, ½ Liter, 12 In.	312.00
Regimental, Roster, 11 Comp., Inft. Regt. No. 110, Griffin Thumblift, Pottery, ½ Liter, 13 In..	312.00
Regimental, Roster, Maschinengewehr, Abt. No. 2, Trier, Eagle Thumblift, c.1913, ½ Liter, 13 In.	1200.00
Regimental, Skull, 5. Esk., Husaren Regt. Nr. 17, Braunschweig, Horse, 1907, ½ Liter.....*Illus*	3240.00
Stoneware, Blue, Salt Glaze, Pewter Lid, Incised Westerwalder Walzenkrug, c.1790, 9 ½ In....	570.00
Stoneware, Creussen Style, Saints, Symbols, Relief, Pewter Lid, c.1900, 1 Liter	240.00
Stoneware, Leaping Stag, Impressed, 1 Liter	47.00
Stoneware, Man, Dachshund, Pewter Lid, Transfer, Enamel, 1 Liter	252.00
Stoneware, Relief, Blue & Brown Salt Glaze, Pewter Lid, 2 Liter	930.00
Stoneware, Third Reich, Komp., I.R. 42, Hof, Pewter Lid, Relief Initials FP, ½ Liter.........*Illus*	276.00
Tankard, Burl, Lion, Loop Handle, Animal Feet, Lid, 10 In.	978.00
Wood, Figural Stag Head Lid, Shield, Opens In 2 Parts, Glass Eyes, ½ Liter.....................*Illus*	690.00

STEREO CARDS that were made for stereoscope viewers became popular after 1840. Two almost identical pictures were mounted on a stiff cardboard backing so that, when viewed through a stereoscope, a three-dimensional picture could be seen. Value is determined by maker and by subject. These cards were made in quantity through the 1930s.

3 Wise Men, Adoration Des Mages, 1850s, 3 ⅜ x 6 ¾ In.	125.00
Great Fire, Portland, Maine, Soule, 1866	29.00
Hampton Beach, New Hampshire, Summer Cottages, Hobbs	39.00
Looking North On Broadway, New York City	5.00
Lower Falls, Yellowstone National Park	12.00
Montezuma, Colorado Ghost Silver Mining Town, Collier	249.00
Moosehead Lake, Maine Indian Camp	249.00
New York City, Woolworth Building, City Hall Park, c.1914	45.00
New York Railroad Bridge	24.00
Palace Of Mines, St. Louis World's Fair, 1904	15.00
Pillsbury A-Mill, Minneapolis, Minnesota, Vanderwarker & Nally	29.00
Place D'Espagne, Rome, Italy	19.00
Queen Victoria, Her Majesty	10.00
San Francisco Earthquake & Fire, Box, 50 Cards	413.00
San Francisco, California, 30 Cards	413.00
St. Louis, Shaw Gardens, 1904 World's Fair, 96 Cards	236.00
White House, Blue Room, Washington, D.C., J.F. Jarvis	19.00
Zeppelin, Flying Over German Town	8.00

STEREOSCOPES were used for viewing stereo cards. The hand viewer was invented by Oliver Wendell Holmes, although more complicated table models were used before his was produced in 1859. Do not confuse the stereoscope with the stereopticon, a magic lantern that used glass slides.

Burl Walnut, Ebony Trim, Magnifier, Collapsible, Victorian, 8 ½ In.	325.00
Burl Walnut, Lockable Top Shutters, State Capital Buildings, Knobs, Victorian, 21 ½ x 10 In...	2714.00
Burl Walnut, Magnifier, Victorian, 10 x 15 In.	472.00
Ebony, Collapsible, Magnifier, Victorian, 8 ¾ In.	413.00
Graphoscope, Wood, 6 Cards, Patented USA Apr. 23, 1889, Fitted Box	168.00
Perfecscope, Underwood & Underwood, Hand Held, 1880s.....................*Illus*	48.00

Stein, Regimental, Feld Backer Abthlg., Train Batl. Nr. 13, Porcelain, Gargoyle Thumblift, c.1885, 1 Liter
$1,020.00

The Stein Auction Co.

Stein, Regimental, Roster, 2 Komp, 10 Lothring, Inftr., Regt. Nr. 174, Names, Scenes, 1907, ½ Liter
$19,320.00

The Stein Auction Co.

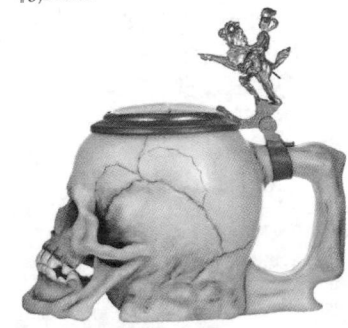

Stein, Regimental, Skull, 5 Esk., Husaren Regt. Nr. 17, Braunschweig, Horse, 1907, ½ Liter
$3,240.00

The Stein Auction Co.

S

Stein, Stoneware, Third Reich, Komp., I.R. 42, Hof, Pewter Lid, Relief Initials FP, ½ Liter
$276.00

The Stein Auction Co.

Stein, Wood, Figural Stag Head Lid, Shield, Opens In 2 Parts, Glass Eyes, ½ Liter
$690.00

Fox Auctions

Stereoscope, Perfecscope, Underwood & Underwood, Hand Held, 1880s
$48.00

Victorian Casino Antiques

S

> **TIP**
>
> *A dealer told us although Steuben Glass has closed, he thought it would take ten years before Steuben glass would go up in price. Watch for it at thrift shops and yard sales. He found a bowl for $8.50.*

Walnut, Bird's-Eye Maple, Portable, Victorian, c.1880, 14 x 9 In.	360.00
Wood, Metal, Monarch, Cards, c.1895, 12 x 6 In.	30.00

STERLING SILVER, *see Silver-Sterling category.*

STEUBEN glass was made at the Steuben Glass Works of Corning, New York. The factory, founded by Frederick Carder and T.G. Hawkes, Sr., was purchased by the Corning Glass Company. Corning continued to make glass called Steuben. Many types of art glass were made at Steuben. Schottenstein Stores Inc. bought 80 percent of the business in 2008. The factory closed in 2011 and no more of this quality glass will be made. Additional pieces may be found in the Cluthra and Perfume Bottle categories.

Basket, Applied Rosettes, Blue Aurene, 3 ⅛ x 2 ¼ x 3 ¼ In.	2875.00
Basket, Applied Rosettes, Gold Aurene Over Calcite, 5 ½ In.	748.00
Bonbon, Verre-De-Soie, Stretch Border, Iridescent, Footed, Ruffled Rim, 2 ¼ In.	173.00
Bowl, Amethyst, Rolled Rim, Optic Swirl, Signed, Fleur-De-Lis, 7 In.	58.00
Bowl, Aurene On Calcite, Signed F. Carder, 3 ½ x 10 In.	356.00
Bowl, Blue Aurene, c.1910, 12 ½ In.	720.00
Bowl, Blue Grotesque, c.1920, 6 x 11 ½ In.	189.00
Bowl, Canton, Plum Jade Acid Cut Back, Acid Stamped, Fleur-De-Lis, 8 In.	1380.00
Bowl, Clear Etched, Green Footed Base, 6 ¼ x 9 ¾ In.	415.00
Bowl, Clear, Flared, Black Threaded Horizontal Design, 5 ¼ x 12 In.	546.00
Bowl, Clear, Flared, Hollow Knob Foot, Engraved, c.1985, 15 ½ In.	540.00
Bowl, Clear, Footed, John Dreves, 1949, 8 In.	212.00
Bowl, Clear, Footed, Round, 8 In.	79.00
Bowl, Dimpled Foot, 7 ¼ x 16 ¼ In.	304.00
Bowl, Flared Rim, Onion Skin Border, Blue Aurene Over Calcite, 3 ¾ x 9 ¼ In.	374.00
Bowl, Flared, Aurene & Calcite, 3 ½ x 9 ¾ In.	356.00
Bowl, Glass Footed, 4 x 11 In.	117.00
Bowl, Gold Aurene & Calcite, Flared, 3 x 10 In.	288.00
Bowl, Gold, Flared Foldover Rim, Ring Foot, Signed, Aurene, 12 In.	546.00
Bowl, Gold, Ruffled Edge, Aurene, 2 ¼ x 5 In.	235.00
Bowl, Grape, Green Jade Acid Cut Back, Oval, Rolled Rim, 7 ½ In.	311.00
Bowl, Green Jade, Alabaster Spread Foot, Wide Flat Rim, 12 In. Diam.	413.00
Bowl, Green Jade, Melon Ribbed, Flaring Ruffled Rim, 5 ¼ x 10 In.	230.00
Bowl, Ice Skaters, Etched, Signed, 2 ¼ x 7 ½ In.	360.00
Bowl, Iridescent Blue, Flared Rim, Ring Foot, Aurene, 8 In.	431.00
Bowl, Jade Glass, Signed F. Carder, 4 ½ x 8 In.	711.00
Bowl, Jadeite, Translucent, Low Base, 7 ⅛ In.	173.00
Bowl, Lens, Concentric Circles, Walter Dorwin Teague, Etched, c.1932, 2 ¼ x 12 In.	3220.00
Bowl, Lid, Applied Gazelle Finial, Clear, Flared, Signed, 6 ¼ In.	189.00
Bowl, Low, Rolled Flared Rim, Blue Aurene On Calcite, 14 ½ In.	489.00
Bowl, Matzu Pattern, Jade Color, White Blossoming Branches, Oval Shape, Signed, 7 In.	748.00
Bowl, Plum Jade, Opalescent Interior, Shallow, Inverted Rim, 10 ½ In.	518.00
Bowl, Ring Foot, Flaring Rim, Gold Aurene Over Calcite, 5 x 14 In.	144.00
Bowl, Round, Pedestal Foot, 8-Scroll Base, c.1961, 15 ⅜ In.	750.00
Bowl, Spiral, Signed, 3 ½ x 7 In.	360.00
Bowl, Stretched Border, Ring Foot, Blue Aurene, Signed, 5 In.	1093.00
Bowl, Threaded Blue, Scalloped Rim Bubble Glass, Oval, 2 ¾ x 14 In.	230.00
Bowl, Yellow Pulled Horizontal Threading, Green Footed Base, 5 ½ x 8 ¾ In.	243.00
Candelabrum, Ivory, 3 Ribbed Flower Stems, Rigaree Base, Textured Leaf Cups, 10 ½ In.	1035.00
Candle Whimsy, Rosaline, Swirled Stems, Alabaster Ends, 10 In., Pair	374.00
Candleholder, Ivrene, Double Ribbed, Swirling Stems, Iridescent Foot, Signed, 8 ¼ In.	345.00
Candlestick, Cone Shape Foot, Flaring Flared Rim, Gold Aurene, 6 In.	230.00
Candlestick, Green Jade, Alabaster, Stems, Vines, Grapes, Bell Foot, Flared Foldover Rim, 12 In.	1150.00
Candlestick, Pomona Green Socket & Foot, Etched Amber Stem, Tapered, c.1920, 10 In.	480.00
Candlestick, Rope Crystal Stem, Topaz, Ribbed Foot & Cup, Spread Base, 12 In., Pair	460.00
Candlestick, Teardrop, Crystal, 8 ¾ In., Pair	900.00
Candlestick, Twist Stem, Gold Aurene, Signed, 7 In., Pair	863.00
Candlestick, Twist Stem, Saucer Foot, Blue Aurene, Iridescent, Signed, 8 In., Pair	1150.00
Candlestick, Twisted Stem, Inverted Saucer Foot, Blue Iridescent, Gold Aurene, 8 In., Pair	690.00
Candlestick, Yellow, Footed, Signed, 3 ¾ In., Pair	356.00
Centerpiece, Light Blue Jade, Translucent, Wide Rim, Ring Foot, 3 ¾ x 10 In.	374.00
Centerpiece, Wide Flat Rim, Ribbed Body, Bell Shape Base, Green & Amber, Fleur-De-Lis, 12 ¼ In.	546.00
Cigarette Box, Translucent Citron, Frosted Lid, Etched Flowers, Signed, 2 ¾ x 6 In.	403.00
Cocktail, Teardrop, Signed, Box, 4 ¾ In., 8 Piece	1080.00
Cologne Bottle, Blue Aurene, Stopper	1265.00

Steuben, Compote, Gold Aurene, c.1910, 8 x 6 In.
$780.00

DuMouchelles Art Gallery

Steuben, Jar, Lid, Pear Finial, Bristol, Yellow, 6 ½ In.
$460.00

Early Auction Co.

Steuben, Lamp Base, Cintra, Shouldered, Stylized Blossoms, 28 In.
$460.00

Early Auction Co.

Steuben, Lamp Base, Green Jade, Black Acid Cut Flowers, 12 In.
$690.00

Cottone Auctions

Steuben, Perfume Atomizer, Blue, Embossed Fittings, Aurene, 9 ½ In.
$518.00

Early Auction Co.

Steuben, Perfume Bottle, Jade, Alabaster, Melon Ribbed, 8 In.
$173.00

Early Auction Co.

Steuben, Vase, Brown Pulled Feather, Pink & Blue Highlights, Gold Aurene, Signed, 11 ½ In.
$8,050.00

James D. Julia Auctioneers

Steuben, Vase, Corset Shape, Scalloped Rim, Red Iridescent, Gold Hearts & Vines, Aurene, 8 In.
$20,700.00

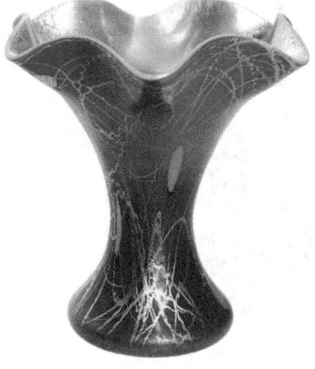

Early Auction Co,

Steuben, Vase, Fan, Bristol, Yellow, 8 ½ In.
$104.00

Early Auction Co.

Cologne Bottle, Melon Ribbed, Squat, Flame Stopper, Blue Aurene, Rockwell Gallery Label, 4 ¾ In.		460.00
Cologne Bottle, Tapered, Elongated Stopper, Blue Aurene, Signed, 6 ¾ In.		460.00
Compote, Aurene On Calcite, 6 In.		173.00
Compote, Dome Lid, Finial, Yellow Jade, Baluster Stem, Pedestal, Flared Rim, 10 In.		748.00
Compote, Frosted, Spreading Flower Center, Cinnamon & Pink, Pedestal Foot, 6 In.		3220.00
Compote, Gold Aurene, c.1910, 8 x 6 In.	*Illus*	780.00
Compote, Optic Ribs, Footed, Gold Aurene On Calcite, 10 In.		288.00
Compote, Pedestal Foot, Blue Aurene On Calcite, 2 ¾ x 6 ¼ In.		316.00
Compote, Ribbed, Footed, Stretch Border, Gold Aurene On Calcite, 3 ½ x 6 In.		345.00
Compote, Shell Shape, Twist Stem, Saucer Foot, Orange Amber Aurene, Signed, 7 In.		1495.00
Compote, Stretch Border, Gold Aurene On Calcite, 5 ½ In.		173.00
Compote, Twisted Stem, Scalloped Rim, Stretched Onionskin Border, Gold Aurene, 6 x 6 In.		748.00
Compote, Wide Flared Rim, Pedestal, Round Foot, Gold Aurene, 3 x 6 In.		316.00
Compote, Wide Undulated Rim, Twist Stem, Round Foot, Blue Aurene, Signed, 6 In.		920.00
Cordial, Spanish Green, Reeded Stem, Side Cabochons, 6 In., Pair		115.00
Creamer, Pomona Green, Topaz Round Foot & Loop Handle, Conical, Flared Spout, 4 ½ In.		259.00
Cup, Jade Green, Swirl Ribbing, Opalescent Twisted Stem, Round Foot, 6 In.		690.00
Decanter, Teardrop Shape, Teardrop In Stopper, Signed, 10 ½ In.		270.00
Decanter, Vermouth, Tapered Neck, Shield Stopper, 7 ¾ In., Pair		180.00
Domed Shade, Hanging, Calcite, Leafy Vine, Geometric Starburst, 3 Chains, Hardware, 14 In.		403.00
Figurine, Arctic Fisherman, Signed, Red Fitted Case, 6 ⅜ x 6 In.		3240.00
Figurine, Bear, Seated, Signed, 6 In.		300.00
Figurine, Blow Fish, Signed, 7 In.		150.00
Figurine, Castle Of Dreams, Signed, Box, 6 x 10 x 5 ½ In.		1920.00
Figurine, Cat, Seated, Signed, 8 ½ In.		270.00
Figurine, Duck, Long Neck, 8 In.		270.00
Figurine, Eagle, On Ball, Clear, Wood Stand, 7 x 12 In.		446.00
Figurine, Elephant, Trunk Raised, c.1950, 7 In.		563.00
Figurine, Frog, Clear, Gold Crown, 6 ¼ In.		1944.00
Figurine, Giraffe, Lloyd Atkins, Signed, 15 x 4 In.		900.00
Figurine, Kitten, Lloyd Atkins, 1955, 3 x 4 In.		240.00
Figurine, Octopus, Signed, 4 x 10 In.		900.00
Figurine, Owl, Clear, Signed, 5 ½ In.		122.00
Figurine, Partridge In Pear Tree, Glass Pear, 18K Yellow Gold Bird, Lloyd Atkins, Steuben, 6 In.		1800.00
Figurine, Penguin, 6 ¾ x 3 ½ In.		270.00
Figurine, Rabbit, Signed, 4 ¼ In.		240.00
Figurine, Rooster, Clear, 10 In.		327.00
Figurine, Snail, Vermeil, Stamped, Paul Shulze, 3 ½ x 6 ½ In.		1200.00
Figurine, Thistle Rock, Cut, Gilt Thistles, Signed, Red Fitted Case, 7 ½ x 3 ½ In.		2160.00
Figurine, Unicorn, Signed, 7 x 5 ½ In.		2040.00
Glass, Martini, Cone Shape, Wide Stem, Internal Airtwist, Round Foot, Inscribed, 3 ½ In., 6 Piece		243.00
Goblet, Amethyst Color, Etched Flowers, Leaves, Blown Hollow Stem, Round Foot, 8 ¼ In.		201.00
Goblet, Teardrop, Signed, 7 In., 8 Piece		1080.00
Goblet, Yellow Bowl, Blue Stem & Foot, 1930s, 16 x 11 ½ In.		625.00
Jar, Dome Lid, Dark Amethyst, Egg Shape, Pedestal Foot, Ball Stem, Clear Finial, 14 In.		1062.00
Jar, Lid, Pear Finial, Bristol, Yellow, 6 ½ In.	*Illus*	460.00
Lamp Base, Cintra, Shouldered, Stylized Blossoms, 28 In.	*Illus*	460.00
Lamp Base, Green Jade, Black Acid Cut Flowers, 12 In.	*Illus*	690.00
Lamp Base, Supino, Opal Over Green Cintra, Flowers, Acid Cut Back, 12 In.		1150.00
Lamp, Acid Cut Ivory, Primrose, Bulbous Stick Shape, Scroll Feet, Acanthus Bronze Collar, 23 In.		403.00
Lamp, Floor, Torchere, Amber Shades, Pierced, Reed & Rope Stem, Scalloped Base, 67 In., Pair		1265.00
Lamp, Grape, Ivrene, Acid Cut Back, Bulbous Stick Shape, Bronze Scrolling Feet, 23 In.		403.00
Nut Dish, Stretched Border, Gold Aurene Over Calcite, 3 ½ In.		86.00
Olive Dish, Flared, Scroll Handle, 1939, 6 ¼ In.		264.00
Olive Dish, Striated Curled Handle, 5 In.		150.00
Parfait, Blue Jade, Flared Rim, Alabaster Foot, Signed, J. Carder, 4 ½ In.		147.00
Perfume Atomizer, Blue, Embossed Fittings, Aurene, 9 ½ In.	*Illus*	518.00
Perfume Bottle, Jade, Alabaster, Melon Ribbed, 8 In.	*Illus*	173.00
Perfume Bottle, Tapered, Jeweled Finial, Blue Aurene, 10 In.		345.00
Plate, Jadeite, Acid Stamped, 8 ½ In., 5 Piece		253.00
Plate, Onionskin Border, Orange, Brown, Gold Aurene Over Calcite, 8 ½ In.		173.00
Plate, Scroll, 8 ½ In.		450.00
Plate, Service, Oriental Poppy, 8 ½ In.		173.00
Plate, Service, Wisteria, 8 ½ In.		144.00
Ring Tray, Blue Aurene, Ruffled Edge, Shallow Tray, Blue Aurene Hand, 4 ¼ In.		1150.00
Salt & Pepper, Faceted, Cylindrical Shape, Blue Aurene, 3 ¼ In., Pair		3565.00

Salt & Pepper, Faceted, Cylindrical Shape, Gold Aurene, 3 In., Pair	403.00
Salt Cellar, Gold, Round Foot, Flared Rim, Rainbow Highlights, Aurene, 1 ⅝ x 2 ½ In.	219.00
Shade, Calcite Glass, Etched Scrolling, 9 x 9 In.	180.00
Shade, Calcite, Green & Gold Pulled Feather, Ruffled Rim, 5 In., Pair	480.00
Shade, Intarzia Band, Bell Shape, Gold Iridescent, 10 In.	5312.00
Shade, Waves, Bell Shape, Gold Iridescent, Gold Aurene, 5 x 5 In.	75.00
Sherbet, Oriental Poppy, Pink Striated Bowl, Green Foot, Standard, Footed, 5 In.	920.00
Sherbet, Underplate, Onionskin Border, Gold Aurene, Calcite, Iridescent, 4 & 6 In., 12 Piece..	400.00
Urn, Flared Lip, Double Scroll Handles, Block Shape Base, Signed, 10 ½ x 6 In.	420.00
Vase, 3-Prong Stump, Iridescent Blue, Wavy Base, Aurene, 6 ¼ In.	978.00
Vase, Acid Cut Back, Double Etched, Chinese Pheasant, Blue Aurene Over Pomona Green, 13 In. .	3738.00
Vase, Acid Cut, Rosaline, Alabaster, Flower Design, Shouldered, Rolled Rim, 10 In.	575.00
Vase, Blue Flowers, Caramel Color, Trailing Vines, Baluster, Round Foot, Aurene, 1975, 3 In...	316.00
Vase, Blue Jade, Cylindrical, Ribbed, Pinched Neck, Flared Rim, Signed, 8 ½ In.	1035.00
Vase, Blue, Cylindrical, Ruffled Rim, Rounded Spread Foot, Signed, Aurene, 12 In.	690.00
Vase, Brown Pulled Feather, Pink & Blue Highlights, Gold Aurene, Signed, 11 ½ In..........*Illus*	8050.00
Vase, Bud, 3 Prongs, Pomona Green, 1920s, 6 ½ In., Pair	500.00
Vase, Bud, Lily, Ruffled Rim, Spread Foot, Gold Aurene, 6 In.	863.00
Vase, Bud, Stick, Saucer Foot, Blue Aurene, 6 ¼ In.	259.00
Vase, Bud, Tapered, Air Bubble In Base, Signed, 8 ¼ In., Pair	150.00
Vase, Bud, Tree Stump Design, 3 Cylindrical Tree Shaped Containers, Gold Aurene, 1910s, 6 x 4 In.	1000.00
Vase, Bud, Vine & Flower Design, Gold Aurene, U.S.A., 1900s, 7 ⅜ In.	2360.00
Vase, Celeste Blue, Optic Diamond, Amber Threading At Rim, Conical, Signed, 12 In.	173.00
Vase, Cintra, Green Satin, Oval, Flared, 2 Opalescent M-Handles, 11 In.	1955.00
Vase, Clear To Amethyst, Grotesque Cone Shape, Ruffled Rim, Spread Foot, 9 In.	144.00
Vase, Corset Shape, Scalloped Rim, Red Iridescent, Gold Hearts & Vines, Aurene, 8 In. .....*Illus*	20700.00
Vase, Custard Glass, Vase Shape, Double Black Handles, Carder, 10 ¼ In.	960.00
Vase, Double Gourd, Ring Foot, Blue Aurene, Signed, 12 ¼ In.	750.00
Vase, Double Lobed, Flower Ribbed, Wavy Rim, Blue Aurene, Signed, 6 In.	604.00
Vase, Dragon, Greek Key, Celeste Blue, Mirror Black, Acid Cut, Shouldered, 14 In.	7188.00
Vase, Elongated Trumpet, Scalloped Rim, Saucer Foot, Gold Aurene, Signed, 12 In.	460.00
Vase, Fan, Bristol, Yellow, 8 ½ In..........*Illus*	104.00
Vase, Fan, Green Heart, Vine Band, Footed, Gold Aurene, Signed, 8 ¾ In.	1725.00
Vase, Feathering, Pear Shape, Spread Foot, Gold, Aurene, 1979, 9 In.	115.00
Vase, Finger, Flared Body, 4 Divided Openings, Blue Aurene, Signed, 9 ¼ In.	748.00
Vase, Flared, Sidney Waugh, 6 ¾ x 9 In.	270.00
Vase, Flemish Blue, Melon Ribbed, Flower Shape Rim, 6 In.	115.00
Vase, Florentia, Green, Urn Shape, Silver Aventurine, Lime Green, Opal Leaves, Footed, 7 In...	2070.00
Vase, Flower Shape, Blue Aurene Iridescent, Signed, 3 x 8 In.	1500.00
Vase, Flower Shape, Round Onionskin Foot, Gold Aurene, 9 ¼ In.	3565.00
Vase, Flower Shape, Twisted Stem, Scalloped Rim, Blue Aurene, Signed, 12 ½ In..........*Illus*	1610.00
Vase, Flowers, Cut Back, Green & Blue Aurene, 6 ½ In.	3770.00
Vase, Gilt Leaves & Vines, Bulbous, Flared Rim, Blue Aurene, 10 ½ x 10 In.	4255.00
Vase, Gold Leaves & Vines, Shouldered, Pinched Neck, Green Aurene, 7 ½ In.	9488.00
Vase, Gold, Purple Foot Rim, Corset Shape, Flared Ruffled Rim, Iridescence, Signed, Aurene, 6 In.	431.00
Vase, Green Hearts & Vines, Millefiori, Gourd Shape, Round Foot, Gold Aurene, 6 ½ In.	3335.00
Vase, Green Jade Glass, Opaque Handles, Signed F. Carder, 10 In.	1154.00
Vase, Green Jade, Urn Shape, M-Handles, Rolled Rim, Ring Foot, 10 In.	431.00
Vase, Green, Stump Shape, Disc Foot, 3 Prongs, 6 ¼ In.	460.00
Vase, Grotesque, Gold Ruby Shaded To Clear, 5 ¼ In.	173.00
Vase, Grotesque, Shaded Blue To Clear, Footed, Steuben Acid Stamp, 11 In.	288.00
Vase, Handkerchief, Signed, 5 x 7 In.	270.00
Vase, Heart & Vine, Ivory, Corset Shape, Gold Aurene, 6 ½ In.	374.00
Vase, Heart & Vine, Platinum Iridescent, Millefiori, Gold Aurene, Signed, 10 In..............*Illus*	6900.00
Vase, Hellenic Urn, Robert Cassetti, 9 ½ x 7 ¼ In.	780.00
Vase, Intarsia, Translucent, Green Heart, Vines, Shouldered, Oval, 5 In.	4600.00
Vase, Iridescent, Concave, Spreading Foot, Flared, Rippled Rim, Marked, Aurene 5 x 5 In.	236.00
Vase, Jack-In-The-Pulpit, Stretched Border, Gold Aurene, Iridescent, 6 ¾ In.	1380.00
Vase, Jack-In-The-Pulpit, Stretched Glass, Gold Aurene, Signed, 10 ½ In. ....*Illus*	2875.00
Vase, Jade Green, Rectangular, Swirl Pattern, 9 ¼ In.	184.00
Vase, King Tut Pattern, Blue Baluster, Round Foot, Aurene, 1974, 3 In.	288.00
Vase, Leaves, Tapered, Ribbed, Flared Scallop Rim, Green & Gold Aurene, Signed, 11 In.	8050.00
Vase, Lily, Spreading Undulating Rim, Onionskin Border, Gold Aurene On Calcite, 6 In.	403.00
Vase, Millefiori, Green, Heart & Vine, Platinum, White, Pear Shape, Rolled Rim, 3 ⅞ In.	2990.00
Vase, Millefiori, Green, White Blossoms, Gold Aurene, Label, 5 ½ In.	2588.00
Vase, Millefiori, Iridescent, Pulled Vines, Inlaid Flowers, Shouldered, Flared, 5 In.	1645.00

Steuben, Vase, Flower Shape, Twisted Stem, Scalloped Rim, Blue Aurene, Signed, 12 ½ In.
$1,610.00

Early Auction Co.

Steuben, Vase, Heart & Vine, Platinum Iridescent, Millefiori, Gold Aurene, Signed, 10 In.
$6,900.00

Early Auction Co.

Steuben, Vase, Jack-In-The-Pulpit, Stretched Glass, Gold Aurene, Signed, 10 ½ In.
$2,875.00

James D. Julia Auctioneers

S

Steuben, Vase, Peacocks, Flowers, Acid Cut, Drilled, Aurene Cut To Green Jade, 12 ½ In.
$3,738.00

Early Auction Co.

Steuben, Vase, Pedestal, Round Foot, Blue Aurene, c.1910, 8 In.
$1,200.00

DuMouchelles Art Gallery

Steuben, Vase, Ribbed, Flared Rim, Blue Aurene, Marked, 4 ¾ In.
$633.00

Early Auction Co.

Vase, Nimbus, Paul Schulze, 6 x 6 In.	360.00
Vase, Optic Diamond, Flared, Random Crimson Threading, 6 In.	86.00
Vase, Oriental Poppy, Fuchsia To Pink, Opalescent Banding, Shouldered, Pinched Neck, Flared, 5 In.	805.00
Vase, Oriental Poppy, Vertical Opalescent Stripes, Cylindrical, 7 In.	690.00
Vase, Oval, Pinched Neck, Flared Rim, Footed, Blue Aurene, 12 In.	1333.00
Vase, Oval, Squat, Flared Rim, Blue Aurene, 2 ½ In.	420.00
Vase, Peacocks, Flowers, Acid Cut, Drilled, Aurene Cut To Green Jade, 12 ½ In. ....*Illus*	3738.00
Vase, Pedestal, Round Foot, Blue Aurene, c.1910, 8 In. ....*Illus*	1200.00
Vase, Plum Jade, Canton Pattern, Squat, Marked Enva, 8 ½ x 10 In. 1547.00 to	2380.00
Vase, Purple Iridescent Highlights, Spread Foot, Wide Ruffled Rim, Blue Aurene, 9 x 8 ½ In.	805.00
Vase, Ribbed Twist, Blue, Pulled Leaves, Rippling Water Design, Aurene, 1981, 9 ⅛ In.	316.00
Vase, Ribbed, Flared Rim, Blue Aurene, Marked, 4 ¾ In. ....*Illus*	633.00
Vase, Ring Foot, Swollen Collar, Frosted, Green Leaves, Opal, Florentia, 6 ¾ In.	2530.00
Vase, Rosaline, Dragon, Cherry Blossoms, Shouldered, Flared Rim, 8 ½ x 6 In.	625.00
Vase, Ruffled Rim, Footed, Signed, Gold Aurene, 11 ¼ In. ....*Illus*	1232.00
Vase, Sculptured, Acid Cut, Green Jade Glass, Early 20th Century, 7 x 8 In.	2160.00
Vase, Shade, Gold Aurene, Flared, Crimped Rim, Ribbing, Footed, 6 ¼ In.	518.00
Vase, Silverina, Clear, Diamond Quilted, Flared Neck, Beaker Shape, 12 In.	797.00
Vase, Silverina, Diamond Quilted, Footed Urn Shape, Flared Rim, 7 In.	460.00
Vase, Spanish Green, Triple Lobed, Ring Foot, Bowl Shape, Art Deco, 7 In.	201.00
Vase, Stump, Iridescent, Pulled Prunts, Signed, 8 ½ In.	690.00
Vase, Textured Alabaster, Pink Flowers, Branch, Leaves, Ball Shape, Nedra Pattern, 7 In.	1150.00
Vase, Trumpet, Round Foot, Blue Aurene, 8 In.	633.00
Vase, Trumpet, Round Foot, White To Green, Bubble Design, 10 In.	460.00
Vase, Turquoise, Gold Hooked Feather Decoration, Oval, Shouldered, Aurene, 3 In. ....*Illus*	4140.00
Vase, Urn Shape, 3 Handles, Footed, Gold Iridescent, Aurene, c.1924, 6 ¼ In.	1000.00
Vase, Urn Shape, Optic Diamond, Signed Aurene, Gold Aurene, Label, 4 ½ In.	518.00
Vase, Urn Shape, Reeded Handles, Footed, Blue Aurene, 11 ½ In.	1150.00
Vase, Vertical Ribbing, Cylindrical, Ruffled Rim, Spread Foot, Gold Aurene, 10 In.	345.00
Vase, Vertoise, Pink Threading, Bulbous, Flared Rim, 6 ½ In.	230.00
Vase, Yellow Jade, Black Handles, Signed F. Carder, 9¼ In.	1067.00
Vase, Yellow Jade, Stamford Pattern, Shouldered, Pinched Neck, Rolled Rim, Cameo, 10 ½ In.	1380.00

STEVENGRAPHS are woven pictures made like fancy ribbons. They were manufactured by Thomas Stevens of Coventry, England, and became popular in 1862. Most are marked *Woven in silk by Thomas Stevens* or were mounted on a cardboard that tells the story of the Stevengraph. Other similar ribbon pictures have been made in England and Germany.

Are You Ready?, Boating Team, Frame, 9 x 6 In.	525.00
Called To The Rescue, Men In Boat, Frame, c.1880, 8 ¾ x 5 ¾ In.	575.00
Dick Turpin's Last Ride, Show Jumping, Frame, c.1880, 5 x 8 In.	295.00
Landing Of Columbus, Oct. 12, 1492, Multicolor, 7 x 2 In.	215.00
Taylor, Man, Teasing A Woman With Pipe, Black & White, Wood Frame Mount, 16 x 21 In.	12.00
The Angelus, Farmers In Field, Silk, Frame, 11 x 13 In.	165.00
U.S. Grant, Richmond, Vicksburg, Fort Donelson, Blue Tassel, Silk, 1868, 1 ⅝ x 5 ¼ In.	126.00

STEVENS & WILLIAMS of Stourbridge, England, made many types of glass, including layered, etched, cameo, and art glass, between the 1830s and 1930s. Some pieces are signed *S & W*. Many pieces are decorated with flowers, leaves, and other designs based on nature.

Basket, Crimped Edge, Red, Yellow, Thorn Handle, Square, 6 x 6 x 5 In.	210.00
Biscuit Jar, Lid, Jade Green, Polished Pontil, 9 In.	375.00
Bottle, Dresser, Green, Clear, Flower Design, Cut Overlay, Globular, c.1900, 4 ½ In.	142.00
Bowl, Flowers, Engraved, Clear, 1930s, 7 x 3 In.	75.00
Bowl, Orange, Applied Crystal Leaves, Oval, Pierced Rim, S-Scroll Feet, 8 In.	115.00
Bowl, Peachblow, Applied Amber Glass Branch & 2 Blue Plums, 3 ½ In. ....*Illus*	173.00
Bowl, Rainbow, Mother-Of-Pearl, Squat, Footed, Scalloped Rim, 3 ¼ x 6 In.	575.00
Compote, Apricot, Alabaster Stem & Foot, 3 ¼ In.	250.00
Compote, Yellow Jade, Alabaster Stem & Foot, 3 ¼ In.	250.00
Dish, Milk Glass, Pink Overlay, Ruffled & Folded Rim, 6 ½ x 2 In.	195.00
Ewer, Peacock Pattern, Multicolor, Clear Handle	266.00
Ewer, Pompeiian Swirl, Gilt Leaves, Amber Handle, Swollen Neck, Ruffled Spout, 11 In.	2990.00
Finger Bowl, Underplate, Blue, Marked, c.1910	300.00
Goblet, Olive Green, Engraved Flower Branch, 4 ½ In., 8 Piece	500.00
Jar, Blue Jade, Alabaster Knob & Foot, Flared Lip, 4 ½ x 5 In.	450.00
Lamp, Kerosene, 3-Footed, Threaded, Amber, 7 x 6 ½ In.	750.00

S

Perfume Bottle, Pompeiian Swirl, Green Shaded To Red, Sterling Twist Lid, 5 ½ In.......*Illus*	1495.00
Pitcher, Opaline, Yellow, Tricorner Spout, Threaded Pink, 3 ½ In..............................	85.00
Pitcher, Peach To Vaseline, Gathered Neck, 8 In...	625.00
Salt, Rainbow Insert, Looping White Enamel, Silver Plate Holder, c.1900, 2 x 3 In..........	550.00
Tumbler, Pompeiian Swirl, Gold Tracery Rim, 3 ¾ In...	86.00
Tumbler, Yellow Jade, 3 ⅞ In..	275.00
Vase, Cameo, Signed J. Millward, 10 In..	2252.00
Vase, Mother-Of-Pearl, Crimped Rim, Pink, Iridescent Green, Air Trap, Moire Pattern, 9 In..... *Illus*	2588.00
Vase, Osiris, Stick Neck, Yellow, Orange, c.1887, 13 In.....................................	3495.00
Vase, Peachblow, Applied Flower, Leaves, Ruffled Rim, 6 ½ x 5 In............................	25.00
Vase, Peachblow, Green, Yellow Leaves, c.1850, 4 In., Pair..................................	180.00
Vase, Pompeiian Swirl, Pink, Yellow, Green, Squatty Stick Shape, 7 ¼ In......................	403.00
Vase, Pompeiian Swirl, Purple Mother-Of-Pearl, Gilt Fern, 17 In..................*Illus*	920.00
Vase, Pompeiian Swirl, Shaded Rose To Blue, Cylindrical, Crimped Ruffled Rim, 8 In...........	2300.00
Vase, Silver Foil, Puckered, Multicolor, Glass Strands, 13 In...................*Illus*	5175.00
Vase, Trumpet, Cream To Amber, Pleated Foldover Rim, Thorn Handles, 6 In......................	180.00
Vase, White Opaque, Pink Cased, Ruffled, Applied Flowers, 9 ½ In............................	285.00
Vase, White, Pink Interior, Applied Multicolor Leaves, Fruit, Ruffled Top, 14 x 7 In.........	98.00

STIEGEL TYPE glass is listed here. It is almost impossible to be sure a piece was actually made by Stiegel, so the knowing collector refers to this glass as "Stiegel type." Henry William Stiegel, a colorful immigrant to the colonies, started his first factory in Pennsylvania in 1763. He remained in business until 1774. Glassware was made in a style popular in Europe at that time and was similar to the glass of many other makers. It was made of clear or colored glass and was decorated with enamel colors, mold blown designs, or etching.

Bottle, Bride's, White Opaque Enamel, Red, Green, Blue, Yellow Flowers, Paneled, 5 In..........	24.00
Mug, Barrel Shape, Applied Loop Handle, Crimped Terminus, Multicolor Flowers, 4 In...........	153.00
Tumbler, Temples & Buildings, Flowers, Enamel, Broken Pontil, 3 In...................*Illus*	295.00

STONE includes those articles made of stones, coral, shells, and some other natural materials not listed elsewhere in this book. Micro mosaics (small decorative designs made by setting pieces of stone into a pattern), urns, vases, and other pieces made of natural stone are listed here. Stoneware is pottery and is listed in the Stoneware category. Alabaster, Jade, Malachite, Marble, and Soapstone are in their own categories.

Bead, Agate, Dzi, Barrel Shape, 2 Eyes, Scrolling Red Bands, Inclusions, Tibet, 1 ½ In............	3450.00
Bonsai Tree, Jade, White, Spinach Jade Leaves, Cloisonne Urn, Chinese, 1800s, 6 ½ x 4 ½ In.	115.00
Boulder, Kuan Yin, Seated In Grotto, Holding Ruyi Scepters, Lotus Blossoms, Pine Branches, 8 In.....	486.00
Bowl, Agate, Cameo, Carved, Lotus Leaf, Bats, Coins, Amber, Butterscotch, Wood Stand, 3 ¾ x 7 ¾ In.	4025.00
Brushpot, Agate, Lavender Gray, Carved, Birds, Flowering Tree, Cranes, Wood Stand, 5 ¾ x 4 ¼ In.....	2300.00
Bust, George Washington, Limestone, Portrait Composite, c.1876, 20 In.........................	2655.00
Cigarette Box, Agate, Silver Mounted, Cylindrical, Hinged Lid, Dog Finial, 1900s, 6 ½ In......	325.00
Ewer, Agate, Lavender Gray, Carved Dragons, Jump Ring, Dragon Handle, Wood Stand, 4 ¼ x 7 In.....	4543.00
Figure, Dog, Lying Down, Hardstone, Carved, Crossed Paws, Flowers, Oriental, 4 x 9 In..........	150.00
Figure, Foo Dog, Carved, Wood Stand, 7 In., Pair...	1080.00
Figure, Kuan Yin, Coral, Seated, Branches, Birds, Wood Stand, Chinese, 4 In..................	1126.00
Figure, Kuan Yin, Coral, Standing On Lotus, Chinese, 4 In....................................	2133.00
Figure, Mountain, Agate, 2 Figures, Houses, Pine Trees, Red, Yellow, Chinese, 4 In............	830.00
Figure, Phoenix, Agate, Perched On Flowering Branch, Chinese, 6 ½ In.........................	657.00
Figure, Pig, Tiger's Eye, Carved, 2 ½ In..	24.00
Figure, Rooster, Rouge Color, Stone Polished, Carved Wood Stand, 9 x 8 In....................	138.00
Figure, Stelae, Vishnu, Durga, Steatite, Carved, Nepal, 1800s, 5 ¾ & 5 ¼ In., Pair...........	86.00
Figure, Woman, Shona, Holding Vessel, Stone Incised K. Musekewa, 21 ½ x 9 ¾ In...............	115.00
Fruit, Carved Agate, Painted, Woven Vine Basket, Cloth Border, 1 ¼ To 6 In., 14 Piece.........	325.00
Happy Hoite Buddha, Lapis Lazuli, Holding Ruyi Scepter, 2 ½ In..............................	148.00
Inkstone, Black, Graded Surface, Engraved, Signed, Wood Box, Chinese, 6 x 1 ¾ In.......*Illus*	2015.00
Jar, Lapis Lazuli, Flattened, Scrolling Lotus, Elephant Head Handles, Dome Lid, Bud Finial, 14 In.	4556.00
Jewelry Box, Onyx, Bronze Dore, Canted Corners, Beaded Trim, Paw Feet, 1800s, 4 ¼ x 5 ½ In.....	956.00
Master Salt, Shell, Mother-Of-Pearl, Pink Iridescent, Basket Shape, Handle, Shell Base, 2 ⅜ x 3 ¾ In.	58.00
Obelisk, Black Slate, Inlaid Semiprecious Stones, Colored Marble, 9 ¾ In., Pair...............	414.00
Obelisk, Tapered, Gray Stone, Wood Base, 8 x 2 In...	213.00
Petrified Wood, Pink Red, Triassic Period, 4 x 5 ½ x 4 In...................................	138.00
Picture, Pietra Dura, Ducks By Pond, Multicolor, Gilt Frame, 3 x 4 ¾ In......................	115.00
Plaque, Rooster & Hen, Pietra Dura, Ebonized Frame, 19 x 22 ½ In.................*Illus*	2900.00
Sculpture, Eagle, Spread Wing, Pebble Base, 30 x 36 In......................................	300.00

Steuben, Vase, Ruffled Rim, Footed, Signed, Gold Aurene, 11 ¼ In.
$1,232.00

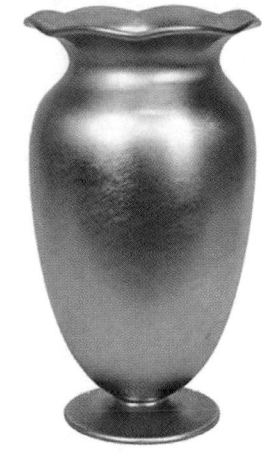

Victorian Casino Antiques

Steuben, Vase, Turquoise, Gold Hooked Feather Decoration, Oval, Shouldered, Aurene, 3 In.
$4,140.00

Early Auction Co.

Stevens & Williams, Bowl, Peachblow, Applied Amber Glass Branch & 2 Blue Plums, 3 ½ In.
$173.00

Early Auction Co.

S

TIP

Never try to fix the inlay on an old metal spur. It takes an expert.

Stevens & Williams, Perfume Bottle, Pompeiian Swirl, Green Shaded To Red, Sterling Twist Lid, 5 ½ In.
$1,495.00

Early Auction Co.

Stevens & Williams, Vase, Mother-Of-Pearl, Crimped Rim, Pink, Iridescent Green, Air Trap, Moire Pattern, 9 In.
$2,588.00

Early Auction Co.

Stevens & Williams, Vase, Pompeiian Swirl, Purple Mother-Of-Pearl, Gilt Fern, 17 In.
$920.00

Early Auction Co.

> **TIP**
> *Don't use ammonia on glasses with gold or silver decorations.*

Sculpture, Gardener, Man, Foot On Shovel, Haddonstone, c.1990, 54 x 14 In.	1062.00
Tabletop, Micro Mosaic, St. Peter's Square, Marble Specimen Band, Italy, 21 In.	13200.00
Tabletop, Pietra Dora Slate, Scenic, Brown Mottled Marble Border, Butterflies, Castle, 36 x 20 In.	144.00
Tobacco Flask, Shell, Turquoise Neck, Turquoise & Mother-Of-Pearl, Silver Trim............*Illus*	303.00
Trinket Box, Agate, Silver Frame, 10 Amethysts, Velvet Lined, M. Buccellati, Italy, 1900s, ⅞ x 5 ¼ In.	2328.00
Trinket Box, Malachite, Bronze, Urn Of Flowers, Hinged Lid, Pad Feet, 1900s, 2 x 12 ¾ In.	600.00

STONEWARE is a coarse, glazed, and fired potter's ceramic that is used to make crocks, jugs, bowls, etc. It is often decorated with cobalt blue decorations. In the nineteenth and early twentieth centuries, potters often decorated crocks with blue numbers indicating the size of the container. A *2* meant 2 gallons. Stoneware is still being made. American stoneware is listed here.

Ale Mug, Incised, Cobalt Blue Flower, Leaves, Coggles, Wingender, Haddonfield, c.1890, 4 ⅛ In.	2070.00
Bank, Cobalt Blue Flowers, Stepped Finial, c.1860, 3 ¾ In.	2370.00
Bank, Cobalt Blue Strokes, Flower, 2 Carved Slots, Finial, Dated 1852, 6 ½ In.	920.00
Bank, Dome Lid, Cobalt Blue Fuchsia Vines, Multicolor Stripes, Squat Shape, Tooled, c.1875, 5 In.	5750.00
Bank, Manganese Glaze, Turnip Shaped Body, Cone Finial, 3 ½ x 4 In.	47.00
Bank, Presentation, Nellie B. Wilson's Bank From Uncle Jack, Ct., 1896, Albany Slip, 3 ¾ In.	345.00
Barrel, 6 Parallel Cobalt Blue Lines At Top, Bottom, Oval, Manganese Glaze Interior, 20 x 14 In.	71.00
Batter Pail, Cobalt Blue Flowers, Slip Trail, Tube Spout, Oval, Handles, White's, Utica, c.1890, 4 Qt.	173.00
Batter Pail, Cobalt Blue Grapes & Bird With Flower, Cowden & Wilcox, c.1865, 8 In.	14950.00
Batter Pail, Cobalt Blue Stencil, F.H. Cowden, Tubular Pouring Spout, Bail Handle, c.1880, Gal.	776.00
Boot, Figural, Blue, Salt Glaze, Marked Gerz 202, 1 Liter, 10 ¼ In. ....*Illus*	264.00
Bottle, Rooney, Cylindrical, Marked, 9 ⅞ In.	230.00
Bowl, Cobalt Blue Sponge, Coggle Rim, Vote Tomorrow, Left Handed Russell Henry, 1974, 2 x 8 In.	47.00
Bowl, Cobalt Blue Tulip, Glaze, Flattened Rim, Central Pa., c.1880, Gal.	86.00
Bowl, Cobalt Blue Tulip, Tooled Shoulder, Flat Rim, Stamped Cowden & Wilcox, Gal.	201.00
Bowl, Coggle Rim, Honest Abe Spinning In His Grave, Left Handed Russell Henry, 1974, 2 x 9 In.	35.00
Bowl, Cylindrical Foot, Wide Rim, Stripe Design, Glazed, McIntosh, c.1952, 3 x 4 ¾ In.	1063.00
Bowl, Milk, Flared Rim, Manganese Glaze, Depressed Spout, 4 ¾ x 16 ¾ In.	94.00
Bowl, Red, 7 Sages Of Bamboo Grove, Brocade Design, Poem, Signed, 1800s, 8 ½ In.	73.00
Bowl, Salt Glazed, Footed, Susan Frackelton, 2 ½ x 5 ½ In. ....*Illus*	875.00
Bowl, Trumpet Shape, Ring Foot, Swirl Design, Children, Flowers, Celadon Glaze, 7 ¾ In.	553.00
Chalice, Cobalt Blue Design, c.1850, 4 ¾ In.	1007.00
Chamber Pot, Cobalt Blue Bird, Flowers, Flat Rim, Handle, 8 ¾ In.	2242.00
Chamber Pot, Cobalt Blue Clover, Leaves, Oval, Tooled, Strap Handle, Baltimore, c.1840, 5 x 7 In.	920.00
Chicken Waterer, Beehive Shape, Blue Slip, Trough, Lug Handles, Tooled Finial, 2 Gal., 14 In.	345.00
Chicken Waterer, Cobalt Blue Strokes, c.1865, 2 Gal.	86.00
Churn, Bird On Branch, Banner In Beak, Cobalt Blue, Ear Handles, Ohio, c.1870, 6 Gal.	28200.00
Churn, Cobalt Blue Bird, Slip Trailed, Tooled, Flared Rim, Lug Handles, W. Roberts, c.1870, 5 Gal.	575.00
Churn, Cobalt Blue Flower Design, Ear Handles, Rolled Rim, U.S.A., c.1850	362.00
Churn, Cobalt Blue Quail, Leaves, Lug Handles, Tapered, J. Burger, Jr., N.Y., c.1885, 5 Gal.	575.00
Churn, Cobalt Blue Rooster, Ear Handles, John Burger, Rochester, 6 Gal., 20 In.	59800.00
Churn, Cobalt Blue Tulip, Slip Trails, Oval, Sloped, Stamped Darrow & Sons, N.Y., c.1865, 3 Gal.	431.00
Churn, Lid, Dasher, Pennsylvania Style, Jar Shape, Blue Band, 13 In.	173.00
Churn, Lid, Design, Cobalt Blue, Salt Glaze, c.1850, 2 Gal., 14 In.	531.00
Churn, Table, Cobalt Blue Flowers, Flared Rim, Oval, c.1840, Gal.	403.00
Compote, Striped Bowl, Cylindrical Pedestal Foot, Brown, c.1950, 5 ½ x 6 ½ In.	625.00
Cooler, Cobalt Blue Bird, Name, Bung Hole, P.H. Smith & Sons, Ohio., c.1865, 6 Gal., 15 In.....*Illus*	1085.00
Cooler, Lid, Cobalt Blue Sponge Bands, 3, Straight-Sided, Spigot Hole, 13 ½ x 11 In.	236.00
Cooler, Oval Keg Shape, Flowers, Leaves, Stump, 5, Cobalt Blue, c.1870, 15 In.	690.00
Cooler, Relief Molded Bands, Cobalt Blue, Barrel Shape, Spigot Hole, 14 In.	83.00
Crock, Applied Handles, Brushed Cobalt Tulip, Green & Hale, Ohio, c.1870, 14 ½ In.	353.00
Crock, Applied Handles, Cobalt Blue Design, McCarel & Burns, Richmond, Ohio, c.1850, 15 ½ In.	823.00
Crock, Baluster Shape, Cobalt Blue Tulip, Tall Collar, Rounded Foot, Remmey, c.1875, 2 Gal.	259.00
Crock, Bird, Cobalt Blue, 2 Ear Handles, White's, Utica, 2, 11 x 8 ½ In.	177.00
Crock, Bird, Flowers, Cobalt Blue, Lug Handles, Michigan Bar, T. Gaffney, c.1850, 5 Gal., 11 ½ In.	295.00
Crock, Bird, Incised, Impressed Warne & Letts, 1807, New Jersey, 7 ¾ In.	18960.00
Crock, Blossoming Tree Branch, Cobalt Blue, 2 Handles, 1840s, 8 ¾ x 9 ¾ In.	323.00
Crock, Bulbous, Blue Incised 2, John Hones, Philadelphia, 11 In.	295.00
Crock, Butter, Cobalt Blue Slip Trailed Leaves, Cylindrical, Tooled Shoulder, N.J., c.1880, ½ Gal.	115.00
Crock, Butter, Cobalt Blue Tulip, Tab Handles, Cylindrical, Stamped D.P. Shenfelder, c.1875, 1 ½ Gal.	115.00
Crock, Butter, Cobalt Blue Tulips, Wavy Stripes, Tooled Shoulder, Remmey Pottery, c.1850, 8 In.	460.00
Crock, Butter, Cover, Cobalt Blue Flowers, Pa., 1800s, 8 ½ x 12 In.	729.00
Crock, Butter, Stenciled Sun, Rounded Sides, Tooled, Western Pa., c.1875, 4 ¾ x 7 In.	259.00
Crock, Cake, Cobalt Blue Chain Stencil, Straight Sides, Round, Dome Stirrup Knob Lid, 5 x 7 In.	118.00
Crock, Cake, Cobalt Blue Flowers, Eagle, Cylindrical, Lug Handles, Henry Remmey, c.1835	316.00

S

Crock,	Cake, Cobalt Blue Flowers, Leafy Stem, Lug Handles, Cylindrical, c.1870, 2 Gal.	230.00
Crock,	Cake, Cobalt Blue Scallop Leaves, Tooled Shoulder, Semi-Round Rim, N.J., c.1880, Gal.	230.00
Crock,	Cake, Cobalt Blue Tulip, Manganese Glazed Interior, Shenfelder, Reading, Pa., 5 x 7 ⅝ In.	212.00
Crock,	Cake, Flower, Blue, Lug Handles, Funkhouser & Co., c.1875, 3 Gal., 8 x 11 In.	403.00
Crock,	Cake, Flowering Vines, Cobalt Blue, Squared Rim, Lug Handles, c.1835, 11 In. Diam.	316.00
Crock,	Cake, Lid, Cobalt Blue Flowers, Cylindrical, Lug Handles, Chester Co., Pa., c.1875, Gal.	316.00
Crock,	Cake, Lid, Cobalt Blue Tulips, Ribbed Lug Handles, Remmey, Philadelphia, 2 Gal.	115.00
Crock,	Cake, Lid, Cobalt Blue, Clover Plant, Streaks, c.1875, 2 Gal.	259.00
Crock,	Cake, Lid, Finial, Cobalt Blue Flowers, Leaves, Ribbed Lug Handles, R. Remmey, c.1865	230.00
Crock,	Cake, Scratchware, Lily, Tooled Shoulder, Squared Rim, Applied Lug Handles, 3 x 2 ⅛ In.	863.00
Crock,	Chicken Pecking Corn, Cobalt Blue, Cylindrical, Tooled Shoulder, Lug Handles, c.1859	690.00
Crock,	Cobalt Blue 2 Birds, Flowers, Impressed White's, Utica, c.1860, 4 Gal., 11 ½ In.	1337.00
Crock,	Cobalt Blue Bird On Flower, John Burger, 6 Gal. .... *Illus*	2300.00
Crock,	Cobalt Blue Bird On Sunflower, Edmands & Co., 3, Salt Glaze, c.1860, 10 ⅝ In. ...... *Illus*	345.00
Crock,	Cobalt Blue Bird, Branch, C-Scroll Handles, Salt Glaze, Vt., c.1850, 4 Gal., 11 x 11 ½ In.	201.00
Crock,	Cobalt Blue Bird, Flowers, Impressed W. Roberts, Binghamton, N.Y., 5 Gal., 13 ½ In.	1778.00
Crock,	Cobalt Blue Bird, Oval, Open Handle, Ohio, c.1860, 8 Gal.	144.00
Crock,	Cobalt Blue Bird, Super Fine, Cylindrical, Handles, Seymour & Bosworth, c.1875, 2 Gal.	863.00
Crock,	Cobalt Blue Brushed 8-Point Star, Tapering Oval, Lug Handles, Face, c.1860, 12 In.	3318.00
Crock,	Cobalt Blue Brushed Leaves, Cylindrical, Tooled Shoulder, Squared, Grier, c.1880, 2 Gal.	144.00
Crock,	Cobalt Blue Chicken Pecking Corn, Cylindrical, P. Sweet, Bull's Head, 4 Gal.	403.00
Crock,	Cobalt Blue Chicken Pecking Corn, Lug Handles, Stamped Riedinger & Caire, c.1860, 4 Gal.	259.00
Crock,	Cobalt Blue Daisies, H.M. Whitman, Havana, N.Y., 6 Gal., 13 ½ In.	826.00
Crock,	Cobalt Blue Date, Wreath, Stamped J.A. & C.W. Underwood, c.1867, 4 Gal.	518.00
Crock,	Cobalt Blue Decoration, Impressed Gilson & Co., Reading, Pa., 1800s, 9 In.	711.00
Crock,	Cobalt Blue Design, Oval, Handles, c.1850, 12 In.	176.00
Crock,	Cobalt Blue Double Birds, Branch, Lug Handles, Stamped Ottman Bros. & Co., c.1880, 4 Gal.	230.00
Crock,	Cobalt Blue Double Grape Clusters, Bosworth, Hartford, Conn., 2, c.1875, 12 In. .... *Illus*	546.00
Crock,	Cobalt Blue Double Tree, Tapered Sides, Crescent Handles, Rim Bead, 7 ¾ x 8 ½ In.	47.00
Crock,	Cobalt Blue Dove, Olive Branch, Cylindrical, Lug Handles, c.1880, 4 Gal., 7 ¾ x 7 In.	316.00
Crock,	Cobalt Blue Fan Flowers, Swags, Ribbed Lug Handles, c.1860, 4 Gal.	230.00
Crock,	Cobalt Blue Federal Eagle, Motto, Cylindrical, Lug Handles, Macquoid & Co., c.1869	3738.00
Crock,	Cobalt Blue Flower Basket, Cylindrical, Open Handle, N.Y. Stoneware Co., c.1875, 2 Gal.	575.00
Crock,	Cobalt Blue Flower, Cylindrical, Tooled Shoulder, R.J. Grier, Mt. Jordan Pottery, c.1880, 3 Gal.	2530.00
Crock,	Cobalt Blue Flower, Flared Rim, Cylindrical, Stamped Courtland, c.1860, Gal.	173.00
Crock,	Cobalt Blue Flower, Lug Handles, Stamped Burger & Burger, Rochester, N.Y., c.1878, 3 Gal.	575.00
Crock,	Cobalt Blue Flower, Ribbed Lug Handles, Oval, Huntingdon County, Pa., c.1860, 6 Gal.	86.00
Crock,	Cobalt Blue Flowers, 2, Crescent Handles, Molded Rim, N.A. White & Son, Utica, 9 x 10 In.	59.00
Crock,	Cobalt Blue Flowers, Cylindrical, Lug Handles, Midwest, c.1870, 6 Gal.	316.00
Crock,	Cobalt Blue Flowers, Cylindrical, M. & T. Miller, c.1870, 5 Gal.	489.00
Crock,	Cobalt Blue Flowers, Dot Trails, Lug Handles, Stamped Adam Green, N.J., c.1875, 3 Gal.	374.00
Crock,	Cobalt Blue Flowers, Flared Rim, Cylindrical, Stamped J.M. Harris, Easton, Pa., c.1885, Gal.	259.00
Crock,	Cobalt Blue Flowers, Grapes, 5 Birds, Loop Handles, Baltimore, c.1815, 3 Gal.	5175.00
Crock,	Cobalt Blue Flowers, H.M. Whitman, Havana, Lug Handles, 6 Gal., 13 ½ In.	826.00
Crock,	Cobalt Blue Flowers, Impressed J. Weaver, Beaver Pa., c.1860, 6 Gal., 16 In.	504.00
Crock,	Cobalt Blue Flowers, Leaves, Cylindrical, Baltimore, c.1845, 1 ½ Gal.	345.00
Crock,	Cobalt Blue Flowers, Leaves, Lug Handles, Stamped, Wells & Richards, Pa., c.1845, 4 Gal.	460.00
Crock,	Cobalt Blue Flowers, Lug Handles, H. Clark, Athens, N.Y., c.1835, 3 Gal., 10 ¼ In.	325.00
Crock,	Cobalt Blue Flowers, Oval, Flared Rim, Lug Handles, Thomas D. Chollar, N.Y., c.1840, 2 Gal.	201.00
Crock,	Cobalt Blue Flowers, Slip Trail, Oval, Lug Handles, C. Hart, Sherburne, c.1860, 6 Gal.	144.00
Crock,	Cobalt Blue Flowers, Slip Trails, Cylindrical, Lug Handles, Evan Jones, Pa., c.1875, 3 Gal.	86.00
Crock,	Cobalt Blue Flowers, Squared Rim, Tab Handles, John Walker, Washington, D.C., Gal., 10 In.	1035.00
Crock,	Cobalt Blue Flowers, Swag, Applied Tab Handles, Baltimore, c.1860, 2 Gal.	115.00
Crock,	Cobalt Blue Flowers, Tab Handles, Paul Cushman, N.Y., c.1810, Gal.	690.00
Crock,	Cobalt Blue Flowers, Tapered Cylinder, Lug Handles, c.1840, 3 Gal.	403.00
Crock,	Cobalt Blue Flowers, Tooled Shoulder, Cylinder, Enoch Burnett, c.1860, ½ Gal.	144.00
Crock,	Cobalt Blue Flowers, Trails, Incised M, Cylindrical, H. Smith & Co., Va., c.1825, Gal.	2415.00
Crock,	Cobalt Blue Flowers, Vines, Lug Handles, James River, Virginia, c.1830, 2 Gal.	230.00
Crock,	Cobalt Blue Flowers, Vines, Tooled Shoulder, Lug Handles, Western Pa., c.1865, 6 Gal.	460.00
Crock,	Cobalt Blue Free Hand, Beaded Rim, Crescent Handles, Manganese Lining, 12 x 12 In.	83.00
Crock,	Cobalt Blue Fruit Compote, Impressed A.O. Whittemore, Havana, N.Y, 1800s, 13 In., 6 Gal.	444.00
Crock,	Cobalt Blue Grapes, Oval, Applied Lug Handles, Stamped Cowden & Wilcox, c.1875, 6 Gal.	345.00
Crock,	Cobalt Blue Horizontal Flowers, Applied Tab Handles, Baltimore, c.1840, 2 Gal.	201.00
Crock,	Cobalt Blue Horizontal Tulips, Ribbed Lug Handles, Baltimore, c.1825, Gal.	230.00
Crock,	Cobalt Blue Leaf & Band, Western Pa., 14 ¾ In., 4 Gal.	443.00
Crock,	Cobalt Blue Leaf & Dragonfly, Cylindrical, Stamped N. Clark Jr., c.1860, 2 Gal.	259.00

TIP

An old hand-engraved monogram or decoration adds value to a piece of silver.

Stevens & Williams, Vase, Silver Foil, Puckered, Multicolor, Glass Strands, 13 In.
$5,175.00

Humler & Nolan

Stiegel Type, Tumbler, Temples & Buildings, Flowers, Enamel, Broken Pontil, 3 In.
$295.00

Conestoga Auction Co., Inc.

Stone, Inkstone, Black, Graded Surface, Engraved, Signed, Wood Box, Chinese, 6 x 1 ¾ In.
$2,015.00

Skinner, Inc.

Stone, Plaque, Rooster & Hen, Pietra Dura, Ebonized Frame, 19 x 22 ½ In. $2,900.00

Skinner, Inc.

Stone, Tobacco Flask, Shell, Turquoise Neck, Turquoise & Mother-Of-Pearl, Silver Trim $303.00

Old Barn Auction

Stoneware, Boot, Figural, Blue, Salt Glaze, Marked Gerz 202, 1 Liter, 10 ¼ In. $264.00

The Stein Auction Co.

Stoneware, Bowl, Salt Glazed, Footed, Susan Frackelton, 2 ½ x 5 ½ In. $875.00

Rago Arts & Auction Center

Crock, Cobalt Blue Leaf, Cylindrical, Lug Handles, Connolly & Palmer, 2 Gal.	259.00
Crock, Cobalt Blue Leaf, Slip Trailed, Cylindrical, Lug Handles, Adam Caire, c.1880, 3 Gal.	58.00
Crock, Cobalt Blue Leaf, Straight Sides, Short Neck, Square Mouth Rim, 10 ¼ x 6 ½ In.	177.00
Crock, Cobalt Blue Leafy Design, Cylindrical, Ear Handles, U.S.A., c.1850, 13 x 12 ½ In.	264.00
Crock, Cobalt Blue Leaves, Impressed Miller Newport, Pa., c.1850, 4 Gal., 12 ¾ In.	790.00
Crock, Cobalt Blue Leaves, Tooled Shoulder, Lug Handles, A.E. Smith, Peck Slip, c.1840, N.Y., 4 Gal.	431.25
Crock, Cobalt Blue Man-In-The-Moon, Handles, Stamped Cowden & Wilcox, c.1865, 2 Gal.	6038.00
Crock, Cobalt Blue Owl, Squared Rim, Applied Lug Handles, Ohio, c.1850, 4 Gal.	374.00
Crock, Cobalt Blue Paddle Tail Bird On Branch, c.1835, 9 x 10 In.	264.00
Crock, Cobalt Blue Parrot, Leafy Branch, Stamped F.B. Norton, Ma., c.1870, 5 Gal.	403.00
Crock, Cobalt Blue Plant, Stylized Leaf, Flared Rim, Applied Tab Handles, Signed J. Swann, c.1820, Gal.	6325.00
Crock, Cobalt Blue Spitting Tulip, Cowden & Wilcox, 11 ¾ In., 3 Gal.	94.00
Crock, Cobalt Blue Stencil, Thos. Johnston, Manu'fr Of Stoneware, Handles, c.1875, 5 Gal.	604.00
Crock, Cobalt Blue Stylized Flower, Cowden & Wilcox, Harrisburg, Pa., Wide Rim, 8 In.	354.00
Crock, Cobalt Blue Stylized Flower, Impressed BC Milburn, c.1830, 10 In.	1175.00
Crock, Cobalt Blue Stylized Flower, Tooled Foot, Tab Handles, Hugh R. Marshall, c.1820, 3 Gal.	316.00
Crock, Cobalt Blue Stylized Slip Trailed Flower, Lug Handles, J. Fisher, c.1880, 7 ½ x 4 ½ In.	58.00
Crock, Cobalt Blue Swags & Sloops, Reeded Band, Stirrup Handles, Flanged Rim, 7 In.	443.00
Crock, Cobalt Blue Swipe, Flared, Lug Handles, Shenandoah Valley, 7 x 8 ¾ In., 1 Gal.	115.00
Crock, Cobalt Blue Tulip, 2, Cylindrical, Flared Rim, Lug Handles, c.1868, 2 Gal.	144.00
Crock, Cobalt Blue Tulip, Flat Rim, Lug Handles, Philip Kabus, c.1875, 3 Gal.	86.00
Crock, Cobalt Blue Tulip, Jug Handles, Pa., c.1850, 4 Gal., 14 ½ In.	444.00
Crock, Cobalt Blue Tulips, Oval, Lug Handles, Stamped John Bell, Pa., c.1860, 13 In., 6 Gal.	748.00
Crock, Cobalt Blue Tulips, Tooled Shoulder, Lug Handles, Augusta County, Va., c.1875, 3 Gal.	374.00
Crock, Cobalt Blue Tulips, Vines, Oval, Applied Lug Handles, c.1835, 3 Gal.	460.00
Crock, Cobalt Blue Urn, Watch Spring Decoration, Captain James Morgan, c.1780, 9 ¼ In.	1823.00
Crock, Cobalt Blue Woman, Trees, Cylindrical, Tooled Bands, Uniontown, c.1865, 4 Gal.	2875.00
Crock, Cobalt Blue, 1832, In Wreath, Tapered, Stamped Clark & Fox, Gal.	633.00
Crock, Cobalt Blue, Daisies, Tooled Shoulder, Oval, Tab Handles, Baltimore, c.1845, 3 Gal.	374.00
Crock, Cobalt Blue, Double Fern Leaf, Berger & Co., c.1870, 11 ½ In.	201.00
Crock, Cobalt Blue, Feather & Swag, Cylinder, S. Bell & Son, c.1890, 2 Gal., 12 x 8 In.	127.00
Crock, Cobalt Blue, Flower Basket, Lug Handles, Straight-Sided, A.K. Ballard, 6 Gal., 13 In.	800.00
Crock, Cobalt Blue, Flowers, Cowden & Wilcox, Pa., c.1850, 4 Gal., 17 ¾ In.	2844.00
Crock, Cobalt Blue, Flowers, J. Young & Co, Harrisburg, Pa., 4 Gal., 18 In.	2370.00
Crock, Cobalt Blue, Flowers, Remmey, Phil., 1800s, 10 ¼ In.	207.00
Crock, Cobalt Blue, Inscribed Johashan E. Buck, Lug Handles, c.1830, 4 In.	652.00
Crock, Cobalt Blue, Jas. Hamilton & Co., Greensboro, Pa., 1800s, 3 Gal., 13 ¾ In.	334.00
Crock, Flared Rim, Applied Lug Handles, Oval, Stamped Boone & Son, Brooklyn, N.Y., 2 Gal.	431.00
Crock, Flower, Stylized, Lug Handles, Rolled Rim, U.S.A., c.1877-79, 13 In.	235.00
Crock, Goodwill's, Barrel Shape, Leaf Neck Reinforcement, Stopper, Wire Bail, c.1895, 8 x 11 In.	106.00
Crock, Hamilton & Jones, Greensboro, Pa., Cobalt Blue Stencils, No. 2, 10 x 9 In.	94.00
Crock, Ice Water, 6, Wreath, Flowers, 14 ¾ x 11 ¼ In.	295.00
Crock, Impressed Richey & Hamilton, Cobalt Blue Flowers, Leaves, Palatine, W.V., 3 Gal., 14 In.	652.00
Crock, Inscribed War With Spain, 7 ¾ In.	948.00
Crock, Leaf, Manganese, Yellow Glaze, c.1850, 2 Gal., 10 ¾ In.	711.00
Crock, Lid, Cobalt Blue Leaves, Lug Handles, Pa., c.1865, 6 ½ x 10 In.	267.00
Crock, Lid, Cobalt Blue Tulips, Swags, Ribbed Lug Handles, R. Remmey, c.1870, Gal.	431.00
Crock, Orange & Green Splotches, Straight-Sided, Banded Rim, Incised 3, 12 In.	59.00
Crock, P. Herrmann, Straight-Sided, Molded Under Rim, Cobalt Blue Tulips, 1 ½ Gal., 11 x 7 In.	83.00
Crock, Stencil, J.M. Pruden, N.J., 2 Gal., 13 In.	267.00
Crock, Straight-Sided, Lug Handles, Bird On Branch, c.1850, 2 Gal., 8 ¼ In.	267.00
Crock, Tapered Body, 2 Lug Handles, Rolled Rim, U.S.A., 1800s, 20 ½ In.	413.00
Cuspidor, Cobalt Blue Flowers, c.1850, 4 x 7 In.	362.00
Cuspidor, Cobalt Blue Leaves, Concave Sides, Stamped Harrisburg, Pa., Wm. Moyer, c.1858	288.00
Cuspidor, Coved Body, Rounded Foot, Opening, Slot, Remmey Pottery, c.1865, 4 x 8 ¼ In.	173.00
Feeder, Cobalt Blue Flowers, Leaves, Pa.1800s, 7 In.	830.00
Figurine, Cat, Seated, Bow, Cobalt Blue Sponging, Bristol Slip Glaze, c.1890, 4 ¼ In.	1495.00
Figurine, Dog, Spaniel, Seated, Chocolate Albany Slip, c.1890, 7 ½ In.	115.00
Figurine, Dog, Spaniel, Seated, Manganese Drip Glaze, Octagonal Base, 10 In.	142.00
Flask, Fox Head Shape, Brown Mottled, Gloss Salt Glaze, Bottle Top At Neck, 1800s, 7 ¼ In.	63.00
Flowerpot, Ruffled Base, Applied Rope Twist Handles, Incised E.E.L., W.J. & E.G. Schrop, 8 In.	323.00
Flowerpot, Seedling, Salt Glazed, Blue Stripes, Tapered, Drain Hole, Albany Slip Glaze, 3 In.	58.00
Flowerpot, Tray, Hanging, Cobalt Blue Stencil, Circles, Oval, Flared, Ripple Rim, 6 x 10 ½ In.	153.00
Ginger Jar, Green Glaze, Incised Designs, Long Life Symbol, Chinese, c.1890, 7 ⅜ x 8 ½ In.	106.00
Ginger Jar, Lid, Musicians, White Flowers, Asia, 6 ½ x 5 ½ In.	24.00
Inkstand, Cobalt Blue Heart Shape, Swags, Dotted Stars, Crosshatch, c.1835, 5 ¾ x 2 In.	31050.00

Inkwell, Blue Coggled Circle, Leaves, Swags, Round, Coved, Nathan Clark, c.1840, 5 ½ x 2 ⅝ In..... 1265.00
Inkwell, Cylindrical, 4 Quill Holes, Cobalt Blue Brushed Rim, Moses B. Tyler, c.1820, 2 x 4 ⅝ In..... 3200.00
Jar, Apple, Tornado Design, Cobalt Blue, c.1880, 8 In........ 529.00
Jar, Blue Loop & Dots, Molded Under Rim, Base Band, Flared Rim, Loop Handles, 9 x 8 ½ In..... 83.00
Jar, Canning, Blue-Gray Glaze, Threaded, Rim, Cylindrical, Stamped John Bell, c.1875, 7 In..... 604.00
Jar, Canning, Green Glaze, Tapered, Flared Rim, Stamped Zigler, Newville, Pa., c.1855, 7 In....... 259.00
Jar, Canning, Lid, Quinces, Squat, Oval, Lug Handles, Squared Rim, Rockingham County, 5 ¾ In.. 690.00
Jar, Canning, Manganese Glaze, Applied Crescent Handles, 12 x 12 ½ In........ 12.00
Jar, Canning, Salt Glazed, Cylindrical, Flared Rim, Stamped H.H. Zigler, Newville, Pa., c.1855, 9 In. 259.00
Jar, Canning, Top Hat, Wax Sealer, Squat, Stenciled A.P. Donaghho, c.1880, 5 ½ In........ 374.00
Jar, Canning, Wax Sealer, 3 Cobalt Blue Horizontal Stripes, Cylindrical, Tooled, c.1875........ 230.00
Jar, Cobalt Blue Chain Link, Tassels Band, Cylindrical, Tooled Collar, B.C. Milburn, c.1850, Gal., 7 In... 805.00
Jar, Cobalt Blue Conical Flower, Lug Handles, Stamped Cowden & Wilcox, Pa., c.1865, Gal......... 173.00
Jar, Cobalt Blue Daisies, Swags, Cylindrical, Henry Remmey, c.1830, Gal......... 575.00
Jar, Cobalt Blue Eagle, Arrows, Hamilton & Jones, Stenciled, Lug Handles, Pa., c.1875, 14 x 8 In. 575.00
Jar, Cobalt Blue Flower Vine, Lug Handles, Oval, Va., c.1835, 4 Gal., 15 x 6 In. 4313.00
Jar, Cobalt Blue Flower, Accents, Oval, Lug Handles, Connecticut, c.1820, 2 Gal...... 201.00
Jar, Cobalt Blue Flower, Oval, Lug Handles, Strasburg, Va., c.1835, 4 Gal., 15 x 8 In. 9775.00
Jar, Cobalt Blue Flower, Oval, Lug Handles, Strasburg, Va., c.1835, Gal., 11 x 6 ¼ In. 633.00
Jar, Cobalt Blue Flower, Squat, Oval, Tooled Shoulder, Open Handles, Rolled Rim, c.1800, 9 In.. 259.00
Jar, Cobalt Blue Flowers, Dated 1840, Smith & Day, Ct., 2 Gal. 575.00
Jar, Cobalt Blue Flowers, Lug Handles, Cylinder, W.H. Lehew & Co., Va., c.1865, 3 Gal., 14 x 9 In. 288.00
Jar, Cobalt Blue Flowers, Lug Handles, Stamped I. Seymour, N.Y., c.1825, 4 Gal...... 288.00
Jar, Cobalt Blue Flowers, Slip Trail, Oval, Flared Collar, Lug Handles, c.1860, Gal...... 316.00
Jar, Cobalt Blue Flowers, Tooled Shoulder, Solomon Bell, Strasburg, Va., c.1875, 2 Gal...... 259.00
Jar, Cobalt Blue Hanging Flower, Flattened Rim, Stamped J.H. Dipple, Lewistown, c.1880, 2 Gal. 230.00
Jar, Cobalt Blue Label, Stencil, Buckeye Store, Pomeroy, O., c.1870, 10 In. 705.00
Jar, Cobalt Blue Pomegranates, 2, Squat, Handles, Kemple Pottery, N.J., c.1750, 11 In. 10350.00
Jar, Cobalt Blue Swag, Rounded Tooled Shoulder, Cylindrical, Richard Remmey, c.1875, 7 In.... 173.00
Jar, Cobalt Blue Swags, Baluster, Flared Rim, Oval, Applied Lug Handles, Philadelphia, c.1870, Gal. 173.00
Jar, Cobalt Blue Tassel Swag, Applied Loop Handle, C. Crollius, c.1820, Gal. 316.00
Jar, Cobalt Blue Tulip, Leaves, Lug Handles, Cowden & Wilcox, Harrisburg, Pa., c.1865, 4 Gal. ... 230.00
Jar, Cobalt Blue Tulips, Wavy Stripes, Footed, Flared Collar, Lug Handles, H. Remmey, c.1840, Gal... 115.00
Jar, Cobalt Blue, Cylinder, E.B. Taylor, Va., c.1874, 12 x 8 In. 259.00
Jar, Coerlears Hook, Incised Leaves, Thomas Commeraw, New York, c.1790, 11 ⅝ In. 24150.00
Jar, Coggled Column & Sawtooth Design, 2 Open Loop Handles, Oval, Leaves, c.1815...... 1035.00
Jar, Cream, Cobalt Blue Flower, Stamped H.B. Pfaltzgraff, Pa., c.1875, Gal....... 173.00
Jar, Cream, Dot & Swag Design, Cobalt Blue, Squat, Tooled Shoulder, Rolled Rim, c.1855, 6 x 9 In. 115.00
Jar, Grape Clusters, Wide Mouth, Risley, c.1850, 10 ¾ In....... 948.00
Jar, Green Brown Alkaline Glaze, Oval, Rounded Rim, Handles, Initials R.M., N.C., 1800s, 3 Gal. 173.00
Jar, Impressed Heart, Loop Handles, Charlestown, Ma., c.1820, 3 Gal...... 431.00
Jar, Incised Rings, Impressed Mark, J, Dillon, Ohio, c.1860, 10 ¼ In...... 118.00
Jar, Lid, Cobalt Blue Leaves, Slip Trailed Vining, Fenton & Hancock, Vt., 9 ¾ In...... 58.00
Jar, Oval Shape, Flower Heads, Aquamarine Drip Glaze, Persia, c.1800, 15 In...... 518.00
Jar, Pickle, Cylindrical Sides, Impressed, Pickles, C. Crolius, 6 ⅝ In...... 2252.00
Jar, Round, Tooled Shoulder, Manganese Glaze, Made By J. Letts, South Amboy, 8 ¼ In...... 1093.00
Jar, Storage, Green Glazed, Oval, Low Wide Rim, Stamped No. 2, Southern, 11 ¼ In...... 189.00
Jar, Tapered, Collared Rim, Impressed Mark, Handles, Rambo, Muskingum County, Ohio, 9 ½ In.... 382.00
Jar, Vertical Handles, Cobalt Watchspring, Oval, Tooled Shoulder, c.1780, 9 ⅛ In...... 805.00
Jar, Worcester Dove, On Branch, Cobalt Blue, Lug Handles, c.1865, 10 ¾ In...... 178.00
Jardiniere, Square, Curved Rim, Raku Fired, U.S.A., 1960s, 18 ¾ x 22 In., Pair...... 2000.00
Jug, Applied Handle, Cobalt Blue 2, Impressed Mark, H.H. Melick, Roseville, Ohio, c.1870, 13 In. 147.00
Jug, Cobalt Blue 1834, Oval, New Jersey, 2 Gal. 374.00
Jug, Cobalt Blue Bird Perched On Branch, Straight-Sided, Loop Handle, c.1895, 15 ½ In........... 1185.00
Jug, Cobalt Blue Bird, Branch, Tulip, Inscribed Edmonds & Co., Ma., 2 Gal., 15 In. 911.00
Jug, Cobalt Blue Bird, Flowers, Impressed Cowden & Wilcox, 1800s, 13 ¾ In. 4977.00
Jug, Cobalt Blue Bird, Impressed W. Roberts, Binghampton, N.Y., c.1845, 5 Gal., 19 In. 2015.00
Jug, Cobalt Blue Bird, Leaf Branch, Sloped Shoulder, Stamped Edmands & Co., c.1860, Gal. 115.00
Jug, Cobalt Blue Bird, Square Rim, Stamped Troy, N.J., c.1875, 2 Gal. 345.00
Jug, Cobalt Blue Bird, Stump, Inscribed Fort Edward Pottery Co., N.Y., c.1850, 2 Gal., 13 ¾ In... 4977.00
Jug, Cobalt Blue Bird, Stump, Inscribed J. Fleming, Fourth St., Troy, N.Y., 5 Gal., 18 ½ In........... 2015.00
Jug, Cobalt Blue Brushed Tulip, Leaves, Oval, Strap Handle, c.1850, 14 ½ In. 617.00
Jug, Cobalt Blue Cherries, Cowden & Wilcox, Pa., c.1850, 16 ½ In...... 444.00
Jug, Cobalt Blue Crested Bird, Branch, Cylindrical, Stamped New York Stoneware, c.1875, Gal. 345.00
Jug, Cobalt Blue Daisy, Bull's-Eye Center, Stamped Cowden & Wilcox, Pa., c.1865, 4 Gal. 661.00
Jug, Cobalt Blue Designs, Redinger & Claire, Poughkeepsie, 2 Gal., 12 ¼ In........... 224.00

TIP
To be sure your clean iron pan is dry, heat it on a stove burner for a minute.

Stoneware, Cooler, Cobalt Blue Bird, Name, Bung Hole, P.H. Smith & Sons, Ohio., c.1865, 6 Gal., 15 In. $1,085.00

Garth's Auctioneers & Appraisers

Stoneware, Crock, Cobalt Blue Bird On Flower, John Burger, 6 Gal. $2,300.00

Cottone Auctions

Stoneware, Crock, Cobalt Blue Bird On Sunflower, Edmands & Co., 3, Salt Glaze, c.1860, 10 ⅝ In. $345.00

Glass Works Auctions

Stoneware, Crock, Cobalt Blue Double Grape Clusters, Bosworth, Hartford, Conn., 2, c.1875, 12 In.
$546.00

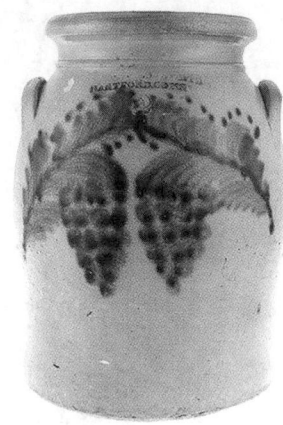

Glass Works Auctions

Stoneware, Jug, Cobalt Blue Ring-Necked Pheasant, Incised, Pulled Reeded Handle, 3 Gal., 14 ½ In.
$2,400.00

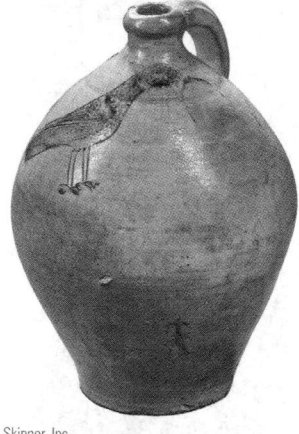

Skinner, Inc.

Stoneware, Jug, Flower, Leaf, 2, Cobalt Blue, Salt Glazed, John Burger, Rochester, New York, c.1870, 2 Gal.
$863.00

Glass Works Auctions

Jug, Cobalt Blue Dots, Semioval, Short Spout, c.1880, 3 ½ In.	403.00
Jug, Cobalt Blue Draped Flowers, Oval, Handle, C. Crolius, N.Y., c.1820, Gal.	259.00
Jug, Cobalt Blue Federal Eagle, Symbols, Narrow Spout, Eagle Pottery, Pa., c.1875, 3 Gal.	546.00
Jug, Cobalt Blue Flower, Gilson & Co., Reading, Pa., 1800s, 15 ½ In.	356.00
Jug, Cobalt Blue Flower, Script, Square Spout, Mabbett & Anthone, Poughkeepsie, c.1840, 3 Gal.	173.00
Jug, Cobalt Blue Flowers, Impressed Cowden & Wilcox, Harrisburg, 1800s, 3 Gal., 15 In.	1067.00
Jug, Cobalt Blue Flowers, Impressed D.P. Shenfelder, Reading, Pa., 11 In.	425.00
Jug, Cobalt Blue Flowers, Impressed D.P. Shenfelder, Reading, Pa., 1800s, 15 In.	444.00
Jug, Cobalt Blue Flowers, Impressed M & T Miller, c.1860, 3 Gal., 14 ½ In.	4740.00
Jug, Cobalt Blue Flowers, J. Mantell, Penn Yan, 15 ½ In., 3 Gal.	153.00
Jug, Cobalt Blue Flowers, Leaves, Cowden & Wilcox, Harrisburg, Pa, c.1865, 2 Gal.	431.00
Jug, Cobalt Blue Flowers, Loop Handle, Stamped S.L. Pewtress & Co., c.1820, 10 ½ In.	84.00
Jug, Cobalt Blue Flowers, Oval, 4 Loop Handles At Shoulder, c.1820-35, 7 ½ In.	9775.00
Jug, Cobalt Blue Flowers, Redinger & Caire, Poughkeepsie, 12 ¼ In.	224.00
Jug, Cobalt Blue Flowers, Salt Glaze, White & Stone, Impressed 5, Utica, N.Y., c.1870, 17 ½ In.	1610.00
Jug, Cobalt Blue Flowers, Slip Trailed Tulip, Sloped Cylinder, c.1860, 2 Gal.	115.00
Jug, Cobalt Blue Flowers, Slope Shoulder, c.1850, 16 In.	94.00
Jug, Cobalt Blue Flowers, Slope Shoulder, Squared Spout, W.H. Farrar & Co., N.Y., c.1860, 3 Gal.	288.00
Jug, Cobalt Blue Flowers, Strap Handle, Impressed Taunton, Mass., c.1830, 14 ½ In., 3 Gal.	189.00
Jug, Cobalt Blue Flowers, Swag, Oval, Rounded Spout, Stamped Cowden & Wilcox, c.1865, Gal.	374.00
Jug, Cobalt Blue Grapes, Vines, Stamped Cowden & Wilcox, c.1865, 3 Gal.	891.00
Jug, Cobalt Blue Hawk, Salt Glaze, C.W. Braun, Buffalo, N.Y., c.1860, 3 Gal., 15 ¾ In.	1652.00
Jug, Cobalt Blue Leaf Design, 2, Oval, Narrow Rim, c.1840, 2 Gal.	173.00
Jug, Cobalt Blue Leaf, Stamped Cowden & Wilcox, c.1875, 3 Gal.	230.00
Jug, Cobalt Blue Leaves, Incised Circles, Tooled Spout, Handle, J. Crolius, c.1775, ½ Gal., 10 In.	805.00
Jug, Cobalt Blue Leaves, Oval, Tooled Spout, Signed Morgan Maker, Baltimore, c.1825, 12 In.	546.00
Jug, Cobalt Blue Man In The Moon, Impressed Cowden & Wilcox, Pa., 1800s, 2 Gal., 13 In.	4503.00
Jug, Cobalt Blue Man's Head, Wavy Lines, Handles, Ohio, c.1875, 6 Gal., 18 ¾ In.	316.00
Jug, Cobalt Blue Oval, Stepped Spout, Ribbed Handle, C. Crolius, N.Y., c.1820, 10 Gal., 9 ¾ In.	460.00
Jug, Cobalt Blue Paddle Tail Bird, Inscribed N.A. White & Sons, Utica, N.Y., 4 Gal., 17 In.	2607.00
Jug, Cobalt Blue Pheasant, Leaf, Incised, Rounded Spout, Ribbed Handle, N.Y., c.1800, 14 ¾ In.	5175.00
Jug, Cobalt Blue Ring-Necked Pheasant, Incised, Pulled Reeded Handle, 3 Gal., 14 ½ In. .... *Illus*	2400.00
Jug, Cobalt Blue Rose Design, Oval, Incised Lines At Neck & Shoulder, Handles, c.1795, 10 In.	770.00
Jug, Cobalt Blue Running Bird, Slip Trail, Wreath, Handle, White's, Utica, c.1860, 5 Gal., 19 In.	1150.00
Jug, Cobalt Blue Script, R.H. Jones, 805 Penn St., Reading, Pa., 1800s, 14 ½ In.	59.00
Jug, Cobalt Blue Slip Tailed Flowers, Thick Spout, Oval, N. Clark & Co., N.Y., c.1845, 3 Gal.	2185.00
Jug, Cobalt Blue Sponge Ware, Inscribed J.E. Merser, 1800s, 11 ½ In.	1185.00
Jug, Cobalt Blue Spotted Bird, Flowers, Inscribed Edmonds & Co., 4 Gal., 18 In.	1422.00
Jug, Cobalt Blue Stag, Salt Glaze, Nathan Clark & Co., Rochester, N.Y., 4 Gal., 17 ¾ In.	4720.00
Jug, Cobalt Blue Stenciled Cross, Tulips, Spout, F.H. Cowden, Harrisburg, c.1880, 2 Gal.	288.00
Jug, Cobalt Blue Stylized Flower, Cowden & Wilcox, Harrisburg, Pa., 11 In.	384.00
Jug, Cobalt Blue Stylized Flowers, c.1875, Gal., 11 ½ In.	533.00
Jug, Cobalt Blue Sunflower, J.W. Cowden, c.1850, 2 Gal., 14 In.	3318.00
Jug, Cobalt Blue Sunflower, Wreaths, Slope Shoulder, Stamped, J.W. Cowden, Pa, c.1860, 2 Gal.	546.00
Jug, Cobalt Blue Swan, Leaves, Ear Handle, U.S.A., c.1855-58, 13 In.	1998.00
Jug, Cobalt Blue Tornado, Slope Shoulder, Tooled Spout, Ottman Bros., N.Y., c.1875, Gal.	144.00
Jug, Cobalt Blue Tulip, Bud, Sloped, Square Spout, Stamped A. Lobdell & Co., c.1860, 3 Gal.	345.00
Jug, Cobalt Blue Tulip, Dash Border, Oval, Rounded Spout, Cowden & Wilcox, c.1865, Gal.	748.00
Jug, Cobalt Blue Tulip, Oval, Strap Handle, c.1850, 18 In.	323.00
Jug, Cobalt Blue Tulip, Slip Trail, Rounded Spout, Oval, Handle, C.W. Braun, N.Y., c.1860, 3 Gal.	460.00
Jug, Cobalt Blue Tulip, Stamped Moyer Harrisburg, Pa., Slump To Neck, Oval, c.1858, 2 Gal	546.00
Jug, Cobalt Blue Tulip, Tapered Cylinder, Handle, Pa., 1800s, 14 ¾ In.	425.00
Jug, Cobalt Blue, Bird, Perched On Branch, Brushed Design, Handle, c.1855, 14 In.	470.00
Jug, Cobalt Blue, Brush, 1796, Straight-Sided, Ribbed Strap Handle, 6 ⅞ In.	3450.00
Jug, Cobalt Blue, Fruit, Cowden & Wilcox, Pa., c.1850, 10 ½ In.	711.00
Jug, Dog Holding Basket, Cowden & Wilcox, 1800s, 4 Gal, 15 ¼ In.	49770.00
Jug, Eagle, Swan, Impressed, Gardiner, Maine, 1800s, 19 In.	296.00
Jug, Face, Green Eyes, Edwin Meaders, 10 ¼ In.	2066.00
Jug, Face, Olive Alkaline Glaze, Angry, Crossed Eyes, Pointed Nose, Cleater Meader, c.1988, Gal.	374.00
Jug, Flower, Leaf, 2, Cobalt Blue, Salt Glazed, John Burger, Rochester, New York, c.1870, 2 Gal. ...*Illus*	863.00
Jug, Gemel, Cobalt Blue Lovebirds, Double Spout, Handle, c.1800, 5 ¼ In.	42660.00
Jug, Gray Blue Swag, Tassel, Impressed, Ribbed Handle, c.1810, Gal., 12 In.	690.00
Jug, Green Loop Design, Incised Liberty Forever Warne Letts 1807, New Jersey, 13 In.	8295.00
Jug, Harvest, Cobalt Blue Flowers, Stenciled Kelly & Harr, Pa., Loop Handle, c.1855, 9 ½ In.	2760.00
Jug, Incised Bird, Oval, Applied Reeded Handle, Israel Seymour & Co., c.1800, 2 Gal., 13 In.	1422.00
Jug, Incised Fish, Oval, Applied Handle, Ribbing, James Morgan, Jacob Van Wickle, c.1840, 12 In.	805.00

S

Jug, O.L. Gregory Vinegar Co., Paducah, Ky., Pure Apple Juice Vinegar, 3 x 2 ¼ In. .... *Illus* 143.00
Jug, Oval Shaped, Incised Lines, Codfish, Cobalt Blue, Loop Handle At Neck, c.1795, 9 ⅝ In. 2489.00
Jug, Robt. Schwartz, Nanticoke, Loop Handle, Evan R. Jones, Pittston, Pa., 10 x 7 In. 106.00
Jug, Salt Glazed, Squat, Applied Loop Handle, 5 ½ In. 47.00
Jug, Stenciled Ernest W. Miller, Seeds & Poultry Supplies, Hagerstown, Md., c.1900, 4 In. 253.00
Jug, Syrup, Cobalt Blue M.H. Brown, Brookfield, N.Y., Squat, Flared Pinched Spout, c.1880, Gal. 316.00
Jug, Tan, Incised Bird Decoration, Blue Bands, Pear Shape, Spigot, 12 In. 863.00
Jug, Vinegar, Albany Slip Glaze, Incised, Compliments Of H.F. Sheesley, Oval, c.1880, 6 ¼ In. 201.00
Jug, Water, Lovebirds, Cobalt Blue, Bung Hole, Stopper, Ear Handle, c.1835, 13 ½ In. 1293.00
Jug, Whiskey, Brown Slip, Paper Label, Ritter & Spillman Dealers, Winchester, Va., c.1910, 11 In. 403.00
Jug, Whiskey, Wm. Foust, Distiller, Glen Rock, Pa., Stoneware, Manganese Dip Neck, 5 ½ In. 83.00
Keg, Albany Slip Glaze, Wheel Thrown, Footed, 2 Spouts, Wood Graining, c.1860, 10 x 8 ¾ In. 115.00
Keg, Cobalt Blue Bands Incised Flowers, Somerset Potters Works, c.1850, 10 Gal., 19 In. 345.00
Keg, Cobalt Blue Bands, Semioval Shape, Tooled, Spout At Midsection, c.1815, 10 In. 546.00
Lid, Cobalt Blue Dotted Tulips, White Slip, Stamped Waynesboro, c.1880, 9 In. 173.00
Match Safe, American Brew Co., Flying Eagle, Shield, White's, Utica, N.Y., 6 ¾ In. 460.00
Matchbox, Striker, Brown, Removable Lid, Winged Man, Eagle, 1 ¼ x 3 ½ In. 35.00
Milk Pan, Cobalt Blue Banana Swag, Spout, Ear Handles, Va., c.1825, 2 Gal., 5 ¾ x 14 ½ In. 173.00
Milk Pan, Cobalt Blue Flowers, Tapered, Flattened Rim, Pouring Spout, R.J. Grier, c.1880, Gal. . 489.00
Milk Pan, Cobalt Blue Flowers, Tapered, Pinched Spout, Grier, Chester County, Pa., c.1890, Gal. 230.00
Milk Pan, Cobalt Blue Hanging Flower, Swag, Flared, Lug Handles, Va., c.1870, ½ Gal., 6 x 12 In. .. 316.00
Moonpot, Glazed, Ball Shape, Cream & White, Artist's Monogram, 1982, 10 ⅛ In. 5000.00
Mug, Berry's Famous Root Beer, Dragons, Vines, White's, Utica, N.Y., c.1880, 4 ¼ In. 173.00
Mug, Cobalt Blue Bands, Barrel Shaped, Incised Lines, Loop Handle, Shenfelder, 4 ½ x 3 In. 153.00
Mug, Cobalt Blue Bands, Wide, Inscribed C. Harry Fletcher, 4 ¼ In. 267.00
Mug, Cobalt Blue Flower, Presentation, Inscribed Charles Krick, Shenfelder, 1800s, 4 ¼ In. 2370.00
Mug, Cobalt Blue Flowers, Incised, Coggle Bead Base, Wingender Pottery, c.1890, 4 In. 345.00
Mug, Cobalt Blue Flowers, Shenfelder, Pa., 1800s, 4 ½ In. 1541.00
Mug, Cobalt Blue Leaves, Flowers, Striped Accents On Handle, Inscribed E.E. Hipple, 1800s, 4 In. 356.00
Mug, Cobalt Blue Stripes, Applied Stag, Incised New Ulm Jager Club, Minnesota, c.1880, 4 ½ In. 1265.00
Mug, Cobalt Blue Tulips, Stenciled Compliments Of John Stock, c.1890, 5 In. 1035.00
Mug, Sgraffito Elk, Trees, Water, Leaf Border, Albany Slip Glaze, Impressed J.H., 1874, 6 In. 345.00
Oyster Jug, Cobalt Blue Thomas Norton, Spout, Strap Handle, c.1875, 8 ⅝ In. 58.00
Pitcher, Albany Slip Dashes, Tanware, Flared Rim, New Geneva, Pa., c.1875, 9 ¼ In. 460.00
Pitcher, Albany Slip, Lined, Ribbed Handle, Oval, Stamped, C. Crolius, N.Y., c.1815, Gal., 10 ¾ In. .. 690.00
Pitcher, Blue & White Salt Glaze, Tankard Shape, Raised Doe & Fawn, c.1900, 8 ⅜ In. 29.00
Pitcher, Brown Alkaline Glaze, Oval, Flared Collar, Ribbed Handle, Southeastern, c.1890, 10 In. 115.00
Pitcher, Brown, Stamped E.V. Zirkel, Wines & Liquors Baltimore, Md., Handle, c.1900, 8 In. 58.00
Pitcher, Cobalt Blue 2 Stem Flower, Oval, Rounded Foot, Tooled Collar, c.1865, 3 Gal. 1725.00
Pitcher, Cobalt Blue 2 Tulips, Leaves, Squat, Round Foot, Tooled Shoulder, c.1865, 8 ½ In. 2185.00
Pitcher, Cobalt Blue Bands, Bristol Slip Glaze, Oval, c.1900, 2 ¾ In. 115.00
Pitcher, Cobalt Blue Clover, Presentation, Stamped Katie, Footed, Tooled, Handle, c.1850, 4 In. .. 5980.00
Pitcher, Cobalt Blue Clover, Swags, Flared Base, P. Herrmann, Balt., c.1870, Gal., 10 In. 633.00
Pitcher, Cobalt Blue Daisies, Basket, Vines, Scalloped Rim, Baltimore, c.1820, 14 In. 7110.00
Pitcher, Cobalt Blue Daisy, Bud, Leaf, Stamped Cowden & Wilcox, c.1865, Gal. 345.00
Pitcher, Cobalt Blue Flower, Handle, Pa., 1800s, 5 In. 711.00
Pitcher, Cobalt Blue Flower, Pa., 1800s, 2 Gal., 13 ¼ In. 385.00
Pitcher, Cobalt Blue Flowers & Chain Links, Handles, c.1850, 11 In. 331.00
Pitcher, Cobalt Blue Flowers, 1800s, 7 ¾ In. 237.00
Pitcher, Cobalt Blue Flowers, Band, Elongated Oval, Shaped Rim, c.1870, 10 ¾ x 5 In. 633.00
Pitcher, Cobalt Blue Flowers, Clover Plants, Tooled Collar, Oval, Maryland, c.1850, 2 Gal. 1035.00
Pitcher, Cobalt Blue Flowers, Maryland, 19th Century, 2 Gal., 13 ¼ In. 652.00
Pitcher, Cobalt Blue Flowers, Pa., 1800s, 12 In. 1185.00
Pitcher, Cobalt Blue Flowers, Presentation, Incised John N. Carley 1894, R. Remmey, 9 In. 4888.00
Pitcher, Cobalt Blue Flowers, Remmey, 1800s, Pa., 8 ¼ In. 395.00
Pitcher, Cobalt Blue Flowers, Swags, Oval, Tooled Collar, c.1865, Gal. 288.00
Pitcher, Cobalt Blue Leaves, Richard Remmey, Pa., c.1875, Gal. 230.00
Pitcher, Cobalt Blue Leaves, Rounded Foot, Tooled Spout, N.J., c.1880, ½ Gal., 8 In. 288.00
Pitcher, Cobalt Blue Panels, Westerwald Shape, Incised Leaves, Pulled Spout, 9 In. 35.00
Pitcher, Cobalt Blue Swag, Albany Slip, Cylindrical, Round Shoulder, Flared Collar, c.1890, Gal. ... 144.00
Pitcher, Cobalt Blue Tulip, Flower Wreath, Squat, Oval, Rounded Foot, Henry Glazier, c.1840, 6 In. 3680.00
Pitcher, Cobalt Blue Tulip, Swags, Richard Remmey, c.1885, Qt., 7 ¼ In. 1035.00
Pitcher, Cobalt Blue Tulips & Leaves, Loop Handle, Narrow Spout, c.1850, 10 ¼ In. 705.00
Pitcher, Cobalt Blue Tulips, Incised Lines, Rounded, B.C. Milburn, Va., c.1850, 2 Gal., 13 In. 3450.00
Pitcher, Cobalt Blue Tulips, Leaves, Handle, Remmey Pottery, c.1875, Gal. 259.00
Pitcher, Cobalt Blue Tulips, Leaves, Tooled Rim, Mauden Perine, c.1860, Gal. 403.00

Stoneware, Jug, O.L. Gregory Vinegar Co., Paducah, Ky., Pure Apple Juice Vinegar, 3 x 2 ¼ In.
$143.00

Wm Morford Antiques

TIP
If you want to keep your collections free from harm, always clean and dust them yourself.

Stoneware, Vase, Bud, Olive Drip Glaze Over Mirrored Auburn, Incised Frans Wildenhain, 6 ¼ x 5 ½ In.
$500.00

Rago Arts & Auction Center

Stoneware, Vase, Art Deco, Gray Brown, Spirals, Bands, Primavera, Lourioux, France, c.1930, 12 ½ In.
$1,080.00

Skinner, Inc.

S

Cold Weather Stoves

In 1932 Admiral Richard Byrd came to Beaver Dam, Wisconsin, and assisted in designing a Monarch coal-wood stove to be used in his second exploration of the South Pole. The range performed so perfectly that Admiral Byrd asked for an oil-burning Monarch range to be built for use on his third trip to Antarctica in 1940. Both stoves are still in use there today (from www.monarchrange.com/history.html).

Stoneware, Vase, Faceted, Warren MacKenzie, 2002, 15 x 8 ½ In. $660.00

Cowans + Clark + DelVecchio

Stoneware, Vase, Moon, Brown Glazes, Incised TT, Toshiko Takaezu, 9 x 11 In. $3,186.00

Brunk Auctions

TIP

Stuff hats with acid-free tissue for storage. Try to make the stuffing deep enough so the hat brim does not touch the shelf.

Pitcher, Cobalt Blue Tulips, Pa., c.1850, 10 ¼ In.	267.00
Pitcher, Cobalt Blue Tulips, Swags, Oval, Richard Remmey, c.1870, Gal.	920.00
Pitcher, Cobalt Blue Tulips, Vines Allover, Huntingdon County, Pa., c.1880, 14 In.	1265.00
Pitcher, Cobalt Blue, Splotched, Bulbous, Pulled Spout, Loop Handle, RH Stamp, 1978, 5 In.	35.00
Pitcher, Cobalt Blue, Sponging, Tapered, Straight-Sided, Molded Foot, Rim, Loop Handle, 9 In.	106.00
Pitcher, Fish Shape, Open Mouth Forming Spout, Curved Tail Handle, Water Base, c.1865, 13 In.	5405.00
Pitcher, Fish, Curled Tail, Open Mouth, Bristol Slip Glaze, Brown, Blue Sponge, c.1880, 10 In.	633.00
Pitcher, Flowering Plant, Cobalt Blue, Spatter Border, Cylindrical, Loop Handle, c.1890, 9 ½ In.	173.00
Pitcher, Milk, Gray, Blue Stylized Flowers, Stand-Up Neck, Penn., 13 x 11 In.	1553.00
Pitcher, Molded Eagle Panels, Black, c.1835, 10 In.	474.00
Pitcher, Running Stag, Dog, Flowers, Handle, Bristol Slip Glaze, Ohio, c.1880, 9 In.	144.00
Pitcher, Straight-Sided, Flower, Pulled Spout, Loop Handle, Russell Henry, 1984, 5 In.	59.00
Planter, D. Cressey, Rectangle Texture Design, Wide Rim, c.1965, 31 x 40 In.	6875.00
Planter, Manganese Glaze, Applied Flower With Stem, Bulbous, Footed, 9 In.	177.00
Pot, Boston Baked Beans, Cobalt Blue, Children Eating, Daisy Finial, White's, Utica, c.1890, 8 In.	86.00
Punch Bowl, Cobalt Blue Raised Leaves, Draping, Bristol Slip, White's, Utica, c.1890, 10 x 19 In.	891.00
Sander, Duck Shape, Cobalt Blue Highlights, Punched Holes, N.C., 4 ⅝ x 5 ½ In.	288.00
Stein, Cobalt Blue Initials, Pewter Lid, Straight-Sided, I.S., Applied Loop Handle, 7 x 3 In.	885.00
Teapot, Lid, Bamboo Shaped Handle, Leaves, Cicada Finial, 1919, 3 ¼ In.	2588.00
Umbrella Stand, Painted, Portrait Of Woman, Red Velvet & Ermine Robe, 20 ½ In.	30.00
Urn, Teapot, Applied Ram's Head, Vase Shape, Rounded Handle, Strap Handle, N.C., c.1900, 11 In.	230.00
Vase, Bud, Olive Drip Glaze Over Mirrored Auburn, Incised Frans Wildenhain, 6 ¼ x 5 ½ In. *Illus*	500.00
Vase, Art Deco, Gray Brown, Spirals, Bands, Primavera, Lourioux, France, c.1930, 12 ½ In. *Illus*	1080.00
Vase, Double Gourd, Incised Flowers, Waves, Pale Gray Crackle Glaze, Chinese, 1800s, 13 ⅝ In.	861.00
Vase, Faceted, Warren MacKenzie, 2002, 15 x 8 ½ In. *Illus*	660.00
Vase, Flowers, Vines, Leaves, Green, White, Bulbous, Ring Foot, Rolled Rim, c.1890, 9 x 11 ½ In.	236.00
Vase, Jugenstil Style, Flowers, Yellow, Blue Matte Glaze, Double Handles, Dutch, 6 ½ x 7 ½ In.	1254.00
Vase, Moon, Brown Glazes, Incised TT, Toshiko Takaezu, 9 x 11 In. *Illus*	3186.00
Vase, Moose, Walking, Pine Trees, Tapered Oval, Ring Foot, Flat Rim, c.1910, 13 ¼ In.	8050.00
Vase, Prunus Tree Trunk Shape, Poem, Blue Green Glaze, Pink Flowers, c.1900, 28 x 17 In.	461.00
Vase, Rim, Horn Handles, Orange, Blue, Yellow, Paint, Italy, 17 x 13 In., Pair	210.00
Vase, Rounded Bottom, Wavy Shaped Rim, Textured, Green & Brown, c.1980, 13 ¾ x 8 In.	5000.00
Vase, Squared, Trumpet Rim, Crackleware, Foo Dogs, Dragons, Multicolor, Chinese, c.1900, 24 In.	2300.00
Vase, Textured, Raised Crackle, Cream, Green Accents, Applied Loop Handle, 20 ½ x 11 ½ In.	83.00
Water Cooler, Blue, Green, Orange Sailing Ship, Blue, White Lid, M.A. Hadley, c.1945, 12 ¾ In.	115.00
Water Cooler, Cobalt Blue Flowers, 2-Sided, Applied Lug Handles, Philadelphia, c.1835, 5 Gal.	978.00
Water Cooler, Cobalt Blue Flowers, Dotted Leaves, Ohio, c.1850, 10 Gal., 19 ½ In.	2185.00
Water Cooler, Cobalt Blue Flowers, Doves, Stamped J.T. Winslow, Portland, c.1850, 6 Gal., 5 In.	354.00
Water Cooler, Cobalt Blue Flowers, July 12, 1809, Brown, Handles, WV Stoneware, c.1875, 19 In.	3105.00
Water Cooler, Cobalt Blue Flowers, Leaves, Open Handles, Oval, Baltimore, c.1825, 2 Gal.	805.00
Water Cooler, Cobalt Blue Tulips, Lug Handles, 1800s, 12 ½ In.	2133.00
Water Cooler, Double Cornucopia, Oval, Ribbed Handles, Thompson & Co., c.1840, 11 In.	748.00
Water Cooler, Ribbed Lug Handles, Impressed John Brelsford, c.1850, 4 Gal.	2645.00

STORE fixtures, cases, cutters, and other items that have no advertising as part of the decoration are listed here. Most items found in an old store are listed in the Advertising category in this book.

Accounting Register System, Oak, Shaped Cabinet, Tambour Roll Top, Drawers, 32 x 23 In.	236.00
Automaton, Bakery Man, Composition Head, Molded Hands, White Attire, Red Scarf, Spoon, 33 In.	1243.00
Back Counter, Mixed Wood, 2 Sections, 32 Drawers, 2 Shelves, 15 Upper Shelves, 94 x 176 In.	295.00
Bin, 2 Tiers, Slant Front, Glass Paned Doors, Lift Top, Interior Bins, Footed, 40 x 44 x 22 In.	295.00
Bin, Feed, Pine, Slant Front, Short Turned Legs, 28 ½ x 51 In.	334.00
Bin, Grain, Pine, Shaped Gallery, Raised Panel Doors, Lift Top, Bracket Feet, c.1800, 43 x 49 In.	1880.00
Bin, Telescope Flour Receiver, Brown Paint, Metal, 40 x 18 ½ In.	2040.00
Cabinet, Display, Oak, Glass Sides, Shelves, Iron Paw Feet, Egg & Dart Cornice, c.1900, 42 x 24 In.	563.00
Cabinet, Hardware, Pine, Octagonal, 104 Drawers, Porcelain Knobs, Wheel Base, c.1890, 73 x 30 In.	1298.00
Cabinet, Nuts & Bolts, 8-Sided, Revolving, 80 Drawers, Metal Stand, 65 x 31 In.	728.00
Cabinet, White Top, Carved Wood Panel, Chevron Flower Carvings, 3 Back Doors, c.1880, 33 x 98 In.	960.00
Case, Display, Hardwood, Glass Panels, 3 Glass Shelves, 31 x 12 In.	142.00
Case, Oak, Beveled Glass Top & Side Panels, Sliding Rear Doors, c.1960, 40 x 72 In.	480.00
Chair, Shoe Shine Station, Curled & Twisted Metal	173.00
Chest, Pine, 36 Drawers, Paneled Base, Yellow Paint, 7 Lift Tops, 2 Sections, c.1890, 46 x 127 In.	4519.00
Cigar Cutter, Artie, Iron, Man, On Chimney, Pulls Cigar From Mouth, Sticks Tongue Out, 10 In.	2300.00
Cigar Cutter, Brass, Half Spherical, Textured Dome Body, 3 Legs, Tubular, Plunger, 5 ¼ In.	71.00
Cigar Cutter, Elephant, Figural, Brown, Black, Iron, 5 x 2 x 8 In.	495.00
Cigar Cutter, Horse, Standing, Nickel Plated, Shield Molded Base, Tail Is Cutter, 7 x 8 ½ In.	590.00

Cigar Cutter, Plug Tobacco, Iron, c.1900, 9 ½ x 9 ⅝ In........................	250.00
Cigar Cutter, Tobacco Plug, Imp On Elongated Handle, Shaped Base, Iron............	78.00
Cigar Cutter, Woman Lifts Leg To Cut, Bronze, Marble Base, Signed C. Kauba, c.1900, 8 ½ x 7 x 5 In.	1344.00
Coffee Grinders are listed in the Coffee Mill category.	
Counter, Bean, Oak, 21 Glass Display Windows, 2 Drawers, 104 x 34 In..........	3300.00
Counter, Bean, Oak, 6 Cupboard Drawers, Glass Fronts, 50 x 37 In.	390.00
Counter, Display, Curved Glass, Nickel, 71 x 13 In.	678.00
Counter, Elm, Drawers, Open Shelves, Molded Openings, Square Feet, Chinese, c.1890, 35 x 58 In.	235.00
Counter, Paneled Oak, 3 Framed Diagonally Boarded Panels, 35 x 168 In.	767.00
Counter, Poplar, Pine Stain, Panels, Turned Columns, Stepped Baseboard, c.1885, 36 x 90 In. .	2000.00
Counter, Quarter Round, Oak, Glass Front, Top, Mid Shelf, Concave Rear Doors, 42 x 72 In...	354.00
Counter, Walnut, Pine, 20 Drawers, 36 x 132 In.	266.00
Display Case, Oak, Curved Glass Top, Hinged, Panel Back, Holds 78 Canes, 35 ½ x 46 ½ In. ..	288.00
Display, Genie, Floating From Lamp, Eyes Closed, Smiling, Paint, Composition, 1940s, 21 In.	300.00
Display, Man, Bug Eyes, Large Hand Gesturing, Paint, Composition, 1930s, 21 In............	1200.00
Display, Pigs At Table, Cook, Wood, Composition, Electric, 20 Movements, Decamps, c.1923, 42 x 36 In.	2723.00
Display, Round, Glass, Oak & Brass Pedestal Base, Brass Crown Molding, 72 x 33 In.	4480.00
Display, Seeds, Wood, Pull-Up Tin Boxes, 15 x 30 x 12 In..................	230.00
Figure, Bell Boy, Mouth Open, Holds Tray, Head Moves Side To Side, Clockwork, 23 In.	780.00
Figure, Black Man, Tan Suit, Paint, Composition, c.1960, 31 ½ In....................	1920.00
Grocery Bag Sorter, Sectioned, Wood, Paint, Inscribed Troy, New York Grocers, c.1875, 15 x 16 In.	744.00
Grocery Grabber, Wood Pole, Aluminum, Squeeze Handle & Gripper	150.00
Hand & Face, Sani-Dri, Dryer, Porcelain, Foot Operated, Painted White, Scrolling Graphics, 47 In.	248.00
Hand Dryer, Sani-Dri, Porcelain, Floor Press, Chicago Hardware Foundry Co.	1120.00
Hat Mannequin, Painted Hair, Halter Top, Papier-Mache, 1930s, 28 In..............	510.00
Hat Model, Man's Head, Smoky Eyes, Paint, Plaster, 1930s, 20 In..............	2400.00
Hat Mold, Figural, Head, Stylized Face, Zinc, c.1910, 10 ½ In......................*Illus*	584.00
Lighter, Cigar, Counter, Pot Metal, Urn Style, Handle, Green Glass Globe	168.00
Lighter, Cigar, Russian Eagle, Countertop, Bronze, 4 ½ x 7 ½ x 3 In................	336.00
Lion, Nodder, Glass Eyes, Open Mouth, Papier-Mache, Wood, Clockwork, 23 In............	575.00
Man In Green Suit, Pink Tie, Paint, Carved Wood, 1940s, 21 ½ In..............	900.00
Man, Dark Suit, Hands On Hips, Carved, Wood, Menswear, 1930s	1200.00
Man, Large Eyes, Pointing Finger, Crossed Legs, Hard Rubber, 1940s, 14 ½ In..........	1200.00
Man, Leaning, Suit, Trousers, Composition, Wood Base, Menswear, 10 In..............	900.00
Man, Striding, Black Suit, Bowler, Flat Back, Wood, Paint, 1930s, 23 In............	840.00
Man, Striding, Hat, Suit, Flat Back, Carved, Paint, Wood, 16 In..................	1140.00
Man, Suit, Spats, Holding Cigar, Paint, Metal, Wood Base, Menswear, 1930s, 36 In........	1560.00
Mannequin, Bust, Man's, Suit Jacket, Vest, Shirt, Wood, Quatrefoil Base................	1232.00
Mannequin, Male Youth, Wax Head, Porcelain Teeth, Human Hair, Composition, Germany..*Illus*	7200.00
Mannequin, Woman, Blue Slip, Paint, Composition, 1960s, 30 ½ In..................	1140.00
Mannequin, Woman, Gold Painted Dress, Papier-Mache, c.1960s, 29 In..............	206.00
Man's Head, Smiling, Molded Collar, Composition, Men's Department Tie Display, 1930s, 8 In.....	360.00
Milkshake Mixer, Cast Iron, Floor Model, Hand Crank Wheel, Wood Base	2400.00
Milkshake Mixer, Coles Shaker, Porcelain, Red, Hand Crank Wheel, 2 Shakers, Countertop ..	2040.00
Milkshake Mixer, Hamilton Beach, Chrome, Electric, Countertop, White Porcelain Base, 17 In..	168.00
Milkshake Mixer, Soda Fountain, Hamilton Beach, Cardboard Milkshake Sign Top	168.00
Post Office Window Section, Build-In, Grill, Counter, Metal Doors, Letter Slot, 44 Cubbies, 40 x 34 In.	118.00
Shoeshine Stand, Twisted Frame, 2 Foot Rests, Wrought, Iron Drawer, Seat, Arms, 53 x 16 ¾ In.	207.00
Showcase, Curved Glass, Metal Frame, Double Tower Top, Excelsior, 27 x 72 In.	6160.00
Showcase, Oak Frame, Bent Glass, Label J. Riswig, Chicago, Mirror Back, Counter, 9 ½ x 18 ½ In..	649.00
Sign, Antiques Ahead, 1 Mile, Hand With Pointing Finger Shape, Wood, 15 x 33 In.	78.00
Sign, Antiques, Stained Leaded Glass, Red, Black, Cream Ground, Frame, 23 x 33 In.	168.00
Sign, Apothecary, Mortar & Pestle, Gilding On White Paint, Wooden Plinth, c.1810, 27 ½ In.. *Illus*	649.00
Sign, Apothecary, Mortar & Pestle, Gold Paint, Tin, 39 ½ In..................	144.00
Sign, Asylum For The Insane, Window Panel, Gold Letters, Reverse Paint, 18 x 29 In............	1003.00
Sign, Beauty Salon, Flange, Porcelain, White, Black Letters, 12 x 22 In.	364.00
Sign, Beaver, Pine, Paint, 14 ½ x 39 In.	5832.00
Sign, Board & Rooms, Pine, 2-Sided, Signed Draper, 10 ½ x 27 ¾ In................	1007.00
Sign, Cafe, Iron, Enamel Border, Inset Bulbs, Light-Up, 2-Sided, c.1900, 24 x 70 In........	2640.00
Sign, Cocktails, Martini Glass, Light-Up, 1960s	795.00
Sign, Cod Fish, Trade, Tin, 21 ½ In....................	516.00
Sign, Crab Shape, Pine, Orange, White, Wrought Iron Brackets, c.1900, 39 x 46 In.	4025.00
Sign, Danger, Keep Out, Caution, Safe To Enter, Red, Yellow, Green, Lights, Metal, 18 In........	300.00
Sign, Do Not Enter, Black & White, Porcelain, Jewel Letters, 34 x 34 In..................	115.00
Sign, Doctor, Scaled Snake, Teeth, Tongue, Scrolls, Torch, Cast Iron, Painted, c.1890, 23 In....	115.00
Sign, Drinks, Neon, Blue Metal Letters, Yellow Bar, 16 x 54 In.	5480.00

Store, Hat Mold, Figural, Head, Stylized Face, Zinc, c.1910, 10 ½ In.
$584.00

Skinner, Inc.

Store, Mannequin, Male Youth, Wax Head, Porcelain Teeth, Human Hair, Composition, Germany
$7,200.00

Showtime Auction Sevices

The edited listings of the current prices in this *Kovels' Antiques & Collectibles Price Guide* aren't available on any website. Readers can visit **Kovels.com** to check thousands of past prices and sign up for free information on trends, tips, reproductions, marks, and more.

TIP
Wrap books in acid-free tissue for storage.

Store, Sign, Apothecary, Mortar & Pestle, Gilding On White Paint, Wooden Plinth, c.1810, 27 ½ In.
$649.00

Brunk Auctions

Store, Sign, Home Made Pies Cake Orders Taken, 2-Sided, c.1910, 11 ¾ x 30 ¼ In.
$1,422.00

Skinner, Inc.

Store, Sign, Optician, Spectacles, Banner, H.N. Weil Optical Parlor, Applied Molding, c.1900, 10 x 22 In.
$2,040.00

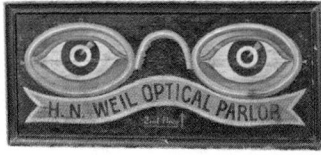
Skinner, Inc.

Store, Sign, Safety Pin, Painted, Pennsylvania, c.1880, 32 ½ x 10 x 1 ½ In.
$660.00

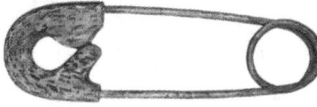
Showtime Auction Sevices

Sign, Drugs, Cigars, Jewel Lights, Mortar, Pestle Shape, Steel, 2-Sided, Electric, 36 x 57 In.	5500.00
Sign, Eyeglasses, Cast Zinc Frame, Advertising, Paint, Hanging Hooks, 35 In.	1936.00
Sign, Eyeglasses, Reverse Painted, 2-Sided, Blue, Black, 23 x 10 In.	345.00
Sign, Fish, Embossed, Tin, 2 Mounting Holes, 26 In.	3025.00
Sign, Fish, Grouper, Metal, Full Bodied, Crimped Sheet Fins, 1900s, 16 ½ x 32 ½ In.	345.00
Sign, Fish, Sheet Iron, Brass Eyes, 39 x 18 In.	834.00
Sign, Fish, Tin, 38 x 12 In.	316.00
Sign, Flies, Fishing, Red, White Paint, Wood, c.1910, 41 x 10 In.	374.00
Sign, Fresh Eggs, Tin, 1930s, 15 ½ x 12 ½ In.	230.00
Sign, Garrison Inn, White Ground, Black Letters, Arrow, Newburyport, Mass., 12 ¼ x 36 In.	354.00
Sign, General Claim Agent, N.A. Calkins, Pension, Bounty, Blue, Red, Black, c.1880, 21 x 14 In.	863.00
Sign, Hardware, Outdoor, Wood, 97 x 16 In.	770.00
Sign, Harness Shop, Pine, Painted, White, Black Lettering, Outline, Arrow Shape, c.1910, 48 In.	148.00
Sign, Home Made Pies Cake Orders Taken, 2-Sided, c.1910, 11 ¾ x 30 ¼ In. ...*Illus*	1422.00
Sign, Hunting Strictly Forbidden On These Premises, Wood, Paint, c.1900, 12 x 30 In.	1126.00
Sign, Ice, Block, Tongs, Slate, Iron, c.1915, 13 x 18 ½ In.	173.00
Sign, Laundry, Sand Paint, 2-Sided, c.1900, 16 ½ x 29 ½ In.	345.00
Sign, Lumber, Pine, Painted, Hendrickson & Dilatush, Robbinsville, N.J., 1800s, 14 ¾ x 38 ¾ In.	533.00
Sign, Mortar & Pestle, Forged, Sheet Iron, Chain Hangers, Salmon, Black, c.1810, 18 x 15 In.	1955.00
Sign, Optician, Spectacles, Banner, H.N. Weil Optical Parlor, Applied Molding, c.1900, 10 x 22 In. ...*Illus*	2040.00
Sign, Pig, Sheet Iron, 4 Mounted Rivets, Old Green Paint, c.1780, 21 x 34 In.	1093.00
Sign, Pineapple, Wood, Carved, Painted, 48 x 28 In.	1180.00
Sign, Please Don't Park, We Need Space For Deliveries, Car, Truck, Porcelain, 18 x 24 In.	266.00
Sign, Pocket Watch, Zinc, Painted, Stennes, 29 In.	1422.00
Sign, Pool-Billiards, Entrance, Stained Glass, Green, Black, Light-Up, 28 x 42 In.	840.00
Sign, Private Beach Keep Off, Red, Black, White, Paint, Tin, 8 ¼ x 11 ½ In.	173.00
Sign, Safety Pin, Gray Paint, Pa., 1880, 32 ½ x 10 In.	660.00
Sign, Safety Pin, Painted, Pennsylvania, c.1880, 32 ½ x 10 x 1 ½ In. ...*Illus*	660.00
Sign, Shoe, Composition, Painted Silver, 20th Century, 12 x 29 In.	243.00
Sign, Tavern, Eastern Inn, Scrolled Crest, Apron, Wrought Iron Hardware, c.1829, 75 x 45 In.	1610.00
Sign, Tavern, Guinness, Painted, Lobster, Wearing German Helmet, 1900s, 43 x 26 In.	2070.00
Sign, Tin, Painted, Saul Felter & Co., Inc. General Merchandise, 508, 30 x 36 ½ In.	593.00
Sign, Tobacco, Scissors, Cut Plug, Wood, Paint, c.1900, 12 x 33 In.	288.00
Sign, Unlawful To Litter $100 Fine, Black & White, Tin, Bullet Holes, 36 x 42 In. ...*Illus*	90.00
Sign, Valet Parking Only, Violators Will Be Towed, Spade Shape, Sahara Hotel	952.00
Sign, Warning Landing Field For Airplanes, No Trespassing, Blue & White, Porcelain, 32 x 27 In.	560.00
Sign, Watch & Clock Repair, Black Sand Paint, Gold Lettering, Pine Frame, c.1890, 7 x 25 ½ In.	288.00
Sign, Watch, Centennial Minutes, Composition, c.1850, 21 x 30 In.	288.00
Sign, Whipping Cream 75 Cents Quart, Pine Board, Bread Board Ends, 2-Sided, 11 ½ x 27 ½ In.	115.00
Sign, Wiring Fixtures Radio, Pine, Molded Edges, Blue, White Lettering, c.1925, 14 ½ x 30 ½ In.	58.00
Spice Box, Metal, Blue, Gold Shield, Red, Paint, c.1900, 11 ½ x 8 In.	75.00
Sporting Goods Model, Man, Running, Hand Extended, Paint, Wood, 1930s, 19 In.	540.00
Strawholder, Dome Lid, Finial, Smokestack Foot, Pressed Glass, 12 ⅝ x 4 ½ In.	220.00
String Dispenser, Ball Shape, Hinged, Painted, Iron, 5 ½ In.	385.00
Ticket Booth, Wood, Painted, Get Tickets Here, Blue, Orange, Square Feet, c.1890, 40 ¾ x 24 In.	3600.00
Ticket Dispenser, Takacheck, Numbered Tickets, Red, Loaf Shape, Metal Case, Spring, 9 x 16 In.	83.00
Tie Head, Pince Nez, Molded Collar, Paint, Composition, Metal Stand, 1930s, 19 ½ In.	360.00
Tin, Biscuit, Lift Top, Ship, Normandie, 3 Funnels, Yellow, Black, Red, Lithograph, France, 17 ½ In.	3038.00
Tobacco Cutter, Figural, Boy Thumbing His Nose, Cast Iron, Scrolled Handle, 13 In. ...*Illus*	177.00
Tobacco Cutter, Figural, General Washington & Horse, Cast Iron, On Plank, 14 ¾ In. ...*Illus*	177.00
Twine Holder, Sphere, Pierced, Iron, Painted Black, 1800s, 4 x 3 In.	36.00
Whip Holder Display, Hanging, Cast Iron, Round, Leather Buggy Whip, 13 ¾ In.	118.00

STOVES have been used in America for heating since the eighteenth century and for cooking since the nineteenth century. Most types of wood, coal, gas, kerosene, and even some electric stoves are collected.

Cook, C.W. Warnick, Cast Iron, Patented 1840, 18 ½ x 29 In.	178.00
Cook, Columbian, Tan & Green, Enamel, 3 Burner, Gas, 54 x 28 x 16 In. ...*Illus*	212.00
Cook, Dayton Manufacturing Company, Gasoline Insurance, Metal, Black Enamel, 63 x 40 In.	413.00
Cook, Majestic, Enamel, Cast Iron, Wood, 48 x 43 x 26 In. ...*Illus*	189.00
Cook, Marvel, Cast Iron, 6 Burners, Side Warmer, Copper Accents, Scroll, Cabriole Feet, 20 x 16 ½ In.	460.00
Cook, Menzel & Kempf, Cast Iron, Ornate, 44 x 62 In.	170.00
Cook, Universal Electric, Porcelain, 2 Burners, Oven, Inset Thermometer, c.1920, 38 x 19 In.	236.00
Door, Oven, Jason & Golden Fleece, Cast Iron, c.1850, 28 x 29 In.	690.00
Heating, Dakota Queen, No. 12, Cast Iron	1008.00
Heating, Estate Air Tight Oak Radiator, No. 512, Kahn & Bros., Cast Iron, Square, 1894	560.00

Heating, Fred Schultz, Patented April 1851, Embossed, Cast Iron, 27 x 25 In.	89.00
Heating, Gloria Light Co., Portable, Gas, Chicago, 14 x 16 In.	468.00
Heating, Isabella Furnace, Cast Iron, 2 Doors, Stand, Pa., 40 In.	593.00
Heating, Palace Oak, Ornate, Cast Iron, Brass Urn Top, Lansing, Mi., 25 x 64 In.	763.00
Heating, Reliable, No. 606, Cast Iron, Inset Jewels, Schneider & Trenkamp Co., Cleveland	1560.00
Heating, Tyson Furnace, Cast Iron, Ship Design, 32 x 24 In.	118.00
Heating, Victorian, Figural Panels, Hoof Feet, Cast Iron, 24 x 12 x 27 In.	226.00
Parlor, Cast Iron, Pin Hinged Door, Maple Handle, Octagonal Legs, Penny Feet, c.1840, 23 x 33 In.	8307.00
Parlor, Cast Iron, Wedgewood, Oak, No.11, Jas. Graham Mfg., 32 In.	288.00
Parlor, Garland Oak, Model 6E, Front Flue ....*Illus*	1560.00
Stove Base, Trestle, 4 Rosettes, Cast Iron, Virginia, c.1820, 14 x 12 In.	173.00
Stove Plate, Abraham & Isaac, Cast Iron, c.1750, 24 x 17 In.	178.00
Stove Plate, Cain & Abel 1741, 27 x 27 In.	395.00
Stove Plate, Central Heart, Side Tulips, Cast Iron, 1762, 27 x 20 In.	385.00
Stove Plate, Dance Of Death, Cast Iron, 1750, 22 ¼ x 23 ½ In.	2370.00
Stove Plate, Death Of Absalom, Cast Iron, c.1750, 27 x 28 In.	830.00
Stove Plate, Depart From Evil Of 1764, Cast Iron, 24 x 27 In.	178.00
Stove Plate, Elijah & The Ravens Of Kingston, c.1750, 24 x 19 ½ In.	356.00
Stove Plate, Figure, Potted Urns, Cast Iron, c.1750, 21 ¾ x 27 ¼ In.	474.00
Stove Plate, Flight Into Egypt, Cast Iron, c.1750, 23 x 25 In.	711.00
Stove Plate, George Ross Mary Ann Furnace, Plate 220, Cast Iron, c.1750, 22 x 24 In.	948.00
Stove Plate, Hearts, Tulips, 5 Plate, Cast Iron, G. Ross, Mary Ann Furnace, Pa., 1766, 24 x 19 In.	33180.00
Stove Plate, Jacob Kiblinger 1787, Cast Iron, 24 ¾ x 15 In.	385.00
Stove Plate, John Potts, Cast Iron, Inscribed Warwick Furnace, 1763, 19 ¼ x 21 ½ In.	729.00
Stove Plate, Judge Not Of 1751, Cast Iron, 26 ½ x 22 ½ In.	178.00
Stove Plate, Judge Not Of 1756, Cast Iron, 23 ¼ x 25 ½ In.	593.00
Stove Plate, Judge Not Of S.F., Cast Iron, 24 x 20 ½ In.	474.00
Stove Plate, Pine Grove, Figure In Mourning, Pa., 19th Century, 22 x 29 In.	119.00
Stove Plate, Samson & Delilah, Cast Iron, c.1750, 25 x 25 In.	395.00
Stove Plate, The Wedding Dance 1746, Cast Iron, 26 x 22 In.	1422.00
Stove Plate, Treasure Of 1758, Cast Iron, c.1770, 22 x 23 ¾ In.	504.00
Stove Plate, Tulips, Hearts, Arched Columns, German Verse, Cast Iron, 27 x 29 In.	885.00
Stove Plate, Tulips, Hearts, Arches, c.1750, 24 ½ x 28 In.	770.00
Stove Plate, Tulips, Hearts, Columns, George Ross Over Mary Ann Furnace, 24 x 26 In.	885.00
Stove Plate, Wedding Fable, Cast Iron, c.1750, 24 x 26 In.	385.00
Stove Plate, Wedding, Cast Iron, c.1750, 26 ½ x 29 In.	563.00
Stove Plate, Wedding, Marlboro, 1768, Cast Iron, 24 x 20 In.	3081.00
Stove Plate, Wicked Borrower, Cast Iron, 18th Century, 22 ¼ x 23 ¾ In.	237.00

STRETCH GLASS is named for the strange stretch marks in the glass. It was made by many glass companies in the United States from about 1900 to the 1920s. It is iridescent. Most American stretch glass is molded; most European pieces are blown and may have a pontil mark.

Bowl, Cupped, Blue, 1 ¾ x 7 In.	16.00
Bowl, Gold Iridescent, Pedestal, 4 x 7 ¼ In.	50.00
Bowl, White Pearlized, Flared, US Glass, 9 ⅝ x 2 In.	77.00
Candy Dish, Lid, Vaseline, Paneled, Footed, 6 In.	110.00
Compote, Celestial Blue, 4 ¼ x 7 ½ In.	45.00
Plate, Vaseline, Pontil, 6 ½ In.	32.00
Plate, Vaseline, Topaz Yellow, 5 ¼ In., 12 Piece	96.00
Rose Bowl, Blue Milk Glass, Turned-In Rim, 6 ½ x 2 In.	60.00
Vase, Green, Swirled White, Pinched Ruffled Rim, 7 ½ In.	45.00

SUMIDA is a Japanese pottery that was made from about 1895 to 1941. Pieces are usually everyday objects—vases, jardinieres, bowls, teapots, and decorative tiles. Most pieces have a very heavy orange-red, blue, brown, black, green, purple, or off-white glaze, with raised three-dimensional figures as decorations. The unglazed part is painted red, green, black, or orange. Sumida is sometimes mistakenly called Sumida gawa, but true Sumida gawa is a softer pottery made in the early 1800s.

Creamer, Man Reading, Snail, Red, Black, Handle, 3 ½ In.	285.00
Humidor, 3 Figures, Holding Pearl, Red, 6 In.	278.00
Incense Burner, Children Playing, Monkey, c.1940, 3 ½ x 4 In.	85.00
Lamp, Figures, Wearing Robes, Figural Finial, Signed On Cartouche, 19 x 38 In. ....*Illus*	480.00
Pot, Boy, Chasing Stone, Black, Red, c.1875, 2 ½ x 2 In.	105.00
Vase, Figures, Basket Weave Center, Red, 18 In.	1495.00
Vase, Man On Ladder, Boys, Trumpet, Red, 8 ¼ In.	550.00

Store, Sign, Unlawful To Litter $100 Fine, Black & White, Tin, Bullet Holes, 36 x 42 In.
$90.00

Victorian Casino Antiques

Store, Tobacco Cutter, Figural, Boy Thumbing His Nose, Cast Iron, Scrolled Handle, 13 In.
$177.00

Conestoga Auction Co., Inc.

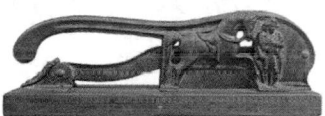

Store, Tobacco Cutter, Figural, General Washington & Horse, Cast Iron, On Plank, 14 ¾ In.
$177.00

Conestoga Auction Co., Inc.

TIP

Don't take your car to a flea market if you have another option. Instead, take your van, truck, or station wagon when you go to a farm auction, flea market, or out-of-town show. You never know when you'll find the dining room table of your dreams.

S

Stove, Cook, Columbian, Tan & Green, Enamel, 3 Burner, Gas, 54 x 28 x 16 In. $212.00

Conestoga Auction Co., Inc.

Stove, Cook, Majestic, Enamel, Cast Iron, Wood, 48 x 43 x 26 In. $189.00

Conestoga Auction Co., Inc.

Stove, Parlor, Garland Oak, Model 6E, Front Flue $1,560.00

Showtime Auction Sevices

SUNBONNET BABIES were introduced in 1900 in the book *The Sunbonnet Babies.* The stories were by Eulalie Osgood Grover, illustrated by Bertha Corbett. The children's faces were completely hidden by the sunbonnets. The children had been pictured in black and white before this time, but the color pictures in the book were immediately successful. The Royal Bayreuth China Company made a full line of children's dishes decorated with the Sunbonnet Babies. Some Sunbonnet Babies plates have been reproduced, but are clearly marked.

Creamer, Friday, Sweeping, Blue Mark	145.00
Dish, Monday, Washing, Molly & May, c.1910, 6 ⅓ In.	50.00
Dish, Tuesday, Ironing, Curled Edges, 5 x 3 ¾ In.	95.00
Figurine, Saturday, Baking, Yellow, Red Dresses, 4 x 6 ⅝ In.	45.00
Pin Dish, Wednesday, Mending, Spade Shape, 4 ¾ x 4 ½ In.	68.00
Plate, Friday, Sweeping, 7 ¼ In.	199.00
Plate, Monday, Washing, 7 ¼ In.	70.00 to 199.00
Plate, Monday, Washing, Pewter Border, 11 ¼ In.	75.00
Plate, Playtime Series, Playing Catch, 7 In.	175.00
Plate, Playtime Series, Round Dance, 7 In.	225.00
Plate, Playtime Series, Swinging, 7 In.	180.00
Plate, Saturday, Baking, 7 ¼ In.	199.00
Plate, Sunday, Fishing, 7 ¼ In.	199.00
Plate, Thursday, Scrubbing, 7 ¼ In.	195.00
Plate, Tuesday, Ironing, 7 ½ In.	110.00
Trinket Box, Tuesday, Ironing, 4 ¾ x 3 ⅞ In.	48.00

SUNDERLAND luster is a name given to a special type of pink luster made by Leeds, Newcastle, and other English firms during the nineteenth century. The luster glaze is metallic and glossy and appears to have bubbles in it. Other pieces of luster are listed in the Luster category.

Bowl, Pink Luster, Family Verse, Dixon Phillips & Co., c.1830, 4 x 8 In.	332.00
Bowl, Pink Luster, Ship, Poem, c.1830, 8 In. Diam.	195.00
Bowl, Verse, Lovers Biding Goodbye, Black Transfer, Pink Luster Bands, c.1810, 7 ¼ In.	413.00
Chamber Pot, Pink Luster, Strap Handles, Prayer, c.1825, 8 x 5 In.	1550.00
Cup & Saucer, Pink Luster, Pearlware, House, Valley, c.1940	82.00
Jug, Pink Luster, Iron Bridge, Masonic Verse, c.1850, 7 ¼ In.	535.00
Jug, Ship, Northumberland, Black Transfer, Enamel, Pink Luster, c.1820, 8 ½ In.	767.00
Mug, Interior Molded Frog, Ship, Fairy Of The Sea, Transfer, Orange Luster, c.1825, 4 In.	267.00
Pitcher, Pink Luster, Poem, c.1820, 5 In.	372.00
Plate, Pink Luster, Ship, Black Transfer, Gray's Pottery, c.1920, 8 In., 3 Piece	105.00

SUPERMAN was created by two seventeen-year-olds in 1938. The first issue of Action comics had the strip. Superman remains popular and became the hero of a radio show in 1940, cartoons in the 1940s, a television series, and several major movies.

Ad Card, Thanksgiving Day Parade, Superman Radio Show, 1940, 3 ½ x 5 ¼ In.	390.00
Belt, Box, 1940s, 8 ¾ In.	240.00
Box, Kellogg's Pep Cereal, Superman, Moon Mullins, Orphan Annie Pins, 1940s, 8 ½ x 6 In.	360.00
Button, Superman Film Serial, Hoyts Suburban Theatres, Flying, Red, White, Blue, c.1948, 1 In.	173.00
Charm, Sterling Silver, Bent Leg, Arm Extended, Holding Fastener Ring, Del Weston, c.1947, 1 In.	168.00
Comic Art, Book, No. 9, Yellow Ground, 1941	1080.00
Comic Book, Christmas Adventure Book, Macy's Premium, 1940, 10 x 7 ½ In.	1140.00
Comic Book, No. 30, 1944	510.00
Comic Book, Superman Stopping Car, Old Woman, Policeman, Cream Pages, No. 46, 1947	330.00
Comic Book, Three Dimension Adventures, With 3-D Glasses, 1953	80.00
Display Stand, 12 Wallets, Trifold, Yellow Vinyl, Superman Breaking Chain, 17 x 19 In.	421.00
Display, String Puppets, Super Heroes, Wonder Woman, Batman, Electric Animation, 12 x 25 In.	421.00
Doll, Lois Lane, Porcelain, Painted, Rooted Hair, Fabric Clothes, R. Tonner, 1997, 19 & 16 In., Pair	370.00
Figure, Superman, Carnival, 1940, 15 ¾ In.	120.00
Lunch Box, Superman Fighting Giant Robot, Slot For Name, Universal, 1954	661.00
Matches, Safety, Superman Flying, Paper Label, 1940s, 1 ½ x 2 ¼ In.	173.00
Membership Kit, Supermen Of America, Envelope, Secret Code, Button, Certificate, c.1959	153.00
Patch, Fabric, Superman Of America Strength, Courage, Justice, 1940, 2 ½ x 2 In.	1440.00
Pennant, Superman Flying, Navy Ground, 1966, 29 In.	120.00
Pin, Action Comics Superman, Lithograph, 1942, 1 In.	90.00
Pin, Portrait, 1950s, ¾ In.	30.00
Pin, Read Superman Action Comics Magazine, White Ground, Blue, Red, 1939, ⅞ In.	476.00
Pin, Supermen Of America, 1961, 1 ¼ In.	60.00

Poster, Atom Man Vs. Superman, 27 x 4 In.	255.00
Poster, Send Superman To War, Send Comic Books To Soldiers, AEWS, c.1944, 18 x 17 In.	690.00
Projector, Movie, Hand, Film, Box, 1947, 7 ½ x 4 In.	180.00
Puzzle, Over The City, Stands Alone, Springs Into Action, Saves A Life, Box, 8 ½ x 11 In., 500 Piece	336.00
Ring, Action, Flying Superman, Yellow, Blue Red, Rectangular, 1966	144.00
Ring, Contest Prize, DC Comics, Breaking Chains, Lightning Bolts, Silver, Enamel, 1940	2296.00
Ring, Secret Chamber, Superman Breaking Chain, Star, Planet, Lighting Bolt, Brass, 1941	8855.00
Ring, Superman Tim, Silver Luster, Symbols, Flying, Initials ST, 1940s	690.00
School Bookbag, Canvas, Photo Of Him Flying Over City, Brown, Blue & Red, 1940, 11 x 14 In.	685.00
Sign, KECO Radio Station, Town Talk Bread Promo, Die Cut, 4 ½ In.	240.00
Table Lighter, Figural, Cast Metal, Hands On Hips, Cape, Bakelite Plastic Base, c.1940, 3 x 4 ½ In.	2013.00
Toy, Superman Rollover Plane, Tin Lithograph, Clockwork, Marx, 6 In.	863.00
T-Shirt, Lois & Clark, New Adventures Of Superman, Screen Worn, Hanes, 1993-97 ...... *Illus*	190.00
TV Guide Cover, Superman, Actor Photo, Story About TV Show, 1953, 5 x 2 ½ In.	450.00
Wrapper, Gum Card, 1940, 6 x 4 ½ In.	540.00
Wristwatch, Chromed Metal, Comic Book Title Logo, Lightning Bolt Hands, Ingraham, 1950s, 1 In.	305.00

SUSIE COOPER began as a designer in 1925 working for the English firm A.E. Gray & Company. In 1932 she formed Susie Cooper Pottery, Ltd. In 1950 it became Susie Cooper China, Ltd., and the company made china and earthenware. In 1966 it was acquired by Josiah Wedgwood & Sons, Ltd. The name *Susie Cooper /* appears with the company names on many pieces of ceramics.

Coffeepot, Lid, Pansies, Brown On White, 8 ½ In.	150.00
Cup & Saucer, Pansies, Shades Of Brown, Can Shape, Demitasse	25.00
Cup & Saucer, Pink Coral, Swirl, Pineapple, Leaves, Demitasse	15.00
Jam Jar, Feather, Blue Ground, Oval, 3 ⅛ x 2 In.	35.00
Mug, Cornpoppy, Red Flowers, White Ground, 4 Piece	28.00
Plate, Stylized Flowers, Yellow, 9 In.	35.00

SWANKYSWIGS are small drinking glasses. In 1933, the Kraft Food Company began to market cheese spreads in these decorated, reusable glass tumblers. They were discontinued from 1941 to 1946, then made again from 1947 to 1958. Then plain glasses were used for most of the cheese, although a few special decorated Swankyswigs have been made since that time. For more prices, go to kovels.com.

Archies, Sabrina Calls The Plays, Red, 1973, 8 Oz., 4 ¼ In.	11.00
Bachelor Button, Red & White Flowers, Green Leaves, 3 ¾ In.	9.00
Bicentennial Tulip, Red, Thumbprint Mark, 3 ¾ In.	28.00
Bustlin' Betsy, Brown, 3 ¾ In.	9.00

SWASTIKA KERAMOS is a line of art pottery made from 1906 to 1908 by the Owen China Company of Minerva, Ohio. Many pieces were made with an iridescent glaze.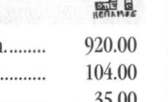

Pitcher, Trees, Nightfall, Purple, Red, Green, Trumpet Bottom, Handle At Neck, 10 ¾ In.	920.00
Vase, Gray Tan, Cylinder Paper, Label, 15 In.	104.00
Vase, Pink Speckled Gray Glaze, Handles, 8 In.	35.00

SWORDS of all types that are of interest to collectors are listed here. The military dress sword with elaborate handle is probably the most wanted. A tsuba is a hand guard fitted to a Japanese sword between the handle and the blade. Be sure to display swords in a safe way, out of reach of children.

Artillery, Motif Blade, Etched, Ebonized Grip, Wire Wrap, Scabbard, Germany, Austria, 37 In.	196.00
Artillery, Straight Blade With Fullers, Marked, Germany, 19 In.	236.00
Basket, Straight Blade, Marked, J.J. Runkel Dolingen, Rayskin Grip, Scotland, c.1790, 39 In.	1121.00
Bayonet, Plug, Hand Forged, Wood Handle, Early 18th Century, 15 In.	115.00
Bayonet, Steel Blade, Wood Handle, Painted Metal Sheath, Circle Emblem, Japan, 15 ¾ In.	63.00
Cavalry, Officer's, Parade, Curved Blade, Nickel Plated Iron Scabbard, Germany, 32 In.	118.00
Cavalry, Saber, Brass Guard, Leather Grip, Mansfield & Lamb, c.1862, 42 ½ In.	452.00
Ceremonial, Steel Hammered Blade, Ebonized Wood, Wire Grip, Gilt Shield, Silver Sheath, 35 In.	138.00
Ceremonial, Tag, Ebonized Grip, Wire & Gilt Handle, Silvered Sheath, Japan, 37 In.	150.00
Executioner's, Konda, Triangular Point, Shaped Wood Grip, c.1890, 14 ¾ In.	875.00
Imperial, Reverse P Guard, Black Enameled Scabbard, Celluloid Grip, Horster, Germany	142.00
Infantry Officer's, M1889, Folding Guard, Black Enamel Scabbard, Twisted Silver Wire, Prussia	153.00
Infantry, Plated Honeysuckle Pierced Hilt, Shark Skin Grip, Scrolling Leaves, c.1897, 32 In.	385.00
Katana, Straight Temper Line, Painted Iron Scabbard, Tsuba, Ray Skin Grip, Menuki, 26 In.	295.00

Sumida, Lamp, Figures, Wearing Robes, Figural Finial, Signed On Cartouche, 19 x 38 In.
$480.00

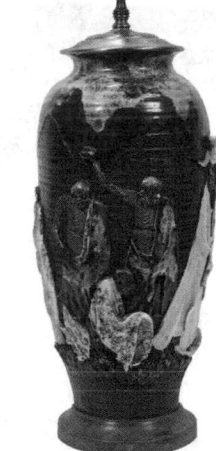

DuMouchelles Art Gallery

Superman, T-Shirt, Lois & Clark, New Adventures Of Superman, Screen Worn, Hanes, 1993-97
$190.00

Hake's Americana & Collectibles

Tea Caddy, Fruitwood, Apple Shape, 4 ¼ x 4 ¾ In.
$1,098.00

Neal Auction Co.

S

TIP
When away on a trip, lower the ring of your telephone so that it can't be heard outside.

Tea Caddy, Lacquer, Chinese Life Scenes, Compartments, Paktong & Ivory Fitted Lids, Chinese, 8 x 14 In.
$2,440.00

Neal Auction Co.

Tea Caddy, Tortoiseshell, Regency, Rounded Corners, 2 Compartments, Brass Ball Feet, 4 ½ x 6 In.
$635.00

Leslie Hindman Auctioneers

Teco, Vase, Green Matte Glaze, Blackened, Impressed, Incised, 6 ½ In.
$920.00

Humler & Nolan

Light Cavalry, M1822, Curved Bright Blade, Brass Hilt, Leather Grip, France, 1823, 36 In.	212.00
Lined Pattern, Round Humps, Brass Mounts, Silk Wrap & Cord, 38 In.	944.00
Militia, Brass Hilt, Stars, Bars, Bow Tie Guard, Bone Grip, Ribbed, U.S.A., c.1850, 25 In.	435.00
Naval Cutlass, Engraved RBT Chateuelleroult, Anchors, Metal Grip, Leather Scabbard, c.1833, 32 In.	759.00
Naval Officer's, M1852, Brass, Leather Scabbard, Straight Blade, Sharkskin Wrap Grip, 29 In.	130.00
Officer's, Dumb Bell Blade, Plated Brass Hilt, Etched Trophies, c.1897, 32 ⅝ In.	425.00
Officer's, Iron P Form Guard, Short Langets, Germany, c.1880, 34 In.	365.00
Officer's, Parade, Nickel Plated Black, Wood Grip, Silver Mon, Nickel Plated Scabbard, Japan, 33 In.	236.00
Saber, Cavalry, Oval Cartouche, Brass Guard, Wire & Scabbard, U.S.A., Marked, c.1850, 35 ¾ In.	531.00
Samurai, Ceremonial, Gendai-To Showa, Signed, Ray Skin Handle, Japan, 1900s, 40 In.	2099.00
Samurai, Ebonized Scabbard, Japan, 1900s, 24 ¾ In.	770.00
Shearing, Double Edge, Hand Forged, Flexible Straight Blade, Carved Wood Grip, 33 In.	861.00
Staff, Medical, M1840, Engraved Straight Blade, Elliptical Cross Section, Brass Hilt, 28 In.	944.00
Steel Blade, Carved Bone Handle, Sheath, c.1945, Japan, 16 In.	230.00
U.S. Navy, Officer's, Engraved Francis A. Hill, Sharkskin Grip, Wire Wrap, Emblems, 39 In.	483.00
U.S. Navy, Officer's, Silver Grip, Wire Wrap, Engraved, Vining, Dolphin Heads, Collins & Co., 35 In.	1553.00
Wakizashi, Mounted Hilt, Resting Scabbard, Japan, 34 In.	399.00
Wakizashi, Wavy Temper Lie, Copper Habaki, Wood Scabbard, Iron Hanger, Tsuba, Menuki, 17 ¼ In.	325.00

SYRACUSE is a trademark used by the Onondaga Pottery of Syracuse, New York. The company was established in 1871. The name became the Syracuse China Company in 1966. Syracuse China closed in 2009. It was known for fine dinnerware and restaurant china.

SYRACUSE
China

Accent, Creamer	14.00
Accent, Cup & Saucer	8.00
Accent, Platter, Oval, 12 ½ In.	33.00
Alcora, Cup & Saucer, Footed, Black Trim	23.00
Alpine, Bowl, Vegetable, Oval, 8 ¼ In.	45.00
Alpine, Cup & Saucer, Demitasse	34.00
Bamboo, Plate, Bread & Butter, 6 ¼ In.	9.00
Bamboo, Plate, Dinner, 10 In.	8.00
Belmont, Cup & Saucer, Footed, 3 In.	23.00
Belmont, Platter, Oval, 16 In.	119.00
Bone Dish, Half Moon, Daisies, c.1950, 6 ½ x 3 In.	10.00
Bridal Rose, Bowl, Fruit, 5 In.	21.00
Bridal Rose, Plate, Dinner, 10 ⅝ In.	12.00
Caprice, Creamer, 4 In.	15.00
Caprice, Gravy Boat, Underplate	55.00
Caprice, Platter, Oval, 12 ½ In.	49.00
Charm, Plate, Dinner, Swirled Ribs, Scalloped Edge, 10 ⅜ In.	24.00
Clover, Creamer, Swirled, Ribbing	24.00
Clover, Plate, Bread & Butter, Scalloped, 6 ⅜ In.	9.00
Dorian, Chop Plate, 12 In.	74.00
Dorian, Coffeepot, Lid, 3 Cup, 7 ½ In.	94.00
Dorian, Plate, Dinner, 10 ⅝ In.	20.00
Grace, Bowl, Cereal, Lugged, 6 In.	64.00
Grace, Cup & Saucer, Footed	26.00
Grace, Platter, Oval, 16 In.	179.00
Inspiration, Cup & Saucer, Footed	10.00
Inspiration, Platter, Oval, 16 In.	148.00
Jefferson, Bowl, Cereal, Rimmed, 6 ¼ In.	26.00
Jefferson, Cup & Saucer, Footed	18.00
Jefferson, Plate, Dinner, 10 ¼ In.	17.00
Montego, Coffeepot, Lid, 5 Cup, 7 ¼ In.	41.00
Montego, Creamer, 8 Oz., 3 ⅝ In.	8.00
Montego, Cup & Saucer	9.00
Nordic, Butter, Cover, ¼ Lb.	33.00
Nordic, Mug, 3 ⅜ In.	49.00
Old Ivory, Plate, 10 ¼ In., 12 Piece	182.00
Prelude, Bowl, Cereal, Lugged, 5 ⅜ In.	11.00
Prelude, Chop Plate, Round, 11 In.	64.00
Puritan, Bowl, Vegetable, Round, 7 In.	25.00
Puritan, Cup & Saucer	7.00
Puritan, Pitcher, 32 Oz., 6 ⅞ In.	35.00
Selma, Chop Plate, Round, 12 In.	69.00

TIP
It is said that for the best deals at a flea market or show, you should arrive early (perhaps pay the early bird admission) for best selection and leave late for best deals. But don't forget to look for things displayed on the ground or under shelves. They are often overlooked.

S

Selma, Plate, Dinner, 9 ¾ In.	14.00
Selma, Sugar, Lid, Footed, 2 ¾ In.	26.00
Sharon, Bowl, Vegetable, Lid, Round, 9 In.	109.00
Sharon, Cup & Saucer, Footed	17.00
Sharon, Platter, Oval, 14 In.	39.00
Sherwood, Gravy Boat, Underplate, Oval	41.00
Sherwood, Plate, Dinner, 9 ¾ In.	25.00
Stardust, Plate, Bread & Butter, 6 ½ In.	7.00
Stardust, Platter, Oval, 14 In.	59.00
Vintage, Bowl, Vegetable, Divided, Oval, 10 In.	16.00
Vintage, Celery Dish, 12 In.	15.00
Vintage, Creamer, 8 Oz., 4 ¼ In.	15.00
Vintage, Plate, Dinner, 10 In.	12.00
Wayside, Bowl, Vegetable, Round, 8 In.	69.00
Wayside, Cup & Saucer	9.00
Wayside, Plate, Dinner, 10 In.	19.00
Westvale, Plate, Dinner, 10 ⅝ In.	33.00
Westvale, Soup, Dish, Rimmed, 8 In.	23.00
Woodbine, Gravy Boat, Underplate	15.00
Woodbine, Mug, 3 ⅜ In.	68.00
Woodbine, Platter, Oval, 11 In.	16.00
Yellow Roses, Chop Plate, Round, 11 In.	45.00
Yellow Roses, Creamer, 8 Oz., 4 In.	15.00
Yellow Roses, Sugar, Lid, 2 ⅝ In.	16.00

TAPESTRY, *Porcelain, see Rose Tapestry category.*

TEA CADDY is the name for a small box made to hold tea leaves. In the eighteenth century, tea was very expensive and it was stored under lock and key. The first tea caddies were made with locks. By the nineteenth century, tea was more plentiful and the tea caddy was larger. Often there were two sections, one for green tea, one for black tea.

Ash, Elm, Walnut, Georgian, Inlaid, Brass Lion Handles, Paw Feet, 7 x 11 In.	354.00
Bentwood, Green Paint, Round, Stenciled Tea, Flourishes, c.1875, 7 ¾ x 3 ¾ In.	201.00
Calamander, Brass, Ivory Tag, Dome, Escutcheons, Compartments, William IV, c.1835, 9 x 10 In.	1722.00
Enamel Over Silver, Pagoda Shape, Beads, Jadeite Band, Chinese, c.1925, 5 In.	1225.00
Enamel, Courting Scene, Flowers, Scrolls, Pink Ground, Continental, 1800s, 4 ½ In.	486.00
Enamel, Silver, Hinged Lid, Tabernacle Shape, 1800s, 6 In.	650.00
Fruitwood, Apple Shape, 4 ¼ x 4 ¾ In. *...Illus*	1098.00
Fruitwood, Apple Shape, George III, c.1810, 5 ½ In.	1003.00
Fruitwood, Apple Shape, George III, c.1810, 5 In.	3068.00
Fruitwood, Hinged Lid, Pear Shape, George III, c.1800, 7 x 4 x 4 In.	1440.00
Fruitwood, Hinged Lid, Shell Inlay, c.1800, 4 ½ x 7 ⅛ In.	237.00
Fruitwood, Melon Shape, Carved, Ribs, Stem, Orange Mottled, Green Patina, George III, c.1780, 5 In.	4130.00
Fruitwood, Pear Shape, George III, c.1810, 6 ¼ In.	2360.00
Fruitwood, Pear Shape, Orange Shaded, George III, c.1780, 5 ⅝ In.	1121.00
Gilt, Black Lacquer, Figural Panels, Flower Borders, Pewter Canisters, Chinese, c.1850, 9 In.	561.00
Japan, Canted Corners, Gold Figural Panels, 5 ½ In.	124.00
Lacquer, Black, Gilt, Allover Figures, Scrolls, Flowers, Paw Feet, Chinese, c.1820, 7 ½ In.	649.00
Lacquer, Chinese Life Scenes, Compartments, Paktong & Ivory Fitted Lids, Chinese, 8 x 14 In. *...Illus*	2440.00
Lacquer, Figural Landscape, Rectangular, Fitted Pewter Interior, Chinese, c.1820, 9 ¾ In.	325.00
Lacquer, Gilt, Figural Reserves, Leaf Borders, Lobed, Hinged, Winged Dragon Feet, c.1900	2813.00
Mahogany, Barber Pole Inlay, Bail Handle, Rosette, Diamond Shape Escutcheon, c.1815, 5 ½ x 5 In.	584.00
Mahogany, Bombe Shape, Barber Pole Inlay, Brass Bail Handle, England, c.1800, 6 x 10 In.	783.00
Mahogany, Coffin Shape, Ivory Knobs, Bun Feet, Lion's Head Pulls, William IV, c.1835, 7 x 12 In.	615.00
Mahogany, Coffin Shape, Regency, c.1810, 6 ¾ x 12 In.	118.00
Mahogany, Coffin Shape, String Inlay, Brass Pull, Ball Feet, England, Regency, 1800s, 6 x 11 In.	207.00
Mahogany, Dome Lid, England, c.1840, 6 x 7 ¾ x 4 In.	450.00
Mahogany, Flower & Matchstick Inlays, George III, c.1800, 4 ½ x 4 ½ In.	119.00
Mahogany, Hinged Lid, Fitted Interior, Bracket Feet, Victorian, England, 9 ¾ x 5 ½ In.	288.00
Mahogany, Hinged Lid, Veneer, Inlaid, Crossbanded, Fans, Kite Shape Escutcheon, c.1800, 4 ⅝ x 10 In.	356.00
Mahogany, Inlaid Stringing, 2 Compartments, Drawer, Turned Legs, Regency Style, c.1890, 24 x 17 In.	922.00
Mahogany, Inlays, George III, c.1770, 4 ½ x 7 ¼ In.	504.00
Mahogany, Leaf Inlays, George III, 4 ½ x 5 In.	267.00
Mahogany, Lozenge Shape Escutcheon, Brass Ball & Claw Feet, Regency, c.1815, 5 x 8 ¾ In.	369.00
Mahogany, Marquetry, Flowers, Rope Twist Borders, George III, c.1900, 4 ½ x 7 In.	944.00
Mahogany, Patera Inlays, George III, 6 x 9 In.	415.00

TIP

Dolls with inset eyes should be stored face down.

Teco, Vase, Indian Heads, Footed, Terra Cotta, Green Matte Glaze, Stamped, c.1910, 16 In.
$11,875.00

Rago Arts & Auction Center

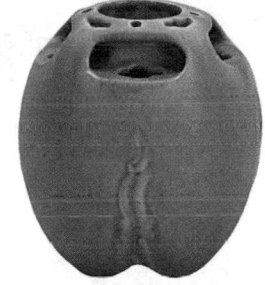

Teco, Vase, Openwork, Pooled Charcoaling, Green Matte Glaze, Stamped, c.1905, 6 ½ x 5 ½ In.
$3,125.00

Rago Arts & Auction Center

Teddy Bear, Steiff, Beige, Jointed, Button, Silk Bow, Original Tag, c.1950, 6 In.
$89.00

Bertoia Auctions

T

Teddy Bear, Steiff, Mohair, Blond, Glass Eyes, Fully Jointed, c.1920, 13 In. $531.00

Eldred's Auction and Appraisal Services

Teddy Bear, Steiff, Mohair, Blond, Shoebutton Eyes, Ear Button, c.1910, 13 In. $885.00

Eldred's Auction and Appraisal Services

Teddy Bear, Steiff, Mohair, Gold, Shoebutton Eyes, Fully Jointed, Ear Button, c.1904-05, 13 In. $944.00

Eldred's Auction and Appraisal Services

Button in Ear
The Steiff "Button in Ear" trademark was first used in 1905.

Mahogany, Satinwood, Conch Shell Inlay, Fitted Interior, George III, c.1780, 5 x 9 ½ In.	322.00
Mahogany, Shell Inlaid Oval Panels, Fitted Interior, 5 x 9 ⅞ In.	708.00
Mahogany, Stepped Lid, Brass Hardware, Georgian, c.1865, 6 ½ x 9 ¼ In.	178.00
Mahogany, Tapered Sides & Lid, Inlaid Bone Escutcheon, England, c.1815, 6 x 10 ½ In.	411.00
Mahogany, Veneer, Hinged Lid, Coffin Shape, 2 Compartments, Bone Handles, 12 x 6 In.	138.00
Mahogany, Veneer, Molded Hinged Lid, Brass Pull, Fitted Interior, Bracket Feet, c.1750, 5 ½ x 9 ½ In.	267.00
Mixed Woods, Inlays, 3 Compartments, Regency, c.1805, 5 ½ x 10 ½ In.	502.00
Mixed Woods, Shell Inlay, 2 Lidded Compartments, England, 1800s, 4 ¾ x 6 ½ In.	374.00
Mother-Of-Pearl, Rosewood, Carved Bird Lid, 8-Sided, Wood & Gilt Bands, Victorian, 4 x 5 In.	201.00
Palasander, Veneer, Coffin Shape, Inlaid Stringing, Brass Mask Handles, Ball Feet, 5 x 8 In.	375.00
Papier-Mache, Lid, Block Front, Mother-Of-Pearl Inlay, Flowers, Victorian, c.1850, 4 x 6 In.	153.00
Pottery, Dome Lid, Flowering Branches, 4 Paneled Sides, Tapered, 9 ½ In.	1446.00
Rolled Paper, Quillwork, Oval, Ivory Escutcheon, Regency, England, 5 ½ x 8 In.	1150.00
Rosewood, 2 Compartments, Shelf, Hinged, Regency, c.1825, 6 x 12 x 6 In.	184.00
Rosewood, Bombay Form, Inlaid, Brass Paw Feet, 7 ½ x 8 In.	460.00
Rosewood, Coffin Shape, 2 Lidded Compartments, Bun Feet, Regency, c.1835, 7 x 12 In.	110.00
Rosewood, Coffin Shape, Tapering, Brass Ball Feet, Regency, 6 x 4 x 7 In.	427.00
Rosewood, Inset Cut Paperwork Panels, England, 5 ½ In.	413.00
Rosewood, Trapezoidal Base & Lid, Egg & Dart Trim, Flattened Bun Feet, 7 x 10 ½ In.	288.00
Satinwood, Inlaid, Plum Pudding Mahogany, Engraved, Cut Glass Bowl, Regency, c.1810, 8 x 12 In.	590.00
Satinwood, Lid, Inlaid Conch Shell, Fans, Regency, England, 6 x 12 In.	690.00
Satinwood, Paper, Hexagonal, Leaf Panels, Girl's Portrait, c.1790, 5 ⅜ x 7 In.	1875.00
Satinwood, Rosewood, Dome Lid, Banded Design, Victorian, c.1835, 3 ¾ x 5 In.	276.00
Silver, Bowl, Footed, Oval, Georg Jensen, c.1930, 4 ¾ x 3 ½ In.	563.00
Silver, Enamel, Urn Shape, Gold Wash, Forget-Me-Not Flowers, Scrolling Leaves, 5 ½ In.	1041.00
Silver, Flower, Scroll Cartouche, Raised Scroll Feet, Germany, 8 In.	476.00
Silver, Flowers, Scroll, Engraved, George III, 1772, 3 ¾ In.	1080.00
Silver, Square, Woman Embossed, Dutch, c.1900, 4 x 2 ¾ In.	313.00
Stand, Chinoiserie, Gilt, Leafy Stems, Square Tapered Legs, Casters, c.1800, 41 x 18 ½ In.	1220.00
Tiger Maple Veneer, Banded, Shell Inlays, Brass Cornucopia Handles, c.1820, 5 x 12 In.	531.00
Tiger Maple, Hinged Dome Lid, 2 Interior Compartments, England, 5 ½ x 8 In.	263.00
Tiger Maple, Hinged Lid, Fitted Interior, England, 5 ½ x 8 In.	268.00
Tole, Black, Gilt Banding, Fruit & Leaves, U.S.A., c.1815, 4 In.	181.00
Tortoiseshell, Dome Lid, Rectangular, Brass Feet, c.1830, 5 x 4 ½ In.	443.00
Tortoiseshell, Dome Lid, Regency, Inlaid, Pierced Brass Strapwork, Shield, c.1835, 5 x 9 In.	1476.00
Tortoiseshell, Ivory Stringing, c.1840, 6 ½ x 8 In.	2280.00
Tortoiseshell, Mother-Of-Pearl, Hinged Lid, Ivory Escutcheon, Disc Feet, George III, c.1800, 4 x 6 In.	657.00
Tortoiseshell, Pagoda Style Lid, Fluted Front, Compressed Bun Feet, 1800s, 5 x 6 ¾ x 4 ¾ In.	2125.00
Tortoiseshell, Regency, Rounded Corners, 2 Compartments, Brass Ball Feet, 4 ½ x 6 In. ....*Illus*	635.00
Tortoiseshell, Regency, Slant Lid, Ball Feet, Double Lidded Compartments, England, 6 x 8 In.	1610.00
Tortoiseshell, Stepped Lid, Divided Interior, Rectangular, George III, c.1820, 7 ½ In.	767.00
Turnbridge Ware, Flower Panel Lid, Inlaid Geometric Borders, 1800s, 4 ¾ x 9 In.	767.00
Walnut, Hexagonal, Barber Pole Inlaid Feet, 6 x 5 In.	575.00
Walnut, Lid, Coffin Shape, Ivory Knobs, Lion's Head Handles, George III, c.1800, 7 x 9 In.	359.00
Wood, Apple Shape, Red Stain, Turned Wood Stem, Hinged Lid, England, c.1800, 4 ¼ In.	2015.00
Wood, Asian Scene, Gilt, Black Ground, Japanned, Labeled C Imperial, c.1850, 18 ¼ In.	270.00
Wood, Dome Lid, Windsor Castle, Ebonized, Mother-Of-Pearl, Shaped Feet, 9 x 16 In.	1599.00
Wood, Inlay, Painted, Cut Corner, Flowers, Garlands, Brass Ball Feet, c.1820, 7 ¼ x 11 ¾ In.	830.00
Wood, Lacquer, Hinged Lid, Double, Octagonal, Gold Design, Pagoda, Landscape, Chinese, 5 x 8 In.	374.00
Wood, Tortoiseshell, Clad, White Painted Edges, Hinged Lid, Silver Handle, 4 x 5 In.	345.00

TEA LEAF IRONSTONE dishes are named for their decorations. There was a superstition that it was lucky if a whole tea leaf unfolded at the bottom of your cup. This idea was translated into the pattern of dishes known as "tea leaf." By 1850 at least twelve English factories were making this pattern, and by the 1870s it was a popular pattern in many countries. The tea leaf was always a luster glaze on early wares, although now some pieces are made with a brown tea leaf. There are many variations of tea leaf designs, such as Teaberry, Pepper Leaf, and Gold Leaf. The designs were used on many different white ironstone shapes, such as Bamboo, Lily of the Valley, Empress, and Cumbow.

Basin, Ewer, Cable, Anthony Shaw	35.00
Basin, Ewer, Fish Hook, Alfred Meakin	50.00 to 60.00
Bowl, Moss Rose, Scalloped, Alfred Meakin, 9 ¾ In.	75.00
Bowl, Vegetable, Oval, Wilkinson, 8 ¾ In.	88.00
Bowl, Vegetable, Scalloped, Anthony Shaw, 10 ⅝ In.	60.00

Bowl, Vegetable, Wedgwood, 8 x 8 In.	109.00
Bowl, Vegetable, Wilkinson, 7 x 7 In.	119.00
Brush Tray, Lid, Lily Of The Valley, Anthony Shaw	60.00
Butter, Cover, Bowl, Insert, Cable, Anthony Shaw	55.00
Cake Plate, Bullet, Anthony Shaw, 8 In.	70.00
Cake Plate, Cable, Oval, Anthony Shaw	10.00
Cake Plate, Fleur-De-Lis, Oval, Mellor Taylor	30.00
Cake Plate, Peerless, John Edwards	40.00
Cake Plate, Simplicity, Anthony Shaw, Round	140.00
Chamber Pot, Lid, Cable, Anthony Shaw	40.00
Coffeepot, Lid, Square, Footed, Wilkinson, 4 Cup, 6 ½ In.	278.00
Coffeepot, Lid, Wedgwood, 7 Cup, 7 In.	189.00
Creamer, Brocade, Alfred Meakin, 6 ¼ In.	30.00
Creamer, Chelsea, Johnson Bros., 5 ⅜ In.	40.00
Dish, Pickle, Morning Glory, Portland Shape, Elsmore & Forster	375.00
Eggcup, Empress, William Adams, Pair	50.00
Gravy Boat, Embossed, Anthony Shaw	78.00
Gravy Boat, Lily Of The Valley, Anthony Shaw	35.00
Mug, Bullet, Anthony Shaw	210.00
Mug, Cable, Anthony Shaw, 3 ¼ In.	40.00
Mug, Moss Rose, Taylor & Knowles	65.00
Mug, Scroll, Alfred Meakin	40.00
Nappy, Wedgwood, 4 ⅜ In.	21.00
Nappy, Wedgwood, Round, 6 Piece	18.00
Plate, Bread & Butter, Wilkinson, 6 ⅞ In.	26.00
Plate, Dinner, Embossed, Anthony Shaw, 9 ⅞ In.	31.00
Plate, Lunch, Wedgwood, 8 ¾ In.	26.00
Plate, Ribbed Rim, Anthony Shaw, 8 ¾ In.	31.00
Plate, Salad, Anthony Shaw, 8 In.	14.00
Plate, Salad, Embossed, Anthony Shaw, 7 ¾ In.	11.00
Plate, Salad, Wilkinson, 9 In.	23.00
Platter, Lily Of The Valley, Anthony Shaw, Oval, 15 In. & 17 In.	25.00
Platter, Oval, Anthony Shaw, 15 In.	112.00
Platter, Oval, Wilkinson, 16 ½ In.	249.00
Platter, Rectangular, Anthony Shaw, 14 ½ In.	98.00
Platter, Rectangular, Ribbed Edge, Wedgwood, 13 ⅞ In.	118.00
Punch Bowl, Basket Weave, Square, 5 ¾ x 8 x 8 In.	110.00
Sugar, Lid, Basket Weave, Anthony Shaw, 6 ¼ In.	25.00
Sugar, Lid, Coronet, W. & E. Corn	20.00
Teapot, Lid, Fish Hook, Alfred Meakin, 9 In.	40.00
Teapot, Lid, Lily Of The Valley, Anthony Shaw, 9 ¼ In.	70.00

TECO is the mark used on the art pottery line made by the American Terra Cotta and Ceramic Company of Terra Cotta and Chicago, Illinois. The company was an offshoot of the firm founded by William D. Gates in 1881. The Teco line was first made in 1885 but was not sold commercially until 1902. It continued in production until 1922. Over 500 designs were made in a variety of colors, shapes, and glazes. The company closed in 1930.

Bowl, Buttressed, Squat, Green Matte Glaze, Stamped, c.1910, 3 ¼ x 9 In.	1125.00
Bowl, Footed, Gray Matte Glaze, Fritz Albert, 7 x 3 In.	400.00
Bowl, Footed, Tapered Globe, Gray Matte Glaze, Fritz Albert, 7 x 3 ½ In.	488.00
Bowl, Grape Pattern, Round, Green Matte Glaze, Signed Fritz Albert, 14 ½ x 5 ½ In.	2318.00
Bowl, Leaf & Berry Design, Green Matte Glaze, Charcoal Highlights, Fritz Albert, 9 x 2 In.	375.00
Bowl, Leaf, Berry, Mottled Green Glaze, 2 ¼ x 9 ¼ In.	236.00
Bowl, Roman Salad, Conical, Footed, Green Matte Glaze, Holmes Smith, 12 x 6 In.	1830.00
Bowl, Salad, 4-Footed, Green Matte Glaze, Holmes Smith, 12 x 6 In.	1500.00
Jardiniere, Molded Pond Lilies, Bulbous, Green Matte Glaze, 9 ¾ x 10 ½ In.	27500.00
Jardiniere, Water Lilies, Leaves, Carved, 8 Handles, Green Matte Glaze, W.J. Dodd, 11 x 9 In.	12500.00
Planter, Round, 4 Column Feet, Green Matte Glaze, 4 x 7 ½ In.	1250.00
Urn, 2 Handles At Neck, Narrow Neck, Green Matte Glaze, Stamped, c.1910, 9 x 5 In.	1625.00
Vase, 3-Footed, Green Matte Glaze, Fritz Albert, 7 x 9 In.	1125.00
Vase, 4 Angular Buttresses, Brown Matte Glaze, 7 ¼ x 4 ½ In.	2500.00
Vase, 4 Buttress Handles, Green Matte Glaze, Impressed W.B. Mundie, 8 x 8 In.	3375.00
Vase, 4 Buttress Shape, Pink Matte Glaze, Impressed, W.D. Gates, 2 ½ x 7 In.	854.00
Vase, 4 Buttresses, Pink Matte Glaze, Marked, W.D. Gates, 2 ½ x 7 In.	700.00

Teco

Teddy Bear, Steiff, Mohair, Golden, Felt Paws, Stitched Nose, 24 In.
$10,030.00

James D. Julia Auctioneers

Teddy Bear, Steiff, Mohair, Jointed, Button, c.1904-08, 12 In.
$1,062.00

Bertoia Auctions

Telephone, American Bell Telephone Co., Candlestick, Copper, Bakelite, Roycroft, c.1912, 12 In.
$281.00

Rago Arts & Auction Center

T

Telephone, Gamewell, Call Box, Police Telegraph, Blue, 105 In.
$1,170.00

Showtime Auction Sevices

Telephone, Garfield, Painted, Prototype, Tyco Toys, 1980s, 6 ¾ x 11 In.
$240.00

Hake's Americana & Collectibles

Telephone, Rotary Phone, Bronze Stand, Swivel, Man & Woman Pictured In Number Pad, 28 In.
$288.00

Victorian Casino Antiques

Vase, 4 Curved Buttresses, Gray Matte Glaze, Tapered, c.1910, 6 ½ x 6 In.	1875.00
Vase, 4 Handles, Green Matte Glaze, J. K. Caddy, 9 ½ x 11 In.	7500.00
Vase, 4 Round Column Handles, Trumpet Neck, Bulbous Bottom, Brown Matte Glaze, 6 ⅝ In.	1265.00
Vase, Bottle Shape, Round Foot, Green Matte Glaze, c.1910, 5 ½ x 4 ½ In.	813.00
Vase, Bulbous Bottom, Straight Neck, 2 Buttressed Handles, Green Matte Glaze, 5 ½ In.	4688.00
Vase, Bulbous, 2 Twist Loop Handles, Ring Foot, Green Matte Glaze, Stamped, c.1910, 11 x 6 In.	2875.00
Vase, Bulbous, Squared Rim, Pinched Corners, Green Matte Glaze, 6 ¾ x 7 ½ In.	4688.00
Vase, Carved Lily, Tapered, Dark Green Matte Glaze, George Dean, 19 x 29 ½ In.	11250.00
Vase, Carved Tulip Shape, Blue Matte Glaze, Signed Fernand Moreau, 6 x 12 In.	1875.00
Vase, Charcoal Highlights, Ear Of Corn, Green Matte Glaze, Fritz Albert, 6 x 14 In.	25000.00
Vase, Conical, Turquoise Matte Glaze, 12 ½ x 26 In.	1830.00
Vase, Flat Shape, Green Matte Glaze, Impressed, Fritz Albert, 5 ½ x 12 In.	3125.00
Vase, Folded Rim, Tulip Shape, Blue Matte Glaze, Fernand Moreau, Impressed, 5 x 12 In.	2074.00
Vase, Footed Smokestack, Lilies Encircling Rim, Green Matte Glaze, Charcoaling Effect, 13 In.	1380.00
Vase, Green Matte Glaze, Blackened, Impressed, Incised, 6 ½ In. ....*Illus*	920.00
Vase, Indian Heads, Footed, Terra Cotta, Green Matte Glaze, Stamped, c.1910, 16 In. ......*Illus*	11875.00
Vase, Openwork, Pooled Charcoaling, Green Matte Glaze, Stamped, c.1905, 6 ½ x 5 ½ In. .....*Illus*	3125.00
Vase, Pinched & Folded Buttresses, Shaped Rim, Green Matte Glaze, 14 x 6 In.	5000.00
Vase, Reed Design, Scalloped Top, Tapered, Green Matte Glaze, Blanche Ostertag, 5 x 12 In.	2375.00
Vase, Ribbed, Indented Sides, Green Matte Glaze, William Gates, 3 x 4 In.	500.00
Vase, Ribbed, Indented Sides, Green Matte Glaze, William Gates, Impressed, 3 ½ x 4 In.	610.00
Vase, Shouldered Cylinder, Recessed Handles, Gray Matte Glaze, Signed Fritz Albert, 5 x 14 In.	5000.00
Vase, Square, Rounded Bottom, 2 Handles, Green Matte Glaze, Stamped, c.1910, 5 x 3 In.	1500.00
Vase, Tall, Rounded Bottom, 4 Buttress, Squared Handles, Green Matte Glaze, Stamped, c.1910, 11 In.	5000.00
Vase, Tapered, Green Matte Glaze, 6 x 3 ½ In.	438.00
Vase, Tulip Shape, Blue Matte Glaze, Fernand Moreau, Impressed Mark, 5 x 12 In.	1700.00
Vase, Tulip Shape, Green Matte Glaze, Fernand Moreau, Impressed, Paper Label, 5 x 12 In.	3416.00
Vase, Tulip Shape, Green Matte Glaze, Fernand Moreau, Paper Label, 5 x 12 In.	2800.00
Wall Pocket, Geometric Design, Round, Impressed, W.D. Gates, 6 ½ x 6 ½ In.	671.00
Wall Pocket, Round, Geometric Design, Green Matte Glaze, W.D. Gates, Marked, 6 x 6 In.	550.00

TEDDY BEARS were named for a president of the United States. The first teddy bear was a cuddly toy said to be inspired by a hunting trip made by Teddy Roosevelt in 1902. Morris and Rose Michtom started selling their stuffed bears as "teddy bears" and the name stayed. The Michtoms founded the Ideal Novelty and Toy Company. The German version of the teddy bear was made about the same time by the Steiff Company. There are many types of teddy bears and all are collected. The old ones are being reproduced. Other bears are listed in the Toy section.

Growler, Brown, On Wheels, Glass Eyes, Wire Frame, Red Metal Wheels, Pull Ring, 18 x 26 In.	106.00
Harmonica, Honey Color, Plush, Applied Eyes, Red Felt Hat, Green Collar, Box, Germany, 9 In.	148.00
Hermann, Growler, Humpback, Cream Color, Swivel Neck, Jointed, Stitched Nose, 36 In.	207.00
Ideal, Baseball, Plush, Batting Helmet, Bat, Sportswear, 29 In.	255.00
Ideal, Golden Mohair, Stitched Nose, Felt Pads, Black Bead Eyes, Straw Filled, 1904-06, 12 In.	354.00
Ideal, Honey Color, Stitched Paws, Mouth, Nose, 1904-10, 12 In.	325.00
Janus, 2-Faced, Brown Plush Fur, Jointed, Swivel Head, Tongue Out, Googly Eyes, Germany, 3 In.	336.00
Mohair, Cinnamon Brown, Swivel Head, Humpback, Amber Glass Eyes, Germany, c.1925, 15 In.	728.00
Mohair, Golden, Jointed, Shoebutton Eyes, c.1910, 12 In.	266.00
Mohair, Golden, Plastic Eyes, Jointed, Germany, c.1930, 17 In.	118.00
Mohair, Golden, Shoebutton Eyes, Germany, 13 In.	153.00
Mohair, Golden, Shoebutton Eyes, Jointed, Germany, c.1920, 16 In.	1003.00
Mohair, Honey Color, Swivel Neck, Joints, Felt Pads, Shoebutton Eyes, Stitched Nose, 36 In.	207.00
Mohair, Plush, Red Jacket, Stitched Nose, Applied Plastic Eyes, Leather Pads, 1930s, 13 In.	118.00
Schuco, Mohair, Panda, Swivel Head, Yes-No, Amber Glass Eyes, Germany, c.1935, 13 In.	1568.00
Steiff, Beige, Jointed, Button, Silk Bow, Original Tag, c.1950, 6 In. ....*Illus*	89.00
Steiff, Blond, Glass Eyes, Jointed, Button, Tag, c.1950, 9 ½ In.	106.00
Steiff, Display, Red Bow, Tag, Ear Button, 1981, 40 In.	182.00
Steiff, Glass Eyes, Jointed, Button, Tag, c.1950, 9 ½ In.	106.00
Steiff, Mohair, Blond, Glass Eyes, Fully Jointed, c.1920, 13 In. ....*Illus*	531.00
Steiff, Mohair, Blond, Plastic Eyes, c.1920, 13 In.	826.00
Steiff, Mohair, Blond, Shoebutton Eyes, c.1920, 14 In.	502.00
Steiff, Mohair, Blond, Shoebutton Eyes, Ear Button, c.1910, 13 In. ....*Illus*	885.00
Steiff, Mohair, Blond, Shoebutton Eyes, Jointed, Button In Ear, 1920s, 13 In.	767.00
Steiff, Mohair, Blond, Shoebutton Eyes, Jointed, Button In Ear, c.1910, 9 In.	472.00
Steiff, Mohair, Blond, Shoebutton Eyes, Jointed, c.1920, 13 In.	354.00
Steiff, Mohair, Blond, Shoebutton Eyes, Jointed, Ear Button, c.1910, 9 In.	472.00
Steiff, Mohair, Blond, Shoebutton Eyes, Jointed, Knit Hat & Sweater, c.1910, 12 In.	531.00
Steiff, Mohair, Blond, Shoebutton Eyes, Pajamas, Slippers, 22 In.	177.00
Steiff, Mohair, Blond, Shoebutton Eyes, Peach Hat, Sweater, Jointed, Ear Button, c.1900, 12 In.	531.00

T

Steiff, Mohair, Brown, Shoebutton Eyes, Jointed, Button In Ear, c.1910, 8 In.	531.00
Steiff, Mohair, Brown, Shoebutton Eyes, Jointed, c.1920, 12 In.	502.00
Steiff, Mohair, Brown, Shoebutton Eyes, Jointed, Ear Button, c.1910, 8 In.	531.00
Steiff, Mohair, Felt Paw Pads, Jointed Head, Hips, Shoebutton Eyes, Plump, 14 In.	1380.00
Steiff, Mohair, Gold, Shoebutton Eyes, Fully Jointed, Ear Button, c.1904-05, 13 In. ....*Illus*	944.00
Steiff, Mohair, Golden, Felt Paws, Stitched Nose, 24 In. ....*Illus*	10030.00
Steiff, Mohair, Golden, Shoebutton Eyes, Jointed, Blank Button, c.1905, 13 In.	944.00
Steiff, Mohair, Jointed, Button, c.1904-08, 12 In. ....*Illus*	1062.00
Steiff, Mohair, Light Brown, Swivel Head, Black Shoebutton Eyes, c.1910, 12 In.	616.00
Steiff, Mohair, Shoebutton Eyes, Swivel Head, c.1905, 16 In.	3402.00
Steiff, Mohair, Swivel Head, Jointed Limbs, Bead Eyes, c.1930, 4 In.	448.00
Steiff, White, Snowflake Tinsel Necklace, Pink Dress, Button Eyes, 1906-08, 12 In.	1003.00
Teddy B. Roosevelt, Blond, Costume, Reddish Nose, Mouth, 1906-10, 11 In.	1534.00
Teddy Roosevelt Costume, Pin, U.S.A., 1904-10, 12 In.	767.00

TELEPHONES are wanted by collectors if the phones are old enough or unusual enough. The first telephone may have been made in Havana, Cuba, in 1849, but it was not patented. The first publicly demonstrated phone was used in Frankfurt, Germany, in 1860. The phone made by Alexander Graham Bell was shown at the Centennial Exhibition in Philadelphia in 1876, but it was not until 1877 that the first private phones were installed. Collectors today want all types of old phones, phone parts, and advertising. Even recent figural phones are popular.

American Bell Telephone Co., Candlestick, Copper, Bakelite, Roycroft, c.1912, 12 In. ....*Illus*	281.00
Automatic Electric, Wall, Coin, Rotary, Chrome, Cast Metal, 16 x 9 In.	148.00
Automatic Electric, Wall, Coin, Rotary, Chrome, Cast Metal, 18 x 9 In.	106.00
Badge, Southern California Telephone Co., 1707, Brass, Blue, Bell Shape, 1930s, 2 ⅜ In.	89.00
Booth, Bell Telephone, Oak, Seat, Operating Phone, Light, Fan, Rotary Dial, c.1930, 83 x 31 In.	1541.00
Booth, Oak, Folding Door, Coin-Operated, Red Paint, 81 x 31 In.	780.00
Booth, Western Electric, Oak, Lobby Booth, Telephone, Sliding Doors, Lights, 84 x 32 In.	944.00
European Style, Black Metal Case, Painted White, Rotary Dial, Top Bell, Gutta Percha, 8 ½ x 10 In.	59.00
Gamewell, Call Box, Police Telegraph, Blue, 105 In. ....*Illus*	1170.00
Garfield, Painted, Prototype, Tyco Toys, 1980s, 6 ¾ x 11 In. ....*Illus*	240.00
Graybar Electric, Hand Crank, Wood, Bakelite Speakers, 20 x 9 In.	147.00
Kellogg S. & S. Co., Candlestick Phone Receiver, Accordion, Wall Mount, Nickel Plate, 25 x 11 In.	83.00
Ladder, Western Electric, Oak, Angled Steps, Hand Rail, Steel Mounts, Putnam, c.1900, 132 In.	239.00
Pin, Pennsylvania State Telephone, Round, Black & White, Dial Shape, c.1931, 2 ½ In.	57.00
Rotary Phone, Bronze Stand, Swivel, Man & Woman Pictured In Number Pad, 28 In. ..*Illus*	288.00
Sign, Pay Here, Candlestick Phone, Black, Cream, Paper, Frame, c.1940, 31 x 14 In.	540.00
Sign, Payphone, Wes-Tex Co-Op, Stanton, Tex., Dial Phone, Round, Yellow, Porcelain, 12 In. Diam.	495.00
Sign, Public Telephone, Bell System On Bell, Blue, White, Square, Metal, Flange, 18 In.	150.00
Sign, Public Telephone, Southwestern States, Porcelain, 2-Sided, 8 x 11 In. ....*Illus*	231.00
Stromberg-Carlson, Black Plastic, Oval Base, Push Dial, Intercom, 5 ½ In.	805.00
Stromberg-Carlson, Wall, Oak Cast, c.1900, 26 x 11 In.	100.00
Wall, Alexander Graham Bell, 3 Box, Enamel Sign, Blake Microphone, Crank, Sweden, 1880, 30 In.	2846.00
Wall, Wood Case, Metal Battery Lid, Handset, L.M. Ericsson, Sweden.	712.00
Western Electric, Candlestick, Black, 11 ½ x 6 ½ In.	176.00
Western Electric, Candlestick, Pedestal Mount, Accordion Receiver, Painted Black, 25 x 14 In.	94.00

TELEVISION sets are twentieth-century collectibles. Although the first television transmission took place in England in 1925, collectors find few sets that pre-date 1946. The first sets had only five channels, but by 1949 the additional UHF channels were included. The first color television set became available in 1951.

Airline, Portable, 6-In. Screen	130.00
Philco, Predicta, Stand ....*Illus*	168.00
Philco, Predicta, Wide Oval Screen, 1940s	224.00
RCA Victor, Console, 1950s, 36 x 20 x 24 In.	395.00
RCA Victor, Model 21-S-501, c.1950, 16 x 23 x 20 In.	200.00
RCA, Swivel Stand, Coaxial Video Connection, Model GJR660T, 1980, 25 In. Screen	53.00
Sharp, Black & White, Model 3S111R, Red Plastic, UHF, VHF, 1970s, 9 x 8 x 8 In.	255.00
Sony, Micro Transistor Television, Model, 5-305UW, AC Cord, Earphone, 1965, 5-In. Screen.	525.00

TEPLITZ refers to art pottery manufactured by a number of companies in the Teplitz-Turn area of Bohemia during the late nineteenth and early twentieth centuries. Two of these companies were the Alexandra Works founded by Ernst Wahliss, and the Amphora Porcelain Works, run by Riessner, Stellmacher, and Kessel.

Bowl, Fates, Heads In Diagonal Swirls, E. Stellmacher, Shouldered, Amphora, 6 x 9 In.	1875.00

Telephone, Sign, Public Telephone, Southwestern States, Porcelain, 2-Sided, 8 x 11 In.
$231.00

Wm Morford Antiques

Television, Philco, Predicta, Stand
$168.00

Victorian Casino Antiques

Teplitz, Vase, Butterfly, Blossoms, Enamel, Riessner, Stellmacher & Kessel, c.1905, 6 x 4 ¼ In.
$1,500.00

Rago Arts & Auction Center

Teplitz, Vase, Pine Tree, Applied Pinecones, Paul Dachsel, Amphora, c.1908, 8 ½ x 6 In.
$2,375.00

Rago Arts & Auction Center

T

Teplitz, Vase, Portrait, Allegory Of Germany, Amphora, Red Mark, RStK Logo, 7 In.
$3,910.00

Humler & Nolan

Teplitz, Vase, Stylized Trees, Elephant Head Handles, Amphora, Impressed Logo, 10 ½ In.
$316.00

Humler & Nolan

Terra-Cotta, Figurine, Elephant, Glazed, c.1910, 18 ½ x 22 x 8 In.
$1,250.00

Rago Arts & Auction Center

TIP

Rub lemon juice and salt on rust spots on white textiles. Then put the cloth in the sun.

Bust, Woman, Art Nouveau, Yellow Cape & Hat, Amphora, E. Wahliss, c.1900, 16 In.	250.00
Centerpiece, Peach Speckle Glaze, Diamond Shape, Applied Seahorse, Handles, Czech, 16 x 11 In.	316.00
Compote, Organic Designs, Cream, Green Frit Dust Glaze, Geometric, Amphora, 10 x 8 In.	915.00
Compote, Poppies, Gilt, Stem Handles, Pedestal, Round Foot, Stamped, 11 ½ In.	460.00
Ewer, Multicolor, Baluster Shape, Figural Handle, Stamped, 9 ¾ x 5 ½ In., Pair	600.00
Figurine, Bedouin On Horseback, Amphora, Riessner, Stellmacher & Kessel, c.1910, 22 In.	625.00
Figurine, Couple, Basket, 1820s Attire, Impressed Amphora, 16 In.	168.00
Figurine, Man, On Camel, c.1900, 24 x 25 In.	700.00
Pitcher, Applied Enamel Drops, Stick Neck, Double Handle, Openwork Rim, Dachsel, 10 In.	1500.00
Plate, Portrait, Amicitia, Amoroga, Brown, Green Iridescent Border, Gilt, Royal Vienna, 9 ½ In., Pair.	615.00
Urn, Confetti, Gold Ribs & Neck, Gourd Form, Amphora, Extended Handles, 15 x 12 In.	1500.00
Urn, Stylized Leaves, Gold Trim, Bulbous, 6 Handles, Amphora, P. Dachsel, RStK, 1903, 12 In.	1500.00
Vase, 2-Wing Dragon, Green, Brown Matte Glaze, Handles, Amphora, 14 x 17 In.	8540.00
Vase, Art Nouveau, Gilt Pebble Ground, Jewels, Lobed Neck, Bottle Shape, Loop Handle, c.1900, 11 In.	1434.00
Vase, Butterfly, Blossoms, Enamel, Riessner, Stellmacher & Kessel, c.1905, 6 x 4 ¼ In. .....*Illus*	1500.00
Vase, Calla Lily, Woman, Seated, On Flowers, Eduard Stellmacher, Amphora, 10 x 23 In.	5490.00
Vase, Dragon, Spread Wings, Wrapped Around, Baluster, Bronze Iridescent, Amphora, 14 In.	10350.00
Vase, Etched Leaves, Pale Green, Flower Shape, 5 Handles, Rolled Ribbed Rim, c.1910, 16 x 6 ½ In.	2125.00
Vase, Figural, Woman, Holding Water Jug, Blue Glaze, Gilt, Amphora, 14 ½ x 8 In.	270.00
Vase, Flowers, Buttressed Handle, Spout, Bulbous, Footed, Blue Underglaze Mark, 12 ½ x 7 In..	86.00
Vase, Freeform, Blue Iridescent Glaze Ground, Applied Cherries, Leaves, 8 x 6 In.	196.00
Vase, Green, Brown Matte Glaze, Organic Shape, Handles, Paul Dachsel, Amphora, 10 ½ x 11 ½ In.	1220.00
Vase, Handle, Carved & Applied Iris, Multicolor, Amphora, 18 In.	1200.00
Vase, Iris, Carved, Applied, Green, Peach Glaze, Twisted Handle, Amphora, 7 ½ x 18 In.	1464.00
Vase, Leaves, Berries, Spiral Neck, 4 Waist Openings, Bulbous Base, Amphora, 9 ½ x 16 In.	438.00
Vase, Maiden, Blossoms In Hair, Gold & White, Flattened, Square Rolled Rim, 1890s, 5 ½ x 4 In.	938.00
Vase, Mushroom Rim, Applied Lizard, Cream Color, Amphora, c.1905, 15 ¾ x 9 ½ In.	3125.00
Vase, Pine Tree, Applied Pinecones, Paul Dachsel, Amphora, c.1908, 8 ½ x 6 In. .....*Illus*	2375.00
Vase, Portrait, Allegory Of Germany, Amphora, Red Mark, RStK Logo, 7 In. .....*Illus*	3910.00
Vase, Portrait, Bust, Art Nouveau Woman, Flowers, Tapered, Gold Trim, RStK, c.1900, 6 In.	2375.00
Vase, Reticulated Clover Band, Green, Swollen Top, 4 Handles, Stellmacher, 7 ½ In.	375.00
Vase, Rooster, Blue & Green Ground, Bulbous, Flared Rim, Riessner & Kessel, 7 x 8 In.	313.00
Vase, Squat, Figural, Seminude Woman, Reclining, Stretched Arms, Blue & Yellow, c.1900, 8 x 6 In.	1500.00
Vase, Stylized Leaves, Bulbous, Footed, Imperial Amphora, 8 x 9 In.	313.00
Vase, Stylized Trees, Elephant Head Handles, Amphora, Impressed Logo, 10 ½ In. .....*Illus*	316.00
Vase, Thistle, Tapered, 3 Square Feet, Amphora, Austria, 1900s, 16 ½ x 9 ½ In.	313.00
Vase, Water Lily, Blue, Gold, 4 Handles, Paul Dachsel, Amphora, 8 ½ x 17 In.	915.00
Vase, White Raspberries, Leaves, Gold Highlights, 4 Loop Handles, Squat, Cylindrical Neck, 10 In.	431.00
Vase, Woman's Portrait, Landscape, Multicolor, Marked, Amphora, 6 ½ x 10 ¾ In.	1625.00
Vase, Yellow, Oval, Blossom Band, Metal Collar, Jewel Cabochons, Amphora, 16 In.	750.00

TERRA-COTTA is a special type of pottery. It ranges from pale orange to dark reddish-brown in color. The color comes from the clay, which is fired but not always glazed in the finished piece.

Bust, Emotive Woman, W. Yerke, 14 x 12 In.	120.00
Bust, Greek Philosopher, Socle, 18 ¼ x 9 ½ In.	263.00
Bust, Man, Short Curled Hair, Head Band, Square Base, c.1950, 20 ½ In., Pair	1845.00
Bust, Woman, Classical, Long Wavy Hair, Impressed Mark, 18 ½ In.	615.00
Bust, Woman, Curly Hair, Side Glance, Plinth, France, c.1850, 13 ¼ In.	750.00
Bust, Woman, Headband, Full Lips, Eyes Closed, 11 ⅛ In.	288.00
Card Carrier, Blackamoor, Standing Male Figure, Holding Tray, Round Base, 16 x 6 ½ In.	215.00
Censer, Outscrolled Ribbed Handles, Faceted Legs, Turquoise Glaze, 8 ¼ x 9 In.	236.00
Charger, White & Brown Glaze, Islamic Script Border, Segmented Circle, Middle East, 15 In.	1353.00
Figurine, Art Nouveau, Apres Le Bal, Man, In Tux, Kissing Woman, Gown, c.1910, 26 In.	250.00
Figurine, Bacchantes Harvesting Grapes, Fernando Ciancianaino, c.1920, 13 In.	1298.00
Figurine, Bacchus, Falling Down, Spilling Wine, Brown Finish, Wood Platform, 18 x 10 In.	897.00
Figurine, Bear, Seated, Holding Shield, Company Display, Northwest, 6 x 11 In.	854.00
Figurine, Bear, Sitting, 6 x 11 In.	700.00
Figurine, Camel Boy, Amber Glaze, Hardwood Base, Chinese, c.1960, 23 ½ In.	1840.00
Figurine, Cobbler, Paint, Austria, c.1890, 12 ¾ In.	108.00
Figurine, Cupid, Column, Doves, Heart, France, 1800s, 17 ¾ x 16 In.	2000.00
Figurine, Dog, Mastiff, Multicolor, Glass Eyes, Painted Brown, Red Collar, c.1880, 15 In., Pair.	230.00
Figurine, Dog, Reclining, Collar, Alert Ears, 9 x 7 In., Pair	840.00
Figurine, Dog, Terrier, Seated, Alert Expression, Painted, 26 x 16 ½ In., Pair	1353.00
Figurine, Elephant, Glazed, c.1910, 18 ½ x 22 x 8 In. .....*Illus*	1250.00
Figurine, Girl, On Dolphin, Signed Edgardo Simone, Chicago, March 1937, 28 ½ x 21 In.	468.00
Figurine, Girl, Stylized, Seated, Hands On Head, Tan Skin, Speckled Body, Hungary, 17 In.	450.00

Figurine, Gnome, On Tree Stump, Majolica Glaze, Marked, B.U., 1803, 13 In. ....*Illus*	180.00
Figurine, Hen, On Nest, Black & White Paint, Basket Weave Base, 12 ½ x 13 ½ In.	922.00
Figurine, Knight In Armor, On Horseback, Multicolor, Marked Mariomi P., Italy, 17 x 17 In. ..	106.00
Figurine, Lion, Seated, Gastelnaudary Fabrique Ceramiques, France, c.1910, 29 x 11 ½ In.	780.00
Figurine, Man Saint, Standing, Paint, Gilt, Red & Green Robes, Hand Raised, Italy, c.1800, 57 In.	3250.00
Figurine, Napoleon, Standing, Stepped Round Base, Painted, c.1870, 24 In.	300.00
Figurine, Nude Man, Stealing Panther Cub, Square Base, c.1950, 17 ¼ In.	538.00
Figurine, Owl, On Book, Open Wings, Marked, J.M., 20 In.	1680.00
Figurine, Putti, Reclining, Holding Urn, Henri Dasson, 14 ½ x 19 In.	1170.00
Figurine, Satyr & Nymph, Basket Of Grapes, Tambourine, Pipes, France, 1767, 15 In.	4148.00
Figurine, The Kiss, E. Cavacos, c.1950, 11 In.	246.00
Figurine, Woman, Seated, Painted, Signed, 15 ½ x 6 x 7 ½ In.	144.00
Group, 2 Putti, c.1880, 23 In.	2015.00
Group, Bacchante, Offering Grapes To Cherub, Clodion, France, c.1800, 17 x 13 ½ In............	604.00
Group, Bloch, Bernard, Courtyard Confession, Woman With Fan, Traveling Friar, 10 x 13 In.	259.00
Group, Satyr & Child, Reclining On Rock, Holding Child, Playing Flute, c.1865, 13 x 19 In.	1476.00
Group, Satyr, Nymph, Putto, Raised Base, After Clodion, France, 20 ½ In. ....*Illus*	688.00
Group, Satyr, Sleeping Nymph, Round Base, Leaves, France, c.1800, 13 x 8 ½ In.	7072.00
Humidor, Lid, Art Nouveau, 3 Gray Elephant Heads, White Floral Ground, Austria, 9 ½ In.	144.00
Jar, Confit, Loop Handles, Flared Lip, Yellow, Brown, Amber Glaze, c.1900, 11 x 11 ½ In., Pair	338.00
Jar, Small Round Foot, Indented Neck, Ring Handles, Yellow Glaze, Guatemala, 6 x 6 In.........	23.00
Jug, Ebonized Figures, Scenes, Loop Handle At Neck, Gilt Striped Highlights, c.1885, 9 In., Pair	153.00
Olive Jar, Bulbous, Rolled Lip, 39 In...	3107.00
Panel, Multicolor, Arched Top, Relief, Christ, Angels, Cherub Head, 25 x 20 In.	483.00
Pitcher, Dragon Encircled Handle, Black, Japanese Studio, 9 ½ x 6 ½ In.	121.00
Planter, Bacchanal, Relief, Cherubs, Goats, Grapevines, Round, 6 x 10 In.	104.00
Planter, Molded, Classical Cherubs, 7 ½ x 14 ½ In.	86.00
Planter, Vase Shape, Turned, Swags, Medallions, Green, Brown, Mottled, 21 x 14 In., Pair......	553.00
Planter, Vase Shaped, Green Mottled Glaze, Turned Foot, France, 23 ½ x 10 ¾ In.	110.00
Plaque, Madonna & Child, Arched, Molded Border, Italy, 13 ¾ x 12 In.	944.00
Plaque, Neoclassical, Thorvaldsen Style, Faux Tortoise Frame, Denmark, c.1865, 14 x 24 In..	738.00
Plaque, Portrait, Man, Eugene Borilier, Oval, Hanging Bail, France, 1888, 8 ¼ x 8 In.	345.00
Plaque, Relief, Putti, On Dolphins, Twist Edge, Italy, 21 In.	420.00
Statue, Woman Saint, Standing, Long Robe, Holding Book, Hexagonal Base, Italy, 1800s, 58 In..	2600.00
Urn, Lid, Glazed, Flowers, Swags, Raised Heads, Handles, Orange, Yellow, Italy, 45 x 23 In.......	510.00
Urn, Neoclassical Style, Palmettes, Leaves, Banding, Black Enamel, 11 In., Pair......................	236.00
Vase, Abstract, Bulbous, 2 Handles, Narrow Neck, White Paint, 22 x 18 In............................	234.00
Vase, Art Nouveau, White Flowers, Green Mottled, Red, Cylinder, Rolled Rim, c.1900, 12 In., Pair..	875.00
Vase, Lid, Ribbed Bands, Buttress Base, c.1920, 28 x 24 In.	360.00

TEXTILES listed here include many types of printed fabrics and table and household linens. Some other textiles will be found under Clothing, Coverlet, Rug, Quilt, etc.

Altar Cloth, Embroidered Silk, Brocade Border, Flowers, Gold Thread, Chinese, 1800s, 36 x 74 In.	9225.00
Bag Face, Oriental Nomadic, Geometric Motifs, 29 x 24 In..	767.00
Bedspread, Chenille, Pink, Hearts, Blocks, Diamonds, Swirls & Knots, Fringe, 1950s, 96 x 78 In...	110.00
Bedspread, Chenille, White Cotton, Race Car Center, Racing Flag, Red Trim, 1950s, 68 x 101 In..	55.00
Bedspread, Trapunto, Round Medallion, Scrolling Flower Border, White Cotton, 80 x 78 In...	118.00
Blanket, Horse, Lions, Fish, Geometric, Multicolor, Hand Woven, Northern China, 1800s, 42 x 26 In.	390.00
Blanket, Hudson Bay, 4-Point, Wool, Red, Black Bands, Label, 80 x 69 In. ....*Illus*	150.00
Blanket, Hudson Bay, White Ground, Red, Black & Gray Stripes, Label, 1930s, 62 x 82 In.	315.00
Blanket, Trapper Point, Wool, Black, Red, Green & Yellow Stripes, c.1920, 88 x 67 In.............	115.00
Chenille, Bird Of Paradise, Velvet, Yellow, Red, Blue, Flowering Branch, Frame, 18 x 23 In.	47.00
Curtain, Tent, Diamond Design, Red Field, c.1940, 28 x 49 In..	214.00
Fabric, Woven, Multicolor Horizontal Stripes, Middle East, 73 x 17 In., 19 x 12 In., 2 Piece	59.00
Flag, American, 8 Stars, In Medallion, Secession, Glazed Cotton, Virginia, 1861, 3 x 5 In........	1020.00
Flag, American, 9 Stars, On Stick, Frame, 1861-65, 8 x 4 In..	546.00
Flag, American, 13 Stars, 14 Stripes, Parade, Printed, Gauze, Canada, c.1890, 18 x 27 In.	1140.00
Flag, American, 13 Stars, Naval Jack, Worsted Wool, Cotton, Civil War, 23 x 45 In...................	940.00
Flag, American, 13 Stars, Naval Jack, Worsted Wool, Cotton, Tassels, 29 x 52 In.	4500.00
Flag, American, 13 Stars, On Stick, Frame, 11 x 6 In.	201.00
Flag, American, 18 Stars, Double Applique, Caroline Whiting, 2nd Div., c.1815, 61 x 100 In. ... *Illus*	32862.00
Flag, American, 30 Stars, Frame, 14 ½ x 22 In..	3105.00
Flag, American, 32 Stars, 13 Stripes, Cotton, Wool, 1858, 27 x 40 ½ In..............................	2350.00
Flag, American, 32 Stars, c.1860, 22 ½ x 45 In...	2950.00
Flag, American, 34 Stars, Eagle, Banner, Blood Stripe, Cotton, Civil War, 37 x 75 In.	11163.00
Flag, American, 36 Stars, By Hufford Family, Lancaster, Pa., c.1865, 69 ½ x 78 ½ In.	4617.00

Terra-Cotta, Figurine, Gnome, On Tree Stump, Majolica Glaze, Marked, B.U., 1803, 13 In.
$180.00

The Stein Auction Co.

Terra-Cotta, Group, Satyr, Nymph, Putto, Raised Base, After Clodion, France, 20 ½ In.
$688.00

Leslie Hindman Auctioneers

T

TEXTILE

Textile, Blanket, Hudson Bay, 4-Point, Wool, Red, Black Bands, Label, 80 x 69 In.
$150.00

Allard Auctions

Textile, Flag, American, 18 Stars, Double Applique, Caroline Whiting, 2nd Div., c.1815, 61 x 100 In.
$32,862.00

Neal Auction Co.

Textile, Flag, American, 36 Stars, Hand Sewn, Wool, Cotton Stars, Annin & Co., New York, 27 x 48 In.
$3,000.00

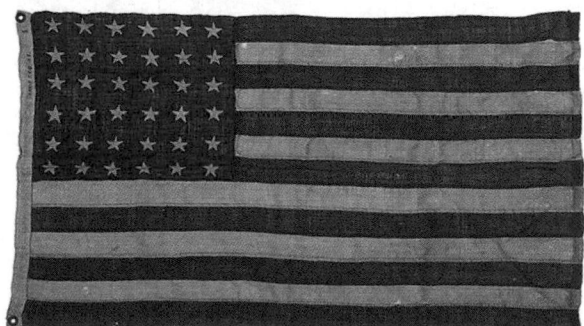

Cowan's Auctions

Textile, Tapestry, Military Rank Badge, Slit Weave, Bear, Clouds, Waves, Chinese, 1700s, 11 ⅝ x 12 In.
$2,214.00

Neal Auction Co.

Textile, Tapestry, Woman, Swirls, Jute Fiber, Alexander Calder, 1974, 84 x 56 In.
$5,313.00

Rago Arts & Auction Center

T

Flag, American, 36 Stars, Grant, Wilson, Red & White, Cotton, 1872, 5 x 7 In............................	1771.00
Flag, American, 36 Stars, Hand Sewn, Wool, Cotton Stars, Annin & Co., New York, 27 x 48 In. ....*Illus*	3000.00
Flag, American, 38 Stars, 1776, 1876 Shape, Machine Sewn, Wool, Centennial, 47 ½ x 46 ½ In.	9440.00
Flag, American, 38 Stars, Colorado 1877, Frame, 23 x 30 ½ In...	460.00
Flag, American, 39 Stars, Frame, 29 x 18 In.	374.00
Flag, American, 39 Stars, North Dakota, Frame, 15 ¼ x 24 In...............................	259.00
Flag, American, 39 Stars, Prior To Dakotas Being Admitted, c.1889, 27 x 46 In.	1323.00
Flag, American, 42 Stars, Printed, Cotton, Frame, c.1890, 12 x 17 In.	153.00
Flag, American, 45 Stars, Frame, 13 ½ x 9 In.	173.00
Flag, American, 48 Stars, c.1920, 41 x 68 In.	144.00
Flag, American, 48 Stars, New Mexico, Arizona Reunion, Frame, 1949, 15 x 23 In................	173.00
Flag, American, U.S. Navy, Signal, 13 Stars, 23 ½ x 36 ½ In.	805.00
Flag, Parade, Eagle, Clutching Flag, Blue, Cream Divided Ground, 38 x 31 In.....................	212.00
Flag, The Hero Of Manila Admiral Dewey, c.1898, 23 ¼ x 24 ½ In.	144.00
Flag, Union Jack, England, c.1900, 70 x 135 In.	86.00
Fragment, Eagle & Shield, Column, Flowers, Leaves, Cotton, Print, Frame, c.1815, 13 x 11 In.	369.00
Panel, Applique, Dancing Figures, Scrolled Leaves, Mirror Jewels, Sequins, Frame, c.1900, 72 x 21 In.	240.00
Panel, Embroidered, Dragon, Pearl, Clouds, Bats, Lotus Scrolls, Yellow, Gold, 1800s, 58 x 43 In.	2065.00
Panel, Linen, Painted, Prince, Animals, Yellow, Amber, Cream, India, c.1950, 76 x 55 In.........	330.00
Panel, Locomotive, Green, Red, Brown, Blue, Mahogany Frame, 10 ½ x 8 In..........................	12.00
Panel, Needlework, Courting Couple, Woods, Cupid, Clouds, Frame, 1700s, 29 ½ x 23 ½ In....	625.00
Panel, Silk Damask, Figural & Architectural Vignettes, Blue, Green, Cream, 1900s, 51 x 48 In..	354.00
Panel, Silk, Embroidered, Elephants, Lotus, Tendrils, Yellow, Chinese, c.1900, 240 In.	5629.00
Panel, Silk, Embroidered, Hundred Birds Pattern, Frame, 1800s, 25 ½ x 24 ½ In.....................	4059.00
Panel, Silk, Embroidered, Lion, Clouds, Flames, Mountains, Blue, Gold, 1800s, 14 x 14 In......	7290.00
Panel, Silk, Yellow, Dragon, Conch Shell, Claw & Pearl, Rolling Wave Border, Chinese, c.1900, 48 In.	1541.00
Panel, Velvet, Chinoiserie, Figures, Garden, Painted, Gilt, 25 x 23 In.	118.00
Panel, Wool, Adam & Eve, Apple, Snake, Black & White, Woven, Mexico, 1960s, 84 x 35 ½ In.	7500.00
Panel, Wool, Darning, Samples, C.M. Chadwick, c.1850, 44 ½ x 5 In.	533.00
Panel, Yellow Silk, Roundels, Facing Dragons, Brocade, Chinese, 27 x 180 In.......................	1476.00
Piano Scarf, Arts & Crafts, Flowers, Fringe, Silk, 62 x 62 In	336.00
Piano Scarf, Dusty Rose Silk, Embroidered Flowers, Fringe, 1920s, 60 x 60 In......................	305.00
Piano Scarf, Paisley, Red, White, Green Flower Stripes, Hand Woven, c.1900, 52 x 104 In.......	71.00
Piano Scarf, Silk, Flowers, Fringe, Arts & Crafts, 62 x 62 In.	275.00
Piano Scarf, Silk, Rose, Green, Woven, Gold Silk Backing, Fringe, 46 x 46 In.	92.00
Pillow Cover, Peacock, Embroidered, Linen, Arts & Crafts, 22 x 23 In.	219.00
Pillow Cover, Pierced, Flying Goose Border, 18 ½ x 26 ½ In., Pair...........................	1126.00
Pillow Cover, Pocahontas, Color, Lithograph, Linen, Bernhard Ulmann Co., 1908, 23 x 22 In.	179.00
Pillow, Velvet, Chenille, Tasseled Fringe Border, 33 x 17 In., Pair	215.00
Pillow, Velvet, Metallic Embroidered, Leafy Vine Design, Beading, 9 ½ x 9 ½ In., Pair.............	110.00
Pillow, Velvet, Tapestry, Moss Green, Metallic Fringe, 1700s, 14 x 11 In.	799.00
Show Towel, Embroidered, Inscribed Rebeca Martin, Pa., c.1855, 55 x 19 In..........................	1185.00
Show Towel, Silk & Wool On Linen, Potted Flowers, Peacocks & Trees, Fringe, 1854, 60 x 17 In..	705.00
Show Towel, Silk, Embroidered, Inscribed Catherine Fass Stowe, Pa., 1848, 60 x 17 In.	948.00
Tablecloth, G. Stickley, Blossom, Stylized Flowers, Linen, 15 ¾ x 15 ¾ In.	1875.00
Tapestry, Arabic Scene, Woven, Belgium, c.1900, 51 x 47 In..	307.00
Tapestry, Aubusson, Dancing Couples, Landscape, France, 1700s, 102 x 84 In........................	1750.00
Tapestry, Aubusson, Oriental Garden, Pavilion, France, 1900s, 97 x 43 In.	615.00
Tapestry, Depicting Couples, 18th Century Garden Scene, Woven, c.1920, 29 x 24 In...............	108.00
Tapestry, Lions, Cranes, River Landscape, c.1890, 46 x 65 In......................................	1534.00
Tapestry, Military Rank Badge, Slit Weave, Bear, Clouds, Waves, Chinese, 1700s, 11 ⅝ x 12 In. .. *Illus*	2214.00
Tapestry, Scenic, Heron, Wading, Village In Background, 80 x 80 In.	4773.00
Tapestry, Storks, Wooded Landscape, Buildings In Distance, Wrought Iron Rod, 40 x 60 In....	604.00
Tapestry, Village Scene, Clock Tower, Fountain, Cobblestone Street, Loomed, France, 22 x 21 In. ...	84.00
Tapestry, Woman, Swirls, Jute Fiber, Alexander Calder, 1974, 84 x 56 In. ....*Illus*	5313.00
Tapestry, Wool, Figures, In Wooded Landscape, Cupid Watching, Village, 79 x 84 ¾ In.	3048.00
Throne Cover, Silk, Embroidered, Dragons, Clouds, Pearl, Flowers, Gold, Chinese, 1800s, 128 x 60 In.	8295.00
Valance, Embroidered, Gold Dragons, Celestial Pearl, Tan Ground, Scrolling Waves, 27 x 117 In..	1610.00
Wall Hanging, Asian Style, Silk Embroidered, Birds, Floral Branches, Frame, 58 x 48 In., Pair	3861.00
Wall Hanging, Silk Embroidered, Goddess, Deer, Multiple Borders, Chinese, c.1910, 141 x 57 In. .*Illus*	1600.00
Weaving, Woman, Seated, Wool, Holding Head, Brown, Edwin Scheier, 1960s, 42 x 38 In........	5313.00

Textile, Wall Hanging, Silk Embroidered, Goddess, Deer, Multiple Borders, Chinese, c.1910, 141 x 57 In.
$1,600.00

Skinner, Inc.

Thermometer, Calumet Baking Powder, Wooden, Paper Label, 22 x 5 ¾ In.
$908.00

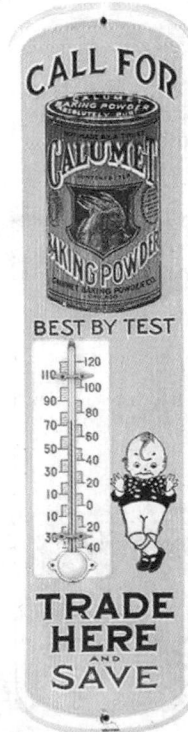

Wm Morford Antiques

THERMOMETER is a name that comes from the Greek word for heat. The thermometer was invented in 1731 to measure the temperature of either water or air. All kinds of thermometers are collected, but those with advertising messages are the most popular.

7Up, Green, Blue, Red, Round, Ohio, 12 In.	144.00

Tiffany, Box, Lid, Figures, Wreaths, Brass Medallion, Marked, Mson Boissier, c.1900, 3 x 4 In. $615.00

New Orleans Auction Galleries, Inc.

Tiffany, Candlestick, Snuffer, Double, Bronze, Purple Iridescent Glass, Hook, Leaf Base, c.1910, 9 x 7 In. $4,444.00

Skinner, Inc.

Tiffany, Compote, Bronze, Enamel Flowers, Leaves, Handles, Signed, Louis C. Tiffany Furnaces, 12 In. $460.00

Early Auction Co.

Tiffany, Frame, Frank Lloyd Wright Window Design, Enamel Accents, Silver Grid, 3 ⅜ x 5 ⅞ In. $2,400.00

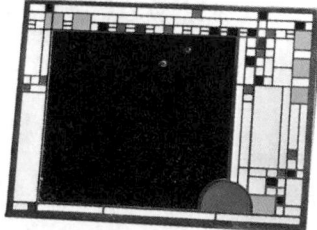

Skinner, Inc.

AC Spark Plug, Sparky The Donkey, Tin	3600.00
Ace High, Wil-Flo Motor Oil, Porcelain, Blue, 39 x 8 In.	3100.00
Art Nouveau, Figural, Woman's Face, Tabletop, Cast Metal, 10 In.	85.00
Black Boy Peering Around, Multi Products, c.1949, 3 ⅜ x 2 In.	75.00
Butte Brewing Co., Girl In Scant Dress & Black Stockings, On Bike, Montana, 1950s, 8 x 9 In.	168.00
Calumet Baking Powder, Wooden, Paper Label, 22 x 5 ¾ In. ....*Illus*	908.00
Campbell's Tomato Soup, Can Shape, Porcelain, Round Gauge, 7 x 12 x 11 In.	15400.00
Dad's, Old Fashioned Root Beer, Embossed, Tin Litho, King Size Junior, 1940s, 10 x 26 In.	474.00
Desk, Sterling Cased, Flowers & Scrolls, Monogram, c.1909, 6 ½ In.	237.00
Dr. A.C. Daniels' Famous Veterinary Medicines, Black Paint, White Ground, 24 In.	189.00
Dr. Legear's Prescriptions, Tin Lithograph, Red, Yellow, 25 x 9 In.	330.00
Drink Double Cola You'll Like It, Tin, 17 x 5 In.	94.00
Fatima Cigarettes, Yellow, White, Metal, c.1930, 27 In.	570.00
Genuine Hires Root Beer, Bottle Shape, Tin, 29 x 8 In.	212.00
Grand Tour, Bronze, Obelisk Shaped, Galleried Black Marble Base, France, c.1898, 8 In.	246.00
Hills Bros. Coffee, Red Ground, Tin, 1920s, 20 ¾ In.	960.00
Hire's, Bottle Shape, Tin, 1950s, 28 ½ In.	108.00
Mail Pouch Tobacco, Treat Yourself To The Best Chew, Porcelain, 39 x 8 In.	384.00
Mail Pouch, Porcelain, Blue, Yellow, White Lettering, Treat Yourself To The Best, 74 x 20 In.	748.00
Nature's Remedy To-Night Tomorrow Alright, Come In, Porcelain, 27 x 7 In.	325.00
Nesbitt's Soda, Black, Yellow, Tin, 27 In.	270.00
NR All Vegetable Laxative Tums, 27 x 7 In.	212.00
Oilzum, The Choice Of Champion Race Drivers, Tin, Red, White, 15 x 8 In.	679.00
Prestone Anti-Freeze, You're Set Safe Sure, Porcelain, White, 36 x 9 In.	148.00
Ramon's Brownie Pills, Ramon's Pink Pills, Tin, Paint, The Little Doctor, 1930s, 9 x 21 In.	160.00
Ramon's Brownie Pills, Yellow Ground, Tin, 1940s, 21 In.	660.00
Regal Beer, Aluminum, Red, Rectangular, c.1945, 25 ¾ In.	270.00
Tusk, Carved Oval Fluted Base, 16 ¼ In.	413.00
Valvoline Motor Oil, Porcelain, Green, 1951, 29 x 7 In.	472.00

TIFFANY is a name that appears on items made by Louis Comfort Tiffany, the American glass designer who worked from about 1879 to 1933. His work included iridescent glass, Art Nouveau styles of design, and original contemporary styles. He was also noted for stained glass windows, unusual lamps, bronze work, pottery, and silver. Tiffany & Company, often called "Tiffany," is also listed in this section. The company was started by Charles Lewis Tiffany and Teddy Young in 1837 in New York City. In 1853 the name was changed to Tiffany & Company. Louis Tiffany (1848–1933), Charles Tiffany's son, started his own business in 1879. It was named Louis Comfort Tiffany and Associated American Artists. In 1902 the name was changed to Tiffany Studios. Tiffany & Company is still working today and is best known for silver and fine jewelry. Louis worked for his father's company as a decorator in 1900 but at the same time was working for his Tiffany Studios. Other types of Tiffany are listed under Tiffany Glass, Tiffany Gold, Tiffany Pottery, or Tiffany Silver. The famous Tiffany lamps are listed in this section. Tiffany jewelry is listed in the Jewelry and Wristwatch categories. Some Tiffany Studio desk sets have matching clocks. They are listed here. Clocks made by Tiffany & Co. are listed in the Clock category. Reproductions of some types of Tiffany are being made.

Louis C. Tiffany

Blotter Ends, Zodiac, Cast Bronze, Stamped Tiffany Studios, 19 x 2 In., Pair	138.00
Bookmark, Dog, Terrier, Green Enamel Collar, Ruby Eye, 14K Gold, 5 ⅜ In.	1007.00
Bookmark, Owl, Figural, Red Stone Eyes, 14K Gold Clip, Monogram, 1930, 3 In., Pair	1304.00
Bowl, Bronze Dore, Marked Tiffany Studios, 7 ¼ In.	150.00
Bowl, Spun Metal, Flared, 9 In.	210.00
Box, Handkerchief, Grapevine, Metal, Etched, Striated Glass Panels, Bun Feet, 8 x 8 In.	1035.00
Box, Handkerchief, Pine Needle, Metal, Etched, Brown Striated Glass, Beading, Bun Feet, 8 x 8 In.	1208.00
Box, Ivory, Carved, Scrolling Vines, Sapphire Cabochons, 18K Gold Mount, Round, 2 In.	8400.00
Box, Lid, Figures, Wreaths, Brass Medallion, Marked, Mson Boissier, c.1900, 3 x 4 In. .....*Illus*	615.00
Box, Pine Needle, Bronze, Favrile Glass, Round, 2 ½ x 4 ¼ In.	750.00
Box, Pine Needle, Bronze, Green, White Glass, 8 x 2 ¾ In.	610.00
Box, Stamp, Bronze, Green Mottled Slag Glass, Ball Feet, Impressed, c.1910, 4 x 2 ¼ In.	720.00
Box, Stamp, Spider Web, Bronze, Slag Glass, 1 ¼ x 4 In.	474.00
Candelabrum, 3-Light, Bronze, Straight Arm, Center Stem, Round Base, Stamped, 8 In., Pair.	593.00
Candelabrum, 6-Light, Bronze, Center Stem, 2 Branches, 6 Candle Cups, Marked, 15 x 21 In.	4148.00
Candelabrum, 6-Light, Bronze, Green Glass Cups, Center Stem, Footed, Art Nouveau, 15 x 21 In.	4600.00
Candelabrum, 6-Light, Bronze, Pulled Feather Shades, Spread Foot, 15 x 22 In.	10625.00
Candelabrum, 12-Light, Gilt Bronze, Scrolling Arms, Leaves, Masks, c.1890, 20 x 30 In., Pair	720.00
Candlestick, Bronze Stem, Enamel Foot & Bobeche, 4 ¾ x 10 In., Pair	1464.00
Candlestick, Bronze, Gold Dore, Urn Cup, 3 Buttresses, Spread Foot, 18 In., Pair	1120.00
Candlestick, Bronze, Green Favrile Glass, Bulbous Cup, Slender Stem, Round Base, 17 ⅜ In.	1207.00
Candlestick, Green Panels, Bronze, Base, Standard, 17 In.	565.00

T

Candlestick, Snuffer, Double, Bronze, Purple Iridescent Glass, Hook, Leaf Base, c.1910, 9 x 7 In. *Illus*		4444.00
Cane, Sterling, L-Shape Handle, Hook At End, Rosewood, Iron Ferrule, Marked, c.1920, 33 In.		1495.00
Chandelier, 7-Light, Engraved Central & 6 Lily Shades, Bronze Frame, c.1910, 23 x 13 In.		37500.00
Cigar Box, Gilt Bronze, Enamel, Blue Geometric Border, Ball Feet, Art Deco, Lid, c.1920, 2 x 6 In.		2125.00
Cigar Box, Zodiac Pattern, Rectangular, Bronze, c.1920, 2 x 3 ¼ In.		250.00
Cigarette Box, Bronze, Blue Favrile, Turtle Back, Cylindrical, Twist Border, Ball Feet, 1910, 5 x 4 In.		2625.00
Cigarette Box, Medallion Pattern, Blue & Green Enamel, Gold, Wood Interior, Signed, 3 x 4 ½ In.		575.00
Clock, Carriage, Brass, Beveled Glass, Corniche Case, Repeating, Enamel Face, France, 5 ¼ In.		1062.00
Clock, Modeled Design, Bronze Dore, Speckled, Tapered Column, Greek Key Corners, 6 In.		1020.00
Clock, Shelf, Brass, Glass, c.1910, 11 x 6 In.		240.00
Compote, Bronze, Enamel Flowers, Leaves, Handles, Signed, Louis C. Tiffany Furnaces, 12 In. *Illus*		460.00
Desk Set, Bronze Dore, Glass Beads, Letter Holder, Inkwell, Notepad, 9th Century, 6 In., 7 Piece		3851.00
Desk Set, Bronze, Clock, Blotter Ends, Calendar, Pen Tray, Spain, c.1910, 1 To 19 In., 9 Piece		10328.00
Desk Set, Venetian, Bronze Dore, Letter Holder, 2 Inkwells, c.1910, ½ To 19 ¼ In., 9 Piece		1823.00
Desk Set, Zodiac, Bronze, Patina, Blotter Ends, Tray, Inkwell, 6-In. Letter Holder, 8 Piece		1875.00
Dish, Nesting, Bronze, Oval Lotus Shape, Largest 5 ½ x 4 In., 4 Piece		717.00
Frame, Bronze, Abalone, Gold Dore, Reverse Signed, 9 ¼ In.		2128.00
Frame, Grapevine, Green Favrile Glass, Gilt Bronze, Beaded Border, Stamped, 12 ⅜ x 9 ¾ In. *Illus*		1625.00
Frame, Pine Needle, Bronze, Green Glass, Beaded Edge, Signed, 12 x 14 ½ In. *Illus*		4313.00
Frame, Frank Lloyd Wright Window Design, Enamel Accents, Silver Grid, 3 ⅜ x 5 ⅞ In. *Illus*		2400.00
Glass, Vase, Cobalt Blue, Leaves, Bulbous, Knopped Stem, Bronze Foot, Stamped, 1920s, 11 In.		1250.00
Inkwell, Grapevine, Green Slag Glass, Glass Liner, Black Insert, Round, 7 x 3 ¾ In.		1006.00
Inkwell, Nautical, Bronze, Gold Dore, Ship Panels, 4 Dolphin Feet, 3 x 5 In.		1875.00
Inkwell, Ninth Century, Bronze Dore, Green, Blue Glass Bead Accents, Hinged Lid, 3 ¾ In.		674.00
Inkwell, Zodiac, No. 842, Signed, 4 In.		325.00
Jewelry Box, Pine Needle, Bronze, Green Slag Glass, 3 x 9 x 6 In.		1298.00
Lamp, 3-Lily Light, Favrile Glass Shades, Drooped, Bronze Stem Base, c.1920., 12 ⅞ x 4 ½ In.		3438.00
Lamp, Acorn, Leaded Glass, Gold & Green, Signed, 16 x 24 In. *Illus*		8800.00
Lamp, American Indian, Bronze Base, Multicolor Geometric Tile Shade, c.1910, 17 x 13 In.		92500.00
Lamp, Apple Blossom Shade, Slag Glass, Bronze Pillow Base, 4-Footed, 24 x 16 In.		21250.00
Lamp, Apple Blossom, Leaded Glass, Patinated Bronze Tree Base, c.1902, 29 x 25 In.		212500.00
Lamp, Arrowroot Shade, Green Slag Glass, Green Rookwood Pottery Base, 24 x 20 In.		35000.00
Lamp, Bell Shade, Iridescent Blue, Amber, White Heart, Vine, Bronze Harp Frame, c.1920, 16 x 5 In.		1250.00
Lamp, Bronze, Leaded Shade, Dragonflies, Yellow, Orange, Red, Spread Foot, c.1990, 31 In.		413.00
Lamp, Chandelier, Turtleback Tile Shade, Favrile Glass, Patinated Bronze, c.1905, 47 x 24 In.		200500.00
Lamp, Desk, Domed Shade, Green Iridescent, Blue Enamel, Dore, Tiffany Furnaces, c.1905, 15 In.		8990.00
Lamp, Desk, Grapevine, Bronze, Harp Base, Ribbed Foot, Signed, 17 ¾ In. *Illus*		3450.00
Lamp, Desk, Pine Needle, Bronze Dore, No. 552, 7 In.		2415.00
Lamp, Dogwood, Jeweled, Bronze Fringe Shade, Favrile, Green Glass Base, c.1905, 22 x 16 In.		98500.00
Lamp, Domed Favrile Tile Shade, Amber, Bronze Standard, Foot, c.1910, 21 ½ x 6 ½ In.		7500.00
Lamp, Dragonfly, Leaded Blue, Green, Yellow Shade, Claw Footed Bronze Base, c.1910, 26 x 20 In.		74500.00
Lamp, Favrile Fabrique Shade, Double Scroll Bronze Base, c.1915, 28 x 19 ½ In.		21250.00
Lamp, Favrile Glass, Domed Blue Damascene Shade, Red, Gold, Bronze Zodiac Base, 8 x 13 In.		4025.00
Lamp, Favrile Glass, Turtleback Tile Base, Bronze, Urn Shape, Geometric, c.1905, 22 In.		43800.00
Lamp, Floor, Blue Favrile Shade, Carved Insect, Bronze Base, Harp Shape, c.1910, 57 x 12 In.		34375.00
Lamp, Floor, Weight-Balance, Gold Damascene Shade, Bronze Frame, Marked, c.1920, 56 x 10 In.		9688.00
Lamp, Green & Amber Iridescent Shade, Bronze Frame, Lobed Foot, Favrile, L.C.T., c.1910, 17 ⅛ In.		8100.00
Lamp, Green Damascene Shade, Bronze, Bead & Ropework, Adjustable Arm, Oil, 23 In.		6600.00
Lamp, Green Translucent Shade, Ribbed, Bronze Candlestick Frame, Stone Insets, Leaf Feet, 17 In.		3125.00
Lamp, Hanging, Satin Glass Onion Shape Pendant Shade, Bronze Collar, c.1910, 8 ½ x 14 ¼ In.		1778.00
Lamp, Lily, 3 Light, Bronze, Triform Stem, Ribbed Base, Green Favrile Shades, 13 In.		1845.00
Lamp, Lily, 3-Light, Favrile Glass, Gilt Bronze Base, c.1910, L.C.T., 22 ½ In.		5000.00
Lamp, Lily, 3-Light, Gold Favrile Shades, Bronze, Cylindrical Stem, Ribbed Base, c.1910, 16 In.		4029.00
Lamp, Lily, 3-Light, Gold Favrile Shades, Signed Base, 11 x 9 In.		4880.00
Lamp, Lily, 10-Light, Favrile Glass, Bronze Base, Stems, Lily Pads Foot, L.C.T., c.1910, 20 In.		37500.00
Lamp, Lily, 12-Light, Favrile, Engraved Shades, Patinated Bronze Base, c.1910, 21 In.		31250.00
Lamp, Lily, 12-Light, Lily, Favrile Shades, Patinated Bronze Lily Pad Base, Signed L.C.T., 21 In.		5925.00
Lamp, Nasturtium, Multicolor Leaded Shade, Bronze Base, Impressed, c.1910, 31 x 23 In.		98500.00
Lamp, Nautilus Shell Shade, Bronze Sinewy Stem, Pillow Base, c.1900, 14 x 8 In.		10625.00
Lamp, Poppy, Bronze Collar Shade, Favrile, Leaded Glass, Turtleback Tile Base, c.1900, 18 x 17 In.		230500.00
Lamp, Slag Glass, Elongated Dome Shade, Grapevine, Gilt Bronze, Curled Arm, 8 In.		2750.00
Lamp, Stained Glass Shade, Cast Gilt Bronze Base, Flower Buds On Shaft, 3 Sockets, 65 In.		518.00
Lamp, Student, Double, Gold Favrile Pleated Shade, Pierced, Bronze, c.1910, 19 ⅞ In. *Illus*		5036.00
Lamp, Student, Double, Satin Glass Shades, Bronze, Ribbed & Beaded Base, 26 In.		7800.00
Lamp, Tulip, Leaded Multicolor Shade, Bronze Leaf Base, c.1905, 19 x 14 In.		37500.00
Lamp, Turtleback Glass Shade, Bronze Baluster Stem, Domed Base, Ball Feet, 23 In.		16250.00

Tiffany, Frame, Grapevine, Green Favrile Glass, Gilt Bronze, Beaded Border, Stamped, 12 ⅜ x 9 ¾ In. $1,625.00

Leslie Hindman Auctioneers

Tiffany, Frame, Pine Needle, Bronze, Green Glass, Beaded Edge, Signed, 12 x 14 ½ In. $4,313.00

James D. Julia Auctioneers

Tiffany, Lamp, Acorn, Leaded Glass, Gold & Green, Signed, 16 x 24 In. $8,800.00

Showtime Auction Sevices

T

Tiffany, Lamp, Desk, Grapevine, Bronze, Harp Base, Ribbed Foot, Signed, 17 ¾ In.
$3,450.00

James D. Julia Auctioneers

Tiffany, Lamp, Student, Double, Gold Favrile Pleated Shade, Pierced, Bronze, c.1910, 19 ⅞ In.
$5,036.00

Skinner, Inc.

Tiffany, Lamp, Turtleback, Bronze, Rope & Beaded, Green Jeweled Base, Monogram, c.1925, 14 In.
$10,665.00

Skinner, Inc.

Tiffany, Lamp, Venetian, Leaded Glass, Green Glass Jewels, Intricate, Signed, 18 In.
$103,500.00

James D. Julia Auctioneers

Tiffany, Sconce, Bronze, 2-Light, Favrile Glass Shades, Etched L.C.T., 1900s, 13 ½ In.
$5,313.00

Rago Arts & Auction Center

Tiffany Glass, Vase, Blue, Feathers, Favrile, Etched, 1901, 2 ¾ x 4 In.
$3,125.00

Rago Arts & Auction Center

Tiffany Glass, Vase, Flower Shape, Gold Iridescent, Ribbed, Favrile, Signed, c.1910, 11 ⅜ In.
$830.00

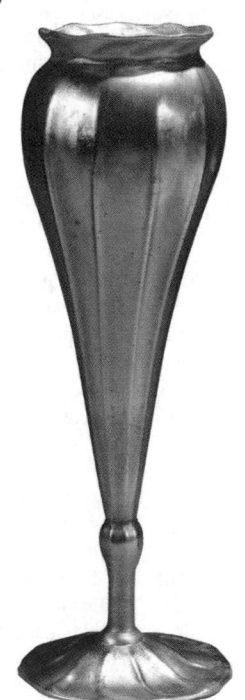

Skinner, Inc.

T

Lamp, Turtleback, Bronze, Rope & Beaded, Green Jeweled Base, Monogram, c.1925, 14 In. .. *Illus*	10665.00
Lamp, Turtleback, Graduate, Adjustable, Bronze, 3 Favrile Glass Tiles, Marked, c.1915, 6 ¾ x 11 In.	3438.00
Lamp, Venetian, Leaded Glass, Green Glass Jewels, Intricate, Signed, 18 In. ....*Illus*	103500.00
Lamp, Weight-Balance, Bronze Verdigris, Favrile Glass, Bell Shape Gold Iridescent Shade, 14 In...	3308.00
Lamp, Weight-Balance, Favrile Glass, Bronze, Arm, Green Fabrique Shade, c.1915, 15 In.	7500.00
Lamp, Weight-Balance, Pulled Feather Shade, Adjustable, Bronze Base, Lily Pad Feet, 53 In...	6038.00
Letter Holder, Chinese, 3 Tiers, Bronze, Marked, 8 x 11 ¾ In.	938.00
Money Clip, 18K Yellow Gold, Basket Weave Design, Signed, 2 ¼ In.	345.00
Paper Rack, Bronze, Gold Dore, Graduate, 2 Compartments, Stamped, 5 ¼ x 9 ½ In.............	403.00
Paperweight, Apple, Clear, 3 ½ In.	45.00
Pen Tray, Bronze, Venetian Pattern, Band Of Otters, Green Enamel Highlights, Marked, 10 In.	460.00
Perfume Bottle, Laydown, Double Ended, Faceted, Silver Plate Lid, 4 ½ In.	179.00
Planter, Abalone, Round, Stamped, c.1900, 9 In.	600.00
Sconce, 4-Light, Round Mount, Bead Trimmed Horizontal Branch, 6 Bronze Sockets, 16 In...	7110.00
Sconce, Bronze, 2-Light, Favrile Glass Shades, Etched L.C.T., 1900s, 13 ½ In. ....*Illus*	5313.00
Tile, Glass, Gold Favrile Iridescent, Turtle Back, L. C. Tiffany, 4 ½ x 6 In.	625.00
Tray, Sandwich, Chased, Repousse, Pierced Rim, Shell Shape, c.1900, 16 In.	40463.00
Vase, Amber, Gold Iridescent, Tapered, Enameled Dome Base, Stamped, 1920s, 13 In.	406.00
Vase, Jack-In-The-Pulpit, Amber Flower, Green Stem, Puffed Foot, Signed, c.1920, 12 In........	531.00

TIFFANY GLASS

Bowl, Blue, Gold Favrile Pull, Blue Interior, Oval, Flared Rim, 3 x 7 In........................	2726.00
Bowl, Favrile, Flared Lip, Tapered Waist, Flared Base, Etched L.C. Tiffany, 7 x 2 In...................	253.00
Bowl, Favrile, Gold Iridescent, Ruffled Edge, Footed, Signed, c.1915, 3 ¾ x 6 In................	1045.00
Bowl, Gold Favrile, Flared, Signed, 3 ¼ x 9 ¾ In.	805.00
Bowl, Gold Favrile, Purple Iridescent, Orange Interior, Underplate, Signed, 2 x 5 In.	345.00
Bowl, Gold Favrile, Side Pulled Prunt Handles, Signed L.C.T., c.1907, 6 In.	403.00
Bowl, Gold Favrile, Stretched & Stepped, Blue & Purple Iridescent, Foldover Rim, 8 In...........	230.00
Bowl, Gold Iridescent, Wide Rim, Footed, 2 x 5 ⅞ In.	267.00
Bowl, Gold, Carved, Lotus Leaf Design, Favrile, c.1900, 14 In.	470.00
Bowl, Lava, Gold, Purple, Favrile, Engraved, c.1905, 3 ⅝ x 6 ½ In.	46875.00
Bowl, Lily Pads, Gold Favrile, Signed Base, 9 ¾ In.	486.00
Bowl, Pulled Peacock Feather, Etched L.C.T., Favrile, c.1910, 6 In.	5000.00
Candlestand, Twist Ribs, Blue Iridescent, Green, Rounded Spread Foot, 7 In.	403.00
Candlestick, Opalescent Foot, Reeded Stem, Purple Onionskin Rim, Signed, 11 In.................	863.00
Compote, Blue Favrile, Pedestal, Bulbous, Wide Ruffle Rim, Round Foot, 1900s, 4 x 5 ½ In. ..	938.00
Compote, Blue Favrile, Ribbed Foot, Double Gourd Shape, Scalloped Rim, c.1909, 6 In.	1725.00
Compote, Blue Favrile, Ribbed, Scalloped Shallow Dish, Tapered Stem, Iridescent Foot, 6 In..	1438.00
Compote, Favrile, Purple Iridescent, Pink, Green, Round Pedestal Foot, Ruffle, Rim, 2 x 4 In....	920.00
Compote, Favrile, Purple Iridescent, Platinum, Saucer Foot, Pedestal, Flat Rim, 3 ½ x 6 In....	460.00
Compote, Favrile, Round Foot, Narrow Stem, Flower Shape, Butterfly, Blue, Green, c.1905, 5 In..	4400.00
Compote, Gold Favrile, Blue Iridescent, Pedestal, Wavy Rim, Spread Foot, Signed, 3 ½ x 6 ½ In...	748.00
Compote, Green, Optic Ribbed Shape, Scalloped Onionskin Rim, Footed, Signed, 7 ½ In........	288.00
Finger Bowl, Underplate, Pastel, Blue, Opalescent Ribbing, Onionskin Border, 2 ½ x 6 ½ In..	518.00
Flower Frog Bowl, Blue Favrile, Iridescent Red, Green, Lily Pad, Border, c.1918, 10 In..........	805.00
Flower Frog Insert, Double, Gold Favrile, Footed, 2 Rows, 8 Loops, Cased Center, c.1917, 4 In.	374.00
Goblet, Gold Iridescence, Footed, 3 ¾ In., Pair..	160.00
Goblet, Gold Iridescent, Prunts On Sides, Spread Foot, Favrile, c.1900, 3 ½ x 3 In.	563.00
Inkwell, Grapevine, Verdigris, Applied Beads, Ball Feet, 3 ½ x 4 In., Pair......................	644.00
Lamp, Candle, Rainbow Iridescent, Twisted Stem, Bulbous Shade, Favrile, 12 In......................	920.00
Perfume Bottle, Cobalt Blue, Favrile Hooked Swag Design, Bulbous Finial, Signed, 9 ½ In....	7475.00
Plate, Pastel, Blue Shaded To Clear, Opalescent Snowflake, Ribbed, Signed, 10 ½ In................	633.00
Pokal, Lid, Footed, Captured Air Bubbles, Finial, Knop, 11 ½ x 5 ¼ In...........................	98.00
Ring Tray, Gold Favrile, Blue Accents, Scalloped Rim, Flower Shape, Signed, 4 ¼ In.............	230.00
Salt Cellar, Yellow, Gold Iridescent, Kettle Style, Ribbed, Pulled Feet, 1 ¼ x 2 ½ In.............	431.00
Salt, Gold Favrile, Pink Iridescent, Gold Highlights, Squat, Footed, Signed, 1 ½ x 2 In............	316.00
Salt, Gold Favrile, Ribbed, Flaring Mouth, Iridescent, Footed, Signed, 1 ½ x 2 ½ In............	201.00
Salt, Open, Gold Favrile, Pig Tail Prunts, Signed L.C.T., 2 In.	230.00
Sherbet, Gold Iridescent, Pedestal, Round Foot, Wide Rim, 3 ½ x 4 ½ In.	196.00
Tumbler, Gold Favrile, Gold Threading, Cylindrical, Signed L.C.T., 3 ¼ In.	259.00
Vase, Amber Translucent, To Gold Iridescent, Flared Rim, Cinched Waist, 8 ⅝ In.	500.00
Vase, Amber, Gold, Translucent, Trumpet, Knopped Stem, Domed Ribbed Foot, c.1917, 10 In..	625.00
Vase, Blue Favrile, Bulbous, Stick, Signed, 5 ¾ In.	748.00
Vase, Blue Favrile, Gold Hooked Feather Design, Cylindrical, Pinched Neck, Signed, c.1895, 3 In...	3450.00
Vase, Blue Favrile, Ribbed Trumpet Shape, Footed, Purple Overtones, Signed, 10 In................	14950.00
Vase, Blue Favrile, Trumpet, Tapering, Ribbed Accents, Round Domed Foot, Signed, 10 ¾ In..	1750.00
Vase, Blue Iridescent, Shouldered, Cylindrical Collar, Gold Favrile Bands, Intarsia, 9 ¼ In......	6900.00

Tiffany Glass, Vase, Green Pulled Feather, Gold Iridescent, Favrile, Button Pontil, Signed, c.1910, 8 In. $1,659.00

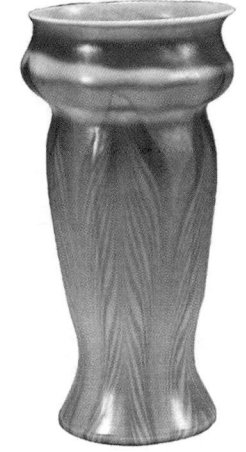

Skinner, Inc.

Tiffany Glass, Vase, Green To Blue Green, Gold Leaves, Iridescent, White Millefiori, Favrile, c.1909, 6 ½ In. $5,463.00

Early Auction Co.

Tiffany Glass, Vase, Lava, Gold Iridescent Drips, Etched L.C. Tiffany, c.1909, 5 ⅛ In. $10,625.00

Leslie Hindman Auctioneers

Tiffany Glass, Vase, Paperweight, Flowers, Favrille, Signed, 11 ½ x 4 ½ In. $11,960.00

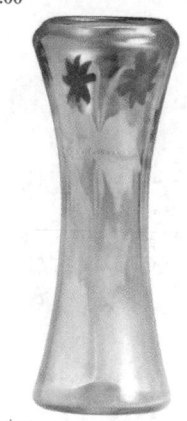

Cottone Auctions

Tiffany Glass, Vase, Prunts, Iridescent, Favrile, Marked, 1906, 2 ¼ x 1 ¾ In. $1,375.00

Rago Arts & Auction Center

Tiffany Glass, Vase, Tel El Amarna, Blue, Favrile, Paper Label, 1900s, 8 ½ x 4 ¾ In. $9,375.00

Rago Arts & Auction Center

TIP
You can tell a piece of jade by the feel. It will be cold, even in warm weather.

Vase, Blue Iridescent, Squat, Lobed, Signed, 3 ½ x 5 ½ In.	516.00
Vase, Blue Iridescent, Tapered, Paneled, Favrile, Paper Label, 6 ¾ In.	944.00
Vase, Blue, Feathers, Favrile, Etched, 1901, 2 ¾ x 4 In. ....*Illus*	3125.00
Vase, Blue, Rust, Yellow, Cup Top, Long Stem, Footed, Favrile, Etched L.C.T., c.1910, 15 ¾ In. .	1250.00
Vase, Bud, Flower Form, White, Acid Etched, Favrile, Gilt Bronze Base, 17 x 5 In.	1375.00
Vase, Bud, Gold Favrile, Green Pulled Feathers, Trumpet Shape, Round Foot, Signed, 8 In.	863.00
Vase, Bud, Gold Favrile, Iridescent, Magenta, Green, Tapered Neck, Signed, c.1917, 6 x 2 ¼ In. .	489.00
Vase, Bud, Gold To Green Iridescent, Pulled Feather, Tubular, Bronze Base, 18 In.	877.00
Vase, Bud, Iridescent, Pulled Feather, Lobed, 1900s, 4 ½ x 3 ½ In.	10625.00
Vase, Cabinet, Blue Favrile, 8 Extending Ribs, Squat Body, Square Mouth, 2 x 4 In.	518.00
Vase, Cobalt, Blue Iridescent, Ribbed, Knop Stem, Domed Foot, Signed Tiffany-Favrile, 12 In.	1375.00
Vase, Dark Green & Gold English Ivy, Embossed Pulled Pattern, Signed, 7 ½ In.	3680.00
Vase, Favrile, Bottle Shape, Red, Orange, Lavender, Pulled Design, 6 ½ In.	8750.00
Vase, Favrile, Bottle Shape, Ribbed Neck, Yellow & Pink, Signed, 8 In.	1250.00
Vase, Favrile, Frosted Amber, Leaves & Vines, Yellow Flowers, Pinched Waist, c.1908, 7 In.	7475.00
Vase, Favrile, Green Iridescent, Gold Pulled Feather Design, Trumpet Foot, Stick, Signed, 10 In.	1495.00
Vase, Favrile, Pulled Ribbing, Purple Iridescent, Platinum, Bulbous, Elongated Neck, 9 In.	920.00
Vase, Flower Form, Green Pulled Feather, Milky Ground, Gold & White Foot, 13 In.	9000.00
Vase, Flower Form, Green Pulled Feathers & Stem, Gold Iridescent Foot, 12 In.	7200.00
Vase, Flower Shape, Gold Iridescent, Ribbed, Favrile, Signed, c.1910, 11 ⅜ In. ....*Illus*	830.00
Vase, Frosted, Clear, Blossoms, Leaves, Cylindrical, Signed L.C. Tiffany-Favrile, c.1910, 13 In. .	8750.00
Vase, Goblet Shape, Scalloped Rim, Amber, Iridescent Pulled Feather, Footed, 8 In.	575.00
Vase, Gold Favrile Glass, Gilt Metal, Trumpet Shape, Pulled Feather, Signed, c.1900, 14 ¾ In. .	540.00
Vase, Gold Favrile, Bottle Shape, Twist Design, Flared Rim, N.Y., 1900s, 8 ¾ x 4 In.	875.00
Vase, Gold Favrile, Figure 8 Chain, Blue & Red Highlights, Oval, c.1910, Signed, 5 ¾ In.	748.00
Vase, Gold Favrile, Heart & Vine, Swirling, Shouldered, Tapered, Rolled Rim, Signed, 8 ½ In. .	4888.00
Vase, Gold Favrile, Intaglio Carved Grape Leaf Rim, Trumpet Shape, Signed, c.1917, 14 In.	863.00
Vase, Gold Favrile, Iridescent Foot, Knopped Stem, Flower Shape, Wavy Rim, Signed, 16 In.	1610.00
Vase, Gold Favrile, Iridescent, Footed, Paper Label, Signed, 4 In.	518.00
Vase, Gold Favrile, Iridescent, Ribbed, Flower Shape, Scalloped Rim, Signed, 11 ½ In.	1380.00
Vase, Gold Favrile, Pinched Waist, Wide Crimped Rim, Round Foot, Signed, 4 In.	230.00
Vase, Gold Favrile, Purple Accents, Ribbed, Shaped Body, Flat Rim, Signed, 4 In.	575.00
Vase, Gold Favrile, Ribbed Elongated Oval, Flare Rim, Round Ribbed Foot, 12 ¾ In.	1265.00
Vase, Gold Favrile, Ribbed, Iridescent Gold, Pink, Saucer Foot, Flared Scallop Rim, Signed, 8 In. .	1150.00
Vase, Gold Favrile, Ribbed, Round Foot, Bulbous Scalloped Rim, Signed, 15 In.	2013.00
Vase, Gold Favrile, Ribbed, Squat, Pinched Neck, Flower Petal Rim, Signed, 3 In.	518.00
Vase, Gold Favrile, Shouldered, Melon Ribbed, N.Y., 1900s, 4 ¾ x 3 ½ In.	1063.00
Vase, Gold Favrile, Swirling, Textured, Swollen, Tapering, Signed, 11 In.	863.00
Vase, Gold Favrile, Trumpet, Ribbed Foot, Balled Standard, Signed, c.1906, 15 ¾ In.	1495.00
Vase, Gold Iridescent, Melon Ribbed, Scalloped Rim, Swollen, 5 ¾ In.	460.00
Vase, Gold Iridescent, Opalescence, Green Ribbing, Shouldered, Tapered, Round Foot, 7 ¾ In. .	2875.00
Vase, Gold, Green, Long Neck, Tapered, Signed Louis Comfort Tiffany, c.1905, 10 In.	3720.00
Vase, Golden Opalescent, Pulled Green Feather, Knopped Stem, Ribbed Flower Shape, 9 ½ In.	4600.00
Vase, Green & Gold Foliage, English Ivy, Vines, Pulled Pattern, Marked, 7 ½ In.	3680.00
Vase, Green Favrile, Low Bowl, White Heart, Vines, Signed L.C.T., 7 ½ In.	230.00
Vase, Green Pulled Feather, Gold Iridescent, Favrile, Button Pontil, Signed, c.1910, 8 In. ..*Illus*	1659.00
Vase, Green To Blue Green, Gold Leaves, Iridescent, White Millefiori, Favrile, c.1909, 6 ½ In. ..*Illus*	5463.00
Vase, Heart & Vine, Stick Neck, To Bulbous Base, Gold Favrile, 6 In.	1154.00
Vase, Heart, Vine, Swirl Gold & Green, Favrile, Paper Label, 5 ⅜ In.	668.00
Vase, Iridescent Gold Favrile, Pulled Shape, Signed L.C. Tiffany, 3 ¼ x 6 In.	915.00
Vase, Iridescent Gold, Favrile, Grape & Vine Etched, Cinched Cylinder, Signed L.C. Tiffany, 4 In.	237.00
Vase, Lava, Gold Iridescent Drips, Etched L.C. Tiffany, c.1909, 5 ⅛ In. ....*Illus*	10625.00
Vase, Lava, Purple, Blue, Gold Flecks, Pock Marked, Ribbed, Flared Rim, Round, 3 x 3 ¼ In. .	472.00
Vase, Leaf & Vine, Tapered, Purple Favrile, Signed, 7 ⅞ In.	3318.00
Vase, Paperweight, Flowers, Favrille, Signed, 11 ½ x 4 ½ In. ....*Illus*	11960.00
Vase, Paperweight, Jonquils, Engraved L.C.T., c.1915, 10 In.	22500.00
Vase, Peacock Feathers, Platinum, Green Ground, Sapphire Blue, Shouldered, Signed, 19 ½ In.	8625.00
Vase, Prunts, Iridescent, Favrile, Marked, 1906, 2 ¼ x 1 ¾ In. ....*Illus*	1375.00
Vase, Pulled Design, Gold Favrile, Iridescence, Faceted Base, Signed, 3 x 4 In.	406.00
Vase, Pulled Flames Design, Clouds, Gold, Pink, Shouldered, Slight Taper, Ring Foot, 4 ½ In. .	805.00
Vase, Purple Iridescent, Shouldered, Footed, Favrile, Signed, c.1900, 6 ¾ In.	767.00
Vase, Red Favrile, Green Swirl, Cylindrical, Everted Rim, Signed, 8 ¾ In.	3565.00
Vase, Red, Orange, Favrile, Engraved L.C.T., c.1895, 14 ¼ In.	9375.00
Vase, Ribbed, Hobnail, Etched, Blue, Gold Favrile, 3 x 2 ½ In.	354.00
Vase, Rose, Iridescent, Tapered, Flared, Signed 1886, 9 ½ In.	384.00
Vase, Royal Blue To Purple, Platinum, Swollen Stick, Round Foot, Trefoil Fold Rim, Signed, 11 In. .	2415.00
Vase, Sherbet Favrile, Clear, Lavender, Flower Shape, Ruffled, Foot, Signed, 1938, 5 ¼ In.	1380.00

Vase, Stick, Gold Iridescent, Pulled Leaves & Vines, Millefiori, Squat Base, 6 In.	2530.00
Vase, Tel El Amarna, Blue, Favrile, Paper Label, 1900s, 8 ½ x 4 ¾ In. ....*Illus*	9375.00
Vase, Tel El Amarna, Gilt Bronze, Stand, Engraved L.C. Tiffany-Favrile, c.1915, 9 ⅞ In.	7500.00
Vase, Trumpet, Gold Favrile, Bronze Base, Signed, 14 In.	1071.00
Vase, Trumpet, Gold Iridescent, Footed, Signed Louis C. Tiffany, 14 ¾ In.	1126.00
Vase, Trumpet, Gold Iridescent, Pulled Vine, Ball Knop, Domed Foot, 1900, 10 In.	1375.00
Vase, Yellow Favrile, Red Cameo Leaves, Bulbous, Urn Shape, Signed L.C. Tiffany, 8 ¼ In.	12075.00
Vase, Yellow Rim, Pulled Red, Blue Threads, Favrile, Signed, 4 In.	28440.00
Whiskey, Gold Favrile, Classic Shape, 8 Extruded Prunts, Signed L.C.T., 2 ¼ In.	230.00
Wine, Gold Favrile, Phantom Luster, Translucent Stem & Foot, 6 ¼ In.	230.00

TIFFANY GOLD

Compact, Rays, Colored Stone, Art Deco, 2 ⅜ x 2 ⅜ In.	351.00
Cuff Links, Gold Rope Work, Union Square Box, c.1865	3776.00
Cuff Links, Scrolled, 18K Gold, Onyx Cross, Signed	708.00
Letter Opener, Spanish Pattern, Gold Dore, Brown Enamel, Red Highlights, Signed, 1884, 10 In.	920.00
Pitcher, Green Leaves & Vines, Favrile, Signed, 6 ½ In. ....*Illus*	2185.00

TIFFANY POTTERY

Vase, Lily Of The Valley, Old Ivory Glaze, Incised LCT, c.1905, 6 x 2 ¾ In. ....*Illus*	1875.00
Vase, Milkweed, Glazed, Etched Tiffany Favrile, 1900s, 10 x 4 In. ....*Illus*	42500.00

TIFFANY SILVER

Asparagus Tongs, Atlantis, E P Monogram, Engraved, Reticulated, 7 ¼ In.	690.00
Basket, Pierced, Reticulated Handle, Oval, Winged Claw Feet, c.1910, 4 ½ In.	420.00
Basket, Reticulated, Pierced, Hexagonal, Straight Handles, 3 ¾ x 10 ¾ In.	875.00
Basket, Strawberry, 3 ½ x 5 ¾ In.	6875.00
Berry Fork, Strawberry Pattern, 2 Prongs, 4 ½ In., 6 Piece	1020.00
Berry Spoon, Kidney Shaped Bowl, Antoine Heller, 1878, 9 ⅜ In.	406.00
Bonbon Spoon, Round Handle, Putti, Gilt Coquille Bowl, Monogram, c.1900, 5 ¼ In.	338.00
Bonbon, Chrysanthemum Pattern, Monogram Center, c.1895, 7 ¾ In.	450.00
Bonbon, Shell Shape, Raised Leaf Border, Handles, Stamped, 1940s, 6 In.	420.00
Bowl, Bell Shape, Monogram, c.1910, 4 ⅜ x 9 In., Pair	1989.00
Bowl, Cloverleaf Border, Flared Out Rim, 2 ¾ x 10 In.	690.00
Bowl, Embossed, Scalloped Rim, Clear Glass Insert, 12 In.	357.00
Bowl, Flared Scalloped Rim, Conforming Base, Hammered, 4 x 9 In.	1180.00
Bowl, Flowers & Leaves, Fluted Panels, Trumpet Foot, Repousse, 1875-91, 8 ⅞ Diam.	1896.00
Bowl, Fluted, Reeded Rim & Base, Monogram, c.1935, 9 In.	590.00
Bowl, Fruit, Clover Pattern, Octagonal, Lobed, Openwork Rim, c.1900, 2 ¼ x 10 In.	861.00
Bowl, Fruit, Molded Shape Rim, Cast Flower Design, 1907-38, 12 ½ In. Diam.	1593.00
Bowl, Fruit, Scrolling Leaf Rim, Fluted, Footed, 1873-91, 8 ¼ In. Diam.	1348.00
Bowl, Half Ribbed, Cherub Band, Pedestal Base, 5 ½ In.	1062.00
Bowl, Leaf Shape, Pierced Handle, Stamped Tiffany & Co., 3 ¼ x 2 ½ In., Pair	144.00
Bowl, Monteith, Gold Wash, Footed, 5 ¼ x 9 ¼ In.	944.00
Bowl, Pierced Rim, Monogram, 1 ½ x 6 ⅜ In., Pair	288.00
Bowl, Pierced, Reticulated, Overlapped Rim, Round, Stepped Foot, c.1910, 12 ½ In.	1750.00
Bowl, Reticulated Rim, Cast Flowering Clover, Monogram, c.1905, 9 In.	600.00
Bowl, Scalloped Rim, Reticulated, Round, Domed Stepped Foot, c.1960, 5 ½ x 9 ½ In.	750.00
Bowl, Scalloped Rim, Wide Border, Round, Monogram, c.1930, 2 ¼ x 10 ¾ In.	875.00
Bowl, Shallow, Round, Flattened Rim, 3 Reeded S-Scroll Feet, 1947-56, 11 ⅞ In. Diam.	1007.00
Bowl, Vegetable, Lid, Leaf Rim & Finial, Oval, c.1900, 11 In.	2125.00
Bowl, Wavy Rim, Clover Border, Tiffany, 9 In. Diam.	575.00
Breakfast Set, Coffeepot, Sugar, Creamer, Tray, Stylized Leaf Berry Band, Tray 10 In., 4 Piece	1500.00
Butter, Dome Cover, Scrolled Acanthus Border, Shell & Wave Finial, 6 In.	1416.00
Cake Plate, Flower Shape, Molded Edge, Flowers & Leaves, Spread Foot, 1875-91, 11 In. Diam.	1659.00
Cake Plate, Reticulated, Monogram, 9 ½ In.	298.00
Candleholder, Hexagonal, C Monogram, c.1928, 4 ¼ In.	431.00
Candlestick, Bone Pattern, Elsa Peretti, Signed, 15 In., Pair ....*Illus*	2640.00
Candlestick, Pierced Cast Flowers, Drip Cup, Knopped Domed Foot, c.1945, 9 ½ In., Pair	2813.00
Centerpiece, Bands Of Flowers, Urn Form, Stepped Foot, 5 ½ x 9 ¼ In.	738.00
Centerpiece, Roses, Scallops, Flared Rim, Chassed, Repousse, Footed, c.1900, 13 ¾ In.	2160.00
Chafing Dish, Stand, Ivory Handles, Knop, Early 20th Century, 9 In.	300.00
Chocolate Pot, Olympian, Bacchus, Dancing Nudes, Cherubs, Scroll Handle, Marked 1902, Pt.	2142.00
Cigar Box, Applied Horse, Galloping, Hinged Lid, Rectangular, 1 ¾ x 9 In.	1875.00
Cigar Box, Presentation, Engraved Names On Lid, 1947-56, 1 ⅝ x 6 ⅞ In.	830.00
Cigarette Box, Footed, 2 x 8 In.	833.00
Claret Spoon, Chrysanthemum, Spiral Center, 1800s, 18 ½ In.	430.00
Coffee Set, Tapered, Wood Scroll Handle, c.1965, 10-In. Coffeepot, 3 Piece	1080.00
Coffeepot, Dome Lid, Urn Finial, Baluster, Hollow Handle, c.1960, 11 ⅜ In.	625.00

Tiffany Gold, Pitcher, Green Leaves & Vines, Favrile, Signed, 6 ½ In. $2,185.00

Early Auction Co.

TIP

Check every collectible before you buy. For glass, look for chips, cracks, flaws, mismatched lids, and faded color. For furniture, look under and inside to see if parts fit, if hardware is original (an extra set of holes will tell), or if it is a "marriage" (two pieces that were put together). Take the drawers out to look for damage, poor fit, worm holes, or faked painted patina.

Tiffany Pottery, Vase, Lily Of The Valley, Old Ivory Glaze, Incised, LCT, c.1905, 6 x 2 ¾ In. $1,875.00

Rago Arts & Auction Center

Tiffany Pottery, Vase, Milkweed, Glazed, Marked, Tiffany Favrile, 1900s, 10 x 4 In. $42,500.00

Rago Arts & Auction Center

Tiffany Silver, Candlestick, Bone Pattern, Elsa Peretti, Signed, 15 In., Pair $2,640.00

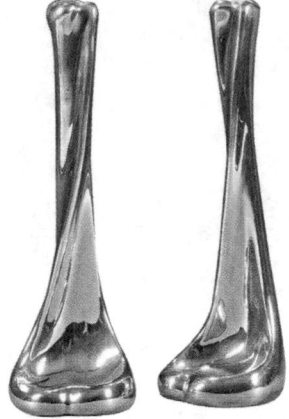

Skinner, Inc.

Tiffany Silver, Tray, Applied Border, Engraved, Leaf & Grape, Footed, Marked, c.1860, 15 x 11 In. $1,416.00

Brunk Auctions

TIP
Be careful how you handle clean silver. Fingerprints will show and eventually tarnish.

Coffeepot, Hinged Onion Dome Lid, Saracenic, Oval, Slender Neck, Swan Spout, 1882, 10 In.	2337.00
Coffeepot, Lobed, Trumpet Shape Lid, Quatrefoil Finial, Ear Shape Handle, Ivory, c.1885, 9 In.	593.00
Compact, Case, Radiating Engraved Design, Art Deco Closure, Square, c.1930, 3 x 3 In., 2 Piece	723.00
Compote, Repousse Border, Knop Standard, Square Base, Paw Feet, c.1900, 5 x 10 In., Pair	3438.00
Cordial Set, Tray, Gilt Lined Cups, Tray 6 In., 3 Piece	165.00
Corkscrew, Art Deco Style, 3 ½ In.	240.00
Cruet Set, Richelieu, Palmettes, Beaded, Paw Feet, 2 Cut Glass Bottles, 8 In.	1586.00
Cup, Applied Handle, Monogram P.B.D., 2 ¾ In.	130.00
Cup, Christening, Baluster, Flower Foot Ring, Caterpillar Handle, Engraved, 1881, 4 x 3 In.	246.00
Dish, Leaf Shape, 2 Ball Shape Feet, Stamped, 6 In.	210.00
Dish, Pierced Rim, Leaves, Footed, Monogram, 6 In.	247.00
Dish, Undulating Rim, Lobed, Pierced Sides, Oval, 10 ¾ x 8 ¾ In.	529.00
Dresser Box, Hinged Lid, Molded Edge, 1 ⅞ x 4 ¼ In.	385.00
Dresser Tray, Engraved, Islamic Design, Geometric Medallions, Borders, Marked, c.1880, 9 In.	767.00
Fish Serving Set, Chrysanthemum, Marked, 1873-91, 9 ½ & 12 ½ In.	885.00
Fruit Knives, Stamped Tiffany & Co., 7 In., 4 Piece	121.00
Gravy Ladle, Olympian, Paris Scene On Ahdnel, 1878, 7 ½ In.	415.00
Gumbo Spoon, Gramercy Pattern, Monogram, 13 In., 10 Piece	676.00
Humidor, Engine Turned Sides, Lid Plaque, Cedar Lining, 1936, 3 x 9 x 6 In.	3286.00
Ice Cream Slice, Grapevine, Gilt Leaf Shape Blade, Monogram, c.1872, 13 In.	522.00
Ice Cream Spoon, Chrysanthemum, Tiffany & Co., 9 ¼ In.	410.00
Ice Cream Spoon, Pastry Fork, Gold Washed, Monogram, Tiffany & Co., 6 ¼ & 6 In., 12 Piece	720.00
Inkwell, Hammered Finish, Applied Initials, Glass Lined, Signed, 2 ⅓ In.	230.00
Lighter, Cigar, Shaped Horn Handle, c.1900, 9 ¼ In.	649.00
Loving Cup, Rocaille Neck Band, 3 Handles, 3 Paw Feet, c.1895, 9 ⅛ In.	3125.00
Mug, Cylindrical, Beaded Band, Acanthus Leaf Band, Child's, 3 ½ In.	173.00
Mug, Handle, Round Foot, Bulbous Bottom, Reeded Rim, Inscribed, Tiffany, 3 ½ In.	150.00
Mustache Comb, Black Leather Pouch, 2 ¾ In.	121.00
Nut Shovel, Cast Flowers, Ribbon Handle, Tiffany & Co., c.1905, 3 ¾ In.	330.00
Oyster Server, Atlantis Pattern, Free-Form Bowl, Stylized Leaf Handle, c.1900, 8 In.	356.00
Pastry Tongs, Olympian, 7 ½ In.	995.00
Pitcher, Allover Chased Flowers, Ferns, Globe Shape, c.1880, 7 ¾ In.	3125.00
Pitcher, Engraved Griffins, Urns, Flowers, Woman's Head Handle, 9 x 7 ½ In.	3510.00
Pitcher, Hammered Honeycomb, Applied Crab, Shells, Seaweed, c.1880, 7 ⅛ In.	8775.00
Pitcher, Moorish Engravings, Die Rolled Rims, c.1880, 8 In.	2300.00
Pitcher, Pear Shape, Squat, Bands Of Waves, Ear Shape Handle, 1885, 7 ¼ In.	1422.00
Pitcher, Water, Cavetto Shoulder, Waisted Collar, Leaf Banding, Wide Spout, 1800s, 11 x 8 In.	2460.00
Pitcher, Wave Band, c.1890, Tiffany & Co., 7 ¾ In.	1800.00
Plate, Plain Border, 11 In., 12 Piece	10000.00
Plateau, Block & Scroll Feet, 10 ¼ In. Diam.	826.00
Platter, Molded Rim, Recessed Plateau, Monogram, Tiffany & Co., c.1926, 12 In. Diam.	738.00
Porringer, Marked On Handle, 4 ⅛ x 1 ⅝ In.	184.00
Ring Box, Figural Apple, Gilt Interior, Signed, 1960s, 2 ¼ x 1 ⅓ In.	200.00
Salad Servers, Flemish Pattern, 2 Piece	387.00
Salt, Chalice, Elk Head Handles, Engraved, Monogram, Leaf Band, Stamped, 2 ½ x 5 In., Pair	178.00
Salt, Gold Flash Lined, Half Sphere Bowl, Stepped Rim, Crescent Legs, c.1850, 1 x 23 In., Pair	177.00
Salver, Armorial Engraving, Bands Of Leaves, Trees, Scrollwork, Corinthian Feet, 10 In. Diam.	1185.00
Sauce Ladle, Berry, Leaf Engraved Handle	295.00
Sauce Ladle, Colonial, Coquille Bowl, Monogram, c.1895, 7 ¼ In.	153.00
Saucepan, Warming, Ivory Handle, Spoon, Wavy Flowers, Leaves, c.1900, Pt.	1800.00
Serving Bowl, Stylized Basket Wave, Beaded Rim, Square, 9 x 9 In.	702.00
Serving Set, Italian, 4-Tine Fork, Spoon, Chased Flowers, Stamped, 8 In.	390.00
Shaker, Figural, Owl, Glass Eyes, 2 ¼ In.	360.00
Smoking Set, Tray, Rectangular, 5 Wells, Match Stand, 3 Round Ashtrays, Tray 13 ⅜ In.	875.00
Soap Box, Rounded Rectangle, Gold Wash Interior, Signed, 4 x 2 ¾ In.	173.00
Soup Ladle, Tomato Vine Pattern, Scalloped Bowl, c.1890, 11 ½ In.	1007.00
Stuffing Spoon, Olympian Pattern, Paris Scene, Golden Apple, Venus, Juno, c.1878-91, 11 In.	889.00
Tazza, Chased Flowers, Footed, 3 ¾ x 7 ½ In.	652.00
Tazza, Pedestal, Scored Rim Lines, Stamped, 3 ½ x 5 ⅛ In., Pair	414.00
Tea & Coffee Set, Baluster, Wood Handles, E.J. Greenberg, London, 1928, 5 Piece	2390.00
Tea & Coffee, Hampton, Heating Stand, Coffeepot, Teapot, Sugar, Creamer, Bowl	5227.00
Tea Set, Etched Bands, Black Handle, Teapot, Sugar, Creamer, Tray, Monogram	1035.00
Tray, Applied Border, Engraved, Leaf & Grape, Footed, Marked, c.1860, 15 x 11 In. ....*Illus*	1416.00
Tray, Canted Corners, Pierced Handles, Rectangular, Engraved, 1931, 24 ¾ In.	4375.00
Tray, Central Geometric, Angled Oval, Cutout Handles, 20 x 26 In.	4740.00
Tray, Round, Border Enamel Flag, 15 ⅛ In.	1169.00
Tray, Round, Die Rolled Border, Engraved Moths, Scroll & Block Feet, c.1860, 1 x 8 ½ In.	5900.00

T

Trophy, Golf, Bowl Shape, Round, Tiffany & Co., 1907-38, 6 ½ In.	600.00
Tureen, Underplate, Gold Washed Interior, Elsa Peretti, 11 ½ & 16 In.	5400.00
Vase, Art Deco, Lined Sides, Flowers At Base, Trumpet Shape, Domed Foot, c.1950, 11 In.	1500.00
Vase, Oval Cartouches, Laurel & Bellflower Swags, Trumpet Shape, Banded Foot, 1912, 9 In.	430.00
Vase, Pierced Inverted Rim, Trumpet Shape, Lattice, Scrolls, Flowers, Domed Foot, 12 x 5 In.	1722.00
Vase, Trumpet Shaped, Spread Foot, Openwork, Wavy Rim, Glass Liner, c.1905, 10 x 5 In.	590.00
Water Jug, Chased, Repousse, Footed, c.1910, 8 ½ In.	4200.00
Yo-Yo, Plain Finish, Signed, 2 ⅓ In.	92.00

TIFFIN Glass Company of Tiffin, Ohio, was a subsidiary of the United States Glass Co. of Pittsburgh, Pennsylvania, in 1892. The U.S. Glass Co. went bankrupt in 1963, and the Tiffin plant employees purchased the building and the inventory. They continued running it from 1963 to 1966, when it was sold to Continental Can Company. In 1969, it was sold to Interpace, and in 1980, it was closed. The black satin glass, made from 1923 to 1926, and the stemware of the last twenty years are the best-known products.

Athens, Cocktail, Gold Band, c.1941, 4 ¾ In.	17.00
Butterfly & Daisy, Champagne, 4 ⅝ In.	45.00
Carla, Wine, Stem, 5 In.	12.00
Cerise, Ashtray, Octagonal, c.1940, 3 ¾ x 2 ¼ In.	30.00
Cerise, Goblet, 7 Oz., 7 ⅞ In.	10.00
Cherokee Rose, Plate, Dessert, 8 In.	10.00
Cherokee Rose, Shaker, Clear	45.00
Cherokee Rose, Sherbet, Stem, 4 ¼ In.	10.00
Flanders, Bowl, Console, 13 In.	35.00
Flanders, Plate, Dessert, 8 In.	8.00
Fuchsia, Bowl, Console, Flared, Scalloped Rim, 13 x 3 In.	54.00
Fuchsia, Vase, Trophy, Handles, Square Footed, 11 ⅜ In.	225.00
Jack Frost, Vase, Open Work, Bulbous, Footed, 8 In.	65.00
June Night, Bowl, Crimped, Beaded, 5 Points, 12 x 4 ¾ In.	100.00
June Night, Candlestick, 2-Light, 5 ¼ x 7 ½ In., Pair	110.00
June Night, Champagne, 6 ⅛ In.	23.00
June Night, Relish, 3 Sections, 12 x 10 In.	80.00
Killarney, Creamer, Green, Clear Handle & Foot, 5 ¼ In.	32.00
King's Crown, Bell, Ruby, 8 In.	35.00
King's Crown, Highball, Cranberry, 5 ½ In., 8 Piece	80.00
King's Crown, Sugar & Creamer, Cranberry	45.00
Minton, Cordial, Gold Band, 3 ⅞ In., 4 Piece	79.00
Minton, Plate, Dessert, Gold Rim, 7 In., 6 Piece	40.00
Rambler Rose, Bowl, Console, Undulating Rim, 4-Footed, 11 x 7 In.	30.00
Rambler Rose, Cocktail, Stem, 5 ¼ In., Pair	24.00
Rosalind, Decanter, Yellow, Footed, Stick Neck	375.00
Tile, Williamsburg, Console, 13 ¾ In.	50.00
Twilight, Vase, Teardrop, Wisteria Line, Turns Pink To Blue, 1950s-60s, 9 In.	160.00

TILES have been used in most countries of the world as a sturdy building material for floors, roofs, fireplace surrounds, and surface toppings. The cuerda seca (dry cord) technique of decoration uses a greasy pigment to separate different glaze colors during firing. In cuenca (raised line) decorated tiles, the design is impressed, leaving ridges that separate the glaze colors. Many of the American tiles are listed in this book under the factory name.

2 White Geese, Blue Sky, Harris Strong, England, 6 x 6 In.	52.00
Arkansas Traveler's Series, Squatter & Demijohn, Henry Mercer, 13 x 12 In., Pair	1067.00
Castle By The Sea, Mosaic, Herman Carl Mueller, Zanesville, Oh., Stamped, 1905, 13 x 10 ½ In. ..*Illus*	5312.00
Deer, Jumping, Branches, Cream, Wood Frame, 10 ¼ x 11 In.	52.00
Delft, Multicolor Enamel, Vase, Flowers, Grape Cluster, Holland, 1600s, 5 x 5 In., 2 Piece	132.00
Dog, Pointer Pose, Tree, Blue Sky, 9 x 9 In.	92.00
Elephant, Warrior, Multicolor, Chinese, 14 x 13 In.	119.00
Fish, Swirling Water, Squeeze Bag, Autumnal Glaze, Maw & Company, England, 6 In. ....*Illus*	115.00
Fountain, Blue, Brown Glaze, Impressed Design, Faience, Boston, 3 ½ In.	122.00
Gleaners, Wood Frame, Fake Sevres Mark, Early 1900s, 8 In. Square ....*Illus*	125.00
Grapes, 6 Varieties, Ground, Signed, Douriez Freres Macon Mai '56, Frame, 58 x 42 In., 35 Piece	690.00
Hen, On Eggs, Sgraffito, Glazed Ceramic, Sol Sant Vicens, Gilt Frame, Linen Liner, 7 ¾ x 7 ¾ In.	75.00
Persian, Woman, Cloak, Flowering Stems, Earthenware, Multicolor Enamel, 13 x 10 ½ In.	144.00
Pictorial, 2 Men, Period Clothing, 1 On Bull, Multicolor Enamel, Glazed, Metal Frame, 11 x 11 ⅜ In.	196.00
Pinecones, Needles, Branch, Green Matte, Turquoise, Brown, Oak Frame, Faience, 5 ⅞ x 7 ⅝ In.	920.00
Roof, Ceramic, Man Riding On Eagle, Multicolor, Acrylic Stand, K.Y. Lin, Chinese, 1900s, 13 x 14 In.	390.00
Roof, Figural, Guardian, Crouching, Sancai, Glazed, Chinese, Late 1800s, 12 x 9 In. ......*Illus*	598.00

Trash to Treasure
Pierced-tin wall shrines for saints were made from tin cans left behind by soldiers in New Mexico and nearby areas during the 1840s and 1850s.

Tile, Castle By The Sea, Mosaic, Herman Carl Mueller, Zanesville, Oh., Stamped, 1905, 13 x 10 ½ In.
$5,312.00

Rago Arts & Auction Center

Tile, Fish, Swirling Water, Squeeze Bag, Autumnal Glaze, Maw & Company, England, 6 In.
$115.00

Humler & Nolan

Tile, Gleaners, Wood Frame, Fake Sevres Mark, Early 1900s, 8 In. Square
$125.00

T

Tile, Roof, Figural, Guardian, Crouching, Sancai, Glazed, Chinese, Late 1800s, 12 x 9 In. $598.00

Neal Auction Co.

Tobacco Jar, Man With Top Hat, Terra-Cotta, Marked, 10 ½ In. $324.00

The Stein Auction Co.

Tobacco Jar, Munich Child, Sitting On Box, Drinking From Stein, Terra-Cotta, Jon Maresch $489.00

Fox Auctions

Roof, Fish, Asian, 8 ½ x 10 ¼ In., Pair	173.00
Scrolls, Stylized Leaves, Blue, Green, Orange, Mauve Outlines, Frame, Portugal, 11 ½ x 11 ½ In.	115.00
Stylized Shore Scene, Rocks, Green, White, Brown, Wayne Higby, 1990, 6 ¾ x 5 ½ In.	976.00
Underglaze Blue, Turquoise, White Enamel, Purple Outlines, Persia, 8 ½ x 8 ½ In.	253.00

TINWARE containers for household use have been made in America since the seventeenth century. The first tin utensils were brought from Europe, but by 1798, tin plate was imported and local tinsmiths made the wares. Painted tin is called tole and is listed separately. Some tin kitchen items may be found listed under Kitchen. The lithographed tin containers used to hold food and tobacco are listed in the Advertising category under Tin.

Box, Wriggle Work, Bird, Flower, Lid, Pa., 2 ½ x 8 In.	1094.00
Bread Basket, Elliptical, White Rim, Leaves & Berries, Crystalline Bottom, c.1800, 2 ¾ x 10 ¼ In.	415.00
Coffeepot, Conical Lid, Lighthouse Shape, Spout Perpendicular To Handle, Flowers, c.1800, 12 In.	720.00
Coffeepot, Hinged Lid, Brass Knop, Gooseneck Spout, Fruit Design, c.1800, 10 ½ In.	1126.00
Coffeepot, Stamped P.G. Mowrey, Pottstown, Pa., 19th Century, 9 ¼ In.	59.00
Coffeepot, Wriggle Work, Bird, Tulip, Pa., 1800s, 11 ½ In.	1541.00
Coffeepot, Wriggle Work, Hearts, Flowers, Pa., 1800s, 10 In.	533.00
Coffeepot, Wriggle Work, Potted Flowers, Vines, Pa., c.1850, 11 In.	2252.00
Foot Warmer, Embossed, Octagonal Body, Wood Treads, Lift Lid, Bail Handle, 6 x 11 In.	71.00
Horn, Coaching, Handle, c.1890, 56 In.	207.00
House, Squirrel's, 2-Part Steeple, Flag, Sliding Lid, Treadwheel, 24 x 18 In.	590.00
Mold, Candle, 24 Tube, Gallery Top, Applied Loop Handles, 10 x 20 In.	189.00
Mold, Candle, 24 Tube, Ribbed Base, Loop Handle, 10 ¼ x 9 ¾ In.	106.00
Mold, Candle, 36 Tube, Paint, Stencil, c.1840, 12 x 13 ½ In.	2300.00
Mold, Cheese, Heart Shape, Punched, Tapered, Folded Legs, 4 x 4 ½ x 4 ¼ In., Pair	325.00
Roof Ornament, Chucker Partridge, Paint, c.1950, 15 ½ In.	325.00
Sconce, 1-Light, Candle, Oval Pan, Crimped Edges, Reeded Support, c.1815, 16 ½ x 9 ½ In.	600.00
Sconce, 1-Light, Wall, Mirrored, Segments, Crimped Drip Pan, 1800s, 9 ¾ x 9 In.	504.00
Shaving Bowl, White Flower, Red Ground, Holding Ring, 11 x 5 ½ In.	92.00
Tray, Bird, Flower Decoupage, Blue, Ground, Shaped, Mahogany Stand, 27 x 29 In.	174.00
Tray, Bird, Flowers, Wreath, Salmon Ground, c.1890, 19 x 26 In.	182.00
Tray, Watermelon, Corn, Tomato, Pear, Black Ground, Yellow Pinstripe, c.1850, 28 x 20 In.	4977.00
Watering Can, Punched Heart Design, 14 In.	1007.00

TOBACCO CUTTERS *may be listed in either the Advertising or Store categories.*

TOBACCO JAR collectors search for those made in odd shapes and colors. Because tobacco needs special conditions of humidity and air, it has been stored in special containers since the eighteenth century.

Arab Head, Porcelain, Painted, c.1890, 5 In.	90.00
Band Of Animals, Pale Green, Cream, Bulbous, Lid, Spread Foot, Weller, Humidor, 6 In.	92.00
Bears, Smoking Pipe, Majolica, 6 ½ In.	177.00
Black Boy's Head, Smiling, Pink Shirt, Green Cap, Humidor, 9 In.	75.00
Black Man, Cargo Box, Top Hat, Composition, Lid, Habana Colorado, Humidor, 8 In.	380.00
Blackamoor Head Finial, Round, Beaded Moldings, Leaf Design, c.1790, 4 ⅛ In. Diam.	86.00
Boy, Black, Shining Shoe, Match Holder & Striker, 11 In.	149.00
Boy, On Chamber Pot, Multicolor, Lid, Terra-Cotta, Bernard Bloch, 9 In.	121.00
Brass, Impressed, Fish, Shells, 5 x 4 ⅞ In.	229.00
Chinaman Head, Rosy Cheeks, White Hat Lid, Austria, c.1900, 5 In.	150.00
Cigar Bundle, Terra-Cotta, c.1900, 4 ½ x 4 In.	229.00
Circus Drum, Bonzo, Pup, Germany, c.1930, 6 In.	350.00
Cloisonne, Birds, Butterflies, Silver Foil, 6 ⅛ In.	395.00
Cobalt Blue, Pegasus, Gilt, Crown Devon, 1950s, 5 ½ x 6 In.	50.00
Cut Glass, Sterling Lid, Paneled, France, c.1914, 8 In.	795.00
Devil Head, Multicolor, Terra-Cotta, Johann Maresch, 5 ¼ In.	322.00
Dog, Double Head, Black, White, Staffordshire, 6 x 4 In.	298.00
Fox On Hen House, Majolica, 6 ¼ x 6 ¼ x 4 In.	375.00
Gnome, Leaning On Apple, Multicolor, Terra-Cotta, Johann Maresch, 9 ½ In.	196.00
Jasperware, Pewter Rim & Top, Tobacco In Script, 4 ⅝ x 3 ¼ In.	250.00
Man With Top Hat, Terra-Cotta, Marked, 10 ½ In. ....*Illus*	324.00
Man, On Chest, Terra-Cotta, Wilhelm Schiller, 7 x 9 ½ In.	195.00
Man, Smoking Pipe, Bas Relief, Mocha, c.1850, 7 x 6 In.	275.00
Man's Head, Black, Cigar Hole In Mouth, Terra-Cotta, Signed Bernard Block, 3 ½ In.	208.00
Munich Child, Sitting On Box, Drinking From Stein, Terra-Cotta, Jon Maresch ....*Illus*	489.00
Relief, 5 Scenes, Erotic Figures, Bronze, Humidor, 10 In.	2400.00

T

Steel, Etched, Sawtooth, Lion Head, Goat Head Handle, Humidor, c.1930, 6 x 10 In.	25000.00
Stoneware, Taback, Man & Native Holding Sack, c.1870, 11 ½ In. ....*Illus*	1380.00

TOBY JUG is the name of a very special form of pitcher. It is shaped like the full figure of a man or woman. A pitcher that shows just the top half of a person is not correctly called a toby. More examples of toby jugs can be found under Royal Doulton and other factory names.

Man, Seated, Blue Hat & Coat, Signed Germany, c.1905, 8 In.	403.00
Man, Seated, Hat, Mug, England, 10 In.	177.00

TOLE is painted tin. It is sometimes called japanned ware, pontypool, or toleware. Most nineteenth-century tole is painted with an orange-red or black background and multicolored decorations. Many recent versions of toleware are made and sold. Related items may be listed in the Tinware category.

Bin, Grape Gathering, Canvas Shoulder Strap, Yellow Paint, France, c.1900, 34 x 17 ½ In., Pair ...	840.00
Box, Document, Black, Peaches, Strawberries, Apples, Spiral Ribbon Border, c.1830, 5 x 8 ¾ In.	633.00
Box, Document, Fruit, Leaves, Red Ground, Handle, Domed, 1800s, 5 x 8 ¾ In.	7110.00
Box, Dome Lid, Fruit, Stylized Leaves, Oval, c.1825, 5 ½ x 7 ¼ In.	1007.00
Box, Dome Lid, Painted, Pa., 1800s, 4 ½ x 8 In.	119.00
Box, Dome Lid, Wire Handle, White Band, Multicolor, Flowers, c.1825, 7 x 9 x 6 In.	830.00
Bread Tray, Red Ground, Green, Blue, Yellow, Black Flowers, Leaves, 19th Century, 8 x 13 In.	59.00
Cachepot, Flared Rim, Classical Figures, Red, Gilt Accents, Paw Feet, c.1820, 10 In., Pair	1380.00
Canister, Lid, Black, Armorial Crest, Gilt Border, England, 1800s, 18 In. ....*Illus*	240.00
Canister, Lid, Multicolor Fruit, Flowers, Black Ground, 1800s, 7 ½ x 7 ¾ In.	356.00
Canister, Warrior, Garden, Black, Gilt, England, 1800s, 14 In., Pair	2360.00
Cheese Trolley, Curved, Painted, Oval Reserves, Leaves, Square Base, 1900s, 4 ⅞ x 13 ½ In. ...	767.00
Coal Scuttle, Flowers, Black Ground, Painted, c.1875, 24 ½ x 12 x 11 In.	177.00
Coffeepot, Fruit, Black Ground, Painted, Pa., c.1850, 8 ½ In.	593.00
Coffeepot, Fruit, Painted, Pa., c.1850, 8 ¾ In.	207.00
Coffeepot, Green, Red, Yellow Flower, Black Ground, Tulip Lid, Pa., 8 In.	288.00
Coffeepot, Hinged, Gooseneck Spout, Leaves, Fruit, Lighthouse Shape, c.1875, 9 ¾ In.	2133.00
Coffeepot, Red, Gooseneck Spout, Multicolor Flowers, 1800s, 10 ½ In.	830.00
Coffeepot, Red, Green Flower, Black Ground, Pa., c.1845, 8 ½ In.	3081.00
Coffeepot, Red, Yellow Flowers, Black Ground, c.1820, 8 ½ In.	1185.00
Coffeepot, Red, Yellow Fruit, Black Ground, Side Spout, 7 ¾ In.	1422.00
Coffeepot, Sunburst, Red Ground, Painted, c.1865, 5 ¼ In.	1007.00
Dresser Box, Flowers, Yellow Ground, c.1850, 2 ½ x 6 ½ In.	267.00
Humidor, Figure Amidst Architecture, Flowers, Parrot, Casket Shape, c.1830, 8 x 9 In.	345.00
Jewelry Box, Sheraton Knob, Brass Paw Feet, Sarcophagus Shape, c.1815, 6 ½ x 11 In.	215.00
Mug, Red, Yellow Fruit, Black Ground, c.1850, 4 In.	1659.00
Syrup, Multicolor Fruit, Black Ground, 1800s, 4 In.	593.00
Teakettle, George III, Pontypool, Bouquets, Pink, Blue, Green, Mottled Red, c.1780, 11 In.	413.00
Tray, Apple, Red, Yellow, Tan, Brown Flowers, Leaves, 13 x 8 In.	71.00
Tray, Arched Fruit Design, Flower, Grape Border, Gilt, Beaded Trim, Round, Painted, 27 In.	345.00
Tray, Cloisonne, Asian Figures, Garden, Red Ground, Gilt Border, Accents, c.1820, 31 x 22 In.	575.00
Tray, George III, Battle Scene, Oak Leaf Border, Gilt Accents, 30 x 21 ¼ In.	1150.00
Tray, Multicolor Flowers, Crystalline Center, Black Ground, Octagonal, Pa., 1800s, 8 ⅝ x 12 ½ In.	326.00
Tray, Painted Courting Scene, Canted Corners, France, 1800s, 22 x 32 ½ In.	889.00
Tray, Painted Scene, Death Of Lord Nelson At Battle Of Trafalgar, Oval, 1800s, 30 In.	649.00
Tray, Painted, Bottle, Glass, Cigarette, Geometric Diamond Pattern, Rounded, 2-Sided, 21 ½ x 28 In..	230.00
Tray, Pastoral Scene, Seaside, Oval Gallery, Georgian, c.1790, 30 x 22 ½ In. ....*Illus*	956.00
Tray, Red Gilt, Bamboo Stand, Octagonal, Stretcher Finial, 22 x 22 In.	531.00
Tray, Red, Yellow, Green Fruit, Flowers, Black Ground, Crystalline Center, c.1860, 12 ¾ x 8 In..	3081.00
Tray, Regency, Architectural Ruins, Mustard Color, Oval, Cutout Handles, 29 x 22 In.	633.00
Tray, Ship, Boats, Portrait, Lighthouse Painted, Oval, Marked, 23 x 27 In.	604.00
Tray, Stand, Painted Flower Sprays, Shaped Oval, Victorian, 20 x 31 In.	550.00
Tray, Vermilion Ground, Classical Scene In Cartouche, Leafy Bands, Pierced Handles, 20 In...	854.00
Tray, Yellow Flowers, Red Ground, Pa., c.1820, 2 ½ x 12 ¾ In.	1422.00
Urn, Lid, Regency, Asian Scenic Design, Lion's Head & Ring Handles, Oval Base, 12 In., Pair ..	1093.00
Urn, Lid, Spire Finial, Ring Handles, Lion Mask, U-Shaped, 1800s, 12 In., Pair	300.00

TOM MIX was born in 1880 and died in 1940. He was the hero of over 100 silent movies from 1910 to 1929, and 25 sound films from 1929 to 1935. There was a Ralston Tom Mix radio show from 1933 to 1950, but the original Tom Mix was not in the show. Tom Mix comics were published from 1942 to 1953.

Badge, Prototype, Blue Checkerboard Ralston Logo, Wrangler	345.00

Tobacco Jar, Stoneware, Taback, Man & Native Holding Sack, c.1870, 11 ½ In. $1,380.00

Glass Works Auctions

Tole, Canister, Lid, Black, Armorial Crest, Gilt Border, England, 1800s, 18 In. $240.00

DuMouchelles Art Gallery

Tole, Tray, Pastoral Scene, Seaside, Oval Gallery, Georgian, c.1790, 30 x 22 ½ In. $956.00

Neal Auction Co.

The edited listings of the current prices in this *Kovels' Antiques & Collectibles Price Guide* aren't available on any website. Readers can visit **Kovels.com** to check thousands of past prices and sign up for free information on trends, tips, reproductions, marks, and more.

Tool, Safe, Bank, Cannonball, Steel, Time Lock, Pay Safe, Mosler Safe Co., Oh., 1917, 53 x 27 In.
$3,240.00

Cowan's Auctions

Tool, Bench, Cobbler's, Pine, Leather Upholstery, Drawer, Dividers, 1800s, 47 ½ x 24 In.
$236.00

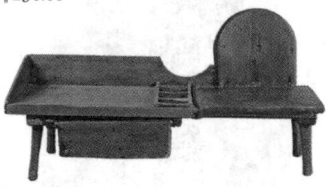

Brunk Auctions

Tool, Dibble, Seed Planting, Blue Paint, Wood, 1800s, 14 x 6 ¼ In.
$711.00

Skinner, Inc.

Badge, Straight Shooters Of America, No. 6540, 2 In.	65.00
Book, In The Range War, Big Little Books, No. 1166, 1937	25.00
Game, Tom Mix In Texas, Board, Box, 15 ¼ x 10 ¾ In.	60.00
Gun, Revolving Cylinder, Wood, Cardboard Covered Handles, 1936, 8 In.	190.00
Patch, Logo, Cloth, Red, White, Blue, 2 x 2 In.	49.00
Postcard, Tom Mix In Timberline, On Horse	15.00
Poster, Circus & Wild West, Frame, 38 ½ x 26 ½ In.	120.00 to 180.00
Poster, Sells Floto Presents Tom Mix, Movie Star On Horseback, c.1930, 40 x 27 In.	600.00
Ring, Stamped Brass, Crossed Guns, Cereal Premium, 1946, Kids Size 2	68.00
Songbook, Western Songs, Soft Cover, 64 Page, M.M. Cole Publishing, 1935, 9 x 11 In.	39.00
Telescope, Ralston Straight Shooters, Decal, 1937, 4 In.	149.00

TOOLS of all sorts are listed here, but most are related to industry. Other tools may be found listed under Iron, Kitchen, Tinware, and Wooden.

Anvil, Coach Maker's, Marked, Kirkstall Forge, 11 ½ x 22 In.	590.00
Ax, Hewing, 3 Forge Lines, Wooden Handle, Oval Mark, France, 19 x 13 ½ In.	295.00
Ax, Ship Building, Placed Oakum Rope Between Boards, Mounted, c.1910	58.00
Bench, Cobbler's, Pine, Leather Upholstery, Drawer, Dividers, 1800s, 47 ½ x 24 In. *...Illus*	236.00
Bench, Harness Maker's, Wood, Leather Strap, Pa., c.1840, 42 In.	59.00
Book Press, Mahogany, Vertical Supports, Threaded Screw, Handled Bolt, 21 In.	354.00
Box, Bird's-Eye Maple, Star Inlay, Lid, Swinging Iron Handles, c.1890, 19 x 21 In.	403.00
Carrier, Carpenter's, Drawer, Knob, Lock, Heart Handle, Green Paint, c.1890, 22 x 11 ½ In.	115.00
Carrying Tray, Wood, Raised Center Board, Oblong Hand Hole, Painted Blue, 28 x 12 In.	71.00
Cheese Press, Weighted Arm, Screw, Iron, 1800s, 67 x 26 In.	360.00
Chest, Threading Device, Oak, Hinged Lid, c.1900	69.00
Corn Sheller, Cast Iron, Gaisser's Red Chief, Brinly-Hardy Co., Louisville, Ky., 1899, 15 In.	83.00
Cranberry Scoop, Wood, Black Paint, Metal Bottom, P.L. Buchingham Mfg., Ma., 22 x 20 In.	354.00
Cranberry Scoop, Wood, Cape Cod, 1800s, 20 x 20 ½ In.	325.00
Dibble, Seed Planting, Blue Paint, Wood, 1800s, 14 x 6 ¼ In. *...Illus*	711.00
Disc Harrow, 4 Rows Of 9 Discs, Brass Frame, Saddle Seat, Lever, 6 x 14 In.	5175.00
Drill, Barn Beam, Wood, Cast Iron, c.1870, 26 x 30 In.	176.00
Easel, Artist's, Oak, Quartered, Painter's Box, Brass Label, c.1900, 87 In.	531.00
Feather Curling Device, Metal, Wood Handle, Ruffled Edge, c.1900, 4 x 11 In.	101.00
Grain Probe Moisture Tester, Brass, Tube Inside A Tube, 8 Windows, Dean Garnet Mfg., 49 In.	59.00
Grain Separator, Wooden, Hand Crank, Paddle Mechanism, Mesh Screen, Drawer, 13 x 16 ½ In.	1840.00
Grinding Station, Brass, Wood Base, 3 Tiers, Flywheels, Grinding Wheel, Copper Flash, 13 x 6 ½ In.	1265.00
Hand Truck, Oak, Red Paint, England, c.1850, 40 In.	59.00
Hat Sizer, Milliner's, Head Size Marking Cards, Bumper Feet, Marked Allie Maillard, 6 x 12 ¾ In.	384.00
Hatchel, Wood, Painted Cover, Initial HS, Pa., 1804, 8 ¾ x 17 In.	4266.00
Hatchet, Camp, Retractable Cover, Marble's, Gladstone, Mich., 1898, 10 x 4 ½ In.	185.00
Hay Baler, Metal, Electric, Conveyor Belt, Incline, Chute, Wheeled Base, 66 x 11 In.	2588.00
Hay Loader, Wood, Spoke Wheels, Gear Mechanism, 26 ½ x 18 In.	5750.00
Hay Press, Eli, No. 10, Salesman's Sample	10200.00
Hay Press, Wood, Nickel, 4 Spoked Wheels, Spring Loaded Mechanism, Chute, Case, 19 ½ x 4 ½ In.	3750.00
Hay Rake, Wiard Plow Co., Wooden, 2 Spoked Wheels, Seat, Curved Tines, Foot Pedals, 13 x 6 ½ In.	4543.00
Hook, Meat, Hanging, Galvanized Metal, c.1930, 56 x 25 In., Pair	300.00
Horse Model, Saddle & Harness Maker's, Horsehair, Wood, Plaster, Iron, c.1890, 80 x 94 In. *...Illus*	8813.00
Ice Shaver, Iron, Quarter Round Bin, Plunger, Crank, G.C. Glawson's Snow King, 21 x 22 In.	177.00
Lamp, Surveyor's, Metal, Tripod, Warren Knight Company Phila., c.1940, 71 x 6 In.	450.00
Lawnmower, Cast Iron, Wood Handle, Salesman's Sample, 15 x 6 In. *...Illus*	144.00
Learning, Child's, Wall Mount, Oak, Rolling Paper Charts, Compartments, 20 x 20 ½ In.	41.00
Mold, Spoon, Bronze, For Making Pewter, Cast, Trifid Handle Terminal, Rattail Bowl, 8 ¾ In.	118.00
Mortise Scribe, No. 77, Rosewood, 2 Brass Adjusting Thumb Screws, Stanley, 1900s, 7 ½ In.	70.00
Nail Bin, Round, 8 Sections, Square Rotating Stand, Union Foundry & Mfg. Co., 1800s, 19 ½ x 4 In.	633.00
Ox Yoke, Double, Hand Hewed Wood, 56 x 29 x 8 In. *...Illus*	540.00
Pipe Tongs, Wrought Iron, 1699, 17 ¼ In.	1003.00
Planter, Lister, Cast Iron, Wood, Steel, Front Traction Wheel, Hopper, Marked Boston, 21 x 16 In.	1955.00
Plow, Forged Steel, Curved Wood Handles, Red & Black, Marked, J.F. Hime, 1873, 36 x 17 In.	2588.00
Plow, Mackerel, Fish Shape, Woman's Leg, Boot, Compass Handle, Maine, 8 & 7 ¾ In., 2 Piece	805.00
Plow, Riding Spoke Wheels, Cast Iron Frame, Pierced Seat, Steel Blade, 2 Levers, 10 ½ x 15 ½ In.	575.00
Plow, Steel, Spoked Wheels, Spring Loaded Lever, 21 In.	4025.00
Press, Baseball, Maple, c.1900, 18 In.	563.00
Press, Wood, Carved, Elephant Base, T-Handle, 13 ½ x 11 In.	173.00
Printing Press, Offset, Painted Black, Gold Lettering, Wood Base, Iron, Kelsey & Co., 1873, 5 x 9 In.	71.00
Roller, Tennis Court, Carved Limestone, Wrought Iron Handle, c.1890, 38 ½ In.	210.00
Rule, Ivory, 4-Fold, J. Gleave & Son, England, 19th Century, 24 In.	132.00

Rule, No. 58, 6-Fold, c.1900	650.00
Safe, Bank, Cannonball, Steel, Time Lock, Pay Safe, Mosler Safe Co., Oh., 1917, 53 x 27 In... *Illus*	3240.00
Sawhorse, Wood, Salesman's Sample, 4 ¾ x 8 In.	138.00
Scribe, Mortise, Stanley, No. 77, Rosewood, 3 Scribing Points, Early 1900s, 7 ½ In.	70.00
Seeder, E.A. Havens, Nickel Plated, Spoked Wheels, Seat, Wood Hopper, 6 Curved Blades, 11 x 18 In...	7475.00
Shovel, Grain, Wood, Painted Winter Landscape, c.1900, 36 In.	147.00
Thread Plug Gauge Set, Pratt & Whitney, ½ To ¹⁄₆₄ In., 5 x 7 x 6 In.	46.00
Tobacco Tongs, Spring Action, Tapered Tamper, Penny Terminals, Iron, 17 ½ In.	531.00
Tool Chest, Lid, Carpenter's, Parquetry, Exotic Woods, Stylized Zigzag, Flag, Stars, 23 x 39 In.	230.00
Tray, Walnut, Dovetailed, Shaped Board Divider, Applied Turned Handle, 8 ½ x 35 In.	325.00
Trencher, Wood, Hole Inside, 5 x 17 ¼ In.	295.00
Wagon Jack, Conestoga, Oak, Iron, Initials, Peter Brunner, Lancaster County, Pa., 1829, 20 In. *Illus*	331.00
Wagon Jack, Conestoga, Oak, Wrought Iron, Casper Brunner Initials, Lancaster County, 1850, 20 In.	235.00
Wagon Jack, Conestoga, Wood Metal, 1822	213.00
Wagon Jack, Oak, Iron, 1831, 25 ¼ In.	148.00
Wheat Cleaner, Wood, Sifter, Hand Crank, Wire Mesh Bed, Case, 17 x 19 In.	863.00
Wheel, Cog, Oak, Pine, Central Axle, c.1900, 6 x 77 In.	150.00
Wheelbarrow, Wood, Iron Mounts, 24 x 29 In.	410.00
Wick Trimmer, Wrought Iron, Maryland, c.1780, 6 ¾ In.	144.00
Wrench, Double Ended, Aluminum, Kenosha Transport & Tre-Clover, c.1970, 14 In.	55.00
Wrench, Fingertip, RCA, For Hard To Reach Nuts On TV, 1950s, 2 x 5 In., Set Of 5	45.00

TOOTHBRUSH HOLDERS were part of every bowl and pitcher set in the late nineteenth century. Most were oblong covered dishes. About 1920, manufacturers started to make children's toothbrush holders shaped like animals or cartoon characters. A few modern toothbrush holders are still being made.

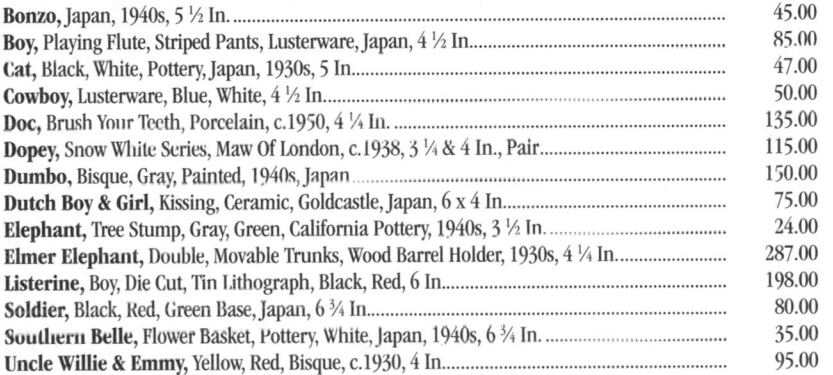

Bonzo, Japan, 1940s, 5 ½ In.	45.00
Boy, Playing Flute, Striped Pants, Lusterware, Japan, 4 ½ In.	85.00
Cat, Black, White, Pottery, Japan, 1930s, 5 In.	47.00
Cowboy, Lusterware, Blue, White, 4 ½ In.	50.00
Doc, Brush Your Teeth, Porcelain, c.1950, 4 ¼ In.	135.00
Dopey, Snow White Series, Maw Of London, c.1938, 3 ¼ & 4 In., Pair	115.00
Dumbo, Bisque, Gray, Painted, 1940s, Japan	150.00
Dutch Boy & Girl, Kissing, Ceramic, Goldcastle, Japan, 6 x 4 In.	75.00
Elephant, Tree Stump, Gray, Green, California Pottery, 1940s, 3 ½ In.	24.00
Elmer Elephant, Double, Movable Trunks, Wood Barrel Holder, 1930s, 4 ¼ In.	287.00
Listerine, Boy, Die Cut, Tin Lithograph, Black, Red, 6 In.	198.00
Soldier, Black, Red, Green Base, Japan, 6 ¾ In.	80.00
Southern Belle, Flower Basket, Pottery, White, Japan, 1940s, 6 ¾ In.	35.00
Uncle Willie & Emmy, Yellow, Red, Bisque, c.1930, 4 In.	95.00

TOOTHPICK HOLDERS are sometimes called *toothpicks* by collectors. The variously shaped containers used to hold small wooden toothpicks are made of glass, china, or metal. Most of the toothpick holders are made of Victorian pressed glass. Additional items may be found in other categories, such as Bisque, Silver Plate, Slag Glass, etc.

Azalea, 6-Sided, Pedestal Base	61.00
Baby Bird, Nest, Clear, Wright Glass Co., 2 In.	32.00
Baker, Orange & Red Shirt, Tie, Apron, Goldcastle, Japan, 5 In.	65.00
Custard, Blue Roses, Scalloped Rim, Fenton, 2 ½ In.	25.00
Cut Glass, Amethyst, c.1960, 4 In.	15.00
Diamond Sheephead, Green Opalescent Glass	45.00
Gaelic, Stained Flowers, Glass	35.00
Glass, Heart Shape, Ball Border, Footed, Green, Boyd Glass Co., 2 ¼ In.	26.00
Glass, Inverted Fan & Feather, Red, 4-Footed, Northwood, 2 ½ In.	13.00
Hawaiian Lei, Clear	25.00
Hobstar, Marigold, Octagonal, Imperial Glass, 2 ½ In.	22.00
Iris With Meander, Green, Gold, Glass	15.00
Jefferson Iris, Meander, Blue, Glass	45.00
Jefferson Iris, Meander, Wine, Glass	45.00
Kentucky, Emerald Green, Glass	35.00
Kings Royal, Ruby Stain, Glass	15.00
Minnesota, Green, Glass	65.00
Murano, Latticinio Ribbons, Multicolor, Ruffled Rim, 2 In.	150.00
Ohio Star, Glass	10.00
Paddlewheel, Gold	25.00

Tool, Horse Model, Saddle & Harness Maker's, Horsehair, Wood, Plaster, Iron, c.1890, 80 x 94 In.
$8,813.00

Garth's Auctioneers & Appraisers

Tool, Lawnmower, Cast Iron, Wood Handle, Salesman's Sample, 15 x 6 In.
$144.00

Victorian Casino Antiques

Tool, Ox Yoke, Double, Hand Hewed Wood, 56 x 29 x 8 In.
$540.00

Showtime Auction Services

Early Construction Tools
Early construction tools include axes, adzes, saws, planes, chisels, drills, turning tools, hammers, vises, wrenches, screwdrivers, rules, and much more. Some nineteenth- and twentieth-century tools can be dated by the marks, usually the name of the company or person who made them.

T

Tool, Wagon Jack, Conestoga, Oak, Iron, Initials, Peter Brunner, Lancaster County, Pa., 1829, 20 In. **$331.00**

Garth's Auctioneers & Appraisers

Tortoiseshell, Box, Writing, Lid, Inlays, Silk, Divided, Drawer With Pen Tray, Ink Bottles, c.1850, 13 x 9 In. **$7,285.00**

Garth's Auctioneers & Appraisers

Tortoiseshell, Brushpot, Reticulated, 4 x 3 ⅛ In. **$600.00**

DuMouchelles Art Gallery

Tortoiseshell, Humidor, Hinged Lid, Brass, Painted Metal Interior, 6 Compartments, Paw Feet, 12 x 8 ⅝ In. **$8,400.00**

Skinner, Inc.

Porcelain, Bird, Flowers, Gilt Handles, c.1900, 3 In.	35.00
Porcelain, Cobalt, Topeka, Kansas, c.1905, 2 ¼ In.	38.00
Prize, Ruby Stained	75.00
Punty & Diamond Point, Glass	165.00
Roman Figure Head, White Slag Glass, 2 ½ In.	28.00
Saddle, Over Barrel, Ruby	120.00
Silver Plate, Cat, Tilting Barrel, c.1875, 3 x 4 In.	215.00
Silver, Farm Boy, Sheaf Of Wheat, c.1885	150.00
Texas Star, Glass	24.00
Umbrella Shape, Silver Plate, 4 ½ In.	39.00

TORQUAY is the name given to ceramics by several potteries working near Torquay, England, from 1870 until 1962. Until about 1900, the potteries used local red clay to make classical-style art pottery vases and figurines. Then they turned to making souvenir wares. Items were dipped in colored slip and decorated with painted slip and sgraffito designs. They often had mottoes or proverbs, and scenes of cottages, ships, birds, or flowers. The Scandy design was a symmetrical arrangement of brushstrokes and spots done in colored slips. Potteries included Watcombe Pottery (1870–1962), Torquay Terra-Cotta Company (1875–1905), Aller Vale (1881–1924), Torquay Pottery (1908–1940), and Longpark (1883–1957). **TORQUAY**

Inkwell, Us Be Always Glad Tu Yer Frum E, Scandy, 2 ½ In.	56.00
Vase, Wildflowers, 4 Necks, Dark Green, c.1925, 3 ⅝ In.	70.00

TORTOISESHELL is the shell of the tortoise. It has been used as inlay and to make small decorative objects since the seventeenth century. Some species of tortoise are now on the endangered species list, and old or new objects made from these shells cannot be sold legally.

Box, Blond, Silver, Flower, Urn, Flower Head Ground, France, c.1800, 3 In.	502.00
Box, Carved, Figures In Palace Garden, Chinese, 1800s, 3 ¼ In.	2214.00
Box, Dome Lid, Oval, 1 ½ x 3 ½ In.	210.00
Box, Edwardian, Ivory Lined, Turned Ivory Feet, c.1900, 1 ½ x 5 In.	615.00
Box, Ivory Inlays, Shaped Sides, Lid, Ball Feet, c.1860, 3 ¾ x 5 In.	826.00
Box, Silver Mounted, Inscribed Lid Plaque, Hinged, Engraved, 1750, 3 x 8 In.	6136.00
Box, Writing, Lid, Inlays, Silk, Divided, Drawer With Pen Tray, Ink Bottles, c.1850, 13 x 9 In. ... *Illus*	7285.00
Brushpot, Hexagonal, Phoenix, Clouds, Marked, Chinese, 1800s, 5 ⅛ In.	582.00
Brushpot, Reticulated, 4 x 3 ⅛ In. *Illus*	600.00
Card Case, Ivory, Silver Mounts, Victorian, 4 x 2 ¾ In.	120.00
Cigar Case, Church Spires, Rose Windows, c.1850, 5 ¼ In.	717.00
Etui, Dark Brown, Silver Pique, c.1800	695.00
Fan, Figures, Landscape, c.1875, 7 x 13 In.	2572.00
Humidor, Hinged Lid, Brass, Painted Metal Interior, 6 Compartments, Paw Feet, 12 x 8 ⅝ In. .. *Illus*	8400.00
Jewelry Casket, Ivory, Octagonal, Filigree, Fretwork, Flower Borders, Footed, 6 x 12 In.	4715.00
Plaque, 2 Dragons, Flaming Pearl, Carved, Chinese, c.1900, 3 ⅛ In.	474.00
Screen, Cranes, Clouds, Lotus Openwork Wood Frame, Chinese, 1800s, 14 ¼ In.	563.00
Tea Box, 2 Lids, Foil Lined Compartments, Brass Feet, England, 1800s, 6 ½ In. *Illus*	1770.00
Trinket Box, Georgian, Mirror, Drawer, Brass Ball & Claw Feet, Hinged Lid, 6 x 10 ½ In.	1380.00

TORTOISESHELL GLASS was made during the 1800s and after by the Sandwich Glass Works of Massachusetts and some firms in Germany. Tortoiseshell glass is, of course, named for its resemblance to real shell from a tortoise. It has been reproduced.

Bowl, Ground Pontil, England, c.1900, 9 x 4 ¾ In.	180.00
Decanter, Bell Shape, Flared Rim, 9 ¾ In.	104.00
Ewer, Bulbous, Ruffled Rim, 1950s, 8 In.	50.00
Figurine, Turtle, Murano, 9 x 4 In.	195.00
Perfume Bottle, Squat, Dabber, 5 x 4 ¼ In.	28.00
Urn, Shouldered, 10 In.	200.00
Vase, Flared Oval Top, c.1900, 8 In.	178.00
Vase, Mottled, Applied Amber Accents, 4 In. *Illus*	58.00

TOY collectors have special clubs, magazines, and shows. Toys are designed to entice children, and today they have attracted new interest among adults who are still children at heart. All types of toys are collected. Tin toys, iron toys, battery-operated toys, and many others are collected by specialists. Dolls, Games, Teddy Bears, and Bicycles are listed in their own categories. Other toys may be found under company or celebrity names.

Action Figure, Bionic Woman, Blue Eyes, Posable, Track Suit, Sneakers, Kennar, 1976, 12 In.	115.00
Action Figure, Spider-Man, Posable, Circle Suit, Box, 1972, 8 In.	513.00

T

Action Figure, Wonder Woman, Super Queens, Box, Ideal, 1967, 6 x 15 In.	4164.00	
Adam 689, Delivery Man, Red Cap, Blue Smock, Red, Pants, Handcart, Tin Litho, c.1910, 8 x 5 In.	538.00	
Airplane, America, Tri-Motor, Cast Iron, Gray, Stars, Red Trim, Pilot, Hubley, 14 In.	1495.00	
Airplane, Army, Mounted Machine Guns, Friction, Tin Lithograph, Sanitoy, Japan, 1950s, 6 x 7 In.	158.00	
Airplane, B-24 Recognition Spotter, Cruver, Marked US July '42 British Liberator, 18 x 11 In.	121.00	
Airplane, Biplane, Wire Frame Body, Propeller, Seated Pilot, Clockwork, Germany, 7-In. Wingspan	1062.00	
Airplane, Biplanes, Airships, Revolving Structure, Tin, Banners, Flag, Germany, c.1910, 16 In.	3920.00	
Airplane, Dagwood In Cockpit, Solo Flight, Tin Litho, Windup, Marx, c.1941, 8 ½ x 11 In.	547.00	*Illus*
Airplane, Dornier Do-X, Iron, 6 Engine, Rubber Tire, Hubley, 3-In. Wingspan	201.00	*Illus*
Airplane, Flying Fortress, Machine Guns, Tin Litho Red, Yellow, Windup, Box, Marx, 1941, 13 x 18 In.	443.00	
Airplane, Fokker, Cast Iron, Green, Orange, Vindex, 5 ¼ In.	6900.00	
Airplane, Ikarus, Paper Wings, Tin Lithograph, Clockwork, Lehmann, 14 In.	1452.00	
Airplane, Lucky Boy, Highwing, Blue, Silver Paint, Cast Iron, 4-In. Wingspan	212.00	
Airplane, Monocoupe, Iron, Black Fuselage, Orange Pressed Steel Wings, Arcade, 9 In.	748.00	
Airplane, Monocoupe, Tin, Nickel Plated, Black & Orange Paint, Arcade, 8 ½ In.	403.00	
Airplane, Pressed Steel, Green, Orange & Red Paint, Turner, Dayton, 1920s, 22 In.	353.00	
Airplane, Seagull, Amphibian, Nickel Motor, Embossed, Iron, Kilgore, c.1930, 8 ½ In.	708.00	*Illus*
Airplane, Seaplane, Seagull, Cast Iron, Red, Green Wings, Kilgore, 4 ¼ In.	748.00	
Airplane, Seaplane, Top-Mount Props, Pontoons, Clockwork, Bing, 16-In. Wingspan	2070.00	*Illus*
Airplane, Tri Motor, White, Black Paint, Marklin, 22 In.	420.00	
Airplane, UX166, Stars, Circles, White Rubber Tires, Green Paint, Cast Iron, Hubley, 6 In.	390.00	
Airship, Tin Lithograph, Yellow, Blue, Spectators, Penny Toy, Ges Gesch, Germany, 4 ½ In.	336.00	
Ali & The Flying Carpet, Tin Lithograph, Windup, 5 In.	130.00	
Ambulance, Hausser, Red, Brown Paint, Tin, Clockwork, 11 ½ In.	1140.00	
Ambulance, Horse Drawn, Red Cross, Van Body, Iron, Nickel Plated, Kenton, 1905, 15 In.	1495.00	
Ambulance, Horse Drawn, Soldier Driver, Flag, Wheeled Platform, Tin, Lionel, 10 In.	300.00	
Ambulance, Iron, Nickel Plated, Embossed Sides, Spoke Wheels, Kenton, c.1915, 7 In.	518.00	
Ambulance, Tin, Painted, White, Red, Tonka, 5 In.	16.00	
Ambulance, Yellow Paint, Pressed Steel, Keystone Packard, 28 In.	840.00	
Amos, Windup, Rocking Walking Motion, Tin Litho, Built-In Key, Marx, 1930, 11 ½ In.	334.00	
Astroman, Green, Red, Plastic, Battery Operated, Dux, West Germany, Box, 12 In.	570.00	
Astronaut, Cragstan, Tin Lithograph, Windup, Yonezawa, 10 In.	295.00	
Astronaut, Red, Silver, Tin Lithograph, Battery Operated, Daiya, Japan, Box, 10 ½ In.	3000.00	
Attache Case, Secret Agent 007, James Bond, Black Plastic Case, Accessories, 1965, 11 x 17 In.	288.00	
Baby, In High Chair, Tin Lithograph, Penny Toy, Fischer, Germany, 2 ½ In.	173.00	
Badge, Captain America, Die Cut Shield Shape, Sentinels Of Liberty, Brass Finish, 1941, 1 ½ In.	316.00	
Badge, Junior Fire Fighter Club, Brass Luster, Eagle Crest, 1930s, 1 ⅝ In.	75.00	
Badge, Junior Pilot, Western Air Lines, Wings, Metal, 2 ⅛ In.	49.00	
Banjo Player, Black, Seated, Movable Head, Arms, Paint, Tin, Windup, Germany, 6 ¾ In.	1020.00	
Barnacle Bill, Punching Bag, Tin Figure Punches Celluloid Bag, Lithograph, Chein, 7 In.	690.00	
Barnacle Bill, Walker, Tin, J. Chein, 1930s, 6 ¼ In.	193.00	
Barney Google & Sparkplug, Wood, Jointed, Cloth Blanket, Schoenhut, 8 In.	518.00	
Barney Google Riding Sparkplug, Tin Lithograph, Clockwork, Fischer, Germany, 7 In.	633.00	
Bath, Doll's, Happy Time, Yellow Vinyl, Folding, Sears, Roebuck & Co., 1950s, 32 x 21 In.	65.00	
Bears are also listed in the Teddy Bears category.		
Bear, Bobby Drinking, Cola Bottle, Tin Litho, Drinks, Walks, Opens Mouth, Eyes Light, Battery, 10 In.	230.00	
Bear, Polar, Drinks, Fur, Papier-Mache, Metal Bottle, Clockwork, Switch, Decamps, 13 In.	1150.00	
Bear, Polar, Wood, Jointed, Glass Eyes, Leather Ears, Schoenhut, 8 In.	726.00	
Bed, Doll's, English Style, Formed Hood, Carved Headboard & Footboard, Casters, 11 x 21 In.	173.00	
Bed, Doll's, Four-Poster, Columns, Canopy, Drapes, Bedding, c.1830, 37 x 33 x 21 In.	805.00	*Illus*
Betty Shako, Walker, Windup, Tin, Lindstrom, 1930s	295.00	
Bicycles that are large enough to ride are listed in the Bicycle category.		
Binoculars, Secret Sam Bomb, Plastic, Shoots Bomb, Topper Toys, Box, 1960s, 7 ¾ In.	85.00	
Bird, Pine, Yellow, Brown Paint, c.1850, 8 ½ In.	59.00	
Bird, String, Lithograph Paper Wings, Painted, Tin, Lehmann, 7 In.	666.00	
Bison, Jointed, Cloth Mane, Leather Ears, Rope Tail, Schoenhut, 8 In.	431.00	
Blimp, Los Angeles, Iron, Yellow Paint, Nickel Plated Wheels, Kenton, 7 ½ In.	201.00	
Blinky Clown, Eyes Light Up, Walks, Plays Xylophone, Battery Operated, Amico, Japan, 1950s, 10 In.	455.00	
Blocks, ABC, Pictures, Hollow, Rattle, Lithographed, 20 Blocks, Box, c.1890, 15 x 14 In.	224.00	*Illus*
Blushing Willy, Pours Drink, Rolls Eyes, Light-Up, Battery Operated, Yonezawa, Box, 1960s, 10 ½ In.	125.00	
Boat, Battleship, 2 Cage Masts, 2 Funnels, 4 Lifeboats, Gray, Brown Paint, Bing, c.1914, 19 In.	577.00	
Boat, Battleship, Blue, 3 Funnels, Tin Lithograph, Penny Toy, Fischer, Germany, 4 In.	668.00	
Boat, Battleship, Cast Iron, Single Mast, Turret On Deck, Wheels, 6 ¼ In.	546.00	
Boat, Battleship, Gun Turrets, Crow's Nest, Clockwork, Fleischmann, Germany, Box, c.1936, 8 In.	1035.00	
Boat, Battleship, Guns, Funnels, Paint, Tin, Putt Putt Engine, Sutcliff, England, Box, 1930s, 12 In.	851.00	
Boat, Battleship, St. Vincent, Red, Tin Lithograph, Lehmann, Germany, Box, 13 ½ In.	1448.00	

Tortoiseshell, Tea Box, 2 Lids, Foil Lined Compartments, Brass Feet, England, 1800s, 6 ½ In.
$1,770.00

Brunk Auctions

Tortoiseshell Glass, Vase, Mottled, Applied Amber Accents, 4 In.
$58.00

Early Auction Co.

Toy, Airplane, Dagwood In Cockpit, Solo Flight, Tin Litho, Windup, Marx, c.1941, 8 ½ x 11 In.
$547.00

Hake's Americana & Collectibles

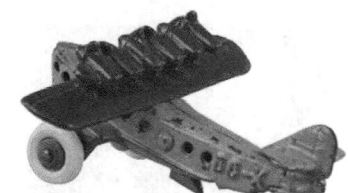

Toy, Airplane, Dornier Do-X, Iron, 6 Engine, Rubber Tire, Hubley, 3-In. Wingspan
$201.00

Bertoia Auctions

Toy, Airplane, Seagull, Amphibian, Nickel Motor, Embossed, Iron, Kilgore, c.1930, 8 ½ In.
$708.00

Bertoia Auctions

Toy, Airplane, Seaplane, Top-Mount Props, Pontoons, Clockwork, Bing, 16-In. Wingspan
$2,070.00

Bertoia Auctions

Toy, Bed, Doll's, Four-Poster, Columns, Canopy, Drapes, Bedding, c.1830, 37 x 33 x 21 In.
$805.00

James D. Julia Auctioneers

Toy, Blocks, ABC, Pictures, Hollow, Rattle, Lithographed, 20 Blocks, Box, c.1890, 15 x 14 In.
$224.00

Theriault's

Boat, Battleship, Wilmington, Funnel, Paint, Putt Putt Engine, Tin, Marklin, c.1915, 9 In.	5468.00
Boat, Cruiser, Iowa, Original Crew, Mast, 2 Decks, Funnels, Red, Gray, Clockwork, Marklin, 20 In.	54675.00
Boat, Cruiser, Red, Cream, Side Guns, 2 Funnels, Tin Lithograph, Windup, Orobr, Germany, 11 In.	920.00
Boat, Destroyer, Gun Turrets & Stations, Bridge, Tin Litho, Fleischmann, Germany, 1950s, 15 In. *Illus*	1380.00
Boat, Destroyer, K-55, Tin Lithograph, Friction, Box, Japan, 8 ½ In.	71.00
Boat, Ferry, Flywheel Friction, Lifeboats, Smokestacks, Pressed Steel, c.1900, 8 x 13 In.	178.00
Boat, Ferry, Paddlewheel, Union, Removable Stack, Key, Bing, Germany, 12 In. *Illus*	2070.00
Boat, Ferry, Wood Stack, Bell, Pressed Steel, Clockwork, Floor Toy, Walbert, Box, c.1925, 13 In.	690.00
Boat, Green, Cream, Paint, Tin, Windup, Ives, Germany, 9 ½ In.	240.00
Boat, Gunboat, Funnel, Deck Flywheel, Tin Lithograph, Floor Toy, Hess, c.1910, 12 In.	790.00
Boat, Gunboat, Gray, Red Paint, Clockwork, Staudt, Germany, Box, c.1907, 14 In.	4600.00
Boat, Gunboat, HMS Alexandra, Blue, Paint, Turrets, Clockwork, Marklin, Germany, 1909, 15 In.	27600.00
Boat, Gunboat, Pirate, 2 Stacks, Rigging, Deck Guns, Paper Litho, Pull Toy, Bliss, 25 In. *Illus*	920.00
Boat, Gunboat, Rail Deck, Automatic Cannon & Rudder, Gray, Clockwork, Bing, Box, c.1910, 15 In.	3340.00
Boat, Launch, Pilot, Canopy, Blue, White, Tin Lithograph, Penny, Fischer, 7 In.	1944.00
Boat, Launch, Putt Putt Steamer, Gray, White, Marklin, Germany, c.1925, 9 In.	6900.00
Boat, Launch, Red, White, Blue, Railed, Mast, Wheels, Penny Toy, Fischer, Germany, 4 In.	395.00
Boat, Launch, Steam, Yellow, Red Paint, Open Hull, Schoenner, 18 In.	4025.00
Boat, Lifeboat, White, Black Paint, Tin, Bench Seating, Marklin, Germany, 5 In.	2300.00
Boat, Moby Dick Whaling, Tin, Lights, Sirens, Linemar, 1950s, 4 ½ x 3 In.	300.00
Boat, Ocean Liner, 3 Funnels, Clockwork, Tin Litho, Husch, Czechoslovakia, c.1930, 10 In.	851.00
Boat, Ocean Liner, 3 Red Funnels, Black, Yellow, Tin Lithograph, Penny Toy, 4 In.	608.00
Boat, Ocean Liner, Blue, White, Mast, Smokestack, Tin Litho, Windup, Arnold, Germany, 1950s, 6 In.	518.00
Boat, Ocean Liner, Copper Hull, Red, Yellow, Blue, Rail, 3 Funnels, Bing, Germany, Box, c.1930, 10 In.	2588.00
Boat, Ocean Liner, Fitted Deck, 3 Funnels, Red, Blue, Tin Lithograph, Clockwork, Arnold, c.1950, 16 In.	3341.00
Boat, Ocean Liner, Kaiserin Augusta Victoria, Red, Black, 10 Lifeboats, Marklin, Germany, 46 In.	14580.00
Boat, Ocean Liner, Le Touriste, Rails, Funnels, Red, White, Black, Clockwork, Marklin, c.1920, 18 In.	10328.00
Boat, Ocean Liner, Mast, Flying Bridge, Tin Litho, Fleischmann, Germany, c.1936, 7 In. *Illus*	863.00
Boat, Ocean Liner, Red, Black Hull, Clockwork, Arnold, U.S. Zone, Germany, Box, 1950s, 13 In.	1495.00
Boat, Ocean Liner, Red, Black, Deck, Masts, Clockwork, Fleischmann, Germany, c.1945, 19 In.	4860.00
Boat, Ocean Liner, Red, White, Tin Lithograph, Clockwork, Bing, Germany, Box, c.1927, 6 In.	863.00
Boat, Ocean Liner, Smokestacks, Masts, Lifeboats, Wheel Turns Rudder, Bing, 25 In. *Illus*	3450.00
Boat, Ocean Liner, Stacks, Hand Lever, Single Propeller, Windup, Bing, Tin Tag, 10 In. *Illus*	345.00
Boat, Ocean Liner, Steam, Series II, Roof Opens, Bing, Germany, c.1912, 20 In. *Illus*	2300.00
Boat, Ocean Liner, Tin Lithograph, Ventilators, Lifeboats, Germany, Arnold, Box, 1950s, 16 In.	3163.00
Boat, Ocean Liner, U.S., Tin Litho, Clockwork, Marusan, Japan, Box, 15 In. *Illus*	805.00
Boat, Ocean Liner, Upper Deck Cabin, Tin Litho, Flags, Fischer, Germany, Penny Toy, 6 In. *Illus*	403.00
Boat, Ocean Liner, Yellow Funnels, Decking, Clockwork, Bing, Germany, c.1912, 25 In.	6075.00
Boat, On Wheels, Soldiers, Cannons, Carved, Painted, Pull Toy, Germany, 8 x 9 In.	1185.00
Boat, Outboard Motor, Driver, Passengers, Orange, Red, Tin Litho, Arnold, Germany, 1920s, 8 In.	6325.00
Boat, Paddlewheel, Funnel, Canopy, Yellow, Red, Clockwork, Tin, Uebelacher, Germany, Box, c.1900	2430.00
Boat, Paddlewheel, Funnels, Canopy, Railings, Clockwork, Marklin, Germany, c.1925, 18 In. *Illus*	28750.00
Boat, Paddlewheel, Gold, Red, Center Flywheel, Tin Lithograph, Hess, Germany, 10 In.	1944.00
Boat, Paddlewheel, Kaiser Wilhelm, Masthead, Orange, Steam, Rock & Graner, c.1875, 21 In.	48600.00
Boat, Paddlewheel, Lettered State Of New York, Paint, Cast Iron, 15 In.	330.00
Boat, Paddlewheel, Ocean, Funnel, Chain Rigging, Clockwork, Rock & Graner, c.1875, 15 In. *Illus*	11500.00
Boat, Paddlewheel, Single Deck, Funnel, Red, Tin, Clockwork Bing, Germany, c.1912, 7 In.	1337.00
Boat, Paddlewheel, Tin Litho, Clockwork, Windup, Fleischmann, Germany, c.1936, 8 In. *Illus*	403.00
Boat, River Steamer, Canopy, Gold, Black, Brown Paint, 15 In.	4556.00
Boat, River Steamer, Canopy, Red, White, Clockwork, Bing, Germany, c.1913, 20 In.	5770.00
Boat, Riverboat, Blenheim, Passengers, Canopy, Mast, Red, Clockwork, Marklin, c.1909, 13 In.	29768.00
Boat, Riverboat, Koln, Red, White, Clockwork, Bing, Germany, c.1913, 20 In.	5463.00
Boat, Riverboat, Rowers, Orange, Green, Tin Litho, Clockwork, Arnold, Germany, c.1920, 9 In.	1093.00
Boat, Riverboat, Stern Flag, Orange, Internal Flywheel, Carette, Schooner, Box, c.1880, 13 In.	4556.00
Boat, Riverboat, Tin, Open Hull, Steam Powered, Paint, Union Mfg., c.1860, 18 In. *Illus*	403.00
Boat, Rowboat, Man Rowing, Sculling Uniform, Windup, Arnold, Germany, 1920s, 8 In. *Illus*	575.00
Boat, Rowboat, Rower, Oars, Stern Flag, Green, Yellow, Tin Litho, Clockwork, Germany, 6 In.	850.00
Boat, Sailboat, Bisque Sailor, Blue, Red, Tin Litho, Clockwork, Issmayer, Germany, Box, 6 In.	4556.00
Boat, Sailboat, Blue, Gold Hull, White Sails, Wood Deck, Schoenhut, Box, 20 In.	3645.00
Boat, Sailboat, Center Mast, Rigging, Soldiers, Rifles, Painted, Buchner, Germany, c.1810, 5 In. *Illus*	1093.00
Boat, Sailboat, Red, White Hull, Cloth Sails, Clockwork, Fleischmann, Germany, c.1908, 6 In.	2300.00
Boat, Sailboat, Tin Litho, Cardboard Sails, Flywheel, Hess, Germany, 9 In. *Illus*	345.00
Boat, Scull, 4 Men Rowing, Coxswain, Tin Litho, Clockwork, Gunthermann, Germany, 22 In. *Illus*	12650.00
Boat, Scull, 8 Men, Coxswain, Multicolor, Tin Litho, Gunthermann, 29 In.	33413.00
Boat, Scull, Oarsman, Oars, Hull Wheels, Clockwork, Floor Toy, Gunthermann, 14 In.	4253.00
Boat, Showboat, Cast Iron, White, Green, Red, Bell Rings, Arcade, 10 In.	1150.00

T

Toy, Boat, Destroyer, Gun Turrets & Stations, Bridge, Tin Litho, Fleischmann, Germany, 1950s, 15 In.
$1,380.00

Bertoia Auctions

Toy, Boat, Ferry, Paddlewheel, Union, Removable Stack, Key, Bing, Germany, 12 In.
$2,070.00

Bertoia Auctions

Toy, Boat, Gunboat, Pirate, 2 Stacks, Rigging, Deck Guns, Paper Litho, Pull Toy, Bliss, 25 In.
$920.00

Bertoia Auctions

Toy, Boat, Ocean Liner, Mast, Flying Bridge, Tin Litho, Fleischmann, Germany, c.1936, 7 In.
$863.00

Bertoia Auctions

Toy, Boat, Ocean Liner, Smokestacks, Masts, Lifeboats, Wheel Turns Rudder, Bing, 25 In.
$3,450.00

James D. Julia Auctioneers

Toy, Boat, Ocean Liner, Stacks, Hand Lever, Single Propeller, Windup, Bing, Tin Tag, 10 In.
$345.00

James D. Julia Auctioneers

Toy, Boat, Ocean Liner, Steam, Series II, Roof Opens, Bing, Germany, c.1912, 20 In.
$2,300.00

Bertoia Auctions

Toy, Boat, Ocean Liner, U.S., Tin Litho, Clockwork, Marusan, Japan, Box, 15 In.
$805.00

Toy, Boat, Ocean Liner, Upper Deck Cabin, Tin Litho, Flags, Fischer, Germany, Penny Toy, 6 In.
$403.00

Bertoia Auctions

Toy, Boat, Paddlewheel, Funnels, Canopy, Railings, Clockwork, Marklin, Germany, c.1925, 18 In.
$28,750.00

Bertoia Auctions

Toy, Boat, Paddlewheel, Ocean, Funnel, Chain Rigging, Clockwork, Rock & Graner, c.1875, 15 In.
$11,500.00

Bertoia Auctions

Bertoia Auctions

Toy, Boat, Paddlewheel, Tin Litho, Clockwork, Windup, Fleischmann, Germany, c.1936, 8 In. $403.00

Bertoia Auctions

Toy, Boat, Riverboat, Tin, Open Hull, Steam Powered, Paint, Union Mfg., c.1860, 18 In. $403.00

Bertoia Auctions

Toy, Boat, Rowboat, Man Rowing, Sculling Uniform, Windup, Arnold, Germany, 1920s, 8 In. $575.00

Bertoia Auctions

Toy, Boat, Sailboat, Center Mast, Rigging, Soldiers, Rifles, Painted, Buchner, Germany, c.1810, 5 In. $1,093.00

Bertoia Auctions

TIP
Do not put wax on a wooden toy to preserve it. The wax may yellow and disturb any markings or paper decoration.

Boat, Side Wheeler, Puritan, Cast Iron, White, Black Smokestack, Wilkens, 11 In.	374.00
Boat, Side Wheeler, Wheels, Paint, Cast Iron, A.C. Williams, 15 In.	259.00
Boat, Speedboat, 2 Seated Drivers, White Hull, Crank Motor, Arnold, c.1920, 8 In.	911.00
Boat, Speedboat, Driver, White, Gray, Red, Steam Power, Bing, Germany, Box, 18 In.	3341.00
Boat, Speedboat, Driver, Yellow, Red, Pressed Steel, Clockwork, Ruban Bleu, France, 1930s, 12 In.	748.00
Boat, Speedboat, Miss America, Windup, Mengel Playthings, Louisville, Ky., 1920s, 4 x 14 In.	550.00
Boat, Speedboat, Penn Yan, Iron, Blue, 4 Passengers, Wheels, Hubley, c.1938, 14 In.	4313.00
Boat, Speedboat, Pilot, Rear Spoke Wheels, Tin Litho, Penny Toy, Fischer, Germany, c.1905, 6 In.	288.00
Boat, Speedboat, Pilot, Spoke Wheels, Tin Lithograph, Windup, Distler, Germany, 4 ¾ In.	668.00
Boat, Speedboat, Polly-Wog, Steam, 2 Cylinder Motor, Aluminum, Wood, Boucher, c.1930, 23 In.	1438.00
Boat, Speedboat, Robot Driver, Red, Gray, Tin Lithograph, Japan, 12 ½ In.	660.00
Boat, Speedboat, Venture, Blue, White Paint, Pressed Steel, Clockwork, Hornby, Box, 16 In.	850.00
Boat, Steam Launch, Brass Boiler, Stack, Paint, Falk, Germany, Box, c.1910, 20 In.	2430.00
Boat, Steam, City Of New York, Side-Wheeler, Iron, Wilkins, New Hampshire, 5 ½ x 15 In.	590.00
Boat, Steamboat, Bell Rings, Wheels, Tin Lithograph, Orobr, Germany, c.1915, 10 In. ....*Illus*	1610.00
Boat, Steamboat, Red Hull, Gray Deck, Canopy, Tin Litho, Pull Toy, Orobr, Germany, c.1915, 10 In..	1701.00
Boat, Torpedo, Gray, Red Hull, Funnel, Steam, Stand, Bing, Germany, Box, c.1905, 15 In.	7898.00
Boat, Torpedo, Rail Deck, Guns, 4 Funnels, Clockwork, Marklin, c.1924, 21 ½ In.	17001.00
Boat, Torpedo, Railing, Mast, Cannon, Pulley, Black, Green, Marklin, Germany, c.1905, 20 In.	10935.00
Boat, Torpedo, Red, Black, Railed Deck, 4 Funnels, Clockwork, Marklin, Germany, c.1924, 21 ½ In.	16100.00
Boat, Tugboat, Brown, Orange, Red Trim, Eagle On Pilot House, Bing, Germany, c.1912, 9 In.	4888.00
Boat, Wood Deck & Roof, Evinrude Motor, Japan, Box, 9 ½ In.	175.00
Box, Cricket, Wood, Arched Lid Screen Sides, Handle, Latch, Oriental, c.1900, 12 x 16 x 13 In.	90.00
Boxers, Rap & Tap, 2 Boxers, Tin Lithograph, Wood Floor In Ring, Windup, Strauss, 7 ¾ In.	316.00
Boy, On Tricycle, Linen Head, Cotton Clothing, Tin Clockwork, Windup, c.1870, 11 x 8 In.	1150.00
Boy, On Tricycle, Wonder Cyclist, Bell Rings, Tin Litho, Marx, Box, 1940s, 7 ½ In.	259.00
Bridge, Hellgate, Tin Lithograph, Lionel, O Gauge, 29 x 11 In.	203.00
Bridge, Suspension, Wood, East River, Interlocking Blocks, Lid, c.1881, 15 ½ x 6 In.	345.00
Bucket Loader, Red, Green, Orange, Doepke, c.1950, 18 In.	350.00
Buddy Bronc, Pull String, Wood, Applied Paper Labels, Fisher-Price, No. 430, 1938, 3 ½ x 8 x 8 In.	313.00
Building, Warehouse, Cardboard Boxes, Wood Fork Lift, Lithograph, Keystone, 1940s, 14 x 16 In.	165.00
Bulldozer, Driver, Spoke Metal Wheels, Paint, Cast Iron, Arcade, 9 In.	1560.00
Bump Army Car, Pop-Up Soldier, Tin Litho, Cloth, Rubber, Box, Wakasco, Japan, 1950s, 3 x 7 In.	173.00
Bump Ball, Milton Bradley, Box, 1968.	35.00
Bus, Coast To Coast, Chevy, Pressed Steel, Pull Handle, White Paint, Keystone, 1930s, 33 In.	4950.00
Bus, Coast To Coast, Cor-Cor, Orange Paint, Pressed Steel, 1930s, 24 In.	523.00
Bus, Coast To Coast, GMC, Cast Iron, Blue & White, White Rubber Tires, Arcade, Box, 9 In.	575.00
Bus, Double-Decker, Berliet Parisian, Tin, Glass Windows, Lamps, Horn, Pinard, c.1905, 19 In.	9568.00
Bus, Double-Decker, Cast Iron, Green, Gold Trim On Roof, 2 Figures, Arcade, Box, 8 In.	316.00
Bus, Double-Decker, Cast Iron, White, Bench Seats, Red Spoke Wheels, Kenton, c.1912, 8 In.	1725.00
Bus, Double-Decker, Ford's Automobile, Tin Litho, Gunthermann, 1930s, 9 ½ In. ....*Illus*	2006.00
Bus, Double-Decker, Tin Litho, Rear Staircase, Bing, Germany, 7 In. ....*Illus*	2300.00
Bus, Greyhound Scenicruiser, Painted Blue, Silver, Slush Metal Casting, Tootsietoy, 6 ¾ In.	12.00
Bus, Greyhound, Blue, White Paint, Pressed Steel, Windup, Buddy L, Box, 1940s, 16 In.	600.00
Bus, Greyhound, GMC, Cast Iron, Blue, White, Tractor & Trailer Style, Arcade, Box, 10 In.	431.00
Bus, Greyhound, Ride 'Em, Electric Headlights, No. 980, Keystone, 22 ½ In.	15400.00
Bus, Greyhound, Windup, Chein, U.S.A., 1950s, 6 In.	95.00
Bus, Inter-City, Pressed Steel, Green Paint, Red Wheels, Steelcraft, 1930s, 24 In.	390.00
Bus, Inter-State, Double-Decker, Green, Yellow, Tin, Windup, Key, Strauss, c.1920, 5 x 10 In.	288.00
Bus, Jackie Gleason Honeymooners' Special, Tin, Friction, Wolverine, Box, 1950s, 14 In.	840.00
Bus, Parlor Coach, Cast Iron, Orange, Black, Nickel Driver, Arcade, c.1926, 13 In.	9775.00
Bus, Pickwick Nite Coach, Cast Iron, Green, Red Stripe, Disc Wheels, Kenton, 9 In.	748.00
Bus, Safety Coach, Blue Paint, Cast Iron, Arcade, c.1930, 12 In.	165.00
Bus, Safety Coach, Driver, Red, Cast Iron, Rubber Tires, Arcade Mfg. & Co., 12 In.	575.00
Bus, Silver, Red Fenders, Rubber Tires, Cast Iron, Hubley, 7 ½ In.	230.00
Bus, Supercoach, Eastern Pacific System, White, Blue, Cast Iron, Arcade, 1937, 9 In.	325.00
Bus, Trailways, Cream, Red, Aluminum, Realister, 9 In.	94.00
Bus, Yellow Coach, Double-Decker, Black, Brown Accents, Cast Iron, Arcade, 13 In.	1062.00
Bus, Yellow, Wood Wheels, Wyandotte, 1940s, 4 In.	45.00
Buttercup & Spareribsy, Holding Broom, Tin Lithograph, Pull Toy, c.1920, 7 ½ In.	230.00
Cabbage Patch Kid, Girl, Holding I Love You, Plastic, C.A.A. Inc., Hong Kong, 1984, 2 x 1 In. ..*Illus*	4.00
Cable Car, San Francisco, Tin Lithograph, Box, 1950s, 9 In.	240.00
Calliope, Overland Circus, Cast Iron, 2 White Horses, Riders, 14 In.	748.00
Camel, 2 Humps, Glass Eyes, Leather Ears, Rope Tail, Wood, Fur, Schoenhut, c.1910, 7 In. .. *Illus*	896.00
Camel, Brown, Movable Legs, Head, Wood, Schoenhut, 7 In.	180.00
Cannon, Admiral Dewey, 2 Flags, Naval Deck Carriage, Iron, Kenton, c.1898, 11 In.	1035.00

Cannon, Pressed Steel, Buddy L, 1950s, 9 ½ In.	145.00
Cap Gun, Atomic Disintegrator, Futuristic Design, Metal Plastic Grip, Hubley, 8 In.	345.00
Cap Gun, Repeating, Die Cast, Plastic, Space Style, Hubley, 8 In.	345.00
Capt. Video Mysto-Decoder, Photo, Brass, Pocket Clip, Plastic, Power House Candy, c.1951, 1 ½ In.	298.00
Car, 2-Tone Blue, Orange Roof, Pressed Steel, Friction, Dayton, 18 In.	270.00
Car, Alphonse & Gaston, Iron, Orange, Figures Bow While Pulled, Kenton, c.1911, 8 In.	1265.00
Car, Andy Gump, Cast Iron, Painted, Red, Silver Grille, Disc Wheels, Arcade, 7 In.	384.00
Car, Arcade Reo, Yellow Paint, Nickel Plated Grill, Rumble Seat, Spare Tires, 1930s, 9 In.	1610.00
Car, Aston Martin, James Bond, DB5, Gold, Roof Opens, Ejector Seat, Box, Corgi, 1965, 3 ¾ In.	491.00
Car, Atom Jet, Green, Tin Lithograph, Yonezawa, Japan, 27 In.	5700.00
Car, Buick, 1927 Model, Sedan, Iron, Green, Black, Silver Trim, Spoke Wheels, Arcade, 1927, 8 In.	5175.00
Car, Buick, Coupe, Cast Iron, Blue, Nickel Spare Tire On Trunk, Arcade, 1929, 8 ½ In.	2300.00
Car, Buick, Tin, Battery Operated, Japan, Box, 1954, 6 In.	110.00
Car, Buick, Toledo, Green, Orange Trim, Pressed Steel, 28 ½ In. ....*Illus*	8250.00
Car, Chevrolet, Coupe, Black, Gray, Arcade, 1929, 8 ½ In.	1250.00
Car, Chevrolet, Coupe, Nickel Driver, Mesh Grille, Paint, Cast Iron, Arcade, 7 In.	660.00
Car, Chevrolet, Coupe, Utility, Logo, Iron, Nickel Driver, Spare Tire, Arcade, c.1925, 6 ¾ In.	403.00
Car, Chevrolet, Utility Coupe, Cast Iron, Black Paint, Gold Stripe, Driver, Arcade, 1925, 7 In.	403.00
Car, Chrysler, Airflow, Green Paint, Headlights, Battery Operated, Grill, Iron, Hubley, 7 ¾ In.	1440.00
Car, Chrysler, Airflow, Orange, Cast Iron, Hubley, 6 In.	106.00
Car, Chrysler, Airflow, Sedan, Cast Iron, Red Paint, Nickel Grille & Chassis, Hubley, 6 In.	230.00
Car, Circus, Tin, Windup, Japan, 1950s	120.00
Car, Convertible, White, Red Wheels, Rear Mount Spare Tire, Pressed Steel, 18 In.	390.00
Car, Convertible, Windup, Metal, Mettoy Of England, 1950s, 8 In.	275.00
Car, Coupe, Chief, Nickel Wheels, Red Paint, Cast Iron, Kenton, 5 ¾ In.	443.00
Car, Coupe, Flat Top, Pressed Steel, Buddy L, 6 x 10 In.	770.00
Car, Coupe, Passengers, Spring Mount, Painted, Nickel Spoke Wheels, Cast Iron, Kilgore, 1920s, 6 In.	259.00
Car, Coupe, Red, Rubber Tires, Hubley, 1930s, 4 ½ In.	110.00
Car, Dagwood, Driver, Tin Lithograph, Clockwork, Marx, 8 In. ....*Illus*	403.00
Car, Driver, 2 Seats, Silver, Black, Pressed Steel, Windup, Converse, 9 ¾ In.	360.00
Car, Driver, Glass Windshield, Tin Lithograph, Windup, Germany, 9 ¼ In.	600.00
Car, Elmer Fudd, Fire Chief, Wood, Bell, Pull Toy, c.1950, 9 In.	204.00
Car, Falcon, Coupe, Tin Lithograph, Friction, Marx, 20 In.	142.00
Car, Fire Chief, Tin, Box, Cortland Mfg., 7 ¼ In.	220.00
Car, Fire Chief, Tin, Spare Tire, Cortland, Box, 7 ¼ In. ....*Illus*	468.00
Car, Firebird, Pontiac, Red, Wipers, Bandai, Box, 10 In.	225.00
Car, Flywheel, Black, Yellow Wheels, Pressed Steel, Scheible, 17 ½ In.	420.00
Car, Ford, 1923 Model, Touring Sedan, Cast Iron, Black, Spoke Wheels, Driver, Arcade, 6 ¼ In.	518.00
Car, Ford, 1935 Model, Coupe, Cast Iron, Orange, Black, Rubber Tires, A.C. Williams, 6 ½ In.	2300.00
Car, Ford, Model A, Coupe, Cast Iron, Red, Driver, Spoke Wheels, Arcade, 6 ½ In.	403.00
Car, Ford, Model A, Red, Cast Iron, Arcade, 5 In.	130.00
Car, Ford, Model T, 4-Door Sedan, Cast Iron, Green Paint, Driver, Rubber Tires, Arcade, 6 ½ In.	863.00
Car, Ford, Model T, Coupe, Iron, Black Gold Trim, Nickel Spokes, Driver, Arcade, 1920s, 7 In.	1035.00
Car, Ford, Mustang, Tin, Friction, Japan, 1960s, 8 ¼ In.	145.00
Car, Ford, Sedan, Center Door, Nickel Plated Driver, Arcade, 1920s	525.00
Car, Ford, Torino, Plastic, Promotional, 1969, 8 ½ In. ....*Illus*	105.00
Car, Green, Tan Roof, Red Wheels, Pressed Steel, Friction, Dayton, 18 In.	570.00
Car, Greyhound Escorter, Box, Open Cart, Yellow Seats, Friction, c.1964, 6 x 4 In.	230.00
Car, Happy Hooligan, Open Soap Box, Chimney Pipe, Comic Driver, Iron, Kenton, 7 In.	230.00
Car, Improved Chevy Coupe, Cast Iron, Gray, Black Roof, Disc Wheels, Arcade, 8 In.	1840.00
Car, Limousine, Driver, Windows, Rack, Lanterns, Tin Litho, Clockwork, Carette, 12 In. ...*Illus*	3450.00
Car, Mercedes-Benz 250SE, Friction, Tin Litho, Cardboard, Box, Ichimura, Japan, 1960s, 7 x 2 In.	86.00
Car, Metropolitan, Convertible, Red, Hubley, 6 In.	345.00
Car, Nifty Station Wagon, Wood, Plastic, Removable Roof, Pull Toy, Fisher-Price, Box, c.1960, 13 ½ In.	173.00
Car, Packard, 1933 Model, Sedan, Shovel Nose, Cast Iron, Green, Rubber Tires, A.C. Williams, 7 In.	805.00
Car, Packard, Sedan, Cast Iron, Orange Paint, Rubber Tires, A.C. Williams, 6 ¾ In.	316.00
Car, Packard, Sedan, Straight 8, Green, Hood Opens, Cast Iron, 1920s, 11 In.	7475.00
Car, Pierce Arrow, Sedan, Cast Iron, Molding, Painted, Silver Body, Red Trim, Arcade, c.1934, 7 In.	944.00
Car, Plymouth, Tin, Friction, Japan, 1956, 6 ½ In.	275.00
Car, Pontiac, Roadster, Green, Cast Iron, Rumble Seat, Vindex, Salesman's Sample, 1929, 5 In.	1265.00
Car, Pontiac, Safari, Station Wagon, Tailgate, Rubber Tires, Blue, White, Tootsietoy, Box, 1956, 7 In.	285.00
Car, Racing, Agajanian Special, Tin, Yellow, Chrome Steering Wheel, Yonezawa, 1950s, 20 In.	3738.00
Car, Racing, Brown Paint, White Wall Tires, Cast Iron, c.1930, 5 x 3 In.	59.00
Car, Racing, Cobalt Blue, Nickel Driver, White Rubber Tires, Cast Iron, A.C. Williams, 8 ½ In.	374.00
Car, Racing, Driver, 36, Green, Red Paint, Tin Lithograph, Windup, France, c.1920, 14 ½ In.	330.00
Car, Racing, Driver, Green, Orange, White, Race Car Graphics, Tin, Marx, 12 In.	1150.00

TIP

Collectors pay higher prices for most plastic space-gun toys than for lithographed tin guns. The newer plastic toys have more futuristic designs.

Toy, Boat, Sailboat, Tin Litho, Cardboard Sails, Flywheel, Hess, Germany, 9 In. $345.00

Bertoia Auctions

Toy, Boat, Scull, 4 Men Rowing, Coxswain, Tin Litho, Clockwork, Gunthermann, Germany, 22 In. $12,650.00

Bertoia Auctions

Toy, Boat, Steamboat, Bell Rings, Wheels, Tin Lithograph, Orobr, Germany, c.1915, 10 In. $1,610.00

Bertoia Auctions

Toy, Bus, Double-Decker, Ford's Automobile, Tin Litho, Gunthermann, 1930s, 9 ½ In. $2,006.00

Bertoia Auctions

T

Toy, Bus, Double-Decker, Tin Litho, Rear Staircase, Bing, Germany, 7 In.
$2,300.00

James D. Julia Auctioneers

Toy, Cabbage Patch Kid, Girl, Holding I Love You, Plastic, C.A.A. Inc., Hong Kong, 1984, 2 x 1 In.
$4.00

Toy, Camel, 2 Humps, Glass Eyes, Leather Ears, Rope Tail, Wood, Fur, Schoenhut, c.1910, 7 In.
$896.00

Theriault's

Toy, Car, Buick, Toledo, Green, Orange Trim, Pressed Steel, 28 ½ In.
$8,250.00

Showtime Auction Sevices

Car, Racing, Driver, Tin Lithograph, Green Paint, Flywheel, Germany, 5 ¼ In.	660.00
Car, Racing, Gray Paint, Cast Iron, Arcade, c.1930, 5 ½ In.	35.00
Car, Racing, Indianapolis Speedway, 2 Drivers, Red Paint, Iron, c.1930, 2 x 6 In.	59.00
Car, Racing, No. 5, Fin Tail, Cast Iron, Light Blue, 2 Figures, Arcade, 1936, 7 ¾ In.	633.00
Car, Racing, No. 9, Bullet Design, Cast Iron, Yellow, Nickel Side Pipes, Arcade, 8 In.	1955.00
Car, Racing, No. 136, Red, Yellow, Tin, J. Chein, 1940s, 6 ½ In.	165.00
Car, Racing, Red, Plastic, Windup, Rite Spot, 9 x 3 In.	30.00
Car, Racing, Red, Silver Paint, Die Cast, Iron, c.1930, 7 ½ x 2 ½ In.	41.00
Car, Racing, Silver, Red Trim, Articulated Pistons, Tail Fin, Cast Iron, Hubley, 8 ½ In.	259.00
Car, Racing, Sport, Cast Iron, Yellow Paint, Driver, Disc Wheels, Kenton, c.1927, 8 ¾ In.	1610.00
Car, Racing, Yellow, Cast Iron, Speedway, c.1930, 4 ½ x 1 ½ In.	30.00
Car, Reo, Coupe, Nickel Grill, Yellow, Red Trim, Cast Iron, Arcade, 9 In.	856.00
Car, Roadster, Electric Headlights, White Tires, Red Paint, Pressed Steel, Wyandotte, 8 In.	60.00
Car, Roadster, Nickel Driver, Disc Wheels, Rumble Seat, Cast Iron, Red Paint, Kilgore, 6 In.	316.00
Car, Roadster, Pressed Steel, Red, Blue Running Boards, Rubber Wheels, Meccano, 1930, 12 In.	990.00
Car, Rumble Seat Coupe, Nickel Grill, Green Paint, Cast Iron, Arcade, 6 ½ In.	510.00
Car, Rumble Seat, Red, Black, Paint, Pressed Steel, Chein, 18 In.	360.00
Car, Runabout, Cast Iron, Red Paint, Yellow Spoke Wheels, Driver With Tiller, Kenton, 6 In.	374.00
Car, Secret Service, Green Hornet, Tin Litho, Bump & Go, Flashing Lights, Box, Aoshin, 11 In.	1120.00
Car, Sedan, Cast Iron, Orange, Red Spokes, Rear Mounted Spare Tire, Kenton, c.1925, 10 In.	1265.00
Car, Sedan, Cast Iron, Red, Black Running Boards, Silver Wheels, Driver, Kenton, Sears, 13 In.	1725.00
Car, Sedan, Nickel Grill, Red, Green Paint, Cast Iron, A.C. Williams, 7 ¾ In.	840.00
Car, Sedan, Orange, Nickel Plated Spoke Wheels, Vindex, Salesman's Sample, c.1929, 5 ½ In.	2185.00
Car, Sedan, Trailer, Pressed Steel, Red, Yellow Roof, All-Metal Prod. Co., Wyandotte, Mich., 26 In.	495.00
Car, Soopa Coopa, Metallic Dark Blue, Matchbox, Box	15.00
Car, Studebaker, Town Car, Cast Iron, Red, Nickeled Chassis, Grille & Headlights, Hubley, 7 In.	403.00
Car, Tippco Phantom, Tin, Electric Light, Clockwork, Driver, Germany, 1956, 13 ¾ In.	1595.00
Car, Touring, Arrow Coupe, Pressed Steel, Windup, Bell, Lights, Girard Mfg. Co., 5 x 14 In.	296.00
Car, Touring, Cast Iron, Yellow, Red Wheels, Driver, Passenger, Kenton, c.1920, 11 ½ In.	633.00
Car, Touring, Convertible, Driver, Passenger, Red, Silver, Kenton For Sears, 9 In. ....*Illus*	431.00
Car, Touring, Driver, Red Spoke Wheels, Paint, Cast Iron, Dent, 11 ½ In.	900.00
Car, Touring, Sedan, Steel, Blue, Composition Tires, Wyandotte, c.1939, 5 In.	125.00
Car, Touring, Yellow Body, Red Wheels, Paint, Cast Iron, Hubley, 4 ½ In.	480.00
Car, Uncle Wiggly, Tin Lithograph, Multicolor, Clockwork, Louis Marx, Box, 7 In.	633.00
Car, Vis-A-Vis, Driver, Tin Litho, Rubber Tires, Spoke Wheels, Gunthermann, c.1895, 6 ½ In. *Illus*	2950.00
Car, Volvo, Tin, Friction, Japan, 1950s, 7 ½ In.	295.00
Car, What's Wrong, Boy Driver, Tin Lithograph, Clockwork, Distler, Germany, 7 ¼ In. ......*Illus*	1003.00
Car, Wrecker, Yellow, Cast Iron, 11 In.	826.00
Carousel, 4 Animals, Riders, Chariot, Tin, Paint, Pinstripes, Windup, Germany, c.1900, 15 x 9 In.	1150.00
Carousel, Hand Crank, Articulated Necks, Cloth Canopy Paint, Wood, 21 x 24 In.	272.00
Carousel, Riders, Watchers, Glass, Canopy, Tin, Crank, Steam, Marklin, c.1910, 16 x 21 In.	218500.00
Carriage, Baby With Doll, Tin Lithograph, Spoke Wheels, Penny Toy, Meier, Germany, 3 ¾ In.	805.00
Carriage, Doll's, Accordion Canopy, Wood Wheels, Frame, Paint, 36 In.	141.00
Carriage, Doll's, Painted Pony Design, Metal, Wood Wheels, Frame, 35 In.	170.00
Carriage, Doll's, Tin, Spoke Wheels, Gilt Crest, Curved Handles, Sunshade, Pink, c.1900, 12 In.	4200.00
Cart, Egyptian, Drawn By Wild Boar, Cast Iron, Orange, Driver, Kenton, 8 In.	489.00
Cart, Goat, Yellow Kid Driver, Cast Iron, Red Spoke Wheels, Kenton, 7 ½ In.	374.00
Cart, Horse Drawn, Wheels, Yellow, Red Paint, Cast Iron, Ives, 9 ¾ In.	1080.00
Cart, Horse Drawn, Wood, Wire, Paint, Pull Toy, c.1910, 20 In.	296.00
Cart, Oxen, Black Paint, Cast Iron, 14 ½ In.	136.00
Cart, Pine, Metal, Open Slat Sides, Pull Handle, Spoke Wheels, 1800s, 52 x 46 x 29 ½ In. ....*Illus*	192.00
Castle, 3 Tiers, Removable Tower, Storage, Revolving, Tin, Marklin, Germany, c.1895, 19 x 23 In. *Illus*	28175.00
Cat, Felix, Chasing Mice, Tin, J. Chein, 3 ¾ x 6 In.	1320.00
Cat, Felix, On Scooter, Tin Litho, Painted, Windup, Gunthermann, Germany, c.1922, 8 In. ....*Illus*	658.00
Cat, Felix, Scooter, Tin, J. Chein, 7 ½ In.	770.00
Cat, Gray Tabby, Fur, Bow & Bell, Wheels, Windup, Germany, c.1900, 10 In.	288.00
Chair, Doll's, Chippendale Style, Mahogany, Pierced Splat, Carved, c.1885, 8 ¾ In.	504.00
Chair, Doll's, Wing, Pine, Painted Ocher, Paper Label, Inscribed, New England, 1964, 12 ½ In.	3540.00
Champion Motorcycle, Cast Iron, Attached Policeman Rider, 1930s, 5 x 3 In.	415.00
Chariot, Hippodrome, 2 Horses, Female Driver, Tin, Dress, Clockwork, Ives, 1893, 14 In. ...*Illus*	69000.00
Chariot, Horse Drawn, Composition, Tin, Soldier Standing, Brevete Invictus, Windup, 14 ½ In.	518.00
Chariot, Swan, Iron, Child, Shell Seat, Articulated Wings, Painted, J. & E. Stevens, 1890s, 10 In.	1770.00
Chest, Doll's, Blanket, Walnut, Hinge Top, Panel Front, Shaped Bench Feet, 11 ½ x 5 In.	230.00
Chicken House, Chicken Inside, Hinged Door, Wood, Wire, Paint, Squeak Toy, c.1910, 6 x 8 In.	207.00
Chicken Snatcher, Black Man, Holding Chicken, Dog, Tin Litho, Clockwork, Marx, c.1934, 8 ½ In.	847.00

Chief Robot Man, Silver, Red, Yellow, Tin Litho, Battery Operated, Ko Yoshiya, Japan, Box, 11 ¾ In...	1200.00
Child, On Chamber Pot, Knitting, Hand Turns, Papier-Mache, Bellows, Squeak, c.1850, 5 In. .....*Illus*	896.00
Chinese Man, Seated, Holding Parasol, Wheeled Platform, Tin Litho, Distler, Germany, 3 ½ In. . *Illus*	460.00
Circus Dude, Black Man, Masked Face, Schoenhut, 8 ½ In. ....*Illus*	460.00
Circus Monkey, Wood, Jointed, Felt Suit & Hat, Fringe, Rope Tail, Schoenhut, 8 In.	374.00
Circus Tent, Humpty Dumpty Circus, Oval, Cloth, Lithograph, Schoenhut, 28 x 42 In.	2588.00
Clever Typist, Miss Bear, Tin Lithograph, Battery Operated, Showa, Japan, c.1965..................	285.00
Climbing Fireman, Ladder, Wind-Up, Tin Lithograph, Painted, Box, 1930s, 7 ¼ In.	158.00
Clock, Take-A-Part, Wood, Bell, Doepke, 1957, 7 x 6 In..	75.00
Clock, Talking, Tells Time Every 5 Minutes, Mod Images, Battery Operated, 1969, 14 x 14 In..	70.00
Clown, Happy, Eyes Move, Body Rises, Tin Litho, Clockwork, Distler, Germany, Box, 6 In.	230.00
Clown, Artist, Seated At Easel, Sketches Picture, Crank, 6 Discs, Vielmetter, Germany, 1800s, 6 In.	3245.00
Clown, Band, Tin Lithograph, Clockwork, Signed THN, 8 ¼ In...	287.00
Clown, Circus, Wood, Jointed Limbs, Red & White Costume, 7 In.	144.00
Clown, Cyclist, Windup, Tin Lithograph, Technofix, U.S. Zone, Germany, 5 ½ In.	660.00
Clown, Drummer, Cymbals, Black, Tin, Felt, Windup, Plays Drum, Cymbals, Schuco, 4 ½ In..	546.00
Clown, Hat, Red Car, Tin, Celluloid, Lithograph, Japan, c.1932, 7 ¾ In.............................	510.00
Clown, Ko-Ko The Inkwell, Original Clothes, Schoenhut, 1920s, 11 In. ....*Illus*	3450.00
Clown, Orchestra, Rings Bells When Piano Is Played, Tin, Wood, Victor Bonnet, France, 10 In. . *Illus*	1265.00
Clown, Riding Bicycle, Chimes Barrel, Wood, Paper, Rubber Tires, Schoenhut, 11 In.............	1035.00
Clown, Rocking Piglet, Circus Blanket, Clown Bounces, Tin Litho, Windup, Germany, c.1915, 5 In.	1904.00
Clown, Roly Poly, Celluloid, Red, Yellow, c.1945, 8 ¾ In...	30.00
Clown, Roly Poly, Composition, Painted, Roly Toys, 15 ¾ In...	201.00
Clown, Sharecropper, Bell Toy, Tin, Iron, 6 In.	180.00
Clown, Tricycle, Big Front Wheel, Tin Lithograph, Clockwork, Marx, 9 In.	575.00
Clown, Walker, Tin, No. 76, J. Chein, c.1925, 5 ½ In..	510.00
Clown, Weight Lifter, 100 Lb. Weight, In Mouth, Cloth, Tin Lithograph, Clockwork, 7 In.	1150.00
Coast Defense, 3 Anti-Aircraft Guns, Revolving Plane, Hangar Base, Tin, Louis Marx, 9 In. ...	633.00
Couple & Dog, Walking Down Broadway, Tin Litho, Flywheel, Cogwheel, Lehmann, 6 In. ... *Illus*	3835.00
Couple, Waltzing, Felt Outfits, Stroll Motion, Tin, Fernand Martin, France, 8 In. ....*Illus*	2588.00
Cow, Bell Collar, Brown, Pull Toy, 5 ½ In.	60.00
Cow, Brown & Cream Hide, Glass Eyes, Papier-Mache Horns & Udder, Neck Bell, 1800s, 36 In. . *Illus*	1232.00
Cow, Hide, Glass Eyes, Platform, 16 In.	90.00
Cow, Pewter Wheels, Head Bobs, Pull Toy, Germany, 1880, 18 x 10 In.	570.00
Cow, Riding, Brown, White Mohair, Button Eyes, Iron Frame, Wood Wheels, c.1969, 20 x 27 In.	316.00
Cradle, Doll's, Molded Hood, Painted Yellow, Applied Rockers, New England, 20 In..............	295.00
Cradle, Doll's, Wood, Scalloped Rim, Paint, Jacob Weber, Pa., c.1850, 8 ½ In.	504.00
Cradle, Red Pinstripe, Yellow Ground, Heart Cutout Handles, 1800s, 4 ¾ x 6 In.	1422.00
Cradle, Stylized Flower Ends, Leaf Design Sides, Jonas Weber, Pa., c.1840, 5 x 8 ½ In.	1185.00
Crane, Overhead, Clam Shell, Pressed Steel, Buddy L, 1930s, 11 x 27 In...........................	2040.00
Crane, Red, Tin Lithograph, Box, Japan, 7 ½ In..	83.00
Cupboard, Doll's, Linen, 2 Glass Doors, Drawers, Shaped Crest, Shaped Apron, Block Feet, 11 x 21 In.	86.00
Deep Sea Diver, Yellow Suit, Helmet, Propeller Blades, Clockwork, Lithograph, Germany, 7 In. ... *Illus*	5750.00
Dinner Set, Cat, Felix, White With Black Applied Decals Of Felix Walking, Hunting, 1920s	287.00
Dinner Set, Exotic Birds, Black Rims, Soft Paste, c.1885, 6-In. Pieces ....*Illus*	1232.00
Dirigible, Flying Zeppelin, Aluminum Windup, Strauss, Box, 15 ¾ In.................................	518.00
Dirigible, Shenandoah, Tin Litho, Clockwork, 2 Gondolas, Celluloid Propellers, Box, Lehmann, 7 In.	2588.00
Doctor's Cart, Horse Drawn, Paint, Tin, Cast Iron Wheels, George Brown, 9 ¼ In..................	1029.00
Dog Whistle, 3-Way Mystery, Capt. Midnight Premium From Ovaltine, 1940, 3 x 4 In............	196.00
Dog, Airedale, Rideable, Barks, Stuffed, Black Spots, Wire Frame, Wood Wheels, Pull Toy, 20 x 24 In.	71.00
Dog, Bulldog, Brown, White, Painted Eye, Leather Ears, Schoenhut, 6 In.	484.00
Dog, Bulldog, Papier-Mache, Barking, Glass Eyes, Flocked, Chain Leash, Straw Collar, France, 17 In.	1150.00
Dog, Cocker Spaniel, Cockie, Sitting, Brown, Beige, Mohair, Button Eyes, Steiff, 1951, 6 x 5 ½ In..	195.00
Dog, Flippo, Windup, Guntermann, 6 x 5 In.	81.00
Dog, Fox Terrier, Straw Stuffed, Mohair, Yarn Nose, Painted Spots, Steiff, 13 In......................	70.00
Dog, German Shepherd, Arco, Mohair, Ears Up, Orange Eyes, Steiff, 1950, 8 ½ In................	175.00
Dog, Jockey, On Platform, Paint, Tin, Cast Iron Wheels, Fallows, 9 ½ In.	575.00
Dog, Kennel, Moves In & Out, Penny Toy, 2 ⅝ In...	431.00
Dog, On Scooter, Tin, Pull Toy, J. Chein, 7 In. ....*Illus*	720.00
Dog, Poodle, Jointed, Wood, Cloth Mane, Glass Eyes, Cord Tail, Schoenhut, 7 In. ....*Illus*	431.00
Dog, Poodle, White, Movable Head, Legs, Paint, Wood, Schoenhut, 7 ½ In..........................	90.00
Dog, Poodle, Wood, Jointed, White, Painted Eyes, Rope Tail, Schoenhut, 7 ¼ In....................	230.00
Dog, Spotted, Wood, Paint, Platform, Wheels, Leather Collar, Saddle, Pull Toy, 23 x 23 In........	748.00
Doggy Racer, Dog Driver, Felt-Like Arms, Steering Wheel, No. 7, Pull Toy, Fisher-Price, 9 ¾ In. ...*Illus*	390.00
Dolls are listed in the Doll category.	

Toy, Car, Fire Chief, Tin, Spare Tire, Cortland, Box, 7 ¼ In.
$468.00

Showtime Auction Sevices

Toy, Car, Ford, Torino, Plastic, Promotional, 1969, 8 ½ In.
$105.00

Matthews Auctions, LLC

Toy, Car, Limousine, Driver, Windows, Rack, Lanterns, Tin Litho, Clockwork, Carette, 12 In.
$3,450.00

Bertoia Auctions

Toy, Car, Touring, Convertible, Driver, Passenger, Red, Silver, Kenton For Sears, 9 In.
$431.00

Bertoia Auctions

TIP

Old metal toy trucks were made of iron or tin, not brass or aluminum, the metals favored by some reproductions.

T

Toy, Car, Vis-A-Vis, Driver, Tin Litho, Rubber Tires, Spoke Wheels, Gunthermann, c.1895, 6 ½ In. $2,950.00

Bertoia Auctions

Toy, Car, What's Wrong, Boy Driver, Tin Lithograph, Clockwork, Distler, Germany, 7 ¼ In. $1,003.00

Bertoia Auctions

Toy, Car, Yellow Cab, Black Trim, Spare Tire, Rear Door, Cast Iron, Hubley, 8 In. $590.00

Bertoia Auctions

Toy, Cart, Pine, Metal, Open Slat Sides, Pull Handle, Spoke Wheels, 1800s, 52 x 46 x 29 ½ In. $192.00

Gray's Auctioneers LLC

Dollhouse Furniture, Candelabra, Fantasia, Petite Princess Fantasy Furniture, Box		10.00
Dollhouse Furniture, Dining Set, Iron, Cream Paint, Table, 2 Benches, Arcade, Box, 4 ½ In.		201.00
Dollhouse Furniture, Dressing Tables, Settee, Chairs, Bed, Desk, Tynietoy, c.1930, 1 In., 7 Piece *Illus*		728.00
Dollhouse Furniture, Grand Piano, Music, Metronome, Petite Princess Fantasy Furniture, Box		32.00
Dollhouse Furniture, Hoosier Cabinet, Iron, Door Opens, Dough Board, Arcade, 1930s		125.00
Dollhouse Furniture, Salon Wing Chair, Brocade, Petite Princess Fantasy Furniture, Box		20.00
Dollhouse, 2 Rooms, Folding, Heavy Board Frame, Litho, McLoughlin Bros., c.1890, 18 In. *Illus*		896.00
Dollhouse, 2 Rooms, Wood, Paper Litho, Balcony, Gottschalk, Germany, c.1890, 17 In. *Illus*		4480.00
Dollhouse, 2 Story, Paper Lithograph, Wood, Wallpaper, Front Door Opens, Bliss, 13 x 17 In.		767.00
Dollhouse, 2 Story, Upper Balcony, Porch, Stork & Nest Atop Chimney, Gottschalk, c.1912, 22 x 17 In.		920.00
Dollhouse, 3 Story, Dormers, 4 Rooms, Wood, Cardboard, Flip Roof, Schoenhut, c.1931, 20 x 18 In.		345.00
Dollhouse, 3 Story, Removable Mansard Roof, Brick Porch, Hinged Wall, c.1890, 31 x 25 x 26 In.		2420.00
Dollhouse, 4 Rooms, Wood, Paper Litho, Front Porch, Balcony, Gingerbread, Bliss, c.1890, 20 In. *Illus*		1120.00
Donkey, Plush, Wire Frame, Leather Saddle, Rein, Black Mane, Wood Wheels, Steiff, 21 x 20 In.		295.00
Dresser, Doll's, Bowfront, Oval Mirror, Turned Pulls, Shaped Apron, Carved Brackets, 19 x 13 In.		148.00
Dresser, Doll's, Empire Style, 6 Drawers, Mirror, 13 x 17 ½ In. *Illus*		345.00
Dresser, Doll's, Empire, Grain Painted, Deck Top Drawers, Maine, c.1850, 21 x 18 In.		1840.00
Duck, Dr. Doodle, Wood Hat, Wheels, No. 100, Pull Toy, Fisher-Price, 1932, 7 In.		360.00
Duck, Granny Doodle, Oilcloth Cap, No. 101, Pull Toy, Fisher-Price, 1932, 8 In.		600.00
Duck, Hillclimber, Inertia Powered, Pressed Steel, Painted, 3 Wheels, c.1910, 7 ¾ x 7 ½ In.		127.00
Duck, Quacky Doodle, Mama 12 ½ In., Baby 5 ½ In., 2 Piece		575.00
Eagle, Bell, Red, White, Blue, Iron, Heart Shape Spokes, Gong Bell Mfg. Co., 4 x 5 ½ In. *Illus*		1560.00
Elephant, Baby, Plush, Standing, Smiling, Shag Tail Tip, Tag, Steiff, 48 x 38 ½ In.		805.00
Elephant, Gray Felt, White Tusks, Red Blanket, Wheels, Push Pull, Steiff, 6 ½ x 9 In.		546.00
Elephant, Whirligig, On Ball, Blue Celluloid Platform, Tin Wheels, Japan, 1930s, 7 ½ In.		265.00
Elsie The Cow, Rubber Head, Stuffed Felt, Borden, 1930s, 22 In.		300.00
Farm Set, Dairy Council, Barn, Animals, Milk Truck, Wood, Case, c.1940, 33 x 51 In.		720.00
Farm Set, Tractor, Accessories, Cast Iron, Arcade, Box, c.1939, 11 x 15 In.		1840.00
Ferdinand The Bull, Head, Ceramic, Paint, Black & White, c.1938, 4 ½ x 3 ¾ In.		442.00
Ferdinand The Bull, Tail Spins, Head Moves, Tin, Silk Flower, Clockwork, Marx, 5 ¾ In.		374.00
Ferris Wheel, Revolves, Musical, Tin, 12 Seats, Papier-Mache Passengers, Ticket Booth, 1925, 28 In.		3640.00
Ferris Wheel, Revolves, Tin, Painted, Papier-Mache Passengers, 6 Seats, Tower, Flags, 1893, 20 In.		4760.00
Figure, Safari Native, Cotton Shorts, Plaid Sash, Spear, Schoenhut, 7 ½ In.		3738.00
Figure, Safari Native, Drum, Head Wrap, Holding Drumsticks, Schoenhut, 7 ½ In.		3450.00
Figure, Safari Native, Orange Bowl On Head, Loincloth Shorts, Sash, Schoenhut, 7 ½ In.		4025.00
Figurine, 3 Little Pigs, Playing Instruments, Hats, c.1950, 4 In., 3 Piece		230.00
Fire House, Pressed Steel, Kingsbury, 1920s, 10 x 9 In.		443.00
Fire House, Pumper, Bell Rings, Doors Open, Iron, Wood, Clockwork, Ives, c.1900, 8 ½ x 16 ½ In.		5750.00
Fire Pumper, Horse Drawn, Open Frame, Cast Iron, Nickel Plated, Kenton, 18 In.		633.00
Fire Pumper, Horse Drawn, Tin, Paint, Gilt Stencil, Clockwork, Spoke Wheels, 15 In.		4025.00
Fire Station Playset, Building, Figures, Cars, Marx, Box, 1954		1634.00
Fire Station, Bell, Garage, Truck, Hoses, Keystone, Paper Label, 1940s, 16 x 10 In.		165.00
Fire Station, No. 8, Pressed Steel, Red Paint, Kingsbury, 10 x 13 In.		384.00
Fire Station, Tin, Red, Yellow, Louis Marx, Nov. 8, 1938, 17 x 4 In.		390.00
Fire Truck, Aerial Ladder, Die Cast, Tootsietoy, 9 In.		150.00
Fire Truck, Aerial Ladder, Red, Yellow, Kingsbury, 1941, 24 In.		295.00
Fire Truck, Aerial Ladders, Pressed Steel, Red Paint, Buddy L, 38 In.		770.00
Fire Truck, American LaFrance, Water Tower, Pressed Steel, Paint, Sturditoy, 1930s, 35 In.		1210.00
Fire Truck, City Fire Department, Red Paint, Pressed Steel, Black Ladders, Structo, 25 In.		495.00
Fire Truck, Driver, Red, Cast Iron, Kenton, 7 In.		106.00
Fire Truck, Driver, Removable Lantern Bars, Red, Gold Trim, Iron, Kenton, 6 ½ In. *Illus*		767.00
Fire Truck, Extension Ladder, Pressed Steel, Red Paint, Kingsbury, Restored, 1920s, 38 In.		1650.00
Fire Truck, Fire Department, 2 Ladders, Hose Spool, Bell, Water Tank, Structo, 1930s, 24 In.		288.00
Fire Truck, Hook & Ladder, Hubley, c.1929, 10 In.		850.00
Fire Truck, Hose Reel, Ladder, Ride 'Em Seat, Handle, Pressed Steel, Keystone, 1930s, 27 In.		880.00
Fire Truck, Hose, Cast Iron, Yellow, Red Spoke Wheels, Kenton, 8 In.		1265.00
Fire Truck, Ladder, Black Rubber Tires, Red Paint, Cast Iron, Hubley, 13 In.		420.00
Fire Truck, Ladder, Cast Iron, Open Body, Gold Trim, Wood Ladders, Driver, Kenton, 11 In.		1093.00
Fire Truck, Ladder, Cast Iron, Red, Nickel Grill, Hubley, Diamond T, 6 ½ In.		185.00
Fire Truck, Ladder, Cast Iron, Red, Open Body, Silver Lights, Hubley, 1930s, 7 ¾ In.		633.00
Fire Truck, Ladder, Cast Iron, Red, Silver Dashboard, Nickel Driver, Hubley, 13 In.		374.00
Fire Truck, Ladder, Headlights, Scene, Red, Yellow, Tin Litho, Mizuno, Japan, c.1950, 4 x 9 In.		173.00
Fire Truck, Ladder, Hillclimber, 2 Drivers, Yellow, Red, Black Paint, c.1915, 19 In.		510.00
Fire Truck, Ladder, Red Paint, Die Cast Metal, Plastic, Doepke Rossmoyne, Ohio, c.1955		460.00
Fire Truck, Ladders, Driver, Black Rubber Tires, Red Paint, Cast Iron, Hubley, 15 In.		224.00
Fire Truck, Mack, Chemical, Cast Iron, Red, Gold Trim, Hose Reel, Side Ladders, Arcade, 12 In.		1840.00
Fire Truck, Merryweather, Red, Wheel Clips, Spoke Wheels, Matchbox, Box		55.00

Toy, Castle, 3 Tiers, Removable Tower, Storage, Revolving, Tin, Marklin, Germany, c.1895, 19 x 23 In.
$28,175.00

RSL Auction

Toy, Cat, Felix, On Scooter, Tin Litho, Painted, Windup, Gunthermann, Germany, c.1922, 8 In.
$658.00

Hake's Americana & Collectibles

Toy, Chariot, Hippodrome, 2 Horses, Female Driver, Tin, Dress, Clockwork, Ives, 1893, 14 In.
$69,000.00

James D. Julia Auctioneers

Toy, Child, On Chamber Pot, Knitting, Hand Turns, Papier-Mache, Bellows, Squeak, c.1850, 5 In.
$896.00

Theriault's

Toy, Chinese Man, Seated, Holding Parasol, Wheeled Platform, Tin Litho, Distler, Germany, 3 ½ In.
$460.00

Bertoia Auctions

Toy, Circus Dude, Black Man, Masked Face, Schoenhut, 8 ½ In.
$460.00

James D. Julia Auctioneerse

Toy, Clown, Ko-Ko The Inkwell, Original Clothes, Schoenhut, 1920s, 11 In.
$3,450.00

Bertoia Auctions

Toy, Clown, Orchestra, Rings Bells When Piano Is Played, Tin, Wood, Victor Bonnet, France, 10 In.
$1,265.00

Bertoia Auctionsa

T

Toy, Couple & Dog, Walking Down Broadway, Tin Litho, Flywheel, Cogwheel, Lehmann, 6 In.
$3,835.00

Bertoia Auctions

Toy, Couple, Waltzing, Felt Outfits, Stroll Motion, Tin, Fernand Martin, France, 8 In.
$2,588.00

Bertoia Auctions

Toy, Cow, Brown & Cream Hide, Glass Eyes, Papier-Mache Horns & Udder, Neck Bell, 1800s, 36 In.
$1,232.00

Theriault's

Toy, Car, Dagwood, Driver, Tin Lithograph, Clockwork, Marx, 8 In.
$403.00

Bertoia Auctions

Toy, Deep Sea Diver, Yellow Suit, Helmet, Propeller Blades, Clockwork, Lithograph, Germany, 7 In.
$5,750.00

Bertoia Auctions

Toy, Dinner Set, Exotic Birds, Black Rims, Soft Paste, c.1885, 6-In. Pieces
$1,232.00

Theriault's

Toy, Dog, On Scooter, Tin, Pull Toy, J. Chein, 7 In.
$720.00

Showtime Auction Sevices

Toy, Dog, Poodle, Jointed, Wood, Cloth Mane, Glass Eyes, Cord Tail, Schoenhut, 7 In.
$431.00

Bertoia Auctions

Toy, Doggy Racer, Dog Driver, Felt-Like Arms, Steering Wheel, No. 7, Pull Toy, Fisher-Price, 9 ¾ In.
$390.00

Showtime Auction Sevices

Toy, Dollhouse Furniture, Dressing Tables, Settee, Chairs, Bed, Desk, Tynietoy, c.1930, 1 In., 7 Piece
$728.00

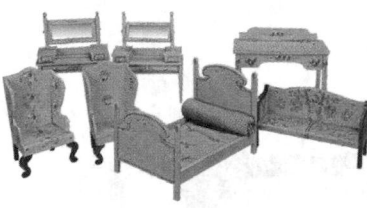

Theriault's

Toy, Dollhouse, 2 Rooms, Folding, Heavy Board Frame, Litho, McLoughlin Bros., c.1890, 18 In.
$896.00

Theriault's

T

Fire Truck, Open Frame, Ladder Supports, Tin Ladders, Driver, Cast Iron, Kenton, 1930s, 17 In.	266.00
Fire Truck, Pumper, Cast Iron, Red Paint, Nickel Boiler, Rubber Tires, Hubley, 1930s, 13 In...	978.00
Fire Truck, Pumper, Cast Iron, Red, Silver Boiler, Nickel Driver, Tool Kit, Hubley, 11 In...........	518.00
Fire Truck, Pumper, Pontiac, 6 Men, Cast Iron, Red, Silver, Rubber Tires, Arcade, 1940s, 13 In.	1610.00
Fire Truck, Pumper, Pressed Steel, No. 7, American LaFrance, Sturditoy, 1930s, 27 In.............	1210.00
Fire Truck, Pumper, Pressed Steel, Red, Silver, Gold Paint, Kingsbury, 22 In.	708.00
Fire Truck, Pumper, Steam, Red, Black, Germany, 7 In.	720.00
Fire Truck, Steamer, Driver, Red Paint, Cast Iron, Rubber Wheels, Hubley, 11 In.	523.00
Fire Truck, Steamer, Pressed Steel, Pull Handle, Kelmut, 1920s, 24 In.	960.00
Fire Truck, Steamer, Pull Handle, Red Paint, Pressed Steel, Kelmut, Restored, 1920s, 24 In.....	960.00
Fire Truck, Steamer, Windup, Tin, Gold, Red, Black Paint, Cast Iron Driver, 11 In.	360.00
Fire Wagon, 2 Horses, Driver, Red, Black Paint, Cast Iron, 20 In........	468.00
Fire Wagon, 2 Horses, Ladder, Open Frame, Iron, Spoke Wheels, 2 Figures, Hubley, 20 In.	144.00
Fire Wagon, 3 Horses, Steamer, Driver, Black, Red, Gold Paint, 18 ½ In........	510.00
Fire Wagon, Chief, Horse Drawn, Blue, Gold Trim, Red Spoke Wheels, Iron, Kenton, 12 In.	748.00
Fire Wagon, Fire Patrol, Wood, Steel Wheels, Red, Gold Lettering, PMC, 48 In.	5500.00
Fire Wagon, Horse Drawn, Driver, Gray, Orange Paint, Cast, Iron, c.1900, 16 x 6 ½ In.	236.00
Fire Wagon, Horse Drawn, Hose Reel, Open Frame, Blue, Silver Hose Reel, Kenton, 12 In.......	546.00
Fire Wagon, Horse Drawn, Hose, Cast Iron, Railed Open Bed, Kenton, 14 In.	460.00
Fire Wagon, Horse, Hose Reel, Cast Iron, Paint, c.1900, 13 ¼ In........	354.00
Foxy Grandpa, Holding Hat & Cane, Painted, Clockwork, Gunthermann, Germany, 8 In. *Illus*	1652.00
Foxy Grandpa, Wood, Jointed, Papier-Mache Head, Fabric Clothing, Grotesque, 9 In.	1495.00
Frog, Butterfly On Wire, Green, Yellow, Tin Lithograph, CKO, 4 ¾ In.	510.00
Frog, Wearing Suit, Hat, Clockwork, Tin, Painted, Germany, 7 x 2 ½ In. ....*Illus*	633.00
Gaston, Felt, Elongated Torso, Shoebutton-Style Eyes, Jointed, Steiff, 18 In. ....*Illus*	690.00
G.I. Joe, British Commando M.P., Khaki Uniform, Helmet, Duffle Bag, Hasbro, 1960s, 12 In. ..*Illus*	224.00
G.I. Joe, Japanese Imperial Soldier, Order Of Kite Medal, Soldiers Of World, Hasbro, c.1965, 11 In...*Illus*	173.00
G.I. Joe, Sailor, Painted Hair, Denim Shirt, Pants, Boots, Sailor Cap, Box, Hasbro, 1960s, 12 In. ...*Illus*	112.00
Games are listed in the Game category.	
Garage, Cars, Gasoline Pump, Lights, 2 Bays, Keystone, 10 x 5 In.	248.00
Gas Pump, Green Paint, Embossed Gas On Globe, Dial Turns, Cast Iron, Arcade, 6 In.............	431.00
Gas Pump, Red Paint, Embossed, Gas, Dials, Cast Iron, Arcade, 6 In.	230.00
Gas Pump, U.S. Gas, Crank, Red, Yellow, Tin Lithograph, c.1930, 7 ¼ In........................	116.00
Geese, In Coop, Pecking, Trough, Tin Litho, Windup, Meier, Germany, 2 x 1 ¼ In. ....*Illus*	345.00
Gilbert Electric Eye, Electronic Science Set, Red Metal Case, 1949, 16 x 8 x 2 ¾ In	135.00
Giraffe, Metal Articulated, Composition, Rope Tail, Ball Bearing, Switzerland, c.1925, 11 In. .	4704.00
Giraffe, Movable Legs, Head, Brown, Tan Paint, Wood, Schoenhut, 11 In.........................	300.00
Giraffe, Wood, Jointed, Yellow, Brown Paint, Schoenhut, 11 In..................................	165.00
Girl, Feeding Pecking Chicken, Mechanical, Penny Toy, 3 ¾ In.	431.00
Girl, In Rocking Chair, Holding Bunny, Tin, Penny Toy, Meier, Germany, Prewar, 2 ½ In....*Illus*	472.00
Golfer, Wood, Painted Metal, Club, Activating Lever, Marked Schoenhut, 35 In......................	242.00
Goose, On Platform, Articulated Neck, Tin Litho, Spoke Wheels, Penny Toy, Distler, Germany, 2 ¼ In.	403.00
Gorilla, Applied Face, Painted Features, Jointed Shoulders, Legs, Wood, Schoenhut, c.1910, 8 In. ..*Illus*	1344.00
Grasshopper, Iron Body, Aluminum Legs, Green, Rubber Tires, Articulated, Pull Toy, 10 In. ..	472.00
Grasshopper, Top Hat, Green Felt, Wooden Eyes, Wire Antennae, Lenci, c.1960, 7 In. ......*Illus*	336.00
Groggy Auto, Celluloid Comic Character, Tin Lithograph Car, Occupied Japan, 4 ½ In.	345.00
Guitar Player, Man, Tin Lithograph, Clockwork, Distler, Germany, Box, 8 ¼ In.	690.00
Gun & Holster, Wagon Train, Plastic, Sheriff, Store Card, 1958, 7 x 11 ½ In.	172.00
Gun, BB, Target Special, Model 118, Steel, Blued Finish, Daisy, 1920s	135.00
Gun, Squirt, Aluminum, Blue Plastic, Buddy L, Box	235.00
Ham & Sam Minstrel Band, 2 Musicians, Piano, Horn, Tin, Clockwork, Strauss, 7 In.	403.00
Handcar, 2 Men Pushing, Painted, Embossed Tin Litho, Windup, Bing, Germany, 4 ½ In.	333.00
Handcar, 2 Men Pushing, Red Blue Paint, Tin, Windup, O Gauge, Bing, 5 ¼ In.	303.00
Handcar, Moon Mullins & Kayo, Railroad Car, Tin Litho, Windup, c.1930, 6 ¼ x 6 ¼ In.	230.00
Hansom Cab, Horse, Black Driver, Turning Bar & Wheel, Paint, Cast Iron, 12 In....................	900.00
Happy Hooligan, Can On Head, Plaid Jacket, Smirk, Comic Character, Schoenhut, 9 In.........	690.00
Happy Hooligan, Walker, Green Jacket, Tin Lithograph, Clockwork, Chein, 6 ¼ In.	259.00
Harold Lloyd, Scissors, Tin Lithograph, Die Cut, 8 In. ....*Illus*	89.00
Harold Lloyd, Standing, Movable Eyes, Face, Brown, Cream, Tin Litho, Windup, Germany, 6 ½ In.	570.00
Henry, Riding Swan, Celluloid, Tin, Paint, Windup, Key, Japan, 1930s, 8 ½ In.	930.00
Hobbyhorse, Carved Painted, c.1895, 32 x 38 In........	334.00
Hobbyhorse, Carved, Painted, Inset Glass Eyes, Iron Clad Wheels, Iron Spokes, c.1890, 41 x 12 In. ...	1185.00
Hobbyhorse, Carved, White, Red Paint, 36 x 39 In.........................	144.00
Hobbyhorse, Gray Speckle, Red Saddle, Paint, Wood Stand, c.1890, 30 x 37 In.....................	267.00
Hobbyhorse, Mobo Bronco, Metal, D. Sebel & Co. Ltd., England, 1940s ....*Illus*	390.00

Toy, Dollhouse, 2 Rooms, Wood, Paper Litho, Balcony, Gottschalk, Germany, c.1890, 17 In.
$4,480.00

Theriault's

Toy, Dollhouse, 4 Rooms, Wood, Paper Litho, Front Porch, Balcony, Gingerbread, Bliss, c.1890, 20 In.
$1,120.00

Theriault's

Toy, Dresser, Doll's, Empire Style, 6 Drawers, Mirror, 13 x 17 ½ In.
$345.00

James D. Julia Auctioneers

Toy, Eagle, Bell, Red, White, Blue, Iron, Heart Shape Spokes, Gong Bell Mfg. Co., 4 x 5 ½ In.
$1,560.00

Skinner, Inc.

Toy, Fire Truck, Driver, Removable Lantern Bars, Red, Gold Trim, Iron, Kenton, 6 ½ In.
$767.00

Bertoia Auctions

Toy, Foxy Grandpa, Holding Hat & Cane, Painted, Clockwork, Gunthermann, Germany, 8 In.
$1,652.00

Bertoia Auctions

Toy, Frog, Wearing Suit, Hat, Clockwork, Tin, Painted, Germany, 7 x 2 ½ In.
$633.00

Bertoia Auctions

Hobbyhorse, White, Brown, Seascape, Ship Base, Carved, Painted, c.1865, 26 x 47 In.	1185.00
Hobo On Bicycle, Balance, Tin Lithograph, Wire, A.C. Gilbert, 1920s, 7 ¼ In.	173.00
Hobo, Brown Coat, Schoenhut, 7 ¾ In.	150.00
Hobo, Wood, Jointed, Brown Felt Jacket, Black Hat, Wine Bottle, Schoenhut, 8 In.	259.00
Horse & Cart, Driver, Coal, Embossed, Cast Iron, Kenton, 7 In.	690.00
Horse & Cart, Paint, Wood, Gibbs, 19 In.	69.00
Horse & Cart, Wood, Red, Black, Yellow Paint, 26 In.	130.00
Horse & Driver, Sulky, Composition, Metal, Germany, 6 In.	100.00
Horse & Plow, Driver, Lever, Red, Yellow Paint, Cast Iron, Tin, 9 In.	5700.00
Horse & Wagon, 2 Horses, Drivers, Overland Circus Band, Paint, Iron, 1930s, 15 ½ In.	259.00
Horse & Wagon, Abbott's Milk, Crate, 10 Bottles, Schoenhut, 12 In.	590.00
Horse & Wagon, Beer, Iron, Green Open Bed, Bench Seat, Driver, 2 Horses, Kenton, 14 In.	288.00
Horse & Wagon, Black Driver, Front End, Yellow, Black Paint, Cast Iron, 10 ½ In.	360.00
Horse & Wagon, Bond Bread, Driver, Wheeled Platform, Green Paint, Schoenhut, 22 In.	3900.00
Horse & Wagon, Confectionery, Tin, Paint, Driver, Awning, Spoke Wheels, 14 ½ In.	2818.00
Horse & Wagon, Driver, Barrels, Wilkens Farm, Red, Cast Iron, 10 ½ In.	130.00
Horse & Wagon, Driver, Red, White, Green Paint, Cast Iron, 16 x 6 In.	71.00
Horse & Wagon, Farm, Ride On, Pressed Steel, Yellow, Gray Paint, Buddy L, 24 In.	330.00
Horse & Wagon, Hood's Dairy, Driver, Harness, Milk Bottle Case, Schoenhut, 23 In.	2070.00
Horse & Wagon, Milk, Borden's, Golden Crest, Tin, Wood, Pull Toy, Rich Toys, Iowa, 20 In. *Illus*	165.00
Horse & Wagon, Milk, Driver, Cast Iron, Kenton, 13 In.	124.00
Horse & Wagon, Pressed Steel, Maroon, Yellow Spoke Wheels, Wilkins, 16 In.	2875.00
Horse, Feet Move As Horse Is Pulled, Painted Slab Base, Metal, 4 Wheels, 10 x 9 x 4 In.	3600.00
Horse, Felt, Leather Saddle, Wheeled Stand, Pull Toy, c.1890, 22 x 19 ¾ In.	486.00
Horse, Full Body, Balanced Between Wheels, Rocks, Tin, George Brown, 8 x 7 In. *Illus*	5175.00
Horse, Harness Racer, Wood Jockey, Metal Sulky, Painted, Spring Seat, 25 x 42 In.	220.00
Horse, Hide Covered, Wood, Platform, Wheels, Glass Eyes, Horsehair Mane & Tail, Pull Toy, 14 In.	1232.00
Horse, Leather, Glass Eyes, Saddle, Wool Blanket, Shearling Mane & Tail, 10 In.	68.00
Horse, Plush, Glass Eyes, Fur Mane, Mohair Tail, Vinyl Trim, Wheeled Base, 14 In.	145.00
Horse, Rider, Platform, Black Horse, Trotting, Tin, Spoke Wheels, 15 x 12 ½ In.	1380.00
Horse, Rocking, American Shield, Green Ground, c.1890, 21 x 35 In.	243.00
Horse, Rocking, Brown, Cream Painted, Carved, 43 x 70 In.	300.00
Horse, Rocking, Carved, Gesso, Dapple Paint, Leather, Martingale, Saddle, c.1865, 42 x 48 In.	353.00
Horse, Rocking, Hide Covered, Painted Blue, 1800s, 31 ½ x 64 In.	830.00
Horse, Rocking, Pine, Painted, Seat Between 2 Horses, c.1900, 18 ½ x 40 In.	89.00
Horse, Rocking, Running, Wood Frame, White Paint, Hair Mane, Glass Eyes, 37 x 44 In.	531.00
Horse, Rocking, Victorian, Wood, White, Black Paint, Square Base, 33 x 23 ½ In.	192.00
Horse, Rocking, Wood, Black, White Paint, Trians Bros., England, c.1900, 39 x 43 In.	295.00
Horse, Rocking, Wood, Carved, Paint, 1800s, 27 x 25 In.	2530.00
Horse, Rocking, Wood, Carved, Painted, Horsehair Mane, Tail, Leather Saddle, c.1850, 23 In.	2128.00
Horse, Rocking, Wood, Carved, White, Brown Paint, c.1845, 49 In.	115.00
Horse, Wood, Composition, Paint, Pull Toy, Germany, c.1925, 12 x 11 In.	138.00
Hott & Tott Musical Band, Piano, Guitar, Unique Art Co., 1920s	775.00
Humphrey Mobile, Humphrey Riding An Outhouse Bike, Tin Litho, Clockwork, Wyandotte, 6 In. *Illus*	316.00
Hyena, Wood, Jointed, Stripes, Leather Ears, Rope Tail, Schoenhut, 6 ½ In.	489.00
Indians Set, Metal, Painted, Standing Warriors, Shield, Tomahawk Bearers, Pony, 3 & 4 In., 6 Piece	35.00
Jazzbo Jim & Fiddler, Dances, Arm Moves, Tin Lithograph, Clockwork, Unique Art, 10 In.	403.00
Jazzbo Jim, Dancing Figure On Cabin, Tin Lithograph, Clockwork, F. Strauss, 9 ½ In.	259.00
Jeep, U.S. Army, World War II, Wood, Green Paint, Wheels, 1950s, 9 x 15 ½ x 9 In. *Illus*	280.00
Jigger, Dutch Boy & Girl, Papier-Mache Heads, Dutch Costumes, Multicolor, Schoenhut, 21 x 16 In.	1208.00
Jigger, Tombo The Alabama Coon, Dances, Moving Arms, Legs, Tin Litho, Windup, c.1918, 5 x 7 In.	460.00
Joe Palooka Boxing Set, Glove, Helmet, Bop Bag, Vinyl, Air Pump, Fisher Art, c.1952, 5 Piece	173.00
Junior Florist Set, Plastic Tools, Pots, Seeds, Box, Worcester Toy Co., Mass., 13 x 13 In., 2 Piece	47.00
Kangaroo, Wood, Jointed, Glass Eyes, Leather Ears, Schoenhut, 7 In.	1725.00
Kitchen, Built-In Chimney, Stove, 3 Walls, Grain Paint, Accessories, Nuremberg, c.1850, 22 x 14 In.	3920.00
Kitty, In A Shoe, Tin, Windup, Shoe Moves Forwards, Yanoman Japan, 1960s, 5 ¾ In.	90.00
Lamb, On Wheeled Base, Plush, Painted Features, Glass Eyes, Brass Bell, Wire Frame, 18 x 19 In.	35.00
Li'l Abner Dogpatch Band, Tin, Windup, Unique Art, 1945	316.00 to 506.00
Lion Larry, Plush, Felt Fabric, Pull String, Mattel, 1960s, 11 In.	90.00
Lion, Marilyn Neuhart, Embroidered Cotton, Yarn Mane, c.1962, 8 x 11 In. *Illus*	1063.00
Lion, Movable Legs, Head, Brown Paint, Wood, Schoenhut, 5 ½ In.	210.00
Little King, Roller Figure, Wood, Painted, Wheel Spool Base, Jaymar, KFS, Box, 1939, 2 x 3 ¾ In.	139.00
Little Tot Building Blocks, Wood, Schoenhut, Box, 18 In.	86.00
Llama, Pushmi-Pullyu, 2 Heads, Plush, Synthetic Fur, Glass Eyes, Standing, Steiff, 67 x 75 In.	2070.00
Lucky Monk, On Riding Cart, Orange Paint, Pull Toy, No. 109, Fisher-Price, 1932, 10 In.	1100.00
Maggie & Jiggs, Dueling, Maggie & Rolling Pin, Jiggs & Cane, Windup, Litho, Nifty, 8 In. *Illus*	633.00

T

Magic Slate, Chandu The Magician, Instructions, Ernst Kern, 1930s, 6 ½ x 9 In.	403.00
Man From Mars, Yellow, Green Dome, Plastic, Windup, Irwin, Box, 10 In.............................	1440.00
Man, Naturalist, Safari Clothes, Wood, Jointed, Painted Face, Schoenhut, 9 In.	968.00
Man, Naturalist, Safari Clothing, Mustache, Ammo Belt, Schoenhut, 7 ½ In..........................	1888.00
Merry-Go-Round, 4 Horses, Riders, Cloth Canopy, Clockwork, Bing, Germany, 24 In. ...*Illus*	2242.00
Merry-Go-Round, Children On Horses, Tin, Clockwork, Wolverine, 12 In...............................	173.00
Merrymakers Band, Mice, Tin Litho, Clockwork, Marx, c.1929, 9 ½ In............................*Illus*	633.00
Metro Sunday Comics, Punch-Out Figures, Die Cut, Display, 27 Characters, 1952	759.00
Model Kit, Addams Family, Haunted House, Instructions, Color, Aurora, Box, 1964, 9 x 12 ½ In. ..	436.00
Model Kit, King Kong, Aurora, Cellophane Wrap, Box, R.K.O., 1964	831.00
Model Kit, U.S. Army Patton Tank, Monogram Co., Red Box, Unopened, 1959.....................	80.00
Monkey Beats Drum, Band Uniform, Moves Head, Tail, Tin Litho, Distler, Germany, c.1920 .	448.00
Monkey Beats Drum, Tin Lithograph, Clockwork, Distler, 8 In.......................................	431.00
Monkey Cyclist, Tricycle, Tin Lithograph, Windup, Lever, Box, Marx, c.1940, 5 ¾ In..............	115.00
Monkey Shines, Tin Litho, Cardboard, Steel, Emporium Specialties, 1950s, 7 x 18 In.............	115.00
Monkey, Climbing, Red, Pants, Cap, Gray Coat, Yellow Vest, Rope, Box, Lehmann, Germany, 7 In.	248.00
Monkey, Climbing, Spiral Pole, Tin Litho, Penny Toy, Germany, 11 In..............................	345.00
Monkey, Coconut Bell Nut, Paint, Cast Iron, Pull Toy, 6 ¼ In.	212.00
Monkey, Jocko, Jointed Hips & Shoulders, Glass Inset Eyes, Steiff, 1950s, 33 In..................	460.00
Mork From Ork Eggship, Mork Inside, Plastic, 1979, 5 x 3 In.	25.00
Mother Goose Rocker, Tin Litho, Multicolor, Windup, Rocks, Hops, Cat Riders, Marx, 7 x 9 In....	413.00
Motorcycle & Rider, Halloh, Tin Litho, Clockwork, Lehmann, 8 ¾ In. ....*Illus*	1725.00
Motorcycle & Rider, Tetsujin, Multicolor, Tin Lithograph, Friction, Japan, 7 In.	1200.00
Motorcycle Cop, Indian Decal, 4 Cylinder Nickel Engine, Rubber Tires, Iron, Hubley, 9 In. ....*Illus*	1416.00
Motorcycle, Champion, Policeman, Blue Suit, Gold Badge On Cap, Iron, 1920s, 5 x 3 In........	415.00
Motorcycle, Highway Patrol, Driver, Battery Operated, Modern Toys, Japan, 11 ½ In. ......*Illus*	489.00
Motorcycle, Indian, 4 Cylinder, Green Paint, Cast Iron, Hubley, 9 ¼ In.............................	660.00
Motorcycle, Indian, Cast Iron, Green, 4 Nickel Cylinders, Pull Cord, Hubley, 1930s, 9 ½ In.	518.00
Motorcycle, Military Rider, Friction, Tin Litho, Rubber Tires, Siren, Nomura, 1950s, 6 ½ x 4 ¾ In.	139.00
Motorcycle, Police, Blue Uniform, Iron, Red, Rubber Tires, Spokes, Globe, 8 ¾ In..................	2300.00
Motorcycle, Police, Tin, Yellow, Windup, Tips Over, Driver, Unique Art, 8 In.	365.00
Motorcycle, Policeman, Paint, Cast Iron, Hubley, 5 In., Pair.....................................	450.00
Motorcycle, Policeman, Tin Litho, Indian, Headdress On Tank, Key, Linemar, 1950s, 6 ¾ x 4 In...	330.00
Motorcycle, Rookie Cop, Flopping Motion, Siren, Tin Litho, Louis Marx, 8 ½ In..................	230.00
Motorcycle, Sidecar, Cop, Red, Blue, Hubley, 4 In...	250.00
Motorcycle, Sidecar, Driver, Passenger, Green Paint, Iron, Harley-Davidson, 9 In.	550.00
Mr. Hustler, Walks, Light-Up, Battery Operated, Tin Lithograph, Japan, Box, 11 ½ In.............	840.00
Mr. Magoo, Tin Litho, Black Cloth Roof, Box, Battery Operated, Hubley, 1961, 9 x 8 In...........	405.00
Mr. Mechanical Brain, Battery Operated, Windup, Bulbs, Alps, Japan, Box, 7 ¾ In................	1140.00
Mule Team, Wagon, Driver, Paint, Cast Iron, Wood Barrel, Kenton, c.1900, 14 In.	230.00
Mystery Ball, Spiral Action, Tin Litho, Figure At Last Stop, Fernand Martin, France, 14 In. ...*Illus*	863.00
Noah's Ark, Pine, Stencil, Painted, 8 Human, 31 Pairs Animals, 8 Singles, Germany, c.1900, 20 In.	452.00
Nodder, Foxy Grandpa Driver, Carriage, Horse Drawn, Uncle Sam, Kenton, 17 In....................	748.00
Nursemaid, Black, White Infant, Wood, Papier-Mache, Old Aunt Chloe, Ives, Blakeslee, c.1875 ...*Illus*	11638.00
Office Desk, Chair, Painted Green, Nickeled Top, Opening Drawers, Iron, Kenton, 2 ½ x 3 In.	354.00
Old Woman, Cane, Eyeglasses, Basket On Back, Walking, Tin, Clockwork, Gunthermann, 7 In. ...*Illus*	690.00
Omnibus, Mechanical, Tin Litho, Compagnie Generale Des Omibus, Driver, France, Rossignol, 12 In.	3360.00
Organ Grinder, Felt Suit, Painted Head, Tin Litho, Clockwork, Fernand Martin, France, 9 In. ...*Illus*	1725.00
Ostrich, Movable Legs, Head, Gray, Black Paint, Wood, Schoenhut, 7 In.	210.00
Ox Cart, Driver, 2 Oxen, Yellow, Red, Cast Iron, Kyser & Rex, 13 ½ In..............................	266.00
Paddy & Pig, Tin Lithograph, Lehmann, 1920s, 6 In. ....*Illus*	1150.00
Paint & Coloring Set, Skippy, Hinged Box, American Toy Works, N.Y., 12 x 17 In....................	115.00
Parrot, Cage, Composition, Squeak, c.1890, 7 ½ In..	178.00
Peacock, Hinged Legs, 3 Feather Panels, Tin Litho, Windup, Germany, Blomer & Schuler, 9 In. ...*Illus*	5824.00
Pedal Car, Airplane, Red, Yellow Paint, Louis Meyers, Rolls Racer Airmail, 1920s, 24 x 43 In..	791.00
Pedal Car, Chevrolet, Tan & Orange, Steel Wheels, Rubber Tires, Steelcraft, 1937, 36 In.	2128.00
Pedal Car, Covered Wagon, 2 Horses, Pressed Steel, 45 In.......................................	330.00
Pedal Car, Estate Wagon, Faux Wood Sides, Green, Whitewall Tires, c.1950, 20 x 41 In.	900.00
Pedal Car, Fire Hose Reel Truck, Red, Whitewall Tires, Bell, American National, 68 In.	4400.00
Pedal Car, Fire Truck, Metal, Red, Black, Ladders, Bell, Steelcraft, 1930s	1650.00
Pedal Car, Fire Truck, Skippy DeSoto Airflow, Siren, Bucket, American National, c.1935, 36 In.	3300.00
Pedal Car, Fire Truck, Toledo No. 6, Chemical, 1924, 64 In.	1925.00
Pedal Car, Fire Truck, Wood, Metal, Red, Black Paint, American National Fire Ladder, 1918, 75 In. ..	4675.00
Pedal Car, Garton Space Cruiser, Spaceship, White, Red Trim, Pressed Steel, 47 In................	1550.00
Pedal Car, Green Frame, Red Hub Caps, Seat, Triang, England, 1930s, 42 In.........................	3600.00
Pedal Car, Green, Triang, England, 1930s, 42 In. ....*Illus*	3600.00

Toy, Gaston, Felt, Elongated Torso, Shoebutton-Style Eyes, Jointed, Steiff, 18 In.
$690.00

James D. Julia Auctioneers

Toy, G.I. Joe, British Commando M.P., Khaki Uniform, Helmet, Duffle Bag, Hasbro, 1960s, 12 In.
$224.00

Theriault's

Toy, G.I. Joe, Japanese Imperial Soldier, Order Of Kite Medal, Soldiers Of World, Hasbro, c.1965, 11 In.
$173.00

Hake's Americana & Collectibles

T

Toy, G.I. Joe, Sailor, Painted Hair, Denim Shirt, Pants, Boots, Sailor Cap, Box, Hasbro, 1960s, 12 In.
$112.00

Theriault's

Toy, Geese, In Coop, Pecking, Trough, Tin Litho, Windup, Meier, Germany, 2 x 1 ¼ In.
$345.00

Bertoia Auctions

Toy, Girl, In Rocking Chair, Holding Bunny, Tin, Penny Toy, Meier, Germany, Prewar, 2 ½ In.
$472.00

Bertoia Auctions

Toy, Gorilla, Applied Face, Painted Features, Jointed Shoulders, Legs, Wood, Schoenhut, c.1910, 8 In.
$1,344.00

Theriault's

Pedal Car, Horse, Black Beauty, Black, Red Paint, 39 In.	1650.00
Pedal Car, Jeep, Metal, U.S. Army Decoration	224.00
Pedal Car, Locomotive, No. 9, Wood Frame, Red, Black Paint, American National, 1927, 46 In.	6875.00
Pedal Car, McCormick Farmall 400, Red Paint, Double Front Wheels, 1960s, 39 x 28 In. ....*Illus*	632.00
Pedal Car, Metal, Red Paint, Steelcraft, 1930s, 46 In.	791.00
Pedal Car, Murray, Convertible, Green, White Paint, 1950s, 35 In.	325.00
Pedal Car, Oldsmobile, Steel, Pierced Wheels, Rubber Tires, Siren, Steelcraft, 1941, 40 In. .. *Illus*	1955.00
Pedal Car, Orange Crate Body, Metal Wheels, 1911 Chicago Sidewalk Riding Permit, 1910, 46 In.	600.00
Pedal Car, Painted, Red, Yellow Striping, Wire Spoke Wheels, Kirk-Latty, 1928, 40 In.	1430.00
Pedal Car, Red, Rounded Frame, Red Paint, Kirk-Latty, c.1932, 36 In.	2090.00
Pedal Car, Scooter, 3 Wheels, Young Lion, 1947, 36 x 24 In.	236.00
Pedal Car, Space Cruiser, Silver, Red Paint, Pressed Steel, 47 In.	360.00
Pedal Car, Steel, Rubber Tires, Luggage Rack, Wood Grill With Jordan, Gendron, 1929, 50 In. .. *Illus*	6325.00
Pedal Car, Thunderbird Jr., Electric, Leather Seats, Power Car Co.	180.00
Pedal Car, Tin Lizzie, Green, Yellow Detail, Garton, 21 x 38 In.	266.00
Pedal Car, Toledo Studebaker, Windshield, Black, Red Striping, White Wheels, 1925	2200.00
Pedal Car, Tractor & Wagon, Red, Pressed Steel, c.1955, 37 In.	180.00
Pedal Car, Tractor, Castelli, Joanne, Metal, Red, 3 Wheels, 1940s	224.00
Pedal Car, Train, LMS, Bell, Wood, Red Paint, Triang Toys, c.1942-43, 42 In. ....*Illus*	823.00
Pedal Car, Wagon, Dump, Wood, Metal, Red Paint, Speed Line, American National, 47 In.	1320.00
Pedal Car, Willys-Knight, Wood Frame, Wood Spoke Wheels, Gendron, 1917, 48 In.	4803.00
Pedal Car, Wood Frame, Hand Crank, Headlights, Black, Red Trim, Wilkerson, c.1915, 44 In.	3575.00
Pedal Carriage, Horse Drawn, France, 1920s	495.00
Peter Rabbit Chick-Mobile, Handcar, Metal, Composition, Clockwork, Lionel, Box, 9 ½ In. .	2723.00
Piano, Grand, Bench, Iron, Painted, Folding Music Stand, Arcade, 5 In., 2 Piece ....*Illus*	575.00
Piano, Pink Bench, Music Stand Folds, Blue Paint, Cast Iron, Arcade, 5 In.	575.00
Piano, Woman Player, Composition, Wood, Metal Hands, Clockwork, Secor & Ives, 10 x 8 In..	1331.00
Pig, Holding Beer Stein, Felt Body, Blue Pants, Clockwork, Marked, Schuco, Germany, 4 ½ In. ..*Illus*	236.00
Pillow, Spider-Man, Swinging Over Cityscape, Inflatable, Vinyl, Clear, c.1968, 13 ½ x 23 ½ In...	696.00
Plane, Fighter, Landing Gear, Die Cast, Red, Silver, Hubley, Box	275.00
Plane, Passenger, 6 Windows, Detachable Wing & Propeller, Tin, Orobr, Germany, Box, c.1930, 14 In.	728.00
Planter, Yellow Paint, Cast Iron, 4 x 4 In.	30.00
Play Golf, Tin Litho, Metal Base, Spring Drive Motor, Golfer, Glass Balls, Strauss, 6 ¾ x 12 In.	561.00
Play House, Yellow Roof, Blue & White House, Wood, Fisher-Price, No. 952, 1969, 15 x 9 In...	85.00
Plow, Red Paint, Cast Iron, c.1900, 6 x 4 In.	30.00
Plow, Steel, Gale Chilled, Albion, Michigan, Salesman's Sample, Pat. Dates 1874-76, 26 x 11 In. ....*Illus*	8625.00
Pokey Joe, Nosco's Ding Dong Fire Truck, Pull String, Hard Plastic, Box, 4 ½ x 10 x 5 In.	115.00
Pond Dredger, Buddy L	360.00
Pool Player, Table, Tin Lithograph, Windup, Germany, 6 ¼ In.	180.00
Porter, Trunk On Hand Cart, Dog Pops Out, Luggage, Red Cap, Tin, Strauss, 6 ½ In.	690.00
Porter, With Luggage, Tin Lithograph, Penny Toy, 3 ¼ In.	403.00
Pounding Bench, Maple, Pegs, Hammer, Doepke, 1957, 6 ½ In.	75.00
Powerful Katrinka, Lifting Jimmy, Tin Litho, Clockwork, c.1923, Fontaine Fox, 5 ½ In. ....*Illus*	2588.00
Powerful Katrinka, Jimmy, Wheelbarrow, Tin Litho, Clockwork, Fontaine Fox, c.1923, 6 ½ In.	1093.00
Puppy, Ginny's, Vinyl Plaid Blankets, Bell, Leash, Steiff	81.00
Puzzle Box, Our Darlings, Children Holding Hands, Milton Bradley Co., 13 x 18 In., 5 Piece..	23.00
Puzzle Cubes, Battleship, Lithograph, Paper, Cardboard, 6 Guide Sheets, McLoughlin, 13 x 11 In..	1380.00
Rabbit, Cart, Tall Rabbit Pulling Small Rabbit In Cart, Tin, Wyandotte, Box, 10 In.	431.00
Rabbit, Mohair, Blond, Boy, Standing, Glass Eyes, Shirt, Felt Lederhosen, Steiff, c.1950, 30 ½ In. ..	118.00
Rabbit, Mohair, Dress, Pink Felt Lined Ears, Amber, Black Glass Eyes, Black Thread Nose, 18 ½ In.	35.00
Rabbit, On Cart, Tin Lithograph, Penny Toy, Meier, Germany, 2 ¾ In.	345.00
Rabbit, On Wheels, Plastic, Friction, Pink, Yellow & Blue Ball, Molded, 1960s	16.00
Rabbit, Wood, Brown Paint, Painted Eyes, Leather Ears, Schoenhut, 4 ¾ In.	805.00
Racing Game, Mechanical Horses, Case, France, 7 x 15 In.	326.00
Range Rider, Cowboy, Lasso, Horse, Rocker Base, Tin Litho, Clockwork, Marx, 11 In.	230.00
Rattle, Wood, Bell In Cylinder, Doepke, 1957, 8 In.	35.00
Red Ranger Ride 'Em Cowboy, Tin Litho, Box, Windup, Wyandotte, 1950s, 6 ½ x 6 ½ In.	144.00
Refrigerator, GE, Iron, Green, Door Opens, Interior Shelves, Nickel Ice Tray, Hubley, 7 In.	460.00
Refrigerator, Steel, Shelves, Tin Pan, Wyandotte, Salesman's Sample, 5 ¼ x 9 ½ In. ....*Illus*	420.00
Reindeer, Plush Body, Velvet Antlers, Leatherette Hooves, Shag Mane & Beard, Steiff, 70 x 68 In...	345.00
Rex Mars Planet Patrol, Sparkling Space Tank, Wind-Up, Box, Marx, 1950s, 5 ¼ x 10 In.....	386.00
Rickshaw, Dog Pushing Monkey, Umbrella, Tin Litho, Windup, Germany, c.1900, 5 ½ x 4 In.	1689.00
Ride A Rocket, Revolving Rocket Cars, Tin Litho, Windup, Chein, c.1950, 18 x 11 In.	538.00
Ring, Magic, Rin Tin Tin, Brilliant Luster Nabisco Premium, Adjustable, Hinged, Pencil, 1954.	86.00
Ring, Rocket, Space Patrol, Plastic, Translucent Blue, Glow-In-Dark, Ralston Premium, 1952 ..*Illus*	403.00
Ringmaster, Red Coat, Hat, White Pants, Paint, Schoenhut, 8 ½ In.	180.00

Road Builder's Set, Signs, Trucks, Iron, Arcade, No. 432, Box, c.1938, 8 x 11 In. 546.00
Road Roller, Mechanical, Striped, Courtland, 9 x 3 In. 299.00
Robot, Astroman, Glow In Dark Head, Walks, Bends, Plastic, Box, c.1962, 4 x 11 ½ In. 403.00
Robot, Atomic Man, Tin Lithograph, Windup, Japan, Box, 5 In. 2160.00
Robot, Atomic Man, Tin, Violet, Clockwork, Japan, 5 ¼ In. 518.00
Robot, Big Loo Moon, Cone Head, Smiling, Green, Plastic, 37 ½ In. 1320.00
Robot, Busy Cart, Construction Hat, Wheelbarrow, Tin Lithograph, Horikawa, Japan, 11 ½ In. 960.00
Robot, Cone Head, Blue, Red Paint, Tin Lithograph, Windup, Yonezawa, Japan, 8 ½ In. 2040.00
Robot, Cragstan Ranger, Plastic, Painted Tin, Battery Operated, Daiya, Japan, Box, 10 ¼ In. 2160.00
Robot, Gray, Red Paint, Windup, Tin Litho, Japan, Box, 9 ½ In. 2700.00
Robot, Gray, Red, Tin Lithograph, Battery Operated, Horikawa, Japan, Box, 11 ¼ In. 540.00
Robot, Krome Dome, Plastic, Battery, Yonezawa, Japan, 11 In. 600.00
Robot, Lost In Space, Plastic, Battery, Remco, Box, Space Productions, 1966, 6 x 9 x 12 In. ... *Illus* 397.00
Robot, Mars King, Gray, Tin Lithograph, Horikawa, Japan, Box, 9 ½ In. 1140.00
Robot, Martian, Attacking, Black, Green, Tin Litho, Battery Operated, Horikawa, Japan, Box, 11 ½ In. 450.00
Robot, Mechanical, Walking, Sparking, Tin, Plastic, Windup, Linemar, Japan, Box, 5 ¾ In. 1200.00
Robot, Moon Explorer, Red, Blue Paint, Tin Lithograph, Yoshiya, Japan, Box, 7 In. 450.00
Robot, Planet Robot, Tin, Black, Plastic Helmet, Tool Hands, Sparks, Yoshiya, Japan, 9 In. 345.00
Robot, R7, Flashy Jim, Walks, Eyes Light Up, Battery Operated, Remote Control, Japan, 7 ½ In. 431.00
Robot, Radar, Tin, Blue, Gray, Nickel Trim, Battery Operated, Nomura, 8 In. 403.00
Robot, Robby, Metallic Blue, Graphics On Chest, Tin, Battery Operated, Yonezawa, Japan, 8 In. ... *Illus* 575.00
Robot, Space Commando, Tin, Gray, Celluloid Dome, Japan, 8 In. 633.00
Robot, Space Explorer, Green Eyes, Tin Litho, Battery Operated, Yonezawa, Japan, Box, 8 In. 1080.00
Robot, Space Trooper, Crank Wind, Clear, Red, Plastic, Metal, Yoshiya, Japan, Box, 6 ½ In. 960.00
Robot, Space, X-70, Silver, Orange, Blue, Tin Litho, Battery Operated, Nomura, Japan, 12 ½ In. 4800.00
Robot, Sparky, Khaki, Tin Lithograph, Windup, Yoshiya, Japan, Box, 7 ¾ In. 1020.00 to 2880.00
Robot, Super Giant Rotomatic, Tin Litho, Plastic, Battery Operated, Horikawa, Japan, Box, 16 In. 120.00
Robot, Swinging Baby, Opens & Closes Mouth, Tin Lithograph, Yellow, Clockwork, 6 In. 230.00
Robot, Thunder, Painted, Tin Lithograph, Asakusa Toy Co., Japan, Box, 10 ¾ In. 10200.00
Robot, Zoomer, Silver, Nickel, Red Celluloid Eyes, Antenna On Backpack, Nomura, 1954, 8 In. 316.00
Rocket Ship, Moon ZX 18, Tin Lithograph, Marusan, 9 ¼ In. 431.00
Rocket, Space Patrol, Tin Litho, Windup, Marked Asashi, Japan, Box, 5 ½ In. 660.00
Roller Coaster, Yellow Paint, Tin, Chein, Box 192.00
Rollo Chair, Riding The Boardwalk, Atlantic City, Man Pushing Chair, Tin, Clockwork, 7 In. 920.00
Roly Poly, Black Man, Paint, Papier-Mache, Germany, c.1925, 9 ½ In. 300.00
Rooster, Composition, Paint, Wire, Wood Base, Squeak, c.1850, 10 In. 711.00
Rooster, Wheeled Platform, Pecking, Tin Lithograph, Embossed, Penny Toy, Meier, 3 In. 575.00
Rowers, Collegiate, Coxswain, Tin Litho, Scull On Platform, Meier, Penny Toy, Germany, 3 ½ In. ... *Illus* 863.00
Runabout, Driver, Painted, Red, Yellow, Cast Iron, Kenton, 5 ½ In. 374.00
Safe, Green, Combination Tag, SH, Japan, Box, c.1960, 4 In. 50.00
Sailor, Dancing, Tin, Columbia Hat Band, Cloth Outfit, Clockwork, Lehmann, 7 ½ In. 288.00
Sam The Hobo, Balancing On Bicycle, Rides String Wire, Tin Litho, A.C. Gilbert, 1920s, 7 In. ... *Illus* 173.00
Sand Loader, Driver, Red, Yellow Scoop, Spoke Wheels, Iron, Arcade, 8 ½ In. ... *Illus* 2655.00
Sand, Scoop, Painted, Cast Iron, Wood Box, Lid, J. & E. Stevens, 11 ½ In. 840.00
Saxophone Player, Man, Tin Lithograph, Clockwork, Distler, Germany, Box, 8 In. 518.00
Saxophone, White Body, Red & Blue Keys, Proll Toys, Newark, N.J., 1960s, 14 In. 50.00
Scrappy, Playing Xylophone, Musical, Wood, Tin Arms, Pull Toy, c.1930, 9 ¼ In. 153.00
Scull, Crew, 5 Members, Wheels, Red, Yellow, Blue Paint, U.S. Hardware, c.1905, 10 In. 1823.00
Scull, Crew, 9 Members, Wheels, Yellow, Green, Paint, Cast Iron, U.S. Hardware, c.1905, 14 ¼ In. 2370.00
Seesaw, Busy Mike, Figures, Tin, J. Chein, 1930, 7 ½ x 7 In. 165.00
Service Station, Roadside Rest, Tin Litho, Electrified, Louis Marx, 1940s, 14 x 6 In. 1020.00
Sewing Machine, Casige, Pressed Steel, Black, Flowers, 1920s, 7 x 4 In. 145.00
Sewing Machine, Painted Black, Iron Chassis, Nickel Plated Flywheel, Decals, 7 x 7 In. 94.00
Sewing Machine, Treadle Base, Moving Needle, Dog & Cart Logo, Penny Toy, Meier, 3 In. 144.00
Sheep, Fleece Over Papier-Mache, Leather Muzzle, Ears, Glass Eyes, Pull Toy, 15 x 17 In. ... *Illus* 560.00
Sheep, Pull Toy, Label, G.A. Schwarz, c.1900, 8 ½ x 11 In. 652.00
Sheep, Walks, Moves Head, Fur, Papier-Mache, Clockwork, Decamps, 11 In. 968.00
Sheep, White Wool, Glass Eye, Wood Wheels, Pull Toy, 18 In. 180.00
Sideboard, Doll's, Shaped Shelves, Drawers, Gallery, Mirrored Back, c.1860, 30 x 24 In. 104.00
Sign, Safety Sal, School Zone, 15 MPH, Die Cast, Yellow Outfit, 7 ½ In. 546.00
Sign, Traffic, Slow School, Yellow, Black, 29 In. 150.00
Sign, Traffic, Stop, Red, White, 29 In. 180.00
Ski Rolf, Blue Suit, White Cap, Tin Litho, Clockwork, Lehmann, Germany, 7 In. ... *Illus* 2070.30
Skittles Set, Camel, Reclining, Man, Figure Pins, French Woman Queen Pin, Germany, c.1900, 19 In. 2300.00
Skittles Set, German Shepherd, 8 Animals & 1 Clown Pin, Painted, Glass Eyes, Germany, 21 In. 1150.00
Skittles Set, Rooster, Wheels, 9 Clown Chicks, Papier-Mache, 19 ½ x 15 ½ In. 14950.00

Toy, Grasshopper, Top Hat, Green Felt, Wooden Eyes, Wire Antennae, Lenci, c.1960, 7 In.
$336.00

Theriault's.

Toy, Harold Lloyd, Scissors, Tin Lithograph, Die Cut, 8 In.
$89.00

Bertoia Auctions

Toy, Hobbyhorse, Mobo Bronco, Metal, D. Sebel & Co. Ltd., England, 1940s
$390.00

Victorian Casino Antiques

Toy, Horse & Wagon, Milk, Borden's, Golden Crest, Tin, Wood, Pull Toy, Rich Toys, Iowa, 20 In.
$165.00

Showtime Auction Sevices

Toy, Horse, Full Body, Balanced Between Wheels, Rocks, Tin, George Brown, 8 x 7 In. $5,175.00

James D. Julia Auctioneers

Toy, Humphrey Mobile, Humphrey Riding An Outhouse Bike, Tin Litho, Clockwork, Wyandotte, 6 In. $316.00

Bertoia Auctions

Toy, Jeep, U.S. Army, World War II, Wood, Green Paint, Wheels, 1950s, 9 x 15 ½ x 9 In. $280.00

V & M

Toy, Lion, Marilyn Neuhart, Embroidered Cotton, Yarn Mane, c.1962, 8 x 11 In. $1,063.00

Los Angeles Modern Auctions (LAMA)

Skittles Set, Vegetable Figures, Cabbage, Tomato, Composition, 13 In., 11 Piece ....*Illus*	7670.00
Sled, Doll's, Pine, Flowers, Red Paint, 14 In.	474.00
Sled, Red, Green Paint, Wood, Metal, Fleetwing, 1930s, 41 In.	30.00
Sled, Runner, Wood, Blue Paint, Dated 1878, 31 In.	192.00
Sled, Stand Up, Wood, Iron, Gant Hall, 45 In.	193.00
Sled, Swan Finials, Running Horse Scene, White, Brown Paint, c.1850, 33 In.	354.00
Sled, Wood Runner, Green, Red Paint, 38 In.	85.00
Sled, Wood, Iron, Flowers, Painted, 34 In.	118.00
Sled, Wood, Painted Flowers, Red Ground, c.1835, 41 x 11 In.	165.00
Sled, Wood, Runner Strips, Stencil, Paint, c.1910, 10 ¾ x 35 ½ In.	288.00
Sled, Wood, Upholstery Seat, Handle, White Paint, 33 x 16 In.	89.00
Sleigh, Rococo, Carved, Fleur-De-Lis Panel Seat, Upholstery, Tub Shape, Painted, 41 x 29 In.	702.00
Sleigh, Victorian Style, Cast Iron, 8 x 6 In.	41.00
Sleigh, Victorian, White, Wood, Paint, Upholstery, 47 In.	115.00
Sleigh, Wood, Flowers, Yellow Pinstripes, Red Ground, c.1890, 15 x 4 ¾ In.	1422.00
Snake Trick, Carved, Painted, Multicolor, Protruding Snake, 2 ½ x 3 In.	356.00
Sofa, Doll's, Wood, Carved Dolphins, Caned Back, Arms, 16 ½ In.	711.00
Soldier On Motorcycle, Uniform, Camouflaged Cycle, Tin, Clockwork, Marx, 8 ½ In.	288.00
Soldier Set, Grenadier Guards, Metal, 3 Firing Positions, England, 2 Boxes, 2 ½ In., 16 Piece	118.00
Soldier Set, Lead, Painted, Castle Scene, 30 Figures, Horseback, Haffner, Germany, Box, c.1890	896.00
Soldier Set, Military Academy, c.1954	836.00
Soldier Set, Military School Cadets, Marching, Pot Metal, Painted, Carrying Rifles, 3 ½ In., 5 Piece	12.00
Soldier Set, Parade Group, Cast Metal, Blue Coats, Britains Ltd., 2 ¼ In., 10 Piece	35.00
Soldier Set, Sailors, Marching, Dress Whites, 3 ¼ In., 7 Piece	24.00
Soldier, Cloth Suit, Holding Rifle, Windup, Martin, France, c.1895, 8 In. ....*Illus*	4025.00
Soldier, Tin, Windup, Ohio Art, 1950s, 8 In.	145.00
Space Commando, Battery Operated, Green Paint, Tin Lithograph, Modern Toys, Japan, Box, 7 ½ In.	3600.00
Space Conqueror, Green, Tin Lithograph, Battery Operated, Daiya, Japan, 10 ¾ In.	3300.00
Space Dog, Red, Plastic, Tin Lithograph, Friction, Japan, Box, 6 In.	780.00
Space Scout, Radar Scope, Tin Litho, Plastic, Battery Operated, Horikawa, Japan, 9 In.	270.00
Space Station KTS, Tin Litho, Plastic Antenna, Battery Operated, Japan, 11 In.	489.00
Spaceman, Blue, Orange, Tin Lithograph, Battery Operated, Nomura, Japan, Box, 11 In.	1920.00
Spaceship X-5, Tin Lithograph, Turquoise, Orange, Yellow, Modern Toys, Japan, 12 In.	403.00
Spaceship, Rocket Fighter, Tin, Red, Yellow, Louis Marx, 12 In.	259.00
Sparkler, Cat, Felix, Black & White, Tin Litho, Copr. Pat Sullivan, Chein, 5 In. ....*Illus*	259.00
Sparkler, Cat, Felix, Tin, Black & White, Chein, 5 In.	259.00
Sparkler, Clown, Tin Lithograph, Red, Blue, 5 ¼ In.	55.00
Sparkler, Harold Lloyd, Moon-Like Face, Tin Lithograph, Germany, 1920s, 6 In.	230.00
Sparkler, Harold Lloyd, Tin Lithograph, Germany, 1920s, 5 ½ In. ....*Illus*	230.00
Sparkler, Old Woman, Tin Litho, Sparks Shoot From Mouth, 5 ⅜ x 2 In. ....*Illus*	154.00
Speed Boy Delivery Cycle, Open Bed Wagon, 3 Disc Wheels, Tin, Clockwork, Marx, 10 In.	489.00
Stable, Wood, Painted Green, Paper Lithograph, 2 Stalls, Composition Horses, Gottschalk, 14 In.	384.00
Stan Laurel, Bobbin Head, Holding Hat, Right Hand Behind Back, Germany, 1930s, 7 ¼ In.	490.00
Steam Shovel, Pressed Steel, Orange, Black Paint, Keystone, 18 In.	118.00
Steamroller, Robot Operator, Tin Lithograph, Showa, Japan, 10 ½ In.	960.00
Stove, Cook, Cast Iron, Cylinder, Bail Handle, Footed, Pexto, No. 782, c.1924, 14 x 8 In.	150.00
Stove, Gas Range, Kent, Nickel, Painted Blue, Embossed Kent, 1927, 10 In.	354.00
Stove, Hotpoint Electric, White Paint, Cast Iron, Arcade, 6 ¼ In.	130.00
Stove, Little Lady Range, Electric, Metal, Cream, Green, 4 Legs, Kokomo, Indiana	140.00
Stove, Marklin, Tin, Nickel, Doors Open, Chimney, Utensils, Germany, c.1890, 21 In. ......*Illus*	7840.00
Stove, Marvel, 5 Burners, 2 Ovens, Grill Plate, Scuttle Bucket, Iron, Nickel Plated, 19 In.	173.00
Stove, Marvel, 6 Burners, Cast Iron, Copper Oxide Finish, 20 x 16 ½ In.	460.00
Stove, Pot, Green Paint, Cast Iron, Crown, 9 x 12 In.	480.00
Stove, Spark, Pot Belly, Cast Iron, 8 x 14 x 9 In. ....*Illus*	77.00
Stove, The Queen, 6 Burners, Accessories, Cast Iron, 6 ½ In.	275.00
Stove, Tin, Incised Decoration, Brass Door & Burner Grate, Pot, Pan, Germany, 9 In.	88.00
Stroller, Spoke Wheels, Cast Iron, Hubley, 1900s, 4 ½ x 4 x 2 In.	115.00
Submarine, Green Hull, Red Rudder, Clockwork, Marklin, Germany, 11 In.	3738.00
Submarine, Maroon, Gray Dive Fins, Rubber Band Powered, France, Box, c.1900, 7 ½ In.	1265.00
Submarine, Railed Deck, Flags, Paint, Clockwork, Marklin, Germany, c.1930s, 13 In.	1458.00
Submarine, Railing, Screw Cap, Clockwork, Fleischmann, Germany, c.1936, 8 In. ....*Illus*	288.00
Submarine, Stenciled Graphics, Paint, Tin, Clockwork, Marklin, Germany, 16 In.	3948.00
Submarine, Tin, Mast, Observation Deck, Clockwork, Bing, Germany, c.1912	748.00
Submarine, TM-300, Flywheel Motor, Tin Lithograph, Box, 11 In.	142.00
Suitcase, Canvas, Leather Trim, Buckles, 2 ½ In.	226.00
Sunny & Fun Fair, Swings, Chutes, Balls, Tin Litho, Paint, 1930s, 13 ¾ x 5 ½ In.	221.00

T

Toy, Maggie & Jiggs, Dueling, Maggie &
Rolling Pin, Jiggs & Cane, Windup, Litho, Nifty,
8 In.
$633.00

James D. Julia Auctioneers

Toy, Merry-Go-Round, 4 Horses, Riders, Cloth
Canopy, Clockwork, Bing, Germany, 24 In.
$2,242.00

Bertoia Auctions

Toy, Merrymakers Band, Mice, Tin Litho,
Clockwork, Marx, c.1929, 9 ½ In.
$633.00

Bertoia Auctions

Toy, Motorcycle & Rider, Halloh, Tin Litho,
Clockwork, Lehmann, 8 ¾ In.
$1,725.00

Bertoia Auctions

Toy, Motorcycle Cop, Indian Decal, 4 Cylinder
Nickel Engine, Rubber Tires, Iron, Hubley,
9 In.
$1,416.00

Bertoia Auctions

Toy, Motorcycle, Highway Patrol, Driver,
Battery Operated, Modern Toys, Japan, 11 ½ In.
$489.00

Bertoia Auctions

Toy, Mystery Ball, Spiral Action, Tin Litho,
Figure At Last Stop, Fernand Martin, France,
14 In.
$863.00

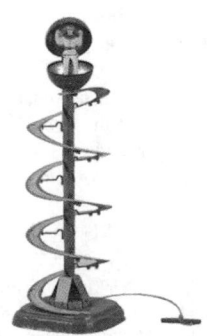

Bertoia Auctions

Toy, Nursemaid, Black, White Infant, Wood,
Papier-Mache, Old Aunt Chloe, Ives, Blakeslee,
c.1875
$11,638.00

RSL Auction

Toy, Old Woman, Cane, Eyeglasses, Basket On
Back, Walking, Tin, Clockwork, Gunthermann,
7 In.
$690.00

Bertoia Auctions

Toy, Organ Grinder, Felt Suit, Painted Head,
Tin Litho, Clockwork, Fernand Martin, France,
9 In.
$1,725.00

Bertoia Auctions

Toy, Paddy & Pig, Tin Lithograph, Lehmann, 1920s, 6 In.
$1,150.00

James D. Julia Auctioneers

Toy, Peacock, Hinged Legs, 3 Feather Panels, Tin Litho, Windup, Germany, Blomer & Schuler, 9 In.
$5,824.00

Theriault's

Toy, Pedal Car, Green, Triang, England, 1930s, 42 In.
$3,600.00

Showtime Auction Sevices

Toy, Pedal Car, McCormick Farmall 400, Red Paint, Double Front Wheels, 1960s, 39 x 28 In.
$632.00

James D. Julia Auctioneers

Supercar, Cockpit Bust, Flight Path Selectors, Battery Operated, Box, Remco, 1963, 9 x 12 In.	582.00
Surrey, Horse Drawn, Iron, Blue, Red Cloth Canopy, 2 Figures, Kenton, 12 In.	230.00
Swamp Buggy, Plastic, Green, Orange, Windup, Box, Ideal, 1960, 11 In.	185.00
Tank, Camouflage, Shoots, Arcade, c.1937, 8 In.	600.00
Tank, Cannon, Tin, Clockwork, Green, Black, Germany, 9 In.	600.00
Taxi, Amos 'n' Andy, Fresh Air, Orange Jalopy, Dog, Horseshoe Ornament, Windup, Box, 1930s, 8 ¼ In.	885.00
Taxi, Amos 'n' Andy, Fresh Air, Tin Lithograph, Louis Marx, 8 In.	690.00
Taxi, Uniform Driver, Die Cut Lamps, For Hire Sign, Penny Toy, Distler, Germany, 3 In.	431.00
Taxi, Yellow Cab, Black Trim, Spare Tire, Rear Door, Cast Iron, Hubley, 8 In. ....*Illus*	590.00
Taxi, Yellow Cab, No. 3, Arcade, 5 In.	750.00
Taxi, Yellow, Black, Main 7570, Tin, Windup, J. Chein, 1920s, 6 In.	270.00
Taxi, Yellow, Black, Pressed Steel, Converse, Flywheel, 10 In.	360.00
Tea Set, Doll's, Porcelain, Gold, Teapot, Sugar, Creamer, 2 Cups, Saucers, Tray, c.1880, 3 ½ In. ..*Illus*	168.00
Tea Set, Pewter, Pot, Sugar, Creamer, Cups, Saucers, Spoons, Tongs, Lined Box, c.1890, 11 x 7 In.	280.00
Tea Tray, Children Driving Car, 2 Others With Doll & Pull Toy, Tin Litho, 9 x 6 In. ....*Illus*	173.00
Teddy Bears are also listed in the Teddy Bear category.	
Three Little Pigs, Musicians, Tin Bodies, Felt, Clockwork, Schuco, Germany, 4 In., 3 Piece ...*Illus*	546.00
Threshing Machine, McCormick-Deering, Paint, Cast Iron, Arcade, 12 x 4 In.	236.00
Ticket Booth, Railroad, Tin, Brick, Shingle Design, Destination Sign, Windows, Bing, 1912, 6 ½ In.	2240.00
Tiger, White, Plush, Black Stripes, Shag Mane, Belly, Felt Open Mouth, Crouching, 40 x 72 In.	345.00
Tightrope Walker, Miss Blondin, Walking Stick, Tin Lithograph, Lehmann, Germany, Box, 9 ½ In.	4500.00
Tom Tom Canoe, 2 Indians, Tin, Friction, Japan, Box, 1950s, 9 In.	225.00
Tool Chest, Boy's Union, 2 Saws, Level, Auger, Scribe, Miter Box, R. Bliss Co., c.1900, 6 x 19 In.	450.00
Toonerville Trolley, Cast Iron, Painted, Green, Orange, Fontaine Fox, Dent, Box, 5 ¾ In.	690.00
Toonerville Trolley, Tin Lithograph, Clockwork Action, Fontaine Fox, c.1922, 7 In.	431.00
Toonerville Trolley, Tin Lithograph, Fontaine Fox, Clockwork, Nifty, Box, 7 In. ....*Illus*	1725.00
Tractor, Allis Chalmers, Cast Iron, Persian Orange, Rubber Tires, Decal, Arcade, c.1940, 7 In.	863.00
Tractor, Allis Chalmers, Driver, Decal, Painted, Arcade, c.1940, 7 In.	863.00
Tractor, Driver, Red, Yellow Paint, Rubber Wheels, Die Cast, c.1950, 7 x 4 ½ In.	30.00
Tractor, Driver, Rubber Wheels, Paint, Iron, Marked Allis-Chalmers, Hubley, 6 ½ In.	240.00
Tractor, Farmall A Cultivision, Iron, Red, Nickel Driver & Drawbar, Arcade, 7 In.	920.00
Tractor, Fordson, Cast Iron, Gray, Gold Trim, Red Spoke Wheels, Driver, Arcade, Box, 5 ½ In.	1265.00
Tractor, Fordson, Driver, Red, Cast Iron, 6 ½ In.	200.00
Tractor, John Deere, 3 Wheels, Attached Wagon, Ertl Co., Iowa, 24 x 60 In.	390.00
Tractor, John Deere, Driver, Nickel, Vindex Toy, Paint, Cast Iron, 6 ¼ In.	1080.00
Tractor, John Deere, Model D, Cast Iron, Green, Yellow Wheels, Vindex, 6 In.	3738.00
Tractor, McCormick Deering, Cast Iron, Blue, Nickel Driver, Kilgore, 5 ½ In.	2185.00
Tractor, Oh Boy, Driver, Embossed, Blue, Wheel Frame, Rubber Tread, Iron, Kilgore, 6 In. .. *Illus*	3835.00
Tractor, Oliver, Driver, Cast Iron, Red, Green, Hubley, 5 ½ In.	350.00
Tractor, Orange Paint, Cast Iron, c.1930, 3 x 5 In.	30.00
Tractor, Spreader, Green Paint, Metal, c.1950, 10 x 3 ½ In.	30.00
Tractor, Spreader, McCormick-Deering, Red Paint, c.1950, 11 x 3 In.	35.00
Tractor, W & F Fordson, Driver, Cast Iron, Hubley, 5 ½ In.	71.00
Tractor, Yellow, Caterpillar, Iron, Nickel Plated Driver, Arcade, 8 In. ....*Illus*	1150.00
Traffic Policeman, Arms Raise, Light, Pressed Steel, Die Cut, Blue Uniform, Box, 7 ⅜ In.	230.00
Trailer, Circus, K-Japan, 1950s, 18 In., 3 Piece	375.00
Trailer, Mullins Red Cap, Green, Arcade, 1936, 3 ½ In.	375.00 to 450.00
Train Accessory, Station, Cafe, Tin, Figures, Marklin, Germany, c.1905, 16 x 11 In. ....*Illus*	18375.00
Train Accessory, Station, Tin, Glass Roof, Green, Columns, Stencils, Marklin, c.1907, 10 x 8 In.	6490.00
Train Car, American Tin, Locomotive, Boss, Painted, Red, Black, Cast Iron Wheels, Ives	545.00
Train Car, American Tin, Locomotive, Flash Stencil, Red, Black, Iron Wheels, George Brown, 10 ½ In.	1815.00
Train Car, American Tin, Locomotive, Puck, Painted, Cast Iron Wheels, Althof-Bergmann, 8 In.	666.00
Train Car, Arcade, Streamline, Railplane, Green Paint, Cast Iron, 10 In.	142.00
Train Car, Buddy L, Hopper Car, Outdoor, Pressed Steel, Black Paint, 1930s, 22 In.	900.00
Train Car, Buddy L, Locomotive, Pressed Steel, 1930s, 26 In. ....*Illus*	1200.00
Train Car, Buddy L, Tanker, Outdoor, Pressed Steel, Yellow Paint, 1930s, 19 In.	1320.00
Train Car, Gunthermann, Red, Black Paint, Tin, Clockwork, 13 In.	303.00
Train Car, Hopper Loader, Pressed Steel, Green Paint, Lamar-Marx, 6 x 10 In.	165.00
Train Car, Horse, Tracks, Driver, Passenger, Wood, c.1910, 9 ½ x 26 In.	504.00
Train Car, Ideal, Stock Car, Cast Iron, Nickel Plated, 4 Horses Inside, 14 In.	288.00
Train Car, J.W. Kensett, Sleeper, Brass, Cast Iron Wheels, Yellow, Red, Gold, 24 In.	1573.00
Train Car, Kenton, Caboose, L.S. & M.S., Red, Green Roof, Cast Iron, 7 ¼ In.	115.00
Train Car, Keystone, Locomotive, Sit & Ride, Pressed Steel, Red, Black Paint, 1930s, 26 In.	880.00
Train Car, Keystone, Pullman Car, Ride 'Em Handle, Pressed Steel, Paint, 1930s, 26 In.	495.00
Train Car, Lionel Lines, Floodlight, 2 Spots, 2 ¾ x 9 In.	79.00
Train Car, Lionel, Crane, Lifting, 4 x 13 In.	96.00

Toy, Pedal Car, Steel, Rubber Tires, Luggage Rack, Wood Grill With Jordan, Gendron, 1929, 50 In.
$6,325.00

James D. Julia Auctioneers

Toy, Pedal Car, Oldsmobile, Steel, Pierced Wheels, Rubber Tires, Siren, Steelcraft, 1941, 40 In.
$1,955.00

James D. Julia Auctioneers

Toy, Pedal Car, Train, LMS, Bell, Wood, Red Paint, Triang Toys, c.1942-43, 42 In.
$823.00

Victorian Casino Antiques

Toy, Piano, Grand, Bench, Iron, Painted, Folding Music Stand, Arcade, 5 In., 2 Piece
$575.00

Bertoia Auctions

Toy, Pig, Holding Beer Stein, Felt Body, Blue Pants, Clockwork, Marked, Schuco, Germany, 4 ½ In.
$236.00

Bertoia Auctions

Toy, Plow, Steel, Gale Chilled, Albion, Michigan, Salesman's Sample, Pat. Dates 1874-76, 26 x 11 In.
$8,625.00

James D. Julia Auctioneers

Toy, Powerful Katrinka, Lifting Jimmy, Tin Litho, Clockwork, c.1923, Fontaine Fox, 5 ½ In.
$2,588.00

Bertoia Auctions

Toy, Refrigerator, Steel, Shelves, Tin Pan, Wyandotte, Salesman's Sample, 5 ¼ x 9 ½ In.
$420.00

Showtime Auction Sevices

T

Toy, Ring, Rocket, Space Patrol, Plastic, Translucent Blue, Glow-In-Dark, Ralston Premium, 1952
$403.00

Hake's Americana & Collectibles

Toy, Robot, Lost In Space, Plastic, Battery, Remco, Box, Space Productions, 1966, 6 x 9 x 12 In.
$397.00

Hake's Americana & Collectibles

Toy, Robot, Robby, Metallic Blue, Graphics On Chest, Tin, Battery Operated, Yonezawa, Japan, 8 In.
$575.00

Bertoia Auctions

Toy, Rowers, Collegiate, Coxswain, Tin Litho, Scull On Platform, Meier, Penny Toy, Germany, 3 ½ In.
$863.00

Toy, Sam The Hobo, Balancing On Bicycle, Rides String Wire, Tin Litho, A.C. Gilbert, 1920s, 7 In.
$173.00

Bertoia Auctions

Toy, Sand Loader, Driver, Red, Yellow Scoop, Spoke Wheels, Iron, Arcade, 8 ½ In.
$2,655.00

Bertoia Auctions

Toy, Sheep, Fleece Over Papier-Mache, Leather Muzzle, Ears, Glass Eyes, Pull Toy, 15 x 17 In.
$560.00

James D. Julia Auctioneers

Toy, Ski Rolf, Blue Suit, White Cap, Tin Litho, Clockwork, Lehmann, Germany, 7 In.
$2,070.30

Bertoia Auctions

Toy, Skittles Set, Vegetable Figures, Cabbage, Tomato, Composition, 13 In., 11 Piece
$7,670.00

Bertoia Auctionss

Toy, Soldier, Cloth Suit, Holding Rifle, Windup, Martin, France, c.1895, 8 In.
$4,025.00

Bertoia Auctions

T

Train Car, Locomotive, Santa Fe, Diesel, Orange, Silver, Black	345.00
Train Car, Locomotive, Traction Engine, Tin, Cast Iron Wheels, 7 In.	424.00
Train Car, Locomotive, Wood, Tin, Clockwork, George Brown, Orion, 9 ½ In. ......*Illus*	4025.00
Train Car, Marklin, Passenger, 4 Axles, Wheels, Interior, 8 Figures, O Gauge, c.1930, 11 ½ In.	618.00
Train Car, Marklin, Sleeper, Tin Lithograph, Interior, 4 Axles, 4 Opening Doors, c.1925, 15 ¾ In. .	1005.00
Train Car, Marklin, Steam, Rear Burner, Black Paint, Germany, 8 In.	1080.00
Train Car, Model, Locomotive, Carved Turned Wood, Iron Wheels, Paint, U.S.A., 13 x 26 In.	723.00
Train Car, Steam Engine, Traction, Brass Boiler, Smoke Stack, Whistle, Schoener, Black, 11 In.	1200.00
Train Car, Tin, Push, Japan, 1950s, 12 In.	145.00
Train Set, American Tin, Skip, Painted, 22 In., 4 Piece	393.00
Train Set, Baby Blue, Passenger Car, Loco, Tender, Nickel Plated Trim, O Gauge, c.1930s	690.00
Train Set, Buddy L, Locomotive, Tender, Cattle Car, Black, Red, Silver Trim, Decals, 27 In.	2013.00
Train Set, Denver & Rio Grande, Locomotive, Tender, Cowcatcher, Smokestack, Box, 27 In.	230.00
Train Set, Karl Bub, Locomotive, 2 Cars, Tin Lithograph, Windup, Germany, c.1930, 4 In.	280.00
Train Set, Kenton, Empire State Express, Locomotive, Tender, Iron, Black, c.1899, 18 In.	403.00
Train Set, Kenton, Vanderbilt, Locomotive, Tender, Coach, Wagner Buffet, Cast Iron, 59 In.	2185.00
Train Set, Marx, Honeymoon Express, 3 Trains, Tunnels, Round, Tin, Box, 9 ½ In.	230.00
Train Set, Marx, Smoking, Caboose, Rail Car, Tracks, 1940, 10 x 15 In.	95.00
Train Set, Welker & Crosby, Locomotive, Tender, Iron, Wood, c.1890, 11 In.	2185.00
Train Station, Lionel City, With Train Stop, Box	180.00
Tray, Alice In Wonderland, Mad Hatters Party, Characters, Texagen, England, c.1953, 12 In.	86.00
Trick Box, Mahogany, Inlaid Hound, Shield, Slide Door, Black Snake Reveal, c.1900, 2 ½ x 3 ½ In.	1067.00
Tricycle, American National Trike, 1920s, 27 x 17 In.	413.00
Tricycle, Gyro-Cycle, Tin, Balloon Tires, Celluloid Rider, Pull String, Triang, 8 In.	201.00
Tricycle, Handicap, Metal Frame, Cloth Seat, Wood Pull Handle, c.1905, 46 In.	275.00
Tricycle, Metal, Red, Yellow Paint, American National Trike, 1920s, 27 x 17 In.	413.00
Tricycle, Racer, Steel, Wood, Skip Sprocket Drive, Low Basket, Speedway, 44 In.	540.00
Trolley, Blue, Yellow, Lights, Reverse Action, Tin Litho, Clockwork, Orobr, Germany, Box, 10 In.	1093.00
Trolley, Double-Decker, Red, Upper Seats, Tin Litho, Clockwork, Bing, Germany, 9 ¼ In.	4313.00
Trolley, Etoile Porte-Maillot, Open End Platforms, Clockwork, Charles Rossignol, France, 9 In.	1380.00
Trolley, Horse Drawn, 2 White Horses, Stenciled, Scalloped Platform, Iron Wheels, 9 In.	1416.00
Trolley, Horse Drawn, Driver, Upper Deck Seating, Tin Litho, Windup, Orobr, 8 ¾ In.	1094.00
Trolley, Horse Drawn, Spoke Wheels, Multicolor, Tin Litho, Richter, Germany, 12 In.	1944.00
Trolley, Incline Layout, Station House, Tin Litho, Bell, Clockwork, Issmeyer, Germany, 78 In.	8625.00
Trolley, Lead Spoke Wheels, Platforms, Inertia Flywheel, Rossignol, Frame, Penny Toy, 3 In.	345.00
Trolley, Metropolitan, Battery Operated, Japan, 1950s, 14 In.	245.00
Trolley, Motorman, Multicolor, Clockwork, Tin Lithograph, Richter, 6 ½ In.	1580.00
Trolley, Roof Pole, Enclosed Platform, Red, Blue, Tin Lithograph, Clockwork, Orobr, Box, 8 ½ In.	1337.00
Trolley, Tramway Co., Yellow, Red, Tin Litho, Clockwork, Geppert & Kelch, 6 ¾ In.	851.00
Trolley, Wood, Wire, Painted, c.1910, 8 x 13 ½ In.	237.00
Trolley, Yellow & Black, Stenciling, Windows, Doors, Motorized Unit, Lionel, 1930s, 19 ½ In. .	4600.00
Truck, Aerial Ladder, Driver, Gold, Red Paint, Cast Iron, Arcade Mfg., 21 In.	963.00
Truck, Aerial, Pressed Steel, Red Paint, 29 In.	560.00
Truck, Allied Van Lines, Tin, Friction, Linemar, 12 In.	195.00
Truck, American Railway Express, Open Cab, Cage Cap, Tires, Keystone, c.1920s, 26 ½ In. ... *Illus*	747.00
Truck, Arctic Ice Cream, Cast Iron, White Paint, Decals, Motorcade Toys, 7 ½ In.	230.00
Truck, Army, Pressed Steel, Green, Yellow Canvas, Keystone, 1930s, 28 In.	450.00
Truck, Bell Telephone, Cast Iron, Olive Green, Embossed Sides, Hubley, 1930s, 7 In.	748.00
Truck, Camper, Blue Truck, White Camper Top, Tonka, 1960s, 8 x 14 In.	60.00
Truck, Car Carrier, Cast Iron, Red Cab, 2 Blue Buick Cars, Hubley, 1932, 10 In.	546.00
Truck, Cement Mixer, Crawler Treads, Pressed Steel, Gray Paint, Buddy L, c.1930, 16 In.	3300.00
Truck, Cement Mixer, Horse Drawn, Driver, Paint, Cast Iron, 12 ½ In.	1560.00
Truck, Champion Panel, Rubber Wheels, Blue Paint, Cast Iron, 7 ¾ In.	660.00
Truck, Coal, High Lift, Red, Cast Iron, Arcade, 10 In.	679.00
Truck, Coal, Mack, Cast Iron, Red, Open Bed, Stencils, Nickel Lever, Arcade, 10 In.	748.00
Truck, Dan-Dee Oil, Mack Cab, Tin, Orange, Green, Windup, Chein, 1930s, 8 ¾ In.	345.00
Truck, Delivery, Borden's Milk, Cream, Cast Iron, White, Spoke Wheels, Hubley, 8 In.	4025.00
Truck, Delivery, Breyer's Ice Cream, Iron, Orange, Black Roof, 3 Doors, Dent, 9 In.	1093.00
Truck, Delivery, Butter, Meadow Gold, Yellow, Pressed Steel, Metalcraft, c.1920, 13 In.	413.00
Truck, Delivery, Express Line, Black, Pressed Steel, Buddy L, 24 ½ In.	900.00
Truck, Delivery, Hathaway's Bakery, Logo, Iron, Painted Black, White, Arcade, 9 In.	1035.00
Truck, Delivery, Ice, Black, Yellow Paint, Pressed Steel, Buddy L, 26 In.	1080.00
Truck, Delivery, Ice, Tongs, Ride On, Pressed Steel, Blue White Paint, Prototype, Buddy L, 1930s, 29 In.	5775.00
Truck, Delivery, Iowana, White, Pressed Steel, Metalcraft, c.1925, 13 In.	207.00
Truck, Delivery, Lyons' Confectionery, Tin Lithograph Black & Yellow Paint, c.1920, 7 In.	4830.00
Truck, Delivery, Rider Seat, Pressed Steel, Blue, White Paint, Buddy L, 1930s, 22 In.	440.00

Toy, Sparkler, Cat, Felix, Black & White, Tin Litho, Copr. Pat Sullivan, Chein, 5 In. $259.00

Bertoia Auctions

Toy, Sparkler, Harold Lloyd, Tin Lithograph, Germany, 1920s, 5 ½ In. $230.00

Bertoia Auctions

Toy, Sparkler, Old Woman, Tin Litho, Sparks Shoot From Mouth, 5 ⅜ x 2 In. $154.00

Wm Morford Antiques

Restoration, Good or Bad?
Restoration adds value to pressed steel toys like Buddy "L" according to one collector. But the question of restoration has plagued collectors in many fields and sometimes the rules change. Carousel horses have been stripped and repainted for years and it has added to the value. Now the "park paint" horses are starting to sell for more than restored examples.

T

Toy, Stove, Marklin, Tin, Nickel, Doors Open, Chimney, Utensils, Germany, c.1890, 21 In.
$7,840.00

Theriault's

Toy, Stove, Spark, Pot Belly, Cast Iron, 8 x 14 x 9 In.
$77.00

Showtime Auction Sevices

Toy, Submarine, Railing, Screw Cap, Clockwork, Fleischmann, Germany, c.1936, 8 In.
$288.00

Bertoia Auctions

Toy, Tea Set, Doll's, Porcelain, Gold, Teapot, Sugar, Creamer, 2 Cups, Saucers, Tray, c.1880, 3 ½ In.
$168.00

Theriault's

Toy, Tea Tray, Children Driving Car, 2 Others With Doll & Pull Toy, Tin Litho, 9 x 6 In.
$173.00

James D. Julia Auctioneers

Toy, Three Little Pigs, Musicians, Tin Bodies, Felt, Clockwork, Schuco, Germany, 4 In., 3 Piece
$546.00

Bertoia Auctions

Toy, Toonerville Trolley, Tin Lithograph, Fontaine Fox, Clockwork, Nifty, Box, 7 In.
$1,725.00

Bertoia Auctions

Toy, Tractor, Oh Boy, Driver, Embossed, Blue, Wheel Frame, Rubber Tread, Iron, Kilgore, 6 In.
$3,835.00

Bertoia Auctions

Toy, Tractor, Yellow, Caterpillar, Iron, Nickel Plated Driver, Arcade, 8 In.
$1,150.00

Bertoia Auctions

TIP
Action figures and small toys can be washed in the dishwasher, but in a lingerie bag on the top shelf.

Toy, Train Accessory, Station, Cafe, Tin, Figures, Marklin, Germany, c.1905, 16 x 11 In.
$18,375.00

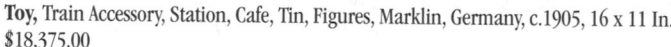

RSL Auction

Truck, Delivery, Wood, Cass, 1910, 16 In.	87.00
Truck, Diamond Gas, Nickel Grille, Rubber Tires, Painted, Iron, Hubley, 7 In.	345.00
Truck, Dump, Blue, Gray, Wyandotte, 1938, 21 In.	175.00
Truck, Dump, Cast Iron, Arcade, 1940, 11 In.	200.00
Truck, Dump, Cast Iron, Red & Green, Door Decals, Rubber Tires, Arcade, 9 In.	920.00
Truck, Dump, Driver, Embossed Coal, Lever Activated, Paint, Cast Iron, Kenton, 10 In.	1320.00
Truck, Dump, Green Paint, Pressed Steel, Sturditoy Co., 27 ½ In.	720.00
Truck, Dump, Hydraulic Lift, Black, Red, Silver, Buddy L, 9 ½ x 24 ½ In.	575.00
Truck, Dump, International, Nickel Driver, Iron, Arcade, 1930, 10 In. ....*Illus*	748.00
Truck, Dump, Mack C Cab, Iron, Red & Blue, Nickel Disc Wheels, Champion, 8 In.	546.00
Truck, Dump, Mack, T-Bar Pulley System, Cast Iron, Blue, Decal, Arcade, 12 In.	805.00
Truck, Dump, Motor, Pivoting Axle, Make Men Of Boys, Red, Clockwork, Structo, 18 In.	460.00
Truck, Dump, Open Cab, Black Paint, Flivver, Pressed Steel, Buddy L, 12 In.	450.00
Truck, Dump, Packard, Mechanical Lift, Red, Green, Steel, Keystone, 1930s, 18 In.	236.00
Truck, Dump, Pressed Steel, Black, Red Chassis, Wheel Hubs, Keystone, 1930s, 27 In.	440.00
Truck, Dump, Red Baby II, Arcade	1250.00
Truck, Dump, Red Mach, Paint, Steelcraft, 26 In.	1100.00
Truck, Dump, Red, Black Paint, Buddy L, 24 In.	266.00
Truck, Dump, Red, Green Paint, Metal, Wyandotte Toys, c.1930, 6 x 8 In.	30.00
Truck, Dump, Red, Green Paint, Pressed Steel, Strucate, 24 In.	390.00
Truck, Dump, Ride 'Em, Handle, Pressed Steel, Green, Cream Paint, Keystone, 1930s, 25 In.	550.00
Truck, Dump, Silver, Red, Wood Wheels, Windup, Marx, 1940, 4 ½ In.	135.00
Truck, Dump, Tip Top, Open Bench Seat, Driver, Tin, Windup, Strauss, 10 In.	1610.00
Truck, Dump, White Paint, Pressed Steel, Turner, 29 In.	210.00
Truck, Dump, Wood Wheels, Silver, Red, Windup, Marx, c.1940, 4 ½ In.	135.00
Truck, Dump, Yellow Paint, Buddy L, c.1930, 22 x 7 In.	89.00
Truck, Front Plow, Back Digger, Yellow Paint, Ford, 5550, Pressed Steel, 29 ½ In.	90.00
Truck, Garbage, Tin Lithograph, Whitewall Tires, Steel, Marx, c.1950, 13 In.	285.00
Truck, Gas, Wood Wheels, Green, Wyandotte, 1940s, 4 In.	45.00
Truck, Gasoline, Oil-Gas, Green, Embossed Cans, Iron, Kenton, 10 In. ....*Illus*	1534.00
Truck, Green, Open Stake Body, Nickel Grille, Rubber Tires, Cast Iron, Arcade, 11 In. .....*Illus*	1265.00
Truck, Hauling Cracker Jack Box, Metal Body, 9 x 4 ¼ In. ....*Illus*	468.00
Truck, Hillclimber, Metal, Yellow Paint, Continental, c.1915, 19 In.	330.00
Truck, Hoisting Tower, Pressed Steel, Black Paint, Buddy L, 1930s, 37 In.	840.00
Truck, Ice Cream, Mechanical, Courtland, 9 In.	199.00
Truck, Ice, Black Cab, Yellow Bed, Canvas, Ice Tong, Buddy L, 26 In.	1980.00
Truck, Ice, Cubes, Pressed Steel, Marx, 1950s, 18 In.	345.00
Truck, Ice, Studebaker, Cube & Tongs, Hubley, 8 In.	550.00
Truck, International Delivery, Iron, Red, Decal, Beaver Tail Rear, Arcade, 1930s, 9 In.	4600.00
Truck, Lift, Dan-Dee, J. Chein, Box, 9 In.	720.00
Truck, Livestock, Trailer, Cast Iron, Kenton, 8 In.	177.00
Truck, McCormick-Deering Manure Spreader, Iron, Open Body, Decal, Vindex, 15 In.	1840.00
Truck, McCormick-Deering Thresher, Iron, Gray, Red Trim, Fold Down Chute, Arcade, 12 In.	489.00
Truck, Mechanical, Easter Greetings, Rabbit Driving, Courtland, 9 In.	375.00
Truck, Merry-Go-Round, Moves, Bell Rings, Friction, Tin Litho, Nomura, Japan, 1950s, 4 x 8 x 4 In.	146.00
Truck, Milk Farms, Rack, Bottles, Wood, Buddy L, 13 ½ In.	358.00
Truck, Milk, Borden Farm Products, Cream, Brown, Wood, Tin, 12 ¾ In.	510.00
Truck, Milk, Borden's Milk, Cream, Embossed, Painted, Cast Iron, Hubley, 8 In.	4025.00
Truck, Milk, Paneled, Green, Red, Steel, Steelcraft, 18 In.	236.00
Truck, Mobile TV, RCA-NBC, Cameraman, Tin Litho, Battery Operated, Yonezawa, Japan, 8 ½ In.	960.00
Truck, Motor Express, Red, Silver, Embossed, Rubber Tires, Iron, Hubley, 7 In. ....*Illus*	354.00
Truck, Moving Van, Red, Green, Buddy L, 1925, 25 In.	875.00
Truck, Moving Van, Son-Ny Long Distance, Red, Black Paint, Buddy L, 26 In.	826.00
Truck, Nu-Car Transport, Iron, Open Cab, Overhead Ramp, Trailer, 4 Cars, Hubley, 16 In.	748.00
Truck, Overland Circus, Cage, Yellow Cast Iron, Kenton, 9 In.	431.00
Truck, Panama Digger, Nickel Scoop, White Rubber Tires, Paint, Cast Iron, Hubley, 12 In.	960.00
Truck, Pickup, Cast Iron, Yellow, Decals, Rubber Tires, Arcade, 1940s, 9 ½ In.	1380.00
Truck, Pile Driver, Pressed Steel, Red, Black Paint, Buddy L, 1930s, 21 In.	550.00
Truck, Police Patrol, Open Cab, Steerable, Mesh Sides, Benches, Disc Tires, Keystone, 28 In.	690.00
Truck, Red, Green Paint, Pressed Steel, Electrified, Robo-Toy, Buddy L, Box, 1930s, 21 In.	1540.00
Truck, Sand Conveyer, Pressed Steel, Red Paint, Kelmet, 1930s, 22 In.	440.00
Truck, Skip, Red, Metallic Gray, Yellow, Matchbox, Box	63.00
Truck, Stake, International, Cast Iron, Arcade, 11 ½ In.	177.00
Truck, Stake, International, Cast Iron, Green Paint, Rubber Tires, Decals, Arcade, 11 In.	1265.00
Truck, Stake, Yellow & Green, Wood Wheels, Wyandotte, 1930s, 7 In.	60.00
Truck, Steam Shovel, Treads, Pressed Steel, Red Paint, Buddy L, c.1930, 24 In.	1760.00
Truck, Steam Shovel, Yellow, Pressed Steel, Buddy L, 32 In.	443.00

Hot Wheels

The number on the base of a Hot Wheels car is the year it was copyrighted, not the year the car was made.

Toy, Train Car, Locomotive, Wood, Tin, Clockwork, George Brown, Orion, 9 ½ In.
$4,025.00

James D. Julia Auctioneers

Toy, Train Car, Buddy L, Locomotive, Pressed Steel, 1930s, 26 In.
$1,200.00

Showtime Auction Services

Toy, Truck, American Railway Express, Open Cab, Cage Cap, Tires, Keystone, c.1920s, 26 ½ In.
$747.00

James D. Julia Auctioneers

Toy, Truck, Dump, International, Nickel Driver, Iron, Arcade, 1930, 10 In.
$748.00

Bertoia Auctions

The edited listings of the current prices in this *Kovels' Antiques & Collectibles Price Guide* aren't available on any website. Readers can visit **Kovels.com** to check thousands of past prices and sign up for free information on trends, tips, reproductions, marks, and more.

T

TIP

Don't buy a Fisher-Price toy with a broken part. It is difficult to find a replacement. The parts that break are the easiest to damage and the least available to use for repairs. Newly made parts are too new-looking to be suitable.

Toy, Truck, Gasoline, Oil-Gas, Green, Embossed Cans, Iron, Kenton, 10 In. $1,534.00

Bertoia Auctions

Toy, Truck, Green, Open Stake Body, Nickel Grille, Rubber Tires, Cast Iron, Arcade, 11 In. $1,265.00

Bertoia Auctions

Toy, Truck, Hauling Cracker Jack Box, Metal Body, 9 x 4 ¼ In. $468.00

Wm Morford Antiques

Toy, Truck, Motor Express, Red, Silver, Embossed, Rubber Tires, Iron, Hubley, 7 In. $354.00

Bertoia Auctions

Truck, Suburban Pumper, No. 5, Red, Fire Hydrant, Tonka, 1950s	1932.00
Truck, Sunshine Biscuit, Yellow, Pressed Steel, Metalcraft, 12 In.	390.00
Truck, Tanker, Black Red Paint, Kelmet, 25 In.	590.00
Truck, Tanker, Black, Green Orange, Keystone, 27 In.	1800.00
Truck, Tanker, Mack, Gas, Iron, Blue, Tin, Wire Bracketed Fill Cap, Arcade, 13 In.	978.00
Truck, Tanker, Oil, Red Paint, Pressed Steel, Windup, Box, 15 In.	660.00
Truck, Tanker, Ride On, Handle, Pressed Steel, Red, Orange Paint, Strutco, 1930s, 22 In.	450.00
Truck, Tanker, Texaco, Rubber Tires, Iron, Kenton, 9 In.	1685.00
Truck, Telephone, Bell, Plastic, Olive, Tools, Box, Hubley, 6 In.	95.00
Truck, Telephone, Red, Cast Iron, 9 ½ In.	443.00
Truck, Tow, Boom, Hook, Open Cab, Red, Black Paint, Pressed Steel, Buddy L, 29 In.	2040.00
Truck, Tow, Mack, Iron, Red, Green Weaver Crane, Stencils, Arcade, 12 In.	1610.00
Truck, Tow, Pressed Steel, Keystone, 1930s, 26 In.	1020.00
Truck, Tow, Red, White, Tonka, 1963, 14 In.	95.00
Truck, Tow, Ride On, Pressed Steel, Yellow, Paint, Buddy L, 1930s, 28 In.	1100.00
Truck, Toy Town Delivery, Cast Iron, Kilgore, 6 In.	502.00
Truck, Trailer, Red Metal, Tonka Toy Transport	420.00
Truck, Trench Digger, Pressed Steel, Red, Yellow Paint, Buddy L, c.1930, 24 In.	4675.00
Truck, U.S. Army, 6 Wheel Transport, Cloth Top, Pressed Steel, Marx, 18 In.	325.00
Truck, U.S. Mail, Pressed Steel, Screen Side, Blue Paint Red Wheels, Sturditoy, 26 In.	3575.00
Truck, Water Sprinkler, Tin, Blue Cab, Yellow Tank, Windup, Strauss, 10 In.	431.00
Truck, Winch, Steam Shovel, Paint, Gray, Blue, Yellow, Wyandotte, c.1949, 25 In.	175.00
Turtle & Frog, Bell In Frog Head, Wheels, Green, Paint, Cast Iron, 6 ½ In.	182.00
Turtle, Green, Yellow, Pull Cord, Red Wheels, Steiff, 20 ½ In.	356.00
Tut Tut, Tin Litho Key, Bellows Mechanism, Horn Sound, Lehmann, 6 ¾ In.	601.00
TV Magic Kit, Marshall Brodien As Wizzo The Wizard, 50 Tricks, 1960s	40.00
Typewriter, Berwin Gold, Children's, Box	55.00
Ukulele, Harold Teen, Wood, Mother-Of-Pearl Look, Characters, c.1930, 21 In.	354.00
Van, Delivery, Nickel Plated, Iron, Green, Black Paint, Driver, Arcade, Wyman's, 8 In.	920.00
Van, NBC Camera, Roof Mount Cameraman, Battery Operated, Japan, Yonezawa, 8 In.	345.00
Velocipede, Carved Wood Horse, 3-Wheels, Iron, Horsehair Mane & Tail, c.1890, 28 x 35 In.	646.00
View-Master Reel, 3-D, Full Color Reel Of Pike's Peak 1949, 3 ½ x 3 ½ In.	10.00
Violinist, Tin, Windup, Body Vibrates, T.P.S., Japan, 1956, 5 In.	385.00
Wagon, Circus Calliope, Horse Drawn, White Horses, Riders, Drivers, Iron, Kenton, 13 ¾ In.	266.00
Wagon, Circus, Cage, Lion, 2 Parade Horses, Spoke Wheels, Wood, Steel, Arcade, 14 In.	288.00
Wagon, Circus, Cage, Wood, Bars, Marquee, Humpty Dumpty Circus, Schoenhut, 12 In.	575.00
Wagon, Circus, Green, Embossed Eagle, Yellow Spokes, 2 Gray Horses, Hubley, 8 In.	288.00
Wagon, Circus, Overland, Band, Cast Iron, Musicians, 2 Parade Horses, 15 In.	748.00
Wagon, Circus, Overland, Cage, Bear, 2 Horses, Driver, Iron, Kenton, 14 In.	353.00 to 633.00
Wagon, City Dairy, Rich's Little Milk Man, Tin, Wood, Pull Toy, Rich Toys, Clinton, Iowa, 20 In.	880.00
Wagon, Coal, Ox, Cast Iron, Red, Yellow Spoke Wheels, Driver, Hubley, 13 In.	345.00
Wagon, Cyclone, Wood Frame, Cast Iron Wheels, Rims, c.1890, 15 x 34 In.	212.00
Wagon, Express, Stenciled, Wood, Cast Iron Supports, Wheels, c.1890, 15 x 34 In.	236.00
Wagon, Good Will Soap, Wood, Wrought Iron, Painted, c.1900, 21 x 38 In. *Illus*	264.00
Wagon, Ice, Horse Drawn, Cast Iron, Nickel, Red Spoke Wheels, Hubley, 13 In.	230.00
Wagon, Ladders, Tin, Paint, 4 Lights Hanging Off Coiled Wires, Bell, 7 ½ In.	3163.00
Wagon, Log, Cast Iron, Plantation Worker, 2 Horses, Kenton, 15 In.	316.00
Wagon, Milk, Borden's, Wood, Tin, Glass Bottles, Wire Holder, Pull Toy, 9 x 20 In.	100.00
Wagon, Mule Drawn, Cast Iron, Red Sides, Tin Floor, Driver, 13 ½ In.	460.00
Wagon, Wood, Green, Red Wheels, Handles, Birdsell, South Bend, In., c.1900, 36 x 16 In.	4400.00
Walkie-Talkie, Space Ranger, Model 13-027, Battery, Transette, Midland International, Box, 1960s	90.00
Washing Machine, Busy Betty, Hoge Mfg., Metal, Glass, Salesman's Sample, 10 In.	448.00
Washing Machine, Hillsdale Electric, Round Tub, Green, Cream, Lift Top, Paddle, 11 x 7 In.	115.00
Washtub, 3 Little Pigs, Dancing, Doing Laundry, Ironing, Tin Litho, c.1934, 6 ½ x 3 In.	244.00
Western Town Playset, Plastic Figures, Animals, Stage Coach, Buildings, Marx, 1960s, 10 x 15 In.	177.00
Wheelbarrow, Wood, Red Trim, Stamped Paris Mfg., 14 x 41 In.	177.00
Whistle, Steamboat, Figure, Spirit Painted Hull, Propeller, Penny Toy, Germany, 4 In.	690.00
Whistler, Black Porter, Carrying Suitcase, Wood Carved, Paint, Key, Windup, 13 ½ In.	660.00
Wild Boar, Pulling Cart, Seated Figure, Cast Iron, Kenton, 8 In.	489.00
Windmill, Wood, Pressed Steel, Decals, Painted, Red, White, Blue, Arcade, 26 In.	201.00
Witch, Sitting In Rocker, Stirs, Rocks, Wood, Cloth, Clockwork, Summerbell, 10 ½ In.	454.00
Wolf, Wood, Jointed, Brown, Open Mouth, Schoenhut, 8 ½ In.	726.00 to 1035.00
Yellow Kid, Goat Cart, Cast Iron, Tin, Red Nightshirt, Kenton, c.1900, 7 x 4 In.	329.00
Yeti, Abominable Snow Man, Walks, Raises Arms, Battery, Remote, Marx, Box, 1964, 11 In. *Illus*	1468.00
Zebra, Movable Arms, Legs, Brown, Orange, Wood, Schoenhut, 8 In.	180.00
Zeppelin, Chicago, Tin, Die Cut Windows, Clockwork, Strauss, 9 ½ In.	144.00

Zeppelin, Hindenburg, Tin Litho, Metal Propeller, Clockwork, Tippco, Germany, 11 In. ..*Illus*	1265.00
Zeppelin, Propellers, Gondolas, Enclosed Cabin, Clockwork Motor, Tin, Paint, Marklin, c.1900, 15 In.	4600.00
Zilotone, Figure Plays, 9 Records Spin, Tin, Pressed Steel, Clockwork, Wolverine, 8 In.	431.00
Zilotone, With Farmer In The Dell Disc, Red & Blue, Player In Red & Black, Wolverine, 7 x 8 In.	140.00
Zulu Man, Yellow Cart, Ostrich Pulled, Tin Lithograph, Lehmann, Germany, 6 ½ In...............	600.00

TRADE CARD, *see Card, Advertising.*

TRAMP ART is a form of folk art made since the Civil War. It is usually made from chip-carved cigar boxes. Examples range from small boxes and picture frames to full-sized pieces of furniture.

Bank, Chip Carved, Layered Strips, Recessed Panels, Rosettes, Drawer, 5 x 4 x 4 In.	35.00
Box, 2 Graduated Layer Pyramids, Double Pedestal, Chip Carved, Loop Handle, Footed, 14 x 14 In.	502.00
Box, 6 & 7 Layer Pyramids, Painted Black, Lift Lid, Brass Knob, Hinges, Drawer, 10 ¼ x 10 In...	177.00
Box, Chip Carved, Tuned Knob Feet, Finials, Applied Oak Leaves, Acorns, Lined, 9 x 13 In.	94.00
Box, Cigar, Chip Carved, Pieced Wood, Shaped Skirt, Signed, John Henry, 1894, 8 ¾ x 6 ¼ In.	71.00
Box, Hinged Lid, Heart Frame, Porcelain Buttons, Pierced Word Souvenir, 5 x 11 ¾ In. ..*Illus*	59.00
Box, Hinged Lid, Painted White, Lock, Hasp, Padded Knit Fabric, 10 x 6 In...............................	71.00
Box, Hinged Lid, Velvet Interior, Mirror, Key, Swedish, 1900s, 10 x 8 x 6 ½ In.	176.00
Box, Lid, Desk, Wood, Chip Carved Strips, Red Paint, Blue Silk Lining, 4 x 7 In.......................	59.00
Box, Lid, Walnut, Star Shape Tacks, Brass Drop Pull ....*Illus*	142.00
Box, Lock, Brass Medallion, Lid, c.1900, 6 x 8 ½ In.	181.00
Box, Pedestal, Red & Green Paint, 10 x 7 ½ In. ....*Illus*	502.00
Box, Pyramids, Geometric Symbols, Cloth Lining, Mirror, Flared Base, 8 x 5 x 4 In.	359.00
Box, Recessed Lid, Chip Carved, Pyramids, 8-Sided, 4 ⅝ x 9 ½ In.	12.00
Box, Sewing, Ornaments, c.1890, 11 x 8 x 8 In..	240.00
Box, Shaving Mirror, Lift Lid, Paper Lined, Hinged Mirror, Stands On Rails, 7 ½ x 10 In..........	142.00
Box, Slide Lid, 2 Compartments, Layered Chip Carved Strips, Diamond Shape Plaque, 11 x 6 In...	83.00
Box, Wall, Wood, Carved, Oval Mirror, Drawer, 16 x 9 In...	189.00
Box, Wall, Wood, Open Pocket, Diamond Carvings, c.1905, 8 In.	115.00
Cabinet, Hanging, Wood, Chip Carved, Diamonds, Stars, Mushroom Pull, 3 Shelves, 17 x 8 In.	443.00
Chest, Chip Carved, 4 Drawers, Turned Knobs, Triangular Backsplash, Base, 10 x 10 In.	83.00
Chest, Hinged Lid, Rising Sun, Scalloped Crest, Zigzag Molding, Applied Scrolls, Drawers, 18 x 8 In. ..	71.00
Chest, Mirror, Applied Rows Of Diamonds, Jewelry Compartment, Drawers, 36 x 17 In.	2300.00
Clock Hutch, Carved Horseshoe, Heart, Shield, c.1919, 15 x 17 ¾ In.........................	356.00
Compote, 4 Layered Pyramids On Sides, Tapered Pedestal, 8-Sided, 6 x 10 In.........................	502.00
Cross, Gold Paint, Chip Carved, Canted Corners	850.00
Crucifix, Ladder, Keys, Spear, Sponge, Pedestal, Glass Dome, Isadore De Smet, c.1890, 21 x 9 In...	120.00
Desk, Tabletop, Hinged Top, Fitted Interior, Mirror, Masonic Symbols, Drawers, 24 ½ x 19 In.	1610.00
Dresser Box, Chip Carved Strip, Shaped Pyramids, Mushroom Knob, 5 ⅝ x 9 ½ In.................	295.00
Dresser Box, Chip Carved, Labeled Mattie, Dark Stain, Applied Shapes, 7 x 12 In.	59.00
Dresser Box, Pincushion, Hinged Lid, Chip Carved, Layered Strips, Rosettes, Paw Feet, 11 x 7 In.	153.00
Dresser, 2 Drawers, Gallery, Chip Carved, 10 x 11 In...	295.00
Dresser, 2 Step Back Drawers, 3 Lower Drawers, Raised Diamonds, Doll's, c.1900, 23 x 12 ¼ In....	243.00
Fern Stand, Oak, Twisted Bead Pedestal, Gargoyle Feet, 42 In....................................	248.00
Frame, Chip Carved, Light Stain, 8 ½ x 10 In.	65.00
Frame, Mirror, Chip Carved, 4 Tiers, Bread Loaf Shape, 14 x 22 In.	47.00
Frame, Mirror, Chip Carved, Painted Red, Black, Silver, 12 ½ x 10 In.............................	384.00
Frame, Notched Carvings, Photo Openings, Signed, c.1929, 25 x 19 In...........................	264.00
Frame, Walnut, Chip Carved, Shield Shape Frame, Oval Port, 2 Halberds, 12 x 9 In.................	35.00
Jewelry Box, Hinged Lid, Chip Carved, Stepped Geometric Design, c.1900, 10 ¼ x 8 In.	86.00
Lamp, Inlaid Design, 6 Disguised Drawers, Embossed Paper Shade, c.1915, 29 x 16 ½ In. ..... *Illus*	353.00
Pincushion, 2 Pyramids, Stacked Panels, Chip Carved, Cloth Cushion, Lace Trim, 5 x 7 ½ In. ....*Illus*	71.00
Plant Stand, Painted Red, Chip Carved, Faux Puzzle, Open Box, 4 Legs, 6 x 4 ⅝ In.................	59.00
Puzzle Cane, Hardwood, Brass Ferrule, c.1890, 34 In.	1610.00
Shaving Stand, Bureau Top, Gothic Arch Pediment, Drawer, 26 x 14 In............................	130.00
Shelf, Chip Carved, Red, White, Green, Triangle Shape, Rosettes..	750.00
Statuette Shrine, Chip Carved, Oval Window Frames, Towers, 16 x 10 In.	106.00
Table, Wood, Chip Carved, Dark Stain, 27 x 30 In.	63.00
Tea Caddy, Metal Corners, Monogram, BH, c.1900, 6 x 6 x 6 In..	160.00
Trinket Box, Chip Carved, Lift Lid, Dark Stain, 7 ½ x 9 ½ In..	94.00
Trinket Box, Dome Lid, Inlay, Heart, Gum Drops, Circles, Diamonds, Felt Lined, 5 ¾ x 7 In. ...*Illus*	325.00
Trinket Box, Hinged Lid, Chip Carved, Matchstick, 6-Point Star, Cross, Shoe Feet, 5 x 7 ¼ In. ..*Illus*	47.00
Trinket Box, Lid, Stacked & Carved Strips, Red Wool Panels, 6 ⅛ x 10 ¼ In. ....*Illus*	35.00
Trinket Box, Lift Lid, Chip Carved, Recessed Strips At Corners, Scalloped Base, 4 x 6 In.	35.00
Trinket Box, Lock, Brass Paw Feet, Marbleized Lining, 7 x 12 x 9 In.	118.00

Toy, Wagon, Good Will Soap, Wood, Wrought Iron, Painted, c.1900, 21 x 38 In. $264.00

Garth's Auctioneers & Appraisers

Toy, Yeti, Abominable Snow Man, Walks, Raises Arms, Battery, Remote, Marx, Box, 1964, 11 In. $1,468.00

Hake's Americana & Collectibles

Toy, Zeppelin, Hindenburg, Tin Litho, Metal Propeller, Clockwork, Tippco, Germany, 11 In. $1,265.00

Bertoia Auctions

Tramp Art, Box, Hinged Lid, Heart Frame, Porcelain Buttons, Pierced Word Souvenir, 5 x 11 ¾ In. $59.00

Conestoga Auction Co., Inc.

T

TIP

When you work with an antique mirror, be careful. Mercury drops may be found at the bottom of the glass and exposure to mercury vapor can be toxic.

Tramp Art, Box, Lid, Walnut, Star Shape Tacks, Brass Drop Pull
$142.00

Conestoga Auction Co., Inc.

Tramp Art, Box, Pedestal, Red & Green Paint, 10 x 7 ½ In.
$502.00

Conestoga Auction Co., Inc.

Tramp Art, Lamp, Inlaid Design, 6 Disguised Drawers, Embossed Paper Shade, c.1915, 29 x 16 ½ In.
$353.00

Garth's Auctioneers & Appraisers

Tramp Art, Pincushion, 2 Pyramids, Stacked Panels, Chip Carved, Cloth Cushion, Lace Trim, 5 x 7 ½ In.
$71.00

Conestoga Auction Co., Inc.

Trinket Box, Matchstick Covered, Hinged Lid, Stacked Bracket Feet, Wallpaper Lining, 3 ¾ x 9 In.	47.00
Wall Vanity, Matchstick, Overhanging Eave, Bracketed Shelf, Framed Mirror, Hanger, 13 x 6 In. ..	24.00
Wardrobe, Mirror, Chip Carved, Shaped Crest, Lower Drawer, Miniature, 8 ½ x 4 ¾ In.	83.00
Watch Hutch, Chip Carved, 3 Tiers, Crisscross Frame, Hinged Door, Round Port, 9 ¾ x 9 ½ In.	47.00

TRAPS for animals may be handmade. One of the most unusual is the mousetrap made so that when the mouse entered the trap, it was hit on the head with a mallet. Other traps were commercially manufactured and often are marked with the name of the manufacturer. Many traps were designed to be as humane as possible, and they would trap the live animal so it could be released in the woods.

Animal, Jump, Victor Oneida, No. 4, Chain, 1909, 10 x 6 ¾ In...	68.00
Ant, Lilly's Ant Trap, Tin, Red, Yellow, Round, 1960s, 2 ⅛ x ½ In.	14.00
Bear, Newhouse No. 5, c.1900, 35 x 13 In.	1450.00
Critter, Wood, Tunnel Shaped Box, Spring Loaded, Trip Wire, John Curtis, c.1867, 12 x 8 ½ In.	748.00
Critter, Wooden Box, 2 Doors, Counterweights, Wm. Biddle, c.1839, 5 x 7 ¼ In.	863.00
Eel, Woven Bamboo, 23 x 7 In.	175.00
Fly, Glass, Bottle, 3 Footed, Embossed Flies, c.1900, 6 ½ In.	80.00
Fly, Glass, Bottle, Bulbous, Stick Neck, c.1880, 7 ¼ x 5 ¾ In.	70.00
Fly, Metal, Central Cylinder, Balance Scale Mechanism, 2 Mesh Traps, 1871, 8 ¾ x 10 In........	633.00
Fly, Tin, Fluted Wood Base, Spring Loaded, Pull Back Plunger, Sweeping Arm, 1878, 9 ½ x 3 In.....	575.00
Fly, Tin, Painted, Open Top, Turntable, Side Box, Sweeping Pediment, 1868, 4 ½ x 12 In........	633.00
Fly, Tin, Squat, Teapot Shape, Hand Crank, Sweeping Arm, Covered Spout, c.1876, 10 ½ x 4 ½ In.	748.00
Gopher, Nickel, Wood Case, Spring Loaded, 6 Impaling Spikes, 8 ½ In...................................	690.00
Gopher, Wooden, Animal Trap Co., 6 x 3 ¾ x 2 In.	30.00
Mole, Wooden, Pedestal, Bar Stool, Spiked Plunger, Tag, 1871, 8 ¼ In.	748.00
Mouse, A Ketch-All No. 2, Kness Mfg. Co., Metal, Black, 1940s, 4 x 2 In..................................	30.00
Mouse, Cardboard, Wood Finish, End-O-Mice, Oneida Community Ltd., 3 x 1 ½ In.	12.00
Mouse, Metal, Bakelite, Victor, 4 Hole Choker, Woodstream Corp., 4 x 4 In.	50.00
Mouse, Wood, Metal, 4 Ways, Animal Trap Co., Box, 1955, 3 ⅞ x 1 ⅞ In., Pair	24.00
Mouse, Wood, Sure Catch, Lovell Manufacturing Company..	40.00
Queen Bee, Wood, Tin Strips, 12 x 5 In.	50.00
Snare, Wood, Turnstile, Spiked Entryway, H.F. Lushbaugh, 4 ½ x 11 In.	518.00
Squirrel, Cage, 2 Front Figures By Wheel, Wire, Wood, Paint, 11 ¼ x 12 In...........................	661.00

TREEN, *see Wooden category.*

TRENCH ART is a form of folk art made by soldiers. Metal casings from bullets and mortar shells were cut and decorated to form useful objects, such as vases.

Tazza, Artillery Shell, Brass Soldier, Machine Gun, Field, Marble Foot, c.1920, 2 ½ x 4 ¾ In. ..	94.00
Vase, Brass Shell Casing, Scalloped Top, Hammered Design, 3 Footed, c.1917, 3 x 3 ½ In........	460.00
Watch Hutch, Tall Case Clock Shape, Walnut, Bonnet Door, Sawtooth Opening, Scallops, 21 x 6 In. .	295.00

TRIVETS are now used to hold hot dishes. Most trivets of the late nineteenth and early twentieth centuries were made to hold hot irons. Iron or brass reproductions are being made of many of the old styles.

Brass, Heart Shape, Shield Cutout, Applied Tubular Feet, 1800s, 4 ½ In. ....*Illus*	71.00
Brass, Iron, Pierced Top, 3 Legs, England, 1800s, 14 ½ x 15 ½ In.	122.00
Brass, Iron, Pierced Top, Engraved, Urn, Mythological Creatures, Rectangular	649.00
Brass, Iron, Turned Wood Handle, Pierced Top, 3 Legs, 19th Century, 13 x 13 ½ In..................	24.00
Brass, Scrolled Design, 1950s	50.00
Bronze, 3 Hearts, 3-Footed, 8 x 4 ½ x 1 ¼ In.	70.00
Cast Iron, Good Luck To All Who Use This Stand, 6-Pointed Star, 8 x 4 In.	35.00
Cast Iron, Porcelain, Jack & Jill, Zigzag Border, Japan, 1930s..	22.00
Cast Iron, Tassel & Grain, Twisted Border, Virginia Metalcrafters, 1930s, 8 x 5 In.	30.00
Cast Iron, Teapot Shape, Homestead, Winter Scene, Japan, 1950s, 8 x 6 In.	15.00
Crowned Lion, Unicorn, On Hind Legs, Brass, Pierced, Iron Base, England, 12 x 7 In.............	212.00
Flower & Leaf, Yellow, Green, Black, Square, Rookwood, c.1925, 5 ¾ In.	115.00
Hearth, Brass & Iron, Pierced Medallion Top, Tripod Feet, c.1800, 9 ⅞ x 7 ⅝ In.	207.00
Horseshoe Shape, Boot Feet, Iron, c.1810, 3 x 5 ½ In.	3555.00
Mosaic Tiles, 3 Flower Central Design, White, Orange, 1960s	12.00
Punched Star, Wrought Iron, Pa., 1843, 1 ¾ x 4 ¾ In..	1896.00
Tile, Windmill In Landscape, Relief, Blue & Gray Glaze, Bracket Feet, Rookwood, c.1919, 5 ½ In....	104.00
Wood, Tile, Butterflies, 4-Footed, 1970s, 8 In. Diam..	20.00
Wrought Iron, Heart Shape, 2 x 7 ½ In...	118.00
Wrought Iron, Heart Shape, Scroll Handle & Feet, Punch Border Design, c.1800, 2 ⅝ x 9 ½ In....	720.00

TRUNKS of many types were made. The nineteenth-century sea chest was often handmade of unpainted wood. Brass-fitted camphorwood chests were brought back from the Orient. Leather-covered trunks were popular from the late eighteenth to mid-nineteenth centuries. By 1895, trunks were covered with canvas or decorated sheet metal. Embossed metal coverings were used from 1870 to 1910. By 1925, trunks were covered with vulcanized fiber or undecorated metal. Suitcases are listed here.

Campaign, Camphorwood, Hinged Lid, Fitted Carrying Handles, Brass Bound, c.1810, 41 x 21 In.	1239.00
Camphorwood, Brass Bound, Bail Handles, 20 ¼ x 41 In.	1416.00
Camphorwood, Marine Officer's, Brass Bound, Flat Top, Inscribed, Chinese, 18 x 42 In.	2714.00
Conestoga, Pine, Wrought Iron Hardware, Original Lock, Early 19th Century, 14 x 23 In.	431.00
Dome Top, Grain Painted, New Hampshire, 12 x 28 In.	531.00
Dome Top, Horizontal Reeded Panels, Blue, Yellow, Red Paint, c.1829, 9 x 16 In.	2370.00
Dome Top, Iron, Inlaid Metal, Geometric, Flowers, Ring Handles, Islam, 38 ⅝ x 26 ½ In.	911.00
Dome Top, Laced Edges, Flower Tooling, Leather, c.1900, 18 x 26 x 16 In.	478.00
Dome Top, Oak, Blue Paint, Iron Straps, Handles, 1700s, 22 ½ x 36 ½ In.	230.00
Dome Top, Oak, Flowers, Blue Paint, Bracket Feet, 30 ¼ x 22 In.	288.00
Dome Top, Painted, Decorated, Success To America, 17 x 42 In.	2242.00
Dome Top, Pennsylvania Dutch, Scrolling Vines, Birds, Tulips, Multicolor, 1856, 15 x 30 In.	590.00
Dome Top, Pine, Hinged Lid, Green Paint, c.1820, 14 x 24 In.	115.00
Dome Top, Pine, Painted, Inscribed Jacob Brahm, Philadelphia, 19 ½ x 35 ¼ In.	148.00
Dome Top, Storage, Grained & Painted, 12 x 28 ¼ In.	531.00
Dome Top, Wood, Iron Strap Hinges, Handles, c.1830, 21 x 35 In.	120.00
Drew & Sons, Travel Case, Leather, Fitted, Ivory, Silver Accessories, England, 11 ¾ x 15 ½ In.	277.00
Fendi, Duffle, Shoulder Strap, Key, 11 x 24 In.	153.00
Gucci, Briefcase, Monogram, Canvas, Stamped, 15 ½ x 16 ½ In.	150.00
Gucci, Carry-On, Monogram, Canvas, Exterior Pocket, Shoulder Strap, Marked, 11 ½ x 16 x 7 In.	270.00
Hide Covered, Hinged Lid, Brass Swing Handle, Tacks, Iron Latch, Paper Lined, c.1800, 6 x 12 In.	119.00
Humpback, Wood, Metal, Victorian, 22 x 30 x 17 In.	270.00
Immigrant's, Dome Top, Pine, Painted Blue, Iron Straps, W. Haman, c.1890, 18 x 34 In.	147.00
Immigrant's, Pine, Painted Blue, Continental, 1800s, 20 x 30 In.	89.00
Leather Cover, Mixed Woods, Oval Brass Tacks, Metal Bail Handles, Ball Feet, c.1890, 21 x 39 In.	176.00
Leather Lid, Brass Studs, Brass Swing Handle, Holding Beads, John B. Baker, Boston, 10 x 7 In.	148.00
Leather, Black, Flowers, Handles, Chinese, 10 ½ x 25 In.	767.00
Leather, Brass Hardware, Copper Rivets, Handles, Saks Fifth Avenue, c.1900, 14 ½ x 37 In.	837.00
Leather, Red, Camphorwood Interior, Stand, Chinese, c.1900, 18 ½ x 30 In.	750.00
Louis Vuitton, Briefcase, Green Epi Leather, Brass Hardware, Pouch	1659.00
Louis Vuitton, Case, Leather Edge, Lined, Tray, Bottle Straps, Mirror, Label, 1900s, 8 x 16 In. ..*Illus*	1968.00
Louis Vuitton, Cat Carrier, Canvas, Leather, Brown Logo, Applied Leather Oval, 16 In.	354.00
Louis Vuitton, Garment Bag, Leather, Canvas, Monogram	270.00
Louis Vuitton, Portfolio, Monogram, Canvas, 21 x 17 In.	450.00
Louis Vuitton, Red Vuittonite Car Trunk, 40 x 20 x 11 In.	2300.00
Louis Vuitton, Steamer, Damier Canvas, Brass Hardware, c.1900, 23 x 43 x 22 In.	4600.00
Louis Vuitton, Steamer, Hangers, Drawers, Key, Painted Monogram, 1930s, 44 x 21 ½ x 22 In. ..*Illus*	8610.00
Louis Vuitton, Steamer, Leather Bound, Wardrobe, c.1900, 45 x 46 In.	4000.00
Louis Vuitton, Steamer, Logo Canvas, Brass Hardware, Label, c.1900, 22 x 43 x 22 In.	8625.00
Louis Vuitton, Steamer, Tray, Basket, Brass Hardware, Rivets, Wheels, c.1920, 21 ½ x 23 ¾ In. ..*Illus*	6274.00
Louis Vuitton, Steamer, Wardrobe, Drawers, Leather Handles, Interior Quilted, c.1910, 24 x 40 In.	34500.00
Louis Vuitton, Steamer, Woven Fabric, Straps, Leather Strips, c.1910, 27 x 36 In.	6900.00
Louis Vuitton, Suitcase, Brown Logo, Initials, 32 & 24 In., 2 Piece	2124.00
Louis Vuitton, Suitcase, Hard Side, Leather Handle, Monogram WW, Key, 9 x 26 In.	1298.00
Louis Vuitton, Suitcase, Leather, Brown, Leather Handle, Saks Fifth Avenue Tag, 20 x 26 In.	295.00
Louis Vuitton, Suitcase, Leather, Canvas, Monogram, 20 x 26 In.	270.00
Louis Vuitton, Suitcase, Leather, Handle, 7 x 28 In.	885.00
Louis Vuitton, Suitcase, Soft Sides, Canvas, Leather Trim, Monogram, 23 x 18 ½ In. ......*Illus*	270.00
Louis Vuitton, Travel Bag, Canvas, Monogram, 16 x 8 ½ In.	600.00
Louis Vuitton, Trunk, Leather, Brass Tacks, Quilted Liner, Wheels, 22 ½ x 34 In.	3346.00
Louis Vuitton, Wood Strapped, Cloth Bound, Monogram Pattern, Tiered Interior, 21 x 40 x 21 In.	5100.00
Oak, Wood Dowels, Wrought Iron Fittings, Lock, Key, c.1800, 51 x 25 x 29 In.	430.00
Oshkosh, Travel, Monogram, c.1939, 43 x 30 In.	1955.00
Pine, Gray, Black Paint, 1800s, 23 x 48 In.	59.00
Steamer, Damier Canvas, Brass Hardware, New Bond St., London, c.1900, 23 x 40 In.	5175.00
Suitcase, Canvas & Tan Leather, Zippered Opening, Chocolate Brown, Label, 21 x 25 In.	492.00
Teak, Scroll, Flower Carved, Brass Bound, Handles, c.1850, 19 ½ x 41 ¾ In.	1062.00
Walnut, Brass Trimmed, Handles, Molded Base, England, 1800s, 18 x 41 In.	323.00
Wood, Iron Hardware, Chinese, c.1910, 22 x 35 In.	236.00
Wood, Mother-Of-Pearl Inlay, Geometric Pattern, Block Feet, Lid, Egypt, 15 ½ x 25 ¼ In.	359.00
Wood, Mother-Of-Pearl Inlay, Hinged Door, Arabesque Design, Syria, 1800s, 34 ½ x 49 ½ In.	896.00

Tramp Art, Trinket Box, Dome Lid, Inlay, Heart, Gum Drops, Circles, Diamonds, Felt Lined, 5 ¾ x 7 In.
$325.00

Conestoga Auction Co., Inc.

Tramp Art, Trinket Box, Hinged Lid, Chip Carved, Matchstick, 6-Point Star, Cross, Shoe Feet, 5 x 7 ¼ In.
$47.00

Conestoga Auction Co., Inc.

Tramp Art, Trinket Box, Lid, Stacked & Carved Strips, Red Wool Panels, 6 ⅛ x 10 ¼ In.
$35.00

Conestoga Auction Co., Inc.

Trivet, Brass, Heart Shape, Shield Cutout, Applied Tubular Feet, 1800s, 4 ½ In.
$71.00

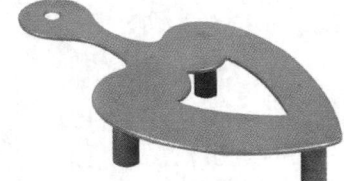

Conestoga Auction Co., Inc.

T

Trunk, Louis Vuitton, Case, Leather Edge, Lined, Tray, Bottle Straps, Mirror, Label, 1900s, 8 x 16 In.
$1,968.00

Neal Auction Co.

Trunk, Louis Vuitton, Steamer, Hangers, Drawers, Key, Painted Monogram, 1930s, 44 x 21 ½ x 22 In.
$8,610.00

Neal Auction Co.

Trunk, Louis Vuitton, Steamer, Tray, Basket, Brass Hardware, Rivets, Wheels, c.1920, 21 ½ x 23 ¾ In.
$6,274.00

Neal Auction Co.

TIP

To be collectible, trunks must be in good condition. Refinishing destroys the trunk's value as an antique. Trunks in poor condition can be refinished to be attractive and useful as pieces of furniture, but they will no longer be of interest to serious trunk collectors.

TUTHILL Cut Glass Company of Middletown, New York, worked from 1902 to 1923. Of special interest are the finely cut pieces of stemware and tableware.

Basket, Cosmos, Hobstar Chain Border, Double Notched Handle, 6 x 8 In.	275.00
Bowl, 5-Point Star Center, Engraved Flowers, Hobstar Chain Border, 6 In.	175.00
Bowl, Engraved, Vintage, 6 Fruit Panels, Geometric Pillars, 2 x 10 In.	250.00
Bowl, Poppy & Russian Sections, Notched Scalloped Edge, 3 ½ x 8 In.	1800.00
Bowl, Rex, Notched Edge, 3 ¼ x 8 In.	1100.00
Bowl, Triangular Hobstar Cluster, Strawberry Diamond & Fan Border, 8 In.	50.00
Bowl, Vintage Pattern, 3 ¾ x 8 In.	250.00
Bowl, Wild Rose, Shaped Rim, 2 x 8 In.	1500.00
Candlestick, Teardrop Stem, Flashed Rayed Base, 12 In., Pair	175.00
Card Tray, Phlox, Geometrics, Square, 6 ¾ In.	150.00
Card Tray, Rosemere, Square, 6 ¾ In.	275.00
Compote, Grape & Blackberry, 5 x 7 In.	450.00
Compote, Hobstar & Prism, Teardrop Stem, Punty Highlights, Rolled Rim, 9 x 5 In., Pair	175.00
Compote, Hobstar, Kite & Fan, 5-Sided, Notched Stem, Rayed Base, 9 x 6 In.	25.00
Compote, Vintage & Pear, Engraved, Shaped Rim, 3 ½ x 7 ¾ In.	275.00
Cruet, Wheat, Tapered, Pattern Cut Stopper, 9 ½ In.	500.00
Decanter, Primrose, Vertical Hobstar & Crosshatched Bands, Oval, Marked, 11 ½ In.	1850.00
Dish, Mayonnaise, Underplate, Hobstar Chain, Engraved Flower Border, 7 In.	225.00
Dresser Box, Hobstar, Block & Lattice, Hobstar Chain Base, Round, 4 x 7 ½ In.	900.00
Plate, Orient, Scalloped, 7 In.	450.00
Sugar & Creamer, Wild Rose, Marked, c.1900	195.00
Tray, Hobstar Border, Tab Handles, Signed, 13 ½ x 8 ⅝ In.	2350.00
Tray, Poppy, Round, Wafer Base, 10 In.	300.00
Tray, Vintage, Geometric Border, Signed, 9 ¾ In.	550.00
Tumbler, Primrose, 3 ⅝ x 3 In.	25.00
Vase, Leaf Flower, Trumpet, c.1880, 11 ¾ In.	225.00
Vase, Sweet Pea, Engraved Wood Lily, Ruffled, Footed, American Brilliant, 5 ½ x 8 In.	100.00

TYPEWRITER collectors divide typewriters into two main classifications: the index machine, which has a pointer and a dial for letter selection, and the keyboard machine, most commonly seen today. The first successful typewriter was made by Sholes and Glidden in 1874.

Blickensderfer, No. 6, DHIATE Keyboard, Oak Case, c.1906	385.00
Blickensderfer, No. 7, Case, c.1897	455.00
Corona Four, Leather Carrying Case, Touch Typewriting Chart, Cleaning Brush, 1898	58.00
Englewood Williams, 3-Row Typebar, Grasshopper Mechanism, c.1897	614.00
Franklin, No. 9, Typebar Machine, Round Ideal Keyboard, 1898	1075.00
L.C. Smith, No. 2, c.1903, 14 x 15 x 9 In.	900.00
Olivetti, Valentine, Red Plastic, Metal, Rubber, Ettore Sottsass, Red Case, 1969, 13 ½ x 14 In.	625.00
Olympia, 2-Tone Gray, Germany, 1970s, 5 x 12 x 12 In.	105.00
Remington, Model 5, Touch Regulator, Streamlined, Art Moderne, Case, c.1940	225.00
Royal, Quiet Deluxe, Tweed Case, 1950s	68.00
Underwood, 4 Bank, Camouflage, c.1929, 9 x 10 x 10 In.	265.00
Underwood, Deluxe, Portable, Case, c.1954, 13 ½ x 13 ½ x 6 ½ In.	200.00
Underwood, Simulated Wood, Manual, c.1928, 9 x 10 x 10 In.	325.00
Ward's, S-100A, Brown, Metal Case, Portable, 1950s, 11 x 12 In.	140.00

TYPEWRITER RIBBON TINS are now being collected. The lithographed tin containers have been used since the 1870s. Most popular with collectors are tins with pictorial graphics.

Beaver Superb, M. B. Cook Co., 2 ½ In.	26.00
Burroughs Old Bellaire, Black, White, 2 ⅝ In.	12.00
Burroughs, Silver, Orange, Brown, 2 ½ In.	14.00
Carter's, Ideal, Blue, Flower Border, 2 ½ In.	30.00
Carter's, Ideal, Woman's Silhouette, Blue, Silver, Tin, Cardboard, 2 ¾ In. Diam.	22.00
Carter's, Midnight, Stars, Planet, Blue, White	12.00
Deluxe Secretarial, Geometric Design, Gold, Black, Green, 2 ½ In.	20.00
Elk, Miller Line, Blue, Yellow, 2 ⅝ x 2 ⅝ In.	19.00
Globe, Geometric Design, Logo, Crown Ribbon Mfg., 2 ½ In.	30.00
Hallmark, M.C. Smith-Elite Type, 1940s, 2 ¾ x 2 ¾ In.	6.00
Silver Brand, Silver, Gold, 2 ½ In.	10.00
Stenno, Silver Medal, Hand Holding Torch, 1st Prize, Stenno Ribbon Corp., 2 ½ In.	18.00
Tagger, Red, Yellow, 2 ¼ In.	10.00
Thurobred, Red, White.	20.00

T

Typebar Brand, Blue, White, Red, Square, 2 ½ In.	16.00
Webster, Star, Gold, Red, Black, Hinged	18.00

UHL POTTERY was made in Evansville, Indiana, in 1854. The pottery moved to Huntingburg, Indiana, in 1908. Stoneware and glazed pottery were made until the mid-1940s.

Boot, Star, 4 ⅛ In.	160.00
Cookie Jar, Yellow Daisies, Red Ground, 9 In.	75.00
Crock, Blue Glaze, 3 x 14 In.	50.00
Decanter, Blue Glaze, Ringed Base, Ball Stopper, Art Deco, 8 In.	50.00
Jug, Merry Christmas, 2 Handles, 1940	100.00

UMBRELLA collectors like rain or shine. The first known umbrella was owned by King Louis XIII of France in 1637. The earliest umbrellas were sunshades, not designed to be used in the rain. The umbrella was embellished and redesigned many times. In 1852, the fluted steel rib style was developed and it has remained the most useful style.

Bakelite Knob Handle, Brown, Silver Stripes, Gentleman's, 1940s, 123 In.	85.00
Bamboo, Paper, Japanese Style, c.1940, 18 In.	98.00
Bubble, Vinyl, Clear, Red Trim, 1960s, 31 In.	48.00
Ivory Handle, Silk, Embroidered, Dragons, Japanese, c.1900	850.00
Knotty Wood Handle, Line, Lace, Tassel, Wood Beads, 37 In.	395.00
Lucite & Bamboo Handle, Fabric, Plaid, Multicolor, c.1940, 26 In.	65.00
Lucite Handle, Navy Blue, Silver Trim, Box, 1950s, 28 In.	165.00
Maroon, White Stripes, Pagoda Shape, c.1940, 34 In.	110.00
Parasol, Carriage, Ivory Handle, Dog, Lion Mask Black Chantilly Lace, Tan Lining, Scalloped, 21 In.	200.00
Parasol, Eagle Talon & Ball Handle, Carved, Aubergine, Silk Tassel, Bakelite, 28 ¼ In.	144.00
Parasol, Embroidered Netting, Lace Trim, Bows, Appliques, Ecru Stationary	50.00
Parasol, Ivory Handle, Silk, Black, Fringe, c.1858, 16 In.	305.00
Parasol, Plaid, Blue, Peach, White, Rayon, c.1945, 17 In.	48.00
Plastic Red Knob Handle, Red & White, Stripes, c.1960, 20 In.	125.00
White With Allover Pattern Of Children, Red & Turquoise, Japan, 1950s, 12 x 21 In.	30.00
Wood Handle, Black & White, Ruffles, c.1960, 30 In.	65.00
Wood Handle, Carved, Silk, Striped Interior, Brass Finial & Nameplate, W. Ellery, c.1815, 37 ¾ In.	518.00
Wood Handle, Louis Vuitton, Monogram, Nylon, 35 In.	390.00
Yellow & Blue Polka Dots, Retro, Curved Handle, c.1960, 26 In.	185.00

UNION PORCELAIN WORKS was originally William Boch & Brothers, located in Greenpoint, New York. Thomas C. Smith bought the company in 1861 and renamed it Union Porcelain Works. The company went through a series of ownership changes and finally closed about 1922. The company made a fine quality white porcelain that was often decorated in clear, bright colors. Don't confuse this company with its competitor, Charles Cartlidge and Company, also in Greenpoint.

Bowl, Vegetable, Flower Sprig, Red & Blue Flowers, Shaker, N.Y., 8 x 6 In.	*Illus*	848.00
Match Striker, White, Printed Brasco's, 1800s, 2 ½ x 3 ½ In.		152.00
Oyster Plate, 5 Wells, Nautical Symbols, Gold, White, Oval, 8 ¼ x 6 ¼ In.		245.00
Oyster Plate, 5 Wells, Sea Life, c.1881, 8 ½ x 6 ½ In.		395.00
Oyster Shooter, 1 Well, Pink Ground, Pink, Orange Flowers, c.1880, 4 ½ x 3 ½ In.		425.00
Water Cooler, Lid, Blue, White Molded Border, Red, Black Designs, c.1880, 17 ¼ In.		243.00

UNIVERSITY CITY POTTERY, of University, Missouri, worked from 1909 to 1915. Well-known artists, including Taxile Doat, Adelaide Alsop Robineau, and Frederick Hurten Rhead, worked there.

Vase, Bud, Carved Acanthus Leaves, White Ground, Marked, 1912, 5 x 3 ½ In.	*Illus*	1750.00
Vase, Bud, Stylized Cypresses, Enamel, Frederick Rhead, 1911, 4 ¾ x 2 In.	*Illus*	5938.00
Vase, Crystalline Glaze, Tan & Green Design, Tapered Rectangle, Marked, 3 ½ In.		1265.00
Vase, White Matte Glaze, Tapered Square, Rounded Top, Flat Rim, Marked, c.1914, 2 x 3 In.		633.00

UNIVERSITY OF NORTH DAKOTA, *see North Dakota School of Mines category.*

VAL ST. LAMBERT Cristalleries of Belgium was founded by Messieurs Kemlin and Lelievre in 1825. The company is still in operation. All types of table glassware and decorative glassware have been made. Pieces are often decorated with cut designs.

Cake Plate, Pompeii Blue Cut To Rose Cut To Clear, Clear Pedestal, 3 x 9 ½ In.	850.00
Centerpiece, Cut Crystal, Pedestal, Signed VSL, 6 x 10 In.	72.00
Centerpiece, Green, Cut To Clear, Diamond, Lop Design, Marked, 9 x 12 In.	298.00

Trunk, Louis Vuitton, Suitcase, Soft Sides, Canvas, Leather Trim, Monogram, 23 x 18 ½ In.
$270.00

DuMouchelles Art Gallery

Union Porcelain Works, Bowl, Vegetable, Flower Sprig, Red & Blue Flowers, Shaker, N.Y., 8 x 6 In.
$848.00

Willis Henry Auctions, Inc.

University City, Vase, Bud, Carved Acanthus Leaves, White Ground, Marked, 1912, 5 x 3 ½ In.
$1,750.00

Rago Arts & Auction Center

University City, Vase, Bud, Stylized Cypresses, Enamel, Frederick Rhead, 1911, 4 ¾ x 2 In.
$5,938.00

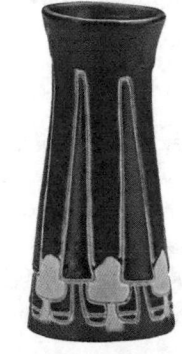

Rago Arts & Auction Center

U
V

Vallerysthal, Vase, Daffodils, Acid Etched, Enamel, Cameo, Signed, 1880s, 10 x 3 ¼ In.
$813.00

Rago Arts & Auction Center

Van Briggle, Figurine, Frog, Turquoise Glaze, Marked, 9 In.
$480.00

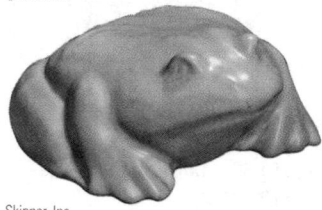

Skinner, Inc.

Van Briggle, Vase, Lavender Glaze, Spider, Diagonal Banding, Marked, 1902, 5 In.
$1,823.00

Skinner, Inc.

TIP

Use denture cleaning tablets to remove a stain from a ceramic teapot. Follow the directions for use with false teeth.

Decanter, Green Cut To Vaseline, Strawberry Diamond & Fan, Pyramid Shape, 16 In.	425.00
Figurine, Eagle, Wings Outstretched, Square Wood Base, Signed, c.1965, 9 ½ In.	180.00
Goblet, Clear, Footed, 6 In., 6 Piece	174.00
Goblet, Crosscut & Strawberry Diamond, Star & Fan, Green Cut To Clear, 10 In.	70.00
Goblet, Water, State Plain, Signed VSL, 6 ¼ In., 8 Piece	480.00
Lantern, Hall, Engraved & Etched, Brass Founts, Smoke Shade, 1880s, 23 x 11 In.	369.00
Trinket Box, Glass, Lid, Classical Figures, Conforming Base, Signed, France, 6 ½ In.	125.00
Vase, Blown, Clear To Green, Shaped Base, Signed, 8 x 4 In.	98.00
Vase, Clear, Frosted Gilt Classical Figures Band, Square Base, 15 In.	268.00
Vase, Green Cut To Clear, Signed, 15 x 8 In.	240.00
Vase, Green, Lavender, Green Leaves, White Flowers, Fold-In Rim, Round Foot, c.1900, 10 x 4 In..	5313.00
Vase, Pompeii Blue Cut To Rose Cut To Clear, Flared, Pedestal Base, 10 In.	1100.00
Vase, Red Cut To Clear, 21 ½ In.	375.00
Vase, Royal Figure, Seated, Cobalt Blue Over White, Cylindrical, Footed, 8 In.	1152.00

VALLERYSTHAL GLASSWORKS was founded in 1836 in Lorraine, France. In 1854, the firm became Klenglin et Cie. It made table and decorative glass, opaline, cameo, and art glass. A line of covered, pressed glass animal dishes was made in the nineteenth century. The firm is still working.

Vase, Berries, Insects, Acid Etched, Enameled, Gilt Trim, Pinch Waist, 1880s, 13 ½ In.	1125.00
Vase, Daffodils, Acid Etched, Enamel, Cameo, Signed, 1880s, 10 x 3 ¼ In. ....*Illus*	813.00

VAN BRIGGLE POTTERY was started by Artus Van Briggle in Colorado Springs, Colorado, after 1901. Van Briggle had been a decorator at Rookwood Pottery of Cincinnati, Ohio. He died in 1904 and his wife took over managing the pottery. One of the employees, Kenneth Stevenson, took over the company in 1969. He died in 1990 and his wife and son ran the pottery. She died in 2010 and her children are trying to sell the company. The wares usually had modeled relief decorations and a soft, dull glaze.

Bookends, Owl, Cranberry Glaze, 5 In., Pair	384.00
Bookends, Peacock, Brown, Marked, 5 In.	92.00
Bowl, Arrowroot Design, Mulberry Matte Glaze, Squat Smokestack, 4 ⅞ x 9 ½ In.	316.00
Bowl, Blue, Green, Side Mermaid, Shell Flower Frog, Signed, c.1920, 8 ¾ x 14 ¾ In.	649.00
Bowl, Blue, Petal Shape, 6 In.	35.00
Bowl, Dragonfly, Frog, Blue Green Glaze, c.1910, 3 x 9 In.	200.00
Bowl, Embossed Flowers, Blue Glaze, Incised, c.1902, 6 ½ In.	240.00
Bowl, Flower, Frog, Honey Gold Glaze, Green Trim, Marked, 1900, 7 ¾ In.	175.00
Bowl, Mermaid, Nude Reclining, Nautilus Flower Frog, Turquoise Glaze, 1920s, 8 x 14 In.	500.00
Bowl, Textured Matte Green Glaze, Smokestack, Round Foot, c.1905, 5 x 10 ½ In.	518.00
Centerpiece, Lady Of Lake, Gazing In Pool, Turtle Flower Form, Turquoise, Cobalt, 11 In.	313.00
Figurine, Frog, Turquoise Glaze, Marked, 9 In. ....*Illus*	480.00
Figurine, Woman, Wishing At Well, Green Matte Glaze, 6 In.	85.00
Incense Burner, Smiling Gnome, Seated, Tray, c.1920, 4 ¼ x 4 In.	200.00
Jardiniere, Indigo Over Light Blue, Incised Rim, 2 Angular Handles, 1910, 6 x 16 In.	625.00
Mug, Green, Handle, Marked 1906, 4 ½ In.	173.00
Paperweight, Indian Face, Red Brown Glaze, Oval, c.1913, 4 x 2 ¼ In.	190.00
Vase, 2 Bears At Top, Blue Matte To Green Glaze, 1930s, 15 ½ In.	1770.00
Vase, Blue Glaze, Yellow, Poppies, Cylindrical, Swollen Shoulder, c.1907, 7 ¼ In.	1000.00
Vase, Bulbous, Maroon Matte Glaze, Incised Mark, c.1925, 12 In.	350.00
Vase, Coneflowers, Blue Matte Glaze, Green Bottom Design, Tapered, Shouldered, Marked, 12 In.	460.00
Vase, Cylindrical, Aqua, c.1970, 9 In.	125.00
Vase, Daffodil, Green Matte Glaze, Cream, Twist Design, Garlic Mouth, 1902, 10 ¾ x 4 In.	1375.00
Vase, Dandelion, Swirling Mulberry Glaze, Bulbous, Tapered, Marked, 1915, 10 ⅜ x 12 In.	1610.00
Vase, Dark Purple Glaze, Bell Shape, Narrow Mouth, 1903, 3 ¼ x 2 ½ In.	1250.00
Vase, Despondency, Pink Shaded To Blue Glaze, Baluster, c.1918, 10 In.	1500.00
Vase, Embossed Flower, Green, Shaped Rim, 8 ¼ In.	81.00
Vase, Embossed Stylized Tulips, Cylindrical, Tapered, Spread Foot, 1920s, 16 In.	259.00
Vase, Flower Design, Green Matte Glaze, Rounded Bottom, Narrow Neck, Flared Rim, c.1915, 12 ⅛ In.	1035.00
Vase, Flowers, Stylized, Green Matte Glaze, Ribbed, Melon Shape, 1907, 6 x 5 ½ In.	1250.00
Vase, Flowers, Stylized, Green, Blue, 6 In.	127.00
Vase, Indian Head, Mountain Craig Brown, Swollen Top, Spread Foot, 11 x 4 In.	469.00
Vase, Iris, Carved, Maroon, Blue Matte Glaze, Incised, 1920s, 7 x 14 In.	732.00
Vase, Iris, Maroon & Blue Matte Glaze, Incised Mark, 1920s, 14 In.	600.00
Vase, Irises, Mountain Craig Brown, Tapered, Low Handles, c.1930, 11 In.	344.00
Vase, Lady Of The Lily, Blue Green Glaze, Reclining Nude Woman, Flared Rim, 1920s, 11 x 9 ¾ In.	1500.00
Vase, Lavender Glaze, Spider, Diagonal Banding, Marked, 1902, 5 In. ....*Illus*	1823.00

Vase, Leaves & Flowers, Mulberry Glaze, Rounded Square Shape, Waisted Neck, Handles, 10 In. ...	431.00
Vase, Leaves Stylized, Stems, Purple Rose Matte, Incised, 1905, 13 In.	1020.00
Vase, Lid, Soft Green, Brown Glaze, Squat, Impressed, 1915, 5 x 3 ½ In.	225.00
Vase, Lily, Blue Green Glaze, Nude Woman, Reclining, Flower Shape Rim, 1920s, 11 x 9 ¾ In...	1500.00
Vase, Lorelei, Aubergine & Green Glaze, 10 ¾ In.	277.00
Vase, Matte Maroon Glaze, Bulbous, Incised, c.1925, 7 ½ x 12 In.	427.00
Vase, Mauve, Embossed Flower, Cylinder, 5 ¾ In.	328.00
Vase, Molded Flowers, Wavy Stems, Mulberry Matte Glaze, Tapered, Round Bottom, 1914, 12 In. ..	863.00
Vase, Morning Glories, Pink Glaze, Bronze Handles, Yosakichi Asano, 1903, 11 In. ....*Illus*	40000.00
Vase, Morning Glory, Red Glaze, Green Overspray, Squat, Flat Rim, Marked, 1905, 6 ¾ In.......	1725.00
Vase, Peacock Feather, Mottled Blue, Cylindrical, Swollen Rim, Marked, 1903, 12 ⅞ In.	3680.00
Vase, Poppy, Carved, Blue Matte Glaze, 1903, 6 x 9 ½ In.	5313.00
Vase, Purple Matte Glaze, Squat, 4 ¼ x 3 In.	425.00
Vase, Round, Tapered, Brown, 1906, 4 x 5 ½ In.	300.00
Vase, Round, Tapered, Yellow, 1906, 4 x 5 ½ In.	375.00
Vase, Spider, Indian Symbols, Blue Glaze, Bulbous, Stand-Up Rim, 4 ¾ x 4 In.	1125.00
Vase, Stylized Flowers, Purple & Green Matte Glaze, Signed AA 1903, 6 ½ x 4 In. ....*Illus*	2125.00
Vase, Swirl, Cranberry, To Clear, Free-Form, 9 ¾ In.	230.00
Vase, Woman, Grasping Rim, Flowing Gown & Hair, Squat, Long Neck, Wavy Rim, Blue Glaze, 11 In.	403.00

VASA MURRHINA is the name of a glassware made by the Vasa Murrhina Art Glass Company of Sandwich, Massachusetts, about 1884. The glassware was transparent and was embedded with small pieces of colored glass and metallic flakes. The mica flakes were coated with silver, gold, copper, or nickel. Some of the pieces were cased. The same type of glass was made in England. Collectors often confuse Vasa Murrhina glass with aventurine, spatter, or spangle glass. There is uncertainty about what actually was made by the Vasa Murrhina factory. Related pieces may be listed under Spangle Glass.

Vase, Gold Mica Flecks Over Tortoiseshell, Amber & Coral Shards, 10 In. ....*Illus*	81.00

VASELINE GLASS is a greenish-yellow glassware resembling petroleum jelly. Pressed glass of the 1870s was often made of vaseline-colored glass. Some vaseline glass is still being made in old and new styles. Additional pieces of vaseline glass may also be listed under Pressed Glass in this book.

Bowl, Blown, Opalescent, Fluted Edge, 1 ⅝ x 8 ⅝ In.	35.00
Box, Melon Shape, Rayed Base, Stem Finial, c.1890, 4 x 5 ¼ In.	92.00
Spooner, Scalloped Edge, Bird Base, 1930s, 4 x 6 In. ....*Illus*	68.00
Vase, Pressed Stemmed Flowers, Egerman, 5 In.	58.00
Vase, Urn Shape, Tapered, Brick Red, Gray, Stylized Flowers, Stems, 1920s, 14 x 8 ½ In.	750.00

VENETIAN GLASS, *see Glass-Venetian category.*

VENINI GLASS, *see Glass-Venetian category.*

VERLYS glass was made in Rouen, France, by the Societe Holophane Français, a company that started in 1920. It was made in Newark, Ohio, from 1935 to 1951. The art glass is either blown or molded. The American glass is signed with a diamond-point-scratched name, but the French pieces are marked with a molded signature. The designs resemble those used by Lalique.

Verlys

Charger, 3 Flying Birds, Fish, Frosted, Marked, 13 ¾ In.	72.00
Vase, Etched Mother Holding Infant, Oval, Signed, 8 x 4 x 7 In.	60.00
Vase, Mandarin, Molded, Frosted Relief, Flower Vase, Key Fret At Base, Engraved, 9 ¼ x 5 In...	92.00

VERNON KILNS was the name used by Vernon Potteries, Ltd. The company, which started in 1931 in Vernon, California, made dinnerware and figurines until it went out of business in 1958. The molds were bought by Metlox, which continued to make some patterns. Collectors search for the brightly colored dinnerware and the pieces designed by Rockwell Kent, Walt Disney, and Don Blanding. For more prices, go to kovels.com.

Anytime, Creamer, 12 Oz., 4 ¼ In.	10.00
Anytime, Plate, 7 ⅝ In.	8.00
Arcadia, Chop Plate, 12 ¼ In.	18.00
Arcadia, Plate, 6 ½ In.	4.00
Arcadia, Platter, Oval, 13 ⅞ In.	16.00
Azure, Bowl, Cereal, 6 In.	8.00
Barkwood, Bowl, Vegetable, Divided, 11 ⅝ In.	18.00

Van Briggle, Vase, Morning Glories, Pink Glaze, Bronze Handles, Yosakichi Asano, 1903, 11 In.
$40,000.00

Rago Arts & Auction Center

Van Briggle, Vase, Stylized Flowers, Purple & Green Matte Glaze, Signed AA 1903, 6 ½ x 4 In.
$2,125.00

Rago Arts & Auction Center

Vasa Murrhina, Vase, Gold Mica Flecks Over Tortoiseshell, Amber & Coral Shards, 10 In.
$81.00

Humler & Nolan

U
V

Vaseline Glass, Spooner, Scalloped Edge, Bird Base, 1930s, 4 x 6 In.
$68.00

Ruby Lane, Inc.

Volkstedt, Figurine, Minerva, Standing, Marked, c.1910, 16 x 6 In.
$450.00

DuMouchelles Art Gallery

Watch, Clock, Thomas Tompion, Champleve Dial, Internal Bell, Pierced Gilt Case, London, c.1700, 2 In.
$14,760.00

Skinner, Inc.

U
V

Barkwood, Chop Plate, 13 ½ In.	30.00
Barkwood, Cup & Saucer	9.00
Butterscotch, Cup & Saucer	8.00
Cape Cod, Bowl, Fruit, 6 ¼ In.	9.00
Cape Cod, Bowl, Vegetable, 10 In.	16.00
Cape Cod, Plate, Dinner, 10 ½ In.	14.00
Chintz, Cup & Saucer	16.00
Chintz, Plate, Dinner, 10 ½ In.	22.00
Chintz, Soup, Dish, 8 In.	60.00
Figurine, Centaur, Fantasia, Ceramic, Marked Disney, 1940, 10 In.	390.00
Gigi, Mug, 3 ¾ In.	40.00
Gigi, Plate, Dinner, 10 ½ In.	42.00
Gigi, Platter, Oval, 13 ½ In.	34.00
Gigi, Salt & Pepper	16.00
Heyday, Bowl, Vegetable, Divided, 11 ⅝ In.	30.00
Heyday, Butter, Cover, ¼ Lb.	26.00
Heyday, Pitcher, 16 Oz., 6 ⅛ In.	22.00
Heyday, Plate, Dinner, 10 ¼ In.	8.00
Linda, Cup & Saucer	8.00
Linda, Salt & Pepper, Jug Shape, 3 In.	17.00
Mesa, Creamer, 10 Oz., 3 ⅜ In.	28.00
Mesa, Platter, Oval, 13 In.	46.00
Pepper Tree, Bowl, Vegetable, Oval, 10 ⅞ In.	20.00
Pepper Tree, Plate, Dinner, 10 ⅝ In.	11.00
Pepper Tree, Sugar, Lid, 2 ½ In.	15.00
Sandflower, Coffeepot, Lid, 6 Cup, 7 In.	56.00
Sandflower, Cup & Saucer, 2 ⅜ In.	9.00
Sandflower, Gravy Boat	43.00
Sandflower, Salt & Pepper	21.00
Sherwood, Bowl, Fruit, 5 ¾ In.	7.00
Sherwood, Pitcher, 24 Oz., 6 In.	40.00
Sherwood, Pitcher, 56 Oz., 9 ¾ In.	33.00
Tulips, Gravy Boat, Underplate	21.00
Tulips, Plate, Dinner, 10 ⅜ In.	15.00

VERRE DE SOIE glass was first made by Frederick Carder at the Steuben Glass Works from about 1905 to 1930. It is an iridescent glass of soft white or very, very pale green. The name means "glass of silk," and it does resemble silk. Other factories have made verre de soie, and some of the English examples were made of different colors. Verre de soie is an art glass and is not related to the iridescent, pressed, white carnival glass mistakenly called by its name. Related pieces may be found in the Steuben category.

Bowl, Low Base, Flared Lip, Opalescent, Steuben, 6 In.	92.00
Bowl, Ribbed Body, Rose Bowl Shape, Scalloped Rim, Steuben, 7 In.	115.00
Bowl, Shallow, Round, Inverted Rim, Paper Label, Steuben, 9 ½ In.	86.00
Perfume Bottle, Saucer Foot, Tapered, Teardrop Stopper, Steuben, 7 ½ In.	104.00
Tumble-Up, Engraved Flower Garland, Signed, F. Carder, Steuben, 6 ½ In.	350.00
Vase, Bulbous, Tapered, Iridescent, Steuben, 12 In.	207.00
Vase, Green Leaves & Vines, Austria, 14 ¾ In.	239.00
Vase, Iridescent, Green Threading, Flared Rim, Steuben, 6 ¼ In.	115.00

VIENNA, *see Beehive category.*

VIENNA ART plates are round metal serving trays produced at the turn of the century. The designs, copied from Royal Vienna porcelain plates, usually featured a portrait of a woman encircled by a wide, ornate border. Many were used as advertising or promotional items and were produced in Coshocton, Ohio, by J. F. Meeks Tuscarora Advertising Co. and H.D. Beach's Standard Advertising Co.

Plate, Arabian, Camels, Pyramids, Royal Saxony, c.1910, 10 ¼ In.	150.00
Plate, Gypsy, Long Hair, Egyptian Border, Royal Saxony, 10 ⅛ In.	95.00
Plate, Puppies, In Basket, Flower Border, Kaufman & Strauss, 9 ¾ In.	125.00
Plate, Sappho, Pink Gown, Holding Lyre, 8 ⅞ In.	65.00
Plate, Under The Sea, Fish, Blue, Green, Orange, Meek Co., c.1908, 9 ¾ In.	195.00
Plate, Woman, Holding Vase Of Flowers, H.D. Beach, c.1907, 10 In.	135.00
Plate, Woman, Seated, Tree, Cupid, Filigree Border, 10 In.	60.00

VILLEROY & BOCH POTTERY of Mettlach was founded in 1836. The firm made many types of wares, including the famous Mettlach steins. Collectors can be confused because although Villeroy & Boch made most of its pieces in the city of Mettlach, Germany, the company also had factories in other locations. The dating code impressed on the bottom of most pieces makes it possible to determine the age of the piece. Additional items, including steins and earthenware pieces marked with the famous castle mark or the word *Mettlach*, may be found in the Mettlach category.

Mug, Young Girl, Kitten Under Bush, 2 ½ In.	24.00
Pitcher, Salmon, Over Glazed Cherries & Leaves, 6 In.	66.00
Plate, Asparagus Stalks, Brown, Green, Relief, c.1900, 9 In.	125.00
Platter, 3 Sections, Galleon, Men On Decks, Seagulls, Border, 11 In.	95.00
Salt & Pepper, Tulips	16.00
Stein, Minstrel, Playing Mandolin, Pewter Lid & Finial, c.1845, Liter	525.00
Stein, Turkish Man, Smoking Pipe, Pewter Rim, Signed R. Buch, c.1887, 8 In.	240.00
Tea Set, Teapot, Creamer, Sugar, Flapper, Parasol, Multicolor, c.1925, 5 In., 3 Piece	60.00
Tile, Adam & Eve, Garden Of Eden, Frame, 4 ⅞ x 4 ⅞ In.	20.00

VOLKMAR POTTERY was made by Charles Volkmar of New York from 1879 to about 1911. He was associated with several firms, including the Volkmar Ceramic Company, Volkmar and Cory, and Charles Volkmar and Son. He was hired by Durant Kilns of Bedford Village, New York, in 1910 to oversee production. Volkmar bought the business and after 1930 only the Volkmar name was used as a mark. Volkmar had been a painter, and his designs often look like oil paintings drawn on pottery.

Tile, Landscape, Shepherd, Sheep, Fumed Oak Frame, E.A. Richardson, 1890, 7 x 15 In.	1375.00

VOLKSTEDT was a soft-paste porcelain factory started in 1760 by Georg Heinrich Macheleid at Volkstedt, Thuringia. Volkstedt-Rudolstadt was a porcelain factory started at Volkstedt-Rudolstadt by Beyer and Bock in 1890. Most pieces seen in shops today are from the later factory.

Figurine, Courting Couple, Goat, 5 ½ x 7 In.	118.00
Figurine, Dancer, Lace Dress, Hand Raised, 1962, 9 ½ In.	238.00
Figurine, Minerva, Standing, Marked, c.1910, 16 x 6 In. ....*Illus*	450.00
Figurine, Woman, Bonnet, Floral Dress, 5 ¾ x 6 In.	295.00
Vase, Boot Shape, Spur, Folded Cuff, c.1860, 11 x 7 In.	185.00

WADE pottery is made by the Wade Group of Potteries started in 1810 near Burslem, England. Several potteries merged to become George Wade & Son, Ltd., early in the twentieth century, and other potteries have been added through the years. The best-known Wade pieces are the small figurines called Whimsies. They were first were made in 1954. Special Whimsies were given away with Red Rose Tea beginning in 1967. The Disney figures are listed in this book in the Disneyana category.

Dish, Green, Center Spiral Design, Ribbed Rim, 10 ⅞ In.	40.00
Figurine, Angel Fish	10.00
Figurine, Blue Bird, White, Open Wings, 1 x 1 ¼ In.	12.00
Figurine, Brown Bear, Ball, Hat, On Base	6.00
Figurine, Butterfly, 1 ¾ In.	13.00
Figurine, Cairn Terrier, 1969, 2 ½ In.	40.00
Figurine, Colt, Eating Grass, 1950s, 1 ½ In.	130.00
Figurine, Colt, Tail In Air, 1 ¾ In.	130.00
Figurine, Gingerbread Man, 1 ½ In.	20.00
Figurine, Humpty Dumpty, 1 ½ In.	12.00
Figurine, Irish Setter, 2 ½ x 2 ½ In.	40.00
Figurine, Kathleen, 3 ½ In.	25.00
Figurine, Koala Bear, In Tree, Tan, 1 ⅜ In.	4.00
Figurine, Little Miss Muffet, 1 ½ In.	18.00
Figurine, Old Lady In Shoe, 1 ½ x 1 In.	8.00
Figurine, Old Nannie, c.1935, 9 In.	450.00
Figurine, Puppy, In Basket, Brown, 1970s, 2 ½ x 3 In.	49.00
Figurine, Queen Of Hearts, Hearts On Hat & Dress, 1 ¾ In.	10.00
Figurine, Raccoon, Brown, Tan, 1 ½ In.	9.00
Figurine, Service Station, 1 ½ x 1 ½ In.	25.00
Figurine, Ship, Serpent Shape, 7 ½ In.	40.00
Figurine, Squirrel, Brown, 1 ½ In.	20.00
Figurine, The Picture Palace, 2 ⅛ x 2 ½ In.	35.00
Figurine, Tiger, Sitting, Tan, 1 ¼ In.	4.00
Figurine, Tom Piper, 2 ¾ In.	25.00
Figurine, Tom Tucker, 3 In.	50.00

Watch, Elgin, Father Time, Open Face, Stem Wind, Nickel Movement, 21 Jewel, Size 18
$1,541.00

Skinner, Inc.

Watch, Elgin, Veritas, Double Sunk Dial, Gold Jewel Settings, 21 Jewel, Gold-Filled Case, Size 18
$711.00

Skinner, Inc.

Watch, Jno. Bayley, 22K, Pierced, Engraved, Porcelain, Repeater, Cleopatra & Anthony, c.1735, 1 ⅞ In.
$7,995.00

Skinner, Inc.

Watch, Silver, Open Face, Porcelain Dial, Painted Scene, Gilt Figure, Head Rotates, Swiss, c.1810, 2 ¼ In.
$8,610.00

Skinner, Inc.

W

637

WADE

Watch, Swiss, Silver, Triple Calendar, Stem-Wound, Gilt Brass, Enameled, 4 Dials, 1800s, 1 ¾ In.
$486.00

Skinner, Inc.

Weather Vane, Banner, Lyre, Cutout Design, Gilt, Copper, Zinc Arrow, Stand, c.1890, 23 x 59 In.
$10,073.00

Skinner, Inc.

Weather Vane, Butterfly, Copper Wire Antennae & Legs, Copper Pierced, J.W. Fiske, c.1890, 20 x 22 In.
$41,475.00

Skinner, Inc.

> **TIP**
> Replace a broken watch crystal immediately to avoid letting dust or moisture into the watch works.

Figurine, Turtle, 2 ⅞ In., Pair	20.00
Figurine, Viking Ship, Serpent Head, Green, Brown, 7 ½ x 3 In.	40.00
Group, 3 Musicians, Period Dress, Gilt Plinth, Germany, 11 x 13 In.	325.00
Mug, Yellow, Car, Duesenberg, 4 ⅝ In.	22.00
Pitcher, Ribbed, Diagonal Stripe, Orange, Yellow, 1940s, 5 ¼ In.	115.00
Salt & Pepper, Yellow, Green, 2 ⅜ In.	22.00
Tankard, Barrel, Chrome Hoops & Handle, 4 ⅞ In.	13.00
Teapot, Police Station, 7 ¼ In.	25.00
Trinket Box, Father Tortoise, Marked, Brown, Blue, 4 In.	18.00
Trinket Box, Tortoise Shape, 4 In.	18.00

WAHPETON POTTERY, *see Rosemeade category.*

WALL POCKETS were popular in the 1930s. They were made by many American and European factories. Glass, pottery, porcelain, majolica, chalkware, and metal wall pockets can be found in many fanciful shapes.

Bird Shape, Holding Urn, White, Flower Garlands, Porcelain, 8 In., Pair	119.00
Ceramic, Green, Carved Geometric Designs, Oakwood, 8 x 5 x 10 In.	500.00
Clear Glass, Art Deco, Ribbed, 6 ½ x 3 In.	69.00
Colonial Woman, Blue & Orange Dress, 7 ½ x 4 ½ In.	121.00
Faience, Basket Weave, Flowers, Multicolor, Gien, c.1890, 10 In.	65.00
Flower Medallions, Cobalt Blue Ground, Cloisonne, Japan, 19th Century, 6 ¼ In.	250.00
Genie, Yellow, Blue, 5 ¾ In.	63.00
Hat, Flowers, Bow, Blue, 5 ¼ x 4 ¾ In.	20.00
Nun, Watering Flowers, Brick Wall, Sanmyro, Japan, 4 ½ x 3 ¾ In.	35.00
Parrot, Multicolor, Chain, Acmeware, Japan, 1950s, 7 ¼ In.	36.00
Peacock, Open Feathers, Pink, USA, 6 ½ x 5 ½ In.	25.00
Pierced, Wood, Gilt Detail, Dragons, Fish, Oriental Designs, Chinese, 18 In., Pair	177.00
Sunbonnet Girl, Ivory, 7 ½ In.	22.00
Woman's Flapper Head, Wavy Blond, Japan, 1930s, 3 In.	85.00

WALLACE NUTTING *photographs are listed under Print, Nutting. His reproduction furniture is listed under Furniture.*

WALRATH was a potter who worked in New York City; Rochester, New York; and at the Newcomb Pottery in New Orleans, Louisiana. Frederick Walrath died in 1920. Pieces listed here are from his Rochester period.

Walrath
Pottery

Chocolate Pot, Stylized Trees, Green, Peach, Brown Glaze, 1910s, 8 ½ x 7 In.	5000.00
Mug, Green Matte Glaze, Stylized Art Deco Decoration, 5 ¼ x 5 ¾ In.	1375.00
Mug, Green, Beige Matte Glaze, Flowers, Initials VON, Arts & Crafts, c.1910, 5 ⅛ In.	1955.00
Vase, Carved Flower, Tan, Double Gourd Shape, F. Walrath, Alfred, 1902, 9 x 4 In.	1250.00
Vase, Fan Shape, Majolica Crane, Insect, Ledge, 14 x 10 In.	268.00
Vase, Stylized Flowers, Leaves, Blue, Red Matte Glaze, 3 Handles, Marked, 1919, 4 x 5 ½ In.	2125.00

WALT DISNEY, *see Disneyana category.*

WALTER, *see A. Walter category.*

WARWICK china was made in Wheeling, West Virginia, in a pottery working from 1887 to 1951. Many pieces were made with hand painted or decal decorations. The most familiar Warwick has a shaded brown background. The name *Warwick* is part of the mark and sometimes the mysterious word *IOGA* is also included.

Casserole, Lid, Purple Flowers, Leaves, Gold Trim, c.1887, 10 ½ x 7 In.	85.00
Cheese Keeper, Lid, Tan Ground, Pink Flowers, Top Handle, c.1900, 6 x 10 In.	50.00
Pitcher, Jovial Monk, Brown, Gilt Rim, Marked, 8 In.	127.00
Vase, Berry Design, Loop Handles, Marked, 7 x 5 x 7 In.	60.00

WATCH pockets held the pocket watch that was important in Victorian times because it was not until World War I that the wristwatch was used. All types of watches are collected: silver, gold, or plated. Watches are listed here by company name or by style. Wristwatches are a separate category.

Breitling, Hunting Case, 18K Gold, Swiss, Pocket, 1 ½ In.	1062.00
Clock, Thomas Tompion, Champleve Dial, Internal Bell, Pierced Gilt Case, London, c.1700, 2 In. . *Illus*	14760.00
Coach, Enamel Dial, Blued Steel Bands, Bailey, Banks & Biddle Co., c.1900, 3 ⅛ In., Pocket	230.00

Dudley, 14K White Gold, Open Face, Scrolling Design, Silvered Dial, Masonic Symbol, 1900s, 1 ⅞ In.	5875.00
Dueber-Hampden, Open Face, 14K Yellow Gold, Silvertone Dial, Geometric Font Numerals ..	472.00
E. Howard & Co., 14K Yellow Gold, 17 Jewel, White Face, Seconds Dial, 1 ¾ In.	649.00
Elgin, 14K Yellow Gold, Open Face, Engraved Roman Numeral, Scrolls, 15 Jewel, c.1920	661.00
Elgin, Duber Gold Filled Case, 17 Jewel, Second Hand, 1917, 1 ⁹⁄₁₆ In.	177.00
Elgin, Father Time, Open Face, Stem Wind, Nickel Movement, 21 Jewel, Size 18 ....*Illus*	1541.00
Elgin, Hunting Case, 14K Gold, 2 ¾ In., Pocket	1645.00
Elgin, Hunting Case, Gold, Engraved Flowers, Locomotive Scenes, c.1889	209.00
Elgin, Hunting Case, No. 7, 10K Gold Plate, 1895, 1 ¾ In.	236.00
Elgin, Open Face, Military, 24-Hour Dial, 1 ¾ In., Pocket	295.00
Elgin, Veritas, Double Sunk Dial, Gold Jewel Settings, 21 Jewel, Gold-Filled Case, Size 18 ... *Illus*	711.00
Elgin, White Enamel Face, Signed, 14K Gold, Pocket, 2 In.	1000.00
Everbrite Watch Co., Dizzy Dean, Baseball Player, Pitching, 1935, 2 In. Diam., Pocket	575.00
Gruen, Open Face, Octagon Shape, 17 Jewel, Pocket, 1 ¾ In.	148.00
H.L. Matile, Engraved Patriotic Profiles, Symbols, 18K Gold, Swiss, 2 ⅓ In., Pocket	2844.00
Hamilton, Model 912, 17 Jewel, 14K Gold, 10 Side Case, 1 ⁹⁄₁₆ In.	148.00
Hamilton, Open Face, Railway Special, 10K Gold, 21 Jewel, 1 ¾ In.	325.00
Hamilton, Railway Special, Open Face, Gold Filled, Double Sunk Porcelain Dial, c.1954	403.00
Hermes, Kelly, Padlock Case & Mount, Dot Numerals, 17 Jewel, Gold, Leather, Woman's	593.00
Hunting Case, Charles Jacot, 18K Gold, Engraved, White Enamel Dial, Roman Numerals	1140.00
Hunting Case, Patek Philippe, 18K Gold, White Porcelain Dial, Roman Numerals, Box	2640.00
Illinois, Bunn Special 163, 23 Jewel, 60-Hour, Gold Case, Blued Steel Spade Hands, c.1931	1438.00
Illinois, Exhibition Back, Open Face, White Metal, Double Sunk Porcelain Dial, J. Miller, c.1912 ..	196.00
Illinois, Garfield, Open Face, 14K Gold, c.1923, 1 ⁹⁄₁₆ In.	118.00
Jno. Bayley, 22K, Pierced, Engraved, Porcelain, Repeater, Cleopatra & Anthony, c.1735, 1 ⅞ In. ..*Illus*	7995.00
John Mayer, Chain Fusee Verge Escapement, Silver, Brass, Key Wind, Cover, Signed, c.1780, 2 In..	791.00
Lewis Jewelry Co., Hunter's Case, 14K Yellow Gold, Scrolling, Woman's	345.00
Movado, Art Deco, Calendar, Self-Winding, Leather Case, Man's, 3 x 1 ½ In., Pocket	1180.00
Movado, Brushed Silver Case, Square, Pearlized Dial, Art Deco, Swiss, c.1935, 2 ¾ x 1 ¼ In..	575.00
Movado, Chronometer, Sterling Case, Square, Enamel Dial, Arabic Chapter Ring, Marked, 3 x 1 ¼ In..	345.00
Open Face, 18K, Applied Pink Gold Roman Numerals, Flowers, England, 1800s	1150.00
Patek Philippe, Open Face, 18 Jewel, 18K Gold, Engraved, Pocket	2938.00
Pendant, 18K Yellow Gold, Open Face, Tiffany & Co., Switzerland, c.1900, 1 ⁵⁄₁₆ In.	944.00
Piaget, Open Face, 18K White Gold, Florentine Finish, Roman Numerals, 18 Jewel, 1 ½ In.	1200.00
RCA Victor, His Master's Voice, Nipper, Open Face, Pocket	196.00
Silver, Open Face, Porcelain Dial, Painted Scene, Gilt Figure, Head Rotates, Swiss, c.1810, 2 ¼ In. *Illus*	8610.00
South Bend, Open Face, Gold Filled, Cobalt Blue Dial, 17 Jewel, Model 211	190.00
Swiss, Repeater, Ivory Enamel Dial, Masonic Symbol, 1800s, 2 In.	512.00
Swiss, Silver, Triple Calendar, Stem-Wound, Gilt Brass, Enameled, 4 Dials, 1800s, 1 ¾ In. ... *Illus*	486.00
Theodore Starr, Hunter's Case, 18K Gold, Pocket	2596.00
Tiffany & Co., 18K Gold, Open Face, Round Case, White Dial, 1 ¾ In., Pocket	1380.00
Tiffany, Open Face, Silvertone Dial, Roman Numerals, 19 Jewel, Art Deco, 1 ½ In.	1080.00
Triple Calendar, 18K Gold, Moon Face, Roman Numerals, Swiss, 19th Century, 2 In.	7800.00
Vacheron & Constantin, Open Face, 18K Gold, 20 Jewel, Corp Of Engineers, c.1920, 2 In., Pocket	4956.00
Waltham, Crest Street, Railroad Grade, 21 Jewel, 1 ¾ In.	207.00
Waltham, Deck, Arabic Numbers, Stem Wind, 8 x 7 In.	790.00
Waltham, Hunting Case, 14K Gold, c.1895, 0 Size, Pocket	369.00
Waltham, Hunting Case, Chased & Engraved, Enamel Dial, Roman Numerals, 1900s, 2 ⅛ In..	1446.00
Waltham, Hunting Case, Coin Silver, Key Wind, PJ Bartlett, 1 ¾ In., Pocket	266.00
Waltham, Hunting Case, Engraved, White Porcelain Dial, 14K Yellow Gold	863.00
Waltham, Hunting Case, Gold, 1 ⁹⁄₁₆ In., Pocket	1300.00
Waltham, Vanguard, Open Face, 23 Jewel, Wind Indicator, c.1908, 1 ¾ In.	1121.00

WATCH FOBS were worn on watch chains. They were popular during Victorian times and after. Many styles, especially advertising designs, are still made today.

All Tourney, Basketball, 2 Players, 1 ¼ In.	80.00
Allis-Chalmers Tractor, Brass, 1 ½ x 2 In.	35.00
American Flag, Stars, Shield Shape, Nickel, 1 ¼ x 1 ½ In.	39.00
Apollo, Killing Serpent, Celluloid, Silver Metal, 1 ½ In.	245.00
Ball, Compass, 14K Yellow Gold, ½ In.	450.00
Battle Ax Shoes, Sterling Silver, Shield Shape, 1 ¾ x 1 ½ In.	65.00
Carnelian, Onyx, Leaves, ¾ In.	50.00
Cruise Ship, Brass, 1930s, 1 ¼ x 1 ¼ In.	30.00
Enlisted Men's Olympics, Sterling Silver, Man Receiving Award, 1919	225.00
Fat Mail, Another Pair If They Don't Wear, Union Made, Locomotive, 1 ¾ In.	75.00
Globe Feed, Makes 'Em Lay, Hen, Metal, Celluloid, 1 x 1 In.	165.00

Weather Vane, Dog, Setter, Flattened Full Body, Gilt Copper, Rod With Stand, 16 ⅜ x 33 ½ In.
$9,600.00

Skinner, Inc.

Weather Vane, Female, Nude, Wings On Feet, Animal Ears, Caduceus, Full Body, Copper, Arrow, c.1890, 90 In.
$8,400.00

Skinner, Inc.

Weather Vane, Girl, Holding Umbrella, Dog, Sheet Iron, Black Paint, Wood Base, c.1925, 37 ½ x 32 In.
$1,062.00

Brunk Auctions

W

Weather Vane, Horse, Jockey, Steeplechase, Copper, Gilt, Zinc, c.1890, 24 x 31 ½ In.
$13,225.00

James D. Julia Auctioneers

Weather Vane, Horse, Running, Flat Body, Applied Tail, Copper, Molded, Iron, Zinc Head, c.1890, 19 x 27 In.
$3,318.00

Skinner, Inc.

Weather Vane, Locomotive, Full Round, Sheet Copper, Painted, Copper Rod, c.1900, 26 x 24 ½ In.
$900.00

Skinner, Inc.

Weather Vane, Pig, Full Body, Flattened, Copper, Cast Zinc Head, Metal Stand, c.1890, 21 x 36 In.
$36,000.00

Skinner, Inc.

Grand Lodge Of England, Sterling, Enamel, Dinosaur, 1923, 1 ¼ x 1 ½ In.	165.00
Horse, Leather, Horse Hair Chain, c.1900, 1 ½ x 1 ½ In.	120.00
John Deere Emblem, Leaping Deer, Shell Shape, Mother-Of-Pearl, Leather, c.1935, 1 ½ In.	350.00
Locket, Carnelian, Agate, Gold Filled	225.00
Mecca, Sterling Silver, Arabic Text, 1 x 1 In.	125.00
National Sportsman, Raised Moose, Brass, 1 ½ In.	25.00
Pistol, Gold Tone, Rotating Cylinder, Pearl Handle, c.1900, ¾ In.	65.00
Red Diamond Union Made Overalls, Celluloid, Fiberboard Backing, Top Strap, c.1910, 2 In.	58.00
Scrolled Leaves, 18K Yellow Gold, Art Nouveau, Maison G. Deshazeille, 5 ¼ In.	2133.00
Silvertone, 2 Men Wrestling, Leather Strap, 1 ¾ In.	30.00
Sphere, 18K Yellow Gold, Garnets, c.1850, 4 ½ In.	475.00

WATERFORD type glass resembles the famous glass made from 1783 to 1851 in the Waterford Glass Works in Ireland. It is a clear glass that was often decorated by cutting. Modern glass is being made again in Waterford, Ireland, and is marketed under the name Waterford. Waterford merged with Wedgwood in 1986 to form the Waterford Wedgwood Group. Most Waterford Wedgwood assets were bought by KPS Capital Partners of New York in 2009 and became part of WWRD Holdings.

Biscuit Jar, Lid, 6 ¾ In.	28.00
Bowl, Emily, Scalloped, 7 ¾ x 5 x 2 ¼ In.	170.00
Champagne, Eileen, 4 ½ In., 8 Piece	58.00
Compote, Clear, Cut, Footed, 8 ¼ x 10 ½ In.	180.00
Compote, Glandore, 3 ¾ x 6 ¼ In.	40.00
Compote, Hobnail, Ruffled Rim, Paper Label, 5 x 5 ½ In.	120.00
Compote, Shell Border, Footed, Round, 5 ¼ In.	28.00
Decanter, Kylemore, 10 ¼ In.	238.00
Decanter, Lismore, Roly Poly Shape, 10 ½ In.	380.00
Decanter, Ship, Alana, 10 In.	150.00
Decanter, Stopper, Large Handle, Footed, 12 In.	51.00
Figurine, Fish, Base, 8 ½ In.	115.00
Fruit Stand, Oval, Footed, 9 x 13 In.	57.00
Goblet Set, Colleen, 6 Wine, 16 Water, 4 ¾ & 5 ⅛ In.	720.00
Honey Jar, Dome Lid, Cut, Cylindrical, Faceted Finial, 5 x 3 ½ In.	58.00
Ice Bucket, Millennium, Molded, Footed, 10 ½ x 9 ½ In.	330.00
Lamp, Clear, Table, Cone Shade, Signed, 14 x 30 In., Pair	357.00
Lamp, Crystal, Urn Shape, 20th Century, 34 ½ In., Pair	207.00
Lamp, Electric, Hurricane Shade & Base, 22 ¼ x 6 ¾ In.	345.00
Lamp, Hurricane, Pompeii Collection, Brass & Marble Base, 16 In.	146.00
Lamp, Hurricane, Squat, Bulbous Shade, Flaring Rim, Candlestick Base, 1900s, 14 In., Pair	173.00
Liqueur, Tramore, Footed, 4 In., 8 Piece	150.00
Relish Tray, 3 Sections, Scalloped, 9 ¼ In.	28.00
Salt & Pepper, 6 In.	41.00
Salt & Pepper, Tapered, Footed, 6 ¼ In.	17.00 to 28.00
Tumbler, Colleen, 3 ½ In., 12 Piece	327.00
Tumbler, Colleen, 4 ½ In., 12 Piece	417.00
Vase, Lismore, Tapered, Footed, 10 In.	120.00
Vase, Marquise, Cased, Amber, Teal, Blue, 15 ¾ In., 3 Piece	155.00
Wine, Colleen, Signed, 4 ¼ In., 10 Piece	230.00
Wine, Overture, Acid Etch Mark, 8 In., 22 Piece	1200.00
Wine, Tramore, Footed, 5 In., 8 Piece	150.00

WATT family members bought the Globe pottery of Crooksville, Ohio, in 1922. They made pottery mixing bowls and tableware of the type made by Globe. In 1935 they changed the production and made the pieces with the freehand decorations that are popular with collectors today. Apple, Starflower, Rooster, Tulip, and Autumn Foliage are the best-known patterns. Pansy, also called Rio Rose, was the earliest pattern. Apple, the most popular pattern, can be dated from the leaves. Originally, the apples had three leaves; after 1958 two leaves were used. The plant closed in 1965. For more prices, go to kovels.com.

Apple, Bean Cup, 2 ⅜ In.	379.00
Apple, Bowl, No. 96, 3-Leaf, 8 ½ In.	50.00
Apple, Bowl, Spaghetti, c.1952, 13 ½ x 3 In.	99.00
Apple, Canister, No. 82, Thornton, Iowa, Hatchery, Wayne Feeds, 5 In.	68.00
Apple, Casserole, No. 18, 3-Leaf, 5 ¼ In.	59.00
Apple, Cookie Jar, No. 503, 3-Leaf	250.00
Apple, Creamer, No. 62, 3-Leaf	75.00

W

Apple, Mixing Bowl, 3-Leaf, 7 ½ In.	75.00
Apple, Mixing Bowl, No. 8, 2-Leaf	50.00
Apple, Mug, 3 ¾ In.	169.00
Apple, Mug, No. 121, 3-Leaf, 3 ¾ In.	42.00
Apple, Pitcher, No. 15, 3-Leaf	95.00
Apple, Pitcher, No. 16, 2-Leaf	95.00
Apple, Pitcher, No. 62, 3-Leaf	65.00
Apple, Pitcher, Water, No. 17	149.00
Autumn Foliage, Pitcher, No. 16, Leaves	50.00
Autumn Foliage, Sugar, No. 98	35.00
Cherry, Bowl, No. 39	75.00
Cherry, Bowl, No. 51	38.00
Cherry, Casserole, No. 18, 4 ¼ In.	38.00
Cookie Jar, Berries, Weave, Leaves, Embossed, Wood Grain	125.00
Pansy, Bowl, Spaghetti, 13 In.	65.00
Pansy, Casserole, Lid, Handle	40.00
Pansy, Casserole, Lid, No. 18	16.00
Pansy, Mixing Bowl, No. 7	12.00
Pansy, Mixing Bowl, No. 9	38.00
Pansy, Pitcher, No. 34, Yellow	90.00
Pansy, Platter, No. 49, 12 In.	35.00
Rooster, Pitcher, No. 16	50.00
Starflower, Bowl, Spaghetti, 11 ½ x 4 ¼ In.	90.00
Starflower, Bowl, Vegetable, No. 60, 6 ⅛ In.	38.00
Starflower, Bowl, Vegetable, No. 66, 5-Petal, 7 ¼ In.	38.00 to 50.00
Starflower, Mug, No. 61	170.00
Starflower, Mug, No. 61, 5-Petal	83.00
Starflower, Pitcher, No. 15, 4-Petal, 16 Oz., 5 ½ In.	65.00 to 139.00
Starflower, Pitcher, No. 16, 4-Petal, 32 Oz., 6 ½ In.	51.00
Tear Drop, Casserole, 2 ½ Qt.	65.00
Tulip, Casserole, Lid, No. 600, Ribbed	115.00
Tulip, Creamer, No. 62, 4 ⅜ In., 12 Oz.	69.00 to 209.00
Tulip, Pitcher, No. 16	18.00
Tulip, Pitcher, Water, No. 17, 5 Pt.	125.00

WAVE CREST glass is an opaque white glassware manufactured by the Pairpoint **WAVE CREST** Manufacturing Company of New Bedford, Massachusetts, and some French factories. **WARE** It was decorated by the C.F. Monroe Company of Meriden, Connecticut. The glass was painted in pastel colors and decorated with flowers. The name Wave Crest was used starting in 1892.

Biscuit Barrel, White, Floral Bouquets, Molded Vining, Silver Lid, Handle, c.1900, 12 x 5 ¼ In.	96.00
Bonbon, Pink, Blue Flowers, Bail Handle, Marked Nakara, C.F.M. Co., 5 ¾ In.	193.00
Box, Country Road, Trees, Round, Squat, Hinged Lid, Cameo, 3 x 8 In.	1610.00
Box, Daisies, Enameled, Round, Silk Liner, 4 Footed, 7 x 7 In.	518.00
Cardholder, Pink Flowers, White Ground, Metal Frame, Egg Crate, 5 ¾ x 4 In.	220.00
Cardholder, Playing Cards, Opal, Enameled Blossoms, Metal Collar, Marked, 2 ½ x 4 ¼ In.	173.00
Cigarette Holder, White, Blue Flowers, Ormolu Scrollwork, Footed, 3 Cylinders, 4 x 8 In.	196.00
Dresser Box, Baroque Shell Shape, Blue Ribbon, White Daisy Cluster, Oval, 6 ½ In.	316.00
Dresser Box, Collars & Cuffs, Egg Crate Shape, Flower Spray, 6 ½ In.	949.00
Dresser Box, Round, Opal, Molded, Enameled Blossoms, Metal Band Rim, 7 ½ In.	115.00
Dresser Box, White, Flower Top, Hand Painted, Pink Satin Liner, Square, Key, Signed, 9 In.	367.00
Dresser Box, White, Flowers, Raised Shell Design, Hinged, Round, 3 ½ In.	124.00
Glove Box, Blossoms, Rocaille, Claret Ground, Silk Interior, Gilt Mounts, c.1910, 5 ½ x 10 In.	688.00
Humidor, Cigar, Pink Flowers, Blue Ground, Round, Marked Kelva	480.00
Postcard Holder, Egg Crate Shape, Pink Enameled Flowers, Metal Frame, 5 ¾ x 4 x 3 In.	220.00
Shaker, Opal, Yellow Flowers, 2 ½ In., Pair	35.00
Sugar & Creamer, Cover, Helmschmied Swirl, Pansies, Meat, 3 ½ In.	115.00
Sugar Shaker, Tan, Free-Form Medallions, Helmschmied Swirl, 3 ¼ In.	115.00
Vase, Enameled Stem Daisy, White, Yellow, Narrow Baluster, Round Foot, Cylindrical Neck, 10 In.	144.00
Vase, Green & Opal, Red Clusters, Flowers, Ormolu Handles & Feet, Scroll, 8 In.	288.00

WEAPONS listed here include instruments of combat other than guns, knives, rifles, or swords and clothing worn in combat. Firearms are not listed in this book. Knives and Swords are listed in their own categories.

Battle Ax, Wood Haft, Iron Head, Semi Crescent Blade, c.1860, 23 In.	550.00
Blasting Machine, No. 50, Dynamite Plunger, Oak Dovetailed Case, E.I. du Pont, 1930s, 13 x 8 In.	472.00

Weather Vane, Ram, Full Body, Gilt Copper, Molded, Hammered, Stand, c.1900, 24 ⅜ x 28 In.
$7,703.00

Skinner, Inc.

Weather Vane, Rooster, Full Body, Embossed Comb & Tail, Copper, Molded, Mounted, On Rod, c.1900, 14 ⅝ In.
$5,925.00

Skinner, Inc.

Webb, Perfume Bottle, Panels, Flowers, White Over Red Cameo, Ball Stopper, Acid Stamp, 5 In.
$2,645.00

Early Auction Co.

Webb, Vase, Bird On Flowering Dogwood Branch, Gold, Silver, Yellow Ground, Opal Interior, 4 ¼ In.
$460.00

Early Auction Co.

W

Webb, Vase, Ivory, Moorish Design, Flowers, Scrolls, Cameo, Signed, 9 In. $2,875.00

Early Auction Co.

Webb, Vase, Wild Rose, Yellow Amber, 2 Butterflies On Reverse, Impressed, Cameo, c.1888, 7 ¾ In. $3,555.00

Skinner, Inc.

Webb Burmese, Charger, Taj Mahal, Yellow To Pink, Gilt Moorish Design Border, 12 In. $8,338.00

Early Auction Co.

Webb Burmese, Fairy Lamp, Ruffled Rim, Double Crystal Insert, 3-Part, Signed Clarkes Cricklite, 6 ¼ In. $546.00

Early Auction Co.

Buckle, Rhino Hide, Cone Shape, Beads, Reeded Bands, c.1850, 8 ¼ In.	425.00
Cartridge Box, Militia, Shoulder Strap, Leather, American Eagle, Brass, Leather, 1800s, 6 x 3 In.	403.00
Crossbow, Georgian, Wrought Iron Hinged Sight, Bow, Nut, Trigger, Walnut Tiller, 1700s, 27 In.	2160.00
Crossbow, Wood, Canon, Inlaid Wheel, Sickle, Decorative Escutcheon, 35 x 30 In.	265.00
Lance, Tilting, Wood, Fluted, Forged Iron Tip, 91 ½ In.	2900.00
Mace, Iron, 6 Scored Flanges, Hollow Shaft, Wrist Loop, 21 ¾ In.	8900.00
Shield, Hide, Bronze Sunflower Bosses, Leaves, Tendrils, Buds, North Indian, c.1850, 24 In. Diam.	2250.00
Shield, Horseman's, Iron, Domed, Rolled Edge, Scalloped Edge Bosses, Leaves, c.1850, 18 In.	395.00
Trident, Iron, Twisted Spike, Wood Haft, Chinese, c.1899, 96 ¼ In.	675.00
War Club, Wood Handle, Rawhide Cording, American Indian, 15 ¾ In.	269.00

WEATHER VANES were used in seventeenth-century Boston. The direction of the wind was an indication of coming weather, important to the seafaring and farming communities. By the mid-nineteenth century, commercial weather vanes were made of metal. Many were shaped like animals. Ethan Allen, Dexter, and St. Julian are famous horses that were depicted. Today's collectors often consider weather vanes to be examples of folk art, even though they may not have been handmade.

Airplane, Full Body, Zinc, Copper, Iron Wirework, Stand, c.1930, 18 ⅝ x 27 In.	1422.00
Airplane, Low Wing, Single Engine, Copper, 13 x 33 In.	215.00
Angel Gabriel, Blowing Horn, Wood, Paint, Black Stand, 51 x 13 ½ In.	3910.00
Angel, Profile, Holding Tray, Sheet Iron, 21 x 28 In.	374.00
Arrow, Crimped Tail, Copper, Iron, Black Paint, Metal Stand, c.1900, 21 x 48 In.	2015.00
Automobile, Full Body, Rotating Wheels, Spare, Copper, Gilt, Painted, Rod & Stand, 18 ⅛ x 24 ¼ In.	5036.00
Banner Scroll, Copper, Directionals, Stand, 26 x 57 In.	1770.00
Banner Style, Horizontal Tube, Cast Arrowhead, Iron, Painted Gold, 25 x 48 In.	165.00
Banner, Blossoms, Pierced S Monogram, Ball Terminals, Copper, Molded, c.1900, 34 x 37 In.	2607.00
Banner, Copper, Verdigris, Wrought Iron, Black Stand, 1800s, 36 In.	889.00
Banner, Cutout & Scroll Design, Ball Terminals, Painted, c.1900, 16 x 50 In.	948.00
Banner, Cutout Numerals, 1819, Scroll Supports, Sheet & Wrought Iron, 17 x 36 In.	2489.00
Banner, Fleur-De-Lis, Pierced, Arrow Point, Balls, Sheet Copper, c.1895, 35 ½ x 33 In.	1778.00
Banner, Lyre, Cutout Design, Gilt, Copper, Zinc Arrow, Stand, c.1890, 23 x 59 In. ....*Illus*	10073.00
Banner, Pierced Date, Copper, Wrought Iron, 1894, 34 x 57 In.	1298.00
Banner, White Paint, Arrow Point, Scroll & Tulip, Openwork, Sheet Copper, c.1865, 7 ½ x 36 In.	1896.00
Beaver, Cutout Teeth, Claws, Ears, Sheet Tin, Hammered, Crimped Flanges, c.1910, 12 x 32 In.	1553.00
Bicycle, High Wheel, Rider, Arrow Shape Base, Copper, Zinc, Gilt, c.1910, 33 x 40 In.	12650.00
Blacksmith, Working At Anvil, Demanding Customer, Sheet Iron, c.1880, 34 x 53 In.	1438.00
Bull, Applied Ears, Horns & Tail, Copper, Molded Relief, 18 ½ x 16 In.	118.00
Butterfly, Copper Wire Antennae & Legs, Copper Pierced, J.W. Fiske, c.1890, 20 x 22 In. .*Illus*	41475.00
Car, Driver, Convertible, Man In Driving Gear, 15 x 7 In.	605.00
Car, Driver, Directional, Copper, 15 x 7 In.	605.00
Cardinal, On Arrow, Painted, Wrought Iron, Mounted On Wood Cupola, 17 x 24 In.	330.00
Cat, Ready To Pounce Bird, Pole, Directionals, Black Sheet Metal, c.1950, 38 ½ x 44 In.	130.00
Chicken, Red, Black, White Painted, White Pedestal Base, Wood, Tin, c.1950, 22 ½ x 32 In.	649.00
Chinook Salmon, Full Body, Sheet Steel, c.1950, 33 In.	723.00
Cockeral, Green, Gilt, Sheet Tin, c.1890, 24 x 22 In.	948.00
Codfish, Copper, Gilt, c.1890, 26 In.	4029.00
Codfish, Full Body, Articulated Fins, Gills, Copper, Verdigris, Cushing & White, 9 x 25 In.	10350.00
Codfish, Full Body, Articulated Fins, Open Mouth, Rib Tail, Gilt, Verdigris, 12 ¾ x 26 In.	3163.00
Codfish, Full Body, Copper, Verdigris, c.1900, 12 x 26 In.	1298.00
Codfish, Full Body, Crimped Fins, Copper, Molded, Stand, c.1900, 13 x 26 In.	1185.00
Codfish, Gold Leaf, Copper, Sheet Fins, J.W. Fiske & Co., New York, c.1890, 16 x 38 In.	40290.00
Codfish, Silhouette, Open Mouth, Lead, Sheet Metal Trim, c.1925, 8 x 24 In.	518.00
Cow, Copper, Directionals, Harris & Company, 19th Century, 14 x 24 In.	2600.00
Cow, Flattened Full Body, Molded, Cone Arrow, Copper, Wood Stand, c.1900, 25 ½ x 33 In.	9480.00
Cow, Full Body, Copper, c.1890, 23 x 19 In.	5451.00
Cow, Standing, Copper, Cast Iron Head & Horns, Box Stand, c.1900, 19 x 33 In.	1840.00
Cupid, Standing, Bow, Black Paint, Wrought Iron, Wood Base, 1800s, 18 ¾ x 13 ½ In.	474.00
Deer, Buck, Full Body, Leaping, Copper, Zinc Head & Antlers, 27 x 24 In.	8100.00
Directional Letters, Brass, Copper Ball, Iron Base, 24 In.	153.00
Doctor, Flying, Silhouette, Top Hat, Tails, Pine, c.1875, 14 x 25 In.	2360.00
Dog, Irish Setter, Full Body, Flattened, Gilt Copper, Textured, Rod & Stand, c.1900, 18 x 32 ¼ In.	4740.00
Dog, Setter, Flattened Full Body, Gilt Copper, Rod With Stand, 16 ⅜ x 33 ½ In. ....*Illus*	9600.00
Dog, Setter, Standing, Copper, Gold Leaf, H.L. Washburn & Co., Mass., c.1890, 18 x 34 In.	40290.00
Dog, Setter, Walking, Verdigris, Washburn, 32 x 16 In.	9488.00

Dory, Man, Fish Inside Boat, Verdigris, 29 x 11 In.	4255.00
Dragon, Scrolling Serpent, Detailed Wing, Cast Iron, Gilt, 1800s, 19 x 28 In.	5462.00
Eagle, Copper, Arrow, Directionals, Stand, c.1910, 76 x 23 ½ In.	236.00
Eagle, Copper, Directional, Round Base, c.1900, 68 In.	1375.00
Eagle, Cutout Spread Wings, Copper, Zinc Head, Gilt, c.1895, 22 In.	1763.00
Eagle, Flying, On Ball, Arrow, Directionals, Gilt Copper, Black Stand, c.1920, 24 x 30 In.	1380.00
Eagle, Full Body, Open Beak, Spread Wings, Copper, Gold Paint, Wood Base, c.1900, 24 In.	649.00
Eagle, Spread Wings, Arrow, Finders, Copper, Wood Stand, c.1910, 76 In.	472.00
Eagle, Spread Wings, Copper Sphere, Directionals, Wrought Iron, 1800s, 52 x 36 In.	720.00
Eagle, Spread Wings, Copper, Cast Iron Directional, c.1890, 62 ½ In.	474.00
Eagle, Spread Wings, Full Body, Copper, Molded, Mounted On Sphere, Gilt, c.1900, 19 ¼ x 24 In.	1541.00
Eagle, Winged, Arrow, Directionals, Copper, Verdigris, 20 ½ In.	1422.00
Equestrian, Woman Rider, Full Dress, High Hat, Prancing Horse, Verdigris, Copper, Zinc, 27 x 28 In.	8050.00
Ewe, Full Body, Copper, Verdigris, Sheet Copper Ears, c.1935, 16 ½ x 22 In.	6490.00
Female, Nude, Wings On Feet, Animal Ears, Caduceus, Full Body, Copper, Arrow, c.1890, 90 In. …*Illus*	8400.00
Fire Pumper, Horse Drawn, Sheet Iron, c.1900, 16 x 36 ¾ In.	326.00
Fish, Directionals, Copper, Yellow Paint, 33 x 12 In.	1612.00
Fish, Full Body, Copper, Verdigris, J.W. Fiske, 1900s, 25 ½ In.	3540.00
Fish, Striped Bass, Wood, Paint, Black Stand, c.1960, 45 In.	885.00
Fish, Wood, White Paint, Metal Stand, c.1900, 39 ½ In.	1121.00
Fox & Hound, Full Body, Copper, Verdigris, Gilt Trace, Cushing & Sons, 1880, 15 x 35 In.	11500.00
Fox, Running, Copper, c.1910, 40 In.	1185.00
Gamecock, Copper, Gilt, c.1900, 22 ½ x 17 In.	4503.00
Gamecock, Full Body, Copper, Zinc, Molded, Orb, Stand, c.1870, 23 ½ x 16 ½ In.	4148.00
Gamecock, Full Body, Zinc Comb, Copper, Stand, U.S.A., 1900s, 28 In.	940.00
Girl, Holding Umbrella, Dog, Sheet Iron, Black Paint, Wood Base, c.1925, 37 ½ x 32 In. …*Illus*	1062.00
Goddess Of Liberty, Flag, Full Body, Copper, Gilt, Cushing & White, c.1875, 43 x 28 In.	29325.00
Goddess Of Liberty, Full Body, Flag On Pole, Copper, Stand, c.1890, 25 x 18 In.	6900.00
Goose, Flying, Copper, Brass Directionals & Ball, 37 x 42 In.	472.00
Goose, Spread Wings, Arrow, Cast Iron, White Paint, Rectangular Wood Mount	112.00
Grasshopper, Copper, Molded, Verdigris, 1900s, 24 In.	472.00
Grasshopper, Full Body, Copper, c.1910, 40 ½ In.	10665.00
Harpoon, Wave Shape Tail Section, Center Spire, Wrought Sheet Iron, c.1900, 16 ¾ x 44 In.	345.00
Horse & Groom, Full Body, Copper, Sheet Copper, Iron Base, A.L. Jewell Co., c.1890, 23 x 32 In.	4600.00
Horse & Rider, Jumping, Fence, 32 x 21 ½ In.	8000.00
Horse & Sulky, Rider, Whip, Copper, Verdigris, c.1950, 33 In.	403.00
Horse, Cart, Rider, Copper, Cast Zinc, Yellow Paint, Harris Co. & Son, Ma., 47 x 21 ½ In.	7763.00
Horse, Dexter, Full Body, Copper, Zinc, Gilt, U.S.A., c.1900, 33 In.	1293.00
Horse, Dexter, Galloping, Full Body, Gilt Copper, Zinc, Stand, Cushing & White, c.1895, 26 ¾ x 47 In.	7110.00
Horse, Ethan Allen, Cushing, Copper, Verdigris, 25 x 13 In.	2070.00
Horse, Ethan Allen, Galloping, Full Body, Copper, Patinated, Zinc Ears, 26 In.	2242.00
Horse, Ethan Allen, Running, Full Body, Copper, Verdigris, 18 ½ x 26 In.	4484.00
Horse, Gilt Tin, Iron Directional, c.1850, 17 In.	385.00
Horse, Hackney, Trotting, Copper, 32 x 24 In.	8050.00
Horse, High Wheel Sulky, Driver, Full Body, Copper, Verdigris, c.1920, 19 x 32 In.	441.00
Horse, Jockey, Steeplechase, Copper, Gilt, Zinc, c.1890, 24 x 31 ½ In. …*Illus*	13225.00
Horse, Prancing, Black Hawk, Full Body, Flattened, Sheet Copper, Mounted, c.1895, 17 ⅜ x 23 In.	9480.00
Horse, Prancing, Copper Body, Zinc Head, Gold Leaf, A.L. Jewell & Co., c.1865, 15 x 18 In.	26070.00
Horse, Prancing, Copper, Full Body, Gilt, Stand, c.1895, 19 ½ x 26 In.	3254.00
Horse, Prancing, Copper, Gold Leaf, Black Bar, A.L. Jewell & Co., c.1880, 30 x 27 In.	29160.00
Horse, Prancing, Red Paint, Sheet Iron, Arrow, c.1845, 14 ½ x 35 In.	770.00
Horse, Running, Black Hawk, Hollow Body, Copper, Verdigris, New England, 1800s, 25 ½ In.	2133.00
Horse, Running, Colonel Patchen, Copper, Gilt, c.1900, 23 In.	748.00
Horse, Running, Copper, 32 x 16 In.	2750.00
Horse, Running, Copper, Verdigris, 16 x 31 In.	3318.00
Horse, Running, Dexter, Directionals, Copper, Verdigris, Harris & Co., 1800s, 12 x 25 ½ In.	5214.00
Horse, Running, Body, Applied Tail, Copper, Molded, Iron, Cast Zinc Head, c.1890, 19 x 27 In. *Illus*	3318.00
Horse, Running, Full Body, Copper, Cast Head, 19 x 33 In.	5688.00
Horse, Running, Full Body, Copper, Verdigris, Stand, c.1890, 13 x 27 In.	1687.00
Horse, Running, Full Body, Copper, Zinc, Gilt, A.L. Jewell & Co., 17 x 28 In.	2065.00
Horse, Running, Full Body, Flattened, Copper, Zinc, Molded, Verdigris, Stand, c.1900, 18 x 34 In.	1778.00
Horse, Running, Full Body, Gilt Copper, Rod, Ball, Stand, c.1900, 21 x 29 ¾ In.	2400.00
Horse, Running, Full Body, Gold Paint, Copper, Stand, c.1895, 17 ½ x 28 In.	1808.00
Horse, Running, Full Body, Jockey Wearing Cap, Holding Reins, Stand, c.1885, 32 x 19 In.	4140.00
Horse, Running, Full Body, Sheet Metal, Gold Paint, Stand, c.1900, 24 x 33 In.	392.00

Wedgwood
The real Wedgwood company run by Josiah Wedgwood is spelled WEDGWOOD. Another English company took advantage of the name by using the mark WEDGE-WOOD.

Webb Burmese, Vase, Bud, Long Neck, Prunus Blossoms, Pinched Body, Paper Label, c.1887, 9 In., Pair
$819.00

Norman C. Heckler & Company

Wedgwood, Barber Bottle, Jasper Dip, Tricolor, White Relief, Bacchus Head, c.1875, 9 ⅝ In., Pair
$960.00

Skinner, Inc.

Wedgwood, Barber Bottle, Lid, Jasper Dip, Green, Lilac Medallions, Bacchus Heads, c.1850, 10 ½ In.
$2,726.00

Skinner, Inc.

W

Wedgwood, Biscuit Jar, Lilac, Jasper Dip, Classical Figures, Silver Plated Rim, Handle, c.1869, 5 ¾ In.
$215.00

Skinner, Inc.

Wedgwood, Bowl, Butterfly, Luster, Mottled Orange Exterior, Blue & Purple, Footed, c.1920, 8 ¾ In.
$711.00

Skinner, Inc.

Wedgwood, Bowl, Fairyland Luster, Tyford Garlands, Fairy Gondola Interior, Pedestal, Signed, 10 ¾ In.
$10,350.00

James D. Julia Auctioneers

Wedgwood, Candleholder, Jasperware, White, Bacchanalian Child, Impressed Mark, c.1800, 12 ½ In., Pair
$5,400.00

Skinner, Inc.

Horse, Running, Gilt Metal, c.1850, 21 x 31 In.	652.00
Horse, Running, Sheet Iron, c.1850, 14 ½ x 25 In.	326.00
Horse, Running, Sulky, Copper, Zinc, Directional, 65 x 45 In.	3125.00
Horse, Running, Yellow Paint, Metal, A.L. Jewell Co., Ma., 28 x 16 ¾ In.	2300.00
Horse, Smuggler, Full Body, Copper, Gilt, Verdigris, c.1890, 18 x 33 In.	1092.00
Horse, Smuggler, Running, Hollow Body, Copper, Gilt Surface, 1800s, 32 In.	1778.00
Horse, Standing, Sheet Iron, Pierced, 31 x 42 In.	354.00
Horse, Sulky, Driver, Copper, c.1900, 43 In.	4374.00
Horse, Trotter, High Wheel Sulky, Driver, Full Body, Copper, Gilt, c.1915, 19 x 34 In.	6756.00
Horse, Trotting, Directional, Iron, Copper, 45 x 22 In.	360.00
Horse, Trotting, Full Body, Copper, Gold Paint, c.1895, 18 x 27 In.	881.00
Horse, Woman Riding Sidesaddle, Full Body, Copper, 1900s, 28 x 28 ½ In.	2360.00
Hound, Chasing Deer, Copper, Zinc Antlers, J. W. Fiske, N.Y., c.1900, 25 x 51 In.	8050.00 to 14950.00
Hunter, Dog, Cutout Silhouette, Sheet Iron, 1900s, 31 ½ x 24 ½ In.	770.00
Indian Warrior, On Horse, Upraised Hatchet, Sheet Iron, Painted, 27 x 37 In.	2760.00
Indian, Bow & Arrow, Full Body, Copper, 1900s, 28 In.	646.00
Indian, Bow & Arrow, Sheet Iron, c.1950, 22 ¼ In.	533.00
Indian, Running, Bow & Arrow, Sheet Iron, c.1910, 15 ¾ x 20 In.	770.00
Indian, Shooting Bow & Arrow, Sheet Iron, Red, Salmon Paint, Pa., 34 ¾ In.	3792.00
Jockey, Running Horse, Full Body, Copper, Verdigris Patina, c.1890, 17 ¼ x 28 In.	1205.00
Locomotive, Full Round, Sheet Copper, Painted, Copper Rod, c.1900, 26 x 24 ½ In. ......*Illus*	900.00
Mobile Pegasus, Die Cut, Brass	3000.00
Mother Goose, Hollow, Copper, c.1950, 25 In.	279.00
Neptune, Seahorse, Copper, c.1850, 28 x 34 In.	266.00
Peacock, Gilt Copper, A.L. Jewell & Co., Ma., c.1860, 33 x 37 In.	39680.00
Peacock, Swollen Belly, Copper, Gilt, Verdigris, Stand, c.1890, 20 x 35 In.	8295.00
Pig, Full Body, Flattened, Copper, Cast Zinc Head, Metal Stand, c.1890, 21 x 36 In. ....*Illus*	36000.00
Plow, Silhouette, Cutout, Sheet Copper, Copper Rod, Wall Mount, c.1900, 15 ½ x 33 In.	2133.00
Quill Pen, Sheet Iron, Yellow Paint, Tube Shaft, Black Iron Base, 22 x 58 In.	767.00
Quill, Copper, Rigged, Gilt, Stand, c.1895, 16 x 36 In.	4700.00
Ram, Full Body, Gilt Copper, Molded, Hammered, Stand, c.1900, 24 ⅜ x 28 In. ....*Illus*	7703.00
Rooster, Cast Iron & Sheet Metal, Old Black Paint, 31 x 32 In.	2530.00
Rooster, Cast, Sheet Iron, Rochester Ironworks, New Hampshire, c.1880, 24 x 23 In.	2478.00
Rooster, Copper, Verdigris, Zinc Legs, c.1900, 29 x 26 In.	4551.00
Rooster, Curlwork Base, Directionals, Wrought Iron, 30 x 36 In.	173.00
Rooster, Flattened Full Body, On Ball, Gilt Copper, Molded, Verdigris, 34 x 25 In.	8888.00
Rooster, Full Body, Copper, c.1890, 21 x 24 In.	2607.00
Rooster, Full Body, Copper, Gilding, Wood Mount, c.1890, 22 x 18 In.	1770.00
Rooster, Full Body, Embossed Comb & Tail, Copper, Molded, Mounted, On Rod, c.1900, 14 ⅝ In. .. *Illus*	5925.00
Rooster, Full Body, Iron, Head Down, Wrought Rod, Wooden Mount, c.1900, 14 x 19 ½ In.	413.00
Rooster, Full Body, Perched On Arrow, Gilt, Copper, Iron Base, c.1890, 27 In.	1416.00
Rooster, Full Body, Tail Support Bar, Copper Gilt, France, c.1790, 31 In.	748.00
Rooster, Iron, Gold Paint, Wood Base, 1800s, 30 ¾ In.	1694.00
Rooster, Standing, Flattened Full Body, Copper, Zinc, Stand, c.1860, 27 x 24 ¼ In.	11850.00
Schooner, 3-Masted, Copper, Cast Zinc Directional, 1890s, 52 In.	300.00
Ship, Wood, Green Paint, Wire Rigging, c.1900, 25 ¾ x 36 ½ In.	1541.00
Sloop, Directional, Spacer Ball, Copper, Brass, c.1950, 29 x 30 In.	590.00
Squirrel, Eating A Nut, Full Body, Copper, L.W. Cushing & Sons, 1900s, 18 x 22 In.	4248.00
Squirrel, Seated, Eating A Nut, Upright Tail, Copper, Zinc Ears, Stand, c.1910, 24 x 20 In.	4888.00
Squirrel, Sitting Up, Eating Nut, Copper, Early 20th Century, 17 x 21 In.	14220.00
Stag, Leaping, Copper, Verdigris, c.1880, 33 x 37 In.	71100.00
Stag, Leaping, Full Body, Copper, Gilt, Stand, c.1890, 27 x 30 In.	13513.00
Stag, Leaping, Full Body, Copper, Zinc Head, Antlers, Tail, Rock, Cushing & White, c.1870, 18 x 27 In..	9775.00
Stag, Leaping, Full Body, Directionals, Copper, Zinc Head, Antlers, 26 ¾ x 29 In.	6900.00
Stag, Leaping, Gilt Copper, Ma., c.1880, 30 x 31 In.	19840.00
Stag, Leaping, Over Brush, Gilt Copper, L.W. Cushing & Sons, Ma., 22 x 19 ½ In.	7475.00
Stag, Running, Sheet Iron, 1800s, 29 x 33 ½ In.	4740.00
Stag, Standing, Full Body, Copper, Gilt, Zinc, Cushing & White, c.1870, 29 x 23 In.	10350.00
Stag, Standing, Zinc, c.1850, 43 In.	729.00
Steer, Copper, Green Patina, Zinc Head, Cushing & White, Waltham, Mass., c.1900, 18 x 30 In.	35550.00
Steer, Full Body, Copper, Molded, Rod & Ball, c.1900, 24 x 29 ½ In.	18000.00
Steer, Standing, Copper, Gilt, c.1870, 12 x 23 In.	4030.00
Turkey, Shot Holes, Copper, Patina, c.1890, 20 ½ In.	443.00
Whale, Silhouette, Pine, Iron Bracket, Maine, c.1900, 12 x 42 In.	382.00
Wolf Baying, Crescent Moon, Finders, Pole, Copper, 35 ½ In.	1298.00

WEBB glass was made by Thomas Webb & Sons of Ambelcot, England. Many types of art and cameo glass were made by them during the Victorian era. Production ceased by 1991 and the factory was demolished in 1995. Webb Burmese and Webb Peachblow are special colored glasswares of the Victorian era. They are listed at the end of this section. Glassware that is not Burmese or Peachblow is included here.

Webb

Bowl, Citron Yellow, White, Cameo Cut Morning Glories, Vines, Inverted Rim, 4 x 8 ¼ In. 3555.00

Bowl, Prussian Blue, White Stemmed Leafy Flowers, Squat, Bulbous, 4 ¼ In. 1783.00

Perfume Bottle, Panels, Flowers, White Over Red Cameo, Ball Stopper, Acid Stamp, 5 In. .. *Illus* 2645.00

Perfume Bottle, Swan's Head, White Cut To Blue, Cameo, 8 ¾ In. 5750.00

Perfume Bottle, White Leaves, Flowers, Red, Silver Mounts, Stopper, Cameo, c.1900, 5 ¾ In. 1875.00

Perfume, Yellow, Mums, Leaves, Teardrop Shape, Embossed Sterling Lid, Cameo, Stopper, 8 ½ In. 1438.00

Rose Bowl, Amber To Rose, Diamond Quilted, Ball Shaped, Scalloped Rim, 4 In. 230.00

Underplate, Alexandrite, Ruffled Edge, 5 ½ In. 546.00

Vase, Bird On Flowering Dogwood Branch, Gold, Silver, Yellow Ground, Opal Interior, 4 ¼ In. ..*Illus* 460.00

Vase, Blue, Thorny Primrose Bush, Butterflies, Oval, Shouldered, Cameo, 7 ¾ In. 2415.00

Vase, Blue, White Blossoming Branches, Shell Swags, Bulbous, Stick Neck, Garlic Mouth, 9 ¼ In.. 2300.00

Vase, Blue, White Flowers & Leaves, Oval, Flared Rim, Cameo, 6 In. 823.00

Vase, Citron, White Overlay, Carved, Passion Flower Spray, Vine, Butterfly, Cameo, c.1890, 7 ½ In. 2124.00

Vase, Cornflower Blue, Flared, Baluster Shape, White, Carved Flowers, Border, Cameo, 10 In.. 2844.00

Vase, Deep Red, White Leaves, Flowers, Bulbous, Elongated Neck, Swollen, Flared Lip, Cameo, 7 In. 3565.00

Vase, Diamond Quilted, Mother-Of-Pearl, Birds, Fuchsia, Yellow, Double Gourd, Cameo, 13 In. 4888.00

Vase, Double Gourd, Emulating Ivory, Cameo Cut, Stylized Medial Frieze, Dragon Heads, 11 ½ In. 2844.00

Vase, Flared Rim, Multicolor, Honeycomb, 4 ¼ In. 2500.00

Vase, Ivory, Moorish Design, Flowers, Scrolls, Cameo, Signed, 9 In. .... *Illus* 2875.00

Vase, Morning Glories, Blue, White, Bulbous, Cameo, 4 In. 1900.00

Vase, Raised Burnished Gilding, Bird, Spider & Web, Peachblow, c.1880, 10 ½ In., Pair 920.00

Vase, Red & White Flowers, Green Ground, White Rim, Bottle Shape, Cameo, 9 In. 1845.00

Vase, Red Roses, Blue & Peach Butterfly, Star Shape Gilt Rim, 6 ½ In. 185.00

Vase, Red, Cascading Morning Glory, Butterfly, Oval, Acid Stamp, Cameo, 8 ½ In. 920.00

Vase, Red, White Morning Glories, Butterflies, Yellow Glass Ground, 5 x 8 ¾ In. 938.00

Vase, Stick, Bulbous Bottom, Yellow, White Leafy Bell Flowers, Butterflies, Cameo, Marked, 13 In.. 2645.00

Vase, Textured Crystal, Red Lilies & Leaves, Pinched Waist, Flared Rim, Signed, 9 In. 345.00

Vase, Tulips, Stems, Leaves, Rain Texture, Yellow, Trumpet Shape, 9 ¼ In. 316.00

Vase, White, Cased Yellow, Orange, Flower Medallions, Stars, Geometric Cuts, Bulbous, Stick, 7 In. 920.00

Vase, Wild Rose, Yellow Amber, 2 Butterflies On Reverse, Impressed, Cameo, c.1888, 7 ¾ In. ... *Illus* 3555.00

Vase, Yellow, Red Overlay, Carved, Persian Flowers, Arabesques, Cameo, 1890, 4 ¾ In. 2360.00

Vase, Yellow, White & Red Cascading Morning Glory Vine, Butterfly, Bulbous, Flared Rim, 12 In... 7590.00

WEBB BURMESE is a shaded Victorian glass made by Thomas Webb & Sons of Stourbridge, England, from 1886. Pieces are shades of pink to yellow.

Charger, Taj Mahal, Yellow To Pink, Gilt Moorish Design Border, 12 In. .... *Illus* 8338.00

Fairy Lamp, Domed Satin Shade, Fluted Base, Stamped Clarke, 5 ½ In. 900.00

Fairy Lamp, Domed Shade, Berries Leaves, Crimped, c.1887, 6 ¼ In. 2550.00

Fairy Lamp, Ruffled Rim, Double Crystal Insert, 3-Part, Signed Clarkes Cricklite, 6 ¼ In. .... *Illus* 546.00

Finger Bowl, Glossy, Rigaree Collar, Metal Caddy, 6 x 6 In. 316.00

Perfume Bottle, Cream To Pink, Gold Ginko Design, Ball Shape, Metal Cap, 4 ¼ In. 546.00

Perfume Bottle, Enameled Flowers, Leaves, Silver Screws Lid, Blossoms, 4 In. 950.00

Rose Bowl, Ball Shape, Crimped Folded In Rim, Flowers, Leaves, Pink, Peach, 3 In. 316.00

Rose Bowl, Ball Shape, Pinched Crimp Rim, Leaf & Berry, 2 ¼ In. 230.00

Salt, Crimped Rim, Grapes, Leaves, c.1887, 1 ¼ In. 1250.00

Shaker, Cylindrical, c.1890, 3 ¼ In., Pair 270.00

Vase, Birds In Flight, Bulbous, Trumped Neck, Crimped Rim, Pedestal Foot, 4 ½ In. 173.00

Vase, Bud, Long Neck, Prunus Blossoms, Pinched Body, Paper Label, c.1887, 9 In., Pair ...*Illus* 819.00

Vase, Bulbous, Square Top, Flowers, Leaves, 3 ⅞ In. 370.00

Vase, Enameled Blossoms & Vines, Globular, Flared Ruffled Rim, Footed, 3 In. 288.00

Vase, Flowers, Leaves, 5-Point Star, 3 ½ In. 460.00

Vase, Hawthorne, Stick, Bulbous, Elongated Neck, 7 In. 518.00

Vase, Peacock Eye Pattern, Red Flowers, Leafy Stems, Cream To Peach, Smokestack, 8 In. 7475.00

Vase, Petal Glass Top, Pink To Yellow, 3 x 3 ½ In. 60.00

Vase, Virginia Creeper Vine, Bulbous, Fold In Petal Top, Cream, Pink, 3 ⅛ In. 288.00

WEBB PEACHBLOW is a shaded Victorian glass made by Thomas Webb & Sons of Stourbridge, England, from 1885.

Biscuit Jar, Lid, Swing Handle, Quilted, Silver Plate .... 260.00 to 295.00

Pitcher, Diamond Quilted, Clear Handle, 7 ½ In. 250.00

Wedgwood, Cheese Dish, Lid, Jasper Dip, Dark Blue, Applied White Classical Figures, c.1890, 11 In.
$533.00

Skinner, Inc.

Wedgwood, Cheese Keeper, Lid, Jasper Dip, Blue, Figures, Oak Leaf Banded Border, c.1890, 10 x 10 ⅝ In.
$600.00

Skinner, Inc.

Wedgwood, Dish, Shell Shape, Scalloped, Mother & Child Scene, Emile Lessore, c.1870, 8 ¼ x 8 In.
$540.00

DuMouchelles Art Gallery

Wedgwood, Group, Country Lovers, Queen's Ware, Seated Couple, Marked, c.1940, 12 In.
$1,020.00

Skinner, Inc.

Wedgwood, Pastille Burner, Lid, Jasper Dip, Black, 3 White Dolphin Supports, c.1850, 5 In.
$1,896.00

Skinner, Inc.

Wedgwood, Potpourri, Moonlight Luster, Mottled Pink, Purple, Orange Glaze, c.1810, 14 In.
$1,778.00

Skinner, Inc.

Wedgwood, Sardine Box, Majolica, Sardines On Lid, Leaves, Blue Border, Wedgwood, 1800s, 7 x 8 In.
$780.00

DuMouchelles Art Gallery

W

Tarnish Prevention
We prefer the modern tarnish-preventing polishes. There is more time between cleanings.

Wedgwood, Vase, Classical Figures, Jasper Dip, 3 Colors, Quatrefoil Band, Handles, c.1790, 9 ¾ In.
$4,305.00

Skinner, Inc.

Wedgwood, Vase, Fairyland Luster, Candlemas, Blue Band Framing, Black, c.1920, 7 ¼ In.
$4,500.00

Skinner, Inc.

Wedgwood, Vase, Fairyland Luster, Flame, Sycamore Tree, Bridge, Ship & Tree, c.1920, 8 In.
$13,035.00

Skinner, Inc.

Wedgwood, Vase, Fish, Luster, Blue, Gilded Design, c.1915, 9 ½ In.
$711.00

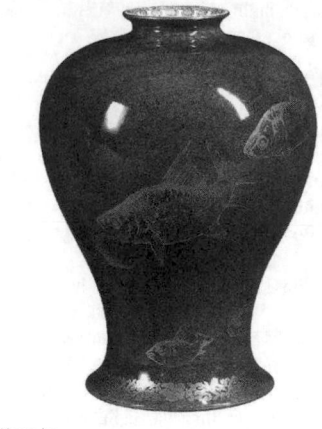

Skinner, Inc.

Wedgwood, Vase, Jasper Dip, Black, Portland, Classical Figures, Handles, 1800s, 6 ⅞ In.
$593.00

Skinner, Inc.

Wedgwood, Vase, Lid, Jasperware, Applied Lilac & Green Relief, Zodiac Border, Medallions, c.1890, 11 In.
$4,148.00

Skinner, Inc.

Pitcher, Vine Applied Handle, Ruffled Rim, 5 In.	420.00
Vase, Shouldered, Branches, Leaves, 5 ½ In.	375.00

WEDGWOOD, one of the world's most successful potteries, was founded by Josiah WEDGWOOD Wedgwood, who was considered a cripple by his brother and was forbidden to work at the family business. The pottery was established in England in 1759. The company used a variety of marks, including Wedgwood, Wedgwood & Bentley, Wedgwood & Sons, and Wedgwood's Stone China. A large variety of wares has been made, including the well-known jasperware, basalt, creamware, and even a limited amount of porcelain. There are two kinds of jasperware. One is made from two colors of clay, the other is made from one color of clay with a color dip to create the contrast in design. In 1986 Wedgwood and Waterford Crystal merged to form the Waterford Wedgwood Group. Most Waterford Wedgwood assets were bought by KPS Capital Partners of New York in 2009 and became part of WWRD Holdings. Some manufacturing will be transferred to Germany, Indonesia, and Slovakia. Other Wedgwood pieces may be listed under Flow Blue, Majolica, Tea Leaf Ironstone, or in other porcelain categories.

Barber Bottle, Jasper Dip, Tricolor, White Relief, Bacchus Head, c.1875, 9 ⅝ In., Pair ...*Illus*	960.00
Barber Bottle, Lid, Jasper Dip, Bacchus Heads, Garland, Black & White, c.1850, 11 In., Pair..	1896.00
Barber Bottle, Lid, Jasper Dip, Green, Lilac Medallions, Bacchus Heads, c.1850, 10 ½ In. ....*Illus*	2726.00
Biscuit Jar, Lid, Jasper Dip, Green, Lilac Border, White Figures, Flowers, Bail Handle, 5 In.	563.00
Biscuit Jar, Lilac, Jasper Dip, Classical Figures, Silver Plated Rim, Handle, c.1869, 5 ¾ In. ....*Illus*	215.00
Bough Pot, Lid, Jasperware, Green Leaves, Lilac Bellflowers, Pierced Lid, Spread Foot, 1891, 7 In.	2133.00
Bowl, Black Basalt, Classical Aidens, 4 x 8 In.	237.00
Bowl, Butterfly, Luster, Mottled Orange Exterior, Blue & Purple, Footed, c.1920, 8 ¾ In. ...*Illus*	711.00
Bowl, Fairyland Luster, Flame, Black, Gilt Highlighted Scene, Woodland Bridge, 10 ¾ In.	3728.00
Bowl, Fairyland Luster, Gold Birds, Mottled Blue Exterior, Orange Interior, Footed, 8 x 6 In.	688.00
Bowl, Fairyland Luster, Large Hat Pattern, Blue Water, Flame Sky, Woodland Bridge, Elves, 6 ½ In.	5750.00
Bowl, Fairyland Luster, Moorish, Octagonal, Daisy Makeig-Jones, c.1920, 4 x 8 In.	2875.00
Bowl, Fairyland Luster, Red, Gilded Firbolgs, Ring Foot, Mother-Of-Pearl Interior, c.1920, 9 ¾ In.	2370.00
Bowl, Fairyland Luster, Thumbelina, K'Ang Hsi, Footed, Daisy Makeig-Jones, c.1925, 3 ¾ x 8 ¼ In.	1725.00
Bowl, Fairyland Luster, Tyford Garlands, Fairy Gondola Interior, Pedestal, Signed, 10 ¾ In. .....*Illus*	10350.00
Bowl, Fairyland Luster, Village Scenes, Gilt Trim, Octagonal Shape, Round Foot, 1920s, 4 ½ x 9 ½ In.	3125.00
Bowl, Fairyland Luster, Woodland Bridge, Poplar Trees, Mermaid, Gilt, Footed, c.1930, 11 x 6 In.	2875.00
Bowl, Jasperware, Blue, Bas Relief Acanthus Leaves, Bell Flowers, Oak Leaf Border, 4 x 10 In..	189.00
Bowl, Jasperware, Strapwork, Wide Flared Rim, Basketweave Design, Blue, White, 7 ¾ In.	4740.00
Bowl, Lid, Pearlware, Wheat Design, Green, Rectangular, 4 ½ x 9 ¾ In., Pair	259.00
Bowl, Lid, Undertray, Moonlight Luster, Purple, Orange, Shell Shape, Impressed, 6 In.	900.00
Box, Blue Mottled Luster Ground, Hummingbirds, Orange Mottled, Gilt, Signed, 2 ¾ x 7 In.	437.00
Cachepot, Black Basalt, Figures, Grape Swags, Lion Masks, Leaf Border, 7 x 7 ¾ In.	184.00
Cake Stand, Lid, Light Blue, Neoclassical Angels Playing Instruments, Acorns, Leaves, 10 In.	374.00
Candleholder, Jasperware, White, Bacchanalian Child, Impressed Mark, c.1800, 12 ½ In., Pair ...*Illus*	5400.00
Candlestick, Chamber, Jasper Dip, Crimson, White Classical Figures, Leaf Border, c.1920, 6 ¼ In.	830.00
Candlestick, Jasperware, Gilt Bronze, Hanging Lusters, Round Spread Foot, c.1785, 10 In., Pair..	8500.00
Centerpiece, Majolica, Pink, White Glaze, Nautilus Bowl, Dolphin Base, c.1860, 17 In.	649.00
Cheese Dish, Lid, Jasper Dip, Dark Blue, Applied White Classical Figures, c.1890, 11 In. ..*Illus*	533.00
Cheese Keeper, Lid, Dark Blue, Oak Leaf & Acorn Garlands, 8 x 11 ½ In.	259.00
Cheese Keeper, Lid, Jasper Dip, Blue, Figures, Oak Leaf Banded Border, c.1890, 10 x 10 ⅝ In. ..*Illus*	600.00
Coffeepot, Lid, Lighthouse Shape, Loop Handle, Blue, White, Spaniel Finial, Figures, c.1860, 9 ½ In.	711.00
Creamer, Black Basalt, Shell Design Below Spout, Long Squared Handle, c.1820, 2 ¾ x 5 ¾ In.	125.00
Creamer, Jasperware, Blue, White, 5 ¼ In.	47.00
Cup & Saucer, Creamware Transfer, Brown Leaf Sprig, Banner Borders, c.1780, 1 ½ x 3 In.	86.00
Cup, Jasper Dip, Crimson, White Figures, Scrolled Leaves, Cylindrical, 3 Handles, c.1920, 4 ½ In.	2015.00
Dish, Moonlight Luster, Oval, Shell Shape, Mottled Purple, Orange, Marked, c.1800, 11 ¼ In.	474.00
Dish, Shell Shape, Scalloped, Mother & Child Scene, Emile Lessore, c.1870, 8 ¼ x 8 In. ..*Illus*	540.00
Figurine, Bison, Celadon Glaze, Impressed Sculptor & Mark, Skeaping, c.1927, 11 In.	960.00
Figurine, Duck, Painted, Multicolor Enamel, H.W. Palliser, c.1940, 6 ¼ In.	1200.00
Figurine, Queen's Ware, Bridal Group, Multicolor Enamels, Arnold Machin, c.1941, 10 ¾ In.	2280.00
Figurine, Queen's Ware, Leopard, On Tree Stump, Pink Luster, Arnold Machin, c.1945, 6 ⅞ In.	960.00
Group, Country Lovers, Queen's Ware, Seated Couple, Marked, c.1940, 12 In. ....*Illus*	1020.00
Group, Cupid & Psyche, Black Basalt, Seated, Rocky Oval Base, 7 ¾ In.	2726.00
Jardiniere, Jasper Dip, Black, White Leaves, Blue Florets, Banded Border, Ring Foot, c.1850, 8 ¼ In.	2844.00
Jug, Jasper Dip, Yellow, White Figures, Trees, Flower Festoon Borders, Marked, c.1900, 5 ¾ In.	267.00
Jug, Rosso Antico, Gilt Transfer, Flower & Leaf Banding, Landscapes, Square Handle, c.1890, 7 ⅜ In..	593.00
Pastille Burner, Lid, Jasper Dip, Black, 3 White Dolphin Supports, c.1850, 5 In. ....*Illus*	1896.00
Pie Dish, Lid, Caneware, Oval, Piecrust Border, Band Of Grapevines, Marked, c.1800, 7 ¼ In.	1126.00
Pitcher, Jasper Dip, Yellow, White Figures, Bulbous, Loop Handle, Ring Foot, c.1900, 7 ¾ In.	385.00
Plate, American Clipper Ship, Brown Transfer, c.1950, 9 ½ In., 12 Piece	1888.00
Plate, Dinner, West Point Pattern, Blue & White, 10 ½ In., 12 Piece	420.00

Wedgwood, Vase, Portland, Crimson, Jasper Dip, Classical Figures, Impressed Mark, c.1920, 7 In.
$4,200.00

Skinner, Inc.

Wedgwood, Vase, Potpourri, Jasper Dip, 3 Colors, Classical Figures, Festoons, c.1890, 14 ¼ In.
$2,520.00

Skinner, Inc.

Wedgwood, Vase, Spill, Jasperware, Blue, White Relief, Bamboo Shape, 3 Spouts, Marked, c.1790, 8 ½ In.
$3,120.00

Skinner, Inc.

W

Weller, Chase, Vase, Horse & Rider, Hounds, White Slip, Dark Blue Ground, Marked, 11 ¾ In.
$173.00

Humler & Nolan

Weller, Etched Matte, Vase, Brown Iris, Pea Green Matte, Impressed, 12 In.
$805.00

Humler & Nolan

Weller, Figurine, Dog, Pop-Eye, Painted Accents, Incised, 10 In.
$1,495.00

Humler & Nolan

Weller, Figurine, Dog, Pop-Eye, White, Painted Features, Script Mark, 4 ⅛ In.
$288.00

Humler & Nolan

Plate, Fairyland Luster, Medallion, Persian Man, Cutting Tree, Gilded Trim, Mother-Of-Pearl, 3 ¾ In.	1553.00
Plate, Hunt Scenes, Fluted Border, Gold Trim, 9 In., 12 Piece	1180.00
Plate, Kutani Crane, 10 ¾ In., 24 Piece	450.00
Plate, Mug, Balmoral Hunt, Ralph Lauren, 10 ¾ In., 18 Piece	840.00
Platter, Elongated Oval, Ocean Plants, Shells, 19 ½ In.	109.00
Potpourri, Lid, Moonlight Luster, Mottled Pink, Purple, Orange Glaze, Marked, c.1810, 14 In. .....*Illus*	1778.00
Potpourri, Pierced Lid, Jasper Dip, Blue, Upturned Handles, White Figures, Leaves, c.1850, 10 In.	474.00
Potpourri, Pierced Lid, White, Gilt Ram's Heads, Flowers, Festoons, Egg Shape, 1800s, 12 ⅜ In.	2918.00
Salt, Figural, Boy, Scantily Clad, Holding Basket, Turquoise Glaze, c.1880, 5 ½ In.	122.00
Sardine Box, Majolica, Sardines On Lid, Leaves, Blue Border, Wedgwood, 1800s, 7 x 8 In. ... *Illus*	780.00
Sauce, Majolica, Argenta Strawberry, Ribbon & Bow, Handle, Footed, Marked, 6 ½ In., Pair ...	63.00
Table Lighter, Jasperware, Blue, 4 Seasons Pattern, Dancing Cherubs, 1964, 3 ½ x 3 In.	65.00
Urn, Gilt Fruit Garlands, Ram's Heads, Leaves, Trophies, Baluster Shape, c.1891, 11 ¼ In.	1188.00
Urn, Jasperware, Light Blue, Classical, Engraved, Made For Mr. Charles Bellows, c.1911, 14 ½ In.	236.00
Urn, Lid, Fairyland Luster, Malfrey, Candlemas, Daisy Makeig-Jones, c.1920, 8 ½ In.	5865.00
Urn, Lid, Jasperware, Green, White, Classical Figures, Handles, Impressed, c.1910, 12 ½ x 8 ½ In.	207.00
Vase, Annular Ware, Blue Glaze, Globe Shape, Concentric Rings, Keith Murray, c.1940, 7 ¼ In.	480.00
Vase, Black Basalt, Baluster, Loop Handles At Neck, Round Foot, Flat Rim, c.1800, 13 ⅜ In.	2963.00
Vase, Black Basalt, Bottle Shape, Side Handle, Iron Red, White & Black Enamel, Woman, 1800s, 6 In.	2430.00
Vase, Caneware, Fluted Body, Leaves, Berries, Outcurved Handles, Ring Foot, Marked, 1700s, 5 ⅛ In.	1126.00
Vase, Classical Figures, Jasper Dip, 3 Colors, Quatrefoil Band, Handles, c.1790, 9 ¾ In. ...*Illus*	4305.00
Vase, Fairyland Luster, Candlemas, Blue Band Framing, Black, c.1920, 7 ¼ In. ....*Illus*	4500.00
Vase, Fairyland Luster, Flame, Gilt Highlighted Scene, Imps On Bridge, 9 In.	4600.00
Vase, Fairyland Luster, Flame, Sycamore Tree, Bridge, Ship & Tree, c.1920, 8 In. ....*Illus*	13035.00
Vase, Fairyland Luster, Pheasant, Mottled Blue, Red, Gold, Green, Gilt, Flared Rim, c.1920, 8 In.	5206.00
Vase, Fairyland Luster, Pillar Pattern, Shouldered, Cylindrical Collar, 14 In.	10925.00
Vase, Fairyland Luster, Trumpet Shape, Butterfly Woman, Black Sky, c.1920, 9 ½ In.	6738.00
Vase, Fish, Luster, Blue, Gilded Design, c.1915, 9 ½ In. ....*Illus*	711.00
Vase, Green Ground, Gold, White Classical Swags, Hexagonal Neck, 6 ½ In.	330.00
Vase, Jasper Dip, Black, Portland, Classical Figures, Handles, 1800s, 6 ⅞ In. ....*Illus*	593.00
Vase, Jasperware, Jug Shape, Loop Handles At Neck, Ring Foot, Black, White, Figures, 1800s, 10 In.	1659.00
Vase, Lid, Jasperware, Applied Lilac & Green Relief, Zodiac Border, Medallions, c.1890, 11 In. .....*Illus*	4148.00
Vase, Luster, Snarling Gold Dragon, Mottled Blue, Pear Shape, Flared Rim, Round Foot, 8 ⅞ In.	374.00
Vase, Portland, Crimson, Jasper Dip, Classical Figures, Impressed Mark, c.1920, 7 In. ......*Illus*	4200.00
Vase, Potpourri, Jasper Dip, 3 Colors, Classical Figures, Festoons, c.1890, 14 ¼ In. ....*Illus*	2520.00
Vase, Spill, Jasperware, Blue, White Relief, Bamboo Shape, 3 Spouts, Marked, c.1790, 8 ½ In. ...*Illus*	3120.00
Vase, Stick, Pink To Fuchsia, Gold Dragonfly, Flowers, Branches, Berries, Ring Foot, 7 In.	173.00
Vase, Trumpet, Spread Foot, Gilded Butterflies, Mother-Of-Pearl, Orange Interior, c.1920, 8 In.	1067.00
Vase, Urn Shape, Black Basalt, 2 Scroll Handles, Square Base, Laurel Festoons, c.1790, 5 ⅜ In.	972.00
Vase, Women, Trees, Cameo, Shouldered, 2 Handles, 19th Century, 10 ¾ In.	1888.00

WELLER pottery was first made in 1872 in Fultonham, Ohio. The firm moved to Zanesville, Ohio, in 1882. Artwares were introduced in 1893. Hundreds of lines of pottery were produced, including Louwelsa, Eocean, Dickens Ware, and Sicardo, before the pottery closed in 1948.

LOUWELSA WELLER

Alvin, Vase, Tree Trunk Shape, Brown, Green, Paper Label, 8 ½ In.	80.00
Art Nouveau, Vase, Poppy Design, Scalloped Rim, Long Neck, 5 ½ x 13 In.	438.00
Baldin, Jardiniere, Pedestal, Carved, Flowers, Leaves, Tree Standard, Marked, 29 In.	460.00
Besline, Goblet, Orange, Footed, Handles, 6 ½ In.	29.00
Blossom, Vase, Handles, Pink Flower, Green Ground, Wavy Rim, 12 ¼ In.	40.00
Bouquet, Vase, Cylindrical, Flower Sprig, Scalloped Rim, 12 ¼ In.	17.00
Brighton, Figurine, Bluebird, Red Head, Yellow Breast, 1 ⅝ x 3 ½ In.	316.00
Brighton, Flower Frog, Ducks, White, Green, 5 ¾ In.	150.00
Burnt Wood, Candlestick, Stylized Flowers, Tapered, 8 ½ In.	29.00
Cameo, Vase, White Flowers, Green Ground, Flared, Handles, Marked, 11 ½ In.	35.00
Cameo, Vase, White Flowers, Leaves, Blue Ground, Shoulder Handles, Round, Marked, 7 ¾ In.	46.00
Chase, Vase, Horse & Rider, Hounds, White Slip, Dark Blue Ground, Marked, 11 ¾ In. .....*Illus*	173.00
Chase, Vase, Hunter, Horse, Dogs, Blue White, 7 In.	110.00
Claywood, Vase, Fish, Brown, 2 ¼ In.	23.00
Coppertone, Bowl, Crouching Frog At One End, Marked, 5 ½ In.	348.00
Coppertone, Bowl, Flower Center, Red Splotches, Green Ground, Petal Edges, Round, 12 ½ In.	244.00
Coppertone, Bowl, Green Lily Pad Shape, Perched Frog On Rim, Copper Accents, 3 ¾ x 11 In.	230.00
Coppertone, Centerpiece, Frog, Lily Pads, Label, 4 x 15 In.	575.00
Coppertone, Figurine, Frog, Seated, Signed, 6 ½ x 7 In.	472.00
Coppertone, Vase, Frog, Looking Up, 9 In.	431.00
Coppertone, Vase, Mottled Green, Brown Matte Glaze, Tapered Cylinder, 12 In.	767.00

W

Coppertone, Vase, Mottled Green, Tapered, 8 ½ In.	161.00
Coppertone, Vase, Open Handles, 6 ¾ x 8 In.	165.00
Coppertone, Vase, Verdigris, 4 ⅞ In.	103.00
Cretone, Vase, Green Leaves, Flowers, Animal, Cream Ground, Signed William Long, 5 ½ In.	368.00
Dealer Sign, Name & Profile Of Vase, White On Blue Ground, Marked, 2 x 5 ½ In.	596.00
Dechiwo, Jardiniere, Children Playing, Balloons, Round, Tapered, Tan, Brown, Marked, 7 x 5 In.	161.00
Dickens Ware, Jug, Smiling Bald Man, Brown, 5 ¾ In.	150.00
Dickens Ware, Lamp Base, Flowers, Marked, 9 ¾ In.	40.00
Dickens Ware, Pitcher, Hollow Horn Bear, Indian, E.L. Pickens, 6 ½ x 12 In.	750.00
Dickens Ware, Tobacco Jar, Lid, The Chinaman, 6 In.	253.00
Dickens Ware, Vase, Dragon, Blue Ground, Painted, 11 ¾ In.	403.00
Dickens Ware, Vase, Monk Profile, Blue Ground, Signed Helen Smith, 14 In.	316.00
Dickens Ware, Vase, Seated Horned Animal, Brown, Green, Flask Shape, 6 ¾ In.	253.00
Double Crane, Planter, Green, 13 ½ In.	23.00
Eocean, Jardiniere, Dark Green, 11 ½ In.	58.00
Eocean, Tankard, Ruby Red Peonies, Arched Stems, Tapered Cylinder, Loop Handle, Green, 12 In.	230.00
Eocean, Vase, Bud, Late Line, Daisy, Brown Glaze, Marked, 6 ¾ In.	58.00
Eocean, Vase, Cherries, 5 ¼ In.	29.00
Eocean, Vase, Cylindrical, Iris, 6 Handles, Marked, 16 In.	600.00
Eocean, Vase, Daffodil, Gray Ground, Tapered, 9 ½ In.	276.00
Eocean, Vase, Holly, Green Ground, 10 ¼ In.	357.00
Eocean, Vase, Iris Design, Cylindrical, 6 Handles, 6 ½ x 16 In.	732.00
Eocean, Vase, Pansies, Cream, Dark Blue Ground, 9 In.	173.00
Etched Matte, Vase, Brown Iris, Pea Green Matte, Impressed, 12 In. ....*Illus*	805.00
Etched Matte, Vase, White Dogwood Flowers, Pale Green, Tapered Cylinder, Rolled Rim, 7 ⅝ In.	138.00
Etna, Vase, Flowers, Mauve, Green Matte, 10 ¼ In.	40.00
Etna, Vase, Thistle, Gray, Dark Blue Ground, Marked, 10 ¼ In.	230.00
Figurine, Dog, Pop-Eye, Painted Accents, Incised, 10 In. ....*Illus*	1495.00
Figurine, Dog, Pop-Eye, White, Painted Features, Script Mark, 4 ⅛ In. ....*Illus*	288.00
Flemish, Bowl, Basket Shape, Green, 2 Handles, 9 ½ In.	62.00
Flemish, Jardiniere & Pedestal, 31 x 13 In.	563.00
Flemish, Jardiniere, Stylized Red Trees, Green Ground, 7 ½ In.	127.00
Flemish, Vase, Magnolia, Dark Blue Ground, 14 In. ....*Illus*	316.00
Flemish, Vase, Rose, Bow, Yellow Ground, 8 ¾ In.	23.00
Fleron, Vase, Ruffled Rim, Mint Green, Lug Handles, 9 ¾ In.	69.00
Floretta Grape Matte, Tankard, Yellow To Purple, 11 In.	58.00
Forest, Bowl, Embossed Squirrel, Branches, Scalloped Rim, 3 In.	81.00
Foxy Grandpa, Incense Burner, Man, Seated, Wiping Brow, Marked, 4 ½ In.	150.00
Frosted Matte, Vase, Mottled Green & Navy Blue, Shouldered, 14 ½ In.	805.00
Fru Russet, Vase, Holly Leaves, Berries, Green Matte Glaze, Handles, 5 x 5 In.	250.00
Fruitone, Vase, Green To Orange, 9 ½ In.	92.00
Gardenware, Flower Frog, Big Turtle, Lily Pad On Back, Impressed, 9 ¾ In. ....*Illus*	546.00
Gardenware, Pan With Rabbit, Coppertone, Impressed Script Logo, 13 ⅝ In. ....*Illus*	3450.00
Gardenware, Rooster, Red, Turquoise, Yellow, Matte Glaze, Incised, 12 ⅞ In. ....*Illus*	1150.00
Gardenware, Sprinkler, Ducks, 2 Happy Yellow Ducks, Coppertone Mound, Marked, 14 ⅝ In. ...*Illus*	6325.00
Gardenware, Sprinkler, Frog, Coppertone Glaze, Inkstamp, 8 ¼ In. ....*Illus*	2990.00
Glendale, Vase, Green Leaves, Bird, Orange Ground, High Gloss, 5 ¼ x 4 ½ In.	187.00
Greora, Vase, Pair Of Handles Cross Itself, Copper Glaze, Marked, 8 ¾ In.	172.00
Hudson, Vase, Apple Blossoms, Pale Blue Ground, Marked, 5 ½ In.	173.00
Hudson, Vase, Ball, Pink Flowers, Green To Pink Ground, Shoulder Handles, 6 ½ In.	288.00
Hudson, Vase, Cherry Blossoms, Cream Ground, Painted, Cylindrical, 6 ½ x 15 ½ In.	531.00
Hudson, Vase, Flowers, Dark Blue Ground, Cylindrical, 7 ¾ In.	104.00
Hudson, Vase, Flowers, Leaves, Gloss Green, 11 ½ In.	489.00
Hudson, Vase, Flowers, Leaves, Tie Band, Dark Blue Ground, 13 ¾ In.	322.00
Hudson, Vase, Flowers, Leaves, White, Yellow, Triangular, 6 ¼ In.	69.00
Hudson, Vase, Gray To Cream Flowers, Yellow, Green, Impressed Mark, 9 In.	384.00
Hudson, Vase, Iris, Blue Ground, Hester Pillsbury, 15 In.	1150.00
Hudson, Vase, Iris, Blue Ground, Stamped L. Morris, 9 ½ In.	253.00
Hudson, Vase, Lilacs, Leaves, Swollen Cylinder, Flare Rim, Rolled Foot, Blue, Green, Cream, 11 ⅞ In.	219.00
Hudson, Vase, Multicolor Flowers, Landscape, Blue Ground, 7 ½ In.	138.00
Hudson, Vase, Pansies, Green Ground, Cylindrical, 8 ¾ In.	201.00
Hudson, Vase, Perfecto, Pink Flowers, Blue To Pink Ground, Signed Leffler, 12 ½ In.	334.00
Hudson, Vase, Seascape, Ships, Yellow Ground, Round, Shouldered, 8 ½ x 9 ½ In.	1875.00
Hudson, Vase, White Roses, Gray To Pink Ground, Signed H.P., 10 In.	380.00
Hudson, Vase, White, Pink Flowers, Blue Ground, Handles, Signed McLaughlin, Marked, 9 ¾ In.	575.00
Hudson, Vase, Windmill, Sailboats, Blue Ground, McLaughlin, 11 In.	920.00
Hudson, Vase, Yellow Daisies, Blue Ground, Signed Hester Pillsbury, 11 ½ In.	396.00
Hudson, Vase, Yellow Ground, Purple Pansies, Flared, 6 ½ In.	136.00

Weller, Flemish, Vase, Magnolia, Dark Blue Ground, 14 In.
$316.00

Humler & Nolan

Weller, Gardenware, Flower Frog, Big Turtle, Lily Pad On Back, Impressed, 9 ¾ In.
$546.00

Humler & Nolan

Weller, Gardenware, Pan With Rabbit, Coppertone, Impressed Script Logo, 13 ⅝ In.
$3,450.00

Humler & Nolan

TIP
Wind your watch clockwise. Don't wind it while it is on your wrist.

WELLER

W

Weller, Gardenware, Rooster, Red, Turquoise, Yellow, Matte Glaze, Incised, 12 ⅞ In.
$1,150.00

Humler & Nolan

Weller, Gardenware, Sprinkler, Ducks, 2 Happy Yellow Ducks, Coppertone Mound, Marked, 14 ⅝ In.
$6,325.00

Humler & Nolan

Weller, Gardenware, Sprinkler, Frog, Coppertone Glaze, Inkstamp, 8 ¼ In.
$2,990.00

Humler & Nolan

Weller, Lasa, Vase, River Scene, Trees, Clouds, 11 ¼ In.
$633.00

Humler & Nolan

Hudson, Vase, Yellow, Blue Iris, Cylindrical, Signed Hood, 8 ¾ In.		311.00
Hudson, Vase, Yellow, Cream Flowers, Blue Ground, Handles, Pillsbury, 6 In.		334.00
Ivory, Jardiniere, Beige, Carved Squirrels, Branches, Marked, 7 ¼ In.		35.00
Jap Birdimal, Vase, Brown Glaze, Man, Standing, Squeezebag Portrait, 2 ½ x 5 ½ In.		610.00
Jap Birdimal, Vase, Pillow, Geisha, Parasol, Rhead Faience		403.00
Jap Birdimal, Vase, White Bird, Dark Brown, 6 ¼ In.		242.00
Jardiniere, Flowers & Vegetation, Red Ground, Metallic Glaze, Squat, 7 x 8 ½ In.		723.00
Jardiniere, Militaris In Banner, Brown Ground, Tripod Base, Figures, Glazed, 9 ½ x 10 In.		180.00
Jardiniere, On Stand, Ivory, Carved, c.1910, 26 x 11 In.		210.00
Jardiniere, Raised White Classical Figure, Blue Ground, Pink Flower Border, c.1935, 9 ½ In.		189.00
Juno, Vase, Oxblood, Neck Handles, Marked, 7 ¼ x 6 ¼ In.		99.00
Kenova, Bowl, Dragonflies, Wings Spread, Brown On Green Matte, Squat, Rolled Rim, 3 ¼ x 5 ½ In.		345.00
Knifewood, Vase, Daisies, 7 ¼ In.		219.00
Knifewood, Vase, Peacock, Trees, Blue, Brown, Green, 9 ¼ In.		155.00
Knifewood, Vase, Squat, Daisies, 4 ½ In.		98.00
Knifewood, Vase, Squirrels, Brown, Tan, 11 ¼ In.		104.00
Lasa, Vase, Forest, Iridescent Red, Green & Gold, Swollen Cylinder, 6 In.		118.00
Lasa, Vase, Landscape, Palm Trees, Signed, 1920-25, 7 ¼ In.		472.00
Lasa, Vase, Metallic Iridescent, Lake Scene, Summer Trees, Clouds, Signed, 8 ¼ In.		431.00
Lasa, Vase, River Scene, Trees, Clouds, 11 ¼ In.	*Illus*	633.00
Lasa, Vase, Stick, Spread Foot, Slight Flare Rim, Lake, Pine Trees, Red Sky, 7 ⅜ In.		546.00
Lasa, Vase, Sunrise, Gold Tones, Squat Base, Tall Neck, 12 In.		235.00
Lasa, Vase, Trees, Leaves, Lake, Rainbow Iridescent, Cylindrical, Tapered, Spread Foot, Flare Rim, 8 In.		633.00
Lavonia, Bowl, Pink, White, Ribbed, Scalloped, 15 ¼ In.		69.00
Lonhuda, Jardiniere, Flowers, Flared Rim, 6 ¾ In.		23.00
Lotus, Flower Frog, Black Slip, Frog Emerging From Blossom, 2 ¾ In.		256.00
Louella, Vase, Bud, Flowers, Reeded, Scalloped Rim, Tan Ground, 7 ½ In.		35.00
Louwelsa, Candlestick, Chamber, Yellow Flowers, Brown Glaze, Spread Base, Handle, 8 x 5 In.		72.00
Louwelsa, Humidor, Native American, Brown Glaze Ground, Signed Anthony Dunlavy, 5 ½ In.		267.00
Louwelsa, Mug, Painted Face, Brown Glaze, 6 ¾ In.		75.00
Louwelsa, Pedestal, Water Lily, Footed, Dark Brown, 18 In.		75.00
Louwelsa, Pitcher, Monk, Brown Glaze, 5 ½ x 6 In.		156.00
Louwelsa, Tankard, Silver Overlay, Berries, Grapes, Signed E.R., 10 In.		748.00
Louwelsa, Vase, Daffodil, Josephine Imlay, Marked, 8 x 4 ½ In.		210.00
Louwelsa, Vase, Dark Brown, Gold Flower, Handle, Marked, 4 In.		63.00
Louwelsa, Vase, Leaves, Flowers, Eugene Roberts, c.1890, 50 In.		4444.00
Luster, Compote, Purple Glaze, 3-Legged Stick Base, 4 ¼ In.		35.00
Malverne, Vase, Waisted, Applied Green Leaves, Marked, 5 ¾ In.		35.00
Marbleized, Vase, Green, Tan, Tapered, 10 ¼ In.		63.00
Marengo, Vase, Pink, Mauve Flowers, Pale Yellow Ground, 9 In.		265.00
Marvo, Vase, Embossed Leaves, Baluster Shape, 9 x 7 In., Pair		374.00
Matte Ware, Vase, Frosted, Cylindrical, 6 In.		75.00
Matte Ware, Vase, Molded Arrowroot Plant, Swollen, 15 ⅞ In.		633.00
Matte Ware, Vase, White Daisies, Squat, Loop Handles, 3 ¼ x 5 ⅜ In.		150.00
Matte Ware, Wall Pocket, Green, Tapered, 15 In.		184.00
Melrose, Vase, Pink, Applied Twigs, Flowers, Handle, Scalloped Rim, 7 ¼ In.		92.00
Muskota, Bowl, Trio Of White Swans Round Rim, Marked, 7 ⅜ In.		195.00
Muskota, Figure, Dog, Labrador Retriever, Tan Glaze, 5 ½ x 5 x 3 ¼ In.		531.00
Muskota, Flower Frog, Duck, Sitting, 3 Holes, 4 ¾ In.		46.00
Narona, Jardiniere, 2 Cream Classical Figures, Black Ground, 8 ½ In.		81.00
Ollas, Water Bottle, Underplate, Lid, Red, Tan, Pear Shape, Marked, 12 ½ x 8 ¼ In.		14.00
Orris, Flower Frog, Green, 3 ½ In.		17.00
Orris, Vase, Green, Incised Design, Cylindrical, 10 In.		115.00
Pearl, Vase, Swags, Cream Ground, 5 ¾ In.		81.00
Perfecto, Vase, Flowering Thistle, Oval, c.1900, 13 ¼ In.		240.00
Rhead Faience, Vase, Geisha, Seated, Formal Dress, Trees, Squeezebag, Incised, 6 ⅞ In.	*Illus*	460.00
Roma, Basket, Hanging, Garlands, 4 ¼ In.		12.00
Roma, Doorstop, Fruit Basket, Purple, Green, Cream, 9 ¾ In.		58.00
Roma, Vase, Stick Neck, Carved Sides, Base, 13 ¾ In.		81.00
Sicardo, Jardiniere, Marked Airabelle, 2 ¼ In.		75.00
Sicardo, Vase, Clover Design, Metallic Glaze, Iridescent, Tapered, Signed, 3 x 5 In.		305.00
Sicardo, Vase, Clovers, Metallic Glaze, 3 x 5 In.		250.00
Sicardo, Vase, Embossed Green Leaves, Signed, 4 ¾ In.		345.00
Sicardo, Vase, Flowers & Leaves, Green Iridescent, Pink, Yellow, Elongated Oval, Rolled Rim, 8 ⅞ In.		403.00
Sicardo, Vase, Flowers, Iridescent Colors, Smokestack Shape, Marked, 4 ¾ In.		575.00
Sicardo, Vase, Flowers, Iridescent, Gold, Purple, Red & Green, Incised, 4 In.	*Illus*	978.00
Sicardo, Vase, Flowers, Metallic Glaze, Iridescence, Signed, 3 ½ x 10 ½ In.		2074.00
Sicardo, Vase, Gold Slip, Allover Leaves & Flowers, c.1905, 33 In.	*Illus*	7763.00

Sicardo, Vase, Leaves, Dandelion Weed, Rainbow Iridescent, Pear Shape, Signed, 3 ⅛ In. 374.00
Sicardo, Vase, Metallic Luster Glaze, Cylindrical, Flat Collar, Multicolor, Signed, 16 In. 575.00
Sicardo, Vase, Smokestack, 4 Lobes On Rim, Iridescent Glaze, Signed, 5 ⅜ In. 836.00
Sicardo, Vase, Stylized Flowers & Swirls, Metallic Glaze, Tapered, 8 ¾ In. 783.00
Sicardo, Vase, Stylized Flowers, Metallic Glaze, Signed, 10 In. 1700.00
Silvertone, Bowl, Frog, Pink Flowers, Branches, Blue Ground, 12 ¼ In. 121.00
Sydonia, Vase, Wall, 4 Buds, Green, 9 ¾ In. 81.00
Toadstool, Flower Frog, Green, Pink, 4 In. 104.00
Trellis, Wall Pocket, Yellow, Green, Tapered, 11 ½ In. 92.00
Vase, Indian Chief, Baluster, Rolled Rim, Marked, 12 ½ In. 2794.00
Vase, Lily Pads, Frog Heads, Green, Trumpet Shape, Stamp, 11 ½ In. 708.00
Vase, Stylized Flowers, Green Matte Glaze, 2 Handles, 7 In. 425.00
Warwick, Vase, Tree Trunk Shape, Applied Leaves, Marked, 10 ½ In. 17.00
Woodcraft, Muskota, Fisher Boy, Seated, Bucket, Pole, 7 ¼ In. 161.00
Woodcraft, Planter, 3 Foxes, In Tree Trunk, Green, Brown, 5 ½ In. 127.00
Woodcraft, Planter, 3 Foxes, Looking Out From Den, Circular, 4 ⅜ x 7 In. 219.00
Woodcraft, Vase, Apple Tree, Green, Tan, Branches, Leaves, Red Fruit, Stamped, 9 In., Pair 59.00
Woodcraft, Vase, Double Bud, Green, Brown, 6 In. 98.00
Woodcraft, Vase, Fan, 8 ¼ In. 127.00
Woodcraft, Vase, Pillow, 3 Kittens, Tree Trunk, Marked, 5 ½ In. 150.00
Woodcraft, Wall Pocket, Squirrel, Black Slip, Marked, 9 ½ In. 180.00
Woodrose, Vase, Bucket Shape, Rose Blossoms, Black Bands, Marked, 5 ¼ In. ....*Illus* 35.00
Zona, Pitcher, Embossed Leaves, Berries, 6 ¾ In. 23.00
Zona, Pitcher, King Fisher, Branch Handle, 8 ¼ In. 106.00

WEMYSS ware was first made in 1882 by Robert Heron, the owner of Fife Pottery in Kirkaldy, Scotland. Large colorful flowers, hearts, and other symbols were hand painted on figurines, inkstands, jardinieres, candlesticks, buttons, pots, and other items. Fife Pottery closed in 1932. The molds and designs were used by a series of potteries until 1957. In 1985 the Wemyss name and designs were obtained by Griselda Hill. The Wemyss Ware trademark was registered in 1994. Modern Wemyss Ware in old styles is still being made.

Cake Plate, Cabbage Roses, Leaves, 10 In. 208.00
Candlestick, Tapering, Cylindrical, Square Base, Cabbage Rose, c.1910, 11 In., Pair 1012.00
Figurine, Pig, Sitting, Shamrocks, Green, 4 ¼ x 6 ½ In. 739.00
Jug, Canterbury Bells Pattern, 5 ½ In. 42.00
Plate, Cabbage Roses, Leaves, 5 ½ In. 112.00

WESTMORELAND GLASS was made by the Westmoreland Glass Company of Grapeville, Pennsylvania, from 1890 to 1984. The company made clear and colored glass of many varieties, such as milk glass, pressed glass, and slag glass.

Candy Dish, Lamb Cover, Figural, Turquoise, 1940s, 5 x 4 In. 80.00
Dish, Hen On Nest Cover, Milk Glass, Red Head, Triple Marked, 5 In. 29.00

WHEATLEY POTTERY was established in 1880. Thomas J. Wheatley had worked in Cincinnati, Ohio, with the founders of the art pottery movement, including M. Louise McLaughlin of the Rookwood Pottery. Wheatley Pottery was purchased by the Cambridge Tile Manufacturing Company in 1927.

Jardiniere, 4 Handles, Green Matte Glaze, Footed, 15 x 12 In. 475.00
Vase, Cobalt Blue Glaze, Applied Dogwood Flowers, Leaves, Formed Handle, Signed, c.1880, 15 x 12 In. 1375.00
Vase, Leaves, Curdled Matte Green Glaze, Signed, 7 ¼ x 8 In. ....*Illus* 1000.00
Vase, Pillow, Yellow Daisies, 1880, 11 ½ In. 115.00

WHIELDON was an English potter who worked alone and with Josiah Wedgwood in eighteenth-century England. Whieldon made many pieces in natural shapes, like cauliflowers or cabbages, and they are almost always unmarked. Do not confuse it with F. Winkle & Co., which made a dinnerware pattern marked *Whieldon Ware*.

Plate, Tortoiseshell Glaze, Brown, Green, Scalloped, 18th Century, 9 In. 575.00

WILLETS MANUFACTURING COMPANY of Trenton, New Jersey, began work in 1879. The company made belleek in the late 1880s and 1890s in shapes similar to those used by the Irish Belleek factory. It stopped working about 1912. A variety of marks were used, all including the name Willets.

Bowl, Gold Dragon Handles, Belleek, 9 In. 57.00
Bowl, Stand, Dragon Handles, 3 x 5 In. ....*Illus* 120.00

Weller, Rhead Faience, Vase, Geisha, Seated, Formal Dress, Trees, Squeezebag, Incised, 6 ⅞ In.
$460.00

Humler & Nolan

Weller, Sicardo, Vase, Flowers, Iridescent, Gold, Purple, Red & Green, Incised, 4 In.
$978.00

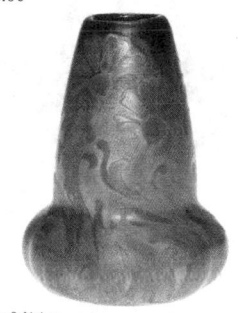

Humler & Nolan

Weller, Sicardo, Vase, Gold Slip, Allover Leaves & Flowers, c.1905, 33 In.
$7,763.00

Humler & Nolan

Weller, Woodrose, Vase, Bucket Shape, Rose Blossoms, Black Bands, Marked, 5 ¼ In.
$35.00

Conestoga Auction Co., Inc.

Wheatley, Vase, Leaves, Curdled Matte Green Glaze, Signed, 7 ¼ x 8 In. $1,000.00

Rago Arts & Auction Center

Willets, Bowl, Stand, Dragon Handles, 3 x 5 In. $120.00

DuMouchelles Art Gallery

Willets, Vase, 6 Peacocks, Multicolor, Fired On Gold, Marked, Belleek, 18 ⅛ In. $1,150.00

Humler & Nolan

Willets, Vase, Art Deco Flowers, Enamel, Dorothea Warren O'Hara, Belleek, 7 x 4 ¾ In. $938.00

Rago Arts & Auction Center

Pitcher, Painted, Monks Making Wine, Tapered, Handle, c.1900, 14 In.	150.00
Vase, 6 Peacocks, Multicolor, Fired On Gold, Marked, Belleek, 18 ⅛ In. ....*Illus*	1150.00
Vase, Art Deco Flowers, Enamel, Dorothea Warren O'Hara, Belleek, 7 x 4 ¾ In. ....*Illus*	938.00
Vase, Painted, Flowers, Pink, Blue, Green, Gold Scrolling Handles, Pedestal Base, c.1900, 18 In.	480.00
Vase, Painted, Pink Flowers, Blue Gray Ground, c.1900, 15 ¾ x 5 ¼ In.	120.00

WILLOW pattern has been made in England since 1780. The pattern has been copied by factories in many countries, including Germany, Japan, and the United States. It is still being made. Willow was named for a pattern that pictures a bridge, birds, willow trees, and a Chinese landscape. Most pieces are blue and white. Some made after 1900 are pink and white.

Bowl, Bakewell Brothers, 5 In.	8.00
Bowl, Ribbed, Flared, Japan, 10 In.	40.00
Bowl, Vegetable, Lid, John Steventon, c.1920, 7 ¾ x 7 ¾ In.	240.00
Butter, Cover, 7 ¾ x 6 ¼ In.	75.00
Canister, Knob Handle, Johnson Brothers, 6 ¾ In.	95.00
Casserole, Lid, Transfer, Handles, Octagonal, 11 ⅝ In.	68.00
Cruet, Oil & Vinegar, Bulbous, Paper Label, Japan, 1900s, 5 ¾ In.	145.00
Cup & Saucer, Fluted, Copeland, Demitasse	55.00
Cup & Saucer, Gilt Trim, Gilman Collamore	75.00
Cup & Saucer, Pink Willow, 4 In.	75.00
Dish, Shell Shape, Scalloped Edge, Royal Albert, 1930s, 5 x 5 In.	45.00
Eggcup, Double, 4 In.	12.00
Ginger Jar, Lid, Shouldered, 1950s, 6 x 4 ¼ In.	48.00
Gravy Boat, 9 ¼ In.	45.00
Grill Plate, 3 Sections, 1920s, 10 ½ In.	12.00
Lamp, Oil, Gilt Base, 11 x 5 ¼ In.	175.00
Napkin Holder, 4 ½ x 4 ½ x 2 In.	42.00
Oil Bottle, Stick Neck, 4 ¾ In.	15.00
Pepper Shaker, Pedestal Style, Flat Top, c.1850, 3 ½ In.	148.00
Pitcher, Ashworth Brothers, c.1910, 6 ¼ In.	54.00
Pitcher, Milk, Enamelware, c.1875, 6 ½ In.	75.00
Plate, Dinner, Churchill, England, 10 ⅜ In.	12.00
Plate, Dinner, Scalloped Rim, 10 In.	25.00
Platter, C.T. Mailing, c.1875	40.00
Platter, English Blue, Oval, 13 x 10 In.	350.00
Platter, Oval, Bourne & Leigh, c.1895, 12 ⅜ x 8 ⅞ In.	60.00
Relish, Diamond Shape, Adderleys, c.1900, 9 ⅝ x 5 ¾ In.	45.00
Salt & Pepper, Barrel Shape, Royal China Co., 1 ¾ x 2 ¼ In.	25.00
Salt & Pepper, Hexagonal, 3 In.	25.00
Soup, Dish, Pink Willow, Homer Laughlin, 1960s, 8 ¼ In.	18.00
Sugar, Lid, Curved Handles, c.1940, 4 ½ In.	20.00
Tankard, Gilt Trim, c.1930, 8 In.	200.00
Teapot, Lid, Royal China Co., c.1945, 10 x 4 In.	72.00
Thimble, Gilt Rim, Staffordshire, England	16.00
Toaster, Electric, 4-Footed, Toastrite	2100.00
Washbasin, Pitcher, c.1835, 4 x 11 In., 9 ½ x 4 ½ In.	338.00

WINDOW glass that was stained and beveled was popular for houses during the late nineteenth and early twentieth centuries. The old windows became popular with collectors in the 1970s; today, old and new examples are seen.

Arts & Crafts, Landscape Scene, Arched, 65 x 14 ½ In.	350.00
Fan, 13 Panes, 1800s, 28 x 45 x 7 ½ In., Pair ....*Illus*	133.00
Fan, 16 Radiuses & Sectioned Panes, 16 x 102 In.	83.00
Fan, Half Round, 13 Panes, 19th Century, 28 x 45 x 7 ½ In.	152.00
Fan, Stained, Jamb Frame, 25 Panes, Blue Slag Glass	212.00
Leaded, Beveled, Blue Rectangular Panels, Red Accented Corners, Gilt Frame, c.1910, 36 x 16 In.	210.00
Leaded, Chevron Design, Wood Frame, Frank Lloyd Wright, 1909, 20 ½ x 37 In., Pair	16250.00
Leaded, Dutch Style, Carved Framed Panels, c.1900, 63 x 20 In., Pair	431.00
Leaded, Oak Frames, 44 ½ x 17 In., 2 Piece	108.00
Leaded, Scrolling Geometric Design, Faceted Jewels Accent, 43 ½ x 23 ⅜ In.	508.00
Leaded, Slag, Cattails, Abstract, Brown, Green, Tan, 25 x 60 In.	232.00
Leaded, Stained, 3 Women, Cloak On Child, Virtue Symbols, c.1865, 29 x 15 ½ In.	240.00
Leaded, Stained, Angel, Cross, Dove, Lilies, Arched Frame, c.1890, 40 x 125 In.	2599.00
Leaded, Stained, Angel, Hovering, 3 Women, c.1880, 144 x 5 ½ In.	1200.00
Leaded, Stained, Angel, Jeweled Crown, Arched, c.1890, 40 x 111 In.	1695.00

Leaded, Stained, Blue, Purple, Green, Yellow, Red, Geometric, 46 x 24 In.		240.00
Leaded, Stained, Fruits, Vegetables, Footed Vase, Frame, c.1920, 26 x 46 In.		420.00
Leaded, Stained, Good Shepherd, Jesus Holding Lamb, 2 Sheep, Crook, 82 x 42 ⅜ In.		1250.00
Leaded, Stained, Purple, Blue, Red, Yellow, Green Abstract, Frame, 10 ¾ x 14 In.		42.00
Leaded, Stained, Scrolling, Acanthus, 1900s, 15 x 49 In.		360.00
Leaded, Stained, Stylized Trees, Topiary, Leafy Lines, 38 ½ x 32 ⅛ In.		1230.00
Leaded, Stained, Tulip, Heart, Frame, Dard Hunter, Roycroft, 1909, 33 ½ x 28 In.	*Illus*	18750.00
Leaded, Wood Frame, Scrolling Leaf, Center Circle 2728, 34 x 25 In.		112.00
Louver, Gothic Arch, Paint, 42 ½ x 40 In., Pair		633.00
Stained, Chief Joseph, Nez Pierce Warrior, Flowers, White Ground, Frame, c.1910, 74 x 48 In.		16500.00
Stained, French Coat Of Arms, Medallion, Rosettes, Leaves, Grotesques, 1800s, 17 ½ In., 4 Piece		1207.00
Stained, Jesus, Holding Lamb, Staff, c.1880, 68 x 36 In.		720.00
Stained, Leaded, Jewel, Vase With Flower, Scrolling, Frame, 29 x 27 In.		141.00
Stained, Leaded, Textured, Beveled Leaves, Branch, c.1900, 54 x 31 ½ In.		475.00
Stained, Leafy Vine, Pink Flowers, Green Purple Ground, Art Nouveau, c.1910, 20 x 22 In.		2963.00
Stained, Slag, 2 Plumes, Yellow, 19 x 32 In.		162.00
Stained, St. George, Rearing White Horse, Germany, c.1860, 9 x 9 ¼ In.		840.00
Stained, Vase, Flower, Jewel On Top, 28 ¾ x 27 In.		141.00
Stained, Vase, Poppies, Red, Green, c.1900, 7 x 10 In.		96.00
Stained, Vertical Vine, Leaves, Daisies, Blue Ribbon, Art Nouveau, 40 x 10 In.		1896.00
Transom, Wood, Arched, 33 Panes, Paint, c.1855, 30 ½ x 59 ½ In.		546.00

WOOD CARVINGS and wooden pieces are listed separately in this book. There are also wooden pieces found in other categories, such as Folk Art, Kitchen, and Tool.

Alligator, Painted, Jointed Tail & Legs, Early 1900s, 29 In.		326.00
Angel, Gilt, Kneeling, Arms Crossed, Hands In Prayer, Italy, 1800s, 15 ¼ In., Pair		1586.00
Angel, Giltwood, Crown, Robes, Wings, Square Base, c.1700, 23 In., Paint		1500.00
Angel, Giltwood, Kneeling, Tasseled Cushion, c.1800, 23 In., Pair		10350.00
Angel, Kneeling, Blue Tunic, Painted, Gilded, Continental, 1800s, 18 ¼ In.	*Illus*	729.00
Angel, Multicolor Paint, Rectangular Plinth, c.1790, 44 In.		4688.00
Angel, Standing, Paint, c.1880, 49 x 15 In.		1440.00
Angel, Wings, Red, Blue, Gold Paint, c.1850, 14 ¾ In.		273.00
Armrest, Hardwood, 3 Supports, Carved, Chinese, c.1850, 13 x 5 In.		1265.00
Bacchic Putto, Pine, Cluster Of Grapes, Chalice, Pedestal Base, 61 In.		875.00
Bag Stamp, Reversed Letters, Herman Long, Hearts, Painted, Pa., c.1860, 5 ¼ In.		1580.00
Baltimore Oriole, Orange, Black Paint, Wood Stump, c.1910, 7 ¾ In.		1033.00
Bass, Painted, Mounted, Pine Oval Board, Lawrence C. Irvine, 1970s, 22 In.		1150.00
Bass, Striped, Glass Eyes, Iron, Wood Base, 18 In.		118.00
Baton, Turned, Tapered, Red, White, Blue, Painted, Gilt Ball Finial, 54 In.		5938.00
Bear, Black Forest, Glass Eyes, 5 ½ In., Pair		492.00
Bear, Black Forest, Standing, Outstretched Forearms, Glass Eyes, 1800s, 41 x 44 In.		920.00
Bear, Standing Upright, c.1920, 10 ¼ In.		130.00
Bear, Standing, Black Forest, Open Mouth, Switzerland, c.1890, 35 ½ In.	*Illus*	1610.00
Bear, Standing, Open Mouth, Staff, Chainsaw, Carved, c.1985, 37 In.		127.00
Bear, Standing, Walnut, Red Tongue, Teeth, c.1900, 7 In.		356.00
Bird, Giltwood, In Flight, Draped Sash, 15 ½ In.		375.00
Bird, Green, Orange Paint, c.1890, 5 ¼ In.		365.00
Bird, Maple, Cream, Black, Paint, Perched On Acorn Finial, Conn., 1869, 8 ½ In., Pair		10073.00
Birds, Bamboo Leaves, Giltwood, Hook, Pole Mount, 81 In.		446.00
Bison, Cut Tree Base, Polish, Inscription, Paper Label, c.1950		71.00
Blue Jay, Wire Legs, Blue Paint, Wood Perch, c.1925, 8 ⅞ In.		948.00
Bowl, Spalted Maple, Rounded Sides, Edward Moulthrop, 9 ½ x 15 In.		590.00
Bracket, Beech, Cherub, S-Scroll Design, Shelf, France, c.1800, 49 x 44 In.		2689.00
Brook Trout, Plaque, Leaping, Painted, 1900s, 75 In.		230.00
Brushpot, 8 Immortals, Bamboo, Squared, Rosewood Base & Lip, Chinese, 10 ¾ In.		492.00
Brushpot, Bamboo, Carved, Herons Feeding, Cylindrical, Chinese, 5 ¾ In.		236.00
Brushpot, Bamboo, Pierced, Immortal Holding Lamp, 2 Cranes, Mountains, 1900s, 8 ½ In.		338.00
Brushpot, Rosewood, 2 Lotus Leaves, Stems, Buds, Pods, Immortals, Cresting Waves, 1800s, 9 In.		1045.00
Buddha, Gold Leaf, Jeweled Red Stones, Mirrors, Black Painted Base, Hands Move, Thailand, 47 In.		720.00
Buddha, Laughing, Seated, Open Robes, Holding Cup, Zitan, Chinese, 7 ¼ x 9 In.		1195.00
Buddha, Reclining, Robed, Carved Couch, Dragon Pierced Back, Paw Feet, 1900s, 22 In.		676.00
Buddha, Robed, Holding Pearl Of Wisdom, Seated On Lotus Throne, Waves, 1900s, 22 ½ In.		738.00
Bull, Fruitwood, Stamped, Franz Hagenauer, Austria, 1930s, 4 x 11 In.	*Illus*	1625.00
Bust, Caesar, Walnut, Carved, Inscribed Thuma, 23 ½ In.		150.00
Bust, Man, Mahogany, Hat, Jacket, Metal Tack Buttons, Glass Eyes, 1800s, 6 ¾ x 4 ⅝ In.		1659.00

Window, Fan, 13 Panes, 1800s, 28 x 45 x 7 ½ In., Pair
$133.00

Conestoga Auction Co., Inc.

Window, Leaded, Stained, Tulip, Heart, Frame, Dard Hunter, Roycroft, 1909, 33 ½ x 28 In.
$18,750.00

Rago Arts & Auction Center

Wood Carving, Angel, Kneeling, Blue Tunic, Painted, Gilded, Continental, 1800s, 18 ¼ In.
$729.00

Skinner, Inc.

The edited listings of the current prices in this *Kovels' Antiques & Collectibles Price Guide* aren't available on any website. Readers can visit **Kovels.com** to check thousands of past prices and sign up for free information on trends, tips, reproductions, marks, and more.

W

Wood Carving, Bear, Standing, Black Forest, Open Mouth, Switzerland, c.1890, 35 ½ In.
$1,610.00

James D. Julia Auctioneers

Wood Carving, Bull, Fruitwood, Stamped, Franz Hagenauer, Austria, 1930s, 4 x 11 In.
$1,625.00

Rago Arts & Auction Center

Wood Carving, Eagle, Spread Wings, 4 Arrows, Gilt Gesso, c.1890, 24 x 17 In.
$4,410.00

Skinner, Inc.

Wood Carving, Letter H, Painted, Gilded, Mica Flakes, Recessed Flowers, c.1890, 18 x 21 ½ In.
$1,185.00

Skinner, Inc.

Wood Carving, Man, Emaciated, Seated, Loose Robe, Chinese, 1800s, 4 ¾ In.
$6,518.00

Skinner, Inc.

Wood Carving, Native Figure, Guanacastle, Rope, Edwin & Mary Scheier, Signed, 1968, 29 x 19 In.
$10,000.00

Rago Arts & Auction Center

Wood Carving, Plaque, Eagle, Don't Give Up The Ship, Flag, John Haley Bellamy, 28 x 9 ¾ In.
$518.00

James D. Julia Auctioneers

Wood Carving, Plaque, Whale, Painted, Signed, Impressed CV Voorhees, Vermont, c.1960, 6 x 18 In.
$2,489.00

Skinner, Inc.

Wood Carving, Ruyi, Scepter, Figures, Pine Trees, Clouds, Incised Characters, Chinese, c.1900, 14 In.
$100.00

Skinner, Inc.

Wood Carving, Sheaf Of Wheat, Relief, Gilt, Half Round, 1800s, 10 ½ x 9 In.
$1,304.00

Skinner, Inc.

Bust, William Shakespeare, Mahogany, Mounted, Carved Base, 1800s, 6 ½ In.	2370.00
Bust, Woman, Walnut, Turned Pedestal, Platform Base, Luisa Depp, 1800s, 7 ¼ In.	118.00
California Quail, Male, Grassy Terrain, Glass Dome, c.1900, 14 x 11 In.	230.00
Cat, Seated, Black Paint, c.1915, 11 ¾ In.	1067.00
Cherub Head, Walnut, On Panel, Scrolling Leaves, c.1900, 32 x 15 In.	330.00
Chickadee, On Driftwood Base, Painted, Signed James Lapham, Life Size	708.00
Chickadee, Perched On Rock, Brown, Yellow, Signed, J.B., c.1947, 1 ⅞ In.	385.00
Church Model, Steeple, Fitted Interior, Painted, 43 ½ In.	119.00
Cigar Box, Terrier Shape, Hinged Head, Googly Eyes, Italy, c.1870, 8 In.	270.00
Cigarette Dispenser, Goldfinch Perched On Barrel, Painted, c.1910, 5 ¼ x 8 ¼ In.	89.00
Corpus Christi, Wood, Gesso, Spain, c.1800, 41 x 32 In.	885.00
Cupid, Arm Raised, Gold Wings & Short Pants, Plinth, 37 In., Pair	938.00
Curtain Panels, For Hearse, Painted, 1800s, 42 ½ x 19 ½ In., Pair	593.00
Dancing Couple, Black Forest, Square Plinth, Germany, 10 In.	60.00
Deer, Standing, Black Forest, Switzerland, c.1880, 28 x 19 In., Pair	2933.00
Dog, Old Silver Radiator Paint, Rectangular Base, 11 In.	443.00
Dog, Spaniel, Standing, Red Brown Paint, Wilhelm Schimmel, c.1885, 2 ½ x 4 ¼ In.	13035.00
Dog, Whippet, Seated, Silver Leaf Collar, Tail Up, Gold Leaf Finish, Gilt, c.1900, 31 x 17 In.	615.00
Dove, Glass Eyes, Standing On Base, Stamped Signature, Frank Finney, 4 ½ In.	470.00
Duck, Mallard, Drake, Head Turned, Painted, Paul Gibson, 1978, 13 In.	565.00
Duck, Preening, c.1910, 4 ⅜ In.	24.00
Duck, Redhead, Standing, Painted, Rock Shaped Base, Signed, J.B., c.1965, 3 ½ In.	652.00
Eagle, Flag Plaque, Paint, Gilt, Pa., 54 In.	5546.00
Eagle, Flapping Wings, Standing, On Craggy Base, 17 x 18 In.	472.00
Eagle, Gesso Paint, Signed, PL Libbey, 72 x 17 In.	19550.00
Eagle, Half Round, Spread Wings, Pedestal, Gilded, c.1875, 42 x 23 x 12 In.	1659.00
Eagle, In Flight, Giltwood, 18 x 21 ½ In.	566.00
Eagle, Louisburg, Spread Wings, Shield, Gilded, Painted, Artistic Carving Co., 44 In.	3422.00
Eagle, Mahogany, Mirrored Crest, c.1900, 8 In.	176.00
Eagle, Pine On Orb, c.1910, 42 ½ In.	2844.00
Eagle, Pine, Plaque, c.1900, 22 In.	711.00
Eagle, Pine, Primitive, Whitewash, Round Base, c.1950, 33 In.	207.00
Eagle, Pine, Spread Wings, Banner, W. Zollman, 1978, 12 x 33 ½ In.	546.00
Eagle, Semi-Spread Wings, Gilded, Rocky Outcrop Base, c.1830, 17 x 30 In.	1610.00
Eagle, Shield, American Flags, Banner, Union Now & Forever, Scroll Leaf Border, Painted, 13 x 65 In.	2640.00
Eagle, Shield, Arrows, Paint, Hanging Mount, c.1910, 18 x 29 In.	633.00
Eagle, Shield, Gilt Gesso, On Plaque, c.1895, 19 x 40 ½ In.	7110.00
Eagle, Spread Wings, 4 Arrows, Gilt Gesso, c.1890, 24 x 17 In. ....*Illus*	4410.00
Eagle, Spread Wings, Black Paint, Gilt Talons, c.1890, 26 x 39 In.	972.00
Eagle, Spread Wings, Delineated Head, Talons, Gilded, Plaque, c.1900, 9 x 23 ½ In.	1007.00
Eagle, Spread Wings, On Branch, Brown Stain, c.1890, 36 ¾ x 15 In.	978.00
Eagle, Spread Wings, On Perch, Giltwood, 12 ½ x 29 In.	3540.00
Eagle, Spread Wings, Perched On Rocks, Glass Outs, Walnut, c.1895, 23 x 16 In.	2252.00
Eagle, Spread Wings, Perched On Tree Trunk, c.1900, 17 x 14 ½ In.	1265.00
Eagle, Spread Wings, Scrolled Acanthus Leaves, Gilded, Plaque, 1800s, 18 x 47 In.	3081.00
Eagle, Spread Wings, Shield Crest, Mahogany, Carved, Painted, c.1890, 43 x 96 In.	8888.00
Eagle, Spread Wings, Shield, Arrow, Oak, Rocky Plinth, Phil., c.1850, 22 x 32 In.	4029.00
Eagle, Standing, Pine, Art Deco, c.1900, 9 ¾ In.	118.00
Eagle, Union Shield, Relief Carved, Painted Gold, 1800s, 43 x 70 In.	6518.00
Egret, Standing, White Paint, Flat Body, Glass Eyes, Wire Legs, Driftwood Base, c.1940, 22 In.	1659.00
Ewe, Modernist, Leo Gervais, 4 ¼ x 7 In.	173.00
Finial, Pine, Pineapple Shape, Socle Base, 21 In.	826.00
Fishmonger, Holding Fish, Japan, 20th Century, 16 ¾ In.	213.00
Flask, Painted, Roses, Leaves, Pinsk Monastery, Russia, 1915, 12 ¾ x 7 ½ In.	120.00
Foo Dog, Pups Climbing On Adult, Red & Gilt Paint, Shaped Base, 1900s, 12 In., Pair	399.00
Fox, Walking, Leg Raised, Painted, 19 x 30 In.	660.00
Frog, Crouching, Upturned Head, Paint, Green, 10 ½ x 26 In.	154.00
Fruit Basket, Mahogany, Wood Base, 1800s, 9 ½ x 10 ¾ In.	1541.00
Fruit Basket, Pineapple, Grapes, Plums, Pears, Cherries, Ribbon, Pine, c.1835, 17 x 14 In.	492.00
Gabriel, Trumpet, Wings, Flying, Iron Stand, 28 x 31 In.	615.00
Gentleman, Top Hat, Tails, Paint, Ley, Windup, Whistler, Germany, 15 In.	495.00
God Of Longevity, Small Companion, Rootwood, Ivory Inlays, Chinese, 16 ¾ In.	259.00
Goddess, Riding Running Fox, Holding Water Buckets, Paint, Japan, 17 ½ x 22 In.	403.00
Goldfinch, Paint, Scratch Feather, Perched, Rock Shaped Base, Signed, J.B., Number, c.1965, 2 ¾ In.	510.00
Gong Stand, Dragons, Clouds, Suspended Metal Gong, 21 x 17 In.	180.00
Good Shepard, Santo, Painted, 17 ¾ In.	239.00

Wooden, Bowl, Ash Burl, Turned, 19th Century, 17 ½ In.
$2,468.00

Garth's Auctioneers + Appraisers

Wooden, Bowl, Elm Burl, Turned, Patina, c.1800s, 10 ¾ x 3 ½ In.
$236.00

Conestoga Auction Co., Inc.

Wooden, Clock Dial, Painted Noah's Ark Scene, Inscription, S. Hoadley, Plymouth, c.1810, 16 x 12 In.
$1,067.00

Skinner, Inc.

Wooden, Firkin, Lid, Pine, Copper Tacks, Wooden Pegs, Hingham, 3 x 2 ⅞ In.
$936.00

Willis Henry Auctions, Inc.

W

Wooden, Firkin, Lid, Pine, Green Paint, Stamped, C. Wilder & Son, So. Hingham, Mass., 1800s, 10 x 9 In. $1,053.00

Willis Henry Auctions, Inc.

Wooden, Propeller, Airplane, Sinsinich Bros., HP 35, RPM 2550, Marked, 72 In. $748.00

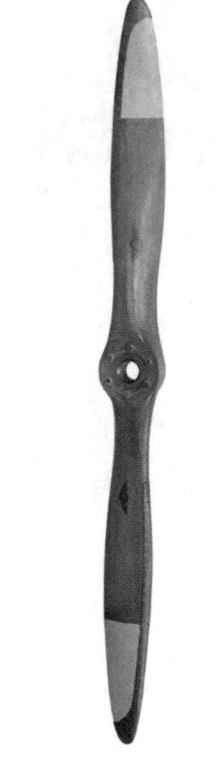

Victorian Casino Antiques

Worcester, Basket, Openwork, Flowers, Twisted Handles, Dr. Wall, 9 ¼ In. $469.00

Leslie Hindman Auctioneers

Grosbeak, Rose Breasted, Perched On Rock Shaped Base, Painted, Signed, J.B., No. 32, c.1965, 2 ½ In.	1080.00
Grotto, Painted Religious Scenes, 3 Niches, Mexico, 42 x 26 In.	240.00
Group, 3 Men Singing, Painted, Jailhouse Carvers, 5 ¼ x 5 ½ In.	504.00
Group, Boy & Girl, Playing With Ball, Boxwood, Base, c.1960, 4 x 7 In.	735.00
Group, Britannia, Standing, Lion In Chains, Painted, 11 ½ In.	649.00
Guanyin, Standing, Loose Robes, Holding Hand Up, Mudra Blessing, Lotus Base, 1900s, 33 ½ In.	922.00
Hand, Outstretched, Gilt, Red Stain, 19 In.	649.00
Head, Grotesque Face, Hat, Eyes Closed, Open Mouth, Display Stand, Square Base, 9 ½ In.	575.00
Headrest, Taoist, Heavenly Twins, Pigment On Lips, 1940s, 8 ½ x 4 x 5 In., Pair	104.00
Horse Head, Bridle, Painted, c.1900, 16 In.	1003.00
Horse, Applied Tin Ears, Mane, Pieced Legs, Horsehair Tail, 8 ¼ x 11 ½ In.	266.00
Horse, Flying, Carved, Painted Gray Dapple, Yellow Glass Eyes, Saddle, Bridle, 28 x 50 In.	1180.00
Horse, Horsehair Mane & Tail, Oval Base, c.1905, 9 ½ x 9 ½ In.	273.00
Horse, Prancing, Pine, Plinth Base, Painted, Gilt, 14 ½ x 12 ½ In.	397.00
Horse, Standing, Black, Red Paint, Pa., 5 ½ x 7 ¾ In.	1337.00
Horse, Standing, Chestnut Brown, Saddle, Reins, Base, c.1890, 33 x 34 In.	16590.00
House Wren, Perched, Rock Shaped Base, Signed, J.B., c.1965, 3 ⅛ In.	889.00
Hummingbird, In Flight, Feathers, Painted, c.1990, 5 In.	711.00
Hummingbird, Ruby Throat, On Perch, Painted, Jess Blackstone, No. 3, c.1950, 4 ⅜ In.	840.00
Immortals, Chained Foo Dogs, Rosewood, Glass Eyes, 1800s, 13 In, Pair.	215.00
Indian Warrior, Standing, Holding Spear, Paint, c.1890, 19 ¼ In.	444.00
John The Baptist, Baroque, Paint, 39 x 13 In.	1112.00
Kuan Ti, God Of War, Lacquer, Chinese, 1800s, 9 ¼ In.	215.00
Kylin, Standing, Backward Glancing, Gilt, Red Lacquer, 10 x 14 ¼ In.	2530.00
Lake Trout, Painted, Mounted, Simulated Birch Oval Board, Lawrence C. Irvine, c.1974, 34 In.	2588.00
Letter H, Painted, Gilded, Mica Flakes, Recessed Flowers, c.1890, 18 x 21 ½ In. ....*Illus*	1185.00
Lion, Fruitwood, Resting On Plinth, Mounted On Base, England, 1900s, 6 x 7 ½ In.	184.00
Lion, Guardian, Zitan, Glass Eyes, Ivory Teeth, 1800s, 24 ½ In., Pair	1955.00
Lion, Resting, Oval Base, Paint, 1800s, England, 12 ½ In.	1750.00
Lion, Roaring, Teeth Exposed, Painted, Inscribed Karl Stoltz, York, Pa., 1892, 10 In.	1659.00
Madonna & Child, Paint, Gilt, Italy, 7 In.	302.00
Madonna, Child, Germany, c.1920, 16 ½ In.	210.00
Madonna, Child, Gothic Style, Germany, 26 In.	1320.00
Madonna, Child, Pointing To Heart, Deep Folds, Paint, 1800s, 48 In.	865.00
Man In The Moon, Smiling, Oak, Beech, High Relief, Big Cheeks, 3 Sections, 41 x 34 In.	3738.00
Man, Asian, Fishing Net, 54 In.	480.00
Man, Bull, Signed Alb. Huggler, Swiss, c.1950, 14 ¾ x 17 ¾ In.	1185.00
Man, Elderly, Long Flowing Beard, 2 Side Knots, Partially Robed, Holding Leaf, 1900s, 18 ½ In.	215.00
Man, Emaciated, Seated, Loose Robe, Chinese, 1800s, 4 ¾ In. ....*Illus*	6518.00
Man, Lying On Back, Raised Platform, Papua New Guinea, 7 ½ x 18 ½ In.	123.00
Man, Scrolled Paper In Hand, Period Attire, Paint, White Pine, c.1820, 38 In.	4650.00
Mask, Pine, Face, Frilled Collar, Paint, c.1850, 13 ½ x 27 In.	948.00
Mermaid, Reclining, Painted, Carved, 48 In.	2714.00
Milkmaid, Standing, Wearing Yoke, Buckets, Ivory, 1800s, 4 ⅜ In.	296.00
Model, Eiffel Tower, Fruitwood, Stained, France, c.1930, 49 ¾ In.	875.00
Model, Stagecoach, Diamond Tally-Ho, Red, Yellow, Black Paint, 12 ¾ x 31 In.	1304.00
Monkey, Peach, Boxwood, Japan, 1800s, 2 ½ In.	184.00
Monkey, Standing, Wearing Dress, Glass Eyes, Square Base, 22 ½ In.	3000.00
Monkey, Teak, Long Arms, Denmark, 1950s, 18 x 19 In.	4375.00
Mountain Goats, Black Forest, J. Baud, Switzerland, 1800s, 18 x 9 In.	1610.00
Napoleon, Hat With Plume, Rifle, Sword, Arms Extend, Square Base, Pull Tab, 1800s, 21 In.	625.00
Native Figure, Guanacastle, Rope, Edwin & Mary Scheier, Signed, 1968, 29 x 19 In. ......*Illus*	10000.00
Nut Dish, Carved Oak Leaf & Acorn, 2 Squirrel Handles, 1900s, 5 x 16 ½ x 10 ½ In.	1062.00
Nuthatch, Painted, Scratch Feather, Perched On Branch, Signed, JB, Numbered, c.1835, 3 ⅛ In.	840.00
Ostrich, Pine, Painted, Oval Base, 9 ½ In.	563.00
Owl, Barn, Painted, Mounted On Driftwood, Wood Base, Stamped, 1950, 5 ¼ In.	796.00
Owl, Great Snowy, Paint, Signed Skinner, 33 ¼ In.	3068.00
Owl, Mouse, Wire Feet, c.1900, 11 In.	767.00
Owl, Painted, Perched On Branch, Round Base, Enoch Benner, c.1890, 8 ⅜ In.	1140.00
Owl, Perched On Pole, Gray, Mottled, Black, Red Paint, c.1850, 12 ¼ In.	1659.00
Owl, Snowy, Painted, Yellow Glass Eyes, Mounted On Tree Stump, 1900s, 21 In.	1610.00
Painted, Cocked Hat, Holding Scabbard, Square Base, Marcel Clesinger, c.1800, 15 ¾ In.	1188.00
Panel, Western Landscape, Cowboy, Log Cabin, Multicolor Paint, 32 x 47 In.	294.00
Parrot, Pueblo, Rio Grande, Black Stand, c.1895, 4 x 9 In.	1116.00
Parrot, Standing, Pine, Green, Brown, Black Painted, c.1890, 14 In.	1896.00
Penguin, Painted, Black, White, Charles Hart, Gloucester, Mass., 6 ½ In.	708.00

W

Pheasant, Yellow, Orange, Blue, Green Paint, Base, c.1910	948.00
Phoenix, Giltwood, Perched, Fruit Festoon, c.1865, 18 x 7 ½ In., Pair.........	1476.00
Pigeon, Painted, c.1900, 5 ¼ In..........	668.00
Pigeon, Painted, Glass Eyes, Cast Iron Bill, Delineated Wings, Stand, c.1895, 11 ½ x 12 ½ In.	415.00
Plaque, Bull's Head, Black Forest, c.1890, 13 ½ In.	2430.00
Plaque, Clenched Fist, Fabric Knot, Pine, 1800s, 9 ¼ x 18 ¼ In.	385.00
Plaque, Coat-Of-Arms, Giltwood, Rampant Lions, Swags, England, 24 ½ x 17 ½ In......	944.00
Plaque, Deer Head, White Tailed, 8-Point Rack, Branches, c.1900, 27 ½ x 16 ½ In.	3555.00
Plaque, Dog's Head, Collar, Scrolled Leaves, Flowers, Scroll Border, c.1895, 10 x 8 In.	2489.00
Plaque, Eagle, Don't Give Up The Ship, Flag, John Haley Bellamy, 28 x 9 ¾ In. ....*Illus*	518.00
Plaque, Eagle, Pine, Clutching Shield, Brace Of Arrows, Gilding, Paint, Plaque, 26 In..........	295.00
Plaque, Eagle, Spread Wings, Clutching Flag, Banner, Painted, Peter Libbey Westbrook, 60 In..	9480.00
Plaque, Fox Head, Carved, Painted, c.1880, 8 ¼ In.	486.00
Plaque, George Washington, Profile, Giltwood, c.1885, 16 In.	1185.00
Plaque, Gold Leaf Decoration, Birds, Flowering Branches, Thailand, 16 x 12 In.	270.00
Plaque, Painted, Partially Furled American Flag, 16 5-Point Stars, c.1880, 20 x 7 ½ In.	978.00
Plaque, Pine, House, In Woods, Signed Rupert P. Kreider, Frame, 9 ¾ x 31 In.	2015.00
Plaque, Quail, Paint, Oval, c.1920, 14 ¼ In..........	148.00
Plaque, Relief, Gilded, Chinese, 20th Century, 18 x 11 ½ In..........	243.00
Plaque, St. Sebastian, Tied To Tree, Loincloth, Molded Frame, 1800s, 11 x 6 ¼ In..........	173.00
Plaque, Whale, Humpback, Black & White Paint, Signed, C. Voorhees, c.1965, 5 x 18 In.	1920.00
Plaque, Whale, Killer, Black & White Paint, Signed, Voorhees, c.1965, 7 ¼ x 18 ¼ In..............	5206.00
Plaque, Whale, Narwhal, Horn, White Paint, Tan, Mottled, Design, Signed, C. Voorhees, c.1965, 23 In.	3600.00
Plaque, Whale, Painted, Signed, Impressed CV Voorhees, Vermont, c.1960, 6 x 18 In. .....*Illus*	2489.00
Plaque, Whale, Sperm, Black Paint, Signed, Voorhees, 1900s, 6 x 17 ¼ In.	2844.00
Plaque, Whale, Sperm, Mouth Open, Black, Paint, Clark Voorhees, Signed, c.1965, 6 ¼ x 17 ½ In.	3318.00
Plaque, Wire Inlaid Hardwood, Carved Immortal, Coiled Dragon, Japan, c.1890, 31 x 22 In...	1300.00
Punch, Red Suit, Hat, Black Buckle Shoes, 57 In..........	600.00
Rooster, Standing, Pine, Wilhelm Schimmel, Cumberland Valley, Pa., 8 ½ In..........	3658.00
Ruyi Scepter, Figures, Pine Trees, Clouds, Incised Characters, Chinese, c.1900, 14 In. ...*Illus*	100.00
Ruyi Scepter, High Relief, Flowering Plum Braches, Chinese, 1800s, 13 ¾ In.	1498.00
Ruyi Scepter, Monkeys & Peaches, Chinese, Agalwood, 15 ⅞ In.	7110.00
Sailor, Telescope, Hat Inscribed H.M.S. Glasgow, 2 Shelves, Paint, c.1900, 28 In.	2015.00
Saint, Bishop, Holding Bible, Bearded, Baroque, Painted, 54 x 21 In.	2223.00
Saint, Man, Kneeling On One Knee, Pointing To Thigh Wound, Paint, 27 x 12 In.	1872.00
Saint, Woman, Multicolor, Germany, c.1690, 34 ¼ In.	3750.00
Saint, Woman, Oak, Crown, Rhine Valley, 34 ¼ In......	1750.00
Salmon, Oak Board Mount, Painted, Caught Isle Of Mull, 1914, 18 x 43 In..........	2875.00
Santo, Madonna, Metal Halo, Paint, 28 x 13 In.	863.00
Santo, Saint, Bone Hands, Paint, 27 In..........	489.00
Scroll Weight, 2 Dragons, Flaming Pearl, Scrolling Border, Chinese, 1800s, 13 In.	2309.00
Scroll Weight, Sandalwood, Tree Branch, Squirrel, Grapevine, Clusters, 11 In., Pair..........	676.00
Sea Gull, White Paint, c.1930, 19 In., Pair	1364.00
Sea Gull, White, Black & White Wings, Yellow Beak, Octagonal Base, 15 ½ In.	561.00
Seahorse, White Paint, New Jersey, 14 ½ x 26 In.	354.00
Sheaf Of Wheat, Relief, Gilt, Half Round, 1800s 10 ½ x 9 In. ......*Illus*	1304.00
Shelf, Figural, King Of Hearts, Painted, Peter Hunt, 33 ¾ In......	550.00
Shield, Armorial, Painted, Washington, D.C., 19 ½ In......	4484.00
Shield, Walnut, Relief, Scrolls, 35 x 22 In..........	1062.00
Smoking Stand, Figural, Draped Woman, 26 In..........	71.00
Snake, Coiled, Blue Paint, c.1900..........	948.00
Snipe, Shorebird, Boomerang Shape, Iron Nail Bill, Metal Stand, Painted, c.1900, 12 x 9 In...	4740.00
Snowflake, Geometric, Gold, White, Red Paint, John Scholl, Pa., 31 In......	17775.00
Song Bird, Wood Mount, Red, Black, Yellow Paint, c.1890, 7 ½ In......	207.00
Squirrel, Seated, Eating Nut, Wood Base, c.1900, 4 ½ In.	735.00
St. Ann, Holding Mary, Green Robes, Paint, 73 In..........	1670.00
St. Francis, Bird In Hand, 9 In..........	40.00
Stag, Reclining, Painted, 13 ½ x 11 ½ In..........	153.00
Steer Head, Walnut Plaque, Incised Scrolling Flowers, H. Leach, Boston, 1869, 19 x 17 In.	3450.00
Swallow Nest, Confidence, Poplar, Carved, Painted, Pa., c.1900, 4 ½ x 5 In..........	711.00
Swan, White, Black Paint, c.1905, 22 x 28 In.	1659.00
Swordfish, 2-Sided, Indigo, Teal, c.1910, 84 x 37 In..........	1438.00
Tabernacle, Giltwood, Columns, Swags, c.1820, 53 x 34 In..........	1320.00
Tavern Scene, Woman, 9 Men, Dog, Painted, Glass Case, Jailhouse Carvers, c.1930, 11 x 19 In. ...	3555.00
Temple, Doric Columns, Domed Roof, Gilt Pinecone Finial, Stepped Round Base, 25 x 16 In..	1845.00
Tiger, Orange, Black Paint, c.1900, 6 x 10 ½ In..........	2252.00

Worcester, Coffeepot, Lid, Rock Strata, Coastal Landscape, Blue, Crescent Mark, c.1770-75, 9 ½ In.
$296.00

Skinner, Inc.

Worcester, Jug, Cabbage Leaf & Mask, Flower Sprays, Molded Body, c.1785, 8 ¾ In.
$182.00

Skinner, Inc.

World War II, Box, Adolf, Pig Bank, Save & Make Him Squeal, Tom Lamb, Otis-Lawson, N.Y., 4 x 6 In.
$230.00

Hake's Americana & Collectibles

TIP

Do not wrap or store scrapbooks in anything made of PVC plastic or vinyl.

W

World War II, Cup & Saucer, Adolf Hitler, Transfer, Porcelain, 3 ½ In. $144.00

The Stein Auction Co.

World War II, Pin, Remember Pearl Harbor, Rebus, Simulated Pearl, Sterling Silver, Embossed Letters, 2 ¼ In. $95.00

Hake's Americana & Collectibles

World War II, Pin, Remember Pearl Harbor, Red, White, Blue, American Flag, 3 ½ In. $174.00

Hake's Americana & Collectibles

World War II, Poster, Bits Of Careless Talk, Hand, Swastika Ring, Puzzle, Stevan Dohanos, 20 x 28 In. $173.00

Hake's Americana & Collectibles

Toad, Inset Glass Eyes, Marked Japan, 3 ½ x 8 In.	1600.00
Tortoise, Diamond Pattern On Back, Painted, c.1905, 3 ¾ x 7 ¾ In.	1154.00
Tray, Green & Black Paint, Cedar Staves, Knuckle Handles, Oval, 1800s, 4 ⅞ x 15 ½ x 25 In.	2280.00
Trophy, Center Shield, Bladed Weapons, 38 ½ In.	1250.00
Trout, Jumping, On Panel, Stained, Integral Frame, c.1900, 16 ¾ x 23 In.	1185.00
Turkey, Tom, Paint, Oval Wood Base, Signed James Lapham, Miniature	443.00
Turtle Dove, Mahogany, Sliding Compartment Base, 5 x 11 ½ In.	201.00
Urn, Gilt, Neoclassical, Leaf, Lion Mask Carved, Rings, Square Plinth, 15 In.	688.00
Virgin Mary, Standing, Wearing Robes, Fruitwood, 1800s, 25 In.	177.00
Warbler, Perched On Rock, Black & Blue, Signed, Jess Blackstone, c.1965, 2 In.	1007.00
Watch Hutch, 2 Soldiers, Holding Nest, Eagle, Germany, 1800s, 12 x 8 In.	237.00
Whale, Sperm, Wood Stand, Signed, Robert J. Innis, Cape Cod, 11 ¾ In.	325.00
Whale, Tail Up, Mouth Open, Painted, Clark Voorhees, 35 ¾ In.	4366.00
Wine Cooler, William IV, Giltwood, Mahogany, Flowers, Leaves, Tapered, Metal Liner, 23 x 40 In.	2691.00
Woman Warming Herself, Seated, Long Dress, Square Base, A. Cornu, c.1890, 28 ½ x 26 ½ In.	1830.00
Woman, Nude, Hands To Breasts, Square Base, Signed, Saleh, 23 In.	82.00
Woman, Princess Zhaojun, Bamboo Root, Holding Lute, Wrapped In Bamboo, 29 In.	5175.00
Woman, Victorian, Standing, Hand Out, 40 In.	128.00
Woman's Torso, Head, Silver Hair, Art Deco, 10 ½ x 27 In.	173.00
Woodpecker, Green, Red Paint, Bark Base, George Miller, Pa., c.1890, 5 x 11 ½ In.	2309.00
Woodsman, Carrying Barrel, Vine Staff, Fruitwood, Silver Base, Sweden, c.1850, 10 In.	1610.00
Wrist Rest, Rosewood, Bamboo, Figure, Lake, Pavilions, Bridge, Pagoda, Mountains, c.1915, 10 In.	307.00
Wrist Rest, Zitan, Stem, Cluster Of Bamboo, Leaves, Poem, Chinese, 2 ½ x 10 ¼ In.	276.00
Yellow Kid, Lift Cane, Hat Tips, Metal, Cloth, 10 ¼ In.	3600.00
Yellowlegs, Driftwood Base, Paint, Signed James Lapham, Ma., Miniature	472.00
Zhongkui Demon Queller, Stag Antler, Standing On Waves, Chinese, 1800s, 5 ¾ In.	2370.00

WOODEN wares were used in all parts of the home. Wood was used for many containers and tools. Small wooden pieces are called *treenware* in England, but the term *woodenware* is more common in the United States. Additional pieces may be found in the Advertising, Kitchen, and Tool categories.

Artist's Model, Articulated, Jointed, Pegged, Stained, 32 In.	2772.00
Backpack, Pine, Painted, New England, 19th Century, 21 In.	356.00
Barrel, Staved, Painted Blue, Hinged Cover, Iron Hoops, 29 x 20 In.	944.00
Barrel, Wine, Cheroot, Painted, Grapes, Chateau Trotanoy, Merlot, Pomerol, Gironde, 43 x 15 In.	1495.00
Blessing Board, Inscribed Built By John & Sarah Kendage, 1823, 15 x 33 In.	207.00
Book Cover, Ivory Mounts, c.1850, 12 x 9 In.	119.00
Bowl, Ash Burl, Turned Collar, Round, 21 In. Diam.	4148.00
Bowl, Ash Burl, Turned, 19th Century, 17 ½ In. *Illus*	2468.00
Bowl, Ash, Burl, Turned Incised Collar, c.1800, 20 ¾ In. Diam.	3120.00
Bowl, Ash, Oval, c.1810, 9 x 21 In.	3720.00
Bowl, Blue Green Paint, New Jersey, c.1790, 16 ½ In.	356.00
Bowl, Burl, Carved, New England, c.1850, 5 x 10 In.	708.00
Bowl, Burl, Carved, Rounded Sides, 19th Century, 4 ½ x 18 x 13 In.	1304.00
Bowl, Burl, Elliptical, Hand Hewn, Carved Handle, c.1800, 7 x 17 ¼ In.	1041.00
Bowl, Burl, Footed Base, Tooled, c.1820, 7 ¾ x 1 ⅜ In.	690.00
Bowl, Burl, Indian, Raised Ends, Oval, c.1800, 14 x 10 ¼ In.	1840.00
Bowl, Burl, Iron Staple Repair, 1800s, 4 x 18 In.	999.00
Bowl, Burl, Lid, New England, c.1810, 7 ½ x 9 In.	3318.00
Bowl, Burl, New England, 5 ½ x 17 In.	1151.00
Bowl, Burl, Oblong, Open Handles, 8 x 19 In.	4340.00
Bowl, Burl, Patina, 19th Century, 3 x 12 ½ In.	353.00
Bowl, Burl, Rectangular, Chip Carved Bands, Pierced Semicircles, U.S.A., 1800s, 4 ½ x 6 ¼ In.	2772.00
Bowl, Burl, Shallow, Round, c.1820, 11 ¾ x 3 ⅓ In.	863.00
Bowl, Burl, Tooled Foot, c.1810, 7 ½ x 2 In.	748.00
Bowl, Burl, Turned Base, Flared Sides, c.1820, 4 ½ x 2 In.	920.00
Bowl, Carved, Double Acorn Handle, Initials, 6 x 3 ½ In.	59.00
Bowl, Cherry, Rudd Osolnik Studio, 11 In.	79.00
Bowl, Elm Burl, Turned, Patina, c.1800s, 10 ¾ x 3 ½ In. *Illus*	236.00
Bowl, Maple, Painted Blue Exterior, Brown Interior, Lathe Turned, c.1800, 5 x 15 ½ In.	920.00
Bowl, Salad, Turned, 1800s, 16 x 4 ½ In.	118.00
Bowl, Turned, Painted Red, Round, Colonial, 21 In.	590.00
Bowl, Turned, Painted, c.1890, 16 In.	89.00
Bowl, Turned, Red Stain Surface, 19th Century, 4 x 13 ¼ In.	326.00
Brush Rest, Carved, Scholar, Base Of Pine Tree, Chinese, 1800s, 8 ⅜ In.	972.00
Brush Washer, Carved, Peach Shape, Scrolling Branches, Leaves, Chinese, 1800s, 4 ⅞ In.	182.00

Brushpot, Bamboo, Carved, Fisherman, Boat, River, Mountains, Cylindrical, Chinese, 1800s, 5 ¼ In.		200.00
Brushpot, Bamboo, Carved, Immortals In Pine Grove, Chinese, 1800s, 6 ⅜ In.		326.00
Brushpot, Bamboo, Fishermen, Farmers, Scholars, Signed, 18th Century, 5 x 4 In.		365.00
Brushpot, Bamboo, Immortals, Attendants, Pine Trees, Mountains, Chinese, 1800s, 6 ⅝ In. ..		1944.00
Brushpot, Bamboo, Mountain Landscape, Scholars In Boat, Calligraphy, Cylindrical, 1800s, 5 ¾ In.		4740.00
Brushpot, Cylindrical, 8 ¾ In.		263.00
Brushpot, Historical Scene, Black, Gold & Red Lacquer, Chinese, 1900s, 8 ¼ In.		338.00
Brushpot, Pearl Inlay, Branches, Clouds, Birds, Rocks, Chinese, 1800s, 8 ¾ x 8 ⅞ In.		2133.00
Brushpot, Pearl, Hardstone, Ivory, Inlay, Birds, Flowering Branches, Rocks, c.1900, 6 ⅞ In....		2726.00
Brushpot, Stone Overlay, Mother-Of-Pearl, Birds, Prunus Trees, 8 ¾ In.		439.00
Brushpot, Vases Of Flowers, Pearl, Lapis Lazuli, Jade, Malachite, Inlay, Hexagonal, c.1900, 6 In.		1067.00
Brushpot, Zitan, Scholar, Attendant, Hut, 3 Friends Of Winter, Pine, Bamboo, 1800s, 5 In.		2370.00
Bucket, Berry, Green Paint, c.1855, 5 ¾ x 7 In.		425.00
Bucket, Pine, Yellow Paint, 14 ½ x 15 In.		91.00
Bucket, Vine & Leaf Bands, Swing Handle, Salmon Grain Paint, J. Lehn, c.1850, 9 ⅜ x 11 ½ In....		1896.00
Bucket, Wire Banded Staves, Red Swirled Paint, Tapered Sides, Wire Swing Bail, 12 x 14 In....		59.00
Candlebox, Oak, Slide, Pa., c.1910, 4 x 10 In.		61.00
Canister, Spice, Lid, Turned Maple, Cut Sponge Decoration, Bone Finial, Treen, 1800s, 3 ⅜ x 3 ½ In..		295.00
Cigarette Dispenser, Swami, Push Plunger, Cigarette Exits Mouth, Kindel & Graham, 1920s		672.00
Clock Dial, Painted Noah's Ark Scene, Inscription, S. Hoadley, Plymouth, c.1810, 16 x 12 In. ...*Illus*		1067.00
Clothespins, Handmade, Box, 3 ¾ x 1 In.		24.00
Coffer, Rounded Corners, Hinged Lid, Bamboo & Bird Design, Carved, 24 x 41 In.		307.00
Compote, Hardwood, Turned, Dark Color, Treen, c.1800, 8 x 13 In.		147.00
Cup, Libation, Flowering Plum Branches, Carved, Handle, Zitan, Chinese, 1800s, 2 ⅞ In.		613.00
Cup, Spice, Lid, Poplar, Yellow, Green Flowers, Red Paint, Treen, Elizabeth Sheely 1859, 4 x 3 In..		1612.00
Dish, Sycamore, Rounded, Wavy Rim, Alexandre Noll, c.1950, 2 ⅛ x 19 ⅝ In.		5000.00
Dummy Board, Pine, Woman, With Broom, Man, With Dog, Paint, c.1810, 61 In., 2 Piece.....		6900.00
Easel, Artist, 2-Sided, Adjustable, 1800s, 94 x 27 In..		1920.00
Easel, Artist, Adjustable Support, Castors, c.1920, 90 x 26 In.		420.00
Firkin, Blue Paint, Handle, 15 In.		374.00
Firkin, Handle, Green Paint, Signed, Reuben Hersey, 1859, 2 ¼ x 2 ¼ In.		10530.00
Firkin, Lid, Pine, Copper Tacks, Wooden Pegs, Hingham, 3 x 2 ⅞ In. ....*Illus*		936.00
Firkin, Lid, Pine, Green Paint, Stamped, C. Wilder & Son, So. Hingham, Mass., 1800s, 10 x 9 In. ...*Illus*		1053.00
Firkin, Paint, Pink Flowers, Green Ground, Swing Handle, c.1850, 11 ½ In.		92.00
Firkin, Painted Orange, Cone Shape, Swing Bail, Wood Grip, Cover, 9 ¾ x 11 In.		130.00
Firkin, Pine, Blue, Paint, Reddish Brown Handle, Pa., c.1850, 12 In...............................		563.00
Firkin, Pine, Green Paint, Stamped S.H., 5 ½ x 5 ½ In.		2844.00
Firkin, Pine, Mustard Yellow Paint, 1800s, 8 ¾ In.		652.00
Firkin, Red, Black Paint, Handle, Marked Kittie, 13 In.		489.00
Firkin, Softwood, Tongue & Groove Staves, Metal Bands, Wire Bail, Wood Grip, 1800s, 10 ½ x 11 In.		295.00
Grain Bin, Side Handles, Salmon Paint, 1800s, 6 x 27 In.		316.00
Half Barrel, Oak, Diagonal Handles, Painted, Crest, Chateau Mauvezin, France, 1800s, 16 x 38 In.		403.00
Hat Mold, Shape Stand, 17 x 12 In.		210.00
Humidor, Bulldog Shape, Hardwood, Hinged, Googly Eyes, c.1900, 8 ¾ In.		1778.00
Humidor, Figural, Man, Seated On Cigar Bundle, Stovepipe Hat, Striped Pants, c.1900, 10 In....		1495.00
Humidor, Mahogany, Brass, Bail Handles, Interior Mirror, France, c.1890, 7 x 15 In.		518.00
Incense Holder, Bamboo, Carved, Official On Horseback, Attendants, Signed, Chinese, 1800s, 9 In. ..		1007.00
Jar, Lid, Turned, Stained, Straight Sides, Tapered Mouth, Knob Handle, 7 x 6 In.		201.00
Jar, Maple, Bulbous, Lid, Finial, Peaseware, 4 In.		323.00
Juggling Pin, Circus, Black, Red Paint, Inscribed, 26 In., Pair		2187.00
Keg, Iron Bands, c.1850, 12 ½ In.		46.00
Mannequin, Arms, Hands, Wire Form, Cast Iron Base, Royal Label, 64 x 21 In.		660.00
Mold, Candle, 24 Tube, Bootjack Ends, Red Stain, c.1860, 18 x 22 In.		633.00
Pail, Lid, Stave Construction, Iron Hoops, Painted Red, Wire Bail Handle, c.1875, 11 ½ In......		415.00
Pail, Stave Construction, Iron Hoops, Painted Yellow, Swing Bail, Wood Handle, 1800s, 4 ½ In.		385.00
Piggin, Pine, Ash, Button Lap Banded, Painted, Mustard, Ocher, Heart Handle, c.1790, 11 ¼ x 8 In.		1610.00
Pipe Rack, Scroll Top, Vines, Rooster, Applied Pipe, Canoe Paddles, 1925, 10 ½ x 11 ¾ In.		805.00
Pitcher, Mahogany, Pinched Neck, Cutout Handle, A. Knoll, France, 1950s, 10 x 7 x 5 In.		5000.00
Plaque, Yale University, 1872, Head Of The Charles, Race, Paint, c.1950, 27 x 45 In.		413.00
Platter, Pyrographic, Painted, Bretons, Landscape, Church, Border, Paul Foullien, 19 ½ In....		426.00
Propeller, Airplane, Sinsinich Bros., HP 35, RPM 2550, Marked, 72 In. ....*Illus*		748.00
Rack, Spoon, Poplar, 3 Tiers, Paint, New Jersey, c.1800, 23 x 9 In................................		6820.00
Receipt Register, Cabinet, Oak, 2 Drawers, Metal Handles, Salesman's Sample, 11 ¼ x 13 ¾ In.		1375.00
Saddle Holder, 52 ½ x 32 In.		403.00
Saffron Cup, Poplar, Turned, Dome Lid, Finial, Footed Pedestal Base, Multicolor Flowers, 5 In.		708.00
Scoop, Burl, New England, 1800s, 10 In.		296.00

World War II, Trade Stimulator, Hitler Gum Target, Satisfy Your Desire, Pistol Shot, Paul Bennett & Co., c.1940 $1,062.00

Victorian Casino Antiques

World's Fair, Badge, 1933, Chicago, Century Of Progress, Employee, Silvered Brass, Enamel, 2 ¼ In. $108.00

Hake's Americana & Collectibles

World's Fair, Salt & Pepper, 1893, Chicago, Government Building, Opaline, Ring Neck, Marked, 3 ¾ In. $144.00

Early Auction Co.

W

World's Fair, Scarf, 1876, Philadelphia, Smithsonian Reproduction, 25 ½ x 25 ½ In.
$25.00

WPA, Figurine, Walrus & Carpenter, Through The Looking Glass, Marked, Eckhardt, 6 In.
$575.00

Humler & Nolan

WPA, Sign, WPA Project, Highway Improvement, New York, Double Sided, Wood, 30 x 18 In.
$72.00

Victorian Casino Antiques

Cocktail Watches Are Back in Style

Vintage watches, called cocktail watches, are back in style. The tiny watch face is hard to read and the watch must be wound each day, but it is worn with blue jeans or cocktail dresses as a vintage bracelet. Jeweled watches by name companies sell for thousands of dollars. Knock-off costume jewelry watches are inexpensive but have the same look.

Shield, Painted 13-Star Flag, 23 x 30 ½ In.	277.00
Sign, The Fish Feeding Is Discontinued, Script, Paint, c.1890, 9 ¼ x 25 In.	5382.00
Sugar, Bucket, Lid, Maple Burl, Turned, c.1800, 7 ¼ x 6 ¼ In.	3720.00
Tray, Hardwood, Mother-Of-Pearl Inlay, Landscape, Figures, Oval, Chinese, c.1890, 20 x 31 In.	1126.00
Tray, Mahogany Veneered Rim, Needlework Insert, Pink Poppies, Handles, Round, c.1880, 22 In.	300.00
Tray, Red Paint, New England, c.1850, 28 x 20 In.	144.00
Tray, Serving, Mahogany, Marquetry Inlay, Flowers & Ribbons, Handles, c.1900, 28 In.	115.00
Tray, Silver Plate Gallery, Handles, Bun Feet, Painted Bellflower Swags, Center Ornament, 23 x 14 In.	357.00
Trencher, Maple, Carved, Oval, 21 ¼ x 12 In.	132.00
Trencher, Oval, 17 ½ In.	116.00
Tub, Red Stain, Stamped, Samuel Hersey, Miniature, 1 ¾ x 2 ¼ In.	8775.00
Urn, Mahogany, Urn Shape, Ring Handles, Lion Mask, Carved, Metal Feet, Finial, 29 In.	150.00
Wagon Seat, Red, Blue Paint, 19 ½ x 29 ½ In.	207.00
Wall Pocket, Black Forest Style, Applied Flowers, Deer's Head, Dove, Hinged, 23 x 13 ½ In.	708.00
Wall Shelf, Shield Shaped, God Bless America, Eagle, Stars & Stripes, Painted, c.1950, 14 ½ x 9 ¾ In.	300.00
Watch Hutch, George III Style, Oak, Mahogany, Parquetry, Tall Case Clock Shape, 18 In.	826.00

WORCESTER porcelains were made in Worcester, England, from 1751. The firm went through many name changes and eventually, in 1862, became The Royal Worcester Porcelain Company Ltd. Collectors often refer to Dr. Wall, Barr, Flight, and other names that indicate time periods or artists at the factory. It became part of Royal Worcester Spode Ltd. in 1976. The company was bought by the Portmeirion Group in 2009. Related pieces may be found in the Royal Worcester category.

Basket, Openwork, Flowers, Twisted Handles, Dr. Wall, 9 ¼ In. *Illus*	469.00
Basket, Painted, Rose, Purple, Red, Green, Yellow, Bouquet, Pierced, Applied Detail, c.1770, 8 ¼ In.	2242.00
Coffeepot, Lid, Pear Shaped, Blue Transfer, c.1785, 8 ¾ In.	326.00
Coffeepot, Lid, Rock Strata, Coastal Landscape, Blue, Crescent Mark, c.1770-75, 9 ½ In. *Illus*	296.00
Cup & Saucer, Scolopendrium Pattern, Leaves, Flower, Spiraled, c.1775, 2 ½ x 5 ⅜ In.	3068.00
Dish, Dessert, Earl Dalhousie, Multicolor Landscape & House, Fluted, 1780-90, 8 ½ In.	325.00
Dish, Junket, Molded Shell Body, Blue Transfer, Fruit & Flowers, Marked, c.1765, 9 ⅝ In.	533.00
Jug, Cabbage Leaf & Mask, Flower Sprays, Molded Body, c.1785, 8 ¾ In. *Illus*	182.00
Jug, Milk, Peony Panels, Gilt Diaperwork, Red, Orange, Loop Handle, Pear Shape, c.1773, 3 ⅜ In.	236.00
Mug, Parrot Pecking Fruit, Second Version Pattern, Blue, White Transfer, c.1775, 4 ½ In., Pair.	531.00
Pitcher, Cabbage Leaf Molded, Scroll Handle, Bacchic Mask Spout, c.1780, 9 ¼ In.	240.00
Plate Set, Luncheon, Imari Color Flowers, Gilt, Impressed Mark, 9 In., 6 Piece	196.00
Plate, Birds, Berry Sprigs, Branches, Scalloped, c.1770, 12 In.	944.00
Plate, Blind Earl Pattern, Green Rose Leaves, Flowers, Scalloped Gilt Rim, c.1775, 7 ½ In., Pair	2124.00
Plate, Dessert, Carnations & Fruit Sprigs, Blue, White Transfer, c.1775, 11 ¾ In.	590.00
Plate, Junket, Urn, Flowers, Mask, Blue, Gilt Scalloped Rim, c.1770, 10 In.	3068.00
Sauceboat, Crane, Flower Garden, Green, Blue, Red, Yellow, Shell Molded Spout, c.1755, 6 ½ In.	1534.00
Sauceboat, Famille Rose Reserves, Relief Scrolls, 3 ¾ x 7 ¾ In., Pair	1112.00
Sauceboat, Lettuce Leaf Molded, Pink, Green, Curled Handle, c.1760, 7 ¼ In., Pair	531.00
Teapot, Blue & White, Spherical, Dome Lid, Flower Head Finial, Dr. Wall, c.1770, 5 ½ x 7 In.	215.00
Teapot, Lid, Boy In A Buffalo Pattern, Black, White Transfer, c.1755, 4 ⅜ In.	1180.00
Teapot, Lid, Fisherman Pattern, Blue Transfer, Coastal Landscape, Globe Shape, c.1780, 6 ⅜ In.	326.00
Teapot, Lid, Mother, Child, Dignitary Scene, Chinoiserie, c.1775, 5 ⅜ In.	354.00
Teapot, Lid, Queen Charlotte, Globe Shape, Flowers & Leaves, Gilt Trim, Marked, c.1770, 8 In.	296.00
Yoke, Brass, Paint, Marked 1674, 40 In.	138.00

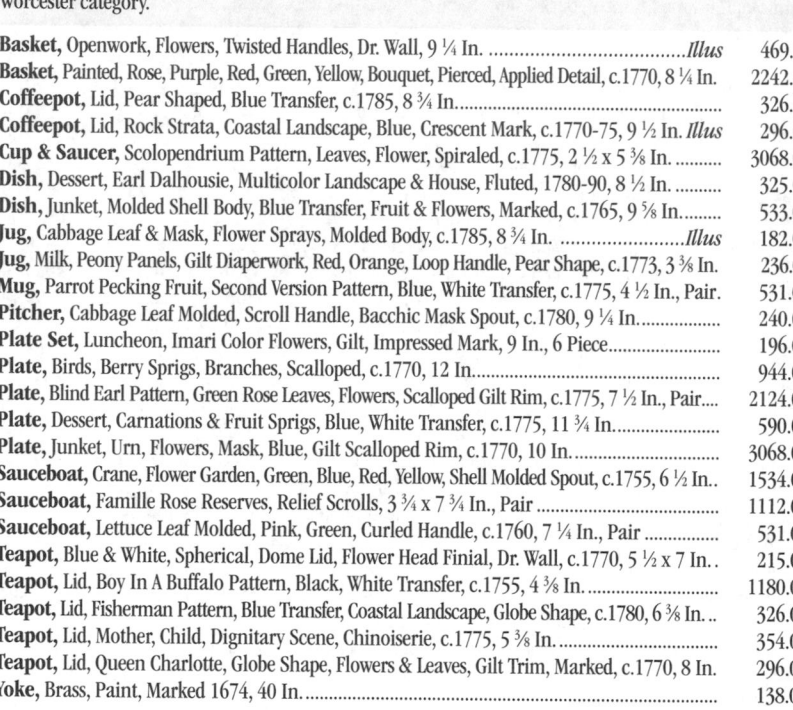

WORLD WAR I and World War II souvenirs are collected today. Be careful not to store anything that includes live ammunition. Your local police will tell you how to dispose of the explosives. See also Sword and Trench Art.

WORLD WAR I

Badge, Award, To Wm. Thomas, From Co-Workers, U.S. Fuel Co., Eagle, Flags, Shield, 2 ¼ In.	278.00
Badge, Son In Service, Enamel, Brass, Photo Frame, Soldier, Bar Pin, 1917, 1 ½ In.	82.00
Button, Peace November 11, 1918, U.S.A., Dove, 2 ¼ In.	75.00
Button, Pressed Copper, Exempt U.S., Whitehead & Hoag, ⅝ In.	29.00
Helmet, Doughboy, Leather Liner, Camp Hunt Etched	94.00
Helmet, Leather, Metal, Leather Strap, France	94.00
Poster, 2nd Liberty Loan Of 1917, Patriotic Image Of Children Holding Flag, 20 x 29 In.	100.00
Poster, America Is Ready, Wilson Portrait, Lithograph, 1917, 40 x 27 In.	2800.00
Poster, Buy Liberty Bonds, Statue Of Liberty, Pennell, 1918, 40 ½ x 28 In.	120.00
Poster, Buy Your Victory Bonds, Soldier, Pointing, 1917, 50 x 35 In.	1300.00
Poster, Enlist, Woman, Baby, Underwater, Fred Spear, Sackett & Wilhelms, 1915, 32 x 22 In.	19000.00
Poster, Everyone Should Do His Bit/Enlist Now, Boy Scout, Baron Low, London, 1915, 28 x 19 In.	450.00

W

Poster, Fight Or Buy Bonds Third Liberty Loan, Girl, Flag, Soldiers, Howard Christy, 30 x 20 In..... 201.00
Poster, For Your Boy, United War Work Campaign, Arthur William Brown, Frame, 18 x 28 In. 193.00
Poster, Forward Enlist Now, Rider, Sword Drawn, Horse, Lucy K. Walsh, 1915, 27 x 19 In. 800.00
Poster, Gee I Wish I Were A Man, Woman In Navy Suit, Howard Chandler Christy, Frame, 29 x 25 In. 1560.00
Poster, Harriman National Bank Urges Faith Courage And Patience, 1918, 26 x 19 In. 100.00
Poster, I Want You For The Navy, Woman In Uniform, H.W. Christy, 1917, Frame, 41 x 26 In.. 1116.00
Poster, I Want You For U.S. Army, Uncle Sam, Pointing, James M. Flagg, 1917, 40 x 29 In...... 11000.00
Poster, Men Wanted For The Army, Cavalry Scene, Michael P. Whelan, c.1915, 30 x 41 In. 369.00
Poster, Navy Needs You Don't Read American History Make It, Montgomery, 1918, 40 x 26 In.. 1000.00
Poster, Now, Back The Bayonets, War Savings, C. Richard, Wynne Nevinson, 1918, 29 x 18 In. . 3400.00
Poster, Preserve, Uncle Sam, Hatless, Holding Apple Buckets, C. Housh, c.1918.40 x 27 In. 1100.00
Poster, Preserve, Woman, In White, Holding Food Tray, C. Housh, c.1918, 39 x 27 In........... 1600.00
Poster, Recruiting, Boys & Girls, You Can Help Your Uncle Sam Win The War, Lithograph...... 123.00
Poster, Save The Products Of The Land, Eat More Fish, C. Bull, U.S. Food Admin., c.1918, 30 x 20 In.. 850.00
Poster, Sure We'll Finish The Job, Victory Liberty Loan Paper, Gerrit A. Beneker, Frame, 26 x 37 In.... 193.00
Poster, Take Up The Sword Of Justice, Woman, Arms Raised, Bernard Partridge, c.1914, 21 x 19 In. . 750.00
Poster, Victory Liberty Loan, Finish The Job, Farmer In Overalls, Gerrit A. Beneker, 1918, 26 x 37 In. 193.00
Poster, Victory Liberty Loan, Howard Chandler Christy, 1919, 40 x 27 In.................. 300.00
Poster, Victory Liberty Loan, They Thought We Couldn't Fight, Frame, 33 ½ x 23 In. 300.00
Poster, YMCA, United War Work Campaign, For Your Boy, Arthur William Brown, 1918, 18 x 28 In... 193.00
Poster, You Are Wanted By The U.S. Army, White Horse, Soldier Rider, K.M. Bara, c.1918, 41 x 27 In.. 4600.00
Uniform, Doughboy, Lieutenant's, Parade & Campaign Hats, Jacket, Trousers, Shirts, Spats... 265.00

WORLD WAR II

Badge, Luftwaffe Observers', Marked F.W. Assmann & Sohne D.R.G.M., Germany 384.00
Badge, U.S. Maritime Service Officer, Eagle, Wreath, Anchor, Silver, Hilborn-Hamburger, 2 x 2 In. 54.00
Box, Adolf, Pig Bank, Save & Make Him Squeal, Tom Lamb, Otis-Lawson, N.Y., 4 x 6 In. ...*Illus* 230.00
Button, Aid The Soviet Union, Defeat Hitler, Aid Great Britain, Red & White, 1 ⅛ In. 75.00
Case, Artillery Instrument, Leather, Oblong, Strap Handle, 13 x 8 In. 86.00
Cup & Saucer, Adolf Hitler, Transfer, Porcelain, 3 ½ In. ....*Illus* 144.00
Dagger, Hitler Youth, Nazi Insignia, Blut Und Ehre, Scabbard, Germany, 5 In. 120.00
Dagger, Nazi SA, Scabbard, Anton Wingen Jr., Germany.. 561.00
Dime Register, Bank, Keep 'Em Rolling, Firing Tank, Red, White, Tin Lithograph, 2 ½ x 2 ½ In.. 312.00
Doll, WAAC, Soldier, Freundlich, Composition, Jointed, Molded Heads, Uniform, 1940s, 15 In., Pair 209.00
Figure, Skunk, Hitler Head, Mussolini & Hirohito On Tail, Arrow, Cast Metal, 5 In. 138.00
License Plate Attachment, Victory V, Morse Code, Red, White, Blue, Painted Enamel, 5 x 5 ½ In. 168.00
Medal, Bronze Star, Slot Brooch, Ribbon Bar, Case 106.00
Pin, 7th Field Artillery, Metal, Cross Arms, 7, A, 2 x 1 ⅝ In... 125.00
Pin, Hitler, Wanted For Murder, Evil Portrait, Swastikas, Adolf Schickelgruber, 3 ½ In. 138.00
Pin, PT 109, Ship, Silvertone Metal, Pinback, 1 ¾ In... 19.00
Pin, Remember Pearl Harbor, Propeller Shape, Silvered White Metal, 3 In............................... 127.00
Pin, Remember Pearl Harbor, Pearl On Hand, Holding Dagger, 3 ½ In.. 214.00
Pin, Remember Pearl Harbor, Rebus, Simulated Pearl, Sterling Silver, Embossed Letters, 2 ¼ In. ...*Illus* 95.00
Pin, Remember Pearl Harbor, Red, White, Blue, American Flag, 3 ½ In. ....*Illus* 174.00
Pin, Remember Pearl Harbor, Thumbs Up, Sterling Silver, 1 ¼ In...................................... 429.00
Pin, Remember Pearl Harbor, Uncle Sam With Bayonet Rifle, Freihofer's, 1 ¼ In..................... 115.00
Pin, Remember Pearl Harbor, White, Red Lettering, Red, White, Blue Ribbon, 1 ¼ In.............. 63.00
Pin, Tojo As Snake, Buck Teeth, For Freedom's Sake, We'll Crush The Snake, 1 ½ In............... 417.00
Pincushion, Hitler, Stooped Over, Inset Tuft On Butt, Plaster, Painted, 4 ½ x 1 ½ In............... 190.00
Poster, Americans All, Tank, Names, Gov. Printing Office, Wash., D.C., 1942, 40 x 27 In......... 1755.00
Poster, Attack Attack Attack, Buy War Bonds, Color, c.1942, 40 x 28 In. 270.00
Poster, Avec De Gaulle, French Sailor, Shaking Finger At English Rowboat, c.1941, 47 x 31 In.. 2400.00
Poster, Bits Of Careless Talk, Hand, Swastika Ring, Puzzle, Stevan Dohanos, 20 x 28 In. .....*Illus* 173.00
Poster, Books Cannot Be Killed By Fire, Books Are Weapons In The War On Ideas, 1942, 27 x 20 In. 550.00
Poster, Careless Talk Got There First, Paratrooper, Frame, 1944, 30 ¾ x 22 ½ In..................... 270.00
Poster, Careless Word, Needless Sinking, Office Of War, Anton Otto Fischer, 1942, 37 x 28 In... 210.00
Poster, Defend Your Country, Enlist Now, Uncle Sam, Rolling Up Sleeves, 38 x 25 In. 510.00
Poster, Fighting Filipinos, Tattered Warrior, Flag Aloft, Manuel Rey Isip, 1943, 40 x 27 In....... 700.00
Poster, Fly, For Her Liberty & Yours, Flyer, Girl, H.C. Christy, 1943, 38 x 25 In. 700.00
Poster, Here Is The Culprit, Jewish Man, Parting Curtain, Homil, 1941, 22 x 16 In. 3600.00
Poster, Hit Em Again, Attacking Airplane, U.S. Government Printing, 1942, 40 x 28 In............ 1100.00
Poster, Jews Balance Roosevelt, Churchill, 3 Men, Teeter-Totter, 1941, 27 x 19 In. 2800.00
Poster, Join The Submarine Service, Flaming Japanese Ships, U.S. Govt. Printing, 1944, 27 x 21 In. 950.00
Poster, Keep Us Flying, Buy War Bonds, Black Parachutist, 1943, 27 x 20 In............................ 3800.00
Poster, Marines Have Landed, G.I. Wading, Gun Raised, James M. Flagg, 1942, 39 x 29 In....... 1000.00
Poster, Navy Admiral, That's The Spot To Hit, Give Us The Stuff & We'll Hit It, 1944, 10 x 14 ¼ In. 173.00
Poster, Prevent This, Flaming Swastika, General Electric, 1942, 49 x 38 In............................... 1700.00

Wristwatch, Buckle Design Over Face, Retro, Gold Tone Dial, Diamonds, 17 Jewel, Manual, 14K, 6 ¼ In.
$1,304.00

Skinner, Inc.

Wristwatch, Cartier, Silvered Dial, Blued Steel Hands, 18K Gold, Back Wind & Set, Jaeger LeCoultre
$4,029.00

Skinner, Inc.

Wristwatch, Concord, Saratoga, Pearl, Diamonds, Quartz, Bezel Set, 18K, Link Band, Woman's
$2,489.00

W

Skinner, Inc.

Wristwatch, Patek Philippe, Calatrava, Gubelin, Secondary Dial, Manual, 18K Gold, Woven Link Bracelet, Box
$5,629.00

Skinner, Inc.

Wristwatch, Pery, Diamond, Crescent-Shaped Links, 2-Tone, 14K Gold, 17 Jewel, Swiss, 7 In.
$531.00

Brunk Auctions

Wristwatch, Rolex, Oyster, Perpetual Datejust, 18K Gold, Man's
$4,025.00

Cottone Auctions

> **TIP**
> *Clean the plastic crystal of a vintage watch with silver polish.*

W

Poster, Propaganda, Recruitment, 5 Sullivan Brothers Missing, c.1943, 40 x 28 In.	210.00
Poster, Starve Squander Bug, Buy War Bonds, Bug, Eating Money, Dr. Seuss, c.1943, 13 x 11 In.	400.00
Poster, This Is The Enemy, SS Officer, Hangman Reflection, K. Koehler, V. Ancona, 1942, 34 x 24 In.	6500.00
Poster, WAAC, This Is My War Too, Dan V. Smith, 1943, 36 x 23 In.	700.00
Poster, War Bonds, Lincoln Quotation, World Can Never Forget, 1940s, 9 ¼ x 14 ⅜ In.	115.00
Tin, Poison Container, Painted Picture Of Hitler Skull & Crossbones, Screw Top, Spout	95.00
Trade Stimulator, Hitler Gum Target, Satisfy Your Desire, Pistol, Paul Bennett, c.1940 .*Illus*	1062.00
Uniform, USS Iowa, Cap, Neckerchief, Shirt, Trousers, G.A. Moseley, c.1917	75.00

WORLD'S FAIR souvenirs from all of the fairs are collected. The first fair was the Great Exhibition of 1851 in London. Some other important exhibitions and fairs include Philadelphia, 1876 (Centennial); Chicago, 1893 (World's Columbian); Buffalo, 1901 (Pan-American); St. Louis, 1904 (Louisiana Purchase); Portland, 1905 (Lewis & Clark Centennial Exposition); San Francisco, 1915 (Panama-Pacific); Philadelphia, 1926 (Sesquicentennial); Chicago, 1933 (Century of Progress); Cleveland, 1936 (Great Lakes); San Francisco, 1939 (Golden Gate International); New York, 1939 (World of Tomorrow); Seattle, 1962 (Century 21); New York, 1964; Montreal, 1967; Knoxville (Energy Turns the World) 1982; New Orleans, 1984; Tsukuba, Japan, 1985; Vancouver, Canada, 1986; Brisbane, Australia, 1988; Seville, Spain, 1992; Genoa, Italy, 1992; Seoul, South Korea, 1993; Lisbon, Portugal, 1998; Hanover, Germany, 2000; and Aichi, Japan, 2005. Memorabilia of fairs include directories, pictures, fabrics, ceramics, etc. Memorabilia from other similar celebrations may be listed in the Souvenir category.

Badge, 1933, Chicago, Century Of Progress, Employee, Silvered Brass, Enamel, 2 ¼ In. .*Illus*	108.00
Badge, 1939, New York, Official Host, North Carolina Day, Yellow, Blue, Aluminum, 1 ½ In.	91.00
Cane, 1939, New York, Trylon & Perisphere, Fireworks, 28 In.	115.00
Charm, 1964, New York, Sterling, ¾ In.	15.00
Deco Lamp, 1939, New York, Glass Shade, White, Building Images, 9 ½ In.	190.00
Fan, 1876, Philadelphia, Pierced & Carved Bone, Silk, 3 Buildings, 17 In.	29.00
Glass Holder, 1909, Seattle, Alaska-Yukon-Pacific Expo, Metal, Totem Pole, Mt. Ranier, 4 In.	45.00
License Plate Attachment, 1964, New York, See Dodge Auto Thrill Show, Orange, Blue, 6 x 12 In.	190.00
Match Safe, 1904, St. Louis, Eagle, Flag, Map, Celluloid, 2 ¼ x 1 ⅕ In.	330.00
Mirror, 1901, Buffalo, Pan-American Exposition, Round, 2 ⅛ In.	158.00
Mirror, 1901, Buffalo, Pan-American Exposition, Simulated Alaskan Visit, Round, 1 ¾ In.	301.00
Mirror, 1904, Louisiana Purchase Exposition, Miss Liberty, Color Of Nations, 1 ¾ In. .*Illus*	287.00
Mug, 1893, World's Columbian, Stoneware, Incised Blue Design, 1893, 4 ¾ x 3 In.	330.00
Needle Book, 1939, New York, World Of Tomorrow, 3 ¾ x 7 In.	15.00
Paperweight, 1904, St. Louis, Bear, To Bear In Mind, Iron, Bronze, Celluloid Overlay, 3 x 2 In.	244.00
Pin, 1901, Buffalo, Pan-American Exposition, Angelic Woman, Trumpet, Wreath, 1901, 2 ⅛ In.	139.00
Pin, 1901, Buffalo, Pan-American Exposition, Bull Fight, McGarvie's Streets Of Mexico, 1 ¼ In.	146.00
Pin, 1901, Pan-American, Spirit Of Niagara, Niagara Falls, Buxom Woman, W&H, 1 ¼ In.	306.00
Pin, 1909, Seattle Alaska-Yukon-Pacific Expo, Flying Maiden, I Do Pennant, 1 ¼ In.	127.00
Pin, 1939, San Francisco, Golden Gate International Exposition, Enamel Sailboat, 1 ½ In.	75.00
Pin, 1940 New York, Ford Day, 37th Anniversary, June 16th, Black, White, 1 ¾ In.	209.00
Pitcher, 1904, St. Louis, Ruby, Clear Cut Glass, Engraved Carrie Wilson, 11 In.	119.00
Plate, 1893 Chicago, Santa Maria, Enameled Picture, A.E. Smith, Signed, Libbey, 6 In.	259.00
Plate, 1933, Chicago, Brass, Buckingham Fountain, Sky Ride, Century Art Works, 4 In.	30.00
Plate, 1939, New York, Man, Seated, Capital & Labor, Pale Blue, 7 In.	81.00
Plate, 1964, New York, Plastic, Crimped Edge, Red, 10 ⅝ In.	25.00
Plate, 1964, New York, Unisphere, 8 ⅛ In.	18.00
Plate, 1968, San Antonio, Hemisfair, 10 ¼ In.	7.50
Poster, 1901, Pan-American Exposition Buffalo, Spirit Of Niagara, Evelyn Rumsey Cary, 46 x 23 In.	3200.00
Poster, 1937, Paris, Exposition Internationale, Paul Colin, 39 x 24 In.	500.00
Poster, 1937, Paris, Exposition Internationale, Woman's Profile, Flags, Jean Carlu, 63 x 46 In.	950.00
Poster, 1939, New York, World Of Tomorrow, Joseph Binder, 30 x 20 In.	2000.00
Potholder, 1964, New York, Yellow Green, Red, Cotton, 6 x 6 In.	18.00
Program, 1901, Pan-American Exposition, President's Day, Notation McKinley Shot 4:07 PM	252.00
Quilt, 1933, Chicago, Pieced & Appliqued, Flags Of The World, Multicolor, Cotton, 80 x 71 In.	2489.00
Ring, 1934, Chicago, Century Of Progress, Red, White, Blue Enamel, Uncas	158.00
Rose Bowl, 1893, Chicago, Fuchsia To Pink, Round, Zigzag Rim, Gold Enamel Flowers, 3 ½ In.	81.00
Salt & Pepper, 1893, Chicago, Government Building, Opaline, Ring Neck, Marked, 3 ¾ In. ...*Illus*	144.00
Scarf, 1876, Philadelphia, Smithsonian Reproduction, 25 ½ x 25 ½ In. .*Illus*	25.00
Sewing Machine, 1901, Buffalo, Pan-American Exposition, Singer, Brass, 29 x 25 In.	2006.00
Shoehorn, 1904, New York, Red Raven, Bird Holding Bottle, Tin, 4 ⅝ In.	358.00
Spoon, 1939, New York, Silver Plate, 6 In.	10.00
Tape Measure, 1901, Buffalo, Pan-American Expo, Flag, Women Shaped Americas, Celluloid, 1 ¾ In.	75.00
Tape Measure, 1901, Buffalo, Pig, Brass, Figural, Wire Tail Serves As Crank, 2 ⅜ In.	160.00

Toy, 1936, Cleveland, Great Lakes Expo, Tractor Trailer, Arcade, 10 ½ In. 489.00
Toy, 1939, New York, Bus & Tram, Driver, Red, Blue Stripe Awning, Cast Iron, Arcade, 7 In. 207.00
Toy, 1939, New York, Bus, Greyhound, Visit World's Fair, Cast Iron, Arcade, 9 In. 1093.00
Toy, 1939, New York, Tractor Train Bus, Cast Iron, Blue, Orange, 11 ½ In. 345.00
Toy, 1939, New York, Tractor Train, Greyhound Co., Driver, Arcade, Box, 16 In. 825.00
Watch, 1939, New York, Lapel Pin, Ingraham, Box 390.00

WPA is the abbreviation for Works Progress Administration, a program created by executive order in 1935 to provide jobs for millions of unemployed Americans. Artists were hired to create murals, paintings, drawings, and sculptures for public buildings. Pieces are marked *WPA* and may have the artist's name on them.

Drawing, Nude, Pen & Ink, Bruno Mankowski, 15 x 12 In. 150.00
Figurine, Cat, Abstract, Bronze, Brass, Wood Base, Si Gordon, 7 In. 290.00
Figurine, Walrus & Carpenter, Through The Looking Glass, Marked, Eckhardt, 6 In. .....*Illus* 575.00
Lithograph, Dog, Sitting In Straw, Cane, Chas. R. Knight, 5 x 7 ½ In. 165.00
Picture, Watercolor, Old Woman, In Bed, Reading Magazine, 10 x 15 In. 250.00
Poster, Moments With Genius, Barnum Radio Players, Illinois Writers, D. Shubow, c.1936, 22 x 14 In. 375.00
Print, Woman, Nude, Woven Paper, Edward Hagedorn, 11 x 15 In. 195.00
Print, Woodblock, Allan A.F. Thomas, Men, Working In Garden, 21 x 18 In. 395.00
Sign, WPA Project, Highway Improvement, New York, Double Sided, Wood, 30 x 18 In. ...*Illus* 72.00

WRISTWATCHES came into use during World War I. Wristwatches are listed here by manufacturer or as advertising or character watches. Wristwatches may also be listed in other categories. Pocket watches are listed in the Watch category.

Atlas, Sterling, Round Case, Roman Numerals, Silver Dial, Black Leather Strap, Tiffany & Co... 426.00
Audemars Piguet, Royal Oak, 18K Gold, Brown Dotted Dial, Octagonal Bezel, 8 Screws 4029.00
Baume & Mercier, 14K Yellow Gold, Sapphire Cabochon, Geneve 1062.00
Baume & Mercier, 18K Gold, Oval Case, Black Alligator Band, Woman's, 8 In. 345.00
Baume & Mercier, 18K Gold, Round Case, Black Crocodile Band, 7 ½ In. 1150.00
Baume & Mercier, 18K Yellow Gold, Steel, 12-Sided Case, Stretch Band, Woman's 717.00
Baume & Mercier, Square, Dial, Brown Leather Band, Battery 236.00
Breguet, 18K Yellow Gold, Chronograph, Round Case, Ribbed Band, 21 Jewel Movement 11500.00
Breitling, Antares World, Stainless Steel Case, Rotational Bezel, Gold Accents, Automatic 1093.00
Breitling, Premier, 18K Rose Gold, White Face 1725.00
Buckle Design Over Face, Retro, Goldtone Dial, Diamonds, 17 Jewel, Manual, 14K, 6 ¼ In. .....*Illus* 1304.00
Bueche Girod, Mercedes Grille, 18K White Gold Case, Logo, Date Aperture, Lizard Band 1898.00
Bulova, 14K Rose Gold Case, Double Chain Bracelet, Diamonds, Rubies, Woman's, 5 ½ In. 518.00
Bulova, 14K White Gold, Elongated Case, Wheat Design Bracelet, Diamonds, Woman's, 6 In.. 460.00
Bulova, Accutron Spaceview, Clear Face, Battery, Brown Leather Band, c.1965 .... 266.00
Bulova, Round Face, 23 Jewel Movement, Textured, Woven Band, 14 K Gold, 1970, 6 In. 469.00
Cartier, 21 Chronoscaph, Stainless Steel, Logo Dial, Luminous Batons 2133.00
Cartier, Panther, 18K Gold Case, Diamond Set Bezel, Bracelet, Silvertone Dial, Signed, Woman's.. 6325.00
Cartier, Panther, 18K Yellow Gold Case, Silvertone Dial, Signed, Woman's, 6 ½ In. 4600.00
Cartier, Silvered Dial, Blued Steel Hands, 18K Gold, Back Wind & Set, Jaeger LeCoultre ...*Illus* 4029.00
Character, Boris Badenov, Holding TNT, 25 Jewel, Morflex Expansion Band, c.1972, 1 ⅛ In. 173.00
Character, Mary Poppins, Flying With Umbrella, White Vinyl Band, Plastic Box, c.1964, 6 In. 139.00
Character, Woody Woodpecker, Time Teacher, Ingraham, Box, 1940s, 2 ⅜ x 5 ¾ In. 690.00
Chopard, Happy Sport, Rose Gold, Stainless Steel, Diamonds, Brickwork Links 5100.00
Concord, Saratoga, Pearl, Diamonds, Quartz, Bezel Set, 18K, Link Band, Woman's ....*Illus* 2489.00
Cyma, 14K Yellow Gold, Oblong Case, Double Twist Chain Bracelet, Woman's, 7 In. 265.00
Ebel, 1911 Series, Stainless Steel Case, Rubies, Diamonds, Pearl Dial, Woman's.... 719.00 to 1006.00
Ebel, Model L 1911, Blue Square Dial, Automatic, Leather Band 719.00
Elgin, 14K White Gold, Navette Shape, Diamond Set Bezel, Silvertone Dial, Signed, Woman's. 276.00
F. Muller, Casablanca, Stainless Steel, Silver Dial, Luminous Arabic Numerals 4029.00
Gruen, Precision, 14K Yellow Gold, Round Case, Silvertone Dial, Waterproof, Patent Band 230.00
Hamilton, 14K Yellow Gold, Square Case, Flat Bezel, Brushed Silver Dial, Textured Leather Band 449.00
Hamilton, Art Deco, Platinum Case, Diamonds, Silvertone Dial, Black Arabic Numerals, Woman's. 506.00
Hamilton, Platinum, Diamond, Round Ivory Dial, Foldover Clasp, Woman's, 6 ½ In. 944.00
Hamilton, Platinum, Diamond, Square Case, Box Link Band, Art Deco, Woman's, 1940s 777.00
Hamilton, White Dial, Platinum, Diamonds, 17 Jewel Movement, Woman's, 1940s, 6 ¾ In. 690.00
Jaeger LeCoultre, 18K Yellow Gold, Goldtone Dial, Applied Lapis, 17 Jewel, Black Band 834.00
LeCoultre, 14K Yellow Gold, Rectangular Case, Fluted Bezel, 17 Jewel, Leather Band 414.00
LeCoultre, 14K Yellow Gold, Round Case, Integral Bracelet, Silvertone, Open Link Bracelet, 6 ½ In.... 564.00
LeCoultre, Futurematic, 14K Gold Filled, 9 In. 719.00
Link Band, Round Face, 14K Gold, Cresaux, Bigelow Kennard, Woman's 531.00

Paper Savings Bonds Gone

No paper U.S. savings bonds were issued after January 1, 2012. All of the "paperwork" for the bonds is now electronic. Sounds like a savings bond will be a disappointing birthday present—a note on a computer screen, not even a fancy picture to go with it.

Wristwatch, Tiffany & Co., Citrine Crystal, Rubies, Diamonds, 18 Jewel, Manual, 14K, Link Bracelet, 6 ¼ In.
$1,304.00

Skinner, Inc.

TIP

Watch out for price tags that harm the items they're stuck on. Sticky labels leave a residue that discolors over time. They're especially harmful to paper and painted tin. Felt markers should not be used on unglazed pottery or porcelain. Some of the ink will be absorbed and never come off. And watch out for a label that covers a ship or other decorations.

Zsolnay, Figurine, Owl, Book, Eosin Glaze, Stamped, c.1900, 12 ½ x 8 x 8 ½ In. $4,375.00

Rago Arts & Auction Center

Zsolnay, Figurine, Polar Bears, Iridescent, Glazed, 4 ½ x 8 In. $374.00

Cottone Auctions

Zsolnay, Figurine, Stylized Dog, Glazed, 7 In. $345.00

Cottone Auctions

TIP
To clean terminals on batteries, use a standard pencil eraser.

Lotus, 14K Yellow Gold, Diamond, Oval Case, Round Face, Gold Mesh Strap, Woman's	657.00
Louis Vuitton, Tambour, Diving, Automatic, Stainless Steel, Round Case	2013.00
Movado, 14K Yellow Gold, Mesh Band, White Square Face, Marked, Woman's	649.00
Movado, 18K Yellow Gold, Diamond Set Dial, Black Leather Band, Woman's	633.00
Movado, Opalescent Dial, Baton Numerals, 28 Jewel, 14K Gold Mesh Band, Tiffany	1150.00
Movado, Triple Date Calendar, Bicolor Dial, Arabic Numerals & Dots, 14K Gold, 1940s	1659.00
Omega, 18K Gold, Herringbone Mesh Bracelet, 6 ¾ In., Woman's	546.00
Omega, Gold, Automatic Sea Master, Round Face, Link Style Band	570.00
Omega, Seamaster De Ville, Automatic, 14K Yellow Gold, Brushed Silvertone Dial, Round Case	518.00
Patek Philippe, 18K Yellow Gold Case, Inscribed Initials, Tapered Mesh Band, 8 In.	5103.00
Patek Philippe, Calatrava, Gubelin, Secondary Dial, Manual, 18K, Link Bracelet, Box ..*Illus*	5629.00
Paul Et Pere, Diamond, 14K Gold, Signed, Woman's, 6 ¼ In.	322.00
Perreaux, Art Deco Style, Diamonds, 14K White Gold, Signed, 6 In.	531.00
Pery, Diamond, Crescent-Shaped Links, 2-Tone, 14K Gold, 17 Jewel, Swiss, 7 In. ..*Illus*	531.00
Piaget, Diamond, Yellow Gold, Woman's, 6 ⅞ In.	3600.00
Piaget, Lapis Dial, 17 Jewel, Tapered Mesh Link Band, Lapis Tablets, Woman's	2500.00
Robert Cart, 18K Gold, Brown Leather Band, Swiss	266.00
Rolex, Cellini Model, Round Dial, Brushed Gold, Mesh Band, 7 In.	1840.00
Rolex, Oyster Brevet, 1935	748.00
Rolex, Oyster, Perpetual Datejust, 18K Gold, Man's ..*Illus*	4025.00
Rolex, Oyster, Perpetual Datejust, Stainless Steel, Brass Band, Case, Case, Box	2006.00
Rolex, Oyster, Perpetual, 2-Tone, Stainless Steel, 18K Gold Case, Jubilee Bracelet, Woman's	2415.00
Rolex, Stainless Steel, 18 K, Diamond, Mother-Of-Pearl Dial, Oyster Band, 7 ¾ In.	3851.00
Seiko, Quartz, Chronograph, Moon Dial, Flexible Bicolor Band	177.00
Tiffany & Co., Citrine Crystal, Rubies, Diamonds, 18 Jewel, Manual, 14K, Link Bracelet, 6 ¼ In. *Illus*	1304.00
Tiffany & Co., Diamonds, Platinum, Enamel, White Dial, Black Numerals, Art Deco, Woman's	4740.00
Tiffany & Co., IWC, 18K Yellow Gold, Oval Case, Silvertone Dial, Deco, Arabic Numerals, Woman's.	633.00
Ulysse Nardin, Chronometer, Round Dial, Black Leather Band	325.00
Vacheron & Constantin, 18K Yellow Gold, Engraved Inscription, 1920	5700.00
Van Cleef & Arpels, Wood, Leather, Goldtone, Arabic Numbers, Manual Wind, Box, Woman's	1304.00

YELLOWWARE is a heavy earthenware made of a yellowish clay. It varies in color from light yellow to orange-yellow. Many nineteenth- and twentieth-century kitchen bowls and jugs were made of yellowware. It was made in England and in the United States. Another form of pottery that is sometimes classed as yellowware is listed in this book in the Mocha category.

Bowl, 5 Brown & White Bands, c.1850, 15 In. Diam	328.00
Bowl, Brown Stripes, 8 x 4 In.	35.00
Bowl, Mustard Beige With 2 Mauve Bands, 1930s, 4 ¾ x 8 ½ In.	70.00
Bowl, Pink & Blue Bands, Square Base, c.1925, 5 In. Diam.	55.00
Butter Tub, Drippy Manganese Glaze, Washtub Form, High Pierced Handles, 5 x 10 In.	24.00
Crock, White Band, c.1925, 9 ½ x 6 In.	195.00
Dog Bowl, Brown Rim, 1920s, 8 x 2 ½ In.	75.00
Figurine, Bull, Manganese Spatter & Drip, Rectangular Base, 14 x 16 In.	153.00
Ice Bucket, Rockingham Drip Glaze, Crescent Handles, Molded Rim & Base, 6 x 9 In.	71.00
Jar, Lid, Rockingham Glaze, Straight Sides, Stirrup Handles, Foot Bead, 6 x 4 ½ In.	201.00
Nappy, c.1850, 10 In. Diam.	125.00
Pitcher, Columbus Landing In New World, 7 ¾ In.	129.00
Pitcher, Embossed Birds, Rabbit, Flowers, Rockingham Glaze, Hound Handle, 8 In.	71.00
Pitcher, Green Glaze, Embossed Grapes, 8 ¼ In.	90.00
Sugar, Dome Lid, Footed Base, Blue Bands, c.1855, 4 ¼ In.	201.00

ZANESVILLE Art Pottery was founded in 1900 by David Schmidt in Zanesville, Ohio. The firm made faience umbrella stands, jardinieres, and pedestals. The company closed in 1962. Many pieces are marked with just the words *La Moro*.

LA MORO

Bowl, Art, 8-Sided, Embossed Flowers, White Gloss, 6 In.	60.00
Bowl, Rose Glaze, 14 Panels, 6 x 2 In.	45.00
Candleholder, Pinecone, Green, Yellow Brown, 4 ¾ In., Pair	288.00
Candlestick, Green Matte Glaze, Tapering Sides, Hexagon, c.1928, 9 ¼ In.	68.00
Cookie Jar, Brown Glaze, Barrel Shape, Tab Handles, Flower Decal, 1940s, 8 ½ In.	70.00
Crock, Liver Pudding, Z.P. Co., 9 x 5 In.	95.00
Jardiniere, Handles, Banded, 7 In.	95.00
Pitcher, Green Gloss, Ribbed, 8 ½ In.	95.00
Planter, Duck, Turquoise, 5 ½ x 3 In.	45.00
Urn, Green Luster, Double Handle, 17 In.	295.00
Vase, Blue Glaze, Tobacco Leaf, Shouldered, 8 ½ In.	225.00

Vase, Brick Pattern, Purple Ground, 11 In.	138.00
Vase, Bulbous, Green Glaze, 7 In.	65.00
Vase, Cornflower Blue, Flower, Leaves, 1930s, 8 ½ In.	120.00
Vase, Fan Shape, Handles, Pink Gloss, Wavy, 5 ⅛ In.	60.00
Vase, Green Glaze, Embossed Tulip, c.1935, 8 ¼ In.	85.00
Vase, Green Glaze, Footed, Squat, 5 x 6 In.	18.00
Vase, Green Gloss, Ruffled Rim, 4 In.	70.00
Vase, Green Gloss, Triangular, 4 x 5 In.	32.00
Vase, Lavender Matte Glaze, Bell Shape, Marked, 3 x 4 ½ In.	36.00
Vase, Lion's Head Embossed, Yellow Glaze, Handles, 25 ½ In.	374.00
Vase, Mottled Rose & Beige, 2 Handles, 1930s, 6 In.	115.00
Vase, Stoneware Rumble Ware, White, 9 ¾ In.	23.00
Wall Pocket, Duck, Cattails, Turquoise, Red, 7 In., Pair	32.00

ZSOLNAY pottery was made in Hungary after 1853 and was characterized by Persian, Art Nouveau, or Hungarian motifs. A series of new Zsolnay figurines with green-gold luster finish is available in many shops today. Early Zsolnay was not marked, but by 1878 the tower trademark was used.

Bowl, 2 Birds On Rim, Green Shaded To Gold Shaded To Blue, c.1900, 7 x 7 1/12 In.	3250.00
Bowl, Curvy Shape, Dragons Rim, Green & Purple Iridescent, c.1900, 3 ½ x 11 ½ In.	3375.00
Bowl, Embossed Leaves, Round, 2 ½ x 7 In.	58.00
Bowl, Squat, Red Swirl Design Rim, Figural, Maiden, Standing, c.1900, 6 ¼ x 6 ½ In.	2625.00
Bowl, Woman, Nude Holding Shell, 5 In.	288.00
Cachepot, Trailing Tree, Organic Form, Iridescent Copper & Purple Glaze, 6 x 5 In.	3000.00
Compote, Stylized Water, Flowers, Grass Sprouts, Eosin Base, Draped Female, 10 In.	4800.00
Ewer, Reticulated, Boat Shape, High Handle, 5 In.	52.00
Figurine, Bison, On Base, Painted, 5 ½ In.	84.00
Figurine, Fig Seller, Woman, Scarf, Basket, Arabic Script, Eosin Glaze, c.1914, 16 ½ In.	4253.00
Figurine, Fish, Green Iridescent, 4 ½ x 7 In., Pair	120.00
Figurine, Hungarian Peasant Girl, Feeding Duck, 7 In.	60.00
Figurine, Hungarian Shepherdess, Painted, Embroidered Apron, Sack On Pole, Dog, 13 In.	120.00
Figurine, Nude Woman, Kneeling, Green Iridescent Glaze, Pedestal Base, 9 ½ In.	86.00
Figurine, Nude Woman, Kneeling, Languorous Pose, Green Iridescent Glaze, 9 ½ In.	311.00
Figurine, Owl, Book, Eosin Glaze, Stamped, c.1900, 12 ½ x 8 x 8 ½ In. *Illus*	4375.00
Figurine, Polar Bears, Iridescent, Glazed, 4 ½ x 8 In. *Illus*	374.00
Figurine, Reclining Nude Woman, Iridescent Glaze, Shaped Plinth Base, 8 In.	1107.00
Figurine, Stylized Dog, Glazed, 7 In. *Illus*	345.00
Pitcher, Green & Red Eosin Glaze, Ribbed Organic Form, Art Nouveau, c.1900, 6 In.	1046.00
Tile, Art Nouveau Flowers, Green & Rose Glaze, Majolica, Steeple Mark, 1911, 16 x 10 In.	308.00
Tile, Woman, Headdress, Green & Cream Glaze, Majolica, 5 Churches Mark, 1885, 17 x 8 In.	338.00
Vase, Bird In Flight, Multicolor Eosin Glaze, Tapered, Shouldered, c.1900, 10 x 6 ¾ In.	5625.00
Vase, Bulbous, Green & Purple Glaze, Marked, 10 ½ In.	125.00
Vase, Chrysanthemums, Fence, Blue Ground, Eosin Glaze, Gourd Shape, 1898, 9 ½ x 5 In.	6250.00
Vase, Cylindrical, Molded Leaf Design, Red, Gold, Eosin Glaze, c.1900, 10 x 4 In.	8125.00
Vase, Double Gourd, 2 Handles, Green & Blue Eosin Glaze, Marked, 11 In.	5000.00
Vase, Double Gourd, Green, Yellow & Purple Eosin Glaze, Marked, 15 In.	350.00
Vase, Fish, Pike, Iridescent, Pecs, Hungary, Medallion Stamp, c.1902, 16 x 10 In. *Illus*	6250.00
Vase, Green, Blue, Iridescent, Eosin Glaze, Double Gourd Shape, Handles, 6 ¼ x 11 ¼ In.	6100.00
Vase, Green, Purple Glaze, Iridescent, Marked, 4 ½ x 10 ½ In.	153.00
Vase, Iridescence, Green, Yellow, Purple, Eosin Glaze, Long Neck, Double Gourd, 7 ½ x 15 In.	427.00
Vase, Leaves, Pink, Gold, Green Ground, Eosin Glaze, Squat, c.1900, 2 ¼ x 4 In.	688.00
Vase, Lions, Eosin Glaze, Marked, c.1897, 6 x 4 ½ In. *Illus*	3625.00
Vase, Raised Nymphs, Swirls, Green Shaded To Gold, Eosin Glaze, Crumpled Rim, 12 In.	4375.00
Vase, Red Flambe Irregular Dots, Yellow Ground, Rolled Rim, c.1910, 7 ¼ In.	677.00
Vase, Rooster, Figural, Brown Crystalline Glaze, 8 ½ In.	492.00
Vase, Rounded Bottom, Ring Foot, Tapered, Swollen, Blooming Trees, Eosin Glaze, c.1900, 9 ½ In.	6875.00
Vase, Snails, Green, Gold, Eosin Glaze, Naturalistic Design, 5 Churches Mark, 8 x 6 In.	4688.00
Vase, Volcanic Glaze, Crystalline Designs, Marked, c.1902, 10 In. *Illus*	861.00

Zsolnay, Vase, Fish, Pike, Iridescent, Pecs, Hungary, Medallion Stamp, c.1902, 16 x 10 In.
$6,250.00

Rago Arts & Auction Center

Zsolnay, Vase, Lions, Eosin Glaze, Marked, c.1897, 6 x 4 ½ In.
$3,625.00

Rago Arts & Auction Center

Zsolnay, Vase, Volcanic Glaze, Crystalline Designs, Marked, c.1902, 10 In.
$861.00

Skinner, Inc.

INDEX

This index is computer-generated, making it as complete and accurate as possible. References in uppercase type are category listings. Those in lowercase letters refer to additional pages where pieces can be found. There is also an internal cross-referencing system used in the main part of the book, so if you look for a Kewpie doll in the Doll category, you will be told it is in its own category. There is additional information at the end of many paragraphs about where to find prices of pieces similar to yours.

A

A. WALTER 1
ABC 1, 85
ABINGDON 1
ADAMS 2, 585
Admiral Dewey 111, 129, 591, 608
ADVERTISING 2–19, 79, 108–109, 132, 163, 179, 300, 422, 578
AGATA 19
Airplane 32, 89, 112, 125, 179, 368, 578, 605, 617, 642, 659, 661
AKRO AGATE 19, 378
ALABASTER 20, 110, 112, 357–358, 379, 564, 566–568
Album 99, 435, 505
Alexandrite 429, 645
Almanac 345
ALUMINUM 3, 5, 20, 45, 49–50, 65, 78, 97, 105, 110, 123, 127, 130, 133, 171, 183–184, 189, 191, 198, 210, 213–214, 218, 233, 236, 259–260, 264–265, 280, 351, 358, 360, 367, 373, 405, 408, 413, 426, 428–429, 515, 558, 577, 592, 603, 608, 611, 615
AMBER GLASS 21, 145, 294, 361, 397, 522, 568
AMBERINA 21, 85, 138, 181, 311, 367
Ambrotype 435
AMERICAN ENCAUSTIC TILING COMPANY 21
AMETHYST GLASS 21–22, 47, 121, 380, 397
Amos 'n' Andy 46, 622
Amphora, see Teplitz
Andiron, see Fireplace; also 186, 510
ANIMAL TROPHY 22
ANIMATION ART 22–23
ANNA POTTERY 23
Apothecary 9, 51, 383–384, 424, 577
ARABIA 23
ARCHITECTURAL 23–26, 242, 358, 374, 469, 550, 591, 601
AREQUIPA POTTERY 26
ARITA 26

ART DECO 1, 21, 25–26, 29–30, 36, 44, 46, 48–50, 66, 69, 72, 80, 100, 104, 110–111, 117, 119, 127, 132, 137, 144–145, 170–171, 175, 177, 186, 188, 198, 202, 208–209, 212, 218, 227, 233, 240, 251, 254, 260, 265, 267, 270, 272, 277, 288–289, 300, 302, 345, 357–358, 363, 365–368, 372, 377, 409, 411–413, 421, 429, 448, 455–456, 461, 464, 475, 480, 484–485, 497, 505, 511–512, 516, 531–532, 538, 542, 546, 576, 597–599, 638–639, 652, 655, 658, 663–664
Art Glass, see Glass-Art
ART NOUVEAU 1, 20, 23–26, 46, 66, 71–72, 77, 81, 87, 89, 91–92, 109, 134, 147, 176–177, 179, 187, 193, 208, 254, 260, 262, 270, 292, 307, 334, 358, 366, 370, 388, 394, 416, 429, 431–432, 467, 494–495, 499, 508, 511, 536, 539–541, 544, 549–551, 556, 588–589, 592, 640, 648, 665
ARTS & CRAFTS 27, 84, 87, 89, 112, 115, 134, 149, 174, 185–188, 200–205, 208, 214, 218, 221, 232–233, 236, 240, 247–248, 251, 254, 256, 258, 260, 264, 272, 276, 280–281, 304, 331–332, 356, 358, 360–361, 400, 402, 416, 467, 511, 539, 547, 549, 591, 652
Ashtray 2, 19–20, 27, 46–47, 69, 71, 83–84, 103, 106, 135, 155, 176, 180–181, 192, 194–195, 303, 306–307, 310, 325, 344, 389, 393, 405, 410–411, 415, 428, 431, 436, 444, 471, 475, 484, 491, 499, 510, 519, 529–530, 599
Atomizer 31, 137, 145, 283, 396, 429, 566
Aunt Jemima 32, 46–47, 286
Austria, see Royal Dux; Porcelain
AUTO 27–30, 105, 444, 615, 662
Automaton 46, 163, 291, 576
AUTUMN LEAF 30, 308
Avon, see Bottle, Avon
AZALEA 31, 148, 156, 603

B

Babe Ruth 63, 557
BACCARAT 31–32, 359
Backbar 23, 64
BADGE 32, 78, 93, 107, 131, 155, 161, 182, 196, 371, 415, 445, 451, 484, 501, 557–558, 587, 591, 601–602, 605, 660–662
BANK 16, 19, 23, 32–36, 80, 82, 104, 190, 341, 428, 445, 454, 487, 497, 525, 558, 560–561, 570, 603, 629, 661
Banner 2, 27–29, 55, 67, 122, 179, 182, 365, 445, 462, 464, 532, 570, 642, 650

BARBER 3, 9, 36–37, 51, 380, 389, 485, 543, 583–584, 647
BAROMETER 37, 389, 424, 522
BASALT 38, 323, 647–648
Baseball, see Card, Baseball; Sports
BASKET 20–21, 38–39, 42, 69–70, 92–93, 101, 133, 138, 141, 170–172, 180–181, 187, 192, 196, 303, 319, 365, 374, 380, 384, 387, 392–393, 415, 419, 424, 455, 471, 480, 523, 525–526, 533–537, 543–544, 546–547, 549–552, 554–555, 557, 564, 568, 581, 597, 600, 632, 655, 660
BATCHELDER 39
Bathtub 19, 23
BATMAN 39, 90
BATTERSEA 39
BAUER 40, 363
BAVARIA 40, 388
Bayonet 581
Beaded Bag, see Purse
BEATLES 40, 394, 504
Bed Warmer 69, 133, 325, 554
BEEHIVE 32, 34, 40–41, 86–87, 110, 112, 138, 310, 324–325, 570
Beer 2, 4, 6, 9–13, 16, 19, 35, 41, 51, 65, 143, 389, 446, 527, 549, 592, 616, 618
Beer Bottle, see Bottle, Beer
BEER CAN 41
BELL 23, 41–42, 44, 49, 51, 80, 84, 105, 122, 141, 182, 293, 314, 346, 391, 405, 484, 497, 548, 558
BELLEEK 42, 651
Belt Buckle 182, 319, 329–330, 394, 523, 548, 557
BENNINGTON 23, 43, 424
BERLIN 43, 73
BESWICK 43–44, 161
BETTY BOOP 44
BICYCLE 12–13, 18, 34, 44–45, 100, 129, 135, 191, 356, 381, 388, 461, 464, 502, 527, 562, 611, 616, 619, 642
BING & GRONDAHL 45–46
BINOCULARS 46, 605
BIRDCAGE 46
Biscuit Barrel 543, 641
Biscuit Jar 42, 79, 133, 135, 139, 283, 294, 370, 372, 389, 396, 402, 419, 431, 474, 508–509, 511, 519, 568, 640, 645, 647
BISQUE 33, 46–47, 80, 105, 163–169, 346–347, 410, 436, 442, 444, 452, 603, 606
BLACK 9–11, 15, 18, 32, 34–35, 46–47, 73, 90, 94, 109, 111, 125, 133, 163–165, 169, 172, 185, 190–191, 246, 259, 291, 300, 366, 374, 381–382, 410, 418, 555, 577, 592, 600, 605, 610–611, 615–616, 619
Blanket 218–220, 319, 484, 508, 589, 610–611, 618

BLENKO GLASS COMPANY 47–48
Blown Glass, see Glass-Blown
Blue Glass, see Cobalt Blue
Blue Onion, see Onion Pattern
Blue Willow, see Willow
BOCH FRERES 48, 358
BOEHM 48–49, 131
BONE 49, 61, 91, 97, 150, 178–179, 204, 212, 214, 226, 264, 317, 320, 350, 352, 366, 406–407, 473, 480, 525, 582, 584, 662
BONE DISH 49, 107, 133, 160, 497, 582
Book 3, 20, 22, 39, 46, 49–50, 68, 78, 80, 104, 122, 132–133, 161, 172, 190, 195, 198, 291, 309, 313, 316, 324, 332, 345–346, 352, 388, 418, 420, 422, 426, 455, 491, 501, 532, 545, 550, 557, 561, 580–581, 589, 602, 658, 661–662, 665
BOOKENDS 47, 49–50, 83, 136, 141, 144, 178, 195, 297, 314, 346, 354, 368, 445, 491–492, 499, 530, 634
BOOKMARK 50, 122, 137, 444–445, 592
BOSSONS 50–51
Boston & Sandwich Co., see Sandwich Glass
BOTTLE 4–5, 7, 11–13, 15, 23–24, 27, 39, 43, 47, 51–65, 98, 101, 104–105, 118–119, 122–126, 138, 143, 145, 149, 174, 183, 190, 197, 256, 283, 293–294, 297, 312, 350, 354, 370, 380, 382, 389, 392–393, 405, 424, 428–429, 444–445, 469, 471, 496, 508, 521, 535, 544, 568–570, 601, 605, 627, 630, 647, 650, 652
BOTTLE CAP 10, 65, 429
BOTTLE OPENER 65, 106, 122, 126, 135, 428
BOX 2–3, 21, 26, 28, 39, 43, 47, 49, 65–71, 93, 98–99, 101, 105, 107, 118, 134, 141, 144–145, 155, 161, 174, 176–177, 179, 182–183, 186–189, 285, 287, 303, 309, 313, 320, 322, 327, 329, 344–351, 353–354, 365, 368, 371–372, 374, 376–377, 380, 383–384, 389, 391, 393, 396–398, 400, 403, 405–407, 412, 423, 429, 442–443, 445, 454–457, 474, 480, 493, 496, 508, 519–520, 522–527, 537–538, 542–544, 547–551, 559, 564, 569–570, 580, 592–593, 597–598, 600–602, 604, 608, 618, 625, 629–630, 634–635, 638, 641–642, 647–648, 655, 661
BOY SCOUT 68, 660
BRADLEY & HUBBARD 49, 68–69, 170, 172, 174, 185, 381

PHOTO CREDITS

We have included the name of the auction house or photographer with each pictured object. This is a list of the addresses of those who have contributed photographs and information for this book. Every dealer or auction house has to buy antiques to have items to sell. Call or email a dealer or auction house if you want to discuss buying or selling. If you need an appraisal or advice, remember that appraising is part of their business and fees may be charged.

A.H. Wilkens
299 Queen St. East
Toronto, Ontario M5A 1S7
Canada
www.ahwilkens.com
416-360-7600

Aleph-Bet Books
85 Old Mill River Road
Pound Ridge, NY 10576
www.alephbet.com
914-764-7410

Allard Auctions
P.O. Box 1030
St. Ignatius, MT 59865
www.allardauctions.com
406-745-0500

American Bottle Auctions
2523 J St., Suite 203
Sacramento, CA 95816
www.americanbottle.com
800-806-7722

American Glass Gallery
P.O. Box 227
New Hudson, MI 48165
www.americanglassgallery.com
248-486-0530

Anderson Americana
P.O. Box 644
Troy, OH 45373
www.anderson-auction.com
937-339-0850

Auction Team Breker
Otto-Hahn St. 10
50997 Cologne, Germany
www.breker.com
703-796-5544 (U.S.)

Bertoia Auctions
2141 DeMarco Dr.
Vineland, NJ 08360
www.bertoiaauctions.com
856-692-1881

Bloomsbury House
24 Maddox St.
London W1S 1PP, England
www.bloomsburyauctions.com
+44(0) 20 7495 9494

Bob Courtney Auctions
Route 122A
12 Providence St.
Millbury, MA 01527
www.bobcourtneyauctions.com
508-865-1009

Bonhams
580 Madison Ave.
New York, NY 10022
www.bonhams.com
212-644-9001

Bonhams
7601 W. Sunset Blvd.
Los Angeles, CA 90046
www.bonhams.com
323-850-7500

Brian Lebel's Old West Show & Auction
3201 Zafarano Dr., Suite C585
Santa Fe, NM 87507
www.codyoldwest.com
480-779-9378

Brunk Auctions
P.O. Box 2135
Asheville, NC 28802
www.brunkauctions.com
828-254-6846

Charlton Hall Auctions
7 Lexington Dr.
West Columbia, SC 29170
www.charltonhallauctions.com
803-779-5678

Coeur d'Alene Art Auction
8836 Hess St.
Hayden Lake, ID 83835
www.cdaartauction.com
208-772-9009

Conestoga Auction Co.
P.O. Box 1
Manheim, PA 17545
www.conestogaauction.com
717-898-7284

Copake Auction
266 Route 7A
Copake, NY 12516
www.copakeauction.com
518-329-1142

Cottone Auctions
120 Court St.
Geneseo, NY 14454
www.cottoneauctions.com
585-243-3100

Cowan's Auctions and Cowans + Clark + DelVecchio
6270 Este Ave.
Cincinnati, OH 45232
www.cowanauctions.com
513-871-1670

Crossroads Angling Auction
Attn: Steve Starrantino
P.O. Box 755
Hillburn, NY 10931
www.crossroadsanglingauction.com
845-598-0888

Decoys Unlimited
P.O. Box 206
2320 Main St.
West Barnstable, MA 02668
www.decoysunlimitedinc.net
508-362-2766

Doyle New York
175 East 87th St.
New York, NY 10128
www.doylenewyork.com
212-427-2730

DuMouchelles Art Gallery
409 East Jefferson Ave.
Detroit, MI 48226
www.dumouchelles.com
313-963-6255

Early American History Auctions
P.O. Box 3507
Rancho Santa Fe, CA 92067
www.earlyamerican.com
858-759-3290

Early Auction Co.
123 Main St.
Milford, OH 45150
www.earlyauctionco.com
513-831-4833

Eldred's Auction
P.O. Box 796
1483 Route 6A
East Dennis, MA 02641
www.eldreds.com
508-385-3116

Elite Decorative Arts
1034 Gateway Blvd., Suite 106
Boynton Beach, FL 33426
www.eliteauction.com
561-200-0893

Fontaine's Auction Gallery
1485 W. Housatonic St.
Pittsfield, MA 01201
www.fontainesauction.com
413-448-8922

Fox Auctions
P.O. Box 4069
Vallejo, CA 94590
www.foxauctionsonline.com
631-553-3841

Garth's Auctioneers & Appraisers
P.O. Box 369
Delaware, OH 43015
www.garths.com
740-362-4771

Glass Works Auctions
P.O. Box 180
East Greenville, PA 18041
www.glswrk-auction.com
215-679-5849

Goldin Auctions
423 Commerce Lane, Suite 4
West Berlin, NJ 08091
www.goldinauctions.com
856-767-8550

Gray's Auctioneers
10717 Detroit Ave.
Cleveland, OH 44102
www.graysauctioneers.com
216-458-7695

Guyette, Schmidt & Deeter
24718 Beverly Road
St. Michaels, MD 21663
www.guyetteandschmidt.com
410-745-0485

Hake's Americana & Collectibles
P.O. Box 12001
York, PA 17402
www.hakes.com
717-434-1600

Heritage Auctions
3500 Maple Ave., 17th Floor
Dallas, TX 75219-3941
www.ha.com
800-872-6467 / 214-528-3500

Holabird-Kagin Americana
3555 Airway Dr., Suite 308
Reno, NV 89511
www.holabirdamericana.com
877-852-8822

Hollywood Poster Auction
The Last Moving Picture Co.
10535 Chillicothe Road
Kirtland, OH 44094
www.hollywoodposterauction.com
440-256-3660

Humler & Nolan
225 E. Sixth St., 4th Floor
Cincinnati, OH 45202
www.humlernolan.com
513-381-2041

Hunt Auctions
256 Welsh Pool Road
Exton, PA 19341
www.huntauctions.com
610-524-0822

Ivey-Selkirk Auctioneers
7447 Forsyth Blvd.
St. Louis, MO 63105
www.iveyselkirk.com
314-726-5515

James D. Julia Auctioneers
203 Skowhegan Road
Fairfield, Maine 04937
www.jamesdjulia.com
207-453-7125

Jeffrey S. Evans & Associates
P.O. Box 2638
Harrisonburg, VA 22801
www.jeffreysevans.com
540-434-3939

Kestenbaum & Co.
242 West 30th St., 12th Floor
New York, NY 10001
www.kestenbaum.net
212-366-1197

Lang's Auction
663 Pleasant Valley Road
Waterville, NY 13480
www.langsauction.com
315-841-4623

Leighton Galleries
6 Pearl Court, Suite C
Allendale, NJ 07401
www.leightongalleries.com
201-327-8800

Leland Little Auction
620 Cornerstone Ct.
Hillsborough, NC 27278
www.llauctions.com
919-644-1243

Leslie Hindman Auctioneers
1338 West Lake St.
Chicago, IL 60607
www.lesliehindman.com
312-280-1212

**Los Angeles Modern Auctions
(LAMA)**
16145 Hart St.
Van Nuys, CA 91406
www.lamodern.com
323-904-1950

Marbeth Schon Gallery
415 Main St.
Natchez, MS 39120
www.mschon.com
228-424-7274

Martin Auction Co.
P.O. Box 2
100 Lick Creek Road
Anna, IL 62906
www.martinauctionco.com
618-833-3589

Matthews Auctions
19186 Nokomis Road
Nokomis, IL 62075
www.matthewsauctions.com
217-563-8880 / 877-968-8880

McMasters Harris Auction Co.
1625 West Church St.
Newark, OH 43055
www.mcmastersharris.com
800-842-3526

Morphy Auctions
2000 North Reading Road
Denver, PA 17517
www.morphyauctions.com
717-335-3435

Mosby & Co. Auctions
905 W. 7th St., #228
Frederick, MD 21701
mosbyauctions.com
240-629-8139

Neal Auction Co.
4038 Magazine St.
New Orleans, LA 70115
www.nealauction.com
800-467-5329

New Orleans Auction Galleries
801 Magazine St.
New Orleans, LA 70130
www.neworleansauction.com
800-501-0277

Noel Barrett Antiques & Auctions
6183 Carversville Road
Carversville, PA 18913
www.noelbarrett.com
215-297-5109

Norman C. Heckler & Co.
79 Bradford Corner Road
Woodstock Valley, CT 06282
www.hecklerauction.com
860-974-1634

Northeast Auctions
93 Pleasant St.
Portsmouth, NH 03801
www.northeastauctions.com
603-433-8400

Old Barn Auction
10040 State Route 224
Findlay, OH 45840
www.oldbarn.com
419-422-8531

Past Tyme Pleasures
5424 Sunol Blvd., #10-242
Pleasanton, CA 94566
www.pasttyme1.com
925-484-6442

Philip Weiss Auctions
74 Merrick Road
Lynbrook, NY 11563
www.weissauctions.com
516-594-0731

Potteries Specialist Auctions
271 Waterloo Road
Cobridge, Stoke On Trent ST6 3HR
England
www.potteriesauctions.com
+44(0)1782 286622

Rago Arts and Auction Center
333 North Main St.
Lambertville, NJ 08530
www.ragoarts.com
609-397-9374

Rich Penn Auctions
P.O. Box 1355
Waterloo, IA 50704
www.richpennauctions.com
319-291-6688

Rock Island Auction Co.
7819 42nd St. West
Rock Island, IL 61201
www.rockislandauction.com
800-238-8022

RSL Auction
P.O. Box 635
Oldwick, NJ 08858
www.rslauctions.com
908-823-4049

Ruby Lane
381 Bush St., Suite 400
San Francisco, CA 94104
www.rubylane.com
415-362-7611

Seeck Auctions
P.O. Box 377
Mason City, IA 50402
www.seeckauction.com
641-424-1116

Serious Toyz
1 Baltic Place
Croton-on-Hudson, NY 10520
www.serioustoyz.com
866-653-8699

Showtime Auction Services
22619 Monterey Dr.
Woodhaven, MI 48183
www.showtimeauctions.com
951-453-2415

Skinner, Inc.
274 Cedar Hill St.
Marlborough, MA 01752
www.skinnerinc.com
508-970-3000

Sloans & Kenyon
7034 Wisconsin Ave.
Chevy Chase, MD 20815
www.sloansandkenyon.com
301-634-2330

Sotheby's
1334 York Ave.
New York, NY 10021
www.sothebys.com
212-606-7000

The Stein Auction Co.
P.O. Box 136
Palatine, IL 60078
www.garykirsnerauctions.com
847-991-5927

Strawser Auction Group
P.O. Box 332
200 North Main St.
Wolcottville, IN 46795
www.strawserauctions.com
260-854-2859

Theriault's
P.O. Box 151
Annapolis, MD 21404
www.theriaults.com
800-638-0422

Tom Harris Auctions
203 South 18th Ave.
Marshalltown, IA 50108
www.tomharrisauctions.com
641-754-4890

Treadway Toomey Galleries
c/o Treadway Gallery
2029 Madison Road
Cincinnati, OH 45208
www.treadwaygallery.com
513-321-6742

V & M
270 Lafayette St., Suite 1400
New York, NY 10012
www.VandM.com
212-993-6430
800-618-2960

Victorian Casino Antiques
4520 Arville St, #1
Las Vegas, NV 89103
www.vcaauction.com
702-382-2466

White's Auctions
250 N. Main St.
Middleboro, MA 02346
www.whitesauctions.com
508-947-9281

William H. Bunch Auctions
1 Hillman Dr.
Chadds Ford, PA 19317
www.williambunchauctions.com
610-558-1800

William Morford Antiques
RD #2 Cobb Hill Road
Cazenovia, NY 13035
www.morfauction.com
315-662-7625

Willis Henry Auctions
22 Main St.
Marshfield, MA 02050
www.willishenry.com
781-834-7774

Woody Auction
P.O. Box 618
317 S. Forrest
Douglass, KS 67039
woodyauction.com
316-747-2694

Wright
1440 W. Hubbard
Chicago, IL 60642
www.wright20.com
312-563-0020

For more than 50 years...

Kovels' price guides, newsletters, syndicated columns, TV shows, and website have been the ultimate sources for reliable information about antiques & collectibles—go to Kovels.com to learn more

KOVELS.com
the go-to source for antiques and collectibles information since 1953

Tap into the Kovels' resources and expertise online! Terry Kovel and her team of experts write about what's hot and what's not and explain how to buy, sell, trade, and display your antiques and collectibles.

Visit Today – Register at Kovels.com to receive our FREE weekly news email, *Kovels Komments*. Read collecting news and tips, along with the identification of a "mystery mark" and a collector's Q&A.

Prices, Prices, Prices – Access more than fourteen years' worth of prices for more than 900,000 antiques and collectibles—from colonial-era furniture and folk art to twentieth-century toys and pop culture memorabilia—for FREE, simply by registering on Kovels.com.

The Best Business Directory – Kovels.com includes a nationwide business directory of antiques-related businesses: auction houses; collectors clubs and publications; museums and archives of interest; and appraisal, restoration, repair, and matching services.

Events You Can't Miss – Looking for the next big flea market? Check out our calendar of events or post your organization's sale!

An Online Community – Enjoy the collective knowledge of the entire Kovels community of antiques collectors—post a question, join a conversation, or start a thread of your own in the Kovels.com Forums.

Archive of reference articles – Find useful information on antiques and collectibles in our extensive searchable archive of articles.

Marks – Use our exclusive database of marks for pottery, porcelain, silver, and other metals. Identify and date your items.

The Most Trusted Name in ANTIQUES & COLLECTIBLES

Kovels.com offers Essential Tools Every Collector Needs

Free Basic Registration: Receive *Kovels Komments* weekly, enjoy access to the huge database of prices, and participate in the Forums.

Premium Subscriber: Get access to thousands of researched articles, news, current sales reports, alerts about fakes, trends, marks, and more actual prices. Includes digital access to *Kovels on Antiques and Collectibles* and its archives, the most trusted newsletter in the field.

Premium Plus Subscriber: In addition, you'll be able to access the Kovels' extensive, searchable database of pottery, porcelain, silver and other metal marks that includes makers, artists, materials, countries, dates, and more.

HOW TO GET ANTIQUE PRICING INFORMATION
∞ That Changes Monthly ∞

Some markets are more volatile than others.

Auctions, trends, and the economy impact prices each year.

Are you a dealer or a collector who NEEDS to know what is happening?

SUBSCRIBE NOW to our award-winning monthly newsletter, *Kovels on Antiques and Collectibles*.

This is **THE SOURCE** that helps **COLLECTORS and DEALERS** keep up with the fast-changing world of antiques and collectibles.

- Learn about prices at the latest sales and auctions

- Spot tomorrow's emerging trends so you can cash in TODAY

- Discover the true value of dozens of collectibles as prices change month to month

- Find out how to avoid fakes and frauds and what is being faked right now!

✂ -

Become a more successful collector! Try Kovels on Antiques and Collectibles for just $27 a year (40% off the regular price). To subscribe, visit Kovels.com, call, or send this order form to the address below.

Name _____

Street _____

City _____ State _____ Zip _____

Telephone (____) _____

☐ MasterCard ☐ Visa ☐ AmEx ☐ Discover ☐ Check *(payable to Kovels)* ☐ Bill me *(option only available in USA)*

Card No. _____

Signature _____

Email address _____

KOVELS
P.O. Box 8534
Big Sandy, TX 75755-8534

(800) 829-9158 (mention offer **6YFKAPB**)

6YFKAPB